Collins

BESTSELLING BILINGUAL DICTIONARIES

Spanish
Dictionary

Collins

HarperCollins Publishers
Westerhill Road
Bishopbriggs
Glasgow
G64 2QT
Great Britain

Sixth Edition 2010

Reprint 10 9 8 7 6 5 4 3 2 1

© HarperCollins Publishers 1997, 2000, 2004, 2006, 2008, 2010

ISBN 978-0-00-732317-3

Collins® is a registered trademark of
HarperCollins Publishers Limited

www.collinslanguage.com

A catalogue record for this book is available
from the British Library

HarperCollins Publishers,
10 East 53rd Street,
New York, NY 10022

COLLINS SPANISH CONCISE DICTIONARY.
Sixth US Edition 2010

ISBN 978-0-06-199864-5

Library of Congress Cataloging-in-Publication
Data has been applied for

www.harpercollins.com

HarperCollins books may be purchased for
educational, business, or sales promotional
use. For information, please write to:
Special Markets Department,
HarperCollins Publishers,
10 East 53rd Street,
New York, NY 10022

Typeset by Davidson Publishing Solutions,
Glasgow

Printed in Italy by
LEGO S.p.A., Lavis (Trento)

Acknowledgements
We would like to thank those authors and
publishers who kindly gave permission for
copyright material to be used in the Collins
Word Web. We would also like to thank
Times Newspapers Ltd for providing valuable
data.

MANAGING EDITOR
Gaëlle Amiot-Cadey

PROJECT MANAGEMENT
Genevieve Gerrard

CONTRIBUTORS
Jeremy Butterfield, Mike González,
Gerry Breslin, Teresa Álvarez García,
Brian Steel, Ana Cristina Llompart,
José Miguel Galván Déniz, Val McNulty,
Sharon Hunter, Tracy Lomas,
Enrique González Sandinero,
Caitlin McMahon

TECHNICAL SUPPORT
Thomas Callan

SERIES EDITOR
Rob Scriven

Índice de materias

Contents

William Collins' dream of knowledge for all began with the publication of his first book in 1819. A self-educated mill worker, he not only enriched millions of lives, but also founded a flourishing publishing house. Today, staying true to this spirit, Collins books are packed with inspiration, innovation, and practical expertise. They place you at the centre of a world of possibility and give you exactly what you need to explore it.

Language is the key to this exploration, and at the heart of Collins Dictionaries is language as it is really used. New words, phrases, and meanings spring up every day, and all of them are captured and analysed by the Collins Word Web. Constantly updated, and with over 2.5 billion entries, this living language resource is unique to our dictionaries.

Words are tools for life. And a Collins Dictionary makes them work for you.

Collins. Do more.

Introduction

You may be starting Spanish for the first time, or you may wish to extend your knowledge of the language. Perhaps you want to read and study Spanish books, newspapers and magazines, or perhaps simply have a conversation with Spanish speakers. Whatever the reason, whether you're a student, a tourist or want to use Spanish for business, this is the ideal book to help you understand and communicate. This modern, user-friendly dictionary gives priority to everyday vocabulary and the language of current affairs, business, computing and tourism, and, as in all Collins dictionaries, the emphasis is firmly placed on contemporary language and expressions.

How to use the dictionary

Below you will find an outline of how information is presented in your dictionary. Our aim is to give you the maximum amount of detail in the clearest and most helpful way.

Entries

A typical entry in your dictionary will be made up of the following elements:

Phonetic transcription

Phonetics appear in square brackets immediately after the headword. They are shown using the International Phonetic Alphabet (IPA), and a complete list of the symbols used in this system can be found on page x. The pronunciation given is for Castilian Spanish except where a word is solely used in Latin America, when we give the Latin American pronunciation. A further guide to the differences in types of Spanish pronunciation is given on page x.

Grammatical information

All words belong to one of the following parts of speech: noun, verb, adjective, adverb, pronoun, article, conjunction, preposition, abbreviation. Nouns can be singular or plural and, in Spanish, masculine or feminine. Verbs can be transitive, intransitive, reflexive or impersonal. Parts of speech appear in *italics* immediately after the phonetic spelling of the headword. The gender of the translation also appears in *italics* immediately following the key element of the translation, except where this is a regular masculine singular noun ending in "o", or a regular feminine singular noun ending in "a".

Often a word can have more than one part of speech. Just as the English word **chemical** can be an adjective or a noun, the Spanish word **conocido** can be an adjective ("(well-)known") or a noun ("acquaintance"). In the same way the verb **to walk** is sometimes transitive, ie it takes an object ("to walk the dog") and sometimes intransitive, ie it doesn't take an object ("to walk to school"). To help you find the meaning you are looking for quickly and for clarity of presentation, the different part of speech categories are separated by a shaded square ■.

Meaning divisions

Most words have more than one meaning. Take, for example, **punch** which can be, amongst other things, a blow with the fist or an object used for making holes. Other words are translated differently depending on the context in which they are used. The transitive verb **to put on**, for example, can be translated by "ponerse", "encender" etc depending on *what* it is you are putting on. To help you select the most appropriate translation in every context, entries are divided according to meaning. Each different meaning is introduced by an "indicator" in *italics* and in brackets. Thus, the examples given above will be shown as follows:

punch [pʌntʃ] n *(blow)* golpe *m*, puñetazo; *(tool)* punzón *m*

Likewise, some words can have a different meaning when used to talk about a specific subject area or field. For example **bishop**, which in a religious context means a high-ranking clergyman, is also the name of a chess piece. To show English speakers which translation to use, we have added "subject field labels" in brackets, in this case *(Chess)*:

bishop [ˈbɪʃəp] n obispo; *(Chess)* alfil *m*

Field labels are often shortened to save space. You will find a complete list of abbreviations used in the dictionary on pages viii and ix.

Translations

Most English words have a direct translation in Spanish and vice versa, as shown in the examples given above. Sometimes, however, no exact equivalent exists in the target language. In such cases we have given an approximate equivalent, indicated by the sign ≈. An example is **Health Service**, the Spanish equivalent of which is "Insalud". There is no exact equivalent since the bodies in the two countries are quite different:

Health Service n *(Brit)* servicio de salud pública, ≈ Insalud *m (SP)*

On occasion it is impossible to find even an approximate equivalent. This may be the case, for example, with the names of types of food:

fabada [faˈβaða] nf *bean and sausage stew*

Here the translation (which doesn't exist) is replaced by an explanation. For increased clarity, the explanation, or "gloss", is shown in *italics*.

It is often the case that a word, or a particular meaning of a word, cannot be translated in isolation. The translation of **Dutch**, for example, is "holandés/esa". However, the phrase **to go Dutch** is rendered by "pagar cada uno lo suyo". Even an expression as simple as **washing powder** needs a separate translation since it translates as "detergente (en polvo)", not "polvo para lavar". This is where your dictionary will prove to be particularly informative and useful since it contains an abundance of compounds, phrases and idiomatic expressions.

Levels of formality and familiarity

In English you instinctively know when to say **I'm broke** or **I'm a bit short of cash** and when to say **I don't have any money**. When you are trying to understand someone who is speaking Spanish, however, or when you yourself try to speak Spanish, it is important to know what is polite and what is less so, and what you can say in a relaxed situation but not in a formal context. To help you with this, on the Spanish-English side we have added the label *(fam)* to show that a Spanish meaning or expression is colloquial, while those meanings or expressions which are vulgar are given an exclamation mark *(fam!)*, warning you they can cause serious offence. Note also that on the English-Spanish side, translations which are vulgar are followed by an exclamation mark in brackets.

Keywords

Words labelled in the text as KEYWORDS, such as **have** and **do** or their Spanish equivalents **tener** and **hacer**, have been given special treatment because they form the basic elements of the language. This extra help will ensure that you know how to use these complex words with confidence.

Cultural Information

Entries which are marked in the main text by a column of dots explain aspects of culture in Spanish and English-speaking countries. Subject areas covered include politics, education, media and national festivals.

Spanish alphabetical order

In 1994 the **Real Academia Española** and the Spanish American language academies jointly decided to stop treating CH and LL as separate letters in Spanish, thereby bringing it into line with European spelling norms. This means that **chapa** and **lluvia** will appear in letters C and L respectively. Of course, it should also be remembered that words like **cancha** and **callar**, with **ch** and **ll** in the middle of the words, will also have changed places alphabetically, now being found after **cáncer** and **cáliz** respectively. Spanish, however still has one more letter than English with Ñ treated separately, between N and O.

Abreviaturas / Abbreviations

abreviatura	*ab(b)r*	abbreviation
adjetivo, locución adjetiva	*adj*	adjective, adjectival phrase
administración, lenguaje administrativo	*Admin*	administration
adverbio, locución adverbial	*adv*	adverb, adverbial phrase
agricultura	*Agr*	agriculture
alguien	*algn*	
América Latina	*Am*	Latin America
anatomía	*Anat*	anatomy
arquitectura	*Arq, Arch*	architecture
astrología, astronomía	*Astro*	astrology, astronomy
el automóvil	*Aut(o)*	the motor car and motoring
aviación, viajes en avión	*Aviat*	flying, air travel
biología	*Bio(l)*	biology
botánica, flores	*Bot*	botany
inglés británico	*Brit*	British English
química	*Chem*	chemistry
cine	*Cine*	cinema
lenguaje familiar (! vulgar)	*col (!)*	colloquial usage (! particularly offensive)
comercio, finanzas, banca	*Com(m)*	commerce, finance, banking
informática	*Comput*	computing
conjunción	*conj*	conjunction
construcción	*Constr*	building
compuesto	*cpd*	compound element
cocina	*Culin*	cookery
economía	*Econ*	economics
electricidad, electrónica	*Elec*	electricity, electronics
enseñanza, sistema escolar	*Escol*	schooling, schools
España	*Esp*	Spain
especialmente	*esp*	especially
exclamación, interjección	*excl*	exclamation, interjection
femenino	*f*	feminine
lenguaje familiar (! vulgar)	*fam (!)*	colloquial usage (! particularly offensive)
ferrocarril	*Ferro*	railways
uso figurado	*fig*	figurative use
fotografía	*Foto*	photography
(verbo inglés) del cual la partícula es inseparable	*fus*	(phrasal verb) where the particle is inseparable
generalmente	*gen*	generally
geografía, geología	*Geo*	geography, geology
geometría	*Geom*	geometry
informática	*Inform*	computing
invariable	*inv*	invariable
irregular	*irreg*	irregular
lo jurídico	*Jur*	law
América Latina	*LAm*	Latin America
gramática, lingüística	*Ling*	grammar, linguistics

literatura	Lit	literature
masculino	m	masculine
matemáticas	Mat(h)	mathematics
medicina	Med	medical term, medicine
masculino/femenino	m/f	masculine/feminine
lo militar, el ejército	Mil	military matters
música	Mus	music
sustantivo	n	noun
navegación, náutica	Naut	sailing, navigation
sustantivo no empleado en el plural	no pl	collective (uncountable) noun, not used in plural
sustantivo numérico	num	numeral noun
complemento	obj	(grammatical) object
	o.s.	oneself
peyorativo	pey, pej	derogatory, pejorative
fotografía	Phot	photography
fisiología	Physiol	physiology
plural	pl	plural
política	Pol	politics
participio de pasado	pp	past participle
prefijo	pref	prefix
preposición	prep	preposition
pronombre	pron	pronoun
psicología, psiquiatría	Psico, Psych	psychology, psychiatry
tiempo pasado	pt	past tense
ferrocarril	Rail	railways
religión, lo eclesiástico	Rel	religion, church service
	sb	somebody
enseñanza, sistema escolar	Scol	schooling, schools
singular	sg	singular
España	SP	Spain
	sth	something
subjuntivo	subjun	subjunctive
sujeto	su(b)j	(grammatical) subject
sufijo	suff	suffix
tauromaquia	Taur	bullfighting
también	tb	also
teatro	Teat	
técnica, tecnología	Tec(h)	technical term, technology
telecomunicaciones	Telec, Tel	telecommunications
	Theat	theatre
imprenta, tipografía	Tip, Typ	typography, printing
televisión	TV	television
sistema universitario	Univ	universities
inglés norteamericano	US	American English
verbo	vb	verb
verbo intransitivo	vi	intransitive verb
verbo pronominal	vr	reflexive verb
verbo transitivo	vt	transitive verb
zoología, animales	Zool	zoology
marca registrada	®	registered trademark
indica un equivalente cultural	≈	introduces a cultural equivalent

Spanish Pronunciation

Consonants

b	[b]	See notes on v below	bomba
	[β]		labor
c	[k]	c before a, o or u is pronounced as in cat	caja
ce, ci	[θe,θi]	c before e or i is pronounced as in thin and as s	cero, cielo
	[se,siʾ]	in sin in Latin America and parts of Spain	vocero, noticiero
ch	[tʃ]	ch is pronounced as ch in chair	chiste
d	[d]	at the beginning of a word or after l or n,	danés
	[ð]	d is pronounced as in English. In any other position it is like th in the	ciudad
g	[g]	g before a, o or u is pronounced as in gap if	gafas, guerra
	[ɣ]	at the beginning of a word or after n. In other positions the sound is softened.	paga
ge, gi	[xe, xi]	g before e or i is pronounced similar to ch in Scottish loch	gente, girar
h		h is always silent in Spanish	haber
j	[x]	j is pronounced like ch in Scottish loch	jugar
ll	[ʎ]	ll is pronounced like the lli in million	talle
ñ	[ɲ]	ñ is pronounced like the ni in onion	niño
q	[k]	q is pronounced as k in king	que
r, rr	[r]	r is always pronounced in Spanish, unlike	quitar
	[rr]	the r in dancer. rr and r at the beginning of a word are trilled, like a Scottish r	garra
s	[s]	s is usually pronounced as in pass, but before	quizás
	[z]	b, d, g, l, m or n it is pronounced as in rose	isla
v	[b]	v is pronounced something like b. At the	vía
	[β]	beginning of a word or after m or n it is pronounced as b in boy. In any other position it is pronounced with the lips in position to pronounce b of boy, but not meeting	dividir
w	[b]	pronounced either like Spanish b, or like	wáter
	[w]	English w	whiskey
x			

z	[θ]	z is pronounced as *th* in *th*in and as *s* in *s*in in	tenaz
	[s']	Latin America and parts of Spain	izada
	[ks]	x is pronounced as in toxin except in informal	tóxico
	[s]	Spanish or at the beginning of a word	xenofobia

f, k, l, m, n, p and *t* are pronounced as in English
' Only shown in Latin American entries.

Vowels

a	[a]	Not as long as *a* in *far*. When followed by a consonant in the same syllable (ie in a closed syllable), as in am*a*nte, the *a* is short as in b*a*t	p*a*ta
e	[e]	like *e* in *they*. In a closed syllable, as in g*e*nte, the *e* is short as in p*e*t	m*e*
i	[i]	as in m*ea*n or mach*i*ne	p*i*no
o	[o]	as in l*o*cal. In a closed syllable, as in c*o*ntrol, the *o* is short as in c*o*t	l*o*
u	[u]	As in r*u*le. It is silent after *q*, and in *gue, qui*, unless marked *güe, güi* eg antig*ü*edad, when it is pronounced like *w* in *wolf*	l*u*nes

Semi-vowels

| i, y | [j] | pronounced like *y* in *yes* | b*i*en, h*i*elo, *y*unta |
| u | [w] | unstressed *u* between consonant and vowel is pronounced like *w* in *well*. See also notes on *u* above | h*u*evo, f*u*ente, antig*ü*edad |

Diphthongs

ai, ay	[ai]	as *i* in r*i*de	b*ai*le
au	[au]	as *ou* in *shout*	*au*to
ei, ey	[ei]	as *ey* in gr*ey*	bu*ey*
eu	[eu]	both elements pronounced independently [e] + [u]	d*eu*da
oi, oy	[oi]	as *oy* in t*oy*	h*oy*

Stress

The rules of stress in Spanish are as follows:

(a)   when a word ends in a vowel or in *n* or *s*, the second last syllable is stressed: pa*tat*a, pa*tat*as, *com*e, *com*en

(b)   when a word ends in a consonant other than *n* or *s*, the stress falls on the last syllable: pa*red*, ha*blar*

(c)   when the rules set out in (a) and (b) are not applied, an acute accent appears over the stressed vowel: común, geografía, inglés

In the phonetic transcription, the symbol ['] precedes the syllable on which the stress falls.

In general, we give the pronunciation of each entry in square brackets after the word in question.

Spanish Verb Forms

1 Gerund **2** Imperative **3** Present **4** Preterite **5** Future **6** Present subjunctive **7** Imperfect subjunctive **8** Past participle **9** Imperfect

acertar 2 acierta 3 acierto, aciertas, acierta, aciertan 6 acierte, aciertes, acierte, acierten
acordar 2 acuerda 3 acuerdo, acuerdas, acuerda, acuerdan 6 acuerde, acuerdes, acuerde, acuerden
advertir 1 advirtiendo 2 advierte 3 advierto, adviertes, advierte, advierten 4 advirtió, advirtieron 6 advierta, adviertas, advierta, advirtamos, advirtáis, adviertan 7 advirtiera etc
agradecer 3 agradezco 6 agradezca etc
andar 4 anduve, anduviste, anduvo, anduvimos, anduvisteis, anduvieron 7 anduviera or anduviese etc
aparecer 3 aparezco 6 aparezca etc
aprobar 2 aprueba 3 apruebo, apruebas, aprueba, aprueban 6 apruebe, apruebes, apruebe, aprueben
atravesar 2 atraviesa 3 atravieso, atraviesas, atraviesa, atraviesan 6 atraviese, atravieses, atraviese, atraviesen
caber 3 quepo 4 cupe, cupiste, cupo, cupimos, cupisteis, cupieron 5 cabré etc 6 quepa etc 7 cupiera etc
caer 1 cayendo 3 caigo 4 cayó, cayeron 6 caiga etc 7 cayera etc
calentar 2 calienta 3 caliento, calientas, calienta, calientan 6 caliente, calientes, caliente, calienten
cerrar 2 cierra 3 cierro, cierras, cierra, cierran 6 cierre, cierres, cierre, cierren
COMER 1 comiendo 2 come, comed 3 como, comes, come, comemos, coméis, comen 4 comí, comiste, comió, comimos, comisteis, comieron 5 comeré, comerás, comerá, comeremos, comeréis, comerán 6 coma, comas, coma, comamos, comáis, coman 7 comiera, comieras, comiera, comiéramos, comierais, comieran 8 comido 9 comía, comías, comía, comíamos, comíais, comían
conocer 3 conozco 6 conozca etc
contar 2 cuenta 3 cuento, cuentas, cuenta, cuentan 6 cuente, cuentes, cuente, cuenten
costar 2 cuesta 3 cuesto, cuestas, cuesta, cuestan 6 cueste, cuestes, cueste, cuesten
dar 3 doy 4 di, diste, dio, dimos, disteis, dieron 7 diera etc
decir 2 di 3 digo 4 dije, dijiste, dijo, dijimos, dijisteis, dijeron 5 diré etc 6 diga etc 7 dijera etc 8 dicho

despertar 2 despierta 3 despierto, despiertas, despierta, despiertan 6 despierte, despiertes, despierte, despierten
divertir 1 divirtiendo 2 divierte 3 divierto, diviertes, divierte, divierten 4 divirtió, divirtieron 6 divierta, diviertas, divierta, divirtamos, divirtáis, diviertan 7 divirtiera etc
dormir 1 durmiendo 2 duerme 3 duermo, duermes, duerme, duermen 4 durmió, durmieron 6 duerma, duermas, duerma, durmamos, durmáis, duerman 7 durmiera etc
empezar 2 empieza 3 empiezo, empiezas, empieza, empiezan 4 empecé 6 empiece, empieces, empiece, empecemos, empecéis, empiecen
entender 2 entiende 3 entiendo, entiendes, entiende, entienden 6 entienda, entiendas, entienda, entiendan
ESTAR 2 está 3 estoy, estás, está, están 4 estuve, estuviste, estuvo, estuvimos, estuvisteis, estuvieron 6 esté, estés, esté, estén 7 estuviera etc
HABER 3 he, has, ha, hemos, habéis, han 4 hube, hubiste, hubo, hubimos, hubisteis, hubieron 5 habré etc 6 haya etc 7 hubiera etc
HABLAR 1 hablando 2 habla, hablad 3 hablo, hablas, habla, hablamos, habláis, hablan 4 hablé, hablaste, habló, hablamos, hablasteis, hablaron 5 hablaré, hablarás, hablará, hablaremos, hablaréis, hablarán 6 hable, hables, hable, hablemos, habléis, hablen 7 hablara or hablase, hablaras or hablases, hablara or hablase, habláramos or hablásemos, hablarais or hablaseis, hablaran or hablasen 8 hablado 9 hablaba, hablabas, hablaba, hablábamos, hablabais, hablaban
hacer 2 haz 3 hago 4 hice, hiciste, hizo, hicimos, hicisteis, hicieron 5 haré etc 6 haga etc 7 hiciera etc 8 hecho
instruir 1 instruyendo 2 instruye 3 instruyo, instruyes, instruye, instruyen 4 instruyó, instruyeron 6 instruya etc 7 instruyera etc
ir 1 yendo 2 ve 3 voy, vas, va, vamos, vais, van 4 fui, fuiste, fue, fuimos, fuisteis, fueron 6 vaya, vayas, vaya, vayamos, vayáis, vayan 7 fuera etc 9 iba, ibas, iba, íbamos, ibais, iban

jugar 2 juega 3 juego, juegas, juega, juegan 4 jugué 6 juegue *etc*
leer 1 leyendo 4 leyó, leyeron 7 leyera *etc*
morir 1 muriendo 2 muere 3 muero, mueres, muere, mueren 4 murió, murieron 6 muera, mueras, muera, muramos, muráis, mueran 7 muriera *etc* 8 muerto
mostrar 2 muestra 3 muestro, muestras, muestra, muestran 6 muestre, muestres, muestre, muestren
mover 2 mueve 3 muevo, mueves, mueve, mueven 6 mueva, muevas, mueva, muevan
negar 2 niega 3 niego, niegas, niega, niegan 4 negué 6 niegue, niegues, niegue, neguemos, neguéis, nieguen
ofrecer 3 ofrezco 6 ofrezca *etc*
oír 1 oyendo 2 oye 3 oigo, oyes, oye, oyen 4 oyó, oyeron 6 oiga *etc* 7 oyera *etc*
oler 2 huele 3 huelo, hueles, huele, huelen 6 huela, huelas, huela, huelan
parecer 3 parezco 6 parezca *etc*
pedir 1 pidiendo 2 pide 3 pido, pides, pide, piden 4 pidió, pidieron 6 pida *etc* 7 pidiera *etc*
pensar 2 piensa 3 pienso, piensas, piensa, piensan 6 piense, pienses, piense, piensen
perder 2 pierde 3 pierdo, pierdes, pierde, pierden 6 pierda, pierdas, pierda, pierdan
poder 1 pudiendo 2 puede 3 puedo, puedes, puede, pueden 4 pude, pudiste, pudo, pudimos, pudisteis, pudieron 5 podré *etc* 6 pueda, puedas, pueda, puedan 7 pudiera *etc*
poner 2 pon 3 pongo 4 puse, pusiste, puso, pusimos, pusisteis, pusieron 5 pondré *etc* 6 ponga *etc* 7 pusiera *etc* 8 puesto
preferir 1 prefiriendo 2 prefiere 3 prefiero, prefieres, prefiere, prefieren 4 prefirió, prefirieron 6 prefiera, prefieras, prefiera, prefiramos, prefiráis, prefieran 7 prefiriera *etc*
querer 2 quiere 3 quiero, quieres, quiere, quieren 4 quise, quisiste, quiso, quisimos, quisisteis, quisieron 5 querré *etc* 6 quiera, quieras, quiera, quieran 7 quisiera *etc*
reír 2 ríe 3 río, ríes, ríe, ríen 4 rió, rieron 6 ría, rías, ría, riamos, riáis, rían 7 riera *etc*
repetir 1 repitiendo 2 repite 3 repito, repites, repite, repiten 4 repitió, repitieron 6 repita *etc* 7 repitiera *etc*
rogar 2 ruega 3 ruego, ruegas, ruega, ruegan 4 rogué 6 ruegue, ruegues, ruegue, roguemos, roguéis, rueguen

saber 3 sé 4 supe, supiste, supo, supimos, supisteis, supieron 5 sabré *etc* 6 sepa *etc* 7 supiera *etc*
salir 2 sal 3 salgo 5 saldré *etc* 6 salga *etc*
seguir 1 siguiendo 2 sigue 3 sigo, sigues, sigue, siguen 4 siguió, siguieron 6 siga *etc* 7 siguiera *etc*
sentar 2 sienta 3 siento, sientas, sienta, sientan 6 siente, sientes, siente, sienten
sentir 1 sintiendo 2 siente 3 siento, sientes, siente, sienten 4 sintió, sintieron 6 sienta, sientas, sienta, sintamos, sintáis, sientan 7 sintiera *etc*
SER 2 sé 3 soy, eres, es, somos, sois, son 4 fui, fuiste, fue, fuimos, fuisteis, fueron 6 sea *etc* 7 fuera *etc* 9 era, eras, era, éramos, erais, eran
servir 1 sirviendo 2 sirve 3 sirvo, sirves, sirve, sirven 4 sirvió, sirvieron 6 sirva *etc* 7 sirviera *etc*
soñar 2 sueña 3 sueño, sueñas, sueña, sueñan 6 sueñe, sueñes, sueñe, sueñen
tener 2 ten 3 tengo, tienes, tiene, tienen 4 tuve, tuviste, tuvo, tuvimos, tuvisteis, tuvieron 5 tendré *etc* 6 tenga *etc* 7 tuviera *etc*
traer 2 trayendo 3 traigo 4 traje, trajiste, trajo, trajimos, trajisteis, trajeron 6 traiga *etc* 7 trajera *etc*
valer 2 val 3 valgo 5 valdré *etc* 6 valga *etc*
venir 2 ven 3 vengo, vienes, viene, vienen 4 vine, viniste, vino, vinimos, vinisteis, vinieron 5 vendré *etc* 6 venga *etc* 7 viniera *etc*
ver 3 veo 6 vea *etc* 8 visto 9 veía *etc*
vestir 1 vistiendo 2 viste 3 visto, vistes, viste, visten 4 vistió, vistieron 6 vista *etc* 7 vistiera *etc*
VIVIR 1 viviendo 2 vive, vivid 3 vivo, vives, vive, vivimos, vivís, viven 4 viví, viviste, vivió, vivimos, vivisteis, vivieron 5 viviré, vivirás, vivirá, viviremos, viviréis, vivirán 6 viva, vivas, viva, vivamos, viváis, vivan 7 viviera *or* viviese, viviera *or* viviese, viviéramos *or* viviésemos, vivierais *or* vivieseis, vivieran *or* viviesen 8 vivido 9 vivía, vivías, vivía, vivíamos, vivíais, vivían
volcar 2 vuelca 3 vuelco, vuelcas, vuelca, vuelcan 4 volqué 6 vuelque, vuelques, vuelque, volquemos, volquéis, vuelquen
volver 2 vuelve 3 vuelvo, vuelves, vuelve, vuelven 6 vuelva, vuelvas, vuelva, vuelvan 8 vuelto

For additional information on Spanish verb formation, see pp 6 – 161 of the Grammar section.

Números

Numbers

uno (un, una)*	1	one
dos	2	two
tres	3	three
cuatro	4	four
cinco	5	five
seis	6	six
siete	7	seven
ocho	8	eight
nueve	9	nine
diez	10	ten
once	11	eleven
doce	12	twelve
trece	13	thirteen
catorce	14	fourteen
quince	15	fifteen
dieciséis	16	sixteen
diecisiete	17	seventeen
dieciocho	18	eighteen
diecinueve	19	nineteen
veinte	20	twenty
veintiuno(-un, -una)*	21	twenty-one
veintidós	22	twenty-two
treinta	30	thirty
treinta y uno(un, una)*	31	thirty-one
treinta y dos	32	thirty-two
cuarenta	40	forty
cincuenta	50	fifty
sesenta	60	sixty
setenta	70	seventy
ochenta	80	eighty
noventa	90	ninety
cien(ciento)**	100	a hundred, one hundred
ciento uno(un, una)*	101	a hundred and one
ciento dos	102	a hundred and two
ciento cincuenta y seis	156	a hundred and fifty-six
doscientos(-as)	200	two hundred
trescientos(-as)	300	three hundred
quinientos(-as)	500	five hundred
mil	1,000	a thousand
mil tres	1,003	a thousand and three
dos mil	2,000	two thousand
un millón	1,000,000	a million

*'uno' (+'veintiuno' etc) agrees in gender (but not number) with its noun: **treinta y una personas**; the masculine form is shortened to 'un' unless it stands alone: **veintiún caballos, veintiuno.**

'ciento' is used in compound numbers, except when it multiplies: **ciento diez, but **cien mil**. 'Cien' is used before nouns: **cien hombres, cien casas.**

Números

Numbers

primero (primer, primera) 1º, 1er/1ª, 1era	first, 1st
segundo(-a) 2º/2ª	second, 2nd
tercero (tercer, tercera) 3º, 3er/3ª, 3era	third, 3rd
cuarto(-a) 4º/4ª	fourth, 4th
quinto(-a)	fifth, 5th
sexto(-a)	sixth, 6th
séptimo(-a)	seventh
octavo(-a)	eighth
noveno(-a); nono(-a)	ninth
décimo(-a)	tenth
undécimo(-a)	eleventh
duodécimo(-a)	twelfth
decimotercero(-a)	thirteenth
decimocuarto(-a)	fourteenth
decimoquinto(-a)	fifteenth
decimosexto(-a)	sixteenth
decimoséptimo(-a)	seventeenth
decimoctavo(-a)	eighteenth
decimonoveno(-a)	nineteenth
vigésimo(-a)	twentieth
vigésimo(-a) primero(-a)	twenty-first
vigésimo(-a) segundo(-a)	twenty-second
trigésimo(-a)	thirtieth
trigésimo(-a) primero(-a)	thirty-first
trigésimo(-a) segundo(-a)	thirty-second
cuadragésimo(-a)	fortieth
quincuagésimo(-a)	fiftieth
sexagésimo(-a)	sixtieth
septuagésimo(-a)	seventieth
octogésimo(-a)	eightieth
nonagésimo(-a)	ninetieth
centésimo(-a)	hundredth
centésimo(-a) primero(-a)	hundred-and-first
milésimo(-a)	thousandth

La hora

¿qué hora es?	what time is it?
es la una	it's one o'clock
son las cuatro	it's four o'clock
medianoche, las doce de la noche	midnight
la una (de la madrugada)	one o'clock (in the morning), one (a.m.)
la una y cinco	five past one
la una y diez	ten past one
la una y cuarto or quince	a quarter past one, one fifteen
la una y veinticinco	twenty-five past one, one twenty-five
la una y media or treinta	half past one, one thirty
las dos menos veinticinco, la una treinta y cinco	twenty-five to two, one thirty-five
las dos menos veinte, la una cuarenta	twenty to two, one forty
las dos menos cuarto, la una cuarenta y cinco	a quarter to two, one forty-five
las dos menos diez, la una cincuenta	ten to two, one fifty
mediodía, las doce (de la mañana)	twelve o'clock, midday, noon
la dos (de la tarde) two o'clock (in the afternoon)	two (p.m.)
la siete (de la tarde), seven o'clock (in the evening)	seven (p.m.)
¿a qué hora?	at what time?
a medianoche	at midnight
a las siete	at seven o'clock
a la una	at one o'clock
en veinte minutos	in twenty minutes
hace diez minutos	ten minutes ago

La fecha

hoy	today
mañana	tomorrow
pasado mañana	the day after tomorrow
ayer	yesterday
antes de ayer, anteayer	the day before yesterday
la víspera	the day before, the previous day
el día siguiente	the next or following day
la mañana	morning
la tarde	evening
esta mañana	this morning
esta tarde	this evening, this afternoon
ayer por la mañana	yesterday morning
ayer por la tarde	yesterday evening

The time

The date

mañana por la mañana	tomorrow morning
mañana por la tarde	tomorrow evening, tomorrow afternoon
en la noche del sábado al domingo	during Saturday night, during the night of Saturday to Sunday
vendrá el sábado	he's coming on Saturday
los sábados	on Saturdays
todos los sábados	every Saturday
el sábado pasado	last Saturday
el sábado que viene, el próximo sábado	next Saturday
ocho días a partir del sábado	a week on Saturday
quince días a partir del sábado	a fortnight or two weeks on Saturday
de lunes a sábado	from Monday to Saturday
todos las días	every day
una vez a la semana	once a week
una vez al mes	once a month
dos veces a la semana	twice a week
hace una semana u ocho días	a week ago
hace quince días	a fortnight or two weeks ago
el año pasado	last year
dentro de dos días	in two days
dentro de ocho días o una semana	in a week
dentro de quince días	in a fortnight or two weeks
el mes que viene, el próximo mes	next month
el año que viene, el próximo año	next year
¿a qué o a cuántos estamos?	*what day is it?*
el 1/22 octubre de 2008	the 1st/22nd of October 2008, October 1st/22nd 2008
en 2008	in 2008
mil novicientos noventa y cinco	nineteen ninety-five
44 a. de J.C.	44 BC
14 d. de J.C.	14 AD
en el (siglo) XIX	in the nineteenth century
en los años treinta	in the thirties
érase una vez ...	once upon a time ...

A, a [a] *nf* (*letra*) A, a; **A de Antonio** A for
Andrew (*Brit*) *o* Able (*US*)
A. *abr* (*Escol*: = *aprobado*) pass

 PALABRA CLAVE

a [a] *prep* (a + el = al) **1** (*dirección*) to; **fueron a
Madrid/Grecia** they went to Madrid/Greece;
me voy a casa I'm going home
2 (*distancia*): **está a 15 km de aquí** it's 15 kms
from here
3 (*posición*): **estar a la mesa** to be at table;
al lado de next to, beside; **a la derecha/
izquierda** on the right/left; *ver tb* **puerta**
4 (*tiempo*): **a las 10/a medianoche** at 10/
midnight; **¿a qué hora?** (at) what time?;
a la mañana siguiente the following
morning; **a los pocos días** after a few days;
estamos a 9 de julio it's the 9th of July; **a
los 24 años** at the age of 24; **ocho horas al
día** eight hours a day; **al año/a la semana**
(*Am*) a year/week later
5 (*manera*): **a la francesa** the French way; **a
caballo** on horseback; **a oscuras** in the dark;
a rayas striped; **le echaron a patadas** they
kicked him out
6 (*medio, instrumento*): **a lápiz** in pencil; **a
mano** by hand; **cocina a gas** gas stove
7 (*razón*): **a dos euros el kilo** at two euros
a kilo; **a más de 50 kms por hora** at more
than 50 kms per hour; **poco a poco** little by
little
8 (*dativo*): **se lo di a él** I gave it to him; **se lo
compré a él** I bought it from him
9 (*complemento directo*): **vi al policía** I saw the
policeman
10 (*tras ciertos verbos*): **voy a verle** I'm going
to see him; **empezó a trabajar** he started
working *o* to work; **sabe a queso** it tastes of
cheese
11 (+*infin*): **al verle, le reconocí
inmediatamente** when I saw him I
recognized him at once; **el camino a**

recorrer the distance we (*etc*) have to travel;
¡a callar! keep quiet!; **¡a comer!** let's eat!
12 (a+*que*): **¡a que llueve!** I bet it's going to
rain!; **¿a qué viene eso?** what's the meaning
of this?; **¿a que sí va a venir?** he IS coming,
isn't he?; **¿a que no lo haces?** — **¡a que sí!**
bet you don't do it! — yes, I WILL!

AA *nfpl abr* = **Aerolíneas Argentinas**
AA EE *abr* (= *Asuntos Exteriores*): **Min. de** ~ = FO
(*Brit*)
ab. *abr* (= *abril*) Apr
abad, esa [a'βað, 'ðesa] *nm/f* abbot/abbess
abadía [aβa'ðia] *nf* abbey
abajo [a'βaxo] *adv* (*situación*) (down) below,
underneath; (*en edificio*) downstairs;
(*dirección*) down, downwards; ~ **de** *prep*
below, under; **el piso de** ~ the downstairs
flat; **la parte de** ~ the lower part; **¡~ el
gobierno!** down with the government!;
cuesta/río ~ downhill/downstream; **de
arriba** ~ from top to bottom; **el** ~ **firmante**
the undersigned; **más** ~ lower *o* further
down
abalance *etc* [aβa'lanθe] *vb ver* **abalanzarse**
abalanzarse [aβalan'θarse] *vr*: ~ **sobre** *o*
contra to throw o.s. at
abalear [aβale'ar] *vt* (*Am fam*) to shoot
abalorios [aβa'lorjos] *nmpl* (*chucherías*)
trinkets
abanderado [aβande'raðo] *nm* standard
bearer
abandonado, -a [aβando'naðo, a] *adj*
derelict; (*desatendido*) abandoned; (*desierto*)
deserted; (*descuidado*) neglected
abandonar [aβando'nar] *vt* to leave; (*persona*)
to abandon, desert; (*cosa*) to abandon, leave
behind; (*descuidar*) to neglect; (*renunciar a*)
to give up; (*Inform*) to quit; **abandonarse**
vr: **abandonarse a** to abandon o.s. to;
abandonarse al alcohol to take to drink
abandono [aβan'dono] *nm* (*acto*) desertion,
abandonment; (*estado*) abandon, neglect;

(*renuncia*) withdrawal, retirement; **ganar por** ~ to win by default
abanicar [aβaniˈkar] *vt* to fan
abanico [aβaˈniko] *nm* fan; (*Naut*) derrick; **en** ~ fan-shaped
abanique *etc* [aβaˈnike] *vb ver* **abanicar**
abaratar [aβaraˈtar] *vt* to lower the price of ◼ *vi*, **abaratarse** *vr* to go *o* come down in price
abarcar [aβarˈkar] *vt* to include, embrace; (*contener*) to comprise; (*Am*) to monopolize; **quien mucho abarca poco aprieta** don't bite off more than you can chew
abarque *etc* [aˈβarke] *vb ver* **abarcar**
abarrotado, -a [aβarroˈtaðo, a] *adj* packed; ~ **de** packed *o* bursting with
abarrote [aβaˈrrote] *nm* packing; **abarrotes** *nmpl* (*Am*) groceries, provisions
abarrotería [aβarroteˈria] *nf* (*Am*) grocery store
abarrotero, -a [aβarroˈtero, a] *nm/f* (*Am*) grocer
abastecedor, a [aβasteθeˈðor, a] *adj* supplying ◼ *nm/f* supplier
abastecer [aβasteˈθer] *vt*: ~ (**de**) to supply (with)
abastecimiento [aβasteθiˈmjento] *nm* supply
abastezca *etc* [aβasˈteθka] *vb ver* **abastecer**
abasto [aˈβasto] *nm* supply; (*abundancia*) abundance; **no dar** ~ **a algo** not to be able to cope with sth
abatible [aβaˈtiβle] *adj*: **asiento** ~ tip-up seat
abatido, -a [aβaˈtiðo, a] *adj* dejected, downcast; **estar muy** ~ to be very depressed
abatimiento [aβatiˈmjento] *nm* (*depresión*) dejection, depression
abatir [aβaˈtir] *vt* (*muro*) to demolish; (*pájaro*) to shoot *o* bring down; (*fig*) to depress; **abatirse** *vr* to get depressed; **abatirse sobre** to swoop *o* pounce on
abdicación [aβðikaˈθjon] *nf* abdication
abdicar [aβðiˈkar] *vi* to abdicate; ~ **en algn** to abdicate in favour of sb
abdique *etc* [aβˈðike] *vb ver* **abdicar**
abdomen [aβˈðomen] *nm* abdomen
abdominal [aβðomiˈnal] *adj* abdominal ◼ *nm*: **abdominales** (*Deporte*) abdominals; (*Anat*) abdominals, stomach muscles
abecedario [aβeθeˈðarjo] *nm* alphabet
abedul [aβeˈðul] *nm* birch
abeja [aˈβexa] *nf* bee; (*fig: hormiguita*) hard worker
abejorro [aβeˈxorro] *nm* bumblebee
aberración [aβerraˈθjon] *nf* aberration
aberrante [aβeˈrrante] *adj* (*disparatado*) ridiculous

abertura [aβerˈtura] *nf* = **apertura**
abertzale [aβerˈtʃale] *adj, nm/f* Basque nationalist
abeto [aˈβeto] *nm* fir
abierto, -a [aˈβjerto, a] *pp de* **abrir** ◼ *adj* open; (*fig: carácter*) frank
abigarrado, -a [aβiɣaˈrraðo, a] *adj* multicoloured; (*fig*) motley
abismal [aβisˈmal] *adj* (*fig*) vast, enormous
abismar [aβisˈmar] *vt* to humble, cast down; **abismarse** *vr* to sink; (*Am*) to be amazed; **abismarse en** (*fig*) to be plunged into
abismo [aˈβismo] *nm* abyss; **de sus ideas a las mías hay un** ~ our views are worlds apart
abjurar [aβxuˈrar] *vt* to abjure, forswear ◼ *vi*: ~ **de** to abjure, forswear
ablandar [aβlanˈdar] *vt* to soften up; (*conmover*) to touch; (*Culin*) to tenderize ◼ *vi*, **ablandarse** *vr* to get softer
abnegación [aβneɣaˈθjon] *nf* self-denial
abnegado, -a [aβneˈɣaðo, a] *adj* self-sacrificing
abobado, -a [aβoˈβaðo, a] *adj* silly
abobamiento [aβoβaˈmjento] *nm* (*asombro*) bewilderment
abocado, -a [aβoˈkaðo, a] *adj*: **verse** ~ **al desastre** to be heading for disaster
abochornar [aβotʃorˈnar] *vt* to embarrass; **abochornarse** *vr* to get flustered; (*Bot*) to wilt; **abochornarse de** to get embarrassed about
abofetear [aβofeteˈar] *vt* to slap (in the face)
abogacía [aβoɣaˈθia] *nf* legal profession; (*ejercicio*) practice of the law
abogado, -a [aβoˈɣaðo, a] *nm/f* lawyer; (*notario*) solicitor; (*asesor*) counsel; (*en tribunal*) barrister, advocate, attorney (*US*); ~ **defensor** defence lawyer *o* attorney (*US*); ~ **del diablo** devil's advocate
abogar [aβoˈɣar] *vi*: ~ **por** to plead for; (*fig*) to advocate
abogue *etc* [aˈβoɣe] *vb ver* **abogar**
abolengo [aβoˈlengo] *nm* ancestry, lineage
abolición [aβoliˈθjon] *nf* abolition
abolir [aβoˈlir] *vt* to abolish; (*cancelar*) to cancel
abolladura [aβoʎaˈðura] *nf* dent
abollar [aβoˈʎar] *vt* to dent
abominable [aβomiˈnaβle] *adj* abominable
abominación [aβominaˈθjon] *nf* abomination
abonado, -a [aβoˈnaðo, a] *adj* (*deuda*) paid (-up) ◼ *nm/f* subscriber
abonar [aβoˈnar] *vt* to pay; (*deuda*) to settle; (*terreno*) to fertilize; (*idea*) to endorse; **abonarse** *vr* to subscribe; ~ **dinero en una cuenta** to pay money into an account, credit

money to an account

abono [a'βono] nm payment; fertilizer; subscription

abordable [aβor'ðaβle] adj (persona) approachable

abordar [aβor'ðar] vt (barco) to board; (asunto) to broach; (individuo) to approach

aborigen [aβo'rixen] nm/f aborigine

aborrecer [aβorre'θer] vt to hate, loathe

aborrezca etc [aβo'rreθka] vb ver **aborrecer**

abortar [aβor'tar] vi (malparir) to have a miscarriage; (deliberadamente) to have an abortion

aborto [a'βorto] nm miscarriage; abortion

abotagado, -a [aβota'ɣaðo, a] adj swollen

abotonar [aβoto'nar] vt to button (up), do up

abovedado, -a [aβoβe'ðaðo, a] adj vaulted, domed

abr. abr (= abril) Apr

abrace etc [a'βraθe] vb ver **abrazar**

abrasar [aβra'sar] vt to burn (up); (Agr) to dry up, parch

abrazadera [aβraθa'ðera] nf bracket

abrazar [aβra'θar] vt to embrace, hug; **abrazarse** vr to embrace, hug each other

abrazo [a'βraθo] nm embrace, hug; **un ~** (en carta) with best wishes

abrebotellas [aβreβo'teλas] nm inv bottle opener

abrecartas [aβre'kartas] nm inv letter opener

abrelatas [aβre'latas] nm inv tin (Brit) o can (US) opener

abrevadero [aβreβa'ðero] nm watering place

abreviar [aβre'βjar] vt to abbreviate; (texto) to abridge; (plazo) to reduce ■ vi: **bueno, para ~** well, to cut a long story short

abreviatura [aβreβja'tura] nf abbreviation

abridor [aβri'ðor] nm (de botellas) bottle opener; (de latas) tin (Brit) o can (US) opener

abrigar [aβri'ɣar] vt (proteger) to shelter; (suj: ropa) to keep warm; (fig) to cherish; **abrigarse** vr (con ropa) to cover (o.s.) up; **abrigarse (de)** to take shelter (from), protect o.s. (from); **¡abrígate bien!** wrap up well!

abrigo [a'βriɣo] nm (prenda) coat, overcoat; (lugar protegido) shelter; **al ~ de** in the shelter of

abrigue etc [a'βriɣe] vb ver **abrigar**

abril [a'βril] nm April; ver tb **julio**

abrillantar [aβriλan'tar] vt (pulir) to polish; (fig) to enhance

abrir [a'βrir] vt to open (up); (camino etc) to open up; (apetito) to whet; (lista) to head ■ vi to open; **abrirse** vr to open (up); (extenderse) to open out; (cielo) to clear; **~ un negocio** to start up a business; **en un ~ y cerrar de ojos** in the twinkling of an eye; **abrirse paso** to find o force a way through

abrochar [aβro'tʃar] vt (con botones) to button (up); (zapato, con broche) to do up; **abrocharse** vr: **abrocharse los zapatos** to tie one's shoelaces

abrogación [aβroɣa'θjon] nf repeal

abrogar [aβro'ɣar] vt to repeal

abrumador, a [aβruma'ðor, a] adj (mayoría) overwhelming

abrumar [aβru'mar] vt to overwhelm; (sobrecargar) to weigh down

abrupto, -a [a'βrupto, a] adj abrupt; (empinado) steep

absceso [aβs'θeso] nm abscess

absentismo [aβsen'tismo] nm (de obreros) absenteeism

absolución [aβsolu'θjon] nf (Rel) absolution; (Jur) acquittal

absoluto, -a [aβso'luto, a] adj absolute; (total) utter, complete; **en ~** adv not at all

absolver [aβsol'βer] vt to absolve; (Jur) to pardon; (: acusado) to acquit

absorbente [aβsor'βente] adj absorbent; (interesante) absorbing, interesting; (exigente) demanding

absorber [aβsor'βer] vt to absorb; (embeber) to soak up; **absorberse** vr to become absorbed

absorción [aβsor'θjon] nf absorption; (Com) takeover

absorto, -a [aβ'sorto, a] pp de **absorber** ■ adj absorbed, engrossed

abstemio, -a [aβs'temjo, a] adj teetotal

abstención [aβsten'θjon] nf abstention

abstendré etc [aβsten'dre] vb ver **abstenerse**

abstenerse [aβste'nerse] vr: **~ (de)** to abstain o refrain (from)

abstenga etc [aβs'tenga] vb ver **abstenerse**

abstinencia [aβsti'nenθja] nf abstinence; (ayuno) fasting

abstracción [aβstrak'θjon] nf abstraction

abstracto, -a [aβ'strakto, a] adj abstract; **en ~** in the abstract

abstraer [aβstra'er] vt to abstract; **abstraerse** vr to be o become absorbed

abstraído, -a [aβstra'iðo, a] adj absent-minded

abstraiga etc [aβs'traiɣa], **abstraje** etc [aβs'traxe], **abstrayendo** etc [aβstra'jendo] vb ver **abstraer**

abstuve etc [aβs'tuβe] vb ver **abstenerse**

absuelto [aβ'swelto] pp de **absolver**

absurdo, -a [aβ'surðo, a] adj absurd; **lo ~ es que ...** the ridiculous thing is that ... ■ nm absurdity

abuchear [aβutʃe'ar] vt to boo

abucheo [aβu'tʃeo] nm booing; **ganarse un ~** (Teat) to be booed

abuela [a'βwela] nf grandmother;

¡**cuéntaselo a tu ~!** (*fam!*) do you think I was
born yesterday? (*fam*); **no tener/necesitar**
~ (*fam*) to be full of o.s./blow one's own
trumpet
abuelita [aβwe'lita] *nf* granny
abuelo [a'βwelo] *nm* grandfather;
(*antepasado*) ancestor; **abuelos** *nmpl*
grandparents
abulense [aβu'lense] *adj* of Ávila ■ *nm/f*
native *o* inhabitant of Ávila
abulia [a'βulja] *nf* lethargy
abúlico, -a [a'βuliko, a] *adj* lethargic
abultado, -a [aβul'taðo, a] *adj* bulky
abultar [aβul'tar] *vt* to enlarge; (*aumentar*) to
increase; (*fig*) to exaggerate ■ *vi* to be bulky
abundancia [aβun'danθja] *nf*: **una ~ de**
plenty of; **en ~** in abundance
abundante [aβun'dante] *adj* abundant,
plentiful
abundar [aβun'dar] *vi* to abound, be
plentiful; **~ en una opinión** to share an
opinion
aburguesarse [aβurɣe'sarse] *vr* to become
middle-class
aburrido, -a [aβu'rriðo, a] *adj* (*hastiado*)
bored; (*que aburre*) boring
aburrimiento [aβurri'mjento] *nm* boredom,
tedium
aburrir [aβu'rrir] *vt* to bore; **aburrirse** *vr* to
be bored, get bored; **aburrirse como una**
almeja *u* **ostra** to be bored stiff
abusar [aβu'sar] *vi* to go too far; **~ de** to abuse
abusivo, -a [aβu'siβo, a] *adj* (*precio*)
exorbitant
abuso [a'βuso] *nm* abuse; **~ de confianza**
betrayal of trust
abyecto, -a [aβ'jekto, a] *adj* wretched, abject
a. C. *abr* (= *antes de Cristo*) B.C.
a/c *abr* (= *al cuidado de*) c/o; (= *a cuenta*) on
account
acá [a'ka] *adv* (*lugar*) here; **pasearse de acá**
para allá to walk up and down; **¡vente para**
acá! come over here!; **¿de cuándo acá?** since
when?
acabado, -a [aka'βaðo, a] *adj* finished,
complete; (*perfecto*) perfect; (*agotado*) worn
out; (*fig*) masterly ■ *nm* finish
acabar [aka'βar] *vt* (*llevar a su fin*) to finish,
complete; (*consumir*) to use up; (*rematar*) to
finish off ■ *vi* to finish, end; (*morir*) to die;
acabarse *vr* to finish, stop; (*terminarse*) to be
over; (*agotarse*) to run out; **~ con** to put an
end to; **~ mal** to come to a sticky end; **esto**
~á conmigo this will be the end of me; **~**
de llegar to have just arrived; **acababa de**
hacerlo I had just done it; **~ haciendo** *o*
por hacer algo to end up (by) doing sth; **¡se**

acabó! (*¡basta!*) that's enough!; (*se terminó*)
it's all over!; **se me acabó el tabaco** I ran out
of cigarettes
acabóse [aka'βose] *nm*: **esto es el ~** this is
the limit
acacia [a'kaθja] *nf* acacia
academia [aka'ðemja] *nf* academy; (*Escol*)
private school; *ver tb* **colegio**
académico, -a [aka'ðemiko, a] *adj* academic
acaecer [akae'θer] *vi* to happen, occur
acaezca *etc* [aka'eθka] *vb ver* **acaecer**
acallar [aka'ʎar] *vt* (*silenciar*) to silence;
(*calmar*) to pacify
acalorado, -a [akalo'raðo, a] *adj* (*discusión*)
heated
acalorarse [akalo'rarse] *vr* (*fig*) to get heated
acampada [akam'paða] *nf*: **ir de ~** to go
camping
acampanado, -a [akampa'naðo, a] *adj*
flared
acampar [akam'par] *vi* to camp
acanalado, -a [akana'laðo, a] *adj* (*hierro*)
corrugated
acanalar [akana'lar] *vt* to groove; (*ondular*) to
corrugate
acantilado [akanti'laðo] *nm* cliff
acaparador, a [akapara'ðor, a] *nm/f*
monopolizer
acaparar [akapa'rar] *vt* to monopolize;
(*acumular*) to hoard
acápite [a'kapite] *nm* (*Am*) paragraph; **punto**
~ full stop, new paragraph
acaramelado, -a [akarame'laðo, a] *adj*
(*Culin*) toffee-coated; (*fig*) sugary
acariciar [akari'θjar] *vt* to caress; (*esperanza*)
to cherish
acarrear [akarre'ar] *vt* to transport; (*fig*)
to cause, result in; **le acarreó muchos**
disgustos it brought him lots of problems
acaso [a'kaso] *adv* perhaps, maybe ■ *nm*
chance; **¿~ es mi culpa?** (*Am fam*) what
makes you think it's my fault?; **(por) si ~**
(just) in case
acatamiento [akata'mjento] *nm* respect;
(*de la ley*) observance
acatar [aka'tar] *vt* to respect; (*ley*) to obey,
observe
acatarrarse [akata'rrarse] *vr* to catch a cold
acaudalado, -a [akauða'laðo, a] *adj* well-off
acaudillar [akauði'ʎar] *vt* to lead, command
acceder [akθe'ðer] *vi* to accede, agree; **~ a**
(*Inform*) to access
accesible [akθe'siβle] *adj* accessible; **~ a**
open to
accésit [ak'θesit] (*pl* **accésits** [ak'θesits]) *nm*
consolation prize
acceso [ak'θeso] *nm* access, entry; (*camino*)

access road; (*Med*) attack, fit; (*de cólera*) fit; (*Pol*) accession; (*Inform*) access; ~ **aleatorio/ directo/secuencial** o **en serie** (*Inform*) random/direct/sequential o serial access; **de ~ múltiple** multi-access

accesorio, -a [akθe'sorjo, a] *adj* accessory ■ *nm* accessory; **accesorios** *nmpl* (*Auto*) accessories, extras; (*Teat*) props

accidentado, -a [akθiðen'taðo, a] *adj* uneven; (*montañoso*) hilly; (*azaroso*) eventful ■ *nm/f* accident victim

accidental [akθiðen'tal] *adj* accidental; (*empleo*) temporary

accidentarse [akθiðen'tarse] *vr* to have an accident

accidente [akθi'ðente] *nm* accident; **por ~** by chance; **accidentes** *nmpl* unevenness *sg*, roughness *sg*

acción [ak'θjon] *nf* action; (*acto*) action, act; (*Teat*) plot; (*Com*) share; (*Jur*) action, lawsuit; **capital en acciones** share capital; **~ liberada/ordinaria/preferente** fully-paid/ordinary/preference share

accionamiento [akθjona'mjento] *nm* (*de máquina*) operation

accionar [akθjo'nar] *vt* to work, operate

accionista [akθjo'nista] *nm/f* shareholder

acebo [a'θeβo] *nm* holly; (*árbol*) holly tree

acechanza [aθe'tʃanθa] *nf* = **acecho**

acechar [aθe'tʃar] *vt* to spy on; (*aguardar*) to lie in wait for

acecho [a'θetʃo] *nm*: **estar al ~ (de)** to lie in wait (for)

acedera [aθe'ðera] *nf* sorrel

aceitar [aθei'tar] *vt* to oil, lubricate

aceite [a'θeite] *nm* oil; (*de oliva*) olive oil; **~ de hígado de bacalao** cod-liver oil

aceitera [aθei'tera] *nf* oilcan

aceitoso, -a [aθei'toso, a] *adj* oily

aceituna [aθei'tuna] *nf* olive

aceitunado, -a [aθeitu'naðo, a] *adj* olive *cpd*; **de tez aceitunada** olive-skinned

acelerador [aθelera'ðor] *nm* accelerator

acelerar [aθele'rar] *vt* to accelerate; **acelerarse** *vr* to hurry

acelga [a'θelɣa] *nf* chard, beet

acendrado, -a [aθen'draðo, a] *adj*: **de ~ carácter español** typically Spanish

acendrar [aθen'drar] *vt* to purify

acento [a'θento] *nm* accent; (*acentuación*) stress; **~ cerrado** strong o thick accent

acentuar [aθen'twar] *vt* to accent; to stress; (*fig*) to accentuate

acepción [aθep'θjon] *nf* meaning

aceptación [aθepta'θjon] *nf* acceptance; (*aprobación*) approval

aceptar [aθep'tar] *vt* to accept; to approve

acequia [a'θekja] *nf* irrigation ditch

acera [a'θera] *nf* pavement (*Brit*), sidewalk (*US*)

acerado, -a [aθe'raðo, a] *adj* steel; (*afilado*) sharp; (*fig: duro*) steely; (: *mordaz*) biting

acerbo, -a [a'θerβo, a] *adj* bitter; (*fig*) harsh

acerca [a'θerka]: **~ de** *prep* about, concerning

acercar [aθer'kar] *vt* to bring o move nearer; **acercarse** *vr* to approach, come near

acerico [aθe'riko] *nm* pincushion

acero [a'θero] *nm* steel; **~ inoxidable** stainless steel

acerque *etc* [a'θerke] *vb ver* **acercar**

acérrimo, -a [a'θerrimo, a] *adj* (*partidario*) staunch; (*enemigo*) bitter

acertado, -a [aθer'taðo, a] *adj* correct; (*apropiado*) apt; (*sensato*) sensible

acertar [aθer'tar] *vt* (*blanco*) to hit; (*solución*) to get right; (*adivinar*) to guess ■ *vi* to get it right, be right; **~ a** to manage to; **~ con** to happen o hit on

acertijo [aθer'tixo] *nm* riddle, puzzle

acervo [a'θerβo] *nm* heap; **~ común** undivided estate

achacar [atʃa'kar] *vt* to attribute

achacoso, -a [atʃa'koso, a] *adj* sickly

achantar [atʃan'tar] *vt* (*fam*) to scare, frighten; **achantarse** *vr* to back down

achaque *etc* [a'tʃake] *vb ver* **achacar** ■ *nm* ailment

achatar [atʃa'tar] *vt* to flatten

achicar [atʃi'kar] *vt* to reduce; (*humillar*) to humiliate; (*Naut*) to bale out; **achicarse** *vr* (*ropa*) to shrink; (*fig*) to humble o.s.

achicharrar [atʃitʃa'rrar] *vt* to scorch, burn

achicoria [atʃi'korja] *nf* chicory

achinado, -a [atʃi'naðo, a] *adj* (*ojos*) slanting; (*Am*) half-caste

achique *etc* [a'tʃike] *vb ver* **achicar**

acholado, -a [atʃo'laðo, a] *adj* (*Am*) half-caste

achuchar [atʃu'tʃar] *vt* to crush

achuchón [atʃu'tʃon] *nm* shove; **tener un ~** (*Med*) to be poorly

achuras [a'tʃuras] *nf* (*Am, Culin*) offal

aciago, -a [a'θjaɣo, a] *adj* ill-fated, fateful

acicalar [aθika'lar] *vt* to polish; (*adornar*) to bedeck; **acicalarse** *vr* to get dressed up

acicate [aθi'kate] *nm* spur; (*fig*) incentive

acidez [aθi'ðeθ] *nf* acidity

ácido, -a ['aθiðo, a] *adj* sour, acid ■ *nm* acid; (*fam: droga*) LSD

acierto *etc* [a'θjerto] *vb ver* **acertar** ■ *nm* success; (*buen paso*) wise move; (*solución*) solution; (*habilidad*) skill, ability; (*al adivinar*) good guess; **fue un ~ suyo** it was a sensible choice on his part

aclamación [aklama'θjon] *nf* acclamation; (*aplausos*) applause

aclamar [akla'mar] vt to acclaim; to applaud
aclaración [aklara'θjon] nf clarification, explanation
aclarar [akla'rar] vt to clarify, explain; (ropa) to rinse ■ vi to clear up; **aclararse** vr (suj: persona: explicarse) to understand; (fig: asunto) to become clear; **aclararse la garganta** to clear one's throat
aclaratorio, -a [aklara'torjo, a] adj explanatory
aclimatación [aklimata'θjon] nf acclimatization
aclimatar [aklima'tar] vt to acclimatize; **aclimatarse** vr to become o get acclimatized; **aclimatarse a algo** to get used to sth
acné [ak'ne] nm acne
ACNUR nm abr (= Alto Comisionado de las Naciones Unidas para los Refugiados) UNHCR f
acobardar [akoβar'ðar] vt to daunt, intimidate; **acobardarse** vr (atemorizarse) to be intimidated; (echarse atrás): **acobardarse (ante)** to shrink back (from)
acodarse [ako'ðarse] vr: ~ **en** to lean on
acogedor, a [akoxe'ðor, a] adj welcoming; (hospitalario) hospitable
acoger [ako'xer] vt to welcome; (abrigar) to shelter; **acogerse** vr to take refuge; **acogerse a** (pretexto) to take refuge in; (ley) to resort to
acogida [ako'xiða] nf reception; refuge
acoja etc [a'koxa] vb ver **acoger**
acojonante [akoxo'nante] adj (Esp fam) tremendous
acolchar [akol'tʃar] vt to pad; (fig) to cushion
acólito [a'kolito] nm (Rel) acolyte; (fig) minion
acometer [akome'ter] vt to attack; (emprender) to undertake
acometida [akome'tiða] nf attack, assault
acomodado, -a [akomo'ðaðo, a] adj (persona) well-to-do
acomodador, a [akomoða'ðor, a] nm/f usher(ette)
acomodar [akomo'ðar] vt to adjust; (alojar) to accommodate; **acomodarse** vr to conform; (instalarse) to install o.s.; (adaptarse) to adapt o.s.; **¡acomódese a su gusto!** make yourself comfortable!
acomodaticio, -a [akomoða'tiθjo, a] adj (pey) accommodating, obliging; (manejable) pliable
acompañamiento [akompaɲa'mjento] nm (Mus) accompaniment
acompañante, -a [akompa'ɲante, a] nm/f companion
acompañar [akompa'ɲar] vt to accompany, go with; (documentos) to enclose; ¿quieres

que te acompañe? do you want me to come with you?; ~ **a algn a la puerta** to see sb to the door o out; **le acompaño en el sentimiento** please accept my condolences
acompasar [akompa'sar] vt (Mus) to mark the rhythm of
acomplejado, -a [akomple'xaðo, a] adj neurotic
acomplejar [akomple'xar] vt to give a complex to; **acomplejarse** vr: **acomplejarse (con)** to get a complex (about)
acondicionado, -a [akondiθjo'naðo, a] adj (Tec) in good condition
acondicionador [akondiθjona'ðor] nm conditioner
acondicionar [akondiθjo'nar] vt to get ready, prepare; (pelo) to condition
acongojar [akongo'xar] vt to distress, grieve
aconsejable [akonse'xaβle] adj advisable
aconsejar [akonse'xar] vt to advise, counsel; **aconsejarse** vr: **aconsejarse con o de** to consult
acontecer [akonte'θer] vi to happen, occur
acontecimiento [akonteθi'mjento] nm event
acontezca etc [akon'teθka] vb ver **acontecer**
acopiar [ako'pjar] vt (recoger) to gather; (Com) to buy up
acopio [a'kopjo] nm store, stock
acoplador [akopla'ðor] nm: ~ **acústico** (Inform) acoustic coupler
acoplamiento [akopla'mjento] nm coupling, joint
acoplar [ako'plar] vt to fit; (Elec) to connect; (vagones) to couple
acoquinar [akoki'nar] vt to scare; **acoquinarse** vr to get scared
acorazado, -a [akora'θaðo, a] adj armour-plated, armoured ■ nm battleship
acordar [akor'ðar] vt (resolver) to agree, resolve; **acordarse** vr to agree; **acordarse (de algo)** to remember (sth)
acorde [a'korðe] adj (Mus) harmonious; ~ **con** (medidas etc) in keeping with ■ nm chord
acordeón [akorðe'on] nm accordion
acordonado, -a [akorðo'naðo, a] adj (calle) cordoned-off
acorralar [akorra'lar] vt to round up, corral; (fig) to intimidate
acortar [akor'tar] vt to shorten; (duración) to cut short; (cantidad) to reduce; **acortarse** vr to become shorter
acosar [ako'sar] vt to pursue relentlessly; (fig) to hound, pester; ~ **a algn a preguntas** to pester sb with questions
acoso [a'koso] nm relentless pursuit; (fig) hounding; ~ **sexual** sexual harassment

acostar [akos'tar] *vt* (*en cama*) to put to bed; (*en suelo*) to lay down; (*barco*) to bring alongside; **acostarse** *vr* to go to bed; to lie down

acostumbrado, -a [akostum'braðo, a] *adj* (*habitual*) usual; **estar ~ a (hacer) algo** to be used to (doing) sth

acostumbrar [akostum'brar] *vt*: **~ a algn a algo** to get sb used to sth ▪ *vi*: **~ (a hacer algo)** to be in the habit (of doing sth); **acostumbrarse** *vr*: **acostumbrarse a** to get used to

acotación [akota'θjon] *nf* (*apunte*) marginal note; (*Geo*) elevation mark; (*de límite*) boundary mark; (*Teat*) stage direction

acotar [ako'tar] *vt* (*terreno*) to mark out; (*fig*) to limit; (*caza*) to protect

acotejar [akote'xar] *vt* (*Am*) to put in order, arrange

ácrata ['akrata] *adj, nm/f* anarchist

acre ['akre] *adj* (*sabor*) sharp, bitter; (*olor*) acrid; (*fig*) biting ▪ *nm* acre

acrecentar [akreθen'tar] *vt* to increase, augment

acreciente *etc* [akre'θjente] *vb ver* **acrecentar**

acreditado, -a [akreði'taðo, a] *adj* (*Pol*) accredited; (*Com*): **una casa acreditada** a reputable firm

acreditar [akreði'tar] *vt* (*garantizar*) to vouch for, guarantee; (*autorizar*) to authorize; (*dar prueba de*) to prove; (*Com: abonar*) to credit; (*embajador*) to accredit; **acreditarse** *vr* to become famous; (*demostrar valía*) to prove one's worth; **acreditarse de** to get a reputation for

acreedor, a [akree'ðor, a] *adj*: **~ a** worthy of ▪ *nm/f* creditor; **~ común/diferido/con garantía** (*Com*) unsecured/deferred/secured creditor

acribillar [akriβi'ʎar] *vt*: **~ a balazos** to riddle with bullets

acrimonia [akri'monja], **acritud** [akri'tuð] *nf* acrimony

acrobacia [akro'βaθja] *nf* acrobatics; **~ aérea** aerobatics

acróbata [a'kroβata] *nm/f* acrobat

acta ['akta] *nf* certificate; (*de comisión*) minutes *pl*, record; **~ de nacimiento/de matrimonio** birth/marriage certificate; **~ notarial** affidavit; **levantar ~** (*Jur*) to make a formal statement *o* deposition

actitud [akti'tuð] *nf* attitude; (*postura*) posture; **adoptar una ~ firme** to take a firm stand

activar [akti'βar] *vt* to activate; (*acelerar*) to speed up

actividad [aktiβi'ðað] *nf* activity; **estar en**

plena ~ to be in full swing

activo, -a [ak'tiβo, a] *adj* active; (*vivo*) lively ▪ *nm* (*Com*) assets *pl*; **~ y pasivo** assets and liabilities; **~ circulante/fijo/inmaterial/ invisible** (*Com*) current/fixed/intangible/ invisible assets; **~ realizable** liquid assets; **activos congelados** *o* **bloqueados** frozen assets; **~ tóxico** toxic asset; **estar en ~** (*Mil*) to be on active service

acto ['akto] *nm* act, action; (*ceremonia*) ceremony; (*Teat*) act; **en el ~** immediately; **hacer ~ de presencia** (*asistir*) to attend (formally)

actor [ak'tor] *nm* actor; (*Jur*) plaintiff

actora [ak'tora] *adj*: **parte ~** prosecution; (*demandante*) plaintiff

actriz [ak'triθ] *nf* actress

actuación [aktwa'θjon] *nf* action; (*comportamiento*) conduct, behaviour; (*Jur*) proceedings *pl*; (*desempeño*) performance

actual [ak'twal] *adj* present(-day), current; **el 6 del ~** the 6th of this month

actualice *etc* [aktwa'liθe] *vb ver* **actualizar**

actualidad [aktwali'ðað] *nf* present; **actualidades** *nfpl* news *sg*; **en la ~** nowadays, at present; **ser de gran ~** to be current

actualización [aktwaliθa'θjon] *nf* updating, modernization

actualizar [aktwali'θar] *vt* to update, modernize

actualmente [aktwal'mente] *adv* at present; (*hoy día*) nowadays

actuar [ak'twar] *vi* (*obrar*) to work, operate; (*actor*) to act, perform ▪ *vt* to work, operate; **~ de** to act as

actuario, -a [ak'twarjo, a] *nm/f* clerk; (*Com*) actuary

acuarela [akwa'rela] *nf* watercolour

acuario [a'kwarjo] *nm* aquarium; **A~** (*Astro*) Aquarius

acuartelar [akwarte'lar] *vt* (*Mil: alojar*) to quarter

acuático, -a [a'kwatiko, a] *adj* aquatic

acuchillar [akutʃi'ʎar] *vt* (*Tec*) to plane (down), smooth

acuciar [aku'θjar] *vt* to urge on

acuclillarse [akukli'ʎarse] *vr* to crouch down

ACUDE [a'kuðe] *nf abr* = **Asociación de Consumidores y Usuarios de España**

acudir [aku'ðir] *vi* to attend, turn up; **~ a** to turn to; **~ en ayuda de** to go to the aid of; **~ a una cita** to keep an appointment; **~ a una llamada** to answer a call; **no tener a quién ~** to have nobody to turn to

acuerdo *etc* [a'kwerðo] *vb ver* **acordar** ▪ *nm* agreement; (*Pol*) resolution; **~ de**

7

pago respectivo (*Com*) knock-for-knock agreement; **A~ general sobre aranceles aduaneros y comercio** (*Com*) General Agreement on Tariffs and Trade; **tomar un ~** to pass a resolution; **¡de ~!** agreed!; **de ~ con** (*persona*) in agreement with; (*acción, documento*) in accordance with; **de común ~** by common consent; **estar de ~** (*persona*) to agree; **llegar a un ~** to come to an understanding

acueste *etc* [a'kweste] *vb ver* **acostar**

acullá [aku'ʎa] *adv* over there

acumular [akumu'lar] *vt* to accumulate, collect

acunar [aku'nar] *vt* to rock (to sleep)

acuñar [aku'ɲar] *vt* (*moneda*) to mint; (*frase*) to coin

acuoso, -a [a'kwoso, a] *adj* watery

acupuntura [akupun'tura] *nf* acupuncture

acurrucarse [akurru'karse] *vr* to crouch; (*ovillarse*) to curl up

acurruque *etc* [aku'rruke] *vb ver* **acurrucarse**

acusación [akusa'θjon] *nf* accusation

acusado, -a [aku'saðo, a] *adj* (*Jur*) accused; (*marcado*) marked; (*acento*) strong

acusar [aku'sar] *vt* to accuse; (*revelar*) to reveal; (*denunciar*) to denounce; (*emoción*) to show; **~ recibo** to acknowledge receipt; **su rostro acusó extrañeza** his face registered surprise; **acusarse** *vr*: **acusarse (de)** to confess (to)

acuse [a'kuse] *nm*: **~ de recibo** acknowledgement of receipt

acústico, -a [a'kustiko, a] *adj* acoustic ▪ *nf* (*de una sala etc*) acoustics *pl*; (*ciencia*) acoustics *sg*

ADA ['aða] *nf abr* (*Esp*: = *Ayuda del Automovilista*) ≈ AA, RAC (*Brit*), AAA (*US*)

adagio [a'ðaxjo] *nm* adage; (*Mus*) adagio

adalid [aða'lið] *nm* leader, champion

adaptación [aðapta'θjon] *nf* adaptation

adaptador [aðapta'ðor] *nm* (*Elec*) adapter; **~ universal** universal adapter

adaptar [aðap'tar] *vt* to adapt; (*acomodar*) to fit; (*convertir*): **~ (para)** to convert (to)

adecentar [aðeθen'tar] *vt* to tidy up

adecuado, -a [aðe'kwaðo, a] *adj* (*apto*) suitable; (*oportuno*) appropriate; **el hombre ~ para el puesto** the right man for the job

adecuar [aðe'kwar] *vt* (*adaptar*) to adapt; (*hacer apto*) to make suitable

adefesio [aðe'fesjo] *nm* (*fam*): **estaba hecha un ~** she looked a sight

a. de J.C. *abr* (= *antes de Jesucristo*) B.C.

adelantado, -a [aðelan'taðo, a] *adj* advanced; (*reloj*) fast; **pagar por ~** to pay in advance

adelantamiento [aðelanta'mjento] *nm*

advance, advancement; (*Auto*) overtaking

adelantar [aðelan'tar] *vt* to move forward; (*avanzar*) to advance; (*acelerar*) to speed up; (*Auto*) to overtake ▪ *vi* (*ir delante*) to go ahead; (*progresar*) to improve; **adelantarse** *vr* (*tomar la delantera*) to go forward, advance; **adelantarse a algn** to get ahead of sb; **adelantarse a los deseos de algn** to anticipate sb's wishes

adelante [aðe'lante] *adv* forward(s), onward(s), ahead ▪ *excl* come in!; **de hoy en ~** from now on; **más ~** later on; (*más allá*) further on

adelanto [aðe'lanto] *nm* advance; (*mejora*) improvement; (*progreso*) progress; (*dinero*) advance; **los adelantos de la ciencia** the advances of science

adelgace *etc* [aðel'ɣaθe] *vb ver* **adelgazar**

adelgazar [aðelɣa'θar] *vt* to thin (down); (*afilar*) to taper ▪ *vi* to get thin; (*con régimen*) to slim down, lose weight

ademán [aðe'man] *nm* gesture; **ademanes** *nmpl* manners; **en ~ de** as if to

además [aðe'mas] *adv* besides; (*por otra parte*) moreover; (*también*) also; **~ de** besides, in addition to

ADENA [a'ðena] *nf abr* (*Esp*: = *Asociación para la Defensa de la Naturaleza*) organization for nature conservation

adentrarse [aðen'trarse] *vr*: **~ en** to go into, get inside; (*penetrar*) to penetrate (into)

adentro [a'ðentro] *adv* inside, in; **mar ~** out at sea; **tierra ~** inland ▪ *nm*: **dijo para sus adentros** he said to himself

adepto, -a [a'ðepto, a] *nm/f* supporter

aderece *etc* [aðe'reθe] *vb ver* **aderezar**

aderezar [aðere'θar] *vt* (*ensalada*) to dress; (*comida*) to season

aderezo [aðe'reθo] *nm* dressing; seasoning

adeudar [aðeu'ðar] *vt* to owe; **adeudarse** *vr* to run into debt; **~ una suma en una cuenta** to debit an account with a sum

adherirse [aðe'rirse] *vr*: **~ a** to adhere to; (*fig*) to follow

adhesión [aðe'sjon] *nf* adhesion; (*fig*) adherence

adhesivo, -a [aðe'siβo, a] *adj* adhesive ▪ *nm* sticker

adhiera *etc* [a'ðjera], **adhiriendo** *etc* [aði'rjendo] *vb ver* **adherirse**

adicción [aðik'θion] *nf* addiction

adición [aði'θjon] *nf* addition

adicional [aðiθjo'nal] *adj* additional; (*Inform*) add-on

adicionar [aðiθjo'nar] *vt* to add

adicto, -a [a'ðikto, a] *adj*: **~ a** (*droga etc*) addicted to; (*dedicado*) devoted to ▪ *nm/f* supporter, follower; (toxicómano etc) addict

adiestrar [aðjes'trar] vt to train, teach; (conducir) to guide, lead; **adiestrarse** vr to practise; (aprender) to train o.s.

adinerado, -a [aðine'raðo, a] adj wealthy

adiós [a'ðjos] excl (para despedirse) goodbye!, cheerio!; (al pasar) hello!

aditivo [aði'tiβo] nm additive

adivinanza [aðiβi'nanθa] nf riddle

adivinar [aðiβi'nar] vt (profetizar) to prophesy; (conjeturar) to guess

adivino, -a [aði'βino, a] nm/f fortune-teller

adj abr (= adjunto) encl; (= adjetivo) adj

adjetivo [aðxe'tiβo] nm adjective

adjudicación [aðxuðika'θjon] nf award; (Com) adjudication

adjudicar [aðxuði'kar] vt to award; **adjudicarse** vr: to appropriate

adjudique etc [aðxu'ðike] vb ver **adjudicar**

adjuntar [aðxun'tar] vt to attach, enclose

adjunto, -a [að'xunto, a] adj attached, enclosed ■ nm/f assistant

adminículo [aðmi'nikulo] nm gadget

administración [aðministra'θjon] nf administration; (dirección) management; **~ pública** civil service; **A~ de Correos** General Post Office

administrador, a [aðministra'ðor, a] nm/f administrator; manager(ess)

administrar [aðminis'trar] vt to administer

administrativo, -a [aðministra'tiβo, a] adj administrative

admirable [aðmi'raβle] adj admirable

admiración [aðmira'θjon] nf admiration; (asombro) wonder; (Ling) exclamation mark

admirar [aðmi'rar] vt to admire; (extrañar) to surprise; **admirarse** vr to be surprised; **se admiró de saberlo** he was amazed to hear it; **no es de ~ que ...** it's not surprising that ...

admisible [aðmi'siβle] adj admissible

admisión [aðmi'sjon] nf admission; (reconocimiento) acceptance

admitir [aðmi'tir] vt to admit; (aceptar) to accept; (dudas) to leave room for; **esto no admite demora** this must be dealt with immediately

admón. abr (= administración) admin

admonición [aðmoni'θjon] nf warning

ADN nm abr (= acido desoxirribonucleico) DNA

adobar [aðo'βar] vt (preparar) to prepare; (cocinar) to season

adobe [a'ðoβe] nm adobe, sun-dried brick

adocenado, -a [aðoθe'naðo, a] adj (fam) mediocre

adoctrinar [aðoktri'nar] vt to indoctrinate

adolecer [aðole'θer] vi: **~ de** to suffer from

adolescente [aðoles'θente] nm/f adolescent, teenager ■ adj adolescent, teenage

adolezca etc [aðo'leθka] vb ver **adolecer**

adonde [a'ðonde] adv (to) where

adónde [a'ðonde] adv = **dónde**

adondequiera [aðonde'kjera] adv wherever

adopción [aðop'θjon] nf adoption

adoptar [aðop'tar] vt to adopt

adoptivo, -a [aðop'tiβo, a] adj (padres) adoptive; (hijo) adopted

adoquín [aðo'kin] nm paving stone

adorar [aðo'rar] vt to adore

adormecer [aðorme'θer] vt to put to sleep; **adormecerse** vr to become sleepy; (dormirse) to fall asleep

adormezca etc [aðor'meθka] vb ver **adormecer**

adormilarse [aðormi'larse] vr to doze

adornar [aðor'nar] vt to adorn

adorno [a'ðorno] nm adornment; (decoración) decoration

adosado, -a [aðo'saðo, a] adj (casa) semidetached

adquiera etc [að'kjera] vb ver **adquirir**

adquirir [aðki'rir] vt to acquire, obtain

adquisición [aðkisi'θjon] nf acquisition; (compra) purchase

adrede [a'ðreðe] adv on purpose

Adriático [að'rjatiko] nm: **el (Mar) ~** the Adriatic (Sea)

adscribir [aðskri'βir] vt to appoint; **estuvo adscrito al servicio de ...** he was attached to ...

adscrito [að'skrito] pp de **adscribir**

ADSL nm abr ADSL

aduana [a'ðwana] nf customs pl; (impuesto) (customs) duty

aduanero, -a [aðwa'nero, a] adj customs cpd ■ nm/f customs officer

aducir [aðu'θir] vt to adduce; (dar como prueba) to offer as proof

adueñarse [aðwe'narse] vr: **~ de** to take possession of

adulación [aðula'θjon] nf flattery

adular [aðu'lar] vt to flatter

adulterar [aðulte'rar] vt to adulterate ■ vi to commit adultery

adulterio [aðul'terjo] nm adultery

adúltero, -a [a'ðultero, a] adj adulterous ■ nm/f adulterer/adulteress

adulto, -a [a'ðulto, a] adj, nm/f adult

adusto, -a [a'ðusto, a] adj stern; (austero) austere

aduzca etc [a'ðuθka] vb ver **aducir**

advenedizo, -a [aðβene'ðiθo, a] nm/f upstart

advenimiento [aðβeni'mjento] nm arrival; (al trono) accession

adverbio [að'βerβjo] *nm* adverb
adversario, -a [aðβer'sarjo, a] *nm/f* adversary
adversidad [aðβersi'ðað] *nf* adversity; (*contratiempo*) setback
adverso, -a [að'βerso, a] *adj* adverse; (*suerte*) bad
advertencia [aðβer'tenθja] *nf* warning; (*prefacio*) preface, foreword
advertir [aðβer'tir] *vt* (*observar*) to notice; (*avisar*): ~ **a algn de** to warn sb about o of
Adviento [að'βjento] *nm* Advent
advierta *etc* [að'βjerta], **advirtiendo** *etc* [aðβir'tjendo] *vb ver* **advertir**
adyacente [aðja'θente] *adj* adjacent
aéreo, -a [a'ereo, a] *adj* aerial; (*tráfico*) air *cpd*
aerobic [ae'roβik] *nm* aerobics *sg*
aerodeslizador [aeroðesliθa'ðor] *nm* hovercraft
aerodinámico, -a [aeroði'namiko, a] *adj* aerodynamic
aeródromo [ae'roðromo] *nm* aerodrome
aerograma [aero'ɣrama] *nm* airmail letter
aeromodelismo [aeromoðe'lismo] *nm* model aircraft making, aeromodelling
aeromozo, -a [aero'moso, a] *nm/f* (*Am*) flight attendant, air steward(ess)
aeronáutico, -a [aero'nautiko, a] *adj* aeronautical
aeronave [aero'naβe] *nm* spaceship
aeroplano [aero'plano] *nm* aeroplane
aeropuerto [aero'pwerto] *nm* airport
aerosol [aero'sol] *nm* aerosol, spray
a/f *abr* (= *a favor*) in favour
afabilidad [afaβili'ðað] *nf* affability, pleasantness
afable [a'faβle] *adj* affable, pleasant
afamado, -a [afa'maðo, a] *adj* famous
afán [a'fan] *nm* hard work; (*deseo*) desire; **con** ~ keenly
afanar [afa'nar] *vt* to harass; (*fam*) to pinch; **afanarse** *vr*: **afanarse por** to strive to
afanoso, -a [afa'noso, a] *adj* (*trabajo*) hard; (*trabajador*) industrious
AFE ['afe] *nf abr* (= *Asociación de Futbolistas Españoles*) ≈ F.A
afear [afe'ar] *vt* to disfigure
afección [afek'θjon] *nf* affection; (*Med*) disease
afectación [afekta'θjon] *nf* affectation
afectado, -a [afek'taðo, a] *adj* affected
afectar [afek'tar] *vt* to affect, have an effect on; (*Am*: *dañar*) to hurt; **por lo que afecta a esto** as far as this is concerned
afectísimo, -a [afek'tisimo, a] *adj* affectionate; **suyo** ~ yours truly
afectivo, -a [afek'tiβo, a] *adj* affective

afecto, -a [a'fekto, a] *adj*: ~ **a** fond of; (*Jur*) subject to ■ *nm* affection; **tenerle** ~ **a algn** to be fond of sb
afectuoso, -a [afek'twoso, a] *adj* affectionate
afeitar [afei'tar] *vt* to shave; **afeitarse** *vr* to shave
afeminado, -a [afemi'naðo, a] *adj* effeminate
aferrar [afe'rrar] *vt* to moor; (*fig*) to grasp ■ *vi* to moor; **aferrarse** *vr* (*agarrarse*) to cling on; **aferrarse a un principio** to stick to a principle; **aferrarse a una esperanza** to cling to a hope
Afganistán [afɣanis'tan] *nm* Afghanistan
afgano, -a [af'ɣano, a] *adj, nm/f* Afghan
afiance *etc* [a'fjanθe] *vb ver* **afianzar**
afianzamiento [afjanθa'mjento] *nm* strengthening; security
afianzar [afjan'θar] *vt* to strengthen, secure; **afianzarse** *vr* to steady o.s.; (*establecerse*) to become established
afiche [a'fitʃe] *nm* (*Am*) poster
afición [afi'θjon] *nf*: ~ **a** fondness o liking for; **la** ~ the fans *pl*; **pinto por** ~ I paint as a hobby
aficionado, -a [afiθjo'naðo, a] *adj* keen, enthusiastic; (*no profesional*) amateur ■ *nm/f* enthusiast, fan; amateur
aficionar [afiθjo'nar] *vt*: ~ **a algn a algo** to make sb like sth; **aficionarse** *vr*: **aficionarse a algo** to grow fond of sth
afilado, -a [afi'laðo, a] *adj* sharp
afilador [afila'ðor] *nm* knife grinder
afilalápices [afila'lapiθes] *nm inv* pencil sharpener
afilar [afi'lar] *vt* to sharpen; **afilarse** *vr* (*cara*) to grow thin
afiliación [afilja'θjon] *nf* (*de sindicatos*) membership
afiliado, -a [afi'ljaðo, a] *adj* subsidiary ■ *nm/f* affiliate
afiliarse [afi'ljarse] *vr* to affiliate
afín [a'fin] *adj* (*parecido*) similar; (*conexo*) related
afinar [afi'nar] *vt* (*Tec*) to refine; (*Mus*) to tune ■ *vi* to play/sing in tune
afincarse [afin'karse] *vr* to settle
afinidad [afini'ðað] *nf* affinity; (*parentesco*) relationship; **por** ~ by marriage
afirmación [afirma'θjon] *nf* affirmation
afirmar [afir'mar] *vt* to affirm, state; (*sostener*) to strengthen; **afirmarse** *vr* (*recuperar el equilibrio*) to steady o.s.; **afirmarse en lo dicho** to stand by what one has said
afirmativo, -a [afirma'tiβo, a] *adj* affirmative

aflicción [aflik'θjon] *nf* affliction; (*dolor*) grief

afligir [afli'xir] *vt* to afflict; (*apenar*) to distress; **afligirse** *vr*: **afligirse (por** *o* **con** *o* **de**) to grieve (about *o* at); **no te aflijas tanto** you must not let it affect you like this

aflija *etc* [a'flixa] *vb ver* **afligir**

aflojar [aflo'xar] *vt* to slacken; (*desatar*) to loosen, undo; (*relajar*) to relax ▪ *vi* (*amainar*) to drop; (*bajar*) to go down; **aflojarse** *vr* to relax

aflorar [aflo'rar] *vi* (*Geo*,*fig*) to come to the surface, emerge

afluencia [aflu'enθja] *nf* flow

afluente [aflu'ente] *adj* flowing ▪ *nm* (*Geo*) tributary

afluir [aflu'ir] *vi* to flow

afluya *etc* [a'fluja], **afluyendo** *etc* [aflu'jendo] *vb ver* **afluir**

afmo., -a. *abr* (= *afectísimo, a suyo, a*) Yours

afónico, -a [a'foniko, a] *adj*: **estar ~** to have a sore throat; to have lost one's voice

aforar [afo'rar] *vt* (*Tec*) to gauge; (*fig*) to value

aforo [a'foro] *nm* (*Tec*) gauging; (*de teatro etc*) capacity; **el teatro tiene un ~ de 2,000** the theatre can seat 2,000

afortunado, -a [afortu'naðo, a] *adj* fortunate, lucky

afrancesado, -a [afranθe'saðo, a] *adj* francophile; (*pey*) Frenchified

afrenta [a'frenta] *nf* affront, insult; (*deshonra*) dishonour (*Brit*), dishonor (*US*), shame

afrentoso, -a [afren'toso, a] *adj* insulting; shameful

África ['afrika] *nf* Africa; **África del Sur** South Africa

africano, -a [afri'kano, a] *adj, nm/f* African

afrontar [afron'tar] *vt* to confront; (*poner cara a cara*) to bring face to face

after ['after] (*pl* **afters** *o* **~**) *nm*, **afterhours** ['afterauars] *nm inv* after-hours club

afuera [a'fwera] *adv* out, outside; **por ~** on the outside; **afueras** *nfpl* outskirts

ag. *abr* (= *agosto*) Aug

agachar [aɣa'tʃar] *vt* to bend, bow; **agacharse** *vr* to stoop, bend

agalla [a'ɣaʎa] *nf* (*Zool*) gill; **agallas** *nfpl* (*Med*) tonsillitis *sg*; (*Anat*) tonsils; **tener agallas** (*fam*) to have guts

agarradera [aɣarra'ðera] *nf* (*Am*), **agarradero** [aɣarra'ðero] *nm* handle; **agarraderas** *nfpl* pull *sg*, influence *sg*

agarrado, -a [aɣa'rraðo, a] *adj* mean, stingy

agarrar [aɣa'rrar] *vt* to grasp, grab; (*Am*) to take, catch ▪ *vi* (*planta*) to take root; **agarrarse** *vr* to hold on (tightly); (*meterse*

uno con otro*) to grapple (with each other); **agarrársela con algn** (*Am*) to pick on sb; **agarró y se fue** (*esp Am fam*) he upped and went

agarrotar [aɣarro'tar] *vt* (*lío*) to tie tightly; (*persona*) to squeeze tightly; (*reo*) to garrotte; **agarrotarse** *vr* (*motor*) to seize up; (*Med*) to stiffen

agasajar [aɣasa'xar] *vt* to treat well, fête

agave [a'ɣaβe] *nf* agave

agazapar [aɣaθa'par] *vt* (*coger*) to grab hold of; **agazaparse** *vr* (*agacharse*) to crouch down

agencia [a'xenθja] *nf* agency; **~ de créditos/ publicidad/viajes** credit/advertising/travel agency; **~ inmobiliaria** estate agent's (office) (*Brit*), real estate office (*US*); **~ matrimonial** marriage bureau

agenciar [axen'θjar] *vt* to bring about; **agenciarse** *vr* to look after o.s.; **agenciarse algo** to get hold of sth

agenda [a'xenda] *nf* diary; **~ electrónica** PDA; **~ telefónica** telephone directory

agente [a'xente] *nm* agent; (*de policía*) policeman; **~ femenino** policewoman; **~ de bolsa** stockbroker; **~ inmobiliario** estate agent (*Brit*), realtor (*US*); **~ de negocios** (*Com*) business agent; **~ de seguros** insurance broker; **~ de viajes** travel agent; **agentes sociales** social partners

ágil ['axil] *adj* agile, nimble

agilidad [axili'ðað] *nf* agility, nimbleness

agilizar [axili'θar] *vt* to speed up

agitación [axita'θjon] *nf* (*de mano etc*) shaking, waving; (*de líquido etc*) stirring; agitation

agitar [axi'tar] *vt* to wave, shake; (*líquido*) to stir; (*fig*) to stir up, excite; **agitarse** *vr* to get excited; (*inquietarse*) to get worried *o* upset

aglomeración [aɣlomera'θjon] *nf*: **~ de tráfico/gente** traffic jam/mass of people

aglomerar [aɣlome'rar] *vt*, **aglomerarse** *vr* to crowd together

agnóstico, -a [aɣ'nostiko, a] *adj, nm/f* agnostic

agobiante [aɣo'βjante] *adj* (*calor*) oppressive

agobiar [aɣo'βjar] *vt* to weigh down; (*oprimir*) to oppress; (*cargar*) to burden; **sentirse agobiado por** to be overwhelmed by

agobio [a'ɣoβjo] *nm* (*peso*) burden; (*fig*) oppressiveness

agolpamiento [aɣolpa'mjento] *nm* crush

agolparse [aɣol'parse] *vr* to crowd together

agonía [aɣo'nia] *nf* death throes *pl*; (*fig*) agony, anguish

agonice *etc* [aɣo'niθe] *vb ver* **agonizar**

agonizante [aɣoni'θante] *adj* dying

agonizar [aɣoni'θar] *vi* (*tb:* **estar**

agonizando) to be dying
agorero, -a [aɣo'rero, a] adj ominous ■ nm/f soothsayer; **ave agorera** bird of ill omen
agostar [aɣo'star] vt (quemar) to parch; (fig) to wither
agosto [a'ɣosto] nm August; (fig) harvest; **hacer su** ~ to make one's pile; ver tb **julio**
agotado, -a [aɣo'taðo, a] adj (persona) exhausted; (acabado) finished; (Com) sold out; (: libros) out of print; (pila) flat
agotador, a [aɣota'ðor, a] adj exhausting
agotamiento [aɣota'mjento] nm exhaustion
agotar [aɣo'tar] vt to exhaust; (consumir) to drain; (recursos) to use up, deplete; **agotarse** vr to be exhausted; (acabarse) to run out; (libro) to go out of print
agraciado, -a [aɣra'θjaðo, a] adj (atractivo) attractive; (en sorteo etc) lucky
agraciar [aɣra'θjar] vt (Jur) to pardon; (con premio) to reward; (hacer más atractivo) to make more attractive
agradable [aɣra'ðaβle] adj pleasant, nice
agradar [aɣra'ðar] vt, vi to please; **agradarse** vr to like each other
agradecer [aɣraðe'θer] vt to thank; (favor etc) to be grateful for; **le ~ía me enviara ...** I would be grateful if you would send me ...; **agradecerse** vr: **¡se agradece!** much obliged!
agradecido, -a [aɣraðe'θiðo, a] adj grateful; **¡muy ~!** thanks a lot!
agradecimiento [aɣraðeθi'mjento] nm thanks pl; gratitude
agradezca etc [aɣra'ðeθka] vb ver **agradecer**
agrado [a'ɣraðo] nm: **ser de tu** etc ~ to be to your etc liking
agrandar [aɣran'dar] vt to enlarge; (fig) to exaggerate; **agrandarse** vr to get bigger
agrario, -a [a'ɣrarjo, a] adj agrarian, land cpd; (política) agricultural, farming cpd
agravante [aɣra'βante] adj aggravating ■ nf complication; **con la ~ de que ...** with the further difficulty that ...
agravar [aɣra'βar] vt (pesar sobre) to make heavier; (irritar) to aggravate; **agravarse** vr to worsen, get worse
agraviar [aɣra'βjar] vt to offend; (ser injusto con) to wrong; **agraviarse** vr to take offence
agravio [a'ɣraβjo] nm offence; wrong; (Jur) grievance
agraz [a'ɣraθ] nm (uva) sour grape; **en** ~ (fig) immature
agredir [aɣre'ðir] vt to attack
agregado [aɣre'ɣaðo] nm aggregate; (persona) attaché; (profesor) assistant professor
agregar [aɣre'ɣar] vt to gather; (añadir) to add; (persona) to appoint

agregue etc [a'ɣreɣe] vb ver **agregar**
agresión [aɣre'sjon] nf aggression; (ataque) attack
agresivo, -a [aɣre'siβo, a] adj aggressive
agreste [a'ɣreste] adj (rural) rural; (fig) rough
agriar [a'ɣrjar] vt (fig) to (turn) sour; **agriarse** vr to turn sour
agrícola [a'ɣrikola] adj farming cpd, agricultural
agricultor, a [aɣrikul'tor, a] nm/f farmer
agricultura [aɣrikul'tura] nf agriculture, farming
agridulce [aɣri'ðulθe] adj bittersweet; (Culin) sweet and sour
agrietarse [aɣrje'tarse] vr to crack; (la piel) to chap
agrimensor, a [aɣrimen'sor, a] nm/f surveyor
agringado, -a [aɣrin'gaðo, a] adj gringolike
agrio, -a ['aɣrjo, a] adj bitter
agronomía [aɣrono'mia] nf agronomy, agriculture
agrónomo, -a [a'ɣronomo, a] nm/f agronomist, agricultural expert
agropecuario, -a [aɣrope'kwarjo, a] adj farming cpd, agricultural
agrupación [aɣrupa'θjon] nf group; (acto) grouping
agrupar [aɣru'par] vt to group; (Inform) to block; **agruparse** vr (Pol) to form a group; (juntarse) to gather
agua ['aɣwa] nf water; (Naut) wake; (Arq) slope of a roof; **aguas** nfpl (de joya) water sg, sparkle sg; (Med) water sg, urine sg; (Naut) waters; **aguas abajo/arriba** downstream/upstream; ~ **bendita/destilada/potable** holy/distilled/drinking water; ~ **caliente** hot water; ~ **corriente** running water; ~ **de colonia** eau de cologne; ~ **mineral (con/sin gas)** (fizzy/non-fizzy) mineral water; **aguas jurisdiccionales** territorial waters; **aguas mayores** excrement sg; ~ **pasada no mueve molino** it's no use crying over spilt milk; **estar con el** ~ **al cuello** to be up to one's neck; **venir como** ~ **de mayo** to be a godsend
aguacate [aɣwa'kate] nm avocado (pear)
aguacero [aɣwa'θero] nm (heavy) shower, downpour
aguachirle [aɣwa'tʃirle] nm (bebida) slops pl
aguado, -a [a'ɣwaðo, a] adj watery, watered down ■ nf (Agr) watering place; (Naut) water supply; (Arte) watercolour
aguafiestas [aɣwa'fjestas] nm/f inv spoilsport
aguafuerte [aɣwa'fwerte] nf etching
aguaitar [aɣwai'tar] vt (Am) to watch
aguanieve [aɣwa'njeβe] nf sleet

aguantable [aɣwan'taβle] *adj* bearable, tolerable

aguantar [aɣwan'tar] *vt* to bear, put up with; (*sostener*) to hold up ▪ *vi* to last; **aguantarse** *vr* to restrain o.s.; **no sé cómo aguanta** I don't know how he can take it

aguante [a'ɣwante] *nm* (*paciencia*) patience; (*resistencia*) endurance; (*Deporte*) stamina

aguar [a'ɣwar] *vt* to water down; (*fig*): ~ **la fiesta a algn** to spoil sb's fun

aguardar [aɣwar'ðar] *vt* to wait for

aguardentoso, -a [aɣwarðen'toso, a] *adj* (*pey*: *voz*) husky, gruff

aguardiente [aɣwar'ðjente] *nm* brandy, liquor

aguarrás [aɣwa'rras] *nm* turpentine

aguce *etc* [a'ɣuθe] *vb ver* **aguzar**

agudeza [aɣu'ðeθa] *nf* sharpness; (*ingenio*) wit

agudice *etc* [aɣu'ðiθe] *vb ver* **agudizar**

agudizar [aɣuði'θar] *vt* to sharpen; (*crisis*) to make worse; **agudizarse** *vr* to worsen, deteriorate

agudo, -a [a'ɣuðo, a] *adj* sharp; (*voz*) high-pitched, piercing; (*dolor, enfermedad*) acute

agüe *etc* ['aɣwe] *vb ver* **aguar**

agüero [a'ɣwero] *nm*: **buen/mal** ~ good/bad omen; **ser de buen** ~ to augur well; **pájaro de mal** ~ bird of ill omen

aguerrido, -a [aɣe'rriðo, a] *adj* hardened; (*fig*) experienced

aguijar [aɣi'xar] *vt* to goad; (*incitar*) to urge on ▪ *vi* to hurry along

aguijón [aɣi'xon] *nm* sting; (*fig*) spur

aguijonear [aɣixone'ar] *vt* = **aguijar**

águila ['aɣila] *nf* eagle; (*fig*) genius

aguileño, -a [aɣi'leɲo, a] *adj* (*nariz*) aquiline; (*rostro*) sharp-featured

aguinaldo [aɣi'naldo] *nm* Christmas box

aguja [a'ɣuxa] *nf* needle; (*de reloj*) hand; (*Arq*) spire; (*Tec*) firing-pin; **agujas** *nfpl* (*Zool*) ribs; (*Ferro*) points

agujerear [aɣuxere'ar] *vt* to make holes in; (*penetrar*) to pierce

agujero [aɣu'xero] *nm* hole; (*Com*) deficit

agujetas [aɣu'xetas] *nfpl* stitch *sg*; (*rigidez*) stiffness *sg*

aguzar [aɣu'θar] *vt* to sharpen; (*fig*) to incite; ~ **el oído** to prick up one's ears

aherrumbrarse [aerrum'brarse] *vr* to get rusty

ahí [a'i] *adv* there; (*allá*) over there; **de ahí que** so that, with the result that; **ahí llega** here he comes; **por ahí** (*dirección*) that way; **¡hasta ahí hemos llegado!** so it has come to this!; **¡ahí va!** (*objeto*) here it comes!; (*individuo*) there he goes!; **ahí donde le ve** as

sure as he's standing there

ahijado, -a [ai'xaðo, a] *nm/f* godson/daughter

ahijar [ai'xar] *vt*: ~ **algo a algn** (*fig*) to attribute sth to sb

ahínco [a'inko] *nm* earnestness; **con** ~ eagerly

ahíto, -a [a'ito, a] *adj*: **estoy** ~ I'm full up

ahogado, -a [ao'ɣaðo, a] *adj* (*en agua*) drowned; (*emoción*) pent-up; (*grito*) muffled

ahogar [ao'ɣar] *vt* (*en agua*) to drown; (*asfixiar*) to suffocate, smother; (*fuego*) to put out; **ahogarse** *vr* (*en agua*) to drown; (*por asfixia*) to suffocate

ahogo [a'oɣo] *nm* (*Med*) breathlessness; (*fig*) distress; (*problema económico*) financial difficulty

ahogue *etc* [a'oɣe] *vb ver* **ahogar**

ahondar [aon'dar] *vt* to deepen, make deeper; (*fig*) to go deeply into ▪ *vi*: ~ **en** to go deeply into

ahora [a'ora] *adv* now; (*hace poco*) a moment ago, just now; (*dentro de poco*) in a moment; ~ **voy** I'm coming; ~ **mismo** right now; ~ **bien** now then; **por** ~ for the present

ahorcado, -a [aor'kaðo, a] *nm/f* hanged person

ahorcar [aor'kar] *vt* to hang; **ahorcarse** *vr* to hang o.s.

ahorita [ao'rita], **ahoritita** [aori'tita] *adv* (*esp Am*: *fam*) right now

ahorque *etc* [a'orke] *vb ver* **ahorcar**

ahorrar [ao'rrar] *vt* (*dinero*) to save; (*esfuerzos*) to save, avoid; **ahorrarse** *vr*: **ahorrarse molestias** to save o.s. trouble

ahorrativo, -a [aorra'tiβo, a] *adj* thrifty

ahorro [a'orro] *nm* (*acto*) saving; (*frugalidad*) thrift; **ahorros** *nmpl* savings

ahuecar [awe'kar] *vt* to hollow (out); (*voz*) to deepen ▪ *vi*: **¡ahueca!** (*fam*) beat it! (*fam*); **ahuecarse** *vr* to give o.s. airs

ahueque *etc* [a'weke] *vb ver* **ahuecar**

ahumar [au'mar] *vt* to smoke, cure; (*llenar de humo*) to fill with smoke ▪ *vi* to smoke; **ahumarse** *vr* to fill with smoke

ahuyentar [aujen'tar] *vt* to drive off, frighten off; (*fig*) to dispel

AI *nf abr* (= *Amnistía Internacional*) AI

aimara [ai'mara], **aimará** [aima'ra] *adj, nm/f* Aymara

aindiado, -a [aindi'aðo, a] *adj* (*Am*) Indian-like

airado, -a [ai'raðo, a] *adj* angry

airar [ai'rar] *vt* to anger; **airarse** *vr* to get angry

aire ['aire] *nm* air; (*viento*) wind; (*corriente*) draught; (*Mus*) tune; **aires** *nmpl*: **darse**

aires to give o.s. airs; **al ~ libre** in the open air; **~ aclimatizado** *o* **acondicionado** air conditioning; **tener ~ de** to look like; **estar de buen/mal ~** to be in a good/bad mood; **estar en el ~** (*Radio*) to be on the air; (*fig*) to be up in the air

airear [aire'ar] *vt* to ventilate; (*fig*: *asunto*) to air; **airearse** *vr* to take the air

airoso, -a [ai'roso, a] *adj* windy; draughty; (*fig*) graceful

aislado, -a [ais'laðo, a] *adj* (*remoto*) isolated; (*incomunicado*) cut off; (*Elec*) insulated

aislante [ais'lante] *nm* (*Elec*) insulator

aislar [ais'lar] *vt* to isolate; (*Elec*) to insulate; **aislarse** *vr* to cut o.s. off

ajar [a'xar] *vt* to spoil; (*fig*) to abuse; **ajarse** *vr* to get crumpled; (*fig*: *piel*) to get wrinkled

ajardinado, -a [axarði'naðo, a] *adj* landscaped

ajedrez [axe'ðreθ] *nm* chess

ajenjo [a'xenxo] *nm* (*bebida*) absinth(e)

ajeno, -a [a'xeno, a] *adj* (*que pertenece a otro*) somebody else's; **~ a** foreign to; **~ de** free from, devoid of; **por razones ajenas a nuestra voluntad** for reasons beyond our control

ajetreado, -a [axetre'aðo, a] *adj* busy

ajetrearse [axetre'arse] *vr* (*atarearse*) to bustle about; (*fatigarse*) to tire o.s. out

ajetreo [axe'treo] *nm* bustle

ají [a'xi] *nm* chil(l)i, red pepper; (*salsa*) chil(l)i sauce

ajiaco [axi'ako] *nm* (*Am*) potato and chil(l)i stew

ajilimoje [axili'moxe] *nm* sauce of garlic and pepper; **ajilimojes** *nmpl* (*fam*) odds and ends

ajo ['axo] *nm* garlic; **~ porro** *o* **puerro** leek; **(tieso) como un ~** (*fam*) snobbish; **estar en el ~** to be mixed up in it

ajorca [a'xorka] *nf* bracelet

ajuar [a'xwar] *nm* household furnishings *pl*; (*de novia*) trousseau; (*de niño*) layette

ajustado, -a [axus'taðo, a] *adj* (*tornillo*) tight; (*cálculo*) right; (*ropa*) tight(-fitting); (*Deporte*: *resultado*) close

ajustar [axus'tar] *vt* (*adaptar*) to adjust; (*encajar*) to fit; (*Tec*) to engage; (*Tip*) to make up; (*apretar*) to tighten; (*concertar*) to agree (on); (*reconciliar*) to reconcile; (*cuenta*) to settle ▪ *vi* to fit

ajuste [a'xuste] *nm* adjustment; (*Costura*) fitting; (*acuerdo*) compromise; (*de cuenta*) settlement

al [al] = **a+el**; *ver* **a**

ala ['ala] *nf* wing; (*de sombrero*) brim; (*futbolista*) winger; **~ delta** hang-glider; **andar con el ~ caída** to be downcast; **cortar** las **alas a algn** to clip sb's wings; **dar alas a algn** to encourage sb

alabanza [ala'βanθa] *nf* praise

alabar [ala'βar] *vt* to praise

alacena [ala'θena] *nf* cupboard (*Brit*), closet (*US*)

alacrán [ala'kran] *nm* scorpion

ALADI [a'laði] *nf abr* = **Asociación Latinoamericana de Integración**

alado, -a [a'laðo, a] *adj* winged

ALALC [a'lalk] *nf abr* (= *Asociación Latinoamericana de Libre Comercio*) LAFTA

alambicado, -a [alambi'kaðo, a] *adj* distilled; (*fig*) affected

alambicar [alambi'kar] *vt* to distil

alambique *etc* [alam'bike] *vb ver* **alambicar** ▪ *nm* still

alambrada [alam'braða] *nf*, **alambrado** [alam'braðo] *nm* wire fence; (*red*) wire netting

alambre [a'lambre] *nm* wire; **~ de púas** barbed wire

alambrista [alam'brista] *nm/f* tightrope walker

alameda [ala'meða] *nf* (*plantío*) poplar grove; (*lugar de paseo*) avenue, boulevard

álamo ['alamo] *nm* poplar; **álamo temblón** aspen

alano [a'lano] *nm* mastiff

alarde [a'larðe] *nm* show, display; **hacer ~ de** to boast of

alardear [alarðe'ar] *vi* to boast

alargador [alarɣa'ðor] *nm* extension cable *o* lead

alargar [alar'ɣar] *vt* to lengthen, extend; (*paso*) to hasten; (*brazo*) to stretch out; (*cuerda*) to pay out; (*conversación*) to spin out; **alargarse** *vr* to get longer

alargue *etc* [a'larɣe] *vb ver* **alargar**

alarido [ala'riðo] *nm* shriek

alarma [a'larma] *nf* alarm; **voz de ~** warning note; **dar la ~** to raise the alarm

alarmante [alar'mante] *adj* alarming

alarmar [alar'mar] *vt* to alarm; **alarmarse** *vr* to get alarmed

alavés, -esa [ala'βes, esa] *adj* of Álava ▪ *nm/f* native *o* inhabitant of Álava

alba ['alβa] *nf* dawn

albacea [alβa'θea] *nm/f* executor/executrix

albaceteño, -a [alβaθe'teɲo, a] *adj* of Albacete ▪ *nm/f* native *o* inhabitant of Albacete

albahaca [al'βaka] *nf* (*Bot*) basil

Albania [al'βanja] *nf* Albania

albañal [alβa'ɲal] *nm* drain, sewer

albañil [alβa'ɲil] *nm* bricklayer; (*cantero*) mason

albarán [alβa'ran] *nm (Com)* invoice
albarda [al'βarða] *nf* packsaddle
albaricoque [alβari'koke] *nm* apricot
albedrío [alβe'ðrio] *nm*: **libre** ~ free will
alberca [al'βerka] *nf* reservoir; *(Am)* swimming pool
albergar [alβer'ɣar] *vt* to shelter; *(esperanza)* to cherish; **albergarse** *vr (refugiarse)* to shelter; *(alojarse)* to lodge
albergue *etc* [al'βerɣe] *vb ver* **albergar** ▪ *nm* shelter, refuge; ~ **de juventud** youth hostel
albis ['alβis] *adv*: **quedarse en** ~ not to have a clue
albóndiga [al'βondiɣa] *nf* meatball
albor [al'βor] *nm* whiteness; *(amanecer)* dawn
alborada [alβo'raða] *nf* dawn; *(diana)* reveille
alborear [alβore'ar] *vi* to dawn
albornoz [alβor'noθ] *nm (de los árabes)* burnous; *(para el baño)* bathrobe
alboroce *etc* [alβo'roθe] *vb ver* **alborozar**
alborotar [alβoro'tar] *vi* to make a row ▪ *vt* to agitate, stir up; **alborotarse** *vr* to get excited; *(mar)* to get rough
alboroto [alβo'roto] *nm* row, uproar
alborozar [alβoro'θar] *vt* to gladden; **alborozarse** *vr* to rejoice, be overjoyed
alborozo [alβo'roθo] *nm* joy
albricias [al'βriθjas] *nfpl*: ¡~! good news!
álbum ['alβum] *(pl* **álbums** *o* **álbumes)** *nm* album
albumen [al'βumen] *nm* egg white, albumen
alcabala [alka'βala] *nf (Am)* roadblock
alcachofa [alka'tʃofa] *nf* (globe) artichoke; *(Tip)* golf ball; *(de ducha)* shower head
alcahueta [alka'weta] *nf* procuress
alcahuete [alka'wete] *nm* pimp
alcalde, -esa [al'kalde, alkal'desa] *nm/f* mayor(ess)
alcaldía [alkal'dia] *nf* mayoralty; *(lugar)* mayor's office
álcali ['alkali] *nm (Química)* alkali
alcance *etc* [al'kanθe] *vb ver* **alcanzar** ▪ *nm (Mil: Radio)* range; *(fig)* scope; *(Com)* adverse balance, deficit; **estar al/fuera del** ~ **de algn** to be within/beyond one's reach; *(fig)* to be within one's powers/over one's head; **de gran** ~ *(Mil)* long-range; *(fig)* far-reaching
alcancía [alkan'θia] *nf* money box
alcanfor [alkan'for] *nm* camphor
alcantarilla [alkanta'riʎa] *nf (de aguas cloacales)* sewer; *(en la calle)* gutter
alcanzar [alkan'θar] *vt (algo: con la mano, el pie)* to reach; *(alguien: en el camino etc)* to catch up (with); *(autobús)* to catch; *(suj: bala)* to hit, strike ▪ *vi (ser suficiente)* to be enough; ~ **algo a algn** to hand sth to sb; **alcánzame la sal, por favor** pass the salt please; ~ **a hacer** to

manage to do
alcaparra [alka'parra] *nf (Bot)* caper
alcatraz [alka'traθ] *nm* gannet
alcayata [alka'jata] *nf* hook
alcázar [al'kaθar] *nm* fortress; *(Naut)* quarter-deck
alce *etc* ['alθe] *vb ver* **alzar**
alcista [al'θista] *adj (Com: Econ)*: **mercado** ~ bull market; **la tendencia** ~ the upward trend ▪ *nm* speculator
alcoba [al'koβa] *nf* bedroom
alcohol [al'kol] *nm* alcohol; **no bebe** ~ he doesn't drink (alcohol)
alcoholemia [alkoo'lemia] *nf* blood alcohol level; **prueba de la** ~ breath test
alcoholice *etc* [alko'liθe] *vb ver* **alcoholizarse**
alcohólico, -a [al'koliko, a] *adj, nm/f* alcoholic
alcoholímetro [alko'limetro] *nm* Breathalyser®, drunkometer *(US)*
alcoholismo [alko'lismo] *nm* alcoholism
alcoholizarse [alkoli'θarse] *vr* to become an alcoholic
alcornoque [alkor'noke] *nm* cork tree; *(fam)* idiot
alcotana [alko'tana] *nf* pickaxe; *(Deporte)* ice-axe
alcurnia [al'kurnja] *nf* lineage
alcuza [al'kusa] *nf (Am)* cruet
aldaba [al'daβa] *nf* (door) knocker
aldea [al'dea] *nf* village
aldeano, -a [alde'ano, a] *adj* village *cpd* ▪ *nm/f* villager
ale ['ale] *excl* come on!, let's go!
aleación [alea'θjon] *nf* alloy
aleatorio, -a [alea'torjo, a] *adj* random, contingent; **acceso** ~ *(Inform)* random access
aleccionador, a [alekθjona'ðor, a] *adj* instructive
aleccionar [alekθjo'nar] *vt* to instruct; *(adiestrar)* to train
aledaño, -a [ale'ðaɲo, a] *adj*: ~ **a** bordering on ▪ *nmpl*: **aledaños** outskirts
alegación [aleɣa'θjon] *nf* allegation
alegar [ale'ɣar] *vt (dificultad etc)* to plead; *(Jur)* to allege ▪ *vi (Am)* to argue; ~ **que** ... to give as an excuse that ...
alegato [ale'ɣato] *nm (Jur)* allegation; *(escrito)* indictment; *(declaración)* statement; *(Am)* argument
alegoría [aleɣo'ria] *nf* allegory
alegrar [ale'ɣrar] *vt (causar alegría)* to cheer (up); *(fuego)* to poke; *(fiesta)* to liven up; **alegrarse** *vr (fam)* to get merry *o* tight; **alegrarse de** to be glad about
alegre [a'leɣre] *adj* happy, cheerful; *(fam)* merry, tight; *(licencioso)* risqué, blue

alegría [ale'ɣria] nf happiness; merriment;
~ **vital** joie de vivre
alegrón [ale'ɣron] nm (fig) sudden joy
alegue etc [a'leɣe] vb ver **alegar**
alejamiento [alexa'mjento] nm removal;
(distancia) remoteness
alejar [ale'xar] vt to move away, remove; (fig)
to estrange; **alejarse** vr to move away
alelado, -a [ale'laðo, a] adj (bobo) foolish
alelar [ale'lar] vt to bewilder
aleluya [ale'luja] nm (canto) hallelujah
alemán, -ana [ale'man, ana] adj, nm/f
German ▪ nm (lengua) German
Alemania [ale'manja] nf Germany; ~
Occidental/Oriental West/East Germany
alentador, a [alenta'ðor, a] adj encouraging
alentar [alen'tar] vt to encourage
alergia [a'lerxja] nf allergy
alero [a'lero] nm (de tejado) eaves pl; (de foca,
Deporte) flipper; (Auto) mudguard
alerta [a'lerta] adj inv, nm alert
aleta [a'leta] nf (de pez) fin; (de ave) wing;
(de coche) mudguard
aletargar [aletar'ɣar] vt to make drowsy;
(entumecer) to make numb; **aletargarse** vr
to grow drowsy; to become numb
aletargue etc [ale'tarɣe] vb ver **aletargar**
aletear [alete'ar] vi to flutter; (ave) to flap its
wings; (individuo) to wave one's arms
alevín [ale'βin] nm fry, young fish
alevosía [aleβo'sia] nf treachery
alfabetización [alfaβetiθa'θjon] nf:
campaña de ~ literacy campaign
alfabeto [alfa'βeto] nm alphabet
alfajor [alfa'xor] nm (Esp: polvorón) cake eaten at
Christmas time
alfalfa [al'falfa] nf alfalfa, lucerne
alfaque [al'fake] nm (Naut) bar, sandbank
alfar [al'far] nm (taller) potter's workshop;
(arcilla) clay
alfarería [alfare'ria] nf pottery; (tienda)
pottery shop
alfarero [alfa'rero] nm potter
alféizar [al'feiθar] nm window-sill
alférez [al'fereθ] nm (Mil) second lieutenant;
(Naut) ensign
alfil [al'fil] nm (Ajedrez) bishop
alfiler [alfi'ler] nm pin; (broche) clip; (pinza)
clothes peg (Brit) o pin (US); ~ **de gancho**
(Am) safety pin; **prendido con alfileres**
shaky
alfiletero [alfile'tero] nm needle case
alfombra [al'fombra] nf carpet; (más pequeña)
rug
alfombrar [alfom'brar] vt to carpet
alfombrilla [alfom'briʎa] nf rug, mat;
(Inform) mouse mat o pad

alforja [al'forxa] nf saddlebag
alforza [al'forθa] nf pleat
algarabía [alɣara'βia] nf (fam) gibberish;
(griterío) hullabaloo
algarada [alɣa'raða] nf outcry; **hacer** o
levantar una ~ to kick up a tremendous fuss
Algarbe [al'ɣarβe] nm: **el ~** the Algarve
algarroba [alɣa'rroβa] nf carob
algarrobo [alɣa'rroβo] nm carob tree
algas ['alɣas] nfpl seaweed sg
algazara [alɣa'θara] nf din, uproar
álgebra ['alxeβra] nf algebra
álgido, -a ['alxiðo, a] adj icy; (momento etc)
crucial, decisive
algo ['alɣo] pron something; (en frases
interrogativas) anything ▪ adv somewhat,
rather; **por ~ será** there must be some
reason for it; **es ~ difícil** it's a bit awkward
algodón [alɣo'ðon] nm cotton; (planta) cotton
plant; ~ **de azúcar** candy floss (Brit), cotton
candy (US); ~ **hidrófilo** cotton wool (Brit),
absorbent cotton (US)
algodonero, -a [alɣoðo'nero, a] adj cotton
cpd ▪ nm/f cotton grower ▪ nm cotton plant
algoritmo [alɣo'ritmo] nm algorithm
alguacil [alɣwa'θil] nm bailiff; (Taur)
mounted official
alguien ['alɣjen] pron someone, somebody;
(en frases interrogativas) anybody
alguno, -a [al'ɣuno, a] adj (antes de nmsg
algún) some; (después de n): **no tiene talento**
~ he has no talent, he hasn't any talent
▪ pron (alguien) someone, somebody; **algún**
que otro libro some book or other; **algún**
día iré I'll go one o some day; **sin interés ~**
without the slightest interest; ~ **que otro**
an occasional one; **algunos piensan** some
(people) think; ~ **de ellos** one of them
alhaja [a'laxa] nf jewel; (tesoro) precious
object, treasure
alhelí [ale'li] nm wallflower, stock
aliado, -a [a'ljaðo, a] adj allied
alianza [a'ljanθa] nf (Pol etc) alliance; (anillo)
wedding ring
aliar [a'ljar] vt to ally; **aliarse** vr to form an
alliance
alias ['aljas] adv alias
alicaído, -a [alika'iðo, a] adj (Med) weak; (fig)
depressed
alicantino, -a [alikan'tino, a] adj of Alicante
▪ nm/f native o inhabitant of Alicante
alicatar [alika'tar] vt to tile
alicate [ali'kate] nm, **alicates** [ali'kates]
nmpl pliers pl; ~**(s) de uñas** nail clippers
aliciente [ali'θjente] nm incentive; (atracción)
attraction
alienación [aljena'θjon] nf alienation

aliento *etc* [a'ljento] *vb ver* **alentar** ▪ *nm* breath; (*respiración*) breathing; **sin** ~ breathless; **de un** ~ in one breath; (*fig*) in one go

aligerar [alixe'rar] *vt* to lighten; (*reducir*) to shorten; (*aliviar*) to alleviate; (*mitigar*) to ease

alijo [a'lixo] *nm* (*Naut*) unloading; (*contrabando*) smuggled goods

alimaña [ali'maɲa] *nf* pest

alimentación [alimenta'θjon] *nf* (*comida*) food; (*acción*) feeding; (*tienda*) grocer's (shop); ~ **continua** (*en fotocopiadora etc*) stream feed

alimentador [alimenta'ðor] *nm*: ~ **de papel** sheet-feeder

alimentar [alimen'tar] *vt* to feed; (*nutrir*) to nourish; **alimentarse** *vr*: **alimentarse (de)** to feed (on)

alimenticio, -a [alimen'tiθjo, a] *adj* food *cpd*; (*nutritivo*) nourishing, nutritious

alimento [ali'mento] *nm* food; (*nutrición*) nourishment; **alimentos** *nmpl* (*Jur*) alimony *sg*

alimón [ali'mon]: **al** ~ *adv* jointly, together

alineación [alinea'θjon] *nf* alignment; (*Deporte*) line-up

alineado, -a [aline'aðo, a] *adj*: **(no)** ~ (un)justified; ~ **a la izquierda/derecha** ranged left/right

alinear [aline'ar] *vt* to align; (*Tip*) to justify; **alinearse** *vr* to line up; **alinearse en** to fall in with

aliñar [ali'ɲar] *vt* (*Culin*) to dress

aliño [ali'ɲo] *nm* (*Culin*) dressing

alisar [ali'sar] *vt* to smooth

aliso [a'liso] *nm* alder

alistamiento [alista'mjento] *nm* recruitment

alistar [ali'star] *vt* to recruit; **alistarse** *vr* to enlist; (*inscribirse*) to enrol; (*Am: prepararse*) to get ready

aliviar [ali'βjar] *vt* (*carga*) to lighten; (*persona*) to relieve; (*dolor*) to relieve, alleviate

alivio [a'liβjo] *nm* alleviation, relief; ~ **de luto** half-mourning

aljibe [al'xiβe] *nm* cistern

allá [a'ʎa] *adv* (*lugar*) there; (*por ahí*) over there; (*tiempo*) then; **allá abajo** down there; **más allá** further on; **más allá de** beyond; **¡allá tú!** that's your problem!

allanamiento [aʎana'mjento] *nm* (*Am Policía*) raid, search; ~ **de morada** housebreaking

allanar [aʎa'nar] *vt* to flatten, level (out); (*igualar*) to smooth (out); (*fig*) to subdue; (*Jur*) to burgle, break into; (*Am Policía*) to raid, search; **allanarse** *vr* to fall down; **allanarse a** to submit to, accept

allegado, -a [aʎe'ɣaðo, a] *adj* near, close ▪ *nm/f* relation

allende [a'ʎenðe] *adv* on the other side ▪ *prep*: ~ **los mares** beyond the seas

allí [a'ʎi] *adv* there; **allí mismo** right there; **por allí** over there; (*por ese camino*) that way

alma ['alma] *nf* soul; (*persona*) person; (*Tec*) core; **se le cayó el** ~ **a los pies** he became very disheartened; **entregar el** ~ to pass away; **estar con el** ~ **en la boca** to be scared to death; **lo siento en el** ~ I am truly sorry; **tener el** ~ **en un hilo** to have one's heart in one's mouth; **estar como** ~ **en pena** to suffer; **ir como** ~ **que lleva el diablo** to go at breakneck speed

almacén [alma'θen] *nm* (*depósito*) warehouse, store; (*Mil*) magazine; (*Am*) grocer's shop, food store, grocery store (US); **(grandes) almacenes** *nmpl* department store *sg*; ~ **depositario** (*Com*) depository

almacenaje [almaθe'naxe] *nm* storage; ~ **secundario** backup storage

almacenamiento [almaθena'mjento] *nm* (*Inform*) storage; ~ **temporal en disco** disk spooling

almacenar [almaθe'nar] *vt* to store, put in storage; (*Inform*) to store; (*proveerse*) to stock up with

almacenero [almaθe'nero] *nm* warehouseman; (*Am*) grocer, shopkeeper

almanaque [alma'nake] *nm* almanac

almeja [al'mexa] *nf* clam

almenas [al'menas] *nfpl* battlements

almendra [al'menðra] *nf* almond

almendro [al'menðro] *nm* almond tree

almeriense [alme'rjense] *adj* of Almería ▪ *nm/f* native *o* inhabitant of Almería

almiar [al'mjar] *nm* haystack

almíbar [al'miβar] *nm* syrup

almidón [almi'ðon] *nm* starch

almidonado, -a [almiðo'naðo, a] *adj* starched

almidonar [almiðo'nar] *vt* to starch

almirantazgo [almiran'taɣo] *nm* admiralty

almirante [almi'rante] *nm* admiral

almirez [almi're0] *nm* mortar

almizcle [al'miθkle] *nm* musk

almizclero [almiθ'klero] *nm* musk deer

almohada [almo'aða] *nf* pillow; (*funda*) pillowcase

almohadilla [almoa'ðiʎa] *nf* cushion; (*Tec*) pad; (*Am*) pincushion; (*Inform*) hash key

almohadillado, -a [almoaði'ʎaðo, a] *adj* (*acolchado*) padded

almohadón [almoa'ðon] *nm* large pillow

almorcé [almor'θe], **almorcemos** *etc* [almor'θemos] *vb ver* **almorzar**

almorranas [almo'rranas] *nfpl* piles, haemorrhoids (*Brit*), hemorrhoids (*US*)

almorzar [almor'θar] *vt*: ~ **una tortilla** to have an omelette for lunch ■ *vi* to (have) lunch
almuerce *etc* [al'mwerθe] *vb ver* **almorzar**
almuerzo *etc* [al'mwerθo] *vb ver* **almorzar** ■ *nm* lunch
aló [a'lo] *excl* (*esp Am Telec*) hello!
alocado, -a [alo'kaðo, a] *adj* crazy
alojamiento [aloxa'mjento] *nm* lodging(s) (*pl*); (*viviendas*) housing
alojar [alo'xar] *vt* to lodge; **alojarse** *vr*: **alojarse en** to stay at; (*bala*) to lodge in
alondra [a'londra] *nf* lark, skylark
alpaca [al'paka] *nf* alpaca
alpargata [alpar'ɣata] *nf* espadrille
Alpes ['alpes] *nmpl*: **los** ~ the Alps
alpinismo [alpi'nismo] *nm* mountaineering, climbing
alpinista [alpi'nista] *nm/f* mountaineer, climber
alpino, -a [al'pino, a] *adj* alpine
alpiste [al'piste] *nm* (*semillas*) birdseed; (*Am fam*: *dinero*) dough; (*fam*: *alcohol*) booze
alquería [alke'ria] *nf* farmhouse
alquilar [alki'lar] *vt* (*suj: propietario*: *inmuebles*) to let, rent (out); (: *coche*) to hire out; (: *TV*) to rent (out); (*suj: alquilador*: *inmuebles, TV*) to rent; (: *coche*) to hire; **"se alquila casa"** "house to let (*Brit*) o to rent (*US*)"
alquiler [alki'ler] *nm* renting, letting; hiring; (*arriendo*) rent; hire charge; **de** ~ for hire; ~ **de automóviles** car hire
alquimia [al'kimja] *nf* alchemy
alquitrán [alki'tran] *nm* tar
alrededor [alreðe'ðor] *adv* around, about; **alrededores** *nmpl* surroundings; ~ **de** *prep* around, about; **mirar a su** ~ to look (round) about one
Alsacia [al'saθja] *nf* Alsace
alta ['alta] *nf* (certificate of) discharge; **dar a algn de** ~ to discharge sb; **darse de** ~ (*Mil*) to join, enrol; (*Deporte*) to declare o.s. fit
altanería [altane'ria] *nf* haughtiness, arrogance
altanero, -a [alta'nero, a] *adj* haughty, arrogant
altar [al'tar] *nm* altar
altavoz [alta'βoθ] *nm* loudspeaker; (*amplificador*) amplifier
alteración [altera'θjon] *nf* alteration; (*alboroto*) disturbance; ~ **del orden público** breach of the peace
alterar [alte'rar] *vt* to alter; to disturb; **alterarse** *vr* (*persona*) to get upset
altercado [alter'kaðo] *nm* argument
alternar [alter'nar] *vt* to alternate ■ *vi*, **alternarse** *vr* to alternate; (*turnar*) to take turns; ~ **con** to mix with

alternativo, -a [alterna'tiβo, a] *adj* alternative; (*alterno*) alternating ■ *nf* alternative; (*elección*) choice; **alternativas** *nfpl* ups and downs; **tomar la alternativa** (*Taur*) to become a fully-qualified bullfighter
alterno, -a [al'terno, a] *adj* (*Bot*: *Mat*) alternate; (*Elec*) alternating
alteza [al'teθa] *nf* (*tratamiento*) highness
altibajos [alti'βaxos] *nmpl* ups and downs
altillo [al'tiʎo] *nm* (*Geo*) small hill; (*Am*) attic
altiplanicie [altipla'niθje] *nf*, **altiplano** [alti'plano] *nm* high plateau
altisonante [altiso'nante] *adj* high-flown, high-sounding
altitud [alti'tuð] *nf* altitude, height; **a una** ~ **de** at a height of
altivez [alti'βeθ] *nf* haughtiness, arrogance
altivo, -a [al'tiβo, a] *adj* haughty, arrogant
alto, -a ['alto, a] *adj* high; (*persona*) tall; (*sonido*) high, sharp; (*noble*) high, lofty; (*Geo, clase*) upper ■ *nm* halt; (*Mus*) alto; (*Geo*) hill; (*Am*) pile ■ *adv* (*estar*) high; (*hablar*) loud, loudly ■ *excl* halt!; **la pared tiene dos metros de** ~ the wall is two metres high; **en alta mar** on the high seas; **en voz alta** in a loud voice; **las altas horas de la noche** the small (*Brit*) o wee (*US*) hours; **en lo** ~ **de** at the top of; **pasar por** ~ to overlook; **altos y bajos** ups and downs; **poner la radio más** ~ to turn the radio up; **¡más** ~, **por favor!** louder, please!
altoparlante [altopar'lante] *nm* (*Am*) loudspeaker
altramuz [altra'muθ] *nm* lupin
altruismo [al'truismo] *nm* altruism
altura [al'tura] *nf* height; (*Naut*) depth; (*Geo*) latitude; **la pared tiene 1.80 de** ~ the wall is 1 metre 80 (cm) high; **a esta** ~ **del año** at this time of the year; **estar a la** ~ **de las circunstancias** to rise to the occasion; **ha sido un partido de gran** ~ it has been a terrific match
alubia [a'luβja] *nf* French bean, kidney bean
alucinación [aluθina'θjon] *nf* hallucination
alucinante [aluθi'nante] *adj* (*fam*: *estupendo*) great, super
alucinar [aluθi'nar] *vi* to hallucinate ■ *vt* to deceive; (*fascinar*) to fascinate
alud [a'luð] *nm* avalanche; (*fig*) flood
aludir [alu'ðir] *vi*: ~ **a** to allude to; **darse por aludido** to take the hint; **no te des por aludido** don't take it personally
alumbrado [alum'braðo] *nm* lighting
alumbramiento [alumbra'mjento] *nm* lighting; (*Med*) childbirth, delivery
alumbrar [alum'brar] *vt* to light (up) ■ *vi* (*iluminar*) to give light; (*Med*) to give birth

aluminio [alu'minjo] *nm* aluminium (*Brit*), aluminum (*US*)

alumnado [alum'naðo] *nm* (*Univ*) student body; (*Escol*) pupils *pl*

alumno, -a [a'lumno, a] *nm/f* pupil, student

alunice *etc* [alu'niθe] *vb ver* **alunizar**

alunizar [aluni'θar] *vi* to land on the moon

alusión [alu'sjon] *nf* allusion

alusivo, -a [alu'siβo, a] *adj* allusive

aluvión [alu'βjon] *nm* (*Geo*) alluvium; (*fig*) flood; ~ **de improperios** torrent of abuse

alvéolo [al'βeolo] *nm* (*Anat*) alveolus; (*fig*) network

alza ['alθa] *nf* rise; (*Mil*) sight; **alzas fijas/graduables** fixed/adjustable sights; **al** *o* **en ~** (*precio*) rising; **jugar al ~** to speculate on a rising *o* bull market; **cotizarse** *o* **estar en ~** to be rising

alzado, -a [al'θaðo, a] *adj* (*gen*) raised; (*Com: precio*) fixed; (*: quiebra*) fraudulent; **por un tanto ~** for a lump sum ■ *nf* (*de caballos*) height; (*Jur*) appeal

alzamiento [alθa'mjento] *nm* (*aumento*) rise, increase; (*acción*) lifting, raising; (*mejor postura*) higher bid; (*rebelión*) rising; (*Com*) fraudulent bankruptcy

alzar [al'θar] *vt* to lift (up); (*precio, muro*) to raise; (*cuello de abrigo*) to turn up; (*Agr*) to gather in; (*Tip*) to gather; **alzarse** *vr* to get up, rise; (*rebelarse*) to revolt; (*Com*) to go fraudulently bankrupt; (*Jur*) to appeal; **alzarse con el premio** to carry off the prize

a.m. *abr* (*Am: = ante meridiem*) a.m.

ama ['ama] *nf* lady of the house; (*dueña*) owner; (*institutriz*) governess; (*madre adoptiva*) foster mother; ~ **de casa** housewife; ~ **de cría** *o* **de leche** wet-nurse; ~ **de llaves** housekeeper

amabilidad [amaβili'ðað] *nf* kindness; (*simpatía*) niceness

amabilísimo, -a [amaβi'lisimo, a] *adj* *superlativo de* **amable**

amable [a'maβle] *adj* kind; nice

amaestrado, -a [amaes'traðo, a] *adj* (*animal*) trained; (*: en circo etc*) performing

amaestrar [amaes'trar] *vt* to train

amagar [ama'ɣar] *vt, vi* to threaten

amago [a'maɣo] *nm* threat; (*gesto*) threatening gesture; (*Med*) symptom

amague *etc* [a'maɣe] *vb ver* **amagar**

amainar [amai'nar] *vt* (*Naut*) to lower, take in; (*fig*) to calm ■ *vi*, **amainarse** *vr* to drop, die down; **el viento amaina** the wind is dropping

amalgama [amal'ɣama] *nf* amalgam

amalgamar [amalɣa'mar] *vt* to amalgamate; (*combinar*) to combine, mix

amamantar [amaman'tar] *vt* to suckle, nurse

amancebarse [amanθe'βarse] *vr* (*pareja*) to live together

amanecer [amane'θer] *vi* to dawn; (*fig*) to appear, begin to show ■ *nm* dawn; **el niño amaneció afiebrado** the child woke up with a fever

amanerado, -a [amane'raðo, a] *adj* affected

amanezca *etc* [ama'neθka] *vb ver* **amanecer**

amansar [aman'sar] *vt* to tame; (*persona*) to subdue; **amansarse** *vr* (*persona*) to calm down

amante [a'mante] *adj*: ~ **de** fond of ■ *nm/f* lover

amanuense [ama'nwense] *nm* (*escribiente*) scribe; (*copista*) copyist; (*Pol*) secretary

amañar [ama'ɲar] *vt* (*gen*) to do skilfully; (*pey: resultado*) to alter

amaño [a'maɲo] *nm* (*habilidad*) skill; **amaños** *nmpl* (*Tec*) tools; (*fig*) tricks

amapola [ama'pola] *nf* poppy

amar [a'mar] *vt* to love

amargado, -a [amar'ɣaðo, a] *adj* bitter; embittered

amargar [amar'ɣar] *vt* to make bitter; (*fig*) to embitter; **amargarse** *vr* to become embittered

amargo, -a [a'marɣo, a] *adj* bitter

amargor [amar'ɣor] *nm* (*sabor*) bitterness; (*fig*) grief

amargue *etc* [a'marɣe] *vb ver* **amargar**

amargura [amar'ɣura] *nf* = **amargor**

amarillento, -a [amari'ʎento, a] *adj* yellowish; (*tez*) sallow

amarillismo [amari'ʎismo] *nm* (*de prensa*) sensationalist journalism

amarillo, -a [ama'riʎo, a] *adj, nm* yellow

amarra [a'marra] *nf* (*Naut*) mooring line; **amarras** *nfpl* (*fig*) protection *sg*; **tener buenas amarras** to have good connections; **soltar amarras** to set off

amarrar [ama'rrar] *vt* to moor; (*sujetar*) to tie up

amartillar [amarti'ʎar] *vt* (*fusil*) to cock

amasar [ama'sar] *vt* to knead; (*mezclar*) to mix, prepare; (*confeccionar*) to concoct

amasijo [ama'sixo] *nm* kneading; mixing; (*fig*) hotchpotch

amateur ['amatur] *nm/f* amateur

amatista [ama'tista] *nf* amethyst

amazacotado, -a [amaθako'taðo, a] *adj* (*terreno, arroz etc*) lumpy

amazona [ama'θona] *nf* horsewoman

Amazonas [ama'θonas] *nm*: **el (Río) ~** the Amazon

ambages [am'baxes] *nmpl*: **sin ~** in plain language

ámbar ['ambar] *nm* amber
Amberes [am'beres] *nm* Antwerp
ambición [ambi'θjon] *nf* ambition
ambicionar [ambiθjo'nar] *vt* to aspire to
ambicioso, -a [ambi'θjoso, a] *adj* ambitious
ambidextro, -a [ambi'ðekstro, a] *adj* ambidextrous
ambientación [ambjenta'θjon] *nf* (*Cine: Lit etc*) setting; (*Radio etc*) sound effects *pl*
ambientador [ambjenta'ðor] *nm* air freshener
ambientar [ambjen'tar] *vt* (*gen*) to give an atmosphere to; (*Lit etc*) to set
ambiente [am'bjente] *nm* (*tb fig*) atmosphere; (*medio*) environment; (*Am*) room
ambigüedad [ambiɣwe'ðað] *nf* ambiguity
ambiguo, -a [am'biɣwo, a] *adj* ambiguous
ámbito ['ambito] *nm* (*campo*) field; (*fig*) scope
ambos, -as ['ambos, as] *adj pl, pron pl* both
ambulancia [ambu'lanθja] *nf* ambulance
ambulante [ambu'lante] *adj* travelling, itinerant; (*biblioteca*) mobile
ambulatorio [ambula'torio] *nm* state health-service clinic
ameba [a'meβa] *nf* amoeba
amedrentar [ameðren'tar] *vt* to scare
amén [a'men] *excl* amen; ~ **de** *prep* besides, in addition to; **en un decir** ~ in the twinkling of an eye; **decir** ~ **a todo** to have no mind of one's own
amenace *etc* [ame'naθe] *vb ver* **amenazar**
amenaza [ame'naθa] *nf* threat
amenazar [amena'θar] *vt* to threaten ■ *vi*: ~ **con hacer** to threaten to do
amenidad [ameni'ðað] *nf* pleasantness
ameno, -a [a'meno, a] *adj* pleasant
América [a'merika] *nf* (*continente*) America, the Americas; (*EEUU*) America; (*Hispanoamérica*) Latin *o* South America; ~ **del Norte/del Sur** North/South America; ~ **Central/Latina** Central/Latin America
americanismo [amerika'nismo] *nm* Americanism
americano, -a [ameri'kano, a] *adj, nm/f ver* **América** American; Latin *o* South American ■ *nf* coat, jacket
americe *etc* [ame'riθe] *vb ver* **amerizar**
amerindio, -a [ame'rindjo, a] *adj, nm/f* Amerindian, American Indian
amerizaje [ameri'θaxe] *nm* (*Aviat*) landing (on the sea)
amerizar [ameri'θar] *vi* (*Aviat*) to land (on the sea)
ametralladora [ametraʎa'ðora] *nf* machine gun
amianto [a'mjanto] *nm* asbestos
amigable [ami'ɣaβle] *adj* friendly

amígdala [a'miɣðala] *nf* tonsil
amigdalitis [amiɣða'litis] *nf* tonsillitis
amigo, -a [a'miɣo, a] *adj* friendly ■ *nm/f* friend; (*amante*) lover; ~ **de lo ajeno** thief; ~ **corresponsal** penfriend; **hacerse amigos** to become friends; **ser** ~ **de** to like, be fond of; **ser muy amigos** to be close friends
amigote [ami'ɣote] *nm* mate (Brit), buddy
amilanar [amila'nar] *vt* to scare; **amilanarse** *vr* to get scared
aminorar [amino'rar] *vt* to diminish; (*reducir*) to reduce; ~ **la marcha** to slow down
amistad [amis'tað] *nf* friendship; **amistades** *nfpl* friends
amistoso, -a [amis'toso, a] *adj* friendly
amnesia [am'nesja] *nf* amnesia
amnistía [amnis'tia] *nf* amnesty
amnistiar [amnis'tjar] *vt* to amnesty, grant an amnesty to
amo ['amo] *nm* owner; (*jefe*) boss
amodorrarse [amoðo'rrarse] *vr* to get sleepy
amolar [amo'lar] *vt* to annoy
amoldar [amol'dar] *vt* to mould; (*adaptar*) to adapt
amonestación [amonesta'θjon] *nf* warning; **amonestaciones** *nfpl* marriage banns
amonestar [amone'star] *vt* to warn; to publish the banns of
amoniaco [amo'njako] *nm* ammonia
amontonar [amonto'nar] *vt* to collect, pile up; **amontonarse** *vr* (*gente*) to crowd together; (*acumularse*) to pile up; (*datos*) to accumulate; (*desastres*) to come one on top of another
amor [a'mor] *nm* love; (*amante*) lover; **hacer el** ~ to make love; ~ **interesado** cupboard love; ~ **propio** self-respect; **por (el)** ~ **de Dios** for God's sake; **estar al** ~ **de la lumbre** to be close to the fire
amoratado, -a [amora'taðo, a] *adj* purple, blue with cold; (*con cardenales*) bruised
amordace *etc* [amor'ðaθe] *vb ver* **amordazar**
amordazar [amorða'θar] *vt* to muzzle; (*fig*) to gag
amorfo, -a [a'morfo, a] *adj* amorphous, shapeless
amorío [amo'rio] *nm* (*fam*) love affair
amoroso, -a [amo'roso, a] *adj* affectionate, loving
amortajar [amorta'xar] *vt* (*fig*) to shroud
amortice *etc* [amor'tiθe] *vb ver* **amortizar**
amortiguador [amortiɣwa'ðor] *nm* shock absorber; (*parachoques*) bumper; (*silenciador*) silencer; **amortiguadores** *nmpl* (*Auto*) suspension *sg*
amortiguar [amorti'ɣwar] *vt* to deaden; (*ruido*) to muffle; (*color*) to soften

amortigüe etc [amor'tiɣwe] vb ver **amortiguar**

amortización [amortiθa'θjon] nf redemption; repayment; (Com) capital allowance

amortizar [amorti'θar] vt (Econ: bono) to redeem; (: capital) to write off; (: préstamo) to pay off

amoscarse [amos'karse] vr to get cross

amosque etc [a'moske] vb ver **amoscarse**

amotinar [amoti'nar] vt to stir up, incite (to riot); **amotinarse** vr to mutiny

amparar [ampa'rar] vt to protect; **ampararse** vr to seek protection; (de la lluvia etc) to shelter

amparo [am'paro] nm help, protection; **al ~ de** under the protection of

amperímetro [ampe'rimetro] nm ammeter

amperio [am'perjo] nm ampère, amp

ampliable [am'pljaβle] adj (Inform) expandable

ampliación [amplja'θjon] nf enlargement; (extensión) extension

ampliar [am'pljar] vt to enlarge; to extend

amplificación [amplifika'θjon] nf enlargement

amplificador [amplifika'ðor] nm amplifier

amplificar [amplifi'kar] vt to amplify

amplifique etc [ampli'fike] vb ver **amplificar**

amplio, -a ['ampljo, a] adj spacious; (falda etc) full; (extenso) extensive; (ancho) wide

amplitud [ampli'tuð] nf spaciousness; extent; (fig) amplitude; **~ de miras** broadmindedness; **de gran ~** far-reaching

ampolla [am'poʎa] nf blister; (Med) ampoule

ampolleta [ampo'ʎeta] nf (Am) (light) bulb

ampuloso, -a [ampu'loso, a] adj bombastic, pompous

amputar [ampu'tar] vt to cut off, amputate

amueblar [amwe'βlar] vt to furnish

amuleto [amu'leto] nm (lucky) charm

amurallar [amura'ʎar] vt to wall up o in

anacarado, -a [anaka'raðo, a] adj mother-of-pearl cpd

anacardo [ana'karðo] nm cashew (nut)

anaconda [ana'konda] nf anaconda

anacronismo [anakro'nismo] nm anachronism

ánade ['anaðe] nm duck

anagrama [ana'ɣrama] nm anagram

anales [a'nales] nmpl annals

analfabetismo [analfaβe'tismo] nm illiteracy

analfabeto, -a [analfa'βeto, a] adj, nm/f illiterate

analgésico [anal'xesiko] nm painkiller, analgesic

analice etc [ana'liθe] vb ver **analizar**

análisis [a'nalisis] nm inv analysis; **~ de costos-beneficios** cost-benefit analysis; **~ de mercados** market research; **~ de sangre** blood test

analista [ana'lista] nm/f (gen) analyst; (Pol: Historia) chronicler; **~ de sistemas** (Inform) systems analyst

analizar [anali'θar] vt to analyse

analogía [analo'xia] nf analogy; **por ~ con** on the analogy of

analógico, -a [ana'loxico, a] adj analogue

análogo, -a [a'naloɣo, a] adj analogous, similar

ananá [ana'na], **ananás** [ana'nas] nm pineapple

anaquel [ana'kel] nm shelf

anaranjado, -a [anaran'xaðo, a] adj orange (-coloured)

anarquía [anar'kia] nf anarchy

anarquismo [anar'kismo] nm anarchism

anarquista [anar'kista] nm/f anarchist

anatematizar [anatemati'θar] vt (Rel) to anathematize; (fig) to curse

anatemice etc [anate'miθe] vb ver **anatemizar**

anatomía [anato'mia] nf anatomy

anca ['anka] nf rump, haunch; **ancas** nfpl (fam) behind sg; **llevar a algn en ancas** to carry sb behind one

ancestral [anθes'tral] adj (costumbre) age-old

ancho, -a ['antʃo, a] adj wide; (falda) full; (fig) liberal ■ nm width; (Ferro) gauge; **le viene muy ~ el cargo** (fig) the job is too much for him; **ponerse ~** to get conceited; **quedarse tan ~** to go on as if nothing had happened; **estar a sus anchas** to be at one's ease

anchoa [an'tʃoa] nf anchovy

anchura [an'tʃura] nf width; (amplitud) wideness

anchuroso, -a [antʃu'roso, a] adj wide

anciano, -a [an'θjano, a] adj old, aged ■ nm/f old man/woman ■ nm elder

ancla ['ankla] nf anchor; **levar anclas** to weigh anchor

ancladero [ankla'ðero] nm anchorage

anclar [an'klar] vi to (drop) anchor

andadas [an'daðas] nfpl (aventuras) adventures; **volver a las ~** to backslide

andaderas [anda'ðeras] nfpl baby-walker sg

andadura [anda'ðura] nf gait; (de caballo) pace

Andalucía [andalu'θia] nf Andalusia

andaluz, a [anda'luθ, a] adj, nm/f Andalusian

andamio [an'damjo] nm, **andamiaje** [anda'mjaxe] nm scaffold(ing)

andanada [anda'naða] nf (fig) reprimand;

soltarle a algn una ~ to give sb a rocket
andante [an'dante] *adj:* **caballero ~** knight errant
andar [an'dar] *vt* to go, cover, travel ■ *vi* to go, walk, travel; *(funcionar)* to go, work; *(estar)* to be ■ *nm* walk, gait, pace; **andarse** *vr (irse)* to go away o off; **~ a pie/a caballo/en bicicleta** to go on foot/on horseback/by bicycle; **¡anda!** *(sorpresa)* go on!; **anda en o por los 40** he's about 40; **¿en qué andas?** what are you up to?; **andamos mal de dinero/tiempo** we're badly off for money/ we're short of time; **andarse por las ramas** to beat about the bush; **no andarse con rodeos** to call a spade a spade *(fam)*; **todo se ~á** all in good time; **anda por aquí** it's round here somewhere; **~ haciendo algo** to be doing sth
andariego, -a [anda'rjeɣo, a] *adj* fond of travelling
andas ['andas] *nfpl* stretcher *sg*
andén [an'den] *nm (Ferro)* platform; *(Naut)* quayside; *(Am: acera)* pavement *(Brit)*, sidewalk *(US)*
Andes ['andes] *nmpl:* **los ~** the Andes
andinismo [andin'ismo] *nm (Am)* mountaineering, climbing
andino, -a [an'dino, a] *adj* Andean, of the Andes
Andorra [an'dorra] *nf* Andorra
andrajo [an'draxo] *nm* rag
andrajoso, -a [andra'xoso, a] *adj* ragged
andurriales [andu'rrjales] *nmpl* out-of-the-way place *sg*, the sticks; **en esos ~** in that godforsaken spot
anduve [an'duβe], **anduviera** *etc* [andu'βjera] *vb ver* **andar**
anécdota [a'nekðota] *nf* anecdote, story
anegar [ane'ɣar] *vt* to flood; *(ahogar)* to drown; **anegarse** *vr* to drown; *(hundirse)* to sink
anegue *etc* [a'neɣe] *vb ver* **anegar**
anejo, -a [a'nexo, a] *adj* attached ■ *nm (Arq)* annexe
anemia [a'nemja] *nf* anaemia
anestesia [anes'tesja] *nf* anaesthetic; **~ general/local** general/local anaesthetic
anestesiar [aneste'sjar] *vt* to anaesthetize *(Brit)*, anesthetize *(US)*
anestésico [anes'tesiko] *nm* anaesthetic
anexar [anek'sar] *vt* to annex; *(documento)* to attach; *(Inform)* to append
anexión [anek'sjon] *nf*, **anexionamiento** [aneksjona'mjento] *nm* annexation
anexionar [aneksjo'nar] *vt* to annex; **anexionarse** *vr:* **anexionarse un país** to annex a country

anexo, -a [a'nekso, a] *adj* attached ■ *nm* annexe
anfetamina [anfeta'mina] *nf* amphetamine
anfibio, -a [an'fiβjo, a] *adj* amphibious ■ *nm* amphibian
anfiteatro [anfite'atro] *nm* amphitheatre; *(Teat)* dress circle
anfitrión, -ona [anfi'trjon, ona] *nm/f* host(ess)
ángel ['anxel] *nm* angel; **ángel de la guarda** guardian angel; **tener ángel** to have charm
Ángeles ['anxeles] *nmpl:* **los Ángeles** Los Angeles
angélico, -a [an'xeliko, a], **angelical** [anxeli'kal] *adj* angelic(al)
angina [an'xina] *nf (Med):* **~ de pecho** angina; **tener anginas** to have a sore throat
o throat infection
anglicano, -a [angli'kano, a] *adj, nm/f* Anglican
anglicismo [angli'θismo] *nm* anglicism
anglosajón, -ona [anglosa'xon, 'xona] *adj, nm/f* Anglo-Saxon
Angola [an'gola] *nf* Angola
angoleño, -a [ango'leɲo, a] *adj, nm/f* Angolan
angosto, -a [an'gosto, a] *adj* narrow
anguila [an'gila] *nf* eel; **anguilas** *nfpl* slipway *sg*
angula [an'gula] *nf* elver, baby eel
ángulo ['angulo] *nm* angle; *(esquina)* corner; *(curva)* bend
angustia [an'gustja] *nf* anguish
angustiar [angus'tjar] *vt* to distress, grieve; **angustiarse** *vr:* **angustiarse (por)** to be distressed (at, on account of)
anhelante [ane'lante] *adj* eager; *(deseoso)* longing
anhelar [ane'lar] *vt* to be eager for; to long for, desire ■ *vi* to pant, gasp
anhelo [a'nelo] *nm* eagerness; desire
anhídrido [a'niðriðo] *nm:* **~ carbónico** carbon dioxide
anidar [ani'ðar] *vt (acoger)* to take in, shelter ■ *vi* to nest; *(fig)* to make one's home
anilina [ani'lina] *nf* aniline
anilla [a'niʎa] *nf* ring; **(las) anillas** *(Deporte)* the rings
anillo [a'niʎo] *nm* ring; **~ de boda** wedding ring; **~ de compromiso** engagement ring; **venir como ~ al dedo** to suit to a tee
ánima ['anima] *nf* soul; **las ánimas** the Angelus (bell) *sg*
animación [anima'θjon] *nf* liveliness; *(vitalidad)* life; *(actividad)* bustle
animado, -a [ani'maðo, a] *adj (vivo)* lively; *(vivaz)* animated; *(concurrido)* bustling; *(alegre)* in high spirits; **dibujos animados** cartoon *sg*

animador, a [anima'ðor, a] *nm/f* (*TV*) host(ess) ■ *nf* (*Deporte*) cheerleader
animadversión [animaðβer'sjon] *nf* ill-will, antagonism
animal [ani'mal] *adj* animal; (*fig*) stupid ■ *nm* animal; (*fig*) fool; (*bestia*) brute
animalada [anima'laða] *nf* (*gen*) silly thing (to do *o* say); (*ultraje*) disgrace
animar [ani'mar] *vt* (*Bio*) to animate, give life to; (*fig*) to liven up, brighten up, cheer up; (*estimular*) to stimulate; **animarse** *vr* to cheer up, feel encouraged; (*decidirse*) to make up one's mind
ánimo ['animo] *nm* soul, mind; (*valentía*) courage ■ *excl* cheer up!; **cobrar ánimo** to take heart; **dar ánimo(s) a** to encourage
animoso, -a [ani'moso, a] *adj* brave; (*vivo*) lively
aniñado, -a [ani'ɲaðo, a] *adj* (*facción*) childlike; (*carácter*) childish
aniquilar [aniki'lar] *vt* to annihilate, destroy
anís [a'nis] *nm* (*grano*) aniseed; (*licor*) anisette
aniversario [aniβer'sarjo] *nm* anniversary
Ankara [an'kara] *nf* Ankara
ano ['ano] *nm* anus
anoche [a'notʃe] *adv* last night; **antes de ~** the night before last
anochecer [anotʃe'θer] *vi* to get dark ■ *nm* nightfall, dark; **al ~** at nightfall
anochezca *etc* [ano'tʃeθka] *vb ver* **anochecer**
anodino, -a [ano'ðino, a] *adj* dull, anodyne
anomalía [anoma'lia] *nf* anomaly
anonadado, -a [anona'ðaðo, a] *adj* stunned
anonimato [anoni'mato] *nm* anonymity
anónimo, -a [a'nonimo, a] *adj* anonymous; (*Com*) limited ■ *nm* (*carta*) anonymous letter; (*: maliciosa*) poison-pen letter
anorak [ano'rak] (*pl* **anoraks**) *nm* anorak
anorexia [ano'reksja] *nf* anorexia
anormal [anor'mal] *adj* abnormal
anotación [anota'θjon] *nf* note; annotation
anotar [ano'tar] *vt* to note down; (*comentar*) to annotate
anquilosado, -a [ankilo'saðo, a] *adj* (*fig*) stale, out of date
anquilosamiento [ankilosa'mjento] *nm* (*fig*) paralysis, stagnation
ansia ['ansja] *nf* anxiety; (*añoranza*) yearning
ansiar [an'sjar] *vt* to long for
ansiedad [ansje'ðað] *nf* anxiety
ansioso, -a [an'sjoso, a] *adj* anxious; (*anhelante*) eager; **~ de** *o* **por algo** greedy for sth
antagónico, -a [anta'yoniko, a] *adj* antagonistic; (*opuesto*) contrasting
antagonista [antayo'nista] *nm/f* antagonist
antaño [an'taɲo] *adv* long ago

Antártico [an'tartiko] *nm*: **el (océano) ~** the Antarctic (Ocean)
Antártida [an'tartiða] *nf* Antarctica
ante ['ante] *prep* before, in the presence of; (*encarado con*) faced with ■ *nm* suede; **~ todo** above all
anteanoche [antea'notʃe] *adv* the night before last
anteayer [antea'jer] *adv* the day before yesterday
antebrazo [ante'βraθo] *nm* forearm
antecámara [ante'kamara] *nf* (*Arq*) anteroom; (*antesala*) waiting room; (*Pol*) lobby
antecedente [anteθe'ðente] *adj* previous ■ *nm*: **antecedentes** *nmpl* (*profesionales*) background *sg*; **antecedentes penales** criminal record; **no tener antecedentes** to have a clean record; **estar en antecedentes** to be well-informed; **poner a algn en antecedentes** to put sb in the picture
anteceder [anteθe'ðer] *vt* to precede, go before
antecesor, a [anteθe'sor, a] *nm/f* predecessor
antedicho, -a [ante'ðitʃo, a] *adj* aforementioned
antelación [antela'θjon] *nf*: **con ~** in advance
antemano [ante'mano]: **de ~** *adv* beforehand, in advance
antena [an'tena] *nf* antenna; (*de televisión etc*) aerial
anteojeras [anteo'xeras] *nfpl* blinkers (*Brit*), blinders (*US*)
anteojo [ante'oxo] *nm* eyeglass; **anteojos** *nmpl* (*esp Am*) glasses, spectacles
antepasados [antepa'saðos] *nmpl* ancestors
antepecho [ante'petʃo] *nm* guardrail, parapet; (*repisa*) ledge, sill
antepondré *etc* [antepon'dre] *vb ver* **anteponer**
anteponer [antepo'ner] *vt* to place in front; (*fig*) to prefer
anteponga *etc* [ante'ponya] *vb ver* **anteponer**
anteproyecto [antepro'jekto] *nm* preliminary sketch; (*fig*) blueprint; (*Pol*): **~ de ley** draft bill
antepuesto, -a [ante'pwesto, a] *pp de* **anteponer**
antepuse *etc* [ante'puse] *vb ver* **anteponer**
anterior [ante'rjor] *adj* preceding, previous
anterioridad [anterjori'ðað] *nf*: **con ~ a** prior to, before
anteriormente [anterjor'mente] *adv* previously, before
antes ['antes] *adv* sooner; (*primero*) first; (*con anterioridad*) before; (*hace tiempo*) previously, once; (*más bien*) rather ■ *prep*: **~ de** before

23

■ *conj*: ~ **(de) que** before; ~ **bien** (but) rather; **dos días** ~ two days before *o* previously; **mucho/poco** ~ long/shortly before; ~ **muerto que esclavo** better dead than enslaved; **tomo el avión** ~ **que el barco** I take the plane rather than the boat; **cuanto** ~, **lo** ~ **posible** as soon as possible; **cuanto** ~ **mejor** the sooner the better
antesala [ante'sala] *nf* anteroom
antiadherente [antiaðe'rente] *adj* non-stick
antiaéreo, -a [antia'ereo, a] *adj* anti-aircraft
antialcohólico, -a [antial'koliko, a] *adj*: **centro** ~ (*Med*) detoxification unit
antibalas [anti'βalas] *adj inv*: **chaleco** ~ bulletproof jacket
antibiótico [anti'βjotiko] *nm* antibiotic
anticiclón [antiθi'klon] *nm* (*Meteorología*) anti-cyclone
anticipación [antiθipa'θjon] *nf* anticipation; **con 10 minutos de** ~ 10 minutes early
anticipado, -a [antiθi'paðo, a] *adj* (in) advance; **por** ~ in advance
anticipar [antiθi'par] *vt* to anticipate; (*adelantar*) to bring forward; (*Com*) to advance; **anticiparse** *vr*: **anticiparse a su época** to be ahead of one's time
anticipo [anti'θipo] *nm* (*Com*) advance
anticonceptivo, -a [antikonθep'tiβo, a] *adj, nm* contraceptive; **métodos anticonceptivos** methods of birth control
anticongelante [antikonxe'lante] *nm* antifreeze
anticonstitucional [antikonstituθjo'nal] *adj* unconstitutional
anticuado, -a [anti'kwaðo, a] *adj* out-of-date, old-fashioned; (*desusado*) obsolete
anticuario [anti'kwarjo] *nm* antique dealer
anticuerpo [anti'kwerpo] *nm* (*Med*) antibody
antidemocrático, -a [antiðemo'kratiko, a] *adj* undemocratic
antideportivo, -a [antiðepor'tiβo, a] *adj* unsporting
antidepresivo [antiðepre'siβo] *nm* antidepressant
antideslumbrante [antiðeslum'brante] *adj* (*Inform*) anti-dazzle
antidoping [anti'ðopin] *adj inv* anti-drug
antídoto [an'tiðoto] *nm* antidote
antidroga [anti'ðroɣa] *adj inv* anti-drug; **brigada** ~ drug squad
antiestético, -a [anties'tetiko, a] *adj* unsightly
antifaz [anti'faθ] *nm* mask; (*velo*) veil
antigás [anti'gas] *adj inv*: **careta** ~ gas mask
antiglobalización [antiglobaliθa'θjon] *n* anti-globalization; **manifestantes** ~ anti-globalization protesters

antigualla [anti'ɣwaʎa] *nf* antique; (*reliquia*) relic; **antiguallas** *nfpl* old things
antiguamente [antiɣwa'mente] *adv* formerly; (*hace mucho tiempo*) long ago
antigüedad [antiɣwe'ðað] *nf* antiquity; (*artículo*) antique; (*rango*) seniority
antiguo, -a [an'tiɣwo, a] *adj* old, ancient; (*que fue*) former; **a la antigua** in the old-fashioned way
antihigiénico, -a [anti'xjeniko, a] *adj* unhygienic
antihistamínico, -a [antista'miniko, a] *adj, nm* antihistamine
antiinflacionista [antinflaθjo'nista] *adj* anti-inflationary, counter-inflationary
antillano, -a [anti'ʎano, a] *adj, nm/f* West Indian
Antillas [an'tiʎas] *nfpl*: **las** ~ the West Indies, the Antilles; **el mar de las** ~ the Caribbean Sea
antílope [an'tilope] *nm* antelope
antimonopolios [antimono'poljos] *adj inv*: **ley** ~ anti-trust law
antinatural [antinatu'ral] *adj* unnatural
antiparras [anti'parras] *nfpl* (*fam*) specs
antipatía [antipa'tia] *nf* antipathy, dislike
antipático, -a [anti'patiko, a] *adj* disagreeable, unpleasant
Antípodas [an'tipoðas] *nfpl*: **las** ~ the Antipodes
antiquísimo, -a [anti'kisimo, a] *adj* ancient
antirreglamentario, -a [antirreɣlamen'tarjo, a] *adj* (*gen*) unlawful; (*Pol etc*) unconstitutional
antirrobo [anti'rroβo] *nm* (*tb*: **dispositivo antirrobo**: *para casas etc*) burglar alarm; (*para coches*) car alarm
antisemita [antise'mita] *adj* anti-Semitic
■ *nm/f* anti-Semite
antiséptico, -a [anti'septiko, a] *adj, nm* antiseptic
antiterrorista [antiterro'rista] *adj* antiterrorist; **la lucha** ~ the fight against terrorism
antítesis [an'titesis] *nf inv* antithesis
antivírico, -a [anti'βiriko, a] *adj* (*Med*) antiviral
antojadizo, -a [antoxa'ðiθo, a] *adj* capricious
antojarse [anto'xarse] *vr* (*desear*): **se me antoja comprarlo** I have a mind to buy it; (*pensar*): **se me antoja que** I have a feeling that
antojo [an'toxo] *nm* caprice, whim; (*rosa*) birthmark; (*lunar*) mole; **hacer a su** ~ to do as one pleases
antología [antolo'xia] *nf* anthology
antonomasia [antono'masja] *nf*: **por** ~ par excellence

antorcha [an'tortʃa] *nf* torch
antro ['antro] *nm* cavern; **~ de corrupción** (*fig*) den of iniquity
antropófago, -a [antro'pofaɣo, a] *adj, nm/f* cannibal
antropología [antropolo'xia] *nf* anthropology
antropólogo, -a [antro'poloɣo, a] *nm/f* anthropologist
anual [a'nwal] *adj* annual
anualidad [anwali'ðað] *nf* annuity, annual payment; **~ vitalicia** life annuity
anuario [a'nwarjo] *nm* yearbook
anublado, -a [anu'βlaðo, a] *adj* overcast
anudar [anu'ðar] *vt* to knot, tie; (*unir*) to join; **anudarse** *vr* to get tied up; **se me anudó la voz** I got a lump in my throat
anulación [anula'θjon] *nf* annulment; cancellation; repeal
anular [anu'lar] *vt* to annul, cancel; (*suscripción*) to cancel; (*ley*) to repeal ■ *nm* ring finger
anunciación [anunθja'θjon] *nf* announcement; **A~** (*Rel*) Annunciation
anunciante [anun'θjante] *nm/f* advertiser
anunciar [anun'θjar] *vt* to announce, (*proclamar*) to proclaim; (*Com*) to advertise
anuncio [a'nunθjo] *nm* announcement; (*señal*) sign; (*Com*) advertisement; (*cartel*) poster; (*Teat*) bill; **anuncios por palabras** classified ads
anverso [am'berso] *nm* obverse
anzuelo [an'θwelo] *nm* hook; (*para pescar*) fish hook; **tragar el ~** to swallow the bait
añadido [aɲa'ðiðo] *nm* addition
añadidura [aɲaði'ðura] *nf* addition, extra; **por ~** besides, in addition
añadir [aɲa'ðir] *vt* to add
añejo, -a [a'ɲexo, a] *adj* old; (*vino*) vintage; (*jamón*) well-cured
añicos [a'ɲikos] *nmpl*: **hacer ~** to smash, shatter; **hacerse ~** to smash, shatter
añil [a'ɲil] *nm* (*Bot, color*) indigo
año ['aɲo] *nm* year; **¡Feliz A~ Nuevo!** Happy New Year!; **tener 15 años** to be 15 (years old); **los años 80** the eighties; **~ bisiesto/escolar** leap/school year; **~ fiscal** fiscal *o* tax year; **estar de buen ~** to be in good shape; **en el ~ de la nana** in the year dot; **el ~ que viene** next year
añoranza [aɲo'ranθa] *nf* nostalgia; (*anhelo*) longing
añorar [aɲo'rar] *vt* to long for
añoso, -a [a'ɲoso, a] *adj* ancient, old
aovado, -a [ao'βaðo, a] *adj* oval
aovar [ao'βar] *vi* to lay eggs
apabullar [apaβu'ʎar] *vt* (*lit, fig*) to crush

apacentar [apaθen'tar] *vt* to pasture, graze
apacible [apa'θiβle] *adj* gentle, mild
apaciente *etc* [apa'θjente] *vb ver* **apacentar**
apaciguar [apaθi'ɣwar] *vt* to pacify, calm (down)
apacigüe *etc* [apa'θiɣwe] *vb ver* **apaciguar**
apadrinar [apaðri'nar] *vt* to sponsor, support; (*Rel*) to act as godfather to
apagado, -a [apa'ɣaðo, a] *adj* (*volcán*) extinct; (*color*) dull; (*voz*) quiet; (*sonido*) muted, muffled; (*persona: apático*) listless; **estar ~** (*fuego, luz*) to be out; (*radio, TV etc*) to be off
apagar [apa'ɣar] *vt* to put out; (*color*) to tone down; (*sonido*) to silence, muffle; (*sed*) to quench; (*Inform*) to toggle off; **apagarse** *vr* (*luz, fuego*) to go out; (*sonido*) to die away; (*pasión*) to wither; **~ el sistema** (*Inform*) to close *o* shut down
apagón [apa'ɣon] *nm* blackout, power cut
apague *etc* [a'paɣe] *vb ver* **apagar**
apaisado, -a [apai'saðo, a] *adj* (*papel*) landscape *cpd*
apalabrar [apala'βrar] *vt* to agree to; (*obrero*) to engage
Apalaches [apa'latʃes] *nmpl*: **(Montes) ~** Appalachians
apalear [apale'ar] *vt* to beat, thrash; (*Agr*) to winnow
apañado, -a [apa'ɲaðo, a] *adj* (*mañoso*) resourceful; (*arreglado*) tidy; (*útil*) handy
apañar [apa'ɲar] *vt* to pick up; (*asir*) to take hold of, grasp; (*reparar*) to mend, patch up; **apañarse** *vr* to manage, get along; **apañárselas por su cuenta** to look after number one (*fam*)
apaño [a'paɲo] *nm* (*Costura*) patch; (*maña*) skill; **esto no tiene ~** there's no answer to this one
aparador [apara'ðor] *nm* sideboard; (*escaparate*) shop window
aparato [apa'rato] *nm* apparatus; (*máquina*) machine; (*doméstico*) appliance; (*boato*) ostentation; (*Inform*) device; **al ~** (*Telec*) speaking; **~ de facsímil** facsimile (machine), fax; **~ respiratorio** respiratory system; **aparatos de mando** (*Aviat etc*) controls
aparatoso, -a [apara'toso, a] *adj* showy, ostentatious
aparcamiento [aparka'mjento] *nm* car park (*Brit*), parking lot (*US*)
aparcar [apar'kar] *vt, vi* to park
aparear [apare'ar] *vt* (*objetos*) to pair, match; (*animales*) to mate; **aparearse** *vr* to form a pair; to mate
aparecer [apare'θer] *vi*, **aparecerse** *vr* to appear; **apareció borracho** he turned up drunk

aparejado, -a [apare'xaðo, a] *adj* fit, suitable; **ir ~ con** to go hand in hand with; **llevar** *o* **traer ~** to involve
aparejador, a [aparexa'ðor, a] *nm/f* (*Arq*) quantity surveyor
aparejar [apare'xar] *vt* to prepare; (*caballo*) to saddle, harness; (*Naut*) to fit out, rig out
aparejo [apa'rexo] *nm* preparation; (*de caballo*) harness; (*Naut*) rigging; (*de poleas*) block and tackle
aparentar [aparen'tar] *vt* (*edad*) to look; (*fingir*): **~ tristeza** to pretend to be sad
aparente [apa'rente] *adj* apparent; (*adecuado*) suitable
aparezca *etc* [apa'reθka] *vb ver* **aparecer**
aparición [apari'θjon] *nf* appearance; (*de libro*) publication; (*de fantasma*) spectre
apariencia [apa'rjenθja] *nf* (outward) appearance; **en ~** outwardly, seemingly
aparque *etc* [a'parke] *vb ver* **aparcar**
apartado, -a [apar'taðo, a] *adj* separate; (*lejano*) remote ■ *nm* (*tipográfico*) paragraph; **~ (de correos)** post office box
apartamento [aparta'mento] *nm* apartment, flat (*Brit*)
apartamiento [aparta'mjento] *nm* separation; (*aislamiento*) remoteness; (*Am*) apartment, flat (*Brit*)
apartar [apar'tar] *vt* to separate; (*quitar*) to remove; (*Mineralogía*) to extract; **apartarse** *vr* (*separarse*) to separate, part; (*irse*) to move away; (*mantenerse aparte*) to keep away
aparte [a'parte] *adv* (*separadamente*) separately; (*además*) besides ■ *prep*: **~ de** apart from ■ *nm* (*Teat*) aside; (*tipográfico*) new paragraph; **"punto y ~"** "new paragraph"
apasionado, -a [apasjo'naðo, a] *adj* passionate; (*pey*) biassed, prejudiced ■ *nm/f* admirer
apasionante [apasjo'nante] *adj* exciting
apasionar [apasjo'nar] *vt* to arouse passion in; **apasionarse** *vr* to get excited; **le apasiona el fútbol** she's crazy about football
apatía [apa'tia] *nf* apathy
apático, -a [a'patiko, a] *adj* apathetic
apátrida [a'patriða] *adj* stateless
Apdo. *nm abr* (= *Apartado (de Correos)*) P.O. Box
apeadero [apea'ðero] *nm* halt, stopping place
apearse [ape'arse] *vr* (*jinete*) to dismount; (*bajarse*) to get down *o* out; (*de coche*) to get out, alight; **no ~ del burro** to refuse to climb down
apechugar [apetʃu'ɣar] *vi*: **~ con algo** to face up to sth

apechugue *etc* [ape'tʃuɣe] *vb ver* **apechugar**
apedrear [apeðre'ar] *vt* to stone
apegarse [ape'ɣarse] *vr*: **~ a** to become attached to
apego [a'peɣo] *nm* attachment, devotion
apegue *etc* [a'peɣe] *vb ver* **apegarse**
apelación [apela'θjon] *nf* appeal
apelar [ape'lar] *vi* to appeal; **~ a** (*fig*) to resort to
apelativo [apela'tiβo] *nm* (*Ling*) appellative; (*Am*) surname
apellidar [apeʎi'ðar] *vt* to call, name; **apellidarse** *vr*: **se apellida Pérez** her (sur)name's Pérez
apellido [ape'ʎiðo] *nm* surname; *see note*

● **APELLIDO**

● In the Spanish-speaking world most
● people use two *apellidos*, the first being
● their father's first surname, and the
● second their mother's first surname:
● eg the children of Juan García López,
● married to Carmen Pérez Rodríguez
● would have as their surname García
● Pérez. Married women retain their own
● surname(s) and sometimes add their
● husband's first surname on to theirs: eg
● Carmen Pérez de García. She could also
● be referred to as (la) Señora de García. In
● Latin America it is usual for the second
● surname to be shortened to an initial in
● correspondence eg: Juan García L.

apelmazado, -a [apelma'θaðo, a] *adj* compact, solid
apelotonar [apeloto'nar] *vt* to roll into a ball; **apelotonarse** *vr* (*gente*) to crowd together
apenar [ape'nar] *vt* to grieve, trouble; (*Am: avergonzar*) to embarrass; **apenarse** *vr* to grieve; (*Am*) to be embarrassed
apenas [a'penas] *adv* scarcely, hardly ■ *conj* as soon as, no sooner
apéndice [a'pendiθe] *nm* appendix
apendicitis [apendi'θitis] *nf* appendicitis
Apeninos [ape'ninos] *nmpl* Apennines
apercibimiento [aperθiβi'mjento] *nm* (*aviso*) warning
apercibir [aperθi'βir] *vt* to prepare; (*avisar*) to warn; (*Jur*) to summon; (*Am*) to notice, see; **apercibirse** *vr* to get ready; **apercibirse de** to notice
aperitivo [aperi'tiβo] *nm* (*bebida*) aperitif; (*comida*) appetizer
apero [a'pero] *nm* (*Agr*) implement; **aperos** *nmpl* farm equipment *sg*
apertura [aper'tura] *nf* (*gen*) opening;

(Pol) openness, liberalization; (Teat etc) beginning; ~ **de un juicio hipotecario** (Com) foreclosure

aperturismo [apertu'rismo] nm (Pol) (policy of) liberalization

apesadumbrar [apesaðum'brar] vt to grieve, sadden; **apesadumbrarse** vr to distress o.s.

apestar [apes'tar] vt to infect ■ vi: ~ **(a)** to stink (of)

apestoso, -a [apes'toso, a] adj (hediondo) stinking; (asqueroso) sickening

apetecer [apete'θer] vt: ¿**te apetece una tortilla?** do you fancy an omelette?

apetecible [apete'θiβle] adj desirable; (comida) tempting

apetezca etc [ape'teθka] vb ver **apetecer**

apetito [ape'tito] nm appetite

apetitoso, -a [apeti'toso, a] adj (gustoso) appetizing; (fig) tempting

apiadarse [apja'ðarse] vr: ~ **de** to take pity on

ápice ['apiθe] nm apex; (fig) whit, iota; **ni un ápice** not a whit; **no ceder un ápice** not to budge an inch

apicultor, a [apikul'tor, a] nm/f beekeeper, apiarist

apicultura [apikul'tura] nf beekeeping

apiladora [apila'ðora] nf (para máquina Impresora) stacker

apilar [api'lar] vt to pile o heap up; **apilarse** vr to pile up

apiñado, -a [api'ɲaðo, a] adj (apretado) packed

apiñar [api'ɲar] vt to crowd; **apiñarse** vr to crowd o press together

apio ['apjo] nm celery

apisonadora [apisona'ðora] nf (máquina) steamroller

aplacar [apla'kar] vt to placate; **aplacarse** vr to calm down

aplace etc [a'plaθe] vb ver **aplazar**

aplanamiento [aplana'mjento] nm smoothing, levelling

aplanar [apla'nar] vt to smooth, level; (allanar) to roll flat, flatten; **aplanarse** vr (edificio) to collapse; (persona) to get discouraged

aplaque etc [a'plake] vb ver **aplacar**

aplastar [aplas'tar] vt to squash (flat); (fig) to crush

aplatanarse [aplata'narse] vr to get lethargic

aplaudir [aplau'ðir] vt to applaud

aplauso [a'plauso] nm applause; (fig) approval, acclaim

aplazamiento [aplaθa'mjento] nm postponement

aplazar [apla'θar] vt to postpone, defer

aplicación [aplika'θjon] nf application; (esfuerzo) effort; **aplicaciones de gestión** business applications

aplicado, -a [apli'kaðo, a] adj diligent, hard-working

aplicar [apli'kar] vt (gen) to apply; (poner en vigor) to put into effect; (esfuerzos) to devote; **aplicarse** vr to apply o.s.

aplique etc [a'plike] vb ver **aplicar** ■ nm wall light o lamp

aplomo [a'plomo] nm aplomb, self-assurance

apocado, -a [apo'kaðo, a] adj timid

apocamiento [apoka'mjento] nm timidity; (depresión) depression

apocarse [apo'karse] vr to feel small o humiliated

apocopar [apoko'par] vt (Ling) to shorten

apócope [a'pokope] nf apocopation; **gran es ~ de grande** "gran" is the shortened form of "grande"

apócrifo, -a [a'pokrifo, a] adj apocryphal

apodar [apo'ðar] vt to nickname

apoderado [apoðe'raðo] nm agent, representative

apoderar [apoðe'rar] vt to authorize, empower; (Jur) to grant (a) power of attorney to; **apoderarse** vr: **apoderarse de** to take possession of

apodo [a'poðo] nm nickname

apogeo [apo'xeo] nm peak, summit

apolillado, -a [apoli'Aaðo, a] adj moth-eaten

apolillarse [apoli'Aarse] vr to get moth-eaten

apología [apolo'xia] nf eulogy; (defensa) defence

apoltronarse [apoltro'narse] vr to get lazy

apoplejía [apople'xia] nf apoplexy, stroke

apoque etc [a'poke] vb ver **apocarse**

apoquinar [apoki'nar] vt (fam) to cough up, fork out

aporrear [aporre'ar] vt to beat (up)

aportación [aporta'θjon] nf contribution

aportar [apor'tar] vt to contribute ■ vi to reach port

aposentar [aposen'tar] vt to lodge, put up

aposento [apo'sento] nm lodging; (habitación) room

apósito [a'posito] nm (Med) dressing

aposta [a'posta] adv on purpose

apostar [apos'tar] vt to bet, stake; (tropas etc) to station, post ■ vi to bet

apostatar [aposta'tar] vi (Rel) to apostatize; (fig) to change sides

a posteriori [apos'terjori] adv at a later date o stage; (Lógica) a posteriori

apostilla [apos'tiAa] nf note, comment

apóstol [a'postol] nm apostle

apóstrofo [a'postrofo] nm apostrophe

27

apostura [apos'tura] *nf* neatness, elegance
apoteósico, -a [apote'osiko, a] *adj* tremendous
apoyar [apo'jar] *vt* to lean, rest; (*fig*) to support, back; **apoyarse** *vr*: **apoyarse en** to lean on
apoyo [a'pojo] *nm* support, backing
apreciable [apre'θjaβle] *adj* considerable; (*fig*) esteemed
apreciación [apreθja'θjon] *nf* appreciation; (*Com*) valuation
apreciar [apre'θjar] *vt* to evaluate, assess; (*Com*) to appreciate, value ▪ *vi* (*Econ*) to appreciate
aprecio [a'preθjo] *nm* valuation, estimate; (*fig*) appreciation
aprehender [apreen'der] *vt* to apprehend, detain; (*ver*) to see, observe
aprehensión [apreen'sjon] *nf* detention, capture
apremiante [apre'mjante] *adj* urgent, pressing
apremiar [apre'mjar] *vt* to compel, force ▪ *vi* to be urgent, press
apremio [a'premjo] *nm* urgency; **~ de pago** demand note
aprender [apren'der] *vt, vi* to learn; **~ a conducir** to learn to drive; **aprenderse** *vr*: **aprenderse algo** to learn sth (off) by heart
aprendiz, a [apren'diθ, a] *nm/f* apprentice; (*principiante*) learner, trainee; **~ de comercio** business trainee
aprendizaje [aprendi'θaxe] *nm* apprenticeship
aprensión [apren'sjon] *nm* apprehension, fear
aprensivo, -a [apren'siβo, a] *adj* apprehensive
apresar [apre'sar] *vt* to seize; (*capturar*) to capture
aprestar [apres'tar] *vt* to prepare, get ready; (*Tec*) to prime, size; **aprestarse** *vr* to get ready
apresto [a'presto] *nm* (*gen*) preparation; (*sustancia*) size
apresurado, -a [apresu'raðo, a] *adj* hurried, hasty
apresuramiento [apresura'mjento] *nm* hurry, haste
apresurar [apresu'rar] *vt* to hurry, accelerate; **apresurarse** *vr* to hurry, make haste; **me apresuré a sugerir que ...** I hastily suggested that ...
apretado, -a [apre'taðo, a] *adj* tight; (*escritura*) cramped
apretar [apre'tar] *vt* to squeeze, press; (*mano*) to clasp; (*dientes*) to grit; (*Tec*) to tighten;

(*presionar*) to press together, pack ▪ *vi* to be too tight; **apretarse** *vr* to crowd together; **~ la mano a algn** to shake sb's hand; **~ el paso** to quicken one's step
apretón [apre'ton] *nm* squeeze; **~ de manos** handshake
aprieto *etc* [a'prjeto] *vb ver* **apretar** ▪ *nm* squeeze; (*dificultad*) difficulty, jam; **estar en un ~** to be in a jam; **ayudar a algn a salir de un ~** to help sb out of trouble
a priori [apri'ori] *adv* beforehand; (*Lógica*) a priori
aprisa [a'prisa] *adv* quickly, hurriedly
aprisionar [aprisjo'nar] *vt* to imprison
aprobación [aproβa'θjon] *nf* approval
aprobado [apro'βaðo] *nm* (*nota*) pass mark
aprobar [apro'βar] *vt* to approve (of); (*examen, materia*) to pass ▪ *vi* to pass
apropiación [apropja'θjon] *nf* appropriation
apropiado, -a [apro'pjaðo, a] *adj* appropriate
apropiarse [apro'pjarse] *vr*: **~ de** to appropriate
aprovechado, -a [aproβe'tʃaðo, a] *adj* industrious, hardworking; (*económico*) thrifty; (*pey*) unscrupulous
aprovechamiento [aproβetʃa'mjento] *nm* use, exploitation
aprovechar [aproβe'tʃar] *vt* to use; (*explotar*) to exploit; (*experiencia*) to profit from; (*oferta, oportunidad*) to take advantage of ▪ *vi* to progress, improve; **aprovecharse** *vr*: **aprovecharse de** to make use of; (*pey*) to take advantage of; **¡que aproveche!** enjoy your meal!
aprovisionar [aproβisjo'nar] *vt* to supply
aproximación [aproksima'θjon] *nf* approximation; (*de lotería*) consolation prize
aproximadamente [aproksimaða'mente] *adv* approximately
aproximado, -a [aproksi'maðo, a] *adj* approximate
aproximar [aproksi'mar] *vt* to bring nearer; **aproximarse** *vr* to come near, approach
apruebe *etc* [a'prweβe] *vb ver* **aprobar**
aptitud [apti'tuð] *nf* aptitude; (*capacidad*) ability; **~ para los negocios** business sense
apto, -a ['apto, a] *adj* (*hábil*) capable; (*apropiado*): **~ (para)** fit (for), suitable (for); **~/no ~ para menores** (*Cine*) suitable/unsuitable for children
apuesto, -a *etc* [a'pwesto, a] *vb ver* **apostar** ▪ *adj* neat, elegant ▪ *nf* bet, wager
apuntador [apunta'ðor] *nm* prompter
apuntalar [apunta'lar] *vt* to prop up
apuntar [apun'tar] *vt* (*con arma*) to aim at; (*con dedo*) to point at o to; (*anotar*) to note (down); (*datos*) to record; (*Teat*) to prompt;

a

apuntarse vr (Deporte: tanto, victoria) to score; (Escol) to enrol; **~ una cantidad en la cuenta de algn** to charge a sum to sb's account; **apuntarse en un curso** to enrol on a course; **¡yo me apunto!** count me in!

apunte [a'punte] nm note; (Teat: voz) prompt; (: texto) prompt book

apuñalar [apuɲa'lar] vt to stab

apurado, -a [apu'raðo, a] adj needy; (difícil) difficult; (peligroso) dangerous; (Am) hurried, rushed; **estar en una situación apurada** to be in a tight spot; **estar ~** to be in a hurry

apurar [apu'rar] vt (agotar) to drain; (recursos) to use up; (molestar) to annoy; **apurarse** vr (preocuparse) to worry; (esp Am: darse prisa) to hurry

apuro [a'puro] nm (aprieto) fix, jam; (escasez) want, hardship; (vergüenza) embarrassment; (Am) haste, urgency

aquejado, -a [ake'xaðo, a] adj: **~ de** (Med) afflicted by

aquejar [ake'xar] vt (afligir) to distress; **le aqueja una grave enfermedad** he suffers from a serious disease

aquel, aquella, aquellos, -as [a'kel, a'keʎa, a'keʎos, as] adj that, those pl

aquél, aquélla, aquéllos, -as [a'kel, a'keʎa, a'keʎos, as] pron that (one), those (ones) pl

aquello [a'keʎo] pron that, that business

aquí [a'ki] adv (lugar) here; (tiempo) now; **aquí arriba** up here; **aquí mismo** right here; **aquí yace** here lies; **de aquí a siete días** a week from now

aquietar [akje'tar] vt to quieten (down), calm (down)

Aquisgrán [akis'ɣran] nm Aachen, Aix-la-Chapelle

A.R. abr (= Alteza Real) R.H.

ara ['ara] nf (altar) altar; **en aras de** for the sake of

árabe ['araβe] adj Arab, Arabian, Arabic ■ nm/f Arab ■ nm (Ling) Arabic

Arabia [a'raβja] nf Arabia; **~ Saudí** o **Saudita** Saudi Arabia

arábigo, -a [a'raβiɣo, a] adj Arab, Arabian, Arabic

arácnido [a'rakniðo] nm arachnid

arado [a'raðo] nm plough

aragonés, -esa [araɣo'nes, esa] adj, nm/f Aragonese ■ nm (Ling) Aragonese

arancel [aran'θel] nm tariff, duty; **~ de aduanas** (customs) duty

arandela [aran'dela] nf (Tec) washer; (chorrera) frill

araña [a'raɲa] nf (Zool) spider; (lámpara) chandelier

arañar [ara'ɲar] vt to scratch

arañazo [ara'ɲaθo] nm scratch

arar [a'rar] vt to plough, till

araucano, -a [arau'kano, a] adj, nm/f Araucanian

arbitraje [arβi'traxe] nm arbitration

arbitrar [arβi'trar] vt to arbitrate in; (recursos) to bring together; (Deporte) to referee ■ vi to arbitrate

arbitrariedad [arβitrarje'ðað] nf arbitrariness; (acto) arbitrary act

arbitrario, -a [arβi'trarjo, a] adj arbitrary

arbitrio [ar'βitrjo] nm free will; (Jur) adjudication, decision; **dejar al ~ de algn** to leave to sb's discretion

árbitro ['arβitro] nm arbitrator; (Deporte) referee; (Tenis) umpire

árbol ['arβol] nm (Bot) tree; (Naut) mast; (Tec) axle, shaft

arbolado, -a [arβo'laðo, a] adj wooded; (camino) tree-lined ■ nm woodland

arboladura [arβola'ðura] nf rigging

arbolar [arβo'lar] vt to hoist, raise

arboleda [arβo'leða] nf grove, plantation

arbusto [ar'βusto] nm bush, shrub

arca ['arka] nf chest, box; **A~ de la Alianza** Ark of the Covenant; **A~ de Noé** Noah's Ark

arcada [ar'kaða] nf arcade; (de puente) arch, span; **arcadas** nfpl retching sg

arcaico, -a [ar'kaiko, a] adj archaic

arce ['arθe] nm maple tree

arcén [ar'θen] nm (de autopista) hard shoulder; (de carretera) verge

archiconocido, -a [artʃikono'θiðo, a] adj extremely well-known

archipiélago [artʃi'pjelaɣo] nm archipelago

archisabido, -a [artʃisa'βiðo, a] adj extremely well-known

archivador [artʃiβa'ðor] nm filing cabinet; **~ colgante** suspension file

archivar [artʃi'βar] vt to file (away); (Inform) to archive

archivo [ar'tʃiβo] nm archive(s) (pl); (Inform) file; **A~ Nacional** Public Record Office; **archivos policíacos** police files; **nombre de ~** (Inform) filename; **~ adjunto** (Inform) attachment; **~ de seguridad** (Inform) backup file

arcilla [ar'θiʎa] nf clay

arco ['arko] nm arch; (Mat) arc; (Mil: Mus) bow; (Am Deporte) goal; **~ iris** rainbow

arcón [ar'kon] nm large chest

arder [ar'ðer] vt to burn; **~ sin llama** to smoulder; **estar que arde** (persona) to fume

ardid [ar'ðið] nm ruse

ardiente [ar'ðjente] adj ardent

ardilla [ar'ðiʎa] nf squirrel

ardor [ar'ðor] nm (calor) heat, warmth; (fig)

ardour; ~ **de estómago** heartburn

ardoroso, -a [arðo'roso, a] adj passionate

arduo, -a ['arðwo, a] adj arduous

área ['area] nf area; (Deporte) penalty area

arena [a'rena] nf sand; (de una lucha) arena

arenal [are'nal] nm (arena movediza) quicksand

arenga [a'renga] nf (fam) sermon

arengar [aren'gar] vt to harangue

arengue etc [a'renge] vb ver **arengar**

arenillas [are'niʎas] nfpl (Med) stones

arenisca [are'niska] nf sandstone; (cascajo) grit

arenoso, -a [are'noso, a] adj sandy

arenque [a'renke] nm herring

arepa [a'repa] nf (Am) corn pancake

arete [a'rete] nm earring

argamasa [arɣa'masa] nf mortar, plaster

Argel [ar'xel] n Algiers

Argelia [ar'xelja] nf Algeria

argelino, -a [arxe'lino, a] adj, nm/f Algerian

Argentina [arxen'tina] nf: **(la)** ~ the Argentine, Argentina

argentino, -a [arxen'tino, a] adj Argentinian; (de plata) silvery ▪ nm/f Argentinian

argolla [ar'ɣoʎa] nf (large) ring; (Am: de matrimonio) wedding ring

argot [ar'ɣo] nm (pl **argots** [ar'ɣo, ar'ɣos]) slang

argucia [ar'ɣuθja] nf subtlety, sophistry

argüir [ar'ɣwir] vt to deduce; (discutir) to argue; (indicar) to indicate, imply; (censurar) to reproach ▪ vi to argue

argumentación [arɣumenta'θjon] nf (line of) argument

argumentar [arɣumen'tar] vt, vi to argue

argumento [arɣu'mento] nm argument; (razonamiento) reasoning; (de novela etc) plot; (Cine: TV) storyline

arguyendo etc [arɣu'jendo] vb ver **argüir**

aria ['arja] nf aria

aridez [ari'ðeθ] nf aridity, dryness

árido, -a ['ariðo, a] adj arid, dry; **áridos** nmpl dry goods

Aries ['arjes] nm Aries

ariete [a'rjete] nm battering ram

ario, -a ['arjo, a] adj Aryan

arisco, -a [a'risko, a] adj surly; (insociable) unsociable

aristocracia [aristo'kraθja] nf aristocracy

aristócrata [aris'tokrata] nm/f aristocrat

aristocrático, -a [aristo'kratiko, a] adj aristocratic

aritmética [arit'metika] nf arithmetic

aritmético, -a [arit'metiko, a] adj arithmetic(al) ▪ nm/f arithmetician

arma ['arma] nf arm; **armas** nfpl arms;

~ **blanca** blade, knife; (espada) sword; ~ **de fuego** firearm; **armas cortas** small arms; **armas de destrucción masiva** weapons of mass destruction; **rendir las armas** to lay down one's arms; **ser de armas tomar** to be somebody to be reckoned with

armada [ar'maða] nf armada; (flota) fleet; ver tb **armado**

armadillo [arma'ðiʎo] nm armadillo

armado, -a [ar'maðo, a] adj armed; (Tec) reinforced

armador [arma'ðor] nm (Naut) shipowner

armadura [arma'ðura] nf (Mil) armour; (Tec) framework; (Zool) skeleton; (Física) armature

armamentista [armamen'tista], **armamentístico, a** [armamen'tistiko, a] adj arms cpd

armamento [arma'mento] nm armament; (Naut) fitting-out

armar [ar'mar] vt (soldado) to arm; (máquina) to assemble; (navío) to fit out; **armarla, ~ un lío** to start a row; **armarse** vr: **armarse de valor** to summon up one's courage

armario [ar'marjo] nm wardrobe; **salir del ~** to come out (of the closet)

armatoste [arma'toste] nm (mueble) monstrosity; (máquina) contraption

armazón [arma'θon] nf o m body, chassis; (de mueble etc) frame; (Arq) skeleton

Armenia [ar'menja] nf Armenia

armería [arme'ria] nf (museo) military museum; (tienda) gunsmith's

armiño [ar'miɲo] nm stoat; (piel) ermine

armisticio [armis'tiθjo] nm armistice

armonía [armo'nia] nf harmony

armónica [ar'monika] nf harmonica; ver tb **armónico**

armonice etc [armo'niθe] vb ver **armonizar**

armónico, -a [ar'moniko, a] adj harmonic

armonioso, -a [armo'njoso, a] adj harmonious

armonizar [armoni'θar] vt to harmonize; (diferencias) to reconcile ▪ vi to harmonize; ~ **con** (fig) to be in keeping with; (colores) to tone in with

arnés [ar'nes] nm armour; **arneses** nmpl harness sg

aro ['aro] nm ring; (tejo) quoit; (Am: pendiente) earring; **entrar por el ~** to give in

aroma [a'roma] nm aroma

aromaterapia [aromate'rapja] nf aromatherapy

aromático, -a [aro'matiko, a] adj aromatic

arpa ['arpa] nf harp

arpegio [ar'pexjo] nm (Mus) arpeggio

arpía [ar'pia] nf (fig) shrew

arpillera [arpi'ʎera] nf sacking, sackcloth

arpón [ar'pon] nm harpoon

arquear [arke'ar] vt to arch, bend; arquearse vr to arch, bend

arqueo [ar'keo] nm (gen) arching; (Naut) tonnage

arqueología [arkeolo'xia] nf archaeology

arqueológico, -a [arkeo'loxiko, a] adj archaeological

arqueólogo, -a [arke'oloɣo, a] nm/f archaeologist

arquero [ar'kero] nm archer, bowman; (Am Deporte) goalkeeper

arquetipo [arke'tipo] nm archetype

arquitecto, -a [arki'tekto, a] nm/f architect; ~ paisajista o de jardines landscape gardener

arquitectónico, -a [arkitek'toniko, a] adj architectural

arquitectura [arkitek'tura] nf architecture

arrabal [arra'βal] nm suburb; arrabales nmpl outskirts

arrabalero, -a [arraβa'lero, a] adj (fig) common, coarse

arracimarse [arraθi'marse] vr to cluster together

arraigado, -a [arrai'ɣaðo, a] adj deep-rooted; (fig) established

arraigar [arrai'ɣar] vt to establish ■ vi, arraigarse vr to take root; (persona) to settle

arraigo [a'rraiɣo] nm (raíces) roots pl; (bienes) property; (influencia) hold; hombre de ~ man of property

arraigue etc [a'rraiɣe] vb ver arraigar

arrancada [arran'kaða] nf (arranque) sudden start

arrancar [arran'kar] vt (sacar) to extract, pull out; (arrebatar) to snatch (away); (pedazo) to tear off; (página) to rip out; (suspiro) to heave; (Auto) to start; (Inform) to boot; (fig) to extract ■ vi (Auto, máquina) to start; (ponerse en marcha) to get going; ~ información a algn to extract information from sb; ~ de to stem from

arranque etc [a'rranke] vb ver arrancar ■ nm sudden start; (Auto) start; (fig) fit, outburst

arras ['arras] nfpl pledge sg, security sg

arrasar [arra'sar] vt (aplanar) to level, flatten; (destruir) to demolish

arrastrado, -a [arras'traðo, a] adj poor, wretched

arrastrador [arrastra'ðor] nm (en máquina impresora) tractor

arrastrar [arras'trar] vt to drag (along); (fig) to drag down, degrade; (suj: agua, viento) to carry away ■ vi to drag, trail on the ground; arrastrarse vr to crawl; (fig) to grovel; llevar algo arrastrado to drag sth along

arrastre [a'rrastre] nm drag, dragging; (Deporte) crawl; estar para el ~ (fig) to have had it

array [a'rrai] nm (Inform) array; ~ empaquetado (Inform) packed array

arrayán [arra'jan] nm myrtle

arre ['arre] excl gee up!

arrear [arre'ar] vt to drive on, urge on ■ vi to hurry along

arrebañar [arreβa'ɲar] vt (juntar) to scrape together

arrebatado, -a [arreβa'taðo, a] adj rash, impetuous; (repentino) sudden, hasty

arrebatar [arreβa'tar] vt to snatch (away), seize; (fig) to captivate; arrebatarse vr to get carried away, get excited

arrebato [arre'βato] nm fit of rage, fury; (éxtasis) rapture; en un ~ de cólera in an outburst of anger

arrebolar [arreβo'lar] vt to redden; arrebolarse vr (enrojecer) to blush

arrebujar [arreβu'xar] vt (objetos) to jumble together; arrebujarse vr to wrap o.s. up

arrechar [arre'tʃar] (Am) vt to arouse, excite; arrecharse vr to become aroused

arrechucho [arre'tʃutʃo] nm (Med) turn

arreciar [arre'θjar] vi to get worse; (viento) to get stronger

arrecife [arre'θife] nm reef

arredrar [arre'ðrar] vt (hacer retirarse) to drive back; arredrarse vr (apartarse) to draw back; arredrarse ante algo to shrink away from sth

arreglado, -a [arre'ɣlaðo, a] adj (ordenado) neat, orderly; (moderado) moderate, reasonable

arreglar [arre'ɣlar] vt (poner orden) to tidy up; (algo roto) to fix, repair; (problema) to solve; arreglarse vr to reach an understanding; arreglárselas (fam) to get by, manage

arreglo [a'rreɣlo] nm settlement; (orden) order; (acuerdo) agreement; (Mus) arrangement, setting; (Inform) array; con ~ a in accordance with; llegar a un ~ to reach a compromise

arrellanarse [arreʎa'narse] vr to sprawl; ~ en el asiento to lie back in one's chair

arremangar [arreman'ɡar] vt to roll up, turn up; arremangarse vr to roll up one's sleeves

arremangue etc [arre'manɡe] vb ver arremangar

arremeter [arreme'ter] vt to attack, assault; ~ contra algn to attack sb

arremetida [arreme'tiða] nf assault

arremolinarse [arremoli'narse] vr to crowd around, mill around; (corriente) to swirl, eddy

arrendador, -a [arrenda'ðor, a] nm/f landlord/lady

arrendamiento [arrenda'mjento] *nm*
letting; (*el alquilar*) hiring; (*contrato*) lease;
(*alquiler*) rent

arrendar [arren'dar] *vt* to let; to hire; to lease;
to rent

arrendatario, -a [arrenda'tarjo, a] *nm/f*
tenant

arreos [a'rreos] *nmpl* harness *sg*, trappings

arrepentido, -a [arrepen'tiðo, a] *nm/f* (*Pol*)
reformed terrorist

arrepentimiento [arrepenti'mjento] *nm*
regret, repentance

arrepentirse [arrepen'tirse] *vr* to repent;
~ **de (haber hecho) algo** to regret (doing) sth

arrepienta *etc* [arre'pjenta], **arrepintiendo**
etc [arrepin'tjendo] *vb ver* **arrepentirse**

arrestar [arres'tar] *vt* to arrest; (*encarcelar*)
to imprison

arresto [a'rresto] *nm* arrest; (*Mil*) detention;
(*audacia*) boldness, daring; ~ **domiciliario**
house arrest

arriar [a'rrjar] *vt* (*velas*) to haul down;
(*bandera*) to lower, strike; (*un cable*) to pay out

arriate [a'rrjate] *nm* (*Bot*) bed; (*camino*) road

 PALABRA CLAVE

arriba [a'rriβa] *adv* **1** (*posición*) above; **desde
arriba** from above; **arriba del todo** at the
very top, right on top; **Juan está arriba**
Juan is upstairs; **lo arriba mencionado** the
aforementioned; **aquí/allí arriba** up here/
there; **está hasta arriba de trabajo** (*fam*)
he's up to his eyes in work (*fam*)

2 (*dirección*) up, upwards; **más arriba** higher
o further up; **calle arriba** up the street

3: **de arriba abajo** from top to bottom;
mirar a algn de arriba abajo to look sb up
and down

4: **para arriba**: **de 50 euros para arriba**
from 50 euros up(wards); **de la cintura
(para) arriba** from the waist up

■ *adj*: **de arriba**: **el piso de arriba** the
upstairs flat (*Brit*) *o* apartment; **la parte de
arriba** the top *o* upper part

■ *prep*: **arriba de** (*Am*) above; **arriba de 200
dólares** more than 200 dollars

■ *excl*: **¡arriba!** up!; **¡manos arriba!** hands
up!; **¡arriba España!** long live Spain!

arribar [arri'βar] *vi* to put into port; (*esp Am*:
llegar) to arrive

arribista [arri'βista] *nm/f* parvenu(e), upstart

arribo [a'rriβo] *nm* (*esp Am*) arrival

arriendo *etc* [a'rrjendo] *vb ver* **arrendar** ■ *nm*
= **arrendamiento**

arriero [a'rrjero] *nm* muleteer

arriesgado, -a [arrjes'γaðo, a] *adj* (*peligroso*)
risky; (*audaz*) bold, daring

arriesgar [arrjes'γar] *vt* to risk; (*poner en
peligro*) to endanger; **arriesgarse** *vr* to take
a risk

arriesgue *etc* [a'rrjesγe] *vb ver* **arriesgar**

arrimar [arri'mar] *vt* (*acercar*) to bring close;
(*poner de lado*) to set aside; **arrimarse** *vr* to
come close *o* closer; **arrimarse a** to lean on;
(*fig*) to keep company with; (*buscar ayuda*)
to seek the protection of; **arrímate a mí**
cuddle up to me

arrinconado, -a [arrinko'naðo, a] *adj*
forgotten, neglected

arrinconar [arrinko'nar] *vt* to put in a
corner; (*fig*) to put on one side; (*abandonar*)
to push aside

arriscado, -a [arris'kaðo, a] *adj* (*Geo*) craggy;
(*fig*) bold, resolute

arroba [a'rroβa] *nf* (*peso*) 25 pounds; (*Inform*: *en
dirección electrónica*) at sign, @; **tiene talento
por arrobas** he has loads *o* bags of talent

arrobado, -a [arro'βaðo, a] *adj* entranced,
enchanted

arrobamiento [arroβa'mjento] *nm* ecstasy

arrobar [arro'βar] *vt* to enchant; **arrobarse**
vr to be enraptured; (*místico*) to go into a
trance

arrodillarse [arroði'ʎarse] *vr* to kneel (down)

arrogancia [arro'γanθja] *nf* arrogance

arrogante [arro'γante] *adj* arrogant

arrojar [arro'xar] *vt* to throw, hurl; (*humo*)
to emit, give out; (*Com*) to yield, produce;
arrojarse *vr* to throw *o* hurl o.s.

arrojo [a'rroxo] *nm* daring

arrollador, a [arroʎa'ðor, a] *adj* crushing,
overwhelming

arrollar [arro'ʎar] *vt* (*enrollar*) to roll up; (*suj*:
inundación) to wash away; (*Auto*) to run over;
(*Deporte*) to crush

arropar [arro'par] *vt* to cover (up), wrap up;
arroparse *vr* to wrap o.s. up

arrostrar [arros'trar] *vt* to face (up to);
arrostrarse *vr*: **arrostrarse con algn** to face
up to sb

arroyo [a'rrojo] *nm* stream; (*de la calle*) gutter;
poner a algn en el ~ to turn sb onto the
streets

arroz [a'rroθ] *nm* rice; ~ **con leche** rice
pudding

arrozal [arro'θal] *nm* paddy field

arruga [a'rruγa] *nf* fold; (*de cara*) wrinkle;
(*de vestido*) crease

arrugar [arru'γar] *vt* to fold; to wrinkle; to
crease; **arrugarse** *vr* to get wrinkled; to get
creased

arrugue *etc* [a'rruγe] *vb ver* **arrugar**

arruinar [arrwi'nar] vt to ruin, wreck;
  arruinarse vr to be ruined
arrullar [arru'ʎar] vi to coo ■ vt to lull to
  sleep
arrumaco [arru'mako] nm (caricia) caress;
  (halago) piece of flattery
arrumbar [arrum'bar] vt (objeto) to discard;
  (individuo) to silence
arrurruz [arru'rruθ] nm arrowroot
arsenal [arse'nal] nm naval dockyard; (Mil)
  arsenal
arsénico [ar'seniko] nm arsenic
arte ['arte] nm (gen m en sg, f en pl) art; (maña)
  skill, guile; **por ~ de magia** (as if) by magic;
  no tener ~ ni parte en algo to have nothing
  whatsoever to do with sth; **artes** nfpl arts;
  Bellas Artes Fine Art sg; **artes y oficios** arts
  and crafts
artefacto [arte'fakto] nm appliance;
  (Arqueología) artefact
arteria [ar'terja] nf artery
arterial [arte'rjal] adj arterial; (presión) blood
  cpd
arterioesclerosis [arterjoeskle'rosis],
  arteriosclerosis [arterjoskle'rosis] nf inv
  hardening of the arteries, arteriosclerosis
artesa [ar'tesa] nf trough
artesanía [artesa'nia] nf craftsmanship;
  (artículos) handicrafts pl
artesano, -a [arte'sano, a] nm/f artisan,
  craftsman/woman
ártico, -a ['artiko, a] adj Arctic ■ nm:
  el (océano) Ártico the Arctic (Ocean)
articulación [artikula'θjon] nf articulation;
  (Med: Tec) joint
articulado, -a [artiku'laðo, a] adj
  articulated; jointed
articular [artiku'lar] vt to articulate; to join
  together
articulista [artiku'lista] nm/f columnist,
  contributor (to a newspaper)
artículo [ar'tikulo] nm article; (cosa) thing,
  article; (TV) feature, report; **~ de fondo**
  leader, editorial; **artículos** nmpl goods;
  artículos de marca (Com) proprietary goods
artífice [ar'tifiθe] nm artist, craftsman; (fig)
  architect
artificial [artifi'θjal] adj artificial
artificio [arti'fiθjo] nm art, skill; (artesanía)
  craftsmanship; (astucia) cunning
artillería [artiʎe'ria] nf artillery
artillero [arti'ʎero] nm artilleryman, gunner
artilugio [arti'luxjo] nm gadget
artimaña [arti'maɲa] nf trap, snare; (astucia)
  cunning
artista [ar'tista] nm/f (pintor) artist, painter;
  (Teat) artist, artiste

artístico, -a [ar'tistiko, a] adj artistic
artritis [ar'tritis] nf arthritis
artrosis [ar'trosis] nf osteoarthritis
arveja [ar'βexa] nf (Am) pea
Arz. abr (= Arzobispo) Abp
arzobispo [arθo'βispo] nm archbishop
as [as] nm ace; **as del fútbol** star player
asa ['asa] nf handle; (fig) lever
asado [a'saðo] nm roast (meat); (Am: barbacoa)
  barbecue
asador [asa'ðor] nm (varilla) spit; (aparato) spit
  roaster
asadura [asa'ðura] nf, **asaduras** [asa'ðuras]
  nfpl entrails pl, offal sg; (Culin) chitterlings pl
asaetear [asaete'ar] vt (fig) to bother
asalariado, -a [asala'rjaðo, a] adj paid,
  wage-earning, salaried ■ nm/f wage earner
asaltador, a [asalta'ðor, a], **asaltante**
  [asal'tante] nm/f assailant
asaltar [asal'tar] vt to attack, assault; (fig)
  to assail
asalto [a'salto] nm attack, assault; (Deporte)
  round
asamblea [asam'blea] nf assembly; (reunión)
  meeting
asar [a'sar] vt to roast; **~ al horno/a la**
  parrilla to bake/grill; **asarse** vr (fig): **me aso**
  de calor I'm roasting; **aquí se asa uno vivo**
  it's boiling hot here
asbesto [as'βesto] nm asbestos
ascendencia [asθen'denθja] nf ancestry;
  de ~ francesa of French origin
ascender [asθen'der] vi (subir) to ascend,
  rise; (ser promovido) to gain promotion ■ vt to
  promote; **~ a** to amount to
ascendiente [asθen'djente] nm influence
  ■ nm/f ancestor
ascensión [asθen'sjon] nf ascent; **la A~** the
  Ascension
ascenso [as'θenso] nm ascent; (promoción)
  promotion
ascensor [asθen'sor] nm lift (Brit), elevator (US)
ascético, -a [as'θetiko, a] adj ascetic
ascienda etc [as'θjenda] vb ver **ascender**
asco ['asko] nm: **el ajo me da ~** I hate o loathe
  garlic; **hacer ascos de algo** to turn up one's
  nose at sth; **estar hecho un ~** to be filthy;
  poner a algn de ~ to call sb all sorts of names
  o every name under the sun; **¡qué ~!** how
  revolting o disgusting!
ascua ['askwa] nf ember; **arrimar el ~ a su**
  sardina to look after number one; **estar en**
  ascuas to be on tenterhooks
aseado, -a [ase'aðo, a] adj clean; (arreglado)
  tidy; (pulcro) smart
asear [ase'ar] vt (lavar) to wash; (ordenar) to
  tidy (up)

33

asechanza [ase'tʃanθa] nf trap, snare
asediar [ase'ðjar] vt (Mil) to besiege, lay siege
  to; (fig) to chase, pester
asedio [a'seðjo] nm siege; (Com) run
asegurado, a [aseɣu'raðo, a] adj insured
asegurador, -a [aseɣura'ðor, a] nm/f insurer
asegurar [aseɣu'rar] vt (consolidar) to secure,
  fasten; (dar garantía de) to guarantee;
  (preservar) to safeguard; (afirmar: dar por cierto)
  to assure, affirm; (tranquilizar) to reassure;
  (hacer un seguro) to insure; **asegurarse** vr to
  assure o.s., make sure
asemejarse [aseme'xarse] vr to be alike;
  ~ **a** to be like, resemble
asentado, -a [asen'taðo, a] adj established,
  settled
asentar [asen'tar] vt (sentar) to seat, sit down;
  (poner) to place, establish; (alisar) to level,
  smooth down o out; (anotar) to note down
  ■ vi to be suitable, suit
asentimiento [asenti'mjento] nm assent,
  agreement
asentir [asen'tir] vi to assent, agree
aseo [a'seo] nm cleanliness; **aseos** nmpl
  toilet sg (Brit), restroom sg (US), cloakroom sg
aséptico, -a [a'septiko, a] adj germ-free, free
  from infection
asequible [ase'kiβle] adj (precio) reasonable;
  (meta) attainable; (persona) approachable
aserradero [aserra'ðero] nm sawmill
aserrar [ase'rrar] vt to saw
asesinar [asesi'nar] vt to murder; (Pol) to
  assassinate
asesinato [asesi'nato] nm murder;
  assassination
asesino, -a [ase'sino, a] nm/f murderer,
  killer; (Pol) assassin
asesor, a [ase'sor, a] nm/f adviser,
  consultant; (Com) assessor, consultant;
  ~ **administrativo** management consultant
asesorar [aseso'rar] vt (Jur) to advise, give
  legal advice to; (Com) to act as consultant to;
  asesorarse vr: **asesorarse con** o **de** to take
  advice from, consult
asesoría [aseso'ria] nf (cargo) consultancy;
  (oficina) consultant's office
asestar [ases'tar] vt (golpe) to deal; (arma)
  to aim; (tiro) to fire
aseverar [aseβe'rar] vt to assert
asfaltado, -a [asfal'taðo, a] adj asphalted
  ■ nm (pavimiento) asphalt
asfalto [as'falto] nm asphalt
asfixia [as'fiksja] nf asphyxia, suffocation
asfixiar [asfik'sjar] vt to asphyxiate,
  suffocate
asga etc ['asɣa] vb ver **asir**
así [a'si] adv (de esta manera) in this way, like

this, thus; (aunque) although; (tan pronto
como) as soon as; **así que** so; **así como** as
well as; **así y todo** even so; **¿no es así?** isn't
it?, didn't you? etc; **así de grande** this big;
¡así sea! so be it!; **así es la vida** such is life,
that's life
Asia ['asja] nf Asia
asiático, -a [a'sjatiko, a] adj, nm/f Asian,
  Asiatic
asidero [asi'ðero] nm handle
asiduidad [asiðwi'ðað] nf assiduousness
asiduo, -a [a'siðwo, a] adj assiduous;
  (frecuente) frequent ■ nm/f regular
  (customer)
asiento etc [a'sjento] vb ver **asentar; asentir**
  ■ nm (mueble) seat, chair; (de coche, en tribunal
  etc) seat; (localidad) seat, place; (fundamento)
  site; ~ **delantero/trasero** front/back seat
asierre etc [a'sjerre] vb ver **aserrar**
asignación [asiɣna'θjon] nf (atribución)
  assignment; (reparto) allocation; (Com)
  allowance; ~ **(semanal)** pocket money;
  ~ **de presupuesto** budget appropriation
asignar [asiɣ'nar] vt to assign, allocate
asignatura [asiɣna'tura] nf subject; (curso)
  course; ~ **pendiente** (fig) matter pending
asilado, -a [asi'laðo, a] nm/f refugee
asilo [a'silo] nm (refugio) asylum, refuge;
  (establecimiento) home, institution; ~ **político**
  political asylum
asimilación [asimila'θjon] nf assimilation
asimilar [asimi'lar] vt to assimilate
asimismo [asi'mismo] adv in the same way,
  likewise
asintiendo etc [asin'tjendo] vb ver **asentir**
asir [a'sir] vt to seize, grasp; **asirse** vr to take
  hold; **asirse a** o **de** to seize
asistencia [asis'tenθja] nf presence; (Teat)
  audience; (Med) attendance; (ayuda)
  assistance; ~ **social** social o welfare work
asistente, -a [asis'tente, a] nm/f assistant
  ■ nm (Mil) orderly ■ nf daily help; **los**
  asistentes those present; ~ **social** social
  worker
asistido, -a [asis'tiðo, a] adj (Auto: dirección)
  power-assisted; ~ **por ordenador** computer-
  assisted
asistir [asis'tir] vt to assist, help ■ vi: ~ **a**
  to attend, be present at
asma ['asma] nf asthma
asno ['asno] nm donkey; (fig) ass
asociación [asoθja'θjon] nf association;
  (Com) partnership
asociado, -a [aso'θjaðo, a] adj associate
  ■ nm/f associate; (Com) partner
asociar [aso'θjar] vt to associate; **asociarse**
  vr to become partners

asolar [aso'lar] *vt* to destroy
asolear [asole'ar] *vt* to put in the sun;
asolearse *vr* to sunbathe
asomar [aso'mar] *vt* to show, stick out ◼ *vi*
to appear; **asomarse** *vr* to appear, show up;
~ la cabeza por la ventana to put one's head
out of the window
asombrar [asom'brar] *vt* to amaze,
astonish; **asombrarse** *vr*: **asombrarse (de)**
(*sorprenderse*) to be amazed (at); (*asustarse*) to
be frightened (at)
asombro [a'sombro] *nm* amazement,
astonishment
asombroso, -a [asom'broso, a] *adj* amazing,
astonishing
asomo [a'somo] *nm* hint, sign; **ni por ~** by
no means
asonancia [aso'nanθja] *nf* (*Lit*) assonance;
(*fig*) connection; **no tener ~ con** to bear no
relation to
asorocharse [asoro'tʃarse] *vr* (*Am*) to get
mountain sickness
aspa ['aspa] *nf* (*cruz*) cross; (*de molino*) sail;
en ~ X-shaped
aspaviento [aspa'βjento] *nm* exaggerated
display of feeling; (*fam*) fuss
aspecto [as'pekto] *nm* (*apariencia*) look,
appearance; (*fig*) aspect; **bajo ese ~** from
that point of view
aspereza [aspe'reθa] *nf* roughness; (*de fruta*)
sharpness; (*de carácter*) surliness
áspero, -a ['aspero, a] *adj* rough; sharp;
harsh
aspersión [asper'sjon] *nf* sprinkling; (*Agr*)
spraying
aspersor [asper'sor] *nm* sprinkler
aspiración [aspira'θjon] *nf* breath,
inhalation; (*Mus*) short pause; **aspiraciones**
nfpl aspirations
aspiradora [aspira'ðora] *nf* vacuum cleaner,
Hoover®
aspirante [aspi'rante] *nm/f* (*candidato*)
candidate; (*Deporte*) contender
aspirar [aspi'rar] *vt* to breathe in ◼ *vi*: **~ a**
to aspire to
aspirina [aspi'rina] *nf* aspirin
asquear [aske'ar] *vt* to sicken ◼ *vi* to be
sickening; **asquearse** *vr* to feel disgusted
asquerosidad [askerosi'ðað] *nf* (*suciedad*)
filth; (*dicho*) obscenity; (*faena*) dirty trick
asqueroso, -a [aske'roso, a] *adj* disgusting,
sickening
asta ['asta] *nf* lance; (*arpón*) spear; (*mango*)
shaft, handle; (*Zool*) horn; **a media ~** at half
mast
astado, -a [as'taðo, a] *adj* horned ◼ *nm* bull
asterisco [aste'risko] *nm* asterisk

asteroide [aste'roiðe] *nm* asteroid
astigmatismo [astiɣma'tismo] *nm*
astigmatism
astilla [as'tiʎa] *nf* splinter; (*pedacito*) chip;
astillas *nfpl* firewood *sg*
astillarse [asti'ʎarse] *vr* to splinter; (*fig*)
to shatter
astillero [asti'ʎero] *nm* shipyard
astringente [astrin'xente] *adj, nm* astringent
astro ['astro] *nm* star
astrología [astrolo'xia] *nf* astrology
astrólogo, -a [as'troloɣo, a] *nm/f* astrologer
astronauta [astro'nauta] *nm/f* astronaut
astronave [astro'naβe] *nm* spaceship
astronomía [astrono'mia] *nf* astronomy
astronómico, -a [astro'nomiko, a] *adj* (*tb fig*)
astronomical
astrónomo, -a [as'tronomo, a] *nm/f*
astronomer
astroso, -a [as'troso, a] *adj* (*desaliñado*)
untidy; (*vil*) contemptible
astucia [as'tuθja] *nf* astuteness; (*destreza*)
clever trick
asturiano, -a [astu'rjano, a] *adj, nm/f*
Asturian
Asturias [as'turjas] *nfpl* Asturias; **Príncipe
de ~** crown prince
astuto, -a [as'tuto, a] *adj* astute; (*taimado*)
cunning
asueto [a'sweto] *nm* holiday; (*tiempo libre*)
time off; **día de ~** day off; **tarde de ~** (*trabajo*)
afternoon off; (*Escol*) half-holiday
asumir [asu'mir] *vt* to assume
asunción [asun'θjon] *nf* assumption
asunto [a'sunto] *nm* (*tema*) matter, subject;
(*negocio*) business; **¡eso es ~ mío!** that's my
business!; **asuntos exteriores** foreign
affairs; **asuntos a tratar** agenda *sg*
asustadizo, -a [asusta'ðiθo, a] *adj* easily
frightened
asustar [asus'tar] *vt* to frighten; **asustarse**
vr to be/become frightened
atacante [ata'kante] *nm/f* attacker
atacar [ata'kar] *vt* to attack
atadura [ata'ðura] *nf* bond, tie
atajar [ata'xar] *vt* (*gen*) to stop; (*ruta de fuga*)
to cut off; (*discurso*) to interrupt ◼ *vi* to take
a short cut
atajo [a'taxo] *nm* short cut; (*Deporte*) tackle
atalaya [ata'laja] *nf* watchtower
atañer [ata'ɲer] *vi*: **~ a** to concern; **en lo que
atañe a eso** with regard to that
ataque *etc* [a'take] *vb ver* **atacar** ◼ *nm* attack;
~ cardíaco heart attack
atar [a'tar] *vt* to tie, tie up; **~ la lengua a algn**
(*fig*) to silence sb
atardecer [atarðe'θer] *vi* to get dark ◼ *nm*

evening; (*crepúsculo*) dusk
atardezca *etc* [atar'ðeθka] *vb ver* **atardecer**
atareado, -a [atare'aðo, a] *adj* busy
atascar [atas'kar] *vt* to clog up; (*obstruir*) to
jam; (*fig*) to hinder; **atascarse** *vr* to stall;
(*cañería*) to get blocked up; (*fig*) to get bogged
down; (*en discurso*) to dry up
atasco [a'tasko] *nm* obstruction; (*Auto*)
traffic jam
atasque *etc* [a'taske] *vb ver* **atascar**
ataúd [ata'uð] *nm* coffin
ataviar [ata'βjar] *vt* to deck, array; **ataviarse**
vr to dress up
atavío [ata'βio] *nm* attire, dress; **atavíos**
nmpl finery *sg*
ateísmo [ate'ismo] *nm* atheism
atemorice *etc* [atemo'riθe] *vb ver* **atemorizar**
atemorizar [atemori'θar] *vt* to frighten,
scare; **atemorizarse** *vr* to get frightened *o*
scared
Atenas [a'tenas] *nf* Athens
atención [aten'θjon] *nf* attention; (*bondad*)
kindness ◾ *excl* (be) careful!, look out!;
en ~ a esto in view of this
atender [aten'der] *vt* to attend to, look after;
(*Tec*) to service; (*enfermo*) to care for; (*ruego*)
to comply with ◾ *vi* to pay attention;
~ a to attend to; (*detalles*) to take care of
atendré *etc* [aten'dre] *vb ver* **atenerse**
atenerse [ate'nerse] *vr:* **~ a** to abide by,
adhere to
atenga *etc* [a'tenga] *vb ver* **atenerse**
ateniense [ate'njense] *adj, nm/f* Athenian
atentado [aten'taðo] *nm* crime, illegal act;
(*asalto*) assault; (*terrorista*) attack; **~ contra la
vida de algn** attempt on sb's life; **~ golpista**
attempted coup; **~ suicida** suicide bombing,
suicide attack
atentamente [atenta'mente] *adv:* **le saluda
~** Yours faithfully
atentar [aten'tar] *vi:* **~ a** *o* **contra** to commit
an outrage against
atento, -a [a'tento, a] *adj* attentive,
observant; (*cortés*) polite, thoughtful; **su
atenta (carta)** (*Com*) your letter
atenuante [ate'nwante] *adj:* **circunstancias
atenuantes** extenuating *o* mitigating
circumstances ◾ *nfpl:* **atenuantes**
extenuating *o* mitigating circumstances
atenuar [ate'nwar] *vt* to attenuate; (*disminuir*)
to lessen, minimize
ateo, -a [a'teo, a] *adj* atheistic ◾ *nm/f* atheist
aterciopelado, -a [aterθjope'laðo, a] *adj*
velvety
aterido, -a [ate'riðo, a] *adj:* **~ de frío** frozen
stiff
aterrador, a [aterra'ðor, a] *adj* frightening

aterrar [ate'rrar] *vt* to frighten; (*aterrorizar*)
to terrify; **aterrarse** *vr* to be frightened;
to be terrified
aterrice *etc* [ate'rriθe] *vb ver* **aterrizar**
aterrizaje [aterri'θaxe] *nm* landing; **~
forzoso** forced landing
aterrizar [aterri'θar] *vi* to land
aterrorice *etc* [aterro'riθe] *vb ver* **aterrorizar**
aterrorizar [aterrori'θar] *vt* to terrify
atesorar [ateso'rar] *vt* to hoard, store up
atestado, -a [ates'taðo, a] *adj* packed ◾ *nm*
(*Jur*) affidavit
atestar [ates'tar] *vt* to pack, stuff; (*Jur*) to
attest, testify to
atestiguar [atesti'ɣwar] *vt* to testify to, bear
witness to
atestigüe *etc* [ates'tiɣwe] *vb ver* **atestiguar**
atiborrar [atiβo'rrar] *vt* to fill, stuff;
atiborrarse *vr* to stuff o.s.
atice *etc* [a'tiθe] *vb ver* **atizar**
ático ['atiko] *nm* attic; **~ de lujo** penthouse
flat
atienda *etc* [a'tjenda] *vb ver* **atender**
atildar [atil'dar] *vt* to criticize; (*Tip*) to put a
tilde over; **atildarse** *vr* to spruce o.s. up
atinado, -a [ati'naðo, a] *adj* correct; (*sensato*)
sensible
atinar [ati'nar] *vi* (*acertar*) to be right; **~ con** *o*
en (*solución*) to hit upon; **~ a hacer**
to manage to do
atípico, -a [a'tipiko, a] *adj* atypical
atiplado, -a [ati'plaðo, a] *adj* (*voz*) high-
pitched
atisbar [atis'βar] *vt* to spy on; (*echar ojeada*)
to peep at
atizar [ati'θar] *vt* to poke; (*horno etc*) to stoke;
(*fig*) to stir up, rouse
atlántico, -a [at'lantiko, a] *adj* Atlantic
◾ *nm:* **el (océano) A~** the Atlantic (Ocean)
atlas ['atlas] *nm inv* atlas
atleta [at'leta] *nm/f* athlete
atlético, -a [at'letiko, a] *adj* athletic
atletismo [atle'tismo] *nm* athletics *sg*
atmósfera [at'mosfera] *nf* atmosphere
atmosférico, -a [atmos'feriko, a] *adj*
atmospheric
atol [a'tol], **atole** [a'tole] *nm* (*Am*) cornflour
drink
atolladero [atoʎa'ðero] *nm:* **estar en un ~**
to be in a jam
atollarse [ato'ʎarse] *vr* to get stuck; (*fig*)
to get into a jam
atolondrado, -a [atolon'draðo, a] *adj*
scatterbrained
atolondramiento [atolondra'mjento] *nm*
bewilderment; (*insensatez*) silliness
atómico, -a [a'tomiko, a] *adj* atomic

a

atomizador [atomiθa'ðor] nm atomizer
átomo ['atomo] nm atom
atónito, -a [a'tonito, a] adj astonished, amazed
atontado, -a [aton'taðo, a] adj stunned; (bobo) silly, daft
atontar [aton'tar] vt to stun; **atontarse** vr to become confused
atorar [ato'rar] vt to obstruct; **atorarse** vr (atragantarse) to choke
atormentar [atormen'tar] vt to torture; (molestar) to torment; (acosar) to plague, harass
atornillar [atorni'ʎar] vt to screw on o down
atorón [ato'ron] nm (Am) traffic jam
atosigar [atosi'ɣar] vt to harass
atosigue etc [ato'siɣe] vb ver **atosigar**
atrabiliario, -a [atraβi'ljarjo, a] adj bad-tempered
atracadero [atraka'ðero] nm pier
atracador, a [atraka'ðor, a] nm/f robber
atracar [atra'kar] vt (Naut) to moor; (robar) to hold up, rob ■ vi to moor; **atracarse** vr (hartarse) to stuff o.s.
atracción [atrak'θjon] nf attraction
atraco [a'trako] nm holdup, robbery
atracón [atra'kon] nm: **darse** o **pegarse un ~ (de)** (fam) to pig out (on)
atractivo, -a [atrak'tiβo, a] adj attractive ■ nm attraction; (belleza) attractiveness
atraer [atra'er] vt to attract; **dejarse ~ por** to be tempted by
atragantarse [atraɣan'tarse] vr: **~ (con algo)** to choke (on sth); **se me ha atragantado el chico ese/el inglés** I don't take to that boy/English
atraiga etc [a'traiɣa], **atraje** etc [a'traxe] vb ver **atraer**
atrancar [atran'kar] vt (con tranca, barra) to bar, bolt
atranque etc [a'tranke] vb ver **atrancar**
atrapar [atra'par] vt to trap; (resfriado etc) to catch
atraque etc [a'trake] vb ver **atracar**
atrás [a'tras] adv (movimiento) back(wards); (lugar) behind; (tiempo) previously; **ir hacia ~** to go back(wards); to go to the rear; **estar ~** to be behind o at the back
atrasado, -a [atra'saðo, a] adj slow; (pago) overdue, late; (país) backward
atrasar [atra'sar] vi to be slow; **atrasarse** vr to remain behind; (llegar tarde) to arrive late
atraso [a'traso] nm slowness; lateness, delay; (de país) backwardness; **atrasos** nmpl arrears
atravesado, -a [atraβe'saðo, a] adj: **un tronco ~ en la carretera** a tree trunk lying across the road

atravesar [atraβe'sar] vt (cruzar) to cross (over); (traspasar) to pierce; (período) to go through; (poner al través) to lay o put across; **atravesarse** vr to come in between; (intervenir) to interfere
atraviese etc [atra'βjese] vb ver **atravesar**
atrayendo [atra'jendo] vb ver **atraer**
atrayente [atra'jente] adj attractive
atreverse [atre'βerse] vr to dare; (insolentarse) to be insolent
atrevido, -a [atre'βiðo, a] adj daring; insolent
atrevimiento [atreβi'mjento] nm daring; insolence
atribución [atriβu'θjon] nf (Lit) attribution; **atribuciones** nfpl (Pol) functions; (Admin) responsibilities
atribuir [atriβu'ir] vt to attribute; (funciones) to confer
atribular [atriβu'lar] vt to afflict, distress
atributo [atri'βuto] nm attribute
atribuya etc [atri'βuja], **atribuyendo** etc [atriβu'jendo] vb ver **atribuir**
atril [a'tril] nm lectern; (Mus) music stand
atrincherarse [atrintʃe'rarse] vr (Mil) to dig (o.s.) in; **~ en** (fig) to hide behind
atrio ['atrjo] nm (Rel) porch
atrocidad [atroθi'ðað] nf atrocity, outrage
atrofiado, -a [atro'fjaðo, a] adj (extremidad) withered
atrofiarse [atro'fjarse] vr (tb fig) to atrophy
atronador, a [atrona'ðor, a] adj deafening
atropellar [atrope'ʎar] vt (derribar) to knock over o down; (empujar) to push (aside); (Auto) to run over o down; (agraviar) to insult; **atropellarse** vr to act hastily
atropello [atro'peʎo] nm (Auto) accident; (empujón) push; (agravio) wrong; (atrocidad) outrage
atroz [a'troθ] adj atrocious, awful
A.T.S. nm/f abr (= Ayudante Técnico Sanitario) nurse
attrezzo [a'treθo] nm props pl
atuendo [a'twendo] nm attire
atufar [atu'far] vt (suj: olor) to overcome; (molestar) to irritate; **atufarse** vr (fig) to get cross
atún [a'tun] nm tuna, tunny
aturdir [atur'ðir] vt to stun; (suj: ruido) to deafen; (fig) to dumbfound, bewilder
aturrullar, aturullar [atur(r)u'ʎar] vt to bewilder
atusar [atu'sar] vt (cortar) to trim; (alisar) to smooth (down)
atuve etc [a'tuβe] vb ver **atenerse**
audacia [au'ðaθja] nf boldness, audacity
audaz [au'ðaθ] adj bold, audacious

audible [au'ðiβle] adj audible
audición [auði'θjon] nf hearing; (Teat) audition; ~ **radiofónica** radio concert
audiencia [au'ðjenθja] nf audience; (Jur) high court; (Pol): ~ **pública** public inquiry
audífono [au'ðifono] nm hearing aid
audiovisual [auðjoβi'swal] adj audio-visual
auditivo, -a [auði'tiβo, a] adj hearing cpd; (conducto, nervio) auditory
auditor [auði'tor] nm (Jur) judge-advocate; (Com) auditor
auditoría [auðito'ria] nf audit; (profesión) auditing
auditorio [auði'torjo] nm audience; (sala) auditorium
auge ['auxe] nm boom; (clímax) climax; (Econ) expansion; **estar en** ~ to thrive
augurar [auɣu'rar] vt to predict; (presagiar) to portend
augurio [au'ɣurjo] nm omen
aula ['aula] nf classroom
aullar [au'ʎar] vi to howl, yell
aullido [au'ʎiðo] nm howl, yell
aumentar [aumen'tar] vt to increase; (precios) to put up; (producción) to step up; (con microscopio, anteojos) to magnify ■ vi, **aumentarse** vr to increase, be on the increase
aumento [au'mento] nm increase; rise
aún [a'un] adv still, yet
aun [a'un] adv even
aunque [a'unke] conj though, although, even though
aúpa [a'upa] excl up!, come on!; (fam): **una función de** ~ a slap-up do; **una paliza de** ~ a good hiding
aupar [au'par] vt (levantar) to help up; (fig) to praise
aura ['aura] nf (atmósfera) aura
aureola [aure'ola] nf halo
auricular [auriku'lar] nm earpiece, receiver; **auriculares** nmpl headphones
aurora [au'rora] nf dawn; ~ **boreal(is)** northern lights pl
auscultar [auskul'tar] vt (Med: pecho) to listen to, sound
ausencia [au'senθja] nf absence
ausentarse [ausen'tarse] vr to go away; (por poco tiempo) to go out
ausente [au'sente] adj absent ■ nm/f (Escol) absentee; (Jur) missing person
auspiciar [auspi'sjar] vt (Am) to back, sponsor
auspicios [aus'piθjos] nmpl auspices; (protección) protection sg
austeridad [austeri'ðað] nf austerity
austero, -a [aus'tero, a] adj austere
austral [aus'tral] adj southern ■ nm monetary

unit of Argentina (1985-1991)
Australia [aus'tralja] nf Australia
australiano, -a [austra'ljano, a] adj, nm/f Australian
Austria ['austrja] nf Austria
austriaco, -a [aus'trjako, a], **austríaco a** [aus'triako, a] adj, nm/f Austrian
autenticar [autenti'kar] vt to authenticate
auténtico, -a [au'tentiko, a] adj authentic
autentificar [autentifi'kar] vt to authenticate
autentique etc [auten'tike] vb ver **autenticar**
auto ['auto] nm (coche) car; (Jur) edict, decree; (: orden) writ; **autos** nmpl (Jur) proceedings; (: acta) court record sg; ~ **de comparecencia** summons, subpoena; ~ **de ejecución** writ of execution
autoadhesivo, -a [autoaðe'siβo, a] adj self-adhesive; (sobre) self-sealing
autoalimentación [autoalimenta'θjon] nf (Inform): ~ **de hojas** automatic paper feed
autobiografía [autoβjoɣra'fia] nf autobiography
autobronceador [autoβronθea'ðor] adj self-tanning
autobús [auto'βus] nm bus (Brit), (passenger) bus (US)
autocar [auto'kar] nm coach; ~ **de línea** intercity coach
autocomprobación [autokomproβa'θjon] nf (Inform) self-test
autóctono, -a [au'toktono, a] adj native, indigenous
autodefensa [autoðe'fensa] nf self-defence
autodeterminación [autoðetermina'θjon] nf self-determination
autodidacta [autoði'ðakta] adj self-taught ■ nm/f: **ser un(a)** ~ to be self-taught
autoescuela [autoes'kwela] nf driving school
autofinanciado, -a [autofinan'θjaðo, a] adj self-financing
autogestión [autoxes'tjon] nf self-management
autógrafo [au'toɣrafo] nm autograph
automación [automa'θjon] nf = **automatización**
autómata [au'tomata] nm automaton
automáticamente [auto'matikamente] adv automatically
automatice etc [automa'tiθe] vb ver **automatizar**
automático, -a [auto'matiko, a] adj automatic ■ nm press stud
automatización [automatiθa'θjon] nf: ~ **de fábricas** factory automation; ~ **de oficinas** office automation

automatizar [automati'θar] *vt* to automate

automontable [automon'taßle] *adj* self-assembly

automotor, -triz [automo'tor, 'triz] *adj* self-propelled ■ *nm* diesel train

automóvil [auto'moßil] *nm* (motor) car (Brit), automobile (US)

automovilismo [automoßi'lismo] *nm* (Deporte) (sports) car racing

automovilista [automoßi'lista] *nm/f* motorist, driver

automovilístico, -a [automoßi'listiko, a] *adj* (industria) car *cpd*

autonomía [autono'mia] *nf* autonomy; (Esp Pol) autonomy, self-government; (: comunidad) autonomous region

autonómico, -a [auto'nomiko, a] *adj* (Esp Pol) relating to autonomy, autonomous; **gobierno ~** autonomous government

autónomo, -a [au'tonomo, a] *adj* autonomous; (Inform) stand-alone, offline

autopista [auto'pista] *nf* motorway (Brit), freeway (US)

autopsia [au'topsja] *nf* autopsy

autor, a [au'tor, a] *nm/f* author; **los autores del atentado** those responsible for the attack

autorice *etc* [auto'riθe] *vb ver* **autorizar**

autoridad [autori'ðað] *nf* authority; **~ local** local authority

autoritario, -a [autori'tarjo, a] *adj* authoritarian

autorización [autoriθa'θjon] *nf* authorization

autorizado, -a [autori'θaðo, a] *adj* authorized; (aprobado) approved

autorizar [autori'θar] *vt* to authorize; to approve

autorretrato [autorre'trato] *nm* self-portrait

autoservicio [autoser'ßiθjo] *nm* self-service shop o store; (restaurante) self-service restaurant

autostop [auto'stop] *nm* hitch-hiking; **hacer ~** to hitch-hike

autostopista [autosto'pista] *nm/f* hitch-hiker

autosuficiencia [autosufi'θjenθja] *nf* self-sufficiency

autosuficiente [autosufi'θjente] *adj* self-sufficient; (pey) smug

autosugestión [autosuxes'tjon] *nf* autosuggestion

autovía [auto'ßia] *nf* ≈ dual carriageway (Brit), ≈ separated highway (US)

auxiliar [auksi'ljar] *vt* to help ■ *nm/f* assistant

auxilio [auk'siljo] *nm* assistance, help; **primeros auxilios** first aid *sg*

Av *abr* (= Avenida) Av(e)

a/v *abr* (Com: = a vista) at sight

aval [a'ßal] *nm* guarantee; (persona) guarantor

avalancha [aßa'lantʃa] *nf* avalanche

avalar [aßa'lar] *vt* (Com etc) to underwrite; (fig) to endorse

avalista [aßa'lista] *nm* (Com) endorser

avance *etc* [a'ßanθe] *vb ver* **avanzar** ■ *nm* advance; (pago) advance payment; (Cine) trailer

avanzado, -a [aßan'θaðo, a] *adj* advanced; **de edad avanzada, ~ de edad** elderly

avanzar [aßan'θar] *vt, vi* to advance

avaricia [aßa'riθja] *nf* avarice, greed

avaricioso, -a [aßari'θjoso, a] *adj* avaricious, greedy

avaro, -a [a'ßaro, a] *adj* miserly, mean ■ *nm/f* miser

avasallar [aßasa'ʎar] *vt* to subdue, subjugate

avatar [aßa'tar] *nm* change; **avatares** ups and downs

Avda *abr* (= Avenida) Av(e)

AVE ['aße] *nm abr* (= Alta Velocidad Española) ≈ Bullet train

ave ['aße] *nf* bird; **~ de rapiña** bird of prey

avecinarse [aßeθi'narse] *vr* (tormenta, fig) to approach, be on the way

avejentar [aßexen'tar] *vt, vi*, **avejentarse** *vr* to age

avellana [aße'ʎana] *nf* hazelnut

avellano [aße'ʎano] *nm* hazel tree

avemaría [aßema'ria] *nm* Hail Mary, Ave Maria

avena [a'ßena] *nf* oats *pl*

avendré *etc* [aßen'dre], **avenga** *etc* [a'ßenga] *vb ver* **avenir**

avenida [aße'niða] *nf* (calle) avenue

avenir [aße'nir] *vt* to reconcile; **avenirse** *vr* to come to an agreement, reach a compromise

aventado, -a [aßen'taðo, a] *adj* (Am) daring

aventajado, -a [aßenta'xaðo, a] *adj* outstanding

aventajar [aßenta'xar] *vt* (sobrepasar) to surpass, outstrip

aventar [aßen'tar] *vt* to fan, blow; (grano) to winnow; (Am fam: echar) to chuck out

aventón [aßen'ton] *nm* (Am) push; **pedir ~** to hitch a lift

aventura [aßen'tura] *nf* adventure; **~ sentimental** love affair

aventurado, -a [aßentu'raðo, a] *adj* risky

aventurar [aßentu'rar] *vt* to risk; **aventurarse** *vr* to dare; **aventurarse a hacer algo** to venture to do sth

aventurero, -a [aßentu'rero, a] *adj* adventurous

39

avergoncé [aβeɾɣonˈθe], **avergoncemos** *etc* [aβeɾɣonˈθemos] *vb ver* **avergonzar**

avergonzar [aβeɾɣonˈθar] *vt* to shame; *(desconcertar)* to embarrass; **avergonzarse** *vr* to be ashamed; to be embarrassed

avergüence *etc* [aβeɾˈɣwenθe] *vb ver* **avergonzar**

avería [aβeˈria] *nf (Tec)* breakdown, fault

averiado, -a [aβeˈrjaðo, a] *adj* broken-down

averiar [aβeˈrjar] *vt* to break; **averiarse** *vr* to break down

averiguación [aβeɾiɣwaˈθjon] *nf* investigation

averiguar [aβeɾiˈɣwar] *vt* to investigate; *(descubrir)* to find out, ascertain

averigüe *etc* [aβeˈriɣwe] *vb ver* **averiguar**

aversión [aβeɾˈsjon] *nf* aversion, dislike; **cobrar ~ a** to take a strong dislike to

avestruz [aβesˈtruθ] *nm* ostrich

aviación [aβjaˈθjon] *nf* aviation; *(fuerzas aéreas)* air force

aviado, -a [aˈβjaðo, a] *adj*: **estar ~** to be in a mess

aviador, a [aβjaˈðor, a] *nm/f* aviator, airman/woman

aviar [aˈβjar] *vt* to prepare, get ready

avícola [aˈβikola] *adj* poultry *cpd*

avicultura [aβikulˈtura] *nf* poultry farming

avidez [aβiˈðeθ] *nf* avidity, eagerness

ávido, -a [ˈaβiðo, a] *adj* avid, eager

aviente *etc* [aˈβjente] *vb ver* **aventar**

avieso, -a [aˈβjeso, a] *adj (torcido)* distorted; *(perverso)* wicked

avinagrado, -a [aβinaˈɣraðo, a] *adj* sour, acid

avinagrarse [aβinaˈɣrarse] *vr* to go o turn sour

avine *etc* [aˈβine] *vb ver* **avenir**

Aviñón [aβiˈɲon] *nm* Avignon

avío [aˈβio] *nm* preparation; **avíos** *nmpl* gear *sg*, kit *sg*

avión [aˈβjon] *nm* aeroplane; *(ave)* martin; **~ de reacción** jet (plane); **por ~** *(Correos)* by air mail

avioneta [aβjoˈneta] *nf* light aircraft

avisar [aβiˈsar] *vt (advertir)* to warn, notify; *(informar)* to tell; *(aconsejar)* to advise, counsel

aviso [aˈβiso] *nm* warning; *(noticia)* notice; *(Com)* demand note; *(Inform)* prompt; **~ escrito** notice in writing; **sin previo ~** without warning; **estar sobre ~** to be on the look-out

avispa [aˈβispa] *nf* wasp

avispado, -a [aβisˈpaðo, a] *adj* sharp, clever

avispero [aβisˈpero] *nm* wasp's nest

avispón [aβisˈpon] *nm* hornet

avistar [aβisˈtar] *vt* to sight, spot

avitaminosis [aβitamiˈnosis] *nf inv* vitamin deficiency

avituallar [aβitwaˈʎar] *vt* to supply with food

avivar [aβiˈβar] *vt* to strengthen, intensify; **avivarse** *vr* to revive, acquire new life

avizor [aβiˈθor] *adj*: **estar ojo ~** to be on the alert

avizorar [aβiθoˈrar] *vt* to spy on

axila [akˈsila] *nf* armpit

axioma [akˈsjoma] *nm* axiom

ay [ai] *excl (dolor)* ow!, ouch!; *(aflicción)* oh!, oh dear!; **¡ay de mí!** poor me!

aya [ˈaja] *nf* governess; *(niñera)* nanny

ayer [aˈjer] *adv, nm* yesterday; **antes de ~** the day before yesterday; **~ por la tarde** yesterday afternoon/evening

aymara, aymará [aiˈmara] [aimaˈra] *adj, nm/f* Aymara

ayo [ˈajo] *nm* tutor

ayote [aˈjote] *nm (Am)* pumpkin

Ayto. *abr* = **Ayuntamiento**

ayuda [aˈjuða] *nf* help, assistance; *(Med)* enema ■ *nm* page; **~ humanitaria** humanitarian aid

ayudante, -a [ajuˈðante, a] *nm/f* assistant, helper; *(Escol)* assistant; *(Mil)* adjutant

ayudar [ajuˈðar] *vt* to help, assist

ayunar [ajuˈnar] *vi* to fast

ayunas [aˈjunas] *nfpl*: **estar en ~** *(no haber comido)* to be fasting; *(ignorar)* to be in the dark

ayuno [aˈjuno] *nm* fasting

ayuntamiento [ajuntaˈmjento] *nm (consejo)* town/city council; *(edificio)* town/city hall; *(cópula)* sexual intercourse

azabache [aθaˈβatʃe] *nm* jet

azada [aˈθaða] *nf* hoe

azafata [aθaˈfata] *nf* air hostess *(Brit)* o stewardess

azafate [asaˈfate] *nm (Am)* tray

azafrán [aθaˈfran] *nm* saffron

azahar [aθaˈar] *nm* orange/lemon blossom

azalea [aθaˈlea] *nf* azalea

azar [aˈθar] *nm (casualidad)* chance, fate; *(desgracia)* misfortune, accident; **por ~** by chance; **al ~** at random

azaroso, -a [aθaˈroso, a] *adj (arriesgado)* risky; *(vida)* eventful

Azerbaiyán [aθerbaˈjan] *nm* Azerbaijan

azerbaiyano, -a [aθerbaˈjano, a], **azerí** [aθeˈri] *adj, nm/f* Azerbaijani, Azeri

azogue [aˈθoɣe] *nm* mercury

azor [aˈθor] *nm* goshawk

azoramiento [aθoraˈmjento] *nm* alarm; *(confusión)* confusion

azorar [aθoˈrar] *vt* to alarm; **azorarse** *vr* to get alarmed

Azores [a'θores] *nfpl*: **las (Islas)** ~ the Azores

azotaina [aθo'taina] *nf* beating

azotar [aθo'tar] *vt* to whip, beat; (*pegar*) to spank

azote [a'θote] *nm* (*látigo*) whip; (*latigazo*) lash, stroke; (*en las nalgas*) spank; (*calamidad*) calamity

azotea [aθo'tea] *nf* (flat) roof

azteca [aθ'teka] *adj*, *nm/f* Aztec

azúcar [a'θukar] *nm* sugar

azucarado, -a [aθuka'raðo, a] *adj* sugary, sweet

azucarero, -a [aθuka'rero, a] *adj* sugar *cpd* ■ *nm* sugar bowl

azuce *etc* [a'θuθe] *vb ver* **azuzar**

azucena [aθu'θena] *nf* white lily

azufre [a'θufre] *nm* sulphur

azul [a'θul] *adj*, *nm* blue; ~ **celeste/marino** sky/navy blue

azulejo [aθu'lexo] *nm* tile

azulgrana [aθul'ɣrana] *adj inv* of Barcelona Football Club ■ *nm*: **los A** ~ the Barcelona Γ.C. players *o* team

azuzar [aθu'θar] *vt* to incite, egg on

41

Bb

B, b (*Esp*) [be] (*Am*) [be'larɣa] *nf* (*letra*) B, b;
B de Barcelona B for Benjamin (*Brit*) o Baker
(*US*)

baba ['baβa] *nf* spittle, saliva; **se le caía la ~**
(*fig*) he was thrilled to bits

babear [baβe'ar] *vi* (*echar saliva*) to slobber;
(*niño*) to dribble; (*fig*) to drool, slaver

babel [ba'βel] *nm o f* bedlam

babero [ba'βero] *nm* bib

Babia ['baβja] *nf*: **estar en ~** to be
daydreaming

bable ['baβle] *nm* Asturian (dialect)

babor [ba'βor] *nm* port (side); **a ~** to port

babosada [baβo'saða] *nf*: **decir babosadas**
(*Am fam*) to talk rubbish

baboso, -a [ba'βoso, a] *adj* slobbering; (*Zool*)
slimy; (*Am*) silly ■ *nm/f* (*Am*) fool

babucha [ba'βutʃa] *nf* slipper

baca ['baka] *nf* (*Auto*) luggage o roof rack

bacalao [baka'lao] *nm* cod(fish)

bacanal [baka'nal] *nf* orgy

bache ['batʃe] *nm* pothole, rut; (*fig*) bad patch

bachillerato [batʃiʎe'rato] *nm* two-year
secondary school course; *ver tb* **sistema educativo**

bacilo [ba'θilo] *nm* bacillus, germ

bacinica [baθi'nika] *nf*, **bacinilla** [baθi'niʎa]
nf chamber pot

bacteria [bak'terja] *nf* bacterium, germ

bacteriológico, -a [bakterjo'loxico, a] *adj*
bacteriological; **guerra bacteriológica**
germ warfare

báculo ['bakulo] *nm* stick, staff; (*fig*) support

badajo [ba'ðaxo] *nm* clapper (*of a bell*)

bádminton ['baðminton] *nm* badminton

bafle ['bafle], **baffle** ['baffle] *nm* (*Elec*)
speaker

bagaje [ba'ɣaxe] *nm* baggage; (*fig*)
background

bagatela [baɣa'tela] *nf* trinket, trifle

Bahama [ba'ama]: **las (Islas) ~, las
Bahamas** *nfpl* the Bahamas

bahía [ba'ia] *nf* bay

bailar [bai'lar] *vt, vi* to dance

bailarín, -ina [baila'rin, ina] *nm/f* dancer;
(*de ballet*) ballet dancer

baile ['baile] *nm* dance; (*formal*) ball

baja ['baxa] *nf* drop, fall; (*Econ*) slump;
(*Mil*) casualty; (*paro*) redundancy; **dar de ~**
(*soldado*) to discharge; (*empleado*) to dismiss,
sack; **darse de ~** (*retirarse*) to drop out; (*Med*)
to go sick; (*dimitir*) to resign; **estar de ~**
(*enfermo*) to be off sick; (*Bolsa*) to be dropping
o falling; **jugar a la ~** (*Econ*) to speculate on a
fall in prices; *ver tb* **bajo**

bajada [ba'xaða] *nf* descent; (*camino*) slope;
(*de aguas*) ebb

bajamar [baxa'mar] *nf* low tide

bajar [ba'xar] *vi* to go o come down;
(*temperatura, precios*) to drop, fall ■ *vt* (*cabeza*)
to bow; (*escalera*) to go o come down; (*radio
etc*) to turn down; (*precio, voz*) to lower; (*llevar
abajo*) to take down; **bajarse** *vr* (*de vehículo*)
to get out; (*de autobús*) to get off; **~ de** (*coche*)
to get out of; (*autobús*) to get off; **bajarle los
humos a algn** (*fig*) to cut sb down to size;
bajarse algo de Internet to download sth
from the Internet

bajeza [ba'xeθa] *nf* baseness; (*una bajeza*) vile
deed

bajío [ba'xio] *nm* shoal, sandbank; (*Am*)
lowlands *pl*

bajista [ba'xista] *nm/f* (*Mus*) bassist ■ *adj*
(*Bolsa*) bear *cpd*

bajo, -a ['baxo, a] *adj* (*terreno*) low(-lying);
(*mueble, número, precio*) low; (*piso*) ground *cpd*;
(*de estatura*) small, short; (*color*) pale; (*sonido*)
faint, soft, low; (*voz, tono*) deep; (*metal*) base
■ *adv* (*hablar*) softly, quietly; (*volar*) low ■ *prep*
under, below, underneath ■ *nm* (*Mus*) bass;
hablar en voz baja to whisper; **~ la lluvia**
in the rain

bajón [ba'xon] *nm* fall, drop

bajura [ba'xura] *nf*: **pesca de ~** coastal
fishing

bakalao [baka'lao] *nm* (*Mus*) rave music

bala ['bala] *nf* bullet; **~ de goma** plastic bullet

balacera [bala'sera] *nf* (*Am*) shoot-out
balada [ba'laða] *nf* ballad
baladí [bala'ði] *adj* trivial
baladronada [balaðro'naða] *nf* (*dicho*) boast,
brag; (*hecho*) piece of bravado
balance [ba'lanθe] *nm* (*Com*) balance; (: *libro*)
balance sheet; (: *cuenta general*) stocktaking;
~ **de comprobación** trial balance; ~
consolidado consolidated balance sheet;
hacer ~ to take stock
balancear [balanθe'ar] *vt* to balance ∎ *vi*,
balancearse *vr* to swing (to and fro); (*vacilar*)
to hesitate
balanceo [balan'θeo] *nm* swinging
balandro [ba'landro] *nm* yacht
balanza [ba'lanθa] *nf* scales *pl*, balance; ~
comercial balance of trade; ~ **de pagos/**
de poder(es) balance of payments/of power;
(*Astro*): **B~ Libra**
balar [ba'lar] *vi* to bleat
balaustrada [balaus'traða] *nf* balustrade;
(*pasamanos*) banister
balazo [ba'laθo] *nm* (*tiro*) shot; (*herida*) bullet
wound
balboa [bal'βoa] *nf* Panamanian currency unit
balbucear [balβuθe'ar] *vi*, *vt* to stammer,
stutter
balbuceo [balβu'θeo] *nm* stammering,
stuttering
balbucir [balβu'θir] *vi*, *vt* to stammer, stutter
balbuzca *etc* [bal'βuθka] *vb ver* **balbucir**
Balcanes [bal'kanes] *nmpl*: **los (Montes)**
~ the Balkans, the Balkan Mountains; **la**
Península de los ~ the Balkan Peninsula
balcánico, -a [bal'kaniko, a] *adj* Balkan
balcón [bal'kon] *nm* balcony
balda ['balda] *nf* (*estante*) shelf
baldar [bal'dar] *vt* to cripple; (*agotar*) to
exhaust
balde ['balde] *nm* (*esp Am*) bucket, pail; **de** ~
adv (for) free, for nothing; **en** ~ *adv* in vain
baldío, -a [bal'dio, a] *adj* uncultivated;
(*terreno*) waste; (*inútil*) vain ∎ *nm* wasteland
baldosa [bal'dosa] *nf* (*azulejo*) floor tile;
(*grande*) flagstone
baldosín [baldo'sin] *nm* wall tile
balear [bale'ar] *adj* Balearic, of the Balearic
Islands ∎ *nm/f* native *o* inhabitant of the
Balearic Islands ∎ *vt* (*Am*) to shoot (at)
Baleares [bale'ares] *nfpl*: **las (Islas)** ~ the
Balearics, the Balearic Islands
balido [ba'liðo] *nm* bleat, bleating
balín [ba'lin] *nm* pellet; **balines** *nmpl*
buckshot *sg*
balística [ba'listika] *nf* ballistics *pl*
baliza [ba'liθa] *nf* (*Aviat*) beacon; (*Naut*) buoy
ballena [ba'ʎena] *nf* whale

ballenero, -a [baʎe'nero, a] *adj*: **industria**
ballenera whaling industry ∎ *nm* (*pescador*)
whaler; (*barco*) whaling ship
ballesta [ba'ʎesta] *nf* crossbow; (*Auto*)
spring
ballet (*pl* **ballets**) [ba'le, ba'les] *nm* ballet
balneario, -a [balne'arjo, a] *adj*: **estación**
balnearia (bathing) resort ∎ *nm* spa, health
resort
balompié [balom'pje] *nm* football
balón [ba'lon] *nm* ball
baloncesto [balon'θesto] *nm* basketball
balonmano [balon'mano] *nm* handball
balonred [balon'reð] *nm* netball
balonvolea [balombo'lea] *nm* volleyball
balsa ['balsa] *nf* raft; (*Bot*) balsa wood
bálsamo ['balsamo] *nm* balsam, balm
balsón [bal'son] *nm* (*Am*) swamp, bog
báltico, -a ['baltiko, a] *adj* Baltic; **el (Mar) B~**
the Baltic (Sea)
baluarte [ba'lwarte] *nm* bastion, bulwark
bambolearse [bambole'arse] *vr* to swing,
sway; (*silla*) to wobble
bamboleo [bambo'leo] *nm* swinging,
swaying; wobbling
bambú [bam'bu] *nm* bamboo
banal [ba'nal] *adj* banal, trivial
banana [ba'nana] *nf* (*Am*) banana
bananal [bana'nal] *nm* (*Am*) banana
plantation
banano [ba'nano] *nm* (*Am*) banana tree
banasta [ba'nasta] *nf* large basket, hamper
banca ['banka] *nf* bench; (*Com*) banking
bancario, -a [ban'karjo, a] *adj* banking *cpd*,
bank *cpd*; **giro** ~ bank draft
bancarrota [banka'rrota] *nf* bankruptcy;
declararse en *o* **hacer** ~ to go bankrupt
banco ['banko] *nm* bench; (*Escol*) desk;
(*Com*) bank; (*Geo*) stratum; ~ **comercial**
o **mercantil** commercial bank; ~ **por**
acciones joint-stock bank; ~ **de crédito/de**
ahorros credit/savings bank; ~ **de arena**
sandbank; ~ **de datos** (*Inform*) data bank;
~ **de hielo** iceberg
banda ['banda] *nf* band; (*cinta*) ribbon;
(*pandilla*) gang; (*Mus*) brass band; (*Naut*) side,
edge; **la** ~ **ancha** broadband; **la B~ Oriental**
Uruguay; ~ **sonora** soundtrack;
~ **transportadora** conveyor belt
bandada [ban'daða] *nf* (*de pájaros*) flock;
(*de peces*) shoal
bandazo [ban'daθo] *nm*: **dar bandazos**
(*coche*) to veer from side to side
bandeja [ban'dexa] *nf* tray; ~ **de entrada/**
salida in-tray/out-tray
bandera [ban'dera] *nf* (*de tela*) flag;
(*estandarte*) banner; **izar la** ~ to hoist the flag

b

banderilla [bande'riʎa] *nf* banderilla; (*tapa*) *savoury appetizer* (*served on a cocktail stick*)

banderín [bande'rin] *nm* pennant, small flag

banderola [bande'rola] *nf* (*Mil*) pennant

bandido [ban'diðo] *nm* bandit

bando ['bando] *nm* (*edicto*) edict, proclamation; (*facción*) faction; **pasar al otro ~** to change sides; **los bandos** (*Rel*) the banns

bandolera [bando'lera] *nf*: **bolsa de ~** shoulder bag

bandolero [bando'lero] *nm* bandit, brigand

bandoneón [bandone'on] *nm* (*Am*) large accordion

banquero [ban'kero] *nm* banker

banqueta [ban'keta] *nf* stool; (*Am: acera*) pavement (*Brit*), sidewalk (*US*)

banquete [ban'kete] *nm* banquet; (*para convidados*) formal dinner; **~ de boda** wedding breakfast

banquillo [ban'kiʎo] *nm* (*Jur*) dock, prisoner's bench; (*banco*) bench; (*para los pies*) footstool

bañadera [baɲa'ðera] *nf* (*Am*) bath(tub)

bañado [ba'ɲaðo] *nm* (*Am*) swamp

bañador [baɲa'ðor] *nm* swimming costume (*Brit*), bathing suit (*US*)

bañar [ba'ɲar] *vt* (*niño*) to bath, bathe; (*objeto*) to dip; (*de barniz*) to coat; **bañarse** *vr* (*en el mar*) to bathe, swim; (*en la bañera*) to have a bath

bañero, -a [ba'ɲero, a] *nm/f* lifeguard ■ *nf* bath(tub)

bañista [ba'ɲista] *nm/f* bather

baño ['baɲo] *nm* (*en bañera*) bath; (*en río, mar*) dip, swim; (*cuarto*) bathroom; (*bañera*) bath(tub); (*capa*) coating; **ir a tomar los baños** to take the waters

baptista [bap'tista] *nm/f* Baptist

baqueano, -a, baquiano, -a [bake'ano, a] [baki'ano, a] *nm/f* (*Am*) guide

baqueta [ba'keta] *nf* (*Mus*) drumstick

bar [bar] *nm* bar

barahúnda [bara'unda] *nf* uproar, hubbub

baraja [ba'raxa] *nf* pack (of cards); *see note*

barajar [bara'xar] *vt* (*naipes*) to shuffle; (*fig*) to jumble up

baranda [ba'randa], **barandilla** [baran'diʎa] *nf* rail, railing

baratija [bara'tixa] *nf* trinket; (*fig*) trifle; **baratijas** *nfpl* (*Com*) cheap goods

baratillo [bara'tiʎo] *nm* (*tienda*) junk shop; (*subasta*) bargain sale; (*conjunto de cosas*) second-hand goods *pl*

barato, -a [ba'rato, a] *adj* cheap ■ *adv* cheap, cheaply

baratura [bara'tura] *nf* cheapness

baraúnda [bara'unda] *nf* = **barahúnda**

barba ['barβa] *nf* (*mentón*) chin; (*pelo*) beard; **tener ~** to be unshaven; **hacer algo en las barbas de algn** to do sth under sb's very nose; **reírse en las barbas de algn** to laugh in sb's face

barbacoa [barβa'koa] *nf* (*parrilla*) barbecue; (*carne*) barbecued meat

barbaridad [barβari'ðað] *nf* barbarity; (*acto*) barbarism; (*atrocidad*) outrage; **una ~ de** (*fam*) loads of; **¡qué ~!** (*fam*) how awful!; **cuesta una ~** (*fam*) it costs a fortune

barbarie [bar'βarje] *nf*, **barbarismo** [barβa'rismo] *nm* barbarism; (*crueldad*) barbarity

bárbaro, -a ['barβaro, a] *adj* barbarous, cruel; (*grosero*) rough, uncouth ■ *nm/f* barbarian ■ *adv*: **lo pasamos ~** (*fam*) we had a great time; **¡qué ~!** (*fam*) how marvellous!; **un éxito ~** (*fam*) a terrific success; **es un tipo ~** (*fam*) he's a great bloke

barbecho [bar'βetʃo] *nm* fallow land

barbero [bar'βero] *nm* barber, hairdresser

barbilampiño [barβilam'piɲo] *adj* smooth-faced; (*fig*) inexperienced

barbilla [bar'βiʎa] *nf* chin, tip of the chin

barbitúrico [barβi'turiko] *nm* barbiturate

barbo ['barβo] *nm*: **~ de mar** red mullet

barbotar [barβo'tar], **barbotear** [barβote'ar] *vt, vi* to mutter, mumble

barbudo, -a [bar'βuðo, a] *adj* bearded

barbullar [barβu'ʎar] *vi* to jabber away

barca ['barka] *nf* (small) boat; **~ pesquera** fishing boat; **~ de pasaje** ferry

barcaza [bar'kaθa] *nf* barge; **~ de desembarco** landing craft

Barcelona [barθe'lona] *nf* Barcelona

barcelonés, -esa [barθelo'nes, esa] *adj* of *o* from Barcelona ■ *nm/f* native *o* inhabitant of Barcelona

barco ['barko] *nm* boat; (*buque*) ship; (*Com etc*) vessel; **~ de carga** cargo boat; **~ de guerra** warship; **~ de vela** sailing ship; **ir en ~** to go by boat

baremo [ba'remo] *nm* scale; (*tabla de cuentas*)

ready reckoner
barítono [ba'ritono] nm baritone
barman ['barman] nm barman
Barna abr = **Barcelona**
barnice etc [bar'niθe] vb ver **barnizar**
barniz [bar'niθ] nm varnish; (en la loza) glaze; (fig) veneer
barnizar [barni'θar] vt to varnish; (loza) to glaze
barómetro [ba'rometro] nm barometer
barón [ba'ron] nm barón
baronesa [baro'nesa] nf baroness
barquero [bar'kero] nm boatman
barquilla [bar'kiʎa] nf (Naut) log
barquillo [bar'kiʎo] nm cone, cornet
barra ['barra] nf bar, rod; (Jur) rail; (: banquillo) dock; (de un bar, café) bar; (de pan) French loaf; (palanca) lever; **~ de carmín** o **de labios** lipstick; **~ de herramientas** (Inform) toolbar; **~ de espaciado** (Inform) space bar; **~ inversa** backslash; **~ libre** free bar; **no pararse en barras** to stick o stop at nothing
barrabasada [barraβa'saða] nf (piece of) mischief
barraca [ba'rraka] nf hut, cabin; (en Valencia) thatched farmhouse; (en feria) booth
barracón [barra'kon] nm (caseta) big hut
barragana [barra'ɣana] nf concubine
barranca [ba'rranka] nf ravine, gully
barranco [ba'rranko] nm ravine; (fig) difficulty
barrena [ba'rrena] nf drill
barrenar [barre'nar] vt to drill (through), bore
barrendero, -a [barren'dero, a] nm/f street-sweeper
barreno [ba'rreno] nm large drill
barreño [ba'rreɲo] nm washing-up bowl
barrer [ba'rrer] vt to sweep; (quitar) to sweep away; (Mil: Naut) to sweep, rake (with gunfire) ■ vi to sweep up
barrera [ba'rrera] nf barrier; (Mil) barricade; (Ferro) crossing gate; **poner barreras a** to hinder; **~ arancelaria** (Com) tariff barrier; **~ comercial** (Com) trade barrier
barriada [ba'rrjaða] nf quarter, district
barricada [barri'kaða] nf barricade
barrida [ba'rriða] nf, **barrido** [ba'rriðo] nm sweep, sweeping
barriga [ba'rriɣa] nf belly; (panza) paunch; (vientre) guts pl; **echar ~** to get middle-age spread
barrigón, -ona [barri'ɣon, ona], **barrigudo, -a** [barri'ɣuðo, a] adj potbellied
barril [ba'rril] nm barrel, cask; **cerveza de ~** draught beer
barrio ['barrjo] nm (vecindad) area,

neighborhood (US); (en las afueras) suburb; **barrios bajos** poor quarter sg; **~ chino** red-light district
barriobajero, -a [barrjobβa'xero, a] adj (vulgar) common
barro ['barro] nm (lodo) mud; (objetos) earthenware; (Med) pimple
barroco, -a [ba'rroko, a] adj Baroque; (fig) elaborate ■ nm Baroque
barrote [ba'rrote] nm (de ventana etc) bar
barruntar [barrun'tar] vt (conjeturar) to guess; (presentir) to suspect
barrunto [ba'rrunto] nm guess; suspicion
bartola [bar'tola]: **a la ~** adv: **tirarse a la ~** to take it easy, be lazy
bártulos ['bartulos] nmpl things, belongings
barullo [ba'ruʎo] nm row, uproar
basa ['basa] nf (Arq) base
basamento [basa'mento] nm base, plinth
basar [ba'sar] vt to base; **basarse** vr: **basarse en** to be based on
basca ['baska] nf nausea
báscula ['baskula] nf (platform) scales pl
base ['base] nf base; **a ~ de** on the basis of, based on; (mediante) by means of; **a ~ de bien** in abundance; **~ de conocimiento** knowledge base; **~ de datos** database
básico, -a ['basiko, a] adj basic
Basilea [basi'lea] nf Basle
basílica [ba'silika] nf basilica
basilisco [basi'lisko] nm (Am) iguana; **estar hecho un ~** to be hopping mad
basket, básquet ['basket] nm basketball

🔘 PALABRA CLAVE

bastante [bas'tante] adj 1 (suficiente) enough; **bastante dinero** enough o sufficient money; **bastantes libros** enough books
2 (valor intensivo): **bastante gente** quite a lot of people; **tener bastante calor** to be rather hot; **hace bastante tiempo que ocurrió** it happened quite o rather a long time ago
■ adv: **bastante bueno/malo** quite good/ rather bad; **bastante rico** pretty rich; **(lo) bastante inteligente (como) para hacer algo** clever enough o sufficiently clever to do sth; **voy a tardar bastante** I'm going to be a while o quite some time

bastar [bas'tar] vi to be enough o sufficient; **bastarse** vr to be self-sufficient; **~ para** to be enough to; **¡basta!** (that's) enough!
bastardilla [bastar'ðiʎa] nf italics pl
bastardo, -a [bas'tarðo, a] adj, nm/f bastard
bastidor [basti'ðor] nm frame; (de coche) chassis; (Arte) stretcher; (Teat) wing; **entre**

bastidores behind the scenes
basto, -a ['basto, a] *adj* coarse, rough ▪ *nmpl*: **bastos** (*Naipes*) one of the suits in the Spanish card deck; *ver tb* **baraja española**
bastón [bas'ton] *nm* stick, staff; (*para pasear*) walking stick; **~ de mando** baton
bastonazo [basto'naθo] *nm* blow with a stick
bastoncillo [baston'θiʎo] *nm* (*tb*: **bastoncillo de algodón**) cotton bud
basura [ba'sura] *nf* rubbish, refuse (*Brit*), garbage (*US*) ▪ *adj*: **comida/televisión ~** junk food/TV
basurero [basu'rero] *nm* (*hombre*) dustman (*Brit*), garbage collector *o* man (*US*); (*lugar*) rubbish dump; (*cubo*) (rubbish) bin (*Brit*), trash can (*US*)
bata ['bata] *nf* (*gen*) dressing gown; (*cubretodo*) smock, overall; (*Med: Tec etc*) lab(oratory) coat
batacazo [bata'kaθo] *nm* bump
batalla [ba'taʎa] *nf* battle; **de ~** for everyday use
batallar [bata'ʎar] *vi* to fight
batallón [bata'ʎon] *nm* battalion
batata [ba'tata] *nf* (*Am: Culin*) sweet potato
bate ['bate] *nm* (*Deporte*) bat
batea [ba'tea] *nf* (*Am*) washing trough
bateador [batea'ðor] *nm* (*Deporte*) batter, batsman
batería [bate'ria] *nf* battery; (*Mus*) drums *pl*; (*Teat*) footlights *pl*; **~ de cocina** kitchen utensils *pl*
batiburrillo [batiβu'rriʎo] *nm* hotchpotch
batido, -a [ba'tiðo, a] *adj* (*camino*) beaten, well-trodden ▪ *nm* (*Culin*) batter; **~ (de leche)** milk shake ▪ *nf* (*Am*) (police) raid
batidora [bati'ðora] *nf* beater, mixer; **~ eléctrica** food mixer, blender
batir [ba'tir] *vt* to beat, strike; (*vencer*) to beat, defeat; (*revolver*) to beat, mix; (*pelo*) to back-comb; **batirse** *vr* to fight; **~ palmas** to clap, applaud
baturro, -a [ba'turro, a] *nm/f* Aragonese peasant
batuta [ba'tuta] *nf* baton; **llevar la ~** (*fig*) to be the boss
baudio ['bauðjo] *nm* (*Inform*) baud
baúl [ba'ul] *nm* trunk; (*Am Auto*) boot (*Brit*), trunk (*US*)
bautice *etc* [bau'tiθe] *vb ver* **bautizar**
bautismo [bau'tismo] *nm* baptism, christening
bautista [bau'tista] *adj, nm/f* Baptist
bautizar [bauti'θar] *vt* to baptize, christen; (*fam: diluir*) to water down; (*dar apodo*) to dub
bautizo [bau'tiθo] *nm* baptism, christening
bávaro, -a ['baβaro, a] *adj, nm/f* Bavarian
Baviera [ba'βjera] *nf* Bavaria

baya ['baja] *nf* berry; *ver tb* **bayo**
bayeta [ba'jeta] *nf* (*trapo*) floor cloth; (*Am: pañal*) nappy (*Brit*), diaper (*US*)
bayo, -a ['bajo, a] *adj* bay
bayoneta [bajo'neta] *nf* bayonet
baza ['baθa] *nf* trick; **meter ~** to butt in
bazar [ba'θar] *nm* bazaar
bazo ['baθo] *nm* spleen
bazofia [ba'θofja] *nf* pigswill (*Brit*), hogwash (*US*); (*libro etc*) trash
BCE *nm abr* (= *Banco Central Europeo*) ECB
beatificar [beatifi'kar] *vt* to beatify
beato, -a [be'ato, a] *adj* blessed; (*piadoso*) pious
bebe (*Am*) (*pl* **bebes**) ['beβe, 'beβes], **bebé** (*pl* **bebés**) [be'βe, be'βes] *nm* baby; **~ de diseño** designer baby
bebedero, -a [beβe'ðero, a] *nm* (*para animales*) drinking trough
bebedizo, -a [beβe'ðiθo, a] *adj* drinkable ▪ *nm* potion
bebedor, a [beβe'ðor, a] *adj* hard-drinking
bebé-probeta [be'βe-pro'βeta] (*pl* **bebés-probeta**) *nm/f* test-tube baby
beber [be'βer] *vt, vi* to drink; **~ a sorbos/tragos** to sip/gulp; **se lo bebió todo** he drank it all up
bebido, -a [be'βiðo, a] *adj* drunk ▪ *nf* drink
beca ['beka] *nf* grant, scholarship
becado, -a [be'kaðo, a] *nm/f*, **becario, a** [be'karjo, a] *nm/f* scholarship holder
becerro [be'θerro] *nm* yearling calf
bechamel [betʃa'mel] *nf* = **besamel**
becuadro [be'kwaðro] *nm* (*Mus*) natural sign
bedel [be'ðel] *nm* porter, janitor
beduino, -a [be'ðwino, a] *adj, nm/f* Bedouin
befarse [be'farse] *vr*: **~ de algo** to scoff at sth
beige ['beix], **beis** ['beis] *adj, nm* beige
béisbol ['beisβol] *nm* baseball
bejuco [be'xuko] *nm* (*Am*) reed, liana
beldad [bel'dað] *nf* beauty
Belén [be'len] *nm* Bethlehem; **belén** (*de Navidad*) nativity scene, crib
belga ['belɣa] *adj, nm/f* Belgian
Bélgica ['belxika] *nf* Belgium
Belgrado [bel'ɣraðo] *nm* Belgrade
Belice [be'liθe] *nm* Belize
bélico, -a ['beliko, a] *adj* (*actitud*) warlike
belicoso, -a [beli'koso, a] *adj* (*guerrero*) warlike; (*agresivo*) aggressive, bellicose
beligerante [belixe'rante] *adj* belligerent
bellaco, -a [be'ʎako, a] *adj* sly, cunning ▪ *nm* villain, rogue
belladona [beʎa'ðona] *nf* deadly nightshade
bellaquería [beʎake'ria] *nf* (*acción*) dirty trick; (*calidad*) wickedness
belleza [be'ʎeθa] *nf* beauty

bello, -a ['beʎo, a] adj beautiful, lovely;
  Bellas Artes Fine Art sg
bellota [be'ʎota] nf acorn
bemol [be'mol] nm (Mus) flat; **esto tiene**
  bemoles (fam) this is a tough one
bencina [ben'sina] nf (Am) petrol (Brit), gas
  (US)
bendecir [bende'θir] vt to bless; **~ la mesa**
  to say grace
bendición [bendi'θjon] nf blessing
bendiga etc [ben'diɣa], **bendije** etc [ben'dixe]
  vb ver **bendecir**
bendito, -a [ben'dito, a] pp de **bendecir** ▪ adj
  (santo) blessed; (agua) holy; (afortunado) lucky;
  (feliz) happy; (sencillo) simple ▪ nm/f simple
  soul; **¡~ sea Dios!** thank goodness!; **es un ~**
  he's sweet; **dormir como un ~** to sleep like
  a log
benedictino, -a [beneðik'tino, a] adj, nm
  Benedictine
benefactor, a [benefak'tor, a] nm/f
  benefactor/benefactress
beneficencia [benefi'θenθja] nf charity
beneficiar [benefi'θjar] vt to benefit, be of
  benefit to; **beneficiarse** vr to benefit, profit
beneficiario, -a [benefi'θjarjo, a] nm/f
  beneficiary; (de cheque) payee
beneficio [bene'fiθjo] nm (bien) benefit,
  advantage; (Com) profit, gain; **a ~ de** for
  the benefit of; **en ~ propio** to one's own
  advantage; **~ bruto/neto** gross/net profit;
  ~ por acción earnings pl per share
beneficioso, -a [benefi'θjoso, a] adj
  beneficial
benéfico, -a [be'nefiko, a] adj charitable;
  sociedad benéfica charity (organization)
benemérito, -a [bene'merito, a] adj
  meritorious ▪ nf: **la Benemérita** (Esp) the
  Civil Guard; ver tb **Guardia Civil**
beneplácito [bene'plaθito] nm approval,
  consent
benevolencia [beneβo'lenθja] nf
  benevolence, kindness
benévolo, -a [be'neβolo, a] adj benevolent,
  kind
Bengala [ben'gala] nf Bengal; **el Golfo de ~**
  the Bay of Bengal
bengala [ben'gala] nf (Mil) flare; (fuego)
  Bengal light; (materia) rattan
bengalí [benga'li] adj, nm/f Bengali
benignidad [beniɣni'ðað] nf (afabilidad)
  kindness; (suavidad) mildness
benigno, -a [be'niɣno, a] adj kind; (suave)
  mild; (Med: tumor) benign, non-malignant
benjamín [benxa'min] nm youngest child
beodo, -a [be'oðo, a] adj drunk ▪ nm/f
  drunkard

berberecho [berβe'retʃo] nm cockle
berenjena [beren'xena] nf aubergine (Brit),
  eggplant (US)
berenjenal [berenxe'nal] nm (Agr) aubergine
  bed; (fig) mess; **en buen ~ nos hemos**
  metido we've got ourselves into a fine mess
bergantín [berɣan'tin] nm brig(antine)
Berlín [ber'lin] nm Berlin
berlinés, -esa [berli'nes, esa] adj of o from
  Berlin ▪ nm/f Berliner
bermejo, -a [ber'mexo, a] adj red
bermellón [berme'ʎon] nm vermilion
bermudas [ber'muðas] nfpl Bermuda shorts
berrear [berre'ar] vi to bellow, low
berrido [be'rriðo] nm bellow(ing)
berrinche [be'rrintʃe] nm (fam) temper,
  tantrum
berro ['berro] nm watercress
berza ['berθa] nf cabbage; **~ lombarda** red
  cabbage
besamel [besa'mel], **besamela** [besa'mela]
  nf (Culin) white sauce, bechamel sauce
besar [be'sar] vt to kiss; (fig: tocar) to graze;
  besarse vr to kiss (one another)
beso ['beso] nm kiss
bestia ['bestja] nf beast, animal; (fig) idiot;
  ~ de carga beast of burden; **¡~!** you idiot!; **¡no**
  seas ~! (bruto) don't be such a brute!; (idiota)
  don't be such an idiot!
bestial [bes'tjal] adj bestial; (fam) terrific
bestialidad [bestjali'ðað] nf bestiality; (fam)
  stupidity
besugo [be'suɣo] nm sea bream; (fam) idiot
besuguera [besu'ɣera] nf (Culin) fish pan
besuquear [besuke'ar] vt to cover with
  kisses; **besuquearse** vr to kiss and cuddle
bético, -a ['betiko, a] adj Andalusian
betún [be'tun] nm shoe polish; (Química)
  bitumen, asphalt
Bib. abr = **Biblioteca**
biberón [biβe'ron] nm feeding bottle
Biblia ['biβlja] nf Bible
bíblico, -a ['biβliko, a] adj biblical
bibliografía [biβljoɣra'fia] nf bibliography
biblioteca [biβljo'teka] nf library; (estantes)
  bookcase, bookshelves pl; **~ de consulta**
  reference library
bibliotecario, -a [biβljote'karjo, a] nm/f
  librarian
B.I.C. [bik] nf abr (= Brigada de Investigación
  Criminal) ≈ CID (Brit), FBI (US)
bicarbonato [bikarβo'nato] nm bicarbonate
bíceps ['biθeps] nm inv biceps
bicho ['bitʃo] nm (animal) small animal;
  (sabandija) bug, insect; (Taur) bull; **~ raro**
  (fam) queer fish
bici ['biθi] nf (fam) bike

bicicleta [biθi'kleta] *nf* bicycle, cycle;
~ **estática/de montaña** exercise/mountain
bike
bicoca [bi'koka] *nf* (*Esp fam*) cushy job
bidé [bi'ðe] *nm* bidet
bidireccional [biðirekθjo'nal] *adj*
bidirectional
bidón [bi'ðon] *nm* (*grande*) drum; (*pequeño*) can
Bielorrusia [bjelo'rrusja] *nf* Belarus,
Byelorussia
bielorruso, -a [bjelo'rruso, a] *adj, nm/f*
Belarussian, Belorussian ■ *nm* (*Ling*)
Belarussian, Belorussian

🔵 PALABRA CLAVE

bien [bjen] *nm* **1** (*bienestar*) good; **te lo digo
por tu bien** I'm telling you for your own
good; **el bien y el mal** good and evil
2 (*posesión*): **bienes** goods; **bienes de
consumo/equipo** consumer/capital
goods; **bienes inmuebles** *o* **raíces/bienes
muebles** real estate *sg*/personal property *sg*
■ *adv* **1** (*de manera satisfactoria, correcta etc*) well;
trabaja/come bien she works/eats well;
contestó bien he answered correctly; **oler
bien** to smell nice *o* good; **me siento bien** I
feel fine; **no me siento bien** I don't feel very
well; **se está bien aquí** it's nice here
2 (*frases*): **hiciste bien en llamarme** you
were right to call me
3 (*valor intensivo*) very; **un cuarto bien
caliente** a nice warm room; **bien de veces**
lots of times; **bien se ve que ...** it's quite
clear that ...
4: **estar bien**: **estoy muy bien aquí** I feel
very happy here; **¿te encuentras bien?**
are you all right?; **te está bien la falda** (*ser
la talla*) the skirt fits you; (*sentar*) the skirt
suits you; **el libro está muy bien** the book
is really good; **está bien que vengan** it's all
right for them to come; **¡está bien! lo haré**
oh all right, I'll do it; **ya está bien de quejas**
that's quite enough complaining
5 (*de buena gana*): **yo bien que iría pero ...**
I'd gladly go but ...
■ *excl*: **¡bien!** (*aprobación*) OK!; **¡muy bien!**
well done!; **¡qué bien!** great!; **bien, gracias,
¿y usted?** fine thanks, and you?
■ *adj inv*: **niño bien** rich kid; **gente bien**
posh people
■ *conj* **1**: **bien ... bien**: **bien en coche bien
en tren** either by car or by train
2: **no bien** (*esp Am*): **no bien llegue te
llamaré** as soon as I arrive I'll call you
3: **si bien** even though; *ver tb* **más**

bienal [bje'nal] *adj* biennial
bienaventurado, -a [bjenaβentu'raðo, a]
adj (*feliz*) happy; (*afortunado*) fortunate; (*Rel*)
blessed
bienestar [bjenes'tar] *nm* well-being;
estado de ~ welfare state
bienhechor, a [bjene'tʃor, a] *adj* beneficent
■ *nm/f* benefactor/benefactress
bienio ['bjenjo] *nm* two-year period
bienvenido, -a [bjembe'niðo, a] *adj* welcome
■ *excl* welcome! ■ *nf* welcome; **dar la
bienvenida a algn** to welcome sb
bies ['bjes] *nm*: **falda al** ~ bias-cut skirt;
cortar al ~ to cut on the bias
bifásico, -a [bi'fasiko, a] *adj* (*Elec*) two-phase
bife ['bife] *nm* (*Am*) steak
bifocal [bifo'kal] *adj* bifocal
bifurcación [bifurka'θjon] *nf* fork; (*Ferro:
Inform*) branch
bifurcarse [bifur'karse] *vr* to fork
bigamia [bi'ɣamja] *nf* bigamy
bígamo, -a ['biɣamo, a] *adj* bigamous ■ *nm/f*
bigamist
bígaro ['biɣaro] *nm* winkle
bigote [bi'ɣote] *nm* (*tb:* **bigotes**) moustache
bigotudo, -a [biɣo'tuðo, a] *adj* with a big
moustache
bigudí [biɣu'ði] *nm* (hair-)curler
bikini [bi'kini] *nm* bikini; (*Culin*) toasted
cheese and ham sandwich
bilateral [bilate'ral] *adj* bilateral
bilbaíno, -a [bilβa'ino, a] *adj* of *o* from Bilbao
■ *nm/f* native *o* inhabitant of Bilbao
bilingüe [bi'lingwe] *adj* bilingual
bilis ['bilis] *nf inv* bile
billar [bi'ʎar] *nm* billiards *sg*; (*lugar*) billiard
hall; (*galería de atracciones*) amusement
arcade; ~ **americano** pool
billete [bi'ʎete] *nm* ticket; (*de banco*) banknote
(*Brit*), bill (*US*); (*carta*) note; ~ **sencillo**, ~ **de
ida solamente/**~ **de ida y vuelta** single (*Brit*)
o one-way (*US*) ticket/return (*Brit*) *o* round-
trip (*US*) ticket; **sacar** (**un**) ~ to get a ticket;
un ~ **de cinco libras** a five-pound note
billetera [biʎe'tera] *nf*, **billetero** [biʎe'tero]
nm wallet
billón [bi'ʎon] *nm* billion
bimensual [bimen'swal] *adj* twice monthly
bimestral [bimes'tral] *adj* bimonthly
bimestre [bi'mestre] *nm* two-month period
bimotor [bimo'tor] *adj* twin-engined ■ *nm*
twin-engined plane
binario, -a [bi'narjo, a] *adj* (*Inform*) binary
bingo ['bingo] *nm* (*juego*) bingo; (*sala*) bingo
hall
binóculo [bi'nokulo] *nm* pince-nez
binomio [bi'nomjo] *nm* (*Mat*) binomial

biodegradable [bioðeɣra'ðaβle] *adj* biodegradable

biodiversidad [bioðiβersi'ðað] *nf* biodiversity

biografía [bjoɣra'fia] *nf* biography

biográfico, -a [bio'ɣrafiko, a] *adj* biographical

biógrafo, -a [bi'oɣrafo, a] *nm/f* biographer

biología [biolo'xia] *nf* biology

biológico, -a [bio'loxiko, a] *adj* biological; (*cultivo, producto*) organic; **guerra biológica** biological warfare

biólogo, -a [bi'oloɣo, a] *nm/f* biologist

biombo ['bjombo] *nm* (folding) screen

biopsia [bi'opsja] *nf* biopsy

bioquímico, -a [bio'kimiko, a] *adj* biochemical ◼ *nm/f* biochemist ◼ *nf* biochemistry

biosfera [blos'feɹa] *nf* biosphere

bioterrorismo [bioterro'rismo] *nm* bioterrorism

bióxido [bi'oksiðo] *nm* dioxide

bipartidismo [biparti'ðismo] *nm* (*Pol*) two-party system

biquini [bi'kini] *nm* = **bikini**

birlar [bir'lar] *vt* (*fam*) to pinch

birlibirloque [birliβir'loke] *nm*: **por arte de ~** (as if) by magic

Birmania [bir'manja] *nf* Burma

birmano, -a [bir'mano, a] *adj, nm/f* Burmese

birrete [bi'rrete] *nm* (*Jur*) judge's cap

birria ['birrja] *nf* (*fam*): **ser una ~** to be rubbish; **ir hecho una ~** to be o look a sight

bis [bis] *excl* encore! ◼ *nm* encore ◼ *adv* (*dos veces*) twice; **viven en el 27 ~** they live at 27a

bisabuelo, -a [bisa'βwelo, a] *nm/f* great-grandfather/mother; **bisabuelos** *nmpl* great-grandparents

bisagra [bi'saɣra] *nf* hinge

bisbisar [bisβi'sar], **bisbisear** [bisβise'ar] *vt* to mutter, mumble

bisbiseo [bisβi'seo] *nm* muttering

biselar [bise'lar] *vt* to bevel

bisexual [bisek'swal] *adj, nm/f* bisexual

bisiesto [bi'sjesto] *adj*: **año ~** leap year

bisnieto, -a [bis'njeto, a] *nm/f* great-grandson/daughter; **bisnietos** *nmpl* great-grandchildren

bisonte [bi'sonte] *nm* bison

bisoñé [biso'ɲe] *nm* toupee

bisoño, -a [bi'soɲo, a] *adj* green, inexperienced

bistec [bis'tek], **bisté** [bis'te] *nm* steak

bisturí [bistu'ri] *nm* scalpel

bisutería [bisute'ria] *nf* imitation o costume jewellery

bit [bit] *nm* (*Inform*) bit; **~ de parada** stop bit; **~ de paridad** parity bit

bizantino, -a [biθan'tino, a] *adj* Byzantine; (*fig*) pointless

bizarría [biθa'rria] *nf* (*valor*) bravery; (*generosidad*) generosity

bizarro, -a [bi'θarro, a] *adj* brave; generous

bizco, -a ['biθko, a] *adj* cross-eyed

bizcocho [biθ'kotʃo] *nm* (*Culin*) sponge cake

biznieto, -a [biθ'njeto, a] *nm/f* = **bisnieto**

bizquear [biθke'ar] *vi* to squint

blanco, -a ['blanko, a] *adj* white ◼ *nm/f* white man/woman, white ◼ *nm* (*color*) white; (*en texto*) blank; (*Mil, fig*) target ◼ *nf* (*Mus*) minim; **en ~** blank; **cheque en ~** blank cheque; **votar en ~** to spoil one's vote; **quedarse en ~** to be disappointed; **noche en ~** sleepless night; **ser el ~ de las burlas** to be the butt of jokes; **sin blanca** broke

blancura [blan'kura] *nf* whiteness

blandengue [blan'denge] *adj* (*fam*) soft, weak

blandir [blan'dir] *vt* to brandish

blando, -a ['blando, a] *adj* soft; (*tierno*) tender, gentle; (*carácter*) mild; (*fam*) cowardly ◼ *nm/f* (*Pol etc*) soft-liner

blandura [blan'dura] *nf* softness; tenderness; mildness

blanquear [blanke'ar] *vt* to whiten; (*fachada*) to whitewash; (*paño*) to bleach; (*dinero*) to launder ◼ *vi* to turn white

blanquecino, -a [blanke'θino, a] *adj* whitish

blanqueo [blan'keo] *nm* (*de pared*) whitewashing; (*de dinero*) laundering

blasfemar [blasfe'mar] *vi* to blaspheme; (*fig*) to curse

blasfemia [blas'femja] *nf* blasphemy

blasfemo, -a [blas'femo, a] *adj* blasphemous ◼ *nm/f* blasphemer

blasón [bla'son] *nm* coat of arms; (*fig*) honour

blasonar [blaso'nar] *vt* to emblazon ◼ *vi* to boast, brag

bledo ['bleðo] *nm*: **(no) me importa un ~** I couldn't care less

blindado, -a [blin'daðo, a] *adj* (*Mil*) armour-plated; (*antibalas*) bulletproof; **coche** o (*Am*) **carro ~** armoured car; **puertas blindadas** security doors

blindaje [blin'daxe] *nm* armour, armour-plating

bloc (*pl* **blocs**) [blok, blos] *nm* writing pad; (*Escol*) jotter; **~ de dibujos** sketch pad

blog [bloɣ] (*pl* **blogs**) *nm* blog

blogging ['bloɣin] *nm* blogging

bloguear [bloɣe'ar] *vi* to blog

bloque ['bloke] *nm* (*tb Inform*) block; (*Pol*) bloc; **~ de cilindros** cylinder block

bloquear [bloke'ar] *vt* (*Naut etc*) to blockade; (*aislar*) to cut off; (*Com, Econ*) to freeze; **fondos bloqueados** frozen assets

bloqueo [blo'keo] *nm* blockade; (*Com*) freezing, blocking
bluejean [blu'jin] *nm* (*Am*) jeans *pl*, denims *pl*
blusa ['blusa] *nf* blouse
B.° *abr* (*Finanzas*: = *banco*) bank; (*Com*: = *beneficiario*) beneficiary
boa ['boa] *nf* boa
boato [bo'ato] *nm* show, ostentation
bobada [bo'βaða] *nf* foolish action (*o* statement); **decir bobadas** to talk nonsense
bobalicón, -ona [boβali'kon, ona] *adj* utterly stupid
bobería [boβe'ria] *nf* = **bobada**
bobina [bo'βina] *nf* (*Tec*) bobbin; (*Foto*) spool; (*Elec*) coil, winding
bobo, -a ['boβo, a] *adj* (*tonto*) daft, silly; (*cándido*) naïve ∎ *nm/f* fool, idiot ∎ *nm* (*Teat*) clown, funny man
boca ['boka] *nf* mouth; (*de crustáceo*) pincer; (*de cañón*) muzzle; (*entrada*) mouth, entrance; **bocas** *nfpl* (*de río*) mouth *sg*; **~ abajo/arriba** face down/up; **a ~ jarro** point-blank; **se me hace la ~ agua** my mouth is watering; **todo salió a pedir de ~** it all turned out perfectly; **en ~ de** (*esp Am*) according to; **la cosa anda de ~ en ~** the story is going the rounds; **¡cállate la ~!** (*fam*) shut up!; **quedarse con la ~ abierta** to be dumbfounded; **no abrir la ~** to keep quiet; **~ del estómago** pit of the stomach; **~ de metro** tube (*Brit*) *o* subway (*US*) entrance
bocacalle [boka'kaʎe] *nf* side street; **la primera ~** the first turning *o* street
bocadillo [boka'ðiʎo] *nm* sandwich
bocado [bo'kaðo] *nm* mouthful, bite; (*de caballo*) bridle; **~ de Adán** Adam's apple
bocajarro [boka'xarro] **a ~** *adv* (*Mil*) at point-blank range; **decir algo a ~** to say sth bluntly
bocanada [boka'naða] *nf* (*de vino*) mouthful, swallow; (*de aire*) gust, puff
bocata [bo'kata] *nm* (*fam*) sandwich
bocazas [bo'kaθas] *nm/f inv* (*fam*) bigmouth
boceto [bo'θeto] *nm* sketch, outline
bocha ['botʃa] *nf* bowl; **bochas** *nfpl* bowls *sg*
bochinche [bo'tʃintʃe] *nm* (*fam*) uproar
bochorno [bo'tʃorno] *nm* (*vergüenza*) embarrassment; (*calor*): **hace ~** it's very muggy
bochornoso, -a [botʃor'noso, a] *adj* muggy; embarrassing
bocina [bo'θina] *nf* (*Mus*) trumpet; (*Auto*) horn; (*para hablar*) megaphone; **tocar la ~** (*Auto*) to sound *o* blow one's horn
bocinazo [boθi'naθo] *nm* (*Auto*) toot
bocio ['boθjo] *nm* (*Med*) goitre
boda ['boða] *nf* (*tb*: **bodas**) wedding, marriage; (*fiesta*) wedding reception; **bodas**

de plata/de oro silver/golden wedding *sg*
bodega [bo'ðeɣa] *nf* (*de vino*) (wine) cellar; (*bar*) bar; (*restaurante*) restaurant; (*depósito*) storeroom; (*de barco*) hold
bodegón [boðe'ɣon] *nm* (*Arte*) still life
bodrio [bo'ðrio] *nm*: **el libro es un ~** the book is awful *o* rubbish
B.O.E. ['boe] *nm abr* = **Boletín Oficial del Estado**
bofe ['bofe] *nm* (*tb*: **bofes**: *de res*) lights *pl*; **echar los bofes** to slave (away)
bofetada [bofe'taða] *nf* slap (in the face); **dar de bofetadas a algn** to punch sb
bofetón [bofe'ton] *nm* = **bofetada**
boga ['boɣa] *nf*: **en ~** in vogue
bogar [bo'ɣar] *vi* (*remar*) to row; (*navegar*) to sail
bogavante [boɣa'βante] *nm* (*Naut*) stroke, first rower; (*Zool*) lobster
Bogotá [boɣo'ta] *n* Bogota
bogotano, -a [boɣo'tano, a] *adj* of *o* from Bogota ∎ *nm/f* native *o* inhabitant of Bogota
bogue *etc* ['boɣe] *vb ver* **bogar**
bohemio, -a [bo'emjo, a] *adj, nm/f* Bohemian
boicot [boi'ko(t)] (*pl* **boicots**) *nm* boycott
boicotear [boikote'ar] *vt* to boycott
boicoteo [boiko'teo] *nm* boycott
boina ['boina] *nf* beret
bola ['bola] *nf* ball; (*canica*) marble; (*Naipes*) (grand) slam; (*betún*) shoe polish; (*mentira*) tale, story; **bolas** *nfpl* (*Am*) bolas; **~ de billar** billiard ball; **~ de nieve** snowball
bolchevique [boltʃe'βike] *adj, nm/f* Bolshevik
boleadoras [bolea'ðoras] *nfpl* (*Am*) bolas *sg*
bolera [bo'lera] *nf* skittle *o* bowling alley
bolero [bo'lero] *nm* bolero
boleta [bo'leta] *nf* (*Am: permiso*) pass, permit; (*: para votar*) ballot
boletería [bolete'ria] *nf* (*Am*) ticket office
boletero, -a [bole'tero, a] *nm/f* (*Am*) ticket seller
boletín [bole'tin] *nm* bulletin; (*periódico*) journal, review; **~ escolar** (*Esp*) school report; **~ de noticias** news bulletin; **~ de pedido** application form; **~ de precios** price list; **~ de prensa** press release; *see note*

⊙ **BOLETÍN**

⊙ The *Boletín Oficial del Estado*, abbreviated
⊙ to BOE, is the official government record
⊙ of all laws and resolutions passed by
⊙ *las Cortes* (Spanish Parliament). It is
⊙ widely consulted, mainly because it
⊙ also publishes the announcements
⊙ for the *oposiciones* (public competitive
⊙ examinations).

boleto [bo'leto] *nm* (*esp Am*) ticket; ~ **de apuestas** betting slip
boli ['boli] *nm* Biro®
boliche [bo'litʃe] *nm* (*bola*) jack; (*juego*) bowls *sg*; (*lugar*) bowling alley; (*Am: tienda*) small grocery store
bólido ['boliðo] *nm* meteorite; (*Auto*) racing car
bolígrafo [bo'liɣrafo] *nm* ball-point pen, Biro®
bolillo [bo'liʎo] *nm* (*Costura*) bobbin (for lacemaking)
bolívar [bo'liβar] *nm* monetary unit of Venezuela
Bolivia [bo'liβja] *nf* Bolivia
boliviano, -a [boli'βjano, a] *adj, nm/f* Bolivian
bollo ['boʎo] *nm* (*de pan*) roll; (*dulce*) scone; (*chichón*) bump, lump; (*abolladura*) dent; **bollos** *nmpl* (*Am*) troubles
bolo ['bolo] *nm* skittle; (*píldora*) (large) pill; (**juego de) bolos** skittles *sg*
Bolonia [bo'lonja] *nf* Bologna
bolsa ['bolsa] *nf* (*cartera*) purse; (*saco*) bag; (*Am*) pocket; (*Anat*) cavity, sac; (*Com*) stock exchange; (*Minería*) pocket; ~ **de agua caliente** hot water bottle; ~ **de aire** air pocket; ~ **de (la) basura** bin-liner; ~ **de dormir** (*Am*) sleeping bag; ~ **de papel** paper bag; ~ **de plástico** plastic (*o* carrier) bag; "**B~ de la propiedad**" "Property Mart"; ~ **de trabajo** employment bureau; **jugar a la ~** to play the market
bolsillo [bol'siʎo] *nm* pocket; (*cartera*) purse; **de ~** pocket *cpd*; **meterse a algn en el ~** to get sb eating out of one's hand
bolsista [bol'sista] *nm/f* stockbroker
bolso ['bolso] *nm* (*bolsa*) bag; (*de mujer*) handbag
boludo, -a [bo'luðo, a] (*Am fam!*) *adj* stupid ■ *nm/f* prat (!)
bomba ['bomba] *nf* (*Mil*) bomb; (*Tec*) pump; (*Am: borrachera*) drunkenness ■ *adj* (*fam*): **noticia ~** bombshell ■ *adv* (*fam*): **pasarlo ~** to have a great time; ~ **atómica/de humo/de retardo** atomic/smoke/time bomb; ~ **de gasolina** petrol pump; ~ **de incendios** fire engine
bombacho, -a [bom'batʃo, a] *adj* baggy
bombardear [bombarðe'ar] *vt* to bombard; (*Mil*) to bomb
bombardeo [bombar'ðeo] *nm* bombardment; bombing
bombardero [bombar'ðero] *nm* bomber
bombear [bombe'ar] *vt* (*agua*) to pump (out *o* up); (*Mil*) to bomb; (*Fútbol*) to lob; **bombearse** *vr* to warp
bombero [bom'bero] *nm* fireman; (**cuerpo de) bomberos** fire brigade

bombilla [bom'biʎa] *nf* (*Esp*), **bombillo** [bom'biʎo] *nm* (*Am*) (light) bulb
bombín [bom'bin] *nm* bowler hat
bombo ['bombo] *nm* (*Mus*) bass drum; (*Tec*) drum; (*fam*) exaggerated praise; **hacer algo a ~ y platillo** to make a great song and dance about sth; **tengo la cabeza hecha un ~** I've got a splitting headache
bombón [bom'bon] *nm* chocolate; (*belleza*) gem
bombona [bom'bona] *nf*: ~ **de butano** gas cylinder
bombonería [bombone'ria] *nf* sweetshop
bonachón, -ona [bona'tʃon, ona] *adj* good-natured
bonaerense [bonae'rense] *adj* of *o* from Buenos Aires ■ *nm/f* native *o* inhabitant of Buenos Aires
bonancible [bonan'θiβle] *adj* (*tiempo*) fair, calm
bonanza [bo'nanθa] *nf* (*Naut*) fair weather; (*fig*) bonanza; (*Minería*) rich pocket *o* vein
bondad [bon'dað] *nf* goodness, kindness; **tenga la ~ de** (please) be good enough to
bondadoso, -a [bonda'ðoso, a] *adj* good, kind
bongo ['bonɣo] *nm* large canoe
boniato [bo'njato] *nm* sweet potato, yam
bonificación [bonifika'θjon] *nf* (*Com*) allowance, discount; (*pago*) bonus; (*Deporte*) extra points *pl*
bonito, -a [bo'nito, a] *adj* (*lindo*) pretty; (*agradable*) nice ■ *adv* (*Am fam*) well ■ *nm* (*atún*) tuna (fish)
bono ['bono] *nm* voucher; (*Finanzas*) bond; ~ **de billetes de metro** booklet of metro tickets; ~ **del Tesoro** treasury bill
bonobús [bono'βus] *nm* (*Esp*) bus pass
Bono Loto, bonoloto [bono'loto] *nm o f* (*Esp*) state-run weekly lottery; *ver tb* **lotería**
boom (*pl* **booms**) [bum, bums] *nm* boom
boquear [boke'ar] *vi* to gasp
boquerón [boke'ron] *nm* (*pez*) (kind of) anchovy; (*agujero*) large hole
boquete [bo'kete] *nm* gap, hole
boquiabierto, -a [bokia'βjerto, a] *adj* open-mouthed (in astonishment); **quedar ~** to be left aghast
boquilla [bo'kiʎa] *nf* (*de riego*) nozzle; (*de cigarro*) cigarette holder; (*Mus*) mouthpiece
borbollar [borβo'ʎar], **borbollear** [borβoʎe'ar] *vi* to bubble
borbollón [borβo'ʎon] *nm* bubbling; **hablar a borbollones** to gabble; **salir a borbollones** (*agua*) to gush out
borbotar [borβo'tar] *vi* = **borbollar**
borbotón [borβo'ton] *nm*: **salir a borbotones** to gush out

b

borda ['borða] nf (Naut) gunwale; **echar** o **tirar algo por la ~** to throw sth overboard
bordado [bor'ðaðo] nm embroidery
bordar [bor'ðar] vt to embroider
borde ['borðe] nm edge, border; (de camino etc) side; (en la costura) hem; **al ~ de** (fig) on the verge o brink of; **ser ~** (Esp fam) to be a pain in the neck
bordear [borðe'ar] vt to border
bordillo [bor'ðiʎo] nm kerb (Brit), curb (US)
bordo ['borðo] nm (Naut) side; **a ~** on board
Borgoña [bor'ɣoɲa] nf Burgundy
borgoña [bor'ɣoɲa] nm burgundy
boricua [bo'rikwa], **borinqueño, -a** [borin'keɲo, a] adj, nm/f Puerto Rican
borla ['borla] nf (gen) tassel; (de gorro) pompon
borra ['borra] nf (pelusa) fluff; (sedimento) sediment
borrachera [borra'tʃera] nf (ebriedad) drunkenness; (orgía) spree, binge
borracho, -a [bo'rratʃo, a] adj drunk ■ nm/f (que bebe mucho) drunkard, drunk; (temporalmente) drunk, drunk man/woman ■ nm (Culin) cake soaked in liqueur or spirit
borrador [borra'ðor] nm (escritura) first draft, rough sketch; (cuaderno) scribbling pad; (goma) rubber (Brit), eraser; (Com) daybook; (para pizarra) duster; **hacer un nuevo ~ de** (Com) to redraft
borrar [bo'rrar] vt to erase, rub out; (tachar) to delete; (cinta) to wipe out; (Inform: archivo) to delete, erase; (Pol etc: eliminar) to deal with
borrasca [bo'rraska] nf (Meteorología) storm
borrascoso, -a [borras'koso, a] adj stormy
borrego, -a [bo'rreɣo, a] nm/f lamb; (oveja) sheep; (fig) simpleton
borricada [borri'kaða] nf foolish action/statement
borrico, -a [bo'rriko, a] nm donkey; (fig) stupid man ■ nf she-donkey; (fig) stupid woman
borrón [bo'rron] nm (mancha) stain; **~ y cuenta nueva** let bygones be bygones
borroso, -a [bo'rroso, a] adj vague, unclear; (escritura) illegible; (escrito) smudgy; (Foto) blurred
Bósforo ['bosforo] nm: **el (Estrecho del) ~** the Bosp(h)orus
Bosnia ['bosnja] nf Bosnia
bosnio, -a ['bosnjo, a] adj, nm/f Bosnian
bosque ['boske] nm wood; (grande) forest
bosquejar [boske'xar] vt to sketch
bosquejo [bos'kexo] nm sketch
bosta ['bosta] nf dung, manure
bostece etc [bos'teθe] vb ver **bostezar**
bostezar [boste'θar] vi to yawn
bostezo [bos'teθo] nm yawn

bota ['bota] nf (calzado) boot; (de vino) leather wine bottle; **ponerse las botas** (fam) to strike it rich
botadura [bota'ðura] nf launching
botanas [bo'tanas] nfpl (Am) hors d'œuvres
botánico, -a [bo'taniko, a] adj botanical ■ nm/f botanist ■ nf botany
botar [bo'tar] vt to throw, hurl; (Naut) to launch; (esp Am fam) to throw out ■ vi to bounce
botarate [bota'rate] nm (imbécil) idiot
bote ['bote] nm (salto) bounce; (golpe) thrust; (vasija) tin, can; (embarcación) boat; **de ~ en ~** packed, jammed full; **~ salvavidas** lifeboat; **dar un ~** to jump; **dar botes** (Auto etc) to bump; **~ de la basura** (Am) dustbin (Brit), trash can (US)
botella [bo'teʎa] nf bottle; **~ de vino** (contenido) bottle of wine; (recipiente) wine bottle
botellero [bote'ʎero] nm wine rack
botellín [bote'ʎin] nm small bottle
botellón [bote'ʎon] nm (Esp: fam) outdoor drinking session (involving groups of young people)
botica [bo'tika] nf chemist's (shop) (Brit), pharmacy
boticario, -a [boti'karjo, a] nm/f chemist (Brit), pharmacist
botijo [bo'tixo] nm (earthenware) jug; (tren) excursion train
botín [bo'tin] nm (calzado) half boot; (polaina) spat; (Mil) booty; (de ladrón) loot
botiquín [boti'kin] nm (armario) medicine chest; (portátil) first-aid kit
botón [bo'ton] nm button; (Bot) bud; (de florete) tip; **~ de arranque** (Auto etc) starter; **~ de oro** buttercup; **pulsar el ~** to press the button
botones [bo'tones] nm inv bellboy, bellhop (US)
botulismo [botu'lismo] nm botulism, food poisoning
bóveda ['boβeða] nf (Arq) vault
bovino, -a [bo'βino, a] adj bovine; (Agr): **ganado ~** cattle
box [boks] nm (Am) boxing
boxeador [boksea'ðor] nm boxer
boxear [bokse'ar] vi to box
boxeo [bok'seo] nm boxing
boya ['boja] nf (Naut) buoy; (flotador) float
boyante [bo'jante] adj (Naut) buoyant; (feliz) buoyant; (próspero) prosperous
bozal [bo'θal] nm (de caballo) halter; (de perro) muzzle
bozo ['boθo] nm (pelusa) fuzz; (boca) mouth
bracear [braθe'ar] vi (agitar los brazos) to wave one's arms

bracero [bra'θero] *nm* labourer; (*en el campo*) farmhand

braga ['braɣa] *nf* (*cuerda*) sling, rope; (*de bebé*) nappy, diaper (*US*); **bragas** *nfpl* (*de mujer*) panties

braguero [bra'ɣero] *nm* (*Med*) truss

bragueta [bra'ɣeta] *nf* fly (*Brit*), flies *pl* (*Brit*), zipper (*US*)

braguetazo [braɣe'taθo] *nm* marriage of convenience

braille [bɾeil] *nm* braille

bramante [bra'mante] *nm* twine, string

bramar [bra'mar] *vi* to bellow, roar

bramido [bra'miðo] *nm* bellow, roar

branquias ['brankjas] *nfpl* gills

brasa ['brasa] *nf* live *o* hot coal; **carne a la ~** grilled meat; **dar la ~** (*col: dar la lata, molestar*) to be a pain (*col*); **dar la ~ a algn** to go on at sb (*col*); **¡deja de darme la ~!** stop going on at me! (*col*)

brasero [bra'sero] *nm* brazier; (*Am: chimenea*) fireplace

Brasil [bra'sil] *nm*: (**el**) **~** Brazil

brasileño, -a [brasi'leɲo, a] *adj, nm/f* Brazilian

bravata [bra'βata] *nf* boast

braveza [bra'βeθa] *nf* (*valor*) bravery; (*ferocidad*) ferocity

bravío, -a [bra'βio, a] *adj* wild; (*feroz*) fierce

bravo, -a ['braβo, a] *adj* (*valiente*) brave; (*bueno*) fine, splendid; (*feroz*) ferocious; (*salvaje*) wild; (*mar etc*) rough, stormy; (*Culin*) hot, spicy ■ *excl* bravo!

bravucón, -ona [braβu'kon, ona] *adj* swaggering ■ *nm/f* braggart

bravura [bra'βura] *nf* bravery; ferocity; (*pey*) boast

braza ['braθa] *nf* fathom; **nadar a la ~** to swim (the) breast-stroke

brazada [bra'θaða] *nf* stroke

brazalete [braθa'lete] *nm* (*pulsera*) bracelet; (*banda*) armband

brazo ['braθo] *nm* arm; (*Zool*) foreleg; (*Bot*) limb, branch; **brazos** *nmpl* (*braceros*) hands, workers; **~ derecho** (*fig*) right-hand man; **a ~ partido** hand-to-hand; **cogidos** *etc* **del ~** arm in arm; **no dar su ~ a torcer** not to give way easily; **huelga de brazos caídos** sit-down strike

brea ['brea] *nf* pitch, tar

brebaje [bre'βaxe] *nm* potion

brecha ['bretʃa] *nf* breach; (*hoyo vacío*) gap, opening

brécol ['brekol] *nm* broccoli

brega ['breɣa] *nf* (*lucha*) struggle; (*trabajo*) hard work

bregar [bre'ɣar] *vi* (*luchar*) to struggle; (*trabajar mucho*) to slog away

bregue *etc* ['breɣe] *vb ver* **bregar**

breña ['breɲa] *nf* rough ground

Bretaña [bre'taɲa] *nf* Brittany

brete ['brete] *nm* (*cepo*) shackles *pl*; (*fig*) predicament; **estar en un ~** to be in a jam

breteles [bre'teles] *nmpl* (*Am*) straps

bretón, -ona [bre'ton, ona] *adj, nm/f* Breton

breva ['breβa] *nf* (*Bot*) early fig; (*puro*) flat cigar; **¡no caerá esa ~!** no such luck!

breve ['breβe] *adj* short, brief; **en ~** (*pronto*) shortly; (*en pocas palabras*) in short ■ *nf* (*Mus*) breve

brevedad [breβe'ðað] *nf* brevity, shortness; **con o a la mayor ~** as soon as possible

breviario [bre'βjarjo] *nm* (*Rel*) breviary

brezal [bre'θal] *nm* moor(land), heath

brezo ['breθo] *nm* heather

bribón, -ona [bri'βon, ona] *adj* idle, lazy ■ *nm/f* (*vagabundo*) vagabond; (*pícaro*) rascal, rogue

bricolaje [briko'laxe] *nm* do-it-yourself, DIY

brida ['briða] *nf* bridle, rein; (*Tec*) clamp; **a toda ~** at top speed

bridge [britʃ] *nm* (*Naipes*) bridge

brigada [bri'ɣaða] *nf* (*unidad*) brigade; (*trabajadores*) squad, gang ■ *nm* warrant officer

brigadier [briɣa'ðjer] *nm* brigadier(-general)

brillante [bri'ʎante] *adj* brilliant; (*color*) bright; (*joya*) sparkling ■ *nm* diamond

brillantez [briʎan'teθ] *nf* (*de color etc*) brightness; (*fig*) brilliance

brillar [bri'ʎar] *vi* (*tb fig*) to shine; (*joyas*) to sparkle; **~ por su ausencia** to be conspicuous by one's absence

brillo ['briʎo] *nm* shine; (*brillantez*) brilliance; (*fig*) splendour; **sacar ~ a** to polish

brilloso, -a [bri'ʎoso, a] *adj* (*Am*) = **brillante**

brincar [brin'kar] *vi* to skip about, hop about, jump about; **está que brinca** he's hopping mad

brinco ['brinko] *nm* jump, leap; **a brincos** by fits and starts; **de un ~** at one bound

brindar [brin'dar] *vi*: **~ a o por** to drink (a toast) to ■ *vt* to offer, present; **le brinda la ocasión de** it offers o affords him the opportunity to; **brindarse a: brindarse a hacer algo** to offer to do sth

brindis ['brindis] *nm inv* toast; (*Taur*) (ceremony of) dedication

brinque *etc* ['brinke] *vb ver* **brincar**

brío ['brio] *nm* spirit, dash

brioso, -a [bri'oso, a] *adj* spirited, dashing

brisa ['brisa] *nf* breeze

británico, -a [bri'taniko, a] *adj* British ■ *nm/f* Briton, British person; **los británicos** the British

b

brizna ['briθna] *nf* (*hebra*) strand, thread; (*de hierba*) blade; (*trozo*) piece

broca ['broka] *nf* (*Costura*) bobbin; (*Tec*) drill bit; (*clavo*) tack

brocado [bro'kaðo] *nm* brocade

brocal [bro'kal] *nm* rim

brocha ['brotʃa] *nf* (large) paintbrush; ~ **de afeitar** shaving brush; **pintor de ~ gorda** painter and decorator; (*fig*) poor painter

brochazo [bro'tʃaθo] *nm* brush-stroke; **a grandes brochazos** (*fig*) in general terms

broche ['brotʃe] *nm* brooch

broma ['broma] *nf* joke; (*inocentada*) practical joke; **en ~** in fun, as a joke; **gastar una ~ a algn** to play a joke on sb; **tomar algo a ~** to take sth as a joke

bromear [brome'ar] *vi* to joke

bromista [bro'mista] *adj* fond of joking ■ *nm/f* joker, wag

bromuro [bro'muro] *nm* bromide

bronca ['bronka] *nf* row; (*regañada*) ticking-off; **armar una ~** to kick up a fuss; **echar una ~ a algn** to tell sb off

bronce ['bronθe] *nm* bronze; (*latón*) brass

bronceado, -a [bronθe'aðo, a] *adj* bronze *cpd*; (*por el sol*) tanned ■ *nm* (sun)tan; (*Tec*) bronzing

bronceador [bronθea'ðor] *nm* suntan lotion

broncearse [bronθe'arse] *vr* to get a suntan

bronco, -a ['bronko, a] *adj* (*manera*) rude, surly; (*voz*) harsh

bronquios ['bronkjos] *nmpl* bronchial tubes

bronquitis [bron'kitis] *nf inv* bronchitis

brotar [bro'tar] *vt* (*tierra*) to produce ■ *vi* (*Bot*) to sprout; (*aguas*) to gush (forth); (*lágrimas*) to well up; (*Med*) to break out

brote ['brote] *nm* (*Bot*) shoot; (*Med, fig*) outbreak

broza ['broθa] *nf* (*Bot*) dead leaves *pl*; (*fig*) rubbish

bruces ['bruθes]: **de ~** *adv*: **caer** *o* **dar de ~** to fall headlong, fall flat

bruja ['bruxa] *nf* witch

Brujas ['bruxas] *nf* Bruges

brujería [bruxe'ria] *nf* witchcraft

brujo ['bruxo] *nm* wizard, magician

brújula ['bruxula] *nf* compass

bruma ['bruma] *nf* mist

brumoso, -a [bru'moso, a] *adj* misty

bruñendo *etc* [bru'ɲendo] *vb ver* **bruñir**

bruñido [bru'ɲiðo] *nm* polish

bruñir [bru'ɲir] *vt* to polish

brusco, -a ['brusko, a] *adj* (*súbito*) sudden; (*áspero*) brusque

Bruselas [bru'selas] *nf* Brussels

brusquedad [bruske'ðað] *nf* suddenness; brusqueness

brutal [bru'tal] *adj* brutal

brutalidad [brutali'ðað] *nf* brutality

bruto, -a ['bruto, a] *adj* (*idiota*) stupid; (*bestial*) brutish; (*peso*) gross ■ *nm* brute; **a la bruta**, **a lo ~** roughly; **en ~** raw, unworked

Bs. *abr* = **bolívares**

Bs.As. *abr* = **Buenos Aires**

bucal [bu'kal] *adj* oral; **por vía ~** orally

bucanero [buka'nero] *nm* buccaneer

bucear [buθe'ar] *vi* to dive ■ *vt* to explore

buceo [bu'θeo] *nm* diving; (*fig*) investigation

buche ['butʃe] *nm* (*de ave*) crop; (*Zool*) maw; (*fam*) belly

bucle ['bukle] *nm* curl; (*Inform*) loop

budín [bu'ðin] *nm* pudding

budismo [bu'ðismo] *nm* Buddhism

budista [bu'ðista] *adj, nm/f* Buddhist

buen [bwen] *adj ver* **bueno**

buenamente [bwena'mente] *adv* (*fácilmente*) easily; (*voluntariamente*) willingly

buenaventura [bwenaβen'tura] *nf* (*suerte*) good luck; (*adivinación*) fortune; **decir** *o* **echar la ~ a algn** to tell sb's fortune

 PALABRA CLAVE

bueno, -a ['bweno, a] (*antes de nmsg* **buen**) *adj*
1 (*excelente etc*) good; (*Med*) well; **es un libro bueno, es un buen libro** it's a good book; **hace bueno, hace buen tiempo** the weather is fine, it is fine; **es buena persona** he's a good sort; **el bueno de Paco** good old Paco; **fue muy bueno conmigo** he was very nice *o* kind to me; **ya está bueno** he's fine now

2 (*apropiado*): **ser bueno para** to be good for; **creo que vamos por buen camino** I think we're on the right track

3 (*irónico*): **le di un buen rapapolvo** I gave him a good *o* real ticking off; **¡buen conductor estás hecho!** some driver *o* a fine driver you are!; **¡estaría bueno que ...!** a fine thing it would be if ...!

4 (*atractivo, sabroso*): **está bueno este bizcocho** this sponge is delicious; **Julio está muy bueno** (*fam*) Julio is a bit of alright

5 (*grande*) good, big; **un buen número de ...** a good number of ...; **un buen trozo de ...** a nice big piece of ...

6 (*saludos*): **¡buen día!** (*Am*), **¡buenos días!** (good) morning!; **¡buenas (tardes)!** good afternoon!; (*más tarde*) good evening!; **¡buenas noches!** good night!

7 (*otras locuciones*): **estar de buenas** to be in a good mood; **por las buenas o por las malas** by hook or by crook; **de buenas a primeras** all of a sudden

■ *excl*: ¡bueno! all right!; **bueno, ¿y qué?** well, so what?; **bueno, lo que pasa es que** ... well, the thing is ...; **pero ¡bueno!** well, I like that!; **bueno, pues** ... right, (then) ...

Buenos Aires [bweno'saires] *nm* Buenos Aires
buey [bwei] *nm* ox
búfalo ['bufalo] *nm* buffalo
bufanda [bu'fanda] *nf* scarf
bufar [bu'far] *vi* to snort
bufete [bu'fete] *nm* (*despacho de abogado*) lawyer's office; **establecer su ~** to set up in legal practice
buffer ['bufer] *nm* (*Inform*) buffer
bufón [bu'fon] *nm* clown
bufonada [bufo'naða] *nf* (*dicho*) jest; (*hecho*) piece of buffoonery; (*Teat*) farce
buhardilla [buar'ðiʎa] *nf* attic
búho ['buo] *nm* owl; (*fig*) hermit, recluse
buhonero [buo'nero] *nm* pedlar
buitre ['bwitre] *nm* vulture
bujía [bu'xia] *nf* (*vela*) candle; (*Elec*) candle (power); (*Auto*) spark plug
bula ['bula] *nf* (*papal*) bull
bulbo ['bulβo] *nm* (*Bot*) bulb
bulevar [bule'βar] *nm* boulevard
Bulgaria [bul'ɣarja] *nf* Bulgaria
búlgaro, -a ['bulɣaro, a] *adj, nm/f* Bulgarian
bulimia [bu'limja] *nf* bulimia
bulla ['buʎa] *nf* (*ruido*) uproar; (*de gente*) crowd; **armar ~ meter ~** to kick up a row
bullendo *etc* [bu'ʎendo] *vb ver* **bullir**
bullicio [bu'ʎiθjo] *nm* (*ruido*) uproar; (*movimiento*) bustle
bullicioso, -a [buʎi'θjoso, a] *adj* (*ruidoso*) noisy; (*calle*) busy; (*situación*) turbulent
bullir [bu'ʎir] *vi* (*hervir*) to boil; (*burbujear*) to bubble; (*moverse*) to move, stir; (*insectos*) to swarm; **~ de** (*fig*) to teem o seethe with
bulo ['bulo] *nm* false rumour
bulto ['bulto] *nm* (*paquete*) package; (*fardo*) bundle; (*tamaño*) size, bulkiness; (*Med*) swelling, lump; (*silueta*) vague shape; (*estatua*) bust, statue; **hacer ~** to take up space; **escurrir el ~** to make o.s. scarce; (*fig*) to dodge the issue
buñuelo [bu'ɲwelo] *nm* ≈ doughnut, ≈ donut (US)
buque ['buke] *nm* ship, vessel; **~ de guerra** warship; **~ mercante** merchant ship; **~ de vela** sailing ship
burbuja [bur'βuxa] *nf* bubble; **hacer burbujas** to bubble; (*gaseosa*) to fizz
burbujear [burβuxe'ar] *vi* to bubble
burdel [bur'ðel] *nm* brothel

Burdeos [bur'ðeos] *nm* Bordeaux
burdo, -a ['burðo, a] *adj* coarse, rough
burgalés, -esa [burɣa'les, esa] *adj* of o from Burgos ■ *nm/f* native o inhabitant of Burgos
burgués, -esa [bur'ɣes, esa] *adj* middle-class, bourgeois; **pequeño ~** lower middle-class; (*Pol, pey*) petty bourgeois
burguesía [burɣe'sia] *nf* middle class, bourgeoisie
burla ['burla] *nf* (*mofa*) gibe; (*broma*) joke; (*engaño*) trick; **hacer ~ de** to make fun of
burladero [burla'ðero] *nm* (*bullfighter's*) refuge
burlador, a [burla'ðor, a] *adj* mocking ■ *nm/f* mocker; (*bromista*) joker ■ *nm* (*libertino*) seducer
burlar [bur'lar] *vt* (*engañar*) to deceive; (*seducir*) to seduce ■ *vi*, **burlarse** *vr* to joke; **burlarse de** to make fun ot
burlesco, -a [bur'lesko, a] *adj* burlesque
burlón, -ona [bur'lon, ona] *adj* mocking
buró [bu'ro] *nm* bureau
burocracia [buro'kraθja] *nf* bureaucracy
burócrata [bu'rokrata] *nm/f* bureaucrat
buromática [buro'matika] *nf* office automation
burrada [bu'rraða] *nf* stupid act; **decir burradas** to talk nonsense
burro, -a ['burro, a] *nm/f* (*Zool*) donkey; (*fig*) ass, idiot ■ *adj* stupid; **caerse del ~** to realise one's mistake; **no ver tres en un ~** to be as blind as a bat
bursátil [bur'satil] *adj* stock-exchange *cpd*
bus [bus] *nm* bus
busca ['buska] *nf* search, hunt ■ *nm* bleeper, pager; **en ~ de** in search of
buscador, a [buska'ðor, a] *nm/f* searcher ■ *nm* (*Internet*) search engine
buscapiés [buska'pjes] *nm inv* jumping jack (Brit), firecracker (US)
buscapleitos [buska'pleitos] *nm/f inv* troublemaker
buscar [bus'kar] *vt* to look for; (*objeto perdido*) to have a look for; (*beneficio*) to seek; (*enemigo*) to seek out; (*traer*) to bring, fetch; (*provocar*) to provoke; (*Inform*) to search ■ *vi* to look, search, seek; **ven a buscarme a la oficina** come and pick me up at the office; **buscarle 3 o 4 pies al gato** to split hairs; **"~ y reemplazar"** (*Inform*) "search and replace"; **se busca secretaria** secretary wanted; **se la buscó** he asked for it
buscavidas [buska'βiðas] *nm/f inv* snooper; (*persona ambiciosa*) go-getter
buscona [bus'kona] *nf* whore
busilis [bu'silis] *nm inv* (*fam*) snag
busque *etc* ['buske] *vb ver* **buscar**

búsqueda ['buskeða] *nf* = **busca**

busto ['busto] *nm* (*Anat: Arte*) bust

butaca [bu'taka] *nf* armchair; (*de cine, teatro*) stall, seat

butano [bu'tano] *nm* butane (gas); **bombona de ~** gas cylinder

butifarra [buti'farra] *nf* Catalan sausage

buzo ['buθo] *nm* diver; (*Am: chandal*) tracksuit

buzón [bu'θon] *nm* (*gen*) letter box; (*en la calle*) pillar box (*Brit*); (*Telec*) mailbox; **echar al ~** to post

buzonear [buθone'ar] *vt* to leaflet

byte [bait] *nm* (*Inform*) byte

Cc

C, c [θe] [se] (*esp Am*) *nf* (*letra*) C, c; **C de Carmen** C for Charlie
C. *abr* (= *centígrado*) C.; (= *compañía*) Co
c. *abr* (= *capítulo*) ch
C/ *abr* (= *calle*) St, Rd
c/ *abr* (*Com*: = *cuenta*) a/c
ca [ka] *excl* not a bit of it!
c.a. *abr* (= *corriente alterna*) A.C.
cabal [ka'βal] *adj* (*exacto*) exact; (*correcto*) right, proper; (*acabado*) finished, complete; **cabales** *nmpl*: **estar en sus cabales** to be in one's right mind
cábala ['kaβala] *nf* (*Rel*) cab(b)ala; (*fig*) cabal, intrigue; **cábalas** *nfpl* guess *sg*, supposition *sg*
cabalgadura [kaβalɣa'ðura] *nf* mount, horse
cabalgar [kaβal'ɣar] *vt, vi* to ride
cabalgata [kaβal'ɣata] *nf* procession; *ver tb* **Reyes Magos**
cabalgue *etc* [ka'βalɣe] *vb ver* **cabalgar**
cabalístico, -a [kaβa'listiko, a] *adj* (*fig*) mysterious
caballa [ka'βaʎa] *nf* mackerel
caballeresco, -a [kaβaʎe'resko, a] *adj* noble, chivalrous
caballería [kaβaʎe'ria] *nf* mount; (*Mil*) cavalry
caballeriza [kaβaʎe'riθa] *nf* stable
caballerizo [kaβaʎe'riθo] *nm* groom, stableman
caballero [kaβa'ʎero] *nm* gentleman; (*de la orden de caballería*) knight; (*trato directo*) sir; **"Caballeros"** "Gents"
caballerosidad [kaβaʎerosi'ðað] *nf* chivalry
caballete [kaβa'ʎete] *nm* (*Agr*) ridge; (*Arte*) easel
caballito [kaβa'ʎito] *nm* (*caballo pequeño*) small horse, pony; (*juguete*) rocking horse; **caballitos** *nmpl* merry-go-round *sg*; **~ de mar** seahorse; **~ del diablo** dragonfly
caballo [ka'βaʎo] *nm* horse; (*Ajedrez*) knight; (*Naipes*) ≈ queen; **~ de vapor** *o* **de fuerza** horsepower; **es su ~ de batalla** it's his

hobby-horse; **~ blanco** (*Com*) backer; *ver tb* **Baraja Española**
cabaña [ka'βaɲa] *nf* (*casita*) hut, cabin
cabaré, cabaret (*pl* **cabarets**) [kaβa're, kaβa'res] *nm* cabaret
cabecear [kaβeθe'ar] *vi* to nod
cabecera [kaβe'θera] *nf* (*gen*) head; (*de distrito*) chief town; (*de cama*) headboard; (*Imprenta*) headline
cabecilla [kaβe'θiʎa] *nm* ringleader
cabellera [kaβe'ʎera] *nf* (head of) hair; (*de cometa*) tail
cabello [ka'βeʎo] *nm* (*tb*: **cabellos**) hair *sg*
cabelludo [kaβe'ʎuðo] *adj ver* **cuero**
caber [ka'βer] *vi* (*entrar*) to fit, go; **caben tres más** there's room for three more; **cabe preguntar si... one might ask whether...**; **cabe que venga más tarde** he may come later
cabestrillo [kaβes'triʎo] *nm* sling
cabestro [ka'βestro] *nm* halter
cabeza [ka'βeθa] *nf* head; (*Pol*) chief, leader ■ *nm/f*: **~ rapada** skinhead; **caer de ~** to fall head first; **sentar la ~** to settle down; **~ de lectura/escritura** read/write head; **~ impresora** *o* **de impresión** printhead
cabezada [kaβe'θaða] *nf* (*golpe*) butt; **dar una ~** to nod off
cabezal [kaβe'θal] *nm*: **~ impresor** print head
cabezazo [kaβe'θaθo] *nm* (*golpe*) headbutt; (*Fútbol*) header
cabezón, -ona [kaβe'θon, ona] *adj* with a big head; (*vino*) heady; (*obstinado*) obstinate, stubborn
cabezota [kaβe'θota] *adj inv* obstinate, stubborn
cabezudo, -a [kaβe'θuðo, a] *adj* with a big head; (*obstinado*) obstinate, stubborn
cabida [ka'βiða] *nf* space; **dar ~ a** to make room for; **tener ~ para** to have room for
cabildo [ka'βildo] *nm* (*de iglesia*) chapter; (*Pol*) town council

cabina [ka'βina] nf (de camión) cabin;
~ **telefónica** (tele)phone box (Brit) o booth
cabizbajo, -a [kaβiθ'βaxo, a] adj crestfallen
cable ['kaβle] nm cable; (de aparato) lead;
~ **aéreo** (Elec) overhead cable; **conectar
con** ~ (Inform) to hardwire
cabo ['kaβo] nm (de objeto) end, extremity;
(Mil) corporal; (Naut) rope, cable; (Geo) cape;
(Tec) thread; **al** ~ **de tres días** after three
days; **de** ~ **a rabo** o ~ from beginning to
end; (libro: leer) from cover to cover; **llevar a**
~ to carry out; **atar cabos** to tie up the loose
ends; **C~ de Buena Esperanza** Cape of Good
Hope; **C~ de Hornos** Cape Horn; **las Islas de
C~ Verde** the Cape Verde Islands
cabra ['kaβra] nf goat; **estar como una** ~
(fam) to be nuts
cabré etc [ka'βre] vb ver **caber**
cabrear [kaβre'ar] vt to annoy; **cabrearse** vr
to fly off the handle
cabrío, -a [ka'βrio, a] adj goatish; **macho** ~
(he-)goat, billy goat
cabriola [ka'βrjola] nf caper
cabritilla [kaβri'tiʎa] nf kid, kidskin
cabrito [ka'βrito] nm kid
cabrón [ka'βron] nm (fig: fam!) bastard (!)
cabronada [kaβro'naða] nf (fam!): **hacer una**
~ **a algn** to be a bastard to sb
caca ['kaka] nf (palabra de niños) pooh ■ excl:
no toques, ¡~! don't touch, it's dirty!
cacahuete [kaka'wete] nm (Esp) peanut
cacao [ka'kao] nm cocoa; (Bot) cacao
cacarear [kakare'ar] vi (persona) to boast;
(gallina) to cackle
cacatúa [kaka'tua] nf cockatoo
cacereño, -a [kaθe'reɲo, a] adj of o from
Cáceres ■ nm/f native o inhabitant of
Cáceres
cacería [kaθe'ria] nf hunt
cacerola [kaθe'rola] nf pan, saucepan
cacha ['katʃa] nf (mango) handle; (nalga)
buttock
cachalote [katʃa'lote] nm sperm whale
cacharro [ka'tʃarro] nm (cazo) pot; (cerámica)
piece of pottery; (fam) useless object;
cacharros nmpl pots and pans
cachear [katʃe'ar] vt to search, frisk
cachemir [katʃe'mir] nm cashmere
cacheo [ka'tʃeo] nm searching, frisking
cachete [ka'tʃete] nm (Anat) cheek; (bofetada)
slap (in the face)
cachimba [ka'tʃimba] nf, **cachimbo**
[ka'tʃimbo] nm (Am) pipe
cachiporra [katʃi'porra] nf truncheon
cachivache [katʃi'βatʃe] nm piece of junk;
cachivaches nmpl trash sg, junk sg
cacho ['katʃo] nm (small) bit; (Am: cuerno)

horn
cachondearse [katʃonde'arse] vr: ~ **de algn**
to tease sb
cachondeo [katʃon'deo] nm (fam) farce, joke;
(guasa) laugh
cachondo, -a [ka'tʃondo, a] adj (Zool) on heat;
(caliente) randy, sexy; (gracioso) funny
cachorro, -a [ka'tʃorro, a] nm/f (de perro) pup,
puppy; (de león) cub
cachucha [ka'tʃutʃa] (Méx fam) nf cap
cacique [ka'θike] nm chief, local ruler; (Pol)
local party boss; (fig) despot
caco ['kako] nm pickpocket
cacofonía [kakofo'nia] nf cacophony
cacto ['kakto] nm, **cactus** ['kaktus] nm inv
cactus
cada ['kaða] adj inv each; (antes de número)
every; ~ **día** each day, every day; ~ **dos días**
every other day; ~ **uno/a** each one, every one;
~ **vez más/menos** more and more/less and
less; **uno de** ~ **diez** one out of every ten;
¿~ cuánto? how often?
cadalso [ka'ðalso] nm scaffold
cadáver [ka'ðaβer] nm (dead) body, corpse
cadavérico, -a [kaða'βeriko, a] adj
cadaverous; (pálido) deathly pale
cadena [ka'ðena] nf chain; (TV) channel;
reacción en ~ chain reaction; **trabajo en**
~ assembly line work; ~ **midi/mini** (Mus)
midi/mini system; ~ **perpetua** (Jur) life
imprisonment; ~ **de caracteres** (Inform)
character string
cadencia [ka'ðenθja] nf cadence, rhythm
cadera [ka'ðera] nf hip
cadete [ka'ðete] nm cadet
Cádiz ['kaðiθ] nm Cadiz
caducar [kaðu'kar] vi to expire
caducidad [kaðuθi'ðað] nf: **fecha de** ~ expiry
date; (de comida) sell-by date
caduco, -a [ka'ðuko, a] adj (idea etc) outdated,
outmoded; **de hoja caduca** deciduous
caduque etc [ka'ðuke] vb ver **caducar**
caer [ka'er] vi to fall; (premio) to go; (sitio) to
be, lie; (pago) to fall due; **caerse** vr to fall
(down); **dejar** ~ to drop; **estar al** ~ to be due
to happen; (persona) to be about to arrive; **me
cae bien/mal** I like/don't like him; ~ **en la
cuenta** to catch on; **su cumpleaños cae en
viernes** her birthday falls on a Friday; **se me
ha caído el guante** I've dropped my glove
café (pl ~**s**) [ka'fe, ka'fes] nm (bebida, planta)
coffee; (lugar) café ■ adj (color) brown; **café
con leche** white coffee; **café solo, café
negro** (Am) (small) black coffee
cafeína [kafe'ina] nf caffein(e)
cafetal [kafe'tal] nm coffee plantation
cafetera [kafe'tera] nf ver **cafetero**

cafetería [kafete'ria] *nf* cafe
cafetero, -a [kafe'tero, a] *adj* coffee *cpd* ■ *nf* coffee pot; **ser muy ~** to be a coffee addict
cagalera [kaɣa'lera] *nf* (*fam!*): **tener ~** to have the runs
cagar [ka'ɣar] (*fam!*) *vt* to shit (!); (*fig*) to bungle, mess up ■ *vi* to have a shit (!); **cagarse** *vr*: **¡me cago en diez** *etc*! Christ! (!)
cague *etc* ['kaɣe] *vb ver* **cagar**
caído, -a [ka'iðo, a] *adj* fallen; (*Inform*) down ■ *nf* fall; (*declive*) slope; (*disminución*) fall, drop; **~ del cielo** out of the blue; **a la caída del sol** at sunset; **sufrir una caída** to have a fall
caiga *etc* ['kaiɣa] *vb ver* **caer**
caimán [kai'man] *nm* alligator
Cairo ['kairo] *nm*: **el ~** Cairo
caja ['kaxa] *nf* box; (*ataúd*) coffin, casket (*US*); (*para reloj*) case; (*de ascensor*) shaft; (*Com*) cash box; (*Econ*) fund; (*donde se hacen los pagos*) cashdesk; (*en supermercado*) checkout, till; (*Tip*) case; (*de parking*) pay station; **~ de ahorros** savings bank; **~ de cambios** gearbox; **~ fuerte, ~ de caudales** safe, strongbox; **ingresar en ~** to be paid in
cajero, -a [ka'xero, a] *nm/f* cashier; (*en banco*) teller ■ *nm*. **~ automático** cash dispenser, automatic telling machine, ATM
cajetilla [kaxe'tiʎa] *nf* (*de cigarrillos*) packet
cajista [ka'xista] *nm/f* typesetter
cajón [ka'xon] *nm* big box; (*de mueble*) drawer
cajuela [kax'wela] (*Méx*) *nf* (*Auto*) boot (*Brit*), trunk (*US*)
cal [kal] *nf* lime; **cerrar algo a ~ y canto** to shut sth firmly
cal. *abr* (= *caloría(s)*) cal. (= *calorie(s)*)
cala ['kala] *nf* (*Geo*) cove, inlet; (*de barco*) hold
calabacín [kalaβa'θin] *nm* (*Bot*) baby marrow, courgette, zucchini (*US*)
calabaza [kala'βaθa] *nf* (*Bot*) pumpkin; **dar calabazas a** (*candidato*) to fail
calabozo [kala'βoθo] *nm* (*cárcel*) prison; (*celda*) cell
calado, -a [ka'laðo, a] *adj* (*prenda*) lace *cpd* ■ *nm* (*Tec*) fretwork; (*Naut*) draught ■ *nf* (*de cigarrillo*) puff; **estar ~ (hasta los huesos)** to be soaked (to the skin)
calamar [kala'mar] *nm* squid
calambre [ka'lambre] *nm* (*tb*: **calambres**) cramp
calamidad [kalami'ðað] *nf* calamity, disaster; (*persona*): **es una ~** he's a dead loss
calamina [kala'mina] *nf* calamine
cálamo ['kalamo] *nm* (*Bot*) stem; (*Mus*) reed
calaña [ka'laɲa] *nf* model, pattern; (*fig*) nature, stamp
calar [ka'lar] *vt* to soak, drench; (*penetrar*) to pierce, penetrate; (*comprender*) to see through; (*vela, red*) to lower; **calarse** *vr* (*Auto*) to stall; **calarse las gafas** to stick one's glasses on
calavera [kala'βera] *nf* skull
calcañal [kalka'ɲal], **calcañar** [kalka'ɲar] *nm* heel
calcar [kal'kar] *vt* (*reproducir*) to trace; (*imitar*) to copy
calce *etc* ['kalθe] *vb ver* **calzar**
cal. cen. *abr* = **calefacción central**
calceta [kal'θeta] *nf* (knee-length) stocking; **hacer ~** to knit
calcetín [kalθe'tin] *nm* sock
calcinar [kalθi'nar] *vt* to burn, blacken
calcio ['kalθjo] *nm* calcium
calco ['kalko] *nm* tracing
calcomanía [kalkoma'nia] *nf* transfer
calculador, a [kalkula'ðor, a] *adj* calculating ■ *nf* calculator
calcular [kalku'lar] *vt* (*Mat*) to calculate, compute; **~ que ...** to reckon that ...
cálculo ['kalkulo] *nm* calculation; (*Med*) (gall)stone; (*Mat*) calculus; **~ de costo** costing; **~ diferencial** differential calculus; **obrar con mucho ~** to act cautiously
caldear [kalde'ar] *vt* to warm (up), heat (up); (*metales*) to weld
caldera [kal'dera] *nf* boiler
calderero [kalde'rero] *nm* boilermaker
calderilla [kalde'riʎa] *nf* small change
caldero [kal'dero] *nm* small boiler
caldo ['kaldo] *nm* stock; (*consomé*) consommé; **~ de cultivo** (*Bio*) culture medium; **poner a ~ a algn** to tear sb off a strip; **los caldos jerezanos** sherries
caidoso, -a [kal'doso, a] *adj* (*guisado*) juicy; (*sopa*) thin
calé [ka'le] *adj* gipsy *cpd*
calefacción [kalefak'θjon] *nf* heating; **~ central** central heating
caleidoscopio [kaleiðos'kopjo] *nm* kaleidoscope
calendario [kalen'darjo] *nm* calendar
calentador [kalenta'ðor] *nm* heater
calentamiento [kalenta'mjento] *nm* (*Deporte*) warm-up
calentar [kalen'tar] *vt* to heat (up); (*fam: excitar*) to turn on; (*Am: enfurecer*) to anger; **calentarse** *vr* to heat up, warm up; (*fig: discusión etc*) to get heated
calentón, -ona [kalen'ton, ona] (*RPl fam*) *adj* (*sexualmente*) horny, randy (*Brit*)
calentura [kalen'tura] *nf* (*Med*) fever, (high) temperature; (*de boca*) mouth sore
calenturiento, -a [kalentu'rjento, a] *adj* (*mente*) overactive

calibrar [kali'βrar] vt to gauge, measure
calibre [ka'liβre] nm (de cañón) calibre, bore;
(diámetro) diameter; (fig) calibre
calidad [kali'ðað] nf quality; **de** ~ quality cpd;
~ **de borrador** (Inform) draft quality; ~ **de
carta** o **de correspondencia** (Inform) letter
quality; ~ **texto** (Inform) text quality; ~ **de
vida** quality of life; **en** ~ **de** in the capacity of
cálido, -a ['kaliðo, a] adj hot; (fig) warm
caliente etc [ka'ljente] vb ver **calentar**
■ adj hot; (fig) fiery; (disputa) heated; (fam:
cachondo) randy
califa [ka'lifa] nm caliph
calificación [kalifika'θjon] nf qualification;
(de alumno) grade, mark; ~ **de sobresaliente**
first-class mark
calificar [kalifi'kar] vt to qualify; (alumno)
to grade, mark; ~ **de** to describe as
calificativo, -a [kalifika'tiβo, a] adj
qualifying ■ nm qualifier, epithet
califique etc [kali'fike] vb ver **calificar**
californiano, -a [kalifor'njano, a] adj, nm/f
Californian
caligrafía [kaliɣra'fia] nf calligraphy
calima [ka'lima] nf mist
calina [ka'lina] nf haze
cáliz ['kaliθ] nm (Bot) calyx; (Rel) chalice
caliza [ka'liθa] nf limestone
callado, -a [ka'ʎaðo, a] adj quiet, silent
callar [ka'ʎar] vt (asunto delicado) to keep quiet
about, say nothing about; (omitir) to pass
over in silence; (persona, oposición) to silence
■ vi, **callarse** vr to keep quiet, be silent; (dejar
de hablar) to stop talking; **¡calla!** be quiet!;
¡cállate!, ¡cállese! shut up!; **¡cállate la boca!**
shut your mouth!
calle ['kaʎe] nf street; (Deporte) lane; ~ **arriba/
abajo** up/down the street; ~ **de sentido
único** one-way street; **poner a algn (de
patitas) en la** ~ to kick sb out
calleja [ka'ʎexa] nf alley, narrow street
callejear [kaʎexe'ar] vi to wander (about) the
streets
callejero, -a [kaʎe'xero, a] adj street cpd
■ nm street map
callejón [kaʎe'xon] nm alley, passage; (Geo)
narrow pass; ~ **sin salida** cul-de-sac; (fig)
blind alley
callejuela [kaʎe'xwela] nf side-street, alley
callista [ka'ʎista] nm/f chiropodist
callo ['kaʎo] nm callus; (en el pie) corn; **callos**
nmpl (Culin) tripe sg
callosidad [kaʎosi'ðað] nf (de pie) corn;
(de mano) callus
calloso, -a [ka'ʎoso, a] adj horny, rough
calma ['kalma] nf calm; (pachorra) slowness;
(Com: Econ) calm, lull; ~ **chicha** dead calm;

¡~!, ¡con ~! take it easy!
calmante [kal'mante] adj soothing ■ nm
sedative, tranquillizer
calmar [kal'mar] vt to calm, calm down;
(dolor) to relieve ■ vi, **calmarse** vr (tempestad)
to abate; (mente etc) to become calm
calmoso, -a [kal'moso, a] adj calm, quiet
caló [ka'lo] nm (de gitanos) gipsy language,
Romany; (argot) slang
calor [ka'lor] nm heat; (calor agradable)
warmth; **entrar en** ~ to get warm; **tener** ~
to be o feel hot
caloría [kalo'ria] nf calorie
calorífero, -a [kalo'rifero, a] adj heat-
producing, heat-giving ■ nm heating system
calque etc ['kalke] vb ver **calcar**
calumnia [ka'lumnja] nf slander; (por escrito)
libel
calumniar [kalum'njar] vt to slander; to libel
calumnioso, -a [kalum'njoso, a] adj
slanderous; libellous
caluroso, -a [kalu'roso, a] adj hot; (sin exceso)
warm; (fig) enthusiastic
calva ['kalβa] nf bald patch; (en bosque)
clearing
calvario [kal'βarjo] nm stations pl of the
cross; (fig) cross, heavy burden
calvicie [kal'βiθje] nf baldness
calvo, -a ['kalβo, a] adj bald; (terreno) bare,
barren; (tejido) threadbare ■ nm bald man
calza ['kalθa] nf wedge, chock
calzado, -a [kal'θaðo, a] adj shod ■ nm
footwear ■ nf roadway, highway
calzador [kalθa'ðor] nm shoehorn
calzar [kal'θar] vt (zapatos etc) to wear; (un
mueble) to put a wedge under; (Tec: rueda etc)
to scotch; **calzarse** vr: **calzarse los zapatos**
to put on one's shoes; **¿qué (número) calza?**
what size do you take?
calzón [kal'θon] nm (tb: **calzones**) shorts pl;
(Am: de hombre) pants pl; (: de mujer) panties pl
calzoncillos [kalθon'θiʎos] nmpl underpants
cama ['kama] nf bed; (Geo) stratum; ~
individual/de matrimonio single/double
bed; **guardar** ~ to be ill in bed
camada [ka'maða] nf litter; (de personas)
gang, band
camafeo [kama'feo] nm cameo
camaleón [kamale'on] nm chameleon
cámara ['kamara] nf (Pol etc) chamber;
(habitación) room; (Cine) hall; (Cine) cine
camera; (fotográfica) camera; ~ **de aire** inner
tube; ~ **alta/baja** upper/lower house; ~ **de
comercio** chamber of commerce; ~ **digital**
digital camera; ~ **de gas** gas chamber; ~
de video video camera; **a** ~ **lenta** in slow
motion

camarada [kama'raða] nm comrade, companion

camaradería [kamaraðe'ria] nf comradeship

camarero, -a [kama'rero, a] nm waiter ■ nf (en restaurante) waitress; (en casa, hotel) maid

camarilla [kama'riʎa] nf (clan) clique; (Pol) lobby

camarín [kama'rin] nm (Teat) dressing room

camarón [kama'ron] nm shrimp

camarote [kama'rote] nm (Naut) cabin

cambiable [kam'bjaβle] adj (variable) changeable, variable; (intercambiable) interchangeable

cambiante [kam'bjante] adj variable

cambiar [kam'bjar] vt to change; (trocar) to exchange ■ vi to change; **cambiarse** vr (mudarse) to move; (de ropa) to change; **~(se) de ...** to change one's ; **~ de idea/de ropa** to change one's mind/clothes

cambiazo [kam'bjaθo] nm: **dar el ~ a algn** to swindle sb

cambio ['kambjo] nm change; (trueque) exchange; (Com) rate of exchange; (oficina) bureau de change; (dinero menudo) small change; **en ~** on the other hand; (en lugar de eso) instead; **~ de divisas** (Com) foreign exchange; **~ de línea** (Inform) line feed; **~ de página** (Inform) form feed; **~ a término** (Com) forward exchange; **~ de velocidades** gear lever; **~ de vía** points pl

cambista [kam'bista] nm (Com) exchange broker

Camboya [kam'boja] nf Cambodia, Kampuchea

camboyano, -a [kambo'jano, a] adj, nm/f Cambodian, Kampuchean

camelar [kame'lar] vt (con mujer) to flirt with; (persuadir) to cajole

camelia [ka'melja] nf camellia

camello [ka'meʎo] nm camel; (fam: traficante) pusher

camelo [ka'melo] nm: **me huele a ~** it smells fishy

camerino [kame'rino] nm (Teat) dressing room

camilla [ka'miʎa] nf (Med) stretcher

caminante [kami'nante] nm/f traveller

caminar [kami'nar] vi (marchar) to walk, go; (viajar) to travel, journey ■ vt (recorrer) to cover, travel

caminata [kami'nata] nf long walk

camino [ka'mino] nm way, road; (sendero) track; **a medio ~** halfway (there); **en el ~** on the way, en route; **~ de** on the way to; **~ particular** private road; **~ vecinal** country road; **Caminos, Canales y Puertos** (Univ) Civil Engineering; **ir por buen ~** (fig) to be on the right track; **C~ de Santiago** see note

CAMINO DE SANTIAGO

The Camino de Santiago is a medieval pilgrim route stretching from the Pyrenees to Santiago de Compostela in north-west Spain, where tradition has it the body of the Apostle James is buried. Nowadays it is a popular tourist route as well as a religious one. The concha (cockleshell) is a symbol of the Camino de Santiago, because it is said that when St James' body was found it was covered in shells.

camión [ka'mjon] nm lorry, truck (US); (Am: autobús) bus; **~ de bomberos** fire engine

camionero [kamjo'nero] nm lorry o truck (US) driver, trucker (esp US)

camioneta [kamjo'neta] nf van, translɩ®

camionista [kamjo'nista] nmf lorry o truck driver

camisa [ka'misa] nf shirt; (Bot) skin; **~ de dormir** nightdress; **~ de fuerza** straitjacket

camisería [kamise'ria] nf outfitter's (shop)

camiseta [kami'seta] nf tee-shirt; (ropa interior) vest; (de deportista) top

camisón [kami'son] nm nightdress, nightgown

camomila [kamo'mila] nf camomile

camorra [ka'morra] nf: **armar ~** to kick up a row; **buscar ~** to look for trouble

camorrista [kamo'rrista] nm/f thug

camote [ka'mote] nm (Am) sweet potato

campal [kam'pal] adj: **batalla ~** pitched battle

campamento [kampa'mento] nm camp

campana [kam'pana] nf bell

campanada [kampa'naða] nf peal

campanario [kampa'narjo] nm belfry

campanilla [kampa'niʎa] nf small bell

campante [kam'pante] adj: **siguió tan ~** he went on as if nothing had happened

campaña [kam'paɲa] nf (Mil: Pol) campaign; **hacer ~ (en pro de/contra)** to campaign (for/against); **~ de venta** sales campaign

campechano, -a [kampe'tʃano, a] adj open

campeón, -ona [kampe'on, ona] nm/f champion

campeonato [kampeo'nato] nm championship

campesino, -a [kampe'sino, a] adj country cpd, rural; (gente) peasant cpd ■ nm/f countryman/woman; (agricultor) farmer

campestre [kam'pestre] adj country cpd, rural

camping ['kampin] nm camping; (lugar) campsite; **ir de o hacer ~** to go camping

campiña [kam'piɲa] nf countryside

campista [kam'pista] *nm/f* camper
campo ['kampo] *nm* (*fuera de la ciudad*) country, countryside; (*Agr: Elec: Inform*) field; (*de fútbol*) pitch; (*de golf*) course; (*Mil*) camp; ~ **de batalla** battlefield; ~ **de minas** minefield; ~ **petrolífero** oilfield; ~ **visual** field of vision; ~ **de concentración/de internación/de trabajo** concentration/ internment/labour camp
camposanto [kampo'santo] *nm* cemetery
campus ['kampus] *nm inv* (*Univ*) campus
camuflaje [kamu'flaxe] *nm* camouflage
camuflar [kamu'flar] *vt* to camouflage
can [kan] *nm* dog, mutt (*fam*)
cana ['kana] *nf ver* **cano**
Canadá [kana'ða] *nm* Canada
canadiense [kana'ðjense] *adj, nm/f* Canadian ∎ *nf* fur-lined jacket
canal [ka'nal] *nm* canal; (*Geo*) channel, strait; (*de televisión*) channel; (*de tejado*) gutter; **C~ de la Mancha** English Channel; **C~ de Panamá** Panama Canal
canalice *etc* [kana'liθe] *vb ver* **canalizar**
canalizar [kanali'θar] *vt* to channel
canalla [ka'naʎa] *nf* rabble, mob ∎ *nm* swine
canallada [kana'ʎaða] *nf* (*hecho*) dirty trick
canalón [kana'lon] *nm* (*conducto vertical*) drainpipe; (*del tejado*) gutter; **canalones** *nmpl* (*Culin*) cannelloni
canapé (*pl* ~**s**) [kana'pe, kana'pes] *nm* sofa, settee; (*Culin*) canapé
Canarias [ka'narjas] *nfpl*: **las (Islas)** ~ the Canaries, the Canary Isles
canario, -a [ka'narjo, a] *adj* of o from the Canary Isles ∎ *nm/f* native o inhabitant of the Canary Isles ∎ *nm* (*Zool*) canary
canasta [ka'nasta] *nf* (*round*) basket
canastilla [kanas'tiʎa] *nf* small basket; (*de niño*) layette
canasto [ka'nasto] *nm* large basket
cancela [kan'θela] *nf* (wrought-iron) gate
cancelación [kanθela'θjon] *nf* cancellation
cancelar [kanθe'lar] *vt* to cancel; (*una deuda*) to write off
cáncer ['kanθer] *nm* (*Med*) cancer; **C~** (*Astro*) Cancer
cancerígeno, -a [kanθe'rixeno, a] *adj* carcinogenic
cancha ['kantʃa] *nf* (*de baloncesto, tenis etc*) court; (*Am: de fútbol etc*) pitch
canciller [kanθi'ʎer] *nm* chancellor; **C~** (*Am*) Foreign Minister, ≈ Foreign Secretary (*Brit*)
Cancillería [kansiʎe'ria] *nf* (*Am*) Foreign Ministry, ≈ Foreign Office (*Brit*)
canción [kan'θjon] *nf* song; ~ **de cuna** lullaby
cancionero [kanθjo'nero] *nm* song book

candado [kan'daðo] *nm* padlock
candela [kan'dela] *nf* candle
candelabro [kande'laβro] *nm* candelabra
candelero [kande'lero] *nm* (*para vela*) candlestick; (*de aceite*) oil lamp
candente [kan'dente] *adj* red-hot; (*tema*) burning
candidato, -a [kandi'ðato, a] *nm/f* candidate; (*para puesto*) applicant
candidatura [kandiða'tura] *nf* candidature
candidez [kandi'ðeθ] *nf* (*sencillez*) simplicity; (*simpleza*) naiveté
cándido, -a ['kandiðo, a] *adj* simple; naive
candil [kan'dil] *nm* oil lamp
candilejas [kandi'lexas] *nfpl* (*Teat*) footlights
candor [kan'dor] *nm* (*sinceridad*) frankness; (*inocencia*) innocence
canela [ka'nela] *nf* cinnamon
canelo [ka'nelo] *nm*: **hacer el** ~ to act the fool
canelones [kane'lones] *nmpl* cannelloni
cangrejo [kan'grexo] *nm* crab
canguro [kan'guro] *nm* (*Zool*) kangaroo; (*de niños*) baby-sitter; **hacer de** ~ to baby-sit
caníbal [ka'niβal] *adj, nm/f* cannibal
canica [ka'nika] *nf* marble
caniche [ka'nitʃe] *nm* poodle
canícula [ka'nikula] *nf* midsummer heat
canijo, -a [ka'nixo, a] *adj* frail, sickly
canilla [ka'niʎa] *nf* (*Tec*) bobbin
canino, -a [ka'nino, a] *adj* canine ∎ *nm* canine (tooth)
canje [kan'xe] *nm* exchange; (*trueque*) swap
canjear [kanxe'ar] *vt* to exchange; (*trocar*) to swap
cano, -a ['kano, a] *adj* grey-haired, white-haired ∎ *nf* (*tb:* **canas**) white o grey hair; **tener canas** to be going grey
canoa [ka'noa] *nf* canoe
canon ['kanon] *nm* canon; (*pensión*) rent; (*Com*) tax
canonice *etc* [kano'niθe] *vb ver* **canonizar**
canónico, -a [ka'noniko, a] *adj*: **derecho** ~ canon law
canónigo [ka'noniɣo] *nm* canon
canonizar [kanoni'θar] *vt* to canonize
canoro, -a [ka'noro, a] *adj* melodious
canoso, -a [ka'noso, a] *adj* (*pelo*) grey (*Brit*), gray (*US*); (*persona*) grey-haired
cansado, -a [kan'saðo, a] *adj* tired, weary; (*tedioso*) tedious, boring; **estoy ~ de hacerlo** I'm sick of doing it
cansancio [kan'sanθjo] *nm* tiredness, fatigue
cansar [kan'sar] *vt* (*fatigar*) to tire, tire out; (*aburrir*) to bore; (*fastidiar*) to bother; **cansarse** *vr* to tire, get tired; (*aburrirse*) to get bored

cantábrico, -a [kan'taβriko, a] *adj*
Cantabrian; **Mar C~** Bay of Biscay; **(Montes)**
Cantábricos, Cordillera Cantábrica
Cantabrian Mountains

cántabro, -a ['kantaβro, a] *adj, nm/f*
Cantabrian

cantante [kan'tante] *adj* singing ■ *nm/f*
singer

cantaor, a [kanta'or, a] *nm/f* Flamenco
singer

cantar [kan'tar] *vt* to sing ■ *vi* to sing;
(insecto) to chirp; *(rechinar)* to squeak; *(fam:*
criminal) to squeal ■ *nm (acción)* singing;
(canción) song; *(poema)* poem; **~ a algn las**
cuarenta to tell sb a few home truths; **~ a**
dos voces to sing a duet

cántara ['kantara] *nf* large pitcher

cántaro ['kantaro] *nm* pitcher, jug

cantautor, a [kantau'tor, a] *nm/f* singer-
songwriter

cante ['kante] *nm*: **~ jondo** flamenco singing

cantera [kan'tera] *nf* quarry

cantidad [kanti'ðaθ] *nf* quantity, amount;
(Econ) sum ■ *adv (fam)* a lot; **~ alzada** lump
sum; **~ de** lots of

cantilena [kanti'lena] *nf* = **cantinela**

cantimplora [kantim'plora] *nf* water bottle

cantina [kan'tina] *nf* canteen; *(de estación)*
buffet; *(esp Am)* bar

cantinela [kanti'nela] *nf* ballad, song

canto ['kanto] *nm* singing; *(canción)* song;
(borde) edge, rim; *(de un cuchillo)* back; **~**
rodado boulder

cantón [kan'ton] *nm* canton

cantor, a [kan'tor, a] *nm/f* singer

canturrear [kanturre'ar] *vi* to sing softly

canutas [ka'nutas] *nfpl*: **pasarlas ~** *(fam)* to
have a rough time (of it)

canuto [ka'nuto] *nm (tubo)* small tube; *(fam:*
porro) joint

caña ['kana] *nf (Bot: tallo)* stem, stalk; *(carrizo)*
reed; *(vaso)* tumbler; *(de cerveza)* glass of
beer; *(Anat)* shinbone; *(Am: aguardiente)* cane
liquor; **~ de azúcar** sugar cane; **~ de pescar**
fishing rod

cañada [ka'naða] *nf (entre dos montañas)* gully,
ravine; *(camino)* cattle track

cáñamo ['kanamo] *nm (Bot)* hemp

cañaveral [kanaβe'ral] *nm (Bot)* reedbed;
(Agr) sugar-cane field

cañería [kane'ria] *nf* piping; *(tubo)* pipe

caño ['kano] *nm (tubo)* tube, pipe; *(de aguas*
servidas) sewer; *(Mus)* pipe; *(Naut)* navigation
channel; *(de fuente)* jet

cañón [ka'non] *nm (Mil)* cannon; *(de fusil)*
barrel; *(Geo)* canyon, gorge

cañonazo [kano'naθo] *nm (Mil)* gunshot

cañonera [kano'nera] *nf (tb:* **lancha**
cañonera) gunboat

caoba [ka'oβa] *nf* mahogany

caos ['kaos] *nm* chaos

caótico, -a [ka'otiko, a] *adj* chaotic

C.A.P. *nm abr* (= *Certificado de Aptitud Pedagógica)*
teaching certificate

cap. *abr* (= *capítulo)* ch.

capa ['kapa] *nf* cloak, cape; *(Culin)* coating;
(Geo) layer, stratum; *(de pintura)* coat; **de ~ y**
espada cloak-and-dagger; **so ~ de** under the
pretext of; **~ de ozono** ozone layer; **capas**
sociales social groups

capacho [ka'patʃo] *nm* wicker basket

capacidad [kapaθi'ðað] *nf (medida)* capacity;
(aptitud) capacity, ability; **una sala con ~**
para 900 a hall seating 900; **~ adquisitiva**
purchasing power

capacitación [kapaθita'θjon] *nf* training

capacitar [kapaθi'tar] *vt*: **~ a algn para algo**
to qualify sb for sth; *(Tec)* to train sb for sth;
capacitarse *vr*: **capacitarse para algo** to
qualify for sth

capar [ka'par] *vt* to castrate, geld

caparazón [kapara'θon] *nm (Zool)* shell

capataz [kapa'taθ] *nm* foreman, charge hand

capaz [ka'paθ] *adj* able, capable; *(amplio)*
capacious, roomy; **es ~ que venga mañana**
(Am) he'll probably come tomorrow

capcioso, -a [kap'θjoso, a] *adj* wily, deceitful;
pregunta capciosa trick question

capea [ka'pea] *nf (Taur)* bullfight with young
bulls

capear [kape'ar] *vt (dificultades)* to dodge;
~ el temporal to weather the storm

capellán [kape'ʎan] *nm* chaplain; *(sacerdote)*
priest

caperuza [kape'ruθa] *nf* hood; *(de bolígrafo)*
cap

capi ['kapi] *nf (esp Am fam)* capital (city)

capicúa [kapi'kua] *nf* reversible number, e.g. 1441

capilar [kapi'lar] *adj* hair *cpd*

capilla [ka'piʎa] *nf* chapel

capital [kapi'tal] *adj* capital ■ *nm (Com)*
capital ■ *nf (de nación)* capital (city); *(tb:*
capital de provincia) provincial capital,
≈ county town; **~ activo/en acciones**
working/share *o* equity capital; **~**
arriesgado venture capital; **~ autorizado** *o*
social authorised capital; **~ emitido** issued
capital; **~ improductivo** idle money;
~ invertido *o* **utilizado** capital employed;
~ pagado paid-up capital; **~ de riesgo** risk
capital; **~ social** equity *o* share capital;
inversión de capitales capital investment;
ver tb **provincia**

capitalice *etc* [kapita'liθe] *vb ver* **capitalizar**

capitalino, -a [kapita'lino, a] adj (Am) of o from the capital ∎ nm/f native o inhabitant of the capital

capitalismo [kapita'lismo] nm capitalism

capitalista [kapita'lista] adj, nm/f capitalist

capitalizar [kapitali'θar] vt to capitalize

capitán [kapi'tan] nm captain; (fig) leader

capitana [kapi'tana] nf flagship

capitanear [kapitane'ar] vt to captain

capitanía [kapita'nia] nf captaincy

capitel [kapi'tel] nm (Arq) capital

capitolio [kapi'toljo] nm capitol

capitulación [kapitula'θjon] nf (rendición) capitulation, surrender; (acuerdo) agreement, pact; **capitulaciones matrimoniales** marriage contract sg

capitular [kapitu'lar] vi to come to terms, make an agreement; (Mil) to surrender

capítulo [ka'pitulo] nm chapter

capo [ka'po] nm drugs baron

capó [ka'po] nm (Auto) bonnet (Brit), hood (US)

capón [ka'pon] nm capon

caporal [kapo'ral] nm chief, leader

capota [ka'pota] nf (de mujer) bonnet; (Auto) hood (Brit), top (US)

capote [ka'pote] nm (abrigo: de militar) greatcoat; (de torero) cloak

capricho [ka'pritʃo] nm whim, caprice

caprichoso, -a [kapri'tʃoso, a] adj capricious

Capricornio [kapri'kornjo] nm Capricorn

cápsula ['kapsula] nf capsule; **~ espacial** space capsule

captar [kap'tar] vt (comprender) to understand; (Radio) to pick up; (atención, apoyo) to attract

captura [kap'tura] nf capture; (Jur) arrest

capturar [kaptu'rar] vt to capture; (Jur) to arrest; (datos) to input

capucha [ka'putʃa] nf hood, cowl

capullo [ka'puʎo] nm (Zool) cocoon; (Bot) bud; (fam!) berk (Brit), jerk (US)

caqui ['kaki] nm khaki

cara ['kara] nf (Anat, de moneda) face; (aspecto) appearance; (de disco) side; (fig) boldness; (descaro) cheek, nerve ∎ prep: **~ a** facing; **de ~ a** opposite, facing; **dar la ~** to face the consequences; **echar algo en ~ a algn** to reproach sb for sth; **¿~ o cruz?** heads or tails?; **¡qué ~ más dura!** what a nerve!; **de una ~** (disquete) single-sided

carabina [kara'βina] nf carbine, rifle; (persona) chaperone

carabinero [karaβi'nero] nm (de aduana) customs officer; (Am) gendarme

Caracas [ka'rakas] nm Caracas

caracol [kara'kol] nm (Zool) snail; (concha) (sea)shell; **escalera de ~** spiral staircase

caracolear [karakole'ar] vi (caballo) to prance about

carácter (pl **caracteres**) [ka'rakter, karak'teres] nm character; **caracteres de imprenta** (Tip) type(face) sg; **~ libre** (Inform) wildcard character; **tener buen/mal ~** to be good-natured/bad tempered

caracterice etc [karakte'riθe] vb ver **caracterizar**

característico, -a [karakte'ristiko, a] adj characteristic ∎ nf characteristic

caracterizar [karakteri'θar] vt (distinguir) to characterize, typify; (honrar) to confer a distinction on

caradura [kara'ðura] nm/f cheeky person; **es un ~** he's got a nerve

carajillo [kara'xiʎo] nm black coffee with brandy

carajo [ka'raxo] nm (esp Am fam!): **¡~!** shit! (!); **¡qué ~!** what the hell!; **me importa un ~** I don't give a damn

caramba [ka'ramba] excl well!, good gracious!

carámbano [ka'rambano] nm icicle

carambola [karam'bola] nf: **por ~** by a fluke

caramelo [kara'melo] nm (dulce) sweet; (azúcar fundido) caramel

carantoñas [karan'toɲas] nfpl: **hacer ~ a algn** to (try to) butter sb up

caraqueño, -a [kara'keɲo, a] adj of o from Caracas ∎ nm/f native o inhabitant of Caracas

carátula [ka'ratula] nf (máscara) mask; (Teat): **la ~** the stage

caravana [kara'βana] nf caravan; (fig) group; (de autos) tailback

carbón [kar'βon] nm coal; **~ de leña** charcoal; **papel ~** carbon paper

carbonatado, -a [karβona'taðo, a] adj carbonated

carbonato [karβo'nato] nm carbonate; **~ sódico** sodium carbonate

carboncillo [karβon'θiʎo] nm (Arte) charcoal

carbonice etc [karβo'niθe] vb ver **carbonizar**

carbonilla [karβo'niʎa] nf coal dust

carbonizar [karβoni'θar] vt to carbonize; (quemar) to char; **quedar carbonizado** (Elec) to be electrocuted

carbono [kar'βono] nm carbon

carburador [karβura'ðor] nm carburettor

carburante [karβu'rante] nm fuel

carca ['karka] adj, nm/f inv reactionary

carcajada [karka'xaða] nf (loud) laugh, guffaw

carcajearse [karkaxe'arse] vr to roar with laughter

cárcel ['karθel] nf prison, jail; (Tec) clamp

carcelero, -a [karθe'lero, a] adj prison cpd ∎ nm/f warder

carcoma [kar'koma] *nf* woodworm
carcomer [karko'mer] *vt* to bore into, eat into; (*fig*) to undermine; **carcomerse** *vr* to become worm-eaten; (*fig*) to decay
carcomido, -a [karko'miðo, a] *adj* worm-eaten; (*fig*) rotten
cardar [kar'ðar] *vt* (*Tec*) to card, comb
cardenal [karðe'nal] *nm* (*Rel*) cardinal; (*Med*) bruise
cárdeno, -a ['karðeno, a] *adj* purple; (*lívido*) livid
cardiaco, -a [kar'ðjako, a], **cardíaco, a** [kar'ðiako, a] *adj* cardiac; (*ataque*) heart *cpd*
cardinal [karði'nal] *adj* cardinal
cardiólogo, -a [karðj'oloyo, a] *nm/f* cardiologist
cardo ['karðo] *nm* thistle
carear [kare'ar] *vt* to bring face to face; (*comparar*) to compare; **carearse** *vr* to come face to face, meet
carecer [kare'θer] *vi*: ~ **de** to lack, be in need of
carencia [ka'renθja] *nf* lack; (*escasez*) shortage; (*Med*) deficiency
carente [ka'rente] *adj*: ~ **de** lacking in, devoid of
carestía [kares'tia] *nf* (*escasez*) scarcity, shortage; (*Com*) high cost; **época de** ~ period of shortage
careta [ka'reta] *nf* mask
carey [ka'rei] *nm* (*tortuga*) turtle; (*concha*) tortoiseshell
carezca *etc* [ka'reθka] *vb ver* **carecer**
carga ['karya] *nf* (*peso*, *Elec*) load; (*de barco*) cargo, freight; (*Finanzas*) tax, duty; (*Mil*) charge; (*Inform*) loading; (*obligación*, *responsabilidad*) duty, obligation; ~ **aérea** (*Com*) air cargo; ~ **útil** (*Com*) payload; **la** ~ **fiscal** the tax burden
cargadero [karya'ðero] *nm* goods platform, loading bay
cargado, -a [kar'yaðo, a] *adj* loaded; (*Elec*) live; (*café*, *té*) strong; (*cielo*) overcast
cargador, a [karya'ðor, a] *nm/f* loader; (*Naut*) docker ■ *nm* (*Inform*): ~ **de discos** disk pack; (*Telec*: *del móvil*) charger
cargamento [karya'mento] *nm* (*acción*) loading; (*mercancías*) load, cargo
cargante [kar'yante] *adj* (*persona*) trying
cargar [kar'yar] *vt* (*barco*, *arma*) to load; (*Elec*) to charge; (*impuesto*) to impose; (*Com*: *algo en cuenta*) to charge, debit; (*Mil*: *enemigo*) to charge ■ *vi* (*Auto*) to load (up); (*inclinarse*) to lean; (*Inform*) to load, feed in; ~ **con** to pick up, carry away; **cargarse** *vr* (*fam*: *estropear*) to break; (: *matar*) to bump off; (*Elec*) to become charged
cargo ['karyo] *nm* (*Com etc*) charge, debit;

(*puesto*) post, office; (*responsabilidad*) duty, obligation; (*fig*) weight, burden; (*Jur*) charge; **altos cargos** high-ranking officials; **una cantidad en** ~ **a algn** a sum chargeable to sb; **hacerse** ~ **de** to take charge of o responsibility for
cargue *etc* ['karye] *vb ver* **cargar**
carguero [kar'yero] *nm* freighter, cargo boat; (*avión*) freight plane
Caribe [ka'riβe] *nm*: **el** ~ the Caribbean
caribeño, -a [kari'βeɲo, a] *adj* Caribbean
caricatura [karika'tura] *nf* caricature
caricia [ka'riθja] *nf* caress; (*a animal*) pat, stroke
caridad [kari'ðað] *nf* charity
caries ['karjes] *nf inv* (*Med*) tooth decay
cariño [ka'riɲo] *nm* affection, love; (*caricia*) caress; (*en carta*) love ...
cariñoso, -a [kari'ɲoso, a] *adj* affectionate
carioca [ka'rjoka] *adj* (*Am*) of o from Rio de Janeiro ■ *nm/f* native o inhabitant of Rio de Janeiro
carisma [ka'risma] *nm* charisma
carismático, -a [karis'matiko, a] *adj* charismatic
caritativo, -a [karita'tiβo, a] *adj* charitable
cariz [ka'riθ] *nm*: **tener** o **tomar buen/mal** ~ to look good/bad
carmesí [karme'si] *adj*, *nm* crimson
carmín [kar'min] *nm* (*color*) carmine; ~ **(de labios)** lipstick
carnal [kar'nal] *adj* carnal; **primo** ~ first cousin
carnaval [karna'βal] *nm* carnival; *see note*

carne ['karne] *nf* flesh; (*Culin*) meat; ~ **de cerdo/de cordero/de ternera/de vaca** pork/lamb/veal/beef; ~ **picada** mince; ~ **de gallina** (*fig*) gooseflesh
carné [kar'ne] *nm* = **carnet**

carnero [kar'nero] *nm* sheep, ram; *(carne)* mutton

carnet *(pl* **carnets**) [kar'ne, kar'nes] *nm*: ~ **de conducir** driving licence; ~ **de identidad** identity card; *ver tb* **Documento Nacional de Identidad**

carnicería [karniθe'ria] *nf* butcher's (shop); *(fig: matanza)* carnage, slaughter

carnicero, -a [karni'θero, a] *adj* carnivorous ■ *nm/f (tb fig)* butcher ■ *nm* carnivore

carnívoro, -a [kar'niβoro, a] *adj* carnivorous ■ *nm* carnivore

carnoso, -a [kar'noso, a] *adj* beefy, fat

caro, -a ['karo, a] *adj* dear; *(Com)* dear, expensive ■ *adv* dear, dearly; **vender** ~ to sell at a high price

carpa ['karpa] *nf (pez)* carp; *(de circo)* big top; *(Am: de camping)* tent

carpeta [kar'peta] *nf* folder, file

carpintería [karpinte'ria] *nf* carpentry

carpintero [karpin'tero] *nm* carpenter; **pájaro** ~ woodpecker

carraspear [karraspe'ar] *vi (aclararse la garganta)* to clear one's throat

carraspera [karras'pera] *nf* hoarseness

carrera [ka'rrera] *nf (acción)* run(ning); *(espacio recorrido)* run; *(certamen)* race; *(trayecto)* course; *(profesión)* career; *(Escol: Univ)* course; *(de taxi)* ride; *(en medias)* ladder; **a la** ~ at (full) speed; **caballo de** ~**(s)** racehorse; ~ **de armamentos** arms race

carrerilla [karre'riʎa] *nf*: **decir algo de** ~ to reel sth off; **tomar** ~ to get up speed

carreta [ka'rreta] *nf* wagon, cart

carrete [ka'rrete] *nm* reel, spool; *(Tec)* coil

carretera [karre'tera] *nf (main)* road, highway; ~ **nacional** ≈ A road *(Brit)*, ≈ state highway *(US)*; ~ **de circunvalación** ring road

carretilla [karre'tiʎa] *nf* trolley; *(Agr)* (wheel)barrow

carril [ka'rril] *nm* furrow; *(de autopista)* lane; *(Ferro)* rail

carril bici [karil'βiθi] *(pl* **carriles bici** [kariles'βiθi]) *nm* cycle lane, bikeway *(US)*

carrillo [ka'rriʎo] *nm (Anat)* cheek; *(Tec)* pulley

carro ['karro] *nm* cart, wagon; *(Mil)* tank; *(Am: coche)* car; *(Tip)* carriage; ~ **blindado** armoured car

carrocería [karroθe'ria] *nf* body, bodywork *no pl (Brit)*

carroña [ka'rroɲa] *nf* carrion *no pl*

carroza [ka'rroθa] *nf (vehículo)* coach ■ *nm/f (fam)* old fogey

carruaje [ka'rrwaxe] *nm* carriage

carrusel [karru'sel] *nm* merry-go-round, roundabout *(Brit)*

carta ['karta] *nf* letter; *(Culin)* menu; *(naipe)* card; *(mapa)* map; *(Jur)* document; ~ **de crédito** credit card; ~ **de crédito documentaria** *(Com)* documentary letter of credit; ~ **de crédito irrevocable** *(Com)* irrevocable letter of credit; ~ **certificada/ urgente** registered/special delivery letter; ~ **marítima** chart; ~ **de pedido** *(Com)* order; ~ **verde** *(Auto)* green card; ~ **de vinos** wine list; **echar una** ~ **al correo** to post a letter; **echar las cartas a algn** to tell sb's fortune

cartabón [karta'βon] *nm* set square

cartearse [karte'arse] *vr* to correspond

cartel [kar'tel] *nm (anuncio)* poster, placard; *(Escol)* wall chart; *(Com)* cartel

cartelera [karte'lera] *nf* hoarding, billboard; *(en periódico etc)* listings *pl*, entertainments guide; **"en ~"** "showing"

cartera [kar'tera] *nf (de bolsillo)* wallet; *(de colegial, cobrador)* satchel; *(Am: de señora)* handbag *(Brit)*, purse *(US)*; *(para documentos)* briefcase; **ministro sin ~** *(Pol)* minister without portfolio; **ocupa la ~ de Agricultura** he is Minister of Agriculture; ~ **de pedidos** *(Com)* order book; **efectos en ~** *(Econ)* holdings

carterista [karte'rista] *nm/f* pickpocket

cartero [kar'tero] *nm* postman

cartílago [kar'tilaɣo] *nm* cartilage

cartilla [kar'tiʎa] *nf (Escol)* primer, first reading book; ~ **de ahorros** bank book

cartografía [kartoɣra'fia] *nf* cartography

cartón [kar'ton] *nm* cardboard

cartucho [kar'tutʃo] *nm (Mil)* cartridge; *(bolsita)* paper cone; ~ **de datos** *(Inform)* data cartridge; ~ **de tinta** ink cartridge

cartulina [kartu'lina] *nf* fine cardboard, card

CASA ['kasa] *nf abr (Esp Aviat)* = **Construcciones Aeronáuticas S.A.**

casa ['kasa] *nf* house; *(hogar)* home; *(edificio)* building; *(Com)* firm, company; ~ **consistorial** town hall; ~ **de huéspedes** ≈ guest house; ~ **de socorro** first aid post; ~ **de citas** *(fam)* brothel; ~ **independiente** detached house; ~ **rural** *(de alquiler)* holiday cottage; *(pensión)* rural B&B; **ir a** ~ to go home; **salir de** ~ to go out; *(para siempre)* to leave home; **echar la** ~ **por la ventana** *(gastar)* to spare no expense; *ver tb* **hotel**

casadero, -a [kasa'ðero, a] *adj* marriageable

casado, -a [ka'saðo, a] *adj* married ■ *nm/f* married man/woman

casamiento [kasa'mjento] *nm* marriage, wedding

casar [ka'sar] *vt* to marry; *(Jur)* to quash, annul; **casarse** *vr* to marry, get married;

casarse por lo civil to have a civil wedding, get married in a registry office (*Brit*)
cascabel [kaska'βel] *nm* (small) bell; (*Zool*) rattlesnake
cascada [kas'kaða] *nf* waterfall
cascajo [kas'kaxo] *nm* gravel, stone chippings *pl*
cascanueces [kaska'nweθes] *nm inv*: **un ~** a pair of nutcrackers
cascar [kas'kar] *vt* to split; (*nuez*) to crack ■ *vi* to chatter; **cascarse** *vr* to crack, split, break (open)
cáscara ['kaskara] *nf* (*de huevo, fruta seca*) shell; (*de fruta*) skin; (*de limón*) peel
cascarón [kaska'ron] *nm* (broken) eggshell
cascarrabias [kaska'rraβjas] *nm/f inv* (*fam*) hothead
casco ['kasko] *nm* (*de bombero, soldado*) helmet; (*cráneo*) skull; (*Naut: de barco*) hull; (*Zool: de caballo*) hoof; (*botella*) empty bottle; (*de ciudad*): **el ~ antiguo** the old part; **el ~ urbano** the town centre; **los cascos azules** the UN peace-keeping force, the blue helmets
cascote [kas'kote] *nm* piece of rubble; **cascotes** *nmpl* rubble *sg*
caserío [kase'rio] *nm* hamlet, group of houses; (*casa*) country house
casero, -a [ka'sero] *adj*: **ser muy ~** (*persona*) to be homeloving; **"comida casera"** "home cooking" ■ *nm/f* (*propietario*) landlord/lady; (*Com*) house agent
caserón [kase'ron] *nm* large (ramshackle) house
caseta [ka'seta] *nf* hut; (*para bañista*) cubicle; (*de feria*) stall
casete [ka'sete] *nm o f* cassette; **~ digital** digital audio tape, DAT
casi ['kasi] *adv* almost; **~ nunca** hardly ever, almost never; **~ nada** next to nothing; **~ te caes** you almost o nearly fell
casilla [ka'siʎa] *nf* (*casita*) hut, cabin; (*Teat*) box office; (*para cartas*) pigeonhole; (*Ajedrez*) square; **C~ postal** o **de Correo(s)** (*Am*) P.O. Box; **sacar a algn de sus casillas** to drive sb round the bend (*fam*), make sb lose his temper
casillero [kasi'ʎero] *nm* pigeonholes
casino [ka'sino] *nm* club; (*de juego*) casino
caso ['kaso] *nm* case; (*suceso*) event; **en ~ de ...** in case of ...; **el ~ es que** the fact is that; **en el mejor de los casos** at best; **en ese ~** in that case; **en todo ~** in any case; **en último ~** as a last resort; **hacer ~ a** to pay attention to; **hacer ~ omiso de** to fail to mention, pass over; **hacer** o **venir al ~** to be relevant
caspa ['kaspa] *nf* dandruff

Caspio ['kaspjo] *adj*: **Mar ~** Caspian Sea
casque *etc* ['kaske] *vb ver* **cascar**
casquillo [kas'kiʎo] *nm* (*de bombilla*) fitting; (*de bala*) cartridge case
cassette [ka'set] *nf o m* = **casete**
casta ['kasta] *nf* caste; (*raza*) breed
castaña [kas'taɲa] *nf ver* **castaño**
castañetear [kastaɲete'ar] *vi* (*dientes*) to chatter
castaño, -a [kas'taɲo, a] *adj* chestnut (-coloured), brown ■ *nm* chestnut tree ■ *nf* chestnut; (*fam: golpe*) punch; **~ de Indias** horse chestnut tree
castañuelas [kasta'ɲwelas] *nfpl* castanets
castellano, -a [kaste'ʎano, a] *adj* Castilian; (*fam*) Spanish ■ *nm/f* Castilian; (*fam*) Spaniard ■ *nm* (*Ling*) Castilian, Spanish; *see note*

● CASTELLANO

The term *castellano* is now the most widely used term in Spain and Spanish America to refer to the Spanish language, since *español* is too closely associated with Spain as a nation. Of course some people maintain that *castellano* should only refer to the type of Spanish spoken in Castilla.

castellonense [kasteʎo'nense] *adj* of o from Castellón de la Plana ■ *nm/f* native o inhabitant of Castellón de la Plana
castidad [kasti'ðað] *nf* chastity, purity
castigar [kasti'ɣar] *vt* to punish; (*Deporte*) to penalize; (*afligir*) to afflict
castigo [kas'tiɣo] *nm* punishment; (*Deporte*) penalty
castigue *etc* [kas'tiɣe] *vb ver* **castigar**
Castilla [kas'tiʎa] *nf* Castile
castillo [kas'tiʎo] *nm* castle
castizo, -a [kas'tiθo, a] *adj* (*Ling*) pure; (*de buena casta*) purebred, pedigree; (*auténtico*) genuine
casto, -a ['kasto, a] *adj* chaste, pure
castor [kas'tor] *nm* beaver
castrar [kas'trar] *vt* to castrate; (*gato*) to doctor; (*Bot*) to prune
castrense [kas'trense] *adj* army *cpd*, military
casual [ka'swal] *adj* chance, accidental
casualidad [kaswali'ðað] *nf* chance, accident; (*combinación de circunstancias*) coincidence; **¡qué ~!** what a coincidence!
casualmente [kaswal'mente] *adv* by chance
cataclismo [kata'klismo] *nm* cataclysm
catador [kata'ðor] *nm* taster
catadura [kata'ðura] *nf* (*aspecto*) looks *pl*
catalán, -ana [kata'lan, ana] *adj, nm/f*

Catalan ▪ *nm* (*Ling*) Catalan; *ver tb* **lenguas cooficiales**

catalejo [kata'lexo] *nm* telescope

catalizador [katali'θa'ðor] *nm* catalyst; (*Auto*) catalytic converter

catalogar [katalo'ɣar] *vt* to catalogue; ~ **(de)** (*fig*) to classify as

catálogo [ka'taloɣo] *nm* catalogue

catalogue *etc* [kata'loɣe] *vb ver* **catalogar**

Cataluña [kata'luɲa] *nf* Catalonia

cataplasma [kata'plasma] *nf* (*Med*) poultice

catapulta [kata'pulta] *nf* catapult

catar [ka'tar] *vt* to taste, sample

catarata [kata'rata] *nf* (*Geo*) (water)fall; (*Med*) cataract

catarro [ka'tarro] *nm* catarrh; (*constipado*) cold

catarsis [ka'tarsis] *nf* catharsis

catastro [ka'tastro] *nm* property register

catástrofe [ka'tastrofe] *nf* catastrophe

catear [kate'ar] *vt* (*fam*) to flunk

catecismo [kate'θismo] *nm* catechism

cátedra ['kateðra] *nf* (*Univ*) chair, professorship; (*Escol*) principal teacher's post; **sentar ~ sobre un argumento** to take one's stand on an argument

catedral [kate'ðral] *nf* cathedral

catedrático, -a [kate'ðratiko, a] *nm/f* professor; (*Escol*) principal teacher

categoría [kateɣo'ria] *nf* category; (*rango*) rank, standing; (*calidad*) quality; **de ~** (*hotel*) top-class; **de baja ~** (*oficial*) low-ranking; **de segunda ~** second-rate; **no tiene ~** he has no standing

categórico, -a [kate'ɣoriko, a] *adj* categorical

catequesis [kate'kesis] *nf* catechism lessons

caterva [ka'terβa] *nf* throng, crowd

cateto, -a [ka'teto, a] *nm/f* yokel

cátodo ['katoðo] *nm* cathode

catolicismo [katoli'θismo] *nm* Catholicism

católico, -a [ka'toliko, a] *adj, nm/f* Catholic

catorce [ka'torθe] *num* fourteen

catre ['katre] *nm* camp bed (*Brit*), cot (*US*); (*fam*) pit

Cáucaso ['kaukaso] *nm* Caucasus

cauce ['kauθe] *nm* (*de río*) riverbed; (*fig*) channel

caucho ['kautʃo] *nm* rubber; (*Am: llanta*) tyre

caución [kau'θjon] *nf* bail

caucionar [kauθjo'nar] *vt* (*Jur*) to bail (out), go bail for

caudal [kau'ðal] *nm* (*de río*) volume, flow; (*fortuna*) wealth; (*abundancia*) abundance

caudaloso, -a [kauða'loso, a] *adj* (*río*) large; (*persona*) wealthy, rich

caudillaje [kauði'ʎaxe] *nm* leadership

caudillo [kau'ðiʎo] *nm* leader, chief

causa ['kausa] *nf* cause; (*razón*) reason; (*Jur*) lawsuit, case; **a o por ~ de** because of, on account of

causar [kau'sar] *vt* to cause

cáustico, -a ['kaustiko, a] *adj* caustic

cautela [kau'tela] *nf* caution, cautiousness

cauteloso, -a [kaute'loso, a] *adj* cautious, wary

cautivar [kauti'βar] *vt* to capture; (*fig*) to captivate

cautiverio [kauti'βerjo] *nm*, **cautividad** [kautiβi'ðað] *nf* captivity

cautivo, -a [kau'tiβo, a] *adj, nm/f* captive

cauto, -a ['kauto, a] *adj* cautious, careful

cava ['kaβa] *nf* (*bodega*) (wine) cellar ▪ *nm* (*vino*) champagne-type wine

cavar [ka'βar] *vt* to dig; (*Agr*) to dig over

caverna [ka'βerna] *nf* cave, cavern

cavernoso, -a [kaβer'noso, a] *adj* cavernous; (*voz*) resounding

caviar [ka'βjar] *nm* caviar(e)

cavidad [kaβi'ðað] *nf* cavity

cavilación [kaβila'θjon] *nf* deep thought

cavilar [kaβi'lar] *vt* to ponder

cayado [ka'jaðo] *nm* (*de pastor*) crook; (*de obispo*) crozier

cayendo *etc* [ka'jendo] *vb ver* **caer**

caza ['kaθa] *nf* (*acción: gen*) hunting; (*: con fusil*) shooting; (*una caza*) hunt, chase; (*animales*) game; **coto de ~** hunting estate ▪ *nm* (*Aviat*) fighter

cazabe [ka'saβe] *nm* (*Am*) cassava bread *o* flour

cazador, a [kaθa'ðor, a] *nm/f* hunter/huntress ▪ *nf* jacket

cazaejecutivos [kaθaexeku'tiβos] *nm inv* (*Com*) headhunter

cazar [ka'θar] *vt* to hunt; (*perseguir*) to chase; (*prender*) to catch; **cazarlas al vuelo** to be pretty sharp

cazasubmarinos [kaθasuβma'rinos] *nm inv* (*Naut*) destroyer; (*Aviat*) anti-submarine craft

cazo ['kaθo] *nm* saucepan

cazuela [ka'θwela] *nf* (*vasija*) pan; (*guisado*) casserole

cazurro, -a [ka'θurro, a] *adj* surly

CC *nm abr* (*Pol*: = *Comité Central*) Central Committee

c/c. *abr* (*Com*: = *cuenta corriente*) current account

CCAA *abr* (*Esp*) = **Comunidades Autónomas**

CCI *nf abr* (*Com*: = *Cámara de Comercio Internacional*) ICC

CC.OO. *nfpl abr* = **Comisiones Obreras**

c/d *abr* (= *en casa de*) c/o, care of

CD *nm abr* (= *compact disc*) CD ▪ *abr* (*Pol*: = *Cuerpo Diplomático*) CD (= *Diplomatic Corps*)

CDN nm abr (= Centro Dramático Nacional)
≈ RADA (Brit)

CD-Rom nm abr CD-Rom

CE nm abr (= Consejo de Europa) Council of
Europe ■ nf abr (= Comunidad Europea) EC

cebada [θe'βaða] nf barley

cebar [θe'βar] vt (animal) to fatten (up); (anzuelo)
to bait; (Mil: Tec) to prime; **cebarse** vr: **cebarse
en** to vent one's fury on, take it out on

cebo ['θeβo] nm (gen: para animales) feed, food;
(para peces, fig) bait; (de arma) charge

cebolla [θe'βoʎa] nf onion

cebolleta [θebo'ʎeta] nf spring onion

cebollino [θeβo'ʎino] nm spring onion

cebón, -ona [θe'βon, ona] adj fat, fattened

cebra ['θeβra] nf zebra; **paso de** ~ zebra
crossing

CECA ['θeka] nf abr (= Comunidad Europea del
Carbón y del Acero) ECSC

ceca ['θeka] nf: **andar** o **ir de la** ~ **a la Meca**
to chase about all over the place

cecear [θeθe'ar] vi to lisp

ceceo [θe'θeo] nm lisp

cecina [θe'θina] nf cured o smoked meat

cedazo [θe'ðaθo] nm sieve

ceder [θe'ðer] vt (entregar) to hand over;
(renunciar a) to give up, part with ■ vi
(renunciar) to give in, yield; (disminuir) to
diminish, decline; (romperse) to give way;
(viento) to drop; (fiebre etc) to abate; **"ceda el
paso"** (Auto) "give way"

cederom [θeðe'rom] nm CD-ROM

cedro ['θeðro] nm cedar

cédula ['θeðula] nf certificate, document;
~ **de identidad** (Am) identity card; ~ **en
blanco** blank cheque; ver tb **Documento
Nacional de Identidad**

CEE nf abr (= Comunidad Económica Europea) EEC

cegar [θe'ɣar] vt to blind; (tubería etc) to block
up, stop up ■ vi to go blind; **cegarse** vr:
cegarse (de) to be blinded (by)

cegué etc [θe'ɣe] vb ver **cegar**

ceguera [θe'ɣera] nf blindness

CEI nf abr (= Comunidad de Estados Independientes)
CIS

Ceilán [θei'lan] nm Ceylon, Sri Lanka

ceja ['θexa] nf eyebrow; **cejas pobladas**
bushy eyebrows; **arquear las cejas** to raise
one's eyebrows; **fruncir las cejas** to frown

cejar [θe'xar] vi (fig) to back down; **no** ~ to
keep it up, stick at it

cejijunto, -a [θexi'xunto, a] adj with bushy
eyebrows; (fig) scowling

celada [θe'laða] nf ambush, trap

celador, a [θela'ðor, a] nm/f (de edificio)
watchman; (de museo etc) attendant; (de cárcel)
warder

celda ['θelda] nf cell

celebérrimo, -a [θele'βerrimo, a] adj
superlativo de **célebre**

celebración [θeleβra'θjon] nf celebration

celebrar [θele'βrar] vt to celebrate; (alabar)
to praise ■ vi to be glad; **celebrarse** vr to
occur, take place

célebre ['θeleβre] adj celebrated, renowned

celebridad [θeleβri'ðað] nf fame; (persona)
celebrity

celeridad [θeleri'ðað] nf: **con** ~ promptly

celeste [θe'leste] adj sky-blue; (cuerpo etc)
heavenly ■ nm sky blue

celestial [θeles'tjal] adj celestial, heavenly

celibato [θeli'βato] nm celibacy

célibe ['θeliβe] adj, nm/f celibate

celo ['θelo] nm zeal; (Rel) fervour; (pey) envy;
celos nmpl jealousy sg; **dar celos a algn** to
make sb jealous; **tener celos de algn** to be
jealous of sb; **en** ~ (animales) on heat

celofán [θelo'fan] nm Cellophane®

celosía [θelo'sia] nf lattice (window)

celoso, -a [θe'loso, a] adj (envidioso) jealous;
(trabajador) zealous; (desconfiado) suspicious

celta ['θelta] adj Celtic ■ nm/f Celt

célula ['θelula] nf cell

celular [θelu'lar] adj: **tejido** ~ cell tissue

celulitis [θelu'litis] nf (enfermedad) cellulitis;
(grasa) cellulite

celuloide [θelu'loiðe] nm celluloid

celulosa [θelu'losa] nf cellulose

cementerio [θemen'terjo] nm cemetery,
graveyard; ~ **de coches** scrap yard

cemento [θe'mento] nm cement; (hormigón)
concrete; (Am: cola) glue

CEN nm abr (Esp) = **Consejo de Economía
Nacional**

cena ['θena] nf evening meal, dinner

cenagal [θena'ɣal] nm bog, quagmire

cenar [θe'nar] vt to have for dinner, dine on
■ vi to have dinner, dine

cencerro [θen'θerro] nm cowbell; **estar
como un** ~ (fam) to be round the bend

cenicero [θeni'θero] nm ashtray

ceniciento, -a [θeni'θjento, a] adj ash-
coloured, ashen

cenit [θe'nit] nm zenith

ceniza [θe'niθa] nf ash, ashes pl

censar [θen'sar] vt to take a census of

censo ['θenso] nm census; ~ **electoral**
electoral roll

censor [θen'sor] nm censor; ~ **de cuentas**
(Com) auditor; ~ **jurado de cuentas**
chartered (Brit) o certified public (US)
accountant

censura [θen'sura] nf (Pol) censorship; (moral)
censure, criticism

censurable [θensuˈraβle] adj reprehensible
censurar [θensuˈrar] vt (idea) to censure; (cortar: película) to censor
centavo [θenˈtaβo] nm hundredth (part); (Am) cent
centella [θenˈteʎa] nf spark
centellear [θenteʎeˈar] vi (metal) to gleam; (estrella) to twinkle; (fig) to sparkle
centelleo [θenteˈʎeo] nm gleam(ing); twinkling; sparkling
centena [θenˈtena] nf hundred
centenar [θenteˈnar] nm hundred
centenario, -a [θenteˈnarjo, a] adj one hundred years old ■ nm centenary
centeno [θenˈteno] nm rye
centésimo, -a [θenˈtesimo, a] adj, nm hundredth
centígrado [θenˈtiɣraðo] adj centigrade
centigramo [θentiˈɣramo] nm centigramme
centilitro [θentiˈlitro] nm centilitre (Brit), centiliter (US)
centímetro [θenˈtimetro] nm centimetre (Brit), centimeter (US)
céntimo, -a [ˈθentimo, a] adj hundredth ■ nm cent
centinela [θentiˈnela] nm sentry, guard
centollo, -a [θenˈtoʎo, a] nm/f large (o spider) crab
central [θenˈtral] adj central ■ nf head office; (Tec) plant; (Telec) exchange; ~ nuclear nuclear power station
centralice etc [θentraˈliθe] vb ver **centralizar**
centralita [θentraˈlita] nf switchboard
centralización [θentraliθaˈθjon] nf centralization
centralizar [θentraliˈθar] vt to centralize
centrar [θenˈtrar] vt to centre
céntrico, -a [ˈθentriko, a] adj central
centrifugar [θentrifuˈɣar] vt (ropa) to spin-dry
centrífugo, -a [θenˈtrifuɣo, a] adj centrifugal
centrifugue etc [θentriˈfuɣe] vb ver **centrifugar**
centrista [θenˈtrista] adj centre cpd
centro [ˈθentro] nm centre; **ser de** ~ (Pol) to be a moderate; ~ **de acogida (para niños)** children's home; ~ **de beneficios** (Com) profit centre; ~ **cívico** community centre; ~ **comercial** shopping centre; ~ **de informática** computer centre; ~ **(de determinación) de costos** (Com) cost centre; ~ **delantero** (Deporte) centre forward; ~ **docente** teaching institution; ~ **juvenil** youth club; ~ **de llamadas** call centre; ~ **social** community centre
centroafricano, -a [θentroafriˈkano, a] adj: **la República Centroafricana** the Central

African Republic
centroamericano, -a [θentroameriˈkano, a] adj, nm/f Central American
centrocampista [θentrokamˈpista] nm/f (Deporte) midfielder
ceñido, -a [θeˈɲiðo, a] adj tight
ceñir [θeˈɲir] vt (rodear) to encircle, surround; (ajustar) to fit (tightly); (apretar) to tighten; **ceñirse** vr: **ceñirse algo** to put sth on; **ceñirse al asunto** to stick to the matter in hand
ceño [ˈθeɲo] nm frown, scowl; **fruncir el** ~ to frown, knit one's brow
CEOE nf abr (= Confederación Española de Organizaciones Empresariales) ≈ CBI (Brit)
cepa [ˈθepa] nf (de vid, fig) stock; (Bio) strain
CEPAL [θeˈpal] nf abr (= Comisión Económica de las Naciones Unidas para la América Latina) ECLA
cepillar [θepiˈʎar] vt to brush; (madera) to plane (down)
cepillo [θeˈpiʎo] nm brush; (para madera) plane; (Rel) poor box, alms box; ~ **de dientes** toothbrush
cepo [ˈθepo] nm (de caza) trap
CEPSA [ˈθepsa] nf abr (Com) = **Compañía Española de Petróleos, S.A.**
CEPYME nf abr = **Confederación Española de la Pequeña y Mediana Empresa**
cera [ˈθera] nf wax; ~ **de abejas** beeswax
cerámica [θeˈramika] nf pottery; (arte) ceramics sg
ceramista [θeraˈmista] nm/f potter
cerbatana [θerβaˈtana] nf blowpipe
cerca [ˈθerka] nf fence ■ adv near, nearby, close; **por aquí** ~ nearby ■ prep: ~ **de** (cantidad) nearly, about; (distancia) near, close to ■ nmpl: **cercas** foreground sg
cercado [θerˈkaðo] nm enclosure
cercanía [θerkaˈnia] nf nearness, closeness; **cercanías** nfpl outskirts, suburbs; **tren de cercanías** commuter o local train
cercano, -a [θerˈkano, a] adj close, near; (pueblo etc) nearby; **C~ Oriente** Near East
cercar [θerˈkar] vt to fence in; (rodear) to surround
cerciorar [θerθjoˈrar] vt (asegurar) to assure; **cerciorarse** vr: **cerciorarse (de)** (descubrir) to find out (about); (asegurarse) to make sure (of)
cerco [ˈθerko] nm (Agr) enclosure; (Am) fence; (Mil) siege
cerda [ˈθerða] nf (de cepillo) bristle; (Zool) sow
cerdada [θerˈðaða] nf (fam): **hacer una** ~ **a algn** to play a dirty trick on sb
Cerdeña [θerˈðeɲa] nf Sardinia
cerdo [ˈθerðo] nm pig; **carne de** ~ pork
cereal [θereˈal] nm cereal; **cereales** nmpl cereals, grain sg

cerebral [θere'βral] *adj* (*tb fig*) cerebral; (*tumor*) brain *cpd*

cerebro [θe'reβro] *nm* brain; (*fig*) brains *pl*; **ser un ~** (*fig*) to be brilliant

ceremonia [θere'monja] *nf* ceremony; **reunión de ~** formal meeting; **hablar sin ~** to speak plainly

ceremonial [θeremo'njal] *adj, nm* ceremonial

ceremonioso, -a [θeremo'njoso, a] *adj* ceremonious; (*cumplido*) formal

cereza [θe'reθa] *nf* cherry

cerezo [θe'reθo] *nm* cherry tree

cerilla [θe'riʎa] *nf*, **cerillo** [se'riʎo] *nm* (*Am*) match

cerner [θer'ner] *vt* to sift, sieve; **cernerse** *vr* to hover

cero ['θero] *nm* nothing, zero; (*Deporte*) nil; **8 grados bajo ~** 8 degrees below zero; **a partir de ~** from scratch

cerque *etc* ['θerke] *vb ver* **cercar**

cerrado, -a [θe'rraðo, a] *adj* closed, shut; (*con llave*) locked; (*tiempo*) cloudy, overcast; (*curva*) sharp; (*acento*) thick, broad; **a puerta cerrada** (*Jur*) in camera

cerradura [θerra'ðura] *nf* (*acción*) closing; (*mecanismo*) lock

cerrajería [θerraxe'ria] *nf* locksmith's craft; (*tienda*) locksmith's (shop)

cerrajero, -a [θerra'xero, a] *nm/f* locksmith

cerrar [θe'rrar] *vt* to close, shut; (*paso, carretera*) to close; (*grifo*) to turn off; (*trato, cuenta, negocio*) to close ■ *vi* to close, shut; (*la noche*) to come down; **~ con llave** to lock; **~ el sistema** (*Inform*) to close o shut down the system; **~ un trato** to strike a bargain; **cerrarse** *vr* to close, shut; (*herida*) to heal

cerro ['θerro] *nm* hill; **andar por las cerros de Úbeda** to wander from the point, digress

cerrojo [θe'rroxo] *nm* (*herramienta*) bolt; (*de puerta*) latch

certamen [θer'tamen] *nm* competition, contest

certero, -a [θer'tero, a] *adj* accurate

certeza [θer'teθa], **certidumbre** [θerti'ðumbre] *nf* certainty

certificación [θertifika'θjon] *nf* certification; (*Jur*) affidavit

certificado, -a [θertifi'kaðo, a] *adj* certified; (*Correos*) registered ■ *nm* certificate

certificar [θertifi'kar] *vt* (*asegurar, atestar*) to certify

certifique *etc* [θerti'fike] *vb ver* **certificar**

cervatillo [θerβa'tiʎo] *nm* fawn

cervecería [θerβeθe'ria] *nf* (*fábrica*) brewery; (*taberna*) public house

cerveza [θer'βeθa] *nf* beer; **~ de barril** draught beer

cervical [θerβi'kal] *adj* cervical

cerviz [θer'βiθ] *nf* nape of the neck

cesación [θesa'θjon] *nf* cessation, suspension

cesante [θe'sante] *adj* redundant; (*Am*) unemployed; (*ministro*) outgoing; (*diplomático*) recalled ■ *nm/f* redundant worker

cesantía [θesan'tia] *nf* (*Am*) unemployment

cesar [θe'sar] *vi* to cease, stop; (*de un trabajo*) to leave ■ *vt* (*en el trabajo*) to dismiss; (*alto cargo*) to remove from office

cesárea [θe'sarea] *nf* Caesarean (section)

cese ['θese] *nm* (*de trabajo*) dismissal; (*de pago*) suspension

CESID [θe'siθ] *nm abr* (*Esp*: = *Centro Superior de Investigación de la Defensa Nacional*) military intelligence service

cesión [θe'sjon] *nf*: **~ de bienes** surrender of property

césped ['θespeð] *nm* grass, lawn

cesta ['θesta] *nf* basket

cesto ['θesto] *nm* (*large*) basket, hamper

cetrería [θetre'ria] *nf* falconry

cetrino, -a [θe'trino, a] *adj* (*tez*) sallow

cetro ['θetro] *nm* sceptre

Ceuta [θe'uta] *nf* Ceuta

ceutí [θeu'ti] *adj* of o from Ceuta ■ *nm/f* native o inhabitant of Ceuta

C.F. *nm abr* (= *Club de Fútbol*) F.C.

CFC *nm abr* (= *clorofluorocarbono*) CFC

cfr *abr* (= *confróntese, compárese*) cf

cg *abr* (= *centigramo*) cg

CGPJ *nm abr* (= *Consejo General del Poder Judicial*) governing body of Spanish legal system

CGS *nm abr* (*Guatemala*: *El Salvador*) = **Confederación General de Sindicatos**

CGT *nf abr* (*Colombia*: *México*: *Nicaragua*: *Esp*: = **Confederación General de Trabajadores**) (*Argentina*: = **Confederación General del Trabajo**)

Ch, ch [tʃe] *nf* former letter in the Spanish alphabet

chabacano, -a [tʃaβa'kano, a] *adj* vulgar, coarse

chabola [tʃa'βola] *nf* shack; **chabolas** *nfpl* shanty town *sg*

chabolismo [tʃaβo'lismo] *nm*: **el problema del ~** the problem of substandard housing, the shanty town problem

chacal [tʃa'kal] *nm* jackal

chacarero [tʃaka'rero] *nm* (*Am*) small farmer

chacha ['tʃatʃa] *nf* (*fam*) maid

cháchara ['tʃatʃara] *nf* chatter; **estar de ~** to chatter away

chacra ['tʃakra] *nf* (*Am*) smallholding

chafar [tʃa'far] *vt* (*aplastar*) to crush, flatten; (*arruinar*) to ruin

C

71

chaflán [tʃaˈflan] *nm* (*Tec*) bevel
chal [tʃal] *nm* shawl
chalado, -a [tʃaˈlaðo, a] *adj* (*fam*) crazy
chalé (*pl* ~**s**) [tʃaˈle, tʃaˈles] *nm* = **chalet**
chaleco [tʃaˈleko] *nm* waistcoat, vest (*US*); ~
antibala bulletproof vest; ~ **salvavidas** life
jacket; ~ **reflectante** (*Aut*) high-visibility
vest
chalet (*pl* **chalets**) [tʃaˈle, tʃaˈles] *nm* villa,
≈ detached house; ~ **adosado** semi-detached
house
chalupa [tʃaˈlupa] *nf* launch, boat
chamaco, -a [tʃaˈmako, a] *nm/f* (*Am*) boy/girl
chamarra [tʃaˈmarra] *nf* sheepskin jacket;
(*Am*: *poncho*) blanket
champán [tʃamˈpan] *nm*, **champaña**
[tʃamˈpaɲa] *nm* champagne
champiñón [tʃampiˈɲon] *nm* mushroom
champú [tʃamˈpu] (*pl* ~**es** *o* ~**s**) *nm* shampoo
chamuscar [tʃamusˈkar] *vt* to scorch, singe
chamusque *etc* [tʃaˈmuske] *vb ver* **chamuscar**
chamusquina [tʃamusˈkina] *nf* singeing
chance [ˈtʃanθe] *nm* (*a veces nf*) (*Am*) chance,
opportunity
chanchada [tʃanˈtʃaða] *nf* (*Am fam*) dirty trick
chancho, -a [ˈtʃantʃo, a] *nm/f* (*Am*) pig
chanchullo [tʃanˈtʃuʎo] *nm* (*fam*) fiddle,
wangle
chancla [ˈtʃankla] *nf*, **chancleta** [tʃanˈkleta]
nf flip-flop; (*zapato viejo*) old shoe
chandal [tʃanˈdal] *nm* tracksuit; ~ **(de tactel)**
shellsuit
chantaje [tʃanˈtaxe] *nm* blackmail; **hacer ~ a**
uno to blackmail sb
chanza [ˈtʃanθa] *nf* joke
chao [tʃao] *excl* (*fam*) cheerio
chapa [ˈtʃapa] *nf* (*de metal*) plate, sheet; (*de
madera*) board, panel; (*de botella*) bottle top;
(*insignia*) (*lapel*) badge; (*Am*: *Auto*: *tb*: **chapa de
matrícula**) number (*Brit*) *o* license (*US*) plate;
(*Am*: *cerradura*) lock; **de 3 chapas** (*madera*)
3-ply
chapado, -a [tʃaˈpaðo, a] *adj* (*metal*) plated;
(*muebles etc*) finished
chaparro, -a [tʃaˈparro, a] *adj* squat; (*Am*:
bajito) short
chaparrón [tʃapaˈrron] *nm* downpour,
cloudburst
chapotear [tʃapoteˈar] *vt* to sponge down
■ *vi* (*fam*) to splash about
chapucero, -a [tʃapuˈθero, a] *adj* rough,
crude ■ *nm/f* bungler
chapurrar [tʃapurˈrar], **chapurrear**
[tʃapurreˈar] *vt* (*idioma*) to speak badly
chapuza [tʃaˈpuθa] *nf* botched job
chapuzón [tʃapuˈθon] *nm*: **darse un ~** to go
for a dip

chaqué [tʃaˈke] *nm* morning coat
chaqueta [tʃaˈketa] *nf* jacket; **cambiar la ~**
(*fig*) to change sides
chaquetón [tʃakeˈton] *nm* three-quarter-
length coat
charca [ˈtʃarka] *nf* pond, pool
charco [ˈtʃarko] *nm* pool, puddle
charcutería [tʃarkuteˈria] *nf* (*tienda*) *shop
selling chiefly pork meat products*; (*productos*)
cooked pork meats *pl*
charla [ˈtʃarla] *nf* talk, chat; (*conferencia*)
lecture
charlar [tʃarˈlar] *vi* to talk, chat
charlatán, -ana [tʃarlaˈtan, ana] *nm/f*
chatterbox; (*estafador*) trickster
charol¹ [tʃaˈrol] *nm* varnish; (*cuero*) patent
leather
charol² [tʃaˈrol] *nm* (*Am*), **charola** [tʃaˈrola]
nf (*Am*) tray
charqui [ˈtʃarki] *nm* (*Am*) dried beef, jerky (*US*)
charro, -a [ˈtʃarro, a] *adj* Salamancan; (*Am*)
Mexican; (*ropa*) loud, gaudy; (*Am*: *costumbres*)
traditional ■ *nm/f* Salamancan; Mexican
chárter [ˈtʃarter] *adj inv*: **vuelo ~** charter
flight
chascarrillo [tʃaskaˈrriʎo] *nm* (*fam*) funny
story
chasco [ˈtʃasko] *nm* (*broma*) trick, joke;
(*desengaño*) disappointment
chasis [ˈtʃasis] *nm inv* (*Auto*) chassis; (*Foto*)
plate holder
chasquear [tʃaskeˈar] *vt* (*látigo*) to crack;
(*lengua*) to click
chasquido [tʃasˈkiðo] *nm* (*de lengua*) click;
(*de látigo*) crack
chat [tʃat] *nm* (*Internet*) chat room
chatarra [tʃaˈtarra] *nf* scrap (metal)
chatero, -a [tʃaˈtero, a] *adj* chat *cpd* ■ *nm/f*
chat-room user
chato, -a [ˈtʃato, a] *adj* flat; (*nariz*) snub ■ *nm*
wine tumbler; **beber unos chatos** to have a
few drinks
chau [tʃau], **chaucito** [tʃauˈsito] *excl* (*fam*)
cheerio
chauvinismo [tʃoβiˈnismo] *nm* chauvinism
chauvinista [tʃoβiˈnista] *adj, nm/f* chauvinist
chaval, a [tʃaˈβal, a] *nm/f* kid (*fam*), lad/lass
chavo [ˈtʃaβo] *nm* (*Am*: *fam*) bloke (*Brit*), guy
checo, -a [ˈtʃeko, a] *adj, nm/f* Czech ■ *nm*
(*Ling*) Czech
checoeslovaco, -a [tʃekoesloˈβako, a],
checoslovaco, -a [tʃekosloˈβako, a] *adj, nm/f*
Czech, Czechoslovak
Checoeslovaquia [tʃekoesloˈβakja],
Checoslovaquia [tʃekosloˈβakja] *nf*
Czechoslovakia
chepa [ˈtʃepa] *nf* hump

cheque ['tʃeke] nm cheque (Brit), check (US); ~ **abierto/en blanco/cruzado** open/blank/crossed cheque; ~ **al portador** cheque payable to bearer; ~ **de viajero** traveller's cheque

chequeo [tʃe'keo] nm (Med) check-up; (Auto) service

chequera [tʃe'kera] nf (Am) chequebook (Brit), checkbook (US)

chévere ['tʃeβere] adj (Am) great, fabulous (fam)

chicano, -a [tʃi'kano, a] adj, nm/f chicano, Mexican-American

chicha ['tʃitʃa] nf (Am) maize liquor

chícharo ['tʃitʃaro] nm (Am) pea

chicharra [tʃi'tʃarra] nf harvest bug, cicada

chicharrón [tʃitʃa'rron] nm (pork) crackling

chichón [tʃi'tʃon] nm bump, lump

chicle ['tʃikle] nm chewing gum

chico, -a ['tʃiko, a] adj small, little ■ nm/f child; (muchacho) boy; (muchacha) girl

chicote [tʃi'kote] nm (Am) whip

chiflado, -a [tʃi'flaðo, a] adj (fam) crazy, round the bend ■ nm/f nutcase

chiflar [tʃi'flar] vt to hiss, boo ■ vi (esp Am) to whistle

Chile ['tʃile] nm Chile

chile ['tʃile] nm chilli, pepper

chileno, -a [tʃi'leno, a] adj, nm/f Chilean

chillar [tʃi'ʎar] vi (persona) to yell, scream; (animal salvaje) to howl; (cerdo) to squeal; (puerta) to creak

chillido [tʃi'ʎiðo] nm (de persona) yell, scream; (de animal) howl; (de frenos) screech(ing)

chillón, -ona [tʃi'ʎon, ona] adj (niño) noisy; (color) loud, gaudy

chimenea [tʃime'nea] nf chimney; (hogar) fireplace

chimpancé (pl ~s) [tʃimpan'θe, tʃimpan'θes] nm chimpanzee

China ['tʃina] nf: (**la**) ~ China

china ['tʃina] nf pebble

chinchar [tʃin'tʃar] (fam) vt to pester, annoy; **chincharse** vr to get cross; **¡chínchate!** tough!

chinche ['tʃintʃe] nf bug; (Tec) drawing pin (Brit), thumbtack (US) ■ nm/f nuisance, pest

chincheta [tʃin'tʃeta] nf drawing pin (Brit), thumbtack (US)

chinchorro [tʃin'tʃorro] nm (Am) hammock

chingado, -a [tʃin'gaðo, a] adj (esp Am fam!) lousy, bloody (!); **hijo de la chingada** bastard (!), son of a bitch (US!)

chingar [tʃin'gar] vt (Am: fam!) to fuck (up) (!), screw (up) (!); **chingarse** vr (Am: emborracharse) to get pissed (Brit), get plastered (!: fracasar) to fail

chingue etc ['tʃinge] vb ver **chingar**

chino, -a ['tʃino, a] adj, nm/f Chinese ■ nm (Ling) Chinese; (Culin) chinois, conical strainer

chip [tʃip] nm (Inform) chip

chipirón [tʃipi'ron] nm squid

Chipre ['tʃipre] nf Cyprus

chipriota [tʃi'prjota], **chipriote** [tʃi'prjote] adj Cypriot, Cyprian ■ nm/f Cypriot

chiquillada [tʃiki'ʎaða] nf childish prank; (Am: chiquillos) kids pl

chiquillo, -a [tʃi'kiʎo, a] nm/f kid (fam), youngster, child

chiquito, -a [tʃi'kito, a] adj very small, tiny ■ nm/f kid (fam)

chirigota [tʃiri'ɣota] nf joke

chirimbolo [tʃirim'bolo] nm thingummyjig (fam)

chirimoya [tʃiri'moja] nf custard apple

chiringuito [tʃirin'gito] nm refreshment stall o stand

chiripa [tʃi'ripa] nf fluke; **por** ~ by chance

chirona [tʃi'rona], **chirola** (Am) [tʃi'rola] nf (fam) clink, jail

chirriar [tʃi'rrjar] vi (goznes) to creak, squeak; (pájaros) to chirp, sing

chirrido [tʃi'rriðo] nm creak(ing), squeak(ing); (de pájaro) chirp(ing)

chis [tʃis] excl sh!

chisme ['tʃisme] nm (habladurías) piece of gossip; (fam: objeto) thingummyjig

chismoso, -a [tʃis'moso, a] adj gossiping ■ nm/f gossip

chispa ['tʃispa] nf spark; (fig) sparkle; (ingenio) wit; (fam) drunkenness

chispeante [tʃispe'ante] adj (tb fig) sparkling

chispear [tʃispe'ar] vi to spark; (lloviznar) to drizzle

chisporrotear [tʃisporrote'ar] vi (fuego) to throw out sparks; (leña) to crackle; (aceite) to hiss, splutter

chistar [tʃistar] vi: **no** ~ not to say a word

chiste ['tʃiste] nm joke, funny story; ~ **verde** blue joke

chistera [tʃis'tera] nf top hat

chistoso, -a [tʃis'toso, a] adj (gracioso) funny, amusing; (bromista) witty

chistu ['tʃistu] nm = **txistu**

chivarse [tʃi'βarse] vr (fam) to grass

chivatazo [tʃiβa'taθo] nm (fam) tip-off; **dar** ~ to inform

chivo, -a ['tʃiβo, a] nm/f (billy/nanny-)goat; ~ **expiatorio** scapegoat

chocante [tʃo'kante] adj startling; (extraño) odd; (ofensivo) shocking

chocar [tʃo'kar] vi (coches etc) to collide, crash; (Mil, fig) to clash ■ vt to shock; (sorprender) to startle; **~ con** to collide with; (fig) to run into, run up against; **¡chócala!** (fam) put it there!

chochear [tʃoˈtʃeˈar] vi to dodder, be senile

chocho, -a [ˈtʃotʃo, a] adj doddering, senile; (fig) soft, doting

chocolate [tʃokoˈlate] adj chocolate ■ nm chocolate; (fam) dope, marijuana

chocolatería [tʃokolateˈria] nf chocolate factory (o shop)

chófer [ˈtʃofer], **chofer** [tʃoˈfer] (esp Am) nm driver

chollo [ˈtʃoʎo] nm (fam) bargain, snip

chomba [ˈtʃomba], **chompa** [ˈtʃompa] nf (Am) jumper, sweater

chopo [ˈtʃopo] nm black poplar

choque etc [ˈtʃoke] vb ver **chocar** ■ nm (impacto) impact; (golpe) jolt; (Auto) crash; (fig) conflict

chorizo [tʃoˈriθo] nm hard pork sausage (type of salami); (ladrón) crook

chorra [ˈtʃorra] nf luck

chorrada [tʃoˈrraða] nf (fam): **¡es una ~!** that's crap! (!); **decir chorradas** to talk crap (!)

chorrear [tʃorreˈar] vt to pour ■ vi to gush (out), spout (out); (gotear) to drip, trickle

chorreras [tʃoˈrreras] nfpl frill sg

chorro [ˈtʃorro] nm jet; (caudalito) dribble, trickle; (fig) stream; **salir a chorros** to gush forth; **con propulsión a ~** jet-propelled

chotearse [tʃoteˈarse] vr to joke

choto [ˈtʃoto] nm (cabrito) kid

chovinismo [tʃoβiˈnismo] nm = **chauvinismo**

chovinista [tʃoβiˈnista] adj, nm/f = **chauvinista**

choza [ˈtʃoθa] nf hut, shack

chubasco [tʃuˈβasko] nm squall

chubasquero [tʃuβasˈkero] nm oilskins pl

chuchería [tʃutʃeˈria] nf trinket

chucho [ˈtʃutʃo] nm (Zool) mongrel

chufa [ˈtʃufa] nf chufa, earth almond, tiger nut; **horchata de chufas** drink made from chufas

chuleta [tʃuˈleta] nf chop, cutlet; (Escol etc: fam) crib

chulo, -a [ˈtʃulo, a] adj (encantador) charming; (aire) proud; (pey) fresh; (fam: estupendo) great, fantastic ■ nm (pícaro) rascal; (madrileño) working-class Madrilenian; (rufián: tb: **chulo de putas**) pimp

chumbera [tʃumˈbera] nf prickly pear

chungo, -a [ˈtʃungo, a] (fam) adj lousy ■ nf: **estar de chunga** to be in a merry mood

chupa [ˈtʃupa] nf (fam) jacket

chupado, -a [tʃuˈpaðo, a] adj (delgado) skinny, gaunt; **está ~** (fam) it's simple, it's dead easy

chupar [tʃuˈpar] vt to suck; (absorber) to absorb; **chuparse** vr to grow thin; **para chuparse los dedos** mouthwatering

chupatintas [tʃupaˈtintas] nm inv penpusher

chupe [ˈtʃupe] nm (Am) stew

chupete [tʃuˈpete] nm dummy (Brit), pacifier (US)

chupetón [tʃupeˈton] nm suck

churrasco [tʃuˈrrasko] nm (Am) barbecue, barbecued meat

churrería [tʃurreˈria] nf stall or shop which sells "churros"

churrete [tʃuˈrrete] nm grease spot

churretón [tʃurreˈton] nm stain

churrigueresco, -a [tʃurrigeˈresko, a] adj (Arq) baroque; (fig) excessively ornate

churro, -a [ˈtʃurro, a] adj coarse ■ nm (Culin) (type of) fritter; see note; (chapuza) botch, mess

● **CHURRO**

Churros, long fritters made with flour and water, are very popular in much of Spain and are often eaten with thick hot chocolate, either for breakfast or as a snack. In Madrid, they eat a thicker variety of churro called porra.

churruscar [tʃurrusˈkar] vt to fry crisp

churrusque etc [tʃuˈrruske] vb ver **churruscar**

churumbel [tʃurumˈbel] nm (fam) kid

chus [tʃus] excl: **no decir ni ~ ni mus** not to say a word

chusco, -a [ˈtʃusko, a] adj funny

chusma [ˈtʃusma] nf rabble, mob

chutar [tʃuˈtar] vi (Deporte) to shoot (at goal); **esto va que chuta** it's going fine

chuzo [ˈtʃuθo] nm: **llueve a chuzos, llueven chuzos de punta** it's raining cats and dogs

C.I. nm abr = **coeficiente intelectual** o **de inteligencia**

Cía abr (= compañía) Co.

cianuro [θjaˈnuro] nm cyanide

ciática [ˈθjatika] nf sciatica

cibercafé [θiβerkaˈfe] nm cybercafé

ciberespacio [θiβeresˈpaθjo] nm cyberspace

cibernauta [θiβerˈnauta] nmf cybernaut

cibernética [θiβerˈnetika] nf cybernetics sg

cicatrice etc [θikaˈtriθe] vb ver **cicatrizar**

cicatriz [θikaˈtriθ] nf scar

cicatrizar [θikatriˈθar] vt to heal; **cicatrizarse** vr to heal (up), form a scar

cíclico, -a [ˈθikliko, a] adj cyclical

ciclismo [θiˈklismo] nm cycling

ciclista [θiˈklista] nm/f cyclist

ciclo [ˈθiklo] nm cycle

ciclomotor [θiklomoˈtor] nm moped

ciclón [θi'klon] *nm* cyclone
cicloturismo [θiklotu'rismo] *nm* touring by bicycle
cicuta [θi'kuta] *nf* hemlock
ciego, -a *etc* ['θjeɣo, a] *vb ver* **cegar** ■ *adj* blind ■ *nm/f* blind man/woman; **a ciegas** blindly; **me puse ciega mariscos** *(fam)* I stuffed myself with seafood
ciegue *etc* ['θjeɣe] *vb ver* **cegar**
cielo ['θjelo] *nm* sky; *(Rel)* heaven; *(Arq: tb:* **cielo raso)** ceiling; **¡cielos!** good heavens!; **ver el ~ abierto** to see one's chance
ciempiés [θjem'pjes] *nm inv* centipede
cien [θjen] *num ver* **ciento**
ciénaga ['θjenaɣa] *nf* marsh, swamp
ciencia ['θjenθja] *nf* science; **ciencias** *nfpl* science *sg*; **saber algo a ~ cierta** to know sth for certain
ciencia-ficción ['θjenθjafik'θjon] *nf* science fiction
cieno ['θjeno] *nm* mud, mire
científico, -a [θjen'tifiko, a] *adj* scientific ■ *nm/f* scientist
ciento ['θjento], **cien** *num* hundred; **pagar al 10 por ~** to pay at 10 per cent
cierne *etc* ['θjerne] *vb ver* **cerner** ■ *nm*: **en ~** in blossom; **en ~(s)** *(fig)* in its infancy
cierre *etc* ['θjerre] *vb ver* **cerrar** ■ *nm* closing, shutting; *(con llave)* locking; *(Radio: TV)* close down; **~ de cremallera** zip (fastener); **precios de ~** *(Bolsa)* closing prices; **~ del sistema** *(Inform)* system shutdown
cierto, -a ['θjerto, a] *adj* sure, certain; *(un tal)* a certain; *(correcto)* right, correct; **~ hombre** a certain man; **ciertas personas** certain *o* some people; **sí, es ~** yes, that's correct; **por ~** by the way; **lo ~ es que ...** the fact is that ...; **estar en lo ~** to be right
ciervo ['θjerβo] *nm (Zool)* deer; *(: macho)* stag
cierzo ['θjerθo] *nm* north wind
CIES *nm abr* = **Consejo Interamericano Económico y Social**
cifra ['θifra] *nf* number, figure; *(cantidad)* number, quantity; *(secreta)* code; **~ global** lump sum; **~ de negocios** *(Com)* turnover; **en cifras redondas** in round figures; **~ de referencia** *(Com)* bench mark; **~ de ventas** *(Com)* sales figures
cifrado, -a [θi'fraðo, a] *adj* in code
cifrar [θi'frar] *vt* to code, write in code; *(resumir)* to abridge; *(calcular)* to reckon
cigala [θi'ɣala] *nf* Norway lobster
cigarra [θi'ɣarra] *nf* cicada
cigarrera [θiɣa'rrera] *nf* cigar case
cigarrillo [θiɣa'rriʎo] *nm* cigarette
cigarro [θi'ɣarro] *nm* cigarette; *(puro)* cigar
cigüeña [θi'ɣweɲa] *nf* stork

cilíndrico, -a [θi'lindriko, a] *adj* cylindrical
cilindro [θi'lindro] *nm* cylinder
cima ['θima] *nf (de montaña)* top, peak; *(de árbol)* top; *(fig)* height
címbalo ['θimbalo] *nm* cymbal
cimbrear [θimbre'ar] *vt* to brandish; **cimbrearse** *vr* to sway
cimentar [θimen'tar] *vt* to lay the foundations of; *(fig: reforzar)* to strengthen; *(: fundar)* to found
cimiento *etc* [θi'mjento] *vb ver* **cimentar** ■ *nm* foundation
cinc [θink] *nm* zinc
cincel [θin'θel] *nm* chisel
cincelar [θinθe'lar] *vt* to chisel
cincha ['θintʃa] *nf* girth, saddle strap
cincho ['θintʃo] *nm* sash, belt
cinco ['θinko] *num* five; *(fecha)* fifth; **las ~** five o'clock; **no estar en sus ~** *(fam)* to be off one's rocker
cincuenta [θin'kwenta] *num* fifty
cincuentón, -ona [θinkwen'ton, ona] *adj, nm/f* fifty-year-old
cine ['θine] *nm* cinema; **el ~ mudo** silent films *pl*; **hacer ~** to make films
cineasta [θine'asta] *nm/f (director de cine)* film-maker *o* director
cine-club ['θine'klub] *nm* film club
cinéfilo, -a [θi'nefilo, a] *nm/f* film buff
cinematográfico, -a [θinemato'ɣrafiko, a] *adj* cine-, film *cpd*
cínico, -a ['θiniko, a] *adj* cynical; *(descarado)* shameless ■ *nm/f* cynic
cinismo [θi'nismo] *nm* cynicism
cinta ['θinta] *nf* band, strip; *(de tela)* ribbon; *(película)* reel; *(de máquina de escribir)* ribbon; *(métrica)* tape measure; *(magnetofónica)* tape; **~ adhesiva** sticky tape; **~ aislante** insulating tape; **~ de carbón** carbon ribbon; **~ magnética** *(Inform)* magnetic tape; **~ métrica** tape measure; **~ de múltiples impactos** *(en impresora)* multistrike ribbon; **~ de tela** *(para máquina de escribir)* fabric ribbon; **~ transportadora** conveyor belt
cinto ['θinto] *nm* belt, girdle
cintura [θin'tura] *nf* waist; *(medida)* waistline
cinturón [θintu'ron] *nm* belt; *(fig)* belt, zone; **~ salvavidas** lifebelt; **~ de seguridad** safety belt
ciña *etc* ['θiɲa], **ciñendo** *etc* [θi'ɲenðo] *vb ver* **ceñir**
ciprés [θi'pres] *nm* cypress (tree)
circo ['θirko] *nm* circus
circuito [θir'kwito] *nm* circuit; *(Deporte)* lap; **TV por ~ cerrado** closed-circuit TV; **~ experimental** *(Inform)* breadboard; **~ impreso** printed circuit; **~ lógico** *(Inform)*

logical circuit

circulación [θirkula'θjon] *nf* circulation; *(Auto)* traffic; **"cerrado a la ~ rodada"** "closed to vehicles"

circular [θirku'lar] *adj, nf* circular ■ *vt* to circulate ■ *vi* to circulate; *(dinero)* to be in circulation; *(Auto)* to drive; *(autobús)* to run

círculo ['θirkulo] *nm* circle; *(centro)* clubhouse; *(Pol)* political group

circuncidar [θirkunθi'dar] *vt* to circumcise

circunciso, -a [θirkun'θiso, a] *pp de* **circuncidar**

circundante [θirkun'dante] *adj* surrounding

circundar [θirkun'dar] *vt* to surround

circunferencia [θirkunfe'renθja] *nf* circumference

circunloquio [θirkun'lokjo] *nm* circumlocution

circunscribir [θirkunskri'βir] *vt* to circumscribe; **circunscribirse** *vr* to be limited

circunscripción [θirkunskrip'θjon] *nf* division; *(Pol)* constituency

circunscrito [θirkuns'krito] *pp de* **circunscribir**

circunspección [θirkunspek'θjon] *nf* circumspection, caution

circunspecto, -a [θirkuns'pekto, a] *adj* circumspect, cautious

circunstancia [θirkuns'tanθja] *nf* circumstance; **circunstancias agravantes/ extenuantes** aggravating/extenuating circumstances; **estar a la altura de las circunstancias** to rise to the occasion

circunvalación [θirkumbala'θjon] *nf*: **carretera de ~** ring road

cirio ['θirjo] *nm* (wax) candle

cirrosis [θi'rrosis] *nf* cirrhosis (of the liver)

ciruela [θi'rwela] *nf* plum; **~ pasa** prune

ciruelo [θi'rwelo] *nm* plum tree

cirugía [θiru'xia] *nf* surgery; **~ estética** o **plástica** plastic surgery

cirujano [θiru'xano] *nm* surgeon

cisco ['θisko] *nm*: **armar un ~** to kick up a row; **estar hecho ~** to be a wreck

cisma ['θisma] *nm* schism; *(Pol etc)* split

cisne ['θisne] *nm* swan; **canto de ~** swan song

cisterna [θis'terna] *nf* cistern, tank

cistitis [θis'titis] *nf* cystitis

cita ['θita] *nf* appointment, meeting; *(de novios)* date; *(referencia)* quotation; **acudir/ faltar a una ~** to turn up for/miss an appointment

citación [θita'θjon] *nf* (Jur) summons *sg*

citadino, -a [sita'ðino, a] *(Am) adj* urban ■ *nm/f* urban o city dweller

citar [θi'tar] *vt* to make an appointment with, arrange to meet; *(Jur)* to summons; *(un autor, texto)* to quote; **citarse** *vr*: **citarse con algn** to arrange to meet sb; **se citaron en el cine** they arranged to meet at the cinema

cítara ['θitara] *nf* zither

citología [θitolo'xia] *nf* smear test

cítrico, -a ['θitriko, a] *adj* citric ■ *nm*: **cítricos** citrus fruits

CiU *nm abr* (Pol) = **Convergència i Unió**

ciudad [θju'ðað] *nf* town; *(capital de país etc)* city; **~ universitaria** university campus; **C~ del Cabo** Cape Town; **la C~ Condal** Barcelona

ciudadanía [θjuðaða'nia] *nf* citizenship

ciudadano, -a [θjuða'ðano, a] *adj* civic ■ *nm/f* citizen

ciudadrealeño, -a [θjuðaðrea'leɲo, a] *adj* of o from Ciudad Real ■ *nm/f* native o inhabitant of Ciudad Real

cívico, -a ['θiβiko, a] *adj* civic; *(fig)* public-spirited

civil [θi'βil] *adj* civil ■ *nm* (guardia) policeman

civilice *etc* [θiβi'liθe] *vb ver* **civilizar**

civilización [θiβiliθa'θjon] *nf* civilization

civilizar [θiβili'θar] *vt* to civilize

civismo [θi'βismo] *nm* public spirit

cizaña [θi'θaɲa] *nf* (fig) discord; **sembrar ~** to sow discord

cl *abr* (= *centilitro*) cl.

clamar [kla'mar] *vt* to clamour for, cry out for ■ *vi* to cry out, clamour

clamor [kla'mor] *nm* (grito) cry, shout; *(fig)* clamour, protest

clamoroso, -a [klamo'roso, a] *adj* (éxito etc) resounding

clan [klan] *nm* clan; *(de gángsters)* gang

clandestinidad [klandestini'ðað] *nf* secrecy

clandestino, -a [klandes'tino, a] *adj* clandestine; *(Pol)* underground

clara ['klara] *nf* (de huevo) egg white

claraboya [klara'βoja] *nf* skylight

clarear [klare'ar] *vi* (el día) to dawn; (el cielo) to clear up, brighten up; **clarearse** *vr* to be transparent

clarete [kla'rete] *nm* rosé (wine)

claridad [klari'ðað] *nf* (del día) brightness; (de estilo) clarity

clarificar [klarifi'kar] *vt* to clarify

clarifique *etc* [klari'fike] *vb ver* **clarificar**

clarín [kla'rin] *nm* bugle

clarinete [klari'nete] *nm* clarinet

clarividencia [klariβi'ðenθja] *nf* clairvoyance; *(fig)* far-sightedness

claro, -a ['klaro, a] *adj* clear; *(luminoso)* bright; *(color)* light; *(evidente)* clear, evident; *(poco espeso)* thin ■ *nm* (en bosque) clearing

■ *adv* clearly ■ *excl* of course!; **hablar ~** (*fig*) to speak plainly; **a las claras** openly; **no sacamos nada en ~** we couldn't get anything definite

clase ['klase] *nf* class; (*tipo*) kind, sort; (*Escol etc*) class; (: *aula*) classroom; ~ **alta/media/obrera** upper/middle/working class; **dar clases** to teach

clásico, -a ['klasiko, a] *adj* classical; (*fig*) classic

clasificable [klasifi'kaβle] *adj* classifiable

clasificación [klasifika'θjon] *nf* classification; (*Deporte*) league (table); (*Com*) ratings *pl*

clasificador [klasifika'ðor] *nm* filing cabinet

clasificar [klasifi'kar] *vt* to classify; (*Inform*) to sort; **clasificarse** *vr* (*Deporte: en torneo*) to qualify

clasifique *etc* [klasi'fike] *vb ver* **clasificar**

clasista [kla'sista] *adj* (*fam: actitud*) snobbish

claudicar [klauði'kar] *vi* (*fig*) to back down

claudique *etc* [klau'ðike] *vb ver* **claudicar**

claustro ['klaustro] *nm* cloister; (*Univ*) staff; (*junta*) senate

claustrofobia [klaustro'foβja] *nf* claustrophobia

cláusula ['klausula] *nf* clause; ~ **de exclusión** (*Com*) exclusion clause

clausura [klau'sura] *nf* closing, closure

clausurar [klausu'rar] *vt* (*congreso etc*) to close, bring to a close; (*Pol etc*) to adjourn; (*cerrar*) to close (down)

clavado, -a [kla'βaðo, a] *adj* nailed ■ *excl* exactly!, precisely!

clavar [kla'βar] *vt* (*tablas etc*) to nail (together); (*con alfiler*) to pin; (*clavo*) to hammer in; (*cuchillo*) to stick, thrust; (*mirada*) to fix; (*fam: estafar*) to cheat

clave ['klaβe] *nf* key; (*Mus*) clef ■ *adj inv* key *cpd*; ~ **de acceso** password

clavel [kla'βel] *nm* carnation

clavicémbalo [klaβi'θembalo] *nm* harpsichord

clavicordio [klaβikor'ðjo] *nm* clavicord

clavícula [kla'βikula] *nf* collar bone

clavija [kla'βixa] *nf* peg, pin; (*Mus*) peg; (*Elec*) plug

clavo ['klaβo] *nm* (*de metal*) nail; (*Bot*) clove; **dar en el ~** (*fig*) to hit the nail on the head

claxon ['klakson] (*pl* **claxons**) *nm* horn; **tocar el ~** to sound one's horn

clemencia [kle'menθja] *nf* mercy, clemency

clemente [kle'mente] *adj* merciful, clement

cleptómano, -a [klep'tomano, a] *nm/f* kleptomaniac

clerical [kleri'kal] *adj* clerical

clérigo ['kleriɣo] *nm* priest, clergyman

clero ['klero] *nm* clergy

clic [klik] *nm* click; **hacer ~/doble ~ en algo** to click/double-click on sth

clicar [kli'kar] *vi* (*Inform*) to click; **clica en el icono** click on the icon

cliché [kli'tʃe] *nm* cliché; (*Tip*) stencil; (*Foto*) negative

cliente, -a ['kljente, a] *nm/f* client, customer

clientela [kljen'tela] *nf* clientele, customers *pl*; (*Com*) goodwill; (*Med*) patients *pl*

clima ['klima] *nm* climate

climatizado, -a [klimati'θaðo, a] *adj* air-conditioned

clímax ['klimaks] *nm inv* climax

clínico, -a ['kliniko, a] *adj* clinical ■ *nf* clinic; (*particular*) private hospital

clip (*pl* **clips**) [klip, klis] *nm* paper clip

cliquear [klike'ar] *vi* (*Inform*) to click; **cliquea en el icono** click on the icon

clítoris ['klitoris] *nm inv* clitoris

cloaca [klo'aka] *nf* sewer, drain

clonación [klona'θjon] *nf* cloning

clorhídrico, -a [klo'ridriko, a] *adj* hydrochloric

cloro ['kloro] *nm* chlorine

clorofila [kloro'fila] *nf* chlorophyl(l)

cloroformo [kloro'formo] *nm* chloroform

cloruro [klo'ruro] *nm* chloride; ~ **sódico** sodium chloride

club (*pl* **clubs** *o* **clubes**) [klub, klus, 'kluβes] *nm* club; ~ **de jóvenes** youth club

cm *abr* (= *centímetro*) cm

C.N.T. *nf abr* (*Esp*: = *Confederación Nacional de Trabajo*) *Anarchist Union Confederation*; (*Am*) = **Confederación Nacional de Trabajadores**

coacción [koak'θjon] *nf* coercion, compulsion

coaccionar [koakθjo'nar] *vt* to coerce, compel

coagular [koaɣu'lar] *vt*, **coagularse** *vr* (*sangre*) to clot; (*leche*) to curdle

coágulo [ko'aɣulo] *nm* clot

coalición [koali'θjon] *nf* coalition

coartada [koar'taða] *nf* alibi

coartar [koar'tar] *vt* to limit, restrict

coba [ko'βa] *nf*: **dar ~ a algn** to soft-soap sb

cobarde [ko'βarðe] *adj* cowardly ■ *nm/f* coward

cobardía [koβar'ðia] *nf* cowardice

cobaya [ko'βaja] *nf* guinea pig

cobertizo [koβer'tiθo] *nm* shelter

cobertor [koβer'tor] *nm* bedspread

cobertura [koβer'tura] *nf* cover; (*Com*) coverage; ~ **de dividendo** (*Com*) dividend cover; **estar fuera de ~** (*Telec*) to be out of range; **no tengo ~** (*Telec*) I'm out of range

cobija [ko'βixa] *nf* (*Am*) blanket

cobijar [koβi'xar] *vt* (*cubrir*) to cover; (*abrigar*) to shelter; **cobijarse** *vr* to take shelter
cobijo [ko'βixo] *nm* shelter
cobra ['koβra] *nf* cobra
cobrador, a [koβra'ðor, a] *nm/f* (*de autobús*) conductor/conductress; (*de impuestos, gas*) collector
cobrar [ko'βrar] *vt* (*cheque*) to cash; (*sueldo*) to collect, draw; (*objeto*) to recover; (*precio*) to charge; (*deuda*) to collect ■ *vi* to draw one's pay; **cobrarse** *vr* to recover, get on well; **cóbrese al entregar** cash on delivery (COD) (*Brit*), collect on delivery (COD) (US); **a** ~ (*Com*) receivable; **cantidades por** ~ sums due
cobre ['koβre] *nm* copper; (*Am fam*) cent
cobrizo, -a [ko'βriθo, a] *adj* coppery
cobro ['koβro] *nm* (*de cheque*) cashing; (*pago*) payment; **presentar al** ~ to cash; *ver tb* **llamada**
coca ['koka] *nf* coca; (*droga*) coke
cocaína [koka'ina] *nf* cocaine
cocainómano, -a [kokai'nomano, a] *nm/f* cocaine addict
cocción [kok'θjon] *nf* (*Culin*) cooking; (*el hervir*) boiling
cocear [koθe'ar] *vi* to kick
cocer [ko'θer] *vt, vi* to cook; (*en agua*) to boil; (*en horno*) to bake
coche ['kotʃe] *nm* (*Auto*) car, automobile (US); (*de tren, de caballos*) coach, carriage; (*para niños*) pram (*Brit*), baby carriage (US); ~ **de bomberos** fire engine; ~ **celular** Black Maria, prison van; ~ **(comedor)** (*Ferro*) (dining) car; ~ **fúnebre** hearse
coche-bomba ['kotʃe'βomba] (*pl* **coches-bomba**) *nm* car bomb
coche-cama ['kotʃe'kama] (*pl* **coches-cama**) *nm* (*Ferro*) sleeping car, sleeper
coche-escuela ['kotʃees'kwela] *nm inv* learner car
cochera [ko'tʃera] *nf* garage; (*de autobuses, trenes*) depot
coche-restaurante ['kotʃerestau'rante] (*pl* **coches-restaurante**) *nm* (*Ferro*) dining-car
cochinada [kotʃi'naða] *nf* dirty trick
cochinillo [kotʃi'niʎo] *nm* piglet, suckling pig
cochino, -a [ko'tʃino, a] *adj* filthy, dirty ■ *nm/f* pig
cocido, -a [ko'θiðo, a] *adj* boiled; (*fam*) plastered ■ *nm* stew
cociente [ko'θjente] *nm* quotient
cocina [ko'θina] *nf* kitchen; (*aparato*) cooker, stove; (*actividad*) cookery; ~ **casera** home cooking; ~ **eléctrica** electric cooker; ~ **francesa** French cuisine; ~ **de gas** gas cooker
cocinar [koθi'nar] *vt, vi* to cook
cocinero, -a [koθi'nero, a] *nm/f* cook

coco ['koko] *nm* coconut; (*fantasma*) bogeyman; (*fam: cabeza*) nut; **comer el ~ a algn** (*fam*) to brainwash sb
cocodrilo [koko'ðrilo] *nm* crocodile
cocotero [koko'tero] *nm* coconut palm
cóctel ['koktel] *nm* (*bebida*) cocktail; (*reunión*) cocktail party; ~ **Molotov** Molotov cocktail, petrol bomb
coctelera [kokte'lera] *nf* cocktail shaker
cod. *abr* (= *código*) code
codazo [ko'ðaθo] *nm*: **dar un ~ a algn** to nudge sb
codear [koðe'ar] *vi* to elbow, jostle; **codearse** *vr*: **codearse con** to rub shoulders with
códice ['koðiθe] *nm* manuscript, codex
codicia [ko'ðiθja] *nf* greed; (*fig*) lust
codiciar [koði'θjar] *vt* to covet
codicioso, -a [koði'θjoso, a] *adj* covetous
codificador [koðifika'ðor] *nm* (*Inform*) encoder; ~ **digital** digitizer
codificar [koðifi'kar] *vt* (*mensaje*) to (en)code; (*leyes*) to codify
código ['koðiyo] *nm* code; ~ **de barras** (*Com*) bar code; ~ **binario** binary code; ~ **de caracteres** (*Inform*) character code; ~ **de (la) circulación** highway code; ~ **civil** common law; ~ **de control** (*Inform*) control code; ~ **máquina** (*Inform*) machine code; ~ **militar** military law; ~ **de operación** (*Inform*) operational o machine code; ~ **penal** penal code; ~ **de práctica** code of practice
codillo [ko'ðiʎo] *nm* (*Zool*) knee; (*Tec*) elbow
codo ['koðo] *nm* (*Anat, de tubo*) elbow; (*Zool*) knee; **hablar por los codos** to talk nineteen to the dozen
codorniz [koðor'niθ] *nf* quail
coeficiente [koefi'θjente] *nm* (*Mat*) coefficient; (*Econ etc*) rate; ~ **intelectual** o **de inteligencia** I.Q.
coerción [koer'θjon] *nf* coercion
coercitivo, -a [koerθi'tiβo, a] *adj* coercive
coetáneo, -a [koe'taneo, a] *nm/f*: **coetáneos** contemporaries
coexistencia [koeksis'tenθja] *nf* coexistence
coexistir [koeksis'tir] *vi* to coexist
cofia ['kofja] *nf* (*de enfermera*) (white) cap
cofradía [kofra'ðia] *nf* brotherhood, fraternity; *ver tb* **Semana Santa**
cofre ['kofre] *nm* (*baúl*) trunk; (*de joyas*) box; (*Am Auto*) bonnet (*Brit*), hood (US)
cogedor [koxe'ðor] *nm* dustpan
coger [ko'xer] *vt* (*Esp*) to take (hold of); (*objeto caído*) to pick up; (*frutas*) to pick, harvest; (*resfriado, ladrón, pelota*) to catch; (*Am fam!*) to lay (!) ■ *vi*: ~ **por el buen camino** to take the right road; **cogerse** *vr* (*el dedo*) to catch;

~ **a algn desprevenido** to take sb unawares;
cogerse a algo to get hold of sth

cogida [ko'xiða] *nf* gathering, harvesting;
(*de peces*) catch; (*Taur*) goring

cogollo [ko'ɣoʎo] *nm* (*de lechuga*) heart; (*fig*)
core, nucleus

cogorza [ko'ɣorθa] *nf* (*fam*): **agarrar una** ~
to get smashed

cogote [ko'ɣote] *nm* back o nape of the neck

cohabitar [koaβi'tar] *vi* to live together,
cohabit

cohecho [ko'etʃo] *nm* (*acción*) bribery;
(*soborno*) bribe

coherencia [koe'renθja] *nf* coherence

coherente [koe'rente] *adj* coherent

cohesión [koe'sjon] *nm* cohesion

cohete [ko'ete] *nm* rocket

cohibido, -a [koi'βiðo, a] *adj* (*Psico*) inhibited;
(*tímido*) shy; **sentirse** ~ to feel embarrassed

cohibir [koi'βir] *vt* to restrain, restrict;
cohibirse *vr* to feel inhibited

COI *nm abr* (= *Comité Olímpico Internacional*) IOC

coima ['koima] *nf* (*Am fam*) bribe

coincidencia [koinθi'ðenθja] *nf* coincidence

coincidir [koinθi'ðir] *vi* (*en idea*) to coincide,
agree; (*en lugar*) to coincide

coito ['koito] *nm* intercourse, coitus

cojear [koxe'ar] *vi* (*persona*) to limp, hobble;
(*mueble*) to wobble, rock

cojera [ko'xera] *nf* lameness; (*andar cojo*) limp

cojín [ko'xin] *nm* cushion

cojinete [koxi'nete] *nm* small cushion, pad;
(*Tec*) (ball) bearing

cojo, -a *etc* ['koxo, a] *vb ver* **coger** ■ *adj* (*que no
puede andar*) lame, crippled; (*mueble*) wobbly
■ *nm/f* lame person, cripple

cojón [ko'xon] *nm* (*fam!*) ball (!), testicle;
¡cojones! shit! (!)

cojonudo, -a [koxo'nuðo, a] *adj* (*Esp fam*)
great, fantastic

col [kol] *nf* cabbage; **coles de Bruselas**
Brussels sprouts

cola ['kola] *nf* tail; (*de gente*) queue; (*lugar*)
end, last place; (*para pegar*) glue, gum; (*de
vestido*) train; **hacer** ~ to queue (up)

colaboración [kolaβora'θjon] *nf* (*gen*)
collaboration; (*en periódico*) contribution

colaborador, a [kolaβora'ðor, a] *nm/f*
collaborator; contributor

colaborar [kolaβo'rar] *vi* to collaborate

colación [kola'θjon] *nf*: **sacar a** ~ to bring up

colado, -a [ko'laðo, a] *adj* (*metal*) cast ■ *nf*:
hacer la colada to do the washing

colador [kola'ðor] *nm* (*de té*) strainer; (*para
verduras etc*) colander

colapsar [kolap'sar] *vt* (*tráfico etc*) to bring to
a standstill

colapso [ko'lapso] *nm* collapse; ~ **nervioso**
nervous breakdown

colar [ko'lar] *vt* (*líquido*) to strain off; (*metal*)
to cast ■ *vi* to ooze, seep (through); **colarse**
vr to jump the queue; (*en mitin*) to sneak in;
(*equivocarse*) to slip up; **colarse en** to get into
without paying; (*en una fiesta*) to gatecrash

colateral [kolate'ral] *nm* collateral

colcha ['koltʃa] *nf* bedspread

colchón [kol'tʃon] *nm* mattress; ~ **inflable**
inflatable mattress

colchoneta [koltʃo'neta] *nf* (*en gimnasio*)
mattress; ~ **hinchable** airbed

colear [kole'ar] *vi* (*perro*) to wag its tail

colección [kolek'θjon] *nf* collection

coleccionar [kolekθjo'nar] *vt* to collect

coleccionista [kolekθjo'nista] *nm/f* collector

colecta [ko'lekta] *nf* collection

colectivo, -a [kolek'tiβo, a] *adj* collective,
joint ■ *nm* (*Am: autobús*) (small) bus; (*taxi*)
collective taxi

colector [kolek'tor] *nm* collector; (*sumidero*)
sewer

colega [ko'leɣa] *nm/f* colleague

colegiado, -a [kole'xjaðo, a] *adj* (*profesional*)
registered ■ *nm/f* referee

colegial, a [kole'xjal, a] *adj* (*Escol etc*) school
cpd, college *cpd* ■ *nm/f* schoolboy/girl

colegio [ko'lexjo] *nm* college; (*escuela*) school;
(*de abogados etc*) association; ~ **de internos**
boarding school; **ir al** ~ to go to school;
see note

◉ **COLEGIO**

  A *colegio* is normally a private primary
  or secondary school. In the state system
  it means a primary school although
  these are also called *escuela*. State
  secondary schools are called *institutos*.
  Extracurricular subjects, such as
  computing or foreign languages, are
  offered in private schools called *academias*.

colegir [kole'xir] *vt* (*juntar*) to collect, gather;
(*deducir*) to infer, conclude

cólera ['kolera] *nf* (*ira*) anger; **montar en** ~
to get angry ■ *nm* (*Med*) cholera

colérico, -a [ko'leriko, a] *adj* angry, furious

colesterol [koleste'rol] *nm* cholesterol

coleta [ko'leta] *nf* pigtail

coletazo [kole'taθo] *nm*: **dar un** ~ (*animal*) to
flap its tail; **los últimos coletazos** death
throes

coletilla [kole'tiʎa] *nf* (*en carta*) postscript;
(*en conversación*) filler phrase

colgado, -a [kol'ɣaðo, a] *pp de* **colgar** ■ *adj*

hanging; (*ahorcado*) hanged; **dejar ~ a algn** to let sb down

colgajo [kol'ɣaxo] *nm* tatter

colgante [kol'ɣante] *adj* hanging; *ver* **puente** ■ *nm* (*joya*) pendant

colgar [kol'ɣar] *vt* to hang (up); (*tender: ropa*) to hang out ■ *vi* to hang; (*teléfono*) to hang up; **no cuelgue** please hold

colgué [kol'ɣe], **colguemos** *etc* [kol'ɣemos] *vb ver* **colgar**

colibrí [koli'βri] *nm* hummingbird

cólico ['koliko] *nm* colic

coliflor [koli'flor] *nf* cauliflower

coligiendo *etc* [koli'xjenðo] *vb ver* **colegir**

colija *etc* [ko'lixa] *vb ver* **colegir**

colilla [ko'liʎa] *nf* cigarette end, butt

colina [ko'lina] *nf* hill

colindante [kolin'dante] *adj* adjacent, neighbouring

colindar [kolin'dar] *vi* to adjoin, be adjacent

colisión [koli'sjon] *nf* collision; **~ de frente** head-on crash

colitis [ko'litis] *nf inv*: **tener ~** to have diarrhoea

collar [ko'ʎar] *nm* necklace; (*de perro*) collar

colmado, -a [kol'maðo, a] *adj* full ■ *nm* grocer's (*shop*) (*Brit*), grocery store (*US*)

colmar [kol'mar] *vt* to fill to the brim; (*fig*) to fulfil, realize

colmena [kol'mena] *nf* beehive

colmillo [kol'miʎo] *nm* (*diente*) eye tooth; (*de elefante*) tusk; (*de perro*) fang

colmo ['kolmo] *nm* height, summit; **para ~ de desgracias** to cap it all; **¡eso es ya el ~!** that's beyond a joke!

colocación [koloka'θjon] *nf* (*acto*) placing; (*empleo*) job, position; (*situación*) place, position; (*Com*) placement

colocar [kolo'kar] *vt* to place, put, position; (*poner en empleo*) to find a job for; **~ dinero** to invest money; **colocarse** *vr* to place o.s.; (*conseguir trabajo*) to find a job

colofón [kolo'fon] *nm*: **como ~ de las conversaciones** as a sequel to o following the talks

Colombia [ko'lombja] *nf* Colombia

colombiano, -a [kolom'bjano, a] *adj, nm/f* Colombian

colon ['kolon] *nm* colon

colón [ko'lon] *nm* (*Am*) *monetary unit of Costa Rica and El Salvador*

Colonia [ko'lonja] *nf* Cologne

colonia [ko'lonja] *nf* colony; (*de casas*) housing estate; (*agua de colonia*) cologne; **~ escolar** summer camp (for schoolchildren)

colonice *etc* [kolo'niθe] *vb ver* **colonizar**

colonización [koloniθa'θjon] *nf* colonization

colonizador, a [koloniθa'ðor, a] *adj* colonizing ■ *nm/f* colonist, settler

colonizar [koloni'θar] *vt* to colonize

colono [ko'lono] *nm* (*Pol*) colonist, settler; (*Agr*) tenant farmer

coloque *etc* [ko'loke] *vb ver* **colocar**

coloquial [kolo'kjal] *adj* colloquial

coloquio [ko'lokjo] *nm* conversation; (*congreso*) conference

color [ko'lor] *nm* colour; **a todo ~** in full colour; **verlo todo ~ de rosa** to see everything through rose-coloured spectacles; **le salieron los colores** she blushed

colorado, -a [kolo'raðo, a] *adj* (*rojo*) red; (*Am: chiste*) rude, blue; **ponerse ~** to blush

colorante [kolo'rante] *nm* colouring (matter)

colorar [kolo'rar] *vt* to colour; (*teñir*) to dye

colorear [kolore'ar] *vt* to colour

colorete [kolo'rete] *nm* blusher

colorido [kolo'riðo] *nm* colour(ing)

coloso [ko'loso] *nm* colossus

columbrar [kolum'brar] *vt* to glimpse, spy

columna [ko'lumna] *nf* column; (*pilar*) pillar; (*apoyo*) support; **~ blindada** (*Mil*) armoured column; **~ vertebral** spine, spinal column

columpiar [kolum'pjar] *vt*, **columpiarse** *vr* to swing

columpio [ko'lumpjo] *nm* swing

colza ['kolθa] *nf* rape; **aceite de ~** rapeseed oil

coma ['koma] *nf* comma ■ *nm* (*Med*) coma

comadre [ko'maðre] *nf* (*madrina*) godmother; (*vecina*) neighbour; (*chismosa*) gossip

comadrear [komaðre'ar] *vi* (*esp Am*) to gossip

comadreja [koma'ðrexa] *nf* weasel

comadrona [koma'ðrona] *nf* midwife

comandancia [koman'danθja] *nf* command

comandante [koman'dante] *nm* commandant; (*grado*) major

comandar [koman'dar] *vt* to command

comando [ko'mando] *nm* (*Mil: mando*) command; (*: grupo*) commando unit; (*Inform*) command; **~ de búsqueda** search command

comarca [ko'marka] *nf* region; *ver tb* **provincia**

comarcal [komar'kal] *adj* local

comba ['komba] *nf* (*curva*) curve; (*en viga*) warp; (*cuerda*) skipping rope; **saltar a la ~** to skip

combar [kom'bar] *vt* to bend, curve

combate [kom'bate] *nm* fight; (*fig*) battle; **fuera de ~** out of action

combatiente [komba'tjente] *nm* combatant

combatir [komba'tir] *vt* to fight, combat

combatividad [kombatiβi'ðað] *nf* (*actitud*) fighting spirit; (*agresividad*) aggressiveness

combativo, -a [komba'tiβo, a] *adj* full of fight
combi ['kombi] *nm* fridge-freezer
combinación [kombina'θjon] *nf* combination; (*Química*) compound; (*bebida*) cocktail; (*plan*) scheme, setup; (*prenda*) slip
combinado, -a [kombi'naðo, a] *adj*: **plato ~** main course served with vegetables
combinar [kombi'nar] *vt* to combine; (*colores*) to match
combustible [kombus'tiβle] *nm* fuel
combustión [kombus'tjon] *nf* combustion
comedia [ko'meðja] *nf* comedy; (*Teat*) play, drama; (*fig*) farce
comediante [kome'ðjante] *nm/f* (comic) actor/actress
comedido, -a [kome'ðiðo, a] *adj* moderate
comedirse [kome'ðirse] *vr* to behave moderately; (*ser cortés*) to be courteous
comedor, a [kome'ðor, a] *nm/f* (*persona*) glutton ■ *nm* (*habitación*) dining room; (*restaurante*) restaurant; (*cantina*) canteen
comencé [komen'θe], **comencemos** *etc* [komen'θemos] *vb ver* **comenzar**
comensal [komen'sal] *nm/f* fellow guest/ diner
comentar [komen'tar] *vt* to comment on; (*fam*) to discuss; **comentó que...** he made the comment that...
comentario [komen'tarjo] *nm* comment, remark; (*Lit*) commentary; **comentarios** *nmpl* gossip *sg*; **dar lugar a comentarios** to cause gossip
comentarista [komenta'rista] *nm/f* commentator
comenzar [komen'θar] *vt, vi* to begin, start, commence; **~ a hacer algo** to begin *o* start doing *o* to do sth
comer [ko'mer] *vt* to eat; (*Damas: Ajedrez*) to take, capture ■ *vi* to eat; (*almorzar*) to have lunch; **comerse** *vr* to eat up; (*párrafo etc*) to skip; **~ el coco a** (*fam*) to brainwash; **¡a ~!** food's ready!
comercial [komer'θjal] *adj* commercial; (*relativo al negocio*) business *cpd*
comerciante [komer'θjante] *nm/f* trader, merchant; (*tendero*) shopkeeper; **~ exclusivo** (*Com*) sole trader
comerciar [komer'θjar] *vi* to trade, do business
comercio [ko'merθjo] *nm* commerce, trade; (*negocio*) business; (*grandes empresas*) big business; (*fig*) dealings *pl*; **~ autorizado** (*Com*) licensed trade; **~ electrónico** e-commerce; **~ exterior** foreign trade
comestible [komes'tiβle] *adj* eatable, edible ■ *nm*: **comestibles** food *sg*, foodstuffs; (*Com*) groceries

cometa [ko'meta] *nm* comet ■ *nf* kite
cometer [kome'ter] *vt* to commit
cometido [kome'tiðo] *nm* (*misión*) task, assignment; (*deber*) commitment
comezón [kome'θon] *nf* itch, itching
cómic (*pl* **cómics**) ['komik, 'komiks] *nm* comic
comicios [ko'miθjos] *nmpl* elections; (*voto*) voting *sg*
cómico, -a ['komiko, a] *adj* comic(al) ■ *nm/f* comedian; (*de teatro*) (comic) actor/actress
comida *etc* [ko'miða] *vb ver* **comedirse** ■ *nf* (*alimento*) food; (*almuerzo, cena*) meal; (*de mediodía*) lunch; (*Am*) dinner
comidilla [komi'ðiʎa] *nf*: **ser la ~ de la ciudad** to be the talk of the town
comience *etc* [ko'mjenθe] *vb ver* **comenzar**
comienzo *etc* [ko'mjenθo] *vb ver* **comenzar** ■ *nm* beginning, start; **dar ~ a un acto** to begin a ceremony; **~ del archivo** (*Inform*) top-of-file
comillas [ko'miʎas] *nfpl* quotation marks
comilón, -ona [komi'lon, ona] *adj* greedy ■ *nf* (*fam*) blow-out
comino [ko'mino] *nm* cumin (*seed*); **no me importa un ~** I don't give a damn!
comisaría [komisa'ria] *nf* police station, precinct (US); (*Mil*) commissariat
comisario [komi'sarjo] *nm* (*Mil etc*) commissary; (*Pol*) commissar
comisión [komi'sjon] *nf* (*Com: pago*) commission, rake-off (*fam*); (*: junta*) board; (*encargo*) assignment; **~ mixta/permanente** joint/standing committee; **Comisiones Obreras** (*Esp*) *formerly* Communist Union Confederation
comisura [komi'sura] *nf*: **~ de los labios** corner of the mouth
comité (*pl* **~s**) *nm* [komi'te, komi'tes] committee; **comité de empresa** works council
comitiva [komi'tiβa] *nf* suite, retinue
como ['komo] *adv* as; (*tal como*) like; (*aproximadamente*) about, approximately ■ *conj* (*ya que, puesto que*) as, since; (*en seguida que*) as soon as; (*si:* +*subjun*) if; **¡~ no!** of course!; **~ no lo haga hoy** unless he does it today; **~ si** as if; **es tan alto ~ ancho** it is as high as it is wide
cómo ['komo] *adv* how?, why? ■ *excl* what?, I beg your pardon? ■ *nm*: **el ~ y el porqué** the whys and wherefores; **¿~ está Ud?** how are you?; **¿~ no?** why not?; **¡~ no!** (*esp Am*) of course!; **¿~ son?** what are they like?
cómoda ['komoða] *nf* chest of drawers
comodidad [komoði'ðað] *nf* comfort; **venga a su ~** come at your convenience

comodín [komo'ðin] nm joker; (Inform) wild card; **símbolo ~** wild-card character

cómodo, -a ['komoðo, a] adj comfortable; (práctico, de fácil uso) convenient

comodón, -ona [komo'ðon, ona] adj comfort-loving ∎ nm/f: **ser un(a) ~/ona** to like one's home comforts

comoquiera [como'kjera] conj: **~ que** (+subjun) in whatever way; **~ que sea eso** however that may be

comp. abr (= compárese) cp

compacto, -a [kom'pakto, a] adj compact

compadecer [kompaðe'θer] vt to pity, be sorry for; **compadecerse** vr: **compadecerse de** to pity, be sorry for

compadezca etc [kompa'ðeθka] vb ver **compadecer**

compadre [kom'paðre] nm (padrino) godfather; (esp Am: amigo) friend, pal

compaginar [kompaxi'nar] vt: **~ A con B** to bring A into line with B; **compaginarse** vr: **compaginarse con** to tally with, square with

compañerismo [kompaɲe'rismo] nm comradeship

compañero, -a [kompa'ɲero, a] nm/f companion; (novio) boyfriend/girlfriend; **~ de clase** classmate

compañía [kompa'ɲia] nf company; **~ afiliada** associated company; **~ concesionaria** franchiser; **~ (no) cotizable** (un)listed company; **~ inversionista** investment trust; **hacer ~ a algn** to keep sb company

comparación [kompara'θjon] nf comparison; **en ~ con** in comparison with

comparar [kompa'rar] vt to compare

comparativo, -a [kompara'tiβo, a] adj comparative

comparecencia [kompare'θenθja] nf (Jur) appearance (in court); **orden de ~** summons sg

comparecer [kompare'θer] vi to appear (in court)

comparezca etc [kompa're θka] vb ver **comparecer**

comparsa [kom'parsa] nm/f extra

compartimento [komparti'mento], **compartimiento** [komparti'mjento] nm (Ferro) compartment; (de mueble, cajón) section; **~ estanco** (fig) watertight compartment

compartir [kompar'tir] vt to divide (up), share (out)

compás [kom'pas] nm (Mus) beat, rhythm; (Mat) compasses pl; (Naut etc) compass; **al ~** in time

compasión [kompa'sjon] nf compassion, pity

compasivo, -a [kompa'siβo, a] adj compassionate

compatibilidad [kompatiβili'ðað] nf (tb Inform) compatibility

compatible [kompa'tiβle] adj compatible

compatriota [kompa'trjota] nm/f compatriot, fellow countryman/woman

compendiar [kompen'djar] vt to summarize; (libro) to abridge

compendio [kom'pendjo] nm summary; abridgement

compenetración [kompenetra'θjon] nf (fig) mutual understanding

compenetrarse [kompene'trarse] vr (fig): **~ (muy) bien** to get on (very) well together

compensación [kompensa'θjon] nf compensation; (Jur) damages pl; (Com) clearing

compensar [kompen'sar] vt to compensate; (pérdida) to make up for

competencia [kompe'tenθja] nf (incumbencia) domain, field; (Com) receipt; (Jur, habilidad) competence; (rivalidad) competition

competente [kompe'tente] adj (Jur, persona) competent; (conveniente) suitable

competer [kompe'ter] vi: **~ a** to be the responsibility of, fall to

competición [kompeti'θjon] nf competition

competidor, a [kompeti'ðor, a] nm/f competitor

competir [kompe'tir] vi to compete

competitivo, -a [kompeti'tiβo, a] adj competitive

compilación [kompila'θjon] nf compilation; **tiempo de ~** (Inform) compile time

compilador [kompila'ðor] nm compiler

compilar [kompi'lar] vt to compile

compinche [kom'pintʃe] nm/f (fam) crony

compita etc [kom'pita] vb ver **competir**

complacencia [kompla'θenθja] nf (placer) pleasure; (satisfacción) satisfaction; (buena voluntad) willingness

complacer [kompla'θer] vt to please; **complacerse** vr to be pleased

complaciente [kompla'θjente] adj kind, obliging, helpful

complazca etc [kom'plaθka] vb ver **complacer**

complejo, -a [kom'plexo, a] adj, nm complex

complementario, -a [komplemen'tarjo, a] adj complementary

complemento [komple'mento] nm (de moda, diseño) accessory; (Ling) complement

completar [komple'tar] vt to complete

completo, -a [kom'pleto, a] adj complete; (perfecto) perfect; (lleno) full ∎ nm full complement

complexión [komple'ksjon] nf constitution
complicación [komplika'θjon] nf
complication
complicado, -a [kompli'kaðo, a] adj
complicated; **estar ~ en** to be involved in
complicar [kompli'kar] vt to complicate
cómplice ['kompliθe] nm/f accomplice
complique etc [kom'plike] vb ver **complicar**
complot (pl **complots**) [kom'plo(t), kom'plos]
nm plot; (conspiración) conspiracy
compondré etc [kompon'dre] vb ver **componer**
componenda [kompo'nenda] nf
compromise; (pey) shady deal
componente [kompo'nente] adj, nm
component
componer [kompo'ner] vt to make up, put
together; (Mus: Lit: Imprenta) to compose;
(algo roto) to mend, repair; (adornar) to adorn;
(arreglar) to arrange; (reconciliar) to reconcile;
componerse vr: **componerse de** to consist
of; **componérselas para hacer algo** to
manage to do sth
componga etc [kom'ponga] vb ver **componer**
comportamiento [komporta'mjento] nm
behaviour, conduct
comportarse [kompor'tarse] vi to behave
composición [komposi'θjon] nf composition
compositor, a [komposi'tor, a] nm/f
composer
compostelano, -a [komposte'lano, a]
adj of o from Santiago de Compostela
■ nm/f native o inhabitant of Santiago de
Compostela
compostura [kompos'tura] nf (reparación)
mending, repair; (composición) composition;
(acuerdo) agreement; (actitud) composure
compota [kom'pota] nf compote, preserve
compra ['kompra] nf purchase; **compras**
nfpl purchases, shopping sg; **hacer la ~/ir de
compras** to do the/go shopping; **~ a granel**
(Com) bulk buying; **~ proteccionista** (Com)
support buying
comprador, a [kompra'ðor, a] nm/f buyer,
purchaser
comprar [kom'prar] vt to buy, purchase;
~ deudas (Com) to factor
compraventa [kompra'βenta] nf (Jur)
contract of sale
comprender [kompren'der] vt to
understand; (incluir) to comprise, include
comprensible [kompren'siβle] adj
understandable
comprensión [kompren'sjon]
nf understanding; (totalidad)
comprehensiveness
comprensivo, -a [kompren'siβo, a] adj
comprehensive; (actitud) understanding

compresa [kom'presa] nf compress; **~
higiénica** sanitary towel (Brit) o napkin (US)
compresión [kompre'sjon] nf compression
comprimido, -a [kompri'miðo] adj
compressed ■ nm (Med) pill, tablet; **en
caracteres comprimidos** (Tip) condensed
comprimir [kompri'mir] vt to compress; (fig)
to control; (Inform) to pack
comprobación [komproβa'θjon] nf: **~
general de cuentas** (Com) general audit
comprobante [kompro'βante] nm proof;
(Com) voucher; **~ (de pago)** receipt
comprobar [kompro'βar] vt to check; (probar)
to prove; (Tec) to check, test
comprometedor, a [kompromete'ðor, a] adj
compromising
comprometer [komprome'ter] vt to
compromise; (exponer) to endanger;
comprometerse vr to compromise o.s.;
(involucrarse) to get involved
comprometido, -a [komprome'tiðo, a] adj
(situación) awkward; (escritor etc) committed
compromiso [kompro'miso] nm (obligación)
obligation; (cita) engagement, date;
(cometido) commitment; (convenio)
agreement; (dificultad) awkward situation;
libre de ~ (Com) without obligation
comprueba etc [kom'prweβa] vb ver
comprobar
compuerta [kom'pwerta] nf (en canal) sluice,
floodgate; (Inform) gate
compuesto, -a [kom'pwesto, a] pp de
componer ■ adj: **~ de** composed of, made up
of ■ nm compound; (Med) preparation
compulsar [kompul'sar] vt (cotejar) to collate,
compare; (Jur) to make an attested copy of
compulsivo, -a [kompul'siβo, a] adj
compulsive
compungido, -a [kompun'xiðo, a] adj
remorseful
compuse etc [com'puse] vb ver **componer**
computador [komputa'ðor] nm,
computadora [komputa'ðora] nf
computer; **~ central** mainframe computer;
~ especializado dedicated computer; **~
personal** personal computer
computar [kompu'tar] vt to calculate,
compute
cómputo ['komputo] nm calculation
comulgar [komul'ɣar] vi to receive
communion
comulgue etc [ko'mulɣe] vb ver **comulgar**
común [ko'mun] adj (gen) common; (corriente)
ordinary; **por lo ~** generally ■ nm: **el ~** the
community
comuna [ko'muna] nf commune; (Am)
district

83

comunicación [komunika'θjon] *nf* communication; (*informe*) report

comunicado [komuni'kaðo] *nm* announcement; ~ **de prensa** press release

comunicar [komuni'kar] *vt* to communicate; (*Arq*) to connect ◼ *vi* to communicate; to send a report; **comunicarse** *vr* to communicate; **está comunicando** (*Telec*) the line's engaged (*Brit*) *o* busy (*US*)

comunicativo, -a [komunika'tiβo, a] *adj* communicative

comunidad [komuni'ðað] *nf* community; ~ **autónoma** autonomous region; ~ **de vecinos** residents' association; **C~ Económica Europea (CEE)** European Economic Community (EEC); *see note*

⬤ **COMUNIDAD**

The 1978 Constitution provides for a degree of self-government for the 19 regions, called *comunidades autónomas* or *autonomías*. Some, such as Catalonia and the Basque Country, with their own language, history and culture, have long felt separate from the rest of Spain. This explains why some of the autonomías have more devolved powers than others, in all matters except foreign affairs and national defence. The regions are: Andalucía, Aragón, Asturias, Islas Baleares, Canarias, Cantabria, Castilla y León, Castilla-La Mancha, Cataluña, Extremadura, Galicia, Madrid, Murcia, Navarra, País Vasco, La Rioja, Comunidad Valenciana, Ceuta, Melilla.

comunión [komu'njon] *nf* communion

comunique *etc* [komu'nike] *vb ver* **comunicar**

comunismo [komu'nismo] *nm* communism

comunista [komu'nista] *adj, nm/f* communist

comunitario, -a [komuni'tarjo, a] *adj* (*de la CE*) Community *cpd*, EC *cpd*

 PALABRA CLAVE

con [kon] *prep* **1** (*medio, compañía, modo*) with; **comer con cuchara** to eat with a spoon; **café con leche** white coffee; **estoy con un catarro** I've got a cold; **pasear con algn** to go for a walk with sb; **con habilidad** skilfully

2 (*a pesar de*): **con todo, merece nuestros respetos** all the same *o* even so, he deserves our respect

3 (*para con*): **es muy bueno para con los**

niños he's very good with (the) children

4 (+*infin*): **con llegar tan tarde se quedó sin comer** by arriving *o* because he arrived so late he missed out on eating; **con estudiar un poco apruebas** with a bit of studying you should pass

5 (*queja*): **¡con las ganas que tenía de ir!** and I really wanted to go (too)!

◼ *conj*: **con que: será suficiente con que le escribas** it will be enough if you write to her

conato [ko'nato] *nm* attempt; ~ **de robo** attempted robbery

cóncavo, -a ['konkaβo, a] *adj* concave

concebir [konθe'βir] *vt* to conceive; (*imaginar*) to imagine ◼ *vi* to conceive

conceder [konθe'ðer] *vt* to concede

concejal, a [konθe'xal, a] *nm/f* town councillor

concejo [kon'θexo] *nm* council

concentración [konθentra'θjon] *nf* concentration

concentrar [konθen'trar] *vt*, **concentrarse** *vr* to concentrate

concéntrico, -a [kon'θentriko, a] *adj* concentric

concepción [konθep'θjon] *nf* conception

concepto [kon'θepto] *nm* concept; **por ~ de** as, by way of; **tener buen ~ de algn** to think highly of sb; **bajo ningún ~** under no circumstances

conceptuar [konθep'twar] *vt* to judge

concernir [konθer'nir] *vi*: **en lo que concierne a** concerning

concertar [konθer'tar] *vt* (*Mus*) to harmonize; (*acordar: precio*) to agree; (: *tratado*) to conclude; (*trato*) to arrange, fix up; (*combinar: esfuerzos*) to coordinate; (*reconciliar: personas*) to reconcile ◼ *vi* to harmonize, be in tune

concesión [konθe'sjon] *nf* concession; (*Com: fabricación*) licence

concesionario, -a [konθesjo'narjo, a] *nm/f* (*Com*) (licensed) dealer, agent, concessionaire; (: *de venta*) franchisee; (: *de transportes etc*) contractor

concha ['kontʃa] *nf* shell; (*Am fam!*) cunt (*!*)

conchabarse [kontʃa'βarse] *vr*: ~ **contra** to gang up on

conciencia [kon'θjenθja] *nf* (*moral*) conscience; (*conocimiento*) awareness; **libertad de ~** freedom of worship; **tener/ tomar ~ de** to be/become aware of; **tener la ~ limpia** *o* **tranquila** to have a clear conscience; **tener plena ~ de** to be fully aware of

concienciar [konθjen'θjar] *vt* to make aware; **concienciarse** *vr* to become aware

concienzudo, -a [konθjen'θuðo, a] *adj*
conscientious
concierne *etc* [kon'θjerne] *vb ver* **concernir**
concierto *etc* [kon'θjerto] *vb ver* **concertar**
■ *nm* concert; (*obra*) concerto
conciliación [konθilja'θjon] *nf* conciliation
conciliar [konθi'ljar] *vt* to reconcile ■ *adj*
(*Rel*) of a council; ~ **el sueño** to get to sleep
concilio [kon'θiljo] *nm* council
concisión [konθi'sjon] *nf* conciseness
conciso, -a [kon'θiso, a] *adj* concise
conciudadano, -a [konθjuða'ðano, a] *nm/f*
fellow citizen
concluir [konklu'ir] *vt* (*acabar*) to conclude;
(*inferir*) to infer, deduce ■ *vi*, **concluirse** *vr*
to conclude; **todo ha concluido** it's all over
conclusión [konklu'sjon] *nf* conclusion;
llegar a la ~ de que ... to come to the
conclusion that ...
concluya *etc* [kon'kluja] *vb ver* **concluir**
concluyente [konklu'jente] *adj* (*prueba*,
información) conclusive
concordancia [konkor'ðanθja] *nf* agreement
concordar [konkor'ðar] *vt* to reconcile ■ *vi*
to agree, tally
concordia [kon'korðja] *nf* harmony
concretamente [konkreta'mente] *adv*
specifically, to be exact
concretar [konkre'tar] *vt* to make concrete,
make more specific; (*problema*) to pinpoint;
concretarse *vr* to become more definite
concreto, -a [kon'kreto, a] *adj, nm* (*Am*)
concrete; **en ~** (*en resumen*) to sum up;
(*específicamente*) specifically; **no hay nada en
~** there's nothing definite
concubina [konku'βina] *nf* concubine
concuerde *etc* [kon'kwerðe] *vb ver* **concordar**
concupiscencia [konkupis'θenθja] *nf*
(*avaricia*) greed; (*lujuria*) lustfulness
concurrencia [konku'rrenθja] *nf* turnout
concurrido, -a [konku'rriðo, a] *adj* (*calle*)
busy; (*local: reunión*) crowded
concurrir [konku'rrir] *vi* (*juntarse: ríos*) to
meet, come together; (: *personas*) to gather,
meet
concursante [konkur'sante] *nm* competitor
concursar [konkur'sar] *vi* to compete
concurso [kon'kurso] *nm* (*de público*) crowd;
(*Escol: Deporte, competición*) competition;
(*Com*) invitation to tender; (*examen*) open
competition; (*TV etc*) quiz; (*ayuda*) help,
cooperation
condado [kon'daðo] *nm* county
condal [kon'dal] *adj*: **la ciudad ~** Barcelona
conde [ˈkonde] *nm* count
condecoración [kondekora'θjon] *nf* (*Mil*)
medal, decoration

condecorar [kondeko'rar] *vt* to decorate
condena [kon'dena] *nf* sentence; **cumplir
una ~** to serve a sentence
condenación [kondena'θjon] *nf*
condemnation; (*Rel*) damnation
condenado, -a [konde'naðo, a] *adj* (*Jur*)
condemned; (*fam: maldito*) damned ■ *nm/f*
(*Jur*) convicted person
condenar [konde'nar] *vt* to condemn; (*Jur*)
to convict; **condenarse** *vr* (*Jur*) to confess
(one's guilt); (*Rel*) to be damned
condensar [konden'sar] *vt* to condense
condesa [kon'desa] *nf* countess
condescendencia [kondesθen'denθja] *nf*
condescension; **aceptar algo por ~** to accept
sth so as not to hurt feelings
condescender [kondesθen'der] *vi* to
acquiesce, comply
condescienda *etc* [kondes'θjenda] *vb ver*
condescender
condición [kondi'θjon] *nf* (*gen*) condition;
(*rango*) social class; **condiciones** *nfpl*
(*cualidades*) qualities; (*estado*) condition;
a ~ de que ... on condition that ...; **las
condiciones del contrato** the terms of
the contract; **condiciones de trabajo**
working conditions; **condiciones de venta**
conditions of sale
condicional [kondiθjo'nal] *adj* conditional
condicionamiento [kondiθjona'mjento] *nm*
conditioning
condicionar [kondiθjo'nar] *vt* (*acondicionar*)
to condition; **~ algo a algo** to make sth
conditional o dependent on sth
condimento [kondi'mento] *nm* seasoning
condiscípulo, -a [kondis'θipulo, a] *nm/f*
fellow student
condolerse [kondo'lerse] *vr* to sympathize
condominio [kondo'minjo] *nm* (*Com*) joint
ownership; (*Am*) condominium, apartment
condón [kon'don] *nm* condom
condonar [kondo'nar] *vt* (*Jur: reo*) to reprieve;
(*Com: deuda*) to cancel
cóndor [ˈkondor] *nm* condor
conducente [kondu'θente] *adj*: **~ a** conducive
to, leading to
conducir [kondu'θir] *vt* to take, convey;
(*Elec etc*) to carry; (*Auto*) to drive; (*negocio*)
to manage ■ *vi* to drive; (*fig*) to lead;
conducirse *vr* to behave
conducta [kon'dukta] *nf* conduct, behaviour
conducto [kon'dukto] *nm* pipe, tube; (*fig*)
channel; (*Elec*) lead; **por ~ de** through
conductor, a [konduk'tor, a] *adj* leading,
guiding ■ *nm* (*Física*) conductor; (*de vehículo*)
driver
conduela *etc* [kon'dwela] *vb ver* **condolerse**

conduje etc [kon'duxe] vb ver **conducir**

conduzca etc [kon'duθka] vb ver **conducir**

conectado, -a [konek'taðo, a] adj (Elec) connected, plugged in; (Inform) on-line

conectar [konek'tar] vt to connect (up), plug in; (Inform) to toggle on; **conectarse** vr (Inform) to log in or on

conejillo [kone'xiʎo] nm: ~ **de Indias** guinea pig

conejo [ko'nexo] nm rabbit

conexión [konek'sjon] nf connection; (Inform) logging in or on

confabularse [konfaβu'larse] vr: ~ **(para hacer algo)** to plot o conspire (to do sth)

confección [konfek'θjon] nf (preparación) preparation, making-up; (industria) clothing industry; (producto) article; **de** ~ (ropa) off-the-peg

confeccionar [konfe(k)θjo'nar] vt to make (up)

confederación [konfeðera'θjon] nf confederation

conferencia [konfe'renθja] nf conference; (lección) lecture; (Telec) call; ~ **de cobro revertido** (Telec) reversed-charge (Brit) o collect (US) call; ~ **cumbre** summit (conference)

conferenciante [konferen'θjante] nm/f lecturer

conferir [konfe'rir] vt to award

confesar [konfe'sar] vt (admitir) to confess, admit; (error) to acknowledge; (crimen) to own up to

confesión [konfe'sjon] nf confession

confesionario [konfesjo'narjo] nm confessional

confeso, -a [kon'feso, a] adj (Jur etc) self-confessed

confeti [kon'feti] nm confetti

confiado, -a [kon'fjaðo, a] adj (crédulo) trusting; (seguro) confident; (presumido) conceited, vain

confianza [kon'fjanθa] nf trust; (aliento, confidencia) confidence; (familiaridad) intimacy, familiarity; (pey) vanity, conceit; **margen de** ~ credibility gap; **tener** ~ **con algn** to be on close terms with sb

confiar [kon'fjar] vt to entrust ■ vi (fiarse) to trust; (contar con) to rely; **confiarse** vr to put one's trust in

confidencia [konfi'ðenθja] nf confidence

confidencial [konfiðen'θjal] adj confidential

confidente [konfi'ðente] nm/f confidant/confidante; (policial) informer

confiera etc [kon'fjera] vb ver **conferir**

confiese etc [kon'fjese] vb ver **confesar**

configuración [konfiɣura'θjon] nf (tb Inform) configuration; **la** ~ **del terreno** the lie of the land; ~ **de bits** (Inform) bit pattern

configurar [konfiɣu'rar] vt to shape, form

confín [kon'fin] nm limit; **confines** nmpl confines, limits

confinar [konfi'nar] vi to confine; (desterrar) to banish

confiriendo etc [konfi'rjendo] vb ver **conferir**

confirmación [konfirma'θjon] nf confirmation; (Rel) Confirmation

confirmar [konfir'mar] vt to confirm; (Jur etc) to corroborate; **la excepción confirma la regla** the exception proves the rule

confiscar [konfis'kar] vt to confiscate

confisque etc [kon'fiske] vb ver **confiscar**

confitado, -a [konfi'taðo, a] adj: **fruta confitada** crystallized fruit

confite [kon'fite] nm sweet (Brit), candy (US)

confitería [konfite'ria] nf confectionery; (tienda) confectioner's (shop)

confitura [konfi'tura] nf jam

conflagración [konflaɣra'θjon] nf conflagration

conflictivo, -a [konflik'tiβo, a] adj (asunto, propuesta) controversial; (país, situación) troubled

conflicto [kon'flikto] nm conflict; (fig) clash; (: dificultad): **estar en un** ~ to be in a jam; ~ **laboral** labour dispute

confluir [konflu'ir] vi (ríos etc) to meet; (gente) to gather

confluya etc [kon'fluja] vb ver **confluir**

conformar [konfor'mar] vt to shape, fashion ■ vi to agree; **conformarse** vr to conform; (resignarse) to resign o.s.

conforme [kon'forme] adj alike, similar; (de acuerdo) agreed, in agreement; (satisfecho) satisfied ■ adv as ■ excl agreed! ■ nm agreement ■ prep: ~ **a** in accordance with

conformidad [konformi'ðað] nf (semejanza) similarity; (acuerdo) agreement; (resignación) resignation; **de/en** ~ **con** in accordance with; **dar su** ~ to consent

conformismo [konfor'mismo] nm conformism

conformista [konfor'mista] nm/f conformist

confort (pl **conforts**) [kon'for, kon'for(t)s] nm comfort

confortable [konfor'taβle] adj comfortable

confortar [konfor'tar] vt to comfort

confraternidad [konfraterni'ðað] nf brotherhood; **espíritu de** ~ feeling of unity

confraternizar [konfraterni'θar] vi to fraternize

confrontación [konfronta'θjon] nf confrontation

confrontar [konfron'tar] vt to confront; (dos personas) to bring face to face; (cotejar) to compare ■ vi to border

confundir [konfun'dir] vt (borrar) to blur; (equivocar) to mistake, confuse; (mezclar) to mix; (turbar) to confuse; **confundirse** vr (hacerse borroso) to become blurred; (turbarse) to get confused; (equivocarse) to make a mistake; (mezclarse) to mix

confusión [konfu'sjon] nf confusion

confusionismo [konfusjo'nismo] nm confusion, uncertainty

confuso, -a [kon'fuso, a] adj (gen) confused; (recuerdo) hazy; (estilo) obscure

congelación [konxela'θjon] nf freezing; ~ **de créditos** credit freeze

congelado, -a [konxe'laðo, a] adj frozen ■ nmpl: **congelados** frozen food sg o foods

congelador [konxela'ðor] nm freezer, deep freeze

congelar [konxe'lar] vt to freeze; **congelarse** vr (sangre, grasa) to congeal

congénere [kon'xenere] nm/f: **sus congéneres** his peers

congeniar [konxe'njar] vi to get on (Brit) o along (US) (well)

congénito, -a [kon'xenito, a] adj congenital

congestión [konxes'tjon] nf congestion

congestionado, a [konxestjo'naðo, a] adj congested

congestionar [konxestjo'nar] vt to congest; **congestionarse** vr to become congested; **se le congestionó la cara** his face became flushed

conglomerado [konglome'raðo] nm conglomerate

Congo ['kongo] nm: **el ~** the Congo

congoja [kon'goxa] nf distress, grief

congraciarse [kongra'θjarse] vr to ingratiate o.s.

congratular [kongratu'lar] vt to congratulate

congregación [kongreɣa'θjon] nf congregation

congregar [kongre'ɣar] vt, **congregarse** vr to gather together

congregue etc [kon'greɣe] vb ver **congregar**

congresista [kongre'sista] nm/f delegate, congressman/woman

congreso [kon'greso] nm congress; **C~ de los Diputados** (Esp Pol) ≈ House of Commons (Brit), House of Representatives (US); ver tb **Las Cortes (españolas)**

congrio ['kongrjo] nm conger (eel)

congruente [kon'grwente] adj congruent, congruous

conífera [ko'nifera] nf conifer

conjetura [konxe'tura] nf guess; (Com) guesstimate

conjeturar [konxetu'rar] vt to guess

conjugación [konxuɣa'θjon] nf conjugation

conjugar [konxu'ɣar] vt to combine, fit together; (Ling) to conjugate

conjugue etc [kon'xuɣe] vb ver **conjugar**

conjunción [konxun'θjon] nf conjunction

conjunctivitis [konxunti'βitis] nf conjunctivitis

conjunto, -a [kon'xunto, a] adj joint, united ■ nm whole; (Mus) band; (de ropa) ensemble; (Inform) set; **en ~** as a whole; **~ integrado de programas** (Inform) integrated software suite

conjura [kon'xura] nf plot, conspiracy

conjurar [konxu'rar] vt (Rel) to exorcise; (peligro) to ward off ■ vi to plot

conjuro [kon'xuro] nm spell

conllevar [konʎe'βar] vt to bear; (implicar) to imply, involve

conmemoración [konmemora'θjon] nf commemoration

conmemorar [konmemo'rar] vt to commemorate

conmigo [kon'miɣo] pron with me

conminar [konmi'nar] vt to threaten

conmiseración [konmisera'θjon] nf pity, commiseration

conmoción [konmo'θjon] nf shock; (Pol) disturbance; (fig) upheaval; **~ cerebral** (Med) concussion

conmovedor, a [konmoβe'ðor, a] adj touching, moving; (emocionante) exciting

conmover [konmo'βer] vt to shake, disturb; (fig) to move; **conmoverse** vr (fig) to be moved

conmueva etc [kon'mweβa] vb ver **conmover**

conmutación [konmuta'θjon] nf (Inform) switching; **~ de mensajes** message switching; **~ por paquetes** packet switching

conmutador [konmuta'ðor] nm switch; (Am Telec) switchboard

conmutar [konmu'tar] vt (Jur) to commute

connivencia [konni'βenθja] nf: **estar en ~ con** to be in collusion with

connotación [konnota'θjon] nf connotation

cono ['kono] nm cone; **C~ Sur** Southern Cone

conocedor, a [konoθe'ðor, a] adj expert, knowledgeable ■ nm/f expert, connoisseur

conocer [kono'θer] vt to know; (por primera vez) to meet, get to know; (entender) to know about; (reconocer) to recognize; **conocerse** vr (una persona) to know o.s.; (dos personas) to (get to) know each other; **darse a ~** (presentarse) to make o.s. known; **se conoce que ...** (parece) apparently ...

conocido, -a [kono'θiðo, a] adj (well-)known ■ nm/f acquaintance

conocimiento [konoθi'mjento] *nm*
knowledge; (*Med*) consciousness; (*Naut*:
tb: **conocimiento de embarque**) bill of
lading; **conocimientos** *nmpl* (*personas*)
acquaintances; (*saber*) knowledge *sg*;
hablar con ~ de causa to speak from
experience; **~ (de embarque) aéreo** (*Com*)
air waybill

conozca *etc* [ko'noθka] *vb ver* **conocer**

conque ['konke] *conj* and so, so then

conquense [kon'kense] *adj* of *o* from Cuenca
■ *nm/f* native *o* inhabitant of Cuenca

conquista [kon'kista] *nf* conquest

conquistador, a [konkista'ðor, a] *adj*
conquering ■ *nm* conqueror

conquistar [konkis'tar] *vt* (*Mil*) to conquer;
(*puesto, simpatía*) to win; (*enamorar*) to win the
heart of

consabido, -a [konsa'βiðo, a] *adj* (*frase etc*)
old; (*pey*): **las consabidas excusas** the same
old excuses

consagrado, -a [konsa'ɣraðo, a] *adj* (*Rel*)
consecrated; (*actor*) established

consagrar [konsa'ɣrar] *vt* (*Rel*) to consecrate;
(*fig*) to devote

consciente [kons'θjente] *adj* conscious; **ser** *o*
estar ~ to be aware of

consecución [konseku'θjon] *nf* acquisition;
(*de fin*) attainment

consecuencia [konse'kwenθja] *nf*
consequence, outcome; (*firmeza*) consistency;
de ~ of importance

consecuente [konse'kwente] *adj* consistent

consecutivo, -a [konseku'tiβo, a] *adj*
consecutive

conseguir [konse'ɣir] *vt* to get, obtain;
(*sus fines*) to attain

consejería [konsexe'ria] *nf* (*Pol*) ministry
(*in a regional government*)

consejero, -a [konse'xero, a] *nm/f* adviser,
consultant; (*Pol*) minister (*in a regional
government*); (*Com*) director; (*en comisión*)
member

consejo [kon'sexo] *nm* advice; (*Pol*) council;
(*Com*) board; **un ~** a piece of advice; **~ de
administración** board of directors; **~
de guerra** court-martial; **C~ de Europa**
Council of Europe

consenso [kon'senso] *nm* consensus

consentido, -a [konsen'tiðo, a] *adj* (*mimado*)
spoiled

consentimiento [konsenti'mjento] *nm*
consent

consentir [konsen'tir] *vt* (*permitir, tolerar*)
to consent to; (*mimar*) to pamper, spoil
■ *vi* to agree, consent; **~ que algn haga algo**
to allow sb to do sth

conserje [kon'serxe] *nm* caretaker; (*portero*)
porter

conserva [kon'serβa] *nf*: **en ~** (*alimentos*)
tinned (*Brit*), canned; **conservas** tinned *o*
canned foods

conservación [konserβa'θjon] *nf*
conservation; (*de alimentos, vida*) preservation

conservador, a [konserβa'ðor, a] *adj* (*Pol*)
conservative ■ *nm/f* conservative

conservadurismo [konserβaðu'rismo] *nm*
(*Pol etc*) conservatism

conservante [konser'βante] *nm* preservative

conservar [konser'βar] *vt* (*gen*) to preserve;
(*recursos*) to conserve, keep; (*alimentos, vida*) to
preserve; **conservarse** *vr* to survive

conservas [kon'serβas] *nfpl*: **~ (alimenticias)**
tinned (*Brit*) *o* canned goods

conservatorio [konserβa'torjo] *nm* (*Mus*)
conservatoire; (*Am*) greenhouse

considerable [konsiðe'raβle] *adj*
considerable

consideración [konsiðera'θjon] *nf*
consideration; (*estimación*) respect; **de ~**
important; **De mi** *o* **nuestra (mayor) ~** (*Am*)
Dear Sir(s) *o* Madam; **tomar en ~** to take into
account

considerado, -a [konsiðe'raðo, a] *adj* (*atento*)
considerate; (*respetado*) respected

considerar [konsiðe'rar] *vt* (*gen*) to consider;
(*meditar*) to think about; (*tener en cuenta*) to
take into account

consienta *etc* [kon'sjenta] *vb ver* **consentir**

consigna [kon'siɣna] *nf* (*orden*) order,
instruction; (*para equipajes*) left-luggage
office (*Brit*), checkroom (*US*)

consignación [konsiɣna'θjon] *nf*
consignment; **~ de créditos** allocation of
credits

consignador [konsiɣna'ðor] *nm* (*Com*)
consignor

consignar [konsiɣ'nar] *vt* (*Com*) to send;
(*créditos*) to allocate

consignatario, -a [konsiɣna'tarjo, a] *nm/f*
(*Com*) consignee

consigo *etc* [kon'siɣo] *vb ver* **conseguir** ■ *pron*
(*m*) with him; (*f*) with her; (*usted*) with you;
(*reflexivo*) with o.s.

consiguiendo *etc* [konsi'ɣjendo] *vb ver*
conseguir

consiguiente [konsi'ɣjente] *adj* consequent;
por ~ and so, therefore, consequently

consintiendo *etc* [konsin'tjendo] *vb ver*
consentir

consistente [konsis'tente] *adj* consistent;
(*sólido*) solid, firm; (*válido*) sound; **~ en**
consisting of

consistir [konsis'tir] *vi*: **~ en** (*componerse de*)

to consist of; (*ser resultado de*) to be due to

consola [kon'sola] *nf* console, control panel; (*mueble*) console table; **~ de juegos** games console; **~ de mandos** (*Inform*) control console; **~ de visualización** visual display console

consolación [konsola'θjon] *nf* consolation

consolar [konso'lar] *vt* to console

consolidar [konsoli'ðar] *vt* to consolidate

consomé (*pl* **~s**) [konso'me, konso'mes] *nm* consommé, clear soup

consonancia [konso'nanθja] *nf* harmony; **en ~ con** in accordance with

consonante [konso'nante] *adj* consonant, harmonious ■ *nf* consonant

consorcio [kon'sorθjo] *nm* (*Com*) consortium, syndicate

consorte [kon'sorte] *nm/f* consort

conspicuo, -a [kons'pikwo, a] *adj* conspicuous

conspiración [konspira'θjon] *nf* conspiracy

conspirador, a [konspira'ðor, a] *nm/f* conspirator

conspirar [konspi'rar] *vi* to conspire

constancia [kons'tanθja] *nf* (*gen*) constancy; (*certeza*) certainly; **dejar ~ de algo** to put sth on record

constante [kons'tante] *adj, nf* constant

constar [kons'tar] *vi* (*evidenciarse*) to be clear o evident; **~ (en)** to appear (in); **~ de** to consist of; **hacer ~** to put on record; **me consta que ...** I have evidence that ...; **que conste que lo hice por ti** believe me, I did it for your own good

constatar [konsta'tar] *vt* (*controlar*) to check; (*observar*) to note

constelación [konstela'θjon] *nf* constellation

consternación [konsterna'θjon] *nf* consternation

constipado, -a [konsti'paðo, a] *adj*: **estar ~** to have a cold ■ *nm* cold

constiparse [konsti'parse] *vr* to catch a cold

constitución [konstitu'θjon] *nf* constitution; **Día de la C~** (*Esp*) Constitution Day (*6th December*)

constitucional [konstituθjo'nal] *adj* constitutional

constituir [konstitu'ir] *vt* (*formar, componer*) to constitute, make up; (*fundar, erigir, ordenar*) to constitute, establish; (*ser*) to be; **constituirse** *vr* (*Pol etc*) to be composed; (: *fundarse*) to be established

constitutivo, -a [konstitu'tiβo, a] *adj* constitutive, constituent

constituya *etc* [konsti'tuja] *vb ver* **constituir**

constituyente [konstitu'jente] *adj* constituent

constreñir [konstre'ɲir] *vt* (*obligar*) to compel, oblige; (*restringir*) to restrict

constriño *etc* [kons'triɲo], **constriñendo** *etc* [konstri'ɲendo] *vb ver* **constreñir**

construcción [konstruk'θjon] *nf* construction, building

constructivo, -a [konstruk'tiβo, a] *adj* constructive

constructor, a [konstruk'tor, a] *nm/f* builder

construir [konstru'ir] *vt* to build, construct

construyendo *etc* [konstru'jendo] *vb ver* **construir**

consuelo *etc* [kon'swelo] *vb ver* **consolar** ■ *nm* consolation, solace

consuetudinario, -a [konswetuði'narjo, a] *adj* customary; **derecho ~** common law

cónsul ['konsul] *nm* consul

consulado [konsu'laðo] *nm* (*sede*) consulate; (*cargo*) consulship

consulta [kon'sulta] *nf* consultation; (*Med: consultorio*) consulting room; (*Inform*) enquiry; **horas de ~** surgery hours; **obra de ~** reference book

consultar [konsul'tar] *vt* to consult; **~ un archivo** (*Inform*) to interrogate a file

consultor, a [konsul'tor, a] *nm*: **~ en dirección de empresas** management consultant

consultorio [konsul'torjo] *nm* (*Med*) surgery

consumado, -a [konsu'maðo, a] *adj* perfect; (*bribón*) out-and-out

consumar [konsu'mar] *vt* to complete, carry out; (*crimen*) to commit; (*sentencia*) to carry out

consumición [konsumi'θjon] *nf* consumption; (*bebida*) drink; (*comida*) food; **~ mínima** cover charge

consumido, -a [konsu'miðo, a] *adj* (*flaco*) skinny

consumidor, a [konsumi'ðor, a] *nm/f* consumer

consumir [konsu'mir] *vt* to consume; **consumirse** *vr* to be consumed; (*persona*) to waste away

consumismo [konsu'mismo] *nm* (*Com*) consumerism

consumo [kon'sumo] *nm* consumption; **bienes de ~** consumer goods

contabilice *etc* [kontaβi'liθe] *vb ver* **contabilizar**

contabilidad [kontaβili'ðað] *nf* accounting, book-keeping; (*profesión*) accountancy; (*Com*): **~ analítica** variable costing; **~ de costos** cost accounting; **~ de doble partida** double-entry book-keeping; **~ de gestión** management accounting; **~ por partida simple** single-entry book-keeping

contabilizar [kontaβi'liθar] *vt* to enter in the accounts

contable [kon'taβle] *nm/f* bookkeeper; *(licenciado)* accountant; ~ **de costos** *(Com)* cost accountant

contactar [kontak'tar] *vi:* ~ **con algn** to contact sb

contacto [kon'takto] *nm* contact; **lentes de** ~ contact lenses; **estar en** ~ **con** to be in touch with

contado, -a [kon'taðo, a] *adj:* **contados** *(escasos)* numbered, scarce, few ■ *nm:* **al** ~ for cash; **pagar al** ~ to pay (in) cash; **precio al** ~ cash price

contador [konta'ðor] *nm (aparato)* meter; *(Am: contable)* accountant

contaduría [kontaðu'ria] *nf* accountant's office

contagiar [konta'xjar] *vt (enfermedad)* to pass on, transmit; *(persona)* to infect; **contagiarse** *vr* to become infected

contagio [kon'taxjo] *nm* infection

contagioso, -a [konta'xjoso, a] *adj* infectious; *(fig)* catching

contaminación [kontamina'θjon] *nf (gen)* contamination; *(del ambiente etc)* pollution

contaminar [kontami'nar] *vt (gen)* to contaminate; *(aire, agua)* to pollute; *(fig)* to taint

contante [kon'tante] *adj:* **dinero** ~ **(y sonante)** hard cash

contar [kon'tar] *vt (páginas, dinero)* to count; *(anécdota etc)* to tell ■ *vi* to count; **contarse** *vr* to be counted, figure; ~ **con** to rely on, count on; **sin** ~ not to mention; **le cuento entre mis amigos** I reckon him among my friends

contemplación [kontempla'θjon] *nf* contemplation; **no andarse con contemplaciones** not to stand on ceremony

contemplar [kontem'plar] *vt* to contemplate; *(mirar)* to look at

contemporáneo, -a [kontempo'raneo, a] *adj, nm/f* contemporary

contemporizar [kontempori'θar] *vi:* ~ **con** to keep in with

contención [konten'θjon] *nf (Jur)* suit; **muro de** ~ retaining wall

contencioso, -a [konten'θjoso, a] *adj (Jur etc)* contentious ■ *nm (Pol)* conflict, dispute

contender [konten'der] *vi* to contend; *(en un concurso)* to compete

contendiente [konten'djente] *nm/f* contestant

contendrá *etc* [konten'dra] *vb ver* **contener**

contenedor [kontene'ðor] *nm* container; *(de escombros)* skip; ~ **de (la) basura** wheelie-bin

(Brit); ~ **de vidrio** bottle bank

contener [konte'ner] *vt* to contain, hold; *(risa etc)* to hold back, contain; **contenerse** *vr* to control *o* restrain o.s.

contenga *etc* [kon'tenga] *vb ver* **contener**

contenido, -a [konte'niðo, a] *adj (moderado)* restrained; *(risa etc)* suppressed ■ *nm* contents *pl*, content

contentar [konten'tar] *vt (satisfacer)* to satisfy; *(complacer)* to please; *(Com)* to endorse; **contentarse** *vr* to be satisfied

contento, -a [kon'tento, a] *adj* contented, content; *(alegre)* pleased; *(feliz)* happy

contestación [kontesta'θjon] *nf* answer, reply; ~ **a la demanda** *(Jur)* defence plea

contestador [kontesta'ðor] *nm:* ~ **automático** answering machine

contestar [kontes'tar] *vt* to answer (back), reply; *(Jur)* to corroborate, confirm

contestatario, -a [kontesta'tarjo, a] *adj* anti-establishment, nonconformist

contexto [kon'teksto] *nm* context

contienda [kon'tjenda] *nf* contest, struggle

contiene *etc* [kon'tjene] *vb ver* **contener**

contigo [kon'tiɣo] *pron* with you

contiguo, -a [kon'tiɣwo, a] *adj (de al lado)* next; *(vecino)* adjacent, adjoining

continental [kontinen'tal] *adj* continental

continente [konti'nente] *adj, nm* continent

contingencia [kontin'xenθja] *nf* contingency; *(riesgo)* risk; *(posibilidad)* eventuality

contingente [kontin'xente] *adj* contingent ■ *nm* contingent; *(Com)* quota

continuación [kontinwa'θjon] *nf* continuation; **a** ~ then, next

continuamente [kon'tinwamente] *adv (sin interrupción)* continuously; *(a todas horas)* constantly

continuar [konti'nwar] *vt* to continue, go on with; *(reanudar)* to resume ■ *vi* to continue, go on; ~ **hablando** to continue talking *o* to talk

continuidad [kontinwi'ðað] *nf* continuity

continuo, -a [kon'tinwo, a] *adj (sin interrupción)* continuous; *(acción perseverante)* continual

contonearse [kontone'arse] *vr (hombre)* to swagger; *(mujer)* to swing one's hips

contorno [kon'torno] *nm* outline; *(Geo)* contour; **contornos** *nmpl* neighbourhood *sg*, surrounding area *sg*

contorsión [kontor'sjon] *nf* contortion

contra ['kontra] *prep* against; *(Com: giro)* on ■ *adv* against ■ *adj, nm/f (Pol fam)* counter-revolutionary ■ *nm* con ■ *nf:* **la C~ (nicaragüense)** the Contras *pl*

contraalmirante [kontraalmi'rante] nm rear admiral

contraanálisis [kontraa'nalisis] nm follow-up test, countertest

contraataque [kontraa'take] nm counterattack

contrabajo [kontra'βaxo] nm double bass

contrabandista [kontraβan'dista] nm/f smuggler

contrabando [kontra'βando] nm (acción) smuggling; (mercancías) contraband; **~ de armas** gun-running

contracción [kontrak'θjon] nf contraction

contrachapado [kontratʃa'paðo] nm plywood

contracorriente [kontrako'rrjente] nf cross-current

contradecir [kontraðe'θir] vt to contradict

contradicción [kontraðik'θjon] nf contradiction; **espíritu de ~** contrariness

contradicho [kontra'ðitʃo] pp de **contradecir**

contradiciendo etc [kontraði'θjendo] vb ver **contradecir**

contradictorio, -a [kontraðik'torjo, a] adj contradictory

contradiga etc [kontra'ðiɣa], **contradije** [kontra'ðixe], **contradirá** etc [kontraði'ra] vb ver **contradecir**

contraer [kontra'er] vt to contract; (hábito) to acquire; (limitar) to restrict; **contraerse** vr to contract; (limitarse) to limit o.s.

contraespionage [kontraespjo'naxe] nm counter-espionage

contrafuerte [kontra'fwerte] nm (Arq) buttress

contragolpe [kontra'ɣolpe] nm backlash

contrahacer [kontraa'θer] vb (copiar) to copy, imitate; (moneda) to counterfeit; (documento) to forge, fake; (libro) to pirate

contrahaga etc [kontra'aɣa], **contraharé** etc [kontraa're] vb ver **contrahacer**

contrahecho, -a [kontra'etʃo, a] pp de **contrahacer** ▪ adj fake; (Anat) hunchbacked

contrahice etc [kontra'iθe] vb ver **contrahacer**

contraiga etc [kon'traiɣa] vb ver **contraer**

contraindicaciones [kontraindika'θjones] nfpl (Med) contraindications

contraje etc [kon'traxe] vb ver **contraer**

contralor [kontra'lor] nm (Am) government accounting inspector

contraluz [kontra'luθ] nf (Foto etc) back lighting; **a ~** against the light

contramaestre [kontrama'estre] nm foreman

contraofensiva [kontraofen'siβa] nf counteroffensive

contraorden [kontra'orðen] nf counter-order, countermand

contrapartida [kontrapar'tiða] nf (Com) balancing entry; **como ~ (de)** in return (for), as o in compensation (for)

contrapelo [kontra'pelo]: **a ~** adv the wrong way

contrapesar [kontrape'sar] vt to counterbalance; (fig) to offset

contrapeso [kontra'peso] nm counterweight; (fig) counterbalance; (Com) makeweight

contrapondré etc [kontrapon'dre] vb ver **contraponer**

contraponer [kontrapo'ner] vt (cotejar) to compare; (oponer) to oppose

contraponga etc [kontra'ponga] vb ver **contraponer**

contraportada [kontrapor'taða] nf (de revista) back page

contraproducente [kontraproðu'θente] adj counterproductive

contrapuesto [kontra'pwesto] pp de **contraponer**

contrapunto [kontra'punto] nm counterpoint

contrapuse etc [kontra'puse] vb ver **contraponer**

contrariar [kontra'rjar] vt (oponerse) to oppose; (poner obstáculo) to impede; (enfadar) to vex

contrariedad [kontrarje'ðað] nf (oposición) opposition; (obstáculo) obstacle, setback; (disgusto) vexation, annoyance

contrario, -a [kon'trarjo, a] adj contrary; (persona) opposed; (sentido, lado) opposite ▪ nm/f enemy, adversary; (Deporte) opponent; **al ~, por el ~** on the contrary; **de lo ~** otherwise

Contrarreforma [kontrarre'forma] nf Counter-Reformation

contrarreloj [kontrarre'lo(x)] nf (tb: **prueba contrarreloj**) time trial

contrarrestar [kontrarres'tar] vt to counteract

contrarrevolución [kontrarreβolu'θjon] nf counter-revolution

contrasentido [kontrasen'tiðo] nm contradiction; **es un ~ que él ...** it doesn't make sense for him to ...

contraseña [kontra'seɲa] nf countersign; (frase) password

contrastar [kontras'tar] vt to resist ▪ vi to contrast

contraste [kon'traste] nm contrast

contrata [kon'trata] nf (Jur) written contract; (empleo) hiring contratar [kontra'tar] vt (firmar un acuerdo para) to contract for; (empleados, obreros) to hire, engage; (Deporte) to sign up; contratarse vr to sign on

contratiempo [kontra'tjempo] nm (revés) setback; (accidente) mishap; a ~ (Mus) off-beat

contratista [kontra'tista] nm/f contractor

contrato [kon'trato] nm contract; ~ de compraventa contract of sale; ~ a precio fijo fixed-price contract; ~ a término forward contract; ~ de trabajo contract of employment o service

contravalor [kontraβa'lor] nm exchange value

contravención [kontraβen'θjon] nf contravention, violation

contravendré etc [kontraβen'dre], contravenga etc [kontra'βenga] vb ver contravenir

contravenir [kontraβe'nir] vi: ~ a to contravene, violate

contraventana [kontraβen'tana] nf shutter

contraviene etc [kontra'βjene], contraviniendo etc [kontraβi'njendo] vb ver contravenir

contrayendo [kontra'jendo] vb ver contraer

contribución [kontriβu'θjon] nf (municipal etc) tax; (ayuda) contribution; exento de contribuciones tax-free

contribuir [kontriβu'ir] vt, vi to contribute; (Com) to pay (in taxes)

contribuyendo etc [kontriβu'jendo] vb ver contribuir

contribuyente [kontriβu'jente] nm/f (Com) taxpayer; (que ayuda) contributor

contrincante [kontrin'kante] nm opponent, rival

control [kon'trol] nm control; (inspección) inspection, check; (Com): ~ de calidad quality control; ~ de cambios exchange control; ~ de costos cost control; ~ de créditos credit control; ~ de existencias stock control; ~ de precios price control

controlador, a [kontrola'ðor, a] nm/f controller; ~ aéreo air-traffic controller

controlar [kontro'lar] vt to control; to inspect, check; (Com) to audit

controversia [kontro'βersja] nf controversy

contubernio [kontu'βernjo] nm ring, conspiracy

contumaz [kontu'maθ] adj obstinate, stubbornly disobedient

contundente [kontun'dente] adj (prueba) conclusive; (fig: argumento) convincing; instrumento ~ blunt instrument

contusión [kontu'sjon] nf bruise

contuve etc [kon'tuβe] vb ver contener

convalecencia [kombale'θenθja] nf convalescence

convalecer [kombale'θer] vi to convalesce, get better

convaleciente [kombale'θjente] adj, nm/f convalescent

convalezca etc [komba'leθka] vb ver convalecer

convalidar [kombali'ðar] vt (título) to recognize

convencer [komben'θer] vt to convince; (persuadir) to persuade

convencimiento [kombenθi'mjento] nm (acción) convincing; (persuasión) persuasion; (certidumbre) conviction; tener el ~ de que ... to be convinced that ...

convención [komben'θjon] nf convention

convencional [kombenθjo'nal] adj conventional

convendré etc [komben'dre], convenga etc [kom'benga] vb ver convenir

conveniencia [kombe'njenθja] nf suitability; (conformidad) agreement; (utilidad, provecho) usefulness; conveniencias nfpl conventions; (Com) property sg; ser de la ~ de algn to suit sb

conveniente [kombe'njente] adj suitable; (útil) useful; (correcto) fit, proper; (aconsejable) advisable

convenio [kom'benjo] nm agreement, treaty; ~ de nivel crítico threshold agreement

convenir [kombe'nir] vi (estar de acuerdo) to agree; (ser conveniente) to suit, be suitable; "sueldo a ~" "salary to be agreed"; conviene recordar que ... it should be remembered that ...

convento [kom'bento] nm monastery; (de monjas) convent

convenza etc [kom'benθa] vb ver convencer

convergencia [komber'xenθja] nf convergence

converger [komber'xer], convergir [komber'xir] vi to converge; sus esfuerzos convergen a un fin común their efforts are directed towards the same objective

converja etc [kom'berxa] vb ver converger; convergir

conversación [kombersa'θjon] nf conversation

conversar [komber'sar] vi to talk, converse

conversión [komber'sjon] nf conversion

converso, -a [kom'berso, a] nm/f convert

convertir [komber'tir] vt to convert; (transformar) to transform, turn; (Com) to (ex)change; convertirse vr (Rel) to convert

convexo, -a [kom'bekso, a] adj convex

convicción [kombik'θjon] *nf* conviction

convicto, -a [kom'bikto, a] *adj* convicted; (*condenado*) condemned

convidado, -a [kombi'ðaðo, a] *nm/f* guest

convidar [kombi'ðar] *vt* to invite

conviene *etc* [kom'bjene] *vb ver* **convenir**

convierta *etc* [kom'bjerta] *vb ver* **convertir**

convincente [kombin'θente] *adj* convincing

conviniendo *etc* [kombi'njendo] *vb ver* **convenir**

convirtiendo *etc* [kombir'tjendo] *vb ver* **convertir**

convite [kom'bite] *nm* invitation; (*banquete*) banquet

convivencia [kombi'βenθja] *nf* coexistence, living together

convivir [kombi'βir] *vi* to live together; (Pol) to coexist

convocar [kombo'kar] *vt* to summon, call (together)

convocatoria [komboka'torja] *nf* summons *sg*; (*anuncio*) notice of meeting; (Escol) examination session

convoque *etc* [kom'boke] *vb ver* **convocar**

convoy [kom'boj] *nm* (Ferro) train

convulsión [kombul'sjon] *nf* convulsion; (Pol etc) upheaval

conyugal [konju'ɣal] *adj* conjugal; **vida ~** married life

cónyuge ['konjuxe] *nm/f* spouse, partner

coña ['koɲa] *nf*: **tomar algo a ~** (fam!) to take sth as a joke

coñac (*pl* **coñacs**) ['koɲa(k), 'koɲas] *nm* cognac, brandy

coñazo [ko'ɲaθo] *nm* (fam) pain; **dar el ~** to be a real pain

coño ['koɲo] (fam!) *nm* cunt (!); (Am pey) Spaniard ■ *excl* (enfado) shit (!); (sorpresa) bloody hell (!); **¡qué ~!** what a pain in the arse! (!)

cookie ['kuki] *nm* (Inform) cookie

cooperación [koopera'θjon] *nf* cooperation

cooperar [koope'rar] *vi* to cooperate

cooperativo, -a [koopera'tiβo, a] *adj* cooperative ■ *nf* cooperative

coordenada [koorðe'naða] *nf* (Mat) coordinate; (fig): **coordenadas** *nfpl* guidelines, framework *sg*

coordinación [koorðina'θjon] *nf* coordination

coordinador, a [koorðina'ðor, a] *nm/f* coordinator ■ *nf* coordinating committee

coordinar [koorði'nar] *vt* to coordinate

copa ['kopa] *nf* (tb Deporte) cup; (vaso) glass; (de árbol) top; (de sombrero) crown; **copas** *nfpl* (Naipes) one of the suits in the Spanish card deck; **(tomar una) ~** (to have a) drink; **ir de copas** to go out for a drink; *ver tb* **Baraja Española**

copar [ko'par] *vt* (puestos) to monopolize

coparticipación [kopartiθipa'θjon] *nf* (Com) co-ownership

COPE *nf abr* (= Cadena de Ondas Populares Españolas) Spanish radio network

Copenhague [kope'naɣe] *n* Copenhagen

copete [ko'pete] *nm* tuft (of hair); **de alto ~** aristocratic, upper-crust (fam)

copia ['kopja] *nf* copy; (Arte) replica; (Com etc) duplicate; (Inform): **~ impresa** hard copy; **~ de respaldo** o **de seguridad** backup copy; **hacer ~ de seguridad** to back up; **~ de trabajo** working copy

copiadora [kopja'ðora] *nf* photocopier

copiar [ko'pjar] *vt* to copy; **~ al pie de la letra** to copy word for word

copiloto [kopi'loto] *nm* (Aviat) co-pilot; (Auto) co-driver

copioso, -a [ko'pjoso, a] *adj* copious, plentiful

copita [ko'pita] *nf* (small) glass; (Golf) tee

copla ['kopla] *nf* verse; (canción) (popular) song

copo ['kopo] *nm*: **copos de maíz** cornflakes; **~ de nieve** snowflake

coprocesador [koproθesa'ðor] *nm* (Inform) co-processor

coproducción [koproðuk'θjon] *nf* (Cine etc) joint production

copropietarios [kopropje'tarjos] *nmpl* (Com) joint owners

cópula ['kopula] *nf* copulation

copular [kopu'lar] *vi* to copulate

coqueta [ko'keta] *adj* flirtatious, coquettish ■ *nf* (mujer) flirt

coquetear [kokete'ar] *vi* to flirt

coraje [ko'raxe] *nm* courage; (ánimo) spirit; (ira) anger

coral [ko'ral] *adj* choral ■ *nf* choir ■ *nm* (Zool) coral

Corán [ko'ran] *nm*: **el ~** the Koran

coraza [ko'raθa] *nf* (armadura) armour; (blindaje) armour plating

corazón [kora'θon] *nm* heart; (Bot) core; **corazones** *nmpl* (Naipes) hearts; **de buen ~** kind-hearted; **de todo ~** wholeheartedly; **estar mal del ~** to have heart trouble

corazonada [koraθo'naða] *nf* impulse; (presentimiento) presentiment, hunch

corbata [kor'βata] *nf* tie

corbeta [kor'βeta] *nf* corvette

Córcega ['korθeɣa] *nf* Corsica

corcel [kor'θel] *nm* steed

corchea [kor'tʃea] *nf* quaver

corchete [kor'tʃete] *nm* catch, clasp; **corchetes** *nmpl* (Tip) square brackets corcho ['kortʃo] nm cork; (Pesca) float

corcovado, -a [korko'βaðo, a] adj hunchbacked ▪ nm/f hunchback

cordel [kor'ðel] nm cord, line

cordero [kor'ðero] nm lamb; (piel) lambskin

cordial [kor'ðjal] adj cordial ▪ nm cordial, tonic

cordialidad [korðjali'ðað] nf warmth, cordiality

cordillera [korði'ʎera] nf range (of mountains)

Córdoba ['korðoβa] nf Cordova

cordobés, -esa [korðo'βes, esa] adj, nm/f Cordovan

cordón [kor'ðon] nm (cuerda) cord, string; (de zapatos) lace; (Elec) flex, wire (US); (Mil etc) cordon

cordura [kor'ðura] nf (Med) sanity; (fig) good sense

Corea [ko'rea] nf Korea; ~ del Norte/Sur North/South Korea

coreano, -a [kore'ano, a] adj, nm/f Korean

corear [kore'ar] vt to chorus

coreografía [koreoɣra'fia] nf choreography

corista [ko'rista] nf (Teat etc) chorus girl

cornada [kor'naða] nf (Taur etc) butt, goring

córner (pl córners) ['korner, 'korners] nm corner (kick)

corneta [kor'neta] nf bugle

cornisa [kor'nisa] nf cornice

Cornualles [kor'nwaʎes] nm Cornwall

cornudo, -a [kor'nuðo, a] adj (Zool) horned; (marido) cuckolded

coro ['koro] nm chorus; (conjunto de cantores) choir

corolario [koro'larjo] nm corollary

corona [ko'rona] nf crown; (de flores) garland

coronación [korona'θjon] nf coronation

coronar [koro'nar] vt to crown

coronel [koro'nel] nm colonel

coronilla [koro'niʎa] nf (Anat) crown (of the head); estar hasta la ~ (de) to be utterly fed up (with)

corpiño [kor'piɲo] nm bodice; (Am: sostén) bra

corporación [korpora'θjon] nf corporation

corporal [korpo'ral] adj corporal, bodily

corporativo, -a [korpora'tiβo, a] adj corporate

corpulento, -a [korpu'lento, a] adj (persona) well-built

corral [ko'rral] nm (patio) farmyard; (Agr: de aves) poultry yard; (redil) pen

correa [ko'rrea] nf strap; (cinturón) belt; (de perro) lead, leash; ~ transportadora conveyor belt

correaje [ko'rreaxe] nm (Agr) harness

corrección [korrek'θjon] nf correction; (reprensión) rebuke; (cortesía) good manners; (Inform): ~ por líneas line editing; ~ en pantalla screen editing; ~ (de pruebas) (Tip) proofreading

correccional [korrekθjo'nal] nm reformatory

correcto, -a [ko'rrekto, a] adj correct; (persona) well-mannered

corrector, a [korrek'tor, a] nm/f: ~ de pruebas proofreader

corredera [korre'ðera] nf: puerta de ~ sliding door

corredizo, -a [korre'ðiθo, a] adj (puerta etc) sliding; (nudo) running

corredor, a [korre'ðor, a] adj running; (rápido) fast ▪ nm/f (Deporte) runner ▪ nm (pasillo) corridor; (balcón corrido) gallery; (Com) agent, broker; ~ de bienes raíces real-estate broker; ~ de bolsa stockbroker; ~ de seguros insurance broker

corregir [korre'xir] vt (error) to correct; (amonestar, reprender) to rebuke, reprimand; corregirse vr to reform

correo [ko'rreo] nm post, mail; (persona) courier; Correos nmpl Post Office sg; ~ aéreo airmail; ~ basura (por carta) junk mail; (por Internet) spam; ~ certificado registered mail; ~ electrónico email, electronic mail; ~ urgente special delivery; a vuelta de ~ by return (of post)

correr [ko'rrer] vt to run; (viajar) to cover, travel; (riesgo) to run; (aventura) to have; (cortinas) to draw; (cerrojo) to shoot ▪ vi to run; (líquido) to run, flow; (rumor) to go round; correrse vr to slide, move; (colores) to run; (fam: tener orgasmo) to come; echar a ~ to break into a run; ~ con los gastos to pay the expenses; eso corre de mi cuenta I'll take care of that

correspondencia [korrespon'denθja] nf correspondence; (Ferro) connection; (reciprocidad) return; ~ directa (Com) direct mail

corresponder [korrespon'der] vi to correspond; (convenir) to be suitable; (pertenecer) to belong; (tocar) to concern; (favor) to repay; corresponderse vr (por escrito) to correspond; (amarse) to love one another; "a quien corresponda" "to whom it may concern"

correspondiente [korrespon'djente] adj corresponding; (respectivo) respective

corresponsal [korrespon'sal] nm/f (newspaper) correspondent; (Com) agent

corretaje [korre'taxe] nm (Com) brokerage

corretear [korrete'ar] vi to loiter

corrido, -a [ko'rriðo, a] adj (avergonzado) abashed; (fluido) fluent ▪ nf run, dash;

(*de toros*) bullfight; **de** ~ fluently; **tres noches corridas** three nights running; **un kilo** ~ a good kilo

corriente [ko'rrjente] *adj* (*agua*) running; (*fig*) flowing; (*cuenta etc*) current; (*común*) ordinary, normal ■ *nf* current; (*fig: tendencia*) course ■ *nm* current month; ~ **de aire** draught; ~ **eléctrica** electric current; **las corrientes modernas del arte** modern trends in art; **estar al ~ de** to be informed about

corrigiendo *etc* [korri'xjendo] *vb ver* **corregir**

corrija *etc* [ko'rrixa] *vb ver* **corregir**

corrillo [ko'rriʎo] *nm* ring, circle (of people); (*fig*) clique

corro ['korro] *nm* ring, circle (of people); (*baile*) ring-a-ring-a-roses; **la gente hizo** ~ the people formed a ring

corroborar [korroβo'rar] *vt* to corroborate

corroer [korro'er] *vt* (*tb fig*) to corrode, eat away; (*Geo*) to erode

corromper [korrom'per] *vt* (*madera*) to rot; (*fig*) to corrupt

corrompido, -a [korrom'piðo, a] *adj* corrupt

corrosivo, -a [korro'siβo, a] *adj* corrosive

corroyendo *etc* [korro'jendo] *vb ver* **corroer**

corrupción [korrup'θjon] *nf* rot, decay; (*fig*) corruption

corrupto, -a [ko'rrupto, a] *adj* corrupt

corsario [kor'sarjo] *nm* privateer, corsair

corsé [kor'se] *nm* corset

corso, -a ['korso, a] *adj, nm/f* Corsican

cortacésped [korta'θespeð] *nm* lawn mower

cortado, -a [kor'taðo, a] *adj* (*con cuchillo*) cut; (*leche*) sour; (*confuso*) confused; (*desconcertado*) embarrassed; (*tímido*) shy ■ *nm* white coffee (with a little milk)

cortadora [korta'ðora] *nf* cutter, slicer

cortadura [korta'ðura] *nf* cut

cortalápices [korta'lapiθes], **cortalápiz** [korta'lapiθ] *nm inv* (*pencil*) sharpener

cortante [kor'tante] *adj* (*viento*) biting; (*frío*) bitter

cortapisa [korta'pisa] *nf* (*restricción*) restriction; (*traba*) snag

cortar [kor'tar] *vt* to cut; (*suministro*) to cut off; (*un pasaje*) to cut out; (*comunicación, teléfono*) to cut off ■ *vi* to cut; (*Am Telec*) to hang up; **cortarse** *vr* (*turbarse*) to become embarrassed; (*leche*) to turn, curdle; ~ **por lo sano** to settle things once and for all; **cortarse el pelo** to have one's hair cut; **se cortó la línea** *o* **el teléfono** I got cut off

cortauñas [korta'uɲas] *nm inv* nail clippers *pl*

corte ['korte] *nm* cut, cutting; (*filo*) edge; (*de tela*) piece, length; (*Costura*) tailoring ■ *nf* (*real*) (royal) court; ~ **y confección** dressmaking; ~ **de corriente** *o* **luz** power

cut; ~ **de pelo** haircut; **me da** ~ **pedírselo** I'm embarrassed to ask him for it; **¡qué** ~ **le di!** I left him with no comeback!; **C~ Internacional de Justicia** International Court of Justice; **las Cortes** the Spanish Parliament *sg*; **hacer la** ~ **a** to woo, court; *see note*

cortejar [korte'xar] *vt* to court

cortejo [kor'texo] *nm* entourage; ~ **fúnebre** funeral procession, cortège

cortés [kor'tes] *adj* courteous, polite

cortesano, -a [korte'sano, a] *adj* courtly

cortesía [korte'sia] *nf* courtesy

corteza [kor'teθa] *nf* (*de árbol*) bark; (*de pan*) crust; (*de fruta*) peel, skin; (*de queso*) rind

cortijo [kor'tixo] *nm* farmhouse

cortina [kor'tina] *nf* curtain; ~ **de humo** smoke screen

corto, -a ['korto, a] *adj* short; (*tímido*) bashful; ~ **de luces** not very bright; ~ **de oído** hard of hearing; ~ **de vista** short-sighted; **estar** ~ **de fondos** to be short of funds

cortocircuito [kortoθir'kwito] *nm* short-circuit

cortometraje [kortome'traxe] *nm* (*Cine*) short

Coruña [ko'ruɲa] *nf*: **La** ~ Corunna

coruñés, -esa [koru'ɲes, esa] *adj* of *o* from Corunna ■ *nm/f* native *o* inhabitant of Corunna

corvo, -a ['korβo, a] *adj* curved; (*nariz*) hooked ■ *nf* back of knee

cosa ['kosa] *nf* thing; (*asunto*) affair; ~ **de** about; **eso es** ~ **mía** that's my business; **es poca** ~ it's not important; **¡qué** ~ **más rara!** how strange!

cosaco, -a [ko'sako, a] *adj, nm/f* Cossack

coscorrón [kosko'rron] *nm* bump on the head

cosecha [ko'setʃa] *nf* (*Agr*) harvest; (*acto*) harvesting; (*de vino*) vintage; (*producción*) yield

cosechadora [kosetʃa'ðora] *nf* combine harvester
cosechar [kose'tʃar] *vt* to harvest, gather (in)
coser [ko'ser] *vt* to sew; (*Med*) to stitch (up)
cosido [ko'siðo] *nm* sewing
cosmético, -a [kos'metiko, a] *adj, nm* cosmetic ■ *nf* cosmetics *pl*
cosmopolita [kosmopo'lita] *adj* cosmopolitan
cosmos ['kosmos] *nm* cosmos
coso ['koso] *nm* bullring
cosquillas [kos'kiʎas] *nfpl*: **hacer ~** to tickle; **tener ~** to be ticklish
cosquilleo [koski'ʎeo] *nm* tickling (sensation)
costa ['kosta] *nf* (*Geo*) coast; **C~ Brava** Costa Brava; **C~ Cantábrica** Cantabrian Coast; **C~ de Marfil** Ivory Coast; **C~ del Sol** Costa del Sol; **a ~** (*Com*) at cost; **a ~ de** at the expense of; **a toda ~** at any price
costado [kos'taðo] *nm* side; **de ~** (*dormir*) on one's side; **español por los 4 costados** Spanish through and through
costal [kos'tal] *nm* sack
costalada [kosta'laða] *nf* bad fall
costanera [kosta'nera] *nf* (*Am*) (seaside) promenade
costar [kos'tar] *vt* (*valer*) to cost; **me cuesta hablarle** I find it hard to talk to him; **¿cuánto cuesta?** how much does it cost?
Costa Rica [kosta'rika] *nf* Costa Rica
costarricense [kostarri'θense],
costarriqueño, -a [kostarri'keɲo, a] *adj, nm/f* Costa Rican
coste ['koste] *nm* (*Com*): **~ promedio** average cost; **costes fijos** fixed costs; *ver tb* **costo**
costear [koste'ar] *vt* to pay for; (*Com etc*) to finance; (*Naut*) to sail along the coast of; **costearse** *vr* (*negocio*) to pay for itself, cover its costs
costeño, -a [kos'teɲo, a] *adj* coastal
costero [kos'tero, a] *adj* coastal, coast *cpd*
costilla [kos'tiʎa] *nf* rib; (*Culin*) cutlet
costo ['kosto] *nm* cost, price; **~ directo** direct cost; **~ de expedición** shipping charges; **~ de sustitución** replacement cost; **~ unitario** unit cost; **~ de la vida** cost of living
costoso, -a [kos'toso, a] *adj* costly, expensive
costra ['kostra] *nf* (*corteza*) crust; (*Med*) scab
costumbre [kos'tumbre] *nf* custom, habit; **como de ~** as usual
costura [kos'tura] *nf* sewing, needlework; (*confección*) dressmaking; (*zurcido*) seam
costurera [kostu'rera] *nf* dressmaker
costurero [kostu'rero] *nm* sewing box *o* case
cota ['kota] *nf* (*Geo*) height above sea level; (*fig*) height

cotarro [ko'tarro] *nm*: **dirigir el ~** (*fam*) to rule the roost
cotejar [kote'xar] *vt* to compare
cotejo [ko'texo] *nm* comparison
cotice *etc* [ko'tiθe] *vb ver* **cotizar**
cotidiano, -a [koti'ðjano, a] *adj* daily, day to day
cotilla [ko'tiʎa] *nf* busybody, gossip
cotillear [kotiʎe'ar] *vi* to gossip
cotilleo [koti'ʎeo] *nm* gossip(ing)
cotización [kotiθa'θjon] *nf* (*Com*) quotation, price; (*de club*) dues *pl*
cotizado, -a [koti'θaðo, a] *adj* (*fig*) highly-prized
cotizar [koti'θar] *vt* (*Com*) to quote, price; **cotizarse** *vr* (*fig*) to be highly prized; **cotizarse a** to sell at, fetch; (*Bolsa*) to stand at, be quoted at
coto ['koto] *nm* (*terreno cercado*) enclosure; (*de caza*) reserve; (*Com*) price-fixing agreement; **poner ~ a** to put a stop to
cotorra [ko'torra] *nf* (*Zool: loro*) parrot; (*fam: persona*) windbag
coyote [ko'jote] *nm* coyote, prairie wolf
coyuntura [kojun'tura] *nf* (*Anat*) joint; (*fig*) juncture, occasion; **esperar una ~ favorable** to await a favourable moment
coz [koθ] *nf* kick
CP *nm abr* (= *computador personal*) PC
C.P. *abr* (*Esp*) = **Caja Postal**
C.P.A. *nf abr* (= *Caja Postal de Ahorros*) Post Office Savings Bank
CP/M *nm abr* (= *Programa de control para microprocesadores*) CP/M
CPN *nm abr* (*Esp*) = **Cuerpo de la Policía Nacional**
cps *abr* (= *caracteres por segundo*) c.p.s.
crac [krak] *nm* (*Econ*) crash
cráneo ['kraneo] *nm* skull, cranium
crápula ['krapula] *nf* drunkenness
cráter ['krater] *nm* crater
creación [krea'θjon] *nf* creation
creador, a [krea'ðor, a] *adj* creative ■ *nm/f* creator
crear [kre'ar] *vt* to create, make; (*originar*) to originate; (*Inform: archivo*) to create; **crearse** *vr* (*comité etc*) to be set up
creativo, -a [krea'tiβo, a] *adj* creative
crecer [kre'θer] *vi* to grow; (*precio*) to rise; **crecerse** *vr* (*engreírse*) to get cocky
creces ['kreθes]: **con ~** *adv* amply, fully
crecido, -a [kre'θiðo, a] *adj* (*persona, planta*) full-grown; (*cantidad*) large ■ *nf* (*de río*) spate, flood
creciente [kre'θjente] *adj* growing; (*cantidad*) increasing; (*luna*) crescent ■ *nm* crescent
crecimiento [kreθi'mjento] *nm* growth;

(*aumento*) increase; (*Com*) rise

credenciales [kreðen'θjales] *nfpl* credentials

crédito ['kreðito] *nm* credit; **a ~** on credit; **dar ~ a** to believe (in); **~ al consumidor** consumer credit; **~ rotativo** *o* **renovable** revolving credit

credo ['kreðo] *nm* creed

crédulo, -a ['kreðulo, a] *adj* credulous

creencia [kre'enθja] *nf* belief

creer [kre'er] *vt, vi* to think, believe; (*considerar*) to think, consider; **creerse** *vr* to believe o.s. (to be); **~ en** to believe in; **¡ya lo creo!** I should think so!

creíble [kre'iβle] *adj* credible, believable

creído, -a [kre'iðo, a] *adj* (*engreído*) conceited

crema ['krema] *adj inv* cream (coloured) ■ *nf* cream; (*natillas*) custard; **la ~ de la sociedad** the cream of society

cremallera [krema'ʎera] *nf* zip (fastener) (*Brit*), zipper (*US*)

crematorio [krema'torjo] *nm* crematorium (*Brit*), crematory (*US*)

cremoso, -a [kre'moso, a] *adj* creamy

crepitar [krepi'tar] *vi* (*fuego*) to crackle

crepúsculo [kre'puskulo] *nm* twilight, dusk

crespo, -a ['krespo, a] *adj* (*pelo*) curly

crespón [kres'pon] *nm* crêpe

cresta ['kresta] *nf* (*Geo: Zool*) crest

Creta ['kreta] *nf* Crete

cretino, -a [kre'tino, a] *adj* cretinous ■ *nm/f* cretin

creyendo *etc* [kre'jendo] *vb ver* **creer**

creyente [kre'jente] *nm/f* believer

crezca *etc* ['kreθka] *vb ver* **crecer**

cría *etc* ['kria] *vb ver* **criar** ■ *nf ver* **crío, a**

criada [kri'aða] *nf ver* **criado, a**

criadero [kria'ðero] *nm* nursery; (*Zool*) breeding place

criadillas [kria'ðiʎas] *nfpl* (*Culin*) bull's (*o* sheep's) testicles

criado, -a [kri'aðo, a] *nm* servant ■ *nf* servant, maid

criador [kria'ðor] *nm* breeder

crianza [kri'anθa] *nf* rearing, breeding; (*fig*) breeding; (*Med*) lactation

criar [kri'ar] *vt* (*amamantar*) to suckle, feed; (*educar*) to bring up; (*producir*) to grow, produce; (*animales*) to breed; **criarse** *vr* to grow (up); **~ cuervos** to nourish a viper in one's bosom; **Dios los cría y ellos se juntan** birds of a feather flock together

criatura [kria'tura] *nf* creature; (*niño*) baby, (small) child

criba ['kriβa] *nf* sieve

cribar [kri'βar] *vt* to sieve

crimen ['krimen] *nm* crime; **~ pasional** crime of passion

criminal [krimi'nal] *adj, nm/f* criminal

crin [krin] *nf* (*tb:* **crines**) mane

crío, -a ['krio, a] *nm/f* (*fam: chico*) kid ■ *nf* (*de animales*) rearing, breeding; (*animal*) young

criollo, -a [kri'oʎo, a] *adj* (*gen*) Creole; (*Am*) native (to America), national ■ *nm/f* (*gen*) Creole; (*Am*) native American

cripta ['kripta] *nf* crypt

crisis ['krisis] *nf inv* crisis; **~ nerviosa** nervous breakdown

crisma ['krisma] *nf*: **romperle la ~ a algn** (*fam*) to knock sb's block off

crisol [kri'sol] *nm* (*Tec*) crucible; (*fig*) melting pot

crispación [krispa'θjon] *nf* tension

crispar [kris'par] *vt* (*músculo*) to cause to contract; (*nervios*) to set on edge

cristal [kris'tal] *nm* crystal; (*de ventana*) glass, pane; (*lente*) lens; **de ~** glass *cpd*; **~ ahumado/tallado** smoked/cut glass

cristalería [kristale'ria] *nf* (*tienda*) glassware shop; (*objetos*) glassware

cristalice *etc* [krista'liθe] *vb ver* **cristalizar**

cristalino, -a [krista'lino, a] *adj* crystalline; (*fig*) clear ■ *nm* lens of the eye

cristalizar [kristali'θar] *vt, vi* to crystallize

cristiandad [kristjan'dað] *nf*, **cristianismo** [kristja'nismo] *nm* Christianity

cristiano, -a [kris'tjano, a] *adj, nm/f* Christian; **hablar en ~** to speak proper Spanish; (*fig*) to speak clearly

Cristo ['kristo] *nm* (*dios*) Christ; (*crucifijo*) crucifix

Cristóbal [kris'toβal] *nm*: **~ Colón** Christopher Columbus

criterio [kri'terjo] *nm* criterion; (*juicio*) judgement; (*enfoque*) attitude, approach; (*punto de vista*) view, opinion; **~ de clasificación** (*Inform*) sort criterion

criticar [kriti'kar] *vt* to criticize

crítico, -a ['kritiko, a] *adj* critical ■ *nm* critic ■ *nf* criticism; (*Teat etc*) review, notice; **la crítica** the critics *pl*

critique *etc* [kri'tike] *vb ver* **criticar**

Croacia [kro'aθja] *nf* Croatia

croar [kro'ar] *vi* to croak

croata [kro'ata] *adj, nm/f* Croat(ian) ■ *nm* (*Ling*) Croat(ian)

croissan, croissant [krwa'san] *nm* croissant

crol ['krol] *nm* crawl

cromado [kro'maðo] *nm* chromium plating, chrome

cromo ['kromo] *nm* chrome; (*Tip*) coloured print

cromosoma [kromo'soma] *nm* chromosome

crónico, -a ['kroniko, a] *adj* chronic ■ *nf* chronicle, account; (*de periódico*) feature, article

cronología [kronolo'xia] *nf* chronology
cronológico, -a [krono'loxiko, a] *adj* chronological
cronometraje [kronome'traxe] *nm* timing
cronometrar [kronome'trar] *vt* to time
cronómetro [kro'nometro] *nm* (*Deporte*) stopwatch; (*Tec etc*) chronometer
croqueta [kro'keta] *nf* croquette, rissole
croquis ['krokis] *nm inv* sketch
cruce *etc* ['kruθe] *vb ver* **cruzar** ■ *nm* crossing; (*de carreteras*) crossroads; (*Auto etc*) junction, intersection; (*Bio: proceso*) crossbreeding; **luces de ~** dipped headlights
crucero [kru'θero] *nm* (*Naut: barco*) cruise ship; (*: viaje*) cruise
crucial [kru'θjal] *adj* crucial
crucificar [kruθifi'kar] *vt* to crucify; (*fig*) to torment
crucifijo [kruθi'fixo] *nm* crucifix
crucifique *etc* [kruθi'fike] *vb ver* **crucificar**
crucigrama [kruθi'ɣrama] *nm* crossword (puzzle)
crudeza [kru'ðeθa] *nf* (*rigor*) harshness; (*aspereza*) crudeness
crudo, -a ['kruðo, a] *adj* raw; (*no maduro*) unripe; (*petróleo*) crude; (*rudo, cruel*) cruel; (*agua*) hard; (*clima etc*) harsh ■ *nm* crude (oil)
cruel [krwel] *adj* cruel
crueldad [krwel'ðað] *nf* cruelty
cruento, -a ['krwento, a] *adj* bloody
crujido [kru'xiðo] *nm* (*de madera etc*) creak
crujiente [kru'xjente] *adj* (*galleta etc*) crunchy
crujir [kru'xir] *vi* (*madera etc*) to creak; (*dedos*) to crack; (*dientes*) to grind; (*nieve, arena*) to crunch
cruz [kruθ] *nf* cross; (*de moneda*) tails *sg*; (*fig*) burden; **~ gamada** swastika; **C~ Roja** Red Cross
cruzado, -a [kru'θaðo, a] *adj* crossed ■ *nm* crusader ■ *nf* crusade
cruzar [kru'θar] *vt* to cross; (*palabras*) to exchange; **cruzarse** *vr* (*líneas etc*) to cross, intersect; (*personas*) to pass each other; **cruzarse de brazos** to fold one's arms; (*fig*) not to lift a finger to help; **cruzarse con algn en la calle** to pass sb in the street
CSIC [θe'sik] *nm abr* (*Esp Escol*) = **Consejo Superior de Investigaciones Científicas**
cta, c.ᵗᵃ *nf abr* (= *cuenta*) a/c
cta. cto. *abr* (= *carta de crédito*) L.C.
cte. *abr* (= *corriente, de los corrientes*) inst.
CTNE *nf abr* (*Telec*) = **Compañía Telefónica Nacional de España**
c/u *abr* (= *cada uno*) ea
cuaco ['kwako] *nm* (*Am*) nag
cuaderno [kwa'ðerno] *nm* notebook; (*de escuela*) exercise book; (*Naut*) logbook

cuadra ['kwaðra] *nf* (*caballeriza*) stable; (*Am*) (city) block
cuadrado, -a [kwa'ðraðo, a] *adj* square ■ *nm* (*Mat*) square
cuadragésimo, -a [kwaðra'xesimo, a] *num* fortieth
cuadrángulo [kwa'ðrangulo] *nm* quadrangle
cuadrante [kwa'ðrante] *nm* quadrant
cuadrar [kwa'ðrar] *vt* to square; (*Tip*) to justify ■ *vi*: **~ con** (*cuenta*) to square with, tally with; **cuadrarse** *vr* (*soldado*) to stand to attention; **~ por la derecha/izquierda** to right-/left-justify
cuadrícula [kwa'ðrikula] *nf* (*Tip etc*) grid, ruled squares
cuadriculado, -a [kwaðriku'laðo, a] *adj*: **papel ~** squared *o* graph paper
cuadrilátero [kwaðri'latero] *nm* (*Deporte*) boxing ring; (*Geom*) quadrilateral
cuadrilla [kwa'ðriʎa] *nf* (*de amigos*) party, group; (*de delincuentes*) gang; (*de obreros*) team
cuadro ['kwaðro] *nm* square; (*Pintura*) painting; (*Teat*) scene; (*diagrama: tb*: **cuadro sinóptico**) chart, table, diagram; (*Deporte: Med*) team; (*Pol*) executive; **~ de mandos** control panel; **a cuadros** check *cpd*
cuadruplicarse [kwaðrupli'karse] *vr* to quadruple
cuádruplo, -a ['kwaðruplo, a], **cuádruple** ['kwaðruple] *adj* quadruple
cuajado, -a [kwa'xaðo, a] *adj*: **~ de** (*fig*) full of ■ *nf* (*de leche*) curd
cuajar [kwa'xar] *vt* to thicken; (*leche*) to curdle; (*sangre*) to congeal; (*adornar*) to adorn; (*Culin*) to set ■ *vi* (*nieve*) to lie; (*fig*) to become set, become established; (*idea*) to be received, be acceptable; **cuajarse** *vr* to curdle; to congeal; (*llenarse*) to fill up
cuajo ['kwaxo] *nm*: **arrancar algo de ~** to tear sth out by its roots
cual [kwal] *adv* like, as ■ *pron*: **el ~** *etc* which; (*persona: sujeto*) who; (*: objeto*) whom; **lo ~** (*relativo*) which; **allá cada ~** every man to his own taste; **son a ~ más gandul** each is as idle as the other; **cada ~** each one ■ *adj* such as; **tal ~** just as it is
cuál [kwal] *pron interrogativo* which (one), what
cualesquier [kwales'kjer], **cualesquiera** [kwales'kjera] *adj pl, pron pl de* **cualquier; cualquiera**
cualidad [kwali'ðað] *nf* quality
cualificado, -a [kwalifi'kaðo, a] *adj* (*obrero*) skilled, qualified
cualquiera [kwal'kjera], **cualquier** [kwal'kjer] (*pl* **cualesquier(a)**) *adj* any ■ *pron* anybody, anyone; (*quienquiera*) whoever;

en cualquier momento any time; **en cualquier parte** anywhere; ~ **que sea** whichever it is; (*persona*) whoever it is

cuán [kwan] *adv* how

cuando ['kwando] *adv* when; (*aún si*) if, even if ■ *conj* (*puesto que*) since ■ *prep*: **yo, ~ niño** ... when I was a child *o* as a child I ...; ~ **no sea así** even if it is not so; ~ **más** at (the) most; ~ **menos** at least; ~ **no** if not, otherwise; **de ~ en ~** from time to time; **ven ~ quieras** come when(ever) you like

cuándo ['kwando] *adv* when; **¿desde ~?, ¿de ~ acá?** since when?

cuantía [kwan'tia] *nf* (*alcance*) extent; (*importancia*) importance

cuantioso, -a [kwan'tjoso, a] *adj* substantial

 PALABRA CLAVE

cuanto, -a ['kwanto, a] *adj* **1** (*todo*): **tiene todo cuanto desea** he's got everything he wants; **le daremos cuantos ejemplares necesite** we'll give him as many copies as *o* all the copies he needs; **cuantos hombres la ven** all the men who see her
2: **unos cuantos: había unos cuantos periodistas** there were (quite) a few journalists
3 (+*más*): **cuanto más vino bebas peor te sentirás** the more wine you drink the worse you'll feel; **cuantos más, mejor** the more the merrier
■ *pron*: **tiene cuanto desea** he has everything he wants; **tome cuanto/ cuantos quiera** take as much/many as you want
■ *adv*: **en cuanto: en cuanto profesor** as a teacher; **en cuanto a mí** as for me; *ver tb* **antes**
■ *conj* **1**: **cuanto más gana menos gasta** the more he earns the less he spends; **cuanto más joven se es más se es confiado** the younger you are the more trusting you are
2: **en cuanto: en cuanto llegue/llegué** as soon as I arrive/arrived

cuánto, -a ['kwanto, a] *adj* (*exclamación*) what a lot of; (*interrogativo: sg*) how much?; (: *pl*) how many? ■ *pron, adv* how; (*interrogativo: sg*) how much?; (: *pl*) how many? ■ *excl*: **¡~ me alegro!** I'm so glad!; **¡~ gente!** what a lot of people!; **¿~ tiempo?** how long?; **¿~ cuesta?** how much does it cost?; **¿a ~s estamos?** what's the date?; **¿~ hay de aquí a Bilbao?** how far is it from here to Bilbao?; **Señor no sé ~s** Mr. So-and-So

cuarenta [kwa'renta] *num* forty

cuarentena [kwaren'tena] *nf* (*Med etc*) quarantine; (*conjunto*) forty(-odd)

cuarentón, -ona [kwaren'ton, ona] *adj* forty-year-old, fortyish ■ *nm/f* person of about forty

cuaresma [kwa'resma] *nf* Lent

cuarta ['kwarta] *nf ver* **cuarto**

cuartear [kwarte'ar] *vt* to quarter; (*dividir*) to divide up; **cuartearse** *vr* to crack, split

cuartel [kwar'tel] *nm* (*de ciudad*) quarter, district; (*Mil*) barracks *pl*; ~ **general** headquarters *pl*

cuartelazo [kwarte'laθo] *nm* coup, military uprising

cuarteto [kwar'teto] *nm* quartet

cuartilla [kwar'tiʎa] *nf* (*hoja*) sheet (of paper); **cuartillas** *nfpl* (*Tip*) copy *sg*

cuarto, -a ['kwarto, a] *adj* fourth ■ *nm* (*Mat*) quarter, fourth; (*habitación*) room ■ *nf* (*Mat*) quarter, fourth; (*palmo*) span; ~ **de baño** bathroom; ~ **de estar** living room; ~ **de hora** quarter (of an) hour; ~ **de kilo** quarter kilo; **no tener un ~** to be broke (*fam*)

cuarzo ['kwarθo] *nm* quartz

cuatrero [kwa'trero] *nm* (*Am*) rustler, stock thief

cuatrimestre [kwatri'mestre] *nm* four month period

cuatro ['kwatro] *num* four; **las ~** four o'clock; **el ~ de octubre** (on) the fourth of October; *ver tb* **seis**

cuatrocientos, -as [kwatro'θjentos, as] *num* four hundred; *ver tb* **seiscientos**

Cuba ['kuβa] *nf* Cuba

cuba ['kuβa] *nf* cask, barrel; **estar como una ~** (*fam*) to be sloshed

cubalibre [kuβa'liβre] *nm* (white) rum and coke®

cubano, -a [ku'βano, a] *adj, nm/f* Cuban

cubata [ku'βata] *nm* = **cubalibre**

cubertería [kuβerte'ria] *nf* cutlery

cúbico, -a ['kuβiko, a] *adj* cubic

cubierto, -a [ku'βjerto, a] *pp de* **cubrir** ■ *adj* covered; (*cielo*) overcast ■ *nm* cover; (*en la mesa*) place ■ *nf* cover, covering; (*neumático*) tyre; (*Naut*) deck; **cubiertos** *nmpl* cutlery *sg*; **a ~ de** covered with *o* in; **precio del ~** cover charge

cubil [ku'βil] *nm* den

cubilete [kuβi'lete] *nm* (*en juegos*) cup

cubito [ku'βito] *nm*: ~ **de hielo** ice cube

cubo ['kuβo] *nm*: ~ **cube**; (*balde*) bucket, tub; (*Tec*) drum; ~ **de (la) basura** dustbin

cubrecama [kuβre'kama] *nm* bedspread

cubrir [ku'βrir] *vt* to cover; (*vacante*) to fill; (*Bio*) to mate with; (*gastos*) to meet; **cubrirse** *vr* (*cielo*) to become overcast; (*Com: gastos*) to

be met o paid; (: *deuda*) to be covered;
~ **las formas** to keep up appearances; **lo cubrieron las aguas** the waters closed over it; **el agua casi me cubría** I was almost out of my depth

cucaracha [kuka'ratʃa] *nf* cockroach

cuchara [ku'tʃara] *nf* spoon; (*Tec*) scoop

cucharada [kutʃa'raða] *nf* spoonful; ~ **colmada** heaped spoonful

cucharadita [kutʃara'ðita] *nf* teaspoonful

cucharilla [kutʃa'riʎa] *nf* teaspoon

cucharita [kutʃa'rita] *nf* teaspoon

cucharón [kutʃa'ron] *nm* ladle

cuchichear [kutʃitʃe'ar] *vi* to whisper

cuchicheo [kutʃi'tʃeo] *nm* whispering

cuchilla [ku'tʃiʎa] *nf* (large) knife; (*de arma blanca*) blade; ~ **de afeitar** razor blade; **pasar a** ~ to put to the sword

cuchillada [kutʃi'ʎaða] *nf* (*golpe*) stab; (*herida*) knife o stab wound

cuchillo [ku'tʃiʎo] *nm* knife

cuchitril [kutʃi'tril] *nm* hovel; (*habitación etc*) pigsty

cuclillas [ku'kliʎas] *nfpl*: **en** ~ squatting

cuco, -a ['kuko, a] *adj* pretty; (*astuto*) sharp ■ *nm* cuckoo

cucurucho [kuku'rutʃo] *nm* paper cone, cornet

cuece *etc* ['kweθe] *vb ver* **cocer**

cuele *etc* ['kwele] *vb ver* **colar**

cuelgue *etc* ['kwelɣe] *vb ver* **colgar**

cuello ['kweʎo] *nm* (*Anat*) neck; (*de vestido, camisa*) collar

cuenca ['kwenka] *nf* (*Anat*) eye socket; (*Geo: valle*) bowl, deep valley; (: *fluvial*) basin

cuenco ['kwenko] *nm* (earthenware) bowl

cuenta *etc* ['kwenta] *vb ver* **contar** ■ *nf* (*cálculo*) count, counting; (*en café, restaurante*) bill; (*Com*) account; (*de collar*) bead; (*fig*) account; **a fin de ~s** in the end; **en resumidas ~s** in short; **caer en la** ~ to catch on; **dar** ~ **a algn de sus actos** to account to sb for one's actions; **darse** ~ **de** to realize; **tener en** ~ to bear in mind; **echar ~s** to take stock; ~ **atrás** countdown; ~ **corriente/de ahorros/a plazo (fijo)** current/savings/deposit account; ~ **de caja** cash account; ~ **de capital** capital account; ~ **por cobrar** account receivable; ~ **de correo** (*Internet*) email account; ~ **de crédito** credit o loan account; ~ **de gastos e ingresos** income and expenditure account; ~ **por pagar** account payable; **abonar una cantidad en** ~ **a algn** to credit a sum to sb's account; **ajustar** o **liquidar una** ~ to settle an account; **pasar la** ~ to send the bill

cuentagotas [kwenta'ɣotas] *nm inv* (*Med*)

dropper; **a** o **con** ~ (*fam, fig*) drop by drop, bit by bit

cuentakilómetros [kwentaki'lometros] *nm inv* (*de distancias*) ≈ milometer, clock; (*velocímetro*) speedometer

cuentista [kwen'tista] *nm/f* gossip; (*Lit*) short-story writer

cuento *etc* ['kwento] *vb ver* **contar** ■ *nm* story; (*Lit*) short story; ~ **de hadas** fairy story; **es el** ~ **de nunca acabar** it's an endless business; **eso no viene a** ~ that's irrelevant

cuerda ['kwerða] *nf* rope; (*hilo*) string; (*de reloj*) spring; (*Mus: de violín etc*) string; (*Mat*) chord; (*Anat*) cord; ~ **floja** tightrope; **cuerdas vocales** vocal cords; **dar** ~ **a un reloj** to wind up a clock

cuerdo, -a ['kwerðo, a] *adj* sane; (*prudente*) wise, sensible

cuerear [kwere'ar] *vt* (*Am*) to skin

cuerno ['kwerno] *nm* (*Zool: gen*) horn; (: *de ciervo*) antler; **poner los cuernos a** (*fam*) to cuckold; **saber a** ~ **quemado** to leave a nasty taste

cuero ['kwero] *nm* (*Zool*) skin, hide; (*Tec*) leather; **en cueros** stark naked; ~ **cabelludo** scalp

cuerpo ['kwerpo] *nm* body; (*cadáver*) corpse; (*fig*) main part; ~ **de bomberos** fire brigade; ~ **diplomático** diplomatic corps; **luchar** ~ **a** ~ to fight hand-to-hand; **tomar** ~ (*plan etc*) to take shape

cuervo ['kwerβo] *nm* (*Zool*) raven, crow; *ver* **criar**

cuesta *etc* ['kwesta] *vb ver* **costar** ■ *nf* slope; (*en camino etc*) hill; ~ **arriba/abajo** uphill/downhill; **a ~s** on one's back

cuestión [kwes'tjon] *nf* matter, question, issue; (*riña*) quarrel, dispute; **eso es otra** ~ that's another matter

cuestionar [kwestjo'nar] *vt* to question

cuestionario [kwestjo'narjo] *nm* questionnaire

cueva ['kweβa] *nf* cave

cueza *etc* ['kweθa] *vb ver* **cocer**

cuidado [kwi'ðaðo] *nm* care, carefulness; (*preocupación*) care, worry ■ *excl* careful!, look out!; **eso me tiene sin** ~ I'm not worried about that

cuidadoso, -a [kwiða'ðoso, a] *adj* careful; (*preocupado*) anxious

cuidar [kwi'ðar] *vt* (*Med*) to care for; (*ocuparse de*) to take care of, look after; (*detalles*) to pay attention to ■ *vi*: ~ **de** to take care of, look after; **cuidarse** *vr* to look after o.s.; **cuidarse de hacer algo** to take care to do something

cuita ['kwita] nf (preocupación) worry, trouble; (pena) grief

culata [ku'lata] nf (de fusil) butt

culatazo [kula'taθo] nm kick, recoil

culebra [ku'leβra] nf snake; ~ **de cascabel** rattlesnake

culebrear [kuleβre'ar] vi to wriggle along; (río) to meander

culebrón [kule'βron] nm (fam) soap (opera)

culinario, -a [kuli'narjo, a] adj culinary, cooking cpd

culminación [kulmina'θjon] nf culmination

culminante [kulmi'nante] adj: **momento ~** climax, highlight, highspot

culminar [kulmi'nar] vi to culminate

culo ['kulo] nm (fam: asentaderas) bottom, backside, bum (Brit), (: ano) arse(hole) (Brit!), ass(hole) (US!); (de vaso) bottom

culpa ['kulpa] nf fault; (Jur) guilt; **culpas** nfpl sins; **por ~ de** through, because of; **tener la ~ (de)** to be to blame (for)

culpabilidad [kulpaβili'ðað] nf guilt

culpable [kul'paβle] adj guilty ■ nm/f culprit; **confesarse ~** to plead guilty; **declarar ~ a algn** to find sb guilty

culpar [kul'par] vt to blame; (acusar) to accuse

cultivadora [kultiβa'ðora] nf cultivator

cultivar [kulti'βar] vt to cultivate; (cosecha) to raise; (talento) to develop

cultivo [kul'tiβo] nm (acto) cultivation; (plantas) crop; (Bio) culture

culto, -a ['kulto, a] adj (cultivado) cultivated; (que tiene cultura) cultured, educated ■ nm (homenaje) worship; (religión) cult; (Pol etc) cult

cultura [kul'tura] nf culture

cultural [kultu'ral] adj cultural

culturismo [kultu'rismo] nm body-building

cumbre ['kumbre] nf summit, top; (fig) top, height; **conferencia (en la) ~** summit (conference)

cumpleaños [kumple'aɲos] nm inv birthday

cumplido, -a [kum'pliðo, a] adj complete, perfect; (abundante) plentiful; (cortés) courteous ■ nm compliment; **visita de ~** courtesy call

cumplidor, a [kumpli'ðor, a] adj reliable

cumplimentar [kumplimen'tar] vt to congratulate; (órdenes) to carry out

cumplimiento [kumpli'mjento] nm (de un deber) fulfilment, execution, performance; (acabamiento) completion; (Com) expiry, end

cumplir [kum'plir] vt (orden) to carry out, obey; (promesa) to carry out, fulfil; (condena) to serve; (años) to reach, attain ■ vi (pago) to fall due; (plazo) to expire; **cumplirse** vr (plazo) to expire; (plan etc) to be fulfilled; (vaticinio) to come true; **hoy cumple**
dieciocho años he is eighteen today; ~ **con** (deber) to carry out, fulfil

cúmulo ['kumulo] nm (montón) heap; (nube) cumulus

cuna ['kuna] nf cradle, cot; **canción de ~** lullaby

cundir [kun'dir] vi (noticia, rumor, pánico) to spread; (rendir) to go a long way

cuneta [ku'neta] nf ditch

cuña ['kuɲa] nf (Tec) wedge; (Com) advertising spot; (Med) bedpan; **tener cuñas** to have influence

cuñado, -a [ku'ɲaðo, a] nm/f brother/sister-in-law

cuño ['kuɲo] nm (Tec) die-stamp; (fig) stamp

cuota ['kwota] nf (parte proporcional) share; (cotización) fee, dues pl; ~ **inicial** (Com) down payment

cupo etc ['kupo] vb ver **caber** ■ nm quota, share; (Com): ~ **de importación** import quota; ~ **de ventas** sales quota

cupón [ku'pon] nm coupon; ~ **de la ONCE** o **de los ciegos** ONCE lottery ticket; ver tb **lotería**

cúpula ['kupula] nf (Arq) dome

cura ['kura] nf (curación) cure; (método curativo) treatment ■ nm priest; ~ **de emergencia** emergency treatment

curación [kura'θjon] nf cure; (acción) curing

curado, -a [ku'raðo, a] adj (Culin) cured; (pieles) tanned

curandero, -a [kuran'dero, a] nm/f healer

curar [ku'rar] vt (Med: herida) to treat, dress; (: enfermo) to cure; (Culin) to cure, salt; (cuero) to tan ■ vi, **curarse** vr to get well, recover

curda ['kurða] (fam) nm drunk ■ nf: **agarrar una/estar ~** to get/be sloshed

curiosear [kurjose'ar] vt to glance at, look over ■ vi to look round, wander round; (explorar) to poke about

curiosidad [kurjosi'ðað] nf curiosity

curioso, -a [ku'rjoso, a] adj curious; (aseado) neat ■ nm/f bystander, onlooker; **¡qué ~!** how odd!

curita [ku'rita] nf (Am) sticking plaster

currante [ku'rrante] nm/f (fam) worker

currar [ku'rrar] vi (fam), **currelar** [kurre'lar] vi (fam) to work

currículo [ku'rrikulo] nm, **currículum** [ku'rrikulum] nm curriculum vitae

curro ['kurro] nm (fam) work, job

cursar [kur'sar] vt (Escol) to study

cursi ['kursi] adj (fam) pretentious; (: amanerado) affected

cursilada [kursi'laða] nf: **¡qué ~!** how tacky!

cursilería [kursile'ria] nf (vulgaridad) bad taste; (amaneramiento) affectation

cursillo [kur'siʎo] *nm* short course

cursiva [kur'siβa] *nf* italics *pl*

curso ['kurso] *nm* (*dirección*) course; (*fig*) progress; (*Escol*) school year; (*Univ*) academic year; **en ~** (*año*) current; (*proceso*) going on, under way; **moneda de ~ legal** legal tender

cursor [kur'sor] *nm* (*Inform*) cursor; (*Tec*) slide

curtido, -a [kur'tiðo, a] *adj* (*cara etc*) weather-beaten; (*fig: persona*) experienced

curtir [kur'tir] *vt* (*piel*) to tan; (*fig*) to harden

curvo, -a ['kurβo, a] *adj* (*gen*) curved; (*torcido*) bent ■ *nf* (*gen*) curve, bend; **curva de rentabilidad** (*Com*) break-even chart

cúspide ['kuspiðe] *nf* (*Geo*) summit, peak; (*fig*) top, pinnacle

custodia [kus'toðja] *nf* (*cuidado*) safekeeping; (*Jur*) custody

custodiar [kusto'ðjar] *vt* (*conservar*) to keep, take care of; (*vigilar*) to guard

custodio [kus'toðjo] *nm* guardian, keeper

cutáneo, -a [ku'taneo, a] *adj* skin *cpd*

cutícula [ku'tikula] *nf* cuticle

cutis ['kutis] *nm inv* skin, complexion

cutre ['kutre] *adj* (*fam: lugar*) grotty; (: *persona*) naff

cuyo, -a ['kujo, a] *pron* (*de quien*) whose; (*de que*) whose, of which; **la señora en cuya casa me hospedé** the lady in whose house I stayed; **el asunto cuyos detalles conoces** the affair the details of which you know; **por ~ motivo** for which reason

C.V. *abr* (= *Curriculum Vitae*) CV; (= *caballos de vapor*) H.P.

Dd

D, d [de] *nf* (*letra*) D, d; **D de Dolores** D for David (*Brit*), D for Dog (*US*)

D. *abr* = **Don**

D.ª *abr* = **Doña**

dactilar [dakti'lar] *adj*: **huellas dactilares** fingerprints

dactilógrafo, -a [dakti'loɣrafo, a] *nm/f* typist

dádiva ['daðiβa] *nf* donation; (*regalo*) gift

dadivoso, -a [daði'βoso, a] *adj* generous

dado, -a ['daðo, a] *pp de* **dar** ▪ *nm* die; **dados** *nmpl* dice ▪ *adj*: **en un momento ~** at a certain point; **ser ~ a (hacer algo)** to be very fond of (doing sth); **~ que** *conj* given that

daga ['daɣa] *nf* dagger

daltónico, -a [dal'toniko, a] *adj* colour-blind

daltonismo [dalto'nismo] *nm* colour blindness

dama ['dama] *nf* (*gen*) lady; (*Ajedrez*) queen; **damas** *nfpl* draughts; **primera ~** (*Teat*) leading lady; (*Pol*) president's wife, first lady (*US*); **~ de honor** (*de reina*) lady-in-waiting; (*de novia*) bridesmaid

damasco [da'masko] *nm* (*tela*) damask; (*Am*: *árbol*) apricot tree; (: *fruta*) apricot

damnificado, -a [damnifi'kaðo, a] *nm/f*: **los damnificados** the victims

damnificar [damnifi'kar] *vt* to harm; (*persona*) to injure

damnifique *etc* [damni'fike] *vb ver* **damnificar**

dance *etc* ['danθe] *vb ver* **danzar**

danés, -esa [da'nes, esa] *adj* Danish ▪ *nm/f* Dane ▪ *nm* (*Ling*) Danish

Danubio [da'nuβjo] *nm* Danube

danza ['danθa] *nf* (*gen*) dancing; (*una danza*) dance

danzar [dan'θar] *vt, vi* to dance

danzarín, -ina [danθa'rin, ina] *nm/f* dancer

dañar [da'ɲar] *vt* (*objeto*) to damage; (*persona*) to hurt; (*estropear*) to spoil; **dañarse** *vr* (*objeto*) to get damaged

dañino, -a [da'ɲino, a] *adj* harmful

daño ['daɲo] *nm* (*a un objeto*) damage; (*a una persona*) harm, injury; **daños y perjuicios** (*Jur*) damages; **hacer ~ a** to damage; (*persona*) to hurt, injure; **hacerse ~** to hurt o.s.

dañoso, -a [da'ɲoso, a] *adj* harmful

DAO *abr* (= *Diseño Asistido por Ordenador*) CAD

 PALABRA CLAVE

dar [dar] *vt* **1** (*gen*) to give; (*obra de teatro*) to put on; (*film*) to show; (*fiesta*) to have; **dar algo a algn** to give sb sth o sth to sb; **dar una patada a algn/algo** to kick sb/sth, give sb/sth a kick; **dar un susto a algn** to give sb a fright; **dar de beber a algn** to give sb a drink; **dar de comer** to feed

2 (*intereses*) to yield; (*fruta*) to produce

3 (*locuciones +n*): **da gusto escucharle** it's a pleasure to listen to him; **me da pena/asco** it frightens/sickens me; *ver tb* **paseo** *y otros sustantivos*

4 (*considerar*): **dar algo por descontado/ entendido** to take sth for granted/as read; **dar algo por concluido** to consider sth finished; **le dieron por desaparecido** they gave him up as lost

5 (*hora*): **el reloj dio las seis** the clock struck six (o'clock)

6: **me da lo mismo** it's all the same to me; *ver tb* **igual; más**

7: **¡y dale!** (*¡otra vez!*) not again!; **estar/ seguir dale que dale** o **dale que te pego** o (*Am*) **dale y dale** to go/keep on and on

▪ *vi* **1**: **dar a** (*habitación*) to overlook, look on to; (*accionar: botón etc*) to press, hit

2: **dar con: dimos con él dos horas más tarde** we came across him two hours later; **al final di con la solución** I eventually came up with the answer

3: **dar en** (*blanco, suelo*) to hit; **el sol me da en la cara** the sun is shining (right) in my face

4: **dar de sí** (*zapatos etc*) to stretch, give

5: **dar para** to be enough for; **nuestro**

presupuesto no da para más our budget's really tight
6: **dar por**: **le ha dado por estudiar música** now he's into studying music
7: **dar que hablar** to set people talking; **una película que da que pensar** a thought-provoking film
darse *vr* **1**: **darse un baño** to have a bath; **darse un golpe** to hit o.s.
2: **darse por vencido** to give up; **con eso me doy por satisfecho** I'd settle for that
3 (*ocurrir*): **se han dado muchos casos** there have been a lot of cases
4: **darse a**: **se ha dado a la bebida** he's taken to drinking
5: **se me dan bien/mal las ciencias** I'm good/bad at science
6: **dárselas de**: **se las da de experto** he fancies himself *o* poses as an expert

dardo ['darðo] *nm* dart
dársena ['darsena] *nf* (*Naut*) dock
datar [da'tar] *vi*: **~ de** to date from
dátil ['datil] *nm* date
dativo [da'tiβo] *nm* (*Ling*) dative
dato ['dato] *nm* fact, piece of information; (*Mat*) datum; **datos** *nmpl* (*Inform*) data; **datos de entrada/salida** input/output data; **datos personales** personal particulars
dcha. *abr* (= *derecha*) r (= *right*)
d. de J. C. *abr* (= *después de Jesucristo*) A.D. (= *Anno Domini*)

 PALABRA CLAVE

de [de] *prep* (*de+el = del*) **1** (*posesión, pertenencia*) of; **la casa de Isabel/mis padres** Isabel's/my parents' house; **es de ellos/ella** it's theirs/hers; **un libro de Unamuno** a book by Unamuno
2 (*origen, distancia, con números*) from; **soy de Gijón** I'm from Gijón; **de 8 a 20** from 8 to 20; **5 metros de largo** 5 metres long; **salir del cine** to go out of *o* leave the cinema; **de ... en ...** from ... to ...; **de 2 en 2** 2 by 2, 2 at a time; **9 de cada 10** 9 out of every 10
3 (*valor descriptivo*): **una copa de vino** a glass of wine; **una silla de madera** a wooden chair; **la mesa de la cocina** the kitchen table; **un viaje de dos días** a two-day journey; **un billete de 50 euros** a 50-euro note; **un niño de tres años** a three-year-old (child); **una máquina de coser** a sewing machine; **la ciudad de Madrid** the city of Madrid; **el tonto de Juan** that idiot Juan; **ir vestido de gris** to be dressed in grey; **la niña del vestido azul** the girl in the blue

dress; **la chica del pelo largo** the girl with long hair; **trabaja de profesora** she works as a teacher; **de lado** sideways; **de atrás/delante** rear/front
4 (*hora, tiempo*): **a las 8 de la mañana** at 8 o'clock in the morning; **de día/noche** by day/night; **de hoy en ocho días** a week from now; **de niño era gordo** as a child he was fat
5 (*comparaciones*): **más/menos de cien personas** more/less than a hundred people; **el más caro de la tienda** the most expensive in the shop; **menos/más de lo pensado** less/more than expected
6 (*causa*): **del calor** from the heat; **de puro tonto** out of sheer stupidity
7 (*tema*) about; **clases de inglés** English classes; **¿sabes algo de él?** do you know anything about him?; **un libro de física** a physics book
8 (*adj+de+infin*): **fácil de entender** easy to understand
9 (*oraciones pasivas*): **fue respetado de todos** he was loved by all
10 (*condicional+infin*) if; **de ser posible** if possible; **de no terminarlo hoy** if I *etc* don't finish it today

dé [de] *vb ver* **dar**
deambular [deambu'lar] *vi* to stroll, wander
debajo [de'βaxo] *adv* underneath; **~ de** below, under; **por ~ de** beneath
debate [de'βate] *nm* debate
debatir [deβa'tir] *vt* to debate; **debatirse** *vr* to struggle
debe ['deβe] *nm* (*en cuenta*) debit side; **~ y haber** debit and credit
deber [de'βer] *nm* duty ■ *vt* to owe ■ *vi*: **debe (de)** it must, it should; **deberse** *vr*: **deberse a** to be owing *o* due to; **deberes** *nmpl* (*Escol*) homework *sg*; **debo hacerlo** I must do it; **debe de ir** he should go; **¿qué *o* cuánto le debo?** how much is it?
debidamente [deβiða'mente] *adv* properly; (*rellenar*) duly
debido, -a [de'βiðo, a] *adj* proper, due; **~ a** due to, because of; **en debida forma** duly
débil ['deβil] *adj* weak; (*persona: físicamente*) feeble; (*salud*) poor; (*voz, ruido*) faint; (*luz*) dim
debilidad [deβili'ðað] *nf* weakness; feebleness; dimness; **tener ~ por algn** to have a soft spot for sb
debilitar [deβili'tar] *vt* to weaken; **debilitarse** *vr* to grow weak
débito ['deβito] *nm* debit; (*deuda*) debt
debutante [deβu'tante] *nm/f* beginner
debutar [deβu'tar] *vi* to make one's debut

década ['dekaða] nf decade
decadencia [deka'ðenθja] nf (estado) decadence; (proceso) decline, decay
decadente [deca'ðente] adj decadent
decaer [deka'cr] vi (declinar) to decline; (debilitarse) to weaken; (salud) to fail; (negocio) to fall off
decaído, -a [deka'iðo, a] adj: estar ~ (persona) to be down
decaiga etc [de'kaiɣa] vb ver **decaer**
decaimiento [dekai'mjento] nm (declinación) decline; (desaliento) discouragement; (Med: depresión) depression
decanato [deka'nato] nm (cargo) deanship; (despacho) dean's office
decano, -a [de'kano, a] nm/f (Univ etc) dean; (de grupo) senior member
decantar [dekan'tar] vt (vino) to decant
decapitar [dekapi'tar] vt to behead
decayendo etc [deka'jendo] vb ver **decaer**
decena [de'θena] nf: una ~ ten (or so)
decencia [de'θenθja] nf (modestia) modesty; (honestidad) respectability
decenio [de'θenjo] nm decade
decente [de'θente] adj (correcto) proper; (honesto) respectable
decepción [deθep'θjon] nf disappointment
decepcionante [deθepθjo'nante] adj disappointing
decepcionar [deθepθjo'nar] vt to disappoint
decibelio [deθi'βeljo] nm decibel
decidido, -a [deθi'ðiðo, a] adj decided; (resuelto) resolute
decidir [deθi'ðir] vt (persuadir) to convince, persuade; (resolver) to decide ■ vi to decide; **decidirse** vr: **decidirse a** to make up one's mind to; **decidirse por** to decide o settle on, choose
decimal [deθi'mal] adj, nm decimal
décimo, -a ['deθimo, a] num tenth ■ nf (Mat) tenth; **tiene unas décimas de fiebre** he has a slight temperature
decimoctavo, -a [deθimok'taβo, a] num eighteenth; ver tb **sexto**
decimocuarto, -a [deθimo'kwarto, a] num fourteenth; ver tb **sexto**
decimonoveno, -a [deθimono'βeno, a] num nineteenth; ver tb **sexto**
decimoquinto, -a [deθimo'kinto, a] num fifteenth; ver tb **sexto**
decimoséptimo, -a [deθimo'septimo, a] num seventeenth; ver tb **sexto**
decimosexto, -a [deθimo'seksto, a] num sixteenth; ver tb **sexto**
decimotercero, -a [deθimoter'θero, a] num thirteenth; ver tb **sexto**
decir [de'θir] vt (expresar) to say; (contar) to tell; (hablar) to speak; (indicar) to show; (revelar) to reveal; (fam: nombrar) to call ■ nm saying; **decirse** vr: **se dice** it is said, they say; (se cuenta) the story goes; **¿cómo se dice en inglés "cursi"?** what's the English for "cursi"?; ~ **para** o **entre sí** to say to o.s.; ~ **por** ~ to talk for talking's sake; **dar que** ~ **(a la gente)** to make people talk; **querer** ~ to mean; **es** ~ that is to say, namely; **ni que** ~ **tiene que** ... it goes without saying that ...; **como quien dice** so to speak; **¡quién lo diría!** would you believe it!; **el qué dirán** gossip; **¡diga!, ¡dígame!** (en tienda etc) can I help you?; (Telec) hello?; **le dije que fuera más tarde** I told her to go later; **es un** ~ it's just a phrase
decisión [deθi'sjon] nf decision; (firmeza) decisiveness; (voluntad) determination
decisivo, -a [deθi'siβo, a] adj decisive
declamar [dekla'mar] vt, vi to declaim; (versos etc) to recite
declaración [deklara'θjon] nf (manifestación) statement; (explicación) explanation; (Jur: testimonio) evidence; ~ **de derechos** bill of rights; ~ **de impuestos** (Com) tax return; ~ **de ingresos** o **de la renta** income tax return; ~ **jurada** affidavit; **falsa** ~ (Jur) misrepresentation
declarar [dekla'rar] vt to declare ■ vi to declare; (Jur) to testify; **declararse** vr (a una chica) to propose; (guerra, incendio) to break out; ~ **culpable/inocente a algn** to find sb guilty/not guilty; **declararse culpable/ inocente** to plead guilty/not guilty
declinación [deklina'θjon] nf (decaimiento) decline; (Ling) declension
declinar [dekli'nar] vt (gen, Ling) to decline; (Jur) to reject ■ vi (el día) to draw to a close
declive [de'kliβe] nm (cuesta) slope; (inclinación) incline; (fig) decline; (Com: tb: **declive económico**) slump
decodificador [dekoðifika'ðor] nm (Inform) decoder
decolorarse [dekolo'rarse] vr to become discoloured
decomisar [dekomi'sar] vt to seize, confiscate
decomiso [deko'miso] nm seizure
decoración [dekora'θjon] nf decoration; (Teat) scenery, set; ~ **de escaparates** window dressing
decorado [deko'raðo] nm (Cine, Teat) scenery, set
decorador, a [dekora'ðor, a] nm/f (de interiores) (interior) decorator; (Teat) stage o set designer
decorar [deko'rar] vt to decorate

decorativo, -a [dekora'tiβo, a] adj
ornamental, decorative
decoro [de'koro] nm (respeto) respect;
(dignidad) decency; (recato) propriety
decoroso, -a [deko'roso, a] adj (decente)
decent; (modesto) modest; (digno) proper
decrecer [dekre'θer] vi to decrease, diminish;
(nivel de agua) to go down; (días) to draw in
decrépito, -a [de'krepito, a] adj decrepit
decretar [dekre'tar] vt to decree
decreto [de'kreto] nm decree; (Pol) act
decreto-ley [dekreto'lei] (pl **decretos-leyes**)
nm decree
decrezca etc [de'kreθka] vb ver **decrecer**
decúbito [de'kuβito] nm (Med): ~ **prono/**
supino prone/supine position
dedal [de'ðal] nm thimble
dedalera [deða'lera] nf foxglove
dédalo ['deðalo] nm (laberinto) labyrinth; (fig)
tangle, mess
dedicación [deðika'θjon] nf dedication; **con**
~ **exclusiva** o **plena** full-time
dedicar [deði'kar] vt (libro) to dedicate;
(tiempo, dinero) to devote; **dedicarse** vr:
dedicarse a (hacer algo) to devote o.s. to
(doing sth); (carrera, estudio) to go in for (doing
sth), take up (doing sth); **¿a qué se dedica**
usted? what do you do (for a living)?
dedicatoria [deðika'torja] nf (de libro)
dedication
dedillo [de'ðiʎo] nm: **saber algo al** ~ to have
sth at one's fingertips
dedique etc [de'ðike] vb ver **dedicar**
dedo ['deðo] nm finger; (de vino etc) drop;
~ **(del pie)** toe; ~ **pulgar** thumb; ~ **índice**
index finger; ~ **mayor** o **cordial** middle
finger; ~ **anular** ring finger; ~ **meñique**
little finger; **contar con los dedos** to count
on one's fingers; **comerse los dedos** to
get very impatient; **entrar a** ~ to get a job
by pulling strings; **hacer** ~ (fam) to hitch
(a lift); **poner el** ~ **en la llaga** to put one's
finger on it; **no tiene dos dedos de frente**
he's pretty dim
deducción [deðuk'θjon] nf deduction
deducir [deðu'θir] vt (concluir) to deduce,
infer; (Com) to deduct
deduje etc [de'ðuxe], **dedujera** etc
[deðu'xera], **deduzca** etc [de'ðuθka] vb ver
deducir
defección [defek'θjon] nf defection,
desertion
defecto [de'fekto] nm defect, flaw; (de cara)
imperfection; ~ **de pronunciación** speech
defect; **por** ~ (Inform) default; ~ **latente**
(Com) latent defect
defectuoso, -a [defek'twoso, a] adj

defective, faulty
defender [defen'der] vt to defend; (ideas)
to uphold; (causa) to champion; (amigos) to
stand up for; **defenderse** vr to defend o.s.;
defenderse bien to give a good account of
o.s.; **me defiendo en inglés** (fig) I can get by
in English
defendible [defen'diβle] adj defensible
defensa [de'fensa] nf defence; (Naut) fender
■ nm (Deporte) back; **en** ~ **propia** in self-
defence
defensivo, -a [defen'siβo, a] adj defensive
■ nf: **a la defensiva** on the defensive
defensor, -a [defen'sor, a] adj defending
■ nm/f (abogado defensor) defending counsel;
(protector) protector; ~ **del pueblo** (Esp)
≈ ombudsman
deferente [defe'rente] adj deferential
deferir [defe'rir] vt (Jur) to refer, delegate
■ vi: ~ **a** to defer to
deficiencia [defi'θjenθja] nf deficiency
deficiente [defi'θjente] adj (defectuoso)
defective; ~ **en** lacking o deficient in
■ nm/f: **ser un** ~ **mental** to be mentally
handicapped
déficit (pl **déficits**) ['defiθit] nm (Com) deficit;
(fig) lack, shortage; ~ **presupuestario**
budget deficit
deficitario, -a [defiθi'tarjo, a] adj (Com) in
deficit; (: empresa) loss-making
defienda etc [de'fjenda] vb ver **defender**
defiera etc [de'fjera] vb ver **deferir**
definición [defini'θjon] nf definition;
(Inform: de pantalla) resolution
definido, -a [defi'niðo, a] adj (tb Ling)
definite; **bien** ~ well o clearly defined; ~ **por**
el usuario (Inform) user-defined
definir [defi'nir] vt (determinar) to determine,
establish; (decidir, Inform) to define; (aclarar)
to clarify
definitivo, -a [defini'tiβo, a] adj (edición, texto)
definitive; (fecha) definite; **en definitiva**
definitively; (en conclusión) finally; (en
resumen) in short
defiriendo etc [defi'rjendo] vb ver **deferir**
deflacionario, -a [deflaθjo'narjo, a],
deflacionista [deflaθjo'nista] adj
deflationary
deflector [deflek'tor] nm (Tec) baffle
deforestación [deforesta'θjon] nf
deforestation
deformación [deforma'θjon] nf (alteración)
deformation; (Radio etc) distortion
deformar [defor'mar] vt (gen) to deform;
deformarse vr to become deformed
deforme [de'forme] adj (informe) deformed;
(feo) ugly; (mal hecho) misshapen

deformidad [deformi'ðað] nf (forma anormal) deformity; (fig: defecto) (moral) shortcoming

defraudar [defrau'ðar] vt (decepcionar) to disappoint; (estafar) to cheat; to defraud; ~ **impuestos** to evade tax

defunción [defun'θjon] nf decease, demise

degeneración [dexenera'θjon] nf (de las células) degeneration; (moral) degeneracy

degenerar [dexene'rar] vi to degenerate; (empeorar) to get worse

deglutir [deɣlu'tir] vt, vi to swallow

degolladero [deɣoʎa'ðero] nm (Anat) throat; (cadalso) scaffold; (matadero) slaughterhouse

degollar [deɣo'ʎar] vt to slaughter

degradar [deɣra'ðar] vt to debase, degrade; (Inform: datos) to corrupt; **degradarse** vr to demean o.s.

degüelle etc [de'ɣweʎe] vb ver **degollar**

degustación [deɣusta'θjon] nf sampling, tasting

deificar [deifi'kar] vt (persona) to deify

deifique etc [dei'fike] vb ver **deificar**

dejadez [dexa'ðeθ] nf (negligencia) neglect; (descuido) untidiness, carelessness

dejado, -a [de'xaðo, a] adj (desaliñado) slovenly; (negligente) careless; (indolente) lazy

dejar [de'xar] vt (gen) to leave; (permitir) to allow, let; (abandonar) to abandon, forsake; (actividad, empleo) to give up; (beneficios) to produce, yield ■ vi: ~ **de** (parar) to stop; **dejarse** vr (abandonarse) to let o.s. go, **no puedo ~ de fumar** I can't give up smoking; **no dejes de visitarles** don't fail to visit them; **no dejes de comprar un billete** make sure you buy a ticket; ~ **a un lado** to leave o set aside; ~ **caer** to drop; ~ **entrar/salir** to let in/out; ~ **pasar** to let through; **¡déjalo!** (no te preocupes) don't worry about it; **te dejo en tu casa** I'll drop you off at your place; **deja mucho que desear** it leaves a lot to be desired; **dejarse persuadir** to allow o.s. to o let o.s. be persuaded; **¡déjate de tonterías!** stop messing about!

deje ['dexe] nm (trace of) accent

dejo ['dexo] nm (Ling) accent

del [del] = **de + el**; ver **de**

del. abr (Admin: = Delegación) district office

delantal [delan'tal] nm apron

delante [de'lante] adv in front; (enfrente) opposite; (adelante) ahead ■ prep: ~ **de** in front of, before; **la parte de** ~ the front part; **estando otros** ~ with others present

delantero, -a [delan'tero, a] adj front; (patas de animal) fore ■ nm (Deporte) forward ■ nf (de vestido, casa etc) front part; (Teat) front row; (Deporte) forward line; **llevar la delantera (a algn)** to be ahead (of sb)

delatar [dela'tar] vt to inform on o against, betray; **los delató a la policía** he reported them to the police

delator, -a [dela'tor, a] nm/f informer

delegación [deleɣa'θjon] nf (acción: delegados) delegation; (Com: oficina) district office, branch; ~ **de poderes** (Pol) devolution; ~ **de policía** police station

delegado, -a [dele'ɣaðo, a] nm/f delegate; (Com) agent

delegar [dele'ɣar] vt to delegate

delegue etc [de'leɣe] vb ver **delegar**

deleitar [delei'tar] vt to delight; **deleitarse** vr: **deleitarse con** o **en** to delight in, take pleasure in

deleite [de'leite] nm delight, pleasure

deletrear [deletre'ar] vt (tb fig) to spell (out)

deletreo [dele'treo] nm spelling; (fig) interpretation, decipherment

deleznable [deleθ'naβle] adj (frágil) fragile; (fig: malo) poor; (: excusa) feeble

delfín [del'fin] nm dolphin

delgadez [delɣa'ðeθ] nf thinness, slimness

delgado, -a [del'ɣaðo, a] adj thin; (persona) slim, thin; (tierra) poor; (tela etc) light, delicate ■ adv: **hilar (muy)** ~ (fig) to split hairs

deliberación [deliβera'θjon] nf deliberation

deliberar [deliβe'rar] vt to debate, discuss ■ vi to deliberate

delicadeza [delika'ðeθa] nf delicacy; (refinamiento, sutileza) refinement

delicado, -a [deli'kaðo, a] adj delicate; (sensible) sensitive; (rasgos) dainty; (gusto) refined; (situación: difícil) tricky; (: violento) embarrassing; (punto, tema) sore; (persona: difícil de contentar) hard to please; (: sensible) touchy, hypersensitive; (: atento) considerate

delicia [de'liθja] nf delight

delicioso, -a [deli'θjoso, a] adj (gracioso) delightful; (exquisito) delicious

delictivo, -a [delik'tiβo, a] adj criminal cpd

delimitar [delimi'tar] vt to delimit

delincuencia [delin'kwenθja] nf: ~ **juvenil** juvenile delinquency; **cifras de la** ~ crime rate

delincuente [delin'kwente] nm/f delinquent; (criminal) criminal; ~ **sin antecedentes** first offender; ~ **habitual** hardened criminal

delineante [deline'ante] nm/f draughtsman

delinear [deline'ar] vt to delineate; (dibujo) to draw; (contornos, fig) to outline; ~ **un proyecto** to outline a project

delinquir [delin'kir] vi to commit an offence

delirante [deli'rante] adj delirious

delirar [deli'rar] vi to be delirious, rave; (fig: desatinar) to talk nonsense

delirio [de'lirjo] nm (Med) delirium; (palabras insensatas) ravings pl; ~ **de grandeza** megalomania; ~ **de persecución** persecution mania; **con** ~ (fam) madly; **¡fue el ~!** (fam) it was great!

delito [de'lito] nm (gen) crime; (infracción) offence

delta ['delta] nm delta

demacrado, -a [dema'kraðo, a] adj emaciated

demagogia [dema'ɣoxja] nf demagogy, demagoguery

demagogo [dema'ɣoɣo] nm demagogue

demanda [de'manda] nf (pedido, Com) demand; (petición) request; (pregunta) inquiry; (reivindicación) claim; (Jur) action, lawsuit; (Teat) call; (Elec) load; ~ **de pago** demand for payment; **escribir en ~ de ayuda** to write asking for help; **entablar** ~ (Jur) to sue; **presentar ~ de divorcio** to sue for divorce; ~ **final** final demand; ~ **indirecta** derived demand; ~ **de mercado** market demand

demandado, -a [deman'daðo, a] nm/f defendant; (en divorcio) respondent

demandante [deman'dante] nm/f claimant; (Jur) plaintiff

demandar [deman'dar] vt (gen) to demand; (Jur) to sue, file a lawsuit against, start proceedings against; ~ **a algn por calumnia/daños y perjuicios** to sue sb for libel/damages

demarcación [demarka'θjon] nf (de terreno) demarcation

demás [de'mas] adj: **los ~ niños** the other children, the remaining children ▪ pron: **los/las ~** the others, the rest (of them); **lo ~** the rest (of it); **por ~** moreover; (en vano) in vain; **y ~** etcetera

demasía [dema'sia] nf (exceso) excess, surplus; **comer en ~** to eat to excess

demasiado, -a [dema'sjaðo, a] adj: ~ **vino** too much wine ▪ adv (antes de adj, adv) too; **demasiados libros** too many books; **¡es ~!** it's too much!; **es ~ pesado para levantar** it is too heavy to lift; ~ **lo sé** I know it only too well; **hace ~ calor** it's too hot

demencia [de'menθja] nf (locura) madness

demencial [demen'θjal] adj crazy

demente [de'mente] adj mad, insane ▪ nm/f lunatic

democracia [demo'kraθja] nf democracy

demócrata [de'mokrata] nm/f democrat

democratacristiano, -a [demokratakris'tjano, a], **democristiano, -a** [demokris'tjano, a] adj, nm/f Christian Democrat

democrático, -a [demo'kratiko, a] adj democratic

demográfico, -a [demo'ɣrafiko, a] adj demographic, population cpd; **la explosión demográfica** the population explosion

demoledor, a [demole'ðor, a] adj (fig: argumento) overwhelming; (: ataque) shattering

demoler [demo'ler] vt to demolish; (edificio) to pull down

demolición [demoli'θjon] nf demolition

demonio [de'monjo] nm devil, demon; **¡demonios!** hell!; **¿cómo demonios?** how the hell?; **¿qué demonios será?** what the devil can it be?; **¿dónde ~ lo habré dejado?** where the devil can I have left it?; **tener el ~ en el cuerpo** (no parar) to be always on the go

demora [de'mora] nf delay

demorar [demo'rar] vt (retardar) to delay, hold back; (dilatar) to hold up ▪ vi to linger, stay on; **demorarse** vr to linger, stay on; (retrasarse) to take a long time; **demorarse en hacer algo** (esp Am) to take time doing sth

demos ['demos] vb ver **dar**

demostración [demostra'θjon] nf (gen, Mat) demonstration; (de cariño, fuerza) show; (de teorema) proof; (de amistad) gesture; (de cólera, gimnasia) display; ~ **comercial** commercial exhibition

demostrar [demos'trar] vt (probar) to prove; (mostrar) to show; (manifestar) to demonstrate

demostrativo, -a [demostra'tiβo, a] adj demonstrative

demudado, -a [demu'ðaðo, a] adj (rostro) pale; (fig) upset; **tener el rostro ~** to look pale

demudar [demu'ðar] vt to change, alter; **demudarse** vr (expresión) to alter; (perder color) to change colour

demuela etc [de'mwela] vb ver **demoler**

demuestre etc [de'mwestre] vb ver **demostrar**

den [den] vb ver **dar**

denegación [deneɣa'θjon] nf refusal

denegar [dene'ɣar] vt (rechazar) to refuse; (negar) to deny; (Jur) to reject

denegué [dene'ɣe], **deneguemos** etc [dene'ɣemos], **deniego** etc [de'njeɣo], **deniegue** etc [de'njeɣe] vb ver **denegar**

dengue ['denɣe] nm dengue o breakbone fever

denigrante [deni'ɣrante] adj (injurioso) insulting; (deshonroso) degrading

denigrar [deni'ɣrar] vt (desacreditar) to denigrate; (injuriar) to insult

denodado, -a [deno'ðaðo, a] adj bold, brave

denominación [denomina'θjon] nf (acto) naming; (clase) denomination; see note

DENOMINACIÓN

The *denominación de origen*, often abbreviated to *D.O.*, is a prestigious product classification given to designated regions by the awarding body, the *Consejo Regulador de la Denominación de Origen*, when their produce meets the required quality and production standards. It is often associated with *manchego* cheeses and many of the wines from the Rioja and Ribera de Duero regions.

denominador [denomina'ðor] *nm*: ~ **común** common denominator

denostar [denos'tar] *vt* to insult

denotar [deno'tar] *vt* (*indicar*) to indicate, denote

densidad [densi'ðað] *nf* (*Física*) density; (*fig*) thickness

denso, -a ['denso, a] *adj* (*apretado*) solid; (*espeso, pastoso*) thick; (*fig*) heavy

dentado, -a [den'taðo, a] *adj* (*rueda*) cogged; (*filo*) jagged; (*sello*) perforated; (*Bot*) dentate

dentadura [denta'ðura] *nf* (*set of*) teeth *pl*; ~ **postiza** false teeth *pl*

dental [den'tal] *adj* dental

dentellada [dente'ʎaða] *nf* (*mordisco*) bite, nip; (*señal*) tooth mark; **partir algo a dentelladas** to sever sth with one's teeth

dentera [den'tera] *nf* (*sensación desagradable*) the shivers *pl*

dentición [denti'θjon] *nf* (*acto*) teething; (*Anat*) dentition; **estar con la ~** to be teething

dentífrico, -a [den'tifriko, a] *adj* dental, tooth *cpd* ■ *nm* toothpaste; **pasta dentífrica** toothpaste

dentista [den'tista] *nm/f* dentist

dentro ['dentro] *adv* inside ■ *prep*: ~ **de** in, inside, within; **allí ~** in there; **mirar por ~** to look inside; ~ **de lo posible** as far as possible; ~ **de todo** all in all; ~ **de tres meses** within three months

denuedo [de'nweðo] *nm* boldness, daring

denuesto [de'nwesto] *nm* insult

denuncia [de'nunθja] *nf* (*delación*) denunciation; (*acusación*) accusation; (*de accidente*) report; **hacer o poner una ~** to report an incident to the police

denunciable [denun'θjaβle] *adj* indictable, punishable

denunciante [denun'θjante] *nm/f* accuser; (*delator*) informer

denunciar [denun'θjar] *vt* to report; (*delatar*) to inform on *o* against

Dep. *abr* (= *Departamento*) Dept.; (= *Depósito*) dep.

deparar [depa'rar] *vt* (*brindar*) to provide *o* furnish with; (*futuro, destino*) to have in store for; **los placeres que el viaje nos deparó** the pleasures which the trip afforded us

departamento [departa'mento] *nm* (*sección*) department, section; (*Am: piso*) flat (*Brit*), apartment (*US*); (*distrito*) department, province; ~ **de envíos** (*Com*) dispatch department; ~ **de máquinas** (*Naut*) engine room

departir [depar'tir] *vi* to talk, converse

dependencia [depen'denθja] *nf* dependence; (*Pol*) dependency; (*Com*) office, section; (*sucursal*) branch office; (*Arq: cuarto*) room; **dependencias** *nfpl* outbuildings

depender [depen'der] *vi*: ~ **de** to depend on; (*contar con*) to rely on; (*autoridad*) to be under, be answerable to; **depende** it (all) depends; **no depende de mí** it's not up to me

dependienta [depen'djenta] *nf* saleswoman, shop assistant

dependiente [depen'djente] *adj* dependent ■ *nm* salesman, shop assistant

depilación [depila'θjon] *nf* hair removal

depilar [depi'lar] *vt* (*con cera: piernas*) to wax; (*cejas*) to pluck

depilatorio, -a [depila'torjo, a] *adj* depilatory ■ *nm* hair remover

deplorable [deplo'raβle] *adj* deplorable

deplorar [deplo'rar] *vt* to deplore

dependré *etc* [depon'dre] *vb ver* **deponer**

deponer [depo'ner] *vt* (*armas*) to lay down; (*rey*) to depose; (*gobernante*) to oust; (*ministro*) to remove from office ■ *vi* (*Jur*) to give evidence; (*declarar*) to make a statement

deponga *etc* [de'ponga] *vb ver* **deponer**

deportación [deporta'θjon] *nf* deportation

deportar [depor'tar] *vt* to deport

deporte [de'porte] *nm* sport

deportista [depor'tista] *adj* sports *cpd* ■ *nm/f* sportsman(-woman)

deportivo, -a [depor'tiβo, a] *adj* (*club, periódico*) sports *cpd* ■ *nm* sports car

deposición [deposi'θjon] *nf* (*de funcionario etc*) removal from office; (*Jur: testimonio*) evidence

depositante [deposi'tante] *nm/f* depositor

depositar [deposi'tar] *vt* (*dinero*) to deposit; (*mercaderías*) to put away, store; **depositarse** *vr* to settle; ~ **la confianza en algn** to place one's trust in sb

depositario, -a [deposi'tarjo, a] *nm/f* trustee; ~ **judicial** official receiver

depósito [de'posito] *nm* (*gen*) deposit; (*de mercaderías*) warehouse, store; (*de animales, coches*) pound; (*de agua, gasolina etc*) tank; (*en retrete*) cistern; ~ **afianzado** bonded warehouse; ~ **bancario** bank deposit; ~ **de**

cadáveres mortuary; ~ **de maderas** timber yard; ~ **de suministro** feeder bin

depravar [depra'βar] vt to deprave, corrupt; **depravarse** vr to become depraved

depreciación [depreθja'θjon] nf depreciation

depreciar [depre'θjar] vt to depreciate, reduce the value of; **depreciarse** vr to depreciate, lose value

depredador, a [depreða'ðor, a] (Zool) adj predatory ■ nm predator

depredar [depre'ðar] vt to pillage

depresión [depre'sjon] nf (gen, Med) depression; (hueco) hollow; (en horizonte, camino) dip; (merma) drop; (Econ) slump, recession; ~ **nerviosa** nervous breakdown

deprimente [depri'mente] adj depressing

deprimido, -a [depri'miðo, a] adj depressed

deprimir [depri'mir] vt to depress; **deprimirse** vr (persona) to become depressed

deprisa [de'prisa] adv ver **prisa**

depuesto [de'pwesto] pp de **deponer**

depuración [depura'θjon] nf purification; (Pol) purge

depurador [depura'ðor] nm purifier

depuradora [depura'ðora] nf (de agua) water-treatment plant; (tb: **depuradora de aguas residuales**) sewage farm

depurar [depu'rar] vt to purify; (purgar) to purge

depuse etc [de'puse] vb ver **deponer**

der., der.° abr (= derecho) r

der.ª abr (= derecha) r

derecha [de'retʃa] nf ver **derecho, a**

derechazo [dere'tʃaθo] nm (Boxeo) right; (Tenis) forehand drive; (Taur) a pass with the cape

derechista [dere'tʃista] (Pol) adj right-wing ■ nm/f right-winger

derecho, -a [de'retʃo, a] adj right, right-hand ■ nm (privilegio) right; (título) claim, title; (lado) right(-hand) side; (leyes) law ■ nf right(-hand) side ■ adv straight, directly; **derechos** nmpl dues; (profesionales) fees; (impuestos) taxes; (de autor) royalties; **la(s) derecha(s)** (Pol) the Right; **derechos civiles** civil rights; **derechos de patente** patent rights; **derechos portuarios** (Com) harbour dues; ~ **de propiedad literaria** copyright; ~ **de timbre** (Com) stamp duty; ~ **de votar** right to vote; ~ **a voto** voting right; **Facultad de D~** Faculty of Law; **a derechas** rightly, correctly; **de derechas** (Pol) right-wing; **"reservados todos los derechos"** "all rights reserved"; **¡no hay ~!** it's not fair!; **tener ~ a** to have a right to; **a la derecha** on the right; (dirección) to the right; **siga todo ~** carry o (Brit) go straight on

deriva [de'riβa] nf: **ir** o **estar a la** ~ to drift, be adrift

derivación [deriβa'θjon] nf derivation

derivado, -a [deri'βaðo, a] adj derived ■ nm (Ling) derivative; (Industria, Química) by-product

derivar [deri'βar] vt to derive; (desviar) to direct ■ vi, **derivarse** vr to derive, be derived; ~**(se) de** (consecuencia) to spring from

dermatólogo, -a [derma'toloɣo, a] nm/f dermatologist

dérmico, -a ['dermiko, a] adj skin cpd

dermoprotector, a [dermoprotek'tor, a] adj protective

derogación [deroɣa'θjon] nf repeal

derogar [dero'ɣar] vt (ley) to repeal; (contrato) to revoke

derogue etc [de'roɣe] vb ver **derogar**

derramamiento [derrama'mjento] nm (dispersión) spilling; (fig) squandering; ~ **de sangre** bloodshed

derramar [derra'mar] vt to spill; (verter) to pour out; (esparcir) to scatter; **derramarse** vr to pour out; ~ **lágrimas** to weep

derrame [de'rrame] nm (de líquido) spilling; (de sangre) shedding; (de tubo etc) overflow; (pédida) leakage; (Med) discharge; (declive) slope; ~ **cerebral** brain haemorrhage; ~ **sinovial** water on the knee

derrapar [derra'par] vi to skid

derredor [derre'ðor] adv: **al** o **en ~ de** around, about

derrengado, -a [derren'gaðo, a] adj (torcido) bent; (cojo) crippled; **estar ~** (fig) to ache all over; **dejar ~ a algn** (fig) to wear sb out

derretido, -a [derre'tiðo, a] adj melted; (metal) molten; **estar ~ por algn** (fig) to be crazy about sb

derretir [derre'tir] vt (gen) to melt; (nieve) to thaw; (fig) to squander; **derretirse** vr to melt

derribar [derri'βar] vt to knock down; (construcción) to demolish; (persona, gobierno, político) to bring down

derribo [de'rriβo] nm (de edificio) demolition; (Lucha) throw; (Aviat) shooting down; (Pol) overthrow; **derribos** nmpl rubble sg, debris sg

derrita etc [de'rrita] vb ver **derretir**

derrocar [derro'kar] vt (gobierno) to bring down, overthrow; (ministro) to oust

derrochador, a [derrotʃa'ðor, a] adj, nm/f spendthrift

derrochar [derro'tʃar] vt (dinero, recursos) to squander; (energía, salud) to be bursting with o full of

derroche [de'rrotʃe] nm (despilfarro) waste, squandering; (exceso) extravagance; **con un**

~ **de buen gusto** with a fine display of good
taste

derroque etc [de'rroke] vb ver **derrocar**

derrota [de'rrota] nf (Naut) course; (Mil)
defeat, rout; **sufrir una grave** ~ (fig) to
suffer a grave setback

derrotar [derro'tar] vt (gen) to defeat

derrotero [derro'tero] nm (rumbo) course;
tomar otro ~ (fig) to adopt a different course

derrotista [derro'tista] adj, nm/f defeatist

derruir [derru'ir] vt to demolish, tear down

derrumbamiento [derrumba'mjento] nm
(caída) plunge; (demolición) demolition;
(desplome) collapse; ~ **de tierra** landslide

derrumbar [derrum'bar] vt to throw down;
(despeñar) to fling o hurl down; (volcar) to
upset; **derrumbarse** vr (hundirse) to collapse;
(: techo) to fall in, cave in; (fig: esperanzas) to
collapse

derrumbe [de'rrumbe] nm = **derrumbamiento**

derruyendo etc [derru'jendo] vb ver **derruir**

des [des] vb ver **dar**

desabastecido, -a [desaβaste'θiðo, a] adj:
estar ~ de algo to be short of o out of sth

desabotonar [desaβoto'nar] vt to
unbutton, undo ■ vi (flores) to blossom;
desabotonarse vr to come undone

desabrido, -a [desa'βriðo, a] adj (comida)
insipid, tasteless; (persona: soso) dull;
(: antipático) rude, surly; (respuesta) sharp;
(tiempo) unpleasant

desabrigado, -a [desaβri'yaðo, a] adj (sin
abrigo) not sufficiently protected; (fig) exposed

desabrigar [desaβri'yar] vt (quitar ropa a) to
remove the clothing of; (descubrir) to uncover;
(fig) to deprive of protection; **desabrigarse**
vr: **me desabrigué en la cama** the
bedclothes came off

desabrigue etc [desa'βriye] vb ver **desabrigar**

desabrochar [desaβro'tʃar] vt (botones, broches)
to undo, unfasten; **desabrocharse** vr (ropa
etc) to come undone

desacatar [desaka'tar] vt (ley) to disobey

desacato [desa'kato] nm (falta de respeto)
disrespect; (Jur) contempt

desacertado, -a [desaθer'taðo, a] adj
(equivocado) mistaken; (inoportuno) unwise

desacierto [desa'θjerto] nm (error) mistake,
error; (dicho) unfortunate remark

desaconsejable [desakonse'xaβle] adj
inadvisable

desaconsejado, -a [desakonse'xaðo, a] adj
ill-advised

desaconsejar [desakonse'xar] vt: ~ **algo a
algn** to advise sb against sth

desacoplar [desako'plar] vt (Elec) to
disconnect; (Tec) to take apart

desacorde [desa'korðe] adj (Mus) discordant;
(fig: opiniones) conflicting; **estar ~ con algo** to
disagree with sth

desacreditar [desakreði'tar] vt (desprestigiar)
to discredit, bring into disrepute; (denigrar)
to run down

desactivar [desakti'βar] vt to deactivate;
(bomba) to defuse

desacuerdo [desa'kwerðo] nm (conflicto)
disagreement, discord; (error) error, blunder;
en ~ out of keeping

desafiante [desa'fjante] adj (insolente) defiant;
(retador) challenging ■ nm/f challenger

desafiar [desa'fjar] vt (retar) to challenge;
(enfrentarse a) to defy

desafilado, -a [desafi'laðo, a] adj blunt

desafinado, -a [desafi'naðo, a] adj: **estar ~**
to be out of tune

desafinar [desafi'nar] vi to be out of tune;
desafinarse vr to go out of tune

desafío [desa'fio] nm (reto) challenge;
(combate) duel; (resistencia) defiance

desaforadamente [desaforaða'mente] adv:
gritar ~ to shout one's head off

desaforado, -a [desafo'raðo, a] adj (grito) ear-
splitting; (comportamiento) outrageous

desafortunadamente [desafortunaða'mente]
adv unfortunately

desafortunado, -a [desafortu'naðo, a] adj
(desgraciado) unfortunate, unlucky

desagradable [desayra'ðaβle] adj (fastidioso,
enojoso) unpleasant; (irritante) disagreeable;
ser ~ con algn to be rude to sb

desagradar [desayra'ðar] vi (disgustar) to
displease; (molestar) to bother

desagradecido, -a [desayraðe'θiðo, a] adj
ungrateful

desagrado [desa'yraðo] nm (disgusto)
displeasure; (contrariedad) dissatisfaction;
con ~ unwillingly

desagraviar [desayra'βjar] vt to make
amends to

desagravio [desa'yraβjo] nm (satisfacción)
amends; (compensación) compensation

desaguadero [desaywa'ðero] nm drain

desagüe [de'saywe] nm (de un líquido)
drainage; (cañería: tb: **tubo de desagüe**)
drainpipe; (salida) outlet, drain

desaguisado, -a [desayi'saðo, a] adj illegal
■ nm outrage

desahogado, -a [desao'yaðo, a] adj (holgado)
comfortable; (espacioso) roomy

desahogar [desao'yar] vt (aliviar) to ease,
relieve; (ira) to vent; **desahogarse** vr
(distenderse) to relax; (desfogarse) to let off
steam (fam); (confesarse) to confess, get sth off
one's chest (fam)

desahogo [desa'oɣo] *nm* (*alivio*) relief; (*comodidad*) comfort, ease; **vivir con ~** to be comfortably off

desahogue *etc* [desa'oɣe] *vb ver* **desahogar**

desahuciado, -a [desau'θjaðo, a] *adj* hopeless

desahuciar [desau'θjar] *vt* (*enfermo*) to give up hope for; (*inquilino*) to evict

desahucio [de'sauθjo] *nm* eviction

desairado, -a [desai'raðo, a] *adj* (*menospreciado*) disregarded; (*desgarbado*) shabby; (*sin éxito*) unsuccessful; **quedar ~** to come off badly

desairar [desai'rar] *vt* (*menospreciar*) to slight, snub; (*cosa*) to disregard; (*Com*) to default on

desaire [des'aire] *nm* (*menosprecio*) slight; (*falta de garbo*) unattractiveness; **dar** *o* **hacer un ~ a algn** to offend sb; **¿me va usted a hacer ese ~?** I won't take no for an answer!

desajustar [desaxus'tar] *vt* (*desarreglar*) to disarrange; (*desconcertar*) to throw off balance; (*fig: planes*) to upset; **desajustarse** *vr* to get out of order; (*aflojarse*) to loosen

desajuste [desa'xuste] *nm* (*de máquina*) disorder; (*avería*) breakdown; (*situación*) imbalance; (*desacuerdo*) disagreement

desalentador, -a [desalenta'ðor, a] *adj* discouraging

desalentar [desalen'tar] *vt* (*desanimar*) to discourage; **desalentarse** *vr* to get discouraged

desaliento *etc* [desa'ljento] *vb ver* **desalentar** ▪ *nm* discouragement; (*abatimiento*) depression

desaliñado, -a [desali'ɲaðo, a] *adj* (*descuidado*) slovenly; (*raído*) shabby; (*desordenado*) untidy; (*negligente*) careless

desaliño [desa'liɲo] *nm* (*descuido*) slovenliness; (*negligencia*) carelessness

desalmado, -a [desal'maðo, a] *adj* (*cruel*) cruel, heartless

desalojar [desalo'xar] *vt* (*gen*) to remove, expel; (*expulsar, echar*) to eject; (*abandonar*) to move out of ▪ *vi* to move out; **la policía desalojó el local** the police cleared people out of the place

desalquilar [desalki'lar] *vt* to vacate, move out; **desalquilarse** *vr* to become vacant

desamarrar [desama'rrar] *vt* to untie; (*Naut*) to cast off

desamor [desa'mor] *nm* (*frialdad*) indifference; (*odio*) dislike

desamparado, -a [desampa'raðo, a] *adj* (*persona*) helpless; (*lugar: expuesto*) exposed; (: *desierto*) deserted

desamparar [desampa'rar] *vt* (*abandonar*) to desert, abandon; (*Jur*) to leave defenceless; (*barco*) to abandon

desamparo [desam'paro] *nm* (*acto*) desertion; (*estado*) helplessness

desamueblado, -a [desamwe'βlaðo, a] *adj* unfurnished

desandar [desan'dar] *vt*: **~ lo andado** *o* **el camino** to retrace one's steps

desanduve *etc* [desan'duβe], **desanduviera** *etc* [desandu'βjera] *vb ver* **desandar**

desangelado, -a [desanxe'laðo, a] *adj* (*habitación, edificio*) lifeless

desangrar [desan'grar] *vt* to bleed; (*fig: persona*) to bleed dry; (*lago*) to drain; **desangrarse** *vr* to lose a lot of blood; (*morir*) to bleed to death

desanimado, -a [desani'maðo, a] *adj* (*persona*) downhearted; (*espectáculo, fiesta*) dull

desanimar [desani'mar] *vt* (*desalentar*) to discourage; (*deprimir*) to depress; **desanimarse** *vr* to lose heart

desánimo [de'sanimo] *nm* despondency; (*abatimiento*) dejection; (*falta de animación*) dullness

desanudar [desanu'ðar] *vt* to untie; (*fig*) to clear up

desapacible [desapa'θiβle] *adj* unpleasant

desaparecer [desapare'θer] *vi* to disappear; (*el sol, la luz*) to vanish; (*desaparecer de vista*) to drop out of sight; (*efectos, señales*) to wear off ▪ *vt* (*esp Am Pol*) to cause to disappear; (: *eufemismo*) to murder

desaparecido, -a [desapare'θiðo, a] *adj* missing; (*especie*) extinct ▪ *nm/f* (*Am Pol*) kidnapped *o* missing person

desaparezca *etc* [desapa'reθka] *vb ver* **desaparecer**

desaparición [desapari'θjon] *nf* disappearance; (*de especie etc*) extinction

desapasionado, -a [desapasjo'naðo, a] *adj* dispassionate, impartial

desapego [desa'peɣo] *nm* (*frialdad*) coolness; (*distancia*) detachment

desapercibido, -a [desaperθi'βiðo, a] *adj* unnoticed; (*desprevenido*) unprepared; **pasar ~** to go unnoticed

desaplicado, -a [desapli'kaðo, a] *adj* slack, lazy

desaprensivo, -a [desapren'siβo, a] *adj* unscrupulous

desaprobar [desapro'βar] *vt* (*reprobar*) to disapprove of; (*condenar*) to condemn; (*no consentir*) to reject

desaprovechado, -a [desaproβe'tʃaðo, a] *adj* (*oportunidad, tiempo*) wasted; (*estudiante*) slack

desaprovechar [desaproβe'tʃar] *vt* to waste; (*talento*) not to use to the full ▪ *vi* (*perder terreno*) to lose ground

desapruebe etc [desa'prweβe] vb ver
desaprobar
desarmar [desar'mar] vt (Mil, fig) to disarm;
(Tec) to take apart, dismantle
desarme [de'sarme] nm disarmament
desarraigado, -a [desarrai'ɣaðo, a] adj
(persona) without roots, rootless
desarraigar [desarrai'ɣar] vt to uproot; (fig:
costumbre) to root out; (: persona) to banish
desarraigo [desa'rraiɣo] nm uprooting
desarraigue etc [desa'rraiɣe] vb ver
desarraigar
desarrapado, -a [desarra'paðo, a] adj
ragged; **(de aspecto)** ~ shabby
desarreglado, -a [desarre'ɣlaðo, a] adj
(desordenado) disorderly, untidy; (hábitos)
irregular
desarreglar [desarre'ɣlar] vt to mess up;
(desordenar) to disarrange; (trastocar) to upset,
disturb
desarreglo [desa'rreɣlo] nm (de casa, persona)
untidiness; (desorden) disorder; (Tec) trouble;
(Med) upset; **viven en el mayor** ~ they live in
complete chaos
desarrollado, -a [desarro'ʎaðo, a] adj
developed
desarrollar [desarro'ʎar] vt (gen) to develop;
(extender) to unfold; (teoría) to explain;
desarrollarse vr to develop, (extenderse) to
open (out); (film) to develop; (fig) to grow;
(tener lugar) to take place; **aquí desarrollan
un trabajo muy importante** they carry on
o out very important work here; **la acción se
desarrolla en Roma** (Cine etc) the scene is
set in Rome
desarrollo [desa'rroʎo] nm development;
(de acontecimientos) unfolding; (de industria,
mercado) expansion, growth; **país en vías de
~** developing country; **la industria está en
pleno ~** industry is expanding steadily; **~
sostenible** sustainable development
desarrugar [desarru'ɣar] vt (alisar) to smooth
(out); (ropa) to remove the creases from
desarrugue etc [desa'rruɣe] vb ver **desarrugar**
desarticulado, -a [desartiku'laðo, a] adj
disjointed
desarticular [desartiku'lar] vt (huesos) to
dislocate, put out of joint; (objeto) to take
apart; (grupo terrorista etc) to break up
desaseado, -a [desase'aðo, a] adj (sucio) dirty;
(desaliñado) untidy
desaseo [desa'seo] nm (suciedad) dirtiness;
(desarreglo) untidiness
desasga etc [de'sasɣa] vb ver **desasir**
desasir [desa'sir] vt to loosen; **desasirse** vr
to extricate o.s.; **desasirse de** to let go, give up
desasosegar [desasose'ɣar] vt (inquietar) to

disturb, make uneasy; **desasosegarse** vr
to become uneasy
desasosegué [desasose'ɣe], **desasoseguemos**
etc [desasose'ɣemos] vb ver **desasosegar**
desasosiego etc [desaso'sjeɣo] vb ver
desasosegar ■ nm (intranquilidad)
uneasiness, restlessness; (ansiedad) anxiety;
(Pol etc) unrest
desasosiegue etc [desaso'sjeɣe] vb ver
desasosegar
desastrado, -a [desas'traðo, a] adj
(desaliñado) shabby; (sucio) dirty
desastre [de'sastre] nm disaster; **¡un ~!** how
awful!; **la función fue un ~** the show was a
shambles
desastroso, -a [desas'troso, a] adj disastrous
desatado, -a [desa'taðo, a] adj (desligado)
untied; (violento) violent, wild
desatar [desa'tar] vt (nudo) to untie; (paquete)
to undo; (perro, odio) to unleash; (misterio)
to solve; (separar) to detach; **desatarse** vr
(zapatos) to come untied; (tormenta) to break;
(perder control de sí mismo) to lose self-control;
desatarse en injurias to pour out a stream
of insults
desatascar [desatas'kar] vt (cañería) to
unblock, clear
desatasque etc [desa'taske] vb ver **desatascar**
desatención [desaten'θjon] nf (descuido)
inattention; (distracción) absent-mindedness
desatender [desaten'der] vt (no prestar atención
a) to disregard; (abandonar) to neglect
desatento, -a [desa'tento, a] adj (distraído)
inattentive; (descortés) discourteous
desatienda etc [desa'tjenda] vb ver
desatender
desatinado, -a [desati'naðo, a] adj foolish,
silly
desatino [desa'tino] nm (idiotez) foolishness,
folly; (error) blunder; **desatinos** nmpl
nonsense sg; **¡qué ~!** how silly!, what
rubbish!
desatornillar [desatorni'ʎar] vt to unscrew
desatrancar [desatran'kar] vt (puerta) to
unbolt; (cañería) to unblock
desatranque etc [desa'tranke] vb ver
desatrancar
desautorice etc [desauto'riθe] vb ver
desautorizar
desautorizado, -a [desautori'θaðo, a] adj
unauthorized
desautorizar [desautori'θar] vt (oficial) to
deprive of authority; (informe) to deny
desavendré etc [desaβen'dre] vb ver
desavenir
desavenencia [desaβe'nenθja] nf (desacuerdo)
disagreement; (discrepancia) quarrel

desavenga etc [desa'βenga] vb ver **desavenir**
desavenido, -a [desaβe'niðo, a] adj (opuesto) contrary; (reñido) in disagreement; **ellos están desavenidos** they are at odds
desavenir [desaβe'nir] vt (enemistar) to make trouble between; **desavenirse** vr to fall out
desaventajado, -a [desaβenta'xaðo, a] adj (inferior) inferior; (poco ventajoso) disadvantageous
desaviene etc [desa'βjene], **desaviniendo** etc [desaβi'njendo] vb ver **desavenir**
desayunar [desaju'nar] vi, **desayunarse** vr to have breakfast ■ vt to have for breakfast; **~ con café** to have coffee for breakfast; **~ con algo** (fig) to get the first news of sth
desayuno [desa'juno] nm breakfast
desazón [desa'θon] nf (angustia) anxiety; (Med) discomfort; (fig) annoyance
desazonar [desaθo'nar] vt (fig) to annoy, upset; **desazonarse** vr (enojarse) to be annoyed; (preocuparse) to worry, be anxious
desbancar [desβan'kar] vt (quitar el puesto a) to oust; (suplantar) to supplant (in sb's affections)
desbandada [desβan'daða] nf rush; **~ general** mass exodus; **a la ~** in disorder
desbandarse [desβan'darse] vr (Mil) to disband; (fig) to flee in disorder
desbanque etc [des'βanke] vb ver **desbancar**
desbarajuste [desβara'xuste] nm confusion, disorder; **¡qué ~!** what a mess!
desbaratar [desβara'tar] vt (gen) to mess up; (plan) to spoil; (deshacer, destruir) to ruin ■ vi to talk nonsense; **desbaratarse** vr (máquina) to break down; (persona: irritarse) to fly off the handle (fam)
desbarrar [desβa'rrar] vi to talk nonsense
desbloquear [desβloke'ar] vt (negociaciones, tráfico) to get going again; (Com: cuenta) to unfreeze
desbocado, -a [desβo'kaðo, a] adj (caballo) runaway; (herramienta) worn
desbocar [desβo'kar] vt (vasija) to break the rim of; **desbocarse** vr (caballo) to bolt; (persona: soltar injurias) to let out a stream of insults
desboque etc [des'βoke] vb ver **desbocar**
desbordamiento [desβorða'mjento] nm (de río) overflowing; (Inform) overflow; (de cólera) outburst; (de entusiasmo) upsurge
desbordar [desβor'ðar] vt (sobrepasar) to go beyond; (exceder) to exceed ■ vi, **desbordarse** vr (líquido, río) to overflow; (entusiasmo) to erupt; (persona: exaltarse) to get carried away
desbravar [desβra'βar] vt (caballo) to break in; (animal) to tame
descabalgar [deskaβal'ɣar] vi to dismount

descabalgue etc [deska'βalɣe] vb ver **descabalgar**
descabellado, -a [deskaβe'ʎaðo, a] adj (disparatado) wild, crazy; (insensato) preposterous
descabellar [deskaβe'ʎar] vt to ruffle; (Taur: toro) to give the coup de grace to
descabezado, -a [deskaβe'θaðo, a] adj (sin cabeza) headless; (insensato) wild
descafeinado, -a [deskafei'naðo, a] adj decaffeinated ■ nm decaffeinated coffee, de-caff
descalabrar [deskala'βrar] vt to smash; (persona) to hit; (: en la cabeza) to hit on the head; (Naut) to cripple; (dañar) to harm, damage; **descalabrarse** vr to hurt one's head
descalabro [deska'laβro] nm blow; (desgracia) misfortune
descalce etc [des'kalθe] vb ver **descalzar**
descalificación [deskalifika'θjon] nf disqualification; **descalificaciones** nfpl discrediting sg
descalificar [deskalifi'kar] vt to disqualify; (desacreditar) to discredit
descalifique etc [deskali'fike] vb ver **descalificar**
descalzar [deskal'θar] vt (persona) to take the shoes off
descalzo, -a [des'kalθo, a] adj barefoot(ed); (fig) destitute; **estar (con los pies) ~(s)** to be barefooted
descambiar [deskam'bjar] vt to exchange
descaminado, -a [deskami'naðo, a] adj (equivocado) on the wrong road; (fig) misguided; **en eso no anda usted muy ~** you're not far wrong there
descamisado, -a [deskami'saðo, a] adj barechested
descampado [deskam'paðo] nm open space, piece of empty ground; **comer al ~** to eat in the open air
descansado, -a [deskan'saðo, a] adj (gen) rested; (que tranquiliza) restful
descansar [deskan'sar] vt (gen) to rest; (apoyar): **~ (sobre)** to lean (on) ■ vi to rest, have a rest; (echarse) to lie down; (cadáver, restos) to lie; **¡que usted descanse!** sleep well!; **~ en** (argumento) to be based on
descansillo [deskan'siʎo] nm (de escalera) landing
descanso [des'kanso] nm (reposo) rest; (alivio) relief; (pausa) break; (Deporte) interval, half time; **día de ~** day off; **~ de enfermedad/ maternidad** sick/maternity leave; **tomarse unos días de ~** to take a few days' leave o rest
descapitalizado, -a [deskapitali'θaðo, a] adj undercapitalized

descapotable [deskapo'taβle] *nm* (*tb*: **coche descapotable**) convertible

descarado, -a [deska'raðo, a] *adj* (*sin vergüenza*) shameless; (*insolente*) cheeky

descarga [des'karɣa] *nf* (*Arq, Elec, Mil*) discharge; (*Naut*) unloading; (*Inform*) download

descargable [deskar'ɣaβle] *adj* downloadable

descargador [deskarɣa'ðor] *nm* docker

descargar [deskar'ɣar] *vt* to unload; (*golpe*) to let fly; (*arma*) to fire; (*Elec*) to discharge; (*pila*) to run down; (*conciencia*) to relieve; (*Com*) to take up; (*persona: de una obligación*) to release; (: *de una deuda*) to free; (*Jur*) to clear ■ *vi* (*río*): ~ **(en)** to flow (into); **descargarse** *vr* to unburden o.s.; **descargarse de algo** to get rid of sth; **descargarse algo de Internet** to download sth from the Internet

descargo [des'karɣo] *nm* (*de obligación*) release; (*Com: recibo*) receipt; (: *de deuda*) discharge; (*Jur*) evidence; ~ **de una acusación** acquittal on a charge

descargue *etc* [des'karɣe] *vb ver* **descargar**

descarnado, -a [deskar'naðo, a] *adj* scrawny; (*fig*) bare; (*estilo*) straightforward

descaro [des'karo] *nm* nerve

descarriar [deska'rrjar] *vt* (*descaminar*) to misdirect; (*fig*) to lead astray; **descarriarse** *vr* (*perderse*) to lose one's way; (*separarse*) to stray; (*pervertirse*) to err, go astray

descarrilamiento [deskarrila'mjento] *nm* (*de tren*) derailment

descarrilar [deskarri'lar] *vi* to be derailed

descartable [deskar'taβle] *adj* (*Inform*) temporary

descartar [deskar'tar] *vt* (*rechazar*) to reject; (*eliminar*) to rule out; **descartarse** *vr* (*Naipes*) to discard; **descartarse de** to shirk

descascarar [deskaska'rar] *vt* (*naranja, limón*) to peel; (*nueces, huevo duro*) to shell; **descascararse** *vr* to peel (off)

descascarillado, -a [deskaskari'ʎaðo, a] *adj* (*paredes*) peeling

descendencia [desθen'denθja] *nf* (*origen*) origin, descent; (*hijos*) offspring; **morir sin dejar** ~ to die without issue

descendente [desθen'dente] *adj* (*cantidad*) diminishing; (*Inform*) top-down

descender [desθen'der] *vt* (*bajar: escalera*) to go down ■ *vi* to descend; (*temperatura, nivel*) to fall, drop; (*líquido*) to run; (*cortina etc*) to hang; (*fuerzas, persona*) to fail, get weak; ~ **de** to be descended from

descendiente [desθen'djente] *nm/f* descendant

descenso [des'θenso] *nm* descent; (*de temperatura*) drop; (*de producción*) downturn; (*de calidad*) decline; (*Minería*) collapse; (*bajada*) slope; (*fig: decadencia*) decline; (*de empleado etc*) demotion

descentrado, -a [desθen'traðo, a] *adj* (*pieza de una máquina*) off-centre; (*rueda*) out of true; (*persona*) bewildered; (*desequilibrado*) unbalanced; (*problema*) out of focus; **todavía está algo** ~ he is still somewhat out of touch

descentralice *etc* [desθentra'liθe] *vb ver* **descentralizar**

descentralizar [desθentrali'θar] *vt* to decentralize

descerrajar [desθerra'xar] *vt* (*puerta*) to break open

descienda *etc* [des'θjenda] *vb ver* **descender**

descifrable [desθi'fraβle] *adj* (*gen*) decipherable; (*letra*) legible

descifrar [desθi'frar] *vt* (*escritura*) to decipher; (*mensaje*) to decode; (*problema*) to puzzle out; (*misterio*) to solve

descocado, -a [desko'kaðo, a] *adj* (*descarado*) cheeky; (*desvergonzado*) brazen

descoco [des'koko] *nm* (*descaro*) cheek; (*atrevimiento*) brazenness

descodificador [deskoðifika'ðor] *nm* decoder

descodificar [deskoðifi'kar] *vt* to decode

descolgar [deskol'ɣar] *vt* (*bajar*) to take down; (*desde una posición alta*) to lower; (*de una pared etc*) to unhook; (*teléfono*) to pick up; **descolgarse** *vr* to let o.s. down; **descolgarse por** (*bajar escurriéndose*) to slip down; (*pared*) to climb down; **dejó el teléfono descolgado** he left the phone off the hook

descolgué [deskol'ɣe] *etc vb ver* **descolgar**

descollar [desko'ʎar] *vi* (*sobresalir*) to stand out; (*montaña etc*) to rise; **la obra que más descuella de las suyas** his most outstanding work

descolocado, -a [deskolo'kaðo, a] *adj*: **estar** ~ (*cosa*) to be out of place; (*criada*) to be unemployed

descolorido, -a [deskolo'riðo, a] *adj* (*color, tela*) faded; (*pálido*) pale; (*fig: estilo*) colourless

descompaginar [deskompaxi'nar] *vt* (*desordenar*) to disarrange, mess up

descompasado, -a [deskompa'saðo, a] *adj* (*sin proporción*) out of all proportion; (*excesivo*) excessive; (*hora*) unearthly

descompensar [deskompen'sar] *vt* to unbalance

descompondré *etc* [deskompon'dre] *vb ver* **descomponer**

descomponer [deskompo'ner] *vt* (*gen, Ling, Mat*) to break down; (*desordenar*) to disarrange, disturb; (*materia orgánica*) to rot, decompose; (*Tec*) to put out of order; (*facciones*) to distort; (*estómago etc*) to upset;

(: *planes*) to mess up; (*persona: molestar*) to
upset; (*irritar*) to annoy; **descomponerse**
vr (*corromperse*) to rot, decompose; (*estómago*)
to get upset; (*el tiempo*) to change (for the
worse); (*Tec*) to break down
descomponga *etc* [deskom'ponga] *vb ver*
descomponer
descomposición [deskomposi'θjon] *nf* (*gen*)
breakdown; (*de fruta etc*) decomposition;
(*putrefacción*) rotting; (*de cara*) distortion;
~ **de vientre** (*Med*) stomach upset, diarrhoea
descompostura [deskompos'tura] *nf* (*Tec*)
breakdown; (*desorganización*) disorganization;
(*desorden*) untidiness
descompuesto, -a [deskom'pwesto, a]
pp de **descomponer** ▪ *adj* (*corrompido*)
decomposed; (*roto*) broken (down)
descompuse *etc* [deskom'puse] *vb ver*
descomponer
descomunal [deskomu'nal] *adj* (*enorme*)
huge; (*fam: excelente*) fantastic
desconcertado, -a [deskonθer'taðo, a] *adj*
disconcerted, bewildered
desconcertar [deskonθer'tar] *vt* (*confundir*)
to baffle; (*incomodar*) to upset, put out; (*orden*)
to disturb; **desconcertarse** *vr* (*turbarse*) to be
upset; (*confundirse*) to be bewildered
desconchado, -a [deskon'tʃaðo, a] *adj*
(*pintura*) peeling
desconchar [deskon'tʃar] *vt* (*pared*) to strip
off; (*loza*) to chip off
desconcierto [deskon'θjerto] *vb ver*
desconcertar ▪ *nm* (*gen*) disorder;
(*desorientación*) uncertainty; (*inquietud*)
uneasiness; (*confusión*) bewilderment
desconectado, -a [deskonek'taðo, a] *adj*
(*Elec*) disconnected, switched off; (*Inform*)
offline; **estar ~ de** (*fig*) to have no contact
with
desconectar [deskonek'tar] *vt* to disconnect;
(*desenchufar*) to unplug; (*radio, televisión*) to
switch off; (*Inform*) to toggle off
desconfiado, -a [deskon'fjaðo, a] *adj*
suspicious
desconfianza [deskon'fjanθa] *nf* distrust
desconfiar [deskon'fjar] *vi* to be distrustful;
~ **de** (*sospechar*) to mistrust, suspect; (*no tener
confianza en*) to have no faith o confidence in;
desconfío de ello I doubt it; **desconfíe de
las imitaciones** (*Com*) beware of imitations
desconforme [deskon'forme] *adj*
= **disconforme**
descongelar [deskonxe'lar] *vt* (*nevera*) to
defrost; (*comida*) to thaw; (*Auto*) to de-ice;
(*Com, Pol*) to unfreeze
descongestionar [deskonxestjo'nar] *vt*
(*cabeza, tráfico*) to clear; (*calle, ciudad*) to relieve

congestion in; (*fig: despejar*) to clear
desconocer [deskono'θer] *vt* (*ignorar*) not to
know, be ignorant of; (*no aceptar*) to deny;
(*repudiar*) to disown
desconocido, -a [deskono'θiðo, a] *adj*
unknown; (*que no se conoce*) unfamiliar; (*no
reconocido*) unrecognized ▪ *nm/f* stranger;
(*recién llegado*) newcomer; **está ~** he is hardly
recognizable
desconocimiento [deskonoθi'mjento] *nm*
(*falta de conocimientos*) ignorance; (*repudio*)
disregard
desconozca *etc* [desko'noθka] *vb ver*
desconocer
desconsiderado, -a [deskonsiðe'raðo, a] *adj*
inconsiderate; (*insensible*) thoughtless
desconsolado, -a [deskonso'laðo, a] *adj*
(*afligido*) disconsolate; (*cara*) sad; (*desanimado*)
dejected
desconsolar [deskonso'lar] *vt* to distress;
desconsolarse *vr* to despair
desconsuelo *etc* [deskon'swelo] *vb ver*
desconsolar ▪ *nm* (*tristeza*) distress;
(*desesperación*) despair
descontado, -a [deskon'taðo, a] *adj*: **por ~** of
course; **dar por ~ (que)** to take it for granted
(that)
descontar [deskon'tar] *vt* (*deducir*) to take
away, deduct; (*rebajar*) to discount
descontento, -a [deskon'tento, a] *adj*
dissatisfied ▪ *nm* dissatisfaction, discontent
descontrol [deskon'trol] *nm* (*fam*) lack of
control
descontrolado, -a [deskontro'laðo, a] *adj*
uncontrolled
descontrolarse [deskontro'larse] *vr* (*persona*)
to lose control
desconvenir [deskombe'nir] *vi* (*personas*)
to disagree; (*no corresponder*) not to fit; (*no
convenir*) to be inconvenient
desconvocar [deskombo'kar] *vt* to call off
descorazonar [deskoraθo'nar] *vt* to
discourage, dishearten; **descorazonarse** *vr*
to get discouraged, lose heart
descorchador [deskortʃa'ðor] *nm* corkscrew
descorchar [deskor'tʃar] *vt* to uncork, open
descorrer [desko'rrer] *vt* (*cortina, cerrojo*) to
draw back; (*velo*) to remove
descortés [deskor'tes] *adj* (*mal educado*)
discourteous; (*grosero*) rude
descortesía [deskorte'sia] *nf* discourtesy;
(*grosería*) rudeness
descoser [desko'ser] *vt* to unstitch;
descoserse *vr* to come apart (at the seams);
(*fam: descubrir un secreto*) to blurt out a secret;
descoserse de risa to split one's sides
laughing

descosido, -a [desko'siðo, a] *adj* (*costura*) unstitched; (*desordenado*) disjointed ∎ *nm*: **como un ~** (*obrar*) wildly; (*beber, comer*) to excess; (*estudiar*) like mad

descoyuntar [deskojun'tar] *vt* (*Anat*) to dislocate; (*hechos*) to twist; **descoyuntarse** *vr*: **descoyuntarse un hueso** (*Anat*) to put a bone out of joint; **descoyuntarse de risa** (*fam*) to split one's sides laughing; **estar descoyuntado** (*persona*) to be double-jointed

descrédito [des'kreðito] *nm* discredit; **caer en ~** to fall into disrepute; **ir en ~ de** to be to the discredit of

descreído, -a [deskre'iðo, a] *adj* (*incrédulo*) incredulous; (*falto de fe*) unbelieving

descremado, -a [deskre'maðo, a] *adj* skimmed

descremar [deskre'mar] *vt* (*leche*) to skim

describir [deskri'βir] *vt* to describe

descripción [deskrip'θjon] *nf* description

descrito [des'krito] *pp de* **describir**

descuajar [deskwa'xar] *vt* (*disolver*) to melt; (*planta*) to pull out by the roots; (*extirpar*) to eradicate, wipe out; (*desanimar*) to dishearten

descuajaringarse [deskwaxarin'garse] *vr* to fall to bits

descuajaringue *etc* [deskwaxa'rinɣe] *vb ver* **descuajaringarse**

descuartice *etc* [deskwar'tiθe] *vb ver* **descuartizar**

descuartizar [deskwarti'θar] *vt* (*animal*) to carve up, cut up; (*fig: hacer pedazos*) to tear apart

descubierto, -a [desku'βjerto, a] *pp de* **descubrir** ∎ *adj* uncovered, bare; (*persona*) bare-headed; (*cielo*) clear; (*coche*) open; (*campo*) treeless ∎ *nm* (*lugar*) open space; (*Com: en el presupuesto*) shortage; (*: bancario*) overdraft; **al ~** in the open; **poner al ~** to lay bare; **quedar al ~** to be exposed; **estar en ~** to be overdrawn

descubridor, a [desku'βri'ðor, a] *nm/f* discoverer

descubrimiento [deskuβri'mjento] *nm* (*hallazgo*) discovery; (*de criminal, fraude*) detection; (*revelación*) revelation; (*de secreto etc*) disclosure; (*de estatua etc*) unveiling

descubrir [desku'βrir] *vt* to discover, find; (*petróleo*) to strike; (*inaugurar*) to unveil; (*vislumbrar*) to detect; (*sacar a luz: crimen*) to bring to light; (*revelar*) to reveal, show; (*poner al descubierto*) to expose to view; (*naipes*) to lay down; (*quitar la tapa de*) to uncover; (*cacerola*) to take the lid off; (*enterarse de: causa, solución*) to find out; (*divisar*) to see, make out; (*delatar*) to give away, betray; **descubrirse** *vr* to reveal o.s.; (*quitarse sombrero*) to take off one's

hat; (*confesar*) to confess; (*fig: salir a luz*) to come out o to light

descuelga *etc* [des'kwelɣa], **descuelgue** *etc* [des'kwelɣe] *vb ver* **descolgar**

descuelle *etc* [des'kweʎe] *vb ver* **descollar**

descuento *etc* [des'kwento] *vb ver* **descontar** ∎ *nm* discount; **~ del 3%** 3% off; **con ~** at a discount; **~ por pago al contado** (*Com*) cash discount; **~ por volumen de compras** (*Com*) volume discount

descuidado, -a [deskwi'ðaðo, a] *adj* (*sin cuidado*) careless; (*desordenado*) untidy; (*olvidadizo*) forgetful; (*dejado*) neglected; (*desprevenido*) unprepared

descuidar [deskwi'ðar] *vt* (*dejar*) to neglect; (*olvidar*) to overlook ∎ *vi*, **descuidarse** *vr* (*distraerse*) to be careless; (*estar desaliñado*) to let o.s. go; (*desprevenirse*) to drop one's guard; **¡descuida!** don't worry!

descuido [des'kwiðo] *nm* (*dejadez*) carelessness; (*olvido*) negligence; (*un descuido*) oversight; **al ~** casually; (*sin cuidado*) carelessly; **al menor ~** if my *etc* attention wanders for a minute; **con ~** thoughtlessly; **por ~** by an oversight

 PALABRA CLAVE

desde ['desðe] *prep* **1** (*lugar*) from; **desde Burgos hasta mi casa hay 30 km** it's 30 kms from Burgos to my house; **desde lejos** from a distance

2 (*posición*): **hablaba desde el balcón** she was speaking from the balcony

3 (*tiempo: +adv, n*): **desde ahora** from now on; **desde entonces/la boda** since then/the wedding; **desde niño** since I *etc* was a child; **desde tres años atrás** since three years ago

4 (*tiempo: +vb*) since; for; **nos conocemos desde 1978/desde hace 20 años** we've known each other since 1978/for 20 years; **no le veo desde 1983/desde hace 5 años** I haven't seen him since 1983/for 5 years; **¿desde cuándo vives aquí?** how long have you lived here?

5 (*gama*): **desde los más lujosos hasta los más económicos** from the most luxurious to the most reasonably priced

6: **desde luego (que no)** of course (not) ∎ *conj*: **desde que**: **desde que recuerdo** for as long as I can remember; **desde que llegó no ha salido** he hasn't been out since he arrived

desdecir [desðe'θir] *vi*: **~ de** (*no merecer*) to be unworthy of; (*no corresponder*) to clash with; **desdecirse** *vr*: **desdecirse de** to go back on

desdén [des'ðen] *nm* scorn
desdentado, -a [desðen'taðo, a] *adj*
toothless
desdeñable [desðe'ɲaβle] *adj* contemptible;
nada ~ far from negligible, considerable
desdeñar [desðe'ɲar] *vt* (*despreciar*) to scorn
desdeñoso, -a [desðe'ɲoso, a] *adj* scornful
desdibujar [desðiβu'xar] *vt* to blur (the
outlines of); **desdibujarse** *vr* to get blurred,
fade (away); **el recuerdo se ha desdibujado**
the memory has become blurred
desdichado, -a [desði'tʃaðo, a] *adj* (*sin suerte*)
unlucky; (*infeliz*) unhappy; (*día*) ill-fated
■ *nm/f* (*pobre desgraciado*) poor devil
desdicho, -a [des'ðitʃo, a] *pp de* **desdecir**
■ *nf* (*desgracia*) misfortune; (*infelicidad*)
unhappiness
desdiciendo *etc* [desði'θjendo] *vb ver* **desdecir**
desdiga *etc* [des'ðiɣa], **desdije** *etc* [des'dixe]
vb ver **desdecir**
desdoblado, -a [desðo'βlaðo, a] *adj*
(*personalidad*) split
desdoblar [desðo'βlar] *vt* (*extender*) to spread
out; (*desplegar*) to unfold
deseable [dese'aβle] *adj* desirable
desear [dese'ar] *vt* to want, desire, wish for;
¿qué desea la señora? (*tienda etc*) what can
I do for you, madam?; **estoy deseando que
esto termine** I'm longing for this to finish
desecar [dese'kar] *vt*, **desecarse** *vr* to dry up
desechable [dese'tʃaβle] *adj* (*envase etc*)
disposable
desechar [dese'tʃar] *vt* (*basura*) to throw out *o*
away; (*ideas*) to reject, discard; (*miedo*) to cast
aside; (*plan*) to drop
desecho [de'setʃo] *nm* (*desprecio*) contempt;
(*lo peor*) dregs *pl*; **desechos** *nmpl* rubbish *sg*,
waste *sg*; **de** ~ (*hierro*) scrap; (*producto*) waste;
(*ropa*) cast-off
desembalar [desemba'lar] *vt* to unpack
desembarace *etc* [desemba'raθe] *vb ver*
desembarazar
desembarazado, -a [desembara'θaðo, a] *adj*
(*libre*) clear, free; (*desenvuelto*) free and easy
desembarazar [desembara'θar] *vt* (*desocupar*)
to clear; (*desenredar*) to free; **desembarazarse**
vr: **desembarazarse de** to free o.s. of, get
rid of
desembarazo [desemba'raθo] *nm* (*acto*)
clearing; (*Am: parto*) birth; (*desenfado*) ease
desembarcadero [desembarka'ðero] *nm*
quay
desembarcar [desembar'kar] *vt* (*personas*)
to land; (*mercancías etc*) to unload ■ *vi*,
desembarcarse *vr* (*de barco, avión*) to
disembark
desembarco [desem'barko] *nm* landing

desembargar [desembar'ɣar] *vt* (*gen*) to free;
(*Jur*) to remove the embargo on
desembargue *etc* [desem'βarɣe] *vb ver*
desembargar
desembarque *etc* [desem'barke] *vb ver*
desembarcar ■ *nm* disembarkation; (*de
pasajeros*) landing; (*de mercancías*) unloading
desembocadura [desemboka'ðura] *nf* (*de río*)
mouth; (*de calle*) opening
desembocar [desembo'kar] *vi*: ~ **en** to flow
into; (*fig*) to result in
desemboce *etc* [desem'boθe] *vb ver*
desembozar
desembolsar [desembol'sar] *vt* (*pagar*) to pay
out; (*gastar*) to lay out
desembolso [desem'bolso] *nm* payment
desemboque *etc* [desem'boke] *vb ver*
desembocar
desembozar [desembo'θar] *vt* to unmask
desembragar [desembra'ɣar] *vt* (*Tec*) to
disengage, release ■ *vi* (*Auto*) to declutch
desembrague *etc* [desem'βraɣe] *vb ver*
desembragar
desembrollar [desembro'ʎar] *vt* (*madeja*) to
unravel; (*asunto, malentendido*) to sort out
desembuchar [desembu'tʃar] *vt* to disgorge;
(*fig*) to come out with ■ *vi* (*confesar*) to spill
the beans (*fam*); **¡desembucha!** out with it!
desemejante [deseme'xante] *adj* dissimilar;
~ **de** different from, unlike
desemejanza [deseme'xanθa] *nf*
dissimilarity
desempacar [desempa'kar] *vt* (*esp Am*)
to unpack
desempañar [desempa'ɲar] *vt* (*cristal*)
to clean, demist
desempaque *etc* [desem'pake] *vb ver*
desempacar
desempaquetar [desempake'tar] *vt*
to unpack, unwrap
desempatar [desempa'tar] *vi* to break a tie;
volvieron a jugar para ~ they held a play-off
desempate [desem'pate] *nm* (*Fútbol*) play-off;
(*Tenis*) tie-break(er)
desempeñar [desempe'ɲar] *vt* (*cargo*) to hold;
(*papel*) to play; (*deber, función*) to perform, carry
out; (*lo empeñado*) to redeem; **desempeñarse**
vr to get out of debt; ~ **un papel** (*fig*) to play
(a role)
desempeño [desem'peɲo] *nm* occupation;
(*de lo empeñado*) redeeming; **de mucho** ~ very
capable
desempleado, -a [desemple'aðo, a]
adj unemployed, out of work ■ *nm/f*
unemployed person
desempleo [desem'pleo] *nm* unemployment
desempolvar [desempol'βar] *vt* (*muebles etc*)

to dust; (lo olvidado) to revive

desencadenar [desenkaðe'nar] vt to unchain; (ira) to unleash; (provocar) to cause, set off; **desencadenarse** vr to break loose; (tormenta) to burst; (guerra) to break out; **se desencadenó una lucha violenta** a violent struggle ensued

desencajar [desenka'xar] vt (hueso) to put out of joint; (mandíbula) to dislocate; (mecanismo, pieza) to disconnect, disengage

desencantar [desenkan'tar] vt to disillusion, disenchant

desencanto [desen'kanto] nm disillusionment, disenchantment

desenchufar [desentʃu'far] vt to unplug, disconnect

desenfadado, -a [desenfa'ðaðo, a] adj (desenvuelto) uninhibited; (descarado) forward; (en el vestir) casual

desenfado [desen'faðo] nm (libertad) freedom; (comportamiento) free and easy manner; (descaro) forwardness; (desenvoltura) self-confidence

desenfocado, -a [desenfo'kaðo, a] adj (Foto) out of focus

desenfrenado, -a [desenfre'naðo, a] adj (descontrolado) uncontrolled; (inmoderado) unbridled

desenfrenarse [desenfre'narse] vr (persona: desmandarse) to lose all self-control; (multitud) to run riot; (tempestad) to burst; (viento) to rage

desenfreno [desen'freno] nm (vicio) wildness; (falta de control) lack of self-control; (de pasiones) unleashing

desenganchar [desengan'tʃar] vt (gen) to unhook; (Ferro) to uncouple; (Tec) to disengage

desengañar [desenga'ɲar] vt to disillusion; (abrir los ojos a) to open the eyes of; **desengañarse** vr to become disillusioned; **¡desengáñate!** don't you believe it!

desengaño [desen'gaɲo] nm disillusionment; (decepción) disappointment; **sufrir un ~ amoroso** to be disappointed in love

desengrasar [desengra'sar] vt to degrease

desenlace etc [desen'laθe] vb ver **desenlazar** ∎ nm outcome; (Lit) ending

desenlazar [desenla'θar] vt (desatar) to untie; (problema) to solve; (aclarar: asunto) to unravel; **desenlazarse** vr (desatarse) to come undone; (Lit) to end

desenmarañar [desenmara'ɲar] vt (fig) to unravel

desenmascarar [desenmaska'rar] vt to unmask, expose

desenredar [desenre'ðar] vt to resolve

desenrollar [desenro'ʎar] vt to unroll, unwind

desenroscar [desenros'kar] vt (tornillo etc) to unscrew

desenrosque etc [desen'roske] vb ver **desenroscar**

desentenderse [desenten'derse] vr: ~ **de** to pretend not to know about; (apartarse) to have nothing to do with

desentendido, -a [desenten'diðo, a] adj: **hacerse el** ~ to pretend not to notice; **se hizo el** ~ he didn't take the hint

desenterrar [desente'rrar] vt to exhume; (tesoro, fig) to unearth, dig up

desentierre etc [desen'tjerre] vb ver **desenterrar**

desentonar [desento'nar] vi (Mus) to sing (o play) out of tune; (no encajar) to be out of place; (color) to clash

desentorpecer [desentorpe'θer] vt (miembro) to stretch; (fam: persona) to polish up

desentorpezca etc [desentor'peθka] vb ver **desentorpecer**

desentrañar [desentra'ɲar] vt (misterio) to unravel

desentrenado, -a [desentre'naðo, a] adj out of training

desentumecer [desentume'θer] vt (pierna etc) to stretch; (Deporte) to loosen up

desentumezca etc [desentu'meθka] vb ver **desentumecer**

desenvainar [desembai'nar] vt (espada) to draw, unsheathe

desenvoltura [desembol'tura] nf (libertad, gracia) ease; (descaro) free and easy manner; (al hablar) fluency

desenvolver [desembol'βer] vt (paquete) to unwrap; (fig) to develop; **desenvolverse** vr (desarrollarse) to unfold, develop; (suceder) to go off; (prosperar) to prosper; (arreglárselas) to cope

desenvolvimiento [desembolβi'mjento] nm (desarrollo) development; (de idea) exposition

desenvuelto, -a [desem'bwelto, a] pp de **desenvolver** ∎ adj (suelto) easy; (desenfadado) confident; (al hablar) fluent; (pey) forward

desenvuelva etc [desem'buelβa] vb ver **desenvolver**

deseo [de'seo] nm desire, wish; ~ **de saber** thirst for knowledge; **buen** ~ good intentions pl; **arder en deseos de algo** to yearn for sth

deseoso, -a [dese'oso, a] adj: **estar** ~ **de hacer** to be anxious to do

deseque etc [de'seke] vb ver **desecar**

desequilibrado, -a [desekili'βraðo, a] adj unbalanced ∎ nm/f unbalanced person; ~ **mental** mentally disturbed person

desequilibrar [desekili'βrar] vt (*mente*) to
unbalance; (*objeto*) to throw out of balance;
(*persona*) to throw off balance

desequilibrio [deseki'liβrio] nm (*mental*)
unbalance; (*entre cantidades*) imbalance;
(*Med*) unbalanced mental condition

desertar [deser'tar] vt (*Jur: derecho de apelación*)
to forfeit ■ vi to desert; ~ **de sus deberes** to
neglect one's duties

desértico, -a [de'sertiko, a] adj desert cpd;
(*vacío*) deserted

desertor, a [deser'tor, a] nm/f deserter

desesperación [desespera'θjon] nf
desperation, despair; (*irritación*) fury; **es una**
~ it's maddening; **es una ~ tener que** ... it's
infuriating to have to ...

desesperado, -a [desespe'raðo, a] adj
(*persona: sin esperanza*) desperate; (*caso,
situación*) hopeless; (*esfuerzo*) furious ■ nm:
como un ~ like mad ■ nf: **hacer algo a la
desesperada** to do sth as a last resort o in
desperation

desesperance etc [desespe'ranθe] vb ver
desesperanzar

desesperante [desespe'rante] adj
(*exasperante*) infuriating; (*persona*) hopeless

desesperanzar [desesperan'θar] vt to drive
to despair; **desesperanzarse** vr to lose hope,
despair

desesperar [desespe'rar] vt to drive to
despair; (*exasperar*) to drive to distraction
■ vi: ~ **de** to despair of; **desesperarse** vr
to despair, lose hope

desespero [deses'pero] nm (*Am*) despair

desestabilice etc [desestaβi'liθe] vb ver
desestabilizar

desestabilizar [desestaβili'θar] vt to
destabilize

desestimar [desesti'mar] vt (*menospreciar*)
to have a low opinion of; (*rechazar*) to reject

desfachatez [desfatʃa'teθ] nf (*insolencia*)
impudence; (*descaro*) rudeness

desfalco [des'falko] nm embezzlement

desfallecer [desfaʎe'θer] vi (*perder las fuerzas*)
to become weak; (*desvanecerse*) to faint

desfallecido, -a [desfaʎe'θiðo, a] adj (*débil*)
weak

desfallezca etc [desfa'ʎeθka] vb ver
desfallecer

desfasado, -a [desfa'saðo, a] adj (*anticuado*)
old-fashioned; (*Tec*) out of phase

desfasar [desfa'sar] vt to phase out

desfase [des'fase] nm (*diferencia*) gap

desfavorable [desfaβo'raβle] adj
unfavourable

desfavorecer [desfaβore'θer] vt (*sentar mal*)
not to suit

desfavorezca etc [desfaβo'reθka] vb ver
desfavorecer

desfiguración [desfiɣura'θjon] nf,
desfiguramiento [desfiɣura'mjento] nm
(*de persona*) disfigurement; (*de monumento*)
defacement; (*Foto*) blurring

desfigurar [desfiɣu'rar] vt (*cara*) to disfigure;
(*cuerpo*) to deform; (*cuadro, monumento*) to
deface; (*Foto*) to blur; (*sentido*) to twist;
(*suceso*) to misrepresent

desfiladero [desfila'ðero] nm gorge, defile

desfilar [desfi'lar] vi to parade; **desfilaron
ante el general** they marched past the
general

desfile [des'file] nm procession; (*Mil*) parade;
~ **de modelos** fashion show

desflorar [desflo'rar] vt (*mujer*) to deflower;
(*arruinar*) to tarnish; (*asunto*) to touch on

desfogar [desfo'ɣar] vt (*fig*) to vent ■ vi
(*Naut: tormenta*) to burst; **desfogarse** vr (*fig*)
to let off steam

desfogue etc [des'foɣe] vb ver **desfogar**

desgajar [desɣa'xar] vt (*arrancar*) to tear off;
(*romper*) to break off; (*naranja*) to split into
segments; **desgajarse** vr to come off

desgana [des'ɣana] nf (*falta de apetito*) loss of
appetite; (*renuencia*) unwillingness; **hacer
algo a** ~ to do sth unwillingly

desganado, -a [desɣa'naðo, a] adj: **estar** ~
(*sin apetito*) to have no appetite; (*sin entusiasmo*)
to have lost interest

desgañitarse [desɣaɲi'tarse] vr to shout o.s.
hoarse

desgarbado, -a [desɣar'βaðo, a] adj (*sin
gracia*) clumsy, ungainly

desgarrador, a [desɣarra'ðor, a] adj
heartrending

desgarrar [desɣa'rrar] vt to tear (up); (*fig*)
to shatter

desgarro [des'ɣarro] nm (*en tela*) tear;
(*aflicción*) grief; (*descaro*) impudence

desgastar [desɣas'tar] vt (*deteriorar*)
to wear away o down; (*estropear*) to spoil;
desgastarse vr to get worn out

desgaste [des'ɣaste] nm wear (and tear);
(*de roca*) erosion; (*de cuerda*) fraying; (*de metal*)
corrosion; ~ **económico** drain on one's
resources

desglosar [desɣlo'sar] vt to detach

desgobernar [desɣoβer'nar] vb (*Pol*) to
misgovern, misrule; (*asunto*) to handle
badly; (*Anat*) to dislocate

desgobierno etc [desɣo'βjerno] vb ver
desgobernar ■ nm (*Pol*) misgovernment,
misrule

desgracia [des'ɣraθja] nf misfortune;
(*accidente*) accident; (*vergüenza*) disgrace;

(*contratiempo*) setback; **por ~** unfortunately; **en el accidente no hay que lamentar desgracias personales** there were no casualties in the accident; **caer en ~** to fall from grace; **tener la ~ de** to be unlucky enough to

desgraciadamente [desɣraθjaða'mente] *adv* unfortunately

desgraciado, -a [desɣra'θjaðo, a] *adj* (*sin suerte*) unlucky, unfortunate; (*miserable*) wretched; (*infeliz*) miserable ▪ *nm/f* (*malvado*) swine; (*infeliz*) poor creature; **¡esa radio desgraciada!** (*esp Am*) that lousy radio!

desgraciar [desɣra'θjar] *vt* (*estropear*) to spoil; (*ofender*) to displease

desgranar [desɣra'nar] *vt* (*trigo*) to thresh; (*guisantes*) to shell; **~ un racimo** to pick the grapes from a bunch; **~ mentiras** to come out with a string of lies

desgravación [desɣraβa'θjon] *nf* (*Com*): **~ de impuestos** tax relief; **~ personal** personal allowance

desgravar [desɣra'βar] *vt* (*producto*) to reduce the tax o duty on

desgreñado, -a [desɣre'ɲaðo, a] *adj* dishevelled

desguace [des'ɣwaθe] *nm* (*de coches*) scrapping; (*lugar*) scrapyard

desguazar [desɣwa'θar] *vt* (*coche*) to scrap

deshabitado, -a [desaβi'taðo, a] *adj* uninhabited

deshabitar [desaβi'tar] *vt* (*casa*) to leave empty; (*despoblar*) to depopulate

deshacer [desa'θer] *vt* (*lo hecho*) to undo, unmake; (*proyectos: arruinar*) to spoil; (*casa*) to break up; (*Tec*) to take apart; (*enemigo*) to defeat; (*diluir*) to melt; (*contrato*) to break; (*intriga*) to solve; (*cama*) to strip; (*maleta*) to unpack; (*paquete*) to unwrap; (*nudo*) to untie; (*costura*) to unpick; **deshacerse** *vr* (*desatarse*) to come undone; (*estropearse*) to be spoiled; (*descomponerse*) to fall to pieces; (*disolverse*) to melt; (*despedazarse*) to come apart o undone; **deshacerse de** to get rid of; (*Com*) to dump, unload; **deshacerse en** (*cumplidos, elogios*) to be lavish with; **deshacerse en lágrimas** to burst into tears; **deshacerse por algo** to be crazy about sth

deshaga *etc* [de'saɣa], **desharé** *etc* [desa're] *vb ver* **deshacer**

desharrapado, -a [desarra'paðo, a] *adj* = **desarrapado**

deshecho, -a [de'setʃo, a] *pp de* **deshacer** ▪ *adj* (*lazo, nudo*) undone; (*roto*) smashed; (*despedazado*) in pieces; (*cama*) unmade; (*Med: persona*) weak, emaciated; (*: salud*) broken; **estoy ~** I'm shattered

deshelar [dese'lar] *vt* (*cañería*) to thaw; (*heladera*) to defrost

desheredar [desere'ðar] *vt* to disinherit

deshice *etc* [de'siθe] *vb ver* **deshacer**

deshidratación [desiðrata'θjon] *nf* dehydration

deshidratar [desiðra'tar] *vt* to dehydrate

deshielo *etc* [des'jelo] *vb ver* **deshelar** ▪ *nm* thaw

deshilachar [desila'tʃar] *vt*, **deshilacharse** *vr* to fray

deshilar [desi'lar] *vt* (*tela*) to unravel

deshilvanado, -a [desilβa'naðo, a] *adj* (*fig*) disjointed, incoherent

deshinchar [desin'tʃar] *vt* (*neumático*) to let down; (*herida etc*) to reduce (the swelling of); **deshincharse** *vr* (*neumático*) to go flat; (*hinchazón*) to go down

deshojar [deso'xar] *vt* (*árbol*) to strip the leaves off; (*flor*) to pull the petals off; **deshojarse** *vr* to lose its leaves *etc*

deshollinar [desoʎi'nar] *vt* (*chimenea*) to sweep

deshonesto, -a [deso'nesto, a] *adj* (*no honrado*) dishonest; (*indecente*) indecent

deshonor [deso'nor] *nm* dishonour, disgrace; (*un deshonor*) insult, affront

deshonra [de'sonra] *nf* (*deshonor*) dishonour; (*vergüenza*) shame

deshonrar [deson'rar] *vt* to dishonour

deshonroso, -a [deson'roso, a] *adj* dishonourable, disgraceful

deshora [de'sora]: **a ~** *adv* at the wrong time; (*llegar*) unexpectedly; (*acostarse*) at some unearthly hour

deshuesar [deswe'sar] *vt* (*carne*) to bone; (*fruta*) to stone

desidia [de'siðja] *nf* (*pereza*) idleness

desierto, -a [de'sjerto, a] *adj* (*casa, calle, negocio*) deserted; (*paisaje*) bleak ▪ *nm* desert

designación [desiɣna'θjon] *nf* (*para un cargo*) appointment; (*nombre*) designation

designar [desiɣ'nar] *vt* (*nombrar*) to designate; (*indicar*) to fix

designio [de'siɣnjo] *nm* plan; **con el ~ de** with the intention of

desigual [desi'ɣwal] *adj* (*lucha*) unequal; (*diferente*) different; (*terreno*) uneven; (*tratamiento*) unfair; (*cambiadizo: tiempo*) changeable; (*: carácter*) unpredictable

desigualdad [desiɣwal'ðað] *nf* (*Econ, Pol*) inequality; (*de carácter, tiempo*) unpredictability; (*de escritura*) unevenness; (*de terreno*) roughness

desilusión [desilu'sjon] *nf* disillusionment; (*decepción*) disappointment

desilusionar [desilusjo'nar] *vt* to disillusion;

121

(*decepcionar*) to disappoint; **desilusionarse** *vr* to become disillusioned

desinencia [desi'nenθja] *nf* (*Ling*) ending

desinfectar [desinfek'tar] *vt* to disinfect

desinfestar [desinfes'tar] *vt* to decontaminate

desinflación [desinfla'θjon] *nf* (*Com*) disinflation

desinflar [desin'flar] *vt* to deflate; **desinflarse** *vr* (*neumático*) to go down *o* flat

desintegración [desinteɣra'θjon] *nf* disintegration; ~ **nuclear** nuclear fission

desintegrar [desinte'ɣrar] *vt* (*gen*) to disintegrate; (*átomo*) to split; (*grupo*) to break up; **desintegrarse** *vr* to disintegrate; to split; to break up

desinterés [desinte'res] *nm* (*objetividad*) disinterestedness; (*altruismo*) unselfishness

desinteresado, -a [desintere'saðo, a] *adj* (*imparcial*) disinterested; (*altruista*) unselfish

desintoxicar [desintoksi'kar] *vt* to detoxify; **desintoxicarse** *vr* (*drogadicto*) to undergo treatment for drug addiction; **desintoxicarse de** (*rutina, trabajo*) to get away from

desintoxique *etc* [desintok'sike] *vb ver* **desintoxicar**

desistir [desis'tir] *vi* (*renunciar*) to stop, desist; ~ **de** (*empresa*) to give up; (*derecho*) to waive

deslavazado, -a [deslaβa'θaðo, a] *adj* (*lacio*) limp; (*desteñido*) faded; (*insípido*) colourless; (*incoherente*) disjointed

desleal [desle'al] *adj* (*infiel*) disloyal; (*Com*: *competencia*) unfair

deslealtad [desleal'tað] *nf* disloyalty

desleído, -a [desle'iðo, a] *adj* weak, woolly

desleír [desle'ir] *vt* (*líquido*) to dilute; (*sólido*) to dissolve

deslenguado, -a [deslen'gwaðo, a] *adj* (*grosero*) foul-mouthed

deslía *etc* [des'lia] *vb ver* **desleír**

desliar [des'ljar] *vt* (*desatar*) to untie; (*paquete*) to open; **desliarse** *vr* to come undone

deslice *etc* [des'liθe] *vb ver* **deslizar**

desliendo *etc* [desli'endo] *vb ver* **desleír**

desligar [desli'ɣar] *vt* (*desatar*) to untie, undo; (*separar*) to separate; **desligarse** *vr* (*de un compromiso*) to extricate o.s.

desligue *etc* [des'liɣe] *vb ver* **desligar**

deslindar [deslin'dar] *vt* (*señalar las lindes de*) to mark out, fix the boundaries of; (*fig*) to define

desliz [des'liθ] *nm* (*fig*) lapse; ~ **de lengua** slip of the tongue; **cometer un** ~ to slip up

deslizar [desli'θar] *vt* to slip, slide; **deslizarse** *vr* (*escurrirse: persona*) to slip, slide; (: *coche*) to skid; (*aguas mansas*) to flow gently;

(*error*) to creep in; (*tiempo*) to pass; (*persona: irse*) to slip away; **deslizarse en un cuarto** to slip into a room

deslomar [deslo'mar] *vt* (*romper el lomo de*) to break the back of; (*fig*) to wear out; **deslomarse** *vr* (*fig, fam*) to work one's guts out

deslucido, -a [deslu'θiðo, a] *adj* dull; (*torpe*) awkward, graceless; (*deslustrado*) tarnished; (*fracasado*) unsuccessful; **quedar** ~ to make a poor impression

deslucir [deslu'θir] *vt* (*deslustrar*) to tarnish; (*estropear*) to spoil, ruin; (*persona*) to discredit; **la lluvia deslució el acto** the rain ruined the ceremony

deslumbrar [deslum'brar] *vt* (*con la luz*) to dazzle; (*cegar*) to blind; (*impresionar*) to dazzle; (*dejar perplejo a*) to puzzle, confuse

deslustrar [deslus'trar] *vt* (*vidrio*) to frost; (*quitar lustre a*) to dull; (*reputación*) to sully

desluzca *etc* [des'luθka] *vb ver* **deslucir**

desmadrarse [desma'ðrarse] *vr* (*fam*) to run wild

desmadre [des'maðre] *nm* (*fam*: *desorganización*) chaos; (: *jaleo*) commotion

desmán [des'man] *nm* (*exceso*) outrage; (*abuso de poder*) abuse

desmandarse [desman'darse] *vr* (*portarse mal*) to behave badly; (*excederse*) to get out of hand; (*caballo*) to bolt

desmano [des'mano]: **a** ~ *adv*: **me coge** *o* **pilla a desmano** it's out of my way

desmantelar [desmante'lar] *vt* (*deshacer*) to dismantle; (*casa*) to strip; (*organización*) to disband; (*Mil*) to raze; (*andamio*) to take down; (*Naut*) to unrig

desmaquillador [desmakiʎa'ðor] *nm* make-up remover

desmaquillarse [desmaki'ʎarse] *vr* to take off one's make-up

desmarcarse [desmar'karse] *vr*: ~ **de** (*Deporte*) to get clear of; (*fig*) to distance o.s. from

desmayado, -a [desma'jaðo, a] *adj* (*sin sentido*) unconscious; (*carácter*) dull; (*débil*) faint, weak; (*color*) pale

desmayar [desma'jar] *vi* to lose heart; **desmayarse** *vr* (*Med*) to faint

desmayo [des'majo] *nm* (*Med: acto*) faint; (*estado*) unconsciousness; (*depresión*) dejection; (*de voz*) faltering; **sufrir un** ~ to have a fainting fit

desmedido, -a [desme'ðiðo, a] *adj* excessive; (*ambición*) boundless

desmejorado, -a [desmexo'raðo, a] *adj*: **está muy desmejorada** (*Med*) she's not looking too well

desmejorar [desmexo'rar] vt (dañar) to impair, spoil; (Med) to weaken

desmembración [desmembra'θjon] nf dismemberment; (fig) break-up

desmembrar [desmem'brar] vt (Med) to dismember; (fig) to separate

desmemoriado, -a [desmemo'rjaðo, a] adj forgetful, absent-minded

desmentir [desmen'tir] vt (contradecir) to contradict; (refutar) to deny; (rumor) to scotch ■ vi: ~ **de** to refute; **desmentirse** vr to contradict o.s.

desmenuce etc [desme'nuθe] vb ver **desmenuzar**

desmenuzar [desmenu'θar] vt (deshacer) to crumble; (carne) to chop; (examinar) to examine closely

desmerecer [desmere'θer] vt to be unworthy of ■ vi (deteriorarse) to deteriorate

desmerezca etc [desme'reθka] vb ver **desmerecer**

desmesurado, -a [desmesu'raðo, a] adj (desmedido) disproportionate; (enorme) enormous; (ambición) boundless; (descarado) insolent

desmiembre etc [des'mjembre] vb ver **desmembrar**

desmienta etc [des'mjenta] vb ver **desmentir**

desmigajar [desmiɣa'xar], **desmigar** [desmi'ɣar] vt to crumble

desmigue etc [des'miɣe] vb ver **desmigar**

desmilitarice etc [desmilita'riθe] vb ver **desmilitarizar**

desmilitarizar [desmilitari'θar] vt to demilitarize

desmintiendo etc [desmin'tjendo] vb ver **desmentir**

desmochar [desmo'tʃar] vt (árbol) to lop; (texto) to cut, hack about

desmontable [desmon'taβle] adj (que se quita) detachable; (en compartimientos) sectional; (que se puede plegar etc) collapsible

desmontar [desmon'tar] vt (deshacer) to dismantle; (motor) to strip down; (máquina) to take apart; (escopeta) to uncock; (tienda de campaña) to take down; (tierra) to level; (quitar los árboles a) to clear; (jinete) to throw ■ vi to dismount

desmonte [des'monte] nm (de tierra) levelling; (de árboles) clearing; (terreno) levelled ground; (Ferro) cutting

desmoralice etc [desmora'liθe] vb ver **desmoralizar**

desmoralizador, a [desmoraliθa'ðor, a] adj demoralizing

desmoralizar [desmorali'θar] vt to demoralize

desmoronado, -a [desmoro'naðo, a] adj (casa, edificio) dilapidated

desmoronamiento [desmorona'mjento] nm (tb fig) crumbling

desmoronar [desmoro'nar] vt to wear away, erode; **desmoronarse** vr (edificio, dique) to fall into disrepair; (economía) to decline

desmovilice etc [desmoβi'liθe] vb ver **desmovilizar**

desmovilizar [desmoβili'θar] vt to demobilize

desnacionalización [desnaθjonaliθa'θjon] nf denationalization

desnacionalizado, -a [desnaθjonali'θaðo, a] adj (industria) denationalized; (persona) stateless

desnatado, -a [desna'taðo, a] adj skimmed; (yogur) low-fat

desnatar [desna'tar] vt (leche) to skim; **leche sin** ~ whole milk

desnaturalice etc [desnatura'liθe] vb ver **desnaturalizar**

desnaturalizado, -a [desnaturali'θaðo, a] adj (persona) unnatural; **alcohol** ~ methylated spirits

desnaturalizar [desnaturali'θar] vt (Química) to denature; (corromper) to pervert; (sentido de algo) to distort; **desnaturalizarse** vr (perder la nacionalidad) to give up one's nationality

desnivel [desni'βel] nm (de terreno) unevenness; (Pol) inequality; (diferencia) difference

desnivelar [desniβe'lar] vt (terreno) to make uneven; (fig: desequilibrar) to unbalance; (balanza) to tip

desnuclearizado, -a [desnukleari'θaðo, a] adj: **región desnuclearizada** nuclear-free zone

desnudar [desnu'ðar] vt (desvestir) to undress; (despojar) to strip; **desnudarse** vr (desvestirse) to get undressed

desnudez [desnu'ðeθ] nf (de persona) nudity; (fig) bareness

desnudo, -a [des'nuðo, a] adj (cuerpo) naked; (árbol, brazo) bare; (paisaje) flat; (estilo) unadorned; (verdad) plain ■ nm/f nude; ~ **de** devoid o bereft of; **la retrató al** ~ he painted her in the nude; **poner al** ~ to lay bare

desnutrición [desnutri'θjon] nf malnutrition

desnutrido, -a [desnu'triðo, a] adj undernourished

desobedecer [desoβeðe'θer] vt, vi to disobey

desobedezca etc [desoβe'ðeθka] vb ver **desobedecer**

desobediencia [desoβe'ðjenθja] nf disobedience

desocupación [desokupa'θjon] nf (Am)
unemployment

desocupado, -a [desoku'paðo, a] adj
at leisure; (desempleado) unemployed;
(deshabitado) empty, vacant

desocupar [desoku'par] vt to vacate;
desocuparse vr (quedar libre) to be free; **se
ha desocupado aquella mesa** that table's
free now

desodorante [desoðo'rante] nm deodorant

desoiga etc [de'soiɣa] vb ver **desoír**

desoír [deso'ir] vt to ignore, disregard

desolación [desola'θjon] nf (de lugar)
desolation; (fig) grief

desolar [deso'lar] vt to ruin, lay waste

desollar [deso'ʎar] vt (quitar la piel a) to skin;
(criticar): ~ **vivo a** to criticize unmercifully

desorbitado, -a [desorβi'taðo, a] adj (excesivo)
excessive; (precio) exorbitant; **con los ojos
desorbitados** pop-eyed

desorbitar [desorβi'tar] vt (exagerar) to
exaggerate; (interpretar mal) to misinterpret;
desorbitarse vr (persona) to lose one's sense
of proportion; (asunto) to get out of hand

desorden [de'sorðen] nm confusion; (de casa,
cuarto) mess; (político) disorder; **desórdenes**
nmpl (alborotos) disturbances; (excesos)
excesses; **en ~** (gente) in confusion

desordenado, -a [desorðe'naðo, a] adj
(habitación, persona) untidy; (objetos revueltos) in
a mess, jumbled; (conducta) disorderly

desordenar [desorðe'nar] vt (gen) to
disarrange; (pelo) to mess up; (cuarto) to
make a mess in; (causar confusión a) to throw
into confusion

desorganice etc [desorɣa'niθe] vb ver
desorganizar

desorganizar [desorɣani'θar] vt to
disorganize

desorientar [desorjen'tar] vt (extraviar) to
mislead; (confundir, desconcertar) to confuse;
desorientarse vr (perderse) to lose one's way

desovar [deso'βar] vi (peces) to spawn;
(insectos) to lay eggs

desoyendo etc [deso'jendo] vb ver **desoír**

despabilado, -a [despaβi'laðo, a] adj
(despierto) wide-awake; (fig) alert, sharp

despabilar [despaβi'lar] vt (despertar) to wake
up; (fig: persona) to liven up; (trabajo) to get
through quickly ■ vi, **despabilarse** vr to
wake up; (fig) to get a move on

despachar [despa'tʃar] vt (negocio) to do,
complete; (resolver: problema) to settle;
(correspondencia) to deal with; (fam: comida) to
polish off; (: bebida) to knock back; (enviar)
to send, dispatch; (vender) to sell, deal in;
(Com: cliente) to attend to; (billete) to issue;

(mandar ir) to send away ■ vi (decidirse) to
get things settled; (apresurarse) to hurry up;
despacharse vr to finish off; (apresurarse) to
hurry up; **despacharse de algo** to get rid
of sth; **despacharse a su gusto con algn**
to give sb a piece of one's mind; **¿quién
despacha?** is anybody serving?

despacho [des'patʃo] nm (oficina) office; (: en
una casa) study; (de paquetes) dispatch; (Com:
venta) sale (of goods); (comunicación) message;
~ **de billetes** o **boletos** (Am) booking office;
~ **de localidades** box office; **géneros sin** ~
unsaleable goods; **tener buen** ~ to find a
ready sale

despachurrar [despatʃu'rrar] vt (aplastar) to
crush; (persona) to flatten

despacio [des'paθjo] adv (lentamente) slowly;
(esp Am: en voz baja) softly; **¡~!** take it easy!

despacito [despa'θito] adv (fam) slowly;
(suavemente) softly

despampanante [despampa'nante] adj (fam:
chica) stunning

desparejado, -a [despare'xaðo, a] adj odd

desparpajo [despar'paxo] nm (desenvoltura)
self-confidence; (pey) nerve

desparramar [desparra'mar] vt (esparcir) to
scatter; (líquido) to spill

despatarrarse [despata'rrarse] vr (abrir las
piernas) to open one's legs wide; (caerse) to
tumble; (fig) to be flabbergasted

despavorido, -a [despaβo'riðo, a] adj
terrified

despecho [des'petʃo] nm spite; **a ~ de** in spite
of; **por ~** out of (sheer) spite

despectivo, -a [despek'tiβo, a] adj
(despreciativo) derogatory; (Ling) pejorative

despedace etc [despe'ðaθe] vb ver **despedazar**

despedazar [despeða'θar] vt to tear to pieces

despedida [despe'ðiða] nf (adiós) goodbye,
farewell; (antes de viaje) send-off; (en carta)
closing formula; (de obrero) sacking; (Inform)
logout; **cena/función de** ~ farewell dinner/
performance; **regalo de** ~ parting gift; ~ **de
soltero/soltera** stag/hen party

despedir [despe'ðir] vt (visita) to see off, show
out; (empleado) to dismiss; (inquilino) to evict;
(objeto) to hurl; (olor etc) to give out o off;
despedirse vr (dejar un empleo) to give up one's
job; (Inform) to log out o off; **despedirse de**
to say goodbye to; **se despidieron** they said
goodbye to each other

despegado, -a [despe'ɣaðo, a] adj (separado)
detached; (persona: poco afectuoso) cold,
indifferent ■ nm/f: **es un** ~ he has cut
himself off from his family

despegar [despe'ɣar] vt to unstick; (sobre) to
open ■ vi (avión) to take off; (cohete) to blast

off; **despegarse** vr to come loose, come
unstuck; **sin ~ los labios** without uttering
a word
despego [des'peɣo] nm detachment
despegue etc [des'peɣe] vb ver **despegar**
■ nm takeoff; (de cohete) blast-off
despeinado, -a [despei'naðo, a] adj
dishevelled, unkempt
despeinar [despei'nar] vt (pelo) to ruffle; ¡**me
has despeinado todo!** you've completely
ruined my hairdo!
despejado, -a [despe'xaðo, a] adj (lugar)
clear, free; (cielo) clear; (persona) wide-awake,
bright
despejar [despe'xar] vt (gen) to clear; (misterio)
to clarify, clear up; (Mat: incógnita) to find
■ vi (el tiempo) to clear; **despejarse** vr (tiempo,
cielo) to clear (up); (misterio) to become clearer;
(cabeza) to clear; ¡**despejen!** (moverse) move
along!; (salirse) everybody out!
despeje [des'pexe] nm (Deporte) clearance
despellejar [despeʎe'xar] vt (animal) to skin;
(criticar) to criticize unmercifully; (fam:
arruinar) to fleece
despelotarse [despelo'tarse] vr (fam) to strip
off; (fig) to let one's hair down
despelote [despe'lote] nm (Am: fam: lío) mess;
¡**qué** o **vaya ~!** what a riot o laugh!
despenalizar [despenali'θar] vt to
decriminalize
despensa [des'pensa] nf (armario) larder;
(Naut) storeroom; (provisión de comestibles)
stock of food
despeñadero [despeɲa'ðero] nm (Geo) cliff,
precipice
despeñar [despe'ɲar] vt (arrojar) to fling
down; **despeñarse** vr to fling o.s. down;
(caer) to fall headlong
desperdiciar [desperði'θjar] vt (comida,
tiempo) to waste; (oportunidad) to throw away
desperdicio [desper'ðiθjo] nm (despilfarro)
squandering; (residuo) waste; **desperdicios**
nmpl (basura) rubbish sg, refuse sg, garbage
sg (US); (residuos) waste sg; **desperdicios de
cocina** kitchen scraps; **el libro no tiene ~**
the book is excellent from beginning to end
desperdigar [desperði'ɣar] vt (esparcir) to
scatter; (energía) to dissipate; **desperdigarse**
vr to scatter
desperdigue etc [desper'ðiɣe] vb ver
desperdigar
desperece etc [despe'reθe] vb ver
desperezarse
desperezarse [despere'θarse] vr to stretch
desperfecto [desper'fekto] nm (deterioro)
slight damage; (defecto) flaw, imperfection
despertador [desperta'ðor] nm alarm clock;

~ de viaje travelling clock
despertar [desper'tar] vt (persona) to wake
up; (recuerdos) to revive; (esperanzas) to raise;
(sentimiento) to arouse ■ vi, **despertarse**
vr to awaken, wake up ■ nm awakening;
despertarse a la realidad to wake up to
reality
despiadado a [despja'ðaðo, a] adj (ataque)
merciless; (persona) heartless
despido etc [des'piðo] vb ver **despedir** ■ nm
dismissal, sacking; **~ improcedente** o
injustificado wrongful dismissal; **~ injusto**
unfair dismissal; **~ libre** right to hire and
fire; **~ voluntario** voluntary redundancy
despierto, -a [des'pjerto, a] pp de **despertar**
■ adj awake; (fig) sharp, alert
despilfarrar [despilfa'rrar] vt (gen) to waste;
(dinero) to squander
despilfarro [despil'farro] nm (derroche)
squandering; (lujo desmedido) extravagance
despintar [despin'tar] vt (quitar pintura a) to
take the paint off; (hechos) to distort ■ vi: **A
no despinta a B** A is in no way inferior to B;
despintarse vr (desteñir) to fade
despiojar [despjo'xar] vt to delouse
despistado, -a [despis'taðo, a] adj (distraído)
vague, absent-minded; (poco práctico)
unpractical; (confuso) confused; (desorientado)
off the track ■ nm/f (persona distraída)
scatterbrain, absent-minded person
despistar [despis'tar] vt to throw off the
track o scent; (fig) to mislead, confuse;
despistarse vr to take the wrong road; (fig)
to become confused
despiste [des'piste] nm (Auto etc) swerve;
(error) slip; (distracción) absent-mindedness;
tiene un terrible ~ he's terribly absent-
minded
desplace etc [des'plaθe] vb ver **desplazar**
desplante [des'plante] nm: **hacer un ~ a
algn** to be rude to sb
desplazado, -a [despla'θaðo, a] adj (pieza)
wrongly placed ■ nm/f (inadaptado) misfit;
sentirse un poco ~ to feel rather out of place
desplazamiento [desplaθa'mjento] nm
displacement; (viaje) journey; (de opinión,
votos) shift, swing; (Inform) scrolling; **~ hacia
arriba/abajo** (Inform) scroll up/down
desplazar [despla'θar] vt (gen) to move;
(Física, Naut, Tec) to displace; (tropas) to
transfer; (suplantar) to take the place of;
(Inform) to scroll; **desplazarse** vr (persona,
vehículo) to travel, go; (objeto) to move, shift;
(votos, opinión) to shift, swing
desplegar [desple'ɣar] vt (tela, papel) to
unfold, open out; (bandera) to unfurl; (alas) to
spread; (Mil) to deploy; (manifestar) to display

desplegué [desple'ye], **despleguemos** *etc*
[desple'yemos] *vb ver* **desplegar**
despliegue *etc* [des'pljeɣe] *vb ver* **desplegar**
■ *nm* unfolding, opening; deployment,
display
desplomarse [desplo'marse] *vr (edificio,*
gobierno, persona) to collapse; *(derrumbarse)* to
topple over; *(precios)* to slump; **se ha**
desplomado el techo the ceiling has fallen in
desplumar [desplu'mar] *vt (ave)* to pluck;
(fam: estafar) to fleece
despoblado, -a [despo'βlaðo, a] *adj (sin*
habitantes) uninhabited; *(con pocos habitantes)*
depopulated; *(con insuficientes habitantes)*
underpopulated ■ *nm* deserted spot
despojar [despo'xar] *vt (a alguien: de sus bienes)*
to divest of, deprive of; *(casa)* to strip, leave
bare; *(de su cargo)* to strip of; **despojarse** *vr*
(desnudarse) to undress; **despojarse de** *(ropa,*
hojas) to shed; *(poderes)* to relinquish
despojo [des'poxo] *nm (acto)* plundering;
(objetos) plunder, loot; **despojos** *nmpl (de ave,*
res) offal *sg*
desposado, -a [despo'saðo, a] *adj, nm/f*
newly-wed
desposar [despo'sar] *vt (sacerdote: pareja)* to
marry; **desposarse** *vr (casarse)* to marry, get
married
desposeer [despose'er] *vt (despojar)* to
dispossess; **~ a algn de su autoridad** to strip
sb of his authority
desposeído, -a [despose'iðo, a] *nm/f*: **los**
desposeídos the have-nots
desposeyendo *etc* [despose'jendo] *vb ver*
desposeer
desposorios [despo'sorjos] *nmpl (esponsales)*
betrothal *sg*; *(boda)* marriage ceremony *sg*
déspota ['despota] *nm/f* despot
despotismo [despo'tismo] *nm* despotism
despotricar [despotri'kar] *vi*: **~ contra** to
moan *o* complain about
despotrique *etc* [despo'trike] *vb ver*
despotricar
despreciable [despre'θjaβle] *adj (moralmente)*
despicable; *(objeto)* worthless; *(cantidad)*
negligible
despreciar [despre'θjar] *vt (desdeñar)* to
despise, scorn; *(afrentar)* to slight
despreciativo, -a [despreθja'tiβo, a] *adj*
(observación, tono) scornful, contemptuous;
(comentario) derogatory
desprecio [des'preθjo] *nm* scorn, contempt;
slight
desprender [despren'der] *vt (soltar)* to loosen;
(separar) to separate; *(desatar)* to unfasten;
(olor) to give off; **desprenderse** *vr (botón:*
caerse) to fall off; *(: abrirse)* to unfasten; *(olor,*

perfume) to be given off; **desprenderse de** to
follow from; **desprenderse de algo** *(ceder)* to
give sth up; *(desembarazarse)* to get rid of sth;
se desprende que … it transpires that …
desprendido, -a [despren'dido, a] *adj (pieza)*
loose; *(sin abrochar)* unfastened; *(desinteresado)*
disinterested; *(generoso)* generous
desprendimiento [desprendi'mjento]
nm (gen) loosening; *(generosidad)*
disinterestedness; *(indiferencia)* detachment;
(de gas) leak; *(de tierra, rocas)* landslide
despreocupado, -a [despreoku'paðo, a] *adj*
(sin preocupación) unworried, unconcerned;
(tranquilo) nonchalant; *(en el vestir)* casual;
(negligente) careless
despreocuparse [despreoku'parse] *vr* to be
carefree; *(dejar de inquietarse)* to stop worrying;
(ser indiferente) to be unconcerned; **~ de** to
have no interest in
desprestigiar [despresti'xjar] *vt (criticar)*
to run down, disparage; *(desacreditar)* to
discredit
desprestigio [despres'tixjo] *nm (denigración)*
disparagement; *(impopularidad)* unpopularity
desprevenido, -a [despreβe'niðo, a] *adj (no*
preparado) unprepared, unready; **coger** *(Esp) o*
agarrar *(Am)* **a algn ~** to catch sb unawares
desproporción [despropor'θjon] *nf*
disproportion, lack of proportion
desproporcionado, -a [desproporθjo'naðo,
a] *adj* disproportionate, out of proportion
despropósito [despro'posito] *nm (salida de*
tono) irrelevant remark; *(disparate)* piece of
nonsense
desprovisto, -a [despro'βisto, a] *adj*: **~ de**
devoid of; **estar ~ de** to lack
después [des'pwes] *adv* afterwards, later;
(desde entonces) since (then); *(próximo paso)*
next; **poco ~** soon after; **un año ~** a year
later; **~ se debatió el tema** next the matter
was discussed ■ *prep*: **~ de** *(tiempo)* after,
since; *(orden)* next (to); **~ de comer** after
lunch; **~ de corregido el texto** after the text
had been corrected; **~ de esa fecha** *(pasado)*
since that date; *(futuro)* from *o* after that date;
~ de todo after all; **~ de verlo** after seeing it,
after I *etc* saw it; **mi nombre está ~ del tuyo**
my name comes next to yours ■ *conj*: **~ (de)**
que after; **~ (de) que lo escribí** after *o* since I
wrote it, after writing it
despuntar [despun'tar] *vt (lápiz)* to blunt
■ *vi (Bot: plantas)* to sprout; *(: flores)* to bud;
(alba) to break; *(día)* to dawn; *(persona:*
descollar) to stand out
desquiciar [deski'θjar] *vt (puerta)* to take off
its hinges; *(descomponer)* to upset; *(persona:*
turbar) to disturb; *(: volver loco a)* to unhinge

desquitarse [deski'tarse] *vr* to obtain satisfaction; (*Com*) to recover a debt; (*fig*: *vengarse de*) to get one's own back; **~ de una pérdida** to make up for a loss

desquite [des'kite] *nm* (*satisfacción*) satisfaction; (*venganza*) revenge

Dest. *abr* = **destinatario**

destacado, -a [desta'kaðo, a] *adj* outstanding

destacamento [destaka'mento] *nm* (*Mil*) detachment

destacar [desta'kar] *vt* (*Arte*: *hacer resaltar*) to make stand out; (*subrayar*) to emphasize, point up; (*Mil*) to detach, detail; (*Inform*) to highlight ■ *vi*, **destacarse** *vr* (*resaltarse*) to stand out; (*persona*) to be outstanding *o* exceptional; **quiero ~ que...** I wish to emphasize that...; **~(se) contra** *o* **en** *o* **sobre** to stand out *o* be outlined against

destajo [des'taxo] *nm*: **a ~** (*por pieza*) by the job; (*con afán*) eagerly; **trabajar a ~** to do piecework; (*fig*) to work one's fingers to the bone

destapar [desta'par] *vt* (*botella*) to open; (*cacerola*) to take the lid off; (*descubrir*) to uncover; **destaparse** *vr* (*descubrirse*) to get uncovered; (*revelarse*) to reveal one's true character

destape [des'tape] *nm* nudity; (*fig*) permissiveness; **el ~ español** *the process of liberalization in Spain after Franco's death*

destaque *etc* [des'take] *vb ver* **destacar**

destartalado, -a [destarta'laðo, a] *adj* (*desordenado*) untidy; (*casa etc*: *grande*) rambling; (: *ruinoso*) tumbledown

destellar [deste'ʎar] *vi* (*diamante*) to sparkle; (*metal*) to glint; (*estrella*) to twinkle

destello [des'teʎo] *nm* (*de diamante*) sparkle; (*de metal*) glint; (*de estrella*) twinkle; (*de faro*) signal light; **no tiene un ~ de verdad** there's not a grain of truth in it

destemplado, -a [destem'plaðo, a] *adj* (*Mus*) out of tune; (*voz*) harsh; (*Med*) out of sorts; (*Meteorología*) unpleasant, nasty

destemplar [destem'plar] *vt* (*Mus*) to put out of tune; (*alterar*) to upset; **destemplarse** *vr* (*Mus*) to lose its pitch; (*descomponerse*) to get out of order; (*persona*: *irritarse*) to get upset; (*Med*) to get out of sorts

desteñir [deste'ɲir] *vt* to fade ■ *vi*, **desteñirse** *vr* to fade; **esta tela no destiñe** this fabric will not run

desternillarse [desterni'ʎarse] *vr*: **~ de risa** to split one's sides laughing

desterrado, -a [deste'rraðo, a] *nm/f* (*exiliado*) exile

desterrar [deste'rrar] *vt* (*exilar*) to exile; (*fig*) to banish, dismiss

destetar [deste'tar] *vt* to wean

destiempo [des'tjempo]: **a ~** *adv* at the wrong time

destierro *etc* [des'tjerro] *vb ver* **desterrar** ■ *nm* exile; **vivir en el ~** to live in exile

destilar [desti'lar] *vt* to distil; (*pus, sangre*) to ooze; (*fig*: *rebosar*) to exude; (: *revelar*) to reveal ■ *vi* (*gotear*) to drip

destilería [destile'ria] *nf* distillery; **~ de petróleo** oil refinery

destinar [desti'nar] *vt* (*funcionario*) to appoint, assign; (*fondos*) to set aside; **es un libro destinado a los niños** it is a book (intended *o* meant) for children; **una carta que viene destinada a usted** a letter for you, a letter addressed to you

destinatario, -a [destina'tarjo, a] *nm/f* addressee; (*Com*) payee

destino [des'tino] *nm* (*suerte*) destiny; (*de viajero*) destination; (*función*) use; (*puesto*) post, placement; **~ público** public appointment; **salir con ~ a** to leave for; **con ~ a Londres** (*avión, barco*) (bound) for London; (*carta*) to London

destiña *etc* [des'tiɲa], **destiñendo** *etc* [desti'ɲendo] *vb ver* **desteñir**

destitución [destitu'θjon] *nf* dismissal, removal

destituir [destitu'ir] *vt* (*despedir*) to dismiss; (: *ministro, funcionario*) to remove from office

destituyendo *etc* [destitu'jendo] *vb ver* **destituir**

destornillador [destorniʎa'ðor] *nm* screwdriver

destornillar [destorni'ʎar] *vt*, **destornillarse** *vr* (*tornillo*) to unscrew

destreza [des'treθa] *nf* (*habilidad*) skill; (*maña*) dexterity

destripar [destri'par] *vt* (*animal*) to gut; (*reventar*) to mangle

destroce *etc* [des'troθe] *vb ver* **destrozar**

destronar [destro'nar] *vt* (*rey*) to dethrone; (*fig*) to overthrow

destroncar [destron'kar] *vt* (*árbol*) to chop off, lop; (*proyectos*) to ruin; (*discurso*) to interrupt

destronque *etc* [des'tronke] *vb ver* **destroncar**

destrozar [destro'θar] *vt* (*romper*) to smash, break (up); (*estropear*) to ruin; (*nervios*) to shatter; **~ a algn en una discusión** to crush sb in an argument

destrozo [des'troθo] *nm* (*acción*) destruction; (*desastre*) smashing; **destrozos** *nmpl* (*pedazos*) pieces; (*daños*) havoc *sg*

destrucción [destruk'θjon] *nf* destruction

destructor, a [destruk'tor, a] *adj* destructive ■ *nm* (*Naut*) destroyer

destruir [destru'ir] *vt* to destroy; (*casa*)
to demolish; (*equilibrio*) to upset; (*proyecto*)
to spoil; (*esperanzas*) to dash; (*argumento*)
to demolish

destruyendo *etc* [destru'jendo] *vb ver*
destruir

desuelle *etc* [de'sweʎe] *vb ver* **desollar**

desueve *etc* [de'sweβe] *vb ver* **desovar**

desunión [desu'njon] *nf* (*separación*)
separation; (*discordia*) disunity

desunir [desu'nir] *vt* to separate; (*Tec*) to
disconnect; (*fig*) to cause a quarrel *o* rift
between

desuso [de'suso] *nm* disuse; **caer en ~** to
fall into disuse, become obsolete; **una
expresión caída en ~** an obsolete expression

desvaído, -a [desβa'iðo, a] *adj* (*color*) pale;
(*contorno*) blurred

desvalido, -a [desβa'liðo, a] *adj* (*desprotegido*)
destitute; (*sin fuerzas*) helpless; **niños
desvalidos** waifs and strays

desvalijar [desβali'xar] *vt* (*persona*) to rob;
(*casa, tienda*) to burgle; (*coche*) to break into

desvalorice *etc* [desβalo'riθe] *vb ver*
desvalorizar

desvalorizar [desβalori'θar] *vt* to devalue

desván [des'βan] *nm* attic

desvanecer [desβane'θer] *vt* (*disipar*) to
dispel; (*recuerdo, temor*) to banish; (*borrar*) to
blur; **desvanecerse** *vr* (*humo etc*) to vanish,
disappear; (*duda*) to be dispelled; (*color*) to
fade; (*recuerdo, sonido*) to fade away; (*Med*) to
pass out

desvanecido, -a [desβane'θiðo, a] *adj* (*Med*)
faint; **caer ~** to fall in a faint

desvanecimiento [desβaneθi'mjento]
nm (*desaparición*) disappearance; (*de dudas*)
dispelling; (*de colores*) fading; (*evaporación*)
evaporation; (*Med*) fainting fit

desvanezca *etc* [desβa'neθka] *vb ver*
desvanecer

desvariar [desβa'rjar] *vi* (*enfermo*) to be
delirious; (*delirar*) to talk nonsense

desvarío [desβa'rio] *nm* delirium; (*desatino*)
absurdity; **desvaríos** *nmpl* ravings

desvelar [desβe'lar] *vt* to keep awake;
desvelarse *vr* (*no poder dormir*) to stay awake;
(*vigilar*) to be vigilant *o* watchful; **desvelarse
por algo** (*inquietarse*) to be anxious about sth;
(*poner gran cuidado*) to take great care over sth

desvelo [des'βelo] *nm* lack of sleep; (*insomnio*)
sleeplessness; (*fig*) vigilance; **desvelos** *nmpl*
(*preocupación*) anxiety *sg*, effort *sg*

desvencijado, -a [desβenθi'xaðo, a] *adj* (*silla*)
rickety; (*máquina*) broken-down

desvencijar [desβenθi'xar] *vt* (*romper*) to
break; (*soltar*) to loosen; (*persona: agotar*) to

exhaust; **desvencijarse** *vr* to come apart

desventaja [desβen'taxa] *nf* disadvantage;
(*inconveniente*) drawback

desventajoso, -a [desβenta'xoso, a] *adj*
disadvantageous, unfavourable

desventura [desβen'tura] *nf* misfortune

desventurado, -a [desβentu'raðo, a] *adj*
(*desgraciado*) unfortunate; (*de poca suerte*) ill-
fated

desvergonzado, -a [desβerɣon'θaðo, a] *adj*
(*sin vergüenza*) shameless; (*descarado*) insolent
■ *nm/f* shameless person

desvergüenza [desβer'ɣwenθa] *nf* (*descaro*)
shamelessness; (*insolencia*) impudence; (*mala
conducta*) effrontery; **esto es una ~** this is
disgraceful; **¡qué ~!** what a nerve!

desvestir [desβes'tir] *vt*, **desvestirse** *vr*
to undress

desviación [desβja'θjon] *nf* deviation;
(*Auto: rodeo*) diversion, detour; (: *carretera de
circunvalación*) ring road (*Brit*), circular route
(*US*); **~ de la circulación** traffic diversion;
es una ~ de sus principios it is a departure
from his usual principles

desviar [des'βjar] *vt* to turn aside; (*balón,
flecha, golpe*) to deflect; (*pregunta*) to parry;
(*ojos*) to avert, turn away; (*río*) to alter
the course of; (*navío*) to divert, re-route;
(*conversación*) to sidetrack; **desviarse** *vr*
(*apartarse del camino*) to turn aside; (: *barco*) to
go off course; (*Auto: dar un rodeo*) to make a
detour; **desviarse de un tema** to get away
from the point

desvincular [desβinku'lar] *vt* to free, release;
desvincularse *vr* (*aislarse*) to be cut off;
(*alejarse*) to cut o.s. off

desvío *etc* [des'βio] *vb ver* **desviar** ■ *nm*
(*desviación*) detour, diversion; (*fig*)
indifference

desvirgar [desβir'ɣar] *vt* to deflower

desvirtuar [desβir'twar] *vt* (*estropear*) to spoil;
(*argumento, razonamiento*) to detract from;
(*efecto*) to counteract; (*sentido*) to distort;
desvirtuarse *vr* to spoil

desvistiendo *etc* [desβis'tjendo] *vb ver*
desvestir

desvitalizar [desβitali'θar] *vt* (*nervio*) to
numb

desvivirse [desβi'βirse] *vr*: **~ por** to long for,
crave for; **~ por los amigos** to do anything
for one's friends

detalladamente [detaʎaða'mente] *adv*
(*en detalle*) in detail; (*extensamente*) at great
length

detallar [deta'ʎar] *vt* to detail; (*asunto por
asunto*) to itemize

detalle [de'taʎe] *nm* detail; (*fig*) gesture,

token; **al ~** in detail; (*Com*) retail *cpd*; **comercio al ~** retail trade; **vender al ~** to sell retail; **no pierde ~** he doesn't miss a trick; **me observaba sin perder ~** he watched my every move; **tiene muchos detalles** she is very considerate

detallista [deta'ʎista] *nm/f* retailer ■ *adj* (*meticuloso*) meticulous; **comercio ~** retail trade

detectar [detek'tar] *vt* to detect

detective [detek'tiβe] *nm/f* detective; **~ privado** private detective

detector [detek'tor] *nm* (*Naut, Tec etc*) detector; **~ de mentiras/de minas** lie/mine detector

detención [deten'θjon] *nf* (*acción*) stopping; (*estancamiento*) stoppage; (*retraso*) holdup, delay; (*Jur; arresto*) arrest; (*cuidado*) care; **~ de juego** (*Deporte*) stoppage of play; **~ ilegal** unlawful detention

detendré *etc* [deten'dre] *vb ver* **detener**

detener [dete'ner] *vt* (*gen*) to stop; (*Jur: arrestar*) to arrest; (*: encarcelar*) to detain; (*objeto*) to keep; (*retrasar*) to hold up, delay; (*aliento*) to hold; **detenerse** *vr* to stop; **detenerse en** (*demorarse*) to delay over, linger over

detenga *etc* [de'tenga] *vb ver* **detener**

detenidamente [deteniða'mente] *adv* (*minuciosamente*) carefully; (*extensamente*) at great length

detenido, -a [dete'niðo, a] *adj* (*arrestado*) under arrest; (*minucioso*) detailed; (*examen*) thorough; (*tímido*) timid ■ *nm/f* person under arrest, prisoner

detenimiento [deteni'mjento] *nm* care; **con ~** thoroughly

detentar [deten'tar] *vt* to hold; (*sin derecho: título*) to hold unlawfully; (*: puesto*) to occupy unlawfully

detergente [deter'xente] *adj, nm* detergent

deteriorado, -a [deterjo'raðo, a] *adj* (*estropeado*) damaged; (*desgastado*) worn

deteriorar [deterjo'rar] *vt* to spoil, damage; **deteriorarse** *vr* to deteriorate

deterioro [dete'rjoro] *nm* deterioration

determinación [determina'θjon] *nf* (*empeño*) determination; (*decisión*) decision; (*de fecha, precio*) settling, fixing

determinado, -a [determi'naðo, a] *adj* (*preciso*) fixed, set; (*Ling: artículo*) definite; (*persona: resuelto*) determined; **un día ~** on a certain day; **no hay ningún tema ~** there is no particular theme

determinar [determi'nar] *vt* (*plazo*) to fix; (*precio*) to settle; (*daños, impuestos*) to assess; (*pleito*) to decide; (*causar*) to cause;

determinarse *vr* to decide; **el reglamento determina que ...** the rules lay it down *or* state that ...; **aquello determinó la caída del gobierno** that brought about the fall of the government; **esto le determinó** this decided him

detestable [detes'taβle] *adj* (*persona*) hateful; (*acto*) detestable

detestar [detes'tar] *vt* to detest

detonación [detona'θjon] *nf* detonation; (*sonido*) explosion

detonante [deto'nante] *nm* (*fig*) trigger

detonar [deto'nar] *vi* to detonate

detractor, a [detrak'tor, a] *adj* disparaging ■ *nm/f* detractor

detrás [de'tras] *adv* behind; (*atrás*) at the back ■ *prep*: **~ de** behind; **por ~ de algn** (*fig*) behind sb's back; **salir de ~** to come out from behind; **por ~** behind

detrasito [detra'sito] *adv* (*Am fam*) behind

detrimento [detri'mento] *nm*: **en ~ de** to the detriment of

detuve *etc* [de'tuβe] *vb ver* **detener**

deuda [de'uða] *nf* (*condición*) indebtedness, debt; (*cantidad*) debt; **~ a largo plazo** long-term debt; **~ exterior/pública** foreign/national debt; **~ incobrable o morosa** bad debt; **deudas activas/pasivas** assets/liabilities; **contraer deudas** to get into debt

deudor, a [deu'ðor, a] *nm/f* debtor; **~ hipotecario** mortgager; **~ moroso** slow payer

devaluación [deβalwa'θjon] *nf* devaluation

devaluar [deβalu'ar] *vt* to devalue

devanar [deβa'nar] *vt* (*hilo*) to wind; **devanarse** *vr*: **devanarse los sesos** to rack one's brains

devaneo [deβa'neo] *nm* (*Med*) delirium; (*desatino*) nonsense; (*fruslería*) idle pursuit; (*amorío*) flirtation

devastar [deβas'tar] *vt* (*destruir*) to devastate

devendré *etc* [deβen'dre], **devenga** *etc* [de'βenga] *vb ver* **devenir**

devengar [deβen'gar] *vt* (*salario: ganar*) to earn; (*: tener que cobrar*) to be due; (*intereses*) to bring in, accrue, earn

devengue *etc* [de'βenge] *vb ver* **devengar**

devenir [deβe'nir] *vi*: **~ en** to become, turn into ■ *nm* (*movimiento progresivo*) process of development; (*transformación*) transformation

deviene *etc* [de'βjene], **deviniendo** *etc* [deβi'njendo] *vb ver* **devenir**

devoción [deβo'θjon] *nf* devotion; (*afición*) strong attachment

devolución [deβolu'θjon] *nf* (*reenvío*) return, sending back; (*reembolso*) repayment; (*Jur*) devolution

129

devolver [deβol'βer] vt (lo extraviado, prestado) to give back; (a su sitio) to put back; (carta al correo) to send back; (Com) to repay, refund; (visita, la palabra) to return; (salud, vista) to restore; (fam: vomitar) to throw up ■ vi (fam) to be sick; **devolverse** vr (Am) to return; ~ **mal por bien** to return ill for good; ~ **la pelota a algn** to give sb tit for tat

devorar [deβo'rar] vt to devour; (comer ávidamente) to gobble up; (fig: fortuna) to run through; **todo lo devoró el fuego** the fire consumed everything; **le devoran los celos** he is consumed with jealousy

devoto, -a [de'βoto, a] adj (Rel: persona) devout; (: obra) devotional; (amigo): ~ **(de algn)** devoted (to sb) ■ nm/f admirer; **los devotos** nmpl (Rel) the faithful; **su muy ~** your devoted servant

devuelto [de'βwelto], **devuelva** etc [de'βwelβa] vb ver **devolver**

D.F. abr (México) = **Distrito Federal**

dg abr (= decigramo) dg

D.G. abr (= Dirección General, Director General) DG

DGT nf abr (= Dirección General de Tráfico) = Dirección General de Turismo

di [di] vb ver **dar; decir**

día ['dia] nm day; ~ **de asueto** day off; ~ **feriado** (Am) o **festivo** (public) holiday; ~ **hábil/inhábil** working/non-working day; ~ **lunes** (Am) Monday; ~ **lectivo** teaching day; ~ **libre** day off; **D~ de Reyes** Epiphany (6 January); **¿qué ~ es?** what's the date?; **estar/poner al** ~ to be/keep up to date; **el ~ de hoy/de mañana** today/tomorrow; **el ~ menos pensado** when you least expect it; **al ~ siguiente** on the following day; **todos los días** every day; **un ~ sí y otro no** every other day; **vivir al** ~ to live from hand to mouth; **de** ~ during the day, by day; **es de** ~ it's daylight; **del** ~ (estilos) fashionable; (menú) today's; **de un** ~ **para otro** any day now; **en pleno** ~ in full daylight; **en su** ~ in due time; **¡hasta otro ~!** so long!

diabetes [dja'betes] nf diabetes sg

diabético, -a [dja'betiko, a] adj, nm/f diabetic

diablo ['djaβlo] nm (tb fig) devil; **pobre ~** poor devil; **hace un frío de todos los diablos** it's hellishly cold

diablura [dja'βlura] nf prank; (travesura) mischief

diabólico, -a [dja'βoliko, a] adj diabolical

diadema [dja'ðema] nf (para el pelo) Alice band, headband; (joya) tiara

diáfano, -a ['djafano, a] adj (tela) diaphanous; (agua) crystal-clear

diafragma [dja'fraɣma] nm diaphragm

diagnosis [djaɣ'nosis] nf inv, **diagnóstico** [djaɣ'nostiko] nm diagnosis

diagnosticar [djaɣnosti'kar] vt to diagnose

diagonal [djaɣo'nal] adj diagonal ■ nf (Geom) diagonal; **en** ~ diagonally

diagrama [dja'ɣrama] nm diagram; ~ **de barras** (Com) bar chart; ~ **de dispersión** (Com) scatter diagram; ~ **de flujo** (Inform) flowchart

dial [di'al] nm dial

dialecto [dja'lekto] nm dialect

dialogar [djalo'ɣar] vt to write in dialogue form ■ vi (conversar) to have a conversation; ~ **con** (Pol) to hold talks with

diálogo ['djaloɣo] nm dialogue

dialogue etc [dja'loɣe] vb ver **dialogar**

diamante [dja'mante] nm diamond

diametralmente [djametral'mente] adv diametrically; ~ **opuesto a** diametrically opposed to

diámetro [di'ametro] nm diameter; ~ **de giro** (Auto) turning circle; **faros de gran ~** wide-angle headlights

diana ['djana] nf (Mil) reveille; (de blanco) centre, bull's-eye

diantre ['djantre] nm: **¡~!** (fam) oh hell!

diapasón [djapa'son] nm (instrumento) tuning fork; (de violín etc) fingerboard; (de voz) tone

diapositiva [djaposi'tiβa] nf (Foto) slide, transparency

diario, -a ['djarjo, a] adj daily ■ nm newspaper; (libro diario) diary; (: Com) daybook; (Com: gastos) daily expenses; ~ **de navegación** (Naut) logbook; ~ **hablado** (Radio) news (bulletin); ~ **de sesiones** parliamentary report; **a** ~ daily; **de** o **para** ~ everyday

diarrea [dja'rrea] nf diarrhoea

diatriba [dja'triβa] nf diatribe, tirade

dibujante [diβu'xante] nm/f (de bosquejos) sketcher; (de dibujos animados) cartoonist; (de moda) designer; ~ **de publicidad** commercial artist

dibujar [diβu'xar] vt to draw, sketch; **dibujarse** vr (emoción) to show; **dibujarse contra** to be outlined against

dibujo [di'βuxo] nm drawing; (Tec) design; (en papel, tela) pattern; (en periódico) cartoon; (fig) description; **dibujos animados** cartoons; ~ **del natural** drawing from life

dic., dic.ᵉ abr (= diciembre) Dec.

diccionario [dikθjo'narjo] nm dictionary

dicharachero, -a [ditʃara'tʃero, a] adj talkative ■ nm/f (con ingenio) wit; (parlanchín) chatterbox

dicho, -a ['ditʃo, a] pp de **decir** ■ adj (susodicho) aforementioned ■ nm saying; (proverbio) proverb; (ocurrencia) bright remark

■ *nf* (*buena suerte*) good luck; **mejor** ~ rather; ~ **y hecho** no sooner said than done

dichoso, -a [di'tʃoso, a] *adj* (*feliz*) happy; (*afortunado*) lucky; **¡aquel ~ coche!** (*fam*) that blessed car!

diciembre [di'θjembre] *nm* December; *ver tb* **julio**

diciendo *etc* [di'θjendo] *vb ver* **decir**

dictado [dik'taðo] *nm* dictation; **escribir al ~** to take dictation; **los dictados de la conciencia** (*fig*) the dictates of conscience

dictador [dikta'ðor] *nm* dictator

dictadura [dikta'ðura] *nf* dictatorship

dictáfono® [dik'tafono] *nm* Dictaphone®

dictamen [dik'tamen] *nm* (*opinión*) opinion; (*informe*) report; ~ **contable** auditor's report; ~ **facultativo** (*Med*) medical report

dictar [dik'tar] *vt* (*carta*) to dictate; (*Jur: sentencia*) to pass; (*decreto*) to issue; (*Am: clase*) to give; (*: conferencia*) to deliver

didáctico, -a [di'ðaktiko, a] *adj* didactic; (*material*) teaching *cpd*; (*juguete*) educational

diecinueve [djeθi'nweβe] *num* nineteen; (*fecha*) nineteenth; *ver tb* **seis**

dieciochesco, -a [djeθio'tʃesko, a] *adj* eighteenth-century

dieciocho [djeθi'otʃo] *num* eighteen; (*fecha*) eighteenth; *ver tb* **seis**

dieciséis [djeθi'seis] *num* sixteen; (*fecha*) sixteenth; *ver tb* **seis**

diecisiete [djeθi'sjete] *num* seventeen; (*fecha*) seventeenth; *ver tb* **seis**

diente ['djente] *nm* (*Anat, Tec*) tooth; (*Zool*) fang; (*: de elefante*) tusk; (*de ajo*) clove; ~ **de león** dandelion; **dientes postizos** false teeth; **enseñar los dientes** (*fig*) to show one's claws; **hablar entre dientes** to mutter, mumble; **hincar el ~ en** (*comida*) to bite into

diera *etc* ['djera] *vb ver* **dar**

diéresis [di'eresis] *nf* diaeresis

dieron ['djeron] *vb ver* **dar**

diesel ['disel] *adj*: **motor ~** diesel engine

diestro, -a ['djestro, a] *adj* (*derecho*) right; (*hábil*) skilful; (*: con las manos*) handy ■ *nm* (*Taur*) matador ■ *nf* right hand; **a ~ y siniestro** (*sin método*) wildly

dieta ['djeta] *nf* diet; **dietas** *nfpl* expenses; **estar a ~** to be on a diet

dietético, -a [dje'tetiko, a] *adj* dietetic ■ *nm/f* dietician ■ *nf* dietetics *sg*

dietista [dje'tista] *nm/f* dietician

diez [djeθ] *num* ten; (*fecha*) tenth; **hacer las ~ de últimas** (*Naipes*) to sweep the board; *ver tb* **seis**

diezmar [djeθ'mar] *vt* to decimate

difamación [difama'θjon] *nf* slander; libel

difamar [difa'mar] *vt* (*Jur: hablando*) to slander; (*: por escrito*) to libel

difamatorio, -a [difama'torjo, a] *adj* slanderous; libellous

diferencia [dife'renθja] *nf* difference; **a ~ de** unlike; **hacer ~ entre** to make a distinction between; ~ **salarial** (*Com*) wage differential

diferencial [diferen'θjal] *nm* (*Auto*) differential

diferenciar [diferen'θjar] *vt* to differentiate between ■ *vi* to differ; **diferenciarse** *vr* to differ, be different; (*distinguirse*) to distinguish o.s.

diferente [dife'rente] *adj* different

diferido [dife'riðo] *nm*: **en ~** (*TV etc*) recorded

diferir [dife'rir] *vt* to defer

difícil [di'fiθil] *adj* difficult; (*tiempos, vida*) hard; (*situación*) delicate; **es un hombre ~** he's a difficult man to get on with

difícilmente [di'fiθilmente] *adv* (*con dificultad*) with difficulty; (*apenas*) hardly

dificultad [difikul'taθ] *nf* difficulty; (*problema*) trouble; (*objeción*) objection

dificultar [difikul'tar] *vt* (*complicar*) to complicate, make difficult; (*estorbar*) to obstruct; **las restricciones dificultan el comercio** the restrictions hinder trade

dificultoso, -a [difikul'toso, a] *adj* (*difícil*) difficult, hard; (*fam: cara*) odd, ugly; (*persona: exigente*) fussy

difiera *etc* [di'fjera], **difiriendo** *etc* [difi'rjendo] *vb ver* **diferir**

difuminar [difumi'nar] *vt* to blur

difundir [difun'dir] *vt* (*calor, luz*) to diffuse; (*Radio*) to broadcast; **difundirse** *vr* to spread (out); ~ **una noticia** to spread a piece of news

difunto, a [di'funto, a] *adj* dead, deceased ■ *nm/f*: **el ~** the deceased

difusión [difu'sjon] *nf* (*de calor, luz*) diffusion; (*de noticia, teoría*) dissemination; (*de programa*) broadcasting; (*programa*) broadcast

difuso, -a [di'fuso, a] *adj* (*luz*) diffused; (*conocimientos*) widespread; (*estilo, explicación*) wordy

diga *etc* ['diɣa] *vb ver* **decir**

digerir [dixe'rir] *vt* to digest; (*fig*) to absorb; (*reflexionar sobre*) to think over

digestión [dixes'tjon] *nf* digestion; **corte de ~** indigestion

digestivo, -a [dixes'tiβo, a] *adj* digestive ■ *nm* (*bebida*) liqueur, digestif

digiera *etc* [di'xjera], **digiriendo** *etc* [dixi'rjendo] *vb ver* **digerir**

digital [dixi'tal] *adj* (*Inform*) digital; (*dactilar*) finger *cpd* ■ *nf* (*Bot*) foxglove; (*droga*) digitalis

d

digitalizador [dixitaliθa'ðor] *nm* (*Inform*) digitizer

dignarse [diɣ'narse] *vr* to deign to

dignidad [diɣni'ðað] *nf* dignity; (*honra*) honour; (*rango*) rank; (*persona*) dignitary; **herir la ~ de algn** to hurt sb's pride

dignificar [diɣnifi'kar] *vt* to dignify

dignifique *etc* [diɣni'fike] *vb ver* **dignificar**

digno, -a ['diɣno, a] *adj* worthy; (*persona: honesto*) honourable; **~ de elogio** praiseworthy; **~ de mención** worth mentioning; **es ~ de verse** it is worth seeing; **poco ~** unworthy

digresión [diɣre'sjon] *nf* digression

dije *etc* ['dixe], **dijera** *etc* [di'xera] *vb ver* **decir**

dilación [dila'θjon] *nf* delay; **sin ~** without delay, immediately

dilapidar [dilapi'ðar] *vt* to squander, waste

dilatación [dilata'θjon] *nf* (*expansión*) dilation

dilatado, -a [dila'taðo, a] *adj* dilated; (*período*) long drawn-out; (*extenso*) extensive

dilatar [dila'tar] *vt* (*gen*) to dilate; (*prolongar*) to prolong; (*aplazar*) to delay; **dilatarse** *vr* (*pupila etc*) to dilate; (*agua*) to expand

dilema [di'lema] *nm* dilemma

diligencia [dili'xenθja] *nf* diligence; (*rapidez*) speed; (*ocupación*) errand, job; (*carruaje*) stagecoach; **diligencias** *nfpl* (*Jur*) formalities; **diligencias judiciales** judicial proceedings; **diligencias previas** inquest *sg*

diligente [dili'xente] *adj* diligent; **poco ~** slack

dilucidar [diluθi'ðar] *vt* (*aclarar*) to elucidate, clarify; (*misterio*) to clear up

diluir [dilu'ir] *vt* to dilute; (*aguar, fig*) to water down

diluviar [dilu'βjar] *vi* to pour with rain

diluvio [di'luβjo] *nm* deluge, flood; **un ~ de cartas** (*fig*) a flood of letters

diluyendo *etc* [dilu'jendo] *vb ver* **diluir**

dimanar [dima'nar] *vi:* **~ de** to arise o spring from

dimensión [dimen'sjon] *nf* dimension; **dimensiones** *nfpl* size *sg*; **tomar las dimensiones de** to take the measurements of

dimes ['dimes] *nmpl:* **andar en ~ y diretes con algn** to bicker o squabble with sb

diminutivo [diminu'tiβo] *nm* diminutive

diminuto, -a [dimi'nuto, a] *adj* tiny, diminutive

dimisión [dimi'sjon] *nf* resignation

dimitir [dimi'tir] *vt* (*cargo*) to give up; (*despedir*) to sack ■ *vi* to resign

dimos ['dimos] *vb ver* **dar**

Dinamarca [dina'marka] *nf* Denmark

dinamarqués, -esa [dinamar'kes, esa] *adj* Danish ■ *nm/f* Dane ■ *nm* (*Ling*) Danish

dinámico, -a [di'namiko, a] *adj* dynamic ■ *nf* dynamics *sg*

dinamita [dina'mita] *nf* dynamite

dinamitar [dinami'tar] *vt* to dynamite

dinamo [di'namo], **dínamo** ['dinamo] *nf, nm en AM* dynamo

dinastía [dinas'tia] *nf* dynasty

dineral [dine'ral] *nm* fortune

dinero [di'nero] *nm* money; (*dinero en circulación*) currency; **~ caro** (*Com*) dear money; **~ contante (y sonante)** hard cash; **~ de curso legal** legal tender; **~ efectivo** cash, ready cash; **es hombre de ~** he is a man of means; **andar mal de ~** to be short of money; **ganar ~ a espuertas** to make money hand over fist

dinosaurio [dino'saurjo] *nm* dinosaur

dintel [din'tel] *nm* lintel; (*umbral*) threshold

diñar [di'ɲar] *vt* (*fam*) to give; **diñarla** to kick the bucket

dio [djo] *vb ver* **dar**

diócesis ['djoθesis] *nf inv* diocese

Dios [djos] *nm* God; **~ mediante** God willing; **a ~ gracias** thank heaven; **a la buena de ~** any old how; **una de ~ es Cristo** an almighty row; **~ los cría y ellos se juntan** birds of a feather flock together; **como ~ manda** as is proper; **¡~ mío!** (oh) my God!; **¡por ~!** for God's sake!; **¡válgame ~!** bless my soul!

dios [djos] *nm* god

diosa ['djosa] *nf* goddess

Dip. *abr* (= *Diputación*) ≈ CC

diploma [di'ploma] *nm* diploma

diplomacia [diplo'maθja] *nf* diplomacy; (*fig*) tact

diplomado, -a [diplo'maðo, a] *adj* qualified ■ *nm/f* holder of a diploma; (*Univ*) graduate; *ver tb* **licenciado**

diplomático, -a [diplo'matiko, a] *adj* (*cuerpo*) diplomatic; (*que tiene tacto*) tactful ■ *nm/f* diplomat

diptongo [dip'tongo] *nm* diphthong

diputación [diputa'θjon] *nf* deputation; **~ permanente** (*Pol*) standing committee; **~ provincial** ≈ county council

diputado, -a [dipu'taðo, a] *nm/f* delegate; (*Pol*) ≈ member of parliament (*Brit*), ≈ representative (*US*); *ver tb* **Corte**

dique ['dike] *nm* dyke; (*rompeolas*) breakwater; **~ de contención** dam

Dir. *abr* = **dirección**; (= *director*) Mgr

diré *etc* [di're] *vb ver* **decir**

dirección [direk'θjon] *nf* direction; (*fig: tendencia*) trend; (*señas, tb Inform*) address; (*Auto*) steering; (*gerencia*) management; (*de periódico*) editorship; (*en escuela*)

headship; (Pol) leadership; (junta)
board of directors; (despacho) director's/
manager's/headmaster's/editor's office;
~ **administrativa** office management;
~ **asistida** power-assisted steering; **D~
General de Seguridad/Turismo** State
Security/Tourist Office; ~ **única** o **prohibida**
one-way; **tomar la ~ de una empresa** to
take over the running of a company
direccionamiento [direkθjona'mjento] nm
(Inform) addressing
directivo,-a [direk'tiβo, a] adj (junta)
managing; (función) administrative ■ nm/f
(Com) manager ■ nf (norma) directive; (tb:
junta directiva) board of directors
directo,-a [di'rekto, a] adj direct; (línea)
straight; (inmediato) immediate; (tren)
through; (TV) live; **programa en ~** live
programme; **transmitir en ~** to broadcast
live
director, a [direk'tor, a] adj leading
■ nm/f director; (Escol) head (teacher)
(Brit), principal (US); (gerente) manager/
manageress; (de compañía) president; (jefe)
head; (Prensa) editor; (de prisión) governor;
(Mus) conductor; ~ **adjunto** assistant
manager; ~ **de cine** film director; ~
comercial marketing manager; ~ **ejecutivo**
executive director; ~ **de empresa** company
director; ~ **general** general manager; ~
gerente managing director; ~ **de sucursal**
branch manager
directorio [direk'torjo] nm (Inform) directory
directrices [direk'triθes] nfpl guidelines
dirigente [diri'xente] adj leading ■ nm/f (Pol)
leader; **los dirigentes del partido** the party
leaders
dirigible [diri'xiβle] adj (Aviat, Naut) steerable
■ nm airship
dirigir [diri'xir] vt to direct; (acusación) to
level; (carta) to address; (obra de teatro, film)
to direct; (Mus) to conduct; (comercio) to
manage; (expedición) to lead; (sublevación)
to head; (periódico) to edit; (guiar) to guide;
dirigirse vr: **dirigirse a** to go towards, make
one's way towards; (hablar con) to speak to;
dirigirse a algn solicitando algo to apply to
sb for sth; **"diríjase a ..."** "apply to ..."
dirigismo [diri'xismo] nm management,
control; ~ **estatal** state control
dirija etc [di'rixa] vb ver **dirigir**
dirimir [diri'mir] vt (contrato, matrimonio) to
dissolve
discado [dis'kaðo] nm: ~ **automático**
autodial
discernir [disθer'nir] vt to discern ■ vi to
distinguish

discierna etc [dis'θjerna] vb ver **discernir**
disciplina [disθi'plina] nf discipline
disciplinar [disθipli'nar] vt to discipline;
(enseñar) to school; (Mil) to drill; (azotar) to
whip
discípulo,-a [dis'θipulo, a] nm/f disciple;
(seguidor) follower; (Escol) pupil
Discman® ['diskman] nm Discman®,
personal CD player
disco ['disko] nm disc (Brit), disk (US);
(Deporte) discus; (Telec) dial; (Auto: semáforo)
light; (Mus) record; (Inform) disk; ~ **de
arranque** boot disk; ~ **compacto** compact
disc; ~ **de densidad sencilla/doble** single/
double density disk; ~ **de larga duración**
long-playing record (LP); ~ **flexible** o
floppy floppy disk; ~ **de freno** brake disc; ~
maestro master disk; ~ **de reserva** backup
disk; ~ **rígido** hard disk; ~ **de una cara/dos
caras** single-/double-sided disk; ~ **virtual**
RAMdisk
discóbolo [dis'koβolo] nm discus thrower
discográfico,-a [dis'koɣrafiko, a] adj record
cpd; **casa discográfica** record company;
sello - label
díscolo,-a ['diskolo, a] adj (rebelde) unruly
disconforme [diskon'forme] adj differing;
estar ~ (con) to be in disagreement (with)
discontinuo,-a [diskon'tinwo, a] adj
discontinuous; (Auto: línea) broken
discordar [diskor'ðar] vi (Mus) to be out of
tune; (estar en desacuerdo) to disagree; (colores,
opiniones) to clash
discorde [dis'korðe] adj (sonido) discordant;
(opiniones) clashing
discordia [dis'korðja] nf discord
discoteca [disko'teka] nf disco(theque)
discreción [diskre'θjon] nf discretion;
(reserva) prudence; **¡a ~!** (Mil) stand easy!;
añadir azúcar a ~ (Culin) add sugar to taste;
comer a ~ to eat as much as one wishes
discrecional [diskreθjo'nal] adj (facultativo)
discretionary; **parada ~** request stop
discrepancia [diskre'panθja] nf (diferencia)
discrepancy; (desacuerdo) disagreement
discrepante [diskre'pante] adj divergent;
hubo varias voces discrepantes there were
some dissenting voices
discrepar [diskre'par] vi to disagree
discreto,-a [dis'kreto, a] adj (diplomático)
discreet; (sensato) sensible; (reservado) quiet;
(sobrio) sober; (mediano) fair, fairly good; **le
daremos un plazo ~** we'll allow him a
reasonable time
discriminación [diskrimina'θjon] nf
discrimination
discriminar [diskrimi'nar] vt to discriminate

against; (*diferenciar*) to discriminate between

discuerde *etc* [dis'kwerðe] *vb ver* **discordar**

disculpa [dis'kulpa] *nf* excuse; (*pedir perdón*) apology; **pedir disculpas a/por** to apologize to/for

disculpar [diskul'par] *vt* to excuse, pardon; **disculparse** *vr* to excuse o.s.; to apologize

discurrir [disku'rrir] *vt* to contrive, think up ▪ *vi* (*pensar, reflexionar*) to think, meditate; (*recorrer*) to roam, wander; (*río*) to flow; (*el tiempo*) to pass, flow by

discurso [dis'kurso] *nm* speech; ~ **de clausura** closing speech; **pronunciar un ~** to make a speech; **en el ~ del tiempo** with the passage of time

discusión [disku'sjon] *nf* (*diálogo*) discussion; (*riña*) argument; **tener una ~** to have an argument

discutible [disku'tiβle] *adj* debatable; **de mérito ~** of dubious worth

discutido, -a [disku'tiðo, a] *adj* controversial

discutir [disku'tir] *vt* (*debatir*) to discuss; (*pelear*) to argue about; (*contradecir*) to argue against ▪ *vi* to discuss; (*disputar*) to argue; **~ de política** to argue about politics; **¡no discutas!** don't argue!

disecar [dise'kar] *vt* (*para conservar: animal*) to stuff; (*: planta*) to dry

diseminar [disemi'nar] *vt* to disseminate, spread

disentir [disen'tir] *vi* to dissent, disagree

diseñador, a [disepa'dor, a] *nm/f* designer

diseñar [dise'par] *vt* to design

diseño [di'sepo] *nm* (*Tec*) design; (*Arte*) drawing; (*Costura*) pattern; **de ~ italiano** Italian-designed; **~ asistido por ordenador** computer-assisted design, CAD

diseque *etc* [di'seke] *vb ver* **disecar**

disertar [diser'tar] *vi* to speak

disfrace *etc* [dis'fraθe] *vb ver* **disfrazar**

disfraz [dis'fraθ] *nm* (*máscara*) disguise; (*traje*) fancy dress; (*excusa*) pretext; **bajo el ~ de** under the cloak of

disfrazado, -a [disfra'θaðo, a] *adj* disguised; **ir ~ de** to masquerade as

disfrazar [disfra'θar] *vt* to disguise; **disfrazarse** *vr* to dress (o.s.) up; **disfrazarse de** to disguise o.s. as

disfrutar [disfru'tar] *vt* to enjoy ▪ *vi* to enjoy o.s.; **¡que disfrutes!** have a good time!; **~ de** to enjoy, possess; **~ de buena salud** to enjoy good health

disfrute [dis'frute] *nm* (*goce*) enjoyment; (*aprovechamiento*) use

disgregar [disɣre'ɣar] *vt* (*desintegrar*) to disintegrate; (*manifestantes*) to disperse; **disgregarse** *vr* to disintegrate, break up

disgregue *etc* [dis'ɣreɣe] *vb ver* **disgregar**

disgustar [disɣus'tar] *vt* (*no gustar*) to displease; (*contrariar, enojar*) to annoy; to upset; **disgustarse** *vr* to be annoyed; (*dos personas*) to fall out; **estaba muy disgustado con el asunto** he was very upset about the affair

disgusto [dis'ɣusto] *nm* (*repugnancia*) disgust; (*contrariedad*) annoyance; (*desagrado*) displeasure; (*tristeza*) grief; (*riña*) quarrel; (*desgracia*) misfortune; **hacer algo a ~** to do sth unwillingly; **matar a algn a disgustos** to drive sb to distraction

disidente [disi'ðente] *nm* dissident

disienta *etc* [di'sjenta] *vb ver* **disentir**

disimulado, -a [disimu'laðo, a] *adj* (*solapado*) furtive, underhand; (*oculto*) covert; **hacerse el ~** to pretend not to notice

disimular [disimu'lar] *vt* (*ocultar*) to hide, conceal ▪ *vi* to dissemble

disimulo [disi'mulo] *nm* (*fingimiento*) dissimulation; **con ~** cunningly

disipar [disi'par] *vt* (*duda, temor*) to dispel; (*esperanza*) to destroy; (*fortuna*) to squander; **disiparse** *vr* (*nubes*) to vanish; (*dudas*) to be dispelled; (*indisciplinarse*) to dissipate

diskette [dis'ket] *nm* (*Inform*) diskette, floppy disk

dislate [dis'late] *nm* (*absurdo*) absurdity; **dislates** *nmpl* nonsense *sg*

dislexia [dis'leksja] *nf* dyslexia

dislocar [dislo'kar] *vt* (*gen*) to dislocate; (*tobillo*) to sprain

disloque *etc* [dis'loke] *vb ver* **dislocar** ▪ *nm*: **es el ~** (*fam*) it's the last straw

disminución [disminu'θjon] *nf* diminution

disminuido, -a [disminu'iðo, a] *nm/f*: **~ mental/físico** mentally/physically-handicapped person

disminuir [disminu'ir] *vt* to decrease, diminish; (*estrechar*) to lessen; (*temperatura*) to lower; (*gastos, raciones*) to cut down; (*dolor*) to relieve; (*autoridad, prestigio*) to weaken; (*entusiasmo*) to damp ▪ *vi* (*días*) to grow shorter; (*precios, temperatura*) to drop, fall; (*velocidad*) to slacken; (*población*) to decrease; (*beneficios, número*) to fall off; (*memoria, vista*) to fail

disminuyendo *etc* [disminu'jendo] *vb ver* **disminuir**

disociar [diso'θjar] *vt* to disassociate; **disociarse** *vr* to disassociate o.s.

disoluble [diso'luβle] *adj* soluble

disolución [disolu'θjon] *nf* (*acto*) dissolution; (*Química*) solution; (*Com*) liquidation; (*moral*) dissoluteness

disoluto, -a [diso'luto, a] *adj* dissolute

disolvente [disol'βente] *nm* solvent, thinner
disolver [disol'βer] *vt* (*gen*) to dissolve;
(*manifestación*) to break up; **disolverse** *vr* to
dissolve; (*Com*) to go into liquidation
disonar [diso'nar] *vb* (*Mus*) to be out of tune;
(*no armonizar*) to lack harmony; ~ **con** to be
out of keeping with, clash with
dispar [dis'par] *adj* (*distinto*) different;
(*irregular*) uneven
disparado, -a [dispa'raðo, a] *adj*: **entrar** ~
to shoot in; **salir** ~ to shoot out; **ir** ~ to go
like mad
disparador [dispara'ðor] *nm* (*de arma*) trigger;
(*Foto, Tec*) release; ~ **atómico** aerosol; ~ **de
bombas** bomb release
disparar [dispa'rar] *vt*, *vi* to shoot, fire;
dispararse *vr* (*arma de fuego*) to go off;
(*persona: marcharse*) to rush off; (: *enojarse*) to
lose control; (*caballo*) to bolt
disparatado, -a [dispara'taðo, a] *adj* crazy
disparate [dispa'rate] *nm* (*tontería*) foolish
remark; (*error*) blunder; **decir disparates** to
talk nonsense; **¡qué ~!** how absurd!; **costar
un ~** to cost a hell of a lot
disparo [dis'paro] *nm* shot; (*acto*) firing;
disparos *nmpl* shooting *sg*, exchange *sg* of
shots, shots; ~ **inicial** (*de cohete*) blast-off
dispendio [dis'pendjo] *nm* waste
dispensar [dispen'sar] *vt* to dispense; (*ayuda*)
to give; (*honores*) to grant; (*disculpar*) to
excuse; **¡usted dispense!** I beg your pardon!;
~ **a algn de hacer algo** to excuse sb from
doing sth
dispensario [dispen'sarjo] *nm* (*clínica*)
community clinic; (*de hospital*) outpatients'
department
dispersar [disper'sar] *vt* to disperse;
(*manifestación*) to break up; **dispersarse** *vr* to
scatter
disperso, -a [dis'perso, a] *adj* scattered
displicencia [displi'θenθja] *nf* (*mal humor*)
peevishness; (*desgana*) lack of enthusiasm
displicente [displi'θente] *adj* (*malhumorado*)
peevish; (*poco entusiasta*) unenthusiastic
dispondré *etc* [dispon'dre] *vb ver* **disponer**
disponer [dispo'ner] *vt* (*arreglar*) to arrange;
(*ordenar*) to put in order; (*preparar*) to
prepare, get ready ■ *vi*: ~ **de** to have, own;
disponerse *vr*: **disponerse para** to prepare
to, prepare for; **la ley dispone que ...** the law
provides that ...; **no puede ~ de esos bienes**
she cannot dispose of those properties
disponga *etc* [dis'ponga] *vb ver* **disponer**
disponibilidad [disponiβili'ðað] *nf*
availability; **disponibilidades** *nfpl* (*Com*)
resources, financial assets
disponible [dispo'niβle] *adj* available;

(*tiempo*) spare; (*dinero*) on hand
disposición [disposi'θjon] *nf* arrangement,
disposition; (*de casa, Inform*) layout; (*ley*)
order; (*cláusula*) provision; (*aptitud*) aptitude;
~ **de ánimo** attitude of mind; **última** ~ last
will and testament; **a la ~ de** at the disposal
of; **a su** ~ at your service
dispositivo [disposi'tiβo] *nm* device,
mechanism; ~ **de alimentación** hopper; ~
de almacenaje storage device; ~ **periférico**
peripheral (device); ~ **de seguridad** safety
catch; (*fig*) security measure
dispuesto, -a [dis'pwesto, a] *pp de* **disponer**
■ *adj* (*arreglado*) arranged; (*preparado*)
disposed; (*persona: dinámico*) bright; **estar ~/
poco ~ a hacer algo** to be inclined/reluctant
to do sth
dispuse *etc* [dis'puse] *vb ver* **disponer**
disputa [dis'puta] *nf* (*discusión*) dispute,
argument; (*controversia*) controversy
disputar [dispu'tar] *vt* (*discutir*) to dispute,
question; (*contender*) to contend for ■ *vi* to
argue
disquete [dis'kete] *nm* (*Inform*) diskette,
floppy disk
disquetera [diske'tera] *nf* disk drive
Dist. *abr* (= *Distrito*) dist.
distancia [dis'tanθja] *nf* distance; (*de tiempo*)
interval; ~ **de parada** braking distance; ~
del suelo (*Auto etc*) height off the ground; **a
gran** *o* **a larga** ~ long-distance; **mantenerse
a** ~ to keep one's distance; (*fig*) to remain
aloof; **guardar las distancias** to keep one's
distance
distanciado, -a [distan'θjaðo, a] *adj* (*remoto*)
remote; (*fig: alejado*) far apart; **estamos
distanciados en ideas** our ideas are poles
apart
distanciamiento [distanθja'mjento] *nm*
(*acto*) spacing out; (*estado*) remoteness; (*fig*)
distance
distanciar [distan'θjar] *vt* to space out;
distanciarse *vr* to become estranged
distante [dis'tante] *adj* distant
distar [dis'tar] *vi*: **dista 5 kms de aquí** it is
5 kms from here; **¿dista mucho?** is it far?;
dista mucho de la verdad it's very far from
the truth
diste ['diste], **disteis** ['disteis] *vb ver* **dar**
distensión [disten'sjon] *nf* distension; (*Pol*)
détente; ~ **muscular** (*Med*) muscular strain
distinción [distin'θjon] *nf* distinction;
(*elegancia*) elegance; (*honor*) honour; **a ~ de**
unlike; **sin** ~ indiscriminately; **sin ~ de
edades** irrespective of age
distinga *etc* [dis'tinga] *vb ver* **distinguir**
distinguido, -a [distin'giðo, a] *adj*

distinguished; (famoso) prominent, well-known; (elegante) elegant

distinguir [distin'gir] vt to distinguish; (divisar) to make out; (escoger) to single out; (caracterizar) to mark out; **distinguirse** vr to be distinguished; (destacarse) to distinguish o.s.; **a lo lejos no se distingue** it's not visible from a distance

distintivo, -a [distin'tiβo, a] adj distinctive; (signo) distinguishing ■ nm (de policía etc) badge; (fig) characteristic

distinto, -a [dis'tinto, a] adj different; (claro) clear; **distintos** several, various

distorsión [distor'sjon] nf (Anat) twisting; (Radio etc) distortion

distorsionar [distorsjo'nar] vt, vi to distort

distracción [distrak'θjon] nf distraction; (pasatiempo) hobby, pastime; (olvido) absent-mindedness, distraction

distraer [distra'er] vt (atención) to distract; (divertir) to amuse; (fondos) to embezzle ■ vi to be relaxing; **distraerse** vr (entretenerse) to amuse o.s.; (perder la concentración) to allow one's attention to wander; **~ a algn de su pensamiento** to divert sb from his train of thought; **el pescar distrae** fishing is a relaxation

distraído, -a [distra'iðo, a] adj (gen) absent-minded; (desatento) inattentive; (entretenido) amusing ■ nm: **hacerse el ~** to pretend not to notice; **con aire ~** idly; **me miró distraída** she gave me a casual glance

distraiga etc [dis'traiɣa], **distraje** etc [dis'traxe], **distrajera** etc [distra'xera], **distrayendo** [distra'jendo] vb ver **distraer**

distribución [distriβu'θjon] nf distribution; (entrega) delivery; (en estadística) distribution, incidence; (Arq) layout; **~ de premios** prize giving; **la ~ de los impuestos** the incidence of taxes

distribuidor, a [distriβui'ðor, a] nm/f (persona: gen) distributor; (: Correos) sorter; (: Com) dealer; **su ~ habitual** your regular dealer

distribuir [distriβu'ir] vt to distribute; (prospectos) to hand out; (cartas) to deliver; (trabajo) to allocate; (premios) to award; (dividendos) to pay; (peso) to distribute; (Arq) to plan

distribuyendo etc [distriβu'jendo] vb ver **distribuir**

distrito [dis'trito] nm (sector, territorio) region; (barrio) district; **~ electoral** constituency; **~ postal** postal district

disturbio [dis'turβjo] nm disturbance; (desorden) riot; **los disturbios** nmpl the troubles

disuadir [diswa'ðir] vt to dissuade

disuasión [diswa'sjon] nf dissuasion; (Mil) deterrent; **~ nuclear** nuclear deterrent

disuasivo, -a [diswa'siβo, a] adj dissuasive; **arma disuasiva** deterrent

disuasorio, -a [diswa'sorjo, a] adj = **disuasivo**

disuelto [di'swelto] pp de **disolver**

disuelva etc [di'swelβa] vb ver **disolver**

disuene etc [di'swene] vb ver **disonar**

disyuntiva [disjun'tiβa] nf (dilema) dilemma

DIU ['diu] nm abr (= dispositivo intrauterino) IUD

diurno, -a ['djurno, a] adj day cpd, diurnal

diva ['diβa] nf prima donna

divagar [diβa'ɣar] vi (desviarse) to digress

divague etc [di'βaɣe] vb ver **divagar**

diván [di'βan] nm divan

divergencia [diβer'xenθja] nf divergence

divergir [diβer'xir] vi (líneas) to diverge; (opiniones) to differ; (personas) to disagree

diverja etc [di'βerxa] vb ver **divergir**

diversidad [diβersi'ðað] nf diversity, variety

diversificación [diβersifika'θjon] nf (Com) diversification

diversificar [diβersifi'kar] vt to diversify

diversifique etc [diβersi'fike] vb ver **diversificar**

diversión [diβer'sjon] nf (gen) entertainment; (actividad) hobby, pastime

diverso, -a [di'βerso, a] adj diverse; (diferente) different ■ nm: **diversos** (Com) sundries; **diversos libros** several books

divertido, -a [diβer'tiðo, a] adj (chiste) amusing, funny; (fiesta etc) enjoyable; (película, libro) entertaining; **está ~** (irónico) this is going to be fun

divertir [diβer'tir] vt (entretener, recrear) to amuse, entertain; **divertirse** vr (pasarlo bien) to have a good time; (distraerse) to amuse o.s.

dividendo [diβi'ðendo] nm (Com): **dividendos** nmpl dividends; **dividendos por acción** earnings per share; **~ definitivo** final dividend

dividir [diβi'ðir] vt (gen) to divide; (separar) to separate; (distribuir) to distribute, share out

divierta etc [di'βjerta] vb ver **divertir**

divinidad [diβini'ðað] nf (esencia divina) divinity; **la D~** God

divino, -a [di'βino, a] adj divine; (fig) lovely

divirtiendo etc [diβir'tjendo] vb ver **divertir**

divisa [di'βisa] nf (emblema) emblem, badge; **divisas** nfpl currency sg; (Com) foreign exchange sg; **control de divisas** exchange control; **~ de reserva** reserve currency

divisar [diβi'sar] vt to make out

división [diβi'sjon] nf division; (de partido) split; (de país) partition

divisorio, -a [diβi'sorjo, a] *adj* (*línea*)
dividing; **línea divisoria de las aguas**
watershed

divorciado, -a [diβor'θjaðo, a] *adj* divorced;
(*opinión*) split ■ *nm/f* divorcé(e)

divorciar [diβor'θjar] *vt* to divorce;
divorciarse *vr* to get divorced

divorcio [di'βorθjo] *nm* divorce; (*fig*) split

divulgación [diβulɣa'θjon] *nf* (*difusión*)
spreading; (*popularización*) popularization

divulgar [diβul'ɣar] *vt* (*desparramar*) to spread;
(*popularizar*) to popularize; (*hacer circular*) to
divulge, circulate; **divulgarse** *vr* (*secreto*) to
leak out; (*rumor*) to get about

divulgue *etc* [di'βulɣe] *vb ver* **divulgar**

dizque ['diske] *adv* (*Am fam*) apparently

Dls., dls *abr* (*Am*) = **dólares**

dm *abr* (= *decímetro*) dm

DNI *nm abr* (*Esp*) = **Documento Nacional de
Identidad**

Dña. *abr* (= *Doña*) Mrs

do [do] *nm* (*Mus*) C

D.O. *abr* = **Denominación de Origen**; *ver*
denominación

dobladillo [doβla'ðiʎo] *nm* (*de vestido*) hem;
(*de pantalón: vuelta*) turn-up (Brit), cuff (US)

doblaje [do'βlaxe] *nm* (*Cine*) dubbing

doblar [do'βlar] *vt* to double; (*papel*) to fold;
(*cano*) to bend; (*la esquina*) to turn, go round;
(*film*) to dub ■ *vi* to turn; (*campana*) to toll;
doblarse *vr* (*plegarse*) to fold (up), crease;
(*encorvarse*) to bend

doble ['doβle] *adj* (*gen*) double; (*de dos aspectos*)
dual; (*cuerda*) thick; (*fig*) two-faced ■ *nm*
double ■ *nm/f* (*Teat*) double, stand-in;
dobles *nmpl* (*Deporte*) doubles *sg*; **~ o nada**
double or quits; **~ página** double-page
spread; **con ~ sentido** with a double
meaning; **el ~** twice the quantity *o* as much;
su sueldo es el ~ del mío his salary is twice
(as much as) mine; (*Inform*): **~ cara** double-
sided; **~ densidad** double density; **~ espacio**
double spacing

doblegar [doβle'ɣar] *vt* to fold, crease;
doblegarse *vr* to yield

doblegue *etc* [do'βleɣe] *vb ver* **doblegar**

doblez [do'βleθ] *nm* (*pliegue*) fold, hem ■ *nf*
(*falsedad*) duplicity

doc. *abr* (= *docena*) doz.; (= *documento*) doc.

doce ['doθe] *num* twelve; (*fecha*) twelfth; **las ~**
twelve o'clock; *ver tb* **seis**

docena [do'θena] *nf* dozen; **por docenas** by
the dozen

docente [do'θente] *adj*: **centro/personal ~**
teaching institution/staff

dócil ['doθil] *adj* (*pasivo*) docile; (*manso*) gentle;
(*obediente*) obedient

docto, -a ['dokto, a] *adj* learned, erudite
■ *nm/f* scholar

doctor, a [dok'tor, a] *nm/f* doctor; **~ en
filosofía** Doctor of Philosophy

doctorado [dokto'raðo] *nm* doctorate

doctorarse [dokto'rarse] *vr* to get a doctorate

doctrina [dok'trina] *nf* doctrine, teaching

documentación [dokumenta'θjon] *nf*
documentation; (*de identidad etc*) papers *pl*

documental [dokumen'tal] *adj, nm*
documentary

documentar [dokumen'tar] *vt* to document;
documentarse *vr* to gather information

documento [doku'mento] *nm* (*certificado*)
document; (*Jur*) exhibit; **documentos** *nmpl*
papers; **~ adjunto** (*Inform*) attachment;
~ justificativo voucher; **D~ Nacional de
Identidad** national identity card; *see note*

> ● DOCUMENTO
>
> ● A laminated plastic ID card with
> ● the holder's personal details and
> ● photograph, the *Documento Nacional de
> ● Identidad* is renewed every 10 years. People
> ● are required to carry it at all times and
> ● to produce it on request for the police. In
> ● Spain it is commonly known as the DNI
> ● or *carnet de identidad*. In Spanish America
> ● a similar card is called the *cédula (de
> ● identidad)*.

dogma ['doɣma] *nm* dogma

dogmático, -a [doɣ'matiko, a] *adj* dogmatic

dogo ['doɣo] *nm* bulldog

dólar ['dolar] *nm* dollar

dolencia [do'lenθja] *nf* (*achaque*) ailment;
(*dolor*) ache

doler [do'ler] *vt, vi* to hurt; (*fig*) to grieve;
dolerse *vr* (*de su situación*) to grieve, feel
sorry; (*de las desgracias ajenas*) to sympathize;
(*quejarse*) to complain; **me duele el brazo** my
arm hurts; **no me duele el dinero** I don't
mind about the money; **¡ahí le duele!** you've
put your finger on it!

doliente [do'ljente] *adj* (*enfermo*) sick;
(*dolorido*) aching; (*triste*) sorrowful; **la
familia ~** the bereaved family

dolor [do'lor] *nm* pain; (*fig*) grief, sorrow; **~ de
cabeza** headache; **~ de estómago** stomach
ache; **~ de oídos** earache; **~ sordo** dull ache

dolorido, -a [dolo'riðo, a] *adj* (*Med*) sore; **la
parte dolorida** the part which hurts

doloroso, -a [dolo'roso, a] *adj* (*Med*) painful;
(*fig*) distressing

dom. *abr* (= *domingo*) Sun.

domar [do'mar] *vt* to tame

domesticado, -a [domesti'kaðo, a] *adj*
(*amansado*) tame

domesticar [domesti'kar] *vt* to tame

doméstico, -a [do'mestiko, a] *adj* domestic
■ *nm/f* servant; **economía doméstica** home
economy; **gastos domésticos** household
expenses

domestique *etc* [domes'tike] *vb ver*
domesticar

domiciliación [domiθilja'θjon] *nf*: ~ **de
pagos** (*Com*) direct debit

domiciliar [domiθi'ljar] *vt* to domicile;
domiciliarse *vr* to take up (one's) residence

domiciliario, -a [domiθi'ljarjo, a] *adj*:
arresto ~ house arrest

domicilio [domi'θiljo] *nm* home; ~
particular private residence; ~ **social** (*Com*)
head office, registered office; **servicio a** ~
delivery service; **sin** ~ **fijo** of no fixed abode

dominante [domi'nante] *adj* dominant;
(*person*) domineering

dominar [domi'nar] *vt* (*gen*) to dominate;
(*países*) to rule over; (*adversario*) to overpower;
(*caballo, nervios, emoción*) to control; (*incendio,
epidemia*) to bring under control; (*idiomas*)
to be fluent in ■ *vi* to dominate, prevail;
dominarse *vr* to control o.s.

domingo [do'mingo] *nm* Sunday; **D~ de
Ramos** Palm Sunday; **D~ de Resurrección**
Easter Sunday; *ver tb* **sábado**; **Semana Santa**

dominguero, -a [domin'gero, a] *adj* Sunday
cpd

dominical [domini'kal] *adj* Sunday *cpd*;
periódico ~ Sunday newspaper

dominicano, -a [domini'kano, a] *adj, nm/f*
Dominican

dominio [do'minjo] *nm* (*tierras*) domain; (*Pol*)
dominion; (*autoridad*) power, authority;
(*supremacía*) supremacy; (*de las pasiones*)
grip, hold; (*de idioma*) command; **ser del** ~
público to be widely known

dominó [domi'no] *nm* (*pieza*) domino; (*juego*)
dominoes

don [don] *nm* (*talento*) gift; **D~ Juan Gómez**
Mr Juan Gómez, Juan Gómez Esq. (*Brit*);
tener ~ **de gentes** to know how to handle
people; ~ **de lenguas** gift for languages;
~ **de mando** (qualities of) leadership;
~ **de palabra** gift of the gab; *see note*

● **DON**

● Don or doña is a term used before
● someone's first name – eg Don Diego,
● Doña Inés – when showing respect or
● being polite to someone of a superior
● social standing or to an older person.

● It is becoming somewhat rare, but it does
● however continue to be used with names
● and surnames in official documents
● and in correspondence: eg Sr. D. Pedro
● Rodríguez Hernández, Sra. Dña Inés
● Rodríguez Hernández.

donación [dona'θjon] *nf* donation

donaire [do'naire] *nm* charm

donante [do'nante] *nm/f* donor; ~ **de sangre**
blood donor

donar [do'nar] *vt* to donate

donativo [dona'tiβo] *nm* donation

doncella [don'θeʎa] *nf* (*criada*) maid

donde ['donde] *adv* where ■ *prep*: **el coche
está allí** ~ **el farol** the car is over there by
the lamppost *o* where the lamppost is; **por** ~
through which; **a** ~ to where, to which; **en**
~ where, in which; **es a** ~ **vamos nosotros**
that's where we're going

dónde ['donde] *adv interrogativo* where?; **¿a** ~
vas? where are you going (to)?; **¿de** ~ **vienes?**
where have you come from?; **¿en** ~? where?;
¿por ~? where?, whereabouts?; **¿por** ~ **se va
al estadio?** how do you get to the stadium?

dondequiera [donde'kjera] *adv* anywhere
■ *conj*: ~ **que** wherever; **por** ~ everywhere, all
over the place

donostiarra [donos'tjarra] *adj* of *o* from San
Sebastián ■ *nm/f* native *o* inhabitant of San
Sebastián

doña ['doɲa] *nf*: **D~ Carmen Gómez** Mrs
Carmen Gómez; *ver tb* **don**

dopar [do'par] *vt* to dope, drug

doping ['dopin] *nm* doping, drugging

doquier [do'kjer] *adv*: **por** ~ all over,
everywhere

dorado, -a [do'raðo, a] *adj* (*color*) golden;
(*Tec*) gilt

dorar [do'rar] *vt* (*Tec*) to gild; (*Culin*) to brown,
cook lightly; ~ **la píldora** to sweeten the pill

dormilón, -ona [dormi'lon, ona] *adj* fond of
sleeping ■ *nm/f* sleepyhead

dormir [dor'mir] *vt*: ~ **la siesta por la tarde**
to have an afternoon nap ■ *vi* to sleep;
dormirse *vr* (*persona, brazo, pierna*) to fall
asleep; **dormirla** (*fam*) to sleep it off;
~ **la mona** (*fam*) to sleep off a hangover;
~ **como un lirón** *o* **tronco** to sleep like a log;
~ **a pierna suelta** to sleep soundly

dormitar [dormi'tar] *vi* to doze

dormitorio [dormi'torjo] *nm* bedroom;
~ **común** dormitory

dorsal [dor'sal] *adj* dorsal ■ *nm* (*Deporte*)
number

dorso ['dorso] *nm* back; **escribir algo al** ~
to write sth on the back; **"vease al** ~**"** "see

other side", "please turn over"

DOS nm abr (= sistema operativo de disco) DOS

dos [dos] num two; (fecha) second; **los ~** the two of them, both of them; **cada ~ por tres** every five minutes; **de ~ en ~** in twos; **estamos a ~** (Tenis) the score is deuce; ver tb **seis**

doscientos, -as [dos'θjentos, as] num two hundred

dosel [do'sel] nm canopy

dosificar [dosifi'kar] vt (Culin, Med, Química) to measure out; (no derrochar) to be sparing with

dosifique etc [dosi'fike] vb ver **dosificar**

dosis ['dosis] nfinv dose, dosage

dossier [do'sjer] nm dossier, file

dotación [dota'θjon] nf (acto, dinero) endowment; (plantilla) staff; (Naut) crew; **la ~ es insuficiente** we are understaffed

dotado, -a [do'taðo, a] adj gifted; **~ de** (persona) endowed with; (máquina) equipped with

dotar [do'tar] vt to endow; (Tec) to fit; (barco) to man; (oficina) to staff

dote ['dote] nf (de novia) dowry; **dotes** nfpl (talentos) gifts

doy [doj] vb ver **dar**

Dpto. abr (~ Departamento) dept.

Dr., Dra. abr (= Doctor, Doctora) Dr

draga ['draɣa] nf dredge

dragado [dra'ɣaðo] nm dredging

dragar [dra'ɣar] vt to dredge; (minas) to sweep

dragón [dra'ɣon] nm dragon

drague etc ['draɣe] vb ver **dragar**

drama ['drama] nm drama; (obra) play

dramático, -a [dra'matiko, a] adj dramatic ■ nm/f dramatist; (actor) actor; **obra dramática** play

dramaturgo, -a [drama'turɣo, a] nm/f dramatist, playwright

dramón [dra'mon] nm (Teat) melodrama; **¡qué ~!** what a scene!

drástico, -a ['drastiko, a] adj drastic

drenaje [dre'naxe] nm drainage

drenar [dre'nar] vt to drain

droga ['droɣa] nf drug; (Deporte) dope; **el problema de la ~** the drug problem

drogadicto, -a [droɣa'ðikto, a] nm/f drug addict

drogar [dro'ɣar] vt to drug; (Deporte) to dope; **drogarse** vr to take drugs

drogodependencia [droɣoðepen'denθja] nf drug addiction

drogue etc ['droɣe] vb ver **drogar**

droguería [droɣe'ria] nf ~ hardware shop (Brit) o store (US)

dromedario [drome'ðarjo] nm dromedary

Dto. abr = descuento

Dtor., Dtora. abr (= Director, Directora) Dir.

ducado [du'kaðo] nm duchy, dukedom

ducha ['dutʃa] nf (baño) shower; (Med) douche

ducharse [du'tʃarse] vr to take a shower

ducho, -a ['dutʃo, a] adj: **~ en** (experimentado) experienced in; (hábil) skilled at

dúctil ['duktil] adj (metal) ductile; (persona) easily influenced

duda ['duða] nf doubt; **sin ~** no doubt, doubtless; **¡sin ~!** of course!; **no cabe ~** there is no doubt about it; **no le quepa ~** make no mistake about it; **no quiero poner en ~ su conducta** I don't want to call his behaviour into question; **sacar a algn de la ~** to settle sb's doubts; **tengo una ~** I have a query

dudar [du'ðar] vt to doubt ■ vi to doubt, have doubts; **~ acerca de algo** to be uncertain about sth; **dudó en comprarlo** he hesitated to buy it; **dudan que sea verdad** they doubt whether o if it's true

dudoso, -a [du'ðoso, a] adj (incierto) hesitant; (sospechoso) doubtful; (conducta) dubious

duelo etc ['dwelo] vb ver **doler** ■ nm (combate) duel; (luto) mourning; **batirse en** etc to fight a duel

duende ['dwende] nm imp, goblin; **tiene ~** he's got real soul

dueño, -a ['dweɲo, a] nm/f (propietario) owner; (de pensión, taberna) landlord(-lady); (de casa, perro) master/mistress; (empresario) employer; **ser ~ de sí mismo** to have self-control; (libre) to be one's own boss; **eres ~ de hacer como te parezca** you're free to do as you think fit; **hacerse ~ de una situación** to take command of a situation

duerma etc ['dwerma] vb ver **dormir**

duermevela [dwerme'βela] nf (fam) nap, snooze

Duero ['dwero] nm Douro

dulce ['dulθe] adj sweet; (carácter, clima) gentle, mild ■ adv gently, softly ■ nm sweet

dulcificar [dulθifi'kar] vt (fig) to soften

dulcifique etc [dulθi'fike] vb ver **dulcificar**

dulzón, -ona [dul'θon, ona] adj (alimento) sickly-sweet, too sweet; (canción etc) gooey

dulzura [dul'θura] nf sweetness; (ternura) gentleness

duna ['duna] nf dune

Dunquerque [dun'kerke] nm Dunkirk

dúo ['duo] nm duet, duo

duodécimo, -a [duo'ðeθimo, a] adj twelfth; ver tb **sexto, a**

dup., dup.[do] abr (= duplicado) duplicated

dúplex ['dupleks] nm inv (piso) duplex (apartment); (Telec) link-up; (Inform): **~ integral** full duplex

duplicar [dupli'kar] vt (hacer el doble de) to duplicate; (cantidad) to double; **duplicarse** vr to double

duplique *etc* [du'plike] *vb ver* **duplicar**
duque ['duke] *nm* duke
duquesa [du'kesa] *nf* duchess
durable [du'raβle] *adj* durable
duración [dura'θjon] *nf* duration, length; (*de
máquina*) life; ~ **media de la vida** average life
expectancy; **de larga** ~ (*enfermedad*) lengthy;
(*pila*) long-life; (*disco*) long-playing; **de poca**
~ short
duradero, -a [dura'ðero, a] *adj* (*tela*) hard-
wearing; (*fe, paz*) lasting
durante [du'rante] *adv* during; ~ **toda la
noche** all night long; **habló ~ una hora** he
spoke for an hour
durar [du'rar] *vi* (*permanecer*) to last; (*recuerdo*)
to remain; (*ropa*) to wear (well)
durazno [du'rasno] *nm* (*Am: fruta*) peach;
(: *árbol*) peach tree
durex ['dureks] *nm* (*Am: tira adhesiva*)
Sellotape® (*Brit*), Scotch tape® (*US*)
dureza [du'reθa] *nf* (*cualidad*) hardness;
(*de carácter*) toughness
durmiendo *etc* [dur'mjendo] *vb ver* **dormir**
durmiente [dur'mjente] *adj* sleeping ■ *nm/f*
sleeper
duro, -a ['duro, a] *adj* hard; (*carácter*) tough;
(*pan*) stale; (*cuello, puerta*) stiff; (*clima, luz*)
harsh ■ *adv* hard ■ *nm* (*moneda*) five peseta
coin; **el sector ~ del partido** the hardliners
pl in the party; **ser ~ con algn** to be tough
with o hard on sb; ~ **de mollera** (*torpe*)
dense; ~ **de oído** hard of hearing; **trabajar ~**
to work hard; **estar sin un ~** to be broke
DVD *nm abr* (= *disco de vídeo digital*) DVD

Ee

E, e [e] *nf* (*letra*) E, e; **E de Enrique** E for
Edward (*Brit*) *o* Easy (*US*)

E *abr* (= *este*) E

e [e] *conj* (*delante de* **i- e hi-** *pero no* **hie-**) and;
ver tb **y**

e/ *abr* (*Com*: = *envío*) shpt.

EA *abr* = **Ejército del Aire**

EAU *nmpl abr* (= *Emiratos Árabes Unidos*) UAE

ebanista [eβa'nista] *nm/f* cabinetmaker

ébano ['eβano] *nm* ebony

ebrio, -a ['eβrjo, a] *adj* drunk

Ebro ['eβro] *nm* Ebro

ebullición [eβuʎi'θjon] *nf* boiling; **punto
de ~** boiling point

eccema [ek'θema] *nm* (*Med*) eczema

echar [e'tʃar] *vt* to throw; (*agua, vino*) to pour
(out); (*Culin*) to put in, add; (*dientes*) to cut;
(*discurso*) to give; (*empleado: despedir*) to fire,
sack; (*hojas*) to sprout; (*cartas*) to post; (*humo*)
to emit, give out; (*reprimenda*) to deal out;
(*cuenta*) to make up; (*freno*) to put on ■ *vi*:
~ a correr/llorar to break into a run/burst
into tears; **~ a reír** to burst out laughing;
echarse *vr* to lie down; **~ abajo** (*gobierno*) to
overthrow; (*edificio*) to demolish; **~ la
buenaventura a algn** to tell sb's fortune;
~ la culpa a to lay the blame on; **~ de menos**
to miss; **~ una mirada** to give a look; **~ sangre**
to bleed; **echarse atrás** to throw o.s.
back(wards); (*fig*) to go back on what one has
said; **echarse una novia** to get o.s. a girlfriend;
echarse una siestecita to have a nap

echarpe [e'tʃarpe] *nm* (woman's) stole

eclesiástico, -a [ekle'sjastiko, a] *adj*
ecclesiastical; (*autoridades etc*) church *cpd*
■ *nm* clergyman

eclipsar [eklip'sar] *vt* to eclipse; (*fig*) to
outshine, overshadow

eclipse [e'klipse] *nm* eclipse

eco ['eko] *nm* echo; **encontrar un ~ en**
to produce a response from; **hacerse ~ de
una opinión** to echo an opinion; **tener ~**
to catch on

ecografía [ekoɣra'fia] *nf* ultrasound

ecología [ekolo'xia] *nf* ecology

ecológico, -a [eko'loxiko, a] *adj* ecological;
(*producto, método*) environmentally-friendly;
(*agricultura*) organic

ecologista [ekolo'xista] *adj* environmental,
conservation *cpd* ■ *nm/f* environmentalist

economato [ekono'mato] *nm* cooperative
store

economía [ekono'mia] *nf* (*sistema*) economy;
(*cualidad*) thrift; **~ dirigida** planned
economy; **~ doméstica** housekeeping;
~ de mercado market economy; **~ mixta**
mixed economy; **~ sumergida** black
economy; **hacer economías** to economize;
economías de escala economies of scale

economice *etc* [ekono'miθe] *vb ver*
economizar

económico, -a [eko'nomiko, a] *adj* (*barato*)
cheap, economical; (*persona*) thrifty; (*Com*:
año etc) financial; (: *situación*) economic

economista [ekono'mista] *nm/f* economist

economizar [ekonomi'θar] *vt* to economize
on ■ *vi* (*ahorrar*) to save up; (*pey*) to be miserly

ecosistema [ekosis'tema] *nm* ecosystem

ecu ['eku] *nm* ecu

ecuación [ekwa'θjon] *nf* equation

ecuador [ekwa'ðor] *nm* equator; **(el) E~**
Ecuador

ecuánime [e'kwanime] *adj* (*carácter*) level-
headed; (*estado*) calm

ecuatorial [ekwato'rjal] *adj* equatorial

ecuatoriano, -a [ekwato'rjano, a] *adj, nm/f*
Ecuador(i)an

ecuestre [e'kwestre] *adj* equestrian

eczema [ek'θema] *nm* = **eccema**

ed. *abr* (= *edición*) ed.

edad [e'ðað] *nf* age; **¿qué ~ tienes?** how
old are you?; **tiene ocho años de ~** he is
eight (years old); **de ~ corta** young; **ser de
~ mediana/avanzada** to be middle-aged/
getting on; **ser mayor de ~** to be of age;
llegar a mayor ~ to come of age; **ser menor**

de ~ to be under age; **la E~ Media** the Middle Ages; **la E~ de Oro** the Golden Age

Edén [e'ðen] *nm* Eden

edición [eði'θjon] *nf (acto)* publication; *(ejemplar)* edition; **"al cerrar la ~"** *(Tip)* "stop press"

edicto [e'ðikto] *nm* edict, proclamation

edificante [eðifi'kante] *adj* edifying

edificar [eðifi'kar] *vt (Arq)* to build

edificio [eði'fiθjo] *nm* building; *(fig)* edifice, structure

edifique *etc* [eði'fike] *vb ver* **edificar**

Edimburgo [eðim'burɣo] *nm* Edinburgh

editar [eði'tar] *vt (publicar)* to publish; *(preparar textos, tb Inform)* to edit

editor, a [eði'tor, a] *nm/f (que publica)* publisher; *(redactor)* editor ▪ *adj:* **casa editora** publishing company

editorial [eðito'rjal] *adj* editorial ▪ *nm* leading article, editorial ▪ *nf (tb:* **casa editorial**) publisher

editorialista [eðitorja'lista] *nm/f* leader-writer

edredón [eðre'ðon] *nm* eiderdown, quilt; **~ nórdico** continental quilt, duvet

educación [eðuka'θjon] *nf* education; *(crianza)* upbringing; *(modales)* (good) manners *pl; (formación)* training; **sin ~** ill-mannered; **¡qué falta de ~!** how rude!

educado, -a [eðu'kaðo, a] *adj* well-mannered; **mal ~** ill-mannered

educar [eðu'kar] *vt* to educate; *(criar)* to bring up; *(voz)* to train

educativo, -a [eðuka'tiβo, a] *adj* educational; *(política)* education *cpd*

eduque *etc* [e'ðuke] *vb ver* **educar**

EE UU *nmpl abr* (= *Estados Unidos*) USA

efectista [efek'tista] *adj* sensationalist

efectivamente [efektiβa'mente] *adv (como respuesta)* exactly, precisely; *(verdaderamente)* really; *(de hecho)* in fact

efectivo, -a [efek'tiβo, a] *adj* effective; *(real)* actual, real ▪ *nm:* **pagar en ~** to pay (in) cash; **hacer ~ un cheque** to cash a cheque

efecto [e'fekto] *nm* effect, result; *(objetivo)* purpose, end; **efectos** *nmpl (personales)* effects; *(bienes)* goods; *(Com)* assets; *(Econ)* bills, securities; **~ 2000** millennium bug; **~ invernadero** greenhouse effect; **efectos de consumo** consumer goods; **efectos a cobrar** bills receivable; **efectos especiales** special effects; **efectos personales** personal effects; **efectos secundarios** *(Com)* spin-off effects; **efectos sonoros** sound effects; **hacer o surtir ~** to have the desired effect; **hacer ~** *(impresionar)* to make an impression; **llevar algo a ~** to carry sth out; **en ~** in fact; *(respuesta)* exactly, indeed

efectuar [efek'twar] *vt* to carry out; *(viaje)* to make

efervescente [eferβes'θente] *adj (bebida)* fizzy, bubbly

eficacia [efi'kaθja] *nf (de persona)* efficiency; *(de medicamento etc)* effectiveness

eficaz [efi'kaθ] *adj (persona)* efficient; *(acción)* effective

eficiencia [efi'θjenθja] *nf* efficiency

eficiente [efi'θjente] *adj* efficient

efigie [e'fixje] *nf* effigy

efímero, -a [e'fimero, a] *adj* ephemeral

EFTA *sigla f* = **Asociación Europea de Libre Comercio**

efusión [efu'sjon] *nf* outpouring; *(en el trato)* warmth; **con ~** effusively

efusivo, -a [efu'siβo, a] *adj* effusive; **mis más efusivas gracias** my warmest thanks

EGB *nf abr (Esp Escol:* = *Educación General Básica)* primary education for six- to fourteen-year olds; *ver tb* **sistema educativo**

Egeo [e'xeo] *nm:* **(Mar)** ~ Aegean (Sea)

egipcio, -a [e'xipθjo, a] *adj, nm/f* Egyptian

Egipto [e'xipto] *nm* Egypt

egocéntrico, -a [eɣo'θentriko, a] *adj* self-centred

egoísmo [eɣo'ismo] *nm* egoism

egoísta [eɣo'ista] *adj* egoistical, selfish ▪ *nm/f* egoist

ególatra [e'ɣolatra] *adj* big-headed

egregio, -a [e'ɣrexjo, a] *adj* eminent, distinguished

egresado, -a [eɣre'saðo, a] *nm/f (Am)* graduate

egresar [eɣre'sar] *vi (Am)* to graduate

eh [e] *excl* hey!, hi!

Eire ['eire] *nm* Eire

ej. *abr* (= *ejemplo*) ex.

eje ['exe] *nm (Geo, Mat)* axis; *(Pol, fig)* axis, main line; *(de rueda)* axle; *(de máquina)* shaft, spindle

ejecución [exeku'θjon] *nf* execution; *(cumplimiento)* fulfilment; *(actuación)* performance; *(Jur: embargo de deudor)* attachment

ejecutar [exeku'tar] *vt* to execute, carry out; *(matar)* to execute; *(cumplir)* to fulfil; *(Mus)* to perform; *(Jur: embargar)* to attach, distrain; *(deseos)* to fulfil; *(Inform)* to run

ejecutivo, -a [exeku'tiβo, a] *adj, nm/f* executive; **el (poder) ~** the Executive (Power)

ejecutor [exeku'tor] *nm (tb:* **ejecutor testamentario**) executor

ejecutoria [exeku'torja] *nf (Jur)* final judgment

ejemplar [exem'plar] *adj* exemplary ▪ *nm* example; *(Zool)* specimen; *(de libro)* copy;

(de periódico) number, issue; **~ de regalo** complimentary copy; **sin ~** unprecedented

ejemplificar [exemplifi'kar] vt to exemplify, illustrate

ejemplifique etc [exempli'fike] vb ver **ejemplificar**

ejemplo [e'xemplo] nm example; (caso) instance; **por ~** for example; **dar ~** to set an example

ejercer [exer'θer] vt to exercise; (funciones) to perform; (negocio) to manage; (influencia) to exert; (un oficio) to practise; (poder) to wield ■ vi: **~ de** to practise as

ejercicio [exer'θiθjo] nm exercise; (Mil) drill; (Com) fiscal o financial year; (período) tenure; **~ acrobático** (Aviat) stunt; **~ comercial** business year; **ejercicios espirituales** (Rel) retreat sg; **hacer ~** to take exercise

ejercitar [exerθi'tar] vt to exercise; (Mil) to drill

ejército [e'xerθito] nm army; **E~ del Aire/de Tierra** Air Force/Army; **~ de ocupación** army of occupation; **~ permanente** standing army; **entrar en el ~** to join the army, join up

ejerza etc [e'xerθa] vb ver **ejercer**

ejote [e'xote] nm (Am) green bean

⭕ **PALABRA CLAVE**

el, la, lo [el, la] (pl **los, las**) artículo definido

1 the; **el libro/la mesa/los estudiantes/las flores** the book/table/students/flowers; **me gusta el fútbol** I like football; **está en la cama** she's in bed

2 (con n abstracto o propio: no se traduce): **el amor/ la juventud** love/youth; **el Conde Drácula** Count Dracula

3 (posesión: se traduce a menudo por adj posesivo): **romperse el brazo** to break one's arm; **levantó la mano** he put his hand up; **se puso el sombrero** she put her hat on

4 (valor descriptivo): **tener la boca grande/los ojos azules** to have a big mouth/blue eyes

5 (con días) on; **me iré el viernes** I'll leave on Friday; **los domingos suelo ir a nadar** on Sundays I generally go swimming

6 (lo + adj): **lo difícil/caro** what is difficult/ expensive; (cuán): **no se da cuenta de lo pesado que es** he doesn't realize how boring he is

■ pron demostrativo 1: **mi libro y el de usted** my book and yours; **las de Pepe son mejores** Pepe's are better; **no la(s) blanca(s) sino la(s) gris(es)** not the white one(s) but the grey one(s)

2: **lo de: lo de ayer** what happened

yesterday; **lo de las facturas** that business about the invoices

■ pron relativo: **el que** etc 1 (indef): **el (los) que quiera(n) que se vaya(n)** anyone who wants to can leave; **llévese el/la que más le guste** take the one you like best

2 (def): **el que compré ayer** the one I bought yesterday; **los que se van** those who leave

3: **lo que: lo que pienso yo/más me gusta** what I think/like most

■ conj: **el que: el que lo diga** the fact that he says so; **el que sea tan vago me molesta** his being so lazy bothers me

■ excl: **¡el susto que me diste!** what a fright you gave me!

■ pron personal 1 (persona: m) him; (: f) her; (: pl) them; **lo/las veo** I can see him/them

2 (animal, cosa: sg) it; (: pl) them; **lo (o la) veo** I can see it; **los (o las) veo** I can see them

3: **lo** (como sustituto de frase): **no lo sabía** I didn't know; **ya lo entiendo** I understand now

él [el] pron (persona) he; (cosa) it; (después de prep: persona) him; (: cosa) it; **mis libros y los de él** my books and his

elaboración [elaβora'θjon] nf (producción) manufacture; **~ de presupuestos** (Com) budgeting

elaborar [elaβo'rar] vt (producto) to make, manufacture; (preparar) to prepare; (madera, metal etc) to work; (proyecto etc) to work on o out

elasticidad [elastiθi'ðað] nf elasticity

elástico, -a [e'lastiko, a] adj elastic; (flexible) flexible ■ nm elastic; (gomita) elastic band

elección [elek'θjon] nf election; (selección) choice, selection; **elecciones parciales** by-election sg; **elecciones generales** general election sg

electo, -a [e'lekto, a] adj elect; **el presidente ~** the president-elect

electorado [elekto'raðo] nm electorate, voters pl

electoral [elekto'ral] adj electoral

electrice etc [elek'triθe] vb ver **electrizar**

electricidad [elektriθi'ðað] nf electricity

electricista [elektri'θista] nm/f electrician

eléctrico, -a [e'lektriko, a] adj electric

electrificar [elektrifi'kar] vt to electrify

electrizar [elektri'θar] vt (Ferro, fig) to electrify

electro... [elektro] pref electro...

electrocardiograma [elektrokarðjo'γrama] nm electrocardiogram

electrocución [elektroku'θjon] nf electrocution

electrocutar [elektroku'tar] vt to electrocute

electrodo [elek'troðo] nm electrode

electrodomésticos [elektroðo'mestikos] *nmpl* (electrical) household appliances; (*Com*) white goods

electroimán [electroi'man] *nm* electromagnet

electromagnético, -a [elektromaɣ'netiko, a] *adj* electromagnetic

electrón [elek'tron] *nm* electron

electrónico, -a [elek'troniko, a] *adj* electronic ■ *nf* electronics *sg*

electrotecnia [elektro'teknja] *nf* electrical engineering

electrotécnico, -a [elektro'tekniko, a] *nm/f* electrical engineer

electrotren [elektro'tren] *nm* express electric train

elefante [ele'fante] *nm* elephant

elegancia [ele'ɣanθja] *nf* elegance, grace; (*estilo*) stylishness

elegante [ele'ɣante] *adj* elegant, graceful; (*traje etc*) smart; (*decoración*) tasteful

elegía [ele'xia] *nf* elegy

elegir [ele'xir] *vt* (*escoger*) to choose, select; (*optar*) to opt for; (*presidente*) to elect

elemental [elemen'tal] *adj* (*claro, obvio*) elementary; (*fundamental*) elemental, fundamental

elemento [ele'mento] *nm* element; (*fig*) ingredient; (*Am*) person, individual; (*tipo raro*) odd person; (*de pila*) cell; **elementos** *nmpl* elements, rudiments; **estar en su ~** to be in one's element; **vino a verle un ~** someone came to see you

elenco [e'lenko] *nm* catalogue, list; (*Teat*) cast; (*Am: equipo*) team

elevación [eleβa'θjon] *nf* elevation; (*acto*) raising, lifting; (*de precios*) rise; (*Geo etc*) height, altitude

elevado, -a [ele'βaðo, a] *pp de* **elevar** ■ *adj* high

elevador [eleβa'ðor] *nm* (*Am*) lift (Brit), elevator (US)

elevar [ele'βar] *vt* to raise, lift (up); (*precio*) to put up; (*producción*) to step up; (*informe etc*) to present; **elevarse** *vr* (*edificio*) to rise; (*precios*) to go up; (*transportarse, enajenarse*) to get carried away; **la cantidad se eleva a ...** the total amounts to ...

eligiendo *etc* [eli'xjenðo], **elija** *etc* [e'lixa] *vb ver* **elegir**

eliminar [elimi'nar] *vt* to eliminate, remove; (*olor, persona*) to get rid of; (*Deporte*) to eliminate, knock out

eliminatoria [elimina'torja] *nf* heat, preliminary (round)

elite [e'lite], **élite** ['elite] *nf* elite, élite

elitista [eli'tista] *adj* elitist

elixir [elik'sir] *nm* elixir; (*tb*: **elixir bucal**) mouthwash

ella ['eʎa] *pron* (*persona*) she; (*cosa*) it; (*después de prep*: *persona*) her; (*cosa*) it; **de ~** hers

ellas ['eʎas] *pron ver* **ellos**

ello ['eʎo] *pron neutro* it; **es por ~ que ...** that's why ...

ellos, -as ['eʎos, as] *pron personal pl* they; (*después de prep*) them; **de ~** theirs

elocuencia [elo'kwenθja] *nf* eloquence

elocuente [elo'kwente] *adj* eloquent; (*fig*) significant; **un dato ~** a fact which speaks for itself

elogiar [elo'xjar] *vt* to praise, eulogize

elogio [e'loxjo] *nm* praise; **queda por encima de todo ~** it's beyond praise; **hacer ~ de** to sing the praises of

elote [e'lote] *nm* (*Am*) corn on the cob

El Salvador *nm* El Salvador

eludir [elu'ðir] *vt* (*evitar*) to avoid, evade; (*escapar*) to escape, elude

Em.ª *abr* (= *Eminencia*) Mgr

email ['imeil] *nm* (*gen*) email *m*; (*dirección*) email address; **mandar un ~ a algn** to email sb, send sb an email

emanar [ema'nar] *vi*: **~ de** to emanate from, come from; (*derivar de*) to originate in

emancipar [emanθi'par] *vt* to emancipate; **emanciparse** *vr* to become emancipated, free o.s.

embadurnar [embaður'nar] *vt* to smear

embajada [emba'xaða] *nf* embassy

embajador, a [embaxa'ðor, a] *nm/f* ambassador/ambassadress

embaladura [embala'ðura] *nf* (*Am*), **embalaje** [emba'laxe] *nm* packing

embalar [emba'lar] *vt* (*envolver*) to parcel, wrap (up); (*envasar*) to package ■ *vi* to sprint

embalsamar [embalsa'mar] *vt* to embalm

embalsar [embal'sar] *vt* (*río*) to dam (up); (*agua*) to retain

embalse [em'balse] *nm* (*presa*) dam; (*lago*) reservoir

embarace *etc* [emba'raθe] *vb ver* **embarazar**

embarazada [embara'θaða] *adj f* pregnant ■ *nf* pregnant woman

embarazar [embara'θar] *vt* to obstruct, hamper; **embarazarse** *vr* to become embarrassed; (*confundirse*) to get into a mess

embarazo [emba'raθo] *nm* (*de mujer*) pregnancy; (*impedimento*) obstacle, obstruction; (*timidez*) embarrassment

embarazoso, -a [embara'θoso, a] *adj* (*molesto*) awkward; (*violento*) embarrassing

embarcación [embarka'θjon] *nf* (*barco*) boat, craft; (*acto*) embarkation; **~ de arrastre** trawler; **~ de cabotaje** coasting vessel

embarcadero [embarka'ðero] nm pier, landing stage

embarcar [embar'kar] vt (cargamento) to ship, stow; (persona) to embark, put on board; (fig): **~ a algn en una empresa** to involve sb in an undertaking; **embarcarse** vr to embark, go on board; (marinero) to sign on; (Am: en tren etc) to get on, get in

embargar [embar'ɣar] vt (frenar) to restrain; (sentidos) to overpower; (Jur) to seize, impound

embargo [em'barɣo] nm (Jur) seizure; (Com etc) embargo; **sin ~** still, however, nonetheless

embargue etc [em'barɣe] vb ver **embargar**

embarque etc [em'barke] vb ver **embarcar** ■ nm shipment, loading

embarrancar [embarran'kar] vt, vi (Naut) to run aground; (Auto etc) to run into a ditch

embarranque etc [emba'rranke] vb ver **embarrancar**

embarullar [embaru'ʎar] vt to make a mess of

embate [em'bate] nm (de mar, viento) beating, violence

embaucador, a [embauka'ðor, a] nm/f (estafador) trickster; (impostor) impostor

embaucar [embau'kar] vt to trick, fool

embauque etc [em'bauke] vb ver **embaucar**

embeber [embe'βer] vt (absorber) to absorb, soak up; (empapar) to saturate ■ vi to shrink; **embeberse** vr: **embeberse en un libro** to be engrossed o absorbed in a book

embelesado, -a [embele'saðo, a] adj spellbound

embelesar [embele'sar] vt to enchant; **embelesarse** vr: **embelesarse (con)** to be enchanted (by)

embellecer [embeʎe'θer] vt to embellish, beautify

embellezca etc [embe'ʎeθka] vb ver **embellecer**

embestida [embes'tiða] nf attack, onslaught; (carga) charge

embestir [embes'tir] vt to attack, assault; to charge, attack ■ vi to attack

embistiendo etc [embis'tjendo] vb ver **embestir**

emblanquecer [emblanke'θer] vt to whiten, bleach; **emblanquecerse** vr to turn white

emblanquezca etc [emblan'keθka] vb ver **emblanquecer**

emblema [em'blema] nm emblem

embobado, -a [embo'βaðo, a] adj (atontado) stunned, bewildered

embobar [embo'βar] vt (asombrar) to amaze; (fascinar) to fascinate; **embobarse** vr:

embobarse con o **de** o **en** to be amazed at; to be fascinated by

embocadura [emboka'ðura] nf narrow entrance; (de río) mouth; (Mus) mouthpiece

embolado [embo'laðo] nm (Teat) bit part, minor role; (fam) trick

embolia [em'bolja] nf (Med) embolism; **~ cerebral** clot on the brain

émbolo ['embolo] nm (Auto) piston

embolsar [embol'sar] vt to pocket

emboquillado, -a [emboki'ʎaðo, a] adj (cigarrillo) tipped, filter cpd

emborrachar [emborra'tʃar] vt to make drunk; **emborracharse** vr to get drunk

emboscada [embos'kaða] nf (celada) ambush

embotar [embo'tar] vt to blunt, dull; **embotarse** vr (adormecerse) to go numb

embotellamiento [emboteʎa'mjento] nm (Auto) traffic jam

embotellar [embote'ʎar] vt to bottle; **embotellarse** vr (circulación) to get into a jam

embozo [em'boθo] nm muffler, mask; (de sábana) turnover

embragar [embra'ɣar] vt (Auto, Tec) to engage; (partes) to connect ■ vi to let in the clutch

embrague etc [em'braɣe] vb ver **embragar** ■ nm (tb: **pedal de embrague**) clutch

embravecer [embraβe'θer] vt to enrage, infuriate; **embravecerse** vr to become furious; (mar) to get rough; (tormenta) to rage

embravecido, -a [embraβe'θiðo, a] adj (mar) rough; (persona) furious

embriagador, a [embrjaɣa'ðor, a] adj intoxicating

embriagar [embrja'ɣar] vt (emborrachar) to make drunk; (alegrar) to delight; **embriagarse** vr (emborracharse) to get drunk

embriague etc [em'brjaɣe] vb ver **embriagar**

embriaguez [embrja'ɣeθ] nf (borrachera) drunkenness

embrión [em'brjon] nm embryo

embrionario, -a [embrjo'narjo, a] adj embryonic

embrollar [embro'ʎar] vt (asunto) to confuse, complicate; (persona) to involve, embroil; **embrollarse** vr (confundirse) to get into a muddle o mess

embrollo [em'broʎo] nm (enredo) muddle, confusion; (aprieto) fix, jam

embromado, -a [embro'maðo, a] adj (Am fam) tricky, difficult

embromar [embro'mar] vt (burlarse de) to tease, make fun of; (Am fam: molestar) to annoy

embrujado, -a [embru'xaðo, a] adj (persona) bewitched; **casa embrujada** haunted house

embrujo [em'bruxo] *nm* (*de mirada etc*) charm, magic

embrutecer [embrute'θer] *vt* (*atontar*) to stupefy; **embrutecerse** *vr* to be stupefied

embrutezca *etc* [embru'teθka] *vb ver* **embrutecer**

embudo [em'buðo] *nm* funnel

embuste [em'buste] *nm* trick; (*mentira*) lie; (*humorístico*) fib

embustero, -a [embus'tero, a] *adj* lying, deceitful ■ *nm/f* (*tramposo*) cheat; (*mentiroso*) liar; (*humorístico*) fibber

embutido [embu'tiðo] *nm* (*Culin*) sausage

embutir [embu'tir] *vt* to insert; (*Tec*) to inlay; (*llenar*) to pack tight, cram

emergencia [emer'xenθja] *nf* emergency; (*surgimiento*) emergence

emergente [emer'xente] *adj* resultant, consequent; (*nación*) emergent; (*Inform*) pop-up *cpd*; **menú/ventana ~** pop-up menu/window

emerger [emer'xer] *vi* to emerge, appear

emeritense [emeri'tense] *adj* of o from Mérida ■ *nm/f* native o inhabitant of Mérida

emerja *etc* [e'merxa] *vb ver* **emerger**

emigración [emiɣra'θjon] *nf* emigration; (*de pájaros*) migration

emigrado, -a [emi'ɣraðo, a] *nm/f* emigrant; (*Pol etc*) émigré(e)

emigrante [emi'ɣrante] *adj, nm/f* emigrant

emigrar [emi'ɣrar] *vi* (*personas*) to emigrate; (*pájaros*) to migrate

eminencia [emi'nenθja] *nf* eminence; (*en títulos*): **Su E~** His Eminence; **Vuestra E~** Your Eminence

eminente [emi'nente] *adj* eminent, distinguished; (*elevado*) high

emisario [emi'sarjo] *nm* emissary

emisión [emi'sjon] *nf* (*acto*) emission; (*Com etc*) issue; (*Radio, TV: acto*) broadcasting; (*: programa*) broadcast, programme, program (*US*); **~ de acciones** (*Com*) share issue; **~ gratuita de acciones** (*Com*) rights issue; **~ de valores** (*Com*) flotation

emisor, a [emi'sor, a] *nm* transmitter ■ *nf* radio o broadcasting station

emitir [emi'tir] *vt* (*olor etc*) to emit, give off; (*moneda etc*) to issue; (*opinión*) to express; (*voto*) to cast; (*señal*) to send out; (*Radio*) to broadcast; **~ una señal sonora** to beep

emoción [emo'θjon] *nf* emotion; (*excitación*) excitement; (*sentimiento*) feeling; **¡qué ~!** how exciting!; (*irónico*) what a thrill!

emocionado, -a [emoθjo'naðo, a] *adj* deeply moved, stirred

emocionante [emoθjo'nante] *adj* (*excitante*) exciting, thrilling

emocionar [emoθjo'nar] *vt* (*excitar*) to excite, thrill; (*conmover*) to move, touch; (*impresionar*) to impress; **emocionarse** *vr* to get excited

emoticón [emoti'kon] *nm* smiley, emoticon

emotivo, -a [emo'tiβo, a] *adj* emotional

empacar [empa'kar] *vt* (*gen*) to pack; (*en caja*) to bale, crate

empacharse [empa'tʃarse] *vr* (*Med*) to get indigestion

empacho [em'patʃo] *nm* (*Med*) indigestion; (*fig*) embarrassment

empadronamiento [empaðrona'mjento] *nm* census; (*de electores*) electoral register

empadronarse [empaðro'narse] *vr* (*Pol: como elector*) to register

empalagar [empala'ɣar] *vt* (*comida*) to cloy; (*hartar*) to pall on ■ *vi* to pall

empalagoso, -a [empala'ɣoso, a] *adj* cloying; (*fig*) tiresome

empalague *etc* [empa'laɣe] *vb ver* **empalagar**

empalizada [empali'θaða] *nf* fence; (*Mil*) palisade

empalmar [empal'mar] *vt* to join, connect ■ *vi* (*dos caminos*) to meet, join

empalme [em'palme] *nm* joint, connection; (*de vías*) junction; (*de trenes*) connection

empanada [empa'naða] *nf* pie, pasty

empanar [empa'nar] *vt* (*Culin*) to cook o roll in breadcrumbs o pastry

empantanarse [empanta'narse] *vr* to get swamped; (*fig*) to get bogged down

empañarse [empa'ɲarse] *vr* (*nublarse*) to get misty, steam up

empapar [empa'par] *vt* (*mojar*) to soak, saturate; (*absorber*) to soak up, absorb; **empaparse** *vr*: **empaparse de** to soak up

empapelar [empape'lar] *vt* (*paredes*) to paper

empaque *etc* [em'pake] *vb ver* **empacar**

empaquetar [empake'tar] *vt* to pack, parcel up; (*Com*) to package

emparedado [empare'ðaðo] *nm* sandwich

emparejar [empare'xar] *vt* to pair ■ *vi* to catch up

emparentar [emparen'tar] *vi*: **~ con** to marry into

empariente *etc* [empa'rjente] *vb ver* **emparentar**

empastar [empas'tar] *vt* (*embadurnar*) to paste; (*diente*) to fill

empaste [em'paste] *nm* (*de diente*) filling

empatar [empa'tar] *vi* to draw, tie

empate [em'pate] *nm* draw, tie; **un ~ a cero** a no-score draw

empecé [empe'θe], **empecemos** *etc* [empe'θemos] *vb ver* **empezar**

empecinado, -a [empeθi'naðo, a] *adj* stubborn

empedernido, -a [empeðer'niðo, a] *adj* hard, heartless; *(fijado)* hardened, inveterate; **un fumador ~** a heavy smoker

empedrado, -a [empe'ðraðo, a] *adj* paved ■ *nm* paving

empedrar [empe'ðrar] *vt* to pave

empeine [em'peine] *nm (de pie, zapato)* instep

empellón [empe'ʎon] *nm* push, shove; **abrirse paso a empellones** to push *o* shove one's way past *o* through

empeñado, -a [empe'ɲaðo, a] *adj (persona)* determined; *(objeto)* pawned

empeñar [empe'ɲar] *vt (objeto)* to pawn, pledge; *(persona)* to compel; **empeñarse** *vr (obligarse)* to bind o.s., pledge o.s.; *(endeudarse)* to get into debt; **empeñarse en hacer** to be set on doing, be determined to do

empeño [em'peɲo] *nm (determinación)* determination; *(cosa prendada)* pledge; **casa de empeños** pawnshop; **con ~** insistently; *(con celo)* eagerly; **tener ~ en hacer algo** to be bent on doing sth

empeoramiento [empeora'mjento] *nm* worsening

empeorar [empeo'rar] *vt* to make worse, worsen ■ *vi* to get worse, deteriorate

empequeñecer [empekeɲe'θer] *vt* to dwarf; *(fig)* to belittle

empequeñezca *etc* [empeke'ɲeθka] *vb ver* **empequeñecer**

emperador [empera'ðor] *nm* emperor

emperatriz [empera'triθ] *nf* empress

emperrarse [empe'rrarse] *vr* to get stubborn; **~ en algo** to persist in sth

empezar [empe'θar] *vt, vi* to begin, start; **empezó a llover** it started to rain; **bueno, para ~** well, to start with

empiece *etc* [em'pjeθe] *vb ver* **empezar**

empiedre *etc* [em'pjeðre] *vb ver* **empedrar**

empiezo *etc* [em'pjeθo] *vb ver* **empezar**

empinado, -a [empi'naðo, a] *adj* steep

empinar [empi'nar] *vt* to raise; *(botella)* to tip up; **empinarse** *vr (persona)* to stand on tiptoe; *(animal)* to rear up; *(camino)* to climb steeply; **~ el codo** to booze *(fam)*

empingorotado, -a [empingoro'taðo, a] *adj (fam)* stuck-up

empírico, -a [em'piriko, a] *adj* empirical

emplace *etc* [em'plaθe] *vb ver* **emplazar**

emplaste [em'plaste], **emplasto** [em'plasto] *nm (Med)* plaster

emplazamiento [emplaθa'mjento] *nm* site, location; *(Jur)* summons *sg*

emplazar [empla'θar] *vt (ubicar)* to site, place, locate; *(Jur)* to summons; *(convocar)* to summon

empleado, -a [emple'aðo, a] *nm/f (gen)*

employee; *(de banco etc)* clerk; **~ público** civil servant

emplear [emple'ar] *vt (usar)* to use, employ; *(dar trabajo a)* to employ; **emplearse** *vr (conseguir trabajo)* to be employed; *(ocuparse)* to occupy o.s.; **~ mal el tiempo** to waste time; **¡te está bien empleado!** it serves you right!

empleo [em'pleo] *nm (puesto)* job; *(puestos: colectivamente)* employment; *(uso)* use, employment; **"modo de ~"** "instructions for use"

emplumar [emplu'mar] *vt (estafar)* to swindle

empobrecer [empoβre'θer] *vt* to impoverish; **empobrecerse** *vr* to become poor *o* impoverished

empobrecimiento [empoβreθi'mjento] *nm* impoverishment

empobrezca *etc* [empo'βreθka] *vb ver* **empobrecer**

empollar [empo'ʎar] *vt* to incubate; *(Escol fam)* to swot (up) ■ *vi (gallina)* to brood; *(Escol fam)* to swot

empollón, -ona [empo'ʎon, ona] *nm/f (Escol fam)* swot

empolvar [empol'βar] *vt (cara)* to powder; **empolvarse** *vr* to powder one's face; *(superficie)* to get dusty

emponzoñar [emponθo'ɲar] *vt (esp fig)* to poison

emporio [em'porjo] *nm* emporium, trading centre; *(Am: gran almacén)* department store

empotrado, -a [empo'traðo, a] *adj (armario etc)* built-in

empotrar [empo'trar] *vt* to embed; *(armario etc)* to build in

emprendedor, a [emprende'ðor, a] *adj* enterprising

emprender [empren'der] *vt* to undertake; *(empezar)* to begin, embark on; *(acometer)* to tackle, take on; **~ marcha a** to set out for

empresa [em'presa] *nf* enterprise; *(Com: sociedad)* firm, company; *(: negocio)* business; *(esp Teat)* management; **~ filial** *(Com)* affiliated company; **~ matriz** *(Com)* parent company

empresarial [empresa'rjal] *adj (función, clase)* managerial; **sector ~** business sector

empresariales [empresa'rjales] *nfpl* business studies

empresario, -a [empre'sarjo, a] *nm/f (Com)* businessman(-woman), entrepreneur; *(Tec)* manager; *(Mus: de ópera etc)* impresario; **~ de pompas fúnebres** undertaker *(Brit)*, mortician *(US)*

empréstito [em'prestito] *nm* (public) loan; *(Com)* loan capital

empujar [empu'xar] vt to push, shove

empuje [em'puxe] nm thrust; (presión) pressure; (fig) vigour, drive

empujón [empu'xon] nm push, shove; **abrirse paso a empujones** to shove one's way through

empuñadura [empuɲa'ðura] nf (de espada) hilt; (de herramienta etc) handle

empuñar [empu'ɲar] vt (asir) to grasp, take (firm) hold of; ~ **las armas** (fig) to take up arms

emulación [emula'θjon] nf emulation

emular [emu'lar] vt to emulate; (rivalizar) to rival

émulo, -a ['emulo, a] nm/f rival, competitor

emulsión [emul'sjon] nf emulsion

 PALABRA CLAVE

en [en] prep **1** (posición) in; (: sobre) on; **está en el cajón** it's in the drawer; **en Argentina/La Paz** in Argentina/La Paz; **en el colegio/la oficina** at school/the office; **en casa** at home; **está en el suelo/quinto piso** it's on the floor/the fifth floor; **en el periódico** in the paper

2 (dirección) into; **entró en el aula** she went into the classroom; **meter algo en el bolso** to put sth into one's bag; **ir de puerta en puerta** to go from door to door

3 (tiempo) in; on; **en 1605/3 semanas/invierno** in 1605/3 weeks/winter; **en (el mes de) enero** in (the month of) January; **en aquella ocasión/época** on that occasion/at that time

4 (precio) for; **lo vendió en 20 dólares** he sold it for 20 dollars

5 (diferencia) by; **reducir/aumentar en una tercera parte/un 20 por ciento** to reduce/increase by a third/20 per cent

6 (manera, forma): **en avión/autobús** by plane/bus; **escrito en inglés** written in English; **en serio** seriously; **en espiral/círculo** in a spiral/circle

7 (después de vb que indica gastar etc) on; **han cobrado demasiado en dietas** they've charged too much to expenses; **se le va la mitad del sueldo en comida** half his salary goes on food

8 (tema, ocupación): **experto en la materia** expert on the subject; **trabaja en la construcción** he works in the building industry

9 (adj + en + infin): **lento en reaccionar** slow to react

enagua [ena'ɣwa] nf, **enaguas** [ena'ɣwas] nfpl (esp Am) petticoat

enajenación [enaxena'θjon] nf, **enajenamiento** [enaxena'mjento] ■ nm alienation; (fig: distracción) absent-mindedness; (: embelesamiento) rapture, trance; ~ **mental** mental derangement

enajenar [enaxe'nar] vt to alienate; (fig) to carry away

enamorado, -a [enamo'raðo, a] adj in love ■ nm/f lover; **estar ~ (de)** to be in love (with)

enamorar [enamo'rar] vt to win the love of; **enamorarse** vr: **enamorarse (de)** to fall in love (with)

enano, -a [e'nano, a] adj tiny, dwarf ■ nm/f dwarf; (pey) runt

enarbolar [enarβo'lar] vt (bandera etc) to hoist; (espada etc) to brandish

enardecer [enarðe'θer] vt (pasiones) to fire, inflame; (persona) to fill with enthusiasm; **enardecerse** vr to get excited; **enardecerse por** to get enthusiastic about

enardezca etc [enar'deθka] vb ver **enardecer**

encabece etc [enka'βeθe] vb ver **encabezar**

encabezado [enkaβe'θaðo] nm (Com) header

encabezamiento [enkaβeθa'mjento] nm (de carta) heading; (Com) billhead, letterhead; (de periódico) headline; (preámbulo) foreword, preface; ~ **normal** (Tip etc) running head

encabezar [enkaβe'θar] vt (movimiento, revolución) to lead, head; (lista) to head; (carta) to put a heading to; (libro) to entitle

encadenar [enkaðe'nar] vt to chain (together); (poner grilletes a) to shackle

encajar [enka'xar] vt (ajustar): ~ **en** to fit (into); (meter a la fuerza) to push in; (máquina etc) to house; (partes) to join; (fam: golpe) to give, deal; (entremeter) to insert ■ vi to fit (well); (fig: corresponder a) to match; **encajarse** vr: **encajarse en un sillón** to squeeze into a chair

encaje [en'kaxe] nm (labor) lace

encajonar [enkaxo'nar] vt to box (up), put in a box

encalar [enka'lar] vt (pared) to whitewash

encallar [enka'ʎar] vi (Naut) to run aground

encaminado, -a [enkami'naðo, a] adj: **medidas encaminadas a ...** measures designed to o aimed at ...

encaminar [enkami'nar] vt to direct, send; **encaminarse** vr: **encaminarse a** to set out for; ~ **por** (expedición etc) to route via

encandilar [enkandi'lar] vt to dazzle; (persona) to daze, bewilder

encanecer [enkane'θer] vi, **encanecerse** vr (pelo) to go grey

encanezca etc [enka'neθka] vb ver **encanecer**

encantado, -a [enkan'taðo, a] *adj* delighted;
¡~! how do you do!, pleased to meet you

encantador, a [enkanta'ðor, a] *adj*
charming, lovely ∎ *nm/f* magician,
enchanter/enchantress

encantar [enkan'tar] *vt* to charm, delight;
(*cautivar*) to fascinate; (*hechizar*) to bewitch,
cast a spell on

encanto [en'kanto] *nm* (*magia*) spell, charm;
(*fig*) charm, delight; (*expresión de ternura*)
sweetheart; **como por ~** as if by magic

encapotado, -a [enkapo'taðo, a] *adj* (*cielo*)
overcast

encapricharse [enkapri'tʃarse] *vr*: **se ha
encaprichado con ir** he's taken it into
his head to go; **se ha encaprichado** he's
digging his heels in

encaramar [enkara'mar] *vt* (*subir*) to raise,
lift up; **encaramarse** *vr* (*subir*) to perch;
encaramarse a (*árbol etc*) to climb

encararse [enka'rarse] *vr*: **~ a** o **con** to
confront, come face to face with

encarcelar [enkarθe'lar] *vt* to imprison, jail

encarecer [enkare'θer] *vt* to put up the price
of ∎ *vi*, **encarecerse** *vr* to get dearer

encarecidamente [enkareθiða'mente] *adv*
earnestly

encarecimiento [enkareθi'mjento] *nm* price
increase

encarezca *etc* [enka'reθka] *vb ver* **encarecer**

encargado, -a [enkar'ɣaðo, a] *adj* in charge
∎ *nm/f* agent, representative; (*responsable*)
person in charge

encargar [enkar'ɣar] *vt* to entrust; (*Com*)
to order; (*recomendar*) to urge, recommend;
encargarse *vr*: **encargarse de** to look after,
take charge of; **~ algo a algn** to put sb in
charge of sth

encargo [en'karɣo] *nm* (*pedido*) assignment,
job; (*responsabilidad*) responsibility;
(*recomendación*) recommendation; (*Com*) order

encargue *etc* [en'karɣe] *vb ver* **encargar**

encariñarse [enkari'ɲarse] *vr*: **~ con** to grow
fond of, get attached to

encarnación [enkarna'θjon] *nf* incarnation,
embodiment

encarnado, -a [enkar'naðo, a] *adj* (*color*) red;
ponerse ~ to blush

encarnar [enkar'nar] *vt* to personify;
(*Teat: papel*) to play ∎ *vi* (*Rel etc*) to become
incarnate

encarnizado, -a [enkarni'θaðo, a] *adj* (*lucha*)
bloody, fierce

encarrilar [enkarri'lar] *vt* (*tren*) to put back
on the rails; (*fig*) to correct, put on the right
track

encasillar [enkasi'ʎar] *vt* (*Teat*) to typecast;
(*clasificar: pey*) to pigeonhole

encasquetar [enkaske'tar] *vt* (*sombrero*)
to pull down o on; **encasquetarse** *vr*:
encasquetarse el sombrero to pull one's
hat down o on; **~ algo a algn** to offload sth
onto sb

encauce *etc* [en'kauθe] *vb ver* **encauzar**

encausar [enkau'sar] *vt* to prosecute, sue

encauzar [enkau'θar] *vt* to channel; (*fig*) to
direct

encendedor [enθende'ðor] *nm* lighter

encender [enθen'der] *vt* (*con fuego*) to light;
(*incendiar*) to set fire to; (*luz, radio*) to put on,
switch on; (*Inform*) to toggle on, switch on;
(*avivar: pasiones etc*) to inflame; (*despertar:
entusiasmo*) to arouse; (*odio*) to awaken;
encenderse *vr* to catch fire; (*excitarse*) to get
excited; (*de cólera*) to flare up; (*el rostro*) to
blush

encendidamente [enθendiða'mente] *adv*
passionately

encendido, -a [enθen'diðo, a] *adj* alight;
(*aparato*) (switched) on; (*mejillas*) glowing;
(*cara: por el vino etc*) flushed; (*mirada*)
passionate ∎ *nm* (*Auto*) ignition; (*de faroles*)
lighting

encerado, -a [enθe'raðo, a] *adj* (*suelo*) waxed,
polished ∎ *nm* (*Escol*) blackboard; (*hule*)
oilcloth

encerar [enθe'rar] *vt* (*suelo*) to wax, polish

encerrar [enθe'rrar] *vt* (*confinar*) to shut in
o up; (*con llave*) to lock in o up; (*comprender,
incluir*) to include, contain; **encerrarse** *vr*
to shut o lock o.s. up o in

encerrona [enθe'rrona] *nf* trap

encestar [enθes'tar] *vi* to score a basket

encharcar [entʃar'kar] *vt* to swamp, flood;
encharcarse *vr* to become flooded

encharque *etc* [en'tʃarke] *vb ver* **encharcar**

enchufar [entʃu'far] *vt* (*Elec*) to plug in; (*Tec*)
to connect, fit together; (*Com*) to merge

enchufe [en'tʃufe] *nm* (*Elec: clavija*) plug;
(: *toma*) socket; (*de dos tubos*) joint, connection;
(*fam: influencia*) contact, connection; (*puesto*)
cushy job; **~ de clavija** jack plug; **tiene un
~ en el ministerio** he can pull strings at the
ministry

encía [en'θia] *nf* (*Anat*) gum

enciclopedia [enθiklo'peðja] *nf*
encyclopaedia

encienda *etc* [en'θjenda] *vb ver* **encender**

encierro *etc* [en'θjerro] *vb ver* **encerrar** ∎ *nm*
shutting in o up; (*calabozo*) prison; (*Agr*) pen;
(*Taur*) penning

encima [en'θima] *adv* (*sobre*) above, over;
(*además*) besides; **~ de** (*en*) on, on top of;
(*sobre*) above, over; (*además de*) besides, on top

of; **por ~ de** over; **¿llevas dinero ~?** have you (got) any money on you?; **se me vino ~** it took me by surprise

encina [en'θina] *nf* (holm) oak

encinta [en'θinta] *adj f* pregnant

enclave [en'klaβe] *nm* enclave

enclenque [en'klenke] *adj* weak, sickly

encoger [enko'xer] *vt* (*gen*) to shrink, contract; (*fig: asustar*) to scare; (: *desanimar*) to discourage; **encogerse** *vr* to shrink, contract; (*fig*) to cringe; **encogerse de hombros** to shrug one's shoulders

encoja *etc* [en'koxa] *vb ver* **encoger**

encolar [enko'lar] *vt* (*engomar*) to glue, paste; (*pegar*) to stick down

encolerice *etc* [enkole'riθe] *vb ver* **encolerizar**

encolerizar [enkoleri'θar] *vt* to anger, provoke; **encolerizarse** *vr* to get angry

encomendar [enkomen'dar] *vt* to entrust, commend; **encomendarse** *vr*: **encomendarse a** to put one's trust in

encomiar [enko'mjar] *vt* to praise, pay tribute to

encomienda *etc* [enko'mjenda] *vb ver* **encomendar ■** *nf* (*encargo*) charge, commission; (*elogio*) tribute; (*Am*) parcel, package; **~ postal** (*Am*) parcel post

encomio [en'komjo] *nm* praise, tribute

encono [en'kono] *nm* (*rencor*) rancour, spite

encontrado, -a [enkon'traðo, a] *adj* (*contrario*) contrary, conflicting; (*hostil*) hostile

encontrar [enkon'trar] *vt* (*hallar*) to find; (*inesperadamente*) to meet, run into; **encontrarse** *vr* to meet (each other); (*situarse*) to be (situated); (*persona*) to find o.s., be; (*entrar en conflicto*) to crash, collide; **encontrarse con** to meet; **encontrarse bien (de salud)** to feel well; **no se encuentra aquí en este momento** he's not in at the moment

encontronazo [enkontro'naθo] *nm* collision, crash

encorvar [enkor'βar] *vt* to curve; (*inclinar*) to bend (down); **encorvarse** *vr* to bend down, bend over

encrespado, -a [enkres'paðo, a] *adj* (*pelo*) curly; (*mar*) rough

encrespar [enkres'par] *vt* (*cabellos*) to curl; (*fig*) to anger, irritate; **encresparse** *vr* (*el mar*) to get rough; (*fig*) to get cross o irritated

encrucijada [enkruθi'xaða] *nf* crossroads *sg*; (*empalme*) junction

encuadernación [enkwaðerna'θjon] *nf* binding; (*taller*) binder's

encuadernador, a [enkwaðerna'ðor, a] *nm/f* bookbinder

encuadrar [enkwa'ðrar] *vt* (*retrato*) to frame; (*ajustar*) to fit, insert; (*encerrar*) to contain

encubierto [enku'βjerto] *pp de* **encubrir**

encubrir [enku'βrir] *vt* (*ocultar*) to hide, conceal; (*criminal*) to harbour, shelter; (*ayudar*) to be an accomplice in

encuentro *etc* [en'kwentro] *vb ver* **encontrar ■** *nm* (*de personas*) meeting; (*Auto etc*) collision, crash; (*Deporte*) match, game; (*Mil*) encounter

encuesta [en'kwesta] *nf* inquiry, investigation; (*sondeo*) public opinion poll; **~ judicial** post-mortem

encumbrado, -a [enkum'braðo, a] *adj* eminent, distinguished

encumbrar [enkum'brar] *vt* (*persona*) to exalt; **encumbrarse** *vr* (*fig*) to become conceited

endeble [en'deβle] *adj* (*argumento, excusa, persona*) weak

endémico, -a [en'demiko, a] *adj* endemic

endemoniado, -a [endemo'njaðo, a] *adj* possessed (of the devil); (*travieso*) devilish

enderece *etc* [ende'reθe] *vb ver* **enderezar**

enderezar [endere'θar] *vt* (*poner derecho*) to straighten (out); (: *verticalmente*) to set upright; (*fig*) to straighten o sort out; (*dirigir*) to direct; **enderezarse** *vr* (*persona sentada*) to sit up straight

endeudarse [endeu'ðarse] *vr* to get into debt

endiablado, -a [endja'βlaðo, a] *adj* devilish, diabolical; (*humorístico*) mischievous

endibia [en'diβja] *nf* endive

endilgar [endil'γar] *vt* (*fam*): **~ algo a algn** to lumber sb with sth; **~ un sermón a algn** to give sb a lecture

endilgue *etc* [en'dilγe] *vb ver* **endilgar**

endiñar [endi'ɲar] *vt*: **~ algo a algn** to land sth on sb

endomingarse [endomin'garse] *vr* to dress up, put on one's best clothes

endomingue *etc* [endo'minge] *vb ver* **endomingarse**

endosar [endo'sar] *vt* (*cheque etc*) to endorse

endulce *etc* [en'dulθe] *vb ver* **endulzar**

endulzar [endul'θar] *vt* to sweeten; (*suavizar*) to soften

endurecer [endure'θer] *vt* to harden; **endurecerse** *vr* to harden, grow hard

endurecido, -a [endure'θiðo, a] *adj* (*duro*) hard; (*fig*) hardy, tough; **estar ~ a algo** to be hardened o used to sth

endurezca *etc* [endu're θka] *vb ver* **endurecer**

ene. *abr* (= *enero*) Jan.

enemigo, -a [ene'miγo, a] *adj* enemy, hostile **■** *nm/f* enemy **■** *nf* enmity, hostility; **ser ~ de** (*persona*) to dislike; (*tendencia*) to be inimical to

enemistad [enemis'taδ] *nf* enmity

enemistar [enemis'tar] *vt* to make enemies of, cause a rift between; **enemistarse** *vr* to become enemies; *(amigos)* to fall out

energético, -a [ener'xetiko, a] *adj*: **política energética** energy policy

energía [ener'xia] *nf (vigor)* energy, drive; *(Tec, Elec)* energy, power; ~ **atómica/eléctrica/ eólica** atomic/electric/wind power; **energías renovables** renewable energy sources

enérgico, -a [e'nerxiko, a] *adj (gen)* energetic; *(ataque)* vigorous; *(ejercicio)* strenuous; *(medida)* bold; *(voz, modales)* forceful

energúmeno, -a [ener'ɣumeno, a] *nm/f* madman(-woman); **ponerse como un ~ con algn** to get furious with sb

enero [e'nero] *nm* January; *ver tb* **julio**

enervar [ener'βar] *vt (poner nervioso a)* to get on sb's nerves

enésimo, -a [e'nesimo, a] *adj (Mat)* nth; **por enésima vez** *(fig)* for the umpteenth time

enfadado, -a [enfa'δaδo, a] *adj* angry, annoyed

enfadar [enfa'δar] *vt* to anger, annoy; **enfadarse** *vr* to get angry *o* annoyed

enfado [en'faδo] *nm (enojo)* anger, annoyance; *(disgusto)* trouble, bother

énfasis ['enfasis] *nm* emphasis, stress; **poner énfasis en** to stress

enfático, -a [en'fatiko, a] *adj* emphatic

enfatizado, -a [enfati'θaδo, a] *adj*: **en caracteres enfatizados** *(Inform)* emphasized

enfermar [enfer'mar] *vt* to make ill ■ *vi* to fall ill, be taken ill; **su actitud me enferma** his attitude makes me sick; ~ **del corazón** to develop heart trouble

enfermedad [enferme'δaδ] *nf* illness; ~ **venérea** venereal disease

enfermera [enfer'mera] *nf ver* **enfermero**

enfermería [enferme'ria] *nf* infirmary; *(de colegio etc)* sick bay

enfermero, -a [enfer'mero, a] *nm* (male) nurse ■ *nf* nurse; **enfermera jefa** matron

enfermizo, -a [enfer'miθo, a] *adj (persona)* sickly, unhealthy; *(fig)* unhealthy

enfermo, -a [en'fermo, a] *adj* ill, sick ■ *nm/f* invalid, sick person; *(en hospital)* patient

enfilar [enfi'lar] *vt (aguja)* to thread; *(calle)* to go down

enflaquecer [enflake'θer] *vt (adelgazar)* to make thin; *(debilitar)* to weaken

enflaquezca *etc* [enfla'keθka] *vb ver* **enflaquecer**

enfocar [enfo'kar] *vt (foto etc)* to focus; *(problema etc)* to consider, look at

enfoque *etc* [en'foke] *vb ver* **enfocar** ■ *nm* focus; *(acto)* focusing; *(óptica)* approach

enfrascado, -a [enfras'kaδo, a] *adj*: **estar ~ en algo** *(fig)* to be wrapped up in sth

enfrascarse [enfras'karse] *vr*: ~ **en un libro** to bury o.s. in a book

enfrasque *etc* [en'fraske] *vb ver* **enfrascarse**

enfrentamiento [enfrenta'mjento] *nm* confrontation

enfrentar [enfren'tar] *vt (peligro)* to face (up to), confront; *(oponer)* to bring face to face; **enfrentarse** *vr (dos personas)* to face *o* confront each other; *(Deporte: dos equipos)* to meet; **enfrentarse a** *o* **con** to face up to, confront

enfrente [en'frente] *adv* opposite; ~ **de** *prep* opposite, facing; **la casa de** ~ the house opposite, the house across the street

enfriamiento [enfria'mjento] *nm* chilling, refrigeration; *(Med)* cold, chill

enfriar [enfri'ar] *vt (alimentos)* to cool, chill; *(algo caliente)* to cool down; *(habitación)* to air, freshen; *(entusiasmo)* to dampen; **enfriarse** *vr* to cool down; *(Med)* to catch a chill; *(amistad)* to cool

enfurecer [enfure'θer] *vt* to enrage, madden; **enfurecerse** *vr* to become furious, fly into a rage; *(mar)* to get rough

enfurezca *etc* [enfu'reθka] *vb ver* **enfurecer**

engalanar [engala'nar] *vt (adornar)* to adorn; *(ciudad)* to decorate; **engalanarse** *vr* to get dressed up

enganchar [engan'tʃar] *vt* to hook; *(ropa)* to hang up; *(dos vagones)* to hitch up; *(Tec)* to couple, connect; *(Mil)* to recruit; *(fam: atraer: persona)* to rope into; **engancharse** *vr (Mil)* to enlist, join up; **engancharse (a)** *(drogas)* to get hooked (on)

enganche [en'gantʃe] *nm* hook; *(Tec)* coupling, connection; *(acto)* hooking (up); *(Mil)* recruitment, enlistment; *(Am: depósito)* deposit

engañar [enga'nar] *vt* to deceive; *(estafar)* to cheat, swindle ■ *vi*: **las apariencias engañan** appearances are deceptive; **engañarse** *vr (equivocarse)* to be wrong; *(asimismo)* to deceive *o* kid o.s.; **engaña a su mujer** he's unfaithful to *o* cheats on his wife

engaño [en'gano] *nm* deceit; *(estafa)* trick, swindle; *(error)* mistake, misunderstanding; *(ilusión)* delusion

engañoso, -a [enga'noso, a] *adj (tramposo)* crooked; *(mentiroso)* dishonest, deceitful; *(aspecto)* deceptive; *(consejo)* misleading

engarce *etc* [en'garθe] *vb ver* **engarzar**

engarzar [engar'θar] *vt (joya)* to set, mount; *(fig)* to link, connect

engatusar [engatu'sar] *vt (fam)* to coax

engendrar [enxen'drar] vt to breed; (*procrear*) to beget; (*fig*) to cause, produce

engendro [en'xendro] nm (*Bio*) foetus; (*fig*) monstrosity; (: *idea*) brainchild

englobar [englo'βar] vt (*comprender*) to include, comprise; (*incluir*) to lump together

engomar [engo'mar] vt to glue, stick

engordar [engor'ðar] vt to fatten ■ vi to get fat, put on weight

engorro [en'gorro] nm bother, nuisance

engorroso, -a [engo'rroso, a] adj bothersome, trying

engranaje [engra'naxe] nm (*Auto*) gear; (*juego*) gears pl

engrandecer [engrande'θer] vt to enlarge, magnify; (*alabar*) to praise, speak highly of; (*exagerar*) to exaggerate

engrandezca etc [engran'deθka] vb ver **engrandecer**

engrasar [engra'sar] vt (*Tec: poner grasa*) to grease; (: *lubricar*) to lubricate, oil; (*manchar*) to make greasy

engrase [en'grase] nm greasing, lubrication

engreído, -a [engre'iðo, a] adj vain, conceited

engrosar [engro'sar] vt (*ensanchar*) to enlarge; (*aumentar*) to increase; (*hinchar*) to swell

engrudo [en'gruðo] nm paste

engruese etc [en'grwese] vb ver **engrosar**

engullir [engu'ʎir] vt to gobble, gulp (down)

enhebrar [ene'βrar] vt to thread

enhiesto, -a [e'njesto, a] adj (*derecho*) erect; (*bandera*) raised; (*edificio*) lofty

enhorabuena [enora'βwena] excl congratulations

enigma [e'niɣma] nm enigma; (*problema*) puzzle; (*misterio*) mystery

enigmático, -a [eniɣ'matiko, a] adj enigmatic

enjabonar [enxaβo'nar] vt to soap; (*barba*) to lather; (*fam: adular*) to soft-soap; (: *regañar*) to tick off

enjalbegar [enxalβe'ɣar] vt (*pared*) to whitewash

enjalbegue etc [enxal'βeɣe] vb ver **enjalbegar**

enjambre [en'xambre] nm swarm

enjaular [enxau'lar] vt to (put in a) cage; (*fam*) to jail, lock up

enjuagar [enxwa'ɣar] vt (*ropa*) to rinse (out)

enjuague etc [en'xwaɣe] vb ver **enjuagar** ■ nm (*Med*) mouthwash; (*de ropa*) rinse, rinsing

enjugar [enxu'ɣar] vt to wipe (off); (*lágrimas*) to dry; (*déficit*) to wipe out

enjugue etc [en'xuɣe] vb ver **enjugar**

enjuiciar [enxwi'θjar] vt (*Jur: procesar*) to prosecute, try; (*fig*) to judge

enjuto, -a [en'xuto, a] adj dry, dried up; (*fig*) lean, skinny

enlace etc [en'laθe] vb ver **enlazar** ■ nm link, connection; (*relación*) relationship; (*tb:* ~ **matrimonial**) marriage; (*de trenes*) connection; ~ **de datos** data link; ~ **sindical** shop steward; ~ **telefónico** telephone link-up

enlazar [enla'θar] vt (*unir con lazos*) to bind together; (*atar*) to tie; (*conectar*) to link, connect; (*Am*) to lasso

enlodar [enlo'ðar] vt to cover in mud; (*fig: manchar*) to stain; (: *rebajar*) to debase

enloquecer [enloke'θer] vt to drive mad ■ vi, **enloquecerse** vr to go mad

enloquezca etc [enlo'keθka] vb ver **enloquecer**

enlutado, -a [enlu'taðo, a] adj (*persona*) in mourning

enlutar [enlu'tar] vt to dress in mourning; **enlutarse** vr to go into mourning

enmarañar [enmara'ɲar] vt (*enredar*) to tangle up, entangle; (*complicar*) to complicate; (*confundir*) to confuse; **enmarañarse** vr (*enredarse*) to become entangled; (*confundirse*) to get confused

enmarcar [enmar'kar] vt (*cuadro*) to frame; (*fig*) to provide a setting for

enmarque etc [en'marke] vb ver **enmarcar**

enmascarar [enmaska'rar] vt to mask; (*intenciones*) to disguise; **enmascararse** vr to put on a mask

enmendar [enmen'dar] vt to emend, correct; (*constitución etc*) to amend; (*comportamiento*) to reform; **enmendarse** vr to reform, mend one's ways

enmienda etc [en'mjenda] vb ver **enmendar** ■ nf correction; amendment; reform

enmohecerse [enmoe'θerse] vr (*metal*) to rust, go rusty; (*muro, plantas*) to go mouldy

enmohezca etc [enmo'eθka] vb ver **enmohecerse**

enmudecer [enmuðe'θer] vt to silence ■ vi, **enmudecerse** vr (*perder el habla*) to fall silent; (*guardar silencio*) to remain silent; (*por miedo*) to be struck dumb

enmudezca etc [enmu'ðeθka] vb ver **enmudecer**

ennegrecer [enneɣre'θer] vt (*poner negro*) to blacken; (*oscurecer*) to darken; **ennegrecerse** vr to turn black; (*oscurecerse*) to get dark, darken

ennegrezca etc [enne'ɣreθka] vb ver **ennegrecer**

ennoblecer [ennoβle'θer] vt to ennoble

ennoblezca etc [enno'βleθka] vb ver **ennoblecer**

en.° *abr* (= *enero*) Jan.

enojadizo, -a [enoxa'ðiθo, a] *adj* irritable, short-tempered

enojar [eno'xar] (*esp Am*) *vt* (*encolerizar*) to anger; (*disgustar*) to annoy, upset; **enojarse** *vr* to get angry; to get annoyed

enojo [e'noxo] *nm* (*esp Am*: *cólera*) anger; (*irritación*) annoyance; **enojos** *nmpl* trials, problems

enojoso, -a [eno'xoso, a] *adj* annoying

enorgullecerse [enorɣuʎe'θerse] *vr* to be proud; **de** to pride o.s. on, be proud of

enorgullezca *etc* [enorɣu'ʎeθka] *vb ver* **enorgullecerse**

enorme [e'norme] *adj* enormous, huge; (*fig*) monstrous

enormidad [enormi'ðað] *nf* hugeness, immensity

enraice *etc* [en'raiθe] *vb ver* **enraizar**

enraizar [enrai'θar] *vi* to take root

enrarecido, -a [enrare'θiðo, a] *adj* rarefied

enredadera [enreða'ðera] *nf* (*Bot*) creeper, climbing plant

enredar [enre'ðar] *vt* (*cables, hilos etc*) to tangle (up), entangle; (*situación*) to complicate, confuse; (*meter cizaña*) to sow discord among o between; (*implicar*) to embroil, implicate; **enredarse** *vr* to get entangled, get tangled (up); (*situación*) to get complicated; (*persona*) to get embroiled

enredo [en'reðo] *nm* (*maraña*) tangle; (*confusión*) mix-up, confusion; (*intriga*) intrigue; (*apuro*) jam; (*amorío*) love affair

enrejado [enre'xaðo] *nm* grating; (*de ventana*) lattice; (*en jardín*) trellis

enrevesado, -a [enreβe'saðo, a] *adj* (*asunto*) complicated, involved

enriquecer [enrike'θer] *vt* to make rich; (*fig*) to enrich; **enriquecerse** *vr* to get rich

enriquezca *etc* [enri'keθka] *vb ver* **enriquecer**

enrojecer [enroxe'θer] *vt* to redden ■ *vi*, **enrojecerse** *vr* (*persona*) to blush

enrojezca *etc* [enro'xeθka] *vb ver* **enrojecer**

enrolar [enro'lar] *vt* (*Mil*) to enlist; (*reclutar*) to recruit; **enrolarse** *vr* (*Mil*) to join up; (*afiliarse*) to enrol, sign on

enrollar [enro'ʎar] *vt* to roll (up), wind (up); **enrollarse** *vr*: **enrollarse con algn** to get involved with sb

enroque [en'roke] *nm* (*Ajedrez*) castling

enroscar [enros'kar] *vt* (*torcer, doblar*) to twist; (*arrollar*) to coil (round), wind; (*tornillo, rosca*) to screw in; **enroscarse** *vr* to coil, wind

enrosque *etc* [en'roske] *vb ver* **enroscar**

ensalada [ensa'laða] *nf* salad; (*lío*) mix-up

ensaladilla [ensala'ðiʎa] *nf* (*tb*: **ensaladilla rusa**) ≈ Russian salad

ensalce *etc* [en'salθe] *vb ver* **ensalzar**

ensalzar [ensal'θar] *vt* (*alabar*) to praise, extol; (*exaltar*) to exalt

ensamblador [ensambla'ðor] *nm* (*Inform*) assembler

ensambladura [ensambla'ðura] *nf*, **ensamblaje** [ensam'blaxe] *nm* assembly; (*Tec*) joint

ensamblar [ensam'blar] *vt* (*montar*) to assemble; (*madera etc*) to join

ensanchar [ensan'tʃar] *vt* (*hacer más ancho*) to widen; (*agrandar*) to enlarge, expand; (*Costura*) to let out; **ensancharse** *vr* to get wider, expand; (*pey*) to give o.s. airs

ensanche [en'santʃe] *nm* (*de calle*) widening; (*de negocio*) expansion

ensangrentado, -a [ensangren'taðo, a] *adj* bloodstained, covered with blood

ensangrentar [ensangren'tar] *vt* to stain with blood

ensangriente *etc* [ensan'grjente] *vb ver* **ensangrentar**

ensañarse [ensa'ɲarse] *vr*: **~ con** to treat brutally

ensartar [ensar'tar] *vt* (*gen*) to string (together); (*carne*) to spit, skewer

ensayar [ensa'jar] *vt* to test, try (out); (*Teat*) to rehearse

ensayista [ensa'jista] *nm/f* essayist

ensayo [en'sajo] *nm* test, trial; (*Química*) experiment; (*Teat*) rehearsal; (*Deporte*) try; (*Escol, Lit*) essay; **pedido de ~** (*Com*) trial order; **~ general** (*Teat*) dress rehearsal; (*Mus*) full rehearsal

enseguida [ense'ɣiða] *adv* at once, right away; **~ termino** I've nearly finished, I shan't be long now

ensenada [ense'naða] *nf* inlet, cove

enseña [en'seɲa] *nf* ensign, standard

enseñante [ense'ɲante] *nm/f* teacher

enseñanza [ense'ɲanθa] *nf* (*educación*) education; (*acción*) teaching; (*doctrina*) teaching, doctrine; **~ primaria/secundaria/ superior** primary/secondary/higher education

enseñar [ense'ɲar] *vt* (*educar*) to teach; (*instruir*) to teach, instruct; (*mostrar, señalar*) to show

enseres [en'seres] *nmpl* belongings

ensillar [ensi'ʎar] *vt* to saddle (up)

ensimismarse [ensimis'marse] *vr* (*abstraerse*) to become lost in thought; (*estar absorto*) to be lost in thought; (*Am*) to become conceited

ensopar [enso'par] *vt* (*Am*) to soak

ensordecer [ensorðe'θer] *vt* to deafen ■ *vi* to go deaf

ensordezca *etc* [ensor'ðeθka] *vb ver* **ensordecer**

ensortijado, -a [ensorti'xaðo, a] *adj (pelo)*
curly

ensuciar [ensu'θjar] *vt (manchar)* to dirty, soil;
(fig) to defile; **ensuciarse** *vr (mancharse)* to
get dirty; *(niño)* to dirty *(o wet)* o.s.

ensueño [en'sweŋo] *nm (sueño)* dream,
fantasy; *(ilusión)* illusion; *(soñando despierto)*
daydream; **de ~** dream-like

entablado [enta'βlaðo] *nm (piso)* floorboards
pl; *(armazón)* boarding

entablar [enta'βlar] *vt (recubrir)* to board (up);
(Ajedrez, Damas) to set up; *(conversación)* to
strike up; *(Jur)* to file ■ *vi* to draw

entablillar [entaβli'ʎar] *vt (Med)* to (put in
a) splint

entallado, -a [enta'ʎaðo, a] *adj* waisted

entallar [enta'ʎar] *vt (traje)* to tailor ■ *vi*:
el traje entalla bien the suit fits well

ente ['ente] *nm (organización)* body,
organization; *(compañía)* company; *(fam:
persona)* odd character; *(ser)* being; **~ público**
(Esp) state(-owned) body

entender [enten'der] *vt (comprender)* to
understand; *(darse cuenta)* to realize; *(querer
decir)* to mean ■ *vi* to understand; *(creer)* to
think, believe ■ *nm*: **a mi ~** in my opinion;
~ de to know all about; **~ algo de** to know
a little about; **~ en** to deal with, have to do
with; **entenderse** *vr (comprenderse)* to be
understood; *(2 personas)* to get on together;
(ponerse de acuerdo) to agree, reach an
agreement; **dar a ~ que ...** to lead to believe
that ...; **entenderse mal** to get on badly;
¿entiendes? (do you) understand?

entendido, -a [enten'diðo, a] *adj
(comprendido)* understood; *(hábil)* skilled;
(inteligente) knowledgeable ■ *nm/f (experto)*
expert ■ *excl* agreed!

entendimiento [entendi'mjento] *nm
(comprensión)* understanding; *(inteligencia)*
mind, intellect; *(juicio)* judgement

enterado, -a [ente'raðo, a] *adj* well-
informed; **estar ~ de** to know about, be
aware of; **no darse por ~** to pretend not to
understand

enteramente [entera'mente] *adv* entirely,
completely

enterarse [ente'rarse] *vr*: **~ (de)** to find out
(about); **para que te enteres ...** *(fam)* for
your information ...

entereza [ente'reθa] *nf (totalidad)* entirety;
(fig: de carácter) strength of mind; *(honradez)*
integrity

enternecedor, a [enterneθe'ðor, a] *adj*
touching

enternecer [enterne'θer] *vt (ablandar)*
to soften; *(apiadar)* to touch, move;

enternecerse *vr* to be touched, be moved

enternezca *etc* [enter'neθka] *vb ver*
enternecer

entero, -a [en'tero, a] *adj (total)* whole,
entire; *(fig: recto)* honest; *(: firme)* firm,
resolute ■ *nm (Mat)* integer; *(Com: punto)*
point; *(Am: pago)* payment; **las acciones han
subido dos enteros** the shares have gone up
two points

enterrador [enterra'ðor] *nm* gravedigger

enterrar [ente'rrar] *vt* to bury; *(fig)* to forget

entibiar [enti'βjar] *vt (enfriar)* to cool;
(calentar) to warm; **entibiarse** *vr (fig)* to cool

entidad [enti'ðað] *nf (empresa)* firm,
company; *(organismo)* body; *(sociedad)* society;
(Filosofía) entity

entienda *etc* [en'tjenda] *vb ver* **entender**

entierro *etc* [en'tjerro] *vb ver* **enterrar** ■ *nm
(acción)* burial; *(funeral)* funeral

entomología [entomolo'xia] *nf* entomology

entomólogo, -a [ento'moloɣo, a] *nm/f*
entomologist

entonación [entona'θjon] *nf (Ling)*
intonation; *(fig)* conceit

entonar [ento'nar] *vt (canción)* to intone;
(colores) to tone; *(Med)* to tone up ■ *vi* to be in
tune; **entonarse** *vr (engreírse)* to give o.s. airs

entonces [en'tonθes] *adv* then, at that time;
desde ~ since then; **en aquel ~** at that time;
(pues) ~ and so; **el ~ embajador de España**
the then Spanish ambassador

entornar [entor'nar] *vt (puerta, ventana)* to
half close, leave ajar; *(los ojos)* to screw up

entorno [en'torno] *nm* setting, environment;
~ de redes *(Inform)* network environment

entorpecer [entorpe'θer] *vt (entendimiento)* to
dull; *(impedir)* to obstruct, hinder; *(: tránsito)*
to slow down, delay

entorpezca *etc* [entor'peθka] *vb ver*
entorpecer

entrado, -a [en'traðo, a] *adj*: **~ en años**
elderly; **(una vez) ~ el verano** in the
summer(time), when summer comes ■ *nf
(acción)* entry, access; *(sitio)* entrance, way
in; *(principio)* beginning; *(Com)* receipts *pl*,
takings *pl*; *(Culin)* entrée; *(Deporte)* innings
sg; *(Teat)* house, audience; *(para el cine etc)*
ticket; *(Inform)* input; *(Econ)*: **entradas**
nfpl income *sg*; **entradas brutas** gross
receipts; **entradas y salidas** *(Com)* income
and expenditure; **entrada de aire** *(Tec)*
air intake *o* inlet; **de entrada** right away;
"entrada gratis" "admission free"; **tiene
entradas** he's losing his hair

entrante [en'trante] *adj* next, coming; *(Pol)*
incoming ■ *nm* inlet; *(Culin)* starter; **mes/
año ~** next month/year

entraña [en'traɲa] *nf* (*fig: centro*) heart, core; (*raíz*) root; **entrañas** *nfpl* (*Anat*) entrails; (*fig*) heart *sg*

entrañable [entra'ɲaβle] *adj* (*persona, lugar*) dear; (*relación*) close; (*acto*) intimate

entrañar [entra'ɲar] *vt* to entail

entrar [en'trar] *vt* (*introducir*) to bring in; (*persona*) to show in; (*Inform*) to input ■ *vi* (*meterse*) to go o come in, enter; (*comenzar*): ~ **diciendo** to begin by saying; **entré en** o **a** (*Am*) **la casa** I went into the house; **le entraron ganas de reír** he felt a sudden urge to laugh; **no me entra** I can't get the hang of it

entre ['entre] *prep* (*dos*) between; (*en medio de*) among(st); (*por*): **se abrieron paso ~ la multitud** they forced their way through the crowd; **~ una cosa y otra** what with one thing and another; **~ más estudia más aprende** (*Am*) the more he studies the more he learns

entreabierto [entrea'βjerto] *pp de* **entreabrir**

entreabrir [entrea'βrir] *vt* to half-open, open halfway

entreacto [entre'akto] *nm* interval

entrecano, -a [entre'kano, a] *adj* greying; **ser ~** (*persona*) to be going grey

entrecejo [entre'θexo] *nm*: **fruncir el ~** to frown

entrechocar [entret∫o'kar] *vi* (*dientes*) to chatter

entrechoque *etc* [entre't∫oke] *vb ver* **entrechocar**

entrecomillado, -a [entrekomi'ʎaðo, a] *adj* in inverted commas

entrecortado, -a [entrekor'taðo, a] *adj* (*respiración*) laboured, difficult; (*habla*) faltering

entrecot [entre'ko(t)] *nm* (*Culin*) sirloin steak

entrecruce *etc* [entre'kruθe] *vb ver* **entrecruzarse**

entrecruzarse [entrekru'θarse] *vr* (*Bio*) to interbreed

entredicho [entre'ðit∫o] *nm* (*Jur*) injunction; **poner en ~** to cast doubt on; **estar en ~** to be in doubt

entrega [en'treɣa] *nf* (*de mercancías*) delivery; (*de premios*) presentation; (*de novela etc*) instalment; **"~ a domicilio"** "door-to-door delivery service"

entregar [entre'ɣar] *vt* (*dar*) to hand (over), deliver; (*ejercicios*) to hand in; **entregarse** *vr* (*rendirse*) to surrender, give in, submit; **entregarse a** (*dedicarse*) to devote o.s. to; **a ~** (*Com*) to be supplied

entregue *etc* [en'treɣe] *vb ver* **entregar**

entrelace *etc* [entre'laθe] *vb ver* **entrelazar**

entrelazar [entrela'θar] *vt* to entwine

entremedias [entre'meðjas] *adv* (*en medio*) in between, halfway

entremeses [entre'meses] *nmpl* hors d'œuvres

entremeter [entreme'ter] *vt* to insert, put in; **entremeterse** *vr* to meddle, interfere

entremetido, -a [entreme'tiðo, a] *adj* meddling, interfering

entremezclar [entreme0'klar] *vt*, **entremezclarse** *vr* to intermingle

entrenador, a [entrena'ðor, a] *nm/f* trainer, coach

entrenamiento [entrena'mjento] *nm* training

entrenar [entre'nar] *vt* (*Deporte*) to train; (*caballo*) to exercise ■ *vi*, **entrenarse** *vr* to train

entrepierna [entre'pjerna] *nf* (*tb:* **entrepiernas**) crotch, crutch

entresacar [entresa'kar] *vt* to pick out, select

entresaque *etc* [entre'sake] *vb ver* **entresacar**

entresuelo [entre'swelo] *nm* mezzanine, entresol; (*Teat*) dress o first circle

entretanto [entre'tanto] *adv* meanwhile, meantime

entretejer [entrete'xer] *vt* to interweave

entretela [entre'tela] *nf* (*de ropa*) interlining; **entretelas** *nfpl* heartstrings

entretención [entreten'sjon] *nf* (*Am*) entertainment

entretendré *etc* [entreten'dre] *vb ver* **entretener**

entretener [entrete'ner] *vt* (*divertir*) to entertain, amuse; (*detener*) to hold up, delay; (*mantener*) to maintain; **entretenerse** *vr* (*divertirse*) to amuse o.s.; (*retrasarse*) to delay, linger; **no le entretengo más** I won't keep you any longer

entretenga *etc* [entre'tenga] *vb ver* **entretener**

entretenido, -a [entrete'niðo, a] *adj* entertaining, amusing

entretenimiento [entreteni'mjento] *nm* entertainment, amusement; (*mantenimiento*) upkeep, maintenance

entretiempo [entre'tjempo] *nm*: **ropa de ~** clothes for spring and autumn

entretiene *etc* [entre'tjene], **entretuve** *etc* [entre'tuβe] *vb ver* **entretener**

entreveía *etc* [entreβe'ia] *vb ver* **entrever**

entrever [entre'βer] *vt* to glimpse, catch a glimpse of

entrevista [entre'βista] *nf* interview

entrevistar [entreβis'tar] *vt* to interview; **entrevistarse** *vr*: **entrevistarse con** to have an interview with, see; **el ministro**

155

se entrevistó con el Rey ayer the minister had an audience with the King yesterday

entrevisto [entre'βisto] pp de **entrever**

entristecer [entriste'θer] vt to sadden, grieve; **entristecerse** vr to grow sad

entristezca etc [entris'teθka] vb ver **entristecer**

entrometerse [entrome'terse] vr: ~ **(en)** to interfere (in o with)

entrometido, -a [entrome'tiðo, a] adj interfering, meddlesome

entroncar [entron'kar] vi to be connected o related

entronque etc [en'tronke] vb ver **entroncar**

entuerto [en'twerto] nm wrong, injustice; **entuertos** nmpl (Med) afterpains

entumecer [entume'θer] vt to numb, benumb; **entumecerse** vr (por el frío) to go o become numb

entumecido, -a [entume'θiðo, a] adj numb, stiff

entumezca etc [entu'meθka] vb ver **entumecer**

enturbiar [entur'βjar] vt (el agua) to make cloudy; (fig) to confuse; **enturbiarse** vr (oscurecerse) to become cloudy; (fig) to get confused, become obscure

entusiasmar [entusjas'mar] vt to excite, fill with enthusiasm; (gustar mucho) to delight; **entusiasmarse** vr: **entusiasmarse con** o **por** to get enthusiastic o excited about

entusiasmo [entu'sjasmo] nm enthusiasm; (excitación) excitement

entusiasta [entu'sjasta] adj enthusiastic ■ nm/f enthusiast

enumerar [enume'rar] vt to enumerate

enunciación [enunθja'θjon] nf, **enunciado** [enun'θjaðo] nm enunciation; (declaración) declaration, statement

enunciar [enun'θjar] vt to enunciate; to declare, state

envainar [embai'nar] vt to sheathe

envalentonar [embalento'nar] vt to give courage to; **envalentonarse** vr (pey: jactarse) to boast, brag

envanecer [embane'θer] vt to make conceited; **envanecerse** vr to grow conceited

envanezca etc [emba'neθka] vb ver **envanecer**

envasar [emba'sar] vt (empaquetar) to pack, wrap; (enfrascar) to bottle; (enlatar) to can; (embolsar) to pocket

envase [em'base] nm packing, wrapping; bottling; canning; pocketing; (recipiente) container; (paquete) package; (botella) bottle; (lata) tin (Brit), can

envejecer [embexe'θer] vt to make old, age ■ vi, **envejecerse** vr (volverse viejo) to grow old; (parecer viejo) to age

envejecido, -a [embexe'θiðo, a] adj old, aged; (de aspecto) old-looking

envejezca etc [embe'xeθka] vb ver **envejecer**

envenenar [embene'nar] vt to poison; (fig) to embitter

envergadura [emberɣa'ðura] nf (expansión) expanse; (Naut) breadth; (fig) scope; **un programa de gran** ~ a wide-ranging programme

envés [em'bes] nm (de tela) back, wrong side

enviado, -a [em'bjaðo, a] nm/f (Pol) envoy; ~ **especial** (de periódico, TV) special correspondent

enviar [em'bjar] vt to send; ~ **un mensaje a algn** (por móvil) to text sb, send sb a text message

enviciar [embi'θjar] vt to corrupt ■ vi (trabajo etc) to be addictive; **enviciarse** vr: **enviciarse (con** o **en)** to get addicted (to)

envidia [em'biðja] nf envy; **tener** ~ **a** to envy, be jealous of

envidiar [embi'ðjar] vt (desear) to envy; (tener celos de) to be jealous of

envidioso, -a [embi'ðjoso, a] adj envious, jealous

envío [em'bio] nm (acción) sending; (de mercancías) consignment; (de dinero) remittance; (en barco) shipment; **gastos de** ~ postage and packing; ~ **contra reembolso** COD shipment

enviudar [embju'ðar] vi to be widowed

envoltura [embol'tura] nf (cobertura) cover; (embalaje) wrapper, wrapping

envolver [embol'βer] vt to wrap (up); (cubrir) to cover; (enemigo) to surround; (implicar) to involve, implicate

envuelto [em'bwelto], **envuelva** etc [em'bwelβa] vb ver **envolver**

enyesar [enje'sar] vt (pared) to plaster; (Med) to put in plaster

enzarzarse [enθar'θarse] vr: ~ **en algo** to get mixed up in sth

epa ['epa], **épale** ['epale] (Am) excl hey!, wow!

E.P.D. abr (= en paz descanse) RIP

epicentro [epi'θentro] nm epicentre

épico, -a ['epiko, a] adj epic ■ nf epic (poetry)

epidemia [epi'ðemja] nf epidemic

epidémico, -a [epi'ðemiko, a] adj epidemic

epidermis [epi'ðermis] nf epidermis

epifanía [epifa'nia] nf Epiphany

epilepsia [epi'lepsja] nf epilepsy

epiléptico, -a [epi'leptiko, a] adj, nm/f epileptic

epílogo [e'piloɣo] nm epilogue

episcopado [episko'paðo] *nm* (*cargo*) bishopric; (*obispos*) bishops *pl* (*collectively*)

episodio [epi'soðjo] *nm* episode; (*suceso*) incident

epístola [e'pistola] *nf* epistle

epitafio [epi'tafjo] *nm* epitaph

epíteto [e'piteto] *nm* epithet

época ['epoka] *nf* period, time; (*temporada*) season; (*Historia*) age, epoch; **hacer ~** to be epoch-making

equidad [eki'ðað] *nf* equity, fairness

equilibrar [ekili'βrar] *vt* to balance

equilibrio [eki'liβrjo] *nm* balance, equilibrium; **~ político** balance of power

equilibrista [ekili'βrista] *nm/f* (*funámbulo*) tightrope walker; (*acróbata*) acrobat

equinoccio [eki'nokθjo] *nm* equinox

equipaje [eki'paxe] *nm* luggage (*Brit*), baggage (*US*); (*avíos*) equipment, kit; **~ de mano** hand luggage; **hacer el ~** to pack

equipar [eki'par] *vt* (*proveer*) to equip

equiparar [ekipa'rar] *vt* (*igualar*) to put on the same level; (*comparar*): **~ con** to compare with; **equipararse** *vr*: **equipararse con** to be on a level with

equipo [e'kipo] *nm* (*conjunto de cosas*) equipment; (*Deporte, grupo*) team; (*de obreros*) shift; (*de máquinas*) plant; (*turbinas etc*) set; **~ de caza** hunting gear; **~ físico** (*Inform*) hardware; **~ médico** medical team; **~ de música** music centre

equis ['ekis] *nf* (the letter) X

equitación [ekita'θjon] *nf* (*acto*) riding; (*arte*) horsemanship

equitativo, -a [ekita'tiβo, a] *adj* equitable, fair

equivaldré *etc* [ekiβal'dre] *vb ver* **equivaler**

equivalencia [ekiβa'lenθja] *nf* equivalence

equivalente [ekiβa'lente] *adj, nm* equivalent

equivaler [ekiβa'ler] *vi*: **~ a** to be equivalent *o* equal to; (*en rango*) to rank as

equivalga *etc* [eki'βalɣa] *vb ver* **equivaler**

equivocación [ekiβoka'θjon] *nf* mistake, error; (*malentendido*) misunderstanding

equivocado, -a [ekiβo'kaðo, a] *adj* wrong, mistaken

equivocarse [ekiβo'karse] *vr* to be wrong, make a mistake; **~ de camino** to take the wrong road

equívoco, -a [e'kiβoko, a] *adj* (*dudoso*) suspect; (*ambiguo*) ambiguous ■ *nm* ambiguity; (*malentendido*) misunderstanding

equivoque *etc* [eki'βoke] *vb ver* **equivocarse**

era ['era] *vb ver* **ser** ■ *nf* era, age; (*Agr*) threshing floor

erais ['erais], **éramos** ['eramos], **eran** ['eran] *vb ver* **ser**

erario [e'rarjo] *nm* exchequer, treasury

eras ['eras], **eres** ['eres] *vb ver* **ser**

erección [erek'θjon] *nf* erection

ergonomía [erɣono'mia] *nf* ergonomics *sg*, human engineering

erguir [er'ɣir] *vt* to raise, lift; (*poner derecho*) to straighten; **erguirse** *vr* to straighten up

erice *etc* [e'riθe] *vb ver* **erizarse**

erigir [eri'xir] *vt* to erect, build; **erigirse** *vr*: **erigirse en** to set o.s. up as

erija *etc* [e'rixa] *vb ver* **erigir**

erizado, -a [eri'θaðo, a] *adj* bristly

erizarse [eri'θarse] *vr* (*pelo: de perro*) to bristle; (: *de persona*) to stand on end

erizo [e'riθo] *nm* hedgehog; **~ de mar** sea urchin

ermita [er'mita] *nf* hermitage

ermitaño, -a [ermi'taɲo, a] *nm/f* hermit

erosión [ero'sjon] *nf* erosion

erosionar [erosjo'nar] *vt* to erode

erótico, -a [e'rotiko, a] *adj* erotic

erotismo [ero'tismo] *nm* eroticism

erradicar [erraði'kar] *vt* to eradicate

erradique *etc* [erra'ðike] *vb ver* **erradicar**

errado, -a [e'rraðo, a] *adj* mistaken, wrong

errante [e'rrante] *adj* wandering, errant

errar [e'rrar] *vi* (*vagar*) to wander, roam; (*equivocarse*) to be mistaken ■ *vt*: **~ el camino** to take the wrong road; **~ el tiro** to miss

errata [e'rrata] *nf* misprint

erre ['erre] *nf* (the letter) R; **~ que ~** stubbornly

erróneo, -a [e'rroneo, a] *adj* (*equivocado*) wrong, mistaken; (*falso*) false, untrue

error [e'rror] *nm* error, mistake; (*Inform*) bug; **~ de imprenta** misprint; **~ de lectura/escritura** (*Inform*) read/write error; **~ sintáctico** syntax error; **~ judicial** miscarriage of justice

Ertzaintza [er'tʃantʃa] *nf* Basque police; *ver tb* **policía**

eructar [eruk'tar] *vt* to belch, burp

eructo [e'rukto] *nm* belch

erudición [eruði'θjon] *nf* erudition, learning

erudito, -a [eru'ðito, a] *adj* erudite, learned ■ *nm/f* scholar; **los eruditos en esta materia** the experts in this field

erupción [erup'θjon] *nf* eruption; (*Med*) rash; (*de violencia*) outbreak; (*de ira*) outburst

es [es] *vb ver* **ser**

E/S *abr* (*Inform*: = *entrada/salida*) I/O

esa ['esa], **esas** ['esas] *adj demostrativo ver* **ese**

ésa ['esa], **ésas** ['esas] *pron ver* **ése**

esbelto, -a [es'βelto, a] *adj* slim, slender

esbirro [es'βirro] *nm* henchman

esbozar [esβo'θar] *vt* to sketch, outline

esbozo [es'βoθo] *nm* sketch, outline

157

escabeche [eska'βetʃe] *nm* brine; *(de aceitunas etc)* pickle; **en ~** pickled

escabechina [eskaβe'tʃina] *nf* (*batalla*) massacre; **hacer una ~** (*Escol*) to fail a lot of students

escabroso, -a [eska'βroso, a] *adj* (*accidentado*) rough, uneven; (*fig*) tough, difficult; (: *atrevido*) risqué

escabullirse [eskaβu'ʎirse] *vr* to slip away; (*largarse*) to clear out

escacharrar [eskatʃa'rrar] *vt* (*fam*) to break; **escacharrarse** *vr* to get broken

escafandra [eska'fandra] *nf* (*buzo*) diving suit; (*escafandra espacial*) spacesuit

escala [es'kala] *nf* (*proporción, Mus*) scale; (*de mano*) ladder; (*Aviat*) stopover; (*de colores etc*) range; **~ de tiempo** time scale; **~ de sueldos** salary scale; **una investigación a ~ nacional** a nationwide inquiry; **reproducir a ~** to reproduce to scale; **hacer ~ en** to stop off o over at

escalada [eska'laða] *nf* (*de montaña*) climb; (*de pared*) scaling

escalafón [eskala'fon] *nm* salary o wage scale

escalar [eska'lar] *vt* to climb, scale ■ *vi* (*Mil, Pol*) to escalate

escaldar [eskal'dar] *vt* (*quemar*) to scald; (*escarmentar*) to teach a lesson

escalera [eska'lera] *nf* stairs *pl*, staircase; (*escala*) ladder; (*Naipes*) run; (*de camión*) tailboard; **~ mecánica** escalator; **~ de caracol** spiral staircase; **~ de incendios** fire escape

escalerilla [eskale'riʎa] *nf* (*de avión*) steps *pl*

escalfar [eskal'far] *vt* (*huevos*) to poach

escalinata [eskali'nata] *nf* staircase

escalofriante [eskalo'frjante] *adj* chilling

escalofrío [eskalo'frio] *nm* (*Med*) chill; **escalofríos** *nmpl* (*fig*) shivers

escalón [eska'lon] *nm* step, stair; (*de escalera*) rung; (*fig: paso*) step; (*al éxito*) ladder

escalonar [eskalo'nar] *vt* to spread out; (*tierra*) to terrace; (*horas de trabajo*) to stagger

escalope [eska'lope] *nm* (*Culin*) escalope

escama [es'kama] *nf* (*de pez, serpiente*) scale; (*de jabón*) flake; (*fig*) resentment

escamar [eska'mar] *vt* (*pez*) to scale; (*producir recelo*) to make wary

escamotear [eskamote'ar] *vt* (*fam: robar*) to lift, swipe; (*hacer desaparecer*) to make disappear

escampar [eskam'par] *vb impersonal* to stop raining

escanciar [eskan'θjar] *vt* (*vino*) to pour (out)

escandalice *etc* [eskanda'liθe] *vb ver* **escandalizar**

escandalizar [eskandali'θar] *vt* to scandalize, shock; **escandalizarse** *vr* to be shocked; (*ofenderse*) to be offended

escándalo [es'kandalo] *nm* scandal; (*alboroto, tumulto*) row, uproar; **armar un ~** to make a scene; **¡es un ~!** it's outrageous!

escandaloso, -a [eskanda'loso, a] *adj* scandalous, shocking; (*risa*) hearty; (*niño*) noisy

Escandinavia [eskandi'naβja] *nf* Scandinavia

escandinavo, -a [eskandi'naβo, a] *adj, nm/f* Scandinavian

escaneo [es'kaneo] *nm* scanning

escáner [es'kaner] *nm* scanner

escaño [es'kaɲo] *nm* bench; (*Pol*) seat

escapada [eska'paða] *nf* (*huida*) escape, flight; (*Deporte*) breakaway; (*viaje*) quick trip

escapar [eska'par] *vi* (*gen*) to escape, run away; (*Deporte*) to break away; **escaparse** *vr* to escape, get away; (*agua, gas, noticias*) to leak (out); **se me escapa su nombre** his name escapes me

escaparate [eskapa'rate] *nm* shop window; (*Com*) showcase; **ir de escaparates** to go window shopping

escapatoria [eskapa'torja] *nf*: **no tener ~** (*fig*) to have no way out

escape [es'kape] *nm* (*huida*) escape; (*de agua, gas*) leak; (*de motor*) exhaust; **salir a ~** to rush out

escapismo [eska'pismo] *nm* escapism

escaquearse [eskake'arse] *vr* (*fam*) to duck out

escarabajo [eskara'βaxo] *nm* beetle

escaramuza [eskara'muθa] *nf* skirmish; (*fig*) brush

escarbar [eskar'βar] *vt* (*gallina*) to scratch; (*fig*) to inquire into, investigate

escarceos [eskar'θeos] *nmpl*: **en sus ~ con la política** in his occasional forays into politics; **~ amorosos** flirtations

escarcha [es'kartʃa] *nf* frost

escarlata [eskar'lata] *adj inv* scarlet

escarlatina [eskarla'tina] *nf* scarlet fever

escarmentar [eskarmen'tar] *vt* to punish severely ■ *vi* to learn one's lesson; **¡para que escarmientes!** that'll teach you!

escarmiento *etc* [eskar'mjento] *vb ver* **escarmentar** ■ *nm* (*ejemplo*) lesson; (*castigo*) punishment

escarnio [es'karnjo] *nm* mockery; (*injuria*) insult

escarola [eska'rola] *nf* (*Bot*) endive

escarpado, -a [eskar'paðo, a] *adj* (*pendiente*) sheer, steep; (*rocas*) craggy

escasamente [eskasa'mente] *adv* (*insuficientemente*) scantily; (*apenas*) scarcely

escasear [eskase'ar] vi to be scarce

escasez [eska'seθ] nf (falta) shortage, scarcity; (pobreza) poverty; **vivir con** ~ to live on the breadline

escaso, -a [es'kaso, a] adj (poco) scarce; (raro) rare; (ralo) thin, sparse; (limitado) limited; (recursos) scanty; (público) sparse; (posibilidad) slim; (visibilidad) poor

escatimar [eskati'mar] vt (limitar) to skimp (on), be sparing with; **no ~ esfuerzos (para)** to spare no effort (to)

escayola [eska'jola] nf plaster

escayolar [eskajo'lar] vt to put in plaster

escena [es'θena] nf scene; (decorado) scenery; (escenario) stage; **poner en** ~ to put on

escenario [esθe'narjo] nm (Teat) stage; (Cine) set; (fig) scene; **el ~ del crimen** the scene of the crime; **el ~ político** the political scene

escenografía [esθenoɣra'fia] nf set o stage design

escepticismo [esθepti'θismo] nm scepticism

escéptico, -a [es'θeptiko, a] adj sceptical ■ nm/f sceptic

escindir [esθin'dir] vt to split; **escindirse** vr (facción) to split off; **escindirse en** to split into

escisión [esθi'sjon] nf (Med) excision; (fig, Pol) split; ~ **nuclear** nuclear fission

esclarecer [esklare'θer] vt (iluminar) to light up, illuminate; (misterio, problema) to shed light on

esclarezca etc [eskla'reθka] vb ver **esclarecer**

esclavice etc [eskla'βiθe] vb ver **esclavizar**

esclavitud [esklaβi'tuð] nf slavery

esclavizar [esklaβi'θar] vt to enslave

esclavo, -a [es'klaβo, a] nm/f slave

esclusa [es'klusa] nf (de canal) lock; (compuerta) floodgate

escoba [es'koβa] nf broom; **pasar la** ~ to sweep up

escobazo [esko'βaθo] nm (golpe) blow with a broom; **echar a algn a escobazos** to kick sb out

escobilla [esko'βiʎa] nf brush

escocer [esko'θer] vi to burn, sting; **escocerse** vr to chafe, get chafed

escocés, -esa [esko'θes, esa] adj Scottish; (whisky) Scotch ■ nm/f Scotsman(-woman), Scot ■ nm (Ling) Scots sg; **tela escocesa** tartan

Escocia [es'koθja] nf Scotland

escoger [esko'xer] vt to choose, pick, select

escogido, -a [esko'xiðo, a] adj chosen, selected; (calidad) choice, select; (persona): **ser muy** ~ to be very fussy

escoja etc [es'koxa] vb ver **escoger**

escolar [esko'lar] adj school cpd ■ nm/f schoolboy(-girl), pupil

escolaridad [eskolari'ðað] nf schooling; **libro de** ~ school record

escolarización [eskolariθa'θjon] nf: ~ **obligatoria** compulsory education

escolarizado, -a [eskolari'θaðo, a] adj, nm/f: **los escolarizados** those in o attending school

escollo [es'koʎo] nm (arrecife) reef, rock; (fig) pitfall

escolta [es'kolta] nf escort

escoltar [eskol'tar] vt to escort; (proteger) to guard

escombros [es'kombros] nmpl (basura) rubbish sg; (restos) debris sg

esconder [eskon'der] vt to hide, conceal; **esconderse** vr to hide

escondidas [eskon'diðas] nfpl (Am) hide-and-seek sg; **a** ~ secretly; **hacer algo a** ~ **de algn** to do sth behind sb's back

escondite [eskon'dite] nm hiding place; (juego) hide-and-seek

escondrijo [eskon'drixo] nm hiding place, hideout

escopeta [esko'peta] nf shotgun; ~ **de aire comprimido** air gun

escoria [es'korja] nf (desecho mineral) slag; (fig) scum, dregs pl

Escorpio [es'korpjo] nm (Astro) Scorpio

escorpión [eskor'pjon] nm scorpion

escotado, -a [esko'taðo, a] adj low-cut

escotar [esko'tar] vt (vestido: ajustar) to cut to fit; (cuello) to cut low

escote [es'kote] nm (de vestido) low neck; **pagar a** ~ to share the expenses

escotilla [esko'tiʎa] nf (Naut) hatchway

escotillón [eskoti'ʎon] nm trapdoor

escozor [esko'θor] nm (dolor) sting(ing)

escribano, -a [eskri'βano, a], **escribiente** [eskri'βjente] nm/f clerk; (secretario judicial) court o lawyer's clerk

escribir [eskri'βir] vt, vi to write; ~ **a máquina** to type; **¿cómo se escribe?** how do you spell it?

escrito, -a [es'krito, a] pp de **escribir** ■ adj written, in writing; (examen) written ■ nm (documento) document; (manuscrito) text, manuscript; **por** ~ in writing

escritor, a [eskri'tor, a] nm/f writer

escritorio [eskri'torjo] nm desk; (oficina) office

escritura [eskri'tura] nf (acción) writing; (caligrafía) (hand)writing; (Jur: documento) deed; (Com) indenture; ~ **de propiedad** title deed; **Sagrada E~** (Holy) Scripture; ~ **social** articles pl of association

escroto [es'kroto] nm scrotum

escrúpulo [es'krupulo] nm scruple; (minuciosidad) scrupulousness

escrupuloso, -a [eskrupu'loso, a] *adj*
scrupulous

escrutar [eskru'tar] *vt* to scrutinize,
examine; *(votos)* to count

escrutinio [eskru'tinjo] *nm (examen atento)*
scrutiny; *(Pol: recuento de votos)* count(ing)

escuadra [es'kwaðra] *nf (Tec)* square; *(Mil etc)*
squad; *(Naut)* squadron; *(de coches etc)* fleet

escuadrilla [eskwa'ðriʎa] *nf (de aviones)*
squadron

escuadrón [eskwa'ðron] *nm* squadron

escuálido, -a [es'kwaliðo, a] *adj* skinny,
scraggy; *(sucio)* squalid

escucha [es'kutʃa] *nf (acción)* listening ■ *nm*
(Telec: sistema) monitor; *(oyente)* listener;
estar a la ~ to listen in; **estar de ~** to spy;
escuchas telefónicas (phone)tapping *sg*

escuchar [esku'tʃar] *vt* to listen to; *(consejo)*
to heed; *(esp Am: oír)* to hear ■ *vi* to listen;
escucharse *vr:* **se escucha muy mal** *(Telec)*
it's a very bad line

escudarse [esku'ðarse] *vr:* **~ en** *(fig)* to hide
behind

escudería [eskuðe'ria] *nf:* **la ~ Ferrari** the
Ferrari team

escudero [esku'ðero] *nm* squire

escudilla [esku'ðiʎa] *nf* bowl, basin

escudo [es'kuðo] *nm* shield; **~ de armas** coat
of arms

escudriñar [eskuðri'ɲar] *vt (examinar)* to
investigate, scrutinize; *(mirar de lejos)* to scan

escuece *etc* [es'kweθe] *vb ver* **escocer**

escuela [es'kwela] *nf (tb fig)* school; **~ normal**
teacher training college; **~ técnica superior**
*university offering five-year courses in engineering
and technical subjects;* **~ universitaria** *university
offering three-year diploma courses;* **~ de párvulos**
kindergarten; *ver tb* **colegio**

escueto, -a [es'kweto, a] *adj* plain; *(estilo)*
simple; *(explicación)* concise

escueza *etc* [es'kweθa] *vb ver* **escocer**

escuincle [es'kwinkle] *nm (Am fam)* kid

esculpir [eskul'pir] *vt* to sculpt; *(grabar)* to
engrave; *(tallar)* to carve

escultor, a [eskul'tor, a] *nm/f* sculptor

escultura [eskul'tura] *nf* sculpture

escupidera [eskupi'ðera] *nf* spittoon

escupir [esku'pir] *vt* to spit (out) ■ *vi* to spit

escupitajo [eskupi'taxo] *nm (fam)* gob of spit

escurreplatos [eskurre'platos] *nm inv* plate
rack

escurridizo, -a [eskurri'ðiθo, a] *adj* slippery

escurrir [esku'rrir] *vt (ropa)* to wring out;
(verduras, platos) to drain ■ *vi (los líquidos)*
to drip; **escurrirse** *vr (secarse)* to drain;
(resbalarse) to slip, slide; *(escaparse)* to slip away

ese¹ ['ese] *nf* (the letter) S; **hacer eses**

(carretera) to zigzag; *(borracho)* to reel about

ese² ['ese], **esa** ['esa], **esos** ['esos], **esas**
['esas] *adj demostrativo* that *sg*, those *pl*

ése ['ese], **ésa** ['esa], **ésos** ['esos], **ésas**
['esas] *pron* that (one) *sg*, those (ones) *pl*; **ése
... éste ...** the former ... the latter ...; **¡no me
vengas con ésas!** don't give me any more of
that nonsense!

esencia [e'senθja] *nf* essence

esencial [esen'θjal] *adj* essential; *(principal)*
chief; **lo ~** the main thing

esfera [es'fera] *nf* sphere; *(de reloj)* face; **~ de
acción** scope; **~ terrestre** globe

esférico, -a [es'feriko, a] *adj* spherical

esfinge [es'finxe] *nf* sphinx

esforcé [esfor'θe], **esforcemos** *etc*
[esfor'θemos] *vb ver* **esforzarse**

esforzado, -a [esfor'θaðo, a] *adj (enérgico)*
energetic, vigorous

esforzarse [esfor'θarse] *vr* to exert o.s., make
an effort

esfuerce *etc* [es'fwerθe] *vb ver* **esforzarse**

esfuerzo *etc* [es'fwerθo] *vb ver* **esforzarse**
■ *nm* effort; **sin ~** effortlessly

esfumarse [esfu'marse] *vr (apoyo, esperanzas)*
to fade away; *(persona)* to vanish

esgrima [es'ɣrima] *nf* fencing

esgrimidor [esɣrimi'ðor] *nm* fencer

esgrimir [esɣri'mir] *vt (arma)* to brandish;
(argumento) to use ■ *vi* to fence

esguince [es'ɣinθe] *nm (Med)* sprain

eslabón [esla'βon] *nm* link; **~ perdido** *(Bio,
fig)* missing link

eslabonar [eslaβo'nar] *vt* to link, connect

eslálom [es'lalom] *nm* slalom

eslavo, -a [es'laβo, a] *adj* Slav, Slavonic
■ *nm/f* Slav ■ *nm (Ling)* Slavonic

eslogan [es'loɣan] *nm (pl* **eslogans***)* slogan

eslora [es'lora] *nf (Naut)* length

eslovaco, -a [eslo'βako, a] *adj, nm/f* Slovak,
Slovakian ■ *nm (Ling)* Slovak, Slovakian

Eslovaquia [eslo'βakja] *nf* Slovakia

Eslovenia [eslo'βenja] *nf* Slovenia

esloveno, -a [eslo'βeno, a] *adj, nm/f* Slovene,
Slovenian ■ *nm (Ling)* Slovene, Slovenian

esmaltar [esmal'tar] *vt* to enamel

esmalte [es'malte] *nm* enamel; **~ de uñas**
nail varnish *o* polish

esmerado, -a [esme'raðo, a] *adj* careful, neat

esmeralda [esme'ralda] *nf* emerald

esmerarse [esme'rarse] *vr (aplicarse)* to take
great pains, exercise great care; *(afanarse)* to
work hard; *(hacer lo mejor)* to do one's best

esmero [es'mero] *nm* (great) care

esmirriado, -a [esmi'rrjaðo, a] *adj* puny

esmoquin [es'mokin] *nm* dinner jacket (Brit),
tuxedo (US)

esnob [es'nob] *adj inv (persona)* snobbish; *(coche etc)* posh ■ *nm/f* snob

esnobismo [esno'βismo] *nm* snobbery

eso ['eso] *pron* that, that thing *o* matter; **~ de su coche** that business about his car; **~ de ir al cine** all that about going to the cinema; **a ~ de las cinco** at about five o'clock; **en ~** thereupon, at that point; **por ~** therefore; **~ es** that's it; **nada de ~** far from it; **¡~ sí que es vida!** now this is really living!; **por ~ te lo dije** that's why I told you; **y ~ que llovía** in spite of the fact it was raining

esófago [e'sofaγo] *nm (Anat)* oesophagus

esos ['esos] *adj demostrativo ver* **ese**

ésos ['esos] *pron ver* **ése**

esotérico, -a [eso'teriko, a] *adj* esoteric

esp. *abr (= español)* Sp., Span.; = **especialmente**

espabilado, -a [espaβi'laðo, a] *adj* quick-witted

espabilar [espaβi'lar] *vt,* **espabilarse** *vr* = **despabilar(se)**

espachurrar [espatʃu'rrar] *vt* to squash; **espachurrarse** *vr* to get squashed

espaciado [espa'θjaðo] *nm (Inform)* spacing

espacial [espa'θjal] *adj (del espacio)* space *cpd*

espaciar [espa'θjar] *vt* to space (out)

espacio [es'paθjo] *nm* space; *(Mus)* interval; *(Radio, TV)* programme, program *(US)*; **el ~** space; **ocupar mucho ~** to take up a lot of room; **a dos espacios, a doble ~** *(Tip)* double-spaced; **por ~ de** during, for

espacioso, -a [espa'θjoso, a] *adj* spacious, roomy

espada [es'paða] *nf* sword ■ *nm* swordsman; *(Taur)* matador; **espadas** *nfpl (Naipes)* one of the suits in the Spanish card deck; **estar entre la ~ y la pared** to be between the devil and the deep blue sea; *ver tb* **baraja española**

espadachín [espaða'tʃin] *nm (esgrimidor)* skilled swordsman

espaguetis [espa'γetis] *nmpl* spaghetti *sg*

espalda [es'palda] *nf (gen)* back; *(Natación)* backstroke; **espaldas** *nfpl (hombros)* shoulders; **a espaldas de algn** behind sb's back; **estar de espaldas** to have one's back turned; **tenderse de espaldas** to lie (down) on one's back; **volver la ~ a algn** to cold-shoulder sb

espaldarazo [espalda'raθo] *nm (tb fig)* slap on the back

espaldilla [espal'ðiʎa] *nf* shoulder blade

espantadizo, -a [espanta'ðiθo, a] *adj* timid, easily frightened

espantajo [espan'taxo] *nm,* **espantapájaros** [espanta'paxaros] *nm inv* scarecrow

espantar [espan'tar] *vt (asustar)* to frighten, scare; *(ahuyentar)* to frighten off; *(asombrar)* to horrify, appal; **espantarse** *vr* to get frightened *o* scared; to be appalled

espanto [es'panto] *nm (susto)* fright; *(terror)* terror; *(asombro)* astonishment; **¡qué ~!** how awful!

espantoso, -a [espan'toso, a] *adj* frightening, terrifying; *(ruido)* dreadful

España [es'paɲa] *nf* Spain; **la ~ de pandereta** touristy Spain

español, a [espa'ɲol, a] *adj* Spanish ■ *nm/f* Spaniard ■ *nm (Ling)* Spanish; *ver tb* **castellano**

españolice *etc* [espaɲo'liθe] *vb ver* **españolizar**

españolizar [espaɲoli'θar] *vt* to make Spanish, Hispanicize; **españolizarse** *vr* to adopt Spanish ways

esparadrapo [espara'ðrapo] *nm (sticking) plaster, Band-Aid® (US)*

esparcido, -a [espar'θiðo, a] *adj* scattered

esparcimiento [esparθi'mjento] *nm (dispersión)* spreading; *(derramamiento)* scattering; *(fig)* cheerfulness

esparcir [espar'θir] *vt* to spread; *(derramar)* to scatter; **esparcirse** *vr* to spread (out); to scatter; *(divertirse)* to enjoy o.s.

espárrago [es'parraγo] *nm (tb:* **espárragos)** asparagus; **estar hecho un ~** to be as thin as a rake; **¡vete a freír espárragos!** *(fam)* go to hell!

esparto [es'parto] *nm* esparto (grass)

esparza *etc* [es'parθa] *vb ver* **esparcir**

espasmo [es'pasmo] *nm* spasm

espátula [es'patula] *nf (Med)* spatula; *(Arte)* palette knife; *(Culin)* fish slice

especia [es'peθja] *nf* spice

especial [espe'θjal] *adj* special

especialidad [espeθjali'ðað] *nf* speciality, specialty *(US)*; *(Escol: ramo)* specialism

especialista [espeθja'lista] *nm/f* specialist; *(Cine)* stuntman(-woman)

especializado, -a [espeθjali'θaðo, a] *adj* specialized; *(obrero)* skilled

especialmente [espeθjal'mente] *adv* particularly, especially

especie [es'peθje] *nf (Bio)* species; *(clase)* kind, sort; **pagar en ~** to pay in kind

especificar [espeθifi'kar] *vt* to specify

específico, -a [espe'θifiko, a] *adj* specific

especifique *etc* [espeθi'fike] *vb ver* **especificar**

espécimen [es'peθimen] *(pl* **especímenes)** *nm* specimen

espectáculo [espek'takulo] *nm (gen)* spectacle; *(Teat etc)* show; *(función)* performance; **dar un ~** to make a scene

espectador, a [espekta'ðor, a] *nm/f* spectator; *(de incidente)* onlooker; **los**

espectadores *nmpl* (*Teat*) the audience *sg*

espectro [es'pektro] *nm* ghost; (*fig*) spectre

especulación [espekula'θjon] *nf* speculation; ~ **bursátil** speculation on the Stock Market

especular [espeku'lar] *vt, vi* to speculate

especulativo, -a [espekula'tiβo, a] *adj* speculative

espejismo [espe'xismo] *nm* mirage

espejo [es'pexo] *nm* mirror; (*fig*) model; ~ **retrovisor** rear-view mirror; **mirarse al** ~ to look (at o.s.) in the mirror

espeleología [espeleolo'xia] *nf* potholing

espeluznante [espeluθ'nante] *adj* horrifying, hair-raising

espera [es'pera] *nf* (*pausa, intervalo*) wait; (*Jur: plazo*) respite; **en** ~ **de** waiting for; (*con expectativa*) expecting; **en** ~ **de su contestación** awaiting your reply

esperance *etc* [espe'ranθe] *vb ver* **esperanzar**

esperanza [espe'ranθa] *nf* (*confianza*) hope; (*expectativa*) expectation; **hay pocas esperanzas de que venga** there is little prospect of his coming

esperanzador, a [esperanθa'ðor, a] *adj* hopeful, encouraging

esperanzar [esperan'θar] *vt* to give hope to

esperar [espe'rar] *vt* (*aguardar*) to wait for; (*tener expectativa de*) to expect; (*desear*) to hope for ■ *vi* to wait; to expect; to hope; **esperarse** *vr*: **como podía esperarse** as was to be expected; **hacer** ~ **a uno** to keep sb waiting; **ir a** ~ **a uno** to go and meet sb; ~ **un bebé** to be expecting (a baby)

esperma [es'perma] *nf* sperm

espermatozoide [espermato'θoiðe] *nm* spermatozoid

esperpento [esper'pento] *nm* (*persona*) sight (*fam*); (*disparate*) (piece of) nonsense

espesar [espe'sar] *vt* to thicken; **espesarse** *vr* to thicken, get thicker

espeso, -a [es'peso, a] *adj* thick; (*bosque*) dense; (*nieve*) deep; (*sucio*) dirty

espesor [espe'sor] *nm* thickness; (*de nieve*) depth

espesura [espe'sura] *nf* (*de bosque*) thicket

espetar [espe'tar] *vt* (*reto, sermón*) to give

espía [es'pia] *nm/f* spy

espiar [espi'ar] *vt* (*observar*) to spy on ■ *vi*: ~ **para** to spy for

espiga [es'piɣa] *nf* (*Bot: de trigo etc*) ear; (: *de flores*) spike

espigado, -a [espi'ɣaðo, a] *adj* (*Bot*) ripe; (*fig*) tall, slender

espigón [espi'ɣon] *nm* (*Bot*) ear; (*Naut*) breakwater

espina [es'pina] *nf* thorn; (*de pez*) bone;

~ **dorsal** (*Anat*) spine; **me da mala** ~ I don't like the look of it

espinaca [espi'naka] *nf* (*tb*: **espinacas**) spinach

espinar [espi'nar] *nm* (*matorral*) thicket

espinazo [espi'naθo] *nm* spine, backbone

espinilla [espi'niʎa] *nf* (*Anat: tibia*) shin(bone); (: *en la piel*) blackhead

espino [es'pino] *nm* hawthorn

espinoso, -a [espi'noso, a] *adj* (*planta*) thorny, prickly; (*fig*) bony; (*problema*) knotty

espionaje [espjo'naxe] *nm* spying, espionage

espiral [espi'ral] *adj, nf* spiral; **la** ~ **inflacionista** the inflationary spiral

espirar [espi'rar] *vt, vi* to breathe out, exhale

espiritista [espiri'tista] *adj, nm/f* spiritualist

espíritu [es'piritu] *nm* spirit; (*mente*) mind; (*inteligencia*) intelligence; (*Rel*) spirit, soul; **E~ Santo** Holy Ghost; **con** ~ **amplio** with an open mind

espiritual [espiri'twal] *adj* spiritual

espita [es'pita] *nf* tap (*Brit*), faucet (*US*)

esplendidez [esplendi'ðeθ] *nf* (*abundancia*) lavishness; (*magnificencia*) splendour

espléndido, -a [es'plendiðo, a] *adj* (*magnífico*) magnificent, splendid; (*generoso*) generous, lavish

esplendor [esplen'dor] *nm* splendour

espliego [es'pljeɣo] *nm* lavender

espolear [espole'ar] *vt* to spur on

espoleta [espo'leta] *nf* (*de bomba*) fuse

espolvorear [espolβore'ar] *vt* to dust, sprinkle

esponja [es'ponxa] *nf* sponge; (*fig*) sponger

esponjoso, -a [espon'xoso, a] *adj* spongy

esponsales [espon'sales] *nmpl* betrothal *sg*

espontaneidad [espontanei'ðað] *nf* spontaneity

espontáneo, -a [espon'taneo, a] *adj* spontaneous; (*improvisado*) impromptu; (*persona*) natural

espora [es'pora] *nf* spore

esporádico, -a [espo'raðiko, a] *adj* sporadic

esposa [es'posa] *nf ver* **esposo**

esposar [espo'sar] *vt* to handcuff

esposo, -a [es'poso, a] *nm* husband ■ *nf* wife; **esposas** *nfpl* handcuffs

espuela [es'pwela] *nf* spur; (*fam: trago*) one for the road

espuerta [es'pwerta] *nf* basket, pannier

espuma [es'puma] *nf* foam; (*de cerveza*) froth, head; (*de jabón*) lather; (*de olas*) surf

espumadera [espuma'ðera] *nf* skimmer

espumarajo [espuma'raxo] *nm* froth, foam; **echar espumarajos (de rabia)** to splutter with rage

espumoso, -a [espu'moso, a] *adj* frothy, foamy; (*vino*) sparkling

esputo [es'puto] *nm* (*de saliva*) spit; (*Med*) sputum

esqueje [es'kexe] *nm* (*Bot*) cutting

esquela [es'kela] *nf*: ~ **mortuoria** announcement of death

esquelético, -a [eske'letiko, a] *adj* (*fam*) skinny

esqueleto [eske'leto] *nm* skeleton; (*lo esencial*) bare bones (of a matter); **en** ~ unfinished

esquema [es'kema] *nm* (*diagrama*) diagram; (*dibujo*) plan; (*plan*) scheme; (*Filosofía*) schema

esquemático, -a [eske'matiko, a] *adj* schematic; **un resumen** ~ a brief outline

esquí [es'ki] (*pl* ~s) *nm* (*objeto*) ski; (*deporte*) skiing; ~ **acuático** water-skiing; **hacer** ~ to go skiing

esquiador, a [eskja'ðor, a] *nm/f* skier

esquiar [es'kjar] *vi* to ski

esquila [es'kila] *nf* (*campanilla*) small bell; (*encerro*) cowbell

esquilar [eski'lar] *vt* to shear

esquimal [eski'mal] *adj, nm/f* Eskimo

esquina [es'kina] *nf* corner; **doblar la** ~ to turn the corner

esquinazo [eski'naθo] *nm*: **dar** ~ **a algn** to give sb the slip

esquirla [es'kirla] *nf* splinter

esquirol [eski'rol] *nm* blackleg

esquivar [eski'βar] *vt* to avoid; (*evadir*) to dodge, elude

esquivo, -a [es'kiβo, a] *adj* (*altanero*) aloof; (*desdeñoso*) scornful, disdainful

esquizofrenia [eskiθo'frenja] *nf* schizophrenia

esta ['esta] *adj demostrativo ver* **este**

ésta ['esta] *pron ver* **éste**

está [es'ta] *vb ver* **estar**

estabilice *etc* [estaβi'liθe] *vb ver* **estabilizar**

estabilidad [estaβili'ðað] *nf* stability

estabilización [estaβiliθa'θjon] *nf* (*Com*) stabilization

estabilizar [estaβili'θar] *vt* to stabilize; (*fijar*) to make steady; (*precios*) to peg; **estabilizarse** *vr* to become stable

estable [es'taβle] *adj* stable

establecer [estaβle'θer] *vt* to establish; (*fundar*) to set up; (*colonos*) to settle; (*récord*) to set (up); **establecerse** *vr* to establish o.s.; (*echar raíces*) to settle (down); (*Com*) to start up

establecimiento [estaβleθi'mjento] *nm* establishment; (*fundación*) institution; (*de negocio*) start-up; (*de colonias*) settlement; (*local*) establishment; ~ **comercial** business house

establezca *etc* [esta'βleθka] *vb ver* **establecer**

establo [es'taβlo] *nm* (*Agr*) stall; (: *esp Am*) barn

estaca [es'taka] *nf* stake, post; (*de tienda de campaña*) peg

estacada [esta'kaða] *nf* (*cerca*) fence, fencing; (*palenque*) stockade; **dejar a algn en la** ~ to leave sb in the lurch

estación [esta'θjon] *nf* station; (*del año*) season; ~ **de autobuses/ferrocarril** bus/railway station; ~ **balnearia (de turistas)** seaside resort; ~ **de servicio** service station; ~ **terminal** terminus; ~ **de trabajo** (*Com*) work station; ~ **transmisora** transmitter; ~ **de visualización** display unit

estacionamiento [estaθjona'mjento] *nm* (*Auto*) parking; (*Mil*) stationing

estacionar [estaθjo'nar] *vt* (*Auto*) to park; (*Mil*) to station

estacionario, -a [estaθjo'narjo, a] *adj* stationary; (*Com: mercado*) slack

estada [es'taða], **estadía** [esta'ðia] *nf* (*Am*) stay

estadio [es'taðjo] *nm* (*fase*) stage, phase; (*Deporte*) stadium

estadista [esta'ðista] *nm* (*Pol*) statesman; (*Estadística*) statistician

estadística [esta'ðistika] *nf* (*una estadística*) figure, statistic; (*ciencia*) statistics *sg*

estado [es'taðo] *nm* (*Pol: condición*) state; ~ **civil** marital status; ~ **de cuenta(s)** bank statement, statement of accounts; ~ **de excepción** (*Pol*) state of emergency; ~ **financiero** (*Com*) financial statement; ~ **mayor** (*Mil*) staff; ~ **de pérdidas y ganancias** (*Com*) profit and loss statement, operating statement; **Estados Unidos (EE. UU.)** United States (of America) (USA); **estar en** ~ **(de buena esperanza)** to be pregnant

estadounidense [estaðouni'ðense] *adj* United States *cpd*, American ■ *nm/f* United States citizen, American

estafa [es'tafa] *nf* swindle, trick; (*Com etc*) racket

estafar [esta'far] *vt* to swindle, defraud

estafeta [esta'feta] *nf* (*oficina de correos*) post office; ~ **diplomática** diplomatic bag

estalactita [estalak'tita] *nf* stalactite

estalagmita [estalaɣ'mita] *nf* stalagmite

estallar [esta'ʎar] *vi* to burst; (*bomba*) to explode, go off; (*volcán*) to erupt; (*vidrio*) to shatter; (*látigo*) to crack; (*epidemia, guerra, rebelión*) to break out; ~ **en llanto** to burst into tears

estallido [esta'ʎiðo] *nm* explosion; (*de látigo, trueno*) crack; (*fig*) outbreak

estambre [es'tambre] *nm* (*tela*) worsted; (*Bot*) stamen

Estambul [estam'bul] *nm* Istanbul

estamento [esta'mento] *nm* (social) class

estampa [es'tampa] *nf* (*impresión, imprenta*) print, engraving; (*imagen, figura: de persona*) appearance

estampado, -a [estam'paðo, a] *adj* printed ▪ *nm* (*impresión: acción*) printing; (: *efecto*) print; (*marca*) stamping

estampar [estam'par] *vt* (*imprimir*) to print; (*marcar*) to stamp; (*metal*) to engrave; (*poner sello en*) to stamp; (*fig*) to stamp, imprint

estampida [estam'piða] *nf* stampede

estampido [estam'piðo] *nm* bang, report

estampilla [estam'piʎa] *nf* (*sello de goma*) (rubber) stamp; (*Am*) (postage) stamp

están [es'tan] *vb ver* **estar**

estancado, -a [estan'kaðo, a] *adj* (*agua*) stagnant

estancamiento [estanka'mjento] *nm* stagnation

estancar [estan'kar] *vt* (*aguas*) to hold up, hold back; (*Com*) to monopolize; (*fig*) to block, hold up; **estancarse** *vr* to stagnate

estancia [es'tanθja] *nf* (*permanencia*) stay; (*sala*) room; (*Am*) farm, ranch

estanciero [estan'sjero] *nm* (*Am*) farmer, rancher

estanco, -a [es'tanko, a] *adj* watertight ▪ *nm* tobacconist's (shop); *see note*

● **ESTANCO**

● Cigarettes, tobacco, postage stamps
● and official forms are all sold under
● state monopoly and usually through a
● shop called an *estanco*. Tobacco products
● are also sold in *quioscos* and bars but are
● generally more expensive. The number of
● *estanco* licences is regulated by the state.

estándar [es'tandar] *adj, nm* standard

estandarice *etc* [estanda'riθe] *vb ver* **estandarizar**

estandarizar [estandari'θar] *vt* to standardize

estandarte [estan'darte] *nm* banner, standard

estanque *etc* [es'tanke] *vb ver* **estancar** ▪ *nm* (*lago*) pool, pond; (*Agr*) reservoir

estanquero, -a [estan'kero, a] *nm/f* tobacconist

estante [es'tante] *nm* (*armario*) rack, stand; (*biblioteca*) bookcase; (*anaquel*) shelf; (*Am*) prop

estantería [estante'ria] *nf* shelving, shelves *pl*

estaño [es'taɲo] *nm* tin

○ **PALABRA CLAVE**

estar [es'tar] *vi* **1** (*posición*) to be; **está en la plaza** it's in the square; **¿está Juan?** is Juan in?; **estamos a 30 km de Junín** we're 30 kms from Junín

2 (+ *adj o adv: estado*) to be; **estar enfermo** to be ill; **está muy elegante** he's looking very smart; **estar lejos** to be far (away); **¿cómo estás?** how are you keeping?

3 (+ *gerundio*) to be; **estoy leyendo** I'm reading

4 (*uso pasivo*): **está condenado a muerte** he's been condemned to death; **está envasado en ...** it's packed in ...

5: **estar a**: **¿a cuántos estamos?** what's the date today?; **estamos a 9 de mayo** it's the 9th of May; **las manzanas están a 1,50 euros** apples are (selling at) 1.5 euros; **estamos a 25 grados** it's 25 degrees today

6 (*locuciones*): **¿estamos?** (*¿de acuerdo?*) okay?; (*¿listo?*) ready?; **¡ya está bien!** that's enough!; **¿está la comida?** is dinner ready?; **¡ya está!**, **¡ya estuvo!** (*Am*) that's it!

7: **estar con**: **está con gripe** he's got (the) flu

8: **estar de**: **estar de vacaciones/viaje** to be on holiday/away o on a trip; **está de camarero** he's working as a waiter

9: **estar para**: **está para salir** he's about to leave; **no estoy para bromas** I'm not in the mood for jokes

10: **estar por** (*propuesta etc*) to be in favour of; (*persona etc*) to support, side with; **está por limpiar** it still has to be cleaned; **¡estoy por dejarlo!** I think I'm going to leave this!

11 (+ *que*): **está que rabia** (*fam*) he's hopping mad (*fam*); **estoy que me caigo de sueño** I'm terribly sleepy, I can't keep my eyes open

12: **estar sin**: **estar sin dinero** to have no money; **está sin terminar** it isn't finished yet

estarse *vr*: **se estuvo en la cama toda la tarde** he stayed in bed all afternoon; **¡estáte quieto!** stop fidgeting!

---

estárter [es'tarter] *nm* (*Auto*) choke

estas ['estas] *adj demostrativo ver* **este**

éstas ['estas] *pron ver* **éste**

estás [es'tas] *vb ver* **estar**

estatal [esta'tal] *adj* state *cpd*

estático, -a [es'tatiko, a] *adj* static

estatua [es'tatwa] *nf* statue

estatura [esta'tura] *nf* stature, height

estatus [es'tatus] *nm inv* status

estatutario, -a [estatu'tarjo, a] *adj* statutory

estatuto [esta'tuto] *nm* (*Jur*) statute; (*de*

ciudad) bye-law; (*de comité*) rule; **estatutos sociales** (*Com*) articles of association

este¹ ['este] *adj* (*lado*) east; (*dirección*) easterly
■ *nm* east; **en la parte del ~** in the eastern part

este² ['este], **esta** ['esta], **estos** ['estos], **estas** ['estas] *adj demostrativo* this *sg*, these *pl*; (*Am*: *como muletilla*) er, um

éste ['este], **ésta** ['esta], **éstos** ['estos], **éstas** ['estas] *pron* this (one) *sg*, these (ones) *pl*; **ése ... éste ...** the former ... the latter ...

esté [es'te] *vb ver* **estar**

estela [es'tela] *nf* wake, wash; (*fig*) trail

estelar [este'lar] *adj* (*Astro*) stellar; (*Teat*) star *cpd*

estén [es'ten] *vb ver* **estar**

estenografía [estenoɣra'fia] *nf* shorthand

estentóreo, -a [esten'toreo, a] *adj* (*sonido*) strident; (*voz*) booming

estepa [es'tepa] *nf* (*Geo*) steppe

estera [es'tera] *nf* (*alfombra*) mat; (*tejido*) matting

estercolero [esterko'lero] *nm* manure heap, dunghill

estéreo [es'tereo] *adj inv, nm* stereo

estereofónico, -a [estereo'foniko, a] *adj* stereophonic

estereotipar [estereoti'par] *vt* to stereotype

estereotipo [estereo'tipo] *nm* stereotype

estéril [es'teril] *adj* sterile, barren; (*fig*) vain, futile

esterilice *etc* [esteri'liθe] *vb ver* **esterilizar**

esterilizar [esterili'θar] *vt* to sterilize

esterilla [este'riʎa] *nf* (*alfombrilla*) small mat

esterlina [ester'lina] *adj*: **libra ~** pound sterling

esternón [ester'non] *nm* breastbone

estero [es'tero] *nm* (*Am*) swamp

estertor [ester'tor] *nm* death rattle

estés [es'tes] *vb ver* **estar**

esteta [es'teta] *nm/f* aesthete

esteticienne [esteti'θjen] *nf* beautician

estético, -a [es'tetiko, a] *adj* aesthetic
■ *nf* aesthetics *sg*

estetoscopio [estetos'kopjo] *nm* stethoscope

estibador [estiβa'ðor] *nm* stevedore

estibar [esti'βar] *vt* (*Naut*) to stow

estiércol [es'tjerkol] *nm* dung, manure

estigma [es'tiɣma] *nm* stigma

estigmatice *etc* [estiɣma'tiθe] *vb ver* **estigmatizar**

estigmatizar [estiɣmati'θar] *vt* to stigmatize

estilarse [esti'larse] *vr* (*estar de moda*) to be in fashion; (*usarse*) to be used

estilice *etc* [esti'liθe] *vb ver* **estilizar**

estilizar [estili'θar] *vt* to stylize; (*Tec*) to design

estilo [es'tilo] *nm* style; (*Tec*) stylus; (*Natación*) stroke; **~ de vida** lifestyle; **al ~ de** in the style of; **algo por el ~** something along those lines

estilográfica [estilo'ɣrafika] *nf* fountain pen

estima [es'tima] *nf* esteem, respect

estimación [estima'θjon] *nf* (*evaluación*) estimation; (*aprecio, afecto*) esteem, regard

estimado, -a [esti'maðo, a] *adj* esteemed; **"E- Señor"** "Dear Sir"

estimar [esti'mar] *vt* (*evaluar*) to estimate; (*valorar*) to value; (*apreciar*) to esteem, respect; (*pensar, considerar*) to think, reckon

estimulante [estimu'lante] *adj* stimulating
■ *nm* stimulant

estimular [estimu'lar] *vt* to stimulate; (*excitar*) to excite; (*animar*) to encourage

estímulo [es'timulo] *nm* stimulus; (*ánimo*) encouragement

estío [es'tio] *nm* summer

estipendio [esti'pendjo] *nm* salary; (*Com*) stipend

estipulación [estipula'θjon] *nf* stipulation, condition

estipular [estipu'lar] *vt* to stipulate

estirado, -a [esti'raðo, a] *adj* (*tenso*) (stretched *o* drawn) tight; (*fig: persona*) stiff, pompous; (*engreído*) stuck-up

estirar [esti'rar] *vt* to stretch; (*dinero, suma etc*) to stretch out; (*cuello*) to crane; (*discurso*) to spin out; **~ la pata** (*fam*) to kick the bucket; **estirarse** *vr* to stretch

estirón [esti'ron] *nm* pull, tug; (*crecimiento*) spurt, sudden growth; **dar un ~** (*niño*) to shoot up

estirpe [es'tirpe] *nf* stock, lineage

estival [esti'βal] *adj* summer *cpd*

esto ['esto] *pron* this, this thing *o* matter; (*como muletilla*) er, um; **~ de la boda** this business about the wedding; **en ~** at this *o* that point; **por ~** for this reason

estocada [esto'kaða] *nf* (*acción*) stab; (*Taur*) death blow

Estocolmo [esto'kolmo] *nm* Stockholm

estofa [es'tofa] *nf*: **de baja ~** poor-quality

estofado [esto'faðo] *nm* stew

estofar [esto'far] *vt* (*bordar*) to quilt; (*Culin*) to stew

estoico, -a [es'toiko, a] *adj* (*Filosofía*) stoic(al); (*fig*) cold, indifferent

estomacal [estoma'kal] *adj* stomach *cpd*; **trastorno ~** stomach upset

estómago [es'tomaɣo] *nm* stomach; **tener ~** to be thick-skinned

Estonia [es'tonja] *nf* Estonia

estonio, -a [es'tonjo, a] *adj, nm/f* Estonian
■ *nm* (*Ling*) Estonian

estoque [es'toke] *nm* rapier, sword
estorbar [estor'βar] *vt* to hinder, obstruct; (*fig*) to bother, disturb ■ *vi* to be in the way
estorbo [es'torβo] *nm* (*molestia*) bother, nuisance; (*obstáculo*) hindrance, obstacle
estornino [estor'nino] *nm* starling
estornudar [estornu'ðar] *vi* to sneeze
estornudo [estor'nuðo] *nm* sneeze
estos ['estos] *adj demostrativo ver* **este**
éstos ['estos] *pron ver* **éste**
estoy [es'toi] *vb ver* **estar**
estrabismo [estra'βismo] *nm* squint
estrado [es'traðo] *nm* (*tarima*) platform; (*Mus*) bandstand; **estrados** *nmpl* law courts
estrafalario, -a [estrafa'larjo, a] *adj* odd, eccentric; (*desarreglado*) slovenly, sloppy
estrago [es'trayo] *nm* ruin, destruction; **hacer estragos en** to wreak havoc among
estragón [estra'yon] *nm* (*Culin*) tarragon
estrambótico, -a [estram'botiko, a] *adj* odd, eccentric
estrangulación [estrangula'θjon] *nf* strangulation
estrangulador, -a [estrangula'ðor, a] *nm/f* strangler ■ *nm* (*Tec*) throttle; (*Auto*) choke
estrangulamiento [estrangula'mjento] *nm* (*Auto*) bottleneck
estrangular [estrangu'lar] *vt* (*persona*) to strangle; (*Med*) to strangulate
estraperlista [estraper'lista] *nm/f* black marketeer
estraperlo [estra'perlo] *nm* black market
estratagema [estrata'xema] *nf* (*Mil*) stratagem; (*astucia*) cunning
estratega [estra'teya] *nm/f* strategist
estrategia [estra'texja] *nf* strategy
estratégico, -a [estra'texiko, a] *adj* strategic
estratificar [estratifi'kar] *vt* to stratify
estratifique *etc* [estrati'fike] *vb ver* **estratificar**
estrato [es'trato] *nm* stratum, layer
estratosfera [estratos'fera] *nf* stratosphere
estrechar [estre'tʃar] *vt* (*reducir*) to narrow; (*vestido*) to take in; (*persona*) to hug, embrace; **estrecharse** *vr* (*reducirse*) to narrow, grow narrow; (*2 personas*) to embrace; **~ la mano** to shake hands
estrechez [estre'tʃeθ] *nf* narrowness; (*de ropa*) tightness; (*intimidad*) intimacy; (*Com*) want o shortage of money; **estrecheces** *nfpl* financial difficulties
estrecho, -a [es'tretʃo, a] *adj* narrow; (*apretado*) tight; (*íntimo*) close, intimate; (*miserable*) mean ■ *nm* strait; **~ de miras** narrow-minded; **E~ de Gibraltar** Straits of Gibraltar
estrella [es'treʎa] *nf* star; **~ fugaz** shooting

star; **~ de mar** starfish; **tener (buena)/ mala ~** to be lucky/unlucky
estrellado, -a [estre'ʎaðo, a] *adj* (*forma*) star-shaped; (*cielo*) starry; (*huevos*) fried
estrellar [estre'ʎar] *vt* (*hacer añicos*) to smash (to pieces); (*huevos*) to fry; **estrellarse** *vr* to smash; (*chocarse*) to crash; (*fracasar*) to fail
estrellato [estre'ʎato] *nm* stardom
estremecer [estreme'θer] *vt* to shake; **estremecerse** *vr* to shake, tremble; **~ de** (*horror*) to shudder with; (*frío*) to shiver with
estremecimiento [estremeθi'mjento] *nm* (*temblor*) trembling, shaking
estremezca *etc* [estre'meθka] *vb ver* **estremecer**
estrenar [estre'nar] *vt* (*vestido*) to wear for the first time; (*casa*) to move into; (*película, obra de teatro*) to present for the first time; **estrenarse** *vr* (*persona*) to make one's début; (*película*) to have its première; (*Teat*) to open
estreno [es'treno] *nm* (*primer uso*) first use; (*Cine etc*) première
estreñido, -a [estre'niðo, a] *adj* constipated
estreñimiento [estreni'mjento] *nm* constipation
estreñir [estre'nir] *vt* to constipate
estrépito [es'trepito] *nm* noise, racket; (*fig*) fuss
estrepitoso, -a [estrepi'toso, a] *adj* noisy; (*fiesta*) rowdy
estrés [es'tres] *nm* stress
estresante [estre'sante] *adj* stressful
estría [es'tria] *nf* groove; **estrías (en el cutis)** stretchmarks
estribación [estriβa'θjon] *nf* (*Geo*) spur; **estribaciones** *nfpl* foothills
estribar [estri'βar] *vi*: **~ en** to rest on, be supported by; **la dificultad estriba en el texto** the difficulty lies in the text
estribillo [estri'βiʎo] *nm* (*Lit*) refrain; (*Mus*) chorus
estribo [es'triβo] *nm* (*de jinete*) stirrup; (*de coche, tren*) step; (*de puente*) support; (*Geo*) spur; **perder los estribos** to fly off the handle
estribor [estri'βor] *nm* (*Naut*) starboard
estricnina [estrik'nina] *nf* strychnine
estricto, -a [es'trikto, a] *adj* (*riguroso*) strict; (*severo*) severe
estridente [estri'ðente] *adj* (*color*) loud; (*voz*) raucous
estro ['estro] *nm* inspiration
estrofa [es'trofa] *nf* verse
estropajo [estro'paxo] *nm* scourer
estropeado, -a [estrope'aðo, a] *adj*: **está ~** it's not working
estropear [estrope'ar] *vt* (*arruinar*) to spoil;

(*dañar*) to damage; (*: máquina*) to break; **estropearse** *vr* (*objeto*) to get damaged; (*coche*) to break down; (*la piel etc*) to be ruined
estropicio [estro'piθjo] *nm* (*rotura*) breakage; (*efectos*) harmful effects *pl*
estructura [estruk'tura] *nf* structure
estruendo [es'trwendo] *nm* (*ruido*) racket, din; (*fig: alboroto*) uproar, turmoil
estrujar [estru'xar] *vt* (*apretar*) to squeeze; (*aplastar*) to crush; (*fig*) to drain, bleed
estuario [es'twarjo] *nm* estuary
estuche [es'tutʃe] *nm* box, case
estudiante [estu'ðjante] *nm/f* student
estudiantil [estuðjan'til] *adj inv* student *cpd*
estudiantina [estuðjan'tina] *nf* student music group
estudiar [estu'ðjar] *vt* to study; (*propuesta*) to think about *o* over; **~ para abogado** to study to become a lawyer
estudio [es'tuðjo] *nm* study; (*encuesta*) research; (*proyecto*) plan; (*piso*) studio flat; (*Cine, Arte, Radio*) studio; **estudios** *nmpl* studies; (*erudición*) learning *sg*; **cursar** *o* **hacer estudios** to study; **~ de casos prácticos** case study; **~ de desplazamientos y tiempos** (*Com*) time and motion study; **estudios de motivación** motivational research *sg*; **~ del trabajo** (*Com*) work study; **~ de viabilidad** (*Com*) feasibility study
estudioso, -a [estu'ðjoso, a] *adj* studious
estufa [es'tufa] *nf* heater, fire
estulticia [estul'tiθja] *nf* foolishness
estupefaciente [estupefa'θjente] *adj, nm* narcotic
estupefacto, -a [estupe'fakto, a] *adj* speechless, thunderstruck
estupendamente [estupenda'mente] *adv* (*fam*): **estoy ~** I feel great; **le salió ~** he did it very well
estupendo, -a [estu'pendo, a] *adj* wonderful, terrific; (*fam*) great; **¡~!** that's great!, fantastic!
estupidez [estupi'ðeθ] *nf* (*torpeza*) stupidity; (*acto*) stupid thing (to do); **fue una ~ mía** that was a silly thing for me to do *o* say
estúpido, -a [es'tupiðo, a] *adj* stupid, silly
estupor [estu'por] *nm* stupor; (*fig*) astonishment, amazement
estupro [es'tupro] *nm* rape
estuve *etc* [es'tuβe], **estuviera** *etc* [estu'βjera] *vb ver* **estar**
esvástica [es'βastika] *nf* swastika
ET *abr* = **Ejército de Tierra**
ETA ['eta] *nf abr* (*Pol: = Euskadi Ta Askatasuna*) ETA
etapa [e'tapa] *nf* (*de viaje*) stage; (*Deporte*) leg; (*parada*) stopping place; (*fig*) stage, phase; **por etapas** gradually, in stages
etarra [e'tarra] *adj* ETA *cpd* ■ *nm/f* member of ETA
etc. *abr* (*= etcétera*) etc
etcétera [et'θetera] *adv* etcetera
etéreo, -a [e'tereo, a] *adj* ethereal
eternice *etc* [eter'niθe] *vb ver* **eternizarse**
eternidad [eterni'ðað] *nf* eternity
eternizarse [eterni'θarse] *vr*: **~ en hacer algo** to take ages to do sth
eterno, -a [e'terno, a] *adj* eternal, everlasting; (*despectivo*) never-ending
ético, -a ['etiko, a] *adj* ethical ■ *nf* ethics
etimología [etimolo'xia] *nf* etymology
etiqueta [eti'keta] *nf* (*modales*) etiquette; (*rótulo*) label, tag; **de ~** formal
etnia ['etnja] *nf* ethnic group
étnico, -a ['etniko, a] *adj* ethnic
ETS *sigla f* (*= Enfermedad de Transmisión Sexual*) STD
EU(A) *nmpl abr* (*esp Am: = Estados Unidos (de América)*) US(A)
eucalipto [euka'lipto] *nm* eucalyptus
Eucaristía [eukaris'tia] *nf* Eucharist
eufemismo [eufe'mismo] *nm* euphemism
euforia [eu'forja] *nf* euphoria
eufórico, -a [eu'foriko, a] *adj* euphoric
eunuco [eu'nuko] *nm* eunuch
euro ['euro] *nm* (*moneda*) euro
eurodiputado, -a [euroðipu'taðo, a] *nm/f* Euro MP, MEP
Eurolandia [euro'landja] *nf* Euroland
Europa [eu'ropa] *nf* Europe
europeice *etc* [euro'peiθe] *vb ver* **europeizar**
europeizar [europei'θar] *vt* to Europeanize; **europeizarse** *vr* to become Europeanized
europeo, -a [euro'peo, a] *adj, nm/f* European
Eurotúnel [euro'tunel] *nm* (*estructura*) Channel Tunnel
eurozona [euro'θona] *nf* Eurozone
Euskadi [eus'kaði] *nm* the Basque Provinces *pl*
euskera, eusquera [eus'kera] *nm* (*Ling*) Basque; *ver tb* **Lengua**
eutanasia [euta'nasja] *nf* euthanasia
evacuación [eβakwa'θjon] *nf* evacuation
evacuar [eβa'kwar] *vt* to evacuate
evadir [eβa'ðir] *vt* to evade, avoid; **evadirse** *vr* to escape
evaluación [eβalwa'θjon] *nf* evaluation, assessment
evaluar [eβa'lwar] *vt* to evaluate, assess
evangélico, -a [eβan'xeliko, a] *adj* evangelical
evangelio [eβan'xeljo] *nm* gospel
evaporación [eβapora'θjon] *nf* evaporation
evaporar [eβapo'rar] *vt* to evaporate;

e

evaporarse vr to vanish
evasión [eβa'sjon] nf escape, flight; (fig) evasion; ~ **fiscal** o **tributaria** tax evasion
evasivo, -a [eβa'siβo, a] adj evasive, non-committal ■ nf (pretexto) excuse; **contestar con evasivas** to avoid giving a straight answer
evento [e'βento] nm event; (eventualidad) eventuality
eventual [eβen'twal] adj possible, conditional (upon circumstances); (trabajador) casual, temporary
Everest [eβe'rest] nm: **el (Monte) ~** (Mount) Everest
evidencia [eβi'ðenθja] nf evidence, proof; **poner en ~** to make clear; **ponerse en ~** (persona) to show o.s. up
evidenciar [eβiðen'θjar] vt (hacer patente) to make evident; (probar) to prove, show; **evidenciarse** vr to be evident
evidente [eβi'ðente] adj obvious, clear, evident
evitar [eβi'tar] vt (evadir) to avoid; (impedir) to prevent; (peligro) to escape; (molestia) to save; (tentación) to shun; **si puedo evitarlo** if I can help it
evocador, a [eβoka'ðor, a] adj (sugestivo) evocative
evocar [eβo'kar] vt to evoke, call forth
evolución [eβolu'θjon] nf (desarrollo) evolution, development; (cambio) change; (Mil) manoeuvre
evolucionar [eβoluθjo'nar] vi to evolve; (Mil, Aviat) to manoeuvre
evoque etc [e'βoke] vb ver **evocar**
ex [eks] adj ex-; **el ex ministro** the former minister, the ex-minister
exabrupto [eksa'βrupto] nm interjection
exacción [eksak'θjon] nf (acto) exaction; (de impuestos) demand
exacerbar [eksaθer'βar] vt to irritate, annoy
exactamente [eksakta'mente] adv exactly
exactitud [eksakti'tuð] nf exactness; (precisión) accuracy; (puntualidad) punctuality
exacto, -a [ek'sakto, a] adj exact; accurate; punctual; **¡~!** exactly!; **eso no es del todo ~** that's not quite right; **para ser ~** to be precise
exageración [eksaxera'θjon] nf exaggeration
exagerado, -a [eksaxe'raðo, a] adj (relato) exaggerated; (precio) excessive; (persona) over-demonstrative; (gesto) theatrical
exagerar [eksaxe'rar] vt to exaggerate; (exceder) to overdo
exaltado, -a [eksal'taðo, a] adj (apasionado) over-excited, worked up; (exagerado) extreme;

(fanático) hot-headed; (discurso) impassioned ■ nm/f (fanático) hothead; (Pol) extremist
exaltar [eksal'tar] vt to exalt, glorify; **exaltarse** vr (excitarse) to get excited o worked up
examen [ek'samen] nm examination; (de problema) consideration; ~ **de** (encuesta) inquiry into; ~ **de ingreso** entrance examination; ~ **de conducir** driving test; ~ **eliminatorio** qualifying examination
examinar [eksami'nar] vt to examine; (poner a prueba) to test; (inspeccionar) to inspect; **examinarse** vr to be examined, take an examination
exánime [ek'sanime] adj lifeless; (fig) exhausted
exasperar [eksaspe'rar] vt to exasperate; **exasperarse** vr to get exasperated, lose patience
Exc.ª abr = **Excelencia**
excarcelar [ekskarθe'lar] vt to release (from prison)
excavador, a [ekskaβa'ðor, a] nm/f (persona) excavator ■ nf (Tec) digger
excavar [ekska'βar] vt to excavate, dig (out)
excedencia [eksθe'ðenθja] nf (Mil) leave; (Escol) sabbatical
excedente [eksθe'ðente] adj, nm excess, surplus
exceder [eksθe'ðer] vt to exceed, surpass; **excederse** vr (extralimitarse) to go too far; (sobrepasarse) to excel o.s.
excelencia [eksθe'lenθja] nf excellence; **E~** Excellency; **por ~** par excellence
excelente [eksθe'lente] adj excellent
excelso, -a [eks'θelso, a] adj lofty, sublime
excentricidad [eksθentriθi'ðað] nf eccentricity
excéntrico, -a [eks'θentriko, a] adj, nm/f eccentric
excepción [eksθep'θjon] nf exception; **la ~ confirma la regla** the exception proves the rule
excepcional [eksθepθjo'nal] adj exceptional
excepto [eks'θepto] adv excepting, except (for)
exceptuar [eksθep'twar] vt to except, exclude
excesivo, -a [eksθe'siβo, a] adj excessive
exceso [eks'θeso] nm excess; (Com) surplus; ~ **de equipaje/peso** excess luggage/weight; ~ **de velocidad** speeding; **en** o **por ~** excessively
excitación [eksθita'θjon] nf (sensación) excitement; (acción) excitation
excitado, -a [eksθi'taðo, a] adj excited; (emociones) aroused

excitante [eksθi'tante] *adj* exciting; (*Med*) stimulating ▪ *nm* stimulant

excitar [eksθi'tar] *vt* to excite; (*incitar*) to urge; (*emoción*) to stir up; (*esperanzas*) to raise; (*pasión*) to arouse; **excitarse** *vr* to get excited

exclamación [eksklama'θjon] *nf* exclamation

exclamar [ekskla'mar] *vi* to exclaim; **exclamarse** *vr*: **exclamarse (contra)** to complain (about)

excluir [eksklu'ir] *vt* to exclude; (*dejar fuera*) to shut out; (*solución*) to reject; (*posibilidad*) to rule out

exclusión [eksklu'sjon] *nf* exclusion

exclusiva [eksklu'siβa] *nf ver* **exclusivo**

exclusive [eksklu'siβe] *prep* exclusive of, not counting

exclusivo, -a [eksklu'siβo, a] *adj* exclusive ▪ *nf* (*Prensa*) exclusive, scoop; (*Com*) sole right o agency; **derecho ~** sole o exclusive right

excluyendo *etc* [eksklu'jendo] *vb ver* **excluir**

Excma., Excmo. *abr* (= *Excelentísima, Excelentísimo*) *courtesy title*

excombatiente [ekskomba'tjente] *nm* ex-serviceman, war veteran (*US*)

excomulgar [ekskomul'ɣar] *vt* (*Rel*) to excommunicate

excomulgue *etc* [eksko'mulɣe] *vb ver* **excomulgar**

excomunión [ekskomu'njon] *nf* excommunication

excoriar [eksko'rjar] *vt* to flay, skin

excremento [ekskre'mento] *nm* excrement

exculpar [ekskul'par] *vt* to exonerate; (*Jur*) to acquit; **exculparse** *vr* to exonerate o.s.

excursión [ekskur'sjon] *nf* excursion, outing; **ir de ~** to go (off) on a trip

excursionista [ekskursjo'nista] *nm/f* (*turista*) sightseer

excusa [eks'kusa] *nf* excuse; (*disculpa*) apology; **presentar sus excusas** to excuse o.s.

excusado, -a [eksku'saðo, a] *adj* unnecessary; (*disculpado*) excused, forgiven

excusar [eksku'sar] *vt* to excuse; (*evitar*) to avoid, prevent; **excusarse** *vr* (*disculparse*) to apologize

execrable [ekse'kraβle] *adj* appalling

exención [eksen'θjon] *nf* exemption

exento, -a [ek'sento, a] *pp de* **eximir** ▪ *adj* exempt

exequias [ek'sekjas] *nfpl* funeral rites

exfoliar [eksfo'ljar] *vt* to exfoliate

exhalación [eksala'θjon] *nf* (*del aire*) exhalation; (*de vapor*) fumes *pl*, vapour; (*rayo*) shooting star; **salir como una ~** to shoot out

exhalar [eksa'lar] *vt* to exhale, breathe out; (*olor etc*) to give off; (*suspiro*) to breathe, heave

exhaustivo, -a [eksaus'tiβo, a] *adj* exhaustive

exhausto, -a [ek'sausto, a] *adj* exhausted, worn-out

exhibición [eksiβi'θjon] *nf* exhibition; (*demostración*) display, show; (*de película*) showing; (*de equipo*) performance

exhibicionista [eksiβiθjo'nista] *adj, nm/f* exhibitionist

exhibir [eksi'βir] *vt* to exhibit; to display, show; (*cuadros*) to exhibit; (*artículos*) to display; (*pasaporte*) to show; (*película*) to screen; (*mostrar con orgullo*) to show off; **exhibirse** *vr* (*mostrarse en público*) to show o.s. off, (*fam: indecentemente*) to expose o.s.

exhortación [eksorta'θjon] *nf* exhortation

exhortar [eksor'tar] *vt*: **~ a** to exhort to sb

exhumar [eksu'mar] *vt* to exhume

exigencia [eksi'xenθja] *nf* demand, requirement

exigente [eksi'xente] *adj* demanding; (*profesor*) strict; **ser ~ con algn** to be hard on sb

exigir [eksi'xir] *vt* (*gen*) to demand, require; (*impuestos*) to exact, levy; **~ el pago** to demand payment

exiguo, -a [ek'siɣwo, a] *adj* (*cantidad*) meagre; (*objeto*) tiny

exija *etc* [e'ksixa] *vb ver* **exigir**

exiliado, -a [eksi'ljaðo, a] *adj* exiled, in exile ▪ *nm/f* exile

exiliar [eksi'ljar] *vt* to exile; **exiliarse** *vr* to go into exile

exilio [ek'siljo] *nm* exile

eximio, -a [ek'simjo, a] *adj* (*eminente*) distinguished, eminent

eximir [eksi'mir] *vt* to exempt

existencia [eksis'tenθja] *nf* existence; **existencias** *nfpl* stock *sg*; **~ de mercancías** (*Com*) stock-in-trade; **tener en ~** to have in stock; **amargar la ~ a algn** to make sb's life a misery

existir [eksis'tir] *vi* to exist, be

éxito [ek'sito] *nm* (*resultado*) result, outcome; (*triunfo*) success; (*Mus, Teat*) hit; **éxito editorial** bestseller; **éxito rotundo** smash hit; **tener éxito** to be successful

exitoso, -a [eksi'toso, a] *adj* (*esp Am*) successful

éxodo ['eksoðo] *nm* exodus; **el éxodo rural** the drift from the land

ex oficio [ekso'fiθjo] *adj, adv* ex officio

exonerar [eksone'rar] *vt* to exonerate; **~ de una obligación** to free from an obligation

exorcice *etc* [eksor'θiθe] *vb ver* **exorcizar**

exorcismo [eksor'θismo] *nm* exorcism

exorcizar [eksorθi'θar] *vt* to exorcize
exótico, -a [ek'sotiko, a] *adj* exotic
expandido, -a [ekspan'diðo, a] *adj*: **en caracteres expandidos** (*Inform*) double width
expandir [ekspan'dir] *vt* to expand; (*Com*) to expand, enlarge; **expandirse** *vr* to expand, spread
expansión [ekspan'sjon] *nf* expansion; (*recreo*) relaxation; **la ~ económica** economic growth; **economía en ~** expanding economy
expansionarse [ekspansjo'narse] *vr* (*dilatarse*) to expand; (*recrearse*) to relax
expansivo, -a [ekspan'siβo, a] *adj* expansive; (*efusivo*) communicative
expatriado, -a [ekspa'trjaðo, a] *nm/f* (*emigrado*) expatriate; (*exiliado*) exile
expatriarse [ekspa'trjarse] *vr* to emigrate; (*Pol*) to go into exile
expectación [ekspekta'θjon] *nf* (*esperanza*) expectation; (*ilusión*) excitement
expectativa [ekspekta'tiβa] *nf* (*espera*) expectation; (*perspectiva*) prospect; **~ de vida** life expectancy; **estar a la ~** to wait and see (what will happen)
expedición [ekspeði'θjon] *nf* (*excursión*) expedition; **gastos de ~** shipping charges
expedientar [ekspeðjen'tar] *vt* to open a file on; (*funcionario*) to discipline, start disciplinary proceedings against
expediente [ekspe'ðjente] *nm* expedient; (*Jur: procedimento*) action, proceedings *pl*; (: *papeles*) dossier, file, record; **~ judicial** court proceedings *pl*; **~ académico** (student's) record
expedir [ekspe'ðir] *vt* (*despachar*) to send, forward; (*pasaporte*) to issue; (*cheque*) to make out
expedito, -a [ekspe'ðito, a] *adj* (*libre*) clear, free
expeler [ekspe'ler] *vt* to expel, eject
expendedor, a [ekspende'ðor, a] *nm/f* (*vendedor*) dealer; (*Teat*) ticket agent ■ *nm* (*aparato*) (vending) machine; **~ de cigarrillos** cigarette machine
expendeduría [ekspendedu'ria] *nf* (*estanco*) tobacconist's (shop) (*Brit*), cigar store (*US*)
expendio [eks'pendjo] *nm* (*Am*) small shop (*Brit*) o store (*US*)
expensas [eks'pensas] *nfpl* (*Jur*) costs; **a ~ de** at the expense of
experiencia [ekspe'rjenθja] *nf* experience
experimentado, -a [eksperimen'taðo, a] *adj* experienced
experimentar [eksperimen'tar] *vt* (*en laboratorio*) to experiment with; (*probar*) to test, try out; (*notar, observar*) to experience;

(*deterioro, pérdida*) to suffer; (*aumento*) to show; (*sensación*) to feel
experimento [eksperi'mento] *nm* experiment
experto, -a [eks'perto, a] *adj* expert ■ *nm/f* expert
expiar [ekspi'ar] *vt* to atone for
expida *etc* [eks'piða] *vb ver* **expedir**
expirar [ekspi'rar] *vi* to expire
explanada [ekspla'naða] *nf* (*paseo*) esplanade; (*a orillas del mar*) promenade
explayarse [ekspla'jarse] *vr* (*en discurso*) to speak at length; **~ con algn** to confide in sb
explicación [eksplika'θjon] *nf* explanation
explicar [ekspli'kar] *vt* to explain; (*teoría*) to expound; (*Univ*) to lecture in; **explicarse** *vr* to explain (o.s.); **no me lo explico** I can't understand it
explícito, -a [eks'pliθito, a] *adj* explicit
explique *etc* [eks'plike] *vb ver* **explicar**
exploración [eksplora'θjon] *nf* exploration; (*Mil*) reconnaissance
explorador, a [eksplora'ðor, a] *nm/f* (*pionero*) explorer; (*Mil*) scout ■ *nm* (*Med*) probe; (*radar*) (radar) scanner
explorar [eksplo'rar] *vt* to explore; (*Med*) to probe; (*radar*) to scan
explosión [eksplo'sjon] *nf* explosion
explosivo, -a [eksplo'siβo, a] *adj* explosive
explotación [eksplota'θjon] *nf* exploitation; (*de planta etc*) running; (*de mina*) working; (*de recurso*) development; **~ minera** mine; **gastos de ~** operating costs
explotar [eksplo'tar] *vt* to exploit; (*planta*) to run, operate; (*mina*) to work ■ *vi* (*bomba etc*) to explode, go off
expondré *etc* [ekspon'dre] *vb ver* **exponer**
exponer [ekspo'ner] *vt* to expose; (*cuadro*) to display; (*vida*) to risk; (*idea*) to explain; (*teoría*) to expound; (*hechos*) to set out; **exponerse** *vr*: **exponerse a (hacer) algo** to run the risk of (doing) sth
exponga *etc* [eks'ponga] *vb ver* **exponer**
exportación [eksporta'θjon] *nf* (*acción*) export; (*mercancías*) exports *pl*
exportador, a [eksporta'ðor, a] *adj* (*país*) exporting ■ *nm/f* exporter
exportar [ekspor'tar] *vt* to export
exposición [eksposi'θjon] *nf* (*gen*) exposure; (*de arte*) show, exhibition; (*Com*) display; (*feria*) show, fair; (*explicación*) explanation; (*de teoría*) exposition; (*narración*) account, statement
exprés [eks'pres] *adj inv* (*café*) espresso ■ *nm* (*Ferro*) express (train)
expresamente [ekspresa'mente] *adv* (*concretamente*) expressly; (*a propósito*) on purpose

expresar [ekspre'sar] vt to express; (redactar) to phrase, put; (emoción) to show; **expresarse** vr to express o.s.; (dato) to be stated; **como abajo se expresa** as stated below

expresión [expre'sjon] nf expression; ~ **familiar** colloquialism

expresivo, -a [ekspre'siβo, a] adj expressive; (cariñoso) affectionate

expreso, -a [eks'preso, a] adj (explícito) express; (claro) specific, clear; (tren) fast ■ nm (Ferro) fast train ■ adv: **mandar ~** to send by express (delivery)

exprimidor [eksprimi'ðor] nm (lemon) squeezer

exprimir [ekspri'mir] vt (fruta) to squeeze; (zumo) to squeeze out

ex profeso [ekspro'feso] adv expressly

expropiar [ekspro'pjar] vt to expropriate

expuesto, -a [eks'pwesto, a] pp de **exponer** ■ adj exposed; (cuadro etc) on show, on display; **según lo ~ arriba** according to what has been stated above

expulsar [ekspul'sar] vt (echar) to eject, throw out; (alumno) to expel; (despedir) to sack, fire; (Deporte) to send off

expulsión [ekspul'sjon] nf expulsion; sending-off

expurgar [ekspur'γar] vt to expurgate

expuse etc [eks'puse] vb ver **exponer**

exquisito, -a [ekski'sito, a] adj exquisite; (comida) delicious; (afectado) affected

Ext. abr (= Exterior) ext.; (= Extensión) ext.

éxtasis ['ekstasis] nm (tb droga) ecstasy

extemporáneo, -a [ekstempo'raneo, a] adj unseasonal

extender [eksten'der] vt to extend; (los brazos) to stretch out, hold out; (mapa, tela) to spread (out), open (out); (mantequilla) to spread; (certificado) to issue; (cheque, recibo) to make out; (documento) to draw up; **extenderse** vr to extend; (terreno) to stretch o spread (out); (persona: en el suelo) to stretch out; (en el tiempo) to extend, last; (costumbre, epidemia) to spread; (guerra) to escalate; **extenderse sobre un tema** to enlarge on a subject

extendido, -a [eksten'diðo, a] adj (abierto) spread out, open; (brazos) outstretched; (costumbre etc) widespread

extensible [eksten'siβle] adj extending

extensión [eksten'sjon] nf (de terreno, mar) expanse, stretch; (Mus) range; (de conocimientos) extent; (de programa) scope; (de tiempo) length, duration; (Telec) extension; ~ **de plazo** (Com) extension; **en toda la ~ de la palabra** in every sense of the word; **de ~** (Inform) add-on

extenso, -a [eks'tenso, a] adj extensive

extenuar [ekste'nwar] vt (debilitar) to weaken

exterior [ekste'rjor] adj (de fuera) external; (afuera) outside, exterior; (apariencia) outward; (deuda, relaciones) foreign ■ nm exterior, outside; (aspecto) outward appearance; (Deporte) wing(er); (países extranjeros) abroad; **asuntos exteriores** foreign affairs; **al ~** outwardly, on the outside; **en el ~** abroad; **noticias del ~** foreign o overseas news

exteriorice etc [ekste'rjoriθe] vb ver **exteriorizar**

exteriorizar [eksterjori'θar] vt (emociones) to show, reveal

exteriormente [eksterjor'mente] adv outwardly

exterminar [ekstermi'nar] vt to exterminate

exterminio [ekster'minjo] nm extermination

externo, -a [eks'terno, a] adj (exterior) external, outside; (superficial) outward ■ nm/f day pupil

extienda etc [eks'tjenda] vb ver **extender**

extinción [ekstin'θjon] nf extinction

extinga etc [eks'tinga] vb ver **extinguir**

extinguido, -a [ekstin'giðo, a] adj (animal, volcán) extinct; (fuego) out, extinguished

extinguir [ekstin'gir] vt (fuego) to extinguish, put out; (raza, población) to wipe out; **extinguirse** vr (fuego) to go out; (Bio) to die out, become extinct

extinto, -a [eks'tinto, a] adj extinct

extintor [ekstin'tor] nm (fire) extinguisher

extirpar [ekstir'par] vt (vicios) to eradicate, stamp out; (Med) to remove (surgically)

extorsión [ekstor'sjon] nf blackmail

extra ['ekstra] adj inv (tiempo) extra; (vino) vintage; (chocolate) good-quality; (gasolina) high-octane ■ nm/f extra ■ nm (bono) bonus; (periódico) special edition

extracción [ekstrak'θjon] nf extraction; (en lotería) draw; (de carbón) mining

extracto [eks'trakto] nm extract

extractor [ekstrak'tor] nm (tb: **extractor de humos**) extractor fan

extradición [ekstraði'θjon] nf extradition

extraditar [ekstraði'tar] vt to extradite

extraer [ekstra'er] vt to extract, take out

extrafino, -a [ekstra'fino, a] adj extra-fine; **azúcar ~** caster sugar

extraiga etc [eks'traiγa], **extraje** etc [eks'traxe], **extrajera** etc [ekstra'xera] vb ver **extraer**

extralimitarse [ekstralimi'tarse] vr to go too far

extranjerismo [ekstranxe'rismo] nm foreign word o phrase etc

e

extranjero, -a [ekstran'xero, a] *adj* foreign ■ *nm/f* foreigner ■ *nm* foreign lands *pl*; **en el ~** abroad

extrañamiento [ekstraɲa'mjento] *nm* estrangement

extrañar [ekstra'ɲar] *vt* (*sorprender*) to find strange *o* odd; (*echar de menos*) to miss; **extrañarse** *vr* (*sorprenderse*) to be amazed, be surprised; (*distanciarse*) to become estranged, grow apart; **me extraña** I'm surprised

extrañeza [ekstra'ɲeθa] *nf* (*rareza*) strangeness, oddness; (*asombro*) amazement, surprise

extraño, -a [eks'traɲo, a] *adj* (*extranjero*) foreign; (*raro, sorprendente*) strange, odd

extraoficial [ekstraofi'θjal] *adj* unofficial, informal

extraordinario, -a [ekstraorði'narjo, a] *adj* extraordinary; (*edición, número*) special ■ *nm* (*de periódico*) special edition; **horas extraordinarias** overtime *sg*

extrarradio [ekstra'rraðjo] *nm* suburbs *pl*

extrasensorial [ekstrasenso'rjal] *adj*: **percepción ~** extrasensory perception

extraterrestre [ekstrate'rrestre] *adj* of *o* from outer space ■ *nm/f* creature from outer space

extravagancia [ekstraβa'ɣanθja] *nf* oddness; outlandishness; (*rareza*) peculiarity; **extravagancias** *nfpl* (*tonterías*) nonsense *sg*

extravagante [ekstraβa'ɣante] *adj* (*excéntrico*) eccentric; (*estrafalario*) outlandish

extraviado, -a [ekstra'βjaðo, a] *adj* lost, missing

extraviar [ekstra'βjar] *vt* to mislead, misdirect; (*perder*) to lose, misplace; **extraviarse** *vr* to lose one's way, get lost;

(*objeto*) to go missing, be mislaid

extravío [ekstra'βio] *nm* loss; (*fig*) misconduct

extrayendo [ekstra'jendo] *vb ver* **extraer**

extremado, -a [ekstre'maðo, a] *adj* extreme, excessive

Extremadura [ekstrema'ðura] *nf* Estremadura

extremar [ekstre'mar] *vt* to carry to extremes; **extremarse** *vr* to do one's utmost, make every effort

extremaunción [ekstremaun'θjon] *nf* extreme unction, last rites *pl*

extremidad [ekstremi'ðað] *nf* (*punta*) extremity; (*fila*) edge; **extremidades** *nfpl* (*Anat*) extremities

extremista [ekstre'mista] *adj, nm/f* extremist

extremo, -a [eks'tremo, a] *adj* extreme; (*más alejado*) furthest; (*último*) last ■ *nm* end; (*situación*) extreme; **E~ Oriente** Far East; **en último ~** as a last resort; **pasar de un ~ a otro** (*fig*) to go from one extreme to the other; **con ~** in the extreme; **la extrema derecha** (*Pol*) the far right; **~ derecho/izquierdo** (*Deporte*) outside right/left

extrínseco, -a [eks'trinseko, a] *adj* extrinsic

extrovertido, -a [ekstroβer'tiðo, a] *adj* extrovert, outgoing ■ *nm/f* extrovert

exuberancia [eksuβe'ranθja] *nf* exuberance

exuberante [eksuβe'rante] *adj* exuberant; (*fig*) luxuriant, lush

exudar [eksu'ðar] *vt, vi* to exude

exultar [eksul'tar] *vi*: **~ (en)** to exult (in); (*pey*) to gloat (over)

exvoto [eks'βoto] *nm* votive offering

eyaculación [ejakula'θjon] *nf* ejaculation

eyacular [ejaku'lar] *vt, vi* to ejaculate

Ff

F, f ['efe] *nf* (*letra*) F, f; **F de Francia** F for Frederick (*Brit*), F for Fox (*US*)

fa [fa] *nm* (*Mus*) F

f.ª *abr* (*Com*: = *factura*) Inv.

fabada [fa'βaða] *nf bean and sausage stew*

fábrica ['faβrika] *nf* factory; **~ de moneda** mint; **marca de ~** trademark; **precio de ~** factory price

fabricación [faβrika'θjon] *nf* (*manufactura*) manufacture; (*producción*) production; **de ~ casera** home-made; **de ~ nacional** home produced; **~ en serie** mass production

fabricante [faβri'kante] *nm/f* manufacturer

fabricar [faβri'kar] *vt* (*manufacturar*) to manufacture, make; (*construir*) to build; (*cuento*) to fabricate, devise; **~ en serie** to mass-produce

fabril [fa'βril] *adj*: **industria ~** manufacturing industry

fabrique *etc* [fa'βrike] *vb ver* **fabricar**

fábula ['faβula] *nf* (*cuento*) fable; (*chisme*) rumour; (*mentira*) fib

fabuloso, -a [faβu'loso, a] *adj* fabulous, fantastic

facción [fak'θjon] *nf* (*Pol*) faction; **facciones** *nfpl* (*del rostro*) features

faceta [fa'θeta] *nf* facet

facha ['fatʃa] (*fam*) *nm/f* fascist, right-wing extremist ■ *nf* (*aspecto*) look; (*cara*) face; **¡qué ~ tienes!** you look a sight!

fachada [fa'tʃaða] *nf* (*Arq*) façade, front; (*Tip*) title page; (*fig*) façade, outward show

facial [fa'θjal] *adj* facial

fácil ['faθil] *adj* (*simple*) easy; (*sencillo*) simple, straightforward; (*probable*) likely; (*respuesta*) facile; **~ de usar** (*Inform*) user-friendly

facilidad [faθili'ðað] *nf* (*capacidad*) ease; (*sencillez*) simplicity; (*de palabra*) fluency; **facilidades** *nfpl* facilities; **"facilidades de pago"** (*Com*) "credit facilities", "payment terms"

facilitar [faθili'tar] *vt* (*hacer fácil*) to make easy; (*proporcionar*) to provide; (*documento*) to

issue; **le agradecería me facilitara ...** I would be grateful if you could let me have ...

fácilmente ['faθilmente] *adv* easily

facsímil [fak'simil] *nm* (*documento*) facsimile; **enviar por ~** to fax

factible [fak'tiβle] *adj* feasible

factor [fak'tor] *nm* factor; (*Com*) agent; (*Ferro*) freight clerk

factoría [fakto'ria] *nf* (*Com: fábrica*) factory

factura [fak'tura] *nf* (*cuenta*) bill; (*nota de pago*) invoice; (*hechura*) manufacture; **presentar ~ a** to invoice

facturación [faktura'θjon] *nf* (*Com*) invoicing; (: *ventas*) turnover; **~ de equipajes** luggage check-in; **~ online** online check-in

facturar [faktu'rar] *vt* (*Com*) to invoice, charge for; (*Aviat*) to check in; (*equipaje*) to register, check (*US*)

facultad [fakul'tað] *nf* (*aptitud, Escol etc*) faculty; (*poder*) power

facultativo, -a [fakulta'tiβo, a] *adj* optional; (*de un oficio*) professional; **prescripción facultativa** medical prescription

FAD *nm abr* (*Esp*) = **Fondo de Ayuda y Desarrollo**

faena [fa'ena] *nf* (*trabajo*) work; (*quehacer*) task, job; **faenas domésticas** housework *sg*

faenar [fae'nar] *vi* to fish

fagot [fa'yot] *nm* (*Mus*) bassoon

faisán [fai'san] *nm* pheasant

faja ['faxa] *nf* (*para la cintura*) sash; (*de mujer*) corset; (*de tierra*) strip

fajo ['faxo] *nm* (*de papeles*) bundle; (*de billetes*) role, wad

falange [fa'lanxe] *nf*: **la F~** (*Pol*) the Falange

falda ['falda] *nf* (*prenda de vestir*) skirt; (*Geo*) foothill; **~ escocesa** kilt

fálico, -a ['faliko, a] *adj* phallic

falla ['faʎa] *nf* (*defecto*) fault, flaw

fallar [fa'ʎar] *vt* (*Jur*) to pronounce sentence on; (*Naipes*) to trump ■ *vi* (*memoria*) to fail; (*plan*) to go wrong; (*motor*) to miss; **~ a algn** to let sb down

Fallas ['faʎas] *nfpl see note*

In the week of the 19th of March (the feast of St Joseph, San José), Valencia honours its patron saint with a spectacular *fiesta* called *las Fallas*. The *Fallas* are huge sculptures, made of wood, cardboard, paper and cloth, depicting famous politicians and other targets for ridicule, which are set alight and burned by the *falleros*, members of the competing local groups who have just spent months preparing them.

fallecer [faʎe'θer] *vi* to pass away, die
fallecido, -a [faʎe'θiðo, a] *adj* late ■ *nm/f* deceased
fallecimiento [faʎeθi'mjento] *nm* decease, demise
fallero, -a [fa'ʎero, a] *nm/f* maker of "Fallas"
fallezca *etc* [fa'ʎeθka] *vb ver* **fallecer**
fallido, -a [fa'ʎiðo, a] *adj* vain; (*intento*) frustrated, unsuccessful
fallo ['faʎo] *nm* (*Jur*) verdict, ruling; (*decisión*) decision; (*de jurado*) findings; (*fracaso*) failure; (*Deporte*) miss; (*Inform*) bug
falo ['falo] *nm* phallus
falsear [false'ar] *vt* to falsify; (*firma etc*) to forge ■ *vi* (*Mus*) to be out of tune
falsedad [false'ðað] *nf* falseness; (*hipocresía*) hypocrisy; (*mentira*) falsehood
falsificación [falsifika'θjon] *nf* (*acto*) falsification; (*objeto*) forgery
falsificar [falsifi'kar] *vt* (*firma etc*) to forge; (*voto etc*) to rig; (*moneda*) to counterfeit
falsifique *etc* [falsi'fike] *vb ver* **falsificar**
falso, -a ['falso, a] *adj* false; (*erróneo*) wrong, mistaken; (*firma, documento*) forged; (*moneda etc*) fake; **en ~** falsely; **dar un paso en ~** to trip; (*fig*) to take a false step
falta ['falta] *nf* (*defecto*) fault, flaw; (*privación*) lack, want; (*ausencia*) absence; (*carencia*) shortage; (*equivocación*) mistake; (*Jur*) default; (*Deporte*) foul; (*Tenis*) fault; **~ de ortografía** spelling mistake; **~ de respeto** disrespect; **echar en ~** to miss; **hacer ~ hacer algo** to be necessary to do sth; **me hace ~ una pluma** I need a pen; **sin ~** without fail; **por ~ de** through o for lack of
faltar [fal'tar] *vi* (*escasear*) to be lacking, be wanting; (*ausentarse*) to be absent, be missing; **¿falta algo?** is anything missing?; **falta mucho todavía** there's plenty of time yet; **¿falta mucho?** is there long to go?; **faltan dos horas para llegar** there are two hours to go till arrival; **~ (al respeto) a algn** to be disrespectful to sb; **~ a una cita** to miss

an appointment; **~ a la verdad** to lie; **¡no faltaba más!** that's the last straw!
falto, -a ['falto, a] *adj* (*desposeído*) deficient, lacking; (*necesitado*) poor, wretched; **estar ~ de** to be short of
fama ['fama] *nf* (*renombre*) fame; (*reputación*) reputation
famélico, -a [fa'meliko, a] *adj* starving
familia [fa'milja] *nf* family; **~ política** in-laws *pl*
familiar [fami'ljar] *adj* (*relativo a la familia*) family *cpd*; (*conocido, informal*) familiar; (*estilo*) informal; (*Ling*) colloquial ■ *nm/f* relative, relation
familiarice *etc* [familja'riθe] *vb ver* **familiarizarse**
familiaridad [familjari'ðað] *nf* familiarity; (*informalidad*) homeliness
familiarizarse [familjari'θarse] *vr*: **~ con** to familiarize o.s. with
famoso, -a [fa'moso, a] *adj* (*renombrado*) famous
fan (*pl* **fans**) [fan, fans] *nm* fan
fanático, -a [fa'natiko, a] *adj* fanatical ■ *nm/f* fanatic; (*Cine, Deporte etc*) fan
fanatismo [fana'tismo] *nm* fanaticism
fanfarrón, -ona [fanfa'rron, ona] *adj* boastful; (*pey*) showy
fanfarronear [fanfarrone'ar] *vi* to boast
fango ['fango] *nm* mud
fangoso, -a [fan'goso, a] *adj* muddy
fantasear [fantase'ar] *vi* to fantasize; **~ con una idea** to toy with an idea
fantasía [fanta'sia] *nf* fantasy, imagination; (*Mus*) fantasia; (*capricho*) whim; **joyas de ~** imitation jewellery *sg*
fantasma [fan'tasma] *nm* (*espectro*) ghost, apparition; (*presumido*) show-off
fantástico, -a [fan'tastiko, a] *adj* (*irreal, fam*) fantastic
fanzine [fan'θine] *nm* fanzine
FAO ['fao] *nf abr* (= *Organización de las Naciones Unidas para la Agricultura y la Alimentación*) FAO
faquir [fa'kir] *nm* fakir
faraón [fara'on] *nm* Pharaoh
faraónico, -a [fara'oniko, a] *adj* Pharaonic; (*fig*) grandiose
fardar [far'ðar] *vi* to show off; **~ de** to boast about
fardo ['farðo] *nm* bundle; (*fig*) burden
faringe [fa'rinxe] *nf* pharynx
faringitis [farin'xitis] *nf* pharyngitis
farmacéutico, -a [farma'θeutiko, a] *adj* pharmaceutical ■ *nm/f* chemist (*Brit*), pharmacist
farmacia [far'maθja] *nf* (*ciencia*) pharmacy; (*tienda*) chemist's (shop) (*Brit*), pharmacy,

drugstore (US); ~ **de turno** duty chemist
fármaco ['farmako] nm medicine, drug
faro ['faro] nm (Naut: torre) lighthouse; (señal)
beacon; (Auto) headlamp; **faros antiniebla**
fog lamps; **faros delanteros/traseros**
headlights/rear lights
farol [fa'rol] nm (luz) lantern, lamp; (Ferro)
headlamp; (poste) lamppost; **echarse un ~**
(fam) to show off
farola [fa'rola] nf street lamp (Brit) o light
(US), lamppost
farruco, -a [fa'rruko, a] adj (fam): **estar** o
ponerse ~ to get aggressive
farsa ['farsa] nf farce
farsante [far'sante] nm/f fraud, fake
FASA ['fasa] nf abr (Esp Auto) = **Fábrica de**
Automóviles, S.A.
fascículo [fas'θikulo] nm part, instalment
(Brit), installment (US)
fascinante [fasθi'nante] adj fascinating
fascinar [fasθi'nar] vt to fascinate; (encantar)
to captivate
fascismo [fas'θismo] nm fascism
fascista [fas'θista] adj, nm/f fascist
fase ['fase] nf phase
fastidiar [fasti'ðjar] vt (disgustar) to annoy,
bother; (estropear) to spoil; **fastidiarse**
vr (disgustarse) to get annoyed o cross; **¡no**
fastidies! you're joking!; **¡que se fastidie!**
(fam) he'll just have to put up with it!
fastidio [fas'tiðjo] nm (disgusto) annoyance
fastidioso, -a [fasti'ðjoso, a] adj (molesto)
annoying
fastuoso, -a [fas'twoso, a] adj (espléndido)
magnificent; (banquete etc) lavish
fatal [fa'tal] adj (gen) fatal; (desgraciado) ill-
fated; (fam: malo, pésimo) awful ■ adv terribly;
lo pasó ~ he had a terrible time (of it)
fatalidad [fatali'ðað] nf (destino) fate; (mala
suerte) misfortune
fatídico, -a [fa'tiðiko, a] adj fateful
fatiga [fa'tiɣa] nf (cansancio) fatigue,
weariness; **fatigas** nfpl hardships
fatigar [fati'ɣar] vt to tire, weary; **fatigarse**
vr to get tired
fatigoso, -a [fati'ɣoso, a] adj (que cansa) tiring
fatigue etc [fa'tiɣe] vb ver **fatigar**
fatuo, -a ['fatwo, a] adj (vano) fatuous;
(presuntuoso) conceited
fauces ['fauθes] nfpl (Anat) gullet sg; (fam)
jaws
fauna ['fauna] nf fauna
favor [fa'βor] nm favour (Brit), favor (US);
haga el ~ de ... would you be so good as to ...,
kindly ...; **por ~** please; **a ~** in favo(u)r; **a ~ de**
in favo(u)r of; (Com) to the order of
favorable [faβo'raβle] adj favourable (Brit),

favorable (US); (condiciones etc) advantageous
favorecer [faβore'θer] vt to favour (Brit),
favor (US); (amparar) to help; (vestido etc) to
become, flatter; **este peinado le favorece**
this hairstyle suits him
favorezca etc [faβo'reθka] vb ver **favorecer**
favorito, -a [faβo'rito, a] adj, nm/f favourite
(Brit), favorite (US)
fax [faks] nm inv fax; **mandar por ~** to fax
faz [faθ] nf face; **la ~ de la tierra** the face of
the earth
FBI nm abr FBI
F.C., f.c. abr = **ferrocarril**; (= Fútbol Club) FC
FE nf abr = **Falange Española**
fe [fe] nf (Rel) faith; (confianza) belief;
(documento) certificate; **de buena fe** (Jur)
bona fide; **prestar fe a** to believe, credit;
actuar con buena/mala fe to act in good/
bad faith; **dar fe de** to bear witness to; **fe de**
erratas errata
fealdad [feal'dað] nf ugliness
feb., feb.° abr (= febrero) Feb.
febrero [fe'βrero] nm February; ver tb **julio**
febril [fe'βril] adj feverish; (movido) hectic
fecha ['fetʃa] nf date; **~ límite** o **tope** closing
o last date; **~ límite de venta** (de alimentos)
sell-by date; **~ de caducidad** (de alimentos)
sell-by date; (de contrato) expiry date; **en ~**
próxima soon; **hasta la ~** to date, so far; **~ de**
vencimiento (Com) due date; **~ de vigencia**
(Com) effective date
fechar [fe'tʃar] vt to date
fechoría [fetʃo'ria] nf misdeed
fécula ['fekula] nf starch
fecundación [fekunda'θjon] nf fertilization;
~ in vitro in vitro fertilization, I.V.F.
fecundar [fekun'dar] vt (generar) to fertilize,
make fertile
fecundidad [fekundi'ðað] nf fertility; (fig)
productiveness
fecundo, -a [fe'kundo, a] adj (fértil) fertile;
(fig) prolific; (productivo) productive
FED nm abr (= Fondo Europeo de Desarrollo) EDF
FEDER nm abr (= Fondo Europeo de Desarrollo
Regional) ERDF
federación [feðera'θjon] nf federation
federal [feðe'ral] adj federal
federalismo [feðera'lismo] nm federalism
FEF [fef] nf abr = **Federación Española de**
Fútbol
felicidad [feliθi'ðað] nf (satisfacción, contento)
happiness; **felicidades** nfpl best wishes,
congratulations
felicitación [feliθita'θjon] nf (tarjeta)
greetings card; **felicitaciones** nfpl
(enhorabuena) congratulations; **~ navideña** o
de Navidad Christmas Greetings

felicitar [feliθi'tar] vt to congratulate
feligrés, -esa [feli'ɣres, esa] nm/f parishioner
felino, -a [fe'lino, a] adj cat-like; (Zool) feline
■ nm feline
feliz [fe'liθ] adj (contento) happy; (afortunado) lucky
felonía [felo'nia] nf felony, crime
felpa ['felpa] nf (terciopelo) plush; (toalla) towelling
felpudo [fel'puðo] nm doormat
femenino, -a [feme'nino, a] adj feminine; (Zool etc) female ■ nm (Ling) feminine
feminismo [femi'nismo] nm feminism
feminista [femi'nista] adj, nm/f feminist
fenomenal [fenome'nal] adj phenomenal; (fam) great, terrific
fenómeno [fe'nomeno] nm phenomenon; (fig) freak, accident ■ adv: **lo pasamos** ~ we had a great time ■ excl great!, marvellous!
feo, -a ['feo, a] adj (gen) ugly; (desagradable) bad, nasty ■ nm insult; **hacer un** ~ **a algn** to offend sb; **más** ~ **que Picio** as ugly as sin
féretro ['feretro] nm (ataúd) coffin; (sarcófago) bier
feria ['ferja] nf (gen) fair; (Am: mercado) market; (descanso) holiday, rest day; (Am: cambio) small change; ~ **comercial** trade fair; ~ **de muestras** trade show
feriado, -a [fe'rjaðo, a] (Am) adj: **día** ~ (public) holiday ■ nm (public) holiday
fermentar [fermen'tar] vi to ferment
fermento [fer'mento] nm leaven, leavening
ferocidad [feroθi'ðað] nf fierceness, ferocity
ferocísimo, -a [fero'θisimo, a] adj superlativo de **feroz**
feroz [fe'roθ] adj (cruel) cruel; (salvaje) fierce
férreo, -a ['ferreo, a] adj iron cpd; (Tec) ferrous; (fig) (of) iron
ferretería [ferrete'ria] nf (tienda) ironmonger's (shop) (Brit), hardware store
ferretero [ferre'tero] nm ironmonger
ferrocarril [ferroka'rril] nm railway, railroad (US); ~ **de vía estrecha/única** narrow-gauge/single-track railway o line
ferroviario, -a [ferrovja'rjo, a] adj rail cpd, railway cpd (Brit), railroad cpd (US) ■ nm: **ferroviarios** railway (Brit) o railroad (US) workers
fértil ['fertil] adj (productivo) fertile; (rico) rich
fertilice etc [ferti'liθe] vb ver **fertilizar**
fertilidad [fertili'ðað] nf (gen) fertility; (productividad) fruitfulness
fertilizante [fertili'θante] nm fertilizer
fertilizar [fertili'θar] vt to fertilize
ferviente [fer'βjente] adj fervent
fervor [fer'βor] nm fervour (Brit), fervor (US)
fervoroso, -a [ferβo'roso, a] adj fervent

festejar [feste'xar] vt (agasajar) to wine and dine; (galantear) to court; (celebrar) to celebrate
festejo [fes'texo] nm (diversión) entertainment; (galanteo) courtship; (fiesta) celebration
festín [fes'tin] nm feast, banquet
festival [festi'βal] nm festival
festividad [festiβi'ðað] nf festivity
festivo, -a [fes'tiβo, a] adj (de fiesta) festive; (fig) witty; (Cine, Lit) humorous; **día** ~ holiday
fetiche [fe'titʃe] nm fetish
fetichista [feti'tʃista] adj fetishistic ■ nm/f fetishist
fétido, -a ['fetiðo, a] adj (hediondo) foul-smelling
feto ['feto] nm foetus; (fam) monster
F.E.V.E. nf abr (= Ferrocarriles Españoles de Vía Estrecha) Spanish narrow-gauge railways
FF.AA. nfpl abr (Mil) = **Fuerzas Armadas**
FF.CC. nmpl abr (= Ferrocarriles) ver **ferrocarril**
fiable [fi'aβle] adj (persona) trustworthy; (máquina) reliable
fiado [fi'aðo] nm: **comprar al** ~ to buy on credit; **en** ~ on bail
fiador, a [fia'ðor, a] nm/f (Jur) surety, guarantor; (Com) backer; **salir** ~ **por algn** to stand bail for sb
fiambre ['fjambre] adj (Culin) served cold ■ nm (Culin) cold meat (Brit), cold cut (US); (fam) corpse, stiff
fiambrera [fjam'brera] nf ≈ lunch box, ≈ dinner pail (US)
fianza ['fjanθa] nf surety; (Jur): **libertad bajo** ~ release on bail
fiar [fi'ar] vt (salir garante de) to guarantee; (Jur) to stand bail o bond (US) for; (vender a crédito) to sell on credit; (secreto) to confide ■ vi: ~ **(de)** to trust (in); **ser de** ~ to be trustworthy; **fiarse** vr: **fiarse de** to trust (in), rely on
fiasco ['fjasko] nm fiasco
fibra ['fiβra] nf fibre (Brit), fiber (US); (fig) vigour (Brit), vigor (US); ~ **óptica** (Inform) optical fibre (Brit) o fiber (US)
ficción [fik'θjon] nf fiction
ficha ['fitʃa] nf (Telec) token; (en juegos) counter, marker; (en casino) chip; (Com, Econ) tally, check (US); (Inform) file; (tarjeta) (index) card; (Elec) plug; (en hotel) registration form; ~ **policíaca** police dossier
fichaje [fi'tʃaxe] nm signing(-up)
fichar [fi'tʃar] vt (archivar) to file, index; (Deporte) to sign (up) ■ vi (deportista) to sign (up); (obrero) to clock in o on; **estar fichado** to have a record
fichero [fi'tʃero] nm card index; (archivo) filing cabinet; (Com) box file; (Inform) file, archive; (de policía) criminal records; ~ **activo**

(*Inform*) active file; ~ **archivado** (*Inform*) archived file; ~ **indexado** (*Inform*) index file; ~ **de reserva** (*Inform*) backup file; ~ **de tarjetas** card index; **nombre de** ~ filename

ficticio, -a [fik'tiθjo, a] *adj* (*imaginario*) fictitious; (*falso*) fabricated

ficus ['fikus] *nm inv* (*Bot*) rubber plant

fidedigno, -a [fiðe'ðiɣno, a] *adj* reliable

fideicomiso [fiðeiko'miso] *nm* (*Com*) trust

fidelidad [fiðeli'ðað] *nf* (*lealtad*) fidelity, loyalty; (*exactitud: de dato etc*) accuracy; **alta** ~ high fidelity, hi-fi

fidelísimo, -a [fiðe'lisimo, a] *adj superlativo de* **fiel**

fideos [fi'ðeos] *nmpl* noodles

fiduciario, -a [fiðu'θjarjo, a] *nm/f* fiduciary

fiebre ['fjeβre] *nf* (*Med*) fever; (*fig*) fever, excitement; ~ **amarilla/del heno** yellow/ hay fever; ~ **palúdica** malaria; **tener** ~ to have a temperature

fiel [fjel] *adj* (*leal*) faithful, loyal; (*fiable*) reliable; (*exacto*) accurate ■ *nm* (*aguja*) needle, pointer; **los fieles** *nmpl* the faithful

fieltro ['fjeltro] *nm* felt

fiera ['fjera] *nf ver* **fiero**

fiereza [tje're̞θa] *nf* (*Zool*) wildness; (*bravura*) fierceness

fiero, -a ['fjero, a] *adj* (*cruel*) cruel; (*feroz*) fierce; (*duro*) harsh ■ *nm/f* (*fig*) fiend ■ *nf* (*animal feroz*) wild animal o beast; (*fig*) dragon

fierro ['fjerro] *nm* (*Am*) iron

fiesta ['fjesta] *nf* party; (*de pueblo*) festival; **la** ~ **nacional** bullfighting; (**día de**) ~ (public) holiday; **mañana es** ~ it's a holiday tomorrow; ~ **de guardar** (*Rel*) day of obligation; *see note*

○ **FIESTA**

○ *Fiestas* can be official public holidays
○ (such as the *Día de la Constitución*), or special
○ holidays for each *comunidad autónoma*,
○ many of which are religious feast days.
○ All over Spain there are also special local
○ *fiestas* for a patron saint or the Virgin
○ Mary. These often last several days
○ and can include religious processions,
○ carnival parades, bullfights, dancing and
○ feasts of typical local produce.

FIFA *nf abr* (= *Federación Internacional de Fútbol Asociación*) FIFA

figura [fi'ɣura] *nf* (*gen*) figure; (*forma, imagen*) shape, form; (*Naipes*) face card

figurado, -a [fiɣu'raðo, a] *adj* figurative

figurante [fiɣu'rante] *nm/f* (*Teat*) walk-on part; (*Cine*) extra

figurar [fiɣu'rar] *vt* (*representar*) to represent; (*fingir*) to feign ■ *vi* to figure; **figurarse** *vr* (*imaginarse*) to imagine; (*suponer*) to suppose; **ya me lo figuraba** I thought as much

fijador [fixa'ðor] *nm* (*Foto etc*) fixative; (*de pelo*) gel

fijar [fi'xar] *vt* (*gen*) to fix; (*cartel*) to post, put up; (*estampilla*) to affix, stick (on); (*pelo*) to set; (*fig*) to settle (on), decide; **fijarse** *vr*: **fijarse en** to notice; **¡fíjate!** just imagine!; **¿te fijas?** see what I mean?

fijo, -a ['fixo, a] *adj* (*gen*) fixed; (*firme*) firm; (*permanente*) permanent; (*trabajo*) steady; (*colorfast*) fast ■ *adv*: **mirar** ~ to stare

fila ['fila] *nf* row; (*Mil*) rank; (*cadena*) line; (*en marcha*) file; ~ **india** single file; **ponerse en** ~ to line up, get into line; **primera** ~ front row

filántropo, -a [fi'lantropo, a] *nm/f* philanthropist

filarmónico, a [filar'moniko, a] *adj, nf* philharmonic

filatelia [fila'telja] *nf* philately, stamp collecting

filatelista [filate'lista] *nm/f* philatelist, stamp collector

filete [fi'lete] *nm* (*de carne*) fillet steak; (*de cerdo*) tenderloin; (*pescado*) fillet; (*Mecánica: rosca*) thread

filiación [filja'θjon] *nf* (*Pol etc*) affiliation; (*señas*) particulars *pl*; (*Mil, Policía*) records *pl*

filial [fi'ljal] *adj* filial ■ *nf* subsidiary; (*sucursal*) branch

Filipinas [fili'pinas] *nfpl*: **las (Islas)** ~ the Philippines

filipino, -a [fili'pino, a] *adj, nm/f* Philippine

film [film] (*pl* **films**) *nm* = **filme**

filmación [filma'θjon] *nf* filming, shooting

filmar [fil'mar] *vt* to film, shoot

filme ['filme] *nm* film, movie (*US*)

filmoteca [filmo'teka] *nf* film library

filo ['filo] *nm* (*gen*) edge; **sacar** ~ a to sharpen; **al** ~ **del medio día** at about midday; **de doble** ~ double-edged

filología [filolo'xia] *nf* philology

filólogo, -a [fi'loloɣo, a] *nm/f* philologist

filón [fi'lon] *nm* (*Minería*) vein, lode; (*fig*) gold mine

filoso, -a [fi'loso, a] *adj* (*Am*) sharp

filosofía [filoso'fia] *nf* philosophy

filosófico, -a [filo'sofiko, a] *adj* philosophic(al)

filósofo, -a [fi'losofo, a] *nm/f* philosopher

filtración [filtra'θjon] *nf* (*Tec*) filtration; (*Inform*) sorting; (*fig: de fondos*) misappropriation; (*de datos*) leak

filtrar [fil'trar] *vt, vi* to filter, strain; (*información*) to leak; **filtrarse** *vr* to filter;

f

(fig: dinero) to dwindle
filtro ['filtro] nm (Tec, utensilio) filter
filudo, -a [fi'luðo, a] adj (Am) sharp
fin [fin] nm end; (objetivo) aim, purpose; **a ~ de cuentas** at the end of the day; **al ~ y al cabo** when all's said and done; **a ~ de** in order to; **por ~** finally; **en ~** (resumiendo) in short; **¡en ~!** (resignación) oh, well!; **~ de archivo** (Inform) end-of-file; **~ de semana** weekend; **sin ~** endless(ly)
final [fi'nal] adj final ■ nm end, conclusion ■ nf (Deporte) final
finalice etc [fina'liθe] vb ver **finalizar**
finalidad [finali'ðað] nf finality; (propósito) purpose, aim
finalista [fina'lista] nm/f finalist
finalizar [finali'θar] vt to end, finish ■ vi to end, come to an end; **~ la sesión** (Inform) to log out o off
financiación [finanθja'θjon] nf financing
financiar [finan'θjar] vt to finance
financiero, -a [finan'θjero, a] adj financial ■ nm/f financier
financista [finan'sista] nm/f (Am) financier
finanzas [fi'nanθas] nfpl finances
finca ['finka] nf country estate
finde ['finde] nm abbr (fam: = fin de semana) weekend
fineza [fi'neθa] nf (cualidad) fineness; (de modales) refinement
fingir [fin'xir] vt (simular) to simulate, feign; (pretextar) to sham, fake ■ vi (aparentar) to pretend; **fingirse** vr: **fingirse dormido** to pretend to be asleep
finiquitar [finiki'tar] vt (Econ: cuenta) to settle and close
Finisterre [finis'terre] nm: **el cabo de ~** Cape Finisterre
finja etc ['finxa] vb ver **fingir**
finlandés, -esa [finlan'des, esa] adj Finnish ■ nm/f Finn ■ nm (Ling) Finnish
Finlandia [fin'landja] nf Finland
fino, -a ['fino, a] adj fine; (delgado) slender; (de buenas maneras) polite, refined; (inteligente) shrewd; (punta) sharp; (gusto) discriminating; (oído) sharp; (jerez) fino, dry ■ nm (jerez) dry sherry
finura [fi'nura] nf (calidad) fineness; (cortesía) politeness; (elegancia) elegance; (agudeza) shrewdness
FIP [fip] nf abr (Esp) = **Formación Intensiva Profesional**
firma ['firma] nf signature; (Com) firm, company
firmamento [firma'mento] nm firmament
firmante [fir'mante] adj, nm/f signatory; **los abajo firmantes** the undersigned

firmar [fir'mar] vt to sign; **~ un contrato** (Com: colocarse) to sign on; **firmado y sellado** signed and sealed
firme ['firme] adj firm; (estable) stable; (sólido) solid; (constante) steady; (decidido) resolute; (duro) hard; **¡firmes!** (Mil) attention!; **oferta en ~** (Com) firm offer ■ nm road (surface)
firmemente [firme'mente] adv firmly
firmeza [fir'meθa] nf firmness; (constancia) steadiness; (solidez) solidity
fiscal [fis'kal] adj fiscal ■ nm (Jur) ≈ Crown Prosecutor, ≈ Procurator Fiscal (Escocia), ≈ district attorney (US)
fiscalice etc [fiska'liθe] vb ver **fiscalizar**
fiscalizar [fiskali'θar] vt (controlar) to control; (registrar) to inspect (officially); (fig) to criticize
fisco ['fisko] nm (hacienda) treasury, exchequer; **declarar algo al ~** to declare sth for tax purposes
fisgar [fis'yar] vt to pry into
fisgón, -ona [fis'yon, ona] adj nosey
fisgue etc ['fisye] vb ver **fisgar**
físico, -a ['fisiko, a] adj physical ■ nm physique; (aspecto) appearance, looks pl ■ nm/f physicist ■ nf physics sg
fisioterapeuta [fisjotera'peuta] nm/f physiotherapist
fisioterapia [fisjote'rapja] nf physiotherapy
fisioterapista [fisjotera'pista] nm/f (Am) physiotherapist
fisonomía [fisono'mia] nf physiognomy, features pl
fisonomista [fisono'mista] nm/f: **ser buen ~** to have a good memory for faces
flaccidez [flakθi'ðeθ], **flacidez** [flaθi'ðeθ] nf softness, flabbiness
fláccido, -a ['flakθiðo, a], **flácido, -a** ['flaθiðo, a] adj flabby
flaco, -a ['flako, a] adj (muy delgado) skinny, thin; (débil) weak, feeble
flagrante [fla'yrante] adj flagrant
flamante [fla'mante] adj (fam) brilliant; (: nuevo) brand-new
flamear [flame'ar] vt (Culin) to flambé
flamenco, -a [fla'menko, a] adj (de Flandes) Flemish; (baile, música) gipsy ■ nm/f Fleming; **los flamencos** the Flemish ■ nm (Ling) Flemish; (baile, música) flamenco; (Zool) flamingo
flan [flan] nm creme caramel
flanco ['flanko] nm side; (Mil) flank
Flandes ['flandes] nm Flanders
flanquear [flanke'ar] vt to flank; (Mil) to outflank
flaquear [flake'ar] vi (debilitarse) to weaken; (persona) to slack

flaqueza [fla'keθa] nf (delgadez) thinness, leanness; (fig) weakness

flaquísimo, -a [fla'kisimo, a] adj superlativo de **flaco**

flash [flas] (pl **flashes**) [flas] nm (Foto) flash

flato ['flato] nm: **el** (o **un**) ~ the (o a) stitch

flauta ['flauta] (Mus) nf flute ■ nm/f flautist, flute player; **¡la gran ~!** (Am) my God!; **hijo de la gran ~** (Am fam!) bastard (!), son of a bitch (US!)

flecha ['fletʃa] nf arrow

flechazo [fle'tʃaθo] nm (acción) bowshot; (fam): **fue un ~** it was love at first sight

fleco ['fleko] nm fringe

flema ['flema] nm phlegm

flemático, -a [fle'matiko, a] adj phlegmatic; (tono etc) matter-of-fact

flemón [fle'mon] nm (Med) gumboil

flequillo [fle'kiʎo] nm (de pelo) fringe, bangs (US)

fletar [fle'tar] vt (Com) to charter; (embarcar) to load; (Auto) to lease(-purchase)

flete ['flete] nm (carga) freight; (alquiler) charter; (precio) freightage; ~ **debido** (Com) freight forward; ~ **sobre compras** (Com) freight inward

flexible [flek'siβle] adj flexible; (individuo) compliant

flexión [flek'sjon] nf (Deporte) bend; (: en el suelo) press-up

flexo ['flekso] nm adjustable table lamp

flipper ['fliper] nm pinball machine

flirtear [flirte'ar] vi to flirt

FLN nm abr (Pol: Esp, Perú, Venezuela: = Frente de Liberación Nacional) political party

flojear [floxe'ar] vi (piernas: al andar) to give way; (alumno) to do badly; (cosecha, mercado) to be poor

flojera [flo'xera] nf (Am) laziness; **me da ~** I can't be bothered

flojo, -a ['floxo, a] adj (gen) loose; (sin fuerzas) limp; (débil) weak; (viento) light; (bebida) weak; (trabajo) poor; (actitud) slack; (precio) low; (Com: mercado) dull, slack; (Am) lazy

flor [flor] nf flower; (piropo) compliment; **la ~ y nata de la sociedad** (fig) the cream of society; **en la ~ de la vida** in the prime of life; **a ~ de** on the surface of

flora ['flora] nf flora

florecer [flore'θer] vi (Bot) to flower, bloom; (fig) to flourish

floreciente [flore'θjente] adj (Bot) in flower, flowering; (fig) thriving

Florencia [flo'renθja] nf Florence

florero [flo'rero] nm vase

florezca etc [flo'reθka] vb ver **florecer**

florista [flo'rista] nm/f florist

floristería [floriste'ria] nf florist's (shop)

flota ['flota] nf fleet

flotación [flota'θjon] nf (Com) flotation

flotador [flota'ðor] nm (gen) float; (para nadar) rubber ring; (de cisterna) ballcock

flotante [flo'tante] adj floating; (Inform): **de coma ~** floating-point

flotar [flo'tar] vi to float

flote ['flote] nm: **a ~** afloat; **ponerse a ~** (fig) to get back on one's feet

FLS nm abr (Pol: Nicaragua) = **Frente de Liberación Sandinista**

fluctuación [fluktwa'θjon] nf fluctuation

fluctuante [fluk'twante] adj fluctuating

fluctuar [fluk'twar] vi (oscilar) to fluctuate

fluidez [flui'ðeθ] nf fluidity; (fig) fluency

fluido, -a ['flwiðo, a] adj fluid; (lenguaje) fluent; (estilo) smooth ■ nm (líquido) fluid

fluir [flu'ir] vi to flow

flujo ['fluxo] nm flow; (Pol) swing; (Naut) rising tide; ~ **y reflujo** ebb and flow; ~ **de sangre** (Med) haemorrhage (Brit), hemorrhage (US); ~ **positivo/negativo de efectivo** (Com) positive/negative cash flow

flúor ['fluor] nm fluorine; (en dentífrico) fluoride

fluorescente [flwores'θente] adj fluorescent ■ nm (tb: **tubo fluorescente**) fluorescent tube

fluoruro [flwo'ruro] nm fluoride

fluvial [fluβi'al] adj fluvial, river cpd

fluyendo etc [flu'jendo] vb ver **fluir**

FM nf abr (= Frecuencia Modulada) FM

FMI nm abr (= Fondo Monetario Internacional) IMF

F.N. nf abr (Esp Pol) = **Fuerza Nueva** ■ nm abr = **Frente Nacional**

f.° abr (= folio) fo., fol.

foca ['foka] nf seal

foco ['foko] nm focus; (centro) focal point; (fuente) source; (de incendio) seat; (Elec) floodlight; (Teat) spotlight; (Am) (light) bulb, light

fofo, -a ['fofo, a] adj (esponjoso) soft, spongy; (músculo) flabby

fogata [fo'yata] nf (hoguera) bonfire

fogón [fo'yon] nm (de cocina) ring, burner

fogoso, -a [fo'yoso, a] adj spirited

foja ['foxa] nf (Am) sheet (of paper); ~ **de servicios** record (file)

fol. abr (= folio) fo., fol.

folder, fólder ['folder] nm (Am) folder

folio ['foljo] nm folio; (hoja) leaf

folklore [fol'klore] nm folklore

folklórico, -a [fol'kloriko, a] adj traditional

follaje [fo'ʎaxe] nm foliage

follar [fo'ʎar] vt, vi (fam!) to fuck (!)

folletinesco, -a [foʎetin'esko, a] adj melodramatic

folleto [fo'λeto] *nm* pamphlet; (*Com*) brochure; (*prospecto*) leaflet; (*Escol etc*) handout

follón [fo'λon] *nm* (*fam: lío*) mess; (: *conmoción*) fuss, rumpus, shindy; **armar un** ~ to kick up a fuss; **se armó un** ~ there was a hell of a row

fomentar [fomen'tar] *vt* (*Med*) to foment; (*fig: promover*) to promote, foster; (*odio etc*) to stir up

fomento [fo'mento] *nm* (*fig: ayuda*) fostering; (*promoción*) promotion

fonda ['fonda] *nf* ≈ guest house; *ver tb* **hotel**

fondear [fonde'ar] *vt* (*Naut: sondear*) to sound; (*barco*) to search

fondo ['fondo] *nm* (*de caja etc*) bottom; (*medida*) depth; (*de coche, sala*) back; (*Arte etc*) background; (*reserva*) fund; (*fig: carácter*) nature; **fondos** *nmpl* (*Com*) funds, resources; ~ **de escritorio** (*Inform*) wallpaper; **F~ Monetario Internacional** International Monetary Fund; ~ **del mar** sea bed *o* floor; **una investigación a** ~ a thorough investigation; **en el** ~ at bottom, deep down; **tener buen** ~ to be good-natured

fonética [fo'netika] *nf* phonetics *sg*

fono ['fono] *nm* (*Am*) telephone (number)

fonobuzón [fonoβu'θon] *nm* voice mail

fonógrafo [fo'noγrafo] *nm* (*esp Am*) gramophone, phonograph (US)

fonología [fonolo'xia] *nf* phonology

fontanería [fontane'ria] *nf* plumbing

fontanero [fonta'nero] *nm* plumber

footing ['futin] *nm* jogging; **hacer** ~ to jog

F.O.P. [fop] *nfpl abr* (*Esp*) = **Fuerza del Orden Público**

forajido [fora'xiδo] *nm* outlaw

foráneo, -a [fo'raneo, a] *adj* foreign ■ *nm/f* outsider

forastero, -a [foras'tero, a] *nm/f* stranger

forcé [for'θe] *vb ver* **forzar**

forcejear [forθexe'ar] *vi* (*luchar*) to struggle

forcemos *etc* [for'θemos] *vb ver* **forzar**

fórceps ['forθeps] *nm inv* forceps *pl*

forense [fo'rense] *adj* forensic ■ *nm/f* pathologist

forestal [fores'tal] *adj* forest *cpd*

forjar [for'xar] *vt* to forge; (*formar*) to form

forma ['forma] *nf* (*figura*) form, shape; (*molde*) mould, pattern; (*Med*) fitness; (*método*) way, means; **estar en** ~ to be fit; ~ **de pago** (*Com*) method of payment; **las formas** the conventions; **de** ~ **que** ... so that ...; **de todas formas** in any case

formación [forma'θjon] *nf* (*gen*) formation; (*enseñanza*) training; ~ **profesional** vocational training; ~ **fuera del trabajo** off-the-job training; ~ **en el trabajo** *o* **sobre la práctica** on-the-job training

formal [for'mal] *adj* (*gen*) formal; (*fig: persona*) serious; (: *de fiar*) reliable; (*conducta*) steady

formalice *etc* [forma'liθe] *vb ver* **formalizar**

formalidad [formali'δaδ] *nf* formality; seriousness; reliability; steadiness

formalizar [formali'θar] *vt* (*Jur*) to formalize; (*plan*) to draw up; (*situación*) to put in order, regularize; **formalizarse** *vr* (*situación*) to be put in order, be regularized

formar [for'mar] *vt* (*componer*) to form, shape; (*constituir*) to make up, constitute; (*Escol*) to train, educate ■ *vi* (*Mil*) to fall in; (*Deporte*) to line up; **formarse** *vr* (*Escol*) to be trained (*o* educated); (*cobrar forma*) to form, take form; (*desarrollarse*) to develop

formatear [formate'ar] *vt* (*Inform*) to format

formateo [forma'teo] *nm* (*Inform*) formatting

formato [for'mato] *nm* (*Inform*): **sin** ~ (*disco, texto*) unformatted; ~ **de registro** record format

formidable [formi'δaβle] *adj* (*temible*) formidable; (*asombroso*) tremendous

fórmula ['formula] *nf* formula

formular [formu'lar] *vt* (*queja*) to lodge; (*petición*) to draw up; (*pregunta*) to pose, formulate; (*idea*) to formulate

formulario [formu'larjo] *nm* form; ~ **de solicitud/de pedido** (*Com*) application/order form; **llenar un** ~ to fill in a form; ~ **continuo desplegable** (*Inform*) fanfold paper

fornicar [forni'kar] *vi* to fornicate

fornido, -a [for'niδo, a] *adj* well-built

fornique *etc* [for'nike] *vb ver* **fornicar**

foro ['foro] *nm* (*gen*) forum; (*Jur*) court; ~ **de discusión** (*Internet*) discussion forum

forofo, -a [fo'rofo, a] *nm/f* fan

FORPPA ['forpa] *nm abr* (*Esp*) = **Fondo de Ordenación y Regulación de Productos y Precios Agrarios**

FORPRONU [for'pronu] *nf abr* (= *Fuerza de Protección de las Naciones Unidas*) UNPROFOR

forrado, -a [fo'rraδo, a] *adj* (*ropa*) lined; (*fam*) well-heeled

forrar [fo'rrar] *vt* (*abrigo*) to line; (*libro*) to cover; (*coche*) to upholster; **forrarse** *vr* (*fam*) to line one's pockets

forro ['forro] *nm* (*de cuaderno*) cover; (*costura*) lining; (*de sillón*) upholstery; ~ **polar** fleece

fortalecer [fortale'θer] *vt* to strengthen; **fortalecerse** *vr* to fortify o.s.; (*opinión etc*) to become stronger

fortaleza [forta'leθa] *nf* (*Mil*) fortress, stronghold; (*fuerza*) strength; (*determinación*) resolution

fortalezca etc [forta'leθka] vb ver **fortalecer**

fortificar [fortifi'kar] vt to fortify; (fig) to strengthen

fortifique etc [forti'fike] vb ver **fortificar**

fortísimo, -a [for'tisimo, a] adj superlativo de **fuerte**

fortuito, -a [for'twito, a] adj accidental, chance cpd

fortuna [for'tuna] nf (suerte) fortune, (good) luck; (riqueza) fortune, wealth

forzar [for'θar] vt (puerta) to force (open); (compeler) to compel; (violar) to rape; (ojos etc) to strain

forzoso, -a [for'θoso, a] adj necessary; (inevitable) inescapable; (obligatorio) compulsory

forzudo, -a [for'θuðo, a] adj burly

fosa ['fosa] nf (sepultura) grave; (en tierra) pit; (Med) cavity; **fosas nasales** nostrils

fosfato [fos'fato] nm phosphate

fosforescente [fosfores'θente] adj phosphorescent

fósforo ['fosforo] nm (Química) phosphorus; (esp Am: cerilla) match

fósil ['fosil] adj fossil, fossilized ■ nm fossil

foso ['foso] nm ditch; (Teat) pit; (Auto): **~ de reconocimiento** inspection pit

foto ['foto] nf photo, snap(shot); **sacar una ~** to take a photo o picture

fotocopia [foto'kopja] nf photocopy

fotocopiadora [fotokopja'ðora] nf photocopier

fotocopiar [fotoko'pjar] vt to photocopy

fotogénico, -a [foto'xeniko, a] adj photogenic

fotografía [fotoɣra'fia] nf (arte) photography; (una fotografía) photograph

fotografiar [fotoɣra'fjar] vt to photograph

fotógrafo, -a [fo'toɣrafo, a] nm/f photographer

fotomatón [fotoma'ton] nm (cabina) photo booth

fotómetro [fo'tometro] nm (Foto) light meter

fotonovela [fotono'βela] nf photo-story

foulard [fu'lar] nm (head)scarf

FP nf abr (Esp: Escol, Com) = **Formación Profesional** ■ nm abr (Pol) = **Frente Popular**

FPLP nm abr (Pol: = Frente Popular para la Liberación de Palestina) PFLP

Fr. abr (= Fray) Fr.

fra. abr = **factura**

frac (pl **fracs** o **fraques**) [frak, 'frakes] nm dress coat, tails

fracasar [fraka'sar] vi (gen) to fail; (plan etc) to fall through

fracaso [fra'kaso] nm (desgracia, revés) failure; (de negociaciones etc) collapse, breakdown

fracción [frak'θjon] nf fraction; (Pol) faction, splinter group

fraccionamiento [fraksjona'mjento] nm (Am) housing estate

fractura [frak'tura] nf fracture, break

fragancia [fra'ɣanθja] nf (olor) fragrance, perfume

fragante [fra'ɣante] adj fragrant, scented

fraganti [fra'ɣanti]: **in ~** adv: **coger a algn in fraganti** to catch sb red-handed

fragata [fra'ɣata] nf frigate

frágil ['fraxil] adj (débil) fragile; (Com) breakable; (fig) frail, delicate

fragilidad [fraxili'ðað] nf fragility; (de persona) frailty

fragmento [fraɣ'mento] nm fragment; (pedazo) piece; (de discurso) excerpt; (de canción) snatch

fragor [fra'ɣor] nm (ruido intenso) din

fragua ['fraɣwa] nf forge

fraguar [fra'ɣwar] vt to forge; (fig) to concoct ■ vi to harden

fragüe etc ['fraɣwe] vb ver **fraguar**

fraile ['fraile] nm (Rel) friar; (: monje) monk

frambuesa [fram'bwesa] nf raspberry

francés, -esa [fran'θes, esa] adj French ■ nm/f Frenchman(-woman) ■ nm (Ling) French

Francia ['franθja] nf France

franco, -a ['franko, a] adj (cándido) frank, open; (Com: exento) free ■ nm (moneda) franc; **~ de derechos** duty-free; **~ al costado del buque** (Com) free alongside ship; **~ puesto sobre vagón** (Com) free on rail; **~ a bordo** free on board

francotirador, a [frankotira'ðor, a] nm/f sniper

franela [fra'nela] nf flannel

franja ['franxa] nf fringe; (de uniforme) stripe; (de tierra etc) strip

franquear [franke'ar] vt (camino) to clear; (carta, paquete) to frank, stamp; (obstáculo) to overcome; (Com etc) to free, exempt

franqueo [fran'keo] nm postage

franqueza [fran'keθa] nf frankness

franquicia [fran'kiθja] nf exemption; **~ aduanera** exemption from customs duties

franquismo [fran'kismo] nm: **el ~** (sistema) the Franco system; (período) the Franco years; see note

⬤ **FRANQUISMO**
⬤
⬤ The political reign and style of
⬤ government of Francisco Franco (from
⬤ the end of the Spanish Civil War in 1939
⬤ until his death in 1975) are commonly

called *franquismo*. He was a powerful, authoritarian, right-wing dictator, who promoted a traditional, Catholic and self-sufficient country. From the 1960s Spain gradually opened its doors to the international community, coinciding with a rise in economic growth and internal political opposition. On his death Spain became a democratic constitutional monarchy.

franquista [fran'kista] *adj* pro-Franco ∎ *nm/f* supporter of Franco

frasco ['frasko] *nm* bottle, flask; ~ **al vacío** (vacuum) flask

frase ['frase] *nf* sentence; (*locución*) phrase, expression; ~ **hecha** set phrase

fraternal [frater'nal] *adj* brotherly, fraternal

fraude ['frauðe] *nm* (*cualidad*) dishonesty; (*acto*) fraud, swindle

fraudulento, -a [frauðu'lento, a] *adj* fraudulent

frazada [fra'saða] *nf* (*Am*) blanket

frecuencia [fre'kwenθja] *nf* frequency; **con** ~ frequently, often; ~ **de red** (*Inform*) mains frequency; ~ **del reloj** (*Inform*) clock speed; ~ **telefónica** voice frequency

frecuentar [frekwen'tar] *vt* (*lugar*) to frequent; (*persona*) to see frequently o often; ~ **la buena sociedad** to mix in high society

frecuente [fre'kwente] *adj* frequent; (*costumbre*) common; (*vicio*) rife

fregadero [freɣa'ðero] *nm* (kitchen) sink

fregado, -a [fre'ɣaðo, a] *adj* (*Am fam!*) damn, bloody (*!*)

fregar [fre'ɣar] *vt* (*frotar*) to scrub; (*platos*) to wash (up); (*Am*) to annoy

fregón, -ona [fre'ɣon, ona] *adj* = **fregado** ∎ *nf* (*utensilio*) mop; (*pey: sirvienta*) skivvy

fregué *etc* [fre'ɣe] *vb ver* **fregar**

freidora [frei'ðora] *nf* deep-fat fryer

freír [fre'ir] *vt* to fry

fréjol ['frexol] *nm* = **fríjol**

frenar [fre'nar] *vt* to brake; (*fig*) to check

frenazo [fre'naθo] *nm*: **dar un** ~ to brake sharply

frenesí [frene'si] *nm* frenzy

frenético, -a [fre'netiko, a] *adj* frantic; **ponerse** ~ to lose one's head

freno ['freno] *nm* (*Tec, Auto*) brake; (*de cabalgadura*) bit; (*fig*) check

frente ['frente] *nm* (*Arq, Mil, Pol*) front; (*de objeto*) front part ∎ *nf* forehead, brow; ~ **de batalla** battle front; **hacer** ~ **común con algn** to make common cause with sb; ~ **a** in front of; (*en situación opuesta a*) opposite; **chocar de** ~ to crash head-on; **hacer** ~ **a**

to face up to

fresa ['fresa] *nf* (*Esp: fruta*) strawberry; (*de dentista*) drill

fresco, -a ['fresko, a] *adj* (*nuevo*) fresh; (*huevo*) newly-laid; (*frío*) cool; (*descarado*) cheeky, bad-mannered ∎ *nm* (*aire*) fresh air; (*Arte*) fresco; (*Am: bebida*) fruit juice o drink ∎ *nm/f* (*fam*) shameless person; (*persona insolente*) impudent person; **tomar el** ~ to get some fresh air; **¡qué ~!** what a cheek!

frescor [fres'kor] *nm* freshness

frescura [fres'kura] *nf* freshness; (*descaro*) cheek, nerve; (*calma*) calmness

fresno ['fresno] *nm* ash (tree)

fresón [fre'son] *nm* strawberry

frialdad [frjal'dað] *nf* (*gen*) coldness; (*indiferencia*) indifference

fricción [frik'θjon] *nf* (*gen*) friction; (*acto*) rub(bing); (*Med*) massage; (*Pol, fig etc*) friction, trouble

friega *etc* ['frjeɣa], **friegue** *etc* ['frjeɣe] *vb ver* **fregar**

friendo *etc* [fri'endo] *vb ver* **freír**

frigidez [frixi'ðeθ] *nf* frigidity

frígido, -a ['frixiðo, a] *adj* frigid

frigo ['friɣo] *nm* fridge

frigorífico, -a [friɣo'rifiko, a] *adj* refrigerating ∎ *nm* refrigerator; (*camión*) freezer lorry o truck (*US*); **instalación frigorífica** cold-storage plant

fríjol [fri'xol], **fríjol** ['frixol] *nm* kidney bean

friki (*col*) *adj* weird (*col*); **me pasó una cosa muy** ~ something really weird (*col*) happened to me; **¡qué tío más ~!** What a weirdo! (*col*) ∎ *nmf* weirdo (*col*)

frió [fri'o] *vb ver* **freír**

frío, -a *etc* ['frio, a] *vb ver* **freír** ∎ *adj* cold; (*fig: indiferente*) unmoved, indifferent; (*poco entusiasta*) chilly ∎ *nm* cold(ness); indifference; **¡qué ~!** how cold it is!

friolento, -a [frjo'lento, a], (*Am*) **friolero, -a** [frjo'lero, a] *adj* sensitive to cold

frito, -a ['frito, a] *pp de* **freír** ∎ *adj* fried ∎ *nm* fry; **me trae** ~ **ese hombre** I'm sick and tired of that man; **fritos variados** mixed grill

frívolo, -a ['friβolo, a] *adj* frivolous

frondoso, -a [fron'doso, a] *adj* leafy

frontal [fron'tal] *nm*: **choque** ~ head-on collision

frontera [fron'tera] *nf* frontier; (*línea divisoria*) border; (*zona*) frontier area

fronterizo, -a [fronte'riθo, a] *adj* frontier *cpd*; (*contiguo*) bordering

frontón [fron'ton] *nm* (*Deporte: cancha*) pelota court; (*: juego*) pelota

frotar [fro'tar] *vt* to rub; (*fósforo*) to strike;

frotarse vr: **frotarse las manos** to rub one's hands

fructífero, -a [fruk'tifero, a] adj productive, fruitful

frugal [fru'ɣal] adj frugal

fruncir [frun'θir] vt (Costura) to gather; (ceño) to frown; (labios) to purse

frunza etc ['frunθa] vb ver **fruncir**

frustración [frustra'θjon] nf frustration

frustrar [frus'trar] vt to frustrate; **frustrarse** vr to be frustrated; (plan etc) to fail

fruta ['fruta] nf fruit

frutal [fru'tal] adj fruit-bearing, fruit cpd ■ nm: (**árbol**) ~ fruit tree

frutería [frute'ria] nf fruit shop

frutero, -a [fru'tero, a] adj fruit cpd ■ nm/f fruiterer ■ nm fruit dish o bowl

frutilla [fru'tiʎa] nf (Am) strawberry

fruto ['fruto] nm (Bot) fruit; (fig: resultado) result, outcome; **frutos secos** ≈ nuts and raisins

FSLN nm abr (Pol: Nicaragua) = **Frente Sandinista de Liberación Nacional**

fue [fwe] vb ver **ser; ir**

fuego ['fweɣo] nm (gen) fire; (Culin: gas) burner, ring; (Mil) fire; (fig: pasión) fire, passion; ~ **amigo** friendly fire; **fuegos artificiales** o **de artificio** fireworks; **prender** ~ **a** to set fire to; **a** ~ **lento** on a low flame o gas; **¡alto el ~!** cease fire!; **estar entre dos fuegos** to be in the crossfire; **¿tienes ~?** have you (got) a light?

fuelle ['fweʎe] nm bellows pl

fuel-oil [fuel'oil] nm paraffin (Brit), kerosene (US)

fuente ['fwente] nf fountain; (manantial, fig) spring; (origen) source; (plato) large dish; ~ **de alimentación** (Inform) power supply; **de ~ desconocida/fidedigna** from an unknown/reliable source

fuera etc ['fwera] vb ver **ser; ir** ■ adv out(side); (en otra parte) away; (excepto, salvo) except, save ■ prep: ~ **de** outside; (fig) besides; ~ **de alcance** out of reach; ~ **de combate** out of action; (boxeo) knocked out; ~ **de sí** beside o. s.; **por** ~ (on the) outside; **los de** ~ strangers, newcomers; **estar** ~ (en el extranjero) to be abroad

fuera-borda [fwera'βorða] nm inv outboard engine o motor

fuerce etc ['fwerθe] vb ver **forzar**

fuereño, -a [fwe'reɲo, a] nm/f (Am) outsider

fuero ['fwero] nm (carta municipal) municipal charter; (leyes locales) local o regional law code; (privilegio) privilege; (autoridad) jurisdiction; (fig): **en mi** etc ~ **interno** ... in my etc heart of hearts ..., deep down ...

fuerte ['fwerte] adj strong; (golpe) hard; (ruido) loud; (comida) rich; (lluvia) heavy; (dolor) intense ■ adv strongly; hard; loud(ly) ■ nm (Mil) fort, strongpoint; (fig): **ser** ~ **en** to be good at; **el canto no es mi** ~ singing is not my strong point

fuerza etc ['fwerθa] vb ver **forzar** ■ nf (fortaleza) strength; (Tec, Elec) power; (coacción) force; (violencia) violence; (Mil: tb: **fuerzas**) forces pl; ~ **de arrastre** (Tec) pulling power; ~ **de brazos** manpower; ~ **mayor** force majeure; ~ **bruta** brute force; **F~ Armadas** (FF.AA.) armed forces; **F~ del Orden Público** (F.O.P.) police (forces); ~ **vital** vitality; **a** ~ **de** by (dint of); **cobrar ~s** to recover one's strength; **tener ~s para** to have the strength to; **hacer algo a la** ~ to be forced to do sth; **con** ~ **legal** (Com) legally binding; **a la** ~, **por** ~ of necessity; ~ **de voluntad** willpower

fuete ['fwete] nm (Am) whip

fuga ['fuɣa] nf (huida) flight, escape; (de enamorados) elopement; (de gas etc) leak; ~ **de cerebros** (fig) brain drain

fugarse [fu'ɣarse] vr to flee, escape

fugaz [fu'ɣaθ] adj fleeting

fugitivo, -a [fuxi'tiβo, a] adj fugitive, fleeing ■ nm/f fugitive

fugue etc ['fuɣe] vb ver **fugarse**

fui etc [fwi] vb ver **ser; ir**

fulano, -a [fu'lano, a] nm/f so-and-so, what's-his-name/what's-her-name

fulgor [ful'ɣor] nm brilliance

fulminante [fulmi'nante] adj (pólvora) fulminating; (fig: mirada) withering; (Med) fulminant; (fam) terrific, tremendous

fulminar [fulmi'nar] vt: **caer fulminado por un rayo** to be struck down by lightning; ~ **a algn con la mirada** to look daggers at sb

fumador, a [fuma'ðor, a] nm/f smoker; **no** ~ non-smoker

fumar [fu'mar] vt, vi to smoke; **fumarse** vr (disipar) to squander; ~ **en pipa** to smoke a pipe

fumigar [fumi'ɣar] vt to fumigate

funámbulo, -a [fu'nambulo, a], **funambulista** [funambu'lista] nm/f tightrope walker

función [fun'θjon] nf function; (de puesto) duties pl; (Teat etc) show; **entrar en funciones** to take up one's duties; ~ **de tarde/de noche** matinée/evening performance

funcional [funθjo'nal] adj functional

funcionamiento [funθjona'mjento] nm functioning; (Tec) working; **en** ~ (Com) on stream; **entrar en** ~ to come into operation

183

funcionar [funθjo'nar] *vi* (*gen*) to function; (*máquina*) to work; **"no funciona"** "out of order"

funcionario, -a [funθjo'narjo, a] *nm/f* official; (*público*) civil servant

funda ['funda] *nf* (*gen*) cover; (*de almohada*) pillowcase; ~ **protectora del disco** (*Inform*) disk-jacket

fundación [funda'θjon] *nf* foundation

fundado, -a [fun'daðo, a] *adj* (*justificado*) well-founded

fundamental [fundamen'tal] *adj* fundamental, basic

fundamentalismo [fundamenta'lismo] *nm* fundamentalism

fundamentalista [fundamenta'lista] *adj*, *nm/f* fundamentalist

fundamentar [fundamen'tar] *vt* (*poner base*) to lay the foundations of; (*establecer*) to found; (*fig*) to base

fundamento [funda'mento] *nm* (*base*) foundation; (*razón*) grounds *pl*; **eso carece de** ~ that is groundless

fundar [fun'dar] *vt* to found; (*crear*) to set up; (*fig: basar*): ~ **(en)** to base o found (on); **fundarse** *vr*: **fundarse en** to be founded on

fundición [fundi'θjon] *nf* (*acción*) smelting; (*fábrica*) foundry; (*Tip*) fount (*Brit*), font

fundir [fun'dir] *vt* (*gen*) to fuse; (*metal*) to smelt, melt down; (*Com*) to merge; (*estatua*) to cast; **fundirse** *vr* (*colores etc*) to merge, blend; (*unirse*) to fuse together; (*Elec: fusible, lámpara etc*) to blow; (*nieve etc*) to melt

fúnebre ['funeβre] *adj* funeral *cpd*, funereal

funeral [fune'ral] *nm* funeral

funeraria [fune'rarja] *nf* undertaker's (*Brit*), mortician's (*US*)

funesto, -a [fu'nesto, a] *adj* ill-fated; (*desastroso*) fatal

fungir [fun'xir] *vi*: ~ **de** (*Am*) to act as

furgón [fur'γon] *nm* wagon

furgoneta [furγo'neta] *nf* (*Auto, Com*) (transit) van (*Brit*), pickup (truck) (*US*)

furia ['furja] *nf* (*ira*) fury; (*violencia*) violence

furibundo, -a [furi'βundo, a] *adj* furious

furioso, -a [fu'rjoso, a] *adj* (*iracundo*) furious; (*violento*) violent

furor [fu'ror] *nm* (*cólera*) rage; (*pasión*) frenzy, passion; **hacer** ~ to be a sensation

furtivo, -a [fur'tiβo, a] *adj* furtive ■ *nm* poacher

furúnculo [fu'runkulo] *nm* (*Med*) boil

fuselaje [fuse'laxe] *nm* fuselage

fusible [fu'siβle] *nm* fuse

fusil [fu'sil] *nm* rifle

fusilamiento [fusila'mjento] *nm* (*Jur*) execution by firing squad

fusilar [fusi'lar] *vt* to shoot

fusión [fu'sjon] *nf* (*gen*) melting; (*unión*) fusion; (*Com*) merger, amalgamation

fusionar [fusjo'nar] *vt* to fuse (together); (*Com*) to merge; **fusionarse** *vr* (*Com*) to merge, amalgamate

fusta ['fusta] *nf* (*látigo*) riding crop

fútbol ['futβol] *nm* football

futbolín [futβo'lin] *nm* table football

futbolista [futβo'lista] *nm/f* footballer

fútil ['futil] *adj* trifling

futilidad [futili'ðað], **futileza** [futi'leθa] *nf* triviality

futón [fu'ton] *nm* futon

futuro, -a [fu'turo, a] *adj* future ■ *nm* future; (*Ling*) future tense; **futuros** *nmpl* (*Com*) futures

Gg

G, g [xe] *nf* (*letra*) G, g; **G de Gerona** G for George
gabacho, -a [ga'βatʃo, a] *adj* Pyrenean; (*fam*) Frenchified ■ *nm/f* Pyrenean villager; (*fam*) Frenchy
gabán [ga'βan] *nm* overcoat
gabardina [gaβar'ðina] *nf* (*tela*) gabardine; (*prenda*) raincoat
gabinete [gaβi'nete] *nm* (*Pol*) cabinet; (*estudio*) study; (*de abogados etc*) office; **~ de consulta/ de lectura** consulting/reading room
gacela [ga'θela] *nf* gazelle
gaceta [ga'θeta] *nf* gazette
gacetilla [gaθe'tiʎa] *nf* (*en periódico*) news in brief; (*de personalidades*) gossip column
gachas ['gatʃas] *nfpl* porridge *sg*
gacho, -a ['gatʃo, a] *adj* (*encorvado*) bent down; (*orejas*) drooping
gaditano, -a [gaði'tano, a] *adj* of o from Cadiz ■ *nm/f* native o inhabitant of Cadiz
gaélico, -a [ga'eliko, a] *adj* Gaelic ■ *nm/f* Gael ■ *nm* (*Ling*) Gaelic
gafar [ga'far] *vt* (*fam: traer mala suerte*) to put a jinx on
gafas ['gafas] *nfpl* glasses; **~ oscuras** dark glasses; **~ de sol** sunglasses
gafe ['gafe] *adj*: **ser ~** to be jinxed ■ *nm* (*fam*) jinx
gaita ['gaita] *nf* flute; (*tb*: **gaita gallega**) bagpipes *pl*; (*dificultad*) bother; (*cosa engorrosa*) tough job
gajes ['gaxes] *nmpl* (*salario*) pay *sg*; **los ~ del oficio** occupational hazards; **~ y emolumentos** perquisites
gajo ['gaxo] *nm* (*gen*) bunch; (*de árbol*) bough; (*de naranja*) segment
gala ['gala] *nf* full dress; (*fig: lo mejor*) cream, flower; **galas** *nfpl* finery *sg*; **estar de ~** to be in one's best clothes; **hacer ~ de** to display, show off; **tener algo a ~** to be proud of sth
galaico, -a [ga'laiko, a] *adj* Galician
galán [ga'lan] *nm* lover, gallant; (*hombre atractivo*) ladies' man; (*Teat*): **primer ~** leading man

galante [ga'lante] *adj* gallant; (*atento*) charming; (*cortés*) polite
galantear [galante'ar] *vt* (*hacer la corte a*) to court, woo
galanteo [galan'teo] *nm* (*coqueteo*) flirting; (*de pretendiente*) wooing
galantería [galante'ria] *nf* (*caballerosidad*) gallantry; (*cumplido*) politeness; (*piropo*) compliment
galápago [ga'lapaɣo] *nm* (*Zool*) freshwater tortoise
galardón [galar'ðon] *nm* award, prize
galardonar [galarðo'nar] *vt* (*premiar*) to reward; (*una obra*) to award a prize for
galaxia [ga'laksja] *nf* galaxy
galbana [gal'βana] *nf* (*pereza*) sloth, laziness
galeote [gale'ote] *nm* galley slave
galera [ga'lera] *nf* (*nave*) galley; (*carro*) wagon; (*Med*) hospital ward; (*Tip*) galley
galería [gale'ria] *nf* (*gen*) gallery; (*balcón*) veranda(h); (*de casa*) corridor; (*fam: público*) audience; **~ secreta** secret passage
Gales ['gales] *nm*: (**el País de**) **~** Wales
galés, -esa [ga'les, esa] *adj* Welsh ■ *nm/f* Welshman(-woman) ■ *nm* (*Ling*) Welsh
galgo, -a ['galɣo, a] *nm/f* greyhound
Galia ['galja] *nf* Gaul
Galicia [ga'liθja] *nf* Galicia
galicismo [gali'θismo] *nm* gallicism
Galilea [gali'lea] *nf* Galilee
galimatías [galima'tias] *nm inv* (*asunto*) rigmarole; (*lenguaje*) gibberish, nonsense
gallardía [gaʎar'ðia] *nf* (*galantería*) dash; (*gracia*) gracefulness; (*valor*) bravery; (*elegancia*) elegance; (*nobleza*) nobleness
gallego, -a [ga'ʎeɣo, a] *adj* Galician; (*Am pey*) Spanish ■ *nm/f* Galician; (*Am pey*) Spaniard ■ *nm* (*Ling*) Galician; *ver tb* **Lengua**
galleta [ga'ʎeta] *nf* biscuit; (*fam: bofetada*) whack, slap
gallina [ga'ʎina] *nf* hen ■ *nm* (*fam*) coward; **~ ciega** blind man's buff; **~ llueca** broody hen

gallinazo [ga'ʎi'naso] nm (Am) turkey buzzard

gallinero [gaʎi'nero] nm (criadero) henhouse; (Teat) gods sg, top gallery; (voces) hubbub

gallo ['gaʎo] nm cock, rooster; (Mus) false o wrong note; (cambio de voz) break in the voice; **en menos que canta un ~** in an instant

galo, -a ['galo, a] adj Gallic; (= francés) French ■ nm/f Gaul

galón [ga'lon] nm (Costura) braid; (Mil) stripe; (medida) gallon

galopante [galo'pante] adj galloping

galopar [galo'par] vi to gallop

galope [ga'lope] nm gallop; **al ~** (fig) in great haste; **a ~ tendido** at full gallop

galvanice etc [galβa'niθe] vb ver **galvanizar**

galvanizar [galβani'θar] vt to galvanize

gama ['gama] nf (Mus) scale; (fig) range; (Zool) doe

gamba ['gamba] nf prawn

gamberrada [gambe'rraða] nf act of hooliganism

gamberro, -a [gam'berro, a] nm/f hooligan, lout

gamo ['gamo] nm (Zool) buck

gamuza [ga'muθa] nf chamois; (bayeta) duster; (Am: piel) suede

gana ['gana] nf (deseo) desire, wish; (apetito) appetite; (voluntad) will; (añoranza) longing; **de buena ~** willingly; **de mala ~** reluctantly; **me dan ganas de** I feel like, I want to; **tener ganas de** to feel like; **no me da la (real) ~** I don't (damned well) want to; **son ganas de molestar** they're just trying to be awkward

ganadería [ganaðe'ria] nf (ganado) livestock; (ganado vacuno) cattle pl; (cría, comercio) cattle raising

ganadero, -a [gana'ðero, a] adj stock cpd ■ nm stockman

ganado [ga'naðo] nm livestock; **~ caballar/cabrío** horses pl/goats pl; **~ lanar** u **ovejuno** sheep pl; **~ porcino/vacuno** pigs pl/cattle pl

ganador, -a [gana'ðor, a] adj winning ■ nm/f winner; (Econ) earner

ganancia [ga'nanθja] nf (lo ganado) gain; (aumento) increase; (beneficio) profit; **ganancias** nfpl (ingresos) earnings; (beneficios) profit sg, winnings; **ganancias y pérdidas** profit and loss; **~ bruta/líquida** gross/net profit; **ganancias de capital** capital gains; **sacar ~ de** to draw profit from

ganapán [gana'pan] nm (obrero casual) odd-job man; (individuo tosco) lout

ganar [ga'nar] vt (obtener) to get, obtain; (sacar ventaja) to gain; (Com) to earn; (Deporte, premio) to win; (derrotar) to beat; (alcanzar) to reach; (Mil: objetivo) to take; (apoyo) to gain, win ■ vi (Deporte) to win; **ganarse** vr: **ganarse la vida** to earn one's living; **se lo ha ganado** he deserves it; **~ tiempo** to gain time

ganchillo [gan'tʃiʎo] nm (para croché) crochet hook; (arte) crochet work

gancho ['gantʃo] nm (gen) hook; (colgador) hanger; (pey: revendedor) tout; (fam: atractivo) sex appeal; (Boxeo: golpe) hook

gandul, -a [gan'dul, a] adj, nm/f good-for-nothing

ganga ['ganga] nf (cosa) bargain; (chollo) cushy job

Ganges ['ganxes] nm: **el (Río) ~** the Ganges

ganglio ['gangljo] nm (Anat) ganglion; (Med) swelling

gangrena [gan'grena] nf gangrene

gansada [gan'saða] nf (fam) stupid thing (to do)

ganso, -a ['ganso, a] nm/f (Zool) gander/goose; (fam) idiot

ganzúa [gan'θua] nf skeleton key ■ nm/f burglar

gañán [ga'ɲan] nm farmhand, farm labourer

garabatear [garaβate'ar] vt to scribble, scrawl

garabato [gara'βato] nm (gancho) hook; (garfio) grappling iron; (escritura) scrawl, scribble; (fam) sex appeal

garaje [ga'raxe] nm garage

garajista [gara'xista] nmf mechanic

garante [ga'rante] adj responsible ■ nm/f guarantor

garantía [garan'tia] nf guarantee; (seguridad) pledge; (compromiso) undertaking; (Jur: caución) warranty; **de máxima ~** absolutely guaranteed; **~ de trabajo** job security

garantice etc [garan'tiθe] vb ver **garantizar**

garantizar [garanti'θar] vt (hacerse responsable de) to vouch for; (asegurar) to guarantee

garbanzo [gar'βanθo] nm chickpea

garbeo [gar'βeo] nm: **darse un ~** to go for a walk

garbo ['garβo] nm grace, elegance; (desenvoltura) jauntiness; (de mujer) glamour; **andar con ~** to walk gracefully

garboso, -a [gar'βoso, a] adj graceful, elegant

garete [ga'rete] nm: **irse al ~** to go to the dogs

garfio ['garfjo] nm grappling iron; (gancho) hook; (Alpinismo) climbing iron

gargajo [gar'ɣaxo] nm phlegm, sputum

garganta [gar'ɣanta] nf (interna) throat; (externa, de botella) neck; (Geo: barranco) ravine; (desfiladero) narrow pass

gargantilla [garɣan'tiʎa] nf necklace

gárgara ['garɣara] nf gargle, gargling; **hacer gárgaras** to gargle; **¡vete a hacer gárgaras!** (fam) go to blazes!

gárgola ['garɣola] nf gargoyle
garita [ga'rita] nf cabin, hut; (*Mil*) sentry box; (*puesto de vigilancia*) lookout post
garito [ga'rito] nm (*lugar*) gaming house o den
garra ['garra] nf (*de gato, Tec*) claw; (*de ave*) talon; (*fam*) hand, paw; (*fig: de canción etc*) bite; **caer en las garras de algn** to fall into sb's clutches
garrafa [ga'rrafa] nf carafe, decanter
garrafal [garra'fal] adj enormous, terrific; (*error*) terrible
garrapata [garra'pata] nf (*Zool*) tick
garrotazo [garro'taθo] nm blow with a stick o club
garrote [ga'rrote] nm (*palo*) stick; (*porra*) club, cudgel; (*suplicio*) garrotte
garza ['garθa] nf heron
gas [gas] nm gas; (*vapores*) fumes pl; **gases de escape** exhaust (fumes)
gasa ['gasa] nf gauze; (*de pañal*) nappy liner
gaseoso, -a [gase'oso, a] adj gassy, fizzy ∎ nf lemonade, pop (*fam*)
gasoducto [gaso'ðukto] nm gas pipeline
gasoil [ga'soil], **gasóleo** [ga'soleo] nm diesel (oil)
gasolina [gaso'lina] nf petrol, gas(oline) (*US*); **~ sin plomo** unleaded petrol
gasolinera [gasoli'nera] nf petrol (*Brit*) o gas (*US*) station
gastado, -a [gas'taðo, a] adj (*ropa*) worn out; (*usado: frase etc*) trite
gastar [gas'tar] vt (*dinero, tiempo*) to spend; (*consumir*) to use (up), consume; (*desperdiciar*) to waste; (*llevar*) to wear; **gastarse** vr to wear out; (*terminarse*) to run out; (*estropearse*) to waste; **~ bromas** to crack jokes; **¿qué número gastas?** what size (shoe) do you take?
gasto ['gasto] nm (*desembolso*) expenditure, spending; (*cantidad gastada*) outlay, expense; (*consumo, uso*) use; (*desgaste*) waste; **gastos** nmpl (*desembolsos*) expenses; (*cargos*) charges, costs; **~ corriente** (*Com*) revenue expenditure; **~ fijo** (*Com*) fixed charge; **gastos bancarios** bank charges; **gastos corrientes** running expenses; **gastos de distribución** (*Com*) distribution costs; **gastos generales** overheads; **gastos de mantenimiento** maintenance expenses; **gastos operacionales** operating costs; **gastos de tramitación** (*Com*) handling charge sg; **gastos vencidos** (*Com*) accrued charges; **cubrir gastos** to cover expenses; **meterse en gastos** to incur expense
gastronomía [gastrono'mia] nf gastronomy
gata ['gata] nf (*Zool*) she-cat; **andar a gatas** to go on all fours

gatear [gate'ar] vi to go on all fours
gatillo [ga'tiʎo] nm (*de arma de fuego*) trigger; (*de dentista*) forceps
gato ['gato] nm (*Zool*) cat; (*Tec*) jack; **~ de Angora** Angora cat; **~ montés** wildcat; **dar a algn ~ por liebre** to take sb in; **aquí hay ~ encerrado** there's something fishy here
GATT [gat] sigla m (= *Acuerdo General sobre Aranceles Aduaneros y Comercio*) GATT
gatuno, -a [ga'tuno, a] adj feline
gaucho, -a ['gautʃo, a] adj, nm/f gaucho
gaveta [ga'βeta] nf drawer
gavilán [gaβi'lan] nm sparrowhawk
gavilla [ga'βiʎa] nf sheaf
gaviota [ga'βjota] nf seagull
gay [ge] adj, nm gay, homosexual
gazapo [ga'θapo] nm young rabbit
gaznate [gaθ'nate] nm (*pescuezo*) gullet; (*garganta*) windpipe
gazpacho [gaθ'patʃo] nm gazpacho
gel [xel] nm gel
gelatina [xela'tina] nf jelly; (*polvos etc*) gelatine
gema ['xema] nf gem
gemelo, -a [xe'melo, a] adj, nm/f twin; **gemelos** nmpl (*de camisa*) cufflinks; **gemelos de campo** field glasses, binoculars; **gemelos de teatro** opera glasses
gemido [xe'miðo] nm (*quejido*) moan, groan; (*lamento*) wail, howl
Géminis ['xeminis] nm (*Astro*) Gemini
gemir [xe'mir] vi (*quejarse*) to moan, groan; (*animal*) to whine; (*viento*) to howl
gen [xen] nm gene
gen. abr (*Ling*) = **género**; **genitivo**
gendarme [xen'darme] nm (*Am*) policeman
genealogía [xenealo'xia] nf genealogy
generación [xenera'θjon] nf generation; **primera/segunda/tercera/cuarta ~** (*Inform*) first/second/third/fourth generation
generado, -a [xene'raðo, a] adj (*Inform*): **~ por ordenador** computer generated
generador [xenera'ðor] nm generator; **~ de programas** (*Inform*) program generator
general [xene'ral] adj general; (*común*) common; (*pey: corriente*) rife; (*frecuente*) usual ∎ nm general; **~ de brigada/de división** brigadier-/major-general; **por lo** o **en ~** in general
generalice etc [xenera'liθe] vb ver **generalizar**
generalidad [xenerali'ðað] nf generality
Generalitat [jenerali'tat] nf regional government of Catalonia; **~ Valenciana** regional government of Valencia
generalización [xenerali θa'θjon] nf generalization
generalizar [xenerali'θar] vt to generalize;

g

187

generalizarse *vr* to become generalized, spread; (*difundirse*) to become widely known

generalmente [xeneral'mente] *adv* generally

generar [xene'rar] *vt* to generate

genérico, -a [xe'neriko, a] *adj* generic

género ['xenero] *nm* (*clase*) kind, sort; (*tipo*) type; (*Bio*) genus; (*Ling*) gender; (*Com*) material; **géneros** *nmpl* (*productos*) goods; **~ humano** human race; **~ chico** (*zarzuela*) Spanish operetta; **géneros de punto** knitwear *sg*

generosidad [xenerosi'ðað] *nf* generosity

generoso, -a [xene'roso, a] *adj* generous

genético, -a [xe'netiko, a] *adj* genetic ■ *nf* genetics *sg*

genial [xe'njal] *adj* inspired; (*idea*) brilliant; (*afable*) genial

genialidad [xenjali'ðað] *nf* (*singularidad*) genius; (*acto genial*) stroke of genius; **es una ~ suya** it's one of his brilliant ideas

genio ['xenjo] *nm* (*carácter*) nature, disposition; (*humor*) temper; (*facultad creadora*) genius; **mal ~** bad temper; **~ vivo** quick o hot temper; **de mal ~** bad-tempered

genital [xeni'tal] *adj* genital ■ *nm*: **genitales** genitals, genital organs

genitivo [xeni'tiβo] *nm* (*Ling*) genitive

genocidio [xeno'θiðjo] *nm* genocide

Génova ['xenoβa] *nf* Genoa

genovés, -esa [xeno'βes, esa] *adj, nm/f* Genoese

gente ['xente] *nf* (*personas*) people *pl*; (*raza*) race; (*nación*) nation; (*parientes*) relatives *pl*; **~ bien/baja** posh/lower-class people *pl*; **~ menuda** (*niños*) children *pl*; **es buena ~** (*fam: esp Am*) he's a good sort; **una ~ como Vd** (*Am*) a person like you

gentil [xen'til] *adj* (*elegante*) graceful; (*encantador*) charming; (*Rel*) gentile

gentileza [xenti'leθa] *nf* grace; charm; (*cortesía*) courtesy; **por ~ de** by courtesy of

gentilicio, -a [xenti'liθjo, a] *adj* (*familiar*) family *cpd*

gentío [xen'tio] *nm* crowd, throng

gentuza [xen'tuθa] *nf* (*pey: plebe*) rabble; (: *chusma*) riffraff

genuflexión [xenuflek'sjon] *nf* genuflexion

genuino, -a [xe'nwino, a] *adj* genuine

GEO ['xeo] *nmpl abr* (*Esp*: = *Grupos Especiales de Operaciones*) *Special Police Units used in anti-terrorist operations etc*

geografía [xeoɣra'fia] *nf* geography

geográfico, -a [xeo'ɣrafiko, a] *adj* geographic(al)

geología [xeolo'xia] *nf* geology

geólogo, -a [xe'oloɣo, a] *nm/f* geologist

geometría [xeome'tria] *nf* geometry

geométrico, -a [xeo'metriko, a] *adj* geometric(al)

Georgia [xe'orxja] *nf* Georgia

georgiano, -a [xeor'xjano, a] *adj, nm/f* Georgian ■ *nm* (*Ling*) Georgian

geranio [xe'ranjo] *nm* (*Bot*) geranium

gerencia [xe'renθja] *nf* management; (*cargo*) post of manager; (*oficina*) manager's office

gerente [xe'rente] *nm/f* (*supervisor*) manager; (*jefe*) director

geriatría [xerja'tria] *nf* (*Med*) geriatrics *sg*

geriátrico, -a [xer'jatriko, a] *adj* geriatric

germano, -a [xer'mano, a] *adj* German, Germanic ■ *nm/f* German

germen ['xermen] *nm* germ

germinar [xermi'nar] *vi* to germinate; (*brotar*) to sprout

gerundense [xerun'dense] *adj* of o from Gerona ■ *nm/f* native o inhabitant of Gerona

gerundio [xe'rundjo] *nm* (*Ling*) gerund

gestación [xesta'θjon] *nf* gestation

gesticulación [xestikula'θjon] *nf* (*ademán*) gesticulation; (*mueca*) grimace

gesticular [xestiku'lar] *vi* (*con ademanes*) to gesture; (*con muecas*) to make faces

gestión [xes'tjon] *nf* management; (*diligencia, acción*) negotiation; **hacer las gestiones preliminares** to do the groundwork; **~ de cartera** (*Com*) portfolio management; **~ financiera** (*Com*) financial management; **~ interna** (*Inform*) housekeeping; **~ de personal** personnel management; **~ de riesgos** (*Com*) risk management

gestionar [xestjo'nar] *vt* (*tratar de arreglar*) to try to arrange; (*llevar*) to manage

gesto ['xesto] *nm* (*mueca*) grimace; (*ademán*) gesture; **hacer gestos** to make faces

gestor, a [xes'tor, a] *adj* managing ■ *nm/f* manager; (*promotor*) promoter; (*agente*) business agent

gestoría [xesto'ria] *nf* *agency undertaking business with government departments, insurance companies etc*

Gibraltar [xiβral'tar] *nm* Gibraltar

gibraltareño, -a [xiβralta'reɲo, a] *adj* of o from Gibraltar ■ *nm/f* native o inhabitant of Gibraltar

gigante [xi'ɣante] *adj, nm/f* giant

gijonés, -esa [xixo'nes, esa] *adj* of o from Gijón ■ *nm/f* native o inhabitant of Gijón

gilipollas [xili'poʎas] (*fam*) *adj inv* daft ■ *nm/f* berk

gilipollez [xilipo'ʎeθ] *nf* (*fam*): **es una ~** that's a load of crap (!); **decir gilipolleces** to talk crap (!)

gima *etc* ['xima] *vb ver* **gemir**

gimnasia [xim'nasja] *nf* gymnastics *pl*; **confundir la ~ con la magnesia** to get things mixed up
gimnasio [xim'nasjo] *nm* gym(nasium)
gimnasta [xim'nasta] *nm/f* gymnast
gimnástica [xim'nastika] *nf* gymnastics *sg*
gimotear [ximote'ar] *vi* to whine, whimper; (*lloriquear*) to snivel
Ginebra [xi'neβra] *n* Geneva
ginebra [xi'neβra] *nf* gin
ginecología [xinekolo'xia] *nf* gyn(a)ecology
ginecológico, -a [xineko'loxiko, a] *adj* gyn(a)ecological
ginecólogo, -a [xine'koloyo, a] *nm/f* gyn(a)ecologist
gira ['xira] *nf* tour, trip
girar [xi'rar] *vt* (*dar la vuelta*) to turn (around); (*; rápidamente*) to spin; (*Com: giro postal*) to draw; (*comerciar: letra de cambio*) to issue ■ *vi* to turn (round); (*dar vueltas*) to rotate; (*rápido*) to spin; **la conversación giraba en torno a las elecciones** the conversation centred on the election; **~ en descubierto** to overdraw
giratorio, -a [xira'torjo, a] *adj* (*gen*) revolving; (*puente*) swing *cpd*; (*silla*) swivel *cpd*
giro ['xiro] *nm* (*movimiento*) turn, revolution; (*Ling*) expression; (*Com*) draft; (*de sucesos*) trend, course; **~ bancario** money order, bank giro; **~ de existencias** (*Com*) stock turnover; **~ postal** postal order
gis [xis] *nm* (*Am*) chalk
gitano, -a [xi'tano, a] *adj, nm/f* gypsy
glacial [gla'θjal] *adj* icy, freezing
glaciar [gla'θjar] *nm* glacier
glándula ['glandula] *nf* (*Anat, Bot*) gland
glicerina [gliθe'rina] *nf* (*Tec*) glycerin(e)
global [glo'βal] *adj* (*en conjunto*) global; (*completo*) total; (*investigación*) full; (*suma*) lump *cpd*
globalización [gloβaliθa'θjon] *nf* globalization
globo ['gloβo] *nm* (*esfera*) globe, sphere; (*aeróstato, juguete*) balloon
glóbulo ['gloβulo] *nm* globule; (*Anat*) corpuscle; **~ blanco/rojo** white/red corpuscle
gloria ['glorja] *nf* glory; (*fig*) delight; (*delicia*) bliss
glorieta [glo'rjeta] *nf* (*de jardín*) bower, arbour, arbor (US); (*Auto*) roundabout (Brit), traffic circle (US); (*plaza redonda*) circus; (*cruce*) junction
glorificar [glorifi'kar] *vt* (*enaltecer*) to glorify, praise
glorifique *etc* [glori'fike] *vb ver* **glorificar**
glorioso, -a [glo'rjoso, a] *adj* glorious
glosa ['glosa] *nf* comment; (*explicación*) gloss

glosar [glo'sar] *vt* (*comentar*) to comment on
glosario [glo'sarjo] *nm* glossary
glotón, -ona [glo'ton, ona] *adj* gluttonous, greedy ■ *nm/f* glutton
glotonería [glotone'ria] *nf* gluttony, greed
glúteo ['gluteo] *nm* (*fam: nalga*) buttock
G.N. *abr* (*Nicaragua, Panama*: = *Guardia Nacional*) *police*
gnomo ['nomo] *nm* gnome
gobernación [goβerna'θjon] *nf* government, governing; (*Pol*) Provincial Governor's office; **Ministro de la G~** Minister of the Interior, Home Secretary (Brit)
gobernador, -a [goβerna'ðor, a] *adj* governing ■ *nm/f* governor
gobernanta [goβer'nanta] *nf* (*esp Am*: *niñera*) governess
gobernante [goβer'nante] *adj* governing ■ *nm* ruler ■ *nf* (*en hotel etc*) housekeeper
gobernar [goβer'nar] *vt* (*dirigir*) to guide, direct; (*Pol*) to rule, govern ■ *vi* to govern; (*Naut*) to steer; **~ mal** to misgovern
gobierno *etc* [go'βjerno] *vb ver* **gobernar** ■ *nm* (*Pol*) government; (*gestión*) management; (*dirección*) guidance, direction; (*Naut*) steering; (*puesto*) governorship
goce *etc* ['goθe] *vb ver* **gozar** ■ *nm* enjoyment
godo, -a ['goðo, a] *nm/f* Goth; (*Am pey*) Spaniard
gol [gol] *nm* goal
golear [gole'ar] *vt* (*marcar*) to score a goal against
golf [golf] *nm* golf
golfo, -a ['golfo, a] *nm/f* (*pilluelo*) street urchin; (*vagabundo*) tramp; (*gorrón*) loafer; (*gamberro*) lout ■ *nm* (*Geo*) gulf ■ *nf* (*fam*: *prostituta*) slut, whore, hooker (US)
golondrina [golon'drina] *nf* swallow
golosina [golo'sina] *nf* titbit; (*dulce*) sweet
goloso, -a [go'loso, a] *adj* sweet-toothed; (*fam: glotón*) greedy
golpe ['golpe] *nm* blow; (*de puño*) punch; (*de mano*) smack; (*de remo*) stroke; (*Fútbol*) kick; (*Tenis etc*) hit, shot; (*mala suerte*) misfortune; (*fam: atraco*) job, heist (US); (*fig: choque*) clash; **no dar ~** to be bone idle; **de un ~** with one blow; **de ~** suddenly; **~ (de estado)** coup (d'état); **~ de gracia** coup de grâce (*tb fig*); **~ de fortuna/maestro** stroke of luck/genius; **cerrar una puerta de ~** to slam a door
golpear [golpe'ar] *vt, vi* to strike, knock; (*asestar*) to beat; (*de puño*) to punch; (*golpetear*) to tap; (*mesa*) to bang
golpista [gol'pista] *adj*: **intentona ~** coup attempt ■ *nm/f* participant in a coup (d'état)
golpiza [gol'pisa] *nf*: **dar una ~ a algn** (*Am*) to beat sb up

g

goma ['goma] nf (caucho) rubber; (elástico) elastic; (tira) rubber o elastic (Brit) band; (fam: preservativo) condom; (droga) hashish; (explosivo) plastic explosive; ~ **(de borrar)** eraser, rubber (Brit); ~ **de mascar** chewing gum; ~ **de pegar** gum, glue

goma-espuma [gomaes'puma] nf foam rubber

gomina [go'mina] nf hair gel

gomita [go'mita] nf rubber o elastic (Brit) band

góndola ['gondola] nf (barco) gondola; (de tren) goods wagon

gordo, -a ['gorðo, a] adj (gen) fat; (persona) plump; (agua) hard; (fam) enormous ■ nm/f fat man o woman; **el (premio)** ~ (en lotería) first prize; ¡~! (fam) fatty!

gordura [gor'ðura] nf fat; (corpulencia) fatness, stoutness

gorgojo [gor'ɣoxo] nm (insecto) grub

gorgorito [gorɣi'rito] nm (gorjeo) trill, warble

gorila [go'rila] nm gorilla; (fam) tough, thug; (guardaespaldas) bodyguard

gorjear [gorxe'ar] vi to twitter, chirp

gorjeo [gor'xeo] nm twittering, chirping

gorra ['gorra] nf (gen) cap; (de niño) bonnet; (militar) bearskin; ~ **de montar/de paño/de punto/de visera** riding/cloth/knitted/peaked cap; **andar** o **ir** o **vivir de** ~ to sponge, scrounge; **entrar de** ~ (fam) to gatecrash

gorrión [go'rrjon] nm sparrow

gorro ['gorro] nm cap; (de niño, mujer) bonnet; **estoy hasta el** ~ I am fed up

gorrón, -ona [go'rron, ona] nm pebble; (Tec) pivot ■ nm/f scrounger

gorronear [gorrone'ar] vi (fam) to sponge, scrounge

gota ['gota] nf (gen) drop; (de pintura) blob; (de sudor) bead; (Med) gout; ~ **a** ~ drop by drop; **caer a gotas** to drip

gotear [gote'ar] vi to drip; (escurrir) to trickle; (salirse) to leak; (cirio) to gutter; (lloviznar) to drizzle

gotera [go'tera] nf leak

gótico, -a ['gotiko, a] adj Gothic

gozar [go'θar] vi to enjoy o.s.; ~ **de** (disfrutar) to enjoy; (poseer) to possess; ~ **de buena salud** to enjoy good health

gozne ['goθne] nm hinge

gozo ['goθo] nm (alegría) joy; (placer) pleasure; ¡**mi** ~ **en el pozo!** that's torn it!, just my luck!

g.p. nm abr (= giro postal) m.o.

gr abr (= gramo(s)) g

grabación [graβa'θjon] nf recording

grabado, -a [gra'βaðo, a] adj (Mus) recorded; (en cinta) taped, on tape ■ nm print, engraving; ~ **al agua fuerte** etching; ~ **al**

aguatinta aquatint; ~ **en cobre** copperplate; ~ **en madera** woodcut; ~ **rupestre** rock carving

grabador, -a [graβa'ðor, a] nm/f engraver ■ nf tape-recorder; **grabadora de cassettes** cassette recorder

grabar [gra'βar] vt to engrave; (discos, cintas) to record; (impresionar) to impress

gracejo [gra'θexo] nm (ingenio) wit, humour; (elegancia) grace

gracia ['graθja] nf (encanto) grace, gracefulness; (Rel) grace; (chiste) joke; (humor) humour, wit; ¡**muchas gracias!** thanks very much!; **gracias a** thanks to; **tener** ~ (chiste etc) to be funny; ¡**qué** ~! how funny!; (irónico) what a nerve!; **no me hace** ~ (broma) it's not funny; (plan) I am not too keen; **con gracias anticipadas/repetidas** thanking you in advance/again; **dar las gracias a algn por algo** to thank sb for sth

grácil ['graθil] adj (sutil) graceful; (delgado) slender; (delicado) delicate

gracioso, -a [gra'θjoso, a] adj (garboso) graceful; (chistoso) funny; (cómico) comical; (agudo) witty; (título) gracious ■ nm/f (Teat) comic character, fool; **su graciosa Majestad** His/Her Gracious Majesty

grada ['graða] nf (de escalera) step; (de anfiteatro) tier, row; **gradas** nfpl (de estadio) terraces

gradación [graða'θjon] nf gradation; (serie) graded series

gradería [graðe'ria] nf (gradas) (flight of) steps pl; (de anfiteatro) tiers pl, rows pl; ~ **cubierta** covered stand

grado ['graðo] nm degree; (etapa) stage, step; (nivel) rate; (de parentesco) order of lineage; (de aceite, vino) grade; (grada) step; (Escol) class, year, grade (US); (Univ) degree; (Ling) degree of comparison; (Mil) rank; **de buen** ~ willingly; **en sumo** ~, **en** ~ **superlativo** in the highest degree

graduación [graðwa'θjon] nf (acto) gradation; (clasificación) rating; (del alcohol) proof, strength; (Escol) graduation; (Mil) rank; **de alta** ~ high-ranking

gradual [gra'ðwal] adj gradual

graduar [gra'ðwar] vt (gen) to graduate; (medir) to gauge; (Tec) to calibrate; (Univ) to confer a degree on; (Mil) to commission; **graduarse** vr to graduate; **graduarse la vista** to have one's eyes tested

grafía [gra'fia] nf (escritura) writing; (ortografía) spelling

gráfico, -a ['grafiko, a] adj graphic; (fig: vívido) vivid, lively ■ nm diagram ■ nf graph; ~ **de barras** (Com) bar chart;

~ **de sectores** o **de tarta** (Com) pie chart;
gráficos nmpl (tb Inform) graphics; **gráficos empresariales** (Com) business graphics

grafito [gra'fito] nm (Tec) graphite, black lead

grafología [grafolo'xia] nf graphology

gragea [gra'xea] nf (Med) pill; (caramelo) dragée

grajo ['graxo] nm rook

Gral. abr (Mil: = General) Gen.

gramático, -a [gra'matiko, a] nm/f (persona) grammarian ▪ nf grammar

gramo ['gramo] nm gramme (Brit), gram (US)

gran [gran] adj ver **grande**

grana ['grana] nf (Bot) seedling; (color) scarlet; **ponerse como la** ~ to go as red as a beetroot

granada [gra'naða] nf pomegranate; (Mil) grenade; ~ **de mano** hand grenade; ~ **de metralla** shrapnel shell

granadilla [grana'ðiʎa] nf (Am) passion fruit

granadino, -a [grana'ðino, a] adj of o from Granada ▪ nm/f native o inhabitant of Granada ▪ nf grenadine

granar [gra'nar] vi to seed

granate [gra'nate] adj inv maroon ▪ nm garnet; (color) maroon

Gran Bretaña [grambre'taɲa] nf Great Britain

Gran Canaria [granka'narja] nf Grand Canary

grancanario, -a [granka'narjo, a] adj of o from Grand Canary ▪ nm/f native o inhabitant of Grand Canary

grande ['grande], **gran** adj (de tamaño) big, large; (alto) tall; (distinguido) great; (impresionante) grand ▪ nm grandee; **¿cómo es de ~?** how big is it?, what size is it?; **pasarlo en ~** to have a tremendous time

grandeza [gran'deθa] nf greatness; (tamaño) bigness; (esplendor) grandness; (nobleza) nobility

grandioso, -a [gran'djoso, a] adj magnificent, grand

grandullón, -ona [granðu'ʎon, ona] adj oversized

granel [gra'nel] nm (montón) heap; **a** ~ (Com) in bulk

granero [gra'nero] nm granary, barn

granice etc [gra'niθe] vb ver **granizar**

granito [gra'nito] nm (Agr) small grain; (roca) granite

granizada [grani'θaða] nf hailstorm; (fig) hail; **una ~ de balas** a hail of bullets

granizado [grani'θaðo] nm iced drink; ~ **de café** iced coffee

granizar [grani'θar] vi to hail

granizo [gra'niθo] nm hail

granja ['granxa] nf (gen) farm; ~ **avícola** chicken o poultry farm

granjear [granxe'ar] vt (cobrar) to earn; (ganar) to win; (avanzar) to gain; **granjearse** vr (amistad etc) to gain for o.s.

granjero, -a [gran'xero, a] nm/f farmer

grano ['grano] nm grain; (semilla) seed; (baya) berry; (Med) pimple, spot; (partícula) particle; (punto) speck; **granos** nmpl cereals; ~ **de café** coffee bean; **ir al** ~ to get to the point

granuja [gra'nuxa] nm rogue; (golfillo) urchin

grapa ['grapa] nf staple; (Tec) clamp; (sujetador) clip, fastener; (Arq) cramp

grapadora [grapa'ðora] nf stapler

GRAPO ['grapo] nm abr (Esp Pol) = Grupo de Resistencia Antifascista Primero de Octubre

grasa ['grasa] nf ver **graso**

grasiento, -a [gra'sjento, a] adj greasy; (de aceite) oily; (mugriento) filthy

graso, -a ['graso, a] adj fatty; (aceitoso) greasy, oily ▪ nf (gen) grease; (de cocina) fat, lard; (sebo) suet; (mugre) filth; (Auto) oil; (lubricante) grease; **grasa de ballena** blubber; **grasa de pescado** fish oil

grasoso, -a [gra'soso, a] adj (Am) greasy, sticky

gratificación [gratifika'θjon] nf (propina) tip; (aguinaldo) gratuity; (bono) bonus; (recompensa) reward

gratificar [gratifi'kar] vt (dar propina) to tip; (premiar) to reward; **"se ~á"** "a reward is offered"

gratifique etc [grati'fike] vb ver **gratificar**

gratinar [grati'nar] vt to cook au gratin

gratis ['gratis] adv free, for nothing

gratitud [grati'tuð] nf gratitude

grato, -a ['grato, a] adj (agradable) pleasant, agreeable; (bienvenido) welcome; **nos es ~ informarle que ...** we are pleased to inform you that ...

gratuito, -a [gra'twito, a] adj (gratis) free; (sin razón) gratuitous; (acusación) unfounded

grava ['graβa] nf (guijos) gravel; (piedra molida) crushed stone; (en carreteras) road metal

gravamen [gra'βamen] nm (carga) burden; (impuesto) tax; **libre de** ~ (Econ) free from encumbrances

gravar [gra'βar] vt to burden; (Com) to tax; (Econ) to assess for tax; ~ **con impuestos** to burden with taxes

grave ['graβe] adj heavy; (fig, Med) grave, serious; (importante) important; (herida) severe; (Mus) low, deep; (Ling: acento) grave; **estar** ~ to be seriously ill

gravedad [graβe'ðað] nf gravity; (fig) seriousness; (grandeza) importance; (dignidad) dignity; (Mus) depth grávido, -a ['graβiðo, a] adj (preñada) pregnant

gravilla [gra'βiʎa] nf gravel

gravitación [graβita'θjon] nf gravitation

gravitar [graβi'tar] vi to gravitate; ~ **sobre** to rest on

gravoso, -a [gra'βoso, a] adj (pesado) burdensome; (costoso) costly

graznar [graθ'nar] vi (cuervo) to squawk; (pato) to quack; (hablar ronco) to croak

graznido [graθ'niðo] nm squawk; croak

Grecia ['greθja] nf Greece

gregario, -a [gre'ɣarjo, a] adj gregarious; **instinto** ~ herd instinct

gremio ['gremjo] nm (asociación) professional association, guild

greña ['greɲa] nf (cabellos) shock of hair; (maraña) tangle; **andar a la** ~ to bicker, squabble

greñudo, -a [gre'ɲuðo, a] adj (persona) dishevelled; (pelo) tangled

gresca ['greska] nf uproar; (trifulca) row

griego, -a ['grjeɣo, a] adj Greek, Grecian ■ nm/f Greek ■ nm (Ling) Greek

grieta ['grjeta] nf crack; (hendidura) chink; (quiebra) crevice; (Med) chap; (Pol) rift

grifa ['grifa] nf (fam: droga) marijuana

grifo ['grifo] nm tap (Brit), faucet (US); (Am) petrol (Brit) o gas (US) station

grilletes [gri'ʎetes] nmpl fetters, shackles

grillo ['griʎo] nm (Zool) cricket; (Bot) shoot; **grillos** nmpl shackles, irons

grima ['grima] nf (horror) loathing; (desagrado) reluctance; (desazón) uneasiness; **me da** ~ it makes me sick

gringo, -a ['gringo, a] (Am) adj (pey: extranjero) foreign; (: norteamericano) Yankee; (idioma) foreign ■ nm/f foreigner; Yank

gripa ['gripa] nf (Am) flu, influenza

gripe ['gripe] nf flu, influenza; ~ **porcina** swine flu

gris [gris] adj grey

grisáceo, -a [gri'saθeo, a] adj greyish

grisoso, -a [gri'soso, a] adj (Am) greyish

gritar [gri'tar] vt, vi to shout, yell; **¡no grites!** stop shouting!

grito ['grito] nm shout, yell; (de horror) scream; **a** ~ **pelado** at the top of one's voice; **poner el** ~ **en el cielo** to scream blue murder; **es el último** ~ (de moda) it's all the rage

groenlandés, -esa [groenlan'des, esa] adj Greenland cpd ■ nm/f Greenlander

Groenlandia [groen'landja] nf Greenland

grosella [gro'seʎa] nf (red)currant; ~ **negra** blackcurrant

grosería [grose'ria] nf (actitud) rudeness; (comentario) vulgar comment; (palabrota) swearword

grosero, -a [gro'sero, a] adj (poco cortés) rude, bad-mannered; (ordinario) vulgar, crude

grosor [gro'sor] nm thickness

grotesco, -a [gro'tesko, a] adj grotesque; (absurdo) bizarre

grúa ['grua] nf (Tec) crane; (de petróleo) derrick; ~ **corrediza** o **móvil/de pescante/puente/ de torre** travelling/jib/overhead/tower crane

grueso, -a ['grweso, a] adj thick; (persona) stout; (calidad) coarse ■ nm bulk; (espesor) thickness; (densidad) density; (de gente) main body, mass; **el** ~ **de** the bulk of

grulla ['gruʎa] nf (Zool) crane

grumete [gru'mete] nm (Naut) cabin o ship's boy

grumo ['grumo] nm (coágulo) clot, lump; (masa) dollop

gruñido [gru'ɲiðo] nm grunt, growl; (fig) grumble

gruñir [gru'ɲir] vi (animal) to grunt, growl; (fam) to grumble

gruñón, -ona [gru'ɲon, ona] adj grumpy ■ nm/f grumbler

grupa ['grupa] nf (Zool) rump

grupo ['grupo] nm group; (Tec) unit, set; (de árboles) cluster; ~ **sanguíneo** blood group

gruta ['gruta] nf grotto

Gta. abr (Auto) = **Glorieta**

guaca ['gwaka] nf Indian tomb

guacamole [gwaka'mole] nm (Am) avocado salad

guachimán [gwatʃi'man] nm (Am) night watchman

guadalajareño, -a [gwaðalaxa'reɲo, a] adj of o from Guadalajara ■ nm/f native o inhabitant of Guadalajara

Guadalquivir [gwaðalki'βir] nm: **el (Río)** ~ the Guadalquivir

guadaña [gwa'ðaɲa] nf scythe

guadañar [gwaða'ɲar] vt to scythe, mow

Guadiana [gwa'ðjana] nm: **el (Río)** ~ the Guadiana

guagua ['gwaɣwa] nf (Am, Canarias) bus; (Am: criatura) baby

guajolote [gwaxo'lote] nm (Am) turkey

guano ['gwano] nm guano

guantada [gwan'taða] nf, **guantazo** [gwan'taθo] nm slap

guante ['gwante] nm glove; **se ajusta como un** ~ it fits like a glove; **echar el** ~ **a algn** to catch hold of sb; (fig: policía) to catch sb

guapo, -a ['gwapo, a] adj good-looking; (mujer) pretty, attractive; (hombre) handsome; (elegante) smart ■ nm lover, gallant; (Am fam) tough guy, bully

guaraní [gwara'ni] adj, nm/f Guarani ■ nm (moneda) monetary unit of Paraguay

guarapo [gwa'rapo] *nm* (*Am*) fermented cane juice

guarda ['gwarða] *nm/f* (*persona*) warden, keeper ■ *nf* (*acto*) guarding; (*custodia*) custody; (*Tip*) flyleaf, endpaper; ~ **forestal** game warden

guardaagujas [gwarða'ɣuxas] *nm inv* (*Ferro*) switchman

guardabarros [gwarða'βarros] *nm inv* mudguard (*Brit*), fender (*US*)

guardabosques [gwarða'βoskes] *nm inv* gamekeeper

guardacoches [gwarða'kotʃes] *nm/f inv* (*celador*) parking attendant

guardacostas [gwarða'kostas] *nm inv* coastguard vessel

guardador, a [gwarða'ðor, a] *adj* protective; (*tacaño*) mean, stingy ■ *nm/f* guardian, protector

guardagujas [gwarða'ɣuxas] *nm inv* = **guardaagujas**

guardaespaldas [gwardaes'paldas] *nm/f inv* bodyguard

guardameta [gwarða'meta] *nm* goalkeeper

guardapolvo [gwarða'polβo] *nm* dust cover; (*prenda de vestir*) overalls *pl*

guardar [gwar'ðar] *vt* (*gen*) to keep; (*vigilar*) to guard, watch over; (*conservar*) to put away; (*dinero: ahorrar*) to save; (*promesa etc*) to keep; (*ley*) to observe; (*rencor*) to bear, harbour; (*Inform: archivo*) to save; **guardarse** *vr* (*preservarse*) to protect o.s.; **guardarse de algo** (*evitar*) to avoid sth; (*abstenerse*) to refrain from sth; **guardarse de hacer algo** to be careful not to do sth; **guardársela a algn** to have it in for sb

guardarropa [gwarða'rropa] *nm* (*armario*) wardrobe; (*en establecimiento público*) cloakroom

guardería [gwarðe'ria] *nf* nursery

guardia ['gwarðja] *nf* (*Mil*) guard; (*cuidado*) care, custody ■ *nm/f* guard; (*policía*) policeman(-woman); **estar de** ~ to be on guard; **montar** ~ to mount guard; **la G~ Civil** the Civil Guard; ~ **municipal** *o* **urbana** municipal police; **un** ~ **civil** a Civil Guard(sman); **un(a)** ~ **nacional** a policeman(-woman); ~ **urbano** traffic policeman; *see note*

● **GUARDIA**

● The *Guardia Civil* is a branch of the *Ejército de Tierra* (Army) run along military lines, which fulfils a policing role outside large urban communities and is under the joint control of the Spanish Ministry of Defence and the Ministry of the Interior. It is also known as *La Benemérita*.

guardián, -ana [gwar'ðjan, ana] *nm/f* (*gen*) guardian, keeper

guarecer [gware'θer] *vt* (*proteger*) to protect; (*abrigar*) to shelter; **guarecerse** *vr* to take refuge

guarezca *etc* [gwa'reθka] *vb ver* **guarecer**

guarida [gwa'riða] *nf* (*de animal*) den, lair; (*de persona*) haunt, hideout; (*refugio*) refuge

guarnecer [gwarne'θer] *vt* (*equipar*) to provide; (*adornar*) to adorn; (*Tec*) to reinforce

guarnezca *etc* [gwar'neθka] *vb ver* **guarnecer**

guarnición [gwarni'θjon] *nf* (*de vestimenta*) trimming; (*de piedra*) mount; (*Culin*) garnish; (*arneses*) harness; (*Mil*) garrison

guarrada [gwa'rraða] *nf* (*cosa sucia*) dirty mess; (*acto o dicho obsceno*) obscenity; **hacer una** ~ **a algn** to do the dirty on sb

guarrería [gwarre'ria] *nf* = **guarrada**

guarro, -a ['gwarro, a] *nm/f* (*fam*) pig; (*fig*) dirty *o* slovenly person

guasa ['gwasa] *nf* joke; **con** *o* **de** ~ jokingly, in fun

guasón, -ona [gwa'son, ona] *adj* witty; (*bromista*) joking ■ *nm/f* wit; joker

Guatemala [gwate'mala] *nf* Guatemala

guatemalteco, -a [gwatemal'teko, a] *adj, nm/f* Guatemalan

guateque [gwa'teke] *nm* (*fiesta*) party

guay [gwai] *adj* (*fam*) super, great

guayaba [gwa'jaβa] *nf* (*Bot*) guava

Guayana [gwa'jana] *nf* Guyana, Guiana

gubernamental [guβernamen'tal], **gubernativo, -a** [guβerna'tiβo, a] *adj* governmental

guedeja [ge'ðexa] *nf* long hair

guerra ['gerra] *nf* war; (*arte*) warfare; (*pelea*) struggle; ~ **atómica/bacteriológica/ nuclear/de guerrillas** atomic/germ/ nuclear/guerrilla warfare; **Primera/ Segunda G~ Mundial** First/Second World War; ~ **de precios** (*Com*) price war; ~ **civil/ fría** civil/cold war; ~ **a muerte** fight to the death; **de** ~ military, war *cpd*; **estar en** ~ to be at war; **dar** ~ to be annoying

guerrear [gerre'ar] *vi* to wage war

guerrero, -a [ge'rrero, a] *adj* fighting; (*carácter*) warlike ■ *nm/f* warrior

guerrilla [ge'rriʎa] *nf* guerrilla warfare; (*tropas*) guerrilla band *o* group

guerrillero, -a [gerri'ʎero, a] *nm/f* guerrilla (fighter); (*contra invasor*) partisan

gueto ['geto] *nm* ghetto

guía *etc* ['gia] *vb ver* **guiar** ■ *nm/f* (*persona*) guide ■ *nf* (*libro*) guidebook; (*manual*) handbook; ~ **de ferrocarriles** railway timetable; ~ **telefónica** telephone directory; ~ **del turista/del viajero** tourist/traveller's guide

guiar [gi'ar] *vt* to guide, direct; (*dirigir*) to lead; (*orientar*) to advise; (*Auto*) to steer; **guiarse** *vr*: **guiarse por** to be guided by

guijarro [gi'xarro] *nm* pebble

guillotina [giʎo'tina] *nf* guillotine

guinda ['ginda] *nf* morello cherry; (*licor*) cherry liqueur

guindar [gin'dar] *vt* to hoist; (*fam: robar*) to nick

guindilla [gin'diʎa] *nf* chil(l)i pepper

Guinea [gi'nea] *nf* Guinea

guineo, -a [gi'neo, a] *adj* Guinea *cpd*, Guinean ■ *nm/f* Guinean

guiñapo [gi'ɲapo] *nm* (*harapo*) rag; (*persona*) rogue

guiñar [gi'ɲar] *vi* to wink

guiño ['giɲo] *nm* (*parpadeo*) wink; (*muecas*) grimace; **hacer guiños a** (*enamorados*) to make eyes at

guiñol [gi'ɲol] *nm* (*Teat*) puppet theatre

guión [gi'on] *nm* (*Ling*) hyphen, dash; (*esquema*) summary, outline; (*Cine*) script

guionista [gjo'nista] *nm/f* scriptwriter

guipuzcoano, -a [gipuθko'ano, a] *adj* of o from Guipúzcoa ■ *nm/f* native o inhabitant of Guipúzcoa

guiri ['giri] *nm/f* (*fam, pey*) foreigner

guirigay [giri'gai] *nm* (*griterío*) uproar; (*confusión*) chaos

guirnalda [gir'nalda] *nf* garland

guisa ['gisa] *nf*: **a ~ de** as, like

guisado [gi'saðo] *nm* stew

guisante [gi'sante] *nm* pea

guisar [gi'sar] *vt, vi* to cook; (*fig*) to arrange

guiso ['giso] *nm* cooked dish

guita ['gita] *nf* twine; (*fam: dinero*) dough

guitarra [gi'tarra] *nf* guitar

guitarrista [gita'rrista] *nm/f* guitarist

gula ['gula] *nf* gluttony, greed

gusano [gu'sano] *nm* maggot, worm; (*de mariposa, polilla*) caterpillar; (*fig*) worm; (*ser despreciable*) creep; **~ de seda** silk-worm

gustar [gus'tar] *vt* to taste, sample ■ *vi* to please, be pleasing; **~ de algo** to like o enjoy sth; **me gustan las uvas** I like grapes; **le gusta nadar** she likes o enjoys swimming; **¿gusta Ud?** would you like some?; **como Ud guste** as you wish

gusto ['gusto] *nm* (*sentido, sabor*) taste; (*agrado*) liking; (*placer*) pleasure; **tiene un ~ amargo** it has a bitter taste; **tener buen ~** to have good taste; **sobre gustos no hay nada escrito** there's no accounting for tastes; **de buen/mal ~** in good/bad taste; **sentirse a ~** to feel at ease; **¡mucho o tanto ~ (en conocerle)!** how do you do?, pleased to meet you; **el ~ es mío** the pleasure is mine; **tomar ~ a** to take a liking to; **con ~** willingly, gladly

gustoso, -a [gus'toso, a] *adj* (*sabroso*) tasty; (*agradable*) pleasant; (*con voluntad*) willing, glad; **lo hizo ~** he did it gladly

gutural [gutu'ral] *adj* guttural

guyanés, -esa [gwaja'nes, esa] *adj, nm/f* Guyanese

Hh

H, h ['atʃe] *nf* (*letra*) H, h; **H de Historia** H for Harry (Brit) *o* How (US)

H. *abr* (*Química*: = *Hidrógeno*) H; (= *Hectárea(s)*) ha.

h. *abr* (= *hora(s)*) h., hr(s). ■ *nmpl abr* (= *habitantes*) pop.

ha¹ [a] *vb ver* **haber**

ha² *abr* (= *Hectárea(s)*) ha.

haba ['aβa] *nf* bean; **son habas contadas** it goes without saying; **en todas partes cuecen habas** it's the same (story) the whole world over

Habana [a'βana] *nf*: **la ~** Havana

habanero, -a [aβa'nero, a] *adj* of *o* from Havana ■ *nm/f* native *o* inhabitant of Havana ■ *nf* (*Mus*) habanera

habano [a'βano] *nm* Havana cigar

habeas corpus [a'βeas'korpus] *nm* (*Law*) habeas corpus

○ **PALABRA CLAVE**

haber [a'βer] *vb auxiliar* **1** (*tiempos compuestos*) to have; **había comido** I have/had eaten; **antes/después de haberlo visto** before seeing/after seeing *o* having seen it; **si lo hubiera sabido habría ido** if I had known I would have gone

2: **¡haberlo dicho antes!** you should have said so before!; **¿habráse visto (cosa igual)?** have you ever seen anything like it?

3: **haber de**: **he de hacerlo** I must do it; **ha de llegar mañana** it should arrive tomorrow

■ *vb impersonal* **1** (*existencia: sg*) there is; (: *pl*) there are; **hay un hermano/dos hermanos** there is one brother/there are two brothers; **¿cuánto hay de aquí a Sucre?** how far is it from here to Sucre?; **habrá unos 4 grados** it must be about 4 degrees; **no hay quien te entienda** there's no understanding you

2 (*obligación*): **hay que hacer algo** something must be done; **hay que apuntarlo para acordarse** you have to write it down to remember

3: **¡hay que ver!** well I never!

4: **¡no hay de** *o* **por** (*Am*) **qué!** don't mention it!, not at all!

5: **¿qué hay?** (*¿qué pasa?*) what's up?, what's the matter?; (*¿qué tal?*) how's it going?

■ *vt*: **he aquí unas sugerencias** here are some suggestions; **todos los inventos habidos y por haber** all inventions present and future; **en el encuentro habido ayer** in yesterday's game

haberse *vr*: **habérselas con algn** to have it out with sb

■ *nm* (*en cuenta*) credit side

haberes *nmpl* assets; **¿cuánto tengo en el haber?** how much do I have in my account?; **tiene varias novelas en su haber** he has several novels to his credit

habichuela [aβi'tʃwela] *nf* kidney bean

hábil ['aβil] *adj* (*listo*) clever, smart; (*capaz*) fit, capable; (*experto*) expert; **día ~** working day

habilidad [aβili'ðað] *nf* (*gen*) skill, ability; (*inteligencia*) cleverness; (*destreza*) expertness, expertise; (*Jur*) competence; **~ (para)** fitness (for); **tener ~ manual** to be clever with one's hands

habilitación [aβilita'θjon] *nf* qualification; (*colocación de muebles*) fitting out; (*financiamiento*) financing; (*oficina*) paymaster's office

habilitado [aβili'taðo] *nm* paymaster

habilitar [aβili'tar] *vt* to qualify; (*autorizar*) to authorize; (*capacitar*) to enable; (*dar instrumentos*) to equip; (*financiar*) to finance

hábilmente [aβil'mente] *adv* skilfully, expertly

habitable [aβi'taβle] *adj* inhabitable

habitación [aβita'θjon] *nf* (*cuarto*) room; (*casa*) dwelling, abode; (*Bio: morada*) habitat; **~ sencilla** *o* **individual** single room; **~ doble** *o* **de matrimonio** double room

habitante [aβi'tante] *nm/f* inhabitant
habitar [aβi'tar] *vt* (*residir en*) to inhabit;
(*ocupar*) to occupy ■ *vi* to live
hábitat (*pl* **hábitats**) ['aβitat, 'aβitats] *nm*
habitat
hábito ['aβito] *nm* habit; **tener el ~ de hacer
algo** to be in the habit of doing sth
habitual [aβi'twal] *adj* habitual
habituar [aβi'twar] *vt* to accustom;
habituarse a to get used to
habla ['aβla] *nf* (*capacidad de hablar*) speech;
(*idioma*) language; (*dialecto*) dialect; **perder
el ~** to become speechless; **de ~ francesa**
French-speaking; **estar al ~** to be in contact;
(*Telec*) to be on the line; **¡González al ~!**
(*Telec*) Gonzalez speaking!
hablador, a [aβla'ðor, a] *adj* talkative ■ *nm/f*
chatterbox
habladuría [aβlaðu'ria] *nf* rumour;
habladurías *nfpl* gossip *sg*
hablante [a'βlante] *adj* speaking ■ *nm/f*
speaker
hablar [a'βlar] *vt* to speak, talk ■ *vi* to speak;
hablarse *vr* to speak to each other; **~ con**
to speak to; **¡hable!**, **¡puede ~!** (*Telec*) you're
through!; **de eso ni ~** no way, that's not on;
~ alto/bajo/claro to speak loudly/quietly/
plainly o bluntly; **~ de** to speak of o about;
"se habla inglés" "English spoken here";
no se hablan they are not on speaking terms
habré *etc* [a'βre] *vb ver* **haber**
hacedor, a [aθe'ðor, a] *nm/f* maker
hacendado, -a [aθen'daðo, a] *adj* property-
owning ■ *nm* (*terrateniente*) large landowner
hacendoso, -a [aθen'doso, a] *adj*
industrious, hard-working

 PALABRA CLAVE

hacer [a'θer] *vt* **1** (*fabricar, producir, conseguir*)
to make; (*construir*) to build; **hacer una
película/un ruido** to make a film/noise; **el
guisado lo hice yo** I made o cooked the stew;
hacer amigos to make friends
2 (*ejecutar: trabajo etc*) to do; **hacer la colada**
to do the washing; **hacer la comida** to do
the cooking; **¿qué haces?** what are you
doing?; **¡eso está hecho!** you've got it!;
hacer el tonto/indio to act the fool/clown;
hacer el malo *o* **el papel del malo** (*Teat*) to
play the villain
3 (*estudios, algunos deportes*) to do; **hacer
español/económicas** to do *o* study Spanish/
economics; **hacer yoga/gimnasia** to do
yoga/go to the gym
4 (*transformar, incidir en*): **esto lo hará más
difícil** this will make it more difficult; **salir

te hará sentir mejor** going out will make
you feel better; **te hace más joven** it makes
you look younger
5 (*cálculo*): **2 y 2 hacen 4** 2 and 2 make 4; **éste
hace 100** this one makes 100
6 (+ *sub*): **esto hará que ganemos** this will
make us win; **harás que no quiera venir**
you'll stop him wanting to come
7 (*como sustituto de vb*) to do; **él bebió y yo hice
lo mismo** he drank and I did likewise
8: **no hace más que criticar** all he does is
criticize
■ *vb semi-auxiliar* (+ *infin*) **1** (*directo*): **les hice
venir** I made o had them come; **hacer
trabajar a los demás** to get others to work
2 (*por intermedio de otros*): **hacer reparar algo**
to get sth repaired
■ *vi* **1**: **haz como que no lo sabes** act as if
you don't know; **hiciste bien en decírmelo**
you were right to tell me
2 (*ser apropiado*): **si os hace** if it's alright with
you
3: **hacer de**: **hacer de madre para uno** to
be like a mother to sb; (*Teat*): **hacer de Otelo**
to play Othello; **la tabla hace de mesa** the
board does as a table
■ *vb impersonal* **1**: **hace calor/frío** it's hot/
cold; *ver tb* **bueno**; **sol**; **tiempo**
2 (*tiempo*): **hace tres años** three years ago;
hace un mes que voy/no voy I've been
going/I haven't been for a month; **no le veo
desde hace mucho** I haven't seen him for a
long time
3: **¿cómo has hecho para llegar tan
rápido?** how did you manage to get here so
quickly?
hacerse *vr* **1** (*volverse*) to become; **se hicieron
amigos** they became friends; **hacerse viejo**
to get o grow old; **se hace tarde** it's getting
late
2: **hacerse algo**: **me hice un traje** I got a
suit made
3 (*acostumbrarse*): **hacerse a** to get used to;
hacerse a la idea to get used to the idea
4: **se hace con huevos y leche** it's made
out of eggs and milk; **eso no se hace** that's
not done
5 (*obtener*): **hacerse de** *o* **con algo** to get hold
of sth
6 (*fingirse*): **hacerse el sordo/sueco** to turn a
deaf ear/pretend not to notice

hacha ['atʃa] *nf* axe; (*antorcha*) torch
hachazo [a'tʃaθo] *nm* axe blow
hache ['atʃe] *nf* (the letter) H; **llámele usted
~** call it what you will
hachís [a'tʃis] *nm* hashish

hacia [a'θja] *prep* (*en dirección de, actitud*) towards; (*cerca de*) near; ~ **arriba/abajo** up(wards)/down(wards); ~ **mediodía** about noon

hacienda [a'θjenda] *nf* (*propiedad*) property; (*finca*) farm; (*Am*) ranch; ~ **pública** public finance; **(Ministerio de) H~** Exchequer (*Brit*), Treasury Department (*US*)

hacinar [aθi'nar] *vt* to pile (up); (*Agr*) to stack; (*fig*) to overcrowd

hada ['aða] *nf* fairy; ~ **madrina** fairy godmother

hado ['aðo] *nm* fate, destiny

haga *etc* ['aɣa] *vb ver* **hacer**

Haití [ai'ti] *nm* Haiti

haitiano, -a [ai'tjano, a] *adj, nm/f* Haitian

hala ['ala] *excl* (*vamos*) come on!; (*anda*) get on with it!

halagar [ala'ɣar] *vt* (*lisonjear*) to flatter

halago [a'laɣo] *nm* (*adulación*) flattery

halague *etc* [a'laɣe] *vb ver* **halagar**

halagüeño, -a [ala'ɣweɲo, a] *adj* flattering

halcón [al'kon] *nm* falcon, hawk

hálito ['alito] *nm* breath

halitosis [ali'tosis] *nf* halitosis, bad breath

hallar [a'ʎar] *vt* (*gen*) to find; (*descubrir*) to discover; (*toparse con*) to run into; **hallarse** *vr* to be (situated); (*encontrarse*) to find o.s.; **se halla fuera** he is away; **no se halla** he feels out of place

hallazgo [a'ʎaθɣo] *nm* discovery; (*cosa*) find

halo ['alo] *nm* halo

halógeno, a [a'loxeno, a] *adj*: **faro** ~ halogen lamp

halterofilia [altero'filja] *nf* weightlifting

hamaca [a'maka] *nf* hammock

hambre ['ambre] *nf* hunger; (*carencia*) famine; (*inanición*) starvation; (*fig*) longing; **tener** ~ to be hungry

hambriento, -a [am'brjento, a] *adj* hungry, starving ▪ *nm/f* starving person; **los hambrientos** the hungry; ~ **de** hungry o longing for

hambruna [am'bruna] *nf* famine

Hamburgo [am'burɣo] *nm* Hamburg

hamburguesa [ambur'ɣesa] *nf* hamburger, burger

hampa ['ampa] *nf* underworld

hampón [am'pon] *nm* thug

hámster ['xamster] *nm* hamster

han [an] *vb ver* **haber**

haragán, -ana [ara'ɣan, ana] *adj, nm/f* good-for-nothing

haraganear [araɣane'ar] *vi* to idle, loaf about

harapiento, -a [ara'pjento, a] *adj* tattered, in rags

harapo [a'rapo] *nm* rag

hardware ['xardwer] *nm* (*Inform*) hardware

haré *etc* [a're] *vb ver* **hacer**

harén [a'ren] *nm* harem

harina [a'rina] *nf* flour; **eso es** ~ **de otro costal** that's another kettle of fish

harinero, -a [ari'nero, a] *nm/f* flour merchant

harinoso, -a [ari'noso, a] *adj* floury

hartar [ar'tar] *vt* to satiate, glut; (*fig*) to tire, sicken; **hartarse** *vr* (*de comida*) to gorge o.s.; (*cansarse*): **hartarse de** to get fed up with

hartazgo [ar'taθɣo] *nm* surfeit, glut

harto, -a ['arto, a] *adj* (*lleno*) full; (*cansado*) fed up ▪ *adv* (*bastante*) enough; (*muy*) very; **estar** ~ **de** to be fed up with; **¡estoy** ~ **de decírtelo!** I'm sick and tired of telling you (so)!

hartura [ar'tura] *nf* (*exceso*) surfeit; (*abundancia*) abundance; (*satisfacción*) satisfaction

has¹ [as] *vb ver* **haber**

has² *abr* (= *Hectáreas*) ha.

hasta ['asta] *adv* even ▪ *prep* (*alcanzando a*) as far as, up/down to; (*de tiempo: a tal hora*) till, until; (*: antes de*) before ▪ *conj*: ~ **que** until; ~ **luego** o **ahora/el sábado** (*fam*) see you soon/ on Saturday; ~ **la fecha** (up) to date; ~ **nueva orden** until further notice; ~ **en Valencia hiela a veces** even in Valencia it freezes sometimes

hastiar [as'tjar] *vt* (*gen*) to weary; (*aburrir*) to bore; **hastiarse** *vr*: **hastiarse de** to get fed up with

hastío [as'tio] *nm* weariness; boredom

hatajo [a'taxo] *nm*: **un** ~ **de gamberros** a bunch of hooligans

hatillo [a'tiʎo] *nm* belongings *pl*, kit; (*montón*) bundle, heap

Hawai [a'wai] *nm* (*tb*: **las Islas Hawai**) Hawaii

hawaianas [awa'janas] *nfpl* (*esp Am*) flip-flops (*Brit*), thongs

hawaiano, -a [awa'jano, a] *adj, nm/f* Hawaiian

hay [ai] *vb ver* **haber**

Haya ['aja] *nf*: **la** ~ The Hague

haya *etc* ['aja] *vb ver* **haber** ▪ *nf* beech tree

hayal [a'jal] *nm* beech grove

haz [aθ] *vb ver* **hacer** ▪ *nm* bundle, bunch; (*rayo: de luz*) beam ▪ *nf*: ~ **de la tierra** face of the earth

hazaña [a'θaɲa] *nf* feat, exploit; **sería una** ~ it would be a great achievement

hazmerreír [aθmerre'ir] *nm inv* laughing stock

he [e] *vb ver* **haber** ▪ *adv*: **he aquí** here is, here are; **he aquí por qué ...** that is why ...

hebilla [e'βiʎa] *nf* buckle, clasp

hebra ['eβra] *nf* thread; (*Bot: fibra*) fibre, grain

h

197

hebreo, -a [e'βreo, a] *adj, nm/f* Hebrew ∎ *nm* (*Ling*) Hebrew

Hébridas ['eβriðas] *nfpl*: **las ~** the Hebrides

hechice *etc* [e'tʃiθe] *vb ver* **hechizar**

hechicero, -a [etʃi'θero, a] *nm/f* sorcerer/ sorceress

hechizar [etʃi'θar] *vt* to cast a spell on, bewitch

hechizo [e'tʃiθo] *nm* witchcraft, magic; (*acto de magia*) spell, charm

hecho, -a ['etʃo, a] *pp de* **hacer** ∎ *adj* complete; (*maduro*) mature; (*Costura*) ready-to-wear ∎ *nm* deed, act; (*dato*) fact; (*cuestión*) matter; (*suceso*) event ∎ *excl* agreed!, done!; ¡bien ~! well done!; **de ~** in fact, as a matter of fact; (*Pol etc: adj, adv*) de facto; **de ~ y de derecho** de facto and de jure; **~ a la medida** made-to-measure; **a lo ~, pecho** it's no use crying over spilt milk

hechura [e'tʃura] *nf* making, creation; (*producto*) product; (*forma*) form, shape; (*de persona*) build; (*Tec*) craftsmanship

hectárea [ek'tarea] *nf* hectare

heder [e'ðer] *vi* to stink, smell; (*fig*) to be unbearable

hediondez [eðjon'deθ] *nf* stench, stink; (*cosa*) stinking thing

hediondo, -a [e'ðjondo, a] *adj* stinking

hedor [e'ðor] *nm* stench

hegemonía [exemo'nia] *nf* hegemony

helada [e'laða] *nf* frost

heladera [ela'ðera] *nf* (*Am: refrigerador*) refrigerator

heladería [elaðe'ria] *nf* ice-cream stall (*o* parlour)

helado, -a [e'laðo, a] *adj* frozen; (*glacial*) icy; (*fig*) chilly, cold ∎ *nm* ice-cream; **dejar ~ a algn** to dumbfound sb

helador, a [ela'ðor, a] *adj* (*viento etc*) icy

helar [e'lar] *vt* to freeze, ice (up); (*dejar atónito*) to amaze; (*desalentar*) to discourage ∎ *vi*, **helarse** *vr* to freeze; (*Aviat, Ferro etc*) to ice (up), freeze up; (*líquido*) to set

helecho [e'letʃo] *nm* bracken, fern

hélice ['eliθe] *nf* spiral; (*Tec*) propeller; (*Mat*) helix

helicóptero [eli'koptero] *nm* helicopter

helio ['eljo] *nm* helium

helmántico, -a [el'mantiko, a] *adj* of *o* from Salamanca

helvético, -a [el'βetiko, a] *adj, nm/f* Swiss

hematoma [ema'toma] *nm* bruise

hembra ['embra] *nf* (*Bot, Zool*) female; (*mujer*) woman; (*Tec*) nut; **un elefante ~** a she-elephant

hemeroteca [emero'teka] *nf* newspaper library

hemiciclo [emi'θiklo] *nm*: **el ~** (*Pol*) the floor

hemisferio [emis'ferjo] *nm* hemisphere

hemofilia [emo'filja] *nf* haemophilia (*Brit*), hemophilia (*US*)

hemorragia [emo'rraxja] *nf* haemorrhage (*Brit*), hemorrhage (*US*)

hemorroides [emo'rroiðes] *nfpl* haemorrhoids (*Brit*), hemorrhoids (*US*)

hemos ['emos] *vb ver* **haber**

henar [e'nar] *nm* meadow, hayfield

henchir [en'tʃir] *vt* to fill, stuff; **henchirse** *vr* (*llenarse de comida*) to stuff o.s. (with food); (*inflarse*) to swell (up)

Hendaya [en'daja] *nf* Hendaye

hender [en'der] *vt* to cleave, split

hendidura [endi'ðura] *nf* crack, split; (*Geo*) fissure

henequén [ene'ken] *nm* (*Am*) henequen

heno ['eno] *nm* hay

hepatitis [epa'titis] *nf inv* hepatitis

herbario, -a [er'βarjo, a] *adj* herbal ∎ *nm* (*colección*) herbarium; (*especialista*) herbalist; (*botánico*) botanist

herbicida [erβi'θiða] *nm* weedkiller

herbívoro, -a [er'βiβoro, a] *adj* herbivorous

herboristería [erβoriste'ria] *nf* herbalist's shop

heredad [ere'ðað] *nf* landed property; (*granja*) farm

heredar [ere'ðar] *vt* to inherit

heredero, -a [ere'ðero, a] *nm/f* heir(ess); **~ del trono** heir to the throne

hereditario, -a [ereði'tarjo, a] *adj* hereditary

hereje [e'rexe] *nm/f* heretic

herejía [ere'xia] *nf* heresy

herencia [e'renθja] *nf* inheritance; (*fig*) heritage; (*Bio*) heredity

herético, -a [e'retiko, a] *adj* heretical

herido, -a [e'riðo, a] *adj* injured, wounded; (*fig*) offended ∎ *nm/f* casualty ∎ *nf* injury

herir [e'rir] *vt* to wound, injure; (*fig*) to offend; (*conmover*) to touch, move

hermana [er'mana] *nf ver* **hermano**

hermanación [ermana'θjon] *nf* (*de ciudades*) twinning

hermanado, -a [erma'naðo, a] *adj* (*ciudad*) twinned

hermanar [erma'nar] *vt* to match; (*unir*) to join; (*ciudades*) to twin

hermanastro, -a [erma'nastro, a] *nm/f* stepbrother(-sister)

hermandad [erman'dað] *nf* brotherhood; (*de mujeres*) sisterhood; (*sindicato etc*) association

hermano, -a [er'mano, a] *adj* similar ∎ *nm* brother ∎ *nf* sister; **~ gemelo** twin brother; **~ político** brother-in-law; **~ primo** first cousin; **mis hermanos** my brothers, my brothers and sisters; **hermana política** sister-in-law

hermético, -a [er'metiko, a] *adj* hermetic; *(fig)* watertight

hermoso, -a [er'moso, a] *adj* beautiful, lovely; *(estupendo)* splendid; *(guapo)* handsome

hermosura [ermo'sura] *nf* beauty; *(de hombre)* handsomeness

hernia ['ernja] *nf* hernia, rupture; ~ **discal** slipped disc

herniarse [er'njarse] *vr* to rupture o.s.; *(fig)* to break one's back

héroe ['eroe] *nm* hero

heroicidad [eroiθi'ðað] *nf* heroism; *(una heroicidad)* heroic deed

heroico, -a [e'roiko, a] *adj* heroic

heroína [ero'ina] *nf* (mujer) heroine; *(droga)* heroin

heroinómano, -a [eroi'nomano, a] *nm/f* heroin addict

heroísmo [ero'ismo] *nm* heroism

herpes ['erpes] *nmpl o nfpl* (Med: gen) herpes sg; *(: de la piel)* shingles *sg*

herradura [erra'ðura] *nf* horseshoe

herraje [e'rraxe] *nm* (trabajos) ironwork

herramienta [erra'mjenta] *nf* tool

herrería [erre'ria] *nf* smithy; *(Tec)* forge

herrero [e'rrero] *nm* blacksmith

herrumbre [e'rrumbre] *nf* rust

herrumbroso, -a [errum'broso, a] *adj* rusty

hervidero [erβi'ðero] *nm* (fig) swarm; *(Pol etc)* hotbed

hervir [er'βir] *vi* to boil; *(burbujear)* to bubble; *(fig)*: ~ **de** to teem with; ~ **a fuego lento** to simmer

hervor [er'βor] *nm* boiling; *(fig)* ardour, fervour

heterogéneo, -a [etero'xeneo, a] *adj* heterogeneous

heterosexual [eterosek'swal] *adj, nm/f* heterosexual

hez [eθ] *nf* (tb: **heces**) dregs

hibernar [iβer'nar] *vi* to hibernate

híbrido, -a ['iβriðo, a] *adj* hybrid

hice *etc* ['iθe] *vb ver* **hacer**

hidalgo, -a [i'ðalɣo, a] *adj* noble; *(honrado)* honourable (Brit), honorable (US) ■ *nm/f* noble(man(-woman))

hidratante [iðra'tante] *adj*: **crema** ~ moisturizing cream, moisturizer

hidratar [iðra'tar] *vt* to moisturize

hidrato [i'ðrato] *nm* hydrate; ~ **de carbono** carbohydrate

hidráulico, -a [i'ðrauliko, a] *adj* hydraulic ■ *nf* hydraulics *sg*

hidro... [iðro] *pref* hydro..., water-...

hidroavión [iðroa'βjon] *nm* seaplane

hidrodeslizador [iðrodesliθa'ðor] *nm* hovercraft

hidroeléctrico, -a [iðroe'lektriko, a] *adj* hydroelectric

hidrófilo, -a [i'ðrofilo, a] *adj* absorbent; **algodón** ~ cotton wool (Brit), absorbent cotton (US)

hidrofobia [iðro'foβja] *nf* hydrophobia, rabies

hidrófugo, -a [i'ðrofuɣo, a] *adj* damp-proof

hidrógeno [i'ðroxeno] *nm* hydrogen

hieda *etc* ['jeða] *vb ver* **heder**

hiedra ['jeðra] *nf* ivy

hiel [jel] *nf* gall, bile; *(fig)* bitterness

hielo *etc* ['jelo] *vb ver* **helar** ■ *nm* (gen) ice; *(escarcha)* frost; *(fig)* coldness, reserve; **romper el** ~ *(fig)* to break the ice

hiena ['jena] *nf* (Zool) hyena

hiera *etc* ['jera] *vb ver* **herir**

hierba ['jerβa] *nf* (pasto) grass; *(Culin, Med: planta)* herb; **mala** ~ weed; *(fig)* evil influence

hierbabuena [jerβa'βwena] *nf* mint

hierro ['jerro] *nm* (metal) iron; *(objeto)* iron object; ~ **acanalado** corrugated iron; ~ **colado** o **fundido** cast iron; **de** ~ iron *cpd*

hierva *etc* ['jerβa] *vb ver* **hervir**

hígado ['iɣaðo] *nm* liver; **hígados** *nmpl* (fig) guts; **echar los hígados** to wear o.s. out

higiene [i'xjene] *nf* hygiene

higiénico, -a [i'xjeniko, a] *adj* hygienic

higo ['iɣo] *nm* fig; ~ **seco** dried fig; ~ **chumbo** prickly pear; **de higos a brevas** once in a blue moon

higuera [i'ɣera] *nf* fig tree

hijastro, -a [i'xastro, a] *nm/f* stepson(-daughter)

hijo, -a ['ixo, a] *nm/f* son/daughter, child; *(uso vocativo)* dear; **hijos** *nmpl* children, sons and daughters; **sin hijos** childless; ~/**hija político/a** son-/daughter-in-law; ~ **pródigo** prodigal son; ~ **de papá/mamá** daddy's/mummy's boy; ~ **de puta** (fam!) bastard (!), son of a bitch (!); ~ **único** only child; **cada** ~ **de vecino** any Tom, Dick or Harry

hilacha [i'latʃa] *nf* ravelled thread

hilado, -a [i'laðo, a] *adj* spun

hilandero, -a [ilan'dero, a] *nm/f* spinner

hilar [i'lar] *vt* to spin; *(fig)* to reason, infer; ~ **delgado** to split hairs

hilera [i'lera] *nf* row, file

hilo ['ilo] *nm* thread; *(Bot)* fibre; *(tela)* linen; *(de metal)* wire; *(de agua)* trickle, thin stream; *(de luz)* beam, ray; *(de conversación)* thread, theme; *(de pensamientos)* train; ~ **dental** dental floss; **colgar de un** ~ *(fig)* to hang by a thread; **traje de** ~ linen suit

hilvanar [ilβa'nar] *vt* (Costura) to tack (Brit), baste (US); *(fig)* to do hurriedly

Himalaya [ima'laja] *nm*: **el** ~, **los Montes Himalaya** the Himalayas

himno ['imno] *nm* hymn; ~ **nacional** national anthem

hincapié [inka'pje] *nm*: **hacer hincapié en** to emphasize, stress

hincar [in'kar] *vt* (*gen*) to drive (in), thrust (in); (*diente*) to sink; **hincarse** *vr*: **hincarse de rodillas** (*esp Am*) to kneel down

hincha ['int∫a] *nm/f* (*fam*: *Deporte*) fan

hinchado, -a [in't∫aðo, a] *adj* (*gen*) swollen; (*persona*) pompous ■ *nf* (group of) supporters *o* fans

hinchar [in't∫ar] *vt* (*gen*) to swell; (*inflar*) to blow up, inflate; (*fig*) to exaggerate; **hincharse** *vr* (*inflarse*) to swell up; (*fam*: *llenarse*) to stuff o.s.; (*fig*) to get conceited; **hincharse de reír** to have a good laugh

hinchazón [int∫a'θon] *nf* (*Med*) swelling; (*protuberancia*) bump, lump; (*altivez*) arrogance

hindú [in'du] *adj*, *nm/f* Hindu

hinojo [i'noxo] *nm* fennel

hinque *etc* ['inke] *vb ver* **hincar**

hipar [i'par] *vi* to hiccup

hiper... [iper] *pref* hyper...

hiperactivo, -a [iperak'tiβo, a] *adj* hyperactive

hipermercado [ipermer'kaðo] *nm* hypermarket, superstore

hipersensible [ipersen'siβle] *adj* hypersensitive

hipertensión [iperten'sjon] *nf* high blood pressure, hypertension

hípico, -a ['ipiko, a] *adj* horse *cpd*, equine; **club** ~ riding club

hipnosis [ip'nosis] *nf inv* hypnosis

hipnotice *etc* [ipno'tiθe] *vb ver* **hipnotizar**

hipnotismo [ipno'tismo] *nm* hypnotism

hipnotizar [ipnoti'θar] *vt* to hypnotize

hipo ['ipo] *nm* hiccups *pl*; **quitar el ~ a algn** to cure sb's hiccups

hipocondría [ipokon'dria] *nf* hypochondria

hipocondríaco, -a [ipokon'driako, a] *adj*, *nm/f* hypochondriac

hipocresía [ipokre'sia] *nf* hypocrisy

hipócrita [i'pokrita] *adj* hypocritical ■ *nm/f* hypocrite

hipodérmico, -a [ipo'ðermiko, a] *adj*: **aguja hipodérmica** hypodermic needle

hipódromo [i'poðromo] *nm* racetrack

hipopótamo [ipo'potamo] *nm* hippopotamus

hipoteca [ipo'teka] *nf* mortgage; **redimir una ~** to pay off a mortgage

hipotecar [ipote'kar] *vt* to mortgage; (*fig*) to jeopardize

hipotecario, -a [ipote'karjo, a] *adj* mortgage *cpd*

hipótesis [i'potesis] *nf inv* hypothesis; **es una ~ (nada más)** that's just a theory

hipotético, -a [ipo'tetiko, a] *adj* hypothetic(al)

hiriendo *etc* [i'rjendo] *vb ver* **herir**

hiriente [i'rjente] *adj* offensive, wounding

hirsuto, -a [ir'suto, a] *adj* hairy

hirviendo *etc* [ir'βjendo] *vb ver* **hervir**

hisopo [i'sopo] *nm* (*Rel*) sprinkler; (*Bot*) hyssop; (*de algodón*) swab

hispánico, -a [is'paniko, a] *adj* Hispanic, Spanish

hispanidad [ispani'ðað] *nf* (*cualidad*) Spanishness; (*Pol*) Spanish *o* Hispanic world

hispanista [ispa'nista] *nm/f* (*Univ etc*) Hispan(ic)ist

hispano, -a [is'pano, a] *adj* Hispanic, Spanish, Hispano- ■ *nm/f* Spaniard

Hispanoamérica [ispanoa'merika] *nf* Spanish *o* Latin America

hispanoamericano, -a [ispanoameri'kano, a] *adj*, *nm/f* Spanish *o* Latin American

hispanohablante [ispanoa'βlante], **hispanoparlante** [ispanopar'lante] *adj* Spanish-speaking

histeria [is'terja] *nf* hysteria

histérico, -a [is'teriko, a] *adj* hysterical

histerismo [iste'rismo] *nm* (*Med*) hysteria; (*fig*) hysterics

histograma [isto'γrama] *nm* histogram

historia [is'torja] *nf* history; (*cuento*) story, tale; **historias** *nfpl* (*chismes*) gossip *sg*; **dejarse de historias** to come to the point; **pasar a la ~** to go down in history

historiador, a [istorja'ðor, a] *nm/f* historian

historial [isto'rjal] *nm* record; (*profesional*) curriculum vitae, c.v., résumé (US); (*Med*) case history

histórico, -a [is'toriko, a] *adj* historical; (*fig*) historic

historieta [isto'rjeta] *nf* tale, anecdote; (*de dibujos*) comic strip

histrionismo [istrjo'nismo] *nm* (*Teat*) acting; (*fig*) histrionics *pl*

hito ['ito] *nm* (*fig*) landmark; (*objetivo*) goal, target; (*fig*) milestone

hizo ['iθo] *vb ver* **hacer**

Hna., Hnas. *abr* (= *Hermana(s)*) Sr(s).

Hno., Hnos. *abr* (= *Hermano(s)*) Bro(s).

hocico [o'θiko] *nm* snout; (*fig*) grimace

hockey ['xoki] *nm* hockey; **~ sobre hielo** ice hockey

hogar [o'γar] *nm* fireplace, hearth; (*casa*) home; (*vida familiar*) home life

hogareño, -a [oγa'reɲo, a] *adj* home *cpd*; (*persona*) home-loving

hogaza [o'γaθa] *nf* (*de pan*) large loaf

hoguera [o'γera] *nf* (*gen*) bonfire; (*para herejes*) stake

hoja ['oxa] nf (gen) leaf; (de flor) petal; (de hierba) blade; (de papel) sheet; (página) page; (formulario) form; (de puerta) leaf; ~ **de afeitar** razor blade; ~ **de cálculo electrónica** spreadsheet; ~ **de ruta** road map; ~ **de solicitud** application form; ~ **de trabajo** (Inform) worksheet; **de ~ ancha** broad-leaved; **de ~ caduca/perenne** deciduous/evergreen

hojalata [oxa'lata] nf tin(plate)

hojaldre [o'xaldre] nm (Culin) puff pastry

hojarasca [oxa'raska] nf (hojas) dead o fallen leaves pl; (fig) rubbish

hojear [oxe'ar] vt to leaf through, turn the pages of

hola ['ola] excl hello!

Holanda [o'landa] nf Holland

holandés, -esa [olan'des, esa] adj Dutch ▪ nm/f Dutchman(-woman); **los holandeses** the Dutch ▪ nm (Ling) Dutch

holgado, -a [ol'ɣaðo, a] adj loose, baggy; (rico) well-to-do

holgar [ol'ɣar] vi (descansar) to rest; (sobrar) to be superfluous; **huelga decir que** it goes without saying that

holgazán, -ana [olɣa'θan, ana] adj idle, lazy ▪ nm/f loafer

holgazanear [olɣaθane'ar] vi to laze o loaf around

holgura [ol'ɣura] nf looseness, bagginess; (Tec) play, free movement; (vida) comfortable living, luxury

hollar [o'ʎar] vt to tread (on), trample

hollín [o'ʎin] nm soot

hombre ['ombre] nm man; (raza humana): **el ~ man**(kind) ▪ excl **¡sí ~!** (claro) of course!; (para énfasis) man, old chap; ~ **de negocios** businessman; ~-**rana** frogman; ~ **de bien** o **pro** honest man; ~ **de confianza** right-hand man; ~ **de estado** statesman; **el ~ medio** the average man

hombrera [om'brera] nf shoulder strap

hombro ['ombro] nm shoulder; **arrimar el ~** to lend a hand; **encogerse de hombros** to shrug one's shoulders

hombruno, -a [om'bruno, a] adj mannish

homenaje [ome'naxe] nm (gen) homage; (tributo) tribute; **un partido ~** a benefit match

homeopatía [omeopa'tia] nf hom(o)eopathy

homeopático, -a [omeo'patiko, a] adj hom(o)eopathic

homicida [omi'θiða] adj homicidal ▪ nm/f murderer

homicidio [omi'θiðjo] nm murder, homicide; (involuntario) manslaughter

homologación [omoloɣa'θjon] nf (de sueldo, condiciones) parity

homologar [omolo'ɣar] vt (Com) to standardize; (Escol) to officially approve; (Deporte) to officially recognize; (sueldos) to equalize

homólogo, -a [o'moloɣo, a] nm/f counterpart, opposite number

homónimo [o'monimo] nm (tocayo) namesake

homosexual [omosek'swal] adj, nm/f homosexual

hondo, -a ['ondo, a] adj deep; **lo ~** the depth(s) (pl), the bottom; **con ~ pesar** with deep regret

hondonada [ondo'naða] nf hollow, depression; (cañón) ravine; (Geo) lowland

hondura [on'dura] nf depth, profundity

Honduras [on'duras] nf Honduras

hondureño, -a [ondu'reɲo, a] adj, nm/f Honduran

honestidad [onesti'ðað] nf purity, chastity; (decencia) decency

honesto, -a [o'nesto, a] adj chaste; decent, honest; (justo) just

hongo ['onɡo] nm (Bot: gen) fungus; (: comestible) mushroom; (: venenoso) toadstool; (sombrero) bowler (hat) (Brit), derby (US); **hongos del pie** foot rot sg, athlete's foot sg

honor [o'nor] nm (gen) honour (Brit), honor (US); (gloria) glory; ~ **profesional** professional etiquette; **en ~ a la verdad** to be fair

honorable [ono'raβle] adj honourable (Brit), honorable (US)

honorario, -a [ono'rarjo, a] adj honorary ▪ nm: **honorarios** fees

honorífico, -a [ono'rifiko, a] adj honourable (Brit), honorable (US); **mención honorífica** hono(u)rable mention

honra ['onra] nf (gen) honour (Brit), honor (US); (renombre) good name; **honras fúnebres** funeral rites; **tener algo a mucha ~** to be proud of sth

honradez [onra'ðeθ] nf honesty; (de persona) integrity

honrado, -a [on'raðo, a] adj honest, upright

honrar [on'rar] vt to honour (Brit) o honor (US); **honrarse** vr: **honrarse con algo/de hacer algo** to be honoured by sth/to do sth

honroso, -a [on'roso, a] adj (honrado) honourable (Brit), honorable (US); (respetado) respectable

hora ['ora] nf hour; (tiempo) time; **¿qué ~ es?** what time is it?; **¿a qué ~?** at what time?; **media ~** half an hour; **a la ~ de comer/de recreo** at lunchtime/at playtime; **a primera ~** first thing (in the morning); **a última ~** at

h

the last moment; **"última ~"** "stop press";
noticias de última ~ last-minute news; **a
altas horas** in the small hours; **a la ~ en
punto** on the dot; **¡a buena ~!** about time,
too!; **en mala ~** unluckily; **dar la ~** to strike
the hour; **poner el reloj en ~** to set one's
watch; **horas de oficina/de trabajo** office/
working hours; **horas de visita** visiting
times; **horas extras** o **extraordinarias**
overtime sg; **horas punta** rush hours; **no
ver la ~ de** to look forward to; **¡ya era ~!** and
about time too!

horadar [ora'ðar] vt to drill, bore
horario, -a [o'rarjo, a] adj hourly, hour cpd
■ nm timetable; **~ comercial** business hours
horca ['orka] nf gallows sg; (Agr) pitchfork
horcajadas [orka'xaðas]: **a ~** adv astride
horchata [or'tʃata] nf cold drink made from tiger
nuts and water, tiger nut milk
horda ['orða] nf horde
horizontal [oriθon'tal] adj horizontal
horizonte [ori'θonte] nm horizon
horma ['orma] nf mould; **~ (de calzado)** last;
~ de sombrero hat block
hormiga [or'miɣa] nf ant; **hormigas** nfpl
(Med) pins and needles
hormigón [ormi'ɣon] nm concrete; **~
armado/pretensado** reinforced/prestressed
concrete
hormigueo [ormi'ɣeo] nm (comezón) itch; (fig)
uneasiness
hormiguero [ormi'ɣero] nm (Zool) ant's nest;
era un ~ it was swarming with people
hormona [or'mona] nf hormone
hornada [or'naða] nf batch of loaves (etc)
hornillo [or'niʎo] nm (cocina) portable stove
horno ['orno] nm (Culin) oven; (Tec)
furnace; (para cerámica) kiln; **~ microondas**
microwave (oven); **alto ~** blast furnace; **~
crematorio** crematorium
horóscopo [o'roskopo] nm horoscope
horquilla [or'kiʎa] nf hairpin; (Agr) pitchfork
horrendo, -a [o'rrendo, a] adj horrendous,
frightful
horrible [o'rriβle] adj horrible, dreadful
horripilante [orripi'lante] adj hair-raising,
horrifying
horripilar [orripi'lar] vt: **~ a algn** to horrify
sb; **horripilarse** vr to be horrified
horror [o'rror] nm horror, dread; (atrocidad)
atrocity; **¡qué ~!** (fam) how awful!; **estudia
horrores** he studies a hell of a lot
horrorice etc [orro'riθe] vb ver **horrorizar**
horrorizar [orrori'θar] vt to horrify, frighten;
horrorizarse vr to be horrified
horroroso, -a [orro'roso, a] adj horrifying,
ghastly

hortaliza [orta'liθa] nf vegetable
hortelano, -a [orte'lano, a] nm/f (market)
gardener
hortera [or'tera] adj (fam) vulgar, naff
horterada [orte'raða] nf (fam): **es una ~** it's
really naff
hortícola [or'tikola] adj horticultural
horticultura [ortikul'tura] nf horticulture
hortofrutícola [ortofru'tikola] adj fruit and
vegetable cpd
hosco, -a ['osko, a] adj dark; (persona) sullen,
gloomy
hospedaje [ospe'ðaxe] nm (cost of) board and
lodging
hospedar [ospe'ðar] vt to put up;
hospedarse vr: **hospedarse (con/en)** to stay
o lodge (with/at)
hospedería [ospeðe'ria] nf (edificio) inn;
(habitación) guest room
hospicio [os'piθjo] nm (para niños) orphanage
hospital [ospi'tal] nm hospital
hospitalario, -a [ospita'larjo, a] adj (acogedor)
hospitable
hospitalice etc [ospita'liθe] vb ver
hospitalizar
hospitalidad [ospitali'ðað] nf hospitality
hospitalizar [ospitali'θar] vt to send o take to
hospital, hospitalize
hosquedad [oske'ðað] nf sullenness
hostal [os'tal] nm small hotel; ver tb **hotel**
hostelería [ostele'ria] nf hotel business o
trade
hostia ['ostja] nf (Rel) host, consecrated
wafer; (fam: golpe) whack, punch ■ excl: **¡~(s)!**
(fam!) damn!
hostigar [osti'ɣar] vt to whip; (fig) to harass,
pester
hostigue etc [os'tiɣe] vb ver **hostigar**
hostil [os'til] adj hostile
hostilidad [ostili'ðað] nf hostility
hotel [o'tel] nm hotel; see note

● **HOTEL**

In Spain you can choose from the
following categories of accommodation,
in descending order of quality and price:
hotel (from 5 stars to 1), *hostal, pensión,
casa de huéspedes, fonda*. Quality can vary
widely even within these categories.
The State also runs luxury hotels called
paradores, which are usually sited in places
of particular historical interest and are
often historic buildings themselves.

hotelero, -a [ote'lero, a] adj hotel cpd ■ nm/f
hotelier

hoy [oi] *adv* (*este día*) today; (*en la actualidad*) now(adays) ▪ *nm* present time; **~ (en) día** now(adays); **el día de ~, ~ día** (*Am*) this very day; **~ por ~** right now; **de ~ en ocho días** a week today; **de ~ en adelante** from now on

hoya ['oja] *nf* pit; (*sepulcro*) grave; (*Geo*) valley

hoyo ['ojo] *nm* hole, pit; (*tumba*) grave; (*Golf*) hole; (*Med*) pockmark

hoyuelo [oj'welo] *nm* dimple

hoz [oθ] *nf* sickle

hube *etc* ['uβe] *vb ver* **haber**

hucha ['utʃa] *nf* money box

hueco, -a ['weko, a] *adj* (*vacío*) hollow, empty; (*resonante*) booming; (*sonido*) resonant; (*persona*) conceited; (*estilo*) pompous ▪ *nm* hollow, cavity; (*agujero*) hole; (*de escalera*) well; (*de ascensor*) shaft; (*vacante*) vacancy; **~ de la mano** hollow of the hand

huela *etc* ['wela] *vb ver* **oler**

huelga *etc* ['welɣa] *vb ver* **holgar** ▪ *nf* strike; **declararse en ~** to go on strike, come out on strike; **~ general** general strike; **~ de hambre** hunger strike; **~ oficial** official strike

huelgue *etc* ['welɣe] *vb ver* **holgar**

huelguista [wel'ɣista] *nm/f* striker

huella ['weʎa] *nf* (*acto de pisar, pisada*) tread(ing); (*marca del paso*) footprint, footstep; (*: de animal, máquina*) track; **~ digital** fingerprint; **sin dejar ~** without leaving a trace

huérfano, -a ['werfano, a] *adj* orphan(ed); (*fig*) unprotected ▪ *nm/f* orphan

huerta ['werta] *nf* market garden (*Brit*), truck farm (*US*); (*de Murcia, Valencia*) irrigated region

huerto ['werto] *nm* kitchen garden; (*de árboles frutales*) orchard

hueso ['weso] *nm* (*Anat*) bone; (*de fruta*) stone, pit (*US*); **sin ~** (*carne*) boned; **estar en los huesos** to be nothing but skin and bone; **ser un ~** (*profesor*) to be terribly strict; **un ~ duro de roer** a hard nut to crack

huesoso, -a [we'soso, a] *adj* (*esp Am*) bony

huésped, a ['wespeð, a] *nm/f* (*invitado*) guest; (*habitante*) resident; (*anfitrión*) host(ess)

huesudo, -a [we'suðo, a] *adj* bony, big-boned

huevas ['weβas] *nfpl* eggs, roe *sg*; (*Am: fam!*) balls (!)

huevera [we'βera] *nf* eggcup

huevo ['weβo] *nm* egg; (*fam!*) ball (!), testicle; **~ duro/escalfado/estrellado** o **frito/pasado por agua** hard-boiled/poached/fried/soft-boiled egg; **huevos revueltos** scrambled eggs; **me costó un ~** (*fam!*) it was hard work; **tener huevos** (*fam!*) to have guts

huevón, -ona [we'βon, ona] *nm/f* (*Am fam!*) stupid bastard (!), stupid idiot

huida [u'iða] *nf* escape, flight; **~ de capitales** (*Com*) flight of capital

huidizo, -a [ui'ðiθo, a] *adj* (*tímido*) shy; (*pasajero*) fleeting

huir [u'ir] *vt* (*escapar*) to flee, escape; (*evadir*) to avoid ▪ *vi* to flee, run away

hule ['ule] *nm* (*encerado*) oilskin; (*esp Am*) rubber

hulla ['uʎa] *nf* bituminous coal

humanice *etc* [uma'niθe] *vb ver* **humanizar**

humanidad [umani'ðað] *nf* (*género humano*) man(kind); (*cualidad*) humanity; (*fam: gordura*) corpulence

humanitario, -a [umani'tarjo, a] *adj* humanitarian; (*benévolo*) humane

humanizar [umani'θar] *vt* to humanize; **humanizarse** *vr* to become more human

humano, -a [u'mano, a] *adj* (*gen*) human; (*humanitario*) humane ▪ *nm* human; **ser ~** human being

humareda [uma'reða] *nf* cloud of smoke

humeante [ume'ante] *adj* smoking, smoky

humedad [ume'ðað] *nf* (*del clima*) humidity; (*de pared etc*) dampness; **a prueba de ~** damp-proof

humedecer [umeðe'θer] *vt* to moisten, wet; **humedecerse** *vr* to get wet

humedezca *etc* [ume'ðeθka] *vb ver* **humedecer**

húmedo, -a ['umeðo, a] *adj* (*mojado*) damp, wet; (*tiempo etc*) humid

humildad [umil'dað] *nf* humility, humbleness

humilde [u'milde] *adj* humble, modest; (*clase etc*) low, modest

humillación [umiʎa'θjon] *nf* humiliation

humillante [umi'ʎante] *adj* humiliating

humillar [umi'ʎar] *vt* to humiliate; **humillarse** *vr* to humble o.s., grovel

humo ['umo] *nm* (*de fuego*) smoke; (*gas nocivo*) fumes *pl*; (*vapor*) steam, vapour; **humos** *nmpl* (*fig*) conceit *sg*; **irse todo en ~** (*fig*) to vanish without trace; **bajar los humos a algn** to take sb down a peg or two

humor [u'mor] *nm* (*disposición*) mood, temper; (*lo que divierte*) humour; **de buen/mal ~** in a good/bad mood

humorismo [umo'rismo] *nm* humour

humorista [umo'rista] *nm/f* comic

humorístico, -a [umo'ristiko, a] *adj* funny, humorous

hundimiento [undi'mjento] *nm* (*gen*) sinking; (*colapso*) collapse

hundir [un'dir] *vt* to sink; (*edificio, plan*) to ruin, destroy; **hundirse** *vr* to sink, collapse; (*fig: arruinarse*) to be ruined; (*desaparecer*) to disappear; **se hundió la economía** the economy collapsed; **se hundieron los precios** prices slumped

húngaro, -a ['ungaro, a] *adj, nm/f* Hungarian ∎ *nm* (*Ling*) Hungarian, Magyar

Hungría [un'gria] *nf* Hungary

huracán [ura'kan] *nm* hurricane

huraño, -a [u'raɲo, a] *adj* shy; (*antisocial*) unsociable

hurgar [ur'ɣar] *vt* to poke, jab; (*remover*) to stir (up); **hurgarse** *vr*: **hurgarse (las narices)** to pick one's nose

hurgonear [urɣone'ar] *vt* to poke

hurgue *etc* ['urɣe] *vb ver* **hurgar**

hurón [u'ron] *nm* (*Zool*) ferret

hurra ['urra] *excl* hurray!, hurrah!

hurtadillas [urta'ðiʎas]: **a ~** *adv* stealthily, on the sly

hurtar [ur'tar] *vt* to steal; **hurtarse** *vr* to hide, keep out of the way

hurto ['urto] *nm* theft, stealing; (*lo robado*) (piece of) stolen property, loot

husmear [usme'ar] *vt* (*oler*) to sniff out, scent; (*fam*) to pry into ∎ *vi* to smell bad

huso ['uso] *nm* (*Tec*) spindle; (*de torno*) drum

huy ['ui] *excl* (*dolor*) ow!, ouch!; (*sorpresa*) well!; (*alivio*) phew!; **¡~, perdona!** oops, sorry!

huyendo *etc* [u'jendo] *vb ver* **huir**

I i

I, i [i] *nf* (*letra*) I, i; **I de Inés** I for Isaac (*Brit*) *o* Item (*US*)

IA *abr* = **inteligencia artificial**

iba *etc* ['iβa] *vb ver* **ir**

Iberia [i'βerja] *nf* Iberia

ibérico, -a [i'βeriko, a] *adj* Iberian; **la Península ibérica** the Iberian Peninsula

ibero, -a [i'βero, a], **íbero, -a** ['iβero, a] *adj, nm/f* Iberian

iberoamericano, -a [iβeroameri'kano, a] *adj, nm/f* Latin American

íbice ['iβiθe] *nm* ibex

ibicenco, -a [iβi'θenko, a] *adj* of *o* from Ibiza ■ *nm/f* native *o* inhabitant of Ibiza

Ibiza [i'βiθa] *nf* Ibiza

ice *etc* ['iθe] *vb ver* **izar**

iceberg [iθe'ber] *nm* iceberg

ICONA [i'kona] *nm abr* (*Esp*) = **Instituto Nacional para la Conservación de la Naturaleza**

icono [i'kono] *nm* (*tb Inform*) icon

iconoclasta [ikono'klasta] *adj* iconoclastic ■ *nm/f* iconoclast

ictericia [ikte'riθja] *nf* jaundice

íd. *abr* = **ídem**

I+D *nf abr* (= *Investigación y Desarrollo*) R&D

ida ['iða] *nf* going, departure; **~ y vuelta** round trip, return; **idas y venidas** comings and goings

IDE ['iðe] *nf abr* (= *Iniciativa de Defensa Estratégica*) SDI

idea [i'ðea] *nf* idea; (*impresión*) opinion; (*propósito*) intention; **~ genial** brilliant idea; **a mala ~** out of spite; **no tengo la menor ~** I haven't a clue

ideal [iðe'al] *adj, nm* ideal

idealice *etc* [iðea'liθe] *vb ver* **idealizar**

idealista [iðea'lista] *adj* idealistic ■ *nm/f* idealist

idealizar [iðeali'θar] *vt* to idealize

idear [iðe'ar] *vt* to think up; (*aparato*) to invent; (*viaje*) to plan

ídem ['iðem] *pron* ditto

idéntico, -a [i'ðentiko, a] *adj* identical

identidad [iðenti'ðað] *nf* identity; **~ corporativa** corporate identity *o* image

identificación [iðentifika'θjon] *nf* identification

identificador de llamadas [iðentifika'ðor-] *nm* caller ID

identificar [iðentifi'kar] *vt* to identify; **identificarse** *vr*: **identificarse con** to identify with

identifique *etc* [iðenti'fike] *vb ver* **identificar**

ideología [iðeolo'xia] *nf* ideology

ideológico, -a [iðeo'loxiko, a] *adj* ideological

idílico, -a [i'ðiliko, a] *adj* idyllic

idilio [i'ðiljo] *nm* love affair

idioma [i'ðjoma] *nm* language

idiomático, -a [iðjo'matiko, a] *adj* idiomatic

idiota [i'ðjota] *adj* idiotic ■ *nm/f* idiot

idiotez [iðjo'teθ] *nf* idiocy

idolatrar [iðola'trar] *vt* (*fig*) to idolize

ídolo ['iðolo] *nm* (*tb fig*) idol

idoneidad [iðonei'ðað] *nf* suitability; (*capacidad*) aptitude

idóneo, -a [i'ðoneo, a] *adj* suitable

I.E.S. *nm abr* = **Instituto de Enseñanza Secundaria**

iglesia [i'ɣlesja] *nf* church; **~ parroquial** parish church; **¡con la ~ hemos topado!** now we're really up against it!

iglú [i'ɣlu] *nm* igloo; (*contenedor*) bottle bank

IGME *nm abr* = **Instituto Geográfico y Minero**

ignición [iɣni'θjon] *nf* ignition

ignominia [iɣno'minja] *nf* ignominy

ignominioso, -a [iɣnomi'njoso, a] *adj* ignominious

ignorado, -a [iɣno'raðo, a] *adj* unknown; (*dato*) obscure

ignorancia [iɣno'ranθja] *nf* ignorance; **por ~** through ignorance

ignorante [iɣno'rante] *adj* ignorant, uninformed ■ *nm/f* ignoramus

ignorar [iɣno'rar] *vt* not to know, be ignorant of; (*no hacer caso a*) to ignore; **ignoramos su**

paradero we don't know his whereabouts

ignoto, -a [iɣ'noto, a] *adj* unknown

igual [i'ɣwal] *adj* equal; (*similar*) like, similar; (*mismo*) (the) same; (*constante*) constant; (*temperatura*) even ■ *nm/f* equal; **al ~ que** *prep, conj* like, just like; **~ que** the same as; **sin ~** peerless; **me da** *o* **es ~** I don't care, it makes no difference; **no tener ~** to be unrivalled; **son iguales** they're the same

iguala [i'ɣwala] *nf* equalization; (*Com*) agreement

igualada [iɣwa'laða] *nf* equalizer

igualar [iɣwa'lar] *vt* (*gen*) to equalize, make equal; (*terreno*) to make even; (*Com*) to agree upon; **igualarse** *vr* (*platos de balanza*) to balance out; **igualarse (a)** (*equivaler*) to be equal (to)

igualdad [iɣwal'dað] *nf* equality; (*similaridad*) sameness; (*uniformidad*) uniformity; **en ~ de condiciones** on an equal basis

igualmente [iɣwal'mente] *adv* equally; (*también*) also, likewise ■ *excl* the same to you!

iguana [i'ɣwana] *nf* iguana

ikurriña [iku'rriɲa] *nf* Basque flag

ilegal [ile'ɣal] *adj* illegal

ilegitimidad [ilexitimi'ðað] *nf* illegitimacy

ilegítimo, -a [ile'xitimo, a] *adj* illegitimate

ileso, -a [i'leso, a] *adj* unhurt, unharmed

ilícito, -a [i'liθito, a] *adj* illicit

ilimitado, -a [ilimi'taðo, a] *adj* unlimited

Ilma., Ilmo. *abr* (= *Ilustrísima, Ilustrísimo*) *courtesy title*

ilógico, -a [i'loxiko, a] *adj* illogical

iluminación [ilumina'θjon] *nf* illumination; (*alumbrado*) lighting; (*fig*) enlightenment

iluminar [ilumi'nar] *vt* to illuminate, light (up); (*fig*) to enlighten

ilusión [ilu'sjon] *nf* illusion; (*quimera*) delusion; (*esperanza*) hope; (*emoción*) excitement, thrill; **hacerse ilusiones** to build up one's hopes; **no te hagas ilusiones** don't build up your hopes *o* get too excited

ilusionado, -a [ilusjo'naðo, a] *adj* excited

ilusionar [ilusjo'nar] *vt*: **~ a algn** (*falsamente*) to build up sb's hopes; **ilusionarse** *vr* (*falsamente*) to build up one's hopes; (*entusiasmarse*) to get excited; **me ilusiona mucho el viaje** I'm really excited about the trip

ilusionista [ilusjo'nista] *nm/f* conjurer

iluso, -a [i'luso, a] *adj* gullible, easily deceived ■ *nm/f* dreamer, visionary

ilusorio, -a [ilu'sorjo, a] *adj* (*de ilusión*) illusory, deceptive; (*esperanza*) vain

ilustración [ilustra'θjon] *nf* illustration; (*saber*) learning, erudition; **la I~** the Enlightenment

ilustrado, -a [ilus'traðo, a] *adj* illustrated; learned

ilustrar [ilus'trar] *vt* to illustrate; (*instruir*) to instruct; (*explicar*) to explain, make clear; **ilustrarse** *vr* to acquire knowledge

ilustre [i'lustre] *adj* famous, illustrious

imagen [i'maxen] *nf* (*gen*) image; (*dibujo*, TV) picture; (*Rel*) statue; **ser la viva ~ de** to be the spitting *o* living image of; **a su ~** in one's own image

imaginación [imaxina'θjon] *nf* imagination; (*fig*) fancy; **ni por ~** on no account; **no se me pasó por la ~ que** ... it never even occurred to me that ...

imaginar [imaxi'nar] *vt* (*gen*) to imagine; (*idear*) to think up; (*suponer*) to suppose; **imaginarse** *vr* to imagine; **¡imagínate!** just imagine!, just fancy!; **imagínese que** ... suppose that ...; **me imagino que sí** I should think so

imaginario, -a [imaxi'narjo, a] *adj* imaginary

imaginativo, -a [imaxina'tiβo, a] *adj* imaginative ■ *nf* imagination

imán [i'man] *nm* magnet

imanar [ima'nar], **imantar** [ima'ntar] *vt* to magnetize

imbécil [im'beθil] *nm/f* imbecile, idiot

imbecilidad [imbeθili'ðað] *nf* imbecility, stupidity

imberbe [im'berβe] *adj* beardless

imborrable [imbo'rraβle] *adj* indelible; (*inolvidable*) unforgettable

imbuir [imbu'ir] *vi* to imbue

imbuyendo *etc* [imbu'jendo] *vb ver* **imbuir**

imitación [imita'θjon] *nf* imitation; (*parodia*) mimicry; **a ~ de** in imitation of; **desconfíe de las imitaciones** (*Com*) beware of copies *o* imitations

imitador, a [imita'ðor, a] *adj* imitative ■ *nm/f* imitator; (*Teat*) mimic

imitar [imi'tar] *vt* to imitate; (*parodiar, remedar*) to mimic, ape; (*copiar*) to follow

impaciencia [impa'θjenθja] *nf* impatience

impacientar [impaθjen'tar] *vt* to make impatient; (*enfadar*) to irritate; **impacientarse** *vr* to get impatient; (*inquietarse*) to fret

impaciente [impa'θjente] *adj* impatient; (*nervioso*) anxious

impacto [im'pakto] *nm* impact; (*esp Am: fig*) shock

impagado, -a [impa'ɣaðo, a] *adj* unpaid, still to be paid

impar [im'par] *adj* odd ■ *nm* odd number

imparable [impa'raβle] *adj* unstoppable

imparcial [impar'θjal] *adj* impartial, fair

imparcialidad [imparθjali'ðað] nf impartiality, fairness

impartir [impar'tir] vt to impart, give

impasible [impa'siβle] adj impassive

impávido, -a [im'paβiðo, a] adj fearless, intrepid

IMPE ['impe] nm abr (Esp, Com) = **Instituto de la Mediana y Pequeña Empresa**

impecable [impe'kaβle] adj impeccable

impedido, -a [impe'ðiðo, a] adj: **estar ~** to be an invalid ■ nm/f: **ser un ~ físico** to be an invalid

impedimento [impeði'mento] nm impediment, obstacle

impedir [impe'ðir] vt (obstruir) to impede, obstruct; (estorbar) to prevent; **~ el tráfico** to block the traffic

impeler [impe'ler] vt to drive, propel; (fig) to impel

impenetrabilidad [impenetraβili'ðað] nf impenetrability

impenetrable [impene'traβle] adj impenetrable; (fig) incomprehensible

impensable [impen'saβle] adj unthinkable

impepinable [impepi'naβle] adj (fam) certain, inevitable

imperante [impe'rante] adj prevailing

imperar [impe'rar] vi (reinar) to rule, reign; (fig) to prevail, reign; (precio) to be current

imperativo, -a [impera'tiβo, a] adj (persona) imperious; (urgente, Ling) imperative

imperceptible [imperθep'tiβle] adj imperceptible

imperdible [imper'ðiβle] nm safety pin

imperdonable [imperðo'naβle] adj unforgivable, inexcusable

imperecedero, -a [impereθe'ðero, a] adj undying

imperfección [imperfek'θjon] nf imperfection; (falla) flaw, fault

imperfecto, -a [imper'fekto, a] adj faulty, imperfect ■ nm (Ling) imperfect tense

imperial [impe'rjal] adj imperial

imperialismo [imperja'lismo] nm imperialism

imperialista [imperja'lista] adj imperialist(ic) ■ nm/f imperialist

impericia [impe'riθja] nf (torpeza) unskilfulness; (inexperiencia) inexperience

imperio [im'perjo] nm empire; (autoridad) rule, authority; (fig) pride, haughtiness; **vale un ~** (fig) it's worth a fortune

imperioso, -a [impe'rjoso, a] adj imperious; (urgente) urgent; (imperativo) imperative

impermeable [imperme'aβle] adj (a prueba de agua) waterproof ■ nm raincoat, mac (Brit)

impersonal [imperso'nal] adj impersonal

impertérrito, -a [imper'territo, a] adj undaunted

impertinencia [imperti'nenθja] nf impertinence

impertinente [imperti'nente] adj impertinent

imperturbable [impertur'βaβle] adj imperturbable; (sereno) unruffled; (impasible) impassive

ímpetu ['impetu] nm (impulso) ímpetus, impulse; (impetuosidad) impetuosity; (violencia) violence

impetuosidad [impetwosi'ðað] nf impetuousness; (violencia) violence

impetuoso, -a [impe'twoso, a] adj impetuous; (río) rushing; (acto) hasty

impida etc [im'piða] vb ver **impedir**

impío, -a [im'pio, a] adj impious, ungodly; (cruel) cruel, pitiless

implacable [impla'kaβle] adj implacable, relentless

implantación [implanta'θjon] nf introduction; (Bio) implantation

implantar [implan'tar] vt (costumbre) to introduce; (Bio) to implant; **implantarse** vr to be introduced

implicar [impli'kar] vt to involve; (entrañar) to imply; **esto no implica que ...** this does not mean that ...

implícito, -a [im'pliθito, a] adj (tácito) implicit; (sobreentendido) implied

implique etc [im'plike] vb ver **implicar**

implorar [implo'rar] vt to beg, implore

impondré etc [impon'dre] vb ver **imponer**

imponente [impo'nente] adj (impresionante) impressive, imposing; (solemne) grand ■ nm/f (Com) depositor

imponer [impo'ner] vt (gen) to impose; (tarea) to set; (exigir) to exact; (miedo) to inspire; (Com) to deposit; **imponerse** vr to assert o.s.; (prevalecer) to prevail; (costumbre) to grow up; **imponerse un deber** to assume a duty

imponga etc [im'ponga] vb ver **imponer**

imponible [impo'niβle] adj (Com) taxable, subject to tax; (importación) dutiable, subject to duty; **no ~** tax-free, tax-exempt (US)

impopular [impopu'lar] adj unpopular

importación [importa'θjon] nf (acto) importing; (mercancías) imports pl

importancia [impor'tanθja] nf importance; (valor) value, significance; (extensión) size, magnitude; **no dar ~ a** to consider unimportant; (fig) to make light of; **no tiene ~** it's nothing

importante [impor'tante] adj important; valuable, significant

importar [impor'tar] vt (del extranjero) to

import; (*costar*) to amount to; (*implicar*) to involve ∎ *vi* to be important, matter; **me importa un bledo** I don't give a damn; **¿le importa que fume?** do you mind if I smoke?; **¿te importa prestármelo?** would you mind lending it to me?; **¿qué importa?** what difference does it make?; **no importa** it doesn't matter; **no le importa** he doesn't care, it doesn't bother him; **"no importa precio"** "cost no object"

importe [im'porte] *nm* (*cantidad*) amount; (*valor*) value

importunar [importu'nar] *vt* to bother, pester

importuno, -a [impor'tuno, a] *adj* (*inoportuno, molesto*) inopportune; (*indiscreto*) troublesome

imposibilidad [imposiβili'ðað] *nf* impossibility; **mi ~ para hacerlo** my inability to do it

imposibilitado, -a [imposiβili'taðo, a] *adj*: **verse ~ para hacer algo** to be unable to do sth

imposibilitar [imposiβili'tar] *vt* to make impossible, prevent

imposible [impo'siβle] *adj* impossible; (*insoportable*) unbearable, intolerable; **es ~** it's out of the question; **es ~ de predecir** it's impossible to forecast o predict

imposición [imposi'θjon] *nf* imposition; (*Com*) tax; (*inversión*) deposit; **efectuar una ~** to make a deposit

impostor, a [impos'tor, a] *nm/f* impostor

impostura [impos'tura] *nf* fraud, imposture

impotencia [impo'tenθja] *nf* impotence

impotente [impo'tente] *adj* impotent

impracticable [imprakti'kaβle] *adj* (*irrealizable*) impracticable; (*intransitable*) impassable

imprecar [impre'kar] *vi* to curse

imprecisión [impreθi'sjon] *nf* lack of precision, vagueness

impreciso, -a [impre'θiso, a] *adj* imprecise, vague

impredecible [impreðe'θiβle], **impredictible** [impreðik'tiβle] *adj* unpredictable

impregnar [impreɣ'nar] *vt* to impregnate; (*fig*) to pervade; **impregnarse** *vr* to become impregnated

imprenta [im'prenta] *nf* (*acto*) printing; (*aparato*) press; (*casa*) printer's; (*letra*) print

impreque *etc* [im'preke] *vb ver* **imprecar**

imprescindible [impresθin'diβle] *adj* essential, vital

impresión [impre'sjon] *nf* impression; (*Imprenta*) printing; (*edición*) edition; (*Foto*) print; (*marca*) imprint; **~ digital** fingerprint

impresionable [impresjo'naβle] *adj* (*sensible*) impressionable

impresionado, -a [impresjo'naðo, a] *adj* impressed; (*Foto*) exposed

impresionante [impresjo'nante] *adj* impressive; (*tremendo*) tremendous; (*maravilloso*) great, marvellous

impresionar [impresjo'nar] *vt* (*conmover*) to move; (*afectar*) to impress, strike; (*película fotográfica*) to expose; **impresionarse** *vr* to be impressed; (*conmoverse*) to be moved

impresionista [impresjo'nista] *adj* impressionist(ic); (*Arte*) impressionist ∎ *nm/f* impressionist

impreso, -a [im'preso, a] *pp de* **imprimir** ∎ *adj* printed ∎ *nm* printed paper/book *etc*; **impresos** *nmpl* printed matter *sg*; **~ de solicitud** application form

impresora [impre'sora] *nf* (*Inform*) printer; **~ de chorro de tinta** ink-jet printer; **~ (por) láser** laser printer; **~ de línea** line printer; **~ de matriz (de agujas)** dot-matrix printer; **~ de rueda** *o* **de margarita** daisy-wheel printer

imprevisible [impreβi'siβle] *adj* unforeseeable; (*individuo*) unpredictable

imprevisión [impreβi'sjon] *nf* short-sightedness; (*irreflexión*) thoughtlessness

imprevisto, -a [impre'βisto, a] *adj* unforeseen; (*inesperado*) unexpected ∎ *nm*: **imprevistos** (*dinero*) incidentals, unforeseen expenses

imprimir [impri'mir] *vt* to stamp; (*textos*) to print; (*Inform*) to output, print out

improbabilidad [improβaβili'ðað] *nf* improbability, unlikelihood

improbable [impro'βaβle] *adj* improbable; (*inverosímil*) unlikely

improcedente [improθe'ðente] *adj* inappropriate; (*Jur*) inadmissible

improductivo, -a [improðuk'tiβo, a] *adj* unproductive

impronunciable [impronun'θjaβle] *adj* unpronounceable

improperio [impro'perjo] *nm* insult; **improperios** *nmpl* abuse *sg*

impropiedad [impropje'ðað] *nf* impropriety (of language)

impropio, -a [im'propjo, a] *adj* improper; (*inadecuado*) inappropriate

improvisación [improβisa'θjon] *nf* improvization

improvisado, -a [improβi'saðo, a] *adj* improvised, impromptu

improvisar [improβi'sar] *vt* to improvise; (*comida*) to rustle up ∎ *vi* to improvise; (*Mus*) to extemporize; (*Teat etc*) to ad-lib

improviso [impro'βiso] adv: **de ~** unexpectedly, suddenly; (Mus etc) impromptu

imprudencia [impru'ðenθja] nf imprudence; (indiscreción) indiscretion; (descuido) carelessness

imprudente [impru'ðente] adj imprudent; indiscreet

Impte. abr (= Importe) amt.

impúdico, -a [im'puðiko, a] adj shameless; (lujurioso) lecherous

impudor [impu'ðor] nm shamelessness; (lujuria) lechery

impuesto, -a [im'pwesto, a] pp de **imponer** ■ adj imposed ■ nm tax; **anterior al ~** pretax; **sujeto a ~** taxable; **~ de lujo** luxury tax; **~ de plusvalía** capital gains tax; **~ sobre la propiedad** property tax; **~ sobre la renta** income tax; **~ sobre la renta de las personas físicas (IRPF)** personal income tax; **~ sobre la riqueza** wealth tax; **~ de transferencia de capital** capital transfer tax; **~ de venta** sales tax; **~ sobre el valor añadido (IVA)** value added tax (VAT)

impugnar [impuɣ'nar] vt to oppose, contest; (refutar) to refute, impugn

impulsar [impul'sar] vt to promote

impulsivo, -a [impul'siβo, a] adj impulsive

impulso [im'pulso] nm impulse; (fuerza, empuje) thrust, drive; (fig: sentimiento) urge, impulse; **a impulsos del miedo** driven on by fear

impune [im'pune] adj unpunished

impunemente [impune'mente] adv with impunity

impureza [impu'reθa] nf impurity; (fig) lewdness

impuro, -a [im'puro, a] adj impure; lewd

impuse etc [im'puse] vb ver **imponer**

imputación [imputa'θjon] nf imputation

imputar [impu'tar] vt: **~ a** to attribute to, to impute to

inabordable [inaβor'ðaβle] adj unapproachable

inacabable [inaka'βaβle] adj (infinito) endless; (interminable) interminable

inaccesible [inakθe'siβle] adj inaccessible; (fig: precio) beyond one's reach, prohibitive; (individuo) aloof

inacción [inak'θjon] nf inactivity

inaceptable [inaθep'taβle] adj unacceptable

inactividad [inaktiβi'ðað] nf inactivity; (Com) dullness

inactivo, -a [inak'tiβo, a] adj inactive; (Com) dull; (población) non-working

inadaptación [inaðapta'θjon] nf maladjustment

inadaptado, -a [inaðap'taðo, a] adj maladjusted ■ nm/f misfit

inadecuado, -a [inaðe'kwaðo, a] adj (insuficiente) inadequate; (inapto) unsuitable

inadmisible [inaðmi'siβle] adj inadmissible

inadvertido, -a [inaðβer'tiðo, a] adj (no visto) unnoticed

inagotable [inaɣo'taβle] adj inexhaustible

inaguantable [inaɣwan'taβle] adj unbearable

inalámbrico, -a [ina'lambriko, a] adj cordless, wireless

inalcanzable [inalkan'θaβle] adj unattainable

inalterable [inalte'raβle] adj immutable, unchangeable

inamovible [inamo'βiβle] adj fixed, immovable; (Tec) undetachable

inanición [inani'θjon] nf starvation

inanimado, -a [inani'maðo, a] adj inanimate

inapelable [inape'laβle] adj (Jur) unappealable; (fig) irremediable

inapetencia [inape'tenθja] nf lack of appetite

inaplicable [inapli'kaβle] adj not applicable

inapreciable [inapre'θjaβle] adj invaluable

inarrugable [inarru'ɣaβle] adj creaseresistant

inasequible [inase'kiβle] adj unattainable

inaudito, -a [inau'ðito, a] adj unheard-of

inauguración [inauɣura'θjon] nf inauguration; (de exposición) opening

inaugurar [inauɣu'rar] vt to inaugurate; to open

I.N.B.A. abr (Am) = **Instituto Nacional de Bellas Artes**

inca ['inka] nm/f Inca

INCAE [in'kae] nm abr = **Instituto Centroamericano de Administración de Empresas**

incaico, -a [in'kaiko, a] adj Inca

incalculable [inkalku'laβle] adj incalculable

incandescente [inkandes'θente] adj incandescent

incansable [inkan'saβle] adj tireless, untiring

incapacidad [inkapaθi'ðað] nf incapacity; (incompetencia) incompetence; **~ física/mental** physical/mental disability

incapacitar [inkapaθi'tar] vt (inhabilitar) to incapacitate, handicap; (descalificar) to disqualify

incapaz [inka'paθ] adj incapable; **~ de hacer algo** unable to do sth

incautación [inkauta'θjon] nf seizure, confiscation

209

incautarse [inkau'tarse] *vr*: ~ **de** to seize,
confiscate

incauto, -a [in'kauto, a] *adj* (*imprudente*)
incautious, unwary

incendiar [inθen'djar] *vt* to set fire to; (*fig*)
to inflame; **incendiarse** *vr* to catch fire

incendiario, -a [inθen'djarjo, a] *adj*
incendiary ■ *nm/f* fire-raiser, arsonist

incendio [in'θendjo] *nm* fire; ~
intencionado arson

incentivo [inθen'tiβo] *nm* incentive

incertidumbre [inθerti'ðumbre] *nf*
(*inseguridad*) uncertainty; (*duda*) doubt

incesante [inθe'sante] *adj* incessant

incesto [in'θesto] *nm* incest

incidencia [inθi'ðenθja] *nf* (*Mat*) incidence;
(*fig*) effect

incidente [inθi'ðente] *nm* incident

incidir [inθi'ðir] *vi*: ~ **en** (*influir*) to influence;
(*afectar*) to affect; ~ **en un error** to be
mistaken

incienso [in'θjenso] *nm* incense

incierto, -a [in'θjerto, a] *adj* uncertain

incineración [inθinera'θjon] *nf* incineration;
(*de cadáveres*) cremation

incinerar [inθine'rar] *vt* to burn; to cremate

incipiente [inθi'pjente] *adj* incipient

incisión [inθi'sjon] *nf* incision

incisivo, -a [inθi'siβo, a] *adj* sharp, cutting;
(*fig*) incisive

inciso [in'θiso] *nm* (*Ling*) clause, sentence;
(*coma*) comma; (*Jur*) subsection

incitante [inθi'tante] *adj* (*estimulante*)
exciting; (*provocativo*) provocative

incitar [inθi'tar] *vt* to incite, rouse

incivil [inθi'βil] *adj* rude, uncivil

inclemencia [inkle'menθja] *nf* (*severidad*)
harshness, severity; (*del tiempo*) inclemency

inclemente [inkle'mente] *adj* harsh, severe;
inclement

inclinación [inklina'θjon] *nf* (*gen*)
inclination; (*de tierras*) slope, incline; (*de
cabeza*) nod, bow; (*fig*) leaning, bent

inclinado, -a [inkli'naðo, a] *adj* (*objeto*)
leaning; (*superficie*) sloping

inclinar [inkli'nar] *vt* to incline; (*cabeza*)
to nod, bow; **inclinarse** *vr* to lean, slope;
(*en reverencia*) to bow; (*encorvarse*) to stoop;
inclinarse a (*parecerse*) to take after,
resemble; **inclinarse ante** to bow down to;
me inclino a pensar que ... I'm inclined to
think that ...

incluir [inklu'ir] *vt* to include; (*incorporar*)
to incorporate; (*meter*) to enclose; **todo
incluido** (*Com*) inclusive, all-in

inclusive [inklu'siβe] *adv* inclusive ■ *prep*
including

incluso, -a [in'kluso, a] *adj* included ■ *adv*
inclusively; (*hasta*) even

incluyendo *etc* [inklu'jendo] *vb ver* **incluir**

incobrable [inko'βraβle] *adj* irrecoverable;
(*deuda*) bad

incógnita [in'koɣnita] *nf* (*fig*) mystery

incógnito [in'koɣnito]: **de** ~ *adv* incognito

incoherencia [inkoe'renθja] *nf* incoherence;
(*falta de conexión*) disconnectedness

incoherente [inkoe'rente] *adj* incoherent

incoloro, -a [inko'loro, a] *adj* colourless

incólume [in'kolume] *adj* safe; (*indemne*)
unhurt, unharmed

incombustible [inkombus'tiβle] *adj* (*gen*)
fire-resistant; (*telas*) fireproof

incomodar [inkomo'ðar] *vt* to
inconvenience; (*molestar*) to bother, trouble;
(*fastidiar*) to annoy; **incomodarse** *vr* to put
o.s. out; (*fastidiarse*) to get annoyed; **no se
incomode** don't bother

incomodidad [inkomoði'ðað] *nf*
inconvenience; (*fastidio, enojo*) annoyance;
(*de vivienda*) discomfort

incómodo, -a [in'komoðo, a] *adj*
(*inconfortable*) uncomfortable; (*molesto*)
annoying; (*inconveniente*) inconvenient;
sentirse ~ to feel ill at ease

incomparable [inkompa'raβle] *adj*
incomparable

incomparecencia [inkompare'θenθja] *nf*
(*Jur etc*) failure to appear

incompatible [inkompa'tiβle] *adj* incompatible

incompetencia [inkompe'tenθja] *nf*
incompetence

incompetente [inkompe'tente] *adj*
incompetent

incompleto, -a [inkom'pleto, a] *adj*
incomplete, unfinished

incomprendido, -a [inkompren'diðo, a] *adj*
misunderstood

incomprensible [inkompren'siβle] *adj*
incomprehensible

incomunicado, -a [inkomuni'kaðo, a]
adj (*aislado*) cut off, isolated; (*confinado*) in
solitary confinement

incomunicar [inkomuni'kar] *vt* (*gen*) to cut
off; (*preso*) to put into solitary confinement;
incomunicarse *vr* (*fam*) to go into one's shell

incomunique *etc* [inkomu'nike] *vb ver*
incomunicar

inconcebible [inkonθe'βiβle] *adj*
inconceivable

inconcluso, -a [inkon'kluso, a] *adj*
(*inacabado*) unfinished

incondicional [inkondiθjo'nal] *adj*
unconditional; (*apoyo*) wholehearted;
(*partidario*) staunch

inconexo, -a [inko'nekso, a] *adj* unconnected; (*desunido*) disconnected; (*incoherente*) incoherent

inconfeso, -a [inkon'feso, a] *adj* unconfessed; **un homosexual ~** a closet homosexual

inconformista [inkonfor'mista] *adj, nm/f* nonconformist

inconfundible [inkonfun'diβle] *adj* unmistakable

incongruente [inkon'grwente] *adj* incongruous

inconmensurable [inkonmensu'raβle] *adj* immeasurable, vast

inconsciencia [inkons'θjenθja] *nf* unconsciousness; (*fig*) thoughtlessness

inconsciente [inkons'θjente] *adj* unconscious; thoughtless; (*ignorante*) unaware; (*involuntario*) unwitting

inconsecuencia [inkonse'kwenθja] *nf* inconsistency

inconsecuente [inkonse'kwente] *adj* inconsistent

inconsiderado, -a [inkonsiðe'raðo, a] *adj* inconsiderate

inconsistente [inkonsis'tente] *adj* inconsistent; (*Culin*) lumpy; (*endeble*) weak; (*tela*) flimsy

inconstancia [inkons'tanθja] *nf* inconstancy; (*de tiempo*) changeability; (*capricho*) fickleness

inconstante [inkons'tante] *adj* inconstant; changeable; fickle

incontable [inkon'taβle] *adj* countless, innumerable

incontestable [inkontes'taβle] *adj* unanswerable; (*innegable*) undeniable

incontinencia [inkonti'nenθja] *nf* incontinence

incontrolado, -a [inkontro'laðo, a] *adj* uncontrolled

incontrovertible [inkontroβer'tiβle] *adj* undeniable, incontrovertible

inconveniencia [inkombe'njenθja] *nf* unsuitability, inappropriateness; (*falta de cortesía*) impoliteness

inconveniente [inkombe'njente] *adj* unsuitable; impolite ■ *nm* obstacle; (*desventaja*) disadvantage; **el ~ es que ...** the trouble is that ...; **no hay ~ en** *o* **para hacer eso** there is no objection to doing that; **no tengo ~** I don't mind

incordiar [inkor'ðjar] *vt* (*fam*) to hassle

incorporación [inkorpora'θjon] *nf* incorporation; (*fig*) inclusion

incorporado, -a [inkorpo'raðo, a] *adj* (*Tec*) built-in

incorporar [inkorpo'rar] *vt* to incorporate; (*abarcar*) to embody; (*Culin*) to mix; **incorporarse** *vr* to sit up; **incorporarse a** to join

incorrección [inkorrek'θjon] *nf* incorrectness, inaccuracy; (*descortesía*) bad-mannered behaviour

incorrecto, -a [inko'rrekto, a] *adj* incorrect, wrong; (*comportamiento*) bad-mannered

incorregible [inkorre'xiβle] *adj* incorrigible

incorruptible [inkorrup'tiβle] *adj* incorruptible

incorrupto, -a [inko'rrupto, a] *adj* uncorrupted; (*fig*) pure

incredulidad [inkreðuli'ðað] *nf* incredulity; (*escepticismo*) scepticism

incrédulo, -a [in'kreðulo, a] *adj* incredulous, unbelieving; sceptical

increíble [inkre'iβle] *adj* incredible

incrementar [inkremen'tar] *vt* (*aumentar*) to increase; (*alzar*) to raise; **incrementarse** *vr* to increase

incremento [inkre'mento] *nm* increment; (*aumento*) rise, increase; **~ de precio** rise in price

increpar [inkre'par] *vt* to reprimand

incriminar [inkrimi'nar] *vt* (*Jur*) to incriminate

incruento, -a [in'krwento, a] *adj* bloodless

incrustar [inkrus'tar] *vt* to incrust; (*piedras; en joya*) to inlay; (*fig*) to graft; (*Tec*) to set

incubar [inku'βar] *vt* to incubate; (*fig*) to hatch

incuestionable [inkwestjo'naβle] *adj* unchallengeable

inculcar [inkul'kar] *vt* to inculcate

inculpar [inkul'par] *vt*: **~ de** (*acusar*) to accuse of; (*achacar, atribuir*) to charge with, blame for

inculque *etc* [in'kulke] *vb ver* **inculcar**

inculto, -a [in'kulto, a] *adj* (*persona*) uneducated, uncultured; (*fig: grosero*) uncouth ■ *nm/f* ignoramus

incumbencia [inkum'benθja] *nf* obligation; **no es de mi ~** it is not my field

incumbir [inkum'bir] *vi*: **~ a** to be incumbent upon; **no me incumbe a mí** it is no concern of mine

incumplimiento [inkumpli'mjento] *nm* non-fulfilment; (*Com*) repudiation; **~ de contrato** breach of contract; **por ~** by default

incurable [inku'raβle] *adj* (*enfermedad*) incurable; (*paciente*) incurably ill

incurrir [inku'rrir] *vi*: **~ en** to incur; (*crimen*) to commit; **~ en un error** to make a mistake

indagación [indaγa'θjon] *nf* investigation; (*búsqueda*) search; (*Jur*) inquest

indagar [inda'ɣar] *vt* to investigate; to search; (*averiguar*) to ascertain

indague *etc* [in'daɣe] *vb ver* **indagar**

indebido, -a [inde'βiðo, a] *adj* undue; (*dicho*) improper

indecencia [inde'θenθja] *nf* indecency; (*dicho*) obscenity

indecente [inde'θente] *adj* indecent, improper; (*lascivo*) obscene

indecible [inde'θiβle] *adj* unspeakable; (*indescriptible*) indescribable

indeciso, -a [inde'θiso, a] *adj* (*por decidir*) undecided; (*vacilante*) hesitant

indefenso, -a [inde'fenso, a] *adj* defenceless

indefinido, -a [indefi'niðo, a] *adj* indefinite; (*vago*) vague, undefined

indeleble [inde'leβle] *adj* indelible

indemne [in'demne] *adj* (*objeto*) undamaged; (*persona*) unharmed, unhurt

indemnice *etc* [indem'niθe] *vb ver* **indemnizar**

indemnización [indemniθa'θjon] *nf* (*acto*) indemnification; (*suma*) indemnity; **~ de cese** redundancy payment; **~ de despido** severance pay; **doble ~** double indemnity

indemnizar [indemni'θar] *vt* to indemnify; (*compensar*) to compensate

independencia [indepen'denθja] *nf* independence

independice *etc* [indepen'diθe] *vb ver* **independizar**

independiente [indepen'djente] *adj* (*libre*) independent; (*autónomo*) self-sufficient; (*Inform*) stand-alone

independizar [independi'θar] *vt* to make independent; **independizarse** *vr* to become independent

indescifrable [indesθi'fraβle] *adj* (*Mil: código*) indecipherable; (*fig: misterio*) impenetrable

indeseable [indese'aβle] *adj, nm/f* undesirable

indeterminado, -a [indetermi'naðo, a] *adj* (*tb Ling*) indefinite; (*desconocido*) indeterminate

India ['indja] *nf:* **la ~** India

indiano, -a [in'djano, a] *adj* (Spanish-) American ■ *nm Spaniard who has made good in America*

indicación [indika'θjon] *nf* indication; (*dato*) piece of information; (*señal*) sign; (*sugerencia*) suggestion, hint; **indicaciones** *nfpl* (*Com*) instructions

indicado, -a [indi'kaðo, a] *adj* (*apto*) right, appropriate

indicador [indika'ðor] *nm* indicator; (*Tec*) gauge, meter; (*aguja*) hand, pointer; (*de carretera*) roadsign; **~ de encendido** (*Inform*) power-on indicator

indicar [indi'kar] *vt* (*mostrar*) to indicate, show; (*suj: termómetro etc*) to read, register; (*señalar*) to point to

indicativo, -a [indika'tiβo, a] *adj* indicative ■ *nm* (*Radio*) call sign; **~ de nacionalidad** (*Auto*) national identification plate

índice ['indiθe] *nm* index; (*catálogo*) catalogue; (*Anat*) index finger, forefinger; **~ del coste de (la) vida** cost-of-living index; **~ de crédito** credit rating; **~ de materias** table of contents; **~ de natalidad** birth rate; **~ de precios al por menor (IPM)** (*Com*) retail price index (RPI)

indicio [in'diθjo] *nm* indication, sign; (*en pesquisa etc*) clue

indiferencia [indife'renθja] *nf* indifference; (*apatía*) apathy

indiferente [indife'rente] *adj* indifferent; **me es ~** it makes no difference to me

indígena [in'dixena] *adj* indigenous, native ■ *nm/f* native

indigencia [indi'xenθja] *nf* poverty, need

indigenista [indixe'nista] (*Am*) *adj* pro-Indian ■ *nm/f* (*estudiante*) student of Indian cultures; (*Pol etc*) promoter of Indian cultures

indigestar [indixes'tar] *vt* to cause indigestion to; **indigestarse** *vr* to get indigestion

indigestión [indixes'tjon] *nf* indigestion

indigesto, -a [indi'xesto, a] *adj* undigested; (*indigerible*) indigestible; (*fig*) turgid

indignación [indiɣna'θjon] *nf* indignation

indignante [indiɣ'nante] *adj* outrageous, infuriating

indignar [indiɣ'nar] *vt* to anger, make indignant; **indignarse** *vr:* **indignarse por** to get indignant about

indigno, -a [in'diɣno, a] *adj* (*despreciable*) low, contemptible; (*inmerecido*) unworthy

indio, -a ['indjo, a] *adj, nm/f* Indian

indique *etc* [in'dike] *vb ver* **indicar**

indirecto, -a [indi'rekto, a] *adj* indirect ■ *nf* insinuation, innuendo; (*sugerencia*) hint

indisciplina [indisθi'plina] *nf* (*gen*) lack of discipline; (*Mil*) insubordination

indiscreción [indiskre'θjon] *nf* (*imprudencia*) indiscretion; (*irreflexión*) tactlessness; (*acto*) gaffe, faux pas; **..., si no es ~ ...**, if I may say so

indiscreto, -a [indis'kreto, a] *adj* indiscreet

indiscriminado, -a [indiskrimi'naðo, a] *adj* indiscriminate

indiscutible [indisku'tiβle] *adj* indisputable, unquestionable

indispensable [indispen'saβle] *adj* indispensable

indispondré *etc* [indispon'dre] *vb ver*
indisponer
indisponer [indispo'ner] *vt* to spoil, upset;
(*salud*) to make ill; **indisponerse** *vr* to fall ill;
indisponerse con algn to fall out with sb
indisponga *etc* [indis'ponga] *vb ver*
indisponer
indisposición [indisposi'θjon] *nf*
indisposition; (*desgana*) unwillingness
indispuesto, -a [indis'pwesto, a] *pp de*
indisponer ■ *adj* indisposed; **sentirse ~**
to feel unwell o indisposed
indispuse *etc* [indis'puse] *vb ver* **indisponer**
indistinto, -a [indis'tinto, a] *adj* indistinct;
(*vago*) vague
individual [indiβi'ðwal] *adj* individual;
(*habitación*) single ■ *nm* (*Deporte*) singles *sg*
individuo, -a [indi'βiðwo, a] *adj* individual
■ *nm* individual
Indochina [indo'tʃina] *nf* Indochina
indocumentado, -a [indokumen'taðo, a] *adj*
without identity papers
indoeuropeo, -a [indoeuro'peo, a] *adj, nm/f*
Indo-European
índole ['indole] *nf* (*naturaleza*) nature; (*clase*)
sort, kind
indolencia [indo'lenθja] *nf* indolence,
laziness
indoloro, -a [in'doloro, a] *adj* painless
indomable [indo'maβle] *adj* (*animal*)
untameable; (*espíritu*) indomitable
indómito, -a [in'domito, a] *adj* indomitable
Indonesia [indo'nesja] *nf* Indonesia
indonesio, -a [indo'nesjo, a] *adj, nm/f*
Indonesian
inducción [induk'θjon] *nf* (*Filosofía, Elec*)
induction; **por ~** by induction
inducir [indu'θir] *vt* to induce; (*inferir*) to
infer; (*persuadir*) to persuade; **~ a algn en el
error** to mislead sb
indudable [indu'ðaβle] *adj* undoubted;
(*incuestionable*) unquestionable; **es ~ que ...**
there is no doubt that ...
indulgencia [indul'xenθja] *nf* indulgence;
(*Jur etc*) leniency; **proceder sin ~ contra** to
proceed ruthlessly against
indultar [indul'tar] *vt* (*perdonar*) to pardon,
reprieve; (*librar de pago*) to exempt
indulto [in'dulto] *nm* pardon; exemption
indumentaria [indumen'tarja] *nf* (*ropa*)
clothing, dress
industria [in'dustrja] *nf* industry; (*habilidad*)
skill; **~ agropecuaria** farming and fishing;
~ pesada heavy industry; **~ petrolífera** oil
industry
industrial [indus'trjal] *adj* industrial ■ *nm*
industrialist

industrializar [industrjali'θar] *vt* to
industrialize; **industrializarse** *vr* to become
industrialized
INE ['ine] *nm abr* (*Esp*) = **Instituto Nacional de
Estadística**
inédito, -a [i'neðito, a] *adj* (*libro*)
unpublished; (*nuevo*) unheard-of
inefable [ine'faβle] *adj* ineffable,
indescribable
ineficacia [inefi'kaθja] *nf* (*de medida*)
ineffectiveness; (*de proceso*) inefficiency
ineficaz [inefi'kaθ] *adj* (*inútil*) ineffective;
(*ineficiente*) inefficient
ineludible [inelu'ðiβle] *adj* inescapable,
unavoidable
INEM [i'nem] *nm abr* (*Esp*: = Instituto Nacional
de Empleo) ≈ Department of Employment (*Brit*)
INEN ['inen] *nm abr* (*México*) = **Instituto
Nacional de Energía Nuclear**
inenarrable [inena'rraβle] *adj* inexpressible
ineptitud [inepti'tuð] *nf* ineptitude,
incompetence
inepto, -a [i'nepto, a] *adj* inept, incompetent
inequívoco, -a [ine'kiβoko, a] *adj*
unequivocal; (*inconfundible*) unmistakable
inercia [i'nerθja] *nf* inertia; (*pasividad*) passivity
inerme [i'nerme] *adj* (*sin armas*) unarmed;
(*indefenso*) defenceless
inerte [i'nerte] *adj* inert; (*inmóvil*) motionless
inescrutable [ineskru'taβle] *adj* inscrutable
inesperado, -a [inespe'raðo, a] *adj*
unexpected, unforeseen
inestable [ines'taβle] *adj* unstable
inestimable [inesti'maβle] *adj* inestimable;
de valor ~ invaluable
inevitable [ineβi'taβle] *adj* inevitable
inexactitud [ineksakti'tuð] *nf* inaccuracy
inexacto, -a [inek'sakto, a] *adj* inaccurate;
(*falso*) untrue
inexistente [ineksis'tente] *adj* non-existent
inexorable [inekso'raβle] *adj* inexorable
inexperiencia [inekspe'rjenθja] *nf*
inexperience, lack of experience
inexperto, -a [ineks'perto, a] *adj* (*novato*)
inexperienced
inexplicable [inekspli'kaβle] *adj* inexplicable
inexpresable [inekspre'saβle] *adj*
inexpressible
inexpresivo, -a [inekspre'siβo, a] *adj*
inexpressive; (*ojos*) dull; (*cara*) wooden
inexpugnable [inekspuɣ'naβle] *adj* (*Mil*)
impregnable; (*fig*) firm
infalible [infa'liβle] *adj* infallible; (*indefectible*)
certain, sure; (*plan*) foolproof
infame [in'fame] *adj* infamous
infamia [in'famja] *nf* infamy; (*deshonra*)
disgrace

infancia [in'fanθja] *nf* infancy, childhood; **jardín de la** ~ nursery school
infanta [in'fanta] *nf* (*hija del rey*) infanta, princess
infante [in'fante] *nm* (*hijo del rey*) infante, prince
infantería [infante'ria] *nf* infantry
infantil [infan'til] *adj* child's, children's; (*pueril, aniñado*) infantile; (*cándido*) childlike
infarto [in'farto] *nm* (*tb*: **infarto de miocardio**) heart attack
infatigable [infati'yaβle] *adj* tireless, untiring
infección [infek'θjon] *nf* infection
infeccioso, -a [infek'θjoso, a] *adj* infectious
infectar [infek'tar] *vt* to infect; **infectarse** *vr*: **infectarse (de)** (*tb fig*) to become infected (with)
infecundidad [infekundi'ðað] *nf* (*de tierra*) infertility, barrenness; (*de mujer*) sterility
infecundo, -a [infe'kundo, a] *adj* infertile, barren; sterile
infeliz [infe'liθ] *adj* (*desgraciado*) unhappy, wretched; (*inocente*) gullible ■ *nm/f* (*desgraciado*) wretch; (*inocentón*) simpleton
inferior [infe'rjor] *adj* inferior; (*situación, Mat*) lower ■ *nm/f* inferior, subordinate; **cualquier número ~ a nueve** any number less than o under o below nine; **una cantidad** ~ a lesser quantity
inferioridad [inferjori'ðað] *nf* inferiority; **estar en ~ de condiciones** to be at a disadvantage
inferir [infe'rir] *vt* (*deducir*) to infer, deduce; (*causar*) to cause
infernal [infer'nal] *adj* infernal
infértil [in'fertil] *adj* infertile
infestar [infes'tar] *vt* to infest
infidelidad [infiðeli'ðað] *nf* infidelity, unfaithfulness
infiel [in'fjel] *adj* unfaithful, disloyal; (*falso*) inaccurate ■ *nm/f* infidel, unbeliever
infiera *etc* [in'fjera] *vb ver* **inferir**
infierno [in'fjerno] *nm* hell; **¡vete al ~!** go to hell; **está en el quinto ~** it's at the back of beyond
infiltrar [infil'trar] *vt* to infiltrate; **infiltrarse** *vr* to infiltrate, filter; (*líquidos*) to percolate
ínfimo, -a ['infimo, a] *adj* (*vil*) vile, mean; (*más bajo*) lowest; (*peor*) worst; (*miserable*) wretched
infinidad [infini'ðað] *nf* infinity; (*abundancia*) great quantity; ~ **de** vast numbers of; ~ **de veces** countless times
infinitivo [infini'tiβo] *nm* infinitive
infinito, -a [infi'nito, a] *adj* infinite; (*fig*)

boundless ■ *adv* infinitely ■ *nm* infinite; (*Mat*) infinity; **hasta lo ~** ad infinitum
infiriendo *etc* [infi'rjendo] *vb ver* **inferir**
inflación [infla'θjon] *nf* (*hinchazón*) swelling; (*monetaria*) inflation; (*fig*) conceit
inflacionario, -a [inflaθjo'narjo, a] *adj* inflationary
inflacionismo [inflaθjo'nismo] *nm* (*Econ*) inflation
inflacionista [inflaθjo'nista] *adj* inflationary
inflamar [infla'mar] *vt* to set on fire; (*Med, fig*) to inflame; **inflamarse** *vr* to catch fire; to become inflamed
inflar [in'flar] *vt* (*hinchar*) to inflate, blow up; (*fig*) to exaggerate; **inflarse** *vr* to swell (up); (*fig*) to get conceited
inflexible [inflek'siβle] *adj* inflexible; (*fig*) unbending
infligir [infli'xir] *vt* to inflict
inflija *etc* [in'flixa] *vb ver* **infligir**
influencia [in'flwenθja] *nf* influence
influenciar [inflwen'θjar] *vt* to influence
influir [influ'ir] *vt* to influence ■ *vi* to have influence, carry weight; ~ **en** o **sobre** to influence, affect; (*contribuir a*) to have a hand in
influjo [in'fluxo] *nm* influence; ~ **de capitales** (*Econ etc*) capital influx
influyendo *etc* [influ'jendo] *vb ver* **influir**
influyente [influ'jente] *adj* influential
información [informa'θjon] *nf* information; (*noticias*) news *sg*; (*informe*) report; (*Inform: datos*) data; (*Jur*) inquiry; **I-** (*oficina*) Information; (*Telec*) Directory Enquiries (Brit), Directory Assistance (US); (*mostrador*) Information Desk; **una** ~ a piece of information; **abrir una** ~ (*Jur*) to begin proceedings; ~ **deportiva** (*en periódico*) sports section
informal [infor'mal] *adj* informal
informante [infor'mante] *nm/f* informant
informar [infor'mar] *vt* (*gen*) to inform; (*revelar*) to reveal, make known ■ *vi* (*Jur*) to plead; (*denunciar*) to inform; (*dar cuenta de*) to report on; **informarse** *vr* to find out; **informarse de** to inquire into
informática [infor'matika] *nf ver* **informático**
informatice *etc* [informa'tiθe] *vb ver* **informatizar**
informático, -a [infor'matiko, a] *adj* computer *cpd* ■ *nf* (*Tec*) information technology; computing; (*Escol*) computer science o studies; ~ **de gestión** commercial computing
informativo, -a [informa'tiβo, a] *adj* (*libro*) informative; (*folleto*) information *cpd*;

(Radio, TV) news cpd ■ nm (Radio, TV) news programme

informatización [informatiθa'θjon] nf computerization

informatizar [informati'θar] vt to computerize

informe [in'forme] adj shapeless ■ nm report; (dictamen) statement; (Mil) briefing; (Jur) plea; **informes** nmpl information sg; (datos) data; ~ **anual** annual report; ~ **del juez** summing-up

infortunio [infor'tunjo] nm misfortune

infracción [infrak'θjon] nf infraction, infringement; (Auto) offence

infraestructura [infraestruk'tura] nf infrastructure

in fraganti [infra'ɣanti] adv: **pillar a algn ~** to catch sb red-handed

infranqueable [infranke'aβle] adj impassable; (fig) insurmountable

infrarrojo, -a [infra'rroxo, a] adj infrared

infravalorar [infraβalo'rar] vt to undervalue; (Finanzas) to underestimate

infringir [infrin'xir] vt to infringe, contravene

infrinja etc [in'frinxa] vb ver **infringir**

infructuoso, -a [infruk'twoso, a] adj fruitless, unsuccessful

infundado, -a [infun'daðo, a] adj groundless, unfounded

infundir [infun'dir] vt to infuse, instil; ~ **ánimo a algn** to encourage sb; ~ **miedo a algn** to intimidate sb

infusión [infu'sjon] nf infusion; ~ **de manzanilla** camomile tea

Ing. abr (Am) = **Ingeniero**

ingeniar [inxe'njar] vt to think up, devise; **ingeniarse** vr to manage; **ingeniarse para** to manage to

ingeniería [inxenje'ria] nf engineering; ~ **genética** genetic engineering; ~ **de sistemas** (Inform) systems engineering

ingeniero, -a [inxe'njero, a] nm/f engineer; (Am) courtesy title; ~ **de sonido** sound engineer; ~ **de caminos** civil engineer

ingenio [in'xenjo] nm (talento) talent; (agudeza) wit; (habilidad) ingenuity, inventiveness; (Tec): ~ **azucarero** sugar refinery

ingenioso, -a [inxe'njoso, a] adj ingenious, clever; (divertido) witty

ingente [in'xente] adj huge, enormous

ingenuidad [inxenwi'ðað] nf ingenuousness; (sencillez) simplicity

ingenuo, -a [in'xenwo, a] adj ingenuous

ingerir [inxe'rir] vt to ingest; (tragar) to swallow; (consumir) to consume

ingiera etc [in'xjera], **ingiriendo** etc [inxi'rjenðo] vb ver **ingerir**

Inglaterra [ingla'terra] nf England

ingle ['ingle] nf groin

inglés, -esa [in'gles, esa] adj English ■ nm/f Englishman(-woman) ■ nm (Ling) English; **los ingleses** the English

ingratitud [ingrati'tuð] nf ingratitude

ingrato, -a [in'grato, a] adj ungrateful; (tarea) thankless

ingravidez [ingraβi'ðeθ] nf weightlessness

ingrediente [ingre'ðjente] nm ingredient; **ingredientes** nmpl (Am: tapas) titbits

ingresar [ingre'sar] vt (dinero) to deposit ■ vi to come o go in; ~ **a** (esp Am) to enter; ~ **en** (club) to join; (Mil, Escol) to enrol in; ~ **en el hospital** to go into hospital

ingreso [in'greso] nm (entrada) entry, (: en hospital etc) admission; (Mil, Escol) enrolment; **ingresos** nmpl (dinero) income sg; (: Com) takings pl; ~ **gravable** taxable income sg; **ingresos accesorios** fringe benefits; **ingresos brutos** gross receipts; **ingresos devengados** earned income sg; **ingresos exentos de impuestos** non-taxable income sg; **ingresos personales disponibles** disposable personal income sg

íngrimo, -a ['ingrimo, a] adj (Am: tb: **íngrimo y solo**) all alone

inhábil [i'naβil] adj unskilful, clumsy

inhabilitar [inaβili'tar] vt (Pol, Med): ~ **a algn (para hacer algo)** to disqualify sb (from doing sth)

inhabitable [inaβi'taβle] adj uninhabitable

inhabituado, -a [inaβi'twaðo, a] adj unaccustomed

inhalador [inala'ðor] nm (Med) inhaler

inhalar [ina'lar] vt to inhale

inherente [ine'rente] adj inherent

inhibición [iniβi'θjon] nf inhibition

inhibir [ini'βir] vt to inhibit; (Rel) to restrain; **inhibirse** vr to keep out

inhospitalario, -a [inospita'larjo, a], **inhóspito, -a** [i'nospito, a] adj inhospitable

inhumación [inuma'θjon] nf burial, interment

inhumano, -a [inu'mano, a] adj inhuman

INI ['ini] nm abr = **Instituto Nacional de Industria**

inicial [ini'θjal] adj, nf initial

inicialice etc [iniθja'liθe] vb ver **inicializar**

inicializar [iniθjali'θar] vt (Inform) to initialize

iniciar [ini'θjar] vt (persona) to initiate; (empezar) to begin, commence; (conversación) to start up; ~ **a algn en un secreto** to let sb into a secret; ~ **la sesión** (Inform) to log in o on

iniciativa [iniθja'tiβa] *nf* initiative; (*liderazgo*) leadership; **la ~ privada** private enterprise

inicio [i'niθjo] *nm* start, beginning

inicuo, -a [i'nikwo, a] *adj* iniquitous

inigualado, -a [iniɣwa'laðo, a] *adj* unequalled

ininteligible [ininteli'xiβle] *adj* unintelligible

ininterrumpido, -a [ininterrum'piðo, a] *adj* uninterrupted; (*proceso*) continuous; (*progreso*) steady

injerencia [inxe'renθja] *nf* interference

injertar [inxer'tar] *vt* to graft

injerto [in'xerto] *nm* graft; **~ de piel** skin graft

injuria [in'xurja] *nf* (*agravio, ofensa*) offence; (*insulto*) insult; **injurias** *nfpl* abuse *sg*

injuriar [inxu'rjar] *vt* to insult

injurioso, -a [inxu'rjoso, a] *adj* offensive; insulting

injusticia [inxus'tiθja] *nf* injustice, unfairness; **con ~** unjustly

injusto, -a [in'xusto, a] *adj* unjust, unfair

inmaculado, -a [inmaku'laðo, a] *adj* immaculate, spotless

inmadurez [inmaðu'reθ] *nf* immaturity

inmaduro, -a [inma'ðuro, a] *adj* immature; (*fruta*) unripe

inmediaciones [inmeðja'θjones] *nfpl* neighbourhood *sg*, environs

inmediatez [inmeðja'teθ] *nf* immediacy

inmediato, -a [inme'ðjato, a] *adj* immediate; (*contiguo*) adjoining; (*rápido*) prompt; (*próximo*) neighbouring, next; **de ~** (*esp Am*) immediately

inmejorable [inmexo'raβle] *adj* unsurpassable; (*precio*) unbeatable

inmemorable [inmemo'raβle], **inmemorial** [inmemo'rjal] *adj* immemorial

inmenso, -a [in'menso, a] *adj* immense, huge

inmerecido, -a [inmere'θiðo, a] *adj* undeserved

inmersión [inmer'sjon] *nf* immersion; (*buzo*) dive

inmigración [inmiɣra'θjon] *nf* immigration

inmigrante [inmi'ɣrante] *adj, nm/f* immigrant

inminente [inmi'nente] *adj* imminent, impending

inmiscuirse [inmisku'irse] *vr* to interfere, meddle

inmiscuyendo *etc* [inmisku'jendo] *vb ver* **inmiscuirse**

inmobiliario, -a [inmoβi'ljarjo, a] *adj* real-estate *cpd*, property *cpd* ■ *nf* estate agency

inmolar [inmo'lar] *vt* to immolate, sacrifice

inmoral [inmo'ral] *adj* immoral

inmortal [inmor'tal] *adj* immortal

inmortalice *etc* [inmorta'liθe] *vb ver* **inmortalizar**

inmortalizar [inmortali'θar] *vt* to immortalize

inmotivado, -a [inmoti'βaðo, a] *adj* motiveless; (*sospecha*) groundless

inmóvil [in'moβil] *adj* immobile

inmovilizar [inmoβili'θar] *vt* to immobilize; (*paralizar*) to paralyse; **inmovilizarse** *vr*: **se le ha inmovilizado la pierna** her leg was paralysed

inmueble [in'mweβle] *adj*: **bienes inmuebles** real estate *sg*, landed property *sg* ■ *nm* property

inmundicia [inmun'diθja] *nf* filth

inmundo, -a [in'mundo, a] *adj* filthy

inmune [in'mune] *adj* (*Med*) immune

inmunidad [inmuni'ðað] *nf* immunity; (*fisco*) exemption; **~ diplomática/ parlamentaria** diplomatic/parliamentary immunity

inmunitario, -a [inmuni'tarjo, a] *adj*: **sistema ~** immune system

inmunización [inmuniθa'θjon] *nf* immunization

inmunizar [inmuni'θar] *vt* to immunize

inmutable [inmu'taβle] *adj* immutable; **permaneció ~** he didn't flinch

inmutarse [inmu'tarse] *vr*: **siguió sin ~** he carried on unperturbed

innato, -a [in'nato, a] *adj* innate

innecesario, -a [inneθe'sarjo, a] *adj* unnecessary

innegable [inne'ɣaβle] *adj* undeniable

innoble [in'noβle] *adj* ignoble

innovación [innoβa'θjon] *nf* innovation

innovador, a [innoβa'ðor, a] *adj* innovatory, innovative ■ *nm/f* innovator

innovar [inno'βar] *vt* to introduce

innumerable [innume'raβle] *adj* countless

inocencia [ino'θenθja] *nf* innocence

inocentada [inoθen'taða] *nf* practical joke

inocente [ino'θente] *adj* (*ingenuo*) naive, innocent; (*no culpable*) innocent; (*sin malicia*) harmless ■ *nm/f* simpleton; **día de los (Santos) Inocentes** ≈ April Fool's Day; *see note*

● **INOCENTE**

● The 28th December, *el día de los*
● *(Santos) Inocentes*, is when the Church
● commemorates the story of Herod's
● slaughter of the innocent children of
● Judea in the time of Christ. On this day

Spaniards play *inocentadas* (practical jokes) on each other, much like our April Fools' Day pranks, eg typically sticking a *monigote* (cut-out paper figure) on someone's back, or broadcasting unlikely news stories.

inocuidad [inokwi'ðað] *nf* harmlessness

inocular [inoku'lar] *vt* to inoculate

inocuo, -a [i'nokwo, a] *adj (sustancia)* harmless

inodoro, -a [ino'ðoro, a] *adj* odourless ■ *nm* toilet *(Brit)*, lavatory *(Brit)*, washroom *(US)*

inofensivo, -a [inofen'siβo, a] *adj* inoffensive

inolvidable [inolβi'ðaβle] *adj* unforgettable

inoperante [inope'rante] *adj* ineffective

inopinado, -a [inopi'naðo, a] *adj* unexpected

inoportuno, -a [inopor'tuno, a] *adj* untimely; *(molesto)* inconvenient; *(inapropiado)* inappropriate

inoxidable [inoksi'ðaβle] *adj* stainless; **acero ~** stainless steel

inquebrantable [inkeβran'taβle] *adj* unbreakable; *(fig)* unshakeable

inquiera *etc* [in'kjera] *vb ver* **inquirir**

inquietante [inkje'tante] *adj* worrying

inquietar [inkje'tar] *vt* to worry, trouble; **inquietarse** *vr* to worry, get upset

inquieto, -a [in'kjeto, a] *adj* anxious, worried; **estar ~ por** to be worried about

inquietud [inkje'tuð] *nf* anxiety, worry

inquilino, -a [inki'lino, a] *nm/f* tenant; *(Com)* lessee

inquiriendo *etc* [inki'rjendo] *vb ver* **inquirir**

inquirir [inki'rir] *vt* to enquire into, investigate

insaciable [insa'θjaβle] *adj* insatiable

insalubre [insa'luβre] *adj* unhealthy; *(condiciones)* insanitary

INSALUD [insa'luð] *nm abr (Esp)* = **Instituto Nacional de la Salud**

insano, -a [in'sano, a] *adj (loco)* insane; *(malsano)* unhealthy

insatisfacción [insatisfak'θjon] *nf* dissatisfaction

insatisfecho, -a [insatis'fetʃo, a] *adj (condición)* unsatisfied; *(estado de ánimo)* dissatisfied

inscribir [inskri'βir] *vt* to inscribe; *(en lista)* to put; *(en censo)* to register; **inscribirse** *vr* to register; *(Escol etc)* to enrol

inscripción [inskrip'θjon] *nf* inscription; *(Escol etc)* enrolment; *(en censo)* registration

inscrito [ins'krito] *pp de* **inscribir**

insecticida [insekti'θiða] *nm* insecticide

insecto [in'sekto] *nm* insect

inseguridad [inseɣuri'ðað] *nf* insecurity

inseguro, -a [inse'ɣuro, a] *adj* insecure; *(inconstante)* unsteady; *(incierto)* uncertain

inseminación [insemina'θjon] *nf*: **~ artificial** artificial insemination (A.I.)

inseminar [insemi'nar] *vt* to inseminate, fertilize

insensato, -a [insen'sato, a] *adj* foolish, stupid

insensibilice *etc* [insensiβi'liθe] *vb ver* **insensibilizar**

insensibilidad [insensiβili'ðað] *nf (gen)* insensitivity; *(dureza de corazón)* callousness

insensibilizar [insensiβili'θar] *vt* to desensitize; *(Med)* to anaesthetize *(Brit)*, anesthetize *(US)*; *(eufemismo)* to knock out *o* unconscious

insensible [insen'siβle] *adj (gen)* insensitive; *(movimiento)* imperceptible; *(sin sensación)* numb

inseparable [insepa'raβle] *adj* inseparable

INSERSO [in'serso] *nm abr* (= Instituto Nacional de Servicios Sociales) branch of social services

insertar [inser'tar] *vt* to insert

inservible [inser'βiβle] *adj* useless

insidioso, -a [insi'ðjoso, a] *adj* insidious

insigne [in'siɣne] *adj* distinguished; *(famoso)* notable

insignia [in'siɣnja] *nf (señal distintiva)* badge; *(estandarte)* flag

insignificante [insiɣnifi'kante] *adj* insignificant

insinuar [insi'nwar] *vt* to insinuate, imply; **insinuarse** *vr*: **insinuarse con algn** to ingratiate o.s. with sb

insípido, -a [in'sipiðo, a] *adj* insipid

insistencia [insis'tenθja] *nf* insistence

insistir [insis'tir] *vi* to insist; **~ en algo** to insist on sth; *(enfatizar)* to stress sth

in situ [in'situ] *adv* on the spot, in situ

insobornable [insoβor'naβle] *adj* incorruptible

insociable [inso'θjaβle] *adj* unsociable

insolación [insola'θjon] *nf (Med)* sunstroke

insolencia [inso'lenθja] *nf* insolence

insolente [inso'lente] *adj* insolent

insólito, -a [in'solito, a] *adj* unusual

insoluble [inso'luβle] *adj* insoluble

insolvencia [insol'βenθja] *nf* insolvency

insomne [in'somne] *adj* sleepless ■ *nm/f* insomniac

insomnio [in'somnjo] *nm* insomnia

insondable [inson'daβle] *adj* bottomless

insonorización [insonoriθa'θjon] *nf* soundproofing

insonorizado, -a [insonori'θaðo, a] *adj (cuarto etc)* soundproof

i

insoportable [insopor'taβle] *adj* unbearable
insoslayable [insosla'jaβle] *adj* unavoidable
insospechado, -a [insospe't∫aðo, a] *adj*
(*inesperado*) unexpected
insostenible [insoste'niβle] *adj* untenable
inspección [inspek'θjon] *nf* inspection,
check; **I~** inspectorate; **~ técnica (de
vehículos)** ≈ MOT (test) (*Brit*)
inspeccionar [inspekθjo'nar] *vt* (*examinar*) to
inspect, examine; (*controlar*) to check
inspector, a [inspek'tor, a] *nm/f* inspector
inspectorado [inspekto'raðo] *nm*
inspectorate
inspiración [inspira'θjon] *nf* inspiration
inspirador, a [inspira'ðor, a] *adj* inspiring
inspirar [inspi'rar] *vt* to inspire; (*Med*) to
inhale; **inspirarse** *vr*: **inspirarse en** to be
inspired by
instalación [instala'θjon] *nf* (*equipo*) fittings
pl, equipment; **~ eléctrica** wiring
instalar [insta'lar] *vt* (*establecer*) to instal;
(*erguir*) to set up, erect; **instalarse** *vr* to
establish o.s.; (*en una vivienda*) to move into
instancia [ins'tanθja] *nf* (*solicitud*)
application; (*ruego*) request; (*Jur*) petition;
a ~ de at the request of; **en última ~** in the
last resort
instantáneo, -a [instan'taneo, a] *adj*
instantaneous ◼ *nf* snap(shot); **café ~**
instant coffee
instante [ins'tante] *nm* instant, moment;
en un ~ in a flash
instar [ins'tar] *vt* to press, urge
instaurar [instau'rar] *vt* (*establecer*) to
establish, set up
instigador, a [instiɣa'ðor, a] *nm/f* instigator;
~ de un delito (*Jur*) accessory before the fact
instigar [insti'ɣar] *vt* to instigate
instintivo, -a [instin'tiβo, a] *adj* instinctive
instinto [ins'tinto] *nm* instinct; **por ~**
instinctively
institución [institu'θjon] *nf* institution,
establishment; **~ benéfica** charitable
foundation
instituir [institu'ir] *vt* to establish; (*fundar*)
to found
instituto [insti'tuto] *nm* (*gen*) institute;
I~ Nacional de Enseñanza (*Esp*)
≈ comprehensive (*Brit*) o high (*US*) school;
I~ Nacional de Industria (INI) (*Esp Com*)
≈ National Enterprise Board (*Brit*)
institutriz [institu'triθ] *nf* governess
instituyendo *etc* [institu'jendo] *vb ver*
instituir
instrucción [instruk'θjon] *nf* instruction;
(*enseñanza*) education, teaching; (*Jur*)
proceedings *pl*; (*Mil*) training; (*Deporte*)

coaching; (*conocimientos*) knowledge;
(*Inform*) statement; **instrucciones para el
uso** directions for use; **instrucciones de
funcionamiento** operating instructions
instructivo, -a [instruk'tiβo, a] *adj*
instructive
instructor [instruk'to] *nm* instructor
instruir [instru'ir] *vt* (*gen*) to instruct;
(*enseñar*) to teach, educate; (*Jur: proceso*) to
prepare, draw up; **instruirse** *vr* to learn,
teach o.s.
instrumento [instru'mento] *nm* (*gen*, *Mus*)
instrument; (*herramienta*) tool, implement;
(*Com*) indenture; (*Jur*) legal document; **~
de percusión/cuerda/viento** percussion/
string(ed)/wind instrument
instruyendo *etc* [instru'jendo] *vb ver* **instruir**
insubordinarse [insuβorði'narse] *vr* to rebel
insuficiencia [insufi'θjenθja] *nf* (*carencia*)
lack; (*inadecuación*) inadequacy; **~ cardíaca/
renal** heart/kidney failure
insuficiente [insufi'θjente] *adj* (*gen*)
insufficient; (*Escol: nota*) unsatisfactory
insufrible [insu'friβle] *adj* insufferable
insular [insu'lar] *adj* insular
insulina [insu'lina] *nf* insulin
insulso, -a [in'sulso, a] *adj* insipid; (*fig*) dull
insultar [insul'tar] *vt* to insult
insulto [in'sulto] *nm* insult
insumisión [insumi'sjon] *nf refusal to do
military service or community service*
insumiso, -a [insu'miso, a] *adj* (*rebelde*)
rebellious ◼ *nm/f* (*Pol*) *person who refuses to do
military service or community service*; *ver tb* **mili**
insuperable [insupe'raβle] *adj*
(*excelente*) unsurpassable; (*problema etc*)
insurmountable
insurgente [insur'xente] *adj*, *nm/f* insurgent
insurrección [insurrek'θjon] *nf* insurrection,
rebellion
insustituible [insusti'twiβle] *adj*
irreplaceable
intachable [inta't∫aβle] *adj* irreproachable
intacto, -a [in'takto, a] *adj* (*sin tocar*)
untouched; (*entero*) intact
integrado, -a [inte'ɣraðo, a] *adj* (*Inform*):
circuito ~ integrated circuit
integral [inte'ɣral] *adj* integral; (*completo*)
complete; (*Tec*) built-in; **pan ~** wholemeal
bread
integrante [inte'ɣrante] *adj* integral ◼ *nm/f*
member
integrar [inte'ɣrar] *vt* to make up, compose;
(*Mat*, *fig*) to integrate
integridad [inteɣri'ðað] *nf* wholeness;
(*carácter*, *tb Inform*) integrity; **en su ~**
completely

integrismo [inte'ɣrismo] *nm*
fundamentalism

integrista [inte'ɣrista] *adj, nm/f*
fundamentalist

íntegro, -a ['inteɣro, a] *adj* whole, entire;
(*texto*) uncut, unabridged; (*honrado*) honest

intelectual [intelek'twal] *adj, nm/f*
intellectual

intelectualidad [intelektwali'ðað] *nf*
intelligentsia, intellectuals *pl*

inteligencia [inteli'xenθja] *nf* intelligence;
(*ingenio*) ability; ~ **artificial** artificial
intelligence

inteligente [inteli'xente] *adj* intelligent

inteligible [inteli'xiβle] *adj* intelligible

intemperancia [intempe'ranθja] *nf* excess,
intemperance

intemperie [intem'perje] *nf*: **a la ~** outdoors,
in the open air

intempestivo, -a [intempes'tiβo, a] *adj*
untimely

intención [inten'θjon] *nf* intention, purpose;
con segundas intenciones maliciously;
con ~ deliberately

intencionado, -a [intenθjo'naðo, a] *adj*
deliberate; **bien ~** well-meaning; **mal ~** ill-
disposed, hostile

intendencia [inten'denθja] *nf* management,
administration; (*Mil: tb*: **cuerpo de
intendencia**) ≈ service corps

intensidad [intensi'ðað] *nf* (*gen*) intensity;
(*Elec, Tec*) strength; (*de recuerdo*) vividness;
llover con ~ to rain hard

intensificar [intensifi'kar] *vt*, **intensificarse**
vr to intensify

intensifique *etc* [intensi'fike] *vb ver*
intensificar

intensivo, -a [inten'siβo, a] *adj* intensive;
curso ~ crash course

intenso, -a [in'tenso, a] *adj* intense;
(*impresión*) vivid; (*sentimiento*) profound, deep

intentar [inten'tar] *vt* (*tratar*) to try, attempt

intento [in'tento] *nm* (*intención*) intention,
purpose; (*tentativa*) attempt

intentona [inten'tona] *nf* (*Pol*) attempted
coup

interaccionar [interakθjo'nar] *vi* (*Inform*) to
interact

interactivo, -a [interak'tiβo, a] *adj*
interactive; (*Inform*): **computación
interactiva** interactive computing

intercalación [interkala'θjon] *nf* (*Inform*)
merging

intercalar [interka'lar] *vt* to insert; (*Inform*:
archivos, texto) to merge

intercambiable [interkam'bjaβle] *adj*
interchangeable

intercambio [inter'kambjo] *nm* (*canje*)
exchange; (*trueque*) swap

interceder [interθe'ðer] *vi* to intercede

interceptar [interθep'tar] *vt* to intercept, cut
off; (*Auto*) to hold up

interceptor [interθep'tor] *nm* interceptor;
(*Tec*) trap

intercesión [interθe'sjon] *nf* intercession

interés [inte'res] *nm* (*gen, Com*) interest;
(*importancia*) concern; (*parte*) share, part;
(*pey*) self-interest; ~ **compuesto** compound
interest; ~ **simple** simple interest; **con un ~
de 9 por ciento** at an interest of 9%; **dar a ~**
to lend at interest; **tener ~ en** (*Com*) to hold
a share in; **intereses acumulados** accrued
interest *sg*; **intereses por cobrar** interest
receivable *sg*; **intereses creados** vested
interests; **intereses por pagar** interest
payable *sg*

interesado, -a [intere'saðo, a] *adj* interested;
(*prejuiciado*) prejudiced; (*pey*) mercenary, self-
seeking ■ *nm/f* person concerned; (*firmante*)
the undersigned

interesante [intere'sante] *adj* interesting

interesar [intere'sar] *vt* to interest, be of
interest to ■ *vi* to interest, be of interest;
(*importar*) to be important; **interesarse** *vr*:
interesarse en *o* **por** to take an interest in;
no me interesan los toros bullfighting
does not appeal to me

interestatal [interesta'tal] *adj* inter-state

interface [inter'faθe], **interfase** [inter'fase]
nm (*Inform*) interface; ~ **hombre/máquina/
por menús** man/machine/menu interface

interfaz [inter'faθ] *nm* = **interface**

interferencia [interfe'renθja] *nf*
interference

interferir [interfe'rir] *vt* to interfere with;
(*Telec*) to jam ■ *vi* to interfere

interfiera *etc* [inter'fjera], **interfiriendo** *etc*
[interfi'rjendo] *vb ver* **interferir**

interfono [inter'fono] *nm* intercom

ínterin ['interin] *adv* meanwhile ■ *nm*
interim; **en el ínterin** in the meantime

interino, -a [inte'rino, a] *adj* temporary;
(*empleado etc*) provisional ■ *nm/f* temporary
holder of a post; (*Med*) locum; (*Escol*) supply
teacher; (*Teat*) stand-in

interior [inte'rjor] *adj* inner, inside; (*Com*)
domestic, internal ■ *nm* interior, inside;
(*fig*) soul, mind; (*Deporte*) inside forward;
Ministerio del I~ ≈ Home Office (*Brit*),
Ministry of the Interior; **dije para mi ~**
I said to myself

interjección [interxek'θjon] *nf* interjection

interlínea [inter'linea] *nf* (*Inform*) line feed

interlocutor, a [interloku'tor, a] *nm/f*

219

speaker; (al teléfono) person at the other end (of the line); **mi** ~ the person I was speaking to

intermediario, -a [interme'ðjarjo, a] adj (mediador) mediating ■ nm/f intermediary, go-between; (mediador) mediator

intermedio, -a [inter'meðjo, a] adj intermediate; (tiempo) intervening ■ nm interval; (Pol) recess

interminable [intermi'naβle] adj endless, interminable

intermitente [intermi'tente] adj intermittent ■ nm (Auto) indicator

internacional [internaθjo'nal] adj international

internado [inter'naðo] nm boarding school

internamiento [interna'mjento] nm internment

internar [inter'nar] vt to intern; (en un manicomio) to commit; **internarse** vr (penetrar) to penetrate; **internarse en** to go into o right inside; **internarse en un estudio** to study a subject in depth

internauta [inter'nauta] nmf Internet user

Internet [inter'net] nm o nf Internet

interno, -a [in'terno, a] adj internal, interior; (Pol etc) domestic ■ nm/f (alumno) boarder

interpelación [interpela'θjon] nf appeal, plea

interpelar [interpe'lar] vt (rogar) to implore; (hablar) to speak to; (Pol) to ask for explanations, question formally

interpondré etc [interpon'dre] vb ver **interponer**

interponer [interpo'ner] vt to interpose, put in; **interponerse** vr to intervene

interponga etc [inter'ponga] vb ver **interponer**

interposición [interposi'θjon] nf insertion

interpretación [interpreta'θjon] nf interpretation; (Mus, Teat) performance; **mala** ~ misinterpretation

interpretar [interpre'tar] vt to interpret

intérprete [in'terprete] nm/f (Ling) interpreter, translator; (Mus, Teat) performer, artist(e)

interpuesto [inter'pwesto], **interpuse** etc [inter'puse] vb ver **interponer**

interrogación [interroγa'θjon] nf interrogation; (Ling: tb: **signo de interrogación**) question mark; (Telec) polling

interrogante [interro'γante] adj questioning ■ nm question mark; (fig) question mark, query

interrogar [interro'γar] vt to interrogate, question

interrogatorio [interroγa'torjo] nm interrogation; (Mil) debriefing; (Jur) examination

interrogue etc [inte'rroγe] vb ver **interrogar**

interrumpir [interrum'pir] vt to interrupt; (vacaciones) to cut short; (servicio) to cut off; (tráfico) to block

interrupción [interrup'θjon] nf interruption

interruptor [interrup'tor] nm (Elec) switch

intersección [intersek'θjon] nf intersection; (Auto) junction

interurbano, -a [interur'βano, a] adj inter-city; (Telec) long-distance

intervalo [inter'βalo] nm interval; (descanso) break; **a intervalos** at intervals, every now and then

intervención [interβen'θjon] nf supervision; (Com) audit(ing); (Med) operation; (Telec) tapping; (participación) intervention; ~ **quirúrgica** surgical operation; **la política de no** ~ the policy of non-intervention

intervencionista [interβenθjo'nista] adj: **no** ~ (Com) laissez-faire

intervendré etc [interβen'dre], **intervenga** etc [inter'βenga] vb ver **intervenir**

intervenir [interβe'nir] vt (controlar) to control, supervise; (Com) to audit; (Med) to operate on; (Telec) to tap ■ vi (participar) to take part, participate; (mediar) to intervene

interventor, a [interβen'tor, a] nm/f inspector; (Com) auditor

interviniendo etc [interβi'njendo] vb ver **intervenir**

interviú [inter'βju] nf interview

intestino [intes'tino] nm intestine

inti ['inti] nm monetary unit of Peru

intimar [inti'mar] vt to intimate, announce; (mandar) to order ■ vi, **intimarse** vr to become friendly

intimidad [intimi'ðað] nf intimacy; (familiaridad) familiarity; (vida privada) private life; (Jur) privacy

intimidar [intimi'ðar] vt to intimidate, scare

íntimo, -a ['intimo, a] adj intimate; (pensamientos) innermost; (vida) personal, private; **una boda íntima** a quiet wedding

intolerable [intole'raβle] adj intolerable, unbearable

intolerancia [intole'ranθja] nf intolerance

intoxicación [intoksika'θjon] nf poisoning; ~ **alimenticia** food poisoning

intraducible [intraðu'θiβle] adj untranslatable

intranet [intra'net] nf intranet

intranquilice etc [intranki'liθe] vb ver **intranquilizarse**

intranquilizarse [intrankili'θarse] vr to get worried o anxious

intranquilo, -a [intran'kilo, a] adj worried

intranscendente [intransθen'dente] adj unimportant

intransferible [intransfe'riβle] *adj* not
transferable
intransigente [intransi'xente] *adj*
intransigent
intransitable [intransi'taβle] *adj* impassable
intransitivo, -a [intransi'tiβo, a] *adj*
intransitive
intratable [intra'taβle] *adj* (*problema*)
intractable; (*dificultad*) awkward; (*individuo*)
unsociable
intrepidez [intrepi'ðeθ] *nf* courage, bravery
intrépido, -a [in'trepiðo, a] *adj* intrepid,
fearless
intriga [in'triɣa] *nf* intrigue; (*plan*) plot
intrigar [intri'ɣar] *vt, vi* to intrigue
intrigue *etc* [in'triɣe] *vb ver* **intrigar**
intrincado, -a [intrin'kaðo, a] *adj* intricate
intrínseco, -a [in'trinseko, a] *adj* intrinsic
introducción [introðuk'θjon] *nf*
introduction; (*de libro*) foreword; (*Inform*)
input
introducir [introðu'θir] *vt* (*gen*) to introduce;
(*moneda*) to insert; (*Inform*) to input, enter
introduje *etc* [intro'ðuxe], **introduzca** *etc*
[intro'ðuθka] *vb ver* **introducir**
intromisión [intromi'sjon] *nf* interference,
meddling
introvertido, -a [introβer'tiðo, a] *adj, nm/f*
introvert
intruso, -a [in'truso, a] *adj* intrusive ■ *nm/f*
intruder
intuición [intwi'θjon] *nf* intuition
intuir [intu'ir] *vt* to know by intuition, intuit
intuyendo *etc* [intu'jendo] *vb ver* **intuir**
inundación [inunda'θjon] *nf* flood(ing)
inundar [inun'dar] *vt* to flood; (*fig*) to
swamp, inundate
inusitado, -a [inusi'taðo, a] *adj* unusual
inútil [i'nutil] *adj* useless; (*esfuerzo*) vain,
fruitless
inutilice *etc* [inuti'liθe] *vb ver* **inutilizar**
inutilidad [inutili'ðað] *nf* uselessness
inutilizar [inutili'θar] *vt* to make unusable,
put out of action; (*incapacitar*) to disable;
inutilizarse *vr* to become useless
invadir [imba'ðir] *vt* to invade
invalidar [imbali'ðar] *vt* to invalidate
invalidez [imbali'ðeθ] *nf* (*Med*) disablement;
(*Jur*) invalidity
inválido, -a [im'baliðo, a] *adj* invalid; (*Jur*)
null and void ■ *nm/f* invalid
invariable [imba'rjable] *adj* invariable
invasión [imba'sjon] *nf* invasion
invasor, a [imba'sor, a] *adj* invading ■ *nm/f*
invader
invencible [imben'θiβle] *adj* invincible;
(*timidez, miedo*) unsurmountable

invención [imben'θjon] *nf* invention
inventar [imben'tar] *vt* to invent
inventario [imben'tarjo] *nm* inventory;
(*Com*) stocktaking
inventiva [imben'tiβa] *nf* inventiveness
invento [im'bento] *nm* invention; (*fig*)
brainchild; (*pey*) silly idea
inventor, a [imben'tor, a] *nm/f* inventor
invernadero [imberna'ðero] *nm* greenhouse
invernal [imber'nal] *adj* wintry, winter *cpd*
invernar [imber'nar] *vi* (*Zool*) to hibernate
inverosímil [imbero'simil] *adj* implausible
inversión [imber'sjon] *nf* (*Com*) investment;
~ de capitales capital investment;
inversiones extranjeras foreign
investment *sg*
inverso, a [im'berso, a] *adj* inverse, opposite;
en el orden ~ in reverse order; **a la inversa**
inversely, the other way round
inversor, -a [imber'sor, a] *nm/f* (*Com*)
investor
invertebrado, -a [imberte'βraðo, a] *adj, nm*
invertebrate
invertido, -a [imber'tiðo, a] *adj* inverted;
(*al revés*) reversed; (*homosexual*) homosexual
■ *nm/f* homosexual
invertir [imber'tir] *vt* (*Com*) to invest; (*volcar*)
to turn upside down; (*tiempo etc*) to spend
investigación [imbestiɣa'θjon] *nf*
investigation; (*indagación*) inquiry; (*Univ*)
research; **~ y desarrollo** (*Com*) research and
development (R & D); **~ de los medios de
publicidad** media research; **~ del mercado**
market research
investigador, a [imbestiɣa'ðor, a] *nm/f*
investigator; (*Univ*) research fellow
investigar [imbesti'ɣar] *vt* to investigate;
(*estudiar*) to do research into
investigue *etc* [imbes'tiɣe] *vb ver* **investigar**
investir [imbes'tir] *vt*: **~ a algn con algo**
to confer sth on sb; **fue investido Doctor
Honoris Causa** he was awarded an
honorary doctorate
invicto, -a [im'bikto, a] *adj* unconquered
invidente [imbi'ðente] *adj* sightless ■ *nm/f*
blind person; **los invidentes** the sightless
invierno [im'bjerno] *nm* winter
invierta *etc* [im'bjerta] *vb ver* **invertir**
inviolabilidad [imbjolaβili'ðað] *nf*
inviolability; **~ parlamentaria**
parliamentary immunity
invirtiendo *etc* [imbir'tjendo] *vb ver* **invertir**
invisible [imbi'siβle] *adj* invisible;
exportaciones/importaciones invisibles
invisible exports/imports
invitación [imbita'θjon] *nf* invitation
invitado, -a [imbi'taðo, a] *nm/f* guest

221

invitar [imbi'tar] *vt* to invite; (*incitar*) to entice; ~ **a algn a hacer algo** to invite sb to do sth; ~ **a algo** to pay for sth; **nos invitó a cenar fuera** she took us out for dinner; **invito yo** it's on me

in vitro [im'bitro] *adv* in vitro

invocar [imbo'kar] *vt* to invoke, call on

involucrar [imbolu'krar] *vt*: ~ **algo en un discurso** to bring something irrelevant into a discussion; ~ **a algn en algo** to involve sb in sth; **involucrarse** *vr* (*interesarse*) to get involved

involuntario, -a [imbolun'tarjo, a] *adj* involuntary; (*ofensa etc*) unintentional

invoque *etc* [im'boke] *vb ver* **invocar**

inyección [injek'θjon] *nf* injection

inyectar [injek'tar] *vt* to inject

ión [i'on] *nm* ion

IPC *nm abr* (*Esp*: = *índice de precios al consumo*) CPI

IPM *nm abr* (= *índice de precios al por menor*) RPI

 PALABRA CLAVE

ir [ir] *vi* **1** to go; (*a pie*) to walk; (*viajar*) to travel; **ir caminando** to walk; **fui en tren** I went *o* travelled by train; **voy a la calle** I'm going out; **ir en coche/en bicicleta** to drive/cycle; **ir a pie** to walk, go on foot; **ir de pesca** to go fishing; **¡(ahora) voy!** (I'm just) coming!

2: **ir (a) por**: **ir (a) por el médico** to fetch the doctor

3 (*progresar: persona, cosa*) to go; **el trabajo va muy bien** work is going very well; **¿cómo te va?** how are things going?; **me va muy bien** I'm getting on very well; **le fue fatal** it went awfully badly for him

4 (*funcionar*): **el coche no va muy bien** the car isn't running very well

5 (*sentar*): **me va estupendamente** (*ropa, color*) it suits me really well; (*medicamento*) it works really well for me; **ir bien con algo** to go well with sth

6 (*aspecto*): **iba muy bien vestido** he was very well dressed; **ir con zapatos negros** to wear black shoes

7 (*locuciones*): **¿vino? — ¡que va!** did he come? — of course not!; **vamos, no llores** come on, don't cry; **¡vaya coche!** (*admiración*) what a car!, that's some car!; (*desprecio*) that's a terrible car!; **¡vaya!** (*regular*) so so; (*desagrado*) come on!; **¡vamos!** come on!; **¡que le vaya bien!** (*adiós*) take care!

8: **no vaya a ser**: **tienes que correr, no vaya a ser que pierdas el tren** you'll have to run so as not to miss the train

9: **no me** *etc* **va ni me viene** I *etc* don't care

■ *vb auxiliar* **1**: **ir a**: **voy/iba a hacerlo hoy** I am/was going to do it today

2 (+*gerundio*): **iba anocheciendo** it was getting dark; **todo se me iba aclarando** everything was gradually becoming clearer to me

3 (+*pp* = *pasivo*) **van vendidos 300 ejemplares** 300 copies have been sold so far

irse *vr* **1**: **¿por dónde se va al zoológico?** which is the way to the zoo?

2 (*marcharse*) to leave; **ya se habrán ido** they must already have left *o* gone; **¡vámonos!**, **¡nos fuimos!** (*Am*) let's go!; **¡vete!** go away!; **¡vete a saber!** your guess is as good as mine!, who knows!

IRA ['ira] *nm abr* (= *Irish Republican Army*) IRA

ira ['ira] *nf* anger, rage

iracundo, -a [ira'kundo, a] *adj* irascible

Irak [i'rak] *nm* = **Iraq**

Irán [i'ran] *nm* Iran

iraní [ira'ni] *adj, nm/f* Iranian

Iraq [i'rak] *nm* Iraq

iraquí [ira'ki] *adj, nm/f* Iraqi

irascible [iras'θiβle] *adj* irascible

irguiendo *etc* [ir'ɣjendo] *vb ver* **erguir**

iris ['iris] *nm inv* (*arco iris*) rainbow; (*Anat*) iris

Irlanda [ir'landa] *nf* Ireland; ~ **del Norte** Northern Ireland, Ulster

irlandés, -esa [irlan'des, esa] *adj* Irish ■ *nm/f* Irishman(-woman) ■ *nm* (*Ling*) Gaelic, Irish; **los irlandeses** *nmpl* the Irish

ironía [iro'nia] *nf* irony

irónico, -a [i'roniko, a] *adj* ironic(al)

IRPF *nm abr* (*Esp*) = **impuesto sobre la renta de las personas físicas**

irracional [irraθjo'nal] *adj* irrational

irrazonable [irraθo'naβle] *adj* unreasonable

irreal [irre'al] *adj* unreal

irrealizable [irreali'θaβle] *adj* (*gen*) unrealizable; (*meta*) unrealistic

irrebatible [irreβa'tiβle] *adj* irrefutable

irreconocible [irrekono'θiβle] *adj* unrecognizable

irrecuperable [irrekupe'raβle] *adj* irrecoverable, irretrievable

irreembolsable [irreembol'saβle] *adj* (*Com*) non-returnable

irreflexión [irreflek'sjon] *nf* thoughtlessness; (*ímpetu*) rashness

irregular [irreɣu'lar] *adj* irregular; (*situación*) abnormal, anomalous; **margen izquierdo/derecho** ~ (*texto*) ragged left/right (margin)

irregularidad [irreɣulari'ðað] *nf* irregularity

irremediable [irreme'ðjaβle] *adj* irremediable; (*vicio*) incurable

irreprochable [irrepro'tʃaβle] *adj*

irreproachable

irresistible [irresis'tiβle] *adj* irresistible

irresoluto, -a [irreso'luto, a] *adj* irresolute, hesitant; *(sin resolver)* unresolved

irrespetuoso, -a [irrespe'twoso, a] *adj* disrespectful

irresponsable [irrespon'saβle] *adj* irresponsible

irreverente [irreβe'rente] *adj* disrespectful

irreversible [irreβer'siβle] *adj* irreversible

irrevocable [irreβo'kaβle] *adj* irrevocable

irrigar [irri'ɣar] *vt* to irrigate

irrigue *etc* [i'rriɣe] *vb ver* **irrigar**

irrisorio, -a [irri'sorjo, a] *adj* derisory, ridiculous; *(precio)* bargain *cpd*

irritación [irrita'θjon] *nf* irritation

irritar [irri'tar] *vt* to irritate, annoy; **irritarse** *vr* to get angry, lose one's temper

irrompible [irrom'piβle] *adj* unbreakable

irrumpir [irrum'pir] *vi*: ~ **en** to burst o rush into

irrupción [irrup'θjon] *nf* irruption; *(invasión)* invasion

IRTP *nm abr (Esp:* = *impuesto sobre el rendimiento del trabajo personal)* ≈ PAYE

ISBN *nm abr* (= *International Standard Book Number)* ISBN

isla ['isla] *nf (Geo)* island; **Islas Británicas** British Isles, **Islas Filipinas/Malvinas/ Canarias** Philippines/Falklands/Canaries

Islam [is'lam] *nm* Islam

islámico, -a [is'lamiko, a] *adj* Islamic

islandés, -esa [islan'des, esa] *adj* Icelandic ■ *nm/f* Icelander ■ *nm (Ling)* Icelandic

Islandia [is'landja] *nf* Iceland

isleño, -a [is'leɲo, a] *adj* island *cpd* ■ *nm/f* islander

islote [is'lote] *nm* small island

isotónico, -a [iso'toniko, a] *adj* isotonic

isótopo [i'sotopo] *nm* isotope

Israel [isra'el] *nm* Israel

israelí [israe'li] *adj, nm/f* Israeli

istmo ['istmo] *nm* isthmus; **el I~ de Panamá** the Isthmus of Panama

Italia [i'talja] *nf* Italy

italiano, -a [ita'ljano, a] *adj, nm/f* Italian ■ *nm (Ling)* Italian

itinerante [itine'rante] *adj* travelling; *(embajador)* roving

itinerario [itine'rarjo] *nm* itinerary, route

ITV *nf abr* (= *Inspección Técnica de Vehículos)* ≈ MOT (test) *(Brit)*

IVA ['iβa] *nm abr (Esp Com:* = *Impuesto sobre el Valor Añadido)* VAT

IVP *nm abr* = **Instituto Venezolano de Petroquímica**

izada [i'saða] *nf (Am)* lifting, raising

izar [i'θar] *vt* to hoist

izda, izq.ª *abr* (= *izquierda)* L, l

izdo, izq.º *abr* (= *izquierdo)* L, l

izquierda [iθ'kjerða] *nf ver* **izquierdo**

izquierdista [iθkjer'ðista] *adj* leftist, left-wing ■ *nm/f* left-winger, leftist

izquierdo, -a [iθ'kjerðo, a] *adj* left ■ *nf* left; *(Pol)* left (wing); **a la izquierda** on the left; **es un cero a la izquierda** *(fam)* he is a nonentity; **conducción por la izquierda** left-hand drive

Jj

J, j ['xota] *nf* (*letra*) J, j; **J de José** J for Jack (*Brit*) o Jig (*US*)

J *abr* (= *julio(s)*) J

jabalí [xaβa'li] *nm* wild boar

jabalina [xaβa'lina] *nf* javelin

jabato, -a [xa'βato, a] *adj* brave, bold ■ *nm* young wild boar

jabón [xa'βon] *nm* soap; (*fam: adulación*) flattery; **~ de afeitar** shaving soap; **~ de tocador** toilet soap; **dar ~ a algn** to soft-soap sb

jabonar [xaβo'nar] *vt* to soap

jaca ['xaka] *nf* pony

jacinto [xa'θinto] *nm* hyacinth

jactancia [xak'tanθja] *nf* boasting, boastfulness

jactarse [xak'tarse] *vr*: **~ (de)** to boast o brag (about o of)

jadear [xaðe'ar] *vi* to pant, gasp for breath

jadeo [xa'ðeo] *nm* panting, gasping

jaguar [xa'ɣwar] *nm* jaguar

jalar [xa'lar] *vt* (*Am*) to pull

jalbegue [xal'βeɣe] *nm* whitewash

jalea [xa'lea] *nf* jelly

jaleo [xa'leo] *nm* racket, uproar; **armar un ~** to kick up a racket

jalón [xa'lon] *nm* (*Am*) tug

jalonar [xalo'nar] *vt* to stake out; (*fig*) to mark

Jamaica [xa'maika] *nf* Jamaica

jamaicano, -a [xamai'kano, a] *adj, nm/f* Jamaican

jamás [xa'mas] *adv* never, not ... ever; (*interrogativo*) ever; **¿~ se vio tal cosa?** did you ever see such a thing?

jamón [xa'mon] *nm* ham; **~ (de) York** boiled ham; **~ dulce/serrano** boiled/cured ham

Japón [xa'pon] *nm*: **el ~** Japan

japonés, -esa [xapo'nes, esa] *adj, nm/f* Japanese ■ *nm* (*Ling*) Japanese

jaque ['xake] *nm*: **~ mate** checkmate

jaqueca [xa'keka] *nf* (very bad) headache, migraine

jarabe [xa'raβe] *nm* syrup; **~ para la tos** cough syrup o mixture

jarana [xa'rana] *nf* (*juerga*) spree (*fam*); **andar/ir de ~** to be/go on a spree

jardín [xar'ðin] *nm* garden; **~ botánico** botanical garden; **~ de (la) infancia** (*Esp*) o **de niños** (*Am*) o **infantil** (*Am*) kindergarten, nursery school

jardinaje [xarði'naχe] *nm* gardening

jardinería [xarðine'ria] *nf* gardening

jardinero, -a [xarði'nero, a] *nm/f* gardener

jarra ['xarra] *nf* jar; (*jarro*) jug; (*de leche*) churn; (*de cerveza*) mug; **de** o **en jarras** with arms akimbo

jarro ['xarro] *nm* jug

jarrón [xa'rron] *nm* vase; (*Arqueología*) urn

jaspeado, -a [xaspe'ado, a] *adj* mottled, speckled

jaula ['xaula] *nf* cage; (*embalaje*) crate

jauría [xau'ria] *nf* pack of hounds

jazmín [xaθ'min] *nm* jasmine

J. C. *abr* = **Jesucristo**

jeep® (*pl* **jeeps**) [jip, jips] *nm* jeep®

jefa ['xefa] *nf ver* **jefe**

jefatura [xefa'tura] *nf* (*liderazgo*) leadership; (*sede*) central office; **J~ de la aviación civil** ≈ Civil Aviation Authority; **~ de policía** police headquarters *sg*

jefazo [xe'faθo] *nm* bigwig

jefe, -a ['xefe, a] *nm/f* (*gen*) chief, head; (*patrón*) boss; (*Pol*) leader; (*Com*) manager(ess); **~ de camareros** head waiter; **~ de cocina** chef; **~ ejecutivo** (*Com*) chief executive; **~ de estación** stationmaster; **~ de estado** head of state; **~ de oficina** (*Com*) office manager; **~ de producción** (*Com*) production manager; **~ supremo** commander-in-chief; **ser el ~** (*fig*) to be the boss

JEN [xen] *nf abr* (*Esp*) = **Junta de Energía Nuclear**

jengibre [xen'xiβre] *nm* ginger

jeque ['xeke] *nm* sheik(h)

jerarquía [xerar'kia] nf (orden) hierarchy; (rango) rank

jerárquico, -a [xe'rarkiko, a] adj hierarchic(al)

jerez [xe'reθ] nm sherry; **J- de la Frontera** Jerez

jerezano, -a [xere'θano, a] adj of o from Jerez ■ nm/f native o inhabitant of Jerez

jerga ['xerɣa] nf (tela) coarse cloth; (lenguaje) jargon; ~ **informática** computer jargon

jerigonza [xeri'ɣonθa] nf (jerga) jargon, slang; (galimatías) nonsense, gibberish

jeringa [xe'ringa] nf syringe; (Am) annoyance, bother; ~ **de engrase** grease gun

jeringar [xerin'gar] vt to annoy, bother

jeringue etc [xe'ringe] vb ver **jeringar**

jeringuilla [xerin'guiʎa] nf hypodermic (syringe)

jeroglífico [xero'ɣlifiko] nm hieroglyphic

jersey [xer'sei] (pl **jerseys**) nm jersey, pullover, jumper

Jerusalén [xerusa'len] n Jerusalem

Jesucristo [xesu'kristo] nm Jesus Christ

jesuita [xe'swita] adj, nm Jesuit

Jesús [xe'sus] nm Jesus; ¡~! good heavens!; (al estornudar) bless you!

jet (pl **jets**) [jet, jet] nm jet (plane) ■ nf: **la ~** the jet set

jeta ['xeta] nf (Zool) snout; (fam: cara) mug; ¡que ~ tienes! (fam: insolencia) you've got a nerve!

jíbaro, -a ['xiβaro, a] adj, nm/f Jíbaro (Indian)

jícara ['xikara] nf small cup

jiennense [xjen'nense] adj of o from Jaén ■ nm/f native o inhabitant of Jaén

jilguero [xil'ɣero] nm goldfinch

jinete, -a [xi'nete, a] nm/f horseman(-woman)

jipijapa [xipi'xapa] nm (Am) straw hat

jira ['xira] nf (de tela) strip; (excursión) picnic

jirafa [xi'rafa] nf giraffe

jirón [xi'ron] nm rag, shred

JJ.OO. nmpl abr = **Juegos Olímpicos**

jocosidad [xokosi'ðað] nf humour; (chiste) joke

jocoso, -a [xo'koso, a] adj humorous, jocular

joder [xo'ðer] (fam!) vt to fuck (!), screw (!); (fig: fastidiar) to piss off (!), bug; **joderse** vr (fracasar) to fail; ¡~! damn it!; **se jodió todo** everything was ruined

jodido, -a [xo'ðiðo, a] adj (fam!: difícil) awkward; **estoy ~** I'm knackered

jofaina [xo'faina] nf washbasin

jojoba [xo'xoβa] nf jojoba

jolgorio [xol'ɣorjo] nm (juerga) fun, revelry

jonrón [xon'ron] nm home run

Jordania [xor'ðanja] nf Jordan

jornada [xor'naða] nf (viaje de un día) day's journey; (camino o viaje entero) journey; (día de trabajo) working day; ~ **de 8 horas** 8-hour day; **(trabajar a) ~ partida** (to work a) split shift

jornal [xor'nal] nm (day's) wage

jornalero, -a [xorna'lero, a] nm/f (day) labourer

joroba [xo'roβa] nf hump

jorobado, -a [xoro'βaðo, a] adj hunchbacked ■ nm/f hunchback

jorobar [xoro'βar] vt to annoy, pester, bother; **jorobarse** vr to get cross; ¡hay que **jorobarse!** to hell with it!; **esto me joroba!** ¡I'm fed up with this!

jota ['xota] nf letter J; (danza) Aragonese dance; (fam) jot, iota; **no saber ni ~** to have no idea

joven ['xoβen] adj young ■ nm young man, youth ■ nf young woman, girl

jovencito, -a [xoβen'θito, a] nm/f youngster

jovial [xo'βjal] adj cheerful, jolly

jovialidad [xoβjali'ðað] nf cheerfulness

joya ['xoja] nf jewel, gem; (fig: persona) gem; **joyas de fantasía** imitation jewellery sg

joyería [xoje'ria] nf (joyas) jewellery; (tienda) jeweller's (shop)

joyero [xo'jero] nm (persona) jeweller; (caja) jewel case

Juan [xwan] nm: **Noche de San ~** see note

NOCHE DE SAN JUAN

The Noche de San Juan (evening of the Feast of Saint John) on the 24th June is a fiesta coinciding with the summer solstice, and which has taken the place of other ancient pagan festivals. Traditionally fire plays a major part in these festivities, which can last for days in certain areas. Celebrations and dancing take place around hogueras (bonfires) in towns and villages across the country.

juanete [xwa'nete] nm (del pie) bunion

jubilación [xuβila'θjon] nf (retiro) retirement

jubilado, -a [xuβi'lado, a] adj retired ■ nm/f retired person, pensioner (Brit), senior citizen

jubilar [xuβi'lar] vt to pension off, retire; (fam) to discard; **jubilarse** vr to retire

jubileo [xuβi'leo] nm jubilee

júbilo ['xuβilo] nm joy, rejoicing

jubiloso, -a [xuβi'loso, a] adj jubilant

judaísmo [xuða'ismo] nm Judaism

judía [xu'ðia] nf ver **judío**

judicatura [xuðika'tura] nf (cargo de juez) office of judge; (cuerpo de jueces) judiciary

judicial [xuði'θjal] *adj* judicial

judío, -a [xu'ðio, a] *adj* Jewish ■ *nm* Jew ■ *nf* Jewess, Jewish woman; (*Culin*) bean; **judía blanca** haricot bean; **judía verde** French *o* string bean

juego *etc* ['xweɣo] *vb ver* **jugar** ■ *nm* (*gen*) play; (*pasatiempo, partido*) game; (*en casino*) gambling; (*deporte*) sport; (*conjunto*) set; (*herramientas*) kit; ~ **de azar** game of chance; ~ **de café** coffee set; ~ **de caracteres** (*Inform*) font; ~ **limpio/sucio** fair/foul *o* dirty play; ~ **de mesa** board game; **J~s Olímpicos** Olympic Games; ~ **de programas** (*Inform*) suite of programs; **fuera de** ~ (*Deporte: persona*) offside; (: *pelota*) out of play; **por** ~ in fun, for fun

juegue *etc* ['xweɣe] *vb ver* **jugar**

juerga ['xwerɣa] *nf* binge; (*fiesta*) party; **ir de** ~ to go out on a binge

juerguista [xwer'ɣista] *nm/f* reveller

jueves ['xweβes] *nm inv* Thursday; *ver tb* **sábado**

juez [xweθ] *nm/f* judge; (*Tenis*) umpire; ~ **de línea** linesman; ~ **de paz** justice of the peace; ~ **de salida** starter

jueza [xweθa] *nf ver* **juez**

jugada [xu'ɣaða] *nf* play; **buena** ~ good move (*o* shot *o* stroke) *etc*

jugador, a [xuɣa'ðor, a] *nm/f* player; (*en casino*) gambler

jugar [xu'ɣar] *vt* to play; (*en casino*) to gamble; (*apostar*) to bet ■ *vi* to play; to gamble; (*Com*) to speculate; **jugarse** *vr* to gamble (away); **jugarse el todo por el todo** to stake one's all, go for bust; **¿quién juega?** whose move is it?; **¡me la han jugado!** (*fam*) I've been had!

jugarreta [xuɣa'rreta] *nf* (*mala jugada*) bad move; (*trampa*) dirty trick; **hacer una** ~ **a algn** to play a dirty trick on sb

juglar [xu'ɣlar] *nm* minstrel

jugo ['xuɣo] *nm* (*Bot, de fruta*) juice; (*fig*) essence, substance; ~ **de naranja** (*esp Am*) orange juice

jugoso, -a [xu'ɣoso, a] *adj* juicy; (*fig*) substantial, important

jugué [xu'ɣe], **juguemos** *etc* [xu'ɣemos] *vb ver* **jugar**

juguete [xu'ɣete] *nm* toy

juguetear [xuɣete'ar] *vi* to play

juguetería [xuɣete'ria] *nf* toyshop

juguetón, -ona [xuɣe'ton, ona] *adj* playful

juicio ['xwiθjo] *nm* judgement; (*sana razón*) sanity, reason; (*opinión*) opinion; (*Jur: proceso*) trial; **estar fuera de** ~ to be out of one's mind; **a mi** ~ in my opinion

juicioso, -a [xwi'θjoso, a] *adj* wise, sensible

JUJEM [xu'xem] *nf abr* (*Esp Mil*) = **Junta de Jefes del Estado Mayor**

jul. *abr* (= *julio*) Jul.

julio ['xuljo] *nm* July; **el uno** *o* **el primero de** ~ the first of July; **en el mes de** ~ during July; **en** ~ **del año que viene** in July of next year

jumento, -a [xu'mento, a] *nm/f* donkey

jun. *abr* (= *junio*) Jun.

junco ['xunko] *nm* rush, reed

jungla ['xungla] *nf* jungle

junio ['xunjo] *nm* June; *ver tb* **julio**

junta ['xunta] *nf ver* **junto**

juntar [xun'tar] *vt* to join, unite; (*maquinaria*) to assemble, put together; (*dinero*) to collect; **juntarse** *vr* to join, meet; (*reunirse: personas*) to meet, assemble; (*arrimarse*) to approach, draw closer; **juntarse con algn** to join sb

junto, -a ['xunto, a] *adj* joined; (*unido*) united; (*anexo*) near, close; (*contiguo, próximo*) next, adjacent ■ *nf* (*asamblea*) meeting, assembly; (*comité, consejo*) board, council, committee; (*Mil, Pol*) junta; (*articulación*) joint ■ *adv*: **todo** ~ all at once ■ *prep*: ~ **a** near (to), next to; **juntos** together; **junta constitutiva** (*Com*) statutory meeting; **junta directiva** (*Com*) board of management; **junta general extraordinaria** (*Com*) extraordinary general meeting

juntura [xun'tura] *nf* (*punto de unión*) join, junction; (*articulación*) joint

jura ['xura] *nf* oath, pledge; ~ **de bandera** (ceremony of taking the) oath of allegiance

jurado [xu'raðo] *nm* (*Jur: individuo*) juror; (: *grupo*) jury; (*de concurso: grupo*) panel (of judges); (: *individuo*) member of a panel

juramentar [xuramen'tar] *vt* to swear in, administer the oath to; **juramentarse** *vr* to be sworn in, take the oath

juramento [xura'mento] *nm* oath; (*maldición*) oath, curse; **bajo** ~ on oath; **prestar** ~ to take the oath; **tomar** ~ **a** to swear in, administer the oath to

jurar [xu'rar] *vt, vi* to swear; ~ **en falso** to commit perjury; **jurárselas a algn** to have it in for sb

jurídico, -a [xu'riðiko, a] *adj* legal, juridical

jurisdicción [xurisðik'θjon] *nf* (*poder, autoridad*) jurisdiction; (*territorio*) district

jurisprudencia [xurispru'ðenθja] *nf* jurisprudence

jurista [xu'rista] *nm/f* jurist

justamente [xusta'mente] *adv* justly, fairly; (*precisamente*) just, exactly

justicia [xus'tiθja] *nf* justice; (*equidad*) fairness, justice; **de** ~ deservedly

justiciero, -a [xusti'θjero, a] *adj* just, righteous

justificable [xustifi'kaβle] *adj* justifiable

justificación [xustifika'θjon] *nf*
justification; **~ automática** (*Inform*)
automatic justification

justificado, -a [xustifi'kaðo, a] *adj* (*Tip*): **(no)**
~ (un)justified

justificante [xustifi'kante] *nm* voucher;
~ médico sick note

justificar [xustifi'kar] *vt* (*tb Tip*) to justify;
(*probar*) to verify

justifique *etc* [xusti'fike] *vb ver* **justificar**

justo, -a ['xusto, a] *adj* (*equitativo*) just, fair,
right; (*preciso*) exact, correct; (*ajustado*) tight

■ *adv* (*precisamente*) exactly, precisely; (*apenas*
a tiempo) just in time; ¡~! that's it!, correct!;
llegaste muy ~ you just made it; **vivir muy**
~ to be hard up

juvenil [xuβe'nil] *adj* youthful

juventud [xuβen'tuð] *nf* (*adolescencia*) youth;
(*jóvenes*) young people *pl*

juzgado [xuθ'γaðo] *nm* tribunal; (*Jur*) court

juzgar [xuθ'γar] *vt* to judge; **a ~ por ...**
to judge by ..., judging by ...; **~ mal** to
misjudge; **júzguelo usted mismo** see for
yourself

Kk

K, k [ka] *nf (letra)* K, k; **K de Kilo** K for King
K *abr* (= *1.000*) K; (*Inform*: = *1.024*) K
Kampuchea [kampu'tʃea] *nf* Kampuchea
karaoke [kara'oke] *nm* karaoke
kárate ['karate], **karate** [ka'rate] *nm* karate
KAS *nf abr* (= *Koordinadora Abertzale Sozialista*)
  Basque nationalist umbrella group
Kazajstán [kaθaxs'tan] *nm* Kazakhstan
k/c. *abr* (= *kilociclos*) kc.

Kenia ['kenja] *nf* Kenya
keniata [ke'njata] *adj, nm/f* Kenyan
kepí, kepis [ke'pi, 'kepis] *nm (esp Am)* kepi,
  military hat
kerosene [kero'sene] *nm* kerosene
Kg, kg *abr* (= *kilogramo(s)*) K, kg
KGB *sigla m* KGB
kilate [ki'late] *nm* = **quilate**
kilo ['kilo] *nm* kilo
kilobyte ['kiloβait] *nm (Inform)* kilobyte
kilogramo [kilo'ɣramo] *nm* kilogramme
  (Brit), kilogram (US)
kilolitro [kilo'litro] *nm* kilolitre (Brit),
  kiloliter (US)
kilometraje [kilome'traxe] *nm* distance in
  kilometres, ≈ mileage

kilométrico, -a [kilo'metriko, a] *adj*
  kilometric; (*fam*) very long; **(billete)** ~ (*Ferro*)
  mileage ticket
kilómetro [ki'lometro] *nm* kilometre (Brit),
  kilometer (US)
kiloocteto [kilook'teto] *nm (Inform)*
  kilobyte
kilovatio [kilo'βatjo] *nm* kilowatt
kiosco ['kjosko] *nm* = **quiosco**
Kirguizistán [kirɣiθis'tan] *nm* Kirghizia
kiwi ['kiwi] *nm* kiwi (fruit)
km *abr* (= *kilómetro(s)*) km
km/h *abr* (= *kilómetros por hora*) km/h
knock-out ['nokau], **K.O.** ['kao] *nm*
  knockout; (*golpe*) knockout blow; **dejar** *o*
  poner a algn ~ to knock sb out
kosovar [koso'βar] *adj* Kosovan
Kosovo [koso'βo] *nm* Kosovo
k.p.h. *abr* (= *kilómetros por hora*) km/h
k.p.l. *abr* (= *kilómetros por litro*) ≈ mpg
kurdo, -a ['kurðo, a] *adj* Kurdish ▪ *nm/f*
  Kurd ▪ *nm (Ling)* Kurdish
kuwaití [kuβai'ti] *adj, nm/f* Kuwaiti
kv *abr* (= *kilovatio*) kw
kv/h *abr* (= *kilovatios-hora*) kw-h

Ll

L, l ['ele] nf (letra) L, l; **L de Lorenzo** L for Lucy (Brit) o Love (US)

l abr (= litro(s)) l; (= libro) bk

L/ abr (Com) = **letra**

la [la] artículo definido fsg the ■ pron her; (en relación a usted) you; (en relación a una cosa) it ■ nm (Mus) A; **está en la cárcel** he's in jail; **la del sombrero rojo** the woman/girl/one in the red hat

laberinto [laβe'rinto] nm labyrinth

labia ['laβja] nf fluency; (pey) glibness; **tener mucha ~** to have the gift of the gab

labial [la'βjal] adj labial

labio ['laβjo] nm lip; (de vasija etc) edge, rim; **~ inferior/superior** lower/upper lip

labor [la'βor] nf labour; (Agr) farm work; (tarea) job, task; (Costura) needlework, sewing; (punto) knitting; **~ de equipo** teamwork; **~ de ganchillo** crochet

laborable [laβo'raβle] adj (Agr) workable; **día ~** working day

laboral [laβo'ral] adj (accidente, conflictividad) industrial; (jornada) working; (derecho, relaciones) labour cpd

laboralista [laβora'lista] adj: **abogado ~** labour lawyer

laborar [laβo'rar] vi to work

laboratorio [laβora'torjo] nm laboratory

laborioso, -a [laβo'rjoso, a] adj (persona) hard-working; (trabajo) tough

laborista [laβo'rista] (Pol) adj: **Partido L~** Labour Party ■ nm/f Labour Party member o supporter

labrado, -a [la'βraðo, a] adj worked; (madera) carved; (metal) wrought ■ nm (Agr) cultivated field

Labrador [laβra'ðor] nm Labrador

labrador, a [laβra'ðor, a] nm/f farmer

labranza [la'βranθa] nf (Agr) cultivation

labrar [la'βrar] vt (gen) to work; (madera etc) to carve; (fig) to cause, bring about

labriego, -a [la'βrjeɣo, a] nm/f peasant

laca ['laka] nf lacquer; (de pelo) hairspray; **~**

de uñas nail varnish

lacayo [la'kajo] nm lackey

lacerar [laθe'rar] vt to lacerate

lacio, -a ['laθjo, a] adj (pelo) lank, straight

lacón [la'kon] nm shoulder of pork

lacónico, -a [la'koniko, a] adj laconic

lacra ['lakra] nf (defecto) blemish; **~ social** social disgrace

lacrar [la'krar] vt (cerrar) to seal (with sealing wax)

lacre ['lakre] nm sealing wax

lacrimógeno, -a [lakri'moxeno, a] adj (fig) sentimental; **gas ~** tear gas

lacrimoso, -a [lakri'moso, a] adj tearful

lactancia [lak'tanθja] nf breast-feeding

lactar [lak'tar] vt, vi to suckle, breast-feed

lácteo, -a ['lakteo, a] adj: **productos lácteos** dairy products

ladear [laðe'ar] vt to tip, tilt ■ vi to tilt; **ladearse** vr to lean; (Deporte) to swerve; (Aviat) to bank, turn

ladera [la'ðera] nf slope

ladino, -a [la'ðino, a] adj cunning

lado ['laðo] nm (gen) side; (fig) protection; (Mil) flank; **~ izquierdo** left(-hand) side; **~ a ~** side by side; **al ~ de** next to, beside; **hacerse a un ~** to stand aside; **poner de ~** to put on its side; **poner a un ~** to put aside; **me da de ~** I don't care; **por un ~ ...,** **por otro ~ ...** on the one hand ..., on the other (hand) ...; **por todos lados** on all sides, all round (Brit)

ladrar [la'ðrar] vi to bark

ladrido [la'ðriðo] nm bark, barking

ladrillo [la'ðriʎo] nm (gen) brick; (azulejo) tile

ladrón, -ona [la'ðron, ona] nm/f thief

lagar [la'ɣar] nm (wine/oil) press

lagartija [laɣar'tixa] nf (small) lizard, wall lizard

lagarto [la'ɣarto] nm (Zool) lizard; (Am) alligator

lago ['laɣo] nm lake

Lagos ['laɣos] nm Lagos

lágrima ['laɣrima] nf tear
lagrimal [laɣri'mal] nm (inner) corner of the eye
lagrimear [laɣrime'ar] vi to weep; (ojos) to water
laguna [la'ɣuna] nf (lago) lagoon; (en escrito, conocimientos) gap
laico, -a ['laiko, a] adj lay ■ nm/f layman(-woman)
laja ['laxa] nf rock
lamber [lam'ber] vt (Am) to lick
lambiscón, -ona [lambis'kon, ona] adj flattering ■ nm/f flatterer
lameculos [lame'kulos] nm/f inv (fam) arse licker (!), crawler
lamentable [lamen'taβle] adj lamentable, regrettable; (miserable) pitiful
lamentación [lamenta'θjon] nf lamentation; **ahora no sirven lamentaciones** it's no good crying over spilt milk
lamentar [lamen'tar] vt (sentir) to regret; (deplorar) to lament; **lamentarse** vr to lament; **lo lamento mucho** I'm very sorry
lamento [la'mento] nm lament
lamer [la'mer] vt to lick
lámina ['lamina] nf (plancha delgada) sheet; (para estampar, estampa) plate; (grabado) engraving
laminar [lami'nar] vt (en libro) to laminate; (Tec) to roll
lámpara ['lampara] nf lamp; **~ de alcohol/gas** spirit/gas lamp; **~ de pie** standard lamp
lamparilla [lampa'riʎa] nf night-light
lamparón [lampa'ron] nm (Med) scrofula; (mancha) (large) grease spot
lampiño, -a [lam'piɲo, a] adj (sin pelo) hairless
lana ['lana] nf wool; (tela) woollen (Brit) o woolen (US) cloth; (Am fam: dinero) dough; **(hecho) de ~** wool cpd
lance etc ['lanθe] vb ver **lanzar** ■ nm (golpe) stroke; (suceso) event, incident
lanceta [lan'seta] nf (Am) sting
lancha ['lantʃa] nf launch; **~ motora** motorboat; **~ de pesca** fishing boat; **~ salvavidas/torpedera** lifeboat/torpedo boat; **~ neumática** rubber dinghy
lanero, -a [la'nero, a] adj wool cpd
langosta [lan'gosta] nf (insecto) locust; (crustáceo) lobster; (: de río) crayfish
langostino [langos'tino] nm prawn; (de agua dulce) crayfish
languidecer [langiðe'θer] vi to languish
languidez [langi'ðeθ] nf languor
languidezca etc [langi'ðeθka] vb ver **languidecer**

lánguido, -a ['langiðo, a] adj (gen) languid; (sin energía) listless
lanilla [la'niʎa] nf nap; (tela) thin flannel cloth
lanolina [lano'lina] nf lanolin(e)
lanudo, -a [la'nuðo, a] adj woolly, fleecy
lanza ['lanθa] nf (arma) lance, spear; **medir lanzas** to cross swords
lanzacohetes [lanθako'etes] nm inv rocket launcher
lanzadera [lanθa'ðera] nf shuttle
lanzado, -a [lan'θaðo, a] adj (atrevido) forward; (decidido) determined; **ir ~** (rápido) to fly along
lanzallamas [lanθa'ʎamas] nm inv flamethrower
lanzamiento [lanθa'mjento] nm (gen) throwing; (Naut, Com) launch, launching; **~ de pesos** putting the shot
lanzar [lan'θar] vt (gen) to throw; (con violencia) to fling; (Deporte: pelota) to bowl, to pitch (US) (Naut, Com) to launch; (Jur) to evict; (grito) to give, utter; **lanzarse** vr to throw o.s.; (fig) to take the plunge; **lanzarse a** (fig) to embark upon
Lanzarote [lanθa'rote] nm Lanzarote
lanzatorpedos [lanθator'peðos] nm inv torpedo tube
lapa ['lapa] nf limpet
La Paz nf La Paz
lapicero [lapi'θero] nm pencil; (Am) propelling (Brit) o mechanical (US) pencil; (: bolígrafo) Biro®
lápida ['lapiða] nf stone; **~ conmemorativa** memorial stone; **~ mortuoria** headstone
lapidar [lapi'ðar] vt to stone; (Tec) to polish, lap
lapidario, -a [lapi'ðarjo, a] adj, nm lapidary
lápiz ['lapiθ] nm pencil; **~ de color** coloured pencil; **~ de labios** lipstick; **~ óptico** o **luminoso** light pen
lapón, -ona [la'pon, ona] adj Lapp ■ nm/f Laplander, Lapp ■ nm (Ling) Lapp
Laponia [la'ponja] nf Lapland
lapso ['lapso] nm lapse; (error) error; **~ de tiempo** interval of time
lapsus ['lapsus] nm inv error, mistake
LAR [lar] nf abr (Esp Jur) = **Ley de Arrendamientos Rústicos**
largamente [larɣa'mente] adv for a long time; (relatar) at length
largar [lar'ɣar] vt (soltar) to release; (aflojar) to loosen; (lanzar) to launch; (fam) to let fly; (velas) to unfurl; (Am) to throw; **largarse** vr (fam) to beat it; **largarse a** (Am) to start to
largo, -a ['larɣo, a] adj (longitud) long; (tiempo) lengthy; (persona: alta) tall; (: fig) generous

■ *nm* length; (*Mus*) largo; **dos años largos** two long years; **a ~ plazo** in the long term; **tiene nueve metros de ~** it is nine metres long; **a lo ~** (*posición*) lengthways; **a lo ~ de** along; (*tiempo*) all through, throughout; **a la larga** in the long run; **me dio largas con una promesa** she put me off with a promise; **¡~ de aquí!** (*fam*) clear off!

largometraje [larɣome'traxe] *nm* full-length o feature film

largue *etc* ['larɣe] *vb ver* **largar**

larguero [lar'ɣero] *nm* (*Arq*) main beam, chief support; (*de puerta*) jamb; (*Deporte*) crossbar; (*de cama*) bolster

largueza [lar'ɣeθa] *nf* generosity

larguirucho, -a [larɣi'rutʃo, a] *adj* lanky, gangling

larquísimo, -a [lar'ɣisimo, a] *adj superlativo de* **largo**

largura [lar'ɣura] *nf* length

laringe [la'rinxe] *nf* larynx

laringitis [larin'xitis] *nf* laryngitis

larva ['larβa] *nf* larva

las [las] *artículo definido fpl* the ■ *pron* them; **~ que cantan** the ones/women/girls who sing

lasaña [la'saɲa] *nf* lasagne, lasagna

lasca ['laska] *nf* chip of stone

lascivia [las'θiβja] *nf* lewdness; (*lujuria*) lust; (*fig*) playfulness

lascivo, -a [las'θiβo, a] *adj* lewd

láser ['laser] *nm* laser

Las Palmas *nf* Las Palmas

lástima ['lastima] *nf* (*pena*) pity; **dar ~** to be pitiful; **es una ~ que** it's a pity that; **¡qué ~!** what a pity!; **estar hecho una ~** to be a sorry sight

lastimar [lasti'mar] *vt* (*herir*) to wound; (*ofender*) to offend; **lastimarse** *vr* to hurt o.s.

lastimero, -a [lasti'mero, a] *adj* pitiful, pathetic

lastre ['lastre] *nm* (*Tec, Naut*) ballast; (*fig*) dead weight

lata ['lata] *nf* (*metal*) tin; (*envase*) tin, can; (*fam*) nuisance; **en ~** tinned; **dar (la) ~** to be a nuisance

latente [la'tente] *adj* latent

lateral [late'ral] *adj* side, lateral ■ *nm* (*Teat*) wings *pl*

latido [la'tiðo] *nm* (*del corazón*) beat; (*de herida*) throb(bing)

latifundio [lati'fundjo] *nm* large estate

latifundista [latifun'dista] *nm/f* owner of a large estate

latigazo [lati'ɣaθo] *nm* (*golpe*) lash; (*sonido*) crack; (*fig: regaño*) dressing-down

látigo ['latiɣo] *nm* whip

latiguillo [lati'ɣiʎo] *nm* (*Teat*) hamming

latín [la'tin] *nm* Latin; **saber (mucho) ~** (*fam*) to be pretty sharp

latinajo [lati'naxo] *nm* dog Latin; **echar latinajos** to come out with Latin words

latino, -a [la'tino, a] *adj* Latin

Latinoamérica [latinoa'merika] *nf* Latin America

latinoamericano, -a [latinoameri'kano, a] *adj, nm/f* Latin American

latir [la'tir] *vi* (*corazón, pulso*) to beat

latitud [lati'tuð] *nf* (*Geo*) latitude; (*fig*) breadth, extent

lato, -a ['lato, a] *adj* broad

latón [la'ton] *nm* brass

latoso, -a [la'toso, a] *adj* (*molesto*) annoying; (*aburrido*) boring

latrocinio [latro'θinjo] *nm* robbery

LAU *nf abr* (*Esp Jur*) **= Ley de Arrendamientos Urbanos**

laúd [la'uð] *nm* lute

laudatorio, -a [lauða'torjo, a] *adj* laudatory

laudo ['lauðo] *nm* (*Jur*) decision, finding

laurear [laure'ar] *vt* to honour, reward

laurel [lau'rel] *nm* (*Bot*) laurel; (*Culin*) bay

Lausana [lau'sana] *nf* Lausanne

lava ['laβa] *nf* lava

lavable [la'βaβle] *adj* washable

lavabo [la'βaβo] *nm* (*jofaina*) washbasin; (*retrete*) lavatory (*Brit*), toilet (*Brit*), washroom (*US*)

lavadero [laβa'ðero] *nm* laundry

lavado [la'βaðo] *nm* washing; (*de ropa*) wash, laundry; (*Arte*) wash; **~ de cerebro** brainwashing

lavadora [laβa'ðora] *nf* washing machine

lavanda [la'βanda] *nf* lavender

lavandería [laβande'ria] *nf* laundry; **~ automática** launderette

lavaparabrisas [laβapara'βrisas] *nm inv* windscreen washer

lavaplatos [laβa'platos] *nm inv* dishwasher

lavar [la'βar] *vt* to wash; (*borrar*) to wipe away; **lavarse** *vr* to wash o.s.; **lavarse las manos** to wash one's hands; (*fig*) to wash one's hands of it; **~ y marcar** (*pelo*) to shampoo and set; **~ en seco** to dry-clean

lavativa [laβa'tiβa] *nf* (*Med*) enema

lavavajillas [laβaβa'xiʎas] *nm inv* dishwasher

laxante [lak'sante] *nm* laxative

laxitud [laksi'tuð] *nf* laxity, slackness

lazada [la'θaða] *nf* bow

lazarillo [laθa'riʎo] *nm*: **perro de ~** guide dog

lazo ['laθo] *nm* knot; (*lazada*) bow; (*para animales*) lasso; (*trampa*) snare; (*vínculo*) tie; **~ corredizo** slipknot

lb *abr* **= libra**

LBE *nf abr* (*Esp Jur*) = **Ley Básica de Empleo**

lbs *abr* = **libras**

L/C *abr* (= *Letra de Crédito*) B/E

Lda., Ldo. *abr* = **Licenciado, a**

le [le] *pron* (*directo*) him (*o* her); (: *en relación a usted*) you; (*indirecto*) to him (*o* her *o* it); (: *a usted*) to you

leal [le'al] *adj* loyal

lealtad [leal'taθ] *nf* loyalty

lebrel [le'βrel] *nm* greyhound

lección [lek'θjon] *nf* lesson; **~ práctica** object lesson; **dar lecciones** to teach, give lessons; **dar una ~ a algn** (*fig*) to teach sb a lesson

leche ['letʃe] *nf* milk; (*fam!*) semen, spunk (!); **dar una ~ a algn** (*fam*) to belt sb; **estar de mala ~** (*fam*) to be in a foul mood; **tener mala ~** (*fam*) to be a nasty piece of work; **~ condensada/en polvo** condensed/powdered milk; **~ desnatada** skimmed milk; **~ de magnesia** milk of magnesia; **¡~!** hell!

lechera [le'tʃera] *nf ver* **lechero**

lechería [letʃe'ria] *nf* dairy

lechero, -a [le'tʃero, a] *adj* milk *cpd* ■ *nm* milkman ■ *nf* (*vendedora*) milkwoman; (*recipiente*) milk pan; (*para servir*) milk churn

lecho ['letʃo] *nm* (*cama, de río*) bed; (*Geo*) layer; **~ mortuorio** deathbed

lechón [le'tʃon] *nm* sucking (*Brit*) *o* suckling (*US*) pig

lechoso, -a [le'tʃoso, a] *adj* milky

lechuga [le'tʃuɣa] *nf* lettuce

lechuza [le'tʃuθa] *nf* (*barn*) owl

lectivo, -a [lek'tiβo, a] *adj* (*horas*) teaching *cpd*; **año** *o* **curso ~** (*Escol*) school year; (*Univ*) academic year

lector, a [lek'tor, a] *nm/f* reader; (*Escol, Univ*) (*conversation*) assistant ■ *nm*: **~ óptico de caracteres** (*Inform*) optical character reader ■ *nf*: **lectora de fichas** (*Inform*) card reader

lectura [lek'tura] *nf* reading; **~ de marcas sensibles** (*Inform*) mark sensing

leer [le'er] *vt* to read; **~ entre líneas** to read between the lines

legación [leɣa'θjon] *nf* legation

legado [le'ɣaðo] *nm* (*don*) bequest; (*herencia*) legacy; (*enviado*) legate

legajo [le'ɣaxo] *nm* file, bundle (of papers)

legal [le'ɣal] *adj* legal, lawful; (*persona*) trustworthy

legalice *etc* [leɣa'liθe] *vb ver* **legalizar**

legalidad [leɣali'ðað] *nf* legality

legalizar [leɣali'θar] *vt* to legalize; (*documento*) to authenticate

legaña [le'ɣaɲa] *nf* sleep (*in eyes*)

legar [le'ɣar] *vt* to bequeath, leave

legatario, -a [leɣa'tarjo, a] *nm/f* legatee

legendario, -a [lexen'darjo, a] *adj* legendary

legible [le'xiβle] *adj* legible; **~ por máquina** (*Inform*) machine-readable

legión [le'xjon] *nf* legion

legionario, -a [lexjo'narjo, a] *adj* legionary ■ *nm* legionnaire

legislación [lexisla'θjon] *nf* legislation; (*leyes*) laws *pl*; **~ antimonopolio** (*Com*) anti-trust legislation

legislar [lexis'lar] *vt* to legislate

legislativo, -a [lexisla'tiβo, a] *adj*: (*elecciones*) **legislativas** = general election

legislatura [lexisla'tura] *nf* (*Pol*) period of office

legitimar [lexiti'mar] *vt* to legitimize

legítimo, -a [le'xitimo, a] *adj* (*genuino*) authentic; (*legal*) legitimate, rightful

lego, -a ['leɣo, a] *adj* (*Rel*) secular; (*ignorante*) ignorant ■ *nm* layman

legua ['leɣwa] *nf* league; **se ve** (*o* **nota**) **a la ~** you can tell (it) a mile off

legue *etc* ['leɣe] *vb ver* **legar**

leguleyo [leɣu'lejo] *nm* (*pey*) petty *o* shyster (*US*) lawyer

legumbres [le'ɣumbres] *nfpl* pulses

leído, -a [le'iðo, a] *adj* well-read

lejanía [lexa'nia] *nf* distance

lejano, -a [le'xano, a] *adj* far-off; (*en el tiempo*) distant; (*fig*) remote; **L~ Oriente** Far East

lejía [le'xia] *nf* bleach

lejísimos [le'xisimos] *adv* a long, long way

lejos ['lexos] *adv* far, far away; **a lo ~** in the distance; **de** *o* **desde ~** from a distance; **está muy ~** it's a long way (away); **¿está ~?** is it far?; **~ de** *prep* far from

lelo, -a ['lelo, a] *adj* silly ■ *nm/f* idiot

lema ['lema] *nm* motto; (*Pol*) slogan

lencería [lenθe'ria] *nf* (*telas*) linen, drapery; (*ropa interior*) lingerie

lendakari [lenda'kari] *nm head of the Basque Autonomous Government*

lengua ['lengwa] *nf* tongue; **~ materna** mother tongue; **~ de tierra** (*Geo*) spit *o* tongue of land; **dar a la ~** to chatter; **morderse la ~** to hold one's tongue; **sacar la ~ a algn** (*fig*) to cock a snook at sb; *see note*

● **LENGUA**

●
● Under the Spanish constitution *lenguas*
● *cooficiales* or *oficiales* enjoy the same status
● as *castellano* in those regions which have
● retained their own distinct language,
● ie in Galicia, *gallego*; in the Basque
● Country, *euskera*; in Catalonia and the
● Balearic Islands, *catalán*. The regional
● governments actively promote their own
● language through the media and the

education system. Of the three regions with their own language, Catalonia has the highest number of people who speak the *lengua cooficial*.

lenguado [len'gwaðo] *nm* sole

lenguaje [len'gwaxe] *nm* language; (*forma de hablar*) (mode of) speech; ~ **comercial** business language; ~ **ensamblador** o **de alto nivel** (*Inform*) high-level language; ~ **máquina** (*Inform*) machine language; ~ **original** source language; ~ **periodístico** journalese; ~ **de programación** (*Inform*) programming language; **en ~ llano** ≈ in plain English

lenguaraz [lengwa'raθ] *adj* talkative; (*pey*) foul-mouthed

lengüeta [len'gweta] *nf* (*Anat*) epiglottis; (*de zapatos, Mus*) tongue

lenidad [leni'ðað] *nf* lenience

Leningrado [lenin'graðo] *nm* Leningrad

lente ['lente] *nm o nf* lens; (*lupa*) magnifying glass; **lentes** *nmpl* glasses; **lentes de contacto** contact lenses; **lentes progresivas** varifocal lenses

lenteja [len'texa] *nf* lentil

lentejuela [lente'xwela] *nf* sequin

lentilla [len'tiʎa] *nf* contact lens

lentitud [lenti'tuð] *nf* slowness; **con ~** slowly

lento, -a ['lento, a] *adj* slow

leña ['leɲa] *nf* firewood; **dar ~ a** to thrash; **echar ~ al fuego** to add fuel to the flames

leñador, a [leɲa'ðor, a] *nm/f* woodcutter

leño ['leɲo] *nm* (*trozo de árbol*) log; (*madera*) timber; (*fig*) blockhead

Leo ['leo] *nm* (*Astro*) Leo

león [le'on] *nm* lion; ~ **marino** sea lion

leonera [leo'nera] *nf* (*jaula*) lion's cage; **parece una ~** it's shockingly dirty

leonés, -esa [leo'nes, esa] *adj, nm/f* Leonese ■ *nm* (*Ling*) Leonese

leonino, -a [leo'nino, a] *adj* leonine

leopardo [leo'parðo] *nm* leopard

leotardos [leo'tarðos] *nmpl* tights

lepra ['lepra] *nf* leprosy

leprosería [leprose'ria] *nf* leper colony

leproso, -a [le'proso, a] *nm/f* leper

lerdo, -a ['lerðo, a] *adj* (*lento*) slow; (*patoso*) clumsy

leridano, -a [leri'ðano, a] *adj* of o from Lérida ■ *nm/f* native o inhabitant of Lérida

les [les] *pron* (*directo*) them; (: *en relación a ustedes*) you; (*indirecto*) to them; (: *a ustedes*) to you

lesbiana [les'βjana] *nf* lesbian

lesión [le'sjon] *nf* wound, lesion; (*Deporte*) injury

lesionado, -a [lesjo'naðo, a] *adj* injured ■ *nm/f* injured person

lesionar [lesjo'nar] *vt* (*dañar*) to hurt; (*herir*) to wound; **lesionarse** *vr* to get hurt

letal [le'tal] *adj* lethal

letanía [leta'nia] *nf* litany; (*retahíla*) long list

letárgico, -a [le'tarxiko, a] *adj* lethargic

letargo [le'taryo] *nm* lethargy

letón, -ona [le'ton, ona] *adj, nm/f* Latvian ■ *nm* (*Ling*) Latvian

Letonia [le'tonja] *nf* Latvia

letra ['letra] *nf* letter; (*escritura*) handwriting; (*Com*) letter, bill, draft; (*Mus*) lyrics *pl*; **letras** *nfpl* (*Univ*) arts; ~ **bastardilla/negrilla** italics *pl*/bold type; ~ **de cambio** bill of exchange; ~ **de imprenta** print; ~ **inicial/mayúscula/minúscula** initial/capital/small letter; **lo tomó al pie de la ~** he took it literally; ~ **bancaria** (*Com*) bank draft; ~ **de patente** (*Com*) letters patent *pl*; **escribir cuarto letras a algn** to drop a line to sb

letrado, -a [le'traðo, a] *adj* learned; (*fam*) pedantic ■ *nm/f* lawyer

letrero [le'trero] *nm* (*cartel*) sign; (*etiqueta*) label

letrina [le'trina] *nf* latrine

leucemia [leu'θemja] *nf* leukaemia

leucocito [leuko'θito] *nm* white blood cell, leucocyte

leva ['leβa] *nf* (*Naut*) weighing anchor; (*Mil*) levy; (*Tec*) lever

levadizo, -a [leβa'ðiθo, a] *adj*: **puente ~** drawbridge

levadura [leβa'ðura] *nf* yeast, leaven; ~ **de cerveza** brewer's yeast

levantamiento [leβanta'mjento] *nm* raising, lifting; (*rebelión*) revolt, rising; (*Geo*) survey; ~ **de pesos** weightlifting

levantar [leβan'tar] *vt* (*gen*) to raise; (*del suelo*) to pick up; (*hacia arriba*) to lift (up); (*plan*) to make, draw up; (*mesa*) to clear; (*campamento*) to strike; (*fig*) to cheer up, hearten; **levantarse** *vr* to get up; (*enderezarse*) to straighten up; (*rebelarse*) to rebel; (*sesión*) to be adjourned; (*niebla*) to lift; (*viento*) to rise; **levantarse (de la cama)** to get up, get out of bed; ~ **el ánimo** to cheer up

levante [le'βante] *nm* east; (*viento*) east wind; **el L~** *region of Spain extending from Castellón to Murcia*

levantino, -a [leβan'tino, a] *adj* of o from the *Levante* ■ *nm/f*: **los levantinos** the people of the *Levante*

levar [le'βar] *vi* to weigh anchor

leve ['leβe] *adj* light; (*fig*) trivial; (*mínimo*) slight

levedad [leβe'ðað] *nf* lightness; (*fig*) levity

levita [le'βita] *nf* frock coat

léxico, -a ['leksiko, a] *adj* lexical ◾ *nm* (*vocabulario*) vocabulary; (*Ling*) lexicon

ley [lei] *nf* (*gen*) law; (*metal*) standard; **decreto--** decree law; **de buena ~** (*fig*) genuine; **según la ~** in accordance with the law, by law, in law

leyenda [le'jenda] *nf* legend; (*Tip*) inscription

leyendo *etc* [le'jendo] *vb ver* **leer**

liar [li'ar] *vt* to tie (up); (*unir*) to bind; (*envolver*) to wrap (up); (*enredar*) to confuse; (*cigarrillo*) to roll; **liarse** *vr* (*fam*) to get involved; (*confundirse*) to get mixed up; **liarse a palos** to get involved in a fight

lib. *abr* (= *libro*) bk.

libanés, -esa [liβa'nes, esa] *adj, nm/f* Lebanese

Líbano ['liβano] *nm*: **el ~** the Lebanon

libar [li'βar] *vt* to suck

libelo [li'βelo] *nm* satire, lampoon; (*Jur*) petition

libélula [li'βelula] *nf* dragonfly

liberación [liβera'θjon] *nf* liberation; (*de la cárcel*) release

liberado, -a [liβe'raðo, a] *adj* liberated; (*Com*) paid-up, paid-in (*US*)

liberal [liβe'ral] *adj, nm/f* liberal

liberar [liβe'rar] *vt* to liberate

libertad [liβer'tað] *nf* liberty, freedom; **~ de asociación/de culto/de prensa/ de comercio/de palabra** freedom of association/of worship/of the press/of trade/ of speech; **~ condicional** probation; **~ bajo palabra** parole; **~ bajo fianza** bail; **estar en ~** to be free; **poner a algn en ~** to set sb free

libertador, a [liβerta'ðor, a] *adj* liberating ◾ *nm/f* liberator; **El L~** (*Am*) The Liberator

libertar [liβer'tar] *vt* (*preso*) to set free; (*de una obligación*) to release; (*eximir*) to exempt

libertinaje [liβerti'naxe] *nm* licentiousness

libertino, -a [liβer'tino, a] *adj* permissive ◾ *nm/f* permissive person

Libia ['liβja] *nf* Libya

libidinoso, -a [liβiði'noso, a] *adj* lustful; (*viejo*) lecherous

libido [li'βiðo] *nf* libido

libio, -a ['liβjo, a] *adj, nm/f* Libyan

libra ['liβra] *nf* pound; **L~** (*Astro*) Libra; **~ esterlina** pound sterling

librador, a [liβra'ðor, a] *nm/f* drawer

libranza [li'βranθa] *nf* (*Com*) draft; (*letra de cambio*) bill of exchange

librar [li'βrar] *vt* (*de peligro*) to save; (*batalla*) to wage, fight; (*de impuestos*) to exempt; (*cheque*) to make out; (*Jur*) to exempt; **librarse** *vr*: **librarse de** to escape from, free o.s. from;

de buena nos hemos librado we're well out of that

libre ['liβre] *adj* (*gen*) free; (*lugar*) unoccupied; (*tiempo*) spare; (*asiento*) vacant; (*Com*): **~ a bordo** free on board; **~ de franqueo** post-free; **~ de impuestos** free of tax; **tiro ~** free kick; **los 100 metros ~** the 100 metres freestyle (race); **al aire ~** in the open air; **¿estás ~?** are you free?

librecambio [liβre'kambjo] *nm* free trade

librecambista [liβrekam'bista] *adj* free-trade *cpd* ◾ *nm* free-trader

librería [liβre'ria] *nf* (*tienda*) bookshop; (*estante*) bookcase; **~ de ocasión** secondhand bookshop

librero, -a [li'βrero, a] *nm/f* bookseller

libreta [li'βreta] *nf* notebook; (*pan*) one-pound loaf; **~ de ahorros** savings book

libro ['liβro] *nm* book; **~ de actas** minute book; **~ de bolsillo** paperback; **~ de cabecera** bedside book; **~ de caja** (*Com*) cashbook; **~ de caja auxiliar** (*Com*) petty cash book; **~ de cocina** cookery book (*Brit*), cookbook (*US*); **~ de consulta** reference book; **~ de cuentas** account book; **~ de cuentos** storybook; **~ de cheques** cheque (*Brit*) o check (*US*) book; **~ diario** journal; **~ de entradas y salidas** (*Com*) daybook; **~ de honor** visitors' book; **~ electrónico** e-book; **~ mayor** (*Com*) general ledger; **~ de reclamaciones** complaints book; **~ de texto** textbook

Lic. *abr* = **Licenciado, a**

licencia [li'θenθja] *nf* (*gen*) licence; (*permiso*) permission; **~ por enfermedad/con goce de sueldo** sick/paid leave; **~ de armas/de caza** gun/game licence; **~ de exportación** (*Com*) export licence; **~ poética** poetic licence

licenciado, -a [liθen'θjaðo, a] *adj* licensed ◾ *nm/f* graduate; **L~ en Filosofía y Letras** = Bachelor of Arts; *see note*

◉ **LICENCIADO**

◉
◉ When students finish University after
◉ an average of five years they receive the
◉ degree of *licenciado*. If the course is only
◉ three years such as Nursing, or if they
◉ choose not to do the optional two-year
◉ specialization, they are awarded the
◉ degree of *diplomado*. *Cursos de posgrado*,
◉ postgraduate courses, are becoming
◉ increasingly popular, especially one-year
◉ specialist courses called *masters*.

licenciar [liθen'θjar] *vt* (*empleado*) to dismiss; (*permitir*) to permit, allow; (*soldado*) to discharge; (*estudiante*) to confer a degree upon; **licenciarse** *vr*: **licenciarse en letras** to get an arts degree

licenciatura [liθenθja'tura] *nf* (*título*) degree; (*estudios*) degree course

licencioso, -a [liθen'θjoso, a] *adj* licentious

liceo [li'θeo] *nm* (*esp Am*) (high) school

licitación [liθita'θjon] *nf* bidding; (*oferta*) tender, offer

licitador [liθita'ðor] *nm* bidder

licitar [liθi'tar] *vt* to bid for ■ *vi* to bid

lícito, -a ['liθito, a] *adj* (*legal*) lawful; (*justo*) fair, just; (*permisible*) permissible

licor [li'kor] *nm* spirits *pl* (*Brit*), liquor (*US*); (*con hierbas etc*) liqueur

licra® ['likra] *nf* Lycra®

licuadora [likwa'ðora] *nf* blender

licuar [li'kwar] *vt* to liquidize

lid [lið] *nf* combat; (*fig*) controversy

líder ['liðer] *nm/f* leader

liderato [liðe'rato] *nm* = **liderazgo**

liderazgo [liðe'raθyo] *nm* leadership

lidia ['liðja] *nf* bullfighting; (*una lidia*) bullfight; **toros de** ~ fighting bulls

lidiar [li'ðjar] *vt, vi* to fight

liebre ['ljeβre] *nf* hare; **dar gato por** ~ to con

Lieja ['ljexa] *nf* Liège

lienzo ['ljenθo] *nm* linen; (*Arte*) canvas; (*Arq*) wall

lifting ['liftin] *nm* facelift

liga ['liya] *nf* (*de medias*) garter, suspender; (*confederación*) league; (*Am*: *goma*) rubber band

ligadura [liya'ðura] *nf* bond, tie; (*Med, Mus*) ligature

ligamento [liya'mento] *nm* (*Anat*) ligament; (*atadura*) tie; (*unión*) bond

ligar [li'yar] *vt* (*atar*) to tie; (*unir*) to join; (*Med*) to bind up; (*Mus*) to slur; (*fam*) to get off with, pick up ■ *vi* to mix, blend; (*fam*) to get off with sb; (*2 personas*) to get off with one another; **ligarse** *vr*: **ligarse a** to commit o.s.; ~ **con** (*fam*) to get off with, pick up; **ligarse a algn** to get off with *o* pick up sb

ligereza [lixe'reθa] *nf* lightness; (*rapidez*) swiftness; (*agilidad*) agility; (*superficialidad*) flippancy

ligero, -a [li'xero, a] *adj* (*de peso*) light; (*tela*) thin; (*rápido*) swift, quick; (*ágil*) agile, nimble; (*de importancia*) slight; (*de carácter*) flippant, superficial ■ *adv* quickly, swiftly; **a la ligera** superficially; **juzgar a la ligera** to jump to conclusions

light ['lait] *adj inv* (*cigarrillo*) low-tar; (*comida*) diet *cpd*

ligón [li'yon] *nm* (*fam*) Romeo

ligue *etc* ['liye] *vb ver* **ligar** ■ *nm/f* boyfriend/girlfriend ■ *nm* (*persona*) pick-up

liguero [li'yero] *nm* suspender (*Brit*) *o* garter (*US*) belt

lija ['lixa] *nf* (*Zool*) dogfish; (**papel de**) ~ sandpaper

lijar [li'xar] *vt* to sand

lila ['lila] *adj inv, nf* lilac ■ *nm* (*fam*) twit

lima ['lima] *nf* file; (*Bot*) lime; ~ **de uñas** nail file; **comer como una** ~ to eat like a horse

limar [li'mar] *vt* to file; (*alisar*) to smooth over; (*fig*) to polish up

limbo ['limbo] *nm* (*Rel*) limbo; **estar en el** ~ to be on another planet

limitación [limita'θjon] *nf* limitation, limit; ~ **de velocidad** speed limit

limitado, -a [limi'taðo, a] *adj* limited; **sociedad limitada** (*Com*) limited company

limitar [limi'tar] *vt* to limit; (*reducir*) to reduce, cut down ■ *vi*: ~ **con** to border on; **limitarse** *vr*: **limitarse a** to limit *o* confine o.s. to

límite ['limite] *nm* (*gen*) limit; (*fin*) end; (*frontera*) border; **como** ~ at (the) most; (*fecha*) at the latest; **no tener límites** to know no bounds; ~ **de crédito** (*Com*) credit limit; ~ **de página** (*Inform*) page break; ~ **de velocidad** speed limit

limítrofe [li'mitrofe] *adj* bordering, neighbouring

limón [li'mon] *nm* lemon ■ *adj*: **amarillo** ~ lemon-yellow

limonada [limo'naða] *nf* lemonade

limonero [limo'nero] *nm* lemon tree

limosna [li'mosna] *nf* alms *pl*; **pedir** ~ to beg; **vivir de** ~ to live on charity

limpiabotas [limpja'βotas] *nm/f inv* bootblack (*Brit*), shoeshine boy/girl

limpiacristales [limpjakris'tales] *nm inv* (*detergente*) window cleaner

limpiador, a [limpja'ðor, a] *adj* cleaning, cleansing ■ *nm/f* cleaner

limpiaparabrisas [limpjapara'βrisas] *nm inv* windscreen (*Brit*) *o* windshield (*US*) wiper

limpiar [lim'pjar] *vt* to clean; (*con trapo*) to wipe; (*quitar*) to wipe away; (*zapatos*) to shine, polish; (*casa*) to tidy up; (*Inform*) to debug; (*fig*) to clean up; (*: purificar*) to cleanse, purify; (*Mil*) to mop up; ~ **en seco** to dry-clean

limpieza [lim'pjeθa] *nf* (*estado*) cleanliness; (*acto*) cleaning; (*: de las calles*) cleansing; (*: de zapatos*) polishing; (*habilidad*) skill; (*fig: Policía*) clean-up; (*pureza*) purity; (*Mil*): **operación de** ~ mopping-up operation; ~ **étnica** ethnic cleansing; ~ **en seco** dry cleaning

limpio, -a ['limpjo, a] *adj* clean; (*moralmente*) pure; (*ordenado*) tidy; (*despejado*) clear; (*Com*) clear, net; (*fam*) honest ■ *adv*: **jugar** ~ to play fair; **pasar a** ~ to make a fair copy; **sacar**

235

algo en ~ to get benefit from sth; **~ de** free from

linaje [li'naxe] *nm* lineage, family

linaza [li'naθa] *nf* linseed; **aceite de ~** linseed oil

lince ['linθe] *nm* lynx; **ser un ~** (*fig: observador*) to be very observant; (: *astuto*) to be shrewd

linchar [lin'tʃar] *vt* to lynch

lindante [lin'dante] *adj* adjoining; **~ con** bordering on

lindar [lin'dar] *vi* to adjoin; **~ con** to border on; (*Arq*) to abut on

linde ['linde] *nm o nf* boundary

lindero, -a [lin'dero, a] *adj* adjoining ■ *nm* boundary

lindo, -a ['lindo, a] *adj* pretty, lovely ■ *adv* (*esp Am: fam*) nicely, very well; **canta muy ~** (*Am*) he sings beautifully; **se divertían de lo ~** they enjoyed themselves enormously

línea ['linea] *nf* (*gen, moral, Pol etc*) line; (*talle*) figure; (*Inform*): **en ~** on line; **fuera de ~** off line; **~ de estado** status line; **~ de formato** format line; **~ aérea** airline; **~ de alto el fuego** ceasefire line; **~ de fuego** firing line; **~ de meta** goal line; (*de carrera*) finishing line; **~ de montaje** assembly line; **~ dura** (*Pol*) hard line; **~ recta** straight line; **la ~ de 2008** (*moda*) the 2008 look

lineal [line'al] *adj* linear

lingote [lin'gote] *nm* ingot

lingüista [lin'gwista] *nm/f* linguist

lingüística [lin'gwistika] *nf* linguistics *sg*

linimento [lini'mento] *nm* liniment

lino ['lino] *nm* linen; (*Bot*) flax

linóleo [li'noleo] *nm* lino, linoleum

linterna [lin'terna] *nf* lantern, lamp; **~ eléctrica** *o* **a pilas** torch (*Brit*), flashlight (*US*)

lío ['lio] *nm* bundle; (*desorden*) muddle, mess; (*fam: follón*) fuss; (: *relación amorosa*) affair; **armar un ~** to make a fuss; **meterse en un ~** to get into a jam; **tener un ~ con algn** to be having an affair with sb

lipotimia [lipo'timja] *nf* blackout

liquen ['liken] *nm* lichen

liquidación [likiða'θjon] *nf* liquidation; (*de cuenta*) settlement; **venta de ~** clearance sale

liquidar [liki'ðar] *vt* (*Química*) to liquefy; (*Com*) to liquidate; (*deudas*) to pay off; (*empresa*) to wind up; **~ a algn** to bump sb off, rub sb out (*fam*)

liquidez [liki'ðeθ] *nf* liquidity

líquido, -a ['likiðo, a] *adj* liquid; (*ganancia*) net ■ *nm* liquid; (*Com: efectivo*) ready cash *o* money; (: *ganancia*) net amount *o* profit; **~ imponible** net taxable income

lira ['lira] *nf* (*Mus*) lyre; (*moneda*) lira

lírico, -a ['liriko, a] *adj* lyrical

lirio ['lirjo] *nm* (*Bot*) iris

lirismo [li'rismo] *nm* lyricism; (*sentimentalismo*) sentimentality

lirón [li'ron] *nm* (*Zool*) dormouse; (*fig*) sleepyhead

Lisboa [lis'βoa] *nf* Lisbon

lisboeta [lisβo'eta] *adj* of *o* from Lisbon ■ *nm/f* native *o* inhabitant of Lisbon

lisiado, -a [li'sjaðo, a] *adj* injured ■ *nm/f* cripple

lisiar [li'sjar] *vt* to maim; **lisiarse** *vr* to injure o.s.

liso, -a ['liso, a] *adj* (*terreno*) flat; (*cabello*) straight; (*superficie*) even; (*tela*) plain; **lisa y llanamente** in plain language, plainly

lisonja [li'sonxa] *nf* flattery

lisonjear [lisonxe'ar] *vt* to flatter; (*fig*) to please

lisonjero, -a [lison'xero, a] *adj* flattering; (*agradable*) gratifying, pleasing ■ *nm/f* flatterer

lista ['lista] *nf* list; (*de alumnos*) school register; (*de libros*) catalogue; (*de correos*) poste restante; (*de platos*) menu; (*de precios*) price list; **pasar ~** to call the roll; (*Escol*) to call the register; **~ de correos** poste restante; **~ de direcciones** mailing list; **~ electoral** electoral roll; **~ de espera** waiting list; **tela a listas** striped material

listado, -a [lis'taðo, a] *adj* striped ■ *nm* (*Com, Inform*) listing; **~ paginado** (*Inform*) paged listing

listar [lis'tar] *vt* (*Inform*) to list

listo, -a ['listo, a] *adj* (*perspicaz*) smart, clever; (*preparado*) ready; **~ para usar** ready-to-use; **¿estás ~?** are you ready?; **pasarse de ~** to be too clever by half

listón [lis'ton] *nm* (*de tela*) ribbon; (*de madera, metal*) strip

litera [li'tera] *nf* (*en barco, tren*) berth; (*en dormitorio*) bunk, bunk bed

literal [lite'ral] *adj* literal

literario, -a [lite'rarjo, a] *adj* literary

literato, -a [lite'rato, a] *nm/f* writer

literatura [litera'tura] *nf* literature

litigante [liti'ɣante] *nm/f* litigant, claimant

litigar [liti'ɣar] *vt* to fight ■ *vi* (*Jur*) to go to law; (*fig*) to dispute, argue

litigio [li'tixjo] *nm* (*Jur*) lawsuit; (*fig*): **en ~ con** in dispute with

litigue *etc* [li'tiɣe] *vb ver* **litigar**

litografía [litoɣra'fia] *nf* lithography; (*una litografía*) lithograph

litoral [lito'ral] *adj* coastal ■ *nm* coast, seaboard

litro ['litro] *nm* litre, liter (*US*)

Lituania [li'twanja] *nf* Lithuania

lituano, -a [li'twano, a] *adj, nm/f* Lithuanian ∎ *nm* (*Ling*) Lithuanian

liturgia [li'turxja] *nf* liturgy

liviano, -a [li'βjano, a] *adj* (*persona*) fickle; (*cosa, objeto*) trivial; (*Am*) light

lívido, -a ['liβiðo, a] *adj* livid

living ['liβin] (*pl* **livings**) *nm* (*esp Am*) sitting room

Ll, ll ['eʎe] *nf former letter in the Spanish alphabet*

llaga ['ʎaɣa] *nf* wound

llagar [ʎa'ɣar] *vt* to make sore; (*herir*) to wound

llague *etc* ['ʎaɣe] *vb ver* **llagar**

llama ['ʎama] *nf* flame; (*fig*) passion; (*Zool*) llama; **en llamas** burning, ablaze

llamada [ʎa'maða] *nf* call; (*a la puerta*) knock; (: *al timbre*) ring; **~ a cobro revertido** reverse-charge call; **al orden** call to order; **~ a pie de página** reference note; **~ a procedimiento** (*Inform*) procedure call; **~ interurbana** trunk call

llamado [ʎa'maðo] *nm* (*Am*) (telephone) call; (*llamamiento*) appeal, call

llamamiento [ʎama'mjento] *nm* call; **hacer un ~ a algn para que haga algo** to appeal to sb to do sth

llamar [ʎa'mar] *vt* to call; (*convocar*) to summon; (*invocar*) to invoke; (*atraer con gesto*) to beckon; (*atención*) to attract; (*Telec: tb.* **llamar por teléfono**) to call, ring up, telephone; (*Mil*) to call up ∎ *vi* (*por teléfono*) to phone; (*a la puerta*) to knock (o ring); (*por señas*) to beckon; **llamarse** *vr* to be called, be named; **¿cómo se llama usted?** what's your name?; **¿quién llama?** (*Telec*) who's calling?, who's that?; **no me llama la atención** (*fam*) I don't fancy it

llamarada [ʎama'raða] *nf* (*llamas*) blaze; (*rubor*) flush; (*fig*) flare-up

llamativo, -a [ʎama'tiβo, a] *adj* showy; (*color*) loud

llamear [ʎame'ar] *vi* to blaze

llanamente [ʎana'mente] *adv* (*lisamente*) smoothly; (*sin ostentaciones*) plainly; (*sinceramente*) frankly; *ver tb* **liso**

llaneza [ʎa'neθa] *nf* (*gen*) simplicity; (*honestidad*) straightforwardness, frankness

llano, -a ['ʎano, a] *adj* (*superficie*) flat; (*persona*) straightforward; (*estilo*) clear ∎ *nm* plain, flat ground

llanta ['ʎanta] *nf* (wheel) rim; (*Am: neumático*) tyre; (: *cámara*) (inner) tube

llanto ['ʎanto] *nm* weeping; (*fig*) lamentation; (*canción*) dirge, lament

llanura [ʎa'nura] *nf* (*lisura*) flatness, smoothness; (*Geo*) plain

llave ['ʎaβe] *nf* key; (*de gas, agua*) tap (*Brit*),

faucet (*US*); (*Mecánica*) spanner; (*de la luz*) switch; (*Mus*) key; **~ inglesa** monkey wrench; **~ maestra** master key; **~ de contacto** (*Auto*) ignition key; **~ de paso** stopcock; **echar ~ a** to lock up

llavero [ʎa'βero] *nm* keyring

llavín [ʎa'βin] *nm* latchkey

llegada [ʎe'ɣaða] *nf* arrival

llegar [ʎe'ɣar] *vt* to bring up, bring over ∎ *vi* to arrive; (*bastar*) to be enough; **llegarse** *vr*: **llegarse a** to approach; **~ a** (*alcanzar*) to reach; to manage to, succeed in; **~ a saber** to find out; **~ a ser famoso/el jefe** to become famous/the boss; **~ a las manos** to come to blows; **~ a las manos de** to come into the hands of; **no llegues tarde** don't be late; **esta cuerda no llega** this rope isn't long enough

llegue *etc* ['ʎeɣe] *vb ver* **llegar**

llenar [ʎe'nar] *vt* to fill; (*superficie*) to cover; (*espacio, tiempo*) to fill, take up; (*formulario*) to fill in o out; (*fig*) to heap; **llenarse** *vr* to fill (up); **llenarse de** (*fam*) to stuff o.s. with

lleno, -a ['ʎeno, a] *adj* full, filled; (*repleto*) full up ∎ *nm* (*abundancia*) abundance; (*Teat*) full house; **dar de ~ contra un muro** to hit a wall head-on

llevadero, -a [ʎeβa'ðero, a] *adj* bearable, tolerable

llevar [ʎe'βar] *vt* to take; (*ropa*) to wear; (*cargar*) to carry; (*quitar*) to take away; (*en coche*) to drive; (*transportar*) to transport; (*ruta*) to follow, keep to; (*traer: dinero*) to carry; (*suj: camino etc*): **~ a** to lead to; (*Mat*) to carry; (*aguantar*) to bear; (*negocio*) to conduct, direct; to manage; **llevarse** *vr* to carry off, take away; **llevamos dos días aquí** we have been here for two days; **él me lleva dos años** he's two years older than me; **~ adelante** (*fig*) to carry forward; **~ por delante a uno** (*en coche etc*) to run sb over; (*fig*) to ride roughshod over sb; **~ la ventaja** to be winning o in the lead; **~ los libros** (*Com*) to keep the books; **llevo las de perder** I'm likely to lose; **no las lleva todas consigo** he's not all there; **nos llevó a cenar fuera** she took us out for a meal; **llevarse a uno por delante** (*atropellar*) to run sb over; **llevarse bien** to get on well (together)

llorar [ʎo'rar] *vt* to cry, weep ∎ *vi* to cry, weep; (*ojos*) to water; **~ a moco tendido** to sob one's heart out; **~ de risa** to cry with laughter

lloriquear [ʎorike'ar] *vi* to snivel, whimper

lloro ['ʎoro] *nm* crying, weeping

llorón, -ona [ʎo'ron, ona] *adj* tearful ∎ *nm/f* cry-baby

lloroso, -a [ʎo'roso, a] *adj* (*gen*) weeping,

237

tearful; (*triste*) sad, sorrowful

llover [ʎo'βer] *vi* to rain; ~ **a cántaros** *o* **a cubos** *o* **a mares** to rain cats and dogs, pour (down); **ser una cosa llovida del cielo** to be a godsend; **llueve sobre mojado** it never rains but it pours

llovizna [ʎo'βiθna] *nf* drizzle

lloviznar [ʎoβiθ'nar] *vi* to drizzle

llueve *etc* ['ʎweβe] *vb ver* **llover**

lluvia ['ʎuβja] *nf* rain; (*cantidad*) rainfall; (*fig: de balas etc*) hail, shower; ~ **radioactiva** radioactive fallout; **día de** ~ rainy day; **una** ~ **de regalos** a shower of gifts

lluvioso, -a [ʎu'βjoso, a] *adj* rainy

lo [lo] *artículo definido neutro*: **lo bueno** the good ■ *pron* (*en relación a una persona*) him; (*en relación a una cosa*) it; **lo mío** what is mine; **lo difícil es que** ... the difficult thing about it is that ...; **no saben lo aburrido que es** they don't know how boring it is; **viste a lo americano** he dresses in the American style; **lo de** that matter of; **lo que** what, that which; **toma lo que quieras** take what(ever) you want; **lo que sea** whatever; **¡toma lo que he dicho!** I stand by what I said!

loa ['loa] *nf* praise

loable [lo'aβle] *adj* praiseworthy

LOAPA [lo'apa] *nf abr* (*Esp Jur*) = **Ley Orgánica de Armonización del Proceso Autónomo**

loar [lo'ar] *vt* to praise

lobato [lo'βato] *nm* (*Zool*) wolf cub

lobo ['loβo] *nm* wolf; ~ **de mar** (*fig*) sea dog; ~ **marino** seal

lóbrego, -a ['loβreɣo, a] *adj* dark; (*fig*) gloomy

lóbulo ['loβulo] *nm* lobe

LOC *nm abr* (= *lector óptico de caracteres*) OCR

local [lo'kal] *adj* local ■ *nm* place, site; (*oficinas*) premises *pl*

localice *etc* [loka'liθe] *vb ver* **localizar**

localidad [lokali'ðað] *nf* (*barrio*) locality; (*lugar*) location; (*Teat*) seat, ticket

localizador *nm* (*de un vuelo*) booking reference, reservation code

localizar [lokali'θar] *vt* (*ubicar*) to locate, find; (*encontrar*) to find, track down; (*restringir*) to localize; (*situar*) to place

loción [lo'θjon] *nf* lotion, wash

loco, -a ['loko, a] *adj* mad; (*fig*) wild, mad ■ *nm/f* lunatic, madman(-woman); ~ **de atar**, ~ **de remate**, ~ **rematado** raving mad; **a lo** ~ without rhyme or reason; **ando** ~ **con el examen** the exam is driving me crazy; **estar** ~ **de alegría** to be overjoyed *o* over the moon

locomoción [lokomo'θjon] *nf* locomotion

locomotora [lokomo'tora] *nf* engine, locomotive

locuaz [lo'kwaθ] *adj* loquacious, talkative

locución [loku'θjon] *nf* expression

locura [lo'kura] *nf* madness; (*acto*) crazy act

locutor, a [loku'tor, a] *nm/f* (*Radio*) announcer; (*comentarista*) commentator; (*TV*) newscaster, newsreader

locutorio [loku'torjo] *nm* (*Telec*) telephone box *o* booth; (*negocio*) shop or internet café providing telephone services

lodo ['lodo] *nm* mud

logia ['loxja] *nf* (*Mil, de masones*) lodge; (*Arq*) loggia

lógico, -a ['loxiko, a] *adj* logical; (*correcto*) natural; (*razonable*) reasonable ■ *nm* logician ■ *nf* logic; **es** ~ **que** ... it stands to reason that ...; **ser una lógica aplastante** to be as clear as day

logístico, -a [lo'xistiko, a] *adj* logistical ■ *nf* logistics *pl*

logotipo [loɣo'tipo] *nm* logo

logrado, -a [lo'ɣraðo, a] *adj* accomplished

lograr [lo'ɣrar] *vt* (*obtener*) to get, obtain; (*conseguir*) to achieve, attain; ~ **hacer** to manage to do; ~ **que algn venga** to manage to get sb to come; ~ **acceso a** (*Inform*) to access

logro ['loɣro] *nm* achievement, success; (*Com*) profit

logroñés, -esa [loɣro'ɲes, esa] *adj* of *o* from Logroño ■ *nm/f* native *o* inhabitant of Logroño

Loira ['loira] *nm* Loire

loma ['loma] *nf* hillock, low ridge

Lombardía [lombar'ðia] *nf* Lombardy

lombriz [lom'briθ] *nf* (earth)worm

lomo ['lomo] *nm* (*de animal*) back; (*Culin: de cerdo*) pork loin; (: *de vaca*) rib steak; (*de libro*) spine

lona ['lona] *nf* canvas

loncha ['lontʃa] *nf* = **lonja**

lonche ['lontʃe] *nm* (*Am*) lunch

lonchería [lontʃe'ria] *nf* (*Am*) snack bar, diner (US)

londinense [londi'nense] *adj* London *cpd*, of *o* from London ■ *nm/f* Londoner

Londres ['londres] *nm* London

longaniza [longa'niθa] *nf* pork sausage

longevidad [lonxeβi'ðað] *nf* longevity

longitud [lonxi'tuð] *nf* length; (*Geo*) longitude; **tener tres metros de** ~ to be three metres long; ~ **de onda** wavelength; **salto de** ~ long jump

longitudinal [lonxituði'nal] *adj* longitudinal

lonja ['lonxa] *nf* slice; (*de tocino*) rasher; (*Com*) market, exchange; ~ **de pescado** fish market

lontananza [lonta'nanθa] *nf* background; **en** ~ far away, in the distance

Lorena [lo'rena] *nf* Lorraine

loro ['loro] nm parrot
los [los] artículo definido mpl the ■ pron them;
(en relación a ustedes) you; **mis libros y ~ de
usted** my books and yours
losa ['losa] nf stone; **~ sepulcral** gravestone
lote ['lote] nm portion, share; (Com) lot;
(Inform) batch
lotería [lote'ria] nf lottery; (juego) lotto; **le
tocó la ~** he won a big prize in the lottery;
(fig) he struck lucky; **~ nacional** national
lottery; **~ primitiva** (Esp) type of state-run
lottery; see note

● **LOTERÍA**

● Millions of pounds are spent every year
● on loterías, lotteries. There is the weekly
● Lotería Nacional which is very popular
● especially at Christmas. Other weekly
● lotteries are the Bono Loto and the (Lotería)
● Primitiva. One of the most famous lotteries
● is run by the wealthy and influential
● society for the blind, la ONCE, and the
● form is called el cupón de la ONCE or el cupón
● de los ciegos.

lotero, -a [lo'tero, a] nm/f seller of lottery
tickets
Lovaina [lo'βaina] nf Louvain
loza ['loθa] nf crockery; **~ fina** china
lozanía [loθa'nia] nf (lujo) luxuriance
lozano, -a [lo'θano, a] adj luxuriant;
(animado) lively
LPA sigla f (= Ley del Proceso Autonómico) law for the
autonomy of the regions
LRA sigla f = **Ley de Reforma Agraria**
LRU sigla f = **Ley de Reforma Universitaria**
LSD sigla m (= Dietilamida del Ácido Lisérgico) LSD
lubina [lu'βina] nf (Zool) sea bass
lubricante [luβri'kante] adj, nm lubricant
lubricar [luβri'kar], **lubrificar** [luβrifi'kar] vt
to lubricate
lubrique etc [lu'βrike] vb ver **lubricar**
lucense [lu'θense] adj of o from Lugo ■ nm/f
native o inhabitant of Lugo
Lucerna [lu'θerna] nf Lucerne
lucero [lu'θero] nm (Astro) bright star; (fig)
brilliance; **~ del alba/de la tarde** morning/
evening star
luces ['luθes] nfpl de **luz**
lucha ['lutʃa] nf fight, struggle; **~ de clases**
class struggle; **~ libre** wrestling
luchar [lu'tʃar] vi to fight
lucidez [luθi'ðeθ] nf lucidity
lúcido, -a [lu'θiðo, a] adj (espléndido) splendid,
brilliant; (elegante) elegant; (exitoso)
successful

lúcido, -a ['luθiðo, a] adj lucid
luciérnaga [lu'θjernaya] nf glow-worm
lucimiento [luθi'mjento] nm (brillo)
brilliance; (éxito) success
lucio ['luθjo] nm (Zool) pike
lucir [lu'θir] vt to illuminate, light (up);
(ostentar) to show off ■ vi (brillar) to shine;
(Am: parecer) to look, seem; **lucirse** vr (irónico)
to make a fool of o.s.; (presumir) to show off;
la casa luce limpia the house looks clean
lucrativo, -a [lukra'tiβo, a] adj lucrative,
profitable; **institución no lucrativa** non
profit-making institution
lucro ['lukro] nm profit, gain; **lucros y daños**
(Com) profit and loss sg
luctuoso, -a [luk'twoso, a] adj mournful
lúdico, -a ['luðiko, a] adj playful; (actividad)
recreational
ludopatía [luðopa'tia] nf addiction to
gambling (o videogames)
luego ['lweyo] adv (después) next; (más tarde)
later, afterwards; (Am fam: en seguida) at once,
immediately; **desde ~** of course; **¡hasta ~!**
see you later!, so long!; **¿y ~?** what next?
lugar [lu'yar] nm place; (sitio) spot; (pueblo)
village, town; **en ~ de** instead of; **en primer
~** in the first place, firstly; **dar ~ a** to give
rise to; **hacer ~** to make room; **fuera de ~**
out of place; **tener ~** to take place; **~ común**
commonplace; **yo en su ~** if I were him;
no hay ~ para preocupaciones there is no
cause for concern
lugareño, -a [luya'reno, a] adj village cpd
■ nm/f villager
lugarteniente [luyarte'njente] nm deputy
lúgubre ['luyuβre] adj mournful
lujo ['luxo] nm luxury; (fig) profusion,
abundance; **de ~** luxury cpd, de luxe
lujoso, -a [lu'xoso, a] adj luxurious
lujuria [lu'xurja] nf lust
lumbago [lum'bayo] nm lumbago
lumbre ['lumbre] nf (luz) light; (fuego) fire;
cerca de la ~ near the fire, at the fireside;
¿tienes ~? (para cigarro) have you got a light?
lumbrera [lum'brera] nf luminary; (fig)
leading light
luminoso, -a [lumi'noso, a] adj luminous,
shining; (idea) bright, brilliant
luna ['luna] nf moon; (vidrio: escaparate) plate
glass; (: de un espejo) glass; (: de gafas) lens; (fig)
crescent; **~ creciente/llena/menguante/
nueva** crescent/full/waning/new moon; **~
de miel** honeymoon; **estar en la ~** to have
one's head in the clouds
lunar [lu'nar] adj lunar ■ nm (Anat) mole;
tela a lunares spotted material
lunes ['lunes] nm inv Monday; ver tb **sábado**

luneta [lu'neta] *nf* lens
lupa ['lupa] *nf* magnifying glass
lusitano, -a [lusi'tano, a], **luso, -a** ['luso, a] *adj, nm/f* Portuguese
lustrador [lustra'ðor] *nm* (*Am*) bootblack
lustrar [lus'trar] *vt* (*esp Am: mueble*) to polish; (*zapatos*) to shine
lustre ['lustre] *nm* polish; (*fig*) lustre; **dar ~ a** to polish
lustro ['lustro] *nm* period of five years
lustroso, -a [lus'troso, a] *adj* shining
luterano, -a [lute'rano, a] *adj* Lutheran
luto ['luto] *nm* mourning; (*congoja*) grief, sorrow; **llevar el** *o* **vestirse de ~** to be in mourning
luxación [luksa'θjon] *nf* (*Med*) dislocation; **tener una ~ de tobillo** to have a dislocated ankle
Luxemburgo [luksem'burɣo] *nm* Luxembourg

luz [luθ] (*pl* **luces**) *nf* (*tb fig*) light; (*fam*) electricity; **dar a ~ un niño** to give birth to a child; **sacar a la ~** to bring to light; **dar la ~** to switch on the light; **encender** (*Esp*) *o* **prender** (*Am*)/**apagar la ~** to switch the light on/off; **les cortaron la ~** their (electricity) supply was cut off; **a la ~ de** in the light of; **a todas luces** by any reckoning; **hacer la ~ sobre** to shed light on; **tener pocas luces** to be dim *o* stupid; **~ de la luna/del sol** *o* **solar** moonlight/sunlight; **~ eléctrica** electric light; **~ roja/verde** red/green light; **~ de cruce** (*Auto*) dipped headlight; **~ de freno** brake light; **~ intermitente/trasera** flashing/rear light; **luces de tráfico** traffic lights; **el Siglo de las Luces** the Age of Enlightenment; **traje de luces** bullfighter's costume

Mm

M, m ['eme] *nf* (*letra*) M, m; **M de Madrid** M
for Mike
M. *abr* (*Ferro*) = **Metro**; (= *mujer*) F
m *abr* (= *metro(s)*) m; (= *minuto(s)*) min., m;
(= *masculino*) m., masc
M.ª *abr* = **María**
macabro, -a [ma'kaβro, a] *adj* macabre
macaco [ma'kako] *nm* (*Zool*) rhesus monkey;
(*fam*) runt, squirt
macana [ma'kana] *nf* (*Am: porra*) club;
(: *mentira*) lie, fib; (: *tontería*) piece of nonsense
macanudo, -a [maka'nuðo, a] *adj* (*Am fam*)
great
macarra [ma'karra] *nm* (*fam*) thug
macarrones [maka'rrones] *nmpl* macaroni *sg*
Macedonia [maθe'ðonja] *nf* Macedonia
macedonia [maθe'ðonja] *nf*: ~ **de frutas**
fruit salad
macedonio [maθe'ðonjo] *adj, nm/f*
Macedonian ■ *nm* (*Ling*) Macedonian
macerar [maθe'rar] *vt* (*Culin*) to soak,
macerate; **macerarse** *vr* to soak, soften
maceta [ma'θeta] *nf* (*de flores*) pot of flowers;
(*para plantas*) flowerpot
macetero [maθe'tero] *nm* flowerpot stand
o holder
machacar [matʃa'kar] *vt* to crush, pound;
(*moler*) to grind (up); (*aplastar*) to mash
■ *vi* (*insistir*) to go on, keep on
machacón, -ona [matʃa'kon, ona] *adj*
(*pesado*) tiresome; (*insistente*) insistent;
(*monótono*) monotonous
machamartillo [matʃamar'tiʎo]: **a ~** *adv*:
creer a machamartillo (*firmemente*) to
believe, firmly
machaque *etc* [ma'tʃake] *vb ver* **machacar**
machete [ma'tʃete] *nm* machete, (large)
knife
machismo [ma'tʃismo] *nm* sexism; male
chauvinism
machista [ma'tʃista] *adj, nm* sexist; male
chauvinist
macho ['matʃo] *adj* male; (*fig*) virile ■ *nm*

male; (*fig*) he man, tough guy (US); (*Tec:
perno*) pin, peg; (*Elec*) pin, plug; (*Costura*) hook
macilento, -a [maθi'lento, a] *adj* (*pálido*)
pale; (*ojeroso*) haggard
macizo, -a [ma'θiθo, a] *adj* (*grande*) massive;
(*fuerte, sólido*) solid ■ *nm* mass, chunk; (*Geo*)
massif
macramé [makra'me] *nm* macramé
macrobiótico, -a [makro'βjotiko, a] *adj*
macrobiotic
macrocomando [makroko'mando] *nm*
(*Inform*) macro (command)
macroeconomía [makroekono'mia] *nf* (*Com*)
macroeconomics *sg*
mácula ['makula] *nf* stain, blemish
macuto [ma'kuto] *nm* (*Mil*) knapsack
Madagascar [maðayas'kar] *nm* Madagascar
madeja [ma'ðexa] *nf* (*de lana*) skein, hank
madera [ma'ðera] *nf* wood; (*fig*) nature,
character; (: *aptitud*) aptitude; **una ~ a** piece
of wood; **~ contrachapada** *o* **laminada**
plywood; **tiene buena ~** he's made of solid
stuff; **tiene ~ de futbolista** he's got the
makings of a footballer
maderaje [maðe'raxe], **maderamen**
[maðe'ramen] *nm* timber; (*trabajo*)
woodwork, timbering
maderero [maðe'rero] *nm* timber merchant
madero [ma'ðero] *nm* beam; (*fig*) ship
madrastra [ma'ðrastra] *nf* stepmother
madre ['maðre] *adj* mother *cpd*; (*Am*)
tremendous ■ *nf* mother; (*de vino etc*) dregs
pl; **~ adoptiva/política/soltera** foster
mother/mother-in-law/unmarried mother;
la M~ Patria the Mother Country; **sin ~**
motherless; **¡~ mía!** oh dear!; **¡tu ~!** (*fam!*)
fuck off! (!); **salirse de ~** (*río*) to burst its
banks; (*persona*) to lose all self-control
madreperla [maðre'perla] *nf* mother-of-
pearl
madreselva [maðre'selβa] *nf* honeysuckle
Madrid [ma'ðrið] *n* Madrid
madriguera [maðri'yera] *nf* burrow

madrileño, -a [maðri'leɲo, a] *adj* of o from
Madrid ■ *nm/f* native o inhabitant of
Madrid
Madriles [ma'ðriles] *nmpl*: **Los ~** *(fam)*
Madrid *sg*
madrina [ma'ðrina] *nf* godmother;
(Arg) prop, shore; *(Tec)* brace; **~ de boda**
bridesmaid
madroño [ma'ðroɲo] *nm* *(Bot)* strawberry
tree, arbutus
madrugada [maðru'ɣaða] *nf* early morning,
small hours; *(alba)* dawn, daybreak; **a las
cuarto de la ~** at four o'clock in the morning
madrugador, a [maðruɣa'ðor, a] *adj* early-
rising
madrugar [maðru'ɣar] *vi* to get up early; *(fig)*
to get a head start
madrugue *etc* [ma'ðruɣe] *vb ver* **madrugar**
madurar [maðu'rar] *vt, vi (fruta)* to ripen; *(fig)*
to mature
madurez [maðu'reθ] *nf* ripeness; *(fig)*
maturity
maduro, -a [ma'ðuro, a] *adj* ripe; *(fig)*
mature; **poco ~** unripe
MAE *nm abr (Esp Pol)* = **Ministerio de Asuntos
Exteriores**
maestra [ma'estra] *nf ver* **maestro**
maestría [maes'tria] *nf* mastery; *(habilidad)*
skill, expertise; *(Am)* Master's Degree
maestro, -a [ma'estro, a] *adj* masterly;
(perito) skilled, expert; *(principal)* main;
(educado) trained ■ *nm/f* master/mistress;
(profesor) teacher ■ *nm (autoridad)* authority;
(Mus) maestro; *(obrero)* skilled workman; **~
albañil** master mason; **~ de obras** foreman
mafia ['mafja] *nf* mafia; **la M~** the Mafia
mafioso [ma'fjoso] *nm* gangster
Magallanes [maɣa'ʎanes] *nm*: **Estrecho de ~**
Strait of Magellan
magia ['maxja] *nf* magic
mágico, -a ['maxiko, a] *adj* magic(al) ■ *nm/f*
magician
magisterio [maxis'terjo] *nm (enseñanza)*
teaching; *(profesión)* teaching profession;
(maestros) teachers *pl*
magistrado [maxis'traðo] *nm* magistrate;
Primer M~ *(Am)* President, Prime Minister
magistral [maxis'tral] *adj* magisterial; *(fig)*
masterly
magistratura [maxistra'tura] *nf* magistracy;
M~ del Trabajo *(Esp)* ≈ Industrial Tribunal
magnánimo, -a [maɣ'nanimo, a] *adj*
magnanimous
magnate [maɣ'nate] *nm* magnate, tycoon;
~ de la prensa press baron
magnesio [maɣ'nesjo] *nm (Química)*
magnesium

magnetice *etc* [maɣne'tiθe] *vb ver*
magnetizar
magnético, -a [maɣ'netiko, a] *adj* magnetic
magnetismo [maɣne'tismo] *nm* magnetism
magnetizar [maɣneti'θar] *vt* to magnetize
magnetofón [maɣneto'fon], **magnetófono**
[maɣne'tofono] *nm* tape recorder
magnetofónico, -a [maɣneto'foniko, a] *adj*:
cinta magnetofónica recording tape
magnicidio [maɣni'θiðjo] *nm* assassination
(of an important person)
magnífico, -a [maɣ'nifiko, a] *adj* splendid,
magnificent
magnitud [maɣni'tuð] *nf* magnitude
mago, -a ['maɣo, a] *nm/f* magician, wizard;
los Reyes Magos the Magi, the Three Wise
Men; *ver tb* **Reyes Magos**
magrear [maɣre'ar] *vt (fam)* to touch up
magro, -a ['maɣro, a] *adj (persona)* thin, lean;
(carne) lean
maguey [ma'ɣei] *nm (Bot)* agave
magulladura [maɣuʎa'ðura] *nf* bruise
magullar [maɣu'ʎar] *vt (amoratar)* to bruise;
(dañar) to damage; *(fam: golpear)* to bash, beat
Maguncia [ma'ɣunθja] *nf* Mainz
mahometano, -a [maome'tano, a] *adj*
Mohammedan
mahonesa [mao'nesa] *nf* = **mayonesa**
maicena [mai'θena] *nf* cornflour, corn starch
(US)
mail [meil] *nm (fam)* email
maillot [ma'jot] *nm* swimming costume;
(Deporte) vest
maître ['metre] *nm* head waiter
maíz [ma'iθ] *nm* maize *(Brit)*, corn *(US)*; sweet
corn
maizal [mai'θal] *nm* maize field, cornfield
majadero, -a [maxa'ðero, a] *adj* silly, stupid
majar [ma'xar] *vt* to crush, grind
majareta [maxa'reta] *adj (fam)* cracked, potty
majestad [maxes'tað] *nf* majesty; **Su
M~** His/Her Majesty; **(Vuestra) M~** Your
Majesty
majestuoso, -a [maxes'twoso, a] *adj*
majestic
majo, -a ['maxo, a] *adj* nice; *(guapo)*
attractive, good-looking; *(elegante)* smart
mal [mal] *adv* badly; *(equivocadamente)*
wrongly; *(con dificultad)* with difficulty ■ *adj*
= **malo, a** ■ *nm* evil; *(desgracia)* misfortune;
(daño) harm, damage; *(Med)* illness ■ *conj*:
~ que le pese whether he likes it or not; **me
entendió ~** he misunderstood me; **hablar
~ de algn** to speak ill of sb; **huele ~** it smells
bad; **ir de ~ en peor** to go from bad to worse;
oigo/veo ~ I can't hear/see very well; **si ~ no
recuerdo** if my memory serves me right;

¡menos ~! just as well!; ~ que bien rightly or wrongly; no hay ~ que por bien no venga every cloud has a silver lining; ~ de ojo evil eye

malabarismo [malaβa'rismo] nm juggling

malabarista [malaβa'rista] nm/f juggler

malaconsejado, -a [malakonse'xaðo, a] adj ill-advised

malacostumbrado, -a [malakostum'braðo, a] adj (consentido) spoiled

malacostumbrar [malakostum'brar] vt: ~ a algn to get sb into bad habits

malagueño, -a [mala'ɣeɲo, a] adj of o from Málaga ■ nm/f native o inhabitant of Málaga

Malaisia [ma'laisja] nf Malaysia

malaria [ma'larja] nf malaria

Malasia [ma'lasja] nf Malaysia

malavenido, -a [malaβe'niðo, a] adj incompatible

malayo, -a [ma'lajo, a] adj Malay(an) ■ nm/f Malay ■ nm (Ling) Malay

Malaysia [ma'laisja] nf Malaysia

malcarado, -a [malka'raðo, a] adj ugly, grim-faced

malcriado, -a [mal'krjaðo, a] adj (consentido) spoiled

malcriar [mal'krjar] vt to spoil, pamper

maldad [mal'dað] nf evil, wickedness

maldecir [malde'θir] vt to curse ■ vi: ~ de to speak ill of

maldiciendo etc [maldi'θjendo] vb ver **maldecir**

maldición [maldi'θjon] nf curse; ¡~! curse it!, damn!

maldiga etc [mal'diɣa], **maldije** etc [mal'dixe] vb ver **maldecir**

maldito, -a [mal'dito, a] adj (condenado) damned; (perverso) wicked ■ nm: el ~ the devil; ¡~ sea! damn it!; no le hace ~ (el) caso he doesn't take a blind bit of notice

maleable [male'aβle] adj malleable

maleante [male'ante] adj wicked ■ nm/f criminal, crook

malecón [male'kon] nm pier, jetty

maledicencia [maleði'θenθja] nf slander, scandal

maleducado, -a [maleðu'kaðo, a] adj bad-mannered, rude

maleficio [male'fiθjo] nm curse, spell

malentendido [malenten'diðo] nm misunderstanding

malestar [males'tar] nm (gen) discomfort; (enfermedad) indisposition; (fig: inquietud) uneasiness; (Pol) unrest; siento un ~ en el estómago my stomach is upset

maleta [ma'leta] nf case, suitcase; (Auto) boot

(Brit), trunk (US); hacer la ~ to pack

maletera [male'tera] nf (Am Auto) boot (Brit), trunk (US)

maletero [male'tero] nm (Auto) boot (Brit), trunk (US); (persona) porter

maletín [male'tin] nm small case, bag; (portafolio) briefcase

malevolencia [maleβo'lenθja] nf malice, spite

malévolo, -a [ma'leβolo, a] adj malicious, spiteful

maleza [ma'leθa] nf (malas hierbas) weeds pl; (arbustos) thicket

malgache [mal'ɣatʃe] adj of o from Madagascar ■ nm/f native o inhabitant of Madagascar

malgastar [malɣas'tar] vt (tiempo, dinero) to waste; (recursos) to squander; (salud) to ruin

malhaya [ma'laja] excl (esp Am: fam!) damn (it)! (!); ¡~ sea/sean! damn it/them! (!)

malhechor, a [male'tʃor, a] nm/f delinquent; (criminal) criminal

malherido, -a [male'riðo, a] adj badly injured

malhumorado, -a [malumo'raðo, a] adj bad-tempered

malicia [ma'liθja] nf (maldad) wickedness; (astucia) slyness, guile; (mala intención) malice, spite; (carácter travieso) mischievousness

malicioso, -a [mali'θjoso, a] adj wicked, evil; sly, crafty; malicious, spiteful; mischievous

malignidad [maliɣni'ðað] nf (Med) malignancy; (malicia) malice

maligno, -a [ma'liɣno, a] adj evil; (dañino) pernicious, harmful; (malévolo) malicious; (Med) malignant ■ nm: el ~ the devil

malintencionado, -a [malintenθjo'naðo, a] adj (comentario) hostile; (persona) malicious

malla ['maʎa] nf (de una red) mesh; (red) network; (Am: de baño) swimsuit; (de ballet, gimnasia) leotard; **mallas** nfpl tights; ~ de alambre wire mesh

Mallorca [ma'ʎorka] nf Majorca

mallorquín, -ina [maʎor'kin, ina] adj, nm/f Majorcan ■ nm (Ling) Majorcan

malnutrido, -a [malnu'triðo, a] adj undernourished

malo, -a ['malo, a] adj (mal before nmsg) bad; (calidad) poor; (falso) false; (espantoso) dreadful; (niño) naughty ■ nm/f villain ■ nm (Cine fam) bad guy ■ nf spell of bad luck; estar ~ to be ill; andar a malas con algn to be on bad terms with sb; estar de malas (mal humor) to be in a bad mood; lo ~ es que ... the trouble is that ...

malograr [malo'ɣrar] vt to spoil; (plan) to upset; (ocasión) to waste; **malograrse** vr (*plan etc*) to fail, come to grief; (*persona*) to die before one's time

maloliente [malo'ljente] *adj* stinking, smelly

malparado, -a [malpa'raðo, a] *adj*: **salir ~** to come off badly

malpensado, -a [malpen'saðo, a] *adj* evil-minded

malquerencia [malke'renθja] *nf* dislike

malquistar [malkis'tar] *vt*: **~ a dos personas** to cause a rift between two people; **malquistarse** *vr* to fall out

malsano, -a [mal'sano, a] *adj* unhealthy

malsonante [malso'nante] *adj* (*palabra*) nasty, rude

Malta ['malta] *nf* Malta

malta ['malta] *nf* malt

malteada [malte'aða] *nf* (*Am*) milk shake

maltés, -esa [mal'tes, esa] *adj, nm/f* Maltese

maltraer [maltra'er] *vt* (*abusar*) to insult, abuse; (*maltratar*) to ill-treat

maltratar [maltra'tar] *vt* to ill-treat, mistreat

maltrecho, -a [mal'tretʃo, a] *adj* battered, damaged

malva ['malβa] *nf* mallow; **~ loca** hollyhock; (**de color de**) **~** mauve

malvado, -a [mal'βaðo, a] *adj* evil, villainous

malvavisco [malβa'βisko] *nm* marshmallow

malvender [malβen'der] *vt* to sell off cheap o at a loss

malversación [malβersa'θjon] *nf* embezzlement, misappropriation

malversar [malβer'sar] *vt* to embezzle, misappropriate

Malvinas [mal'βinas] *nfpl*: **Islas ~** Falkland Islands

mama ['mama] (*pl* **mamás**) *nf* (*de animal*) teat; (*de mujer*) breast

mamá [ma'ma] *nf* (*fam*) mum, mummy

mamacita [mama'sita] *nf* (*Am fam*) mum, mummy

mamadera [mama'dera] *nf* (*Am*) baby's bottle

mamagrande [mama'grande] *nf* (*Am*) grandmother

mamar [ma'mar] *vt* (*pecho*) to suck; (*fig*) to absorb, assimilate ■ *vi* to suck; **dar de ~** to (breast-)feed; (*animal*) to suckle

mamarracho [mama'rratʃo] *nm* sight, mess

mambo ['mambo] *nf* (*Mus*) mambo

mamífero, -a [ma'mifero, a] *adj* mammalian, mammal *cpd* ■ *nm* mammal

mamón, -ona [ma'mon, ona] *adj* small, baby *cpd* ■ *nm/f* small baby; (*fam!*) wanker (!)

mamotreto [mamo'treto] *nm* hefty volume; (*fam*) whacking great thing

mampara [mam'para] *nf* (*entre habitaciones*) partition; (*biombo*) screen

mamporro [mam'porro] *nm* (*fam*): **dar un ~ a** to clout

mampostería [mamposte'ria] *nf* masonry

mamut [ma'mut] *nm* mammoth

maná [ma'na] *nm* manna

manada [ma'naða] *nf* (*Zool*) herd; (: *de leones*) pride; (: *de lobos*) pack; **llegaron en manadas** (*fam*) they came in droves

Managua [ma'naɣwa] *n* Managua

manantial [manan'tjal] *nm* spring; (*fuente*) fountain; (*fig*) source

manar [ma'nar] *vt* to run with, flow with ■ *vi* to run, flow; (*abundar*) to abound

manaza [ma'naθa] *nf* big hand ■ *adj, nm/f inv*: **manazas**: **ser un manazas** to be clumsy

mancebo [man'θeβo] *nm* (*joven*) young man

mancha ['mantʃa] *nf* stain, mark; (*de tinta*) blot; (*de vegetación*) patch; (*imperfección*) stain, blemish, blot; (*boceto*) sketch, outline; **la M~** La Mancha

manchado, -a [man'tʃaðo, a] *adj* (*sucio*) dirty; (*animal*) spotted; (*ave*) speckled; (*de tinta*) smudged

manchar [man'tʃar] *vt* to stain, mark; (*Zool*) to patch; (*ensuciar*) to soil, dirty; **mancharse** *vr* to get dirty; (*fig*) to dirty one's hands

manchego, -a [man'tʃeɣo, a] *adj* of o from La Mancha ■ *nm/f* native o inhabitant of La Mancha

mancilla [man'θiʎa] *nf* stain, blemish

mancillar [manθi'ʎar] *vt* to stain, sully

manco, -a ['manko, a] *adj* one-armed; one-handed; (*fig*) defective, faulty; **no ser ~** to be useful o active

mancomunar [mankomu'nar] *vt* to unite, bring together; (*recursos*) to pool; (*Jur*) to make jointly responsible

mancomunidad [mankomuni'ðað] *nf* union, association; (*comunidad*) community; (*Jur*) joint responsibility

mandado [man'daðo] *nm* (*orden*) order; (*recado*) commission, errand

mandamás [manda'mas] *adj, nm/f inv* boss; **ser un ~** to be very bossy

mandamiento [manda'mjento] *nm* (*orden*) order, command; (*Rel*) commandment; **~ judicial** warrant

mandar [man'dar] *vt* (*ordenar*) to order; (*dirigir*) to lead, command; (*país*) to rule over; (*enviar*) to send; (*pedir*) to order, ask for ■ *vi* to be in charge; (*pey*) to be bossy; **mandarse** *vr*: **mandarse mudar** (*Am fam*) to go away, clear off; **¿mande?** pardon?, excuse me? (*US*); **¿manda usted algo más?** is there anything else?; **~ a algn a paseo** o **a la porra** to tell sb to go to hell; **se lo mandaremos por correo** we'll post it to you; ~ **hacer un traje** to have a suit made

mandarín [manda'rin] *nm* petty bureaucrat

mandarina [manda'rina] *nf (fruta)* tangerine, mandarin (orange)

mandatario, -a [manda'tarjo, a] *nm/f (representante)* agent; **primer** ~ *(esp Am)* head of state

mandato [man'dato] *nm (orden)* order; *(Pol: período)* term of office; *(: territorio)* mandate; ~ **judicial** (search) warrant

mandíbula [man'diβula] *nf* jaw

mandil [man'dil] *nm (delantal)* apron

Mandinga [man'dinya] *nm (Am)* Devil

mandioca [man'djoka] *nf* cassava

mando ['mando] *nm (Mil)* command; *(de país)* rule; *(el primer lugar)* lead; *(Pol)* term of office; *(Tec)* control; ~ **a la izquierda** left-hand drive; **los altos mandos** the high command *sg*; ~ **por botón** push-button control; **al** ~ **de** in charge of; **tomar el** ~ to take the lead

mandolina [mando'lina] *nf* mandolin(e)

mandón, -ona [man'don, ona] *adj* bossy, domineering

manecilla [mane'θiʎa] *nf (Tec)* pointer; *(de reloj)* hand

manejable [mane'xaβle] *adj* manageable; *(fácil de usar)* handy

manejar [mane'xar] *vt* to manage; *(máquina)* to work, operate; *(caballo etc)* to handle; *(casa)* to run, manage; *(Am Auto)* to drive ■ *vi (Am Auto)* to drive; **manejarse** *vr (comportarse)* to act, behave; *(arreglárselas)* to manage; "~ **con cuidado**" "handle with care"

manejo [ma'nexo] *nm* management; handling; running; driving; *(facilidad de trato)* ease, confidence; *(de Idioma)* command; **manejos** *nmpl* intrigues; **tengo ~ del francés** I have a good command of French

manera [ma'nera] *nf* way, manner, fashion; *(Arte, Lit etc: estilo)* manner, style; **maneras** *nfpl (modales)* manners; **su ~ de ser** the way he is; *(aire)* his manner; **de mala ~** *(fam)* badly, unwillingly; **de ninguna ~** no way, by no means; **de otra ~** otherwise; **de todas maneras** at any rate; **en gran ~** to a large extent; **sobre ~** exceedingly; **a mi ~ de ver** in my view; **no hay ~ de persuadirle** there's no way of convincing him

manga ['manga] *nf (de camisa)* sleeve; *(de riego)* hose; **de ~ corta/larga** short-/long-sleeved; **andar ~ por hombro** *(desorden)* to be topsy-turvy; **tener ~ ancha** to be easy-going

mangante [man'gante] *adj (descarado)* brazen ■ *nm (mendigo)* beggar

mangar [man'gar] *vt (unir)* to plug in; *(fam:*

birlar) to pinch, nick, swipe; *(mendigar)* to beg

mango ['mango] *nm* handle; *(Bot)* mango; ~ **de escoba** broomstick

mangonear [mangone'ar] *vt* to boss about ■ *vi* to be bossy

mangue *etc* ['mange] *vb ver* **mangar**

manguera [man'gera] *nf (de riego)* hose; *(tubo)* pipe; ~ **de incendios** fire hose

maní [ma'ni] *nm (pl* ~**es** *o* **manises)** *(Am: cacahuete)* peanut; *(: planta)* groundnut plant

manía [ma'nia] *nf (Med)* mania; *(fig: moda)* rage, craze; *(disgusto)* dislike; *(malicia)* spite; **tiene manías** she's a bit fussy; **tener ~ a algn** to dislike sb

maníaco, -a [ma'niako, a] *adj* maniac(al) ■ *nm/f* maniac

maniatar [manja'tar] *vt* to tie the hands of

maniático, -a [ma'njatiko, a] *adj* maniac(al); *(loco)* crazy; *(tiquismiquis)* fussy ■ *nm/f* maniac

manicomio [mani'komjo] *nm* mental hospital (Brit), insane asylum (US)

manicuro, -a [mani'kuro, a] *nm/f* manicurist ■ *nf* manicure

manido, -a [ma'niðo, a] *adj (tema etc)* trite, stale

manifestación [manifesta'θjon] *nf (declaración)* statement, declaration; *(demostración)* show, display; *(Pol)* demonstration

manifestante [manifes'tante] *nm/f* demonstrator

manifestar [manifes'tar] *vt* to show, manifest; *(declarar)* to state, declare; **manifestarse** *vr* to show, become apparent; *(Pol: desfilar)* to demonstrate; *(: reunirse)* to hold a mass meeting

manifiesto, -a *etc* [mani'fjesto, a] *vb ver* **manifestar** ■ *adj* clear, manifest ■ *nm* manifesto; *(Anat, Naut)* manifest; **poner algo de** ~ *(aclarar)* to make sth clear; *(revelar)* to reveal sth; **quedar** ~ to be plain o clear

manija [ma'nixa] *nf* handle

manilla [ma'niʎa] *nf (de reloj)* hand; *(Am)* handle, lever; **manillas (de hierro)** *nfpl* handcuffs

manillar [mani'ʎar] *nm* handlebars *pl*

maniobra [ma'njoβra] *nf* manœuvring; *(manejo)* handling; *(fig: movimiento)* manœuvre, move; *(: estratagema)* trick, stratagem; **maniobras** *nfpl* manœuvres

maniobrar [manio'βrar] *vt* to manœuvre; *(manejar)* to handle ■ *vi* to manœuvre

manipulación [manipula'θjon] *nf* manipulation; *(Com)* handling

manipular [manipu'lar] *vt* to manipulate; *(manejar)* to handle

m

245

maniquí [mani'ki] *nm/f* model ■ *nm* dummy
manirroto, -a [mani'rroto, a] *adj* lavish, extravagant ■ *nm/f* spendthrift
manita [ma'nita] *nf* little hand; **manitas de plata** artistic hands
manitas [ma'nitas] *adj inv* good with one's hands ■ *nm/f inv*: **ser un ~** to be very good with one's hands
manito [ma'nito] *nm* (*Am: en conversación*) mate (*fam*), chum
manivela [mani'βela] *nf* crank
manjar [man'xar] *nm* (tasty) dish
mano¹ ['mano] *nf* hand; (*Zool*) foot, paw; (*de pintura*) coat; (*serie*) lot, series; **a ~** by hand; **a ~ derecha/izquierda** on (*o* to) the right(-hand side)/left(-hand side); **hecho a ~** handmade; **a manos llenas** lavishly, generously; **de primera ~** (at) first hand; **de segunda ~** (at) second hand; **robo a ~ armada** armed robbery; **Pedro es mi ~ derecha** Pedro is my right-hand man; **~ de obra** labour, manpower; **~ de santo** sure remedy; **darse la(s) ~(s)** to shake hands; **echar una ~ to** lend a hand; **echar una ~ a** to lay hands on; **echar ~ de** to make use of; **estrechar la ~ a algn** to shake sb's hand; **traer** *o* **llevar algo entre manos** to deal *o* be busy with sth; **está en tus manos** it's up to you; **se le fue la ~** his hand slipped; (*fig*) he went too far; **¡manos a la obra!** to work!
mano² ['mano] *nm* (*Am fam*) friend, mate
manojo [ma'noxo] *nm* handful, bunch; **~ de llaves** bunch of keys
manómetro [ma'nometro] *nm* (pressure) gauge
manopla [ma'nopla] *nf* (*paño*) flannel; **manoplas** *nfpl* mittens
manoseado, -a [manose'aðo, a] *adj* well-worn
manosear [manose'ar] *vt* (*tocar*) to handle, touch; (*desordenar*) to mess up, rumple; (*insistir en*) to overwork; (*acariciar*) to caress, fondle; (*pey: persona*) to feel *o* touch up
manotazo [mano'taθo] *nm* slap, smack
mansalva [man'salβa]: **a ~** *adv* indiscriminately
mansedumbre [manse'ðumbre] *nf* gentleness, meekness; (*de animal*) tameness
mansión [man'sjon] *nf* mansion
manso, -a ['manso, a] *adj* gentle, mild; (*animal*) tame
manta ['manta] *nf* blanket; (*Am*) poncho
manteca [man'teka] *nf* fat; (*Am*) butter; **~ de cacahuete/cacao** peanut/cocoa butter; **~ de cerdo** lard
mantecado [mante'kaðo] *nm* ice cream
mantecoso, -a [mante'koso, a] *adj* fat, greasy; **queso ~** soft cheese

mantel [man'tel] *nm* tablecloth
mantelería [mantele'ria] *nf* table linen
mantendré *etc* [manten'dre] *vb ver* **mantener**
mantener [mante'ner] *vt* to support, maintain; (*alimentar*) to sustain; (*conservar*) to keep; (*Tec*) to maintain, service; **mantenerse** *vr* (*seguir de pie*) to be still standing; (*no ceder*) to hold one's ground; (*subsistir*) to sustain o.s., keep going; **~ algo en equilibrio** to keep sth balanced; **mantenerse a distancia** to keep one's distance; **mantenerse firme** to hold one's ground
mantenga *etc* [man'tenga] *vb ver* **mantener**
mantenimiento [manteni'mjento] *nm* maintenance; sustenance; (*sustento*) support
mantequería [manteke'ria] *nf* (*ultramarinos*) grocer's (shop)
mantequilla [mante'kiʎa] *nf* butter
mantilla [man'tiʎa] *nf* mantilla; **mantillas** *nfpl* baby clothes; **estar en mantillas** (*persona*) to be terribly innocent; (*proyecto*) to be in its infancy
manto ['manto] *nm* (*capa*) cloak; (*de ceremonia*) robe, gown
mantón [man'ton] *nm* shawl
mantuve *etc* [man'tuβe] *vb ver* **mantener**
manual [ma'nwal] *adj* manual ■ *nm* manual, handbook; **habilidad ~** manual skill
manubrio [ma'nuβrio] *nm* (*Am Auto*) steering wheel
manufactura [manufak'tura] *nf* manufacture; (*fábrica*) factory
manufacturado, -a [manufaktu'raðo, a] *adj* manufactured
manuscrito, -a [manus'krito, a] *adj* handwritten ■ *nm* manuscript
manutención [manuten'θjon] *nf* maintenance; (*sustento*) support
manzana [man'θana] *nf* apple; (*Arq*) block; **~ de la discordia** (*fig*) bone of contention
manzanal [manθa'nal] *nm* apple orchard
manzanilla [manθa'niʎa] *nf* (*planta*) camomile; (*infusión*) camomile tea; (*vino*) manzanilla
manzano [man'θano] *nm* apple tree
maña ['maɲa] *nf* (*gen*) skill, dexterity; (*pey*) guile; (*costumbre*) habit; (*una maña*) trick, knack; **con ~** craftily
mañana [ma'ɲana] *adv* tomorrow ■ *nm* future ■ *nf* morning; **de** *o* **por la ~** in the morning; **¡hasta ~!** see you tomorrow!; **pasado ~** the day after tomorrow; **~ por la ~** tomorrow morning
mañanero, -a [maɲa'nero, a] *adj* early-rising
maño, -a ['maɲo, a] *adj* Aragonese ■ *nm/f*

native o inhabitant of Aragon

mañoso, -a [ma'ɲoso, a] *adj* (*hábil*) skilful; (*astuto*) smart, clever

mapa ['mapa] *nm* map

mapuche, -a [ma'putʃe, a] *adj, nm/f* Mapuche, Araucanian

maqueta [ma'keta] *nf* (scale) model

maquiavélico, -a [makja'βeliko, a] *adj* Machiavellian

maquillador, a [makiʎa'ðor, a] *nm/f* (*Teat etc*) make-up artist

maquillaje [maki'ʎaxe] *nm* make-up; (*acto*) making up

maquillar [maki'ʎar] *vt* to make up; **maquillarse** *vr* to put on (some) make-up

máquina ['makina] *nf* machine; (*de tren*) locomotive, engine; (*Foto*) camera; (*Am: coche*) car; (*fig*) machinery; (*: proyecto*) plan, project; **a toda ~** at full speed; **escrito a ~** typewritten; **~ de afeitar** electric razor; **~ de escribir** typewriter; **~ de coser/lavar** sewing/washing machine; **~ de facsímil** facsimile (machine), fax; **~ de franqueo** franking machine; **~ tragaperras** fruit machine; (*Com*) slot machine

maquinación [makina'θjon] *nf* machination, plot

maquinal [maki'nal] *adj* (*fig*) mechanical, automatic

maquinar [maki'nar] *vt, vi* to plot

maquinaria [maki'narja] *nf* (*máquinas*) machinery; (*mecanismo*) mechanism, works *pl*

maquinilla [maki'niʎa] *nf* small machine; (*torno*) winch; **~ de afeitar** razor; **~ eléctrica** electric razor

maquinista [maki'nista] *nm* (*Ferro*) engine driver (Brit), engineer (US); (*Tec*) operator; (*Naut*) engineer

mar [mar] *nm* sea; **~ de fondo** groundswell; **~ llena** high tide; **~ adentro** o **afuera** out at sea; **en alta ~** on the high seas; **por ~** by sea o boat; **hacerse a la ~** to put to sea; **a mares** in abundance; **un ~ de** lots of; **es la ~ de guapa** she is ever so pretty; **el M~ Negro/Báltico** the Black/Baltic Sea; **el M~ Muerto/Rojo** the Dead/Red Sea; **el M~ del Norte** the North Sea

mar. *abr* (= *marzo*) Mar.

maraca [ma'raka] *nf* maraca

maraña [ma'raɲa] *nf* (*maleza*) thicket; (*confusión*) tangle

maravilla [mara'βiʎa] *nf* marvel, wonder; (*Bot*) marigold; **hacer maravillas** to work wonders; **a (las mil) maravillas** wonderfully well

maravillar [maraβi'ʎar] *vt* to astonish, amaze; **maravillarse** *vr* to be astonished,

be amazed

maravilloso, -a [maraβi'ʎoso, a] *adj* wonderful, marvellous

marbellí [marβe'ʎi] *adj* of o from Marbella ■ *nm/f* native o inhabitant of Marbella

marca ['marka] *nf* mark; (*sello*) stamp; (*Com*) make, brand; (*de ganado*) brand; (*: acto*) branding; (*Deporte*) record; **de ~** excellent; **~ de fábrica** trademark; **~ propia** own brand; **~ registrada** registered trademark

marcación [marka'θjon] *nf* (*Telec*): **~ automática** autodial

marcado, -a [mar'kaðo, a] *adj* marked, strong

marcador [marka'ðor] *nm* marker; (*rotulador*) marker (pen); (*de libro*) bookmark; (*Deporte*) scoreboard; (*: persona*) scorer

marcapasos [marka'pasos] *nm inv* pacemaker

marcar [mar'kar] *vt* to mark; (*número de teléfono*) to dial; (*gol*) to score; (*números*) to record, keep a tally of; (*el pelo*) to set; (*ganado*) to brand; (*suj: termómetro*) to read, register; (*: reloj*) to show; (*tarea*) to assign; (*Com*) to put a price on ■ *vi* (*Deporte*) to score; (*Telec*) to dial; **mi reloj marca las dos** it's two o'clock by my watch; **~ el compás** (*Mus*) to keep time; **~ el paso** (*Mil*) to mark time

marcha ['martʃa] *nf* march; (*Deporte*) walk; (*Tec*) running, working; (*Auto*) gear; (*velocidad*) speed; (*fig*) progress; (*curso*) course; **dar ~ atrás** to reverse, put into reverse; **estar en ~** to be under way, be in motion; **hacer algo sobre la ~** to do sth as you *etc* go along; **poner en ~** to put into gear; **ponerse en ~** to start, get going; **a marchas forzadas** (*fig*) with all speed; **¡en ~!** (*Mil*) forward march!; (*fig*) let's go!; **"~ moderada"** (*Auto*) "drive slowly"; **que tiene** o **de mucha ~** (*fam*) very lively

marchante, -a [mar'tʃante, a] *nm/f* dealer, merchant

marchar [mar'tʃar] *vi* (*ir*) to go; (*funcionar*) to work, go; (*fig*) to go, proceed; **marcharse** *vr* to go (away), leave; **todo marcha bien** everything is going well

marchitar [martʃi'tar] *vt* to wither, dry up; **marchitarse** *vr* (*Bot*) to wither; (*fig*) to fade away

marchito, -a [mar'tʃito, a] *adj* withered, faded; (*fig*) in decline

marchoso, -a [mar'tʃoso, a] *adj* (*fam: animado*) lively; (*: moderno*) modern

marcial [mar'θjal] *adj* martial, military

marciano, -a [mar'θjano, a] *adj* Martian, of o from Mars

marco ['marko] *nm* frame; (*Deporte*) goalposts

pl; (*moneda*) mark; (*fig*) setting; (*contexto*)
framework; ~ **de chimenea** mantelpiece
marea [ma'rea] *nf* tide; (*llovizna*) drizzle; ~
alta/baja high/low tide; ~ **negra** oil slick
mareado, -a [mare'aðo, a] *adj*: **estar** ~ (*con
náuseas*) to feel sick; (*aturdido*) to feel dizzy
marear [mare'ar] *vt* (*fig*: *irritar*) to annoy,
upset; (*Med*): ~ **a algn** to make sb feel sick;
marearse *vr* (*tener náuseas*) to feel sick;
(*desvanecerse*) to feel faint; (*aturdirse*) to feel
dizzy; (*fam*: *emborracharse*) to get tipsy
marejada [mare'xaða] *nf* (*Naut*) swell, heavy
sea
maremágnum [mare'maɣnum] *nm* (*fig*)
ocean, abundance
maremoto [mare'moto] *nm* tidal wave
mareo [ma'reo] *nm* (*náusea*) sick feeling;
(*aturdimiento*) dizziness; (*fam*: *lata*) nuisance
marfil [mar'fil] *nm* ivory
margarina [marɣa'rina] *nf* margarine
margarita [marɣa'rita] *nf* (*Bot*) daisy;
(**rueda**) ~ (*en máquina impresora*) daisy wheel
margen ['marxen] *nm* (*borde*) edge, border;
(*fig*) margin, space ■ *nf* (*de río etc*) bank; ~
de beneficio *o* **de ganancia** profit margin;
~ **comercial** mark-up; ~ **de confianza**
credibility gap; **dar** ~ **para** to give an
opportunity for; **dejar a algn al** ~ to leave sb
out (in the cold); **mantenerse al** ~ to keep
out (of things); **al** ~ **de lo que digas** despite
what you say
marginado, -a [marxi'naðo, a] *nm/f* outcast
marginal [marxi'nal] *adj* (*tema, error*) minor;
(*grupo*) fringe *cpd*; (*anotación*) marginal
marginar [marxi'nar] *vt* to exclude
maría [ma'ria] *nf* (*fam*: *mujer*) housewife
mariachi [ma'rjatʃi] *nm* (*música*) mariachi
music; (*grupo*) mariachi band; (*persona*)
mariachi player
marica [ma'rika] *nm* (*fam*) sissy; (*homosexual*)
queer
Maricastaña [marikas'taɲa] *nf*: **en los días**
o **en tiempos de** ~ way back, in the good old
days
maricón [mari'kon] *nm* (*fam*) queer
marido [ma'riðo] *nm* husband
marihuana [mari'wənə] *nf* marijuana,
cannabis
marimacho [mari'matʃo] *nf* (*fam*) mannish
woman
marimorena [marimo'rena] *nf* fuss, row;
armar una ~ to kick up a row
marina [ma'rina] *nf* navy; ~ **mercante**
merchant navy
marinero, -a [mari'nero, a] *adj* sea *cpd*;
(*barco*) seaworthy ■ *nm* sailor, seaman
marino, -a [ma'rino, a] *adj* sea *cpd*, marine

■ *nm* sailor; ~ **de agua dulce/de cubierta/
de primera** landlubber/deckhand/able
seaman
marioneta [marjo'neta] *nf* puppet
mariposa [mari'posa] *nf* butterfly
mariposear [maripose'ar] *vi* (*revolotear*) to
flutter about; (*ser inconstante*) to be fickle;
(*coquetear*) to flirt
mariquita [mari'kita] *nm* (*fam*) sissy;
(*homosexual*) queer ■ *nf* (*Zool*) ladybird (*Brit*),
ladybug (*US*)
marisco [ma'risko] *nm* (*tb*: **mariscos**)
shellfish, seafood
marisma [ma'risma] *nf* marsh, swamp
marisquería [mariske'ria] *nf* shellfish bar,
seafood restaurant
marítimo, -a [ma'ritimo, a] *adj* sea *cpd*,
maritime
marmita [mar'mita] *nf* pot
mármol ['marmol] *nm* marble
marmóreo, -a [mar'moreo, a] *adj* marble
marmota [mar'mota] *nf* (*Zool*) marmot; (*fig*)
sleepyhead
maroma [ma'roma] *nf* rope
marque *etc* ['marke] *vb ver* **marcar**
marqués, -esa [mar'kes, esa] *nm/f* marquis/
marchioness
marquesina [marke'sina] *nf* (*de parada*) bus-
shelter
marquetería [markete'ria] *nf* marquetry,
inlaid work
marranada [marra'naða] *nf* (*fam*): **es una** ~
that's disgusting; **hacer una** ~ **a algn** to do
the dirty on sb
marrano, -a [ma'rrano, a] *adj* filthy, dirty
■ *nm* (*Zool*) pig; (*malo*) swine; (*sucio*) dirty pig
marras [ma'rras]: **de** ~ *adv*: **es el problema
de** ~ it's the same old problem
marrón [ma'rron] *adj* brown
marroquí [marro'ki] *adj, nm/f* Moroccan
■ *nm* Morocco (leather)
Marruecos [ma'rrwekos] *nm* Morocco
marta ['marta] *nf* (*animal*) (pine) marten;
(*piel*) sable
Marte ['marte] *nm* Mars
martes ['martes] *nm inv* Tuesday; ~ **de
carnaval** Shrove Tuesday; *ver tb* **Carnaval;
sábado**
martillar [marti'ʎar], **martillear**
[martiʎe'ar] *vt* to hammer
martilleo [marti'ʎeo] *nm* hammering
martillo [mar'tiʎo] *nm* hammer; (*de presidente
de asamblea, comité*) gavel; ~ **neumático**
pneumatic drill (*Brit*), jackhammer (*US*)
Martinica [marti'nika] *nf* Martinique
mártir ['martir] *nm/f* martyr
martirice *etc* [marti'riθe] *vb ver* **martirizar**

martirio [mar'tirjo] *nm* martyrdom; *(fig)* torture, torment

martirizar [martiri'θar] *vt* (*Rel*) to martyr; *(fig)* to torture, torment

maruja [ma'ruxa] *nf* (*fam*) = **maría**

marxismo [mark'sismo] *nm* Marxism

marxista [mark'sista] *adj, nm/f* Marxist

marzo ['marθo] *nm* March; **11-M** (= *11 de marzo*) *the Madrid train bombings of 11th March 2004*; *ver tb* **julio**

mas [mas] *conj* but

🔵 **PALABRA CLAVE**

más [mas] *adj, adv* **1**: ~ (**que, de**) *(compar)* more (than), ...+ er (than); ~ **grande/ inteligente** bigger/more intelligent; **trabaja (que yo)** he works more (than me); ~ **de seis** more than six; **es** ~ **de medianoche** it's after midnight; **durar** ~ to last longer; *ver tb* **cada**

2 *(superl)*: **el** ~ the most, ...+ est; **el** ~ **grande/inteligente (de)** the biggest/most intelligent (in)

3 *(negativo)*: **no tengo** ~ **dinero** I haven't got any more money; **no viene** ~ **por aquí** he doesn't come round here any more; **no sé** ~ I don't know any more, that's all I know

4 *(adicional)*: **un kilómetro** ~ one more kilometre; **no le veo** ~ **solución que** ... I see no other solution than to ...; **¿algo** ~**?** anything else?; (*en tienda*) will that be all?; **¿quién** ~**?** anybody else?

5 (+ *adj: valor intensivo*): **¡qué perro** ~ **sucio!** what a filthy dog!; **¡es** ~ **tonto!** he's so stupid!

6 *(locuciones)*: ~ **o menos** more or less; **los** ~ most people; **es** ~ in fact, furthermore; ~ **bien** rather; **¡qué** ~ **da!** what does it matter!; *ver tb* **no**

7: **por** ~: **por más que lo intento** no matter how much o hard I try; **por** ~ **que quisiera ayudar** much as I should like to help

8: **de** ~: **veo que aquí estoy de más** I can see I'm not needed here; **tenemos uno de** ~ we've got one extra

9 (*Am*): **no** ~ only, just; **ayer no** ~ just yesterday ■ *prep*: **2** ~ **2 son 4** 2 and 0 plus 2 are 4

■ *nm inv*: **este trabajo tiene sus** ~ **y sus menos** this job's got its good points and its bad points

masa ['masa] *nf* (*mezcla*) dough; (*volumen*) volume, mass; (*Física*) mass; **en** ~ en masse; **las masas** (*Pol*) the masses

masacrar [masa'krar] *vt* to massacre

masacre [ma'sakre] *nf* massacre

masaje [ma'saxe] *nm* massage; **dar** ~ **a** to massage

masajista [masa'xista] *nm/f* masseur/ masseuse

mascar [mas'kar] *vt, vi* to chew; *(fig)* to mumble, mutter

máscara ['maskara] *nf* (*tb Inform*) mask ■ *nm/f* masked person; ~ **antigás** gas mask

mascarada [maska'raða] *nf* masquerade

mascarilla [maska'riʎa] *nf* mask; (*vaciado*) deathmask; (*de maquillaje*) face pack

mascarón [maska'ron] *nm* large mask; ~ **de proa** figurehead

mascota [mas'kota] *nf* mascot

masculino, -a [masku'lino, a] *adj* masculine; (*Bio*) male ■ *nm* (*Ling*) masculine

mascullar [masku'ʎar] *vt* to mumble, mutter

masificación [masifika'θjon] *nf* overcrowding

masilla [ma'siʎa] *nf* putty

masivo, -a [ma'siβo, a] *adj* (*en masa*) mass

masón [ma'son] *nm* (free)mason

masonería [masone'ria] *nf* (free)masonry

masoquista [maso'kista] *adj* masochistic ■ *nm/f* masochist

masque *etc* ['maske] *vb ver* **mascar**

mastectomía [mastekto'mia] *nf* mastectomy

máster (*pl* **masters**) ['master, 'masters] *nm* postgraduate degree; *ver tb* **licenciado**

masticar [masti'kar] *vt* to chew; *(fig)* to ponder over

mástil ['mastil] *nm* (*de navío*) mast; (*de guitarra*) neck

mastín [mas'tin] *nm* mastiff

mastique *etc* [mas'tike] *vb ver* **masticar**

masturbación [masturβa'θjon] *nf* masturbation

masturbarse [mastur'βarse] *vr* to masturbate

Mat. *abr* = **Matemáticas**

mata ['mata] *nf* (*arbusto*) bush, shrub; (*de hierbas*) tuft; (*campo*) field; (*manojo*) tuft, blade; **matas** *nfpl* scrub *sg*; ~ **de pelo** mop of hair; **a salto de** ~ (*día a día*) from day to day; (*al azar*) haphazardly

matadero [mata'ðero] *nm* slaughterhouse, abattoir

matador, a [mata'ðor, a] *adj* killing ■ *nm/f* killer ■ *nm* (*Taur*) matador, bullfighter

matamoscas [mata'moskas] *nm inv* (*palo*) fly swat

matanza [ma'tanθa] *nf* slaughter

matar [ma'tar] *vt* to kill; (*tiempo, pelota*) to kill ■ *vi* to kill; **matarse** *vr* (*suicidarse*) to kill o.s., commit suicide; (*morir*) to be o get killed;

(*gastarse*) to wear o.s. out; ~ **el hambre** to stave off hunger; ~ **a algn a disgustos** to make sb's life a misery; **matarlas callando** to go about things slyly; **matarse trabajando** to kill o.s. with work; **matarse por hacer algo** to struggle to do sth

matarife [mata'rife] *nm* slaughterman

matasanos [mata'sanos] *nm inv* quack

matasellos [mata'seʎos] *nm inv* postmark

mate ['mate] *adj* (*sin brillo: color*) dull, matt ■ *nm* (*en ajedrez*) (check)mate; (*Am: hierba*) maté; (: *vasija*) gourd

matemático, -a [mate'matiko, a] *adj* mathematical ■ *nm/f* mathematician; **matemáticas** *nfpl* mathematics *sg*

materia [ma'terja] *nf* (*gen*) matter; (*Tec*) material; (*Escol*) subject; **en ~ de** on the subject of; (*en cuanto a*) as regards; ~ **prima** raw material; **entrar en ~** to get down to business

material [mate'rjal] *adj* material; (*dolor*) physical; (*real*) real; (*literal*) literal ■ *nm* material; (*Tec*) equipment; ~ **de construcción** building material; **materiales de derribo** rubble *sg*

materialismo [materja'lismo] *nm* materialism

materialista [materja'lista] *adj* materialist(ic)

materialmente [materjal'mente] *adv* materially; (*fig*) absolutely

maternal [mater'nal] *adj* motherly, maternal

maternidad [materni'ðað] *nf* motherhood, maternity

materno, -a [ma'terno, a] *adj* maternal; (*lengua*) mother *cpd*

matice *etc* [ma'tiθe] *vb ver* **matizar**

matinal [mati'nal] *adj* morning *cpd*

matiz [ma'tiθ] *nm* shade; (*de sentido*) shade, nuance; (*de ironía etc*) touch

matizar [mati'θar] *vt* (*variar*) to vary; (*Arte*) to blend; ~ **de** to tinge with

matón [ma'ton] *nm* bully

matorral [mato'rral] *nm* thicket

matraca [ma'traka] *nf* rattle; (*fam*) nuisance

matraz [ma'traθ] *nm* (*Química*) flask

matriarcado [matrjar'kaðo] *nm* matriarchy

matrícula [ma'trikula] *nf* (*registro*) register; (*Escol: inscripción*) registration; (*Auto*) registration number; (: *placa*) number plate

matricular [matriku'lar] *vt* to register, enrol

matrimonial [matrimo'njal] *adj* matrimonial

matrimonio [matri'monjo] *nm* (*pareja*) (married) couple; (*acto*) marriage; ~ **civil/ clandestino** civil/secret marriage; **contraer ~ (con)** to marry

matriz [ma'triθ] *nf* (*Anat*) womb; (*Tec*) mould; (*Mat*) matrix; **casa ~** (*Com*) head office

matrona [ma'trona] *nf* (*mujer de edad*) matron

matutino, -a [matu'tino, a] *adj* morning *cpd*

maula ['maula] *adj* (*persona*) good-for-nothing ■ *nm/f* (*vago*) idler, slacker ■ *nf* (*persona*) dead loss (*fam*)

maullar [mau'ʎar] *vi* to mew, miaow

maullido [mau'ʎiðo] *nm* mew(ing), miaow(ing)

Mauricio [mau'riθjo] *nm* Mauritius

Mauritania [mauri'tanja] *nf* Mauritania

mausoleo [mauso'leo] *nm* mausoleum

max. *abr* (= *máximo*) max.

maxilar [maksi'lar] *nm* jaw(bone)

máxima ['maksima] *nf ver* **máximo**

máxime ['maksime] *adv* especially

máximo, -a ['maksimo, a] *adj* maximum; (*más alto*) highest; (*más grande*) greatest ■ *nm* maximum ■ *nf* maxim; ~ **jefe** o **líder** (*Am*) President, leader; **como ~** at most; **al ~** to the utmost

maxisingle [maksi'singel] *nm* twelve-inch (single)

maya ['maja] *adj* Mayan ■ *nm/f* Maya(n)

mayo ['majo] *nm* May; *ver tb* **julio**

mayonesa [majo'nesa] *nf* mayonnaise

mayor [ma'jor] *adj* main, chief; (*adulto*) grown-up, adult; (*Jur*) of age; (*de edad avanzada*) elderly; (*Mus*) major; (*comparativo: de tamaño*) bigger; (: *de edad*) older; (*superlativo: de tamaño*) biggest; (*tb fig*) greatest; (: *de edad*) oldest ■ *nm* chief, boss; (*adulto*) adult; **al por ~** wholesale; ~ **de edad** adult; *ver tb* **mayores**

mayoral [majo'ral] *nm* foreman

mayordomo [major'ðomo] *nm* butler

mayoreo [majo'reo] *nm* (*Am*) wholesale (trade)

mayores [ma'jores] *nmpl* grown-ups; **llegar a ~** to get out of hand

mayoría [majo'ria] *nf* majority, greater part; **en la ~ de los casos** in most cases; **en su ~** on the whole

mayorista [majo'rista] *nm/f* wholesaler

mayoritario, -a [majori'tarjo, a] *adj* majority *cpd*; **gobierno ~** majority government

mayúsculo, -a [ma'juskulo, a] *adj* (*fig*) big, tremendous ■ *nf* capital (letter); **mayúsculas** *nfpl* capitals; (*Tip*) upper case *sg*

maza ['maθa] *nf* (*arma*) mace; (*Deporte*) bat; (*Polo*) stick

mazacote [maθa'kote] *nm* hard mass; (*Culin*) dry doughy food; (*Arte, Lit etc*) mess, hotchpotch

mazapán [maθa'pan] *nm* marzipan

mazmorra [maθ'morra] *nf* dungeon

mazo ['maθo] nm (martillo) mallet; (de mortero) pestle; (de flores) bunch; (Deporte) bat

mazorca [ma'θorka] nf (Bot) spike; (de maíz) cob, ear

Mb abr (= megabyte) Mb

MCAC nm abr = **Mercado Común de la América Central**

m.c.d. abr (= mínimo común denominador) lcd

MCI nm abr = **Mercado Común Iberoamericano**

m.c.m. abr = **mínimo común múltiplo**

me [me] pron (directo) me; (indirecto) (to) me; (reflexivo) (to) myself; **¡dámelo!** give it to me!; **me lo compró** (de mí) he bought it from me; (para mí) he bought it for me

meandro [me'andro] nm meander

mear [me'ar] (fam) vt to piss on (!) ■ vi to pee, piss (!), have a piss (!); **mearse** vr to wet o.s.

Meca ['meka] nf: **La** ~ Mecca

mecánica [me'kanika] nf ver **mecánico**

mecanice etc [meka'niθe] vb ver **mecanizar**

mecánico, -a [me'kaniko, a] adj mechanical; (repetitivo) repetitive ■ nm/f mechanic ■ nf (estudio) mechanics sg; (mecanismo) mechanism

mecanismo [meka'nismo] nm mechanism; (engranaje) gear

mecanizar [mekani'θar] vt to mechanize

mecanografía [mekanoɣra'fia] nf typewriting

mecanografiado, -a [mekanoɣra'fjaðo, a] adj typewritten ■ nm typescript

mecanógrafo, -a [meka'noɣrafo, a] nm/f (copy) typist

mecate [me'kate] nm (Am) rope

mecedor [mese'ðor] nm (Am), **mecedora** [meθe'ðora] nf rocking chair

mecenas [me'θenas] nm inv patron

mecenazgo [meθe'naθɣo] nm patronage

mecer [me'θer] vt (cuna) to rock; **mecerse** vr to rock; (rama) to sway

mecha ['metʃa] nf (de vela) wick; (de bomba) fuse; **a toda** ~ at full speed; **ponerse mechas** to streak one's hair

mechero [me'tʃero] nm (cigarette) lighter

mechón [me'tʃon] nm (gen) tuft; (manojo) bundle; (de pelo) lock

medalla [me'ðaʎa] nf medal

media ['meðja] nf ver **medio**

mediación [meða'θjon] nf mediation; **por** ~ **de** through

mediado, -a [me'ðjaðo, a] adj half-full; (trabajo) half-completed; **a mediados de** in the middle of, halfway through

medianamente [meðjana'mente] adv (moderadamente) moderately, fairly; (regularmente) moderately well

mediano, -a [me'ðjano, a] adj (regular) medium, average; (mediocre) mediocre ■ nf (Aut) central reservation, median (US); **(de tamaño)** ~ medium-sized

medianoche [meðja'notʃe] nf midnight

mediante [me'ðjante] adv by (means of), through

mediar [me'ðjar] vi (tiempo) to elapse; (interceder) to mediate, intervene; (existir) to exist; **media el hecho de que ...** there is the fact that ...

medicación [meðika'θjon] nf medication, treatment

medicamento [meðika'mento] nm medicine, drug

medicina [meði'θina] nf medicine

medicinal [meðiθi'nal] adj medicinal

medición [meði'θjon] nf measurement

médico, -a ['meðiko, a] adj medical ■ nm/f doctor; ~ **de cabecera** family doctor; ~ **pediatra** paediatrician; ~ **residente** house physician, intern (US)

medida [me'ðiða] nf measure; (medición) measurement; (de camisa, zapato etc) size, fitting; (moderación) moderation, prudence; **en cierta/gran** ~ up to a point/to a great extent; **un traje a la** ~ made-to-measure suit; ~ **de cuello** collar size; **a** ~ **de** in proportion to; (de acuerdo con) in keeping with; **con** ~ with restraint; **sin** ~ immoderately; **a** ~ **que ...** (at the same time) as ...; **tomar medidas** to take steps

medieval [meðje'βal] adj medieval

medio, -a ['meðjo, a] adj half (a); (punto) mid, middle; (promedio) average ■ adv half-; (esp Am: un tanto) rather, quite ■ nm (centro) middle, centre; (método) means, way; (ambiente) environment ■ nf (prenda de vestir) stocking; (Am) sock; (promedio) average; **medias** nfpl tights; **media hora** half an hour; ~ **litro** half a litre; **las tres y media** half past three; **M~ Oriente** Middle East; **a** ~ **camino** halfway (there); ~ **dormido** half asleep; ~ **enojado** (esp Am) rather annoyed; **lo dejó a medios** he left it half-done; **ir a medios** to go fifty fifty; **a** ~ **terminar** half finished; **en** ~ in the middle; (entre) in between; **por** ~ **de** by (means of), through; **en los medios financieros** in financial circles; **encontrarse en su** ~ to be in one's element; ~ **ambiente** environment; ~ **circulante** (Com) money supply; ver tb **medios**

medioambiental [meðjoambjen'tal] adj environmental

mediocre [me'ðjokre] adj middling, average; (pey) mediocre

m

mediocridad [meðjokri'ðað] nf middling quality; (pey) mediocrity

mediodía [meðjo'ðia] nm midday, noon

mediopensionista [meðjopensjo'nista] nm/f day boy (girl)

medios ['meðjos] nmpl means, resources; **los ~ de comunicación** the media

medir [me'ðir] vt (gen) to measure ■ vi to measure; **medirse** vr (moderarse) to be moderate, act with restraint; **¿cuánto mides? — mido 1.50 m** how tall are you? — I am 1.50 m tall

meditabundo, -a [meðita'βundo, a] adj pensive

meditar [meði'tar] vt to ponder, think over, meditate on; (planear) to think out ■ vi to ponder, think, meditate

mediterráneo, -a [meðite'rraneo, a] adj Mediterranean ■ nm: **el (mar) M~** the Mediterranean (Sea)

medrar [me'ðrar] vi to increase, grow; (mejorar) to improve; (prosperar) to prosper, thrive; (animal, planta etc) to grow

medroso, -a [me'ðroso, a] adj fearful, timid

médula ['meðula] nf (Anat) marrow; (Bot) pith; **~ espinal** spinal cord; **hasta la ~** (fig) to the core

medusa [me'ðusa] nf (Esp) jellyfish

megabyte ['meɣaβait] nm (Inform) megabyte

megafonía [meɣafo'nia] nf PA o public address system

megáfono [me'ɣafono] nm public address system

megalomanía [meɣaloma'nia] nf megalomania

megalómano, -a [meɣa'lomano, a] nm/f megalomaniac

megaocteto [meɣaok'teto] nm (Inform) megabyte

mejicano, -a [mexi'kano, a] adj, nm/f Mexican

Méjico ['mexiko] nm Mexico

mejilla [me'xiʎa] nf cheek

mejillón [mexi'ʎon] nm mussel

mejor [me'xor] adj, adv (comparativo) better; (superlativo) best; **lo ~** the best thing; **lo ~ de la vida** the prime of life; **a lo ~** probably; (quizá) maybe; **~ dicho** rather; **tanto ~** so much the better; **es el ~ de todos** he's the best of all

mejora [me'xora] nf, **mejoramiento** [mexora'mjento] nm improvement

mejorar [mexo'rar] vt to improve, make better ■ vi, **mejorarse** vr to improve, get better; (Com) to do well, prosper; **~ a** to be better than; **los negocios mejoran** business is picking up

mejoría [mexo'ria] nf improvement; (restablecimiento) recovery

mejunje [me'xunxe] nm (pey) concoction

melancolía [melanko'lia] nf melancholy

melancólico, -a [melan'koliko, a] adj (triste) sad, melancholy; (soñador) dreamy

melena [me'lena] nf (de persona) long hair; (Zool) mane

melillense [meli'ʎense] adj of o from Melilla ■ nm/f native o inhabitant of Melilla

mella ['meʎa] nf (rotura) notch, nick; **hacer ~** (fig) to make an impression

mellizo, -a [me'ʎiθo, a] adj, nm/f twin

melocotón [meloko'ton] nm (Esp) peach

melodía [melo'ðia] nf melody; (tonada) tune; (de móvil) ringtone

melodrama [melo'ðrama] nm melodrama

melodramático, -a [meloðra'matiko, a] adj melodramatic

melón [me'lon] nm melon

melopea [melo'pea] nf (fam): **tener una ~** to be sloshed

meloso, -a [me'loso, a] adj honeyed, sweet; (empalagoso) sickly, cloying; (voz) sweet; (zalamero) smooth

membrana [mem'brana] nf membrane

membrete [mem'brete] nm letterhead; **papel con ~** headed notepaper

membrillo [mem'briʎo] nm quince; **carne de ~** quince jelly

memo, -a ['memo, a] adj silly, stupid ■ nm/f idiot

memorable [memo'raβle] adj memorable

memorándum [memo'randum] nm (libro) notebook; (comunicación) memorandum

memoria [me'morja] nf (gen) memory; (artículo) (learned) paper; **memorias** nfpl (de autor) memoirs; **~ anual** annual report; **aprender algo de ~** to learn sth by heart; **si tengo buena ~** if my memory serves me right; **venir a la ~** to come to mind; (Inform): **~ de acceso aleatorio** random access memory, RAM; **~ auxiliar** backing storage; **~ fija** read-only memory, ROM; **~ del teclado** keyboard memory

memorice etc [memo'riθe] vb ver **memorizar**

memorizar [memori'θar] vt to memorize

menaje [me'naxe] nm (muebles) furniture; (utensilios domésticos) household equipment; **~ de cocina** kitchenware

mención [men'θjon] nf mention; **digno de ~** noteworthy; **hacer ~ de** to mention

mencionar [menθjo'nar] vt to mention; (nombrar) to name; **sin ~ ...** let alone ...

mendicidad [mendiθi'ðað] nf begging

mendigar [mendi'ɣar] vt to beg (for)

mendigo, -a [men'diɣo, a] nm/f beggar

mendigue *etc* [men'diɣe] *vb ver* **mendigar**

mendrugo [men'druɣo] *nm* crust

menear [mene'ar] *vt* to move; (*cola*) to wag; (*cadera*) to swing; (*fig*) to handle; **menearse** *vr* to shake; (*balancearse*) to sway; (*moverse*) to move; (*fig*) to get a move on

menester [menes'ter] *nm* (*necesidad*) necessity; **menesteres** *nmpl* (*deberes*) duties; **es ~ hacer algo** it is necessary to do sth, sth must be done

menestra [me'nestra] *nf*: **~ de verduras** vegetable stew

mengano, -a [men'gano, a] *nm/f* Mr (*o* Mrs *o* Miss) So-and-so

mengua ['mengwa] *nf* (*disminución*) decrease; (*falta*) lack; (*pobreza*) poverty; (*fig*) discredit; **en ~ de** to the detriment of

menguante [men'gwante] *adj* decreasing, diminishing; (*luna*) waning; (*marea*) ebb *cpd*

menguar [men'gwar] *vt* to lessen, diminish; (*fig*) to discredit ■ *vi* to diminish, decrease; (*fig*) to decline

mengüe *etc* ['mengwe] *vb ver* **menguar**

menopausia [meno'pausja] *nf* menopause

menor [me'nor] *adj* (*más pequeño: comparativo*) smaller; (*número*) less, lesser; (*: superlativo*) smallest; (*número*) least; (*más joven: comparativo*) younger; (*: superlativo*) youngest; (*Mus*) minor ■ *nm/f* (*joven*) young person, juvenile; **Juanito es ~ que Pepe** Juanito is younger than Pepe; **ella es la ~ de todas** she is the youngest of all; **no tengo la ~ idea** I haven't the faintest idea; **al por ~** retail; **~ de edad** under age

Menorca [me'norka] *nf* Minorca

menorquín, -ina [menor'kin, ina] *adj, nm/f* Minorcan

 PALABRA CLAVE

menos [menos] *adj* **1**: **~ (que/de)** (*compar: cantidad*) less (than); (*: número*) fewer (than); **con ~ entusiasmo** with less enthusiasm; **~ gente** fewer people; *ver tb* **cada**

2 (*superl*): **es el que ~ culpa tiene** he is the least to blame; **donde ~ problemas hay** where there are fewest problems

■ *adv* **1** (*compar*): **~ (que/de)** less (than); **me gusta ~ que el otro** I like it less than the other one; **~ de cinco** less than five; **~ de lo que piensas** less than you think

2 (*superl*): **es el ~ listo (de su clase)** he's the least bright (in his class); **de todas ellas es la que ~ me agrada** out of all of them she's the one I like least; **(por) lo ~** at (the very) least; **es lo ~ que puedo hacer** it's the least I can do; **lo ~ posible** as little as possible

3 (*locuciones*): **no quiero verle y ~ visitarle** I don't want to see him let alone visit him; **tenemos siete (de) ~** we're seven short; **eso es lo de ~** that's the least of it; **¡todo ~ eso!** anything but that!; **al/por lo ~** at (the very) least; **si al ~** if only

■ *prep* except; (*cifras*) minus; **todos ~ él** everyone except (for) him; **5 ~ 2** 5 minus 2; **las 7 ~ 20** (*hora*) 20 to 7

■ *conj*: **a ~ que**: **a menos que venga mañana** unless he comes tomorrow

menoscabar [menoska'βar] *vt* (*estropear*) to damage, harm; (*fig*) to discredit

menospreciar [menospre'θjar] *vt* to underrate, undervalue; (*despreciar*) to scorn, despise

menosprecio [menos'preθjo] *nm* (*subestimación*) underrating, undervaluation; (*desdén*) scorn, contempt

mensaje [men'saxe] *nm* message; **~ de error** (*Inform*) error message; **~ de texto** text message; **~ electrónico** email

mensajero, -a [mensa'xero, a] *nm/f* messenger

menstruación [menstrwa'θjon] *nf* menstruation

menstruar [mens'trwar] *vi* to menstruate

mensual [men'swal] *adj* monthly; **10 euros mensuales** 10 euros a month

mensualidad [menswali'ðað] *nf* (*salario*) monthly salary; (*Com*) monthly payment *o* instalment

menta ['menta] *nf* mint

mentado, -a [men'taðo, a] *adj* (*mencionado*) aforementioned; (*famoso*) well-known ■ *nf*: **hacerle una mentada a algn** (*Am fam*) to (seriously) insult sb

mental [men'tal] *adj* mental

mentalidad [mentali'ðað] *nf* mentality

mentalizar [mentali'θar] *vt* (*sensibilizar*) to make aware; (*convencer*) to convince; (*preparar mentalmente*) to psych up; **mentalizarse** *vr* (*concienciarse*) to become aware; (*prepararse mentalmente*) to get psyched up; **mentalizarse de que ...** (*convencerse*) to get it into one's head that ...

mentar [men'tar] *vt* to mention, name; **~ la madre a algn** to swear at sb

mente ['mente] *nf* mind; (*inteligencia*) intelligence; **no tengo en ~ hacer eso** it is not my intention to do so

mentecato, -a [mente'kato, a] *adj* silly, stupid ■ *nm/f* fool, idiot

mentir [men'tir] *vi* to lie; **¡miento!** sorry, I'm wrong!

mentira [men'tira] *nf* (*una mentira*) lie; (*acto*)

lying; (*invención*) fiction; ~ **piadosa** white lie; **una ~ como una casa** a whopping great lie (*fam*); **parece ~ que ...** it seems incredible that ..., I can't believe that ...

mentiroso, -a [menti'roso, a] *adj* lying; (*falso*) deceptive ■ *nm/f* liar

mentís [men'tis] *nm inv* denial; (*tb:* **dar el mentís a**) to deny

mentón [men'ton] *nm* chin

menú [me'nu] *nm* (*tb Inform*) menu; (*tb:* **menú del día**) set meal; **guiado por menú** (*Inform*) menu-driven

menudear [menuðe'ar] *vt* (*repetir*) to repeat frequently ■ *vi* (*ser frecuente*) to be frequent; (*detallar*) to go into great detail

menudencia [menu'ðenθja] *nf* (*bagatela*) trifle; **menudencias** *nfpl* odds and ends

menudeo [menu'ðeo] *nm* retail sales *pl*

menudillos [menu'ðiʎos] *nmpl* giblets

menudo, -a [me'nuðo, a] *adj* (*pequeño*) small, tiny; (*sin importancia*) petty, insignificant; **¡~ negocio!** (*fam*) some deal!; **a ~** often, frequently

meñique [me'ɲike] *nm* little finger

meollo [me'oʎo] *nm* (*fig*) essence, core

mequetrefe [meke'trefe] *nm* good-for-nothing, whippersnapper

mercader [merka'ðer] *nm* merchant

mercadería [merkaðe'ria] *nf* commodity; **mercaderías** *nfpl* goods, merchandise *sg*

mercado [mer'kaðo] *nm* market; ~ **en baja** falling market; **M~ Común** Common Market; ~ **de demanda/de oferta** seller's/buyer's market; ~ **laboral** labour market; ~ **objetivo** target market; ~ **de productos básicos** commodity market; ~ **de valores** stock market; ~ **exterior/interior** o **nacional/libre** overseas/home/free market

mercancía [merkan'θia] *nf* commodity; **mercancías** *nfpl* goods, merchandise *sg*; **mercancías en depósito** bonded goods; **mercancías perecederas** perishable goods

mercancías [merkan'θias] *nm inv* goods train, freight train (US)

mercantil [merkan'til] *adj* mercantile, commercial

mercenario, -a [merθe'narjo, a] *adj, nm* mercenary

mercería [merθe'ria] *nf* (*artículos*) haberdashery (*Brit*), notions *pl* (US); (*tienda*) haberdasher's shop (*Brit*), drapery (*Brit*), notions store (US)

Mercosur [merko'sur] *nm abr* (*Argentina, Brasil, Paraguay, Uruguay*) = **Mercado Común del Sur**

mercurio [mer'kurjo] *nm* mercury

merecedor, a [mereθe'ðor, a] *adj* deserving; ~ **de confianza** trustworthy

merecer [mere'θer] *vt* to deserve, merit ■ *vi* to be deserving, be worthy; **merece la pena** it's worthwhile

merecido, -a [mere'θiðo, a] *adj* (well) deserved; **llevarse su ~** to get one's deserts

merendar [meren'dar] *vt* to have for tea ■ *vi* to have tea; (*en el campo*) to have a picnic

merendero [meren'dero] *nm* (*café*) tearoom; (*en el campo*) picnic spot

merengue [me'renge] *nm* meringue

merezca *etc* [me'reθka] *vb ver* **merecer**

meridiano [meri'ðjano] *nm* (*Astro, Geo*) meridian; **la explicación es de una claridad meridiana** the explanation is as clear as day

meridional [meriðjo'nal] *adj* Southern ■ *nm/f* Southerner

merienda *etc* [me'rjenda] *vb ver* **merendar** ■ *nf* (light) tea, afternoon snack; (*de campo*) picnic; ~ **de negros** free-for-all

mérito ['merito] *nm* merit; (*valor*) worth, value; **hacer méritos** to make a good impression; **restar ~ a** to detract from

meritorio, -a [meri'torjo, a] *adj* deserving

merluza [mer'luθa] *nf* hake; **coger una ~** (*fam*) to get sozzled

merma ['merma] *nf* decrease; (*pérdida*) wastage

mermar [mer'mar] *vt* to reduce, lessen ■ *vi* to decrease, dwindle

mermelada [merme'laða] *nf* jam; ~ **de naranja** marmalade

mero, -a ['mero, a] *adj* mere, simple; (*Am fam*) real ■ *adv* (*Am*) just, right ■ *nm* (*Zool*) grouper; **el ~ ~** (*Am fam*) the boss

merodear [meroðe'ar] *vi* (*Mil*) to maraud; (*de noche*) to prowl (about); (*curiosear*) to snoop around

mes [mes] *nm* month; (*salario*) month's pay; **el ~ corriente** this o the current month

mesa ['mesa] *nf* table; (*de trabajo*) desk; (*Com*) counter; (*en mitin*) platform; (*Geo*) plateau; (*Arq*) landing; ~ **de noche/de tijera/de operaciones** u **operatoria** bedside/folding/operating table; ~ **redonda** (*reunión*) round table; ~ **digitalizadora** (*Inform*) graph pad; ~ **directiva** board; ~ **y cama** bed and board; **poner/quitar la ~** to lay/clear the table

mesarse [me'sarse] *vr*: ~ **el pelo** o **los cabellos** to tear one's hair

mesera [me'sera] *nf* (*Am*) waitress

mesero [me'sero] *nm* (*Am*) waiter

meseta [me'seta] *nf* (*Geo*) tableland; (*Arq*) landing

mesilla [me'siʎa], **mesita** [me'sita] *nf*: ~ **de noche** bedside table

mesón [me'son] *nm* inn

mestizo, -a [mes'tiθo, a] *adj* half-caste, of mixed race; (*Zool*) crossbred ▪ *nm/f* half-caste

mesura [me'sura] *nf* (*calma*) calm; (*moderación*) moderation, restraint; (*cortesía*) courtesy

mesurar [mesu'rar] *vt* (*contener*) to restrain; **mesurarse** *vr* to restrain o.s.

meta ['meta] *nf* goal; (*de carrera*) finish; (*fig*) goal, aim, objective

metabolismo [metaβo'lismo] *nm* metabolism

metafísico, -a [meta'fisiko, a] *adj* metaphysical ▪ *nf* metaphysics *sg*

metáfora [me'tafora] *nf* metaphor

metafórico, -a [meta'foriko, a] *adj* metaphorical

metal [me'tal] *nm* (*materia*) metal; (*Mus*) brass

metálico, -a [me'taliko, a] *adj* metallic; (*de metal*) metal ▪ *nm* (*dinero contante*) cash

metalurgia [meta'lurxja] *nf* metallurgy

metalúrgico, -a [meta'lurxiko, a] *adj* metallurgic(al); **industria metalúrgica** engineering industry

metamorfosear [metamorfose'ar] *vt*: ~ **(en)** to metamorphose o transform (into)

metamorfosis [metamor'fosis] *nf inv* metamorphosis, transformation

metedura [mete'ðura] *nf*: ~ **de pata** (*fam*) blunder

meteorito [meteo'rito] *nm* meteorite

meteoro [mete'oro] *nm* meteor

meteorología [meteorolo'xia] *nf* meteorology

meteorólogo, -a [meteo'roloyo, a] *nm/f* meteorologist; (*Radio, TV*) weather reporter

meter [me'ter] *vt* (*colocar*) to put, place; (*introducir*) to put in, insert; (*involucrar*) to involve; **meterse** *vr*: **meterse en** to go into, enter; (*fig*) to interfere in, meddle in; **meterse a** to start; **meterse a escritor** to become a writer; **meterse con algn** to provoke sb, pick a quarrel with sb; ~ **prisa a algn** to hurry sb up

meticuloso, -a [metiku'loso, a] *adj* meticulous, thorough

metido, -a [me'tiðo, a] *adj*: **estar muy ~ en un asunto** to be deeply involved in a matter; ~ **en años** elderly; ~ **en carne** plump

metódico, -a [me'toðiko, a] *adj* methodical

metodismo [meto'ðismo] *nm* Methodism

método ['metoðo] *nm* method

metodología [metoðolo'xia] *nf* methodology

metomentodo [metomen'toðo] *nm inv* meddler, busybody

metraje [me'traxe] *nm* (*Cine*) length; **cinta de largo/corto** ~ full-length film/short

metralla [me'traʎa] *nf* shrapnel

metralleta [metra'ʎeta] *nf* sub-machine-gun

métrico, -a ['metriko, a] *adj* metric ▪ *nf* metrics *pl*; **cinta métrica** tape measure

metro ['metro] *nm* metre; (*tren: tb*: **metropolitano**) underground (*Brit*), subway (*US*); (*instrumento*) rule; ~ **cuadrado/cúbico** square/cubic metre

metrópoli [me'tropoli], **metrópolis** [me'tropolis] *nf* (*ciudad*) metropolis; (*colonial*) mother country

mexicano, -a [mexi'kano, a] *adj, nm/f* (*Am*) Mexican

México ['mexiko] *nm* (*Am*) Mexico; **Ciudad de** ~ Mexico City

mezcla ['meθkla] *nf* mixture; (*fig*) blend

mezclar [meθ'klar] *vt* to mix (up); (*armonizar*) to blend; (*combinar*) to merge; **mezclarse** *vr* to mix, mingle; ~ **en** to get mixed up in, get involved in

mezcolanza [meθko'lanθa] *nf* hotchpotch, jumble

mezquindad [meθkin'dað] *nf* (*cicatería*) meanness; (*miras estrechas*) pettiness; (*acto*) mean action

mezquino, -a [meθ'kino, a] *adj* (*cicatero*) mean ▪ *nm/f* (*avaro*) mean person; (*miserable*) petty individual

mezquita [meθ'kita] *nf* mosque

mg *abr* (= *miligramo(s)*) mg

mi [mi] *adj posesivo* my ▪ *nm* (*Mus*) E

mí [mi] *pron* me, myself; **¿y a mí qué?** so what?

miaja ['mjaxa] *nf* crumb; **ni una** ~ (*fig*) not the least little bit

miau [mjau] *nm* miaow

michelín [mitʃe'lin] *nm* (*fam*) spare tyre

mico ['miko] *nm* monkey

micro ['mikro] *nm* (*Radio*) mike, microphone; (*Am: pequeño*) minibus; (: *grande*) coach, bus

microbio [mi'kroβjo] *nm* microbe

microbús [mikro'βus] *nm* minibus

microchip [mikro'tʃip] *nm* microchip

microcomputador [mikrokomputa'ðor] *nm*, **microcomputadora** [mikrokomputa'ðora] *nf* micro(computer)

microeconomía [mikroekono'mia] *nf* microeconomics *sg*

microficha [mikro'fitʃa] *nf* microfiche

microfilm (*pl* **microfilms**) [mikro'film, mikro'films] *nm* microfilm

micrófono [mi'krofono] *nm* microphone

microinformática [mikroinfor'matika] *nf* microcomputing

micrómetro [mi'krometro] *nm* micrometer

microonda [mikro'onda] *nf* microwave;

(horno) microondas microwave (oven)
microordenador [mikroordena'ðor] *nm*
microcomputer
micropastilla [mikropas'tiʎa],
microplaqueta [mikropla'keta] *nf* (*Inform*)
chip, wafer
microplaquita [mikropla'kita] *nf*: ~ **de**
silicio silicon chip
microprocesador [mikroprocesa'ðor] *nm*
microprocessor
microscópico, -a [mikros'kopiko, a] *adj*
microscopic
microscopio [mikros'kopjo] *nm* microscope
midiendo *etc* [mi'ðjendo] *vb ver* **medir**
miedo ['mjeðo] *nm* fear; (*nerviosismo*)
apprehension, nervousness; **meter ~ a** to
scare, frighten; **tener ~** to be afraid; **de ~**
wonderful, marvellous; **¡qué ~!** (*fam*) how
awful!; **me da ~** it scares me; **hace un frío**
de ~ (*fam*) it's terribly cold
miedoso, -a [mje'ðoso, a] *adj* fearful, timid
miel [mjel] *nf* honey; **no hay ~ sin hiel**
there's no rose without a thorn
miembro ['mjembro] *nm* limb; (*socio*)
member; (*de institución*) fellow; **~ viril** penis
mientes *etc* ['mjentes] *vb ver* **mentar; mentir**
∎ *nfpl*: **no parar ~ en** to pay no attention to;
traer a las ~ to recall
mientras ['mjentras] *conj* while; (*duración*) as
long as ∎ *adv* meanwhile; **~ (que)** whereas;
~ tanto meanwhile; **~ más tiene, más**
quiere the more he has, the more he wants
miércoles ['mjerkoles] *nm inv* Wednesday; **~**
de ceniza Ash Wednesday; *ver tb* **Carnaval;**
sábado
mierda ['mjerða] *nf* (*fam!*) shit (*!*); crap (*!*); (*fig*)
filth, dirt; **¡vete a la ~!** go to hell!
mies [mjes] *nf* (ripe) corn, wheat, grain
miga ['miɣa] *nf* crumb; (*fig: meollo*) essence;
hacer buenas migas (*fam*) to get on well;
esto tiene su ~ there's more to this than
meets the eye
migaja [mi'ɣaxa] *nf*: **una ~ de** (*un poquito*) a
little; **migajas** *nfpl* crumbs; (*pey*) left-overs
migración [miɣra'θjon] *nf* migration
migratorio, -a [miɣra'torjo, a] *adj* migratory
mil [mil] *num* thousand; **dos ~ libras** two
thousand pounds
milagro [mi'laɣro] *nm* miracle; **hacer**
milagros (*fig*) to work wonders
milagroso, -a [mila'ɣroso, a] *adj* miraculous
Milán [mi'lan] *nm* Milan
milenario, -a [mile'narjo, a] *adj* millennial;
(*fig*) very ancient
milenio [mi'lenjo] *nm* 'millennium
milésimo, -a [mi'lesimo, a] *num* thousandth
mileurista *nmf* *person earning around a thousand*

euros or less; **un ~ no puede comprar ese piso**
no one on a salary of a thousand euros could
afford that flat ∎ *adj* of (around) a thousand
euros; **un sueldo ~** a salary of (around) a
thousand euros
mili ['mili] *nf*: **hacer la ~** (*fam*) to do one's
military service; *see note*

milicia [mi'liθja] *nf* (*Mil*) militia; (*servicio*
militar) military service
miligramo [mili'ɣramo] *nm* milligram
milímetro [mi'limetro] *nm* millimetre (*Brit*),
millimeter (*US*)
militante [mili'tante] *adj* militant
militar [mili'tar] *adj* military ∎ *nm/f* soldier
∎ *vi* to serve in the army; (*fig*) to militate, fight
militarismo [milita'rismo] *nm* militarism
milla ['miʎa] *nf* mile; **~ marina** nautical mile
millar [mi'ʎar] *num* thousand; **a millares** in
thousands
millón [mi'ʎon] *num* million
millonario, -a [miʎo'narjo, a] *nm/f*
millionaire
millonésimo, -a [miʎo'nesimo, a] *num*
millionth
mimado, -a [mi'maðo, a] *adj* spoiled
mimar [mi'mar] *vt* to spoil, pamper
mimbre ['mimbre] *nm* wicker; **de ~** wicker
cpd, wickerwork
mimetismo [mime'tismo] *nm* mimicry
mímica ['mimika] *nf* (*para comunicarse*) sign
language; (*imitación*) mimicry
mimo ['mimo] *nm* (*caricia*) caress; (*de niño*)
spoiling; (*Teat*) mime; (: *actor*) mime artist
mina ['mina] *nf* mine; (*pozo*) shaft; (*de lápiz*)
lead refill; **hullera o ~ de carbón** coalmine
minar [mi'nar] *vt* to mine; (*fig*) to undermine
mineral [mine'ral] *adj* mineral ∎ *nm* (*Geo*)
mineral; (*mena*) ore
minería [mine'ria] *nf* mining
minero, -a [mi'nero, a] *adj* mining *cpd*
∎ *nm/f* miner

miniatura [minja'tura] *adj inv, nf* miniature
minicadena [minika'ðena] *nf (Mus)* mini hi-fi
minicomputador [minikomputa'ðor] *nm* minicomputer
MiniDisc® [mini'disk] *nm* MiniDisc®
minidisco [mini'ðisko] *nm* diskette
minifalda [mini'falda] *nf* miniskirt
minifundio [mini'fundjo] *nm* smallholding, small farm
minimizar [minimi'θar] *vt* to minimize
mínimo, -a ['minimo, a] *adj* minimum; *(insignificante)* minimal ■ *nm* minimum; **precio/salario ~** minimum price/wage; **lo ~ que pueden hacer** the least they can do
minino, -a [mi'nino, a] *nm/f (fam)* puss, pussy
ministerio [minis'terjo] *nm* ministry *(Brit)*, department *(US)*; **M~ de Asuntos Exteriores** Foreign Office *(Brit)*, State Department *(US)*; **M~ del Comercio e Industria** Department of Trade and Industry; **M~ de (la) Gobernación** *o* **del Interior** ~ Home Office *(Brit)*, Ministry of the Interior; **M~ de Hacienda** Treasury *(Brit)*, Treasury Department *(US)*
ministro, -a [mi'nistro, a] *nm/f* minister, secretary *(esp US)*; **M~ de Hacienda** Chancellor of the Exchequer, Secretary of the Treasury *(US)*; **M~ de (la) Gobernación** *o* **del Interior** ~ Home Secretary *(Brit)*, Secretary of the Interior *(US)*
minoría [mino'ria] *nf* minority
minorista [mino'rista] *nm* retailer
mintiendo *etc* [min'tjendo] *vb ver* **mentir**
minucia [mi'nuθja] *nf (detalle insignificante)* trifle; *(bagatela)* mere nothing
minuciosidad [minuθjosi'ðað] *nf (meticulosidad)* thoroughness, meticulousness
minucioso, -a [minu'θjoso, a] *adj* thorough, meticulous; *(prolijo)* very detailed
minúsculo, -a [mi'nuskulo, a] *adj* tiny, minute ■ *nf* small letter; **minúsculas** *nfpl (Tip)* lower case *sg*
minusvalía [minusβa'lia] *nf* physical handicap; *(Com)* depreciation, capital loss
minusválido, -a [minus'βaliðo, a] *adj* (physically) handicapped *o* disabled ■ *nm/f* disabled person
minuta [mi'nuta] *nf (de comida)* menu; *(de abogado etc)* fee
minutero [minu'tero] *nm* minute hand
minuto [mi'nuto] *nm* minute
Miño ['miɲo] *nm*: **el (río) ~** the Miño
mío, -a ['mio, a] *adj, pron*: **el ~** mine; **un amigo ~** a friend of mine; **lo ~** what is mine; **los míos** my people, my relations
miope ['mjope] *adj* short-sighted

miopía [mjo'pia] *nf* near- *o* short-sightedness
MIR [mir] *nm abr (Pol)* = **Movimiento de Izquierda Revolucionaria**; *(Esp Med)* = **Médico Interno y Residente**
mira ['mira] *nf (de arma)* sight(s) *pl*; *(fig)* aim, intention; **de amplias/estrechas miras** broad-/narrow-minded
mirada [mi'raða] *nf* look, glance; *(expresión)* look, expression; **~ de soslayo** sidelong glance; **~ fija** stare, gaze; **~ perdida** distant look; **echar una ~ a** to glance at; **levantar/bajar la ~** to look up/down; **resistir la ~ de algn** to stare sb out
mirado, -a [mi'raðo, a] *adj (sensato)* sensible; *(considerado)* considerate; **bien/mal ~** well/not well thought of
mirador [mira'ðor] *nm* viewpoint, vantage point
miramiento [mira'mjento] *nm (consideración)* considerateness; **tratar sin miramientos a algn** to ride roughshod over sb
mirar [mi'rar] *vt* to look at; *(observar)* to watch; *(considerar)* to consider, think over; *(vigilar, cuidar)* to watch, look after ■ *vi* to look; *(Arq)* to face; **mirarse** *vr (dos personas)* to look at each other; **~ algo/a algn de reojo** *o* **de través** to look askance at sth/sb; **~ algo/a algn por encima del hombro** to look down on sth/sb; **~ bien/mal** to think highly of/have a poor opinion of; **~ fijamente** to stare *o* gaze at; **~ por** *(fig)* to look after; **~ por la ventana** to look out of the window; **mirarse al espejo** to look at o.s. in the mirror; **mirarse a los ojos** to look into each other's eyes
mirilla [mi'riʎa] *nf (agujero)* spyhole, peephole
mirlo ['mirlo] *nm* blackbird
misa ['misa] *nf* mass; **~ del gallo** midnight mass *(on Christmas Eve)*; **~ de difuntos** requiem mass; **como en ~** in dead silence; **estos datos van a ~** *(fig)* these facts are utterly trustworthy
misántropo [mi'santropo] *nm* misanthrope, misanthropist
miscelánea [misθe'lanea] *nf* miscellany
miserable [mise'raβle] *adj (avaro)* mean, stingy; *(nimio)* miserable, paltry; *(lugar)* squalid; *(fam)* vile, despicable ■ *nm/f (malvado)* rogue
miseria [mi'serja] *nf* misery; *(pobreza)* poverty; *(tacañería)* meanness, stinginess; *(condiciones)* squalor; **una ~** a pittance
misericordia [miseri'korðja] *nf (compasión)* compassion, pity; *(perdón)* forgiveness, mercy
misil [mi'sil] *nm* missile
misión [mi'sjon] *nf* mission; *(tarea)* job,

m

duty; (Pol) assignment; **misiones** nfpl (Rel) overseas missions

misionero, -a [misjo'nero, a] nm/f missionary

mismamente [misma'mente] adv (fam: sólo) only, just

mismísimo, -a [mis'misimo, a] adj superlativo selfsame, very (same)

mismo, -a ['mismo, a] adj (semejante) same; (después de pronombre) -self; (para énfasis) very ■ adv: **aquí/ayer/hoy** ~ right here/only yesterday/this very day; **ahora** ~ right now ■ conj: **lo** ~ **que** just like, just as; **por lo** ~ for the same reason; **el** ~ **traje** the same suit; **en ese** ~ **momento** at that very moment; **vino el** ~ **Ministro** the Minister himself came; **yo** ~ **lo vi** I saw it myself; **lo hizo por sí** ~ he did it by himself; **lo** ~ the same (thing); **da lo** ~ it's all the same; **quedamos en las mismas** we're no further forward

misógino [mi'soxino] nm misogynist

miss [mis] nf beauty queen

misterio [mis'terjo] nm mystery; (lo secreto) secrecy

misterioso, -a [miste'rjoso, a] adj mysterious; (inexplicable) puzzling

misticismo [misti'θismo] nm mysticism

místico, -a ['mistiko, a] adj mystic(al) ■ nm/f mystic ■ nf mysticism

mitad [mi'tað] nf (medio) half; (centro) middle; ~ (y) ~ half-and-half; (fig) yes and no; **a** ~ **de precio** (at) half-price; **en** o **a** ~ **del camino** halfway along the road; **cortar por la** ~ to cut through the middle

mítico, -a ['mitiko, a] adj mythical

mitigar [miti'ɣar] vt to mitigate; (dolor) to relieve; (sed) to quench; (ira) to appease; (preocupación) to allay; (soledad) to alleviate

mitigue etc [mi'tiɣe] vb ver **mitigar**

mitin ['mitin] nm (esp Pol) meeting

mito ['mito] nm myth

mitología [mitolo'xia] nf mythology

mitológico, -a [mito'loxiko, a] adj mythological

mixto, -a ['miksto, a] adj mixed; (comité) joint

ml abr (= mililitro(s)) ml

mill. abr (= millón, millones) M

mm abr (= milímetro(s)) mm

MMS nm abr (= multimedia message service) MMS m

M.N. (Am), **m/n** abr (Econ) = **moneda nacional**

M.° abr (Pol: = Ministerio) Min

m/o abr (Com) = **mi orden**

mobiliario [moβi'ljarjo] nm furniture

mocasín [moka'sin] nm moccasin

mocedad [moθe'ðað] nf youth

mochila [mo'tʃila] nf rucksack (Brit), backpack

moción [mo'θjon] nf motion; ~ **compuesta** (Pol) composite motion

moco ['moko] nm mucus; **limpiarse los mocos** to blow one's nose; **no es** ~ **de pavo** it's no trifle

mocoso, -a [mo'koso, a] adj snivelling; (fig) ill-bred ■ nm/f (fam) brat

moda ['moða] nf fashion; (estilo) style; **de** o **a la** ~ in fashion, fashionable; **pasado de** ~ out of fashion; **vestido a la última** ~ trendily dressed

modal [mo'ðal] adj modal ■ nm: **modales** manners

modalidad [moðali'ðað] nf (clase) kind, variety; (manera) way; (Inform) mode; ~ **de texto** (Inform) text mode

modelar [moðe'lar] vt to model

modelo [mo'ðelo] adj inv model ■ nm/f model ■ nm (patrón) pattern; (norma) standard

módem ['moðem] nm (Inform) modem

moderado, -a [moðe'raðo, a] adj moderate

moderar [moðe'rar] vt to moderate; (violencia) to restrain, control; (velocidad) to reduce; **moderarse** vr to restrain o.s., control o.s

modernice etc [moðer'niθe] vb ver **modernizar**

modernizar [moðerni'θar] vt to modernize; (Inform) to upgrade

moderno, -a [mo'ðerno, a] adj modern; (actual) present-day; (equipo etc) up-to-date

modestia [mo'ðestja] nf modesty

modesto, -a [mo'ðesto, a] adj modest

módico, -a ['moðiko, a] adj moderate, reasonable

modificar [moðifi'kar] vt to modify

modifique etc [moði'fike] vb ver **modificar**

modismo [mo'ðismo] nm idiom

modisto, -a [mo'ðisto, a] nm/f dressmaker

modo ['moðo] nm (manera, forma) way, manner; (Inform, Mus) mode; (Ling) mood; **modos** nmpl manners; **"~ de empleo"** "instructions for use"; ~ **de gobierno** form of government; **a** ~ **de** like; **de este** ~ in this way; **de ningún** ~ in no way; **de todos modos** at any rate; **de un** ~ **u otro** (in) one way or another

modorra [mo'ðorra] nf drowsiness

modoso, -a [mo'ðoso, a] adj (educado) quiet, well-mannered

modulación [moðula'θjon] nf modulation; ~ **de frecuencia** (Radio) frequency modulation, FM

módulo ['moðulo] *nm* module; *(de mueble)* unit

mofarse [mo'farse] *vr*: ~ **de** to mock, scoff at

moflete [mo'flete] *nm* fat cheek, chubby cheek

mogollón [moɣo'ʎon] *(fam) nm*: ~ **de discos** *etc* loads of records *etc* ∎ *adv*: **un** ~ a hell of a lot

mohín [mo'in] *nm (mueca)* (wry) face; *(pucheros)* pout

mohíno, -a [mo'ino, a] *adj (triste)* gloomy, depressed; *(enojado)* sulky

moho ['moo] *nm (Bot)* mould, mildew; *(en metal)* rust

mohoso, -a [mo'oso, a] *adj* mouldy; rusty

mojado, -a [mo'xaðo, a] *adj* wet; *(húmedo)* damp; *(empapado)* drenched

mojar [mo'xar] *vt* to wet; *(humedecer)* to damp(en), moisten; *(calar)* to soak; **mojarse** *vr* to get wet; ~ **el pan en el café** to dip o dunk one's bread in one's coffee

mojigato, -a [moxi'ɣato, a] *adj (hipócrita)* hypocritical; *(santurrón)* sanctimonious; *(gazmoño)* prudish ∎ *nm/f* hypocrite; sanctimonious person; prude

mojón [mo'xon] *nm (hito)* landmark; *(en un camino)* signpost; *(tb:* **mojón kilométrico**) milestone

mol. *abr* (= *molécula*) mol

molar [mo'lar] *nm* molar ∎ *vt (fam)*: **lo que más me mola es** ... what I'm really into is ...; **¿te mola un pitillo?** do you fancy a smoke?

Moldavia [mol'ðaβja], **Moldova** [mol'ðoβa] *nf* Moldavia, Moldova

moldavo, -a [mol'ðaβo, a] *adj, nm/f* Moldavian, Moldovan

molde ['molde] *nm* mould; *(vaciado)* cast; *(de costura)* pattern; *(fig)* model

moldear [molde'ar] *vt* to mould; *(en yeso etc)* to cast

mole ['mole] *nf* mass, bulk; *(edificio)* pile

molécula [mo'lekula] *nf* molecule

moler [mo'ler] *vt* to grind, crush; *(pulverizar)* to pound; *(trigo etc)* to mill; *(cansar)* to tire out, exhaust; ~ **a algn a palos** to give sb a beating

molestar [moles'tar] *vt* to bother; *(fastidiar)* to annoy; *(incomodar)* to inconvenience, put out; *(perturbar)* to trouble, upset ∎ *vi* to be a nuisance; **molestarse** *vr* to bother; *(incomodarse)* to go to a lot of trouble; *(ofenderse)* to take offence; **¿le molesta el ruido?** do you mind the noise?; **siento molestarle** I'm sorry to trouble you

molestia [mo'lestja] *nf* bother, trouble; *(incomodidad)* inconvenience; *(Med)* discomfort; **no es ninguna** ~ it's no trouble at all

molesto, -a [mo'lesto, a] *adj (que fastidia)* annoying; *(incómodo)* inconvenient; *(inquieto)* uncomfortable, ill at ease; *(enfadado)* annoyed; **estar** ~ *(Med)* to be in some discomfort; **estar** ~ **con algn** *(fig)* to be cross with sb; **me sentí** ~ I felt embarrassed

molido, -a [mo'liðo, a] *adj (machacado)* ground; *(pulverizado)* powdered; **estar** ~ *(fig)* to be exhausted o dead beat

molinero [moli'nero] *nm* miller

molinillo [moli'niʎo] *nm* hand mill; ~ **de carne/café** mincer/coffee grinder

molino [mo'lino] *nm (edificio)* mill; *(máquina)* grinder

mollera [mo'ʎera] *nf (Anat)* crown of the head; *(fam: seso)* brains *pl*; **duro de** ~ *(estúpido)* thick

Molucas [mo'lukas] *nfpl*: **las (Islas)** ~ the Moluccas, the Molucca Islands

molusco [mo'lusko] *nm* mollusc

momentáneo, -a [momen'taneo, a] *adj* momentary

momento [mo'mento] *nm (gen)* moment; *(Tec)* momentum; **de** ~ at the moment, for the moment; **en ese** ~ at that moment, just then; **por el** ~ for the time being

momia ['momja] *nf* mummy

mona ['mona] *nf ver* **mono**

Mónaco ['monako] *nm* Monaco

monada [mo'naða] *nf (gracia)* charming habit; *(cosa primorosa)* lovely thing; *(chica)* pretty girl; **¡qué** ~! isn't it cute?

monaguillo [mona'ɣiʎo] *nm* altar boy

monarca [mo'narka] *nm/f* monarch, ruler

monarquía [monar'kia] *nf* monarchy

monárquico, -a [mo'narkiko, a] *nm/f* royalist, monarchist

monasterio [monas'terjo] *nm* monastery

Moncloa [mon'kloa] *nf*: **la** ~ *official residence of the Spanish Prime Minister*

monda ['monda] *nf (poda)* pruning; *(: de árbol)* lopping; *(: de fruta)* peeling; *(cáscara)* skin; **¡es la** ~! *(fam: fantástico)* it's great!; *(: el colmo)* it's the limit!; *(: persona: gracioso)* he's a knockout!

mondadientes [monda'ðjentes] *nm inv* toothpick

mondar [mon'dar] *vt (limpiar)* to clean; *(pelar)* to peel; **mondarse** *vr*: **mondarse de risa** *(fam)* to split one's sides laughing

moneda [mo'neða] *nf (tipo de dinero)* currency, money; *(pieza)* coin; **una** ~ **de 50 céntimos** a 50-cent coin; ~ **de curso** legal tender; ~ **extranjera** foreign exchange; ~ **única** single currency; **es** ~ **corriente** *(fig)* it's common knowledge

monedero [mone'ðero] *nm* purse

monegasco, -a [mone'ɣasko, a] *adj* of o from

m

Monaco, Monegasque ■ nm/f Monegasque

monetario, -a [mone'tarjo, a] adj monetary, financial

monetarista [moneta'rista] adj, nm/f monetarist

mongólico, -a [mon'goliko, a] adj, nm/f Mongol

monigote [moni'ɣote] nm (dibujo) doodle; (de papel) cut-out figure; (pey) wimp; ver tb **inocente**

monitor [moni'tor] nm (Inform) monitor; ~ **en color** colour monitor

monja ['monxa] nf nun

monje ['monxe] nm monk

mono, -a ['mono, a] adj (bonito) lovely, pretty; (gracioso) nice, charming ■ nm/f monkey, ape ■ nm dungarees pl; (traje de faena) overalls pl; (fam: de drogadicto) cold turkey; **una chica muy mona** a very pretty girl; **dormir la** ~ to sleep it off

monóculo [mo'nokulo] nm monocle

monografía [monoɣra'fia] nf monograph

monolingüe [mono'lingwe] adj monolingual

monólogo [mo'noloɣo] nm monologue

monomando [mono'mando] nm (tb: **grifo monomando**) mixer tap

monoparental [monoparen'tal] adj: **familia** ~ single-parent family

monopatín [monopa'tin] nm skateboard

monopolice etc [monopo'liθe] vb ver **monopolizar**

monopolio [mono'poljo] nm monopoly; ~ **total** absolute monopoly

monopolista [monopo'lista] adj, nm/f monopolist

monopolizar [monopoli'θar] vt to monopolize

monosílabo, -a [mono'silaβo, a] adj monosyllabic ■ nm monosyllable

monotonía [monoto'nia] nf (sonido) monotone; (fig) monotony

monótono, -a [mo'notono, a] adj monotonous

mono-usuario, -a [monou'swarjo, a] adj (Inform) single-user

monóxido [mo'noksiðo] nm monoxide; ~ **de carbono** carbon monoxide

Mons. abr (Rel) = **Monseñor**

monseñor [monse'ɲor] nm monsignor

monserga [mon'serɣa] nf (lenguaje confuso) gibberish; (tonterías) drivel

monstruo ['monstrwo] nm monster ■ adj inv fantastic

monstruoso, -a [mons'trwoso, a] adj monstrous

monta ['monta] nf total, sum; **de poca** ~ unimportant, of little account

montacargas [monta'karɣas] nm inv service lift (Brit), freight elevator (US)

montador [monta'ðor] nm (para montar) mounting block; (profesión) fitter; (Cine) film editor

montaje [mon'taxe] nm assembly; (organización) fitting up; (Teat) décor; (Cine) montage

montante [mon'tante] nm (poste) upright; (soporte) stanchion; (Arq: de puerta) transom; (: de ventana) mullion; (suma) amount, total

montaña [mon'taɲa] nf (monte) mountain; (sierra) mountains pl, mountainous area; (Am: selva) forest; ~ **rusa** roller coaster

montañero, -a [monta'ɲero, a] adj mountain cpd ■ nm/f mountaineer, climber

montañés, -esa [monta'ɲes, esa] adj mountain cpd; (de Santander) of o from the Santander region ■ nm/f highlander; native o inhabitant of the Santander region

montañismo [monta'ɲismo] nm mountaineering, climbing

montañoso, -a [monta'ɲoso, a] adj mountainous

montar [mon'tar] vt (subir a) to mount, get on; (caballo etc) to ride; (Tec) to assemble, put together; (negocio) to set up; (colocar) to lift on to; (Cine: película) to edit; (Teat: obra) to stage, put on; (Culin: batir) to whip, beat ■ vi to mount, get on; (sobresalir) to overlap; ~ **en cólera** to get angry; ~ **un número** o **numerito** to make a scene; **tanto monta** it makes no odds

montaraz [monta'raθ] adj mountain cpd, highland cpd; (pey) uncivilized

monte ['monte] nm (montaña) mountain; (bosque) woodland; (área sin cultivar) wild area, wild country; ~ **de piedad** pawnshop; ~ **alto** forest; ~ **bajo** scrub(land)

montera [mon'tera] nf (sombrero) cloth cap; (de torero) bullfighter's hat

monto ['monto] nm total, amount

montón [mon'ton] nm heap, pile; **un** ~ **de** (fig) heaps of, lots of; **a montones** by the score, galore

montura [mon'tura] nf (cabalgadura) mount; (silla) saddle; (arreos) harness; (de joya) mounting; (de gafas) frame

monumental [monumen'tal] adj (tb fig) monumental; **zona** ~ area of historical interest

monumento [monu'mento] nm monument; (de conmemoración) memorial

monzón [mon'θon] nm monsoon

moña ['moɲa] nf hair ribbon

moño ['moɲo] nm (de pelo) bun; **estar hasta**

el ~ (fam) to be fed up to the back teeth

MOPTMA nm abr = **Ministerio de Obras Públicas, Transporte y Medio Ambiente**

moqueta [mo'keta] nf fitted carpet

moquillo [mo'kiʎo] nm (enfermedad) distemper

mora ['mora] nf (Bot) mulberry; (: zarzamora) blackberry; (Com): **en ~** in arrears

morado, -a [mo'raðo, a] adj purple, violet ■ nm bruise ■ nf (casa) dwelling, abode; **pasarlas moradas** to have a tough time of it

moral [mo'ral] adj moral ■ nf (ética) ethics pl; (moralidad) morals pl, morality; (ánimo) morale; **tener baja la ~** to be in low spirits

moraleja [mora'lexa] nf moral

moralice etc [mora'liθe] vb ver **moralizar**

moralidad [morali'ðað] nf morals pl, morality

moralizar [morali'θar] vt to moralize

morar [mo'rar] vi to live, dwell

moratón [mora'ton] nm bruise

moratoria [mora'torja] nf moratorium

morbo ['morβo] nm (fam) morbid pleasure

morbosidad [morβosi'ðað] nf morbidity

morboso, -a [mor'βoso, a] adj morbid

morcilla [mor'θiʎa] nf blood sausage, ≈ black pudding (Brit)

mordaz [mor'ðaθ] adj (crítica) biting, scathing

mordaza [mor'ðaθa] nf (para la boca) gag; (Tec) clamp

morder [mor'ðer] vt to bite; (mordisquear) to nibble; (fig: consumir) to eat away, eat into ■ vi, **morderse** vr to bite; **está que muerde** he's hopping mad; **morderse la lengua** to hold one's tongue

mordida [mor'ðiða] nf (Am fam) bribe

mordisco [mor'ðisko] nm bite

mordisquear [morðiske'ar] vt to nibble at

moreno, -a [mo'reno, a] adj (color) (dark) brown; (de tez) dark; (de pelo moreno) dark-haired; (negro) black ■ nm/f (de tez) dark-skinned man/woman; (de pelo) dark-haired man/woman

morfina [mor'fina] nf morphine

morfinómano, -a [morfi'nomano, a] adj addicted to hard drugs ■ nm/f drug addict

morgue ['morgue] nf (Am) mortuary (Brit), morgue (US)

moribundo, -a [mori'βundo, a] adj dying ■ nm/f dying person

morir [mo'rir] vi to die; (fuego) to die down; (luz) to go out; **morirse** vr to die; (fig) to be dying; (Ferro etc: vías) to end; (calle) to come out; **fue muerto a tiros/en un accidente** he was shot (dead)/was killed in an accident; **~ de frío/hambre** to die of cold/starve to death; **¡me muero de hambre!** (fig) I'm starving!; **morirse por algo** to be dying for sth; **morirse por algn** to be crazy about sb

mormón, -ona [mor'mon, ona] nm/f Mormon

moro, -a ['moro, a] adj Moorish ■ nm/f Moor; **¡hay moros en la costa!** watch out!

moroso, -a [mo'roso, a] adj (lento) slow ■ nm (Com) bad debtor, defaulter; **deudor ~** (Com) slow payer

morral [mo'rral] nm haversack

morriña [mo'rriɲa] nf homesickness; **tener ~** to be homesick

morro ['morro] nm (Zool) snout, nose; (Auto, Aviat) nose; (fam: labio) (thick) lip; **beber a ~** to drink from the bottle; **caer de ~** to nosedive; **estar de morros (con algn)** to be in a bad mood (with sb); **tener ~** to have a nerve

morrocotudo, -a [morroko'tuðo, a] adj (fam: fantástico) smashing; (riña, golpe) tremendous; (fuerte) strong; (pesado) heavy; (difícil) awkward

morsa ['morsa] nf walrus

morse ['morse] nm Morse (code)

mortadela [morta'ðela] nf mortadella, bologna sausage

mortaja [mor'taxa] nf shroud; (Tec) mortise; (Am) cigarette paper

mortal [mor'tal] adj mortal; (golpe) deadly

mortalidad [mortali'ðað], **mortandad** [mortan'dað] nf mortality

mortecino, -a [morte'θino, a] adj (débil) weak; (luz) dim; (color) dull

mortero [mor'tero] nm mortar

mortífero, -a [mor'tifero, a] adj deadly, lethal

mortificar [mortifi'kar] vt to mortify; (atormentar) to torment

mortifique etc [morti'fike] vb ver **mortificar**

mortuorio, -a [mor'tworjo, a] adj mortuary, death cpd

Mosa ['mosa] nm: **el (Río) ~** the Meuse

mosaico [mo'saiko] nm mosaic

mosca ['moska] nf fly; **por si las moscas** just in case; **estar ~** (desconfiar) to smell a rat; **tener la ~ en o detrás de la oreja** to be wary

moscovita [mosko'βita] adj Muscovite, Moscow cpd ■ nm/f Muscovite

Moscú [mos'ku] nm Moscow

mosquear [moske'ar] vt (hacer sospechar) to make suspicious; (fastidiar) to annoy; **mosquearse** vr (enfadarse) to get annoyed; (ofenderse) to take offence

mosquita [mos'kita] nf: **parece una ~ muerta** he looks as though butter wouldn't melt in his mouth

mosquitero [moski'tero] nm mosquito net

mosquito [mos'kito] *nm* mosquito
Mossos ['mosos] *nmpl*: ~ **d'Esquadra** Catalan police; *ver tb* **policía**
mostaza [mos'taθa] *nf* mustard
mosto ['mosto] *nm* unfermented grape juice
mostrador [mostra'ðor] *nm* (*de tienda*) counter; (*de café*) bar
mostrar [mos'trar] *vt* to show; (*exhibir*) to display, exhibit; (*explicar*) to explain; **mostrarse** *vr*: **mostrarse amable** to be kind; to prove to be kind; **no se muestra muy inteligente** he doesn't seem (to be) very intelligent; ~ **en pantalla** (*Inform*) to display
mota ['mota] *nf* speck; (*en diseño*) dot
mote ['mote] *nm* (*apodo*) nickname
motín [mo'tin] *nm* (*del pueblo*) revolt, rising; (*del ejército*) mutiny
motivación [motiβa'θjon] *nf* motivation
motivar [moti'βar] *vt* (*causar*) to cause, motivate; (*explicar*) to explain, justify
motivo [mo'tiβo] *nm* motive, reason; (*Arte, Mus*) motif; **con ~ de** (*debido a*) because of; (*en ocasión de*) on the occasion of; (*con el fin de*) in order to; **sin ~** for no reason at all
moto ['moto] *nf*, **motocicleta** [motoθi'kleta] *nf* motorbike (*Brit*), motorcycle
motociclista [motoθi'klista] *nmf* motorcyclist, biker
motoneta [moto'neta] *nf* (*Am*) Vespa®
motor, a [mo'tor, a] *adj* (*Tec*) motive; (*Anat*) motor ■ *nm* motor, engine; ~ **a chorro** *o* **de reacción/de explosión** jet engine/internal combustion engine; ~ **de búsqueda** (*Internet*) search engine ■ *nf* motorboat
motorismo [moto'rismo] *nm* motorcycling
motorista [moto'rista] *nm/f* (*esp Am: automovilista*) motorist; (: *motociclista*) motorcyclist
motorizado, -a [motori'θaðo, a] *adj* motorized
motosierra [moto'sjerra] *nf* mechanical saw
motriz [mo'triz] *adj*: **fuerza ~** motive power; (*fig*) driving force
movedizo, -a [moβe'ðiθo, a] *adj* (*inseguro*) unsteady; (*fig*) unsettled, changeable; (*persona*) fickle
mover [mo'βer] *vt* to move; (*cambiar de lugar*) to shift; (*cabeza: para negar*) to shake; (: *para asentir*) to nod; (*accionar*) to drive; (*fig*) to cause, provoke; **moverse** *vr* to move; (*mar*) to get rough; (*viento*) to rise; (*fig: apurarse*) to get a move on; (: *transformarse*) to be on the move
movible [mo'βiβle] *adj* (*no fijo*) movable; (*móvil*) mobile; (*cambiadizo*) changeable
movido, -a [mo'βiðo, a] *adj* (*Foto*) blurred;

(*persona: activo*) active; (*mar*) rough; (*día*) hectic ■ *nf* move; **la movida madrileña** the Madrid scene
móvil ['moβil] *adj* mobile; (*pieza de máquina*) moving; (*mueble*) movable ■ *nm* (*motivo*) motive; (*teléfono*) mobile, cellphone (*US*)
movilice *etc* [moβi'liθe] *vb ver* **movilizar**
movilidad [moβili'ðað] *nf* mobility
movilizar [moβili'θar] *vt* to mobilize
movimiento [moβi'mjento] *nm* movement; (*Tec*) motion; (*actividad*) activity; (*Mus*) tempo; **el M~** the Falangist Movement; ~ **de bloques** (*Inform*) block move; ~ **de mercancías** (*Com*) turnover, volume of business; ~ **obrero/sindical** workers'/trade union movement; ~ **sísmico** earth tremor
Mozambique [moθam'bike] *nm* Mozambique
mozambiqueño, -a [moθambi'keɲo, a] *adj, nm/f* Mozambican
mozo, -a ['moθo, a] *adj* (*joven*) young; (*soltero*) single, unmarried ■ *nm/f* (*joven*) youth, young man (girl); (*camarero*) waiter; (*camarera*) waitress; ~ **de estación** porter
MP3 *nm* MP3; **reproductor (de) ~** MP3 player
MPAIAC [emepa'jak] *nm abr* (*Esp Pol*)
= **Movimiento para la Autodeterminación y la Independencia del Archipiélago Canario**
mucama [mu'kama] *nf* (*Am*) maid
muchacho, -a [mu'tʃatʃo, a] *nm/f* (*niño*) boy/girl; (*criado*) servant/servant *o* maid
muchedumbre [mutʃe'ðumbre] *nf* crowd
muchísimo, -a [mu'tʃisimo, a] *adj superlativo de* **mucho** lots and lots of, ever so much ■ *adv* ever so much

 PALABRA CLAVE

mucho, -a ['mutʃo, a] *adj* **1** (*cantidad*) a lot of, much; (*número*) lots of, a lot of, many; ~ **dinero** a lot of money; **hace ~ calor** it's very hot; **muchas amigas** lots *o* a lot of *o* many friends

2 (*sg: fam*): **ésta es mucha casa para él** this house is much too big for him; **había ~ borracho** there were a lot *o* lots of drunks ■ *pron*: **tengo ~ que hacer** I've got a lot to do; **muchos dicen que ...** a lot of people say that ...; *ver tb* **tener**

■ *adv* **1**: **me gusta ~** I like it a lot *o* very much; **lo siento ~** I'm very sorry; **come ~** he eats a lot; **trabaja ~** he works hard; **¿te vas a quedar ~?** are you going to be staying long?; ~ **más/menos** much *o* a lot more/less

2 (*respuesta*) very; **¿estás cansado?** — **¡~!** are you tired? — very!

3 (*locuciones*): **como ~** at (the) most; **el mejor**

con ~ by far the best; ¡ni ~ **menos!** far from
it!; **no es rico ni ~ menos** he's far from
being rich
4: **por ~ que**: **por mucho que le creas**
however much o no matter how much you
believe him

muda ['muða] nf (de ropa) change of clothing;
(Zool) moult; (de serpiente) slough
mudanza [mu'ðanθa] nf (cambio) change;
(de casa) move; **estar de ~** to be moving
mudar [mu'ðar] vt to change; (Zool) to shed
■ vi to change; **mudarse** vr (la ropa) to
change; **mudarse de casa** to move house
mudo, -a ['muðo, a] adj dumb; (callado:
película) silent; (Ling: letra) mute; (: consonante)
voiceless; **quedarse ~ (de)** (fig) to be dumb
with; **quedarse ~ de asombro** to be
speechless
mueble ['mweβle] nm piece of furniture;
muebles nmpl furniture sg
mueble-bar [mweβle'βar] nm cocktail
cabinet
mueca ['mweka] nf face, grimace; **hacer
muecas a** to make faces at
muela etc ['mwela] vb ver **moler** ■ nf (diente)
tooth; (: da atrás) molar; (de molino) millstone;
(de afilar) grindstone; **~ del juicio** wisdom
tooth
muelle ['mweʎe] adj (blando) soft; (fig) soft,
easy ■ nm spring; (Naut) wharf; (malecón)
jetty
muera etc ['mwera] vb ver **morir**
muerda etc ['mwerða] vb ver **morder**
muermo ['mwermo] nm (fam) wimp
muerte ['mwerte] nf death; (homicidio)
murder; **dar ~ a** to kill; **de mala ~** (fam)
lousy, rotten; **es la ~** (fam) it's deadly boring
muerto, -a ['mwerto, a] pp de **morir** ■ adj
dead; (color) dull ■ nm/f dead man(-woman);
(difunto) deceased; (cadáver) corpse; **cargar
con el ~** (fam) to carry the can; **echar el ~ a
algn** to pass the buck; **hacer el ~** (nadando) to
float; **estar ~ de cansancio** to be dead tired
muesca ['mweska] nf nick
muestra etc ['mwestra] vb ver **mostrar**
■ nf (señal) indication, sign; (demostración)
demonstration; (prueba) proof; (estadística)
sample; (modelo) model, pattern; (testimonio)
token; **dar ~s de** to show signs of; **~ al azar**
(Com) random sample
muestrario [mwes'trarjo] nm collection of
samples; (exposición) showcase
muestreo [mwes'treo] nm sample, sampling
mueva etc ['mweβa] vb ver **mover**
mugir [mu'xir] vi (vaca) to moo
mugre ['muɣre] nf dirt, filth, muck

mugriento, -a [mu'ɣrjento, a] adj dirty,
filthy, mucky
mugroso, -a [mu'ɣroso, a] adj (Am) filthy,
grubby
muja etc ['muxa] vb ver **mugir**
mujer [mu'xer] nf woman; (esposa) wife
mujeriego [muxe'rjeɣo] nm womaniser
mula ['mula] nf mule
mulato, -a [mu'lato, a] adj, nm/f mulatto
muleta [mu'leta] nf (para andar) crutch; (Taur)
stick with red cape attached
muletilla [mule'tiʎa] nf (palabra) pet word,
tag; (de cómico) catch phrase
mullido, -a [mu'ʎiðo, a] adj (cama) soft;
(hierba) soft, springy
multa ['multa] nf fine; **echar o poner una
~ a** to fine
multar [mul'tar] vt to fine; (Deporte) to
penalize
multiacceso [multjak'θeso] adj (Inform)
multi-access
multicine [multi'θine] nm multiscreen
cinema
multicolor [multiko'lor] adj multicoloured
multimillonario, -a [multimiʎo'narjo, a]
adj (contrato) multimillion pound o dollar cpd
■ nm/f multimillionaire/ millionairess
multinacional [multinaθjo'nal] adj, nf
multinational
múltiple ['multiple] adj multiple, many
pl, numerous; **de tarea ~** (Inform) multi-
tasking; **de usuario ~** (Inform) multi-user
multiplicar [multipli'kar] vt (Mat) to
multiply; (fig) to increase; **multiplicarse**
vr (Bio) to multiply; (fig) to be everywhere
at once
multiplique etc [multi'plike] vb ver
multiplicar
múltiplo ['multiplo] adj, nm multiple
multitud [multi'tuð] nf (muchedumbre) crowd;
~ de lots of
multitudinario, -a [multituði'narjo, a] adj
(numeroso) multitudinous; (de masas) mass cpd
mundanal [munda'nal] adj worldly;
alejarse del ~ ruido to get away from it all
mundano, -a [mun'dano, a] adj worldly; (de
moda) fashionable
mundial [mun'djal] adj world-wide,
universal; (guerra, récord) world cpd
mundialización [mundjaliθa'θjon] nf
globalization
mundialmente [mundjal'mente] adv
worldwide; **~ famoso** world-famous
mundo ['mundo] nm world; (ámbito) world,
circle; **el otro ~** the next world; **~ del
espectáculo** show business; **todo el ~**
everybody; **tener ~** to be experienced, know

one's way around; **el ~ es un pañuelo** it's a small world; **no es nada del otro ~** it's nothing special; **se le cayó el ~ (encima)** his world fell apart

Munich ['munitʃ] *nm* Munich

munición [muni'θjon] *nf* (*Mil: provisiones*) stores *pl*, supplies *pl*; (*: de armas*) ammunition

municipal [muniθi'pal] *adj* (*elección*) municipal; (*concejo*) town *cpd*, local; (*piscina etc*) public ■ *nm* (*guardia*) policeman

municipio [muni'θipjo] *nm* (*ayuntamiento*) town council, corporation; (*territorio administrativo*) town, municipality

muñeca [mu'ɲeka] *nf* (*Anat*) wrist; (*juguete*) doll

muñeco [mu'ɲeko] *nm* (*figura*) figure; (*marioneta*) puppet; (*fig*) puppet, pawn; (*niño*) pretty little boy; **~ de nieve** snowman

muñequera [muɲe'kera] *nf* wristband

muñón [mu'ɲon] *nm* (*Anat*) stump

mural [mu'ral] *adj* mural, wall *cpd* ■ *nm* mural

muralla [mu'raʎa] *nf* (city) wall(s) *pl*

murciano, -a [mur'θjano, a] *adj* of *o* from Murcia ■ *nm/f* native *o* inhabitant of Murcia

murciélago [mur'θjelaɣo] *nm* bat

murga ['murɣa] *nf* (*banda*) band of street musicians; **dar la ~** to be a nuisance

murmullo [mur'muʎo] *nm* murmur(ing); (*cuchicheo*) whispering; (*de arroyo*) murmur, rippling; (*de hojas, viento*) rustle, rustling; (*ruido confuso*) hum(ming)

murmuración [murmura'θjon] *nf* gossip; (*críticas*) backbiting

murmurador, a [murmura'ðor, a] *adj* gossiping; (*criticón*) backbiting ■ *nm/f* gossip; backbiter

murmurar [murmu'rar] *vi* to murmur, whisper; (*criticar*) to criticize; (*cotillear*) to gossip

muro ['muro] *nm* wall; **~ de contención** retaining wall

mus [mus] *nm card game*

musaraña [musa'raɲa] *nf* (*Zool*) shrew; (*insecto*) creepy-crawly; **pensar en las musarañas** to daydream

muscular [musku'lar] *adj* muscular

músculo ['muskulo] *nm* muscle

musculoso, -a [musku'loso, a] *adj* muscular

museo [mu'seo] *nm* museum; **~ de arte** *o* **pintura** art gallery; **~ de cera** waxworks

musgo ['musɣo] *nm* moss

musical [musi'kal] *adj*, *nm* musical

músico, -a ['musiko, a] *adj* musical ■ *nm/f* musician ■ *nf* music; **irse con la música a otra parte** to clear off

musitar [musi'tar] *vt*, *vi* to mutter, mumble

muslo ['muslo] *nm* thigh; (*de pollo*) leg, drumstick

mustio, -a ['mustjo, a] *adj* (*persona*) depressed, gloomy; (*planta*) faded, withered

musulmán, -ana [musul'man, ana] *nm/f* Moslem, Muslim

mutación [muta'θjon] *nf* (*Bio*) mutation; (*: cambio*) (sudden) change

mutilar [muti'lar] *vt* to mutilate; (*a una persona*) to maim

mutis ['mutis] *nm inv* (*Teat*) exit; **hacer ~** (*Teat: retirarse*) to exit, go off; (*fig*) to say nothing

mutismo [mu'tismo] *nm* silence

mutualidad [mutwali'ðað] *nf* (*reciprocidad*) mutual character; (*asociación*) friendly *o* benefit (US) society

mutuamente [mutwa'mente] *adv* mutually

mutuo, -a ['mutwo, a] *adj* mutual

muy [mwi] *adv* very; (*demasiado*) too; **M~ Señor mío** Dear Sir; **~ bien** (*de acuerdo*) all right; **~ de noche** very late at night; **eso es ~ de él** that's just like him; **eso es ~ español** that's typically Spanish

Nn

N, n ['ene] *nf* (*letra*) N, n; **N de Navarra** N for Nellie (*Brit*) o Nan (*US*)

N *abr* (= *norte*) N

N. *abr* = **carretera nacional** (*Am*: = *moneda nacional*) local currency; **le entregaron sólo N.$2.000** they only gave him $2000 pesos

N.° *abr* (= *número*) No

n. *abr* (Ling: = *nombre*) n; = **nacido, a**

n/ *abr* = **nuestro, a**

nabo ['naβo] *nm* turnip

nácar ['nakar] *nm* mother-of-pearl

nacer [na'θer] *vi* to be born; (*huevo*) to hatch; (*vegetal*) to sprout; (*río*) to rise; (*fig*) to begin, originate, have its origins; **nació para poeta** he was born to be a poet; **nadie nace enseñado** we all have to learn; **nació una sospecha en su mente** a suspicion formed in her mind

nacido, -a [na'θiðo, a] *adj* born; **recién ~** newborn

naciente [na'θjente] *adj* new, emerging; (*sol*) rising

nacimiento [naθi'mjento] *nm* birth; (*fig*) birth, origin; (*de Navidad*) Nativity; (*linaje*) descent, family; (*de río*) source; **ciego de ~** blind from birth

nación [na'θjon] *nf* nation; (*pueblo*) people; **Naciones Unidas** United Nations

nacional [naθjo'nal] *adj* national; (*Com, Econ*) domestic, home *cpd*

nacionalice *etc* [naθjona'liθe] *vb ver* **nacionalizar**

nacionalidad [naθjonali'ðað] *nf* nationality; (*Esp, Pol*) autonomous region

nacionalismo [naθjona'lismo] *nm* nationalism

nacionalista [naθjona'lista] *adj, nm/f* nationalist

nacionalizar [naθjonali'θar] *vt* to nationalize; **nacionalizarse** *vr* (*persona*) to become naturalized

nada ['naða] *pron* nothing ■ *adv* not at all, in no way ■ *nf* nothingness; **no decir ~ (más)** to say nothing (else), not to say anything (else); **¡~ más!** that's all; **de ~** don't mention it; **~ de eso** nothing of the kind; **antes de ~** right away; **como si ~** as if it didn't matter; **no ha sido ~** it's nothing; **la ~** the void

nadador, a [naða'ðor, a] *nm/f* swimmer

nadar [na'ðar] *vi* to swim; **~ en la abundancia** (*fig*) to be rolling in money

nadie ['naðje] *pron* nobody, no-one; **~ habló** nobody spoke; **no había ~** there was nobody there, there wasn't anybody there; **es un don ~** he's a nobody o nonentity

nadita [na'ðita] (*csp Am: fam*) = **nada**

nado ['naðo]: **a ~** *adv*: **pasar a ~** to swim across

nafta ['nafta] *nf* (*Am*) petrol (*Brit*), gas(oline) (*US*)

naftalina [nafta'lina] *nf*: **bolas de ~** mothballs

náhuatl ['nawatl] *adj, nm* Nahuatl

naipe ['naipe] *nm* (playing) card; **naipes** *nmpl* cards

nal. *abr* (= *nacional*) nat

nalgas ['nalɣas] *nfpl* buttocks

Namibia [na'miβja] *nf* Namibia

nana ['nana] *nf* lullaby

napias ['napjas] *nfpl* (*fam*) conk *sg*

Nápoles ['napoles] *nf* Naples

napolitano, -a [napoli'tano, a] *adj* of o from Naples, Neapolitan ■ *nm/f* Neapolitan

naranja [na'ranxa] *adj inv, nf* orange; **media ~** (*fam*) better half; **¡naranjas de la China!** nonsense!

naranjada [naran'xaða] *nf* orangeade

naranjo [na'ranxo] *nm* orange tree

Narbona [nar'βona] *nf* Narbonne

narcisista [narθi'sista] *adj* narcissistic

narciso [nar'θiso] *nm* narcissus

narcotice *etc* [narko'tiθe] *vb ver* **narcotizar**

narcótico, -a [nar'kotiko, a] *adj, nm* narcotic

narcotizar [narkoti'θar] *vt* to drug

narcotraficante [narkotrafi'kante] *nm/f* narcotics o drug trafficker

n

narcotráfico [narko'trafiko] *nm* narcotics *o* drug trafficking

nardo ['narðo] *nm* lily

narices [na'riθes] *nfpl ver* **nariz**

narigón, -ona [nari'ɣon, ona], **narigudo, a** [nari'ɣuðo, a] *adj* big-nosed

nariz [na'riθ] *nf* nose; **narices** *nfpl* nostrils; **¡narices!** *(fam)* rubbish!; **delante de las narices de algn** under one's (very) nose; **estar hasta las narices** to be completely fed up; **meter las narices en algo** to poke one's nose into sth

narración [narra'θjon] *nf* narration

narrador, a [narra'ðor, a] *nm/f* narrator

narrar [na'rrar] *vt* to narrate, recount

narrativo, -a [narra'tiβo, a] *adj* narrative ■ *nf* narrative, story

nasal [na'sal] *adj* nasal

N.ª *abr* = **Nuestra Señora**

nata ['nata] *nf* cream *(tb fig)*; *(en leche cocida etc)* skin; **~ batida** whipped cream

natación [nata'θjon] *nf* swimming

natal [na'tal] *adj* natal; *(país)* native; **ciudad ~** home town

natalicio [nata'liθjo] *nm* birthday

natalidad [natali'ðað] *nf* birth rate

natillas [na'tiʎas] *nfpl (egg)* custard *sg*

natividad [natiβi'ðað] *nf* nativity

nativo, -a [na'tiβo, a] *adj, nm/f* native

nato, -a ['nato, a] *adj* born; **un músico ~** a born musician

natural [natu'ral] *adj* natural; *(fruta etc)* fresh ■ *nm/f* native ■ *nm* disposition, temperament; **buen ~** good nature; **fruta al ~** fruit in its own juice

naturaleza [natura'leθa] *nf* nature; *(género)* nature, kind; **~ muerta** still life

naturalice *etc* [natura'liθe] *vb ver* **naturalizarse**

naturalidad [naturali'ðað] *nf* naturalness

naturalización [naturaliθa'θjon] *nf* naturalization

naturalizarse [naturali'θarse] *vr* to become naturalized; *(aclimatarse)* to become acclimatized

naturalmente [natural'mente] *adv* naturally; **¡~!** of course!

naturista [natu'rista] *adj (Med)* naturopathic ■ *nm/f* naturopath

naufragar [naufra'ɣar] *vi (barco)* to sink; *(gente)* to be shipwrecked; *(fig)* to fail

naufragio [nau'fraxjo] *nm* shipwreck

náufrago, -a ['naufraɣo, a] *nm/f* castaway, shipwrecked person

naufrague *etc* [nau'fraɣe] *vb ver* **naufragar**

náusea ['nausea] *nf* nausea; **me da náuseas** it makes me feel sick

nauseabundo, -a [nausea'βundo, a] *adj* nauseating, sickening

náutico, -a ['nautiko, a] *adj* nautical; **club ~** sailing *o* yacht club ■ *nf* navigation, seamanship

navaja [na'βaxa] *nf (cortaplumas)* clasp knife *(Brit)*, penknife; **~ (de afeitar)** razor

navajazo [naβa'xaθo] *nm (herida)* gash; *(acto)* slash

naval [na'βal] *adj (Mil)* naval; **construcción ~** shipbuilding; **sector ~** shipbuilding industry

Navarra [na'βarra] *nf* Navarre

navarro, -a [na'βarro, a] *adj* of *o* from Navarre, Navarrese ■ *nm/f* Navarrese ■ *nm (Ling)* Navarrese

nave ['naβe] *nf (barco)* ship, vessel; *(Arq)* nave; **~ espacial** spaceship; **quemar las naves** to burn one's boats

navegación [naβeɣa'θjon] *nf* navigation; *(viaje)* sea journey; **~ aérea** air traffic; **~ costera** coastal shipping; **~ fluvial** river navigation

navegador [naβeɣa'ðor] *nm (Inform)* browser; *(de coche)* sat nav

navegante [naβe'ɣante] *nm/f* navigator

navegar [naβe'ɣar] *vi (barco)* to sail; *(avión)* to fly ■ *vt* to sail; to fly; *(dirigir el rumbo de)* to navigate

navegue *etc* [na'βeɣe] *vb ver* **navegar**

navidad [naβi'ðað] *nf* Christmas; **navidades** *nfpl* Christmas time *sg*; **día de ~** Christmas Day; **por navidades** at Christmas (time); **¡felices navidades!** Merry Christmas

navideño, -a [naβi'ðeɲo, a] *adj* Christmas *cpd*

navío [na'βio] *nm* ship

nazi ['naθi] *adj, nm/f* Nazi

nazismo [na'θismo] *nm* Nazism

N. de la R. *abr* (= *nota de la redacción*) editor's note

N. de la T./del T. *abr* (= *nota de la traductora/del traductor*) translator's note

NE *abr* (= *nor(d)este*) NE

neblina [ne'βlina] *nf* mist

nebuloso, -a [neβu'loso, a] *adj* foggy; *(calinoso)* misty; *(indefinido)* nebulous, vague ■ *nf* nebula

necedad [neθe'ðað] *nf* foolishness; *(una necedad)* foolish act

necesario, -a [neθe'sarjo, a] *adj* necessary; **si fuera** *o* **fuese ~** if need(s) be

neceser [neθe'ser] *nm* vanity case; *(bolsa grande)* holdall

necesidad [neθesi'ðað] *nf* need; *(lo inevitable)* necessity; *(miseria)* poverty, need; **en caso de ~** in case of need *o* emergency; **hacer sus necesidades** to relieve o.s.

necesitado, -a [neθesi'taðo, a] *adj* needy, poor; **~ de** in need of

necesitar [neθesi'tar] *vt* to need, require ■ *vi*: **~ de** to have need of; **necesitarse** *vr* to be needed; *(en anuncios)*: **"necesítase coche"** "car wanted"

necio, -a ['neθjo, a] *adj* foolish ■ *nm/f* fool

necrología [nekrolo'xia] *nf* obituary

necrópolis [ne'kropolis] *nf inv* cemetery

néctar ['nektar] *nm* nectar

nectarina [nekta'rina] *nf* nectarine

neerlandés, -esa [neerlan'des, esa] *adj* Dutch ■ *nm/f* Dutchman(-woman) ■ *nm* *(Ling)* Dutch; **los neerlandeses** the Dutch

nefando, -a [ne'fando, a] *adj* unspeakable

nefasto, -a [ne'fasto, a] *adj* ill-fated, unlucky

negación [neɣa'θjon] *nf* negation; *(Ling)* negative; *(rechazo)* refusal, denial

negado, -a [ne'ɣaðo, a] *adj*: **~ para** inept at, unfitted for

negar [ne'ɣar] *vt* *(renegar, rechazar)* to refuse; *(prohibir)* to refuse, deny; *(desmentir)* to deny; **negarse** *vr*: **negarse a hacer algo** to refuse to do sth

negativo, -a [neɣa'tiβo, a] *adj* negative ■ *nm* *(Foto)* negative; *(Mat)* minus ■ *nf* *(gen)* negative; *(rechazo)* refusal, denial; **negativa rotunda** flat refusal

negligencia [neɣli'xenθja] *nf* negligence

negligente [neɣli'xente] *adj* negligent

negociable [neɣo'θjaβle] *adj* negotiable

negociación [neɣoθja'θjon] *nf* negotiation

negociado [neɣo'θjaðo] *nm* department, section

negociante [neɣo'θjante] *nm/f* businessman(-woman)

negociar [neɣo'θjar] *vt, vi* to negotiate; **~ en** to deal in, trade in

negocio [ne'ɣoθjo] *nm* *(Com)* business; *(asunto)* affair, business; *(operación comercial)* deal, transaction; *(Am)* shop, store; *(lugar)* place of business; **los negocios** business *sg*; **hacer ~** to do business; **el ~ del libro** the book trade; **~ autorizado** licensed trade; **hombre de negocios** businessman; **~ sucio** shady deal; **hacer un buen ~** to pull off a profitable deal; **¡mal ~!** it looks bad!

negra ['neɣra] *nf ver* **negro** ■ *nf* *(Mus)* crotchet

negrita [ne'ɣrita] *nf* *(Tip)* bold face; **en ~** in bold (type)

negro, -a ['neɣro, a] *adj* black; *(suerte)* awful, atrocious; *(humor etc)* sad; *(lúgubre)* gloomy ■ *nm* *(color)* black ■ *nm/f* Black person ■ *nf* *(Mus)* crotchet; **~ como la boca del lobo** pitch-black; **estoy ~ con esto** I'm getting desperate about it; **ponerse ~** *(fam)* to get cross

negrura [ne'ɣrura] *nf* blackness

negué [ne'ɣe], **neguemos** *etc* [ne'ɣemos] *vb ver* **negar**

nene, -a ['nene, a] *nm/f* baby, small child

nenúfar [ne'nufar] *nm* water lily

neologismo [neolo'xismo] *nm* neologism

neón [ne'on] *nm* neon

neoyorquino, -a [neojor'kino, a] *adj* New York *cpd* ■ *nm/f* New Yorker

neozelandés, -esa [neoθelan'des, esa] *adj* New Zealand *cpd* ■ *nm/f* New Zealander

nepotismo [nepo'tismo] *nm* nepotism

nervio ['nerβjo] *nm* *(Anat)* nerve; *(: tendón)* tendon; *(fig)* vigour; *(Tec)* rib; **crispar los nervios a algn**, **poner los nervios de punta a algn** to get on sb's nerves

nerviosismo [nerβjo'sismo] *nm* nervousness, nerves *pl*

nervioso, -a [ner'βjoso, a] *adj* nervous; *(sensible)* nervy, highly-strung; *(impaciente)* restless; **¡no te pongas ~!** take it easy!

nervudo, -a [ner'βuðo, a] *adj* tough; *(mano)* sinewy

netiqueta [neti'keta] *n* netiquette

neto, -a ['neto, a] *adj* clear; *(limpio)* clean; *(Com)* net

neumático, -a [neu'matiko, a] *adj* pneumatic ■ *nm* *(Esp)* tyre *(Brit)*, tire *(US)*; **~ de recambio** spare tyre

neumonía [neumo'nia] *nf* pneumonia; **~ asiática** SARS

neura ['neura] *(fam)* *nm/f* *(persona)* neurotic ■ *nf* *(obsesión)* obsession

neuralgia [neu'ralxja] *nf* neuralgia

neurálgico, -a [neu'ralxiko, a] *adj* neuralgic; *(fig: centro)* nerve *cpd*

neurastenia [neuras'tenja] *nf* neurasthenia; *(fig)* excitability

neurasténico, -a [neuras'teniko, a] *adj* neurasthenic; excitable

neurólogo, -a [neu'roloɣo, a] *nm/f* neurologist

neurona [neu'rona] *nf* neuron

neurosis [neu'rosis] *nf inv* neurosis

neurótico, -a [neu'rotiko, a] *adj, nm/f* neurotic

neutral [neu'tral] *adj* neutral

neutralice *etc* [neutra'liθe] *vb ver* **neutralizar**

neutralizar [neutrali'θar] *vt* to neutralize; *(contrarrestar)* to counteract

neutro, -a ['neutro, a] *adj* *(Bio, Ling)* neuter

neutrón [neu'tron] *nm* neutron

nevado, -a [ne'βaðo, a] *adj* snow-covered; *(montaña)* snow-capped; *(fig)* snowy, snow-white ■ *nf* snowstorm; *(caída de nieve)* snowfall

nevar [ne'βar] *vi* to snow ■ *vt* *(fig)* to whiten

nevera [ne'βera] *nf* *(Esp)* refrigerator *(Brit)*, icebox *(US)*

n

nevisca [ne'βiska] *nf* flurry of snow
nexo ['nekso] *nm* link, connection
n/f *abr* (*Com*) = **nuestro favor**
ni [ni] *conj* nor, neither; (*tb*: **ni siquiera**) not even; **ni que** not even if; **ni blanco ni negro** neither white nor black; **ni el uno ni el otro** neither one nor the other
Nicaragua [nika'raɣwa] *nf* Nicaragua
nicaragüense [nikara'ɣwense] *adj, nm/f* Nicaraguan
nicho ['nitʃo] *nm* niche
nick [nik] *nm* (*Internet*) nickname, user name, nick
nicotina [niko'tina] *nf* nicotine
nido ['niðo] *nm* nest; (*fig*) hiding place; ~ **de ladrones** den of thieves
niebla ['njeβla] *nf* fog; (*neblina*) mist; **hay ~** it is foggy
niego *etc* ['njeɣo], **niegue** *etc* ['njeɣe] *vb ver* **negar**
nieto, -a ['njeto, a] *nm/f* grandson/granddaughter; **nietos** *nmpl* grandchildren
nieve *etc* ['njeβe] *vb ver* **nevar** ■ *nf* snow; (*Am*) ice cream; **copo de ~** snowflake
N.I.F. *nm abr* (= *Número de Identificación Fiscal*) ID number used for tax purposes
Nigeria [ni'xerja] *nf* Nigeria
nigeriano, -a [nixe'rjano, a] *adj, nm/f* Nigerian
nigromancia [niɣro'manθja] *nf* necromancy, black magic
nihilista [nii'lista] *adj* nihilistic ■ *nm* nihilist
Nilo ['nilo] *nm*: **el (Río) ~** the Nile
nimbo ['nimbo] *nm* (*aureola*) halo; (*nube*) nimbus
nimiedad [nimje'ðað] *nf* small-mindedness; (*trivialidad*) triviality; (*una nimiedad*) trifle, tiny detail
nimio, -a ['nimjo, a] *adj* trivial, insignificant
ninfa ['ninfa] *nf* nymph
ninfómana [nin'fomana] *nf* nymphomaniac
ninguno, -a [nin'guno, a] *adj* (*antes de nmsg* **ningún**) no ■ *pron* (*nadie*) nobody; (*ni uno*) none, not one; (*ni uno ni otro*) neither; **de ninguna manera** by no means, not at all; **no voy a ninguna parte** I'm not going anywhere
niña ['niɲa] *nf ver* **niño**
niñera [ni'ɲera] *nf* nursemaid, nanny
niñería [niɲe'ria] *nf* childish act
niñez [ni'ɲeθ] *nf* childhood; (*infancia*) infancy
niño, -a ['niɲo, a] *adj* (*joven*) young; (*inmaduro*) immature ■ *nm* (*chico*) boy, child ■ *nf* girl, child; (*Anat*) pupil; **los niños** the children; ~ **bien** rich kid; ~ **expósito** foundling; ~ **de pecho** babe-in-arms; ~ **prodigio** child

prodigy; **de ~** as a child; **ser el ~ mimado de algn** to be sb's pet; **ser la niña de los ojos de algn** to be the apple of sb's eye
nipón, -ona [ni'pon, ona] *adj, nm/f* Japanese; **los nipones** the Japanese
níquel ['nikel] *nm* nickel
niquelar [nike'lar] *vt* (*Tec*) to nickel-plate
níspero ['nispero] *nm* medlar
nitidez [niti'ðeθ] *nf* (*claridad*) clarity; (: *de atmósfera*) brightness; (: *de imagen*) sharpness
nítido, -a ['nitiðo, a] *adj* bright; (*fig*) pure; (*imagen*) clear, sharp
nitrato [ni'trato] *nm* nitrate
nitrógeno [ni'troxeno] *nm* nitrogen
nitroglicerina [nitroɣliθe'rina] *nf* nitroglycerine
nivel [ni'βel] *nm* (*Geo*) level; (*norma*) level, standard; (*altura*) height; ~ **de aceite** oil level; ~ **de aire** spirit level; ~ **de vida** standard of living; **al ~ de** on a level with, at the same height as; (*fig*) on a par with; **a 900m sobre el ~ del mar** at 900m above sea level
nivelado, -a [niβe'laðo, a] *adj* level, flat; (*Tec*) flush
nivelar [niβe'lar] *vt* to level out; (*fig*) to even up; (*Com*) to balance
Niza ['niθa] *nf* Nice
n/l. *abr* (*Com*) = **nuestra letra**
NNE *abr* (= *nornordeste*) NNE
NNO *abr* (= *nornoroeste*) NNW
NN. UU. *nfpl abr* (= *Naciones Unidas*) UN *sg*
NO *abr* (= *noroeste*) NW
no [no] *adv* no; (*con verbo*) not ■ *excl* no!; **no tengo nada** I don't have anything, I have nothing; **no es el mío** it's not mine; **ahora no** not now; **¿no lo sabes?** don't you know?; **no mucho** not much; **no bien termine, lo entregaré** as soon as I finish I'll hand it over; **¡a que no lo sabes!** I bet you don't know!; **¡cómo no!** of course!; **pacto de no agresión** non-aggression pact; **los países no alineados** the non-aligned countries; **el no va más** the ultimate; **la no intervención** non-intervention
n/o *abr* (*Com*) = **nuestra orden**
noble ['noβle] *adj, nm/f* noble; **los nobles** the nobility *sg*
nobleza [noβ'leθa] *nf* nobility
noche ['notʃe] *nf* night, night-time; (*la tarde*) evening; (*fig*) darkness; **de ~**, **por la ~** at night; **ayer por la ~** last night; **esta ~** tonight; **(en) toda la ~** all night; **hacer ~ en un sitio** to spend the night in a place; **se hace de ~** it's getting dark
Nochebuena [notʃe'βwena] *nf* Christmas Eve; *see note*

NOCHEBUENA

On *Nochebuena* in Spanish homes there is normally a large supper when family members come from all over to be together. The more religiously inclined attend *la misa del gallo* at midnight. The tradition of receiving Christmas presents from Santa Claus that night is becoming more and more widespread and gradually replacing the tradition of *los Reyes Magos* (The Three Wise Men) on the 6th of January.

Nochevieja [notʃe'βjexa] *nf* New Year's Eve; *ver tb* **uvas**

noción [no'θjon] *nf* notion; **nociones** *nfpl* elements, rudiments

nocivo, -a [no'θiβo, a] *adj* harmful

noctambulismo [noktambu'lismo] *nm* sleepwalking

noctámbulo, -a [nok'tambulo, a] *nm/f* sleepwalker

nocturno, -a [nok'turno, a] *adj* (*de la noche*) nocturnal, night *cpd*; (*de la tarde*) evening *cpd* ■ *nm* nocturne

Noé [no'e] *nm* Noah

nogal [no'ɣal] *nm* walnut tree; (*madera*) walnut

nómada ['nomaða] *adj* nomadic ■ *nm/f* nomad

nomás [no'mas] *adv* (*Am: gen*) just; (: *tan sólo*) only; **así** ~ (*Am fam*) just like that; **ayer** ~ only yesterday ■ *conj* (*Am: en cuanto*): ~ **se fue se acordó** no sooner had she left than she remembered

nombramiento [nombra'mjento] *nm* naming; (*para un empleo*) appointment; (*Pol etc*) nomination; (*Mil*) commission

nombrar [nom'brar] *vt* (*gen*) to name; (*mencionar*) to mention; (*designar*) to appoint, nominate; (*Mil*) to commission

nombre ['nombre] *nm* name; (*sustantivo*) noun; (*fama*) renown; ~ **y apellidos** name in full; ~ **común/propio** common/proper noun; ~ **de pila/de soltera** Christian/maiden name; ~ **de fichero** (*Inform*) file name; **en** ~ **de** in the name of, on behalf of; **sin** ~ nameless; **su conducta no tiene** ~ his behaviour is utterly despicable

nomenclatura [nomenkla'tura] *nf* nomenclature

nomeolvides [nomeol'βiðes] *nm inv* forget-me-not

nómina ['nomina] *nf* (*lista*) list; (*Com: tb*: **nóminas**) payroll

nominal [nomi'nal] *adj* nominal; (*valor*) face *cpd*; (*Ling*) noun *cpd*, substantival

nominar [nomi'nar] *vt* to nominate

nominativo, -a [nomina'tiβo, a] *adj* (*Ling*) nominative; (*Com*): **un cheque** ~ **a X** a cheque made out to X

non [non] *adj* odd, uneven ■ *nm* odd number; **pares y nones** odds and evens

nonagésimo, -a [nona'xesimo, a] *num* ninetieth

nono, -a ['nono, a] *num* ninth

nordeste [nor'ðeste] *adj* north-east, north-eastern, north-easterly ■ *nm* north-east; (*viento*) north-east wind, north-easterly

nórdico, -a ['norðiko, a] *adj* (*del norte*) northern, northerly; (*escandinavo*) Nordic, Norse ■ *nm/f* northerner; (*escandinavo*) Norseman/-woman ■ *nm* (*Ling*) Norse

noreste [no'reste] *adj, nm* = **nordeste**

noria ['norja] *nf* (*Agr*) waterwheel; (*de carnaval*) big (*Brit*) o Ferris (*US*) wheel

norma ['norma] *nf* standard, norm, rule; (*patrón*) pattern; (*método*) method

normal [nor'mal] *adj* (*corriente*) normal; (*habitual*) usual, natural; (*Tec*) standard; **Escuela N**~ teacher training college; (**gasolina**) ~ two-star petrol

normalice *etc* [norma'liθe] *vb ver* **normalizar**

normalidad [normali'ðað] *nf* normality

normalización [normaliθa'θjon] *nf* (*Com*) standardization

normalizar [normali'θar] *vt* (*reglamentar*) to normalize; (*Com, Tec*) to standardize; **normalizarse** *vr* to return to normal

normalmente [normal'mente] *adv* (*con normalidad*) normally; (*habitualmente*) usually

Normandía [norman'dia] *nf* Normandy

normando, -a [nor'mando, a] *adj, nm/f* Norman

normativo, -a [norma'tiβo, a] *adj*: **es** ~ **en todos los coches nuevos** it is standard in all new cars ■ *nf* regulations *pl*

noroeste [noro'este] *adj* north-west, north-western, north-westerly ■ *nm* north-west; (*viento*) north-west wind, north-westerly

norte ['norte] *adj* north, northern, northerly ■ *nm* north; (*fig*) guide

Norteamérica [nortea'merika] *nf* North America

norteamericano, -a [norteameri'kano, a] *adj, nm/f* (North) American

norteño, -a [nor'teɲo, a] *adj* northern ■ *nm/f* northerner

Noruega [no'rweɣa] *nf* Norway

noruego, -a [no'rweɣo, a] *adj, nm/f* Norwegian ■ *nm* (*Ling*) Norwegian

nos [nos] *pron* (*directo*) us; (*indirecto*) (to) us; (*reflexivo*) (to) ourselves; (*recíproco*) (to) each

n

other; ~ **levantamos a las siete** we get up at seven

nosocomio [noso'komjo] *nm* (*Am*) hospital

nosotros, -as [no'sotros, as] *pron* (*sujeto*) we; (*después de prep*) us; ~ **(mismos)** ourselves

nostalgia [nos'talxja] *nf* nostalgia, homesickness

nostálgico, -a [nos'talxiko, a] *adj* nostalgic, homesick

nota ['nota] *nf* note; (*Escol*) mark; (*de fin de año*) report; (*Univ etc*) footnote; (*Com*) account; ~ **de aviso** advice note; ~ **de crédito/débito** credit/debit note; ~ **de gastos** expenses claim; ~ **de sociedad** gossip column; **tomar notas** to take notes

notable [no'taβle] *adj* noteworthy, notable; (*Escol etc*) outstanding ■ *nm/f* notable

notar [no'tar] *vt* to notice, note; (*percibir*) to feel; (*ver*) to see; **notarse** *vr* to be obvious; **se nota que ...** one observes that ...

notaría [nota'ria] *nf* (*profesión*) profession of notary; (*despacho*) notary's office

notarial [nota'rjal] *adj* (*estilo*) legal; **acta** ~ affidavit

notario [no'tarjo] *nm* notary; (*abogado*) solicitor

noticia [no'tiθja] *nf* (*información*) piece of news; (*TV etc*) news item; **las noticias** the news *sg*; **según nuestras noticias** according to our information; **tener noticias de algn** to hear from sb

noticiario [noti'θjarjo] *nm* (*Cine*) newsreel; (*TV*) news bulletin

noticiero [noti'θjero] *nm* newspaper; (*Am: tb*: **noticiero telediario**) news bulletin

notificación [notifika'θjon] *nf* notification

notificar [notifi'kar] *vt* to notify, inform

notifique *etc* [noti'fike] *vb ver* **notificar**

notoriedad [notorje'ðað] *nf* fame, renown

notorio, -a [no'torjo, a] *adj* (*público*) well-known; (*evidente*) obvious

nov. *abr* (= *noviembre*) Nov.

novatada [noβa'taða] *nf* (*burla*) teasing, hazing (*US*); **pagar la** ~ to learn the hard way

novato, -a [no'βato, a] *adj* inexperienced ■ *nm/f* beginner, novice

novecientos, -as [noβe'θjentos, as] *num* nine hundred

novedad [noβe'ðað] *nf* (*calidad de nuevo*) newness, novelty; (*noticia*) piece of news; (*cambio*) change, (new) development; (*sorpresa*) surprise; **novedades** *nfpl* (*noticia*) latest (news) *sg*

novedoso, -a [noβe'ðoso, a] *adj* novel

novel [no'βel] *adj* new; (*inexperto*) inexperienced ■ *nm/f* beginner

novela [no'βela] *nf* novel; ~ **policíaca** detective story

novelero, -a [noβe'lero, a] *adj* highly imaginative

novelesco, -a [noβe'lesko, a] *adj* fictional; (*romántico*) romantic; (*fantástico*) fantastic

novelista [noβe'lista] *nm/f* novelist

novelística [noβe'listika] *nf*: **la** ~ fiction, the novel

noveno, -a [no'βeno, a] *num* ninth

noventa [no'βenta] *num* ninety

novia ['noβja] *nf ver* **novio**

noviazgo [no'βjaθɣo] *nm* engagement

novicio, -a [no'βiθjo, a] *nm/f* novice

noviembre [no'βjembre] *nm* November; *ver tb* **julio**

novilla [no'βiʎa] *nf* heifer

novillada [noβi'ʎaða] *nf* (*Taur*) bullfight with young bulls

novillero [noβi'ʎero] *nm* novice bullfighter

novillo [no'βiʎo] *nm* young bull, bullock; **hacer novillos** (*fam*) to play truant (*Brit*) o hooky (*US*)

novio, -a [no'βjo, a] *nm/f* boyfriend/girlfriend; (*prometido*) fiancé/fiancée; (*recién casado*) bridegroom/bride; **los novios** the newly-weds

novísimo, -a [no'βisimo, a] *adj superlativo de* **nuevo, a**

NPI *nm abr* (*Inform*: = *número personal de identificación*) PIN

N. S. *abr* = **Nuestro Señor**

ns/nc *abr* = **no sabe(n)/no contesta(n)**

ntra., ntro. *abr* = **nuestra, nuestro**

Ntro. Sr. *abr* = **Nuestro Señor**

NU *nfpl abr* (= *Naciones Unidas*) UN *sg*

nubarrón [nuβa'rron] *nm* storm cloud

nube ['nuβe] *nf* cloud; (*Med: ocular*) cloud, film; (*fig*) mass; **una** ~ **de críticas** a storm of criticism; **los precios están por las nubes** prices are sky-high; **estar en las nubes** to be away with the fairies

nublado, -a [nu'βlaðo, a] *adj* cloudy ■ *nm* storm cloud

nublar [nu'βlar] *vt* (*oscurecer*) to darken; (*confundir*) to cloud; **nublarse** *vr* to cloud over

nuboso, -a [nu'βoso, a] *adj* cloudy

nuca ['nuka] *nf* nape of the neck

nuclear [nukle'ar] *adj* nuclear

nuclearizado, -a [nukleari'θaðo, a] *adj*: **países nuclearizados** countries possessing nuclear weapons

núcleo ['nukleo] *nm* (*centro*) core; (*Física*) nucleus

nudillo [nu'ðiʎo] *nm* knuckle

nudista [nu'dista] *adj, nm/f* nudist

nudo ['nuðo] *nm* knot; (*unión*) bond; (*de problema*) crux; (*Ferro*) junction; (*fig*) lump;

~ **corredizo** slipknot; **con un ~ en la garganta** with a lump in one's throat
nudoso, -a [nu'ðoso, a] *adj* knotty; (*tronco*) gnarled; (*bastón*) knobbly
nueces ['nweθes] *nfpl de* **nuez**
nuera ['nwera] *nf* daughter-in-law
nuestro, -a ['nwestro, a] *adj posesivo* our ■ *pron* ours; ~ **padre** our father; **un amigo** ~ a friend of ours; **es el** ~ it's ours; **los nuestros** our people; (*Deporte*) our *o* the local team *o* side
nueva ['nweβa] *nf ver* **nuevo**
Nueva Escocia *nf* Nova Scotia
nuevamente [nweβa'mente] *adv* (*otra vez*) again; (*de nuevo*) anew
Nueva York [-'jork] *nf* New York
Nueva Zelanda [-θe'landa], **Nueva Zelandia** [-θe'landja] *nf* New Zealand
nueve ['nweβe] *num* nine
nuevo, -a ['nweβo, a] *adj* (*gen*) new ■ *nf* piece of news; **¿qué hay de ~?** (*fam*) what's new?; **de** ~ again
Nuevo Méjico *nm* New Mexico
nuez [nweθ] (*pl* **nueces**) *nf* nut; (*del nogal*) walnut, ~ **de Adán** Adam's apple, ~ **moscada** nutmeg
nulidad [nuli'ðað] *nf* (*incapacidad*) incompetence; (*abolición*) nullity; (*individuo*) nonentity; **es una** ~ he's a dead loss
nulo, -a ['nulo, a] *adj* (*inepto, torpe*) useless; (*Invólido*) (null and) void; (*Deporte*) drawn, tied
núm. *abr* (= *número*) no.
numen ['numen] *nm* inspiration
numeración [numera'θjon] *nf* (*cifras*) numbers *pl*; (*arábiga, romana etc*) numerals *pl*; ~ **de línea** (*Inform*) line numbering
numerador [numera'ðor] *nm* (*Mat*) numerator
numeral [nume'ral] *nm* numeral

numerar [nume'rar] *vt* to number; **numerarse** *vr* (*Mil etc*) to number off
numerario, -a [nume'rarjo, a] *adj* numerary; **profesor** ~ permanent *o* tenured member of teaching staff ■ *nm* hard cash
numérico, -a [nu'meriko, a] *adj* numerical
número ['numero] *nm* (*gen*) number; (*tamaño: de zapato*) size; (*ejemplar: de diario*) number, issue; (*Teat etc*) turn, act, number; **sin** ~ numberless, unnumbered; ~ **binario** (*Inform*) binary number; ~ **de matrícula/de teléfono** registration/telephone number; ~ **personal de identificación** (*Inform etc*) personal identification number; ~ **de serie** (*Com*) serial number; ~ **atrasado** back number
numeroso, -a [nume'roso, a] *adj* numerous; **familia numerosa** large family
numerus ['numerus] *nm*: ~ **clausus** (*Univ*) restricted *o* selective entry
nunca ['nunka] *adv* (*jamás*) never; (*con verbo negativo*) ever; ~ **lo pensé** I never thought it; **no viene** ~ he never comes; ~ **más** never again
nuncio ['nunθjo] *nm* (*Rel*) nuncio
nupcial [nup'θjal] *adj* wedding *cpd*
nupcias ['nupθjas] *nfpl* wedding *sg*, nuptials
nutria ['nutrja] *nf* otter
nutrición [nutri'θjon] *nf* nutrition
nutrido, -a [nu'triðo, a] *adj* (*alimentado*) nourished; (*fig: grande*) large; (*abundante*) abundant; **mal** ~ undernourished; ~ **de** full of
nutrir [nu'trir] *vt* to feed, nourish; (*fig*) to feed, strengthen
nutritivo, -a [nutri'tiβo, a] *adj* nourishing, nutritious
nylon [ni'lon] *nm* nylon

n

Ñ, ñ ['eɲe] *nf* (*letra*) Ñ ñ
ñato, -a ['ɲato, a] *adj* (*Am*) snub-nosed
ñoñería [ɲoɲe'ria], **ñoñez** [ɲo'ɲeθ] *nf*
  insipidness

ñoño, -a ['ɲoɲo, a] *adj* (*soso*) insipid;
  (*persona*: *débil*) spineless
ñoquis ['ɲokis] *nmpl* (*Culin*) gnocchi

Oo

O, o [o] nf (letra) O, o; **O de Oviedo** O for Oliver (Brit) o Oboe (US)

O abr (= oeste) W

o [o] conj or; **o ... o** either ... or; **o sea** that is

ó [o] conj (en números para evitar confusión) or; **cinco ó seis** five or six

o/ nm (Com: = orden) o

OACI nf abr (= Organización de la Aviación Civil Internacional) ICAO

oasis [o'asis] nm inv oasis

obcecado, -a [oβθe'kaðo, a] adj blind; (terco) stubborn

obcecarse [oβθe'karse] vr to be obstinate; **~ en hacer** to insist on doing

obceque etc [oβ'θeke] vb ver **obcecarse**

obedecer [oβeðe'θer] vt to obey; **~ a** (Med etc) to yield to; (fig): **~ a ..., ~ al hecho de que ...** to be due to ..., arise from ...

obedezca etc [oβe'ðeθka] vb ver **obedecer**

obediencia [oβe'ðjenθja] nf obedience

obediente [oβe'ðjente] adj obedient

obertura [oβer'tura] nf overture

obesidad [oβesi'ðað] nf obesity

obeso, -a [o'βeso, a] adj obese

óbice ['oβiθe] nm obstacle, impediment

obispado [oβis'paðo] nm bishopric

obispo [o'βispo] nm bishop

óbito ['oβito] nm demise

objeción [oβxe'θjon] nf objection; **hacer una ~, poner objeciones** to raise objections, object

objetar [oβxe'tar] vt, vi to object

objetivo, -a [oβxe'tiβo, a] adj objective ■ nm objective; (fig) aim; (Foto) lens

objeto [oβ'xeto] nm (cosa) object; (fin) aim

objetor, a [oβxe'tor, a] nm/f objector; **~ de conciencia** conscientious objector; ver tb **mili**

oblea [o'βlea] nf (Rel, fig) wafer

oblicuo, -a [o'βlikwo, a] adj oblique; (mirada) sidelong

obligación [oβliɣa'θjon] nf obligation; (Com) bond, debenture

obligar [oβli'ɣar] vt to force; **obligarse** vr: **obligarse a** to commit o.s. to

obligatorio, -a [oβliɣa'torjo, a] adj compulsory, obligatory

obligue etc [o'βliɣe] vb ver **obligar**

oboe [o'βoe] nm oboe; (músico) oboist

Ob.º abr (= Obispo) Bp

obra ['oβra] nf work; (producción) piece of work; (Arq) construction, building; (libro) book; (Mus) opus; (Teat) play; **~ de arte** work of art; **~ maestra** masterpiece; **~ de consulta** reference book; **obras completas** complete works; **~ benéfica** charity; **"obras"** (en carretera) "men at work"; **obras públicas** public works; **por ~ de** thanks to (the efforts of); **obras son amores y no buenas razones** actions speak louder than words

obrar [o'βrar] vt to work; (tener efecto) to have an effect on ■ vi to act, behave; (tener efecto) to have an effect; **la carta obra en su poder** the letter is in his/her possession

Ob.ᵖᵒ abr = **obispo**

obr. cit. abr (= obra citada) op. cit.

obrero, -a [o'βrero, a] adj working; (movimiento) labour cpd; **clase obrera** working class ■ nm/f (gen) worker; (sin oficio) labourer

obscenidad [oβsθeni'ðað] nf obscenity

obsceno, -a [oβs'θeno, a] adj obscene

obscu... pref = **oscu...**

obsequiar [oβse'kjar] vt (ofrecer) to present; (agasajar) to make a fuss of, lavish attention on

obsequio [oβ'sekjo] nm (regalo) gift; (cortesía) courtesy, attention

obsequioso, -a [oβse'kjoso, a] adj attentive

observación [oβserβa'θjon] nf observation; (reflexión) remark; (objeción) objection

observador, a [oβserβa'ðor, a] adj observant ■ nm/f observer

observancia [oβser'βanθja] nf observance

observar [oβser'βar] vt to observe; (notar) to notice; (leyes) to observe, respect; (reglas) to abide by

observatorio [oβserβa'torjo] nm
observatory; ~ **del tiempo** weather station
obsesión [oβse'sjon] nf obsession
obsesionar [oβsesjo'nar] vt to obsess
obseso, -a [oβ'seso, a] nm/f (sexual) sex
maniac
obsolescencia [oβsoles'θenθja] nf: ~
incorporada (Com) built-in obsolescence
obsoleto, -a [oβso'leto, a] adj obsolete
obstaculice etc [oβstaku'liθe] vb ver
obstaculizar
obstaculizar [oβstakuli'θar] vt (dificultar) to
hinder, hamper
obstáculo [oβs'takulo] nm (gen) obstacle;
(impedimento) hindrance, drawback
obstante [oβs'tante]: **no** ~ adv nevertheless;
(de todos modos) all the same prep in spite of
obstetra [oβs'tetra] nm/f obstetrician
obstetricia [oβste'triθja] nf obstetrics sg
obstinado, -a [oβsti'naðo, a] adj (gen)
obstinate; (terco) stubborn
obstinarse [oβsti'narse] vr to dig one's heels
in; ~ **en** to persist in
obstrucción [oβstruk'θjon] nf obstruction
obstruir [oβstru'ir] vt to obstruct; (bloquear)
to block; (estorbar) to hinder
obstruyendo etc [oβstru'jendo] vb ver
obstruir
obtención [oβten'θjon] nf (Com)
procurement
obtendré etc [oβten'dre] vb ver **obtener**
obtener [oβte'ner] vt (conseguir) to obtain;
(ganar) to gain
obtenga etc [oβ'tenga] vb ver **obtener**
obturación [oβtura'θjon] nf plugging,
stopping; (Foto): **velocidad de** ~ shutter speed
obturador [oβtura'ðor] nm (Foto) shutter
obtuso, -a [oβ'tuso, a] adj (filo) blunt; (Mat,
fig) obtuse
obtuve etc [oβ'tuβe] vb ver **obtener**
obús [o'βus] nm (Mil) shell
obviar [oβ'βjar] vt to obviate, remove
obvio, -a ['oββjo, a] adj obvious
oca ['oka] nf goose; (tb: **juego de la oca**)
≈ snakes and ladders
ocasión [oka'sjon] nf (oportunidad)
opportunity, chance; (momento) occasion,
time; (causa) cause; **de** ~ secondhand; **con** ~
de on the occasion of; **en algunas ocasiones**
sometimes; **aprovechar la** ~ to seize one's
opportunity
ocasionar [okasjo'nar] vt to cause
ocaso [o'kaso] nm sunset; (fig) decline
occidental [okθiðen'tal] adj western ■ nm/f
westerner ■ nm west
occidente [okθi'ðente] nm west; **el O~** the
West

occiso, -a [ok'θiso, a] nm/f: **el** ~ the deceased;
(de asesinato) the victim
O.C.D.E. nf abr (= Organización de Cooperación y
Desarrollo Económicos) OECD
océano [o'θeano] nm ocean; **el** ~ **Índico** the
Indian Ocean
ochenta [o'tʃenta] num eighty
ocho ['otʃo] num eight; (fecha) eighth; ~ **días**
a week
ochocientos, -as [otʃo'θjentos, as] num
eight hundred
OCI ['oθi] nf abr (Pol: Venezuela, Perú) = **Oficina
Central de Información**
ocio ['oθjo] nm (tiempo) leisure; (pey) idleness;
"guía del ~**"** "what's on"
ociosidad [oθjosi'ðað] nf idleness
ocioso, -a [o'θjoso, a] adj (inactivo) idle; (inútil)
useless
oct. abr (= octubre) Oct.
octanaje [okta'naxe] nm: **de alto** ~ high
octane
octano [ok'tano] nm octane
octavilla [okta'βiʎa] nm leaflet, pamphlet
octavo, -a [ok'taβo, a] num eighth
octeto [ok'teto] nm (Inform) byte
octogenario, -a [oktoxe'narjo, a] adj, nm/f
octogenarian
octubre [ok'tuβre] nm October; ver tb **julio**
OCU ['oku] nf abr (Esp: = Organización de
Consumidores y Usuarios) ≈ Consumers'
Association
ocular [oku'lar] adj ocular, eye cpd; **testigo** ~
eyewitness
oculista [oku'lista] nm/f oculist
ocultar [okul'tar] vt (esconder) to hide; (callar)
to conceal; (disfrazar) to screen; **ocultarse** vr
to hide (o.s.); **ocultarse a la vista** to keep
out of sight
oculto, -a [o'kulto, a] adj hidden; (fig) secret
ocupación [okupa'θjon] nf occupation;
(tenencia) occupancy
ocupado, -a [oku'paðo, a] adj (persona) busy;
(plaza) occupied, taken; (teléfono) engaged;
¿**está ocupada la silla?** is that seat taken?
ocupar [oku'par] vt (gen) to occupy; (puesto)
to hold, fill; (individuo) to engage; (obreros)
to employ; (confiscar) to seize; **ocuparse**
vr: **ocuparse de** o **en** to concern o.s. with;
(cuidar) to look after; **ocuparse de lo suyo** to
mind one's own business
ocurrencia [oku'rrenθja] nf (ocasión)
occurrence; (agudeza) witticism
ocurrir [oku'rrir] vi to happen; **ocurrirse**
vr: **se me ocurrió que** ... it occurred to me
that ...; ¿**se te ocurre algo?** can you think
of o come up with anything?; ¿**qué ocurre?**
what's going on?

oda ['oða] nf ode
ODECA [o'ðeka] nf abr = **Organización de Estados Centroamericanos**
odiar [o'ðjar] vt to hate
odio ['oðjo] nm (gen) hate, hatred; (disgusto) dislike
odioso, -a [o'ðjoso, a] adj (gen) hateful; (malo) nasty
odisea [oði'sea] nf odyssey
odontología [oðontolo'xia] nf dentistry, dental surgery
odontólogo, -a [oðon'toloyo, a] nm/f dentist, dental surgeon
odre ['oðre] nm wineskin
O.E.A. nf abr (= Organización de Estados Americanos) O.A.S.
OECE nf abr (= Organización Europea de Cooperación Económica) OEEC
OELA [o'ela] nf abr = **Organización de Estados Latinoamericanos**
oeste [o'este] nm west; **una película del ~** a western
ofender [ofen'der] vt (agraviar) to offend; (insultar) to insult; **ofenderse** vr to take offence
ofensa [o'fensa] nf offence; (insulto) slight
ofensivo, -a [ofen'siβo, a] adj (insultante) insulting; (Mil) offensive ■ nf offensive
oferta [o'ferta] nf offer; (propuesta) proposal; (para contrato) bid, tender; **la ~ y la demanda** supply and demand; **artículos en ~** goods on offer; **~ excedentaria** (Com) excess supply; **~ monetaria** money supply; **~ pública de adquisición (OPA)** (Com) takeover bid; **ofertas de trabajo** (en periódicos) situations vacant column
offset ['ofset] nm offset
oficial [ofi'θjal] adj official ■ nm official; (Mil) officer
oficialista [ofisja'lista] adj (Am) (pro-) government; **el candidato ~** the governing party's candidate
oficiar [ofi'θjar] vt to inform officially ■ vi (Rel) to officiate
oficina [ofi'θina] nf office; **~ de empleo** employment agency; **~ de información** information bureau; **~ de objetos perdidos** lost property office (Brit), lost-and-found department (US); **~ de turismo** tourist office; **~ principal** (Com) head office, main branch
oficinista [ofiθi'nista] nm/f clerk; **los oficinistas** white-collar workers
oficio [o'fiθjo] nm (profesión) profession; (puesto) post; (Rel) service; (función) function; (comunicado) official letter; **ser del ~** to be an old hand; **tener mucho ~** to have a lot of

experience; **~ de difuntos** funeral service; **de ~** officially
oficioso, -a [ofi'θjoso, a] adj (pey) officious; (no oficial) unofficial, informal
ofimática [ofi'matika] nf office automation
ofrecer [ofre'θer] vt (dar) to offer; (proponer) to propose; **ofrecerse** vr (persona) to offer o.s., volunteer; (situación) to present itself; **¿qué se le ofrece?, ¿se le ofrece algo?** what can I do for you?, can I get you anything?
ofrecimiento [ofreθi'mjento] nm offer, offering
ofrendar [ofren'dar] vt to present, contribute
ofrezca etc [o'freθka] vb ver **ofrecer**
oftalmología [oftalmolo'xia] nf ophthalmology
oftalmólogo, -a [oftal'moloyo, a] nm/f ophthalmologist
ofuscación [ofuska'θjon] nf, **ofuscamiento** [ofuska'mjento] nm (fig) bewilderment
ofuscar [ofus'kar] vt (confundir) to bewilder; (enceguecer) to dazzle, blind
ofusque etc [o'fuske] vb ver **ofuscar**
ogro ['oyro] nm ogre
OIC nf abr (= Organización Interamericana del Café: Com) = **Organización Internacional del Comercio**
oída [o'iða] nf: **de oídas** by hearsay
oído [o'iðo] nm (Anat, Mus) ear; (sentido) hearing; **~ interno** inner ear; **de ~** by ear; **apenas pude dar crédito a mis oídos** I could scarcely believe my ears; **hacer oídos sordos a** to turn a deaf ear to
OIEA nm abr (= Organismo Internacional de Energía Atómica) IAEA
oiga etc [o'iya] vb ver **oír**
OIR [o'ir] nf abr (= Organización Internacional para los Refugiados) IRO; = **Organización Internacional de Radiodifusión**
oír [o'ir] vt (gen) to hear; (esp Am: escuchar) to listen to; **¡oye!** (sorpresa) I say!, say! (US); **¡oiga!** (Telec) hullo?; **~ misa** to attend mass; **como quien oye llover** without paying (the slightest) attention
O.I.T. nf abr (= Organización Internacional del Trabajo) ILO
ojal [o'xal] nm buttonhole
ojalá [oxa'la] excl if only (it were so)!, some hope! ■ conj if only...!, would that...!; **ojalá que venga hoy** I hope he comes today; **¡ojalá pudiera!** I wish I could!
ojeada [oxe'aða] nf glance; **echar una ~ a** to take a quick look at
ojera [o'xera] nf: **tener ojeras** to have bags under one's eyes
ojeriza [oxe'riθa] nf ill-will; **tener ~ a** to have a grudge against, have it in for

o

ojeroso, -a [oxe'roso, a] adj haggard

ojete [o'xete] nm eye(let)

ojo ['oxo] nm eye; (de puente) span; (de cerradura) keyhole ◼ excl careful!; **tener ~ para** to have an eye for; **ojos saltones** bulging o goggle eyes; **~ de buey** porthole; **~ por ~** an eye for an eye; **en un abrir y cerrar de ojos** in the twinkling of an eye; **a ojos vistas** openly; (crecer etc) before one's (very) eyes; **a ~ (de buen cubero)** roughly; **ojos que no ven, corazón que no siente** out of sight, out of mind; **ser el ~ derecho de algn** (fig) to be the apple of sb's eye

okupa [o'kupa] nm/f (fam) squatter

OL abr (= onda larga) LW, long wave

ola ['ola] nf wave; **~ de calor/frío** heatwave/ cold spell; **la nueva ~** the latest fashion; (Cine, Mus) (the) new wave

OLADE [o'laðe] nf abr = **Organización Latinoamericana de Energía**

olé [o'le] excl bravo!, olé!

oleada [ole'aða] nf big wave, swell; (fig) wave

oleaje [ole'axe] nm swell

óleo ['oleo] nm oil

oleoducto [oleo'ðukto] nm (oil) pipeline

oler [o'ler] vt (gen) to smell; (inquirir) to pry into; (fig: sospechar) to sniff out ◼ vi to smell; **~ a** to smell of; **huele mal** it smells bad, it stinks

olfatear [olfate'ar] vt to smell; (fig: sospechar) to sniff out; (inquirir) to pry into

olfato [ol'fato] nm sense of smell

oligarquía [oliɣar'kia] nf oligarchy

olimpiada [olim'piaða] nf: **la ~** o **las olimpiadas** the Olympics

olímpicamente [o'limpikamente] adv: **pasar ~ de algo** to totally ignore sth

olímpico, -a [o'limpiko, a] adj Olympian; (deportes) Olympic

oliva [o'liβa] nf (aceituna) olive; **aceite de ~** olive oil

olivar [oli'βar] nm olive grove o plantation

olivo [o'liβo] nm olive tree

olla ['oʎa] nf pan; (para hervir agua) kettle; (comida) stew; **~ a presión** pressure cooker

olmo ['olmo] nm elm (tree)

olor [o'lor] nm smell

oloroso, -a [olo'roso, a] adj scented

OLP nf abr (= Organización para la Liberación de Palestina) PLO

olvidadizo, -a [olβiða'ðiθo, a] adj (desmemoriado) forgetful; (distraído) absent-minded

olvidar [olβi'ðar] vt to forget; (omitir) to omit; (abandonar) to leave behind; **olvidarse** vr (fig) to forget o.s.; **se me olvidó** I forgot

olvido [ol'βiðo] nm oblivion; (acto) oversight;

(descuido) slip; **caer en el ~** to fall into oblivion

O.M. abr (= onda media) MW, medium wave; (= Oriente Medio) Middle East; (Pol) = **Orden Ministerial**

ombligo [om'bliɣo] nm navel

OMI nf abr (= Organización Marítima Internacional) IMO

ominoso, -a [omi'noso, a] adj ominous

omisión [omi'sjon] nf (abstención) omission; (descuido) neglect

omiso, -a [o'miso, a] adj: **hacer caso ~ de** to ignore, pass over

omitir [omi'tir] vt to leave o miss out, omit

ómnibus ['omniβus] nm (Am) bus

omnipotente [omnipo'tente] adj omnipotent

omnipresente [omnipre'sente] adj omnipresent

omnívoro, -a [om'niβoro, a] adj omnivorous

omoplato [omo'plato], **omóplato** [o'moplato] nm shoulder-blade

OMS nf abr (= Organización Mundial de la Salud) WHO

ONCE ['onθe] nf abr (= Organización Nacional de Ciegos Españoles) charity for the blind

once ['onθe] num eleven ◼ nm (Am); **onces** nfpl tea break sg

onda ['onda] nf wave; **~ corta/larga/ media** short/long/medium wave; **ondas acústicas/hertzianas** acoustic/Hertzian waves; **~ sonora** sound wave

ondear [onde'ar] vi to wave; (tener ondas) to be wavy; (agua) to ripple; **ondearse** vr to swing, sway

ondulación [ondula'θjon] nf undulation

ondulado, -a [ondu'laðo, a] adj wavy ◼ nm wave

ondulante [ondu'lante] adj undulating

ondular [ondu'lar] vt (el pelo) to wave ◼ vi, **ondularse** vr to undulate

oneroso, -a [one'roso, a] adj onerous

ONG nf abr (= organización no gubernamental) NGO

onomástico, -a [ono'mastiko, a] adj: **fiesta onomástica** saint's day ◼ nm saint's day

ONU ['onu] nf abr ver **Organización de las Naciones Unidas**

onubense [onu'βense] adj of o from Huelva ◼ nm/f native o inhabitant of Huelva

ONUDI [o'nuði] nf abr (= Organización de las Naciones Unidas para el Desarrollo Industrial) UNIDO (= United Nations Industrial Development Organization)

onza ['onθa] nf ounce

O.P. nfpl abr = **Obras Públicas**; (Com) = **Oficina Principal**

OPA ['opa] *nf abr* (= *Oferta Pública de Adquisición*) takeover bid

opaco, -a [o'pako, a] *adj* opaque; (*fig*) dull

ópalo ['opalo] *nm* opal

opción [op'θjon] *nf* (*gen*) option; (*derecho*) right, option; **no hay ~** there is no alternative

opcional [opθjo'nal] *adj* optional

O.P.E.P. [o'pep] *nf abr* (= *Organización de Países Exportadores de Petróleo*) OPEC

ópera ['opera] *nf* opera; **ópera bufa** o **cómica** comic opera

operación [opera'θjon] *nf* (*gen*) operation; (*Com*) transaction, deal; **~ a plazo** (*Com*) forward transaction; **operaciones accesorias** (*Inform*) housekeeping; **operaciones a término** (*Com*) futures

operador, a [opera'ðor, a] *nm/f* operator; (*Cine: proyección*) projectionist; (: *rodaje*) cameraman

operar [ope'rar] *vt* (*producir*) to produce, bring about; (*Med*) to operate on ■ *vi* (*Com*) to operate, deal; **operarse** *vr* to occur; (*Med*) to have an operation; **se han operado grandes cambios** great changes have been made o have taken place

operario, -a [ope'rarjo, a] *nm/f* worker

opereta [ope'reta] *nf* operetta

opinar [opi'nar] *vt* (*estimar*) to think ■ *vi* (*enjuiciar*) to give one's opinion; **~ bien de** to think well of

opinión [opi'njon] *nf* (*creencia*) belief; (*criterio*) opinion; **la ~ pública** public opinion

opio ['opjo] *nm* opium

opíparo, -a [o'piparo, a] *adj* sumptuous

opondré *etc* [opon'dre] *vb ver* **oponer**

oponente [opo'nente] *nm/f* opponent

oponer [opo'ner] *vt* (*resistencia*) to put up, offer; (*negativa*) to raise; **oponerse** *vr* (*objetar*) to object; (*estar frente a frente*) to be opposed; (*dos personas*) to oppose each other; **~ A a B** to set A against B; **me opongo a pensar que ...** I refuse to believe o think that ...

oponga *etc* [o'ponga] *vb ver* **oponer**

Oporto [o'porto] *nm* Oporto

oporto [o'porto] *nm* port

oportunidad [oportuni'ðað] *nf* (*ocasión*) opportunity; (*posibilidad*) chance

oportunismo [oportu'nismo] *nm* opportunism

oportunista [oportu'nista] *nm/f* opportunist; (*infección*) opportunistic

oportuno, -a [opor'tuno, a] *adj* (*en su tiempo*) opportune, timely; (*respuesta*) suitable; **en el momento ~** at the right moment

oposición [oposi'θjon] *nf* opposition; **oposiciones** *nfpl* public examinations;

ganar un puesto por oposiciones to win a post by public competitive examination; **hacer oposiciones a, presentarse a unas oposiciones a** to sit a competitive examination for; *see note*

● **OPOSICIÓN**
●
● The *oposiciones* are exams held every
● year for posts nationally and locally in
● the public sector, State education, the
● Judiciary etc. These posts are permanent
● and the number of candidates is high
● so the exams are tough. The candidates,
● *opositores*, have to study a great number of
● subjects relating to their field and also
● the Constitution. People can spend years
● studying and resitting exams

opositar [oposi'tar] *vi* to sit a public entrance examination

opositor, -a [oposi'tor, a] *nm/f* (*Admin*) candidate to a public examination; (*adversario*) opponent

opresión [opre'sjon] *nf* oppression

opresivo, -a [opre'siβo, a] *adj* oppressive

opresor, a [opre'sor, a] *nm/f* oppressor

oprimir [opri'mir] *vt* to squeeze; (*asir*) to grasp; (*pulsar*) to press; (*fig*) to oppress

optar [op'tar] *vi* (*elegir*) to choose; **~ a** o **por** to opt for

optativo, -a [opta'tiβo, a] *adj* optional

óptico, -a ['optiko, a] *adj* optic(al) ■ *nm/f* optician ■ *nf* optics *sg*; (*fig*) viewpoint

optimismo [opti'mismo] *nm* optimism

optimista [opti'mista] *nm/f* optimist

óptimo, -a ['optimo, a] *adj* (*el mejor*) very best

opuesto, -a [o'pwesto, a] *pp de* **oponer** ■ *adj* (*contrario*) opposite; (*antagónico*) opposing

opulencia [opu'lenθja] *nf* opulence

opulento, -a [opu'lento, a] *adj* opulent

opuse *etc* [o'puse] *vb ver* **oponer**

ora ['ora] *adv*: **~ tú ~ yo** now you, now me

oración [ora'θjon] *nf* (*Rel*) prayer; (*Ling*) sentence

oráculo [o'rakulo] *nm* oracle

orador, a [ora'ðor, a] *nm/f* orator; (*conferenciante*) speaker

oral [o'ral] *adj* oral; **por vía ~** (*Med*) orally

orangután [orangu'tan] *nm* orang-utan

orar [o'rar] *vi* (*Rel*) to pray

oratoria [ora'torja] *nf* oratory

orbe ['orβe] *nm* orb, sphere; (*fig*) world; **en todo el ~** all over the globe

órbita ['orβita] *nf* orbit; (*Anat: ocular*) (eye-) socket

orden ['orðen] *nm* (*gen*) order; (*Inform*)

o

command; ~ **público** public order, law and
order; (*números*): **del ~ de** about; **de primer**
~ first-rate; **en ~ de prioridad** in order
of priority ■ *nf* (*gen*) order; ~ **bancaria**
banker's order; ~ **de compra** (*Com*) purchase
order; ~ **del día** agenda; **eso ahora está a
la ~ del día** that is now the order of the day;
a la ~ de usted at your service; **dar la ~ de
hacer algo** to give the order to do sth
ordenación [orðena'θjon] *nf* (*estado*) order;
(*acto*) ordering; (*Rel*) ordination
ordenado, -a [orðe'naðo, a] *adj* (*metódico*)
methodical; (*arreglado*) orderly
ordenador [orðena'ðor] *nm* computer; ~
central mainframe computer; ~ **de gestión**
business computer; ~ **portátil** laptop
(computer); ~ **de sobremesa** desktop
computer
ordenamiento [orðena'mjento] *nm*
legislation
ordenanza [orðe'nanθa] *nf* ordinance;
ordenanzas municipales by-laws ■ *nm*
(*Com etc*) messenger; (*Mil*) orderly; (*bedel*)
porter
ordenar [orðe'nar] *vt* (*mandar*) to order; (*poner
orden*) to put in order, arrange; **ordenarse** *vr*
(*Rel*) to be ordained
ordeñadora [orðeɲa'ðora] *nf* milking
machine
ordeñar [orðe'ɲar] *vt* to milk
ordinariez [orðina'rjeθ] *nf* (*cualidad*)
coarseness, vulgarity; (*una ordinariez*) coarse
remark *o* joke *etc*
ordinario, -a [orði'narjo, a] *adj* (*común*)
ordinary, usual; (*vulgar*) vulgar, common
ordinograma [orðino'ɣrama] *nm* flowchart
orear [ore'ar] *vt* to air; **orearse** *vr* (*ropa*) to air
orégano [o'reɣano] *nm* oregano
oreja [o'rexa] *nf* ear; (*Mecánica*) lug, flange
orensano, -a [oren'sano, a] *adj* of *o* from
Orense ■ *nm/f* native *o* inhabitant of Orense
orfanato [orfa'nato] *nm*, **orfanatorio**
[orfana'torjo] *nm* orphanage
orfandad [orfan'dað] *nf* orphanhood
orfebre [or'feβre] *nm* gold-/silversmith
orfebrería [orfeβre'ria] *nf* gold/silver work
orfelinato [orfeli'nato] *nm* orphanage
orfeón [orfe'on] *nm* (*Mus*) choral society
organice *etc* [orɣa'niθe] *vb ver* **organizar**
orgánico, -a [or'ɣaniko, a] *adj* organic
organigrama [orɣani'ɣrama] *nm* flow chart;
(*de organización*) organization chart
organillo [orɣa'niʎo] *nm* barrel organ
organismo [orɣa'nismo] *nm* (*Bio*) organism;
(*Pol*) organization; **O~ Internacional de
Energía Atómica** International Atomic
Energy Agency

organista [orɣa'nista] *nm/f* organist
organización [orɣaniθa'θjon] *nf*
organization; **O~ de las Naciones Unidas
(ONU)** United Nations Organization; **O~ del
Tratado del Atlántico Norte (OTAN)** North
Atlantic Treaty Organization (NATO)
organizador, a [orɣaniθa'ðor, a] *adj*
organizing; **el comité ~** the organizing
committee ■ *nm/f* organizer
organizar [orɣani'θar] *vt* to organize
órgano ['orɣano] *nm* organ
orgasmo [or'ɣasmo] *nm* orgasm
orgía [or'xia] *nf* orgy
orgullo [or'ɣuʎo] *nm* (*altanería*) pride;
(*autorespeto*) self-respect
orgulloso, -a [orɣu'ʎoso, a] *adj* (*gen*) proud;
(*altanero*) haughty
orientación [orjenta'θjon] *nf* (*posición*)
position; (*dirección*) direction; ~ **profesional**
occupational guidance
oriental [orjen'tal] *adj* oriental; (*región etc*)
eastern ■ *nm/f* oriental
orientar [orjen'tar] *vt* (*situar*) to orientate;
(*señalar*) to point; (*dirigir*) to direct; (*guiar*) to
guide; **orientarse** *vr* to get one's bearings;
(*decidirse*) to decide on a course of action
oriente [o'rjente] *nm* east; **el O~** the East, the
Orient; **Cercano/Medio/Lejano O~** Near/
Middle/Far East
orificio [ori'fiθjo] *nm* orifice
origen [o'rixen] *nm* origin; (*nacimiento*)
lineage, birth; **dar ~ a** to cause, give rise to
original [orixi'nal] *adj* (*nuevo*) original;
(*extraño*) odd, strange ■ *nm* original; (*Tip*)
manuscript; (*Tec*) master (copy)
originalidad [orixinali'ðað] *nf* originality
originar [orixi'nar] *vt* to originate;
originarse *vr* to originate
originario, -a [orixi'narjo, a] *adj* (*nativo*)
native; (*primordial*) original; **ser ~ de** to
originate from; **país ~** country of origin
orilla [o'riʎa] *nf* (*borde*) border; (*de río*) bank;
(*de bosque, tela*) edge; (*de mar*) shore; **a orillas
de** on the banks of
orillar [ori'ʎar] *vt* (*bordear*) to skirt, go round;
(*Costura*) to edge; (*resolver*) to wind up; (*tocar:
asunto*) to touch briefly on; (*dificultad*) to avoid
orín [o'rin] *nm* rust
orina [o'rina] *nf* urine
orinal [ori'nal] *nm* (chamber) pot
orinar [ori'nar] *vi* to urinate; **orinarse** *vr* to
wet o.s.
orines [o'rines] *nmpl* urine *sg*
oriundo, -a [o'rjundo, a] *adj*: ~ **de** native of
orla ['orla] *nf* edge, border; (*Escol*) graduation
photograph
ornamentar [ornamen'tar] *vt* (*adornar,*

ataviar) to adorn; *(revestir)* to bedeck

ornar [or'nar] *vt* to adorn

ornitología [ornitolo'xia] *nf* ornithology, bird watching

ornitólogo, -a [orni'toloɣo, a] *nm/f* ornithologist

oro ['oro] *nm* gold; ~ **en barras** gold ingots; **de** ~ gold, golden; **no es** ~ **todo lo que reluce** all that glitters is not gold; **hacerse de** ~ to make a fortune; *ver tb* **oros**

orondo, -a [o'rondo, a] *adj (vasija)* rounded; *(individuo)* smug, self-satisfied

oropel [oro'pel] *nm* tinsel

oros ['oros] *nmpl (Naipes) one of the suits in the Spanish card deck*; *ver tb* **Baraja Española**

orquesta [or'kesta] *nf* orchestra; ~ **de cámara/sinfónica** chamber/symphony orchestra; ~ **de jazz** jazz band

orquestar [orkes'tar] *vt* to orchestrate

orquídea [or'kiðea] *nf* orchid

ortiga [or'tiɣa] *nf* nettle

ortodoncia [orto'ðonθja] *nf* orthodontics *sg*

ortodoxo, -a [orto'ðokso, a] *adj* orthodox

ortografía [ortoɣra'fia] *nf* spelling

ortopedia [orto'peðja] *nf* orthop(a)edics *sg*

ortopédico, -a [orto'peðiko, a] *adj* orthop(a)edic

oruga [o'ruɣa] *nf* caterpillar

orujo [o'ruxo] *nm* type of strong grape liqueur made from grape pressings

orzuelo [or'θwelo] *nm (Med)* stye

os [os] *pron (gen)* you; *(a vosotros)* (to) you; *(reflexivo)* (to) yourselves; *(mutuo)* (to) each other; **vosotros os laváis** you wash yourselves; **¡callaros!** *(fam)* shut up!

osa ['osa] *nf* (she-)bear; **O~ Mayor/Menor** Great/Little Bear, Ursa Major/Minor

osadía [osa'ðia] *nf* daring; *(descaro)* impudence

osamenta [osa'menta] *nf* skeleton

osar [o'sar] *vi* to dare

oscense [os'θense] *adj* of o from Huesca ◼ *nm/f* native o inhabitant of Huesca

oscilación [osθila'θjon] *nf (movimiento)* oscillation; *(fluctuación)* fluctuation; *(vacilación)* hesitation; *(de columpio)* swinging, movement to and fro

oscilar [osθi'lar] *vi* to oscillate; to fluctuate; to hesitate

ósculo ['oskulo] *nm* kiss

oscurecer [oskure'θer] *vt* to darken ◼ *vi* to grow dark; **oscurecerse** *vr* to grow o get dark

oscurezca *etc* [osku'reθka] *vb ver* **oscurecer**

oscuridad [oskuri'ðað] *nf* obscurity; *(tinieblas)* darkness

oscuro, -a [os'kuro, a] *adj* dark; *(fig)* obscure;

(indefinido) confused; *(cielo)* overcast, cloudy; *(futuro etc)* uncertain; **a oscuras** in the dark

óseo, -a ['oseo, a] *adj* bony; *(Med etc)* bone *cpd*

oso ['oso] *nm* bear; ~ **blanco/gris/pardo** polar/grizzly/brown bear; ~ **de peluche** teddy bear; ~ **hormiguero** anteater; **hacer el** ~ to play the fool

Ostende [os'tende] *nm* Ostend

ostensible [osten'siβle] *adj* obvious

ostensiblemente [ostensiβle'mente] *adv* perceptibly, visibly

ostentación [ostenta'θjon] *nf (gen)* ostentation; *(acto)* display

ostentar [osten'tar] *vt (gen)* to show; *(pey)* to flaunt, show off; *(poseer)* to have, possess

ostentoso, -a [osten'toso, a] *adj* ostentatious, showy

osteópata [oste'opata] *nm/f* osteopath

ostra ['ostra] *nf* oyster ◼ *excl:* **¡ostras!** *(fam)* sugar!

ostracismo [ostra'θismo] *nm* ostracism

OTAN ['otan] *nf abr ver* **Organización del Tratado del Atlántico Norte**

OTASE [o'tase] *nf abr* (= *Organización del Tratado del Sudeste Asiático*) SEATO

otear [ote'ar] *vt* to observe; *(fig)* to look into

otero [o'tero] *nm* low hill, hillock

otitis [o'titis] *nf* earache

otoñal [oto'ɲal] *adj* autumnal

otoño [o'toɲo] *nm* autumn, fall (US)

otorgamiento [otorɣa'mjento] *nm* conferring, granting; *(Jur)* execution

otorgar [otor'ɣar] *vt (conceder)* to concede; *(dar)* to grant; *(poderes)* to confer; *(premio)* to award

otorgue *etc* [o'torɣe] *vb ver* **otorgar**

otorrinolaringólogo, -a [otorrinolarin'go loɣo, a] *nm/f (Med: tb:* **otorrino***)* ear, nose and throat specialist

 PALABRA CLAVE

otro, -a ['otro, a] *adj* **1** *(distinto: sg)* another; *(: pl)* other; **otra cosa/persona** something/ someone else; **con otros amigos** with other o different friends; **a/en otra parte** elsewhere, somewhere else

2 *(adicional)*: **tráigame ~ café (más), por favor** can I have another coffee please; **otros 10 días más** another 10 days

◼ *pron* **1** *(sg)* another one; **el** ~ the other one; **(los) otros** (the) others; **¡otra!** *(Mus)* more!; **de** ~ somebody o someone else's; **que lo haga** ~ let somebody o someone else do it; **ni uno ni** ~ neither one nor the other

2 *(recíproco)*: **se odian (la) una a (la) otra** they hate one another o each other

3: ~ **tanto**: **comer otro tanto** to eat the same *o* as much again; **recibió una decena de telegramas y otras tantas llamadas** he got about ten telegrams and as many calls

otrora [o'trora] *adv* formerly; **el ~ señor del país** the one-time ruler of the country
OUA *nf abr* (= *Organización de la Unidad Africana*) OAU
ovación [oβa'θjon] *nf* ovation
ovacionar [oβaθjo'nar] *vt* to cheer
oval [o'βal], **ovalado, a** [oβa'laðo, a] *adj* oval
óvalo ['oβalo] *nm* oval
ovario [o'βarjo] *nm* ovary
oveja [o'βexa] *nf* sheep; ~ **negra** (*fig*) black sheep (of the family)
overol [oβe'rol] *nm* (*Am*) overalls *pl*
ovetense [oβe'tense] *adj* of *o* from Oviedo ▪ *nm/f* native *o* inhabitant of Oviedo

ovillo [o'βiʎo] *nm* (*de lana*) ball; (*fig*) tangle; **hacerse un ~** to curl up (into a ball)
OVNI ['oβni] *nm abr* (= *objeto volante* (*o volador*) *no identificado*) UFO
ovulación [oβula'θjon] *nf* ovulation
óvulo ['oβulo] *nm* ovum
oxidación [oksiða'θjon] *nf* rusting
oxidar [oksi'ðar] *vt* to rust; **oxidarse** *vr* to go rusty; (*Tec*) to oxidize
óxido ['oksiðo] *nm* oxide
oxigenado, -a [oksixe'naðo, a] *adj* (*Química*) oxygenated; (*pelo*) bleached
oxigenar [oksixe'nar] *vt* to oxygenate; **oxigenarse** *vr* to become oxygenated; (*fam*) to get some fresh air
oxígeno [ok'sixeno] *nm* oxygen
oyendo *etc* [o'jendo] *vb ver* **oír**
oyente [o'jente] *nm/f* listener, hearer; (*Escol*) unregistered *o* occasional student

Pp

P, p [pe] *nf* (*letra*) P, p; **P de París** P for Peter
P *abr* (*Rel:* = *padre*) Fr.; = **papa**; (= *pregunta*) Q
p. *abr* (= *página*) p; (*Costura*) = **punto**
p.a. *abr* = **por autorización; por ausencia**
pabellón [paβe'ʎon] *nm* bell tent; (*Arq*)
pavilion; (*de hospital etc*) block, section;
(*bandera*) flag; **~ de conveniencia** (*Com*) flag
of convenience; **~ de la oreja** outer ear
pábilo ['paβilo] *nm* wick
pábulo ['paβulo] *nm* food; **dar ~ a** to feed,
encourage
PAC *nf abr* (= *Política Agrícola Común*) CAP
pacense [pa'θense] *adj* of o from Badajoz
■ *nm/f* native o inhabitant of Badajoz
paceño, -a [pa'θeɲo, a] *adj* of o from La Paz
■ *nm/f* native o inhabitant of La Paz
pacer [pa'θer] *vi* to graze ■ *vt* to graze on
pachá [pa'tʃa] *nm*: **vivir como un pachá** to
live like a king
pachanguero, -a [patʃan'gero, a] *adj* (*pey:
música*) noisy and catchy
pachorra [pa'tʃorra] *nf* (*indolencia*) slowness;
(*tranquilidad*) calmness
pachucho, -a [pa'tʃutʃo, a] *adj* (*fruta*)
overripe; (*persona*) off-colour, poorly
paciencia [pa'θjenθja] *nf* patience; **¡~!** be
patient!; **¡~ y barajar!** don't give up!; **perder
la ~** to lose one's temper
paciente [pa'θjente] *adj, nm/f* patient
pacificación [paθifika'θjon] *nf* pacification
pacificar [paθifi'kar] *vt* to pacify; (*tranquilizar*)
to calm
pacífico, -a [pa'θifiko, a] *adj* peaceful;
(*persona*) peace-loving; (*existencia*) pacific;
el (Océano) P~ the Pacific (Ocean)
pacifique *etc* [paθi'fike] *vb ver* **pacificar**
pacifismo [paθi'fismo] *nm* pacifism
pacifista [paθi'fista] *nm/f* pacifist
pack [pak] *nm* (*de yogures, latas*) pack; (*de
vacaciones*) package
pacotilla [pako'tiʎa] *nf* trash; **de ~** shoddy
pactar [pak'tar] *vt* to agree to, agree on ■ *vi*
to come to an agreement

pacto ['pakto] *nm* (*tratado*) pact; (*acuerdo*)
agreement
padecer [paðe'θer] *vt* (*sufrir*) to suffer;
(*soportar*) to endure, put up with; (*ser víctima
de*) to be a victim of ■ *vi*: **~ de** to suffer from
padecimiento [paðeθi'mjento] *nm* suffering
pádel ['paðel] *nm* paddle tennis
padezca *etc* [pa'ðeθka] *vb ver* **padecer**
padrastro [pa'ðrastro] *nm* stepfather
padre ['paðre] *nm* father ■ *adj* (*fam*): **un
éxito ~** a tremendous success; **padres** *nmpl*
parents; **~ espiritual** confessor; **P~ Nuestro**
Lord's Prayer; **~ político** father-in-law;
García ~ García senior; **¡tu ~!** (*fam!*) up
yours! (*!*)
padrino [pa'ðrino] *nm* godfather; (*fig*)
sponsor, patron; **padrinos** *nmpl* godparents;
~ de boda best man
padrón [pa'ðron] *nm* (*censo*) census, roll; (*de
socios*) register
paella [pa'eʎa] *nf* paella,, dish of rice with meat,
shellfish etc
paga ['paɣa] *nf* (*dinero pagado*) payment;
(*sueldo*) pay, wages *pl*
pagadero, -a [paɣa'ðero, a] *adj* payable; **~ a
la entrega/a plazos** payable on delivery/in
instalments
pagano, -a [pa'ɣano, a] *adj, nm/f* pagan,
heathen
pagar [pa'ɣar] *vt* (*gen*) to pay; (*las compras,
crimen*) to pay for; (*deuda*) to pay (off); (*fig:
favor*) to repay ■ *vi* to pay; **pagarse** *vr*:
pagarse con algo to be content with sth;
¡me las ~ás! I'll get you for this!
pagaré [paɣa're] *nm* I.O.U
página ['paxina] *nf* page; **~ de inicio** (*Inform*)
home page; **~ personal** (*Internet*) personal
web page
páginas amarillas *nfpl* Yellow Pages®;
página web web page
paginación [paxina'θjon] *nf* (*Inform, Tip*)
pagination
paginar [paxi'nar] *vt* (*Inform, Tip*) to paginate

P

pago ['payo] *nm* (*dinero*) payment; (*fig*) return; ~ **anticipado/a cuenta/a la entrega/en especie/inicial** advance payment/payment on account/cash on delivery/payment in kind/down payment; ~ **a título gracioso** ex gratia payment; **en ~ de** in return for

pág(s). *abr* (= *página(s)*) p(p)

pague *etc* ['paye] *vb ver* **pagar**

paila ['paila] *nf* (*Am*) frying pan

país [pa'is] *nm* (*gen*) country; (*región*) land; **los Países Bajos** the Low Countries; **el P~ Vasco** the Basque Country

paisaje [pai'saxe] *nm* countryside, landscape; (*vista*) scenery

paisano, -a [pai'sano, a] *adj* of the same country ■ *nm/f* (*compatriota*) fellow countryman(-woman); **vestir de ~** (*soldado*) to be in civilian clothes; (*guardia*) to be in plain clothes

paja ['paxa] *nf* straw; (*fig*) trash, rubbish; (*en libro, ensayo*) padding, waffle; **riñeron por un quítame allá esas pajas** they quarrelled over a trifle

pajar [pa'xar] *nm* hay loft

pajarita [paxa'rita] *nf* bow tie

pájaro ['paxaro] *nm* bird; (*fam: astuto*) clever fellow; **tener la cabeza a pájaros** to be featherbrained

pajita [pa'xita] *nf* (drinking) straw

pajizo, -a [pa'xiθo, a] *adj* (*de paja*) straw *cpd*; (*techo*) thatched; (*color*) straw-coloured

pakistaní [pakista'ni] *adj, nm/f* Pakistani

pala ['pala] *nf* (*de mango largo*) spade; (*de mango corto*) shovel; (*raqueta etc*) bat; (: *de tenis*) racquet; (*Culin*) slice; ~ **matamoscas** fly swat

palabra [pa'laβra] *nf* (*gen, promesa*) word; (*facultad*) (power of) speech; (*derecho de hablar*) right to speak; **faltar a su ~** to go back on one's word; **quedarse con la ~ en la boca** to stop short; (*en reunión, comité etc*): **tomar la ~** to speak, take the floor; **pedir la ~** to ask to be allowed to speak; **tener la ~** to have the floor; **no encuentro palabras para expresarme** words fail me

palabrería [palaβre'ria] *nf* hot air

palabrota [pala'βrota] *nf* swearword

palacio [pa'laθjo] *nm* palace; (*mansión*) mansion, large house; ~ **de justicia** courthouse; ~ **municipal** town/city hall

palada [pa'laða] *nf* shovelful, spadeful; (*de remo*) stroke

paladar [pala'ðar] *nm* palate

paladear [palaðe'ar] *vt* to taste

palanca [pa'lanka] *nf* lever; (*fig*) pull, influence; ~ **de cambio** (*Auto*) gear lever, gearshift (*US*); ~ **de freno** (*Auto*) brake lever; ~ **de gobierno** *o* **de control** (*Inform*) joystick

palangana [palan'gana] *nf* washbasin

palco ['palko] *nm* box

palenque [pa'lenke] *nm* (*cerca*) stockade, fence; (*área*) arena, enclosure; (*de gallos*) pit

palentino, -a [palen'tino, a] *adj* of *o* from Palencia ■ *nm/f* native *o* inhabitant of Palencia

paleolítico, -a [paleo'litiko, a] *adj* paleolithic

paleontología [paleontolo'xia] *nf* paleontology

Palestina [pales'tina] *nf* Palestine

palestino, -a [pales'tino, a] *adj, nm/f* Palestinian

palestra [pa'lestra] *nf*: **salir *o* saltar a la ~** to come into the spotlight

paleto, -a [pa'leto, a] *nm/f* yokel, hick (*US*) ■ *nf* (*pala*) small shovel; (*Arte*) palette; (*Anat*) shoulder blade; (*Am*) ice lolly

paliar [pa'ljar] *vt* (*mitigar*) to mitigate; (*disfrazar*) to conceal

paliativo [palja'tiβo] *nm* palliative

palidecer [paliðe'θer] *vi* to turn pale

palidez [pali'ðeθ] *nf* paleness

palidezca *etc* [pali'ðeθka] *vb ver* **palidecer**

pálido, -a [pa'liðo, a] *adj* pale

palillo [pa'liʎo] *nm* small stick; (*para dientes*) toothpick; **palillos (chinos)** chopsticks; **estar hecho un ~** to be as thin as a rake

palio ['paljo] *nm* canopy

palique [pa'like] *nm*: **estar de ~** (*fam*) to have a chat

paliza [pa'liθa] *nf* beating, thrashing; **dar *o* propinar > una ~ a algn** (*fam*) to give sb a thrashing

palma ['palma] *nf* (*Anat*) palm; (*árbol*) palm tree; **batir *o* dar palmas** to clap, applaud; **llevarse la ~** to triumph, win

palmada [pal'maða] *nf* slap; **palmadas** *nfpl* clapping *sg*, applause *sg*

Palma de Mallorca *nf* Palma

palmar [pal'mar] *vi* (*tb*: **palmarla**) to die, kick the bucket

palmarés [palma'res] *nm* (*lista*) list of winners; (*historial*) track record

palmear [palme'ar] *vi* to clap

palmero, -a [pal'mero, a] *adj* of the island of Palma ■ *nm/f* native *o* inhabitant of the island of Palma ■ *nm* (*Am*) ■ *nf* palm tree

palmo ['palmo] *nm* (*medida*) span; (*fig*) small amount; ~ **a ~** inch by inch

palmotear [palmote'ar] *vi* to clap, applaud

palmoteo [palmo'teo] *nm* clapping, applause

palo ['palo] *nm* stick; (*poste*) post, pole; (*mango*) handle, shaft; (*golpe*) blow, hit; (*de golf*) club; (*de béisbol*) bat; (*Naut*) mast; (*Naipes*) suit; **vermut a ~ seco** straight vermouth; **de tal ~ tal astilla** like father like son

paloma [pa'loma] *nf* dove, pigeon; ~
mensajera carrier o homing pigeon
palomilla [palo'miʎa] *nf* moth; (*Tec: tuerca*)
wing nut; (*soporte*) bracket
palomitas [palo'mitas] *nfpl* popcorn *sg*
palpable [pal'paβle] *adj* palpable; (*fig*)
tangible
palpar [pal'par] *vt* to touch, feel
palpitación [palpita'θjon] *nf* palpitation
palpitante [palpi'tante] *adj* palpitating; (*fig*)
burning
palpitar [palpi'tar] *vi* to palpitate; (*latir*) to
beat
palta ['palta] *nf* (*Am*) avocado
palúdico, -a [pa'luðiko, a] *adj* marshy
paludismo [palu'ðismo] *nm* malaria
palurdo, -a [pa'lurðo, a] *adj* coarse, uncouth
■ *nm/f* yokel, hick (*US*)
pamela [pa'mela] *nf* sun hat
pampa ['pampa] *nf* (*Am*) pampa(s), prairie
pamplinas [pam'plinas] *nfpl* nonsense *sg*
pamplonés, -esa [pamplo'nes, esa],
pamplonica [pamplo'nika] *adj* of o from
Pamplona ■ *nm/f* native o inhabitant of
Pamplona
pan [pan] *nm* bread; (*una barra*) loaf; ~ **de
molde** sliced loaf; **integral** wholemeal
bread; ~ **rallado** breadcrumbs *pl*; **eso es ~
comido** it's a cinch; **llamar al ~ ~ y al vino
vino** to call a spade a spade
pana ['pana] *nf* corduroy
panadería [panaðe'ria] *nf* baker's (shop)
panadero, -a [pana'ðero, a] *nm/f* baker
panal [pa'nal] *nm* honeycomb
Panamá [pana'ma] *nm* Panama
panameño, -a [pana'meɲo, a] *adj*
Panamanian
pancarta [pan'karta] *nf* placard, banner
pancho, -a ['pantʃo, a] *adj*: **estar tan ~**
to remain perfectly calm
pancito [pan'sito] *nm* (*Am*) (bread) roll
páncreas ['pankreas] *nm* pancreas
panda ['panda] *nm* panda ■ *nf* gang
pandemia [pan'demja] *nf* pandemic
pandereta [pande'reta] *nf* tambourine
pandilla [pan'diʎa] *nf* set, group; (*de
criminales*) gang; (*pey*) clique
pando, -a ['pando, a] *adj* sagging
panecillo [pane'θiʎo] *nm* (bread) roll
panel [pa'nel] *nm* panel; ~ **acústico** acoustic
screen
panera [pa'nera] *nf* bread basket
panfleto [pan'fleto] *nm* (*Pol etc*) pamphlet;
lampoon
pánico ['paniko] *nm* panic
panificadora [panifika'ðora] *nf* bakery
panorama [pano'rama] *nm* panorama;

(*vista*) view
panqué [pan'ke] *nm* (*Am*) pancake
pantaletas [panta'letas] *nfpl* (*Am*) panties
pantalla [pan'taʎa] *nf* (*de cine*) screen;
(*cubreluz*) lampshade; (*Inform*) screen, display;
servir de ~ to be a blind for; ~ **de cristal
líquido** liquid crystal display; ~ **táctil** touch
screen; ~ **de ayuda** help screen
pantalón [panta'lon] *nm*, **pantalones**
[panta'lones] *nmpl* trousers *pl*, pants *pl* (*US*);
pantalones cortos shorts *pl*; **pantalones
vaqueros** jeans *pl*
pantano [pan'tano] *nm* (*ciénaga*) marsh,
swamp; (*depósito: de agua*) reservoir; (*fig*) jam,
fix, difficulty
pantera [pan'tera] *nf* panther
pantis ['pantis] *nmpl* tights
pantomima [panto'mima] *nf* pantomime
pantorrilla [panto'rriʎa] *nf* calf (of the leg)
pantufla [pan'tufla] *nf* slipper
panty ['panti] *nm* = **pantis**
panza ['panθa] *nf* belly, paunch
panzón, -ona [pan'θon, ona], **panzudo, -a**
[pan'θuðo, a] *adj* fat, potbellied
pañal [pa'ɲal] *nm* nappy, diaper (*US*); **estar
todavía en pañales** to be still wet behind
the ears
pañería [paɲe'ria] *nf* (*artículos*) drapery;
(*tienda*) draper's (shop), dry-goods store (*US*)
paño ['paɲo] *nm* (*tela*) cloth; (*pedazo de tela*)
(piece of) cloth; (*trapo*) duster, rag; ~ **de
cocina** dishcloth; ~ **higiénico** sanitary
towel; **paños menores** underclothes;
paños calientes (*fig*) half-measures; **no
andarse con paños calientes** to pull no
punches
pañuelo [pa'ɲwelo] *nm* handkerchief, hanky
(*fam*); (*para la cabeza*) (head)scarf
papa ['papa] *nf* (*Am*) potato ■ *nm*: **el P~** the
Pope
papá [pa'pa] *nm* (*pl* **~s**) (*fam*) dad, daddy, pop
(*US*); **papás** *nmpl* parents; **hijo de papá**
Hooray Henry (*fam*)
papada [pa'paða] *nf* double chin
papagayo [papa'ɣajo] *nm* parrot
papanatas [papa'natas] *nm inv* (*fam*) sucker,
simpleton
paparrucha [papa'rrutʃa] *nf* (*tontería*) piece
of nonsense
papaya [pa'paja] *nf* papaya
papear [pape'ar] *vt, vi* (*fam*) to eat
papel [pa'pel] *nm* (*gen*) paper; (*hoja de papel*)
sheet of paper; (*Teat*) part, role; **papeles**
nmpl identification papers; ~ **de calco/
carbón/de cartas** tracing paper/carbon
paper/stationery; ~ **continuo** (*Inform*)
continuous stationery; ~ **de envolver/de**

empapelar brown paper/wrapping paper/ wallpaper; ~ **de aluminio/higiénico** tinfoil/ toilet paper; ~ **del** *o* **de pagos al Estado** government bonds *pl*; ~ **de lija** sandpaper; ~ **moneda** paper money; ~ **plegado (en abanico** *o* **en acordeón)** fanfold paper; ~ **pintado** wallpaper; ~ **secante** blotting paper; ~ **térmico** thermal paper

papeleo [pape'leo] *nm* red tape

papelera [pape'lera] *nf* (*cesto*) wastepaper basket; (*escritorio*) desk; ~ **de reciclaje** (*Inform*) wastebasket

papelería [papele'ria] *nf* (*tienda*) stationer's (shop)

papeleta [pape'leta] *nf* (*pedazo de papel*) slip *o* bit of paper; (*Pol*) ballot paper; (*Escol*) report; ¡vaya ~! this is a tough one!

paperas [pa'peras] *nfpl* mumps *sg*

papilla [pa'piʎa] *nf* (*de bebé*) baby food; (*pey*) mush; **estar hecho ~** to be dog-tired

paquete [pa'kete] *nm* (*caja*) packet; (*bulto*) parcel; (*Am fam*) nuisance, bore; (*Inform*) package (*of software*); (*de vacaciones*) package tour; ~ **de aplicaciones** (*Inform*) applications package; ~ **integrado** (*Inform*) integrated package; ~ **de gestión integrado** combined management suite; **paquetes postales** parcel post *sg*

paquistaní [pakista'ni] = **pakistaní**

par [par] *adj* (*igual*) like, equal; (*Mat*) even ■ *nm* equal; (*de guantes*) pair; (*de veces*) couple; (*título*) peer; (*Golf, Com*) par ■ *nf* par; **pares o nones** odds or evens; **abrir de ~ en ~** to open wide; **a la ~** par; **sobre/bajo la ~** above/ below par

para ['para] *prep* for; **no es ~ comer** it's not for eating; **decir ~ sí** to say to o.s.; ¿~ **qué lo quieres?** what do you want it for?; **se casaron ~ separarse otra vez** they married only to separate again; ~ **entonces** by then *o* that time; **lo tendré ~ mañana** I'll have it for tomorrow; **ir ~ casa** to go home, head for home; ~ **profesor es muy estúpido** he's very stupid for a teacher; ¿**quién es usted ~ gritar así?** who are you to shout like that?; **tengo bastante ~ vivir** I have enough to live on

parabellum [paraβe'lum] *nm* (automatic) pistol

parabién [para'βjen] *nm* congratulations *pl*

parábola [pa'raβola] *nf* parable; (*Mat*) parabola

parabólica [para'βolika] *nf* (*tb*: **antena parabólica**) satellite dish

parabrisas [para'βrisas] *nm inv* windscreen, windshield (*US*)

paracaídas [paraka'iðas] *nm inv* parachute

paracaidista [parakai'ðista] *nm/f* parachutist; (*Mil*) paratrooper

parachoques [para'tʃokes] *nm inv* bumper, fender (*US*); shock absorber

parada [pa'raða] *nf ver* **parado**

paradero [para'ðero] *nm* stopping-place; (*situación*) whereabouts

parado, -a [pa'raðo, a] *adj* (*persona*) motionless, standing still; (*fábrica*) closed, at a standstill; (*coche*) stopped; (*Am: de pie*) standing (up); (*sin empleo*) unemployed, idle; (*confuso*) confused ■ *nf* (*gen*) stop; (*acto*) stopping; (*de industria*) shutdown, stoppage; (*lugar*) stopping-place; **salir bien ~** to come off well; **parada de autobús** bus stop; **parada discrecional** request stop; **parada en seco** sudden stop; **parada de taxis** taxi rank

paradoja [para'ðoxa] *nf* paradox

paradójico, -a [para'ðoxiko, a] *adj* paradoxical

parador [para'ðor] *nm* (luxury) hotel

parafrasear [parafrase'ar] *vt* to paraphrase

paráfrasis [pa'rafrasis] *nf inv* paraphrase

paraguas [pa'raɣwas] *nm inv* umbrella

Paraguay [para'ɣwai] *nm*: **el ~** Paraguay

paraguayo, -a [para'ɣwajo, a] *adj, nm/f* Paraguayan

paraíso [para'iso] *nm* paradise, heaven; ~ **fiscal** (*Com*) tax haven

paraje [pa'raxe] *nm* place, spot

paralelo, -a [para'lelo, a] *adj, nm* parallel; **en ~** (*Elec, Inform*) (in) parallel

paralice *etc* [para'liθe] *vb ver* **paralizar**

parálisis [pa'ralisis] *nf inv* paralysis; ~ **cerebral** cerebral palsy; ~ **progresiva** creeping paralysis

paralítico, -a [para'litiko, a] *adj, nm/f* paralytic

paralizar [parali'θar] *vt* to paralyse; **paralizarse** *vr* to become paralysed; (*fig*) to come to a standstill

parámetro [pa'rametro] *nm* parameter

paramilitar [paramili'tar] *adj* paramilitary

páramo ['paramo] *nm* bleak plateau

parangón [paran'gon] *nm*: **sin ~** incomparable

paraninfo [para'ninfo] *nm* (*Escol*) assembly hall

paranoia [para'noia] *nf* paranoia

paranoico, -a [para'noiko, a] *adj, nm/f* paranoid

paranormal [paranor'mal] *adj* paranormal

parapetarse [parape'tarse] *vr* to shelter

parapléjico, -a [para'plexiko, a] *adj, nm/f* paraplegic

parar [pa'rar] *vt* to stop; (*progreso etc*) to

check, halt; (golpe) to ward off ■ vi to stop; (hospedarse) to stay, put up; **pararse** vr to stop; (Am) to stand up; **no ~ de hacer algo** to keep on doing sth; **ha parado de llover** it has stopped raining; **van a ~ en la comisaría** they're going to end up in the police station; **no sabemos en qué va a ~ todo esto** we don't know where all this is going to end; **pararse a hacer algo** to stop to do sth; **pararse en** to pay attention to

pararrayos [para'rrajos] nm inv lightning conductor

parásito, -a [pa'rasito, a] nm/f parasite

parasol [para'sol] nm parasol, sunshade

parcela [par'θela] nf plot, piece of ground, smallholding

parche ['partʃe] nm patch

parchís [par'tʃis] nm ludo

parcial [par'θjal] adj (pago) part-; (eclipse) partial; (juez) prejudiced, biased

parcialidad [parθjali'ðað] nf (prejuicio) prejudice, bias

parco, -a ['parko, a] adj (frugal) sparing; (moderado) moderate

pardillo, -a [par'ðiʎo, a] adj (pey) provincial ■ nm/f (pey) country bumpkin ■ nm (Zool) linnet

pardo, -a ['parðo, a] adj (color) brown; (cielo) overcast; (voz) flat, dull

parear [pare'ar] vt (juntar, hacer par) to match, put together; (calcetines) to put into pairs; (Bio) to mate, pair

parecer [pare'θer] nm (opinión) opinion, view; (aspecto) looks pl ■ vi (tener apariencia) to seem, look; (asemejarse) to look like, seem like; (aparecer, llegar) to appear; **parecerse** vr to look alike, resemble each other; **parecerse a** to look like, resemble; **al ~** apparently; **me parece que** I think (that), it seems to me that

parecido, -a [pare'θiðo, a] adj similar ■ nm similarity, likeness, resemblance; **~ a** like, similar to; **bien ~** good-looking, nice-looking

pared [pa'reð] nf wall; **~ divisoria/ medianera** dividing/party wall; **subirse por las paredes** (fam) to go up the wall

paredón [pare'ðon] nm: **llevar a algn al ~** to put sb up against a wall, shoot sb

parejo, -a [pa'rexo, a] adj (igual) equal; (liso) smooth, even ■ nf (dos) pair; (: de personas) couple; (el otro: de un par) other one (of a pair); (: persona) partner; (de Guardias) Civil Guard patrol

parentela [paren'tela] nf relations pl

parentesco [paren'tesko] nm relationship

paréntesis [pa'rentesis] nm inv parenthesis;

(digresión) digression; (en escrito) bracket

parezca etc [pa'reθka] vb ver **parecer**

parida [pa'riða] nf: **~ mental** (fam) dumb idea

paridad [pari'ðað] nf (Econ) parity

pariente, -a [pa'rjente, a] nm/f relative, relation

parihuela [pari'wela] nf stretcher

paripé [pari'pe] nm: **hacer el ~** to put on an act

parir [pa'rir] vt to give birth to ■ vi (mujer) to give birth, have a baby; (yegua) to foal; (vaca) to calve

París [pa'ris] nm Paris

parisiense [pari'sjense] adj, nm/f Parisian

paritario, -a [pari'tarjo, a] adj equal

parking ['parkin] nm car park, parking lot (US)

parlamentar [parlamen'tar] vi (negociar) to parley

parlamentario, -a [parlamen'tarjo, a] adj parliamentary ■ nm/f member of parliament

parlamento [parla'mento] nm (Pol) parliament; (Jur) speech

parlanchín, -ina [parlan'tʃin, ina] adj loose-tongued, indiscreet ■ nm/f chatterbox

parlante [par'lante] nm (Am) loudspeaker

parlar [par'lar] vi to chatter (away)

parlotear [parlote'ar] vi to chatter, prattle

parloteo [parlo'teo] nm chatter, prattle

paro ['paro] nm (huelga) stoppage (of work), strike; (desempleo) unemployment; **~ cardíaco** cardiac arrest; **subsidio de ~** unemployment benefit; **hay ~ en la industria** work in the industry is at a standstill; **~ del sistema** (Inform) system shutdown

parodia [pa'roðja] nf parody

parodiar [paro'ðjar] vt to parody

parpadear [parpaðe'ar] vi (los ojos) to blink; (luz) to flicker

parpadeo [parpa'ðeo] nm (de ojos) blinking, winking; (de luz) flickering

párpado ['parpaðo] nm eyelid

parque ['parke] nm (lugar verde) park; **~ de atracciones/de bomberos/zoológico** fairground/fire station/zoo; **~ infantil** children's playground; **~ temático** theme park

parqué, parquet [par'ke] nm parquet

parqueadero [parkea'ðero] nm (Am) car park, parking lot (US)

parquímetro [par'kimetro] nm parking meter

parra ['parra] nf grapevine

párrafo ['parrafo] nm paragraph; **echar un ~** (fam) to have a chat

parranda [pa'rranda] nf (fam) spree, binge

parrilla [pa'rriʎa] nf (Culin) grill; (Am Auto) roof-rack; ~ **(de salida)** (Auto) starting grid; **carne a la** ~ grilled meat

parrillada [parri'ʎaða] nf barbecue

párroco ['parroko] nm parish priest

parroquia [pa'rrokja] nf parish; (iglesia) parish church; (Com) clientele, customers pl

parroquiano, -a [parro'kjano, a] nm/f parishioner; client, customer

parsimonia [parsi'monja] nf (frugalidad) sparingness; (calma) deliberateness; **con** ~ calmly

parte ['parte] nm message; (informe) report; ~ **meteorológico** weather forecast ∎ nf part; (lado, cara) side; (de reparto) share; (Jur) party; **en alguna** ~ **de Europa** somewhere in Europe; **en cualquier** ~ anywhere; **por ahí no se va a ninguna** ~ that leads nowhere; (fig) this is getting us nowhere; **en** o **por todas partes** everywhere; **en gran** ~ to a large extent; **la mayor** ~ **de los españoles** most Spaniards; **de algún tiempo a esta** ~ for some time past; **de** ~ **de algn** on sb's behalf; **¿de** ~ **de quién?** (Telec) who is speaking?; **por** ~ **de** on the part of; **yo por mi** ~ I for my part; **por una** ~ ... **por otra** ~ on the one hand, ... on the other (hand); **dar** ~ **a algn** to report to sb; **tomar** ~ to take part

partera [par'tera] nf midwife

parterre [par'terre] nm (flower)bed

partición [parti'θjon] nf division, sharing-out; (Pol) partition

participación [partiθipa'θjon] nf (acto) participation, taking part; (parte) share; (Com) share, stock (US); (de lotería) shared prize; (aviso) notice, notification; ~ **en los beneficios** profit-sharing; ~ **minoritaria** minority interest

participante [partiθi'pante] nm/f participant

participar [partiθi'par] vt to notify, inform ∎ vi to take part, participate; ~ **en una empresa** (Com) to invest in an enterprise; **le participo que** ... I have to tell you that ...

partícipe [par'tiθipe] nm/f participant; **hacer** ~ **a algn de algo** to inform sb of sth

participio [parti'θipjo] nm participle; ~ **de pasado/presente** past/present participle

partícula [par'tikula] nf particle

particular [partiku'lar] adj (especial) particular, special; (individual, personal) private, personal ∎ nm (punto, asunto) particular, point; (individuo) individual; **tiene coche** ~ he has a car of his own; **no dijo mucho sobre el** ~ he didn't say much about the matter

particularice etc [partikula'riθe] vb ver **particularizar**

particularidad [partikulari'ðað] nf peculiarity; **tiene la** ~ **de que** ... one of its special features is (that) ...

particularizar [partikulari'θar] vt to distinguish; (especificar) to specify; (detallar) to give details about

partida [par'tiða] nf (salida) departure; (Com) entry, item; (juego) game; (grupo, bando) band, group; **mala** ~ dirty trick; ~ **de nacimiento/matrimonio/defunción** birth/marriage/death certificate; **echar una** ~ to have a game

partidario, -a [parti'ðarjo, a] adj partisan ∎ nm/f (Deporte) supporter; (Pol) partisan

partidismo [parti'ðismo] nm (Jur) partisanship, bias; (Pol) party politics

partido [par'tiðo] nm (Pol) party; (encuentro) game, match; (apoyo) support; (equipo) team; ~ **amistoso** (Deporte) friendly (game); ~ **de fútbol** football match; **sacar** ~ **de** to profit from, benefit from; **tomar** ~ to take sides

partir [par'tir] vt (dividir) to split, divide; (compartir, distribuir) to share (out), distribute; (romper) to break open, split open; (rebanada) to cut (off); (vi: ponerse en camino) to set off, set out; (comenzar) to start (off o out); **partirse** vr to crack o split o break (in two etc); **a** ~ **de** (starting) from; **partirse de risa** to split one's sides (laughing)

partitura [parti'tura] nf score

parto ['parto] nm birth, delivery; (fig) product, creation; **estar de** ~ to be in labour

parvulario [parβu'larjo] nm nursery school, kindergarten

párvulo, -a ['parβulo, a] nm/f infant

pasa ['pasa] nf ver **paso**

pasable [pa'saβle] adj passable

pasada [pa'saða] nf ver **pasado**

pasadizo [pasa'ðiθo] nm (pasillo) passage, corridor; (callejuela) alley

pasado, -a [pa'saðo, a] adj past; (malo: comida, fruta) bad; (muy cocido) overdone; (anticuado) out of date ∎ nm past; (Ling) past (tense) ∎ nf passing, passage; (acción de pulir) rub, polish; ~ **mañana** the day after tomorrow; **el mes** ~ last month; **pasados dos días** after two days; **lo** ~, ~ let bygones be bygones; ~ **de moda** old-fashioned; ~ **por agua** (huevo) boiled; **estar** ~ **de vueltas** o **de rosca** (grifo, tuerca) to be worn; **de pasada** in passing, incidentally; **una mala pasada** a dirty trick

pasador [pasa'ðor] nm (gen) bolt; (de pelo) pin, grip, slide; **pasadores** nmpl (Am: cordones) shoelaces

pasaje [pa'saxe] nm (gen) passage; (pago de

viaje) fare; (los pasajeros) passengers pl; (pasillo) passageway

pasajero, -a [pasa'xero, a] adj passing; (ave) migratory ■ nm/f passenger; (viajero) traveller

pasamanos [pasa'manos] nm inv rail, handrail; (de escalera) banister

pasamontañas [pasamon'taɲas] nm inv balaclava (helmet)

pasaporte [pasa'porte] nm passport

pasar [pa'sar] vt (gen) to pass; (tiempo) to spend; (durezas) to suffer, endure; (noticia) to give, pass on; (película) to show; (persona) to take, conduct; (río) to cross; (barrera) to pass through; (falta) to overlook, tolerate; (contrincante) to surpass, do better than; (coche) to overtake; (contrabando) to smuggle (in/out); (enfermedad) to give, infect with ■ vi (gen) to pass, go; (terminarse) to be over; (ocurrir) to happen; **pasarse** vr (efectos) to pass, be over; (flores) to fade; (comida) to go bad, go off; (fig) to overdo it, go too far o over the top; ~ **la aspiradora** to do the vacuuming o hoovering, to hoover; ~ **de** to go beyond, exceed; **¡pase!** come in!; **nos hicieron** ~ they showed us in; ~ **por** to fetch; ~ **por alto** to skip; ~ **por una crisis** to go through a crisis; **se hace** ~ **por médico** he passes himself off as a doctor; **pasarlo bien/bomba** o **de maravilla** to have a good/great time; **¡que lo pases bien!** have a good time!; **pasarse al enemigo** to go over to the enemy; **pasarse de la raya** to go too far; **¡no te pases!** don't try me!; **se me pasó** I forgot; **se me pasó el turno** I missed my turn; **no se le pasa nada** nothing escapes him, he misses nothing; **ya se te ~á** you'll get over it; **¿qué pasa?** what's happening?, what's going on?, what's up?; **¡cómo pasa el tiempo!** time just flies!; **pase lo que pase** come what may; **el autobús pasa por nuestra casa** the bus goes past our house

pasarela [pasa'rela] nf footbridge; (en barco) gangway

pasatiempo [pasa'tjempo] nm pastime, hobby; (distracción) amusement

Pascua, pascua ['paskwa] nf: ~ **(de Resurrección)** Easter; ~ **de Navidad** Christmas; **Pascuas** nfpl Christmas time sg; **¡felices Pascuas!** Merry Christmas!; **de Pascuas a Ramos** once in a blue moon; **hacer la** ~ **a** (fam) to annoy, bug

pase ['pase] nm pass; (Cine) performance, showing; (Com) permit; (Jur) licence

pasear [pase'ar] vt to take for a walk; (exhibir) to parade, show off ■ vi, **pasearse** vr to walk, go for a walk; ~ **en coche** to go for a drive

paseo [pa'seo] nm avenue; (distancia corta) short walk; ~ **marítimo** promenade; **dar un** ~ to go for a walk; ~ **en bicicleta** (bike) ride; ~ **en barco** boat trip; **mandar a algn a** ~ to tell sb to go to blazes; **¡vete a ~!** get lost!

pasillo [pa'siʎo] nm passage, corridor

pasión [pa'sjon] nf passion

pasional [pasjo'nal] adj passionate; **crimen** ~ crime of passion

pasivo, -a [pa'siβo, a] adj passive; (inactivo) inactive ■ nm (Com) liabilities pl, debts pl; (de cuenta) debit side; ~ **circulante** current liabilities

pasma ['pasma] nm (fam) cop

pasmado, -a [pas'maðo, a] adj (asombrado) astonished; (atontado) bewildered

pasmar [pas'mar] vt (asombrar) to amaze, astonish; **pasmarse** vr to be amazed o astonished

pasmo ['pasmo] nm amazement, astonishment; (fig) wonder, marvel

pasmoso, -a [pas'moso, a] adj amazing, astonishing

paso, -a ['paso, a] adj dried ■ nm (gen, de baile) step; (modo de andar) walk; (huella) footprint; (rapidez) speed, pace, rate; (camino accesible) way through, passage; (cruce) crossing; (pasaje) passing, passage; (Rel) religious float or sculpture; (Geo) pass; (estrecho) strait; (fig) step, measure; (apuro) difficulty ■ nf raisin; **pasa de Corinto/de Esmirna** currant/sultana; ~ **a** ~ step by step; **a ese** ~ (fig) at that rate; **salir al** ~ **de** o **a** to waylay; **salir del** ~ to get out of trouble; **dar un** ~ **en falso** to trip; (fig) to take a false step; **estar de** ~ to be passing through; ~ **atrás** step backwards; (fig) backward step; ~ **elevado/subterráneo** flyover/subway, underpass (US); **prohibido el** ~ no entry; **ceda el** ~ give way; ver tb **Semana Santa**

pasota [pa'sota] adj, nm/f (fam) ≈ dropout; **ser un (tipo)** ~ to be a bit of a dropout; (ser indiferente) not to care about anything

pasotismo [paso'tismo] nm underground o alternative culture

pasta ['pasta] nf (gen) paste; (Culin: masa) dough; (: de bizcochos etc) pastry; (fam) money, dough; (encuadernación) hardback; **pastas** nfpl (bizcochos) pastries, small cakes; (espaguetis etc) pasta sg; ~ **de dientes** o **dentífrica** toothpaste; ~ **de madera** wood pulp

pastar [pas'tar] vt, vi to graze

pastel [pas'tel] nm (dulce) cake; (de carne) pie; (Arte) pastel; (fig) plot; **pasteles** nmpl pastry sg, confectionery sg

pastelería [pastele'ria] nf cake shop, pastry shop

pasteurizado, -a [pasteuri'θaðo, a] *adj* pasteurized

pastilla [pas'tiʎa] *nf* (*de jabón, chocolate*) cake, bar; (*píldora*) tablet, pill

pastizal [pasti'θal] *nm* pasture

pasto ['pasto] *nm* (*hierba*) grass; (*lugar*) pasture, field; (*fig*) food, nourishment

pastor, a [pas'tor, a] *nm/f* shepherd(ess) ■ *nm* clergyman, pastor; (*Zool*) sheepdog; **~ alemán** Alsatian

pastoso, -a [pas'toso, a] *adj* (*material*) doughy, pasty; (*lengua*) furry; (*voz*) mellow

pat. *abr* (= *patente*) pat

pata ['pata] *nf* (*pierna*) leg; (*pie*) foot; (*de muebles*) leg; **patas arriba** upside down; **a cuatro patas** on all fours; **meter la ~** to put one's foot in it; **~ de cabra** (*Tec*) crowbar; **patas de gallo** crow's feet; **tener buena/ mala ~** to be lucky/unlucky

patada [pa'taða] *nf* stamp; (*puntapié*) kick; **a patadas** in abundance; (*trato*) roughly; **echar a algn a patadas** to kick sb out

patagón, -ona [pata'ɣon, ona] *adj, nm/f* Patagonian

Patagonia [pata'ɣonja] *nf*: **la ~** Patagonia

patalear [patale'ar] *vi* to stamp one's feet

pataleo [pata'leo] *nm* stamping

patán [pa'tan] *nm* rustic, yokel

patata [pa'tata] *nf* potato; **patatas fritas** o **a la española** chips, French fries; **patatas a la inglesa** crisps; **ni ~** (*fam*) nothing at all; **no entendió ni ~** he didn't understand a single word

paté [pa'te] *nm* pâté

patear [pate'ar] *vt* (*pisar*) to stamp on, trample (on); (*pegar con el pie*) to kick ■ *vi* to stamp (with rage), stamp one's foot

patentar [paten'tar] *vt* to patent

patente [pa'tente] *adj* obvious, evident; (*Com*) patent ■ *nf* patent

patera [pa'tera] *nf* boat

paternal [pater'nal] *adj* fatherly, paternal

paternalista [paterna'lista] *adj* (*tono, actitud etc*) patronizing

paternidad [paterni'ðað] *nf* fatherhood, parenthood; (*Jur*) paternity

paterno, -a [pa'terno, a] *adj* paternal

patético, -a [pa'tetiko, a] *adj* pathetic, moving

patíbulo [pa'tiβulo] *nm* scaffold, gallows *sg*

patilla [pa'tiʎa] *nf* (*de gafas*) arm; (*de pelo*) sideburn

patín [pa'tin] *nm* skate; (*de tobogán*) runner; **~ de hielo** ice skate; **~ de ruedas** roller skate

patinaje [pati'naxe] *nm* skating

patinar [pati'nar] *vi* to skate; (*resbalarse*) to skid, slip; (*fam*) to slip up, blunder

patinazo [pati'naθo] *nm* (*Auto*) skid; **dar un ~** (*fam*) to blunder

patio ['patjo] *nm* (*de casa*) patio, courtyard; **~ de recreo** playground

pato ['pato] *nm* duck; **pagar el ~** (*fam*) to take the blame, carry the can

patológico, -a [pato'loxiko, a] *adj* pathological

patoso, -a [pa'toso, a] *adj* awkward, clumsy

patraña [pa'traɲa] *nf* story, fib

patria ['patrja] *nf* native land, mother country; **~ chica** home town

patrimonio [patri'monjo] *nm* inheritance; (*fig*) heritage; (*Com*) net worth

patriota [pa'trjota] *nm/f* patriot

patriotero, -a [patrjo'tero, a] *adj* chauvinistic

patriótico, -a [pa'trjotiko, a] *adj* patriotic

patriotismo [patrjo'tismo] *nm* patriotism

patrocinador, a [patroθina'ðor, a] *nm/f* sponsor

patrocinar [patroθi'nar] *vt* to sponsor; (*apoyar*) to back, support

patrocinio [patro'θinjo] *nm* sponsorship; backing, support

patrón, -ona [pa'tron, ona] *nm/f* (*jefe*) boss, chief, master/mistress; (*propietario*) landlord(-lady); (*Rel*) patron saint ■ *nm* (*Costura*) pattern; (*Tec*) standard; **~ oro** gold standard

patronal [patro'nal] *adj*: **la clase ~** management; **cierre ~** lockout

patronato [patro'nato] *nm* sponsorship; (*acto*) patronage; (*Com*) employers' association; (*fundación*) trust; **el ~ de turismo** the tourist board

patrulla [pa'truʎa] *nf* patrol

patrullar [patru'ʎar] *vi* to patrol

paulatino, -a [paula'tino, a] *adj* gradual, slow

paupérrimo, -a [pau'perrimo, a] *adj* very poor, poverty-stricken

pausa ['pausa] *nf* pause; (*intervalo*) break; (*interrupción*) interruption; (*Tec*: *en videograbadora*) hold; **con ~** slowly

pausado, -a [pau'saðo, a] *adj* slow, deliberate

pauta ['pauta] *nf* line, guide line

pavimento [paβi'mento] *nm* (*Arq*) flooring

pavo ['paβo] *nm* turkey; (*necio*) silly thing, idiot; **~ real** peacock; **¡no seas ~!** don't be silly!

pavonearse [paβone'arse] *vr* to swagger, show off

pavor [pa'βor] *nm* dread, terror

payasada [paja'saða] *nf* ridiculous thing (to do); **payasadas** *nfpl* clowning *sg*

payaso, -a [pa'jaso, a] *nm/f* clown

payo, -a ['pajo, a] *adj, nm/f* non-gipsy
paz [paθ] *nf* peace; (*tranquilidad*) peacefulness, tranquillity; **dejar a algn en** ~ to leave sb alone o in peace; **hacer las paces** to make peace; (*fig*) to make up; ¡**haya** ~! stop it!
pazca *etc* ['paθka] *vb ver* **pacer**
PC *nm abr* (*Pol*: = *Partido Comunista*) CP
P.C.E. *nm abr* = **Partido Comunista Español**
PCL *nf abr* (= *pantalla de cristal líquido*) LCD
P.D. *abr* (= *posdata*) P.S.
peaje [pe'axe] *nm* toll; **autopista de** ~ toll motorway, turnpike (US)
peatón [pea'ton] *nm* pedestrian; **paso de peatones** pedestrian crossing, crosswalk (US)
peca ['peka] *nf* freckle
pecado [pe'kaðo] *nm* sin
pecador, a [peka'ðor, a] *adj* sinful ▪ *nm/f* sinner
pecaminoso, -a [pekami'noso, a] *adj* sinful
pecar [pe'kar] *vi* (*Rel*) to sin; (*fig*): ~ **de generoso** to be too generous
pecera [pe'θera] *nf* goldfish bowl
pecho ['petʃo] *nm* (*Anat*) chest; (*de mujer*) breast(s *pl*), bosom; (*corazón*) heart, breast; (*valor*) courage, spirit; **dar el** ~ **a** to breast-feed; **tomar algo a** ~ to take sth to heart; **no le cabía en el** ~ he was bursting with happiness
pechuga [pe'tʃuɣa] *nf* breast (of chicken *etc*)
pecoso, -a [pe'koso, a] *adj* freckled
peculiar [peku'ljar] *adj* special, peculiar; (*característico*) typical, characteristic
peculiaridad [pekuljari'ðað] *nf* peculiarity; special feature, characteristic
pedagogía [peðaɣo'ɣia] *nf* education
pedagogo [peða'ɣoɣo] *nm* pedagogue, teacher
pedal [pe'ðal] *nm* pedal; ~ **de embrague** clutch (pedal); ~ **de freno** footbrake
pedalear [peðale'ar] *vi* to pedal
pédalo ['peðalo] *nm* pedalo, pedal boat
pedante [pe'ðante] *adj* pedantic ▪ *nm/f* pedant
pedantería [peðante'ria] *nf* pedantry
pedazo [pe'ðaθo] *nm* piece, bit; **hacerse pedazos** to fall to pieces; (*romperse*) to smash, shatter; **un** ~ **de pan** a scrap of bread; (*fig*) a terribly nice person
pedernal [peðer'nal] *nm* flint
pedestal [peðes'tal] *nm* base; **tener/poner a algn en un** ~ to put sb on a pedestal
pedestre [pe'ðestre] *adj* pedestrian; **carrera** ~ foot race
pediatra [pe'ðjatra] *nm/f* paediatrician (Brit), pediatrician (US)
pediatría [peðja'tria] *nf* paediatrics *sg* (Brit), pediatrics *sg* (US)

pedicuro, -a [peði'kuro, a] *nm/f* chiropodist (Brit), podiatrist (US)
pedido [pe'ðiðo] *nm* (*Com*: *mandado*) order; (*petición*) request; **pedidos en cartera** (*Com*) backlog *sg*
pedigrí [peði'ɣri] *nm* pedigree
pedir [pe'ðir] *vt* to ask for, request; (*comida, Com*: *mandar*) to order; (*exigir*: *precio*) to ask; (*necesitar*) to need, demand, require ▪ *vi* to ask; ~ **prestado** to borrow; ~ **disculpas** to apologize; **me pidió que cerrara la puerta** he asked me to shut the door; ¿**cuánto piden por el coche?** how much are they asking for the car?
pedo ['peðo] (*fam*) *adj inv*: **estar** ~ to be pissed (!) ▪ *nm* fart (!)
pedrada [pe'ðraða] *nf* throw of a stone; (*golpe*) blow from a stone; **herir a algn de una** ~ to hit sb with a stone
pedrea [pe'ðrea] *nf* (*granizada*) hailstorm; (*de lotería*) minor prizes
pedrisco [pe'ðrisko] *nm* (*granizo*) hail; (*granizada*) hailstorm
Pedro ['peðro] *nm* Peter; **entrar como** ~ **por su casa** to come in as if one owned the place
pega ['peɣa] *nf* (*dificultad*) snag; **de** ~ false, dud; **poner pegas** to raise objections
pegadizo, -a [peɣa'ðiθo, a] *adj* (*canción etc*) catchy
pegajoso, -a [peɣa'xoso, a] *adj* sticky, adhesive
pegamento [peɣa'mento] *nm* gum
pegar [pe'ɣar] *vt* (*papel, sellos*) to stick (on); (*con cola*) to glue; (*cartel*) to post, stick up; (*coser*) to sew (on); (*unir*: *partes*) to join, fix together; (*Inform*) to paste; (*Med*) to give, infect with; (*dar*: *golpe*) to give, deal ▪ *vi* (*adherirse*) to stick, adhere; (*Inform*) to paste; (*ir juntos*: *colores*) to match, go together; (*golpear*) to hit; (*quemar*: *el sol*) to strike hot, burn; (*fig*); **pegarse** *vr* (*gen*) to stick; (*dos personas*) to hit each other, fight; **pegarle a algo** to be a great one for sth; ~ **un grito** to let out a yell; ~ **un salto** to jump (with fright); ~ **fuego** to catch fire; ~ **en** to touch; **pegarse un tiro** to shoot o.s.; **no pega** that doesn't seem right; **ese sombrero no pega con el abrigo** that hat doesn't go with the coat
pegatina [peɣa'tina] *nf* (*Pol etc*) sticker
pego ['peɣo] *nm*: **dar el** ~ (*pasar por verdadero*) to look like the real thing
pegote [pe'ɣote] *nm* (*fig*) patch, ugly mend; **tirarse pegotes** (*fam*) to come on strong
pegue *etc* ['peɣe] *vb ver* **pegar**
peinado [pei'naðo] *nm* (*en peluquería*) hairdo; (*estilo*) hair style

289

peinar [pei'nar] *vt* to comb sb's hair; (*con un cierto estilo*) to style; **peinarse** *vr* to comb one's hair

peine ['peine] *nm* comb

peineta [pei'neta] *nf* ornamental comb

p.ej. *abr* (= *por ejemplo*) e.g.

Pekín [pe'kin] *n* Peking

pela ['pela] *nf* (*Esp fam*) peseta; *ver tb* **pelas**

pelado, -a [pe'laðo, a] *adj* (*cabeza*) shorn; (*fruta*) peeled; (*campo, fig*) bare; (*fam: sin dinero*) broke

pelaje [pe'laxe] *nm* (*Zool*) fur, coat; (*fig*) appearance

pelambre [pe'lambre] *nm* long hair, mop

pelar [pe'lar] *vt* (*fruta, patatas*) to peel; (*cortar el pelo a*) to cut the hair of; (*quitar la piel: animal*) to skin; (*ave*) to pluck; (*habas etc*) to shell; **pelarse** *vr* (*la piel*) to peel off; **corre que se las pela** (*fam*) he runs like nobody's business

pelas ['pelas] *nfpl* (*Esp fam*) dough

peldaño [pel'daɲo] *nm* step; (*de escalera portátil*) rung

pelea [pe'lea] *nf* (*lucha*) fight; (*discusión*) quarrel, row

peleado, -a [pele'aðo, a] *adj*: **estar ~ (con algn)** to have fallen out (with sb)

pelear [pele'ar] *vi* to fight; **pelearse** *vr* to fight; (*reñir*) to fall out, quarrel

pelele [pe'lele] *nm* (*figura*) guy, dummy; (*fig*) puppet

peletería [pelete'ria] *nf* furrier's, fur shop

peliagudo, -a [pelja'ɣuðo, a] *adj* tricky

pelícano [pe'likano] *nm* pelican

película [pe'likula] *nf* (*Cine*) film, movie (*US*); (*cobertura ligera*) film, thin covering; (*Foto: rollo*) roll o reel of film; **~ de dibujos (animados)** cartoon film; **~ muda** silent film; **de ~** (*fam*) astonishing, out of this world

peligrar [peli'ɣrar] *vi* to be in danger

peligro [pe'liɣro] *nm* danger; (*riesgo*) risk; **"~ de muerte"** "danger"; **correr ~ de** to be in danger of; **con ~ de la vida** at the risk of one's life

peligrosidad [peliɣrosi'ðað] *nf* danger, riskiness

peligroso, -a [peli'ɣroso, a] *adj* dangerous; risky

pelirrojo, -a [peli'rroxo, a] *adj* red-haired, red-headed

pellejo [pe'ʎexo] *nm* (*de animal*) skin, hide; **salvar el ~** to save one's skin

pellizcar [peʎiθ'kar] *vt* to pinch, nip

pellizco [pe'ʎiθko] *nm* pinch

pellizque *etc* [pe'ʎiθke] *vb ver* **pellizcar**

pelma ['pelma] *nm/f*, **pelmazo** [pel'maθo] *nm* (*fam*) pest

pelo ['pelo] *nm* (*cabellos*) hair; (*de barba, bigote*) whisker; (*de animal: piel*) fur, coat; (*de perro etc*) hair, coat; (*de ave*) down; (*de tejido*) nap; (*Tec*) fibre; **a ~** bareheaded; (*desnudo*) naked; **al ~** just right; **venir al ~** to be exactly what one needs; **por los pelos** by the skin of one's teeth; **escaparse por un ~** to have a close shave; **se me pusieron los pelos de punta** my hair stood on end; **no tener pelos en la lengua** to be outspoken, not mince words; **tomar el ~ a algn** to pull sb's leg

pelón, -ona [pe'lon, ona] *adj* hairless, bald

pelota [pe'lota] *nf* ball; (*fam: cabeza*) nut (*fam*); **en ~(s)** stark naked; **~ vasca** pelota; **devolver la ~ a algn** (*fig*) to turn the tables on sb; **hacer la ~ (a algn)** to creep (to sb)

pelotera [pelo'tera] *nf* (*fam*) barney

pelotón [pelo'ton] *nm* (*Mil*) squad, detachment

peluca [pe'luka] *nf* wig

peluche [pe'lutʃe] *nm*: **muñeco de ~** soft toy

peludo, -a [pe'luðo, a] *adj* hairy, shaggy

peluquería [peluke'ria] *nf* hairdresser's; (*para hombres*) barber's (shop)

peluquero, -a [pelu'kero, a] *nm/f* hairdresser; barber

peluquín [pelu'kin] *nm* toupée

pelusa [pe'lusa] *nf* (*Bot*) down; (*Costura*) fluff

pelvis ['pelβis] *nf* pelvis

PEMEX [pe'meks] *nm abr* = **Petróleos Mejicanos**

PEN [pen] *nm abr* (*Esp*: = *Plan Energético Nacional: Arg*) = **Poder Ejecutivo Nacional**

pena ['pena] *nf* (*congoja*) grief, sadness; (*remordimiento*) regret; (*dificultad*) trouble; (*dolor*) pain; (*Am: vergüenza*) shame; (*Jur*) sentence; (*Deporte*) penalty; **~ capital** capital punishment; **~ de muerte** death penalty; **~ pecuniaria** fine; **merecer o valer la ~** to be worthwhile; **a duras penas** with great difficulty; **so ~ de** on pain of; **me dan ~** I feel sorry for them; **¿no te da ~ hacerlo?** (*Am*) aren't you embarrassed doing that?; **¡qué ~!** what a shame o pity!

penal [pe'nal] *adj* penal ■ *nm* (*cárcel*) prison

penalidad [penali'ðað] *nf* (*problema, dificultad*) trouble, hardship; (*Jur*) penalty, punishment

penalizar [penali'θar] *vt* to penalize

penalti, penalty [pe'nalti] *nm* (*Deporte*) penalty

penar [pe'nar] *vt* to penalize; (*castigar*) to punish ■ *vi* to suffer

pendejo, -a [pen'dexo, a] *nm/f* (*Am fam!*) wanker (*Brit*) (!), jerk (*US*) (!)

pender [pen'der] *vi* (*colgar*) to hang; (*Jur*) to be pending

pendiente [pen'djente] *adj* pending,

unsettled ∎ *nm* earring ∎ *nf* hill, slope;
tener una asignatura ~ to have to resit a
subject

pendón [pen'don] *nm* banner, standard

péndulo ['pendulo] *nm* pendulum

pene ['pene] *nm* penis

penene [pe'nene] *nm/f* = **PNN**

penetración [penetra'θjon] *nf* (*acto*)
penetration; (*agudeza*) sharpness, insight

penetrante [pene'trante] *adj* (*herida*) deep;
(*persona, arma*) sharp; (*sonido*) penetrating,
piercing; (*mirada*) searching; (*viento, ironía*)
biting

penetrar [pene'trar] *vt* to penetrate, pierce;
(*entender*) to grasp ∎ *vi* to penetrate, go in;
(*líquido*) to soak in; (*emoción*) to pierce

penicilina [peniθi'lina] *nf* penicillin

península [pe'ninsula] *nf* peninsula;
P~ Ibérica Iberian Peninsula

peninsular [peninsu'lar] *adj* peninsular

penique [pe'nike] *nm* penny; **peniques** *nmpl*
pence

penitencia [peni'tenθja] *nf* (*remordimiento*)
penitence; (*castigo*) penance; **en** ~ as a
penance

penitencial [peniten'θjal] *adj* penitential

penitenciaría [penitenθja'ria] *nf* prison,
penitentiary

penitenciario, -a [peniten'θjarjo, a] *adj*
prison *cpd*

penoso, -a [pe'noso, a] *adj* laborious, difficult

pensado, -a [pen'saðo, a] *adj*: **bien/mal** ~
well intentioned/cynical; **en el momento
menos** ~ when least expected

pensador, a [pensa'ðor, a] *nm/f* thinker

pensamiento [pensa'mjento] *nm* (*gen*)
thought; (*mente*) mind; (*idea*) idea; (*Bot*)
pansy; **no se le pasó por el** ~ it never
occurred to him

pensar [pen'sar] *vt* to think; (*considerar*)
to think over, think out; (*proponerse*) to
intend, plan, propose; (*imaginarse*) to think
up, invent ∎ *vi* to think; ~ **en** to think of *o*
about; (*anhelar*) to aim at, aspire to; **dar que
~ a algn** to give sb food for thought

pensativo, -a [pensa'tiβo, a] *adj* thoughtful,
pensive

pensión [pen'sjon] *nf* (*casa*) = guest house;
(*dinero*) pension; (*cama y comida*) board
and lodging; ~ **de jubilación** retirement
pension; ~ **escalada** graduated pension; ~
completa full board; **media** ~ half board

pensionista [pensjo'nista] *nm/f* (*jubilado*)
(old-age) pensioner; (*el que vive en una pensión*)
lodger; (*Escol*) boarder

pentágono [pen'tayono] *nm* pentagon; **el P~**
the Pentagon

pentagrama [penta'yrama] *nm* (*Mus*) stave,
staff

penúltimo, -a [pe'nultimo, a] *adj*
penultimate, second last

penumbra [pe'numbra] *nf* half-light, semi-
darkness

penuria [pe'nurja] *nf* shortage, want

peña ['pena] *nf* (*roca*) rock; (*acantilado*)
cliff, crag; (*grupo*) group, circle; (*Deporte*)
supporters' club

peñasco [pe'nasko] *nm* large rock, boulder

peñón [pe'non] *nm* crag; **el P~** the Rock (of
Gibraltar)

peón [pe'on] *nm* labourer; (*Am*) farm
labourer, farmhand; (*Tec*) spindle, shaft;
(*Ajedrez*) pawn

peonza [pe'onθa] *nf* spinning top

peor [pe'or] *adj* (*comparativo*) worse;
(*superlativo*) worst ∎ *adv* worse; worst; **de
mal en** ~ from bad to worse; **tanto** ~ so
much the worse; **A es** ~ **que B** A is worse
than B; **Z es el** ~ **de todos** Z is the worst of all

pepenar [pepe'nar] *vi* (*Am*) to sift through
rubbish *o* garbage

pepinillo [pepi'niʎo] *nm* gherkin

pepino [pe'pino] *nm* cucumber; **(no) me
importa un** ~ I don't care two hoots

pepita [pe'pita] *nf* (*Bot*) pip; (*Minería*) nugget

pepito [pe'pito] *nm* meat sandwich

peque *etc* ['peke] *vb ver* **pecar**

pequeñez [peke'neθ] *nf* smallness,
littleness; (*trivialidad*) trifle, triviality

pequeño, -a [pe'keno, a] *adj* small, little;
(*cifra*) small, low; (*bajo*) short; ~ **burgués**
lower middle-class

pequinés, -esa [peki'nes, esa] *adj, nm/f*
Pekinese

pera ['pera] *adj inv* classy; **niño** ~ spoiled
upper-class brat ∎ *nf* pear; **eso es pedir
peras al olmo** that's asking the impossible

peral [pe'ral] *nm* pear tree

percance [per'kanθe] *nm* setback,
misfortune

per cápita [per'kapita] *adj*: **renta** ~ per capita
income

percatarse [perka'tarse] *vr*: ~ **de** to notice,
take note of

percebe [per'θeβe] *nm* (*Zool*) barnacle; (*fam*)
idiot

percepción [perθep'θjon] *nf* (*vista*)
perception; (*idea*) notion, idea; (*Com*)
collection

perceptible [perθep'tiβle] *adj* perceptible,
noticeable; (*Com*) payable, receivable

percha ['pertʃa] *nf* (*poste*) pole, support;
(*gancho*) peg; (*de abrigos*) coat stand; (*colgador*)
coat hanger; (*de ave*) perch

P

perchero [per'tʃero] *nm* clothes rack
percibir [perθi'βir] *vt* to perceive, notice; (*ver*)
to see; (*peligro etc*) to sense; (*Com*) to earn,
receive, get
percusión [perku'sjon] *nf* percussion
percusor [perku'sor], **percutor** [perku'tor]
nm (*Tec*) hammer; (*de arma*) firing pin
perdedor, a [perðe'ðor, a] *adj* losing ■ *nm/f*
loser
perder [per'ðer] *vt* to lose; (*tiempo, palabras*)
to waste; (*oportunidad*) to lose, miss; (*tren*) to
miss ■ *vi* to lose; **perderse** *vr* (*extraviarse*)
to get lost; (*desaparecer*) to disappear, be lost
to view; (*arruinarse*) to be ruined; **echar**
a ~ (*comida*) to spoil, ruin; (*oportunidad*) to
waste; **tener buen** ~ to be a good loser; **¡no**
te lo pierdas! don't miss it!; **he perdido la**
costumbre I have got out of the habit
perdición [perði'θjon] *nf* perdition; (*fig*) ruin
pérdida ['perðiða] *nf* loss; (*de tiempo*) waste;
(*Com*) net loss; **pérdidas** *nfpl* (*Com*) losses;
¡no tiene ~! you can't go wrong!; ~ **contable**
(*Com*) book loss
perdido, -a [per'ðiðo, a] *adj* lost; **estar ~**
por to be crazy about; **es un caso** ~ he is a
hopeless case
perdigón [perði'ɣon] *nm* pellet
perdiz [per'ðiθ] *nf* partridge
perdón [per'ðon] *nm* (*disculpa*) pardon,
forgiveness; (*clemencia*) mercy; **¡~!** sorry!, I beg
your pardon!; **con** ~ if I may, if you don't mind
perdonar [perðo'nar] *vt* to pardon, forgive;
(*la vida*) to spare; (*excusar*) to exempt, excuse
■ *vi* to pardon, forgive; **¡perdone (usted)!**
sorry!, I beg your pardon!; **perdone, pero**
me parece que ... excuse me, but I think ...
perdurable [perðu'raβle] *adj* lasting; (*eterno*)
everlasting
perdurar [perðu'rar] *vi* (*resistir*) to last,
endure; (*seguir existiendo*) to stand, still exist
perecedero, -a [pereθe'ðero, a] *adj*
perishable
perecer [pere'θer] *vi* to perish, die
peregrinación [pereɣrina'θjon] *nf* (*Rel*)
pilgrimage
peregrino, -a [pere'ɣrino] *adj* (*extraño*)
strange; (*singular*) rare ■ *nm/f* pilgrim
perejil [pere'xil] *nm* parsley
perenne [pe'renne] *adj* perennial
perentorio, -a [peren'torjo, a] *adj* (*urgente*)
urgent; (*terminante*) peremptory; (*fijo*) set,
fixed
pereza [pe're θa] *nf* (*flojera*) laziness; (*lentitud*)
sloth, slowness
perezca *etc* [pe're θka] *vb ver* **perecer**
perezoso, -a [pere'θoso, a] *adj* lazy; slow,
sluggish

perfección [perfek'θjon] *nf* perfection; **a la** ~
to perfection
perfeccionar [perfekθjo'nar] *vt* to perfect;
(*acabar*) to complete, finish
perfecto, -a [per'fekto, a] *adj* perfect ■ *nm*
(*Ling*) perfect (tense)
perfidia [per'fiðja] *nf* perfidy, treachery
pérfido, -a ['perfiðo, a] *adj* perfidious,
treacherous
perfil [per'fil] *nm* (*parte lateral*) profile; (*silueta*)
silhouette, outline; (*Tec*) (cross) section;
perfiles *nmpl* features; (*fig*) social graces;
~ **del cliente** (*Com*) customer profile; **en** ~
from the side, in profile
perfilado, -a [perfi'laðo, a] *adj* (*bien formado*)
well-shaped; (*largo: cara*) long
perfilar [perfi'lar] *vt* (*trazar*) to outline;
(*dar carácter a*) to shape, give character to;
perfilarse *vr* to be silhouetted (*en* against);
el proyecto se va perfilando the project is
taking shape
perforación [perfora'θjon] *nf* perforation;
(*con taladro*) drilling
perforadora [perfora'ðora] *nf* drill; ~ **de**
fichas card-punch
perforar [perfo'rar] *vt* to perforate; (*agujero*)
to drill, bore; (*papel*) to punch a hole in ■ *vi*
to drill, bore
perfumar [perfu'mar] *vt* to scent, perfume
perfume [per'fume] *nm* perfume, scent
perfumería [perfume'ria] *nf* perfume shop
pergamino [perɣa'mino] *nm* parchment
pericia [pe'riθja] *nf* skill, expertise
periferia [peri'ferja] *nf* periphery; (*de ciudad*)
outskirts *pl*
periférico, -a [peri'feriko, a] *adj* peripheral
■ *nm* (*Inform*) peripheral; (*Am: Auto*) ring
road; **barrio** ~ outlying district
perilla [pe'riʎa] *nf* goatee
perímetro [pe'rimetro] *nm* perimeter
periódico, -a [pe'rjoðiko, a] *adj* periodic(al)
■ *nm* (news)paper; ~ **dominical** Sunday
(news)paper
periodismo [perjo'ðismo] *nm* journalism
periodista [perjo'ðista] *nm/f* journalist
periodístico, -a [perjo'ðistiko, a] *adj*
journalistic
periodo [pe'rjoðo], **período** [pe'rioðo] *nm*
period; ~ **contable** (*Com*) accounting period
peripecias [peri'peθjas] *nfpl* adventures
peripuesto, -a [peri'pwesto, a] *adj* dressed
up; **tan** ~ all dressed up (to the nines)
periquito [peri'kito] *nm* budgerigar, budgie
(*fam*)
perito, -a [pe'rito, a] *adj* (*experto*) expert;
(*diestro*) skilled, skilful ■ *nm/f* expert; skilled
worker; (*técnico*) technician

perjudicar [perxuði'kar] vt (gen) to damage, harm; (fig) to prejudice

perjudicial [perxuði'θjal] adj damaging, harmful; (en detrimento) detrimental

perjudique etc [perxu'ðike] vb ver **perjudicar**

perjuicio [per'xwiθjo] nm damage, harm; **en/sin ~ de** to the detriment of/without prejudice to

perjurar [perxu'rar] vi to commit perjury

perla ['perla] nf pearl; **me viene de perlas** it suits me fine

permanecer [permane'θer] vi (quedarse) to stay, remain; (seguir) to continue to be

permanencia [perma'nenθja] nf (duración) permanence; (estancia) stay

permanente [perma'nente] adj (que queda) permanent; (constante) constant; (comisión etc) standing ■ nf perm; **hacerse una ~** to have one's hair permed

permanezca etc [perma'neθka] vb ver **permanecer**

permisible [permi'siβle] adj permissible, allowable

permiso [per'miso] nm permission; (licencia) permit, licence (Brit), license (US); **con ~** excuse me; **estar de ~** (Mil) to be on leave; **~ de conducir** o **conductor** driving licence (Brit), driver's license (US); **~ de exportación/importación** export/import licence; **~ por asuntos familiares** compassionate leave

permitir [permi'tir] vt to permit, allow; **permitirse** vr: **permitirse algo** to allow o.s. sth; **no me puedo ~ ese lujo** I can't afford that; **¿me permite?** may I?; **si lo permite el tiempo** weather permitting

permuta [per'muta] nf exchange

permutar [permu'tar] vt to switch, exchange; **~ destinos con algn** to swap o exchange jobs with sb

pernicioso, -a [perni'θjoso, a] adj (maligno, Med) pernicious; (persona) wicked

perno ['perno] nm bolt

pernoctar [pernok'tar] vi to stay for the night

pero ['pero] conj but; (aún) yet ■ nm (defecto) flaw, defect; (reparo) objection; **¡no hay ~ que valga!** there are no buts about it

perogrullada [peroɣru'ʎaða] nf platitude, truism

perol [pe'rol] nm, **perola** [pe'rola] nf pan

peronista [pero'nista] adj, nm/f Peronist

perorata [pero'rata] nf long-winded speech

perpendicular [perpendiku'lar] adj perpendicular; **el camino es ~ al río** the road is at right angles to the river

perpetrar [perpe'trar] vt to perpetrate

perpetuamente [perpetwa'mente] adv perpetually

perpetuar [perpe'twar] vt to perpetuate

perpetuo, -a [per'petwo, a] adj perpetual; (Jur etc: condena) life cpd

Perpiñán [perpi'ɲan] nm Perpignan

perplejo, -a [per'plexo, a] adj perplexed, bewildered

perra ['perra] nf bitch; (fam: dinero) money; (: manía) mania, crazy idea; (: rabieta) tantrum; **estar sin una ~** to be flat broke

perrera [pe'rrera] nf kennel

perro ['perro] nm dog; **~ caliente** hot dog; **"~ peligroso"** "beware of the dog"; **ser ~ viejo** to be an old hand; **tiempo de perros** filthy weather; **~ que ladra no muerde** his bark is worse than his bite

persa ['persa] adj, nm/f Persian ■ nm (Ling) Persian

persecución [perseku'θjon] nf pursuit, hunt, chase; (Rel, Pol) persecution

perseguir [perse'ɣir] vt to pursue, hunt; (correr tras) to chase after; (molestar) to pester, annoy; (Rel, Pol) to persecute; (Jur) to prosecute

perseverante [perseβe'rante] adj persevering, persistent

perseverar [perseβe'rar] vi to persevere, persist; **~ en** to persevere in, persist with

persiana [per'sjana] nf (Venetian) blind

persiga etc [per'siɣa] vb ver **perseguir**

persignarse [persiɣ'narse] vr to cross o.s.

persiguiendo etc [persi'ɣjenðo] vb ver **perseguir**

persistente [persis'tente] adj persistent

persistir [persis'tir] vi to persist

persona [per'sona] nf person; **10 personas** 10 people; **tercera ~** third party; (Ling) third person; **en ~** in person o the flesh; **por ~** a head; **es buena ~** he's a good sort

personaje [perso'naxe] nm important person, celebrity; (Teat) character

personal [perso'nal] adj (particular) personal; (para una persona) single, for one person ■ nm (plantilla) personnel, staff; (Naut) crew; (fam: gente) people

personalidad [personali'ðað] nf personality; (Jur) status

personalizar [personali'θar] vt to personalize ■ vi (al hablar) to name names

personarse [perso'narse] vr to appear in person; **~ en** to present o.s. at, report to

personero, -a [perso'nero, a] nm/f (Am) (government) official

personificar [personifi'kar] vt to personify

personifique etc [personi'fike] vb ver **personificar**

perspectiva [perspek'tiβa] *nf* perspective; (*vista, panorama*) view, panorama; (*posibilidad futura*) outlook, prospect; **tener algo en ~** to have sth in view

perspicacia [perspi'kaθja] *nf* discernment, perspicacity

perspicaz [perspi'kaθ] *adj* shrewd

persuadir [perswa'ðir] *vt* (*gen*) to persuade; (*convencer*) to convince; **persuadirse** *vr* to become convinced

persuasión [perswa'sjon] *nf* (*acto*) persuasion; (*convicción*) conviction

persuasivo, -a [perwa'siβo, a] *adj* persuasive; convincing

pertenecer [pertene'θer] *vi*: **~ a** to belong to; (*fig*) to concern

perteneciente [pertene'θjente] *adj*: **~ a** belonging to

pertenencia [perte'nenθja] *nf* ownership; **pertenencias** *nfpl* possessions, property *sg*

pertenezca *etc* [perte'neθka] *vb ver* **pertenecer**

pértiga ['pertiɣa] *nf* pole; **salto de ~** pole vault

pertinaz [perti'naθ] *adj* (*persistente*) persistent; (*terco*) obstinate

pertinente [perti'nente] *adj* relevant, pertinent; (*apropiado*) appropriate; **~ a** concerning, relevant to

pertrechar [pertre'tʃar] *vt* (*gen*) to supply; (*Mil*) to supply with ammunition and stores; **pertrecharse** *vr*: **pertrecharse de algo** to provide o.s. with sth

pertrechos [per'tretʃos] *nmpl* (*gen*) implements; (*Mil*) supplies and stores

perturbación [perturβa'θjon] *nf* (*Pol*) disturbance; (*Med*) upset, disturbance; **~ del orden público** breach of the peace

perturbador, a [perturβa'ðor, a] *adj* (*que perturba*) perturbing, disturbing; (*subversivo*) subversive

perturbar [pertur'βar] *vt* (*el orden*) to disturb; (*Med*) to upset, disturb; (*mentalmente*) to perturb

Perú [pe'ru] *nm*: **el Perú** Peru

peruano, -a [pe'rwano, a] *adj, nm/f* Peruvian

perversión [perβer'sjon] *nf* perversion

perverso, -a [perβerso, a] *adj* perverse; (*depravado*) depraved

pervertido, -a [perβer'tiðo, a] *adj* perverted ■ *nm/f* pervert

pervertir [perβer'tir] *vt* to pervert, corrupt

pervierta *etc* [per'βjerta], **pervirtiendo** *etc* [perβir'tjendo] *vb ver* **pervertir**

pesa ['pesa] *nf* weight; (*Deporte*) shot

pesadez [pesa'ðeθ] *nf* (*calidad de pesado*) heaviness; (*lentitud*) slowness; (*aburrimiento*) tediousness; **es una ~ tener que ...** it's a bind having to ...

pesadilla [pesa'ðiʎa] *nf* nightmare, bad dream; (*fig*) worry, obsession

pesado, -a [pe'saðo, a] *adj* (*gen*) heavy; (*lento*) slow; (*difícil, duro*) tough, hard; (*aburrido*) tedious, boring; (*bochornoso*) sultry ■ *nm/f* bore; **tener el estómago ~** to feel bloated; **¡no seas ~!** come off it!

pesadumbre [pesa'ðumbre] *nf* grief, sorrow

pésame ['pesame] *nm* expression of condolence, message of sympathy; **dar el ~** to express one's condolences

pesar [pe'sar] *vt* to weigh; (*fig*) to weigh heavily on; (*afligir*) to grieve ■ *vi* to weigh; (*ser pesado*) to weigh a lot, be heavy; (*fig: opinión*) to carry weight ■ *nm* (*sentimiento*) regret; (*pena*) grief, sorrow; **a ~ de (que)** in spite of, despite; **no me pesa haberlo hecho** I'm not sorry I did it

pesca ['peska] *nf* (*acto*) fishing; (*cantidad de pescado*) catch; **~ de altura** deep sea/coastal fishing; **ir de ~** to go fishing

pescadería [peskaðe'ria] *nf* fish shop, fishmonger's

pescadilla [peska'ðiʎa] *nf* whiting

pescado [pes'kaðo] *nm* fish

pescador, a [peska'ðor, a] *nm/f* fisherman(-woman)

pescar [pes'kar] *vt* (*coger*) to catch; (*tratar de coger*) to fish for; (*fam: lograr*) to get hold of, land; (*conseguir: trabajo*) to manage to get; (*sorprender*) to catch unawares ■ *vi* to fish, go fishing

pescuezo [pes'kweθo] *nm* neck

pese ['pese] *prep*: **~ a** despite, in spite of

pesebre [pe'seβre] *nm* manger

peseta [pe'seta] *nf* peseta

pesetero, -a [pese'tero, a] *adj* money-grubbing

pesimismo [pesi'mismo] *nm* pessimism

pesimista [pesi'mista] *adj* pessimistic ■ *nm/f* pessimist

pésimo, -a ['pesimo, a] *adj* abominable, vile

peso ['peso] *nm* weight; (*balanza*) scales *pl*; (*Am Com*) monetary unit; (*moneda*) peso; (*Deporte*) shot; **~ bruto/neto** gross/net weight; **~ mosca/pesado** fly-/heavyweight; **de poco ~** light(weight); **levantamiento de pesos** weightlifting; **vender a ~** to sell by weight; **argumento de ~** weighty argument; **eso cae de su ~** that goes without saying

pesque *etc* ['peske] *vb ver* **pescar**

pesquero, -a [pes'kero, a] *adj* fishing *cpd*

pesquisa [pes'kisa] *nf* inquiry, investigation

pestaña [pes'taɲa] *nf* (*Anat*) eyelash; (*borde*) rim

pestañear [pesta'ɲe'ar] vi to blink
peste ['peste] nf plague; (fig) nuisance;
(mal olor) stink, stench; ~ **negra** Black Death;
echar pestes to swear, fume
pesticida [pesti'θiða] nm pesticide
pestilencia [pesti'lenθja] nf (mal olor) stink,
stench
pestillo [pes'tiʎo] nm bolt, latch; (cerrojo)
catch; (picaporte) (door) handle
petaca [pe'taka] nf (de cigarrillos) cigarette
case; (de pipa) tobacco pouch; (Am: maleta)
suitcase
pétalo ['petalo] nm petal
petanca [pe'tanka] nf a game in which metal
bowls are thrown at a target bowl
petardo [pe'tarðo] nm firework, firecracker
petición [peti'θjon] nf (pedido) request, plea;
(memorial) petition; (Jur) plea; **a ~ de** at the
request of; ~ **de aumento de salarios** wage
demand o claim
petirrojo [peti'rroxo] nm robin
peto ['peto] nm (corpiño) bodice; (Taur) horse's
padding
pétreo, -a ['petreo, a] adj stony, rocky
petrificar [petrifi'kar] vt to petrify
petrifique etc [petri'fike] vb ver **petrificar**
PETROVEN [petro'ben] nm abr = **Petróleos de
Venezuela**
petrodólar [petro'ðolar] nm petrodollar
petróleo [pe'troleo] nm oil, petroleum
petrolero, -a [petro'lero, a] adj petroleum cpd
■ nm (Com) oil man; (buque) (oil) tanker
petulancia [petu'lanθja] nf (insolencia) vanity,
opinionated nature
peyorativo, -a [pejora'tiβo, a] adj pejorative
pez [peθ] nm fish; ~ **de colores** goldfish; ~
espada swordfish; **estar como el ~ en el
agua** to feel completely at home
pezón [pe'θon] nm teat, nipple
pezuña [pe'θuɲa] nf hoof
piadoso, -a [pja'ðoso, a] adj (devoto) pious,
devout; (misericordioso) kind, merciful
Piamonte [pja'monte] nm Piedmont
pianista [pja'nista] nm/f pianist
piano ['pjano] nm piano; ~ **de cola** grand
piano
piar [pjar] vi to cheep
piara ['pjara] nf (manada) herd, drove
PIB nm abr (Esp Com: = Producto Interno Bruto) GDP
pibe, -a ['piβe, a] nm/f (Am) boy/girl, kid,
child
pica ['pika] nf (Mil) pike; (Taur) goad; **poner
una ~ en Flandes** to bring off something
difficult
picadero [pika'ðero] nm riding school
picadillo [pika'ðiʎo] nm mince, minced meat
picado, -a [pi'kaðo, a] adj pricked,

punctured; (mar) choppy; (diente) bad;
(tabaco) cut; (enfadado) cross
picador [pika'ðor] nm (Taur) picador; (minero)
faceworker
picadora [pika'ðora] nf mincer
picadura [pika'ðura] nf (pinchazo) puncture;
(de abeja) sting; (de mosquito) bite; (tabaco
picado) cut tobacco
picana [pi'kana] (Am) nf (Agr) cattle prod;
(Pol: para tortura) electric prod
picante [pi'kante] adj (comida, sabor) hot;
(comentario) racy, spicy
picaporte [pika'porte] nm (tirador) handle;
(pestillo) latch
picar [pi'kar] vt (agujerear, perforar) to prick,
puncture; (billete) to punch, clip; (abeja) to
sting; (mosquito, serpiente) to bite; (persona) to
nibble (at); (incitar) to incite, goad; (dañar,
irritar) to annoy, bother; (quemar: lengua) to
burn, sting ■ vi (pez) to bite, take the bait;
(el sol) to burn, scorch; (abeja, Med) to sting;
(mosquito) to bite; **picarse** vr (agriarse) to turn
sour, go off; (mar) to get choppy; (ofenderse)
to take offence; **me pican los ojos** my eyes
sting; **me pica el brazo** my arm itches
picardía [pikar'ðia] nf villainy; (astucia)
slyness, craftiness; (una picardía) dirty trick;
(palabra) rude/bad word o expression
picaresco, -a [pika'resko, a] adj (travieso)
roguish, rascally; (Lit) picaresque
pícaro, -a ['pikaro, a] adj (malicioso)
villainous; (travieso) mischievous ■ nm
(astuto) sly sort; (sinvergüenza) rascal,
scoundrel
picazón [pika'θon] nf (comezón) itch; (ardor)
sting(ing feeling); (remordimiento) pang of
conscience
pichón, -ona [pi'tʃon, ona] nm/f (de paloma)
young pigeon; (apelativo) darling, dearest
pico ['piko] nm (de ave) beak; (punta agudo)
peak, sharp point; (Tec) pick, pickaxe; (Geo)
peak, summit; (labia) talkativeness; **no
abrir el** ~ to keep quiet; ~ **parásito** (Elec)
spike; **y** ~ and a bit; **son las tres y** ~ it's just
after three; **tiene 50 libros y** ~ he has 50-
odd books; **me costó un** ~ it cost me quite
a bit
picor [pi'kor] nm itch; (ardor) sting(ing
feeling)
picota [pi'kota] nf pillory; **poner a algn en
la ~** (fig) to ridicule sb
picotada [piko'taða] nf, **picotazo**
[piko'taθo] nm (de pájaro) peck; (de insecto)
sting, bite
picotear [pikote'ar] vt to peck ■ vi to nibble,
pick
pictórico, -a [pik'toriko, a] adj pictorial;

p

tiene dotes pictóricas she has a talent for painting

picudo, -a [pi'kuðo, a] *adj* pointed, with a point

pidiendo *etc* [pi'ðjendo] *vb ver* **pedir**

pie [pje] (*pl* **pies**) *nm* (*gen*, *Mat*) foot; (*de cama, página, escalera*) foot, bottom; (*Teat*) cue; (*fig*: *motivo*) motive, basis; (: *fundamento*) foothold; **pies planos** flat feet; **ir a ~** to go on foot, walk; **estar de ~** to be standing (up); **ponerse de ~** to stand up; **al ~ de la letra** (*citar*) literally, verbatim; (*copiar*) exactly, word for word; **de pies a cabeza** from head to foot; **en ~ de guerra** on a war footing; **sin pies ni cabeza** pointless, absurd; **dar ~ a** to give cause for; **no dar ~ con bola** to be no good at anything; **saber de qué ~ cojea algn** to know sb's weak spots

piedad [pje'ðað] *nf* (*lástima*) pity, compassion; (*clemencia*) mercy; (*devoción*) piety, devotion; **tener ~ de** to take pity on

piedra ['pjeðra] *nf* stone; (*roca*) rock; (*de mechero*) flint; (*Meteorología*) hailstone; **primera ~** foundation stone; **~ de afilar** grindstone; **~ arenisca/caliza** sand-/limestone

piel [pjel] *nf* (*Anat*) skin; (*Zool*) skin, hide; (*de oso*) fur; (*cuero*) leather; (*Bot*) skin, peel ■ *nm/f*: **~ roja** redskin

pienso *etc* ['pjenso] *vb ver* **pensar** ■ *nm* (*Agr*) feed

piercing ['pjersiŋ] *nm* piercing

pierda *etc* ['pjerða] *vb ver* **perder**

pierna ['pjerna] *nf* leg; **en piernas** bare-legged

pieza ['pjeθa] *nf* piece; (*esp Am*: *habitación*) room; (*Mus*) piece, composition; (*Teat*) work, play; **~ de recambio** *o* **repuesto** spare (part), extra (*US*); **~ de ropa** article of clothing; **quedarse de una ~** to be dumbfounded

pigmento [piɣ'mento] *nm* pigment

pigmeo, -a [piɣ'meo, a] *adj*, *nm/f* pigmy

pijama [pi'xama] *nm* pyjamas *pl*

pijo, -a ['pixo, a] *nm/f* (*fam*) upper-class twit

pijotada [pixo'taða] *nf* nuisance

pila ['pila] *nf* (*Elec*) battery; (*montón*) heap, pile; (*de fuente*) sink; (*Rel*: *tb*: **pila bautismal**) font; **nombre de ~** Christian *o* first name; **tengo una ~ de cosas que hacer** (*fam*) I have heaps *o* stacks of things to do

pilar [pi'lar] *nm* pillar; (*de puente*) pier; (*fig*) prop, mainstay

píldora ['pildora] *nf* pill; **la ~ (anticonceptiva)** the pill; **tragarse la ~** to be taken in

pileta [pi'leta] *nf* basin, bowl; (*Am*: *de cocina*) sink; (: *piscina*) swimming pool

pillaje [pi'ʎaxe] *nm* pillage, plunder

pillar [pi'ʎar] *vt* (*fam*: *coger*) to catch; (: *agarrar*) to grasp, seize; (: *entender*) to grasp, catch on to; (*suj*: *coche etc*) to run over; **~ un resfriado** (*fam*) to catch a cold

pillo, -a ['piʎo, a] *adj* villainous; (*astuto*) sly, crafty ■ *nm/f* rascal, rogue, scoundrel

pilón [pi'lon] *nm* pillar, post; (*Elec*) pylon; (*bebedero*) drinking trough; (*de fuente*) basin

pilotar [pilo'tar] *vt* (*avión*) to pilot; (*barco*) to steer

piloto [pi'loto] *nm* pilot; (*Auto*) rear light, tail light; (*conductor*) driver ■ *adj inv*: **planta ~** pilot plant; **luz ~** side light

piltrafa [pil'trafa] *nf* (*carne*) poor quality meat; (*fig*) worthless object; (: *individuo*) wretch

pimentón [pimen'ton] *nm* (*polvo*) paprika

pimienta [pi'mjenta] *nf* pepper

pimiento [pi'mjento] *nm* pepper, pimiento

pimpante [pim'pante] *adj* (*encantador*) charming; (*tb*: **tan pimpante**) smug, self-satisfied

PIN *nm abr* (*Esp Com*: = *Producto Interior Neto*) net domestic product

pin (*pl* **pins**) [pin, pins] *nm* badge

pinacoteca [pinako'teka] *nf* art gallery

pinar [pi'nar] *nm* pinewood

pincel [pin'θel] *nm* paintbrush

pincelada [pinθe'laða] *nf* brushstroke; **última ~** (*fig*) finishing touch

pinchadiscos [pintʃa'diskos] *nm/f inv* disc jockey, DJ

pinchar [pin'tʃar] *vt* (*perforar*) to prick, pierce; (*neumático*) to puncture; (*incitar*) to prod ■ *vi* (*Mus fam*) to be DJ; **pincharse** *vr* (*con droga*) to inject o.s.; (*neumático*) to burst, puncture; **no ~ ni cortar** (*fam*) to cut no ice; **tener un neumático pinchado** to have a puncture *o* a flat tyre

pinchazo [pin'tʃaθo] *nm* (*perforación*) prick; (*de llanta*) puncture, flat (*US*)

pinche ['pintʃe] *nm* (*de cocina*) kitchen boy, scullion

pinchito [pin'tʃito] *nm* shish kebab

pincho ['pintʃo] *nm* point; (*aguijón*) spike; (*Culin*) savoury (snack); **~ moruno** shish kebab; **~ de tortilla** small slice of omelette

ping-pong ['pimpon] *nm* table tennis

pingüe ['pingwe] *adj* (*cosecha*) bumper *cpd*; (*negocio*) lucrative

pingüino [pin'gwino] *nm* penguin

pinitos [pi'nitos] *nmpl*: **hacer sus primeros ~** to take one's first steps

pino ['pino] *nm* pine (tree); **vivir en el quinto ~** to live at the back of beyond

pinta ['pinta] *nf* spot; (*gota*) spot, drop;

(*aspecto*) appearance, look(s) pl; (*medida*) pint; **tener buena ~** to look good, look well; **por la ~** by the look of it

pintado, -a [pin'taðo, a] *adj* spotted; (*de muchos colores*) colourful ▪ *nf* piece of political graffiti; **pintados** *nfpl* political graffiti *sg*; **me sienta que ni ~, me viene que ni ~** it suits me a treat

pintar [pin'tar] *vt* to paint ▪ *vi* to paint; (*fam*) to count, be important; **pintarse** *vr* to put on make-up; **pintárselas solo para hacer algo** to manage to do sth by o.s.; **no pinta nada** (*fam*) he has no say

pintor, a [pin'tor, a] *nm/f* painter; **~ de brocha gorda** house painter; (*fig*) bad painter

pintoresco, -a [pinto'resko, a] *adj* picturesque

pintura [pin'tura] *nf* painting; **~ a la acuarela** watercolour; **~ al óleo** oil painting; **~ rupestre** cave painting

pinza ['pinθa] *nf* (*Zool*) claw; (*para colgar ropa*) clothes peg, clothespin (*US*); (*Tec*) pincers pl; **pinzas** *nfpl* (*para depilar*) tweezers

piña ['piɲa] *nf* (*fruto del pino*) pine cone; (*fruta*) pineapple; (*fig*) group

piñón [pi'ɲon] *nm* (*Bot*) pine nut; (*Tec*) pinion

PIO *nm abr* (*Esp*: = *Patronato de Igualdad de Oportunidades*) ≈ Equal Opportunities Board

pío, -a ['pio, a] *adj* (*devoto*) pious, devout; (*misericordioso*) merciful ▪ *nm*: **no decir ni ~** not to breathe a word

piojo ['pjoxo] *nm* louse

piojoso, -a [pjo'xoso, a] *adj* lousy; (*sucio*) dirty

piolet (*pl* **piolets**) [pjo'le] *nm* ice axe

pionero, -a [pjo'nero, a] *adj* pioneering ▪ *nm/f* pioneer

pipa ['pipa] *nf* pipe; (*Bot*) seed, pip

pipí [pi'pi] *nm* (*fam*): **hacer pipí** to have a wee(-wee)

pipiolo [pi'pjolo] *nm* youngster; (*novato*) novice, greenhorn

pique *etc* ['pike] *vb ver* **picar** ▪ *nm* (*resentimiento*) pique, resentment; (*rivalidad*) rivalry, competition; **irse a ~** to sink; (*familia*) to be ruined; **tener un ~ con algn** to have a grudge against sb

piqueta [pi'keta] *nf* pick(axe)

piquete [pi'kete] *nm* (*agujerito*) small hole; (*Mil*) squad, party; (*de obreros*) picket; **~ secundario** secondary picket

pirado, -a [pi'raðo, a] *adj* (*fam*) round the bend

piragua [pi'raɣwa] *nf* canoe

piragüismo [pira'ɣwismo] *nm* (*Deporte*) canoeing

pirámide [pi'ramiðe] *nf* pyramid

piraña [pi'raɲa] *nf* piranha

pirarse [pi'rarse] *vr*: **~(las)** (*largarse*) to beat it (*fam*); (*Escol*) to cut class

pirata [pi'rata] *adj*: **edición/disco ~** pirate edition/bootleg record ▪ *nm* pirate; (*tb*: **pirata informático**) hacker

pirenaico, -a [pire'naiko, a] *adj* Pyrenean

Pirineo [piri'neo] *nm*, **Pirineos** [piri'neos] *nmpl* Pyrenees *pl*

pirómano, -a [pi'romano, a] *nm/f* (*Psico*) pyromaniac; (*Jur*) arsonist

piropo [pi'ropo] *nm* compliment, (piece of) flattery; **echar piropos a** to make flirtatious remarks to

pirueta [pi'rweta] *nf* pirouette

piruleta [piru'leta] *nf* lollipop

pirulí [piru'li] *nm* lollipop

pis [pis] *nm* (*fam*) pee; **hacer ~** to have a pee

pisada [pi'saða] *nf* (*paso*) footstep; (*huella*) footprint

pisar [pi'sar] *vt* (*caminar sobre*) to walk on, tread on; (*apretar con el pie*) to press; (*fig*) to trample on, walk all over ▪ *vi* to tread, step, walk; **~ el acelerador** to step on the accelerator; **~ fuerte** (*fig*) to act determinedly

piscifactoría [pisθifakto'ria] *nf* fish farm

piscina [pis'θina] *nf* swimming pool

Piscis ['pisθis] *nm* (*Astro*) Pisces

piso ['piso] *nm* (*suelo; de edificio*) floor; (*Am*) ground; (*apartamento*) flat, apartment; **primer ~** (*Esp*) first o second (*US*) floor; (*Am*) ground o first (*US*) floor

pisotear [pisote'ar] *vt* to trample (on o underfoot); (*fig: humillar*) to trample on

pisotón [piso'ton] *nm* (*con el pie*) stamp

pista ['pista] *nf* track, trail; (*indicio*) clue; (*Inform*) track; **~ de auditoría** (*Com*) audit trail; **~ de aterrizaje** runway; **~ de baile** dance floor; **~ de tenis** tennis court; **~ de hielo** ice rink; **estar sobre la ~ de algn** to be on sb's trail

pisto ['pisto] *nm* (*Culin*) ratatouille; **darse ~** (*fam*) to show off

pistola [pis'tola] *nf* pistol; (*Tec*) spray gun

pistolero, -a [pisto'lero, a] *nm/f* gunman, gangster ▪ *nf* holster

pistón [pis'ton] *nm* (*Tec*) piston; (*Mus*) key

pitar [pi'tar] *vt* (*hacer sonar*) to blow; (*partido*) to referee; (*rechiflar*) to whistle at, boo; (*actor, obra*) to hiss ▪ *vi* to whistle; (*Auto*) to sound o toot one's horn; (*Am*) to smoke; **salir pitando** to beat it

pitido [pi'tiðo] *nm* whistle; (*sonido agudo*) beep; (*sonido corto*) pip

pitillera [piti'ʎera] *nf* cigarette case

pitillo [pi'tiʎo] *nm* cigarette

pito ['pito] *nm* whistle; (*de coche*) horn; (*cigarrillo*) cigarette; (*fam: de marihuana*) joint; (*fam!*) prick (*!*); **me importa un ~** I don't care two hoots

pitón [pi'ton] *nm* (*Zool*) python

pitonisa [pito'nisa] *nf* fortune-teller

pitorrearse [pitorre'arse] *vr:* **~ de** to scoff at, make fun of

pitorreo [pito'rreo] *nm* joke, laugh; **estar de ~** to be in a joking mood

píxel ['piksel] *nm* (*Inform*) pixel

piyama [pi'jama] *nm* (*Am*) pyjamas *pl*, pajamas (*US*) *pl*

pizarra [pi'θarra] *nf* (*piedra*) slate; (*encerado*) blackboard

pizca ['piθka] *nf* pinch, spot; (*fig*) spot, speck, trace; **ni ~** not a bit

pizza ['pitsa] *nf* pizza

placa ['plaka] *nf* plate; (*Med*) dental plate; (*distintivo*) badge; **~ de matrícula** number plate; **~ madre** (*Inform*) mother board

placaje [pla'kaxe] *nm* tackle

placard [pla'kar] *nm* (*Am*) built-in cupboard, (*clothes*) closet (*US*)

placenta [pla'θenta] *nf* placenta, afterbirth

placentero, -a [plaθen'tero, a] *adj* pleasant, agreeable

placer [pla'θer] *nm* pleasure; **a ~** at one's pleasure

plácido, -a ['plaθiðo, a] *adj* placid

plafón [pla'fon] *nm* (*Am*) ceiling

plaga ['plaɣa] *nf* pest; (*Med*) plague; (*fig*) swarm

plagar [pla'ɣar] *vt* to infest, plague; (*llenar*) to fill; **plagado de** riddled with; **han plagado la ciudad de carteles** they have plastered the town with posters

plagiar [pla'gjar] *vt* to plagiarize; (*Am*) to kidnap

plagiario, -a [pla'gjario, a] *nm/f* plagiarist; (*Am*) kidnapper

plagio ['plaxjo] *nm* plagiarism; (*Am*) kidnap

plague *etc* ['plaɣe] *vb ver* **plagar**

plan [plan] *nm* (*esquema, proyecto*) plan; (*idea, intento*) idea, intention; (*de curso*) programme; **~ cotizable de jubilación** contributory pension scheme; **~ de estudios** curriculum, syllabus; **~ de incentivos** (*Com*) incentive scheme; **tener ~** (*fam*) to have a date; **tener un ~** (*fam*) to have an affair; **en ~ de cachondeo** for a laugh; **en ~ económico** (*fam*) on the cheap; **vamos en ~ de turismo** we're going as tourists; **si te pones en ese ~** ... if that's your attitude ...

plana ['plana] *nf ver* **plano**

plancha ['plantʃa] *nf* (*para planchar*) iron; (*rótulo*) plate, sheet; (*Naut*) gangway; (*Culin*)

grill; **pescado a la ~** grilled fish; **~ de pelo** straighteners

planchado, -a [plan'tʃaðo, a] *adj* (*ropa*) ironed; (*traje*) pressed ■ *nm* ironing

planchar [plan'tʃar] *vt* to iron ■ *vi* to do the ironing

planeador [planea'ðor] *nm* glider

planear [plane'ar] *vt* to plan ■ *vi* to glide

planeta [pla'neta] *nm* planet

planetario, -a [plane'tarjo, a] *adj* planetary ■ *nm* planetarium

planicie [pla'niθje] *nf* plain

planificación [planifika'θjon] *nf* planning; **~ corporativa** (*Com*) corporate planning; **~ familiar** family planning; **diagrama de ~** (*Com*) planner

planilla [pla'niʎa] *nf* (*Am*) form

plano, -a ['plano, a] *adj* flat, level, even; (*liso*) smooth ■ *nm* (*Mat, Tec, Aviat*) plane; (*Foto*) shot; (*Arq*) plan; (*Geo*) map; (*de ciudad*) map, street plan ■ *nf* sheet of paper, page; (*Tec*) trowel; **primer ~** close-up; **caer de ~** to fall flat; **rechazar algo de ~** to turn sth down flat; **le daba el sol de ~** (*fig*) the sun shone directly on it; **en primera plana** on the front page; **plana mayor** staff

planta ['planta] *nf* (*Bot, Tec*) plant; (*Anat*) sole of the foot, foot; **~ baja** ground floor

plantación [planta'θjon] *nf* (*Agr*) plantation; (*acto*) planting

plantar [plan'tar] *vt* (*Bot*) to plant; (*puesto*) to put in; (*levantar*) to erect, set up; **plantarse** *vr* to stand firm; **~ a algn en la calle** to chuck sb out; **dejar plantado a algn** (*fam*) to stand sb up; **plantarse en** to reach, get to

plantear [plante'ar] *vt* (*problema*) to pose; (*dificultad*) to raise; **se lo plantearé** I'll put it to him

plantel [plan'tel] *nm* (*fig*) group, set

plantilla [plan'tiʎa] *nf* (*de zapato*) insole; (*personal*) personnel; **ser de ~** to be on the staff

plantío [plan'tio] *nm* (*acto*) planting; (*lugar*) plot, bed, patch

plantón [plan'ton] *nm* (*Mil*) guard, sentry; (*fam*) long wait; **dar (un) ~ a algn** to stand sb up

plañir [pla'ɲir] *vi* to mourn

plasma ['plasma] *nm* plasma

plasmar [plas'mar] *vt* (*dar forma*) to mould, shape; (*representar*) to represent ■ *vi:* **~ en** to take the form of

plasta ['plasta] *nf* soft mass, lump; (*desastre*) botch, mess

plasticidad [plastiθi'ðað] *nf* (*fig*) expressiveness

plástico, -a ['plastiko, a] *adj* plastic ■ *nf* (*art of*) sculpture, modelling ■ *nm* plastic

plastificar [plastifiˈkar] vt (documento) to laminate

plastifique etc [plastiˈfike] vb ver **plastificar**

plastilina [plastiˈlina] nf Plasticine®

plata ['plata] nf (metal) silver; (cosas hechas de plata) silverware; (Am) cash, dough (fam); **hablar en** ~ to speak bluntly o frankly

plataforma [plataˈforma] nf platform; ~ **de lanzamiento/perforación** launch(ing) pad/drilling rig

plátano ['platano] nm (fruta) banana; (árbol) plane tree

platea [plaˈtea] nf (Teat) pit

plateado, -a [plateˈaðo, a] adj silver; (Tec) silver-plated

platense [plaˈtense] (fam) = **ríoplatense**

plática ['platika] nf (Am) talk, chat; (Rel) sermon

platicar [platiˈkar] vi (Am) to talk, chat

platillo [plaˈtiʎo] nm saucer; (de limosnas) collecting bowl; **platillos** nmpl cymbals; ~ **volador** o **volante** flying saucer; **pasar el** ~ to pass the hat round

platina [plaˈtina] nf (Mus) tape deck

platino [plaˈtino] nm platinum; **platinos** nmpl (Auto) (contact) points

platique etc [plaˈtike] vb ver **platicar**

plato ['plato] nm plate, dish; (parte de comida) course; (guiso) dish; ~ **frutero/sopero** fruit/soup dish; **pagar los platos rotos** (fam) to carry the can (fam)

plató [plaˈto] nm set

platónico, -a [plaˈtoniko, a] adj platonic

playa ['plaja] nf beach; (costa) seaside; ~ **de estacionamiento** (Am) car park

playero, -a [plaˈjero, a] adj beach cpd ■ nf (Am: camiseta) T-shirt; **playeras** nfpl canvas shoes; (Tenis) tennis shoes

plaza ['plaθa] nf square; (mercado) market(place); (sitio) room, space; (en vehículo) seat, place; (colocación) post, job; ~ **de abastos** food market; ~ **mayor** main square; ~ **de toros** bullring; **hacer la** ~ to do the daily shopping; **reservar una** ~ to reserve a seat; **el hotel tiene 100 plazas** the hotel has 100 beds

plazca etc ['plaθka] vb ver **placer**

plazo ['plaθo] nm (lapso de tiempo) time, period, term; (fecha de vencimiento) expiry date; (pago parcial) instalment; **a corto/largo** ~ short-/long-term; **comprar a plazos** to buy on hire purchase, pay for in instalments; **nos dan un** ~ **de ocho días** they allow us a week

plazoleta [plaθoˈleta], **plazuela** [plaˈθwela] nf small square

pleamar [pleaˈmar] nf high tide

plebe ['pleβe] nf: **la** ~ the common people pl,

the masses pl; (pey) the plebs pl

plebeyo, -a [pleˈβejo, a] adj plebeian; (pey) coarse, common

plebiscito [pleβisˈθito] nm plebiscite

pleca ['pleka] nf (Inform) backslash

plegable [pleˈɣaβle] adj pliable; (silla) folding

plegar [pleˈɣar] vt (doblar) to fold, bend; (Costura) to pleat; **plegarse** vr to yield, submit

plegaria [pleˈɣarja] nf (oración) prayer

plegué [pleˈɣe], **pleguemos** etc [pleˈɣemos] vb ver **plegar**

pleitear [pleiteˈar] vi (Jur) to plead, conduct a lawsuit; (litigar) to go to law

pleito ['pleito] nm (Jur) lawsuit, case; (fig) dispute, feud; **pleitos** nmpl litigation sg; **entablar** ~ to bring an action o a lawsuit; **poner** ~ to sue

plenario, -a [pleˈnarjo, a] adj plenary, full

plenilunio [pleniˈlunjo] nm full moon

plenitud [pleniˈtuð] nf plenitude, fullness; (abundancia) abundance

pleno, -a ['pleno, a] adj full; (completo) complete ■ nm plenum; **en** ~ as a whole; (por unanimidad) unanimously; **en** ~ **día** in broad daylight; **en** ~ **verano** at the height of summer; **en plena cara** full in the face

pletina nf (Mus) tape deck

pleuresía [pleureˈsia] nf pleurisy

plexiglás [pleksiˈɣlas] nm acrylic

pliego etc ['pljeɣo] vb ver **plegar** ■ nm (hoja) sheet (of paper); (carta) sealed letter/document; ~ **de condiciones** details pl, specifications pl

pliegue etc ['pljeɣe] vb ver **plegar** ■ nm fold, crease; (de vestido) pleat

plisado [pliˈsaðo] nm pleating

plomero [ploˈmero] nm (Am) plumber

plomizo, -a [ploˈmiθo, a] adj leaden, lead-coloured

plomo ['plomo] nm (metal) lead; (Elec) fuse; **caer a** ~ to fall heavily o flat

pluma ['pluma] nf (Zool) feather; ~ **estilográfica**, ~ **fuente** (Am) fountain pen

plumazo [pluˈmaθo] nm (lit, fig) stroke of the pen

plumero [pluˈmero] nm (quitapolvos) feather duster; **ya te veo el** ~ I know what you're up to

plumón [pluˈmon] nm (Am) felt-tip pen

plural [pluˈral] adj plural ■ nm: **en** ~ in the plural

pluralidad [pluraliˈðað] nf plurality; **una** ~ **de votos** a majority of votes

pluriempleo [pluriemˈpleo] nm moonlighting

plus [plus] nm bonus

P

plusmarquista [plusmar'kista] *nm/f* (*Deporte*) record holder

plusvalía [plusβa'lia] *nf* (*mayor valor*) appreciation, added value; (*Com*) goodwill

PM *nf abr* (*Mil:* = *Policía Militar*) MP

p.m. *abr* (= *post meridiem*) p.m.; (= *por minuto*) per minute

PMA *nm abr* (= *Programa Mundial de Alimentos*) World Food Programme

pmo. *abr* (= *próximo*) prox.

PNB *nm abr* (*Esp Com*: = *Producto Nacional Bruto*) GNP

P.N.D. *nm abr* (*Escol:* = *personal no docente*) non-teaching staff

PNN [pe'nene] *nm/f abr* (= *profesor(a) no numerario(-a)*) untenured teacher ■ *nm abr* (*Esp Com*: = *Producto Nacional Neto*) net national product

PNUD *nm abr* (= *Programa de las Naciones Unidas para el Desarrollo*) United Nations Development Programme

PNV *nm abr* (*Esp Pol*) = **Partido Nacional Vasco**

P.° *abr* (= *Paseo*) Av(e).

p.o. *abr* = **por orden**

población [poβla'θjon] *nf* population; (*pueblo, ciudad*) town, city; ~ **activa** working population

poblado, -a [po'βlaðo, a] *adj* inhabited; (*barba*) thick; (*cejas*) bushy ■ *nm* (*aldea*) village; (*pueblo*) (small) town; ~ **de** (*lleno de*) filled with; **densamente** ~ densely populated

poblador, a [poβla'ðor, a] *nm/f* settler, colonist

poblar [po'βlar] *vt* (*colonizar*) to colonize; (*fundar*) to found; (*habitar*) to inhabit; **poblarse** *vr*: **poblarse de** to fill up with; (*irse cubriendo*) to become covered with

pobre ['poβre] *adj* poor ■ *nm/f* poor person; (*mendigo*) beggar; **los pobres** the poor; **¡~!** poor thing!; ~ **diablo** (*fig*) poor wretch *o* devil

pobreza [po'βreθa] *nf* poverty; ~ **energética** fuel poverty

pocho, -a ['potʃo, a] *adj* (*flor, color*) faded, discoloured; (*persona*) pale; (*fruta*) overripe; (*deprimido*) depressed

pocilga [po'θilɣa] *nf* pigsty

pocillo [po'siʎo] *nm* (*Am*) coffee cup

pócima ['poθima], **poción** [po'θjon] *nf* potion; (*brebaje*) concoction, nasty drink

PALABRA CLAVE

poco, -a ['poko, a] *adj* **1** (*sg*) little, not much; ~ **tiempo** little *o* not much time; **de** ~ **interés** of little interest, not very interesting; **poca cosa** not much

2 (*pl*) few, not many; **unos pocos** a few, some; **pocos niños comen lo que les conviene** few children eat what they should

■ *adv* **1** little, not much; **cuesta** ~ it doesn't cost much; ~ **más o menos** more or less

2 (+ *adj: negativo, antónimo*): ~ **amable/inteligente** not very nice/intelligent

3: **por** ~ **me caigo** I almost fell

4 (*tiempo*): ~ **después** soon after that; **dentro de** ~ shortly; **hace** ~ a short time ago, not long ago; **a** ~ **de haberse casado** shortly after getting married

5: ~ **a** ~ little by little

6 (*Am*): **¿a** ~ **no está divino?** isn't it just divine?; **de a** ~ gradually

■ *nm* a little, a bit; **un** ~ **triste/de dinero** a little sad/money

---

poda ['poða] *nf* (*acto*) pruning; (*temporada*) pruning season

podar [po'ðar] *vt* to prune

podcast ['poðkast] *nm* podcast

podcastear [poðkaste'ar] *vi* to podcast

podenco [po'ðenko] *nm* hound

PALABRA CLAVE

poder [po'ðer] *vi* **1** (*capacidad*) can, be able to; **no puedo hacerlo** I can't do it, I'm unable to do it

2 (*permiso*) can, may, be allowed to; **¿se puede?** may I (*o* we)?; **puedes irte ahora** you may go now; **no se puede fumar en este hospital** smoking is not allowed in this hospital

3 (*posibilidad*) may, might, could; **puede llegar mañana** he may *o* might arrive tomorrow; **pudiste haberte hecho daño** you might *o* could have hurt yourself; **¡podías habérmelo dicho antes!** you might have told me before!

4: **puede (ser)** perhaps; **puede que lo sepa Tomás** Tomás may *o* might know

5: **¡no puedo más!** I've had enough!; **no pude menos que dejarlo** I couldn't help but leave it; **es tonto a más no** ~ he's as stupid as they come

6: ~ **con**: **¿puedes con eso?** can you manage that?; **no puedo con este crío** this kid's too much for me

7: **él me puede** (*fam*) he's stronger than me

■ *nm* power; **el** ~ the Government; ~ **adquisitivo** purchasing power; **detentar** *u* **ocupar** *o* **estar en el** ~ to be in power *o* office; **estar** *u* **obrar en** ~ **de** to be in the hands *o* possession of; **por** ~**(es)** by proxy

poderío [poðe'rio] *nm* power; (*autoridad*) authority

poderoso, -a [poðe'roso, a] *adj* powerful

podio ['poðjo] *nm* podium

podólogo, -a [po'ðoloɣo, a] *nm/f* chiropodist (*Brit*), podiatrist (*US*)

podré *etc* [po'ðre] *vb ver* **poder**

podrido, -a [po'ðriðo, a] *adj* rotten, bad; (*fig*) rotten, corrupt

podrir [po'ðrir] = **pudrir**

poema [po'ema] *nm* poem

poesía [poe'sia] *nf* poetry

poeta [po'eta] *nm* poet

poético, -a [po'etiko, a] *adj* poetic(al)

poetisa [poe'tisa] *nf* (woman) poet

póker ['poker] *nm* poker

polaco, -a [po'lako, a] *adj* Polish ▪ *nm/f* Pole ▪ *nm* (*Ling*) Polish

polar [po'lar] *adj* polar

polarice *etc* [pola'riθe] *vb ver* **polarizar**

polaridad [polari'ðað] *nf* polarity

polarizar [polari'θar] *vt* to polarize

polea [po'lea] *nf* pulley

polémica [po'lemika] *nf* polemics *sg*; (*una polémica*) controversy

polemice *etc* [pole'miθe] *vb ver* **polemizar**

polémico, -a [po'lemiko, a] *adj* polemic(al)

polemizar [polemi'θar] *vi* argue

polen ['polen] *nm* pollen

poleo [po'leo] *nm* pennyroyal

poli ['poli] *nm* (*fam*) cop (*fam*) ▪ *nf*: **la ~** the cops *pl* (*fam*)

policía [poli'θia] *nm/f* policeman(-woman) ▪ *nf* police; *see note*

policíaco, -a [poli'θiako, a] *adj* police *cpd*; **novela policíaca** detective story

polideportivo [poliðepor'tiβo] *nm* sports centre

poliéster [poli'ester] *nm* polyester

polietileno [polieti'leno] *nm* polythene (*Brit*), polyethylene (*US*)

polifacético, -a [polifa'θetiko, a] *adj* (*persona, talento*) many-sided, versatile

poligamia [poli'ɣamja] *nf* polygamy

polígamo, -a [po'liɣamo, a] *adj* polygamous ▪ *nm* polygamist

polígono [po'liɣono] *nm* (*Mat*) polygon; (*solar*) building lot; (*zona*) area; (*unidad vecina*) housing estate; **~ industrial** industrial estate

polígrafo [po'liɣrafo] *nm* polygraph

polilla [po'liʎa] *nf* moth

Polinesia [poli'nesja] *nf* Polynesia

polinesio, -a [poli'nesjo, a] *adj, nm/f* Polynesian

polio ['poljo] *nf* polio

Polisario [poli'sarjo] *nm abr* (*Pol*: *tb*: **Frente Polisario**) = **Frente Político de Liberación del Sáhara y Río de Oro**

politécnico [poli'tekniko] *nm* polytechnic

político, -a [po'litiko, a] *adj* political; (*discreto*) tactful; (*pariente*) in-law ▪ *nm/f* politician ▪ *nf* politics *sg*; (*económica, agraria*) policy; **padre ~** father-in-law; **política exterior/de ingresos y precios** foreign/ prices and incomes policy

póliza ['poliθa] *nf* certificate, voucher; (*impuesto*) tax *o* fiscal stamp; **~ de seguro(s)** insurance policy

polizón [poli'θon] *nm* (*Aviat, Naut*) stowaway

pollera [po'ʎera] *nf* (*criadero*) hencoop; (*Am*) skirt, overskirt

pollería [poʎe'ria] *nf* poulterer's (shop)

pollo ['poʎo] *nm* chicken; (*joven*) young man; (*señorito*) playboy; **~ asado** roast chicken

polo ['polo] *nm* (*Geo, Elec*) pole; (*helado*) ice lolly; (*Deporte*) polo; (*suéter*) polo-neck; **P~ Norte/Sur** North/South Pole; **esto es el ~ opuesto de lo que dijo antes** this is the exact opposite of what he said before

Polonia [po'lonja] *nf* Poland

poltrona [pol'trona] *nf* reclining chair, easy chair

polución [polu'θjon] *nf* pollution; **~ ambiental** environmental pollution

polvera [pol'βera] *nf* powder compact

polvo ['polβo] *nm* dust; (*Química, Culin, Med*) powder; (*fam!*) screw (!); **en ~** powdered; **~ de talco** talcum powder; **estar hecho ~** to be worn out *o* exhausted; **hacer algo ~** to smash sth; **hacer ~ a algn** to shatter sb; *ver tb* **polvos**

pólvora ['polβora] *nf* gunpowder; (*fuegos artificiales*) fireworks *pl*; **propagarse como la ~** (*noticia*) to spread like wildfire

polvoriento, -a [polβo'rjento, a] *adj* (*superficie*) dusty; (*sustancia*) powdery

polvorín [polβo'rin] *nm* (*fig*) powder keg

polvorosa [polβo'rosa] *adj* (*fam*): **poner pies en ~** to beat it

polvos ['polβos] *nmpl* powder *sg*

p

polvoso, -a [pol'βoso, a] *adj* (*Am*) dusty
pomada [po'maða] *nf* pomade
pomelo [po'melo] *nm* grapefruit
pómez ['pomeθ] *nf*: **piedra ~** pumice stone
pomo ['pomo] *nm* handle
pompa ['pompa] *nf* (*burbuja*) bubble; (*bomba*) pump; (*esplendor*) pomp, splendour; **pompas fúnebres** funeral *sg*
pomposo, -a [pom'poso, a] *adj* splendid, magnificent; (*pey*) pompous
pómulo ['pomulo] *nm* cheekbone
ponche ['pontʃe] *nm* punch
poncho ['pontʃo] *nm* (*Am*) poncho, cape
ponderar [ponde'rar] *vt* (*considerar*) to weigh up, consider; (*elogiar*) to praise highly, speak in praise of
pondré *etc* [pon'dre] *vb ver* **poner**
ponencia [po'nenθja] *nf* (*exposición*) (learned) paper, communication; (*informe*) report

 PALABRA CLAVE

poner [po'ner] *vt* **1** to put; (*colocar*) to place, set; (*ropa*) to put on; (*problema, la mesa*) to set; (*interés*) to show; (*telegrama*) to send; (*obra de teatro*) to put on; (*película*) to show; **ponlo más alto** turn it up; **¿qué ponen en el Excelsior?** what's on at the Excelsior?; **~ algo a secar** to put sth (out) to dry; **¡no pongas esa cara!** don't look at me like that!
2 (*tienda*) to open; (*instalar: gas etc*) to put in; (*radio, TV*) to switch *o* turn on
3 (*suponer*): **pongamos que ...** let's suppose that ...
4 (*contribuir*): **el gobierno ha puesto otro millón** the government has contributed another million
5 (*Telec*): **póngame con el Sr. López** can you put me through to Mr. López?
6 (*estar escrito*) to say; **¿qué pone aquí?** what does it say here?
7: **~ de, le han puesto de director general** they've appointed him general manager
8 (+*adj*) to make; **me estás poniendo nerviosa** you're making me nervous
9 (*dar nombre*): **al hijo le pusieron Diego** they called their son Diego
■ *vi* (*gallina*) to lay;
ponerse *vr* **1** (*colocarse*): **se puso a mi lado** he came and stood beside me; **tú ponte en esa silla** you go and sit on that chair; **ponerse en camino** to set off
2 (*vestido, cosméticos*) to put on; **¿por qué no te pones el vestido nuevo?** why don't you put on *o* wear your new dress?
3 (*sol*) to set
4 (+*adj*) to get, become; to turn; **ponerse**

enfermo/gordo/triste to get ill/fat/sad; **se puso muy serio** he got very serious; **después de lavarla la tela se puso azul** after washing it the material turned blue; **¡no te pongas así!** don't be like that!;
ponerse cómodo to make o.s. comfortable
5: **ponerse a, se puso a llorar** he started to cry; **tienes que ponerte a estudiar** you must get down to studying
6: **ponerse a bien con algn** to make it up with sb; **ponerse a mal con algn** to get on the wrong side of sb
7 (*Am*): **se me pone que ...** it seems to me that ..., I think that ...

ponga *etc* ['ponga] *vb ver* **poner**
poniente [po'njente] *nm* west
pontevedrés, -esa [ponteβe'ðres, esa] *adj* of *o* from Pontevedra ■ *nm/f* native *o* inhabitant of Pontevedra
pontificado [pontifi'kaðo] *nm* papacy
pontífice [pon'tifiθe] *nm* pope, pontiff; **el Sumo P~** His Holiness the Pope
pontón [pon'ton] *nm* pontoon
ponzoña [pon'θoɲa] *nf* poison, venom
ponzoñoso, -a [ponθo'ɲoso, a] *adj* poisonous, venomous
pop [pop] *adj inv, nm* (*Mus*) pop
popa ['popa] *nf* stern; **a ~** astern, abaft; **de ~ a proa** fore and aft
popular [popu'lar] *adj* popular; (*del pueblo*) of the people
popularice *etc* [popula'riθe] *vb ver* **popularizarse**
popularidad [populari'ðað] *nf* popularity
popularizarse [populari'θarse] *vr* to become popular
poquísimo, -a [po'kisimo, a] *adj superlativo de* **poco** very little, very few *pl*; (*casi nada*) hardly any
poquito [po'kito] *nm*: **un ~** a little bit ■ *adv* a little, a bit; **a poquitos** bit by bit

 PALABRA CLAVE

por [por] *prep* **1** (*objetivo*) for; **luchar ~ la patria** to fight for one's country; **hazlo ~ mí** do it for my sake
2 (+*infin*): **~ no llegar tarde** so as not to arrive late; **~ citar unos ejemplos** to give a few examples
3 (*causa*) out of, because of; **no es ~ eso** that's not the reason; **~ escasez de fondos** through *o* for lack of funds
4 (*tiempo*): **~ la mañana/noche** in the morning/at night; **se queda ~ una semana** she's staying (for) a week

5 (*lugar*): **pasar ~ Madrid** to pass through Madrid; **ir a Guayaquil ~ Quito** to go to Guayaquil via Quito; **caminar ~ la calle** to walk along the street; **~ allí** over there; **se va ~ ahí** we have to go that way; **¿hay un banco ~ aquí?** is there a bank near here?; **¿~ dónde?** which way?; **está ~ el norte** it's somewhere in the north; **~ todo el país** throughout the country

6 (*cambio, precio*): **te doy uno nuevo ~ el que tienes** I'll give you a new one (in return) for the one you've got; **lo vendí ~ 15 dólares** I sold it for 15 dollars

7 (*valor distributivo*): **30 euros ~ hora/cabeza** 30 euros an o per hour/a o per head; **10 ~ ciento** 10 per cent; **80 (kms) ~ hora** 80 (km) an o per hour

8 (*modo, medio*) by; **~ correo/avión** by post/air; **día ~ día** day by day; **~ orden** in order; **entrar ~ la entrada principal** to go in through the main entrance

9 (*agente*) by; **hecho ~ él** done by him; **"dirigido ~"** "directed by"

10: **10 ~ 10 son 100** 10 by 10 is 100

11 (*en lugar de*): **vino él ~ su jefe** he came instead of his boss

12: **~ mí que revienten** as far as I'm concerned they can drop dead

13 (*evidencia*): **~ lo que dicen** judging by o from what they say

14: **estar/quedar ~ hacer** to be still o remain to be done

15: **~ (muy) difícil que sea** however hard it is o may be; **~ más que lo intente** no matter how o however hard I try

16: **~ qué** why?; **¿~ qué?** why?; **¿~?** (*fam*) why (do you ask)?

porcelana [porθe'lana] *nf* porcelain, china
porcentaje [porθen'taxe] *nm* percentage; **~ de actividad** (*Inform*) hit rate
porche ['portʃe] *nm* (*de una plaza*) arcade; (*de casa*) porch
porción [por'θjon] *nf* (*parte*) portion, share; (*cantidad*) quantity, amount
pordiosero, -a [porðjo'sero, a] *nm/f* beggar
porfía [por'fia] *nf* persistence; (*terquedad*) obstinacy
porfiado, -a [por'fjaðo, a] *adj* persistent; obstinate
porfiar [por'fjar] *vi* to persist, insist; (*disputar*) to argue stubbornly
pormenor [porme'nor] *nm* detail, particular
pormenorice *etc* [pormeno'riθe] *vb ver* **pormenorizar**
pormenorizar [pormenori'θar] *vt* to (set out in) detail ▪ *vi* to go into detail

porno ['porno] *adj inv* porno ▪ *nm* porn
pornografía [pornoɣra'fia] *nf* pornography
poro ['poro] *nm* pore
poroso, -a [po'roso, a] *adj* porous
poroto [po'roto] *nm* (*Am*) kidney bean
porque ['porke] *conj* (*a causa de*) because; (*ya que*) since; **~ sí** because I feel like it
porqué [por'ke] *nm* reason, cause
porquería [porke'ria] *nf* (*suciedad*) filth, muck, dirt; (*acción*) dirty trick; (*objeto*) small thing, trifle; (*fig*) rubbish
porqueriza [porke'riθa] *nf* pigsty
porra ['porra] *nf* (*arma*) truncheon; **¡porras!** oh heck!; **¡vete a la ~!** go to heck!
porrazo [po'rraθo] *nm* (*golpe*) blow; (*caída*) bump; **de un ~** in one go
porro ['porro] *nm* joint
porrón [po'rron] *nm* wine jar with a long spout
portaaviones [port(a)a'βjones] *nm inv* aircraft carrier
portada [por'taða] *nf* (*Tip*) title page; (: *de revista*) cover
portador, a [porta'ðor, a] *nm/f* carrier, bearer; (*Com*) bearer, payee; (*Med*) carrier; **ser ~ del virus del sida** to be HIV-positive
portaequipajes [portaeki'paxes] *nm inv* boot (*Brit*), trunk (*US*); (*baca*) luggage rack
portafolio [porta'foljo], **portafolios** [porta'foljos] *nm* (*Am*) briefcase; **~(s) de inversiones** (*Com*) investment portfolio
portal [por'tal] *nm* (*entrada*) vestibule, hall; (*pórtico*) porch, doorway; (*puerta de entrada*) main door; (*Deporte*) goal; **portales** *nmpl* arcade *sg*
portaligas [porta'liɣas] *nm inv* (*Am*) suspender belt
portamaletas [portama'letas] *nm inv* roof rack
portamonedas [portamo'neðas] *nm inv* purse
portar [por'tar] *vt* to carry, bear; **portarse** *vr* to behave, conduct o.s.; **portarse mal** to misbehave; **se portó muy bien conmigo** he treated me very well
portátil [por'tatil] *adj* portable; **(ordenador) ~** laptop (computer)
portaviones [porta'βjones] *nm inv* aircraft carrier
portavoz [porta'βoθ] *nm/f* spokesman(-woman)
portazo [por'taθo] *nm*: **dar un ~** to slam the door
porte ['porte] *nm* (*Com*) transport; (*precio*) transport charges *pl*; (*Correos*) postage; **~ debido** (*Com*) carriage forward; **~ pagado** (*Com*) carriage paid, post-paid

p

portento [por'tento] *nm* marvel, wonder
portentoso, -a [porten'toso, a] *adj*
marvellous, extraordinary
porteño, -a [por'teɲo, a] *adj* of *o* from
Buenos Aires ■ *nm/f* native *o* inhabitant of
Buenos Aires
portería [porte'ria] *nf* (*oficina*) porter's office;
(*gol*) goal
portero, -a [por'tero, a] *nm/f* porter; (*conserje*)
caretaker; (*Deporte*) goalkeeper
pórtico ['portiko] *nm* (*porche*) portico, porch;
(*fig*) gateway; (*arcada*) arcade
portilla [por'tiʎa] *nf*, **portillo** [por'tiʎo] *nm*
gate
portorriqueño, -a [portorri'keɲo, a] *adj, nm/f*
Puerto Rican
portuario, -a [por'twarjo] *adj* (*del puerto*)
port *cpd*, harbour *cpd*; (*del muelle*) dock *cpd*;
trabajador ~ docker
Portugal [portu'ɣal] *nm* Portugal
portugués, -esa [portu'ɣes, esa] *adj, nm/f*
Portuguese ■ *nm* (*Ling*) Portuguese
porvenir [porβe'nir] *nm* future
pos [pos]: **en ~ de** *prep* after, in pursuit of
posada [po'saða] *nf* (*refugio*) shelter, lodging;
(*mesón*) guest house; **dar ~ a** to give shelter
to, take in
posaderas [posa'ðeras] *nfpl* backside *sg*,
buttocks
posar [po'sar] *vt* (*en el suelo*) to lay down, put
down; (*la mano*) to place, put gently ■ *vi* to
sit, pose; **posarse** *vr* to settle; (*pájaro*) to
perch; (*avión*) to land, come down
posdata [pos'ðata] *nf* postscript
pose ['pose] *nf* (*Arte, afectación*) pose
poseedor, a [posee'ðor, a] *nm/f* owner,
possessor; (*de récord, puesto*) holder
poseer [pose'er] *vt* to have, possess, own;
(*ventaja*) to enjoy; (*récord, puesto*) to hold
poseído, -a [pose'iðo, a] *adj* possessed; **estar**
muy ~ de to be very vain about
posesión [pose'sjon] *nf* possession; **tomar ~**
(de) to take over
posesionarse [posesjo'narse] *vr*: **~ de** to take
possession of, take over
posesivo, -a [pose'siβo, a] *adj* possessive
poseyendo *etc* [pose'jendo] *vb ver* **poseer**
posgrado [pos'ɣraðo] *nm* = **postgrado**
posgraduado, -a [posɣra'ðwaðo, a] *adj, nm/f*
= **postgraduado**
posguerra [pos'ɣerra] *nf* = **postguerra**
posibilidad [posiβili'ðað] *nf* possibility;
(*oportunidad*) chance
posibilitar [posiβili'tar] *vt* to make possible,
permit; (*hacer factible*) to make feasible
posible [po'siβle] *adj* possible; (*factible*)
feasible ■ *nm*: **posibles** means; (*bienes*)

funds, assets; **de ser ~** if possible; **en** *o*
dentro de lo ~ as far as possible; **lo antes ~**
as quickly as possible
posición [posi'θjon] *nf* (*gen*) position; (*rango
social*) status
positivo, -a [posi'tiβo, a] *adj* positive ■ *nf*
(*Foto*) print
poso ['poso] *nm* sediment
posoperatorio, -a [posopera'torjo, a] *adj, nm*
= **postoperatorio**
posponer [pospo'ner] *vt* to put behind *o*
below; (*aplazar*) to postpone
posponga *etc* [pos'ponga], **pospuesto**
[pos'pwesto], **pospuse** *etc* [pos'puse] *vb ver*
posponer
post [post] *nm* (*en sitio web*) post
posta ['posta] *nf* (*de caballos*) relay, team;
a ~ on purpose, deliberately
postal [pos'tal] *adj* postal ■ *nf* postcard
poste ['poste] *nm* (*de telégrafos*) post, pole;
(*columna*) pillar
póster (*pl* **posters**) ['poster, 'posters] *nm*
poster
postergar [poster'ɣar] *vt* (*esp Am*) to put off,
postpone, delay
postergue *etc* [pos'terɣe] *vb ver* **postergar**
posteridad [posteri'ðað] *nf* posterity
posterior [poste'rjor] *adj* back, rear; (*siguiente*)
following, subsequent; (*más tarde*) later; **ser**
~ a to be later than
posterioridad [posterjori'ðað] *nf*: **con ~** later,
subsequently
postgrado [post'ɣraðo] *nm*: **curso de ~**
postgraduate course
postgraduado, -a [postɣra'ðwaðo, a] *adj*,
nm/f postgraduate
postguerra [post'ɣerra] *nf* postwar period;
en la ~ after the war
postigo [pos'tiɣo] *nm* (*portillo*) postern;
(*contraventana*) shutter
postín [pos'tin] *nm* (*fam*) elegance; **de ~** posh;
darse ~ to show off
postizo, -a [pos'tiθo, a] *adj* false, artificial;
(*sonrisa*) false, phoney ■ *nm* hairpiece
postoperatorio, -a [postopera'torjo, a] *adj*
postoperative ■ *nm* postoperative period
postor, a [pos'tor, a] *nm/f* bidder; **mejor ~**
highest bidder
postrado, -a [pos'traðo, a] *adj* prostrate
postrar [pos'trar] *vt* (*derribar*) to cast down,
overthrow; (*humillar*) to humble; (*Med*) to
weaken, exhaust; **postrarse** *vr* to prostrate
o.s.
postre ['postre] *nm* sweet, dessert ■ *nf*: **a la**
~ in the end, when all is said and done; **para**
~ (*fam*) to crown it all; **llegar a los postres**
(*fig*) to come too late

postrero, -a [pos'trero, a] *adj* (*antes de nmsg* **postrer**) (*último*) last; (: *que viene detrás*) rear
postrimerías [postrime'rias] *nfpl* final stages
postulado [postu'laðo] *nm* postulate
postulante [postu'lante] *nm/f* petitioner; (*Rel*) postulant
póstumo, -a ['postumo, a] *adj* posthumous
postura [pos'tura] *nf* (*del cuerpo*) posture, position; (*fig*) attitude, position
post-venta [pos'βenta] *adj* (*Com*) after-sales
potable [po'taβle] *adj* drinkable
potaje [po'taxe] *nm* thick vegetable soup
pote ['pote] *nm* pot, jar
potencia [po'tenθja] *nf* power; (*capacidad*) capacity; ~ (**en caballos**) horsepower; **en** ~ potential, in the making; **las grandes potencias** the great powers
potencial [poten'θjal] *adj, nm* potential
potenciar [poten'θjar] *vt* (*promover*) to promote; (*fortalecer*) to boost
potente [po'tente] *adj* powerful
potestad [potes'taδ] *nf* authority; **patria** ~ paternal authority
potosí [poto'si] *nm* fortune; **cuesta un** ~ it costs the earth
potra ['potra] *nf* (*Zool*) filly; **tener** ~ to be lucky
potro ['potro] *nm* (*Zool*) colt; (*Deporte*) vaulting horse
pozo ['poθo] *nm* well; (*de río*) deep pool; (*de mina*) shaft; ~ **negro** cesspool; **ser un** ~ **de ciencia** (*fig*) to be deeply learned
PP *abr* (= *por poderes*) pp; (= *porte pagado*) carriage paid ■ *nm abr* = **Partido Popular**
p.p. *abr* = **por poderes**
p.p.m. *abr* (= *palabras por minuto*) wpm
práctica ['praktika] *nf ver* **práctico**
practicable [prakti'kaβle] *adj* practicable; (*camino*) passable, usable
prácticamente ['praktikamente] *adv* practically
practicante [prakti'kante] *nm/f* (*Med*: *ayudante de doctor*) medical assistant; (: *enfermero*) nurse; (*el que practica algo*) practitioner ■ *adj* practising
practicar [prakti'kar] *vt* to practise; (*deporte*) to go in for, play; (*ejecutar*) to carry out, perform
práctico, -a ['praktiko, a] *adj* (*gen*) practical; (*conveniente*) handy; (*instruído*: *persona*) skilled, expert ■ *nf* practice; (*método*) method; (*arte, capacidad*) skill; **en la práctica** in practice
practique *etc* [prak'tike] *vb ver* **practicar**
pradera [pra'ðera] *nf* meadow; (*de Canadá*) prairie
prado ['praðo] *nm* (*campo*) meadow, field; (*pastizal*) pasture; (*Am*) lawn

Praga ['praɣa] *nf* Prague
pragmático, -a [praɣ'matiko, a] *adj* pragmatic
preámbulo [pre'ambulo] *nm* preamble, introduction; **decir algo sin preámbulos** to say sth without beating about the bush
precalentamiento [prekalenta'mjento] *nm* (*Deporte*) warm-up
precalentar [prekalen'tar] *vt* to preheat
precaliente *etc* [preka'ljente] *vb ver* **precalentar**
precario, -a [pre'karjo, a] *adj* precarious
precaución [prekau'θjon] *nf* (*medida preventiva*) preventive measure, precaution; (*prudencia*) caution, wariness
precaver [preka'βer] *vt* to guard against; (*impedir*) to forestall; **precaverse** *vr*: **precaverse de** o **contra algo** to (be on one's) guard against sth
precavido, -a [preka'βiðo, a] *adj* cautious, wary
precedencia [preθe'ðenθja] *nf* precedence; (*prioridad*) priority; (*superioridad*) greater importance, superiority
precedente [preθe'ðente] *adj* preceding; (*anterior*) former ■ *nm* precedent; **sin ~(s)** unprecedented; **establecer** o **sentar un** ~ to establish o set a precedent
preceder [preθe'ðer] *vt, vi* to precede, go/come before
precepto [pre'θepto] *nm* precept
preceptor [preθep'tor] *nm* (*maestro*) teacher; (: *particular*) tutor
preciado, -a [pre'θjaðo, a] *adj* (*estimado*) esteemed, valuable
preciar [pre'θjar] *vt* to esteem, value; **preciarse** *vr* to boast; **preciarse de** to pride o.s. on
precintar [preθin'tar] *vt* (*local*) to seal off; (*producto*) to seal
precinto [pre'θinto] *nm* (*Com*: *tb*: **precinto de garantía**) seal
precio ['preθjo] *nm* (*de mercado*) price; (*costo*) cost; (*valor*) value, worth; (*de viaje*) fare; ~ **de coste** o **de cobertura** cost price; ~ **al contado** cash price; ~ **al detalle** o **al menor** retail price; ~ **al detallista** trade price; ~ **de entrega inmediata** spot price; ~ **de oferta** offer price; ~ **de oportunidad** bargain price; ~ **de salida** upset price; ~ **tope** top price; ~ **unitario** unit price; **no tener** ~ (*fig*) to be priceless; **"no importa ~"** "cost no object"
preciosidad [preθjosi'ðaδ] *nf* (*valor*) (high) value, (great) worth; (*encanto*) charm; (*cosa bonita*) beautiful thing; **es una** ~ it's lovely, it's really beautiful

P

precioso, -a [pre'θjoso, a] *adj* precious; *(de mucho valor)* valuable; *(fam)* lovely, beautiful

precipicio [preθi'piθjo] *nm* cliff, precipice; *(fig)* abyss

precipitación [preθipita'θjon] *nf* *(prisa)* haste; *(lluvia)* rainfall; *(Química)* precipitation

precipitado, -a [preθipi'taðo, a] *adj* hasty, rash; *(salida)* hasty, sudden ∎ *nm* *(Química)* precipitate

precipitar [preθipi'tar] *vt* *(arrojar)* to hurl, throw; *(apresurar)* to hasten; *(acelerar)* to speed up, accelerate; *(Química)* to precipitate; **precipitarse** *vr* to throw o.s.; *(apresurarse)* to rush; *(actuar sin pensar)* to act rashly; **precipitarse hacia** to rush towards

precisado, -a [preθi'saðo, a] *adj*: **verse ~ a hacer algo** to be obliged to do sth

precisamente [preθisa'mente] *adv* precisely; *(justo)* precisely, exactly, just; **~ por eso** for that very reason; **~ fue él quien lo dijo** as a matter of fact he said it; **no es eso ~** it's not really that

precisar [preθi'sar] *vt* *(necesitar)* to need, require; *(fijar)* to determine exactly, fix; *(especificar)* to specify; *(señalar)* to pinpoint

precisión [preθi'sjon] *nf* *(exactitud)* precision

preciso, -a [pre'θiso, a] *adj* *(exacto)* precise; *(necesario)* necessary, essential; *(estilo, lenguaje)* concise; **es ~ que lo hagas** you must do it

precocidad [prekoθi'ðað] *nf* precociousness, precocity

preconcebido, -a [prekonθe'βiðo, a] *adj* preconceived

preconice *etc* [preko'niθe] *vb ver* **preconizar**

preconizar [prekoni'θar] *vt* *(aconsejar)* to advise; *(prever)* to foresee

precoz [pre'koθ] *adj* *(persona)* precocious; *(calvicie)* premature

precursor, a [prekur'sor, a] *nm/f* precursor

predecesor, a [preðeθe'sor, a] *nm/f* predecessor

predecir [preðe'θir] *vt* to predict, foretell, forecast

predestinado, -a [preðesti'naðo, a] *adj* predestined

predeterminar [preðetermi'nar] *vt* to predetermine

predicado [preði'kaðo] *nm* predicate

predicador, a [preðika'ðor, a] *nm/f* preacher

predicar [preði'kar] *vt, vi* to preach

predicción [preðik'θjon] *nf* prediction; *(pronóstico)* forecast; **~ del tiempo** weather forecast(ing)

predicho [pre'ðitʃo], **prediga** *etc* [pre'ðiɣa], **predije** *etc* [pre'ðixe] *vb ver* **predecir**

predilecto, -a [preði'lekto, a] *adj* favourite

predique *etc* [pre'ðike] *vb ver* **predicar**

prediré *etc* [preði're] *vb ver* **predecir**

predispondré *etc* [preðispon'dre] *vb ver* **predisponer**

predisponer [preðispo'ner] *vt* to predispose; *(pey)* to prejudice

predisponga *etc* [preðis'ponga] *vb ver* **predisponer**

predisposición [preðisposi'θjon] *nf* predisposition, inclination; prejudice, bias; *(Med)* tendency

predispuesto [preðis'pwesto], **predispuse** *etc* [preðis'puse] *vb ver* **predisponer**

predominante [preðomi'nante] *adj* predominant; *(preponderante)* prevailing; *(interés)* controlling

predominar [preðomi'nar] *vt* to dominate ∎ *vi* to predominate; *(prevalecer)* to prevail

predominio [preðo'minjo] *nm* predominance; prevalence

preescolar [preesko'lar] *adj* preschool

preestreno [prees'treno] *nm* preview, press view

prefabricado, -a [prefaβri'kaðo, a] *adj* prefabricated

prefacio [pre'faθjo] *nm* preface

preferencia [prefe'renθja] *nf* preference; **de ~** preferably, for preference; **localidad de ~** reserved seat

preferible [prefe'riβle] *adj* preferable

preferido, a [prefe'riðo, a] *adj, nm/f* favourite, favorite *(US)*

preferir [prefe'rir] *vt* to prefer

prefiera *etc* [pre'fjera] *vb ver* **preferir**

prefijo [pre'fixo] *nm* prefix

prefiriendo *etc* [prefi'rjendo] *vb ver* **preferir**

pregón [pre'ɣon] *nm* proclamation, announcement

pregonar [preɣo'nar] *vt* to proclaim, announce; *(mercancía)* to hawk

pregonero [preɣo'nero] *nm* town crier

pregunta [pre'ɣunta] *nf* question; **~ capciosa** catch question; **hacer una ~** to ask a question; **preguntas frecuentes** FAQs, frequently asked questions

preguntar [preɣun'tar] *vt* to ask; *(cuestionar)* to question ∎ *vi* to ask; **preguntarse** *vr* to wonder; **~ por algn** to ask for sb; **~ por la salud de algn** to ask after sb's health

preguntón, -ona [preɣun'ton, ona] *adj* inquisitive

prehistórico, -a [preis'toriko, a] *adj* prehistoric

prejuicio [pre'xwiθjo] *nm* prejudgement; *(preconcepción)* preconception; *(pey)* prejudice, bias

prejuzgar [prexuθ'ɣar] *vt* *(predisponerse)* to prejudge

prejuzgue *etc* [pre'xuθγe] *vb ver* **prejuzgar**
preliminar [prelimi'nar] *adj, nm* preliminary
preludio [pre'luðjo] *nm* (*Mus, fig*) prelude
premamá [prema'ma] *adj:* **vestido ~**
maternity dress
prematrimonial [prematrimo'njal] *adj:*
relaciones prematrimoniales premarital sex
prematuro, -a [prema'turo, a] *adj* premature
premeditación [premeðita'θjon] *nf*
premeditation
premeditado, -a [premeði'taðo, a] *adj*
premeditated, deliberate; (*intencionado*)
wilful
premeditar [premeði'tar] *vt* to premeditate
premiar [pre'mjar] *vt* to reward; (*en un
concurso*) to give a prize to
premio ['premjo] *nm* reward; prize; (*Com*)
premium; **~ gordo** first prize
premisa [pre'misa] *nf* premise
premonición [premoni'θjon] *nf* premonition
premura [pre'mura] *nf* (*prisa*) haste, urgency
prenatal [prena'tal] *adj* antenatal, prenatal
prenda ['prenda] *nf* (*de ropa*) garment, article
of clothing; (*garantía*) pledge; (*fam*) darling!;
prendas *nfpl* talents, gifts; **dejar algo en
~** to pawn sth; **no soltar ~** to give nothing
away; (*fig*) not to say a word
prendar [pren'dar] *vt* to captivate, enchant;
prendarse de algo to fall in love with sth
prendedor [prende'ðor] *nm* brooch
prender [pren'der] *vt* (*captar*) to catch,
capture; (*detener*) to arrest; (*coser*) to pin,
attach; (*sujetar*) to fasten; (*Am*) to switch
on ■ *vi* to catch; (*arraigar*) to take root;
prenderse *vr* (*encenderse*) to catch fire
prendido, -a [pren'diðo, a] *adj* (*Am: luz*) on
prensa ['prensa] *nf* press; **la P~** the press;
tener mala ~ to have o get a bad press;
la ~ nacional the national press
prensar [pren'sar] *vt* to press
preñado, -a [pre'ɲaðo, a] *adj* (*mujer*)
pregnant; **~ de** pregnant with, full of
preocupación [preokupa'θjon] *nf* worry,
concern; (*ansiedad*) anxiety
preocupado, -a [preoku'paðo, a] *adj*
worried, concerned; anxious
preocupar [preoku'par] *vt* to worry;
preocuparse *vr* to worry; **preocuparse de
algo** (*hacerse cargo de algo*) to take care of sth;
preocuparse por algo to worry about sth
preparación [prepara'θjon] *nf* (*acto*)
preparation; (*estado*) preparedness,
readiness; (*entrenamiento*) training
preparado, -a [prepa'raðo, a] *adj* (*dispuesto*)
prepared; (*Culin*) ready (to serve) ■ *nm* (*Med*)
preparation; **¡preparados, listos, ya!** ready,
steady, go!

preparar [prepa'rar] *vt* (*disponer*) to prepare,
get ready; (*Tec: tratar*) to prepare, process,
treat; (*entrenar*) to teach, train; **prepararse**
vr: **prepararse a** *o* **para hacer algo** to
prepare o get ready to do sth
preparativo, -a [prepara'tiβo] *adj*
preparatory, preliminary ■ *nm:*
preparativos *nmpl* preparations
preparatoria [prepara'torja] *nf* (*Am*) sixth
form college (*Brit*), senior high school (*US*)
preposición [preposi'θjon] *nf* preposition
prepotencia [prepo'tenθja] *nf* abuse of
power; (*Pol*) high-handedness; (*soberbia*)
arrogance
prepotente [prepo'tente] *adj* (*Pol*) high-
handed; (*soberbio*) arrogant
prerrogativa [prerroγa'tiβa] *nf* prerogative,
privilege
presa ['presa] *nf* (*cosa apresada*) catch; (*víctima*)
victim; (*de animal*) prey; (*de agua*) dam; **hacer
~ en** to clutch (on to), seize; **ser ~ de** (*fig*) to
be a prey to
presagiar [presa'xjar] *vt* to threaten
presagio [pre'saxjo] *nm* omen
presbítero [pres'βitero] *nm* priest
prescindir [presθin'dir] *vi:* **~ de** (*privarse de*)
to do without, go without; (*descartar*) to
dispense with; **no podemos ~ de él** we can't
manage without him
prescribir [preskri'βir] *vt* to prescribe
prescripción [preskrip'θjon] *nf* prescription;
~ facultativa medical prescription
prescrito [pres'krito] *pp de* **prescribir**
preseleccionar [preselek'θjo'nar] *vt* (*Deporte*)
to seed
presencia [pre'senθja] *nf* presence; **en ~ de**
in the presence of
presencial [presen'θjal] *adj:* **testigo ~**
eyewitness
presenciar [presen'θjar] *vt* to be present at;
(*asistir a*) to attend; (*ver*) to see, witness
presentación [presenta'θjon] *nf*
presentation; (*introducción*) introduction
presentador, a [presenta'ðor, a] *nm/f*
compère
presentar [presen'tar] *vt* to present; (*ofrecer*)
to offer; (*mostrar*) to show, display; (*renuncia*)
to tender; (*moción*) to propose; (*a una
persona*) to introduce; **presentarse** *vr* (*llegar
inesperadamente*) to appear, turn up; (*ofrecerse:
como candidato*) to run, stand; (*aparecer*) to
show, appear; (*solicitar empleo*) to apply;
~ al cobro (*Com*) to present for payment;
presentarse a la policía to report to the
police
presente [pre'sente] *adj* present ■ *nm*
present; (*Ling*) present (tense); (*regalo*) gift;

los presentes those present; **hacer** ~ to state, declare; **tener** ~ to remember, bear in mind; **la carta** ~, **la** ~ this letter

presentimiento [presenti'mjento] *nm* premonition, presentiment

presentir [presen'tir] *vt* to have a premonition of

preservación [preserβa'θjon] *nf* protection, preservation

preservar [preser'βar] *vt* to protect, preserve

preservativo [preserβa'tiβo] *nm* sheath, condom

presidencia [presi'ðenθja] *nf* presidency; (*de comité*) chairmanship; **ocupar la** ~ to preside, be in o take the chair

presidente [presi'ðente] *nm/f* president; chairman(-woman); (*en parlamento*) speaker; (*Jur*) presiding magistrate

presidiario [presi'ðjarjo] *nm* convict

presidio [pre'siðjo] *nm* prison, penitentiary

presidir [presi'ðir] *vt* (*dirigir*) to preside at, preside over; (: *comité*) to take the chair at; (*dominar*) to dominate, rule ■ *vi* to preside; to take the chair

presienta *etc* [pre'sjenta], **presintiendo** *etc* [presin'tjendo] *vb ver* **presentir**

presión [pre'sjon] *nf* pressure; ~ **arterial** o **sanguínea** blood pressure; **a** ~ under pressure

presionar [presjo'nar] *vt* to press; (*botón*) to push, press; (*fig*) to press, put pressure on ■ *vi*: ~ **para** o **por** to press for

preso, -a ['preso, a] *adj*: **estar** ~ **de terror** o **pánico** to be panic-stricken ■ *nm/f* prisoner; **tomar** o **llevar** ~ **a algn** to arrest sb, take sb prisoner

prestación [presta'θjon] *nf* (*aportación*) lending; (*Inform*) capability; (*servicio*) service; (*subsidio*) benefit; **prestaciones** *nfpl* (*Auto*) performance features; ~ **de juramento** oath-taking; ~ **personal** obligatory service; **P~ Social Sustitutoria** community service for conscientious objectors; *ver tb* **mili**

prestado, -a [pres'taðo, a] *adj* on loan; **dar algo** ~ to lend sth; **pedir** ~ to borrow

prestamista [presta'mista] *nm/f* moneylender

préstamo ['prestamo] *nm* loan; ~ **con garantía** loan against collateral; ~ **hipotecario** mortgage

prestar [pres'tar] *vt* to lend, loan; (*atención*) to pay; (*ayuda*) to give; (*servicio*) to do, render; (*juramento*) to take, swear; **prestarse** *vr* (*ofrecerse*) to offer o volunteer

prestatario, -a [presta'tarjo, a] *nm/f* borrower

presteza [pres'teθa] *nf* speed, promptness

prestidigitador [prestiðixita'ðor] *nm* conjurer

prestigio [pres'tixjo] *nm* prestige; (*reputación*) face; (*renombre*) good name

prestigioso, -a [presti'xjoso, a] *adj* (*honorable*) prestigious; (*famoso, renombrado*) renowned, famous

presto, -a ['presto, a] *adj* (*rápido*) quick, prompt; (*dispuesto*) ready ■ *adv* at once, right away

presumido, -a [presu'miðo, a] *adj* conceited

presumir [presu'mir] *vt* to presume ■ *vi* (*darse aires*) to be conceited; **según cabe** ~ as may be presumed, presumably; ~ **de listo** to think o.s. very smart

presunción [presun'θjon] *nf* presumption; (*sospecha*) suspicion; (*vanidad*) conceit

presunto, -a [pre'sunto, a] *adj* (*supuesto*) supposed, presumed; (*así llamado*) so-called

presuntuoso, -a [presun'twoso, a] *adj* conceited, presumptuous

presupondré *etc* [presupon'dre] *vb ver* **presuponer**

presuponer [presupo'ner] *vt* to presuppose

presuponga *etc* [presu'ponga] *vb ver* **presuponer**

presupuestar [presupwes'tar] *vi* to budget ■ *vt*: ~ **algo** to budget for sth

presupuestario, -a [presupwes'tarjo, a] *adj* (*Finanzas*) budgetary, budget *cpd*

presupuesto [presu'pwesto] *pp de* **presuponer** ■ *nm* (*Finanzas*) budget; (*estimación*: *de costo*) estimate; **asignación de** ~ (*Com*) budget appropriation

presupuse *etc* [presu'puse] *vb ver* **presuponer**

presuroso, -a [presu'roso, a] *adj* (*rápido*) quick, speedy; (*que tiene prisa*) hasty

pretencioso, -a [preten'θjoso, a] *adj* pretentious

pretender [preten'der] *vt* (*intentar*) to try to, seek to; (*reivindicar*) to claim; (*buscar*) to seek, try for; (*cortejar*) to woo, court; ~ **que** to expect that; **¿qué pretende usted?** what are you after?

pretendiente [preten'djente] *nm/f* (*candidato*) candidate, applicant; (*amante*) suitor

pretensión [preten'sjon] *nf* (*aspiración*) aspiration; (*reivindicación*) claim; (*orgullo*) pretension

pretérito, -a [pre'terito, a] *adj* (*Ling*) past; (*fig*) past, former

pretextar [preteks'tar] *vt* to plead, use as an excuse

pretexto [pre'teksto] *nm* pretext; (*excusa*) excuse; **so** ~ **de** under pretext of

pretil [pre'til] *nm* (*valla*) parapet; (*baranda*) handrail

prevalecer [preβale'θer] vi to prevail
prevaleciente [preβale'θjente] adj prevailing, prevalent
prevalezca etc [preβa'leθka] vb ver **prevalecer**
prevención [preβen'θjon] nf (preparación) preparation; (estado) preparedness, readiness; (medida) prevention; (previsión) foresight, forethought; (precaución) precaution
prevendré etc [preβen'dre], **prevenga** etc [pre'βenga] vb ver **prevenir**
prevenido, -a [preβe'niðo, a] adj prepared, ready; (cauteloso) cautious; **estar ~** (preparado) to be ready; **ser ~** (cuidadoso) to be cautious; **hombre ~ vale por dos** forewarned is forearmed
prevenir [preβe'nir] vt (impedir) to prevent; (prever) to foresee, anticipate; (predisponer) to prejudice, bias; (avisar) to warn; (preparar) to prepare, get ready; **prevenirse** vr to get ready, prepare; **prevenirse contra** to take precautions against
preventivo, -a [preβen'tiβo, a] adj preventive, precautionary
prever [pre'βer] vt to foresee; (anticipar) to anticipate
previniendo etc [preβi'njendo] vb ver **prevenir**
previo, -a ['preβjo, a] adj (anterior) previous, prior ■ prep: **~ acuerdo de los otros** subject to the agreement of the others; **~ pago de los derechos** on payment of the fees
previsible [preβi'siβle] adj foreseeable
previsión [preβi'sjon] nf (perspicacia) foresight; (predicción) forecast; (prudencia) caution; **~ de ventas** (Com) sales forecast
previsor, a [preβi'sor, a] adj (precavido) far-sighted; (prudente) thoughtful
previsto [pre'βisto] pp de **prever**
P.R.I. ['pri] nm abr (Am: = Partido Revolucionario Institucional) political party
prieto, -a ['prjeto, a] adj (oscuro) dark; (Am) dark(-skinned); (fig) mean; (comprimido) tight, compressed
prima ['prima] nf ver **primo**
primacía [prima'θia] nf primacy
primar [pri'mar] vi (tener primacía) to occupy first place; **~ sobre** to have priority over
primario, -a [pri'marjo, a] adj primary ■ nf primary education; ver tb **sistema educativo**
primavera [prima'βera] nf (temporada) spring; (período) springtime
primaveral [primaβe'ral] adj spring cpd
Primer Ministro [pri'mer-] nm Prime Minister
primero, -a [pri'mero, a] adj (antes de nmsg **primer**) first; (fig) prime; (anterior) former; (básico) fundamental ■ adv first; (más bien)

sooner, rather ■ nf (Auto) first gear; (Ferro) first class; **de primera** (fam) first-class, first-rate; **de buenas a primeras** suddenly; **primera dama** (Teat) leading lady
primicia [pri'miθja] nf (Prensa) scoop; **primicias** nfpl (tb fig) first fruits
primitivo, -a [primi'tiβo, a] adj primitive; (original) original; (Com: acción) ordinary ■ nf: **(Lotería) Primitiva** weekly state-run lottery; ver tb **lotería**
primo, -a ['primo, a] adj (Mat) prime ■ nm/f cousin; (fam) fool, dupe ■ nf (Com) bonus; (de seguro) premium; (a la exportación) subsidy; **~ hermano** first cousin; **materias primas** raw materials; **hacer el ~** to be taken for a ride
primogénito, -a [primo'xenito, a] adj first-born
primor [pri'mor] nm (cuidado) care; **es un ~** it's lovely
primordial [primor'ðjal] adj basic, fundamental
primoroso, -a [primo'roso, a] adj exquisite, fine
princesa [prin'θesa] nf princess
principado [prinθi'paðo] nm principality
principal [prinθi'pal] adj principal, main; (más destacado) foremost; (piso) first, second (US); (Inform) foreground ■ nm (jefe) chief, principal
príncipe ['prinθipe] nm prince; **~ heredero** crown prince; **P~ de Asturias** King's son and heir to the Spanish throne; **~ de gales** (tela) check
principiante [prinθi'pjante] nm/f beginner; (novato) novice
principio [prin'θipjo] nm (comienzo) beginning, start; (origen) origin; (base) rudiment, basic idea; (moral) principle; **a principios de** at the beginning of; **desde el ~** from the first; **en un ~** at first
pringar [prin'gar] vt (Culin: pan) to dip; (ensuciar) to dirty; **pringarse** vr to get splashed o soiled; **~ a algn en un asunto** (fam) to involve sb in a matter
pringoso, -a [prin'goso, a] adj greasy; (pegajoso) sticky
pringue etc ['pringe] vb ver **pringar** ■ nm (grasa) grease, fat, dripping
prioridad [priori'ðað] nf priority; (Auto) right of way
prioritario, -a [priori'tarjo, a] adj (Inform) foreground
prisa ['prisa] nf (apresuramiento) hurry, haste; (rapidez) speed; (urgencia) (sense of) urgency; **correr ~** to be urgent; **darse ~** to hurry up; **estar de o tener ~** to be in a hurry
prisión [pri'sjon] nf (cárcel) prison; (período de cárcel) imprisonment

P

prisionero, -a [prisjo'nero, a] *nm/f* prisoner
prismáticos [pris'matikos] *nmpl* binoculars
privación [priβa'θjon] *nf* deprivation;
(*falta*) want, privation; **privaciones** *nfpl*
hardships, privations
privado, -a [pri'βaðo, a] *adj* (*particular*)
private; (*Pol: favorito*) favourite (*Brit*),
favorite (*US*); **en** ~ privately, in private; **"~ y
confidencial"** "private and confidential"
privar [pri'βar] *vt* to deprive; **privarse** *vr:*
privarse de (*abstenerse de*) to deprive o.s. of;
(*renunciar a*) to give up
privativo, -a [priβa'tiβo, a] *adj* exclusive
privatizar [priβati'θar] *vt* to privatize
privilegiado, -a [priβile'xjaðo, a] *adj*
privileged; (*memoria*) very good ■ *nm/f*
(*afortunado*) privileged person
privilegiar [priβile'xjar] *vt* to grant a
privilege to; (*favorecer*) to favour
privilegio [priβi'lexjo] *nm* privilege;
(*concesión*) concession
pro [pro] *nm o nf* profit, advantage ■ *prep:*
asociación ~ ciegos association for the blind
■ *pref:* ~ **soviético/americano** pro-Soviet/-
American; **en ~ de** on behalf of, for; **los pros
y los contras** the pros and cons
proa ['proa] *nf* (*Naut*) bow, prow
probabilidad [proβaβili'ðað] *nf* probability,
likelihood; (*oportunidad, posibilidad*) chance,
prospect
probable [pro'βaβle] *adj* probable, likely;
es ~ que (+*subjun*) it is probable o likely that;
es ~ que no venga he probably won't come
probador [proβa'ðor] *nm* (*persona*) taster (*of
wine etc*); (*en una tienda*) fitting room
probar [pro'βar] *vt* (*demostrar*) to prove;
(*someter a prueba*) to test, try out; (*ropa*) to try
on; (*comida*) to taste ■ *vi* to try; **probarse** *vr:*
probarse un traje to try on a suit
probeta [pro'βeta] *nf* test tube
problema [pro'βlema] *nm* problem
procaz [pro'kaθ] *adj* insolent, impudent
procedencia [proθe'ðenθja] *nf* (*principio*)
source, origin; (*lugar de salida*) point of
departure
procedente [proθe'ðente] *adj* (*razonable*)
reasonable; (*conforme a derecho*) proper,
fitting; ~ **de** coming from, originating in
proceder [proθe'ðer] *vi* (*avanzar*) to proceed;
(*actuar*) to act; (*ser correcto*) to be right (and
proper), be fitting ■ *nm* (*comportamiento*)
behaviour, conduct; **no procede obrar así**
it is not right to act like that; ~ **de** to come
from, originate in
procedimiento [proθeði'mjento] *nm*
procedure; (*proceso*) process; (*método*) means,
method; (*trámite*) proceedings *pl*

prócer ['proθer] *nm* (*persona eminente*) worthy;
(*líder*) great man, leader; (*esp Am*) national
hero
procesado, -a [proθe'saðo, a] *nm/f* accused
(person)
procesador [proθesa'ðor] *nm:* ~ **de textos**
(*Inform*) word processor
procesamiento [proθesa'mjento] *nm* (*Inform*)
processing; ~ **de datos** data processing;
~ **por lotes** batch processing; ~ **solapado**
multiprogramming; ~ **de textos** word
processing
procesar [proθe'sar] *vt* to try, put on trial;
(*Inform*) to process
procesión [proθe'sjon] *nf* procession; **la ~ va
por dentro** he keeps his troubles to himself
proceso [pro'θeso] *nm* process; (*Jur*) trial;
(*lapso*) course (of time); (*Inform*): ~
(**automático**) **de datos** (automatic) data
processing; ~ **no prioritario** background
process; ~ **por pasadas** batch processing;
~ **en tiempo real** real-time programming
proclama [pro'klama] *nf* (*acto*) proclamation;
(*cartel*) poster
proclamar [prokla'mar] *vt* to proclaim
proclive [pro'kliβe] *adj:* ~ **(a)** inclined o
prone (to)
procreación [prokrea'θjon] *nf* procreation
procrear [prokre'ar] *vt, vi* to procreate
procurador, a [prokura'ðor, a] *nm/f* attorney,
solicitor
procurar [proku'rar] *vt* (*intentar*) to try,
endeavour; (*conseguir*) to get, obtain;
(*asegurar*) to secure; (*producir*) to produce
prodigar [proði'ɣar] *vt* to lavish; **prodigarse**
vr: **prodigarse en** to be lavish with
prodigio [pro'ðixjo] *nm* prodigy; (*milagro*)
wonder, marvel; **niño ~** child prodigy
prodigioso, -a [proði'xjoso, a] *adj*
prodigious, marvellous
pródigo, -a ['proðiɣo, a] *adj* (*rico*) rich,
productive; **hijo ~** prodigal son
producción [proðuk'θjon] *nf* production;
(*suma de productos*) output; (*producto*) product;
~ **en serie** mass production
producir [proðu'θir] *vt* to produce; (*generar*) to
cause, bring about; (*impresión*) to give; (*Com:
interés*) to bear; **producirse** *vr* (*gen*) to come
about, happen; (*hacerse*) to be produced, be
made; (*estallar*) to break out; (*accidente*) to
take place
productividad [proðuktiβi'ðað] *nf*
productivity
productivo, -a [proðuk'tiβo, a] *adj*
productive; (*provechoso*) profitable
producto [pro'ðukto] *nm* (*resultado*) product;
(*producción*) production; ~ **alimenticio**

foodstuff; ~ **(nacional) bruto** gross
(national) product; ~ **interno bruto** gross
domestic product
productor, a [proðuk'tor, a] *adj* productive,
producing ∎ *nm/f* producer
produje [pro'ðuxe], **produjera** [proðu'xera],
produzca *etc* [pro'ðuθka] *vb ver* **producir**
proeza [pro'eθa] *nf* exploit, feat
profanar [profa'nar] *vt* to desecrate, profane
profano, -a [pro'fano, a] *adj* profane ∎ *nm/f*
(*inexperto*) layman(-woman); **soy ~ en
música** I don't know anything about music
profecía [profe'θia] *nf* prophecy
proferir [profe'rir] *vt* (*palabra, sonido*) to utter;
(*injuria*) to hurl, let fly
profesar [profe'sar] *vt* (*declarar*) to profess;
(*practicar*) to practise
profesión [profe'sjon] *nf* profession;
(*confesión*) avowal; **abogado de ~, de ~
abogado** a lawyer by profession
profesional [profesjo'nal] *adj* professional
profesor, a [profe'sor, a] *nm/f* teacher;
(*instructor*) instructor; ~ **de universidad**
lecturer; ~ **adjunto** assistant lecturer,
associate professor (*US*)
profesorado [profeso'raðo] *nm* (*profesión*)
teaching profession; (*cuerpo*) teaching staff,
faculty (*US*); (*cargo*) professorship
profeta [pro'feta] *nm/f* prophet
profetice *etc* [profe'tiθe] *vb ver* **profetizar**
profetizar [profeti'θar] *vt, vi* to prophesy
profiera *etc* [pro'fjera], **profiriendo** *etc*
[profi'rjendo] *vb ver* **proferir**
profilaxis [profi'laksis] *nf inv* prevention
prófugo, -a ['profuɣo, a] *nm/f* fugitive;
(*desertor*) deserter
profundice *etc* [profun'diθe] *vb ver*
profundizar
profundidad [profundi'ðað] *nf* depth;
tener una ~ de 30 cm to be 30 cm deep
profundizar [profundi'θar] *vt* (*fig*) to go
deeply into, study in depth
profundo, -a [pro'fundo, a] *adj* deep;
(*misterio, pensador*) profound; **poco ~** shallow
profusión [profu'sjon] *nf* (*abundancia*)
profusion; (*prodigalidad*) wealth
progenie [pro'xenje] *nf* offspring
progenitor [proxeni'tor] *nm* ancestor;
progenitores *nmpl* (*fam*) parents
programa [pro'ɣrama] *nm* programme;
(*Inform*) program; ~ **de estudios** curriculum,
syllabus; ~ **verificador de ortografía**
(*Inform*) spelling checker
programación [proɣrama'θjon] *nf* (*Inform*)
programming; ~ **estructurada** structured
programming
programador, a [proɣrama'ðor, a] *nm/f*

(*computer*) programmer; ~ **de aplicaciones**
applications programmer
programar [proɣra'mar] *vt* (*Inform*) to
programme
progre ['proɣre] *adj* (*fam*) liberal
progresar [proɣre'sar] *vi* to progress, make
progress
progresión [proɣres'jon] *nf*: ~ **geométrica/
aritmética** geometric/arithmetic
progression
progresista [proɣre'sista] *adj, nm/f*
progressive
progresivo, -a [proɣre'siβo, a] *adj*
progressive; (*gradual*) gradual; (*continuo*)
continuous
progreso [pro'ɣreso] *nm* (*tb*: **progresos**)
progress; **hacer progresos** to progress,
advance
prohibición [proiβi'θjon] *nf* prohibition,
ban; **levantar la ~ de** to remove the ban on
prohibir [proi'βir] *vt* to prohibit, ban, forbid;
se prohíbe fumar no smoking
prohibitivo, -a [proiβi'tiβo, a] *adj*
prohibitive
prójimo, -a ['proximo, a] *nm* fellow man
∎ *nm/f* (*vecino*) neighbour
prole ['prole] *nf* (*descendencia*) offspring
proletariado [proleta'rjaðo] *nm* proletariat
proletario, -a [prole'tarjo, a] *adj, nm/f*
proletarian
proliferación [prolifera'θjon] *nf*
proliferation; ~ **de armas nucleares** spread
of nuclear arms
proliferar [prolife'rar] *vi* to proliferate
prolífico, -a [pro'lifiko, a] *adj* prolific
prolijo, -a [pro'lixo, a] *adj* long-winded,
tedious; (*Am*) neat
prólogo ['proloɣo] *nm* prologue; (*preámbulo*)
preface, introduction
prolongación [prolonga'θjon] *nf* extension
prolongado, -a [prolon'gaðo, a] *adj* (*largo*)
long; (*alargado*) lengthy
prolongar [prolon'gar] *vt* (*gen*) to extend;
(*en el tiempo*) to prolong; (*calle, tubo*) to make
longer, extend; **prolongarse** *vr* (*alargarse*) to
extend, go on
prolongue *etc* [pro'longe] *vb ver* **prolongar**
prom. *abr* (= *promedio*) av.
promedio [pro'meðjo] *nm* average; (*de
distancia*) middle, mid-point
promesa [pro'mesa] *nf* promise ∎ *adj*:
jugador ~ promising player; **faltar a una ~**
to break a promise
prometer [prome'ter] *vt* to promise ∎ *vi* to
show promise; **prometerse** *vr* (*dos personas*)
to get engaged
prometido, -a [prome'tiðo, a] *adj* promised;

P

engaged ■ nm/f fiancé/fiancée
prominente [promi'nente] adj prominent
promiscuidad [promiskwi'ðað] nf
promiscuity
promiscuo, -a [pro'miskwo, a] adj
promiscuous
promoción [promo'θjon] nf promotion; (año)
class, year; ~ **por correspondencia directa**
(Com) direct mailshot; ~ **de ventas** sales
promotion o drive
promocionar [promoθjo'nar] vt (Com: dar
publicidad) to promote
promontorio [promon'torjo] nm
promontory
promotor [promo'tor] nm promoter;
(instigador) instigator
promover [promo'βer] vt to promote; (causar)
to cause; (juicio) to bring; (motín) to instigate,
stir up
promueva etc [pro'mweβa] vb ver **promover**
promulgar [promul'ɣar] vt to promulgate;
(fig) to proclaim
promulgue etc [pro'mulɣe] vb ver **promulgar**
pronombre [pro'nombre] nm pronoun
pronosticar [pronosti'kar] vt to predict,
foretell, forecast
pronóstico [pro'nostiko] nm prediction,
forecast; (profecía) omen; (Med: diagnóstico)
prognosis; **de ~ leve** slight, not serious;
~ **del tiempo** weather forecast
pronostique etc [pronos'tike] vb ver
pronosticar
prontitud [pronti'tuð] nf speed, quickness
pronto, -a ['pronto, a] adj (rápido) prompt,
quick; (preparado) ready ■ adv quickly,
promptly; (en seguida) at once, right away;
(dentro de poco) soon; (temprano) early ■ nm
urge, sudden feeling; **tener prontos de
enojo** to be quick-tempered; **al ~** at first;
de ~ suddenly; **¡hasta ~!** see you soon!; **lo
más ~ posible** as soon as possible; **por lo ~**
meanwhile, for the present; **tan ~ como** as
soon as
pronunciación [pronunθja'θjon] nf
pronunciation
pronunciado, -a [pronun'θjaðo, a] adj
(marcado) pronounced; (curva etc) sharp;
(facciones) marked
pronunciamiento [pronunθja'mjento] nm
(rebelión) insurrection
pronunciar [pronun'θjar] vt to pronounce;
(discurso) to make, deliver; (Jur: sentencia)
to pass, pronounce; **pronunciarse** vr to
revolt, rise, rebel; (declararse) to declare o.s.;
pronunciarse sobre to pronounce on
propagación [propaɣa'θjon] nf propagation;
(difusión) spread(ing)

propaganda [propa'ɣanda] nf (política)
propaganda; (comercial) advertising; **hacer ~
de** (Com) to advertise
propagar [propa'ɣar] vt to propagate;
(difundir) to spread, disseminate; **propagarse**
vr (Bio) to propagate; (fig) to spread
propague etc [pro'paɣe] vb ver **propagar**
propalar [propa'lar] vt (divulgar) to divulge;
(publicar) to publish an account of
propano [pro'pano] nm propane
propasarse [propa'sarse] vr (excederse) to go
too far; (sexualmente) to take liberties
propensión [propen'sjon] nf inclination,
propensity
propenso, -a [pro'penso, a] adj: ~ **a** prone o
inclined to; **ser ~ a hacer algo** to be inclined
o have a tendency to do sth
propiamente [propja'mente] adv properly;
(realmente) really, exactly; ~ **dicho** real, true
propicio, -a [pro'piθjo, a] adj favourable,
propitious
propiedad [propje'ðað] nf property; (posesión)
possession, ownership; (conveniencia)
suitability; (exactitud) accuracy; ~ **particular**
private property; ~ **pública** (Com) public
ownership; **ceder algo a algn en ~** to
transfer to sb the full rights over sth
propietario, -a [propje'tarjo, a] nm/f owner,
proprietor
propina [pro'pina] nf tip; **dar algo de ~** to
give something extra
propinar [propi'nar] vt (golpe) to strike;
(azotes) to give
propio, -a ['propjo, a] adj own, of one's
own; (característico) characteristic, typical;
(conveniente) proper; (mismo) selfsame, very;
el ~ ministro the minister himself; **¿tienes
casa propia?** have you a house of your own?;
eso es muy ~ de él that's just like him;
tiene un olor muy ~ it has a smell of its own
propondré etc [propon'dre] vb ver **proponer**
proponente [propo'nente] nm proposer,
mover
proponer [propo'ner] vt to propose, put
forward; (candidato) to propose, nominate;
(problema) to pose; **proponerse** vr to propose,
plan, intend
proponga etc [pro'ponga] vb ver **proponer**
proporción [propor'θjon] nf proportion;
(Mat) ratio; (razón, porcentaje) rate;
proporciones nfpl dimensions; (fig) size sg;
en ~ con in proportion to
proporcionado, -a [proporθjo'naðo, a] adj
proportionate; (regular) medium, middling;
(justo) just right; **bien ~** well-proportioned
proporcional [proporθjo'nal] adj
proportional; ~ **a** proportional to

proporcionar [proporθjo'nar] vt (dar) to give, supply, provide; **esto le proporciona una renta anual de ...** this brings him in a yearly income of ...

proposición [proposi'θjon] nf proposition; (propuesta) proposal

propósito [pro'posito] nm (intención) purpose; (intento) aim, intention ■ adv: **a ~** by the way, incidentally; **a ~ de** about, with regard to

propuesto, -a [pro'pwesto, a] pp de **proponer** ■ nf proposal

propugnar [propuɣ'nar] vt to uphold

propulsar [propul'sar] vt to drive, propel; (fig) to promote, encourage

propulsión [propul'sjon] nf propulsion; **~ a chorro o por reacción** jet propulsion

propuse etc [pro'puse] vb ver **proponer**

prorrata [pro'rrata] nf (porción) share, quota, prorate (US) ■ adv (Com) pro rata

prorratear [prorrate'ar] vt (dividir) to share out, prorate (US)

prórroga ['prorroɣa] nf (gen) extension; (Jur) stay; (Com) deferment

prorrogable [prorro'ɣaβle] adj which can be extended

prorrogar [prorro'ɣar] vt (período) to extend; (decisión) to defer, postpone

prorrogue etc [pro'rroɣe] vb ver **prorrogar**

prorrumpir [prorrum'pir] vi to burst forth, break out; **~ en gritos** to start shouting; **~ en lágrimas** to burst into tears

prosa ['prosa] nf prose

prosaico, -a [pro'saiko, a] adj prosaic, dull

proscribir [proskri'βir] vt to prohibit, ban; (desterrar) to exile, banish; (partido) to proscribe

proscripción [proskrip'θjon] nf prohibition, ban; banishment; proscription

proscrito, -a [pros'krito, a] pp de **proscribir** ■ adj (prohibido) banned; (desterrado) outlawed ■ nm/f (exilado) exile; (bandido) outlaw

prosecución [proseku'θjon] nf continuation; (persecución) pursuit

proseguir [prose'ɣir] vt to continue, carry on, proceed with; (investigación, estudio) to pursue ■ vi to continue, go on

prosiga etc [pro'siɣa], **prosiguiendo** etc [prosi'ɣjendo] vb ver **proseguir**

prosista [pro'sista] nm/f (escritor) prose writer

prospección [prospek'θjon] nf exploration; (del petróleo, del oro) prospecting

prospecto [pros'pekto] nm prospectus; (folleto) leaflet, sheet of instructions

prosperar [prospe'rar] vi to prosper, thrive, flourish

prosperidad [prosperi'ðað] nf prosperity; (éxito) success

próspero, -a ['prospero, a] adj prosperous; (que tiene éxito) successful

prostíbulo [pros'tiβulo] nm brothel

prostitución [prostitu'θjon] nf prostitution

prostituir [prosti'twir] vt to prostitute; **prostituirse** vr to prostitute o.s., become a prostitute

prostituta [prosti'tuta] nf prostitute

prostituyendo etc [prostitu'jendo] vb ver **prostituir**

protagonice etc [protaɣo'niθe] vb ver **protagonizar**

protagonista [protaɣo'nista] nm/f protagonist; (Lit: personaje) main character, hero/heroine

protagonizar [protaɣoni'θar] vt to head, take the chief role in

protección [protek'θjon] nf protection

proteccionismo [protekθjo'nismo] nm (Com) protectionism

protector, a [protek'tor, a] adj protective, protecting; (tono) patronizing ■ nm/f protector; (bienhechor) patron; (de la tradición) guardian

proteger [prote'xer] vt to protect; **~ contra grabación** o **contra escritura** (Inform) to write protect

protegido, -a [prote'xiðo, a] nm/f protégé/protégée

proteína [prote'ina] nf protein

proteja etc [pro'texa] vb ver **proteger**

prótesis ['protesis] nf (Med) prosthesis

protesta [pro'testa] nf protest

protestante [protes'tante] adj Protestant

protestar [protes'tar] vt to protest, declare; (fe) to protest ■ vi to protest; (objetar) to object; **cheque protestado por falta de fondos** cheque referred to drawer

protocolo [proto'kolo] nm protocol; **sin protocolos** (formalismo) informal(ly)

protón [pro'ton] nm proton

prototipo [proto'tipo] nm prototype; (ideal) model

protuberancia [protuβe'ranθja] nf protuberance

prov. abr (= provincia) prov.

provecho [pro'βetʃo] nm advantage, benefit; (Finanzas) profit; **¡buen ~!** bon appétit!; **en ~ de** to the benefit of; **sacar ~ de** to benefit from, profit by

provechoso, -a [proβe'tʃoso, a] adj (ventajoso) advantageous; (beneficioso) beneficial, useful; (Finanzas: lucrativo) profitable

proveedor, a [proβee'ðor, a] nm/f (abastecedor) supplier; (distribuidor) dealer; **~ de (acceso a) Internet** Internet Service Provider

proveer [proβe'er] vt to provide, supply;

313

(preparar) to provide, get ready; *(vacante)* to fill; *(negocio)* to transact, dispatch ■ *vi*: ~ **a** to provide for; **proveerse** *vr*: **proveerse de** to provide o.s. with

provendré *etc* [proβen'dre], **provenga** *etc* [pro'βenga] *vb ver* **provenir**

provenir [proβe'nir] *vi*: ~ **de** to come from

Provenza [pro'βenθa] *nf* Provence

proverbial [proβer'βjal] *adj* proverbial; *(fig)* notorious

proverbio [pro'βerβjo] *nm* proverb

proveyendo *etc* [proβe'jendo] *vb ver* **proveer**

providencia [proβi'ðenθja] *nf* providence; *(previsión)* foresight; **providencias** *nfpl* measures, steps

provincia [pro'βinθja] *nf* province; *(Esp: Admin)* ≈ county, ≈ region *(Scot)*; **un pueblo de ~(s)** a country town; *see note*

◉ **PROVINCIA**

Spain is divided up into 55 administrative *provincias*, including the islands, and territories in North Africa. Each one has a *capital de provincia*, which generally bears the same name. *Provincias* are grouped by geography, history and culture into *comunidades autónomas*. It should be noted that the term *comarca* normally has a purely geographical function in Spanish, but in Catalonia it designates administrative boundaries.

provinciano, -a [proβin'θjano, a] *adj* provincial; *(del campo)* country *cpd*

proviniendo *etc* [proβi'njendo] *vb ver* **provenir**

provisión [proβi'sjon] *nf* provision; *(abastecimiento)* provision, supply; *(medida)* measure, step

provisional [proβisjo'nal] *adj* provisional

provisorio, -a [proβi'sorjo, a] *adj (esp Am)* provisional

provisto, -a [pro'βisto, a] *adj*: ~ **de** provided *o* supplied with; *(que tiene)* having, possessing

provocación [proβoka'θjon] *nf* provocation

provocador, a [proβoka'ðor, a] *adj* provocative, provoking

provocar [proβo'kar] *vt* to provoke; *(alentar)* to tempt, invite; *(causar)* to bring about, lead to; *(promover)* to promote; *(estimular)* to rouse, stir, stimulate; *(protesta, explosión)* to cause, spark off; *(Am)*: **¿te provoca un café?** would you like a coffee?

provocativo, -a [proβoka'tiβo, a] *adj* provocative

provoque *etc* [pro'βoke] *vb ver* **provocar**

proxeneta [prokse'neta] *nm/f* go-between; *(de prostitutas)* pimp/procuress

próximamente [proksima'mente] *adv* shortly, soon

proximidad [proksimi'ðað] *nf* closeness, proximity

próximo, -a ['proksimo, a] *adj* near, close; *(vecino)* neighbouring; *(el que viene)* next; **en fecha próxima** at an early date; **el mes ~** next month

proyección [projek'θjon] *nf* projection; *(Cine)* showing; *(diapositiva)* slide, transparency; *(influencia)* influence; **el tiempo de ~ es de 35 minutos** the film runs for 35 minutes

proyectar [projek'tar] *vt (objeto)* to hurl, throw; *(luz)* to cast, shed; *(Cine)* to screen, show; *(planear)* to plan

proyectil [projek'til] *nm* projectile, missile; ~ **(tele)dirigido** guided missile

proyecto [pro'jekto] *nm* plan; *(idea)* project; *(estimación de costo)* detailed estimate; **tener algo en ~** to be planning sth; ~ **de ley** *(Pol)* bill

proyector [projek'tor] *nm (Cine)* projector

prudencia [pru'ðenθja] *nf (sabiduría)* wisdom, prudence; *(cautela)* care

prudente [pru'ðente] *adj* sensible, wise, prudent; *(cauteloso)* careful

prueba *etc* ['prweβa] *vb ver* **probar** ■ *nf* proof; *(ensayo)* test, trial; *(cantidad)* taste, sample; *(saboreo)* testing, sampling; *(de ropa)* fitting; *(Deporte)* event; **a ~** on trial; *(Com)* on approval; **a ~ de** proof against; **a ~ de agua/fuego** waterproof/fireproof; ~ **de capacitación** *(Com)* proficiency test; ~ **de fuego** *(fig)* acid test; ~ **de vallas** hurdles; **someter a ~** to put to the test; **¿tiene usted ~ de ello?** can you prove it?, do you have proof?

prurito [pru'rito] *nm* itch; *(de bebé)* nappy rash; *(anhelo)* urge

psico... [siko] *pref* psycho...

psicoanálisis [sikoa'nalisis] *nm* psychoanalysis

psicoanalista [sikoana'lista] *nm/f* psychoanalyst

psicología [sikolo'xia] *nf* psychology

psicológico, -a [siko'loxiko, a] *adj* psychological

psicólogo, -a [si'koloyo, a] *nm/f* psychologist

psicópata [si'kopata] *nm/f* psychopath

psicosis [si'kosis] *nf inv* psychosis

psicosomático, -a [sikoso'matiko, a] *adj* psychosomatic

psicoterapia [sikote'rapja] *nf* psychotherapy

psiquiatra [si'kjatra] *nm/f* psychiatrist

psiquiátrico, -a [si'kjatriko, a] *adj* psychiatric ■ *nm* mental hospital

psíquico, -a ['sikiko, a] *adj* psychic(al)

PSOE [pe'soe] *nm abr* = **Partido Socialista Obrero Español**
PSS *nf abr* (= *Prestación Social Sustitutoria*) *community service for conscientious objectors*
Pta. *abr* (*Geo:* = *Punta*) Pt.
pta(s). *abr* (*Historia*) = **peseta(s)**
pts. *abr* (*Historia*) = **pesetas**
púa ['pua] *nf* sharp point; (*para guitarra*) plectrum; **alambre de púas** barbed wire
pub [puβ/paβ/paf] *nm* bar
púber, a ['puβer, a] *adj, nm/f* adolescent
pubertad [puβer'tað] *nf* puberty
publicación [puβlika'θjon] *nf* publication
publicar [puβli'kar] *vt* (*editar*) to publish; (*hacer público*) to publicize; (*divulgar*) to make public, divulge
publicidad [puβliθi'ðað] *nf* publicity; (*Com*) advertising; **dar ~ a** to publicize, give publicity to; **~ gráfica** display advertising; **~ en el punto de venta** point-of-sale advertising
publicitar [puβliθi'tar] *vt* to publicize
publicitario, -a [puβliθi'tarjo, a] *adj* publicity *cpd*; advertising *cpd*
público, -a ['puβliko, a] *adj* public ■ *nm* public; (*Teat etc*) audience; (*Deporte*) spectators *pl*, crowd; (*en restaurantes etc*) clients *pl*; **el gran ~** the general public; **hacer ~** to publish; (*difundir*) to disclose; **~ objetivo** (*Com*) target audience
publique *etc* [pu'βlike] *vb ver* **publicar**
pucherazo [putʃe'raθo] *nm* (*fraude*) electoral fiddle; **dar ~** to rig an election
puchero [pu'tʃero] *nm* (*Culin: olla*) cooking pot; (*: guiso*) stew; **hacer pucheros** to pout
pudibundo, -a [puði'βundo, a] *adj* bashful
púdico, -a ['puðiko, a] *adj* modest; (*pudibundo*) bashful
pudiendo *etc* [pu'ðjendo] *vb ver* **poder**
pudiente [pu'ðjente] *adj* (*opulento*) wealthy; (*poderoso*) powerful
pudín [pu'ðin] *nm* pudding
pudor [pu'ðor] *nm* modesty; (*vergüenza*) (sense of) shame
pudoroso, -a [puðo'roso, a] *adj* (*modesto*) modest; (*casto*) chaste
pudrir [pu'ðrir] *vt* to rot; (*fam*) to upset, annoy; **pudrirse** *vr* to rot, decay; (*fig*) to rot, languish
pueblerino, -a [pweβle'rino, a] *adj* (*lugareño*) small-town *cpd*; (*persona*) rustic, provincial ■ *nm/f* (*aldeano*) country person
pueblo *etc* ['pweβlo] *vb ver* **poblar** ■ *nm* people; (*nación*) nation; (*aldea*) village; (*plebe*) common people; (*población pequeña*) small town, country town
pueda *etc* ['pweða] *vb ver* **poder**

puente ['pwente] *nm* (*gen*) bridge; (*Naut: tb*: **puente de mando**) bridge; (*: cubierta*) deck; **~ aéreo** airlift; **~ colgante** suspension bridge; **~ levadizo** drawbridge; **hacer (el) ~** (*fam*) to take a long weekend
puenting ['pwentin] *nm* bungee jumping
puerco, -a ['pwerko, a] *adj* (*sucio*) dirty, filthy; (*obsceno*) disgusting ■ *nm/f* pig/sow
pueril [pwe'ril] *adj* childish
puerro ['pwerro] *nm* leek
puerta ['pwerta] *nf* door; (*de jardín*) gate; (*portal*) doorway; (*fig*) gateway; (*gol*) goal; (*Inform*) port; **a la ~** at the door; **a ~ cerrada** behind closed doors; **~ corredera/giratoria** sliding/swing o revolving door; **~ principal/trasera** o **de servicio** front/back door; **~ (de transmisión en) paralelo/serie** (*Inform*) parallel/serial port; **tomar la ~** (*fam*) to leave
puerto ['pwerto] *nm* (*tb Inform*) port; (*de mar*) seaport; (*paso*) pass; (*fig*) haven, refuge; **llegar a ~** (*fig*) to get over a difficulty
Puerto Rico [pwerto'riko] *nm* Puerto Rico
puertorriqueño, -a [pwertorri'keɲo, a] *adj, nm/f* Puerto Rican
pues [pwes] *adv* (*entonces*) then; (*¡entonces!*) well, well then; (*así que*) so ■ *conj* (*porque*) since; **~ ... no sé** well ... I don't know
puesto, -a ['pwesto, a] *pp de* **poner** ■ *adj* dressed ■ *nm* (*lugar, posición*) place; (*trabajo*) post, job; (*Mil*) post; (*Com*) stall; (*quiosco*) kiosk ■ *conj*: **~ que** since, as ■ *nf* (*apuesta*) bet, stake; **~ de mercado** market stall; **~ de policía** police station; **~ de socorro** first aid post; **puesta en escena** staging; **puesta en marcha** starting; **puesta del sol** sunset; **puesta a cero** (*Inform*) reset
pugna ['puɣna] *nf* battle, conflict
pugnar [puɣ'nar] *vi* (*luchar*) to struggle, fight; (*pelear*) to fight
puja ['puxa] *nf* (*esfuerzo*) attempt; (*en una subasta*) bid
pujante [pu'xante] *adj* strong, vigorous
pujar [pu'xar] *vt* (*precio*) to raise, push up ■ *vi* (*en licitación*) to bid, bid up; (*fig: esforzarse*) to struggle, strain
pulcro, -a ['pulkro, a] *adj* neat, tidy
pulga ['pulɣa] *nf* flea; **tener malas pulgas** to be short-tempered
pulgada [pul'ɣaða] *nf* inch
pulgar [pul'ɣar] *nm* thumb
pulgón [pul'ɣon] *nm* plant louse, greenfly
pulir [pu'lir] *vt* to polish; (*alisar*) to smooth; (*fig*) to polish up, touch up
pulla ['puʎa] *nf* cutting remark
pulmón [pul'mon] *nm* lung; **a pleno ~** (*respirar*) deeply; (*gritar*) at the top of one's voice; **~ de acero** iron lung

P

pulmonía [pulmo'nia] *nf* pneumonia
pulpa ['pulpa] *nf* pulp; (*de fruta*) flesh, soft part
pulpería [pulpe'ria] *nf* (*Am*) small grocery store
púlpito ['pulpito] *nm* pulpit
pulpo ['pulpo] *nm* octopus
pulsación [pulsa'θjon] *nf* beat, pulsation; (*Anat*) throb(bing); (*en máquina de escribir*) tap; (*de pianista, mecanógrafo*) touch; ~ **(de una tecla)** (*Inform*) keystroke; ~ **doble** (*Inform*) strikeover
pulsador [pulsa'ðor] *nm* button, push button
pulsar [pul'sar] *vt* (*tecla*) to touch, tap; (*Mus*) to play; (*botón*) to press, push ■ *vi* to pulsate; (*latir*) to beat, throb
pulsera [pul'sera] *nf* bracelet; **reloj de** ~ wristwatch
pulso ['pulso] *nm* (*Med*) pulse; **hacer algo a** ~ to do sth unaided o by one's own efforts
pulular [pulu'lar] *vi* (*estar plagado*): ~ **(de)** to swarm (with)
pulverice *etc* [pulβe'riθe] *vb ver* **pulverizar**
pulverizador [pulβeriθa'ðor] *nm* spray, spray gun
pulverizar [pulβeri'θar] *vt* to pulverize; (*líquido*) to spray
puna ['puna] *nf* (*Am Med*) mountain sickness
punce *etc* ['punθe] *vb ver* **punzar**
punción [pun'θjon] *nf* (*Med*) puncture
pundonor [pundo'nor] *nm* (*dignidad*) self-respect
punición [puni'θjon] *nf* punishment
punitivo, -a [puni'tiβo, a] *adj* punitive
punki ['punki] *adj, nm/f* punk
punta ['punta] *nf* point, tip; (*extremidad*) end; (*promontorio*) headland; (*Costura*) corner; (*Tec*) small nail; (*fig*) touch, trace; **horas puntas** peak hours, rush hours; **sacar** ~ **a** to sharpen; **de** ~ on end; **de** ~ **a** ~ from one end to the other; **estar de** ~ to be edgy; **ir de** ~ **en blanco** to be all dressed up to the nines; **tener algo en la** ~ **de la lengua** to have sth on the tip of one's tongue; **se le pusieron los pelos de** ~ her hair stood on end
puntada [pun'taða] *nf* (*Costura*) stitch
puntal [pun'tal] *nm* prop, support
puntapié [punta'pje ʃ] (*pl* ~**s**) *nm* kick; **echar a algn a** ~**s** to kick sb out
punteado, -a [punte'aðo, a] *adj* (*moteado*) dotted; (*diseño*) of dots ■ *nm* (*Mus*) twang
puntear [punte'ar] *vt* to tick, mark; (*Mus*) to pluck
puntería [punte'ria] *nf* (*de arma*) aim, aiming; (*destreza*) marksmanship
puntero, -a [pun'tero, a] *adj* leading ■ *nm* (*señal, Inform*) pointer; (*dirigente*) leader
puntiagudo, -a [puntja'ɣuðo, a] *adj* sharp, pointed

puntilla [pun'tiʎa] *nf* (*Tec*) tack, braid; (*Costura*) lace edging; **(andar) de puntillas** (to walk) on tiptoe
puntilloso, -a [punti'ʎoso, a] *adj* (*pundonoroso*) punctilious; (*susceptible*) touchy
punto ['punto] *nm* (*gen*) point; (*señal diminuta*) spot, dot; (*lugar*) spot, place; (*momento*) point, moment; (*en un examen*) mark; (*tema*) item; (*Costura*) stitch; (*Inform: impresora*) pitch; (: *pantalla*) pixel; **a** ~ ready; **estar a** ~ **de** to be on the point of o about to; **llegar a** ~ to come just at the right moment; **al** ~ at once; **en** ~ on the dot; **estar en su** ~ (*Culin*) to be done to a turn; **hasta cierto** ~ to some extent; **hacer** ~ to knit; **poner un motor en** ~ to tune an engine; ~ **de partida/de congelación/de fusión** starting/freezing/melting point; ~ **de vista** point of view, viewpoint; ~ **muerto** dead centre; (*Auto*) neutral (gear); **puntos a tratar** matters to be discussed, agenda *sg*; ~ **final** full stop; **dos puntos** colon; ~ **y coma** semicolon; ~ **acápite** (*Am*) full stop, new paragraph; ~ **de interrogación** question mark; **puntos suspensivos** suspension points; ~ **de equilibrio/de pedido** (*Com*) breakeven/reorder point; ~ **inicial** o **de partida** (*Inform*) home; ~ **de referencia/de venta** (*Com*) benchmark point/point-of-sale
puntocom [punto'kom] *nf inv, adj inv* dotcom, dot.com
puntuación [puntwa'θjon] *nf* punctuation; (*puntos: en examen*) mark(s) *pl*; (: *Deporte*) score
puntual [pun'twal] *adj* (*a tiempo*) punctual; (*cálculo*) exact, accurate; (*informe*) reliable
puntualice *etc* [puntwa'liθe] *vb ver* **puntualizar**
puntualidad [puntwali'ðað] *nf* punctuality; exactness, accuracy; reliability
puntualizar [puntwali'θar] *vt* to fix, specify
puntuar [pun'twar] *vt* (*Ling, Tip*) to punctuate; (*examen*) to mark ■ *vi* (*Deporte*) to score, count
punzada [pun'θaða] *nf* (*puntura*) prick; (*Med*) stitch; (*dolor*) twinge (of pain)
punzante [pun'θante] *adj* (*dolor*) shooting, sharp; (*herramienta*) sharp; (*comentario*) biting
punzar [pun'θar] *vt* to prick, pierce ■ *vi* to shoot, stab
punzón [pun'θon] *nm* (*Tec*) punch
puñado [pu'ɲaðo] *nm* handful (*tb fig*); **a puñados** by handfuls
puñal [pu'ɲal] *nm* dagger
puñalada [puɲa'laða] *nf* stab
puñeta [pu'ɲeta] *nf*: **¡~!, ¡qué ~(s)!** (*fam!*) hell!; **mandar a algn a hacer puñetas** (*fam*) to tell sb to go to hell
puñetazo [puɲe'taθo] *nm* punch

puño ['puɲo] *nm* (*Anat*) fist; (*cantidad*) fistful, handful; (*Costura*) cuff; (*de herramienta*) handle; **como un ~** (*verdad*) obvious; (*palpable*) tangible, visible; **de ~ y letra del poeta** in the poet's own handwriting

pupila [pu'pila] *nf* (*Anat*) pupil

pupitre [pu'pitre] *nm* desk

puré [pu're ʃ] (*pl* ~**s**) *nm* puree; (*sopa*) (thick) soup; **~ de patatas** mashed potatoes; **estar hecho ~** (*fig*) to be knackered

pureza [pu'reθa] *nf* purity

purga ['purɣa] *nf* purge

purgante [pur'ɣante] *adj, nm* purgative

purgar [pur'ɣar] *vt* to purge; (*Pol: depurar*) to purge, liquidate; **purgarse** *vr* (*Med*) to take a purge

purgatorio [purɣa'torjo] *nm* purgatory

purgue *etc* ['purɣe] *vb ver* **purgar**

purificar [purifi'kar] *vt* to purify; (*refinar*) to refine

purifique *etc* [puri'fike] *vb ver* **purificar**

puritano, -a [puri'tano, a] *adj* (*actitud*) puritanical; (*iglesia, tradición*) puritan ■ *nm/f* puritan

puro, -a ['puro, a] *adj* pure; (*depurado*) unadulterated; (*oro*) solid; (*cielo*) clear; (*verdad*) simple, plain ■ *adv*: **de ~ cansado** out of sheer tiredness ■ *nm* cigar; **por pura casualidad** by sheer chance

púrpura ['purpura] *nf* purple

purpúreo, -a [pur'pureo, a] *adj* purple

pus [pus] *nm* pus

puse *etc* ['puse] *vb ver* **poner**

pústula ['pustula] *nf* pimple, sore

puta ['puta] *nf* whore, prostitute

putada [pu'taða] *nf* (*fam!*): **hacer una ~ a algn** to play a dirty trick on sb; **¡qué ~!** what a pain in the arse! (*!*)

putería [pute'ria] *nf* (*prostitución*) prostitution; (*prostíbulo*) brothel

putrefacción [putrefak'θjon] *nf* rotting, putrefaction

pútrido, -a ['putriðo, a] *adj* rotten

puzzle ['puθle] *nm* puzzle

PVP *abr* (*Esp*: = *Precio Venta al Público*) ≈ RRP

PYME ['pime] *nf abr* (= *Pequeña y Mediana Empresa*) SME

Pza *abr* = **plaza**

Qq

Q, q [ku] *nf* (*letra*) Q, q; **Q de Querido** Q for Queen

q.e.p.d. *abr* (= *que en paz descanse*) R.I.P

qm *abr* = **quintal métrico**; **quintales métricos**

qts. *abr* = **quilates**

 PALABRA CLAVE

que [ke] *conj* **1** (*con oración subordinada: muchas veces no se traduce*) that; **dijo que vendría** he said (that) he would come; **espero que lo encuentres** I hope (that) you find it; **dile que me llame** ask him to call me; *ver tb* **el**
2 (*en oración independiente*): **¡que entre!** send him in; **¡que se mejore tu padre!** I hope your father gets better; **¡que lo haga él!** he can do it!; (*orden*) get him to do it!
3 (*enfático*): **¿me quieres? — ¡que sí!** do you love me? — of course!; **te digo que sí** I'm telling you
4 (*consecutivo: muchas veces no se traduce*) that; **es tan grande que no lo puedo levantar** it's so big (that) I can't lift it
5 (*comparaciones*) than; **yo que tú/él** if I were you/him; *ver tb* **más**; **menos**
6 (*valor disyuntivo*): **que le guste o no** whether he likes it or not; **que venga o que no venga** whether he comes or not
7 (*porque*): **no puedo, que tengo que quedarme en casa** I can't, I've got to stay in
8: **siguió toca que toca** he kept on playing ■ *pron* **1** (*cosa*) that, which; (+ *prep*) which; **el sombrero que te compraste** the hat (that o which) you bought; **la cama en que dormí** the bed (that o which) I slept in; **el día (en) que ella nació** the day (when) she was born
2 (*persona: suj*) that, who; (: *objeto*) that, whom; **el amigo que me acompañó al museo** the friend that o who went to the museum with me; **la chica que invité** the girl (that o whom) I invited

qué [ke] *adj* what?, which? ■ *pron* what?; **¡qué divertido/asco!** how funny/revolting!; **¡qué día más espléndido!** what a glorious day!; **¿qué edad tienes?** how old are you?; **¿de qué me hablas?** what are you saying to me?; **¿qué tal?** how are you?, how are things?; **¿qué hay (de nuevo)?** what's new?; **¿qué más?** anything else?

quebrada [ke'βraða] *nf ver* **quebrado**

quebradero [keβra'ðero] *nm*: ~ **de cabeza** headache, worry

quebradizo, -a [keβra'ðiθo, a] *adj* fragile; (*persona*) frail

quebrado, -a [ke'βraðo, a] *adj* (*roto*) broken; (*terreno*) rough, uneven ■ *nm/f* bankrupt ■ *nm* (*Mat*) fraction ■ *nf* ravine; ~ **rehabilitado** discharged bankrupt

quebradura [keβra'ðura] *nf* (*fisura*) fissure; (*Med*) rupture

quebrantamiento [keβranta'mjento] *nm* (*acto*) breaking; (*de ley*) violation; (*estado*) exhaustion

quebrantar [keβran'tar] *vt* (*infringir*) to violate, transgress; **quebrantarse** *vr* (*persona*) to fail in health

quebranto [ke'βranto] *nm* damage, harm; (*decaimiento*) exhaustion; (*dolor*) grief, pain

quebrar [ke'βrar] *vt* to break, smash ■ *vi* to go bankrupt; **quebrarse** *vr* to break, get broken; (*Med*) to be ruptured

quechua ['ketʃua] *adj, nm/f* Quechua

queda ['keða] *nf*: (**toque de**) ~ curfew

quedar [ke'ðar] *vi* to stay, remain; (*encontrarse*) to be; (*restar*) to remain, be left; **quedarse** *vr* to remain, stay (behind); ~ **en** (*acordar*) to agree on/to; (*acabar siendo*) to end up as; ~ **por hacer** to be still to be done; ~ **ciego/mudo** to be left blind/dumb; **no te queda bien ese vestido** that dress doesn't suit you; **quedamos a las seis** we agreed to meet at six; **eso queda muy lejos** that's a long way (away); **nos quedan 12 kms para llegar al pueblo** there are still 12 kms before we get to the village; **no queda otra** there's no alternative; **quedarse (con) algo** to keep sth; **quedarse con algn** (*fam*) to swindle sb; **quedarse en nada** to come to nothing *o* nought; **quedarse sin** to run out of

quedo, -a ['keðo, a] *adj* still ■ *adv* softly, gently

quehacer [kea'θer] *nm* task, job; **quehaceres (domésticos)** household chores

queja ['kexa] *nf* complaint

quejarse [ke'xarse] *vr* (*enfermo*) to moan, groan; (*protestar*) to complain; ~ **de que ...** to complain (about the fact) that ...

quejica [ke'xika] *adj* grumpy, complaining ■ *nm/f* grumbler, whinger

quejido [ke'xiðo] *nm* moan

quejoso, -a [ke'xoso, a] *adj* complaining

quema ['kema] *nf* fire; (*combustión*) burning

quemado, -a [ke'maðo, a] *adj* burnt; (*irritado*) annoyed

quemadura [kema'ðura] *nf* burn, scald; (*de sol*) sunburn; (*de fusible*) blow-out

quemar [ke'mar] *vt* to burn; (*fig: malgastar*) to burn up, squander; (*Com: precios*) to slash, cut; (*fastidiar*) to annoy, bug ■ *vi* to be burning hot; **quemarse** *vr* (*consumirse*) to burn (up); (*del sol*) to get sunburnt

quemarropa [kema'rropa]: **a ~** *adv* point-blank

quemazón [kema'θon] *nf* burn; (*calor*) intense heat; (*sensación*) itch

quena ['kena] *nf* (*Am*) Indian flute

quepo *etc* ['kepo] *vb ver* **caber**

querella [ke'reʎa] *nf* (*Jur*) charge; (*disputa*) dispute

querellarse [kere'ʎarse] *vr* to file a complaint

querencia [ke'renθja] *nf* (*Zool*) homing instinct; (*fig*) homesickness

 PALABRA CLAVE

querer [ke'rer] *vt* **1** (*desear*) to want; **quiero más dinero** I want more money; **quisiera** *o* **querría un té** I'd like a tea; **quiero ayudar/que vayas** I want to help/you to go; **como Vd quiera** as you wish, as you please; **ven cuando quieras** come when you like; **lo hizo sin querer** he didn't mean to do it; **no quiero** I don't want to; **le pedí que me dejara ir pero no quiso** I asked him to let me go but he refused

2 (*preguntas: para pedir u ofrecer algo*): **¿quiere abrir la ventana?** could you open the window?; **¿quieres echarme una mano?** can you give me a hand?; **¿quiere un café?** would you like some coffee?

3 (*amar*) to love; (*tener cariño a*) to be fond of;

quiere mucho a sus hijos he's very fond of his children

4 (*requerir*): **esta planta quiere más luz** this plant needs more light

5: **querer decir** to mean; **¿qué quieres decir?** what do you mean?

querido, -a [ke'riðo, a] *adj* dear ■ *nm/f* darling; (*amante*) lover; **nuestra querida patria** our beloved country

querosén [kero'sen], **querosene** [kero'sene] *nm* (*Am*) kerosene, paraffin

querré *etc* [ke'rre] *vb ver* **querer**

quesería [kese'ria] *nf* dairy; (*fábrica*) cheese factory

quesero, -a [ke'sero, a] *adj*: **la industria quesera** the cheese industry ■ *nm/f* cheesemaker ■ *nf* cheese dish

queso ['keso] *nm* cheese; ~ **rallado** grated cheese; ~ **crema** cream cheese; **dárselas con ~ a algn** (*fam*) to take sb in

quetzal [ket'sal] *nm* monetary unit of Guatemala

quicio ['kiθjo] *nm* hinge; **estar fuera de ~** to be beside o.s.; **sacar a algn de ~** to drive sb up the wall

quid [kið] *nm* gist, crux; **dar en el ~** to hit the nail on the head

quiebra ['kjeβra] *nf* break, split; (*Com*) bankruptcy; (*Econ*) slump

quiebro *etc* ['kjeβro] *vb ver* **quebrar** ■ *nm* (*del cuerpo*) swerve

quien [kjen] *pron relativo* (*suj*) who; (*complemento*) whom; (*indefinido*): ~ **dice eso es tonto** whoever says that is a fool; **hay ~ piensa que** there are those who think that; **no hay ~ lo haga** no-one will do it; ~ **más, ~ menos tiene sus problemas** everybody has problems

quién [kjen] *pron interrogativo* who; (*complemento*) whom; **¿~ es?** who is it?, who's there?; (*Telec*) who's calling?

quienquiera [kjen'kjera] (*pl* **quienesquiera**) *pron* whoever

quiera *etc* ['kjera] *vb ver* **querer**

quieto, -a ['kjeto, a] *adj* still; (*carácter*) placid; **¡estáte ~!** keep still!

quietud [kje'tuð] *nf* stillness

quijada [ki'xaða] *nf* jaw, jawbone

quijote [ki'xote] *nm* dreamer; **Don Q~** Don Quixote

quil. *abr* = **quilates**

quilate [ki'late] *nm* carat

quilla ['kiʎa] *nf* keel

quilo ... ['kilo] = **kilo...**

quimera [ki'mera] *nf* (*sueño*) pipe dream

quimérico, -a [ki'meriko, a] *adj* fantastic

químico, -a ['kimiko, a] *adj* chemical ■ *nm/f*

q

chemist ■ nf chemistry
quimioterapia [kimiote'rapia] nf
chemotherapy
quina ['kina] nf quinine
quincallería [kinkaʎe'ria] nf ironmonger's
(shop), hardware store (US)
quince ['kinθe] num fifteen; ~ **días** a fortnight
quinceañero, -a [kinθea'ɲero, a] adj fifteen-
year-old; (adolescente) teenage ■ nm/f
fifteen-year-old; (adolescente) teenager
quincena [kin'θena] nf fortnight; (pago)
fortnightly pay
quincenal [kinθe'nal] adj fortnightly
quincuagésimo, -a [kinkwa'xesimo, a] num
fiftieth
quiniela [ki'njela] nf football pools pl;
quinielas nfpl pools coupon sg
quinientos, -as [ki'njentos, as] num five
hundred
quinina [ki'nina] nf quinine
quinqué [kin'ke] nm oil lamp
quinquenal [kinke'nal] adj five-year cpd
quinqui ['kinki] nm delinquent
quinta ['kinta] nf ver **quinto**
quintaesencia [kintae'senθja] nf
quintessence
quintal [kin'tal] nm (Castilla: peso) = 46kg;
~ **métrico** = 100kg
quinteto [kin'teto] nm quintet
quinto, -a ['kinto, a] adj fifth ■ nm (Mil)
conscript, draftee ■ nf country house; (Mil)
call-up, draft
quintuplo, -a [kin'tuplo, a] adj quintuple,
five-fold
quiosco ['kjosko] nm (de música) bandstand;
(de periódicos) news stand (also selling sweets,

cigarettes etc)
quirófano [ki'rofano] nm operating theatre
quiromancia [kiro'manθja] nf palmistry
quirúrgico, -a [ki'rurxiko, a] adj surgical
quise etc ['kise] vb ver **querer**
quisque ['kiske] pron (fam): **cada** o **todo** ~
(absolutely) everyone
quisquilloso [kiski'ʎoso, a] adj (susceptible)
touchy; (meticuloso) pernickety
quiste ['kiste] nm cyst
quitaesmalte [kitaes'malte] nm nail polish
remover
quitamanchas [kita'mantʃas] nm inv stain
remover
quitanieves [kita'njeβes] nm inv snowplough
(Brit), snowplow (US)
quitar [ki'tar] vt to remove, take away; (ropa)
to take off; (dolor) to relieve; (vida) to take;
(valor) to reduce; (hurtar) to remove, steal
■ vi: ¡**quita de ahí!** get away!; **quitarse** vr to
withdraw; (mancha) to come off o out; (ropa)
to take off; **me quita mucho tiempo** it
takes up a lot of my time; **el café me quita
el sueño** coffee stops me sleeping; ~ **de
en medio a algn** to get rid of sb; **quitarse
algo de encima** to get rid of sth; **quitarse
del tabaco** to give up smoking; **se quitó el
sombrero** he took off his hat
quitasol [kita'sol] nm sunshade (Brit), parasol
quite ['kite] nm (en esgrima) parry; (evasión)
dodge; **estar al** ~ to be ready to go to sb's aid
Quito ['kito] n Quito
quizá [ki'θa]
quizás [ki'θas] adv perhaps, maybe
quórum ['kworum] (pl **quórums**) ['kworum]
nm quorum

Rr

R, r ['erre] *nf* (*letra*) R, r; **R de Ramón** R for Robert (*Brit*) *o* Roger (*US*)

R. *abr* (*Rel*) = **real; reverendo; Remite, Remitente; río**

rabadilla [raβa'ðiʎa] *nf* base of the spine

rábano ['raβano] *nm* radish; **me importa un ~** I don't give a damn

rabia ['raβja] *nf* (*Med*) rabies *sg*; (*fig: ira*) fury, rage; **¡qué ~!** isn't it infuriating!; **me da ~** it maddens me; **tener ~ a algn** to have a grudge against sb

rabiar [ra'βjar] *vi* to have rabies; to rage, be furious; **~ por algo** to long for sth

rabieta [ra'βjeta] *nf* tantrum, fit of temper

rabino [ra'βino] *nm* rabbi

rabioso, -a [ra'βjoso, a] *adj* rabid; (*fig*) furious

rabo ['raβo] *nm* tail

racanear [rakane'ar] *vi* (*fam*) to skive

rácano ['rakano] *nm* (*fam*) slacker, skiver

RACE ['raθe] *nm abr* (= *Real Automóvil Club de España*) = RAC

racha ['ratʃa] *nf* gust of wind; (*serie*) string, series; **buena/mala ~** spell of good/bad luck

racial [ra'θjal] *adj* racial, race *cpd*

racimo [ra'θimo] *nm* bunch

raciocinio [raθjo'θinjo] *nm* reason; (*razonamiento*) reasoning

ración [ra'θjon] *nf* portion; **raciones** *nfpl* rations

racional [raθjo'nal] *adj* (*razonable*) reasonable; (*lógico*) rational

racionalice *etc* [raθjona'liθe] *vb ver* **racionalizar**

racionalizar [raθjonali'θar] *vt* to rationalize; (*Com*) to streamline

racionamiento [raθjona'mjento] *nm* (*Com*) rationing

racionar [raθjo'nar] *vt* to ration (out)

racismo [ra'θismo] *nm* racialism, racism

racista [ra'θista] *adj, nm/f* racist

radar [ra'ðar] *nm* radar

radiación [raðja'θjon] *nf* radiation; (*Telec*) broadcasting

radiactividad [raðjaktiβi'ðað] *nf* radioactivity

radiactivo, -a [raðjak'tiβo, a] *adj* radioactive

radiado, -a [ra'ðjaðo, a] *adj* radio *cpd*, broadcast

radiador [raðja'ðor] *nm* radiator

radial [ra'ðjal] *adj* (*Am*) radio *cpd*

radiante [ra'ðjante] *adj* radiant

radiar [ra'ðjar] *vt* to radiate; (*Telec*) to broadcast; (*Med*) to give radiotherapy to

radical [raði'kal] *adj, nm/f* radical ■ *nm* (*Ling*) root; (*Mat*) square-root sign

radicar [raði'kar] *vi* to take root, **~ en** to lie *o* consist in; **radicarse** *vr* to establish o.s., put down (one's) roots

radio ['raðjo] *nf* radio; (*aparato*) radio (set) ■ *nm* (*Mat*) radius; (*Am*) radio; (*Química*) radium; **~ de acción** extent of one's authority, sphere of influence

radioaficionado, -a [raðjoafiθjo'naðo, a] *nm/f* radio ham

radiocasete [raðjoka'sete] *nm* radiocassette (player)

radiodifusión [raðjodifu'sjon] *nf* broadcasting

radioemisora [raðjoemi'sora] *nf* transmitter, radio station

radiofónico, -a [raðjo'foniko, a] *adj* radio *cpd*

radiografía [raðjoɣra'fia] *nf* X-ray

radiólogo, -a [ra'ðjoloɣo, a] *nm/f* radiologist

radionovela [raðjono'βela] *nf* radio series

radiotaxi [raðjo'taksi] *nm* radio taxi

radioterapia [raðjote'rapja] *nf* radiotherapy

radioyente [raðjo'jente] *nm/f* listener

radique *etc* [ra'ðike] *vb ver* **radicar**

RAE ['rae] *nf abr* (= *Real Academia Española*) *ver* **real**

ráfaga ['rafaɣa] *nf* gust; (*de luz*) flash; (*de tiros*) burst

raído, -a [ra'iðo, a] *adj* (*ropa*) threadbare; (*persona*) shabby

raigambre [rai'ɣambre] *nf* (*Bot*) roots *pl*; (*fig*) tradition

r

raíz [ra'iθ] (*pl* **raíces**) *nf* root; **~ cuadrada** square root; **a ~ de** as a result of; (*después de*) immediately after

raja ['raxa] *nf* (*de melón etc*) slice; (*hendidura*) slit, split; (*grieta*) crack

rajar [ra'xar] *vt* to split; (*fam*) to slash; **rajarse** *vr* to split, crack; **rajarse de** to back out of

rajatabla [raxa'taβla]: **a ~** *adv* (*estrictamente*) strictly, to the letter

RAL *abr* (*Inform*) = **red de área local**

ralea [ra'lea] *nf* (*pey*) kind, sort

ralenti [ra'lenti] *nm* (*TV etc*) slow motion; (*Auto*) neutral; **al ~** in slow motion; (*Auto*) ticking over

rallador [raʎa'ðor] *nm* grater

rallar [ra'ʎar] *vt* to grate

ralo, -a ['ralo, a] *adj* thin, sparse

RAM [ram] *nf abr* (= *random access memory*) RAM

rama ['rama] *nf* bough, branch; **andarse por las ramas** (*fig: fam*) to beat about the bush

ramaje [ra'maje] *nm* branches *pl*, foliage

ramal [ra'mal] *nm* (*de cuerda*) strand; (*Ferro*) branch line; (*Auto*) branch (road)

rambla ['rambla] *nf* (*avenida*) avenue

ramera [ra'mera] *nf* whore, hooker (*US*)

ramificación [ramifika'θjon] *nf* ramification

ramificarse [ramifi'karse] *vr* to branch out

ramifique *etc* [rami'fike] *vb ver* **ramificarse**

ramillete [rami'ʎete] *nm* bouquet; (*fig*) select group

ramo ['ramo] *nm* branch, twig; (*sección*) department, section; (*sector*) field, sector

rampa ['rampa] *nf* ramp

ramplón, -ona [ram'plon, ona] *adj* uncouth, coarse

rana ['rana] *nf* frog; **salto de ~** leapfrog; **cuando las ranas críen pelos** when pigs fly

ranchero [ran'tʃero] *nm* (*Am*) rancher; (*pequeño propietario*) smallholder

rancho ['rantʃo] *nm* (*Mil*) food; (*Am: grande*) ranch; (: *pequeño*) small farm

rancio, -a ['ranθjo, a] *adj* (*comestibles*) stale, rancid; (*vino*) aged, mellow; (*fig*) ancient

rango ['rango] *nm* rank; (*prestigio*) standing

ranura [ra'nura] *nf* groove; (*de teléfono etc*) slot; **~ de expansión** (*Inform*) expansion slot

rap [rap] *nm* (*Mus*) rap

rapacidad [rapaθi'ðað] *nf* rapacity

rapapolvo [rapa'polβo] *nm*: **echar un ~ a algn** to give sb a ticking off

rapar [ra'par] *vt* to shave; (*los cabellos*) to crop

rapaz [ra'paθ] *adj* (*Zool*) predatory **■** *nm* young boy

rapaza [ra'paθa] *nf* young girl

rape ['rape] *nm* quick shave; (*pez*) angler (fish); **al ~** cropped

rapé [ra'pe] *nm* snuff

rapel [ra'pel] *nm* = **rappel**

rapidez [rapi'ðeθ] *nf* speed, rapidity

rápido, -a ['rapiðo, a] *adj* fast, quick **■** *adv* quickly **■** *nm* (*Ferro*) express; **rápidos** *nmpl* rapids

rapiña [ra'piɲa] *nm* robbery; **ave de ~** bird of prey

rappel [ra'pel] *nm* (*Deporte*) abseiling

raptar [rap'tar] *vt* to kidnap

rapto ['rapto] *nm* kidnapping; (*impulso*) sudden impulse; (*éxtasis*) ecstasy, rapture

raqueta [ra'keta] *nf* racquet

raquítico, -a [ra'kitiko, a] *adj* stunted; (*fig*) poor, inadequate

raquitismo [raki'tismo] *nm* rickets *sg*

rareza [ra'reθa] *nf* rarity; (*fig*) eccentricity

raro, -a ['raro, a] *adj* (*poco común*) rare; (*extraño*) odd, strange; (*excepcional*) remarkable; **¡qué ~!** how (very) odd!; **¡(qué) cosa más rara!** how strange!

ras [ras] *nm*: **a ~ de** level with; **a ~ de tierra** at ground level

rasar [ra'sar] *vt* to level

rascacielos [raska'θjelos] *nm inv* skyscraper

rascar [ras'kar] *vt* (*con las uñas etc*) to scratch; (*raspar*) to scrape; **rascarse** *vr* to scratch (o.s.)

rasgar [ras'ɣar] *vt* to tear, rip (up)

rasgo ['rasɣo] *nm* (*con pluma*) stroke; **rasgos** *nmpl* features, characteristics; **a grandes rasgos** in outline, broadly

rasgue *etc* ['rasɣe] *vb ver* **rasgar**

rasguear [rasɣe'ar] *vt* (*Mus*) to strum

rasguñar [rasɣu'ɲar] *vt* to scratch; (*bosquejar*) to sketch

rasguño [ras'ɣuɲo] *nm* scratch

raso, -a ['raso, a] *adj* (*liso*) flat, level; (*a baja altura*) very low **■** *nm* satin; (*campo llano*) flat country; **cielo ~** clear sky; **al ~** in the open

raspado [ras'paðo] *nm* (*Med*) scrape

raspador [raspa'ðor] *nm* scraper

raspadura [raspa'ðura] *nf* (*acto*) scrape, scraping; (*marca*) scratch; **raspaduras** *nfpl* scrapings

raspar [ras'par] *vt* to scrape; (*arañar*) to scratch; (*limar*) to file **■** *vi* (*manos*) to be rough; (*vino*) to be sharp, have a rough taste

rasque *etc* ['raske] *vb ver* **rascar**

rastra ['rastra] *nf*: **a rastras** by dragging; (*fig*) unwillingly

rastreador [rastrea'ðor] *nm* tracker; **~ de minas** minesweeper

rastrear [rastre'ar] *vt* (*seguir*) to track; (*minas*) to sweep

rastrero, -a [ras'trero, a] *adj* (*Bot: Zool*) creeping; (*fig*) despicable, mean

rastrillar [rastri'ʎar] *vt* to rake

rastrillo [ras'triʎo] nm rake; (Am) safety razor
rastro ['rastro] nm (Agr) rake; (pista) track, trail; (vestigio) trace; (mercado) flea market; **el R~** the Madrid flea market; **perder el ~** to lose the scent; **desaparecer sin ~** to vanish without trace
rastrojo [ras'troxo] nm stubble
rasurador [rasura'ðor] nm, **rasuradora** (Am) [rasura'ðora] ■ nf electric shaver o razor
rasurarse [rasu'rarse] vr to shave
rata ['rata] nf rat
ratear [rate'ar] vt (robar) to steal
ratero, -a [ra'tero, a] adj light-fingered ■ nm/f pickpocket; (Am: de casas) burglar
ratificar [ratifi'kar] vt to ratify
ratifique etc [rati'fike] vb ver **ratificar**
rato ['rato] nm while, short time; **a ratos** from time to time; **al poco ~** shortly after, soon afterwards; **ratos libres** o **de ocio** leisure sg, spare o free time sg; **hay para ~** there's still a long way to go; **pasar el ~** to kill time; **pasar un buen/mal ~** to have a good/rough time
ratón [ra'ton] nm (tb Inform) mouse
ratonera [rato'nera] nf mousetrap
RAU nf abr (= República Árabe Unida) UAR
raudal [rau'ðal] nm torrent; **a raudales** in abundance; **entrar a raudales** to pour in
raya ['raja] nf line; (marca) scratch; (en tela) stripe; (Tip) hyphen; (de pelo) parting; (límite) boundary; (pez) ray; **a rayas** striped; **pasarse de la ~** to overstep the mark; **tener a ~** to keep in check
rayado, -a [ra'jaðo, a] adj (papel) ruled; (tela, diseño) striped
rayar [ra'jar] vt to line; to scratch; (subrayar) to underline ■ vi: **~ en** o **con** to border on; **al ~ el alba** at first light; **~ a algn >** (col) to do sb's head in (col); **está siempre rayándome con esa historia** he's doing my head in with that business (col)
rayo ['rajo] nm (del sol) ray, beam; (de luz) shaft; (en una tormenta) (flash of) lightning; **~ solar** o **de sol** sunbeam; **rayos infrarrojos** infrared rays; **rayos X** X-rays; **como un ~** like a shot; **la noticia cayó como un ~** the news was a bombshell; **pasar como un ~** to flash past
raza ['raθa] nf race; (de animal) breed; **~ humana** human race; **de pura ~** (caballo) thoroughbred; (perro etc) pedigree
razón [ra'θon] nf reason; (justicia) right, justice; (razonamiento) reasoning; (motivo) reason, motive; (proporción) rate; (Mat) ratio; **a ~ de 10 cada día** at the rate of 10 a day; **"~: ..."** "inquiries to ..."; **en ~ de** with regard to; **perder la ~** to go out of one's mind; **dar ~ a**

algn to agree that sb is right; **dar ~ de** to give an account of, report on; **tener/no tener ~** to be right/wrong; **~ directa/inversa** direct/inverse proportion; **~ de ser** raison d'être
razonable [raθo'naβle] adj reasonable; (justo, moderado) fair
razonado, -a [raθo'naðo, a] adj (Com: cuenta etc) itemized
razonamiento [raθona'mjento] nm (juicio) judgement; (argumento) reasoning
razonar [raθo'nar] vt, vi to reason, argue
RDA nf abr (Historia: = República Democrática Alemana) ver **república**
Rdo. abr (Rel: = Reverendo) Rev
RDSI nf abr (= Red Digital de Servicios Integrados) ISDN
re [re] nm (Mus) D
reabierto [rea'βjerto] pp de **reabrir**
reabrir [rea'βrir] vt, **reabrirse** vr to reopen
reacción [reak'θjon] nf reaction; **avión a ~** jet plane; **~ en cadena** chain reaction
reaccionar [reakθjo'nar] vi to react
reaccionario, -a [reakθjo'narjo, a] adj reactionary
reacio, -a [re'aθjo, a] adj stubborn; **ser** o **estar ~ a** to be opposed to
reactivar [reakti'βar] vt to reactivate; **reactivarse** vr (economía) to be on the upturn
reactor [reak'tor] nm reactor; (avión) jet plane; **~ nuclear** nuclear reactor
readaptación [reaðapta'θjon] nf: **~ profesional** industrial retraining
readmitir [reaðmi'tir] vt to readmit
reafirmar [reafir'mar] vt to reaffirm
reagrupar [reagru'par] vt to regroup
reajustar [reaxus'tar] vt (Inform) to reset
reajuste [rea'xuste] nm readjustment; **~ salarial** wage increase; **~ de plantilla** rationalization
real [re'al] adj real; (del rey, fig) royal; (espléndido) grand ■ nm (de feria) fairground; **la R~ Academia Española** see note

● **REAL ACADEMIA ESPAÑOLA**

The *Real Academia Española* (RAE) is the regulatory body for the Spanish language in Spain and was founded in 1713. It produces dictionaries and grammars bearing its own name, and is considered the authority on the language, although it has been criticized for being too conservative. In 1994, along with the Spanish American *academias*, it approved a change to the Spanish alphabet, no longer treating "ch" and "ll" as separate letters. "ñ" continues to be treated separately.

r

realce etc [re'alθe] vb ver **realzar** ■ nm (Tec) embossing; **poner de** ~ to emphasize

real-decreto [re'alde'kreto] (pl **reales-decretos**) nm royal decree

realeza [rea'leθa] nf royalty

realice etc [rea'liθe] vb ver **realizar**

realidad [reali'ðað] nf reality; (verdad) truth; ~ **virtual** virtual reality; **en** ~ in fact

realismo [rea'lismo] nm realism

realista [rea'lista] nm/f realist

realización [realiθa'θjon] nf fulfilment, realization; (Com) selling up (Brit), conversion into money (US); ~ **de plusvalías** profit-taking

realizador, a [realiθa'ðor, a] nm/f (TV etc) producer

realizar [reali'θar] vt (objetivo) to achieve; (plan) to carry out; (viaje) to make, undertake; (Com) to realize; **realizarse** vr to come about, come true; **realizarse como persona** to fulfil one's aims in life

realmente [real'mente] adv really

realojar [realo'xar] vt to rehouse

realquilar [realki'lar] vt (subarrendar) to sublet; (alquilar de nuevo) to relet

realzar [real'θar] vt (Tec) to raise; (embellecer) to enhance; (acentuar) to highlight

reanimar [reani'mar] vt to revive; (alentar) to encourage; **reanimarse** vr to revive

reanudar [reanu'ðar] vt (renovar) to renew; (historia, viaje) to resume

reaparición [reapari'θjon] nf reappearance; (vuelta) return

reapertura [reaper'tura] nf reopening

rearme [re'arme] nm rearmament

reata [re'ata] nf (Am) lasso

reavivar [reaβi'βar] vt (persona) to revive; (fig) to rekindle

rebaja [re'βaxa] nf reduction, lowering; (Com) discount; **"grandes rebajas"** "big reductions", "sale"

rebajar [reβa'xar] vt (bajar) to lower; (reducir) to reduce; (precio) to cut; (disminuir) to lessen; (humillar) to humble; **rebajarse** vr: **rebajarse a hacer algo** to stoop to doing sth

rebanada [reβa'naða] nf slice

rebañar [reβa'ɲar] vt to scrape clean

rebaño [re'βaɲo] nm herd; (de ovejas) flock

rebasar [reβa'sar] vt (tb: **rebasar de**) to exceed; (Auto) to overtake

rebatir [reβa'tir] vt to refute; (rebajar) to reduce; (ataque) to repel

rebato [re'βato] nm alarm; (ataque) surprise attack; **llamar** o **tocar a** ~ (fig) to sound the alarm

rebeca [re'βeka] nf cardigan

rebelarse [reβe'larse] vr to rebel, revolt

rebelde [re'βelde] adj rebellious; (niño) unruly ■ nm/f rebel; **ser** ~ **a** to be in revolt against, rebel against

rebeldía [reβel'dia] nf rebelliousness; (desobediencia) disobedience; (Jur) default

rebelión [reβe'ljon] nf rebellion

rebenque [re'βenke] nm (Am) whip

reblandecer [reβlande'θer] vt to soften

reblandezca etc [reβlan'deθka] vb ver **reblandecer**

rebobinar [reβoβi'nar] vt to rewind

reboce etc [re'βoθe] vb ver **rebozar**

rebosante [reβo'sante] adj: ~ **de** (fig) brimming o overflowing with

rebosar [reβo'sar] vi to overflow; (abundar) to abound, be plentiful; ~ **de salud** to be bursting o brimming with health

rebotar [reβo'tar] vt to bounce; (rechazar) to repel

rebote [re'βote] nm rebound; **de** ~ on the rebound

rebozado, -a [reβo'θaðo, a] adj (Culin) fried in batter o breadcrumbs o flour

rebozar [reβo'θar] vt to wrap up; (Culin) to fry in batter etc

rebozo [reβo'θo] nm: **sin** ~ openly

rebuscado, -a [reβus'kaðo, a] adj affected

rebuscar [reβus'kar] vi (en bolsillo, cajón) to fish; (en habitación) to search high and low

rebuznar [reβuθ'nar] vi to bray

recabar [reka'βar] vt (obtener) to manage to get; ~ **fondos** to collect money

recadero [reka'ðero] nm messenger

recado [re'kaðo] nm message; **dejar/tomar un** ~ (Telec) to leave/take a message

recaer [reka'er] vi (Med) to relapse; ~ **en** to fall to o on; (criminal etc) to fall back into, relapse into; (premio) to go to

recaída [reka'iða] nf relapse

recaiga etc [re'kaiɣa] vb ver **recaer**

recalcar [rekal'kar] vt (fig) to stress, emphasize

recalcitrante [rekalθi'trante] adj recalcitrant

recalentamiento [rekalenta'mjento] nm: ~ **global** global warming

recalentar [rekalen'tar] vt (comida) to warm up, reheat; (demasiado) to overheat; **recalentarse** vr to overheat, get too hot

recaliente etc [reka'ljente] vb ver **recalentar**

recalque etc [re'kalke] vb ver **recalcar**

recámara [re'kamara] nf side room; (Am) bedroom

recamarera [rekama'rera] nf (Am) maid

recambio [re'kambjo] nm spare; (de pluma) refill; **piezas de** ~ spares

recapacitar [rekapaθi'tar] vi to reflect

recapitular [rekapitu'lar] vt to recap
recargable [rekar'ɣaβle] adj (batería, pila) rechargeable; (mechero, pluma) refillable
recargado, -a [rekar'ɣaðo, a] adj overloaded; (exagerado) over-elaborate
recargar [rekar'ɣar] vt to overload; (batería) to recharge; (mechero, pluma) to refill; (tarjeta de móvil) to top up
recargo [re'karɣo] nm surcharge; (aumento) increase
recargue etc [re'karɣe] vb ver **recargar**
recatado, -a [reka'taðo, a] adj (modesto) modest, demure; (prudente) cautious
recato [re'kato] nm (modestia) modesty, demureness; (cautela) caution
recauchutado, -a [rekautʃu'taðo, a] adj remould cpd
recaudación [rekauða'θjon] nf (acción) collection; (cantidad) takings pl; (en deporte) gate; (oficina) tax office
recaudador, a [rekauða'ðor, a] nm/f tax collector
recaudar [rekau'ðar] vt to collect
recaudo [re'kauðo] nm: **estar a buen ~** to be in safekeeping; **poner algo a buen ~** to put sth in a safe place
recayendo etc [reka'jendo] vb ver **recaer**
rece etc ['reθe] vb ver **rezar**
recelar [reθe'lar] vt: **~ que** (sospechar) to suspect that; (temer) to fear that ■ vi: **~(se) de** to distrust
recelo [re'θelo] nm distrust, suspicion
receloso, -a [reθe'loso, a] adj distrustful, suspicious
recepción [reθep'θjon] nf reception; (acto de recibir) receipt
recepcionista [reθepθjo'nista] nm/f receptionist
receptáculo [reθep'takulo] nm receptacle
receptivo, -a [reθep'tiβo, a] adj receptive
receptor, a [reθep'tor, a] nm/f recipient ■ nm (Telec) receiver; **descolgar el ~** to pick up the receiver
recesión [reθe'sjon] nf (Com) recession
receta [re'θeta] nf (Culin) recipe; (Med) prescription
recetar [reθe'tar] vt to prescribe
rechace etc [re'tʃaθe] vb ver **rechazar**
rechazar [retʃa'θar] vt to repel, drive back; (idea) to reject; (oferta) to turn down
rechazo [re'tʃaθo] nm (de fusil) recoil; (rebote) rebound; (negación) rebuff
rechifla [re'tʃifla] nf hissing, booing; (fig) derision
rechinar [retʃi'nar] vi to creak; (dientes) to grind; (máquina) to clank, clatter; (metal seco) to grate; (motor) to hum

rechistar [retʃis'tar] vi: **sin ~** without complaint
rechoncho, -a [re'tʃontʃo, a] adj (fam) stocky, thickset (Brit), heavy-set (US)
rechupete [retʃu'pete]: **de ~** adj (comida) delicious
recibidor [reθiβi'ðor] nm entrance hall
recibimiento [reθiβi'mjento] nm reception, welcome
recibir [reθi'βir] vt to receive; (dar la bienvenida) to welcome; (salir al encuentro de) to go and meet ■ vi to entertain; **recibirse** vr: **recibirse de** to qualify as
recibo [re'θiβo] nm receipt; **acusar ~ de** to acknowledge receipt of
reciclable [reθi'klaβle] adj recyclable
reciclaje [reθi'klaxe] nm recycling; (de trabajadores) retraining; **cursos de ~** refresher courses
reciclar [reθi'klar] vt to recycle; (trabajador) to retrain
recién [re'θjen] adv recently, newly; (Am) just, recently; **~ casado** newly-wed; **el ~ llegado** the newcomer; **el ~ nacido** the newborn child; **~ a las seis** only at six o'clock
reciente [re'θjente] adj recent; (fresco) fresh
recientemente [reθjente'mente] adv recently
recinto [re'θinto] nm enclosure; (área) area, place
recio, -a ['reθjo, a] adj strong, tough; (voz) loud ■ adv hard; loud(ly)
recipiente [reθi'pjente] nm (objeto) container, receptacle; (persona) recipient
reciprocidad [reθiproθi'ðað] nf reciprocity
recíproco, -a [re'θiproko, a] adj reciprocal
recital [reθi'tal] nm (Mus) recital; (Lit) reading
recitar [reθi'tar] vt to recite
reclamación [reklama'θjon] nf claim, demand; (queja) complaint; **libro de reclamaciones** complaints book; **~ salarial** pay claim
reclamar [rekla'mar] vt to claim, demand ■ vi: **~ contra** to complain about; **~ a algn en justicia** to take sb to court
reclamo [re'klamo] nm (anuncio) advertisement; (tentación) attraction
reclinar [rekli'nar] vt to recline, lean; **reclinarse** vr to lean back
recluir [reklu'ir] vt to intern, confine
reclusión [reklu'sjon] nf (prisión) prison; (refugio) seclusion; **~ perpetua** life imprisonment
recluso, -a [re'kluso, a] adj imprisoned; **población reclusa** prison population ■ nm/f (solitario) recluse; (Jur) prisoner
recluta [re'kluta] nm/f recruit ■ nf recruitment

325

reclutamiento [rekluta'mjento] *nm*
recruitment
recluyendo *etc* [reklu'jendo] *vb ver* **recluir**
recobrar [reko'βrar] *vt* (*recuperar*) to recover;
(*rescatar*) to get back; (*ciudad*) to recapture;
(*tiempo*) to make up (for); **recobrarse** *vr* to
recover
recochineo [rekotʃi'neo] *nm* (*fam*) mickey-
taking
recodo [re'koðo] *nm* (*de río, camino*) bend
recogedor, a [rekoxe'ðor, a] *nm/f* picker,
harvester
recoger [reko'xer] *vt* to collect; (*Agr*) to
harvest; (*fruta*) to pick; (*levantar*) to pick up;
(*juntar*) to gather; (*pasar a buscar*) to come for,
get; (*dar asilo*) to give shelter to; (*faldas*) to
gather up; (*mangas*) to roll up; (*pelo*) to put
up; **recogerse** *vr* (*retirarse*) to retire; **me
recogieron en la estación** they picked me
up at the station
recogido, -a [reko'xiðo, a] *adj* (*lugar*) quiet,
secluded; (*pequeño*) small ◼ *nf* (*Correos*)
collection; (*Agr*) harvest; **recogida de datos**
(*Inform*) data capture
recogimiento [rekoxi'mjento] *nm* collection;
(*Agr*) harvesting
recoja *etc* [re'koxa] *vb ver* **recoger**
recolección [rekolek'θjon] *nf* (*Agr*)
harvesting; (*colecta*) collection
recomencé [rekomen'θe], **recomencemos**
etc [rekomen'θemos] *vb ver* **recomenzar**
recomendable [rekomen'daβle] *adj*
recommendable; **poco ~** inadvisable
recomendación [rekomenda'θjon] *nf*
(*sugerencia*) suggestion, recommendation;
(*referencia*) reference; **carta de ~ para** letter of
introduction to
recomendar [rekomen'dar] *vt* to suggest,
recommend; (*confiar*) to entrust
recomenzar [rekomen'θar] *vt, vi* to begin
again, recommence
recomience *etc* [reko'mjenθe] *vb ver*
recomenzar
recomiende *etc* [reko'mjende] *vb ver*
recomendar
recomienzo *etc* [reko'mjenθo] *vb ver*
recomenzar
recompensa [rekom'pensa] *nf* reward,
recompense; (*compensación*): **~ (de una
pérdida)** compensation (for a loss); **como** o
en ~ por in return for
recompensar [rekompen'sar] *vt* to reward,
recompense
recompondré *etc* [rekompon'dre] *vb ver*
recomponer
recomponer [rekompo'ner] *vt* to mend;
(*Inform: texto*) to reformat

recomponga *etc* [rekom'ponga],
recompuesto [rekom'pwesto], **recompuse**
etc [rekom'puse] *vb ver* **recomponer**
reconciliación [rekonθilja'θjon] *nf*
reconciliation
reconciliar [rekonθi'ljar] *vt* to reconcile;
reconciliarse *vr* to become reconciled
recóndito, -a [re'kondito, a] *adj* (*lugar*)
hidden, secret
reconfortar [rekonfor'tar] *vt* to comfort
reconocer [rekono'θer] *vt* to recognize; **~ los
hechos** to face the facts
reconocido, -a [rekono'θiðo, a] *adj*
recognized; (*agradecido*) grateful
reconocimiento [rekonoθi'mjento] *nm*
recognition; (*registro*) search; (*inspección*)
examination; (*gratitud*) gratitude; (*confesión*)
admission; **~ óptico de caracteres** (*Inform*)
optical character recognition; **~ de la voz**
(*Inform*) speech recognition
reconozca *etc* [reko'noθka] *vb ver* **reconocer**
reconquista [rekon'kista] *nf* reconquest
reconquistar [rekonkis'tar] *vt* (*Mil*) to
reconquer; (*fig*) to recover, win back
reconstituyente [rekonstitu'jente] *nm* tonic
reconstruir [rekonstru'ir] *vt* to reconstruct
reconstruyendo *etc* [rekonstru'jendo] *vb ver*
reconstruir
reconversión [rekomber'sjon] *nf*
restructuring, reorganization; (*tb:*
reconversión industrial) rationalization
recopilación [rekopila'θjon] *nf* (*resumen*)
summary; (*compilación*) compilation
recopilar [rekopi'lar] *vt* to compile
récord ['rekorð] *adj inv* record; **cifras ~** record
figures ◼ *nm* (*pl* **records** o **récords**) ['rekorð]
record; **batir el ~** to break the record
recordar [rekor'ðar] *vt* (*acordarse de*) to
remember; (*traer a la memoria*) to recall;
(*recordar a otro*) to remind ◼ *vi* to remember;
recuérdale que me debe cinco dólares
remind him that he owes me five dollars;
que yo recuerde as far as I can remember;
creo ~, si mal no recuerdo if my memory
serves me right
recordatorio [rekorða'torjo] *nm* (*de
fallecimiento*) in memoriam card; (*de bautizo,
comunión*) commemorative card
recorrer [reko'rrer] *vt* (*país*) to cross, travel
through; (*distancia*) to cover; (*registrar*) to
search; (*repasar*) to look over
recorrido [reko'rriðo] *nm* run, journey; **tren
de largo ~** main-line o inter-city (*Brit*) train
recortado, -a [rekor'taðo, a] *adj* uneven,
irregular
recortar [rekor'tar] *vt* (*papel*) to cut out; (*el
pelo*) to trim; (*dibujar*) to draw in outline;

recortarse *vr* to stand out, be silhouetted

recorte [re'korte] *nm* (*acción, de prensa*) cutting; (*de telas, chapas*) trimming; **~ presupuestario** budget cut; **~ salarial** wage cut

recostado, -a [rekos'taðo, a] *adj* leaning; **estar ~** to be lying down

recostar [rekos'tar] *vt* to lean; **recostarse** *vr* to lie down

recoveco [reko'βeko] *nm* (*de camino, río etc*) bend; (*en casa*) cubbyhole

recreación [rekrea'θjon] *nf* recreation

recrear [rekre'ar] *vt* (*entretener*) to entertain; (*volver a crear*) to recreate

recreativo, -a [rekrea'tiβo, a] *adj* recreational

recreo [re'kreo] *nm* recreation; (*Escol*) break, playtime

recriminar [rekrimi'nar] *vt* to reproach ▪ *vi* to recriminate; **recriminarse** *vr* to reproach each other

recrudecer [rekruðe'θer] *vt, vi,* **recrudecerse** *vr* to worsen

recrudecimiento [rekruðeθi'mjento] *nm* upsurge

recrudezca *etc* [recru'ðeθka] *vb ver* recrudecer

recta ['rekta] *nf ver* recto

rectangular [rektangu'lar] *adj* rectangular

rectángulo, -a [rek'tangulo, a] *adj* rectangular ▪ *nm* rectangle

rectificable [rektifi'kaβle] *adj* rectifiable; **fácilmente ~** easily rectified

rectificación [rektifika'θjon] *nf* correction

rectificar [rektifi'kar] *vt* to rectify; (*volverse recto*) to straighten ▪ *vi* to correct o.s.

rectifique *etc* [rekti'fike] *vb ver* rectificar

rectitud [rekti'tuð] *nf* straightness; (*fig*) rectitude

recto, -a ['rekto, a] *adj* straight; (*persona*) honest, upright; (*estricto*) strict; (*juez*) fair; (*juicio*) sound ▪ *nm* rectum; (*Atletismo*) straight ▪ *nf* straight line; **en el sentido ~ de la palabra** in the proper sense of the word; **recta final** *o* **de llegada** home straight

rector, a [rek'tor, a] *adj* governing ▪ *nm/f* head, chief; (*Escol*) rector, president (*US*)

rectorado [rekto'raðo] *nm* (*cargo*) rectorship, presidency (*US*); (*oficina*) rector's office

recuadro [re'kwaðro] *nm* box; (*Tip*) inset

recubrir [reku'βir] *vt* to cover

recuento [re'kwento] *nm* inventory; **hacer el ~ de** to count *o* reckon up

recuerdo *etc* [re'kwerðo] *vb ver* recordar ▪ *nm* souvenir; **recuerdos** *nmpl* memories; **¡~s a tu madre!** give my regards to your mother!;

"**R~ de Mallorca**" "a present from Majorca"; **contar los ~s** to reminisce

recueste *etc* [re'kweste] *vb ver* recostar

recular [reku'lar] *vi* to back down

recuperable [rekupe'raβle] *adj* recoverable

recuperación [rekupera'θjon] *nf* recovery; **~ de datos** (*Inform*) data retrieval

recuperar [rekupe'rar] *vt* to recover; (*tiempo*) to make up; (*Inform*) to retrieve; **recuperarse** *vr* to recuperate

recurrir [reku'rrir] *vi* (*Jur*) to appeal; **~ a** to resort to; (*persona*) to turn to

recurso [re'kurso] *nm* resort; (*medio*) means *pl,* resource; (*Jur*) appeal; **como último ~** as a last resort; **recursos económicos** economic resources; **recursos naturales** natural resources

recusar [reku'sar] *vt* to reject, refuse

red [reð] *nf* net, mesh; (*Ferro: Inform*) network; (*Elec, de agua*) mains, supply system; (*de tiendas*) chain; (*trampa*) trap; **la R~** (*Internet*) the Net; **estar conectado con la ~** to be connected to the mains; **~ local** (*Inform*) local area network; **~ de transmisión** (*Inform*) data network

redacción [reðak'θjon] *nf* (*acción*) writing; (*Escol*) essay, composition; (*limpieza de texto*) editing; (*personal*) editorial staff

redactar [reðak'tar] *vt* to draw up, draft; (*periódico, Inform*) to edit

redactor, a [reðak'tor, a] *nm/f* writer; (*en periódico*) editor

redada [re'ðaða] *nf* (*Pesca*) cast, throw; (*fig*) catch; **~ policial** police raid, round-up

redención [reðen'θjon] *nf* redemption

redentor, a [reðen'tor, a] *adj* redeeming ▪ *nm/f* (*Com*) redeemer

redescubierto [reðesku'βjerto] *pp de* redescubrir

redescubrir [reðesku'βrir] *vt* to rediscover

redesignar [reðesiɣ'nar] *vt* (*Inform*) to rename

redicho, -a [re'ðitʃo, a] *adj* affected

redil [re'ðil] *nm* sheepfold

redimir [reði'mir] *vt* to redeem; (*rehén*) to ransom

redistribución [reðistriβu'θjon] *nf* (*Com*) redeployment

rédito ['reðito] *nm* interest, yield

redoblar [reðo'βlar] *vt* to redouble ▪ *vi* (*tambor*) to play a roll on the drums

redoble [re'ðoβle] *nm* (*Mus*) drumroll, drumbeat; (*de trueno*) roll

redomado, -a [reðo'maðo, a] *adj* (*astuto*) sly, crafty; (*perfecto*) utter

redonda [re'ðonda] *nf ver* redondo

redondear [reðonde'ar] *vt* to round, round off; (*cifra*) to round up

redondel [reðon'del] *nm* (*círculo*) circle; (*Taur*) bullring, arena; (*Auto*) roundabout

redondo, -a [re'ðondo, a] *adj* (*circular*) round; (*completo*) complete ■ *nf*: **a la redonda** around, round about; **en muchas millas a la redonda** for many miles around; **rehusar en ~** to give a flat refusal

reducción [reðuk'θjon] *nf* reduction; **~ del activo** (*Com*) divestment; **~ de precios** (*Com*) price-cutting

reducido, -a [reðu'θiðo, a] *adj* reduced; (*limitado*) limited; (*pequeño*) small; **quedar ~ a** to be reduced to

reducir [reðu'θir] *vt* to reduce, limit; (*someter*) to bring under control; **reducirse** *vr* to diminish; (*Mat*): **~ (a)** to reduce (to), convert (into); **~ las millas a kilómetros** to convert miles into kilometres; **reducirse a** (*fig*) to come *o* boil down to

reducto [re'ðukto] *nm* redoubt

reduje *etc* [re'ðuxe] *vb ver* **reducir**

redundancia [reðun'danθja] *nf* redundancy

reduzca *etc* [re'ðuθka] *vb ver* **reducir**

reedición [re(e)ði'θjon] *nf* reissue

reeditar [re(e)ði'tar] *vt* to reissue

reelección [re(e)lek'θjon] *nf* re-election

reelegir [re(e)le'xir] *vt* to re-elect

reembolsable [re(e)mbol'saβle] *adj* (*Com*) redeemable, refundable

reembolsar [re(e)mbol'sar] *vt* (*persona*) to reimburse; (*dinero*) to repay, pay back; (*depósito*) to refund

reembolso [re(e)m'bolso] *nm* reimbursement; refund; **enviar algo contra ~** to send sth cash on delivery; **contra ~ del flete** freight forward; **~ fiscal** tax rebate

reemplace *etc* [re(e)m'plaθe] *vb ver* **reemplazar**

reemplazar [re(e)mpla'θar] *vt* to replace

reemplazo [re(e)m'plaθo] *nm* replacement; **de ~** (*Mil*) reserve

reencuentro [re(e)n'kwentro] *nm* reunion

reengancharse [re(e)ngan'tʃarse] *vr* (*Mil*) to re-enlist

reestreno [re(e)s'treno] *nm* rerun

reestructurar [re(e)struktu'rar] *vt* to restructure

reexportación [re(e)ksporta'θjon] *nf* (*Com*) re-export

reexportar [re(e)kspor'tar] *vt* (*Com*) to re-export

REF *nm abr* (*Esp Econ*) = **Régimen Económico Fiscal**

Ref.ª *abr* (= *referencia*) ref

refacción [refak'θjon] *nf* (*Am*) repair(s); **refacciones** *nfpl* (*piezas de repuesto*) spare parts

referencia [refe'renθja] *nf* reference; **con ~ a** with reference to; **hacer ~ a** to refer *o* allude to; **~ comercial** (*Com*) trade reference

referéndum [refe'rendum] (*pl* **referéndums**) *nm* referendum

referente [refe'rente] *adj*: **~ a** concerning, relating to

referir [refe'rir] *vt* (*contar*) to tell, recount; (*relacionar*) to refer, relate; **referirse** *vr*: **referirse a** to refer to; **~ al lector a un apéndice** to refer the reader to an appendix; **~ a** (*Com*) to convert into; **por lo que se refiere a eso** as for that, as regards that

refiera *etc* [re'fjera] *vb ver* **referir**

refilón [refi'lon]: **de ~** *adv* obliquely; **mirar a algn de ~** to look out of the corner of one's eye at sb

refinado, -a [refi'naðo, a] *adj* refined

refinamiento [refina'mjento] *nm* refinement; **~ por pasos** (*Inform*) stepwise refinement

refinar [refi'nar] *vt* to refine

refinería [refine'ria] *nf* refinery

refiriendo *etc* [refi'rjendo] *vb ver* **referir**

reflector [reflek'tor] *nm* reflector; (*Elec*) spotlight; (*Aviat: Mil*) searchlight

reflejar [refle'xar] *vt* to reflect; **reflejarse** *vr* to be reflected

reflejo, -a [re'flexo, a] *adj* reflected; (*movimiento*) reflex ■ *nm* reflection; (*Anat*) reflex; (*en el pelo*): **reflejos** *nmpl* highlights; **tiene el pelo castaño con reflejos rubios** she has chestnut hair with blond streaks

reflexión [reflek'sjon] *nf* reflection

reflexionar [refleksjo'nar] *vt* to reflect on ■ *vi* to reflect; (*detenerse*) to pause (to think); **¡reflexione!** you think it over!

reflexivo, -a [reflek'siβo, a] *adj* thoughtful; (*Ling*) reflexive

refluir [reflu'ir] *vi* to flow back

reflujo [re'fluxo] *nm* ebb

refluyendo *etc* [reflu'jendo] *vb ver* **refluir**

reforcé [refor'θe], **reforcemos** *etc* [refor'θemos] *vb ver* **reforzar**

reforma [re'forma] *nf* reform; (*Arq etc*) repair; **~ agraria** agrarian reform

reformar [refor'mar] *vt* to reform; (*modificar*) to change, alter; (*texto*) to revise; (*Arq*) to repair; **reformarse** *vr* to mend one's ways

reformatear [reformate'ar] *vt* (*Inform: disco*) to reformat

reformatorio [reforma'torjo] *nm* reformatory; **~ de menores** remand home

reformista [refor'mista] *adj, nm/f* reformist

reforzamiento [reforθa'mjento] *nm* reinforcement

reforzar [refor'θar] *vt* to strengthen; (*Arq*) to reinforce; (*fig*) to encourage

refractario, -a [refrak'tarjo, a] *adj* (*Tec*) heat-resistant; **ser ~ a una reforma** to resist o be opposed to a reform

refrán [re'fran] *nm* proverb, saying

refregar [refre'ɣar] *vt* to scrub

refrenar [refre'nar] *vt* to check, restrain

refrendar [refren'dar] *vt* (*firma*) to endorse, countersign; (*ley*) to approve

refrescante [refres'kante] *adj* refreshing, cooling

refrescar [refres'kar] *vt* to refresh ■ *vi* to cool down; **refrescarse** *vr* to get cooler; (*tomar aire fresco*) to go out for a breath of fresh air; (*beber*) to have a drink

refresco [re'fresko] *nm* soft drink, cool drink; **"refrescos"** "refreshments"

refresque *etc* [re'freske] *vb ver* **refrescar**

refriega *etc* [re'frjeɣa] *vb ver* **refregar** ■ *nf* scuffle, brawl

refriegue *etc* [re'frjeɣe] *vb ver* **refregar**

refrigeración [refrixera'θjon] *nf* refrigeration; (*de casa*) air-conditioning

refrigerado, -a [refrixe'raðo, a] *adj* cooled; (*sala*) air-conditioned

refrigerador [refrixera'ðor] *nm*, **refrigeradora** (*Am*) [refrixera'ðora] ■ *nf* refrigerator, icebox (US)

refrigerar [refrixe'rar] *vt* to refrigerate; (*sala*) to air-condition

refrito [re'frito] *nm* (*Culin*): **un ~ de cebolla y tomate** sautéed onions and tomatoes; **un ~** (*fig*) a rehash

refuerce *etc* [re'fwerθe] *vb ver* **reforzar**

refuerzo *etc* [re'fwerθo] *vb ver* **reforzar** ■ *nm* reinforcement; (*Tec*) support

refugiado, -a [refu'xjaðo, a] *nm/f* refugee

refugiarse [refu'xjarse] *vr* to take refuge, shelter

refugio [re'fuxjo] *nm* refuge; (*protección*) shelter; (*Auto*) street o traffic island; **~ alpino** o **de montaña** mountain hut; **~ subterráneo** (*Mil*) underground shelter

refulgencia [reful'xenθja] *nf* brilliance

refulgir [reful'xir] *vi* to shine, be dazzling

refulja *etc* [re'fulxa] *vb ver* **refulgir**

refundir [refun'dir] *vt* to recast; (*escrito etc*) to adapt, rewrite

refunfuñar [refunfu'nar] *vi* to grunt, growl; (*quejarse*) to grumble

refunfuñón, -ona [refunfu'non, ona] (*fam*) *adj* grumpy ■ *nm/f* grouch

refutación [refuta'θjon] *nf* refutation

refutar [refu'tar] *vt* to refute

regadera [reɣa'ðera] *nf* watering can; (*Am*) shower; **estar como una ~** (*fam*) to be as mad as a hatter

regadío [reɣa'ðio] *nm* irrigated land

regalado, -a [reɣa'laðo, a] *adj* comfortable, luxurious; (*gratis*) free, for nothing; **lo tuvo ~** it was handed to him on a plate

regalar [reɣa'lar] *vt* (*dar*) to give (as a present); (*entregar*) to give away; (*mimar*) to pamper, make a fuss of; **regalarse** *vr* to treat o.s. to

regalía [reɣa'lia] *nf* privilege, prerogative; (*Com*) bonus; (*de autor*) royalty

regaliz [reɣa'liθ] *nm* liquorice

regalo [re'ɣalo] *nm* (*obsequio*) gift, present; (*gusto*) pleasure; (*comodidad*) comfort

regañadientes [reɣana'ðjentes]: **a ~** *adv* reluctantly

regañar [reɣa'nar] *vt* to scold ■ *vi* to grumble; (*dos personas*) to fall out, quarrel

regañón, -ona [reɣa'non, ona] *adj* nagging

regar [re'ɣar] *vt* to water, irrigate; (*fig*) to scatter, sprinkle

regata [re'ɣata] *nf* (*Naut*) race

regatear [reɣate'ar] *vt* (*Com*) to bargain over; (*escatimar*) to be mean with ■ *vi* to bargain, haggle; (*Deporte*) to dribble; **no ~ esfuerzo** to spare no effort

regateo [reɣa'teo] *nm* bargaining; (*Deporte*) dribbling; (*con el cuerpo*) swerve, dodge

regazo [re'ɣaθo] *nm* lap

regencia [re'xenθja] *nf* regency

regeneración [rexenera'θjon] *nf* regeneration

regenerar [rexene'rar] *vt* to regenerate

regentar [rexen'tar] *vt* to direct, manage; (*puesto*) to hold in an acting capacity; (*negocio*) to be in charge of

regente, -a [re'xente, a] *adj* (*príncipe*) regent; (*director*) managing ■ *nm* (*Com*) manager; (*Pol*) regent

régimen ['reximen] (*pl* **regímenes**) [re'ximenes] *nm* regime; (*reinado*) rule; (*Med*) diet; (*reglas*) (set of) rules *pl*; (*manera de vivir*) lifestyle; **estar a ~** to be on a diet

regimiento [rexi'mjento] *nm* regiment

regio, -a ['rexjo, a] *adj* royal, regal; (*fig: suntuoso*) splendid; (*Am fam*) great, terrific

región [re'xjon] *nf* region; (*área*) area

regional [rexjo'nal] *adj* regional

regir [re'xir] *vt* to govern, rule; (*dirigir*) to manage, run; (*Econ: Jur: Ling*) to govern ■ *vi* to apply, be in force

registrador [rexistra'ðor] *nm* registrar, recorder

registrar [rexis'trar] *vt* (*buscar*) to search; (*en cajón*) to look through; (*inspeccionar*) to inspect; (*anotar*) to register, record; (*Inform: Mus*) to record; **registrarse** *vr* to register; (*ocurrir*) to happen

registro [re'xistro] *nm* (*acto*) registration;

329

(*Mus, libro*) register; (*lista*) list, record; (*Inform*) record; (*inspección*) inspection, search; ~ **civil** registry office; ~ **electoral** voting register; ~ **de la propiedad** land registry (office)

regla ['reɣla] *nf* (*ley*) rule, regulation; (*de medir*) ruler, rule; (*Med: período*) period; (*regla científica*) law, principle; **no hay ~ sin excepción** every rule has its exception

reglamentación [reɣlamenta'θjon] *nf* (*acto*) regulation; (*lista*) rules *pl*

reglamentar [reɣlamen'tar] *vt* to regulate

reglamentario, -a [reɣlamen'tarjo, a] *adj* statutory; **en la forma reglamentaria** in the properly established way

reglamento [reɣla'mento] *nm* rules *pl*, regulations *pl*; ~ **del tráfico** highway code

reglar [re'ɣlar] *vt* (*acciones*) to regulate; **reglarse** *vr*: **reglarse por** to be guided by

regocijarse [reɣoθi'xarse] *vr*: ~ **de** *o* **por** to rejoice at, be glad about

regocijo [reɣo'θixo] *nm* joy, happiness

regodearse [reɣoðe'arse] *vr* to be glad, be delighted; (*pey*): ~ **con** *o* **en** to gloat over

regodeo [reɣo'ðeo] *nm* delight; (*pey*) perverse pleasure

regresar [reɣre'sar] *vi* to come/go back, return; **regresarse** *vr* (*Am*) to return

regresivo, -a [reɣre'siβo, a] *adj* backward; (*fig*) regressive

regreso [re'ɣreso] *nm* return; **estar de** ~ to be back, be home

regué [re'ɣe], **reguemos** etc [re'ɣemos] *vb ver* **regar**

reguero [re'ɣero] *nm* (*de sangre*) trickle; (*de humo*) trail

regulación [reɣula'θjon] *nf* regulation; (*Tec*) adjustment; (*control*) control; ~ **de empleo** redundancies *pl*; ~ **del tráfico** traffic control

regulador [reɣula'ðor] *nm* (*Tec*) regulator; (*de radio etc*) knob, control

regular [reɣu'lar] *adj* regular; (*normal*) normal, usual; (*común*) ordinary; (*organizado*) regular, orderly; (*mediano*) average; (*fam*) not bad, so-so ■ *adv*: **estar** ~ to be so-so *o* alright ■ *vt* (*controlar*) to control, regulate; (*Tec*) to adjust; **por lo** ~ as a rule

regularice etc [reɣula'riθe] *vb ver* **regularizar**

regularidad [reɣulari'ðað] *nf* regularity; **con** ~ regularly

regularizar [reɣulari'θar] *vt* to regularize

regusto [re'ɣusto] *nm* aftertaste

rehabilitación [reaβilita'θjon] *nf* rehabilitation; (*Arq*) restoration

rehabilitar [reaβili'tar] *vt* to rehabilitate; (*Arq*) to restore; (*reintegrar*) to reinstate

rehacer [rea'θer] *vt* (*reparar*) to mend, repair; (*volver a hacer*) to redo, repeat; **rehacerse** *vr*

(*Med*) to recover

rehaga etc [re'aɣa], **reharé** etc [rea're], **rehaz** [re'aθ], **rehecho** [re'etʃo] *vb ver* **rehacer**

rehén [re'en] *nm/f* hostage

rehice etc [re'iθe], **rehizo** [re'iθo] *vb ver* **rehacer**

rehogar [reo'ɣar] *vt* to sauté, toss in oil

rehuir [reu'ir] *vt* to avoid, shun

rehusar [reu'sar] *vt, vi* to refuse

rehuyendo etc [reu'jendo] *vb ver* **rehuir**

reina ['reina] *nf* queen

reinado [rei'naðo] *nm* reign

reinante [rei'nante] *adj* (*fig*) prevailing

reinar [rei'nar] *vi* to reign; (*fig: prevalecer*) to prevail, be general

reincidir [reinθi'ðir] *vi* to relapse; (*criminal*) to repeat an offence

reincorporarse [reinkorpo'rarse] *vr*: ~ **a** to rejoin

reinicializar [reiniθjali'θar] *vt* (*Inform*) to reset

reino ['reino] *nm* kingdom; **el R~ Unido** the United Kingdom

reinserción [reinser'θjon] *nf* rehabilitation

reinsertar [reinser'tar] *vt* to rehabilitate

reintegración [reinteɣra'θjon] *nf* (*Com*) reinstatement

reintegrar [reinte'ɣrar] *vt* (*reconstituir*) to reconstruct; (*persona*) to reinstate; (*dinero*) to refund, pay back; **reintegrarse** *vr*: **reintegrarse a** to return to

reintegro [rein'teɣro] *nm* refund, reimbursement; (*en banco*) withdrawal

reír [re'ir] *vi*, **reírse** *vr* to laugh; **reírse de** to laugh at

reiterado, -a [reite'raðo, a] *adj* repeated

reiterar [reite'rar] *vt* to reiterate; (*repetir*) to repeat

reivindicación [reiβindika'θjon] *nf* (*demanda*) claim, demand; (*justificación*) vindication

reivindicar [reiβindi'kar] *vt* to claim

reivindique etc [reiβin'dike] *vb ver* **reivindicar**

reja ['rexa] *nf* (*de ventana*) grille, bars *pl*; (*en la calle*) grating

rejilla [re'xiʎa] *nf* grating, grille; (*muebles*) wickerwork; (*de ventilación*) vent; (*de coche etc*) luggage rack

rejuvenecer [rexuβene'θer] *vt, vi* to rejuvenate

rejuvenezca etc [rexuβe'neθka] *vb ver* **rejuvenecer**

relación [rela'θjon] *nf* relation, relationship; (*Mat*) ratio; (*lista*) list; (*narración*) report; ~ **costo-efectivo** *o* **costo-rendimiento** (*Com*) cost-effectiveness; **relaciones** *nfpl* (*enchufes*) influential friends, connections; **relaciones carnales** sexual relations; **relaciones**

comerciales business connections; **relaciones empresariales/humanas** industrial/human relations; **relaciones laborales/públicas** labour/public relations; **con ~ a, en ~ con** in relation to; **estar en** o **tener buenas relaciones con** to be on good terms with

relacionar [relaθjo'nar] *vt* to relate, connect; **relacionarse** *vr* to be connected o linked

relajación [rclaxa'θjon] *nf* relaxation

relajado, -a [rela'xaðo, a] *adj* (*disoluto*) loose; (*cómodo*) relaxed; (*Med*) ruptured

relajante [rela'xante] *adj* relaxing; (*Med*) sedative

relajar [rela'xar] *vt*, **relajarse** *vr* to relax

relamerse [rela'merse] *vr* to lick one's lips

relamido, -a [rela'miðo, a] *adj* (*pulcro*) overdressed; (*afectado*) affected

relámpago [re'lampaɣo] *nm* flash of lightning ■ *adj* lightning *cpd*; **como un ~** as quick as lightning, in a flash; **visita/huelga ~** lightning visit/strike

relampaguear [relampaɣe'ar] *vi* to flash

relanzar [relan'θar] *vt* to relaunch

relatar [rela'tar] *vt* to tell, relate

relatividad [relatiβi'ðað] *nf* relativity

relativo, -a [rela'tiβo, a] *adj* relative; **en lo ~ a** concerning

relato [re'lato] *nm* (*narración*) story, tale

relax [re'las] *nm* rest; **"R~"** (*en anuncio*) "Personal services"

relegar [rele'ɣar] *vt* to relegate; **~ algo al olvido** to banish sth from one's mind

relegue *etc* [re'leɣe] *vb ver* **relegar**

relevante [rele'βante] *adj* eminent, outstanding

relevar [rele'βar] *vt* (*sustituir*) to relieve; **relevarse** *vr* to relay; **~ a algn de un cargo** to relieve sb of his post

relevo [re'leβo] *nm* relief; **carrera de relevos** relay race; **coger** o **tomar el ~** to take over, stand in

relieve [re'ljeβe] *nm* (*Arte: Tec*) relief; (*fig*) prominence, importance; **bajo ~** bas-relief; **un personaje de ~** an important man; **dar ~ a** to highlight

religión [reli'xjon] *nf* religion

religioso, -a [reli'xjoso, a] *adj* religious ■ *nm/f* monk/nun

relinchar [relin'tʃar] *vi* to neigh

relincho [re'lintʃo] *nm* neigh; (*acto*) neighing

reliquia [re'likja] *nf* relic; **~ de familia** heirloom

rellano [re'ʎano] *nm* (*Arq*) landing

rellenar [reʎe'nar] *vt* (*llenar*) to fill up; (*Culin*) to stuff; (*Costura*) to pad; (*formulario etc*) to fill in o out

relleno, -a [re'ʎeno, a] *adj* full up; (*Culin*) stuffed ■ *nm* stuffing; (*de tapicería*) padding

reloj [re'lo(x)] *nm* clock; **~ de pie** grandfather clock; **~ (de pulsera)** wristwatch; **~ de sol** sundial; **~ despertador** alarm (clock); **como un ~** like clockwork; **contra (el) ~** against the clock

relojería [reloxe'ria] (*tienda*) watchmaker's (shop); **aparato de ~** clockwork; **bomba de ~** time bomb

relojero, -a [relo'xero, a] *nm/f* clockmaker; watchmaker

reluciente [relu'θjente] *adj* brilliant, shining

relucir [relu'θir] *vi* to shine; (*fig*) to excel; **sacar algo a ~** to show sth off

relumbrante [relum'brante] *adj* dazzling

relumbrar [relum'brar] *vi* to dazzle, shine brilliantly

reluzca *etc* [re'luθka] *vb ver* **relucir**

remachar [rema'tʃar] *vt* to rivet; (*fig*) to hammer home, drive home

remache [re'matʃe] *nm* rivet

remanente [rema'nente] *nm* remainder; (*Com*) balance; (*de producto*) surplus

remangarse [reman'garse] *vr* to roll one's sleeves up

remanso [re'manso] *nm* pool

remar [re'mar] *vi* to row

rematado, -a [rema'taðo, a] *adj* complete, utter; **es un loco ~** he's a raving lunatic

rematar [rema'tar] *vt* to finish off; (*animal*) to put out of its misery; (*Com*) to sell off cheap ■ *vi* to end, finish off; (*Deporte*) to shoot

remate [re'mate] *nm* end, finish; (*punta*) tip; (*Deporte*) shot; (*Arq*) top; (*Com*) auction sale; **de** o **para ~** to crown it all (*Brit*), to top it off

remediable [reme'ðjaβle] *adj*: **fácilmente ~** easily remedied

remediar [reme'ðjar] *vt* (*gen*) to remedy; (*subsanar*) to make good, repair; (*evitar*) to avoid; **sin poder remediarlo** without being able to prevent it

remedio [re'meðjo] *nm* remedy; (*Jur*) recourse, remedy; **poner ~ a** to correct, stop; **no tener más ~** to have no alternative; **¡qué ~!** there's no other way; **como último ~** as a last resort; **sin ~** inevitable; (*Med*) hopeless

remedo [re'meðo] *nm* imitation; (*pey*) parody

remendar [remen'dar] *vt* to repair; (*con parche*) to patch; (*fig*) to correct

remesa [re'mesa] *nf* remittance; (*Com*) shipment

remiendo *etc* [re'mjendo] *vb ver* **remendar** ■ *nm* mend; (*con parche*) patch; (*cosido*) darn; (*fig*) correction

remilgado, -a [remil'ɣaðo, a] *adj* prim; (*afectado*) affected

r

remilgo [re'milɣo] *nm* primness; *(afectación)* affectation

reminiscencia [reminis'θenθja] *nf* reminiscence

remirar [remi'rar] *vt (volver a mirar)* to look at again; *(examinar)* to look hard at

remisión [remi'sjon] *nf (acto)* sending, shipment; *(Rel)* forgiveness, remission; **sin ~** hopelessly

remiso, -a [re'miso, a] *adj* remiss

remite [re'mite] *nm (en sobre)* name and address of sender

remitente [remi'tente] *nm/f (Correos)* sender

remitir [remi'tir] *vt* to remit, send ■ *vi* to slacken

remo ['remo] *nm (de barco)* oar; *(Deporte)* rowing; **cruzar un río a ~** to row across a river

remoce *etc* [re'moθe] *vb ver* **remozar**

remodelación [remodela'θjon] *nf (Pol)*: **~ del gobierno** cabinet reshuffle

remojar [remo'xar] *vt* to steep, soak; *(galleta etc)* to dip, dunk; *(fam)* to celebrate with a drink

remojo [re'moxo] *nm* steeping, soaking; *(por la lluvia)* drenching, soaking; **dejar la ropa en ~** to leave clothes to soak

remojón [remo'xon] *nm* soaking; **darse un ~** *(fam)* to go (in) for a dip

remolacha [remo'latʃa] *nf* beet, beetroot *(Brit)*

remolcador [remolka'ðor] *nm (Naut)* tug; *(Auto)* breakdown lorry

remolcar [remol'kar] *vt* to tow

remolino [remo'lino] *nm* eddy; *(de agua)* whirlpool; *(de viento)* whirlwind; *(de gente)* crowd

remolón, -ona [remo'lon, ona] *adj* lazy ■ *nm/f* slacker, shirker

remolque *etc* [re'molke] *vb ver* **remolcar** ■ *nm* tow, towing; *(cuerda)* towrope; **llevar a ~** to tow

remontar [remon'tar] *vt* to mend; *(obstáculo)* to negotiate, get over; **remontarse** *vr* to soar; **remontarse a** *(Com)* to amount to; *(en tiempo)* to go back to, date from; **~ el vuelo** to soar

rémora ['remora] *nf* hindrance

remorder [remor'ðer] *vt* to distress, disturb

remordimiento [remorði'mjento] *nm* remorse

remotamente [remota'mente] *adv* vaguely

remoto, -a [re'moto, a] *adj* remote

remover [remo'βer] *vt* to stir; *(tierra)* to turn over; *(objetos)* to move round

remozar [remo'θar] *vt (Arq)* to refurbish; *(fig)* to brighten o polish up

remuerda *etc* [re'mwerða] *vb ver* **remorder**

remueva *etc* [re'mweβa] *vb ver* **remover**

remuneración [remunera'θjon] *nf* remuneration

remunerado, -a [remune'raðo, a] *adj*: **trabajo bien/mal ~** well-/badly-paid job

remunerar [remune'rar] *vt* to remunerate; *(premiar)* to reward

renacer [rena'θer] *vi* to be reborn; *(fig)* to revive

renacimiento [renaθi'mjento] *nm* rebirth; **el R~** the Renaissance

renacuajo [rena'kwaxo] *nm (Zool)* tadpole

renal [re'nal] *adj* renal, kidney *cpd*

Renania [re'nanja] *nf* Rhineland

renazca *etc* [re'naθka] *vb ver* **renacer**

rencilla [ren'θiʎa] *nf* quarrel; **rencillas** *nfpl* bickering *sg*

rencor [ren'kor] *nm* rancour, bitterness; *(resentimiento)* ill feeling, resentment; **guardar ~ a** to have a grudge against

rencoroso, -a [renko'roso, a] *adj* spiteful

rendición [rendi'θjon] *nf* surrender

rendido, -a [ren'diðo, a] *adj (sumiso)* submissive; *(agotado)* worn-out, exhausted; *(enamorado)* devoted

rendija [ren'dixa] *nf (hendidura)* crack; *(abertura)* aperture; *(fig)* rift, split; *(Jur)* loophole

rendimiento [rendi'mjento] *nm (producción)* output; *(Com)* yield, profit(s) *(pl)*; *(Tec: Com)* efficiency; **~ de capital** *(Com)* return on capital

rendir [ren'dir] *vt (vencer)* to defeat; *(producir)* to produce; *(dar beneficio)* to yield; *(agotar)* to exhaust ■ *vi* to pay; *(Com)* to yield, produce; **rendirse** *vr (someterse)* to surrender; *(ceder)* to yield; *(cansarse)* to wear o.s. out; **~ homenaje** o **culto a** to pay homage to; **el negocio no rinde** the business doesn't pay

renegado, -a [rene'ɣaðo, a] *adj, nm/f* renegade

renegar [rene'ɣar] *vt (negar)* to deny vigorously ■ *vi (blasfemar)* to blaspheme; **~ de** *(renunciar)* to renounce; *(quejarse)* to complain about

renegué [rene'ɣe], **reneguemos** *etc* [rene'ɣemos] *vb ver* **renegar**

RENFE ['renfe] *nf abr (Esp: Ferro)* = **Red Nacional de Ferrocarriles Españoles**

renglón [ren'glon] *nm (línea)* line; *(Com)* item, article; **a ~ seguido** immediately after

rengo, -a ['rengo, a] *adj (Am)* lame

reniego *etc* [re'njeɣo], **reniegue** *etc* [re'njeɣe] *vb ver* **renegar**

reno ['reno] *nm* reindeer

renombrado, -a [renom'braðo, a] *adj* renowned

renombre [re'nombre] *nm* renown

renovable [reno'βaβle] *adj* renewable

renovación [renoβa'θjon] *nf* (*de contrato*) renewal; (*Arq*) renovation

renovar [reno'βar] *vt* to renew; (*Arq*) to renovate; (*sala*) to redecorate

renquear [renke'ar] *vi* to limp; (*fam*) to get along, scrape by

renta ['renta] *nf* (*ingresos*) income; (*beneficio*) profit; (*alquiler*) rent; **~ gravable** *o* **imponible** taxable income; **~ nacional (bruta)** (gross) national income; **~ no salarial** unearned income; **~ sobre el terreno** (*Com*) ground rent; **~ vitalicia** annuity; **política de rentas** incomes policy; **vivir de sus rentas** to live on one's private income

rentabilizar [rentaβili'θar] *vt* to make profitable

rentable [ren'taβle] *adj* profitable; **no ~** unprofitable

rentar [ren'tar] *vt* to produce, yield; (*Am*) to rent

rentista [ren'tista] *nm/f* (*accionista*) shareholder (*Brit*), stockholder (*US*)

renuencia [re'nwenθja] *nf* reluctance

renuente [re'nwente] *adj* reluctant

renueve *etc* [re'nweβe] *vb ver* **renovar**

renuncia [re'nunθja] *nf* resignation

renunciar [renun'θjar] *vt* to renounce, give up ▪ *vi* to resign; **~ a hacer algo** to give up doing sth

reñido, -a [re'niðo, a] *adj* (*batalla*) bitter, hard-fought; **estar ~ con algn** to be on bad terms with sb; **está ~ con su familia** he has fallen out with his family

reñir [re'nir] *vt* (*regañar*) to scold ▪ *vi* (*estar peleado*) to quarrel, fall out; (*combatir*) to fight

reo ['reo] *nm/f* culprit, offender; (*Jur*) accused

reojo [re'oxo]: **de ~** *adv* out of the corner of one's eye

reorganizar [reorɣani'θar] *vt* to reorganize

Rep *abr* = **República**

reparación [repara'θjon] *nf* (*acto*) mending, repairing; (*Tec*) repair; (*fig*) amends, reparation; **"reparaciones en el acto"** "repairs while you wait"

reparador, -a [repara'ðor, a] *adj* refreshing; (*comida*) fortifying ▪ *nm* repairer

reparar [repa'rar] *vt* to repair; (*fig*) to make amends for; (*suerte*) to retrieve; (*observar*) to observe ▪ *vi*: **~ en** (*darse cuenta de*) to notice; (*poner atención en*) to pay attention to; **sin ~ en los gastos** regardless of the cost

reparo [re'paro] *nm* (*advertencia*) observation; (*duda*) doubt; (*dificultad*) difficulty; (*escrúpulo*) scruple, qualm; **poner reparos (a)** to raise

objections (to); (*criticar*) to criticize; **no tuvo ~ en hacerlo** he did not hesitate to do it

repartición [reparti'θjon] *nf* distribution; (*división*) division

repartidor, a [reparti'ðor, a] *nm/f* distributor; **~ de leche** milkman

repartir [repar'tir] *vt* to distribute, share out; (*Com: Correos*) to deliver; (*Mil*) to partition; (*libros*) to give out; (*comida*) to serve out; (*Naipes*) to deal

reparto [re'parto] *nm* distribution; (*Com: Correos*) delivery; (*Teat, Cine*) cast; (*Am: urbanización*) housing estate (*Brit*), real estate development (*US*); **"~ a domicilio"** "home delivery service"

repasar [repa'sar] *vt* (*Escol*) to revise; (*Mecánica*) to check, overhaul; (*Costura*) to mend

repaso [re'paso] *nm* revision; (*Mecánica*) overhaul, checkup; (*Costura*) mending; **~ general** servicing, general overhaul; **curso de ~** refresher course

repatriar [repa'trjar] *vt* to repatriate; **repatriarse** *vr* to return home

repelente [repe'lente] *adj* repellent, repulsive

repeler [repe'ler] *vt* to repel; (*idea, oferta*) to reject

repensar [repen'sar] *vt* to reconsider

repente [re'pente] *nm* sudden movement; (*fig*) impulse; **de ~** suddenly; **~ de ira** fit of anger

repentice *etc* [repen'tiθe] *vb ver* **repentizar**

repentino, -a [repen'tino, a] *adj* sudden; (*imprevisto*) unexpected

repentizar [repenti'θar] *vi* (*Mus*) to sight-read

repercusión [reperku'sjon] *nf* repercussion; **de amplia** *o* **ancha ~** far-reaching

repercutir [reperku'tir] *vi* (*objeto*) to rebound; (*sonido*) to echo; **~ en** (*fig*) to have repercussions *o* effects on

repertorio [reper'torjo] *nm* list; (*Teat*) repertoire

repesca [re'peska] *nf* (*Escol fam*) resit

repetición [repeti'θjon] *nf* repetition

repetido, -a [repe'tiðo, a] *adj* repeated; **repetidas veces** repeatedly

repetir [repe'tir] *vt* to repeat; (*plato*) to have a second helping of; (*Teat*) to give as an encore, sing *etc* again ▪ *vi* to repeat; (*sabor*) to come back; **repetirse** *vr* to repeat o.s.; (*suceso*) to recur

repetitivo, -a [repeti'tiβo, a] *adj* repetitive, repetitious

repicar [repi'kar] *vi* (*campanas*) to ring (out)

repiense *etc* [re'pjense] *vb ver* **repensar**

r

repipi [re'pipi] *adj* la-di-da ■ *nf*: **es una ~** she's a little madam

repique *etc* [re'pike] *vb ver* **repicar** ■ *nm* pealing, ringing

repiqueteo [repike'teo] *nm* pealing; (*de tambor*) drumming

repisa [re'pisa] *nf* ledge, shelf; **~ de chimenea** mantelpiece; **~ de ventana** windowsill

repitiendo *etc* [repi'tjendo] *vb ver* **repetir**

replantear [replante'ar] *vt* (*cuestión pública*) to readdress; (*problema personal*) to reconsider; (*en reunión*) to raise again; **replantearse** *vr*: **replantearse algo** to reconsider sth

replegarse [reple'ɣarse] *vr* to fall back, retreat

replegué [reple'ɣe], **repleguemos** *etc* [reple'ɣemos] *vb ver* **replegarse**

repleto, -a [re'pleto, a] *adj* replete, full up; **~ de** filled o crammed with

réplica ['replika] *nf* answer; (*Arte*) replica; **derecho de ~** right of o to reply

replicar [repli'kar] *vi* to answer; (*objetar*) to argue, answer back

repliego *etc* [re'pljeɣo] *vb ver* **replegarse**

repliegue *etc* [re'pljeɣe] *vb ver* **replegarse** ■ *nm* (*Mil*) withdrawal

replique *etc* [re'plike] *vb ver* **replicar**

repoblación [repoβla'θjon] *nf* repopulation; (*de río*) restocking; **~ forestal** reafforestation

repoblar [repo'βlar] *vt* to repopulate; to restock

repollo [re'poʎo] *nm* cabbage

repondré *etc* [repon'dre] *vb ver* **reponer**

reponer [repo'ner] *vt* to replace, put back; (*máquina*) to re-set; (*Teat*) to revive; **reponerse** *vr* to recover; **~ que** to reply that

reponga *etc* [re'ponga] *vb ver* **reponer**

reportaje [repor'taxe] *nm* report, article; **~ gráfico** illustrated report

reportar [repor'tar] *vt* (*traer*) to bring, carry; (*conseguir*) to obtain; (*fig*) to check; **reportarse** *vr* (*contenerse*) to control o.s.; (*calmarse*) to calm down; **la cosa no le reportó sino disgustos** the affair brought him nothing but trouble

reportero, -a [repor'tero, a] *nm/f* reporter; **~ gráfico/a** news photographer

reposacabezas [reposaka'βeθas] *nm inv* headrest

reposado, -a [repo'saðo, a] *adj* (*descansado*) restful; (*tranquilo*) calm

reposar [repo'sar] *vi* to rest, repose; (*muerto*) to lie, rest

reposición [reposi'θjon] *nf* replacement; (*Cine*) second showing; (*Teat*) revival

reposo [re'poso] *nm* rest

repostar [repos'tar] *vt* to replenish; (*Auto*) to fill up (with petrol o gasoline)

repostería [reposte'ria] *nf* (*arte*) confectionery, pastry-making; (*tienda*) confectioner's (shop)

repostero, -a [repos'tero, a] *nm/f* confectioner

reprender [repren'der] *vt* to reprimand; (*niño*) to scold

reprensión [repren'sjon] *nf* rebuke, reprimand; (*de niño*) telling-off, scolding

represa [re'presa] *nf* dam; (*lago artificial*) lake, pool

represalia [repre'salja] *nf* reprisal; **tomar represalias** to take reprisals, retaliate

representación [representa'θjon] *nf* representation; (*Teat*) performance; **en ~ de** representing; **por ~** by proxy

representante [represen'tante] *nm/f* (*Pol*: *Com*) representative; (*Teat*) performer

representar [represen'tar] *vt* to represent; (*significar*) to mean; (*Teat*) to perform; (*edad*) to look; **representarse** *vr* to imagine; **tal acto ~ía la guerra** such an act would mean war

representativo, -a [representa'tiβo, a] *adj* representative

represión [repre'sjon] *nf* repression

represivo, -a [repre'siβo, a] *adj* repressive

reprimenda [repri'menda] *nf* reprimand, rebuke

reprimir [repri'mir] *vt* to repress; **reprimirse** *vr*: **reprimirse de hacer algo** to stop o.s. from doing sth

reprobación [reproβa'θjon] *nf* reproval; (*culpa*) blame

reprobar [repro'βar] *vt* to censure, reprove

réprobo, -a ['reproβo, a] *nm/f* reprobate

reprochar [repro'tʃar] *vt* to reproach; (*censurar*) to condemn, censure

reproche [re'protʃe] *nm* reproach

reproducción [reproðuk'θjon] *nf* reproduction

reproducir [reproðu'θir] *vt* to reproduce; **reproducirse** *vr* to breed; (*situación*) to recur

reproductor, a [reproðuk'tor, a] *adj* reproductive ■ *nm*: **~ de discos compactos** CD player; **~ MP3/MP4** MP3/MP4 player

reproduje [repro'ðuxe], **reprodujera** *etc* [reproðu'xera], **reproduzca** *etc* [repro'ðuθka] *vb ver* **reproducir**

repruebe *etc* [re'prweβe] *vb ver* **reprobar**

reptar [rep'tar] *vi* to creep, crawl

reptil [rep'til] *nm* reptile

república [re'puβlika] *nf* republic; **R~ Dominicana** Dominican Republic; **R~ Democrática Alemana (RDA)** German

Democratic Republic; **R~ Federal Alemana (RFA)** Federal Republic of Germany; **R~ Árabe Unida** United Arab Republic

republicano, -a [repuβli'kano, a] adj, nm/f republican

repudiar [repu'ðjar] vt to repudiate; (fe) to renounce

repudio [re'puðjo] nm repudiation

repueble etc [re'pweβle] vb ver **repoblar**

repuesto [re'pwesto] pp de **reponer** ■ nm (pieza de recambio) spare (part); (abastecimiento) supply; **rueda de ~** spare wheel; **y llevamos otro de ~** and we have another as a spare o in reserve

repugnancia [repuɣ'nanθja] nf repugnance

repugnante [repuɣ'nante] adj repugnant, repulsive

repugnar [repuɣ'nar] vt to disgust ■ vi, **repugnarse** vr to contradict each other

repujar [repu'xar] vt to emboss

repulsa [re'pulsa] nf rebuff

repulsión [repul'sjon] nf repulsion, aversion

repulsivo, -a [repul'siβo, a] adj repulsive

repuse etc [re'puse] vb ver **reponer**

reputación [reputa'θjon] nf reputation

reputar [repu'tar] vt to consider, deem

requemado, -a [reke'maðo, a] adj (quemado) scorched; (bronceado) tanned

requemar [reke'mar] vt (quemar) to scorch; (secar) to parch; (Culin) to overdo, burn; (la lengua) to burn, sting

requerimiento [rekeri'mjento] nm request; (demanda) demand; (Jur) summons

requerir [reke'rir] vt (pedir) to ask, request; (exigir) to require; (ordenar) to call for; (llamar) to send for, summon

requesón [reke'son] nm cottage cheese

requete ... [rekete] pref extremely

requiebro [re'kjeβro] nm (piropo) compliment, flirtatious remark

réquiem ['rekjem] nm requiem

requiera etc [re'kjera], **requiriendo** etc [reki'rjendo] vb ver **requerir**

requisa [re'kisa] nf (inspección) survey, inspection; (Mil) requisition

requisar [reki'sar] vt (Mil) to requisition; (confiscar) to seize, confiscate

requisito [reki'sito] nm requirement, requisite; **~ previo** prerequisite; **tener los requisitos para un cargo** to have the essential qualifications for a post

res [res] nf beast, animal

resabio [re'saβjo] nm (maña) vice, bad habit; (dejo) (unpleasant) aftertaste

resaca [re'saka] nf (en el mar) undertow, undercurrent; (fig) backlash; (fam) hangover

resaltar [resal'tar] vi to project, stick out;

(fig) to stand out

resarcir [resar'θir] vt to compensate; (pagar) to repay; **resarcirse** vr to make up for; **~ a algn de una pérdida** to compensate sb for a loss; **~ a algn de una cantidad** to repay sb a sum

resarza etc [re'sarθa] vb ver **resarcir**

resbalada [resβa'laða] nf (Am) slip

resbaladizo, -a [resβala'ðiθo, a] adj slippery

resbalar [resβa'lar] vi, **resbalarse** vr to slip, slide; (fig) to slip (up); **le resbalaban las lágrimas por las mejillas** tears were trickling down his cheeks

resbalón [resβa'lon] nm (acción) slip; (deslizamiento) slide; (fig) slip

rescatar [reska'tar] vt (salvar) to save, rescue; (objeto) to get back, recover; (cautivos) to ransom

rescate [res'kate] nm rescue; (de objeto) recovery; **pagar un ~** to pay a ransom

rescindir [resθin'dir] vt (contrato) to annul, rescind

rescisión [resθi'sjon] nf cancellation

rescoldo [res'koldo] nm embers pl

resecar [rese'kar] vt to dry off, dry thoroughly; (Med) to cut out, remove; **resecarse** vr to dry up

reseco, -a [re'seko, a] adj very dry; (fig) skinny

resentido, -a [resen'tiðo, a] adj resentful; **es un ~** he's bitter

resentimiento [resenti'mjento] nm resentment, bitterness

resentirse [resen'tirse] vr (debilitarse: persona) to suffer; **~ con** to resent; **~ de** (sufrir las consecuencias de) to feel the effects of

reseña [re'seɲa] nf (cuenta) account; (informe) report; (Lit) review

reseñar [rese'ɲar] vt to describe; (Lit) to review

reseque etc [re'seke] vb ver **resecar**

reserva [re'serβa] nf reserve; (reservación) reservation; **a ~ de que ...** unless ...; **con toda ~** in strictest confidence; **de ~** spare; **tener algo de ~** to have sth in reserve; **~ de indios** Indian reservation; (Com): **~ para amortización** depreciation allowance; **~ de caja** o **en efectivo** cash reserves; **reservas del Estado** government stock; **reservas en oro** gold reserves

reservación [reserβa'θjon] nf reservation

reservado, -a [reser'βaðo, a] adj reserved; (retraído) cold, distant ■ nm private room; (Ferro) reserved compartment

reservar [reser'βar] vt (guardar) to keep; (Ferro: Teat etc) to reserve, book; **reservarse** vr to save o.s.; (callar) to keep to o.s.; **~ con exceso** to overbook

335

resfriado [res'friaðo] *nm* cold
resfriarse [res'friarse] *vr* to cool off; (*Med*) to catch (a) cold
resfrío [res'frio] *nm* (*esp Am*) cold
resguardar [resɣwar'ðar] *vt* to protect, shield; **resguardarse** *vr*: **resguardarse de** to guard against
resguardo [res'ɣwarðo] *nm* defence; (*vale*) voucher; (*recibo*) receipt, slip
residencia [resi'ðenθja] *nf* residence; (*Univ*) hall of residence; ~ **para ancianos** *o* **jubilados** rest home
residencial [resiðen'θjal] *adj* residential ■ *nf* (*urbanización*) housing estate (*Brit*), real estate development (*US*)
residente [resi'ðente] *adj*, *nm/f* resident
residir [resi'ðir] *vi* to reside, live; ~ **en** to reside *o* lie in; (*consistir en*) to consist of
residual [resi'ðwal] *adj* residual; **aguas residuales** sewage
residuo [re'siðwo] *nm* residue; **residuos atmosféricos** *o* **radiactivos** fallout *sg*
resienta *etc* [re'sjenta] *vb ver* **resentirse**
resignación [resiɣna'θjon] *nf* resignation
resignarse [resiɣ'narse] *vr*: ~ **a** *o* **con** to resign o.s. to, be resigned to
resina [re'sina] *nf* resin
resintiendo *etc* [resin'tjendo] *vb ver* **resentirse**
resistencia [resis'tenθja] *nf* (*dureza*) endurance, strength; (*oposición*, *Elec*) resistance; **la R~** (*Mil*) the Resistance
resistente [resis'tente] *adj* strong, hardy; (*Tec*) resistant; ~ **al calor** heat-resistant
resistir [resis'tir] *vt* (*soportar*) to bear; (*oponerse a*) to resist, oppose; (*aguantar*) to put up with ■ *vi* to resist; (*aguantar*) to last, endure; **resistirse** *vr*: **resistirse a** to refuse to, resist; **no puedo ~ este frío** I can't bear *o* stand this cold; **me resisto a creerlo** I refuse to believe it; **se le resiste la química** chemistry escapes her
resol [re'sol] *nm* glare of the sun
resollar [reso'ʎar] *vi* to breathe noisily, wheeze
resolución [resolu'θjon] *nf* resolution; (*decisión*) decision; (*moción*) motion; ~ **judicial** legal ruling; **tomar una ~** to take a decision
resoluto, -a [reso'luto, a] *adj* resolute
resolver [resol'βer] *vt* to resolve; (*solucionar*) to solve, resolve; (*decidir*) to decide, settle; **resolverse** *vr* to make up one's mind
resonancia [reso'nanθja] *nf* (*del sonido*) resonance; (*repercusión*) repercussion; (*fig*) wide effect, impact
resonante [reso'nante] *adj* resonant,

resounding; (*fig*) tremendous
resonar [reso'nar] *vi* to ring, echo
resoplar [reso'plar] *vi* to snort; (*por cansancio*) to puff
resoplido [reso'pliðo] *nm* heavy breathing
resorte [re'sorte] *nm* spring; (*fig*) lever
respaldar [respal'dar] *vt* to back (up), support; (*Inform*) to back up; **respaldarse** *vr* to lean back; **respaldarse con** *o* **en** (*fig*) to take one's stand on
respaldo [res'paldo] *nm* (*de sillón*) back; (*fig*) support, backing
respectivo, -a [respek'tiβo, a] *adj* respective; **en lo ~ a** with regard to
respecto [res'pekto] *nm*: **al ~** on this matter; **con ~ a**, ~ **de** with regard to, in relation to
respetable [respe'taβle] *adj* respectable
respetar [respe'tar] *vt* to respect
respeto [res'peto] *nm* respect; (*acatamiento*) deference; **respetos** *nmpl* respects; **por ~ a** out of consideration for; **presentar sus respetos a** to pay one's respects to
respetuoso, -a [respe'twoso, a] *adj* respectful
respingo [res'pingo] *nm* start, jump
respiración [respira'θjon] *nf* breathing; (*Med*) respiration; (*ventilación*) ventilation
respirar [respi'rar] *vt*, *vi* to breathe; **no dejar ~ a algn** to keep on at sb; **estuvo escuchándole sin ~** he listened to him in complete silence
respiratorio, -a [respira'torjo, a] *adj* respiratory
respiro [res'piro] *nm* breathing; (*fig*: *descanso*) respite, rest; (*Com*) period of grace
resplandecer [resplande'θer] *vi* to shine
resplandeciente [resplande'θjente] *adj* resplendent, shining
resplandezca *etc* [resplan'deθka] *vb ver* **resplandecer**
resplandor [resplan'dor] *nm* brilliance, brightness; (*del fuego*) blaze
responder [respon'der] *vt* to answer ■ *vi* to answer; (*fig*) to respond; (*pey*) to answer back; (*corresponder*) to correspond; ~ **a** (*situación etc*) to respond to; ~ **a una pregunta** to answer a question; ~ **a una descripción** to fit a description; ~ **de** *o* **por** to answer for
respondón, -ona [respon'don, ona] *adj* cheeky
responsabilice *etc* [responsaβi'liθe] *vb ver* **responsabilizarse**
responsabilidad [responsaβili'ðað] *nf* responsibility; **bajo mi ~** on my authority; ~ **ilimitada** (*Com*) unlimited liability
responsabilizarse [responsaβili'θarse] *vr* to make o.s. responsible, take charge

responsable [respon'sable] *adj* responsible; **la persona ~** the person in charge; **hacerse ~ de algo** to assume responsibility for sth

respuesta [res'pwesta] *nf* answer, reply; *(reacción)* response

resquebrajar [reskeβra'xar] *vt*, **resquebrajarse** *vr* to crack, split

resquemor [reske'mor] *nm* resentment

resquicio [res'kiθjo] *nm* chink; *(hendidura)* crack

resta ['resta] *nf (Mat)* remainder

restablecer [restaβle'θer] *vt* to re-establish, restore; **restablecerse** *vr* to recover

restablecimiento [restaβleθi'mjento] *nm* re-establishment; *(restauración)* restoration; *(Med)* recovery

restablezca *etc* [resta'βleθka] *vb ver* **restablecer**

restallar [resta'ʎar] *vi* to crack

restante [res'tante] *adj* remaining; **lo ~** the remainder; **los restantes** the rest, those left (over)

restar [res'tar] *vt (Mat)* to subtract; *(descontar)* to deduct; *(fig)* to take away ∎ *vi* to remain, be left

restauración [restaura'θjon] *nf* restoration

restaurador, a [restaura'ðor, a] *nm/f (persona)* restorer

restaurante [restau'rante] *nm* restaurant

restaurar [restau'rar] *vt* to restore

restitución [restitu'θjon] *nf* return, restitution

restituir [restitu'ir] *vt (devolver)* to return, give back; *(rehabilitar)* to restore

restituyendo *etc* [restitu'jendo] *vb ver* **restituir**

resto ['resto] *nm (residuo)* rest, remainder; *(apuesta)* stake; **restos** *nmpl* remains; *(Culin)* leftovers, scraps; **restos mortales** mortal remains

restregar [restre'ɣar] *vt* to scrub, rub

restregué [restre'ɣe], **restreguemos** *etc* [restre'ɣemos] *vb ver* **restregar**

restricción [restrik'θjon] *nf* restriction; **sin ~ de** without restrictions on *o* as to; **hablar sin restricciones** to talk freely

restrictivo, -a [restrik'tiβo, a] *adj* restrictive

restriego *etc* [res'trjeɣo], **restriegue** *etc* [res'trjeɣe] *vb ver* **restregar**

restringir [restrin'xir] *vt* to restrict, limit

restrinja *etc* [res'trinxa] *vb ver* **restringir**

resucitar [resuθi'tar] *vt, vi* to resuscitate, revive

resuello *etc* [re'sweʎo] *vb ver* **resollar** ∎ *nm (aliento)* breath

resuelto, -a [re'swelto, a] *pp de* **resolver** ∎ *adj* resolute, determined; **estar ~ a algo**

to be set on sth; **estar ~ a hacer algo** to be determined to do sth

resuelva *etc* [re'swelβa] *vb ver* **resolver**

resuene *etc* [re'swene] *vb ver* **resonar**

resulta [re'sulta] *nf* result; **de resultas de** as a result of

resultado [resul'taðo] *nm* result; *(conclusión)* outcome; **resultados** *nmpl (Inform)* output *sg*; **dar ~** to produce results

resultante [resul'tante] *adj* resulting, resultant

resultar [resul'tar] *vi (ser)* to be; *(llegar a ser)* to turn out to be; *(salir bien)* to turn out well; *(seguir)* to ensue; **~ a** *(Com)* to amount to; **~ de** to stem from; **~ en** to result in, produce; **resulta que ...** *(en consecuencia)* it follows that ...; *(parece que)* it seems that ...; **el conductor resultó muerto** the driver was killed, **no resultó** it didn't work *o* come off; **me resulta difícil hacerlo** it's difficult for me to do it

resumen [re'sumen] *nm* summary, résumé; **en ~** in short

resumir [resu'mir] *vt* to sum up; *(condensar)* to summarize; *(cortar)* to abridge, cut down; **resumirse** *vr*: **la situación se resume en pocas palabras** the situation can be summed up in a few words

resurgir [resur'xir] *vi (reaparecer)* to reappear

resurrección [resurrek'θjon] *nf* resurrection

retablo [re'taβlo] *nm* altarpiece

retaguardia [reta'ɣwarðja] *nf* rearguard

retahíla [reta'ila] *nf* series, string; *(de injurias)* volley, stream

retal [re'tal] *nm* remnant

retar [re'tar] *vt (gen)* to challenge; *(desafiar)* to defy, dare

retardar [retar'ðar] *vt (demorar)* to delay; *(hacer más lento)* to slow down; *(retener)* to hold back

retardo [re'tarðo] *nm* delay

retazo [re'taθo] *nm* snippet *(Brit)*, fragment

RETD *nf abr (Esp Telec)* = **Red Especial de Transmisión de Datos**

rete ... ['rete] *pref* very, extremely

retén [re'ten] *nm (Am)* roadblock, checkpoint

retención [reten'θjon] *nf* retention; *(de pago)* deduction; **~ de llamadas** *(Telec)* hold facility

retendré *etc* [reten'dre] *vb ver* **retener**

retener [rete'ner] *vt (guardar)* to retain, keep; *(intereses)* to withhold

retenga *etc* [re'tenga] *vb ver* **retener**

reticencia [reti'θenθja] *nf (insinuación)* insinuation, *(malevolent)* suggestion; *(verdad a medias)* half-truth

reticente [reti'θente] *adj (insinuador)*

r

insinuating; (*engañoso*) deceptive

retiene *etc* [re'tjene] *vb ver* **retener**

retina [re'tina] *nf* retina

retintín [retin'tin] *nm* jangle, jingle; **decir algo con ~** to say sth sarcastically

retirado, -a [reti'raðo, a] *adj* (*lugar*) remote; (*vida*) quiet; (*jubilado*) retired ■ *nf* (*Mil*) retreat; (*de dinero*) withdrawal; (*de embajador*) recall; **batirse en retirada** to retreat

retirar [reti'rar] *vt* to withdraw; (*la mano*) to draw back; (*quitar*) to remove; (*dinero*) to take out, withdraw; (*jubilar*) to retire, pension off; **retirarse** *vr* to retreat, withdraw; (*jubilarse*) to retire; (*acostarse*) to retire, go to bed

retiro [re'tiro] *nm* retreat; (*jubilación, tb Deporte*) retirement; (*pago*) pension; (*lugar*) quiet place

reto ['reto] *nm* dare, challenge

retocar [reto'kar] *vt* to touch up, retouch

retoce *etc* [re'toθe] *vb ver* **retozar**

retoño [re'toɲo] *nm* sprout, shoot; (*fig*) offspring, child

retoque *etc* [re'toke] *vb ver* **retocar** ■ *nm* retouching

retorcer [retor'θer] *vt* to twist; (*argumento*) to turn, twist; (*manos, lavado*) to wring; **retorcerse** *vr* to become twisted; (*persona*) to writhe; **retorcerse de dolor** to writhe in *o* squirm with pain

retorcido, -a [retor'θiðo, a] *adj* (*tb fig*) twisted

retorcimiento [retorθi'mjento] *nm* twist, twisting; (*fig*) deviousness

retórico, -a [re'toriko, a] *adj* rhetorical; (*pey*) affected, windy ■ *nf* rhetoric; (*pey*) affectedness

retornable [retor'naβle] *adj* returnable

retornar [retor'nar] *vt* to return, give back ■ *vi* to return, go/come back

retorno [re'torno] *nm* return; **~ del carro** (*Inform: Tip*) carriage return

retortero [retor'tero] *nm*: **andar al ~** to bustle about, have heaps of things to do; **andar al ~ por algn** to be madly in love with sb

retortijón [retorti'xon] *nm* twist, twisting; **~ de tripas** stomach cramp

retorzamos *etc* [retor'θamos] *vb ver* **retorcer**

retozar [reto'θar] *vi* (*juguetear*) to frolic, romp; (*saltar*) to gambol

retozón, -ona [reto'θon, ona] *adj* playful

retracción [retrak'θjon] *nf* retraction

retractarse [retrak'tarse] *vr* to retract; **me retracto** I take that back

retraerse [retra'erse] *vr* to retreat, withdraw

retraído, -a [retra'iðo, a] *adj* shy, retiring

retraiga *etc* [re'traiɣa] *vb ver* **retraerse**

retraimiento [retrai'mjento] *nm* retirement; (*timidez*) shyness

retraje *etc* [re'traxe], **retrajera** *etc* [retra'xera] *vb ver* **retraerse**

retransmisión [retransmi'sjon] *nf* repeat (broadcast)

retransmitir [retransmi'tir] *vt* (*mensaje*) to relay; (*TV etc*) to repeat, retransmit; (*: en vivo*) to broadcast live

retrasado, -a [retra'saðo, a] *adj* late; (*Med*) mentally retarded; (*país etc*) backward, underdeveloped; **estar ~** (*reloj*) to be slow; (*persona, industria*) to be *o* lag behind

retrasar [retra'sar] *vt* (*demorar*) to postpone, put off; (*retardar*) to slow down ■ *vi*, **retrasarse** *vr* (*atrasarse*) to be late; (*reloj*) to be slow; (*producción*) to fall (away); (*quedarse atrás*) to lag behind

retraso [re'traso] *nm* (*demora*) delay; (*lentitud*) slowness; (*tardanza*) lateness; (*atraso*) backwardness; **retrasos** *nmpl* (*Com*) arrears; (*deudas*) deficit *sg*, debts; **llegar con ~** to arrive late; **llegar con 25 minutos de ~** to be 25 minutes late; **llevo un ~ de seis semanas** I'm six weeks behind (with my work *etc*); **~ mental** mental deficiency

retratar [retra'tar] *vt* (*Arte*) to paint the portrait of; (*fotografiar*) to photograph; (*fig*) to depict, describe; **retratarse** *vr* to have one's portrait painted; to have one's photograph taken

retratista [retra'tista] *nm/f* (*Arte*) (portrait) painter; (*Foto*) photographer

retrato [re'trato] *nm* portrait; (*Foto*) photograph; (*descripción*) portrayal, depiction; (*fig*) likeness; **ser el vivo ~ de** to be the spitting image of

retrato-robot [re'tratoro'βo(t)] (*pl* **retratos-robot**) *nm* identikit picture

retrayendo *etc* [retra'jendo] *vb ver* **retraerse**

retreta [re'treta] *nf* retreat

retrete [re'trete] *nm* toilet

retribución [retriβu'θjon] *nf* (*recompensa*) reward; (*pago*) pay, payment

retribuir [retriβu'ir] *vt* (*recompensar*) to reward; (*pagar*) to pay

retribuyendo *etc* [retriβu'jendo] *vb ver* **retribuir**

retro ... [retro] *pref* retro...

retroactivo, -a [retroak'tiβo, a] *adj* retroactive, retrospective; **dar efecto ~ a un pago** to backdate a payment

retroalimentación [retroalimenta'θjon] *nf* (*Inform*) feedback

retroceder [retroθe'ðer] *vi* (*echarse atrás*) to move back(wards); (*fig*) to back down; **no ~** to stand firm; **la policía hizo ~ a la multitud** the police forced the crowd back

retroceso [retro'θeso] *nm* backward

movement; (Med) relapse; (Com) recession, depression; (fig) backing down

retrógrado, -a [retro'yraðo, a] adj retrograde, retrogressive; (Pol) reactionary

retropropulsión [retropropul'sjon] nf jet propulsion

retrospectivo, -a [retrospek'tiβo, a] adj retrospective; **mirada retrospectiva** backward glance

retrovisor [retroβi'sor] nm rear-view mirror

retuerce etc [re'twerθe], **retuerza** etc [re'twerθa] vb ver **retorcer**

retumbante [retum'bante] adj resounding

retumbar [retum'bar] vi to echo, resound; (continuamente) to reverberate

retuve etc [re'tuβe] vb ver **retener**

reuma ['reuma] nm rheumatism

reumático, -a [reu'matiko, a] adj rheumatic

reumatismo [reuma'tismo] nm rheumatism

reunificar [reunifi'kar] vt to reunify

reunifique etc [reuni'fike] vb ver **reunificar**

reunión [reu'njon] nf (asamblea) meeting; (fiesta) party; **~ en la cumbre** summit meeting; **~ de ventas** (Com) sales meeting

reunir [reu'nir] vt (juntar) to reunite, join (together); (recoger) to gather (together); (personas) to bring o get together; (cualidades) to combine; **reunirse** vr (personas: en asamblea) to meet, gather; **reunió a sus amigos para discutirlo** he got his friends together to talk it over

reválida [re'βaliða] nf (Escol) final examination

revalidar [reβali'ðar] vt (ratificar) to confirm, ratify

revalorar [reβalo'rar] vt to revalue, reassess

revalorización [reβaloriθa'θjon], **revaloración** [reβalora'θjon] nf revaluation; (Econ) reassessment

revancha [re'βantʃa] nf revenge; (Deporte) return match; (Boxeo) return fight

revelación [reβela'θjon] nf revelation

revelado [reβe'laðo] nm developing

revelador, a [reβela'ðor, a] adj revealing

revelar [reβe'lar] vt to reveal; (secreto) to disclose; (mostrar) to show; (Foto) to develop

revendedor, a [reβende'ðor, a] nm/f retailer; (pey) ticket tout

revendré etc [reβen'dre], **revenga** etc [re'βenga] vb ver **revenirse**

revenirse [reβe'nirse] vr to shrink; (comida) to go bad o off; (vino) to sour; (Culin) to get tough

reventa [re'βenta] nf resale; (especulación) speculation; (de entradas) touting

reventar [reβen'tar] vt to burst, explode; (molestar) to annoy, rile ■ vi, **reventarse** vr (estallar) to burst, explode; **me revienta**

tener que ponérmelo I hate having to wear it; **~ de** (fig) to be bursting with; **~ por** to be bursting to

reventón [reβen'ton] nm (Auto) blow-out (Brit), flat (US)

reverberación [reβerβera'θjon] nf reverberation

reverberar [reβerβe'rar] vi (luz) to play, be reflected; (superficie) to shimmer; (nieve) to glare; (sonido) to reverberate

reverbero [reβer'βero] nm play; shimmer, shine; glare; reverberation

reverencia [reβe'renθja] nf reverence; (inclinación) bow

reverenciar [reβeren'θjar] vt to revere

reverendo, -a [reβe'rendo, a] adj reverend; (fam) big, awful; **un ~ imbécil** an awful idiot

reverente [reβe'rente] adj reverent

reversible [reβer'siβle] adj reversible

reverso [re'βerso] nm back, other side; (de moneda) reverse

revertir [reβer'tir] vi to revert; **~ en beneficio de** to be to the advantage of; **~ en perjuicio de** to be to the detriment of

revés [re'βes] nm back, wrong side; (fig) reverse, setback; (Deporte) backhand; **al ~** the wrong way round; (de arriba abajo) upside down; (ropa) inside out; **y al ~** and vice versa; **volver algo del ~** to turn sth round; (ropa) to turn sth inside out; **los reveses de la fortuna** the blows of fate

revestir [reβes'tir] vt (poner) to put on; (cubrir) to cover, coat; (cualidad) to have, possess; **revestirse** vr (Rel) to put on one's vestments; (ponerse) to put on; **~ con o de** to arm o.s. with; **el acto revestía gran solemnidad** the ceremony had great dignity

reviejo, -a [re'βjexo, a] adj very old, ancient

reviene etc [re'βjene] vb ver **revenirse**

reviente etc [re'βjente] vb ver **reventar**

revierta etc [re'βjerta] vb ver **revertir**

reviniendo etc [reβi'njendo] vb ver **revenirse**

revirtiendo etc [reβir'tjendo] vb ver **revertir**

revisar [reβi'sar] vt (examinar) to check; (texto etc) to revise; (Jur) to review

revisión [reβi'sjon] nf revision; **~ aduanera** customs inspection; **~ de cuentas** audit

revisor, a [reβi'sor, a] nm/f inspector; (Ferro) ticket collector; **~ de cuentas** auditor

revista etc [re'βista] vb ver **revestir** ■ nf magazine, review; (Teat) revue; (inspección) inspection; **~ literaria** literary review; **~ de libros** book reviews (page); **pasar ~ a** to review, inspect

revivir [reβi'βir] vt (recordar) to revive memories of ■ vi to revive

revocación [reβoka'θjon] nf repeal

revocar [reβo'kar] vt (decisión) to revoke; (Arq) to plaster

revolcar [reβol'kar] vt to knock down, send flying; **revolcarse** vr to roll about

revolcón [reβol'kon] nm tumble

revolotear [reβolote'ar] vi to flutter

revoloteo [reβolo'teo] nm fluttering

revolqué [reβol'ke], **revolquemos** etc [reβol'kemos] vb ver **revolcar**

revoltijo [reβol'tixo] nm mess, jumble

revoltoso, -a [reβol'toso, a] adj (travieso) naughty, unruly

revolución [reβolu'θjon] nf revolution

revolucionar [reβoluθjo'nar] vt to revolutionize

revolucionario, -a [reβoluθjo'narjo, a] adj, nm/f revolutionary

revolver [reβol'βer] vt (desordenar) to disturb, mess up; (agitar) to shake; (líquido) to stir; (mover) to move about; (Pol) to stir up ■ vi: ~ **en** to go through, rummage (about) in; **revolverse** vr (en cama) to toss and turn; (Meteorología) to break, turn stormy; **revolverse contra** to turn on o against; **han revuelto toda la casa** they've turned the whole house upside down

revólver [re'βolβer] nm revolver

revoque etc [re'βoke] vb ver **revocar**

revuelco etc [re'βwelko] vb ver **revolcar**

revuelo [re'βwelo] nm fluttering; (fig) commotion; **armar** o **levantar un gran ~** to cause a great stir

revuelque etc [re'βwelke] vb ver **revolcar**

revuelto, -a [re'βwelto, a] pp de **revolver** ■ adj (mezclado) mixed-up, in disorder; (mar) rough; (tiempo) unsettled ■ nf (motín) revolt; (agitación) commotion; **todo estaba ~** everything was in disorder o was topsy-turvy

revuelva etc [re'βwelβa] vb ver **revolver**

revulsivo [reβul'siβo] nm: **servir de ~** to have a salutary effect

rey [rei] nm king; **los Reyes** the King and Queen; ver tb **Baraja Española**; see note

● REY
●
● The night before the 6th of January (the
● Epiphany), which is a holiday in Spain,
● children go to bed expecting los Reyes
● Magos, the Three Wise Men who visited
● the baby Jesus, to bring them presents.
● Twelfth night processions, known as
● cabalgatas, take place that evening, when
● 3 people dressed as los Reyes Magos arrive in
● the town by land or sea to the delight of
● the children.

reyerta [re'jerta] nf quarrel, brawl

rezagado, -a [reθa'ɣaðo, a] adj: **quedar ~** to be left behind; (estar retrasado) to be late, be behind ■ nm/f straggler

rezagar [reθa'ɣar] vt (dejar atrás) to leave behind; (retrasar) to delay, postpone; **rezagarse** vr (atrasarse) to fall behind

rezague etc [re'θaɣe] vb ver **rezagar**

rezar [re'θar] vi to pray; ~ **con** (fam) to concern, have to do with

rezo ['reθo] nm prayer

rezongar [reθon'gar] vi to grumble; (murmurar) to mutter; (refunfuñar) to growl

rezongue etc [re'θonge] vb ver **rezongar**

rezumar [reθu'mar] vt to ooze ■ vi to leak; **rezumarse** vr to leak out

RFA nf abr (= República Federal Alemana) ver **república**

RI abr = **regimiento de infantería**

ría ['ria] nf estuary

riachuelo [rja'tʃwelo] nm stream

riada [ri'aða] nf flood

ribera [ri'βera] nf (de río) bank; (: área) riverside

ribete [ri'βete] nm (de vestido) border; (fig) addition

ribetear [riβete'ar] vt to edge, border

rice etc ['riθe] vb ver **rizar**

ricino [ri'θino] nm: **aceite de ~** castor oil

rico, -a ['riko, a] adj (adinerado) rich, wealthy; (lujoso) luxurious; (comida) delicious; (niño) lovely, cute ■ nm/f rich person; **nuevo ~** nouveau riche

rictus ['riktus] nm (mueca) sneer, grin; ~ **de amargura** bitter smile

ridiculez [riðiku'leθ] nf absurdity

ridiculice etc [riðiku'liθe] vb ver **ridiculizar**

ridiculizar [riðikuli'θar] vt to ridicule

ridículo, -a [ri'ðikulo, a] adj ridiculous; **hacer el ~** to make a fool of o.s.; **poner a algn en ~** to make a fool of sb; **ponerse en ~** to make a fool of o.s.

riego etc ['rjeɣo] vb ver **regar** ■ nm (aspersión) watering; (irrigación) irrigation

riegue etc ['rjeɣe] vb ver **regar**

riel [rjel] nm rail

rienda ['rjenda] nf rein; (fig) restraint, moderating influence; **dar ~ suelta a** to give free rein to; **llevar las riendas** to be in charge

riendo ['rjendo] vb ver **reír**

riesgo ['rjesɣo] nm risk; **seguro a** o **contra todo ~** comprehensive insurance; ~ **para la salud** health hazard; **correr el ~ de** to run the risk of

Rif [rif] nm Rif(f)

rifa ['rifa] nf (lotería) raffle

rifar [ri'far] *vt* to raffle
rifeño, -a [ri'feɲo, a] *adj* of the Rif(f),
Rif(f)ian ■ *nm/f* Rif(f)ian, Rif(f)
rifle ['rifle] *nm* rifle
rigidez [rixi'ðeθ] *nf* rigidity, stiffness; *(fig)*
strictness
rígido, -a ['rixiðo, a] *adj* rigid, stiff;
(moralmente) strict, inflexible; *(cara)* wooden,
expressionless
rigiendo *etc* [ri'xjendo] *vb ver* **regir**
rigor [ri'yor] *nm* strictness, rigour; *(dureza)*
toughness; *(inclemencia)* harshness;
(meticulosidad) accuracy; **el ~ del verano** the
hottest part of the summer; **con todo ~
científico** with scientific precision; **de ~ de**
rigueur, essential; **después de los saludos
de ~** after the inevitable greetings
riguroso, -a [riyu'roso, a] *adj* rigorous;
(Meteorología) harsh; *(severo)* severe
rija *etc* ['rixa] *vb ver* **regir** ■ *nf* quarrel
rima ['rima] *nf* rhyme; **rimas** *nfpl* verse *sg*;
~ imperfecta assonance; **~ rimando** *(fam)*
merrily
rimar [ri'mar] *vi* to rhyme
rimbombante [rimbom'bante] *adj (fig)*
pompous
rímel, rímmel ['rimel] *nm* mascara
rimero [ri'mero] *nm* stack, pile
Rin [rin] *nm* Rhine
rincón [rin'kon] *nm* corner *(inside)*
rindiendo *etc* [rin'djendo] *vb ver* **rendir**
ring [riŋ] *nm (Boxeo)* ring
rinoceronte [rinoθe'ronte] *nm* rhinoceros
riña ['riɲa] *nf (disputa)* argument; *(pelea)*
brawl
riñendo *etc* [ri'ɲendo] *vb ver* **reñir**
riñón [ri'ɲon] *nm* kidney; **me costó un
~** *(fam)* it cost me an arm and a leg; **tener
riñones** to have guts
río *etc* ['rio] *vb ver* **reír** ■ *nm* river; *(fig)* torrent,
stream; **~ abajo/arriba** downstream/
upstream; **cuando el ~ suena, agua lleva**
there's no smoke without fire
rió [ri'o] *vb ver* **reír**
Río de Janeiro ['rioðexa'neiro] *nm* Rio de
Janeiro
Río de la Plata ['rioðela'plata] *nm* Rio de la
Plata, River Plate
Rioja [ri'oxa] *nf*: **La ~** La Rioja ■ *nm*: **rioja**
rioja wine
riojano, -a [rjo'xano, a] *adj, nm/f* Riojan
rioplatense [riopla'tense] *adj* of o from
the River Plate region ■ *nm/f* native o
inhabitant of the River Plate region
riqueza [ri'keθa] *nf* wealth, riches *pl*;
(cualidad) richness
risa ['risa] *nf* laughter; *(una risa)* laugh; **¡qué**

~! what a laugh!; **caerse** o **morirse de ~** to
split one's sides laughing, die laughing;
tomar algo a ~ to laugh sth off
risco ['risko] *nm* crag, cliff
risible [ri'siβle] *adj* ludicrous, laughable
risotada [riso'taða] *nf* guffaw, loud laugh
ristra ['ristra] *nf* string
ristre ['ristre] *nm*: **en ~** at the ready
risueño, -a [ri'sweɲo, a] *adj (sonriente)*
smiling; *(contento)* cheerful
ritmo ['ritmo] *nm* rhythm; **a ~ lento** slowly;
trabajar a ~ lento to go slow
rito ['rito] *nm* rite
ritual [ri'twal] *adj, nm* ritual
rival [ri'βal] *adj, nm/f* rival
rivalice *etc* [riβa'liθe] *vb ver* **rivalizar**
rivalidad [riβali'ðað] *nf* rivalry, competition
rivalizar [riβali'θar] *vi*: **con** to rival,
compete with
rizado, -a [ri'θaðo, a] *adj (pelo)* curly;
(superficie) ridged; *(terreno)* undulating; *(mar)*
choppy ■ *nm* curls *pl*
rizar [ri'θar] *vt* to curl; **rizarse** *vr (el pelo)*
to curl; *(agua)* to ripple; *(el mar)* to become
choppy
rizo ['riθo] *nm* curl; *(en agua)* ripple
Rma. *abr* (= *Reverendísima*) courtesy title
Rmo. *abr* (= *Reverendísimo*) Rt. Rev.
RNE *nf abr* = **Radio Nacional de España**
R. O. *abr* (= *Real Orden*) royal order
robar [ro'βar] *vt* to rob; *(objeto)* to steal; *(casa
etc)* to break into; *(Naipes)* to draw; *(atención)*
to steal, capture; *(paciencia)* to exhaust
roble ['roβle] *nm* oak
robledal [roβle'ðal], **robledo** [ro'βleðo] *nm*
oakwood
robo ['roβo] *nm* robbery, theft; *(objeto robado)*
stolen article o goods *pl*; **¡esto es un ~!** this is
daylight robbery!
robot [ro'βo(t)] *(pl* **robots***) adj, nm* robot
■ *nm (tb*: **robot de cocina**) food processor
robótica [ro'βotika] *nf* robotics *sg*
robustecer [roβuste'θer] *vt* to strengthen
robustezca *etc* [roβus'teθka] *vb ver*
robustecer
robusto, -a [ro'βusto, a] *adj* robust, strong
ROC *abr* (*Inform.* = *reconocimiento óptico de
caracteres*) OCR
roca ['roka] *nf* rock; **la R~** the Rock (of
Gibraltar)
roce *etc* ['roθe] *vb ver* **rozar** ■ *nm* rub,
rubbing; *(caricia)* brush; *(Tec)* friction; *(en la
piel)* graze; **tener ~ con** to have a brush with
rociar [ro'θjar] *vt* to sprinkle, spray
rocín [ro'θin] *nm* nag, hack
rocío [ro'θio] *nm* dew
rock [rok] *adj inv, nm (Mus)* rock *(cpd)*

r

341

rockero, -a [ro'kero, a] *adj* rock *cpd* ▪ *nm/f* rocker

rocoso, -a [ro'koso, a] *adj* rocky

rodado, -a [ro'ðaðo, a] *adj* (*con ruedas*) wheeled ▪ *nf* rut

rodaja [ro'ðaxa] *nf* (*raja*) slice

rodaje [ro'ðaxe] *nm* (*Cine*) shooting, filming; (*Auto*): **en ~** running in

rodamiento [roða'mjento] *nm* (*Auto*) tread

Ródano ['roðano] *nm* Rhône

rodar [ro'ðar] *vt* (*vehículo*) to wheel (along); (*escalera*) to roll down; (*viajar por*) to travel (over) ▪ *vi* to roll; (*coche*) to go, run; (*Cine*) to shoot, film; (*persona*) to move about (from place to place), drift; **echarlo todo a ~** (*fig*) to mess it all up

Rodas ['roðas] *nf* Rhodes

rodear [roðe'ar] *vt* to surround ▪ *vi* to go round; **rodearse** *vr*: **rodearse de amigos** to surround o.s. with friends

rodeo [ro'ðeo] *nm* (*ruta indirecta*) long way round, roundabout way; (*desvío*) detour; (*evasión*) evasion; (*Am*) rodeo; **dejarse de rodeos** to talk straight; **hablar sin rodeos** to come to the point, speak plainly

rodilla [ro'ðiʎa] *nf* knee; **de rodillas** kneeling

rodillo [ro'ðiʎo] *nm* roller; (*Culin*) rolling-pin; (*en máquina de escribir, impresora*) platen

rododendro [roðo'ðendro] *nm* rhododendron

roedor, a [roe'ðor, a] *adj* gnawing ▪ *nm* rodent

roer [ro'er] *vt* (*masticar*) to gnaw; (*corroer, fig*) to corrode

rogar [ro'ɣar] *vt* (*pedir*) to beg, ask for ▪ *vi* (*suplicar*) to beg, plead; **rogarse** *vr*: **se ruega no fumar** please do not smoke; **~ que** (+*subjun*) to ask to ...; **ruegue a este señor que nos deje en paz** please ask this gentleman to leave us alone; **no se hace de ~** he doesn't have to be asked twice

rogué [ro'ɣe], **roguemos** *etc* [ro'ɣemos] *vb* ver **rogar**

rojizo, -a [ro'xiθo, a] *adj* reddish

rojo, -a ['roxo, a] *adj* red ▪ *nm* red (colour); (*Pol*) red; **ponerse ~** to turn red, blush; **al ~ vivo** red-hot

rol [rol] *nm* list, roll; (*esp Am: papel*) role

rollizo, -a [ro'ʎiθo, a] *adj* (*objeto*) cylindrical; (*persona*) plump

rollo, -a ['roʎo, a] *adj* (*fam*) boring, tedious ▪ *nm* roll; (*de cuerda*) coil; (*de madera*) log; (*fam*) bore; (*discurso*) boring speech; **¡qué ~!** what a carry-on!; **la conferencia fue un ~** the lecture was a big drag

ROM [rom] *nf abr* (= *memoria de sólo lectura*) ROM

Roma ['roma] *nf* Rome; **por todas partes se va a ~** all roads lead to Rome

romance [ro'manθe] *nm* (*Ling*) Romance language; (*Lit*) ballad; **hablar en ~** to speak plainly

románico, -a [ro'maniko, a] *adj, nm* Romanesque

romano, -a [ro'mano, a] *adj* Roman, of Rome ▪ *nm/f* Roman

romanticismo [romanti'θismo] *nm* romanticism

romántico, -a [ro'mantiko, a] *adj* romantic

rombo ['rombo] *nm* (*Geom*) rhombus; (*diseño*) diamond; (*Tip*) lozenge

romería [rome'ria] *nf* (*Rel*) pilgrimage; (*excursión*) trip, outing; *see note*

romero, -a [ro'mero, a] *nm/f* pilgrim ▪ *nm* rosemary

romo, -a ['romo, a] *adj* blunt; (*fig*) dull

rompecabezas [rompeka'βeθas] *nm inv* riddle, puzzle; (*juego*) jigsaw (puzzle)

rompehielos [rompe'jelos] *nm inv* icebreaker

rompeolas [rompe'olas] *nm inv* breakwater

romper [rom'per] *vt* to break; (*hacer pedazos*) to smash; (*papel, tela etc*) to tear, rip; (*relaciones*) to break off ▪ *vi* (*olas*) to break; (*sol, diente*) to break through; **~ un contrato** to break a contract; **~ a** to start (suddenly) to; **~ a llorar** to burst into tears; **~ con algn** to fall out with sb; **ha roto con su novio** she has broken up with her fiancé

rompimiento [rompi'mjento] *nm* (*acto*) breaking; (*fig*) break; (*quiebra*) crack; **~ de relaciones** breaking off of relations

ron [ron] *nm* rum

roncar [ron'kar] *vi* (*al dormir*) to snore; (*animal*) to roar

roncha ['rontʃa] *nf* (*cardenal*) bruise; (*hinchazón*) swelling

ronco, -a ['ronko, a] *adj* (*afónico*) hoarse; (*áspero*) raucous

ronda ['ronda] *nf* (*de bebidas etc*) round; (*patrulla*) patrol; (*de naipes*) hand, game; **ir de ~** to do one's round

rondar [ron'dar] *vt* to patrol; (*a una persona*) to hang round; (*molestar*) to harass; (*a una chica*) to court ▪ *vi* to patrol; (*fig*) to prowl round;

(Mus) to go serenading

rondeño, -a [ron'deɲo, a] adj of o from Ronda
■ nm/f native o inhabitant of Ronda

ronque etc ['ronke] vb ver **roncar**

ronquido [ron'kiðo] nm snore, snoring

ronronear [ronrone'ar] vi to purr

ronroneo [ronro'neo] nm purr

roña ['roɲa] nf (en veterinaria) mange; (mugre)
dirt, grime; (óxido) rust

roñica [ro'ɲika] nm/f (fam) skinflint

roñoso, -a [ro'ɲoso, a] adj (mugriento) filthy;
(tacaño) mean

ropa ['ropa] nf clothes pl, clothing; ~ **blanca**
linen; ~ **de cama** bed linen; ~ **interior**
underwear; ~ **lavada** o **para lavar** washing;
~ **planchada** ironing; ~ **sucia** dirty clothes
pl, washing; ~ **usada** secondhand clothes

ropaje [ro'paxe] nm gown, robes pl

ropero [ro'pero] nm linen cupboard;
(guardarropa) wardrobe

rosa ['rosa] adj inv pink ■ nf rose; (Anat) red
birthmark; ~ **de los vientos** the compass;
estar como una ~ to feel as fresh as a daisy;
(**color**) **de** ~ pink

rosado, -a [ro'saðo, a] adj pink ■ nm rosé

rosal [ro'sal] nm rosebush

rosaleda [rosa'leða] nf rose bed o garden

rosario [ro'sarjo] nm (Rel) rosary; (fig: serie)
string; **rezar el** ~ to say the rosary

rosbif [ros'βif] nm roast beef

rosca ['roska] nf (de tornillo) thread; (de humo)
coil, spiral; (pan, postre) ring-shaped roll/
pastry; **hacer la** ~ **a algn** (fam) to suck up to
sb; **pasarse de** ~ (fig) to go too far

Rosellón [rose'ʎon] nm Roussillon

rosetón [rose'ton] nm rosette; (Arq) rose
window

rosquilla [ros'kiʎa] nf small ring-shaped cake;
(de humo) ring

rosticería [rostise'ria] nf (Am) roast chicken shop

rostro ['rostro] nm (cara) face; (fig) cheek

rotación [rota'θjon] nf rotation; ~ **de
cultivos** crop rotation

rotativo, -a [rota'tiβo, a] adj rotary ■ nm
newspaper

roto, -a ['roto, a] pp de **romper** ■ adj broken;
(en pedazos) smashed; (tela, papel) torn; (vida)
shattered ■ nm (en vestido) hole, tear

rótula ['rotula] nf kneecap; (Tec) ball-and-
socket joint

rotulador [rotula'ðor] nm felt-tip pen

rotular [rotu'lar] vt (carta, documento) to head,
entitle; (objeto) to label

rótulo ['rotulo] nm (título) heading, title;
(etiqueta) label; (letrero) sign

rotundo, -a [ro'tundo, a] adj round; (enfático)
emphatic

rotura [ro'tura] nf (rompimiento) breaking;
(Med) fracture

roturar [rotu'rar] vt to plough

roulote [ru'lote] nf caravan (Brit), trailer (US)

rozado, -a [ro'θaðo, a] adj worn

rozadura [roθa'ðura] nf abrasion, graze

rozar [ro'θar] vt (frotar) to rub; (ensuciar)
to dirty; (Med) to graze; (tocar ligeramente)
to shave, skim; (fig) to touch o border on;
rozarse vr to rub (together); ~ **con** (fam) to
rub shoulders with

Rte. abr = **remite, remitente**

RTVE nf abr (TV) = **Radiotelevisión Española**

Ruán [ru'an] nm Rouen

rubéola [ru'βeola] nf German measles,
rubella

rubí [ru'βi] nm ruby; (de reloj) jewel

rubio, -a ['ruβjo, a] adj fair-haired, blond(e)
■ nm/f blond/blonde; **tabaco** ~ Virginia
tobacco; (**cerveza**) **rubia** lager

rubor [ru'βor] nm (sonrojo) blush; (timidez)
bashfulness

ruborice etc [ruβo'riθe] vb ver **ruborizarse**

ruborizarse [ruβori'θarse] vr to blush

ruboroso, -a [ruβo'roso, a] adj blushing

rúbrica ['ruβrika] nf (título) title, heading;
(de la firma) flourish; **bajo la** ~ **de** under the
heading of

rubricar [ruβri'kar] vt (firmar) to sign with a
flourish; (concluir) to sign and seal

rubrique etc [ru'βrike] vb ver **rubricar**

rudeza [ru'ðeθa] nf (tosquedad) coarseness;
(sencillez) simplicity

rudimentario, -a [ruðimen'tarjo, a] adj
rudimentary, basic

rudo, -a ['ruðo, a] adj (sin pulir) unpolished;
(grosero) coarse; (violento) violent; (sencillo)
simple

rueda ['rweða] nf wheel; (círculo) ring, circle;
(rodaja) slice, round; (en impresora etc) sprocket;
~ **delantera/trasera/de repuesto** front/
back/spare wheel; ~ **impresora** (Inform)
print wheel; ~ **de prensa** press conference

ruedo etc ['rweðo] vb ver **rodar** ■ nm (contorno)
edge, border; (de vestido) hem; (círculo) circle;
(Taur) arena, bullring; (esterilla) (round) mat

ruego etc ['rweɣo] vb ver **rogar** ■ nm request;
a ~ **de** at the request of; "~**s y preguntas**"
"question and answer session"

ruegue etc ['rweɣe] vb ver **rogar**

rufián [ru'fjan] nm scoundrel

rugby ['ruɣβi] nm rugby

rugido [ru'xiðo] nm roar

rugir [ru'xir] vi to roar; (toro) to bellow;
(estómago) to rumble

rugoso, -a [ru'ɣoso, a] adj (arrugado)
wrinkled; (áspero) rough; (desigual) ridged

r

ruibarbo [rwi'βarβo] *nm* rhubarb
ruido ['rwiðo] *nm* noise; (*sonido*) sound;
  (*alboroto*) racket, row; (*escándalo*) commotion,
  rumpus; **~ de fondo** background noise;
  hacer *o* **meter ~** to cause a stir
ruidoso, -a [rwi'ðoso, a] *adj* noisy, loud; (*fig*)
  sensational
ruin [rwin] *adj* contemptible, mean
ruina ['rwina] *nf* ruin; (*hundimiento*) collapse;
  (*de persona*) ruin, downfall; **estar hecho una**
  ~ to be a wreck; **la empresa le llevó a la ~**
  the venture ruined him (financially)
ruindad [rwin'dað] *nf* lowness, meanness;
  (*acto*) low *o* mean act
ruinoso, -a [rwi'noso, a] *adj* ruinous;
  (*destartalado*) dilapidated, tumbledown;
  (*Com*) disastrous
ruiseñor [rwise'ɲor] *nm* nightingale
ruja *etc* ['ruxa] *vb ver* **rugir**
ruleta [ru'leta] *nf* roulette
rulo ['rulo] *nm* (*para el pelo*) curler
rulot [ru'lot], **rulote** [ru'lote] *nf* caravan
  (*Brit*), trailer (*US*)
Rumania [ru'manja] *nf* Rumania
rumano, -a [ru'mano, a] *adj, nm/f* Rumanian
rumba ['rumba] *nf* rumba
rumbo ['rumbo] *nm* (*ruta*) route, direction;
  (*ángulo de dirección*) course, bearing; (*fig*)
  course of events; **con ~ a** in the direction
  of; **ir con ~ a** to be heading for; (*Naut*) to be
  bound for

rumboso, -a [rum'boso, a] *adj* (*generoso*)
  generous
rumiante [ru'mjante] *nm* ruminant
rumiar [ru'mjar] *vt* to chew; (*fig*) to chew
  over ▪ *vi* to chew the cud
rumor [ru'mor] *nm* (*ruido sordo*) low sound;
  (*murmuración*) murmur, buzz
rumorearse [rumore'arse] *vr*: **se rumorea**
  que it is rumoured that
rumoroso, -a [rumo'roso, a] *adj* full of
  sounds; (*arroyo*) murmuring
runrún [run'run] *nm* (*de voces*) murmur,
  sound of voices; (*fig*) rumour; (*de una máquina*)
  whirr
rupestre [ru'pestre] *adj* rock *cpd*; **pintura ~**
  cave painting
ruptura [rup'tura] *nf* (*gen*) rupture; (*disputa*)
  split; (*de contrato*) breach; (*de relaciones*)
  breaking-off
rural [ru'ral] *adj* rural
Rusia ['rusja] *nf* Russia
ruso, -a ['ruso, a] *adj, nm/f* Russian ▪ *nm*
  (*Ling*) Russian
rústico, -a ['rustiko, a] *adj* rustic; (*ordinario*)
  coarse, uncouth ▪ *nm/f* yokel ▪ *nf*: **libro en**
  rústica paperback (book)
ruta ['ruta] *nf* route
rutina [ru'tina] *nf* routine; **~ diaria** daily
  routine; **por ~** as a matter of course
rutinario, -a [ruti'narjo, a] *adj* routine

Ss

S, s ['ese] *nf* (*letra*) S, s; **S de Sábado** S for Sugar
S *abr* (= *san, santo, a*) St.; (= *sur*) S
s. *abr* (*tb*: **S.**: = *siglo*) c.; (= *siguiente*) foll.
s/ *abr* (*Com*) = **su; sus**
S.Sª *abr* (= *Sierra*) Mts
S.A. *abr* (= *Sociedad Anónima*) Ltd., Inc. (US);
    (= *Su Alteza*) H.H.
sáb. *abr* (= *sábado*) Sat.
sábado ['saβaðo] *nm* Saturday; (*de los judíos*)
    Sabbath; **del ~ en ocho días** a week on
    Saturday; **un ~ sí y otro no, cada dos
    sábados** every other Saturday; **S~ Santo**
    Holy Saturday; *ver tb* **Semana Santa**
sabana [sa'βana] *nf* savannah
sábana ['saβana] *nf* sheet; **se le pegan las
    sábanas** he can't get up in the morning
sabandija [saβan'dixa] *nf* (*bicho*) bug; (*fig*)
    louse
sabañón [saβa'ɲon] *nm* chilblain
sabático, -a [sa'βatiko, a] *adj* (*Rel: Univ*)
    sabbatical
sabelotodo [saβelo'toðo] *nm/f inv* know-all
saber [sa'βer] *vt* to know; (*llegar a conocer*)
    to find out, learn; (*tener capacidad de*) to
    know how to ■ *vi:* **~ a** to taste of, taste like
    ■ *nm* knowledge, learning; **saberse** *vr:*
    se sabe que ... it is known that ...; **no se
    sabe** nobody knows; **a ~** namely; **¿sabes
    conducir/nadar?** can you drive/swim?;
    ¿sabes francés? do you *o* can you speak
    French?; **~ de memoria** to know by heart;
    lo sé I know; **hacer ~** to inform, let know;
    que yo sepa as far as I know; **vete o anda a ~**
    your guess is as good as mine, who knows!;
    ¿sabe? (*fam*) you know (what I mean)?; **le
    sabe mal que otro la saque a bailar** it
    upsets him that anybody else should ask her
    to dance
sabido, -a [sa'βiðo, a] *adj* (*consabido*) well-
    known; **como es ~** as we all know
sabiduría [saβiðu'ria] *nf* (*conocimientos*)
    wisdom; (*instrucción*) learning; **~ popular**
    folklore

sabiendas [sa'βjendas]: **a ~** *adv* knowingly;
    a ~ de que ... knowing full well that ...
sabihondo, -a [sa'βjondo, a] *adj, nm/f* know-
    all, know-it-all (US)
sabio, -a ['saβjo, a] *adj* (*docto*) learned;
    (*prudente*) wise, sensible
sablazo [sa'βlaθo] *nm* (*herida*) sword wound;
    (*fam*) sponging; **dar un ~ a algn** to tap sb for
    money
sable [sa'βle] *nm* sabre
sabor [sa'βor] *nm* taste, flavour; (*fig*) flavour;
    sin ~ flavourless
saborear [saβore'ar] *vt* to taste, savour; (*fig*)
    to relish
sabotaje [saβo'taxe] *nm* sabotage
saboteador, a [saβotea'ðor, a] *nm/f* saboteur
sabotear [saβote'ar] *vt* to sabotage
Saboya [sa'βoja] *nf* Savoy
sabré *etc* [sa'βre] *vb ver* **saber**
sabroso, -a [sa'βroso, a] *adj* tasty; (*fig fam*)
    racy, salty
saca ['saka] *nf* big sack; **~ de correo(s)**
    mailbag; (*Com*) withdrawal
sacacorchos [saka'kortʃos] *nm inv* corkscrew
sacapuntas [saka'puntas] *nm inv* pencil
    sharpener
sacar [sa'kar] *vt* to take out; (*fig: extraer*) to
    get (out); (*quitar*) to remove, get out; (*hacer
    salir*) to bring out; (*fondos: de cuenta*) to draw
    out, withdraw; (*obtener: legado etc*) to get;
    (*demostrar*) to show; (*conclusión*) to draw;
    (*novela etc*) to publish, bring out; (*ropa*) to
    take off; (*obra*) to make; (*premio*) to receive;
    (*entradas*) to get; (*Tenis*) to serve; (*Fútbol*) to put
    into play; **~ adelante** (*niño*) to bring up; **~ a
    algn a bailar** to dance with sb; **~ a algn de
    sí** to infuriate sb; **~ una foto** to take a photo;
    ~ la lengua to stick out one's tongue; **~
    buenas/malas notas** to get good/bad marks
sacarina [saka'rina] *nf* saccharin(e)
sacerdote [saθer'ðote] *nm* priest
saciar [sa'θjar] *vt* (*hartar*) to satiate; (*fig*) to
    satisfy; **saciarse** *vr* (*fig*) to be satisfied

saciedad [saθje'ðað] *nf* satiety; **hasta la ~** (*comer*) one's fill; (*repetir*) ad nauseam

saco ['sako] *nm* bag; (*grande*) sack; (*contenido*) bagful; (*Am: chaqueta*) jacket; **~ de dormir** sleeping bag

sacramento [sakra'mento] *nm* sacrament

sacrificar [sakrifi'kar] *vt* to sacrifice; (*animal*) to slaughter; (*perro etc*) to put to sleep; **sacrificarse** *vr* to sacrifice o.s.

sacrificio [sakri'fiθjo] *nm* sacrifice

sacrifique *etc* [sakri'fike] *vb ver* **sacrificar**

sacrilegio [sakri'lexjo] *nm* sacrilege

sacrílego, -a [sa'krileɣo, a] *adj* sacrilegious

sacristán [sakris'tan] *nm* verger

sacristía [sakris'tia] *nf* sacristy

sacro, -a ['sakro, a] *adj* sacred

sacudida [saku'ðiða] *nf* (*agitación*) shake, shaking; (*sacudimiento*) jolt, bump; (*fig*) violent change; (*Pol etc*) upheaval; **~ eléctrica** electric shock

sacudir [saku'ðir] *vt* to shake; (*golpear*) to hit; (*ala*) to flap; (*alfombra*) to beat; **~ a algn** (*fam*) to belt sb

S.A. de C.V. *abr* (*Am:* = *Sociedad Anónima de Capital Variable*) ≈ PLC (Brit), ≈ Corps (US), ≈ Inc. (US)

sádico, -a ['saðiko, a] *adj* sadistic ◼ *nm/f* sadist

sadismo [sa'ðismo] *nm* sadism

sadomasoquismo [saðomaso'kismo] *nm* sadomasochism, S & M

sadomasoquista [saðomaso'kista] *adj* sadomasochistic ◼ *nm/f* sadomasochist

saeta [sa'eta] *nf* (*flecha*) arrow; (*Mus*) *sacred song in flamenco style*

safari [sa'fari] *nm* safari

sagacidad [saɣaθi'ðað] *nf* shrewdness, cleverness

sagaz [sa'ɣaθ] *adj* shrewd, clever

Sagitario [saxi'tarjo] *nm* (*Astro*) Sagittarius

sagrado, -a [sa'ɣraðo, a] *adj* sacred, holy

Sáhara ['saara] *nm:* **el ~** the Sahara (desert)

saharaui [saxa'rawi] *adj* Saharan ◼ *nm/f* native o inhabitant of the Sahara

sajón, -ona [sa'xon, 'xona] *adj, nm/f* Saxon

sal [sal] *vb ver* **salir** ◼ *nf* salt; (*gracia*) wit; (*encanto*) charm; **sales de baño** bath salts; **~ gorda** *o* **de cocina** kitchen o cooking salt

sala ['sala] *nf* (*cuarto grande*) large room; (*tb:* **sala de estar**) living room; (*Teat*) house, auditorium; (*de hospital*) ward; **~ de apelación** court; **~ de conferencias** lecture hall; **~ de espera** waiting room; **~ de embarque** departure lounge; **~ de estar** living room; **~ de fiestas** function room; **~ de juntas** (*Com*) boardroom; **~ VIP** (*en aeropuerto, discoteca*) VIP lounge

salado, -a [sa'laðo, a] *adj* salty; (*fig*) witty,

amusing; **agua salada** salt water

salar [sa'lar] *vt* to salt, add salt to

salariado, -a [sala'rjaðo, a] *adj* (*empleado*) salaried

salarial [sala'rjal] *adj* (*aumento, revisión*) wage *cpd*, salary *cpd*, pay *cpd*

salario [sa'larjo] *nm* wage, pay

salchicha [sal'tʃitʃa] *nf* (*pork*) sausage

salchichón [saltʃi'tʃon] *nm* (*salami-type*) sausage

saldar [sal'dar] *vt* to pay; (*vender*) to sell off; (*fig*) to settle, resolve

saldo ['saldo] *nm* (*pago*) settlement; (*de una cuenta*) balance; (*lo restante*) remnant(s) (*pl*), remainder; (*liquidación*) sale; (*Com*): **~ anterior** balance brought forward; **~ acreedor/deudor** *o* **pasivo** credit/debit balance; **~ final** final balance

saldré *etc* [sal'dre] *vb ver* **salir**

salero [sa'lero] *nm* salt cellar; (*ingenio*) wit; (*encanto*) charm

salga *etc* ['salɣa] *vb ver* **salir**

salida [sa'liða] *nf* (*puerta etc*) exit, way out; (*acto*) leaving, going out; (*de tren, Aviat*) departure; (*Com: Tec*) output, production; (*fig*) way out; (*resultado*) outcome; (*Com: oportunidad*) opening; (*Geo, válvula*) outlet; (*de gas*) escape; (*ocurrencia*) joke; **calle sin ~** cul-de-sac; **a la ~ del teatro** after the theatre; **dar la ~** (*Deporte*) to give the starting signal; **~ de incendios** fire escape; **~ impresa** (*Inform*) hard copy; **no hay ~** there's no way out of it; **no tenemos otra ~** we have no option; **tener salidas** to be witty

salido, -a [sa'liðo, a] *adj* (*fam*) randy

saliente [sa'ljente] *adj* (*Arq*) projecting; (*sol*) rising; (*fig*) outstanding

salina [sa'lina] *nf* salt mine; **salinas** *nfpl* saltworks *sg*

 PALABRA CLAVE

salir [sa'lir] *vi* **1** (*persona*) to come o go out; (*tren, avión*) to leave; **Juan ha salido** Juan has gone out; **salió de la cocina** he came out of the kitchen; **salimos de Madrid a las ocho** we left Madrid at eight (o'clock); **salió corriendo (del cuarto)** he ran out (of the room); **salir de un apuro** to get out of a jam
2 (*pelo*) to grow; (*diente*) to come through; (*disco, libro*) to come out; (*planta, número de lotería*) to come up; **salir a la superficie** to come to the surface; **anoche salió en la tele** she appeared o was on TV last night; **salió en todos los periódicos** it was in all the papers; **le salió un trabajo** he got a job
3 (*resultar*): **la muchacha nos salió muy**

trabajadora the girl turned out to be a very hard worker; **la comida te ha salido exquisita** the food was delicious; **sale muy caro** it's very expensive; **la entrevista que hice me salió bien/mal** the interview I did turned out *o* went well/badly; **nos salió a 5.000 ptas cada uno** it worked out at 5,000 pesetas each; **no salen las cuentas** it doesn't work out *o* add up; **salir ganando** to come out on top; **salir perdiendo** to lose out **4** (*Deporte*) to start; (*Naipes*) to lead **5**: **salir con algn** to go out with sb **6**: **salir adelante**: **no sé como haré para salir adelante** I don't know how I'll get by ◆ **salirse** *vr* **1** (*líquido*) to spill; (*animal*) to escape **2** (*desviarse*): **salirse de la carretera** to leave *o* go off the road; **salirse de lo normal** to be unusual, **salirse del tema** to get off the point **3**: **salirse con la suya** to get one's own way

saliva [sa'liβa] *nf* saliva
salivadera [saliβa'ðera] *nf* (*Am*) spittoon
salmantino, -a [salman'tino, a] *adj* of *o* from Salamanca ◼ *nm/f* native *o* inhabitant of Salamanca
salmo ['salmo] *nm* psalm
salmón [sal'mon] *nm* salmon
salmonete [salmo'nete] *nm* red mullet
salmuera [sal'mwera] *nf* pickle, brine
salón [sa'lon] *nm* living-room, lounge; (*muebles*) lounge suite; **~ de belleza** beauty parlour; **~ de baile** dance hall; **~ de actos/ sesiones** assembly hall
salpicadero [salpika'ðero] *nm* (*Auto*) dashboard
salpicar [salpi'kar] *vt* (*de barro, pintura*) to splash; (*rociar*) to sprinkle, spatter; (*esparcir*) to scatter
salpicón [salpi'kon] *nm* (*acto*) splashing; (*Culin*) meat *o* fish salad
salpimentar [salpimen'tar] *vt* (*Culin*) to season
salpique *etc* [sal'pike] *vb ver* **salpicar**
salsa ['salsa] *nf* sauce; (*con carne asada*) gravy; (*fig*) spice; **~ mayonesa** mayonnaise; **estar en su ~** (*fam*) to be in one's element
saltamontes [salta'montes] *nm inv* grasshopper
saltar [sal'tar] *vt* to jump (over), leap (over); (*dejar de lado*) to skip, miss out ◼ *vi* to jump, leap; (*pelota*) to bounce; (*al aire*) to fly up; (*quebrarse*) to break; (*al agua*) to dive; (*fig*) to explode, blow up; (*botón*) to come off; (*corcho*) to pop out; **saltarse** *vr* (*omitir*) to skip, miss; **salta a la vista** it's obvious; **saltarse todas las reglas** to break all the rules

salteado, -a [salte'aðo, a] *adj* (*Culin*) sauté(ed)
salteador [saltea'ðor] *nm* (*tb*: **salteador de caminos**) highwayman
saltear [salte'ar] *vt* (*robar*) to rob (in a holdup); (*asaltar*) to assault, attack; (*Culin*) to sauté
saltimbanqui [saltim'banki] *nm/f* acrobat
salto ['salto] *nm* jump, leap; (*al agua*) dive; **a saltos** by jumping; **~ de agua** waterfall; **~ de altura** high jump; **~ de cama** negligee; **~ mortal** somersault; (*Inform*): **~ de línea** line feed; **~ de línea automático** wordwrap; **~ de página** formfeed
saltón, -ona [sal'ton, ona] *adj* (*ojos*) bulging, popping; (*dientes*) protruding
salubre [sa'luβre] *adj* healthy, salubrious
salud [sa'luð] *nf* health; **estar bien/mal de ~** to be in good/poor health; **¡(a su) ¡cheers!**, good health!; **beber a la ~ de** to drink (to) the health of
saludable [salu'ðaβle] *adj* (*de buena salud*) healthy; (*provechoso*) good, beneficial
saludar [salu'ðar] *vt* to greet; (*Mil*) to salute; **ir a ~ a algn** to drop in to see sb; **salude de mi parte a X** give my regards to X; **le saluda atentamente** (*en carta*) yours faithfully
saludo [sa'luðo] *nm* greeting; **saludos** (*en carta*) best wishes, regards; **un ~ afectuoso** *o* **cordial** yours sincerely
salva ['salβa] *nf* (*Mil*) salvo; **una ~ de aplausos** thunderous applause
salvación [salβa'θjon] *nf* salvation; (*rescate*) rescue
salvado [sal'βaðo] *nm* bran
salvador [salβa'ðor] *nm* rescuer, saviour; **el S~** the Saviour; **El S~** El Salvador; **San S~** San Salvador
salvadoreño, -a [salβaðo'reɲo, a] *adj, nm/f* Salvadoran, Salvadorian
salvaguardar [salβaɣwar'ðar] *vt* to safeguard; (*Inform*) to back up, make a backup copy of
salvajada [salβa'xaða] *nf* savage deed, atrocity
salvaje [sal'βaxe] *adj* wild; (*tribu*) savage
salvajismo [salβa'xismo] *nm* savagery
salvamento [salβa'mento] *nm* (*acción*) rescue; (*de naufragio*) salvage; **~ y socorrismo** life-saving
salvapantallas [salβapan'taʎas] *nm inv* screensaver
salvar [sal'βar] *vt* (*rescatar*) to save, rescue; (*resolver*) to overcome, resolve; (*cubrir distancias*) to cover, travel; (*hacer excepción*) to except, exclude; (*un barco*) to salvage; **salvarse** *vr* to save o.s., escape; **¡sálvese el que pueda!** every man for himself!

salvavidas [salβa'βiðas] *adj inv*: **bote/ chaleco/cinturón** ~ lifeboat/lifejacket/ lifebelt

salvedad [salβe'ðað] *nf* reservation, qualification; **con la ~ de que ...** with the proviso that ...

salvia ['salβja] *nf* sage

salvo, -a ['salβo, a] *adj* safe ■ *prep* except (for), save; **~ error u omisión** (*Com*) errors and omissions excepted; **a ~** out of danger; **~ que** unless

salvoconducto [salβokon'dukto] *nm* safe- conduct

samba ['samba] *nf* samba

san [san] *n* (*apócope de* **santo**) saint; **~ Juan** St. John; *ver tb* **Juan**

sanar [sa'nar] *vt* (*herida*) to heal; (*persona*) to cure ■ *vi* (*persona*) to get well, recover; (*herida*) to heal

sanatorio [sana'torjo] *nm* sanatorium

sanción [san'θjon] *nf* sanction

sancionar [sanθjo'nar] *vt* to sanction

sancocho [san'kotʃo] *nm* (*Am*) stew

sandalia [san'dalja] *nf* sandal

sándalo ['sandalo] *nm* sandal(wood)

sandez [san'deθ] *nf* (*cualidad*) foolishness; (*acción*) stupid thing; **decir sandeces** to talk nonsense

sandía [san'dia] *nf* watermelon

sandinista [sanði'nista] *adj, nm/f* Sandinist(a)

sandwich ['sandwitʃ] (*pl* **sandwichs** *o* **sandwiches**) *nm* sandwich

saneamiento [sanea'mjento] *nm* sanitation

sanear [sane'ar] *vt* to drain; (*indemnizar*) to compensate; (*Econ*) to reorganize

sanfermines [sanfer'mines] *nmpl see note*

● **SANFERMINES**
●
● The *Sanfermines* are a week of *fiestas* in
● Pamplona, the capital of Navarre, made
● famous by Ernest Hemingway. From
● the 7th of July, the feast of San Fermín,
● crowds of mainly young people take
● to the streets drinking, singing and
● dancing. Early in the morning bulls are
● released along the narrow streets leading
● to the bullring, and people risk serious
● injury by running out in front of them,
● a custom which is also typical of many
● Spanish villages.

sangrar [san'grar] *vt, vi* to bleed; (*texto*) to indent

sangre ['sangre] *nf* blood; **~ fría** sangfroid; **a ~ fría** in cold blood

sangría [san'gria] *nf* (*Med*) bleeding; (*Culin*) sangria, *sweetened drink of red wine with fruit*, ≈ fruit cup

sangriento, -a [san'grjento, a] *adj* bloody

sanguijuela [sangi'xwela] *nf* (*Zool, fig*) leech

sanguinario, -a [sangi'narjo, a] *adj* bloodthirsty

sanguíneo, -a [san'gineo, a] *adj* blood *cpd*

sanidad [sani'ðað] *nf* sanitation; (*calidad de sano*) health, healthiness; **~ pública** public health (department)

sanitario, -a [sani'tarjo, a] *adj* sanitary; (*de la salud*) health *cpd* ■ *nm*: **sanitarios** *nmpl* toilets (*Brit*), restroom *sg* (*US*)

San Marino [sanma'rino] *nm*: (**La República de**) ~ San Marino

sano, -a ['sano, a] *adj* healthy; (*sin daños*) sound; (*comida*) wholesome; (*entero*) whole, intact; **~ y salvo** safe and sound

santanderino, -a [santande'rino, a] *adj* of *o* from Santander ■ *nm/f* native *o* inhabitant of Santander

Santiago [san'tjaɣo] *nm*: ~ (**de Chile**) Santiago

santiamén [santja'men] *nm*: **en un ~** in no time at all

santidad [santi'ðað] *nf* holiness, sanctity

santificar [santifi'kar] *vt* to sanctify

santifique *etc* [santi'fike] *vb ver* **santificar**

santiguarse [santi'ɣwarse] *vr* to make the sign of the cross

santigüe *etc* [san'tiɣwe] *vb ver* **santiguarse**

santo, -a ['santo, a] *adj* holy; (*fig*) wonderful, miraculous ■ *nm/f* saint ■ *nm* saint's day; **hacer su santa voluntad** to do as one jolly well pleases; **¿a ~ de qué ...?** why on earth ...?; **se le fue el ~ al cielo** he forgot what he was about to say; **~ y seña** password; *see note*

■ **SANTO**
●
● As well as celebrating their birthday
● Spaniards have traditionally celebrated
● *el santo*, their Saint's day, when the
● Saint they were called after at birth, eg
● San Pedro or la Virgen de los Dolores, is
● honoured in the Christian calendar. This
● is a custom which is gradually dying out.

santuario [san'twarjo] *nm* sanctuary, shrine

saña ['saɲa] *nf* rage, fury

sapo ['sapo] *nm* toad

saque *etc* ['sake] *vb ver* **sacar** ■ *nm* (*Tenis*) service, serve; (*Fútbol*) throw-in; **~ inicial** kick-off; **~ de esquina** corner (kick); **tener buen ~** to eat heartily

saquear [sake'ar] *vt* (*Mil*) to sack; (*robar*) to loot, plunder; (*fig*) to ransack

saqueo [sa'keo] *nm* sacking; looting, plundering; ransacking

S.A.R. *abr* (= *Su Alteza Real*) HRH

sarampión [saram'pjon] *nm* measles *sg*

sarape [sa'rape] *nm* (*Am*) blanket

sarcasmo [sar'kasmo] *nm* sarcasm

sarcástico, -a [sar'kastiko, a] *adj* sarcastic

sarcófago [sar'kofaɣo] *nm* sarcophagus

sardina [sar'ðina] *nf* sardine

sardo, -a ['sarðo, a] *adj, nm/f* Sardinian

sardónico, -a [sar'ðoniko, a] *adj* sardonic; (*irónico*) ironical, sarcastic

sargento [sar'xento] *nm* sergeant

sarmiento [sar'mjento] *nm* vine shoot

sarna ['sarna] *nf* itch; (*Med*) scabies

sarpullido [sarpu'ʎiðo] *nm* (*Med*) rash

sarro ['sarro] *nm* deposit; (*en dientes*) tartar

sarta ['sarta] *nf* (*fig*): **una ~ de mentiras** a pack of lies

sartén [sar'ten] *nf* frying pan; **tener la ~ por el mango** to rule the roost

sastre ['sastre] *nm* tailor

sastrería [sastre'ria] *nf* (*arte*) tailoring; (*tienda*) tailor's (shop)

Satanás [sata'nas] *nm* Satan

satélite [sa'telite] *nm* satellite

satinado, -a [sati'naðo, a] *adj* glossy
■ *nm* gloss, shine

sátira ['satira] *nf* satire

satírico, -a [sa'tiriko, a] *adj* satiric(al)

sátiro ['satiro] *nm* (*Mitología*) satyr; (*fig*) sex maniac

satisfacción [satisfak'θjon] *nf* satisfaction

satisfacer [satisfa'θer] *vt* to satisfy; (*gastos*) to meet; (*deuda*) to pay; (*Com: letra de cambio*) to honour (*Brit*), honor (*US*); (*pérdida*) to make good; **satisfacerse** *vr* to satisfy o.s., be satisfied; (*vengarse*) to take revenge

satisfaga *etc* [satis'faɣa], **satisfaré** *etc* [satisfa're] *vb ver* **satisfacer**

satisfecho, -a [satis'fetʃo, a] *pp de* **satisfacer**
■ *adj* satisfied; (*contento*) content(ed), happy; (*tb:* **satisfecho de sí mismo**) self-satisfied, smug

satisfice *etc* [satis'fiθe] *vb ver* **satisfacer**

saturación [satura'θjon] *nf* saturation; **llegar a la ~** to reach saturation point

saturar [satu'rar] *vt* to saturate; **saturarse** *vr* (*mercado, aeropuerto*) to reach saturation point; **¡estoy saturado de tanta televisión!** I can't take any more television!

sauce ['sauθe] *nm* willow; **~ llorón** weeping willow

saúco [sa'uko] *nm* (*Bot*) elder

saudí [sau'ði] *adj, nm/f* Saudi

sauna ['sauna] *nf* sauna

savia ['saβja] *nf* sap

saxo ['sakso] *nm* sax

saxofón [sakso'fon] *nm* saxophone

saya ['saja] *nf* (*falda*) skirt; (*enagua*) petticoat

sayo ['sajo] *nm* smock

sazón [sa'θon] *nf* (*de fruta*) ripeness; **a la ~** then, at that time

sazonado, -a [saθo'naðo, a] *adj* (*fruta*) ripe; (*Culin*) flavoured, seasoned

sazonar [saθo'nar] *vt* to ripen; (*Culin*) to flavour, season

s/c *abr* (*Com*: = *su casa*) your firm; (: = *su cuenta*) your account

Sdo. *abr* (*Com*: = *Saldo*) bal

SE *abr* (= *sudeste*) SE

 PALABRA CLAVE

se [se] *pron* **1** (*reflexivo*: *sg: m*) himself; (: *f*) herself; (: *pl*) themselves; (: *cosa*) itself; (: *de Vd*) yourself; (: *de Vds*) yourselves; (*indefinido*) oneself; **se mira en el espejo** he looks at himself in the mirror; **¡siéntese!** sit down!; **se durmió** he fell asleep; **se está preparando** she's getting (herself) ready; (*para usos léxicos del pron ver el vb en cuestión, p.ej.* **arrepentirse**)

2 (*como complemento indirecto*) to him; to her, to them; to it; to you; **se lo dije ayer** (*a Vd*) I told you yesterday; **se compró un sombrero** he bought himself a hat; **se rompió la pierna** he broke his leg; **cortarse el pelo** to get one's hair cut; (*uno mismo*) to cut one's hair; **se comió un pastel** he ate a cake

3 (*uso recíproco*) each other, one another; **se miraron (el uno al otro)** they looked at each other *o* one another

4 (*en oraciones pasivas*): **se han vendido muchos libros** a lot of books have been sold; **"se vende coche"** "car for sale"

5 (*impers*): **se dice que** people say that, it is said that; **allí se come muy bien** the food there is very good, you can eat very well there

sé [se] *vb ver* **saber; ser**

sea *etc* ['sea] *vb ver* **ser**

SEAT ['seat] *nf abr* = **Sociedad Española de Automóviles de Turismo**

sebo ['seβo] *nm* fat, grease

Sec. *abr* (= *Secretario*) Sec

seca ['seka] *vb ver* **seco**

secado [se'kaðo] *nm* drying; **~ a mano** blow-dry

secador [seka'ðor] *nm*: **~ para el pelo** hairdryer

secadora [seka'ðora] *nf* tumble dryer; **~ centrífuga** spin-dryer

secano [se'kano] *nm* (*Agr*: *tb*: **tierra de secano**) dry land *o* region; **cultivo de ~** dry farming

secante [se'kante] *adj* (*viento*) drying ■ *nm* blotting paper

secar [se'kar] *vt* to dry; (*superficie*) to wipe dry; (*frente, suelo*) to mop; (*líquido*) to mop up; (*tinta*) to blot; **secarse** *vr* to dry (off); (*río, planta*) to dry up

sección [sek'θjon] *nf* section; (*Com*) department; **~ deportiva** (*en periódico*) sports page(s)

seco, -a ['seko, a] *adj* dry; (*fruta*) dried; (*persona*: *magro*) thin, skinny; (*carácter*) cold; (*antipático*) disagreeable; (*respuesta*) sharp, curt ■ *nf* dry season; **habrá pan a secas** there will be just bread; **decir algo a secas** to say sth curtly; **parar en ~** to stop dead

secreción [sekre'θjon] *nf* secretion

secretaría [sekreta'ria] *nf* secretariat; (*oficina*) secretary's office

secretariado [sekreta'rjaðo] *nm* (*oficina*) secretariat; (*cargo*) secretaryship; (*curso*) secretarial course

secretario, -a [sekre'tarjo, a] *nm/f* secretary; **~ adjunto** (*Com*) assistant secretary

secreto, -a [se'kreto, a] *adj* secret; (*información*) confidential; (*persona*) secretive ■ *nm* secret; (*calidad*) secrecy

secta ['sekta] *nf* sect

sectario, -a [sek'tarjo, a] *adj* sectarian

sector [sek'tor] *nm* sector (*tb Inform*); (*de opinión*) section; (*fig*: *campo*) area, field; **~ privado/público** (*Com*: *Econ*) private/public sector

secuela [se'kwela] *nf* consequence

secuencia [se'kwenθja] *nf* sequence

secuestrar [sekwes'trar] *vt* to kidnap; (*avión*) to hijack; (*bienes*) to seize, confiscate

secuestro [se'kwestro] *nm* kidnapping; hijack; seizure, confiscation

secular [seku'lar] *adj* secular

secundar [sekun'dar] *vt* to second, support

secundario, -a [sekun'darjo, a] *adj* secondary; (*carretera*) side *cpd*; (*Inform*) background *cpd* ■ *nf* secondary education; *ver tb* **sistema educativo**

sed [seð] *nf* thirst; (*fig*) thirst, craving; **tener ~** to be thirsty

seda ['seða] *nf* silk; **~ dental** dental floss

sedal [se'ðal] *nm* fishing line

sedante [se'ðante] *nm* sedative

sede ['seðe] *nf* (*de gobierno*) seat; (*de compañía*) headquarters *pl*, head office; **Santa S~** Holy See

sedentario, -a [seðen'tarjo, a] *adj* sedentary

SEDIC [se'ðik] *nf abr* = **Sociedad Española de Documentación e Información Científica**

sedición [seði'θjon] *nf* sedition

sediento, -a [se'ðjento, a] *adj* thirsty

sedimentar [seðimen'tar] *vt* to deposit; **sedimentarse** *vr* to settle

sedimento [seði'mento] *nm* sediment

sedoso, -a [se'ðoso, a] *adj* silky, silken

seducción [seðuk'θjon] *nf* seduction

seducir [seðu'θir] *vt* to seduce; (*sobornar*) to bribe; (*cautivar*) to charm, fascinate; (*atraer*) to attract

seductor, a [seðuk'tor, a] *adj* seductive; charming, fascinating; attractive; (*engañoso*) deceptive, misleading ■ *nm/f* seducer

seduje *etc* [se'ðuxe], **seduzca** *etc* [se'ðuθka] *vb ver* **seducir**

sefardí [sefar'ði], **sefardita** [sefar'ðita] *adj* Sephardi(c) ■ *nm/f* Sephardi

segador, a [seɣa'ðor, a] *nm/f* (*persona*) harvester ■ *nf* (*Tec*) mower, reaper

segadora-trilladora [seɣa'ðoratriʎa'ðora] *nf* combine harvester

segar [se'ɣar] *vt* (*mies*) to reap, cut; (*hierba*) to mow, cut; (*esperanzas*) to ruin

seglar [se'ɣlar] *adj* secular, lay

segoviano, -a [seɣo'βjano, a] *adj* of *o* from Segovia ■ *nm/f* native *o* inhabitant of Segovia

segregación [seɣreɣa'θjon] *nf* segregation; **~ racial** racial segregation

segregar [seɣre'ɣar] *vt* to segregate, separate

segregue *etc* [se'ɣreɣe] *vb ver* **segregar**

segué [se'ɣe], **seguemos** *etc* [se'ɣemos] *vb ver* **segar**

seguidamente [seɣiða'mente] *adv* (*sin parar*) without a break; (*inmediatamente después*) immediately after

seguido, -a [se'ɣiðo, a] *adj* (*continuo*) continuous, unbroken; (*recto*) straight ■ *adv* (*directo*) straight (on); (*después*) after; (*Am*: *a menudo*) often ■ *nf*: **en seguida** at once, right away; **cinco días seguidos** five days running, five days in a row; **en seguida termino** I've nearly finished, I shan't be long now

seguimiento [seɣi'mjento] *nm* chase, pursuit; (*continuación*) continuation

seguir [se'ɣir] *vt* to follow; (*venir después*) to follow on, come after; (*proseguir*) to continue; (*perseguir*) to chase, pursue; (*indicio*) to follow up; (*mujer*) to court ■ *vi* (*gen*) to follow; (*continuar*) to continue, carry *o* go on; **seguirse** *vr* to follow; **a ~** to be continued; **sigo sin comprender** I still don't understand; **sigue lloviendo** it's still raining; **sigue** (*en carta*) P.T.O.; (*en libro, TV*)

continued; **"hágase ~"** "please forward";
¡**siga!** (*Am: pase*) come in!
según [se'ɣun] *prep* according to ▪ *adv*:
~ **(y conforme)** it all depends ▪ *conj* as;
~ **esté el tiempo** depending on the weather;
~ **me consta** as far as I know; **está ~ lo
dejaste** it is just as you left it
segundo, -a [se'ɣundo, a] *adj* second; (*en
discurso*) secondly ▪ *nm* (*gen, medida de tiempo*)
second; (*piso*) second floor ▪ *nf* (*sentido*)
second meaning; ~ **(de a bordo)** (*Naut*) first
mate; **segunda (clase)** (*Ferro*) second class;
segunda (marcha) (*Auto*) second (gear);
de segunda mano second hand
seguramente [seɣura'mente] *adv* surely;
(*con certeza*) for sure, with certainty;
(*probablemente*) probably; ¿**lo va a
comprar?** is he going to buy it?
I should think so
seguridad [seɣuri'ðað] *nf* safety; (*del estado,
de casa etc*) security; (*certidumbre*) certainty;
(*confianza*) confidence; (*estabilidad*) stability;
~ **social** social security; ~ **contra incendios**
fire precautions *pl*; ~ **en sí mismo** (self-)
confidence
seguro, -a [se'ɣuro, a] *adj* (*cierto*) sure,
certain; (*fiel*) trustworthy; (*libre de peligro*)
safe; (*bien defendido, firme*) secure; (*datos etc*)
reliable; (*fecha*) firm ▪ *adv* for sure, certainly
▪ *nm* (*dispositivo*) safety device; (*de cerradura*)
tumbler; (*de arma*) safety catch; (*Com*)
insurance; ~ **contra accidentes/incendios**
fire/accident insurance; ~ **contra terceros/
a todo riesgo** third party/comprehensive
insurance; ~ **dotal con beneficios** with-
profits endowment assurance; **S~ de
Enfermedad** = National Insurance; ~
marítimo marine insurance; ~ **mixto**
endowment assurance; ~ **temporal** term
insurance; ~ **de vida** life insurance
seis [seis] *num* six; ~ **mil** six thousand; **tiene
~ años** she is six (years old); **unos** ~ about
six; **hoy es el ~** today is the sixth
seiscientos, -as [seis'θjentos, as] *num* six
hundred
seísmo [se'ismo] *nm* tremor, earthquake
SELA *sigla m* = **Sistema Económico
Latinoamericano**
selección [selek'θjon] *nf* selection; ~
múltiple multiple choice; ~ **nacional**
(*Deporte*) national team
seleccionador, a [selekθjona'ðor, a] *nm/f*
(*Deporte*) selector
seleccionar [selekθjo'nar] *vt* to pick, choose,
select
selectividad [selektiβi'ðað] *nf* (*Univ*)
entrance examination; *see note*

SELECTIVIDAD

School leavers wishing to go on to
University sit the dreaded *selectividad* in
June, with resits in September. When
student numbers are too high for a
particular course only the best students
get their choice. Some of the others then
wait a year to sit the exam again rather
than do a course they don't want.

selecto, -a [se'lekto, a] *adj* select, choice;
(*escogido*) selected
sellado, -a [se'ʎaðo, a] *adj* (*documento oficial*)
sealed; (*pasaporte*) stamped
sellar [se'ʎar] *vt* (*documento oficial*) to seal;
(*pasaporte, visado*) to stamp; (*marcar*) to brand;
(*pacto, labios*) to seal
sello ['seʎo] *nm* stamp; (*precinto*) seal; (*fig: tb:*
sello distintivo) hallmark; ~ **fiscal** revenue
stamp; **sellos de prima** (*Com*) trading
stamps
selva ['selβa] *nf* (*bosque*) forest, woods *pl*;
(*jungla*) jungle; **la S~ Negra** the Black Forest
S.Em. *abr* = **Su Eminencia**
semáforo [se'maforo] *nm* (*Auto*) traffic lights
pl; (*Ferro*) signal
semana [se'mana] *nf* week; ~ **inglesa** five-
day (working) week; ~ **laboral** working
week; **S~ Santa** Holy Week; *see note*; **entre ~**
during the week

SEMANA SANTA

Semana Santa is a holiday in Spain. All
regions take *Viernes Santo*, Good Friday,
Sábado Santo, Holy Saturday, and *Domingo
de Resurrección*, Easter Sunday. Other
holidays at this time vary according
to each region. There are spectacular
procesiones all over the country, with
members of *cofradías* (brotherhoods)
dressing in hooded robes and parading
their *pasos* (religious floats or sculptures)
through the streets. Seville has the most
renowned celebrations, on account of the
religious fervour shown by the locals.

semanal [sema'nal] *adj* weekly
semanario [sema'narjo] *nm* weekly
(magazine)
semántica [se'mantika] *nf* semantics *sg*
semblante [sem'blante] *nm* face; (*fig*) look
sembrar [sem'brar] *vt* to sow; (*objetos*) to
sprinkle, scatter about; (*noticias etc*) to spread
semejante [seme'xante] *adj* (*parecido*)
similar; (*tal*) such; **semejantes** alike,

similar ∎ nm fellow man, fellow creature; **son muy semejantes** they are very much alike; **nunca hizo cosa ~** he never did such a thing

semejanza [seme'xanθa] nf similarity, resemblance; **a ~ de** like, as

semejar [seme'xar] vi to seem like, resemble; **semejarse** vr to look alike, be similar

semen ['semen] nm semen

semental [semen'tal] nm (macho) stud

sementera [semen'tera] nf (acto) sowing; (temporada) seedtime; (tierra) sown land

semestral [semes'tral] adj half-yearly, bi-annual

semestre [se'mestre] nm period of six months; (Univ) semester; (Com) half-yearly payment

semicírculo [semi'θirkulo] nm semicircle

semiconductor [semikonduk'tor] nm semiconductor

semiconsciente [semikons'θjente] adj semiconscious

semidesnatado, -a [semiðesna'taðo, a] adj semi-skimmed

semifinal [semifi'nal] nf semifinal

semiinconsciente [semi(i)nkons'θjente] adj semiconscious

semilla [se'miʎa] nf seed

semillero [semi'ʎero] nm (Agr etc) seedbed; (fig) hotbed

seminario [semi'narjo] nm (Rel) seminary; (Escol) seminar

semiseco [semi'seko] nm medium-dry

semita [se'mita] adj Semitic ∎ nm/f Semite

sémola ['semola] nf semolina

sempiterno, -a [sempi'terno, a] adj everlasting

Sena ['sena] nm: **el ~** the (river) Seine

senado [se'naðo] nm senate; ver tb **Las Cortes (españolas)**

senador, a [sena'ðor, a] nm/f senator

sencillez [senθi'ʎeθ] nf simplicity; (de persona) naturalness

sencillo, -a [sen'θiʎo, a] adj simple; (carácter) natural, unaffected; (billete) single ∎ nm (disco) single; (Am) small change

senda ['senda] nf, **sendero** [sen'dero] nm path, track; **Sendero Luminoso** the Shining Path (guerrilla movement)

senderismo [sende'rismo] nm trekking

sendos, -as ['sendos, as] adj pl: **les dio ~ golpes** he hit both of them

senil [se'nil] adj senile

seno ['seno] nm (Anat) bosom, bust; (fig) bosom; **senos** nmpl breasts; **~ materno** womb

sensación [sensa'θjon] nf sensation; (sentido) sense; (sentimiento) feeling; **causar o hacer ~** to cause a sensation

sensacional [sensaθjo'nal] adj sensational

sensatez [sensa'teθ] nf common sense

sensato, -a [sen'sato, a] adj sensible

sensibilidad [sensiβili'ðað] nf sensitivity; (para el arte) feel

sensibilizar [sensiβili'θar] vt: **~ a la población/opinión pública** to raise public awareness

sensible [sen'sible] adj sensitive; (apreciable) perceptible, appreciable; (pérdida) considerable

sensiblero, -a [sensi'βlero, a] adj sentimental, slushy

sensitivo, -a [sensi'tiβo, a], **sensorial** [senso'rjal] adj sense cpd

sensor [sen'sor] nm: **~ de fin de papel** paper out sensor

sensual [sen'swal] adj sensual

sentado, -a [sen'taðo, a] adj (establecido) settled; (carácter) sensible ∎ nf sitting; (Pol) sit-in, sit-down protest; **dar por ~** to take for granted, assume; **dejar algo ~** to establish sth firmly; **estar ~** to sit, be sitting (down); **de una sentada** at one sitting

sentar [sen'tar] vt to sit, seat; (fig) to establish ∎ vi (vestido) to suit; (alimento): **~ bien/mal a** to agree/disagree with; **sentarse** vr (persona) to sit, sit down; (el tiempo) to settle (down); (los depósitos) to settle; **¡siéntese!** (do) sit down, take a seat

sentencia [sen'tenθja] nf (máxima) maxim, saying; (Jur) sentence; **~ de muerte** death sentence

sentenciar [senten'θjar] vt to sentence

sentido, -a [sen'tiðo, a] adj (pérdida) regrettable; (carácter) sensitive ∎ nm sense; (sentimiento) feeling; (significado) sense, meaning; (dirección) direction; **mi más ~ pésame** my deepest sympathy; **~ del humor** sense of humour; **~ común** common sense; **en el buen ~ de la palabra** in the best sense of the word; **sin ~** meaningless; **tener ~** to make sense; **~ único** one-way (street)

sentimental [sentimen'tal] adj sentimental; **vida ~** love life

sentimiento [senti'mjento] nm (emoción) feeling, emotion; (sentido) sense; (pesar) regret, sorrow

sentir [sen'tir] vt to feel; (percibir) to perceive, sense; (esp Am: oír) to hear; (lamentar) to regret, be sorry for; (música etc) to have a feeling for ∎ vi to feel; (lamentarse) to feel sorry ∎ nm opinion, judgement; **sentirse** vr to feel; **lo siento** I'm sorry; **sentirse mejor/mal** to feel better/ill; **sentirse como en su**

casa to feel at home

seña ['seɲa] *nf* sign; (*Mil*) password; **señas** *nfpl* address *sg*; **señas personales** personal description *sg*; **por más señas** moreover; **dar señas de** to show signs of

señal [se'ɲal] *nf* sign; (*síntoma*) symptom; (*indicio*) indication; (*Ferro: Telec*) signal; (*marca*) mark; (*Com*) deposit; (*Inform*) marker, mark; **en ~ de** as a token of, as a sign of; **dar señales de** to show signs of; **~ de auxilio/de peligro** distress/danger signal; **~ de llamada** ringing tone; **~ para marcar** dialling tone

señalado, -a [seɲa'laðo, a] *adj* (*persona*) distinguished; (*pey*) notorious

señalar [seɲa'lar] *vt* to mark; (*indicar*) to point out, indicate; (*significar*) to denote; (*referirse a*) to allude to; (*fijar*) to fix, settle; (*pey*) to criticize

señalice *etc* [seɲa'liθe] *vb ver* **señalizar**

señalización [seɲaliθa'θjon] *nf* signposting; signals *pl*

señalizar [seɲali'θar] *vt* (*Auto*) to put up road signs on; (*Ferro*) to put signals on; (*Auto: ruta*): **está bien señalizada** it's well signposted

señas ['seɲas] *nfpl ver* **seña**

señor, a [se'ɲor, a] *adj* (*fam*) lordly ■ *nm* (*hombre*) man; (*caballero*) gentleman; (*dueño*) owner, master; (*trato: antes de nombre propio*) Mr; (: *hablando directamente*) sir ■ *nf* (*dama*) lady; (*trato: antes de nombre propio*) Mrs; (: *hablando directamente*) madam; (*esposa*) wife; **los señores González** Mr and Mrs González; **S~ Don Jacinto Benavente** (*en sobre*) Mr J. Benavente, J. Benavente Esq.; **S~ Director ...** (*de periódico*) Dear Sir ...; **~ juez** my lord, your worship (*US*); **~ Presidente** Mr Chairman *o* President; **Muy ~ mío** Dear Sir; **Muy señores nuestros** Dear Sirs; **Nuestro S~** (*Rel*) Our Lord; **¿está la señora?** is the lady of the house in?; **la señora de Smith** Mrs Smith; **Nuestra Señora** (*Rel*) Our Lady

señoría [seɲo'ria] *nf* rule; **su** *o* **vuestra S~** your *o* his/her lordship/ladyship

señorío [seɲo'rio] *nm* manor; (*fig*) rule

señorita [seɲo'rita] *nf* (*gen*) Miss; (*mujer joven*) young lady; (*maestra*) schoolteacher

señorito [seɲo'rito] *nm* young gentleman; (*lenguaje de criados*) master; (*pey*) toff

señuelo [se'ɲwelo] *nm* decoy

Sep. *abr* (= *septiembre*) Sept

sepa *etc* ['sepa] *vb ver* **saber**

separable [sepa'raβle] *adj* separable; (*Tec*) detachable

separación [separa'θjon] *nf* separation; (*división*) division; (*distancia*) gap, distance; **~ de bienes** division of property

separado, -a [sepa'raðo, a] *adj* separate; (*Tec*) detached; **vive ~ de su mujer** he is separated from his wife; **por ~** separately

separador [separa'ðor] *nm* (*Inform*) delimiter

separadora [separa'ðora] *nf*: **~ de hojas** burster

separar [sepa'rar] *vt* to separate; (*silla (de la mesa*)) to move away; (*Tec: pieza*) to detach; (*persona: de un cargo*) to remove, dismiss; (*dividir*) to divide; **separarse** *vr* (*parte*) to come away; (*partes*) to come apart; (*persona*) to leave, go away; (*matrimonio*) to separate

separata [sepa'rata] *nf* offprint

separatismo [separa'tismo] *nm* (*Pol*) separatism

sepelio [se'peljo] *nm* burial, interment

sepia ['sepja] *nf* cuttlefish

Sept. *abr* (= *septiembre*) Sept

septentrional [septentrjo'nal] *adj* north *cpd*, northern

septiembre [sep'tjembre] *nm* September; *ver tb* **julio**

séptimo, -a ['septimo, a] *adj, nm* seventh

septuagésimo, -a [septwa'xesimo, a] *adj* seventieth

sepulcral [sepul'kral] *adj* sepulchral; (*fig*) gloomy, dismal

sepulcro [se'pulkro] *nm* tomb, grave, sepulchre

sepultar [sepul'tar] *vt* to bury; (*en accidente*) to trap; **quedaban sepultados en la caverna** they were trapped in the cave

sepultura [sepul'tura] *nf* (*acto*) burial; (*tumba*) grave, tomb; **dar ~ a** to bury; **recibir ~** to be buried

sepulturero, -a [sepultu'rero, a] *nm/f* gravedigger

seque *etc* ['seke] *vb ver* **secar**

sequedad [seke'ðað] *nf* dryness; (*fig*) brusqueness, curtness

sequía [se'kia] *nf* drought

séquito ['sekito] *nm* (*de rey etc*) retinue; (*Pol*) followers *pl*

SER *nf abr* (*Radio:* = *Sociedad Española de Radiodifusión*) *Spanish radio network*

 PALABRA CLAVE

ser [ser] *vi* **1** (*descripción, identidad*) to be; **es médica/muy alta** she's a doctor/very tall; **la familia es de Cuzco** his (*o* her *etc*) family is from Cuzco; **ser de madera** to be made of wood; **soy Ana** I'm Ana

2 (*propiedad*): **es de Joaquín** it's Joaquín's, it belongs to Joaquín

3 (*horas, fechas, números*): **es la una** it's one o'clock; **son las seis y media** it's half-past six; **es el 1 de junio** it's the first of June; **somos/son seis** there are six of us/them; **2 y 2 son 4** 2 and 2 are o make 4

4 (*suceso*): **¿qué ha sido eso?** what was that?; **la fiesta es en mi casa** the party's at my house; **¿qué será de mí?** what will become of me?; **"érase una vez ..."** "once upon a time ..."

5 (*en oraciones pasivas*): **ha sido descubierto ya** it's already been discovered

6: **es de esperar que ...** it is to be hoped o I etc hope that ...

7 (*locuciones con sub*): **o sea** that is to say; **sea él sea su hermana** either him or his sister; **tengo que irme, no sea que mis hijos estén esperándome** I have to go in case my children are waiting for me

8: **a o de no ser por él ...** but for him ...

9: **a no ser que**: **a no ser que tenga uno ya** unless he's got one already

■ *nm* being; **ser humano** human being; **ser vivo** living creature

Serbia ['serβja] *nf* Serbia
serbio, -a ['serβjo, a] *adj* Serbian ■ *nm/f* Serb
serenarse [sere'narse] *vr* to calm down; (*mar*) to grow calm; (*tiempo*) to clear up
serenidad [sereni'ðað] *nf* calmness
sereno, -a [se'reno, a] *adj* (*persona*) calm, unruffled; (*tiempo*) fine, settled; (*ambiente*) calm, peaceful ■ *nm* night watchman
serial [se'rjal] *nm* serial
serie ['serje] *nf* series; (*cadena*) sequence, succession; (*TV etc*) serial; (*de inyecciones*) course; **fuera de** ~ out of order; (*fig*) special, out of the ordinary; **fabricación en** ~ mass production; (*Inform*): **interface/impresora en** ~ serial interface/printer
seriedad [serje'ðað] *nf* seriousness; (*formalidad*) reliability; (*de crisis*) gravity, seriousness
serigrafía [seriɣra'fia] *nf* silk screen printing
serio, -a ['serjo, a] *adj* serious; reliable, dependable; grave, serious; **poco** ~ (*actitud*) undignified; (*carácter*) unreliable; **en** ~ seriously
sermón [ser'mon] *nm* (*Rel*) sermon
sermonear [sermone'ar] *vt* (*fam*) to lecture ■ *vi* to sermonize
seropositivo, -a [seroposi'tiβo, a] *adj* HIV-positive
serpentear [serpente'ar] *vi* to wriggle; (*camino, río*) to wind, snake
serpentina [serpen'tina] *nf* streamer
serpiente [ser'pjente] *nf* snake; ~ **boa** boa constrictor; ~ **de cascabel** rattlesnake
serranía [serra'nia] *nf* mountainous area

serrano, -a [se'rrano, a] *adj* highland *cpd*, hill *cpd* ■ *nm/f* highlander
serrar [se'rrar] *vt* to saw
serrín [se'rrin] *nm* sawdust
serrucho [se'rrutʃo] *nm* handsaw
Servia ['serβja] *nf* Serbia
servicial [serβi'θjal] *adj* helpful, obliging
servicio [ser'βiθjo] *nm* service; (*Culin etc*) set; **servicios** *nmpl* toilet(s) (*pl*); **estar de** ~ to be on duty; ~ **aduanero** o **de aduana** customs service; ~ **a domicilio** home delivery service; ~ **incluido** (*en hotel etc*) service charge included; ~ **militar** military service; ~ **público** (*Com*) public utility
servidor, a [serβi'ðor, a] *nm/f* servant ■ *nm* (*Inform*) server; **su seguro** ~ (**s.s.s.**) yours faithfully; **un** ~ (*el que habla o escribe*) your humble servant
servidumbre [serβi'ðumbre] *nf* (*sujeción*) servitude; (*criados*) servants *pl*, staff
servil [ser'βil] *adj* servile
servilleta [serβi'ʎeta] *nf* serviette, napkin
servilletero [serβiʎe'tero] *nm* napkin ring
servir [ser'βir] *vt* to serve; (*comida*) to serve out o up; (*Tenis etc*) to serve ■ *vi* to serve; (*camarero*) to serve, wait; (*tener utilidad*) to be of use, be useful; **servirse** *vr* to serve o help o.s.; **¿en qué puedo servirle?** how can I help you?; ~ **vino a algn** to pour out wine for sb; ~ **de guía** to act o serve as a guide; **no sirve para nada** it's no use at all; **servirse de algo** to make use of sth, use sth; **sírvase pasar** please come in
sesenta [se'senta] *num* sixty
sesentón, -ona [sesen'ton, ona] *adj, nm/f* sixty-year-old
sesgado, -a [ses'ɣaðo, a] *adj* slanted, slanting
sesgo ['sesɣo] *nm* slant; (*fig*) slant, twist
sesión [se'sjon] *nf* (*Pol*) session, sitting; (*Cine*) showing; (*Teat*) performance; **abrir/ levantar la** ~ to open/close o adjourn the meeting; **la segunda** ~ the second house
seso ['seso] *nm* brain; (*fig*) intelligence; **sesos** *nmpl* (*Culin*) brains; **devanarse los sesos** to rack one's brains
sesudo, -a [se'suðo, a] *adj* sensible, wise
set (*pl* **sets**) [set, sets] *nm* (*Tenis*) set
Set. *abr* (= *setiembre*) Sept.
seta ['seta] *nf* mushroom; ~ **venenosa** toadstool
setecientos, -as [sete'θjentos, as] *num* seven hundred
setenta [se'tenta] *num* seventy
setiembre [se'tjembre] *nm* = **septiembre**; *ver tb* **julio**
seto ['seto] *nm* fence; ~ **vivo** hedge

seudo... [seuðo] pref pseudo...
seudónimo [seu'ðonimo] nm pseudonym
Seúl [se'ul] nm Seoul
s.e.u.o. abr (= salvo error u omisión) E & O E
severidad [seβeri'ðað] nf severity
severo, -a [se'βero, a] adj severe; (disciplina) strict; (frío) bitter
Sevilla [se'βiʎa] nf Seville
sevillano, -a [seβi'ʎano, a] adj of o from Seville ■ nm/f native o inhabitant of Seville
S.Exc. abr = Su Excelencia
sexagenario, -a [seksaxe'narjo, a] adj sixty-year-old ■ nm/f person in his/her sixties
sexagésimo, -a [seksa'xesimo, a] num sixtieth
sexo ['sekso] nm sex; **el ~ femenino/masculino** the female/male sex
sexto, -a ['seksto, a] num sixth; **Juan S~** John the Sixth
sexual [sek'swal] adj sexual; **vida ~** sex life
sexualidad [sekswali'ðað] nf sexuality
s.f. abr (= sin fecha) no date
s/f abr (Com: = su favor) your favour
sgte(s). abr (= siguiente) foll
si [si] conj if; (en pregunta indirecta) if, whether ■ nm (Mus) B; **si ... si ...** whether ... or ...; **me pregunto si ...** I wonder if o whether ...; **si no** if not, otherwise; **¡si fuera verdad!** if only it were true!; **por si viene** in case he comes
sí [si] adv yes ■ nm consent ■ pron (uso impersonal) oneself; (sg: m) himself; (: f) herself; (: de cosa) itself; (: de usted) yourself; (pl) themselves; (: de ustedes) yourselves; (: recíproco) each other; **él no quiere pero yo sí** he doesn't want to but I do; **ella sí vendrá** she will certainly come, she is sure to come; **claro que sí** of course; **creo que sí** I think so; **porque sí** because that's the way it is; (porque lo digo yo) because I say so; **¡sí que lo es!** I'll say it is!; **¡eso sí que no!** never!; **se ríe de sí misma** she laughs at herself; **cambiaron una mirada entre sí** they gave each other a look; **de por sí** in itself
siamés, -esa [sja'mes, esa] adj, nm/f Siamese
sibarita [siβa'rita] adj sybaritic ■ nm/f sybarite
sicario [si'karjo] nm hired killer
Sicilia [si'θilja] nf Sicily
siciliano, -a [siθi'ljano, a] adj, nm/f Sicilian ■ nm (Ling) Sicilian
SIDA ['siða] nm abr (= síndrome de inmunodeficiencia adquirida) AIDS
siderurgia [siðe'rurxja] nf iron and steel industry
siderúrgico, -a [siðe'rurxico, a] adj iron and steel cpd

sidra ['siðra] nf cider
siega etc ['sjeɣa] vb ver **segar** ■ nf (el cosechar) reaping; (el segar) mowing; (época) harvest (time)
siegue etc ['sjeɣe] vb ver **segar**
siembra etc ['sjembra] vb ver **sembrar** ■ nf sowing
siempre ['sjempre] adv always; (todo el tiempo) all the time; (Am: así y todo) still ■ conj: **~ que** ... (+indic) whenever ...; (+ subjun) provided that ...; **es lo de ~** it's the same old story; **como ~** as usual; **para ~** forever; **~ me voy mañana** (Am) I'm still leaving tomorrow
sien [sjen] nf (Anat) temple
siento etc ['sjento] vb ver **sentar**; **sentir**
sierra etc ['sjerra] vb ver **serrar** ■ nf (Tec) saw; (Geo) mountain range; **S~ Leona** Sierra Leone
siervo, -a ['sjerβo, a] nm/f slave
siesta ['sjesta] nf siesta, nap; **dormir la o echarse una o tomar una ~** to have an afternoon nap o a doze
siete ['sjete] num seven ■ excl (Am fam): **¡la gran ~!** wow!, hell!; **hijo de la gran ~** (fam!) bastard (!), son of a bitch (US!)
sífilis ['sifilis] nf syphilis
sifón [si'fon] nm syphon; **whisky con ~** whisky and soda
siga etc ['siɣa] vb ver **seguir**
sigilo [si'xilo] nm secrecy; (discreción) discretion
sigla ['siɣla] nf initial, abbreviation
siglo ['siɣlo] nm century; (fig) age; **S~ de las Luces** Age of Enlightenment; **S~ de Oro** Golden Age
significación [siɣnifika'θjon] nf significance
significado [siɣnifi'kaðo] nm significance; (de palabra etc) meaning
significar [siɣnifi'kar] vt to mean, signify; (notificar) to make known, express
significativo, -a [siɣnifika'tiβo, a] adj significant
signifique etc [siɣni'fike] vb ver **significar**
signo ['siɣno] nm sign; **~ de admiración** o **exclamación** exclamation mark; **~ igual** equals sign; **~ de interrogación** question mark; **~ de más/de menos** plus/minus sign; **signos de puntuación** punctuation marks
siguiendo etc [si'yjendo] vb ver **seguir**
siguiente [si'yjente] adj following; (próximo) next
silbar [sil'βar] vt, vi to whistle; (silbato) to blow; (Teat etc) to hiss
silbato [sil'βato] nm (instrumento) whistle
silbido [sil'βiðo] nm whistle, whistling; (abucheo) hiss
silenciador [silenθja'ðor] nm silencer

silenciar [silen'θjar] *vt* (*persona*) to silence; (*escándalo*) to hush up

silencio [si'lenθjo] *nm* silence, quiet; **en el ~ más absoluto** in dead silence; **guardar ~** to keep silent

silencioso, -a [silen'θjoso, a] *adj* silent, quiet

sílfide ['silfiðe] *nf* sylph

silicio [si'liθjo] *nm* silicon

silla ['siʎa] *nf* (*asiento*) chair; (*tb*: **silla de montar**) saddle; **~ de ruedas** wheelchair

sillería [siʎe'ria] *nf* (*asientos*) chairs *pl*, set of chairs; (*Rel*) choir stalls *pl*; (*taller*) chairmaker's workshop

sillín [si'ʎin] *nm* saddle, seat

sillón [si'ʎon] *nm* armchair, easy chair

silueta [si'lweta] *nf* silhouette; (*de edificio*) outline; (*figura*) figure

silvestre [sil'βestre] *adj* (*Bot*) wild; (*fig*) rustic, rural

sima ['sima] *nf* abyss, chasm

simbolice *etc* [simbo'liθe] *vb ver* **simbolizar**

simbólico, -a [sim'boliko, a] *adj* symbolic(al)

simbolizar [simboli'θar] *vt* to symbolize

símbolo ['simbolo] *nm* symbol; **~ gráfico** (*Inform*) icon

simetría [sime'tria] *nf* symmetry

simétrico, -a [si'metriko, a] *adj* symmetrical

simiente [si'mjente] *nf* seed

similar [simi'lar] *adj* similar

similitud [simili'tuð] *nf* similarity, resemblance

simio ['simjo] *nm* ape

simpatía [simpa'tia] *nf* liking; (*afecto*) affection; (*amabilidad*) kindness; (*de ambiente*) friendliness; (*de persona, lugar*) charm, attractiveness; (*solidaridad*) mutual support, solidarity; **tener ~ a** to like; **la famosa ~ andaluza** that well-known Andalusian charm

simpatice *etc* [simpa'tiθe] *vb ver* **simpatizar**

simpático, -a [sim'patiko, a] *adj* nice, pleasant; (*bondadoso*) kind; **no le hemos caído muy simpáticos** she didn't much take to us

simpatiquísimo, -a [simpati'kisimo, a] *adj superlativo de* **simpático** ever so nice; ever so kind

simpatizante [simpati'θante] *nm/f* sympathizer

simpatizar [simpati'θar] *vi*: **~ con** to get on well with

simple ['simple] *adj* simple; (*elemental*) simple, easy; (*mero*) mere; (*puro*) pure, sheer ∎ *nm/f* simpleton; **un ~ soldado** an ordinary soldier

simpleza [sim'pleθa] *nf* simpleness; (*necedad*) silly thing

simplicidad [simpliθi'ðað] *nf* simplicity

simplificar [simplifi'kar] *vt* to simplify

simplifique *etc* [simpli'fike] *vb ver* **simplificar**

simplón, -ona [sim'plon, ona] *adj* simple, gullible ∎ *nm/f* simple soul

simposio [sim'posjo] *nm* symposium

simulacro [simu'lakro] *nm* (*apariencia*) semblance; (*fingimiento*) sham

simular [simu'lar] *vt* to simulate; (*fingir*) to feign, sham

simultanear [simultane'ar] *vt*: **~ dos cosas** to do two things simultaneously

simultáneo, -a [simul'taneo, a] *adj* simultaneous

sin [sin] *prep* without; (*a no ser por*) but for ∎ *conj*: **~ que** (*+subjun*) without; **~ decir nada** without a word; **~ verlo yo** without my seeing it; **platos ~ lavar** unwashed *o* dirty dishes; **la ropa está ~ lavar** the clothes are unwashed; **~ que lo sepa él** without his knowing; **~ embargo** however

sinagoga [sina'ɣoɣa] *nf* synagogue

Sinaí [sina'i] *nm*: **El Sinaí** Sinai, the Sinai Peninsula; **el Monte Sinaí** Mount Sinai

sinceridad [sinθeri'ðað] *nf* sincerity

sincero, -a [sin'θero, a] *adj* sincere; (*persona*) genuine; (*opinión*) frank; (*felicitaciones*) heartfelt

síncope ['sinkope] *nm* (*desmayo*) blackout; **~ cardíaco** (*Med*) heart failure

sincronice *etc* [sinkro'niθe] *vb ver* **sincronizar**

sincronizar [sinkroni'θar] *vt* to synchronize

sindical [sindi'kal] *adj* union *cpd*, trade-union *cpd*

sindicalista [sindika'lista] *adj* trade-union *cpd* ∎ *nm/f* trade unionist

sindicar [sindi'kar] *vt* (*obreros*) to organize, unionize; **sindicarse** *vr* (*obrero*) to join a union

sindicato [sindi'kato] *nm* (*de trabajadores*) trade(s) *o* labor (US) union; (*de negociantes*) syndicate

sindique *etc* [sin'dike] *vb ver* **sindicar**

síndrome ['sindrome] *nm* syndrome; **~ de abstinencia** withdrawal symptoms

sine qua non [sine'kwanon] *adj*: **condición ~** sine qua non

sinfín [sin'fin] *nm*: **un ~ de** a great many, no end of

sinfonía [sinfo'nia] *nf* symphony

sinfónico, -a [sin'foniko, a] *adj* (*música*) symphonic; **orquesta sinfónica** symphony orchestra

Singapur [singa'pur] *nm* Singapore

singular [singu'lar] *adj* singular; (*fig*) outstanding, exceptional; (*pey*) peculiar, odd ∎ *nm* (*Ling*) singular; **en ~** in the singular

singularice etc [singula'riθe] vb ver **singularizar**
singularidad [singulari'ðað] nf singularity, peculiarity
singularizar [singulari'θar] vt to single out; **singularizarse** vr to distinguish o.s., stand out
siniestro, -a [si'njestro, a] adj left; (fig) sinister ■ nm (accidente) accident; (desastre) natural disaster
sinnúmero [sin'numero] nm = **sinfín**
sino ['sino] nm fate, destiny ■ conj (pero) but; (salvo) except, save; **no son 8 ~ 9** there are not 8 but 9; **todos ~ él** all except him
sinónimo, -a [si'nonimo, a] adj synonymous ■ nm synonym
sinrazón [sinra'θon] nf wrong, injustice
sinsabor [sinsa'βor] nm (molestia) trouble; (dolor) sorrow; (preocupación) uneasiness
sintaxis [sin'taksis] nf syntax
síntesis ['sintesis] nf inv synthesis
sintetice etc [sinte'tiθe] vb ver **sintetizar**
sintético, -a [sin'tetiko, a] adj synthetic
sintetizador [sintetiθa'ðor] nm synthesizer
sintetizar [sinteti'θar] vt to synthesize
sintiendo etc [sin'tjendo] vb ver **sentir**
síntoma ['sintoma] nm symptom
sintomático, -a [sinto'matiko, a] adj symptomatic
sintonía [sinto'nia] nf (Radio) tuning; (melodía) signature tune
sintonice etc [sinto'niθe] vb ver **sintonizar**
sintonizador [sintoniθa'ðor] nm (Radio) tuner
sintonizar [sintoni'θar] vt (Radio) to tune (in) to, pick up
sinuoso, -a [si'nwoso, a] adj (camino) winding; (rumbo) devious
sinvergüenza [simber'ɣwenθa] nm/f rogue, scoundrel
sionismo [sjo'nismo] nm Zionism
siquiera [si'kjera] conj even if, even though ■ adv (esp Am) at least; **ni ~** not even; **~ bebe algo** at least drink something
sirena [si'rena] nf siren, mermaid; (bocina) siren, hooter
Siria ['sirja] nf Syria
sirio, -a ['sirjo, a] adj, nm/f Syrian
sirviendo etc [sir'βjendo] vb ver **servir**
sirviente, -a [sir'βjente, a] nm/f servant
sisa ['sisa] nf petty theft; (Costura) dart; (sobaquera) armhole
sisar [si'sar] vt (robar) to thieve; (Costura) to take in
sisear [sise'ar] vt, vi to hiss
sísmico, -a ['sismiko, a] adj: **movimiento ~** earthquake

sismógrafo [sis'moɣrafo] nm seismograph
sistema [sis'tema] nm system; (método) method; **~ impositivo** o **tributario** taxation, tax system; **~ pedagógico** educational system; **~ de alerta inmediata** early-warning system; **~ binario** (Inform) binary system; **~ experto** expert system; **~ de facturación** (Com) invoicing system; **~ de fondo fijo** (Com) imprest system; **~ de lógica compartida** (Inform) shared logic system; **~ métrico** metric system; **~ operativo (en disco)** (Inform) (disk based) operating system; see note

● **SISTEMA EDUCATIVO**
●
● The reform of the Spanish sistema
● educativo (education system) begun in
● the early 90s has replaced the courses
● EGB, BUP and COU with the following:
● Primaria a compulsory 6 years; Secundaria
● a compulsory 4 years; Bachillerato an
● optional 2 year secondary school course,
● essential for those wishing to go on to
● higher education.

sistemático, -a [siste'matiko, a] adj systematic
sitiar [si'tjar] vt to besiege, lay siege to
sitio ['sitjo] nm (lugar) place; (espacio) room, space; (Mil) siege; **~ web** website; **¿hay ~?** is there any room?; **hay ~ de sobra** there's plenty of room
situación [sitwa'θjon] nf situation, position; (estatus) position, standing
situado, -a [si'twaðo, a] adj situated, placed; **estar ~** (Com) to be financially secure
situar [si'twar] vt to place, put; (edificio) to locate, situate
S.L. abr (Com: = Sociedad Limitada) Ltd
slip [es'lip] (pl **slips**) nm pants pl, briefs pl
slot [es'lot] (pl **slots**) nm: **~ de expansión** expansion slot
S.M. abr (= Su Majestad) HM
SME nm abr (= Sistema Monetario Europeo) EMS; **(mecanismo de cambios del)** ~ ERM
smoking [(e)'smokin] (pl **smokings**) nm dinner jacket (Brit), tuxedo (US)
SMS nm (mensaje) text (message), SMS (message)
s/n abr (= sin número) no number
snob [es'nob] = **esnob**
SO abr (= suroeste) SW
so [so] excl whoa!; **¡so burro!** you idiot! ■ prep under
s/o abr (Com: = su orden) your order
sobaco [so'βako] nm armpit

S

sobado, -a [so'βaðo, a] adj (ropa) worn; (arrugado) crumpled; (libro) well-thumbed; (Culin: bizcocho) short

sobar [so'βar] vt (tela) to finger; (ropa) to rumple, mess up; (músculos) to rub, massage

soberanía [soβera'nia] nf sovereignty

soberano, -a [soβe'rano, a] adj sovereign; (fig) supreme ■ nm/f sovereign; **los soberanos** the king and queen

soberbio, -a [so'βerβjo, a] adj (orgulloso) proud; (altivo) haughty, arrogant; (fig) magnificent, superb ■ nf pride; haughtiness, arrogance; magnificence

sobornar [soβor'nar] vt to bribe

soborno [so'βorno] nm (un soborno) bribe; (el soborno) bribery

sobra ['soβra] nf excess, surplus; **sobras** nfpl left-overs, scraps; **de ~** surplus, extra; **lo sé de ~** I'm only too aware of it; **tengo de ~** I've more than enough

sobradamente [soβraða'mente] adv amply; (saber) only too well

sobrado, -a [so'βraðo, a] adj (más que suficiente) more than enough; (superfluo) excessive ■ adv too, exceedingly; **sobradas veces** repeatedly

sobrante [so'βrante] adj remaining, extra ■ nm surplus, remainder

sobrar [so'βrar] vt to exceed, surpass ■ vi (tener de más) to be more than enough; (quedar) to remain, be left (over)

sobrasada [soβra'saða] nf ≈ sausage spread

sobre ['soβre] prep (gen) on; (encima) on (top of); (por encima de, arriba de) over, above; (más que) more than; (además) in addition to, besides; (alrededor de) about; (porcentaje) in, out of; (tema) about, on ■ nm envelope; **~ todo** above all; **3 ~ 100** 3 in a 100, 3 out of every 100; **un libro ~ Tirso** a book about Tirso; **~ de ventanilla** window envelope

sobrecama [soβre'kama] nf bedspread

sobrecapitalice etc [soβrekapita'liθe] vb ver **sobrecapitalizar**

sobrecapitalizar [soβrekapitali'θar] vi to overcapitalize

sobrecargar [soβrekar'ɣar] vt (camión) to overload; (Com) to surcharge

sobrecargue etc [soβre'karɣe] vb ver **sobrecargar**

sobrecoger [soβreko'xer] vt (sobresaltar) to startle; (asustar) to scare; **sobrecogerse** vr (sobresaltarse) to be startled; (asustarse) to get scared; (quedar impresionado): **sobrecogerse (de)** to be overawed (by)

sobrecoja etc [soβre'koxa] vb ver **sobrecoger**

sobredosis [soβre'ðosis] nf inv overdose

sobreentender [soβreenten'der] vt to understand; (adivinar) to deduce, infer; **sobreentenderse** vr: **se sobreentiende que ... it is implied that ...**

sobreescribir [soβreeskri'βir] vt (Inform) to overwrite

sobreestimar [soβreesti'mar] vt to overestimate

sobregiro [soβre'xiro] nm (Com) overdraft

sobrehumano, -a [soβreu'mano, a] adj superhuman

sobreimprimir [soβreimpri'mir] vt (Com) to merge

sobrellevar [soβreʎe'βar] vt (fig) to bear, endure

sobremesa [soβre'mesa] nf (después de comer) sitting on after a meal; (Inform) desktop; **conversación de ~** table talk

sobremodo [soβre'moðo] adv very much, enormously

sobrenatural [soβrenatu'ral] adj supernatural

sobrenombre [soβre'nombre] nm nickname

sobrentender [soβrenten'der] vt = sobreentender

sobrepasar [soβrepa'sar] vt to exceed, surpass

sobrepondré etc [soβrepon'dre] vb ver **sobreponer**

sobreponer [soβrepo'ner] vt (poner encima) to put on top; (añadir) to add; **sobreponerse** vr: **sobreponerse a** to overcome

sobreponga etc [soβre'ponga] vb ver **sobreponer**

sobreprima [soβre'prima] nf (Com) loading

sobreproducción [soβreproðuk'θjon] nf overproduction

sobrepuesto [soβre'pwesto], **sobrepuse** etc [soβre'puse] vb ver **sobreponer**

sobresaldré etc [soβresal'dre], **sobresalga** etc [soβre'salɣa] vb ver **sobresalir**

sobresaliente [soβresa'ljente] adj projecting; (fig) outstanding, excellent; (Univ etc) first class ■ nm (Univ etc) first class (mark), distinction

sobresalir [soβresa'lir] vi to project, jut out; (fig) to stand out, excel

sobresaltar [soβresal'tar] vt (asustar) to scare, frighten; (sobrecoger) to startle

sobresalto [soβre'salto] nm (movimiento) start; (susto) scare; (turbación) sudden shock

sobreseer [soβrese'er] vt: **~ una causa** (Jur) to stop a case

sobrestadía [soβresta'ðia] nf (Com) demurrage

sobrestimar [soβresti'mar] vt = sobreestimar

sobretensión [soβreten'sjon] nf (Elec): **~ transitoria** surge

sobretiempo [soβre'tjempo] nm (Am) overtime

sobretodo [soβre'toðo] nm overcoat

sobrevendré etc [soβreβen'dre], **sobrevenga** etc [soβre'βenga] vb ver **sobrevenir**

sobrevenir [soβreβe'nir] vi (ocurrir) to happen (unexpectedly); (resultar) to follow, ensue

sobreviene etc [soβre'βjene], **sobrevine** etc [soβre'βine] vb ver **sobrevenir**

sobreviviente [soβreβi'βjente] adj surviving ■ nm/f survivor

sobrevivir [soβreβi'βir] vi to survive; (persona) to outlive; (objeto etc) to outlast

sobrevolar [soβreβo'lar] vt to fly over

sobrevuele etc [soβre'βwele] vb ver **sobrevolar**

sobriedad [soβrje'ðað] nf sobriety, soberness; (moderación) moderation, restraint

sobrino, -a [so'βrino, a] nm/f nephew/niece

sobrio, -a ['soβrjo, a] adj (moderado) moderate, restrained

socarrón, -ona [soka'rron, ona] adj (sarcástico) sarcastic, ironic(al)

socavar [soka'βar] vt to undermine; (excavar) to dig underneath o below

socavón [soka'βon] nm (en mina) gallery; (hueco) hollow; (en la calle) hole

sociable [so'θjaβle] adj (persona) sociable, friendly; (animal) social

social [so'θjal] adj social; (Com) company cpd

socialdemócrata [soθjalde'mokrata] adj social-democratic ■ nm/f social democrat

socialice etc [soθja'liθe] vb ver **socializar**

socialista [soθja'lista] adj, nm/f socialist

socializar [soθjali'θar] vt to socialize

sociedad [soθje'ðað] nf society; (Com) company; ~ **de ahorro y préstamo** savings and loan society; ~ **anónima (S.A.)** limited company (Ltd) (Brit), incorporated company (Inc) (US); ~ **de beneficiencia** friendly society (Brit), benefit association (US); ~ **de cartera** investment trust; ~ **comanditaria** (Com) co-ownership; ~ **conjunta** (Com) joint venture; ~ **inmobiliaria** building society (Brit), savings and loan (society) (US); ~ **de responsabilidad limitada** (Com) private limited company

socio, -a ['soθjo, a] nm/f (miembro) member; (Com) partner; ~ **activo** active partner; ~ **capitalista** o **comanditario** sleeping o silent (US) partner

socioeconómico, -a [soθjoeko'nomiko, a] adj socio-economic

sociología [soθjolo'xia] nf sociology

sociólogo, -a [so'θjologo, a] nm/f sociologist

socorrer [soko'rrer] vt to help

socorrido, -a [soko'rriðo, a] adj (tienda) well-stocked; (útil) handy; (persona) helpful

socorrismo [soko'rrismo] nm life-saving

socorrista [soko'rrista] nm/f first aider; (en piscina, playa) lifeguard

socorro [so'korro] nm (ayuda) help, aid; (Mil) relief; ¡~! help!

soda ['soða] nf (sosa) soda; (bebida) soda (water)

sódico, -a ['soðiko, a] adj sodium cpd

soez [so'eθ] adj dirty, obscene

sofá [so'fa] nm sofa, settee

sofá-cama [so'fakama] nm studio couch, sofa bed

Sofia ['sofja] nf Sofia

sofisticación [sofistika'θjon] nf sophistication

sofisticado, -a [sofisti'kaðo, a] adj sophisticated

sofocado, -a [sofo'kaðo, a] adj: **estar ~** (fig) to be out of breath; (ahogarse) to feel stifled

sofocar [sofo'kar] vt to suffocate; (apagar) to smother, put out; **sofocarse** vr to suffocate; (fig) to blush, feel embarrassed

sofoco [so'foko] nm suffocation; (azoro) embarrassment

sofocón [sofo'kon] nm: **llevarse** o **pasar un ~** to have a sudden shock

sofreír [sofre'ir] vt to fry lightly

sofría etc [so'fria], **sofriendo** etc [so'frjendo], **sofrito** [so'frito] vb ver **sofreír**

soft ['sof], **software** ['sofwer] nm (Inform) software

soga ['soɣa] nf rope

sois [sois] vb ver **ser**

soja ['soxa] nf soya

sojuzgar [soxuθ'ɣar] vt to subdue, rule despotically

sojuzgue etc [so'xuɣθe] vb ver **sojuzgar**

sol [sol] nm sun; (luz) sunshine, sunlight; (Mus) G; ~ **naciente/poniente** rising/setting sun; **tomar el ~** to sunbathe; **hace ~** it is sunny

solace etc [so'laθe] vb ver **solazar**

solamente [sola'mente] adv only, just

solapa [so'lapa] nf (de chaqueta) lapel; (de libro) jacket

solapado, -a [sola'paðo, a] adj sly, underhand

solar [so'lar] adj solar, sun cpd ■ nm (terreno) plot (of ground); (local) undeveloped site

solaz [so'laθ] nm recreation, relaxation

solazar [sola'θar] vt (divertir) to amuse; **solazarse** vr to enjoy o.s., relax

soldada [sol'daða] nf pay

soldado [sol'daðo] nm soldier; ~ **raso** private

soldador [solda'ðor] nm soldering iron; (persona) welder

soldar [sol'dar] vt to solder, weld; (unir) to join, unite

S

359

soleado, -a [sole'aðo, a] *adj* sunny
soledad [sole'ðað] *nf* solitude; (*estado infeliz*) loneliness
solemne [so'lemne] *adj* solemn; (*tontería*) utter; (*error*) complete
solemnidad [solemni'ðað] *nf* solemnity
soler [so'ler] *vi* to be in the habit of, be accustomed to; **suele salir a las ocho** she usually goes out at 8 o'clock; **solíamos ir todos los años** we used to go every year
solera [so'lera] *nf* (*tradición*) tradition; **vino de** ~ vintage wine
solfeo [sol'feo] *nm* singing of scales; **ir a clases de** ~ to take singing lessons
solicitar [soliθi'tar] *vt* (*permiso*) to ask for, seek; (*puesto*) to apply for; (*votos*) to canvass for; (*atención*) to attract; (*persona*) to pursue, chase after
solícito, -a [so'liθito, a] *adj* (*diligente*) diligent; (*cuidadoso*) careful
solicitud [soliθi'tuð] *nf* (*calidad*) great care; (*petición*) request; (*a un puesto*) application
solidaridad [soliðari'ðað] *nf* solidarity; **por** ~ **con** (*Pol etc*) out of o in solidarity with
solidario, -a [soli'ðarjo, a] *adj* (*participación*) joint, common; (*compromiso*) mutually binding; **hacerse** ~ **de** to declare one's solidarity with
solidarizarse [soliðari'θarse] *vr:* ~ **con algn** to support sb, sympathize with sb
solidez [soli'ðeθ] *nf* solidity
sólido, -a ['soliðo, a] *adj* solid; (*Tec*) solidly made; (*bien construido*) well built
soliloquio [soli'lokjo] *nm* soliloquy
solista [so'lista] *nm/f* soloist
solitario, -a [soli'tarjo, a] *adj* (*persona*) lonely, solitary; (*lugar*) lonely, desolate ■ *nm/f* (*reclusa*) recluse; (*en la sociedad*) loner ■ *nm* solitaire ■ *nf* tapeworm
soliviantar [solißjan'tar] *vt* to stir up, rouse (to revolt); (*enojar*) to anger; (*sacar de quicio*) to exasperate
solloce *etc* [so'ʎoθe] *vb ver* **sollozar**
sollozar [soʎo'θar] *vi* to sob
sollozo [so'ʎoθo] *nm* sob
solo, -a ['solo, a] *adj* (*único*) single, sole; (*sin compañía*) alone; (*Mus*) solo; (*solitario*) lonely; **hay una sola dificultad** there is just one difficulty; **a solas** alone, by o.s.
sólo ['solo] *adv* only, just; (*exclusivamente*) solely; **tan** ~ only just
solomillo [solo'miʎo] *nm* sirloin
solsticio [sols'tiθjo] *nm* solstice
soltar [sol'tar] *vt* (*dejar ir*) to let go of; (*desprender*) to unfasten, loosen; (*librar*) to release, set free; (*amarras*) to cast off; (*Auto: freno etc*) to release; (*suspiro*) to heave; (*risa etc*)

to let out; **soltarse** *vr* (*desanudarse*) to come undone; (*desprenderse*) to come off; (*adquirir destreza*) to become expert; (*en idioma*) to become fluent
soltero, -a [sol'tero, a] *adj* single, unmarried ■ *nm* bachelor ■ *nf* single woman, spinster
solterón [solte'ron] *nm* confirmed bachelor
solterona [solte'rona] *nf* spinster, maiden lady; (*pey*) old maid
soltura [sol'tura] *nf* looseness, slackness; (*de los miembros*) agility, ease of movement; (*en el hablar*) fluency, ease
soluble [so'lußle] *adj* (*Química*) soluble; (*problema*) solvable; ~ **en agua** soluble in water
solución [solu'θjon] *nf* solution; ~ **de continuidad** break in continuity
solucionar [soluθjo'nar] *vt* (*problema*) to solve; (*asunto*) to settle, resolve
solvencia [sol'ßenθja] *nf* (*Com: estado*) solvency; (: *acción*) settlement, payment
solventar [solßen'tar] *vt* (*pagar*) to settle, pay; (*resolver*) to resolve
solvente [sol'ßente] *adj* solvent, free of debt
Somalia [so'malja] *nf* Somalia
sombra ['sombra] *nf* shadow; (*como protección*) shade; **sombras** *nfpl* darkness *sg*, shadows; **sin** ~ **de duda** without a shadow of doubt; **tener buena/mala** ~ (*suerte*) to be lucky/unlucky; (*carácter*) to be likeable/disagreeable
sombrero [som'brero] *nm* hat; ~ **hongo** bowler (hat), derby (*US*); ~ **de copa** o **de pelo** (*Am*) top hat
sombrilla [som'briʎa] *nf* parasol, sunshade
sombrío, -a [som'brio, a] *adj* (*oscuro*) shady; (*fig*) sombre, sad; (*persona*) gloomy
somero, -a [so'mero, a] *adj* superficial
someter [some'ter] *vt* (*país*) to conquer; (*persona*) to subject to one's will; (*informe*) to present, submit; **someterse** *vr* to give in, yield, submit; **someterse a** to submit to; **someterse a una operación** to undergo an operation
sometimiento [someti'mjento] *nm* (*estado*) submission; (*acción*) presentation
somier [so'mjer] (*pl* **somiers**) *nm* spring mattress
somnífero [som'nifero] *nm* sleeping pill o tablet
somnolencia [somno'lenθja] *nf* sleepiness, drowsiness
somos ['somos] *vb ver* **ser**
son [son] *vb ver* **ser** ■ *nm* sound; **en** ~ **de broma** as a joke
sonado, -a [so'naðo, a] *adj* (*comentado*) talked-of; (*famoso*) famous; (*Com: pey*) hyped(-up)

sonajero [sona'xero] *nm* (baby's) rattle
sonambulismo [sonambu'lismo] *nm* sleepwalking
sonámbulo, -a [so'nambulo, a] *nm/f* sleepwalker
sonar [so'nar] *vt* (*campana*) to ring; (*trompeta, sirena*) to blow ▪ *vi* to sound; (*hacer ruido*) to make a noise; (*Ling*) to be sounded, be pronounced; (*ser conocido*) to sound familiar; (*campana*) to ring; (*reloj*) to strike, chime; **sonarse** *vr*: **sonarse (la nariz)** to blow one's nose; **es un nombre que suena** it's a name that's in the news; **me suena ese nombre** that name rings a bell
sonda ['sonda] *nf* (*Naut*) sounding; (*Tec*) bore, drill; (*Med*) probe
sondear [sonde'ar] *vt* to sound; to bore (into), drill; to probe, sound; (*fig*) to sound out
sondeo [son'deo] *nm* sounding; boring, drilling; (*encuesta*) poll, enquiry; **~ de la opinión pública** public opinion poll
sónico, -a ['soniko, a] *adj* sonic, sound *cpd*
sonido [so'niðo] *nm* sound
sonoro, -a [so'noro, a] *adj* sonorous; (*resonante*) loud, resonant; (*Ling*) voiced; **efectos sonoros** sound effects
sonreír [sonre'ir] *vi*, **sonreírse** *vi* to smile
sonría *etc* [son'ria], **sonriendo** *etc* [son'rjendo] *vb ver* **sonreír**
sonriente [son'rjente] *adj* smiling
sonrisa [son'risa] *nf* smile
sonrojar [sonro'xar] *vt*: **~ a algn** to make sb blush; **sonrojarse** *vr*: **sonrojarse (de)** to blush (at)
sonrojo [son'roxo] *nm* blush
sonsacar [sonsa'kar] *vt* to wheedle, coax; **~ a algn** to pump sb for information
sonsaque *etc* [son'sake] *vb ver* **sonsacar**
sonsonete [sonso'nete] *nm* (*golpecitos*) tap(ping); (*voz monótona*) monotonous delivery, singsong (voice)
soñador, a [soɲa'ðor, a] *nm/f* dreamer
soñar [so'ɲar] *vt*, *vi* to dream; **~ con** to dream about o of; **soñé contigo anoche** I dreamed about you last night
soñoliento, -a [soɲo'ljento, a] *adj* sleepy, drowsy
sopa ['sopa] *nf* soup; **~ de fideos** noodle soup
sopero, -a [so'pero, a] *adj* (*plato, cuchara*) soup *cpd* ▪ *nm* soup plate ▪ *nf* soup tureen
sopesar [sope'sar] *vt* to try the weight of; (*fig*) to weigh up
sopetón [sope'ton] *nm*: **de ~** suddenly, unexpectedly
soplar [so'plar] *vt* (*polvo*) to blow away, blow off; (*inflar*) to blow up; (*vela*) to blow out; (*ayudar a recordar*) to prompt; (*birlar*) to nick;

(*delatar*) to split on ▪ *vi* to blow; (*delatar*) to squeal; (*beber*) to booze, bend the elbow
soplete [so'plete] *nm* blowlamp; **~ soldador** welding torch
soplo ['soplo] *nm* blow, puff; (*de viento*) puff, gust
soplón, -ona [so'plon, ona] *nm/f* (*fam*: *chismoso*) telltale; (: *de policía*) informer, grass
soponcio [so'ponθjo] *nm* dizzy spell
sopor [so'por] *nm* drowsiness
soporífero, -a [sopo'rifero, a] *adj* sleep-inducing; (*fig*) soporific ▪ *nm* sleeping pill
soportable [sopor'taβle] *adj* bearable
soportal [sopor'tal] *nm* porch; **soportales** *nmpl* arcade *sg*
soportar [sopor'tar] *vt* to bear, carry; (*fig*) to bear, put up with
soporte [so'porte] *nm* support; (*fig*) pillar, support; (*Inform*) medium; **~ de entrada/ salida** input/output medium
soprano [so'prano] *nf* soprano
sor [sor] *nf*: **S~ María** Sister Mary
sorber [sor'βer] *vt* (*chupar*) to sip; (*inhalar*) to sniff, inhale; (*absorber*) to soak up, absorb
sorbete [sor'βete] *nm* sherbet
sorbo ['sorβo] *nm* (*trago*) gulp, swallow; (*chupada*) sip, **beber a sorbos** to sip
sordera [sor'ðera] *nf* deafness
sórdido, -a ['sorðiðo, a] *adj* dirty, squalid
sordo, -a ['sorðo, a] *adj* (*persona*) deaf; (*ruido*) dull; (*Ling*) voiceless ▪ *nm/f* deaf person; **quedarse ~** to go deaf
sordomudo, -a [sorðo'muðo, a] *adj* deaf and dumb ▪ *nm/f* deaf-mute
soriano, -a [so'rjano, a] *adj* of o from Soria ▪ *nm/f* native o inhabitant of Soria
sorna ['sorna] *nf* (*malicia*) slyness; (*tono burlón*) sarcastic tone
soroche [so'rotʃe] *nm* (*Am Med*) mountain sickness
sorprendente [sorpren'dente] *adj* surprising
sorprender [sorpren'der] *vt* to surprise; (*asombrar*) to amaze; (*sobresaltar*) to startle; (*coger desprevenido*) to catch unawares; **sorprenderse** *vr*: **sorprenderse (de)** to be surprised o amazed (at)
sorpresa [sor'presa] *nf* surprise
sorpresivo, -a [sorpre'siβo, a] *adj* (*Am*) surprising; (*imprevisto*) sudden
sortear [sorte'ar] *vt* to draw lots for; (*rifar*) to raffle; (*dificultad*) to dodge, avoid
sorteo [sor'teo] *nm* (*en lotería*) draw; (*rifa*) raffle
sortija [sor'tixa] *nf* ring; (*rizo*) ringlet, curl
sortilegio [sorti'lexjo] *nm* (*hechicería*) sorcery; (*hechizo*) spell
SOS *sigla m* SOS

S

sosegado, -a [sose'ɣaðo, a] *adj* quiet, calm
sosegar [sose'ɣar] *vt* to quieten, calm; *(el ánimo)* to reassure ∎ *vi* to rest
sosegué *etc* [sose'ɣe] *vb ver* **sosegar**
sosiego *etc* [so'sjeɣo] *vb ver* **sosegar** ∎ *nm* quiet(ness), calm(ness)
sosiegue *etc* [so'sjeɣe] *vb ver* **sosegar**
soslayar [sosla'jar] *vt (preguntas)* to get round
soslayo [sos'lajo]: **de ~** *adv* obliquely, sideways; **mirar de ~** to look out of the corner of one's eye (at)
soso, -a ['soso, a] *adj (Culin)* tasteless; *(fig)* dull, uninteresting
sospecha [sos'petʃa] *nf* suspicion
sospechar [sospe'tʃar] *vt* to suspect ∎ *vi:* **~ de** to be suspicious of
sospechoso, -a [sospe'tʃoso, a] *adj* suspicious; *(testimonio, opinión)* suspect ∎ *nm/f* suspect
sostén [sos'ten] *nm (apoyo)* support; *(sujetador)* bra; *(alimentación)* sustenance, food
sostendré *etc* [sosten'dre] *vb ver* **sostener**
sostener [soste'ner] *vt* to support; *(mantener)* to keep up, maintain; *(alimentar)* to sustain, keep going; **sostenerse** *vr* to support o.s.; *(seguir)* to continue, remain
sostenga *etc* [sos'tenga] *vb ver* **sostener**
sostenido, -a [soste'niðo, a] *adj* continuous, sustained; *(prolongado)* prolonged; *(Mus)* sharp ∎ *nm (Mus)* sharp
sostuve *etc* [sos'tuβe] *vb ver* **sostener**
sota ['sota] *nf (Naipes)* ≈ jack; *ver tb* **baraja española**
sotana [so'tana] *nf (Rel)* cassock
sótano ['sotano] *nm* basement
sotavento [sota'βento] *nm (Naut)* lee, leeward
soterrar [sote'rrar] *vt* to bury; *(esconder)* to hide away
sotierre *etc* [so'tjerre] *vb ver* **soterrar**
soviético, -a [so'βjetiko, a] *adj, nm/f* Soviet; **los soviéticos** the Soviets, the Russians
soy [soi] *vb ver* **ser**
soya ['soja] *nf (Am)* soya (bean)
SP *abr (Auto)* = **servicio público**
SPM *nm abr (= síndrome premenstrual)* PMS
spooling [es'pulin] *nm (Inform)* spooling
sport [es'por(t)] *nm* sport
spot [es'pot] *(pl ~)* *nm (publicitario)* ad
squash [es'kwas] *nm (Deporte)* squash
Sr. *abr (= Señor)* Mr
Sra. *abr (= Señora)* Mrs
Sras. *abr (= Señoras)* Mrs
S.R.C. *abr (= se ruega contestación)* R.S.V.P.
Sres., Srs. *abr (= Señores)* Messrs
Sri Lanka [sri'lanka] *nm* Sri Lanka

Srta. *abr* = **Señorita**
SS *abr (= Santos, Santas)* SS
S.S. *abr (Rel: = Su Santidad)* H.H.; = **Seguridad Social**
ss. *abr (= siguientes)* foll
SSE *abr (= sursudeste)* SSE
SS.MM. *abr (= Sus Majestades)* Their Royal Highnesses
SSO *abr (= sursudoeste)* SSW
Sta. *abr (= Santa)* St; *(= Señorita)* Miss
stand *(pl* **stands)** [es'tan, es'tan(s)] *nm (Com)* stand
stárter [es'tarter] *nm (Auto)* self-starter, starting motor
statu quo [es'tatu'kuo], **status quo** [es'tatus'kuo] *nm* status quo
status ['status, es'tatus] *nm inv* status
Sto. *abr (= Santo)* St
stop *(pl* **stops)** [es'top, es'top(s)] *nm (Auto)* stop sign
su [su] *pron (de él)* his; *(de ella)* her; *(de una cosa)* its; *(de ellos, ellas)* their; *(de usted, ustedes)* your
suave ['swaβe] *adj* gentle; *(superficie)* smooth; *(trabajo)* easy; *(música, voz)* soft, sweet; *(clima, sabor)* mild
suavice *etc* [swa'βiθe] *vb ver* **suavizar**
suavidad [swaβi'ðað] *nf* gentleness; *(de superficie)* smoothness; *(de música)* softness, sweetness
suavizante [swaβi'θante] *nm* conditioner
suavizar [swaβi'θar] *vt* to soften; *(quitar la aspereza)* to smooth (out); *(pendiente)* to ease; *(colores)* to tone down; *(carácter)* to mellow; *(dureza)* to temper
subalimentado, -a [suβalimen'taðo, a] *adj* undernourished
subalterno, -a [suβal'terno, a] *adj (importancia)* secondary; *(personal)* minor, auxiliary ∎ *nm* subordinate
subarrendar [suβarren'dar] *vt (Com)* to lease back
subarriendo [suβa'rrjendo] *nm (Com)* leaseback
subasta [su'βasta] *nf* auction; **poner en** *o* **sacar a pública ~** to put up for public auction; **~ a la rebaja** Dutch auction
subastador, a [suβasta'ðor, a] *nm/f* auctioneer
subastar [suβas'tar] *vt* to auction (off)
subcampeón, -ona [suβkampe'on, ona] *nm/f* runner-up
subconsciente [suβkons'θjente] *adj* subconscious
subcontratar [suβkontra'tar] *vt (Com)* to subcontract
subcontrato [suβkon'trato] *nm (Com)* subcontract

subdesarrollado, -a [suβðesarro'ʎaðo, a] *adj*
underdeveloped
subdesarrollo [suβðesa'rroʎo] *nm*
underdevelopment
subdirector, a [suβðirek'tor, a] *nm/f*
assistant o deputy manager
subdirectorio [suβðirek'torjo] *nm* (*Inform*)
subdirectory
súbdito, -a ['suβðito, a] *nm/f* subject
subdividir [suβðiβi'ðir] *vt* to subdivide
subempleo [suβem'pleo] *nm*
underemployment
subestimar [suβesti'mar] *vt* to
underestimate, underrate
subido, -a [su'βiðo, a] *adj* (*color*) bright,
strong; (*precio*) high ■ *nf* (*de montaña etc*)
ascent, climb; (*de precio*) rise, increase;
(*pendiente*) slope, hill
subíndice [su'βindiθe] *nm* (*Inform, Tip*)
subscript
subir [su'βir] *vt* (*objeto*) to raise, lift up; (*cuesta,
calle*) to go up; (*colina, montaña*) to climb;
(*precio*) to raise, put up; (*empleado etc*) to
promote ■ *vi* to go/come up; (*a un coche*) to
get in; (*a un autobús, tren*) to get on; (*precio*) to
rise, go up; (*en el empleo*) to be promoted; (*río,
marea*) to rise; **subirse** *vr* to get up, climb;
subirse a un coche to get in(to) a car
súbito, -a ['suβito, a] *adj* (*repentino*) sudden;
(*imprevisto*) unexpected
subjetivo, -a [suβxe'tiβo, a] *adj* subjective
subjuntivo [suβxun'tiβo] *nm* subjunctive
(mood)
sublevación [suβleβa'θjon] *nf* revolt, rising
sublevar [suβle'βar] *vt* to rouse to revolt;
sublevarse *vr* to revolt, rise
sublimar [suβli'mar] *vt* (*persona*) to exalt;
(*deseos etc*) to sublimate
sublime [su'βlime] *adj* sublime
subliminal [suβlimi'nal] *adj* subliminal
submarinista [suβmari'nista] *nm/f*
underwater explorer
submarino, -a [suβma'rino, a] *adj*
underwater ■ *nm* submarine
subnormal [suβnor'mal] *adj* subnormal
■ *nm/f* subnormal person
suboficial [suβofi'θjal] *nm* non-
commissioned officer
subordinado, -a [suβorði'naðo, a] *adj, nm/f*
subordinate
subproducto [suβpro'ðukto] *nm* by-product
subrayado [suβra'jaðo] *nm* underlining
subrayar [suβra'jar] *vt* to underline; (*recalcar*)
to underline, emphasize
subrepticio, -a [suβrep'tiθjo, a] *adj*
surreptitious
subrutina [suβru'tina] *nf* (*Inform*) subroutine

subsanar [suβsa'nar] *vt* (*reparar*) to make
good; (*perdonar*) to excuse; (*sobreponerse a*) to
overcome
subscribir [suβskri'βir] *vt* = **suscribir**
subsecretario, -a [suβsekre'tarjo, a] *nm/f*
undersecretary, assistant secretary
subsidiariedad [suβsiðjarie'ðað] *nf* (*Pol*)
subsidiarity
subsidiario, -a [suβsi'ðjarjo, a] *adj*
subsidiary
subsidio [suβ'siðjo] *nm* (*ayuda*) aid, financial
help; (*subvención*) subsidy, grant; (*de
enfermedad, paro etc*) benefit, allowance
subsistencia [suβsis'tenθja] *nf* subsistence
subsistir [suβsis'tir] *vi* to subsist; (*vivir*) to
live; (*sobrevivir*) to survive, endure
subsuelo [suβ'swelo] *nm* subsoil
subte *nm abr* (*CSur*) = **subterráneo**
subterfugio [suβter'fuxjo] *nm* subterfuge
subterráneo, -a [suβte'rraneo, a] *adj*
underground, subterranean ■ *nm*
underpass, underground passage; (*Am*)
underground railway, subway (*US*)
subtitulado, -a [suβtitu'laðo, a] *adj* subtitled
subtítulo [suβ'titulo] *nm* subtitle,
subheading
suburbano, -a [suβur'βano, a] *adj* suburban
suburbio [su'βurβjo] *nm* (*barrio*) slum quarter;
(*afueras*) suburbs *pl*
subvención [suββen'θjon] *nf* subsidy,
subvention, grant; ~ **estatal** state subsidy
o support; ~ **para la inversión** (*Com*)
investment grant
subvencionar [suββenθjo'nar] *vt* to
subsidize
subversión [suββer'sjon] *nf* subversion
subversivo, -a [suββer'siβo, a] *adj*
subversive
subyacente [suβja'θente] *adj* underlying
subyugar [suβju'ɣar] *vt* (*país*) to subjugate,
subdue; (*enemigo*) to overpower; (*voluntad*) to
dominate
subyugue *etc* [suβ'juɣe] *vb ver* **subyugar**
succión [suk'θjon] *nf* suction
succionar [sukθjo'nar] *vt* (*sorber*) to suck;
(*Tec*) to absorb, soak up
sucedáneo, -a [suθe'ðaneo, a] *adj* substitute
■ *nm* substitute (food)
suceder [suθe'ðer] *vi* to happen; ~ **a** (*seguir*)
to succeed, follow; **lo que sucede es que ...**
the fact is that ...; ~ **al trono** to succeed to
the throne
sucesión [suθe'sjon] *nf* succession; (*serie*)
sequence, series; (*hijos*) issue, offspring
sucesivamente [suθesiβa'mente] *adv*: **y así**
~ and so on
sucesivo, -a [suθe'siβo, a] *adj* successive,

S

following; **en lo ~** in future, from now on
suceso [su'θeso] *nm* (*hecho*) event,
 happening; (*incidente*) incident
sucesor, a [suθe'sor, a] *nm/f* successor;
 (*heredero*) heir/heiress
suciedad [suθje'θað] *nf* (*estado*) dirtiness;
 (*mugre*) dirt, filth
sucinto, -a [su'θinto, a] *adj* (*conciso*) succinct,
 concise
sucio, -a ['suθjo, a] *adj* dirty; (*mugriento*)
 grimy; (*manchado*) grubby; (*borroso*) smudged;
 (*conciencia*) bad; (*conducta*) vile; (*táctica*) dirty,
 unfair
Sucre ['sukre] *n* Sucre
sucre ['sukre] *nm* Ecuadorean monetary unit
suculento, -a [suku'lento, a] *adj* (*sabroso*)
 tasty; (*jugoso*) succulent
sucumbir [sukum'bir] *vi* to succumb
sucursal [sukur'sal] *nf* branch (office); (*filial*)
 subsidiary
Sudáfrica [su'ðafrika] *nf* South Africa
sudafricano, -a [suðafri'kano, a] *adj, nm/f*
 South African
Sudamérica [suða'merika] *nf* South America
sudamericano, -a [suðameri'kano, a] *adj,*
 nm/f South American
sudanés, -esa [suða'nes, esa] *adj, nm/f*
 Sudanese
sudar [su'ðar] *vt, vi* to sweat; (*Bot*) to ooze,
 give out *o* off
sudeste [su'ðeste] *adj* south-east(ern);
 (*rumbo, viento*) south-easterly ■ *nm* south-
 east; (*viento*) south-east wind
sudoeste [suðo'este] *adj* south-west(ern);
 (*rumbo, viento*) south-westerly ■ *nm* south-
 west; (*viento*) south-west wind
sudoku [su'ðoku] *nm* sudoku
sudor [su'ðor] *nm* sweat
sudoroso, a [suðo'roso, a] *adj* sweaty,
 sweating
Suecia ['sweθja] *nf* Sweden
sueco, -a ['sweko, a] *adj* Swedish ■ *nm/f*
 Swede ■ *nm* (*Ling*) Swedish; **hacerse el ~**
 to pretend not to hear *o* understand
suegro, -a ['sweɣro, a] *nm/f* father-/mother-
 in-law; **los suegros** one's in-laws
suela ['swela] *nf* (*de zapato, tb pescado*) sole
sueldo *etc* ['sweldo] *vb ver* **soldar** ■ *nm* pay,
 wage(s) (*pl*)
suelo *etc* ['swelo] *vb ver* **soler** ■ *nm* (*tierra*)
 ground; (*de casa*) floor
suelto, -a *etc* ['swelto, a] *vb ver* **soltar** ■ *adj*
 loose; (*libre*) free; (*separado*) detached; (*ágil*)
 quick, agile; (*fue corre*) fluent, flowing ■ *nm*
 (loose) change, small change; **está muy ~ en**
 inglés he is very good at *o* fluent in English
suene *etc* ['swene] *vb ver* **sonar**

sueño *etc* ['sweɲo] *vb ver* **soñar** ■ *nm* sleep;
 (*somnolencia*) sleepiness, drowsiness; (*lo*
 soñado, fig) dream; **~ pesado** *o* **profundo** deep
 o heavy sleep; **tener ~** to be sleepy
suero ['swero] *nm* (*Med*) serum; (*de leche*)
 whey
suerte ['swerte] *nf* (*fortuna*) luck; (*azar*)
 chance; (*destino*) fate, destiny; (*condición*) lot;
 (*género*) sort, kind; **lo echaron a suertes**
 they drew lots *o* tossed up for it; **tener ~** to be
 lucky; **de otra ~** otherwise, if not; **de ~ que**
 so that, in such a way that
suéter ['sweter] (*pl* **suéters**) *nm* sweater
suficiencia [sufi'θjenθja] *nf* (*cabida*) sufficiency;
 (*idoneidad*) suitability; (*aptitud*) adequacy
suficiente [sufi'θjente] *adj* enough,
 sufficient
sufijo [su'fixo] *nm* suffix
sufragar [sufra'ɣar] *vt* (*ayudar*) to help;
 (*gastos*) to meet; (*proyecto*) to pay for
sufragio [su'fraxjo] *nm* (*voto*) vote; (*derecho de*
 voto) suffrage
sufrague *etc* [su'fraɣe] *vb ver* **sufragar**
sufrido, -a [su'friðo, a] *adj* (*de carácter fuerte*)
 tough; (*paciente*) long-suffering; (*tela*) hard-
 wearing; (*color*) that does not show the dirt;
 (*marido*) complaisant
sufrimiento [sufri'mjento] *nm* suffering
sufrir [su'frir] *vt* (*padecer*) to suffer; (*soportar*)
 to bear, stand, put up with; (*apoyar*) to hold
 up, support ■ *vi* to suffer
sugerencia [suxe'renθja] *nf* suggestion
sugerir [suxe'rir] *vt* to suggest; (*sutilmente*) to
 hint; (*idea: incitar*) to prompt
sugestión [suxes'tjon] *nf* suggestion; (*sutil*)
 hint; (*poder*) hypnotic power
sugestionar [suxestjo'nar] *vt* to influence
sugestivo, -a [suxes'tiβo, a] *adj* stimulating;
 (*atractivo*) attractive; (*fascinante*) fascinating
sugiera *etc* [su'xjera], **sugiriendo** *etc*
 [suxi'rjendo] *vb ver* **sugerir**
suicida [sui'θiða] *adj* suicidal ■ *nm/f* suicidal
 person; (*muerto*) suicide, person who has
 committed suicide
suicidarse [suiθi'ðarse] *vr* to commit suicide,
 kill o.s.
suicidio [sui'θiðjo] *nm* suicide
Suiza ['swiθa] *nf* Switzerland
suizo, -a ['swiθo, a] *adj, nm/f* Swiss ■ *nm*
 sugared bun
sujeción [suxe'θjon] *nf* subjection
sujetador [suxeta'ðor] *nm* fastener, clip;
 (*prenda femenina*) bra, brassiere
sujetapapeles [suxetapa'peles] *nm inv* paper
 clip
sujetar [suxe'tar] *vt* (*fijar*) to fasten; (*detener*)
 to hold down; (*fig*) to subject, subjugate;

(*pelo etc*) to keep *o* hold in place; (*papeles*) to fasten together; **sujetarse** *vr* to subject o.s.

sujeto, -a [su'xeto, a] *adj* fastened, secure ■ *nm* subject; (*individuo*) individual; (*fam: tipo*) fellow, character, type, guy (US); ~ **a** subject to

sulfurar [sulfu'rar] *vt* (*Tec*) to sulphurate; (*sacar de quicio*) to annoy; **sulfurarse** *vr* (*enojarse*) to get riled, see red, blow up

sulfuro [sul'furo] *nm* sulphide

suma ['suma] *nf* (*cantidad*) total, sum; (*de dinero*) sum; (*acto*) adding (up), addition; **en ~** in short; **~ y sigue** (*Com*) carry forward

sumador [suma'ðor] *nm* (*Inform*) adder

sumamente [suma'mente] *adv* extremely, exceedingly

sumar [su'mar] *vt* to add (up); (*reunir*) to collect, gather ■ *vi* to add up

sumario, -a [su'marjo, a] *adj* brief, concise ■ *nm* summary

sumergir [sumer'xir] *vt* to submerge; (*hundir*) to sink; (*bañar*) to immerse, dip; **sumergirse** *vr* (*hundirse*) to sink beneath the surface

sumerja *etc* [su'merxa] *vb ver* **sumergir**

sumidero [sumi'ðero] *nm* drain, sewer; (*Tec*) sump

suministrador, a [suministra'ðor, a] *nm/f* supplier

suministrar [suminis'trar] *vt* to supply, provide

suministro [sumi'nistro] *nm* supply; (*acto*) supplying, providing

sumir [su'mir] *vt* to sink, submerge; (*fig*) to plunge; **sumirse** *vr* (*objeto*) to sink; **sumirse en el estudio** to become absorbed in one's studies

sumisión [sumi'sjon] *nf* (*acto*) submission; (*calidad*) submissiveness, docility

sumiso, -a [su'miso, a] *adj* submissive, docile

súmmum ['sumum] *nm inv* (*fig*) height

sumo, -a ['sumo, a] *adj* great, extreme; (*mayor*) highest, supreme ■ *nm* sumo (wrestling); **a lo ~** at most

suntuoso, -a [sun'twoso, a] *adj* sumptuous, magnificent; (*lujoso*) lavish

sup. *abr* (= *superior*) sup

supe *etc* ['supe] *vb ver* **saber**

supeditar [supeði'tar] *vt* to subordinate; (*sojuzgar*) to subdue; (*oprimir*) to oppress; **supeditarse** *vr*: **supeditarse a** to subject o.s. to

super... [super] *pref* super..., over...

súper ['super] *adj* (*fam*) super, great

superable [supe'raβle] *adj* (*dificultad*) surmountable; (*tarea*) that can be performed

superación [supera'θjon] *nf* (*tb*: **superación personal**) self-improvement

superar [supe'rar] *vt* (*sobreponerse a*) to overcome; (*rebasar*) to surpass, do better than; (*pasar*) to go beyond; (*marca, récord*) to break; (*etapa: dejar atrás*) to get past; **superarse** *vr* to excel o.s.

superávit [supe'raβit] (*pl* **superávits**) *nm* surplus

superchería [supertʃe'ria] *nf* fraud, trick, swindle

superficial [superfi'θjal] *adj* superficial; (*medida*) surface *cpd*

superficie [super'fiθje] *nf* surface; (*área*) area; **grandes superficies** (*Com*) superstores

superfluo, -a [su'perflwo, a] *adj* superfluous

superíndice [supe'rindiθe] *nm* (*Inform: Tip*) superscript

superintendente [superinten'dente] *nm/f* supervisor, superintendent

superior [supe'rjor] *adj* (*piso, clase*) upper; (*temperatura, número, nivel*) higher; (*mejor: calidad, producto*) superior, better ■ *nm/f* superior

superiora [supe'rjora] *nf* (*Rel*) mother superior

superioridad [superjori'ðað] *nf* superiority

superlativo, -a [superla'tiβo, a] *adj, nm* superlative

supermercado [supermer'kaðo] *nm* supermarket

superpoblación [superpoβla'θjon] *nf* overpopulation; (*congestionamiento*) overcrowding

superponer [superpo'ner] *vt* (*Inform*) to overstrike

superposición [superposi'θjon] *nf* (*en impresora*) overstrike

superpotencia [superpo'tenθja] *nf* superpower, great power

superproducción [superproðuk'θjon] *nf* overproduction

supersónico, -a [super'soniko, a] *adj* supersonic

superstición [supersti'θjon] *nf* superstition

supersticioso, -a [supersti'θjoso, a] *adj* superstitious

supervisar [superβi'sar] *vt* to supervise; (*Com*) to superintend

supervisor, a [superβi'sor, a] *nm/f* supervisor

supervivencia [superβi'βenθja] *nf* survival

superviviente [superβi'βjente] *adj* surviving ■ *nm/f* survivor

suplantar [suplan'tar] *vt* (*persona*) to supplant; (*hacerse pasar por otro*) to take the place of

suplementario, -a [suplemen'tarjo, a] *adj* supplementary

S

suplemento [suple'mento] *nm* supplement

suplencia [su'plenθja] *nf* substitution, replacement; (*etapa*) period during which one deputizes *etc*

suplente [su'plente] *adj* substitute; (*disponible*) reserve ■ *nm/f* substitute

supletorio, -a [suple'torjo, a] *adj* supplementary; (*adicional*) extra ■ *nm* supplement; **mesa supletoria** spare table

súplica ['suplika] *nf* request; (*Rel*) supplication; (*Jur: instancia*) petition; **súplicas** *nfpl* entreaties

suplicar [supli'kar] *vt* (*cosa*) to beg (for), plead for; (*persona*) to beg, plead with; (*Jur*) to appeal to, petition

suplicio [su'pliθjo] *nm* torture; (*tormento*) torment; (*emoción*) anguish; (*experiencia penosa*) ordeal

suplique *etc* [su'plike] *vb ver* **suplicar**

suplir [su'plir] *vt* to make good, make up for; (*reemplazar*) to replace, substitute ■ *vi*: ~ **a** to take the place of, substitute for

supo *etc* ['supo] *vb ver* **saber**

supondré *etc* [supon'dre] *vb ver* **suponer**

suponer [supo'ner] *vt* to suppose; (*significar*) to mean; (*acarrear*) to involve ■ *vi* to count, have authority; **era de ~ que ...** it was to be expected that ...

suponga *etc* [su'ponga] *vb ver* **suponer**

suposición [suposi'θjon] *nf* supposition

supositorio [suposi'torjo] *nm* suppository

supremacía [supremaθia] *nf* supremacy

supremo, -a [su'premo, a] *adj* supreme

supresión [supre'sjon] *nf* suppression; (*de derecho*) abolition; (*de dificultad*) removal; (*de palabra etc*) deletion; (*de restricción*) cancellation, lifting

suprimir [supri'mir] *vt* to suppress; (*derecho, costumbre*) to abolish; (*dificultad*) to remove; (*palabra etc, Inform*) to delete; (*restricción*) to cancel, lift

supuestamente [supwesta'mente] *adv* supposedly

supuesto, -a [su'pwesto, a] *pp de* **suponer** ■ *adj* (*hipotético*) supposed; (*falso*) false ■ *nm* assumption, hypothesis ■ *conj*: ~ **que** since; **dar por ~ algo** to take sth for granted; **por ~** of course

supurar [supu'rar] *vi* to fester, suppurate

supuse *etc* [su'puse] *vb ver* **suponer**

sur [sur] *adj* southern; (*rumbo*) southerly ■ *nm* south; (*viento*) south wind

Suráfrica *etc* [su'rafrika] = **Sudáfrica** *etc*

Suramérica *etc* [sura'merika] = **Sudamérica** *etc*

surcar [sur'kar] *vt* to plough; (*superficie*) to cut, score

surco ['surko] *nm* groove; (*Agr*) furrow

surcoreano, -a [surkore'ano, a] *adj, nm/f* South Korean

sureño, -a [su'reɲo, a] *adj* southern ■ *nm/f* southerner

sureste [su'reste] = **sudeste**

surf [surf] *nm* surfing

surfear [surfe'ar] *vt*: ~ **el Internet** to surf the internet

surgir [sur'xir] *vi* to arise, emerge; (*dificultad*) to come up, crop up

surja *etc* ['surxa] *vb ver* **surgir**

suroeste [suro'este] = **sudoeste**

surque *etc* ['surke] *vb ver* **surcar**

surrealismo [surrea'lismo] *nm* surrealism

surrealista [surrea'lista] *adj, nm/f* surrealist

surtido, -a [sur'tiðo, a] *adj* mixed, assorted ■ *nm* (*selección*) selection, assortment; (*abastecimiento*) supply, stock

surtidor [surti'ðor] *nm* (*chorro*) jet, spout; (*fuente*) fountain; ~ **de gasolina** petrol (*Brit*) o gas (*US*) pump

surtir [sur'tir] *vt* to supply, provide; (*efecto*) to have, produce ■ *vi* to spout, spurt; **surtirse** *vr*: **surtirse de** to provide o.s. with

susceptible [susθep'tiβle] *adj* susceptible; (*sensible*) sensitive; ~ **de** capable of

suscitar [susθi'tar] *vt* to cause, provoke; (*discusión*) to start; (*duda, problema*) to raise; (*interés, sospechas*) to arouse

suscribir [suskri'βir] *vt* (*firmar*) to sign; (*respaldar*) to subscribe to, endorse; (*Com: acciones*) to take out an option on; **suscribirse** *vr* to subscribe; ~ **a algn a una revista** to take out a subscription to a journal for sb

suscripción [suskrip'θjon] *nf* subscription

suscrito, -a [sus'krito, a] *pp de* **suscribir** ■ *adj*: ~ **en exceso** oversubscribed

sushi ['suʃi] *nm* sushi

susodicho, -a [suso'ditʃo, a] *adj* above-mentioned

suspender [suspen'der] *vt* (*objeto*) to hang (up), suspend; (*trabajo*) to stop, suspend; (*Escol*) to fail

suspense [sus'pense] *nm* suspense

suspensión [suspen'sjon] *nf* suspension; (*fig*) stoppage, suspension; (*Jur*) stay; ~ **de fuego** o **de hostilidades** ceasefire, cessation of hostilities; ~ **de pagos** suspension of payments

suspensivo, -a [suspen'siβo, a] *adj*: **puntos suspensivos** dots, suspension points

suspenso, -a [sus'penso, a] *adj* hanging, suspended; (*Escol*) failed ■ *nm* (*Escol*) fail(ure); **quedar** o **estar en ~** to be pending

suspicacia [suspi'kaθja] *nf* suspicion, mistrust

suspicaz [suspi'kaθ] *adj* suspicious, distrustful

suspirar [suspi'rar] vi to sigh
suspiro [sus'piro] nm sigh
sustancia [sus'tanθja] nf substance; ~
gris (Anat) grey matter; **sin** ~ lacking in
substance, shallow
sustancial [sustan'θjal] adj substantial
sustancioso, -a [sustan'θjoso, a] adj
substantial; (discurso) solid
sustantivo, -a [sustan'tiβo, a] adj
substantive; (Ling) substantival, noun cpd
■ nm noun, substantive
sustentar [susten'tar] vt (alimentar) to
sustain, nourish; (objeto) to hold up, support;
(idea, teoría) to maintain, uphold; (fig) to
sustain, keep going
sustento [sus'tento] nm support; (alimento)
sustenance, food
sustituir [sustitu'ir] vt to substitute, replace
sustituto, a [susti'tuto, a] nm/f substitute,
replacement
sustituyendo etc [sustitu'jendo] vb ver
sustituir
susto ['susto] nm fright, scare; **dar un ~ a
algn** to give sb a fright; **darse o pegarse un
~** (fam) to get a fright
sustraer [sustra'er] vt to remove, take away;
(Mat) to subtract
sustraiga etc [sus'traiɣa], **sustraje** etc
[sus'traxe] vb ver **sustraer**

sustrato [sus'trato] nm substratum
sustrayendo etc [sustra'jendo] vb ver
sustraer
susurrar [susu'rrar] vi to whisper
susurro [su'surro] nm whisper
sutil [su'til] adj (aroma) subtle; (tenue) thin;
(hilo, hebra) fine; (olor) delicate; (brisa) gentle;
(diferencia) fine, subtle; (inteligencia) sharp,
keen
sutileza [suti'leθa] nf subtlety; (delgadez)
thinness; (delicadeza) delicacy; (agudeza)
keenness
sutura [su'tura] nf suture
suturar [sutu'rar] vt to suture; (juntar con
puntos) to stitch
suyo, -a ['sujo, a] adj (con artículo o después del
verbo **ser**: de él) his; (: de ella) hers; (: de ellos,
ellas) theirs; (: de usted, ustedes) yours; (después
de un nombre: de él) of his; (: de ella) of hers;
(: de ellos, ellas) of theirs; (: de usted, ustedes) of
yours; **lo ~** (what is) his; (su parte) his share,
what he deserves; **los suyos** (su familia) one's
family o relations; (sus partidarios) one's own
people o supporters; **~ afectísimo** (en carta)
yours faithfully o sincerely; **de ~** in itself;
eso es muy ~ that's just like him; **hacer de
las suyas** to get up to one's old tricks; **ir a la
suya, ir a lo ~** to go one's own way; **salirse
con la suya** to get one's way

Tt

T, t [te] *nf* (*letra*) T, t; **T de Tarragona** T for Tommy

t *abr* = **tonelada**

T. *abr* (= *Teléfon, Telégrafo*) tel.; (*Com*) = **Tarifa; Tasa**

t. *abr* (= *tomo(s)*) vol(s)

TA *abr* = **traducción automática**

Tabacalera [taβaka'lera] *nf* Spanish state tobacco monopoly

tabaco [ta'βako] *nm* tobacco; (*fam*) cigarettes *pl*

tábano ['taβano] *nm* horsefly

tabaquería [tabake'ria] *nf* tobacconist's (Brit), cigar store (US)

tabarra [ta'βarra] *nf* (*fam*) nuisance; **dar la ~** to be a pain in the neck

taberna [ta'βerna] *nf* bar

tabernero, -a [taβer'nero, a] *nm/f* (*encargado*) publican; (*camarero*) barman/barmaid

tabique [ta'βike] *nm* (*pared*) thin wall; (*para dividir*) partition

tabla ['taβla] *nf* (*de madera*) plank; (*estante*) shelf; (*de anuncios*) board; (*lista, catálogo*) list; (*de vestido*) pleat; (*Arte*) panel; **tablas** *nfpl* (*Taur: Teat*) boards; **hacer tablas** to draw; **~ de consulta** (*Inform*) lookup table

tablado [ta'βlaðo] *nm* (*plataforma*) platform; (*suelo*) plank floor; (*Teat*) stage

tablao [ta'βlao] *nm* (*tb:* **tablao flamenco**) flamenco show

tablero [ta'βlero] *nm* (*de madera*) plank, board; (*pizarra*) blackboard; (*de ajedrez, damas*) board; (*Auto*) dashboard; **~ de gráficos** (*Inform*) graph pad

tableta [ta'βleta] *nf* (*Med*) tablet; (*de chocolate*) bar

tablilla [ta'βliʎa] *nf* small board; (*Med*) splint

tablón [ta'βlon] *nm* (*de suelo*) plank; (*de techo*) beam; (*de anuncios*) notice board

tabú [ta'βu] *nm* taboo

tabulación [taβula'θjon] *nf* (*Inform*) tab(bing)

tabulador [taβula'ðor] *nm* (*Inform: Tip*) tab

tabuladora [taβula'ðora] *nf*: **~ eléctrica** electric accounting machine

tabular [taβu'lar] *vt* to tabulate; (*Inform*) to tab

taburete [taβu'rete] *nm* stool

tacaño, -a [ta'kaɲo, a] *adj* (*avaro*) mean; (*astuto*) crafty

tacha ['tatʃa] *nf* (*defecto*) flaw, defect; (*Tec*) stud; **poner ~ a** to find fault with; **sin ~** flawless

tachar [ta'tʃar] *vt* (*borrar*) to cross out; (*corregir*) to correct; (*criticar*) to criticize; **~ de** to accuse of

tacho ['tatʃo] *nm* (*Am*) bucket, pail

tachón [ta'tʃon] *nm* erasure; (*tachadura*) crossing-out; (*Tec*) ornamental stud; (*Costura*) trimming

tachuela [ta'tʃwela] *nf* (*clavo*) tack

tácito, -a ['taθito, a] *adj* tacit; (*acuerdo*) unspoken; (*Ling*) understood; (*ley*) unwritten

taciturno, -a [taθi'turno, a] *adj* (*callado*) silent; (*malhumorado*) sullen

taco ['tako] *nm* (*Billar*) cue; (*libro de billetes*) book; (*manojo de billetes*) wad; (*Am*) heel; (*tarugo*) peg; (*fam: bocado*) snack; (*: palabrota*) swear word; (*: trago de vino*) swig; (*México*) filled tortilla; **armarse o hacerse un ~** to get into a mess

tacógrafo [ta'koɣrafo] *nm* (*Com*) tachograph

tacón [ta'kon] *nm* heel; **de ~ alto** high-heeled

taconear [takone'ar] *vi* (*dar golpecitos*) to tap with one's heels; (*Mil etc*) to click one's heels

taconeo [tako'neo] *nm* (*heel*) tapping *o* clicking

táctico, -a ['taktiko, a] *adj* tactical ■ *nf* tactics *pl*

tacto ['takto] *nm* touch; (*acción*) touching; (*fig*) tact

TAE *nf abr* (= *tasa anual equivalente*) APR

tafetán [tafe'tan] *nm* taffeta; **tafetanes** *nmpl* (*fam*) frills; **~ adhesivo o inglés** sticking plaster

tafilete [tafi'lete] *nm* morocco leather

tahona [ta'ona] *nf* (*panadería*) bakery; (*molino*) flourmill

tahur [ta'ur] *nm* gambler; (*pey*) cheat

tailandés, -esa [tailan'des, esa] *adj, nm/f* Thai ■ *nm* (*Ling*) Thai

Tailandia [tai'landja] *nf* Thailand

taimado, -a [tai'maðo, a] *adj* (*astuto*) sly; (*resentido*) sullen

taita ['taita] *nm* dad, daddy

tajada [ta'xaða] *nf* slice; (*fam*) rake-off; **sacar ~** to get one's share

tajante [ta'xante] *adj* sharp; (*negativa*) emphatic; **es una persona ~** he's an emphatic person

tajar [ta'xar] *vt* to cut, slice

Tajo ['taxo] *nm* Tagus

tajo ['taxo] *nm* (*corte*) cut; (*filo*) cutting edge; (*Geo*) cleft

tal [tal] *adj* such; **un ~ García** a man called García; **~ vez** perhaps ■ *pron* (*persona*) someone, such a one; (*cosa*) something, such a thing; **~ como** such as; **~ para cual** tit for tat; (*dos iguales*) two of a kind; **hablábamos de que si ~ si cual** we were talking about this, that and the other ■ *adv*: **~ como** (*igual*) just as; **~ cual** (*como es*) just as it is; **~ el padre, cual el hijo** like father, like son; **¿qué ~?** how are things?; **¿qué ~ te gusta?** how do you like it? ■ *conj*: **con ~ (de) que** provided that

tala ['tala] *nf* (*de árboles*) tree felling

taladradora [talaðra'ðora] *nf* drill; **~ neumática** pneumatic drill

taladrar [tala'ðrar] *vt* to drill; (*fig: ruido*) to pierce

taladro [ta'laðro] *nm* (*gen*) drill; (*hoyo*) drill hole; **~ neumático** pneumatic drill

talante [ta'lante] *nm* (*humor*) mood; (*voluntad*) will, willingness

talar [ta'lar] *vt* to fell, cut down; (*fig*) to devastate

talco ['talko] *nm* (*polvos*) talcum powder; (*Mineralogía*) talc

talega [ta'leɣa] *nf* sack

talego [ta'leɣo] *nm* sack; **tener ~** (*fam*) to have money

talento [ta'lento] *nm* talent; (*capacidad*) ability; (*don*) gift

Talgo ['talɣo] *nm abr* (*Ferro*: = *tren articulado ligero Goicoechea-Oriol*) high-speed train

talidomida [taliðo'miða] *nm* thalidomide

talismán [talis'man] *nm* talisman

talla ['taʎa] *nf* (*estatura, fig, Med*) height, stature; (*de ropa*) size, fitting; (*palo*) measuring rod; (*Arte: de madera*) carving; (*de piedra*) sculpture

tallado, -a [ta'ʎaðo, a] *adj* carved ■ *nm* (*de madera*) carving; (*de piedra*) sculpture

tallar [ta'ʎar] *vt* (*trabajar*) to work, carve; (*grabar*) to engrave; (*medir*) to measure; (*repartir*) to deal ■ *vi* to deal

tallarín [taʎa'rin] *nm* noodle

talle ['taʎe] *nm* (*Anat*) waist; (*medida*) size; (*física*) build; (: *de mujer*) figure; (*fig*) appearance; **de ~ esbelto** with a slim figure

taller [ta'ʎer] *nm* (*Tec*) workshop; (*fábrica*) factory; (*Auto*) garage; (*de artista*) studio

tallo ['taʎo] *nm* (*de planta*) stem; (*de hierba*) blade; (*brote*) shoot; (*col*) cabbage; (*Culin*) candied peel

talmente [tal'mente] *adv* (*de esta forma*) in such a way; (*hasta tal punto*) to such an extent; (*exactamente*) exactly

talón [ta'lon] *nm* (*gen*) heel; (*Com*) counterfoil; (*Tec*) rim; **~ de Aquiles** Achilles heel

talonario [talo'narjo] *nm* (*de cheques*) cheque book; (*de billetes*) book of tickets; (*de recibos*) receipt book

tamaño, -a [ta'maɲo, a] *adj* (*tan grande*) such a big; (*tan pequeño*) such a small ■ *nm* size; **de ~ natural** full-size; **¿de qué ~ es?** what size is it?

tamarindo [tama'rindo] *nm* tamarind

tambaleante [tambale'ante] *adj* (*persona*) staggering; (*mueble*) wobbly; (*vehículo*) swaying

tambalearse [tambale'arse] *vr* (*persona*) to stagger; (*mueble*) to wobble; (*vehículo*) to sway

también [tam'bjen] *adv* (*igualmente*) also, too, as well; (*además*) besides; **estoy cansado — yo ~** I'm tired — so am I o me too

tambor [tam'bor] *nm* drum; (*Anat*) eardrum; **~ del freno** brake drum; **~ magnético** (*Inform*) magnetic drum

tamboril [tambo'ril] *nm* small drum

tamborilear [tamborile'ar] *vi* (*Mus*) to drum; (*con los dedos*) to drum with one's fingers

tamborilero [tambori'lero] *nm* drummer

Támesis ['tamesis] *nm* Thames

tamice *etc* [ta'miθe] *vb ver* **tamizar**

tamiz [ta'miθ] *nm* sieve

tamizar [tami'θar] *vt* to sieve

tampoco [tam'poko] *adv* nor, neither; **yo ~ lo compré** I didn't buy it either

tampón [tam'pon] *nm* plug; (*Med*) tampon

tan [tan] *adv* so; **~ es así que** so much so that; **¡qué cosa ~ rara!** how strange!; **no es una idea ~ buena** it is not such a good idea

tanatorio [tana'torjo] *nm* (*privado*) funeral home o parlour; (*público*) mortuary

tanda ['tanda] *nf* (*gen*) series; (*de inyecciones*) course; (*juego*) set; (*turno*) shift; (*grupo*) gang

tándem ['tandem] *nm* tandem; (*Pol*) duo

tanga ['tanga] *nm* (*bikini*) tanga; (*ropa interior*) tanga briefs

t

tangente [tan'xente] nf tangent; **salirse por la ~** to go off at a tangent

Tánger ['tanxer] n Tangier

tangerino, -a [tanxe'rino, a] adj of o from Tangier ■ nm/f native o inhabitant of Tangier

tangible [tan'xiβle] adj tangible

tango ['tango] nm tango

tanino [ta'nino] nm tannin

tankini [tan'kini] nm tankini

tanque ['tanke] nm (gen) tank; (Auto, Naut) tanker

tanqueta [tan'keta] nf (Mil) small tank, armoured vehicle

tantear [tante'ar] vt (calcular) to reckon (up); (medir) to take the measure of; (probar) to test, try out; (tomar la medida: persona) to take the measurements of; (considerar) to weigh up ■ vi (Deporte) to score

tanteo [tan'teo] nm (cálculo aproximado) (rough) calculation; (prueba) test, trial; (Deporte) scoring; (adivinanzas) guesswork; **al ~** by trial and error

tantísimo, -a [tan'tisimo, a] adj so much; **tantísimos** so many

tanto, -a ['tanto, a] adj (cantidad) so much, as much; **tantos** so many, as many; **20 y tantos** 20-odd ■ adv (cantidad) so much, as much; (tiempo) so long, as long; **~ tú como yo** both you and I; **~ como eso** it's not as bad as that; **~ más … cuanto que** it's all the more … because; **~ mejor/peor** so much the better/the worse; **~ si viene como si va** whether he comes or whether he goes; **~ es así que** so much so that; **por ~, por lo ~** therefore; **me he vuelto ronco de o con ~ hablar** I have become hoarse with so much talking ■ conj: **con ~ que** provided (that); **en ~ que** while; **hasta ~ (que)** until such time as ■ nm (suma) certain amount; (proporción) so much; (punto) point; (gol) goal; **~ alzado** agreed price; **~ por ciento** percentage; **al ~** up to date; **estar al ~ de los acontecimientos** to be fully abreast of events; **un ~ perezoso** somewhat lazy; **al ~ de que** because of the fact that ■ pron: **cada uno paga ~** each one pays so much; **uno de tantos** one of many; **a tantos de agosto** on such and such a day in August; **entre ~** meanwhile

tañer [ta'ɲer] vt (Mus) to play; (campana) to ring

TAO nf abr (= traducción asistida por ordenador) MAT

tapa ['tapa] nf (de caja, olla) lid; (de botella) top; (de libro) cover; (de comida) snack

tapacubos [tapa'kuβos] nm inv hub cap

tapadera [tapa'ðera] nf lid, cover

tapado [ta'paðo] nm (Am: abrigo) coat

tapar [ta'par] vt (cubrir) to cover; (envolver) to wrap o cover up; (la vista) to obstruct; (persona, falta) to conceal; (Am) to fill; **taparse** vr to wrap o.s. up

tapete [ta'pete] nm table cover; **estar sobre el ~** (fig) to be under discussion

tapia ['tapja] nf (garden) wall

tapiar [ta'pjar] vt to wall in

tapice etc [ta'piθe] vb ver **tapizar**

tapicería [tapiθe'ria] nf tapestry; (para muebles) upholstery; (tienda) upholsterer's (shop)

tapicero, -a [tapi'θero, a] nm/f (de muebles) upholsterer

tapiz [ta'piθ] nm (alfombra) carpet; (tela tejida) tapestry

tapizar [tapi'θar] vt (pared) to wallpaper; (suelo) to carpet; (muebles) to upholster

tapón [ta'pon] nm (corcho) stopper; (Tec) plug; (Med) tampon; **~ de rosca o de tuerca** screw-top

taponar [tapo'nar] vt (botella) to cork; (tubería) to block

taponazo [tapo'naθo] nm (de tapón) pop

tapujo [ta'puxo] nm (embozo) muffler; (engaño) deceit; **sin tapujos** honestly

taquigrafía [takiɣra'fia] nf shorthand

taquígrafo, -a [ta'kiɣrafo, a] nm/f shorthand writer

taquilla [ta'kiʎa] nf (de estación etc) booking office; (de teatro) box office; (suma recogida) takings pl; (archivador) filing cabinet

taquillero, -a [taki'ʎero, a] adj: **función taquillera** box office success ■ nm/f ticket clerk

taquimecanografía [takimekanoɣra'fia] nf shorthand and typing

taquímetro [ta'kimetro] nm speedometer; (de control) tachymeter

tara ['tara] nf (defecto) defect; (Com) tare

tarado, -a [ta'raðo, a] adj (Com) defective, imperfect; (idiota) stupid; (loco) crazy, nuts ■ nm/f idiot, cretin

tarántula [ta'rantula] nf tarantula

tararear [tarare'ar] vi to hum

tardanza [tar'ðanθa] nf (demora) delay; (lentitud) slowness

tardar [tar'ðar] vi (tomar tiempo) to take a long time; (llegar tarde) to be late; (demorar) to delay; **¿tarda mucho el tren?** does the train take long?; **a más ~** at the (very) latest; **~ en hacer algo** to be slow o take a long time to do sth; **no tardes en venir** come soon, come before long

tarde ['tarðe] adv (hora) late; (fuera de tiempo)

too late ■ *nf* (*de día*) afternoon; (*de noche*) evening; ~ **o temprano** sooner or later; **de ~ en ~** from time to time; **¡buenas tardes!** (*de día*) good afternoon!; (*de noche*) good evening!; **a o por la ~** in the afternoon; in the evening

tardío, -a [tar'ðio, a] *adj* (*retrasado*) late; (*lento*) slow (to arrive)

tardo, -a ['tarðo, a] *adj* (*lento*) slow; (*torpe*) dull; **~ de oído** hard of hearing

tarea [ta'rea] *nf* task; **tareas** *nfpl* (*Escol*) homework *sg*; **~ de ocasión** chore

tarifa [ta'rifa] *nf* (*lista de precios*) price list; (*Com*) tariff; **~ básica** basic rate; **~ completa** all-in cost; **~ a destajo** piece rate; **~ doble** double time

tarima [ta'rima] *nf* (*plataforma*) platform

tarjeta [tar'xeta] *nf* card; **~ postal/de crédito/de Navidad** postcard/credit card/ Christmas card; **~ de circuitos** (*Inform*) circuit board; **~ cliente** loyalty card; **~ comercial** (*Com*) calling card; **~ dinero** cash card; **~ gráficos** (*Inform*) graphics card; **~ monedero** electronic purse *o* wallet; **~ prepago** top-up card; **~ SIM** SIM card

tarot [ta'rot] *nm* tarot

tarraconense [tarrako'nense] *adj* of *o* from Tarragona ■ *nm/f* native *o* inhabitant of Tarragona

tarro ['tarro] *nm* jar, pot

tarta ['tarta] *nf* (*pastel*) cake; (*torta*) tart

tartajear [tartaxe'ar] *vi* to stammer

tartamudear [tartamuðe'ar] *vi* to stutter, stammer

tartamudo, -a [tarta'muðo, a] *adj* stuttering, stammering ■ *nm/f* stutterer, stammerer

tartárico, -a [tar'tariko, a] *adj*: **ácido ~** tartaric acid

tártaro ['tartaro] *adj, nm* Tartar ■ *nm* (*Química*) tartar

tarugo, -a [ta'ruɣo, a] *adj* stupid ■ *nm* (*de madera*) lump

tarumba [ta'rumba] *adj* (*confuso*) confused

tasa ['tasa] *nf* (*precio*) (fixed) price, rate; (*valoración*) valuation; (*medida, norma*) measure, standard; **~ básica** (*Com*) basic rate; **~ de cambio** exchange rate; **de ~ cero** (*Com*) zero-rated; **~ de crecimiento** growth rate; **~ de interés/de nacimiento** rate of interest/birth rate; **~ de rendimiento** (*Com*) rate of return; **tasas universitarias** university fees

tasación [tasa'θjon] *nf* assessment, valuation; (*fig*) appraisal

tasador, a [tasa'ðor, a] *nm/f* valuer; (*Com: de impuestos*) assessor

tasar [ta'sar] *vt* (*arreglar el precio*) to fix a price for; (*valorar*) to value, assess; (*limitar*) to limit

tasca ['taska] *nf* (*fam*) pub

tata ['tata] *nm* (*fam*) dad(dy) ■ *nf* (*niñera*) nanny, maid

tatarabuelo, -a [tatara'βwelo, a] *nm/f* great-great-grandfather/mother; **los tatarabuelos** one's great-great-grandparents

tatuaje [ta'twaxe] *nm* (*dibujo*) tattoo; (*acto*) tattooing

tatuar [ta'twar] *vt* to tattoo

taumaturgo [tauma'turɣo] *nm* miracle-worker

taurino, -a [tau'rino, a] *adj* bullfighting *cpd*

Tauro ['tauro] *nm* Taurus

tauromaquia [tauro'makja] *nf* (art of) bullfighting

tautología [tautolo'xia] *nf* tautology

taxativo, -a [taksa'tiβo, a] *adj* (*restringido*) limited; (*sentido*) specific

taxi ['taksi] *nm* taxi

taxidermia [taksi'ðermja] *nf* taxidermy

taxímetro [tak'simetro] *nm* taximeter

taxista [tak'sista] *nm/f* taxi driver

Tayikistán [tajikis'tan] *nm* Tajikistan

taza ['taθa] *nf* cup; (*de retrete*) bowl; **~ para café** coffee cup

tazón [ta'θon] *nm* mug, large cup; (*escudilla*) basin

TCI *nf abr* (= *tarjeta de circuito impreso*) PCB

te [te] *pron* (*complemento de objeto*) you; (*complemento indirecto*) (to) you; (*reflexivo*) (to) yourself; **¿te duele mucho el brazo?** does your arm hurt a lot?; **te equivocas** you're wrong; **¡cálmate!** calm yourself!

té [te] (*pl* **tés**) *nm* tea; (*reunión*) tea party

tea ['tea] *nf* (*antorcha*) torch

teatral [tea'tral] *adj* theatre *cpd*; (*fig*) theatrical

teatro [te'atro] *nm* theatre; (*Lit*) plays *pl*, drama; **el ~** (*carrera*) the theatre, acting; **~ de aficionados/de variedades** amateur/variety theatre, vaudeville theater (*US*); **hacer ~** (*fig*) to make a fuss

tebeo [te'βeo] *nm* children's comic

techado [te'tʃaðo] *nm* (*techo*) roof; **bajo ~** under cover

techo ['tetʃo] *nm* (*externo*) roof; (*interno*) ceiling

techumbre [te'tʃumbre] *nf* roof

tecla ['tekla] *nf* (*Inform: Mus: Tip*) key; (*Inform*): **~ de anulación/de borrar** cancel/delete key; **~ de control/de edición** control/edit key; **~ con flecha** arrow key; **~ programable** user-defined key; **~ de retorno/de tabulación** return/tab key; **~ del cursor** cursor key; **teclas de control direccional del cursor** cursor control keys

teclado [te'klaðo] *nm* keyboard (*tb Inform*);
~ **numérico** (*Inform*) numeric keypad
teclear [tekle'ar] *vi* to strum; (*fam*) to drum
■ *vt* (*Inform*) to key (in), type in, keyboard
tecleo [te'kleo] *nm* (*Mus: sonido*) strumming;
(: *forma de tocar*) fingering; (*fam*) drumming
tecnicismo [tekni'θismo] *nm* (*carácter técnico*)
technical nature; (*Ling*) technical term
técnico, -a ['tekniko, a] *adj* technical
■ *nm* technician; (*experto*) expert ■ *nf*
(*procedimientos*) technique; (*arte, oficio*) craft
tecnicolor [tekniko'lor] *nm* Technicolor®
tecnócrata [tek'nokrata] *nm/f* technocrat
tecnología [teknolo'xia] *nf* technology;
~ **de estado sólido** (*Inform*) solid-state
technology; ~ **de la información**
information technology
tecnológico, -a [tekno'loxiko, a] *adj*
technological
tecnólogo, -a [tek'noloyo, a] *nm/f*
technologist
tedio ['teðjo] *nm* (*aburrimiento*) boredom;
(*apatía*) apathy; (*fastidio*) depression
tedioso, -a [te'ðjoso, a] *adj* boring; (*cansado*)
wearisome, tedious
Teherán [tee'ran] *nm* Teheran
teja ['texa] *nf* (*azulejo*) tile; (*Bot*) lime (tree)
tejado [te'xaðo] *nm* (tiled) roof
tejano, -a [te'xano, a] *adj, nm/f* Texan ■ *nmpl*:
tejanos (*vaqueros*) jeans
Tejas ['texas] *nm* Texas
tejemaneje [texema'nexe] *nm* (*actividad*)
bustle; (*lío*) fuss, to-do; (*intriga*) intrigue
tejer [te'xer] *vt* to weave; (*tela de araña*) to
spin; (*Am*) to knit; (*fig*) to fabricate ■ *vi*: ~ **y**
destejer to chop and change
tejido [te'xiðo] *nm* fabric; (*estofa, tela*) (knitted)
material; (*Anat*) tissue; (*textura*) texture
tejo ['texo] *nm* (*Bot*) yew (tree)
tel. *abr* (= *teléfono*) tel.
tela ['tela] *nf* (*material*) material; (*de fruta,*
en líquido) skin; (*del ojo*) film; **hay ~ para**
rato there's lots to talk about; **poner en ~**
de juicio to (call in) question; ~ **de araña**
cobweb, spider's web
telar [te'lar] *nm* (*máquina*) loom; (*de teatro*)
gridiron; **telares** *nmpl* textile mill *sg*
telaraña [tela'raɲa] *nf* cobweb, spider's web
tele ... [tele] *pref* tele...
tele ['tele] *nf* (*fam*) TV
telecargar [telekar'yar] *vt* (*Inform*) to
download
telecomunicación [telekomunika'θjon] *nf*
telecommunication
teleconferencia [telekonfe'renθja]
nf (*reunión*) teleconference; (*sistema*)
teleconferencing

telecontrol [telekon'trol] *nm* remote control
telecopiadora [telekopja'ðora] *nf*: ~ **facsímil**
fax copier
telediario [tele'ðjarjo] *nm* television news
teledifusión [teleðifu'sjon] *nf* (television)
broadcast
teledirigido, -a [teleðiri'xiðo, a] *adj* remote-
controlled
teléf. *abr* (= *teléfono*) tel.
teleférico [tele'feriko] *nm* (*tren*) cable-
railway; (*de esquí*) ski-lift
telefilm [tele'film], **telefilme** [tele'filme]
nm TV film
telefonazo [telefo'naθo] *nm* (*fam*) telephone
call; **te daré un** ~ I'll give you a ring
telefonear [telefone'ar] *vi* to telephone
telefónicamente [tele'fonikamente] *adv* by
(tele)phone
telefónico, -a [tele'foniko, a] *adj* telephone
cpd ■ *nf*: **Telefónica** (*Esp*) Spanish national
telephone company, ≈ British Telecom
telefonista [telefo'nista] *nm/f* telephonist
teléfono [te'lefono] *nm* (tele)phone; ~ **móvil**
mobile phone; **está hablando por** ~ he's on
the phone
telefoto [tele'foto] *nf* telephoto
telegrafía [teleyra'fia] *nf* telegraphy
telégrafo [tele'leyrafo] *nm* telegraph; (*fam:*
persona) telegraph boy
telegrama [tele'yrama] *nm* telegram
teleimpresor [teleimpre'sor] *nm* teleprinter
telemática [tele'matika] *nf* telematics *sg*
telémetro [te'lemetro] *nm* rangefinder
telenovela [teleno'βela] *nf* soap (opera)
teleobjetivo [teleobxe'tiβo] *nm* telephoto
lens
telepatía [telepa'tia] *nf* telepathy
telepático, -a [tele'patiko, a] *adj* telepathic
teleproceso [telepro'θeso] *nm* teleprocessing
telescópico, -a [tele'skopiko, a] *adj*
telescopic
telescopio [tele'skopjo] *nm* telescope
telesilla [tele'siʎa] *nm* chairlift
telespectador, a [telespekta'ðor, a] *nm/f*
viewer
telesquí [teles'ki] *nm* ski-lift
teletex [tele'teks], **teletexto** [tele'teksto]
nm teletext
teletipista [teleti'pista] *nm/f* teletypist
teletipo [tele'tipo] *nm* teletype(writer)
teletrabajo [teletra'βaxo] *nm* teleworking
televentas [tele'βentas] *nfpl* telesales
televidente [tele'βiðente] *nm/f* viewer
televisar [teleβi'sar] *vt* to televise
televisión [teleβi'sjon] *nf* television; ~
en color/por satélite colour/satellite
television; ~ **digital** digital television

televisivo, -a [teleβi'siβo, a] *adj* television *cpd*
televisor [teleβi'sor] *nm* television set
télex ['teleks] *nm* telex; **máquina ~** telex
(machine); **enviar por ~** to telex
telón [te'lon] *nm* curtain; **~ de boca/**
seguridad front/safety curtain; **~ de acero**
(*Pol*) iron curtain; **~ de fondo** backcloth,
background
telonero, -a [telo'nero, a] *nm/f* support act;
los teloneros (*Mus*) the support band
tema ['tema] *nm* (*asunto*) subject, topic; (*Mus*)
theme; **temas de actualidad** current affairs
■ *nf* (*obsesión*) obsession; (*manía*) ill-will;
tener ~ a algn to have a grudge against sb
temario [te'marjo] *nm* (*Escol*) set of topics;
(*de una conferencia*) agenda
temático, -a [te'matiko, a] *adj* thematic
■ *nf* subject matter
tembladera [tembla'ðera] *nf* shaking; (*Am*)
quagmire
temblar [tem'blar] *vi* to shake, tremble;
(*de frío*) to shiver
tembleque [tem'bleke] *adj* shaking ■ *nm*
shaking
temblón, -ona [tem'blon, ona] *adj* shaking
temblor [tem'blor] *nm* trembling; (*de tierra*)
earthquake
tembloroso, -a [temblo'roso, a] *adj*
trembling
temer [te'mer] *vt* to fear ■ *vi* to be afraid;
temo que Juan llegue tarde I am afraid
Juan may be late
temerario, -a [teme'rarjo, a] *adj* (*imprudente*)
rash; (*descuidado*) reckless; (*arbitrario*) hasty
temeridad [temeri'ðað] *nf* (*imprudencia*)
rashness; (*audacia*) boldness
temeroso, -a [teme'roso, a] *adj* (*miedoso*)
fearful; (*que inspira temor*) frightful
temible [te'miβle] *adj* fearsome
temor [te'mor] *nm* (*miedo*) fear; (*duda*)
suspicion
témpano ['tempano] *nm* (*Mus*) kettledrum;
~ de hielo ice floe
temperamento [tempera'mento] *nm*
temperament; **tener ~** to be temperamental
temperar [tempe'rar] *vt* to temper, moderate
temperatura [tempera'tura] *nf* temperature
tempestad [tempes'tað] *nf* storm; **~ en un**
vaso de agua (*fig*) storm in a teacup
tempestuoso, -a [tempes'twoso, a] *adj*
stormy
templado, -a [tem'plaðo, a] *adj* (*moderado*)
moderate; (: *en el comer*) frugal; (: *en el beber*)
abstemious; (*agua*) lukewarm; (*clima*) mild;
(*Mus*) in tune, well-tuned
templanza [tem'planθa] *nf* moderation; (*en*
el beber) abstemiousness; (*del clima*) mildness

templar [tem'plar] *vt* (*moderar*) to moderate;
(*furia*) to restrain; (*calor*) to reduce; (*solución*)
to dilute; (*afinar*) to tune (up); (*acero*) to
temper ■ *vi* to moderate; **templarse** *vr* to
be restrained
temple ['temple] *nm* (*humor*) mood; (*coraje*)
courage; (*ajuste*) tempering; (*afinación*)
tuning; (*pintura*) tempera
templo ['templo] *nm* (*iglesia*) church; (*pagano*
etc) temple; **~ metodista** Methodist chapel
temporada [tempo'raða] *nf* time, period;
(*estación, social, Deporte*) season; **en plena ~**
at the height of the season
temporal [tempo'ral] *adj* (*no permanente*)
temporary; (*Rel*) temporal ■ *nm* storm
temporario, -a [tempo'rarjo, a] *adj* (*Am*)
temporary
temporanero. -a [tempra'nero, a] *adj* (*Bot*)
early; (*persona*) early-rising
temprano, -a [tem'prano, a] *adj* early ■ *adv*
early; (*demasiado pronto*) too soon, too early;
lo más ~ posible as soon as possible
ten [ten] *vb ver* **tener**
tenacidad [tenaθi'ðað] *nf* (*gen*) tenacity;
(*dureza*) toughness; (*terquedad*) stubbornness
tenacillas [tena'θiʎas] *nfpl* (*gen*) tongs; (*para*
el pelo) curling tongs; (*Med*) forceps
tenaz [te'naθ] *adj* (*material*) tough; (*persona*)
tenacious; (*pegajoso*) sticky; (*terco*) stubborn
tenaza [te'naθa] *nf*, **tenazas** [te'naθas] *nfpl*
(*Med*) forceps; (*Tec*) pliers; (*Zool*) pincers
tendal [ten'dal] *nm* awning
tendedero [tende'ðero] *nm* (*para ropa*) drying-
place; (*cuerda*) clothes line
tendencia [ten'denθja] *nf* tendency; (*proceso*)
trend; **~ imperante** prevailing tendency;
~ del mercado run of the market; **tener ~ a**
to tend o have a tendency to
tendenciosidad [tendenθjosi'ðað] *nf*
tendentiousness
tendencioso, -a [tenden'θjoso, a] *adj*
tendentious
tender [ten'der] *vt* (*extender*) to spread out;
(*ropa*) to hang out; (*vía férrea, cable*) to lay;
(*cuerda*) to stretch; (*trampa*) to set ■ *vi* to
tend; **tenderse** *vr* to lie down; (*fig: dejarse*
llevar) to let o.s. go; (: *dejar ir*) to let things go;
~ la cama/la mesa (*Am*) to make the bed/lay
the table
ténder ['tender] *nm* (*Ferro*) tender
tenderete [tende'rete] *nm* (*puesto*) stall;
(*carretilla*) barrow; (*exposición*) display of goods
tendero, -a [ten'dero, a] *nm/f* shopkeeper
tendido, -a [ten'diðo, a] *adj* (*acostado*) lying
down, flat; (*colgado*) hanging ■ *nm* (*ropa*)
washing; (*Taur*) front rows *pl* of seats;
(*colocación*) laying; (*Arq: enyesado*) coat of

t

plaster; **a galope** ~ flat out

tendón [ten'don] *nm* tendon

tendré *etc* [ten'dre] *vb ver* **tener**

tenducho [ten'dutʃo] *nm* small dirty shop

tenebroso, -a [tene'βroso, a] *adj (oscuro)* dark; *(fig)* gloomy; *(siniestro)* sinister

tenedor [tene'ðor] *nm (Culin)* fork; *(poseedor)* holder; ~ **de libros** book-keeper; ~ **de acciones** shareholder; ~ **de póliza** policyholder

teneduría [teneðu'ria] *nf* keeping; ~ **de libros** book-keeping

tenencia [te'nenθja] *nf (de casa)* tenancy; *(de oficio)* tenure; *(de propiedad)* possession; ~ **asegurada** security of tenure; ~ **ilícita de armas** illegal possession of weapons

 PALABRA CLAVE

tener [te'ner] *vt* **1** *(poseer, gen)* to have; *(en la mano)* to hold; **¿tienes un boli?** have you got a pen?; **va a tener un niño** she's going to have a baby; **tiene los ojos azules** he's got blue eyes; **¡ten** *(o* **tenga)!**, **¡aquí tienes** *(o* **tiene)!** here you are!

2 *(edad, medidas)* to be; **tiene siete años** she's seven (years old); **tiene 15 cm de largo** it's 15 cm long

3 *(sentimientos, sensaciones)*: **tener sed/ hambre/frío/calor** to be thirsty/hungry/ cold/hot; **tener celos** to be jealous; **tener cuidado** to be careful; **tener razón** to be right; **tener suerte** to be lucky

4 *(considerar)*: **lo tengo por brillante** I consider him to be brilliant; **tener en mucho a algn** to think very highly of sb

5 *(+ pp: + adj: + gerundio)*: **tengo terminada ya la mitad del trabajo** I've done half the work already; **tenía el sombrero puesto** he had his hat on; **tenía pensado llamarte** I had been thinking of phoning you; **nos tiene hartos** we're fed up with him; **me ha tenido tres horas esperando** he kept me waiting three hours

6: **tener que hacer algo** to have to do sth; **tengo que acabar este trabajo hoy** I have to finish this job today

7: **¿qué tienes, estás enfermo?** what's the matter with you, are you ill?

8 *(locuciones)*: **¿conque ésas tenemos?** so it's like that, then?; **no las tengo todas conmigo** I'm a bit unsure (about it); **lo tiene difícil** he'll have a hard job

tenerse *vr* **1**: **tenerse en pie** to stand up

2: **tenerse por** to think o.s.; **se tiene por un gran cantante** he thinks himself a great singer

tenga *etc* ['tenga] *vb ver* **tener**

tenia ['tenja] *nf* tapeworm

teniente [te'njente] *nm* lieutenant; ~ **coronel** lieutenant colonel

tenis ['tenis] *nm* tennis; ~ **de mesa** table tennis

tenista [te'nista] *nm/f* tennis player

tenor [te'nor] *nm (tono)* tone; *(sentido)* meaning; *(Mus)* tenor; **a** ~ **de** on the lines of

tenorio [te'norjo] *nm (fam)* ladykiller, Don Juan

tensar [ten'sar] *vt* to tauten; *(arco)* to draw

tensión [ten'sjon] *nf* tension; *(Tec)* stress; *(Med)*: ~ **arterial** blood pressure; ~ **nerviosa** nervous strain; **tener la** ~ **alta** to have high blood pressure

tenso, -a ['tenso, a] *adj* tense; *(relaciones)* strained

tentación [tenta'θjon] *nf* temptation

tentáculo [ten'takulo] *nm* tentacle

tentador, a [tenta'ðor, a] *adj* tempting ■ *nm/f* tempter/temptress

tentar [ten'tar] *vt (tocar)* to touch, feel; *(seducir)* to tempt; *(atraer)* to attract; *(probar)* to try (out); *(Med)* to probe; ~ **hacer algo** to try to do sth

tentativa [tenta'tiβa] *nf* attempt; ~ **de asesinato** attempted murder

tentempié [tentem'pje] *nm (fam)* snack

tenue ['tenwe] *adj (delgado)* thin, slender; *(alambre)* fine; *(insustancial)* tenuous; *(sonido)* faint; *(neblina)* light; *(lazo, vínculo)* slight

teñir [te'ɲir] *vt* to dye; *(fig)* to tinge; **teñirse el pelo** to dye one's hair

teología [teolo'xia] *nf* theology

teólogo, -a [te'oloɣo, a] *nm/f* theologist, theologian

teorema [teo'rema] *nm* theorem

teoría [teo'ria] *nf* theory; **en** ~ in theory

teóricamente [te'orikamente] *adv* theoretically

teorice *etc* [teo'riθe] *vb ver* **teorizar**

teórico, -a [te'oriko, a] *adj* theoretic(al) ■ *nm/f* theoretician, theorist

teorizar [teori'θar] *vi* to theorize

tequila [te'kila] *nm o f* tequila

TER [ter] *nm abr (Ferro)* = **tren español rápido**

terapeuta [tera'peuta] *nm/f* therapist

terapéutico, -a [tera'peutiko, a] *adj* therapeutic(al) ■ *nf* therapeutics *sg*

terapia [te'rapja] *nf* therapy; ~ **laboral** occupational therapy

tercer [ter'θer] *adj ver* **tercero**

tercermundista [terθermun'dista] *adj* Third World *cpd*

tercero, -a [ter'θero, a] *adj* third *(antes de nmsg* **tercer**) ■ *nm (árbitro)* mediator; *(Jur)* third party

terceto [ter'θeto] *nm* trio
terciado, -a [ter'θjaðo, a] *adj* slanting;
　azúcar ~ brown sugar
terciar [ter'θjar] *vt* (*Mat*) to divide into three;
　(*inclinarse*) to slope; (*llevar*) to wear across
　one's chest ■ *vi* (*participar*) to take part; (*hacer
　de árbitro*) to mediate; **terciarse** *vr* to arise
terciario, -a [ter'θjarjo, a] *adj* tertiary
tercio ['terθjo] *nm* third
terciopelo [terθjo'pelo] *nm* velvet
terco, -a ['terko, a] *adj* obstinate, stubborn;
　(*material*) tough
tergal® [ter'ɣal] *nm* Terylene®
tergiversación [terxiβersa'θjon] *nf*
　(*deformación*) distortion; (*evasivas*)
　prevarication
tergiversar [terxiβer'sar] *vt* to distort ■ *vi*
　to prevaricate
termal [ter'mal] *adj* thermal
termas ['termas] *nfpl* hot springs
térmico, -a ['termiko, a] *adj* thermic,
　thermal, heat *cpd*
terminación [termina'θjon] *nf* (*final*) end;
　(*conclusión*) conclusion, ending
terminal [termi'nal] *adj* terminal ■ *nm*
　(*Elec: Inform*) terminal; ~ **conversacional**
　interactive terminal; ~ **de pantalla** visual
　display unit ■ *nf* (*Aviat. Ferro*) terminal
terminante [termi'nante] *adj* (*final*) final,
　definitive; (*tajante*) categorical
terminar [termi'nar] *vt* (*completar*) to
　complete, finish; (*concluir*) to end ■ *vi* (*llegar
　a su fin*) to end; (*parar*) to stop; (*acabar*) to
　finish; **terminarse** *vr* to come to an end;
　~ **por hacer algo** to end up (by) doing sth
término ['termino] *nm* end, conclusion;
　(*parada*) terminus; (*límite*) boundary; (*en
　discusión*) point; (*Ling: Com*) term; ~ **medio**
　average; (*fig*) middle way; **en otros
　términos** in other words; **en último** ~ (*a fin
　de cuentas*) in the last analysis; (*como último
　recurso*) as a last resort; **en términos de** in
　terms of; **según los términos del contrato**
　according to the terms of the contract
terminología [terminolo'xia] *nf*
　terminology
termita [ter'mita] *nf* termite
termo ['termo] *nm* Thermos® (flask)
termodinámico, -a [termoði'namiko, a] *adj*
　thermodynamic ■ *nf* thermodynamics *sg*
termoimpresora [termoimpre'sora] *nf*
　thermal printer
termómetro [ter'mometro] *nm*
　thermometer
termonuclear [termonukle'ar] *adj*
　thermonuclear
termostato [termos'tato] *nm* thermostat

ternero, -a [ter'nero, a] *nm/f* (*animal*) calf
　■ *nf* (*carne*) veal, beef
terneza [ter'neθa] *nf* tenderness
ternilla [ter'niʎa] *nf* gristle; (*cartílago*)
　cartilage
terno ['terno] *nm* (*traje*) three-piece suit;
　(*conjunto*) set of three
ternura [ter'nura] *nf* (*trato*) tenderness;
　(*palabra*) endearment; (*cariño*) fondness
terquedad [terke'ðað] *nf* obstinacy; (*dureza*)
　harshness
terrado [te'rraðo] *nm* terrace
Terranova [terra'noβa] *nf* Newfoundland
terraplén [terra'plen] *nm* (*Agr*) terrace; (*Ferro*)
　embankment; (*Mil*) rampart; (*cuesta*) slope
terráqueo, -a [te'rrakeo, a] *adj*: **globo** ~ globe
terrateniente [terrate'njente] *nm*
　landowner
terraza [te'rraθa] *nf* (*balcón*) balcony; (*techo*)
　flat roof; (*Agr*) terrace
terremoto [terre'moto] *nm* earthquake
terrenal [terre'nal] *adj* earthly
terreno, -a [te'rreno, a] *adj* (*de la tierra*)
　earthly, worldly ■ *nm* (*tierra*) land; (*parcela*)
　plot; (*suelo*) soil; (*fig*) field; **un** ~ a piece of
　land; **sobre el** ~ on the spot; **ceder/perder** ~
　to give/lose ground; **preparar el** (**a**) (*fig*) to
　pave the way (for)
terrestre [te'rrestre] *adj* terrestrial; (*ruta*)
　land *cpd*
terrible [te'rriβle] *adj* (*espantoso*) terrible;
　(*aterrador*) dreadful; (*tremendo*) awful
territorial [territo'rjal] *adj* territorial
territorio [terri'torjo] *nm* territory; ~ **bajo
　mandato** mandated territory
terrón [te'rron] *nm* (*de azúcar*) lump; (*de tierra*)
　clod, lump; **terrones** *nmpl* land *sg*
terror [te'rror] *nm* terror
terrorífico, -a [terro'rifiko, a] *adj* terrifying
terrorismo [terro'rismo] *nm* terrorism
terrorista [terro'rista] *adj, nm/f* terrorist
terroso, -a [te'rroso, a] *adj* earthy
terruño [te'rruno] *nm* (*pedazo*) clod; (*parcela*)
　plot; (*fig*) native soil; **apego al** ~ attachment
　to one's native soil
terso, -a ['terso, a] *adj* (*liso*) smooth; (*pulido*)
　polished; (*fig: estilo*) flowing
tersura [ter'sura] *nf* smoothness; (*brillo*)
　shine
tertulia [ter'tulja] *nf* (*reunión informal*) social
　gathering; (*grupo*) group, circle; (*sala*)
　clubroom; ~ **literaria** literary circle
tesina [te'sina] *nf* dissertation
tesis ['tesis] *nf inv* thesis
tesón [te'son] *nm* (*firmeza*) firmness;
　(*tenacidad*) tenacity
tesorería [tesore'ria] *nf* treasurership

tesorero, -a [teso'rero, a] *nm/f* treasurer
tesoro [te'soro] *nm* treasure; **T~ público** (*Pol*) Exchequer
test (*pl* **tests**) [tes(t), tes(t)] *nm* test
testaferro [testa'ferro] *nm* figurehead
testamentaría [testamenta'ria] *nf* execution of a will
testamentario, -a [testamen'tarjo, a] *adj* testamentary ■ *nm/f* executor/executrix
testamento [testa'mento] *nm* will
testar [tes'tar] *vi* to make a will
testarada [testa'raða] *nf*, **testarazo** [testa'raθo] *nm*: **darse una ~ o un testarazo** (*fam*) to bump one's head
testarudo, -a [testa'ruðo, a] *adj* stubborn
testículo [tes'tikulo] *nm* testicle
testificar [testifi'kar] *vt* to testify; (*fig*) to attest ■ *vi* to give evidence
testifique *etc* [testi'fike] *vb ver* **testificar**
testigo [tes'tiɣo] *nm/f* witness; **~ de cargo/descargo** witness for the prosecution/defence; **~ ocular** eye witness; **poner a algn por ~** to cite sb as a witness
testimonial [testimo'njal] *adj* (*prueba*) testimonial; (*gesto*) token
testimoniar [testimo'njar] *vt* to testify to; (*fig*) to show
testimonio [testi'monjo] *nm* testimony; **en ~ de** as a token *o* mark of; **falso ~** perjured evidence, false witness
teta ['teta] *nf* (*de biberón*) teat; (*Anat*) nipple; (*fam*) breast; (*fam!*) tit (!)
tétanos ['tetanos] *nm* tetanus
tetera [te'tera] *nf* teapot; **~ eléctrica** (electric) kettle
tetilla [te'tiʎa] *nf* (*Anat*) nipple; (*de biberón*) teat
tétrico, -a ['tetriko, a] *adj* gloomy, dismal
textear [tekste'ar] *vt* to text
textil [teks'til] *adj* textile
texto ['teksto] *nm* text
textual [teks'twal] *adj* textual; **palabras textuales** exact words
textura [teks'tura] *nf* (*de tejido*) texture; (*de mineral*) structure
tez [teθ] *nf* (*cutis*) complexion; (*color*) colouring
tfno. *abr* (= *teléfono*) tel.
ti [ti] *pron* you; (*reflexivo*) yourself
tía ['tia] *nf* (*pariente*) aunt; (*fam: mujer*) girl
Tibet [ti'βet] *nm*: **El ~** Tibet
tibetano, -a [tiβe'tano, a] *adj, nm/f* Tibetan ■ *nm* (*Ling*) Tibetan
tibia ['tiβja] *nf* tibia
tibieza [ti'βjeθa] *nf* (*temperatura*) tepidness; (*fig*) coolness
tibio, -a ['tiβjo, a] *adj* lukewarm, tepid

tiburón [tiβu'ron] *nm* shark
tic [tik] *nm* (*ruido*) click; (*de reloj*) tick; **~ nervioso** (*Med*) nervous tic
tico, -a ['tiko, a] *adj, nm/f* (*Am fam*) Costa Rican
tictac [tik'tak] *nm* (*de reloj*) tick tock
tiemble *etc* ['tjemble] *vb ver* **temblar**
tiempo ['tjempo] *nm* (*gen*) time; (*época, período*) age, period; (*Meteorología*) weather; (*Ling*) tense; (*edad*) age; (*de juego*) half; **a ~** in time; **a un o al mismo ~** at the same time; **al poco ~** very soon (after); **andando el ~** in due course; **cada cierto ~** every so often; **con ~** in time; **con el ~** eventually; **de ~ en ~** from time to time; **en mis tiempos** in my time; **en los buenos tiempos** in the good old days; **hace buen/mal ~** the weather is fine/bad; **estar a ~** to be in time; **hace ~** some time ago; **hacer ~** to while away the time; **¿qué ~ tiene?** how old is he?; **motor de 2 tiempos** two-stroke engine; **~ compartido** (*Inform*) time sharing; **~ de ejecución** (*Inform*) run time; **~ inactivo** (*Com*) downtime; **~ libre** spare time; **~ de paro** (*Com*) idle time; **a ~ partido** (*trabajar*) part-time; **~ preferencial** (*Com*) prime time; **en ~ real** (*Inform*) real time
tienda *etc* ['tjenda] *vb ver* **tender** ■ *nf* shop; (*más grande*) store; (*Naut*) awning; **~ de campaña** tent; **~ de comestibles** grocer's shop (*esp Brit*), grocery (*US*)
tiene *etc* ['tjene] *vb ver* **tener**
tienta ['tjenta] *nf* (*Med*) probe; (*fig*) tact; **andar a tientas** to grope one's way along
tiento *etc* ['tjento] *vb ver* **tentar** ■ *nm* (*tacto*) touch; (*precaución*) wariness; (*pulso*) steady hand; (*Zool*) feeler, tentacle
tierno, -a ['tjerno, a] *adj* tender; (*fresco*) fresh
tierra ['tjerra] *nf* earth; (*suelo*) soil; (*mundo*) world; (*país*) country, land; (*Elec*) earth, ground (*US*); **~ adentro** inland; **~ natal** native land; **echar ~ a un asunto** to hush an affair up; **no es de estas tierras** he's not from these parts; **la T~ Santa** the Holy Land
tieso, -a ['tjeso, a] *adj* (*rígido*) rigid; (*duro*) stiff; (*fig: testarudo*) stubborn; (*fam: orgulloso*) conceited ■ *adv* strongly
tiesto ['tjesto] *nm* flowerpot; (*pedazo*) piece of pottery
tifoidea [tifoi'ðea] *nf* typhoid
tifón [ti'fon] *nm* (*huracán*) typhoon; (*de mar*) tidal wave
tifus ['tifus] *nm* typhus; **~ icteroides** yellow fever
tigre ['tiɣre] *nm* tiger; (*Am*) jaguar
TIJ *sigla m* (= *Tribunal Internacional de Justicia*) ICJ
tijera [ti'xera] *nf* (*una tijera*) (pair of) scissors *pl*; (*Zool*) claw; (*persona*) gossip; **de ~** folding;

tijeras *nfpl* scissors; *(para plantas)* shears; **unas tijeras** a pair of scissors

tijeretear [tixerete'ar] *vt* to snip ■ *vi (fig)* to meddle

tila ['tila] *nf* (Bot) lime tree; *(Culin)* lime flower tea

tildar [til'dar] *vt*: ~ **de** to brand as

tilde ['tilde] *nf (defecto)* defect; *(trivialidad)* triviality; *(Tip)* tilde

tilín [ti'lin] *nm* tinkle

tilo ['tilo] *nm* lime tree

timador, a [tima'ðor, a] *nm/f* swindler

timar [ti'mar] *vt (robar)* to steal; *(estafar)* to swindle; *(persona)* to con; **timarse** *vr (fam)*: **timarse con algn** to make eyes at sb

timbal [tim'bal] *nm* small drum

timbrar [tim'brar] *vt* to stamp; *(sellar)* to seal; *(carta)* to postmark

timbrazo [tim'braθo] *nm* ring; **dar un ~** to ring the bell

timbre ['timbre] *nm (sello)* stamp; *(campanilla)* bell; *(tono)* timbre; *(Com)* stamp duty

timidez [timi'ðeθ] *nf* shyness

tímido, -a ['timiðo, a] *adj* shy, timid

timo ['timo] *nm* swindle; **dar un ~ a algn** to swindle sb

timón [ti'mon] *nm* helm, rudder; *(Am)* steering wheel; **coger el ~** *(fig)* to take charge

timonel [timo'nel] *nm* helmsman

timorato, -a [timo'rato, a] *adj* God-fearing; *(mojigato)* sanctimonious

tímpano ['timpano] *nm (Anat)* eardrum; *(Mus)* small drum

tina ['tina] *nf* tub; *(Am: baño)* bath(tub)

tinaja [ti'naxa] *nf* large earthen jar

tinerfeño, -a [tiner'feɲo, a] *adj* of o from Tenerife ■ *nm/f* native o inhabitant of Tenerife

tinglado [tiŋ'glaðo] *nm (cobertizo)* shed; *(fig: truco)* trick; *(intriga)* intrigue; **armar un ~** to lay a plot

tinieblas [ti'njeβlas] *nfpl* darkness *sg*; *(sombras)* shadows; **estamos en ~ sobre sus proyectos** *(fig)* we are in the dark about his plans

tino ['tino] *nm (habilidad)* skill; *(Mil)* marksmanship; *(juicio)* insight; *(moderación)* moderation; **sin ~** immoderately; **coger el ~** to get the feel o hang of it

tinta ['tinta] *nf* ink; *(Tec)* dye; *(Arte)* colour; **~ china** Indian ink; **tintas** *nfpl (fig)* shades; **medias tintas** *(fig)* half measures; **saber algo de buena ~** to have sth on good authority

tinte ['tinte] *nm (acto)* dyeing; *(fig)* tinge; *(barniz)* veneer

tintero [tin'tero] *nm* inkwell; **se le quedó en el ~** he clean forgot about it

tintinear [tintine'ar] *vt* to tinkle

tinto, -a ['tinto, a] *adj (teñido)* dyed; *(manchado)* stained ■ *nm* red wine

tintorera [tinto'rera] *nf* shark

tintorería [tintore'ria] *nf* dry cleaner's

tintorero [tinto'rero] *nm* dry cleaner('s)

tintura [tin'tura] *nf (acto)* dyeing; *(Química)* dye; *(farmacéutico)* tincture

tiña *etc* ['tiɲa] *vb ver* **teñir** ■ *nf (Med)* ringworm

tío ['tio] *nm (pariente)* uncle; *(fam: hombre)* bloke, guy (US)

tiovivo [tio'βiβo] *nm* roundabout

típico, -a ['tipiko, a] *adj* typical; *(pintoresco)* picturesque

tiple ['tiple] *nm* soprano *(voice)* ■ *nf* soprano

tipo ['tipo] *nm (clase)* type, kind; *(norma)* norm; *(patrón)* pattern; *(fam: hombre)* fellow, bloke, guy (US); *(Anat)* build; *(: de mujer)* figure; *(Imprenta)* type; **~ bancario/de descuento** bank/discount rate; **~ de interés** interest rate; **~ de interés vigente** *(Com)* standard rate; **~ de cambio** exchange rate; **~ base** (Com) base rate; **~ a término** *(Com)* forward rate; **dos tipos sospechosos** two suspicious characters; **~ de letra** *(Inform: Tip)* typeface; **~ de datos** *(Inform)* data type

tipografía [tipoɣra'fia] *nf (tipo)* printing; *(lugar)* printing press

tipográfico, -a [tipo'ɣrafiko, a] *adj* printing

tipógrafo, -a [ti'poɣrafo, a] *nm/f* printer

tique, tíquet ['tike] *(pl* **~(t)s)** ['tikes] *nm* ticket; *(en tienda)* cash slip

tiquismiquis [tikis'mikis] *nm* fussy person ■ *nmpl (querellas)* squabbling *sg*; *(escrúpulos)* silly scruples

tira ['tira] *nf* strip; *(fig)* abundance ■ *nm*: **~ y afloja** give and take; *(cautela)* caution; **la ~ de ...** *(fam)* lots of ...

tirabuzón [tiraβu'θon] *nm* corkscrew; *(rizo)* curl

tiradero [tira'ðero] *nm (Am)* rubbish dump

tirado, -a [ti'raðo, a] *adj (barato)* dirt-cheap; *(fam: fácil)* very easy ■ *nf (acto)* cast, throw; *(distancia)* distance; *(serie)* series; *(Tip)* printing, edition; **de una tirada** at one go; **está ~** *(fam)* it's a cinch

TIR *sigla mpl* = **Transportes internacionales por carretera**

tirador, a [tira'ðor, a] *nm/f (persona)* shooter ■ *nm (mango)* handle; *(Elec)* flex; **~ certero** sniper

tiralíneas [tira'lineas] *nm inv* ruling-pen

tiranía [tira'nia] *nf* tyranny

tiránico, -a [ti'raniko, a] *adj* tyrannical

tiranizar [tirani'θar] vt (pueblo, empleado) to tyrannize

tirano, -a [ti'rano, a] adj tyrannical ■ nm/f tyrant

tirante [ti'rante] adj (cuerda) tight, taut; (relaciones) strained ■ nm (Arq) brace; (Tec) stay; (correa) shoulder strap; **tirantes** nmpl braces, suspenders (US)

tirantez [tiran'teθ] nf tightness; (fig) tension

tirar [ti'rar] vt to throw; (volcar) to upset; (derribar) to knock down o over; (tiro) to fire; (cohete) to launch; (bomba) to drop; (edificio) to pull down; (desechar) to throw out o away; (disipar) to squander; (imprimir) to print; (dar: golpe) to deal ■ vi (disparar) to shoot; (dar un tirón) to pull; (fig) to draw; (interesar) to appeal; (fam: andar) to go; (tender a) to tend to; (Deporte) to shoot; **tirarse** vr to throw o.s.; (fig) to demean o.s.; (fam!) to screw (!); ~ **abajo** to bring down, destroy; **tira más a su padre** he takes more after his father; ~ **de algo** to pull o tug (on) sth; **ir tirando** to manage; ~ **a la derecha** to turn o go right; **a todo** ~ at the most

tirita [ti'rita] nf (sticking) plaster, bandaid (US)

tiritar [tiri'tar] vi to shiver

tiritona [tiri'tona] nf shivering (fit)

tiro ['tiro] nm (lanzamiento) throw; (disparo) shot; (tiroteo) shooting; (Deporte) shot; (Tenis: Golf) drive; (alcance) range; (de escalera) flight (of stairs); (golpe) blow; (engaño) hoax; ~ **al blanco** target practice; **caballo de** ~ cart-horse; **andar de tiros largos** to be all dressed up; **al** ~ (Am) at once; **de a** ~ (Am fam) completely; **se pegó un** ~ he shot himself; **le salió el** ~ **por la culata** it backfired on him

tiroides [ti'roiðes] nm inv thyroid

Tirol [ti'rol] nm: **El** ~ the Tyrol

tirolés, -esa [tiro'les, esa] adj, nm/f Tyrolean

tirón [ti'ron] nm (sacudida) pull, tug; **de un** ~ in one go; **dar un** ~ **a** to pull at, tug at

tirotear [tirote'ar] vt to shoot at; **tirotearse** vr to exchange shots

tiroteo [tiro'teo] nm exchange of shots, shooting; (escaramuza) skirmish

tirria ['tirrja] nf: **tener una** ~ **a algn** to have a grudge against sb

tísico, -a ['tisiko, a] adj, nm/f consumptive

tisis ['tisis] nf consumption, tuberculosis

tít. abr = **título**

titánico, -a [ti'taniko, a] adj titanic

títere ['titere] nm puppet; **no dejar** ~ **con cabeza** to turn everything upside-down

titilar [titi'lar] vi (luz, estrella) to twinkle; (párpado) to flutter

titiritero, -a [titiri'tero, a] nm/f (acróbata) acrobat; (malabarista) juggler

titubeante [tituβe'ante] adj (inestable) shaky, tottering; (farfullante) stammering; (dudoso) hesitant

titubear [tituβe'ar] vi to stagger; (tartamudear) to stammer; (vacilar) to hesitate

titubeo [titu'βeo] nm staggering; stammering; hesitation

titulado, -a [titu'laðo, a] adj (libro) entitled; (persona) titled

titular [titu'lar] adj titular ■ nm/f (de oficina) occupant; (de pasaporte) holder ■ nm headline ■ vt to title; **titularse** vr to be entitled

título ['titulo] nm (gen) title; (de diario) headline; (certificado) professional qualification; (universitario) university degree; (Com) bond; (fig) right; **títulos** nmpl qualifications; **a** ~ **de** by way of; (en calidad de) in the capacity of; **a** ~ **de curiosidad** as a matter of interest; ~ **de propiedad** title deed; **títulos convertibles de interés fijo** (Com) convertible loan stock sg

tiza ['tiθa] nf chalk; **una** ~ a piece of chalk

tizna ['tiθna] nf grime

tiznar [tiθ'nar] vt to blacken; (manchar) to smudge, stain; (fig) to tarnish

tizón [ti'θon], **tizo** ['tiθo] nm brand; (fig) stain

TLC nm abr (= Tratado de Libre Comercio) NAFTA

Tm. abr = **tonelada(s) métrica(s)**

TNT sigla m (= trinitrotolueno) TNT

toalla [to'aʎa] nf towel

tobillo [to'βiʎo] nm ankle

tobogán [toβo'ɣan] nm toboggan; (montaña rusa) switchback; (resbaladilla) chute, slide

toca ['toka] nf headdress

tocadiscos [toka'ðiskos] nm inv record player

tocado, -a [to'kaðo, a] adj (fruta etc) rotten ■ nm headdress; **estar** ~ **de la cabeza** (fam) to be weak in the head

tocador [toka'ðor] nm (mueble) dressing table; (cuarto) boudoir; (neceser) toilet case; (fam) ladies' room

tocante [to'kante]: ~ **a** prep with regard to; **en lo** ~ **a** as for, so far as concerns

tocar [to'kar] vt to touch; (sentir) to feel; (con la mano) to handle; (Mus) to play; (campana) to ring; (tambor) to beat; (trompeta) to blow; (topar con) to run into, strike; (referirse a) to allude to; (estar emparentado con) to be related to ■ vi (a la puerta) to knock (on o at the door); (ser el turno) to fall to, be the turn of; (ser hora) to be due; (atañer) to concern; **tocarse** vr (cubrirse la cabeza) to cover one's head; (tener contacto) to touch (each other); **tocarle a**

algn to fall to sb's lot; ~ **en** (*Naut*) to call at; **por lo que a mí me toca** as far as I am concerned; **esto toca en la locura** this verges on madness

tocateja [toka'texa] (*fam*): **a** ~ *adv* in readies

tocayo, -a [to'kajo, a] *nm/f* namesake

tocino [to'θino] *nm* (bacon) fat; ~ **de panceta** bacon

todavía [toða'βia] *adv* (*aun*) even; (*aún*) still, yet; ~ **más** yet *o* still more; ~ **no** not yet; ~ **en 1970** as late as 1970; **está lloviendo** ~ it's still raining

toditito, -a [toði'tito, a], **todito a** [to'ðito, a] *adj* (*Am fam*) (absolutely) all

 PALABRA CLAVE

todo, -a ['toðo, a] *adj* **1** (*sg*) all; **toda la carne** all the meat; **toda la noche** all night, the whole night; **todo el libro** the whole book; **toda una botella** a whole bottle; **todo lo contrario** quite the opposite; **está toda sucia** she's all dirty; **a toda velocidad** at full speed; **por todo el país** throughout the whole country; **es todo un hombre** he's every inch a man; **soy todo oídos** I'm all ears

2 (*pl*) all; every; **todos los libros** all the books; **todas las noches** every night; **todos los que quieran salir** all those who want to leave; **todos vosotros** all of you

■ *pron* **1** everything, all; **todos** everyone, everybody; **lo sabemos todo** we know everything; **todos querían más tiempo** everybody *o* everyone wanted more time; **nos marchamos todos** all of us left; **corriendo y todo, no llegaron a tiempo** even though they ran, they still didn't arrive in time

2 (*con preposición*): **a pesar de todo** even so, in spite of everything; **con todo él me sigue gustando** even so I still like him; **le llamaron de todo** they called him all the names under the sun; **no me agrada del todo** I don't entirely like it

■ *adv* all; **vaya todo seguido** keep straight on *o* ahead

■ *nm*: **como un todo** as a whole; **arriba del todo** at the very top; **todo a cien** ≈ pound store (*Brit*), ≈ dollar store (*US*)

todopoderoso, -a [toðopoðe'roso, a] *adj* all powerful; (*Rel*) almighty

todoterreno [toðote'rreno] *nm* (*tb*: **vehículo todoterreno**) four-by-four

toga ['toɣa] *nf* toga; (*Escol*) gown

Tokio ['tokjo] *n* Tokyo

toldo ['toldo] *nm* (*para el sol*) sunshade; (*en tienda*) marquee; (*fig*) pride

tole ['tole] *nm* (*fam*) commotion

toledano, -a [tole'ðano, a] *adj* of *o* from Toledo ■ *nm/f* native *o* inhabitant of Toledo

tolerable [tole'raβle] *adj* tolerable

tolerancia [tole'ranθja] *nf* tolerance

tolerante [tole'rante] *adj* tolerant; (*fig*) open-minded

tolerar [tole'rar] *vt* to tolerate; (*resistir*) to endure

Tolón [to'lon] *nm* Toulon

toma ['toma] *nf* (*gen*) taking; (*Med*) dose; (*Elec*: *tb*: **toma de corriente**) socket; (*Mec*) inlet; ~ **de posesión** (*por presidente*) taking up office; ~ **de tierra** (*Aviat*) landing

tomadura [toma'ðura] *nf*: ~ **de pelo** hoax

tomar [to'mar] *vt* (*gen, Cine*: *Foto*: *TV*) to take; (*actitud*) to adopt; (*aspecto*) to take on; (*notas*) to take down; (*beber*) to drink ■ *vi* to take; (*Am*) to drink; **tomarse** *vr* to take; **tomarse por** to consider o.s. to be; **¡toma!** here you are!; ~ **asiento** to sit down; ~ **a algn por loco** to think sb mad; ~ **a bien/a mal** to take well/badly; ~ **en serio** to take seriously; ~ **el pelo a algn** to pull sb's leg; **tomarla con algn** to pick a quarrel with sb; **por escrito** to write down; **toma y daca** give and take

tomate [to'mate] *nm* tomato

tomatera [toma'tera] *nf* tomato plant

tomavistas [toma'βistas] *nm inv* movie camera

tomillo [to'miʎo] *nm* thyme

tomo ['tomo] *nm* (*libro*) volume; (*fig*) importance

ton [ton] *abr* = **tonelada** ■ *nm*: **sin** ~ **ni son** without rhyme or reason

tonada [to'naða] *nf* tune

tonalidad [tonali'ðað] *nf* tone

tonel [to'nel] *nm* barrel

tonelada [tone'laða] *nf* ton; ~(**s**) **métrica(s)** metric ton(s)

tonelaje [tone'laxe] *nm* tonnage

tonelero [tone'lero] *nm* cooper

tongo ['tongo] *nm* (*Deporte*) fix

tónico, -a ['toniko, a] *adj* tonic ■ *nm* (*Med*) tonic ■ *nf* (*Mus*) tonic; (*fig*) keynote

tonificador, a [tonifika'ðor, a], **tonificante** [tonifi'kante] *adj* invigorating, stimulating

tonificar [tonifi'kar] *vt* to tone up

tonifique *etc* [toni'fike] *vb ver* **tonificar**

tonillo [to'niʎo] *nm* monotonous voice

tono ['tono] *nm* (*Mus*) tone; (*altura*) pitch; (*color*) shade; **fuera de** ~ inappropriate; ~ **de llamada** ringtone; ~ **de marcar** (*Telec*) dialling tone; **darse** ~ to put on airs

tontear [tonte'ar] *vi* (*fam*) to fool about; (*enamorados*) to flirt

tontería [tonte'ria] *nf* (*estupidez*) foolishness; (*una tontería*) silly thing; **tonterías** *nfpl* rubbish *sg*, nonsense *sg*

tonto, -a ['tonto, a] *adj* stupid; (*ridículo*) silly ■ *nm/f* fool; (*payaso*) clown; **a tontas y a locas** anyhow; **hacer(se) el ~** to act the fool

topacio [to'paθjo] *nm* topaz

topar [to'par] *vt* (*tropezar*) to bump into; (*encontrar*) to find, come across; (*cabra etc*) to butt ■ *vi*: **~ contra** *o* **en** to run into; **~ con** to run up against; **el problema topa en eso** that's where the problem lies

tope ['tope] *adj* maximum ■ *nm* (*fin*) end; (*límite*) limit; (*Ferro*) buffer; (*Auto*) bumper; **al ~** end to end; **fecha ~** closing date; **precio ~** top price; **sueldo ~** maximum salary; **~ de tabulación** tab stop

tópico, -a ['topiko, a] *adj* topical; (*Med*) local ■ *nm* platitude, cliché; **de uso ~** for external application

topo ['topo] *nm* (*Zool*) mole; (*fig*) blunderer

topografía [topoɣra'fia] *nf* topography

topógrafo, -a [to'poɣrafo, a] *nm/f* topographer; (*agrimensor*) surveyor

toponimia [topo'nimja] *nf* place names *pl*; (*estudio*) study of place names

toque *etc* ['toke] *vb ver* **tocar** ■ *nm* touch; (*Mus*) beat; (*de campana*) ring, chime; (*Mil*) bugle call; (*fig*) crux; **dar un ~ a** to test; **dar el último ~ a** to put the final touch to; **~ de queda** curfew

toquetear [tokete'ar] *vt* to handle; (*fam!*) to touch up

toquilla [to'kiʎa] *nf* (*chal*) shawl

tórax ['toraks] *nm inv* thorax

torbellino [torbe'ʎino] *nm* whirlwind; (*fig*) whirl

torcedura [torθe'ðura] *nf* twist; (*Med*) sprain

torcer [tor'θer] *vt* to twist; (*la esquina*) to turn; (*Med*) to sprain; (*cuerda*) to plait; (*ropa, manos*) to wring; (*persona*) to corrupt; (*sentido*) to distort ■ *vi* (*cambiar de dirección*) to turn; **torcerse** *vr* to twist; (*doblar*) to bend; (*desviarse*) to go astray; (*fracasar*) to go wrong; **~ el gesto** to scowl; **torcerse un pie** to twist one's foot; **el coche torció a la derecha** the car turned right

torcido, -a [tor'θiðo, a] *adj* twisted; (*fig*) crooked ■ *nm* curl

tordo, -a ['torðo, a] *adj* dappled ■ *nm* thrush

torear [tore'ar] *vt* (*fig: evadir*) to dodge; (*toro*) to fight ■ *vi* to fight bulls

toreo [to'reo] *nm* bullfighting

torero, -a [to'rero, a] *nm/f* bullfighter

toril [to'ril] *nm* bullpen

tormenta [tor'menta] *nf* storm; (*fig: confusión*) turmoil

tormento [tor'mento] *nm* torture; (*fig*) anguish

tormentoso, -a [tormen'toso, a] *adj* stormy

tornar [tor'nar] *vt* (*devolver*) to return, give back; (*transformar*) to transform ■ *vi* to go back; **tornarse** *vr* (*ponerse*) to become; (*volver*) to return

tornasol [torna'sol] *nm* (*Bot*) sunflower; **papel de ~** litmus paper

tornasolado, -a [tornaso'laðo, a] *adj* (*brillante*) iridescent; (*reluciente*) shimmering

torneo [tor'neo] *nm* tournament

tornero, -a [tor'nero, a] *nm/f* machinist

tornillo [tor'niʎo] *nm* screw; **apretar los tornillos a algn** to apply pressure on sb; **le falta un ~** (*fam*) he's got a screw loose

torniquete [torni'kete] *nm* (*puerta*) turnstile; (*Med*) tourniquet

torno ['torno] *nm* (*Tec: grúa*) winch; (: *de carpintero*) lathe; (*tambor*) drum; **~ de banco** vice, vise (*US*); **en ~ (a)** round, about

toro ['toro] *nm* bull; (*fam*) he-man; **los toros** bullfighting *sg*

toronja [to'ronxa] *nf* grapefruit

torpe ['torpe] *adj* (*poco hábil*) clumsy, awkward; (*movimiento*) sluggish; (*necio*) dim; (*lento*) slow; (*indecente*) crude; (*no honrado*) dishonest

torpedo [tor'peðo] *nm* torpedo

torpemente [torpe'mente] *adv* (*sin destreza*) clumsily; (*lentamente*) slowly

torpeza [tor'peθa] *nf* (*falta de agilidad*) clumsiness; (*lentitud*) slowness; (*rigidez*) stiffness; (*error*) mistake; (*crudeza*) obscenity

torre ['torre] *nf* tower; (*de petróleo*) derrick; (*de electricidad*) pylon; (*Ajedrez*) rook; (*Aviat: Mil: Naut*) turret

torrefacto, -a [torre'fakto, a] *adj*: **café ~** high roast coffee

torrencial [torren'θjal] *adj* torrential

torrente [to'rrente] *nm* torrent

tórrido, -a ['torriðo, a] *adj* torrid

torrija [to'rrixa] *nf* fried bread; **torrijas** French toast *sg*

torsión [tor'sjon] *nf* twisting

torso ['torso] *nm* torso

torta ['torta] *nf* cake; (*fam*) slap; **~ de huevos** (*Am*) omelette; **no entendió ni ~** he didn't understand a word of it

tortazo [tor'taθo] *nm* (*bofetada*) slap; (*de coche*) crash

tortícolis [tor'tikolis] *nm inv* stiff neck

tortilla [tor'tiʎa] *nf* omelette; (*Am*) maize pancake; **~ francesa/española** plain/potato omelette; **cambiar** *o* **volver la ~ a algn** to turn the tables on sb

tortillera [torti'ʎera] *nf* (*fam!*) lesbian

tórtola ['tortola] nf turtledove
tortuga [tor'tuɣa] nf tortoise; ~ **marina** turtle
tortuoso, -a [tor'twoso, a] adj winding
tortura [tor'tura] nf torture
torturar [tortu'rar] vt to torture
torvo, -a ['torβo, a] adj grim, fierce
torzamos etc [tor'θamos] vb ver **torcer**
tos [tos] nf inv cough; ~ **ferina** whooping cough
Toscana [tos'kana] nf: **La** ~ Tuscany
tosco, -a ['tosko, a] adj coarse
toser [to'ser] vi to cough; **no hay quien le tosa** he's in a class by himself
tostado, -a [tos'taðo, a] adj toasted; (por el sol) dark brown; (piel) tanned ■ nf tan; (pan) piece of toast; **tostadas** nfpl toast sg
tostador [tosta'ðor] nm toaster
tostar [tos'tar] vt to toast; (café) to roast; (al sol) to tan; **tostarse** vr to get brown
tostón [tos'ton] nm: **ser un** ~ to be a drag
total [to'tal] adj total ■ adv in short; (al fin y al cabo) when all is said and done ■ nm total; **en** ~ in all; ~ **que** to cut a long story short; ~ **de comprobación** (Inform) hash total; ~ **debe/haber** (Com) debit/assets total
totalidad [totali'ðað] nf whole
totalitario, -a [totali'tarjo, a] adj totalitarian
totalmente [to'talmente] adv totally
tóxico, -a ['toksiko, a] adj toxic ■ nm poison
toxicómano, -a [toksi'komano, a] adj addicted to drugs ■ nm/f drug addict
toxina [to'ksina] nf toxin
tozudo, -a [to'θuðo, a] adj obstinate
traba ['traβa] nf bond, tie; (cadena) fetter; **poner trabas a** to restrain
trabajador, a [traβaxa'ðor, a] nm/f worker ■ adj hard-working
trabajar [traβa'xar] vt to work; (arar) to till; (empeñarse en) to work at; (empujar: persona) to push; (convencer) to persuade ■ vi to work; (esforzarse) to strive; **¡a** ~! let's get to work!; ~ **por hacer algo** to strive to do sth
trabajo [tra'βaxo] nm work; (tarea) task; (Pol) labour; (fig) effort; **tomarse el** ~ **de** to take the trouble to; ~ **por turno/a destajo** shift work/piecework; ~ **en proceso** (Com) work-in-progress
trabajoso, -a [traβa'xoso, a] adj hard; (Med) pale
trabalenguas [traβa'lengwas] nm inv tongue twister
trabar [tra'βar] vt (juntar) to join, unite; (atar) to tie down, fetter; (agarrar) to seize; (amistad) to strike up; **trabarse** vr to become entangled; (reñir) to squabble; **se le traba la lengua** he gets tongue-tied

trabazón [traβa'θon] nf (Tec) joining, assembly; (fig) bond, link
trabucar [traβu'kar] vt (confundir) to confuse, mix up; (palabras) to misplace
trabuque etc [tra'βuke] vb ver **trabucar**
tracción [trak'θjon] nf traction; ~ **delantera/trasera** front-wheel/rear-wheel drive
trace etc ['traθe] vb ver **trazar**
tractor [trak'tor] nm tractor
trad. abr (= traducido) trans
tradición [traði'θjon] nf tradition
tradicional [traðiθjo'nal] adj traditional
traducción [traðuk'θjon] nf translation; ~ **asistida por ordenador** computer-assisted translation
traducible [traðu'θiβle] adj translatable
traducir [traðu'θir] vt to translate; **traducirse** vr: **traducirse en** (fig) to entail, result in
traductor, a [traðuk'tor, a] nm/f translator
traduzca etc [tra'ðuθka] vb ver **traducir**
traer [tra'er] vt to bring; (llevar) to carry; (ropa) to wear; (incluir) to carry; (fig) to cause; **traerse** vr: **traerse algo** to be up to sth; **traerse bien/mal** to dress well/badly; **traérselas** to be annoying; ~ **consigo** to involve, entail; **es un problema que se las trae** it's a difficult problem
traficante [trafi'kante] nm/f trader, dealer
traficar [trafi'kar] vi to trade; ~ **con** (pey) to deal illegally in
tráfico ['trafiko] nm (Com) trade; (Auto) traffic
trafique etc [tra'fike] vb ver **traficar**
tragaderas [traɣa'ðeras] nfpl (garganta) throat sg, gullet sg; (credulidad) gullibility sg
tragaluz [traɣa'luθ] nm skylight
tragamonedas [traɣamo'neðas] nm inv, **tragaperras** [traɣa'perras] nm inv slot machine
tragar [tra'ɣar] vt to swallow; (devorar) to devour, bolt down; **tragarse** vr to swallow; (tierra) to absorb, soak up; **no le puedo** ~ (persona) I can't stand him
tragedia [tra'xeðja] nf tragedy
trágico, -a ['traxiko, a] adj tragic
trago ['traɣo] nm (de líquido) drink; (comido de golpe) gulp; (fam: de bebida) swig; (desgracia) blow; ~ **amargo** (fig) hard time
trague etc ['traɣe] vb ver **tragar**
traición [trai'θjon] nf treachery; (Jur) treason; (una traición) act of treachery
traicionar [traiθjo'nar] vt to betray
traicionero, -a [traiθjo'nero, a] = **traidor, a**
traída [tra'iða] nf carrying; ~ **de aguas** water supply
traidor, a [trai'ðor, a] adj treacherous ■ nm/f traitor

t

traiga etc ['traiɣa] vb ver **traer**

trailer (pl **trailers**) ['trailer, 'trailer(s)] nm trailer

traje etc ['traxe] vb ver **traer** ■ nm (gen) dress; (de hombre) suit; (traje típico) costume; (fig) garb; ~ **de baño** swimsuit; ~ **de luces** bullfighter's costume; ~ **hecho a la medida** made-to-measure suit

trajera etc [tra'xera] vb ver **traer**

trajín [tra'xin] nm haulage; (fam: movimiento) bustle; **trajines** nmpl goings-on

trajinar [traxi'nar] vt (llevar) to carry, transport ■ vi (moverse) to bustle about; (viajar) to travel around

trama ['trama] nf (fig) link; (: intriga) plot; (de tejido) weft

tramar [tra'mar] vt to plot; (Tec) to weave; **tramarse** vr (fig): **algo se está tramando** there's something going on

tramitar [trami'tar] vt (asunto) to transact; (negociar) to negotiate; (manejar) to handle

trámite ['tramite] nm (paso) step; (Jur) transaction; **trámites** nmpl (burocracia) paperwork sg, procedures; (Jur) proceedings

tramo ['tramo] nm (de tierra) plot; (de escalera) flight; (de vía) section

tramoya [tra'moja] nf (Teat) piece of stage machinery; (fig) trick

tramoyista [tramo'jista] nm/f scene shifter; (fig) trickster

trampa ['trampa] nf trap; (en el suelo) trapdoor; (prestidigitación) conjuring trick; (engaño) trick; (fam) fiddle; **caer en la** ~ to fall into the trap; **hacer trampas** (trampear) to cheat

trampear [trampe'ar] vt, vi to cheat

trampilla [tram'piʎa] nf trap, hatchway

trampolín [trampo'lin] nm trampoline; (de piscina etc) diving board

tramposo, -a [tram'poso, a] adj crooked, cheating ■ nm/f crook, cheat

tranca ['tranka] nf (palo) stick; (viga) beam; (de puerta, ventana) bar; (borrachera) binge; **a trancas y barrancas** with great difficulty

trancar [tran'kar] vt to bar ■ vi to stride along

trancazo [tran'kaθo] nm (golpe) blow

trance ['tranθe] nm (momento difícil) difficult moment; (situación crítica) critical situation; (estado de hipnosis) trance; **estar en ~ de muerte** to be at death's door

tranco ['tranko] nm stride

tranque etc ['tranke] vb ver **trancar**

tranquilamente [tran'kilamente] adv (sin preocupaciones: leer, trabajar) peacefully; (sin enfadarse: hablar, discutir) calmly

tranquilice etc [tranki'liθe] vb ver **tranquilizar**

tranquilidad [trankili'ðað] nf (calma) calmness, stillness; (paz) peacefulness

tranquilizador, a [trankiliθa'ðor, a] adj (música) soothing; (hecho) reassuring

tranquilizante [trankili'θante] nm tranquillizer

tranquilizar [trankili'θar] vt (calmar) to calm (down); (asegurar) to reassure

tranquilo, -a [tran'kilo, a] adj (calmado) calm; (apacible) peaceful; (mar) calm; (mente) untroubled

Trans. abr (Com) = **transferencia**

transacción [transak'θjon] nf transaction

transar [tran'sar] vi (Am) = **transigir**

transatlántico, -a [transat'lantiko, a] adj transatlantic ■ nm (ocean) liner

transbordador [transβorða'ðor] nm ferry

transbordar [transβor'ðar] vt to transfer; **transbordarse** vr to change

transbordo [trans'βorðo] nm transfer; **hacer** ~ to change (trains)

transcender [transθen'der] vt = **trascender**

transcribir [transkri'βir] vt to transcribe

transcurrir [transku'rrir] vi (tiempo) to pass; (hecho) to turn out

transcurso [trans'kurso] nm passing, lapse; **en el ~ de ocho días** in the course of a week

transeúnte [transe'unte] adj transient ■ nm/f passer-by

transexual [transe'kswal] adj, nm/f transsexual

transferencia [transfe'renθja] nf transference; (Com) transfer; ~ **bancaria** banker's order; ~ **de crédito** (Com) credit transfer; ~ **electrónica de fondos** (Com) electronic funds transfer

transferir [transfe'rir] vt to transfer; (aplazar) to postpone

transfiera etc [trans'fjera] vb ver **transferir**

transfigurar [transfiɣu'rar] vt to transfigure

transfiriendo etc [transfi'rjendo] vb ver **transferir**

transformación [transforma'θjon] nf transformation

transformador [transforma'ðor] nm transformer

transformar [transfor'mar] vt to transform; (convertir) to convert

tránsfuga ['transfuɣa] nm/f (Mil) deserter; (Pol) turncoat

transfusión [transfu'sjon] nf (tb: **transfusión de sangre**) (blood) transfusion

transgénico, -a [trans'xeniko, a] adj genetically modified

transgredir [transɣre'dir] vt to transgress

transgresión [transɣre'sjon] nf transgression

transición [transi'θjon] nf transition;
período de ~ transitional period

transido, -a [tran'siðo, a] adj overcome; **~
de angustia** beset with anxiety; **~ de dolor**
racked with pain

transigir [transi'xir] vi to compromise;
(ceder) to make concessions

transija etc [tran'sixa] vb ver **transigir**

Transilvania [transil'βanja] nf Transylvania

transistor [transis'tor] nm transistor

transitable [transi'taβle] adj (camino)
passable

transitar [transi'tar] vi to go (from place to
place)

transitivo, -a [transi'tiβo, a] adj transitive

tránsito ['transito] nm transit; (Auto) traffic;
(parada) stop; **horas de máximo ~** rush
hours; **"se prohíbe el ~"** "no thoroughfare"

transitorio, -a [transi'torjo, a] adj transitory

transmisión [transmi'sjon] nf (Radio: TV)
transmission, broadcast(ing); (transferencia)
transfer; **~ en circuito** hookup; **~ en
directo/exterior** live/outside broadcast;
~ de datos (en paralelo/en serie)
(Inform) (parallel/serial) data transfer o
transmission; **plena/media ~ bidireccional**
(Inform) full/half duplex

transmitir [transmi'tir] vt to transmit;
(Radio: TV) to broadcast; (enfermedad) to give,
pass on

transparencia [transpa'renθja] nf
transparency; (claridad) clearness, clarity;
(foto) slide

transparentar [transparen'tar] vt to reveal
■ vi to be transparent

transparente [transpa'rente] adj
transparent; (aire) clear; (ligero) diaphanous
■ nm curtain

transpirar [transpi'rar] vi to perspire; (fig)
to transpire

transpondré etc [transpon'dre] vb ver
transponer

transponer [transpo'ner] vt to transpose;
(cambiar de sitio) to move about ■ vi
(desaparecer) to disappear; (ir más allá) to go
beyond; **transponerse** vr to change places;
(ocultarse) to hide; (sol) to go down

transponga etc [trans'ponga] vb ver
transponer

transportador [transporta'ðor] nm
(Mecánica): **~ de correa** belt conveyor

transportar [transpor'tar] vt to transport;
(llevar) to carry

transporte [trans'porte] nm transport;
(Com) haulage; **Ministerio de Transportes**
Ministry of Transport

transpuesto [trans'pwesto], **transpuse** etc

[trans'puse] vb ver **transponer**

transversal [transβer'sal] adj transverse,
cross ■ nf (tb: **calle transversal**) cross street

transversalmente [transβersal'mente] adv
obliquely

tranvía [tram'bia] nm tram, streetcar (US)

trapecio [tra'peθjo] nm trapeze

trapecista [trape'θista] nm/f trapeze artist

trapero, -a [tra'pero, a] nm/f ragman

trapicheos [trapi'tʃeos] nmpl (fam) schemes,
fiddles

trapisonda [trapi'sonda] nf (jaleo) row;
(estafa) swindle

trapo ['trapo] nm (tela) rag; (de cocina) cloth;
trapos nmpl (fam: de mujer) clothes, dresses;
a todo ~ under full sail; **soltar el ~** (llorar) to
burst into tears

tráquea ['trakea] nf (trachea, windpipe)

traqueteo [trake'teo] nm (crujido) crack;
(golpeteo) rattling

tras [tras] prep (detrás) behind; (después) after;
~ de besides; **día ~ día** day after day; **uno ~
otro** one after the other

trascendencia [trasθen'denθja] nf
(importancia) importance; (en filosofía)
transcendence

trascendental [trasθenden'tal] adj
important; transcendental

trascender [trasθen'der] vi (oler) to smell;
(noticias) to come out, leak out; (sucesos,
sentimientos) to spread, have a wide effect; **~
a** (afectar) to reach, have an effect on; (oler a)
to smack of; **en su novela todo trasciende
a romanticismo** everything in his novel
smacks of romanticism

trascienda etc [tras'θjenda] vb ver **trascender**

trasegar [trase'ɣar] vt (mover) to move about;
(vino) to decant

trasegué [trase'ɣe], **traseguemos** etc
[trase'ɣemos] vb ver **trasegar**

trasero, -a [tra'sero, a] adj back, rear ■ nm
(Anat) bottom; **traseros** nmpl ancestors

trasfondo [tras'fondo] nm background

trasgo ['trasɣo] nm (duende) goblin

trasgredir [trasɣre'ðir] vt to contravene

trashumante [trasu'mante] adj migrating

trasiego etc [tra'sjeɣo] vb ver **trasegar** ■ nm
(cambiar de sitio) move, switch; (de vino)
decanting; (trastorno) upset

trasiegue etc [tra'sjeɣe] vb ver **trasegar**

trasladar [trasla'ðar] vt to move; (persona) to
transfer; (postergar) to postpone; (copiar) to
copy; (interpretar) to interpret; **trasladarse** vr
(irse) to go; (mudarse) to move; **trasladarse a
otro puesto** to move to a new job

traslado [tras'laðo] nm move; (mudanza)
move, removal; (de persona) transfer; (copia)

copy; ~ **de bloque** (*Inform*) block move, cut-and-paste

traslucir [traslu'θir] *vt* to show; **traslucirse** *vr* to be translucent; (*fig*) to be revealed

trasluz [tras'luθ] *nm* reflected light; **al ~** against *o* up to the light

trasluzca *etc* [tras'luθka] *vb ver* **traslucir**

trasmano [tras'mano]: **a ~** *adv* (*fuera de alcance*) out of reach; (*apartado*) out of the way

trasnochado, -a [trasno'tʃaðo, a] *adj* dated

trasnochador, a [trasnotʃa'ðor, a] *adj* given to staying up late ■ *nm/f* (*fig*) night bird

trasnochar [trasno'tʃar] *vi* (*acostarse tarde*) to stay up late; (*no dormir*) to have a sleepless night; (*pasar la noche*) to stay the night

traspasar [traspa'sar] *vt* (*bala*) to pierce, go through; (*propiedad*) to sell, transfer; (*calle*) to cross over; (*límites*) to go beyond; (*ley*) to break; **"traspaso negocio"** "business for sale"

traspaso [tras'paso] *nm* transfer; (*fig*) anguish

traspié [tras'pje] (*pl* **~s**) *nm* (*caída*) stumble; (*tropezón*) trip; (*fig*) blunder

trasplantar [trasplan'tar] *vt* to transplant

trasplante [tras'plante] *nm* transplant

traspuesto, -a [tras'pwesto, a] *adj*: **quedarse ~** to doze off

trastada [tras'taða] *nf* (*fam*) prank

trastazo [tras'taθo] *nm* (*fam*) bump; **darse un ~** (*persona*) to bump o.s.; (*en coche*) to have a bump

traste ['traste] *nm* (*Mus*) fret; **dar al ~ con algo** to ruin sth; **ir al ~** to fall through

trastero [tras'tero] *nm* lumber room

trastienda [tras'tjenda] *nf* backshop; **obtener algo por la ~** to get sth by underhand means

trasto ['trasto] *nm* (*mueble*) piece of furniture; (*tarro viejo*) old pot; (*pey: cosa*) piece of junk; (: *persona*) dead loss; **trastos** *nmpl* (*Teat*) scenery *sg*; **tirar los trastos a la cabeza** to have a blazing row

trastocar [trasto'kar] *vt* (*papeles*) to mix up

trastornado, -a [trastor'naðo, a] *adj* (*loco*) mad; (*agitado*) crazy

trastornar [trastor'nar] *vt* to overturn, upset; (*fig: ideas*) to confuse; (: *nervios*) to shatter; (: *persona*) to drive crazy; **trastornarse** *vr* (*plan*) to fall through

trastorno [tras'torno] *nm* (*acto*) overturning; (*confusión*) confusion; (*Pol*) disturbance, upheaval; (*Med*) upset; **~ estomacal** stomach upset; **~ mental** mental disorder, breakdown

trasunto [tra'sunto] *nm* copy

trasvase [tras'βase] *nm* (*de río*) diversion

tratable [tra'taβle] *adj* friendly

tratado [tra'taðo] *nm* (*Pol*) treaty; (*Com*) agreement; (*Lit*) treatise

tratamiento [trata'mjento] *nm* treatment; (*Tec*) processing; (*de problema*) handling; **~ de datos** (*Inform*) data processing; **~ de gráficos** (*Inform*) graphics; **~ de márgenes** margin settings; **~ de textos** (*Inform*) word processing; **~ por lotes** (*Inform*) batch processing; **~ de tú** familiar address

tratante [tra'tante] *nm/f* dealer, merchandizer

tratar [tra'tar] *vt* (*ocuparse de*) to treat; (*manejar, Tec*) to handle; (*Inform*) to process; (*Med*) to treat; (*dirigirse a: persona*) to address ■ *vi*: **~ de** (*hablar sobre*) to deal with, be about; (*intentar*) to try to; **~ con** (*Com*) to trade in; (*negociar con*) to negotiate with; (*tener tratos con*) to have dealings with; **tratarse** *vr* to treat each other; **se trata de la nueva piscina** it's about the new pool; **¿de qué se trata?** what's it about?

trato ['trato] *nm* dealings *pl*; (*relaciones*) relationship; (*comportamiento*) manner; (*Com: Jur*) agreement, contract; (*título*) (form of) address; **de ~ agradable** pleasant; **de fácil ~** easy to get on with; **~ equitativo** fair deal; **¡~ hecho!** it's a deal!; **malos tratos** ill-treatment *sg*

trauma ['trauma] *nm* trauma

traumático, -a [trau'matiko, a] *adj* traumatic

través [tra'βes] *nm* (*contratiempo*) reverse; **al ~** across, crossways; **a ~ de** across; (*sobre*) over; (*por*) through; **de ~** across; (*de lado*) sideways

travesaño [traβe'saɲo] *nm* (*Arq*) crossbeam; (*Deporte*) crossbar

travesía [traβe'sia] *nf* (*calle*) cross-street; (*Naut*) crossing

travesti [tra'βesti] *nm/f* transvestite

travesura [traβe'sura] *nf* (*broma*) prank; (*ingenio*) wit

travieso, -a [tra'βjeso, a] *adj* (*niño*) naughty; (*adulto*) restless; (*ingenioso*) witty ■ *nf* crossing; (*Arq*) crossbeam; (*Ferro*) sleeper

trayecto [tra'jekto] *nm* (*ruta*) road, way; (*viaje*) journey; (*tramo*) stretch; (*curso*) course; **final del ~** end of the line

trayectoria [trajek'torja] *nf* trajectory; (*desarrollo*) development, path; **la ~ actual del partido** the party's present line

trayendo *etc* [tra'jendo] *vb ver* **traer**

traza ['traθa] *nf* (*Arq*) plan, design; (*aspecto*) looks *pl*; (*señal*) sign; (*engaño*) trick; (*habilidad*) skill; (*Inform*) trace

trazado, -a [tra'θaðo, a] *adj*: **bien ~** shapely, well-formed ■ *nm* (*Arq*) plan, design; (*fig*)

outline; (de carretera etc) line, route
trazador [traθa'ðor] nm plotter; ~ **plano** flatbed plotter
trazar [tra'θar] vt (Arq) to plan; (Arte) to sketch; (fig) to trace; (itinerario: hacer) to plot; (plan) to follow
trazo ['traθo] nm (línea) line; (bosquejo) sketch; **trazos** nmpl (de cara) lines, features
TRB abr = **toneladas de registro bruto**
trébol ['treβol] nm (Bot) clover; **tréboles** nmpl (Naipes) clubs
trece ['treθe] num thirteen; **estar en sus ~** to stand firm
trecho ['tretʃo] nm (distancia) distance; (de tiempo) while; (fam) piece; **de ~ en ~** at intervals
tregua ['treɣwa] nf (Mil) truce; (fig) lull; **sin ~** without respite
treinta ['treinta] num thirty
treintena [trein'tena] nf (about) thirty
tremendo, -a [tre'mendo, a] adj (terrible) terrible; (imponente: cosa) imposing; (fam: fabuloso) tremendous; (divertido) entertaining
trémulo, -a ['tremulo, a] adj quivering; (luz) flickering
tren [tren] nm (Ferro) train; ~ **de aterrizaje** undercarriage; ~ **directo/expreso/(de) mercancías/de pasajeros/suplementario** through/fast/goods o freight/passenger/relief train; ~ **de vida** way of life
trenca ['trenka] nf duffel coat
trence etc ['trenθe] vb ver **trenzar**
trenza ['trenθa] nf (de pelo) plait
trenzar [tren'θar] vt (el pelo) to plait ■ vi (en baile) to weave in and out; **trenzarse** vr (Am) to become involved
trepa ['trepa] nf (subida) climb; (ardid) trick
trepador, a [trepa'ðor(a)] nm/f (fam): **ser un(a) ~(a)** to be on the make ■ nf (Bot) climber
trepar [tre'par] vt, vi to climb; (Tec) to drill
trepidación [trepiða'θjon] nf shaking, vibration
trepidar [trepi'ðar] vi to shake, vibrate
tres [tres] num three; (fecha) third; **las ~** three o'clock
trescientos, -as [tres'θjentos, as] num three hundred
tresillo [tre'siʎo] nm three-piece suite; (Mus) triplet
treta ['treta] nf (Com etc) gimmick; (fig) trick
tri ... [tri] pref tri..., three-...
tríada ['triaða] nf triad
triangular [trjangu'lar] adj triangular
triángulo [tri'angulo] nm triangle
tribal [tri'βal] adj tribal
tribu ['triβu] nf tribe

tribuna [tri'βuna] nf (plataforma) platform; (Deporte) stand; (fig) public speaking; ~ **de la prensa** press box; ~ **del acusado** (Jur) dock; ~ **del jurado** jury box
tribunal [triβu'nal] nm (en juicio) court; (comisión, fig) tribunal; (Escol: examinadores) board of examiners; **T~ Supremo** High Court, Supreme Court (US); **T~ de Justicia de las Comunidades Europeas** European Court of Justice; ~ **popular** jury
tributar [triβu'tar] vt to pay; (las gracias) to give; (cariño) to show
tributario, -a [triβu'tarjo, a] adj (Geo: Pol) tributary cpd; (Econ) tax cpd, taxation cpd ■ nm (Geo) tributary ■ nm/f (Com) taxpayer; **sistema ~** tax system
tributo [tri'βuto] nm (Com) tax
triciclo [tri'θiklo] nm tricycle
tricornio [tri'kornjo] nm three-cornered hat
tricota [tri'kota] nf (Am) knitted sweater
tricotar [triko'tar] vi to knit
tridimensional [triðimensjo'nal] adj three-dimensional
trienal [trje'nal] adj three-year
trifulca [tri'fulka] nf (fam) row, shindy
trigal [tri'ɣal] nm wheat field
trigésimo, -a [tri'xesimo, a] num thirtieth
trigo ['triɣo] nm wheat; **trigos** nmpl wheat field(s) (pl)
trigueño, -a [tri'ɣeɲo, a] adj (pelo) corn-coloured; (piel) olive-skinned
trillado, -a [tri'ʎaðo, a] adj threshed; (fig) trite, hackneyed
trilladora [triʎa'ðora] nf threshing machine
trillar [tri'ʎar] vt (Agr) to thresh; (fig) to frequent
trillizos, -as [tri'ʎiθos, as] nmpl/nfpl triplets
trilogía [trilo'xia] nf trilogy
trimestral [trimes'tral] adj quarterly; (Escol) termly
trimestre [tri'mestre] nm (Escol) term; (Com) quarter, financial period; (: pago) quarterly payment
trinar [tri'nar] vi (Mus) to trill; (ave) to sing, warble; **está que trina** he's hopping mad
trincar [trin'kar] vt (atar) to tie up; (Naut) to lash; (agarrar) to pinion
trinchante [trin'tʃante] nm (para cortar carne) carving knife; (tenedor) meat fork
trinchar [trin'tʃar] vt to carve
trinchera [trin'tʃera] nf (fosa) trench; (para vía) cutting; (impermeable) trench-coat
trineo [tri'neo] nm sledge
trinidad [trini'ðað] nf trio; (Rel): **la T~** the Trinity
trino ['trino] nm trill
trinque etc ['trinke] vb ver **trincar**

385

trinquete [trin'kete] *nm* (*Tec*) pawl; (*Naut*) foremast

trío ['trio] *nm* trio

tripa ['tripa] *nf* (*Anat*) intestine; (*fig: fam*) belly; **tripas** *nfpl* (*Anat*) insides; (*Culin*) tripe *sg*; **tener mucha** ~ to be fat; **me duelen las tripas** I have a stomach ache

tripartito, -a [tripar'tito, a] *adj* tripartite

triple ['triple] *adj* triple; (*tres veces*) threefold

triplicado, -a [tripli'kaðo, a] *adj*: **por** ~ in triplicate

triplicar [tripli'kar] *vt* to treble

triplo ['triplo] *adj* = **triple**

trípode ['tripoðe] *nm* tripod

Trípoli ['tripoli] *nm* Tripoli

tríptico ['triptiko] *nm* (*Arte*) triptych; (*documento*) three-part document

tripulación [tripula'θjon] *nf* crew

tripulante [tripu'lante] *nm/f* crewman/woman

tripular [tripu'lar] *vt* (*barco*) to man; (*Auto*) to drive

triquiñuela [triki'ɲwela] *nf* trick

tris [tris] *nm* crack; **en un** ~ in an instant; **estar en un** ~ **de hacer algo** to be within an inch of doing sth

triste ['triste] *adj* (*afligido*) sad; (*sombrío*) melancholy, gloomy; (*desolado*) desolate; (*lamentable*) sorry, miserable; (*viejo*) old; (*único*) single; **no queda sino un** ~ **penique** there's just one miserable penny left

tristeza [tris'teθa] *nf* (*aflicción*) sadness; (*melancolía*) melancholy; (*de lugar*) desolation; (*pena*) misery

tristón, -ona [tris'ton, ona] *adj* sad, downhearted

trituradora [tritura'ðora] *nf* shredder

triturar [tritu'rar] *vt* (*moler*) to grind; (*mascar*) to chew; (*documentos*) to shred

triunfador, a [triunfa'ðor, a] *adj* triumphant; (*ganador*) winning ■ *nm/f* winner

triunfal [triun'fal] *adj* triumphant; (*arco*) triumphal

triunfante [triun'fante] *adj* triumphant; (*ganador*) winning

triunfar [triun'far] *vi* (*tener éxito*) to triumph; (*ganar*) to win; (*Naipes*) to be trumps; **triunfan corazones** hearts are trumps; ~ **en la vida** to succeed in life

triunfo [tri'unfo] *nm* triumph; (*Naipes*) trump

trivial [tri'βjal] *adj* trivial

trivialice *etc* [triβja'liθe] *vb ver* **trivializar**

trivializar [triβjali'θar] *vt* to minimize, play down

triza ['triθa] *nf* bit, piece; **hacer algo trizas** to smash sth to bits; (*papel*) to tear sth to shreds

trocar [tro'kar] *vt* (*Com*) to exchange; (*dinero, de lugar*) to change; (*palabras*) to exchange; (*confundir*) to confuse; **trocarse** *vr* (*confundirse*) to get mixed up; (*transformarse*): **trocarse (en)** to change (into)

trocear [troθe'ar] *vt* to cut up

trocha ['trotʃa] *nf* (*sendero*) by-path; (*atajo*) short cut

troche ['trotʃe]: **a** ~ **y moche** *adv* helter-skelter, pell-mell

trofeo [tro'feo] *nm* (*premio*) trophy

trola ['trola] *nf* (*fam*) fib

tromba ['tromba] *nf* whirlwind; ~ **de agua** cloudburst

trombón [trom'bon] *nm* trombone

trombosis [trom'bosis] *nf inv* thrombosis

trompa ['trompa] *nf* (*Mus*) horn; (*de elefante*) trunk; (*trompo*) humming top; (*hocico*) snout; (*Anat*) tube, duct ■ *nm* (*Mus*) horn player; ~ **de Falopio** Fallopian tube; **cogerse una** ~ (*fam*) to get tight

trompada [trom'paða] *nf*, **trompazo** [trom'paθo] *nm* (*choque*) bump, bang; (*puñetazo*) punch

trompeta [trom'peta] *nf* trumpet; (*clarín*) bugle ■ *nm* trumpeter

trompetilla [trompe'tiʎa] *nf* ear trumpet

trompicón [trompi'kon]: **a trompicones** *adv* in fits and starts

trompo ['trompo] *nm* spinning top

trompón [trom'pon] *nm* bump

tronado, -a [tro'naðo, a] *adj* broken-down

tronar [tro'nar] *vt* (*Am*) to shoot, execute ■ *vi* to thunder; (*fig*) to rage; (*fam*) to go broke

tronchar [tron'tʃar] *vt* (*árbol*) to chop down; (*fig: vida*) to cut short; (*esperanza*) to shatter; (*persona*) to tire out; **troncharse** *vr* to fall down; **troncharse de risa** to split one's sides with laughter

tronco ['tronko] *nm* (*de árbol, Anat*) trunk; (*de planta*) stem; **estar hecho un** ~ to be sound asleep

tronera [tro'nera] *nf* (*Mil*) loophole; (*Arq*) small window

trono ['trono] *nm* throne

tropa ['tropa] *nf* (*Mil*) troop; (*soldados*) soldiers *pl*; (*soldados rasos*) ranks *pl*; (*gentío*) mob

tropecé [trope'θe], **tropecemos** *etc* [trope'θemos] *vb ver* **tropezar**

tropel [tro'pel] *nm* (*muchedumbre*) crowd; (*prisa*) rush; (*montón*) throng; **acudir** *etc* **en** ~ to come *etc* in a mad rush

tropelía [trope'lia] *nm* outrage

tropezar [trope'θar] *vi* to trip, stumble; (*fig*) to slip up; **tropezarse** *vr* (*dos personas*) to run into each other; ~ **con** (*encontrar*) to run into; (*topar con*) to bump into

tropezón [trope'θon] *nm* trip; (*fig*) blunder; (*traspié*): **dar un** ~ to trip

tropical [tropi'kal] *adj* tropical

trópico ['tropiko] *nm* tropic

tropiece *etc* [tro'pjeθe] *vb ver* **tropezar**

tropiezo *etc* [tro'pjeθo] *vb ver* **tropezar** ■ *nm* (*error*) slip, blunder; (*desgracia*) misfortune; (*revés*) setback; (*obstáculo*) snag; (*discusión*) quarrel

troqué [tro'ke], **troquemos** *etc* [tro'kemos] *vb ver* **trocar**

trotamundos [trota'mundos] *nm inv* globetrotter

trotar [tro'tar] *vi* to trot; (*viajar*) to travel about

trote ['trote] *nm* trot; (*fam*) travelling; **de mucho** ~ hard-wearing

Troya ['troja] *nf* Troy, **aquí fue** ~ now there's nothing but ruins

trozo ['troθo] *nm* bit, piece; (*Lit: Mus*) passage; **a trozos** in bits

trucha ['trutʃa] *nf* (*pez*) trout; (*Tec*) crane

truco ['truko] *nm* (*habilidad*) knack; (*engaño*) trick; (*Cine*) trick effect o photography; **trucos** *nmpl* billiards *sg*; ~ **publicitario** advertising gimmick

trueco *etc* ['trweko] *vb ver* **trocar**

trueno *etc* ['trweno] *vb ver* **tronar** ■ *nm* (*gen*) thunder; (*estampido*) boom; (*de arma*) bang

trueque *etc* ['trweke] *vb ver* **trocar** ■ *nm* exchange; (*Com*) barter

trufa ['trufa] *nf* (*Bot*) truffle; (*fig: fam*) fib

truhán, -ana [tru'an, ana] *nm/f* rogue

truncado, -a [trun'kaðo, a] *adj* truncated

truncar [trun'kar] *vt* (*cortar*) to truncate; (*la vida etc*) to cut short; (*el desarrollo*) to stunt

trunque *etc* ['trunke] *vb ver* **truncar**

Tte. *abr* (= *Teniente*) Lt.

tu [tu] *adj* your

tú [tu] *pron* you

tubérculo [tu'βerkulo] *nm* (*Bot*) tuber

tuberculosis [tuβerku'losis] *nf inv* tuberculosis

tubería [tuβe'ria] *nf* pipes *pl*, piping; (*conducto*) pipeline

tubo ['tuβo] *nm* tube, pipe; ~ **de desagüe** drainpipe; ~ **de ensayo** test-tube; ~ **de escape** exhaust (pipe); ~ **digestivo** alimentary canal

tuerca ['twerka] *nf* (*Tec*) nut

tuerce *etc* ['twerθe] *vb ver* **torcer**

tuerto, -a ['twerto, a] *adj* (*torcido*) twisted; (*ciego*) blind in one eye ■ *nm/f* one-eyed person ■ *nm* (*ofensa*) wrong; **a tuertas** upside-down

tuerza *etc* ['twerθa] *vb ver* **torcer**

tueste *etc* ['tweste] *vb ver* **tostar**

tuétano ['twetano] *nm* (*Anat: médula*) marrow; (*Bot*) pith; **hasta los tuétanos** through and through, utterly

tufo ['tufo] *nm* vapour; (*fig: pey*) stench

tugurio [tu'ɣurjo] *nm* slum

tul [tul] *nm* tulle

tulipán [tuli'pan] *nm* tulip

tullido, -a [tu'ʎiðo, a] *adj* crippled; (*cansado*) exhausted

tumba ['tumba] *nf* (*sepultura*) tomb; (*sacudida*) shake; (*voltereta*) somersault; **ser (como) una** ~ to keep one's mouth shut

tumbar [tum'bar] *vt* to knock down; (*doblar*) to knock over; (*fam: suj: olor*) to overpower ■ *vi* to fall down; **tumbarse** *vr* (*echarse*) to lie down; (*extenderse*) to stretch out

tumbo ['tumbo] *nm* (*caída*) fall; (*de vehículo*) jolt; (*momento crítico*) critical moment

tumbona [tum'bona] *nf* lounger

tumor [tu'mor] *nm* tumour

tumulto [tu'multo] *nm* turmoil; (*Pol: motín*) riot

tuna ['tuna] *nf* (*Mus*) student music group; *ver tb* **tuno**; *see note*

○ **TUNA**

A *tuna* is made up of university students, or quite often former students, who dress up in costumes from the *Edad de Oro*, the Spanish Golden Age. These musical troupes go through the town playing their guitars, lutes and tambourines and serenade the young ladies in the halls of residence, or make impromptu appearances at weddings or parties singing traditional Spanish songs for a few pesetas.

tunante [tu'nante] *adj* rascally ■ *nm* rogue, villain; **¡~!** you villain!

tunda ['tunda] *nf* (*de tela*) shearing; (*de golpes*) beating

tundir [tun'dir] *vt* (*tela*) to shear; (*hierba*) to mow; (*fig*) to exhaust; (*fam: golpear*) to beat

tunecino, -a [tune'θino, a] *adj, nm/f* Tunisian

túnel ['tunel] *nm* tunnel

Túnez ['tuneθ] *nm* Tunis

túnica ['tunika] *nf* tunic; (*vestido largo*) long dress; (*Anat: Bot*) tunic

Tunicia [tu'niθja] *nf* Tunisia

tuno, -a ['tuno, a] *nm/f* (*fam*) rogue ■ *nm* (*Mus*) member of a "*tuna*"

tuntún [tun'tun]: **al** ~ *adv* thoughtlessly

tupamaro, -a [tupa'maro, a] *adj, nm/f* (*Am*) urban guerrilla tupé [tu'pe] nm quiff

tupí [tu'pi], tupí-guaraní [tupigwara'ni] adj,
nm/f Tupi-Guarani

tupido, -a [tu'piðo, a] adj (denso) dense; (fig:
torpe) dim; (tela) close-woven

turba ['turβa] nf (combustible) turf;
(muchedumbre) crowd

turbación [turβa'θjon] nf (molestia)
disturbance; (preocupación) worry

turbado, -a [tur'βaðo, a] adj (molesto)
disturbed; (preocupado) worried

turbante [tur'βante] nm turban

turbar [tur'βar] vt (molestar) to disturb;
(incomodar) to upset; turbarse vr to be
disturbed

turbina [tur'βina] nf turbine

turbio, -a ['turβjo, a] adj (agua etc) cloudy;
(vista) dim, blurred; (tema) unclear, confused;
(negocio) shady ■ adv indistinctly

turbión [tur'βjon] nf downpour; (fig) shower,
hail

turbo ['turβo] adj inv turbo(-charged) ■ nm
(tb coche) turbo

turbulencia [turβu'lenθja] nf turbulence;
(fig) restlessness

turbulento, -a [turβu'lento, a] adj turbulent;
(fig: intranquilo) restless; (: ruidoso) noisy

turco, -a ['turko, a] adj Turkish ■ nm/f Turk
■ nm (Ling) Turkish

Turena [tu'rena] nf Touraine

turgente [tur'xente], túrgido, a ['turxiðo, a]
adj (tirante) turgid, swollen

Turín [tu'rin] nm Turin

turismo [tu'rismo] nm tourism; (coche)

saloon car; hacer ~ to go travelling (abroad)

turista [tu'rista] nm/f tourist; (vacacionista)
holidaymaker (Brit), vacationer (US)

turístico, -a [tu'ristiko, a] adj tourist cpd

Turkmenistán [turkmeni'stan] nm
Turkmenistan

turnar [tur'nar] vi, turnarse vr to take (it in)
turns

turno ['turno] nm (oportunidad, orden de
prioridad) opportunity; (Deporte etc) turn; es
su ~ it's his turn (next); ~ de día/de noche
(Industria) day/night shift

turolense [turo'lense] adj of o from Teruel
■ nm/f native o inhabitant of Teruel

turquesa [tur'kesa] nf turquoise

Turquía [tur'kia] nf Turkey

turrón [tu'rron] nm (dulce) nougat; (fam)
sinecure, cushy job o number

tute ['tute] nm (Naipes) card game; darse un ~
to break one's back

tutear [tute'ar] vt to address as familiar "tú";
tutearse vr to be on familiar terms

tutela [tu'tela] nf (legal) guardianship;
(instrucción) guidance; estar bajo la ~ de (fig)
to be under the protection of

tutelar [tute'lar] adj tutelary ■ vt to protect

tutor, a [tu'tor, a] nm/f (legal) guardian;
(Escol) tutor; ~ de curso form master/
mistress

tuve etc ['tuβe] vb ver tener

tuyo, -a ['tujo, a] adj yours, of yours ■ pron
yours; los tuyos (fam) your relations, your
family

TVE nf abr = Televisión Española

Uu

U, u [u] *nf (letra)* U, u; **viraje en U** U-turn;
   U de Ulises U for Uncle
u [u] *conj* or
u. *abr* = **unidad**
UAR [war] *nfpl abr (Esp)* = **Unidades
   Antiterroristas Rurales**
ubérrimo, -a [u'βerrimo, a] *adj* very rich,
   fertile
ubicación [uβika'θjon] *nf (esp Am)* place,
   position, location
ubicado, -a [uβi'kaðo, a] *adj (esp Am)* situated
ubicar [uβi'kar] *vt (esp Am)* to place, situate;
   (: *fig*) to install in a post; (: *encontrar*) to find;
   ubicarse *vr* to be situated, be located
ubicuo, -a [u'βikwo, a] *adj* ubiquitous
ubique *etc* [u'βike] *vb ver* **ubicar**
ubre ['uβre] *nf* udder
UCI ['uθi] *sigla f* (= Unidad de Cuidados Intensivos)
   ICU
Ucrania [u'kranja] *nf* Ukraine
ucraniano, -a [ukra'njano, a] *adj, nm/f*
   Ukrainian ■ *nm (Ling)* Ukrainian
ucranio [u'kranjo] *nm (Ling)* Ukrainian
Ud(s) *abr* = **usted(es)**; *ver* **usted**
UDV *sigla f* = **Unidad de Despliegue Visual**
UE *nf abr* (= Unión Europea) EU
UEFA [w'efa] *nf abr* (= Unión de Asociaciones de
   Fútbol Europeo) UEFA
UEO *nf abr* (= Unión Europea Occidental) WEU
UEP *nf abr* = **Unión Europea de Pagos**
UER *sigla f* = **Unión Europea de Radiodifusión**
uf [uf] *excl (cansancio)* phew!; *(repugnancia)* ugh!
ufanarse [ufa'narse] *vr* to boast; **~ de** to pride
   o.s. on
ufano, -a [u'fano, a] *adj (arrogante)* arrogant;
   (presumido) conceited
UGT *nf abr ver* **Unión General de Trabajadores**
UIT *sigla f* = **Unión Internacional de
   Telecomunicaciones**
ujier [u'xjer] *nm* usher; *(portero)* doorkeeper
úlcera ['ulθera] *nf* ulcer
ulcerar [ulθe'rar] *vt* to make sore; **ulcerarse**
   vr to ulcerate

ulterior [ulte'rjor] *adj (más allá)* farther,
   further; *(subsecuente, siguiente)* subsequent
ulteriormente [ulterjor'mente] *adv* later,
   subsequently
últimamente ['ultimamente] *adv*
   (recientemente) lately, recently; *(finalmente)*
   finally; *(como último recurso)* as a last resort
ultimar [ulti'mar] *vt* to finish; *(finalizar)* to
   finalize; *(Am: rematar)* to finish off, murder
ultimátum [ulti'matum] *nm (pl* **ultimátums***)*
   ultimatum
último, -a ['ultimo, a] *adj* last; *(más reciente)*
   latest, most recent; *(más bajo)* bottom; *(más
   alto)* top; *(fig)* final, extreme; **en las últimas**
   on one's last legs; **por último** finally
ultra ['ultra] *adj* ultra ■ *nm/f* extreme right-
   winger
ultracongelar [ultrakonxe'lar] *vt* to deep-
   freeze
ultraderecha [ultraðe'retʃa] *nf* extreme
   right (wing)
ultrajar [ultra'xar] *vt (escandalizar)* to outrage;
   (insultar) to insult, abuse
ultraje [ul'traxe] *nm* outrage; insult
ultraligero [ultrali'xero] *nm* microlight *(Brit)*,
   microlite *(US)*
ultramar [ultra'mar] *nm:* **de** *o* **en ~** abroad,
   overseas; **los países de ~** the overseas
   countries
ultramarino, -a [ultrama'rino, a] *adj*
   overseas, foreign ■ *nmpl:* **ultramarinos**
   groceries; **tienda de ultramarinos** grocer's
   (shop)
ultranza [ul'tranθa]: **a ~** *adv* to the death; *(a
   toda costa)* at all costs; *(completo)* outright; *(Pol
   etc)* out-and-out, extreme; **un nacionalista
   a ~** a rabid nationalist
ultrarrojo, -a [ultra'rroxo, a] *adj* =
   infrarrojo, a
ultrasónico, -a [ultra'soniko, a] *adj*
   ultrasonic
ultratumba [ultra'tumba] *nf:* **la vida de ~**
   the next life; **una voz de ~** a ghostly voice

u

ultravioleta [ultraβjo'leta] *adj inv* ultraviolet
ulular [ulu'lar] *vi* to howl; (*búho*) to hoot
umbilical [umbili'kal] *adj*: **cordón ~** umbilical cord
umbral [um'bral] *nm* (*gen*) threshold; **~ de rentabilidad** (*Com*) break-even point
umbrío, -a [um'brio, a] *adj* shady
UME *nf abr* (= *Unión Monetaria y Económica*) EMU

PALABRA CLAVE

un, una [un, 'una] *artículo indefinido* a; (*antes de vocal*) an; **una mujer/naranja** a woman/an orange
■ *adj* **1**: **unos** (*o* **unas**): **hay unos regalos para ti** there are some presents for you; **hay unas cervezas en la nevera** there are some beers in the fridge
2 (*enfático*): **¡hace un frío!** it's so cold!; **¡tiene una casa!** he's got some house!

U.N.A.M. ['unam] *nf abr* = **Universidad Nacional Autónoma de México**
unánime [u'nanime] *adj* unanimous
unanimidad [unanimi'ðað] *nf* unanimity; **por ~** unanimously
unción [un'θjon] *nf* anointing
uncir [un'θir] *vt* to yoke
undécimo, -a [un'deθimo, a] *adj, nm/f* eleventh
UNED [u'ned] *nf abr* (*Esp Univ*: = *Universidad Nacional de Enseñanza a Distancia*) ≈ Open University (Brit)
UNEF [u'nef] *sigla f* = **Fuerzas de Urgencia de las Naciones Unidas**
UNESCO, Unesco [u'nesko] *sigla f* (= *United Nations Educational, Scientific and Cultural Organization*) UNESCO
ungir [un'xir] *vt* to rub with ointment; (*Rel*) to anoint
ungüento [un'gwento] *nm* ointment; (*fig*) salve, balm
únicamente ['unikamente] *adv* solely; (*solamente*) only
UNICEF, Unicef [uni'θef] *sigla m* (= *United Nations International Children's Emergency Fund*) ≈ UNICEF
unicidad [uniθi'ðað] *nf* uniqueness
único, -a ['uniko, a] *adj* only; (*solo*) sole, single; (*sin par*) unique; **hijo único** only child
unidad [uni'ðað] *nf* unity; (*Tec*) unit; **~ móvil** (*TV*) mobile unit; (*Inform*): **~ central** system unit, central processing unit; **~ de control** control unit; **~ de disco** disk drive; **~ de entrada/salida** input/output device; **~ de información** data item; **~ periférica** peripheral device; **~ de presentación visual**

o **de visualización** visual display unit; **~ procesadora central** central processing unit
unido, -a [u'niðo, a] *adj* joined, linked; (*fig*) united
unifamiliar [unifamil'jar] *adj*: **vivienda ~** single-family home
unificar [unifi'kar] *vt* to unite, unify
unifique *etc* [uni'fike] *vb ver* **unificar**
uniformado, -a [unifor'maðo, a] *adj* uniformed, in uniform
uniformar [unifor'mar] *vt* to make uniform; (*Tec*) to standardize
uniforme [uni'forme] *adj* uniform, equal; (*superficie*) even ■ *nm* uniform
uniformidad [uniformi'ðað] *nf* uniformity; (*llaneza*) levelness, evenness
unilateral [unilate'ral] *adj* unilateral
unión [u'njon] *nf* (*gen*) union; (*acto*) uniting, joining; (*calidad*) unity; (*Tec*) joint; (*fig*) closeness, togetherness; **en ~ con** (together) with, accompanied by; **~ aduanera** customs union; **U~ General de Trabajadores (UGT)** (*Esp*) Socialist Union Confederation; **U~ Europea** European Union; **la U~ Soviética** the Soviet Union; **punto de ~** (*Tec*) junction
unir [u'nir] *vt* (*juntar*) to join, unite; (*atar*) to tie, fasten; (*combinar*) to combine ■ *vi* (*ingredientes*) to mix well; **unirse** *vr* to join together, unite; (*empresas*) to merge; **les une una fuerte simpatía** they are bound by (a) strong affection; **unirse en matrimonio** to marry
unisex [uni'seks] *adj inv* unisex
unísono [u'nisono] *nm*: **al ~** in unison
unitario, -a [uni'tarjo, a] *adj* unitary; (*Rel*) Unitarian ■ *nm/f* (*Rel*) Unitarian
universal [uniβer'sal] *adj* universal; (*mundial*) world *cpd*; **historia ~** world history
universidad [uniβersi'ðað] *nf* university; **~ laboral** polytechnic, poly
universitario, -a [uniβersi'tarjo, a] *adj* university *cpd* ■ *nm/f* (*profesor*) lecturer; (*estudiante*) (university) student
universo [uni'βerso] *nm* universe
unja *etc* ['unxa] *vb ver* **ungir**

PALABRA CLAVE

uno, -a ['uno, a] *adj* one; **es todo uno** it's all one and the same; **unos pocos** a few; **unos cien** about a hundred
■ *pron* **1** one; **quiero uno solo** I only want one; **uno de ellos** one of them; **una de dos** either one or the other; **no doy una hoy** I can't do anything right today
2 (*alguien*) somebody, someone; **conozco a**

uno que se te parece I know somebody o someone who looks like you; **unos querían quedarse** some (people) wanted to stay
3 (*impersonal*) one; **uno mismo** oneself; **uno nunca sabe qué hacer** one never knows what to do
4: **unos ... otros ...** some ... others; **una y otra son muy agradables** they're both very nice; **(los) uno(s) a (los) otro(s)** each other, one another
■ *nf* one; **es la una** it's one o'clock
■ *num* (number) one; **el día uno** the first

untar [un'tar] *vt* (*gen*) to rub; (*engrasar*) to grease, oil; (*Med*) to rub (with ointment); (*fig*) to bribe; **untarse** *vr* (*fig*) to be crooked; **~ el pan con mantequilla** to spread butter on one's bread
unto ['unto] *nm* animal fat; (*Med*) ointment
unza *etc* ['unθa] *vb ver* **uncir**
uña ['uɲa] *nf* (*Anat*) nail; (*del pie*) toenail; (*garra*) claw; (*casco*) hoof; (*arranca* claws; claw; **ser ~ y carne** to be as thick as thieves; **enseñar** o **mostrar** o **sacar las uñas** to show one's claws
UOE *nf abr* (*Esp Mil*) **= Unidad de Operaciones Especiales**
UPA *nf abr* **= Unión Panamericana**
UPC *nf abr* (**= unidad procesadora central**) CPU
uperizado, -a [uperi'θaðo, a] *adj*: **leche uperizada** UHT milk
Urales [u'rales] *nmpl* (*tb*: **Montes Urales**) Urals
uralita® [ura'lita] *nf* corrugated asbestos cement
uranio [u'ranjo] *nm* uranium
urbanidad [urβani'ðað] *nf* courtesy, politeness
urbanismo [urβa'nismo] *nm* town planning
urbanista [urβa'nista] *nm/f* town planner
urbanización [urβaniθa'θjon] *nf* (*colonia, barrio*) estate, housing scheme
urbanizar [urβani'θar] *vt* to develop
urbano, -a [ur'βano, a] *adj* (*de ciudad*) urban, town *cpd*; (*cortés*) courteous, polite
urbe ['urβe] *nf* large city, metropolis
urdimbre [ur'ðimbre] *nf* (*de tejido*) warp; (*intriga*) intrigue
urdir [ur'ðir] *vt* to warp; (*fig*) to plot, contrive
urgencia [ur'xenθja] *nf* urgency; (*prisa*) haste, rush; **salida de ~** emergency exit; **servicios de ~** emergency services
urgente [ur'xente] *adj* urgent; (*insistente*) insistent; **carta ~** registered (*Brit*) o special delivery (*US*) letter
urgir [ur'xir] *vi* to be urgent; **me urge** I'm in a hurry for it; **me urge terminarlo** I must finish it as soon as I can

urinario, -a [uri'narjo, a] *adj* urinary ■ *nm* urinal, public lavatory, comfort station (*US*)
urja *etc* ['urxa] *vb ver* **urgir**
urna ['urna] *nf* urn; (*Pol*) ballot box; **acudir a las urnas** (*fig*: *persona*) to (go and) vote; (: *gobierno*) to go to the country
urología [urolo'xia] *nf* urology
urólogo, -a [u'roloyo, a] *nm/f* urologist
urraca [u'rraka] *nf* magpie
URSS *nf abr* (*Historia*: **= Unión de Repúblicas Socialistas Soviéticas**) USSR
Uruguay [uru'ɣwai] *nm*: **El ~** Uruguay
uruguayo, -a [uru'ɣwajo, a] *adj, nm/f* Uruguayan
usado, -a [u'saðo, a] *adj* (*gen*) used; (*ropa etc*) worn; **muy ~** worn out
usanza [u'sanθa] *nf* custom, usage
usar [u'sar] *vt* to use; (*ropa*) to wear; (*tener costumbre*) to be in the habit of ■ *vi*: **~ de** to make use of; **usarse** *vr* to be used; (*ropa*) to be worn o in fashion
USO ['uso] *nf abr* (*Esp*: **= Unión Sindical Obrera**) workers' union
uso ['uso] *nm* use; (*Mecánica etc*) wear; (*costumbre*) usage, custom; (*moda*) fashion; **al ~** in keeping with custom; **al ~ de** in the style of; **de ~ externo** (*Med*) for external application; **estar en el ~ de la palabra** to be speaking, have the floor; **~ y desgaste** (*Com*) wear and tear
usted [us'teð] *pron* (*sg formal*: *abr* **Ud** o **Vd**) you *sg*; **ustedes** (*pl formal*: *abr* **Uds** o **Vds**) you *pl*; (*Am*: *formal y fam*) you *pl*
usual [u'swal] *adj* usual
usuario, -a [usw'arjo, a] *nm/f* user; **~ final** (*Com*) end user
usufructo [usu'frukto] *nm* use; **~ vitalicio (de)** life interest (in)
usura [u'sura] *nf* usury
usurero, -a [usu'rero, a] *nm/f* usurer
usurpar [usur'par] *vt* to usurp
utensilio [uten'siljo] *nm* tool; (*Culin*) utensil
útero ['utero] *nm* uterus, womb
útil ['util] *adj* useful; (*servible*) usable, serviceable ■ *nm* tool; **día útil** working day, weekday; **es muy útil tenerlo aquí cerca** it's very handy having it here close by
utilice *etc* [uti'liθe] *vb ver* **utilizar**
utilidad [utili'ðað] *nf* usefulness, utility; (*Com*) profit; **utilidades líquidas** net profit *sg*
utilitario [utili'tarjo] *nm* (*Inform*) utility
utilizar [utili'θar] *vt* to use, utilize; (*explotar*) to harness
utopía [uto'pia] *nf* Utopia
utópico, -a [u'topiko, a] *adj* Utopian
UVA *sigla mpl* (**= ultravioleta**) UV, UVA

u

uva ['uβa] *nf* grape; ~ **pasa** raisin; ~ **de Corinto** currant; **estar de mala** ~ to be in a bad mood; *see note*

● **UVA**

● In Spain *Las uvas* play a big part on New Years' Eve (*Nochevieja*), when on the stroke of midnight people from every part of Spain, at home, in restaurants or in the plaza mayor eat a grape for each stroke of the clock of the Puerta del Sol in Madrid. It is said to bring luck for the following year.

uve ['uβe] *nf name of the letter* V; **en forma de** ~ V-shaped; ~ **doble** *name of the letter* W

UVI ['uβi] *nf abr* (*Esp Med*: = *unidad de vigilancia intensiva*) ICU

Vv

V, v (Esp) ['uβe] (Am) [be'korta, bet∫ika] nf
(letra) V, v; **V de Valencia** V for Victor
V. abr = **usted**; (= visto) approved, passed
v. abr (= voltio) v; (= ver, véase) v.; (Lit: = verso) v
va [ba] vb ver **ir**
V.A. abr = **Vuestra Alteza**
vaca ['baka] nf (animal) cow; (carne) beef;
(cuero) cowhide; **vacas flacas/gordas** (fig)
bad/good times
vacaciones [baka'θjones] nfpl holiday(s);
estar/irse o **marcharse de ~** to be/go (away)
on holiday
vacante [ba'kante] adj vacant, empty ■ nf
vacancy
vaciado, -a [ba'θjaðo, a] adj (hecho en molde)
cast in a mould; (hueco) hollow ■ nm cast,
mould(ing)
vaciar [ba'θjar] vt to empty (out); (ahuecar)
to hollow out; (moldear) to cast; (Inform) to
dump ■ vi (río): **~ en** to flow into; **vaciarse**
vr to empty; (fig) to blab, spill the beans
vaciedad [baθje'ðað] nf emptiness
vacilación [baθila'θjon] nf hesitation
vacilante [baθi'lante] adj unsteady; (habla)
faltering; (luz) flickering; (fig) hesitant
vacilar [baθi'lar] vi to be unsteady; to falter;
to flicker; to hesitate, waver; (persona) to
stagger, stumble; (memoria) to fail; (esp Am:
divertirse) to have a great time
vacilón [baθi'lon] nm (esp Am): **estar** o **ir de ~**
to have a great time
vacío, -a [ba'θio, a] adj empty; (puesto)
vacant; (desocupado) idle; (vano) vain; (charla
etc) light, superficial ■ nm emptiness;
(Física) vacuum; (un vacío) (empty) space;
hacer el ~ a algn to send sb to Coventry
vacuna [ba'kuna] nf vaccine
vacunar [baku'nar] vt to vaccinate;
vacunarse vr to get vaccinated
vacuno, -a [ba'kuno, a] adj bovine
vacuo, -a ['bakwo, a] adj empty
vadear [baðe'ar] vt (río) to ford; (problema) to
overcome; (persona) to sound out

vado ['baðo] nm ford; (solución) solution;
(descanso) respite; **"~ permanente"** "keep
clear"
vagabundo, -a [baɣa'βundo, a] adj
wandering; (pey) vagrant ■ nm/f (errante)
wanderer; (vago) tramp, bum (US)
vagamente [baɣa'mente] adv vaguely
vagancia [ba'ɣanθja] nf vagrancy
vagar [ba'ɣar] vi to wander; (pasear) to
saunter up and down; (no hacer nada) to idle
■ nm leisure
vagido [ba'xiðo] nm wail
vagina [ba'xina] nf vagina
vago, -a ['baɣo, a] adj vague; (perezoso) lazy;
(ambulante) wandering ■ nm/f (vagabundo)
tramp, bum (US); (perezoso) lazybones sg, idler
vagón [ba'ɣon] nm (de pasajeros) carriage; (de
mercancías) wagon; **~ cama/restaurante**
sleeping/dining car
vague etc ['baɣe] vb ver **vagar**
vaguear [baɣe'ar] vi to laze around
vaguedad [baɣe'ðað] nf vagueness
vahído [ba'iðo] nm dizzy spell
vaho ['bao] nm (vapor) vapour, steam; (olor)
smell; (respiración) breath; **vahos** nmpl (Med)
inhalation sg
vaina ['baina] nf sheath ■ nm (Am) nuisance
vainilla [bai'niʎa] nf vanilla
vainita [bai'nita] nf (Am) green o French bean
vais [bais] vb ver **ir**
vaivén [bai'βen] nm to-and-fro movement;
(de tránsito) coming and going; **vaivenes**
nmpl (fig) ups and downs
vajilla [ba'xiʎa] nf crockery, dishes pl; (una
vajilla) service; **~ de porcelana** chinaware
val [bal], **valdré** etc [bal'dre] vb ver **valer**
vale ['bale] nm voucher; (recibo) receipt; (pagaré)
I.O.U.; **~ de regalo** gift voucher o token
valedero, -a [bale'ðero, a] adj valid
valenciano, -a [balen'θjano, a] adj, nm/f
Valencian ■ nm (Ling) Valencian
valentía [balen'tia] nf courage, bravery; (pey)
boastfulness; (acción) heroic deed

V

valentísimo, -a [balen'tisimo, a] *adj*
superlativo de **valiente** very brave, courageous
valentón, -ona [balen'ton, ona] *adj*
blustering
valer [ba'ler] *vt* to be worth; (*Mat*) to equal;
(*costar*) to cost; (*amparar*) to aid, protect ▪ *vi*
(*ser útil*) to be useful; (*ser válido*) to be valid;
valerse *vr* to defend o.s. ▪ *nm* worth, value;
~ **la pena** to be worthwhile; **¿vale?** O.K.?;
¡vale! (¡*basta!*) that'll do!; **¡eso no vale!** that
doesn't count!; **no vale nada** it's no good;
(*mercancía*) it's worthless; (*argumento*) it's no
use; **no vale para nada** he's no good at all;
más vale tarde que nunca better late than
never; **más vale que nos vayamos** we'd
better go; **valerse de** to make use of, take
advantage of; **valerse por sí mismo** to help
o manage by o.s.
valga *etc* ['balɣa] *vb ver* **valer**
valía [ba'lia] *nf* worth; **de gran** ~ (*objeto*) very
valuable
validar [bali'ðar] *vt* to validate; (*Pol*) to ratify
validez [bali'ðeθ] *nf* validity; **dar ~ a** to
validate
válido, -a ['baliðo, a] *adj* valid
valiente [ba'ljente] *adj* brave, valiant;
(*audaz*) bold; (*pey*) boastful; (*con ironía*) fine,
wonderful ▪ *nm/f* brave man/woman
valija [ba'lixa] *nf* case; (*Am*) suitcase;
(*mochila*) satchel; (*Correos*) mailbag; ~
diplomática diplomatic bag
valioso, -a [ba'ljoso, a] *adj* valuable; (*rico*)
wealthy
valla ['baʎa] *nf* fence; (*Deporte*) hurdle; (*fig*)
barrier; ~ **publicitaria** billboard
vallar [ba'ʎar] *vt* to fence in
valle ['baʎe] *nm* valley, vale
vallisoletano, -a [baʎisole'tano, a] *adj* of o
from Valladolid ▪ *nm/f* native o inhabitant
of Valladolid
valor [ba'lor] *nm* value, worth; (*precio*) price;
(*valentía*) valour, courage; (*importancia*)
importance; (*cara*) nerve, cheek (*fam*); **sin**
~ worthless; ~ **adquisitivo** o **de compra**
purchasing power; **dar ~ a** to attach
importance to; **quitar ~ a** to minimize the
importance of; (*Com*): ~ **según balance** book
value; ~ **comercial** o **de mercado** market
value; ~ **contable/desglosado** asset/break-
up value; ~ **de escasez** scarcity value; ~
intrínseco intrinsic value; ~ **a la par** par
value; ~ **neto** net worth; ~ **de rescate/de**
sustitución surrender/replacement value;
ver tb **valores**
valoración [balora'θjon] *nf* valuation
valorar [balo'rar] *vt* to value; (*tasar*) to price;
(*fig*) to assess

valores [ba'lores] *nmpl* (*Com*) securities;
~ **en cartera** o **habidos** investments
vals [bals] *nm* waltz
válvula ['balβula] *nf* valve
vamos ['bamos] *vb ver* **ir**
vampiro, -iresa [bam'piro, i'resa] *nm/f*
vampire ▪ *nf* (*Cine*) vamp, femme fatale
van [ban] *vb ver* **ir**
vanagloriarse [banaɣlo'rjarse] *vr* to boast
vandalismo [banda'lismo] *nm* vandalism
vándalo, -a ['bandalo, a] *nm/f* vandal
vanguardia [ban'gwardja] *nf* vanguard; **de ~**
(*Arte*) avant-garde; **estar en** o **ir a la ~ de** (*fig*)
to be in the forefront of
vanguardista [bangwar'ðista] *adj* avant-
garde
vanidad [bani'ðað] *nf* vanity; (*inutilidad*)
futility; (*irrealidad*) unreality
vanidoso, -a [bani'ðoso, a] *adj* vain,
conceited
vano, -a ['bano, a] *adj* (*irreal*) unreal;
(*irracional*) unreasonable; (*inútil*) vain, useless;
(*persona*) vain, conceited; (*frívolo*) frivolous
vapor [ba'por] *nm* vapour; (*vaho*) steam; (*de*
gas) fumes *pl*; (*neblina*) mist; **vapores** *nmpl*
(*Med*) hysterics; **al ~** (*Culin*) steamed
vaporice *etc* [bapo'riθe] *vb ver* **vaporizar**
vaporizador [baporiθa'ðor] *nm* (*de perfume*
etc) spray
vaporizar [bapori'θar] *vt* to vaporize;
(*perfume*) to spray
vaporoso, -a [bapo'roso, a] *adj* vaporous;
(*vahoso*) steamy; (*tela*) light, airy
vapulear [bapule'ar] *vt* to thrash; (*fig*) to
slate
vaquería [bake'ria] *nf* dairy
vaquero, -a [ba'kero, a] *adj* cattle *cpd* ▪ *nm*
cowboy; **vaqueros** *nmpl* jeans
vaquilla [ba'kiʎa] *nf* heifer
vara ['bara] *nf* stick, pole; (*Tec*) rod; ~ **mágica**
magic wand
varado, -a [ba'raðo, a] *adj* (*Naut*) stranded;
estar ~ to be aground
varar [ba'rar] *vt* to beach ▪ *vi*, **vararse** *vr* to
be beached
varear [bare'ar] *vt* to hit, beat; (*frutas*) to
knock down (with poles)
variable [ba'rjaβle] *adj*, *nf* variable (*tb Inform*)
variación [barja'θjon] *nf* variation; **sin ~**
unchanged
variado, -a [ba'rjaðo, a] *adj* varied; (*dulces*,
galletas) assorted; **entremeses variados** a
selection of starters
variante [ba'rjante] *adj* variant ▪ *nf*
(*alternativa*) alternative; (*Auto*) bypass
variar [ba'rjar] *vt* (*cambiar*) to change; (*poner*
variedad) to vary; (*modificar*) to modify;

(*cambiar de posición*) to switch around ▪ *vi* to vary; ~ **de** to differ from; ~ **de opinión** to change one's mind; **para** ~ just for a change
varicela [bari'θela] *nf* chicken pox
varices [ba'riθes] *nfpl* varicose veins
variedad [barje'ðað] *nf* variety
varilla [ba'riʎa] *nf* stick; (*Bot*) twig; (*Tec*) rod; (*de rueda*) spoke; ~ **mágica** magic wand
vario, -a ['barjo, a] *adj* (*variado*) varied; (*multicolor*) motley; (*cambiable*) changeable; **varios** various, several
variopinto, -a [barjo'pinto, a] *adj* diverse; **un público** ~ a mixed audience
varita [ba'rita] *nf*: ~ **mágica** magic wand
varón [ba'ron] *nm* male, man
varonil [baro'nil] *adj* manly
Varsovia [bar'soβja] *nf* Warsaw
vas [bas] *vb ver* **ir**
vasco, -a ['basko, a], **vascongado a** [baskon'gaðo, a] *adj, nm/f* Basque ▪ *nm* (*Ling*) Basque ▪ *nfpl*: **las Vascongadas** the Basque Country *sg o* Provinces
vascuence [bas'kwenθe] *nm* (*Ling*) Basque
vasectomía [basekto'mia] *nf* vasectomy
vaselina [base'lina] *nf* Vaseline®
vasija [ba'sixa] *nf* (*earthenware*) vessel
vaso ['baso] *nm* glass, tumbler; (*Anat*) vessel; (*cantidad*) glass(ful); ~ **de vino** glass of wine; ~ **para vino** wineglass
vástago ['bastaɣo] *nm* (*Bot*) shoot; (*Tec*) rod; (*fig*) offspring
vasto, -a ['basto, a] *adj* vast, huge
váter ['bater] *nm* lavatory, W.C.
Vaticano [bati'kano] *nm*: **el** ~ the Vatican; **la Ciudad del** ~ the Vatican City
vaticinar [batiθi'nar] *vt* to prophesy, predict
vaticinio [bati'θinjo] *nm* prophecy
vatio ['batjo] *nm* (*Elec*) watt
vaya *etc* ['baja] *vb ver* **ir**
Vda. *abr* (= *viuda*) = **viudo**
Vd *abr* = **usted**
Vds *abr* = **ustedes**
ve [be] *vb ver* **ir**; **ver**
vea *etc* ['bea] *vb ver* **ver**
vecinal [beθi'nal] *adj* (*camino, impuesto etc*) local
vecindad [beθin'dað] *nf*, **vecindario** [beθin'darjo] *nm* neighbourhood; (*habitantes*) residents *pl*
vecino, -a [be'θino, a] *adj* neighbouring ▪ *nm/f* neighbour; (*residente*) resident; **somos vecinos** we live next door to one another
vector [bek'tor] *nm* vector
veda ['beða] *nf* prohibition; (*temporada*) close season
vedado [be'ðaðo] *nm* preserve

vedar [be'ðar] *vt* (*prohibir*) to ban, prohibit; (*idea, plan*) to veto; (*impedir*) to stop, prevent
vedette [be'ðet] *nf* (*Teat: Cine*) star(let)
vega ['beɣa] *nf* fertile plain *o* valley
vegetación [bexeta'θjon] *nf* vegetation
vegetal [bexe'tal] *adj, nm* vegetable
vegetar [bexe'tar] *vi* to vegetate
vegetariano, -a [bexeta'rjano, a] *adj, nm/f* vegetarian
vegetativo, -a [bexeta'tiβo, a] *adj* vegetative
vehemencia [bee'menθja] *nf* (*insistencia*) vehemence; (*pasión*) passion; (*fervor*) fervour; (*violencia*) violence
vehemente [bee'mente] *adj* vehement; passionate; fervent; violent
vehículo [be'ikulo] *nm* vehicle; (*Med*) carrier; ~ **de servicio público** public service vehicle; ~ **espacial** spacecraft
veinte ['beinte] *num* twenty; (*orden, fecha*) twentieth; **el siglo** ~ the twentieth century
veintena [bein'tena] *nf*: **una** ~ (about) twenty, a score
vejación [bexa'θjon] *nf* vexation; (*humillación*) humiliation
vejamen [be'xamen] *nm* satire
vejar [be'xar] *vt* (*irritar*) to annoy, vex; (*humillar*) to humiliate
vejatorio, -a [bexa'torjo, a] *adj* humiliating, degrading
vejez [be'xeθ] *nf* old age
vejiga [be'xiɣa] *nf* (*Anat*) bladder
vela ['bela] *nf* (*de cera*) candle; (*Naut*) sail; (*insomnio*) sleeplessness; (*vigilia*) vigil; (*Mil*) sentry duty; (*fam*) snot; **a toda** ~ (*Naut*) under full sail; **estar a dos velas** (*fam*) to be skint; **pasar la noche en** ~ to have a sleepless night
velado, -a [be'laðo, a] *adj* veiled; (*sonido*) muffled; (*Foto*) blurred ▪ *nf* soirée
velador [bela'ðor] *nm* watchman; (*candelero*) candlestick; (*Am*) bedside table
velar [be'lar] *vt* (*vigilar*) to keep watch over; (*cubrir*) to veil ▪ *vi* to stay awake; ~ **por** to watch over, look after
velatorio [bela'torjo] *nm* (*funeral*) wake
veleidad [belei'ðað] *nf* (*ligereza*) fickleness; (*capricho*) whim
velero [be'lero] *nm* (*Naut*) sailing ship; (*Aviat*) glider
veleta [be'leta] *nm/f* fickle person ▪ *nf* weather vane
veliz [be'lis] *nm* (*Am*) suitcase
vello ['beʎo] *nm* down, fuzz
vellón [be'ʎon] *nm* fleece
velloso, -a [be'ʎoso, a] *adj* fuzzy
velludo, -a [be'ʎuðo, a] *adj* shaggy ▪ *nm* plush, velvet

V

395

velo ['belo] *nm* veil; **~ de paladar** (*Anat*) soft palate

velocidad [beloθi'ðað] *nf* speed; (*Tec*) rate, pace, velocity; (*Mecánica: Auto*) gear; **¿a qué ~?** how fast?; **de alta ~** high-speed; **cobrar ~** to pick up *o* gather speed; **meter la segunda ~** to change into second gear; **~ máxima de impresión** (*Inform*) maximum print speed

velocímetro [belo'θimetro] *nm* speedometer

velódromo [be'loðromo] *nm* cycle track

veloz [be'loθ] *adj* fast, swift

ven [ben] *vb ver* **venir**

vena ['bena] *nf* vein; (*fig*) vein, disposition; (*Geo*) seam, vein

venablo [be'naβlo] *nm* javelin

venado [be'naðo] *nm* deer; (*Culin*) venison

venal [be'nal] *adj* (*Anat*) venous; (*pey*) venal

venalidad [benali'ðað] *nf* venality

vencedor, a [benθe'ðor, a] *adj* victorious ◼ *nm/f* victor, winner

vencer [ben'θer] *vt* (*dominar*) to defeat, beat; (*derrotar*) to vanquish; (*superar, controlar*) to overcome, master ◼ *vi* (*triunfar*) to win (through), triumph; (*pago*) to fall due; (*plazo*) to expire; **dejarse ~** to yield, give in

vencido, -a [ben'θiðo, a] *adj* (*derrotado*) defeated, beaten; (*Com*) payable, due ◼ *adv*: **pagar ~** to pay in arrears; **le pagan por meses vencidos** he is paid at the end of the month; **darse por ~** to give up

vencimiento [benθi'mjento] *nm* collapse; (*Com: de plazo*) expiration; **a su ~** when it falls due

venda ['benda] *nf* bandage

vendaje [ben'daxe] *nm* bandage, dressing

vendar [ben'dar] *vt* to bandage; **~ los ojos** to blindfold

vendaval [benda'βal] *nm* (*viento*) gale; (*huracán*) hurricane

vendedor, a [bende'ðor, a] *nm/f* seller; **~ ambulante** hawker, pedlar (*Brit*), peddler (*US*)

vender [ben'der] *vt* to sell; (*comerciar*) to market; (*traicionar*) to sell out, betray; **venderse** *vr* to be sold; **~ al contado/al por mayor/al por menor/a plazos** to sell for cash/wholesale/retail/on credit; **"se vende"** "for sale"; **"véndese coche"** "car for sale"; **~ al descubierto** to sell short

vendimia [ben'dimja] *nf* grape harvest; **la ~ de 1973** the 1973 vintage

vendimiar [bendi'mjar] *vi* to pick grapes

vendré *etc* [ben'dre] *vb ver* **venir**

Venecia [be'neθja] *nf* Venice

veneciano, -a [bene'θjano, a] *adj, nm/f* Venetian

veneno [be'neno] *nm* poison, venom

venenoso, -a [bene'noso, a] *adj* poisonous

venerable [bene'raβle] *adj* venerable

veneración [benera'θjon] *nf* veneration

venerar [bene'rar] *vt* (*reconocer*) to venerate; (*adorar*) to worship

venéreo, -a [be'nereo, a] *adj* venereal

venezolano, -a [beneθo'lano, a] *adj, nm/f* Venezuelan

Venezuela [bene'θwela] *nf* Venezuela

venga *etc* ['benga] *vb ver* **venir**

vengador, a [benga'ðor, a] *adj* avenging ◼ *nm/f* avenger

venganza [ben'ganθa] *nf* vengeance, revenge

vengar [ben'gar] *vt* to avenge; **vengarse** *vr* to take revenge

vengativo, -a [benga'tiβo, a] *adj* (*persona*) vindictive

vengue *etc* ['benge] *vb ver* **vengar**

venia ['benja] *nf* (*perdón*) pardon; (*permiso*) consent; **con su ~** by your leave

venial [be'njal] *adj* venial

venida [be'niða] *nf* (*llegada*) arrival; (*regreso*) return; (*fig*) rashness

venidero, -a [beni'ðero, a] *adj* coming, future; **en lo ~** in (the) future

venir [be'nir] *vi* to come; (*llegar*) to arrive; (*ocurrir*) to happen; **venirse** *vr*: **venirse abajo** to collapse; **~ a menos** (*persona*) to lose status; (*empresa*) to go downhill; **~ bien** to be suitable, come just right; (*ropa, gusto*) to suit; **~ mal** to be unsuitable *o* inconvenient, come awkwardly; **el año que viene** next year; **¡ven acá!** come (over) here!; **¡venga!** (*fam*) come on!

venta ['benta] *nf* (*Com*) sale; (*posada*) inn; **~ a plazos** hire purchase; **~ al contado/al por mayor/al por menor** *o* **al detalle** cash sale/ wholesale/retail; **~ a domicilio** door-to-door selling; **~ y arrendamiento al vendedor** sale and lease back; **~ de liquidación** clearance sale; **estar de** *o* **en ~** to be (up) for sale *o* on the market; **ventas brutas** gross sales; **ventas a término** forward sales

ventaja [ben'taxa] *nf* advantage; **llevar la ~** (*en carrera*) to be leading *o* ahead

ventajoso, -a [benta'xoso, a] *adj* advantageous

ventana [ben'tana] *nf* window; **~ de guillotina/galería** sash/bay window; **~ de la nariz** nostril

ventanilla [benta'niʎa] *nf* (*de taquilla, tb Inform*) window

ventearse [bente'arse] *vr* (*romperse*) to crack; (*Anat*) to break wind

ventilación [bentila'θjon] *nf* ventilation; (*corriente*) draught; (*fig*) airing

ventilador [bentila'ðor] *nm* ventilator; (*eléctrico*) fan

ventilar [benti'lar] *vt* to ventilate; (*poner a secar*) to put out to dry; (*fig*) to air, discuss

ventisca [ben'tiska] *nf* blizzard

ventisquero [bentis'kero] *nm* snowdrift

ventolera [bento'lera] *nf* (*ráfaga*) gust of wind; (*idea*) whim, wild idea; **le dio la ~ de comprarlo** he had a sudden notion to buy it

ventosear [bentose'ar] *vi* to break wind

ventosidad [bentosi'ðað] *nf* flatulence

ventoso, -a [ben'toso, a] *adj* windy ■ *nf* (*Zool*) sucker; (*instrumento*) suction pad

ventrículo [ben'trikulo] *nm* ventricle

ventrílocuo, -a [ben'trilokwo, a] *nm/f* ventriloquist

ventriloquia [bentri'lokja] *nf* ventriloquism

ventura [ben'tura] *nf* (*felicidad*) happiness; (*buena suerte*) luck; (*destino*) fortune; **a la (buena) ~** at random

venturoso, -a [bentu'roso, a] *adj* happy; (*afortunado*) lucky, fortunate

venza *etc* ['benθa] *vb ver* **vencer**

ver [ber] *vt, vi* to see; (*mirar*) to look at, watch; (*investigar*) to look into; (*entender*) to see, understand; **verse** *vr* (*encontrarse*) to meet; (*dejarse ver*) to be seen; (*hallarse: en un apuro*) to find o.s., be ■ *nm* looks *pl*, appearance; **a ~** let's see; **a ~ si …** I wonder if …; **por lo que veo** apparently; **dejarse ~** to become apparent; **no tener nada que ~ con** to have nothing to do with; **a mi modo de ~** as I see it; **merece verse** it's worth seeing; **no lo veo** I can't see it; **¡nos vemos!** see you (later)!; **¡habráse visto!** did you ever! (*fam*); **¡viera(n) o hubiera(n) visto qué casa!** (*Am fam*) if only you'd seen the house!, what a house!; **ya se ve que …** it is obvious that …; **si te vi no me acuerdo** they *etc* just don't want to know

vera ['bera] *nf* edge, verge; (*de río*) bank; **a la ~ de** near, next to

veracidad [beraθi'ðað] *nf* truthfulness

veraneante [berane'ante] *nm/f* holidaymaker, (summer) vacationer (US)

veranear [berane'ar] *vi* to spend the summer

veraneo [bera'neo] *nm*: **estar de ~** to be away on (one's summer) holiday; **lugar de ~** holiday resort

veraniego, -a [bera'njeɣo, a] *adj* summer *cpd*

verano [be'rano] *nm* summer

veras ['beras] *nfpl* truth *sg*; **de ~** really, truly; **esto va de ~** this is serious

veraz [be'raθ] *adj* truthful

verbal [ber'βal] *adj* verbal; (*mensaje etc*) oral

verbena [ber'βena] *nf* street party

verbigracia [berβi'ɣraθja] *adv* for example

verbo ['berβo] *nm* verb

verborrea [berβo'rrea] *nf* verbosity, verbal diarrhoea

verboso, -a [ber'βoso, a] *adj* verbose

verdad [ber'ðað] *nf* (*lo verídico*) truth; (*fiabilidad*) reliability ■ *adv* really; **¿~?, ¿no es ~?** isn't it?, aren't you?, don't you? *etc*; **de ~** *adj* real, proper; **a decir ~, no quiero** to tell (you) the truth, I don't want to; **la pura ~** the plain truth

verdaderamente [berðaðera'mente] *adv* really, indeed, truly

verdadero, -a [berða'ðero, a] *adj* (*veraz*) true, truthful; (*fiable*) reliable; (*fig*) real

verde ['berðe] *adj* green; (*fruta etc*) green, unripe; (*chiste etc*) blue, smutty, dirty ■ *nm* green; **viejo ~** dirty old man; **poner a algn a ~** to give sb a dressing-down

verdear [berðe'ar], **verdecer** [berðe'θer] *vi* to turn green

verdezca *etc* [ber'ðeθka] *vb ver* **verdecer**

verdor [ber'ðor] *nm* (*lo verde*) greenness; (*Bot*) verdure; (*fig*) youthful vigour

verdugo [ber'ðuɣo] *nm* executioner; (*Bot*) shoot; (*cardenal*) weal

verdulero, -a [berðu'lero, a] *nm/f* greengrocer

verdura [ber'ðura] *nf* greenness; **verduras** *nfpl* (*Culin*) greens

vereda [be'reða] *nf* path; (*Am*) pavement, sidewalk (US); **meter a algn en ~** to bring sb into line

veredicto [bere'ðikto] *nm* verdict

vergel [ber'xel] *nm* lush garden

vergonzoso, -a [berɣon'θoso, a] *adj* shameful; (*tímido*) timid, bashful

vergüenza [ber'ɣwenθa] *nf* shame, sense of shame; (*timidez*) bashfulness; (*pudor*) modesty; **tener ~** to be ashamed; **me da ~ decírselo** I feel too shy o it embarrasses me to tell him; **¡qué ~!** (*de situación*) what a disgrace!; (*a persona*) shame on you!

vericueto [beri'kweto] *nm* rough track

verídico, -a [be'riðiko, a] *adj* true, truthful

verificar [berifi'kar] *vt* to check; (*corroborar*) to verify (*tb Inform*); (*testamento*) to prove; (*llevar a cabo*) to carry out; **verificarse** *vr* to occur, happen; (*mitin etc*) to be held; (*profecía etc*) to come o prove true

verifique *etc* [beri'fike] *vb ver* **verificar**

verja ['berxa] *nf* iron gate; (*cerca*) railing(s) (*pl*); (*rejado*) grating

vermut [ber'mu] (*pl* **vermuts**) *nm* vermouth ■ *nf* (*esp Am*) matinée

verosímil [bero'simil] *adj* likely, probable; (*relato*) credible

V

verosimilitud [berosimili'tuð] *nf* likeliness, probability

verruga [be'rruɣa] *nf* wart

versado, -a [ber'saðo, a] *adj*: ~ **en** versed in

Versalles [ber'saʎes] *nm* Versailles

versar [ber'sar] *vi* to go round, turn; ~ **sobre** to deal with, be about

versátil [ber'satil] *adj* versatile

versículo [ber'sikulo] *nm* (*Rel*) verse

versión [ber'sjon] *nf* version; (*traducción*) translation

verso ['berso] *nm* verse; **un** ~ a line of poetry; ~ **libre/suelto** free/blank verse

vértebra ['berteβra] *nf* vertebra

vertebrado, -a [berte'βraðo, a] *adj, nm/f* vertebrate

vertebral [berte'βral] *adj* vertebral; **columna** ~ spine

vertedero [berte'ðero] *nm* rubbish dump, tip

verter [ber'ter] *vt* (*vaciar*) to empty, pour (out); (*tirar*) to dump ■ *vi* to flow

vertical [berti'kal] *adj* vertical; (*postura, piano etc*) upright ■ *nf* vertical

vértice ['bertiθe] *nm* vertex, apex

vertiente [ber'tjente] *nf* slope

vertiginoso, -a [bertixi'noso, a] *adj* giddy, dizzy

vértigo ['bertiɣo] *nm* vertigo; (*mareo*) dizziness; (*actividad*) intense activity; **de** ~ (*fam: velocidad*) giddy; (: *ruido*) tremendous; (: *talento*) fantastic

vesícula [be'sikula] *nf* blister; ~ **biliar** gall bladder

vespa® ['bespa] *nf* (motor) scooter

vespertino, -a [besper'tino, a] *adj* evening *cpd*

vespino® [bes'pino] *nm o f* ≈ moped

vestíbulo [bes'tiβulo] *nm* hall; (*de teatro*) foyer

vestido [bes'tiðo] *nm* (*ropa*) clothes *pl*, clothing; (*de mujer*) dress, frock

vestigio [bes'tixjo] *nm* (*trazo*) trace; (*señal*) sign; **vestigios** *nmpl* remains

vestimenta [besti'menta] *nf* clothing

vestir [bes'tir] *vt* (*poner: ropa*) to put on; (*llevar: ropa*) to wear; (*cubrir*) to clothe, cover; (*pagar: la ropa*) to clothe, pay for the clothing of; (*sastre*) to make clothes for ■ *vi* (*ponerse: ropa*) to dress; (*verse bien*) to look good; **vestirse** *vr* to get dressed, dress o.s.; **traje de** ~ (*formal*) formal suit; **estar vestido de** to be dressed *o* clad in; (*como disfraz*) to be dressed as

vestuario [bes'twarjo] *nm* clothes *pl*, wardrobe; (*Teat: para actores*) dressing room; (: *para público*) cloakroom; (*Deporte*) changing room

Vesubio [be'suβjo] *nm* Vesuvius

veta ['beta] *nf* (*vena*) vein, seam; (*raya*) streak; (*de madera*) grain

vetar [be'tar] *vt* to veto

veterano, -a [bete'rano, a] *adj, nm/f* veteran

veterinario, -a [beteri'narjo, a] *nm/f* vet(erinary surgeon) ■ *nf* veterinary science

veto ['beto] *nm* veto

vetusto, -a [be'tusto, a] *adj* ancient

vez [beθ] *nf* time; (*turno*) turn; **a la** ~ **que** at the same time as; **a su** ~ in its turn; **cada** ~ **más/menos** more and more/less and less; **una** ~ once; **dos veces** twice; **de una** ~ in one go; **de una** ~ **para siempre** once and for all; **en** ~ **de** instead of; **a veces** sometimes; **otra** ~ again; **una y otra** ~ repeatedly; **muchas veces** (*con frecuencia*) often; **pocas veces** seldom; **de** ~ **en cuando** from time to time; **7 veces 9** 7 times 9; **hacer las veces de** to stand in for; **tal** ~ perhaps; **¿lo viste alguna** ~? did you ever see it?; **¿cuántas veces?** how often?; **érase una** ~ once upon a time (there was)

v. g., v. gr. *abr* (= *verbigracia*) viz

VHF *sigla f* (= *Very High Frequency*) VHF

vía ['bia] *nf* (*calle*) road; (*ruta*) track, route; (*Ferro*) line; (*fig*) way; (*Anat*) passage, tube ■ *prep* via, by way of; **por** ~ **bucal** orally; **por** ~ **judicial** by legal means; **por** ~ **oficial** through official channels; **por** ~ **de** by way of; **en vías de** in the process of; **un país en vías de desarrollo** a developing country; ~ **aérea** airway; **V~ Láctea** Milky Way; ~ **pública** public highway *o* thoroughfare; ~ **única** one-way street; **el tren está en la** ~ **8** the train is (standing) at platform 8

viable ['bjaβle] *adj* (*Com*) viable; (*plan etc*) feasible

viaducto [bja'ðukto] *nm* viaduct

viajante [bja'xante] *nm* commercial traveller, traveling salesman (*US*)

viajar [bja'xar] *vi* to travel, journey

viaje ['bjaxe] *nm* journey; (*gira*) tour; (*Naut*) voyage; (*Com: carga*) load; **los viajes** travel *sg*; **estar de** ~ to be on a journey; ~ **de ida y vuelta** round trip; ~ **de novios** honeymoon

viajero, -a [bja'xero, a] *adj* travelling (*Brit*), traveling (*US*); (*Zool*) migratory ■ *nm/f* (*quien viaja*) traveller; (*pasajero*) passenger

vial [bjal] *adj* road *cpd*, traffic *cpd*

vianda ['bjanda] *nf* (*tb*: **viandas**) food

viáticos ['bjatikos] *nmpl* (*Com*) travelling (*Brit*) *o* traveling (*US*) expenses

víbora ['biβora] *nf* viper

vibración [biβra'θjon] *nf* vibration

vibrador [biβra'ðor] *nm* vibrator

vibrante [bi'βrante] *adj* vibrant, vibrating

vibrar [bi'βrar] *vt* to vibrate ■ *vi* to vibrate;

(*pulsar*) to throb, beat, pulsate

vicario [bi'karjo] *nm* curate

vicecónsul [biθe'konsul] *nm* vice-consul

vicegerente [biθexe'rente] *nm/f* assistant manager

vicepresidente [biθepresi'ðente] *nm/f* vice president; (*de comité etc*) vice-chairman

viceversa [biθe'βersa] *adv* vice versa

viciado, -a [bi'θjaðo, a] *adj* (*corrompido*) corrupt; (*contaminado*) foul, contaminated

viciar [bi'θjar] *vt* (*pervertir*) to pervert; (*adulterar*) to adulterate; (*falsificar*) to falsify; (*Jur*) to nullify; (*estropear*) to spoil; (*sentido*) to twist; **viciarse** *vr* to become corrupted; (*aire, agua*) to be(come) polluted

vicio ['biθjo] *nm* (*libertinaje*) vice; (*mala costumbre*) bad habit; (*mimo*) spoiling; (*alabeo*) warp, warping; **de** *o* **por** ~ out of sheer habit

vicioso, -a [bi'θjoso, a] *adj* (*muy malo*) vicious; (*corrompido*) depraved; (*mimado*) spoiled ■ *nm/f* depraved person; (*adicto*) addict

vicisitud [biθisi'tuð] *nf* vicissitude

víctima ['biktima] *nf* victim; (*de accidente etc*) casualty

victimario [bikti'marjo] *nm* (*Am*) killer, murderer

victoria [bik'torja] *nf* victory

victorioso, -a [bikto'rjoso, a] *adj* victorious

vicuña [bi'kuɲa] *nf* vicuna

vid [bið] *nf* vine

vida ['biða] *nf* life; (*duración*) lifetime; (*modo de vivir*) way of life; ¡~!, ¡~ mía! (*saludo cariñoso*) my love!; **de por** ~ for life; **de** ~ **airada** *o* **libre** loose-living; **en la/mi** ~ never; **estar con** ~ to be still alive; **ganarse la** ~ to earn one's living; ¡esto es ~! this is the life!; **le va la** ~ **en esto** his life depends on it

vidente [bi'ðente] *nm/f* (*adivino*) clairvoyant; (*no ciego*) sighted person

vídeo ['biðeo] *nm* video; (*aparato*) video (recorder); **cinta de** ~ videotape; **película de** ~ videofilm; **grabar en** ~ to record, (video)tape; ~ **compuesto/inverso** (*Inform*) composite/reverse video

videocámara [biðeo'kamara] *nf* video camera; (*pequeña*) camcorder

videocassette [biðeoka'set] *nm* video cassette

videoclip [biðeo'klip] *nm* (*music*) video

videoclub [biðeo'klub] *nm* video club; (*tienda*) video shop

videodatos [biðeo'ðatos] *nmpl* (*Com*) viewdata

videojuego [biðeo'xweɣo] *nm* video game

videojugador, -a [biðeoxuɣa'ðor, a] *m/f* gamer

videotex [biðeo'teks], **videotexto** [biðeo'tekso] *nm* Videotex®

vidriero, -a [bi'ðrjero, a] *nm/f* glazier ■ *nf* (*ventana*) stained-glass window; (*Am: de tienda*) shop window; (*puerta*) glass door

vidrio ['biðrjo] *nm* glass; (*Am*) window; ~ **cilindrado/inastillable** plate/splinter-proof glass

vidrioso, -a [bi'ðrjoso, a] *adj* glassy; (*frágil*) fragile, brittle; (*resbaladizo*) slippery

viejo, -a ['bjexo, a] *adj* old ■ *nm/f* old man/woman; **mi** ~/**vieja** (*fam*) my old man/woman; **hacerse** *o* **ponerse** ~ to grow *o* get old

Viena ['bjena] *nf* Vienna

viene *etc* ['bjene] *vb ver* **venir**

viento ['bjento] *nm* wind; **contra** ~ **y marea** at all costs; **ir** ~ **en popa** to go splendidly; (*negocio*) to prosper

vientre ['bjentre] *nm* belly; (*matriz*) womb; **vientres** *nmpl* bowels; **hacer de** ~ to have a movement of the bowels

vier. *abr* (= *viernes*) Fri.

viernes ['bjernes] *nm inv* Friday; **V~ Santo** Good Friday; *ver tb* **Semana Santa; sábado**

vierta *etc* ['bjerta] *vb ver* **verter**

Vietnam [bjet'nam] *nm*: **el** ~ Vietnam

vietnamita [bjetna'mita] *adj, nm/f* Vietnamese

viga ['biɣa] *nf* beam, rafter; (*de metal*) girder

vigencia [bi'xenθja] *nf* validity; (*de contrato etc*) term, life; **estar/entrar en** ~ to be in/come into effect *o* force

vigente [bi'xente] *adj* valid, in force; (*imperante*) prevailing

vigésimo, -a [bi'xesimo, a] *num* twentieth

vigía [bi'xia] *nm* look-out ■ *nf* (*atalaya*) watchtower; (*acción*) watching

vigilancia [bixi'lanθja] *nf* vigilance

vigilante [bixi'lante] *adj* vigilant ■ *nm* caretaker; (*en cárcel*) warder; (*en almacén*) shopwalker (*Brit*), floor-walker (*US*); ~ **jurado** security guard (*licensed to carry a gun*); ~ **nocturno** night watchman

vigilar [bixi'lar] *vt* to watch over; (*cuidar*) to look after, keep an eye on ■ *vi* to be vigilant; (*hacer guardia*) to keep watch

vigilia [vi'xilja] *nf* wakefulness; (*Rel*) fast; **comer de** ~ to fast

vigor [bi'ɣor] *nm* vigour, vitality; **en** ~ in force; **entrar/poner en** ~ to take/put into effect

vigoroso, -a [biɣo'roso, a] *adj* vigorous

VIH *nm abr* (= *virus de inmunodeficiencia humana*) HIV

vil [bil] *adj* vile, low

vileza [bi'leθa] *nf* vileness; (*acto*) base deed

vilipendiar [bilipen'djar] *vt* to vilify, revile

villa ['biʎa] *nf* (*pueblo*) small town;

V

(municipalidad) municipality; **la V~** (Esp) Madrid; **~ miseria** shanty town

villancico [biʎan'θeiko] nm (Christmas) carol

villorrio [bi'ʎorrjo] nm one-horse town, dump; (Am: barrio pobre) shanty town

vilo ['bilo]: **en ~** adv in the air, suspended; (fig) on tenterhooks, in suspense; **estar** o **quedar en ~** to be left in suspense

vinagre [bi'naɣre] nm vinegar

vinagrera [bina'ɣrera] nf vinegar bottle; **vinagreras** nfpl cruet stand sg

vinagreta [bina'ɣreta] nf French dressing

vinatería [binate'ria] nf wine shop

vinatero, -a [bina'tero, a] adj wine cpd ■ nm wine merchant

vinculación [binkula'θjon] nf (lazo) link, bond; (acción) linking

vincular [binku'lar] vt to link, bind

vínculo ['binkulo] nm link, bond

vindicar [bindi'kar] vt to vindicate; (vengar) to avenge; (Jur) to claim

vinícola [bi'nikola] adj (industria) wine cpd; (región) wine-growing cpd

vinicultor, -a [binikul'tor, a] nm/f wine grower

vinicultura [binikul'tura] nf wine growing

vino etc ['bino] vb ver **venir** ■ nm wine; **~ de solera/seco/tinto** vintage/dry/red wine; **~ de Jerez** sherry; **~ de Oporto** port (wine)

viña ['biɲa], **viñedo** [bi'ɲeðo] nm vineyard

viñeta [bi'ɲeta] nf (en historieta) cartoon

viola ['bjola] nf viola

violación [bjola'θjon] nf violation; (Jur) offence, infringement; (estupro): **~ (sexual)** rape; **~ de contrato** (Com) breach of contract

violar [bjo'lar] vt to violate; (Jur) to infringe; (cometer estupro) to rape

violencia [bjo'lenθja] nf (fuerza) violence, force; (embarazo) embarrassment; (acto injusto) unjust act

violentar [bjolen'tar] vt to force; (casa) to break into; (agredir) to assault; (violar) to violate

violento, -a [bjo'lento, a] adj violent; (furioso) furious; (situación) embarrassing; (acto) forced, unnatural; (difícil) awkward; **me es muy ~** it goes against the grain with me

violeta [bjo'leta] nf violet

violín [bjo'lin] nm violin

violón [bjo'lon] nm double bass

violoncelo [bjolon'θelo] nm cello

V.I.P. ['bip] sigla m (= Very Important Person) VIP

virador [bira'ðor] nm (para fotocopiadora) toner

viraje [bi'raxe] nm turn; (de vehículo) swerve; (de carretera) bend; (fig) change of direction

virar [bi'rar] vi to turn; to swerve; to change direction

virgen ['birxen] adj virgin; (cinta) blank

■ nm/f virgin; **la Santísima V~** (Rel) the Blessed Virgin

virginidad [birxini'ðað] nf virginity

Virgo ['birɣo] nm Virgo

viril [bi'ril] adj virile

virilidad [birili'ðað] nf virility

virrey [bi'rrei] nm viceroy

virtual [bir'twal] adj (real) virtual; (en potencia) potential

virtud [bir'tuð] nf virtue; **en ~ de** by virtue of

virtuoso, -a [bir'twoso, a] adj virtuous ■ nm/f virtuoso

viruela [bi'rwela] nf smallpox; **viruelas** nfpl pockmarks; **viruelas locas** chickenpox sg

virulento, -a [biru'lento, a] adj virulent

virus ['birus] nm inv virus

viruta [bi'ruta] nf wood o metal shaving

vis [bis] nf: **~ cómica** sense of humour

visa ['bisa] nf (Am), **visado** [bi'saðo] nm visa; **~ de permanencia** residence permit

visar [bi'sar] vt (pasaporte) to visa; (documento) to endorse

visceral [bisθe'ral] adj (odio) deep-rooted; **reacción ~** gut reaction

viscoso, -a [bis'koso, a] adj viscous

visera [bi'sera] nf visor

visibilidad [bisiβili'ðað] nf visibility

visible [bi'siβle] adj visible; (fig) obvious; **exportaciones/importaciones visibles** (Com) visible exports/imports

visillo [bi'siʎo] nm lace curtain

visión [bi'sjon] nf (Anat) vision, (eye)sight; (fantasía) vision, fantasy; (panorama) view; **ver visiones** to see o be seeing things

visionario, -a [bisjo'narjo, a] adj (que prevé) visionary; (alucinado) deluded ■ nm/f visionary; (chalado) lunatic

visita [bi'sita] nf call, visit; (persona) visitor; **horas/tarjeta de ~** visiting hours/card; **~ de cortesía/de cumplido/de despedida** courtesy/formal/farewell visit; **hacer una ~** to pay a visit; **ir de ~** to go visiting

visitante [bisi'tante] adj visiting ■ nmf visitor

visitar [bisi'tar] vt to visit, call on; (inspeccionar) to inspect

vislumbrar [bislum'brar] vt to glimpse, catch a glimpse of

vislumbre [bis'lumbre] nf glimpse; (centelleo) gleam; (idea vaga) glimmer

viso ['biso] nm (de metal) glint, gleam; (de tela) sheen; (aspecto) appearance; **hay un ~ de verdad en esto** there is an element of truth in this

visón [bi'son] nm mink

visor [bi'sor] nm (Foto) viewfinder

víspera ['bispera] nf eve, day before; **la ~ o en**

vísperas de on the eve of
vista ['bista] *nf* sight, vision; (*capacidad de ver*) (eye)sight; (*mirada*) look(s) (*pl*); (*Foto etc*) view; (*Jur*) hearing ▪ *nm* customs officer; **a primera ~** at first glance; **~ general** overview; **fijar** *o* **clavar la ~ en** to stare at; **hacer la ~ gorda** to turn a blind eye; **volver la ~** to look back; **está a la ~ que** it's obvious that; **a la ~** (*Com*) at sight; **en ~ de** in view of; **en ~ de que** in view of the fact that; **¡hasta la ~!** so long!, see you!; **con vistas a** with a view to; *ver th* **visto, a**
vistazo [bis'taθo] *nm* glance; **dar** *o* **echar un ~ a** to glance at
visto, -a *etc* ['bisto, a] *vb ver* **vestir** ▪ *pp de* **ver** ▪ *adj* seen; (*considerado*) considered ▪ *nm*: **~ bueno** approval; **"~ bueno"** "approved"; **por lo ~** evidently; **dar el ~ bueno a algo** to give sth the go-ahead; **está ~ que** it's clear that; **está bien/mal ~** it's acceptable/unacceptable; **está muy ~** it is very common; **estaba ~** it had to be; **~ que** *conj* since, considering that
vistoso, -a [bis'toso, a] *adj* colourful; (*alegre*) gay; (*pey*) gaudy
visual [bi'swal] *adj* visual
visualice *etc* [biswa'liθe] *vb ver* **visualizar**
visualizador [biswaliθa'ðor] *nm* (*Inform*) display screen, VDU
visualizar [biswali'θar] *vt* (*imaginarse*) to visualize; (*Inform*) to display
vital [bi'tal] *adj* life *cpd*, living *cpd*; (*fig*) vital; (*persona*) lively, vivacious
vitalicio, -a [bita'liθjo, a] *adj* for life
vitalidad [bitali'ðað] *nf* vitality
vitamina [bita'mina] *nf* vitamin
vitaminado, -a [bitami'naðo, a] *adj* with added vitamins
vitamínico, -a [bita'miniko, a] *adj* vitamin *cpd*; **complejos vitamínicos** vitamin compounds
viticultor, a [bitikul'tor, a] *nm/f* vine grower
viticultura [bitikul'tura] *nf* vine growing
vitorear [bitore'ar] *vt* to cheer, acclaim
vítores ['bitores] *nmpl* cheers
vitoriano, -a [bito'rjano, a] *adj* of *o* from Vitoria ▪ *nm/f* native *o* inhabitant of Vitoria
vítreo, -a ['bitreo, a] *adj* vitreous
vitrina [bi'trina] *nf* glass case; (*en casa*) display cabinet; (*Am*) shop window
vituperar [bitupe'rar] *vt* to condemn
vituperio [bitu'perjo] *nm* (*condena*) condemnation; (*censura*) censure; (*insulto*) insult
viudez [bju'ðeθ] *nf* widowhood
viudo, -a ['bjuðo, a] *adj* widowed ▪ *nm* widower ▪ *nf* widow

viva ['biβa] *excl* hurrah! ▪ *nm* cheer; **¡~ el rey!** long live the King!
vivacidad [biβaθi'ðað] *nf* (*vigor*) vigour; (*vida*) vivacity
vivamente [biβa'mente] *adv* in lively fashion; (*describir*) vividly; (*protestar*) sharply; (*emocionarse*) acutely
vivaracho, -a [biβa'ratʃo, a] *adj* jaunty, lively; (*ojos*) bright, twinkling
vivaz [bi'βaθ] *adj* (*que dura*) enduring; (*vigoroso*) vigorous; (*vivo*) lively
vivencia [bi'βenθja] *nf* experience
víveres ['biβeres] *nmpl* provisions
vivero [bi'βero] *nm* (*Horticultura*) nursery; (*para peces*) fishpond; (*:Com*) fish farm
viveza [bi'βeθa] *nf* liveliness; (*agudeza*) sharpness
vividor, a [biβi'ðor, a] *adj* (*pey*) opportunistic ▪ *nm* (*aprovechado*) hustler
vivienda [bi'βjenda] *nf* (*alojamiento*) housing; (*morada*) dwelling; **viviendas protegidas** *o* **sociales** council housing *sg* (*Brit*), public housing *sg* (*US*)
viviente [bi'βjente] *adj* living
vivificar [biβifi'kar] *vt* to give life to
vivifique *etc* [biβi'fike] *vb ver* **vivificar**
vivir [bi'βir] *vt* (*experimentar*) to live *o* go through ▪ *vi* (*gen, Com*): **~ (de)** to live (by, off, on) ▪ *nm* life, living; **¡viva!** hurray!; **¡viva el rey!** long live the king!
vivo, -a ['biβo, a] *adj* living, live, alive; (*fig*) vivid; (*movimiento*) quick; (*color*) bright; (*protesta etc*) strong; (*astuto*) smart, clever; **en ~** (*TV etc*) live; **llegar a lo ~** to cut to the quick
vizcaíno, -a [biθka'ino, a] *adj, nm/f* Biscayan
Vizcaya [biθ'kaja] *nf* Biscay; **el Golfo de ~** the Bay of Biscay
V.M. *abr* = **Vuestra Majestad**
V.O. *abr* = **versión original**
V.°B.° *abr* = **visto bueno**
vocablo [bo'kaβlo] *nm* (*palabra*) word; (*término*) term
vocabulario [bokaβu'larjo] *nm* vocabulary, word list
vocación [boka'θjon] *nf* vocation
vocacional [bokasjo'nal] *nf* (*Am*) ≈ technical college
vocal [bo'kal] *adj* vocal ▪ *nm/f* member (of a committee *etc*) ▪ *nm* non-executive director ▪ *nf* vowel
vocalice *etc* [boka'liθe] *vb ver* **vocalizar**
vocalizar [bokali'θar] *vt* to vocalize
voceador [bosea'ðor] *nm* (*Am*): **~ de periódicos** newspaper vendor *o* seller
vocear [boθe'ar] *vt* (*para vender*) to cry; (*aclamar*) to acclaim; (*fig*) to proclaim ▪ *vi* to yell

vocerío [boθe'rio] nm shouting; (escándalo) hullabaloo

vocero, -a [bo'sero, a] nm/f (Am) spokesman/woman

vociferar [boθife'rar] vt to shout; (jactarse) to proclaim boastfully ■ vi to yell

vocinglero, -a [boθin'glero, a] adj vociferous; (gárrulo) garrulous; (fig) blatant

vodevil [boðe'βil] nm music hall, variety, vaudeville (US)

vodka ['boðka] nm vodka

vodú [bo'ðu] nm voodoo

vol abr = **volumen**

volado, -a [bo'laðo, a] adj: **estar ~** (fam: inquieto) to be worried; (: loco) to be crazy

volador, a [bola'ðor, a] adj flying

voladura [bola'ðura] nf blowing up, demolition; (Minería) blasting

volandas [bo'landas]: **en ~** adv in o through the air; (fig) swiftly

volante [bo'lante] adj flying ■ nm (de máquina, coche) steering wheel; (de reloj) balance; (nota) note; **ir al ~** to be at the wheel, be driving

volar [bo'lar] vt (demoler) to blow up, demolish ■ vi to fly; (fig: correr) to rush, hurry; (fam: desaparecer) to disappear; **voy volando** I must dash; **¡cómo vuela el tiempo!** how time flies!

volátil [bo'latil] adj volatile; (fig) changeable

volcán [bol'kan] nm volcano

volcánico, -a [bol'kaniko, a] adj volcanic

volcar [bol'kar] vt to upset, overturn; (tumbar, derribar) to knock over; (vaciar) to empty out ■ vi to overturn; **volcarse** vr to tip over; (barco) to capsize

voleibol [bolei'βol] nm volleyball

voleo [bo'leo] nm volley; **a(l) ~** haphazardly; **de un ~** quickly

Volga ['bolɣa] nm Volga

volición [boli'θjon] nf volition

volqué [bol'ke], **volquemos** etc [bol'kemos] vb ver **volcar**

volquete [bol'kete] nm dumper, dump truck (US)

voltaje [bol'taxe] nm voltage

voltear [bolte'ar] vt to turn over; (volcar) to knock over; (doblar) to peal ■ vi to roll over; **voltearse** vr (Am) to turn round; **~ a hacer algo** (Am) to do sth again

voltereta [bolte'reta] nf somersault; **~ sobre las manos** handspring; **~ lateral** cartwheel

voltio ['boltjo] nm volt

voluble [bo'luβle] adj fickle

volumen [bo'lumen] nm volume; **~ monetario** money supply; **~ de negocios** turnover; **bajar el ~** to turn down the volume; **poner la radio a todo ~** to turn the radio up full

voluminoso, -a [bolumi'noso, a] adj voluminous; (enorme) massive

voluntad [bolun'taθ] nf will, willpower; (deseo) desire, wish; (afecto) fondness; **a ~** at will; (cantidad) as much as one likes; **buena ~** goodwill; **mala ~** ill will, malice; **por causas ajenas a mi ~** for reasons beyond my control

voluntario, -a [bolun'tarjo, a] adj voluntary ■ nm/f volunteer

voluntarioso, -a [bolunta'rjoso, a] adj headstrong

voluptuoso, -a [bolup'twoso, a] adj voluptuous

volver [bol'βer] vt to turn; (boca abajo) to turn (over); (voltear) to turn round, turn upside down; (poner del revés) to turn inside out; (devolver) to return; (transformar) to change, transform; (manga) to roll up ■ vi to return, go/come back; **volverse** vr to turn round; (llegar a ser) to become; **~ la espalda** to turn one's back; **~ bien por mal** to return good for evil; **~ a hacer** to do again; **~ en sí** to come to o round, regain consciousness; **~ la vista atrás** to look back; **~ loco a algn** to drive sb mad; **volverse loco** to go mad

vomitar [bomi'tar] vt, vi to vomit

vómito ['bomito] nm (acto) vomiting; (resultado) vomit

voracidad [boraθi'ðað] nf voracity

vorágine [bo'raxine] nf whirlpool; (fig) maelstrom

voraz [bo'raθ] adj voracious; (fig) fierce

vórtice ['bortiθe] nm whirlpool; (de aire) whirlwind

VOS abr = **versión original subtitulada**

vos [bos] pron (Am) you

voseo [bo'seo] nm (Am) addressing a person as "vos", familiar usage

Vosgos ['bosɣos] nmpl Vosges

vosotros, -as [bo'sotros, as] pron you pl; (reflexivo) yourselves; **entre ~** among yourselves

votación [bota'θjon] nf (acto) voting; (voto) vote; **~ a mano alzada** show of hands; **someter algo a ~** to put sth to the vote

votar [bo'tar] vt (Pol: partido etc) to vote for; (proyecto: aprobar) to pass; (Rel) to vow ■ vi to vote

voto ['boto] nm vote; (promesa) vow; (maldición) oath, curse; **votos** nmpl (good) wishes; **~ de bloque/de grupo** block/card vote; **~ de censura/de (des)confianza/de gracias** vote of censure/(no) confidence/thanks; **dar su ~** to cast one's vote

voy [boi] vb ver **ir**

voz [boθ] *nf* voice; (*grito*) shout; (*chisme*) rumour; (*Ling*: *palabra*) word; (: *forma*) voice; **dar voces** to shout, yell; **llamar a algn a voces** to shout to sb; **llevar la ~ cantante** (*fig*) to be the boss; **tener la ~ tomada** to be hoarse; **tener ~ y voto** to have the right to speak; **a media ~** in a low voice; **a ~ en cuello** *o* **en grito** at the top of one's voice; **de viva ~** verbally; **en ~ alta** aloud; **~ de mando** command

vozarrón [boθa'rron] *nm* booming voice

vra., vro. *abr* = **vuestra; vuestro**

Vto. *abr* (*Com*) = **vencimiento**

vudú [bu'ðu] *nm* voodoo

vuelco *etc* ['bwelko] *vb ver* **volcar** ■ *nm* spill, overturning; (*fig*) collapse; **mi corazón dio un ~** my heart missed a beat

vuelo *etc* ['bwelo] *vb ver* **volar** ■ *nm* flight; (*encaje*) lace, frill; (*de falda etc*) loose part; (*fig*) importance; **de altos ~s** (*fig*: *plan*) grandiose; (: *persona*) ambitious; **alzar el ~** to take flight; (*fig*) to dash off; **coger al ~** to catch in flight; **~ de bajo coste** low-cost flight; **~ en picado** dive; **~ libre** hang-gliding; **~ regular** scheduled flight; **falda de mucho ~** full *o* wide skirt

vuelque *etc* ['bwelke] *vb ver* **volcar**

vuelta ['bwelta] *nf* turn; (*curva*) bend, curve; (*regreso*) return; (*revolución*) revolution; (*paseo*) stroll; (*circuito*) lap; (*de papel, tela*) reverse; (*de pantalón*) turn-up (*Brit*), cuff (*US*); (*cambio*) change; **~ a empezar** back to square one; **~ al mundo** world trip; **V~ de Francia** Tour de France; **~ cerrada** hairpin bend; **a la ~** (*Esp*) on one's return; **a la ~ de la esquina, a la ~** (*Am*) round the corner; **a ~ de correo** by return of post; **dar vueltas** to turn, revolve; **dar vueltas a una idea** to turn over an idea (in one's mind); **dar una ~** to go for a walk; **dar media ~** (*Auto*) to do a U-turn; (*fam*) to beat it; **estar de ~** (*fam*) to be back; **poner a algn de ~ y media** to heap abuse on sb; **no tiene ~ de hoja** there's no alternative

vueltita [bwel'tita] *nf* (*esp Am fam*) (little) walk; (: *en coche*) (little) drive

vuelto ['bwelto] *pp de* **volver** ■ *nm* (*Am*: *moneda*) change

vuelva *etc* ['bwelβa] *vb ver* **volver**

vuestro, -a ['bwestro, a] *adj* your; (*después de n*) of yours ■ *pron*: **el ~/la vuestra/los vuestros/las vuestras** yours; **lo ~** (what is) yours; **un amigo ~** a friend of yours; **una idea vuestra** an idea of yours

vulgar [bul'ɣar] *adj* (*ordinario*) vulgar; (*común*) common

vulgarice *etc* [bulɣa'riθe] *vb ver* **vulgarizar**

vulgaridad [bulɣari'ðað] *nf* commonness; (*acto*) vulgarity; (*expresión*) coarse expression; **vulgaridades** *nfpl* banalities

vulgarismo [bulɣa'rismo] *nm* popular form of a word

vulgarizar [bulɣari'θar] *vt* to popularize

vulgo ['bulɣo] *nm* common people

vulnerable [bulne'raβle] *adj* vulnerable

vulnerar [bulne'rar] *vt* to harm, damage; (*derechos*) to interfere with; (*Jur: Com*) to violate

vulva ['bulβa] *nf* vulva

V

W *abr* (= *vatio(s)*) w

W, w ['uβe'doβle] (*Am*) ['doβleβe] *nf* (*letra*) W, w; **W de Washington** W for William

walkie-talkie [walki'talki] *nm* walkie-talkie

walkman® ['wal(k)man] *nm* Walkman®

WAP [wap] *adj, nm* WAP; **teléfono ~** WAP phone

wáter ['bater] *nm* lavatory

waterpolo [water'polo] *nm* waterpolo

web [web] *nm o nf* (*página*) website; (*red*) (World Wide) Web

web site ['websait] *nm* website

webcam ['webkam] *nf* webcam

web master ['webmaster] *nm/f* webmaster

whisky ['wiski] *nm* whisky

widget (*pl* **widgets**) [wi'tʃet, s] *nm* (*Inform*) widget

wifi ['waifai] *nm* Wi-Fi

Winchester ['wintʃester] *nm* (*Inform*): **disco ~** Winchester disk

windsurf ['winsurf] *nm* windsurfing

WWW *nm o nf abr* (*Inform*: = World Wide Web) WWW

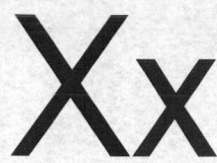

Xx

X, x ['ekis] *nf* (*letra*) X, x; **X de Xiquena** X for Xmas
xenofobia [seno'foβja] *nf* xenophobia
xenófobo, -a [se'nofoβo, a] *adj* xenophobic ■ *nm/f* xenophobe

xerografía [seɾoɣra'fia] *nf* xerography
xilófono [si'lofono] *nm* xylophone
Xunta ['ʃunta] *nf* (*tb*: **Xunta de Galicia**) *regional government of Galicia*

X

Yy

Y, y [i'ɣrjeɣa] *nf* (*letra*) Y, y; **Y de Yegua** Y for Yellow (*Brit*) *o* Yoke (US)

y [i] *conj* and; (*Am fam: pues*) well; (*hora*): **la una y cinco** five past one; **¿y eso?** why?, how so?; **¿y los demás?** what about the others?; **y bueno ...** (*Am*) well ...

ya [ja] *adv* (*gen*) already; (*ahora*) now; (*en seguida*) at once; (*pronto*) soon ■ *excl* all right!; (*por supuesto*) of course! ■ *conj* (*ahora que*) now that; **ya no** not any more, no longer; **ya lo sé** I know; **ya dice que sí, ya dice que no** first he says yes, then he says no; **¡ya, ya!** yes, yes!; (*con impaciencia*) all right!, O.K.!; **¡ya voy!** (*enfático: no se suele traducir*) coming!; **ya que** since

yacer [ja'θer] *vi* to lie

yacimiento [jaθi'mjento] *nm* bed, deposit; **~ petrolífero** oilfield

Yakarta [ja'karta] *nf* Jakarta

yanqui ['janki] *adj* Yankee ■ *nm/f* Yank, Yankee

yate ['jate] *nm* yacht

yazca *etc* ['jaθka] *vb ver* **yacer**

yedra ['jeðra] *nf* ivy

yegua ['jeɣwa] *nf* mare

yema ['jema] *nf* (*del huevo*) yolk; (*Bot*) leaf bud; (*fig*) best part; **~ del dedo** fingertip

Yemen ['jemen] *nm*: **el ~ del Norte** Yemen; **el ~ del Sur** Southern Yemen

yemení [jeme'ni] *adj, nm/f* Yemeni

yendo ['jendo] *vb ver* **ir**

yerba ['jerβa] *nf* = **hierba**

yerbatero, -a [jerβa'tero, a] *adj* (*Am*) maté ■ *nm/f* (*Am*) herbal healer

yerga *etc* ['jerɣa], **yergue** *etc* ['jerɣe] *vb ver* **erguir**

yermo, -a ['jermo, a] *adj* barren; (*de gente*) uninhabited ■ *nm* waste land

yerno ['jerno] *nm* son-in-law

yerre *etc* ['jerre] *vb ver* **errar**

yerto, -a ['jerto, a] *adj* stiff

yesca ['jeska] *nf* tinder

yeso ['jeso] *nm* (*Geo*) gypsum; (*Arq*) plaster

yo [jo] *pron personal* I; **soy yo** it's me, it is I; **yo que tú/usted** if I were you

yodo ['joðo] *nm* iodine

yoga ['joɣa] *nm* yoga

yogur [jo'ɣur], **yogurt** [jo'ɣurt] *nm* yogurt

yogurtera [joɣur'tera] *nf* yogurt maker

yuca ['juka] *nf* yucca

yudo ['juðo] *nm* judo

yugo ['juɣo] *nm* yoke

Yugoslavia [juɣos'laβja] *nf* Yugoslavia

yugoslavo, -a [juɣos'laβo, a] *adj* Yugoslavian ■ *nm/f* Yugoslav

yugular [juɣu'lar] *adj* jugular

yunque ['junke] *nm* anvil

yunta ['junta] *nf* yoke

yuntero [jun'tero] *nm* ploughman

yute ['jute] *nm* jute

yuxtapondré *etc* [jukstapond're] *vb ver* **yuxtaponer**

yuxtaponer [jukstapo'ner] *vt* to juxtapose

yuxtaponga *etc* [juksta'ponga] *vb ver* **yuxtaponer**

yuxtaposición [jukstaposi'θjon] *nf* juxtaposition

yuxtapuesto [juksta'pwesto], **yuxtapuse** *etc* [juksta'puse] *vb ver* **yuxtaponer**

Zz

Z, z ['θeta] (*esp Am*) ['seta] *nf* (*letra*) Z, z; **Z de Zaragoza** Z for Zebra

zafar [θa'far] *vt* (*soltar*) to untie; (*superficie*) to clear; **zafarse** *vr* (*escaparse*) to escape, (*ocultarse*) to hide o.s. away; (*Tec*) to slip off; **zafarse de** (*persona*) to get away from

zafio, -a ['θafjo, a] *adj* coarse

zafiro [θa'firo] *nm* sapphire

zaga ['θaγa] *nf* rear; **a la ~** behind, in the rear

zagal [θa'γal] *nm* boy, lad

zagala [θa'γala] *nf* girl, lass

zaguán [θa'ɣwan] *nm* hallway

zaherir [θae'rir] *vt* (*criticar*) to criticize; (*fig*: *herir*) to wound

zahiera *etc*, **zahiriendo** *etc* [θa'jera, θai'rjendo] *vb ver* **zaherir**

zahorí [θao'ri] *nm* clairvoyant

zaino, -a ['θaino, a] *adj* (*color de caballo*) chestnut; (*pérfido*) treacherous; (*animal*) vicious

zalamería [θalame'ria] *nf* flattery

zalamero, -a [θala'mero, a] *adj* flattering; (*relamido*) suave

zamarra [θa'marra] *nf* (*piel*) sheepskin; (*chaqueta*) sheepskin jacket

Zambeze [θam'beθe] *nm* Zambezi

zambo, -a ['θambo, a] *adj* knock-kneed ▪ *nm/f* (*Am*) half-breed (*of Negro and Indian parentage*); (*mulato*) mulatto ▪ *nf* samba

zambullida [θambu'ʎiða] *nf* dive, plunge

zambullirse [θambu'ʎirse] *vr* to dive; (*ocultarse*) to hide o.s.

zamorano, -a [θamo'rano, a] *adj* of o from Zamora ▪ *nm/f* native o inhabitant of Zamora

zampar [θam'par] *vt* (*esconder*) to hide o put away (hurriedly); (*comer*) to gobble; (*arrojar*) to hurl ▪ *vi* to eat voraciously; **zamparse** *vr* (*chocar*) to bump; (*fig*) to gatecrash

zanahoria [θana'orja] *nf* carrot

zancada [θan'kaða] *nf* stride

zancadilla [θanka'ðiʎa] *nf* trip; (*fig*) stratagem; **echar la ~ a algn** to trip sb up

zancajo [θan'kaxo] *nm* (*Anat*) heel; (*fig*) dwarf

zanco ['θanko] *nm* stilt

zancudo, -a [θan'kuðo, a] *adj* long-legged ▪ *nm* (*Am*) mosquito

zángano ['θangano] *nm* drone; (*holgazán*) idler, slacker

zanja ['θanxa] *nf* (*fosa*) ditch; (*tumba*) grave

zanjar [θan'xar] *vt* (*fosa*) to ditch, trench; (*problema*) to surmount; (*conflicto*) to resolve

zapapico [θapa'piko] *nm* pick, pickaxe

zapata [θa'pata] *nf* half-boot; (*Mecánica*) shoe

zapateado [θapate'aðo] *nm* (*flamenco*) tap dance

zapatear [θapate'ar] *vt* (*tocar*) to tap with one's foot; (*patear*) to kick; (*fam*) to ill-treat ▪ *vi* to tap with one's feet

zapatería [θapate'ria] *nf* (*oficio*) shoemaking; (*tienda*) shoe-shop; (*fábrica*) shoe factory

zapatero, -a [θapa'tero, a] *nm/f* shoemaker; **~ remendón** cobbler

zapatilla [θapa'tiʎa] *nf* slipper; (*Tec*) washer; (*de deporte*) training shoe

zapato [θa'pato] *nm* shoe

zapear [θape'ar] *vi* to flick through the channels

zapping ['θapin] *nm* channel-hopping; **hacer ~** to channel-hop

zar [θar] *nm* tsar, czar

zarabanda [θara'βanda] *nf* saraband; (*fig*) whirl

Zaragoza [θara'ɣoθa] *nf* Saragossa

zaragozano, -a [θaraɣo'θano, a] *adj* of o from Saragossa ▪ *nm/f* native o inhabitant of Saragossa

zaranda [θa'randa] *nf* sieve

zarandear [θarande'ar] *vt* to sieve; (*fam*) to shake vigorously

zarpa ['θarpa] *nf* (*garra*) claw, paw; **echar la ~ a** to claw at; (*fam*) to grab

zarpar [θar'par] *vt* to weigh anchor

zarpazo [θar'paθo] *nm*: **dar un ~** to claw

zarza ['θarθa] *nf* (*Bot*) bramble

zarzal [θar'θal] *nm* (*matorral*) bramble patch

zarzamora [θarθa'mora] *nf* blackberry
zarzuela [θar'θwela] *nf* Spanish light opera;
  la Z~ *home of the Spanish Royal Family*
zigzag [θiɣ'θaɣ] *adj* zigzag
zigzaguear [θiɣθaɣe'ar] *vi* to zigzag
zinc [θink] *nm* zinc
zíper ['siper] *nm* (*Am*) zip, zipper (*US*)
zócalo ['θokalo] *nm* (*Arq*) plinth, base;
  (*de pared*) skirting board
zoco ['θoko] *nm* (*Arab*) market, souk
zodíaco [θo'ðiako] *nm* zodiac; **signo del ~**
  star sign
zona ['θona] *nf* zone; **~ cero** Ground Zero;
  ~ euro Eurozone; **los países de la ~ euro**
  the Eurozone countries; **~ fronteriza** border
  area; **~ del dólar** (*Com*) dollar area; **~ de
  fomento** o **de desarrollo** development area
zonzo, -a ['sonso, a] *adj* (*Am*) silly
zoología [θoolo'xia] *nf* zoology
zoológico, -a [θoo'loxiko, a] *adj* zoological
  ■ *nm* (*tb*: **parque zoológico**) zoo
zoólogo, -a [θo'oloɣo, a] *nm/f* zoologist
zoom [θum] *nm* zoom lens
zopenco, -a [θo'penko, a] (*fam*) *adj* dull,
  stupid ■ *nm/f* clot, nitwit
zopilote [sopi'lote] *nm* (*Am*) buzzard
zoquete [θo'kete] *nm* (*de madera*) block;
  (*de pan*) crust; (*fam*) blockhead
zorro, -a ['θorro, a] *adj* crafty ■ *nm/f* fox/
  vixen ■ *nf* (*fam*) whore, tart, hooker (*US*)

zote ['θote] (*fam*) *adj* dim, stupid ■ *nm/f*
  dimwit
zozobra [θo'θoβra] *nf* (*fig*) anxiety
zozobrar [θoθo'βrar] *vi* (*hundirse*) to capsize;
  (*fig*) to fail
zueco ['θweko] *nm* clog
zulo ['θulo] *nm* (*de armas*) cache
zumbar [θum'bar] *vt* (*burlar*) to tease; (*golpear*)
  to hit ■ *vi* to buzz; (*fam*) to be very close;
  zumbarse *vr*: **zumbarse de** to tease; **me
  zumban los oídos** I have a buzzing o ringing
  in my ears
zumbido [θum'biðo] *nm* buzzing; (*fam*)
  punch; **~ de oídos** buzzing o ringing in the
  ears
zumo ['θumo] *nm* juice; (*ganancia*) profit;
  ~ de naranja (fresh) orange juice
zurcir [θur'θir] *vt* (*coser*) to darn; (*fig*) to put
  together; **¡que las zurzan!** to blazes with
  them!
zurdo, -a ['θurðo, a] *adj* (*mano*) left; (*persona*)
  left-handed
zurrar [θu'rrar] *vt* (*Tec*) to dress; (*fam: pegar
  duro*) to wallop; (: *aplastar*) to flatten; (: *criticar*)
  to criticize harshly
zurriagazo [θurrja'ɣaθo] *nm* lash, stroke;
  (*desgracia*) stroke of bad luck
zurrón [θu'rron] *nm* pouch
zurza *etc* ['θurθa] *vb ver* **zurcir**
zutano, -a [θu'tano, a] *nm/f* so-and-so

Aa

A, a [eɪ] n (letter) A, a; (Scol: mark)
≈ sobresaliente; (Mus): A la m; **A for Andrew,**
(US) **A for Able** A de Antonio; **A road** n (Brit
Aut) ≈ carretera nacional

⭕ KEYWORD

a [ə] indef art (before vowel and silent h **an**) **1** un(a);
a book un libro; **an apple** una manzana;
she's a nurse (ella) es enfermera; **I haven't
got a car** no tengo coche
2 (instead of the number "one") un(a); **a year ago**
hace un año; **a hundred/thousand pounds**
cien/mil libras
3 (in expressing ratios, prices etc): **three a day/
week** tres al día/a la semana; **10 km an hour**
10 km por hora; **£5 a person** £5 por persona;
30p a kilo 30p el kilo; **three times a month**
tres veces al mes

a. abbr = **acre**
A2 n (Brit Scol) segunda parte de los "A levels"
(módulos 4-6)
AA n abbr (Brit: = Automobile Association) ≈ RACE
m (SP); = **Alcoholics Anonymous** A.A.; (US:
= Associate in/of Arts) título universitario; = **anti-
aircraft**
AAA n abbr (= American Automobile Association)
≈ RACE m (SP) ['θriː'eɪz] (Brit: = Amateur
Athletics Association) asociación de atletismo
amateur
A & R n abbr (Mus: = artists and repertoire) nuevos
artistas y canciones; ~ **man** descubridor de jóvenes
talentos
AAUP n abbr (= American Association of University
Professors) asociación de profesores universitarios
AB abbr (Brit) = **able-bodied seaman**; (Canada)
= **Alberta**
aback [ə'bæk] adv: **to be taken** ~ quedar(se)
desconcertado
abandon [ə'bændən] vt abandonar;
(renounce) renunciar a ■ n abandono; (wild
behaviour): **with** ~ con desenfreno; **to** ~ **ship**

abandonar el barco
abandoned [ə'bændənd] adj (child, house
etc) abandonado; (unrestrained: manner)
desinhibido
abase [ə'beɪs] vt: **to** ~ **o.s. (so far as to do ...)**
rebajarse (hasta el punto de hacer ...)
abashed [ə'bæʃt] adj avergonzado
abate [ə'beɪt] vi moderarse; (lessen)
disminuir; (calm down) calmarse
abatement [ə'beɪtmənt] n (of pollution, noise)
disminución f
abattoir ['æbətwɑː'] n (Brit) matadero
abbey ['æbɪ] n abadía
abbot ['æbət] n abad m
abbreviate [ə'briːvɪeɪt] vt abreviar
abbreviation [əbriːvɪ'eɪʃən] n (short form)
abreviatura; (act) abreviación f
ABC n abbr (= American Broadcasting Company)
cadena de televisión
abdicate ['æbdɪkeɪt] vt, vi abdicar
abdication [æbdɪ'keɪʃən] n abdicación f
abdomen ['æbdəmən] n abdomen m
abdominal [æb'dɔmɪnl] adj abdominal
abduct [æb'dʌkt] vt raptar, secuestrar
abduction [æb'dʌkʃən] n rapto, secuestro
abductor [æb'dʌktə'] n raptor(a) m(f),
secuestrador(a) m(f)
Aberdonian [æbə'dəunɪən] adj de Aberdeen
■ n nativo(-a) or habitante m/f de Aberdeen
aberration [æbə'reɪʃən] n aberración f; **in a
moment of mental** ~ en un momento de
enajenación mental
abet [ə'bɛt] vt see **aid**
abeyance [ə'beɪəns] n: **in** ~ (law) en desuso;
(matter) en suspenso
abhor [əb'hɔː'] vt aborrecer, abominar (de)
abhorrent [əb'hɔrənt] adj aborrecible,
detestable
abide [ə'baɪd] vt: **I can't** ~ **it/him** no lo/le
puedo ver or aguantar; **to** ~ **by** vt fus
atenerse a
abiding [ə'baɪdɪŋ] adj (memory etc) perdurable
ability [ə'bɪlɪtɪ] n habilidad f, capacidad f;

(*talent*) talento; **to the best of my** ~ lo mejor que pueda *etc*

abject ['æbdʒekt] *adj* (*poverty*) sórdido; (*apology*) rastrero; (*coward*) vil

ablaze [ə'bleɪz] *adj* en llamas, ardiendo

able ['eɪbl] *adj* capaz; (*skilled*) hábil; **to be ~ to do sth** poder hacer algo

able-bodied ['eɪbl'bɔdɪd] *adj* sano; ~ **seaman** marinero de primera

ably ['eɪblɪ] *adv* hábilmente

ABM *n abbr* = **anti-ballistic missile**

abnormal [æb'nɔːməl] *adj* anormal

abnormality [æbnɔː'mælɪtɪ] *n* (*condition*) anormalidad *f*; (*instance*) anomalía

aboard [ə'bɔːd] *adv* a bordo ■ *prep* a bordo de; ~ **the train** en el tren

abode [ə'bəud] *n* (*old*) morada; (*Law*) domicilio; **of no fixed** ~ sin domicilio fijo

abolish [ə'bɔlɪʃ] *vt* suprimir, abolir

abolition [æbəu'lɪʃən] *n* supresión *f*, abolición *f*

abominable [ə'bɔmɪnəbl] *adj* abominable

aborigine [æbə'rɪdʒɪnɪ] *n* aborigen *m/f*

abort [ə'bɔːt] *vt* abortar; (*Comput*) interrumpir ■ *vi* (*Comput*) interrumpir el programa

abortion [ə'bɔːʃən] *n* aborto (provocado); **to have an** ~ abortar

abortionist [ə'bɔːʃənɪst] *n* persona que practica abortos

abortive [ə'bɔːtɪv] *adj* fracasado

abound [ə'baund] *vi*: **to** ~ **(in** *or* **with)** abundar (de *or* en)

⊙ KEYWORD

about [ə'baut] *adv* **1** (*approximately*) más o menos, aproximadamente; **about a hundred/thousand** *etc* unos (unas) *or* como cien/mil *etc*; **it takes about 10 hours** se tarda unas *or* más o menos 10 horas; **at about two o'clock** sobre las dos; **I've just about finished** casi he terminado
2 (*referring to place*) por todas partes; **to leave things lying about** dejar las cosas (tiradas) por ahí; **to run about** correr por todas partes; **to walk about** pasearse, ir y venir; **is Paul about?** ¿está por aquí Paul?; **it's the other way about** es al revés
3: **to be about to do sth** estar a punto de hacer algo; **I'm not about to do all that for nothing** no pienso hacer todo eso para nada
■ *prep* **1** (*relating to*) de, sobre, acerca de; **a book about London** un libro sobre *or* acerca de Londres; **what is it about?** (*book, film*) ¿de qué se trata?; **we talked about it** hablamos de eso *or* ello; **what** *or* **how about doing**

this? ¿qué tal si hacemos esto?
2 (*referring to place*) por; **to walk about the town** caminar por la ciudad

about face, about turn *n* (*Mil*) media vuelta; (*fig*) cambio radical

above [ə'bʌv] *adv* encima, por encima, arriba ■ *prep* encima de; ~ **mentioned** ~ susodicho; ~ **all** sobre todo; **he's not** ~ **a bit of blackmail** es capaz hasta de hacer chantaje

above board *adj* legítimo

above-mentioned [əbʌv'menʃnd] *adj* susodicho

abrasion [ə'breɪʒən] *n* (*on skin*) abrasión *f*

abrasive [ə'breɪzɪv] *adj* abrasivo

abreast [ə'brest] *adv* uno al lado de otro; **to keep** ~ **of** mantenerse al corriente de

abridge [ə'brɪdʒ] *vt* abreviar

abroad [ə'brɔːd] *adv* (*be*) en el extranjero; (*go*) al extranjero; **there is a rumour** ~ **that ...** corre el rumor de que ...

abrupt [ə'brʌpt] *adj* (*sudden: departure*) repentino; (*manner*) brusco

abruptly [ə'brʌptlɪ] *adv* (*leave*) repentinamente; (*speak*) bruscamente

abscess ['æbsɪs] *n* absceso

abscond [əb'skɔnd] *vi* fugarse

absence ['æbsəns] *n* ausencia; **in the** ~ **of** (*person*) en ausencia de; (*thing*) a falta de

absent ['æbsənt] *adj* ausente; ~ **without leave (AWOL)** ausente sin permiso

absentee [æbsən'tiː] *n* ausente *m/f*

absenteeism [æbsən'tiːɪzəm] *n* absentismo

absent-minded [æbsənt'maɪndɪd] *adj* distraído

absolute ['æbsəluːt] *adj* absoluto; ~ **monopoly** monopolio total

absolutely [æbsə'luːtlɪ] *adv* totalmente; **oh yes, ~!** ¡claro *or* por supuesto que sí!

absolution [æbsə'luːʃən] *n* (*Rel*) absolución *f*

absolve [əb'zɔlv] *vt*: **to** ~ **sb (from)** absolver a algn (de)

absorb [əb'zɔːb] *vt* absorber; **to be absorbed in a book** estar enfrascado en un libro

absorbent [əb'zɔːbənt] *adj* absorbente

absorbent cotton *n* (*US*) algodón *m* hidrófilo

absorbing [əb'zɔːbɪŋ] *adj* absorbente; (*book etc*) interesantísimo

absorption [əb'zɔːpʃən] *n* absorción *f*

abstain [əb'steɪn] *vi*: **to** ~ **(from)** abstenerse (de)

abstemious [əb'stiːmɪəs] *adj* abstemio

abstention [əb'stenʃən] *n* abstención *f*

abstinence ['æbstɪnəns] *n* abstinencia

abstract ['æbstrækt] *adj* abstracto

abstruse [æb'struːs] *adj* abstruso, oscuro

absurd [əb'səːd] *adj* absurdo

absurdity [əb'sə:dɪtɪ] n absurdo
ABTA ['æbtə] n abbr = **Association of British Travel Agents**
abundance [ə'bʌndəns] n abundancia
abundant [ə'bʌndənt] adj abundante
abuse [ə'bju:s] n (insults) insultos mpl, improperios mpl; (misuse) abuso ■ vt [ə'bju:z] (ill-treat) maltratar; (take advantage of) abusar de; **open to ~** sujeto al abuso
abusive [ə'bju:sɪv] adj ofensivo
abysmal [ə'bɪzməl] adj pésimo; (ignorance) supino
abyss [ə'bɪs] n abismo
AC abbr (= alternating current) corriente f alterna
■ n abbr (US) = **athletic club**
a/c abbr (Banking etc: = account, account current) c/c
academic [ækə'dɛmɪk] adj académico, universitario; (pej: issue) puramente teórico
■ n estudioso(-a); (lecturer) profesor(a) m(f) universitario(-a)
academic year n (Univ) año académico
academy [ə'kædəmɪ] n (learned body) academia; (school) instituto, colegio
academy of music n conservatorio
ACAS ['eɪkæs] n abbr (Brit: ~ Advisory, Conciliation and Arbitration Service) = Instituto de Mediación, Arbitraje y Conciliación
accede [æk'si:d] vi: **to ~ to** acceder a
accelerate [æk'sɛləreɪt] vt acelerar
■ vi acelerarse
acceleration [æksɛlə'reɪʃən] n aceleración f
accelerator [æk'sɛləreɪtər] n (Brit) acelerador m
accent ['æksɛnt] n acento
accentuate [æk'sɛntjueɪt] vt (syllable) acentuar; (need, difference etc) recalcar, subrayar
accept [ək'sɛpt] vt aceptar; (approve) aprobar; (concede) admitir
acceptable [ək'sɛptəbl] adj aceptable, admisible
acceptance [ək'sɛptəns] n aceptación f; aprobación f; **to meet with general ~** recibir la aprobación general
access ['æksɛs] n acceso ■ vt (Comput) acceder a; **the burglars gained ~ through a window** los ladrones lograron entrar por una ventana; **to have ~ to** tener acceso a
accessible [æk'sɛsəbl] adj accesible
accession [æk'sɛʃən] n (of monarch) subida, ascenso; (addition) adquisición f
accessory [æk'sɛsərɪ] n accesorio; **toilet accessories** artículos mpl de tocador
access road n carretera de acceso; (to motorway) carril m de acceso
access time n (Comput) tiempo de acceso

accident ['æksɪdənt] n accidente m; (chance) casualidad f; **by ~** (unintentionally) sin querer; (by coincidence) por casualidad; **accidents at work** accidentes mpl de trabajo; **to meet with** or **to have an ~** tener or sufrir un accidente
accidental [æksɪ'dɛntl] adj accidental, fortuito
accidentally [æksɪ'dɛntəlɪ] adv sin querer; por casualidad
accident insurance n seguro contra accidentes
accident-prone ['æksɪdənt'prəun] adj propenso a los accidentes
acclaim [ə'kleɪm] vt aclamar, aplaudir
■ n aclamación f, aplausos mpl
acclamation [æklə'meɪʃən] n (approval) aclamación f; (applause) aplausos mpl; **by ~** por aclamación
acclimatize [ə'klaɪmətaɪz], **acclimate** (US) [ə'klaɪmət] vt: **to become acclimatized** aclimatarse
accolade ['ækəuleɪd] n (prize) premio; (praise) alabanzas fpl, homenaje m
accommodate [ə'kɔmədeɪt] vt alojar, hospedar; (oblige, help) complacer; **this car accommodates four people comfortably** en este coche caben cuatro personas cómodamente
accommodating [ə'kɔmədeɪtɪŋ] adj servicial, complaciente
accommodation n, **accommodations** (US)
■ npl [əkɔmə'deɪʃən(z)] alojamiento; **"~ to let"** "se alquilan habitaciones"; **seating ~** asientos mpl
accompaniment [ə'kʌmpənɪmənt] n acompañamiento
accompanist [ə'kʌmpənɪst] n (Mus) acompañante m/f
accompany [ə'kʌmpənɪ] vt acompañar
accomplice [ə'kʌmplɪs] n cómplice m/f
accomplish [ə'kʌmplɪʃ] vt (finish) acabar; (aim) realizar; (task) llevar a cabo
accomplished [ə'kʌmplɪʃt] adj experto, hábil
accomplishment [ə'kʌmplɪʃmənt] n (ending) conclusión f; (bringing about) realización f; (skill) talento
accord [ə'kɔ:d] n acuerdo ■ vt conceder; **of his own ~** espontáneamente; **with one ~** de or por común acuerdo
accordance [ə'kɔ:dəns] n: **in ~ with** de acuerdo con
according [ə'kɔ:dɪŋ]: **~ to** prep según; (in accordance with) conforme a; **it went ~ to plan** salió según lo previsto
accordingly [ə'kɔ:dɪŋlɪ] adv (thus) por consiguiente

accordion [əˈkɔːdɪən] n acordeón m
accordionist [əˈkɔːdɪənɪst] n acordeonista m/f
accost [əˈkɒst] vt abordar, dirigirse a
account [əˈkaunt] n (Comm) cuenta, factura; (report) informe m; **accounts** npl (Comm) cuentas fpl; **"~ payee only"** "únicamente en cuenta del beneficiario"; **your ~ is still outstanding** su cuenta está todavía pendiente; **of little ~** de poca importancia; **on ~** a crédito; **to buy sth on ~** comprar algo a crédito; **on no ~** bajo ningún concepto; **on ~ of** a causa de, por motivo de; **to take into ~**, **take ~ of** tener en cuenta; **to keep an ~ of** llevar la cuenta de; **to bring sb to ~ for sth/for having done sth** pedirle cuentas a algn por algo/por haber hecho algo
▶ **account for** vt fus (explain) explicar; **all the children were accounted for** no faltaba ningún niño
accountability [əkauntəˈbɪlɪtɪ] n responsabilidad f
accountable [əˈkauntəbl] adj: **~ (for)** responsable (de)
accountancy [əˈkauntənsɪ] n contabilidad f
accountant [əˈkauntənt] n contable m/f, contador(a) m(f) (LAm)
accounting [əˈkauntɪŋ] n contabilidad f
accounting period n período contable, ejercicio financiero
account number n (at bank etc) número de cuenta
account payable n cuenta por pagar
account receivable n cuenta por cobrar
accoutrements [əˈkuːtrəmənts] npl equipo, pertrechos mpl
accredited [əˈkredɪtɪd] adj (agent etc) autorizado, acreditado
accretion [əˈkriːʃən] n acumulación f
accrue [əˈkruː] vi (mount up) aumentar, incrementarse; (interest) acumularse; **to ~ to** corresponder a; **accrued charges** gastos mpl vencidos; **accrued interest** interés m acumulado
accumulate [əˈkjuːmjuleɪt] vt acumular ■ vi acumularse
accumulation [əkjuːmjuˈleɪʃən] n acumulación f
accuracy [ˈækjurəsɪ] n exactitud f, precisión f
accurate [ˈækjurɪt] adj (number) exacto; (answer) acertado; (shot) certero
accurately [ˈækjurɪtlɪ] adv (count, shoot, answer) con precisión
accursed [əˈkəːst] adj maldito
accusation [ækjuˈzeɪʃən] n acusación f
accusative [əˈkjuːzətɪv] n acusativo
accuse [əˈkjuːz] vt acusar; (blame) echar la

culpa a
accused [əˈkjuːzd] n acusado(-a)
accuser [əˈkjuːzər] n acusador(a) m(f)
accustom [əˈkʌstəm] vt acostumbrar; **to ~ o.s. to sth** acostumbrarse a algo
accustomed [əˈkʌstəmd] adj: **~ to** acostumbrado a
AC/DC abbr (= alternating current/direct current) CA/CC
ACE [eɪs] n abbr = **American Council on Education**
ace [eɪs] n as m
acerbic [əˈsəːbɪk] adj acerbo; (fig) mordaz
acetate [ˈæsɪteɪt] n acetato
ache [eɪk] n dolor m ■ vi doler; (yearn): **to ~ to do sth** ansiar hacer algo; **I've got stomach ~** or (US) **a stomach ~** tengo dolor de estómago, me duele el estómago; **my head aches** me duele la cabeza
achieve [əˈtʃiːv] vt (reach) alcanzar; (realize) realizar; (victory, success) lograr, conseguir
achievement [əˈtʃiːvmənt] n (completion) realización f; (success) éxito
Achilles heel [əˈkɪliːz-] n talón m de Aquiles
acid [ˈæsɪd] adj ácido; (bitter) agrio ■ n ácido
acidity [əˈsɪdɪtɪ] n acidez f; (Med) acedía
acid rain n lluvia ácida
acid test n (fig) prueba de fuego
acknowledge [əkˈnɒlɪdʒ] vt (letter: also: **acknowledge receipt of**) acusar recibo de; (fact) reconocer
acknowledgement [əkˈnɒlɪdʒmənt] n acuse m de recibo; reconocimiento; **acknowledgements** (in book) agradecimientos mpl
ACLU n abbr (= American Civil Liberties Union) unión americana por libertades civiles
acme [ˈækmɪ] n súmmum m
acne [ˈæknɪ] n acné m
acorn [ˈeɪkɔːn] n bellota
acoustic [əˈkuːstɪk] adj acústico
acoustics [əˈkuːstɪks] n, npl acústica sg
acquaint [əˈkweɪnt] vt: **to ~ sb with sth** (inform) poner a algn al corriente de algo; **to be acquainted with** (person) conocer; (fact) estar al corriente de
acquaintance [əˈkweɪntəns] n conocimiento; (person) conocido(-a); **to make sb's ~** conocer a algn
acquiesce [ækwɪˈɛs] vi (agree): **to ~ (in)** consentir (en), conformarse (con)
acquire [əˈkwaɪər] vt adquirir
acquired [əˈkwaɪəd] adj adquirido; **it's an ~ taste** es algo a lo que uno se aficiona poco a poco
acquisition [ækwɪˈzɪʃən] n adquisición f
acquisitive [əˈkwɪzɪtɪv] adj codicioso

a

acquit [ə'kwɪt] vt absolver, exculpar; **to ~ o.s. well** defenderse bien

acquittal [ə'kwɪtl] n absolución f, exculpación f

acre ['eɪkəʳ] n acre m

acreage ['eɪkərɪdʒ] n extensión f

acrid ['ækrɪd] adj (smell) acre; (fig) mordaz, sarcástico

acrimonious [ækrɪ'məʊnɪəs] adj (remark) mordaz; (argument) reñido

acrobat ['ækrəbæt] n acróbata m/f

acrobatic [ækrə'bætɪk] adj acrobático

acrobatics [ækrə'bætɪks] npl acrobacias fpl

acronym ['ækrənɪm] n siglas fpl

across [ə'krɔs] prep (on the other side of) al otro lado de; (crosswise) a través de ▪ adv de un lado a otro, de una parte a otra a través, al través; **to run/swim ~** atravesar corriendo/nadando; **~ from** enfrente de; **the lake is 12 km ~** el lago tiene 12 km de ancho; **to get sth ~ to sb** (fig) hacer comprender algo a algn

acrylic [ə'krɪlɪk] adj acrílico

ACT n abbr (= American College Test) prueba de aptitud estándar que por lo general hacen los estudiantes que quieren entrar a la universidad por primera vez

act [ækt] n acto, acción f; (Theat) acto; (in music-hall etc) número; (Law) decreto, ley f ▪ vi (behave) comportarse; (Theat) actuar; (pretend) fingir; (take action) tomar medidas ▪ vt (part) hacer, representar; **~ of God** fuerza mayor; **it's only an ~** es cuento; **to catch sb in the ~** coger a algn in fraganti or con las manos en la masa; **to ~ Hamlet** hacer el papel de Hamlet; **to ~ as** actuar or hacer de; **acting in my capacity as chairman, I ...** en mi calidad de presidente, yo ...; **it acts as a deterrent** sirve para disuadir; **he's only acting** está fingiendo nada más
  ▶ **act on** vt: **to ~ on sth** actuar sobre algo
  ▶ **act out** vt (event) representar; (fantasies) realizar

acting ['æktɪŋ] adj suplente ▪ n: **to do some ~** hacer algo de teatro; **he is the ~ manager** es el gerente en funciones

action ['ækʃən] n acción f, acto; (Mil) acción f; (Law) proceso, demanda ▪ vt (Comm) llevar a cabo; **to put a plan into ~** poner un plan en acción or en marcha; **killed in ~** (Mil) muerto en acto de servicio or en combate; **out of ~** (person) fuera de combate; (thing) averiado, descompuesto; **to take ~** tomar medidas; **to bring an ~ against sb** entablar or presentar demanda contra algn

action replay n (TV) repetición f

activate ['æktɪveɪt] vt activar

active ['æktɪv] adj activo, enérgico; (volcano) en actividad; **to play an ~ part in** colaborar activamente en

active duty n (US Mil) servicio activo

actively ['æktɪvlɪ] adv (participate) activamente; (discourage, dislike) enérgicamente

active partner n (Comm) socio activo

activist ['æktɪvɪst] n activista m/f

activity [æk'tɪvɪtɪ] n actividad f

actor ['æktəʳ] n actor m

actress ['æktrɪs] n actriz f

actual ['æktjʊəl] adj verdadero, real

actually ['æktjʊəlɪ] adv realmente, en realidad

actuary ['æktjʊərɪ] n (Comm) actuario(-a) (de seguros)

actuate ['æktjʊeɪt] vt mover, impulsar

acumen ['ækjʊmən] n perspicacia; **business ~** talento para los negocios

acupuncture ['ækjʊpʌŋktʃəʳ] n acupuntura

acute [ə'kju:t] adj agudo

acutely [ə'kju:tlɪ] adv profundamente, extremadamente

AD adv abbr (= Anno Domini) A.C. ▪ n abbr (US Mil) = **active duty**

ad [æd] n abbr = **advertisement**

adage ['ædɪdʒ] n refrán m, adagio

Adam ['ædəm] n Adán; **~'s apple** n nuez f (de la garganta)

adamant ['ædəmənt] adj firme, inflexible

adapt [ə'dæpt] vt adaptar; (reconcile) acomodar ▪ vi: **to ~ (to)** adaptarse (a), ajustarse (a)

adaptability [ədæptə'bɪlɪtɪ] n (of person, device etc) adaptabilidad f

adaptable [ə'dæptəbl] adj (device) adaptable; (person) acomodadizo, que se adapta

adaptation [ædæp'teɪʃən] n adaptación f

adapter, adaptor [ə'dæptəʳ] n (Elec) adaptador m

ADC n abbr (Mil: = aide-de-camp; US: = Aid to Dependent Children) ayuda para niños dependientes

add [æd] vt añadir, agregar (esp LAm); (figures: also: **add up**) sumar ▪ vi: **to ~ to** (increase) aumentar, acrecentar ▪ n (Internet): **thanks for the ~** gracias por agregarme
  ▶ **add on** vt añadir
  ▶ **add up** vt (figures) sumar ▪ vi (fig): **it doesn't ~ up** no tiene sentido; **it doesn't ~ up to much** es poca cosa, no tiene gran or mucha importancia

addendum [ə'dɛndəm] n ad(d)enda m or f

adder ['ædəʳ] n víbora

addict ['ædɪkt] n (to drugs etc) adicto(-a); (enthusiast) aficionado(-a), entusiasta m/f; **heroin ~** heroinómano(-a)

addicted [ə'dɪktɪd] adj: **to be ~ to** ser adicto a;

413

ser aficionado a

addiction [ə'dɪkʃən] n (*dependence*) hábito morboso; (*enthusiasm*) afición f

addictive [ə'dɪktɪv] adj que causa adicción

adding machine ['ædɪŋ-] n calculadora

Addis Ababa ['ædɪs'æbəbə] n Addis Abeba m

addition [ə'dɪʃən] n (*adding up*) adición f; (*thing added*) añadidura, añadido; **in ~** además, por añadidura; **in ~ to** además de

additional [ə'dɪʃənl] adj adicional

additive ['ædɪtɪv] n aditivo

addled ['ædld] adj (Brit: *rotten*) podrido; (: *fig*) confuso

address [ə'drɛs] n dirección f, señas fpl; (*speech*) discurso; (*Comput*) dirección f ■ vt (*letter*) dirigir; (*speak to*) dirigirse a, dirigir la palabra a; **form of ~** tratamiento; **absolute/relative ~** (*Comput*) dirección f absoluta/relativa; **to ~ o.s. to sth** (*issue, problem*) abordar

address book n agenda (de direcciones)

addressee [ædre'si:] n destinatario(-a)

Aden ['eɪdn] n Adén m

adenoids ['ædɪnɔɪdz] npl vegetaciones fpl (adenoideas)

adept ['ædɛpt] adj: **~ at** experto or ducho en

adequacy ['ædɪkwəsɪ] n idoneidad f

adequate ['ædɪkwɪt] adj (*satisfactory*) adecuado; (*enough*) suficiente; **to feel ~ to a task** sentirse con fuerzas para una tarea

adequately ['ædɪkwɪtlɪ] adv adecuadamente

adhere [əd'hɪər] vi: **to ~ to** adherirse a; (*fig: abide by*) observar

adherent [əd'hɪərənt] n partidario(-a)

adhesion [əd'hi:ʒən] n adherencia

adhesive [əd'hi:zɪv] adj, n adhesivo

adhesive tape n (Brit) cinta adhesiva; (US Med) esparadrapo

ad hoc [æd'hɔk] adj (*decision*) ad hoc; (*committee*) formado con fines específicos ■ adv ad hoc

adieu [ə'dju:] excl ¡vaya con Dios!

ad inf ['æd'ɪnf] adv hasta el infinito

adjacent [ə'dʒeɪsənt] adj: **~ to** contiguo a, inmediato a

adjective ['ædʒɛktɪv] n adjetivo

adjoin [ə'dʒɔɪn] vt estar contiguo a; (*land*) lindar con

adjoining [ə'dʒɔɪnɪŋ] adj contiguo, vecino

adjourn [ə'dʒə:n] vt aplazar; (*session*) suspender, levantar; (US: *end*) terminar ■ vi suspenderse; **the meeting has been adjourned till next week** se ha levantado la sesión hasta la semana que viene; **they adjourned to the pub** (*col*) se trasladaron al bar

adjournment [ə'dʒə:nmənt] n (*period*)

suspensión f; (*postponement*) aplazamiento

Adjt. abbr (Mil) = **adjutant**

adjudicate [ə'dʒu:dɪkeɪt] vi sentenciar ■ vt (*contest*) hacer de árbitro en, juzgar; (*claim*) decidir

adjudication [ədʒu:dɪ'keɪʃən] n fallo

adjudicator [ə'dʒu:dɪkeɪtər] n juez m, árbitro

adjust [ə'dʒʌst] vt (*change*) modificar; (*arrange*) arreglar; (*machine*) ajustar ■ vi: **to ~ (to)** adaptarse (a)

adjustable [ə'dʒʌstəbl] adj ajustable

adjuster [ə'dʒʌstər] n see **loss adjuster**

adjustment [ə'dʒʌstmənt] n modificación f; arreglo; (*of prices, wages*) ajuste m

adjutant ['ædʒətənt] n ayudante m

ad-lib [æd'lɪb] vt, vi improvisar ■ adv: **ad lib** a voluntad, a discreción

adman ['ædmæn] n (*col*) publicista m

admin ['ædmɪn] n abbr (*col*) = **administration**

administer [əd'mɪnɪstər] vt proporcionar; (*justice*) administrar

administration [ədmɪnɪ'streɪʃən] n administración f; (*government*) gobierno; **the A~** (US) la Administración

administrative [əd'mɪnɪstrətɪv] adj administrativo

administrator [əd'mɪnɪstreɪtər] n administrador(a) m(f)

admirable ['ædmərəbl] adj admirable

admiral ['ædmərəl] n almirante m

Admiralty ['ædmərəltɪ] n (Brit) Ministerio de Marina, Almirantazgo

admiration [ædmə'reɪʃən] n admiración f

admire [əd'maɪər] vt admirar

admirer [əd'maɪərər] n admirador(a) m(f); (*suitor*) pretendiente m

admiring [əd'maɪərɪŋ] adj (*expression*) de admiración

admissible [əd'mɪsəbl] adj admisible

admission [əd'mɪʃən] n (*to exhibition, nightclub*) entrada; (*enrolment*) ingreso; (*confession*) confesión f; **"~ free"** "entrada gratis or libre"; **by his own ~** él mismo reconoce que

admit [əd'mɪt] vt dejar entrar, dar entrada a; (*permit*) admitir; (*acknowledge*) reconocer; **"this ticket admits two"** "entrada para dos personas"; **children not admitted** se prohíbe la entrada a (los) menores de edad; **I must ~ that ...** debo reconocer que ...
   ▸ **admit of** vt fus admitir, permitir
   ▸ **admit to** vt fus confesarse culpable de

admittance [əd'mɪtəns] n entrada; **"no ~"** "se prohíbe la entrada", "prohibida la entrada"

admittedly [əd'mɪtədlɪ] adv de acuerdo que

admonish [əd'mɔnɪʃ] vt amonestar; (*advise*) aconsejar

a

ad nauseam [æd'nɔːsɪæm] *adv* hasta la saciedad

ado [ə'duː] *n*: **without (any) more** ~ sin más (ni más)

adolescence [ædəʊ'lɛsns] *n* adolescencia

adolescent [ædəʊ'lɛsnt] *adj, n* adolescente *m/f*

adopt [ə'dɔpt] *vt* adoptar

adopted [ə'dɔptɪd] *adj* adoptivo

adoption [ə'dɔpʃən] *n* adopción *f*

adoptive [ə'dɔptɪv] *adj* adoptivo

adorable [ə'dɔːrəbl] *adj* adorable

adoration [ædə'reɪʃən] *n* adoración *f*

adore [ə'dɔːʳ] *vt* adorar

adoring [ə'dɔːrɪŋ] *adj*: **to his** ~ **public** a un público que le adora *or* le adoraba *etc*

adorn [ə'dɔːn] *vt* adornar

adornment [ə'dɔːnmənt] *n* adorno

ADP *n abbr* = **automatic data processing**

adrenalin [ə'drɛnəlɪn] *n* adrenalina

Adriatic [eɪdrɪ'ætɪk] *n*: **the** ~ **(Sea)** el (Mar) Adriático

adrift [ə'drɪft] *adv* a la deriva; **to come** ~ (*boat*) ir a la deriva, soltarse; (*wire, rope etc*) soltarse

adroit [ə'drɔɪt] *adj* diestro, hábil

ADSL *n abbr* (= *asymmetrical digital subscriber line*) ADSL *m*

ADT *abbr* (US: ~ *Atlantic Daylight Time*) hora de verano de Nueva York

adulation [ædjuˈleɪʃən] *n* adulación *f*

adult ['ædʌlt] *n* adulto(-a) ■ *adj*: ~ **education** educación *f* para adultos

adulterate [ə'dʌltəreɪt] *vt* adulterar

adulterer [ə'dʌltərəʳ] *n* adúltero

adulteress [ə'dʌltrɪs] *n* adúltera

adultery [ə'dʌltərɪ] *n* adulterio

adulthood ['ædʌlthud] *n* edad *f* adulta

advance [əd'vɑːns] *n* adelanto, progreso; (*money*) anticipo; (*Mil*) avance *m* ■ *vt* avanzar, adelantar; (*money*) anticipar ■ *vi* avanzar, adelantarse; **in** ~ por adelantado; (*book*) con antelación; **to make advances to sb** (*gen*) ponerse en contacto con algn; (*amorously*) insinuarse a algn

advanced *adj* avanzado; (*Scol: studies*) adelantado; ~ **in years** entrado en años

Advanced Higher *n* (*Scottish Scol*) titulación que sigue al "*Higher*", = Bachillerato

advancement [əd'vɑːnsmənt] *n* progreso; (*in rank*) ascenso

advance notice *n* previo aviso

advance payment *n* (*part sum*) anticipo

advantage [əd'vɑːntɪdʒ] *n* (*also Tennis*) ventaja; **to take** ~ **of** aprovecharse de; **it's to our** ~ es ventajoso para nosotros

advantageous [ædvən'teɪdʒəs] *adj*

ventajoso, provechoso

advent ['ædvənt] *n* advenimiento; **A~** Adviento

adventure [əd'vɛntʃəʳ] *n* aventura

adventure playground *n* parque *m* infantil

adventurous [əd'vɛntʃərəs] *adj* aventurero; (*bold*) arriesgado

adverb ['ædvəːb] *n* adverbio

adversary ['ædvəsərɪ] *n* adversario, contrario

adverse ['ædvəːs] *adj* adverso, contrario; ~ **to** adverso a

adversity [əd'vəːsɪtɪ] *n* infortunio

advert ['ædvəːt] *n abbr* (*Brit*) = **advertisement**

advertise ['ædvətaɪz] *vi* hacer propaganda; (*in newspaper etc*) poner un anuncio, anunciarse; **to** ~ **for** (*staff*) buscar por medio de anuncios ■ *vt* anunciar

advertisement [əd'vəːtɪsmənt] *n* anuncio

advertiser ['ædvətaɪzəʳ] *n* anunciante *m/f*

advertising ['ædvətaɪzɪŋ] *n* publicidad *f*, propaganda; anuncios *mpl*

advertising agency *n* agencia de publicidad

advertising campaign *n* campaña de publicidad

advice [əd'vaɪs] *n* consejo, consejos *mpl*; (*notification*) aviso; **a piece of** ~ un consejo; **to take legal** ~ consultar a un abogado; **to ask (sb) for** ~ pedir consejo (a algn)

advice note *n* (*Brit*) nota de aviso

advisable [əd'vaɪzəbl] *adj* aconsejable, conveniente

advise [əd'vaɪz] *vt* aconsejar; **to** ~ **sb of sth** (*inform*) informar a algn de algo; **to** ~ **sb against sth/doing sth** desaconsejar algo a algn/aconsejar a algn que no haga algo; **you will be well/ill advised to go** deberías/no deberías ir

advisedly [əd'vaɪzɪdlɪ] *adv* deliberadamente

adviser [əd'vaɪzəʳ] *n* consejero(-a); (*business adviser*) asesor(a) *m(f)*

advisory [əd'vaɪzərɪ] *adj* consultivo; **in an** ~ **capacity** como asesor

advocate ['ædvəkeɪt] *vt* (*argue for*) abogar por; (*give support to*) ser partidario de ■ *n* ['ædvəkɪt] abogado(-a)

advt. *abbr* = **advertisement**

AEA *n abbr* (*Brit*: = *Atomic Energy Authority*) consejo de energía nuclear; (*Brit Scol*: = *Advanced Extension Award*) titulación opcional para los alumnos mejor preparados de los "*A levels*"

AEC *n abbr* (US: = *Atomic Energy Commission*) AEC *f*

Aegean [iːˈdʒiːən] *n*: **the** ~ **(Sea)** el (Mar) Egeo

aegis ['iːdʒɪs] *n*: **under the** ~ **of** bajo la tutela de

aeon ['iːən] *n* eón *m*

aerial ['ɛərɪəl] *n* antena ■ *adj* aéreo

aerie ['ɛərɪ] *n* (US) aguilera

415

aero- ['ɛərəu] *pref* aero-
aerobatics [ɛərəu'bætɪks] *npl* acrobacia aérea
aerobics [ɛə'rəubɪks] *nsg* aerobic *m*, aerobismo (*LAm*)
aerodrome ['ɛərədrəum] *n* (*Brit*) aeródromo
aerodynamic [ɛərəudaɪ'næmɪk] *adj* aerodinámico
aeronautics [ɛərəu'nɔ:tɪks] *nsg* aeronáutica
aeroplane ['ɛərəpleɪn] *n* (*Brit*) avión *m*
aerosol ['ɛərəsɔl] *n* aerosol *m*
aerospace industry ['ɛərəuspeɪs-] *n* industria aeroespacial
aesthetic [i:s'θɛtɪk] *adj* estético
aesthetics [i:s'θɛtɪks] *npl* estética
afar [ə'fɑ:ʳ] *adv* lejos; **from ~** desde lejos
AFB *n abbr* (*US*) = **Air Force Base**
AFDC *n abbr* (*US*: = *Aid to Families with Dependent Children*) *ayuda a familias con hijos menores*
affable ['æfəbl] *adj* afable
affair [ə'fɛəʳ] *n* asunto; (*also:* **love affair**) aventura *f* amorosa; **affairs** (*business*) asuntos *mpl*; **the Watergate ~** el asunto (de) Watergate
affect [ə'fɛkt] *vt* afectar, influir en; (*move*) conmover
affectation [æfɛk'teɪʃən] *n* afectación *f*
affected [ə'fɛktɪd] *adj* afectado
affection [ə'fɛkʃən] *n* afecto, cariño
affectionate [ə'fɛkʃənɪt] *adj* afectuoso, cariñoso
affectionately [ə'fɛkʃənɪtlɪ] *adv* afectuosamente
affidavit [æfɪ'deɪvɪt] *n* (*Law*) declaración *f* jurada
affiliated [ə'fɪlɪeɪtɪd] *adj* afiliado; **~ company** empresa *or* compañía filial *or* subsidiaria
affinity [ə'fɪnɪtɪ] *n* afinidad *f*
affirm [ə'fə:m] *vt* afirmar
affirmation [æfə'meɪʃən] *n* afirmación *f*
affirmative [ə'fə:mətɪv] *adj* afirmativo
affix [ə'fɪks] *vt* (*signature*) estampar; (*stamp*) pegar
afflict [ə'flɪkt] *vt* afligir
affliction [ə'flɪkʃən] *n* enfermedad *f*, aflicción *f*
affluence ['æfluəns] *n* opulencia, riqueza
affluent ['æfluənt] *adj* adinerado, acaudalado; **the ~ society** la sociedad opulenta
afford [ə'fɔ:d] *vt* poder permitirse; (*provide*) proporcionar; **can we ~ a car?** ¿podemos permitirnos el gasto de comprar un coche?
affordable [ə'fɔ:dəbl] *adj* asequible
affray [ə'freɪ] *n* refriega, reyerta
affront [ə'frʌnt] *n* afrenta, ofensa
affronted [ə'frʌntɪd] *adj* ofendido

Afghan ['æfgæn] *adj, n* afgano(-a) *m(f)*
Afghanistan [æf'gænɪstæn] *n* Afganistán *m*
afield [ə'fi:ld] *adv*: **far ~** muy lejos
AFL-CIO *n abbr* (*US*: = *American Federation of Labor and Congress of Industrial Organizations*) *confederación sindicalista*
afloat [ə'fləut] *adv* (*floating*) a flote; (*at sea*) en el mar
afoot [ə'fut] *adv*: **there is something ~** algo se está tramando
aforesaid [ə'fɔ:sɛd] *adj* susodicho; (*Comm*) mencionado anteriormente
afraid [ə'freɪd] *adj*: **to be ~ of** (*person*) tener miedo a; (*thing*) tener miedo de; **to be ~ to** tener miedo de, temer; **I am ~ that** me temo que; **I'm ~ so** ¡me temo que sí!, ¡lo siento, pero es así!; **I'm ~ not** me temo que no
afresh [ə'frɛʃ] *adv* de nuevo, otra vez
Africa ['æfrɪkə] *n* África
African ['æfrɪkən] *adj, n* africano(-a) *m(f)*
Afrikaans [æfrɪ'kɑ:ns] *n* africaans *m*
Afrikaner [æfrɪ'kɑ:nəʳ] *n* africánder *m/f*
Afro-American ['æfrəuə'mɛrɪkən] *adj, n* afroamericano(-a) *m(f)*
AFT *n abbr* (= *American Federation of Teachers*) *sindicato de profesores*
aft [ɑ:ft] *adv* (*be*) en popa; (*go*) a popa
after ['ɑ:ftəʳ] *prep* (*time*) después de; (*place, order*) detrás de, tras ■ *adv* después ■ *conj* después (de) que; **what/who are you ~?** ¿qué/a quién buscas?; **the police are ~ him** la policía le está buscando; **~ having done/he left** después de haber hecho/después de que se marchó; **~ dinner** después de cenar *or* comer; **the day ~ tomorrow** pasado mañana; **to ask ~ sb** preguntar por algn; **~ all** después de todo, al fin y al cabo; **~ you!** ¡Vd primero!; **quarter ~ two** (*US*) las dos y cuarto
afterbirth ['ɑ:ftəbə:θ] *n* placenta
aftercare ['ɑ:ftəkɛəʳ] *n* (*Med*) asistencia postoperatoria
after-effects ['ɑ:ftərɪfɛkts] *npl* secuelas *fpl*, efectos *mpl*
afterlife ['ɑ:ftəlaɪf] *n* vida después de la muerte
aftermath ['ɑ:ftəmɑ:θ] *n* consecuencias *fpl*, resultados *mpl*
afternoon [ɑ:ftə'nu:n] *n* tarde *f*; **good ~!** ¡buenas tardes!
afters ['ɑ:ftəz] *n* (*col: dessert*) postre *m*
after-sales service [ɑ:ftə'seɪlz-] *n* (*Brit Comm: for car, washing machine etc*) servicio de asistencia pos-venta
after-shave ['ɑ:ftəʃeɪv], **after-shave lotion** *n* loción *f* para después del afeitado, aftershave *m*

aftershock ['ɑ:ftəʃɔk] n (of earthquake) pequeño temblor m posterior

aftersun ['ɑ:ftəsʌn], **aftersun lotion** n after-sun m inv

aftertaste ['ɑ:ftəteɪst] n regusto

afterthought ['ɑ:ftəθɔ:t] n ocurrencia (tardía)

afterwards ['ɑ:ftəwədz] adv después, más tarde

again [ə'gɛn] adv otra vez, de nuevo; **to do sth ~** volver a hacer algo; **~ and ~** una y otra vez; **now and ~** de vez en cuando

against [ə'gɛnst] prep (opposed) en contra de; (close to) contra, junto a; **I was leaning ~ the desk** estaba apoyado en el escritorio; **(as) ~** frente a

age [eɪdʒ] n edad f; (old age) vejez f; (period) época ∎ vi envejecer(se) ∎ vt envejecer; **what ~ is he?** ¿qué edad or cuántos años tiene?; **he is 20 years of ~** tiene 20 años; **under ~** menor de edad; **to come of ~** llegar a la mayoría de edad; **it's been ages since I saw you** hace siglos que no te veo

aged [eɪdʒd] adj: **~ 10** de 10 años de edad ∎ npl ['eɪdʒɪd]: **the ~** los ancianos

age group n: **to be in the same ~** tener la misma edad; **the 40 to 50 ~** las personas de 40 a 50 años

ageing ['eɪdʒɪŋ] adj que envejece; (pej) en declive ∎ n envejecimiento

ageless ['eɪdʒlɪs] adj (eternal) eterno; (ever young) siempre joven

age limit n límite m de edad, edad f tope

agency ['eɪdʒənsɪ] n agencia; **through or by the ~ of** por medio de

agenda [ə'dʒɛndə] n orden m del día; **on the ~** (Comm) en el orden del día

agent ['eɪdʒənt] n (gen) agente m/f; (representative) representante m/f delegado(-a)

aggravate ['ægrəveɪt] vt agravar; (annoy) irritar, exasperar

aggravating ['ægrəveɪtɪŋ] adj irritante, molesto

aggravation [ægrə'veɪʃən] n agravamiento

aggregate ['ægrɪgeɪt] n conjunto

aggression [ə'grɛʃən] n agresión f

aggressive [ə'grɛsɪv] adj agresivo; (vigorous) enérgico

aggressiveness [ə'grɛsɪvnɪs] n agresividad f

aggressor [ə'grɛsər] n agresor(a) m(f)

aggrieved [ə'gri:vd] adj ofendido, agraviado

aggro ['ægrəu] n (col: physical violence) bronca; (bad feeling) mal rollo; (hassle) rollo, movida

aghast [ə'gɑ:st] adj horrorizado

agile ['ædʒaɪl] adj ágil

agility [ə'dʒɪlɪtɪ] n agilidad f

agitate ['ædʒɪteɪt] vt (shake) agitar; (trouble)

inquietar; to ~ for hacer campaña en pro de or en favor de

agitated ['ædʒɪteɪtɪd] adj agitado

agitator ['ædʒɪteɪtər] n agitador(a) m(f)

AGM n abbr = **annual general meeting**

agnostic [æg'nɔstɪk] adj, n agnóstico(-a) m(f)

ago [ə'gəu] adv: **two days ~** hace dos días; **not long ~** hace poco; **how long ~?** ¿hace cuánto tiempo?; **as long ~ as 1980** ya en 1980

agog [ə'gɔg] adj (anxious) ansioso; (excited): **(all) ~ (for)** (todo) emocionado (por)

agonize ['ægənaɪz] vi: **to ~ (over)** atormentarse (por)

agonized ['ægənaɪzd] adj angustioso

agonizing ['ægənaɪzɪŋ] adj (pain) atroz; (suspense) angustioso

agony ['ægənɪ] n (pain) dolor m atroz; (distress) angustia: **to be in ~** retorcerse de dolor

agony aunt n (Brit col) consejera sentimental

agony column n consultorio sentimental

agree [ə'gri:] vt (price) acordar, quedar en ∎ vi (statements etc) coincidir, concordar; **to ~ (with)** (person) estar de acuerdo (con), ponerse de acuerdo (con); **to ~ to do** aceptar hacer; **to ~ to sth** consentir en algo; **to ~ that** (admit) estar de acuerdo en que; **it was agreed that ...** se acordó que ...; **garlic doesn't ~ with me** el ajo no me sienta bien

agreeable [ə'gri:əbl] adj agradable; (person) simpático; (willing) de acuerdo, conforme

agreeably [ə'gri:əblɪ] adv agradablemente

agreed [ə'gri:d] adj (time, place) convenido

agreement [ə'gri:mənt] n acuerdo; (Comm) contrato; **in ~** de acuerdo, conforme; **by mutual ~** de común acuerdo

agricultural [ægrɪ'kʌltʃərəl] adj agrícola

agriculture ['ægrɪkʌltʃər] n agricultura

aground [ə'graund] adv: **to run ~** encallar, embarrancar

ahead [ə'hɛd] adv delante; **~ of** delante de; (fig: schedule etc) antes de; **~ of time** antes de la hora; **to be ~ of sb** (fig) llevar ventaja or la delantera a algn; **go right or straight ~** siga adelante; **they were (right) ~ of us** iban (justo) delante de nosotros

ahoy [ə'hɔɪ] excl ¡oiga!

AI n abbr (= Amnesty International) (Comput) = **artificial intelligence**

AIB n abbr (Brit: = Accident Investigation Bureau) oficina de investigación de accidentes

AID n abbr (= artificial insemination by donor) inseminación artificial por donante; (US: = Agency for International Development) Agencia Internacional para el Desarrollo

aid [eɪd] n ayuda, auxilio ∎ vt ayudar, auxiliar; **in ~ of** a beneficio de; **with the ~ of** con la ayuda de; **to ~ and abet** (Law) ser cómplice

aide [eɪd] n (Pol) ayudante m/f
AIDS [eɪdz] n abbr (= acquired immune (or immuno-) deficiency syndrome) SIDA m, sida m
AIH n abbr (= artificial insemination by husband) inseminación artificial por esposo
ailing ['eɪlɪŋ] adj (person, economy) enfermizo
ailment ['eɪlmənt] n enfermedad f, achaque m
aim [eɪm] vt (gun) apuntar; (missile, remark) dirigir; (blow) asestar ▪ vi (also: take aim) apuntar ▪ n puntería; (objective) propósito, meta; **to ~ at** (objective) aspirar a, pretender; **to ~ to do** tener como objetivo hacer, aspirar a hacer
aimless ['eɪmlɪs] adj sin propósito, sin objeto
aimlessly ['eɪmlɪslɪ] adv sin rumbo fijo
ain't [eɪnt] (col) = **am not; aren't; isn't**
air [ɛəʳ] n aire m; (appearance) aspecto ▪ vt (room) ventilar; (clothes, bed, grievances, ideas) airear; (views) hacer público ▪ cpd aéreo; **to throw sth into the ~** (ball etc) lanzar algo al aire; **by ~** (travel) en avión; **to be on the ~** (Radio, TV: programme) estarse emitiendo; (: station) estar emitiendo
airbag ['ɛəbæg] n airbag m inv
air base n (Mil) base f aérea
air bed n (Brit) colchoneta inflable or neumática
airborne ['ɛəbɔːn] adj (in the air) en el aire; (Mil) aerotransportado; **as soon as the plane was ~** tan pronto como el avión estuvo en el aire
air cargo n carga aérea
air-conditioned ['ɛəkən'dɪʃənd] adj climatizado
air conditioning [-kən'dɪʃənɪŋ] n aire m acondicionado
air-cooled ['ɛəkuːld] adj refrigerado por aire
aircraft ['ɛəkrɑːft] n pl inv avión m
aircraft carrier n porta(a)viones m inv
air cushion n cojín m de aire; (Aviat) colchón m de aire
airdrome ['ɛədrəum] n (US) aeródromo
airfield ['ɛəfiːld] n campo de aviación
Air Force n fuerzas aéreas fpl, aviación f
air freight n flete m por avión
air freshener n ambientador m
air gun n escopeta de aire comprimido
air hostess (Brit) n azafata, aeromoza (LAm)
airily ['ɛərɪlɪ] adv muy a la ligera
airing ['ɛərɪŋ] n: **to give an ~ to** (linen) airear; (room) ventilar; (fig: ideas etc) airear, someter a discusión
air letter n (Brit) carta aérea
airlift ['ɛəlɪft] n puente m aéreo
airline ['ɛəlaɪn] n línea aérea
airliner ['ɛəlaɪnəʳ] n avión m de pasajeros

airlock ['ɛəlɔk] n (in pipe) esclusa de aire
airmail ['ɛəmeɪl] n: **by ~** por avión
air mattress n colchón m inflable or neumático
airplane ['ɛəpleɪn] n (US) avión m
air pocket n bolsa de aire
airport ['ɛəpɔːt] n aeropuerto
air rage n conducta agresiva de pasajeros a bordo de un avión
air raid n ataque m aéreo
air rifle n escopeta de aire comprimido
airsick ['ɛəsɪk] adj: **to be ~** marearse (en avión)
airspeed ['ɛəspiːd] n velocidad f de vuelo
airstrip ['ɛəstrɪp] n pista de aterrizaje
air terminal n terminal f
airtight ['ɛətaɪt] adj hermético
air time n (Radio, TV) tiempo en antena
air traffic control n control m de tráfico aéreo
air traffic controller n controlador(a) m(f) aéreo(-a)
airway ['ɛəweɪ] n (Aviat) vía aérea; (Anat) vía respiratoria
airy ['ɛərɪ] adj (room) bien ventilado; (manners) despreocupado
aisle [aɪl] n (of church) nave f lateral; (of theatre, plane) pasillo
ajar [ə'dʒɑːʳ] adj entreabierto
AK abbr (US) = **Alaska**
aka abbr (= also known as) alias
akin [ə'kɪn] adj: **~ to** semejante a
AL abbr (US) = **Alabama**
ALA n abbr = **American Library Association**
Ala. abbr (US) = **Alabama**
alabaster ['æləbɑːstəʳ] n alabastro
à la carte [ælæ'kɑːt] adv a la carta
alacrity [ə'lækrɪtɪ] n: **with ~** con la mayor prontitud
alarm [ə'lɑːm] n alarma; (anxiety) inquietud f ▪ vt asustar, alarmar
alarm clock n despertador m
alarmed [ə'lɑːmd] adj (person) alarmado, asustado; (house, car etc) con alarma
alarming [ə'lɑːmɪŋ] adj alarmante
alarmingly [ə'lɑːmɪŋlɪ] adv de forma alarmante; **~ quickly** a una velocidad alarmante
alarmist [ə'lɑːmɪst] n alarmista m/f
alas [ə'læs] adv desgraciadamente ▪ excl ¡ay!
Alas. abbr (US) = **Alaska**
Alaska [ə'læskə] n Alaska
Albania [æl'beɪnɪə] n Albania
Albanian [æl'beɪnɪən] adj albanés(-esa) ▪ n albanés(-esa) m(f); (Ling) albanés m
albatross ['ælbətrɔs] n albatros m
albeit [ɔːl'biːɪt] conj (although) aunque

album ['ælbəm] n álbum m; (L.P.) elepé m
albumen ['ælbjumɪn] n albúmina
alchemy ['ælkɪmɪ] n alquimia
alcohol ['ælkəhɔl] n alcohol m
alcohol-free adj sin alcohol
alcoholic [ælkə'hɔlɪk] adj, n alcohólico(-a) m(f)
alcoholism ['ælkəhɔlɪzəm] n alcoholismo
alcove ['ælkəuv] n nicho, hueco
Ald. abbr = **alderman**
alderman ['ɔːldəmən] n concejal m
ale [eɪl] n cerveza
alert [ə'lɜːt] adj alerta inv; (sharp) despierto, despabilado ■ n alerta m, alarma ■ vt poner sobre aviso; **to ~ sb (to sth)** poner sobre aviso or alertar a algn (de algo); **to ~ sb to the dangers of sth** poner sobre aviso or alertar a algn de los peligros de algo; **to be on the ~** estar alerta or sobre aviso
alertness [ə'lɜːtnɪs] n vigilancia
Aleutian Islands [ə'luːʃən-] npl Islas fpl Aleutianas
A level n abbr (Brit Scol: = Advanced level) ≈ Bachillerato
Alexandria [ælɪɡ'zuːndrɪə] n Alejandría
alfresco [æl'freskəu] adj, adv al aire libre
algebra ['ældʒɪbrə] n álgebra
Algeria [æl'dʒɪərɪə] n Argelia
Algerian [æl'dʒɪərɪən] adj, n argelino(-a) m(f)
Algiers [æl'dʒɪəz] n Argel m
algorithm ['ælɡərɪðəm] n algoritmo
alias ['eɪlɪəs] adv alias, conocido por ■ n alias m
alibi ['ælɪbaɪ] n coartada
alien ['eɪlɪən] n (foreigner) extranjero(-a) ■ adj: **~ to** ajeno a
alienate ['eɪlɪəneɪt] vt enajenar, alejar
alienation [eɪlɪə'neɪʃən] n alejamiento m
alight [ə'laɪt] adj ardiendo ■ vi apearse, bajar
align [ə'laɪn] vt alinear
alignment [ə'laɪnmənt] n alineación f; **the desks are out of ~** los pupitres no están bien alineados
alike [ə'laɪk] adj semejantes, iguales ■ adv igualmente, del mismo modo; **to look ~** parecerse
alimony ['ælɪmənɪ] n (Law) pensión f alimenticia
alive [ə'laɪv] adj (gen) vivo; (lively) activo
alkali ['ælkəlaɪ] n álcali m

 **KEYWORD**

all [ɔːl] adj todo(-a) sg, todos(-as) pl; **all day** todo el día; **all night** toda la noche; **all men** todos los hombres; **all five came** vinieron los cinco; **all the books** todos los libros; **all the time/his life** todo el tiempo/toda su vida; **for all their efforts** a pesar de todos sus esfuerzos
■ pron **1** todo; **I ate it all, I ate all of it** me lo comí todo; **all of them** todos (ellos); **all of us went** fuimos todos; **all the boys went** fueron todos los chicos; **is that all?** ¿eso es todo?, ¿algo más?; (in shop) ¿algo más?, ¿alguna cosa más?
2 (in phrases): **above all** sobre todo; por encima de todo; **after all** después de todo; **at all: anything at all** lo que sea; **not at all** (in answer to question) en absoluto; (in answer to thanks) ¡de nada!, ¡no hay de qué!; **I'm not at all tired** no estoy nada cansado(-a); **anything at all will do** cualquier cosa viene bien; **all in all** a fin de cuentas
■ adv: **all alone** completamente solo(-a); **to be/feel all in** estar rendido; **it's not as hard as all that** no es tan difícil como lo pintas; **all the more/the better** tanto más/mejor; **all but** casi; **the score is two all** están empatados a dos

all-around ['ɔːlə'raund] adj (US) = **all-round**
allay [ə'leɪ] vt (fears) aquietar, (pain) aliviar
all clear n (after attack etc) fin m de la alerta; (fig) luz f verde
allegation [ælɪ'ɡeɪʃən] n alegato
allege [ə'ledʒ] vt pretender; **he is alleged to have said ...** se afirma que él dijo ...
alleged [ə'ledʒd] adj supuesto, presunto
allegedly [ə'ledʒɪdlɪ] adv supuestamente, según se afirma
allegiance [ə'liːdʒəns] n lealtad f
allegory ['ælɪɡərɪ] n alegoría
all-embracing ['ɔːləm'breɪsɪŋ] adj universal
allergic [ə'lɜːdʒɪk] adj: **~ to** alérgico a
allergy ['ælədʒɪ] n alergia
alleviate [ə'liːvɪeɪt] vt aliviar
alleviation [əliːvɪ'eɪʃən] n alivio
alley ['ælɪ] n (street) callejuela; (in garden) paseo
alleyway ['ælɪweɪ] n callejón m
alliance [ə'laɪəns] n alianza
allied ['ælaɪd] adj aliado; (related) relacionado
alligator ['ælɪɡeɪtəʳ] n caimán m
all-important ['ɔːlɪm'pɔːtənt] adj de suma importancia
all-in ['ɔːlɪn] adj (Brit: also adv: charge) todo incluido
all-in wrestling n lucha libre
alliteration [əlɪtə'reɪʃən] n aliteración f
all-night ['ɔːl'naɪt] adj (café) abierto toda la noche; (party) que dura toda la noche
allocate ['æləkeɪt] vt (share out) repartir; (devote) asignar

419

allocation [ælə'keɪʃən] *n* (*of money*) ración *f*, cuota; (*distribution*) reparto

allot [ə'lɔt] *vt* asignar; **in the allotted time** en el tiempo asignado

allotment [ə'lɔtmənt] *n* porción *f*; (*garden*) parcela

all-out ['ɔ:laut] *adj* (*effort etc*) supremo ■ *adv*: **all out** con todas las fuerzas, a fondo

allow [ə'lau] *vt* (*permit*) permitir, dejar; (*a claim*) admitir; (*sum to spend, time estimated*) dar, conceder; (*concede*): **to ~ that** reconocer que; **to ~ sb to do** permitir a algn hacer; **smoking is not allowed** prohibido or se prohíbe fumar; **he is allowed to ...** se le permite ...; **we must ~ three days for the journey** debemos dejar tres días para el viaje ▸ **allow for** *vt fus* tener en cuenta

allowance [ə'lauəns] *n* concesión *f*; (*payment*) subvención *f*, pensión *f*; (*discount*) descuento, rebaja; **to make allowances for** (*person*) disculpar a; (*thing: take into account*) tener en cuenta

alloy ['ælɔɪ] *n* aleación *f*

all right *adv* (*feel, work*) bien; (*as answer*) ¡de acuerdo!, ¡está bien!

all-round ['ɔ:l'raund] *adj* completo; (*view*) amplio

all-rounder ['ɔ:l'raundə'] *n*: **to be a good ~** ser una persona que hace de todo

allspice ['ɔ:lspaɪs] *n* pimienta inglesa or de Jamaica

all-time ['ɔ:l'taɪm] *adj* (*record*) de todos los tiempos

allude [ə'lu:d] *vi*: **to ~ to** aludir a

alluring [ə'ljuərɪŋ] *adj* seductor(a), atractivo

allusion [ə'lu:ʒən] *n* referencia, alusión *f*

ally *n* ['ælaɪ] aliado(-a) ■ *vt* [ə'laɪ]: **to ~ o.s. with** aliarse con

almanac ['ɔ:lmənæk] *n* almanaque *m*

almighty [ɔ:l'maɪtɪ] *adj* todopoderoso

almond ['ɑ:mənd] *n* (*fruit*) almendra; (*tree*) almendro

almost ['ɔ:lməust] *adv* casi; **he ~ fell** casi or por poco se cae

alms [ɑ:mz] *npl* limosna *sg*

aloft [ə'lɔft] *adv* arriba

alone [ə'ləun] *adj* solo ■ *adv* sólo, solamente; **to leave sb ~** dejar a algn en paz; **to leave sth ~** no tocar algo; **let ~ ...** y mucho menos, y no digamos ...

along [ə'lɔŋ] *prep* a lo largo de, por ■ *adv*: **is he coming ~ with us?** ¿viene con nosotros?; **he was limping ~** iba cojeando; **~ with** junto con; **all ~** (*all the time*) desde el principio

alongside [ə'lɔŋ'saɪd] *prep* al lado de ■ *adv* (*Naut*) de costado; **we brought our boat ~** atracamos nuestro barco

aloof [ə'lu:f] *adj* distante ■ *adv*: **to stand ~** mantenerse a distancia

aloud [ə'laud] *adv* en voz alta

alphabet ['ælfəbɛt] *n* alfabeto

alphabetical [ælfə'bɛtɪkəl] *adj* alfabético; **in ~ order** por orden alfabético

alphanumeric [ælfənju:'mɛrɪk] *adj* alfanumérico

alpine ['ælpaɪn] *adj* alpino, alpestre

Alps [ælps] *npl*: **the ~** los Alpes

already [ɔ:l'rɛdɪ] *adv* ya

alright ['ɔ:l'raɪt] *adv* (*Brit*) = **all right**

Alsatian [æl'seɪʃən] *n* (*dog*) pastor *m* alemán

also ['ɔ:lsəu] *adv* también, además

Alta. *abbr* (*Canada*) = **Alberta**

altar ['ɔltə'] *n* altar *m*

alter ['ɔltə'] *vt* cambiar, modificar ■ *vi* cambiarse, modificarse

alteration [ɔltə'reɪʃən] *n* cambio, modificación *f*; **alterations** *npl* (*Arch*) reformas *fpl*; (*Sewing*) arreglos *mpl*; **timetable subject to ~** el horario puede cambiar

altercation [ɔltə'keɪʃən] *n* altercado

alternate [ɔl'tə:nɪt] *adj* alterno ■ *vi* ['ɔltəneɪt]: **to ~ (with)** alternar (con); **on ~ days** en días alternos

alternately [ɔl'tə:nɪtlɪ] *adv* alternativamente, por turno

alternating ['ɔltəneɪtɪŋ] *adj* (*current*) alterno

alternative [ɔl'tə:nətɪv] *adj* alternativo ■ *n* alternativa

alternatively [ɔl'tə:nətɪvlɪ] *adv*: **~ one could** ... por otra parte se podría ...

alternative medicine *n* medicina alternativa

alternator ['ɔltəneɪtə'] *n* (*Aut*) alternador *m*

although [ɔ:l'ðəu] *conj* aunque, si bien

altitude ['æltɪtju:d] *n* altitud *f*, altura

altitude sickness *n* mal *m* de altura, soroche *m* (*LAm*)

alto ['æltəu] *n* (*female*) contralto *f*; (*male*) alto

altogether [ɔ:ltə'gɛðə'] *adv* completamente, del todo; (*on the whole, in all*) en total, en conjunto; **how much is that ~?** ¿cuánto es todo or en total?

altruism ['æltruɪzəm] *n* altruismo

altruistic [æltru'ɪstɪk] *adj* altruista

aluminium [ælju'mɪnɪəm], **aluminum** (*US*) [ə'lu:mɪnəm] *n* aluminio

always ['ɔ:lweɪz] *adv* siempre

Alzheimer's ['ælts.haɪməz] *n* (*also*: **Alzheimer's disease**) enfermedad *f* de Alzheimer

AM *abbr* (= *amplitude modulation*) A.M. *f* ■ *n abbr* (*Pol: in Wales*) = **Assembly Member**

am [æm] *vb see* **be**

a.m. *adv abbr* (= *ante meridiem*) de la mañana
AMA *n abbr* = **American Medical Association**
amalgam [ə'mælgəm] *n* amalgama
amalgamate [ə'mælgəmeɪt] *vi* amalgamarse ▪ *vt* amalgamar
amalgamation [əmælgə'meɪʃən] *n* (*Comm*) fusión *f*
amass [ə'mæs] *vt* amontonar, acumular
amateur ['æmətə*r*] *n* aficionado(-a), amateur *m/f*; **~ dramatics** dramas *mpl* presentados por aficionados, representación *f* de aficionados
amateurish ['æmətərɪʃ] *adj* (*pej*) torpe, inexperto
amaze [ə'meɪz] *vt* asombrar, pasmar; **to be amazed (at)** asombrarse (de)
amazement [ə'meɪzmənt] *n* asombro, sorpresa; **to my ~** para mi sorpresa
amazing [ə'meɪzɪŋ] *adj* extraordinario, asombroso; (*bargain, offer*) increíble
amazingly [ə'meɪzɪŋlɪ] *adv* extraordinariamente
Amazon ['æməzən] *n* (*Geo*) Amazonas *m*; (*Mythology*) amazona ▪ *cpd*: **the ~ basin/jungle** la cuenca/selva del Amazonas
Amazonian [æmə'zəʊnɪən] *adj* amazónico
ambassador [æm'bæsədə*r*] *n* embajador(a) *m(f)*
amber ['æmbə*r*] *n* ámbar *m*; **at ~** (*Brit Aut*) en amarillo
ambidextrous [æmbɪ'dɛkstrəs] *adj* ambidextro
ambience ['æmbɪəns] *n* ambiente *m*
ambiguity [æmbɪ'gjuɪtɪ] *n* ambigüedad *f*; (*of meaning*) doble sentido
ambiguous [æm'bɪgjuəs] *adj* ambiguo
ambition [æm'bɪʃən] *n* ambición *f*; **to achieve one's ~** realizar su ambición
ambitious [æm'bɪʃəs] *adj* ambicioso; (*plan*) grandioso
ambivalent [æm'bɪvələnt] *adj* ambivalente; (*pej*) equívoco
amble ['æmbl] *vi* (*gen: also:* **amble along**) deambular, andar sin prisa
ambulance ['æmbjuləns] *n* ambulancia
ambulanceman/woman ['æmbjulənsmən/wumən] *n* ambulanciero(-a)
ambush ['æmbuʃ] *n* emboscada ▪ *vt* tender una emboscada a; (*fig*) coger (*SP*) *or* agarrar (*LAm*) por sorpresa
ameba [ə'mi:bə] *n* (*US*) = **amoeba**
ameliorate [ə'mi:lɪəreɪt] *vt* mejorar
amelioration [əmi:lɪə'reɪʃən] *n* mejora
amen [ɑ:'mɛn] *excl* amén
amenable [ə'mi:nəbl] *adj*: **~ to** (*advice etc*) sensible a
amend [ə'mɛnd] *vt* (*law, text*) enmendar;

to make amends (*apologize*) enmendarlo, dar cumplida satisfacción
amendment [ə'mɛndmənt] *n* enmienda
amenities [ə'mi:nɪtɪz] *npl* comodidades *fpl*
amenity [ə'mi:nɪtɪ] *n* servicio
America [ə'mɛrɪkə] *n* América (del Norte)
American [ə'mɛrɪkən] *adj, n* (norte)americano(-a) *m(f)*, estadounidense *m/f*
Americanism [ə'mɛrɪkənɪzəm] *n* americanismo
americanize [ə'mɛrɪkənaɪz] *vt* americanizar
Amerindian [æmər'ɪndɪən] *adj, n* amerindio(-a)
amethyst ['æmɪθɪst] *n* amatista
Amex ['æmɛks] *n abbr* = **American Stock Exchange**
amiable ['eɪmɪəbl] *adj* (*kind*) amable, simpático
amicable ['æmɪkəbl] *adj* amistoso, amigable
amicably ['æmɪkəblɪ] *adv* amigablemente, amistosamente; **to part ~** separarse amistosamente
amid [ə'mɪd], **amidst** [ə'mɪdst] *prep* entre, en medio de
amiss [ə'mɪs] *adv*: **to take sth ~** tomar algo a mal; **there's something ~** pasa algo
ammo ['æməʊ] *n abbr* (*col*) = **ammunition**
ammonia [ə'məʊnɪə] *n* amoníaco
ammunition [æmju'nɪʃən] *n* municiones *fpl*; (*fig*) argumentos *mpl*
ammunition dump *n* depósito de municiones
amnesia [æm'ni:zɪə] *n* amnesia
amnesty ['æmnɪstɪ] *n* amnistía; **to grant an ~ to** amnistiar (a); **A~ International** Amnistía Internacional
amoeba, ameba (*US*) [ə'mi:bə] *n* amiba
amok [ə'mɔk] *adv*: **to run ~** enloquecerse, desbocarse
among [ə'mʌŋ], **amongst** [ə'mʌŋst] *prep* entre, en medio de
amoral [æ'mɔrəl] *adj* amoral
amorous ['æmərəs] *adj* cariñoso
amorphous [ə'mɔ:fəs] *adj* amorfo
amortization [əmɔ:taɪ'zeɪʃən] *n* amortización *f*
amount [ə'maʊnt] *n* (*gen*) cantidad *f*; (*of bill etc*) suma, importe *m* ▪ *vi*: **to ~ to** (*total*) sumar; (*be same as*) equivaler a, significar; **this amounts to a refusal** esto equivale a una negativa; **the total ~** (*of money*) la suma total
amp [æmp], **ampère** ['æmpɛə*r*] *n* amperio; **a 13 ~ plug** un enchufe de 13 amperios
ampersand ['æmpəsænd] *n* signo &, "y" comercial

amphetamine [æm'fɛtəmi:n] n anfetamina

amphibian [æm'fɪbɪən] n anfibio

amphibious [æm'fɪbɪəs] adj anfibio

amphitheatre, amphitheater (US) ['æmfɪθɪətə'] n anfiteatro

ample ['æmpl] adj (spacious) amplio; (abundant) abundante; **to have ~ time** tener tiempo de sobra

amplifier ['æmplɪfaɪə'] n amplificador m

amplify ['æmplɪfaɪ] vt amplificar, aumentar; (explain) explicar

amply ['æmplɪ] adv ampliamente

ampoule, ampule (US) ['æmpu:l] n (Med) ampolla

amputate ['æmpjuteɪt] vt amputar

amputee [æmpju'ti:] n persona que ha sufrido una amputación

Amsterdam ['æmstədæm] n Amsterdam m

amt abbr = **amount**

amuck [ə'mʌk] adv = **amok**

amuse [ə'mju:z] vt divertir; (distract) distraer, entretener; **to ~ o.s. with sth/by doing sth** distraerse con algo/haciendo algo; **he was amused at the joke** le divirtió el chiste

amusement [ə'mju:zmənt] n diversión f; (pastime) pasatiempo; (laughter) risa; **much to my ~** con gran regocijo mío

amusement arcade n salón m de juegos

amusement park n parque m de atracciones

amusing [ə'mju:zɪŋ] adj divertido

an [æn, ən, n] indef art see **a**

ANA n abbr = **American Newspaper Association; American Nurses Association**

anachronism [ə'nækrənɪzəm] n anacronismo

anaemia [ə'ni:mɪə] n anemia

anaemic [ə'ni:mɪk] adj anémico; (fig) flojo

anaesthetic [ænɪs'θɛtɪk] n anestesia; **local/general ~** anestesia local/general

anaesthetist [æ'ni:sθɪtɪst] n anestesista m/f

anagram ['ænəgræm] n anagrama m

anal ['eɪnl] adj anal

analgesic [ænæl'dʒi:sɪk] adj, n analgésico

analogous [ə'næləgəs] adj: **~ to** or **with** análogo a

analogue, analog ['ænələg] adj (watch) analógico

analogy [ə'nælədʒɪ] n analogía; **to draw an ~ between** señalar la analogía entre

analyse ['ænəlaɪz] vt (Brit) analizar

analysis (pl **analyses**) [ə'næləsɪs, -si:z] n análisis m inv

analyst ['ænəlɪst] n (political analyst) analista m/f; (psychoanalyst) psicoanalista m/f

analytic [ænə'lɪtɪk], **analytical** [ænə'lɪtɪkəl] adj analítico

analyze ['ænəlaɪz] vt (US) = **analyse**

anarchic [æ'nɑ:kɪk] adj anárquico

anarchist ['ænəkɪst] adj, n anarquista m/f

anarchy ['ænəkɪ] n anarquía, desorden m

anathema [ə'næθɪmə] n: **that is ~ to him** eso es pecado para él

anatomical [ænə'tɔmɪkəl] adj anatómico

anatomy [ə'nætəmɪ] n anatomía

ANC n abbr = **African National Congress**

ancestor ['ænsɪstə'] n antepasado

ancestral [æn'sɛstrəl] adj ancestral

ancestry ['ænsɪstrɪ] n ascendencia, abolengo

anchor ['æŋkə'] n ancla, áncora ■ vi (also: **to drop anchor**) anclar, echar el ancla ■ vt (fig) sujetar, afianzar; **to weigh ~** levar anclas

anchorage ['æŋkərɪdʒ] n ancladero

anchor man, anchor woman n (Radio, TV) presentador(a) m(f)

anchovy ['æntʃəvɪ] n anchoa

ancient ['eɪnʃənt] adj antiguo; **~ monument** monumento histórico

ancillary [æn'sɪlərɪ] adj (worker, staff) auxiliar

and [ænd] conj y; (before i, hi) e; **~ so on** etcétera; **try ~ come** procure or intente venir; **better ~ better** cada vez mejor

Andalusia [ændə'lu:zɪə] n Andalucía

Andean ['ændɪən] adj andino(-a); **~ high plateau** altiplanicie f, altiplano (LAm)

Andes ['ændi:z] npl: **the ~** los Andes

anecdote ['ænɪkdəut] n anécdota

anemia [ə'ni:mɪə] n (US) = **anaemia**

anemic [ə'ni:mɪk] adj (US) = **anaemic**

anemone [ə'nɛmənɪ] n (Bot) anémone f; **sea ~** anémona

anesthetic [ænɪs'θɛtɪk] adj, n (US) = **anaesthetic**

anesthetist [æ'ni:sθɪtɪst] n (US) = **anaesthetist**

anew [ə'nju:] adv de nuevo, otra vez

angel ['eɪndʒəl] n ángel m

angel dust n polvo de ángel

angelic [æn'dʒɛlɪk] adj angélico

anger ['æŋgə'] n ira, cólera, enojo (LAm) ■ vt enojar, enfurecer

angina [æn'dʒaɪnə] n angina (del pecho)

angle ['æŋgl] n ángulo; **from their ~** desde su punto de vista

angler ['æŋglə'] n pescador(a) m(f) (de caña)

Anglican ['æŋglɪkən] adj, n anglicano(-a)

anglicize ['æŋglɪsaɪz] vt anglicanizar

angling ['æŋglɪŋ] n pesca con caña

Anglo- [æŋgləu] pref anglo...

Angola [æŋ'gəulə] n Angola

Angolan [æŋ'gəulən] adj, n angoleño(-a) m(f)

angrily ['æŋgrɪlɪ] adv enojado, enfadado

angry ['æŋgrɪ] adj enfadado, enojado (esp LAm); **to be ~ with sb/at sth** estar enfadado con algn/por algo; **to get ~** enfadarse, enojarse (esp LAm)

anguish ['æŋgwɪʃ] n (physical) tormentos mpl; (mental) angustia

anguished ['æŋgwɪʃt] adj angustioso

angular ['æŋgjulər] adj (shape) angular; (features) anguloso

animal ['ænɪməl] adj, n animal m

animal rights [-raɪts] npl derechos mpl de los animales

animate vt ['ænɪmeɪt] (enliven) animar; (encourage) estimular, alentar ▪ adj ['ænɪmɪt] vivo, animado

animated ['ænɪmeɪtɪd] adj vivo, animado

animation [ænɪ'meɪʃən] n animación f

animosity [ænɪ'mɔsɪtɪ] n animosidad f, rencor m

aniseed ['ænɪsiːd] n anís m

Ankara ['æŋkərə] n Ankara

ankle ['æŋkl] n tobillo m

ankle sock n calcetín m

annex n ['æneks] (Brit: also: **annexe**: building) edificio anexo ▪ vt [æ'neks] (territory) anexar

annihilate [ə'naɪəleɪt] vt aniquilar

annihilation [ənaɪə'leɪʃən] n aniquilación f

anniversary [ænɪ'vəːsərɪ] n aniversario

annotate ['ænəuteɪt] vt anotar

announce [ə'nauns] vt (gen) anunciar; (inform) comunicar, **he announced that he wasn't going** declaró que no iba

announcement [ə'naunsmənt] n (gen) anuncio; (declaration) declaración f; **I'd like to make an ~** quisiera anunciar algo

announcer [ə'naunsər] n (Radio, TV) locutor(a) m(f)

annoy [ə'nɔɪ] vt molestar, fastidiar, fregar (LAm), embromar (LAm); **to be annoyed (at sth/with sb)** estar enfadado or molesto (por algo/con algn); **don't get annoyed!** ¡no se enfade!

annoyance [ə'nɔɪəns] n enojo; (thing) molestia

annoying [ə'nɔɪɪŋ] adj molesto, fastidioso, fregado (LAm), embromado (LAm); (person) pesado

annual ['ænjuəl] adj anual ▪ n (Bot) anual m; (book) anuario

annual general meeting n junta general anual

annually ['ænjuəlɪ] adv anualmente, cada año

annual report n informe m or memoria anual

annuity [ə'njuːɪtɪ] n renta or pensión f vitalicia

annul [ə'nʌl] vt anular; (law) revocar

annulment [ə'nʌlmənt] n anulación f

annum ['ænəm] n see **per annum**

Annunciation [ənʌnsɪ'eɪʃən] n Anunciación f

anode ['ænəud] n ánodo

anoint [ə'nɔɪnt] vt untar

anomalous [ɔ'nɔmələs] adj anómalo

anomaly [ə'nɔməlɪ] n anomalía

anon. [ə'nɔn] abbr = **anonymous**

anonymity [ænə'nɪmɪtɪ] n anonimato

anonymous [ə'nɔnɪməs] adj anónimo; **to remain ~** quedar en el anonimato

anorak ['ænəræk] n anorak m

anorexia [ænə'reksɪə] n (Med) anorexia

anorexic [ænə'reksɪk] adj, n anoréxico(-a) m(f)

another [ə'nʌðər] adj: **~ book** otro libro; **~ beer?** ¿(quieres) otra cerveza?; **in ~ five years** en cinco años más ▪ pron otro; see also **one**

ANSI n abbr (= American National Standards Institution) oficina de normalización de EEUU

answer ['ɑːnsər] n respuesta, contestación f; (to problem) solución f ▪ vi contestar, responder ▪ vt (reply to) contestar a, responder a; (problem) resolver; **to ~ the phone** contestar el teléfono; **in ~ to your letter** contestando or en contestación a su carta; **to ~ the bell** or **the door** abrir la puerta

▶ **answer back** vi replicar, ser respondón(-ona)

▶ **answer for** vt fus responder de or por

▶ **answer to** vt fus (description) corresponder a

answerable ['ɑːnsərəbl] adj: **~ to sb for sth** responsable ante algn de algo

answering machine ['ɑːnsərɪŋ-] n contestador m automático

ant [ænt] n hormiga

ANTA n abbr = **American National Theater and Academy**

antagonism [æn'tægənɪzəm] n antagonismo m

antagonist [æn'tægənɪst] n antagonista m/f, adversario(-a)

antagonistic [æntægə'nɪstɪk] adj antagónico; (opposed) contrario, opuesto

antagonize [æn'tægənaɪz] vt provocar la enemistad de

Antarctic [ænt'ɑːktɪk] adj antártico ▪ n: **the ~** el Antártico

Antarctica [æn'tɑːktɪkə] n Antártida

Antarctic Circle n Círculo Polar Antártico

Antarctic Ocean n Océano Antártico

ante ['æntɪ] n: **to up the ~** subir la apuesta

ante... ['æntɪ] pref ante...

anteater ['æntiːtər] n oso hormiguero

antecedent [æntɪ'siːdənt] n antecedente m

antechamber ['æntɪtʃeɪmbər] n antecámara

antelope ['æntɪləup] n antílope m
antenatal [æntɪ'neɪtl] adj prenatal
antenatal clinic n clínica prenatal
antenna [æn'tɛnə] (pl antennae [-ni:])
n antena
anteroom ['æntɪrum] n antesala
anthem ['ænθəm] n: national ~ himno
nacional
anthology [æn'θɔlədʒɪ] n antología
anthropologist [ænθrə'pɔlədʒɪst] n
antropólogo(-a)
anthropology [ænθrə'pɔlədʒɪ] n antropología
anti... [æntɪ] pref anti...
anti-aircraft ['æntɪ'ɛəkrɑ:ft] adj antiaéreo
antiballistic [æntɪbə'lɪstɪk] adj antibalístico
antibiotic [æntɪbaɪ'ɔtɪk] adj, n antibiótico
antibody ['æntɪbɔdɪ] n anticuerpo
anticipate [æn'tɪsɪpeɪt] vt (foresee) prever;
(expect) esperar, contar con; (forestall)
anticiparse a, adelantarse a; this is worse
than I anticipated esto es peor de lo que
esperaba; as anticipated según se esperaba
anticipation [æntɪsɪ'peɪʃən] n previsión f;
esperanza; anticipación f
anticlimax [æntɪ'klaɪmæks] n decepción f
anticlockwise [æntɪ'klɔkwaɪz] adv en
dirección contraria a la de las agujas del reloj
antics ['æntɪks] npl payasadas fpl
anticyclone [æntɪ'saɪkləun] n anticiclón m
antidepressant [,æntɪdɪ'presnt] n
antidepresivo
antidote ['æntɪdəut] n antídoto
antifreeze ['æntɪfri:z] n anticongelante m
anti-globalization ['æntɪɡləubəlaɪ'zeɪʃən]
n antiglobalización f; ~ protesters
manifestantes m/fpl antiglobalización
antihistamine [æntɪ'hɪstəmi:n] n
antihistamínico
Antilles [æn'tɪli:z] npl: the ~ las Antillas
antipathy [æn'tɪpəθɪ] n (between people)
antipatía; (to person, thing) aversión f
antiperspirant ['æntɪpə:spɪrənt] n
antitranspirante m
Antipodes [æn'tɪpədi:z] npl: the ~ las
Antípodas
antiquarian [æntɪ'kwɛərɪən] n
anticuario(-a)
antiquated ['æntɪkweɪtɪd] adj anticuado
antique [æn'ti:k] n antigüedad f ■ adj
antiguo
antique dealer n anticuario(-a)
antique shop n tienda de antigüedades
antiquity [æn'tɪkwɪtɪ] n antigüedad f
anti-Semitic ['æntɪsɪ'mɪtɪk] adj antisemita
anti-Semitism [æntɪ'semɪtɪzəm] n
antisemitismo
antiseptic [æntɪ'septɪk] adj, n antiséptico

antisocial [æntɪ'səuʃəl] adj antisocial
antitank [æntɪ'tæŋk] adj antitanque
antithesis (pl antitheses) [æn'tɪθɪsɪs, -si:z] n
antítesis f inv
antitrust [æntɪ'trʌst] adj: ~ legislation
legislación f antimonopolio
antiviral [æntɪ'vaɪər] adj (Med) antivírico
antivirus [æntɪ'vaɪərəs] adj antivirus; ~
software antivirus m
antlers ['æntləz] npl cornamenta
anus ['eɪnəs] n ano
anvil ['ænvɪl] n yunque m
anxiety [æŋ'zaɪətɪ] n (worry) inquietud f;
(eagerness) ansia, anhelo
anxious ['æŋkʃəs] adj (worried) inquieto; (keen)
deseoso; I'm very ~ about you me tienes
muy preocupado
anxiously ['æŋkʃəslɪ] adv con inquietud, de
manera angustiada

 KEYWORD

any ['ɛnɪ] adj 1 (in questions etc) algún/alguna;
have you any butter/children? ¿tienes
mantequilla/hijos?; if there are any
tickets left si quedan billetes, si queda
algún billete
2 (with negative): I haven't any money/books
no tengo dinero/libros
3 (no matter which) cualquier; any excuse
will do valdrá or servirá cualquier excusa;
choose any book you like escoge el libro que
quieras; any teacher you ask will tell you
cualquier profesor al que preguntes te lo dirá
4 (in phrases): in any case de todas formas,
en cualquier caso; any day now cualquier
día (de estos); at any moment en cualquier
momento, de un momento a otro; at any
rate en todo caso; any time: come (at) any
time ven cuando quieras; he might come
(at) any time podría llegar de un momento
a otro
■ pron 1 (in questions etc): have you got any?
¿tienes alguno/a?; can any of you sing?
¿sabe cantar alguno de vosotros/ustedes?
2 (with negative): I haven't any (of them) no
tengo ninguno
3 (no matter which one(s)): take any of those
books (you like) toma el libro que quieras
de ésos
■ adv 1 (in questions etc): do you want any
more soup/sandwiches? ¿quieres más
sopa/bocadillos?; are you feeling any
better? ¿te sientes algo mejor?
2 (with negative): I can't hear him any more
ya no le oigo; don't wait any longer no
esperes más

anybody ['ɛnɪbɔdɪ] *pron* cualquiera, cualquier persona; (*in interrogative sentences*) alguien; (*in negative sentences*): **I don't see** ~ no veo a nadie

anyhow ['ɛnɪhau] *adv* de todos modos, de todas maneras; (*carelessly*) de cualquier manera; (*haphazardly*) de cualquier modo; **I shall go** ~ iré de todas maneras

anyone ['ɛnɪwʌn] = **anybody**

anyplace ['ɛnɪpleɪs] *adv* (US) = **anywhere**

anything ['ɛnɪθɪŋ] *pron* cualquier cosa; (*in interrogative sentences*) algo; (*in negative sentences*) nada; (*everything*) todo; ~ **else?** ¿algo más?; **it can cost** ~ **between £15 and £20** puede costar entre 15 y 20 libras

anytime ['ɛnɪtaɪm] *adv* (*at any moment*) en cualquier momento, de un momento a otro; (*whenever*) no importa cuándo, cuando quiera

anyway ['ɛnɪweɪ] *adv* de todas maneras; de cualquier modo

anywhere ['ɛnɪwɛəʳ] *adv* dondequiera; (*interrogative*) en algún sitio; (*negative sense*) en ningún sitio; (*everywhere*) en or por todas partes; **I don't see him** ~ no le veo en ningún sitio; ~ **in the world** en cualquier parte del mundo

Anzac ['ænzæk] *n abbr* ~ **Australia-New Zealand Army Corps**

apace [ə'peɪs] *adv* aprisa

apart [ə'pɑːt] *adv* aparte, separadamente; **10 miles** ~ separados por 10 millas; **to take** ~ desmontar; ~ **from** *prep* aparte de

apartheid [ə'pɑːteɪt] *n* apartheid *m*

apartment [ə'pɑːtmənt] *n* (US) piso, departamento (*LAm*), apartamento; (*room*) cuarto

apartment block or **building** *n* (US) bloque *m* de pisos

apathetic [æpə'θɛtɪk] *adj* apático, indiferente

apathy ['æpəθɪ] *n* apatía, indiferencia

APB *n abbr* (US: = *all points bulletin: police expression*) *expresión usada por la policía que significa "descubrir y aprehender al sospechoso"*

ape [eɪp] *n* mono ■ *vt* imitar, remedar

Apennines ['æpənaɪnz] *npl*: **the** ~ los Apeninos *mpl*

aperitif [ə'pɛrɪtiːf] *n* aperitivo

aperture ['æpətʃuəʳ] *n* rendija, resquicio; (*Phot*) abertura

APEX ['eɪpɛks] *n abbr* (*Aviat*: = *advance purchase excursion*) APEX *m*

apex ['eɪpɛks] *n* ápice *m*; (*fig*) cumbre *f*

aphid ['eɪfɪd] *n* pulgón *m*

aphorism ['æfərɪzəm] *n* aforismo

aphrodisiac [æfrəu'dɪzɪæk] *adj, n* afrodisíaco

API *n abbr* = **American Press Institute**

apiece [ə'piːs] *adv* cada uno

aplomb [ə'plɔm] *n* aplomo, confianza

APO *n abbr* (US: = *Army Post Office*) *servicio postal del ejército*

Apocalypse [ə'pɔkəlɪps] *n* Apocalipsis *m*

apocryphal [ə'pɔkrɪfəl] *adj* apócrifo

apolitical [eɪpə'lɪtɪkl] *adj* apolítico

apologetic [əpɔlə'dʒɛtɪk] *adj* (*look, remark*) de disculpa

apologetically [əpɔlə'dʒɛtɪkəlɪ] *adv* con aire de disculpa, excusándose, disculpándose

apologize [ə'pɔlədʒaɪz] *vi*: **to** ~ (**for sth to sb**) disculparse (con algn por algo)

apology [ə'pɔlədʒɪ] *n* disculpa, excusa; **please accept my apologies** le ruego me disculpe

apoplectic [æpə'plɛktɪk] *adj* (*Med*) apoplético; (*col*): ~ **with rage** furioso

apoplexy ['æpəplɛksɪ] *n* apoplejía

apostle [ə'pɔsl] *n* apóstol *m/f*

apostrophe [ə'pɔstrəfɪ] *n* apóstrofo *m*

app *n abbr* (*Comput*) = **application**

appal [ə'pɔːl] *vt* horrorizar, espantar

Appalachian Mountains [æpə'leɪʃən-] *npl*: **the** ~ los (Montes) Apalaches

appalling [ə'pɔːlɪŋ] *adj* espantoso; (*awful*) pésimo; **she's an** ~ **cook** es una cocinera malísima

apparatus [æpə'reɪtəs] *n* aparato; (*in gymnasium*) aparatos *mpl*

apparel [ə'pærl] *n* (US) indumentaria

apparent [ə'pærənt] *adj* aparente; (*obvious*) manifiesto, evidente; **it is** ~ **that** está claro que

apparently [ə'pærəntlɪ] *adv* por lo visto, al parecer, dizque (*LAm*)

apparition [æpə'rɪʃən] *n* aparición *f*

appeal [ə'piːl] *vi* (*Law*) apelar ■ *n* (*Law*) apelación *f*; (*request*) llamamiento, llamado (*LAm*); (*plea*) súplica; (*charm*) atractivo, encanto; **to** ~ **for** solicitar; **to** ~ **to** (*person*) rogar a, suplicar a; (*thing*) atraer, interesar; **to** ~ **to sb for mercy** rogarle misericordia a algn; **it doesn't** ~ **to me** no me atrae, no me llama la atención; **right of** ~ derecho de apelación

appealing [ə'piːlɪŋ] *adj* (*nice*) atractivo; (*touching*) conmovedor(a), emocionante

appear [ə'pɪəʳ] *vi* aparecer, presentarse; (*Law*) comparecer; (*publication*) salir (a luz), publicarse; (*seem*) parecer; **it would** ~ **that** parecería que

appearance [ə'pɪərəns] *n* aparición *f*; (*look, aspect*) apariencia, aspecto; **to keep up appearances** salvar las apariencias; **to all appearances** al parecer

appease [ə'piːz] *vt* (*pacify*) apaciguar; (*satisfy*) satisfacer

appeasement [ə'pi:zmənt] *n* (*Pol*) apaciguamiento

append [ə'pɛnd] *vt* (*Comput*) añadir (al final)

appendage [ə'pɛndɪdʒ] *n* añadidura

appendicitis [əpɛndɪ'saɪtɪs] *n* apendicitis *f*

appendix (*pl* **appendices**) [ə'pɛndɪks, -dɪsi:z] *n* apéndice *m*; **to have one's ~ out** operarse de apendicitis

appetite ['æpɪtaɪt] *n* apetito; (*fig*) deseo, anhelo; **that walk has given me an ~** ese paseo me ha abierto el apetito

appetizer ['æpɪtaɪzər] *n* (*drink*) aperitivo; (*food*) tapas *fpl* (*SP*)

appetizing ['æpɪtaɪzɪŋ] *adj* apetitoso

applaud [ə'plɔːd] *vt, vi* aplaudir

applause [ə'plɔːz] *n* aplausos *mpl*

apple ['æpl] *n* manzana

apple tree *n* manzano

appliance [ə'plaɪəns] *n* aparato; **electrical appliances** electrodomésticos *mpl*

applicable [ə'plɪkəbl] *adj* aplicable, pertinente; **the law is ~ from January** la ley es aplicable *or* se pone en vigor a partir de enero; **to be ~ to** referirse a

applicant ['æplɪkənt] *n* candidato(-a); solicitante *m/f*

application [æplɪ'keɪʃən] *n* (*also Comput*) aplicación *f*; (*for a job, a grant etc*) solicitud *f*

application form *n* solicitud *f*

application program *n* (*Comput*) (programa *m* de) aplicación *f*

applications package *n* (*Comput*) paquete *m* de programas de aplicación

applied [ə'plaɪd] *adj* (*science, art*) aplicado

apply [ə'plaɪ] *vt*: **to ~ (to)** aplicar (a); (*fig*) emplear (para) ■ *vi*: **to ~ to** (*ask*) dirigirse a; (*be suitable for*) ser aplicable a; (*be relevant to*) tener que ver con; **to ~ for** (*permit, grant, job*) solicitar; **to ~ the brakes** echar el freno; **to ~ o.s. to** aplicarse a, dedicarse a

appoint [ə'pɔɪnt] *vt* (*to post*) nombrar; (*date, place*) fijar, señalar

appointee [əpɔɪn'ti:] *n* persona nombrada

appointment [ə'pɔɪntmənt] *n* (*engagement*) cita; (*date*) compromiso; (*act*) nombramiento; (*post*) puesto; **to make an ~ (with)** (*doctor*) pedir hora (con); (*friend*) citarse (con); **"appointments"** "ofertas de trabajo"; **by ~** mediante cita

apportion [ə'pɔːʃən] *vt* repartir

appraisal [ə'preɪzl] *n* evaluación *f*

appraise [ə'preɪz] *vt* (*value*) tasar, valorar; (*situation etc*) evaluar

appreciable [ə'pri:ʃəbl] *adj* sensible

appreciably [ə'pri:ʃəblɪ] *adv* sensiblemente, de manera apreciable

appreciate [ə'pri:ʃɪeɪt] *vt* (*like*) apreciar, tener

en mucho; (*be grateful for*) agradecer; (*be aware of*) comprender ■ *vi* (*Comm*) aumentar en valor; **I appreciated your help** agradecí tu ayuda

appreciation [əpri:ʃɪ'eɪʃən] *n* aprecio; reconocimiento, agradecimiento; aumento en valor

appreciative [ə'pri:ʃɪətɪv] *adj* agradecido

apprehend [æprɪ'hɛnd] *vt* percibir; (*arrest*) detener

apprehension [æprɪ'hɛnʃən] *n* (*fear*) aprensión *f*

apprehensive [æprɪ'hɛnsɪv] *adj* aprensivo

apprentice [ə'prɛntɪs] *n* aprendiz(a) *m(f)* ■ *vt*: **to be apprenticed to** estar de aprendiz con

apprenticeship [ə'prɛntɪʃɪp] *n* aprendizaje *m*; **to serve one's ~** hacer el aprendizaje

appro. ['æprəu] *abbr* (*Brit Comm: col*) *see* **approval**

approach [ə'prəutʃ] *vi* acercarse ■ *vt* acercarse a; (*be approximate*) aproximarse a; (*ask, apply to*) dirigirse a; (*problem*) abordar ■ *n* acercamiento; aproximación *f*; (*access*) acceso; (*proposal*) proposición *f*; (*to problem etc*) enfoque *m*; **to ~ sb about sth** hablar con algn sobre algo

approachable [ə'prəutʃəbl] *adj* (*person*) abordable; (*place*) accesible

approach road *n* vía de acceso

approbation [æprə'beɪʃən] *n* aprobación *f*

appropriate [ə'prəuprɪɪt] *adj* apropiado, conveniente ■ *vt* [-rɪeɪt] (*take*) apropiarse de; (*allot*): **to ~ sth for** destinar algo a; **~ for** *or* **to** apropiado para; **it would not be ~ for me to comment** no estaría bien *or* sería pertinente que yo diera mi opinión

appropriation [əprəuprɪ'eɪʃən] *n* asignación *f*

approval [ə'pru:vəl] *n* aprobación *f*, visto bueno; **on ~** (*Comm*) a prueba; **to meet with sb's ~** obtener la aprobación de algn

approve [ə'pru:v] *vt* aprobar

▶ **approve of** *vt fus* aprobar

approved school *n* (*Brit*) correccional *m*

approx. *abbr* (= *approximately*) aprox

approximate [ə'prɔksɪmɪt] *adj* aproximado

approximately [ə'prɔksɪmɪtlɪ] *adv* aproximadamente, más o menos

approximation [əprɔksɪ'meɪʃən] *n* aproximación *f*

Apr. *abbr* (= *April*) abr

apr *n abbr* (= *annual percentage rate*) tasa de interés anual

apricot ['eɪprɪkɔt] *n* albaricoque *m* (*SP*), damasco (*LAm*)

April ['eɪprəl] *n* abril *m*; *see also* **July**

April Fools' Day n = día m de los (Santos) Inocentes; ver nota

● **APRIL FOOLS' DAY**
●
● El 1 de abril es *April Fools' Day* en la
● tradición anglosajona. Tal día se les
● gastan bromas a los más desprevenidos,
● quienes reciben la denominación de
● "April Fool" (= inocente), y tanto la prensa
● escrita como la televisión difunden
● alguna historia falsa con la que sumarse
● al espíritu del día.

apron ['eɪprən] n delantal m; (Aviat) pista
apse [æps] n (Arch) ábside m
APT n abbr (Brit) = **advanced passenger train**
Apt. abbr = **apartment**
apt. [æpt] adj (to the point) acertado, oportuno; (appropriate) apropiado; ~ **to do** (likely) propenso a hacer
aptitude ['æptɪtjuːd] n aptitud f, capacidad f
aptitude test n prueba de aptitud
aptly ['æptlɪ] adj acertadamente
aqualung ['ækwəlʌŋ] n escafandra autónoma
aquarium [ə'kwɛərɪəm] n acuario
Aquarius [ə'kwɛərɪəs] n Acuario
aquatic [ə'kwætɪk] adj acuático
aqueduct ['ækwɪdʌkt] n acueducto
AR abbr (US) = **Arkansas**
ARA n abbr (Brit) = **Associate of the Royal Academy**
Arab ['ærəb] adj, n árabe m/f
Arabia [ə'reɪbɪə] n Arabia
Arabian [ə'reɪbɪən] adj árabe, arábigo
Arabian Desert n Desierto de Arabia
Arabian Sea n Mar m de Omán
Arabic ['ærəbɪk] adj (language, manuscripts) árabe, arábigo ■ n árabe m; ~ **numerals** numeración f arábiga
arable ['ærəbl] adj cultivable
Aragon ['ærəgən] n Aragón m
ARAM n abbr (Brit) = **Associate of the Royal Academy of Music**
arbiter ['ɑːbɪtəʳ] n árbitro
arbitrary ['ɑːbɪtrərɪ] adj arbitrario
arbitrate ['ɑːbɪtreɪt] vi arbitrar
arbitration [ɑːbɪ'treɪʃən] n arbitraje m; **the dispute went to ~** el conflicto laboral fue sometido al arbitraje
arbitrator ['ɑːbɪtreɪtəʳ] n árbitro
ARC n abbr = **American Red Cross**
arc [ɑːk] n arco
arcade [ɑː'keɪd] n (Arch) arcada; (round a square) soportales mpl; (shopping arcade) galería comercial

arch [ɑːtʃ] n arco; (vault) bóveda; (of foot) empeine m ■ vt arquear
archaeological [ɑːkɪə'lɒdʒɪkl] adj arqueológico
archaeologist [ɑːkɪ'ɒlədʒɪst] n arqueólogo(-a)
archaeology [ɑːkɪ'ɒlədʒɪ] n arqueología
archaic [ɑː'keɪɪk] adj arcaico
archangel ['ɑːkeɪndʒəl] n arcángel m
archbishop [ɑːtʃ'bɪʃəp] n arzobispo
arched [ɑːtʃt] adj abovedado
archenemy ['ɑːtʃ'enəmɪ] n enemigo jurado
archeology etc [ɑːkɪ'ɒlədʒɪ] (US) see **archaeology** etc
archer ['ɑːtʃəʳ] n arquero(-a)
archery ['ɑːtʃərɪ] n tiro al arco
archetypal ['ɑːkɪtaɪpəl] adj arquetípico
archetype ['ɑːkɪtaɪp] n arquetipo
archipelago [ɑːkɪ'pɛlɪgəu] n archipiélago
architect ['ɑːkɪtɛkt] n arquitecto(-a)
architectural [ɑːkɪ'tɛktʃərəl] adj arquitectónico
architecture ['ɑːkɪtɛktʃəʳ] n arquitectura
archive ['ɑːkaɪv] n (often pl: also Comput) archivo
archive file n (Comput) fichero archivado
archives ['ɑːkaɪvz] npl archivo sg
archivist ['ɑːkɪvɪst] n archivero(-a)
archway ['ɑːtʃweɪ] n arco, arcada
ARCM n abbr (Brit) = **Associate of the Royal College of Music**
Arctic ['ɑːktɪk] adj ártico ■ n: **the ~** el Ártico
Arctic Circle n Círculo Polar Ártico
Arctic Ocean n Océano (Glacial) Ártico
ARD n abbr (US Med) = **acute respiratory disease**
ardent ['ɑːdənt] adj (desire) ardiente; (supporter, lover) apasionado
ardour, ardor (US) ['ɑːdəʳ] n ardor m, pasión f
arduous ['ɑːdjuəs] adj (gen) arduo; (journey) penoso
are [ɑːʳ] vb see **be**
area ['ɛərɪə] n área; (Math etc) superficie f, extensión f; (zone) región f, zona; **the London ~** la zona de Londres
area code n (US Tel) prefijo
arena [ə'riːnə] n arena; (of circus) pista; (for bullfight) plaza, ruedo
aren't [ɑːnt] = **are not**
Argentina [ɑːdʒən'tiːnə] n Argentina
Argentinian [ɑːdʒən'tɪnɪən] adj, n argentino(-a) m(f)
arguable ['ɑːgjuəbl] adj: **it is ~ whether ...** es dudoso que + subjun
arguably ['ɑːgjuəblɪ] adv: **it is ~ ...** es discutiblemente ...
argue ['ɑːgjuː] vt (debate: case, matter)

mantener, argüir ■ vi (quarrel) discutir;
(reason) razonar, argumentar; **to ~ that**
sostener que; **to ~ about sth (with sb)**
pelearse (con algn) por algo
argument ['ɑːgjumənt] n (reasons)
argumento; (quarrel) discusión f; (debate)
debate m; **~ for/against** argumento en pro/
contra de
argumentative [ɑːgjuˈmɛntətɪv] adj
discutidor(a)
aria ['ɑːrɪə] n (Mus) aria
ARIBA n abbr (Brit) = **Associate of the Royal
Institute of British Architects**
arid ['ærɪd] adj árido
aridity [əˈrɪdɪtɪ] n aridez f
Aries ['ɛərɪz] n Aries m
arise [əˈraɪz] (pt **arose**, pp **arisen** [əˈrɪzn]) vi
(rise up) levantarse, alzarse; (emerge) surgir,
presentarse; **to ~ from** derivar de; **should
the need ~** si fuera necesario
aristocracy [ærɪsˈtɔkrəsɪ] n aristocracia
aristocrat ['ærɪstəkræt] n aristócrata m/f
aristocratic [ərɪstəˈkrætɪk] adj aristocrático
arithmetic [əˈrɪθmətɪk] n aritmética
arithmetical [ærɪθˈmɛtɪkl] adj aritmético
Ariz. abbr (US) = **Arizona**
Ark [ɑːk] n: **Noah's ~** el Arca f de Noé
Ark. abbr (US) = **Arkansas**
arm [ɑːm] n (Anat) brazo ■ vt armar; **~ in ~**
cogidos del brazo; see also **arms**
armaments ['ɑːməmənts] npl (weapons)
armamentos mpl
armchair ['ɑːmtʃɛəʳ] n sillón m, butaca
armed [ɑːmd] adj armado; **the ~ forces** las
fuerzas armadas
armed robbery n robo a mano armada
Armenia [ɑːˈmiːnɪə] n Armenia
Armenian [ɑːˈmiːnɪən] adj armenio ■ n
armenio(-a); (Ling) armenio
armful ['ɑːmful] n brazada
armistice ['ɑːmɪstɪs] n armisticio
armour, armor (US) ['ɑːməʳ] n armadura
armoured car, armored car (US) n coche m
or carro (LAm) blindado
armoury, armory (US) ['ɑːmərɪ] n arsenal m
armpit ['ɑːmpɪt] n sobaco, axila
armrest ['ɑːmrɛst] n reposabrazos m inv,
brazo
arms [ɑːmz] npl (weapons) armas fpl; (Heraldry)
escudo sg
arms control n control m de armamentos
arms race n carrera de armamentos
army ['ɑːmɪ] n ejército
aroma [əˈrəumə] n aroma m, fragancia
aromatherapy [ərəuməˈθɛrəpɪ] n
aromaterapia
aromatic [ærəˈmætɪk] adj aromático,

fragante
arose [əˈrəuz] pt of **arise**
around [əˈraund] adv alrededor; (in the area)
a la redonda ■ prep alrededor de
arousal [əˈrauzəl] n (sexual) excitación f;
(of feelings, interest) despertar m
arouse [əˈrauz] vt despertar
arrange [əˈreɪndʒ] vt arreglar, ordenar;
(programme) organizar; (appointment)
concertar ■ vi: **we have arranged for a taxi
to pick you up** hemos organizado todo para
que le recoja un taxi; **to ~ to do sth** quedar
en hacer algo; **it was arranged that ...**
se quedó en que ...
arrangement [əˈreɪndʒmənt] n arreglo;
(agreement) acuerdo; **arrangements** npl
(plans) planes mpl, medidas fpl; (preparations)
preparativos mpl; **to come to an ~ (with
sb)** llegar a un acuerdo (con algn); **by ~** a
convenir; **I'll make arrangements for you
to be met** haré los preparativos para que le
estén esperando
arrant ['ærənt] adj: **~ nonsense** una
verdadera tontería
array [əˈreɪ] n (Comput) matriz f; **~ of** (things)
serie f or colección f de; (people) conjunto de
arrears [əˈrɪəz] npl atrasos mpl; **in ~** (Comm)
en mora; **to be in ~ with one's rent** estar
retrasado en el pago del alquiler
arrest [əˈrɛst] vt detener; (sb's attention)
llamar ■ n detención f; **under ~** detenido
arresting [əˈrɛstɪŋ] adj (fig) llamativo
arrival [əˈraɪvəl] n llegada, arribo (LAm);
new ~ recién llegado(-a)
arrive [əˈraɪv] vi llegar, arribar (LAm)
arrogance ['ærəgəns] n arrogancia,
prepotencia (LAm)
arrogant ['ærəgənt] adj arrogante,
prepotente (LAm)
arrow ['ærəu] n flecha
arse [ɑːs] n (Brit col!) culo, trasero
arsenal ['ɑːsɪnl] n arsenal m
arsenic ['ɑːsnɪk] n arsénico
arson ['ɑːsn] n incendio provocado
art [ɑːt] n arte m; (skill) destreza; (technique)
técnica; **Arts** npl (Scol) Letras fpl; **work of ~**
obra de arte
art and design n (Brit Scol) arte m y diseño,
dibujo
artefact ['ɑːtɪfækt] n artefacto
arterial [ɑːˈtɪərɪəl] adj (Anat) arterial; (road
etc) principal
artery ['ɑːtərɪ] n (Med: road etc) arteria
artful ['ɑːtful] adj (cunning: person, trick)
mañoso
art gallery n pinacoteca, museo de pintura;
(Comm) galería de arte

arthritis [ɑːˈθraɪtɪs] *n* artritis *f*
artichoke [ˈɑːtɪtʃəuk] *n* alcachofa;
Jerusalem ~ aguaturma
article [ˈɑːtɪkl] *n* artículo, objeto, cosa;
(*in newspaper*) artículo; (*Brit Law: training*);
articles *npl* contrato *sg* de aprendizaje;
articles of clothing prendas *fpl* de vestir
articles of association *npl* (*Comm*) estatutos
mpl sociales, escritura social
articulate *adj* [ɑːˈtɪkjulɪt] (*speech*) claro;
(*person*) que se expresa bien ■ *vi* [ɑːˈtɪkjuleɪt]
articular
articulated lorry *n* (*Brit*) trailer *m*
artifice [ˈɑːtɪfɪs] *n* artificio, truco
artificial [ɑːtɪˈfɪʃəl] *adj* artificial; (*teeth etc*)
postizo
artificial insemination *n* inseminación *f*
artificial
artificial intelligence *n* inteligencia
artificial
artificial respiration *n* respiración *f*
artificial
artillery [ɑːˈtɪlərɪ] *n* artillería
artisan [ˈɑːtɪzæn] *n* artesano(-a)
artist [ˈɑːtɪst] *n* artista *m/f*; (*Mus*) intérprete
m/f
artistic [ɑːˈtɪstɪk] *adj* artístico
artistry [ˈɑːtɪstrɪ] *n* arte *m*, habilidad *f*
(artística)
artless [ˈɑːtlɪs] *adj* (*innocent*) natural, sencillo;
(*clumsy*) torpe
art school *n* escuela de bellas artes
artwork [ˈɑːtwəːk] *n* material *m* gráfico
arty [ˈɑːtɪ] *adj* artistoide
ARV *n abbr* (= *American Revised Version*) traducción
americana de la Biblia
AS *n abbr* (*US Scol*) = **Associate in Science**

⭕ KEYWORD

as [æz] *conj* **1** (*referring to time: while*) mientras;
(: *when*) cuando; **she wept as she told her
story** lloraba mientras contaba lo que le
ocurrió; **as the years go by** a medida que
pasan los años, con el paso de los años; **he
came in as I was leaving** entró cuando me
marchaba; **as from tomorrow** a partir de *or*
desde mañana
2 (*in comparisons*): **as big as** tan grande como;
twice as big as el doble de grande que; **as
much money/many books as** tanto dinero/
tantos libros como; **as soon as** en cuanto, no
bien (*LAm*)
3 (*since, because*) como, ya que; **as I don't
speak German I can't understand him**
como no hablo alemán no le entiendo, no le
entiendo ya que no hablo alemán

4 (*although*): **much as I like them, ...** aunque
me gustan, ...
5 (*referring to manner, way*): **do as you wish**
haz lo que quieras; **as she said** como dijo;
he gave it to me as a present me lo dio de
regalo; **it's on the left as you go in** según se
entra, a la izquierda
6 (*concerning*): **as for** *or* **to that** por *or* en lo que
respecta a eso
7: **as if** *or* **though** como si; **he looked as
if he was ill** parecía como si estuviera
enfermo, tenía aspecto de enfermo; *see also*
long; such; well
■ *prep* (*in the capacity of*): **he works as a
barman** trabaja de barman; **as chairman of
the company, he ...** como presidente de la
compañía, ...

ASA *n abbr* (= *American Standards Association*)
instituto de normalización; (*Brit*: = *Advertising
Standards Association*) departamento de control de
la publicidad; (= *Amateur Swimming Association*)
federación amateur de natación
a.s.a.p. *abbr* (= *as soon as possible*) cuanto antes,
lo más pronto posible
asbestos [æzˈbɛstəs] *n* asbesto, amianto
ascend [əˈsɛnd] *vt* subir, ascender
ascendancy [əˈsɛndənsɪ] *n* ascendiente *m*,
dominio
ascendant [əˈsɛndənt] *n*: **to be in the ~** estar
en auge, ir ganando predominio
Ascension [əˈsɛnʃən] *n*: **the ~** la Ascensión
Ascension Island *n* Isla Ascensión
ascent [əˈsɛnt] *n* subida; (*slope*) cuesta,
pendiente *f*; (*of plane*) ascenso
ascertain [æsəˈteɪn] *vt* averiguar
ascetic [əˈsɛtɪk] *adj* ascético
asceticism [əˈsɛtɪsɪzəm] *n* ascetismo
ASCII [ˈæskiː] *n abbr* (= *American Standard Code
for Information Interchange*) ASCII
ascribe [əˈskraɪb] *vt*: **to ~ sth to** atribuir
algo a
ASCU *n abbr* (*US*) = **Association of State
Colleges and Universities**
ASE *n abbr* = **American Stock Exchange**
ASH [æʃ] *n abbr* (*Brit*: = *Action on Smoking and
Health*) organización anti-tabaco
ash [æʃ] *n* ceniza; (*tree*) fresno
ashamed [əˈʃeɪmd] *adj* avergonzado; **to be ~
of** avergonzarse de
ashcan [ˈæʃkæn] *n* (*US*) cubo *or* bote *m* (*LAm*)
de la basura
ashen [ˈæʃn] *adj* pálido
ashore [əˈʃɔːr] *adv* en tierra
ashtray [ˈæʃtreɪ] *n* cenicero
Ash Wednesday *n* miércoles *m* de ceniza
Asia [ˈeɪʃə] *n* Asia

Asian ['eɪʃən], **Asiatic** [eɪsɪ'ætɪk] *adj, n*
asiático(-a) *m(f)*
aside [ə'saɪd] *adv* a un lado ■ *n* aparte *m*;
~ **from** *prep (as well as)* aparte *or* además de
ask [ɑ:sk] *vt (question)* preguntar; *(demand)*
pedir; *(invite)* invitar ■ *vi*: **to ~ about sth**
preguntar acerca de algo; **to ~ sb sth/to do**
sth preguntar algo a algn/pedir a algn que
haga algo; **to ~ sb about sth** preguntar
algo a algn; **to ~ (sb) a question** hacer
una pregunta (a algn); **to ~ sb the time**
preguntar la hora a algn; **to ~ sb out to**
dinner invitar a cenar a algn
▸ **ask after** *vt fus* preguntar por
▸ **ask for** *vt fus* pedir; **it's just asking for**
trouble *or* **for it** es buscarse problemas
askance [ə'skɑ:ns] *adv*: **to look ~ at sb** mirar
con recelo a algn
askew [ə'skju:] *adv* sesgado, ladeado
asking price *n (Comm)* precio inicial
asleep [ə'sli:p] *adj* dormido; **to fall ~**
dormirse, quedarse dormido
ASLEF ['æzlɛf] *n abbr (Brit: = Associated Society*
of Locomotive Engineers and Firemen) sindicato de
ferroviarios
AS level *n abbr (Brit Scol: = Advanced Subsidiary*
level) título intermedio entre los "GCSEs" y los "A
levels"
asp [æsp] *n* áspid *m*
asparagus [əs'pærəgəs] *n* espárragos *mpl*
ASPCA *n abbr* = **American Society for the**
Prevention of Cruelty to Animals
aspect ['æspɛkt] *n* aspecto, apariencia;
(direction in which a building etc faces)
orientación *f*
aspersions [əs'pə:ʃənz] *npl*: **to cast ~ on**
difamar a, calumniar a
asphalt ['æsfælt] *n* asfalto
asphyxiate [æs'fɪksɪeɪt] *vt* asfixiar
asphyxiation [aesfɪksɪ'eɪʃən] *n* asfixia
aspirate ['æspəreɪt] *vt* aspirar ■ *adj*
['æspərɪt] aspirado
aspirations [æspə'reɪʃənz] *npl* aspiraciones
fpl; *(ambition)* ambición *f*
aspire [əs'paɪəʳ] *vi*: **to ~ to** aspirar a,
ambicionar
aspirin ['æsprɪn] *n* aspirina
aspiring [əs'paɪərɪŋ] *adj*: **an ~ actor** un
aspirante a actor
ass [æs] *n* asno, burro; *(col)* imbécil *m/f*; *(US*
col!) culo, trasero
assailant [ə'seɪlənt] *n* agresor(a) *m(f)*
assassin [ə'sæsɪn] *n* asesino(-a)
assassinate [ə'sæsɪneɪt] *vt* asesinar
assassination [əsæsɪ'neɪʃən] *n* asesinato
assault [ə'sɔ:lt] *n (gen: attack)* asalto, agresión
f ■ *vt* asaltar, agredir; *(sexually)* violar

assemble [ə'sɛmbl] *vt* reunir, juntar; *(Tech)*
montar ■ *vi* reunirse, juntarse
assembly [ə'sɛmblɪ] *n (meeting)* reunión *f*,
asamblea; *(construction)* montaje *m*
assembly language *n (Comput)* lenguaje *m*
ensamblador
assembly line *n* cadena de montaje
Assembly Member *n (in Wales)* miembro *m/f*
de la Asamblea Nacional (de Gales)
assent [ə'sɛnt] *n* asentimiento, aprobación
f ■ *vi* consentir, asentir; **to ~ (to sth)**
consentir (en algo)
assert [ə'sə:t] *vt* afirmar; *(insist on)* hacer
valer; **to ~ o.s.** imponerse
assertion [ə'sə:ʃən] *n* afirmación *f*
assertive [ə'sə:tɪv] *adj* enérgico, agresivo,
perentorio
assess [ə'sɛs] *vt* valorar, calcular; *(tax,*
damages) fijar; *(property etc: for tax)* gravar
assessment [ə'sɛsmənt] *n* valoración *f*;
gravamen *m*; *(judgment)*: ~ **(of)** juicio (sobre)
assessor [ə'sɛsəʳ] *n* asesor(a) *m(f)*; *(of tax)*
tasador(a) *m(f)*
asset ['æsɛt] *n* posesión *f*; *(quality)* ventaja;
assets *npl (funds)* activo *sg*, fondos *mpl*
asset-stripping ['æsɛt'strɪpɪŋ] *n (Comm)*
acaparamiento de activos
assiduous [ə'sɪdjuəs] *adj* asiduo
assign [ə'saɪn] *vt (date)* fijar; *(task)* asignar;
(resources) destinar; *(property)* traspasar
assignment [ə'saɪnmənt] *n* asignación *f*;
(task) tarea
assimilate [ə'sɪmɪleɪt] *vt* asimilar
assimilation [əsɪmɪ'leɪʃən] *n* asimilación *f*
assist [ə'sɪst] *vt* ayudar
assistance [ə'sɪstəns] *n* ayuda, auxilio
assistant [ə'sɪstənt] *n* ayudante *m/f*; *(Brit:*
also: **shop assistant**) dependiente(-a) *m(f)*
assistant manager *n* subdirector(a) *m(f)*
assizes [ə'saɪzɪz] *npl* sesión *f* de un tribunal
associate [*adj, n* ə'səuʃɪɪt, *vt, vi* ə'səuʃɪeɪt] *adj*
asociado ■ *n* socio(-a), colega *m/f*; *(in crime)*
cómplice *m/f*; *(member)* miembro(-a) ■ *vt*
asociar; *(ideas)* relacionar ■ *vi*: **to ~ with sb**
tratar con algn; ~ **director** subdirector(a)
m(f); **associated company** compañía
afiliada
association [əsəusɪ'eɪʃən] *n* asociación *f*;
(Comm) sociedad *f*; **in ~ with** en asociación
con
association football *n (Brit)* fútbol *m*
assorted [ə'sɔ:tɪd] *adj* surtido, variado; **in ~**
sizes en distintos tamaños
assortment [ə'sɔ:tmənt] *n* surtido
Asst. *abbr* = **Assistant**
assuage [ə'sweɪdʒ] *vt* mitigar
assume [ə'sju:m] *vt (suppose)* suponer;

(*responsibilities etc*) asumir; (*attitude, name*) adoptar, tomar

assumed name *n* nombre *m* falso

assumption [ə'sʌmpʃən] *n* (*supposition*) suposición *f*, presunción *f*; (*act*) asunción *f*; **on the ~ that** suponiendo que

assurance [ə'ʃuərəns] *n* garantía, promesa; (*confidence*) confianza, aplomo; (Brit: *insurance*) seguro; **I can give you no assurances** no puedo hacerle ninguna promesa

assure [ə'ʃuəʳ] *vt* asegurar

assured [ə'ʃuəd] *adj* seguro

assuredly [ə'ʃuərɪdlɪ] *adv* indudablemente

AST *abbr* (= *Atlantic Standard Time*) *hora oficial del este del Canadá*

asterisk ['æstərɪsk] *n* asterisco

astern [ə'stəːn] *adv* a popa

asteroid ['æstərɔɪd] *n* asteroide *m*

asthma ['æsmə] *n* asma

asthmatic [æs'mætɪk] *adj, n* asmático(-a) *m(f)*

astigmatism [ə'stɪgmətɪzəm] *n* astigmatismo

astir [ə'stəːʳ] *adv* en acción

astonish [ə'stɒnɪʃ] *vt* asombrar, pasmar

astonishing [ə'stɒnɪʃɪŋ] *adj* asombroso, pasmoso; **I find it ~ that ...** me asombra or pasma que ...

astonishingly [ə'stɒnɪʃɪŋlɪ] *adv* increíblemente, asombrosamente

astonishment [ə'stɒnɪʃmənt] *n* asombro, sorpresa; **to my ~** con gran sorpresa mía

astound [ə'staund] *vt* asombrar, pasmar

astounding [ə'staundɪŋ] *adj* asombroso

astray [ə'streɪ] *adv*: **to go ~** extraviarse; **to lead ~** llevar por mal camino; **to go ~ in one's calculations** equivocarse en sus cálculos

astride [ə'straɪd] *prep* a caballo or horcajadas sobre

astringent [əs'trɪndʒənt] *adj, n* astringente *m*

astrologer [əs'trɒlədʒəʳ] *n* astrólogo(-a)

astrology [əs'trɒlədʒɪ] *n* astrología

astronaut ['æstrənɔːt] *n* astronauta *m/f*

astronomer [əs'trɒnəməʳ] *n* astrónomo(-a)

astronomical [æstrə'nɒmɪkəl] *adj* astronómico

astronomy [əs'trɒnəmɪ] *n* astronomía

astrophysics ['æstrəu'fɪzɪks] *n* astrofísica

astute [əs'tjuːt] *adj* astuto

asunder [ə'sʌndəʳ] *adv*: **to tear ~** hacer pedazos

ASV *n abbr* (= *American Standard Version*) *traducción de la Biblia*

asylum [ə'saɪləm] *n* (*refuge*) asilo; (*hospital*) manicomio; **to seek political ~** pedir asilo político

asymmetric [eɪsɪ'metrɪk], **asymmetrical** [eɪsɪ'metrɪkl] *adj* asimétrico

 KEYWORD

at [æt] *prep* **1** (*referring to position*) en; (*direction*) a; **at the top** en lo alto; **at home/school** en casa/la escuela; **to look at sth/sb** mirar algo/a algn

2 (*referring to time*): **at four o'clock** a las cuatro; **at night** por la noche; **at Christmas** en Navidad; **at times** a veces

3 (*referring to rates, speed etc*): **at £1 a kilo** a una libra el kilo; **two at a time** de dos en dos; **at 50 km/h** a 50 km/h

4 (*referring to manner*): **at a stroke** de un golpe; **at peace** en paz

5 (*referring to activity*): **to be at work** estar trabajando; (*in office*) estar en el trabajo; **to play at cowboys** jugar a los vaqueros; **to be good at sth** ser bueno en algo

6 (*referring to cause*): **shocked/surprised/annoyed at sth** asombrado/sorprendido/fastidiado por algo; **I went at his suggestion** fui a instancias suyas

■ *n* (*symbol* @) arroba

ate [ɛt, eɪt] *pt of* **eat**

atheism ['eɪθɪɪzəm] *n* ateísmo

atheist ['eɪθɪɪst] *n* ateo(-a)

Athenian [ə'θiːnɪən] *adj, n* ateniense *m/f*

Athens ['æθɪnz] *n* Atenas *f*

athlete ['æθliːt] *n* atleta *m/f*

athletic [æθ'letɪk] *adj* atlético

athletics [æθ'letɪks] *n* atletismo

Atlantic [ət'læntɪk] *adj* atlántico ■ *n*: **the ~ (Ocean)** el (Océano) Atlántico

atlas ['ætləs] *n* atlas *m inv*

Atlas Mountains *npl*: **the ~** el Atlas

A.T.M. *n abbr* (= *Automated Telling Machine*) cajero automático

atmosphere ['ætməsfɪəʳ] *n* (*air*) atmósfera; (*fig*) ambiente *m*

atom ['ætəm] *n* átomo

atom bomb *n* bomba atómica

atomic [ə'tɒmɪk] *adj* atómico

atomic bomb *n* bomba atómica

atomic power *n* energía atómica

atomizer ['ætəmaɪzəʳ] *n* atomizador *m*

atone [ə'təun] *vi*: **to ~ for** expiar

atonement [ə'təunmənt] *n* expiación *f*

A to Z® *n* guía alfabética; (*map*) callejero

ATP *n abbr* (= *Association of Tennis Professionals*) *sindicato de jugadores de tenis profesionales*

atrocious [ə'trəuʃəs] *adj* atroz; (*fig*) horrible, infame

atrocity [ə'trɒsɪtɪ] *n* atrocidad *f*

atrophy ['ætrəfɪ] *n* atrofia ■ *vi* atrofiarse
attach [ə'tætʃ] *vt* sujetar; (*stick*) pegar; (*document, email, letter*) adjuntar; **to be attached to sb/sth** (*like*) tener cariño a algn/ algo; **the attached letter** la carta adjunta
attaché [ə'tæʃeɪ] *n* agregado(-a)
attaché case *n* (*Brit*) maletín *m*
attachment [ə'tætʃmənt] *n* (*tool*) accesorio; (*Comput*) archivo *o* documento adjunto; (*love*): ~ **(to)** apego (a), cariño (a)
attack [ə'tæk] *vt* (*Mil*) atacar; (*criminal*) agredir, asaltar; (*task etc*) emprender ■ *n* ataque *m*, asalto; (*on sb's life*) atentado; **heart** ~ infarto (de miocardio)
attacker [ə'tækə'] *n* agresor(a) *m(f)*, asaltante *m/f*
attain [ə'teɪn] *vt* (*also*: **attain to**) alcanzar; (*achieve*) lograr, conseguir
attainments [ə'teɪnmənts] *npl* (*skill*) talento *sg*
attempt [ə'tɛmpt] *n* tentativa, intento; (*attack*) atentado ■ *vt* intentar, tratar de; **he made no ~ to help** ni siquiera intentó ayudar
attempted [ə'tɛmptɪd] *adj*: ~ **murder/ burglary/suicide** tentativa *or* intento de asesinato/robo/suicidio
attend [ə'tɛnd] *vt* asistir a; (*patient*) atender ▶ **attend to** *vt fus* (*needs, affairs etc*) ocuparse de; (*speech etc*) prestar atención a; (*customer*) atender a
attendance [ə'tɛndəns] *n* asistencia, presencia; (*people present*) concurrencia
attendant [ə'tɛndənt] *n* sirviente(-a) *m(f)*, mozo(-a); (*Theat*) acomodador(a) *m(f)* ■ *adj* concomitante
attention [ə'tɛnʃən] *n* atención *f* ■ *excl* (*Mil*) ¡firme(s)!; **for the ~ of ...** (*Admin*) a la atención de ...; **it has come to my ~ that ...** me he enterado de que ...
attentive [ə'tɛntɪv] *adj* atento; (*polite*) cortés
attenuate [ə'tɛnjueɪt] *vt* atenuar
attest [ə'tɛst] *vi*: **to ~ to** dar fe de
attic ['ætɪk] *n* desván *m*, altillo (*LAm*), entretecho (*LAm*)
attitude ['ætɪtjuːd] *n* (*gen*) actitud *f*; (*disposition*) disposición *f*
attorney [ə'tɜːnɪ] *n* (*US: lawyer*) abogado(-a); (*having proxy*) apoderado
Attorney General *n* (*Brit*) ≈ Presidente *m* del Consejo del Poder Judicial (*SP*); (*US*) ≈ ministro de justicia
attract [ə'trækt] *vt* atraer; (*attention*) llamar
attraction [ə'trækʃən] *n* (*gen*) encanto, atractivo; (*Physics*) atracción *f*; (*towards sth*) atracción *f*
attractive [ə'træktɪv] *adj* atractivo

attribute ['ætrɪbjuːt] *n* atributo ■ *vt* [ə'trɪbjuːt]: **to ~ sth to** atribuir algo a; (*accuse*) achacar algo a
attrition [ə'trɪʃən] *n*: **war of ~** guerra de agotamiento *or* desgaste
Atty. Gen. *abbr* = **Attorney General**
ATV *n abbr* (= *all terrain vehicle*) vehículo todo terreno
atypical [eɪ'tɪpɪkl] *adj* atípico
AU *n abbr* (= *African Union*) UA *f* (= *Unión Africana*)
aubergine ['əʊbəʒiːn] *n* (*Brit*) berenjena
auburn ['ɔːbən] *adj* color castaño rojizo
auction ['ɔːkʃən] *n* (*also*: **sale by auction**) subasta ■ *vt* subastar
auctioneer [ɔːkʃə'nɪə'] *n* subastador(a) *m(f)*
auction room *n* sala de subastas
audacious [ɔː'deɪʃəs] *adj* (*bold*) audaz, osado; (*impudent*) atrevido, descarado
audacity [ɔː'dæsɪtɪ] *n* audacia, atrevimiento; (*pej*) descaro
audible ['ɔːdɪbl] *adj* audible, que se puede oír
audience ['ɔːdɪəns] *n* auditorio; (*gathering*) público; (*interview*) audiencia
audio-typist ['ɔːdɪəʊ'taɪpɪst] *n* mecanógrafo(-a) de dictáfono
audiovisual [ɔːdɪəʊ'vɪzjuəl] *adj* audiovisual
audiovisual aid *n* ayuda *or* medio audiovisual
audit ['ɔːdɪt] *vt* revisar, intervenir
audition [ɔː'dɪʃən] *n* audición *f* ■ *vi*: **to ~ for the part of** hacer una audición para el papel de
auditor ['ɔːdɪtə'] *n* interventor(a) *m(f)*, censor(a) *m(f)* de cuentas
auditorium [ɔːdɪ'tɔːrɪəm] *n* auditorio
Aug. *abbr* (= *August*) ag
augment [ɔːg'mɛnt] *vt, vi* aumentar
augur ['ɔːgə'] *vi*: **it augurs well** es de buen agüero
August ['ɔːgəst] *n* agosto; *see also* **July**
august [ɔː'gʌst] *adj* augusto
aunt [ɑːnt] *n* tía
auntie, aunty ['ɑːntɪ] *n diminutive of* **aunt**
au pair ['əʊ'pɛə'] *n* (*also*: **au pair girl**) chica *f* au pair
aura ['ɔːrə] *n* aura; (*atmosphere*) ambiente *m*
auspices ['ɔːspɪsɪz] *npl*: **under the ~ of** bajo los auspicios de
auspicious [ɔːs'pɪʃəs] *adj* propicio, de buen augurio
austere [ɔs'tɪə'] *adj* austero; (*manner*) adusto
austerity [ɔ'stɛrɪtɪ] *n* austeridad *f*
Australasia [ɔːstrə'leɪzɪə] *n* Australasia
Australia [ɔs'treɪlɪə] *n* Australia
Australian [ɔs'treɪlɪən] *adj, n* australiano(-a) *m(f)*
Austria ['ɔstrɪə] *n* Austria

Austrian ['ɒstrɪən] *adj, n* austríaco(-a) *m(f)*
AUT *n abbr* (*Brit*: = *Association of University Teachers*) sindicato de profesores de universidad
authentic [ɔː'θentɪk] *adj* auténtico
authenticate [ɔː'θentɪkeɪt] *vt* autentificar
authenticity [ɔːθen'tɪsɪtɪ] *n* autenticidad *f*
author ['ɔːθəʳ] *n* autor(a) *m(f)*
authoritarian [ɔːθɒrɪ'tɛərɪən] *adj* autoritario
authoritative [ɔː'θɒrɪtətɪv] *adj* autorizado; (*manner*) autoritario
authority [ɔː'θɒrɪtɪ] *n* autoridad *f*; **the authorities** *npl* las autoridades; **to have ~ to do sth** tener autoridad para hacer algo
authorization [ɔːθəraɪ'zeɪʃən] *n* autorización *f*
authorize ['ɔːθəraɪz] *vt* autorizar
authorized capital *n* (*Comm*) capital *m* autorizado *or* social
autistic [ɔː'tɪstɪk] *adj* autista
auto ['ɔːtəu] *n* (*US*) coche *m*, carro (*LAm*), auto (*LAm*), automóvil *m*
autobiographical [ɔːtəbaɪə'græfɪkəl] *adj* autobiográfico
autobiography [ɔːtəbaɪ'ɒɡrəfɪ] *n* autobiografía
autocratic [ɔːtə'krætɪk] *adj* autocrático
Autocue® ['ɔːtəukjuː] *n* autocue *m*, teleapuntador *m*
autograph ['ɔːtəɡrɑːf] *n* autógrafo ■ *vt* firmar; (*photo etc*) dedicar
autoimmune [ɔːtəu'mjuːn] *adj* autoinmune
automat ['ɔːtəmæt] *n* (*US*) restaurante *m* de autoservicio
automate ['ɔːtəmeɪt] *vt* automatizar
automated ['ɔːtəmeɪtɪd] *adj* automatizado
automatic [ɔːtə'mætɪk] *adj* automático ■ *n* (*gun*) pistola automática; (*washing machine*) lavadora
automatically [ɔːtə'mætɪklɪ] *adv* automáticamente
automatic data processing *n* proceso automático de datos
automation [ɔːtə'meɪʃən] *n* automatización *f*
automaton (*pl* **automata**) [ɔː'tɒmətən, -tə] *n* autómata
automobile ['ɔːtəməbiːl] *n* (*US*) coche *m*, carro (*LAm*), auto (*LAm*), automóvil *m*
autonomous [ɔː'tɒnəməs] *adj* autónomo
autonomy [ɔː'tɒnəmɪ] *n* autonomía
autopsy ['ɔːtɒpsɪ] *n* autopsia
autumn ['ɔːtəm] *n* otoño
auxiliary [ɔːɡ'zɪlɪərɪ] *adj* auxiliar
AV *n abbr* (= *Authorized Version*) traducción inglesa de la Biblia ■ *abbr* = **audiovisual**
Av. *abbr* (= *avenue*) Av., Avda
avail [ə'veɪl] *vt*: **to ~ o.s. of** aprovechar(se) de, valerse de ■ *n*: **to no ~** en vano, sin resultado
availability [əveɪlə'bɪlɪtɪ] *n* disponibilidad *f*

available [ə'veɪləbl] *adj* disponible; (*obtainable*) asequible; **to make sth ~ to sb** poner algo a la disposición de algn; **is the manager ~?** ¿está libre el gerente?
avalanche ['ævəlɑːnʃ] *n* alud *m*, avalancha
avant-garde ['ævɑ̃n'ɡɑːd] *adj* de vanguardia
avarice ['ævərɪs] *n* avaricia
avaricious [æve'rɪʃəs] *adj* avaricioso
avdp. *abbr* = **avoirdupois**
Ave. *abbr* (= *avenue*) Av., Avda
avenge [ə'vendʒ] *vt* vengar
avenue ['ævənjuː] *n* avenida; (*fig*) camino, vía
average ['ævərɪdʒ] *n* promedio, media ■ *adj* (*mean*) medio; (*ordinary*) regular, corriente ■ *vt* calcular el promedio de; **on ~** por término medio
  ▶ **average out** *vi*: **to ~ out at** salir a un promedio de
averse [ə'vɜːs] *adj*: **to be ~ to sth/doing** sentir aversión *or* antipatía por algo/por hacer
aversion [ə'vɜːʃən] *n* aversión *f*, repugnancia
avert [ə'vɜːt] *vt* prevenir; (*blow*) desviar; (*one's eyes*) apartar
aviary ['eɪvɪərɪ] *n* pajarera
aviation [eɪvɪ'eɪʃən] *n* aviación *f*
aviator ['eɪvɪeɪtəʳ] *n* aviador(a) *m(f)*
avid ['ævɪd] *adj* ávido, ansioso
avidly ['ævɪdlɪ] *adv* ávidamente, con avidez
avocado [ævə'kɑːdəu] *n* (*Brit*: *also*: **avocado pear**) aguacate *m*, palta (*LAm*)
avoid [ə'vɔɪd] *vt* evitar, eludir
avoidable [ə'vɔɪdəbl] *adj* evitable, eludible
avoidance [ə'vɔɪdəns] *n* evasión *f*
avow [ə'vau] *vt* prometer
avowal [ə'vauəl] *n* promesa, voto
avowed [ə'vaud] *adj* declarado
AVP *n abbr* (*US*) = **assistant vice-president**
avuncular [ə'vʌŋkjuləʳ] *adj* paternal
AWACS ['eɪwæks] *n abbr* (= *airborne warning and control system*) AWACS *m*
await [ə'weɪt] *vt* esperar, aguardar; **long awaited** largamente esperado
awake [ə'weɪk] (*pt* **awoke**, *pp* **awoken** *or* **awaked**) *adj* despierto ■ *vt* despertar ■ *vi* despertarse; **to be ~** estar despierto
awakening [ə'weɪknɪŋ] *n* despertar *m*
award [ə'wɔːd] *n* (*prize*) premio; (*medal*) condecoración *f*; (*Law*) fallo, sentencia; (*act*) concesión *f* ■ *vt* (*prize*) otorgar, conceder; (*Law*: *damages*) adjudicar
aware [ə'wɛəʳ] *adj* consciente; (*awake*) despierto; (*informed*) enterado; **to become ~ of** darse cuenta de, enterarse de; **I am fully ~ that** sé muy bien que
awareness [ə'wɛənɪs] *n* conciencia, conocimiento
awash [ə'wɒʃ] *adj* inundado

433

away [ə'weɪ] *adv* (*gen*) fuera; (*far away*) lejos; **two kilometres** ~ a dos kilómetros (de distancia); **two hours** ~ **by car** a dos horas en coche; **the holiday was two weeks** ~ faltaban dos semanas para las vacaciones; ~ **from** lejos de, fuera de; **he's** ~ **for a week** estará ausente una semana; **he's** ~ **in Barcelona** está en Barcelona; **to take** ~ llevar(se); **to work/pedal** ~ seguir trabajando/pedaleando; **to fade** ~ desvanecerse; (*sound*) apagarse

away game *n* (*Sport*) partido de fuera

awe [ɔː] *n* respeto, temor *m* reverencial

awe-inspiring ['ɔːɪnspaɪərɪŋ], **awesome** ['ɔːsəm] *adj* imponente, pasmoso

awestruck ['ɔːstrʌk] *adj* pasmado

awful ['ɔːfəl] *adj* terrible; **an** ~ **lot of** (*people, cars, dogs*) la mar de, muchísimos

awfully ['ɔːfəlɪ] *adv* (*very*) terriblemente

awhile [ə'waɪl] *adv* (durante) un rato, algún tiempo

awkward ['ɔːkwəd] *adj* (*clumsy*) desmañado, torpe; (*shape, situation*) incómodo; (*difficult: question*) difícil; (*problem*) complicado

awkwardness ['ɔːkwədnɪs] *n* (*clumsiness*) torpeza; (*of situation*) incomodidad *f*

awl [ɔːl] *n* lezna, subilla

awning ['ɔːnɪŋ] *n* (*of shop*) toldo; (*of window etc*) marquesina

awoke [ə'wəuk], **awoken** [ə'wəukən] *pt, pp of* **awake**

AWOL ['eɪwɔl] *abbr* (*Mil etc*) *see* **absent without leave**

awry [ə'raɪ] *adv*: **to be** ~ estar descolocado *or* atravesado; **to go** ~ salir mal, fracasar

axe, ax (US) [æks] *n* hacha ■ *vt* (*employee*) despedir; (*project etc*) cortar; (*jobs*) reducir; **to have an** ~ **to grind** (*fig*) tener un interés creado *or* algún fin interesado

axes ['æksiːz] *npl of* **axis**

axiom ['æksɪəm] *n* axioma *m*

axiomatic [æksɪə'mætɪk] *adj* axiomático

axis (*pl* **axes**) ['æksɪs, -siːz] *n* eje *m*

axle ['æksl] *n* eje *m*, árbol *m*

ay, aye [aɪ] *excl* (*yes*) sí; **the ayes** los que votan a favor

AYH *n abbr* = **American Youth Hostels**

AZ *abbr* (US) = **Arizona**

azalea [ə'zeɪlɪə] *n* azalea

Azerbaijan [æzəbaɪ'dʒɑːn] *n* Azerbaiyán *m*

Azerbaijani [æzəbaɪ'dʒɑːnɪ], **Azeri** [ə'zɛərɪ] *adj, n* azerbaiyano(-a), azerí *m/f*

Azores [ə'zɔːz] *npl*: **the** ~ las (Islas) Azores

AZT *n abbr* (= *azidothymidine*) AZT *m*

Aztec ['æztɛk] *adj, n* azteca *m/f*

azure ['eɪʒər] *adj* celeste

Bb

B, b [biː] n (letter) B, b f; (Scol: mark) N; (Mus) si
m; **B for Benjamin**, (US) **B for Baker**
B de Barcelona; **B road** (Brit Aut) ≈ carretera
secundaria
b. abbr = **born**
BA n abbr = **British Academy**; (Scol) = **Bachelor
of Arts**; see also **Bachelor's Degree**
babble ['bæbl] vi farfullar
babe [beɪb] n criatura
baboon [bə'buːn] n mandril m
baby ['beɪbɪ] n bebé m/f
baby carriage n (US) cochecito
babyish ['beɪbɪʃ] adj infantil
baby-minder ['beɪbɪ'maɪndər] n niñera f
(cualificada)
baby-sit ['beɪbɪsɪt] vi hacer de canguro
baby-sitter ['beɪbɪsɪtər] n canguro m/f
bachelor ['bætʃələr] n soltero; **B~ of Arts/
Science (BA/BSc)** licenciado(-a) en Filosofía
y Letras/Ciencias
bachelor's degree n licenciatura; ver nota

⊙ **BACHELOR'S DEGREE**
⊙
⊙ Se denomina Bachelor's Degree a la
⊙ titulación que se recibe al finalizar el
⊙ primer ciclo universitario, normalmente
⊙ después de un período de estudio de
⊙ tres o cuatro años. Las titulaciones
⊙ más frecuentes son las de Letras, "BA
⊙ (Bachelor of Arts)", Ciencias, "BSc
⊙ (Bachelor of Science)", Educación,
⊙ "BEd (Bachelor of Education)" y Derecho,
⊙ "LLB (Bachelor of Laws)".

back [bæk] n (of person) espalda; (of animal)
lomo; (of hand, page) dorso; (as opposed to front)
parte f de atrás; (of room) fondo; (of chair)
respaldo; (Football) defensa m; **to have one's
~ to the wall** (fig) estar entre la espada y la
pared; **to break the ~ of a job** hacer lo más
difícil de un trabajo; **~ to front** al revés;
at the ~ of my mind was the thought

that ... en el fondo tenía la idea de que
... ◼ vt (candidate: also: **back up**) respaldar,
apoyar; (horse: at races) apostar a; (car) dar
marcha atrás a or con ◼ vi (car etc) dar
marcha atrás ◼ adj (in compounds) de atrás;
~ seats/wheels (Aut) asientos mpl traseros,
ruedas fpl traseras; **~ garden/room** jardín m/
habitación f de atrás; **~ payments** pagos mpl
con efecto retroactivo; **~ rent** renta atrasada;
to take a ~ seat (fig) pasar a segundo
plano ◼ adv (not forward) (hacia) atrás;
he's ~ (returned) ha vuelto; **he ran ~** volvió
corriendo; **throw the ball ~** (restitution)
devuelve la pelota; **can I have it ~?** ¿me
lo devuelve?; **he called ~** (again) volvió a
llamar; **~ and forth** de acá para allá; **as far
as the 13th century** ya en el siglo XIII; **when
will you be ~?** ¿cuándo volverá?
▶ **back down** vi echarse atrás
▶ **back on to** vt fus: **the house backs on to
the golf course** por atrás la casa da al campo
de golf
▶ **back out** vi (of promise) volverse atrás
▶ **back up** vt (support: person) apoyar,
respaldar; (: theory) defender; (car) dar
marcha atrás a; (Comput) hacer una copia de
reserva de
backache ['bækeɪk] n dolor m de espalda
backbencher ['bæk'bentʃər] n (Brit) diputado
sin cargo oficial en el gobierno o la oposición
back benches npl (Brit) ver nota

⊙ **BACK BENCHES**
⊙
⊙ Reciben el nombre genérico de the
⊙ back benches los escaños más alejados
⊙ del pasillo central en la Cámara de los
⊙ Comunes del Parlamento británico, que
⊙ son ocupados por los "backbenchers", los
⊙ miembros de la cámara que no tienen
⊙ cargo en el gobierno o en la oposición.

backbiting ['bækbaɪtɪŋ] n murmuración f

backbone ['bækbəun] *n* columna vertebral; **the ~ of the organization** el pilar de la organización

backchat ['bæktʃæt] *n* réplicas *fpl*

backcloth ['bækklɔθ] *n* telón *m* de fondo

backcomb ['bækkəum] *vt* cardar

backdate [bæk'deɪt] *vt* (*letter*) poner fecha atrasada a; **backdated pay rise** aumento de sueldo con efecto retroactivo

backdrop ['bækdrɔp] *n* = **backcloth**

backer ['bækə'] *n* partidario(-a); (*Comm*) promotor(a) *m(f)*

backfire [bæk'faɪə'] *vi* (*Aut*) petardear; (*plans*) fallar, salir mal

backgammon ['bækgæmən] *n* backgammon *m*

background ['bækgraund] *n* fondo; (*of events*) antecedentes *mpl*; (*basic knowledge*) bases *fpl*; (*experience*) conocimientos *mpl*, educación *f* ■ *cpd* (*noise, music*) de fondo; (*Comput*) secundario; **~ reading** lectura de preparación; **family ~** origen *m*, antecedentes *mpl* familiares

backhand ['bækhænd] *n* (*Tennis: also:* **backhand stroke**) revés *m*

backhanded ['bæk'hændɪd] *adj* (*fig*) ambiguo, equívoco

backhander ['bæk'hændə'] *n* (*Brit: bribe*) soborno

backing ['bækɪŋ] *n* (*fig*) apoyo, respaldo; (*Comm*) respaldo financiero; (*Mus*) acompañamiento

backlash ['bæklæʃ] *n* reacción *f* (en contra)

backlog ['bæklɔg] *n:* **~ of work** trabajo atrasado

back number *n* (*of magazine etc*) número atrasado

backpack ['bækpæk] *n* mochila

backpacker ['bækpækə'] *n* mochilero(-a)

back pay *n* atrasos *mpl*

backpedal ['bækpɛdl] *vi* (*fig*) volverse/echarse atrás

backseat driver ['bæksiːt-] *n pasajero que se empeña en aconsejar al conductor*

backside ['bæksaɪd] *n* (*col*) trasero

backslash ['bækslæʃ] *n* pleca, barra inversa

backslide ['bækslaɪd] *vi* reincidir, recaer

backspace ['bækspeɪs] *vi* (*in typing*) retroceder

backstage [bæk'steɪdʒ] *adv* entre bastidores

back-street ['bækstriːt] *adj* de barrio; **~ abortionist** persona que practica abortos clandestinos

backstroke ['bækstrəuk] *n* espalda

backtrack ['bæktræk] *vi* (*fig*) = **backpedal**

backup ['bækʌp] *adj* (*train, plane*) suplementario; (*Comput: disk, file*) de reserva ■ *n* (*support*) apoyo; (*also:* **backup file**) copia de reserva; (*US: congestion*) embotellamiento, retención *f*

back-up lights *npl* (*US*) luces *fpl* de marcha atrás

backward ['bækwəd] *adj* (*movement*) hacia atrás; (*person, country*) atrasado; (*shy*) tímido

backwardness ['bækwədnɪs] *n* atraso

backwards ['bækwədz] *adv* (*move, go*) hacia atrás; (*read a list*) al revés; (*fall*) de espaldas; **to know sth ~** *or* (*US*) **~ and forwards** (*col*) saberse algo al dedillo

backwater ['bækwɔːtə'] *n* (*fig*) lugar *m* atrasado *or* apartado

backyard [bæk'jɑːd] *n* patio trasero

bacon ['beɪkən] *n* tocino, bacon *m*, beicon *m*

bacteria [bæk'tɪərɪə] *npl* bacterias *fpl*

bacteriology [bæktɪərɪ'ɔlədʒɪ] *n* bacteriología

bad [bæd] *adj* malo; (*serious*) grave; (*meat, food*) podrido, pasado; **to go ~** pasarse; **to have a ~ time of it** pasarlo mal; **I feel ~ about it** (*guilty*) me siento culpable; **~ debt** (*Comm*) cuenta incobrable; **in ~ faith** de mala fe

baddie, baddy ['bædɪ] *n* (*col: Cine etc*) malo(-a)

bade [bæd] [beɪd] *pt of* **bid**

badge [bædʒ] *n* insignia; (*metal badge*) chapa; (*of policeman*) placa; (*stick-on*) pegatina

badger ['bædʒə'] *n* tejón *m*

badly ['bædlɪ] *adv* (*work, dress etc*) mal; **~ wounded** gravemente herido; **he needs it ~** le hace mucha falta; **to be ~ off (for money)** andar mal de dinero; **things are going ~** las cosas van muy mal

bad-mannered ['bæd'mænəd] *adj* mal educado

badminton ['bædmɪntən] *n* bádminton *m*

bad-tempered ['bæd'tɛmpəd] *adj* de mal genio *or* carácter; (*temporary*) de mal humor

baffle ['bæfl] *vt* desconcertar, confundir

baffling ['bæflɪŋ] *adj* incomprensible

bag [bæg] *n* bolsa; (*handbag*) bolso; (*satchel*) mochila; (*case*) maleta; (*of hunter*) caza ■ *vt* (*col: take*) coger (*SP*), agarrar (*LAm*), pescar; **bags of** (*col: lots of*) un montón de; **to pack one's bags** hacer las maletas

bagful ['bægful] *n* saco (lleno)

baggage ['bægɪdʒ] *n* equipaje *m*

baggage claim *n* recogida de equipajes

baggy ['bægɪ] *adj* (*trousers*) ancho, holgado

Baghdad [bæg'dæd] *n* Bagdad *m*

bag lady *n* (*col*) *mujer sin hogar cargada de bolsas*

bagpipes ['bægpaɪps] *npl* gaita *sg*

bag-snatcher ['bægsnætʃə'] *n* (*Brit*) ladrón(-ona) *m(f)* de bolsos

bag-snatching ['bægsnætʃɪŋ] *n* (*Brit*) tirón *m* (de bolsos)

Bahamas [bə'hɑːməz] npl: **the ~** las (Islas) Bahama

Bahrain [bɑː'reɪn] n Bahrein m

bail [beɪl] n fianza ■ vt (prisoner: also: **grant bail to**) poner en libertad bajo fianza; (boat: also: **bail out**) achicar; **on ~** (prisoner) bajo fianza; **to be released on ~** ser puesto en libertad bajo fianza; **to ~ sb out** pagar la fianza de algn; see also **bale**

bailiff ['beɪlɪf] n alguacil m

bait [beɪt] n cebo ■ vt poner el cebo en

bake [beɪk] vt cocer (al horno) ■ vi (cook) cocerse; (be hot) hacer un calor terrible

baked beans npl judías fpl en salsa de tomate

baker ['beɪkər] n panadero(-a)

baker's dozen n docena del fraile

bakery ['beɪkərɪ] n (for bread) panadería; (for cakes) pastelería

baking ['beɪkɪŋ] n (act) cocción f; (batch) hornada

baking powder n levadura (en polvo)

baking tin n molde m (para horno)

balaclava [bælə'klɑːvə] n (also: **balaclava helmet**) pasamontañas m inv

balance ['bæləns] n equilibrio; (Comm: sum) balance m; (remainder) resto, (scales) balanza ■ vt equilibrar; (budget) nivelar; (account) saldar; (compensate) compensar; **~ of trade/ payments** balanza de comercio/pagos; **~ carried forward** balance m pasado a cuenta nueva; **~ brought forward** saldo de hoja anterior; **to ~ the books** hacer el balance

balanced ['bælənst] adj (personality, diet) equilibrado

balance sheet n balance m

balcony ['bælkənɪ] n (open) balcón m; (closed) galería

bald [bɔːld] adj calvo; (tyre) liso

baldness ['bɔːldnɪs] n calvicie f

bale [beɪl] n (Agr) paca, fardo

▶ **bale out** vi (of a plane) lanzarse en paracaídas ■ vt (Naut) achicar; **to ~ sb out of a difficulty** sacar a algn de un apuro

Balearic Islands [bælɪ'ærɪk-] npl: **the ~** las (Islas) Baleares

baleful ['beɪlful] adj (look) triste; (sinister) funesto, siniestro

balk [bɔːk] vi: **to ~ (at)** resistirse (a); (horse) plantarse (ante)

Balkan ['bɔːlkən] adj balcánico ■ n: **the Balkans** los Balcanes

ball [bɔːl] n (sphere) bola; (football) balón m; (for tennis, golf etc) pelota; (dance) baile m; **to be on the ~** (fig: competent) ser un enterado; (: alert) estar al tanto; **to play ~ (with sb)** jugar a la pelota (con algn); (fig) cooperar; **to start the ~ rolling** (fig) empezar; **the ~ is in your court** (fig) le toca a usted

ballad ['bæləd] n balada, romance m

ballast ['bæləst] n lastre m

ball bearing n cojinete m de bolas

ballcock ['bɔːlkɔk] n llave f de bola or de flotador

ballerina [bælə'riːnə] n bailarina

ballet ['bæleɪ] n ballet m

ballet dancer n bailarín(-ina) m(f) (de ballet)

ballistic [bə'lɪstɪk] adj balístico; **intercontinental ~ missile** misil m balístico intercontinental

ballistics [bə'lɪstɪks] n balística

balloon [bə'luːn] n globo; (in comic strip) bocadillo ■ vi dispararse

balloonist [bə'luːnɪst] n aeróstata m/f

ballot ['bælət] n votación f

ballot box n urna (electoral)

ballot paper n papeleta

ballpark ['bɔːlpɑːk] n (US) estadio de béisbol

ball-point pen ['bɔːlpɔɪnt-] n bolígrafo

ballroom ['bɔːlrum] n salón m de baile

balm [bɑːm] n (also fig) bálsamo

balmy ['bɑːmɪ] adj (breeze, air) suave; (col) = **barmy**

BALPA ['bælpə] n abbr (= British Airline Pilots' Association) sindicato de pilotos de líneas aéreas

balsa ['bɔːlsə], **balsa wood** n (madera de) balsa

Baltic ['bɔːltɪk] adj báltico ■ n: **the ~ (Sea)** el (Mar) Báltico

balustrade ['bæləstreɪd] n barandilla

bamboo [bæm'buː] n bambú m

bamboozle [bæm'buːzl] vt (col) embaucar, engatusar

ban [bæn] n prohibición f ■ vt prohibir; (exclude) excluir; **he was banned from driving** le retiraron el carnet de conducir

banal [bə'nɑːl] adj banal, vulgar

banana [bə'nɑːnə] n plátano, banana (LAm)

band [bænd] n (group) banda; (gang) pandilla; (strip) faja, tira; (at a dance) orquesta; (Mil) banda; (rock band) grupo

▶ **band together** vi juntarse, asociarse

bandage ['bændɪdʒ] n venda, vendaje m ■ vt vendar

Band-Aid ® ['bændeɪd] n (US) tirita, curita (LAm)

B & B n abbr = **bed and breakfast**

bandit ['bændɪt] n bandido; **one-armed ~** máquina tragaperras

bandstand ['bændstænd] n quiosco de música

bandwagon ['bændwægən] n: **to jump on the ~** (fig) subirse al carro

bandy ['bændɪ] vt (jokes, insults) intercambiar

bandy-legged ['bændɪ'legd] adj patizambo

437

bane [beɪn] *n*: **it** (*or* **he** *etc*) **is the ~ of my life** me amarga la vida

bang [bæŋ] *n* estallido; (*of door*) portazo; (*blow*) golpe *m* ■ *vt* golpear ■ *vi* estallar ■ *adv*: **to be ~ on time** (*col*) llegar en punto; **to ~ the door** dar un portazo; **to ~ into sth** chocar con algo, golpearse contra algo; *see also* **bangs**

banger ['bæŋəʳ] *n* (*Brit: car: also*: **old banger**) armatoste *m*, cacharro; (*Brit col: sausage*) salchicha; (*firework*) petardo

Bangkok [bæŋ'kɔk] *n* Bangkok *m*

Bangladesh [bæŋgləˈdeʃ] *n* Bangladesh *f*

bangle ['bæŋgl] *n* brazalete *m*, ajorca

bangs [bæŋz] *npl* (*US*) flequillo *sg*

banish ['bænɪʃ] *vt* desterrar

banister ['bænɪstəʳ] *n*, **banisters** ['bænɪstəz] ■ *npl* barandilla *f*, pasamanos *m inv*

banjo (*pl* **banjoes** *or* **banjos**) ['bændʒəu] *n* banjo

bank [bæŋk] *n* (*Comm*) banco; (*of river, lake*) ribera, orilla; (*of earth*) terraplén *m* ■ *vi* (*Aviat*) ladearse; (*Comm*): **to ~ with** tener la cuenta en
▶ **bank on** *vt fus* contar con

bank account *n* cuenta bancaria

bank balance *n* saldo

bank card *n* = **banker's card**

bank charges *npl* comisión *fsg*

bank draft *n* letra de cambio

banker ['bæŋkəʳ] *n* banquero; **~'s card** (*Brit*) tarjeta bancaria; **~'s order** orden *f* bancaria

bank giro *n* giro bancario

bank holiday *n* (*Brit*) día *m* festivo *or* de fiesta; *ver nota*

◉ **BANK HOLIDAY**
◉
◉ El término *bank holiday* se aplica en el
◉ Reino Unido a todo día festivo oficial en
◉ el que cierran bancos y comercios. Los
◉ más destacados coinciden con Navidad,
◉ Semana Santa, finales de mayo y finales
◉ de agosto. Al contrario que en los países
◉ de tradición católica, no se celebran las
◉ festividades dedicadas a los santos.

banking ['bæŋkɪŋ] *n* banca

bank loan *n* préstamo bancario

bank manager *n* director(a) *m(f)* (de sucursal) de banco

banknote ['bæŋknəut] *n* billete *m* de banco

bank rate *n* tipo de interés bancario

bankrupt ['bæŋkrʌpt] *n* quebrado(-a) ■ *adj* quebrado, insolvente; **to go ~** quebrar, hacer bancarrota; **to be ~** estar en quiebra

bankruptcy ['bæŋkrʌptsɪ] *n* quiebra, bancarrota

bank statement *n* extracto de cuenta

banned substance ['bænd -] *n* (*Sport*) sustancia prohibida

banner ['bænəʳ] *n* bandera; (*in demonstration*) pancarta

banns [bænz] *npl* amonestaciones *fpl*

banquet ['bæŋkwɪt] *n* banquete *m*

banter ['bæntəʳ] *n* guasa, bromas *fpl*

baptism ['bæptɪzəm] *n* bautismo; (*act*) bautizo

baptize [bæp'taɪz] *vt* bautizar

bar [bɑːʳ] *n* barra; (*on door*) tranca; (*of window, cage*) reja; (*of soap*) pastilla; (*fig: hindrance*) obstáculo; (*prohibition*) prohibición *f*; (*pub*) bar *m*, cantina (*esp LAm*); (*counter: in pub*) barra, mostrador *m*; (*Mus*) barra ■ *vt* (*road*) obstruir; (*window, door*) atrancar; (*person*) excluir; (*activity*) prohibir; **behind bars** entre rejas; **the B~** (*Law: profession*) la abogacía; (: *people*) el cuerpo de abogados; **~ none** sin excepción

Barbados [bɑː'beɪdɔs] *n* Barbados *m*

barbarian [bɑː'bɛərɪən] *n* bárbaro(-a)

barbaric [bɑː'bærɪk] *adj* bárbaro

barbarity [bɑː'bærɪtɪ] *n* barbaridad *f*

barbarous ['bɑːbərəs] *adj* bárbaro

barbecue ['bɑːbɪkjuː] *n* barbacoa, asado (*LAm*)

barbed wire ['bɑːbd -] *n* alambre *m* de espino

barber ['bɑːbəʳ] *n* peluquero, barbero

barbiturate [bɑː'bɪtjurɪt] *n* barbitúrico

Barcelona [bɑːsɪ'ləunə] *n* Barcelona

bar chart *n* gráfico de barras

bar code *n* código de barras

bare [bɛəʳ] *adj* desnudo; (*head*) descubierto ■ *vt* desnudar; **to ~ one's teeth** enseñar los dientes

bareback ['bɛəbæk] *adv* a pelo

barefaced ['bɛəfeɪst] *adj* descarado

barefoot ['bɛəfut] *adj, adv* descalzo

bareheaded [bɛə'hɛdɪd] *adj* descubierto, sin sombrero

barely ['bɛəlɪ] *adv* apenas

bareness ['bɛənɪs] *n* desnudez *f*

Barents Sea ['bærənts-] *n*: **the ~** el Mar de Barents

bargain ['bɑːgɪn] *n* pacto; (*transaction*) negocio; (*good buy*) ganga ■ *vi* negociar; (*haggle*) regatear; **into the ~** además, por añadidura
▶ **bargain for** *vt fus* (*col*): **he got more than he bargained for** le resultó peor de lo que esperaba

bargaining ['bɑːgənɪŋ] *n* negociación *f*, regateo; **~ table** mesa de negociaciones

bargaining position *n*: **to be in a strong/ weak ~** estar/no estar en una posición de fuerza para negociar

barge [bɑ:dʒ] n barcaza
▸ **barge in** vi irrumpir; (in conversation) entrometerse
▸ **barge into** vt fus dar contra
baritone ['bærɪtəʊn] n barítono
barium meal ['bɛərɪəm-] n (Med) sulfato de bario
bark [bɑ:k] n (of tree) corteza; (of dog) ladrido ■ vi ladrar
barley ['bɑ:lɪ] n cebada
barley sugar n azúcar m cande
barmaid ['bɑ:meɪd] n camarera
barman ['bɑ:mən] n camarero, barman m
barmy ['bɑ:mɪ] adj (col) chiflado, chalado
barn [bɑ:n] n granero; (for animals) cuadra
barnacle ['bɑ:nəkl] n percebe m
barn owl n lechuza
barometer [bə'rɒmɪtər] n barómetro
baron ['bærən] n barón m; (fig) magnate m; **the press barons** los magnates de la prensa
baroness ['bærənɪs] n baronesa
baroque [bə'rɒk] adj barroco
barrack ['bærək] vt (Brit) abuchear
barracking ['bærəkɪŋ] n: **to give sb a ~** (Brit) abuchear a algn
barracks ['bærəks] npl cuartel msg
barrage ['bærɑ:ʒ] n (Mil) cortina de fuego; (dam) presa; (fig: of criticism etc) lluvia, aluvión m; **a ~ of questions** una lluvia de preguntas
barrel ['bærəl] n barril m; (of wine) tonel m, cuba; (of gun) cañón m
barren ['bærən] adj estéril
barricade [bærɪ'keɪd] n barricada ■ vt cerrar con barricadas
barrier ['bærɪər] n barrera; (crash barrier) barrera
barrier cream n crema protectora
barring ['bɑ:rɪŋ] prep excepto, salvo
barrister ['bærɪstər] n (Brit) abogado(-a); ver nota

⊕ **BARRISTER**
⊕
⊕ En el sistema legal inglés barrister es el
⊕ abogado que se ocupa de defender los
⊕ casos de sus clientes en los tribunales
⊕ superiores. El equivalente escocés es
⊕ "advocate". Normalmente actúan según
⊕ instrucciones de un "solicitor", abogado
⊕ de despacho que no toma parte activa en
⊕ los juicios de dichos tribunales. El título
⊕ de barrister lo otorga el órgano colegiado
⊕ correspondiente, "the Inns of Court".

barrow ['bærəʊ] n (cart) carretilla
barstool ['bɑ:stu:l] n taburete m (de bar)
Bart. abbr (Brit) = **baronet**

bartender ['bɑ:tɛndər] n (US) camarero, barman m
barter ['bɑ:tər] vt: **to ~ sth for sth** trocar algo por algo
base [beɪs] n base f ■ vt: **to ~ sth on** basar or fundar algo en ■ adj bajo, infame; **to ~ at** (troops) estacionar en; **I'm based in London** (work) trabajo en Londres
baseball ['beɪsbɔ:l] n béisbol m
base camp n campamento base
Basel ['bɑ:zəl] n Basilea
baseless ['beɪslɪs] adj infundado
baseline ['beɪslaɪn] n (Tennis) línea de fondo
basement ['beɪsmənt] n sótano
base rate n tipo base
bases ['beɪsi:z] npl of **basis** ['beɪsɪz] ■ npl of **base**
bash [bæʃ] n: **I'll have a ~ (at it)** lo intentaré ■ vt (col) golpear
▸ **bash up** vt (col: car) destrozar; (: person) aporrear, vapulear
bashful ['bæʃful] adj tímido, vergonzoso
bashing ['bæʃɪŋ] n (col) paliza; **to go Paki-/queer-~** ir a dar una paliza a los paquistaníes/a los maricas
BASIC ['beɪsɪk] n (Comput) BASIC m
basic ['beɪsɪk] adj (salary etc) básico, (elementary: principles) fundamental
basically ['beɪsɪklɪ] adv fundamentalmente, en el fondo
basic rate n (of tax) base f mínima imponible
basil ['bæzl] n (col) albahaca
basin ['beɪsn] n (vessel) cuenco, tazón m; (Geo) cuenca; (also: **washbasin**) palangana, jofaina; (in bathroom) lavabo
basis ['beɪsɪs] (pl **-ses**) [-si:z] n base f; **on the ~ of what you've said** en base a lo que has dicho
bask [bɑ:sk] vi: **to ~ in the sun** tomar el sol
basket ['bɑ:skɪt] n cesta, cesto
basketball ['bɑ:skɪtbɔ:l] n baloncesto
basketball player n jugador(a) m(f) de baloncesto
basketwork ['bɑ:skɪtwə:k] n cestería
Basle [bɑ:l] n Basilea
basmati rice [bəz'mætɪ-] n arroz m basmati
Basque [bæsk] adj, n vasco(-a) m(f)
Basque Country n Euskadi m, País m Vasco
bass [beɪs] n (Mus) bajo
bass clef n clave f de fa
bassoon [bə'su:n] n fagot m
bastard ['bɑ:stəd] n bastardo(-a); (col!) cabrón m, hijo de puta (!)
baste [beɪst] vt (Culin) rociar (con su salsa)
bastion ['bæstɪən] n bastión m, baluarte m
bat [bæt] n (Zool) murciélago; (for ball games) palo; (for cricket, baseball) bate m; (Brit: for

table tennis) pala; **he didn't ~ an eyelid** ni pestañeó, ni se inmutó

batch [bætʃ] n lote m, remesa; (*of bread*) hornada

bated ['beɪtɪd] adj: **with ~ breath** sin respirar

bath [bɑ:θ, pl bɑ:ðz] n (*act*) baño; (*bathtub*) bañera, tina (*esp LAm*) ▪ vt bañar; **to have a ~** bañarse, darse un baño; *see also* **baths**

bathchair ['bɑ:θtʃeəʳ] n silla de ruedas

bathe [beɪð] vi bañarse; (US) darse un baño, bañarse ▪ vt (*wound etc*) lavar; (US) bañar, dar un baño a

bather ['beɪðəʳ] n bañista m/f

bathing ['beɪðɪŋ] n baño

bathing cap n gorro de baño

bathing costume, bathing suit (US) n bañador m, traje m de baño

bathing trunks npl bañador msg

bathmat ['bɑ:θmæt] n alfombrilla de baño

bathrobe ['bɑ:θrəub] n albornoz m

bathroom ['bɑ:θrum] n (cuarto de) baño

baths [bɑ:ðz] npl piscina sg

bath towel n toalla de baño

bathtub ['bɑ:θtʌb] n bañera

batman ['bætmən] n (Brit) ordenanza m

baton ['bætən] n (Mus) batuta

battalion [bə'tæliən] n batallón m

batten ['bætn] n (Carpentry) listón m; (Naut) junquillo, sable m

▶ **batten down** vt (Naut): **to ~ down the hatches** atrancar las escotillas

batter ['bætəʳ] vt maltratar; (wind, rain) azotar ▪ n batido

battered ['bætəd] adj (hat, pan) estropeado

battery ['bætərɪ] n batería; (of torch) pila

battery charger n cargador m de baterías

battery farming n cría intensiva

battle ['bætl] n batalla; (fig) lucha ▪ vi luchar; **that's half the ~** (col) ya hay medio camino andado; **to fight a losing ~** (fig) luchar por una causa perdida

battlefield ['bætlfi:ld] n campo m de batalla

battlements ['bætlmənts] npl almenas fpl

battleship ['bætlʃɪp] n acorazado

batty ['bætɪ] adj (col: person) chiflado; (: idea) de chiflado

bauble ['bɔ:bl] n chuchería

baud rate n (Comput) velocidad f (de transmisión) en baudios

bauxite ['bɔ:ksaɪt] n bauxita

Bavaria [bə'vɛərɪə] n Baviera

Bavarian [bə'vɛərɪən] adj, n bávaro(-a) m(f)

bawdy ['bɔ:dɪ] adj indecente; (joke) verde

bawl [bɔ:l] vi chillar, gritar

bay [beɪ] n (Geo) bahía; (for parking) parking m, estacionamiento; (loading bay) patio de carga;

(Bot) laurel m ▪ vi aullar; **to hold sb at ~** mantener a alguien a raya

bay leaf n (hoja de) laurel m

bayonet ['beɪənɪt] n bayoneta

bay window n ventana salediza

bazaar [bə'zɑ:ʳ] n bazar m

bazooka [bə'zu:kə] n bazuca

BB n abbr (Brit: = Boys' Brigade) organización juvenil para chicos

BBB n abbr (US: = Better Business Bureau) organismo para la defensa del consumidor

BBC n abbr (= British Broadcasting Corporation) BBC f; ver nota

BBC

La BBC es el organismo público británico de radio y televisión, autónomo en cuanto a su política de programas pero regulado por un estatuto ("BBC charter") que ha de aprobar el Parlamento. Además de cadenas nacionales de televisión y de radio, transmite también un servicio informativo mundial ("BBC World Service"). A no tener publicidad, se financia a través de operaciones comerciales paralelas y del cobro de una licencia anual obligatoria ("TV licence") para los que tienen aparato de televisión.

BBE n abbr (US) = **Benevolent and Protective Order of Elks**

BC adv abbr (= before Christ) a. de J.C. ▪ abbr (Canada) = **British Columbia**

BCG n abbr (= Bacillus Calmette-Guérin) vacuna de la tuberculosis

BD n abbr (= Bachelor of Divinity) Licenciado/a en Teología

B/D abbr = **bank draft**

BDS n abbr (= Bachelor of Dental Surgery) título universitario

 KEYWORD

be [bi:] (pt **was, were,** pp **been**) aux vb **1** (with present participle: forming continuous tenses): **what are you doing?** ¿qué estás haciendo?, ¿qué haces?; **they're coming tomorrow** vienen mañana; **I've been waiting for you for hours** llevo horas esperándote

2 (with pp: forming passives) ser (but often replaced by active or reflexive constructions); **to be murdered** ser asesinado; **the box had been opened** habían abierto la caja; **the thief was nowhere to be seen** no se veía al ladrón por ninguna parte

3 (*in tag questions*): **it was fun, wasn't it?** fue divertido, ¿no? *or* ¿verdad?; **he's good-looking, isn't he?** es guapo, ¿no te parece?; **she's back again, is she?** entonces, ¿ha vuelto?

4 (*+to +infin*): **the house is to be sold** (*necessity*) hay que vender la casa; (*future*) van a vender la casa; **he's not to open it** no tiene que abrirlo; **he was to have come yesterday** debía de haber venido ayer; **am I to understand that ...?** ¿debo entender que ...?

■ *vb +complement* **1** (*with n or num complement*) ser; **he's a doctor** es médico; **2 and 2 are 4** 2 y 2 son 4

2 (*with adj complement: expressing permanent or inherent quality*) ser; (: *expressing state seen as temporary or reversible*) estar; **I'm English** soy inglés(-esa); **she's tall/pretty** es alta/bonita; **he's young** es joven; **be careful/good/quiet** ten cuidado/pórtate bien/cállate; **I'm tired** estoy cansado(-a); **I'm warm** tengo calor; **it's dirty** está sucio(-a)

3 (*of health*) estar; **how are you?** ¿cómo estás?; **he's very ill** está muy enfermo; **I'm better now** ya estoy mejor

4 (*of age*) tener; **how old are you?** ¿cuántos años tienes?; **I'm sixteen (years old)** tengo dieciséis años

5 (*cost*) costar; ser; **how much was the meal?** ¿cuánto fue *or* costó la comida?; **that'll be £5.75, please** son £5.75, por favor; **this shirt is £17** esta camisa cuesta £17

■ *vi* **1** (*exist, occur etc*) existir, haber; **the best singer that ever was** el mejor cantante que existió jamás; **is there a God?** ¿hay un Dios?, ¿existe Dios?; **be that as it may** sea como sea; **so be it** así sea

2 (*referring to place*) estar; **I won't be here tomorrow** no estaré aquí mañana

3 (*referring to movement*): **where have you been?** ¿dónde has estado?

■ *impers vb* **1** (*referring to time*): **it's 5 o'clock** son las 5; **it's the 28th of April** estamos a 28 de abril

2 (*referring to distance*): **it's 10 km to the village** el pueblo está a 10 km

3 (*referring to the weather*): **it's too hot/cold** hace demasiado calor/frío; **it's windy today** hace viento hoy

4 (*emphatic*): **it's me** soy yo; **it was Maria who paid the bill** fue María la que pagó la cuenta

B/E *abbr* = **bill of exchange**
beach [biːtʃ] *n* playa ■ *vt* varar
beach buggy [-bʌgɪ] *n* buggy *m*

beachcomber ['biːtʃkəumər] *n* raquero(-a)
beachwear ['biːtʃweər] *n* ropa de playa
beacon ['biːkən] *n* (*lighthouse*) faro; (*marker*) guía; (*radio beacon*) radiofaro
bead [biːd] *n* cuenta, abalorio; (*of dew, sweat*) gota; **beads** *npl* (*necklace*) collar *m*
beady ['biːdɪ] *adj* (*eyes*) pequeño y brillante
beagle ['biːgl] *n* sabueso pequeño, beagle *m*
beak [biːk] *n* pico
beaker ['biːkər] *n* vaso
beam [biːm] *n* (*Arch*) viga; (*of light*) rayo, haz *m* de luz; (*Radio*) rayo ■ *vi* brillar; (*smile*) sonreír; **to drive on full** *or* **main ~** conducir con las luces largas
beaming ['biːmɪŋ] *adj* (*sun, smile*) radiante
bean [biːn] *n* judía, fríjol/frijol *m* (*esp LAm*); **runner/broad ~** habichuela/haba; **coffee ~** grano de café
beanpole ['biːnpəul] *n* (*col*) espárrago
beansprouts ['biːnsprauts] *npl* brotes *mpl* de soja
bear [bɛər] (*pt* **bore**, *pp* **borne**) *n* oso; (*Stock Exchange*) bajista *m* ■ *vt* (*weight etc*) llevar; (*cost*) pagar; (*responsibility*) tener; (*traces, signs*) mostrar; (*produce: fruit*) dar; (*Comm: interest*) devengar; (*endure*) soportar, aguantar; (*stand up to*) resistir a; (*children*) tener, dar a luz ■ *vi*: **to ~ right/left** torcer a la derecha/izquierda; **I can't ~ him** no le puedo ver, no lo soporto; **to bring pressure to ~ on sb** ejercer presión sobre algn
► **bear on** *vt fus* tener que ver con, referirse a
► **bear out** *vt fus* (*suspicions*) corroborar, confirmar; (*person*) confirmar lo dicho por
► **bear up** *vi* (*cheer up*) animarse; **he bore up well under the strain** resistió bien la presión
► **bear with** *vt fus* (*sb's moods, temper*) tener paciencia con
bearable ['bɛərəbl] *adj* soportable, aguantable
beard [bɪəd] *n* barba
bearded ['bɪədɪd] *adj* con barba
bearer ['bɛərər] *n* (*of news, cheque*) portador(a) *m(f)*; (*of passport*) titular *m/f*
bearing ['bɛərɪŋ] *n* porte *m*; (*connection*) relación *f*; **(ball) bearings** *npl* cojinetes *mpl* a bolas; **to take a ~** marcarse; **to find one's bearings** orientarse
bearskin ['bɛəskɪn] *n* (*Mil*) gorro militar (*de piel de oso*)
beast [biːst] *n* bestia; (*col*) bruto, salvaje *m*
beastly ['biːstlɪ] *adj* bestial; (*awful*) horrible
beat [biːt] (*pt* **~**, *pp* **beaten**) *n* (*of heart*) latido; (*Mus*) ritmo, compás *m*; (*of policeman*) ronda ■ *vt* (*hit*) golpear; (*eggs*) batir; (*defeat*) vencer, derrotar; (*better*) sobrepasar; (*drum*) tocar;

(*rhythm*) marcar ■ *vi* (*heart*) latir; **off the beaten track** aislado; **to ~ about the bush** andarse con rodeos; **to ~ it** largarse; **that beats everything!** (*col*) ¡eso es el colmo!; **to ~ on a door** dar golpes en una puerta

▶ **beat down** *vt* (*door*) derribar a golpes; (*price*) conseguir rebajar, regatear; (*seller*) hacer rebajar el precio ■ *vi* (*rain*) llover a cántaros; (*sun*) caer de plomo

▶ **beat off** *vt* rechazar

▶ **beat up** *vt* (*col: person*) dar una paliza a

beater ['biːtəʳ] *n* (*for eggs, cream*) batidora

beating ['biːtɪŋ] *n* paliza, golpiza (*LAm*); **to take a ~** recibir una paliza

beat-up ['biːtʌp] *adj* (*col*) destartalado

beautiful ['bjuːtɪful] *adj* hermoso, bello, lindo (*esp LAm*)

beautifully ['bjuːtɪfəlɪ] *adv* de maravilla

beautify ['bjuːtɪfaɪ] *vt* embellecer

beauty ['bjuːtɪ] *n* belleza, hermosura; (*concept, person*) belleza; **the ~ of it is that ...** lo mejor de esto es que ...

beauty contest *n* concurso de belleza

beauty queen *n* reina de la belleza

beauty salon *n* salón *m* de belleza

beauty sleep *n*: **to get one's ~** no perder horas de sueño

beauty spot *n* lunar *m* postizo; (*Brit: Tourism*) lugar *m* pintoresco

beaver ['biːvəʳ] *n* castor *m*

becalmed [bɪ'kɑːmd] *adj* encalmado

became [bɪ'keɪm] *pt of* **become**

because [bɪ'kɔz] *conj* porque; **~ of** *prep* debido a, a causa de

beck [bɛk] *n*: **to be at the ~ and call of** estar a disposición de

beckon ['bɛkən] *vt* (*also:* **beckon to**) llamar con señas

become [bɪ'kʌm] (*irreg: like* **come**) *vi* (+*noun*) hacerse, llegar a ser; (+*adj*) ponerse, volverse ■ *vt* (*suit*) favorecer, sentar bien a; **to ~ fat** engordar; **to ~ angry** enfadarse; **it became known that ...** se descubrió que ...

becoming [bɪ'kʌmɪŋ] *adj* (*behaviour*) decoroso; (*clothes*) favorecedor(a)

becquerel [bɛkə'rɛl] *n* becquerelio

BECTU ['bɛktuː] *n abbr* (*Brit*) = **Broadcasting Entertainment Cinematographic and Theatre Union**

BEd *n abbr* (= *Bachelor of Education*) título universitario; *see also* **Bachelor's Degree**

bed [bɛd] *n* cama; (*of flowers*) macizo; (*of sea, lake*) fondo; (*of coal, clay*) capa; **to go to ~** acostarse

▶ **bed down** *vi* acostarse

bed and breakfast *n* ≈ pensión *f*; *ver nota*

Se llama *Bed and Breakfast* a la casa de hospedaje particular, o granja si es en el campo, que ofrece cama y desayuno a tarifas inferiores a las de un hotel. El servicio se suele anunciar con carteles colocados en las ventanas del establecimiento, en el jardín o en la carretera y en ellos aparece a menudo únicamente el símbolo "B & B".

bedbug ['bɛdbʌg] *n* chinche *f*

bedclothes ['bɛdkləuðz] *npl* ropa de cama

bedding ['bɛdɪŋ] *n* ropa de cama

bedeck [bɪ'dɛk] *vt* engalanar, adornar

bedevil [bɪ'dɛvl] *vt* (*dog*) acosar; (*trouble*) fastidiar

bedfellow ['bɛdfɛləu] *n*: **they are strange bedfellows** (*fig*) hacen una pareja rara

bedlam ['bɛdləm] *n* confusión *f*

bedpan ['bɛdpæn] *n* cuña

bedraggled [bɪ'drægld] *adj* desastrado

bedridden ['bɛdrɪdn] *adj* postrado (en cama)

bedrock ['bɛdrɔk] *n* (*Geo*) roca firme; (*fig*) pilar *m*

bedroom ['bɛdrum] *n* dormitorio, alcoba

Beds *abbr* (*Brit*) = **Bedfordshire**

bed settee *n* sofá-cama *m*

bedside ['bɛdsaɪd] *n*: **at sb's ~** a la cabecera de alguien

bedside lamp *n* lámpara de noche

bedsit ['bɛdsɪt], **bedsitter** ['bɛdsɪtəʳ] *n* (*Brit*) estudio

bedspread ['bɛdsprɛd] *n* cubrecama *m*, colcha

bedtime ['bɛdtaɪm] *n* hora de acostarse; **it's ~** es hora de acostarse *or* de irse a la cama

bee [biː] *n* abeja; **to have a ~ in one's bonnet (about sth)** tener una idea fija (de algo)

beech [biːtʃ] *n* haya

beef [biːf] *n* carne *f* de vaca; **roast ~** rosbif *m*

▶ **beef up** *vt* (*col*) reforzar

beefburger ['biːfbəːgəʳ] *n* hamburguesa

beefeater ['biːfiːtəʳ] *n* alabardero de la Torre de Londres

beehive ['biːhaɪv] *n* colmena

bee-keeping ['biːkiːpɪŋ] *n* apicultura

beeline ['biːlaɪn] *n*: **to make a ~ for** ir derecho a

been [biːn] *pp of* **be**

beep [biːp] *n* pitido ■ *vi* pitar

beeper ['biːpəʳ] *n* (*of doctor etc*) busca *m inv*

beer [bɪəʳ] *n* cerveza

beer belly *n* (*col*) barriga (*de bebedor de cerveza*)

beer can *n* bote *m or* lata de cerveza

beet [biːt] *n* (*US*) remolacha

b

beetle ['biːtl] n escarabajo
beetroot ['biːtruːt] n (Brit) remolacha
befall [bɪ'fɔːl] vi, vt (irreg: like **fall**) acontecer (a)
befit [bɪ'fɪt] vt convenir a, corresponder a
before [bɪ'fɔːʳ] prep (of time) antes de; (of space) delante de ■ conj antes (de) que ■ adv (time) antes; (space) delante, adelante; **~ going** antes de marcharse; **~ she goes** antes de que se vaya; **the week ~** la semana anterior; **I've never seen it ~** no lo he visto nunca
beforehand [bɪ'fɔːhænd] adv de antemano, con anticipación
befriend [bɪ'frɛnd] vt ofrecer amistad a
befuddled [bɪ'fʌdld] adj aturdido, atontado
beg [bɛg] vi pedir limosna, mendigar ■ vt pedir, rogar; (entreat) suplicar; **I ~ your pardon** (apologising) perdóneme; (not hearing) ¿perdón?
began [bɪ'gæn] pt of **begin**
beggar ['bɛgəʳ] n mendigo(-a)
begin (pt **began**, pp **begun**) [bɪ'gɪn, -'gæn, -'gʌn] vt, vi empezar, comenzar; **to ~ doing** or **to do sth** empezar a hacer algo; **I can't ~ to thank you** no encuentro palabras para agradecerle; **to ~ with, I'd like to know ...** en primer lugar, quisiera saber ...; **beginning from Monday** a partir del lunes
beginner [bɪ'gɪnəʳ] n principiante m/f
beginning [bɪ'gɪnɪŋ] n principio, comienzo; **right from the ~** desde el principio
begrudge [bɪ'grʌdʒ] vt: **to ~ sb sth** tenerle envidia a alguien por algo
beguile [bɪ'gaɪl] vt (enchant) seducir
beguiling [bɪ'gaɪlɪŋ] adj seductor(a), atractivo
begun [bɪ'gʌn] pp of **begin**
behalf [bɪ'hɑːf] n: **on ~ of**, (US) **in ~ of** en nombre de; (for benefit of) por
behave [bɪ'heɪv] vi (person) portarse, comportarse; (thing) funcionar; (well: also: **behave o.s.**) portarse bien
behaviour, behavior (US) [bɪ'heɪvjəʳ] n comportamiento, conducta
behead [bɪ'hɛd] vt decapitar
beheld [bɪ'hɛld] pt, pp of **behold**
behind [bɪ'haɪnd] prep detrás de ■ adv detrás, por detrás, atrás ■ n trasero; **to be ~ (schedule)** ir retrasado; **~ the scenes** (fig) entre bastidores; **we're ~ them in technology** (fig) nos dejan atrás en tecnología; **to leave sth ~** olvidar or dejarse algo; **to be ~ with sth** estar atrasado en algo; **to be ~ with payments (on sth)** estar atrasado en el pago (de algo)
behold [bɪ'həʊld] (irreg: like **hold**) vt contemplar
beige [beɪʒ] adj (color) beige

being ['biːɪŋ] n ser m; **to come into ~** nacer, aparecer
Beirut [beɪ'ruːt] n Beirut m
Belarus [bɛlə'rus] n Bielorrusia
Belarussian [bɛlə'rʌʃən] adj, n bielorruso(-a) ■ n (Ling) bielorruso
belated [bɪ'leɪtɪd] adj atrasado, tardío
belch [bɛltʃ] vi eructar ■ vt (also: **belch out**: smoke etc) vomitar, arrojar
beleaguered [bɪ'liːgəd] adj asediado
Belfast ['bɛlfɑːst] n Belfast m
belfry ['bɛlfrɪ] n campanario
Belgian ['bɛldʒən] adj, n belga m/f
Belgium ['bɛldʒəm] n Bélgica
Belgrade [bɛl'greɪd] n Belgrado
belie [bɪ'laɪ] vt (give false impression of) desmentir, contradecir
belief [bɪ'liːf] n (opinion) opinión f; (trust, faith) fe f; (acceptance as true) creencia; **it's beyond ~** es increíble; **in the ~ that** creyendo que
believable [bɪ'liːvəbl] adj creíble
believe [bɪ'liːv] vt, vi creer; **to ~ (that)** creer (que); **to ~ in** (God, ghosts) creer en; (method) ser partidario de; **he is believed to be abroad** se cree que está en el extranjero; **I don't ~ in corporal punishment** no soy partidario del castigo corporal
believer [bɪ'liːvəʳ] n (in idea, activity) partidario(-a); (Rel) creyente m/f, fiel m/f
belittle [bɪ'lɪtl] vt despreciar
Belize [bɛ'liːz] n Belice f
bell [bɛl] n campana; (small) campanilla; (on door) timbre m; (animal's) cencerro; (on toy etc) cascabel m; **that rings a ~** (fig) eso me suena
bellboy ['bɛlbɔɪ] n, **bellhop** (US) ['bɛlhɔp] ■ n botones m inv
belligerent [bɪ'lɪdʒərənt] adj (at war) beligerante; (fig) agresivo
bellow ['bɛləʊ] vi bramar; (person) rugir ■ vt (orders) gritar
bellows ['bɛləʊz] npl fuelle msg
bell push n pulsador m de timbre
belly ['bɛlɪ] n barriga, panza
bellyache ['bɛlɪeɪk] n dolor m de barriga or de tripa ■ vi (col) gruñir
bellyful ['bɛlɪful] n: **to have had a ~ of ...** (col) estar más que harto de ...
belong [bɪ'lɔŋ] vi: **to ~ to** pertenecer a; (club etc) ser socio de; **this book belongs here** este libro va aquí
belongings [bɪ'lɔŋɪŋz] npl: **personal ~** pertenencias fpl
Belorussia [bɛləʊ'rʌʃə] n Bielorrusia
Belorussian [bɛləʊ'rʌʃən] adj, n = **Belarussian**
beloved [bɪ'lʌvɪd] adj, n querido(-a) m(f), amado(-a) m(f)

below [bɪ'ləu] *prep* bajo, debajo de ■ *adv* abajo, (por) debajo; **see** ~ véase más abajo

belt [bɛlt] *n* cinturón *m*; (*Tech*) correa, cinta ■ *vt* (*thrash*) golpear con correa; **industrial** ~ cinturón industrial

▶ **belt out** *vt* (*song*) cantar a voz en grito *or* a grito pelado

▶ **belt up** *vi* (*Aut*) ponerse el cinturón de seguridad; (*fig, col*) cerrar el pico

beltway ['bɛltweɪ] *n* (*US Aut*) carretera de circunvalación

bemoan [bɪ'məun] *vt* lamentar

bemused [bɪ'mju:zd] *adj* perplejo

bench [bɛntʃ] *n* banco; **the B~** (*Law*) el tribunal; (*people*) la judicatura

bench mark *n* punto de referencia

bend [bɛnd] *vb* (*pt, pp* **bent**) ■ *vt* doblar; (*body, head*) inclinar ■ *vi* inclinarse; (*road*) curvarse ■ *n* (*Brit: in road, river*) recodo; (*in pipe*) codo; *see also* **bends**

▶ **bend down** *vi* inclinarse, doblarse

▶ **bend over** *vi* inclinarse

bends [bɛndz] *npl* (*Med*) *apoplejía por cambios bruscos de presión*

beneath [bɪ'ni:θ] *prep* bajo, debajo de; (*unworthy of*) indigno de ■ *adv* abajo, (por) debajo

benefactor ['bɛnɪfæktər] *n* bienhechor *m*

benefactress ['bɛnɪfæktrɪs] *n* bienhechora

beneficial [bɛnɪ'fɪʃəl] *adj:* ~ **to** beneficioso para

beneficiary [bɛnɪ'fɪʃərɪ] *n* (*Law*) beneficiario(-a)

benefit ['bɛnɪfɪt] *n* beneficio, provecho; (*allowance of money*) subsidio ■ *vt* beneficiar ■ *vi:* **he'll** ~ **from it** le sacará provecho; **unemployment** ~ subsidio de desempleo

Benelux ['bɛnɪlʌks] *n* Benelux *m*

benevolence [bɪ'nɛvələns] *n* benevolencia

benevolent [bɪ'nɛvələnt] *adj* benévolo

BEng *n abbr* (= *Bachelor of Engineering*) *título universitario*

benign [bɪ'naɪn] *adj* (*person*) benigno; (*Med*) benigno; (*smile*) afable

bent [bɛnt] *pt, pp of* **bend** ■ *n* inclinación *f* ■ *adj* (*wire, pipe*) doblado, torcido; **to be** ~ **on** estar empeñado en

bequeath [bɪ'kwi:ð] *vt* legar

bequest [bɪ'kwɛst] *n* legado

bereaved [bɪ'ri:vd] *adj* afligido ■ *n:* **the** ~ los afligidos *mpl*

bereavement [bɪ'ri:vmənt] *n* aflicción *f*

beret ['bɛreɪ] *n* boina

Bering Sea ['bɛərɪŋ-] *n:* **the** ~ el Mar de Bering

berk [bə:k] *n* (*Brit col*) capullo(-a) (*!*)

Berks *abbr* (*Brit*) = **Berkshire**

Berlin [bə:'lɪn] *n* Berlín *m*; **East/West** ~ Berlín del Este/Oeste

berm [bə:m] *n* (*US Aut*) arcén *m*

Bermuda [bə:'mju:də] *n* las (Islas) Bermudas

Bermuda shorts *npl* bermudas *mpl or fpl*

Bern [bə:n] *n* Berna

berry ['bɛrɪ] *n* baya

berserk [bə'sə:k] *adj:* **to go** ~ perder los estribos

berth [bə:θ] *n* (*bed*) litera; (*cabin*) camarote *m*; (*for ship*) amarradero ■ *vi* atracar, amarrar; **to give sb a wide** ~ (*fig*) evitar encontrarse con algn

beseech (*pt, pp* **besought**) [bɪ'si:tʃ, -'sɔ:t] *vt* suplicar

beset (*pt, pp* ~) [bɪ'sɛt] *vt* (*person*) acosar ■ *adj:* **a policy** ~ **with dangers** una política rodeada de peligros

besetting [bɪ'sɛtɪŋ] *adj:* **his** ~ **sin** su principal falta

beside [bɪ'saɪd] *prep* junto a, al lado de; (*compared with*) comparado con; **to be** ~ **o.s. with anger** estar fuera de sí; **that's** ~ **the point** eso no tiene nada que ver con el asunto

besides [bɪ'saɪdz] *adv* además ■ *prep* (*as well as*) además de; (*except*) excepto

besiege [bɪ'si:dʒ] *vt* (*town*) sitiar; (*fig*) asediar

besmirch [bɪ'smə:tʃ] *vt* (*fig*) manchar, mancillar

besotted [bɪ'sɔtɪd] *adj:* ~ **with** chiflado por

bespoke [bɪ'spəuk] *adj* (*garment*) hecho a la medida; ~ **tailor** sastre *m* que confecciona a la medida

best [bɛst] *adj* (el/la) mejor ■ *adv* (lo) mejor; **the** ~ **part of** (*most*) la mayor parte de; **at** ~ en el mejor de los casos; **to make the** ~ **of sth** sacar el mejor partido de algo; **to do one's** ~ hacer todo lo posible; **to the** ~ **of my knowledge** que yo sepa; **to the** ~ **of my ability** como mejor puedo; **the** ~ **thing to do is ...** lo mejor (que se puede hacer) es ...; **he's not exactly patient at the** ~ **of times** no es que tenga mucha paciencia precisamente

bestial ['bɛstɪəl] *adj* bestial

best man *n* padrino de boda

bestow [bɪ'stəu] *vt* otorgar; (*honour, praise*) dispensar; **to** ~ **sth on sb** conceder *or* dar algo a algn

bestseller ['bɛst'sɛlər] *n* éxito de ventas, best-seller *m*

bet [bɛt] *n* apuesta ■ *vt, vi* (*pt, pp* **bet** *or* **betted**); **to** ~ **(on)** apostar (a); **it's a safe** ~ (*fig*) es cosa segura

Bethlehem ['bɛθlɪhɛm] *n* Belén *m*

betray [bɪ'treɪ] *vt* traicionar; (*inform on*) delatar

betrayal [bɪ'treɪəl] n traición f
better ['bɛtə'] adj mejor ■ adv mejor ■ vt
mejorar; (record etc) superar ■ n: **to get the**
~ of sb quedar por encima de algn; **you had**
~ do it más vale que lo hagas; **he thought ~**
of it cambió de parecer; **to get ~** mejorar(se);
(Med) reponerse; **that's ~!** ¡eso es!; **I had ~**
go tengo que irme; **a change for the ~** una
mejora; **~ off** adj más acomodado
betting ['bɛtɪŋ] n juego, apuestas fpl
betting shop n (Brit) casa de apuestas
between [bɪ'twiːn] prep entre ■ adv (also:
in between: time) mientras tanto; (: place)
en medio; **the road ~ here and London** la
carretera de aquí a Londres; **we only had 5 ~**
us teníamos sólo 5 entre todos
bevel ['bɛvəl] n (also: **bevel edge**) bisel m,
chaflán m
beverage ['bɛvərɪdʒ] n bebida
bevy ['bɛvɪ] n: **a ~ of** una bandada de
bewail [bɪ'weɪl] vt lamentar
beware [bɪ'weə'] vi: **to ~ (of)** tener cuidado
(con) ■ excl ¡cuidado!
bewildered [bɪ'wɪldəd] adj aturdido, perplejo
bewildering [bɪ'wɪldərɪŋ] adj desconcertante
bewitching [bɪ'wɪtʃɪŋ] adj hechicero,
encantador(a)
beyond [bɪ'jɔnd] prep más allá de; (exceeding)
además de, fuera de; (above) superior a ■ adv
más allá, más lejos; **~ doubt** fuera de toda
duda; **~ repair** irreparable
b/f abbr (= brought forward) saldo previo
BFPO n abbr (= British Forces Post Office) servicio
postal del ejército
bhp n abbr (Aut: = brake horsepower) potencia al
freno
bi ... [baɪ] pref bi ...
biannual [baɪ'ænjuəl] adj semestral
bias ['baɪəs] n (prejudice) prejuicio; (preference)
predisposición f
biased, biassed ['baɪəst] adj parcial; **to be**
bias(s)ed against tener perjuicios contra
biathlon [baɪ'æθlən] n biatlón m
bib [bɪb] n babero
Bible ['baɪbl] n Biblia
biblical ['bɪblɪkəl] adj bíblico
bibliography [bɪblɪ'ɔgrəfɪ] n bibliografía
bicarbonate of soda [baɪ'kɑːbənɪt-] n
bicarbonato de soda
bicentenary [baɪsɛn'tiːnərɪ], **bicentennial**
(US) [baɪsɛn'tɛnɪəl] n bicentenario
biceps ['baɪsɛps] n bíceps m
bicker ['bɪkə'] vi reñir
bickering ['bɪkərɪŋ] n riñas fpl, altercados mpl
bicycle ['baɪsɪkl] n bicicleta
bicycle path n camino para ciclistas
bicycle pump n bomba de bicicleta

bid [bɪd] n (at auction) oferta, puja, postura;
(attempt) tentativa, conato ■ vi (pt, pp **bid**)
hacer una oferta ■ vt (pt **bade**) [bæd] (pp
bidden) ['bɪdn] mandar, ordenar; **to ~ sb**
good day dar a algn los buenos días
bidder ['bɪdə'] n: **the highest ~** el mejor
postor
bidding ['bɪdɪŋ] n (at auction) ofertas fpl, puja;
(order) orden f, mandato
bide [baɪd] vt: **to ~ one's time** esperar el
momento adecuado
bidet ['biːdeɪ] n bidet m
bidirectional ['baɪdɪ'rɛkʃənl] adj
bidireccional
biennial [baɪ'ɛnɪəl] adj, n bienal f
bier [bɪə'] n féretro
bifocals [baɪ'fəuklz] npl gafas fpl or anteojos
mpl (LAm) bifocales
big [bɪg] adj grande; **~ business** gran
negocio; **to do things in a ~ way** hacer las
cosas en grande
bigamy ['bɪgəmɪ] n bigamia
big dipper [-'dɪpə'] n montaña rusa
big end n (Aut) cabeza de biela
biggish ['bɪgɪʃ] adj más bien grande; (man)
más bien alto
bigheaded ['bɪg'hɛdɪd] adj engreído
bigot ['bɪgət] n fanático(-a), intolerante m/f
bigoted ['bɪgətɪd] adj fanático, intolerante
bigotry ['bɪgətrɪ] n fanatismo, intolerancia
big toe n dedo gordo (del pie)
big top n (circus) circo; (main tent) carpa
principal
big wheel n (at fair) noria
bigwig ['bɪgwɪg] n (col) pez m gordo
bike [baɪk] n bici f
bike lane n carril m de bicicleta, carril m bici
bikini [bɪ'kiːnɪ] n bikini m
bilateral [baɪ'lætərl] adj (agreement) bilateral
bile [baɪl] n bilis f
bilge [bɪldʒ] n (water) agua de sentina
bilingual [baɪ'lɪŋgwəl] adj bilingüe
bilious ['bɪlɪəs] adj bilioso (also fig)
bill [bɪl] n (gen) cuenta; (invoice) factura; (Pol)
proyecto de ley; (US: banknote) billete m; (of
bird) pico; (notice) cartel m; (Theat) programa
m ■ vt extender or pasar la factura a; **may**
I have the ~ please? ¿puede traerme la
cuenta, por favor?; **~ of exchange** letra
de cambio; **~ of lading** conocimiento de
embarque; **~ of sale** escritura de venta;
"post no bills" "prohibido fijar carteles"
billboard ['bɪlbɔːd] n valla publicitaria
billet ['bɪlɪt] n alojamiento ■ vt: **to ~ sb**
(on sb) alojar a algn (con algn)
billfold ['bɪlfəuld] n (US) cartera
billiards ['bɪljədz] n billar m

b

billion ['bɪljən] n (Brit) billón m; (US) mil millones mpl

billow ['bɪləu] n (of smoke) nube f; (of sail) ondulación f ■ vi (smoke) salir en nubes; (sail) ondear, ondular

billy ['bɪlɪ] n (US) porra

billy goat n macho cabrío

bimbo ['bɪmbəu] n (col) tía buena sin seso

bin [bɪn] n (gen) cubo or bote m (LAm) de la basura; **litterbin** n (Brit) papelera

binary ['baɪnərɪ] adj (Math) binario; ~ **code** código binario

bind (pt, pp **bound**) [baɪnd, baund] vt atar, liar; (wound) vendar; (book) encuadernar; (oblige) obligar

▶ **bind over** vt (Law) obligar por vía legal

▶ **bind up** vt (wound) vendar; **to be bound up in** (work, research etc) estar absorto en; **to be bound up with** (person) estar estrechamente ligado a

binder ['baɪndəʳ] n (file) archivador m

binding ['baɪndɪŋ] adj (contract) vinculante

binge [bɪndʒ] n borrachera, juerga; **to go on a ~** ir de juerga

bingo ['bɪŋgəu] n bingo m

bin-liner ['bɪnlaɪnəʳ] n bolsa de la basura

binoculars [bɪ'nɔkjuləz] npl prismáticos mpl, gemelos mpl

bio [baɪə'] adj (fam) biológico

biochemistry [baɪə'kɛmɪstrɪ] n bioquímica

biodegradable ['baɪəudɪ'greɪdəbl] adj biodegradable

biodiversity ['baɪəudaɪ'və:sɪtɪ] n biodiversidad f

biographer [baɪ'ɔgrəfəʳ] n biógrafo(-a)

biographical [baɪə'græfɪkəl] adj biográfico

biography [baɪ'ɔgrəfɪ] n biografía

biological [baɪə'lɔdʒɪkəl] adj biológico; (products, foodstuffs etc) orgánico(-a)

biological clock n reloj m biológico

biologist [baɪ'ɔlədʒɪst] n biólogo(-a)

biology [baɪ'ɔlədʒɪ] n biología

biophysics ['baɪəu'fɪzɪks] nsg biofísica

biopic ['baɪəupɪk] n filme m biográfico

biopsy ['baɪɔpsɪ] n biopsia

biosphere ['baɪəsfɪəʳ] n biosfera

biotechnology ['baɪəutɛk'nɔlədʒɪ] n biotecnología

bioterrorism ['baɪəu'tɛrərɪzəm] n bioterrorismo

biped ['baɪpɛd] n bípedo

birch [bə:tʃ] n abedul m; (cane) vara

bird [bə:d] n ave f, pájaro; (Brit col: girl) chica

birdcage ['bə:dkeɪdʒ] n jaula

bird flu n gripe aviar

bird of prey n ave f de presa

bird's-eye view ['bə:dzaɪ-] n vista de pájaro

bird watcher n ornitólogo(-a)

Biro® ['baɪrəu] n bolígrafo

birth [bə:θ] n nacimiento; (Med) parto; **to give ~ to** parir, dar a luz a; (fig) dar origen a

birth certificate n partida de nacimiento

birth control n control m de natalidad; (methods) métodos mpl anticonceptivos

birthday ['bə:θdeɪ] n cumpleaños m inv

birthday card n tarjeta de cumpleaños

birthplace ['bə:θpleɪs] n lugar m de nacimiento

birth rate n (tasa de) natalidad f

Biscay ['bɪskeɪ] n: **the Bay of ~** el Mar Cantábrico, el golfo de Vizcaya

biscuit ['bɪskɪt] n (Brit) galleta

bisect [baɪ'sɛkt] vt (also Math) bisecar

bisexual ['baɪ'sɛksjuəl] adj, n bisexual m/f

bishop ['bɪʃəp] n obispo; (Chess) alfil m

bistro ['bi:strəu] n café-bar m

bit [bɪt] pt of **bite** ■ n trozo, pedazo, pedacito; (Comput) bit m; (for horse) freno, bocado; **a ~ of** un poco de; **a ~ mad** algo loco; ~ **by** ~ poco a poco; **to come to bits** (break) hacerse pedazos; **to do one's** ~ aportar su granito de arena; **bring all your bits and pieces** trae todas tus cosas

bitch [bɪtʃ] n (dog) perra; (col!) zorra (!)

bite [baɪt] vt, vi (pt **bit**) [bɪt] (pp **bitten**) ['bɪtn] morder; (insect etc) picar ■ n (wound: of dog, snake etc) mordedura; (of insect) picadura; (mouthful) bocado; **to ~ one's nails** morderse las uñas; **let's have a ~ (to eat)** comamos algo

biting ['baɪtɪŋ] adj (wind) que traspasa los huesos; (criticism) mordaz

bit part n (Theat) papel m sin importancia, papelito

bitten ['bɪtn] pp of **bite**

bitter ['bɪtəʳ] adj amargo; (wind, criticism) cortante, penetrante; (icy: weather) glacial; (battle) encarnizado ■ n (Brit: beer) cerveza típica británica a base de lúpulos

bitterly ['bɪtəlɪ] adv (disappoint, complain, weep) desconsoladamente; (oppose, criticise) implacablemente; (jealous) agriamente; **it's ~ cold** hace un frío glacial

bitterness ['bɪtənɪs] n amargura; (anger) rencor m

bitty ['bɪtɪ] adj deshilvanado

bitumen ['bɪtjumɪn] n betún m

bivouac ['bɪvuæk] n vivac m, vivaque m

bizarre [bɪ'zɑ:ʳ] adj raro, estrafalario

bk abbr = **bank; book**

BL n abbr (= Bachelor of Law(s), Bachelor of Letters) título universitario; (US: = Bachelor of Literature) título universitario

B/L abbr = **bill of lading**

blab [blæb] vi cantar ▪ vt (also: **blab out**) soltar, contar

black [blæk] adj (colour) negro; (dark) oscuro ▪ n (colour) color m negro; (person): **B~** negro(a) ▪ vt (shoes) lustrar; (Brit Industry) boicotear; **to give sb a ~ eye** ponerle a algn el ojo morado; **~ coffee** café m solo; **there it is in ~ and white** (fig) ahí está bien claro; **to be in the ~** (in credit) tener saldo positivo; **~ and blue** adj amoratado
▸ **black out** vi (faint) desmayarse

black belt n (Sport) cinturón m negro; (US: area) zona negra

blackberry ['blækbərɪ] n zarzamora

blackbird ['blækbə:d] n mirlo

blackboard ['blækbɔ:d] n pizarra

black box n (Aviat) caja negra

Black Country n (Brit): **the ~** región industrial del centro de Inglaterra

blackcurrant ['blæk'kʌrənt] n grosella negra

black economy n economía sumergida

blacken ['blækən] vt ennegrecer; (fig) denigrar

Black Forest n: **the ~** la Selva Negra

blackguard ['blægɑ:d] n canalla m, pillo

black hole n (Astro) agujero negro

black ice n hielo invisible en la carretera

blackjack ['blækdʒæk] n (US) veintiuna

blackleg ['blækleg] n (Brit) esquirol m/f

blacklist ['blæklɪst] n lista negra ▪ vt poner en la lista negra

blackmail ['blækmeɪl] n chantaje m ▪ vt chantajear

blackmailer ['blækmeɪlə'] n chantajista m/f

black market n mercado negro, estraperlo

blackness ['blæknɪs] n negrura

blackout ['blækaut] n (TV, Elec) apagón m; (fainting) desmayo, pérdida de conocimiento

Black Sea n: **the ~** el Mar Negro

black sheep n oveja negra

blacksmith ['blæksmɪθ] n herrero

black spot n (Aut) punto negro

bladder ['blædə'] n vejiga

blade [bleɪd] n hoja; (cutting edge) filo; **a ~ of grass** una brizna de hierba

Blairite ['bleərait] n, adj blairista m/f

blame [bleɪm] n culpa ▪ vt: **to ~ sb for sth** echar a algn la culpa de algo; **to be to ~ (for)** tener la culpa (de); **I'm not to ~** yo no tengo la culpa; **and I don't ~ him** y lo comprendo perfectamente

blameless ['bleɪmlɪs] adj (person) inocente

blanch [blɑ:ntʃ] vi (person) palidecer; (Culin) escaldar

bland [blænd] adj suave; (taste) soso

blank [blæŋk] adj en blanco; (shot) de fogueo; (look) sin expresión ▪ n blanco, espacio en blanco; cartucho de fogueo; **to draw a ~** (fig) no conseguir nada

blank cheque, blank check (US) n cheque m en blanco

blanket ['blæŋkɪt] n manta, frazada (LAm), cobija (LAm) ▪ adj (statement, agreement) comprensivo, general; **to give ~ cover** (insurance policy) dar póliza a todo riesgo

blankly ['blæŋklɪ] adv: **she looked at me ~** me miró sin comprender

blare [bleə'] vi (brass band, horns, radio) resonar

blasé ['blɑ:zeɪ] adj de vuelta de todo

blaspheme [blæs'fi:m] vi blasfemar

blasphemous ['blæsfɪməs] adj blasfemo

blasphemy ['blæsfɪmɪ] n blasfemia

blast [blɑ:st] n (of wind) ráfaga, soplo; (of whistle) toque m; (of explosive) carga explosiva; (force) choque m ▪ vt (blow up) volar; (blow open) abrir con carga explosiva ▪ excl (Brit col) ¡maldito sea!; (at) **full ~** (also fig) a toda marcha
▸ **blast off** vi (spacecraft etc) despegar

blast furnace n alto horno

blast-off ['blɑ:stɔf] n (Space) lanzamiento

blatant ['bleɪtənt] adj descarado

blatantly ['bleɪtəntlɪ] adv: **it's ~ obvious** está clarísimo

blather ['blæðə'] vi decir tonterías

blaze [bleɪz] n (fire) fuego; (flames) llamarada; (glow: of fire, sun etc) resplandor m; (fig) arranque m ▪ vi (fire) arder con llamaradas; (fig) brillar ▪ vt: **to ~ a trail** (fig) abrir (un) camino; **in a ~ of publicity** bajo los focos de la publicidad

blazer ['bleɪzə'] n chaqueta de uniforme de colegial o de socio de club

bleach [bli:tʃ] n (also: **household bleach**) lejía ▪ vt (linen) blanquear

bleached [bli:tʃt] adj (hair) de colorado; (clothes) blanqueado

bleachers ['bli:tʃəz] npl (US Sport) gradas fpl

bleak [bli:k] adj (countryside) desierto; (landscape) desolado, desierto; (weather) desapacible; (smile) triste; (prospect, future) poco prometedor(a)

bleary-eyed ['blɪərɪ'aɪd] adj: **to be ~** tener ojos de cansado

bleat [bli:t] vi balar

bleed (pt, pp **bled**) [bli:d, bled] vt sangrar; (brakes, radiator) desaguar ▪ vi sangrar

bleeding ['bli:dɪŋ] adj sangrante

bleep [bli:p] n pitido ▪ vi pitar ▪ vt llamar por el busca

bleeper ['bli:pə'] n (of doctor etc) busca m

blemish ['blemɪʃ] n mancha, tacha

blench [blentʃ] vi (shrink back) acobardarse; (grow pale) palidecer

447

blend [blɛnd] n mezcla ▪ vt mezclar ▪ vi (colours etc) combinarse, mezclarse
blender ['blɛndə'] n (Culin) batidora
bless (pt, pp **blessed** or **blest**) [blɛs, blɛst] vt bendecir
blessed ['blɛsɪd] adj (Rel: holy) santo, bendito; (: happy) dichoso; **every ~ day** cada santo día
blessing ['blɛsɪŋ] n bendición f; (advantage) beneficio, ventaja; **to count one's blessings** agradecer lo que se tiene; **it was a ~ in disguise** no hay mal que por bien no venga
blew [blu:] pt of **blow**
blight [blaɪt] vt (hopes etc) frustrar, arruinar
blimey ['blaɪmɪ] excl (Brit col) ¡caray!
blind [blaɪnd] adj ciego ▪ n (for window) persiana ▪ vt cegar; (dazzle) deslumbrar
blind alley n callejón m sin salida
blind corner n (Brit) esquina or curva sin visibilidad
blind date n cita a ciegas
blinders ['blaɪndəz] npl (US) anteojeras fpl
blindfold ['blaɪndfəuld] n venda ▪ adj, adv con los ojos vendados ▪ vt vendar los ojos a
blinding ['blaɪndɪŋ] adj (flash, light) cegador; (pain) intenso
blindingly ['blaɪndɪŋlɪ] adv: **it's ~ obvious** salta a la vista
blindly ['blaɪndlɪ] adv a ciegas, ciegamente
blindness ['blaɪndnɪs] n ceguera
blind spot n (Aut) ángulo muerto; **to have a ~ about sth** estar ciego para algo
blink [blɪŋk] vi parpadear, pestañear; (light) oscilar; **to be on the ~** (col) estar estropeado
blinkers ['blɪŋkəz] npl (esp Brit) anteojeras fpl
blinking ['blɪŋkɪŋ] adj (col): **this ~ ...** este condenado ...
blip [blɪp] n señal f luminosa; (on graph) pequeña desviación f; (fig) pequeña anomalía
bliss [blɪs] n felicidad f
blissful ['blɪsful] adj dichoso; **in ~ ignorance** feliz en la ignorancia
blissfully ['blɪsfulɪ] adv (sigh, smile) con felicidad; **~ happy** sumamente feliz
blister ['blɪstə'] n ampolla ▪ vi ampollarse
blistering ['blɪstərɪŋ] adj (heat) abrasador(a)
BLit, BLitt n abbr (= Bachelor of Literature) título universitario
blithely ['blaɪðlɪ] adv alegremente, despreocupadamente
blithering ['blɪðərɪŋ] adj (col): **this ~ idiot** este tonto perdido
blitz [blɪts] n bombardeo aéreo; **to have a ~ on sth** (fig) emprenderla con algo
blizzard ['blɪzəd] n ventisca

BLM n abbr (US) = **Bureau of Land Management**
bloated ['bləutɪd] adj hinchado
blob [blɔb] n (drop) gota; (stain, spot) mancha
bloc [blɔk] n (Pol) bloque m
block [blɔk] n bloque m (also Comput); (in pipes) obstáculo; (of buildings) manzana ▪ vt (gen) obstruir, cerrar; (progress) estorbar; (Comput) agrupar; **~ of flats** (Brit) bloque m de pisos; **mental ~** amnesia temporal; **~ and tackle** (Tech) aparejo de polea; **3 blocks from here** a 3 manzanas or cuadras (LAm) de aquí
▶ **block up** vt tapar, obstruir; (pipe) atascar
blockade [blɔ'keɪd] n bloqueo ▪ vt bloquear
blockage ['blɔkɪdʒ] n estorbo, obstrucción f
block booking n reserva en grupo
blockbuster ['blɔkbʌstə'] n (book) best-seller m; (film) éxito de público
block capitals npl mayúsculas fpl
block letters npl letras fpl de molde
block release n (Brit) exención f por estudios
block vote n (Brit) voto por delegación
blog [blɔg] n (Comput) blog m ▪ vi bloguear
blogger ['blɔgə'] n (col: person) blogger mf
blogging ['blɔgɪŋ] n blogging m
bloke [bləuk] n (Brit col) tipo, tío
blond, blonde [blɔnd] adj, n rubio(-a) m(f)
blood [blʌd] n sangre f; **new ~** (fig) gente f nueva
blood bank n banco de sangre
blood count n recuento de glóbulos rojos y blancos
blood donor n donante m/f de sangre
blood group n grupo sanguíneo
bloodhound ['blʌdhaund] n sabueso
bloodless ['blʌdlɪs] adj (pale) exangüe; (revolt etc) sin derramamiento de sangre, incruento
bloodletting ['blʌdlɛtɪŋ] n (Med) sangría; (fig) sangría, carnicería
blood poisoning n septicemia de la sangre
blood pressure n tensión f sanguínea; **to have high/low ~** tener la tensión alta/baja
bloodshed ['blʌdʃɛd] n baño de sangre
bloodshot ['blʌdʃɔt] adj inyectado en sangre
bloodstained ['blʌdsteɪnd] adj manchado de sangre
bloodstream ['blʌdstri:m] n corriente f sanguínea
blood test n análisis m de sangre
bloodthirsty ['blʌdθə:stɪ] adj sanguinario
blood transfusion n transfusión f de sangre
blood type n grupo sanguíneo
blood vessel n vaso sanguíneo
bloody ['blʌdɪ] adj sangriento; (Brit col!): **this ~ ...** este condenado or puñetero or fregado (LAm ...) (!) ▪ adv (Brit col!): **~ strong/good** terriblemente fuerte/bueno

bloody-minded ['blʌdɪ'maɪndɪd] *adj* (*Brit col*) con malas pulgas

bloom [blu:m] *n* floración *f*; **in ~** en flor ■ *vi* florecer

blooming ['blu:mɪŋ] *adj* (*col*): **this ~ ...** este condenado ...

blossom ['blɔsəm] *n* flor *f* ■ *vi* florecer; (*fig*) desarrollarse; **to ~ into** (*fig*) convertirse en

blot [blɔt] *n* borrón *m* ■ *vt* (*dry*) secar; (*stain*) manchar; **to ~ out** *vt* (*view*) tapar; (*memories*) borrar; **to be a ~ on the landscape** estropear el paisaje; **to ~ one's copy book** (*fig*) manchar su reputación

blotchy ['blɔtʃɪ] *adj* (*complexion*) lleno de manchas

blotter ['blɔtər] *n* secante *m*

blotting paper ['blɔtɪŋ-] *n* papel *m* secante

blotto ['blɔtəu] *adj* (*col*) mamado

blouse [blauz] *n* blusa

blow [bləu] (*pt* **blew**, *pp* **blown**) *n* golpe *m* ■ *vi* soplar; (*fuse*) fundirse ■ *vt* (*glass*) soplar; (*fuse*) quemar; (*instrument*) tocar; **to come to blows** llegar a golpes; **to ~ one's nose** sonarse

▶ **blow away** *vt* llevarse, arrancar

▶ **blow down** *vt* derribar

▶ **blow off** *vt* arrebatar

▶ **blow out** *vt* apagar ■ *vi* apagarse; (*tyre*) reventar

▶ **blow over** *vi* amainar

▶ **blow up** *vi* estallar ■ *vt* volar; (*tyre*) inflar; (*Phot*) ampliar

blow-dry ['bləudraɪ] *n* secado con secador de mano ■ *vt* secar con secador de mano

blowlamp ['bləulæmp] *n* (*Brit*) soplete *m*, lámpara de soldar

blown [bləun] *pp of* **blow**

blow-out ['bləuaut] *n* (*of tyre*) pinchazo; (*col: big meal*) banquete *m*, festín *m*

blowtorch ['bləutɔ:tʃ] *n* = **blowlamp**

blow-up ['bləuʌp] *n* (*Phot*) ampliación *f*

BLS *n abbr* (*US*) = **Bureau of Labor Statistics**

blubber ['blʌbə'] *n* grasa de ballena ■ *vi* (*pej*) lloriquear

bludgeon ['blʌdʒən] *vt*: **to ~ sb into doing sth** coaccionar a algn a hacer algo

blue [blu:] *adj* azul; **~ film** película porno; **~ joke** chiste verde; **once in a ~ moon** de higos a brevas; **to come out of the ~** (*fig*) ser completamente inesperado; *see also* **blues**

blue baby *n* niño azul *or* cianótico

bluebell ['blu:bɛl] *n* campanilla, campánula azul

blue-blooded [blu:'blʌdɪd] *adj* de sangre azul

bluebottle ['blu:bɔtl] *n* moscarda, mosca azul

blue cheese *n* queso azul

blue-chip ['blu:tʃɪp] *n*: **~ investment** inversión *f* asegurada

blue-collar worker ['blu:kɔlər-] *n* obrero(-a)

blue jeans *npl* tejanos *mpl*, vaqueros *mpl*

blueprint ['blu:prɪnt] *n* proyecto; **~ (for)** (*fig*) anteproyecto (de)

blues [blu:z] *npl*: **the ~** (*Mus*) el blues; **to have the ~** estar triste

Bluetooth® ['blu:tu:θ] *n* Bluetooth® *f*; **~ technology®** tecnología Bluetooth®

bluff [blʌf] *vi* tirarse un farol, farolear ■ *n* bluff *m*, farol *m*; (*Geo*) precipicio, despeñadero; **to call sb's ~** coger a algn en un renuncio

bluish ['blu:ɪʃ] *adj* azulado

blunder ['blʌndər] *n* patinazo, metedura de pata ■ *vi* cometer un error, meter la pata; **to ~ into sb/sth** tropezar con algn/algo

blunt [blʌnt] *adj* (*knife*) desafilado; (*person*) franco, directo ■ *vt* embotar, desafilar; **this pencil is ~** este lápiz está despuntado; **~ instrument** (*Law*) instrumento contundente

bluntly ['blʌntlɪ] *adv* (*speak*) francamente, de modo terminante

bluntness ['blʌntnɪs] *n* (*of person*) franqueza, brusquedad *f*

blur [blə:'] *n* aspecto borroso ■ *vt* (*vision*) enturbiar; (*memory*) empañar

blurb [blə:b] *n* propaganda

blurred [blə:d] *adj* borroso

blurt [blə:t]: **to ~ out** *vt* (*say*) descolgarse con, dejar escapar

blush [blʌʃ] *vi* ruborizarse, ponerse colorado ■ *n* rubor *m*

blusher ['blʌʃər] *n* colorete *m*

bluster ['blʌstər] *n* fanfarronada, bravata ■ *vi* fanfarronear, echar bravatas

blustering ['blʌstərɪŋ] *adj* (*person*) fanfarrón(-ona)

blustery ['blʌstərɪ] *adj* (*weather*) tempestuoso, tormentoso

Blvd *abbr* = **boulevard**

BM *n abbr* (= *British Museum*; *Univ*: = *Bachelor of Medicine*) título universitario

BMA *n abbr* = **British Medical Association**

BMJ *n abbr* = **British Medical Journal**

BMus *n abbr* (= *Bachelor of Music*) título universitario

BMX *n abbr* (= *bicycle motocross*) BMX *f*; **~ bike** bici(cleta) *f* BMX

bn *abbr* = **billion**

BO *n abbr* (*col*: = *body odour*) olor *m* a sudor; (*US*) = **box office**

boa ['bəuə] *n* boa

boar [bɔ:'] *n* verraco, cerdo

board [bɔ:d] *n* tabla, tablero; (*on wall*) tablón

m; (*for chess etc*) tablero; (*committee*) junta, consejo; (*in firm*) mesa *or* junta directiva; (*Naut, Aviat*): **on ~** a bordo ■ *vt* (*ship*) embarcarse en; (*train*) subir a; **full ~** (*Brit*) pensión *f* completa; **half ~** (*Brit*) media pensión; **~ and lodging** alojamiento y comida; **to go by the ~** (*fig*) irse por la borda; **above ~** (*fig*) sin tapujos; **across the ~** (*fig: adv*) en todos los niveles; (*: adj*) general
▶ **board up** *vt* (*door*) tapar, cegar
boarder ['bɔːdə^r] *n* huésped(a) *m(f)*; (*Scol*) interno(-a)
board game *n* juego de tablero
boarding card ['bɔːdɪŋ-] *n* (*Brit: Aviat, Naut*) tarjeta de embarque
boarding house ['bɔːdɪŋ-] *n* casa de huéspedes
boarding party ['bɔːdɪŋ-] *n* brigada de inspección
boarding pass ['bɔːdɪŋ-] *n* (*US*) = **boarding card**
boarding school ['bɔːdɪŋ-] *n* internado
board meeting *n* reunión *f* de la junta directiva
board room *n* sala de juntas
boardwalk ['bɔːdwɔːk] *n* (*US*) paseo entablado
boast [bəust] *vi*: **to ~ (about *or* of)** alardear (de) ■ *vt* ostentar ■ *n* alarde *m*, baladronada
boastful ['bəustfəl] *adj* presumido
boastfulness ['bəustfulnɪs] *n* fanfarronería, jactancia
boat [bəut] *n* barco, buque *m*; (*small*) barca, bote *m*; **to go by ~** ir en barco
boater ['bəutə^r] *n* (*hat*) canotié *m*
boating ['bəutɪŋ] *n* canotaje *m*
boatman ['bəutmən] *n* barquero
boat people *npl* *refugiados que huyen en barca*
boatswain ['bəusn] *n* contramaestre *m*
bob [bɔb] *vi* (*boat, cork on water: also:* **bob up and down**) menearse, balancearse ■ *n* (*Brit col*) = **shilling**
▶ **bob up** *vi* (re)aparecer de repente
bobbin ['bɔbɪn] *n* (*of sewing machine*) carrete *m*, bobina
bobby ['bɔbɪ] *n* (*Brit col*) poli *m/f*
bobsleigh ['bɔbsleɪ] *n* bob *m*, trineo de competición *f*
bode [bəud] *vi*: **to ~ well/ill (for)** ser de buen/mal agüero (para)
bodice ['bɔdɪs] *n* corpiño
-bodied ['bɔdɪd] *adj suff* de cuerpo ...
bodily ['bɔdɪlɪ] *adj* (*comfort, needs*) corporal; (*pain*) corpóreo ■ *adv* (*in person*) en persona; (*carry*) corporalmente; (*lift*) en peso
body ['bɔdɪ] *n* cuerpo; (*corpse*) cadáver *m*;

(*of car*) caja, carrocería; (*also:* **body stocking**) body *m*; (*fig: organization*) organización *f*; (*: public body*) organismo; (*: quantity*) masa; (*: of speech, document*) parte *f* principal; **ruling ~** directiva; **in a ~** todos juntos, en masa
body blow *n* (*fig*) palo
body-building ['bɔdɪ'bɪldɪŋ] *n* culturismo
bodyguard ['bɔdɪgɑːd] *n* guardaespaldas *m inv*
body language *n* lenguaje *m* gestual
body search *n* cacheo; **to carry out a ~ on sb** registrar a algn; **to submit to *or* undergo a ~** ser registrado
bodywork ['bɔdɪwəːk] *n* carrocería
boffin ['bɔfɪn] *n* (*Brit*) científico(-a)
bog [bɔg] *n* pantano, ciénaga ■ *vt*: **to get bogged down** (*fig*) empantanarse, atascarse
boggle ['bɔgl] *vi*: **the mind boggles!** ¡no puedo creerlo!
Bogotá [bəugə'tɑː] *n* Bogotá
bogus ['bəugəs] *adj* falso, fraudulento; (*person*) fingido
Bohemia [bə'hiːmɪə] *n* Bohemia
Bohemian [bə'hiːmɪən] *adj, n* bohemio(-a) *m(f)*
boil [bɔɪl] *vt* cocer; (*eggs*) pasar por agua ■ *vi* hervir ■ *n* (*Med*) furúnculo, divieso; **to bring to the ~** calentar hasta que hierva; **to come to the** (*Brit*) *or* **a** (*US*) **~** comenzar a hervir; **boiled egg** huevo pasado por agua; **boiled potatoes** patatas *fpl or* papas *fpl* (*LAm*) cocidas
▶ **boil down** *vi* (*fig*): **to ~ down to** reducirse a
▶ **boil over** *vi* (*liquid*) rebosar; (*anger, resentment*) llegar al colmo
boiler ['bɔɪlə^r] *n* caldera
boiler suit *n* (*Brit*) mono, overol *m* (*LAm*)
boiling ['bɔɪlɪŋ] *adj*: **I'm ~ (hot)** (*col*) estoy asado
boiling point *n* punto de ebullición *f*
boil-in-the-bag [bɔɪlɪnðə'bæg] *adj*: **~ meals** platos que se cuecen en su misma bolsa
boisterous ['bɔɪstərəs] *adj* (*noisy*) bullicioso; (*excitable*) exuberante; (*crowd*) tumultuoso
bold [bəuld] *adj* (*brave*) valiente, audaz; (*pej*) descarado; (*outline*) grueso; (*colour*) vivo; **~ type** (*Typ*) negrita
boldly ['bəuldlɪ] *adv* audazmente
boldness ['bəuldnɪs] *n* valor *m*, audacia; (*cheek*) descaro
Bolivia [bə'lɪvɪə] *n* Bolivia
Bolivian [bə'lɪvɪən] *adj, n* boliviano(-a) *m(f)*
bollard ['bɔləd] *n* (*Brit Aut*) poste *m*
Bollywood ['bɔlɪwud] *n* Bollywood *m*
bolshy ['bɔlʃɪ] *adj* (*Brit col*) protestón(-ona); **to be in a ~ mood** tener el día protestón
bolster ['bəulstə^r] *n* travesero, cabezal *m*

▶ **bolster up** vt reforzar; (fig) alentar

bolt [bəult] n (lock) cerrojo; (with nut) perno, tornillo ■ adv: ~ **upright** rígido, erguido ■ vt (door) echar el cerrojo a; (food) engullir ■ vi fugarse; (horse) desbocarse

bomb [bɔm] n bomba ■ vt bombardear

bombard [bɔm'bɑːd] vt bombardear; (fig) asediar

bombardment [bɔm'bɑːdmənt] n bombardeo

bombastic [bɔm'bæstɪk] adj rimbombante; (person) pomposo

bomb disposal n desactivación f de explosivos

bomb disposal expert n artificiero(-a)

bomber ['bɔmər] n (Aviat) bombardero; (terrorist) persona que pone bombas

bombing ['bɔmɪŋ] n bombardeo

bomb scare n amenaza de bomba

bombshell ['bɔmʃɛl] n obús m, granada; (fig) bomba

bomb site n lugar m donde estalló una bomba

bona fide ['bəunə'faɪdɪ] adj genuino, auténtico

bonanza [bə'nænzə] n bonanza

bond [bɔnd] n (binding promise) fianza; (Finance) bono; (link) vínculo, lazo; **in ~** (Comm) en depósito bajo fianza

bondage ['bɔndɪdʒ] n esclavitud f

bonded goods ['bɔndɪd-] npl mercancías fpl en depósito de aduanas

bonded warehouse ['bɔndɪd-] n depósito de aduanas

bone [bəun] n hueso; (of fish) espina ■ vt deshuesar; quitar las espinas a; **~ of contention** manzana de la discordia

bone china n porcelana fina

bone-dry ['bəun'draɪ] adj completamente seco

bone idle adj gandul

bone marrow n médula; **~ transplant** transplante m de médula

boner ['bəunər] n (US col) plancha, patochada

bonfire ['bɔnfaɪər] n hoguera, fogata

bonk [bɔŋk] vt, vi (humorous, col) chingar (!)

bonkers ['bɔŋkəz] adj (Brit col) majareta

Bonn [bɔn] n Bonn m

bonnet ['bɔnɪt] n gorra; (Brit: of car) capó m

bonny ['bɔnɪ] adj (esp Scottish) bonito, hermoso, lindo

bonus ['bəunəs] n (at Christmas etc) paga extraordinaria; (merit award) sobrepaga, prima

bony ['bəunɪ] adj (arm, face) huesudo; (Med: tissue) huesudo; (meat) lleno de huesos; (fish) lleno de espinas; (thin: person) flaco, delgado

boo [buː] vt abuchear

boob [buːb] n (col: mistake) disparate m, sandez f; (: breast) teta

booby prize ['buːbɪ-] n premio de consolación (al último)

booby trap ['buːbɪ-] n (Mil etc) trampa explosiva

book [buk] n libro; (notebook) libreta; (of stamps etc) librillo; **books** (Comm) cuentas fpl, contabilidad f ■ vt (ticket, seat, room) reservar; (driver) fichar; (Football) amonestar; **to keep the books** llevar las cuentas or los libros; **by the ~** según las reglas; **to throw the ~ at sb** echar un rapapolvo a algn

▶ **book in** vi (at hotel) registrarse

▶ **book up** vt: **all seats are booked up** todas las plazas están reservadas; **the hotel is booked up** el hotel está lleno

bookable ['bukəbl] adj: **seats are ~** los asientos se pueden reservar (de antemano)

bookcase ['bukkeɪs] n librería, estante m para libros

booking office ['bukɪŋ-] n (Brit: Rail) despacho de billetes or boletos (LAm); (: Theat) taquilla, boletería (LAm)

book-keeping ['buk'kiːpɪŋ] n contabilidad f

booklet ['buklɪt] n folleto

bookmaker ['bukmeɪkər] n corredor m de apuestas

bookmark ['bukmɑːk] n (Comput) favorito m

bookseller ['buksɛlər] n librero(-a)

bookshelf ['bukʃɛlf] n estante m

bookshop ['bukʃɔp] n librería

bookstall ['bukstɔːl] n quiosco de libros

book store n = **bookshop**

book token n vale m para libros

book value n (Comm) valor m contable

bookworm ['bukwəːm] n (fig) ratón m de biblioteca

boom [buːm] n (noise) trueno, estampido; (in prices etc) alza rápida; (Econ) boom m, auge m ■ vi (cannon) hacer gran estruendo, retumbar; (Econ) estar en alza

boomerang ['buːməræŋ] n bumerang m (also fig) ■ vi: **to ~ on sb** (fig) ser contraproducente para algn

boom town n ciudad f de crecimiento rápido

boon [buːn] n favor m, beneficio

boorish ['buərɪʃ] adj grosero

boost [buːst] n estímulo, empuje m ■ vt estimular, empujar; (increase: sales, production) aumentar; **to give a ~ to** (morale) levantar; **it gave a ~ to his confidence** le dio confianza en sí mismo

booster ['buːstər] n (Med) reinyección f; (TV) repetidor m; (Elec) elevador m de tensión; (also: **booster rocket**) cohete m

b

451

boot [buːt] n bota; (ankle boot) botín m, borceguí m; (Brit: of car) maleta, maletero, baúl m (LAm) ■ vt dar un puntapié a; (Comput) arrancar; **to ~** (in addition) además, por añadidura; **to give sb the ~** (col) despedir a algn, poner a algn en la calle

booth [buːð] n (at fair) barraca; (telephone booth, voting booth) cabina

bootleg ['buːtleg] adj de contrabando; **~ record** disco pirata

booty ['buːtɪ] n botín m

booze [buːz] (col) n bebida ■ vi emborracharse

boozer ['buːzəʳ] n (col: person) bebedor(a) m(f); (: Brit: pub) bar m

border ['bɔːdəʳ] n borde m, margen m; (of a country) frontera ■ adj fronterizo; **the Borders** región fronteriza entre Escocia e Inglaterra
▶ **border on** vt fus lindar con; (fig) rayar en

borderline ['bɔːdəlaɪn] n (fig) frontera

bore [bɔːʳ] pt of **bear** ■ vt (hole) taladrar; (person) aburrir ■ n (person) pelmazo, pesado; (of gun) calibre m

bored [bɔːd] adj aburrido; **he's ~ to tears** or **to death** or **stiff** está aburrido como una ostra, está muerto de aburrimiento

boredom ['bɔːdəm] n aburrimiento

boring ['bɔːrɪŋ] adj aburrido, pesado

born [bɔːn] adj: **to be ~** nacer; **I was ~ in 1960** nací en 1960

born-again [bɔːnə'gɛn] adj: **~ Christian** evangelista m/f

borne [bɔːn] pp of **bear**

Borneo ['bɔːnɪəu] n Borneo

borough ['bʌrə] n municipio

borrow ['bɔrəu] vt: **to ~ sth (from sb)** tomar algo prestado (a alguien); **may I ~ your car?** ¿me prestas tu coche?

borrower ['bɔrəuəʳ] n prestatario(-a)

borrowing ['bɔrəuɪŋ] n préstamos mpl

borstal ['bɔːstl] n (Brit) reformatorio (de menores)

Bosnia ['bɔznɪə] n Bosnia

Bosnia-Herzegovina, Bosnia-Herzegovina ['bɔznɪəhɛrzə'gəuviːnə] n Bosnia-Herzegovina

Bosnian ['bɔznɪən] adj, n bosnio(-a)

bosom ['buzəm] n pecho; (fig) seno

bosom friend n amigo(-a) íntimo(-a) or del alma

boss [bɔs] n jefe(-a) m(f); (employer) patrón(-ona) m(f); (political etc) cacique m ■ vt (also: **boss about** or **around**) mangonear; **stop bossing everyone about!** ¡deja de dar órdenes or de mangonear a todos!

bossy ['bɔsɪ] adj mandón(-ona)

bosun ['bəusn] n contramaestre m

botanical [bə'tænɪkl] adj botánico

botanist ['bɔtənɪst] n botanista m/f

botany ['bɔtənɪ] n botánica

botch [bɔtʃ] vt (also: **botch up**) arruinar, estropear

both [bəuθ] adj, pron ambos(-as), los/las dos; **~ of us went, we ~ went** fuimos los dos, ambos fuimos ■ adv: **~ A and B** tanto A como B

bother ['bɔðəʳ] vt (worry) preocupar; (disturb) molestar, fastidiar, fregar (LAm), embromar (LAm) ■ vi (gen): **~ o.s.** molestarse ■ n: **what a ~!** ¡qué lata! ■ excl ¡maldita sea!, ¡caramba!; **I'm sorry to ~ you** perdona que te moleste; **to ~ doing** tomarse la molestia de hacer; **please don't ~** no te molestes

Botswana [bɔt'swɑːnə] n Botswana

bottle ['bɔtl] n botella; (small) frasco; (baby's) biberón m ■ vt embotellar; **~ of wine/milk** botella de vino/de leche; **wine/milk ~** botella de vino/de leche
▶ **bottle up** vt (fig) contener, reprimir

bottle bank n contenedor m de vidrio, iglú m

bottleneck ['bɔtlnɛk] n embotellamiento

bottle-opener ['bɔtləupnəʳ] n abrebotellas m inv

bottom ['bɔtəm] n (of box, sea) fondo; (buttocks) trasero, culo; (of page, mountain, tree) pie m; (of list) final m ■ adj (lowest) más bajo; (last) último; **to get to the ~ of sth** (fig) llegar al fondo de algo

bottomless ['bɔtəmlɪs] adj sin fondo, insondable

bottom line n: **the ~** lo fundamental; **the ~ is he has to go** el caso es que tenemos que despedirle

botulism ['bɔtjulɪzəm] n botulismo

bough [bau] n rama

bought [bɔːt] pt, pp of **buy**

bouillon cube ['buːjɔn-] n (US) cubito de caldo

boulder ['bəuldəʳ] n canto rodado

bounce [bauns] vi (ball) (re)botar; (cheque) ser rechazado ■ vt hacer (re)botar ■ n (rebound) (re)bote m; **he's got plenty of ~** (fig) tiene mucha energía

bouncer ['baunsəʳ] n (col) forzudo, gorila m

bouncy castle® ['baunsɪ-] n castillo inflable

bound [baund] pt, pp of **bind** ■ n (leap) salto; (gen pl: limit) límite m ■ vi (leap) saltar ■ adj: **~ by** rodeado de; **to be ~ to do sth** (obliged) tener el deber de hacer algo; **he's ~ to come** es seguro que vendrá; **"out of bounds to the public"** "prohibido el paso"; **~ for** con destino a

boundary ['baundrɪ] n límite m, lindero

boundless ['baundlɪs] adj ilimitado

bountiful ['bauntɪful] adj (person) liberal,

generoso; (*God*) bondadoso; (*supply*) abundante

bounty ['bauntɪ] *n* (*generosity*) generosidad *f*; (*reward*) prima

bounty hunter *n* cazarrecompensas *m inv*

bouquet ['bukeɪ] *n* (*of flowers*) ramo, ramillete *m*; (*of wine*) aroma *m*

bourbon ['buəbən] *n* (*US: also:* **bourbon whiskey**) whisky *m* americano, bourbon *m*

bourgeois ['buəʒwa:] *adj, n* burgués(-esa) *m(f)*

bout [baut] *n* (*of malaria etc*) ataque *m*; (*Boxing etc*) combate *m*, encuentro

boutique [bu:'ti:k] *n* boutique *f*, tienda de ropa

bow [bəu] *n* (*knot*) lazo; (*weapon*) arco; (*Mus*) arco [bau] (*of the head*) reverencia; (*Naut: also:* **bows**) proa ■ *vi* [bau] inclinarse, hacer una reverencia, (*yield*): **to ~ to** *or* **before** ceder ante, someterse a; **to ~ to the inevitable** resignarse a lo inevitable

bowels ['bauəlz] *npl* intestinos *mpl*, vientre *m*

bowl [bəul] *n* tazón *m*, cuenco; (*for washing*) palangana, jofaina; (*ball*) bola; (*US: stadium*) estadio ■ *vi* (*Cricket*) arrojar la pelota; *see also* **bowls**

bow-legged ['bəu'legɪd] *adj* estevado

bowler ['bəulə'] *n* (*Cricket*) lanzador *m* (de la pelota); (*Brit: also:* **bowler hat**) hongo, bombín *m*

bowling ['bəulɪŋ] *n* (*game*) bolos *mpl*, bochas *fpl*

bowling alley *n* bolera

bowling green *n* pista para bochas

bowls [bəulz] *n* juego de los bolos, bochas *fpl*

bow tie ['bəu-] *n* corbata de lazo, pajarita

box [bɔks] *n* (*also:* **cardboard box**) caja, cajón *m*; (*for jewels*) estuche *m*; (*for money*) cofre *m*; (*crate*) cofre *m*, arca; (*Theat*) palco ■ *vt* encajonar ■ *vi* (*Sport*) boxear

boxer ['bɔksə'] *n* (*person*) boxeador *m*; (*dog*) bóxer *m*

box file *n* fichero

boxing ['bɔksɪŋ] *n* (*Sport*) boxeo, box *m* (*LAm*)

Boxing Day *n* (*Brit*) día *m* de San Esteban; *ver nota*

● **BOXING DAY**
●
● El día después de Navidad es *Boxing Day*,
● fiesta en todo el Reino Unido, aunque
● si el 26 de diciembre cae en domingo el
● día de descanso se traslada al lunes. En
● dicho día solía ser tradición entregar
● "Christmas boxes" (aguinaldos) a
● empleados, proveedores a domicilio,
● carteros etc.

boxing gloves *npl* guantes *mpl* de boxeo

boxing ring *n* ring *m*, cuadrilátero

box number *n* (*for advertisements*) apartado

box office *n* taquilla, boletería (*LAm*)

boxroom ['bɔksrum] *n* trastero

boy [bɔɪ] *n* (*young*) niño; (*older*) muchacho

boycott ['bɔɪkɔt] *n* boicot *m* ■ *vt* boicotear

boyfriend ['bɔɪfrend] *n* novio

boyish ['bɔɪɪʃ] *adj* de muchacho, inmaduro

boy scout *n* boy scout *m*

bp *abbr* = **bishop**

Br. *abbr* (*Rel*) = **brother**

bra [bra:] *n* sostén *m*, sujetador *m*, corpiño (*LAm*)

brace [breɪs] *n* refuerzo, abrazadera; (*Brit: on teeth*) corrector *m*; (*tool*) berbiquí *m* ■ *vt* asegurar, reforzar; **to ~ o.s. (for)** (*fig*) prepararse (para); *see also* **braces**

bracelet ['breɪslɪt] *n* pulsera, brazalete *m*, pulso (*LAm*)

braces ['breɪsɪz] *npl* (*Brit*) tirantes *mpl*, suspensores *mpl* (*LAm*); (*US: on teeth*) corrector *m*

bracing ['breɪsɪŋ] *adj* vigorizante, tónico

bracken ['brækən] *n* helecho

bracket ['brækɪt] *n* (*Tech*) soporte *m*, puntal *m*; (*group*) clase *f*, categoría; (*also:* **brace bracket**) soporte *m*, abrazadera; (*also:* **round bracket**) paréntesis *m inv*; (*gen*): **square ~** corchete *m* ■ *vt* (*fig: also:* **bracket together**) agrupar; **income ~** nivel *m* económico; **in brackets** entre paréntesis

brackish ['brækɪʃ] *adj* (*water*) salobre

brag [bræg] *vi* jactarse

braid [breɪd] *n* (*trimming*) galón *m*; (*of hair*) trenza

Braille [breɪl] *n* Braille *m*

brain [breɪn] *n* cerebro; **brains** *npl* sesos *mpl*; **she's got brains** es muy lista

brainchild ['breɪntʃaɪld] *n* invención *f*

braindead ['breɪnded] *adj* (*Med*) clínicamente muerto; (*col*) subnormal, tarado

brainless ['breɪnlɪs] *adj* estúpido, insensato

brainstorm ['breɪnstɔ:m] *n* (*fig*) ataque *m* de locura, frenesí *m*; (*US: brainwave*) idea luminosa *or* genial, inspiración *f*

brainstorming ['breɪnstɔ:mɪŋ] *n* *discusión intensa para solucionar problemas*

brainwash ['breɪnwɔʃ] *vt* lavar el cerebro a

brainwave ['breɪnweɪv] *n* idea luminosa *or* genial, inspiración *f*

brainy ['breɪnɪ] *adj* muy listo *or* inteligente

braise [breɪz] *vt* cocer a fuego lento

brake [breɪk] *n* (*on vehicle*) freno ■ *vt, vi* frenar

brake drum *n* tambor *m* de freno

brake fluid *n* líquido de frenos

brake light *n* luz *f* de frenado

brake pedal n pedal m de freno
bramble ['bræmbl] n (fruit) zarza
bran [bræn] n salvado
branch [brɑːntʃ] n rama; (fig) ramo; (Comm) sucursal f ■ vi ramificarse; (fig) extenderse
▶ **branch out** vi ramificarse
branch line n (Rail) ramal m, línea secundaria
branch manager n director(a) m(f) de sucursal
brand [brænd] n marca; (iron) hierro de marcar ■ vt (cattle) marcar con hierro candente
brandish ['brændɪʃ] vt blandir
brand name n marca
brand-new ['brænd'njuː] adj flamante, completamente nuevo
brandy ['brændɪ] n coñac m, brandy m
brash [bræʃ] adj (rough) tosco; (cheeky) descarado
Brasilia [brə'zɪlɪə] n Brasilia
brass [brɑːs] n latón m; **the ~** (Mus) los cobres
brass band n banda de metal
brassière ['bræsɪəʳ] n sostén m, sujetador m, corpiño (LAm)
brass tacks npl: **to get down to ~** ir al grano
brat [bræt] n (pej) mocoso(-a)
bravado [brə'vɑːdəu] n fanfarronería
brave [breɪv] adj valiente, valeroso ■ n guerrero indio ■ vt (challenge) desafiar; (resist) aguantar
bravely ['breɪvlɪ] adv valientemente, con valor
bravery ['breɪvərɪ] n valor m, valentía
bravo [brɑː'vəu] excl ¡bravo!, ¡olé!
brawl [brɔːl] n pendencia, reyerta ■ vi pelearse
brawn [brɔːn] n fuerza muscular; (meat) carne f en gelatina
brawny ['brɔːnɪ] adj fornido, musculoso
bray [breɪ] n rebuzno ■ vi rebuznar
brazen ['breɪzn] adj descarado, cínico ■ vt: **to ~ it out** echarle cara al asunto
brazier ['breɪzɪəʳ] n brasero
Brazil [brə'zɪl] n (el) Brasil
Brazilian [brə'zɪlɪən] adj, n brasileño(-a) m(f)
breach [briːtʃ] vt abrir brecha en ■ n (gap) brecha; (estrangement) ruptura; (breaking): **~ of confidence** abuso de confianza; **~ of contract** infracción f de contrato; **~ of the peace** perturbación f del orden público; **in ~ of** por incumplimiento or infracción de
bread [bred] n pan m; (col: money) pasta, lana (LAm); **~ and butter** n pan con mantequilla; (fig) pan (de cada día) ■ adj común y corriente; **to earn one's daily ~** ganarse el pan; **to know which side one's ~ is buttered (on)** saber dónde aprieta el zapato

breadbin ['bredbɪn] n panera
breadboard ['bredbɔːd] n (Comput) circuito experimental
breadbox ['bredbɒks] n (US) panera
breadcrumbs ['bredkrʌmz] npl migajas fpl; (Culin) pan msg rallado
breadline ['bredlaɪn] n: **on the ~** en la miseria
breadth [brɛtθ] n anchura; (fig) amplitud f
breadwinner ['bredwɪnəʳ] n sostén m de la familia
break [breɪk] vb (pt **broke**, pp **broken**) ■ vt (gen) romper; (promise) no cumplir; (fall) amortiguar; (journey) interrumpir; (law) violar, infringir; (record) batir; (news) comunicar ■ vi romperse, quebrarse; (storm) estallar; (weather) cambiar ■ n (gap) abertura; (crack) grieta; (fracture) fractura; (in relations) ruptura; (rest) descanso; (time) intervalo; (: at school) (período de) recreo; (holiday) vacaciones fpl; (chance) oportunidad f; (escape) evasión f, fuga; **to ~ with sb** (fig) romper con algn; **to ~ even** vi cubrir los gastos; **to ~ free** or **loose** vi escaparse; **lucky ~** (col) chiripa, racha de buena suerte; **to have** or **take a ~** (few minutes) descansar; **without a ~** sin descanso or descansar
▶ **break down** vt (door etc) echar abajo, derribar; (resistance) vencer, acabar con; (figures, data) analizar, descomponer; (undermine) acabar con ■ vi estropearse; (Med) sufrir un colapso; (Aut) averiarse, descomponerse (LAm); (person) romper a llorar
▶ **break in** vt (horse etc) domar ■ vi (burglar) forzar una entrada
▶ **break into** vt fus (house) forzar
▶ **break off** vi (speaker) pararse, detenerse; (branch) partir ■ vt (talks) suspender; (engagement) romper
▶ **break open** vt (door etc) abrir por la fuerza, forzar
▶ **break out** vi estallar; **to ~ out in spots** salir a algn granos
▶ **break through** vi: **the sun broke through** asomó el sol ■ vt fus (defences, barrier, crowd) abrirse paso por
▶ **break up** vi (partnership) disolverse; (friends) romper ■ vt (rocks, ice etc) partir; (crowd) disolver
breakable ['breɪkəbl] adj quebradizo ■ n: **breakables** cosas fpl frágiles
breakage ['breɪkɪdʒ] n rotura; **to pay for breakages** pagar por los objetos rotos
breakaway ['breɪkəweɪ] adj (group etc) disidente
break-dancing ['breɪkdɑːnsɪŋ] n break m

breakdown ['breɪkdaun] n (Aut) avería;
(in communications) interrupción f; (Med:
also: **nervous breakdown**) colapso, crisis f
nerviosa; (of figures) desglose m
breakdown van n (Brit) (camión m) grúa
breaker ['breɪkə'] n rompiente m, ola grande
breakeven ['breɪk'i:vn] cpd: ~ **chart** gráfico
del punto de equilibrio; ~ **point** punto de
break-even or de equilibrio
breakfast ['brɛkfəst] n desayuno
breakfast cereal n cereales mpl para el
desayuno
break-in ['breɪkɪn] n robo con allanamiento
de morada
breaking and entering ['breɪkɪŋənd'ɛntə
rɪŋ] n (Law) violación f de domicilio,
allanamiento de morada
breaking point ['breɪkɪŋ-] n punto de
ruptura
breakthrough ['breɪkθru:] n ruptura; (fig)
avance m, adelanto
break-up ['breɪkʌp] n (of partnership, marriage)
disolución f
break-up value n (Comm) valor m de
liquidación
breakwater ['breɪkwɔ:tə'] n rompeolas m inv
breast [brɛst] n (of woman) pecho, seno; (chest)
pecho; (of bird) pechuga
breast-feed ['brɛstfi:d] vt, vi (irreg: like **feed**)
amamantar, dar el pecho
breaststroke ['brɛststrəuk] n braza de pecho
breath [brɛθ] n aliento, respiración f; **out of**
~ sin aliento, sofocado; **to go out for a ~ of**
air salir a tomar el fresco
Breathalyser® ['brɛθəlaɪzə'] n (Brit)
alcoholímetro m; ~ **test** n prueba de
alcoholemia
breathe [bri:ð] vt, vi respirar; (noisily) resollar;
I won't ~ a word about it no diré ni una
palabra de ello
▸ **breathe in** vt, vi aspirar
▸ **breathe out** vt, vi espirar
breather ['bri:ðə'] n respiro, descanso
breathing ['bri:ðɪŋ] n respiración f
breathing space n (fig) respiro, pausa
breathless ['brɛθlɪs] adj sin aliento,
jadeante; (with excitement) pasmado
breathtaking ['brɛθteɪkɪŋ] adj imponente,
pasmoso
breath test n prueba de la alcoholemia
-bred [brɛd] suff: **to be well/ill~** estar bien/
mal criado
breed [bri:d] vb (pt, pp **bred**) [brɛd] ■ vt criar;
(fig: hate, suspicion) crear, engendrar ■ vi
reproducirse, procrear ■ n raza, casta
breeder ['bri:də'] n (person) criador(a) m(f);
(Physics: also: **breeder reactor**) reactor m

breeding ['bri:dɪŋ] n (of person) educación f
breeze [bri:z] n brisa
breezeblock ['bri:zblɔk] n (Brit) bovedilla
breezy ['bri:zɪ] adj de mucho viento, ventoso;
(person) despreocupado
Breton ['brɛtən] adj bretón(-ona) ■ n
bretón(-ona) m(f); (Ling) bretón m
brevity ['brɛvɪtɪ] n brevedad f
brew [bru:] vt (tea) hacer; (beer) elaborar;
(plot) tramar ■ vi hacerse; elaborarse;
tramarse; (storm) amenazar
brewer ['bru:ə'] n cervecero, fabricante m de
cerveza
brewery ['bru:ərɪ] n fábrica de cerveza
briar ['braɪə'] n (thorny bush) zarza; (wild rose)
escaramujo, rosa silvestre
bribe [braɪb] n soborno ■ vt sobornar,
cohechar; **to ~ sb to do sth** sobornar a algn
para que haga algo
bribery ['braɪbərɪ] n soborno, cohecho
bric-a-brac ['brɪkəbræk] n inv baratijas fpl
brick [brɪk] n ladrillo
bricklayer ['brɪkleɪə'] n albañil m
brickwork ['brɪkwə:k] n enladrillado
brickworks ['brɪkwə:ks] n ladrillar m
bridal ['braɪdl] adj nupcial
bride [braɪd] n novia
bridegroom ['braɪdgru:m] n novio
bridesmaid ['braɪdzmeɪd] n dama de honor
bridge [brɪdʒ] n puente m; (Naut) puente m de
mando; (of nose) caballete m; (Cards) bridge m
■ vt (river) tender un puente sobre
bridgehead ['brɪdʒhɛd] n cabeza de puente
bridging loan ['brɪdʒɪŋ-] n crédito
provisional
bridle ['braɪdl] n brida, freno ■ vt poner la
brida a; (fig) reprimir, refrenar ■ vi (in anger
etc) picarse
bridle path n camino de herradura
brief [bri:f] adj breve, corto ■ n (Law)
escrito ■ vt (inform) informar; (instruct) dar
instrucciones a; **in ~ ...** en resumen ...; **to ~**
sb (about sth) informar a algn (sobre algo)
briefcase ['bri:fkeɪs] n cartera, portafolio(s)
m inv (LAm)
briefing ['bri:fɪŋ] n (Press) informe m
briefly adv (smile, glance) brevemente; (explain,
say) brevemente, en pocas palabras
briefs [bri:fs] npl (for men) calzoncillos mpl;
(for women) bragas fpl
Brig. abbr = **brigadier**
brigade [brɪ'geɪd] n (Mil) brigada
brigadier [brɪgə'dɪə'] n general m de brigada
bright [braɪt] adj claro; (room) luminoso;
(day) de sol; (person: clever) listo, inteligente;
(: lively) alegre, animado; (colour) vivo; **to**
look on the ~ side mirar el lado bueno

455

brighten ['braɪtn] (*also*: **brighten up**) *vt* (*room*) hacer más alegre ▪ *vi* (*weather*) despejarse; (*person*) animarse, alegrarse

brill [brɪl] *adj* (*Brit col*) guay

brilliance ['brɪljəns] *n* brillo, brillantez *f*; (*fig*: *of person*) inteligencia

brilliant ['brɪljənt] *adj* (*light, idea, person, success*) brillante; (*clever*) genial

brilliantly ['brɪljəntlɪ] *adv* brillantemente

brim [brɪm] *n* borde *m*; (*of hat*) ala

brimful ['brɪm'ful] *adj* lleno hasta el borde; (*fig*) rebosante

brine [braɪn] *n* (*Culin*) salmuera

bring (*pt, pp* **brought**) [brɪŋ, brɔ:t] *vt* (*thing*) traer; (*person*) conducir; **to ~ sth to an end** terminar con algo; **I can't ~ myself to sack him** no soy capaz de echarle
  ▶ **bring about** *vt* ocasionar, producir
  ▶ **bring back** *vt* volver a traer; (*return*) devolver
  ▶ **bring down** *vt* bajar; (*price*) rebajar
  ▶ **bring forward** *vt* adelantar; (*Bookkeeping*) sumar y seguir
  ▶ **bring in** *vt* (*harvest*) recoger; (*person*) hacer entrar *or* pasar; (*object*) traer; (*Pol*: *bill, law*) presentar; (*Law*: *verdict*) pronunciar; (*produce*: *income*) producir, rendir
  ▶ **bring off** *vt* (*task, plan*) lograr, conseguir; (*deal*) cerrar
  ▶ **bring out** *vt* (*object*) sacar; (*new product*) sacar; (*book*) publicar
  ▶ **bring round** *vt* (*unconscious person*) hacer volver en sí; (*convince*) convencer
  ▶ **bring up** *vt* (*person*) educar, criar; (*carry up*) subir; (*question*) sacar a colación; (*food: vomit*) devolver, vomitar

brink [brɪŋk] *n* borde *m*; **on the ~ of doing sth** a punto de hacer algo; **she was on the ~ of tears** estaba al borde de las lágrimas

brisk [brɪsk] *adj* (*walk*) enérgico, vigoroso; (*speedy*) rápido; (*wind*) fresco; (*trade*) activo, animado; (*abrupt*) brusco; **business is ~** el negocio va bien *or* a paso activo

brisket ['brɪskɪt] *n* falda de vaca

bristle ['brɪsl] *n* cerda ▪ *vi* erizarse

bristly ['brɪslɪ] *adj* (*beard, hair*) erizado; **to have a ~ chin** tener la barba crecida

Brit [brɪt] *n abbr* (*col*: = *British person*) británico(-a)

Britain ['brɪtən] *n* (*also*: **Great Britain**) Gran Bretaña

British ['brɪtɪʃ] *adj* británico; **the British** *npl* los británicos; **the British Isles** *npl* las Islas Británicas

British Rail *n* ≈ RENFE *f* (*SP*)

British Summer Time *n* hora de verano británica

Briton ['brɪtən] *n* británico(-a)

brittle ['brɪtl] *adj* quebradizo, frágil

Bro. *abbr* (*Rel*) = **brother**

broach [brəʊtʃ] *vt* (*subject*) abordar

broad [brɔ:d] *adj* ancho, amplio; (*accent*) cerrado ▪ *n* (*US col*) tía; **in ~ daylight** en pleno día; **the ~ outlines** las líneas generales

broadband ['brɔ:dbænd] *n* banda ancha

broad bean *n* haba

broadcast ['brɔ:dkɑ:st] (*pt, pp* ~) *n* emisión *f* ▪ *vt* (*Radio*) emitir; (*TV*) transmitir ▪ *vi* emitir; transmitir

broadcaster ['brɔ:dkɑ:stə^r] *n* locutor(a) *m(f)*

broadcasting ['brɔ:dkɑ:stɪŋ] *n* radiodifusión *f*, difusión *f*

broadcasting station *n* emisora

broaden ['brɔ:dn] *vt* ensanchar ▪ *vi* ensancharse

broadly ['brɔ:dlɪ] *adv* en general

broad-minded ['brɔ:d'maɪndɪd] *adj* tolerante, liberal

broadsheet ['brɔ:dʃi:t] *n* (*Brit*) periódico de gran formato (*no sensacionalista*); *see also* **quality press**

brocade [brə'keɪd] *n* brocado

broccoli ['brɒkəlɪ] *n* brécol *m*, bróculi *m*

brochure ['brəʊʃjuə^r] *n* folleto

brogue [brəʊg] *n* (*accent*) acento regional; (*shoe*) (*tipo de*) zapato de cuero grueso

broil [brɔɪl] *vt* (*US*) asar a la parrilla

broiler ['brɔɪlə^r] *n* (*fowl*) pollo (para asar)

broke [brəʊk] *pt of* **break** ▪ *adj* (*col*) pelado, sin una perra; **to go ~** quebrar

broken ['brəʊkən] *pp of* **break** ▪ *adj* (*stick*) roto; (*fig*: *marriage*) deshecho; (: *promise, vow*) violado; **~ leg** pierna rota; **in ~ English** en un inglés chapurreado

broken-down ['brəʊkn'daʊn] *adj* (*car*) averiado; (*machine*) estropeado; (*house*) destartalado

broken-hearted ['brəʊkn'hɑ:tɪd] *adj* con el corazón destrozado

broker ['brəʊkə^r] *n* corredor(a) *m(f)* de bolsa

brokerage ['brəʊkərɪdʒ] *n* corretaje *m*

brolly ['brɒlɪ] *n* (*Brit col*) paraguas *m inv*

bronchitis [brɒŋ'kaɪtɪs] *n* bronquitis *f*

bronze [brɒnz] *n* bronce *m*

bronzed [brɒnzd] *adj* bronceado

brooch [brəʊtʃ] *n* broche *m*

brood [bru:d] *n* camada, cría; (*children*) progenie *f* ▪ *vi* (*hen*) empollar; **to ~ over** dar vueltas a, rumiar

broody ['bru:dɪ] *adj* (*fig*) triste, melancólico

brook [bruk] *n* arroyo

broom [brum] *n* escoba; (*Bot*) retama

broomstick ['brumstɪk] *n* palo de escoba

Bros. *abbr* (*Comm*: = *Brothers*) Hnos

broth [brɔθ] n caldo
brothel ['brɔθl] n burdel m
brother ['brʌðəʳ] n hermano
brotherhood ['brʌðəhud] n hermandad f
brother-in-law ['brʌðərɪn'lɔ:] n cuñado
brotherly ['brʌðəlɪ] adj fraternal
brought [brɔ:t] pt, pp of **bring**
brow [brau] n (forehead) frente f; (of hill) cumbre f
browbeat ['braubi:t] vt (irreg: like **beat**) intimidar
brown [braun] adj marrón; (hair) castaño; (tanned) moreno ■ n (colour) marrón m ■ vt (tan) poner moreno; (Culin) dorar; **to go ~** (person) ponerse moreno; (leaves) dorarse
brown bread n pan m moreno
brownie ['braunɪ] n niña exploradora
brown paper n papel m de estraza
brown rice n arroz m integral
brown sugar n azúcar m moreno
browse [brauz] vi (animal) pacer; (among books) hojear libros; **to ~ through a book** hojear un libro
browser ['brauzəʳ] n (Comput) navegador m
bruise [bru:z] n (on person) cardenal m, hematoma m ■ vt (leg etc) magullar; (fig: feelings) herir
Brum [brʌm] n abbr, **Brummagem** ['brʌmədʒəm] n (col) = **Birmingham**
Brummie ['brʌmɪ] n (col) habitante m/f de Birmingham
brunch [brʌntʃ] n desayuno-almuerzo
brunette [bru:'nɛt] n morena, morocha (LAm)
brunt [brʌnt] n: **to bear the ~ of** llevar el peso de
brush [brʌʃ] n cepillo, escobilla (LAm); (large) escoba; (for painting, shaving etc) brocha; (artist's) pincel m; (Bot) maleza ■ vt cepillar; (gen): **~ past, ~ against** rozar al pasar; **to have a ~ with the police** tener un roce con la policía
▶ **brush aside** vt rechazar, no hacer caso a
▶ **brush up** vt (knowledge) repasar, refrescar
brushed [brʌʃt] adj (nylon, denim etc) afelpado; (Tech: steel, chrome etc) cepillado
brushwood ['brʌʃwud] n (bushes) maleza; (sticks) leña
brusque [bru:sk] adj (person, manner) brusco; (tone) áspero
Brussels ['brʌslz] n Bruselas
Brussels sprout n col f de Bruselas
brutal ['bru:tl] adj brutal
brutality [bru:'tælɪtɪ] n brutalidad f
brutalize ['bru:tələɪz] vt (harden) embrutecer; (ill-treat) tratar brutalmente a
brute [bru:t] n bruto; (person) bestia ■ adj:

by ~ force por la fuerza bruta
brutish ['bru:tɪʃ] adj brutal
BS n abbr (US: = Bachelor of Science) título universitario
bs abbr = **bill of sale**
BSA n abbr (US) = **Boy Scouts of America**
BSc abbr = **Bachelor of Science**; see also **Bachelor's Degree**
BSE n abbr (= bovine spongiform encephalopathy) encefalopatía espongiforme bovina
BSI n abbr (= British Standards Institution) institución británica de normalización
BST n abbr (= British Summer Time) hora de verano británica
Bt. abbr (Brit) = **baronet**
btu n abbr (= British thermal unit) = 1054.2 julios
BTW abbr (= by the way) por cierto
bubble ['bʌbl] n burbuja; (in paint) ampolla ■ vi burbujear, borbotar
bubble bath n espuma para el baño
bubble gum n chicle m
bubblejet printer ['bʌbldʒɛt-] n impresora de inyección por burbujas
bubbly ['bʌblɪ] adj (person) vivaracho; (liquid) con burbujas ■ n (col) champán m
Bucharest [bu:kə'rɛst] n Bucarest m
buck [bʌk] n macho; (US col) dólar m ■ vi corcovear; **to pass the ~ (to sb)** echar (a algn) el muerto
▶ **buck up** vi (cheer up) animarse, cobrar ánimo ■ vt: **to ~ one's ideas up** poner más empeño
bucket ['bʌkɪt] n cubo, balde m (esp LAm) ■ vi: **the rain is bucketing (down)** (col) está lloviendo a cántaros
Buckingham Palace ['bʌkɪŋəm-] n el Palacio de Buckingham; ver nota

● **BUCKINGHAM PALACE**
●
● Buckingham Palace es la residencia oficial
● del monarca británico en Londres. Data
● de 1703 y fue en principio el palacio
● del Duque de Buckingham, para
● pasar a manos de Jorge III en 1762. Fue
● reconstruido el siglo pasado y reformado
● después a principios de este siglo. Hoy
● en día parte del palacio está abierto al
● público.

buckle ['bʌkl] n hebilla ■ vt abrochar con hebilla ■ vi torcerse, combarse
▶ **buckle down** vi poner empeño
Bucks [bʌks] abbr (Brit) = **Buckinghamshire**
bud [bʌd] n brote m, yema; (of flower) capullo ■ vi brotar, echar brotes
Budapest [bju:də'pɛst] n Budapest m

Buddhism ['budɪzm] n Budismo
Buddhist ['budɪst] adj, n budista m/f
budding ['bʌdɪŋ] adj en ciernes, en embrión
buddy ['bʌdɪ] n (US) compañero, compinche m
budge [bʌdʒ] vt mover; (fig) hacer ceder
■ vi moverse
budgerigar ['bʌdʒərɪgaːʳ] n periquito
budget ['bʌdʒɪt] n presupuesto ■ vi: **to ~ for sth** presupuestar algo; **I'm on a tight ~** no puedo gastar mucho; **she works out her ~ every month** planea su presupuesto todos los meses
budgie ['bʌdʒɪ] n = **budgerigar**
Buenos Aires ['bweɪnɔs'aɪrɪz] n Buenos Aires m ■ adj bonaerense, porteño (LAm)
buff [bʌf] adj (colour) color m de ante ■ n (enthusiast) entusiasta m/f
buffalo ['bʌfələu] (pl ~ or **buffaloes**) n (Brit) búfalo; (US: bison) bisonte m
buffer ['bʌfəʳ] n amortiguador m; (Comput) memoria intermedia, buffer m ■ vi (Comput) almacenar temperalmente
buffering ['bʌfərɪŋ] n (Comput) almacenamiento en memoria intermedia
buffer zone n zona (que sirve de) colchón
buffet ['bufeɪ] n (Brit: bar) bar m, cafetería; (food) buffet m ■ vt ['bʌfɪt] (strike) abofetear; (wind etc) golpear
buffet car n (Brit Rail) coche-restaurante m
buffet lunch n buffet m (almuerzo)
buffoon [bə'fuːn] n bufón m
bug [bʌg] n (insect) chinche m; (: gen) bicho, sabandija; (germ) microbio, bacilo; (spy device) micrófono oculto; (Comput) fallo, error m ■ vt (annoy) fastidiar; (room) poner un micrófono oculto en; (phone) pinchar; **I've got the travel ~** (fig) me encanta viajar; **it really bugs me** me fastidia or molesta mucho
bugbear ['bʌgbɛəʳ] n pesadilla
bugle ['bjuːgl] n corneta, clarín m
build [bɪld] n (of person) talle m, tipo ■ vt (pt, pp **built**) [bɪlt] construir, edificar
▶ **build on** vt fus (fig) basar en
▶ **build up** vt (Med) fortalecer; (stocks) acumular; (establish: business) fomentar, desarrollar; (: reputation) crear(se); (increase: production) aumentar; **don't ~ your hopes up too soon** no te hagas demasiadas ilusiones
builder ['bɪldəʳ] n constructor(a) m(f); (contractor) contratista m/f
building ['bɪldɪŋ] n (act) construcción f; (habitation, offices) edificio
building contractor n contratista m/f de obras
building industry n construcción f
building site n solar m (SP), obra (LAm)
building society n (Brit) sociedad f de préstamo inmobiliario; ver nota

building trade n = **building industry**
build-up ['bɪldʌp] n (publicity): **to give sb/sth a good ~** hacer mucha propaganda de algn/ algo
built [bɪlt] pt, pp of **build**
built-in ['bɪlt'ɪn] adj (cupboard) empotrado; (device) interior, incorporado; **~ obsolescence** caducidad f programada
built-up ['bɪltʌp] adj (area) urbanizado
bulb [bʌlb] n (Bot) bulbo; (Elec) bombilla, bombillo (LAm), foco (LAm)
bulbous ['bʌlbəs] adj bulboso
Bulgaria [bʌl'gɛərɪə] n Bulgaria
Bulgarian [bʌl'gɛərɪən] adj búlgaro ■ n búlgaro(-a); (Ling) búlgaro
bulge [bʌldʒ] n bombeo, pandeo; (in birth rate, sales) alza, aumento ■ vi bombearse, pandearse; (pocket etc) hacer bulto
bulimia [bə'lɪmɪə] n bulimia
bulk [bʌlk] n (mass) bulto, volumen m; (major part) grueso; **in ~** (Comm) a granel; **the ~ of** la mayor parte de; **to buy in ~** comprar en grandes cantidades
bulk buying n compra a granel
bulk carrier n (buque m) granelero
bulkhead ['bʌlkhɛd] n mamparo
bulky ['bʌlkɪ] adj voluminoso, abultado
bull [bul] n toro; (Stock Exchange) alcista m/f de bolsa; (Rel) bula
bulldog ['buldɔg] n dogo
bulldoze ['buldəuz] vt mover con excavadora; **I was bulldozed into doing it** (fig col) me obligaron a hacerlo
bulldozer ['buldəuzəʳ] n buldozer m, excavadora
bullet ['bulɪt] n bala; **~ wound** balazo
bulletin ['bulɪtɪn] n comunicado, parte m; (journal) boletín m
bulletin board n (US) tablón m de anuncios; (Comput) tablero de noticias
bulletproof ['bulɪtpruːf] adj a prueba de balas; **~ vest** chaleco antibalas
bullfight ['bulfaɪt] n corrida de toros
bullfighter ['bulfaɪtəʳ] n torero

bullfighting ['bulfaɪtɪŋ] n los toros mpl, el toreo; (art of bullfighting) tauromaquia
bullion ['buljən] n oro or plata en barras
bullock ['bulək] n novillo
bullring ['bulrɪŋ] n plaza de toros
bull's-eye ['bulzaɪ] n blanco, diana
bullshit ['bulʃɪt] (col!) excl chorradas ■ n chorradas fpl ■ vi decir chorradas ■ vt: **to ~ sb** quedarse con algn
bully ['bulɪ] n valentón m, matón m ■ vt intimidar, tiranizar
bum [bʌm] n (Brit: col: backside) culo; (: tramp) vagabundo; (col: esp US: idler) holgazán(-ana) m(f), flojo(-a)
bumble ['bʌmbl] vi (walk unsteadily) andar de forma vacilante; (fig) farfullar, trastabillar
bumblebee ['bʌmblbi:] n abejorro
bumbling ['bʌmblɪŋ] n divagación f
bumf [bʌmf] n (col: forms etc) papeleo
bump [bʌmp] n (blow) tope m, choque m; (jolt) sacudida; (noise) choque m, topetón m; (on road etc) bache m; (on head) chichón m ■ vt (strike) chocar contra, topetar ■ vi dar sacudidas
▶ **bump into** vt fus chocar contra, tropezar con; (person) topar con; (col: meet) tropezar con, toparse con
bumper ['bʌmpəʳ] n (Brit) parachoques m inv ■ adj: **~ crop/harvest** cosecha abundante
bumper cars npl (US) autos or coches mpl de choque
bumph [bʌmf] n = **bumf**
bumptious ['bʌmpʃəs] adj engreído, presuntuoso
bumpy ['bʌmpɪ] adj (road) lleno de baches; (journey, flight) agitado
bun [bʌn] n (Brit: cake) pastel m; (US: bread) bollo; (of hair) moño
bunch [bʌntʃ] n (of flowers) ramo; (of keys) manojo; (of bananas) piña; (of people) grupo; (pej) pandilla
bundle ['bʌndl] n (gen) bulto, fardo; (of sticks) haz m; (of papers) legajo ■ vt (also: **bundle up**) atar, envolver; **to ~ sth/sb into** meter algo/a algn precipitadamente en
bun fight n (Brit col: tea party) merienda; (: function) fiesta oficial
bung [bʌŋ] n tapón m, bitoque m ■ vt (throw: also: **bung into**) arrojar; (also: **bung up**: pipe, hole) tapar; **my nose is bunged up** (col) tengo la nariz atascada or taponada
bungalow ['bʌŋgələu] n bungalow m, chalé m
bungee jumping ['bʌndʒi:'dʒʌmpɪŋ] n puenting m, banyi m
bungle ['bʌŋgl] vt chapucear
bunion ['bʌnjən] n juanete m

bunk [bʌŋk] n litera; **~ beds** npl literas fpl
bunker ['bʌŋkəʳ] n (coal store) carbonera; (Mil) refugio; (Golf) bunker m
bunk off vi: **to ~ school** (Brit col) pirarse las clases; **I'll ~ at 3 this afternoon** me voy a pirar a las 3 esta tarde
bunny ['bʌnɪ] n (also: **bunny rabbit**) conejito
Bunsen burner ['bʌnsn-] n mechero Bunsen
bunting ['bʌntɪŋ] n empavesada, banderas fpl
buoy [bɔɪ] n boya
▶ **buoy up** vt mantener a flote; (fig) animar
buoyancy ['bɔɪənsɪ] n (of ship) flotabilidad f
buoyant ['bɔɪənt] adj (carefree) boyante, optimista; (Comm: market, prices etc) sostenido
BUPA ['bu:pə] n abbr (= British United Provident Association) seguro médico privado
burden ['bə:dn] n carga ■ vt cargar; **to be a ~ to sb** ser una carga para algn
bureau (pl **bureaux**) ['bjuərəu, -z] n (Brit: writing desk) escritorio, buró m; (US: chest of drawers) cómoda; (office) oficina, agencia
bureaucracy [bjuə'rɔkrəsɪ] n burocracia
bureaucrat ['bjuərəkræt] n burócrata m/f
bureaucratic [bjuərə'krætɪk] adj burocrático
burgeon ['bə:dʒən] vi (develop rapidly) crecer, incrementarse; (trade etc) florecer
burger ['bə:gəʳ] n hamburguesa
burglar ['bə:gləʳ] n ladrón(-ona) m(f)
burglar alarm n alarma f contra robo
burglarize ['bə:gləraɪz] vt (US) robar (con allanamiento)
burglary ['bə:glərɪ] n robo con allanamiento or fractura, robo de una casa
burgle ['bə:gl] vt robar (con allanamiento)
Burgundy ['bə:gəndɪ] n Borgoña
burial ['berɪəl] n entierro
burial ground n cementerio
burlap ['bə:læp] n arpillera
burlesque [bə:'lesk] n parodia
burly ['bə:lɪ] adj fornido, membrudo
Burma ['bə:mə] n Birmania; see also **Myanmar**
Burmese [bə:'mi:z] adj birmano ■ n (pl inv) birmano(-a); (Ling) birmano
burn [bə:n] vb (pt, pp **burned** or **burnt**) ■ vt quemar; (house) incendiar ■ vi quemarse, arder; incendiarse; (sting) escocer ■ n (Med) quemadura; **the cigarette burnt a hole in her dress** se ha quemado el vestido con el cigarrillo; **I've burnt myself!** ¡me he quemado!
▶ **burn down** vt incendiar
▶ **burn out** vt (writer etc): **to ~ o.s. out** agotarse
burner ['bə:nəʳ] n (gas) quemador m
burning ['bə:nɪŋ] adj ardiente; (building, forest) en llamas

b

Burns' Night [bəːnz-] *n ver nota*

● **BURNS' NIGHT**

● Cada veinticinco de enero los escoceses
● celebran la llamada *Burns' Night* (noche de
● Burns), en honor al poeta escocés Robert
● Burns (1759-1796). Es tradición hacer una
● cena en la que, al son de la música de la
● gaita escocesa, se sirve "haggis", plato
● tradicional de asadura de cordero cocida
● en el estómago del animal, acompañado
● de nabos y puré de patatas. Durante la
● misma se recitan poemas del autor y
● varios discursos conmemorativos de
● carácter festivo.

burnt [bəːnt] *pt, pp of* **burn**
burp [bəːp] *(col) n* eructo ■ *vi* eructar
burqa ['bəːkə] *n* burka *m*, burqa *m*
burrow ['bʌrəu] *n* madriguera ■ *vt* hacer
una madriguera
bursar ['bəːsəʳ] *n* tesorero; *(Brit: student)*
becario(-a)
bursary ['bəːsərɪ] *n (Brit)* beca
burst [bəːst] *vb (pt, pp* **burst)** ■ *vt (balloon,
pipe)* reventar; *(banks etc)* romper ■ *vi*
reventarse; romperse; *(tyre)* pincharse;
(bomb) ■ *n (explosion)* estallido; *(also:* **burst
pipe)** reventón *m;* **the river has ~ its banks**
el río se ha desbordado; **to ~ into flames**
estallar en llamas; **to ~ out laughing** soltar
la carcajada; **to ~ into tears** deshacerse en
lágrimas; **to be bursting with** reventar de;
a ~ of energy una explosión de energía;
a ~ of applause una salva de aplausos;
a ~ of speed una escapada; **to ~ open**
vi abrirse de golpe
▸ **burst into** *vt fus (room etc)* irrumpir en
bury ['bɛrɪ] *vt* enterrar; *(body)* enterrar,
sepultar; **to ~ the hatchet** enterrar el hacha
(de guerra), echar pelillos a la mar
bus [bʌs] *n* autobús *m*, camión *m (LAm)*
bus boy *n (US)* ayudante *m/f* de camarero
bush [buʃ] *n* arbusto; *(scrub land)* monte *m*
bajo; **to beat about the ~** andar(se) con
rodeos
bushed [buʃt] *adj (col)* molido
bushel ['buʃl] *n (measure: Brit)* = 36,36 *litros;* (US)
= 35,24 *litros*
bush fire *n* incendio en el monte
bushy ['buʃɪ] *adj (beard, eyebrows)* poblado;
(hair) espeso; *(fur)* tupido
busily ['bɪzɪlɪ] *adv* afanosamente
business ['bɪznɪs] *n (matter, affair)* asunto;
(trading) comercio, negocios *mpl; (firm)*
empresa, casa; *(occupation)* oficio; **to be away**

on ~ estar en viaje de negocios; **it's my ~ to
... me toca** *or* **corresponde ...; it's none of
my ~** no es asunto mío; **he means ~** habla
en serio; **he's in the insurance ~** se dedica
a los seguros; **I'm here on ~** estoy aquí por
mi trabajo; **to do ~ with sb** hacer negocios
con algn
business address *n* dirección *f* comercial
business card *n* tarjeta de visita
businesslike ['bɪznɪslaɪk] *adj (company)* serio;
(person) eficiente
businessman ['bɪznɪsmən] *n* hombre *m* de
negocios
business trip *n* viaje *m* de negocios
businesswoman ['bɪznɪswumən] *n* mujer *f*
de negocios
busker ['bʌskəʳ] *n (Brit)* músico(-a)
ambulante
bus route *n* recorrido del autobús
bus station *n* estación *f or* terminal *f* de
autobuses
bus-stop ['bʌsstɔp] *n* parada de autobús,
paradero *(LAm)*
bust [bʌst] *n (Anat)* pecho ■ *adj (col: broken)*
roto, estropeado ■ *vt (col: Police: arrest)*
detener; **to go ~** quebrar
bustle ['bʌsl] *n* bullicio, movimiento
■ *vi* menearse, apresurarse
bustling ['bʌslɪŋ] *adj (town)* animado,
bullicioso
bust-up ['bʌstʌp] *n (col)* riña
busty ['bʌstɪ] *adj (col)* pechugona, con buena
delantera
busy ['bɪzɪ] *adj* ocupado, atareado; *(shop,
street)* concurrido, animado ■ *vt:* **to ~ o.s.
with** ocuparse en; **he's a ~ man** *(normally)*
es un hombre muy ocupado; *(temporarily)*
está muy ocupado; **the line's ~** *(esp US)* está
comunicando
busybody ['bɪzɪbɔdɪ] *n* entrometido(-a)
busy signal *n (US Tel)* señal *f* de comunicando

 KEYWORD

but [bʌt] *conj* **1** pero; **he's not very bright,
but he's hard-working** no es muy
inteligente, pero es trabajador
2 *(in direct contradiction)* sino; **he's not English
but French** no es inglés sino francés; **he
didn't sing but he shouted** no cantó sino
que gritó
3 *(showing disagreement, surprise etc):* **but that's
far too expensive!** ¡pero eso es carísimo!;
but it does work! ¡(pero) sí que funciona!
■ *prep (apart from, except)* menos, salvo; **we've
had nothing but trouble** no hemos tenido
más que problemas; **no-one but him can**

do it nadie más que él puede hacerlo; **the last but one** el penúltimo; **who but a lunatic would do such a thing?** ¡sólo un loco haría una cosa así!; **but for you/your help** si no fuera por ti/tu ayuda; **anything but that** cualquier cosa menos eso ■ adv (just, only): **she's but a child** no es más que una niña; **had I but known** si lo hubiera sabido; **I can but try** al menos lo puedo intentar; **it's all but finished** está casi acabado

butane ['bjuːteɪn] n (also: **butane gas**) (gas m) butano

butch [butʃ] adj (pej: woman) machirula, marimacho; (col: man) muy macho

butcher ['butʃər] n carnicero(-a) ■ vt hacer una carnicería con; (cattle etc for meat) matar; ~'**s (shop)** carnicería

butler ['bʌtlər] n mayordomo

butt [bʌt] n (cask) tonel m; (for rain) tina; (thick end) cabo, extremo; (of gun) culata; (of cigarette) colilla; (Brit fig: target) blanco ■ vt dar cabezadas contra, topetar
▶ **butt in** vi (interrupt) interrumpir

butter ['bʌtər] n mantequilla, manteca (LAm) ■ vt untar con mantequilla

butter bean n judía blanca

buttercup ['bʌtəkʌp] n ranúnculo

butterfingers ['bʌtəfɪŋgəz] n (col) torpe m/f

butterfly ['bʌtəflaɪ] n mariposa; (Swimming: also: **butterfly stroke**) (braza de) mariposa

buttocks ['bʌtəks] npl nalgas fpl

button ['bʌtn] n botón m ■ vt (also: **button up**) abotonar, abrochar ■ vi abrocharse

buttonhole ['bʌtnhəʊl] n ojal m; (flower) flor f que se lleva en el ojal ■ vt obligar a escuchar

buttress ['bʌtrɪs] n contrafuerte m; (fig) apoyo, sostén m

buxom ['bʌksəm] adj (woman) frescachona, rolliza

buy [baɪ] vb (pt, pp **bought**) ■ vt comprar ■ n compra; **to ~ sb sth/sth from sb** comprarle algo a algn; **to ~ sb a drink** invitar a algn a una copa; **a good/bad ~** una buena/mala compra
▶ **buy back** vt volver a comprar
▶ **buy in** vt proveerse or abastecerse de
▶ **buy into** vt fus comprar acciones en
▶ **buy off** vt (col: bribe) sobornar
▶ **buy out** vt (partner) comprar la parte de

buyer ['baɪər] n comprador(a) m(f); ~'**s market** mercado favorable al comprador

buy-out ['baɪaut] n (Comm) adquisición f de (la totalidad de) las acciones

buzz [bʌz] n zumbido; (col: phone call) llamada (telefónica) ■ vt (call on intercom) llamar; (with buzzer) hacer sonar; (Aviat: plane, building) pasar rozando ■ vi zumbar; **my head is buzzing** me zumba la cabeza
▶ **buzz off** vi (Brit col) largarse

buzzard ['bʌzəd] n (Brit) águila ratonera; (US) buitre m, gallinazo (LAm)

buzzer ['bʌzər] n timbre m

buzz word n palabra que está de moda

 KEYWORD

by [baɪ] prep **1** (referring to cause, agent) por; de; **abandoned by his mother** abandonado por su madre; **surrounded by enemies** rodeado de enemigos; **a painting by Picasso** un cuadro de Picasso

2 (referring to method, manner, means): **by bus/car/train** en autobús/coche/tren; **to pay by cheque** pagar con cheque(s); **by moonlight/candlelight** a la luz de la luna/una vela; **by saving hard, he ...** ahorrando, ...

3 (via, through) por; **we came by Dover** vinimos por Dover

4 (close to, past): **the house by the river** la casa junto al río; **she rushed by me** pasó a mi lado como una exhalación; **I go by the post office every day** paso por delante de Correos todos los días

5 (time: not later than) para; (: during): **by daylight** de día; **by 4 o'clock** para las cuatro; **by this time tomorrow** mañana a estas horas; **by the time I got here it was too late** cuando llegué ya era demasiado tarde

6 (amount): **by the metre/kilo** por metro/kilo; **paid by the hour** pagado por hora

7 (in measurements, sums): **to divide/multiply by 3** dividir/multiplicar por 3; **a room 3 metres by 4** una habitación de 3 metros por 4; **it's broader by a metre** es un metro más ancho; **the bus missed me by inches** no me pilló el autobús por un pelo

8 (according to) según, de acuerdo con; **it's 3 o'clock by my watch** según mi reloj, son las tres; **it's all right by me** por mí, está bien

9: **(all) by oneself** etc todo solo; **he did it (all) by himself** lo hizo él solo; **he was standing (all) by himself in a corner** estaba de pie solo en un rincón

10: **by the way** a propósito, por cierto; **this wasn't my idea, by the way** pues, no fue idea mía

■ adv **1** see **go**; **pass** etc

2: **by and by** finalmente; **they'll come back by and by** acabarán volviendo; **by and large** en líneas generales, en general

bye ['baɪ], **bye-bye** ['baɪ'baɪ] excl adiós, hasta luego, chao (esp LAm)

bye-law ['baɪlɔ:] *n see* **by-law**
by-election ['baɪɪlɛkʃən] *n* (Brit) elección *f*
parcial; *ver nota*

● BY-ELECTION
●
●
● Se celebra una *by-election* en el
● Reino Unido y otros países de la
● "Commonwealth" cuando es necesario
● reemplazar a un parlamentario
● ("Member of Parliament") cesado o
● fallecido durante una legislatura. Dichas
● elecciones tienen lugar únicamente en el
● área electoral representada por el citado
● parlamentario, su "constituency".

Byelorussia [bjɛləu'rʌʃə] *n* Bielorrusia
Byelorussian [bjɛləu'rʌʃən] *adj, n*

= **Belorussian**
bygone ['baɪɡɔn] *adj* pasado, del pasado
■ *n*: **let bygones be bygones** lo pasado,
pasado está
by-law ['baɪlɔ:] *n* ordenanza municipal
bypass ['baɪpɑ:s] *n* carretera de,
circunvalación; (Med) (operación *f* de) bypass
m ■ *vt* evitar
by-product ['baɪprɔdʌkt] *n* subproducto,
derivado
bystander ['baɪstændəʳ] *n* espectador(a) *m(f)*
byte [baɪt] *n* (Comput) byte *m*, octeto
byway ['baɪweɪ] *n* camino poco frecuentado
byword ['baɪwə:d] *n*: **to be a ~ for** ser
sinónimo de
by-your-leave ['baɪjɔ:'li:v] *n*: **without so
much as a ~** sin decir nada, sin dar ningún
tipo de explicación

Cc

C, c [si:] n (letter) C, c f; (Mus): **C** do m; **C for Charlie** C de Carmen

C abbr (= Celsius, centigrade) C

c abbr (= century) S.; (= circa) hacia; (US etc) = **cent; cents**

CA n abbr = **Central America**; (Brit) = **chartered accountant**; (US) = **California**

ca. abbr (= circa) c

c/a abbr = **capital account; credit account; current account**

CAA n abbr (Brit: = Civil Aviation Authority) organismo de control y desarrollo de la aviación civil; = **Civil Aeronautics Authority**

CAB n abbr (Brit: = Citizens' Advice Bureau) ≈ Servicio de Información Ciudadana

cab [kæb] n taxi m; (of truck) cabina

cabaret ['kæbəreɪ] n cabaret m

cabbage ['kæbɪdʒ] n col f, berza

cabbie, cabby ['kæbɪ] n (col) taxista m/f

cab driver n taxista m/f

cabin ['kæbɪn] n cabaña; (on ship) camarote m

cabin cruiser n yate m de motor

cabinet ['kæbɪnɪt] n (Pol) consejo de ministros; (furniture) armario; (also: **display cabinet**) vitrina

cabinet-maker ['kæbɪnɪt'meɪkə'] n ebanista m

cabinet minister n ministro(-a) (del gabinete)

cable ['keɪbl] n cable m ∎ vt cablegrafiar

cable-car ['keɪblkɑː'] n teleférico

cablegram ['keɪblgræm] n cablegrama m

cable television n televisión f por cable

cache [kæʃ] n (of drugs) alijo; (of arms) zulo

cackle ['kækl] vi cacarear

cactus (pl **cacti**) ['kæktəs, -taɪ] n cacto

CAD ['kæd] n (= computer-aided design) DAO m

caddie, caddy ['kædɪ] n (Golf) cadi m

cadence ['keɪdəns] n ritmo; (Mus) cadencia

cadet [kə'dɛt] n (Mil) cadete m; **police ~** cadete m de policía

cadge [kædʒ] vt gorronear

cadger ['kædʒə'] n gorrón(-ona) m(f)

cadre ['kædrɪ] n cuadro

Caesarean, Cesarean (US) [si:'zɛərɪən] adj: **~ (section)** cesárea

CAF abbr (Brit: = cost and freight) C y F

café ['kæfeɪ] n café m

cafeteria [kæfɪ'tɪərɪə] n cafetería (con autoservicio para comer)

caffeine ['kæfi:n] n cafeína

cage [keɪdʒ] n jaula ∎ vt enjaular

cagey ['keɪdʒɪ] adj (col) cauteloso, reservado

cagoule [kə'gu:l] n canguro

cahoots [kə'hu:ts] n: **to be in ~ (with sb)** estar conchabado (con algn)

Cairo ['kaɪərəu] n El Cairo

cajole [kə'dʒəul] vt engatusar

cake [keɪk] n pastel m; (of soap) pastilla; **he wants to have his ~ and eat it** (fig) quiere estar en misa y repicando; **it's a piece of ~** (col) es pan comido

caked [keɪkt] adj: **~ with** cubierto de

cake shop n pastelería

Cal. abbr (US) = **California**

calamine ['kæləmaɪn] n calamina

calamitous [kə'læmɪtəs] adj calamitoso

calamity [kə'læmɪtɪ] n calamidad f

calcium ['kælsɪəm] n calcio

calculate ['kælkjuleɪt] vt (estimate: chances, effect) calcular

▶ **calculate on** vt fus: **to ~ on sth/on doing sth** contar con algo/con hacer algo

calculated ['kælkjuleɪtɪd] adj: **we took a ~ risk** calculamos el riesgo

calculating ['kælkjuleɪtɪŋ] adj (scheming) calculador(a)

calculation [kælkju'leɪʃən] n cálculo, cómputo

calculator ['kælkjuleɪtə'] n calculadora

calculus ['kælkjuləs] n cálculo

calendar ['kæləndə'] n calendario; **~ month/ year** n mes m/año civil

calf (pl **calves**) [kɑːf, kɑːvz] n (of cow) ternero, becerro; (of other animals) cría; (also: **calfskin**) piel f de becerro; (Anat) pantorrilla, canilla (LAm)

caliber ['kælɪbəʳ] n (US) = **calibre**
calibrate ['kælɪbreɪt] vt (gun etc) calibrar; (scale of measuring instrument) graduar
calibre, caliber (US) ['kælɪbəʳ] n calibre m
calico ['kælɪkəu] n calicó m
Calif. abbr (US) = **California**
California [kælɪ'fɔːnɪə] n California
calipers ['kælɪpəz] npl (US) = **callipers**
call [kɔːl] vt (gen) llamar; (Tel) llamar; (announce: flight) anunciar; (meeting, strike) convocar ■ vi (shout) llamar; (telephone) llamar (por teléfono), telefonear; (visit: also: **call in, call round**) hacer una visita ■ n (shout) llamada, llamado (LAm); (Tel) llamada, llamado (LAm); (of bird) canto; (appeal) llamamiento, llamado (LAm); (summons: for flight etc) llamada; (fig: lure) llamada; **to be called** (person, object) llamarse; **to ~ sb names** poner verde a algn; **let's ~ it a day** (col) ¡dejémoslo!, ¡ya está bien!; **who is calling?** ¿de parte de quién?; **London calling** (Radio) aquí Londres; **on ~** (nurse, doctor etc) de guardia; **please give me a ~ at seven** despiérteme or llámeme a las siete, por favor; **long-distance ~** conferencia (interurbana); **to make a ~** llamar por teléfono; **port of ~** puerto de escala; **to pay a ~ on sb** pasarse a ver a algn; **there's not much ~ for these items** estos artículos no tienen mucha demanda
  ▶ **call at** vt fus (ship) hacer escala en, tocar en; (train) parar en
  ▶ **call back** vi (return) volver; (Tel) volver a llamar
  ▶ **call for** vt fus (demand) pedir, exigir; (fetch) venir por
  ▶ **call in** vt (doctor, expert, police) llamar
  ▶ **call off** vt suspender; **the strike was called off** se desconvocó la huelga
  ▶ **call on** vt fus (visit) ir a ver; (turn to) acudir a
  ▶ **call out** vi gritar, dar voces ■ vt (doctor) llamar; (police, troops) hacer intervenir
  ▶ **call up** vt (Mil) llamar a filas
Callanetics® [kælə'netɪks] nsg gimnasia de repetición de pequeños ejercicios musculares
callbox ['kɔːlbɔks] n (Brit) cabina telefónica
call centre n (Brit) centro de llamadas
caller ['kɔːləʳ] n visita f; (Tel) usuario(-a); **hold the line, ~!** ¡no cuelgue!
call girl n prostituta
call-in ['kɔːlɪn] n (US) programa de línea abierta al público
calling ['kɔːlɪŋ] n vocación f; (profession) profesión f
calling card n tarjeta de visita
callipers, calipers (US) ['kælɪpəz] npl (Med) aparato ortopédico; (Math) calibrador m

callous ['kæləs] adj insensible, cruel
callousness ['kæləsnɪs] n insensibilidad, crueldad f
callow ['kæləu] adj inexperto, novato
calm [kɑːm] adj tranquilo; (sea) tranquilo, en calma ■ n calma, tranquilidad f ■ vt calmar, tranquilizar
  ▶ **calm down** vi calmarse, tranquilizarse ■ vt calmar, tranquilizar
calmly ['kɑːmlɪ] adv tranquilamente, con calma
calmness ['kɑːmnɪs] n calma
Calor gas® ['kæləʳ-] n butano, camping gas® m inv
calorie ['kælərɪ] n caloría; **low-~ product** producto bajo en calorías
calve [kɑːv] vi parir
calves [kɑːvz] npl of **calf**
CAM n abbr (= computer-aided manufacturing) producción f asistida por ordenador
camber ['kæmbəʳ] n (of road) combadura
Cambodia [kæm'bəudjə] n Camboya
Cambodian [kæm'bəudjən] adj, n camboyano(-a) m(f)
Cambs abbr (Brit) = **Cambridgeshire**
camcorder ['kæmkɔːdəʳ] n videocámara
came [keɪm] pt of **come**
camel ['kæməl] n camello
cameo ['kæmɪəu] n camafeo
camera ['kæmərə] n cámara or máquina fotográfica; (Cine, TV) cámara; (movie camera) cámara, tomavistas m inv; **in ~** a puerta cerrada
cameraman ['kæmərəmən] n cámara m
camera phone n teléfono m con cámara
Cameroon, Cameroun [kæme'ruːn] n Camerún m
camomile tea ['kæməmaɪl-] n manzanilla
camouflage ['kæməflɑːʒ] n camuflaje m ■ vt camuflar
camp [kæmp] n campo, campamento ■ vi acampar ■ adj afectado, afeminado; **to go camping** ir de or hacer camping
campaign [kæm'peɪn] n (Mil, Pol etc) campaña ■ vi: **to ~ (for/against)** hacer campaña (a favor de/en contra de)
campaigner [kæm'peɪnəʳ] n: **~ for** defensor(a) m(f) de; **~ against** persona que hace campaña contra
campbed ['kæmpbed] n (Brit) cama plegable
camper ['kæmpəʳ] n campista m/f; (vehicle) caravana
camping ['kæmpɪŋ] n camping m
campsite ['kæmpsaɪt] n camping m
campus ['kæmpəs] n campus m
camshaft ['kæmʃɑːft] n árbol m de levas
can [kæn] (aux vb see keyword) n (of oil, water)

bidón m; (tin) lata, bote m ■ vt enlatar;
(preserve) conservar en lata; **a ~ of beer** una
lata or un bote de cerveza; **to carry the ~** (col)
pagar el pato

 KEYWORD

can (negative **cannot, can't,** conditional and pt
could) aux vb **1** (be able to) poder; **you can do
it if you try** puedes hacerlo si lo intentas;
I can't see you no te veo; **can you hear me?**
(not translated) ¿me oyes?
2 (know how to) saber; **I can swim/play
tennis/drive** sé nadar/jugar al tenis/
conducir; **can you speak French?** ¿hablas or
sabes hablar francés?
3 (may) poder; **can I use your phone?** ¿me
dejas or puedo usar tu teléfono?; **could
I have a word with you?** ¿podría hablar
contigo un momento?
4 (expressing disbelief, puzzlement etc): **it can't be
true!** ¡no puede ser (verdad)!; **what CAN he
want?** ¿qué querrá?
5 (expressing possibility, suggestion etc): **he
could be in the library** podría estar en la
biblioteca; **she could have been delayed**
puede que se haya retrasado

Canada ['kænədə] n Canadá m
Canadian [kə'neɪdɪən] adj, n canadiense m/f
canal [kə'næl] n canal m
canary [kə'nɛərɪ] n canario
Canary Islands, Canaries [kə'nɛərɪz] npl las
(Islas) Canarias
Canberra ['kænbərə] n Canberra
cancel ['kænsəl] vt cancelar; (train) suprimir;
(appointment, cheque) anular; (cross out) tachar
▶ **cancel out** vt (Math) anular; (fig)
contrarrestar; **they ~ each other out** se
anulan mutuamente
cancellation [kænsə'leɪʃən] n cancelación f;
supresión f
cancer ['kænsə^r] n cáncer m; **C~** (Astro)
Cáncer m
cancerous ['kænsərəs] adj canceroso
cancer patient n enfermo(-a) m(f) de cáncer
cancer research n investigación f del cáncer
C and F abbr (= cost and freight) C y F
candid ['kændɪd] adj franco, abierto
candidacy ['kændɪdəsɪ] n candidatura
candidate ['kændɪdeɪt] n candidato(-a)
candidature ['kændɪdətʃə^r] n (Brit)
= **candidacy**
candidly ['kændɪdlɪ] adv francamente, con
franqueza
candle ['kændl] n vela; (in church) cirio
candle holder n see **candlestick**

candlelight ['kændllaɪt] n: **by ~** a la luz de
una vela
candlestick ['kændlstɪk] n (also: **candle
holder**: single) candelero; (: low) palmatoria;
(bigger, ornate) candelabro
candour, candor (US) ['kændə^r] n franqueza
C & W n abbr = **country and western (music)**
candy ['kændɪ] n azúcar m cande; (US)
caramelo ■ vt (fruit) escarchar
candy-floss ['kændɪflɔs] n (Brit) algodón m
(azucarado)
cane [keɪn] n (Bot) caña; (for baskets, chairs
etc) mimbre m; (stick) vara, palmeta; (for
walking) bastón m ■ vt (Brit Scol) castigar (con
palmeta); **~ liquor** caña
canine ['kænaɪn] adj canino
canister ['kænɪstə^r] n bote m
cannabis ['kænəbɪs] n canabis m
canned [kænd] adj en lata, de lata; (col: music)
grabado; (: drunk) mamado
cannibal ['kænɪbəl] n caníbal m/f,
antropófago(-a)
cannibalism ['kænɪbəlɪzəm] n canibalismo
cannon (pl ~ or **cannons**) ['kænən] n cañón m
cannonball ['kænənbɔːl] n bala (de cañón)
cannon fodder n carne f de cañón
cannot ['kænɔt] = **can not**
canny ['kænɪ] adj avispado
canoe [kə'nuː] n canoa; (Sport) piragua
canoeing [kə'nuːɪŋ] n (Sport) piragüismo
canoeist [kə'nuːɪst] n piragüista m/f
canon ['kænən] n (clergyman) canónigo;
(standard) canon m
canonize ['kænənaɪz] vt canonizar
can opener n abrelatas m inv
canopy ['kænəpɪ] n dosel m, toldo
can't [kænt] = **can not**
Cantab. abbr (Brit: = cantabrigiensis) of Cambridge
cantankerous [kæn'tæŋkərəs] adj arisco,
malhumorado
canteen [kæn'tiːn] n (eating place) comedor m;
(Brit: of cutlery) juego
canter ['kæntə^r] n medio galope ■ vi ir a
medio galope
cantilever ['kæntɪliːvə^r] n viga voladiza
canvas ['kænvəs] n (material) lona; (painting)
lienzo; (Naut) velamen m; **under ~** (camping)
en tienda de campaña
canvass ['kænvəs] vt (Pol: district) hacer
campaña (puerta a puerta) en; (: person) hacer
campaña (puerta a puerta) a favor de; (Comm:
district) sondear el mercado en; (: citizens,
opinions) sondear
canvasser ['kænvəsə^r] n (Pol) representante
m/f electoral; (Comm) corredor(a) m(f)
canyon ['kænjən] n cañón m
CAP n abbr (= Common Agricultural Policy) PAC f

465

cap [kæp] n (hat) gorra; (for swimming) gorro; (of pen) capuchón m; (of bottle) tapón m; (: metal) chapa; (contraceptive) diafragma m ■ vt (outdo) superar; (Brit Sport) seleccionar (para el equipo nacional); **and to ~ it all, he ...** y para colmo, él ...

capability [keɪpə'bɪlɪtɪ] n capacidad f

capable ['keɪpəbl] adj capaz

capacious [kə'peɪʃəs] adj amplio

capacity [kə'pæsɪtɪ] n capacidad f; (position) calidad f; **filled to ~** lleno a reventar; **this work is beyond my ~** este trabajo es superior a mí; **in an advisory ~** como asesor

cape [keɪp] n capa; (Geo) cabo

Cape of Good Hope n Cabo de Buena Esperanza

caper ['keɪpə'] n (Culin: also: **capers**) alcaparra; (prank) travesura

Cape Town n Ciudad f del Cabo

capital ['kæpɪtl] n (also: **capital city**) capital f; (money) capital m; (also: **capital letter**) mayúscula

capital account n cuenta de capital

capital allowance n desgravación f sobre bienes del capital

capital assets n activo fijo

capital expenditure n inversión f de capital

capital gains tax n impuesto sobre la plusvalía

capital goods npl bienes mpl de capital

capital-intensive [kæpɪtlɪn'tɛnsɪv] adj de utilización intensiva de capital

capital investment n inversión f de capital

capitalism ['kæpɪtəlɪzəm] n capitalismo

capitalist ['kæpɪtəlɪst] adj, n capitalista m/f

capitalize ['kæpɪtəlaɪz] vt (Comm: provide with capital) capitalizar

▶ **capitalize on** vt fus (fig) sacar provecho de, aprovechar

capital punishment n pena de muerte

capital transfer tax n impuesto sobre plusvalía de cesión

Capitol ['kæpɪtl] n: **the ~** el Capitolio

◉ **CAPITOL**
◉
◉ El Capitolio (Capitol) es el edificio en el
◉ que se reúne el Congreso de los Estados
◉ Unidos ("Congress"), situado en la ciudad
◉ de Washington. Por extensión, también
◉ se suele llamar así al edificio en el que
◉ tienen lugar las sesiones parlamentarias
◉ de la cámara de representantes de
◉ muchos de los estados.

capitulate [kə'pɪtjuleɪt] vi capitular, rendirse

capitulation [kəpɪtju'leɪʃən] n capitulación f, rendición f

capricious [kə'prɪʃəs] adj caprichoso

Capricorn ['kæprɪkɔ:n] n Capricornio

caps [kæps] abbr (= capital letters) may

capsize [kæp'saɪz] vt volcar, hacer zozobrar ■ vi volcarse, zozobrar

capstan ['kæpstən] n cabrestante m

capsule ['kæpsju:l] n cápsula

Capt. abbr = **Captain**

captain ['kæptɪn] n capitán m ■ vt capitanear, ser el capitán de

caption ['kæpʃən] n (heading) título; (to picture) leyenda, pie m

captivate ['kæptɪveɪt] vt cautivar, encantar

captive ['kæptɪv] adj, n cautivo(-a) m(f)

captivity [kæp'tɪvɪtɪ] n cautiverio

captor ['kæptə'] n captor(a) m(f)

capture ['kæptʃə'] vt capturar; (place) tomar; (attention) captar, llamar ■ n captura; toma; (Comput: also: **data capture**) formulación f de datos

car [kɑ:'] n coche m, carro (LAm), automóvil m, auto (LAm); (US Rail) vagón m; **by ~** en coche

Caracas [kə'rækəs] n Caracas m

carafe [kə'ræf] n garrafa

caramel ['kærəməl] n caramelo

carat ['kærət] n quilate m; **18-~ gold** oro de 18 quilates

caravan ['kærəvæn] n (Brit) caravana, remolque m; (of camels) caravana

caravan site n (Brit) camping m para caravanas

caraway ['kærəweɪ] n: **~ seed** carvi m

carbohydrates [kɑ:bəu'haɪdreɪts] npl (foods) hidratos mpl de carbono

carbolic [kɑ:'bɔlɪk] adj: **~ acid** ácido carbólico, fenol m

car bomb n coche-bomba m

carbon ['kɑ:bən] n carbono

carbonated ['kɑ:bəneɪtɪd] adj (drink) con gas

carbon copy n copia al carbón

carbon dioxide n dióxido de carbono, anhídrido carbónico

carbon footprint n huella de carbono

carbon monoxide n monóxido de carbono

carbon paper n papel m carbón

carbon ribbon n cinta de carbón

car boot sale n mercadillo (de objetos usados expuestos en el maletero del coche)

carburettor, carburetor (US) [kɑ:bju'rɛtə'] n carburador m

carcass ['kɑ:kəs] n (of animal) res f muerta; (dead body) cadáver m

carcinogenic [kɑ:sɪnə'dʒɛnɪk] adj cancerígeno

card [kɑ:d] n (thin cardboard) cartulina; (playing

card) carta, naipe *m*; (*visiting card, greetings card etc*) tarjeta; (*index card*) ficha; **membership ~** carnet *m*; **to play cards** jugar a las cartas *or* los naipes
cardamom ['kɑ:dəməm] *n* cardamomo
cardboard ['kɑ:dbɔːd] *n* cartón *m*, cartulina
cardboard box *n* caja de cartón
cardboard city *n* zona de marginados sin hogar (*que se refugian entre cartones*)
card-carrying member ['kɑ:dkærɪɪŋ-] *n* miembro con carnet
card game *n* juego de naipes *or* cartas
cardiac ['kɑ:dɪæk] *adj* cardíaco
cardigan ['kɑ:dɪgən] *n* chaqueta (de punto), rebeca
cardinal ['kɑ:dɪnl] *adj* cardinal ■ *n* cardenal *m*
cardinal number *n* número cardinal
card index *n* fichero
cardphone ['kɑ:dfəʊn] *n* cabina que funciona con tarjetas telefónicas
cardsharp ['kɑ:dʃɑ:p] *n* fullero(-a)
card vote *n* voto por delegación
CARE [kɛəʳ] *n abbr* (= *Cooperative for American Relief Everywhere*) *sociedad benéfica*
care [kɛəʳ] *n* cuidado; (*worry*) preocupación *f*; (*charge*) cargo, custodia ■ *vi*: **to ~ about** preocuparse por; **~ of (c/o)** en casa de, al cuidado de; (*on letter*) para (entregar a); **in sb's ~** a cargo de algn; **the child has been taken into ~** pusieron al niño bajo custodia del gobierno; **"with ~"** ¡frágil!"; **to take ~ to** cuidarse de, tener cuidado de; **to take ~ of** *vt* cuidar; (*details, arrangements*) encargarse de; **I don't ~** no me importa; **I couldn't ~ less** me trae sin cuidado
  ▸ **care for** *vt fus* cuidar; (*like*) querer
careen [kə'ri:n] *vi* (*ship*) inclinarse, escorar ■ *vt* carenar
career [kə'rɪəʳ] *n* carrera (profesional); (*occupation*) profesión *f* ■ *vi* (*also*: **career along**) correr a toda velocidad
career girl *n* mujer *f* dedicada a su profesión
careers officer *n* consejero(-a) de orientación profesional
carefree ['kɛəfri:] *adj* despreocupado
careful ['kɛəful] *adj* cuidadoso; (*cautious*) cauteloso; **(be) ~!** ¡ten cuidado!; **he's very ~ with his money** mira mucho el dinero; (*pej*) es muy tacaño
carefully ['kɛəfəlɪ] *adv* con cuidado, cuidadosamente
careless ['kɛəlɪs] *adj* descuidado; (*heedless*) poco atento
carelessly ['kɛəlɪslɪ] *adv* sin cuidado, a la ligera

carelessness ['kɛəlɪsnɪs] *n* descuido, falta de atención
carer ['kɛərəʳ] *n persona que cuida de enfermos, ancianos o disminuidos*
caress [kə'rɛs] *n* caricia ■ *vt* acariciar
caretaker ['kɛəteɪkəʳ] *n* portero(-a), conserje *m/f*
caretaker government *n* gobierno provisional
car-ferry ['kɑ:fɛrɪ] *n* transbordador *m* para coches
cargo (*pl* **cargoes**) ['kɑ:gəʊ] *n* cargamento, carga
cargo boat *n* buque *m* de carga, carguero
cargo plane *n* avión *m* de carga
car hire *n* alquiler *m* de coches
Caribbean [kærɪ'bi:ən] *adj* caribe, caribeño; **the ~ (Sea)** el (Mar) Caribe
caricature ['kærɪkətjʊəʳ] *n* caricatura
caring ['kɛərɪŋ] *adj* humanitario
carnage ['kɑ:nɪdʒ] *n* matanza, carnicería
carnal ['kɑ:nl] *adj* carnal
carnation [kɑ:'neɪʃən] *n* clavel *m*
carnival ['kɑ:nɪvəl] *n* carnaval *m*; (*US*) parque *m* de atracciones
carnivore ['kɑ:nɪvɔ:ʳ] *n* carnívoro(-a)
carnivorous [kɑ:'nɪvrəs] *adj* carnívoro
carol ['kærəl] *n*: (**Christmas**) **~** villancico
carouse [kə'rauz] *vi* estar de juerga
carousel [kærə'sɛl] *n* (*US*) tiovivo, caballitos *mpl*
carp [kɑ:p] *n* (*fish*) carpa
  ▸ **carp at** *or* **about** *vt fus* sacar faltas de
car park *n* (*Brit*) aparcamiento, parking *m*, playa de estacionamiento (*LAm*)
carpenter ['kɑ:pɪntəʳ] *n* carpintero
carpentry ['kɑ:pɪntrɪ] *n* carpintería
carpet ['kɑ:pɪt] *n* alfombra ■ *vt* alfombrar; **fitted ~** moqueta
carpet bombing *n* bombardeo de arrasamiento
carpet slippers *npl* zapatillas *fpl*
carpet sweeper [-'swi:pəʳ] *n* cepillo mecánico
car phone *n* teléfono de coche
carping ['kɑ:pɪŋ] *adj* (*critical*) criticón(-ona)
carriage ['kærɪdʒ] *n* coche *m*; (*Brit Rail*) vagón *m*; (*for goods*) transporte *m*; (*of typewriter*) carro; (*bearing*) porte *m*; **~ forward** porte *m* debido; **~ free** franco de porte; **~ paid** porte pagado; **~ inwards/outwards** gastos *mpl* de transporte a cargo del comprador/vendedor
carriage return *n* (*on typewriter etc*) tecla de regreso
carriageway ['kærɪdʒweɪ] *n* (*Brit: part of road*) calzada; **dual ~** autovía

carrier ['kærɪəʳ] n transportista m/f; (company) empresa de transportes; (Med) portador(a) m(f)
carrier bag n (Brit) bolsa de papel or plástico
carrier pigeon n paloma mensajera
carrion ['kærɪən] n carroña
carrot ['kærət] n zanahoria
carry ['kærɪ] vt (person) llevar; (transport) transportar; (a motion, bill) aprobar; (involve: responsibilities etc) entrañar, conllevar; (Comm: stock) tener en existencia; (interest) llevar; (Math: figure) llevarse ▪ vi (sound) oírse; **to get carried away** (fig) entusiasmarse; **this loan carries 10% interest** este empréstito devenga un interés del 10 por ciento
▶ **carry forward** vt (Math, Comm) pasar a la página/columna siguiente
▶ **carry on** vi (continue) seguir (adelante), continuar; (fam: complain) montar el número ▪ vt seguir, continuar
▶ **carry out** vt (orders) cumplir; (investigation) llevar a cabo, realizar
carrycot ['kærɪkɔt] n (Brit) cuna portátil, capazo
carry-on ['kærɪ'ɔn] n (col) follón m
cart [kɑːt] n carro, carreta ▪ vt cargar con
carte blanche ['kɑːt'blɒnʃ] n: **to give sb a ~** dar carta blanca a algn
cartel [kɑː'tɛl] n (Comm) cartel m
cartilage ['kɑːtɪlɪdʒ] n cartílago
cartographer [kɑː'tɔgrəfəʳ] n cartógrafo(-a)
carton ['kɑːtən] n caja (de cartón); (of cigarettes) cartón m
cartoon [kɑː'tuːn] n (Press) chiste m; (comic strip) historieta, tira cómica; (film) dibujos mpl animados
cartoonist [kɑː'tuːnɪst] n humorista m/f gráfico
cartridge ['kɑːtrɪdʒ] n cartucho
cartwheel ['kɑːtwiːl] n: **to turn a ~** dar una voltereta lateral
carve [kɑːv] vt (meat) trinchar; (wood) tallar; (stone) cincelar, esculpir; (on tree) grabar
▶ **carve up** vt dividir, repartir; (meat) trinchar
carving ['kɑːvɪŋ] n (in wood etc) escultura, talla
carving knife n trinchante m
car wash n túnel m de lavado
Casablanca [kæsə'blæŋkə] n Casablanca
cascade [kæs'keɪd] n salto de agua, cascada; (fig) chorro ▪ vi caer a chorros
case [keɪs] n (container) caja; (Med) caso; (for jewels etc) estuche m; (Law) causa, proceso; (Brit: also: **suitcase**) maleta; **lower/upper ~** (Typ) caja baja/alta; **in ~ of** en caso de; **in any ~** en todo caso; **just in ~** por si acaso; **to**

have a good ~ tener buenas razones; **there's a strong ~ for reform** hay razones sólidas para exigir una reforma
case history n (Med) historial m médico, historia clínica
case study n estudio de casos prácticos
cash [kæʃ] n (dinero) efectivo; (col: money) dinero ▪ vt cobrar, hacer efectivo; **to pay (in) ~** pagar al contado; **~ on delivery (COD)** entrega contra reembolso; **~ with order** paga al hacer el pedido; **to be short of ~** estar pelado, estar sin blanca
▶ **cash in** vt (insurance policy etc) cobrar ▪ vi: **to ~ in on sth** sacar partido or aprovecharse de algo
cash account n cuenta de caja
cash and carry n cash and carry m, autoservicio mayorista
cashbook ['kæʃbuk] n libro de caja
cash box n hucha
cash card n tarjeta f de(l) cajero (automático)
cash desk n (Brit) caja
cash discount n descuento por pago al contado
cash dispenser n cajero automático
cashew [kæ'ʃuː] n (also: **cashew nut**) anacardo
cash flow n flujo de fondos, cash-flow m, movimiento de efectivo
cashier [kæ'ʃɪəʳ] n cajero(-a) ▪ vt (Mil) destituir, expulsar
cashmere ['kæʃmɪəʳ] n cachemir m, cachemira
cash payment n pago al contado
cash price n precio al contado
cash register n caja
cash reserves npl reserva en efectivo
cash sale n venta al contado
casing ['keɪsɪŋ] n revestimiento
casino [kə'siːnəu] n casino
cask [kɑːsk] n tonel m, barril m
casket ['kɑːskɪt] n cofre m, estuche m; (US: coffin) ataúd m
Caspian Sea ['kæspɪən-] n: **the ~** el Mar Caspio
cassava [kə'sɑːvə] n mandioca
casserole ['kæsərəul] n (food, pot) cazuela
cassette [kæ'sɛt] n cas(s)et(t)e m or f
cassette deck n platina
cassette player, cassette recorder n cas(s)et(t)e m
cassock ['kæsək] n sotana
cast [kɑːst] vb (pt, pp **cast**) ▪ vt (throw) echar, arrojar, lanzar; (skin) mudar, perder; (metal) fundir; (Theat): **to ~ sb as Othello** dar a algn el papel de Otelo ▪ n (Theat) reparto; (mould) forma, molde m; (also: **plaster cast**) vaciado;

to ~ loose soltar; to ~ one's vote votar
▶ cast aside vt (reject) descartar, desechar
▶ cast away vt desechar
▶ cast down vt derribar
▶ cast off vi (Naut) soltar amarras; (Knitting) cerrar los puntos ■ vt (Knitting) cerrar; to ~ sb off abandonar a algn, desentenderse de algn
▶ cast on vt (Knitting) montar
castanets [kæstə'nɛts] npl castañuelas fpl
castaway ['kɑːstəwəɪ] n náufrago(-a)
caste [kɑːst] n casta
caster sugar ['kɑːstəʳ-] n (Brit) azúcar m en polvo
Castile [kæs'tiːl] n Castilla
Castilian [kæs'tɪlɪən] adj, n castellano(-a) ■ n (Ling) castellano
casting vote ['kɑːstɪŋ-] n (Brit) voto decisivo
cast iron n hierro fundido or colado ■ adj (fig: alibi) irrebatible; (will) férreo
castle ['kɑːsl] n castillo; (Chess) torre f
castor ['kɑːstəʳ] n (wheel) ruedecilla
castor oil n aceite m de ricino
castrate [kæs'treɪt] vt castrar
casual ['kæʒjuːl] adj (by chance) fortuito; (irregular: work etc) eventual, temporero; (unconcerned) despreocupado; (informal: clothes) de sport
casually ['kæʒjulɪ] adv por casualidad; de manera despreocupada
casualty ['kæʒjultɪ] n víctima, herido; (dead) muerto; (Mil) baja; heavy casualties numerosas bajas fpl
casualty ward n urgencias fpl
cat [kæt] n gato
catacombs ['kætəkuːmz] npl catacumbas fpl
Catalan ['kætələn] adj, n catalán(-ana) m(f)
catalogue, catalog (US) ['kætələɡ] n catálogo ■ vt catalogar
Catalonia [kætə'ləunɪə] n Cataluña
catalyst ['kætəlɪst] n catalizador m
catalytic converter [kætə'lɪtɪkkən'vəːtəʳ] n catalizador m
catapult ['kætəpʌlt] n tirachinas m inv
cataract ['kætərækt] n (Med) cataratas fpl
catarrh [kə'tɑːʳ] n catarro
catastrophe [kə'tæstrəfɪ] n catástrofe f
catastrophic [kætə'strɔfɪk] adj catastrófico
catcall ['kætkɔːl] n (at meeting etc) rechifla, silbido
catch [kætʃ] vb (pt, pp caught) ■ vt coger (SP), agarrar (LAm); (arrest) atrapar, coger (SP); (grasp) asir; (breath) recobrar; (person: by surprise) pillar; (attract: attention) captar; (Med) pillar, coger; (also: catch up) alcanzar ■ vi (fire) encenderse; (in branches etc) engancharse ■ n (fish etc) captura; (act of catching) cogida;

(trick) trampa; (of lock) pestillo, cerradura; to ~ fire prenderse; (house) incendiarse; to ~ sight of divisar
▶ catch on vi (understand) caer en la cuenta; (grow popular) tener éxito, cuajar
▶ catch out vt (fig: with trick question) hundir
▶ catch up vi (fig) ponerse al día
catching ['kætʃɪŋ] adj (Med) contagioso
catchment area ['kætʃmənt-] n (Brit) zona de captación
catch phrase n frase f de moda
catch-22 ['kætʃtwɛntɪ'tuː] n: it's a ~ situation es un callejón sin salida, es un círculo vicioso
catchy ['kætʃɪ] adj (tune) pegadizo
catechism ['kætɪkɪzəm] n (Rel) catecismo
categoric [kætɪ'ɡɔrɪk], categorical [kætɪ'ɡɔrɪkəl] adj categórico, terminante
categorically [kætɪ'ɡɔrɪkəlɪ] adv categóricamente, terminantemente
categorize ['kætɪɡəraɪz] vt clasificar
category ['kætɪɡərɪ] n categoría
cater ['keɪtəʳ] vi: to ~ for (Brit) abastecer a; (needs) atender a; (consumers) proveer a
caterer ['keɪtərəʳ] n abastecedor(a) m(f), proveedor(a) m(f)
catering ['keɪtərɪŋ] n (trade) hostelería
caterpillar ['kætəpɪləʳ] n oruga
caterpillar track n rodado de oruga
cat flap n gatera
cathedral [kə'θiːdrəl] n catedral f
cathode-ray tube ['kæθəudreɪ'tjuːb] n tubo de rayos catódicos
catholic ['kæθəlɪk] adj católico; C~ adj, n (Rel) católico(-a) m(f)
CAT scanner [kæt-] (Med) n abbr (= computerized axial tomography scanner) escáner m TAC
cat's-eye ['kætsaɪ] n (Brit Aut) catafaro
catsup ['kætsəp] n (US) ketchup, catsup m
cattle ['kætl] npl ganado sg
catty ['kætɪ] adj malicioso
catwalk ['kætwɔːk] n pasarela
Caucasian [kɔː'keɪzɪən] adj, n caucásico(-a) m(f)
Caucasus ['kɔːkəsəs] n Cáucaso
caucus ['kɔːkəs] n (Pol: local committee) comité m local; (: US: to elect candidates) comité m electoral; (: group) camarilla política
caught [kɔːt] pt, pp of catch
cauliflower ['kɔlɪflauəʳ] n coliflor f
cause [kɔːz] n causa; (reason) motivo, razón f ■ vt causar; (provoke) provocar; to ~ sb to do sth hacer que algn haga algo
causeway ['kɔːzweɪ] n (road) carretera elevada; (embankment) terraplén m
caustic ['kɔːstɪk] adj cáustico; (fig) mordaz

cauterize ['kɔːtəraɪz] vt cauterizar
caution ['kɔːʃən] n cautela, prudencia; (*warning*) advertencia, amonestación f ▪ vt amonestar
cautious ['kɔːʃəs] adj cauteloso, prudente, precavido
cautiously ['kɔːʃəslɪ] adv con cautela
cautiousness ['kɔːʃəsnɪs] n cautela
cavalcade [kævəl'keɪd] n cabalgata
cavalier [kævə'lɪər] n (*knight*) caballero ▪ adj (*pej: offhand: person, attitude*) arrogante, desdeñoso
cavalry ['kævəlrɪ] n caballería
cave [keɪv] n cueva, caverna ▪ vi: **to go caving** ir en una expedición espeleológica
▶ **cave in** vi (*roof etc*) derrumbarse, hundirse
caveman ['keɪvmæn] n cavernícola m
cavern ['kævən] n caverna
cavernous ['kævənəs] adj (*cheeks, eyes*) hundido
caviar, caviare ['kævɪɑːr] n caviar m
cavity ['kævɪtɪ] n hueco, cavidad f
cavity wall insulation n aislamiento térmico
cavort [kə'vɔːt] vi hacer cabrioladas
cayenne [keɪ'ɛn] n: ~ **pepper** pimentón m picante
CB n abbr (= *Citizens' Band (Radio)*) frecuencias de radio usadas para la comunicación privada; (Brit: = *Companion of (the Order of) the Bath*) título de nobleza
CBC n abbr (= *Canadian Broadcasting Corporation*) cadena de radio y televisión
CBE n abbr (Brit: = *Companion of (the Order of) the British Empire*) título de nobleza
CBI n abbr (= *Confederation of British Industry*) ≈ C.E.O.E. f (SP)
CBS n abbr (US: = *Columbia Broadcasting System*) cadena de radio y televisión
CC abbr (Brit) = **county council**
cc abbr (= *cubic centimetres*) cc, cm³; (*on letter etc*) = **carbon copy**
CCA n abbr (US: = *Circuit Court of Appeals*) tribunal de apelación itinerante
CCTV n abbr = **closed-circuit television**
CCU n abbr (*esp US: = coronary care unit*) unidad f de cuidados cardiológicos
CD n abbr (= *compact disc*) CD m; (Mil: = *Civil Defence (Corps*): Brit: = *Civil Defense*: US) ▪ abbr (Brit: = *Corps Diplomatique*) CD
CD burner n tostadora/grabadora f de CDs
CD player n reproductor m de compact disc
CDC n abbr (US) = **center for disease control**
Cdr. abbr = **commander**
CD-ROM ['siː'diː'rɔm] n abbr (= *compact disc read-only memory*) CD-ROM m
CDT n abbr (US: = *Central Daylight Time*) hora de

verano del centro; (Brit: Scol: = *Craft, Design and Technology*) artesanía, diseño y tecnología
CDW n abbr = **collision damage waiver**
CD writer n tostadora/grabadora f de CDs
cease [siːs] vt cesar
ceasefire ['siːsfaɪər] n alto m el fuego
ceaseless ['siːslɪs] adj incesante
ceaselessly ['siːslɪslɪ] adv sin cesar
CED n abbr (US) = **Committee for Economic Development**
cedar ['siːdər] n cedro
cede [siːd] vt ceder
CEEB n abbr (US: = *College Entrance Examination Board*) tribunal para las pruebas de acceso a la universidad
ceilidh ['keɪlɪ] n baile con música y danzas tradicionales escocesas o irlandesas
ceiling ['siːlɪŋ] n techo; (*fig: upper limit*) límite m, tope m
celebrate ['sɛlɪbreɪt] vt celebrar; (*have a party*) festejar ▪ vi: **let's ~!** ¡vamos a celebrarlo!
celebrated ['sɛlɪbreɪtɪd] adj célebre
celebration [sɛlɪ'breɪʃən] n celebración f, festejo
celebrity [sɪ'lɛbrɪtɪ] n celebridad f
celeriac [sə'lɛrɪæk] n apio-nabo
celery ['sɛlərɪ] n apio
celestial [sɪ'lɛstɪəl] adj (*of the sky*) celeste; (*divine*) celestial
celibacy ['sɛlɪbəsɪ] n celibato
cell [sɛl] n celda; (Biol) célula; (Elec) elemento
cellar ['sɛlər] n sótano; (*for wine*) bodega
cellist ['tʃɛlɪst] n violoncelista m/f
cello ['tʃɛləu] n violoncelo
cellophane ['sɛləfeɪn] n celofán m
cellphone ['sɛlfəun] n móvil m
cellular ['sɛljulər] adj celular
celluloid ['sɛljulɔɪd] n celuloide m
cellulose ['sɛljuləus] n celulosa
Celsius ['sɛlsɪəs] adj centígrado
Celt [kɛlt, sɛlt] n celta m/f
Celtic ['kɛltɪk, 'sɛltɪk] adj celta, céltico ▪ n (Ling) celta m
cement [sə'mɛnt] n cemento ▪ vt cementar; (*fig*) cimentar
cement mixer n hormigonera
cemetery ['sɛmɪtrɪ] n cementerio
cenotaph ['sɛnətɑːf] n cenotafio
censor ['sɛnsər] n censor(a) m(f) ▪ vt (*cut*) censurar
censorship ['sɛnsəʃɪp] n censura
censure ['sɛnʃər] vt censurar
census ['sɛnsəs] n censo
cent [sɛnt] n (US: *unit of dollar*) centavo; (*unit of euro*) céntimo; *see also* **per**
centenary [sɛn'tiːnərɪ], **centennial** [sɛn'tɛnɪəl] (US) n centenario

center ['sentər] n (US) = **centre**
centigrade ['sentigreid] adj centígrado
centilitre, centiliter (US) ['sentili:tər] n
centilitro
centimetre, centimeter (US) ['sentimi:tər]
n centímetro
centipede ['sentipi:d] n ciempiés m inv
central ['sentrəl] adj central; (house etc)
céntrico
Central African Republic n República
Centroafricana
Central America n Centroamérica
Central American adj, n centroamericano(-a)
m(f)
central heating n calefacción f central
centralize ['sentrəlaiz] vt centralizar
central processing unit n (Comput) unidad
f procesadora central, unidad f central de
proceso
central reservation n (Brit Aut) mediana
centre, center (US) ['sentər] n centro ■ vt
centrar; **to ~ (on)** (concentrate) concentrar
(en)
centrefold, centerfold (US) ['sentəfəuld] n
página central plegable
centre-forward ['sentə'fɔ:wəd] n (Sport)
delantero centro
centre-half ['sentə'ha:f] n (Sport) medio
centro
centrepiece, centerpiece (US) ['sentəpi:s] n
punto central
centre spread n (Brit) páginas fpl centrales
centre-stage n: **to take ~** pasar a primer
plano
centrifuge ['sentrifju:dʒ] n centrifugadora
century ['sentjuri] n siglo; **20th ~** siglo
veinte; **in the twentieth ~** en el siglo veinte
CEO n abbr = **chief executive officer**
ceramic [si'ræmik] adj de cerámica
ceramics [si'ræmiks] n cerámica
cereal ['si:riəl] n cereal m
cerebral ['seribrəl] adj cerebral
ceremonial [seri'məuniəl] n ceremonial
ceremony ['seriməni] n ceremonia; **to
stand on ~** hacer ceremonias, andarse con
cumplidos
cert [sə:t] n (Brit col): **it's a dead ~** ¡es cosa
segura!
certain ['sə:tən] adj seguro; (correct) cierto;
(particular) cierto; **for ~** a ciencia cierta
certainly ['sə:tənli] adv desde luego, por
supuesto
certainty ['sə:tənti] n certeza, certidumbre
f, seguridad f
certificate [sə'tifikit] n certificado
certified ['sə:tifaid] adj: **~ mail** (US) correo
certificado

certified public accountant n (US) contable
m/f diplomado(-a)
certify ['sə:tifai] vt certificar
cervical ['sə:vikl] adj: **~ cancer** cáncer m
cervical; **~ smear** citología
cervix ['sə:viks] n cerviz f, cuello del útero
Cesarean [si'zɛəriən] adj, n (US) = **Caesarean**
cessation [sə'seiʃən] n cese m, suspensión f
cesspit ['sespit] n pozo negro
CET n abbr (= Central European Time) hora de Europa
central
Ceylon [si'lɔn] n Ceilán m
cf. abbr (= compare) cfr
c/f abbr (Comm) = **carried forward**
CFC n abbr (= chlorofluorocarbon) CFC m
CG n abbr (US) = **coastguard**
cg abbr (= centigram) cg
CH n abbr (Brit: = Companion of Honour) título de
nobleza
ch. abbr (= chapter) cap
Chad [tʃæd] n Chad m
chafe [tʃeif] vt (rub) rozar; (irritate) irritar;
to ~ (against) (fig) irritarse or enojarse (con)
chaffinch ['tʃæfintʃ] n pinzón m (vulgar)
chagrin ['ʃægrin] n (annoyance) disgusto;
(disappointment) desazón f
chain [tʃein] n cadena ■ vt (also: **chain up**)
encadenar
chain reaction n reacción f en cadena
chain-smoke ['tʃeinsməuk] vi fumar un
cigarrillo tras otro
chain store n tienda de una cadena,
≈ grandes almacenes mpl
chair [tʃɛər] n silla; (armchair) sillón m; (of
university) cátedra ■ vt (meeting) presidir; **the
~** (US: electric chair) la silla eléctrica; **please
take a ~** siéntese or tome asiento, por favor
chairlift ['tʃɛəlift] n telesilla m
chairman ['tʃɛəmən] n presidente m
chairperson ['tʃɛəpə:sn] n presidente(-a) m(f)
chairwoman ['tʃɛəwumən] n presidenta
chalet ['ʃælei] n chalet m (de madera)
chalice ['tʃælis] n cáliz m
chalk [tʃɔ:k] n (Geo) creta; (for writing) tiza, gis
m (LAm)
▶ **chalk up** vt apuntar; (fig: success, victory)
apuntarse
challenge ['tʃælindʒ] n desafío, reto ■ vt
desafiar, retar; (statement, right) poner en
duda; **to ~ sb to do sth** retar a algn a que
haga algo
challenger ['tʃælindʒər] n (Sport)
contrincante m/f
challenging ['tʃælindʒiŋ] adj que supone un
reto; (tone) de desafío
chamber ['tʃeimbər] n cámara, sala
chambermaid ['tʃeimbəmeid] n camarera

chamber music n música de cámara
chamber of commerce n cámara de comercio
chamberpot ['tʃeɪmbəpɔt] n orinal m
chameleon [kə'miːlɪən] n camaleón m
chamois ['ʃæmwɑː] n gamuza
champagne [ʃæm'peɪn] n champaña m, champán m
champers ['ʃæmpəz] nsg (col) champán m
champion ['tʃæmpɪən] n campeón(-ona) m(f); (of cause) defensor(a) m(f), paladín m/f ■ vt defender, apoyar
championship ['tʃæmpɪənʃɪp] n campeonato
chance [tʃɑːns] n (coincidence) casualidad f; (luck) suerte f; (fate) azar m; (opportunity) ocasión f, oportunidad f, chance m or f (LAm); (likelihood) posibilidad f; (risk) riesgo ■ vt arriesgar, probar ■ adj fortuito, casual; **to ~ it** arriesgarse, intentarlo; **to take a ~** arriesgarse; **by ~** por casualidad; **it's the ~ of a lifetime** es la oportunidad de su vida; **the chances are that ...** lo más probable es que ...; **to ~ to do sth** (happen) hacer algo por casualidad
▸**chance (up)on** vt fus tropezar(se) con
chancel ['tʃɑːnsəl] n coro y presbiterio
chancellor ['tʃɑːnsələr] n canciller m; **C~ of the Exchequer** (Brit) Ministro de Economía y Hacienda; see also **Downing Street**
chancy ['tʃɑːnsɪ] adj (col) arriesgado
chandelier [ʃændə'lɪər] n araña (de luces)
change [tʃeɪndʒ] vt cambiar; (clothes, house) cambiarse de, mudarse de; (transform) transformar ■ vi cambiar(se); (change trains) hacer transbordo; (be transformed): **to ~ into** transformarse en ■ n cambio; (alteration) modificación f, transformación f; (coins) suelto; (money returned) vuelta, vuelto (LAm); **to ~ one's mind** cambiar de opinión or idea; **to ~ gear** (Aut) cambiar de marcha; **she changed into an old skirt** se puso una falda vieja; **for a ~** para variar; **can you give me ~ for £1?** ¿tiene cambio de una libra?; **keep the ~** quédese con la vuelta
changeable ['tʃeɪndʒəbl] adj (weather) cambiable; (person) variable
changeless ['tʃeɪndʒlɪs] adj inmutable
change machine n máquina de cambio
changeover ['tʃeɪndʒəuvər] n (to new system) cambio
changing ['tʃeɪndʒɪŋ] adj cambiante
changing room n (Brit) vestuario
channel ['tʃænl] n (TV) canal m; (of river) cauce m; (of sea) estrecho; (groove: fig: medium) conducto, medio ■ vt (river etc) encauzar; **to ~ into** (fig: interest, energies) encauzar a, dirigir a; **the (English) C~** el Canal (de la Mancha);

the C~ Islands las Islas Anglonormandas;
channels of communication canales mpl de comunicación; **green/red ~** (Customs) pasillo verde/rojo
Channel Tunnel n: **the ~** el túnel del Canal de la Mancha, el Eurotúnel
chant [tʃɑːnt] n canto; (of crowd) gritos mpl ■ vt cantar; **the demonstrators chanted their disapproval** los manifestantes corearon su desaprobación
chaos ['keɪɔs] n caos m
chaos theory n teoría del caos
chaotic [keɪ'ɔtɪk] adj caótico
chap [tʃæp] n (Brit col: man) tío, tipo; **old ~** amigo (mío)
chapel ['tʃæpəl] n capilla
chaperone ['ʃæpərəun] n carabina
chaplain ['tʃæplɪn] n capellán m
chapped [tʃæpt] adj agrietado
chapter ['tʃæptər] n capítulo
char [tʃɑːr] vt (burn) carbonizar, chamuscar ■ n (Brit) = **charlady**
character ['kærɪktər] n carácter m, naturaleza, índole f; (in novel, film) personaje m; (role) papel m; (individuality) carácter m; (Comput) carácter m; **a person of good ~** una persona de buena reputación
character code n código de caracteres
characteristic [kærɪktə'rɪstɪk] adj característico ■ n característica
characterize ['kærɪktəraɪz] vt caracterizar
charade [ʃə'rɑːd] n farsa, comedia; **charades** (game) charadas fpl
charcoal ['tʃɑːkəul] n carbón m vegetal; (Art) carboncillo
charge [tʃɑːdʒ] n carga; (Law) cargo, acusación f; (cost) precio, coste m; (responsibility) cargo; (task) encargo ■ vt (Law): **to ~ (with)** acusar (de); (gun, battery) cargar; (Mil: enemy) cargar; (price) pedir; (customer) cobrar; (person: with task) encargar ■ vi precipitarse; (make pay) cobrar; **charges** npl: **bank charges** comisiones fpl bancarias; **extra ~** recargo, suplemento; **free of ~** gratis; **to reverse the charges** (Brit Tel) llamar a cobro revertido; **to take ~ of** hacerse cargo de, encargarse de; **to be in ~ of** estar encargado de; **how much do you ~?** ¿cuánto cobra usted?; **to ~ an expense (up) to sb's account** cargar algo a cuenta de algn; **~ it to my account** póngalo or cárguelo a mi cuenta
charge account n (US) cuenta abierta or a crédito
charge card n tarjeta de cuenta
chargé d'affaires ['ʃɑːʒeɪdæ'fɛər] n encargado de negocios

chargehand ['tʃɑːdʒhænd] *n* capataz *m*
charger ['tʃɑːdʒəʳ] *n* (*also*: **battery charger**)
cargador *m* (de baterías)
chariot ['tʃærɪət] *n* carro
charisma [kæ'rɪzmə] *n* carisma *m*
charitable ['tʃærɪtəbl] *adj* caritativo
charity ['tʃærɪtɪ] *n* (*gen*) caridad *f*;
(*organization*) organización *f* benéfica
charlady ['tʃɑːleɪdɪ] *n* (*Brit*) mujer *f* de la
limpieza
charlatan ['ʃɑːlətən] *n* charlatán *m*
charm [tʃɑːm] *n* encanto, atractivo; (*spell*)
hechizo; (*object*) amuleto ■ *vt* encantar;
hechizar
charm bracelet *n* pulsera amuleto
charming ['tʃɑːmɪŋ] *adj* encantador(a);
(*person*) simpático
chart [tʃɑːt] *n* (*table*) cuadro; (*graph*) gráfica;
(*map*) carta de navegación; (*weather chart*)
mapa *m* meteorológico ■ *vt* (*course*) trazar;
(*sales, progress*) hacer una gráfica de; **to be in
the charts** (*record, pop group*) estar en la lista
de éxitos
charter ['tʃɑːtəʳ] *vt* (*bus*) alquilar; (*plane, ship*)
fletar ■ *n* (*document*) estatuto, carta; **on ~ en**
alquiler, alquilado
chartered accountant *n* (*Brit*) contable *m/f*
diplomado(-a)
charter flight *n* vuelo chárter
charwoman ['tʃɑːwumən] *n* = **charlady**
chase [tʃeɪs] *vt* (*pursue*) perseguir; (*hunt*) cazar
■ *n* persecución *f*; caza; **to ~ after** correr tras
▶ **chase up** *vt* (*information*) tratar de
conseguir; **to ~ sb up about sth** recordar
algo a algn
chasm ['kæzəm] *n* abismo
chassis ['ʃæsɪ] *n* chasis *m*
chaste [tʃeɪst] *adj* casto
chastened ['tʃeɪsənd] *adj* escarmentado
chastening ['tʃeɪsnɪŋ] *adj* aleccionador(a)
chastity ['tʃæstɪtɪ] *n* castidad *f*
chat [tʃæt] *vi* (*also*: **have a chat**) charlar;
(*Internet*) chatear ■ *n* charla; (*Internet*) chat *m*
▶ **chat up** *vt* (*col*: *girl*) ligar con, enrollarse con
chatline ['tʃætlaɪn] *n* línea (telefónica)
múltiple, party line *f*
chat room *n* (*internet*) chat *m*, canal *m* de
charla
chat show *n* (*Brit*) programa *m* de entrevistas
chattel ['tʃætl] *n* bien *m* mueble
chatter ['tʃætəʳ] *vi* (*person*) charlar; (*teeth*)
castañetear ■ *n* (*of birds*) parloteo; (*of people*)
charla, cháchara
chatterbox ['tʃætəbɒks] *n* parlanchín(-ina)
m(f)
chattering classes ['tʃætərɪŋ'klɑːsɪz] *npl*:
the ~ (*col, pej*) los intelectualillos

chatty ['tʃætɪ] *adj* (*style*) informal; (*person*)
hablador(a)
chauffeur ['ʃəufəʳ] *n* chófer *m*
chauvinist ['ʃəuvɪnɪst] *n* (*also*: **male
chauvinist**) machista *m*; (*nationalist*)
chovinista *m/f*, patriotero(-a) *m(f)*
ChE *abbr* = **chemical engineer**
cheap [tʃiːp] *adj* barato; (*joke*) de mal gusto,
chabacano; (*poor quality*) malo; (*reduced: ticket*)
económico; (: *fare*) barato ■ *adv* barato
cheapen ['tʃiːpn] *vt* rebajar el precio de,
abaratar
cheaply ['tʃiːplɪ] *adv* barato, a bajo precio
cheat [tʃiːt] *vi* hacer trampa; (*in exam*) copiar
■ *vt* estafar, timar ■ *n* trampa; estafa;
(*person*) tramposo(-a); **he's been cheating
on his wife** ha estado engañando a su
esposa
cheating ['tʃiːtɪŋ] *n* trampa
Chechnia ['tʃɛtʃniːə] *n* Chechenia
check [tʃɛk] *vt* comprobar; (*count*) contar;
(*halt*) frenar; (*restrain*) refrenar, restringir
■ *vi*: **to ~ with sb** consultar con algn; (*official
etc*) informarse por ■ *n* (*inspection*) control *m*,
inspección *f*; (*curb*) freno; (*bill*) nota, cuenta;
(*US*) = **cheque**; (*pattern: gen pl*) cuadro
■ *adj* (*also*: **checked**: *pattern, cloth*) a cuadros;
to keep a ~ on sth/sb controlar algo/a algn
▶ **check in** *vi* (*in hotel*) registrarse; (*at airport*)
facturar ■ *vt* (*luggage*) facturar
▶ **check out** *vi* (*of hotel*) desocupar la
habitación ■ *vt* (*investigate: story*) comprobar;
(: *person*) informarse sobre
▶ **check up** *vi*: **to ~ up on sth** comprobar
algo; **to ~ up on sb** investigar a algn
checkbook ['tʃɛkbuk] *n* (*US*) = **chequebook**
checkered ['tʃɛkəd] *adj* (*US*) = **chequered**
checkers ['tʃɛkəz] *n* (*US*) damas *fpl*
check-in ['tʃɛkɪn] *n* (*also*: **check-in desk**: *at*
airport) mostrador *m* de facturación
checking account ['tʃɛkɪŋ-] *n* (*US*) cuenta
corriente
checklist ['tʃɛklɪst] *n* lista
checkmate ['tʃɛkmeɪt] *n* jaque *m* mate
checkout ['tʃɛkaut] *n* (*in supermarket*) caja
checkpoint ['tʃɛkpɔɪnt] *n* (punto de) control
m, retén *m* (*LAm*)
checkroom ['tʃɛkrum] *n* (*US*) consigna
checkup ['tʃɛkʌp] *n* (*Med*) reconocimiento
general; (*of machine*) revisión *f*
cheek [tʃiːk] *n* mejilla; (*impudence*) descaro
cheekbone ['tʃiːkbəun] *n* pómulo
cheeky ['tʃiːkɪ] *adj* fresco, descarado
cheep [tʃiːp] *n* (*of bird*) pío ■ *vi* piar
cheer [tʃɪəʳ] *vt* vitorear, ovacionar; (*gladden*)
alegrar, animar ■ *vi* dar vivas ■ *n* viva *m*;
cheers *npl* vítores *mpl*; **cheers!** ¡salud!

▶ **cheer on** vt (person etc) animar con aplausos or gritos

▶ **cheer up** vi animarse ■ vt alegrar, animar

cheerful ['tʃɪəful] adj alegre

cheerfulness ['tʃɪəfulnɪs] n alegría

cheering ['tʃɪərɪŋ] n ovaciones fpl, vítores mpl

cheerio [tʃɪərɪ'əu] excl (Brit) ¡hasta luego!

cheerleader ['tʃɪəli:dər] n animador(a) m(f)

cheerless ['tʃɪəlɪs] adj triste, sombrío

cheese [tʃi:z] n queso

cheeseboard ['tʃi:zbɔːd] n tabla de quesos

cheeseburger ['tʃi:zbəːgər] n hamburguesa con queso

cheesecake ['tʃi:zkeɪk] n pastel m de queso

cheetah ['tʃi:tə] n guepardo

chef [ʃɛf] n jefe(-a) m(f) de cocina

chemical ['kɛmɪkəl] adj químico ■ n producto químico

chemist ['kɛmɪst] n (Brit: pharmacist) farmacéutico(-a); (scientist) químico(-a); ~'s (shop) n (Brit) farmacia

chemistry ['kɛmɪstrɪ] n química

chemotherapy [ki:məu'θɛrəpɪ] n quimioterapia

cheque, check (US) [tʃɛk] n cheque m; **to pay by ~** pagar con cheque

chequebook, checkbook (US) ['tʃɛkbuk] n talonario (de cheques), chequera (LAm)

cheque card n (Brit) tarjeta de identificación bancaria

chequered, checkered (US) ['tʃɛkəd] adj (fig) accidentado; (pattern) de cuadros

cherish ['tʃɛrɪʃ] vt (love) querer, apreciar; (protect) cuidar; (hope etc) abrigar

cheroot [ʃə'ru:t] n puro (cortado en los dos extremos)

cherry ['tʃɛrɪ] n cereza

Ches abbr (Brit) = **Cheshire**

chess [tʃɛs] n ajedrez m

chessboard ['tʃɛsbɔːd] n tablero (de ajedrez)

chessman ['tʃɛsmən] n pieza (de ajedrez)

chest [tʃɛst] n (Anat) pecho; (box) cofre m; **to get sth off one's ~** (col) desahogarse; **~ of drawers** n cómoda

chest measurement n talla (de chaqueta etc)

chestnut ['tʃɛsnʌt] n castaña; (also: **chestnut tree**) castaño; (colour) castaño ■ adj (color) castaño inv

chesty ['tʃɛstɪ] adj (cough) de bronquios, de pecho

chew [tʃu:] vt mascar, masticar

chewing gum ['tʃu:ɪŋ-] n chicle m

chic [ʃi:k] adj elegante

chicanery [ʃɪ'keɪnərɪ] n embustes mpl, sofismas mpl

Chicano [tʃɪ'kɑːnəu] adj, n chicano(-a)

chick [tʃɪk] n pollito, polluelo; (US col) chica

chicken ['tʃɪkɪn] n gallina, pollo; (food) pollo; (col: coward) gallina m/f

▶ **chicken out** vi (col) rajarse; **to ~ out of doing sth** rajarse y no hacer algo

chickenpox ['tʃɪkɪnpɔks] n varicela

chickpea ['tʃɪkpi:] n garbanzo

chicory ['tʃɪkərɪ] n (for coffee) achicoria; (salad) escarola

chide [tʃaɪd] vt: **to ~ sb for sth** reprender a algn por algo

chief [tʃi:f] n jefe(-a) m(f) ■ adj principal, esp máximo (LAm); **C~ of Staff** (esp Mil) Jefe m del Estado mayor

chief executive, chief executive officer (US) n director m general

chiefly ['tʃi:flɪ] adv principalmente

chieftain ['tʃi:ftən] n jefe m, cacique m

chiffon ['ʃɪfɔn] n gasa

chilblain ['tʃɪlbleɪn] n sabañón m

child (pl **children**) [tʃaɪld, 'tʃɪldrən] n niño(-a); (offspring) hijo(-a)

child benefit n (Brit) subsidio por cada hijo pequeño

childbirth ['tʃaɪldbəːθ] n parto

childhood ['tʃaɪldhud] n niñez f, infancia

childish ['tʃaɪldɪʃ] adj pueril, infantil

childless ['tʃaɪldlɪs] adj sin hijos

childlike ['tʃaɪldlaɪk] adj de niño, infantil

child minder n (Brit) niñera, madre f de día

child prodigy n niño(-a) prodigio inv

children's home n centro de acogida para niños

child's play n (fig): **this is ~** esto es coser y cantar

Chile ['tʃɪlɪ] n Chile m

Chilean ['tʃɪlɪən] adj, n chileno(-a) m(f)

chill [tʃɪl] n frío; (Med) resfriado ■ adj frío ■ vt enfriar; (Culin) refrigerar

▶ **chill out** vi (esp US col) tranquilizarse

chilli, chili ['tʃɪlɪ] n (Brit) chile m, ají m (LAm)

chilling ['tʃɪlɪŋ] adj escalofriante

chilly ['tʃɪlɪ] adj frío

chime [tʃaɪm] n repique m, campanada ■ vi repicar, sonar

chimney ['tʃɪmnɪ] n chimenea

chimney sweep n deshollinador m

chimpanzee [tʃɪmpæn'zi:] n chimpancé m

chin [tʃɪn] n mentón m, barbilla

China ['tʃaɪnə] n China

china ['tʃaɪnə] n porcelana; (crockery) loza

Chinese [tʃaɪ'ni:z] adj chino ■ n (pl inv) chino(-a); (Ling) chino

chink [tʃɪŋk] n (opening) rendija, hendedura; (noise) tintineo

chintz [tʃɪnts] n cretona

chinwag ['tʃɪnwæg] n (Brit col): **to have a ~** echar una parrafada

chip [tʃɪp] n (gen pl: Culin: Brit) patata or (LAm) papa frita; (: US: also: **potato chip**) patata or (LAm) papa frita; (of wood) astilla; (stone) lasca; (in gambling) ficha; (Comput) chip m ∎ vt (cup, plate) desconchar; **when the chips are down** (fig) a la hora de la verdad
▸ **chip in** vi (col: interrupt) interrumpir, meterse; (: contribute) contribuir
chip and PIN n chip and PIN m (sistema de tarjetas chip con número PIN); ~ **machine** lector m de tarjetas chip and PIN
chipboard ['tʃɪpbɔːd] n madera aglomerada
chipmunk ['tʃɪpmʌŋk] n ardilla listada
chip shop n ver nota

○ **CHIP SHOP**
○
○ Se denomina chip shop o "fish-and-chip
○ shop" a un tipo de tienda popular de
○ comida rápida en la que se despachan
○ platos tradicionales británicos,
○ principalmente filetes de pescado
○ rebozado frito y patatas fritas.

chiropodist [kɪ'rɔpədɪst] n (Brit) podólogo(-a)
chiropody [kɪ'rɔpədɪ] n podología
chirp [tʃəːp] vi gorjear; (cricket) cantar ∎ n (of cricket) canto
chirpy ['tʃəːpɪ] adj alegre, animado
chisel ['tʃɪzl] n (for wood) escoplo; (for stone) cincel m
chit [tʃɪt] n nota
chitchat ['tʃɪttʃæt] n chismes mpl, habladurías fpl
chivalrous ['ʃɪvəlrəs] adj caballeroso
chivalry ['ʃɪvəlrɪ] n caballerosidad f
chives [tʃaɪvz] npl cebollinos mpl
chloride ['klɔːraɪd] n cloruro
chlorinate ['klɔːrɪneɪt] vt clorar
chlorine ['klɔːriːn] n cloro
chock-a-block ['tʃɔkə'blɔk], **chock-full** [tʃɔk'ful] adj atestado
chocolate ['tʃɔklɪt] n chocolate m
choice [tʃɔɪs] n elección f; (preference) preferencia ∎ adj escogido; **I did it by** or **from** ~ lo hice de buena gana; **a wide** ~ un gran surtido, una gran variedad
choir ['kwaɪə'] n coro
choirboy ['kwaɪəbɔɪ] n niño de coro
choke [tʃəuk] vi ahogarse; (on food) atragantarse ∎ vt ahogar; (block) atascar ∎ n (Aut) estárter m
choker ['tʃəukə'] n (necklace) gargantilla
cholera ['kɔlərə] n cólera m
cholesterol [kɔ'lestərəl] n colesterol m
choose [tʃuːz] (pt **chose**) [tʃəuz] (pp **chosen**) [tʃəuzn] vt escoger, elegir; (team) seleccionar;

to ~ **between** elegir or escoger entre; **to** ~ **from** escoger entre
choosy ['tʃuːzɪ] adj remilgado
chop [tʃɔp] vt (wood) cortar, talar; (Culin: also: **chop up**) picar ∎ n tajo, golpe m cortante; (Culin) chuleta; **chops** npl (jaws) boca sg; **to get the** ~ (col: project) ser suprimido; (: person: be sacked) ser despedido
chopper ['tʃɔpə'] n (helicopter) helicóptero
choppy ['tʃɔpɪ] adj (sea) picado, agitado
chopsticks ['tʃɔpstɪks] npl palillos mpl
choral ['kɔːrəl] adj coral
chord [kɔːd] n (Mus) acorde m
chore [tʃɔː'] n faena, tarea; (routine task) trabajo rutinario
choreographer [kɔrɪ'ɔgrəfə'] n coreógrafo(-a)
choreography [kɔrɪ'ɔgrəfɪ] n coreografía
chorister ['kɔrɪstə'] n corista m/f
chortle ['tʃɔːtl] vi reírse satisfecho
chorus ['kɔːrəs] n coro; (repeated part of song) estribillo
chose [tʃəuz] pt of **choose**
chosen ['tʃəuzn] pp of **choose**
chowder ['tʃaudə'] n (esp US) sopa de pescado
Christ [kraɪst] n Cristo
christen ['krɪsn] vt bautizar
christening ['krɪsnɪŋ] n bautizo
Christian ['krɪstɪən] adj, n cristiano(-a) m(f)
Christianity [krɪstɪ'ænɪtɪ] n cristianismo
Christian name n nombre m de pila
Christmas ['krɪsməs] n Navidad f; **Merry** ~! ¡Felices Navidades!, ¡Felices Pascuas!
Christmas card n crismas m inv, tarjeta de Navidad
Christmas Day n día m de Navidad
Christmas Eve n Nochebuena
Christmas Island n Isla Christmas
Christmas tree n árbol m de Navidad
chrome [krəum] n = **chromium plating**
chromium ['krəumɪəm] n cromo; (also: **chromium plating**) cromado
chromosome ['krəuməsəum] n cromosoma m
chronic ['krɔnɪk] adj crónico; (fig: liar, smoker) empedernido
chronicle ['krɔnɪkl] n crónica
chronological [krɔnə'lɔdʒɪkəl] adj cronológico
chrysanthemum [krɪ'sænθəməm] n crisantemo
chubby ['tʃʌbɪ] adj rechoncho
chuck [tʃʌk] vt tirar; **to** ~ (**up** or **in**) vt (Brit) dejar, mandar a paseo
chuckle ['tʃʌkl] vi reírse entre dientes
chuffed [tʃʌft] adj (col): **to be** ~ (**about sth**) estar encantado (con algo)

C

chug [tʃʌg] vi (also: **chug along**: train) ir despacio; (: fig) ir tirando
chum [tʃʌm] n amiguete(-a) m(f), coleguilla m/f
chump [tʃʌmp] n (col) tonto(-a), estúpido(-a)
chunk [tʃʌŋk] n pedazo, trozo
chunky ['tʃʌŋkɪ] adj (furniture etc) achaparrado; (person) fornido; (knitwear) de lana gorda, grueso
Chunnel [tʃʌnl] n = **Channel Tunnel**
church [tʃəːtʃ] n iglesia; **the C~ of England** la Iglesia Anglicana
churchyard ['tʃəːtʃjɑːd] n cementerio, camposanto
churlish ['tʃəːlɪʃ] adj grosero; (mean) arisco
churn [tʃəːn] n (for butter) mantequera; (for milk) lechera
  ▶ **churn out** vt producir en serie
chute [ʃuːt] n (also: **rubbish chute**) vertedero; (Brit: children's slide) tobogán m
chutney ['tʃʌtnɪ] n salsa picante de frutas y especias
CIA n abbr (US: = Central Intelligence Agency) CIA f, Agencia Central de Inteligencia
cicada [sɪ'kɑːdə] n cigarra
CID n abbr (Brit: = Criminal Investigation Department) ≈ B.I.C. f (SP)
cider ['saɪdər] n sidra
CIF abbr (= cost, insurance, and freight) c.s.f.
cigar [sɪ'gɑːr] n puro
cigarette [sɪgə'ret] n cigarrillo, pitillo
cigarette case n pitillera
cigarette end n colilla
cigarette holder n boquilla
C-in-C abbr (= commander-in-chief) comandante mf general
cinch [sɪntʃ] n: **it's a ~** está tirado
Cinderella [sɪndə'relə] n Cenicienta
cinders ['sɪndəz] npl cenizas fpl
cine-camera ['sɪnɪ'kæmərə] n (Brit) cámara cinematográfica
cine-film ['sɪnɪfɪlm] n (Brit) película de cine
cinema ['sɪnəmə] n cine m
cinnamon ['sɪnəmən] n canela
cipher ['saɪfər] n clave f; (fig) cero; **in ~** en clave
circle ['səːkl] n círculo; (in theatre) anfiteatro ■ vi dar vueltas ■ vt (surround) rodear, cercar; (move round) dar la vuelta a
circuit ['səːkɪt] n circuito; (track) pista; (lap) vuelta
circuit board n tarjeta de circuitos
circuitous [səː'kjuɪtəs] adj indirecto
circular ['səːkjulər] adj circular ■ n circular f; (as advertisement) panfleto
circulate ['səːkjuleɪt] vi circular; (person: socially) alternar, circular ■ vt poner en circulación
circulation [səːkju'leɪʃən] n circulación f; (of newspaper etc) tirada
circumcise ['səːkəmsaɪz] vt circuncidar
circumference [sə'kʌmfərəns] n circunferencia
circumscribe ['səːkəmskraɪb] vt circunscribir
circumspect ['səːkəmspɛkt] adj circunspecto, prudente
circumstances ['səːkəmstənsɪz] npl circunstancias fpl; (financial condition) situación f económica; **in the ~** en or dadas las circunstancias; **under no ~** de ninguna manera, bajo ningún concepto
circumstantial [səːkəm'stænʃəl] adj detallado; **~ evidence** prueba indiciaria
circumvent ['səːkəmvent] vt (rule etc) burlar
circus ['səːkəs] n circo; (also: **Circus**: in place names) Plaza
cirrhosis [sɪ'rəusɪs] n (also: **cirrhosis of the liver**) cirrosis f inv
CIS n abbr (= Commonwealth of Independent States) CEI f
cissy ['sɪsɪ] n = **sissy**
cistern ['sɪstən] n tanque m, depósito; (in toilet) cisterna
citation [saɪ'teɪʃən] n cita; (Law) citación f; (Mil) mención f
cite [saɪt] vt citar
citizen ['sɪtɪzn] n (Pol) ciudadano(-a); (of city) habitante m/f
Citizens' Advice Bureau n (Brit) organización voluntaria británica que aconseja especialmente en temas legales o financieros
citizenship ['sɪtɪznʃɪp] n ciudadanía; (Brit Scol) civismo
citric ['sɪtrɪk] adj: **~ acid** ácido cítrico
citrus fruits ['sɪtrəs-] npl cítricos mpl
city ['sɪtɪ] n ciudad f; **the C~** centro financiero de Londres
city centre n centro de la ciudad
City Hall n (US) ayuntamiento
City Technology College n (Brit) ≈ Centro de formación profesional
civic ['sɪvɪk] adj cívico; (authorities) municipal
civic centre n (Brit) centro de administración municipal
civil ['sɪvɪl] adj civil; (polite) atento, cortés; (well-bred) educado
civil defence n protección f civil
civil engineer n ingeniero(-a) de caminos
civil engineering n ingeniería de caminos
civilian [sɪ'vɪlɪən] adj civil; (clothes) de paisano ■ n civil m/f
civilization [sɪvɪlaɪ'zeɪʃən] n civilización f
civilized ['sɪvɪlaɪzd] adj civilizado

civil law n derecho civil
civil liberties npl libertades fpl civiles
civil rights npl derechos mpl civiles
civil servant n funcionario(-a) (del Estado)
Civil Service n administración f pública
civil war n guerra civil
civvies ['sɪvɪz] npl: **in ~** (col) de paisano
CJD n abbr (= Creutzfeldt-Jakob disease) enfermedad de Creutzfeldt-Jakob
cl abbr (= centilitre) cl
clad [klæd] adj: **~ (in)** vestido (de)
claim [kleɪm] vt exigir, reclamar; (rights etc) reivindicar; (assert) pretender ■ vi (for insurance) reclamar ■ n (for expenses) reclamación f; (Law) demanda; (pretension) pretensión f; **to put in a ~ for sth** presentar una demanda por algo
claimant ['kleɪmənt] n (Admin, Law) demandante m/f
claim form n solicitud f
clairvoyant [klɛə'vɔɪənt] n clarividente m/f
clam [klæm] n almeja
 ▶ **clam up** vi (col) cerrar el pico
clamber ['klæmbəʳ] vi trepar
clammy ['klæmɪ] adj (cold) frío y húmedo; (sticky) pegajoso
clamour, clamor (US) ['klæməʳ] n (noise) clamor m; (protest) protesta ■ vi: **to ~ for sth** clamar por algo, pedir algo a voces
clamp [klæmp] n abrazadera; (laboratory clamp) grapa; (wheel clamp) cepo ■ vt afianzar (con abrazadera)
 ▶ **clamp down on** vt fus (government, police) poner coto a
clampdown ['klæmpdaʊn] n restricción f; **there has been a ~ on terrorism** se ha puesto coto al terrorismo
clan [klæn] n clan m
clandestine [klæn'dɛstɪn] adj clandestino
clang [klæŋ] n estruendo ■ vi sonar con estruendo
clanger [klæŋəʳ] n: **to drop a ~** (Brit col) meter la pata
clansman ['klænzmən] n miembro del clan
clap [klæp] vi aplaudir ■ vt (hands) batir ■ n (of hands) palmada; **to ~ one's hands** dar palmadas, batir las palmas; **a ~ of thunder** un trueno
clapping ['klæpɪŋ] n aplausos mpl
claptrap ['klæptræp] n (col) gilipolleces fpl
claret ['klærət] n burdeos m inv
clarification [klærɪfɪ'keɪʃən] n aclaración f
clarify ['klærɪfaɪ] vt aclarar
clarinet [klærɪ'nɛt] n clarinete m
clarity ['klærɪtɪ] n claridad f
clash [klæʃ] n estruendo; (fig) choque m ■ vi enfrentarse; (personalities, interests) oponerse,

chocar; (colours) desentonar; (dates, events) coincidir
clasp [klɑ:sp] n broche m; (on jewels) cierre m ■ vt abrochar; (hand) apretar; (embrace) abrazar
class [klɑ:s] n (gen) clase f; (group, category) clase f, categoría ■ cpd de clase ■ vt clasificar
class-conscious ['klɑ:s'kɔnʃəs] adj clasista, con conciencia de clase
classic ['klæsɪk] adj clásico ■ n (work) obra clásica, clásico; **classics** npl (Univ) clásicas fpl
classical ['klæsɪkəl] adj clásico; **~ music** música clásica
classification [klæsɪfɪ'keɪʃən] n clasificación f
classified ['klæsɪfaɪd] adj (information) reservado
classified advertisement n anuncio por palabras
classify ['klæsɪfaɪ] vt clasificar
classless ['klɑ:slɪs] adj: **~ society** sociedad f sin clases
classmate ['klɑ:smeɪt] n compañero(-a) de clase
classroom ['klɑ:srʊm] n aula
classy ['klɑ:sɪ] adj (col) elegante, con estilo
clatter ['klætəʳ] n ruido, estruendo; (of hooves) trápala ■ vi hacer ruido or estruendo
clause [klɔ:z] n cláusula; (Ling) oración f
claustrophobia [klɔ:strə'fəʊbɪə] n claustrofobia
claustrophobic [klɔ:strə'fəʊbɪk] adj claustrofóbico; **I feel ~** me entra claustrofobia
claw [klɔ:] n (of cat) uña; (of bird of prey) garra; (of lobster) pinza; (Tech) garfio ■ vi: **to ~ at** arañar; (tear) desgarrar
clay [kleɪ] n arcilla
clean [kli:n] adj limpio; (copy) en limpio; (lines) bien definido ■ vt limpiar ■ adv: **he ~ forgot** lo olvidó por completo; **to come ~** (col: admit guilt) confesarlo todo; **to have a ~ driving licence** tener el carnet de conducir sin sanciones; **to ~ one's teeth** lavarse los dientes
 ▶ **clean off** vt limpiar
 ▶ **clean out** vt limpiar (a fondo)
 ▶ **clean up** vt limpiar, asear ■ vi (fig: make profit): **to ~ up on** sacar provecho de
clean-cut ['kli:n'kʌt] adj bien definido; (outline) nítido; (person) de buen parecer
cleaner ['kli:nəʳ] n encargado(-a) m(f) de la limpieza; (also: **dry cleaner**) tintorero(-a)
cleaning ['kli:nɪŋ] n limpieza
cleaning lady n señora de la limpieza, asistenta

477

cleanliness ['klɛnlɪnɪs] n limpieza
cleanse [klɛnz] vt limpiar
cleanser ['klɛnzəʳ] n detergente m; (cosmetic) loción f or crema limpiadora
clean-shaven ['kli:n'ʃeɪvn] adj bien afeitado
cleansing department ['klɛnzɪŋ-] n (Brit) servicio municipal de limpieza
clean sweep n: **to make a ~** (Sport) arrasar, barrer
clear [klɪəʳ] adj claro; (road, way) libre; (profit) neto; (majority) absoluto ■ vt (space) despejar, limpiar; (Law: suspect) absolver; (obstacle) salvar, saltar por encima de; (debt) liquidar; (cheque) aceptar; (site, woodland) desmontar ■ vi (fog etc) despejarse ■ n: **to be in the ~** (out of debt) estar libre de deudas; (out of suspicion) estar fuera de toda sospecha; (out of danger) estar fuera de peligro ■ adv: **~ of** a distancia de; **to make o.s. ~** explicarse claramente; **to make it ~ to sb that ...** hacer entender a algn que ...; **I have a ~ day tomorrow** mañana tengo el día libre; **to keep ~ of sth/sb** evitar algo/a algn; **to ~ a profit of ...** sacar una ganancia de ...; **to ~ the table** recoger or quitar la mesa
  ▶ **clear off** vi (col: leave) marcharse, mandarse mudar (LAm)
  ▶ **clear up** vt limpiar; (mystery) aclarar, resolver
clearance ['klɪərəns] n (removal) despeje m; (permission) acreditación f
clear-cut ['klɪə'kʌt] adj bien definido, claro
clearing ['klɪərɪŋ] n (in wood) claro
clearing bank n (Brit) banco central
clearing house n (Comm) cámara de compensación
clearly ['klɪəlɪ] adv claramente
clearway ['klɪəweɪ] n (Brit) carretera en la que no se puede estacionar
cleaver ['kli:və] n cuchilla (de carnicero)
clef [klɛf] n (Mus) clave f
cleft [klɛft] n (in rock) grieta, hendedura
clemency ['klɛmənsɪ] n clemencia
clench [klɛntʃ] vt apretar, cerrar
clergy ['klə:dʒɪ] n clero
clergyman ['klə:dʒɪmən] n clérigo
clerical ['klɛrɪkəl] adj de oficina; (Rel) clerical; (error) de copia
clerk [klɑ:k] (US) [klə:k] n oficinista m/f; (US) dependiente(-a) m(f), vendedor(a) m(f); **C~ of the Court** secretario(-a) de juzgado
clever ['klɛvəʳ] adj (mentally) inteligente, listo; (skilful) hábil; (device, arrangement) ingenioso
cleverly ['klɛvəlɪ] adv ingeniosamente
clew [klu:] n (US) = **clue**
cliché ['kli:ʃeɪ] n cliché m, frase f hecha

click [klɪk] vt (tongue) chasquear ■ vi (Comput) hacer clic; **to ~ one's heels** taconear
clickable ['klɪkəbl] adj (Comput) cliqueable
client ['klaɪənt] n cliente m/f
clientele [kli:ā:n'tɛl] n clientela
cliff [klɪf] n acantilado
cliffhanger ['klɪfhæŋəʳ] n: **it was a ~** estuvimos etc en ascuas hasta el final
climactic [klaɪ'mæktɪk] adj culminante
climate ['klaɪmɪt] n clima m; (fig) clima m, ambiente m
climax ['klaɪmæks] n punto culminante; (of play etc) clímax m; (sexual climax) orgasmo
climb [klaɪm] vi subir, trepar; (plane) elevarse, remontar el vuelo ■ vt (stairs) subir; (tree) trepar a; (mountain) escalar ■ n subida, ascenso; **to ~ over a wall** saltar una tapia
  ▶ **climb down** vi (fig) volverse atrás
climbdown ['klaɪmdaun] n vuelta atrás
climber ['klaɪməʳ] n escalador(a) m(f)
climbing ['klaɪmɪŋ] n escalada
clinch [klɪntʃ] vt (deal) cerrar; (argument) rematar
clincher ['klɪntʃəʳ] n (col): **that was the ~ for me** eso me hizo decidir
cling [klɪŋ] (pt, pp **clung**) [klʌŋ] vi: **to ~ (to)** agarrarse (a); (clothes) pegarse (a)
clingfilm ['klɪŋfɪlm] n plástico adherente
clinic ['klɪnɪk] n clínica
clinical ['klɪnɪkl] adj clínico; (fig) frío, impasible
clink [klɪŋk] vi tintinear
clip [klɪp] n (for hair) horquilla; (also: **paper clip**) sujetapapeles m inv, clip m; (clamp) grapa ■ vt (cut) cortar; (hedge) podar; (also: **clip together**) unir
clippers ['klɪpəz] npl (for gardening) tijeras fpl de podar; (for hair) maquinilla sg; (for nails) cortauñas m inv
clipping ['klɪpɪŋ] n (from newspaper) recorte m
clique [kli:k] n camarilla
cloak [kləuk] n capa, manto ■ vt (fig) encubrir, disimular
cloakroom ['kləukrum] n guardarropa m; (Brit: WC) lavabo, aseos mpl, baño (esp LAm)
clobber ['klɔbəʳ] n (col) bártulos mpl, trastos mpl ■ vt dar una paliza a
clock [klɔk] n reloj m; (in taxi) taxímetro; **to work against the ~** trabajar contra reloj; **around the ~** las veinticuatro horas; **to sleep round the ~** dormir un día entero; **30,000 on the ~** (Aut) treinta mil millas en el cuentakilómetros
  ▶ **clock in, clock on** vi fichar, picar
  ▶ **clock off, clock out** vi fichar or picar la salida
  ▶ **clock up** vt hacer

clockwise ['klɔkwaɪz] *adv* en el sentido de las agujas del reloj

clockwork ['klɔkwə:k] *n* aparato de relojería ■ *adj* (*toy, train*) de cuerda

clog [klɔg] *n* zueco, chanclo ■ *vt* atascar ■ *vi* atascarse

cloister ['klɔɪstə'] *n* claustro

clone [kləun] *n* clon *m*

close [*adj, adv* kləus, *vb, n* kləuz] *adj* cercano, próximo; (*near*): ~ (**to**) cerca (de); (*print, weave*) tupido, compacto; (*friend*) íntimo; (*connection*) estrecho; (*examination*) detallado, minucioso; (*weather*) bochornoso; (*atmosphere*) sofocante; (*room*) mal ventilado ■ *adv* cerca; ~ **by**, ~ **at hand** *adj, adv* muy cerca; ~ **to** *prep* cerca de; **to have a ~ shave** (*fig*) escaparse por un pelo; **how ~ is Edinburgh to Glasgow?** ¿qué distancia hay de Edimburgo a Glasgow?; **at ~ quarters** de cerca ■ *vt* cerrar; (*end*) concluir, terminar ■ *vi* (*shop etc*) cerrar; (*end*) concluir(se), terminar(se) ■ *n* (*end*) fin *m*, final *m*, conclusión *f*; **to bring sth to a ~** terminar algo
  ▸ **close down** *vi* cerrar definitivamente
  ▸ **close in** *vi* (*hunters*) acercarse rodeando, rodear; (*evening, night*) caer; (*fog*) cerrarse; **to ~ in on sb** rodear or cercar a algn; **the days are closing in** los días son cada vez más cortos
  ▸ **close off** *vt* (*area*) cerrar al tráfico *or* al público

closed [kləuzd] *adj* (*shop etc*) cerrado

closed-circuit ['kləuzd'sə:kɪt] *adj*: ~ **television** televisión *f* por circuito cerrado

closed shop *n* empresa en la que todo el personal está afiliado a un sindicato

close-knit ['kləus'nɪt] *adj* (*fig*) muy unido

closely ['kləuslɪ] *adv* (*study*) con detalle; (*listen*) con atención; (*watch*) de cerca; **we are ~ related** somos parientes cercanos; **a ~ guarded secret** un secreto rigurosamente guardado

close season [kləuz-] *n* (*Football*) temporada de descanso; (*Hunting*) veda

closet ['klɔzɪt] *n* (*cupboard*) armario, placar(d) *m* (*LAm*)

close-up ['kləusʌp] *n* primer plano

closing ['kləuzɪŋ] *adj* (*stages, remarks*) último, final; ~ **price** (*Stock Exchange*) cotización *f* de cierre

closing time *n* hora de cierre

closure ['kləuʒə'] *n* cierre *m*

clot [klɔt] *n* (*gen: also*: **blood clot**) embolia; (*col: idiot*) imbécil *m/f* ■ *vi* (*blood*) coagularse

cloth [klɔθ] *n* (*material*) tela, paño; (*table cloth*) mantel *m*; (*rag*) trapo

clothe [kləuð] *vt* vestir; (*fig*) revestir

clothes [kləuðz] *npl* ropa *sg*; **to put one's ~ on** vestirse, ponerse la ropa; **to take one's ~ off** desvestirse, desnudarse

clothes brush *n* cepillo (para la ropa)

clothes line *n* cuerda (para tender la ropa)

clothes peg, **clothes pin** (*US*) *n* pinza

clothing ['kləuðɪŋ] *n* = **clothes**

clotted cream ['klɔtɪd-] *n* nata muy espesa

cloud [klaud] *n* nube *f*; (*storm cloud*) nubarrón *m* ■ *vt* (*liquid*) enturbiar; **every ~ has a silver lining** no hay mal que por bien no venga; **to ~ the issue** empañar el problema
  ▸ **cloud over** *vi* (*also fig*) nublarse

cloudburst ['klaudbə:st] *n* chaparrón *m*

cloud-cuckoo-land ['klaud'kuku:'lænd] *n* Babia

cloudy ['klaudɪ] *adj* nublado; (*liquid*) turbio

clout [klaut] *n* (*fig*) influencia, peso ■ *vt* dar un tortazo a

clove [kləuv] *n* clavo; ~ **of garlic** diente *m* de ajo

clover ['kləuvə'] *n* trébol *m*

clown [klaun] *n* payaso ■ *vi* (*also*: **clown about**, **clown around**) hacer el payaso

cloying ['klɔɪɪŋ] *adj* (*taste*) empalagoso

club [klʌb] *n* (*society*) club *m*; (*weapon*) porra, cachiporra; (*also*: **golf club**) palo ■ *vt* aporrear ■ *vi*: **to ~ together** (*join forces*) unir fuerzas; **clubs** *npl* (*Cards*) tréboles *mpl*

club car *n* (*US Rail*) coche *m* salón

club class *n* (*Aviat*) clase *f* preferente

clubhouse ['klʌbhaus] *n* local social, sobre todo en clubs deportivos

club soda *n* (*US*) soda

cluck [klʌk] *vi* cloquear

clue [klu:] *n* pista; (*in crosswords*) indicación *f*; **I haven't a ~** no tengo ni idea

clued up, **clued in** (*US*) [klu:d-] *adj* (*col*) al tanto, al corriente

clueless ['klu:lɪs] *adj* (*col*) desorientado

clump [klʌmp] *n* (*of trees*) grupo

clumsy ['klʌmzɪ] *adj* (*person*) torpe; (*tool*) difícil de manejar

clung [klʌŋ] *pt, pp* of **cling**

cluster ['klʌstə'] *n* grupo; (*Bot*) racimo ■ *vi* agruparse, apiñarse

clutch [klʌtʃ] *n* (*Aut*) embrague *m*; (*pedal*) (pedal *m* de) embrague *m*; **to fall into sb's clutches** caer en las garras de algn ■ *vt* agarrar

clutter ['klʌtə'] *vt* (*also*: **clutter up**) atestar, llenar desordenadamente ■ *n* desorden *m*, confusión *f*

CM *abbr* (*US*) = **North Mariana Islands**

cm *abbr* (= *centimetre*) cm

CNAA *n abbr* (*Brit*: = *Council for National Academic Awards*) organismo no universitario que otorga diplomas

CND n abbr (Brit: = Campaign for Nuclear Disarmament) plataforma pro desarme nuclear

CO n abbr = **commanding officer**; (Brit) = **Commonwealth Office** ■ abbr (US) = **Colorado**

Co. abbr = **county; company**

c/o abbr (= care of) c/a, a/c

coach [kəutʃ] n (bus) autocar m (SP), autobús m; (horse-drawn) coche m; (ceremonial) carroza; (of train) vagón m, coche m; (Sport) entrenador(a) m(f), instructor(a) m(f) ■ vt (Sport) entrenar; (student) preparar, enseñar

coach trip n excursión f en autocar

coagulate [kəu'ægjuleɪt] vi coagularse

coal [kəul] n carbón m

coal face n frente m de carbón

coalfield ['kəulfiːld] n yacimiento de carbón

coalition [kəuə'lɪʃən] n coalición f

coal man n carbonero

coalmine ['kəulmaɪn] n mina de carbón

coalminer ['kəulmaɪnəʳ] n minero (de carbón)

coalmining ['keulmaɪnɪŋ] n minería (de carbón)

coarse [kɔːs] adj basto, burdo; (vulgar) grosero, ordinario

coast [kəust] n costa, litoral m ■ vi (Aut) ir en punto muerto

coastal ['kəustl] adj costero

coaster ['kəustəʳ] n buque m costero, barco de cabotaje

coastguard ['kəustgɑːd] n guardacostas m inv

coastline ['kəustlaɪn] n litoral m

coat [kəut] n (jacket) chaqueta, saco (LAm); (overcoat) abrigo; (of animal) pelo, lana; (of paint) mano f, capa ■ vt cubrir, revestir

coat hanger n percha, gancha (LAm)

coating ['kəutɪŋ] n capa, baño

coat of arms n escudo de armas

co-author ['kəu'ɔːθəʳ] n coautor(a) m(f)

coax [kəuks] vt engatusar

cob [kɔb] n see **corn**

cobbler ['kɔbləʳ] n zapatero (remendón)

cobbles ['kɔblz], **cobblestones** ['kɔblstəunz] npl adoquines mpl

COBOL ['kəubɔl] n COBOL m

cobra ['kəubrə] n cobra

cobweb ['kɔbwɛb] n telaraña

cocaine [kə'keɪn] n cocaína

cock [kɔk] n (rooster) gallo; (male bird) macho ■ vt (gun) amartillar

cock-a-hoop [kɔkə'huːp] adj: **to be ~** estar más contento que unas pascuas

cockatoo [kɔkə'tuː] n cacatúa

cockerel ['kɔkərl] n gallito, gallo joven

cock-eyed ['kɔkaɪd] adj bizco; (fig: crooked) torcido; (: idea) disparatado

cockle ['kɔkl] n berberecho

cockney ['kɔknɪ] n habitante de ciertos barrios de Londres

cockpit ['kɔkpɪt] n (in aircraft) cabina

cockroach ['kɔkrəutʃ] n cucaracha

cocktail ['kɔkteɪl] n combinado, cóctel m; **prawn ~** cóctel m de gambas

cocktail cabinet n mueble-bar m

cocktail party n cóctel m

cocktail shaker [-ʃeɪkəʳ] n coctelera

cocky ['kɔkɪ] adj farruco, flamenco

cocoa ['kəukəu] n cacao; (drink) chocolate m

coconut ['kəukənʌt] n coco

cocoon [kə'kuːn] n capullo

cod [kɔd] n bacalao

COD abbr = **cash on delivery**; (US) = **collect on delivery**

code [kəud] n código; (cipher) clave f; (Tel) prefijo; **~ of behaviour** código de conducta; **~ of practice** código profesional

codeine ['kəudiːn] n codeína

codger [kɔdʒəʳ] n (Brit col): **an old ~** un abuelo

codicil ['kɔdɪsɪl] n codicilo

codify ['kəudɪfaɪ] vt codificar

cod-liver oil ['kɔdlɪvəʳ-] n aceite m de hígado de bacalao

co-driver ['kəu'draɪvəʳ] n (in race) copiloto m/f; (of lorry) segundo conductor m

co-ed ['kəuɛd] adj abbr = **coeducational** ■ n abbr (US: = female student) alumna de una universidad mixta; (Brit: school) colegio mixto

coeducational [kəuɛdju'keɪʃənl] adj mixto

coerce [kəu'əːs] vt forzar, coaccionar

coercion [kəu'əːʃən] n coacción f

coexistence ['kəuɪg'zɪstəns] n coexistencia

C. of C. n abbr = **chamber of commerce**

C of E abbr = **Church of England**

coffee ['kɔfɪ] n café m; **white ~**, (US) **~ with cream** café con leche

coffee bar n (Brit) cafetería

coffee bean n grano de café

coffee break n descanso (para tomar café)

coffee cup n taza de café, pocillo (LAm)

coffeepot ['kɔfɪpɔt] n cafetera

coffee table n mesita baja

coffin ['kɔfɪn] n ataúd m

C of I abbr = **Church of Ireland**

C of S abbr = **Church of Scotland**

cog [kɔg] n diente m

cogent ['kəudʒənt] adj lógico, convincente

cognac ['kɔnjæk] n coñac m

cogwheel ['kɔgwiːl] n rueda dentada

cohabit [kəu'hæbɪt] vi (formal): **to ~ (with sb)** cohabitar (con algn)

coherent [kəu'hɪərənt] adj coherente

cohesion [kəu'hiːʒən] n cohesión f

cohesive [kəu'hiːsɪv] adj (fig) cohesivo, unido

COI n abbr (Brit: = Central Office of Information) servicio de información gubernamental

coil [kɔɪl] n rollo; (of rope) vuelta; (of smoke) espiral f; (Aut, Elec) bobina, carrete m; (contraceptive) DIU m ■ vt enrollar

coin [kɔɪn] n moneda ■ vt acuñar; (word) inventar, acuñar

coinage ['kɔɪnɪdʒ] n moneda

coin-box ['kɔɪnbɔks] n (Brit) caja recaudadora

coincide [kəuɪn'saɪd] vi coincidir

coincidence [kəu'ɪnsɪdəns] n casualidad f, coincidencia

coin-operated ['kɔɪn'ɔpəreɪtɪd] adj (machine) que funciona con monedas

Coke® [kəuk] n Coca Cola® f

coke [kəuk] n (coal) coque m

Col. abbr (= colonel) col; (US) = **Colorado**

COLA n abbr (US: = cost-of-living adjustment) reajuste salarial de acuerdo con el coste de la vida

colander ['kɔləndər] n escurridor m

cold [kəuld] adj frío ■ n frío; (Med) resfriado; **it's** ~ hace frío; **to be** ~ tener frío; **to catch a** ~ coger un catarro, resfriarse, acatarrarse; **in** ~ **blood** a sangre fría; **the room's getting** ~ está empezando a hacer frío en la habitación; **to give sb the** ~ **shoulder** tratar a algn con frialdad

cold-blooded ['kəuld'blʌdɪd] adj (Zool) de sangre fría

cold cream n crema

coldly ['kəuldlɪ] adj fríamente

cold sore n calentura, herpes m labial

cold sweat n: **to be in a** ~ (about sth) tener sudores fríos (por algo)

cold turkey n (col) mono

Cold War n: **the** ~ la guerra fría

coleslaw ['kəulslɔ:] n ensalada de col con zanahoria

colic ['kɔlɪk] n cólico

colicky ['kɔlɪkɪ] adj: **to be** ~ tener un cólico

collaborate [kə'læbəreɪt] vi colaborar

collaboration [kəlæbə'reɪʃən] n colaboración f; (Pol) colaboracionismo

collaborator [kə'læbəreɪtər] n colaborador(a) m(f); (Pol) colaboracionista m/f

collage [kɔ'lɑ:ʒ] n collage m

collagen ['kɔlədʒən] n colágeno

collapse [kə'læps] vi (gen) hundirse, derrumbarse; (Med) sufrir un colapso ■ n (gen) hundimiento; (Med) colapso; (of government) caída; (of plans, scheme) fracaso; (of business) ruina

collapsible [kə'læpsəbl] adj plegable

collar ['kɔlər] n (of coat, shirt) cuello; (for dog) collar m; (Tech) collar m ■ vt (col: person) agarrar; (: object) birlar

collarbone ['kɔləbəun] n clavícula

collate [kɔ'leɪt] vt cotejar

collateral [kɔ'lætərəl] n (Comm) garantía subsidiaria

collation [kə'leɪʃən] n colación f

colleague ['kɔli:g] n colega m/f, compañero(-a) m(f)

collect [kə'lɛkt] vt reunir; (as a hobby) coleccionar; (Brit: call and pick up) recoger; (wages) cobrar; (debts) recaudar; (donations, subscriptions) colectar ■ vi (crowd) reunirse ■ adv: **to call** ~ (US Tel) llamar a cobro revertido; **to** ~ **one's thoughts** reponerse, recobrar el dominio de sí mismo; ~ **on delivery (COD)** (US) entrega contra reembolso

collection [kə'lɛkʃən] n colección f; (of fares, wages) cobro; (of post) recogida

collective [kə'lɛktɪv] adj colectivo

collective bargaining n negociación f del convenio colectivo

collector [kə'lɛktər] n coleccionista m/f; (of taxes etc) recaudador(a) m(f); ~**'s item** or **piece** pieza de coleccionista

college ['kɔlɪdʒ] n colegio; (of technology, agriculture etc) escuela

collide [kə'laɪd] vi chocar

collie ['kɔlɪ] n (dog) collie m, perro pastor escocés

colliery ['kɔlɪərɪ] n (Brit) mina de carbón

collision [kə'lɪʒən] n choque m, colisión f; **to be on a** ~ **course** (also fig) ir rumbo al desastre

colloquial [kə'ləukwɪəl] adj coloquial

collusion [kə'lu:ʒən] n confabulación f, connivencia; **in** ~ **with** en connivencia con

Colo. abbr (US) = **Colorado**

cologne [kə'ləun] n (also: **eau de cologne**) (agua de) colonia

Colombia [kə'lɔmbɪə] n Colombia

Colombian [kə'lɔmbɪən] adj, n colombiano(-a) m(f)

colon ['kəulən] n (sign) dos puntos; (Med) colon m

colonel ['kə:nl] n coronel m

colonial [kə'ləunɪəl] adj colonial

colonize ['kɔlənaɪz] vt colonizar

colonnade [kɔlə'neɪd] n columnata

colony ['kɔlənɪ] n colonia

color ['kʌlər] (US) = **colour**

Colorado beetle [kɔlə'rɑ:dəu-] n escarabajo de la patata

colossal [kə'lɔsl] adj colosal

colour, color (US) ['kʌlər] n color m ■ vt colorear, pintar; (dye) teñir ■ vi (blush) sonrojarse; **colours** npl (of party, club) colores mpl

colour bar, color bar (US) n segregación f racial

481

colour-blind, color-blind (US) ['kʌləblaɪnd] adj daltónico

coloured, colored (US) ['kʌləd] adj de color; (photo) en color; (of race) de color

colour film, color film (US) n película en color

colourful, colorful (US) ['kʌləful] adj lleno de color; (person) pintoresco

colouring, coloring (US) ['kʌlərɪŋ] n colorido, color; (substance) colorante m

colourless, colorless (US) ['kʌlələs] adj incoloro, sin color

colour scheme, color scheme (US) n combinación f de colores

colour supplement n (Brit Press) suplemento semanal or dominical

colour television, color television (US) n televisión f en color

colt [kəult] n potro

column ['kɔləm] n columna; (fashion column, sports column etc) sección f, columna; **the editorial ~** el editorial

columnist ['kɔləmnɪst] n columnista m/f

coma ['kəumə] n coma m

comb [kəum] n peine m; (ornamental) peineta ■ vt (hair) peinar; (area) registrar a fondo, peinar

combat ['kɔmbæt] n combate m ■ vt combatir

combination [kɔmbɪ'neɪʃən] n (gen) combinación f

combination lock n cerradura de combinación

combine [kəm'baɪn] vt combinar; (qualities) reunir ■ vi combinarse ■ n ['kɔmbaɪn] (Econ) cartel m; (also: **combine harvester**) cosechadora; **a combined effort** un esfuerzo conjunto

combine harvester n cosechadora

combo ['kɔmbəu] n (jazz etc) conjunto

combustion [kəm'bʌstʃən] n combustión f

 KEYWORD

come [kʌm] (pt **came**, pp **come**) vi **1** (movement towards) venir; **to come running** venir corriendo; **come with me** ven conmigo **2** (arrive) llegar; **he's come here to work** ha venido aquí para trabajar; **to come home** volver a casa; **we've just come from Seville** acabamos de llegar de Sevilla; **coming!** ¡voy! **3** (reach): **to come to** llegar a; **the bill came to £40** la cuenta ascendía a cuarenta libras **4** (occur): **an idea came to me** se me ocurrió una idea; **if it comes to it** llegado el caso **5** (be, become): **to come loose/undone** etc aflojarse/desabrocharse, desatarse etc;

I've come to like him por fin ha llegado a gustarme

▶ **come about** vi suceder, ocurrir

▶ **come across** vt fus (person) encontrarse con; (thing) encontrar ■ vi: **to come across well/badly** causar buena/mala impresión

▶ **come away** vi (leave) marcharse; (become detached) desprenderse

▶ **come back** vi (return) volver; (reply): **can I come back to you on that one?** volvamos sobre ese punto

▶ **come by** vt fus (acquire) conseguir

▶ **come down** vi (price) bajar; (building) derrumbarse; (be demolished) ser derribado

▶ **come forward** vi presentarse

▶ **come from** vt fus (place, source) ser de

▶ **come in** vi (visitor) entrar; (train, report) llegar; (fashion) ponerse de moda; (on deal etc) entrar

▶ **come in for** vt fus (criticism etc) recibir

▶ **come into** vt fus (money) heredar; (be involved) tener que ver con; **to come into fashion** ponerse de moda

▶ **come off** vi (button) soltarse, desprenderse; (attempt) salir bien

▶ **come on** vi (pupil, work, project) marchar; (lights) encenderse; (electricity) volver; **come on!** ¡vamos!

▶ **come out** vi (fact) salir a la luz; (book, sun) salir; (stain) quitarse; **to come out (on strike)** declararse en huelga; **to come out for/against** declararse a favor/en contra de

▶ **come over** vt fus: **I don't know what's come over him!** ¡no sé lo que le pasa!

▶ **come round** vi (after faint, operation) volver en sí

▶ **come through** vi (survive) sobrevivir; (telephone call): **the call came through** recibimos la llamada

▶ **come to** vi (wake) volver en sí; (total) sumar; **how much does it come to?** ¿cuánto es en total?, ¿a cuánto asciende?

▶ **come under** vt fus (heading) entrar dentro de; (influence) estar bajo

▶ **come up** vi (sun) salir; (problem) surgir; (event) aproximarse; (in conversation) mencionarse

▶ **come up against** vt fus (resistance etc) tropezar con

▶ **come up to** vt fus llegar hasta; **the film didn't come up to our expectations** la película no fue tan buena como esperábamos

▶ **come up with** vt fus (idea) sugerir; (money) conseguir

▶ **come upon** vt fus (find) dar con

comeback ['kʌmbæk] n (reaction) reacción f; (response) réplica; **to make a ~** (Theat) volver a las tablas
comedian [kə'miːdɪən] n humorista m
comedienne [kəmiːdɪ'ɛn] n humorista
comedown ['kʌmdaʊn] n revés m
comedy ['kɒmɪdɪ] n comedia
comet ['kɒmɪt] n cometa m
comeuppance [kʌm'ʌpəns] n: **to get one's ~** llevar su merecido
comfort ['kʌmfət] n comodidad f, confort m; (well-being) bienestar m; (solace) consuelo; (relief) alivio ▪ vt consolar; see also **comforts**
comfortable ['kʌmfətəbl] adj cómodo; (income) adecuado; (majority) suficiente; **I don't feel very ~ about it** la cosa me tiene algo preocupado
comfortably ['kʌmfətəblɪ] adv (sit) cómodamente, (live) holgadamente
comforter ['kʌmfətəʳ] n (US: pacifier) chupete m; (: bed cover) colcha
comforts ['kʌmfəts] npl comodidades fpl
comfort station n (US) servicios mpl
comic ['kɒmɪk] adj (also: **comical**) cómico, gracioso ▪ n (magazine) tebeo; (for adults) cómic m
comic strip n tira cómica
coming ['kʌmɪŋ] n venida, llegada ▪ adj que viene; (next) próximo; (future) venidero; **~(s) and going(s)** n(pl) ir y venir m, ajetreo; **in the ~ weeks** en las próximas semanas
Comintern ['kɒmɪntəːn] n Comintern m
comma ['kɒmə] n coma
command [kə'mɑːnd] n orden f, mandato; (Mil: authority) mando; (mastery) dominio; (Comput) orden f, comando ▪ vt (troops) mandar; (give orders to) mandar, ordenar; (be able to get) disponer de; (deserve) merecer; **to have at one's ~** (money, resources etc) disponer de; **to have/take ~ of** estar al/asumir el mando de
command economy n economía dirigida
commandeer [kɒmən'dɪəʳ] vt requisar
commander [kə'mɑːndəʳ] n (Mil) comandante m/f, jefe(-a) m(f)
commanding [kə'mɑːndɪŋ] adj (appearance) imponente; (voice, tone) imperativo; (lead) abrumador(-a); (position) dominante
commanding officer n comandante m
commandment [kə'mɑːndmənt] n (Rel) mandamiento
command module n módulo de mando
commando [kə'mɑːndəʊ] n comando
commemorate [kə'mɛməreɪt] vt conmemorar
commemoration [kəmɛmə'reɪʃən] n conmemoración f

commemorative [kə'mɛmərətɪv] adj conmemorativo
commence [kə'mɛns] vt, vi comenzar
commend [kə'mɛnd] vt (praise) elogiar, alabar; (recommend) recomendar; (entrust) encomendar
commendable [kə'mɛndəbl] adj encomiable
commendation [kɒmɛn'deɪʃən] n (for bravery etc) elogio, encomio
commensurate [kə'mɛnʃərɪt] adj: **~ with** en proporción a
comment ['kɒmɛnt] n comentario ▪ vt: **to ~ that** comentar or observar que ▪ vi: **to ~ (on)** comentar, hacer comentarios (sobre); **"no ~"** "no tengo nada que decir", "sin comentarios"
commentary ['kɒməntərɪ] n comentario
commentator ['kɒmənteɪtəʳ] n comentarista m/f
commerce ['kɒməːs] n comercio
commercial [kə'məːʃəl] adj comercial ▪ n (TV) anuncio
commercial bank n banco comercial
commercial break n intermedio para publicidad
commercialism [kə'məːʃəlɪzəm] n comercialismo
commercial television n televisión f comercial
commercial vehicle n vehículo comercial
commiserate [kə'mɪzəreɪt] vi: **to ~ with** compadecerse de, condolerse de
commission [kə'mɪʃən] n (committee, fee, order for work of art etc) comisión f; (act) perpetración f ▪ vt (Mil) nombrar; (work of art) encargar; **out of ~** (machine) fuera de servicio; **~ of inquiry** comisión f investigadora; **I get 10% ~** me dan el diez por ciento de comisión; **to ~ sb to do sth** encargar a algn que haga algo; **to ~ sth from sb** (painting etc) encargar algo a algn
commissionaire [kəmɪʃə'nɛəʳ] n (Brit) portero, conserje m
commissioner [kə'mɪʃənəʳ] n comisario; (Police) comisario m de policía
commit [kə'mɪt] vt (act) cometer; (to sb's care) entregar; **to ~ o.s. (to do)** comprometerse (a hacer); **to ~ suicide** suicidarse; **to ~ sb for trial** remitir a algn al tribunal
commitment [kə'mɪtmənt] n compromiso
committed [kə'mɪtɪd] adj (writer, politician etc) comprometido
committee [kə'mɪtɪ] n comité m; **to be on a ~** ser miembro(-a) de un comité
committee meeting n reunión f del comité
commodious [kə'məʊdɪəs] adj grande, espacioso

483

commodity [kə'mɔdɪtɪ] n mercancía
commodity exchange n bolsa de productos or de mercancías
commodity market n mercado de productos básicos
commodore ['kɔmədɔːʳ] n comodoro
common ['kɔmən] adj (gen) común; (pej) ordinario ■ n campo común; **in ~** en común; **in ~ use** de uso corriente
common cold n: **the ~** el resfriado
common denominator n común denominador m
commoner ['kɔmənəʳ] n plebeyo(-a)
common land n campo comunal, ejido
common law n ley f consuetudinaria
common-law ['kɔmənlɔː] adj: **~ wife** esposa de hecho
commonly ['kɔmənlɪ] adv comúnmente
Common Market n Mercado Común
commonplace ['kɔmənpleɪs] adj corriente
commonroom ['kɔmənrum] n sala de reunión
Commons ['kɔmənz] npl (Brit Pol): **the ~** (la Cámara de) los Comunes
common sense n sentido común
Commonwealth ['kɔmənwɛlθ] n: **the ~** la Comunidad (Británica) de Naciones, la Commonwealth; ver nota

● **COMMONWEALTH**
●
● La *Commonwealth* es la asociación de
● estados soberanos independientes y
● territorios asociados que formaban parte
● del antiguo Imperio Británico. Éste pasó
● a llamarse así después de la Segunda
● Guerra Mundial, aunque ya desde 1931 se
● le conocía como "British Commonwealth
● of Nations". Todos los estados miembros
● reconocen al monarca británico como
● "Head of the Commonwealth".

commotion [kə'məʊʃən] n tumulto, confusión f
communal ['kɔmju:nl] adj comunal; (kitchen) común
commune ['kɔmju:n] n (group) comuna ■ vi [kə'mju:n]: **to ~ with** comunicarse con
communicate [kə'mju:nɪkeɪt] vt comunicar ■ vi: **to ~ (with)** comunicarse (con)
communication [kəmju:nɪ'keɪʃən] n comunicación f
communication cord n (Brit) timbre m de alarma
communications network n red f de comunicaciones
communications satellite n satélite m de comunicaciones

communicative [kə'mju:nɪkətɪv] adj comunicativo
communion [kə'mju:nɪən] n (also: **Holy Communion**) comunión f
communiqué [kə'mju:nɪkeɪ] n comunicado, parte m
communism ['kɔmjunɪzəm] n comunismo
communist ['kɔmjunɪst] adj, n comunista m/f
community [kə'mju:nɪtɪ] n comunidad f; (large group) colectividad f; (local) vecindario
community centre n centro social
community chest n (US) fondo social
community health centre n centro médico, casa de salud
community spirit n civismo
commutation ticket [kɔmju'teɪʃən-] n (US) billete m de abono
commute [kə'mju:t] vi viajar a diario de casa al trabajo ■ vt conmutar
commuter [kə'mju:təʳ] n persona que viaja a diario de casa al trabajo
compact [kəm'pækt] adj compacto; (style) conciso; (dense) apretado ■ n ['kɔmpækt] (pact) pacto; (also: **powder compact**) polvera
compact disc n compact disc m, disco compacto
compact disc player n lector m or reproductor m de discos compactos
companion [kəm'pænɪən] n compañero(-a)
companionship [kəm'pænjənʃɪp] n compañerismo
companionway [kəm'pænjənweɪ] n (Naut) escalerilla
company ['kʌmpənɪ] n (gen) compañía; (Comm) empresa, compañía; **to keep sb ~** acompañar a algn; **Smith and C~** Smith y Compañía
company car n coche m de la empresa
company director n director(a) m(f) de empresa
company secretary n (Brit) administrador(a) m(f) de empresa
comparable ['kɔmpərəbl] adj comparable
comparative [kəm'pærətɪv] adj (freedom, luxury, cost) relativo; (study, linguistics) comparado
comparatively [kəm'pærətɪvlɪ] adv (relatively) relativamente
compare [kəm'pɛəʳ] vt comparar ■ vi: **to ~ (with)** poder compararse (con); **compared with** or **to** comparado con or a; **how do the prices ~?** ¿cómo son los precios en comparación?
comparison [kəm'pærɪsn] n comparación f; **in ~ (with)** en comparación (con)

compartment [kəm'pɑ:tmənt] n
compartim(i)ento; (Rail) departamento,
compartimento

compass ['kʌmpəs] n brújula; **compasses**
npl compás m; **within the ~ of** al alcance de

compassion [kəm'pæʃən] n compasión f

compassionate [kəm'pæʃənɪt] adj
compasivo; **on ~ grounds** por compasión

compassionate leave n permiso por
asuntos familiares

compatibility [kəmpætɪ'bɪlɪtɪ] n
compatibilidad f

compatible [kəm'pætɪbl] adj compatible

compel [kəm'pɛl] vt obligar

compelling [kəm'pɛlɪŋ] adj (fig: argument)
convincente

compendium [kəm'pɛndɪəm] n compendio

compensate ['kɔmpənseɪt] vt compensar
▪ vi. **to ~ for** compensar

compensation [kɔmpən'seɪʃən] n (for loss)
indemnización f

compère ['kɔmpɛəʳ] n presentador(a) m(f)

compete [kəm'pi:t] vi (take part) competir;
(vie with) competir, hacer la competencia

competence ['kɔmpɪtəns] n capacidad f,
aptitud f

competent ['kɔmpɪtənt] adj competente,
capaz

competing [kəm'pi:tɪŋ] adj (rival)
competidor(-a); (ideas) contrapuesto

competition [kɔmpɪ'tɪʃən] n (contest)
concurso; (Sport) competición f; (Econ: rivalry)
competencia; **in ~ with** en competencia con

competitive [kəm'pɛtɪtɪv] adj (Econ, Sport)
competitivo; (spirit) competidor(a),
de competencia; (selection) por concurso

competitor [kəm'pɛtɪtəʳ] n (rival)
competidor(a) m(f); (participant) concursante
m/f

compile [kəm'paɪl] vt recopilar

complacency [kəm'pleɪsnsɪ] n
autosatisfacción f

complacent [kəm'pleɪsənt] adj
autocomplaciente

complain [kəm'pleɪn] vi (gen) quejarse;
(Comm) reclamar

complaint [kəm'pleɪnt] n (gen) queja; (Comm)
reclamación f; (Law) demanda, querella;
(Med) enfermedad f

complement ['kɔmplɪmənt] n
complemento; (esp ship's crew) dotación f
▪ vt ['kɔmplɪmɛnt] (enhance) complementar

complementary [kɔmplɪ'mɛntərɪ] adj
complementario

complete [kəm'pli:t] adj (full) completo;
(finished) acabado ▪ vt (fulfil) completar;
(finish) acabar; (a form) rellenar; **it's a ~**

disaster es un desastre total

completely [kəm'pli:tlɪ] adv completamente

completion [kəm'pli:ʃən] n (gen) conclusión
f, terminación f; **to be nearing ~** estar a
punto de terminarse; **on ~ of contract**
cuando se realice el contrato

complex ['kɔmplɛks] adj complejo ▪ n (gen)
complejo

complexion [kəm'plɛkʃən] n (of face) tez f,
cutis m; (fig) aspecto

complexity [kəm'plɛksɪtɪ] n complejidad f

compliance [kəm'plaɪəns] n (submission)
sumisión f; (agreement) conformidad f; **in ~
with** de acuerdo con

compliant [kəm'plaɪənt] adj sumiso;
conforme

complicate ['kɔmplɪkeɪt] vt complicar

complicated ['kɔmplɪkeɪtɪd] adj complicado

complication [kɔmplɪ'keɪʃən] n
complicación f

complicity [kəm'plɪsɪtɪ] n complicidad f

compliment ['kɔmplɪmənt] n (formal)
cumplido; (flirtation) piropo ▪ vt felicitar;
compliments npl saludos mpl; **to pay sb
a ~** (formal) hacer cumplidos a algn; (flirt)
piropear, echar piropos a algn; **to ~ sb (on
sth/on doing sth)** felicitar a algn (por algo/
por haber hecho algo)

complimentary [kɔmplɪ'mɛntərɪ] adj
elogioso; (copy) de regalo; **~ ticket** invitación f

compliments slip n saluda m

comply [kəm'plaɪ] vi: **to ~ with** acatar

component [kəm'pəunənt] adj componente
▪ n (Tech) pieza, componente m

compose [kəm'pəuz] vt componer; **to be
composed of** componerse de, constar de;
to ~ o.s. tranquilizarse

composed [kəm'pəuzd] adj sosegado

composer [kəm'pəuzəʳ] n (Mus)
compositor(a) m(f)

composite ['kɔmpəzɪt] adj compuesto; **~
motion** (Comm) moción f compuesta

composition [kɔmpə'zɪʃən] n composición f

compositor [kəm'pɔzɪtəʳ] n (Typ) cajista m/f

compos mentis ['kɔmpəs'mɛntɪs] adj: **to be
~** estar en su sano juicio

compost ['kɔmpɔst] n abono

compost heap n montón de basura orgánica para
abono

composure [kəm'pəuʒəʳ] n serenidad f,
calma

compound ['kɔmpaund] n (Chem)
compuesto; (Ling) término compuesto;
(enclosure) recinto ▪ adj (gen) compuesto;
(fracture) complicado ▪ vt [kəm'paund]
(fig: problem, difficulty) agravar

comprehend [kɔmprɪ'hɛnd] vt comprender

comprehension [kɔmprɪ'hɛnʃən] *n* comprensión *f*

comprehensive [kɔmprɪ'hɛnsɪv] *adj* (*broad*) extenso; (*general*) de conjunto; ~ **(school)** *n* centro estatal de enseñanza secundaria, ≈ Instituto Nacional de Bachillerato (*SP*); *ver nota*

● **COMPREHENSIVE SCHOOL**

En los años 60 se creó un nuevo tipo de centro educativo de enseñanza secundaria (aproximadamente de los once años en adelante) denominado *comprehensive school*, abierto a todos los alumnos independientemente de sus capacidades, con el que se intentó poner fin a la división tradicional entre centros de enseñanzas teóricas para acceder a la educación superior ("grammar schools") y otros de enseñanzas básicamente profesionales ("secondary modern schools").

comprehensive insurance policy *n* seguro a todo riesgo

compress [kəm'prɛs] *vt* comprimir; (*Inform*) comprimir ■ *n* ['kɔmprɛs] (*Med*) compresa

compression [kəm'prɛʃən] *n* compresión *f*

comprise [kəm'praɪz] *vt* (*also*: **be comprised of**) comprender, constar de

compromise ['kɔmprəmaɪz] *n* solución *f* intermedia; (*agreement*) arreglo ■ *vt* comprometer ■ *vi* transigir, transar (*LAm*) ■ *cpd* (*decision, solution*) de término medio

compulsion [kəm'pʌlʃən] *n* obligación *f*; **under** ~ a la fuerza, por obligación

compulsive [kəm'pʌlsɪv] *adj* compulsivo

compulsory [kəm'pʌlsərɪ] *adj* obligatorio

compulsory purchase *n* expropiación *f*

compunction [kəm'pʌŋkʃən] *n* escrúpulo; **to have no ~ about doing sth** no tener escrúpulos en hacer algo

computer [kəm'pju:tər] *n* ordenador *m*, computador *m*, computadora

computer game *n* juego de ordenador

computerize [kəm'pju:təraɪz] *vt* (*data*) computerizar; (*system*) informatizar

computer language *n* lenguaje *m* de ordenador *or* computadora

computer literate *adj*: **to be ~** tener conocimientos de informática a nivel de usuario

computer peripheral *n* periférico

computer program *n* programa *m* informático *or* de ordenador

computer programmer *n* programador(a) *m(f)*

computer programming *n* programación *f*

computer science *n* informática

computing [kəm'pju:tɪŋ] *n* (*activity*) informática

comrade ['kɔmrɪd] *n* compañero(-a)

comradeship ['kɔmrɪdʃɪp] *n* camaradería, compañerismo

comsat® ['kɔmsæt] *n abbr* = **communications satellite**

con [kɔn] *vt* timar, estafar ■ *n* timo, estafa; **to ~ sb into doing sth** (*col*) engañar a algn para que haga algo

concave ['kɔn'keɪv] *adj* cóncavo

conceal [kən'si:l] *vt* ocultar; (*thoughts etc*) disimular

concede [kən'si:d] *vt* reconocer; (*game*) darse por vencido en; (*territory*) ceder ■ *vi* darse por vencido

conceit [kən'si:t] *n* orgullo, presunción *f*

conceited [kən'si:tɪd] *adj* orgulloso

conceivable [kən'si:vəbl] *adj* concebible; **it is ~ that ...** es posible que ...

conceivably [kən'si:vəblɪ] *adv*: **he may ~ be right** es posible que tenga razón

conceive [kən'si:v] *vt, vi* concebir; **to ~ of sth/of doing sth** imaginar algo/imaginarse haciendo algo

concentrate ['kɔnsəntreɪt] *vi* concentrarse ■ *vt* concentrar

concentration [kɔnsən'treɪʃən] *n* concentración *f*

concentration camp *n* campo de concentración

concentric [kən'sɛntrɪk] *adj* concéntrico

concept ['kɔnsɛpt] *n* concepto

conception [kən'sɛpʃən] *n* (*idea*) concepto, idea; (*Biol*) concepción *f*

concern [kən'sə:n] *n* (*matter*) asunto; (*Comm*) empresa; (*anxiety*) preocupación *f* ■ *vt* tener que ver con; (*affect*) atañer, concernir; **to be concerned (about)** interesarse (por), preocuparse (por); **to be concerned with** tratar de; **"to whom it may ~"** "a quien corresponda"; **the department concerned** (*under discussion*) el departamento en cuestión; (*relevant*) el departamento competente; **as far as I am concerned** en cuanto a mí, por lo que a mí se refiere

concerning [kən'sə:nɪŋ] *prep* sobre, acerca de

concert ['kɔnsət] *n* concierto

concerted [kən'sə:təd] *adj* (*efforts etc*) concertado

concert hall *n* sala de conciertos

concertina [kɔnsə'ti:nə] *n* concertina

concerto [kən'tʃə:təu] *n* concierto

concession [kən'sɛʃən] *n* concesión *f*; (*price concession*) descuento; **tax ~** privilegio fiscal

concessionaire [kənsɛʃə'nɛəʳ] n
concesionario(-a)

concessionary [kən'sɛʃənərɪ] adj (ticket, fare)
con descuento, a precio reducido

conciliation [kənsɪlɪ'eɪʃən] n conciliación f

conciliatory [kən'sɪlɪətrɪ] adj conciliador(a)

concise [kən'saɪs] adj conciso

conclave ['kɔnkleɪv] n cónclave m

conclude [kən'kluːd] vt (finish) concluir;
(treaty etc) firmar; (agreement) llegar a; (decide):
to ~ that ... llegar a la conclusión de que ...
■ vi (events) concluir, terminar

concluding [kən'kluːdɪŋ] adj (remarks etc)
final

conclusion [kən'kluːʒən] n conclusión f;
to come to the ~ that llegar a la conclusión
de que

conclusive [kən'kluːsɪv] adj decisivo,
concluyente

conclusively [kən'kluːsɪvlɪ] adv
concluyentemente

concoct [kən'kɔkt] vt (food, drink) preparar;
(story) inventar; (plot) tramar

concoction [kən'kɔkʃən] n (food) mezcla;
(drink) brebaje m

concord ['kɔŋkɔːd] n (harmony) concordia;
(treaty) acuerdo

concourse ['kɔŋkɔːs] n (hall) vestíbulo

concrete ['kɔnkriːt] n hormigón m ■ adj
concreto

concrete mixer n hormigonera

concur [kən'kəːʳ] vi estar de acuerdo

concurrently [kən'kʌrntlɪ] adv al mismo
tiempo

concussion [kən'kʌʃən] n conmoción f
cerebral

condemn [kən'dɛm] vt condenar

condemnation [kɔndɛm'neɪʃən] n (gen)
condena; (blame) censura

condensation [kɔndɛn'seɪʃən] n
condensación f

condense [kən'dɛns] vi condensarse ■ vt
condensar; (text) abreviar

condensed milk n leche f condensada

condescend [kɔndɪ'sɛnd] vi condescender;
to ~ to sb tratar a algn con condescendencia;
to ~ to do sth dignarse hacer algo

condescending [kɔndɪ'sɛndɪŋ] adj superior

condition [kən'dɪʃən] n condición f; (of
health) estado; (disease) enfermedad f ■ vt
condicionar; **on ~ that** a condición (de)
que; **weather conditions** condiciones
atmosféricas; **in good/poor ~** en buenas/
malas condiciones, en buen/mal estado;
conditions of sale condiciones de venta

conditional [kən'dɪʃənl] adj condicional

conditioned reflex [kən'dɪʃənd-] n reflejo
condicionado

conditioner [kən'dɪʃənəʳ] n (for hair)
suavizante m, acondicionador m

condo ['kɔndəu] n abbr (US col)
= **condominium**

condolences [kən'dəulənsɪz] npl pésame msg

condom ['kɔndəm] n condón m

condominium [kɔndə'mɪnɪəm] n (US:
building) bloque m de pisos or apartamentos
(propiedad de quienes lo habitan), condominio
(LAm); (: apartment) piso or apartamento
(en propiedad), condominio (LAm)

condone [kən'dəun] vt condonar

conducive [kən'djuːsɪv] adj: **~ to**
conducente a

conduct ['kɔndʌkt] n conducta,
comportamiento ■ vt [kən'dʌkt] (lead)
conducir; (manage) llevar, dirigir; (Mus)
dirigir ■ vi (Mus) llevar la batuta; **to ~ o.s.**
comportarse

conducted tour n (Brit) visita con guía

conductor [kən'dʌktəʳ] n (of orchestra)
director(a) m(f); (US: on train) revisor(a) m(f);
(on bus) cobrador m; (Elec) conductor m

cone [kəun] n cono; (pine cone) piña; (for ice
cream) cucurucho

confectioner [kən'fɛkʃənəʳ] n (of cakes)
pastelero(-a); (of sweets) confitero(-a); **~'s
(shop)** n pastelería; confitería

confectionery [kən'fɛkʃənrɪ] n pasteles mpl;
dulces mpl

confederate [kən'fɛdrɪt] adj confederado
■ n (pej) cómplice m/f; (US History)
confederado(-a)

confederation [kənfɛdə'reɪʃən] n
confederación f

confer [kən'fəːʳ] vt: **~ (on)** otorgar (a) ■ vi
conferenciar; **to ~ (with sb about sth)**
consultar (con algn sobre algo)

conference ['kɔnfərns] n (meeting) reunión f;
(convention) congreso; **to be in ~** estar en una
reunión

conference room n sala de conferencias

confess [kən'fɛs] vt confesar ■ vi confesar;
(Rel) confesarse

confession [kən'fɛʃən] n confesión f

confessional [kən'fɛʃənl] n confesionario

confessor [kən'fɛsəʳ] n confesor m

confetti [kən'fɛtɪ] n confeti m

confide [kən'faɪd] vi: **to ~ in** confiar en

confidence ['kɔnfɪdns] n (gen: also: **self-
confidence**) confianza; (secret) confidencia;
in ~ (speak, write) en confianza; **to have
(every) ~ that** estar seguro or confiado de
que; **motion of no ~** moción f de censura;
to tell sb sth in strict ~ decir algo a algn de
manera confidencial

confidence trick n timo
confident ['kɔnfɪdənt] adj seguro de sí mismo
confidential [kɔnfɪ'dɛnʃəl] adj confidencial; (secretary) de confianza
confidentiality [kɔnfɪdɛnʃɪ'ælɪtɪ] n confidencialidad f
configuration [kənfɪgju'reɪʃən] n (Comput) configuración f
confine [kən'faɪn] vt (limit) limitar; (shut up) encerrar; **to ~ o.s. to doing sth** limitarse a hacer algo
confined [kən'faɪnd] adj (space) reducido
confinement [kən'faɪnmənt] n (prison) reclusión f; (Med) parto; **in solitary ~** incomunicado
confines ['kɔnfaɪnz] npl confines mpl
confirm [kən'fə:m] vt confirmar
confirmation [kɔnfə'meɪʃən] n confirmación f
confirmed [kən'fə:md] adj empedernido
confiscate ['kɔnfɪskeɪt] vt confiscar
confiscation [kɔnfɪs'keɪʃən] n incautación f
conflagration [kɔnflə'greɪʃən] n conflagración f
conflict ['kɔnflɪkt] n conflicto ■ vi [kən'flɪkt] (opinions) estar reñido; (reports, evidence) contradecirse
conflicting [kən'flɪktɪŋ] adj (reports, evidence, opinions) contradictorio
conform [kən'fɔ:m] vi: **to ~ to** (laws) someterse a; (usages, mores) amoldarse a; (standards) ajustarse a
conformist [kən'fɔ:mɪst] n conformista m/f
confound [kən'faund] vt confundir; (amaze) pasmar
confounded [kən'faundɪd] adj condenado
confront [kən'frʌnt] vt (problems) hacer frente a; (enemy, danger) enfrentarse con
confrontation [kɔnfrən'teɪʃən] n enfrentamiento, confrontación f
confrontational [kɔnfrən'teɪʃənəl] adj conflictivo
confuse [kən'fju:z] vt (perplex) desconcertar; (mix up) confundir
confused [kən'fju:zd] adj confuso; (person) desconcertado; **to get ~** desconcertarse; (muddled up) hacerse un lío
confusing [kən'fju:zɪŋ] adj confuso
confusion [kən'fju:ʒən] n confusión f
congeal [kən'dʒi:l] vi coagularse
congenial [kən'dʒi:nɪəl] adj agradable
congenital [kən'dʒɛnɪtl] adj congénito
congested [kən'dʒɛstɪd] adj (gen) atestado; (telephone lines) saturado
congestion [kən'dʒɛstʃən] n congestión f
congestion charge n, **congestion charges** ■ npl tasa por congestión

conglomerate [kən'glɔmərət] n (Comm, Geo) conglomerado
conglomeration [kənglɔmə'reɪʃən] n conglomeración f
Congo ['kɔŋgəu] n (state) Congo
congratulate [kən'grætjuleɪt] vt felicitar
congratulations [kəngrætju'leɪʃənz] npl: ~ (on) felicitaciones fpl (por); ~! ¡enhorabuena!, ¡felicidades!
congregate ['kɔŋgrɪgeɪt] vi congregarse
congregation [kɔŋgrɪ'geɪʃən] n (in church) fieles mpl
congress ['kɔŋgrɛs] n congreso; (US Pol): **C~** el Congreso (de los Estados Unidos); ver nota

● **CONGRESS**
●
● En el Congreso de los Estados Unidos
● (Congress) se elaboran y aprueban las
● leyes federales. Consta de dos cámaras:
● la Cámara de Representantes ("House of
● Representatives"), cuyos 435 miembros
● son elegidos cada dos años por voto
● popular directo y en número proporcional
● a los habitantes de cada estado, y el
● Senado ("Senate"), con 100 senadores
● ("senators"), 2 por estado, de los que un
● tercio se elige cada dos años y el resto
● cada seis.

congressman ['kɔŋgrɛsmən] n (US) diputado, miembro del Congreso
congresswoman ['kɔŋgrɛswumən] n (US) diputada, miembro f del Congreso
conical ['kɔnɪkl] adj cónico
conifer ['kɔnɪfəʳ] n conífera
coniferous [kə'nɪfərəs] adj (forest) conífero
conjecture [kən'dʒɛktʃəʳ] n conjetura
conjugal ['kɔndʒugl] adj conyugal
conjugate ['kɔndʒugeɪt] vt conjugar
conjunction [kən'dʒʌŋkʃən] n conjunción f; **in ~ with** junto con
conjunctivitis [kəndʒʌŋktɪ'vaɪtɪs] n conjuntivitis f
conjure ['kʌndʒəʳ] vi hacer juegos de manos
▶ **conjure up** vt (ghost, spirit) hacer aparecer; (memories) evocar
conjurer ['kʌndʒərəʳ] n ilusionista m/f
conjuring trick ['kʌndʒərɪŋ-] n juego de manos
conker ['kɔŋkəʳ] n (Brit) castaño de Indias
conk out [kɔŋk-] vi (col) estropearse, fastidiarse, descomponerse (LAm)
con man n timador m
Conn. abbr (US) = Connecticut
connect [kə'nɛkt] vt juntar, unir; (Elec) conectar; (pipes) empalmar; (fig) relacionar,

asociar ■ vi: **to ~ with** (*train*) enlazar con;
to be connected with (*associated*) estar
relacionado con; (*related*) estar emparentado
con; **I am trying to ~ you** (*Tel*) estoy
intentando ponerle al habla
connection [kə'nɛkʃən] *n* juntura, unión
f; (*Elec*) conexión *f*; (*Tech*) empalme *m*;
(*Rail*) enlace *m*; (*Tel*) comunicación *f*; (*fig*)
relación *f*; **what is the ~ between them?**
¿qué relación hay entre ellos?; **in ~ with**
con respecto a, en relación a; **she has many
business connections** tiene muchos
contactos profesionales; **to miss/make a ~**
perder/coger el enlace
connive [kə'naɪv] *vi*: **to ~ at** hacer la vista
gorda a
connoisseur [kɔnɪ'sə:ʳ] *n* experto(-a),
entendido(-a)
connotation [kɔnə'teɪʃən] *n* connotación *f*
conquer ['kɔŋkəʳ] *vt* (*territory*) conquistar;
(*enemy, feelings*) vencer
conqueror ['kɔŋkərəʳ] *n* conquistador(a) *m(f)*
conquest ['kɔŋkwɛst] *n* conquista
cons [kɔnz] *npl see* **convenience; pro**
conscience ['kɔnʃəns] *n* conciencia; **in all ~**
en conciencia
conscientious [kɔnʃɪ'ɛnʃəs] *adj* concienzudo;
(*objection*) de conciencia
conscientious objector *n* objetor *m* de
conciencia
conscious ['kɔnʃəs] *adj* consciente; (*deliberate:
insult, error*) premeditado, intencionado;
to become ~ of sth/that darse cuenta de
algo/de que
consciousness ['kɔnʃəsnɪs] *n* conciencia;
(*Med*) conocimiento
conscript ['kɔnskrɪpt] *n* recluta *m/f*
conscription [kən'skrɪpʃən] *n* servicio
militar (obligatorio)
consecrate ['kɔnsɪkreɪt] *vt* consagrar
consecutive [kən'sɛkjutɪv] *adj* consecutivo;
on 3 ~ occasions en 3 ocasiones consecutivas
consensus [kən'sɛnsəs] *n* consenso; **the ~ of
opinion** el consenso general
consent [kən'sɛnt] *n* consentimiento ■ *vi*:
to ~ to consentir en; **by common ~** de
común acuerdo
consenting adults [kən'sɛntɪŋ-] *npl* adultos
con capacidad de consentir
consequence ['kɔnsɪkwəns] *n* consecuencia;
in ~ por consiguiente
consequently ['kɔnsɪkwəntlɪ] *adv* por
consiguiente
conservation [kɔnsə'veɪʃən] *n* conservación
f; (*of nature*) conservación, protección *f*
conservationist [kɔnsə'veɪʃnɪst] *n*
conservacionista *m/f*

conservative [kən'sə:vətɪv] *adj*
conservador(a); (*cautious*) moderado; **C~** *adj*,
n (*Brit Pol*) conservador(a) *m(f)*; **the C~ Party**
el partido conservador (británico)
conservatory [kən'sə:vətrɪ] *n* (*greenhouse*)
invernadero
conserve [kən'sə:v] *vt* conservar ■ *n*
conserva
consider [kən'sɪdəʳ] *vt* considerar; (*take into
account*) tomar en cuenta; (*study*) estudiar,
examinar; **to ~ doing sth** pensar en (la
posibilidad de) hacer algo; **all things
considered** pensándolo bien; **~ yourself
lucky** ¡date por satisfecho!
considerable [kən'sɪdərəbl] *adj* considerable
considerably [kən'sɪdərəblɪ] *adv* bastante,
considerablemente
considerate [kən'sɪdərɪt] *adj* considerado
consideration [kənsɪdə'reɪʃən] *n*
consideración *f*; (*reward*) retribución *f*; **to be
under ~** estar estudiándose; **my first ~ is
my family** mi primera consideración es mi
familia
considered [kən'sɪdəd] *adj*: **it's my
~ opinion that ...** después de haber
reflexionado mucho, pienso que ...
considering [kən'sɪdərɪŋ] *prep*: **~ (that)**
teniendo en cuenta (que)
consign [kən'saɪn] *vt* consignar
consignee [kɔnsaɪ'ni:] *n* consignatario(-a)
consignment [kən'saɪnmənt] *n* envío
consignment note *n* (*Comm*) talón *m* de
expedición
consignor [kən'saɪnəʳ] *n* remitente *m/f*
consist [kən'sɪst] *vi*: **to ~ of** consistir en
consistency [kən'sɪstənsɪ] *n* (*of person
etc*) consecuencia, coherencia; (*thickness*)
consistencia
consistent [kən'sɪstənt] *adj* (*person, argument*)
consecuente, coherente; (*results*) constante
consolation [kɔnsə'leɪʃən] *n* consuelo
console [kən'səul] *vt* consolar ■ *n* ['kɔnsəul]
(*control panel*) consola
consolidate [kən'sɔlɪdeɪt] *vt* consolidar
consols ['kɔnsɔlz] *npl* (*Brit Stock Exchange*)
valores *mpl* consolidados
consommé [kən'sɔmeɪ] *n* consomé *m*, caldo
consonant ['kɔnsənənt] *n* consonante *f*
consort ['kɔnsɔ:t] *n* consorte *m/f* ■ *vi*
[kən'sɔ:t]: **to ~ with sb** (*often pej*) asociarse
con algn; **prince ~** príncipe *m* consorte
consortium [kən'sɔ:tɪəm] *n* consorcio
conspicuous [kən'spɪkjuəs] *adj* (*visible*)
visible; (*garish etc*) llamativo; (*outstanding*)
notable; **to make o.s. ~** llamar la atención
conspiracy [kən'spɪrəsɪ] *n* conjura,
complot *m*

conspiratorial [kənspɪrə'tɔːrɪəl] *adj* de conspirador

conspire [kən'spaɪəʳ] *vi* conspirar

constable ['kʌnstəbl] *n* (*Brit*) agente *m/f* (de policía); **chief ~ ≈** jefe *m/f* de policía

constabulary [kən'stæbjʊlərɪ] *n* ≈ policía

constancy ['kɔnstənsɪ] *n* constancia; fidelidad *f*

constant ['kɔnstənt] *adj* (*gen*) constante; (*loyal*) leal, fiel

constantly ['kɔnstəntlɪ] *adv* constantemente

constellation [kɔnstə'leɪʃən] *n* constelación *f*

consternation [kɔnstə'neɪʃən] *n* consternación *f*

constipated ['kɔnstɪpeɪtəd] *adj* estreñido

constipation [kɔnstɪ'peɪʃən] *n* estreñimiento

constituency [kən'stɪtjuənsɪ] *n* (*Pol*) distrito electoral; (*people*) electorado; *ver nota*

 CONSTITUENCY

 Constituency es la denominación que recibe un distrito o circunscripción electoral y el grupo de electores registrados en ella en el sistema electoral británico. Cada circunscripción elige a un diputado ("Member of Parliament"), el cual se halla disponible semanalmente para las consultas y peticiones de sus electores durante ciertas horas a la semana, tiempo al que se llama "surgery".

constituency party *n* partido local

constituent [kən'stɪtjuənt] *n* (*Pol*) elector(a) *m(f)*; (*part*) componente *m*

constitute ['kɔnstɪtjuːt] *vt* constituir

constitution [kɔnstɪ'tjuːʃən] *n* constitución *f*

constitutional [kɔnstɪ'tjuːʃənl] *adj* constitucional; **~ monarchy** monarquía constitucional

constrain [kən'streɪn] *vt* obligar

constrained [kən'streɪnd] *adj*: **to feel ~ to ...** sentirse obligado a ...

constraint [kən'streɪnt] *n* (*force*) fuerza; (*limit*) restricción *f*; (*restraint*) reserva; (*embarrassment*) cohibición *f*

constrict [kən'strɪkt] *vt* oprimir

constriction [kən'strɪkʃən] *n* constricción *f*, opresión *f*

construct [kən'strʌkt] *vt* construir

construction [kən'strʌkʃən] *n* construcción *f*; (*fig: interpretation*) interpretación *f*; **under ~** en construcción

construction industry *n* industria de la construcción

constructive [kən'strʌktɪv] *adj* constructivo

construe [kən'struː] *vt* interpretar

consul ['kɔnsl] *n* cónsul *m/f*

consulate ['kɔnsjʊlɪt] *n* consulado

consult [kən'sʌlt] *vt, vi* consultar; **to ~ sb (about sth)** consultar a algn (sobre algo)

consultancy [kən'sʌltənsɪ] *n* (*Comm*) consultoría; (*Med*) puesto de especialista

consultant [kən'sʌltənt] *n* (*Brit Med*) especialista *m/f*; (*other specialist*) asesor(a) *m(f)*, consultor(a) *m(f)*

consultation [kɔnsəl'teɪʃən] *n* consulta; **in ~ with** en consulta con

consultative [kən'sʌltətɪv] *adj* consultivo

consulting room *n* (*Brit*) consulta, consultorio

consume [kən'sjuːm] *vt* (*eat*) comerse; (*drink*) beberse; (*fire etc*) consumir; (*Comm*) consumir

consumer [kən'sjuːməʳ] *n* (*of electricity, gas etc*) consumidor(a) *m(f)*

consumer association *n* asociación *f* de consumidores

consumer credit *n* crédito al consumidor

consumer durables *npl* bienes *mpl* de consumo duraderos

consumer goods *npl* bienes *mpl* de consumo

consumerism [kən'sjuːmərɪzəm] *n* consumismo

consumer society *n* sociedad *f* de consumo

consumer watchdog *n* organización *f* protectora del consumidor

consummate ['kɔnsʌmeɪt] *vt* consumar

consumption [kən'sʌmpʃən] *n* consumo; (*Med*) tisis *f*; **not fit for human ~** no apto para el consumo humano

cont. *abbr* (= *continued*) sigue

contact ['kɔntækt] *n* contacto; (*person: pej*) enchufe *m* ▪ *vt* ponerse en contacto con; **~ lenses** *npl* lentes *fpl* de contacto; **to be in ~ with sb/sth** estar en contacto con algn/algo; **business contacts** relaciones *fpl* comerciales

contagious [kən'teɪdʒəs] *adj* contagioso

contain [kən'teɪn] *vt* contener; **to ~ o.s.** contenerse

container [kən'teɪnəʳ] *n* recipiente *m*; (*for shipping etc*) contenedor *m*

containerize [kən'teɪnəraɪz] *vt* transportar en contenedores

container ship *n* buque *m* contenedor, portacontenedores *m inv*

contaminate [kən'tæmɪneɪt] *vt* contaminar

contamination [kəntæmɪ'neɪʃən] *n* contaminación *f*

cont'd *abbr* (= *continued*) sigue

contemplate ['kɔntəmpleɪt] *vt* (*gen*) contemplar; (*reflect upon*) considerar; (*intend*) pensar

contemplation [kɔntəm'pleɪʃən] n
contemplación f
contemporary [kən'tɛmpərərɪ] adj, n (of the
same age) contemporáneo(-a) m(f)
contempt [kən'tɛmpt] n desprecio; ~ **of
court** (Law) desacato (a los tribunales or a la
justicia)
contemptible [kən'tɛmptɪbl] adj
despreciable, desdeñable
contemptuous [kən'tɛmptjuəs] adj desdeñoso
contend [kən'tɛnd] vt (argue) afirmar ▪ vi
(struggle) luchar; **he has a lot to ~ with** tiene
que hacer frente a muchos problemas
contender [kən'tɛndər] n (Sport)
contendiente m/f
content [kɔn'tɛnt] adj (happy) contento;
(satisfied) satisfecho ▪ vt contentar;
satisfacer ▪ n ['kɔntɛnt] contenido;
contents npl contenido msg; **(table of)
contents** índice m de materias; (in magazine)
sumario; **to be ~ with** conformarse con; **to
~ o.s. with sth/with doing sth** conformarse
con algo/con hacer algo
contented [kən'tɛntɪd] adj contento;
satisfecho
contentedly [kən'tɛntɪdlɪ] adv con aire
satisfecho
contention [kən'tɛnʃən] n discusión f;
(belief) argumento; **bone of ~** manzana de la
discordia
contentious [kən'tɛnʃəs] adj discutible
contentment [kən'tɛntmənt] n satisfacción f
contest ['kɔntɛst] n contienda; (competition)
concurso ▪ vt [kən'tɛst] (dispute) impugnar;
(Law) disputar, litigar; (Pol: election, seat)
presentarse como candidato(-a) a
contestant [kən'tɛstənt] n concursante m/f;
(in fight) contendiente m/f
context ['kɔntɛkst] n contexto; **in/out of ~**
en/fuera de contexto
continent ['kɔntɪnənt] n continente m; **the
C~** (Brit) el continente europeo, Europa; **on
the C~** en el continente europeo, en Europa
continental [kɔntɪ'nɛntl] adj continental;
(Brit: European) europeo
continental breakfast n desayuno estilo
europeo
continental quilt n (Brit) edredón m
contingency [kən'tɪndʒənsɪ] n contingencia
contingent [kən'tɪndʒənt] n (group)
representación f
continual [kən'tɪnjuəl] adj continuo
continually [kən'tɪnjuəlɪ] adv
continuamente
continuation [kəntɪnju'eɪʃən] n
prolongación f; (after interruption)
reanudación f; (of story, episode) continuación f

continue [kən'tɪnjuː] vi, vt seguir, continuar;
continued on page 10 sigue en la página 10
continuing education [kən'tɪnjuɪŋ-] n
educación f continua de adultos
continuity [kɔntɪ'njuɪtɪ] n (also Cine)
continuidad f
continuity girl n (Cine) secretaria de
continuidad
continuous [kən'tɪnjuəs] adj continuo;
~ **performance** (Cine) sesión f continua
continuously [kən'tɪnjuəslɪ] adv
continuamente
contort [kən'tɔːt] vt retorcer
contortion [kən'tɔːʃən] n (movement)
contorsión f
contortionist [kən'tɔːʃənɪst] n
contorsionista m/f
contour ['kɔntuər] n contorno; (also: **contour
line**) curva de nivel
contraband ['kɔntrəbænd] n contrabando
▪ adj de contrabando
contraception [kɔntrə'sɛpʃən] n
contracepción f
contraceptive [kɔntrə'sɛptɪv] adj, n
anticonceptivo
contract [n 'kɔntrækt, vb kən'trækt] n
contrato ▪ cpd ['kɔntrækt] (price, date)
contratado, de contrato; (work) hajo contrato
▪ vi (Comm): **to ~ to do sth** comprometerse
por contrato a hacer algo; (become smaller)
contraerse, encogerse ▪ vt contraer; **to be
under ~ to do sth** estar bajo contrato para
hacer algo; ~ **of employment** or **of service**
contrato de trabajo
  ▶ **contract in** vi tomar parte
  ▶ **contract out** vi: **to ~ out (of)** optar por
  no tomar parte (en); **to ~ out of a pension
  scheme** dejar de cotizar en un plan de
  jubilación
contraction [kən'trækʃən] n contracción f
contractor [kən'træktər] n contratista m/f
contractual [kən'træktjuəl] adj contractual
contradict [kɔntrə'dɪkt] vt (declare to be wrong)
desmentir; (be contrary to) contradecir
contradiction [kɔntrə'dɪkʃən] n
contradicción f; **to be in ~ with** contradecir
contradictory [kɔntrə'dɪktərɪ] adj
(statements) contradictorio; **to be ~ to**
contradecir
contralto [kən'træltəu] n contralto f
contraption [kən'træpʃən] n (pej) artilugio m
contrary ['kɔntrərɪ] adj (opposite, different)
contrario [kən'trɛərɪ] (perverse) terco ▪ n:
on the ~ al contrario; **unless you hear to
the ~** a no ser que le digan lo contrario; ~ **to
what we thought** al contrario de lo que
pensábamos

contrast ['kɔntrɑːst] n contraste m ■ vt
[kən'trɑːst] contrastar; **in ~ to** or **with** a
diferencia de
contrasting [kən'trɑːstɪŋ] adj (opinion)
opuesto; (colour) que hace contraste
contravene [kɔntrə'viːn] vt contravenir
contravention [kɔntrə'venʃən] n: **~ (of)**
contravención f (de)
contribute [kən'trɪbjuːt] vi contribuir
■ vt: **to ~ to** (gen) contribuir a; (newspaper)
colaborar en; (discussion) intervenir en
contribution [kɔntrɪ'bjuːʃən] n (money)
contribución f; (to debate) intervención f;
(to journal) colaboración f
contributor [kən'trɪbjutər] n (to newspaper)
colaborador(a) m(f)
contributory [kən'trɪbjutərɪ] adj (cause)
contribuyente; **it was a ~ factor in ...** fue un
factor que contribuyó en ...
contributory pension scheme n plan m
cotizable de jubilación
contrivance [kən'traɪvəns] n (machine, device)
aparato, dispositivo
contrive [kən'traɪv] vt (invent) idear ■ vi:
to ~ to do lograr hacer; (try) procurar hacer
control [kən'trəul] vt controlar; (traffic
etc) dirigir; (machinery) manejar; (temper)
dominar; (disease, fire) dominar, controlar
■ n (command) control m; (of car) conducción
f; (check) freno; **controls** npl mandos mpl; **to
~ o.s.** controlarse, dominarse; **everything is
under ~** todo está bajo control; **to be in ~ of**
estar al mando de; **the car went out of ~** el
coche se descontroló
control group n (Med, Psych etc) grupo de
control
control key n (Comput) tecla de control
controlled economy n economía dirigida
controller [kən'trəulər] n controlador(a) m(f)
controlling interest [kən'trəulɪŋ-] n
participación f mayoritaria
control panel n (on aircraft, ship, TV etc) tablero
de instrumentos
control point n (puesto de) control m
control room n (Naut, Mil) sala de mandos;
(Radio, TV) sala de control
control tower n (Aviat) torre f de control
control unit n (Comput) unidad f de control
controversial [kɔntrə'vəːʃl] adj polémico
controversy ['kɔntrəvəːsɪ] n polémica
conurbation [kɔnəː'beɪʃən] n conurbación f
convalesce [kɔnvə'les] vi convalecer
convalescence [kɔnvə'lesns] n
convalecencia
convalescent [kɔnvə'lesnt] adj, n
convaleciente m/f
convector [kən'vektər] n calentador m de

convección
convene [kən'viːn] vt (meeting) convocar
■ vi reunirse
convenience [kən'viːnɪəns] n (comfort)
comodidad f; (advantage) ventaja; **at your
earliest ~** (Comm) tan pronto como le sea
posible; **all modern conveniences,** (Brit)
all mod cons todo confort
convenience foods npl platos mpl preparados
convenient [kən'viːnɪənt] adj (useful) útil;
(place) conveniente; (time) oportuno; **if it is ~
for you** si le viene bien
conveniently [kən'viːnɪəntlɪ] adv
(happen) oportunamente; (situated)
convenientemente
convent ['kɔnvənt] n convento
convention [kən'venʃən] n convención f;
(meeting) asamblea
conventional [kən'venʃənl] adj convencional
convent school n colegio de monjas
converge [kən'vəːdʒ] vi converger
conversant [kən'vəːsnt] adj: **to be ~ with**
estar familiarizado con
conversation [kɔnvə'seɪʃən] n conversación f
conversational [kɔnvə'seɪʃənl] adj (familiar)
familiar; (talkative) locuaz; **~ mode** (Comput)
modo de conversación
converse ['kɔnvəːs] n inversa ■ vi [kən'vəːs]
conversar; **to ~ (with sb about sth)**
conversar or platicar (LAm) (con algn de algo)
conversely [kɔn'vəːslɪ] adv a la inversa
conversion [kən'vəːʃən] n conversión f;
(house conversion) reforma, remodelación f
conversion table n tabla de equivalencias
convert [kən'vəːt] vt (Rel, Comm) convertir;
(alter) transformar ■ n ['kɔnvəːt]
converso(-a)
convertible [kən'vəːtəbl] adj convertible
■ n descapotable m; **~ loan stock**
obligaciones fpl convertibles
convex ['kɔn'veks] adj convexo
convey [kən'veɪ] vt transportar; (thanks)
comunicar; (idea) expresar
conveyance [kən'veɪəns] n (of goods)
transporte m; (vehicle) vehículo, medio de
transporte
conveyancing [kən'veɪənsɪŋ] n (Law)
preparación f de escrituras de traspaso
conveyor belt [kən'veɪər-] n cinta
transportadora
convict [kən'vɪkt] vt (gen) condenar; (find
guilty) declarar culpable a ■ n ['kɔnvɪkt]
presidiario(-a)
conviction [kən'vɪkʃən] n condena; (belief)
creencia, convicción f
convince [kən'vɪns] vt convencer; **to ~ sb (of
sth/that)** convencer a algn (de algo/de que)

convinced [kən'vɪnst] *adj*: ~ **of/that** convencido de/de que

convincing [kən'vɪnsɪŋ] *adj* convincente

convincingly [kən'vɪnsɪŋlɪ] *adv* de modo convincente, convincentemente

convivial [kən'vɪvɪəl] *adj* (*person*) sociable; (*atmosphere*) alegre

convoluted ['kɔnvəlu:tɪd] *adj* (*argument etc*) enrevesado; (*shape*) enrollado, enroscado

convoy ['kɔnvɔɪ] *n* convoy *m*

convulse [kən'vʌls] *vt* convulsionar; **to be convulsed with laughter** dislocarse de risa

convulsion [kən'vʌlʃən] *n* convulsión *f*

coo [ku:] *vi* arrullar

cook [kuk] *vt* cocinar; (*stew etc*) guisar; (*meal*) preparar ■ *vi* hacerse; (*person*) cocinar ■ *n* cocinero(-a)

▶ **cook up** *vt* (*col: excuse, story*) inventar

cookbook ['kukbuk] *n* libro de cocina

cooker ['kukəʳ] *n* cocina

cookery ['kukərɪ] *n* cocina

cookery book *n* (*Brit*) = **cookbook**

cookie ['kukɪ] *n* (*US*) galleta; (*Comput*) cookie *m*

cooking ['kukɪŋ] *n* cocina ■ *cpd* (*apples*) para cocinar; (*utensils, salt, foil*) de cocina

cooking chocolate *n* chocolate *m* fondant *or* de hacer

cookout ['kukaut] *n* (*US*) comida al aire libre

cool [ku:l] *adj* fresco; (*not hot*) tibio; (*not afraid*) tranquilo; (*unfriendly*) frío ■ *vt* enfriar ■ *vi* enfriarse; **it is** ~ (*weather*) hace fresco; **to keep sth** ~ *or* **in a** ~ **place** conservar algo fresco *or* en un sitio fresco

▶ **cool down** *vi* enfriarse; (*fig: person, situation*) calmarse

coolant ['ku:lənt] *n* refrigerante *m*

cool box, cooler (*US*) ['ku:ləʳ] *n* nevera portátil

cooling ['ku:lɪŋ] *adj* refrescante

cooling-off period [ku:lɪŋ'ɔf-] *n* (*Industry*) plazo de negociaciones

cooling tower *n* torre *f* de refrigeración

coolly ['ku:lɪ] *adv* (*calmly*) con tranquilidad; (*audaciously*) descaradamente; (*unenthusiastically*) fríamente, con frialdad

coolness ['ku:lnɪs] *n* frescura; tranquilidad *f*; (*hostility*) frialdad *f*; (*indifference*) falta de entusiasmo

coop [ku:p] *n* gallinero ■ *vt*: **to** ~ **up** (*fig*) encerrar

co-op ['kəuɔp] *n abbr* (= *cooperative (society)*) cooperativa

cooperate [kəu'ɔpəreɪt] *vi* cooperar, colaborar; **will he** ~? ¿querrá cooperar?

cooperation [kəuɔpə'reɪʃən] *n* cooperación *f*, colaboración *f*

cooperative [kəu'ɔpərətɪv] *adj* cooperativo; (*person*) dispuesto a colaborar ■ *n* cooperativa

co-opt [kəu'ɔpt] *vt*: **to** ~ **sb into sth** nombrar a algn para algo

coordinate [kəu'ɔ:dɪneɪt] *vt* coordinar ■ *n* [kəu'ɔ:dɪnət] (*Math*) coordenada; **coordinates** *npl* (*clothes*) coordinados *mpl*

coordination [kəuɔ:dɪ'neɪʃən] *n* coordinación *f*

coot [ku:t] *n* focha *f* (común)

co-ownership [kəu'əunəʃɪp] *n* copropiedad *f*

cop [kɔp] *n* (*col*) poli *m*

cope [kəup] *vi*: **to** ~ **with** poder con; (*problem*) hacer frente a

Copenhagen [kəupən'heɪgən] *n* Copenhague *m*

copier ['kɔpɪəʳ] *n* (*photocopier*) (foto)copiadora

co-pilot ['kəu'paɪlət] *n* copiloto *m/f*

copious ['kəupɪəs] *adj* copioso, abundante

copper ['kɔpəʳ] *n* (*metal*) cobre *m*; (*col: policeman*) poli *m*; **coppers** *npl* perras *fpl*; (*small change*) calderilla

coppice ['kɔpɪs], **copse** [kɔps] *n* bosquecillo

copulate ['kɔpjuleɪt] *vi* copular

copulation [kɔpju'leɪʃən] *n* cópula

copy ['kɔpɪ] *n* copia; (*of book*) ejemplar *m*; (*of magazine*) número; (*material: for printing*) original *m* ■ *vt* copiar (*also Comput*), (*imitate*) copiar, imitar; **to make good** ~ (*fig*) ser una noticia de interés; **rough** ~ borrador *m*; **fair** ~ copia en limpio

▶ **copy out** *vt* copiar

copycat ['kɔpɪkæt] *n* (*pej*) imitador(a) *m(f)*

copyright ['kɔpɪraɪt] *n* derechos *mpl* de autor

copy typist *n* mecanógrafo(-a)

coral ['kɔrəl] *n* coral *m*

coral reef *n* arrecife *m* (de coral)

Coral Sea *n*: **the** ~ el Mar del Coral

cord [kɔ:d] *n* cuerda; (*Elec*) cable *m*; (*fabric*) pana; **cords** *npl* (*trousers*) pantalones *mpl* de pana

cordial ['kɔ:dɪəl] *adj* cordial ■ *n* cordial *m*

cordless ['kɔ:dlɪs] *adj* sin hilos; ~ **telephone** teléfono inalámbrico

cordon ['kɔ:dn] *n* cordón *m*

▶ **cordon off** *vt* acordonar

Cordova ['kɔ:dəvə] *n* Córdoba

corduroy ['kɔ:dərɔɪ] *n* pana

CORE [kɔ:ʳ] *n abbr* (*US*) = **Congress of Racial Equality**

core [kɔ:ʳ] *n* (*of earth, nuclear reactor*) centro, núcleo; (*of fruit*) corazón *m*; (*of problem etc*) esencia, meollo ■ *vt* quitar el corazón de

Corfu [kɔ:'fu:] *n* Corfú *m*

coriander [kɔrɪ'ændəʳ] *n* culantro, cilantro

cork [kɔ:k] *n* corcho; (*tree*) alcornoque *m*

corkage ['kɔ:kɪdʒ] *n* precio que se cobra en un restaurante por una botella de vino traída de fuera

corked [kɔːkt] *adj* (*wine*) con sabor a corcho
corkscrew ['kɔːkskruː] *n* sacacorchos *m inv*
cormorant ['kɔːmərnt] *n* cormorán *m*
Corn *abbr* (*Brit*) = **Cornwall**
corn [kɔːn] *n* (*Brit: wheat*) trigo; (*US: maize*)
maíz *m*, choclo (*LAm*); (*on foot*) callo; ~ **on the cob** (*Culin*) maíz en la mazorca
cornea ['kɔːnɪə] *n* córnea
corned beef ['kɔːnd-] *n* carne *f* de vaca acecinada
corner ['kɔːnəʳ] *n* (*outside*) esquina; (*inside*)
rincón *m*; (*in road*) curva; (*Football*) córner *m*,
saque *m* de esquina ■ *vt* (*trap*) arrinconar;
(*Comm*) acaparar ■ *vi* (*in car*) tomar las
curvas; **to cut corners** atajar
corner flag *n* (*Football*) banderola de esquina
corner kick *n* (*Football*) córner *m*, saque *m* de
esquina
cornerstone ['kɔːnəstəun] *n* piedra angular
cornet ['kɔːnɪt] *n* (*Mus*) corneta; (*Brit: of ice cream*) cucurucho
cornflakes ['kɔːnfleɪks] *npl* copos *mpl* de
maíz, cornflakes *mpl*
cornflour ['kɔːnflauəʳ] *n* (*Brit*) harina de maíz
cornice ['kɔːnɪs] *n* cornisa
Cornish ['kɔːnɪʃ] *adj* de Cornualles
corn oil *n* aceite *m* de maíz
cornstarch ['kɔːnstɑːtʃ] *n* (*US*) = **cornflour**
cornucopia [kɔːnjuˈkəupɪə] *n* cornucopia
Cornwall ['kɔːnwəl] *n* Cornualles *m*
corny ['kɔːnɪ] *adj* (*col*) gastado
corollary [kəˈrɔlərɪ] *n* corolario
coronary ['kɔrənərɪ] *n:* ~ **(thrombosis)**
infarto
coronation [kɔrəˈneɪʃən] *n* coronación *f*
coroner ['kɔrənəʳ] *n* juez *m/f* de instrucción
coronet ['kɔrənɪt] *n* corona
Corp. *abbr* = **corporation**
corporal ['kɔːpərl] *n* cabo ■ *adj:*
~ **punishment** castigo corporal
corporate ['kɔːpərɪt] *adj* corporativo
corporate hospitality *n obsequios a los clientes
por cortesía de la empresa*
corporate identity, corporate image *n*
(*of organization*) identidad *f* corporativa
corporation [kɔːpəˈreɪʃən] *n* (*of town*)
ayuntamiento; (*Comm*) corporación *f*
corps [kɔːʳ] (*pl* ~) [kɔːz] *n* cuerpo; **press ~**
gabinete *m* de prensa
corpse [kɔːps] *n* cadáver *m*
corpulent ['kɔːpjulənt] *adj* corpulento(-a)
Corpus Christi ['kɔːpəsˈkrɪstɪ] *n* Corpus *m*
(Christi)
corpuscle ['kɔːpʌsl] *n* corpúsculo
corral [kəˈrɑːl] *n* corral *m*
correct [kəˈrɛkt] *adj* correcto; (*accurate*) exacto
■ *vt* corregir; **you are ~** tiene razón

correction [kəˈrɛkʃən] *n* rectificación *f*;
(*erasure*) tachadura
correlate ['kɔrɪleɪt] *vi:* **to ~ with** tener
correlación con
correlation [kɔrɪˈleɪʃən] *n* correlación *f*
correspond [kɔrɪsˈpɔnd] *vi* (*write*) escribirse;
(*be equal to*) corresponder
correspondence [kɔrɪsˈpɔndəns] *n*
correspondencia
correspondence course *n* curso por
correspondencia
correspondent [kɔrɪsˈpɔndənt] *n*
corresponsal *m/f*
corresponding [kɔrɪsˈpɔndɪŋ] *adj*
correspondiente
corridor ['kɔrɪdɔːʳ] *n* pasillo
corroborate [kəˈrɔbəreɪt] *vt* corroborar
corroboration [kərɔbəˈreɪʃən] *n*
corroboración *f*, confirmación *f*
corrode [kəˈrəud] *vt* corroer ■ *vi* corroerse
corrosion [kəˈrəuʒən] *n* corrosión *f*
corrosive [kəˈrəusɪv] *adj* corrosivo
corrugated ['kɔrəgeɪtɪd] *adj* ondulado
corrugated cardboard *n* cartón *m*
ondulado
corrugated iron *n* chapa ondulada
corrupt [kəˈrʌpt] *adj* corrompido; (*person*)
corrupto ■ *vt* corromper; (*bribe*) sobornar;
(*Comput: data*) degradar; ~ **practices**
(*dishonesty, bribery*) corrupción *f*
corruption [kəˈrʌpʃən] *n* corrupción *f*;
(*Comput: of data*) alteración *f*
corset ['kɔːsɪt] *n* faja; (*old-style*) corsé *m*
Corsica ['kɔːsɪkə] *n* Córcega
Corsican ['kɔːsɪkən] *adj, n* corso(-a) *m(f)*
cortège [kɔːˈteɪʒ] *n* cortejo, comitiva
cortisone ['kɔːtɪzəun] *n* cortisona
cosh [kɔʃ] *n* (*Brit*) cachiporra
cosignatory ['kəuˈsɪgnətərɪ] *n*
cosignatario(-a)
cosine ['kəusaɪn] *n* coseno
cosiness ['kəuzɪnɪs] *n* comodidad *f*;
(*atmosphere*) lo acogedor
cos lettuce [kɔs-] *n* lechuga romana
cosmetic [kɔzˈmɛtɪk] *n* cosmético ■ *adj* (*also
fig*) cosmético; (*surgery*) estético
cosmic ['kɔzmɪk] *adj* cósmico
cosmonaut ['kɔzmənɔːt] *n* cosmonauta *m/f*
cosmopolitan [kɔzməˈpɔlɪtn] *adj*
cosmopolita
cosmos ['kɔzmɔs] *n* cosmos *m*
cosset ['kɔsɪt] *vt* mimar
cost [kɔst] (*pt, pp* ~) *n* (*gen*) coste *m*, costo;
(*price*) precio; **costs** *npl* (*Law*) costas *fpl* ■ *vi*
costar, valer ■ *vt* preparar el presupuesto
de; **how much does it ~?** ¿cuánto cuesta?,
¿cuánto vale?; **what will it ~ to have it**

repaired? ¿cuánto costará repararlo?; **the ~ of living** el coste or costo de la vida; **at all costs** cueste lo que cueste
cost accountant n contable m de costos
co-star ['kəustɑːʳ] n coprotagonista m/f
Costa Rica ['kɔstə'riːkə] n Costa Rica
Costa Rican ['kɔstə'riːkən] adj, n costarriqueño(-a) m(f), costarricense m/f
cost centre n centro (de determinación) de coste
cost control n control m de costes
cost-effective [kɔstɪ'fɛktɪv] adj (Comm) rentable
cost-effectiveness ['kɔstɪ'fɛktɪvnɪs] n relación f coste-rendimiento
costing ['kɔstɪŋ] n cálculo del coste
costly ['kɔstlɪ] adj (expensive) costoso
cost-of-living [kɔstəv'lɪvɪŋ] adj: **~ allowance** n plus m de carestía de vida; **~ index** n índice m del coste de vida
cost price n (Brit) precio de coste
costume ['kɔstjuːm] n traje m; (Brit: also: **swimming costume**) traje de baño
costume jewellery n bisutería
cosy, cozy (US) ['kəuzɪ] adj cómodo, a gusto; (room, atmosphere) acogedor(a)
cot [kɔt] n (Brit: child's) cuna; (US: folding bed) cama plegable
cot death n muerte f en la cuna
Cotswolds ['kɔtswəuldz] npl región de colinas del suroeste inglés
cottage ['kɔtɪdʒ] n casita de campo
cottage cheese n requesón m
cottage industry n industria artesanal
cottage pie n pastel de carne cubierta de puré de patatas
cotton ['kɔtn] n algodón m; (thread) hilo
  ▸ **cotton on** vi (col): **to ~ on (to sth)** caer en la cuenta (de algo)
cotton candy n (US) algodón m (azucarado)
cotton wool n (Brit) algodón m (hidrófilo)
couch [kautʃ] n sofá m; (in doctor's surgery) camilla
couchette [kuːˈʃɛt] n litera
couch potato n (col) persona comodona que no se mueve en todo el día
cough [kɔf] vi toser ■ n tos f
  ▸ **cough up** vt escupir
cough drop n pastilla para la tos
cough mixture n jarabe m para la tos
could [kud] pt of **can**
couldn't ['kudnt] = **could not**
council ['kaunsl] n consejo; **city** or **town ~** ayuntamiento; **C~ of Europe** Consejo de Europa
council estate n (Brit) barriada de viviendas sociales de alquiler

council house n (Brit) vivienda social de alquiler
councillor ['kaunsləʳ] n concejal m/f
council tax n (Brit) contribución f municipal (dependiente del valor de la vivienda)
counsel ['kaunsl] n (advice) consejo; (lawyer) abogado(-a) ■ vt aconsejar; **~ for the defence/the prosecution** abogado(-a) defensor(a)/fiscal; **to ~ sth/sb to do sth** aconsejar algo/a algn que haga algo
counsellor, counselor (US) ['kaunsləʳ] n consejero(-a); (US Law) abogado(-a)
count [kaunt] vt (gen) contar; (include) incluir ■ vi contar ■ n cuenta; (of votes) escrutinio; (nobleman) conde m; (sum) total m, suma; **to ~ the cost of** calcular el coste de; **not counting the children** niños aparte; **10 counting him** diez incluyéndolo a él, diez con él; **~ yourself lucky** date por satisfecho; **that doesn't ~!** ¡eso no vale!; **to ~ (up) to 10** contar hasta diez; **it counts for very little** cuenta poco; **to keep ~ of sth** llevar la cuenta de algo
  ▸ **count on** vt fus contar con; **to ~ on doing sth** contar con hacer algo
  ▸ **count up** vt contar
countdown ['kauntdaun] n cuenta atrás
countenance ['kauntɪnəns] n semblante m, rostro ■ vt (tolerate) aprobar, consentir
counter ['kauntəʳ] n (in shop) mostrador m; (position: in post office, bank) ventanilla; (in games) ficha; (Tech) contador m ■ vt contrarrestar; (blow) parar; (attack) contestar a ■ adv: **~ to** contrario a; **to buy under the ~** (fig) comprar de estraperlo or bajo mano; **to ~ sth with sth/by doing sth** contestar algo con algo/haciendo algo
counteract ['kauntər'ækt] vt contrarrestar
counterattack ['kauntərə'tæk] n contraataque m ■ vi contraatacar
counterbalance ['kauntə'bæləns] n contrapeso
counter-clockwise ['kauntə'klɔkwaɪz] adv en sentido contrario al de las agujas del reloj
counter-espionage ['kauntər'ɛspɪənɑːʒ] n contraespionaje m
counterfeit ['kauntəfɪt] n falsificación f ■ vt falsificar ■ adj falso, falsificado
counterfoil ['kauntəfɔɪl] n (Brit) matriz f, talón m
counterintelligence ['kauntərɪn'tɛlɪdʒəns] n contraespionaje m
countermand ['kauntəmɑːnd] vt revocar
counter-measure ['kauntəmɛʒəʳ] n contramedida
counteroffensive ['kauntərə'fɛnsɪv] n contraofensiva

C

counterpane ['kauntəpeɪn] n colcha
counterpart ['kauntəpɑːt] n (of person)
homólogo(-a)
counter-productive [kauntəprə'dʌktɪv] adj
contraproducente
counterproposal ['kauntəprə'pəuzl] n
contrapropuesta
countersign ['kauntəsaɪn] vt ratificar,
refrendar
countess ['kauntɪs] n condesa
countless ['kauntlɪs] adj innumerable
countrified ['kʌntrɪfaɪd] adj rústico
country ['kʌntrɪ] n país m; (native land) patria;
(as opposed to town) campo; (region) región f,
tierra; **in the ~** en el campo; **mountainous
~** región f montañosa
**country and western, country and
western music** n música country
country dancing n (Brit) baile m regional
country house n casa de campo
countryman ['kʌntrɪmən] n (national)
compatriota m; (rural) hombre m del campo
countryside ['kʌntrɪsaɪd] n campo
countrywide ['kʌntrɪ'waɪd] adj nacional
■ adv por todo el país
county ['kauntɪ] n condado; see also **district
council**
county council n (Brit) ≈ diputación f
provincial
county town n cabeza de partido
coup [kuː] (pl **coups**) [kuːz] n golpe m;
(triumph) éxito; (also: **coup d'état**) golpe de
estado
coupé ['kuːpeɪ] n cupé m
couple ['kʌpl] n (of things) par m; (of people)
pareja; (married couple) matrimonio ■ vt
(ideas, names) unir, juntar; (machinery) acoplar;
a ~ of un par de
couplet ['kʌplɪt] n pareado
coupling ['kʌplɪŋ] n (Rail) enganche m
coupon ['kuːpɔn] n cupón m; (pools coupon)
boleto (de quiniela)
courage ['kʌrɪdʒ] n valor m, valentía
courageous [kə'reɪdʒəs] adj valiente
courgette [kuə'ʒet] n (Brit) calabacín m
courier ['kurɪəʳ] n mensajero(-a); (diplomatic)
correo; (for tourists) guía m/f (de turismo)
course [kɔːs] n (direction) dirección f; (of
river) curso; (Scol) curso; (of ship) rumbo; (fig)
proceder m; (Golf) campo; (part of meal) plato;
of ~ adv desde luego, naturalmente; **of ~!**
¡claro!, ¡cómo no! (LAm); **(no) of ~ not!** ¡claro
que no!, ¡por supuesto que no!; **in due ~**
a su debido tiempo; **in the ~ of the next
few days** durante los próximos días; **we
have no other ~ but to ...** no tenemos más
remedio que ...; **there are 2 courses open**

to us se nos ofrecen dos posibilidades; **the
best ~ would be to ...** lo mejor sería ...; **~ of
treatment** (Med) tratamiento
court [kɔːt] n (royal) corte f; (Law) tribunal
m, juzgado; (Tennis) pista, cancha (LAm)
■ vt (woman) cortejar; (fig: favour, popularity)
solicitar, buscar; (: death, disaster, danger etc)
buscar; **to take to ~** demandar; **~ of appeal**
tribunal m de apelación
courteous ['kəːtɪəs] adj cortés
courtesan [kɔːtɪ'zæn] n cortesana
courtesy ['kəːtəsɪ] n cortesía; **by ~ of** (por)
cortesía de
courtesy light n (Aut) luz f interior
court-house ['kɔːthaus] n (US) palacio de
justicia
courtier ['kɔːtɪəʳ] n cortesano
court martial (pl **courts martial**)
['kɔːt'mɑːʃəl] n consejo de guerra ■ vt
someter a consejo de guerra
courtroom ['kɔːtrum] n sala de justicia
court shoe n zapato de mujer de estilo clásico
courtyard ['kɔːtjɑːd] n patio
cousin ['kʌzn] n primo(-a); **first ~** primo(-a)
carnal
cove [kəuv] n cala, ensenada
covenant ['kʌvənənt] n convenio ■ vt:
to ~ £20 per year to a charity concertar el
pago de veinte libras anuales a una sociedad
benéfica
Coventry ['kɔvəntrɪ] n: **to send sb to ~** (fig)
hacer el vacío a algn
cover ['kʌvəʳ] vt cubrir; (with lid) tapar;
(chairs etc) revestir; (distance) cubrir, recorrer;
(include) abarcar; (protect) abrigar; (journalist)
investigar; (issues) tratar ■ n cubierta; (lid)
tapa; (for chair etc) funda; (for bed) cobertor
m; (envelope) sobre m; (of magazine) portada;
(shelter) abrigo; (insurance) cobertura; **to
take ~** (shelter) protegerse, resguardarse;
under ~ (indoors) bajo techo; **under ~ of
darkness** al amparo de la oscuridad; **under
separate ~** (Comm) por separado; **£10 will ~
everything** con diez libras cubriremos todos
los gastos
▶ **cover up** vt (child, object) cubrir
completamente, tapar; (fig: hide: truth, facts)
ocultar; **to ~ up for sb** (fig) encubrir a algn
coverage ['kʌvərɪdʒ] n alcance m; (in media)
reportaje m; (Insurance) cobertura
coveralls ['kʌvərɔːlz] npl (US) mono sg
cover charge n precio del cubierto
covering ['kʌvərɪŋ] n cubierta, envoltura
covering letter, cover letter (US) n carta de
explicación
cover note n (Insurance) póliza provisional
cover price n precio de cubierta

covert ['kəuvət] adj (secret) secreto, encubierto; (dissembled) furtivo

cover-up ['kʌvərʌp] n encubrimiento

covet ['kʌvɪt] vt codiciar

covetous ['kʌvɪtəs] adj codicioso

cow [kau] n vaca ▪ vt intimidar

coward ['kauəd] n cobarde m/f

cowardice ['kauədɪs] n cobardía

cowardly ['kauədlɪ] adj cobarde

cowboy ['kaubɔɪ] n vaquero

cower ['kauə'] vi encogerse (de miedo)

co-worker ['kəuwə:kə'] n colaborador(a) m(f)

cowshed ['kauʃed] n establo

cowslip ['kauslɪp] n (Bot) primavera, prímula

cox ['kɔks], **coxswain** ['kɔksn] n timonel m

coy [kɔɪ] adj tímido

coyote [kɔɪ'əutɪ] n coyote m

cozy ['kəuzɪ] adj (US) = **cosy**

CP n abbr (= Communist Party) PC m

cp. abbr (= compare) cfr.

CPA n abbr (US) = **certified public accountant**

CPI n abbr (= Consumer Price Index) IPC m

Cpl. abbr (Mil) = **corporal**

c.p.s. abbr (= characters per second) c.p.s.

CPSA n abbr (Brit: = Civil and Public Services Association) sindicato de funcionarios

CPU n abbr = **central processing unit**

cr. abbr = **credit; creditor**

crab [kræb] n cangrejo

crab apple n manzana silvestre

crack [kræk] n grieta; (noise) crujido; (: of whip) chasquido; (joke) chiste m; (col: drug) crack m; (attempt): **to have a ~ at sth** intentar algo ▪ vt agrietar, romper; (nut) cascar; (safe) forzar; (whip etc) chasquear; (knuckles) crujir; (joke) contar; (case: solve) resolver; (code) descifrar ▪ adj (athlete) de primera clase; **to ~ jokes** (col) bromear

▸ **crack down on** vt fus reprimir fuertemente, adoptar medidas severas contra

▸ **crack up** vi sufrir una crisis nerviosa

crackdown ['krækdaun] n: **~ (on)** (on crime) campaña (contra); (on spending) reducción f (en)

cracker ['krækə'] n (biscuit) galleta salada, crácker m; (Christmas cracker) sorpresa (navideña)

crackle ['krækl] vi crepitar

crackling ['kræklɪŋ] n (on radio, telephone) interferencia; (of fire) chisporroteo, crepitación f; (of leaves etc) crujido; (of pork) chicharrón m

crackpot ['krækpɔt] (col) n pirado(-a) ▪ adj de pirado

cradle ['kreɪdl] n cuna ▪ vt (child) mecer, acunar; (object) abrazar

craft [krɑ:ft] n (skill) arte m; (trade) oficio; (cunning) astucia; (boat) embarcación f

craftsman ['krɑ:ftsmən] n artesano

craftsmanship ['krɑ:ftsmənʃɪp] n artesanía

crafty ['krɑ:ftɪ] adj astuto

crag [kræg] n peñasco

craggy ['krægɪ] adj escarpado

cram [kræm] vt (fill): **to ~ sth with** llenar algo (a reventar) de; (put): **to ~ sth into** meter algo a la fuerza en ▪ vi (for exams) empollar

crammed [kræmd] adj atestado

cramp [kræmp] n (Med) calambre m; (Tech) grapa ▪ vt (limit) poner trabas a

cramped [kræmpt] adj apretado; (room) minúsculo

crampon ['kræmpən] n crampón m

cranberry ['krænbərɪ] n arándano

crane [kreɪn] n (Tech) grúa; (bird) grulla ▪ vt, vi: **to ~ forward, to ~ one's neck** estirar el cuello

cranium ['kreɪnɪəm] n cráneo

crank [kræŋk] n manivela; (person) chiflado(-a)

crankshaft ['kræŋkʃɑ:ft] n cigüeñal m

cranky ['kræŋkɪ] adj (eccentric) maniático; (bad-tempered) de mal genio

cranny ['krænɪ] n see **nook**

crap [kræp] n (col!) mierda (!)

crappy ['kræpɪ] adj (col) chungo

craps [kræps] n (US) dados mpl

crash [kræʃ] n (noise) estrépito; (of cars, plane) accidente m; (of business) quiebra; (Stock Exchange) crac m ▪ vt (plane) estrellar ▪ vi (plane) estrellarse; (two cars) chocar; (fall noisily) caer con estrépito; **he crashed the car into a wall** estrelló el coche contra una pared or tapia

crash barrier n (Aut) barrera de protección

crash course n curso acelerado

crash helmet n casco (protector)

crash landing n aterrizaje m forzoso

crass [kræs] adj grosero, maleducado

crate [kreɪt] n caja, cajón m de embalaje; (col) armatoste m

crater ['kreɪtə'] n cráter m

cravat, cravate [krə'væt] n pañuelo

crave [kreɪv] vt, vi: **to ~ (for)** ansiar, anhelar

craving ['kreɪvɪŋ] n (for food, cigarettes etc) ansias fpl; (during pregnancy) antojo

crawl [krɔ:l] vi (drag o.s.) arrastrarse; (child) andar a gatas, gatear; (vehicle) avanzar (lentamente); (col): **to ~ to sb** dar coba a algn, hacerle la pelota a algn ▪ n (Swimming) crol m

crawler lane [krɔ:lə-] n (Brit Aut) carril m para tráfico lento

crayfish ['kreɪfɪʃ] *n pl inv* (*freshwater*) cangrejo (de río); (*saltwater*) cigala
crayon ['kreɪən] *n* lápiz *m* de color
craze [kreɪz] *n* manía; (*fashion*) moda
crazed [kreɪzd] *adj* (*look, person*) loco, demente; (*pottery, glaze*) agrietado, cuarteado
crazy ['kreɪzɪ] *adj* (*person*) loco; (*idea*) disparatado; **to go ~** volverse loco; **to be ~ about sb/sth** (*col*) estar loco por algn/algo
crazy paving *n* pavimento de baldosas irregulares
creak [kri:k] *vi* crujir; (*hinge etc*) rechinar
cream [kri:m] *n* (*of milk*) nata, crema; (*lotion*) crema; (*fig*) flor *f* y nata ■ *adj* (*colour*) color *m* crema; **whipped ~** nata batida
▶ **cream off** *vt* (*fig: best talents, part of profits*) separar lo mejor de
cream cake *n* pastel *m* de nata
cream cheese *n* queso fresco cremoso
creamery ['kri:mərɪ] *n* (*shop*) quesería; (*factory*) central *f* lechera
creamy ['kri:mɪ] *adj* cremoso
crease [kri:s] *n* (*fold*) pliegue *m*; (*in trousers*) raya; (*wrinkle*) arruga ■ *vt* (*fold*) doblar, plegar; (*wrinkle*) arrugar ■ *vi* (*wrinkle up*) arrugarse
crease-resistant ['kri:srɪzɪstənt] *adj* inarrugable
create [kri:'eɪt] *vt* (*also Comput*) crear; (*impression*) dar; (*fuss, noise*) hacer
creation [kri:'eɪʃən] *n* creación *f*
creative [kri:'eɪtɪv] *adj* creativo
creativity [kri:eɪ'tɪvɪtɪ] *n* creatividad *f*
creator [kri:'eɪtəʳ] *n* creador(a) *m(f)*
creature ['kri:tʃəʳ] *n* (*living thing*) criatura; (*animal*) animal *m*; (*insect*) bicho
creature comforts *npl* comodidades *fpl* materiales
crèche, creche [krɛʃ] *n* (*Brit*) guardería (infantil)
credence ['kri:dəns] *n*: **to lend** *or* **give ~ to** creer en, dar crédito a
credentials [krɪ'dɛnʃlz] *npl* credenciales *fpl*; (*letters of reference*) referencias *fpl*
credibility [krɛdɪ'bɪlɪtɪ] *n* credibilidad *f*
credible ['krɛdɪbl] *adj* creíble; (*witness, source*) fidedigno
credit ['krɛdɪt] *n* (*gen*) crédito; (*merit*) honor *m*, mérito ■ *vt* (*Comm*) abonar; (*believe*) creer, dar crédito a ■ *adj* crediticio; **to be in ~** (*person, bank account*) tener saldo a favor; **on ~** a crédito; (*col*) al fiado; **he's a ~ to his family** hace honor a su familia; **to ~ sb with** (*fig*) reconocer a algn el mérito de; *see also* **credits**
creditable ['krɛdɪtəbl] *adj* estimable, digno de elogio
credit account *n* cuenta de crédito
credit agency *n* agencia de informes comerciales
credit balance *n* saldo acreedor
credit card *n* tarjeta de crédito
credit control *n* control *m* de créditos
credit crunch *n* crisis *f* crediticia
credit facilities *npl* facilidades *fpl* de crédito
credit limit *n* límite *m* de crédito
credit note *n* nota de crédito
creditor ['krɛdɪtəʳ] *n* acreedor(a) *m(f)*
credits ['krɛdɪts] *npl* (*Cine*) títulos *mpl or* rótulos *mpl* de crédito, créditos *mpl*
credit transfer *n* transferencia de crédito
creditworthy ['krɛdɪtwə:ðɪ] *adj* solvente
credulity [krɪ'dju:lɪtɪ] *n* credulidad *f*
creed [kri:d] *n* credo
creek [kri:k] *n* cala, ensenada; (*US*) riachuelo
creel [kri:l] *n* nasa
creep [kri:p] (*pt, pp* **crept**) [krɛpt] *vi* (*animal*) deslizarse; (*plant*) trepar; **to ~ up on sb** acercarse sigilosamente a algn; (*fig: old age etc*) acercarse ■ *n* (*col*): **he's a ~** ¡qué lameculos es!; **it gives me the creeps** me da escalofríos
creeper ['kri:pəʳ] *n* enredadera
creepers ['kri:pəz] *npl* (*US: for baby*) pelele *msg*
creepy ['kri:pɪ] *adj* (*frightening*) horripilante
creepy-crawly ['kri:pɪ'krɔ:lɪ] *n* (*col*) bicho
cremate [krɪ'meɪt] *vt* incinerar
cremation [krɪ'meɪʃən] *n* incineración *f*, cremación *f*
crematorium [krɛmə'tɔ:rɪəm] (*pl* **crematoria** [krɛmə'tɔ:rɪə]) *n* crematorio
creosote ['krɪəsəʊt] *n* creosota
crêpe [kreɪp] *n* (*fabric*) crespón *m*; (*also:* **crêpe rubber**) crep(é) *m*
crêpe bandage *n* (*Brit*) venda elástica
crêpe paper *n* papel *m* crep(é)
crêpe sole *n* (*on shoes*) suela de crep(é)
crept [krɛpt] *pt, pp of* **creep**
crescent ['krɛsnt] *n* media luna; (*street*) calle *f* (*en forma de semicírculo*)
cress [krɛs] *n* berro
crest [krɛst] *n* (*of bird*) cresta; (*of hill*) cima, cumbre *f*; (*of helmet*) cimera; (*of coat of arms*) blasón *m*
crestfallen ['krɛstfɔ:lən] *adj* alicaído
Crete [kri:t] *n* Creta
cretin ['krɛtɪn] *n* cretino(-a)
crevasse [krɪ'væs] *n* grieta
crevice ['krɛvɪs] *n* grieta, hendedura
crew [kru:] *n* (*of ship etc*) tripulación *f*; (*Cine etc*) equipo; (*gang*) pandilla, banda; (*Mil*) dotación *f*
crew-cut ['kru:kʌt] *n* corte *m* al rape
crew-neck ['kru:nɛk] *n* cuello de caja
crib [krɪb] *n* pesebre *m* ■ *vt* (*col*) plagiar; (*Scol*) copiar

crick [krɪk] n: ~ **in the neck** tortícolis f inv
cricket ['krɪkɪt] n (insect) grillo; (game) críquet m
cricketer ['krɪkɪtə'] n jugador(a) m(f) de críquet
crime [kraɪm] n crimen m; (less serious) delito
crime wave n ola de crímenes or delitos
criminal ['krɪmɪnl] n criminal m/f, delincuente m/f ▪ adj criminal; (law) penal
Criminal Investigation Department n ≈ Brigada de Investigación Criminal f (SP)
crimp [krɪmp] vt (hair) rizar
crimson ['krɪmzn] adj carmesí
cringe [krɪndʒ] vi encogerse
crinkle ['krɪŋkl] vt arrugar
crinkly ['krɪŋklɪ] adj (hair) rizado, crespo
cripple ['krɪpl] n lisiado(-a), cojo(-a) ▪ vt lisiar, mutilar; (ship, plane) inutilizar; (production, exports) paralizar; **crippled with arthritis** paralizado por la artritis
crippling ['krɪplɪŋ] adj (injury etc) debilitador(a); (prices, taxes) devastador(a)
crisis ['kraɪsɪs] (pl **crises**) ['kraɪsi:z] n crisis f
crisp [krɪsp] adj fresco; (toast, snow) crujiente; (manner) seco
crisps [krɪsps] npl (Brit) patatas fpl fritas
crisscross ['krɪskrɒs] adj entrelazado, entrecruzado ▪ vt entrecruzar(se)
criterion [kraɪ'tɪərɪən] (pl **criteria**) [kraɪ'tɪərɪə] n criterio
critic ['krɪtɪk] n crítico(-a)
critical ['krɪtɪkl] adj (gen) crítico; (illness) grave; **to be ~ of sb/sth** criticar a algn/algo
critically ['krɪtɪklɪ] adv (speak etc) en tono crítico; (ill) gravemente
criticism ['krɪtɪsɪzm] n crítica
criticize ['krɪtɪsaɪz] vt criticar
critique [krɪ'ti:k] n crítica
croak [krəuk] vi (frog) croar; (raven) graznar ▪ n (of raven) graznido
Croat ['krəuæt] adj, n = **Croatian**
Croatia [krəu'eɪʃə] n Croacia
Croatian [krəu'eɪʃən] adj, n croata m/f ▪ n (Ling) croata m
crochet ['krəuʃeɪ] n ganchillo
crock [krɒk] n cántaro; (col: person: also: **old crock**) carcamal m/f, vejestorio; (: car etc) cacharro
crockery ['krɒkərɪ] n (plates, cups etc) loza, vajilla
crocodile ['krɒkədaɪl] n cocodrilo
crocus ['krəukəs] n azafrán m
croft [krɒft] n granja pequeña
crofter ['krɒftə'] n pequeño granjero
croissant ['krwas] n croissant m, medialuna (esp LAm)
crone [krəun] n arpía, bruja

crony ['krəunɪ] n compinche m/f
crook [kruk] n (fam) ladrón(-ona) m(f); (of shepherd) cayado; (of arm) pliegue m
crooked ['krukɪd] adj torcido; (path) tortuoso; (fam) sucio
crop [krɒp] n (produce) cultivo; (amount produced) cosecha; (riding crop) látigo de montar; (of bird) buche m ▪ vt cortar, recortar; (animals: grass) pacer
  ▶ **crop up** vi surgir, presentarse
crop spraying [-'spreɪɪŋ] n fumigación f de los cultivos
croquet ['krəukeɪ] n croquet m
croquette [krə'kɛt] n croqueta (de patata)
cross [krɒs] n cruz f ▪ vt (street etc) cruzar, atravesar; (thwart: person) contrariar, ir contra ▪ vi: **the boat crosses from Santander to Plymouth** el barco hace la travesía de Santander a Plymouth ▪ adj de mal humor, enojado; **it's a ~ between geography and sociology** es una mezcla de geografía y sociología; **to ~ o.s.** santiguarse; **they've got their lines crossed** (fig) hay un malentendido entre ellos; **to be/get ~ with sb (about sth)** estar enfadado/enfadarse con algn (por algo)
  ▶ **cross out** vt tachar
  ▶ **cross over** vi cruzar
crossbar ['krɒsbɑ:'] n travesaño; (of bicycle) barra
crossbow ['krɒsbəu] n ballesta
cross-Channel ferry ['krɒs'tʃænl-] n transbordador m que cruza el Canal de la Mancha
cross-check ['krɒstʃɛk] n verificación f ▪ vt verificar
cross-country ['krɒs'kʌntrɪ], **cross-country race** n carrera a campo traviesa, cross m
cross-dressing [krɒs'drɛsɪŋ] n travestismo
cross-examination ['krɒsɪgzæmɪ'neɪʃən] n interrogatorio
cross-examine ['krɒsɪg'zæmɪn] vt interrogar
cross-eyed ['krɒsaɪd] adj bizco
crossfire ['krɒsfaɪə'] n fuego cruzado
crossing ['krɒsɪŋ] n (on road) cruce m; (Rail) paso a nivel; (sea passage) travesía; (also: **pedestrian crossing**) paso de peatones
crossing guard n (US) persona encargada de ayudar a los niños a cruzar la calle
crossing point n paso; (at border) paso fronterizo
cross purposes npl: **to be at ~ with sb** tener un malentendido con algn
cross-question ['krɒs'kwɛstʃən] vt interrogar
cross-reference ['krɒs'refrəns] n remisión f
crossroads ['krɒsrəudz] nsg cruce m; (fig) encrucijada

cross section n corte m transversal; (of population) muestra (representativa)
crosswalk ['krɔswɔ:k] n (US) paso de peatones
crosswind ['krɔswɪnd] n viento de costado
crossword ['krɔswəːd] n crucigrama m
crotch [krɔtʃ] n (of garment) entrepierna
crotchet ['krɔtʃɪt] n (Brit Mus) negra
crotchety ['krɔtʃɪtɪ] adj (person) arisco
crouch [krautʃ] vi agacharse
croup [kru:p] n (Med) crup m
croupier ['kru:pɪə] n crupier m/f
crouton ['kru:tɔn] n cubito de pan frito
crow [krəu] n (bird) cuervo; (of cock) canto, cacareo ■ vi (cock) cantar; (fig) jactarse
crowbar ['krəubaːʳ] n palanca
crowd [kraud] n muchedumbre f; (Sport) público; (common herd) vulgo ■ vt (gather) amontonar; (fill) llenar ■ vi (gather) reunirse; (pile up) amontonarse; **crowds of people** gran cantidad de gente
crowded ['kraudɪd] adj (full) atestado; (well-attended) concurrido
crowd scene n (Cine, Theat) escena con muchos comparsas
crown [kraun] n corona; (of head) coronilla; (of hat) copa; (of hill) cumbre f ■ vt (also tooth) coronar; **and to ~ it all ...** (fig) y para colmo or remate ...
crown court n (Law) tribunal m superior; ver nota

● **CROWN COURT**
●
● En el sistema legal inglés los delitos
● graves como asesinato, violación o
● atraco son juzgados por un jurado en un
● tribunal superior llamado crown court con
● sede en noventa ciudades. Los jueces de
● paz ("Justice of the Peace") juzgan delitos
● menores e infracciones de la ley en
● juzgados llamados "Magistrates' Courts".
● Es el juez de paz quien decide remitir los
● casos pertinentes a la crown court, que en
● caso de recursos se remite al tribunal de
● apelación, "Court of Appeal".

crowning ['kraunɪŋ] adj (achievement, glory) máximo
crown jewels npl joyas fpl reales
crown prince n príncipe m heredero
crow's feet ['krəuzfiːt] npl patas fpl de gallo
crucial ['kruːʃl] adj crucial, decisivo; **his approval is ~ to the success of the project** su aprobación es crucial para el éxito del proyecto
crucifix ['kruːsɪfɪks] n crucifijo

crucifixion [kruːsɪ'fɪkʃən] n crucifixión f
crucify ['kruːsɪfaɪ] vt crucificar; (fig) martirizar
crude [kruːd] adj (materials) bruto; (fig: basic) tosco; (: vulgar) ordinario ■ n (also: **crude oil**) (petróleo) crudo
crude oil n petróleo crudo
cruel ['kruəl] adj cruel
cruelty ['kruəltɪ] n crueldad f
cruet ['kruːɪt] n vinagreras fpl
cruise [kruːz] n crucero ■ vi (ship) navegar; (holidaymakers) hacer un crucero; (car) ir a velocidad constante
cruise missile n misil m de crucero
cruiser ['kruːzəʳ] n crucero
cruising speed ['kruːzɪŋ-] n velocidad f de crucero
crumb [krʌm] n miga, migaja
crumble ['krʌmbl] vt desmenuzar ■ vi (gen) desmenuzarse; (building) desmoronarse
crumbly ['krʌmblɪ] adj desmenuzable
crummy ['krʌmɪ] adj (col: poor quality) pésimo, cutre (SP); (: unwell) fatal
crumpet ['krʌmpɪt] n ≈ bollo para tostar
crumple ['krʌmpl] vt (paper) estrujar; (material) arrugar
crunch [krʌntʃ] vt (with teeth) ronzar; (underfoot) hacer crujir ■ n (fig) hora de la verdad
crunchy ['krʌntʃɪ] adj crujiente
crusade [kruː'seɪd] n cruzada ■ vi: **to ~ for/against** (fig) hacer una campaña en pro de/en contra de
crusader [kruː'seɪdəʳ] n (fig) paladín m/f
crush [krʌʃ] n (crowd) aglomeración f ■ vt (gen) aplastar; (paper) estrujar; (cloth) arrugar; (grind, break up: garlic, ice) picar; (fruit) exprimir; (grapes) exprimir, prensar; **to have a ~ on sb** estar enamorado de algn
crush barrier n barrera de seguridad
crushing ['krʌʃɪŋ] adj aplastante; (burden) agobiante
crust [krʌst] n corteza
crustacean [krʌs'teɪʃən] n crustáceo
crusty ['krʌstɪ] adj (bread) crujiente; (person) de mal carácter; (remark) brusco
crutch [krʌtʃ] n (Med) muleta; (support) apoyo
crux [krʌks] n: **the ~** lo esencial, el quid
cry [kraɪ] vi llorar; (shout: also: **cry out**) gritar ■ n grito; (of animal) aullido; (weep): **she had a good ~** lloró a lágrima viva; **what are you crying about?** ¿por qué lloras?; **to ~ for help** pedir socorro a voces; **it's a far ~ from ...** (fig) dista mucho de ...
▶ **cry off** vi retirarse
crypt [krɪpt] n cripta
cryptic ['krɪptɪk] adj enigmático

crystal ['krɪstl] n cristal m
crystal-clear ['krɪstl'klɪəʳ] adj claro como el agua; (fig) cristalino
crystallize ['krɪstəlaɪz] vt (fig) cristalizar ■ vi cristalizarse; **crystallized fruits** frutas fpl escarchadas
CSA n abbr (= Confederate States of America, Child Support Agency) organismo que supervisa el pago de la pensión a hijos de padres separados
CSC n abbr (= Civil Service Commission) comisión para la contratación de funcionarios
CS gas n (Brit) gas m lacrimógeno
CST n abbr (US: = Central Standard Time) huso horario
CT, Ct. abbr (US) = **Connecticut**
ct abbr = **cent; court; carat**
CTC n abbr (Brit: = city technology college) ≈ centro de formación profesional
cu. abbr = **cubic**
cub [kʌb] n cachorro; (also: **cub scout**) niño explorador
Cuba ['kju:bə] n Cuba
Cuban ['kju:bən] adj, n cubano(-a) m(f)
cubbyhole ['kʌbɪhəul] n cuchitril m
cube [kju:b] n cubo; (of sugar) terrón m ■ vt (Math) elevar al cubo
cube root n raíz f cúbica
cubic ['kju:bɪk] adj cúbico; ~ **capacity** (Aut) capacidad f cúbica
cubicle ['kju:bɪkl] n (at pool) caseta; (for bed) cubículo
cubism ['kju:bɪzəm] n cubismo
cuckoo ['kuku:] n cuco
cuckoo clock n reloj m de cuco
cucumber ['kju:kʌmbəʳ] n pepino
cuddle ['kʌdl] vt abrazar ■ vi abrazarse
cuddly ['kʌdlɪ] adj mimoso; (toy) de peluche
cudgel ['kʌdʒəl] vt: **to ~ one's brains** devanarse los sesos
cue [kju:] n (snooker cue) taco; (Theat etc) entrada
cuff [kʌf] n (Brit: of shirt, coat etc) puño; (US: of trousers) vuelta; (blow) bofetada ■ vt bofetear; **off the ~** adv improvisado
cufflinks ['kʌflɪŋks] npl gemelos mpl
cu. ft. abbr = **cubic feet**
cu. in. abbr = **cubic inches**
cuisine [kwɪ'zi:n] n cocina
cul-de-sac ['kʌldəsæk] n callejón m sin salida
culinary ['kʌlɪnərɪ] adj culinario
cull [kʌl] vt (select) entresacar; (kill selectively: animals) matar selectivamente ■ n matanza selectiva; **seal ~** matanza selectiva de focas
culminate ['kʌlmɪneɪt] vi: **to ~ in** culminar en
culmination [kʌlmɪ'neɪʃən] n culminación f, colmo

culottes [ku:'lɔts] npl falda f pantalón
culpable ['kʌlpəbl] adj culpable
culprit ['kʌlprɪt] n culpable m/f
cult [kʌlt] n culto; **a ~ figure** un ídolo
cultivate ['kʌltɪveɪt] vt (also fig) cultivar
cultivated ['kʌltɪveɪtɪd] adj culto
cultivation [kʌltɪ'veɪʃən] n cultivo; (fig) cultura
cultural ['kʌltʃərəl] adj cultural
culture ['kʌltʃəʳ] n (also fig) cultura
cultured ['kʌltʃəd] adj culto
cumbersome ['kʌmbəsəm] adj voluminoso
cumin ['kʌmɪn] n (spice) comino
cummerbund ['kʌməbʌnd] n faja, fajín m
cumulative ['kju:mjulətɪv] adj cumulativo
cunning ['kʌnɪŋ] n astucia ■ adj astuto; (clever: device, idea) ingenioso
cunt [kʌnt] n (col!) coño (!); (insult) mamonazo(-a) (!)
cup [kʌp] n taza; (prize, event) copa; **a ~ of tea** una taza de té
cupboard ['kʌbəd] n armario, placar(d) m (LAm)
cup final n (Football) final f de copa
cupful ['kʌpful] n taza
Cupid ['kju:pɪd] n Cupido
cupola ['kju:pələ] n cúpula
cuppa ['kʌpə] n (Brit col) (taza de) té m
cup-tie ['kʌptaɪ] n (Brit) partido de copa
cur [kəːʳ] n perro de mala raza; (person) canalla m
curable ['kjuərəbl] adj curable
curate ['kjuərɪt] n coadjutor m
curator [kjuə'reɪtəʳ] n director(a) m(f)
curb [kəːb] vt refrenar; (powers, spending) limitar ■ n freno; (US: kerb) bordillo
curd cheese [kəːd-] n requesón m
curdle ['kəːdl] vi cuajarse
curds [kəːdz] npl requesón msg
cure [kjuəʳ] vt curar ■ n cura, curación f; **to be cured of sth** curarse de algo; **to take a ~** tomar un remedio
cure-all ['kjuərɔːl] n (also fig) panacea
curfew ['kəːfju:] n toque m de queda
curio ['kjuərɪəu] n curiosidad f
curiosity [kjuərɪ'ɔsɪtɪ] n curiosidad f
curious ['kjuərɪəs] adj curioso; **I'm ~ about him** me intriga
curiously ['kjuərɪəslɪ] adv curiosamente; **~ enough, ...** aunque parezca extraño ...
curl [kəːl] n rizo; (of smoke etc) espiral f, voluta ■ vt (hair) rizar; (paper) arrollar; (lip) fruncir ■ vi rizarse; arrollarse
  ▶ **curl up** vi arrollarse; (person) hacerse un ovillo; (fam) morirse de risa
curler ['kəːləʳ] n bigudí m
curlew ['kəːlu:] n zarapito

curling tongs, curling irons (US) ['kə:lɪŋ-] npl tenacillas fpl

curly ['kə:lɪ] adj rizado

currant ['kʌrnt] n pasa; (black, red) grosella

currency ['kʌrnsɪ] n moneda; **to gain ~** (fig) difundirse

current ['kʌrnt] n corriente f ▪ adj actual; **direct/alternating ~** corriente directa/alterna; **the ~ issue of a magazine** el último número de una revista; **in ~ use** de uso corriente

current account n (Brit) cuenta corriente

current affairs npl (noticias fpl de) actualidad f

current assets npl (Comm) activo disponible

current liabilities npl (Comm) pasivo circulante

currently ['kʌrntlɪ] adv actualmente

curriculum (pl **curriculums** or **curricula**) [kə'rɪkjuləm, -lə] n plan m de estudios

curriculum vitae [-'vi:taɪ] n currículum m (vitae)

curry ['kʌrɪ] n curry m ▪ vt: **to ~ favour with** buscar el favor de

curry powder n curry m en polvo

curse [kə:s] vi echar pestes ▪ vt maldecir ▪ n maldición f; (swearword) palabrota

cursor ['kə:sə'] n (Comput) cursor m

cursory ['kə:sərɪ] adj rápido, superficial

curt [kə:t] adj seco

curtail [kə:'teɪl] vt (cut short) acortar; (restrict) restringir

curtain ['kə:tn] n cortina; (Theat) telón m; **to draw the curtains** (together) cerrar las cortinas; (apart) abrir las cortinas

curtain call n (Theat) llamada a escena

curtain ring n anilla

curtsey, curtsy ['kə:tsɪ] n reverencia ▪ vi hacer una reverencia

curve [kə:v] n curva ▪ vt, vi torcer

curved [kə:vd] adj curvo

cushion ['kuʃən] n cojín m; (Snooker) banda ▪ vt (seat) acolchar; (shock) amortiguar

cushy ['kuʃɪ] adj (col): **a ~ job** un chollo; **to have a ~ time** tener la vida arreglada

custard ['kʌstəd] n (for pouring) natillas fpl

custard powder n polvos mpl para natillas

custodial sentence [kʌs'təudɪəl-] n pena de prisión

custodian [kʌs'təudɪən] n guardián(-ana) m(f); (of museum etc) conservador(a) m(f)

custody ['kʌstədɪ] n custodia; **to take sb into ~** detener a algn; **in the ~ of** al cuidado or cargo de

custom ['kʌstəm] n costumbre f; (Comm) clientela; see also **customs**

customary ['kʌstəmərɪ] adj acostumbrado;

it is ~ to do ... es la costumbre hacer ...

custom-built ['kʌstəm'bɪlt] adj = **custom-made**

customer ['kʌstəmə'] n cliente m/f; **he's an awkward ~** (col) es un tipo difícil

customer profile n perfil m del cliente

customized ['kʌstəmaɪzd] adj (car etc) hecho a encargo

custom-made ['kʌstəm'meɪd] adj hecho a la medida

customs ['kʌstəmz] npl aduana sg; **to go through (the) ~** pasar la aduana

Customs and Excise n (Brit) Aduanas fpl y Arbitrios

customs officer n aduanero(-a), funcionario(-a) de aduanas

cut [kʌt] vb (pt, pp **cut**) ▪ vt cortar; (price) rebajar; (record) grabar; (reduce) reducir; (col: avoid: class, lecture) fumarse, faltar a ▪ vi cortar; (intersect) cruzarse ▪ n corte m; (in skin) corte, cortadura; (with sword) tajo; (of knife) cuchillada; (in salary etc) recorte m; (slice of meat) tajada; **to ~ one's finger** cortarse un dedo; **to get one's hair ~** cortarse el pelo; **to ~ and paste** (Comput) cortar y pegar; **to ~ sb dead** negarle el saludo or cortarle (LAm) a algn; **it cuts both ways** (fig) tiene doble filo; **to ~ a tooth** echar un diente; **power ~** (Brit) apagón m

▸ **cut back** vt (plants) podar; (production, expenditure) reducir

▸ **cut down** vt (tree) cortar, derribar; (consumption, expenses) reducir; **to ~ sb down to size** (fig) bajarle los humos a algn

▸ **cut in** vi: **to ~ in (on)** (interrupt: conversation) interrumpir, intervenir (en); (Aut) cerrar el paso (a)

▸ **cut off** vt cortar; (fig) aislar; (troops) cercar; **we've been ~ off** (Tel) nos han cortado la comunicación

▸ **cut out** vt (shape) recortar; (delete) suprimir

▸ **cut up** vt cortar (en pedazos); (chop: food) trinchar, cortar

cut-and-dried ['kʌtən'draɪd] adj (also: **cut-and-dry**) arreglado de antemano, seguro

cutback ['kʌtbæk] n reducción f

cute [kju:t] adj lindo, mono; (shrewd) listo

cuticle ['kju:tɪkl] n cutícula

cutlery ['kʌtlərɪ] n cubiertos mpl

cutlet ['kʌtlɪt] n chuleta

cutoff ['kʌtɔf] n (also: **cutoff point**) límite m

cutout ['kʌtaut] n (cardboard cutout) recortable m

cut-price ['kʌt'praɪs], **cut-rate** (US) ['kʌt'reɪt] adj a precio reducido

cutthroat ['kʌtθrəut] n asesino(-a) ▪ adj feroz; **~ competition** competencia encarnizada or despiadada

cutting ['kʌtɪŋ] adj (gen) cortante; (remark) mordaz ∎ n (Brit: from newspaper) recorte m; (: Rail) desmonte m; (Cine) montaje m
cutting edge n (of knife) filo; (fig) vanguardia; **a country on** or **at the ~ of space technology** un país puntero en tecnología del espacio
CV n abbr = **curriculum vitae**
cwo abbr (Comm) = **cash with order**
cwt. abbr = **hundredweight(s)**
cyanide ['saɪənaɪd] n cianuro
cybercafé ['saɪbə,kæfeɪ] n cibercafé m
cybernetics [saɪbə'nɛtɪks] nsg cibernética
cyberspace ['saɪbəspeɪs] n ciberespacio
cyberterrorism ['saɪbətɛrərɪzəm] n ciberterrorismo m
cyclamen ['sɪkləmən] n ciclamen m
cycle ['saɪkl] n ciclo; (bicycle) bicicleta ∎ vi ir en bicicleta
cycle lane n carril m de bicicleta, carril m bici
cycle race n carrera ciclista
cycle rack n soporte m para bicicletas
cycling ['saɪklɪŋ] n ciclismo
cycling holiday n vacaciones fpl en bicicleta
cyclist ['saɪklɪst] n ciclista m/f
cyclone ['saɪkləun] n ciclón m
cygnet ['sɪgnɪt] n pollo de cisne

cylinder ['sɪlɪndər] n cilindro
cylinder block n bloque m de cilindros
cylinder head n culata de cilindro
cylinder-head gasket n junta de culata
cymbals ['sɪmblz] npl platillos mpl, címbalos mpl
cynic ['sɪnɪk] n cínico(-a)
cynical ['sɪnɪkl] adj cínico
cynicism ['sɪnɪsɪzəm] n cinismo
cypress ['saɪprɪs] n ciprés m
Cypriot ['sɪprɪət] adj, n chipriota m/f
Cyprus ['saɪprəs] n Chipre f
cyst [sɪst] n quiste m
cystitis [sɪs'taɪtɪs] n cistitis f
CZ n abbr (US: = Canal Zone) zona del Canal de Panamá
czar [zɑːr] n zar m
czarina [zɑː'riːnə] n zarina
Czech [tʃɛk] adj checo ∎ n checo(-a); (Ling) checo; **the ~ Republic** la República Checa
Czechoslovak [tʃɛkə'sləuvæk] adj, n = **Czechoslovakian**
Czechoslovakia [tʃɛkəslə'vækɪə] n Checoslovaquia
Czechoslovakian [tʃɛkəslə'vækɪən] adj, n checoslovaco(-a) m(f)

C

Dd

D, d [di:] *n* (*letter*) D, d; (*Mus*): **D** re *m*; **D for David,** (*US*) **D for Dog** D de Dolores

D *abbr* (*US Pol*) = **democrat; democratic**

d *abbr* (*Brit: old*) = **penny**

d. *abbr* = **died**

DA *n abbr* (*US*) = **district attorney**

dab [dæb] *vt*: **to ~ ointment onto a wound** aplicar pomada sobre una herida; **to ~ with paint** dar unos toques de pintura ■ *n* (*light stroke*) toque *m*; (*small amount*) pizca

dabble ['dæbl] *vi*: **to ~ in** hacer por afición

Dacca ['dækə] *n* Dacca

dachshund ['dækshund] *n* perro tejonero

Dacron® ['deıkrɔn] *n* (*US*) terylene *m*

dad [dæd], **daddy** ['dædı] *n* papá *m*

daddy-long-legs [dædı'lɔŋlɛgz] *n* típula

daffodil ['dæfədıl] *n* narciso

daft [dɑ:ft] *adj* chiflado

dagger ['dægəʳ] *n* puñal *m*, daga; **to look daggers at sb** fulminar a algn con la mirada

dahlia ['deıljə] *n* dalia

daily ['deılı] *adj* diario, cotidiano ■ *n* (*paper*) diario; (*domestic help*) asistenta ■ *adv* todos los días, cada día; **twice ~** dos veces al día

dainty ['deıntı] *adj* delicado; (*tasteful*) elegante

dairy ['dɛərı] *n* (*shop*) lechería; (*on farm*) vaquería ■ *adj* (*cow etc*) lechero

dairy cow *n* vaca lechera

dairy farm *n* vaquería

dairy produce *n* productos *mpl* lácteos

dais ['deııs] *n* estrado

daisy ['deızı] *n* margarita

daisy-wheel printer *n* impresora de margarita

dale [deıl] *n* valle *m*

dally ['dælı] *vi* entretenerse

dalmatian [dæl'meıʃən] *n* (*dog*) (perro) dálmata *m*

dam [dæm] *n* presa; (*reservoir*) embalse ■ *vt* embalsar

damage ['dæmıdʒ] *n* daño; (*fig*) perjuicio; (*to machine*) avería ■ *vt* dañar; perjudicar; averiar; **~ to property** daños materiales

damages ['dæmıdʒız] *npl* (*Law*) daños y perjuicios; **to pay £5000 in ~** pagar £5000 por daños y perjuicios

damaging ['dæmıdʒıŋ] *adj*: **~ (to)** perjudicial (a)

Damascus [də'mɑ:skəs] *n* Damasco

dame [deım] *n* (*title*) dama; (*US col*) tía; (*Theat*) vieja; *see also* **pantomime**

damn [dæm] *vt* condenar; (*curse*) maldecir ■ *n* (*col*): **I don't give a ~** me importa un pito ■ *adj* (*col: also:* **damned**) maldito, fregado (*LAm*); **~ (it)!** ¡maldito sea!

damnable ['dæmnəbl] *adj* (*col: behaviour*) detestable; (*weather*) horrible

damnation [dæm'neıʃən] *n* (*Rel*) condenación *f* ■ *excl* (*col*) ¡maldición!, ¡maldito sea!

damning ['dæmıŋ] *adj* (*evidence*) irrecusable

damp [dæmp] *adj* húmedo, mojado ■ *n* humedad *f* ■ *vt* (*also:* **dampen:** *cloth, rag*) mojar; (*enthusiasm*) enfriar

dampcourse ['dæmpkɔ:s] *n* aislante *m* hidrófugo

damper ['dæmpəʳ] *n* (*Mus*) sordina; (*of fire*) regulador *m* de tiro; **to put a ~ on things** ser un jarro de agua fría

dampness ['dæmpnıs] *n* humedad *f*

damson ['dæmzən] *n* ciruela damascena

dance [dɑ:ns] *n* baile *m* ■ *vi* bailar; **to ~ about** saltar

dance hall *n* salón *m* de baile

dancer ['dɑ:nsəʳ] *n* bailador(a) *m(f)*; (*professional*) bailarín(-ina) *m(f)*

dancing ['dɑ:nsıŋ] *n* baile *m*

D and C *n abbr* (*Med*: = *dilation and curettage*) raspado

dandelion ['dændılaıən] *n* diente *m* de león

dandruff ['dændrəf] *n* caspa

D and T *n abbr* (*Brit Scol*) = **design and technology**

dandy ['dændı] *n* dandi *m* ■ *adj* (*US col*) estupendo

Dane [deɪn] n danés(-esa) m(f)
danger ['deɪndʒəʳ] n peligro; (risk) riesgo; ~!
(on sign) ¡peligro!; **to be in ~ of** correr riesgo
de; **out of ~** fuera de peligro
danger list n (Med): **to be on the ~** estar grave
dangerous ['deɪndʒərəs] adj peligroso
dangerously ['deɪndʒərəslɪ] adv
peligrosamente; **~ ill** gravemente enfermo
danger zone n área or zona de peligro
dangle ['dæŋgl] vt colgar ■ vi pender, estar
colgado
Danish ['deɪnɪʃ] adj danés(-esa) ■ n (Ling)
danés m
Danish pastry n pastel m de almendra
dank [dæŋk] adj húmedo y malsano
dapper ['dæpəʳ] adj pulcro, apuesto
Dardanelles [dɑːdə'nɛlz] npl Dardanelos mpl
dare [dɛəʳ] vt: **to ~ sb to do** desafiar a algn a
hacer ■ vi: **to ~ (to) do sth** atreverse a hacer
algo; **I ~ say** (I suppose) puede ser, a lo mejor;
I ~ say he'll turn up puede ser que or quizás
venga; **I daren't tell him** no me atrevo a
decírselo
daredevil ['dɛədɛvl] n temerario(-a),
atrevido(-a)
Dar-es-Salaam ['dɑːrɛssə'lɑːm] n Dar es
Salaam m
daring ['dɛərɪŋ] adj (person) osado; (plan,
escape) atrevido ■ n atrevimiento, osadía
dark [dɑːk] adj oscuro; (hair, complexion)
moreno; (fig. cheerless) triste, sombrío
■ n (gen) oscuridad f; (night) tinieblas fpl;
~ chocolate chocolate m amargo; **it is/is
getting ~** es de noche/está oscureciendo;
in the ~ about (fig) ignorante de; **after ~**
después del anochecer
darken ['dɑːkn] vt oscurecer; (colour) hacer
más oscuro ■ vi oscurecerse; (cloud over)
nublarse
dark glasses npl gafas fpl oscuras
dark horse n (fig) incógnita
darkly ['dɑːklɪ] adv (gloomily) tristemente;
(sinisterly) siniestramente
darkness ['dɑːknɪs] n (in room) oscuridad f;
(night) tinieblas fpl
darkroom ['dɑːkrum] n cuarto oscuro
darling ['dɑːlɪŋ] adj, n querido(-a) m(f)
darn [dɑːn] vt zurcir
dart [dɑːt] n dardo; (in sewing) pinza ■ vi
precipitarse; **to ~ away/along** salir/marchar
disparado
dartboard ['dɑːtbɔːd] n diana
darts [dɑːts] n dardos mpl
dash [dæʃ] n (small quantity: of liquid) gota,
chorrito; (of solid) pizca; (sign) guión m; (: long)
raya ■ vt (break) romper, estrellar; (hopes)
defraudar ■ vi precipitarse, ir de prisa; **a ~**

of soda un poco or chorrito de sifón or soda
▶ **dash away, dash off** vi marcharse
apresuradamente
dashboard ['dæʃbɔːd] n (Aut) salpicadero
dashing ['dæʃɪŋ] adj gallardo
dastardly ['dæstədlɪ] adj ruin, vil
DAT n abbr (= digital audio tape) cas(s)et(t)e m or
f digital
data ['deɪtə] npl datos mpl
database ['deɪtəbeɪs] n base f de datos
data capture n recogida de datos
data link n enlace m de datos
data processing n proceso or procesamiento
de datos
data transmission n transmisión f de datos
date [deɪt] n (day) fecha; (with friend) cita;
(fruit) dátil m ■ vt fechar; (col: girl etc) salir
con; **what's the ~ today?** ¿qué fecha es hoy?;
~ of birth fecha de nacimiento; **closing ~**
fecha tope; **to ~** adv hasta la fecha; **out of ~**
pasado de moda; **up to ~** moderno; puesto
al día; **to bring up to ~** (correspondence,
information) poner al día; (method) actualizar;
to bring sb up to ~ poner a algn al corriente;
letter dated 5th July or (US) **July 5th** carta
fechada el 5 de julio
dated ['deɪtɪd] adj anticuado
date rape n violación ocurrida durante una cita con
un conocido
date stamp n matasellos m inv; (on fresh foods)
sello de fecha
dative ['deɪtɪv] n dativo
daub [dɔːb] vt embadurnar
daughter ['dɔːtəʳ] n hija
daughter-in-law ['dɔːtərɪnlɔː] n nuera, hija
política
daunting ['dɔːntɪŋ] adj desalentador(-a)
davenport ['dævnpɔːt] n escritorio; (US: sofa)
sofá m
dawdle ['dɔːdl] vi (waste time) perder el
tiempo; (go slowly) andar muy despacio;
to ~ over one's work trabajar muy despacio
dawn [dɔːn] n alba, amanecer m ■ vi
amanecer; (fig): **it dawned on him that ...**
cayó en la cuenta de que ...; **at ~** al amanecer;
from ~ to dusk de sol a sol
dawn chorus n canto de los pájaros al
amanecer
day [deɪ] n día m; (working day) jornada;
the ~ before el día anterior; **the ~ after
tomorrow** pasado mañana; **the ~ before
yesterday** anteayer, antes de ayer; **the ~
after, the following ~** el día siguiente; **by ~**
de día; **~ by ~** día a día; **(on) the ~ that ...** el
día que ...; **to work an eight-hour ~** trabajar
ocho horas diarias or al día; **he works eight
hours a ~** trabaja ocho horas al día; **paid**

by the ~ pagado por día; **these days, in the present** ~ hoy en día

daybook ['deɪbuk] n (Brit) diario or libro de entradas y salidas

daybreak ['deɪbreɪk] n amanecer m

day-care centre ['deɪkeə-] n centro de día; (for children) guardería infantil

daydream ['deɪdriːm] n ensueño ■ vi soñar despierto

daylight ['deɪlaɪt] n luz f (del día)

daylight robbery n: **it's** ~! (fig, col) ¡es un robo descarado!

Daylight Saving Time n (US) hora de verano

day-release course [deɪrɪ'liːs-] n curso de formación de un día a la semana

day return, day return ticket n (Brit) billete m de ida y vuelta (en un día)

day shift n turno de día

daytime ['deɪtaɪm] n día m

day-to-day ['deɪtə'deɪ] adj cotidiano, diario; (expenses) diario; **on a** ~ **basis** día por día

day trip n excursión f (de un día)

day tripper n excursionista m/f

daze [deɪz] vt (stun) aturdir ■ n: **in a** ~ aturdido

dazed [deɪzd] adj aturdido

dazzle ['dæzl] vt deslumbrar

dazzling ['dæzlɪŋ] adj (light, smile) deslumbrante; (colour) fuerte

dB abbr = **decibel**

DBS n abbr (= direct broadcasting by satellite) transmisión vía satélite

DC abbr (Elec) = **direct current**; (US) = **District of Columbia**

DCC® n abbr (= digital compact cassette) cas(s)et(t)e m digital compacto

DD n abbr (= Doctor of Divinity) título universitario ■ abbr = **direct debit**

dd. abbr (Comm) = **delivered**

D-day ['diːdeɪ] n (fig) día m clave

DDS n abbr (US: = Doctor of Dental Science, Doctor of Dental Surgery) títulos universitarios

DDT n abbr (= dichlorodiphenyl trichloroethane) DDT m

DE abbr (US) = **Delaware**

DEA n abbr (US: = Drug Enforcement Administration) brigada especial dedicada a la lucha contra el tráfico de estupefacientes

deacon ['diːkən] n diácono

dead [ded] adj muerto; (limb) dormido; (battery) agotado ■ adv totalmente; (exactly) justo; **he was** ~ **on arrival** ingresó cadáver; **to shoot sb** ~ matar a algn a tiros; ~ **tired** muerto (de cansancio); **to stop** ~ parar en seco; **the line has gone** ~ (Tel) se ha cortado la línea; **the** ~ npl los muertos

dead beat adj: **to be** ~ (col) estar hecho polvo

deaden ['dedn] vt (blow, sound) amortiguar; (pain) calmar, aliviar

dead end n callejón m sin salida

dead-end ['dedend] adj: **a** ~ **job** un trabajo sin porvenir

dead heat n (Sport) empate m

deadline ['dedlaɪn] n fecha tope; **to work to a** ~ trabajar con una fecha tope

deadlock ['dedlɔk] n punto muerto

dead loss n (col): **to be a** ~ (person) ser un inútil; (thing) ser una birria

deadly ['dedlɪ] adj mortal, fatal; ~ **dull** aburridísimo

deadly nightshade [-'naɪtʃeɪd] n belladona

deadpan ['dedpæn] adj sin expresión

Dead Sea n: **the** ~ el Mar Muerto

dead season n (Tourism) temporada baja

deaf [def] adj sordo; **to turn a** ~ **ear to sth** hacer oídos sordos a algo

deaf-aid ['defeɪd] n audífono

deaf-and-dumb ['defən'dʌm] adj (person) sordomudo; (alphabet) para sordomudos

deafen ['defn] vt ensordecer

deafening ['defnɪŋ] adj ensordecedor(-a)

deaf-mute ['defmjuːt] n sordomudo(-a)

deafness ['defnɪs] n sordera

deal [diːl] n (agreement) pacto, convenio; (business) negocio, transacción f; (Cards) reparto ■ vt (pt, pp **dealt**) (gen) dar; **a great** ~ **(of)** bastante, mucho; **it's a** ~! (col) ¡trato hecho!, ¡de acuerdo!; **to do a** ~ **with sb** hacer un trato con algn; **he got a bad/fair** ~ **from them** le trataron mal/bien

▶ **deal in** vt fus tratar en, comerciar en

▶ **deal with** vt fus (people) tratar con; (problem) ocuparse de; (subject) tratar de

dealer ['diːlər] n comerciante m/f; (Cards) mano f

dealership ['diːləʃɪp] n concesionario

dealings ['diːlɪŋz] npl (Comm) transacciones fpl; (relations) relaciones fpl

dealt [delt] pt, pp of **deal**

dean [diːn] n (Rel) deán m; (Scol) decano(-a)

dear [dɪər] adj querido; (expensive) caro ■ n: **my** ~ querido(-a); ~ **me!** ¡Dios mío!; **D~ Sir/Madam** (in letter) Muy señor mío, Estimado señor/Estimada señora, De mi/nuestra (mayor) consideración (esp LAm); **D~ Mr/Mrs X** Estimado(-a) señor(a) X

dearly ['dɪəlɪ] adv (love) mucho; (pay) caro

dearth [dəːθ] n (of food, resources, money) escasez f

death [deθ] n muerte f

deathbed ['deθbed] n lecho de muerte

death certificate n partida de defunción

death duties npl (Brit) derechos mpl de sucesión

deathly ['dɛθlɪ] *adj* mortal; (*silence*) profundo

death penalty *n* pena de muerte

death rate *n* tasa de mortalidad

death row *n*: **to be on ~** (*US*) estar condenado a muerte

death sentence *n* condena a muerte

death squad *n* escuadrón *m* de la muerte

deathtrap ['dɛθtræp] *n* lugar *m* (*or* vehículo *etc*) muy peligroso

deb [dɛb] *n abbr* (*col*) = **debutante**

debacle [deɪ'baːkl] *n* desastre *m*, catástrofe *f*

debar [dɪ'baːʳ] *vt*: **to ~ sb from doing** prohibir a algn hacer

debase [dɪ'beɪs] *vt* degradar

debatable [dɪ'beɪtəbl] *adj* discutible; **it is ~ whether ...** es discutible si ...

debate [dɪ'beɪt] *n* debate *m* ■ *vt* discutir

debauched [dɪ'bɔːtʃt] *adj* vicioso

debauchery [dɪ'bɔːtʃərɪ] *n* libertinaje *m*

debenture [dɪ'bɛntʃəʳ] *n* (*Comm*) bono, obligación *f*

debenture capital *n* capital *m* hipotecario

debilitate [dɪ'bɪlɪteɪt] *vt* debilitar

debilitating [dɪ'bɪlɪteɪtɪŋ] *adj* (*illness etc*) debilitante

debit ['dɛbɪt] *n* debe *m* ■ *vt*: **to ~ a sum to sb** *or* **to sb's account** cargar una suma en cuenta a algn

debit balance *n* saldo deudor *or* pasivo

debit note *n* nota de débito *or* cargo

debonair [dɛbə'nɛəʳ] *adj* jovial, cortés(-esa)

debrief [diː'briːf] *vt* hacer dar parte

debriefing [diː'briːfɪŋ] *n* relación *f* (de un informe)

debris ['dɛbriː] *n* escombros *mpl*

debt [dɛt] *n* deuda; **to be in ~** tener deudas; **debts of £5000** deudas de cinco mil libras; **bad ~** deuda incobrable

debt collector *n* cobrador(a) *m(f)* de deudas

debtor ['dɛtəʳ] *n* deudor(a) *m(f)*

debug ['diː'bʌg] *vt* (*Comput*) depurar

debunk [diː'bʌŋk] *vt* (*col: theory*) desprestigiar, desacreditar; (*claim*) desacreditar; (*person, institution*) desenmascarar

début ['deɪbjuː] *n* presentación *f*

debutante ['dɛbjutænt] *n* debutante *f*

Dec. *abbr* (= *December*) dic

decade ['dɛkeɪd] *n* década, decenio

decadence ['dɛkədəns] *n* decadencia

decadent ['dɛkədənt] *adj* decadente

de-caff ['diː'kæf] *n* (*col*) descafeinado

decaffeinated [dɪ'kæfɪneɪtɪd] *adj* descafeinado

decamp [dɪ'kæmp] *vi* (*col*) escaparse, largarse, rajarse (*LAm*)

decant [dɪ'kænt] *vt* decantar

decanter [dɪ'kæntəʳ] *n* jarra, decantador *m*

decathlon [dɪ'kæθlən] *n* decatlón *m*

decay [dɪ'keɪ] *n* (*fig*) decadencia; (*of building*) desmoronamiento; (*of tooth*) caries *f inv* ■ *vi* (*rot*) pudrirse; (*fig*) decaer

decease [dɪ'siːs] *n* fallecimiento ■ *vi* fallecer

deceased [dɪ'siːst] *adj* difunto

deceit [dɪ'siːt] *n* engaño

deceitful [dɪ'siːtful] *adj* engañoso

deceive [dɪ'siːv] *vt* engañar

decelerate [diː'sɛləreɪt] *vt* moderar la marcha de ■ *vi* decelerar

December [dɪ'sɛmbəʳ] *n* diciembre *m*; *see also* **July**

decency ['diːsənsɪ] *n* decencia

decent ['diːsənt] *adj* (*proper*) decente; (*person*) amable, bueno

decently ['diːsəntlɪ] *adv* (*respectably*) decentemente; (*kindly*) amablemente

decentralization [diːsɛntrəlaɪ'zeɪʃən] *n* descentralización *f*

decentralize [diː'sɛntrəlaɪz] *vt* descentralizar

deception [dɪ'sɛpʃən] *n* engaño

deceptive [dɪ'sɛptɪv] *adj* engañoso

decibel ['dɛsɪbɛl] *n* decibel(io) *m*

decide [dɪ'saɪd] *vt* (*person*) decidir; (*question, argument*) resolver ■ *vi*: **to ~ to do/that** decidir hacer/que; **to ~ on sth** tomar una decisión sobre algo; **to ~ against doing sth** decidir en contra de hacer algo

decided [dɪ'saɪdɪd] *adj* (*resolute*) decidido; (*clear, definite*) indudable

decidedly [dɪ'saɪdɪdlɪ] *adv* decididamente

deciding [dɪ'saɪdɪŋ] *adj* decisivo

deciduous [dɪ'sɪdjuəs] *adj* de hoja caduca

decimal ['dɛsɪməl] *adj* decimal ■ *n* decimal *f*; **to three ~ places** con tres cifras decimales

decimalize ['dɛsɪməlaɪz] *vt* convertir al sistema decimal

decimal point *n* coma decimal

decimal system *n* sistema *m* métrico decimal

decimate ['dɛsɪmeɪt] *vt* diezmar

decipher [dɪ'saɪfəʳ] *vt* descifrar

decision [dɪ'sɪʒən] *n* decisión *f*; **to make a ~** tomar una decisión

decisive [dɪ'saɪsɪv] *adj* (*influence*) decisivo; (*manner, person*) decidido; (*reply*) tajante

deck [dɛk] *n* (*Naut*) cubierta; (*of bus*) piso; (*of cards*) baraja; **cassette ~** platina; **to go up on ~** subir a (la) cubierta; **below ~** en la bodega

deckchair ['dɛktʃɛəʳ] *n* tumbona

deckhand ['dɛkhænd] *n* marinero de cubierta

declaration [dɛklə'reɪʃən] *n* declaración *f*

declare [dɪ'klɛəʳ] *vt* (*gen*) declarar

declassify [diːˈklæsɪfaɪ] vt permitir que salga a la luz

decline [dɪˈklaɪn] n decaimiento, decadencia; (lessening) disminución f ■ vt rehusar ■ vi decaer; disminuir; ~ **in living standards** disminución f del nivel de vida; **to ~ to do sth** rehusar hacer algo

declutch [ˈdiːˈklʌtʃ] vi desembragar

decode [diːˈkəud] vt descifrar

decoder [diːˈkəudəʳ] n (Comput, TV) de(s)codificador m

decompose [diːkəmˈpəuz] vi descomponerse

decomposition [diːkɔmpəˈzɪʃən] n descomposición f

decompression [diːkəmˈprɛʃən] n descompresión f

decompression chamber n cámara de descompresión

decongestant [diːkənˈdʒɛstənt] n descongestionante m

decontaminate [diːkənˈtæmɪneɪt] vt descontaminar

decontrol [diːkənˈtrəul] vt (trade) quitar controles a; (prices) descongelar

décor [ˈdeɪkɔːʳ] n decoración f; (Theat) decorado

decorate [ˈdɛkəreɪt] vt (paint) pintar; (paper) empapelar; (adorn): **to ~ (with)** adornar (de), decorar (de)

decoration [dɛkəˈreɪʃən] n adorno; (act) decoración f; (medal) condecoración f

decorative [ˈdɛkərətɪv] adj decorativo

decorator [ˈdɛkəreɪtəʳ] n (workman) pintor m decorador

decorum [dɪˈkɔːrəm] n decoro

decoy [ˈdiːkɔɪ] n señuelo; **police ~** trampa or señuelo policial

decrease [n ˈdiːkriːs] n disminución f ■ vt [dɪˈkriːs] disminuir, reducir ■ vi reducirse; **to be on the ~** ir disminuyendo

decreasing [dɪˈkriːsɪŋ] adj decreciente

decree [dɪˈkriː] n decreto ■ vt: **to ~ (that)** decretar (que); **~ absolute/nisi** sentencia absoluta/provisional de divorcio

decrepit [dɪˈkrɛpɪt] adj (person) decrépito; (building) ruinoso

decry [dɪˈkraɪ] vt criticar, censurar

dedicate [ˈdɛdɪkeɪt] vt dedicar

dedicated [ˈdɛdɪkeɪtɪd] adj dedicado; (Comput) especializado; **~ word processor** procesador m de textos especializado or dedicado

dedication [dɛdɪˈkeɪʃən] n (devotion) dedicación f; (in book) dedicatoria

deduce [dɪˈdjuːs] vt deducir

deduct [dɪˈdʌkt] vt restar; (from wage etc) descontar, deducir

deduction [dɪˈdʌkʃən] n (amount deducted) descuento; (conclusion) deducción f, conclusión f

deed [diːd] n hecho, acto; (feat) hazaña; (Law) escritura; **~ of covenant** escritura de contrato

deem [diːm] vt (formal) juzgar, considerar; **to ~ it wise to do** considerar prudente hacer

deep [diːp] adj profundo; (voice) bajo; (breath) profundo, a pleno pulmón ■ adv: **the spectators stood 20 ~** los espectadores se formaron de 20 en fondo; **to be four metres ~** tener cuatro metros de profundidad

deepen [ˈdiːpn] vt ahondar, profundizar ■ vi (darkness) intensificarse

deep-freeze [ˈdiːpˈfriːz] n arcón m congelador

deep-fry [ˈdiːpˈfraɪ] vt freír en aceite abundante

deeply [ˈdiːplɪ] adv (breathe) profundamente, a pleno pulmón; (interested, moved, grateful) profundamente, hondamente; **to regret sth ~** sentir algo profundamente

deep-rooted [ˈdiːpˈruːtɪd] adj (prejudice, habit) profundamente arraigado; (affection) profundo

deep-sea [ˈdiːpˈsiː] adj: **~ diver** buzo; **~ diving** buceo de altura

deep-seated [ˈdiːpˈsiːtɪd] adj (beliefs) (profundamente) arraigado

deep-set [ˈdiːpsɛt] adj (eyes) hundido

deep-vein thrombosis n (Med) trombosis f venosa profunda

deer (pl ~) [dɪəʳ] n ciervo

deerstalker [ˈdɪəstɔːkəʳ] n (hat) gorro de cazador

deface [dɪˈfeɪs] vt desfigurar, mutilar

defamation [dɛfəˈmeɪʃən] n difamación f

defamatory [dɪˈfæmətrɪ] adj difamatorio

default [dɪˈfɔːlt] vi faltar al pago; (Sport) no presentarse, no comparecer ■ n (Comput) defecto; **by ~** (Law) en rebeldía; (Sport) por incomparecencia; **to ~ on a debt** dejar de pagar una deuda

defaulter [dɪˈfɔːltəʳ] n (in debt) moroso(-a)

default option n (Comput) opción f por defecto

defeat [dɪˈfiːt] n derrota ■ vt derrotar, vencer; (fig: efforts) frustrar

defeatism [dɪˈfiːtɪzəm] n derrotismo

defeatist [dɪˈfiːtɪst] adj, n derrotista m/f

defecate [ˈdɛfəkeɪt] vi defecar

defect [ˈdiːfɛkt] n defecto ■ vi [dɪˈfɛkt]: **to ~ to the enemy** pasarse al enemigo; **physical ~** defecto físico; **mental ~** deficiencia mental

defective [dɪˈfɛktɪv] adj (gen) defectuoso; (person) anormal

defector [dɪ'fɛktə] n tránsfuga m/f

defence, (US) **defense** [dɪ'fɛns] n defensa;
the Ministry of D~ el Ministerio de
Defensa; **witness for the ~** testigo de
descargo

defenceless [dɪ'fɛnslɪs] adj indefenso

defence spending n gasto militar

defend [dɪ'fɛnd] vt defender; (decision, action)
defender; (opinion) mantener

defendant [dɪ'fɛndənt] n acusado(-a); (in civil
case) demandado(-a)

defender [dɪ'fɛndə'] n defensor(a) m(f)

defending champion [dɪ'fɛndɪŋ-] n (Sport)
defensor(-a) m(f) del título

defending counsel n (Law) abogado defensor

defense [dɪ'fɛns] n (US) = **defence**

defensive [dɪ'fɛnsɪv] adj defensivo ∎ n
defensiva; **on the ~** a la defensiva

defer [dɪ'fə:'] vt (postpone) aplazar; **to ~ to**
diferir a; (submit): **to ~ to sb/sb's opinion**
someterse a algn/a la opinión de algn

deference ['dɛfərəns] n deferencia, respeto;
out of or **in ~ to** por respeto a

deferential [dɛfə'rɛnʃəl] adj respetuoso

deferred [dɪ'fə:d] adj: **~ creditor** acreedor m
diferido

defiance [dɪ'faɪəns] n desafío; **in ~ of** en
contra de

defiant [dɪ'faɪənt] adj (insolent) insolente;
(challenging) retador(a)

defiantly [dɪ'faɪəntlɪ] adv con aire de desafío

deficiency [dɪ'fɪʃənsɪ] n (lack) falta; (Comm)
déficit m; (defect) defecto

deficient [dɪ'fɪʃənt] adj (lacking) insuficiente;
(incomplete) incompleto; (defective) defectuoso;
(mentally) anormal; **~ in** deficiente en

deficit ['dɛfɪsɪt] n déficit m

defile [dɪ'faɪl] vt manchar; (violate) violar

define [dɪ'faɪn] vt (Comput) definir

definite ['dɛfɪnɪt] adj (fixed) determinado;
(clear, obvious) claro; **he was ~ about it** no dejó
lugar a dudas (sobre ello)

definitely ['dɛfɪnɪtlɪ] adv: **he's ~ mad** no cabe
duda de que está loco

definition [dɛfɪ'nɪʃən] n definición f

definitive [dɪ'fɪnɪtɪv] adj definitivo

deflate [di:'fleɪt] vt (gen) desinflar; (pompous
person) quitar or rebajar los humos a; (Econ)
deflacionar

deflation [di:'fleɪʃən] n (Econ) deflación f

deflationary [di:'fleɪʃənrɪ] adj (Econ)
deflacionario

deflect [dɪ'flɛkt] vt desviar

defog [di:'fɔg] vt desempañar

defogger [di:'fɔgə'] n (US Aut) dispositivo
antivaho

deform [dɪ'fɔ:m] vt deformar

deformed [dɪ'fɔ:md] adj deformado

deformity [dɪ'fɔ:mɪtɪ] n deformación f

Defra n abbr (Brit) = **Department for
Environment, Food and Rural Affairs**

defraud [dɪ'frɔ:d] vt estafar; **to ~ sb of sth**
estafar algo a algn

defray [dɪ'freɪ] vt: **to ~ sb's expenses**
reembolsar a algn los gastos

defrost [di:'frɔst] vt (frozen food, fridge)
descongelar

defroster [di:'frɔstə'] n (US) eliminador m
de vaho

deft [dɛft] adj diestro, hábil

defunct [dɪ'fʌŋkt] adj difunto; (organization
etc) ya desaparecido

defuse [di:'fju:z] vt desarmar; (situation)
calmar, apaciguar

defy [dɪ'faɪ] vt (resist) oponerse a; (challenge)
desafiar; (order) contravenir

degenerate [dɪ'dʒɛnəreɪt] vi degenerar ∎ adj
[dɪ'dʒɛnərɪt] degenerado

degradation [dɛgrə'deɪʃən] n degradación f

degrade [dɪ'greɪd] vt degradar

degrading [dɪ'greɪdɪŋ] adj degradante

degree [dɪ'gri:] n grado; (Scol) título; **10
degrees below freezing** 10 grados bajo cero;
to have a ~ in maths ser licenciado(-a) en
matemáticas; **by degrees** (gradually) poco a
poco, por etapas; **to some ~, to a certain ~**
hasta cierto punto; **a considerable ~ of risk**
un gran índice de riesgo

dehydrated [di:haɪ'dreɪtɪd] adj
deshidratado; (milk) en polvo

dehydration [di:haɪ'dreɪʃən] n
deshidratación f

de-ice [di:'aɪs] vt (windscreen) deshelar

de-icer [di:'aɪsə'] n descongelador m

deign [deɪn] vi: **to ~ to do** dignarse hacer

deity ['di:ɪtɪ] n deidad f, divinidad f

déjà vu [deɪʒɑ:'vu:] n: **I had a sense of ~**
sentía como si ya lo hubiera vivido

dejected [dɪ'dʒɛktɪd] adj abatido,
desanimado

dejection [dɪ'dʒɛkʃən] n abatimiento

Del. abbr (US) = **Delaware**

delay [dɪ'leɪ] vt demorar, aplazar; (person)
entretener; (train) retrasar; (payment) aplazar
∎ vi tardar ∎ n demora, retraso; **without ~**
en seguida, sin tardar

delayed-action [dɪleɪd'ækʃən] adj (bomb etc)
de acción retardada

delectable [dɪ'lɛktəbl] adj (person)
encantador(-a); (food) delicioso

delegate ['dɛlɪgɪt] n delegado(-a) ∎ vt
['dɛlɪgeɪt] delegar; **to ~ sth to sb/sb to do
sth** delegar algo en algn/en algn para hacer
algo

d

delegation [dɛlɪ'geɪʃən] n (of work etc)
delegación f
delete [dɪ'liːt] vt suprimir, tachar; (Comput)
suprimir, borrar
Delhi ['dɛlɪ] n Delhi m
deli ['dɛlɪ] n = **delicatessen**
deliberate [dɪ'lɪbərɪt] adj (intentional)
intencionado; (slow) pausado, lento
■ vi [dɪ'lɪbəreɪt] deliberar
deliberately [dɪ'lɪbərɪtlɪ] adv (on purpose)
a propósito; (slowly) pausadamente
deliberation [dɪlɪbə'reɪʃən] n (consideration)
reflexión f; (discussion) deliberación f,
discusión f
delicacy ['dɛlɪkəsɪ] n delicadeza; (choice food)
manjar m
delicate ['dɛlɪkɪt] adj (gen) delicado; (fragile)
frágil
delicately ['dɛlɪkɪtlɪ] adv con delicadeza,
delicadamente; (act, express) con discreción
delicatessen [dɛlɪkə'tɛsn] n tienda
especializada en comida exótica
delicious [dɪ'lɪʃəs] adj delicioso, rico
delight [dɪ'laɪt] n (feeling) placer m, deleite
m; (object) encanto, delicia ■ vt encantar,
deleitar; **to take ~ in** deleitarse en
delighted [dɪ'laɪtɪd] adj: ~ (**at** or **with/to do**)
encantado (con/de hacer); **to be ~ that** estar
encantado de que; **I'd be ~** con mucho or todo
gusto
delightful [dɪ'laɪtful] adj encantador(a),
delicioso
delimit [diː'lɪmɪt] vt delimitar
delineate [dɪ'lɪnɪeɪt] vt delinear
delinquency [dɪ'lɪŋkwənsɪ] n delincuencia
delinquent [dɪ'lɪŋkwənt] adj, n delincuente
m/f
delirious [dɪ'lɪrɪəs] adj (Med: fig) delirante;
to be ~ delirar, desvariar
delirium [dɪ'lɪrɪəm] n delirio
deliver [dɪ'lɪvər] vt (distribute) repartir; (hand
over) entregar; (message) comunicar; (speech)
pronunciar; (blow) lanzar, dar; (Med) asistir
al parto de
deliverance [dɪ'lɪvrəns] n liberación f
delivery [dɪ'lɪvərɪ] n reparto; entrega; (of
speaker) modo de expresarse; (Med) parto,
alumbramiento; **to take ~ of** recibir
delivery note n nota de entrega
delivery van n furgoneta de reparto
delta ['dɛltə] n delta m
delude [dɪ'luːd] vt engañar
deluge ['dɛljuːdʒ] n diluvio ■ vt (fig):
to ~ (with) inundar (de)
delusion [dɪ'luːʒən] n ilusión f, engaño
de luxe [də'lʌks] adj de lujo
delve [dɛlv] vi: **to ~ into** hurgar en

Dem. abbr (US Pol) = **Democrat; Democratic**
demand [dɪ'mɑːnd] vt (gen) exigir; (rights)
reclamar; (need) requerir ■ n (gen) exigencia;
(claim) reclamación f; (Econ) demanda; **to ~
sth (from** or **of sb)** exigir algo (a algn); **to be
in ~** ser muy solicitado; **on ~** a solicitud
demanding [dɪ'mɑːndɪŋ] adj (boss) exigente;
(work) absorbente
demarcation [diːmɑː'keɪʃən] n
demarcación f
demarcation dispute n conflicto de
definición or demarcación del trabajo
demean [dɪ'miːn] vt: **to ~ o.s.** rebajarse
demeanour, demeanor (US) [dɪ'miːnər] n
porte m, conducta, comportamiento
demented [dɪ'mɛntɪd] adj demente
demi- ['dɛmɪ] pref semi..., medio...
demilitarize [diː'mɪlɪtəraɪz] vt
desmilitarizar; **demilitarized zone** zona
desmilitarizada
demise [dɪ'maɪz] n (death) fallecimiento
demist [diː'mɪst] vt (Aut) eliminar el vaho de
demister [diː'mɪstər] n (Aut) eliminador m
de vaho
demo ['dɛməu] n abbr (col: = demonstration)
manifestación f
demobilization [diː'məubɪlaɪ'zeɪʃən] n
desmovilización f
democracy [dɪ'mɔkrəsɪ] n democracia
democrat ['dɛməkræt] n demócrata m/f
democratic [dɛmə'krætɪk] adj democrático;
the D~ Party el partido demócrata
(estadounidense)
demography [dɪ'mɔgrəfɪ] n demografía
demolish [dɪ'mɔlɪʃ] vt derribar, demoler
demolition [dɛmə'lɪʃən] n derribo,
demolición f
demon ['diːmən] n (evil spirit) demonio ■ cpd
temible
demonstrate ['dɛmənstreɪt] vt demostrar
■ vi manifestarse; **to ~ (for/against)**
manifestarse (a favor de/en contra de)
demonstration [dɛmən'streɪʃən] n
(Pol) manifestación f; (proof) prueba,
demostración f; **to hold a ~** (Pol) hacer una
manifestación
demonstrative [dɪ'mɔnstrətɪv] adj (person)
expresivo; (Ling) demostrativo
demonstrator ['dɛmənstreɪtər] n (Pol)
manifestante m/f
demoralize [dɪ'mɔrəlaɪz] vt desmoralizar
demote [dɪ'məut] vt degradar
demotion [dɪ'məuʃən] n degradación f;
(Comm) descenso
demur [dɪ'məːr] vi: **to ~ (at)** hacer objeciones
(a), vacilar (ante) ■ n: **without ~** sin
objeción

demure [dɪˈmjuəʳ] *adj* recatado
demurrage [dɪˈmʌrɪdʒ] *n* sobrestadía
den [dɛn] *n* (*of animal*) guarida; (*study*) estudio
denationalization [diːnæʃnəlaɪˈzeɪʃən] *n* desnacionalización f
denationalize [diːˈnæʃnəlaɪz] *vt* desnacionalizar
denatured alcohol [diːˈneɪtʃəd-] *n* (*US*) alcohol *m* desnaturalizado
denial [dɪˈnaɪəl] *n* (*refusal*) negativa; (*of report etc*) denegación f
denier [ˈdɛnɪəʳ] *n* denier *m*
denim [ˈdɛnɪm] *n* tela vaquera; *see also* **denims**
denim jacket *n* chaqueta vaquera, saco vaquero (*LAm*)
denims [ˈdɛnɪmz] *npl* vaqueros *mpl*
denizen [ˈdɛnɪzn] *n* (*inhabitant*) habitante *m/f*; (*foreigner*) residente *m/f* extranjero(-a)
Denmark [ˈdɛnmɑːk] *n* Dinamarca
denomination [dɪnɔmɪˈneɪʃən] *n* valor *m*; (*Rel*) confesión f
denominator [dɪˈnɔmɪneɪtəʳ] *n* denominador *m*
denote [dɪˈnəut] *vt* indicar, significar
denounce [dɪˈnauns] *vt* denunciar
dense [dɛns] *adj* (*thick*) espeso; (*foliage etc*) tupido; (*stupid*) torpe
densely [ˈdɛnslɪ] *adv*: **~ populated** con una alta densidad de población
density [ˈdɛnsɪtɪ] *n* densidad f; **single/double-~ disk** *n* disco de densidad sencilla/ de doble densidad
dent [dɛnt] *n* abolladura ■ *vt* (*also*: **make a dent in**) abollar
dental [ˈdɛntl] *adj* dental
dental floss [-flɔs] *n* seda dental
dental surgeon *n* odontólogo(-a)
dentifrice [ˈdɛntɪfrɪs] *n* dentífrico
dentist [ˈdɛntɪst] *n* dentista *m/f*; **~'s surgery** (*Brit*) consultorio dental
dentistry [ˈdɛntɪstrɪ] *n* odontología
dentures [ˈdɛntʃəz] *npl* dentadura *sg* (postiza)
denude [dɪˈnjuːd] *vt*: **to ~ of** despojar de
denunciation [dɪnʌnsɪˈeɪʃən] *n* denuncia, denunciación f
deny [dɪˈnaɪ] *vt* negar; (*charge*) rechazar; (*report*) desmentir; **to ~ o.s.** privarse (de); **he denies having said it** niega haberlo dicho
deodorant [diːˈəudərənt] *n* desodorante *m*
depart [dɪˈpɑːt] *vi* irse, marcharse; (*train*) salir; **to ~ from** (*fig: differ from*) apartarse de
departed [dɪˈpɑːtɪd] *adj* (*bygone: days, glory*) pasado; (*dead*) difunto ■ *n*: **the (dear) ~** el/ la/los/las difunto/a/os/as
department [dɪˈpɑːtmənt] *n* (*Comm*) sección f; (*Scol*) departamento; (*Pol*) ministerio;

that's not my ~ (*fig*) no tiene que ver conmigo; **D~ of State** (*US*) Ministerio de Asuntos Exteriores
departmental [diːpɑːtˈmɛntl] *adj* (*dispute*) departamental; (*meeting*) departamental, de departamento; **~ manager** jefe(-a) *m(f)* de sección *or* de departamento *or* de servicio
department store *n* grandes almacenes *mpl*
departure [dɪˈpɑːtʃəʳ] *n* partida, ida; (*of train*) salida; **a new ~** un nuevo rumbo
departure lounge *n* (*at airport*) sala de embarque
depend [dɪˈpɛnd] *vi*: **to ~ (up)on** (*be dependent upon*) depender de; (*rely on*) contar con; **it depends** depende, según; **depending on the result** según el resultado
dependable [dɪˈpɛndəbl] *adj* (*person*) formal, serio
dependant [dɪˈpɛndənt] *n* dependiente *m/f*
dependence [dɪˈpɛndəns] *n* dependencia
dependent [dɪˈpɛndənt] *adj*: **to be ~ (on)** depender (de) ■ *n* = **dependant**
depict [dɪˈpɪkt] *vt* (*in picture*) pintar; (*describe*) representar
depilatory [dɪˈpɪlətrɪ] *n* (*also*: **depilatory cream**) depilatorio
depleted [dɪˈpliːtɪd] *adj* reducido
deplorable [dɪˈplɔːrəbl] *adj* deplorable
deplore [dɪˈplɔː] *vt* deplorar
deploy [dɪˈplɔɪ] *vt* desplegar
depopulate [diːˈpɔpjuleɪt] *vt* despoblar
depopulation [ˈdiːpɔpjuˈleɪʃən] *n* despoblación f
deport [dɪˈpɔːt] *vt* deportar
deportation [diːpɔːˈteɪʃən] *n* deportación f
deportation order *n* orden f de expulsión *or* deportación
deportee [diːpɔːˈtiː] *n* deportado(-a)
deportment [dɪˈpɔːtmənt] *n* comportamiento
depose [dɪˈpəuz] *vt* deponer
deposit [dɪˈpɔzɪt] *n* depósito; (*Chem*) sedimento; (*of ore, oil*) yacimiento ■ *vt* (*gen*) depositar; **to put down a ~ of £50** dejar un depósito de 50 libras
deposit account *n* (*Brit*) cuenta de ahorros
depositor [dɪˈpɔzɪtəʳ] *n* depositante *m/f*, cuentacorrentista *m/f*
depository [dɪˈpɔzɪtərɪ] *n* almacén *m* depositario
depot [ˈdɛpəu] *n* (*storehouse*) depósito; (*for vehicles*) parque *m*
deprave [dɪˈpreɪv] *vt* depravar
depraved [dɪˈpreɪvd] *adj* depravado, vicioso
depravity [dɪˈprævɪtɪ] *n* depravación f, vicio
deprecate [ˈdɛprɪkeɪt] *vt* desaprobar, lamentar

deprecating [ˈdɛprɪkeɪtɪŋ] *adj* (*disapproving*) de desaprobación; (*apologetic*): **a ~ smile** una sonrisa de disculpa

depreciate [dɪˈpriːʃɪeɪt] *vi* depreciarse, perder valor

depreciation [dɪpriːʃɪˈeɪʃən] *n* depreciación *f*

depress [dɪˈprɛs] *vt* deprimir; (*press down*) apretar

depressant [dɪˈprɛsnt] *n* (*Med*) calmante *m*, sedante *m*

depressed [dɪˈprɛst] *adj* deprimido; (*Comm: market, economy*) deprimido; (*area*) deprimido (económicamente); **to get ~** deprimirse

depressing [dɪˈprɛsɪŋ] *adj* deprimente

depression [dɪˈprɛʃən] *n* depresión *f*; **the economy is in a state of ~** la economía está deprimida

deprivation [dɛprɪˈveɪʃən] *n* privación *f*; (*loss*) pérdida

deprive [dɪˈpraɪv] *vt*: **to ~ sb of** privar a algn de

deprived [dɪˈpraɪvd] *adj* necesitado

dept. *abbr* (= *department*) dto

depth [dɛpθ] *n* profundidad *f*; **at a ~ of three metres** a tres metros de profundidad; **to be out of one's ~** (*swimmer*) perder pie; (*fig*) estar perdido; **to study sth in ~** estudiar algo a fondo; **in the depths of** en lo más hondo de

depth charge *n* carga de profundidad

deputation [dɛpjuˈteɪʃən] *n* delegación *f*

deputize [ˈdɛpjutaɪz] *vi*: **to ~ for sb** sustituir a algn

deputy [ˈdɛpjutɪ] *adj*: **~ head** subdirector(-a) *m(f)* ▪ *n* sustituto(-a), suplente *m/f*; (*Pol*) diputado(-a); (*agent*) representante *m/f*

deputy leader *n* vicepresidente(-a) *m(f)*

derail [dɪˈreɪl] *vt*: **to be derailed** descarrilarse

derailment [dɪˈreɪlmənt] *n* descarrilamiento

deranged [dɪˈreɪndʒd] *adj* trastornado

derby [ˈdɑːbɪ] *n* (US) hongo

deregulate [diːˈrɛgjuleɪt] *vt* desreglamentar

deregulation [diːrɛgjuˈleɪʃən] *n* desreglamentación *f*

derelict [ˈdɛrɪlɪkt] *adj* abandonado

deride [dɪˈraɪd] *vt* ridiculizar, mofarse de

derision [dɪˈrɪʒən] *n* irrisión *f*, mofas *fpl*

derisive [dɪˈraɪsɪv] *adj* burlón(-ona)

derisory [dɪˈraɪzərɪ] *adj* (*sum*) irrisorio; (*laughter, person*) burlón(-ona), irónico

derivation [dɛrɪˈveɪʃən] *n* derivación *f*

derivative [dɪˈrɪvətɪv] *n* derivado ▪ *adj* (*work*) poco original

derive [dɪˈraɪv] *vt* derivar ▪ *vi*: **to ~ from** derivarse de

derived [dɪˈraɪvd] *adj* derivado

dermatitis [dɜːməˈtaɪtɪs] *n* dermatitis *f*

dermatology [dɜːməˈtɔlədʒɪ] *n* dermatología

derogatory [dɪˈrɔgətərɪ] *adj* despectivo

derrick [ˈdɛrɪk] *n* torre *f* de perforación

derv [dɜːv] *n* (*Brit*) gasoil *m*

descend [dɪˈsɛnd] *vt, vi* descender, bajar; **to ~ from** descender de; **in descending order of importance** de mayor a menor importancia
▶ **descend on** *vt fus* (*enemy, angry person*) caer sobre; (*misfortune*) sobrevenir; (*gloom, silence*) invadir; **visitors descended on us** las visitas nos invadieron

descendant [dɪˈsɛndənt] *n* descendiente *m/f*

descent [dɪˈsɛnt] *n* descenso; (*Geo*) pendiente *f*, declive *m*; (*origin*) descendencia

describe [dɪsˈkraɪb] *vt* describir

description [dɪsˈkrɪpʃən] *n* descripción *f*; (*sort*) clase *f*, género; **of every ~** de toda clase

descriptive [dɪsˈkrɪptɪv] *adj* descriptivo

desecrate [ˈdɛsɪkreɪt] *vt* profanar

desegregation [diːsɛgrɪˈgeɪʃən] *n* desegregación *f*

desert [*n* ˈdɛzət, *vb* dɪˈzɜːt] *n* desierto ▪ *vt* abandonar, desamparar ▪ *vi* (*Mil*) desertar; *see also* **deserts**

deserter [dɪˈzɜːtər] *n* desertor(-a) *m(f)*

desertion [dɪˈzɜːʃən] *n* deserción *f*

desert island *n* isla desierta

deserts [dɪˈzɜːts] *npl*: **to get one's just ~** llevarse su merecido

deserve [dɪˈzɜːv] *vt* merecer, ser digno de, ameritar (*LAm*)

deservedly [dɪˈzɜːvɪdlɪ] *adv* con razón

deserving [dɪˈzɜːvɪŋ] *adj* (*person*) digno; (*action, cause*) meritorio

desiccated [ˈdɛsɪkeɪtɪd] *adj* desecado

design [dɪˈzaɪn] *n* (*sketch*) bosquejo; (*of dress, car*) diseño; (*pattern*) dibujo ▪ *vt* (*gen*) diseñar; **industrial ~** diseño industrial; **to have designs on sb** tener la(s) mira(s) puesta(s) en algn; **to be designed for sb/sth** estar hecho para algn/algo

design and technology *n* (*Brit Scol*) diseño y tecnología

designate [ˈdɛzɪgneɪt] *vt* (*appoint*) nombrar; (*destine*) designar ▪ *adj* [ˈdɛzɪgnɪt] designado

designation [dɛzɪgˈneɪʃən] *n* (*appointment*) nombramiento; (*name*) denominación *f*

designer [dɪˈzaɪnər] *n* diseñador(-a) *m(f)*; (*fashion designer*) modisto(-a)

designer baby *n* bebé *m* de diseño

desirability [dɪzaɪərəˈbɪlɪtɪ] *n* ventaja, atractivo

desirable [dɪˈzaɪərəbl] *adj* (*proper*) deseable; (*attractive*) atractivo; **it is ~ that** es conveniente que

desire [dɪˈzaɪər] *n* deseo ▪ *vt* desear; **to ~ sth/to do sth/that** desear algo/hacer algo/que

desirous [dɪˈzaɪərəs] adj deseoso
desist [dɪˈzɪst] vi: **to ~ (from)** desistir (de)
desk [dɛsk] n (in office) escritorio; (for pupil) pupitre m; (in hotel, at airport) recepción f; (Brit: in shop, restaurant) caja
desktop computer [ˈdɛsktɔp-] n ordenador m de sobremesa
desktop publishing [ˈdɛsktɔp-] n autoedición f
desolate [ˈdɛsəlɪt] adj (place) desierto; (person) afligido
desolation [dɛsəˈleɪʃən] n (of place) desolación f; (of person) aflicción f
despair [dɪsˈpɛər] n desesperación f ■ vi: **to ~ of** desesperar de; **in ~** desesperado
despatch [dɪsˈpætʃ] n, vt = **dispatch**
desperate [ˈdɛspərɪt] adj desesperado; (fugitive) peligroso; (measures) extremo; **we are getting ~** estamos al borde de desesperación
desperately [ˈdɛspərɪtlɪ] adv desesperadamente; (very) terriblemente, gravemente; **~ ill** gravemente enfermo
desperation [dɛspəˈreɪʃən] n desesperación f; **in ~** desesperado
despicable [dɪsˈpɪkəbl] adj vil, despreciable
despise [dɪsˈpaɪz] vt despreciar
despite [dɪsˈpaɪt] prep a pesar de, pese a
despondent [dɪsˈpɔndənt] adj deprimido, abatido
despot [ˈdɛspɔt] n déspota m/f
dessert [dɪˈzɜːt] n postre m
dessertspoon [dɪˈzɜːtspuːn] n cuchara (de postre)
destabilize [diːˈsteɪbɪlaɪz] vt desestabilizar
destination [dɛstɪˈneɪʃən] n destino
destine [ˈdɛstɪn] vt destinar
destined [ˈdɛstɪnd] adj: **~ for London** con destino a Londres
destiny [ˈdɛstɪnɪ] n destino
destitute [ˈdɛstɪtjuːt] adj desamparado, indigente
destitution [dɛstɪˈtjuːʃən] n indigencia, miseria
destroy [dɪsˈtrɔɪ] vt destruir; (finish) acabar con
destroyer [dɪsˈtrɔɪər] n (Naut) destructor m
destruction [dɪsˈtrʌkʃən] n destrucción f; (fig) ruina
destructive [dɪsˈtrʌktɪv] adj destructivo, destructor(a)
desultory [ˈdɛsəltərɪ] adj (reading) poco metódico; (conversation) inconexo; (contact) intermitente
detach [dɪˈtætʃ] vt separar; (unstick) despegar
detachable [dɪˈtætʃəbl] adj separable; (Tech) desmontable

detached [dɪˈtætʃt] adj (attitude) objetivo, imparcial
detached house n chalé m, chalet m
detachment [dɪˈtætʃmənt] n separación f; (Mil) destacamento; (fig) objetividad f, imparcialidad f
detail [ˈdiːteɪl] n detalle m; (Mil) destacamento ■ vt detallar; (Mil) destacar; **in ~** detalladamente; **to go into ~(s)** entrar en detalles
detailed [ˈdiːteɪld] adj detallado
detain [dɪˈteɪn] vt retener; (in captivity) detener
detainee [diːteɪˈniː] n detenido(-a)
detect [dɪˈtɛkt] vt (discover) descubrir; (Med, Police) identificar; (Mil, Radar, Tech) detectar; (notice) percibir
detection [dɪˈtɛkʃən] n descubrimiento; identificación f; **crime ~** investigación f; **to escape ~** (criminal) escaparse sin ser descubierto; (mistake) pasar inadvertido
detective [dɪˈtɛktɪv] n detective m
detective story n novela policíaca
detector [dɪˈtɛktər] n detector m
détente [deɪˈtɑːnt] n distensión f, detente f
detention [dɪˈtɛnʃən] n detención f, arresto
deter [dɪˈtɜː] vt (dissuade) disuadir; (prevent) impedir; **to ~ sb from doing sth** disuadir a algn de que haga algo
detergent [dɪˈtɜːdʒənt] n detergente m
deteriorate [dɪˈtɪərɪəreɪt] vi deteriorarse
deterioration [dɪtɪərɪəˈreɪʃən] n deterioro
determination [dɪtɜːmɪˈneɪʃən] n resolución f
determine [dɪˈtɜːmɪn] vt determinar; **to ~ to do sth** decidir hacer algo
determined [dɪˈtɜːmɪnd] adj: **to be ~ to do sth** estar decidido or resuelto a hacer algo; **a ~ effort** un esfuerzo enérgico
deterrence [dɪˈtɛrns] n disuasión f
deterrent [dɪˈtɛrənt] n fuerza de disuasión; **to act as a ~** servir para prevenir
detest [dɪˈtɛst] vt aborrecer
detestable [dɪˈtɛstəbl] adj aborrecible
dethrone [diːˈθrəun] vt destronar
detonate [ˈdɛtəneɪt] vi estallar ■ vt hacer detonar
detonator [ˈdɛtəneɪtər] n detonador m, fulminante m
detour [ˈdiːtuər] n (gen: US Aut: diversion) desvío ■ vt (US: traffic) desviar; **to make a ~** dar un rodeo
detract [dɪˈtrækt] vt: **to ~ from** quitar mérito a, restar valor a
detractor [dɪˈtræktər] n detractor(-a) m(f)
detriment [ˈdɛtrɪmənt] n: **to the ~ of** en perjuicio de; **without ~ to** sin detrimento de, sin perjuicio para

detrimental [dɛtrɪ'mɛntl] *adj* perjudicial
deuce [djuːs] *n* (*Tennis*) cuarenta iguales
devaluation [dɪvælju'eɪʃən] *n* devaluación *f*
devalue [dɪ'vælju:] *vt* devaluar
devastate ['dɛvəsteɪt] *vt* devastar; **he was devastated by the news** las noticias le dejaron desolado
devastating ['dɛvəsteɪtɪŋ] *adj* devastador(-a); (*fig*) arrollador(-a)
devastation [dɛvəs'teɪʃən] *n* devastación *f*, ruina
develop [dɪ'vɛləp] *vt* desarrollar; (*Phot*) revelar; (*disease*) contraer; (*habit*) adquirir ■ *vi* desarrollarse; (*advance*) progresar; **this land is to be developed** se va a construir en este terreno; **to ~ a taste for sth** tomar gusto a algo; **to ~ into** transformarse *or* convertirse en
developer [dɪ'vɛləpə^r] *n* (*property developer*) promotor(-a) *m(f)*
developing country *n* país *m* en (vías de) desarrollo
development [dɪ'vɛləpmənt] *n* desarrollo; (*advance*) progreso; (*of affair, case*) desenvolvimiento; (*of land*) urbanización *f*
development area *n* zona de fomento *or* desarrollo
deviant ['di:vɪənt] *adj* anómalo, pervertido
deviate ['di:vɪeɪt] *vi*: **to ~ (from)** desviarse (de)
deviation [di:vɪ'eɪʃən] *n* desviación *f*
device [dɪ'vaɪs] *n* (*scheme*) estratagema, recurso; (*apparatus*) aparato, mecanismo; (*explosive device*) artefacto explosivo
devil ['dɛvl] *n* diablo, demonio
devilish ['dɛvlɪʃ] *adj* diabólico
devil-may-care ['dɛvlmeɪ'kɛə^r] *adj* despreocupado
devil's advocate *n*: **to play (the) ~** hacer de abogado del diablo
devious ['di:vɪəs] *adj* intricado, enrevesado; (*person*) taimado
devise [dɪ'vaɪz] *vt* idear, inventar
devoid [dɪ'vɔɪd] *adj*: **~ of** desprovisto de
devolution [di:və'lu:ʃən] *n* (*Pol*) descentralización *f*
devolve [dɪ'vɔlv] *vi*: **to ~ (up) on** recaer sobre
devote [dɪ'vəut] *vt*: **to ~ sth to** dedicar algo a
devoted [dɪ'vəutɪd] *adj* (*loyal*) leal, fiel; **the book is ~ to politics** el libro trata de política
devotee [dɛvəu'ti:] *n* devoto(-a)
devotion [dɪ'vəuʃən] *n* dedicación *f*; (*Rel*) devoción *f*
devour [dɪ'vauə^r] *vt* devorar
devout [dɪ'vaut] *adj* devoto
dew [dju:] *n* rocío
dexterity [dɛks'tɛrɪtɪ] *n* destreza

dexterous, dextrous ['dɛkstrəs] *adj* (*skilful*) diestro, hábil; (*movement*) ágil
DfEE *n abbr* (*Brit*) = **Department for Education and Employment**
dg *abbr* (= *decigram*) dg
diabetes [daɪə'bi:ti:z] *n* diabetes *f*
diabetic [daɪə'bɛtɪk] *n* diabético(-a) ■ *adj* diabético; (*chocolate, jam*) para diabéticos
diabolical [daɪə'bɔlɪkəl] *adj* diabólico; (*col: dreadful*) horrendo, horroroso
diagnose ['daɪəgnəuz] *vt* diagnosticar
diagnosis (*pl* **diagnoses**) [daɪəg'nəusɪs, -si:z] *n* diagnóstico
diagonal [daɪ'ægənl] *adj* diagonal ■ *n* diagonal *f*
diagram ['daɪəgræm] *n* diagrama *m*, esquema *m*
dial ['daɪəl] *n* esfera; (*of radio*) dial *m*; (*tuner*) sintonizador *m*; (*of phone*) disco ■ *vt* (*number*) marcar, discar (*LAm*); **to ~ a wrong number** equivocarse de número; **can I ~ London direct?** ¿puedo marcar un número de Londres directamente?
dial. *abbr* = **dialect**
dial code *n* (*US*) prefijo
dialect ['daɪəlɛkt] *n* dialecto
dialling code ['daɪəlɪŋ-] *n* (*Brit*) prefijo
dialling tone *n* (*Brit*) señal *f or* tono de marcar
dialogue, (*US*) **dialog** ['daɪəlɔg] *n* diálogo
dial tone *n* (*US*) señal *f or* tono de marcar
dialysis [daɪ'ælɪsɪs] *n* diálisis *f*
diameter [daɪ'æmɪtə^r] *n* diámetro
diametrically [daɪə'mɛtrɪklɪ] *adv*: **~ opposed (to)** diametralmente opuesto (a)
diamond ['daɪəmənd] *n* diamante *m*; **diamonds** *npl* (*Cards*) diamantes *mpl*
diamond ring *n* anillo *or* sortija de diamantes
diaper ['daɪəpə^r] *n* (*US*) pañal *m*
diaphragm ['daɪəfræm] *n* diafragma *m*
diarrhoea, diarrhea (*US*) [daɪə'ri:ə] *n* diarrea
diary ['daɪərɪ] *n* (*daily account*) diario; (*book*) agenda; **to keep a ~** escribir un diario
diatribe ['daɪətraɪb] *n*: **~ (against)** diatriba (contra)
dice [daɪs] *n pl inv* dados *mpl* ■ *vt* (*Culin*) cortar en cuadritos
dicey ['daɪsɪ] *adj* (*col*): **it's a bit ~** (*risky*) es un poco arriesgado; (*doubtful*) es un poco dudoso
dichotomy [daɪ'kɔtəmɪ] *n* dicotomía
dickhead ['dɪkhɛd] *n* (*Brit col!*) gilipollas *m inv*
Dictaphone® ['dɪktəfəun] *n* dictáfono®
dictate [dɪk'teɪt] *vt* dictar ■ *n* ['dɪkteɪt] dictado
▶ **dictate to** *vt fus* (*person*) dar órdenes a;

I won't be dictated to no recibo órdenes de nadie

dictation [dɪk'teɪʃən] n (to secretary etc) dictado; **at ~ speed** para tomar al dictado

dictator [dɪk'teɪtə'] n dictador m

dictatorship [dɪk'teɪtəʃɪp] n dictadura

diction ['dɪkʃən] n dicción f

dictionary ['dɪkʃənrɪ] n diccionario

did [dɪd] pt of **do**

didactic [daɪ'dæktɪk] adj didáctico

diddle ['dɪdl] vt estafar, timar

didn't ['dɪdənt] = **did not**

die [daɪ] vi morir; **to ~ (of or from)** morirse (de); **to be dying** morirse, estar muriéndose; **to be dying for sth/to do sth** morirse por algo/de ganas de hacer algo
  ▶ **die away** vi (sound, light) desvanecerse
  ▶ **die down** vi (gen) apagarse; (wind) amainar
  ▶ **die out** vi desaparecer, extinguirse

diehard ['daɪhɑ:d] n intransigente m/f

diesel ['di:zl] n diesel m

diesel engine n motor m diesel

diesel fuel, diesel oil n gas-oil m

diet ['daɪət] n dieta; (restricted food) régimen m ■ vi (also: **be on a diet**) estar a dieta, hacer régimen; **to live on a ~ of** alimentarse de

dietician [daɪə'tɪʃən] n dietista m/f

differ ['dɪfə'] vi (be different) ser distinto, diferenciarse; (disagree) discrepar

difference ['dɪfrəns] n diferencia; (quarrel) desacuerdo; **it makes no ~ to me** me da igual or lo mismo; **to settle one's differences** arreglarse

different ['dɪfrənt] adj diferente, distinto

differential [dɪfə'renʃəl] n diferencial f

differentiate [dɪfə'renʃɪeɪt] vt distinguir ■ vi diferenciarse; **to ~ between** distinguir entre

differently ['dɪfrəntlɪ] adv de otro modo, en forma distinta

difficult ['dɪfɪkəlt] adj difícil; **~ to understand** difícil de entender

difficulty ['dɪfɪkəltɪ] n dificultad f; **to have difficulties with** (police, landlord etc) tener problemas con; **to be in ~** estar en apuros

diffidence ['dɪfɪdəns] n timidez f, falta de confianza en sí mismo

diffident ['dɪfɪdənt] adj tímido

diffuse [dɪ'fju:s] adj difuso ■ vt [dɪ'fju:z] difundir

dig [dɪg] vt (pt, pp **dug**) [dʌg] (hole) cavar; (ground) remover; (coal) extraer; (nails etc) clavar ■ n (prod) empujón m; (archaeological) excavación f; (remark) indirecta; **to ~ into** (savings) consumir; **to ~ into one's pockets for sth** hurgar en el bolsillo buscando algo; **to ~ one's nails into** clavar las uñas en; see also **digs**

▶ **dig in** vi (also: **dig o.s. in**: Mil) atrincherarse; (col: eat) hincar los dientes ■ vt (compost) añadir al suelo; (knife, claw) clavar; **to ~ in one's heels** (fig) mantenerse en sus trece

▶ **dig out** vt (hole) excavar; (survivors, car from snow) sacar

▶ **dig up** vt desenterrar; (plant) desarraigar

digest [daɪ'dʒest] vt (food) digerir; (facts) asimilar ■ n ['daɪdʒest] resumen m

digestible [daɪ'dʒestəbl] adj digerible

digestion [dɪ'dʒestʃən] n digestión f

digestive [daɪ'dʒestɪv] adj (juices, system) digestivo

digit ['dɪdʒɪt] n (number) dígito; (finger) dedo

digital ['dɪdʒɪtl] adj digital

digital camera n cámara digital

digital compact cassette n cas(s)et(t)e m or f digital compacto

digital TV n televisión f digital

dignified ['dɪgnɪfaɪd] adj grave, solemne; (action) decoroso

dignify ['dɪgnɪfaɪ] vt dignificar

dignitary ['dɪgnɪtərɪ] n dignatario(-a)

dignity ['dɪgnɪtɪ] n dignidad f

digress [daɪ'gres] vi: **to ~ from** apartarse de

digression [daɪ'greʃən] n digresión f

digs [dɪgz] npl (Brit: col) pensión f, alojamiento

dike [daɪk] n = **dyke**

dilapidated [dɪ'læpɪdeɪtɪd] adj desmoronado, ruinoso

dilate [daɪ'leɪt] vt dilatar ■ vi dilatarse

dilatory ['dɪlətərɪ] adj (person) lento; (action) dilatorio

dilemma [daɪ'lemə] n dilema m; **to be in a ~** estar en un dilema

dilettante [dɪlɪ'tæntɪ] n diletante m/f

diligence ['dɪlɪdʒəns] n diligencia

diligent ['dɪlɪdʒənt] adj diligente

dill [dɪl] n eneldo

dilly-dally ['dɪlɪ'dælɪ] vi (hesitate) vacilar; (dawdle) entretenerse

dilute [daɪ'lu:t] vt diluir

dim [dɪm] adj (light) débil; (sight) turbio; (outline) borroso; (stupid) lerdo; (room) oscuro ■ vt (light) bajar; **to take a ~ view of sth** tener una pobre opinión de algo

dime [daɪm] n (US) moneda de diez centavos

dimension [dɪ'menʃən] n dimensión f

-dimensional [dɪ'menʃənl] adj suff: **two-** de dos dimensiones

dimensions [dɪ'menʃənz] npl dimensiones fpl

diminish [dɪ'mɪnɪʃ] vt, vi disminuir

diminished [dɪ'mɪnɪʃt] adj: **~ responsibility** (Law) responsabilidad f disminuida

diminutive [dɪ'mɪnjutɪv] adj diminuto ■ n (Ling) diminutivo

515

dimly ['dɪmlɪ] *adv* débilmente; (*not clearly*) vagamente

dimmer ['dɪməʳ] *n* (*also*: **dimmer switch**) regulador *m* (de intensidad); (*US Aut*) interruptor *m*

dimple ['dɪmpl] *n* hoyuelo

dimwitted ['dɪm'wɪtɪd] *adj* (*col*) lerdo, de pocas luces

din [dɪn] *n* estruendo, estrépito ▪ *vt*: **to ~ sth into sb** (*col*) meter algo en la cabeza a algn

dine [daɪn] *vi* cenar

diner ['daɪnəʳ] *n* (*person: in restaurant*) comensal *m/f*; (*Brit Rail*) = **dining car**; (*US*) restaurante económico

dinghy ['dɪŋgɪ] *n* bote *m*; (*also*: **rubber dinghy**) lancha (neumática)

dingy ['dɪndʒɪ] *adj* (*room*) sombrío; (*dirty*) sucio; (*dull*) deslucido

dining car ['daɪnɪŋ-] *n* (*Brit*) coche-restaurante *m*

dining room ['daɪnɪŋ-] *n* comedor *m*

dinner ['dɪnəʳ] *n* (*evening meal*) cena, comida (*LAm*); (*lunch*) comida; (*public*) cena, banquete *m*; **~'s ready!** ¡la cena está servida!

dinner jacket *n* smoking *m*

dinner party *n* cena

dinner time *n* hora de cenar *or* comer

dinosaur ['daɪnəsɔːʳ] *n* dinosaurio

dint [dɪnt] *n*: **by ~ of (doing) sth** a fuerza de (hacer) algo

diocese ['daɪəsɪs] *n* diócesis *f*

dioxide [daɪ'ɔksaɪd] *n* bióxido; **carbon ~** bióxido de carbono

Dip. *abbr* (*Brit*) = **diploma**

dip [dɪp] *n* (*slope*) pendiente *f*; (*in sea*) chapuzón *m* ▪ *vt* (*in water*) mojar; (*ladle etc*) meter; (*Brit Aut*): **to ~ one's lights** poner la luz de cruce ▪ *vi* inclinarse hacia abajo

diphtheria [dɪf'θɪərɪə] *n* difteria

diphthong ['dɪfθɔŋ] *n* diptongo

diploma [dɪ'pləumə] *n* diploma *m*

diplomacy [dɪ'pləuməsɪ] *n* diplomacia

diplomat ['dɪpləmæt] *n* diplomático(-a) *m(f)*

diplomatic [dɪplə'mætɪk] *adj* diplomático; **to break off ~ relations** romper las relaciones diplomáticas

diplomatic corps *n* cuerpo diplomático

diplomatic immunity *n* inmunidad *f* diplomática

dipstick ['dɪpstɪk] *n* (*Aut*) varilla de nivel (del aceite)

dipswitch ['dɪpswɪtʃ] *n* (*Brit Aut*) interruptor *m*

dire [daɪəʳ] *adj* calamitoso

direct [daɪ'rɛkt] *adj* (*gen*) directo; (*manner, person*) franco ▪ *vt* dirigir; **can you ~ me to ...?** ¿puede indicarme dónde está ...?; **to ~ sb**

to do sth mandar a algn hacer algo

direct cost *n* costo directo

direct current *n* corriente *f* continua

direct debit *n* domiciliación *f* bancaria de recibos; **to pay by ~** domiciliar el pago

direct dialling *n* servicio automático de llamadas

direction [dɪ'rɛkʃən] *n* dirección *f*; **sense of ~** sentido de la orientación; **directions** *npl* (*advice*) órdenes *fpl*, instrucciones *fpl*; (*to a place*) señas *fpl*; **in the ~ of** hacia, en dirección a; **directions for use** modo de empleo; **to ask for directions** preguntar el camino

directional [dɪ'rɛkʃənl] *adj* direccional

directive [daɪ'rɛktɪv] *n* orden *f*, instrucción *f*; **a government ~** una orden del gobierno

direct labour *n* mano *f* de obra directa

directly [dɪ'rɛktlɪ] *adv* (*in straight line*) directamente; (*at once*) en seguida

direct mail *n* correspondencia personalizada

direct mailshot *n* (*Brit*) promoción *f* por correspondencia personalizada

directness [dɪ'rɛktnɪs] *n* (*of person, speech*) franqueza

director [dɪ'rɛktəʳ] *n* director(a) *m(f)*; **managing ~** director(a) *m(f)* gerente

Director of Public Prosecutions *n* ≈ fiscal *m/f* general del Estado

directory [dɪ'rɛktərɪ] *n* (*Tel*) guía (telefónica); (*street directory*) callejero; (*trade directory*) directorio de comercio; (*Comput*) directorio

directory enquiries, (*US*) **directory assistance** *n* (*service*) (servicio *m* de) información

dirt [dəːt] *n* suciedad *f*

dirt-cheap ['dəːt'tʃiːp] *adj* baratísimo

dirt road *n* (*US*) camino sin firme

dirty ['dəːtɪ] *adj* sucio; (*joke*) verde, colorado (*LAm*) ▪ *vt* ensuciar; (*stain*) manchar

dirty trick *n* mala jugada, truco sucio

disability [dɪsə'bɪlɪtɪ] *n* incapacidad *f*

disability allowance *n* pensión *f* de invalidez

disable [dɪs'eɪbl] *vt* (*illness, accident*) dejar incapacitado *or* inválido; (*tank, gun*) inutilizar; (*Law: disqualify*) incapacitar

disabled [dɪs'eɪbld] *adj* minusválido

disabuse [dɪsə'bjuːz] *vt* desengañar

disadvantage [dɪsəd'vɑːntɪdʒ] *n* desventaja, inconveniente *m*

disadvantaged [dɪsəd'vɑːntɪdʒd] *adj* (*person*) desventajado

disadvantageous [dɪsædvən'teɪdʒəs] *adj* desventajoso

disaffected [dɪsə'fɛktɪd] *adj* descontento; **to be ~ (to *or* towards)** estar descontento (de)

disaffection [dɪsə'fɛkʃən] n desafecto, descontento

disagree [dɪsə'griː] vi (differ) discrepar; **to ~ (with)** no estar de acuerdo (con); **I ~ with you** no estoy de acuerdo contigo

disagreeable [dɪsə'grɪəbl] adj desagradable

disagreement [dɪsə'griːmənt] n (gen) desacuerdo; (quarrel) riña; **to have a ~ with sb** estar en desacuerdo con algn

disallow ['dɪsə'lau] vt (goal) anular; (claim) rechazar

disappear [dɪsə'pɪər] vi desaparecer

disappearance [dɪsə'pɪərəns] n desaparición f

disappoint [dɪsə'pɔɪnt] vt decepcionar; (hopes) defraudar

disappointed [dɪsə'pɔɪntɪd] adj decepcionado

disappointing [dɪsə'pɔɪntɪŋ] adj decepcionante

disappointment [dɪsə'pɔɪntmənt] n decepción f

disapproval [dɪsə'pruːvəl] n desaprobación f

disapprove [dɪsə'pruːv] vi: **to ~ of** desaprobar

disapproving [dɪsə'pruːvɪŋ] adj de desaprobación, desaprobador(a)

disarm [dɪs'ɑːm] vt desarmar

disarmament [dɪs'ɑːməmənt] n desarme m

disarmament talks npl conversaciones fpl de or sobre desarme

disarming [dɪs'ɑːmɪŋ] adj (smile) que desarma, encantador(a)

disarray [dɪsə'reɪ] n: **in ~** (troops) desorganizado; (thoughts) confuso; (hair, clothes) desarreglado; **to throw into ~** provocar el caos

disaster [dɪ'zɑːstər] n desastre m

disaster area n zona catastrófica

disastrous [dɪ'zɑːstrəs] adj desastroso

disband [dɪs'bænd] vt disolver ■ vi desbandarse

disbelief [dɪsbə'liːf] n incredulidad f; **in ~** con incredulidad

disbelieve ['dɪsbə'liːv] vt (person, story) poner en duda, no creer

disc [dɪsk] n disco; (Comput) = **disk**

disc. abbr (Comm) = **discount**

discard [dɪs'kɑːd] vt tirar; (fig) descartar

discern [dɪ'səːn] vt percibir, discernir; (understand) comprender

discernible [dɪ'səːnəbl] adj perceptible

discerning [dɪ'səːnɪŋ] adj perspicaz

discharge [dɪs'tʃɑːdʒ] vt (task, duty) cumplir; (ship etc) descargar; (patient) dar de alta; (employee) despedir; (soldier) licenciar; (defendant) poner en libertad; (settle: debt) saldar ■ n ['dɪstʃɑːdʒ] (Elec) descarga;

(vaginal discharge) emisión f vaginal; (dismissal) despedida; (of duty) desempeño; (of debt) pago, descargo; (of gas, chemicals) escape m; **discharged bankrupt** quebrado/a rehabilitado/a

disciple [dɪ'saɪpl] n discípulo(-a)

disciplinary ['dɪsɪplɪnərɪ] adj: **to take ~ action against sb** disciplinar a algn

discipline ['dɪsɪplɪn] n disciplina ■ vt disciplinar; **to ~ o.s. to do sth** obligarse a hacer algo

disc jockey, DJ n pinchadiscos m/f inv

disclaim [dɪs'kleɪm] vt negar tener

disclaimer [dɪs'kleɪmər] n rectificación f; **to issue a ~** hacer una rectificación

disclose [dɪs'kləuz] vt revelar

disclosure [dɪs'kləuʒər] n revelación f

Discman ® ['dɪskmən] n Discman® m

disco ['dɪskəu] n abbr = **discothèque**

discolouration, discoloration (US) [dɪskʌlə'reɪʃən] n descoloramiento, decoloración f

discoloured, discolored (US) [dɪs'kʌləd] adj descolorido

discomfort [dɪs'kʌmfət] n incomodidad f; (unease) inquietud f; (physical) malestar m

disconcert [dɪskən'səːt] vt desconcertar

disconnect [dɪskə'nɛkt] vt (gen) separar; (Elec etc) desconectar; (supply) cortar (el suministro) a

disconsolate [dɪs'kɔnsəlɪt] adj desconsolado

discontent [dɪskən'tɛnt] n descontento

discontented [dɪskən'tɛntɪd] adj descontento

discontinue [dɪskən'tɪnjuː] vt interrumpir; (payments) suspender

discord ['dɪskɔːd] n discordia; (Mus) disonancia

discordant [dɪs'kɔːdənt] adj disonante

discothèque ['dɪskəutɛk] n discoteca

discount ['dɪskaunt] n descuento ■ vt [dɪs'kaunt] descontar; (report etc) descartar; **at a ~** con descuento; **~ for cash** descuento por pago en efectivo; **to give sb a ~ on sth** hacer un descuento a algn en algo

discount house n (Finance) banco de descuento; (Comm: also: **discount store**) = tienda de saldos

discount rate n (Comm) tipo de descuento

discount store n = tienda de saldos

discourage [dɪs'kʌrɪdʒ] vt desalentar; (oppose) oponerse a; (dissuade, deter) desanimar, disuadir

discouragement [dɪs'kʌrɪdʒmənt] n (dissuasion) disuasión f; (depression) desánimo, desaliento; **to act as a ~ to** servir para disuadir

discouraging [dɪsˈkʌrɪdʒɪŋ] *adj* desalentador(a)
discourteous [dɪsˈkəːtɪəs] *adj* descortés
discover [dɪsˈkʌvəʳ] *vt* descubrir
discovery [dɪsˈkʌvərɪ] *n* descubrimiento
discredit [dɪsˈkrɛdɪt] *vt* desacreditar
discreet [dɪˈskriːt] *adj* (*tactful*) discreto; (*careful*) circunspecto, prudente
discreetly [dɪˈskriːtlɪ] *adv* discretamente
discrepancy [dɪˈskrɛpənsɪ] *n* (*difference*) diferencia; (*disagreement*) discrepancia
discretion [dɪˈskrɛʃən] *n* (*tact*) discreción f; (*care*) prudencia, circunspección f; **use your own ~** haz lo que creas oportuno
discretionary [dɪˈskrɛʃənrɪ] *adj* (*powers*) discrecional
discriminate [dɪˈskrɪmɪneɪt] *vi*: **to ~ between** distinguir entre; **to ~ against** discriminar contra
discriminating [dɪˈskrɪmɪneɪtɪŋ] *adj* entendido
discrimination [dɪskrɪmɪˈneɪʃə n] *n* (*discernment*) perspicacia; (*bias*) discriminación f; **racial/sexual ~** discriminación racial/sexual
discus [ˈdɪskəs] *n* disco
discuss [dɪˈskʌs] *vt* (*gen*) discutir; (*a theme*) tratar
discussion [dɪˈskʌʃən] *n* discusión f; **under ~** en discusión
disdain [dɪsˈdeɪn] *n* desdén m ■ *vt* desdeñar
disease [dɪˈziːz] *n* enfermedad f
diseased [dɪˈziːzd] *adj* enfermo
disembark [dɪsɪmˈbaːk] *vt*, *vi* desembarcar
disembarkation [dɪsɛmbaːˈkeɪʃən] *n* desembarque m
disenchanted [dɪsɪnˈtʃaːntɪd] *adj*: **~ (with)** desilusionado (con)
disenfranchise [ˈdɪsɪnˈfræntʃaɪz] *vt* privar del derecho al voto; (*Comm*) privar de franquicias
disengage [dɪsɪnˈgeɪdʒ] *vt* soltar; **to ~ the clutch** (*Aut*) desembragar
disentangle [dɪsɪnˈtæŋgl] *vt* desenredar
disfavour, disfavor (US) [dɪsˈfeɪvəʳ] *n* desaprobación f
disfigure [dɪsˈfɪgəʳ] *vt* desfigurar
disgorge [dɪsˈgɔːdʒ] *vt* verter
disgrace [dɪsˈgreɪs] *n* ignominia; (*downfall*) caída; (*shame*) vergüenza, escándalo ■ *vt* deshonrar
disgraceful [dɪsˈgreɪsful] *adj* vergonzoso; (*behaviour*) escandaloso
disgruntled [dɪsˈgrʌntld] *adj* disgustado, descontento
disguise [dɪsˈgaɪz] *n* disfraz m ■ *vt* disfrazar; (*voice*) disimular; (*feelings etc*) ocultar; **in**
~ disfrazado; to ~ o.s. as disfrazarse de; **there's no disguising the fact that ...** no puede ocultarse el hecho de que ...
disgust [dɪsˈgʌst] *n* repugnancia ■ *vt* repugnar, dar asco a
disgusting [dɪsˈgʌstɪŋ] *adj* repugnante, asqueroso
dish [dɪʃ] *n* (*gen*) plato; **to do** *or* **wash the dishes** fregar los platos
  ▶ **dish out** *vt* (*money, exam papers*) repartir; (*food*) servir; (*advice*) dar
  ▶ **dish up** *vt* servir
dishcloth [ˈdɪʃklɔθ] *n* paño de cocina, bayeta
dishearten [dɪsˈhaːtn] *vt* desalentar
dishevelled, disheveled (US) [dɪˈʃɛvəld] *adj* (*hair*) despeinado; (*clothes, appearance*) desarreglado
dishonest [dɪsˈɔnɪst] *adj* (*person*) poco honrado, tramposo; (*means*) fraudulento
dishonesty [dɪsˈɔnɪstɪ] *n* falta de honradez
dishonour, dishonor (US) [dɪsˈɔnəʳ] *n* deshonra
dishonourable, dishonorable (US) [dɪsˈɔnə rəbl] *adj* deshonroso
dish soap *n* (US) lavavajillas m inv
dishtowel [ˈdɪʃtauəl] *n* (US) trapo de fregar
dishwasher [ˈdɪʃwɔʃəʳ] *n* lavaplatos m inv; (*person*) friegaplatos m/f inv
dishy [ˈdɪʃɪ] *adj* (Brit col) buenón(-ona)
disillusion [dɪsɪˈluːʒən] *vt* desilusionar; **to become disillusioned (with)** quedar desilusionado (con)
disillusionment [dɪsɪˈluːʒənmənt] *n* desilusión f
disincentive [dɪsɪnˈsɛntɪv] *n* freno; **to act as a ~ (to)** actuar de freno (a); **to be a ~ to** ser un freno a
disinclined [ˈdɪsɪnˈklaɪnd] *adj*: **to be ~ to do sth** estar poco dispuesto a hacer algo
disinfect [dɪsɪnˈfɛkt] *vt* desinfectar
disinfectant [dɪsɪnˈfɛktənt] *n* desinfectante m
disinflation [dɪsɪnˈfleɪʃən] *n* desinflación f
disinformation [dɪsɪnfəˈmeɪʃən] *n* desinformación f
disingenuous [dɪsɪnˈdʒɛnjuəs] *adj* poco sincero, falso
disinherit [dɪsɪnˈhɛrɪt] *vt* desheredar
disintegrate [dɪsˈɪntɪgreɪt] *vi* disgregarse, desintegrarse
disinterested [dɪsˈɪntrəstɪd] *adj* desinteresado
disjointed [dɪsˈdʒɔɪntɪd] *adj* inconexo
disk [dɪsk] *n* (*Comput*) disco, disquete m; **single-/double-sided ~** disco de una cara/dos caras
disk drive *n* unidad f (de disco)

diskette [dɪs'kɛt] n diskette m, disquete m, disco flexible

disk operating system n sistema m operativo de discos

dislike [dɪs'laɪk] n antipatía, aversión f ■ vt tener antipatía a; **to take a ~ to sb/sth** cogerle or (LAm) agarrarle antipatía a algn/ algo; **I ~ the idea** no me gusta la idea

dislocate ['dɪsləkeɪt] vt dislocar; **he dislocated his shoulder** se dislocó el hombro

dislodge [dɪs'lɔdʒ] vt sacar; (enemy) desalojar

disloyal [dɪs'lɔɪəl] adj desleal

dismal ['dɪzml] adj (dark) sombrío; (depressing) triste; (very bad) fatal

dismantle [dɪs'mæntl] vt desmontar, desarmar

dismay [dɪs'meɪ] n consternación f ■ vt consternar; **much to my ~** para gran consternación mía

dismiss [dɪs'mɪs] vt (worker) despedir; (official) destituir; (idea) rechazar; (Law) rechazar; (possibility) descartar ■ vi (Mil) romper filas

dismissal [dɪs'mɪsl] n despedida; destitución f

dismount [dɪs'maʊnt] vi apearse; (rider) desmontar

disobedience [dɪsə'bi:dɪəns] n desobediencia

disobedient [dɪsə'bi:dɪənt] adj desobediente

disobey [dɪsə'beɪ] vt desobedecer; (rule) infringir

disorder [dɪs'ɔ:dəʳ] n desorden m; (rioting) disturbio; (Med) trastorno; (disease) enfermedad f; **civil ~** desorden m civil

disorderly [dɪs'ɔ:dəlɪ] adj (untidy) desordenado; (meeting) alborotado; **~ conduct** (Law) conducta escandalosa

disorganized [dɪs'ɔ:gənaɪzd] adj desorganizado

disorientated [dɪs'ɔ:rɪenteɪtəd] adj desorientado

disown [dɪs'əʊn] vt renegar de

disparaging [dɪs'pærɪdʒɪŋ] adj despreciativo; **to be ~ about sth/sb** menospreciar algo/a algn

disparate ['dɪspərɪt] adj dispar

disparity [dɪs'pærɪtɪ] n disparidad f

dispassionate [dɪs'pæʃənɪt] adj (unbiased) imparcial; (unemotional) desapasionado

dispatch [dɪs'pætʃ] vt enviar; (kill) despachar; (deal with: business) despachar ■ n (sending) envío; (speed) prontitud f; (Press) informe m; (Mil) parte m

dispatch department n (Comm) departamento de envíos

dispatch rider n (Mil) correo

dispel [dɪs'pɛl] vt disipar, dispersar

dispensary [dɪs'pɛnsərɪ] n dispensario

dispensation [dɪspɛn'seɪʃən] n (Rel) dispensa

dispense [dɪs'pɛns] vt dispensar, repartir; (medicine) preparar
  ▶ **dispense with** vt fus (make unnecessary) prescindir de

dispenser [dɪs'pɛnsəʳ] n (container) distribuidor m automático

dispensing chemist [dɪs'pɛnsɪŋ-] n (Brit) farmacia

dispersal [dɪs'pə:sl] n dispersión f

disperse [dɪs'pə:s] vt dispersar ■ vi dispersarse

dispirited [dɪ'spɪrɪtɪd] adj desanimado, desalentado

displace [dɪs'pleɪs] vt (person) desplazar; (replace) reemplazar

displaced person n (Pol) desplazado(-a)

displacement [dɪs'pleɪsmənt] n cambio de sitio

display [dɪs'pleɪ] n (exhibition) exposición f; (Comput) visualización f; (Mil) desfile m; (of feeling) manifestación f; (pej) aparato, pompa ■ vt exponer; manifestar; (ostentatiously) lucir; **on ~** (exhibits) expuesto, exhibido; (goods) en el escaparate

display advertising n publicidad f gráfica

displease [dɪs'pli:z] vt (offend) ofender; (annoy) fastidiar; **displeased with** disgustado con

displeasure [dɪs'plɛʒəʳ] n disgusto

disposable [dɪs'pəuzəbl] adj (not reusable) desechable; **~ personal income** ingresos mpl personales disponibles

disposable nappy n pañal m desechable

disposal [dɪs'pəuzl] n (sale) venta; (of house) traspaso; (by giving away) donación f; (arrangement) colocación f; (of rubbish) destrucción f; **at one's ~** a la disposición de algn; **to put sth at sb's ~** poner algo a disposición de algn

disposed [dɪs'pəuzd] adj: **~ to do** dispuesto a hacer

dispose of [dɪs'pəuz] vt fus (time, money) disponer de; (unwanted goods) deshacerse de; (Comm: sell) traspasar, vender; (throw away) tirar

disposition [dɪspə'zɪʃən] n disposición f; (temperament) carácter m

dispossess ['dɪspə'zɛs] vt: **to ~ sb (of)** desposeer a algn (de)

disproportion [dɪsprə'pɔ:ʃən] n desproporción f

disproportionate [dɪsprə'pɔ:ʃənət] adj desproporcionado

disprove [dɪs'pru:v] vt refutar

d

519

dispute [dɪsˈpjuːt] n disputa; (verbal) discusión f; (also: **industrial dispute**) conflicto (laboral) ■ vt (argue) disputar; (question) cuestionar; **to be in** or **under ~** (matter) discutirse; (territory) estar en disputa; (Jur) estar en litigio

disqualification [dɪskwɔlɪfɪˈkeɪʃən] n inhabilitación f; (Sport) descalificación f; (from driving) descalificación f

disqualify [dɪsˈkwɔlɪfaɪ] vt (Sport) desclasificar; **to ~ sb for sth/from doing sth** incapacitar a algn para algo/para hacer algo

disquiet [dɪsˈkwaɪət] n preocupación f, inquietud f

disquieting [dɪsˈkwaɪətɪŋ] adj inquietante

disregard [dɪsrɪˈgɑːd] vt desatender; (ignore) no hacer caso de ■ n (indifference: to feelings, danger, money): **~ (for)** indiferencia (a); **~ (of)** (non-observance: of law, rules) violación f (de)

disrepair [dɪsrɪˈpɛəʳ] n: **to fall into ~** (building) desmoronarse; (street) deteriorarse

disreputable [dɪsˈrɛpjutəbl] adj (person, area) de mala fama; (behaviour) vergonzoso

disrepute [ˈdɪsrɪˈpjuːt] n descrédito, ignominia; **to bring into ~** desacreditar

disrespectful [dɪsrɪˈspɛktful] adj irrespetuoso

disrupt [dɪsˈrʌpt] vt (meeting, public transport, conversation) interrumpir; (plans) desbaratar, alternar, trastornar

disruption [dɪsˈrʌpʃən] n trastorno; desbaratamiento; interrupción f

disruptive [dɪsˈrʌptɪv] adj (influence) disruptivo; (strike action) perjudicial

dissatisfaction [dɪssætɪsˈfækʃən] n disgusto, descontento

dissatisfied [dɪsˈsætɪsfaɪd] adj insatisfecho

dissect [dɪˈsɛkt] vt (also fig) disecar

disseminate [dɪˈsɛmɪneɪt] vt divulgar, difundir

dissent [dɪˈsɛnt] n disensión f

dissenter [dɪˈsɛntəʳ] n (Rel, Pol etc) disidente m/f

dissertation [dɪsəˈteɪʃən] n (Univ) tesina; see also **master's degree**

disservice [dɪsˈsəːvɪs] n: **to do sb a ~** perjudicar a algn

dissident [ˈdɪsɪdnt] adj, n disidente m/f

dissimilar [dɪˈsɪmɪləʳ] adj distinto

dissipate [ˈdɪsɪpeɪt] vt disipar; (waste) desperdiciar

dissipated [ˈdɪsɪpeɪtɪd] adj disoluto

dissipation [dɪsɪˈpeɪʃən] n disipación f (moral), libertinaje m, vicio; (waste) derroche m

dissociate [dɪˈsəʊʃɪeɪt] vt disociar; **to ~ o.s. from** disociarse de

dissolute [ˈdɪsəluːt] adj disoluto

dissolution [dɪsəˈluːʃən] n disolución f

dissolve [dɪˈzɔlv] vt disolver ■ vi disolverse

dissuade [dɪˈsweɪd] vt: **to ~ sb (from)** disuadir a algn (de)

distaff [ˈdɪstæf] n: **~ side** rama femenina

distance [ˈdɪstns] n distancia; **in the ~** a lo lejos; **what ~ is it to London?** ¿qué distancia hay de aquí a Londres?; **it's within walking ~** se puede ir andando

distant [ˈdɪstnt] adj lejano; (manner) reservado, frío

distaste [dɪsˈteɪst] n repugnancia

distasteful [dɪsˈteɪstful] adj repugnante, desagradable

Dist. Atty. abbr (US) = **district attorney**

distemper [dɪsˈtɛmpəʳ] n (of dogs) moquillo

distend [dɪˈstɛnd] vt dilatar, hinchar ■ vi dilatarse, hincharse

distended [dɪˈstɛndɪd] adj (stomach) hinchado

distil, distill (US) [dɪsˈtɪl] vt destilar

distillery [dɪsˈtɪlərɪ] n destilería

distinct [dɪsˈtɪŋkt] adj (different) distinto; (clear) claro; (unmistakeable) inequívoco; **as ~ from** a diferencia de

distinction [dɪsˈtɪŋkʃən] n distinción f; (in exam) sobresaliente m; **a writer of ~** un escritor destacado; **to draw a ~ between** hacer una distinción entre

distinctive [dɪsˈtɪŋktɪv] adj distintivo

distinctly [dɪsˈtɪŋktlɪ] adv claramente

distinguish [dɪsˈtɪŋgwɪʃ] vt distinguir ■ vi: **to ~ (between)** distinguir (entre)

distinguished [dɪsˈtɪŋgwɪʃt] adj (eminent) distinguido; (career) eminente; (refined) distinguido, de categoría

distinguishing [dɪsˈtɪŋgwɪʃɪŋ] adj (feature) distintivo

distort [dɪsˈtɔːt] vt torcer, retorcer; (account, news) desvirtuar, deformar

distortion [dɪsˈtɔːʃən] n deformación f; (of sound) distorsión f; (of truth etc) tergiversación f; (of facts) falseamiento

distract [dɪsˈtrækt] vt distraer

distracted [dɪsˈtræktɪd] adj distraído

distracting [dɪsˈtræktɪŋ] adj que distrae la atención, molesto

distraction [dɪsˈtrækʃən] n distracción f; (confusion) aturdimiento; (amusement) diversión f; **to drive sb to ~** (distress, anxiety) volver loco a algn

distraught [dɪsˈtrɔːt] adj turbado, enloquecido

distress [dɪsˈtrɛs] n (anguish) angustia; (want) miseria; (pain) dolor m; (danger) peligro ■ vt afligir; (*pain*) doler; **in ~** (*ship etc*) en peligro

distressing [dɪs'trɛsɪŋ] *adj* angustioso; doloroso

distress signal *n* señal *f* de socorro

distribute [dɪs'trɪbjuːt] *vt* (*gen*) distribuir; (*share out*) repartir

distribution [dɪstrɪ'bjuːʃən] *n* distribución *f*

distribution cost *n* gastos *mpl* de distribución

distributor [dɪs'trɪbjutəʳ] *n* (*Aut*) distribuidor *m*; (*Comm*) distribuidora

district ['dɪstrɪkt] *n* (*of country*) zona, región *f*; (*of town*) barrio; (*Admin*) distrito

district attorney *n* (*US*) fiscal *m/f*

district council *n* ~ municipio; *ver nota*

● **DISTRICT COUNCIL**
●
● En Inglaterra y Gales, con la excepción
● de Londres, la administración local corre
● a cargo del *district council*, responsable de
● los servicios municipales como vivienda,
● urbanismo, recolección de basuras, salud
● medioambiental etc. La mayoría de sus
● miembros son elegidos a nivel local
● cada cuatro años. Hay un total de 369
● "districts" (distritos), repartidos en 53
● "counties" (condados), que se financian
● a través de los impuestos municipales
● y partidas presupuestarias del Estado.
● Éste controla sus gastos a través de una
● comisión independiente.

district manager *n* representante *m/f* regional

district nurse *n* (*Brit*) enfermera que atiende a pacientes a domicilio

distrust [dɪs'trʌst] *n* desconfianza ▪ *vt* desconfiar de

distrustful [dɪs'trʌstful] *adj* desconfiado

disturb [dɪs'təːb] *vt* (*person: bother, interrupt*) molestar; (*meeting*) interrumpir; (*disorganize*) desordenar; **sorry to ~ you** perdone la molestia

disturbance [dɪs'təːbəns] *n* (*political etc*) disturbio; (*violence*) alboroto; (*of mind*) trastorno; **to cause a ~** causar alboroto, **~ of the peace** alteración *f* del orden público

disturbed [dɪs'təːbd] *adj* (*worried, upset*) preocupado, angustiado; **to be emotionally/mentally ~** tener problemas emocionales/ser un trastornado mental

disturbing [dɪs'təːbɪŋ] *adj* inquietante, perturbador(a)

disuse [dɪs'juːs] *n*: **to fall into ~** caer en desuso

disused [dɪs'juːzd] *adj* abandonado

ditch [dɪtʃ] *n* zanja; (*irrigation ditch*) acequia ▪ *vt* (*col*) deshacerse de

dither ['dɪðəʳ] *vi* vacilar

ditto ['dɪtəu] *adv* ídem, lo mismo

divan [dɪ'væn] *n* diván *m*

divan bed *n* cama turca

dive [daɪv] *n* (*from board*) salto; (*underwater*) buceo; (*of submarine*) inmersión *f*; (*Aviat*) picada ▪ *vi* saltar; bucear; sumergirse; picar

diver ['daɪvəʳ] *n* (*Sport*) saltador(a) *m(f)*; (*underwater*) buzo

diverge [daɪ'vəːdʒ] *vi* divergir

divergent [daɪ'vəːdʒənt] *adj* divergente

diverse [daɪ'vəːs] *adj* diversos(-as), varios(-as)

diversification [daɪvəːsɪfɪ'keɪʃən] *n* diversificación *f*

diversify [daɪ'vəːsɪfaɪ] *vt* diversificar

diversion [daɪ'vɔːʃən] *n* (*Brit Aut*) desviación *f*; (*distraction*) diversión *f*; (*Mil*) diversión *f*

diversionary tactics [daɪ'vəːʃənrɪ-] *npl* tácticas *fpl* de diversión

diversity [daɪ'vəːsɪtɪ] *n* diversidad *f*

divert [daɪ'vɔːt] *vt* (*Brit: train, plane, traffic*) desviar; (*amuse*) divertir

divest [daɪ'vɛst] *vt*: **to ~ sb of sth** despojar a algn de algo

divide [daɪ'vaɪd] *vt* dividir; (*separate*) separar ▪ *vi* dividirse; (*road*) bifurcarse; **to ~ (between, among)** repartir *or* dividir (entre); **40 divided by 5** 40 dividido por 5
▸ **divide out** *vt*: **to ~ out (between, among)** (*sweets, tasks etc*) repartir (entre)

divided [dɪ'vaɪdɪd] *adj* (*country, couple*) dividido, separado; (*opinions*) en desacuerdo

divided highway *n* (*US*) carretera de doble calzada

dividend ['dɪvɪdɛnd] *n* dividendo; (*fig*) beneficio

dividend cover *n* cobertura de dividendo

dividers [dɪ'vaɪdəz] *npl* compás *msg* de puntas

divine [dɪ'vaɪn] *adj* divino ▪ *vt* (*future*) vaticinar; (*truth*) alumbrar; (*water, metal*) descubrir, detectar

diving ['daɪvɪŋ] *n* (*Sport*) salto; (*underwater*) buceo

diving board *n* trampolín *m*

diving suit *n* escafandra

divinity [dɪ'vɪnɪtɪ] *n* divinidad *f*; (*Scol*) teología

divisible [dɪ'vɪzɪbl] *adj* divisible

division [dɪ'vɪʒən] *n* (*also Brit Football*) división *f*; (*sharing out*) repartimiento; (*Brit Pol*) votación *f*; **~ of labour** división *f* del trabajo

divisive [dɪ'vaɪsɪv] *adj* divisivo

divorce [dɪ'vɔːs] *n* divorcio ▪ *vt* divorciarse de

divorced [dɪ'vɔːst] *adj* divorciado

d

divorcee [dɪvɔːˈsiː] n divorciado(-a)
divot [ˈdɪvət] n (Golf) chuleta
divulge [daɪˈvʌldʒ] vt divulgar, revelar
D.I.Y. adj, n abbr (Brit) = **do-it-yourself**
dizziness [ˈdɪzɪnɪs] n vértigo
dizzy [ˈdɪzɪ] adj (person) mareado; (height)
vertiginoso; **to feel ~** marearse; **I feel ~**
estoy mareado
DJ n abbr see **disc jockey**
dj n abbr = **dinner jacket**
Djakarta [dʒəˈkɑːtə] n Yakarta
DJIA n abbr (US Stock Exchange) = **Dow-Jones
Industrial Average**
dl abbr (= decilitre(s)) dl
DLit, DLitt abbr (= Doctor of Literature, Doctor of
Letters) título universitario
dm abbr (= decimetre(s)) dm
DMus abbr (= Doctor of Music) título universitario
DMZ n abbr (= demilitarized zone) zona
desmilitarizada
DNA n abbr (= deoxyribonucleic acid) ADN m
DNA test n prueba f del ADN

 KEYWORD

do [duː] (pt **did**, pp **done**) n **1** (col: party etc):
we're having a little do on Saturday
damos una fiestecita el sábado; **it was
rather a grand do** fue un acontecimiento a
lo grande
2: **the dos and don'ts** lo que se debe y no se
debe hacer
■ aux vb **1** (in negative constructions: not
translated): **I don't understand** no entiendo
2 (to form questions: not translated): **do you
speak English?** ¿habla (usted) inglés?;
didn't you know? ¿no lo sabías?; **what do
you think?** ¿qué opinas?
3 (for emphasis, in polite expressions): **people do
make mistakes sometimes** a veces sí se
cometen errores; **she does seem rather
late** a mí también me parece que se ha
retrasado; **do sit down/help yourself**
siéntate/sírvete por favor; **do take care!** ¡ten
cuidado! ¿eh?; **I DO wish I could ...** ojalá
(que) pudiera ...; **but I DO like it** pero, sí
(que) me gusta
4 (used to avoid repeating vb): **she sings better
than I do** canta mejor que yo; **do you agree?**
— **yes, I do/no, I don't** ¿estás de acuerdo?
— sí (lo estoy)/no (lo estoy); **she lives in
Glasgow — so do I** vive en Glasgow — yo
también; **he didn't like it and neither did
we** no le gustó y a nosotros tampoco; **who
made this mess?** — **I did** ¿quién hizo esta
chapuza? — yo; **he asked me to help him
and I did** me pidió que le ayudara y lo hice

5 (in question tags): **you like him, don't you?**
te gusta, ¿verdad? or ¿no?; **I don't know
him, do I?** creo que no le conozco;
he laughed, didn't he? se rió ¿no?
■ vt **1** (gen): **what are you doing tonight?**
¿qué haces esta noche?; **what can I do for
you?** (in shop) ¿en qué puedo servirle?; **what
does he do for a living?** ¿a qué se dedica?;
I'll do all I can haré todo lo que pueda;
what have you done with my slippers?
¿qué has hecho con mis zapatillas?; **to
do the washing-up/cooking** fregar los
platos/cocinar; **to do one's teeth/hair/
nails** lavarse los dientes/arreglarse el pelo/
arreglarse las uñas
2 (Aut etc): **the car was doing 100** el coche
iba a 100; **we've done 200 km already** ya
hemos hecho 200 km; **he can do 100 in that
car** puede ir a 100 en ese coche
3 (visit: city, museum) visitar, recorrer
4 (cook): **a steak – well done please** un filete
bien hecho, por favor
■ vi **1** (act, behave) hacer; **do as I do** haz
como yo
2 (get on, fare): **he's doing well/badly at
school** va bien/mal en la escuela; **the firm
is doing well** la empresa anda or va bien;
how do you do? mucho gusto; (less formal)
¿qué tal?
3 (suit): **will it do?** ¿sirve?, ¿está or va bien?;
it doesn't do to upset her cuidado en
ofenderla
4 (be sufficient) bastar; **will £10 do?** ¿será
bastante con £10?; **that'll do** así está bien;
that'll do! (in annoyance) ¡ya está bien!, ¡basta
ya!; **to make do (with)** arreglárselas (con)
▸ **do away with** vt fus (kill) eliminar;
(eradicate: disease) eliminar; (abolish: law etc)
abolir; (withdraw) retirar
▸ **do out of** vt fus: **to do sb out of sth** pisar
algo a algn
▸ **do up** vt (laces) atar; (zip, dress, shirt)
abrochar; (renovate: room, house) renovar
▸ **do with** vt fus (need): **I could do with a
drink/some help** no me vendría mal un
trago/un poco de ayuda; (be connected with)
tener que ver con; **what has it got to do
with you?** ¿qué tiene que ver contigo?
▸ **do without** vi: **if you're late for dinner
then you'll do without** si llegas tarde
tendrás que quedarte sin cenar
■ vt fus pasar sin; **I can do without a car**
puedo pasar sin coche

do. abbr = **ditto**
DOA abbr = **dead on arrival**
d.o.b. abbr = **date of birth**

doc [dɔk] n (col) médico(-a)
docile ['dəusaɪl] adj dócil
dock [dɔk] n (Naut: wharf) dársena, muelle m; (Law) banquillo (de los acusados); **docks** npl muelles mpl, puerto sg ∎ vi (enter dock) atracar (en el muelle) ∎ vt (pay etc) descontar
dock dues npl derechos mpl de muelle
docker ['dɔkə'] n trabajador m portuario, estibador m
docket ['dɔkɪt] n (on parcel etc) etiqueta
dockyard ['dɔkjɑːd] n astillero
doctor ['dɔktə'] n médico; (Ph.D etc) doctor(a) m(f) ∎ vt (fig) arreglar, falsificar; (drink etc) adulterar
doctorate ['dɔktərɪt] n doctorado; ver nota

⊙ **DOCTORATE**
⊙
⊙
⊙ El grado más alto que conceden las
⊙ universidades es el doctorado (doctorate),
⊙ tras un período de estudio e investigación
⊙ original no inferior a tres años que
⊙ culmina con la presentación de una
⊙ tesis ("thesis") en la que se exponen los
⊙ resultados. El título más frecuente es el
⊙ de "PhD" ("Doctor of Philosophy"), que se
⊙ obtiene en Letras, Ciencias e Ingeniería,
⊙ aunque también existen otros doctorados
⊙ específicos en Música, Derecho etc.

Doctor of Philosophy n Doctor m (en Filosofía y Letras)
doctrinaire [dɔktrɪ'nɛə'] adj doctrinario
doctrine ['dɔktrɪn] n doctrina
docudrama [dɔkju'drɑːmə] n (TV) docudrama m
document ['dɔkjumənt] n documento ∎ vt documentar
documentary [dɔkju'mɛntərɪ] adj documental ∎ n documental m
documentation [dɔkjumɛn'teɪʃən] n documentación f
DOD n abbr (US: = Department of Defense) Ministerio de Defensa
doddering ['dɔdərɪŋ] adj, **doddery** ['dɔdərɪ] ∎ adj vacilante
doddle ['dɔdl] n: **it's a ~** (Brit col) es pan comido
Dodecanese [dəudəkə'niːz], **Dodecanese Islands** npl Dodecaneso sg
dodge [dɔdʒ] n (of body) regate m; (fig) truco ∎ vt (gen) evadir; (blow) esquivar ∎ vi escabullirse; (Sport) hacer una finta; **to ~ out of the way** echarse a un lado; **to ~ through the traffic** esquivar el tráfico
dodgems ['dɔdʒəmz] npl (Brit) autos or coches mpl de choque

dodgy ['dɔdʒɪ] adj (col: uncertain) dudoso; (shady) sospechoso; (risky) arriesgado
DOE n abbr (Brit) = **Department of the Environment**; (US) = **Department of Energy**
doe [dəu] n (deer) cierva, gama; (rabbit) coneja
does [dʌz] vb see **do**
doesn't ['dʌznt] = **does not**
dog [dɔg] n perro ∎ vt seguir (de cerca); (fig: memory etc) perseguir; **to go to the dogs** (person) echarse a perder; (nation etc) ir a la ruina
dog biscuit n galleta de perro
dog collar n collar m de perro; (fig) alzacuello(s) msg
dog-eared ['dɔgɪəd] adj sobado; (page) con la esquina doblada
dogfish ['dɔgfɪʃ] n cazón m, perro marino
dog food n comida para perros
dogged ['dɔgɪd] adj tenaz, obstinado
doggy ['dɔgɪ] n (col) perrito
doggy bag n bolsa para llevarse las sobras de la comida
dogma ['dɔgmə] n dogma m
dogmatic [dɔg'mætɪk] adj dogmático
do-gooder [duː'gudə'] n (col pej): **to be a ~** ser una persona bien intencionada or un filantropista
dogsbody ['dɔgzbɔdɪ] n (Brit) burro de carga
doily ['dɔɪlɪ] n pañito de adorno
doing ['duːɪŋ] n: **this is your ~** esto es obra tuya
doings ['duːɪŋz] npl (events) sucesos mpl; (acts) hechos mpl
do-it-yourself [duːɪtjɔː'sɛlf] n bricolaje m
doldrums ['dɔldrəmz] npl: **to be in the ~** (person) estar abatido; (business) estar estancado
dole [dəul] n (Brit: payment) subsidio de paro; **on the ~** parado
    ▶ **dole out** vt repartir
doleful ['dəulful] adj triste, lúgubre
doll [dɔl] n muñeca
    ▶ **doll up** vt: **to ~ o.s. up** ataviarse
dollar ['dɔlə'] n dólar m
dollop ['dɔləp] n buena cucharada
dolphin ['dɔlfɪn] n delfín m
domain [də'meɪn] n (fig) campo, competencia; (land) dominios mpl
dome [dəum] n (Arch) cúpula; (shape) bóveda
domestic [də'mɛstɪk] adj (animal, duty) doméstico; (flight, news, policy) nacional
domesticated [də'mɛstɪkeɪtɪd] adj domesticado; (person: home-loving) casero, hogareño
domesticity [dəumɛs'tɪsɪtɪ] n vida casera
domestic servant n sirviente(-a) m(f)
domicile ['dɔmɪsaɪl] n domicilio

dominant ['dɔmɪnənt] *adj* dominante
dominate ['dɔmɪneɪt] *vt* dominar
domination [dɔmɪ'neɪʃən] *n* dominación *f*
domineering [dɔmɪ'nɪərɪŋ] *adj* dominante
Dominican Republic [də'mɪnɪkən-] *n* República Dominicana
dominion [də'mɪnɪən] *n* dominio
domino (*pl* **dominoes**) ['dɔmɪnəu] *n* ficha de dominó
dominoes ['dɔmɪnəuz] *n* (*game*) dominó
don [dɔn] *n* (*Brit*) profesor(a) *m(f)* de universidad
donate [də'neɪt] *vt* donar
donation [də'neɪʃən] *n* donativo
done [dʌn] *pp of* **do**
donkey ['dɔŋkɪ] *n* burro
donkey-work ['dɔŋkɪwə:k] *n* (*Brit col*) trabajo pesado
donor ['dəunəʳ] *n* donante *m/f*
donor card *n* carnet *m* de donante de órganos
don't [dəunt] = **do not**
donut ['dəunʌt] *n* (*US*) = **doughnut**
doodle ['du:dl] *n* garabato ▪ *vi* pintar dibujitos *or* garabatos
doom [du:m] *n* (*fate*) suerte *f*; (*death*) muerte *f* ▪ *vt*: **to be doomed to failure** estar condenado al fracaso
doomsday ['du:mzdeɪ] *n* día *m* del juicio final
door [dɔ:ʳ] *n* puerta; (*of car*) portezuela; (*entry*) entrada; **from ~ to ~** de puerta en puerta
doorbell ['dɔ:bɛl] *n* timbre *m*
door handle *n* tirador *m*; (*of car*) manija
door knocker *n* aldaba
doorman ['dɔ:mən] *n* (*in hotel*) portero
doormat ['dɔ:mæt] *n* felpudo, estera
doorstep ['dɔ:stɛp] *n* peldaño; **on your ~** en la puerta de casa; (*fig*) al lado de casa
door-to-door ['dɔ:tə'dɔ:ʳ] *adj*: **~ selling** venta a domicilio
doorway ['dɔ:weɪ] *n* entrada, puerta; **in the ~** en la puerta
dope [dəup] *n* (*col: person*) imbécil *m/f*; (: *information*) información *f*, informes *mpl* ▪ *vt* (*horse etc*) drogar
dopey ['dəupɪ] *adj* atontado
dormant ['dɔ:mənt] *adj* inactivo; (*latent*) latente
dormer ['dɔ:məʳ] *n* (*also*: **dormer window**) buhardilla
dormitory ['dɔ:mɪtrɪ] *n* (*Brit*) dormitorio; (*US: hall of residence*) residencia, colegio mayor
dormouse (*pl* **dormice**) ['dɔ:maus, -maɪs] *n* lirón *m*
Dors *abbr* (*Brit*) = **Dorset**
DOS [dɔs] *n abbr* = **disk operating system**

dosage ['dəusɪdʒ] *n* (*on medicine bottle*) dosis *f inv*, dosificación *f*
dose [dəus] *n* (*of medicine*) dosis *f inv*; **a ~ of flu** un ataque de gripe ▪ *vt*: **to ~ o.s. with** automedicarse con
dosser ['dɔsəʳ] *n* (*Brit col*) mendigo(-a); (*lazy person*) vago(-a)
doss house ['dɔs-] *n* (*Brit*) pensión *f* de mala muerte
dossier ['dɔsɪeɪ] *n*: **~ (on)** expediente *m* (sobre)
DOT *n abbr* (*US*: = *Department of Transportation*) ministerio de transporte
dot [dɔt] *n* punto; **dotted with** salpicado de; **on the ~** en punto
dotcom ['dɔtkɔm] *n* puntocom *f*
dot command *n* (*Comput*) instrucción *f* (precedida) de punto
dote [dəut]: **to ~ on** *vt fus* adorar, idolatrar
dot-matrix printer [dɔt'meɪtrɪks-] *n* impresora matricial *or* de matriz
dotted line ['dɔtɪd-] *n* línea de puntos; **to sign on the ~** firmar
dotty ['dɔtɪ] *adj* (*col*) disparatado, chiflado
double ['dʌbl] *adj* doble ▪ *adv* (*twice*): **to cost ~** costar el doble ▪ *n* (*gen*) doble *m* ▪ *vt* doblar; (*efforts*) redoblar ▪ *vi* doblarse; (*have two uses etc*): **to ~ as** hacer las veces de; **~ five two six (5526)** (*Telec*) cinco cinco dos seis; **spelt with a ~ "s"** escrito con dos "eses"; **on the ~**, (*Brit*) **at the ~** corriendo
  ▸ **double back** *vi* (*person*) volver sobre sus pasos
  ▸ **double up** *vi* (*bend over*) doblarse; (*share bedroom*) compartir
double bass *n* contrabajo
double bed *n* cama matrimonial
double-breasted ['dʌbl'brɛstɪd] *adj* cruzado
double-check ['dʌbl'tʃɛk] *vt* volver a revisar ▪ *vi*: **I'll ~** voy a revisarlo otra vez
double-click ['dʌbl,klɪk] (*Comput*) *vi* hacer doble clic
double cream *n* nata enriquecida
doublecross ['dʌbl'krɔs] *vt* (*trick*) engañar; (*betray*) traicionar
doubledecker ['dʌbl'dɛkəʳ] *n* autobús *m* de dos pisos
double glazing *n* (*Brit*) doble acristalamiento
double indemnity *n* doble indemnización *f*
double-page ['dʌblpeɪdʒ] *adj*: **~ spread** doble página
double room *n* cuarto para dos
doubles ['dʌblz] *n* (*Tennis*) juego de dobles
double time *n* tarifa doble
double whammy [-'wæmɪ] *n* (*col*) palo doble
doubly ['dʌblɪ] *adv* doblemente
doubt [daut] *n* duda ▪ *vt* dudar; (*suspect*)

dudar de; **to ~ that** dudar que; **there is no ~ that** no cabe duda de que; **without (a) ~** sin duda (alguna); **beyond ~** fuera de duda; **I ~ it very much** lo dudo mucho

doubtful ['dautful] *adj* dudoso; *(arousing suspicion: person)* sospechoso; **to be ~ about sth** tener dudas sobre algo; **I'm a bit ~** no estoy convencido

doubtless ['dautlıs] *adv* sin duda

dough [dəu] *n* masa, pasta; *(col: money)* pasta, lana *(LAm)*

doughnut ['dəunʌt] *n* buñuelo

douse [daus] *vt (drench: with water)* mojar; *(extinguish: flames)* apagar

dove [dʌv] *n* paloma

Dover ['dəuvə^r] *n* Dover

dovetail ['dʌvteıl] *vi (fig)* encajar

dowager ['dauıdʒə^r] *n:* **~ duchess** duquesa viuda

dowdy ['daudı] *adj* desaliñado; *(inelegant)* poco elegante

Dow-Jones average ['daudʒəunz-] *n (US)* índice *m* Dow-Jones

Dow-Jones Index *n (US)* índice *m* Dow-Jones

down [daun] *n (fluff)* pelusa; *(feathers)* plumón *m*, flojel *m*; *(hill)* loma ■ *adv (also:* **downwards)** abajo, hacia abajo; *(on the ground)* por/en tierra ■ *prep* abajo ■ *vt (col: drink)* beberse, tragar(se); **~ with X!** ¡abajo X!; **~ there** allí abajo; **~ here** aquí abajo; **I'll be ~ in a minute** ahora bajo; **England is two goals ~** Inglaterra está perdiendo por dos tantos; **I've been ~ with flu** he estado con gripe; **the price of meat is ~** ha bajado el precio de la carne; **I've got it ~ in my diary** lo he apuntado en mi agenda; **to pay £2 ~** dejar £2 de depósito; **he went ~ the hill** fue cuesta abajo; **~ under** *(in Australia etc)* en Australia/Nueva Zelanda; **to ~ tools** *(fig)* declararse en huelga

down-and-out ['daunəndaut] *n (tramp)* vagabundo(-a)

down-at-heel ['daunət'hi:l] *adj* venido a menos; *(appearance)* desaliñado

downbeat ['daunbi:t] *n (Mus)* compás *m* ■ *adj (gloomy)* pesimista

downcast ['daunka:st] *adj* abatido

downer ['daunə^r] *n (col: drug)* tranquilizante; **to be on a ~** estar pasando un mal bache

downfall ['daunfɔ:l] *n* caída, ruina

downgrade [daun'greıd] *vt (job)* degradar; *(hotel)* bajar de categoría

downhearted [daun'ha:tıd] *adj* desanimado

downhill [daun'hıl] *adv:* **to go ~** ir cuesta abajo; *(business)* estar en declive

Downing Street ['daunıŋ-] *n (Brit)* Downing Street *f*; *ver nota*

● **DOWNING STREET**

Downing Street es la calle de Londres en la que tienen su residencia oficial tanto el Primer Ministro ("Prime Minister") como el Ministro de Economía ("Chancellor of the Exchequer"). El primero vive en el n°10 y el segundo en el n°11. Es una calle cerrada al público que se encuentra en el barrio de Westminster, en el centro de Londres. *Downing Street* se usa también en lenguaje periodístico para referirse al jefe del gobierno británico.

download ['daunləud] *vt (Comput)* transferir, telecargar

downloadable [daun'ləudəbl] *adj (Comput)* descargable

down-market ['daun'ma:kıt] *adj* de escasa calidad

down payment *n* entrada, pago al contado

downplay ['daunpleı] *vt (US)* quitar importancia a

downpour ['daunpɔ:^r] *n* aguacero

downright ['daunraıt] *adj (nonsense, lie)* manifiesto; *(refusal)* terminante

downsize [daun'saız] *vt* reducir la plantilla de

Down's syndrome [daunz] *n* síndrome *m* de Down

downstairs [daun'steəz] *adv (below)* (en el piso de) abajo; *(motion)* escaleras abajo; **to come** *(or* **go) ~** bajar la escalera

downstream [daun'stri:m] *adv* río abajo

downtime ['dauntaım] *n (Comm)* tiempo inactivo

down-to-earth [dauntu'ə:θ] *adj* práctico

downtown [daun'taun] *adv* en el centro de la ciudad

downtrodden ['dauntrɔdn] *adj* oprimido

downward ['daunwəd] *adv* hacia abajo; **face ~** *(person)* boca abajo; *(object)* cara abajo ■ *adj:* **a ~ trend** una tendencia descendente

downwards ['daunwədz] *adv* hacia abajo

dowry ['daurı] *n* dote *f*

doz. *abbr* – **dozen**

doze [dəuz] *vi* dormitar

▶ **doze off** *vi* echar una cabezada

dozen ['dʌzn] *n* docena; **a ~ books** una docena de libros; **dozens of** cantidad de; **dozens of times** cantidad de veces; **80p a ~** 80 peniques la docena

DPh, DPhil *n abbr* (= *Doctor of Philosophy*) título universitario

DPP *n abbr* (Brit) = **Director of Public Prosecutions**

DPT n abbr (Med: = diphtheria, pertussis, tetanus) vacuna trivalente

DPW n abbr (US: = Department of Public Works) ministerio de obras públicas

Dr, Dr. abbr (= doctor) Dr

Dr. abbr (= in street names) = **Drive**

dr abbr (Comm) = **debtor**

drab [dræb] adj gris, monótono

draft [drɑːft] n (first copy: of document, report) borrador m; (Comm) giro; (US: call-up) quinta ▪ vt (write roughly) hacer un borrador de; see also **draught**

draftsman etc ['drɑːftsmən] (US) = **draughtsman** etc

drag [dræg] vt arrastrar; (river) dragar, rastrear ▪ vi arrastrarse por el suelo ▪ n (Aviat: resistance) resistencia aerodinámica; (col) lata; (women's clothing): **in ~** travestido; **to ~ and drop** (Comput) arrastrar y soltar
▸ **drag away** vt: **to ~ away (from)** separar a rastras (de)
▸ **drag on** vi ser interminable

dragnet ['drægnet] n (Naut) rastra; (fig) emboscada

dragon ['drægən] n dragón m

dragonfly ['drægənflaɪ] n libélula

dragoon [drə'guːn] n (cavalryman) dragón m ▪ vt: **to ~ sb into doing sth** forzar a algn a hacer algo

drain [dreɪn] n desaguadero; (in street) sumidero; (drain cover) rejilla del sumidero ▪ vt (land, marshes) desecar; (Med) drenar; (reservoir) desecar; (fig) agotar ▪ vi escurrirse; **to be a ~ on** consumir, agotar; **to feel drained (of energy)** (fig) sentirse agotado

drainage ['dreɪnɪdʒ] n (act) desagüe m; (Med, Agr) drenaje m; (sewage) alcantarillado

draining board ['dreɪnɪŋ-], **drainboard** (US) ['dreɪnbɔːd] n escurridero, escurridor m

drainpipe ['dreɪnpaɪp] n tubo de desagüe

drake [dreɪk] n pato m (macho)

dram [dræm] n (drink) traguito, copita

drama ['drɑːmə] n (art) teatro; (play) drama m

dramatic [drə'mætɪk] adj dramático

dramatist ['dræmətɪst] n dramaturgo(-a)

dramatize ['dræmətaɪz] vt (events etc) dramatizar; (adapt: novel: for TV, cinema) adaptar

drank [dræŋk] pt of **drink**

drape [dreɪp] vt cubrir

draper ['dreɪpər] n (Brit) pañero, mercero

drapes [dreɪps] npl (US) cortinas fpl

drastic ['dræstɪk] adj (measure, reduction) severo; (change) radical

draught, draft (US) [drɑːft] n (of air) corriente f de aire; (drink) trago; (Naut) calado; **on ~** (beer) de barril

draught beer n cerveza de barril

draughtboard ['drɑːftbɔːd] (Brit) n tablero de damas

draughts [drɑːfts] n (Brit) juego de damas

draughtsman, draftsman (US) ['drɑːftsmən] n proyectista m, delineante m

draughtsmanship, draftsmanship (US) ['drɑːftsmənʃɪp] n (drawing) dibujo lineal; (skill) habilidad f para el dibujo

draw [drɔː] vb (pt **drew**, pp **drawn**) ▪ vt (pull) tirar; (take out) sacar; (attract) atraer; (picture) dibujar; (money) retirar; (formulate: conclusion): **to ~ (from)** sacar (de); (comparison, distinction): **to ~ (between)** hacer (entre) ▪ vi (Sport) empatar ▪ n (Sport) empate m; (lottery) sorteo; (attraction) atracción f; **to ~ near** vi acercarse
▸ **draw back** vi: **to ~ back (from)** echarse atrás (de)
▸ **draw in** vi (car) aparcar; (train) entrar en la estación
▸ **draw on** vt (resources) utilizar, servirse de; (imagination, person) recurrir a
▸ **draw out** vi (lengthen) alargarse
▸ **draw up** vi (stop) pararse ▪ vt (document) redactar; (plan) trazar

drawback ['drɔːbæk] n inconveniente m, desventaja

drawbridge ['drɔːbrɪdʒ] n puente m levadizo

drawee [drɔː'iː] n girado, librado

drawer [drɔːr] n cajón m; (of cheque) librador(a) m(f)

drawing ['drɔːɪŋ] n dibujo

drawing board n tablero (de dibujante)

drawing pin n (Brit) chincheta m

drawing room n salón m

drawl [drɔːl] n habla lenta y cansina

drawn [drɔːn] pp of **draw** ▪ adj (haggard: with tiredness) ojeroso; (: with pain) macilento

drawstring ['drɔːstrɪŋ] n cordón m

dread [dred] n pavor m, terror m ▪ vt temer, tener miedo or pavor a

dreadful ['dredful] adj espantoso; **I feel ~!** (ill) ¡me siento fatal or malísimo!; (ashamed) ¡qué vergüenza!

dream [driːm] n sueño ▪ vt, vi (pt, pp **dreamed** or **dreamt**) [dremt] soñar; **to have a ~ about sb/sth** soñar con algn/algo; **sweet dreams!** ¡que sueñes con los angelitos!
▸ **dream up** vt (reason, excuse) inventar; (plan, idea) idear

dreamer ['driːmər] n soñador(a) m(f)

dream world n mundo imaginario or de ensueño

dreamy ['driːmɪ] adj (person) soñador(a), distraído; (music) de sueño

dreary ['drɪərɪ] adj monótono, aburrido

dredge [drɛdʒ] vt dragar
▶ **dredge up** vt sacar con draga; (fig: unpleasant facts) pescar, sacar a luz
dredger ['drɛdʒəʳ] n (ship, machine) draga; (Culin) tamiz m
dregs [drɛgz] npl heces fpl
drench [drɛntʃ] vt empapar; **drenched to the skin** calado hasta los huesos
dress [drɛs] n vestido; (clothing) ropa
■ vt vestir; (wound) vendar; (Culin) aliñar; (shop window) decorar, arreglar ■ vi vestirse; **to ~ o.s., get dressed** vestirse; **she dresses very well** se viste muy bien
▶ **dress up** vi vestirse de etiqueta; (in fancy dress) disfrazarse
dress circle n (Brit) principal m
dress designer n modisto(-a)
dresser ['drɛsəʳ] n (furniture) aparador m; (: US) tocador m; (Theat) camarero(-a)
dressing ['drɛsɪŋ] n (Med) vendaje m; (Culin) aliño
dressing gown n (Brit) bata
dressing room n (Theat) camarín m; (Sport) vestidor m
dressing table n tocador m
dressmaker ['drɛsmeɪkəʳ] n modista, costurera
dressmaking ['drɛsmeɪkɪŋ] n costura
dress rehearsal n ensayo general
dress shirt n camisa de frac
dressy ['drɛsɪ] adj (col) elegante
drew [dru:] pt of **draw**
dribble ['drɪbl] vi gotear, caer gota a gota; (baby) babear ■ vt (ball) driblar, regatear
dried [draɪd] adj (gen) seco; (fruit) paso; (milk) en polvo
drier ['draɪəʳ] n = **dryer**
drift [drɪft] n (of current etc) velocidad f; (of sand) montón m; (of snow) ventisquero; (meaning) significado ■ vi (boat) ir a la deriva; (sand, snow) amontonarse; **to catch sb's ~** cogerle el hilo a algn; **to let things ~** dejar las cosas como están; **to ~ apart** (friends) seguir su camino; (lovers) disgustarse, romper
drifter ['drɪftəʳ] n vagabundo(-a)
driftwood ['drɪftwʊd] n madera flotante
drill [drɪl] n taladro; (bit) broca; (of dentist) fresa; (for mining etc) perforadora, barrena; (Mil) instrucción f ■ vt perforar, taladrar; (soldiers) ejercitar; (pupils: in grammar) hacer ejercicios con ■ vi (for oil) perforar
drilling ['drɪlɪŋ] n (for oil) perforación f
drilling rig n (on land) torre f de perforación; (at sea) plataforma de perforación
drily ['draɪlɪ] adv secamente
drink [drɪŋk] n bebida ■ vt, vi (pt **drank**, pp **drunk**) beber, tomar (LAm); **to have a ~** tomar algo; tomar una copa or un trago; **a ~ of water** un trago de agua; **to invite sb for drinks** invitar a algn a tomar unas copas; **there's food and ~ in the kitchen** hay de comer y de beber en la cocina; **would you like something to ~?** ¿quieres beber or tomar algo?
▶ **drink in** vt (person: fresh air) respirar; (: story, sight) beberse
drinkable ['drɪŋkəbl] adj (not poisonous) potable; (palatable) aguantable
drink-driving [drɪŋk'draɪvɪŋ] n: **to be charged with ~** ser acusado de conducir borracho or en estado de embriaguez
drinker ['drɪŋkəʳ] n bebedor(a) m(f)
drinking ['drɪŋkɪŋ] n (drunkenness) beber m
drinking fountain n fuente f de agua potable
drinking water n agua potable
drip [drɪp] n (act) goteo; (one drip) gota; (Med) gota a gota m; (sound: of water etc) goteo; (col: spineless person) soso(-a) ■ vi gotear, caer gota a gota
drip-dry ['drɪp'draɪ] adj (shirt) de lava y pon
dripping ['drɪpɪŋ] n (animal fat) pringue m
■ adj: **~ wet** calado
drive [draɪv] (pt **drove**, pp **driven**) n paseo (en coche); (journey) viaje m (en coche); (also: **driveway**) entrada; (street) calle; (energy) energía, vigor m; (Psych) impulso; (Sport) ataque m; (Comput: also: **disk drive**) unidad f (de disco) ■ vt (car) conducir, manejar (LAm); (nail) clavar; (push) empujar; (Tech: motor) impulsar ■ vi (Aut: at controls) conducir, manejar (LAm); (: travel) pasearse en coche; **to go for a ~** dar una vuelta en coche; **it's three hours' ~ from London** es un viaje de tres horas en coche desde Londres; **left-/right-hand ~** conducción f a la izquierda/derecha; **front-/rear-wheel ~** tracción f delantera/trasera; **sales ~** promoción f de ventas; **to ~ sb mad** volverle loco a algn; **to ~ sb to (do) sth** empujar a algn a (hacer) algo; **he drives a taxi** es taxista; **he drives a Mercedes** tiene un Mercedes; **can you ~?** ¿sabes conducir or (LAm) manejar?; **to ~ at 50 km an hour** ir a 50km por hora
▶ **drive at** vt fus (fig: intend, mean) querer decir, insinuar
▶ **drive on** vi no parar, seguir adelante ■ vt (incite, encourage) empujar
drive-by ['draɪvbaɪ] n: **~ shooting** tiroteo desde el coche
drive-in ['draɪvɪn] adj (esp US): **~ cinema** autocine m
drivel ['drɪvl] n (col) tonterías fpl
driven ['drɪvn] pp of **drive**

driver ['draɪvəʳ] n conductor(a) m(f), chofer m (LAm); (of taxi) taxista m/f
driver's license n (US) carnet m or permiso de conducir
driveway ['draɪvweɪ] n camino de entrada
driving ['draɪvɪŋ] n conducir m, manejar m (LAm) ▪ adj (force) impulsor(a)
driving instructor n instructor(a) m(f) de autoescuela
driving lesson n clase f de conducir
driving licence n (Brit) carnet m or permiso de conducir
driving school n autoescuela
driving test n examen m de conducir
drizzle ['drɪzl] n llovizna, garúa (LAm) ▪ vi lloviznar
droll [drəul] adj gracioso
dromedary ['drɔmɪdərɪ] n dromedario
drone [drəun] vi (bee, aircraft, engine) zumbar; (also: **drone on**) murmurar sin interrupción ▪ n zumbido; (male bee) zángano
drool [dru:l] vi babear; **to ~ over sb/sth** caérsele la baba por algn/algo
droop [dru:p] vi (fig) decaer, desanimarse
drop [drɔp] n (of water) gota; (fall: in price) bajada; (: in salary) disminución f ▪ vt (allow to fall) dejar caer; (voice, eyes, price) bajar; (set down from car) dejar ▪ vi (price, temperature) bajar; (wind) calmarse, amainar; (numbers, attendance) disminuir; **drops** npl (Med) gotas fpl; **cough drops** pastillas fpl para la tos; **a ~ of 10%** una bajada del 10 por ciento; **to ~ anchor** echar el ancla; **to ~ sb a line** mandar unas líneas a algn
▸ **drop in** vi (col: visit): **to ~ in (on)** pasar por casa (de)
▸ **drop off** vi (sleep) dormirse ▪ vt (passenger) bajar, dejar
▸ **drop out** vi (withdraw) retirarse
droplet ['drɔplɪt] n gotita
dropout ['drɔpaut] n (from society) marginado(-a); (from university) estudiante m/f que ha abandonado los estudios
dropper ['drɔpəʳ] n (Med) cuentagotas m inv
droppings ['drɔpɪŋz] npl excrementos sg
dross [drɔs] n (fig) escoria
drought [draut] n sequía
drove [drəuv] pt of **drive**
drown [draun] vt (also: **drown out**: sound) ahogar ▪ vi ahogarse
drowse [drauz] vi estar medio dormido
drowsy ['drauzɪ] adj soñoliento; **to be ~** tener sueño
drudge [drʌdʒ] n esclavo del trabajo
drudgery ['drʌdʒərɪ] n trabajo pesado or monótono
drug [drʌg] n (Med) medicamento, droga;

(narcotic) droga ▪ vt drogar; **to be on drugs** drogarse; **he's on drugs** se droga
drug addict n drogadicto(-a)
druggist ['drʌgɪst] n (US) farmacéutico(-a)
drug peddler n traficante m/f de drogas
drugstore ['drʌgstɔ:ʳ] n (US) tienda (de comestibles, periódicos y medicamentos)
drug trafficker n narcotraficante m/f
drum [drʌm] n tambor m; (large) bombo; (for oil, petrol) bidón m ▪ vi tocar el tambor; (with fingers) tamborilear ▪ vt: **to ~ one's fingers on the table** tamborilear con los dedos sobre la mesa; **drums** npl batería sg
▸ **drum up** vt (enthusiasm, support) movilizar, fomentar
drummer ['drʌməʳ] n (in military band) tambor m/f; (in jazz/pop group) batería m/f
drumstick ['drʌmstɪk] n (Mus) palillo, baqueta; (chicken leg) muslo (de pollo)
drunk [drʌŋk] pp of **drink** ▪ adj borracho ▪ n (also: **drunkard**) borracho(-a); **to get ~** emborracharse
drunken ['drʌŋkən] adj borracho
drunkenness ['drʌŋkənnɪs] n embriaguez f
dry [draɪ] adj seco; (day) sin lluvia; (climate) árido, seco; (humour) agudo; (uninteresting: lecture) aburrido, pesado ▪ vt secar; (tears) enjugarse ▪ vi secarse; **on ~ land** en tierra firme; **to ~ one's hands/hair/eyes** secarse las manos/el pelo/las lágrimas
▸ **dry up** vi (supply, imagination etc) agotarse; (in speech) atascarse
dry-clean ['draɪ'kli:n] vt limpiar or lavar en seco; **"~ only"** (on label) "limpieza or lavado en seco"
dry-cleaner's ['draɪ'kli:nəz] n tintorería
dry-cleaning ['draɪ'kli:nɪŋ] n lavado en seco
dry dock n (Naut) dique m seco
dryer ['draɪəʳ] n (for hair) secador m; (for clothes) secadora
dry goods npl (Comm) mercería sg
dry goods store n (US) mercería
dry ice n nieve f carbónica, hielo seco
dryness ['draɪnɪs] n sequedad f
dry rot n putrefacción f
dry run n (fig) ensayo
dry ski slope n pista artificial de esquí
DSc n abbr (= Doctor of Science) título universitario
DSS n abbr (Brit) = **Department of Social Security;** see **social security**
DST n abbr (US: = Daylight Saving Time) hora de verano
DT n abbr (Comput) = **data transmission**
DTI n abbr (Brit) = **Department of Trade and Industry**
DTP n abbr = **desktop publishing;** (Med) = **diphtheria, tetanus, pertussis**

DT's *n abbr* (*col*: = *delirium tremens*) delirium *m* tremens

dual ['djuəl] *adj* doble

dual carriageway *n* (*Brit*) ≈ autovía

dual-control ['djuəlkən'trəul] *adj* de doble mando

dual nationality *n* doble nacionalidad *f*

dual-purpose ['djuəl'pə:pəs] *adj* de doble uso

dubbed [dʌbd] *adj* (*Cine*) doblado

dubious ['dju:bɪəs] *adj* indeciso; (*reputation, company*) dudoso; (*character*) sospechoso; **I'm very ~ about it** tengo mis dudas sobre ello

Dublin ['dʌblɪn] *n* Dublín

Dubliner ['dʌblɪnəʳ] *n* dublinés(-esa) *m(f)*

duchess ['dʌtʃɪs] *n* duquesa

duck [dʌk] *n* pato ■ *vi* agacharse ■ *vt* (*plunge in water*) zambullir

duckling ['dʌklɪŋ] *n* patito

duct [dʌkt] *n* conducto, canal *m*

dud [dʌd] *n* (*shell*) obús *m* que no estalla; (*object, tool*): **it's a ~** es una filfa ■ *adj*: **~ cheque** (*Brit*) cheque *m* sin fondos

due [dju:] *adj* (*proper*) debido; (*fitting*) conveniente, oportuno ■ *adv*: **~ north** derecho al norte; **dues** *npl* (*for club, union*) cuota *sg*; (*in harbour*) derechos *mpl*; **in ~ course** a su debido tiempo; **~ to** debido a; **to be ~ to** deberse a; **the train is ~ to arrive at 8.00** el tren tiene (prevista) la llegada a las ocho; **the rent's ~ on the 30th** hay que pagar el alquiler el día 30; **I am ~ six days' leave** me deben seis días de vacaciones; **she is ~ back tomorrow** ella debe volver mañana

due date *n* fecha de vencimiento

duel ['djuəl] *n* duelo

duet [dju:'ɛt] *n* dúo

duff [dʌf] *adj* sin valor

duffel bag ['dʌfl-] *n* macuto

duffel coat ['dʌfl-] *n* trenca

dug [dʌg] *pt, pp of* **dig**

dugout ['dʌgaut] *n* (*canoe*) piragua (*hecha de un solo tronco*); (*Sport*) banquillo; (*Mil*) refugio subterráneo

duke [dju:k] *n* duque *m*

dull [dʌl] *adj* (*light*) apagado; (*stupid*) torpe; (*boring*) pesado; (*sound, pain*) sordo; (*weather, day*) gris ■ *vt* (*pain, grief*) aliviar; (*mind, senses*) entorpecer

duly ['dju:lɪ] *adv* debidamente; (*on time*) a su debido tiempo

dumb [dʌm] *adj* mudo; (*stupid*) estúpido; **to be struck ~** (*fig*) quedar boquiabierto

dumbbell ['dʌmbɛl] *n* (*Sport*) pesa

dumbfounded [dʌm'faundɪd] *adj* pasmado

dummy ['dʌmɪ] *n* (*tailor's model*) maniquí *m*; (*Brit: for baby*) chupete *m* ■ *adj* falso, postizo;

~ run ensayo

dump [dʌmp] *n* (*heap*) montón *m* de basura; (*place*) basurero, vertedero; (*col*) tugurio; (*Mil*) depósito; (*Comput*) copia vaciada ■ *vt* (*put down*) dejar; (*get rid of*) deshacerse de; (*Comput*) tirar (a la papelera); (*Comm: goods*) inundar el mercado de; **to be (down) in the dumps** (*col*) tener murria, estar deprimido

dumping ['dʌmpɪŋ] *n* (*Econ*) dumping *m*; (*of rubbish*): **"no ~"** "prohibido verter basura"

dumpling ['dʌmplɪŋ] *n* bola de masa hervida

dumpy ['dʌmpɪ] *adj* regordete(-a)

dunce [dʌns] *n* zopenco

dune [dju:n] *n* duna

dung [dʌŋ] *n* estiércol *m*

dungarees [dʌŋgə'ri:z] *npl* mono *sg*, overol *msg* (*LAm*)

dungeon ['dʌndʒən] *n* calabozo

dunk [dʌŋk] *vt* mojar

duo ['dju:əu] *n* (*Mus*) dúo

duodenal [dju:ə'di:nl] *adj* (*ulcer*) de duodeno

duodenum [dju:ə'di:nəm] *n* duodeno

dupe [dju:p] *n* (*victim*) víctima ■ *vt* engañar

duplex ['dju:plɛks] *n* (*US: also*: **duplex apartment**) dúplex *m*

duplicate ['dju:plɪkət] *n* duplicado; (*copy of letter etc*) copia ■ *adj* (*copy*) duplicado ■ *vt* ['dju:plɪkeɪt] duplicar; (*on machine*) multicopiar; **in ~** por duplicado

duplicate key *n* duplicado de una llave

duplicating machine ['dju:plɪkeɪtɪŋ-], **duplicator** ['dju:plɪkeɪtəʳ] *n* multicopista *m*

duplicity [dju:'plɪsɪtɪ] *n* doblez *f*, duplicidad *f*

Dur. *abbr* (*Brit*) = **Durham**

durability [djuərə'bɪlɪtɪ] *n* durabilidad *f*

durable ['djuərəbl] *adj* duradero

duration [djuə'reɪʃən] *n* duración *f*

duress [djuə'rɛs] *n*: **under ~** por coacción

Durex® ['djuərɛks] *n* (*Brit*) preservativo

during ['djuərɪŋ] *prep* durante

dusk [dʌsk] *n* crepúsculo, anochecer *m*

dusky ['dʌskɪ] *adj* oscuro; (*complexion*) moreno

dust [dʌst] *n* polvo ■ *vt* (*furniture*) desempolvar; (*cake etc*): **to ~ with** espolvorear de

▶ **dust off** *vt* (*also fig*) desempolvar, quitar el polvo de

dustbin ['dʌstbɪn] *n* (*Brit*) cubo de la basura, balde *m* (*LAm*)

dustbin liner *n* bolsa de basura

duster ['dʌstəʳ] *n* paño, trapo; (*feather duster*) plumero

dust jacket *n* sobrecubierta

dustman ['dʌstmən] *n* (*Brit*) basurero

dustpan ['dʌstpæn] *n* cogedor *m*

dust storm *n* vendaval *m* de polvo

dusty ['dʌstɪ] *adj* polvoriento

Dutch [dʌtʃ] *adj* holandés(-esa) ▪ *n* (*Ling*)
   holandés *m* ▪ *adv*: **to go** ~ pagar a escote;
   the Dutch *npl* los holandeses
Dutch auction *n* subasta a la rebaja
Dutchman ['dʌtʃmən], **Dutchwoman**
   ['dʌtʃwumən] *n* holandés(-esa) *m(f)*
dutiful ['djuːtɪful] *adj* (*child*) obediente;
   (*husband*) sumiso; (*employee*) cumplido
duty ['djuːtɪ] *n* deber *m*; (*tax*) derechos *mpl*
   de aduana; (*Med: in hospital*) servicio, guardia;
   on ~ de servicio; (*at night etc*) de guardia;
   off ~ libre (de servicio); **to make it one's** ~
   to do sth encargarse de hacer algo sin f
   alta; **to pay** ~ **on sth** pagar los derechos
   sobre algo
duty-free [djuːtɪ'friː] *adj* libre de derechos de
   aduana; ~ **shop** tienda libre de impuestos
duty officer *n* (*Mil etc*) oficial *m/f* de guardia
duvet ['duːveɪ] *n* (*Brit*) edredón *m* (nórdico)
DV *abbr* (= *Deo volente*) Dios mediante
DVD *n abbr* (= *digital versatile or video disc*) DVD *m*
DVLA *n abbr* (*Brit*: = *Driver and Vehicle Licensing
   Agency*) organismo encargado de la expedición de
   permisos de conducir y matriculación de vehículos
DVM *n abbr* (*US*: = *Doctor of Veterinary Medicine*)
   título universitario
DVT *n abbr* = **deep-vein thrombosis**
dwarf [dwɔːf] (*pl* **dwarves**) [dwɔːvz] *n* enano
   ▪ *vt* empequeñecer

dwell [dwɛl] (*pt, pp* **dwelt**) [dwɛlt] *vi* morar
   ▸ **dwell on** *vt fus* explayarse en
dweller ['dwɛləʳ] *n* habitante *m*; **city** ~
   habitante *m* de la ciudad
dwelling ['dwɛlɪŋ] *n* vivienda
dwelt [dwɛlt] *pt, pp of* **dwell**
dwindle ['dwɪndl] *vi* menguar, disminuir
dwindling ['dwɪndlɪŋ] *adj* (*strength,
   interest*) menguante; (*resources, supplies*) en
   disminución
dye [daɪ] *n* tinte *m* ▪ *vt* teñir; **hair** ~ tinte *m*
   para el pelo
dying ['daɪɪŋ] *adj* moribundo, agonizante;
   (*moments*) final; (*words*) último
dyke [daɪk] *n* (*Brit*) dique *m*; (*channel*) arroyo,
   acequia; (*causeway*) calzada
dynamic [daɪ'næmɪk] *adj* dinámico
dynamics [daɪ'næmɪks] *n or npl* dinámica *sg*
dynamite ['daɪnəmaɪt] *n* dinamita ▪ *vt*
   dinamitar
dynamo ['daɪnəməu] *n* dinamo *f*, dinamo
   m (*LAm*)
dynasty ['dɪnəstɪ] *n* dinastía
dysentery ['dɪsɪntrɪ] *n* disentería
dyslexia [dɪs'lɛksɪə] *n* dislexia
dyslexic [dɪs'lɛksɪk] *adj, n* disléxico(-a) *m(f)*
dyspepsia [dɪs'pɛpsɪə] *n* dispepsia
dystrophy ['dɪstrəfɪ] *n* distrofia; **muscular** ~
   distrofia muscular

Ee

E, e [i:] n (letter) E, e f; (Mus) mi m; **E for
  Edward,** (US) **E for Easy** E de Enrique
E abbr (= east) E ∎ n abbr (= Ecstasy) éxtasis m
E111 n abbr (= form E111) impreso E111
ea. abbr = **each**
E.A. abbr (US: = educational age) nivel escolar
each [i:tʃ] adj cada inv ∎ pron cada uno; (also:
  each other) el uno al otro; **they hate ~ other**
  se odian (entre ellos or mutuamente); **~ day**
  cada día; **they have two books ~** tienen dos
  libros cada uno; **they cost £5 ~** cuestan cinco
  libras cada uno; **~ of us** cada uno de nosotros
eager ['i:gə'] adj (gen) impaciente; (hopeful)
  ilusionado; (keen) entusiasmado; (pupil)
  apasionado; **to be ~ to do sth** estar deseoso
  de hacer algo; **to be ~ for** ansiar, anhelar
eagerly ['i:gəlɪ] adv con impaciencia; con
  ilusión; con entusiasmo
eagerness ['i:gənɪs] n impaciencia; ilusión f;
  entusiasmo
eagle ['i:gl] n águila
E & OE abbr = **errors and omissions excepted**
ear [ɪə'] n oreja; (sense of hearing) oído; (of corn)
  espiga; **up to the ears in debt** abrumado
  de deudas
earache ['ɪəreɪk] n dolor m de oídos
eardrum ['ɪədrʌm] n tímpano
earful ['ɪəful] n: **to give sb an ~** (col) echar
  una bronca a algn
earl [ə:l] n conde m
early ['ə:lɪ] adv (gen) temprano; (ahead of time)
  con tiempo, con anticipación ∎ adj (gen)
  temprano; (reply) pronto; (man) primitivo;
  (first: Christians, settlers) primero; **to have an
  ~ night** acostarse temprano; **in the ~** or **~ in
  the spring/19th century** a principios de
  primavera/del siglo diecinueve; **you're ~!**
  ¡has llegado temprano or pronto!; **~ in the
  morning/afternoon** a primeras horas de la
  mañana/tarde; **she's in her ~ forties** tiene
  poco más de cuarenta años; **at your earliest
  convenience** (Comm) con la mayor brevedad
  posible; **I can't come any earlier** no puedo
  llegar antes
early retirement n jubilación f anticipada
early warning system n sistema m de alerta
  inmediata
earmark ['ɪəmɑ:k] vt: **to ~ for** reservar para,
  destinar a
earn [ə:n] vt (gen) ganar; (interest) devengar;
  (praise) ganarse; **to ~ one's living** ganarse
  la vida
earned income n renta del trabajo
earnest ['ə:nɪst] adj serio, formal ∎ n (also:
  earnest money) anticipo, señal f; **in ~** adv
  en serio
earnings ['ə:nɪŋz] npl (personal) ingresos mpl;
  (of company etc) ganancias fpl
earphones ['ɪəfəunz] npl auriculares mpl
earplugs ['ɪəplʌgz] npl tapones mpl para los
  oídos
earring ['ɪərɪŋ] n pendiente m, arete m (LAm)
earshot ['ɪəfɔt] n: **out of/within ~** fuera del/
  al alcance del oído
earth [ə:θ] n (gen) tierra; (Brit Elec) toma de
  tierra ∎ vt (Brit Elec) conectar a tierra
earthenware ['ə:θnwεə'] n loza (de barro)
earthly ['ə:θlɪ] adj terrenal, mundano;
  ~ paradise paraíso terrenal; **there is no
  ~ reason to think ...** no existe razón para
  pensar ...
earthquake ['ə:θkweɪk] n terremoto
earth-shattering ['ə:θʃætərɪŋ] adj
  trascendental
earthworm ['ə:θwə:m] n lombriz f
earthy ['ə:θɪ] adj (fig: uncomplicated) sencillo;
  (coarse) grosero
earwig ['ɪəwɪg] n tijereta
ease [i:z] n facilidad f; (comfort) comodidad
  f ∎ vt (task) facilitar; (pain) aliviar; (loosen)
  soltar; (relieve: pressure, tension) aflojar;
  (weight) aligerar; (help pass): **to ~ sth in/out**
  meter/sacar algo con cuidado ∎ vi (situation)
  relajarse; **with ~** con facilidad; **to feel at
  ~/ill at ~** sentirse a gusto/a disgusto; **at ~!**
  (Mil) ¡descansen!

▸ **ease off, ease up** vi (work, business) aflojar; (person) relajarse

easel ['i:zl] n caballete m

easily ['i:zɪlɪ] adv fácilmente

easiness ['i:zɪnɪs] n facilidad f; (of manners) soltura

east [i:st] n este m, oriente m ▪ adj del este, oriental ▪ adv al este, hacia el este; **the E~** el Oriente; (Pol) el Este

Easter ['i:stəʳ] n Pascua (de Resurrección)

Easter egg n huevo de Pascua

Easter holidays npl Semana Santa sg

Easter Island n Isla de Pascua

easterly ['i:stəlɪ] adj (to the east) al este; (from the east) del este

Easter Monday n lunes m de Pascua

eastern ['i:stən] adj del este, oriental; **E~ Europe** Europa del Este; **the E~ bloc** (Pol) los países del Este

Easter Sunday n Domingo de Resurrección

East Germany n (formerly) Alemania Oriental or del Este

eastward ['i:stwəd], **eastwards** ['i:stwədz] adv hacia el este

easy ['i:zɪ] adj fácil; (life) holgado, cómodo; (relaxed) natural ▪ adv: **to take it** or **things ~** (not worry) no preocuparse; (go slowly) tomarlo con calma; (rest) descansar; **payment on ~ terms** (Comm) facilidades de pago; **I'm ~** (col) me da igual, no me importa; **easier said than done** del dicho al hecho hay buen trecho

easy chair n butaca

easy-going ['i:zɪ'gəuɪŋ] adj acomodadizo

easy touch [i:zɪ'tʌtʃ] n: **he's an ~** (col) es fácil de convencer

eat (pt **ate** [i:t, eɪt, 'i:tn] vt comer

▸ **eat away** vt (sea) desgastar; (acid) corroer

▸ **eat into, eat away at** vt fus corroer

▸ **eat out** vi comer fuera

▸ **eat up** vt (meal etc) comerse; **it eats up electricity** devora la electricidad

eatable ['i:təbl] adj comestible

eau de Cologne [əudəkə'ləun] n (agua de) colonia

eaves [i:vz] npl alero sg

eavesdrop ['i:vzdrɔp] vi: **to ~ (on sb)** escuchar a escondidas or con disimulo (a algn)

ebb [ɛb] n reflujo ▪ vi bajar; (fig: also: **ebb away**) decaer; **~ and flow** el flujo y reflujo; **to be at a low ~** (fig: person) estar de capa caída

ebb tide n marea menguante

ebony ['ɛbənɪ] n ébano

e-book ['i:buk] n libro electrónico

ebullient [ɪ'bʌlɪənt] adj entusiasta, animado

e-business [i:bɪznɪs] n (commerce) comercio electrónico; (company) negocio electrónico

ECB n abbr (= European Central Bank) BCE m

eccentric [ɪk'sɛntrɪk] adj, n excéntrico(-a)

ecclesiastical [ɪkli:zɪ'æstɪkəl] adj eclesiástico

ECG n abbr (= electrocardiogram) E.C.G. m

echo (pl **echoes**) ['ɛkəu] n eco m ▪ vt (sound) repetir ▪ vi resonar, hacer eco

ECLA n abbr (= Economic Commission for Latin America) CEPAL f

éclair ['eɪklɛəʳ] n petisú m

eclipse [ɪ'klɪps] n eclipse m ▪ vt eclipsar

ECM n abbr (US: = European Common Market) MCE m

eco- ['i:kəu] pref eco-

eco-friendly ['i:kəufrɛndlɪ] adj ecológico

ecological [i:kə'lɔdʒɪkl] adj ecológico

ecologist [ɪ'kɔlədʒɪst] n ecologista m/f; (scientist) ecólogo(-a) m(f)

ecology [ɪ'kɔlədʒɪ] n ecología

e-commerce ['i:ˌkɔmə:s] n comercio electrónico

economic [i:kə'nɔmɪk] adj (profitable: price) económico; (business etc) rentable

economical [i:kə'nɔmɪkl] adj económico

economically [i:kə'nɔmɪklɪ] adv económicamente

economics [i:kə'nɔmɪks] n economía ▪ npl (financial aspects) finanzas fpl

economic warfare n guerra económica

economist [ɪ'kɔnəmɪst] n economista m/f

economize [ɪ'kɔnəmaɪz] vi economizar, ahorrar

economy [ɪ'kɔnəmɪ] n economía; **economies of scale** economías fpl de escala

economy class n (Aviat etc) clase f turista

economy class syndrome n síndrome m de la clase turista

economy size n tamaño familiar

ecosystem ['i:kəusɪstəm] n ecosistema m

eco-tourism [i:kəu'tuərɪzm] n turismo verde or ecológico

ECSC n abbr (= European Coal and Steel Community) CECA f

ecstasy ['ɛkstəsɪ] n éxtasis m inv

ecstatic [ɛks'tætɪk] adj extático, extasiado

ECT n abbr = **electroconvulsive therapy**

Ecuador ['ɛkwədɔ:ʳ] n Ecuador m

Ecuadoran [ɛkwə'dɔ:rən], **Ecuadorian** [ɛkwə'dɔ:rɪən] adj, n ecuatoriano(-a) m(f)

ecumenical [i:kju'mɛnɪkl] adj ecuménico

eczema ['ɛksɪmə] n eczema m

eddy ['ɛdɪ] n remolino

edge [ɛdʒ] n (of knife etc) filo; (of object) borde m; (of lake etc) orilla ▪ vt (Sewing) ribetear ▪ vi: **to ~ past** pasar con dificultad; **on ~** (fig) = **edgy**; **to ~ away from** alejarse poco a poco de; **to ~ forward** avanzar poco a poco; **to ~ up** subir lentamente

edgeways ['ɛdʒweɪz] *adv:* **he couldn't get a word in** ~ no pudo meter baza
edging ['ɛdʒɪŋ] *n* (*Sewing*) ribete *m*; (*of path*) borde *m*
edgy ['ɛdʒɪ] *adj* nervioso, inquieto
edible ['ɛdɪbl] *adj* comestible
edict ['i:dɪkt] *n* edicto
edifice ['ɛdɪfɪs] *n* edificio
edifying ['ɛdɪfaɪɪŋ] *adj* edificante
Edinburgh ['ɛdɪnbərə] *n* Edimburgo
edit ['ɛdɪt] *vt* (*be editor of*) dirigir; (*re-write*) redactar; (*cut*) cortar; (*Comput*) editar
edition [ɪ'dɪʃən] *n* (*gen*) edición *f*; (*number printed*) tirada
editor ['ɛdɪtəʳ] *n* (*of newspaper*) director(a) *m(f)*; (*of book*) redactor(a) *m(f)*; (*also:* **film editor**) montador(a) *m(f)*
editorial [ɛdɪ'tɔ:rɪəl] *adj* editorial ▪ *n* editorial *m*; ~ **staff** redacción *f*
EDP *n abbr* (= *electronic data processing*) PED *m*
EDT *n abbr* (US: = *Eastern Daylight Time*) hora de verano de Nueva York
educate ['ɛdjukeɪt] *vt* (*gen*) educar; (*instruct*) instruir
educated guess ['ɛdjukeɪtɪd-] *n* hipótesis *f* sólida
education [ɛdju'keɪʃən] *n* educación *f*; (*schooling*) enseñanza; (*Scol: subject etc*) pedagogía; **primary/secondary** ~ enseñanza primaria/secundaria
educational [ɛdju'keɪʃənl] *adj* (*policy etc*) de educación, educativo; (*teaching*) docente; (*instructive*) educativo; ~ **technology** tecnología educacional
Edwardian [ɛd'wɔ:dɪən] *adj* eduardiano
EE *abbr* = **electrical engineer**
EEG *n abbr* = **electroencephalogram**
eel [i:l] *n* anguila
EENT *n abbr* (US Med) = **eye, ear, nose and throat**
EEOC *n abbr* (US: = *Equal Employment Opportunity Commission*) comisión que investiga discriminación racial o sexual en el empleo
eerie ['ɪərɪ] *adj* (*sound, experience*) espeluznante
EET *n abbr* (= *Eastern European Time*) hora de Europa oriental
efface [ɪ'feɪs] *vt* borrar
effect [ɪ'fɛkt] *n* efecto ▪ *vt* efectuar, llevar a cabo; **effects** *npl* (*property*) efectos *mpl*; **to take** ~ (*law*) entrar en vigor or vigencia; (*drug*) surtir efecto; **in** ~ en realidad; **to have an** ~ **on sb/sth** hacerle efecto a algn/afectar algo; **to put into** ~ (*plan*) llevar a la práctica; **his letter is to the** ~ **that** ... su carta viene a decir que ...
effective [ɪ'fɛktɪv] *adj* (*gen*) eficaz; (*striking:*

display, outfit) impresionante; (*real*) efectivo; **to become** ~ (*law*) entrar en vigor; ~ **date** fecha de vigencia
effectively [ɪ'fɛktɪvlɪ] *adv* (*efficiently*) eficazmente; (*strikingly*) de manera impresionante; (*in reality*) en efecto
effectiveness [ɪ'fɛktɪvnɪs] *n* eficacia
effeminate [ɪ'fɛmɪnɪt] *adj* afeminado
effervescent [ɛfə'vɛsnt] *adj* efervescente
efficacy ['ɛfɪkəsɪ] *n* eficacia
efficiency [ɪ'fɪʃənsɪ] *n* (*gen*) eficiencia; (*of machine*) rendimiento
efficient [ɪ'fɪʃənt] *adj* eficiente; (*remedy, product, system*) eficaz; (*machine, car*) de buen rendimiento
effigy ['ɛfɪdʒɪ] *n* efigie *f*
effluent ['ɛfluənt] *n* vertidos *mpl*
effort ['ɛfət] *n* esfuerzo; **to make an** ~ **to do sth** hacer un esfuerzo or esforzarse para hacer algo
effortless ['ɛfətlɪs] *adj* sin ningún esfuerzo
effrontery [ɪ'frʌntərɪ] *n* descaro
effusive [ɪ'fju:sɪv] *adj* efusivo
EFL *n abbr* (*Scol*) = **English as a foreign language**
EFTA ['ɛftə] *n abbr* (= *European Free Trade Association*) EFTA *f*
e.g. *adv abbr* (= *exempli gratia*) p.ej.
egg [ɛg] *n* huevo; **hard-boiled/ soft-boiled/poached** ~ huevo duro or (*LAm*) a la copa or (*LAm*) tibio /pasado por agua/escalfado; **scrambled eggs** huevos revueltos
▸ **egg on** *vt* incitar
eggcup ['ɛgkʌp] *n* huevera
eggnog [ɛg'nɔg] *n* ponche *m* de huevo
eggplant ['ɛgplaːnt] *n* (*esp US*) berenjena
eggshell ['ɛgʃɛl] *n* cáscara de huevo
egg-timer ['ɛgtaɪməʳ] *n* reloj *m* de arena (*para cocer huevos*)
egg white *n* clara de huevo
egg yolk *n* yema de huevo
ego ['iːgəu] *n* ego
egotism ['ɛgəutɪzəm] *n* egoísmo
egotist ['ɛgəutɪst] *n* egoísta *m/f*
ego trip *n:* **to be on an** ~ creerse el centro del mundo
Egypt ['iːdʒɪpt] *n* Egipto
Egyptian [ɪ'dʒɪpʃən] *adj, n* egipcio(-a) *m(f)*
eiderdown ['aɪdədaun] *n* edredón *m*
eight [eɪt] *num* ocho
eighteen [eɪ'tiːn] *num* dieciocho
eighth [eɪtθ] *adj* octavo
eighty ['eɪtɪ] *num* ochenta
Eire ['ɛərə] *n* Eire *m*
EIS *n abbr* (= *Educational Institute of Scotland*) sindicato de profesores escoceses

either ['aɪðəʳ] *adj* cualquiera de los dos ...;
(*both, each*) cada ■ *pron*: ~ **(of them)**
cualquiera (de los dos) ■ *adv* tampoco ■ *conj*:
~ **yes or no** o sí o no; **on** ~ **side** en ambos
lados; **I don't like** ~ no me gusta ninguno de
los dos; **no, I don't** ~ no, yo tampoco
eject [ɪ'dʒekt] *vt* echar; (*tenant*) desahuciar
■ *vi* eyectarse
ejector seat [ɪ'dʒɛktə-] *n* asiento proyectable
eke out [i:k-] *vt fus* (*money*) hacer que llegue
EKG *n abbr* (US) *see* **electrocardiogram**
el [ɛl] *n abbr* (*US col*) = **elevated railroad**
elaborate [*adj* ɪ'læbərɪt, *vb* ɪ'læbəreɪt] *adj*
(*design, pattern*) complicado ■ *vt* elaborar
■ *vi* explicarse con muchos detalles
elaborately [ɪ'læbərɪtlɪ] *adv* de manera
complicada; (*decorated*) profusamente
elaboration [ɪlæbə'reɪʃən] *n* elaboración *f*
elapse [ɪ'læps] *vi* transcurrir
elastic [ɪ'læstɪk] *adj, n* elástico
elastic band *n* (Brit) gomita
elated [ɪ'leɪtɪd] *adj*: **to be** ~ estar eufórico
elation [ɪ'leɪʃən] *n* euforia
elbow ['ɛlbəʊ] *n* codo ■ *vt*: **to** ~ **one's way
through the crowd** abrirse paso a codazos
por la muchedumbre
elbow grease *n* (*col*): **to use some** *or* **a bit of**
~ menearse
elder ['ɛldəʳ] *adj* mayor ■ *n* (*tree*) saúco;
(*person*) mayor; (*of tribe*) anciano
elderly ['ɛldəlɪ] *adj* de edad, mayor ■ *npl*:
the ~ la gente mayor, los ancianos
elder statesman *n* estadista *m* veterano; (*fig*)
figura respetada
eldest ['ɛldɪst] *adj, n* el/la mayor
elect [ɪ'lɛkt] *vt* elegir; (*choose*): **to** ~ **to do**
optar por hacer ■ *adj*: **the president** ~ el
presidente electo
election [ɪ'lɛkʃən] *n* elección *f*; **to hold an** ~
convocar elecciones
election campaign *n* campaña electoral
electioneering [ɪlɛkʃə'nɪərɪŋ] *n* campaña
electoral
elector [ɪ'lɛktəʳ] *n* elector(a) *m(f)*
electoral [ɪ'lɛktərəl] *adj* electoral
electoral college *n* colegio electoral
electoral roll *n* censo electoral
electorate [ɪ'lɛktərɪt] *n* electorado
electric [ɪ'lɛktrɪk] *adj* eléctrico
electrical [ɪ'lɛktrɪkl] *adj* eléctrico
electrical engineer *n* ingeniero(-a)
electricista
electrical failure *n* fallo eléctrico
electric blanket *n* manta eléctrica
electric chair *n* silla eléctrica
electric cooker *n* cocina eléctrica
electric current *n* corriente *f* eléctrica

electric fire *n* estufa eléctrica
electrician [ɪlɛk'trɪʃən] *n* electricista *m/f*
electricity [ɪlɛk'trɪsɪtɪ] *n* electricidad *f*;
to switch on/off the ~ conectar/desconectar
la electricidad
electricity board *n* (Brit) compañía eléctrica
(estatal)
electric light *n* luz *f* eléctrica
electric shock *n* electrochoque *m*
electrification [ɪlɛktrɪfɪ'keɪʃən] *n*
electrificación *f*
electrify [ɪ'lɛktrɪfaɪ] *vt* (Rail) electrificar;
(*fig: audience*) electrizar
electro... [ɪ'lɛktrəʊ] *pref* electro...
electrocardiogram [ɪ'lɛktrə'kɑːdɪəgræm] *n*
electrocardiograma *m*
electrocardiograph [ɪ'lɛktrəʊ'kɑːdɪəgrɑːf] *n*
electrocardiógrafo
electro-convulsive therapy [ɪ'lɛktrə-
kən'vʌlsɪv-] *n* electroterapia
electrocute [ɪ'lɛktrəʊkju:t] *vt* electrocutar
electrode [ɪ'lɛktrəʊd] *n* electrodo
electroencephalogram [ɪ'lɛktrəʊen'sɛfələ-
græm] *n* electroencefalograma *m*
electrolysis [ɪlɛk'trɒlɪsɪs] *n* electrólisis *f inv*
electromagnetic [ɪ'lɛktrəmæg'nɛtɪk] *adj*
electromagnético
electron [ɪ'lɛktrɒn] *n* electrón *m*
electronic [ɪlɛk'trɒnɪk] *adj* electrónico
electronic data processing *n* tratamiento *or*
proceso electrónico de datos
electronic mail *n* correo electrónico
electronics [ɪlɛk'trɒnɪks] *n* electrónica
electron microscope *n* microscopio
electrónico
electroplated [ɪ'lɛktrə'pleɪtɪd] *adj*
galvanizado
electrotherapy [ɪ'lɛktrə'θɛrəpɪ] *n*
electroterapia
elegance ['ɛlɪgəns] *n* elegancia
elegant ['ɛlɪgənt] *adj* elegante
elegy ['ɛlɪdʒɪ] *n* elegía
element ['ɛlɪmənt] *n* (*gen*) elemento;
(*of heater, kettle etc*) resistencia
elementary [ɛlɪ'mɛntərɪ] *adj* elemental;
(*primitive*) rudimentario; (*school, education*)
primario
elementary school *n* (US) escuela de
enseñanza primaria; *ver nota*

⬤ **ELEMENTARY SCHOOL**

⬤ En Estados Unidos y Canadá se llama
⬤ *elementary school* al centro estatal en el que
⬤ los niños reciben los primeros seis u ocho
⬤ años de su educación, también llamado
⬤ "grade school" o "grammar school".

elephant ['ɛlɪfənt] n elefante m
elevate ['ɛlɪveɪt] vt (gen) elevar; (in rank)
ascender
elevated railroad n (US) ferrocarril urbano
elevado
elevation [ɛlɪ'veɪʃən] n elevación f; (rank)
ascenso; (height) altitud f
elevator ['ɛlɪveɪtər] n (US) ascensor m,
elevador m (LAm)
eleven [ɪ'lɛvn] num once
elevenses [ɪ'lɛvnzɪz] npl (Brit) ≈ café m de
media mañana
eleventh [ɪ'lɛvnθ] adj undécimo; **at the ~
hour** (fig) a última hora
elf (pl **elves**) [ɛlf, ɛlvz] n duende m
elicit [ɪ'lɪsɪt] vt: **to ~ sth (from sb)** obtener
algo (de algn)
eligible ['ɛlɪdʒəbl] adj cotizado; **to be ~ for a
pension** tener derecho a una pensión
eliminate [ɪ'lɪmɪneɪt] vt eliminar; (score out)
suprimir; (a suspect, possibility) descartar
elimination [ɪlɪmɪ'neɪʃən] n eliminación f;
supresión f; **by process of ~** por eliminación
elite [eɪ'liːt] n élite f
elitist [eɪ'liːtɪst] adj (pej) elitista
elixir [ɪ'lɪksɪər] n elixir m
Elizabethan [ɪlɪzə'biːθən] adj isabelino
elm [ɛlm] n olmo
elocution [ɛlə'kjuːʃən] n elocución f
elongated ['iːlɔŋgeɪtɪd] adj alargado
elope [ɪ'ləup] vi fugarse
elopement [ɪ'ləupmənt] n fuga
eloquence ['ɛləkwəns] n elocuencia
eloquent ['ɛləkwənt] adj elocuente
else [ɛls] adv: **or ~** si no; **something ~** otra
cosa or algo más; **somewhere ~** en otra
parte; **everywhere ~** en los demás sitios;
everyone ~ todos los demás; **nothing ~** nada
más; **is there anything ~ I can do?** ¿puedo
hacer algo más?; **where ~?** ¿dónde más?,
¿en qué otra parte?; **there was little ~ to do**
apenas quedaba otra cosa que hacer; **nobody
~** nadie más
elsewhere [ɛls'wɛər] adv (be) en otra parte;
(go) a otra parte
ELT n abbr (Scol) = **English Language Teaching**
elucidate [ɪ'luːsɪdeɪt] vt esclarecer, elucidar
elude [ɪ'luːd] vt eludir; (blow, pursuer) esquivar
elusive [ɪ'luːsɪv] adj escurridizo; (answer)
difícil de encontrar; **he is very ~** no es fácil
encontrarlo
elves [ɛlvz] npl of **elf**
emaciated [ɪ'meɪsɪeɪtɪd] adj escuálido
email ['iːmeɪl] n abbr (= electronic mail) email m,
correo electrónico ■ vt: **to ~ sb** mandar un
email or un correo electrónico a algn;
to ~ sb sth mandar algo a algn por Internet,

mandar algo a algn en un email or un correo
electrónico
email account n cuenta de correo
email address n dirección f electrónica,
email m
emanate ['ɛməneɪt] vi emanar, provenir
emancipate [ɪ'mænsɪpeɪt] vt emancipar
emancipated [ɪ'mænsɪpeɪtɪd] adj liberado
emancipation [ɪmænsɪ'peɪʃən] n
emancipación f, liberación f
emasculate [ɪ'mæskjuleɪt] vt castrar; (fig)
debilitar
embalm [ɪm'baːm] vt embalsamar
embankment [ɪm'bæŋkmənt] n (of railway)
terraplén m; (riverside) dique m
embargo (pl **embargoes**) [ɪm'baːgəu] n
prohibición f; (Comm, Naut) embargo; **to put
an ~ on sth** poner un embargo en algo
embark [ɪm'baːk] vi embarcarse ■ vt
embarcar; **to ~ on** (journey) comenzar,
iniciar; (fig) emprender
embarkation [ɛmbaː'keɪʃən] n (of people)
embarco; (of goods) embarque m
embarrass [ɪm'bærəs] vt avergonzar, dar
vergüenza a; (financially etc) poner en un aprieto
embarrassed [ɪm'baerəst] adj azorado,
violento; **to be ~** sentirse azorado or violento
embarrassing [ɪm'bærəsɪŋ] adj (situation)
violento; (question) embarazoso
embarrassment [ɪm'bærəsmənt] n
vergüenza, azoramiento; (financial) apuros mpl
embassy ['ɛmbəsɪ] n embajada
embed [ɪm'bɛd] vt (jewel) empotrar; (teeth
etc) clavar
embellish [ɪm'bɛlɪʃ] vt embellecer; (fig: story,
truth) adornar
embers ['ɛmbəz] npl rescoldo sg, ascuas
embezzle [ɪm'bɛzl] vt desfalcar, malversar
embezzlement [ɪm'bɛzlmənt] n desfalco,
malversación f
embezzler [ɪm'bɛzlər] n malversador(a) m(f)
embitter [ɪm'bɪtər] vt (person) amargar;
(relationship) envenenar
embittered [ɪm'bɪtəd] adj resentido,
amargado
emblem ['ɛmbləm] n emblema m
embody [ɪm'bɔdɪ] vt (spirit) encarnar; (ideas)
expresar
embolden [ɪm'bəuldən] vt envalentonar
embolism ['ɛmbəlɪzəm] n embolia
emboss [ɪm'bɔs] vt estampar en relieve;
(metal, leather) repujar
embossed [ɪm'bost] adj realzado; **~ with …**
con … en relieve
embrace [ɪm'breɪs] vt abrazar, dar un abrazo
a; (include) abarcar; (adopt: idea) adherirse a
■ vi abrazarse ■ n abrazo

embroider [ɪmˈbrɔɪdəʳ] vt bordar; (fig: story) adornar, embellecer

embroidery [ɪmˈbrɔɪdərɪ] n bordado

embroil [ɪmˈbrɔɪl] vt: **to become embroiled (in sth)** enredarse (en algo)

embryo [ˈɛmbrɪəu] n (also fig) embrión m

emcee [ɛmˈsiː] n abbr (US: = master of ceremonies) presentador(a) m(f)

emend [ɪˈmɛnd] vt (text) enmendar

emerald [ˈɛmərəld] n esmeralda

emerge [ɪˈmɜːdʒ] vi (gen) salir; (arise) surgir; **it emerges that** resulta que

emergence [ɪˈmɜːdʒəns] n (of nation) surgimiento

emergency [ɪˈmɜːdʒənsɪ] n (event) emergencia; (crisis) crisis f inv; **in an ~** en caso de urgencia; **(to declare a) state of ~** (declarar) estado de emergencia or de excepción

emergency cord n (US) timbre m de alarma

emergency exit n salida de emergencia

emergency landing n aterrizaje m forzoso

emergency lane n (US) arcén m

emergency meeting n reunión f extraordinaria

emergency service n servicio de urgencia

emergency stop n (Aut) parada en seco

emergent [ɪˈmɜːdʒənt] adj (nation) recientemente independizado

emery board [ˈɛmərɪ-] n lima de uñas

emetic [ɪˈmɛtɪk] n vomitivo, emético

emigrant [ˈɛmɪɡrənt] n emigrante m/f

emigrate [ˈɛmɪɡreɪt] vi emigrar

emigration [ɛmɪˈɡreɪʃən] n emigración f

émigré [ˈɛmɪɡreɪ] n emigrado(-a)

eminence [ˈɛmɪnəns] n eminencia; **to gain** or **win ~** ganarse fama

eminent [ˈɛmɪnənt] adj eminente

eminently [ˈɛmɪnəntlɪ] adv eminentemente

emirate [ˈɛmɪrɪt] n emirato

emission [ɪˈmɪʃən] n emisión f

emit [ɪˈmɪt] vt emitir; (smell, smoke) despedir

emolument [ɪˈmɔljumənt] n (often pl: formal) honorario, emolumento

emoticon [ɪˈməutɪkɔn] n emoticón m

emotion [ɪˈməuʃən] n emoción f

emotional [ɪˈməuʃənl] adj (person) sentimental; (scene) conmovedor(a), emocionante

emotionally [ɪˈməuʃnəlɪ] adv (behave, speak) con emoción; (be involved) sentimentalmente

emotive [ɪˈməutɪv] adj emotivo

empathy [ˈɛmpəθɪ] n empatía; **to feel ~ with sb** sentirse identificado con algn

emperor [ˈɛmpərəʳ] n emperador m

emphasis (pl **emphases**) [ˈɛmfəsɪs, -siːz] n énfasis m inv; **to lay** or **place ~ on sth** (fig) hacer hincapié en algo; **the ~ is on sport** se

da mayor importancia al deporte

emphasize [ˈɛmfəsaɪz] vt (word, point) subrayar, recalcar; (feature) hacer resaltar

emphatic [ɛmˈfætɪk] adj (condemnation) enérgico; (denial) rotundo

emphatically [ɛmˈfætɪklɪ] adv con énfasis

emphysema [ɛmfɪˈsiːmə] n (Med) enfisema m

empire [ˈɛmpaɪəʳ] n imperio

empirical [ɛmˈpɪrɪkl] adj empírico

employ [ɪmˈplɔɪ] vt (give job to) emplear; (make use of: thing, method) emplear, usar; **he's employed in a bank** está empleado en un banco

employee [ɪmplɔɪˈiː] n empleado(-a)

employer [ɪmˈplɔɪəʳ] n patrón(-ona) m(f); (businessman) empresario(-a)

employment [ɪmˈplɔɪmənt] n empleo; **full ~** pleno empleo; **without ~** sin empleo; **to find ~** encontrar trabajo; **place of ~** lugar m de trabajo

employment agency n agencia de colocaciones or empleo

employment exchange n bolsa de trabajo

empower [ɪmˈpauəʳ] vt: **to ~ sb to do sth** autorizar a algn para hacer algo

empress [ˈɛmprɪs] n emperatriz f

emptiness [ˈɛmptɪnɪs] n vacío

empty [ˈɛmptɪ] adj vacío; (street, area) desierto; (threat) vano ∎ n (bottle) envase m ∎ vt vaciar; (place) dejar vacío ∎ vi vaciarse; (house) quedar(se) vacío or desocupado; (place) quedar(se) desierto; **to ~ into** (river) desembocar en

empty-handed [ˈɛmptɪˈhændɪd] adj con las manos vacías

empty-headed [ˈɛmptɪˈhɛdɪd] adj casquivano

EMS n abbr (= European Monetary System) SME m

EMT n abbr (US) = **emergency medical technician**

EMU n abbr (= European Monetary Union, Economic and Monetary Union) UME f

emulate [ˈɛmjuleɪt] vt emular

emulsion [ɪˈmʌlʃən] n emulsión f

enable [ɪˈneɪbl] vt: **to ~ sb to do sth** (allow) permitir a algn hacer algo; (prepare) capacitar a algn para hacer algo

enact [ɪnˈækt] vt (law) promulgar; (play, scene, role) representar

enamel [ɪˈnæməl] n esmalte m

enamel paint n esmalte m

enamoured [ɪˈnæməd] adj: **to be ~ of** (person) estar enamorado de; (activity etc) tener gran afición a; (idea) aferrarse a

enc. abbr (on letters etc: = enclosed, enclosure) adj

encampment [ɪnˈkæmpmənt] n campamento

encase [ɪn'keɪs] vt: **to ~ in** (contain) encajar; (cover) cubrir

encased [ɪn'keɪst] adj: **~ in** (covered) revestido de

enchant [ɪn'tʃɑːnt] vt encantar

enchanting [ɪn'tʃɑːntɪŋ] adj encantador(a)

encircle [ɪn'səːkl] vt (gen) rodear; (waist) ceñir

encl. abbr (= enclosed) adj

enclave ['enkleɪv] n enclave m

enclose [ɪn'kləuz] vt (land) cercar; (with letter etc) adjuntar; (in receptacle): **to ~ (with)** encerrar (con); **please find enclosed** le mandamos adjunto

enclosure [ɪn'kləuʒər] n cercado, recinto; (Comm) carta adjunta

encoder [ɪn'kəudər] n (Comput) codificador m

encompass [ɪn'kʌmpəs] vt abarcar

encore [ɔŋ'kɔːr] excl ¡otra!, ¡bis! ■ n bis m

encounter [ɪn'kauntər] n encuentro ■ vt encontrar, encontrarse con; (difficulty) tropezar con

encourage [ɪn'kʌrɪdʒ] vt alentar, animar; (growth) estimular; **to ~ sb (to do sth)** animar a algn (a hacer algo)

encouragement [ɪn'kʌrɪdʒmənt] n estímulo; (of industry) fomento

encouraging [ɪn'kʌrɪdʒɪŋ] adj alentador(a)

encroach [ɪn'krəutʃ] vi: **to ~ (up)on** (gen) invadir; (time) adueñarse de

encrust [ɪn'krʌst] vt incrustar

encrusted [ɪn'krʌstəd] adj: **~ with** recubierto de

encumber [ɪn'kʌmbər] vt: **to be encumbered with** (carry) estar cargado de; (debts) estar gravado de

encyclopaedia, encyclopedia [ensaɪkləu'piːdɪə] n enciclopedia

end [end] n fin m; (of table) extremo; (of line, rope etc) cabo; (of pointed object) punta; (of town) barrio; (of street) final m; (Sport) lado ■ vt terminar, acabar; (also: **bring to an end, put an end to**) acabar con ■ vi terminar, acabar; **to ~ (with)** terminar (con); **in the ~** al final; **to be at an ~** llegar a su fin; **at the ~ of the day** (fig) al fin y al cabo, a fin de cuentas; **to this ~, with this ~ in view** con este propósito; **from ~ to ~** de punta a punta; **on ~** (object) de punta, de cabeza; **to stand on ~** (hair) erizarse, ponerse de punta; **for hours on ~** hora tras hora

▶ **end up** vi: **to ~ up** terminar en; (place) ir a parar a

endanger [ɪn'deɪndʒər] vt poner en peligro; **an endangered species** (of animal) una especie en peligro de extinción

endear [ɪn'dɪər] vt: **to ~ o.s. to sb** ganarse la simpatía de algn

endearing [ɪn'dɪərɪŋ] adj entrañable

endearment [ɪn'dɪərmənt] n cariño, palabra cariñosa; **to whisper endearments** decir unas palabras cariñosas al oído; **term of ~** nombre m cariñoso

endeavour, endeavor (US) [ɪn'devər] n esfuerzo; (attempt) tentativa ■ vi: **to ~ to do** esforzarse por hacer; (try) procurar hacer

endemic [en'demɪk] adj (poverty, disease) endémico

ending ['endɪŋ] n fin m, final m; (of book) desenlace m; (Ling) terminación f

endive ['endaɪv] n (curly) escarola; (smooth, flat) endibia

endless ['endlɪs] adj interminable, inacabable; (possibilities) infinito

endorse [ɪn'dɔːs] vt (cheque) endosar; (approve) aprobar

endorsee [ɪndɔː'siː] n endorsatario(-a)

endorsement [ɪn'dɔːsmənt] n (approval) aprobación f; (signature) endoso; (Brit: on driving licence) nota de sanción

endorser [ɪn'dɔːsər] n avalista m/f

endow [ɪn'dau] vt (provide with money) dotar; (found) fundar; **to be endowed with** (fig) estar dotado de

endowment [ɪn'daumənt] adj (amount) donación f

endowment mortgage n hipoteca dotal

endowment policy n póliza dotal

end product n (Industry) producto final; (fig) resultado

end result n resultado

endurable [ɪn'djuərəbl] adj soportable, tolerable

endurance [ɪn'djuərəns] n resistencia

endurance test n prueba de resistencia

endure [ɪn'djuər] vt (bear) aguantar, soportar; (resist) resistir ■ vi (last) perdurar; (resist) resistir

enduring [ɪn'djuərɪŋ] adj duradero

end user n (Comput) usuario final

enema ['enɪmə] n (Med) enema m

enemy ['enəmɪ] adj, n enemigo(-a) m(f); **to make an ~ of sb** enemistarse con algn

energetic [enə'dʒetɪk] adj enérgico

energy ['enədʒɪ] n energía

energy crisis n crisis f energética

energy-saving ['enədʒɪseɪvɪŋ] adj (policy) para ahorrar energía; (device) que ahorra energía ■ n ahorro de energía

enervating ['enəveɪtɪŋ] adj deprimente

enforce [ɪn'fɔːs] vt (law) hacer cumplir

enforced [ɪn'fɔːst] adj forzoso, forzado

enfranchise [ɪn'fræntʃaɪz] vt (give vote to) conceder el derecho de voto a; (set free) emancipar

engage [ɪn'geɪdʒ] vt (attention) captar; (in conversation) abordar; (worker, lawyer) contratar ■ vi (Tech) engranar; **to ~ in** dedicarse a, ocuparse en; **to ~ sb in conversation** entablar conversación con algn; **to ~ the clutch** embragar

engaged [ɪn'geɪdʒd] adj (Brit: busy, in use) ocupado; (betrothed) prometido; **to get ~** prometerse; **he is ~ in research** se dedica a la investigación

engaged tone n (Brit Tel) señal f de comunicando

engagement [ɪn'geɪdʒmənt] n (appointment) compromiso, cita; (battle) combate m; (to marry) compromiso; (period) noviazgo; **I have a previous ~** ya tengo un compromiso

engagement ring n anillo de pedida

engaging [ɪn'geɪdʒɪŋ] adj atractivo, simpático

engender [ɪn'dʒɛndəʳ] vt engendrar

engine ['ɛndʒɪn] n (Aut) motor m; (Rail) locomotora

engine driver n (Brit: of train) maquinista m/f

engineer [ɛndʒɪ'nɪəʳ] n ingeniero(-a); (Brit: for repairs) técnico(-a); (US Rail) maquinista m/f; **civil/mechanical ~** ingeniero(-a) de caminos, canales y puertos/industrial

engineering [ɛndʒɪ'nɪərɪŋ] n ingeniería ■ cpd (works, factory) de componentes mecánicos

engine failure, engine trouble n avería del motor

England ['ɪŋglənd] n Inglaterra

English ['ɪŋglɪʃ] adj inglés(-esa) ■ n (Ling) el inglés; **the English** npl los ingleses

English Channel n: **the ~** el Canal de la Mancha

Englishman ['ɪŋglɪʃmən], **Englishwoman** ['ɪŋglɪʃwumən] n inglés(-esa) m(f)

English-speaker ['ɪŋglɪʃspi:kəʳ] n persona de habla inglesa

English-speaking ['ɪŋglɪʃspi:kɪŋ] adj de habla inglesa

engraving [ɪn'greɪvɪŋ] n grabado

engrossed [ɪn'grəust] adj: **~ in** absorto en

engulf [ɪn'gʌlf] vt sumergir, hundir; (fire) devorar

enhance [ɪn'hɑːns] vt (gen) aumentar; (beauty) realzar; (position, reputation) mejorar

enigma [ɪ'nɪgmə] n enigma m

enigmatic [ɛnɪg'mætɪk] adj enigmático

enjoy [ɪn'dʒɔɪ] vt (have: health, fortune) disfrutar de, gozar de; (food) comer con gusto; **I ~ doing ...** me gusta hacer ...; **to ~ o.s.** divertirse, pasarlo bien

enjoyable [ɪn'dʒɔɪəbl] adj (pleasant) agradable; (amusing) divertido

enjoyment [ɪn'dʒɔɪmənt] n (use) disfrute m; (joy) placer m

enlarge [ɪn'lɑːdʒ] vt aumentar; (broaden) extender; (Phot) ampliar ■ vi: **to ~ on** (subject) tratar con más detalles

enlarged [ɪn'lɑːdʒd] adj (edition) aumentado; (Med: organ, gland) dilatado

enlargement [ɪn'lɑːdʒmənt] n (Phot) ampliación f

enlighten [ɪn'laɪtn] vt informar, instruir

enlightened [ɪn'laɪtnd] adj iluminado; (tolerant) comprensivo

enlightening [ɪn'laɪtnɪŋ] adj informativo, instructivo

Enlightenment [ɪn'laɪtnmənt] n (History): **the ~** la Ilustración, el Siglo de las Luces

enlist [ɪn'lɪst] vt alistar; (support) conseguir ■ vi alistarse; **enlisted man** (US Mil) soldado raso

enliven [ɪn'laɪvn] vt (people) animar; (events) avivar, animar

enmity ['ɛnmɪtɪ] n enemistad f

ennoble [ɪ'nəubl] vt ennoblecer

enormity [ɪ'nɔːmɪtɪ] n enormidad f

enormous [ɪ'nɔːməs] adj enorme

enough [ɪ'nʌf] adj: **~ time/books** bastante tiempo/bastantes libros ■ pron: **have you got ~?** ¿tiene usted bastante? ■ adv: **big ~** bastante grande; **he has not worked ~** no ha trabajado bastante; **(that's) ~!** ¡basta ya!, ¡ya está bien!; **that's ~, thanks** con eso basta, gracias; **will five be ~?** ¿bastará con cinco?; **I've had ~** estoy harto; **he was kind ~ to lend me the money** tuvo la bondad or amabilidad de prestarme el dinero; ... **which, funnily ~ ... ...** lo que, por extraño que parezca ...

enquire [ɪn'kwaɪəʳ] vt, vi = **inquire**

enrage [ɪn'reɪdʒ] vt enfurecer

enrich [ɪn'rɪtʃ] vt enriquecer

enrol, enroll (US) [ɪn'rəul] vt (member) inscribir; (Scol) matricular ■ vi inscribirse; (Scol) matricularse

enrolment, enrollment (US) [ɪn'rəulmənt] n inscripción f; matriculación f

en route [ɔn'ruːt] adv durante el viaje; **~ for/ from/to** camino de/de/a

ensconce [ɪn'skɔns] vt: **to ~ o.s.** instalarse cómodamente, acomodarse

ensemble [ɔn'sɔmbl] n (Mus) conjunto

enshrine [ɪn'ʃraɪn] vt recoger

ensign ['ɛnsaɪn] n (flag) bandera; (Naut) alférez m

enslave [ɪn'sleɪv] vt esclavizar

ensue [ɪn'sjuː] vi seguirse; (result) resultar

ensuing [ɪn'sjuːɪŋ] adj subsiguiente

ensure [ɪn'ʃuəʳ] vt asegurar

ENT n abbr (Med: = ear, nose and throat) otorrinolaringología

entail [ɪn'teɪl] vt (imply) suponer; (result in) acarrear

entangle [ɪn'tæŋgl] vt (thread etc) enredar, enmarañar; **to become entangled in sth** (fig) enredarse en algo

entanglement [ɪn'tæŋglmənt] n enredo

enter ['ɛntə'] vt (room, profession) entrar en; (club) hacerse socio de; (army) alistarse en; (sb for a competition) inscribir; (write down) anotar, apuntar; (Comput) introducir ▪ vi entrar; **to ~ for** vt fus presentarse a; **to ~ into** vt fus (relations) establecer; (plans) formar parte de; (debate) tomar parte en; (negotiations) entablar; (agreement) llegar a, firmar; **to ~ (up)on** vt fus (career) emprender

enteritis [ɛntə'raɪtɪs] n enteritis f

enterprise ['ɛntəpraɪz] n empresa; (spirit) iniciativa; **free ~** la libre empresa; **private ~** la iniciativa privada

enterprising ['ɛntəpraɪzɪŋ] adj emprendedor(a)

entertain [ɛntə'teɪn] vt (amuse) divertir; (receive: guest) recibir (en casa); (idea) abrigar

entertainer [ɛntə'teɪnə'] n artista m/f

entertaining [ɛntə'teɪnɪŋ] adj divertido, entretenido ▪ n: **to do a lot of ~** dar muchas fiestas, tener muchos invitados

entertainment [ɛntə'teɪnmənt] n (amusement) diversión f; (show) espectáculo; (party) fiesta

entertainment allowance n (Comm) gastos mpl de representación

enthral [ɪn'θrɔːl] vt embelesar, cautivar

enthralled [ɪn'θrɔːld] adj cautivado

enthralling [ɪn'θrɔːlɪŋ] adj cautivador(a)

enthuse [ɪn'θuːz] vi: **to ~ about** or **over** entusiasmarse por

enthusiasm [ɪn'θuːzɪæzəm] n entusiasmo

enthusiast [ɪn'θuːzɪæst] n entusiasta m/f

enthusiastic [ɪnθuːzɪ'æstɪk] adj entusiasta; **to be ~ about sb/sth** estar entusiasmado con algn/algo

entice [ɪn'taɪs] vt tentar; (seduce) seducir

entire [ɪn'taɪə'] adj entero, todo

entirely [ɪn'taɪəlɪ] adv totalmente

entirety [ɪn'taɪərətɪ] n: **in its ~** en su totalidad

entitle [ɪn'taɪtl] vt: **to ~ sb to sth** dar a algn derecho a algo

entitled [ɪn'taɪtld] adj (book) titulado; **to be ~ to sth/to do sth** tener derecho a algo/a hacer algo

entity ['ɛntɪtɪ] n entidad f

entourage [ɔntu'rɑːʒ] n séquito

entrails ['ɛntreɪlz] npl entrañas fpl; (US: offal) asadura sg, menudos mpl

entrance ['ɛntrəns] n entrada ▪ vt [ɪn'trɑːns] encantar, hechizar; **to gain ~ to** (university etc) ingresar en

entrance examination n (to school) examen m de ingreso

entrance fee n entrada

entrance ramp n (US Aut) rampa de acceso

entrancing [ɪn'trɑːnsɪŋ] adj encantador(a)

entrant ['ɛntrənt] n (in race, competition) participante m/f; (in exam) candidato(-a)

entreat [ɛn'triːt] vt rogar, suplicar

entrenched [ɛn'trɛntʃd] adj: **~ interests** intereses mpl creados

entrepreneur [ɔntrəprə'nəː'] n empresario(-a), capitalista m/f

entrepreneurial [ɔntrəprə'nəːrɪəl] adj empresarial

entrust [ɪn'trʌst] vt: **to ~ sth to sb** confiar algo a algn

entry ['ɛntrɪ] n entrada; (permission to enter) acceso; (in register, diary, ship's log) apunte m; (in account book, ledger, list) partida; **no ~** prohibido el paso; (Aut) dirección prohibida; **single/double ~ book-keeping** contabilidad f simple/por partida doble

entry form n boletín m de inscripción

entry phone n (Brit) portero automático

E-number ['iːnʌmbə'] n número E

enumerate [ɪ'njuːməreɪt] vt enumerar

enunciate [ɪ'nʌnsɪeɪt] vt pronunciar; (principle etc) enunciar

envelop [ɪn'vɛləp] vt envolver

envelope ['ɛnvələup] n sobre m

enviable ['ɛnvɪəbl] adj envidiable

envious ['ɛnvɪəs] adj envidioso; (look) de envidia

environment [ɪn'vaɪərnmənt] n medio ambiente; (surroundings) entorno; **Department of the E~** ministerio del medio ambiente

environmental [ɪnvaɪərn'mɛntl] adj (medio) ambiental; **~ studies** (in school etc) ecología sg

environmentalist [ɪnvaɪərn'mɛntlɪst] n ecologista m/f

environmentally [ɪnvaɪərn'mɛntlɪ] adv: **~ sound/friendly** ecológico

envisage [ɪn'vɪzɪdʒ] vt (foresee) prever; (imagine) concebir

envision [ɪn'vɪʒən] vt imaginar

envoy ['ɛnvɔɪ] n enviado(-a)

envy ['ɛnvɪ] n envidia ▪ vt tener envidia a; **to ~ sb sth** envidiar algo a algn

enzyme ['ɛnzaɪm] n enzima m or f

EPA n abbr (US: = Environmental Protection Agency) Agencia del Medio Ambiente

ephemeral [ɪ'fɛmərl] adj efímero

epic ['ɛpɪk] n epopeya ▪ adj épico

539

epicentre, (US) **epicenter** ['ɛpɪsɛntə^r] n
epicentro
epidemic [ɛpɪ'dɛmɪk] n epidemia
epigram ['ɛpɪgræm] n epigrama m
epilepsy ['ɛpɪlɛpsɪ] n epilepsia
epileptic [ɛpɪ'lɛptɪk] adj, n epiléptico(-a) m(f)
epilogue ['ɛpɪlɒg] n epílogo
episcopal [ɪ'pɪskəpl] adj episcopal
episode ['ɛpɪsəud] n episodio
epistle [ɪ'pɪsl] n epístola
epitaph ['ɛpɪtɑːf] n epitafio
epithet ['ɛpɪθɛt] n epíteto
epitome [ɪ'pɪtəmɪ] n arquetipo
epitomize [ɪ'pɪtəmaɪz] vt representar
epoch ['iːpɒk] n época
eponymous [ɪ'pɒnɪməs] adj epónimo
equable ['ɛkwəbl] adj (climate) estable;
(character) ecuánime
equal ['iːkwl] adj (gen) igual; (treatment)
equitativo ■ n igual m/f ■ vt ser igual a; (fig)
igualar; **to be ~ to** (task) estar a la altura de;
the E~ Opportunities Commission (Brit)
comisión para la igualdad de la mujer en el trabajo
equality [iː'kwɒlɪtɪ] n igualdad f
equalize ['iːkwəlaɪz] vt, vi igualar; (Sport)
empatar
equalizer ['iːkwəlaɪzə^r] n igualada
equally ['iːkwəlɪ] adv igualmente; (share etc)
a partes iguales; **they are ~ clever** son tan
listos uno como otro
equals sign n signo igual
equanimity [ɛkwə'nɪmɪtɪ] n ecuanimidad f
equate [ɪ'kweɪt] vt: **to ~ sth with** equiparar
algo con
equation [ɪ'kweɪʒən] n (Math) ecuación f
equator [ɪ'kweɪtə^r] n ecuador m
equatorial [ɛkwə'tɔːrɪəl] adj ecuatorial
Equatorial Guinea n Guinea Ecuatorial
equestrian [ɪ'kwɛstrɪən] adj ecuestre
■ n jinete m/f
equilibrium [iːkwɪ'lɪbrɪəm] n equilibrio
equinox ['iːkwɪnɒks] n equinoccio
equip [ɪ'kwɪp] vt (gen) equipar; (person)
proveer; **equipped with** (machinery etc)
provisto de; **to be well equipped** estar bien
equipado; **he is well equipped for the job**
está bien preparado para este puesto
equipment [ɪ'kwɪpmənt] n equipo
equitable ['ɛkwɪtəbl] adj equitativo
equities ['ɛkwɪtɪz] npl (Brit Comm) acciones fpl
ordinarias
equity ['ɛkwɪtɪ] n (fairness) equidad f; (Econ: of
debtor) valor m líquido
equity capital n capital m propio,
patrimonio neto
equivalent [ɪ'kwɪvəlnt] adj, n equivalente m;
to be ~ to equivaler a

equivocal [ɪ'kwɪvəkl] adj equívoco
equivocate [ɪ'kwɪvəkeɪt] vi andarse con
ambigüedades
equivocation [ɪkwɪvə'keɪʃən] n
ambigüedad f
ER abbr (Brit: = Elizabeth Regina) la reina Isabel
er [əː] interj (col: in hesitation) esto, este (LAm)
ERA n abbr (US Pol: = Equal Rights Amendment)
enmienda sobre la igualdad de derechos de la mujer
era ['ɪərə] n era, época
eradicate [ɪ'rædɪkeɪt] vt erradicar, extirpar
erase [ɪ'reɪz] vt (Comput) borrar
eraser [ɪ'reɪzə^r] n goma de borrar
erect [ɪ'rɛkt] adj erguido ■ vt erigir, levantar;
(assemble) montar
erection [ɪ'rɛkʃən] n (of building) construcción
f; (of machinery) montaje m; (structure) edificio;
(Med) erección f
ergonomics [əːgə'nɒmɪks] n ergonomía
ERISA n abbr (US: = Employee Retirement Income
Security Act) ley que regula las pensiones de jubilados
Eritrea [ɛrɪ'treɪə] n Eritrea
ERM n abbr (= Exchange Rate Mechanism)
(mecanismo de cambios del) SME m
ermine ['əːmɪn] n armiño
ERNIE ['əːnɪ] n abbr (Brit: = Electronic Random
Number Indicator Equipment) ordenador que elige al
azar los números ganadores de los bonos del Estado
erode [ɪ'rəud] vt (Geo) erosionar; (metal)
corroer, desgastar
erogenous zone [ɪ'rɒdʒənəs-] n zona
erógena
erosion [ɪ'rəuʒən] n erosión f; desgaste m
erotic [ɪ'rɒtɪk] adj erótico
eroticism [ɪ'rɒtɪsɪzm] n erotismo
err [əː^r] vi errar; (Rel) pecar
errand ['ɛrnd] n recado, mandado; **to run
errands** hacer recados; **~ of mercy** misión f
de caridad
errand boy n recadero
erratic [ɪ'rætɪk] adj variable; (results etc)
desigual, poco uniforme
erroneous [ɪ'rəunɪəs] adj erróneo
error ['ɛrə^r] n error m, equivocación f; **typing/
spelling ~** error de mecanografía/ortografía;
in ~ por equivocación; **errors and
omissions excepted** salvo error u omisión
error message n (Comput) mensaje m de error
erstwhile ['əːstwaɪl] adj antiguo, previo
erudite ['ɛrudaɪt] adj erudito
erudition [ɛru'dɪʃən] n erudición f
erupt [ɪ'rʌpt] vi entrar en erupción; (Med)
hacer erupción; (fig) estallar
eruption [ɪ'rʌpʃən] n erupción f; (fig: of anger,
violence) explosión f, estallido
ESA n abbr (= European Space Agency) Agencia
Espacial Europea

escalate ['ɛskəleɪt] *vi* extenderse, intensificarse; (*costs*) aumentar vertiginosamente

escalation clause [ɛskə'leɪʃən-] *n* cláusula de reajuste de los precios

escalator ['ɛskəleɪtəʳ] *n* escalera mecánica

escapade [ɛskə'peɪd] *n* aventura

escape [ɪ'skeɪp] *n* (*gen*) fuga; (*Tech*) escape *m*; (*from duties*) escapatoria; (*from chase*) evasión *f* ■ *vi* (*gen*) escaparse; (*flee*) huir, evadirse ■ *vt* evitar, eludir; (*consequences*) escapar a; **to ~ from** (*place*) escaparse de; (*person*) huir de; (*clutches*) librarse de; **to ~ to** (*another place, freedom, safety*) huir a; **to ~ notice** pasar desapercibido

escape artist *n* artista *m/f* de la evasión

escape clause *n* (*fig: in agreement*) cláusula de excepción

escapee [ɪskeɪ'piː] *n* fugado(-a)

escape hatch *n* (*in submarine, space rocket*) escotilla de salvamento

escape key *n* (*Comput*) tecla de escape

escape route *n* (*from fire*) vía de escape

escapism [ɪ'skeɪpɪzəm] *n* escapismo, evasión *f*

escapist [ɪ'skeɪpɪst] *adj* escapista, de evasión ■ *n* escapista *m/f*

escapologist [ɛskə'pɒlədʒɪst] *n* (*Brit*) = **escape artist**

escarpment [ɪ'skɑːpmənt] *n* escarpa

eschew [ɪs'tʃuː] *vt* evitar, abstenerse de

escort ['ɛskɔːt] *n* acompañante *m/f*; (*Mil*) escolta; (*Naut*) convoy *m* ■ *vt* [ɪ'skɔːt] acompañar; (*Mil, Naut*) escoltar

escort agency *n* agencia de acompañantes

Eskimo ['ɛskɪməu] *adj* esquimal ■ *n* esquimal *m/f*; (*Ling*) esquimal *m*

ESL *n abbr* (*Scol*) = **English as a Second Language**

esophagus [iː'sɒfəgəs] *n* (*US*) = **oesophagus**

esoteric [ɛsəu'tɛrɪk] *adj* esotérico

ESP *n abbr* = **extrasensory perception**; (*Scol:* = *English for Specific (or Special) Purposes*) inglés especializado

esp. *abbr* = **especially**

especially [ɪ'spɛʃlɪ] *adv* (*gen*) especialmente; (*above all*) sobre todo; (*particularly*) en especial

espionage ['ɛspiənɑːʒ] *n* espionaje *m*

esplanade [ɛsplə'neɪd] *n* (*by sea*) paseo marítimo

espouse [ɪ'spauz] *vt* adherirse a

Esq. *abbr* (= *Esquire*) D.

Esquire [ɪ'skwaɪəʳ] *n*: **J. Brown, ~** Sr. D. J. Brown

essay ['ɛseɪ] *n* (*Scol*) redacción *f*; (*: longer*) trabajo

essayist ['ɛseɪɪst] *n* ensayista *m/f*

essence ['ɛsns] *n* esencia; **in ~** esencialmente; **speed is of the ~** es esencial hacerlo con la mayor prontitud

essential [ɪ'sɛnʃl] *adj* (*necessary*) imprescindible; (*basic*) esencial ■ *n* (*often pl*) lo esencial; **it is ~ that** es imprescindible que

essentially [ɪ'sɛnʃlɪ] *adv* esencialmente

EST *n abbr* (*US:* = *Eastern Standard Time*) hora de invierno de Nueva York

est. *abbr* (= *established*) fundado; (= *estimated*) aprox.

establish [ɪ'stæblɪʃ] *vt* establecer; (*prove: fact*) comprobar, demostrar; (*identity*) verificar; (*relations*) entablar

established [ɪ'stæblɪʃt] *adj* (*business*) de buena reputación; (*staff*) de plantilla

establishment [ɪ'stæblɪʃmənt] *n* establecimiento; (*also:* **the Establishment**) la clase dirigente; **a teaching ~** un centro de enseñanza

estate [ɪ'steɪt] *n* (*land*) finca, hacienda; (*property*) propiedad *f*; (*inheritance*) herencia; (*Pol*) estado; **housing ~** (*Brit*) urbanización *f*; **industrial ~** polígono industrial

estate agency *n* (*Brit*) agencia inmobiliaria

estate agent *n* (*Brit*) agente *m/f* inmobiliario(-a)

estate agent's *n* agencia inmobiliaria

estate car *n* (*Brit*) ranchera

esteem [ɪ'stiːm] *n*: **to hold sb in high ~** estimar en mucho a algn ■ *vt* estimar

esthetic [iːs'θɛtɪk] *adj* (*US*) = **aesthetic**

estimate ['ɛstɪmət] *n* estimación *f*; (*assessment*) tasa, cálculo; (*Comm*) presupuesto ■ *vt* ['ɛstɪmeɪt] estimar; tasar, calcular; **to give sb an ~ of** presentar a algn un presupuesto de; **at a rough ~** haciendo un cálculo aproximado; **to ~ for** (*Comm*) hacer un presupuesto de, presupuestar

estimation [ɛstɪ'meɪʃən] *n* opinión *f*, juicio; (*esteem*) aprecio; **in my ~** a mi juicio

Estonia [ɛ'stəunɪə] *n* Estonia

Estonian [ɛ'stəunɪən] *adj* estonio ■ *n* estonio(-a); (*Ling*) estonio

estranged [ɪ'streɪndʒd] *adj* separado

estrangement [ɪ'streɪndʒmənt] *n* alejamiento, distanciamiento

estrogen ['iːstrəudʒən] *n* (*US*) = **oestrogen**

estuary ['ɛstjuərɪ] *n* estuario, ría

ET *n abbr* (*Brit:* = *Employment Training*) plan estatal de formación para los desempleados ■ *abbr* (*US*) = **Eastern Time**

ETA *n abbr* = **estimated time of arrival**

e-tailing ['iːteɪlɪŋ] *n* venta en línea, venta vía or por Internet

et al. *abbr* (= *et alii: and others*) et al.

etc *abbr* (= *et cetera*) etc
etch [ɛtʃ] *vt* grabar al aguafuerte
etching ['ɛtʃɪŋ] *n* aguafuerte *m or f*
ETD *n abbr* = **estimated time of departure**
eternal [ɪ'tə:nl] *adj* eterno
eternity [ɪ'tə:nɪtɪ] *n* eternidad *f*
ether ['i:θəʳ] *n* éter *m*
ethereal [ɪ'θɪərɪəl] *adj* etéreo
ethical ['ɛθɪkl] *adj* ético; (*honest*) honrado
ethics ['ɛθɪks] *n* ética ◼ *npl* moralidad *f*
Ethiopia [i:θɪ'əupɪə] *n* Etiopía
Ethiopian [i:θɪ'əupɪən] *adj, n* etíope *m/f*
ethnic ['ɛθnɪk] *adj* étnico
ethnic cleansing [-klɛnzɪŋ] *n* limpieza étnica
ethos ['i:θɔs] *n* (*of culture, group*) sistema *m* de valores
e-ticket ['i:tɪkɪt] *n* billete electrónico, boleto electrónico (*LAm*)
etiquette ['ɛtɪkɛt] *n* etiqueta
ETV *n abbr* (*US*: = *Educational Television*) televisión escolar
etymology [ɛtɪ'mɔlədʒɪ] *n* etimología
EU *n abbr* (= *European Union*) UE *f*
eucalyptus [ju:kə'lɪptəs] *n* eucalipto
Eucharist ['ju:kərɪst] *n* Eucaristía
eulogy ['ju:lədʒɪ] *n* elogio, encomio
eunuch ['ju:nək] *n* eunuco
euphemism ['ju:fəmɪzm] *n* eufemismo
euphemistic [ju:fə'mɪstɪk] *adj* eufemístico
euphoria [ju:'fɔ:rɪə] *n* euforia
Eurasia [juə'reɪʒə] *n* Eurasia
Eurasian [juə'reɪʃən] *adj, n* eurasiático(-a) *m(f)*
Euratom [juə'rætəm] *n abbr* (= *European Atomic Energy Commission*) Euratom *m*
Euro- *pref* euro-
euro ['juərəu] *n* (*currency*) euro
Eurocheque ['juərəutʃɛk] *n* Eurocheque *m*
Eurocrat ['juərəukræt] *n* eurócrata *m/f*
Eurodollar ['juərəudɔləʳ] *n* eurodólar *m*
Euroland ['juərəulænd] *n* Eurolandia
Europe ['juərəp] *n* Europa
European [juərə'pi:ən] *adj, n* europeo(-a) *m(f)*
European Court of Justice *n* Tribunal *m* de Justicia de las Comunidades Europeas
Euro-sceptic [juərəu'skɛptɪk] *n* euroescéptico(-a)
Eurozone ['juərəuzəun] *n* eurozona, zona euro
euthanasia [ju:θə'neɪzɪə] *n* eutanasia
evacuate [ɪ'vækjueɪt] *vt* evacuar; (*place*) desocupar
evacuation [ɪvækju'eɪʃən] *n* evacuación *f*
evacuee [ɪvækju'i:] *n* evacuado(-a)
evade [ɪ'veɪd] *vt* evadir, eludir
evaluate [ɪ'væljueɪt] *vt* evaluar; (*value*) tasar; (*evidence*) interpretar
evangelical [i:væn'dʒɛlɪkəl] *adj* evangélico

evangelist [ɪ'vændʒəlɪst] *n* evangelista *m*; (*preacher*) evangelizador(a) *m(f)*
evaporate [ɪ'væpəreɪt] *vi* evaporarse; (*fig*) desvanecerse ◼ *vt* evaporar
evaporation [ɪvæpə'reɪʃən] *n* evaporación *f*
evasion [ɪ'veɪʒən] *n* evasión *f*
evasive [ɪ'veɪsɪv] *adj* evasivo
eve [i:v] *n*: **on the ~ of** en vísperas de
even ['i:vn] *adj* (*level*) llano; (*smooth*) liso; (*speed, temperature*) uniforme; (*number*) par; (*Sport*) igual(es) ◼ *adv* hasta, incluso; **~ if**, **~ though** aunque + *subjun*, así + *subjun* (*LAm*); **~ more** aun más; **~ so** aun así; **not ~** ni siquiera; **~ he was there** hasta él estaba allí; **~ on Sundays** incluso los domingos; **~ faster** aún más rápido; **to break ~** cubrir los gastos; **to get ~ with sb** ajustar cuentas con algn; **to ~ out** *vi* nivelarse
even-handed [i:vn'hændɪd] *adj* imparcial
evening ['i:vnɪŋ] *n* tarde *f*; (*dusk*) atardecer *m*; (*night*) noche *f*; **in the ~** por la tarde; **this ~** esta tarde or noche; **tomorrow/yesterday ~** mañana/ayer por la tarde or noche
evening class *n* clase *f* nocturna
evening dress *n* (*man's*) traje *m* de etiqueta; (*woman's*) traje *m* de noche
evenly ['i:vnlɪ] *adv* (*distribute, space, spread*) de modo uniforme; (*divide*) equitativamente
evensong ['i:vnsɔŋ] *n* vísperas *fpl*
event [ɪ'vɛnt] *n* suceso, acontecimiento; (*Sport*) prueba; **in the ~ of** en caso de; **in the ~** en realidad; **in the course of events** en el curso de los acontecimientos; **at all events**, **in any ~** en cualquier caso
eventful [ɪ'vɛntful] *adj* azaroso; (*game*) lleno de emoción; (*journey*) lleno de incidentes
eventing [ɪ'vɛntɪŋ] *n* (*Horseriding*) competición *f*
eventual [ɪ'vɛntʃuəl] *adj* final
eventuality [ɪvɛntʃu'ælɪtɪ] *n* eventualidad *f*
eventually [ɪ'vɛntʃuəlɪ] *adv* (*finally*) por fin; (*in time*) con el tiempo
ever ['ɛvəʳ] *adv* nunca, jamás; (*at all times*) siempre; **for ~** (para) siempre; **the best ~** lo nunca visto; **did you ~ meet him?** ¿llegaste a conocerle?; **have you ~ been there?** ¿has estado allí alguna vez?; **have you ~ seen it?** ¿lo has visto alguna vez?; **better than ~** mejor que nunca; **thank you ~ so much** muchísimas gracias; **yours ~** (*in letters*) un abrazo de; **~ since** *adv* desde entonces ◼ *conj* después de que
Everest ['ɛvərɪst] *n* (*also*: **Mount Everest**) el Everest *m*
evergreen ['ɛvəgri:n] *n* árbol *m* de hoja perenne
everlasting [ɛvə'lɑ:stɪŋ] *adj* eterno, perpetuo

○ KEYWORD

every ['ɛvrɪ] *adj* **1** (*each*) cada; **every one of them** (*persons*) todos ellos(-as); (*objects*) cada uno de ellos(-as); **every shop in the town was closed** todas las tiendas de la ciudad estaban cerradas
2 (*all possible*) todo(-a); **I gave you every assistance** te di toda la ayuda posible; **I have every confidence in him** tiene toda mi confianza; **we wish you every success** te deseamos toda suerte de éxitos
3 (*showing recurrence*) todo(-a); **every day/week** todos los días/todas las semanas; **every other car had been broken into** habían forzado uno de cada dos coches; **she visits me every other/third day** me visita cada dos/tres días, **every now and then** de vez en cuando

everybody ['ɛvrɪbɔdɪ] *pron* todos *pron pl*, todo el mundo; **~ knows about it** todo el mundo lo sabe; **~ else** todos los demás
everyday ['ɛvrɪdeɪ] *adj* (*daily: use, occurrence, experience*) diario, cotidiano; (*usual: expression*) corriente; (*common*) vulgar; (*routine*) rutinario
everyone ['ɛvrɪwʌn] = **everybody**
everything ['ɛvrɪθɪŋ] *pron* todo; **~ is ready** todo está dispuesto; **he did ~ possible** hizo todo lo posible
everywhere ['ɛvrɪwɛər] *adv* (*be*) en todas partes; (*go*) a or por todas partes; **~ you meet ...** en todas partes encontrarás ...
evict [ɪ'vɪkt] *vt* desahuciar
eviction [ɪ'vɪkʃən] *n* desahucio
eviction notice *n* orden *f* de desahucio or desalojo (*LAm*)
evidence ['ɛvɪdəns] *n* (*proof*) prueba; (*of witness*) testimonio; (*facts*) datos *mpl*, hechos *mpl*; **to give ~** prestar declaración, dar testimonio
evident ['ɛvɪdənt] *adj* evidente, manifiesto
evidently ['ɛvɪdəntlɪ] *adv* (*obviously*) obviamente, evidentemente; (*apparently*) por lo visto
evil ['iːvl] *adj* malo; (*influence*) funesto; (*smell*) horrible ■ *n* mal *m*
evildoer ['iːvlduːər] *n* malhechor(a) *m(f)*
evince [ɪ'vɪns] *vt* mostrar, dar señales de
evocative [ɪ'vɔkətɪv] *adj* sugestivo, evocador(a)
evoke [ɪ'vəuk] *vt* evocar; (*admiration*) provocar
evolution [iːvə'luːʃən] *n* evolución *f*, desarrollo
evolve [ɪ'vɔlv] *vt* desarrollar ■ *vi* evolucionar, desarrollarse

ewe [juː] *n* oveja
ex- [ɛks] *pref* (*former: husband, president etc*) ex-; (*out of*): **the price ~works** precio de fábrica
exacerbate [ɛk'sæsəbeɪt] *vt* exacerbar
exact [ɪg'zækt] *adj* exacto ■ *vt*: **to ~ sth (from)** exigir algo (de)
exacting [ɪg'zæktɪŋ] *adj* exigente; (*conditions*) arduo
exactitude [ɪg'zæktɪtjuːd] *n* exactitud *f*
exactly [ɪg'zæktlɪ] *adv* exactamente; (*time*) en punto; **~!** ¡exacto!
exactness [ɪg'zæktnɪs] *n* exactitud *f*
exaggerate [ɪg'zædʒəreɪt] *vt, vi* exagerar
exaggerated [ɪg'zædʒəreɪtɪd] *adj* exagerado
exaggeration [ɪgzædʒə'reɪʃən] *n* exageración *f*
exalt [ɪg'zɔːlt] *vt* (*praise*) ensalzar; (*elevate*) elevar
exalted [ɪg'zɔːltɪd] *adj* (*position*) elevado; (*elated*) enardecido
exam [ɪg'zæm] *n abbr* (*Scol*) = **examination**
examination [ɪgzæmɪ'neɪʃən] *n* (*gen*) examen *m*; (*Law*) interrogación *f*; (*inquiry*) investigación *f*; **to take** or **sit an ~** hacer un examen; **the matter is under ~** se está examinando el asunto
examine [ɪg'zæmɪn] *vt* (*gen*) examinar; (*inspect: machine, premises*) inspeccionar; (*Scol, Law: person*) interrogar; (*at customs: luggage, passport*) registrar; (*Med*) hacer un reconocimiento médico de, examinar
examiner [ɪg'zæmɪnər] *n* examinador(a) *m(f)*
example [ɪg'zɑːmpl] *n* ejemplo; **for ~** por ejemplo; **to set a good/bad ~** dar buen/mal ejemplo
exasperate [ɪg'zɑːspəreɪt] *vt* exasperar, irritar; **exasperated by** or **at** or **with** exasperado por or con
exasperating [ɪg'zɑːspəreɪtɪŋ] *adj* irritante
exasperation [ɪgzɑːspə'reɪʃən] *n* exasperación *f*, irritación *f*
excavate ['ɛkskəveɪt] *vt* excavar
excavation [ɛkskə'veɪʃən] *n* excavación *f*
excavator ['ɛkskəveɪtər] *n* excavadora
exceed [ɪk'siːd] *vt* exceder; (*number*) pasar de; (*speed limit*) sobrepasar; (*limits*) rebasar; (*powers*) excederse en; (*hopes*) superar
exceedingly [ɪk'siːdɪŋlɪ] *adv* sumamente, sobremanera
excel [ɪk'sɛl] *vi* sobresalir; **to ~ o.s.** lucirse
excellence ['ɛksələns] *n* excelencia
Excellency ['ɛksələnsɪ] *n*: **His ~** Su Excelencia
excellent ['ɛksələnt] *adj* excelente
except [ɪk'sɛpt] *prep* (*also*: **except for**, **excepting**) excepto, salvo ■ *vt* exceptuar, excluir; **~ if/when** excepto si/cuando; **~ that** salvo que

exception [ɪk'sɛpʃən] n excepción f; **to take ~ to** ofenderse por; **with the ~ of** a excepción de; **to make an ~** hacer una excepción

exceptional [ɪk'sɛpʃənl] adj excepcional

excerpt ['ɛksɔːpt] n extracto

excess [ɪk'sɛs] n exceso; **in ~ of** superior a; see also **excesses**

excess baggage n exceso de equipaje

excesses npl excesos mpl

excess fare n suplemento

excessive [ɪk'sɛsɪv] adj excesivo

excess supply n exceso de oferta

excess weight n exceso de peso

exchange [ɪks'tʃeɪndʒ] n cambio; (of prisoners) canje m; (of ideas) intercambio; (also: **telephone exchange**) central f (telefónica) ▪ vt intercambiar; **to ~ (for)** cambiar (por); **in ~ for** a cambio de; **foreign ~** (Comm) divisas fpl

exchange control n control m de divisas

exchange rate n tipo de cambio

exchequer [ɪks'tʃɛkəʳ] n: **the ~** (Brit) Hacienda

excisable [ɛk'saɪzəbl] adj sujeto al pago de impuestos sobre el consumo

excise ['ɛksaɪz] n impuestos sobre el consumo interior

excitable [ɪk'saɪtəbl] adj excitable

excite [ɪk'saɪt] vt (stimulate) entusiasmar; (anger) suscitar, provocar; (move) emocionar; **to get excited** emocionarse

excitement [ɪk'saɪtmənt] n emoción f

exciting [ɪk'saɪtɪŋ] adj emocionante

excl. abbr = **excluding**; **exclusive (of)**

exclaim [ɪk'skleɪm] vi exclamar

exclamation [ɛksklə'meɪʃən] n exclamación f

exclamation mark n signo de admiración

exclude [ɪk'skluːd] vt excluir; (except) exceptuar

excluding [ɪks'kluːdɪŋ] prep: **~ VAT** IVA no incluido

exclusion [ɪk'skluːʒən] n exclusión f; **to the ~ of** con exclusión de

exclusion clause n cláusula de exclusión

exclusion zone n zona de exclusión

exclusive [ɪk'skluːsɪv] adj exclusivo; (club, district) selecto; **~ of tax** excluyendo impuestos; **~ of postage/service** franqueo/servicio no incluido; **from 1st to 13th March ~** del 1 al 13 de marzo exclusive

exclusively [ɪk'skluːsɪvlɪ] adv únicamente

excommunicate [ɛkskə'mjuːnɪkeɪt] vt excomulgar

excrement ['ɛkskrəmənt] n excremento

excrete [ɪk'skriːt] vi excretar

excruciating [ɪk'skruːʃɪeɪtɪŋ] adj (pain) agudísimo, atroz

excursion [ɪk'skəːʃən] n excursión f

excursion ticket n billete m (especial) de excursión

excusable [ɪk'skjuːsəbl] adj perdonable

excuse n [ɪk'skjuːs] disculpa, excusa; (evasion) pretexto ▪ vt [ɪk'skjuːz] disculpar, perdonar; (justify) justificar; **to make excuses for sb** presentar disculpas por algn; **to ~ sb from doing sth** dispensar a algn de hacer algo; **to ~ o.s. (for (doing) sth)** pedir disculpas a algn (por (hacer) algo); **~ me!** ¡perdone!; (attracting attention) ¡oiga (, por favor)!; **if you will ~ me** con su permiso

ex-directory ['ɛksdɪ'rɛktərɪ] adj (Brit): **~ (phone) number** número que no figura en la guía (telefónica)

execrable ['ɛksɪkrəbl] adj execrable, abominable; (manners) detestable

execute ['ɛksɪkjuːt] vt (plan) realizar; (order) cumplir; (person) ajusticiar, ejecutar

execution [ɛksɪ'kjuːʃən] n realización f; cumplimiento; ejecución f

executioner [ɛksɪ'kjuːʃənəʳ] n verdugo

executive [ɪg'zɛkjutɪv] n (Comm) ejecutivo(-a); (Pol) poder m ejecutivo ▪ adj ejecutivo; (car, plane, position) de ejecutivo; (offices, suite) de la dirección; (secretary) de dirección

executive director n director(a) m(f) ejecutivo(-a)

executor [ɪg'zɛkjutəʳ] n albacea m, testamentario

exemplary [ɪg'zɛmplərɪ] adj ejemplar

exemplify [ɪg'zɛmplɪfaɪ] vt ejemplificar

exempt [ɪg'zɛmpt] adj: **~ from** exento de ▪ vt: **to ~ sb from** eximir a algn de

exemption [ɪg'zɛmpʃən] n exención f; (immunity) inmunidad f

exercise ['ɛksəsaɪz] n ejercicio ▪ vt ejercer; (patience etc) proceder con; (dog) sacar de paseo ▪ vi hacer ejercicio

exercise bike n bicicleta estática

exercise book n cuaderno de ejercicios

exert [ɪg'zəːt] vt ejercer; (strength, force) emplear; **to ~ o.s.** esforzarse

exertion [ɪg'zəːʃən] n esfuerzo

exfoliant [ɛks'fəʊlɪənt] n exfoliante m

ex gratia [ɛks'greɪʃə] adj: **~ payment** pago a título voluntario

exhale [ɛks'heɪl] vt despedir, exhalar ▪ vi espirar

exhaust [ɪg'zɔːst] n (pipe) (tubo de) escape m; (fumes) gases mpl de escape ▪ vt agotar; **to ~ o.s.** agotarse

exhausted [ɪg'zɔːstɪd] adj agotado

exhausting [ɪgˈzɔːstɪŋ] adj: **an ~ journey/day** un viaje/día agotador
exhaustion [ɪgˈzɔːstʃən] n agotamiento; **nervous ~** agotamiento nervioso
exhaustive [ɪgˈzɔːstɪv] adj exhaustivo
exhibit [ɪgˈzɪbɪt] n (Art) obra expuesta; (Law) objeto expuesto ▪ vt (show: emotions) manifestar; (: courage, skill) demostrar; (paintings) exponer
exhibition [ɛksɪˈbɪʃən] n exposición f
exhibitionist [ɛksɪˈbɪʃənɪst] n exhibicionista m/f
exhibitor [ɪgˈzɪbɪtər] n expositor(a) m(f)
exhilarating [ɪgˈzɪləreɪtɪŋ] adj estimulante, tónico
exhilaration [ɪgzɪləˈreɪʃən] n júbilo
exhort [ɪgˈzɔːt] vt exhortar
exile [ˈɛksaɪl] n exilio; (person) exiliado(-a) ▪ vt desterrar, exiliar
exist [ɪgˈzɪst] vi existir
existence [ɪgˈzɪstəns] n existencia
existentialism [ɛgzɪsˈtɛnʃəlɪzəm] n existencialismo
existing [ɪgˈzɪstɪŋ] adj existente, actual
exit [ˈɛksɪt] n salida ▪ vi (Theat) hacer mutis; (Comput) salir (del sistema)
exit poll n encuesta a la salida de los colegios electorales
exit ramp n (US Aut) vía de acceso
exit visa n visado de salida
exodus [ˈɛksədəs] n éxodo
ex officio [ˈɛksəˈfɪʃɪəʊ] adj de pleno derecho ▪ adv ex oficio
exonerate [ɪgˈzɒnəreɪt] vt: **to ~ from** exculpar de
exorbitant [ɪgˈzɔːbɪtənt] adj (price, demands) exorbitante, excesivo
exorcize [ˈɛksɔːsaɪz] vt exorcizar
exotic [ɪgˈzɒtɪk] adj exótico
expand [ɪkˈspænd] vt ampliar, extender; (number) aumentar ▪ vi (trade etc) ampliarse, expandirse; (gas, metal) dilatarse; **to ~ on** (notes, story etc) ampliar
expanse [ɪkˈspæns] n extensión f
expansion [ɪkˈspænʃən] n ampliación f; aumento; (of trade) expansión f
expansionism [ɪkˈspænʃənɪzəm] n expansionismo
expansionist [ɪkˈspænʃənɪst] adj expansionista
expatriate [ɛksˈpætrɪət] n expatriado(-a)
expect [ɪkˈspɛkt] vt (gen) esperar; (count on) contar con; (suppose) suponer ▪ vi: **to be expecting** estar encinta; **to ~ to do sth** esperar hacer algo; **as expected** como era de esperar; **I ~ so** supongo que sí
expectancy [ɪkˈspɛktənsɪ] n (anticipation)

expectación f; **life ~** esperanza de vida
expectantly [ɪkˈspɛktəntlɪ] adv (look, listen) con expectación
expectant mother [ɪkˈspɛktənt-] n futura madre f
expectation [ɛkspɛkˈteɪʃən] n esperanza, expectativa; **in ~ of** esperando; **against** or **contrary to all ~(s)** en contra de todas las previsiones; **to come** or **live up to sb's expectations** resultar tan bueno como se esperaba; **to fall short of sb's expectations** no cumplir las esperanzas de algn, decepcionar a algn
expedience [ɪkˈspiːdɪəns], **expediency** [ɪkˈspiːdɪənsɪ] n conveniencia
expedient [ɪkˈspiːdɪənt] adj conveniente, oportuno ▪ n recurso, expediente m
expedite [ˈɛkspɪdaɪt] vt (speed up) acelerar; (: progress) facilitar
expedition [ɛkspəˈdɪʃən] n expedición f
expeditionary force [ɛkspəˈdɪʃnrɪ-] n cuerpo expedicionario
expel [ɪkˈspɛl] vt expulsar
expend [ɪkˈspɛnd] vt gastar; (use up) consumir
expendable [ɪkˈspɛndəbl] adj prescindible
expenditure [ɪkˈspɛndɪtʃər] n gastos mpl, desembolso; (of time, effort) gasto
expense [ɪkˈspɛns] n gasto, gastos mpl; (high cost) coste m; **expenses** npl (Comm) gastos mpl; **at the ~ of** a costa de; **to meet the ~ of** hacer frente a sus gastos de
expense account n cuenta de gastos (de representación)
expensive [ɪkˈspɛnsɪv] adj caro, costoso
experience [ɪkˈspɪərɪəns] n experiencia ▪ vt experimentar; (suffer) sufrir; **to learn by ~** aprender con la experiencia
experienced [ɪkˈspɪərɪənst] adj experimentado
experiment [ɪkˈspɛrɪmənt] n experimento ▪ vi hacer experimentos, experimentar; **to perform** or **carry out an ~** realizar un experimento; **as an ~** como experimento; **to ~ with a new vaccine** experimentar con una vacuna nueva
experimental [ɪkspɛrɪˈmɛntl] adj experimental; **the process is still at the ~ stage** el proceso está todavía en prueba
expert [ˈɛkspɜːt] adj experto, perito ▪ n experto(-a), perito(-a); (specialist) especialista m/f; **~ witness** (Law) testigo pericial; **~ in** or **at doing sth** experto or perito en hacer algo; **an ~ on sth** un experto en algo
expertise [ɛkspɜːˈtiːz] n pericia
expiration [ɛkspɪˈreɪʃən] n (gen) expiración f, vencimiento

expire [ɪk'spaɪəʳ] *vi* (*gen*) caducar, vencerse
expiry [ɪk'spaɪərɪ] *n* caducidad *f*, vencimiento
explain [ɪk'spleɪn] *vt* explicar; (*mystery*) aclarar
▶ **explain away** *vt* justificar
explanation [ɛksplə'neɪʃən] *n* explicación *f*; aclaración *f*; **to find an ~ for sth** encontrarle una explicación a algo
explanatory [ɪk'splænətrɪ] *adj* explicativo; aclaratorio
expletive [ɪk'spli:tɪv] *n* imprecación *f*
explicable [ɪk'splɪkəbl] *adj* explicable
explicit [ɪk'splɪsɪt] *adj* explícito
explicitly [ɪk'splɪsɪtlɪ] *adv* explícitamente
explode [ɪk'spləud] *vi* estallar, explotar; (*with anger*) reventar ■ *vt* hacer explotar; (*fig: theory, myth*) demoler
exploit ['ɛksplɔɪt] *n* hazaña ■ *vt* [ɪk'splɔɪt] explotar
exploitation [ɛksplɔɪ'teɪʃən] *n* explotación *f*
exploration [ɛksplə'reɪʃən] *n* exploración *f*
exploratory [ɪk'splɔrətrɪ] *adj* (*fig: talks*) exploratorio, preliminar
explore [ɪk'splɔːʳ] *vt* explorar; (*fig*) examinar, sondear
explorer [ɪk'splɔːrəʳ] *n* explorador(a) *m(f)*
explosion [ɪk'spləuʒən] *n* explosión *f*
explosive [ɪk'spləusɪv] *adj, n* explosivo
exponent [ɪk'spəunənt] *n* partidario(-a); (*of skill, activity*) exponente *m/f*
export *vt* [ɛk'spɔːt] exportar ■ *n* ['ɛkspɔːt] exportación *f* ■ *cpd* de exportación
exportation [ɛkspɔː'teɪʃən] *n* exportación *f*
export drive *n* campaña de exportación
exporter [ɛk'spɔːtəʳ] *n* exportador(a) *m(f)*
export licence *n* licencia de exportación
export manager *n* gerente *m/f* de exportación
export trade *n* comercio exterior
expose [ɪk'spəuz] *vt* exponer; (*unmask*) desenmascarar
exposé [ɪk'spəuzeɪ] *n* revelación *f*
exposed [ɪk'spəuzd] *adj* expuesto; (*land, house*) desprotegido; (*Elec: wire*) al aire; (*pipe, beam*) al descubierto
exposition [ɛkspə'zɪʃən] *n* exposición *f*
exposure [ɪk'spəuʒəʳ] *n* exposición *f*; (*Phot: speed*) (tiempo *m* de) exposición *f*; (: *shot*) fotografía; **to die from ~** (*Med*) morir de frío
exposure meter *n* fotómetro
expound [ɪk'spaund] *vt* exponer; (*theory, text*) comentar; (*one's views*) explicar
express [ɪk'sprɛs] *adj* (*definite*) expreso, explícito; (*Brit: letter etc*) urgente ■ *n* (*train*) rápido ■ *adv* (*send*) por correo extraordinario ■ *vt* expresar; (*squeeze*) exprimir; **to send**

sth ~ enviar algo por correo urgente; **to ~ o.s.** expresarse
expression [ɪk'sprɛʃən] *n* expresión *f*
expressionism [ɪk'sprɛʃənɪzm] *n* expresionismo
expressive [ɪk'sprɛsɪv] *adj* expresivo
expressly [ɪk'sprɛslɪ] *adv* expresamente
expressway [ɪk'sprɛsweɪ] *n* (*US: urban motorway*) autopista
expropriate [ɛks'prəuprieɪt] *vt* expropiar
expulsion [ɪk'spʌlʃən] *n* expulsión *f*
expurgate ['ɛkspəgeɪt] *vt* expurgar
exquisite [ɛk'skwɪzɪt] *adj* exquisito
exquisitely [ɛk'skwɪzɪtlɪ] *adv* exquisitamente
ex-serviceman ['ɛks'sə:vɪsmən] *n* ex-combatiente *m*
ext. *abbr* (*Tel*) = **extension**
extemporize [ɪk'stɛmpəraɪz] *vi* improvisar
extend [ɪk'stɛnd] *vt* (*visit, street*) prolongar; (*building*) ampliar; (*thanks, friendship etc*) extender; (*Comm: credit*) conceder; (*deadline*) prorrogar ■ *vi* (*land*) extenderse; **the contract extends to/for ...** el contrato se prolonga hasta/por ...
extension [ɪk'stɛnʃən] *n* extensión *f*; (*building*) ampliación *f*; (*Tel: line*) extensión *f*; (: *telephone*) supletorio *m*; (*of deadline*) prórroga; **~ 3718** extensión 3718
extension cable *n* (*Elec*) alargador *m*
extensive [ɪk'stɛnsɪv] *adj* (*gen*) extenso; (*damage*) importante; (*knowledge*) amplio
extensively [ɪk'stɛnsɪvlɪ] *adv* (*altered, damaged etc*) extensamente; **he's travelled ~** ha viajado por muchos países
extent [ɪk'stɛnt] *n* (*breadth*) extensión *f*; (*scope: of knowledge, activities*) alcance *m*; (*degree: of damage, loss*) grado; **to some ~** hasta cierto punto; **to a certain ~** hasta cierto punto; **to a large ~** en gran parte; **to the ~ of ...** hasta el punto de ...; **to such an ~ that ...** hasta tal punto que ...; **to what ~?** ¿hasta qué punto?; **debts to the ~ of £5000** deudas por la cantidad de £5000
extenuating [ɪk'stɛnjueɪtɪŋ] *adj*: **~ circumstances** circunstancias *fpl* atenuantes
exterior [ɛk'stɪərɪəʳ] *adj* exterior, externo ■ *n* exterior *m*
exterminate [ɪk'stə:mɪneɪt] *vt* exterminar
extermination [ɪkstə:mɪ'neɪʃən] *n* exterminio
external [ɛk'stə:nl] *adj* externo, exterior ■ *n*: **the externals** la apariencia exterior; **~ affairs** asuntos *mpl* exteriores; **for ~ use only** (*Med*) para uso tópico
externally [ɛk'stə:nəlɪ] *adv* por fuera

extinct [ɪkˈstɪŋkt] *adj* (*volcano*) extinguido, apagado; (*race*) extinguido
extinction [ɪkˈstɪŋkʃən] *n* extinción *f*
extinguish [ɪkˈstɪŋgwɪʃ] *vt* extinguir, apagar
extinguisher [ɪkˈstɪŋgwɪʃəʳ] *n* extintor *m*
extol, extoll (US) [ɪkˈstəʊl] *vt* (*merits, virtues*) ensalzar, alabar; (*person*) alabar, elogiar
extort [ɪkˈstɔːt] *vt* sacar a la fuerza; (*confession*) arrancar
extortion [ɪkˈstɔːʃən] *n* extorsión *f*
extortionate [ɪkˈstɔːʃnət] *adj* excesivo, exorbitante
extra [ˈɛkstrə] *adj* adicional ■ *adv* (*in addition*) más ■ *n* (*addition*) extra *m*, suplemento; (*Theat*) extra *m/f*, comparsa *m/f*; (*newspaper*) edición *f* extraordinaria; **wine will cost ~** el vino se paga aparte; **~ large sizes** tallas extragrandes; *see also* **extras**
extra... [ˈɛkstrə] *pref* extra...
extract *vt* [ɪkˈstrækt] sacar; (*tooth*) extraer; (*confession*) arrancar ■ *n* [ˈɛkstrækt] fragmento; (*Culin*) extracto
extraction [ɪkˈstrækʃən] *n* extracción *f* (*origin*), origen *m*
extractor fan [ɪkˈstræktə-] *n* extractor *m* de humos
extracurricular [ɛkstrəkəˈrɪkjuləʳ] *adj* (*Scol*) extraescolar
extradite [ˈɛkstrədaɪt] *vt* extraditar
extradition [ɛkstrəˈdɪʃən] *n* extradición *f*
extramarital [ɛkstrəˈmærɪtl] *adj* extramatrimonial
extramural [ɛkstrəˈmjuərl] *adj* extra-académico
extraneous [ɪkˈstreɪnɪəs] *adj* extraño, ajeno
extraordinary [ɪkˈstrɔːdnrɪ] *adj* extraordinario; (*odd*) raro; **the ~ thing is that ...** lo más extraordinario es que ...
extraordinary general meeting *n* junta general extraordinaria
extrapolation [ɪkstræpəˈleɪʃən] *n* extrapolación *f*
extras *npl* (*additional expense*) extras *mpl*
extrasensory perception [ˈɛkstrəˈsɛnsərɪ-] *n* percepción *f* extrasensorial
extra time *n* (*Football*) prórroga
extravagance [ɪkˈstrævəgəns] *n* (*excessive spending*) derroche *m*; (*thing bought*) extravagancia
extravagant [ɪkˈstrævəgənt] *adj* (*wasteful*) derrochador(a); (*taste, gift*) excesivamente caro; (*price*) exorbitante; (*praise*) excesivo
extreme [ɪkˈstriːm] *adj* extremo; (*poverty etc*) extremado; (*case*) excepcional ■ *n* extremo; **the ~ left/right** (*Pol*) la extrema izquierda/derecha; **extremes of temperature**

temperaturas extremas
extremely [ɪkˈstriːmlɪ] *adv* sumamente, extremadamente
extremist [ɪkˈstriːmɪst] *adj, n* extremista *m/f*
extremity [ɪkˈstrɛmətɪ] *n* extremidad *f*, punta; (*need*) apuro, necesidad *f*; **extremities** *npl* (*hands and feet*) extremidades *fpl*
extricate [ˈɛkstrɪkeɪt] *vt*: **to ~ o.s. from** librarse de
extrovert [ˈɛkstrəvəːt] *n* extrovertido(-a)
exuberance [ɪgˈzjuːbərns] *n* exuberancia
exuberant [ɪgˈzjuːbərnt] *adj* (*person*) eufórico; (*style*) exuberante
exude [ɪgˈzjuːd] *vt* rezumar
exult [ɪgˈzʌlt] *vi* regocijarse
exultant [ɪgˈzʌltənt] *adj* (*person*) regocijado, jubiloso; (*shout, expression, smile*) de júbilo
exultation [ɛgzʌlˈteɪʃən] *n* regocijo, júbilo
eye [aɪ] *n* ojo ■ *vt* mirar; **to keep an ~ on** vigilar; **as far as the ~ can see** hasta donde alcanza la vista; **with an ~ to doing sth** con vistas *or* miras a hacer algo; **to have an ~ for sth** tener mucha vista *or* buen ojo para algo; **there's more to this than meets the ~** esto tiene su miga
eyeball [ˈaɪbɔːl] *n* globo ocular
eyebath [ˈaɪbɑːθ] *n* baño ocular, lavaojos *m inv*
eyebrow [ˈaɪbraʊ] *n* ceja
eyebrow pencil *n* lápiz *m* de cejas
eye-catching [ˈaɪkætʃɪŋ] *adj* llamativo
eye cup *n* (US) = **eyebath**
eyedrops [ˈaɪdrɒps] *npl* gotas *fpl* para los ojos
eyeful [ˈaɪful] *n* (*col*): **to get an ~ of sth** ver bien algo
eyelash [ˈaɪlæʃ] *n* pestaña
eyelet [ˈaɪlɪt] *n* ojete *m*
eye-level [ˈaɪlɛvl] *adj* a la altura de los ojos
eyelid [ˈaɪlɪd] *n* párpado
eyeliner [ˈaɪlaɪnəʳ] *n* lápiz *m* de ojos
eye-opener [ˈaɪəʊpnəʳ] *n* revelación *f*, gran sorpresa
eyeshadow [ˈaɪʃædəʊ] *n* sombra de ojos
eyesight [ˈaɪsaɪt] *n* vista
eyesore [ˈaɪsɔːʳ] *n* monstruosidad *f*
eyestrain [ˈaɪstreɪn] *n*: **to get ~** cansar la vista *or* los ojos
eyetooth (*pl* **eyeteeth**) [ˈaɪtuːθ, -tiːθ] *n* colmillo; **to give one's eyeteeth for sth/to do sth** (*col, fig*) dar un ojo de la cara por algo/ por hacer algo
eyewash [ˈaɪwɒʃ] *n* (*fig*) disparates *mpl*, tonterías *fpl*
eye witness *n* testigo *m/f* ocular
eyrie [ˈɪərɪ] *n* aguilera

547

Ff

F, f [ɛf] *n* (*letter*) F, f *f*; (*Mus*) fa *m*; **F for Frederick**, (*US*) **F for Fox** F de Francia

F. *abbr* = **Fahrenheit**

FA *n abbr* (*Brit*: = *Football Association*) ≈ AFE *f* (*SP*)

FAA *n abbr* (*US*) = **Federal Aviation Administration**

fable ['feɪbl] *n* fábula

fabric ['fæbrɪk] *n* tejido, tela

fabricate ['fæbrɪkeɪt] *vt* fabricar; (*fig*) inventar

fabrication [fæbrɪ'keɪʃən] *n* fabricación *f*; (*fig*) invención *f*

fabric ribbon *n* (*for typewriter*) cinta de tela

fabulous ['fæbjuləs] *adj* fabuloso

façade [fə'sɑːd] *n* fachada

face [feɪs] *n* (*Anat*) cara, rostro; (*of clock*) esfera, cara; (*side*) cara; (*surface*) superficie *f* ◼ *vt* mirar a; (*fig*) enfrentarse a; ~ **down** (*person, card*) boca abajo; **to lose** ~ desprestigiarse; **to save** ~ salvar las apariencias; **to make** *or* **pull a** ~ hacer muecas; **in the** ~ **of** (*difficulties etc*) en vista de, ante; **on the** ~ **of it** a primera vista; ~ **to** ~ cara a cara; **to** ~ **the fact that ...** reconocer que ...

▶ **face up to** *vt fus* hacer frente a, enfrentarse a

face cloth *n* (*Brit*) toallita

face cream *n* crema (de belleza)

faceless ['feɪslɪs] *adj* (*fig*) anónimo

face lift *n* lifting *m*, estirado facial

face powder *n* polvos *mpl* para la cara

face-saving ['feɪsseɪvɪŋ] *adj* para salvar las apariencias

facet ['fæsɪt] *n* faceta

facetious [fə'siːʃəs] *adj* chistoso

facetiously [fə'siːʃəslɪ] *adv* chistosamente

face value *n* (*of stamp*) valor *m* nominal; **to take sth at** ~ (*fig*) tomar algo en sentido literal, aceptar las apariencias de algo

facial ['feɪʃəl] *adj* de la cara ◼ *n* (*also*: **beauty facial**) tratamiento facial, limpieza

facile ['fæsaɪl] *adj* superficial

facilitate [fə'sɪlɪteɪt] *vt* facilitar

facility [fə'sɪlɪtɪ] *n* facilidad *f*; **facilities** *npl* instalaciones *fpl*; **credit** ~ facilidades de crédito

facing ['feɪsɪŋ] *prep* frente a ◼ *adj* de enfrente

facsimile [fæk'sɪmɪlɪ] *n* facsímil(e) *m*

fact [fækt] *n* hecho; **in** ~ en realidad; **to know for a** ~ **that ...** saber a ciencia cierta que ...

fact-finding ['fæktfaɪndɪŋ] *adj*: **a** ~ **tour/mission** un viaje/una misión de reconocimiento

faction ['fækʃən] *n* facción *f*

factional ['fækʃənl] *adj* (*fighting*) entre distintas facciones

factor ['fæktə^r] *n* factor *m*; (*Comm: person*) agente *m/f* comisionado(-a) ◼ *vi* (*Comm*) comprar deudas; **safety** ~ factor de seguridad

factory ['fæktərɪ] *n* fábrica

factory farming *n* cría industrial

factory floor *n* (*workers*) trabajadores *mpl*, mano *f* de obra directa; (*area*) talleres *mpl*

factory ship *n* buque *m* factoría

factual ['fæktjuəl] *adj* basado en los hechos

faculty ['fækəltɪ] *n* facultad *f*; (*US: teaching staff*) personal *m* docente

fad [fæd] *n* novedad *f*, moda

fade [feɪd] *vi* descolorarse, desteñirse; (*sound, hope*) desvanecerse; (*light*) apagarse; (*flower*) marchitarse

▶ **fade away** *vi* (*sound*) apagarse

▶ **fade in** *vt* (*TV, Cine*) fundir; (*Radio: sound*) mezclar ◼ *vi* (*TV, Cine*) fundirse; (*Radio*) oírse por encima

▶ **fade out** *vt* (*TV, Cine*) fundir; (*Radio*) apagar, disminuir el volumen de ◼ *vi* (*TV, Cine*) desvanecerse; (*Radio*) apagarse, dejarse de oír

faded ['feɪdɪd] *adj* (*clothes, colour*) descolorido; (*flower*) marchito

faeces, feces (*US*) ['fiːsiːz] *npl* excremento *sg*, heces *fpl*

fag [fæg] n (Brit col: cigarette) pitillo (SP), cigarro; (US col: homosexual) maricón m
fag end n (Brit col) colilla
fagged [fægd] adj (Brit col: exhausted) rendido, agotado
Fahrenheit ['fɑːrənhaɪt] n Fahrenheit m
fail [feɪl] vt suspender; (memory etc) fallar a ■ vi suspender; (be unsuccessful) fracasar; (strength, brakes, engine) fallar; **to ~ to do sth** (neglect) dejar de hacer algo; (be unable) no poder hacer algo; **without ~** sin falta; **words ~ me!** ¡no sé qué decir!
failing ['feɪlɪŋ] n falta, defecto ■ prep a falta de; **~ that** de no ser posible eso
failsafe ['feɪlseɪf] adj (device etc) de seguridad
failure ['feɪljəʳ] n fracaso; (person) fracasado(-a); (mechanical etc) fallo; (in exam) suspenso; (of crops) pérdida, destrucción f; **it was a complete ~** fue un fracaso total
faint [feɪnt] adj débil; (smell, breeze, trace) leve; (recollection) vago; (mark) apenas visible ■ n desmayo ■ vi desmayarse; **to feel ~** estar mareado, marearse
faintest ['feɪntɪst] adj: **I haven't the ~ idea** no tengo la más remota idea
faint-hearted ['feɪnt'hɑːtɪd] adj apocado
faintly ['feɪntlɪ] adv débilmente; (vaguely) vagamente
faintness ['feɪntnɪs] n debilidad f; vaguedad f
fair [fɛəʳ] adj justo; (hair, person) rubio; (weather) bueno; (good enough) suficiente; (sizeable) considerable ■ adv: **to play ~** jugar limpio ■ n feria; (Brit: funfair) parque m de atracciones; **it's not ~!** ¡no es justo!, ¡no hay derecho!; **~ copy** copia en limpio; **~ play** juego limpio; **a ~ amount of** bastante; **~ wear and tear** desgaste m natural; **trade ~** feria de muestras
fair game n: **to be ~** ser blanco legítimo
fairground ['fɛəgraund] n recinto ferial
fair-haired [fɛə'hɛəd] adj (person) rubio
fairly ['fɛəlɪ] adv (justly) con justicia; (equally) equitativamente; (quite) bastante; **I'm ~ sure** estoy bastante seguro
fairness ['fɛənɪs] n justicia; (impartiality) imparcialidad f; **in all ~** a decir verdad
fair trade n comercio justo
fairy ['fɛərɪ] n hada
fairy godmother n hada madrina
fairyland ['fɛərɪlænd] n el país de ensueño
fairy lights npl bombillas fpl de colores
fairy tale n cuento de hadas
faith [feɪθ] n fe f; (trust) confianza; (sect) religión f; **to have ~ in sb/sth** confiar en algn/algo
faithful ['feɪθful] adj fiel
faithfully ['feɪθfulɪ] adv fielmente; **yours ~**

(Brit: in letters) le saluda atentamente
faith healer n curador(a) m(f) por fe
fake [feɪk] n (painting etc) falsificación f; (person) impostor(a) m(f) ■ adj falso ■ vt fingir; (painting etc) falsificar
falcon ['fɔːlkən] n halcón m
Falkland Islands ['fɔːlklənd-] npl Islas fpl Malvinas
fall [fɔːl] n caída; (US) otoño; (decrease) disminución f ■ vi (pt fell, pp fallen) ['fɔːlən] caer; (accidentally) caerse; (price) bajar; **falls** npl (waterfall) cataratas fpl, salto sg de agua; **a ~ of earth** un desprendimiento de tierra; **a ~ of snow** una nevada; **to ~ flat** vi (on one's face) caerse de bruces; (joke, story) no hacer gracia; **to ~ short of sb's expectations** decepcionar a algn; **to ~ in love (with sb/sth)** enamorarse (de algn/algo)
▶ **fall apart** vi deshacerse
▶ **fall back** vi retroceder
▶ **fall back on** vt fus (remedy etc) recurrir a; **to have sth to ~ back on** tener algo a que recurrir
▶ **fall behind** vi quedarse atrás; (fig: with payments) retrasarse
▶ **fall down** vi (person) caerse; (building) derrumbarse
▶ **fall for** vt fus (trick) tragar; (person) enamorarse de
▶ **fall in** vi (roof) hundirse; (Mil) alinearse
▶ **fall in with** vt fus: **to ~ in with sb's plans** acomodarse con los planes de algn
▶ **fall off** vi caerse; (diminish) disminuir
▶ **fall out** vi (friends etc) reñir; (Mil) romper filas
▶ **fall over** vi caer(se)
▶ **fall through** vi (plan, project) fracasar
fallacy ['fæləsɪ] n error m
fallback position ['fɔːlbæk-] n posición f de repliegue
fallen ['fɔːlən] pp of **fall**
fallible ['fæləbl] adj falible
falling ['fɔːlɪŋ] adj: **~ market** mercado en baja
falling-off ['fɔːlɪŋ'ɔf] n (reduction) disminución f
Fallopian tube [fə'ləupɪən-] n (Anat) trompa de Falopio
fallout ['fɔːlaut] n lluvia radioactiva
fallout shelter n refugio antinuclear
fallow ['fæləu] adj (land, field) en barbecho
false [fɔːls] adj (gen) falso; (teeth etc) postizo; (disloyal) desleal, traidor(a); **under ~ pretences** con engaños
false alarm n falsa alarma
falsehood ['fɔːlshud] n falsedad f
falsely ['fɔːlslɪ] adv falsamente

false teeth *npl* (*Brit*) dentadura *sg* postiza
falsify ['fɔ:lsɪfaɪ] *vt* falsificar
falter ['fɔ:ltər] *vi* vacilar
fame [feɪm] *n* fama
familiar [fə'mɪliər] *adj* familiar; (*well-known*) conocido; (*tone*) de confianza; **to be ~ with** (*subject*) estar enterado de; **to make o.s. ~ with** familiarizarse con; **to be on ~ terms with sb** tener confianza con algn
familiarity [fəmɪlɪ'ærɪtɪ] *n* familiaridad *f*
familiarize [fə'mɪliəraɪz] *vt*: **to ~ o.s. with** familiarizarse con
family ['fæmɪlɪ] *n* familia
family allowance *n* subsidio que se recibe por cada hijo
family business *n* negocio familiar
family credit *n* (*Brit*) ≈ ayuda familiar
family doctor *n* médico(-a) de cabecera
family life *n* vida doméstica *or* familiar
family man *n* (*home-loving*) hombre *m* casero; (*having family*) padre *m* de familia
family planning *n* planificación *f* familiar
family planning clinic *n* clínica de planificación familiar
family tree *n* árbol *m* genealógico
famine ['fæmɪn] *n* hambre *f*, hambruna
famished ['fæmɪʃt] *adj* hambriento; **I'm ~!** (*col*) ¡estoy muerto de hambre!, ¡tengo un hambre canina!
famous ['feɪməs] *adj* famoso, célebre
famously ['feɪməslɪ] *adv* (*get on*) estupendamente
fan [fæn] *n* abanico; (*Elec*) ventilador *m*; (*person*) aficionado(-a); (*Sport*) hincha *m/f*; (*of pop star*) fan *m/f* ▪ *vt* abanicar; (*fire, quarrel*) atizar
  ▶ **fan out** *vi* desplegarse
fanatic [fə'nætɪk] *n* fanático(-a)
fanatical [fə'nætɪkəl] *adj* fanático
fan belt *n* correa de ventilador
fancied ['fænsɪd] *adj* imaginario
fanciful ['fænsɪful] *adj* (*gen*) fantástico; (*imaginary*) fantasioso; (*design*) rebuscado
fan club *n* club *m* de fans
fancy ['fænsɪ] *n* (*whim*) capricho, antojo; (*imagination*) imaginación *f* ▪ *adj* (*luxury*) de lujo; (*price*) exorbitado ▪ *vt* (*feel like, want*) tener ganas de; (*imagine*) imaginarse, figurarse; **to take a ~ to sb** tomar cariño a algn; **when the ~ takes him** cuando se le antoja; **it took** *or* **caught my ~** me cayó en gracia; **to ~ that ...** imaginarse que ...; **he fancies her** le gusta (ella) mucho
fancy dress *n* disfraz *m*
fancy-dress ball ['fænsɪdrɛs-] *n* baile *m* de disfraces
fancy goods *n* artículos *mpl* de fantasía

fanfare ['fænfɛər] *n* fanfarria (de trompeta)
fanfold paper ['fænfəuld-] *n* papel *m* plegado en abanico *or* en acordeón
fang [fæŋ] *n* colmillo
fan heater *n* calefactor *m* de aire
fanlight ['fænlaɪt] *n* (montante *m* en) abanico
fanny ['fænɪ] *n* (*Brit col!*) chocho (!); (*US col*) pompis *m*, culo (!)
fantasize ['fæntəsaɪz] *vi* fantasear, hacerse ilusiones
fantastic [fæn'tæstɪk] *adj* fantástico
fantasy ['fæntəzɪ] *n* fantasía
fanzine ['fænzi:n] *n* fanzine *m*
FAO *n abbr* (= *Food and Agriculture Organization*) OAA *f*, FAO *f*
FAQ *abbr* (= *free alongside quay*) franco sobre muelle
FAQs *npl abbr* (= *frequently asked questions*) preguntas *fpl* frecuentes
far [fɑ:ʳ] *adj* (*distant*) lejano ▪ *adv* lejos; **the ~ left/right** (*Pol*) la extrema izquierda/derecha; **~ away, ~ off** (a lo) lejos; **~ better** mucho mejor; **~ from** lejos de; **by ~** con mucho; **it's by ~ the best** es con mucho el mejor; **go as ~ as the farm** vaya hasta la granja; **is it ~ to London?** ¿estamos lejos de Londres?, ¿Londres queda lejos?; **it's not ~ (from here)** no está lejos (de aquí); **as ~ as I know** que yo sepa; **how ~ have you got with your work?** ¿hasta dónde has llegado en tu trabajo?
faraway ['fɑ:rəweɪ] *adj* remoto; (*look*) ausente, perdido
farce [fɑ:s] *n* farsa
farcical ['fɑ:sɪkəl] *adj* absurdo
fare [fɛəʳ] *n* (*on trains, buses*) precio (del billete); (*in taxi: cost*) tarifa; (: *passenger*) pasajero; (*food*) comida; **half/full ~** medio billete *m*/billete *m* completo
Far East *n*: **the ~** el Extremo *or* Lejano Oriente
farewell [fɛə'wɛl] *excl, n* adiós *m*
far-fetched [fɑ:'fɛtʃt] *adj* inverosímil
farm [fɑ:m] *n* granja, finca, estancia (*LAm*), chacra (*LAm*), rancho (*LAm*) ▪ *vt* cultivar
  ▶ **farm out** *vt* (*work*): **to ~ out (to sb)** mandar hacer fuera (a algn)
farmer ['fɑ:məʳ] *n* granjero(-a), estanciero(-a) (*LAm*)
farmhand ['fɑ:mhænd] *n* peón *m*
farmhouse ['fɑ:mhaus] *n* granja, casa de hacienda (*LAm*)
farming ['fɑ:mɪŋ] *n* (*gen*) agricultura; (*tilling*) cultivo; **sheep ~** cría de ovejas
farm labourer *n* = **farmhand**
farmland ['fɑ:mlænd] *n* tierra de cultivo
farm produce *n* productos *mpl* agrícolas

farm worker n = **farmhand**

farmyard ['fɑːmjɑːd] n corral m

Faroe Islands ['fɛərəu-], **Faroes** ['fɛərəuz] npl: **the ~** las Islas Feroe

far-reaching [fɑːˈriːtʃɪŋ] adj (reform, effect) de gran alcance

far-sighted [fɑːˈsaɪtɪd] adj previsor(a)

fart [fɑːt] (col!) n pedo (!) ■ vi tirarse un pedo (!)

farther ['fɑːðər] adv más lejos, más allá ■ adj más lejano

farthest ['fɑːðɪst] superlative of **far**

FAS abbr (Brit: = free alongside ship) franco al costado del buque

fascinate ['fæsɪneɪt] vt fascinar

fascinating ['fæsɪneɪtɪŋ] adj fascinante

fascination [fæsɪˈneɪʃən] n fascinación f

fascism ['fæʃɪzəm] n fascismo

fascist ['fæʃɪst] adj, n fascista m/f

fashion ['fæʃən] n moda; (manner) manera ■ vt formar; **in ~** a la moda; **out of ~** pasado de moda; **in the Greek ~** a la griega, al estilo griego; **after a ~** (finish, manage etc) en cierto modo

fashionable ['fæʃnəbl] adj de moda; (writer) de moda, popular; **it is ~ to do** ... está de moda hacer ...

fashion designer n diseñador(a) m(f) de modas, modisto(-a)

fashionista [fæʃəˈnɪstə] n fashionista m/f

fashion show n desfile m de modelos

fast [fɑːst] adj rápido; (dye, colour) sólido; (clock): **to be ~** estar adelantado ■ adv rápidamente, de prisa; (stuck) firmemente ■ n ayuno ■ vi ayunar; **~ asleep** profundamente dormido; **in the ~ lane** (Aut) en el carril de adelantamiento; **my watch is five minutes ~** mi reloj está adelantando cinco minutos; **as ~ as I etc can** lo más rápido posible; **to make a boat ~** amarrar una barca

fasten ['fɑːsn] vt asegurar, sujetar; (coat, belt) abrochar ■ vi cerrarse

▶ **fasten (up)on** vt fus (idea) aferrarse a

fastener ['fɑːsnər] n cierre m; (of door etc) cerrojo; (Brit: also: **zip fastener**) cremallera

fastening ['fɑːsnɪŋ] n = **fastener**

fast food n comida rápida, platos mpl preparados

fastidious [fæsˈtɪdɪəs] adj (fussy) delicado; (demanding) exigente

fat [fæt] adj gordo; (meat) con mucha grasa; (greasy) grasiento ■ n grasa; (on person) carnes fpl; (lard) manteca; **to live off the ~ of the land** vivir a cuerpo de rey

fatal ['feɪtl] adj (mistake) fatal; (injury) mortal; (consequence) funesto

fatalism ['feɪtəlɪzəm] n fatalismo

fatality [fəˈtælɪtɪ] n (road death etc) víctima f mortal

fatally ['feɪtəlɪ] adv: **~ injured** herido de muerte

fate [feɪt] n destino, sino

fated ['feɪtɪd] adj predestinado

fateful ['feɪtful] adj fatídico

fat-free ['fætfriː] adj sin grasa

father ['fɑːðər] n padre m

Father Christmas n Papá m Noel

fatherhood ['fɑːðəhud] n paternidad f

father-in-law ['fɑːðərɪnlɔː] n suegro

fatherland ['fɑːðəlænd] n patria

fatherly ['fɑːðəlɪ] adj paternal

fathom ['fæðəm] n braza ■ vt (unravel) desentrañar; (understand) explicarse

fatigue [fəˈtiːg] n fatiga, cansancio; **metal ~** fatiga del metal

fatness ['fætnɪs] n gordura

fatten ['fætn] vt, vi engordar; **chocolate is fattening** el chocolate engorda

fatty ['fætɪ] adj (food) graso ■ n (fam) gordito(-a), gordinflón(-ona) m(f)

fatuous ['fætjuəs] adj fatuo, necio

faucet ['fɔːsɪt] n (US) grifo, llave f, canilla (LAm)

fault [fɔːlt] n (blame) culpa; (defect: in character) defecto; (in manufacture) desperfecto; (Geo) falla ■ vt criticar; **it's my ~** es culpa mía; **to find ~ with** criticar, poner peros a; **at ~** culpable

faultless ['fɔːltlɪs] adj (action) intachable; (person) sin defectos

faulty ['fɔːltɪ] adj defectuoso

fauna ['fɔːnə] n fauna

faux pas ['fəʊpɑː] n desacierto

favour, favor (US) ['feɪvər] n favor m; (approval) aprobación f ■ vt (proposition) estar a favor de, aprobar; (person etc) preferir; (assist) favorecer; **to ask a ~ of** pedir un favor a; **to do sb a ~** hacer un favor a algn; **to find ~ with sb** (person) caerle bien a algn; (: suggestion) tener buena acogida por parte de algn; **in ~ of** a favor de; **to be in ~ of sth/of doing sth** ser partidario or estar a favor de algo/de hacer algo

favourable, favorable (US) ['feɪvərəbl] adj favorable

favourably, favorably (US) ['feɪvərəblɪ] adv favorablemente

favourite, favorite (US) ['feɪvərɪt] adj, n favorito(-a) m(f), preferido(-a) m(f)

favouritism, favoritism (US) ['feɪvərɪtɪzəm] n favoritismo

fawn [fɔːn] n cervato ■ adj (also: **fawn-coloured**) de color cervato, leonado ■ vi: **to ~ (up)on** adular

fax [fæks] n fax m ▪ vt mandar or enviar por fax

FBI n abbr (US: = Federal Bureau of Investigation) FBI m

FCC n abbr (US) = **Federal Communications Commission**

FCO n abbr (Brit: = Foreign and Commonwealth Office) = Min. de AA. EE

FD n abbr (US) = **fire department**

FDA n abbr (US: = Food and Drug Administration) oficina que se ocupa del control de los productos alimenticios y farmacéuticos

FE n abbr = **further education**

fear [fɪər] n miedo, temor m ▪ vt temer; **for ~ of** por temor a; **~ of heights** vértigo; **to ~ for/that** temer por/que

fearful ['fɪəful] adj temeroso; (awful) espantoso; **to be ~ of** (frightened) tener miedo de

fearfully ['fɪəfulɪ] adv (timidly) con miedo; (col: very) terriblemente

fearless ['fɪəlɪs] adj (gen) sin miedo or temor; (bold) audaz

fearlessly ['fɪəlɪslɪ] adv temerariamente

fearlessness ['fɪəlɪsnɪs] n temeridad f

fearsome ['fɪəsəm] adj (opponent) temible; (sight) espantoso

feasibility [fiːzə'bɪlɪtɪ] n factibilidad f, viabilidad f

feasibility study n estudio de viabilidad

feasible ['fiːzəbl] adj factible, viable

feast [fiːst] n banquete m; (Rel: also: **feast day**) fiesta ▪ vi banquetear

feat [fiːt] n hazaña

feather ['feðər] n pluma ▪ vt: **to ~ one's nest** (fig) hacer su agosto, sacar tajada ▪ cpd (mattress, bed, pillow) de plumas

feather-weight ['feðəweɪt] n (Boxing) peso pluma

feature ['fiːtʃər] n (gen) característica; (Anat) rasgo; (article) reportaje m ▪ vt (film) presentar ▪ vi figurar; **features** npl (of face) facciones fpl; **a (special) ~ on sth/sb** un reportaje (especial) sobre algo/algn; **it featured prominently in ...** tuvo un papel destacado en ...

feature film n largometraje m

Feb. abbr (= February) feb

February ['februərɪ] n febrero; see also **July**

feces ['fiːsiːz] npl (US) = **faeces**

feckless ['feklɪs] adj irresponsable, irreflexivo

Fed [fed] abbr (US) = **federal; federation**

Fed. [fed] n abbr (US col) = **Federal Reserve Board**

fed [fed] pt, pp of **feed**

federal ['fedərəl] adj federal

Federal Republic of Germany n República Federal de Alemania

federation [fedə'reɪʃən] n federación f

fed-up [fed'ʌp] adj: **to be ~ (with)** estar harto (de)

fee [fiː] n (professional) honorarios mpl; (for examination) derechos mpl; (of school) matrícula; (also: **membership fee**) cuota; (also: **entrance fee**) entrada; **for a small ~** por poco dinero

feeble ['fiːbl] adj débil

feeble-minded [fiːbl'maɪndɪd] adj imbécil

feed [fiːd] n (gen) comida; (of animal) pienso; (on printer) dispositivo de alimentación ▪ vt (pp, pt **fed**) (gen) alimentar; (Brit: breastfeed) dar el pecho a; (animal, baby) dar de comer a ▪ vi (baby, animal) comer
▶ **feed back** vt (results) pasar
▶ **feed in** vt (Comput) introducir
▶ **feed into** vt (data, information) suministrar a; **to ~ sth into a machine** introducir algo en una máquina
▶ **feed on** vt fus alimentarse de

feedback ['fiːdbæk] n (from person) reacción f; (Tech) realimentación f, feedback m

feeder ['fiːdər] n (bib) babero

feeding bottle ['fiːdɪŋ-] n (Brit) biberón m

feel [fiːl] n (sensation) sensación f; (sense of touch) tacto ▪ vt (pt, pp **felt**) tocar; (cold, pain etc) sentir; (think, believe) creer; **to get the ~ of sth** (fig) acostumbrarse a algo; **to ~ hungry/cold** tener hambre/frío; **to ~ lonely/better** sentirse solo/mejor; **I don't ~ well** no me siento bien; **it feels soft** es suave al tacto; **it feels colder out here** se siente más frío aquí fuera; **to ~ like** (want) tener ganas de; **I'm still feeling my way** (fig) todavía me estoy orientando; **I ~ that you ought to do it** creo que debes hacerlo; **to ~ about** or **around** vi tantear

feeler ['fiːlər] n (of insect) antena; **to put out feelers** (fig) tantear el terreno

feeling ['fiːlɪŋ] n (physical) sensación f; (foreboding) presentimiento; (impression) impresión f; (emotion) sentimiento; **what are your feelings about the matter?** ¿qué opinas tú del asunto?; **to hurt sb's feelings** herir los sentimientos de algn; **feelings ran high about it** causó mucha controversia; **I got the ~ that ...** me dio la impresión de que ...; **there was a general ~ that ...** la opinión general fue que ...

fee-paying school ['fiːpeɪɪŋ-] n colegio de pago

feet [fiːt] npl of **foot**

feign [feɪn] vt fingir

feigned [feɪnd] adj fingido

feline ['fi:laın] *adj* felino
fell [fɛl] *pt of* **fall** ■ *vt* (*tree*) talar ■ *adj*: **with one ~ blow** con un golpe feroz; **at one ~ swoop** de un solo golpe ■ *n* (*Brit: mountain*) montaña; (*moorland*): **the fells** los páramos
fellow ['fɛləu] *n* tipo, tío (*SP*); (*of learned society*) socio(-a); (*Univ*) *miembro de la junta de gobierno de un colegio* ■ *cpd*: **~ students** compañeros(-as) *m(f)pl* de curso, de curso, condiscípulos(-as) *m(f)pl*
fellow citizen *n* conciudadano(-a)
fellow countryman *n* compatriota *m*
fellow feeling *n* compañerismo
fellow men *npl* semejantes *mpl*
fellowship ['fɛləuʃɪp] *n* compañerismo; (*grant*) beca
fellow traveller *n* compañero(-a) de viaje; (*Pol: with communists*) simpatizante *m/f*
fellow worker *n* colega *m/f*
felon ['fɛlən] *n* criminal *m/f*
felony ['fɛlənı] *n* crimen *m*, delito mayor
felt [fɛlt] *pt, pp of* **feel** ■ *n* fieltro
felt-tip pen ['fɛlttɪp-] *n* rotulador *m*
female ['fi:meıl] *n* (*woman*) mujer *f*; (*Zool*) hembra ■ *adj* femenino
feminine ['femɪnɪn] *adj* femenino
femininity [femɪ'nɪnɪtı] *n* feminidad *f*
feminism ['femɪnɪzəm] *n* feminismo
feminist ['femɪnɪst] *n* feminista *m/f*
fence [fɛns] *n* valla, cerca; (*Racing*) valla ■ *vt* (*also*: **fence in**) cercar ■ *vi* hacer esgrima; **to sit on the ~** (*fig*) nadar entre dos aguas
▶ **fence in** *vt* cercar
▶ **fence off** *vt* separar con cerca
fencing ['fɛnsıŋ] *n* esgrima
fend [fɛnd] *vi*: **to ~ for o.s.** valerse por sí mismo
▶ **fend off** *vt* (*attack, attacker*) rechazar, repeler; (*blow*) desviar; (*awkward question*) esquivar
fender ['fɛndəʳ] *n* pantalla; (*US Aut*) parachoques *m inv*; (*Rail*) trompa
fennel ['fɛnl] *n* hinojo
Fens [fɛnz] *npl* (*Brit*): **the ~** *las tierras bajas de Norfolk* (*antiguamente zona de marismas*)
ferment *vi* [fə'mɛnt] fermentar ■ *n* ['fə:mɛnt] (*fig*) agitación *f*
fermentation [fə:mɛn'teıʃən] *n* fermentación *f*
fern [fə:n] *n* helecho
ferocious [fə'rəuʃəs] *adj* feroz
ferociously [fə'rəuʃəslı] *adv* ferozmente, con ferocidad
ferocity [fə'rɔsıtı] *n* ferocidad *f*
ferret ['fɛrɪt] *n* hurón *m*
▶ **ferret about, ferret around** *vi* rebuscar
▶ **ferret out** *vt* (*secret, truth*) desentrañar

ferry ['fɛrı] *n* (*small*) barca de pasaje, balsa; (*large: also*: **ferryboat**) transbordador *m*, ferry *m* ■ *vt* transportar; **to ~ sth/sb across** or **over** transportar algo/a algn a la otra orilla; **to ~ sb to and fro** llevar a algn de un lado para otro
ferryman ['fɛrımən] *n* barquero
fertile ['fə:taıl] *adj* fértil; (*Biol*) fecundo
fertility [fə'tılıtı] *n* fertilidad *f*; fecundidad *f*
fertility drug *n* medicamento contra la infertilidad
fertilization [fə:tılaı'zeıʃən] *n* fertilización *f*; (*Biol*) fecundación *f*
fertilize ['fə:tılaız] *vt* fertilizar; (*Biol*) fecundar; (*Agr*) abonar
fertilizer ['fə:tılaızəʳ] *n* abono, fertilizante *m*
fervent ['fə:vənt] *adj* ferviente
fervour, fervor (*US*) ['fə:vəʳ] *n* fervor *m*, ardor *m*
fester ['fɛstəʳ] *vi* supurar
festival ['fɛstıvəl] *n* (*Rel*) fiesta; (*Art, Mus*) festival *m*
festive ['fɛstıv] *adj* festivo; **the ~ season** (*Brit: Christmas*) las Navidades
festivities [fɛs'tıvıtız] *npl* festejos *mpl*
festoon [fɛs'tu:n] *vt*: **to ~ with** festonear or engalanar de
fetch [fɛtʃ] *vt* ir a buscar; (*Brit: sell for*) venderse por; **how much did it ~?** ¿por cuánto se vendió?
▶ **fetch up** *vi* ir a parar
fetching ['fɛtʃıŋ] *adj* atractivo
fête [feıt] *n* fiesta
fetid ['fɛtıd] *adj* fétido
fetish ['fɛtıʃ] *n* fetiche *m*
fetter ['fɛtəʳ] *vt* (*person*) encadenar, poner grillos a; (*horse*) trabar; (*fig*) poner trabas a
fetters ['fɛtəz] *npl* grillos *mpl*
fettle ['fɛtl] *n*: **in fine ~** en buenas condiciones
fetus ['fi:təs] *n* (*US*) = **foetus**
feud [fju:d] *n* (*hostility*) enemistad *f*; (*quarrel*) disputa; **a family ~** una pelea familiar
feudal ['fju:dl] *adj* feudal
feudalism ['fju:dəlızəm] *n* feudalismo
fever ['fi:vəʳ] *n* fiebre *f*; **he has a ~** tiene fiebre
feverish ['fi:vərıʃ] *adj* febril
feverishly ['fi:vərıʃlı] *adv* febrilmente
few [fju:] *adj* (*not many*) pocos; (*some*) algunos, unos ■ *pron* algunos; **a ~** *adj* unos pocos; **few people**, poca gente; **a good ~**, **quite a ~** bastantes; **in** or **over the next ~ days** en los próximos días; **every ~ weeks** cada dos o tres semanas; **a ~ more days** unos días más
fewer ['fju:əʳ] *adj* menos
fewest ['fju:ıst] *adj* los/las menos

553

FFA *n abbr* = **Future Farmers of America**
FH *abbr* (Brit) = **fire hydrant**
FHA *n abbr* (US: = *Federal Housing Administration*) oficina federal de la vivienda
fiancé [fɪ'ãːŋseɪ] *n* novio, prometido
fiancée [fɪ'ãːŋseɪ] *n* novia, prometida
fiasco [fɪ'æskəu] *n* fiasco
fib [fɪb] *n* mentirijilla ■ *vi* decir mentirijillas
fibre, fiber (US) ['faɪbəʳ] *n* fibra
fibreboard, fiberboard (US) ['faɪbəbɔːd] *n* fibra vulcanizada
fibreglass, fiberglass (US) ['faɪbəglɑːs] *n* fibra de vidrio
fibrositis [faɪbrə'saɪtɪs] *n* fibrositis *f inv*
FICA *n abbr* (US) = **Federal Insurance Contributions Act**
fickle ['fɪkl] *adj* inconstante
fiction ['fɪkʃən] *n* (gen) ficción f
fictional ['fɪkʃnl] *adj* novelesco
fictionalize ['fɪkʃənəlaɪz] *vt* novelar
fictitious [fɪk'tɪʃəs] *adj* ficticio
fiddle ['fɪdl] *n* (Mus) violín m; (cheating) trampa ■ *vt* (Brit: accounts) falsificar; **tax ~** evasión f fiscal; **to work a ~** hacer trampa
▶ **fiddle with** *vt fus* juguetear con
fiddler ['fɪdləʳ] *n* violinista m/f
fiddly ['fɪdlɪ] *adj* (task) delicado, mañoso; (object) enrevesado
fidelity [fɪ'dɛlɪtɪ] *n* fidelidad f
fidget ['fɪdʒɪt] *vi* moverse (nerviosamente)
fidgety ['fɪdʒɪtɪ] *adj* nervioso
fiduciary [fɪ'duːʃɪərɪ] *n* fiduciario(-a)
field [fiːld] *n* (gen) campo; (Comput) campo; (fig) campo, esfera; (Sport) campo, cancha (LAm); (competitors) competidores mpl ■ *cpd*: **to have a ~ day** (fig) ponerse las botas; **to lead the ~** (Sport, Comm) llevar la delantera; **to give sth a year's trial in the ~** (fig) sacar algo al mercado a prueba por un año; **my particular ~** mi especialidad
field glasses *npl* gemelos *mpl*
field hospital *n* hospital m de campaña
field marshal *n* mariscal m
fieldwork ['fiːldwəːk] *n* (Archaeology, Geo) trabajo de campo
fiend [fiːnd] *n* demonio
fiendish ['fiːndɪʃ] *adj* diabólico
fierce [fɪəs] *adj* feroz; (wind, attack) violento; (heat) intenso; (fighting, enemy) encarnizado
fiercely ['fɪəslɪ] *adv* con ferocidad; violentamente; intensamente; encarnizadamente
fierceness ['fɪəsnɪs] *n* ferocidad f; violencia; intensidad f; encarnizamiento
fiery ['faɪərɪ] *adj* (burning) ardiente; (temperament) apasionado

FIFA ['fiːfə] *n abbr* (= *Fédération Internationale de Football Association*) FIFA f
fifteen [fɪf'tiːn] *num* quince
fifth [fɪfθ] *adj* quinto
fiftieth ['fɪftɪɪθ] *adj* quincuagésimo
fifty ['fɪftɪ] *num* cincuenta; **the fifties** los años cincuenta; **to be in one's fifties** andar por los cincuenta
fifty-fifty ['fɪftɪ'fɪftɪ] *adv*: **to go ~ with sb** ir a medias con algn ■ *adj*: **we have a ~ chance of success** tenemos un cincuenta por ciento de posibilidades de tener éxito
fig [fɪg] *n* higo
fight [faɪt] (pt, pp **fought**) *n* (gen) pelea; (Mil) combate m; (struggle) lucha ■ *vt* luchar contra; (cancer, alcoholism) combatir; (Law): **to ~ a case** defenderse ■ *vi* pelear, luchar; (quarrel): **to ~ (with sb)** pelear (con algn); (fig): **to ~ (for/against)** luchar (por/contra)
▶ **fight back** *vi* defenderse; (after illness) recuperarse ■ *vt* (tears) contener
▶ **fight down** *vt* (anger, anxiety, urge) reprimir
▶ **fight off** *vt* (attack, attacker) rechazar; (disease, sleep, urge) luchar contra
▶ **fight out** *vt*: **to ~ it out** decidirlo en una pelea
fighter ['faɪtəʳ] *n* combatiente m/f; (fig) luchador(a) m(f); (plane) caza m
fighter-bomber ['faɪtəbɔməʳ] *n* cazabombardero
fighter pilot *n* piloto de caza
fighting ['faɪtɪŋ] *n* (gen) el luchar; (battle) combate m; (in streets) disturbios mpl
figment ['fɪgmənt] *n*: **a ~ of the imagination** un producto de la imaginación
figurative ['fɪgjurətɪv] *adj* (meaning) figurado; (Art) figurativo
figure ['fɪgəʳ] *n* (Drawing, Geom) figura, dibujo; (number, cipher) cifra; (person, outline) figura; (body shape) línea; (: attractive) tipo ■ *vt* (esp US: think, calculate) calcular, imaginarse ■ *vi* (appear) figurar; (esp US: make sense) ser lógico; **~ of speech** (Ling) figura retórica; **public ~** personaje m
▶ **figure on** *vt fus* (US) contar con
▶ **figure out** *vt* (understand) comprender
figurehead ['fɪgəhɛd] *n* (fig) figura decorativa
figure skating *n* patinaje m artístico
Fiji ['fiːdʒiː], **Fiji Islands** *npl* (Islas fpl) Fiji
filament ['fɪləmənt] *n* (Elec) filamento
filch [fɪltʃ] *vt* (col: steal) birlar
file [faɪl] *n* (tool) lima; (for nails) lima de uñas; (dossier) expediente m; (folder) carpeta; (in cabinet) archivo; (Comput) fichero; (row) fila ■ *vt* limar; (papers) clasificar; (Law: claim) presentar; (store) archivar; **to open/close a ~** (Comput) abrir/cerrar un fichero; **to ~ in/out**

vi entrar/salir en fila; **to ~ a suit against sb** entablar pleito contra algn; **to ~ past** desfilar ante

file name n (Comput) nombre m de fichero

filibuster ['fɪlɪbʌstəʳ] (esp US Pol) n obstruccionista m/f, filibustero(-a) ■ vi usar maniobras obstruccionistas

filing ['faɪlɪŋ] n: **to do the ~** llevar los archivos

filing cabinet n fichero, archivo

filing clerk n oficinista m/f

fill [fɪl] vt llenar; (tooth) empastar; (vacancy) cubrir ■ n: **to eat one's ~** comer hasta hartarse; **we've already filled that vacancy** ya hemos cubierto esa vacante; **filled with admiration (for)** lleno de admiración (por)
▶ **fill in** vt rellenar; (details, report) completar; **to ~ sb in on sth** (col) poner a algn al corriente or al día sobre algo
▶ **fill out** vt (form, receipt) rellenar
▶ **fill up** vt llenar (hasta el borde) ■ vi (Aut) echar gasolina

fillet ['fɪlɪt] n filete m

fillet steak n filete m de ternera

filling ['fɪlɪŋ] n (Culin) relleno; (for tooth) empaste m

filling station n estación f de servicio

fillip ['fɪlɪp] n estímulo

filly ['fɪlɪ] n potra

film [fɪlm] n película ■ vt (scene) filmar ■ vi rodar

film script n guión m

film star n estrella de cine

filmstrip ['fɪlmstrɪp] n tira de diapositivas

film studio n estudio de cine

Filofax® ['faɪləfæks] n agenda (profesional)

filter ['fɪltəʳ] n filtro ■ vt filtrar
▶ **filter in, filter through** vi filtrarse

filter coffee n café m (molido) para filtrar

filter lane n (Brit) carril m de selección

filter-tipped ['fɪltətɪpt] adj con filtro

filth [fɪlθ] n suciedad f

filthy ['fɪlθɪ] adj sucio; (language) obsceno

fin [fɪn] n (gen) aleta

final ['faɪnl] adj (last) final, último; (definitive) definitivo ■ n (Sport) final f; **finals** npl (Scol) exámenes mpl finales

final demand n (on invoice etc) último aviso

final dividend n dividendo final

finale [fɪ'nɑːlɪ] n final m

finalist ['faɪnəlɪst] n (Sport) finalista m/f

finality [faɪ'nælɪtɪ] n finalidad f; **with an air of ~** en tono resuelto, de modo terminante

finalize ['faɪnəlaɪz] vt ultimar

finally ['faɪnəlɪ] adv (lastly) por último, finalmente; (eventually) por fin; (irrevocably) de modo definitivo; (once and for all) definitivamente

finance [faɪ'næns] n (money, funds) fondos mpl; **finances** npl finanzas fpl ■ cpd (page, section, company) financiero ■ vt financiar

financial [faɪ'nænʃəl] adj financiero

financially [faɪ'nænʃəlɪ] adv económicamente

financial management n gestión f financiera

financial statement n estado financiero

financial year n ejercicio (financiero)

financier [faɪ'nænsɪəʳ] n financiero(-a)

find [faɪnd] vt (pt, pp **found**) [faund] (gen) encontrar, hallar; (come upon) descubrir ■ n hallazgo; descubrimiento; **to ~ sb guilty** (Law) declarar culpable a algn; **I ~ it easy** me resulta fácil
▶ **find out** vt averiguar; (truth, secret) descubrir ■ vi: **to ~ out about sth** enterarse de

findings ['faɪndɪŋz] npl (Law) veredicto sg, fallo sg; (of report) recomendaciones fpl

fine [faɪn] adj (delicate) fino; (beautiful) hermoso ■ adv (well) bien ■ n (Law) multa ■ vt (Law) multar; **the weather is ~** hace buen tiempo; **he's ~** está muy bien; **you're doing ~** lo estás haciendo muy bien; **to cut it ~** (of time, money) calcular muy justo; **to get a ~ for (doing) sth** recibir una multa por (hacer) algo

fine arts npl bellas artes fpl

finely ['faɪnlɪ] adv (splendidly) con elegancia; (chop) en trozos pequeños, fino; (adjust) con precisión

fineness ['faɪnnɪs] n (of cloth) finura

fine print n: **the ~** la letra pequeña or menuda

finery ['faɪnərɪ] n galas fpl

finesse [fɪ'nɛs] n sutileza

fine-tooth comb ['faɪntuːθ-] n: **to go through sth with a ~** revisar algo a fondo

finger ['fɪŋgəʳ] n dedo ■ vt (touch) manosear; (Mus) puntear; **little/index ~** (dedo) meñique m/índice m

fingernail ['fɪŋgəneɪl] n uña

fingerprint ['fɪŋgəprɪnt] n huella dactilar

fingertip ['fɪŋgətɪp] n yema del dedo; **to have sth at one's fingertips** saberse algo al dedillo

finicky ['fɪnɪkɪ] adj (fussy) delicado

finish ['fɪnɪʃ] n (end) fin m; (Sport) meta; (polish etc) acabado ■ vt, vi acabar, terminar; **to ~ doing sth** acabar de hacer algo; **to ~ first/second/third** (Sport) llegar el primero/segundo/tercero; **I've finished with the paper** he terminado con el periódico; **she's finished with him** ha roto or acabado con él
▶ **finish off** vt acabar, terminar; (kill) rematar
▶ **finish up** vt acabar, terminar ■ vi ir a parar, terminar

555

finished ['fɪnɪʃt] adj (product) acabado; (performance) pulido; (col: tired) rendido, hecho polvo

finishing ['fɪnɪʃɪŋ] adj: ~ **touches** toque m final

finishing line n línea de llegada or meta

finishing school n colegio para la educación social de señoritas

finite ['faɪnaɪt] adj finito

Finland ['fɪnlənd] n Finlandia

Finn [fɪn] n finlandés(-esa) m(f)

Finnish ['fɪnɪʃ] adj finlandés(-esa) ■ n (Ling) finlandés m

fiord [fjɔːd] n fiordo

fir [fəːˈ] n abeto

fire ['faɪəˈ] n fuego; (accidental, damaging) incendio ■ vt (gun) disparar; (set fire to) incendiar; (excite) exaltar; (interest) despertar; (dismiss) despedir ■ vi encenderse; (Aut: engine) encender; **electric/gas** ~ estufa eléctrica/de gas; **on** ~ ardiendo, en llamas; **to be on** ~ estar ardiendo; **to catch** ~ prenderse fuego; **to set** ~ **to sth, set sth on** ~ prender fuego a algo; **insured against** ~ asegurado contra incendios; **to be/come under** ~ estar/caer bajo el fuego enemigo

fire alarm n alarma de incendios

firearm ['faɪərɑːm] n arma de fuego

fire brigade, fire department (US) n (cuerpo de) bomberos mpl

fire door n puerta contra incendios

fire drill n (ejercicio de) simulacro de incendio

fire engine n coche m de bomberos

fire escape n escalera de incendios

fire extinguisher n extintor m

fireguard ['faɪəgɑːd] n pantalla (guardallama)

fire hazard n = **fire risk**

fire hydrant n boca de incendios

fire insurance n seguro contra incendios

fireman ['faɪəmən] n bombero

fireplace ['faɪəpleɪs] n chimenea

fireplug ['faɪəplʌg] n (US) boca de incendios

fire practice n = **fire drill**

fireproof ['faɪəpruːf] adj a prueba de fuego; (material) incombustible

fire regulations npl reglamentos mpl contra incendios

fire risk n peligro de incendio

firescreen ['faɪəskriːn] n pantalla refractaria

fireside ['faɪəsaɪd] n: **by the** ~ al lado de la chimenea

fire station n parque m de bomberos

firewall ['faɪəwɔːl] n (Internet) firewall m

firewood ['faɪəwud] n leña

fireworks ['faɪəwəːks] npl fuegos mpl artificiales

firing ['faɪərɪŋ] n (Mil) disparos mpl, tiroteo

firing line n línea de fuego; **to be in the** ~ (fig: liable to be criticised) estar en la línea de fuego

firing squad n pelotón m de ejecución

firm [fəːm] adj firme; (offer, decision) en firme ■ n empresa; **to be a** ~ **believer in sth** ser un partidario convencido de algo; **to stand** ~ or **take a** ~ **stand on sth** (fig) mantenerse firme ante algo

firmly ['fəːmlɪ] adv firmemente

firmness ['fəːmnɪs] n firmeza

first [fəːst] adj primero ■ adv (before others) primero; (when listing reasons etc) en primer lugar, primeramente ■ n (person: in race) primero(-a); (Aut: also: **first gear**) primera; **at** ~ al principio; ~ **of all** ante todo; **the** ~ **of January** el uno or primero de enero; **in the** ~ **instance** en primer lugar; **I'll do it** ~ **thing tomorrow** lo haré mañana a primera hora; **for the** ~ **time** por primera vez; **head** ~ de cabeza; **from the (very)** ~ desde el principio

first aid n primeros auxilios mpl

first aid kit n botiquín m

first aid post, first aid station (US) n puesto de auxilio

first-class ['fəːstklɑːs] adj de primera clase; ~ **ticket** (Rail etc) billete m or (LAm) boleto de primera clase; ~ **mail** correo de primera clase

first-hand [fəːstˈhænd] adj de primera mano

first lady n (esp US) primera dama

firstly ['fəːstlɪ] adv en primer lugar

first name n nombre m de pila

first night n estreno

first-rate [fəːstˈreɪt] adj de primera (clase)

first-time buyer [fəːsttaɪm-] n persona que compra su primera vivienda

fir tree n abeto

fiscal ['fɪskəl] adj fiscal; ~ **year** año fiscal, ejercicio

fish [fɪʃ] n pl inv pez m; (food) pescado ■ vt pescar en ■ vi pescar; **to go fishing** ir de pesca

▶ **fish out** vt (from water, box etc) sacar

fish-and-chip shop n = **chip shop**

fishbone ['fɪʃbəun] n espina

fisherman ['fɪʃəmən] n pescador m

fishery ['fɪʃərɪ] n pesquería

fish factory n fábrica de elaboración de pescado

fish farm n piscifactoría

fish fingers npl (Brit) palitos mpl de pescado (empanado)

fishing boat ['fɪʃɪŋ-] n barca de pesca

fishing industry n industria pesquera

fishing line n sedal m
fishing net n red f de pesca
fishing rod n caña (de pescar)
fishing tackle n aparejo (de pescar)
fish market n mercado de pescado
fishmonger ['fɪʃmʌŋgəʳ] n (Brit) pescadero(-a)
fishmonger's, fishmonger's shop n (Brit) pescadería
fishseller ['fɪʃsɛləʳ] n (US) = **fishmonger**
fish slice n paleta para pescado
fish sticks npl (US) = **fish fingers**
fishstore ['fɪʃstɔːʳ] n (US) = **fishmonger's**
fishy ['fɪʃɪ] adj (fig) sospechoso
fission ['fɪʃən] n fisión f; **atomic/nuclear ~** fisión f atómica/nuclear
fissure ['fɪʃəʳ] n fisura
fist [fɪst] n puño
fistfight ['fɪstfaɪt] n lucha a puñetazos
fit [fɪt] adj (Med, Sport) en (buena) forma; (proper) adecuado, apropiado ■ vt (clothes) quedar bien a; (try on: clothes) probar; (match: facts) cuadrar or corresponder or coincidir con; (: description) estar de acuerdo con; (accommodate) ajustar, adaptar ■ vi (clothes) quedar bien; (in space, gap) caber; (facts) coincidir ■ n (Med) ataque m; (outburst) arranque m; **~ to** apto para; **~ for** apropiado para; **do as you think** or **see ~** haz lo que te parezca mejor; **to keep ~** mantenerse en forma; **to be ~ for work** (after illness) estar en condiciones para trabajar; **~ of coughing** acceso de tos; **~ of anger/enthusiasm** arranque de cólera/entusiasmo; **to have** or **suffer a ~** tener un ataque or acceso; **this dress is a good ~** este vestido me queda bien; **by fits and starts** a rachas
▸ **fit in** vi encajar ■ vt (object) acomodar; (fig: appointment, visitor) encontrar un hueco para; **to ~ in with sb's plans** acomodarse a los planes de algn
▸ **fit out** vt, (Brit) **fit up** equipar
fitful ['fɪtful] adj espasmódico, intermitente
fitfully ['fɪtfəlɪ] adv irregularmente; **to sleep ~** dormir a rachas
fitment ['fɪtmənt] n mueble m
fitness ['fɪtnɪs] n (Med) forma física; (of remark) conveniencia
fitted carpet ['fɪtɪd-] n moqueta
fitted cupboards ['fɪtɪd-] npl armarios mpl empotrados
fitted kitchen ['fɪtɪd-] n cocina amueblada
fitter ['fɪtəʳ] n ajustador(a) m(f)
fitting ['fɪtɪŋ] adj apropiado ■ n (of dress) prueba; see also **fittings**
fitting room n (in shop) probador m
fittings ['fɪtɪŋz] npl instalaciones fpl
five [faɪv] num cinco; **she is ~ (years old)**

tiene cinco años (de edad); **it costs ~ pounds** cuesta cinco libras; **it's ~ (o'clock)** son las cinco
five-day week ['faɪvdeɪ] n semana inglesa
fiver ['faɪvəʳ] n (col: Brit) billete m de cinco libras; (: US) billete m de cinco dólares
fix [fɪks] vt (secure) fijar, asegurar; (mend) arreglar; (make ready: meal, drink) preparar ■ n: **to be in a ~** estar en un aprieto; **to ~ sth in one's mind** fijar algo en la memoria; **the fight was a ~** (col) la pelea estaba amañada
▸ **fix on** vt (decide on) fijar
▸ **fix up** vt (arrange: date, meeting) arreglar; **to ~ sb up with sth** conseguirle algo a algn
fixation [fɪk'seɪʃən] n (Psych) fijación f
fixative ['fɪksətɪv] n fijador m
fixed [fɪkst] adj (prices etc) fijo; **how are you ~ for money?** (col) ¿qué tal andas de dinero?
fixed assets npl activo sg fijo
fixed charge n gasto fijo
fixture ['fɪkstʃəʳ] n (Sport) encuentro; **fixtures** npl instalaciones fpl fijas
fizz [fɪz] vi burbujear
fizzle out ['fɪzl-] vi apagarse; (enthusiasm, interest) decaer; (plan) quedar en agua de borrajas
fizzy ['fɪzɪ] adj (drink) gaseoso
fjord [fjɔːd] n = **fiord**
FL, Fla. abbr (US) = **Florida**
flabbergasted ['flæbəgɑːstɪd] adj pasmado
flabby ['flæbɪ] adj flojo (de carnes); (skin) fofo
flag [flæg] n bandera; (stone) losa ■ vi decaer; **~ of convenience** pabellón m de conveniencia
▸ **flag down** vt: **to ~ sb down** hacer señas a algn para que se pare
flagpole ['flægpəul] n asta de bandera
flagrant ['fleɪgrənt] adj flagrante
flagship ['flægʃɪp] n buque m insignia or almirante
flagstone ['flægstəun] n losa
flag stop n (US) parada discrecional
flair [flɛəʳ] n aptitud f especial
flak [flæk] n (Mil) fuego antiaéreo; (col: criticism) lluvia de críticas
flake [fleɪk] n (of rust, paint) desconchón m; (of snow) copo; (of soap powder) escama ■ vi (also: **flake off**: paint) desconcharse; (skin) descamarse
flaky ['fleɪkɪ] adj (paintwork) desconchado; (skin) escamoso
flaky pastry n (Culin) hojaldre m
flamboyant [flæm'bɔɪənt] adj (dress) vistoso; (person) extravagante
flame [fleɪm] n llama; **to burst into flames** incendiarse; **old ~** (col) antiguo amor m/f
flamingo [flə'mɪŋgəu] n flamenco

flammable ['flæməbl] *adj* inflamable

flan [flæn] *n* (*Brit*) tarta

flank [flæŋk] *n* flanco; (*of person*) costado ∎ *vt* flanquear

flannel ['flænl] *n* (*Brit*: *also*: **face flannel**) toallita; (*fabric*) franela; **flannels** *npl* pantalones *mpl* de franela

flannelette [flænə'lɛt] *n* franela de algodón

flap [flæp] *n* (*of pocket, envelope*) solapa; (*of table*) hoja (plegadiza); (*wing movement*) aletazo; (*Aviat*) flap *m* ∎ *vt* (*wings*) batir ∎ *vi* (*sail, flag*) ondear

flapjack ['flæpdʒæk] *n* (*US*: *pancake*) torta, panqueque *m* (*LAm*)

flare [flɛər] *n* llamarada; (*Mil*) bengala; (*in skirt etc*) vuelo
▶ **flare up** *vi* encenderse; (*fig*: *person*) encolerizarse; (: *revolt*) estallar

flash [flæʃ] *n* relámpago; (*also*: **news flash**) noticias *fpl* de última hora; (*Phot*) flash *m*; (*US*: *torch*) linterna ∎ *vt* (*light, headlights*) lanzar destellos con; (*torch*) encender ∎ *vi* destellar; **in a ~** en un santiamén; **~ of inspiration** ráfaga de inspiración; **to ~ sth about** (*fig, col*: *flaunt*) ostentar algo, presumir con algo; **he flashed by** *or* **past** pasó como un rayo

flashback ['flæʃbæk] *n* flashback *m*, escena retrospectiva

flashbulb ['flæʃbʌlb] *n* bombilla de flash

flash card *n* (*Scol*) tarjeta

flasher ['flæʃər] *n* exhibicionista *m*

flashlight ['flæʃlaɪt] *n* (*US*: *torch*) linterna

flashpoint ['flæʃpɔɪnt] *n* punto de inflamación; (*fig*) punto de explosión

flashy ['flæʃɪ] *adj* (*pej*) ostentoso

flask [flɑːsk] *n* petaca; (*also*: **vacuum flask**) termo

flat [flæt] *adj* llano; (*smooth*) liso; (*tyre*) desinflado; (*battery*) descargado; (*beer*) sin gas; (*Mus*: *instrument*) desafinado ∎ *n* (*Brit*: *apartment*) piso (*SP*), departamento (*LAm*), apartamento; (*Aut*) pinchazo; (*Mus*) bemol *m*; (**to work**) **~ out** (trabajar) a tope; **~ rate of pay** sueldo fijo

flatfooted [flæt'futɪd] *adj* de pies planos

flatly ['flætlɪ] *adv* rotundamente, de plano

flatmate ['flætmeɪt] *n* compañero(-a) de piso

flatness ['flætnɪs] *n* (*of land*) llanura, lo llano

flat pack *n*: **it comes in a ~** viene en un paquete plano para su automontaje

flat-pack *adj*: **~ furniture** muebles *mpl* automontables (*embalados en paquetes planos*)

flat-screen ['flætskriːn] *adj* de pantalla plana

flatten ['flætn] *vt* (*also*: **flatten out**) allanar; (*smooth out*) alisar; (*house, city*) arrasar

flatter ['flætər] *vt* adular, halagar; (*show to advantage*) favorecer

flatterer ['flætərər] *n* adulador(a) *m(f)*

flattering ['flætərɪŋ] *adj* halagador(a); (*clothes etc*) que favorece, favorecedor(a)

flattery ['flætərɪ] *n* adulación *f*

flatulence ['flætjuləns] *n* flatulencia

flaunt [flɔːnt] *vt* ostentar, lucir

flavour, flavor (*US*) ['fleɪvər] *n* sabor *m*, gusto ∎ *vt* sazonar, condimentar; **strawberry flavoured** con sabor a fresa

flavouring, flavoring (*US*) ['fleɪvərɪŋ] *n* (*in product*) aromatizante *m*

flaw [flɔː] *n* defecto

flawless ['flɔːlɪs] *adj* intachable

flax [flæks] *n* lino

flaxen ['flæksən] *adj* muy rubio

flea [fliː] *n* pulga

flea market *n* rastro, mercadillo

fleck [flɛk] *n* mota ∎ *vt* (*with blood, mud etc*) salpicar; **brown flecked with white** marrón con motas blancas

fledgeling, fledgling ['flɛdʒlɪŋ] *n* (*fig*) novato(-a), principiante *m/f*

flee [fliː] (*pt, pp* **fled**) [flɛd] *vt* huir de, abandonar ∎ *vi* huir

fleece [fliːs] *n* (*of sheep*) vellón *m*; (*wool*) lana; (*top*) forro polar ∎ *vt* (*col*) desplumar

fleecy ['fliːsɪ] *adj* (*blanket*) lanoso, lanudo; (*cloud*) algodonoso

fleet [fliːt] *n* flota; (*of cars, lorries etc*) parque *m*

fleeting ['fliːtɪŋ] *adj* fugaz

Flemish ['flɛmɪʃ] *adj* flamenco ∎ *n* (*Ling*) flamenco; **the ~** los flamencos

flesh [flɛʃ] *n* carne *f*; (*of fruit*) pulpa; **of ~ and blood** de carne y hueso

flesh wound *n* herida superficial

flew [fluː] *pt of* **fly**

flex [flɛks] *n* cable *m* ∎ *vt* (*muscles*) tensar

flexibility [flɛksɪ'bɪlɪtɪ] *n* flexibilidad *f*

flexible ['flɛksəbl] *adj* flexible; **~ working hours** horario *sg* flexible

flexitime ['flɛksɪtaɪm] *n* horario flexible

flick [flɪk] *n* golpecito; (*with finger*) capirotazo; (*Brit*: *col*: *film*) película ∎ *vt* dar un golpecito a
▶ **flick off** *vt* quitar con el dedo
▶ **flick through** *vt fus* hojear

flicker ['flɪkər] *vi* (*light*) parpadear; (*flame*) vacilar ∎ *n* parpadeo

flick knife *n* navaja de muelle

flier ['flaɪər] *n* aviador(a) *m(f)*

flies [flaɪz] *npl of* **fly**

flight [flaɪt] *n* vuelo; (*escape*) huida, fuga; (*also*: **flight of steps**) tramo (de escaleras); **to take ~** huir, darse a la fuga; **to put to ~** ahuyentar; **how long does the ~ take?** ¿cuánto dura el vuelo?

flight attendant n (US) auxiliar m/f de vuelo
flight deck n (Aviat) cabina de mandos
flight path n trayectoria de vuelo
flight recorder n registrador m de vuelo
flighty ['flaɪtɪ] adj caprichoso
flimsy ['flɪmzɪ] adj (thin) muy ligero; (excuse) flojo
flinch [flɪntʃ] vi encogerse
fling [flɪŋ] vt (pt, pp **flung**) [flʌŋ] arrojar ▪ n (love affair) aventura amorosa
flint [flɪnt] n pedernal m; (in lighter) piedra
flip [flɪp] vt: **to ~ a coin** echar a cara o cruz
  ▶ **flip over** vt dar la vuelta a
  ▶ **flip through** vt fus (book) hojear; (records) ver de pasada
flippancy ['flɪpənsɪ] n ligereza
flippant ['flɪpənt] adj poco serio
flipper ['flɪpər] n aleta
flip side n (of record) cara B
flirt [flɜːt] vi coquetear, flirtear ▪ n coqueta f
flirtation [flɜː'teɪʃən] n coqueteo, flirteo
flit [flɪt] vi revolotear
float [fləʊt] n flotador m; (in procession) carroza; (sum of money) (dinero suelto para) cambio ▪ vi (Comm: currency) flotar ▪ vt (gen) hacer flotar; (company) lanzar; **to ~ an idea** plantear una idea
floating ['fləʊtɪŋ] adj: **~ vote** voto indeciso; **~ voter** votante m/f indeciso(-a)
flock [flɒk] n (of sheep) rebaño; (of birds) bandada; (of people) multitud f
floe [fləʊ] n: **ice ~** témpano de hielo
flog [flɒg] vt azotar; (col) vender
flood [flʌd] n inundación f; (of words, tears etc) torrente m ▪ vt (Aut: carburettor) inundar; (also: **to flood the market**: Comm) inundar el mercado
flooding ['flʌdɪŋ] n inundación f
floodlight ['flʌdlaɪt] n foco ▪ vt (irreg: like **light**) iluminar con focos
floodlit ['flʌdlɪt] pt, pp of **floodlight** ▪ adj iluminado
flood tide n pleamar f
floodwater ['flʌdwɔːtər] n aguas fpl (de la inundación)
floor [flɔːr] n suelo, piso (LAm); (storey) piso; (of sea, valley) fondo; (dance floor) pista ▪ vt (fig: baffle) dejar anonadado; **ground ~**, (US) **first ~** planta baja; **first ~**, (US) **second ~** primer piso; **top ~** último piso; **to have the ~** (speaker) tener la palabra
floorboard ['flɔːbɔːd] n tabla
flooring ['flɔːrɪŋ] n suelo; (material) solería
floor lamp n (US) lámpara de pie
floor show n cabaret m
floorwalker ['flɔːwɔːkər] n (US Comm) supervisor(a) m(f)

flop [flɒp] n fracaso ▪ vi (fail) fracasar
flora ['flɔːrə] n flora
floral ['flɔːrl] adj floral; (dress, wallpaper) de flores
Florence ['flɒrəns] n Florencia
Florentine ['flɒrəntaɪn] adj, n florentino(-a) m(f)
florid ['flɒrɪd] adj (style) florido
florist ['flɒrɪst] n florista m/f; **~'s (shop)** n floristería
flotation [fləʊ'teɪʃən] n (of shares) emisión f; (of company) lanzamiento
flounce [flaʊns] n volante m
  ▶ **flounce in** vi entrar con gesto exagerado
  ▶ **flounce out** vi salir con gesto airado
flounder ['flaʊndər] vi tropezar ▪ n (Zool) platija
flour ['flaʊər] n harina
flourish ['flʌrɪʃ] vi florecer ▪ n ademán m, movimiento (ostentoso)
flourishing ['flʌrɪʃɪŋ] adj floreciente
flout [flaʊt] vt burlarse de; (order) no hacer caso de, hacer caso omiso de
flow [fləʊ] n (movement) flujo; (direction) curso; (Elec) corriente f ▪ vi correr, fluir
flow chart n organigrama m
flow diagram n organigrama m
flower ['flaʊər] n flor f ▪ vi florecer; **in ~** en flor
flower bed n macizo
flowerpot ['flaʊəpɔt] n tiesto
flowery ['flaʊərɪ] adj florido; (perfume, pattern) de flores
flowing ['fləʊɪŋ] adj (hair, clothes) suelto; (style) fluido
flown [fləʊn] pp of **fly**
flu [fluː] n gripe f
fluctuate ['flʌktjʊeɪt] vi fluctuar
fluctuation [flʌktjʊ'eɪʃən] n fluctuación f
flue [fluː] n cañón m
fluency ['fluːənsɪ] n fluidez f, soltura
fluent ['fluːənt] adj (speech) elocuente; **he speaks ~ French, he's ~ in French** domina el francés
fluently ['fluːəntlɪ] adv con soltura
fluff [flʌf] n pelusa
fluffy ['flʌfɪ] adj lanoso
fluid ['fluːɪd] adj, n fluido, líquido; (in diet) líquido
fluke [fluːk] n (col) chiripa
flummox ['flʌməks] vt desconcertar
flung [flʌŋ] pt, pp of **fling**
flunky ['flʌŋkɪ] n lacayo
fluorescent [flʊə'resnt] adj fluorescente
fluoride ['flʊəraɪd] n fluoruro
fluoride toothpaste n pasta de dientes con flúor

f

flurry ['flʌrɪ] n (of snow) ventisca; (haste) agitación f; ~ **of activity** frenesí m de actividad

flush [flʌʃ] n (on face) rubor m; (fig: of youth, beauty) resplandor m ▪ vt limpiar con agua; (also: **flush out**: game, birds) levantar; (fig: criminal) poner al descubierto ▪ vi ruborizarse ▪ adj: ~ **with** a ras de; **to ~ the toilet** tirar de la cadena (del wáter); **hot flushes** (Med) sofocos mpl

flushed [flʌʃt] adj ruborizado

fluster ['flʌstəʳ] n aturdimiento ▪ vt aturdir

flustered ['flʌstəd] adj aturdido

flute [fluːt] n flauta travesera

flutter ['flʌtəʳ] n (of wings) revoloteo, aleteo; (col: bet) apuesta ▪ vi revolotear; **to be in a ~** estar nervioso

flux [flʌks] n flujo; **in a state of ~** cambiando continuamente

fly [flaɪ] (pt **flew**, pp **flown**) n (insect) mosca; (on trousers: also: **flies**) bragueta ▪ vt (plane) pilotar; (cargo) transportar (en avión); (distance) recorrer (en avión) ▪ vi volar; (passenger) ir en avión; (escape) evadirse; (flag) ondear
  ▸ **fly away** vi (bird, insect) irse volando
  ▸ **fly in** vi (person) llegar en avión; (plane) aterrizar; **he flew in from Bilbao** llegó en avión desde Bilbao
  ▸ **fly off** vi irse volando
  ▸ **fly out** vi irse en avión

fly-fishing ['flaɪfɪʃɪŋ] n pesca con mosca

flying ['flaɪɪŋ] n (activity) (el) volar ▪ adj: ~ **visit** visita relámpago; **with ~ colours** con lucimiento

flying buttress n arbotante m

flying picket n piquete m volante

flying saucer n platillo volante

flying squad n (Police) brigada móvil

flying start n: **to get off to a ~** empezar con buen pie

flyleaf (pl **flyleaves**) ['flaɪliːf, -liːvz] n (hoja de) guarda

flyover ['flaɪəuvəʳ] n (Brit: bridge) paso elevado or (LAm) a desnivel

flypast ['flaɪpɑːst] n desfile m aéreo

flysheet ['flaɪʃiːt] n (for tent) doble techo

flyswatter ['flaɪswɔtəʳ] n matamoscas m inv

flyweight ['flaɪweɪt] adj de peso mosca
  ▪ n peso mosca

flywheel ['flaɪwiːl] n volante m (de motor)

FM abbr (Radio: = frequency modulation) FM; (Brit Mil) = **field marshal**

FMB n abbr (US) = **Federal Maritime Board**

FMCS n abbr (US: = Federal Mediation and Conciliation Services) organismo de conciliación en conflictos laborales

FO n abbr (Brit: = Foreign Office) ≈ Min. de AA. EE

foal [fəul] n potro

foam [fəum] n espuma ▪ vi hacer espuma

foam rubber n goma espuma

FOB abbr (= free on board) f.a.b.

fob [fɔb] n (also: **watch fob**) leontina ▪ vt: **to ~ sb off with sth** deshacerse de algn con algo

foc abbr (Brit: = free of charge) gratis

focal ['fəukəl] adj focal; ~ **point** punto focal; (fig) centro de atención

focus ['fəukəs] (pl **focuses**) n foco ▪ vt (field glasses etc) enfocar ▪ vi: **to ~ (on)** enfocar (a); (issue etc) centrarse en; **in/out of ~** enfocado/desenfocado

fodder ['fɔdəʳ] n pienso

FOE n abbr (= Friends of the Earth) Amigos mpl de la Tierra; (US: = Fraternal Order of Eagles) organización benéfica

foe [fəu] n enemigo

foetus, fetus (US) ['fiːtəs] n feto

fog [fɔg] n niebla

fogbound ['fɔgbaund] adj inmovilizado por la niebla

foggy ['fɔgɪ] adj: **it's ~** hay niebla

fog lamp, fog light (US) n (Aut) faro antiniebla

foible ['fɔɪbl] n manía

foil [fɔɪl] vt frustrar ▪ n hoja; (also: **kitchen foil**) papel m (de) aluminio; (Fencing) florete m

foist [fɔɪst] vt: **to ~ sth on sb** endilgarle algo a algn

fold [fəuld] n (bend, crease) pliegue m; (Agr) redil m ▪ vt doblar; (map etc) plegar; **to ~ one's arms** cruzarse de brazos
  ▸ **fold up** vi plegarse, doblarse; (business) quebrar

folder ['fəuldəʳ] n (for papers) carpeta; (binder) carpeta de anillas; (brochure) folleto

folding ['fəuldɪŋ] adj (chair, bed) plegable

foliage ['fəuliɪdʒ] n follaje m

folio ['fəuliəu] n folio

folk [fəuk] npl gente f ▪ adj popular, folklórico; **folks** npl familia, parientes mpl

folklore ['fəuklɔːʳ] n folklore m

folk music n música folk

folk singer n cantante m/f de música folk

folk song n canción f popular or folk

follow ['fɔləu] vt seguir ▪ vi seguir; (result) resultar; **he followed suit** hizo lo mismo; **to ~ sb's advice** seguir el consejo de algn; **I don't quite ~ you** no te comprendo muy bien; **to ~ in sb's footsteps** seguir los pasos de algn; **it doesn't ~ that ...** no se deduce que ....
  ▸ **follow on** vi seguir; (continue): **to ~ on from** ser la consecuencia lógica de

▶**follow out** vt (*implement: idea, plan*) realizar, llevar a cabo

▶**follow through** vt llevar hasta el fin ▪ vi (*Sport*) dar el remate

▶**follow up** vt (*letter, offer*) responder a; (*case*) investigar

follower ['fɔləuə'] n seguidor(a) m(f); (*Pol*) partidario(-a)

following ['fɔləuɪŋ] adj siguiente ▪ n seguidores mpl

follow-up ['fɔləuʌp] n continuación f

follow-up letter n carta recordatoria

folly ['fɔlɪ] n locura

fond [fɔnd] adj (*loving*) cariñoso; **to be ~ of sb** tener cariño a algn; **she's ~ of swimming** tiene afición a la natación, le gusta nadar

fondle ['fɔndl] vt acariciar

fondly ['fɔndlɪ] adv (*lovingly*) con cariño; **he ~ believed that ...** creía ingenuamente que ...

fondness ['fɔndnɪs] n (*for things*) afición f; (*for people*) cariño

font [fɔnt] n pila bautismal

food [fuːd] n comida

food chain n cadena alimenticia

food mixer n batidora

food poisoning n intoxicación f alimentaria

food processor n robot m de cocina

food stamp n (*US*) vale m para comida

foodstuffs ['fuːdstʌfs] npl comestibles mpl

fool [fuːl] n tonto(-a); (*Culin*) mousse m de frutas ▪ vt engañar, **to make a ~ of o.s.** ponerse en ridículo; **you can't ~ me** a mí no me engañas; *see also* **April Fool's Day**

▶**fool about, fool around** vi hacer el tonto

foolhardy ['fuːlhɑːdɪ] adj temerario

foolish ['fuːlɪʃ] adj tonto; (*careless*) imprudente

foolishly ['fuːlɪʃlɪ] adv tontamente, neciamente

foolproof ['fuːlpruːf] adj (*plan etc*) infalible

foolscap ['fuːlskæp] n ≈ papel m tamaño folio

foot [fut] (pl **feet**) n (*Anat*) pie m; (*of page, stairs, mountain*) pie m; (*measure*) pie (= 304 mm); (*of animal, table*) pata ▪ vt (*bill*) pagar; **on ~** a pie; **to find one's feet** acostumbrarse; **to put one's ~ down** (*say no*) plantarse; (*Aut*) pisar el acelerador

footage ['futɪdʒ] n (*Cine*) imágenes fpl

foot-and-mouth [futənd'mauθ-], **foot-and-mouth disease** n fiebre f aftosa

football ['futbɔːl] n balón m; (*game: Brit*) fútbol m; (*US*) fútbol m americano

footballer ['futbɔːlə'] n (*Brit*) = **football player**

football match n partido de fútbol

football player n futbolista m/f, jugador(a) m(f) de fútbol

footbrake ['futbreɪk] n freno de pie

footbridge ['futbrɪdʒ] n pasarela, puente m para peatones

foothills ['futhɪlz] npl estribaciones fpl

foothold ['futhəuld] n pie m firme

footing ['futɪŋ] n (*fig*) nivel m; **to lose one's ~** perder el equilibrio; **on an equal ~** en pie de igualdad

footlights ['futlaɪts] npl candilejas fpl

footman ['futmən] n lacayo

footnote ['futnəut] n nota (de pie de página)

footpath ['futpɑːθ] n sendero

footprint ['futprɪnt] n huella, pisada

footrest ['futrest] n apoyapiés m inv

footsie ['futsɪ] n: **to play ~ with sb** (*col*) juguetear con los pies de algn

footsore ['futsɔː'] adj con los pies doloridos

footstep ['futstep] n paso

footwear ['futwɛə'] n calzado

FOR abbr (= *free on rail*) franco (puesto sobre) vagón

 KEYWORD

for [fɔː] prep **1** (*indicating destination, intention*) para; **the train for London** el tren para Londres; (*in announcements*) el tren con destino a Londres; **he left for Rome** marchó para Roma; **he went for the paper** fue por el periódico; **is this for me?** ¿es esto para mí?; **it's time for lunch** es la hora de comer

2 (*indicating purpose*) para; **what('s it) for?** ¿para qué (es)?; **what's this button for?** ¿para qué sirve este botón?; **to pray for peace** rezar por la paz

3 (*on behalf of, representing*): **the MP for Hove** el diputado por Hove; **he works for the government/a local firm** trabaja para el gobierno/en una empresa local; **I'll ask him for you** se lo pediré por ti; **G for George** G de Gerona

4 (*because of*) por esta razón; **for fear of being criticized** por temor a ser criticado

5 (*with regard to*) para; **it's cold for July** hace frío para julio; **he has a gift for languages** tiene don de lenguas

6 (*in exchange for*) por; **I sold it for £5** lo vendí por £5; **to pay 50 pence for a ticket** pagar 50 peniques por un billete

7 (*in favour of*): **are you for or against us?** ¿estás con nosotros o contra nosotros?; **I'm all for it** estoy totalmente a favor; **vote for X** vote (a) X

8 (*referring to distance*): **there are roadworks for 5 km** hay obras en 5 km; **we walked for miles** caminamos kilómetros y kilómetros

9 (*referring to time*): **he was away for two**

years estuvo fuera (durante) dos años;
it hasn't rained for three weeks no ha
llovido durante *or* en tres semanas; **I have
known her for years** la conozco desde hace
años; **can you do it for tomorrow?**
¿lo podrás hacer para mañana?

10 (*with infinitive clauses*): **it is not for me to
decide** la decisión no es cosa mía; **it would
be best for you to leave** sería mejor que te
fueras; **there is still time for you to do it**
todavía te queda tiempo para hacerlo; **for
this to be possible ...** para que esto sea
posible ...

11 (*in spite of*) a pesar de; **for all his
complaints** a pesar de sus quejas
■ *conj* (*since, as: rather formal*) puesto que

forage ['fɔrɪdʒ] *n* forraje *m*
foray ['fɔreɪ] *n* incursión *f*
forbid (*pt* **forbad(e)**, *pp* **forbidden**)
[fə'bɪd, -'bæd, -'bɪdn] *vt* prohibir; **to ~ sb to
do sth** prohibir a algn hacer algo
forbidding [fə'bɪdɪŋ] *adj* (*landscape*) inhóspito;
(*severe*) severo
force [fɔːs] *n* fuerza ■ *vt* obligar, forzar;
to ~ o.s. to do hacer un esfuerzo por hacer;
the Forces *npl* (*Brit*) las Fuerzas Armadas;
sales ~ (*Comm*) personal *m* de ventas; **a ~ 5
wind** un viento fuerza 5; **to join forces** unir
fuerzas; **in ~** (*law etc*) en vigor; **to ~ sb to do
sth** obligar a algn a hacer algo
▶ **force back** *vt* (*crowd, enemy*) hacer
retroceder; (*tears*) reprimir
▶ **force down** *vt* (*food*) tragar con esfuerzo
forced [fɔːst] *adj* (*smile*) forzado; (*landing*)
forzoso
force-feed ['fɔːsfiːd] *vt* (*animal, prisoner*)
alimentar a la fuerza
forceful ['fɔːsful] *adj* enérgico
forcemeat ['fɔːsmiːt] *n* (*Culin*) relleno
forceps ['fɔːsɛps] *npl* fórceps *m inv*
forcible ['fɔːsəbl] *adj* (*violent*) a la fuerza;
(*telling*) convincente
forcibly ['fɔːsəblɪ] *adv* a la fuerza
ford [fɔːd] *n* vado ■ *vt* vadear
fore [fɔːʳ] *n*: **to bring to the ~** sacar a la
luz pública; **to come to the ~** empezar a
destacar
forearm ['fɔːrɑːm] *n* antebrazo
forebear ['fɔːbɛəʳ] *n* antepasado
foreboding [fɔː'bəudɪŋ] *n* presentimiento
forecast ['fɔːkɑːst] *n* pronóstico ■ *vt* (*irreg:
like* **cast**) pronosticar; **weather ~** previsión *f*
meteorológica
foreclose [fɔː'kləuz] *vt* (*Law: also:* **foreclose
on**) extinguir el derecho de redimir
foreclosure [fɔː'kləuʒəʳ] *n* apertura de un

juicio hipotecario
forecourt ['fɔːkɔːt] *n* (*of garage*) área de
entrada
forefathers ['fɔːfɑːðəz] *npl* antepasados *mpl*
forefinger ['fɔːfɪŋgəʳ] *n* (dedo) índice *m*
forefront ['fɔːfrʌnt] *n*: **in the ~ of** en la
vanguardia de
forego (*pt* **forewent**, *pp* **foregone**)
[fɔː'gəu, -'wɛnt, -'gɔn] *vt* = **forgo**
foregoing ['fɔːgəuɪŋ] *adj* anterior, precedente
foregone ['fɔːgɔn] *pp of* **forego** ■ *adj*: **it's a ~
conclusion** es una conclusión inevitable
foreground ['fɔːgraund] *n* primer plano *m*
(*also Comput*)
forehand ['fɔːhænd] *n* (*Tennis*) derechazo
directo
forehead ['fɔrɪd] *n* frente *f*
foreign ['fɔrɪn] *adj* extranjero; (*trade*) exterior
foreign currency *n* divisas *fpl*
foreigner ['fɔrɪnəʳ] *n* extranjero(-a)
foreign exchange *n* (*system*) cambio
de divisas; (*money*) divisas *fpl*, moneda
extranjera
foreign investment *n* inversión *f* en el
extranjero; (*money, stock*) inversiones *fpl*
extranjeras
Foreign Minister *n* Ministro(-a) de Asuntos
Exteriores, Canciller *m* (*LAm*)
Foreign Office *n* Ministerio de Asuntos
Exteriores
Foreign Secretary *n* (*Brit*) Ministro(-a) de
Asuntos Exteriores, Canciller *m* (*LAm*)
foreleg ['fɔːlɛg] *n* pata delantera
foreman ['fɔːmən] *n* capataz *m*; (*Law: of jury*)
presidente *m/f*
foremost ['fɔːməust] *adj* principal ■ *adv*:
first and ~ ante todo, antes que nada
forename ['fɔːneɪm] *n* nombre *m* (de pila)
forensic [fə'rɛnsɪk] *adj* forense; **~ scientist**
forense *m/f*
foreplay ['fɔːpleɪ] *n* preámbulos *mpl* (*de
estimulación sexual*)
forerunner ['fɔːrʌnəʳ] *n* precursor(a) *m(f)*
foresee (*pt* **foresaw**, *pp* **foreseen**)
[fɔː'siː, -'sɔː, -'siːn] *vt* prever
foreseeable [fɔː'siːəbl] *adj* previsible
foreshadow [fɔː'ʃædəu] *vt* prefigurar,
anunciar
foreshore ['fɔːʃɔːʳ] *n* playa
foreshorten [fɔː'ʃɔːtn] *vt* (*figure, scene*)
escorzar
foresight ['fɔːsaɪt] *n* previsión *f*
foreskin ['fɔːskɪn] *n* (*Anat*) prepucio
forest ['fɔrɪst] *n* bosque *m*
forestall [fɔː'stɔːl] *vt* anticiparse a
forestry ['fɔrɪstrɪ] *n* silvicultura
foretaste ['fɔːteɪst] *n* anticipo

foretell (*pt, pp* **foretold**) [fɔː'tɛl, -'təuld] *vt* predecir, pronosticar

forethought ['fɔːθɔːt] *n* previsión *f*

forever [fə'rɛvəʳ] *adv* siempre; (*for good*) para siempre

forewarn [fɔː'wɔːn] *vt* avisar, advertir

forewent [fɔː'wɛnt] *pt of* **forego**

foreword ['fɔːwəːd] *n* prefacio

forfeit ['fɔːfɪt] *n* (*in game*) prenda ▪ *vt* perder (derecho a)

forgave [fə'geɪv] *pt of* **forgive**

forge [fɔːdʒ] *n* fragua; (*smithy*) herrería ▪ *vt* (*signature: Brit: money*) falsificar; (*metal*) forjar
▸ **forge ahead** *vi* avanzar mucho

forger ['fɔːdʒəʳ] *n* falsificador(a) *m(f)*

forgery ['fɔːdʒərɪ] *n* falsificación *f*

forget (*pt* **forgot**, *pp* **forgotten**) [fə'gɛt, -'gɒt, -'gɒtn] *vt* olvidar, olvidarse de ▪ *vi* olvidarse

forgetful [fə'gɛtful] *adj* olvidadizo

forget-me-not [fə'gɛtmɪnɒt] *n* nomeolvides *f inv*

forgive (*pt* **forgave**, *pp* **forgiven**) [fə'gɪv, -'geɪv, -'gɪvn] *vt* perdonar; **to ~ sb for sth/for doing sth** perdonar algo a algn/a algn por haber hecho algo

forgiveness [fə'gɪvnɪs] *n* perdón *m*

forgiving [fə'gɪvɪŋ] *adj* compasivo

forgo (*pt* **forwent**, *pp* **forgone**) [fɔː'gəu, -'wɛnt, -'gɒn] *vt* (*give up*) renunciar a; (*go without*) privarse de

forgot [fə'gɒt] *pt of* **forget**

forgotten [fə'gɒtn] *pp of* **forget**

fork [fɔːk] *n* (*for eating*) tenedor *m*; (*for gardening*) horca; (*of roads*) bifurcación *f*; (*in tree*) horcadura ▪ *vi* (*road*) bifurcarse
▸ **fork out** *vt* (*col: pay*) soltar

forked [fɔːkt] *adj* (*lightning*) en zigzag

fork-lift truck ['fɔːklɪft-] *n* máquina elevadora

forlorn [fə'lɔːn] *adj* (*person*) triste, melancólico; (*deserted: cottage*) abandonado; (*desperate: attempt*) desesperado

form [fɔːm] *n* forma; (*Brit Scol*) curso; (*document*) formulario, planilla (*LAm*) ▪ *vt* formar; **in the ~ of** en forma de; **in top ~** en plena forma; **to be in good ~** (*Sport: fig*) estar en plena forma; **to ~ part of sth** formar parte de algo; **to ~ a circle/a queue** hacer una curva/una cola

formal ['fɔːməl] *adj* (*offer, receipt*) por escrito; (*person etc*) correcto; (*occasion, dinner*) ceremonioso; **~ dress** traje *m* de vestir; (*evening dress*) traje *m* de etiqueta

formalities [fɔː'mælɪtɪz] *npl* formalidades *fpl*

formality [fɔː'mælɪtɪ] *n* ceremonia

formalize ['fɔːməlaɪz] *vt* formalizar

formally ['fɔːməlɪ] *adv* oficialmente

format ['fɔːmæt] *n* formato ▪ *vt* (*Comput*) formatear

formation [fɔː'meɪʃən] *n* formación *f*

formative ['fɔːmətɪv] *adj* (*years*) de formación

former ['fɔːməʳ] *adj* anterior; (*earlier*) antiguo; (*ex*) ex; **the ~ ... the latter ...** aquél ... éste ...; **the ~ president** el antiguo *or* ex presidente; **the ~ Yugoslavia/Soviet Union** la antigua *or* ex Yugoslavia/Unión Soviética

formerly ['fɔːməlɪ] *adv* antiguamente

form feed *n* (*on printer*) salto de página

Formica® [fɔː'maɪkə] *n* formica®

formidable ['fɔːmɪdəbl] *adj* formidable

formula ['fɔːmjulə] *n* fórmula; **F~ One** (*Aut*) Fórmula Uno

formulate ['fɔːmjuleɪt] *vt* formular

fornicate ['fɔːnɪkeɪt] *vi* fornicar

forsake (*pt* **forsook**, *pp* **forsaken**) [fə'seɪk, -'suk, -'seɪkən] *vt* (*gen*) abandonar; (*plan*) renunciar a

fort [fɔːt] *n* fuerte *m*; **to hold the ~** (*fig*) quedarse a cargo

forte ['fɔːtɪ] *n* fuerte *m*

forth [fɔːθ] *adv*: **back and ~** de acá para allá; **and so ~** y así sucesivamente

forthcoming [fɔːθ'kʌmɪŋ] *adj* próximo, venidero; (*character*) comunicativo

forthright ['fɔːθraɪt] *adj* franco

forthwith ['fɔːθ'wɪθ] *adv* en el acto, acto seguido

fortification [fɔːtɪfɪ'keɪʃən] *n* fortificación *f*

fortified wine ['fɔːtɪfaɪd-] *n* vino encabezado

fortify ['fɔːtɪfaɪ] *vt* fortalecer

fortitude ['fɔːtɪtjuːd] *n* fortaleza

fortnight ['fɔːtnaɪt] *n* (*Brit*) quincena; **it's a ~ since ...** hace quince días que ...

fortnightly ['fɔːtnaɪtlɪ] *adj* quincenal ▪ *adv* quincenalmente

FORTRAN ['fɔːtræn] *n* FORTRAN *m*

fortress ['fɔːtrɪs] *n* fortaleza

fortuitous [fɔː'tjuːɪtəs] *adj* fortuito

fortunate ['fɔːtʃənɪt] *adj*: **it is ~ that ...** (es una) suerte que ...

fortunately ['fɔːtʃənɪtlɪ] *adv* afortunadamente

fortune ['fɔːtʃən] *n* suerte *f*; (*wealth*) fortuna; **to make a ~** hacer un dineral

fortune-teller ['fɔːtʃəntɛləʳ] *n* adivino(-a)

forty ['fɔːtɪ] *num* cuarenta

forum ['fɔːrəm] *n* (*also fig*) foro

forward ['fɔːwəd] *adj* (*position*) avanzado; (*movement*) hacia delante; (*front*) delantero; (*not shy*) atrevido ▪ *n* (*Sport*) delantero ▪ *vt* (*letter*) remitir; (*career*) promocionar; **to move ~** avanzar; **"please ~"** "remítase al destinatario"

forward contract n contrato a término
forward exchange n cambio a término
forward planning n planificación f por anticipado
forward rate n tipo a término
forwards ['fɔːwədz] adv (hacia) adelante
forward sales npl ventas fpl a término
forwent [fɔː'wɛnt] pt of **forgo**
fossil ['fɔsl] n fósil m
fossil fuel n combustible m fósil
foster ['fɔstəʳ] vt (child) acoger en familia; (idea) fomentar
foster brother n hermano de leche
foster child n hijo(-a) adoptivo(-a)
foster mother n madre f adoptiva
fought [fɔːt] pt, pp of **fight**
foul [faul] adj (gen) sucio, puerco; (weather, smell etc) asqueroso ■ n (Football) falta ■ vt (dirty) ensuciar; (block) atascar; (entangle: anchor, propeller) atascar, enredarse en; (football player) cometer una falta contra
foul play n (Sport) mala jugada; (Law) muerte f violenta
found [faund] pt, pp of **find** ■ vt (establish) fundar
foundation [faun'deɪʃən] n (act) fundación f; (basis) base f; (also: **foundation cream**) base f de maquillaje
foundations [faun'deɪʃənz] npl (of building) cimientos mpl; **to lay the ~** poner los cimientos
foundation stone n: **to lay the ~** poner la primera piedra
founder ['faundəʳ] n fundador(a) m(f) ■ vi irse a pique
founding ['faundɪŋ] adj: **~ fathers** (esp US) fundadores mpl, próceres mpl; **~ member** miembro fundador
foundry ['faundrɪ] n fundición f
fountain ['fauntɪn] n fuente f
fountain pen n (pluma) estilográfica, plumafuente f (LAm)
four [fɔːʳ] num cuatro; **on all fours** a gatas
four-footed [fɔː'futɪd] adj cuadrúpedo
four-letter word ['fɔːlɛtə-] n taco
four-poster ['fɔː'pəustəʳ] n (also: **four-poster bed**) cama de columnas
foursome ['fɔːsəm] n grupo de cuatro personas
fourteen ['fɔː'tiːn] num catorce
fourteenth [fɔː'tiːnθ] adj decimocuarto
fourth [fɔːθ] adj cuarto ■ n (Aut: also: **fourth gear**) cuarta (velocidad)
four-wheel drive ['fɔːwiːl-] n tracción f a las cuatro ruedas
fowl [faul] n ave f (de corral)
fox [fɔks] n zorro ■ vt confundir

fox fur n piel f de zorro
foxglove ['fɔksglʌv] n (Bot) dedalera
fox-hunting ['fɔkshʌntɪŋ] n caza de zorros
foxtrot ['fɔkstrɔt] n fox(trot) m
foyer ['fɔɪeɪ] n vestíbulo
FPA n abbr (Brit: = Family Planning Association) asociación de planificación familiar
Fr. abbr (Rel: = father) P.; (= friar) Fr.
fracas ['frækɑː] n gresca, refriega
fraction ['frækʃən] n fracción f
fractionally ['frækʃnəlɪ] adv ligeramente
fractious ['frækʃəs] adj (person, mood) irascible
fracture ['fræktʃəʳ] n fractura ■ vt fracturar
fragile ['frædʒaɪl] adj frágil
fragment ['frægmənt] n fragmento
fragmentary [fræg'mɛntərɪ] adj fragmentario
fragrance ['freɪgrəns] n fragancia
fragrant ['freɪgrənt] adj fragante, oloroso
frail [freɪl] adj (fragile) frágil, quebradizo; (weak) delicado
frame [freɪm] n (Tech) armazón f; (of picture, door etc) marco; (of spectacles: also: **frames**) montura ■ vt encuadrar; (picture) enmarcar; (reply) formular; **to ~ sb** (col) inculpar por engaños a algn
frame of mind n estado de ánimo
framework ['freɪmwəːk] n marco
France [frɑːns] n Francia
franchise ['fræntʃaɪz] n (Pol) derecho al voto, sufragio; (Comm) licencia, concesión f
franchisee [fræntʃaɪ'ziː] n concesionario(-a)
franchiser ['fræntʃaɪzəʳ] n compañía concesionaria
frank [fræŋk] adj franco ■ vt (Brit: letter) franquear
frankfurter ['fræŋkfəːtəʳ] n salchicha de Frankfurt
frankincense ['fræŋkɪnsɛns] n incienso
franking machine ['fræŋkɪŋ-] n máquina de franqueo
frankly ['fræŋklɪ] adv francamente
frankness ['fræŋknɪs] n franqueza
frantic ['fræntɪk] adj (desperate: need, desire) desesperado; (: search) frenético; (: person) desquiciado
fraternal [frə'təːnl] adj fraterno
fraternity [frə'təːnɪtɪ] n (club) fraternidad f; (US) club m de estudiantes; (guild) gremio
fraternization [frætənaɪ'zeɪʃən] n fraternización f
fraternize ['frætənaɪz] vi confraternizar
fraud [frɔːd] n fraude m; (person) impostor(a) m(f)
fraudulent ['frɔːdjulənt] adj fraudulento
fraught [frɔːt] adj (tense) tenso; **~ with** cargado de

fray [freɪ] n combate m, lucha, refriega
■ vi deshilacharse; **tempers were frayed** el ambiente se ponía tenso
FRB n abbr (US) = **Federal Reserve Board**
FRCM n abbr (Brit) = **Fellow of the Royal College of Music**
FRCO n abbr (Brit) = **Fellow of the Royal College of Organists**
FRCP n abbr (Brit) = **Fellow of the Royal College of Physicians**
FRCS n abbr (Brit) = **Fellow of the Royal College of Surgeons**
freak [fri:k] n (person) fenómeno; (event) suceso anormal; (col: enthusiast) adicto(-a)
■ adj (storm, conditions) anormal; **health ~** (col) maniático(-a) en cuestión de salud
▶ **freak out** vi (col: on drugs) flipar
freakish ['fri:kɪʃ] adj (result) inesperado; (appearance) estrambótico; (weather) cambiadizo
freckle ['frɛkl] n peca
freckled ['frɛkld] adj pecoso, lleno de pecas
free [fri:] adj (person: at liberty) libre; (not fixed) suelto; (gratis) gratuito; (unoccupied) desocupado; (liberal) generoso ■ vt (prisoner etc) poner en libertad; (jammed object) soltar; **to give sb a ~ hand** dar carta blanca a algn; **~ and easy** despreocupado; **is this seat ~?** ¿está libre este asiento?; **~ of tax** libre de impuestos; **admission ~** entrada libre; **~ (of charge), for ~** adv gratis
freebie ['fri:bɪ] n (col): **it's a ~** es gratis
freedom ['fri:dəm] n libertad f; **~ of association** libertad de asociación
freedom fighter n luchador(a) m(f) por la libertad
free enterprise n libre empresa
Freefone® ['fri:fəun] n (Brit) número gratuito
free-for-all ['fri:fərɔ:l] n riña general
free gift n regalo
freehold ['fri:həuld] n propiedad f absoluta
free kick n tiro libre
freelance ['fri:lɑ:ns] adj, adv por cuenta propia; **to do ~ work** trabajar por su cuenta
freely ['fri:lɪ] adv libremente; (liberally) generosamente
free-market economy ['fri:ˈmɑ:kɪt-] n economía de libre mercado
freemason ['fri:meɪsn] n francmasón m
freemasonry ['fri:meɪsnrɪ] n (franc)masonería
freepost ['fri:pəust] n porte m pagado
free-range ['fri:ˈreɪndʒ] adj (hen, egg) de granja
free sample n muestra gratuita
freesia ['fri:ʒə] n fresia

free speech n libertad f de expresión
free trade n libre comercio
freeway ['fri:weɪ] n (US) autopista
freewheel [fri:ˈwi:l] vi ir en punto muerto
freewheeling [fri:ˈwi:lɪŋ] adj libre, espontáneo; (careless) irresponsable
free will n libre albedrío; **of one's own ~** por su propia voluntad
freeze [fri:z] (pt **froze**, pp **frozen**) vi helarse, congelarse ■ vt helar; (prices, food, salaries) congelar ■ n helada; congelación f
▶ **freeze over** vi (lake, river) helarse, congelarse; (window, windscreen) cubrirse de escarcha
▶ **freeze up** vi helarse, congelarse
freeze-dried ['fri:zdraɪd] adj liofilizado
freezer ['fri:zər] n congelador m, congeladora
freezing ['fri:zɪŋ] adj helado
freezing point n punto de congelación; **3 degrees below ~** tres grados bajo cero
freight [freɪt] n (goods) carga; (money charged) flete m
freight car n vagón m de mercancías
freighter ['freɪtər] n buque m de carga; (Aviat) avión m de transporte de mercancías
freight forward n contra reembolso del flete, flete por pagar
freight forwarder [-ˈfɔ:wədər] n agente m expedidor
freight inward n flete sobre compras
freight train n (US) tren m de mercancías
French [frɛntʃ] adj francés(-esa) ■ n (Ling) francés m; **the French** npl los franceses
French bean n judía verde
French bread n pan m francés
French Canadian adj, n francocanadiense m/f
French dressing n (Culin) vinagreta
French fried potatoes, French fries (US) npl patatas fpl or (LAm) papas fpl fritas
French Guiana [-gaɪˈænə] n la Guayana Francesa
French loaf n barra de pan
Frenchman ['frɛntʃmən] n francés m
French Riviera n: **the ~** la Riviera, la Costa Azul
French stick n barra de pan
French window n puertaventana
Frenchwoman ['frɛntʃwumən] n francesa
frenetic [frəˈnɛtɪk] adj frenético
frenzy ['frɛnzɪ] n frenesí m
frequency ['fri:kwənsɪ] n frecuencia
frequency modulation n frecuencia modulada
frequent adj ['fri:kwənt] frecuente ■ vt [frɪˈkwɛnt] frecuentar
frequently ['fri:kwəntlɪ] adv frecuentemente, a menudo

fresco ['freskəu] n fresco
fresh [freʃ] adj (gen) fresco; (new) nuevo; (water) dulce; **to make a ~ start** empezar de nuevo
freshen ['freʃən] vi (wind) arreciar; (air) refrescar
▶ **freshen up** vi (person) refrescarse
freshener ['freʃnəʳ] n: **air ~** ambientador m; **skin ~** tónico
fresher ['freʃəʳ] n (Brit Scol: col) estudiante m/f de primer año
freshly ['freʃlɪ] adv: **~ painted/arrived** recién pintado/llegado
freshman ['freʃmən] n (US Scol) = **fresher**
freshness ['freʃnɪs] n frescura
freshwater ['freʃwɔːtəʳ] adj (fish) de agua dulce
fret [fret] vi inquietarse
fretful ['fretful] adj (child) quejumbroso
Freudian ['frɔɪdɪən] adj freudiano; **~ slip** lapsus m (freudiano)
FRG n abbr (= Federal Republic of Germany) RFA f
Fri. abbr (= Friday) vier
friar ['fraɪəʳ] n fraile m; (before name) fray
friction ['frɪkʃən] n fricción f
friction feed n (on printer) avance m por fricción
Friday ['fraɪdɪ] n viernes m inv; see also **Tuesday**
fridge [frɪdʒ] n (Brit) nevera, frigo, refrigeradora (LAm), heladera (LAm)
fridge-freezer ['frɪdʒ'friːzəʳ] n frigorífico-congelador m, combi m
fried [fraɪd] pt, pp of **fry** ■ adj: **~ egg** huevo frito, huevo estrellado
friend [frend] n amigo(-a) ■ vt (Internet) agregar como amigo
friendliness ['frendlɪnɪs] n simpatía
friendly ['frendlɪ] adj simpático
friendly fire n fuego amigo, disparos mpl del propio bando
friendly society n mutualidad f, montepío
friendship ['frendʃɪp] n amistad f
frieze [friːz] n friso
frigate ['frɪgɪt] n fragata
fright [fraɪt] n susto; **to take ~** asustarse
frighten ['fraɪtn] vt asustar
▶ **frighten away, frighten off** vt (birds, children etc) espantar, ahuyentar
frightened ['fraɪtnd] adj asustado
frightening ['fraɪtnɪŋ] adj: **it's ~** da miedo
frightful ['fraɪtful] adj espantoso, horrible
frightfully ['fraɪtfulɪ] adv terriblemente; **I'm ~ sorry** lo siento muchísimo
frigid ['frɪdʒɪd] adj (Med) frígido
frigidity [frɪ'dʒɪdɪtɪ] n (Med) frigidez f
frill [frɪl] n volante m; **without frills** (fig) sin adornos

frilly ['frɪlɪ] adj con volantes
fringe [frɪndʒ] n (Brit: of hair) flequillo; (edge: of forest etc) borde m, margen m
fringe benefits npl ventajas fpl complementarias
fringe theatre n teatro experimental
Frisbee® ['frɪzbɪ] n frisbee® m
frisk [frɪsk] vt cachear, registrar
frisky ['frɪskɪ] adj juguetón(-ona)
fritter ['frɪtəʳ] n buñuelo
▶ **fritter away** vt desperdiciar
frivolity [frɪ'vɔlɪtɪ] n frivolidad f
frivolous ['frɪvələs] adj frívolo
frizzy ['frɪzɪ] adj crespo
fro [frəu] see **to**
frock [frɔk] n vestido
frog [frɔg] n rana; **to have a ~ in one's throat** tener carraspera
frogman ['frɔgmən] n hombre-rana m
frogmarch ['frɔgmɑːtʃ] vt: **to ~ sb in/out** meter/sacar a algn a rastras
frolic ['frɔlɪk] vi juguetear

 KEYWORD

from [frɔm] prep **1** (indicating starting place) de, desde; **where do you come from?, where are you from?** ¿de dónde eres?; **where has he come from?** ¿de dónde ha venido?; **from London to Glasgow** de Londres a Glasgow; **to escape from sth/sb** escaparse de algo/algn
2 (indicating origin etc) de; **a letter/telephone call from my sister** una carta/llamada de mi hermana; **tell him from me that ...** dígale de mi parte que ...
3 (indicating time): **from one o'clock to** or **until** or **till nine** de la una a las nueve, desde la una hasta las nueve; **from January (on)** a partir de enero; **(as) from Friday** a partir del viernes
4 (indicating distance) de; **the hotel is 1 km from the beach** el hotel está a 1 km de la playa
5 (indicating price, number etc) de; **prices range from £10 to £50** los precios van desde £10 a or hasta £50; **the interest rate was increased from 9% to 10%** el tipo de interés fue incrementado de un 9% a un 10%
6 (indicating difference) de; **he can't tell red from green** no sabe distinguir el rojo del verde; **to be different from sb/sth** ser diferente a algn/algo
7 (because of, on the basis of): **from what he says** por lo que dice; **weak from hunger** debilitado por el hambre

frond [frɔnd] n fronda
front [frʌnt] n (foremost part) parte f delantera; (of house) fachada; (promenade: also: **sea front**) paseo marítimo; (Mil, Pol, Meteorology) frente m; (fig: appearances) apariencia ▪ adj (wheel, leg) delantero; (row, line) primero ▪ vi: **to ~ onto sth** dar a algo; **in ~ (of)** delante (de)
frontage ['frʌntɪdʒ] n (of building) fachada
frontal ['frʌntl] adj frontal
front bench n (Brit: Pol) ver nota

frontbencher ['frʌnt'bentʃəʳ] n (Brit) see **front bench**
front desk n (US) recepción f
front door n puerta principal
frontier ['frʌntɪəʳ] n frontera
frontispiece ['frʌntɪspiːs] n frontispicio
front page n primera plana
front room n (Brit) salón m, sala
front runner n favorito(-a)
front-wheel drive ['frʌntwiːl-] n tracción f delantera
frost [frɔst] n (gen) helada; (also: **hoarfrost**) escarcha ▪ vt (US Culin) escarchar
frostbite ['frɔstbaɪt] n congelación f
frosted ['frɔstɪd] adj (glass) esmerilado; (esp US: cake) glaseado
frosting ['frɔstɪŋ] n (esp US: icing) glaseado
frosty ['frɔstɪ] adj (surface) cubierto de escarcha; (welcome etc) glacial
froth [frɔθ] n espuma
frothy ['frɔθɪ] adj espumoso
frown [fraun] vi fruncir el ceño ▪ n: **with a ~** frunciendo el entrecejo
▶ **frown on** vt fus desaprobar
froze [frəuz] pt of **freeze**
frozen ['frəuzn] pp of **freeze** ▪ adj (food) congelado; (Comm): **~ assets** activos mpl congelados or bloqueados
FRS n abbr (Brit: = Fellow of the Royal Society) miembro de la principal asociación de investigación científica; (US: = Federal Reserve System) banco central de los EE. UU.
frugal ['fruːɡəl] adj (person) frugal

fruit [fruːt] n pl inv fruta
fruiterer ['fruːtərəʳ] n frutero(-a); **~'s (shop)** frutería
fruit fly n mosca de la fruta
fruitful ['fruːtful] adj provechoso
fruition [fruːˈɪʃən] n: **to come to ~** realizarse
fruit juice n jugo or (SP) zumo de fruta
fruitless ['fruːtlɪs] adj (fig) infructuoso, inútil
fruit machine n (Brit) máquina tragaperras
fruit salad n macedonia or (LAm) ensalada de frutas
frump [frʌmp] n espantajo, adefesio
frustrate [frʌsˈtreɪt] vt frustrar
frustrated [frʌsˈtreɪtɪd] adj frustrado
frustrating [frʌsˈtreɪtɪŋ] adj (job, day) frustrante
frustration [frʌsˈtreɪʃən] n frustración f
fry (pt, pp **fried**) [fraɪ, -d] vt freír ▪ n: **small ~** gente f menuda
frying pan ['fraɪɪŋ-] n sartén f, sartén m (LAm)
FT n abbr (Brit: = Financial Times) periódico financiero
ft. abbr = **foot**; **feet**
FTC n abbr (US) = **Federal Trade Commission**
FTSE 100 Index n abbr (= Financial Times Stock Exchange 100 Index) índice bursátil del Financial Times
fuchsia ['fjuːʃə] n fucsia
fuck [fʌk] (col!) vt joder (SP) (!), coger (LAm) (!) ▪ vi joder (SP) (!), coger (LAm) (!); **~ off!** ¡vete a tomar por culo! (!)
fuddled ['fʌdld] adj (muddled) confuso, aturdido; (col: tipsy) borracho
fuddy-duddy ['fʌdɪdʌdɪ] (pej) n carcamal m, carroza m/f ▪ adj chapado a la antigua
fudge [fʌdʒ] n (Culin) caramelo blando ▪ vt (issue, problem) rehuir, esquivar
fuel [fjuəl] n (for heating) combustible m; (coal) carbón m; (wood) leña; (for engine) carburante m ▪ vt (furnace etc) alimentar; (aircraft, ship etc) aprovisionar de combustible
fuel oil n fuel oil m
fuel poverty n pobreza energética
fuel pump n (Aut) surtidor m de gasolina
fuel tank n depósito de combustible
fug [fʌɡ] n aire m viciado
fugitive ['fjuːdʒɪtɪv] n (from prison) fugitivo(-a)
fulfil, fulfill (US) [fulˈfɪl] vt (function) desempeñar; (condition) cumplir; (wish, desire) realizar
fulfilled [fulˈfɪld] adj (person) realizado
fulfilment, fulfillment (US) [fulˈfɪlmənt] n realización f; (of promise) cumplimiento
full [ful] adj lleno; (fig) pleno; (complete) completo; (information) detallado; (price) íntegro, sin descuento ▪ adv: **~ well** perfectamente; **we're ~ up for July** estamos completos para julio; **I'm ~ (up)** estoy lleno;

~ **employment** pleno empleo; ~ **name**
nombre *m* completo; **a ~ two hours** dos
horas enteras; **at ~ speed** a toda velocidad;
in ~ (*reproduce, quote*) íntegramente; **to write**
sth in ~ escribir algo por extenso; **to pay in ~**
pagar la deuda entera
fullback ['fulbæk] *n* (*Football*) defensa *m*;
(*Rugby*) zaguero
full-blooded ['ful'blʌdɪd] *adj* (*vigorous: attack*)
vigoroso; (*pure*) puro
full-cream ['ful'kri:m] *adj*: ~ **milk** leche *f*
entera
full driving licence *n* (*Brit Aut*) carnet *m* de
conducir (*definitivo*); *see also* **L-plates**
full-fledged ['fulflɛdʒd] *adj* (*US*) = **fully-**
fledged
full-grown ['ful'grəun] *adj* maduro
full-length ['ful'lɛŋgθ] *adj* (*portrait*) de cuerpo
entero; (*film*) de largometraje
full moon *n* luna llena, plenilunio
fullness ['fulnɪs] *n* plenitud *f*, amplitud *f*
full-scale ['fulskeɪl] *adj* (*attack, war, search,*
retreat) en gran escala; (*plan, model*) de tamaño
natural
full stop *n* punto
full-time ['fultaɪm] *adj* (*work*) de tiempo
completo ∎ *adv*: **to work ~** trabajar a tiempo
completo
fully ['fulɪ] *adv* completamente; (*at least*) al
menos
fully-fledged ['fulɪ'flɛdʒd], (*US*) **full-fledged**
adj (*teacher, barrister*) diplomado; (*bird*) con
todas sus plumas, capaz de volar; (*fig*) de
pleno derecho
fully-paid ['fulɪpeɪd] *adj*: ~ **share** acción *f*
liberada
fulsome ['fulsəm] *adj* (*pej: praise, gratitude*)
excesivo, exagerado; (*manner*) obsequioso
fumble with ['fʌmbl-] *vt fus* manosear
fume [fju:m] *vi* humear, echar humo
fumes [fju:mz] *npl* humo *sg*, gases *mpl*
fumigate ['fju:mɪgeɪt] *vt* fumigar
fun [fʌn] *n* (*amusement*) diversión *f*; (*joy*)
alegría; **to have ~** divertirse; **for ~** por gusto;
to make ~ of reírse de
function ['fʌŋkʃən] *n* función *f* ∎ *vi*
funcionar; **to ~ as** hacer (las veces) de, fungir
de (*LAm*)
functional ['fʌŋkʃənl] *adj* funcional
function key *n* (*Comput*) tecla de función
fund [fʌnd] *n* fondo; (*reserve*) reserva; **funds**
npl fondos *mpl*
fundamental [fʌndə'mɛntl] *adj*
fundamental ∎ *n*; **fundamentals** *npl*
fundamentos *mpl*
fundamentalism [fʌndə'mɛntəlɪzəm] *n*
fundamentalismo, integrismo

fundamentalist [fʌndə'mɛntəlɪst] *n*
fundamentalista *m/f*, integrista *m/f*
fundamentally [fʌndə'mɛntəlɪ] *adv*
fundamentalmente
funding ['fʌndɪŋ] *n* financiación *f*
fund-raising ['fʌndreɪzɪŋ] *n* recaudación *f*
de fondos
funeral ['fju:nərəl] *n* (*burial*) entierro;
(*ceremony*) funerales *mpl*
funeral director *n* director(a) *m(f)* de pompas
fúnebres
funeral parlour *n* (*Brit*) funeraria
funeral service *n* misa de cuerpo presente
funereal [fju:'nɪərɪəl] *adj* fúnebre
funfair ['fʌnfɛəʳ] *n* (*Brit*) parque *m* de
atracciones; (*travelling*) feria
fungus (*pl* **fungi**) ['fʌŋgəs, -gaɪ] *n* hongo
funicular [fju:'nɪkjuləʳ] *n* (*also*: **funicular**
railway) funicular *m*
funky ['fʌŋkɪ] *adj* (*music*) funky; (*col: good*)
guay
funnel ['fʌnl] *n* embudo; (*of ship*) chimenea
funnily ['fʌnɪlɪ] *adv* de modo divertido,
graciosamente; (*oddly*) de una manera rara;
~ **enough** aunque parezca extraño
funny ['fʌnɪ] *adj* gracioso, divertido; (*strange*)
curioso, raro
funny bone *n* hueso de la alegría
fun run *n* maratón *m* popular
fur [fə:ʳ] *n* piel *f*; (*Brit: on tongue etc*) sarro
fur coat *n* abrigo de pieles
furious ['fjuərɪəs] *adj* furioso; (*effort, argument*)
violento; **to be ~ with sb** estar furioso con algn
furiously ['fjuərɪəslɪ] *adv* con furia
furl [fə:l] *vt* (*sail*) recoger
furlong ['fə:lɔŋ] *n* octava parte de una milla
furlough ['fə:ləu] *n* (*US Mil*) permiso
furnace ['fə:nɪs] *n* horno
furnish ['fə:nɪʃ] *vt* amueblar; (*supply*)
proporcionar; (*information*) facilitar
furnished ['fə:nɪʃt] *adj*: ~ **flat** *or* (*US*)
apartment piso amueblado
furnishings ['fə:nɪʃɪŋz] *npl* mobiliario *sg*
furniture ['fə:nɪtʃəʳ] *n* muebles *mpl*; **piece**
of ~ mueble *m*
furniture polish *n* cera para muebles
furore [fjuə'rɔ:rɪ] *n* (*protests*) escándalo
furrier ['fʌrɪəʳ] *n* peletero(-a)
furrow ['fʌrəu] *n* surco ∎ *vt* (*forehead*) arrugar
furry ['fə:rɪ] *adj* peludo; (*toy*) de peluche
further ['fə:ðəʳ] *adj* (*new*) nuevo; (*place*) más
lejano ∎ *adv* más lejos; (*more*) más; (*moreover*)
además ∎ *vt* hacer avanzar; **how much ~ is**
it? ¿a qué distancia queda?; ~ **to your letter**
of ... (*Comm*) con referencia a su carta de ...;
to ~ one's interests fomentar sus intereses
further education *n* educación *f* postescolar

furthermore [fə:ðə'mɔːʳ] *adv* además
furthermost ['fə:ðəməust] *adj* más lejano
furthest ['fə:ðɪst] *superlative of* **far**
furtive ['fə:tɪv] *adj* furtivo
furtively ['fə:tɪvlɪ] *adv* furtivamente, a escondidas
fury ['fjuərɪ] *n* furia
fuse, *(US)* **fuze** [fju:z] *n* fusible *m*; *(for bomb etc)* mecha ■ *vt (metal)* fundir; *(fig)* fusionar ■ *vi* fundirse; fusionarse; *(Brit Elec)*: **to ~ the lights** fundir los plomos; **a ~ has blown** se ha fundido un fusible
fuse box *n* caja de fusibles
fuselage ['fju:zəlɑ:ʒ] *n* fuselaje *m*
fuse wire *n* hilo fusible
fusillade [fju:zɪ'leɪd] *n* descarga cerrada; *(fig)* lluvia
fusion ['fju:ʒən] *n* fusión *f*
fuss [fʌs] *n (noise)* bulla; *(dispute)* lío, jaleo; *(complaining)* protesta ■ *vi* preocuparse (por pequeñeces) ■ *vt (person)* molestar; **to make a ~** armar jaleo

▶ **fuss over** *vt fus (person)* contemplar, mimar
fusspot ['fʌspɔt] *n (col)* quisquilloso(-a)
fussy ['fʌsɪ] *adj (person)* quisquilloso; **I'm not ~** *(col)* me da igual
fusty ['fʌstɪ] *adj (pej)* rancio; **to smell ~** oler a cerrado
futile ['fju:taɪl] *adj* vano
futility [fju:'tɪlɪtɪ] *n* inutilidad *f*
futon ['fu:tɔn] *n* futón *m*
future ['fju:tʃəʳ] *adj (gen)* futuro; *(coming)* venidero ■ *n* futuro, porvenir; **in ~** de ahora en adelante
futures ['fju:tʃəz] *npl (Comm)* operaciones *fpl* a término, futuros *mpl*
futuristic [fju:tʃə'rɪstɪk] *adj* futurista
fuze [fju:z] *(US)* = **fuse**
fuzzy ['fʌzɪ] *adj (Phot)* borroso; *(hair)* muy rizado
fwd. *abbr* = **forward**
fwy *abbr (US)* = **freeway**
FY *abbr* = **fiscal year**
FYI *abbr* = **for your information**

f

Gg

G, g [dʒiː] n (letter) G, g f; **G** (Mus) sol m; **G for George** G de Gerona

G n abbr (Brit Scol: mark: = good) N; (US Cine: = general audience) todos los públicos

g. abbr (= gram(s), gravity) g

G8 n abbr (Pol: = Group of Eight) G8 m

G20 n abbr (Pol: = Group of Twenty) G20 m

GA abbr (US Post) = **Georgia**

gab [gæb] n: **to have the gift of the ~** (col) tener mucha labia

gabble ['gæbl] vi hablar atropelladamente; (gossip) cotorrear

gaberdine [gæbə'diːn] n gabardina

gable ['geɪbl] n aguilón m

Gabon [gə'bɔn] n Gabón m

gad about [gæd-] vi (col) moverse mucho

gadget ['gædʒɪt] n aparato

gadgetry ['gædʒɪtrɪ] n chismes mpl

Gaelic ['geɪlɪk] adj, n (Ling) gaélico

gaffe [gæf] n plancha, patinazo, metedura de pata

gaffer ['gæfəʳ] n (Brit col) jefe m; ((old) man) vejete m

gag [gæg] n (on mouth) mordaza; (joke) chiste m ■ vt (prisoner etc) amordazar ■ vi (choke) tener arcadas

gaga ['gɑːgɑː] adj: **to go ~** (senile) chochear; (ecstatic) caérsele a algn la baba

gaiety ['geɪtɪ] n alegría

gaily ['geɪlɪ] adv alegremente

gain [geɪn] n ganancia ■ vt ganar ■ vi (watch) adelantarse; **to ~ by sth** ganar con algo; **to ~ ground** ganar terreno; **to ~ 3 lbs (in weight)** engordar 3 libras
▸ **gain (up)on** vt fus alcanzar

gainful ['geɪnful] adj (employment) remunerado

gainfully ['geɪnfulɪ] adv: **to be ~ employed** tener un trabajo remunerado

gait [geɪt] n forma de andar, andares mpl

gala ['gɑːlə] n gala; **swimming ~** certamen m de natación

Galapagos Islands [gə'læpəgəs-] npl: **the ~** las Islas Galápagos

galaxy ['gæləksɪ] n galaxia

gale [geɪl] n (wind) vendaval m; **~ force 10** vendaval de fuerza 10

gall [gɔːl] n (Anat) bilis f, hiel f; (fig: impudence) descaro, caradura ■ vt molestar

gal., gall. abbr = **gallon; gallons**

gallant ['gælənt] adj valeroso; (towards ladies) galante

gallantry ['gæləntrɪ] n valentía; (courtesy) galantería

gall bladder n vesícula biliar

galleon ['gælɪən] n galeón m

gallery ['gælərɪ] n (Theat) galería; (for spectators) tribuna; (also: **art gallery**: state-owned) pinacoteca or museo de arte; (: private) galería de arte

galley ['gælɪ] n (ship's kitchen) cocina; (ship) galera

galley proof n (Typ) prueba de galera, galerada

Gallic ['gælɪk] adj galo

gallon ['gæln] n galón m (= 8 pints; BRIT = 4,546 litros; US = 3,785 litros)

gallop ['gæləp] n galope m ■ vi galopar; **galloping inflation** inflación f galopante

gallows ['gæləuz] n horca

gallstone ['gɔːlstəun] n cálculo biliar

Gallup poll ['gæləp-] n sondeo de opinión

galore [gə'lɔːʳ] adv en cantidad, en abundancia

galvanize ['gælvənaɪz] vt (metal) galvanizar; (fig): **to ~ sb into action** mover or impulsar a algn a actuar

Gambia ['gæmbɪə] n Gambia

gambit ['gæmbɪt] n (fig): **opening ~** táctica inicial

gamble ['gæmbl] n (risk) jugada arriesgada; (bet) apuesta ■ vt: **to ~ on** apostar a; (fig) confiar en que ■ vi jugar; (Comm) especular; **to ~ on the Stock Exchange** jugar a la bolsa

gambler ['gæmbləʳ] n jugador(a) m(f)

gambling ['gæmblɪŋ] n juego

gambol ['gæmbl] vi brincar, juguetear

game [geɪm] n (gen) juego; (match) partido; (of cards) partida; (Hunting) caza ▪ adj valiente; (ready): **to be ~ for anything** estar dispuesto a todo; **games** (Scol) deportes mpl; **big ~** caza mayor

game bird n ave f de caza

gamekeeper ['geɪmki:pə'] n guardabosque m/f

gamely ['geɪmlɪ] adv con decisión

gamer ['geɪmə'] n jugador(a) m(f) de videojuegos, videojugador(a) m(f)

game reserve n coto de caza

games console [geɪmz-] n consola de juegos

game show n programa m concurso inv, concurso

gamesmanship ['geɪmzmənʃɪp] n (uso de) artimañas fpl para ganar

gaming ['geɪmɪŋ] n jugar a videojuegos

gammon ['gæmən] n (bacon) tocino ahumado; (ham) jamón m ahumado

gamut ['gæmət] n (Mus) gama

gander ['gændə'] n ganso

gang [gæŋ] n pandilla; (of criminals etc) banda; (of kids) pandilla; (of colleagues) peña; (of workmen) brigada ▪ vi: **to ~ up on sb** conchabarse contra algn

Ganges ['gændʒi:z] n. the ~ el Ganges

gangland ['gæŋglænd] adj: ~ **bosses** cabecillas mafiosos; ~ **killings** asesinatos entre bandas

gangling ['gæŋglɪŋ] adj larguirucho

gangly ['gæŋglɪ] adj desgarbado

gangplank ['gæŋplæŋk] n pasarela, plancha

gangrene ['gæŋgriːn] n gangrena

gangster ['gæŋstə'] n gángster m

gang warfare n guerra entre bandas

gangway ['gæŋweɪ] n (Brit: in theatre, bus etc) pasillo; (on ship) pasarela

gantry ['gæntrɪ] n (for crane, railway signal) pórtico; (for rocket) torre f de lanzamiento

GAO n abbr (US: = General Accounting Office) tribunal de cuentas

gaol [dʒeɪl] n, vt (Brit): = **jail**

gap [gæp] n hueco; (in trees, traffic) claro; (in market, records) laguna; (in time) intervalo

gape [geɪp] vi mirar boquiabierto

gaping ['geɪpɪŋ] adj (hole) muy abierto

gap year n año sabático

garage ['gærɑ:ʒ] n garaje m

garb [gɑ:b] n atuendo

garbage ['gɑ:bɪdʒ] n (US) basura; (nonsense) bobadas fpl; (fig: film, book etc) basura

garbage can n (US) cubo or balde m (LAm) or bote m (LAm) de la basura

garbage collector n (US) basurero(-a)

garbage disposal unit n triturador m

(de basura)

garbage man n basurero

garbage truck n (US) camión m de la basura

garbled ['gɑ:bld] adj (account, explanation) confuso

garden ['gɑ:dn] n jardín m; **gardens** npl (public) parque m, jardines mpl; (private) huertos mpl

garden centre n centro de jardinería

garden city n (Brit) ciudad f jardín

gardener ['gɑ:dnə'] n jardinero(-a)

gardening ['gɑ:dnɪŋ] n jardinería

garden party n recepción f al aire libre

gargle ['gɑ:gl] vi hacer gárgaras, gargarear (LAm)

gargoyle ['gɑ:gɔɪl] n gárgola

garish ['geərɪʃ] adj chillón(-ona)

garland ['gɑ:lənd] n guirnalda

garlic ['gɑ:lɪk] n ajo

garment ['gɑ:mənt] n prenda (de vestir)

garner ['gɑ:nə'] vt hacer acopio de

garnish ['gɑ:nɪʃ] vt adornar; (Culin) aderezar

garret ['gærɪt] n desván m, buhardilla

garrison ['gærɪsn] n guarnición f ▪ vt guarnecer

garrulous ['gærjuləs] adj charlatán(-ana)

garter ['gɑ:tə'] n (US) liga

garter belt n (US) liguero, portaligas m inv

gas [gæs] n gas m; (US: gasoline) gasolina ▪ vt asfixiar con gas; **Calor ~®** (gas m) butano

gas chamber n cámara de gas

gas cooker n (Brit) cocina de gas

gas cylinder n bombona de gas

gaseous ['gæsɪəs] adj gaseoso

gas fire n estufa de gas

gas-fired ['gæsfaɪəd] adj de gas

gash [gæʃ] n brecha, raja; (from knife) cuchillada ▪ vt rajar; (with knife) acuchillar

gasket ['gæskɪt] n (Aut) junta

gas mask n careta antigás

gas meter n contador m de gas

gasoline ['gæsəliːn] n (US) gasolina

gasp [gɑ:sp] n grito sofocado ▪ vi (pant) jadear

▸ **gasp out** vt (say) decir jadeando

gas pedal n (esp US) acelerador m

gas ring n hornillo de gas

gas station n (US) gasolinera

gas stove n cocina de gas

gassy ['gæsɪ] adj con mucho gas

gas tank n (US Aut) depósito (de gasolina)

gas tap n llave f del gas

gastric ['gæstrɪk] adj gástrico

gastric ulcer n úlcera gástrica

gastroenteritis ['gæstrəuentə'raɪtɪs] n gastroenteritis f

gasworks ['gæswə:ks] nsg or npl fábrica de gas

gate [geɪt] *n* (*also at airport*) puerta; (*Rail: at level crossing*) barrera; (*metal*) verja
gâteau (*pl* **gâteaux**) ['gætəu, z] *n* tarta
gatecrash ['geɪtkræʃ] *vt* colarse en
gatecrasher ['geɪtkræʃə'] *n* intruso(-a)
gatehouse ['geɪthaus] *n* casa del guarda
gateway ['geɪtweɪ] *n* puerta
gather ['gæðə'] *vt* (*flowers, fruit*) coger (*SP*), recoger (*LAm*); (*assemble*) reunir; (*pick up*) recoger; (*Sewing*) fruncir; (*understand*) sacar en consecuencia ■ *vi* (*assemble*) reunirse; (*dust*) acumularse; (*clouds*) cerrarse; **to ~ speed** ganar velocidad; **to ~ (from/that)** deducir (por/que); **as far as I can ~** por lo que tengo entendido
gathering ['gæðərɪŋ] *n* reunión *f*, asamblea
GATT [gæt] *n abbr* (= *General Agreement on Tariffs and Trade*) GATT *m*
gauche [gəuʃ] *adj* torpe
gaudy ['gɔːdɪ] *adj* chillón(-ona)
gauge, gage (*US*) [geɪdʒ] *n* calibre *m*; (*Rail*) ancho de vía, entrevía; (*instrument*) indicador *m* ■ *vt* medir; (*fig: sb's capabilities, character*) juzgar, calibrar; **petrol ~** indicador *m* (del nivel) de gasolina; **to ~ the right moment** elegir el momento (oportuno)
gaunt [gɔːnt] *adj* descarnado; (*fig*) adusto
gauntlet ['gɔːntlɪt] *n* (*fig*): **to run the ~ of sth** exponerse a algo; **to throw down the ~** arrojar el guante
gauze [gɔːz] *n* gasa
gave [geɪv] *pt of* **give**
gawk [gɔːk] *vi* mirar pasmado
gawky ['gɔːkɪ] *adj* desgarbado
gay [geɪ] *adj* (*colour, person*) alegre; (*homosexual*) gay
gaze [geɪz] *n* mirada fija ■ *vi*: **to ~ at sth** mirar algo fijamente
gazelle [gə'zɛl] *n* gacela
gazette [gə'zɛt] *n* (*newspaper*) gaceta; (*official publication*) boletín *m* oficial
gazetteer [gæzə'tɪə'] *n* índice geográfico
gazump [gə'zʌmp] *vti* (*Brit*) *echarse atrás en la venta ya acordada de una casa por haber una oferta más alta*
GB *abbr* (= *Great Britain*) GB
GBH *n abbr* (*Brit Law: col*) = **grievous bodily harm**
GC *n abbr* (*Brit*: = *George Cross*) *distinción honorífica*
GCE *n abbr* (*Brit*: = *General Certificate of Education*) ≈ certificado de bachillerato
GCHQ *n abbr* (*Brit*: = *Government Communications Headquarters*) *centro de intercepción de las telecomunicaciones internacionales*
GCSE *n abbr* (*Brit*: = *General Certificate of Secondary Education*) *certificado del último ciclo de la enseñanza secundaria obligatoria*

Gdns. *abbr* (= *gardens*) jdns
GDP *n abbr* (= *gross domestic product*) PIB *m*
GDR *n abbr* (= *German Democratic Republic*) RDA *f*
gear [gɪə'] *n* equipo; (*Tech*) engranaje *m*; (*Aut*) velocidad *f*, marcha ■ *vt* (*fig: adapt*): **to ~ sth to** adaptar *or* ajustar algo a; **top** *or* (*US*) **high/low ~** cuarta/primera; **in ~** con la marcha metida; **our service is geared to meet the needs of the disabled** nuestro servicio va enfocado a responder a las necesidades de los minusválidos
▶ **gear up** *vi* prepararse
gear box *n* caja de cambios
gear lever, gear shift (*US*) *n* palanca de cambio
gear wheel *n* rueda dentada
GED *n abbr* (*US Scol*) = **general educational development**
geese [giːs] *npl of* **goose**
geezer ['giːzə'] *n* (*Brit col*) tipo, maromo (*SP*)
Geiger counter ['gaɪgə-] *n* contador *m* Geiger
gel [dʒɛl] *n* gel *m*
gelatin, gelatine ['dʒɛləti:n] *n* gelatina
gelignite ['dʒɛlɪgnaɪt] *n* gelignita
gem [dʒɛm] *n* gema, piedra preciosa; (*fig*) joya
Gemini ['dʒɛmɪnaɪ] *n* Géminis *m*
gen [dʒɛn] *n* (*Brit col*): **to give sb the ~ on sth** poner a algn al tanto de algo
Gen. *abbr* (*Mil*: = *General*) Gen., Gral
gen. *abbr* (= *general*) grl.; = **generally**
gender ['dʒɛndə'] *n* género
gene [dʒiːn] *n* gen(e) *m*
genealogy [dʒiːnɪ'ælədʒɪ] *n* genealogía
general ['dʒɛnərl] *n* general *m* ■ *adj* general; **in ~** en general; **~ audit** auditoría general; **the ~ public** el gran público
general anaesthetic, general anesthetic (*US*) *n* anestesia general
general delivery *n* (*US*) lista de correos
general election *n* elecciones *fpl* generales
generalization [dʒɛnrəlaɪ'zeɪʃən] *n* generalización *f*
generalize ['dʒɛnrəlaɪz] *vi* generalizar
generally ['dʒɛnrəlɪ] *adv* generalmente, en general
general manager *n* director(a) *m(f)* general
general practitioner *n* médico(-a) de medicina general
general strike *n* huelga general
generate ['dʒɛnəreɪt] *vt* generar
generation [dʒɛnə'reɪʃən] *n* (*of electricity etc*) generación *f*
generator ['dʒɛnəreɪtə'] *n* generador *m*
generic [dʒɪ'nɛrɪk] *adj* genérico
generosity [dʒɛnə'rɒsɪtɪ] *n* generosidad *f*
generous ['dʒɛnərəs] *adj* generoso; (*copious*) abundante

generously ['dʒɛnərəslı] *adv* generosamente; abundantemente

genesis ['dʒɛnısıs] *n* génesis *f*

genetic [dʒɪ'nɛtɪk] *adj* genético

genetically modified organism [dʒɪ'nɛtɪkə lı] *n* organismo genéticamente modificado, organismo transgénico

genetic engineering *n* ingeniería genética

genetic fingerprinting [-'fɪŋgəprɪntɪŋ] *n* identificación *f* genética

genetics [dʒɪ'nɛtɪks] *n* genética

Geneva [dʒɪ'niːvə] *n* Ginebra

genial ['dʒiːnɪəl] *adj* afable

genitals ['dʒɛnɪtlz] *npl* (órganos *mpl*) genitales *mpl*

genitive ['dʒɛnɪtɪv] *n* genitivo

genius ['dʒiːnɪəs] *n* genio

Genoa ['dʒɛnəuə] *n* Génova

genocide ['dʒɛnəusaɪd] *n* genocidio

gent [dʒɛnt] *n abbr* (*Brit col*) = **gentleman**

genteel [dʒɛn'tiːl] *adj* fino, distinguido

gentle ['dʒɛntl] *adj* (*sweet*) dulce; (*touch etc*) ligero, suave

gentleman ['dʒɛntlmən] *n* señor *m*; (*well-bred man*) caballero; **~'s agreement** acuerdo entre caballeros

gentlemanly ['dʒɛntlmənlı] *adj* caballeroso

gentleness ['dʒɛntlnıs] *n* dulzura; (*of touch*) suavidad *f*

gently ['dʒɛntlı] *adv* suavemente

gentrification [dʒɛntrıfı'keıʃən] *n* aburguesamiento

gentry ['dʒɛntrı] *npl* pequeña nobleza *sg*

gents [dʒɛnts] *n* servicios *mpl* (de caballeros)

genuine ['dʒɛnjuɪn] *adj* auténtico; (*person*) sincero

genuinely ['dʒɛnjuɪnlı] *adv* sinceramente

geographer [dʒɪ'ɔgrəfər] *n* geógrafo(-a)

geographic [dʒɪə'græfɪk], **geographical** [dʒɪə'græfɪkl] *adj* geográfico

geography [dʒɪ'ɔgrəfı] *n* geografía

geological [dʒɪə'lɔdʒɪkl] *adj* geológico

geologist [dʒɪ'ɔlədʒɪst] *n* geólogo(-a)

geology [dʒɪ'ɔlədʒı] *n* geología

geometric [dʒɪə'mɛtrɪk], **geometrical** [dʒɪə'mɛtrɪkl] *adj* geométrico

geometry [dʒɪ'ɔmətrı] *n* geometría

Geordie ['dʒɔːdı] *n* habitante *m/f* de Tyneside

Georgia ['dʒɔːdʒə] *n* Georgia

Georgian ['dʒɔːdʒən] *adj* georgiano ■ *n* georgiano(-a); (*Ling*) georgiano

geranium [dʒɪ'reınjəm] *n* geranio

gerbil ['dʒɛrbl] *n* gerbo

geriatric [dʒɛrı'ætrɪk] *adj*, *n* geriátrico(-a) *m(f)*

germ [dʒəːm] *n* (*microbe*) microbio, bacteria; (*seed*) germen *m*

German ['dʒəːmən] *adj* alemán(-ana) ■ *n* alemán(-ana) *m(f)*; (*Ling*) alemán *m*

German Democratic Republic *n* República Democrática Alemana

germane [dʒəː'meın] *adj*: **~ (to)** pertinente (a)

German measles *n* rubeola, rubéola

German Shepherd *n* (*dog*) pastor *m* alemán

Germany ['dʒəːmənı] *n* Alemania; **East/West ~** Alemania Oriental *or* Democrática/Occidental *or* Federal

germination [dʒəːmı'neıʃən] *n* germinación *f*

germ warfare *n* guerra bacteriológica

gesticulate [dʒɛs'tɪkjuleıt] *vi* gesticular

gesticulation [dʒɛstɪkju'leıʃən] *n* gesticulación *f*

gesture ['dʒɛstjər] *n* gesto; **as a ~ of friendship** en señal de amistad

 KEYWORD

get [gɛt] (*pt, pp* **got**) (*US*) (*pp* **gotten**) *vi*
1 (*become, be*) ponerse, volverse; **to get old/tired** envejecer/cansarse; **to get drunk** emborracharse; **to get dirty** ensuciarse; **to get ready/washed** prepararse/lavarse; **to get married** casarse; **when do I get paid?** ¿cuándo me pagan *or* se me paga?; **it's getting late** se está haciendo tarde
2 (*go*): **to get to/from** llegar a/de; **to get home** llegar a casa; **he got under the fence** pasó por debajo de la barrera
3 (*begin*) empezar a; **to get to know sb** (llegar a) conocer a algn; **I'm getting to like him** me está empezando a gustar; **let's get going** *or* **started** ¡vamos (a empezar)!
4 (*modal aux vb*): **you've got to do it** tienes que hacerlo

■ *vt* **1**: **to get sth done** (*finish*) hacer algo; (*have done*) mandar hacer algo; **to get one's hair cut** cortarse el pelo; **to get the car going** *or* **to go** arrancar el coche; **to get sb to do sth** conseguir *or* hacer que algn haga algo; **to get sth/sb ready** preparar algo/a algn
2 (*obtain: money, permission, results*) conseguir; (*find: job, flat*) encontrar; (*fetch: person, doctor*) buscar; (*object*) ir a buscar, traer; **to get sth for sb** conseguir algo para algn; **get me Mr Jones, please** (*Tel*) póngame *or* (*LAm*) comuníqueme con el Sr. Jones, por favor; **can I get you a drink?** ¿quieres algo de beber?
3 (*receive: present, letter*) recibir; (*acquire: reputation*) alcanzar; (*: prize*) ganar; **what did you get for your birthday?** ¿qué te regalaron por tu cumpleaños?; **how much did you get for the painting?** ¿cuánto sacaste por el cuadro?

g

4 (catch) coger (SP), agarrar (LAm); (hit: target etc) dar en; **to get sb by the arm/throat** coger or agarrar a algn por el brazo/cuello; **get him!** ¡cógelo! (SP), ¡atrápalo! (LAm); **the bullet got him in the leg** la bala le dio en la pierna
5 (take, move) llevar; **to get sth to sb** hacer llegar algo a algn; **do you think we'll get it through the door?** ¿crees que lo podremos meter por la puerta?
6 (catch, take: plane, bus etc) coger (SP), tomar (LAm); **where do I get the train for Birmingham?** ¿dónde se coge or se toma el tren para Birmingham?
7 (understand) entender; (hear) oír; **I've got it!** ¡ya lo tengo!, ¡eureka!; **I don't get your meaning** no te entiendo; **I'm sorry, I didn't get your name** lo siento, no me he enterado de tu nombre
8 (have, possess): **to have got** tener
9 (col: annoy) molestar; (: thrill) chiflar
▶ **get about** vi salir mucho; (news) divulgarse
▶ **get across** vt (message, meaning) lograr comunicar
■ vi: **to get across to sb** hacer que algn comprenda
▶ **get along** vi (agree) llevarse bien; (depart) marcharse; (manage) = **get by**
▶ **get at** vt fus (attack) meterse con; (reach) alcanzar; (the truth) descubrir; **what are you getting at?** ¿qué insinúas?
▶ **get away** vi marcharse; (escape) escaparse
▶ **get away with** vt fus hacer impunemente
▶ **get back** vi (return) volver
■ vt recobrar
▶ **get back at** vt fus (col): **to get back at sb (for sth)** vengarse de algn (por algo)
▶ **get by** vi (pass) (lograr) pasar; (manage) arreglárselas; **I can get by in Dutch** me defiendo en holandés
▶ **get down** vi bajar(se)
■ vt fus bajar
■ vt bajar; (depress) deprimir
▶ **get down to** vt fus (work) ponerse a
▶ **get in** vi entrar; (train) llegar; (arrive home) volver a casa, regresar; (political party) salir
■ vt (bring in: harvest) recoger; (: coal, shopping, supplies) comprar, traer; (insert) meter
▶ **get into** vt fus entrar en; (vehicle) subir a; **to get into a rage** enfadarse
▶ **get off** vi (from train etc) bajar(se); (depart: person, car) marcharse
■ vt (remove) quitar; (send off) mandar; (have as leave: day, time) tener libre
■ vt fus (train, bus) bajar(se) de; **to get off to a good start** (fig) empezar muy bien or con buen pie

▶ **get on** vi (at exam etc): **how are you getting on?** ¿cómo te va?; (agree): **to get on (with)** llevarse bien (con)
■ vt fus subir(se) a
▶ **get on to** vt fus (deal with) ocuparse de; (col: contact on phone etc) hablar con
▶ **get out** vi salir; (of vehicle) bajar(se); (news) saberse
■ vt sacar
▶ **get out of** vt fus salir de; (duty etc) escaparse de; (gain from: pleasure, benefit) sacar de
▶ **get over** vt fus (illness) recobrarse de
▶ **get round** vt fus rodear; (fig: person) engatusar a
■ vi: **to get round to doing sth** encontrar tiempo para hacer algo
▶ **get through** vt fus (finish) acabar
■ vi (Tel) (lograr) comunicar
▶ **get through to** vt fus (Tel) comunicar con
▶ **get together** vi reunirse
■ vt reunir, juntar
▶ **get up** vi (rise) levantarse
■ vt fus subir; **to get up enthusiasm for sth** cobrar entusiasmo por algo
▶ **get up to** vt fus (reach) llegar a; (prank) hacer

getaway ['gɛtəweɪ] n fuga
getaway car n: **the thieves' ~** el coche en que huyeron los ladrones
get-together ['gɛttəgɛðəʳ] n reunión f; (party) fiesta
get-up ['gɛtʌp] n (Brit col: outfit) atavío, atuendo
get-well card [gɛt'wɛl-] n tarjeta en la que se desea a un enfermo que se mejore
geyser ['giːzəʳ] n (water heater) calentador m de agua; (Geo) géiser m
Ghana ['gɑːnə] n Ghana
Ghanaian [gɑːˈneɪən] adj, n ghanés(-esa) m(f)
ghastly ['gɑːstlɪ] adj horrible; (pale) pálido
gherkin ['gəːkɪn] n pepinillo
ghetto ['gɛtəu] n gueto
ghetto blaster [-ˈblɑːstəʳ] n radiocas(s)et(t)e m portátil (de gran tamaño)
ghost [gəust] n fantasma m ■ vt (book) escribir por otro
ghostly ['gəustlɪ] adj fantasmal
ghost story n cuento de fantasmas
ghostwriter ['gəustraɪtəʳ] n negro(-a)
ghoul [guːl] n espíritu m necrófago
GHQ n abbr (Mil: = general headquarters) cuartel m general
GI n abbr (US col: = government issue) soldado del ejército norteamericano
giant ['dʒaɪənt] n gigante m/f ■ adj gigantesco, gigante; **~ (size) packet** paquete m (de tamaño) gigante or familiar

giant killer n (Sport) matagigantes m inv
gibber ['dʒɪbəʳ] vi farfullar
gibberish ['dʒɪbərɪʃ] n galimatías m
gibe [dʒaɪb] n pulla
giblets ['dʒɪblɪts] npl menudillos mpl
Gibraltar [dʒɪ'brɔːltəʳ] n Gibraltar m
giddiness ['gɪdɪnɪs] n mareo
giddy ['gɪdɪ] adj (dizzy) mareado; (height, speed)
vertiginoso; **it makes me ~** me marea; **I feel
~** me siento mareado
gift [gɪft] n (gen) regalo; (Comm: also: **free gift**)
obsequio; (ability) don m; **to have a ~ for sth**
tener dotes para algo
gifted ['gɪftɪd] adj dotado
gift token, gift voucher n vale-regalo m
gig [gɪg] n (col: concert) actuación f
gigabyte ['dʒɪgəbaɪt] n gigabyte m
gigantic [dʒaɪ'gæntɪk] adj gigantesco
giggle ['gɪgl] vi reírse tontamente ◼ n risilla
GIGO ['gaɪgəu] abbr (Comput: col) = **garbage in,
garbage out**
gill [dʒɪl] n (measure) 0.25 pints (BRIT = 0,148 litros;
US = 0,118 litros.)
gills [gɪlz] npl (of fish) branquias fpl, agallas fpl
gilt [gɪlt] adj, n dorado
gilt-edged ['gɪltedʒd] adj (Comm: stocks,
securities) de máxima garantía
gimlet ['gɪmlɪt] n barrena de mano
gimmick ['gɪmɪk] n reclamo; **sales ~** reclamo
promocional
gimmicky ['gɪmɪkɪ] adj de reclamo
gin [dʒɪn] n (liquor) ginebra
ginger ['dʒɪndʒəʳ] n jengibre m
ginger ale n ginger ale m
ginger beer n refresco m de jengibre
gingerbread ['dʒɪndʒəbred] n pan m de
jengibre
ginger-haired [dʒɪndʒə'hɛəd] adj pelirrojo
gingerly ['dʒɪndʒəlɪ] adv con pies de plomo
ginseng ['dʒɪnsɛn] n ginseng m
gipsy ['dʒɪpsɪ] n gitano(-a)
giraffe [dʒɪ'rɑːf] n jirafa
girder ['gəːdəʳ] n viga
girdle ['gəːdl] n (corset) faja ◼ vt ceñir
girl [gəːl] n (small) niña; (young woman) chica,
joven f, muchacha; **an English ~** una (chica)
inglesa
girlfriend ['gəːlfrend] n (of girl) amiga; (of boy)
novia
Girl Guide n exploradora
girlish ['gəːlɪʃ] adj de niña
Girl Scout n (US) = **Girl Guide**
giro ['dʒaɪrəu] n (Brit: bank giro) giro bancario;
(post office giro) giro postal
girth [gəːθ] n circunferencia; (of saddle)
cincha
gist [dʒɪst] n lo esencial

give [gɪv] (pt **gave**, pp **given**) [geɪv, 'gɪvn] vt
dar; (deliver) entregar; (as gift) regalar ◼ vi
(break) romperse; (stretch: fabric) dar de sí;
to ~ sb sth, ~ sth to sb dar algo a algn;
how much did you ~ for it? ¿cuánto pagaste
por él?; **12 o'clock, ~ or take a few minutes**
más o menos las doce; **~ them my regards**
dales recuerdos de mi parte; **I can ~ you 10
minutes** le puedo conceder 10 minutos;
to ~ way (Brit Aut) ceder el paso; **to ~ way to
despair** ceder a la desesperación
▶ **give away** vt (give free) regalar; (betray)
traicionar; (disclose) revelar
▶ **give back** vt devolver
▶ **give in** vi ceder ◼ vt entregar
▶ **give off** vt despedir
▶ **give out** vt distribuir ◼ vi (be exhausted:
supplies) agotarse; (fail: engine) averiarse;
(strength) fallar
▶ **give up** vi rendirse, darse por vencido
◼ vt renunciar a; **to ~ up smoking** dejar de
fumar; **to ~ o.s. up** entregarse
give-and-take ['gɪvənd'teɪk] n (col) toma y
daca m
giveaway ['gɪvəweɪ] n (col): **her expression
was a ~** su expresión la delataba; **the exam
was a ~!** ¡el examen estaba tirado! ◼ cpd:
~ prices precios mpl de regalo
given ['gɪvn] pp of **give** ◼ adj (fixed: time,
amount) determinado ◼ conj: **~ (that)** ... dado
(que) ...; **~ the circumstances** ... dadas las
circunstancias ...
glacial ['gleɪsɪəl] adj glacial
glacier ['glæsɪəʳ] n glaciar m
glad [glæd] adj contento; **to be ~ about sth/
that** alegrarse de algo/de que; **I was ~ of his
help** agradecí su ayuda
gladden ['glædn] vt alegrar
glade [gleɪd] n claro
gladiator ['glædɪeɪtəʳ] n gladiador m
gladioli [glædɪ'əulaɪ] npl gladiolos mpl
gladly ['glædlɪ] adv con mucho gusto
glamorous ['glæmərəs] adj con encanto,
atractivo
glamour ['glæməʳ] n encanto, atractivo
glance [glɑːns] n ojeada, mirada ◼ vi: **to ~ at**
echar una ojeada a
▶ **glance off** vt fus (bullet) rebotar en
glancing ['glɑːnsɪŋ] adj (blow) oblicuo
gland [glænd] n glándula
glandular ['glændjuləʳ] adj: **~ fever**
mononucleosis f infecciosa
glare [glɛəʳ] n deslumbramiento, brillo
◼ vi deslumbrar; **to ~ at** mirar con odio
glaring ['glɛərɪŋ] adj (mistake) manifiesto
glass [glɑːs] n vidrio, cristal m; (for drinking) vaso;
(with stem) copa; (also: **looking glass**) espejo

glass-blowing ['glɑːsbləuɪŋ] n soplado de vidrio

glass ceiling n (fig) techo or barrera invisible (que impide ascender profesionalmente a las mujeres o miembros de minorías étnicas)

glasses ['glɑːsəs] npl gafas fpl, anteojos mpl (LAm)

glass fibre, (US) **glass fiber** n fibra de vidrio

glasshouse ['glɑːshaus] n invernadero

glassware ['glɑːswɛəʳ] n cristalería

glassy ['glɑːsɪ] adj (eyes) vidrioso

Glaswegian [glæs'wiːdʒən] adj de Glasgow
■ n nativo(-a) or habitante m(f) de Glasgow

glaze [gleɪz] vt (window) acristalar; (pottery) vidriar; (Culin) glasear ■ n barniz m; (Culin) glaseado

glazed [gleɪzd] adj (eye) vidrioso; (pottery) vidriado

glazier ['gleɪzɪəʳ] n vidriero(-a)

gleam [gliːm] n destello ■ vi relucir; **a ~ of hope** un rayo de esperanza

gleaming ['gliːmɪŋ] adj reluciente

glean [gliːn] vt (gather: information) recoger

glee [gliː] n alegría, regocijo

gleeful ['gliːful] adj alegre

glen [glɛn] n cañada

glib [glɪb] adj (person) de mucha labia; (comment) fácil

glibly ['glɪblɪ] adv (explain) con mucha labia

glide [glaɪd] vi deslizarse; (Aviat: bird) planear

glider ['glaɪdəʳ] n (Aviat) planeador m

gliding ['glaɪdɪŋ] n (Aviat) vuelo sin motor

glimmer ['glɪməʳ] n luz f tenue

glimpse [glɪmps] n vislumbre m ■ vt vislumbrar, entrever; **to catch a ~ of** vislumbrar

glint [glɪnt] n destello; (in the eye) chispa ■ vi centellear

glisten ['glɪsn] vi relucir, brillar

glitter ['glɪtəʳ] vi relucir, brillar ■ n brillo

glittering ['glɪtərɪŋ] adj reluciente, brillante

glitz [glɪts] n (col) vistosidad f

gloat [gləut] vi: **to ~ over** regodearse con

global ['gləubl] adj (world-wide) mundial; (comprehensive) global

globalization ['gləubəlaɪzeɪʃən] n globalización f, mundialización f

global warming [-'wɔːmɪŋ] n (re)calentamiento global or de la tierra

globe [gləub] n globo, esfera; (model) bola del mundo; globo terráqueo

globetrotter ['gləubtrɔtəʳ] n trotamundos m inv

globule ['glɔbjuːl] n glóbulo

gloom [gluːm] n penumbra; (sadness) desaliento, melancolía

gloomily ['gluːmɪlɪ] adv tristemente;

de modo pesimista

gloomy ['gluːmɪ] adj (dark) oscuro; (sad) triste; (pessimistic) pesimista; **to feel ~** sentirse pesimista

glorification [glɔːrɪfɪ'keɪʃən] n glorificación f

glorify ['glɔːrɪfaɪ] vt glorificar

glorious ['glɔːrɪəs] adj glorioso; (weather, sunshine) espléndido

glory ['glɔːrɪ] n gloria

Glos abbr (Brit) = **Gloucestershire**

gloss [glɔs] n (shine) brillo; (also: **gloss paint**) (pintura) esmalte m
▶ **gloss over** vt fus restar importancia a; (omit) pasar por alto

glossary ['glɔsərɪ] n glosario

glossy ['glɔsɪ] adj (hair) brillante; (photograph) con brillo; (magazine) de papel satinado or cuché

glove [glʌv] n guante m

glove compartment n (Aut) guantera

glow [gləu] vi (shine) brillar ■ n brillo

glower ['glauəʳ] vi: **to ~ at** mirar con ceño

glowing ['gləuɪŋ] adj (fire) vivo; (complexion) encendido; (fig: report, description) entusiasta

glow-worm ['gləuwəːm] n luciérnaga

glucose ['gluːkəus] n glucosa

glue [gluː] n pegamento, cemento (LAm) ■ vt pegar

glue-sniffing ['gluːsnɪfɪŋ] n inhalación f de pegamento or (LAm) cemento

glum [glʌm] adj (mood) abatido; (person, tone) melancólico

glut [glʌt] n superabundancia

glutinous ['gluːtɪnəs] adj glutinoso, pegajoso

glutton ['glʌtn] n glotón(-ona) m(f); **~ for punishment** masoquista m/f

gluttony ['glʌtənɪ] n gula, glotonería

glycerin, glycerine ['glɪsəriːn] n glicerina

GM adj abbr (= genetically-modified) transgénico

gm abbr (= gram) g

GMAT n abbr (US: = Graduate Management Admissions Test) examen de admisión al segundo ciclo de la enseñanza superior

GMB n abbr (Brit) = **General, Municipal, and Boilermakers (Union)**

GMo n abbr (= genetically modified organism) organismo transgénico, OGM m

GMT abbr (= Greenwich Mean Time) GMT

gnarled [nɑːld] adj nudoso

gnash [næʃ] vt: **to ~ one's teeth** hacer rechinar los dientes

gnat [næt] n mosquito

gnaw [nɔː] vt roer

gnome [nəum] n gnomo

GNP n abbr (= gross national product) PNB m

GNVQ n abbr (Brit: = general national vocational qualification) título general de formación profesional

go [gəu] *vb* (*pt* **went**, *pp* **gone**) ■ *vi* ir; (*travel*) viajar; (*depart*) irse, marcharse; (*work*) funcionar, marchar; (*be sold*) venderse; (*time*) pasar; (*become*) ponerse; (*break etc*) estropearse, romperse; (*fit, suit*): **to go with** hacer juego con ■ *n* (*pl* **goes**); **to have a go (at)** probar suerte (con); **to be on the go** no parar; **whose go is it?** ¿a quién le toca?; **to go by car/on foot** ir en coche/a pie; **he's going to do it** va a hacerlo; **to go for a walk** ir a dar un paseo; **to go dancing** ir a bailar; **to go looking for sth/sb** ir a buscar algo/a algn; **to make sth go, get sth going** poner algo en marcha; **my voice has gone** he perdido la voz; **the cake is all gone** se acabó la tarta; **the money will go towards our holiday** el dinero es para (ayuda de) nuestras vacaciones; **how did it go?** ¿qué tal salió *or* resultó?, ¿cómo ha ido?; **the meeting went well** la reunión salió bien; **to go and see sb** ir a ver a algn; **to go to sleep** dormirse; **I'll take whatever is going** acepto lo que haya; **... to go** (US: *food*) ... para llevar; **to go round the back** pasar por detrás

▶ **go about** *vi* (*rumour*) propagarse; (*also*: **go round**: *wander about*) andar (de un sitio para otro) ■ *vt fus*: **how do I go about this?** ¿cómo me las arreglo para hacer esto?; **to go about one's business** ocuparse de sus asuntos

▶ **go after** *vt fus* (*pursue*) perseguir; (*job, record etc*) andar tras

▶ **go against** *vt fus* (*be unfavourable to*: *results*) ir en contra de; (*be contrary to*: *principles*) ser contrario a

▶ **go ahead** *vi* seguir adelante

▶ **go along** *vi* ir; **as you go along** sobre la marcha ■ *vt fus* bordear

▶ **go along with** *vt fus* (*accompany*) acompañar; (*agree with*: *idea*) estar de acuerdo con

▶ **go around** *vi* = **go round**

▶ **go away** *vi* irse, marcharse

▶ **go back** *vi* volver

▶ **go back on** *vt fus* (*promise*) faltar a

▶ **go by** *vi* (*years, time*) pasar ■ *vt fus* guiarse por

▶ **go down** *vi* bajar; (*ship*) hundirse; (*sun*) ponerse ■ *vt fus* bajar por; **that should go down well with him** eso le va a gustar; **he's gone down with flu** ha cogido la gripe

▶ **go for** *vt fus* (*fetch*) ir por; (*like*) gustar; (*attack*) atacar

▶ **go in** *vi* entrar

▶ **go in for** *vt fus* (*competition*) presentarse a

▶ **go into** *vt fus* entrar en; (*investigate*) investigar; (*embark on*) dedicarse a

▶ **go off** *vi* irse, marcharse; (*food*) pasarse; (*lights etc*) apagarse; (*explode*) estallar; (*event*) realizarse ■ *vt fus* perder el interés por; **the party went off well** la fiesta salió bien

▶ **go on** *vi* (*continue*) seguir, continuar; (*lights*) encenderse; (*happen*) pasar, ocurrir; (*be guided by*: *evidence etc*) partir de; **to go on doing sth** seguir haciendo algo; **what's going on here?** ¿qué pasa aquí?

▶ **go on at** *vt fus* (*nag*) soltarle el rollo a

▶ **go out** *vi* salir; (*fire, light*) apagarse; (*ebb*: *tide*) bajar, menguar; **to go out with sb** salir con algn

▶ **go over** *vi* (*ship*) zozobrar ■ *vt fus* (*check*) revisar; **to go over sth in one's mind** repasar algo mentalmente

▶ **go round** *vi* (*circulate*: *news, rumour*) correr; (*suffice*) alcanzar, bastar; (*revolve*) girar, dar vueltas; (*visit*): **to go round (to sb's)** pasar a ver (a algn); **to go round (by)** (*make a detour*) dar la vuelta (por)

▶ **go through** *vt fus* (*town etc*) atravesar; (*search through*) revisar; (*perform*: *ceremony*) realizar; (*examine*: *list, book*) repasar

▶ **go through with** *vt fus* (*plan, crime*) llevar a cabo; **I couldn't go through with it** no pude llevarlo a cabo

▶ **go together** *vi* entenderse

▶ **go under** *vi* (*sink*: *ship, person*) hundirse; (*fig*: *business, firm*) quebrar

▶ **go up** *vi* subir; **to go up in flames** estallar en llamas

▶ **go without** *vt fus* pasarse sin

goad [gəud] *vt* aguijonear

go-ahead ['gəuəhɛd] *adj* emprendedor(a) ■ *n* luz *f* verde; **to give sth/sb the ~** dar luz verde a algo/algn

goal [gəul] *n* meta, arco (LAm); (*score*) gol *m*

goal difference *n* diferencia por goles

goalie ['gəulı] *n* (*col*) = **goalkeeper**

goalkeeper ['gəulki:pə'] *n* portero, guardameta *m/f*, arquero (LAm)

goal post *n* poste *m* (de la portería)

goat [gəut] *n* cabra *f*

gobble ['gɔbl] *vt* (*also*: **gobble down, gobble up**) engullir

go-between ['gəubɪtwi:n] *n* intermediario(-a)

Gobi Desert ['gəubı-] *n* Desierto de Gobi

goblet ['gɔblɪt] *n* copa

goblin ['gɔblɪn] *n* duende *m*

go-cart ['gəukɑ:t] *n* = **go-kart**

god [gɔd] *n* dios *m*; **G~** Dios *m*

god-awful [gɔd'ɔ:fəl] *adj* (*col*) de puta pena

godchild ['gɔdtʃaɪld] *n* ahijado(-a)

goddamn ['gɔddæm] *adj* (*col*: *also*: **goddamned**) maldito, puñetero ■ *excl*: **~!** ¡cagüen diez!

g

goddess ['gɔdɪs] *n* diosa
godfather ['gɔdfɑːðəʳ] *n* padrino
god-fearing ['gɔdfɪərɪŋ] *adj* temeroso de Dios
god-forsaken ['gɔdfəseɪkən] *adj* dejado de la mano de Dios
godmother ['gɔdmʌðəʳ] *n* madrina
godparents ['gɔdpɛərənts] *npl*: **the** ~ los padrinos
godsend ['gɔdsɛnd] *n*: **to be a** ~ venir como llovido del cielo
godson ['gɔdsʌn] *n* ahijado
goes [gəuz] *vb see* **go**
gofer ['gəufəʳ] *n* (*col*) chico(-a) para todo
go-getter ['gəugɛtəʳ] *n* ambicioso(-a)
goggle ['gɔgl] *vi*: **to** ~ (**at**) mirar con ojos desorbitados
goggles ['gɔglz] *npl* (*Aut*) gafas *fpl*, anteojos *mpl* (*LAm*); (*diver's*) gafas *fpl* submarinas
going ['gəuɪŋ] *n* (*conditions*) cosas *fpl* ■ *adj*: **the** ~ **rate** la tarifa corriente *or* en vigor; **it was slow** ~ las cosas iban lentas
going-over [gəuɪŋ'əuvəʳ] *n* revisión *f*; (*col*: *beating*) paliza
goings-on ['gəuɪŋz'ɔn] *npl* (*col*) tejemanejes *mpl*
go-kart ['gəukɑːt] *n* kart *m*
gold [gəuld] *n* oro ■ *adj* (*reserves*) de oro
golden ['gəuldn] *adj* (*made of gold*) de oro; (*golden in colour*) dorado
Golden Age *n* Siglo de Oro
golden handshake *n* cuantiosa gratificación por los servicios prestados
golden rule *n* regla de oro
goldfish ['gəuldfɪʃ] *n* pez *m* de colores
gold leaf *n* pan *m* de oro
gold medal *n* (*Sport*) medalla de oro
goldmine ['gəuldmaɪn] *n* mina de oro
gold-plated ['gəuld'pleɪtɪd] *adj* chapado en oro
goldsmith ['gəuldsmɪθ] *n* orfebre *m/f*
gold standard *n* patrón *m* oro
golf [gɔlf] *n* golf *m*
golf ball *n* (*for game*) pelota de golf; (*on typewriter*) esfera impresora
golf club *n* club *m* de golf; (*stick*) palo (de golf)
golf course *n* campo de golf
golfer ['gɔlfəʳ] *n* jugador(a) *m(f)* de golf, golfista *m/f*
golfing ['gɔlfɪŋ] *n*: **to go** ~ jugar al golf
gondola ['gɔndələ] *n* góndola
gondolier [gɔndə'lɪəʳ] *n* gondolero
gone [gɔn] *pp of* **go**
goner ['gɔnəʳ] *n* (*col*): **to be a** ~ estar en las últimas
gong [gɔŋ] *n* gong *m*
gonorrhea [gɔnə'rɪə] *n* gonorrea
good [gud] *adj* bueno; (*before m sing n*) buen;

(*well-behaved*) educado ■ *n* bien *m*; ~! ¡qué bien!; **he's** ~ **at it** se le da bien; **to be** ~ **for** servir para; **it's** ~ **for you** te hace bien; **would you be** ~ **enough to ...?** ¿podría hacerme el favor de ...?, ¿sería tan amable de ...?; **that's very** ~ **of you** es usted muy amable; **to feel** ~ sentirse bien; **it's** ~ **to see you** me alegro de verte; **a** ~ **deal (of)** mucho; **a** ~ **many** muchos; **to make** ~ reparar; **it's no** ~ **complaining** no sirve de nada quejarse; **is this any** ~? (*will it do?*) ¿sirve esto?; (*what's it like?*) ¿qué tal es esto?; **it's a** ~ **thing you were there** menos mal que estabas allí; **for** ~ (*for ever*) para siempre, definitivamente; ~ **morning/afternoon** ¡buenos días/buenas tardes!; ~ **evening!** ¡buenas noches!; ~ **night!** ¡buenas noches!; **he's up to no** ~ está tramando algo; **for the common** ~ para el bien común; *see also* **goods**
goodbye [gud'baɪ] *excl* ¡adiós!; **to say** ~ (**to**) (*person*) despedirse (de)
good faith *n* buena fe *f*
good-for-nothing ['gudfənʌθɪŋ] *n* inútil *m/f*
Good Friday *n* Viernes *m* Santo
good-humoured ['gud'hjuːməd] *adj* (*person*) afable, de buen humor; (*remark, joke*) bien intencionado
good-looking ['gud'lukɪŋ] *adj* guapo
good-natured ['gud'neɪtʃəd] *adj* (*person*) de buen carácter; (*discussion*) cordial
goodness ['gudnɪs] *n* (*of person*) bondad *f*; **for** ~ **sake!** ¡por Dios!; ~ **gracious!** ¡madre mía!
goods [gudz] *npl* bienes *mpl*; (*Comm etc*) géneros *mpl*, mercancías *fpl*, artículos *mpl*; **all his** ~ **and chattels** todos sus bienes
goods train *n* (*Brit*) tren *m* de mercancías
goodwill [gud'wɪl] *n* buena voluntad *f*; (*Comm*) fondo de comercio; (*customer connections*) clientela
goody-goody ['gudɪgudɪ] *n* (*pej*) santurrón(-ona) *m(f)*
gooey ['guːɪ] *adj* (*Brit col*) pegajoso; (*cake, behaviour*) empalagoso
google® ['gugl] *vi*, *vt* googlear
goose, geese [guːs, giːs] *n* ganso, oca
gooseberry ['guzbərɪ] *n* grosella espinosa *or* silvestre
gooseflesh ['guːsfleʃ] *n*, **goosepimples** ['guːspɪmplz] *npl* carne *f* de gallina
goose step *n* (*Mil*) paso de la oca
GOP *n abbr* (*US Pol*: *col*: = *Grand Old Party*) Partido Republicano
gopher ['gəufəʳ] *n* = **gofer**
gore [gɔːʳ] *vt* dar una cornada a, cornear ■ *n* sangre *f*
gorge [gɔːdʒ] *n* garganta ■ *vr*: **to** ~ **o.s. (on)** atracarse (de)

gorgeous ['gɔːdʒəs] *adj* precioso; (*weather*) estupendo; (*person*) guapísimo

gorilla [gə'rɪlə] *n* gorila *m*

gormless ['gɔːmlɪs] *adj* (*col*) ceporro, zoquete

gorse [gɔːs] *n* tojo

gory ['gɔːrɪ] *adj* sangriento

go-slow ['gəu'sləu] *n* (*Brit*) huelga de celo

gospel ['gɔspl] *n* evangelio

gossamer ['gɔsəmər] *n* gasa

gossip ['gɔsɪp] *n* cotilleo; (*person*) cotilla *m/f* ■ *vi* cotillear, comadrear (*LAm*); **a piece of ~** un cotilleo

gossip column *n* ecos *mpl* de sociedad

got [gɔt] *pt, pp of* **get**

Gothic ['gɔθɪk] *adj* gótico

gotten ['gɔtn] (*US*) *pp of* **get**

gouge [gaudʒ] *vt* (*also:* **gouge out**: *hole etc*) excavar; (: *initials*) grabar; **to ~ sb's eyes out** sacar los ojos a algn

goulash ['guːlæʃ] *n* g(o)ulash *m*

gourd [guəd] *n* calabaza

gourmet ['guəmeɪ] *n* gastrónomo(-a) *m(f)*

gout [gaut] *n* gota

govern ['gʌvən] *vt* (*gen*) gobernar; (*event, conduct*) regir

governess ['gʌvənɪs] *n* institutriz *f*

governing ['gʌvənɪŋ] *adj* (*Pol*) de gobierno, gubernamental; **~ body** organismo de gobierno

government ['gʌvnmənt] *n* gobierno; **local ~** administración *f* municipal

governmental [gʌvn'mentl] *adj* gubernamental

government stock *n* papel *m* del Estado

governor ['gʌvənər] *n* gobernador(a) *m(f)*; (*of jail*) director(a) *m(f)*

Govt *abbr* (= *Government*) gobno

gown [gaun] *n* vestido; (*of teacher*: *Brit*: *of judge*) toga

GP *n abbr* (*Med*) = **general practitioner**

GPMU *n abbr* (*Brit*: = *Graphical, Paper and Media Union*) *sindicato de trabajadores del sector editorial*

GPO *n abbr* (*Brit*: *old*: = *General Post Office*) (*US*) = **Government Printing Office**

GPS *n abbr* (= *global positioning system*) GPS *m*

gr. *abbr* (*Comm*: = *gross*) bto

grab [græb] *vt* coger (*SP*) *or* agarrar; **to ~ at** intentar agarrar

grace [greɪs] *n* (*Rel*) gracia; (*gracefulness*) elegancia, gracia; (*graciousness*) cortesía, gracia ■ *vt* (*favour*) honrar; (*adorn*) adornar; **5 days' ~** un plazo de 5 días; **to say ~** bendecir la mesa; **his sense of humour is his saving ~** lo que le salva es su sentido del humor

graceful ['greɪsful] *adj* elegante

gracious ['greɪʃəs] *adj* amable ■ *excl*: **good ~!** ¡Dios mío!

grade [greɪd] *n* (*quality*) clase *f*, calidad *f*; (*in hierarchy*) grado; (*US Scol*) curso; (: *gradient*) pendiente *f*, cuesta ■ *vt* clasificar; **to make the ~** (*fig*) dar el nivel; *see also* **high school**

grade crossing *n* (*US*) paso a nivel

grade school *n* (*US*) escuela primaria; *see also* **elementary school**

gradient ['greɪdɪənt] *n* pendiente *f*

gradual ['grædjuəl] *adj* gradual

gradually ['grædjuəlɪ] *adv* gradualmente

graduate *n* ['grædjuɪt] licenciado(-a), graduado(-a), egresado(-a) (*LAm*); (*US Scol*) bachiller *m/f* ■ *vi* ['grædjueɪt] licenciarse, graduarse, recibirse (*LAm*); (*US*) obtener el título de bachillerato

graduated pension ['grædjueɪtɪd-] *n* pensión *f* escalonada

graduation [grædju'eɪʃən] *n* graduación *f*; (*US Scol*) entrega de los títulos de bachillerato

graffiti [grə'fiːtɪ] *npl* pintadas *fpl*

graft [grɑːft] *n* (*Agr, Med*) injerto; (*bribery*) corrupción *f* ■ *vt* injertar; **hard ~** (*col*) trabajo duro

grain [greɪn] *n* (*single particle*) grano; (*no pl*: *cereals*) cereales *mpl*; (*US*: *corn*) trigo; (*in wood*) veta

gram [græm] *n* (*US*) gramo

grammar ['græmər] *n* gramática

grammar school *n* (*Brit*) ≈ instituto (de segunda enseñanza); (*US*) escuela primaria; *see also* **comprehensive school**

grammatical [grə'mætɪkl] *adj* gramatical

gramme [græm] *n* = **gram**

gramophone ['græməfəun] *n* (*Brit*) gramófono

granary ['grænərɪ] *n* granero

grand [grænd] *adj* grandioso ■ *n* (*US*: *col*) mil dólares *mpl*

grandchildren ['græntʃɪldrən] *npl* nietos *mpl*

granddad ['grændæd] *n* yayo, abuelito

granddaughter ['grændɔːtər] *n* nieta

grandeur ['grændjər] *n* grandiosidad *f*

grandfather ['grænfɑːðər] *n* abuelo

grandiose ['grændɪəuz] *adj* grandioso; (*pej*) pomposo

grand jury *n* (*US*) jurado de acusación

grandma ['grænmɑː] *n* yaya, abuelita

grandmother ['grænmʌðər] *n* abuela

grandpa ['grænpɑː] *n* = **granddad**

grandparents ['grændpɛərənts] *npl* abuelos *mpl*

grand piano *n* piano de cola

Grand Prix ['grɑː'priː] *n* (*Aut*) gran premio, Grand Prix *m*

grandson ['grænsʌn] *n* nieto

grandstand ['grændstænd] *n* (*Sport*) tribuna

grand total *n* suma total, total *m*

granite ['grænɪt] n granito
granny ['grænɪ] n abuelita, yaya
grant [grɑ:nt] vt (concede) conceder; (admit):
　to ~ (that) reconocer (que) ■ n (Scol) beca;
　to take sth for granted dar algo por sentado
granulated sugar ['grænjuleɪtɪd-] n (Brit)
　azúcar m granulado
granule ['grænju:l] n gránulo
grape [greɪp] n uva; **sour grapes** (fig)
　envidia sg; **a bunch of grapes** un racimo
　de uvas
grapefruit ['greɪpfru:t] n pomelo, toronja
grape juice n jugo or (SP) zumo de uva
grapevine ['greɪpvaɪn] n vid f, parra; **I heard
　it on the ~** (fig) me enteré, me lo contaron
graph [grɑ:f] n gráfica
graphic ['græfɪk] adj gráfico
graphic designer n diseñador(a) m(f)
　gráfico(-a)
graphic equalizer n ecualizador m gráfico
graphics ['græfɪks] n (art, process) artes fpl
　gráficas ■ npl (drawings: Comput) gráficos mpl
graphite ['græfaɪt] n grafito
graph paper n papel m cuadriculado
grapple ['græpl] vi (also: **to grapple with a
　problem**) enfrentarse a un problema
grappling iron ['græplɪŋ-] n (Naut) rezón m
grasp [grɑ:sp] vt agarrar, asir; (understand)
　comprender ■ n (grip) asimiento; (reach)
　alcance m; (understanding) comprensión f;
　to have a good ~ of (subject) dominar
　▶ **grasp at** vt fus (rope etc) tratar de agarrar;
　(fig: opportunity) aprovechar
grasping ['grɑ:spɪŋ] adj avaro
grass [grɑ:s] n hierba; (lawn) césped m;
　(pasture) pasto; (col: informer) soplón(-ona) m(f)
grasshopper ['grɑ:shɔpər] n saltamontes
　m inv
grassland ['grɑ:slænd] n pradera, pampa
　(LAm)
grass roots adj de base ■ npl (Pol) bases fpl
grass snake n culebra
grassy ['grɑ:sɪ] adj cubierto de hierba
grate [greɪt] n parrilla ■ vi chirriar, rechinar
　■ vt (Culin) rallar
grateful ['greɪtful] adj agradecido
gratefully ['greɪtfəlɪ] adv con
　agradecimiento
grater ['greɪtər] n rallador m
gratification [grætɪfɪ'keɪʃən] n satisfacción f
gratify ['grætɪfaɪ] vt complacer; (whim)
　satisfacer
gratifying ['grætɪfaɪɪŋ] adj gratificante
grating ['greɪtɪŋ] n (iron bars) rejilla ■ adj
　(noise) chirriante
gratitude ['grætɪtju:d] n agradecimiento
gratuitous [grə'tju:ɪtəs] adj gratuito

gratuity [grə'tju:ɪtɪ] n gratificación f
grave [greɪv] n tumba ■ adj serio, grave
gravedigger ['greɪvdɪgər] n sepulturero(-a)
gravel ['grævl] n grava
gravely ['greɪvlɪ] adv seriamente; **~ ill** muy
　grave
gravestone ['greɪvstəun] n lápida
graveyard ['greɪvjɑ:d] n cementerio,
　camposanto
gravitate ['grævɪteɪt] vi gravitar
gravitation [grævɪ'teɪʃən] n gravitación f
gravity ['grævɪtɪ] n gravedad f; (seriousness)
　seriedad f
gravy ['greɪvɪ] n salsa de carne
gravy boat n salsera
gravy train n (esp US: col): **to get on the ~**
　coger un chollo
gray [greɪ] adj (US) = **grey**
graze [greɪz] vi pacer ■ vt (touch lightly, scrape)
　rozar ■ n (Med) rozadura
grazing ['greɪzɪŋ] n (for livestock) pastoreo
grease [gri:s] n (fat) grasa; (lubricant)
　lubricante m ■ vt engrasar; **to ~ the skids**
　(US: fig) engrasar el mecanismo
grease gun n pistola engrasadora
greasepaint ['gri:speɪnt] n maquillaje m
greaseproof ['gri:spru:f] adj a prueba de
　grasa; (Brit: paper) de grasa
greasy ['gri:sɪ] adj (hands, clothes) grasiento;
　(road, surface) resbaladizo
great [greɪt] adj grande; (before n sing) gran;
　(col) estupendo, macanudo (LAm), regio
　(LAm); (pain, heat) intenso; **we had a ~ time**
　nos lo pasamos muy bien; **they're ~ friends**
　son íntimos or muy amigos; **the ~ thing
　is that ...** lo bueno es que ...; **it was ~!** ¡fue
　estupendo!
Great Barrier Reef n Gran Barrera de Coral
Great Britain n Gran Bretaña
greater ['greɪtər] adj mayor; **G~ London** el
　área metropolitana de Londres
greatest ['greɪtɪst] adj (el/la) mayor
great-grandchild (pl **-children**)
　[greɪt'grændtʃaɪld, 'tʃɪldrən] n bisnieto(-a)
great-grandfather [greɪt'grændfɑ:ðər] n
　bisabuelo
great-grandmother [greɪt'grændmʌðər] n
　bisabuela
Great Lakes npl: **the ~** los Grandes Lagos
greatly ['greɪtlɪ] adv sumamente, muy
greatness ['greɪtnɪs] n grandeza
Greece [gri:s] n Grecia
greed [gri:d] n (also: **greediness**) codicia;
　(for food) gula
greedily ['gri:dɪlɪ] adv con avidez
greedy ['gri:dɪ] adj codicioso; (for food)
　glotón(-ona)

Greek [gri:k] *adj* griego ■ *n* griego(-a); (*Ling*) griego; **ancient/modern ~** griego antiguo/moderno

green [gri:n] *adj* verde; (*inexperienced*) novato ■ *n* verde *m*; (*stretch of grass*) césped *m*; (*of golf course*) campo, "green" *m*; **the G~ party** (*Pol*) el partido verde; **greens** *npl* verduras *fpl*; **to have ~ fingers** (*fig*) tener buena mano para las plantas

green belt *n* cinturón *m* verde

green card *n* (*Aut*) carta verde

greenery ['gri:nəri] *n* vegetación *f*

greenfly ['gri:nflaɪ] *n* pulgón *m*

greengage ['gri:ngeɪdʒ] *n* (ciruela) claudia

greengrocer ['gri:ngrəusə'] *n* (*Brit*) frutero(-a), verdulero(-a)

greenhouse ['gri:nhaus] *n* invernadero

greenhouse effect *n*: **the ~** el efecto invernadero

greenhouse gas *n* gas *m* que produce el efecto invernadero

greenish ['gri:nɪʃ] *adj* verdoso

Greenland ['gri:nlənd] *n* Groenlandia

Greenlander ['gri:nləndə'] *n* groenlandés(-esa) *m(f)*

green light *n* luz *f* verde

green pepper *n* pimiento verde

greet [gri:t] *vt* saludar; (*news*) recibir

greeting ['gri:tɪŋ] *n* (*gen*) saludo; (*welcome*) bienvenida; **greetings** saludos *mpl*; **season's greetings** Felices Pascuas

greeting card, greetings card *n* tarjeta de felicitación

gregarious [grə'gɛərɪəs] *adj* gregario

grenade [grə'neɪd] *n* (*also*: **hand grenade**) granada

grew [gru:] *pt of* **grow**

grey [greɪ] *adj* gris; **to go ~** salirle canas

grey-haired [greɪ'hɛəd] *adj* canoso

greyhound ['greɪhaund] *n* galgo

grid [grɪd] *n* rejilla; (*Elec*) red *f*

griddle ['grɪdl] *n* (*esp US*) plancha

gridiron ['grɪdaɪən] *n* (*Culin*) parrilla

gridlock ['grɪdlɔk] *n* (*esp US*) retención *f*

grief [gri:f] *n* dolor *m*, pena; **to come to ~** (*plan*) fracasar, ir al traste; (*person*) acabar mal, desgraciarse

grievance ['gri:vəns] *n* (*cause for complaint*) motivo de queja, agravio

grieve [gri:v] *vi* afligirse, acongojarse ■ *vt* afligir, apenar; **to ~ for** llorar por; **to ~ for sb** (*dead person*) llorar la pérdida de algn

grievous ['gri:vəs] *adj* grave; (*loss*) cruel; **~ bodily harm** (*Law*) daños *mpl* corporales graves

grill [grɪl] *n* (*on cooker*) parrilla ■ *vt* (*Brit*) asar a la parrilla; (*question*) interrogar; **grilled meat** carne *f* (asada) a la parrilla *or* plancha

grille [grɪl] *n* rejilla

grim [grɪm] *adj* (*place*) lúgubre; (*person*) adusto

grimace [grɪ'meɪs] *n* mueca ■ *vi* hacer muecas

grime [graɪm] *n* mugre *f*

grimly ['grɪmlɪ] *adv* (*say*) sombríamente

grimy ['graɪmɪ] *adj* mugriento

grin [grɪn] *n* sonrisa abierta ■ *vi*: **to ~ (at)** sonreír abiertamente (a)

grind [graɪnd] (*pt, pp* **ground**) *vt* (*coffee, pepper etc*) moler; (*US: meat*) picar; (*make sharp*) afilar; (*polish: gem, lens*) esmerilar ■ *vi* (*car gears*) rechinar ■ *n*: **the daily ~** (*col*) la rutina diaria; **to ~ one's teeth** hacer rechinar los dientes; **to ~ to a halt** (*vehicle*) pararse con gran estruendo de frenos; (*fig: talks, scheme*) interrumpirse; (*work, production*) paralizarse

grinder ['graɪndə'] *n* (*machine: for coffee*) molinillo

grindstone ['graɪndstəun] *n*: **to keep one's nose to the ~** trabajar sin descanso

grip [grɪp] *n* (*hold*) asimiento; (*of hands*) apretón *m*; (*handle*) asidero; (*of racquet etc*) mango; (*understanding*) comprensión *f* ■ *vt* agarrar; **to get to grips with** enfrentarse con; **to lose one's ~** (*fig*) perder el control; **he lost his ~ of the situation** la situación se le fue de las manos

gripe [graɪp] *n* (*col: complaint*) queja ■ *vi* (*col: complain*): **to ~ (about)** quejarse (de); **gripes** *npl* retortijones *mpl*

gripping ['grɪpɪŋ] *adj* absorbente

grisly ['grɪzlɪ] *adj* horripilante, horrible

gristle ['grɪsl] *n* cartílago

grit [grɪt] *n* gravilla; (*courage*) valor *m* ■ *vt* (*road*) poner gravilla en; **I've got a piece of ~ in my eye** tengo una arenilla en el ojo; **to ~ one's teeth** apretar los dientes

grits [grɪts] *npl* (*US*) maíz *msg* a medio moler

grizzle ['grɪzl] *vi* (*cry*) lloriquear

grizzly ['grɪzlɪ] *n* (*also*: **grizzly bear**) oso pardo

groan [grəun] *n* gemido, quejido ■ *vi* gemir, quejarse

grocer ['grəusə'] *n* tendero (de ultramarinos); **~'s (shop)** *n* tienda de ultramarinos *or* (*LAm*) de abarrotes

groceries ['grəusərɪz] *npl* comestibles *mpl*

grocery ['grəusərɪ] *n* (*shop*) tienda de ultramarinos

grog [grɔg] *n* (*Brit*) grog *m*

groggy ['grɔgɪ] *adj* atontado

groin [grɔɪn] *n* ingle *f*

groom [gru:m] *n* mozo(-a) de cuadra; (*also*: **bridegroom**) novio ■ *vt* (*horse*) almohazar; **well-groomed** acicalado

groove [gru:v] *n* ranura; (*of record*) surco

grope [grəup] *vi* ir a tientas; **to ~ for** buscar
a tientas

gross [grəus] *adj* grueso; (*Comm*) bruto
■ *vt* (*Comm*) recaudar en bruto

gross domestic product *n* producto interior
bruto

gross income *n* ingresos *mpl* brutos

grossly ['grəuslı] *adv* (*greatly*) enormemente

gross national product *n* producto nacional
bruto

gross profit *n* beneficios *mpl* brutos

gross sales *npl* ventas *fpl* brutas

grotesque [grə'tesk] *adj* grotesco

grotto ['grɔtəu] *n* gruta

grotty ['grɔtı] *adj* asqueroso

grouch [grautʃ] *vi* (*col*) refunfuñar ■ *n* (*col*:
person) refunfuñón(-ona) *m(f)*

ground [graund] *pt, pp of* **grind** ■ *n* suelo,
tierra; (*Sport*) campo, terreno; (*reason: gen pl*)
motivo, razón *f*; (*US: also*: **ground wire**) tierra
■ *vt* (*plane*) mantener en tierra; (*US Elec*)
conectar con tierra ■ *vi* (*ship*) varar, encallar
■ *adj* (*coffee etc*) molido; **grounds** *npl* (*of coffee
etc*) poso *sg*; (*gardens etc*) jardines *mpl*, parque
m; **on the ~** en el suelo; **common ~** terreno
común; **to gain/lose ~** ganar/perder terreno;
to the ~ al suelo; **below ~** bajo tierra;
he covered a lot of ~ in his lecture abarcó
mucho en la clase

ground cloth *n* (*US*) = **groundsheet**

ground control *n* control *m* desde tierra

ground floor *n* (*Brit*) planta baja

grounding ['graundıŋ] *n* (*in education*)
conocimientos *mpl* básicos

groundkeeper ['graundki:pər] *n*:
groundsman

groundless ['graundlıs] *adj* infundado, sin
fundamento

groundnut ['graundnʌt] *n* cacahuete *m*

ground rent *n* alquiler *m* del terreno

ground rules *npl* normas básicas

groundsheet ['graundʃi:t] (*Brit*) *n* tela
impermeable

groundsman ['graundzmən],
groundskeeper (*US*) ['graundzki:pər] *n*
(*Sport*) encargado de pista de deportes

ground staff *n* personal *m* de tierra

ground swell *n* mar *m or f* de fondo; (*fig*) ola

ground-to-air ['grauntə'ɛə] *adj* tierra-aire

ground-to-ground ['grauntə'graund] *adj*
tierra-tierra

groundwork ['graundwə:k] *n* trabajo
preliminar

Ground Zero *n* zona cero

group [gru:p] *n* grupo; (*Mus: pop group*)
conjunto, grupo; (*vb: also*: **group together**)
■ *vt* agrupar ■ *vi* agruparse

groupie ['gru:pı] *n* groupie *f*

group therapy *n* terapia de grupo

grouse [graus] *n* (*pl inv: bird*) urogallo
■ *vi* (*complain*) quejarse

grove [grəuv] *n* arboleda

grovel ['grɔvl] *vi* (*fig*) arrastrarse

grow (*pt* **grew**, *pp* **grown**) [grəu, gru:, grəun]
vi crecer; (*increase*) aumentar; (*expand*)
desarrollarse; (*become*) volverse ■ *vt*
cultivar; (*hair, beard*) dejar crecer; **to ~ rich/
weak** enriquecerse/debilitarse; **to ~ tired of
waiting** cansarse de esperar
  ▶ **grow apart** *vi* (*fig*) alejarse uno del otro
  ▶ **grow away from** *vt fus* (*fig*) alejarse de
  ▶ **grow on** *vt fus*: **that painting is growing
on me** ese cuadro me gusta cada vez más
  ▶ **grow out of** *vt fus* (*clothes*): **I've grown out
of this shirt** esta camisa se me ha quedado
pequeña; (*habit*) perder
  ▶ **grow up** *vi* crecer, hacerse hombre/mujer

grower ['grəuər] *n* (*Agr*) cultivador(a) *m(f)*,
productor(a) *m(f)*

growing ['grəuıŋ] *adj* creciente; **~ pains** (*also
fig*) problemas *mpl* de crecimiento

growl [graul] *vi* gruñir

grown [grəun] *pp of* **grow**

grown-up [grəun'ʌp] *n* adulto(-a), mayor *m/f*

growth [grəuθ] *n* crecimiento, desarrollo;
(*what has grown*) brote *m*; (*Med*) tumor *m*

growth rate *n* tasa de crecimiento

grub [grʌb] *n* gusano; (*col: food*) comida

grubby ['grʌbı] *adj* sucio, mugriento,
mugroso (*LAm*)

grudge [grʌdʒ] *n* rencor ■ *vt*: **to ~ sb sth**
dar algo a algn de mala gana; **to bear sb a ~**
guardar rencor a algn; **he grudges (giving)
the money** da el dinero de mala gana

grudgingly ['grʌdʒıŋlı] *adv* de mala gana

gruelling, grueling (*US*) ['gruəlıŋ] *adj*
agotador

gruesome ['gru:səm] *adj* horrible

gruff [grʌf] *adj* (*voice*) ronco; (*manner*) brusco

grumble ['grʌmbl] *vi* refunfuñar, quejarse

grumpy ['grʌmpı] *adj* gruñón(-ona)

grunge [grʌndʒ] *n* (*Mus: fashion*) grunge *m*

grunt [grʌnt] *vi* gruñir ■ *n* gruñido

G-string ['dʒi:strıŋ] *n* tanga *m*

GSUSA *n abbr* = **Girl Scouts of the United
States of America**

GT *abbr* (*Aut*: = *gran turismo*) GT

GU *abbr* (*US Post*) = **Guam**

guarantee [gærən'ti:] *n* garantía ■ *vt*
garantizar; **he can't ~ (that) he'll come** no
está seguro de poder venir

guarantor [gærən'tɔ:r] *n* garante *m/f*,
fiador(a) *m(f)*

guard [gɑ:d] *n* guardia; (*person*) guarda

m/f; (Brit Rail) jefe m de tren; (safety device: on machine) cubierta de protección; (protection) protección f; (fireguard) pantalla; (mudguard) guardabarros m inv ■ vt guardar; **to ~ (against** or **from)** proteger (de); **to be on one's ~** (fig) estar en guardia

▸ **guard against** vi: **to ~ against doing sth** guardarse de hacer algo

guard dog n perro guardián

guarded ['gɑːdɪd] adj (fig) cauteloso

guardian ['gɑːdɪən] n guardián(-ana) m(f); (of minor) tutor(a) m(f)

guardrail ['gɑːdreɪl] n pretil m

guard's van n (Brit Rail) furgón m del jefe de tren

Guatemala [gwɑːtəˈmɑːlə] n Guatemala

Guatemalan [gwɑːtəˈmɑːlən] adj, n guatemalteco(-a) m(f)

Guernsey ['gɜːnzɪ] n Guernsey m

guerrilla [gəˈrɪlə] n guerrillero(-a)

guerrilla warfare n guerra de guerrillas

guess [gɛs] vi, vt (gen) adivinar; (suppose) suponer ■ n suposición f, conjetura; **I ~ you're right** (esp US) supongo que tienes razón; **to keep sb guessing** mantener a algn a la expectativa; **to take** or **have a ~** tratar de adivinar; **my ~ is that ...** yo creo que ...

guesstimate ['gɛstɪmɪt] n cálculo aproximado

guesswork ['gɛswɜːk] n conjeturas fpl; **I got the answer by ~** acerté a ojo de buen cubero

guest [gɛst] n invitado(-a); (in hotel) huésped(a) m(f); **be my ~** (col) estás en tu casa

guest-house ['gɛsthaʊs] n casa de huéspedes, pensión f

guest room n cuarto de huéspedes

guff [gʌf] n (col) bobadas fpl

guffaw [gʌˈfɔː] n carcajada ■ vi reírse a carcajadas

guidance ['gaɪdəns] n (gen) dirección f; (advice) consejos mpl; **marriage/vocational ~** orientación f matrimonial/profesional

guide [gaɪd] n (person) guía m/f; (book) guía f; (fig) guía f; (also: **girl guide**) exploradora ■ vt guiar; **to be guided by sb/sth** dejarse guiar por algn/algo

guidebook ['gaɪdbʊk] n guía f

guided missile ['gaɪdɪd-] n misil m teledirigido

guide dog n perro guía

guidelines ['gaɪdlaɪnz] npl (fig) directrices fpl

guild [gɪld] n gremio

guildhall ['gɪldhɔːl] n (Brit: town hall) ayuntamiento

guile [gaɪl] n astucia

guileless ['gaɪllɪs] adj cándido

guillotine ['gɪlətiːn] n guillotina

guilt [gɪlt] n culpabilidad f

guilty ['gɪltɪ] adj culpable; **to feel ~ (about)** sentirse culpable (de); **to plead ~/not ~** declararse culpable/inocente

Guinea ['gɪnɪ] n: **Republic of ~** República de Guinea

guinea ['gɪnɪ] n (Brit: old) guinea (21 chelines: en la actualidad ya no se usa esta moneda)

guinea pig n cobaya; (fig) conejillo de Indias

guise [gaɪz] n: **in** or **under the ~ of** bajo la apariencia de

guitar [gɪˈtɑːʳ] n guitarra

guitarist [gɪˈtɑːrɪst] n guitarrista m/f

gulch [gʌltʃ] n (US) barranco

gulf [gʌlf] n golfo; (abyss) abismo; **the G~** el Golfo (Pérsico)

Gulf States npl: **the ~** los países del Golfo

Gulf Stream n: **the ~** la Corriente del Golfo

gull [gʌl] n gaviota

gullet ['gʌlɪt] n esófago

gullibility [gʌlɪˈbɪlɪtɪ] n credulidad f

gullible ['gʌlɪbl] adj crédulo

gully ['gʌlɪ] n barranco

gulp [gʌlp] vi tragar saliva ■ vt (also: **gulp down**) tragarse ■ n (of liquid) trago; (of food) bocado; **in** or **at one ~** de un trago

gum [gʌm] n (Anat) encía; (glue) goma, cemento (LAm); (sweet) gominola; (also: **chewing-gum**) chicle m ■ vt pegar con goma

▸ **gum up** vt: **to ~ up the works** (col) entorpecerlo todo

gumboots ['gʌmbuːts] npl (Brit) botas fpl de goma

gumption ['gʌmpʃən] n (col) iniciativa

gum tree n árbol m gomero

gun [gʌn] n (small) pistola; (shotgun) escopeta; (rifle) fusil m; (cannon) cañón m ■ vt (also: **gun down**) abatir a tiros; **to stick to one's guns** (fig) mantenerse firme or en sus trece

gunboat ['gʌnbəʊt] n cañonero

gun dog n perro de caza

gunfire ['gʌnfaɪəʳ] n disparos mpl

gung-ho [gʌŋˈhəʊ] adj (col) patriotero

gunk [gʌŋk] n (col) masa viscosa

gunman ['gʌnmən] n pistolero

gunner ['gʌnəʳ] n artillero

gunpoint ['gʌnpɔɪnt] n: **at ~** a mano armada

gunpowder ['gʌnpaʊdəʳ] n pólvora

gunrunner ['gʌnrʌnəʳ] n traficante m/f de armas

gunrunning ['gʌnrʌnɪŋ] n tráfico de armas

gunshot ['gʌnʃɒt] n disparo

gunsmith ['gʌnsmɪθ] n armero

583

gurgle ['gə:gl] *vi* gorgotear
guru ['gu:ru:] *n* guru *m*
gush [gʌʃ] *vi* chorrear; (*fig*) deshacerse en efusiones
gushing ['gʌʃɪŋ] *adj* efusivo
gusset ['gʌsɪt] *n* (*in tights, pants*) escudete *m*
gust [gʌst] *n* (*of wind*) ráfaga
gusto ['gʌstəu] *n* entusiasmo
gusty ['gʌstɪ] *adj* racheado
gut [gʌt] *n* intestino; (*Mus etc*) cuerda de tripa ▪ *vt* (*poultry, fish*) destripar; (*building*): **the blaze gutted the entire building** el fuego destruyó el edificio entero
gut reaction *n* reacción *f* instintiva
guts [gʌts] *npl* (*courage*) agallas *fpl*, valor *m*; (*col: innards: of people, animals*) tripas *fpl*; **to hate sb's ~** odiar a algn (a muerte)
gutsy ['gʌtsɪ] *adj*: **to be ~** (*col*) tener agallas
gutted ['gʌtɪd] *adj* (*col: disappointed*): **I was ~** me quedé hecho polvo
gutter ['gʌtə'] *n* (*of roof*) canalón *m*; (*in street*) cuneta; **the ~** (*fig*) el arroyo
gutter press *n* (*col*): **the ~** la prensa sensacionalista *or* amarilla; *see also* **tabloid press**
guttural ['gʌtərl] *adj* gutural
guy [gaɪ] *n* (*also*: **guyrope**) viento, cuerda; (*col: man*) tío (SP), tipo
Guyana [gaɪ'ænə] *n* Guayana
Guy Fawkes' Night [gaɪ'fɔ:ks-] *n*

● **GUY FAWKES' NIGHT**
●
● La noche del cinco de noviembre, *Guy*
● *Fawkes' Night*, se celebra el fracaso de una
● conspiración de la pólvora ("Gunpowder
● Plot"), el intento fallido de volar el
● parlamento de Jaime 1 en 1605. Esa noche
● se lanzan fuegos artificiales y se queman
● en muchas hogueras muñecos de trapo
● que representan a "Guy Fawkes", uno de
● los cabecillas. Días antes los niños tienen
● por costumbre pedir a los viandantes "a
● penny for the guy", dinero para comprar
● los cohetes.

guzzle ['gʌzl] *vi* tragar ▪ *vt* engullir
gym [dʒɪm] *n* (*also*: **gymnasium**) gimnasio; (*also*: **gymnastics**) gimnasia
gymkhana [dʒɪm'kɑ:nə] *n* gincana
gymnast ['dʒɪmnæst] *n* gimnasta *m/f*
gymnastics [dʒɪm'næstɪks] *n* gimnasia
gym shoes *npl* zapatillas *fpl* de gimnasia
gym slip *n* (Brit) pichi *m*
gynaecologist, (US) **gynecologist** [gaɪnɪ'kɔlədʒɪst] *n* ginecólogo(-a)
gynaecology, (US) **gynecology** [gaɪnə'kɔlə dʒɪ] *n* ginecología
gypsy ['dʒɪpsɪ] *n* = **gipsy**
gyrate [dʒaɪ'reɪt] *vi* girar
gyroscope ['dʒaɪrəskəup] *n* giroscopio

Hh

H, h [eɪtʃ] n (letter) H, h f; **H for Harry,**
(US) **H for How** H de Historia
habeas corpus ['heɪbɪəs'kɔːpəs] n (Law)
hábeas corpus m
haberdashery ['hæbə'dæʃərɪ] n (Brit) mercería;
(US: men's clothing) prendas fpl de caballero
habit ['hæbɪt] n hábito, costumbre f; **to get
out of/into the ~ of doing sth** perder la
costumbre de/acostumbrarse a hacer algo
habitable ['hæbɪtəbl] adj habitable
habitat ['hæbɪtæt] n hábitat m
habitation [hæbɪ'teɪʃən] n habitación f
habitual [hə'bɪtjuəl] adj acostumbrado,
habitual; (drinker, liar) empedernido
habitually [hə'bɪtjuəlɪ] adv por costumbre
hack [hæk] vt (cut) cortar, (slice) tajar
■ n corte m; (axe blow) hachazo; (pej. writer)
escritor(a) m(f) a sueldo; (old horse) jamelgo
hacker ['hækəʳ] n (Comput) pirata m informático
hackles ['hæklz] npl: **to make sb's ~ rise** (fig)
poner furioso a algn
hackney cab ['hæknɪ-] n coche m de alquiler
hackneyed ['hæknɪd] adj trillado, gastado
hacksaw ['hæksɔː] n sierra para metales
had [hæd] pt, pp of **have**
haddock (pl ~ or **haddocks**) ['hædək] n especie
de merluza
hadn't ['hædnt] = **had not**
haematology, hematology (US)
['hiːmə'tɔlədʒɪ] n hematología
haemoglobin, hemoglobin (US)
['hiːmə'gləubɪn] n hemoglobina
haemophilia, hemophilia (US) ['hiːmə'fɪlɪə]
n hemofilia
haemorrhage, hemorrhage (US)
['hɛmərɪdʒ] n hemorragia
haemorrhoids, hemorrhoids (US) ['hɛmə-
rɔɪdz] npl hemorroides fpl, almorranas fpl
hag [hæg] n (ugly) vieja fea, tarasca; (nasty)
bruja; (witch) hechicera
haggard ['hægəd] adj ojeroso
haggis ['hægɪs] n (Scottish) asadura de cordero

cocida; see also **Burns' Night**
haggle ['hægl] vi (argue) discutir; (bargain)
regatear
haggling ['hæglɪŋ] n regateo
Hague [heɪg] n: **The ~** La Haya
hail [heɪl] n (weather) granizo ■ vt saludar;
(call) llamar a ■ vi granizar; **to ~ (as)**
aclamar (como), celebrar (como); **he hails
from Scotland** es natural de Escocia
hailstone ['heɪlstəun] n (piedra de) granizo
hailstorm ['heɪlstɔːm] n granizada
hair [hɛəʳ] n (gen) pelo, cabellos mpl; (one hair)
pelo, cabello; (head of hair) pelo, cabellera; (on
legs etc) vello; **to do one's ~** arreglarse el pelo;
grey ~ canas fpl
hairbrush ['hɛəbrʌʃ] n cepillo (para el pelo)
haircut ['hɛəkʌt] n corte m de pelo
hairdo ['hɛəduː] n peinado
hairdresser ['hɛədrɛsəʳ] n peluquero(-a);
~'s peluquería
hair-dryer ['hɛədraɪəʳ] n secador m (de pelo)
-haired [hɛəd] adj suff: **fair/long~** (de pelo)
rubio or (LAm) güero/de pelo largo
hairgrip ['hɛəgrɪp] n horquilla
hairline ['hɛəlaɪn] n nacimiento del pelo
hairline fracture n fractura muy fina
hairnet ['hɛənɛt] n redecilla
hair oil n brillantina
hairpiece ['hɛəpiːs] n trenza postiza
hairpin ['hɛəpɪn] n horquilla
hairpin bend, (US) **hairpin curve** n curva
muy cerrada
hair-raising ['hɛəreɪzɪŋ] adj espeluznante
hair remover n depilatorio
hair's breadth n: **by a ~** por un pelo
hair spray n laca
hairstyle ['hɛəstaɪl] n peinado
hairy ['hɛərɪ] adj peludo, velludo
Haiti ['heɪtɪ] n Haití m
hake [heɪk] n merluza
halcyon ['hælsɪən] adj feliz
hale [heɪl] adj: **~ and hearty** sano y fuerte

half [hɑːf] n (pl **halves**) [hɑːvz] mitad f; (Sport: of match) tiempo, parte f; (: of ground) campo ▪ adj medio ▪ adv medio, a medias; **~-an-hour** media hora; **two and a ~** dos y media; **~ a dozen** media docena; **~ a pound** media libra, ≈ 250 gr.; **to cut sth in ~** cortar algo por la mitad; **to go halves (with sb)** ir a medias (con algn); **halfempty/closed** medio vacío/ entreabierto; **~ asleep** medio dormido; **~ past 3** las 3 y media

half-back ['hɑːfbæk] n (Sport) medio

half-baked ['hɑːfbeɪkt] adj (col: idea, scheme) mal concebido or pensado

half-breed ['hɑːfbriːd] n = **half-caste**

half-brother ['hɑːfbrʌðəʳ] n hermanastro

half-caste ['hɑːfkɑːst] n mestizo(-a)

half-hearted ['hɑːfhɑːtɪd] adj indiferente, poco entusiasta

half-hour [hɑːf'auəʳ] n media hora

half-mast ['hɑːf'mɑːst] n: **at ~** (flag) a media asta

halfpenny ['heɪpnɪ] n medio penique m

half-price ['hɑːf'praɪs] adj a mitad de precio

half term n (Brit Scol) vacaciones de mediados del trimestre

half-time [hɑːf'taɪm] n descanso

halfway ['hɑːf'weɪ] adv a medio camino; **to meet sb ~** (fig) llegar a un acuerdo con algn

halfway house n centro de readaptación de antiguos presos; (fig) solución f intermedia

half-wit ['hɑːfwɪt] n (col) zoquete m

half-yearly [hɑːf'jɪəlɪ] adv semestralmente ▪ adj semestral

halibut ['hælɪbət] n (pl inv) halibut m

halitosis [hælɪ'təusɪs] n halitosis f

hall [hɔːl] n (for concerts) sala; (entrance way) entrada, vestíbulo

hallmark ['hɔːlmɑːk] n (mark) rasgo distintivo; (seal) sello

hallo [hə'ləu] excl = **hello**

hall of residence n (Brit) colegio mayor, residencia universitaria

Hallowe'en [hæləu'iːn] n víspera de Todos los Santos; ver nota

● dé un pequeño regalo (como golosinas o
● dinero).

hallucination [həluːsɪ'neɪʃən] n alucinación f

hallucinogenic [həluːsɪnəu'dʒɛnɪk] adj alucinógeno

hallway ['hɔːlweɪ] n vestíbulo

halo ['heɪləu] n (of saint) aureola

halt [hɔːlt] n (stop) alto, parada; (Rail) apeadero ▪ vt parar ▪ vi pararse; (process) interrumpirse; **to call a ~ (to sth)** (fig) poner fin (a algo)

halter ['hɔːltəʳ] n (for horse) cabestro

halterneck ['hɔːltənɛk] adj de espalda escotada

halve [hɑːv] vt partir por la mitad

halves [hɑːvz] pl of **half**

ham [hæm] n jamón m (cocido); (col: also: **radio ham**) radioaficionado(-a) m(f); (: also: **ham actor**) comicastro

hamburger ['hæmbəːgəʳ] n hamburguesa

ham-fisted ['hæm'fɪstɪd] adj torpe, desmañado

hamlet ['hæmlɪt] n aldea

hammer ['hæməʳ] n martillo ▪ vt (nail) clavar; **to ~ a point home to sb** remacharle un punto a algn
▶ **hammer out** vt (metal) forjar a martillo; (fig: solution, agreement) elaborar (trabajosamente)

hammock ['hæmək] n hamaca

hamper ['hæmpəʳ] vt estorbar ▪ n cesto

hamster ['hæmstəʳ] n hámster m

hand [hænd] n mano f; (of clock) aguja, manecilla; (writing) letra; (worker) obrero; (measurement: of horse) palmo ▪ vt (give) dar, pasar; (deliver) entregar; **to give sb a ~** echar una mano a algn, ayudar a algn; **to force sb's ~** forzarle la mano a algn; **at ~** a mano; **in ~** entre manos; **we have the matter in ~** tenemos el asunto entre manos; **to have in one's ~** (knife, victory) tener en la mano; **to have a free ~** tener carta blanca; **on ~** (person, services) a mano, al alcance; **to ~** (information etc) a mano; **on the one ~ ...**, **on the other ~ ...** por una parte ... por otra (parte) ...
▶ **hand down** vt pasar, bajar; (tradition) transmitir; (heirloom) dejar en herencia; (US: sentence, verdict) imponer
▶ **hand in** vt entregar
▶ **hand out** vt (leaflets, advice) repartir, distribuir
▶ **hand over** vt (deliver) entregar; (surrender) ceder
▶ **hand round** vt (Brit: information, papers) pasar (de mano en mano); (: chocolates etc) ofrecer

handbag ['hændbæg] n bolso, cartera (LAm)

hand baggage n = **hand luggage**
handball ['hændbɔːl] n balonmano
handbasin ['hændbeɪsn] n lavabo
handbook ['hændbuk] n manual m
handbrake ['hændbreɪk] n freno de mano
hand cream n crema para las manos
handcuffs ['hændkʌfs] npl esposas fpl
handful ['hændful] n puñado
hand-held ['hænd'held] adj de mano
handicap ['hændɪkæp] n desventaja; (Sport) hándicap m ■ vt estorbar
handicapped ['hændɪkæpt] adj: **to be mentally** ~ ser deficiente m/f mental; **to be physically** ~ ser minusválido(-a)
handicraft ['hændɪkrɑːft] n artesanía
handiwork ['hændɪwəːk] n manualidad(es) f(pl); (fig) obra; **this looks like his** ~ (pej) es obra de él, parece
handkerchief ['hæŋkətʃɪf] n pañuelo
handle ['hændl] n (of door etc) pomo; (of cup etc) asa; (of knife etc) mango; (for winding) manivela ■ vt (touch) tocar; (deal with) encargarse de; (treat: people) manejar; **"~ with care"** "(manéjese) con cuidado"; **to fly off the** ~ perder los estribos
handlebar ['hændlbɑːʳ] n, **handlebars** ['hændlbɑːz] npl manillar msg
handling ['hændlɪŋ] n (Aut) conducción f; **his** ~ **of the matter** su forma de llevar el asunto
handling charges npl gastos mpl de tramitación
hand luggage n equipaje m de mano
handmade ['hændmeɪd] adj hecho a mano
handout ['hændaut] n (distribution) repartición f; (charity) limosna; (leaflet) folleto, octavilla; (press handout) nota
hand-picked ['hænd'pɪkt] adj (produce) escogido a mano; (staff etc) seleccionado cuidadosamente
handrail ['hændreɪl] n (on staircase etc) pasamanos m inv, barandilla
handset ['hændset] n (Tel) auricular m
handsfree ['hændzfriː] adj (Tel: telephone, kit) manos libres
handshake ['hændʃeɪk] n apretón m de manos; (Comput) coloquio
handsome ['hænsəm] adj guapo
hands-on ['hændz'ɔn] adj práctico; **she has a very** ~ **approach** le gusta tomar parte activa; ~ **experience** (Comput) experiencia práctica
handstand ['hændstænd] n voltereta, salto mortal
hand-to-mouth ['hændtə'mauθ] adj (existence) precario
handwriting ['hændraɪtɪŋ] n letra
handwritten ['hændrɪtn] adj escrito a mano, manuscrito

handy ['hændɪ] adj (close at hand) a mano; (useful: machine, tool etc) práctico; (skilful) hábil, diestro; **to come in** ~ venir bien
handyman ['hændɪmæn] n manitas m inv
hang (pt, pp **hung**) [hæŋ, hʌŋ] vt colgar; (head) bajar; (criminal) (pt, pp **hanged**) ahorcar; **to get the** ~ **of sth** (col) coger el tranquillo a algo
▶ **hang about** vi haraganear
▶ **hang back** vi (hesitate): **to** ~ **back (from doing)** vacilar (en hacer)
▶ **hang on** vi (wait) esperar ■ vt fus (depend on: decision etc) depender de; **to** ~ **on to** (keep) guardar, quedarse con
▶ **hang out** vt (washing) tender, colgar ■ vi (col: live) vivir; (: often be found) moverse; **to** ~ **out of sth** colgar fuera de algo
▶ **hang together** vi (cohere: argument etc) sostenerse
▶ **hang up** vt (coat) colgar ■ vi (Tel) colgar; **to** ~ **up on sb** colgarle a algn
hangar ['hæŋəʳ] n hangar m
hangdog ['hæŋdɔg] adj (guilty: look, expression) avergonzado
hanger ['hæŋəʳ] n percha
hanger-on [hæŋər'ɔn] n parásito
hang glider ['hæŋglaɪdəʳ] n ala delta
hang-gliding ['hæŋglaɪdɪŋ] n vuelo con ala delta
hanging ['hæŋɪŋ] n (execution) ejecución f (en la horca)
hangman ['hæŋmən] n verdugo
hangover ['hæŋəuvəʳ] n (after drinking) resaca
hang-up ['hæŋʌp] n complejo
hanker ['hæŋkəʳ] vi: **to** ~ **after** (miss) echar de menos; (long for) añorar
hankie, hanky ['hæŋkɪ] n abbr = **handkerchief**
Hansard ['hænsɑːd] n actas oficiales de las sesiones del parlamento británico
Hants abbr (Brit) = **Hampshire**
haphazard [hæp'hæzəd] adj fortuito
hapless ['hæplɪs] adj desventurado
happen ['hæpən] vi suceder, ocurrir; (take place) tener lugar, realizarse; **as it happens** da la casualidad de que; **what's happening?** ¿qué pasa?
▶ **happen (up)on** vt fus tropezar or dar con
happening ['hæpnɪŋ] n suceso, acontecimiento
happily ['hæpɪlɪ] adv (luckily) afortunadamente; (cheerfully) alegremente
happiness ['hæpɪnɪs] n (contentment) felicidad f; (joy) alegría
happy ['hæpɪ] adj feliz; (cheerful) alegre; **to be** ~ **(with)** estar contento (con); **yes, I'd be** ~ **to** sí, con mucho gusto; **H~ Christmas!** ¡Feliz

h

Navidad!; **H~ New Year!** ¡Feliz Año Nuevo!;
~ birthday! ¡felicidades!, ¡feliz cumpleaños!
happy-go-lucky ['hæpɪɡəʊ'lʌkɪ] *adj*
despreocupado
happy hour *n* *horas en las que la bebida es más*
barata en un bar
harangue [hə'ræŋ] *vt* arengar
harass ['hærəs] *vt* acosar, hostigar
harassed ['hærəst] *adj* agobiado, presionado
harassment ['hærəsmənt] *n* persecución *f*,
acoso; (*worry*) preocupación *f*
harbour, harbor (US) ['hɑːbə*ʳ*] *n* puerto ■ *vt*
(*hope etc*) abrigar; (*hide*) dar abrigo a; (*retain:*
grudge etc) guardar
harbour dues, harbor dues (US) *npl*
derechos *mpl* portuarios
hard [hɑːd] *adj* duro; (*difficult*) difícil; (*person*)
severo ■ *adv* (*work*) mucho, duro; (*think*)
profundamente; **to look ~ at sb/sth** clavar
los ojos en algn/algo; **to try ~** esforzarse;
no ~ feelings! ¡sin rencor(es)!; **to be ~ of**
hearing ser duro de oído; **to be ~ done by**
ser tratado injustamente; **to be ~ on sb** ser
muy duro con algn; **I find it ~ to believe**
that ... me cuesta trabajo creer que ...
hard-and-fast ['hɑːdən'fɑːst] *adj* rígido,
definitivo
hardback ['hɑːdbæk] *n* libro de tapas duras
hard cash *n* dinero en efectivo
hard copy *n* (*Comput*) copia impresa
hard-core ['hɑːd'kɔː*ʳ*] *adj* (*pornography*) duro;
(*supporters*) incondicional
hard court *n* (*Tennis*) pista *or* cancha (de tenis)
de cemento
hard disk *n* (*Comput*) disco duro
harden ['hɑːdn] *vt* endurecer; (*steel*) templar;
(*fig*) curtir; (: *determination*) fortalecer ■ *vi*
(*substance*) endurecerse
hardened ['hɑːdnd] *adj* (*criminal*) habitual;
to be ~ to sth estar acostumbrado a algo
hard-headed ['hɑːd'hɛdɪd] *adj* poco
sentimental, realista
hard-hearted ['hɑːd'hɑːtɪd] *adj* insensible
hard-hitting ['hɑːd'hɪtɪŋ] *adj* (*speech, article*)
contundente
hard labour *n* trabajos *mpl* forzados
hardliner [hɑːd'laɪnə*ʳ*] *n* partidario(-a) de la
línea dura
hard-luck story ['hɑːdlʌk-] *n* dramón *m*
hardly ['hɑːdlɪ] *adv* (*scarcely*) apenas; **that can**
~ be true eso difícilmente puede ser cierto;
~ ever casi nunca; **I can ~ believe it** apenas
me lo puedo creer
hardness ['hɑːdnɪs] *n* dureza
hard-nosed ['hɑːd'nəʊzd] *adj* duro, sin
contemplaciones
hard-pressed ['hɑːd'prɛst] *adj* en apuros

hard sell *n* publicidad *f* agresiva; ~
techniques técnicas *fpl* agresivas de venta
hardship ['hɑːdʃɪp] *n* (*troubles*) penas *fpl*;
(*financial*) apuro
hard shoulder *n* (*Aut*) arcén *m*
hard-up [hɑːd'ʌp] *adj* (*col*) sin un duro (SP),
sin plata (LA*m*)
hardware ['hɑːdwɛə*ʳ*] *n* ferretería; (*Comput*)
hardware *m*
hardware shop *n* ferretería
hard-wearing [hɑːd'wɛərɪŋ] *adj* resistente,
duradero; (*shoes*) resistente
hard-won ['hɑːd'wʌn] *adj* ganado con
esfuerzo
hard-working [hɑːd'wəːkɪŋ] *adj*
trabajador(a)
hardy ['hɑːdɪ] *adj* fuerte; (*plant*) resistente
hare [hɛə*ʳ*] *n* liebre *f*
hare-brained ['hɛəbreɪnd] *adj* atolondrado
harelip ['hɛəlɪp] *n* labio leporino
harem [hɑː'riːm] *n* harén *m*
haricot ['hærɪkəʊ], **haricot bean** *n* alubia
hark back [hɑːk-] *vi*: **to ~ to** (*former days, earlier*
occasion) recordar
harm [hɑːm] *n* daño, mal *m* ■ *vt* (*person*)
hacer daño a; (*health, interests*) perjudicar;
(*thing*) dañar; **out of ~'s way** a salvo; **there's**
no ~ in trying no se pierde nada con
intentar
harmful ['hɑːmful] *adj* (*gen*) dañino;
(*reputation*) perjudicial
harmless ['hɑːmlɪs] *adj* (*person*) inofensivo;
(*drug*) inocuo
harmonica [hɑː'mɔnɪkə] *n* armónica
harmonious [hɑː'məʊnɪəs] *adj* armonioso
harmonize ['hɑːmənaɪz] *vt, vi* armonizar
harmony ['hɑːmənɪ] *n* armonía
harness ['hɑːnɪs] *n* arreos *mpl* ■ *vt* (*horse*)
enjaezar; (*resources*) aprovechar
harp [hɑːp] *n* arpa ■ *vi*: **to ~ on (about)**
machacar (con)
harpoon [hɑː'puːn] *n* arpón *m*
harrow ['hærəʊ] *n* grada ■ *vt* gradar
harrowing ['hærəʊɪŋ] *adj* angustioso
harry ['hærɪ] *vt* (*Mil*) acosar; (*person*) hostigar
harsh [hɑːʃ] *adj* (*cruel*) duro, cruel; (*severe*)
severo; (*words*) hosco; (*colour*) chillón(-ona);
(*contrast*) violento
harshly ['hɑːʃlɪ] *adv* (*say*) con aspereza; (*treat*)
con mucha dureza
harshness ['hɑːʃnɪs] *n* dureza
harvest ['hɑːvɪst] *n* cosecha; (*of grapes*)
vendimia ■ *vt, vi* cosechar
harvester ['hɑːvɪstə*ʳ*] *n* (*machine*)
cosechadora; (*person*) segador(a) *m(f)*;
combine ~ segadora trilladora
has [hæz] *vb see* **have**

has-been ['hæzbi:n] n (col: person) persona acabada; (: thing) vieja gloria

hash [hæʃ] n (Culin) picadillo; (fig: mess) lío

hashish ['hæʃɪʃ] n hachís m

hasn't ['hæznt] = **has not**

hassle ['hæsl] n (col) lío, rollo ▪ vt incordiar

haste [heɪst] n prisa

hasten ['heɪsn] vt acelerar ▪ vi darse prisa; **I ~ to add that ...** me apresuro a añadir que ...

hastily ['heɪstɪlɪ] adv de prisa

hasty ['heɪstɪ] adj apresurado

hat [hæt] n sombrero

hatbox ['hætbɒks] n sombrerera

hatch [hætʃ] n (Naut: also: **hatchway**) escotilla ▪ vi salir del cascarón ▪ vt incubar; (fig: scheme, plot) idear, tramar

hatchback ['hætʃbæk] n (Aut) tres or cinco puertas m

hatchet ['hætʃɪt] n hacha

hatchet job n (col) varapalo

hatchet man n (col) ejecutor de faenas desagradables por cuenta de otro

hate [heɪt] vt odiar, aborrecer ▪ n odio; **I ~ to trouble you, but ...** siento or lamento molestarle, pero ...

hateful ['heɪtful] adj odioso

hater ['heɪtə^r] n: **cop-hater** persona que siente aversión a la policía; **woman-hater** misógino

hatred ['heɪtrɪd] n odio

hat trick n: **to score a ~** (Brit Sport) marcar tres tantos (or triunfos) seguidos

haughty ['hɔːtɪ] adj altanero, arrogante

haul [hɔːl] vt tirar, jalar (LAm) ▪ n (of fish) redada; (of stolen goods etc) botín m

haulage ['hɔːlɪdʒ] n (Brit) transporte m; (costs) gastos mpl de transporte

haulage contractor n (firm) empresa de transportes; (person) transportista m/f

haulier ['hɔːlɪə^r], **hauler** (US) ['hɔːlə^r] n transportista m/f

haunch [hɔːntʃ] n anca; (of meat) pierna

haunt [hɔːnt] vt (ghost) aparecer en; (frequent) frecuentar; (obsess) obsesionar ▪ n guarida

haunted ['hɔːntɪd] adj (castle etc) embrujado; (look) de angustia

haunting ['hɔːntɪŋ] adj (sight, music) evocativo

Havana [hə'vɑːnə] n La Habana

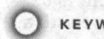 KEYWORD

have [hæv] (pt, pp **had**) aux vb **1** (gen) haber; **to have arrived/eaten** haber llegado/comido; **having finished** or **when he had finished, he left** cuando hubo acabado, se fue

2 (in tag questions): **you've done it, haven't you?** lo has hecho, ¿verdad? or ¿no?

3 (in short answers and questions): **I haven't** no;

so I have pues, es verdad; **we haven't paid — yes we have!** no hemos pagado — ¡sí que hemos pagado!; **I've been there before, have you?** he estado allí antes, ¿y tú?

▪ modal aux vb (be obliged): **to have (got) to do sth** tener que hacer algo; **you haven't to tell her** no hay que or no debes decírselo

▪ vt **1** (possess) tener; **he has (got) blue eyes/dark hair** tiene los ojos azules/el pelo negro

2 (referring to meals etc): **to have breakfast/lunch/dinner** desayunar/comer/cenar; **to have a drink/a cigarette** tomar algo/fumar un cigarrillo

3 (receive) recibir; (obtain) obtener; **may I have your address?** ¿puedes darme tu dirección?; **you can have it for £5** te lo puedes quedar por £5; **I must have it by tomorrow** lo necesito para mañana; **to have a baby** tener un niño or bebé

4 (maintain, allow): **I won't have it!** ¡no lo permitiré!; **I won't have this nonsense!** ¡no permitiré estas tonterías!; **we can't have that** no podemos permitir eso

5: to have sth done hacer or mandar hacer algo; **to have one's hair cut** cortarse el pelo; **to have sb do sth** hacer que algn haga algo

6 (experience, suffer): **to have a cold/flu** tener un resfriado/la gripe; **she had her bag stolen/her arm broken** le robaron el bolso/se rompió un brazo; **to have an operation** operarse

7 (+ noun): **to have a swim/walk/bath/rest** nadar/dar un paseo/darse un baño/descansar; **let's have a look** vamos a ver; **to have a meeting/party** celebrar una reunión/una fiesta; **let me have a try** déjame intentarlo

▶ **have in** vt: **to have it in for sb** (col) tenerla tomada con algn

▶ **have on** vt: **have you anything on tomorrow?** ¿vas a hacer algo mañana?; **I don't have any money on me** no llevo dinero (encima); **to have sb on** (Brit col) tomarle el pelo a algn

▶ **have out** vt: **to have it out with sb** (settle a problem etc) dejar las cosas en claro con algn

haven ['heɪvn] n puerto; (fig) refugio

haven't ['hævnt] = **have not**

haversack ['hævəsæk] n macuto

haves [hævz] npl: **the ~ and the have-nots** los ricos y los pobres

havoc ['hævək] n estragos mpl; **to play ~ with sth** hacer estragos en algo

Hawaii [hə'waɪiː] n (Islas fpl) Hawai m

Hawaiian [hə'waɪjən] adj, n hawaiano(-a) m(f)

hawk [hɔːk] n halcón m ■ vt (goods for sale) pregonar
hawkish ['hɔːkɪʃ] adj beligerante
hawthorn ['hɔːθɔːn] n espino
hay [heɪ] n heno
hay fever n fiebre f del heno
haystack ['heɪstæk] n almiar m
haywire ['heɪwaɪəʳ] adj (col): **to go ~** (person) volverse loco; (plan) irse al garete
hazard ['hæzəd] n riesgo; (danger) peligro ■ vt (remark) aventurar; (one's life) arriesgar; **to be a health ~** ser un peligro para la salud; **to ~ a guess** aventurar una respuesta or hipótesis
hazardous ['hæzədəs] adj (dangerous) peligroso; (risky) arriesgado
hazard warning lights npl (Aut) señales fpl de emergencia
haze [heɪz] n neblina
hazel ['heɪzl] n (tree) avellano ■ adj (eyes) color m de avellano
hazelnut ['heɪzlnʌt] n avellana
hazy ['heɪzɪ] adj brumoso; (idea) vago
H-bomb ['eɪtʃbɒm] n bomba H
h & c abbr (Brit) = **hot and cold (water)**
HD abbr (= **high definition**) HD m
HDTV abbr (= **high definition television**) HDTV f
HE abbr = **high explosive**; (Rel, Diplomacy: = His (or Her) Excellency) S. Exc\ª
he [hiː] pron él; **he who ...** aquél que ..., quien ...
head [hɛd] n cabeza; (leader) jefe(-a) m(f) ■ vt (list) encabezar; (group) capitanear; **heads (or tails)** cara (o cruz); **~ first** de cabeza; **~ over heels** patas arriba; **~ over heels in love** perdidamente enamorado; **it was above** or **over their heads** no alcanzaron a entenderlo; **to come to a ~** (fig: situation etc) llegar a un punto crítico; **to have a ~ for business** tener talento para los negocios;
to have no ~ for heights no resistir las alturas; **to lose/keep one's ~** perder la cabeza/mantener la calma; **to sit at the ~ of the table** sentarse a la cabecera de la mesa; **to ~ the ball** cabecear (el balón)
▸ **head for** vt fus dirigirse a
▸ **head off** vt (threat, danger) evitar
headache ['hɛdeɪk] n dolor m de cabeza; **to have a ~** tener dolor de cabeza
headband ['hɛdbænd] n cinta (para la cabeza), vincha (LAm)
headboard ['hɛdbɔːd] n cabecera
headdress ['hɛddrɛs] n (of bride, Indian) tocado
headed notepaper ['hɛdɪd-] n papel m con membrete
header ['hɛdəʳ] n (Brit col: Football) cabezazo; (: fall) caída de cabeza

headfirst [hɛd'fəːst] adv de cabeza
headhunt ['hɛdhʌnt] vt: **to be headhunted** ser seleccionado por un cazatalentos
headhunter ['hɛdhʌntəʳ] n (fig) cazaejecutivos m inv
heading ['hɛdɪŋ] n título
headlamp ['hɛdlæmp] n (Brit) = **headlight**
headland ['hɛdlənd] n promontorio
headlight ['hɛdlaɪt] n faro
headline ['hɛdlaɪn] n titular m
headlong ['hɛdlɒŋ] adv (fall) de cabeza; (rush) precipitadamente
headmaster/mistress [hɛd'mɑːstəʳ/mɪstrɪs] n director(a) m(f) (de escuela)
head office n oficina central, central f
head-on [hɛd'ɒn] adj (collision) de frente
headphones ['hɛdfəʊnz] npl auriculares mpl
headquarters ['hɛdkwɔːtəz] npl sede f central; (Mil) cuartel m general
head-rest ['hɛdrɛst] n reposa-cabezas m inv
headroom ['hɛdrum] n (in car) altura interior; (under bridge) (límite m de) altura
headscarf ['hɛdskɑːf] n pañuelo
headset ['hɛdsɛt] n cascos mpl
headstone ['hɛdstəʊn] n lápida
headstrong ['hɛdstrɒŋ] adj testarudo
head waiter n maître m
headway ['hɛdweɪ] n: **to make ~** (fig) hacer progresos
headwind ['hɛdwɪnd] n viento contrario
heady ['hɛdɪ] adj (experience, period) apasionante; (wine) fuerte
heal [hiːl] vt curar ■ vi cicatrizar
health [hɛlθ] n salud f
health care n asistencia sanitaria
health centre n ambulatorio, centro médico
health food n, **health foods** npl alimentos mpl orgánicos
health hazard n riesgo para la salud
Health Service n (Brit) servicio de salud pública, ≈ Insalud m (SP)
healthy ['hɛlθɪ] adj (gen) sano; (economy, bank balance) saludable
heap [hiːp] n montón m ■ vt amontonar; (plate) colmar; **heaps (of)** (col: lots) montones (de); **to ~ favours/praise/gifts** etc **on sb** colmar a algn de favores/elogios/regalos etc
hear (pt, pp **heard**) [hɪəʳ, həːd] vt oír; (perceive) sentir; (listen to) escuchar; (lecture) asistir a; (Law: case) ver ■ vi oír; **to ~ about** oír hablar de; **to ~ from sb** tener noticias de algn; **I've never heard of that book** nunca he oído hablar de ese libro
▸ **hear out** vt: **to ~ sb out** dejar que algn termine de hablar
hearing ['hɪərɪŋ] n (sense) oído; (Law) vista; **to give sb a ~** dar a algn la oportunidad de

hablar, escuchar a algn
hearing aid n audífono
hearsay ['hɪəseɪ] n rumores mpl, habladurías fpl
hearse [hɜːs] n coche m fúnebre
heart [hɑːt] n corazón m; **hearts** npl (Cards)
corazones mpl; **at ~** en el fondo; **by ~** (learn,
know) de memoria; **to have a weak ~** tener
el corazón débil; **to set one's ~ on sth/on
doing sth** anhelar algo/hacer algo; **I did
not have the ~ to tell her** no tuve valor para
decírselo; **to take ~** cobrar ánimos; **the ~
of the matter** lo esencial or el meollo del
asunto
heartache ['hɑːteɪk] n angustia
heart attack n infarto (de miocardio)
heartbeat ['hɑːtbiːt] n latido (del corazón)
heartbreak ['hɑːtbreɪk] n angustia, congoja
heartbreaking ['hɑːtbreɪkɪŋ] adj
desgarrador(a)
heartbroken ['hɑːtbrəukən] adj: **she was ~
about it** le partió el corazón
heartburn ['hɑːtbəːn] n acedía
-hearted ['hɑːtɪd] adj suff: **a kind~ person**
una persona bondadosa
heartening ['hɑːtnɪŋ] adj alentador(a)
heart failure n (Med) paro cardíaco
heartfelt ['hɑːtfelt] adj (cordial) cordial;
(deeply felt) sincero
hearth [hɑːθ] n (gen) hogar m; (fireplace)
chimenea
heartily ['hɑːtɪlɪ] adv sinceramente,
cordialmente; (laugh) a carcajadas; (eat)
con buen apetito; **to be ~ sick of** estar
completamente harto de
heartland ['hɑːtlænd] n zona interior or
central; (fig) corazón m
heartless ['hɑːtlɪs] adj despiadado
heartstrings ['hɑːtstrɪŋz] npl: **to tug (at)
sb's ~** tocar la fibra sensible de algn
heart-throb ['hɑːtθrɔb] n ídolo
heart-to-heart ['hɑːttə'hɑːt] n (also: **heart-
to-heart talk**) conversación f íntima
heart transplant n transplante m de corazón
hearty ['hɑːtɪ] adj cordial
heat [hiːt] n (gen) calor m; (Sport: also:
qualifying heat) prueba eliminatoria; (Zool):
in or **on ~** en celo ■ vt calentar
▶ **heat up** vi (gen) calentarse
heated ['hiːtɪd] adj caliente; (fig) acalorado
heater ['hiːtəʳ] n calentador m
heath [hiːθ] n (Brit) brezal m
heathen ['hiːðn] adj, n pagano(-a) m(f)
heather ['hɛðəʳ] n brezo
heating ['hiːtɪŋ] n calefacción f
heat-resistant ['hiːtrɪzɪstənt] adj refractario
heat-seeking ['hiːtsiːkɪŋ] adj guiado por
infrarrojos, termoguiado

heatstroke ['hiːtstrəuk] n insolación f
heatwave ['hiːtweɪv] n ola de calor
heave [hiːv] vt (pull) tirar; (push) empujar con
esfuerzo; (lift) levantar (con esfuerzo) ■ vi
(water) subir y bajar ■ n tirón m; empujón m;
(effort) esfuerzo; (throw) echada; **to ~ a sigh**
dar or echar un suspiro, suspirar
▶ **heave to** vi (Naut) ponerse al pairo
heaven ['hɛvn] n cielo; (Rel) paraíso; **thank
~!** ¡gracias a Dios!; **for ~'s sake!** (pleading)
¡por el amor de Dios!, ¡por lo que más quiera!;
(protesting) ¡por Dios!
heavenly ['hɛvnlɪ] adj celestial; (Rel) divino
heavenly body n cuerpo celeste
heavily ['hɛvɪlɪ] adv pesadamente; (drink,
smoke) en exceso; (sleep, sigh) profundamente
heavy ['hɛvɪ] adj pesado; (work) duro;
(sea, rain, meal) fuerte; (drinker, smoker)
empedernido; (eater) comilón(-ona)
heavy-duty ['hɛvɪ'djuːtɪ] adj resistente
heavy goods vehicle n (Brit) vehículo pesado
heavy-handed ['hɛvɪ'hændɪd] adj (clumsy,
tactless) torpe
heavy industry n industria pesada
heavy metal n (Mus) heavy m (metal)
heavy-set [hɛvɪ'sɛt] adj (esp US) corpulento,
fornido
heavy user n consumidor m intensivo
heavyweight ['hɛvɪweɪt] n (Sport) peso pesado
Hebrew ['hiːbruː] adj, n (Ling) hebreo
Hebrides ['hɛbrɪdiːz] npl: **the ~** las Hébridas
heck [hɛk] n (col): **why the ~ ...?** ¿por qué
porras ...?; **a ~ of a lot of** cantidad de
heckle ['hɛkl] vt interrumpir
heckler ['hɛkləʳ] n el/la que interrumpe a un orador
hectare ['hɛktɑːʳ] n (Brit) hectárea
hectic ['hɛktɪk] adj agitado; (busy) ocupado
hector ['hɛktəʳ] vt intimidar con bravatas
he'd [hiːd] = **he would; he had**
hedge [hɛdʒ] n seto ■ vt cercar (con un
seto) ■ vi contestar con evasivas; **as a ~
against inflation** como protección contra la
inflación; **to ~ one's bets** (fig) cubrirse
hedgehog ['hɛdʒhɔg] n erizo
hedgerow ['hɛdʒrəu] n seto vivo
hedonism ['hiːdənɪzəm] n hedonismo
heed [hiːd] vt (also: **take heed of**: pay attention)
hacer caso de; (bear in mind) tener en cuenta;
to pay (no) ~ to, take (no) ~ of (no) hacer
caso a, (no) tener en cuenta
heedless ['hiːdlɪs] adj desatento
heel [hiːl] n talón m ■ vt (shoe) poner tacón
a; **to take to one's heels** (col) poner pies en
polvorosa; **to bring to ~** meter en cintura;
see also **dig**
hefty ['hɛftɪ] adj (person) fornido; (piece)
grande; (price) alto

heifer ['hɛfə'] n novilla, ternera
height [haɪt] n (of person) talla f; (of building)
altura; (high ground) cerro; (altitude) altitud f;
what ~ are you? ¿cuánto mides?; **of average
~** de estatura mediana; **to be afraid of
heights** tener miedo a las alturas; **it's the ~
of fashion** es el último grito en moda
heighten ['haɪtn] vt elevar; (fig) aumentar
heinous ['heɪnəs] adj atroz, nefasto
heir [ɛə'] n heredero
heir apparent n presunto heredero
heiress ['ɛərɛs] n heredera
heirloom ['ɛəluːm] n reliquia de familia
heist [haɪst] n (col: hold-up) atraco a mano
armada
held [hɛld] pt, pp of **hold**
helicopter ['hɛlɪkɔptə'] n helicóptero
heliport ['hɛlɪpɔːt] n (Aviat) helipuerto
helium ['hiːlɪəm] n helio
hell [hɛl] n infierno; **oh ~!** (col) ¡demonios!,
¡caramba!
he'll [hiːl] = **he will; he shall**
hellbent [hɛl'bɛnt] adj (col): **he was ~ on
going** se le metió entre ceja y ceja ir
hellish ['hɛlɪʃ] adj infernal; (col) horrible
hello [hə'ləu] excl ¡hola!; (surprise) ¡caramba!;
(Tel) ¡dígame! (esp SP), ¡aló! (LAm)
helm [hɛlm] n (Naut) timón m
helmet ['hɛlmɪt] n casco
helmsman ['hɛlmzmən] n timonel m
help [hɛlp] n ayuda; (charwoman) criada,
asistenta ▪ vt ayudar; **~!** ¡socorro!; **with the
~ of** con la ayuda de; **can I ~ you?** (in shop)
¿qué desea?; **to be of ~ to sb** servir a algn;
to ~ sb (to) do sth echarle una mano or
ayudar a algn a hacer algo; **~ yourself**
sírvete; **he can't ~ it** no lo puede evitar
helper ['hɛlpə'] n ayudante m/f
helpful ['hɛlpful] adj útil; (person) servicial
helping ['hɛlpɪŋ] n ración f
helping hand n: **to give sb a ~** echar una
mano a algn
helpless ['hɛlplɪs] adj (incapable) incapaz;
(defenceless) indefenso
helpline ['hɛlplaɪn] n teléfono de asistencia
al público
Helsinki ['hɛlsɪŋkɪ] n Helsinki m
helter-skelter ['hɛltə'skɛltə'] n (in funfair)
tobogán m
hem [hɛm] n dobladillo ▪ vt poner or coser el
dobladillo a
▸ **hem in** vt cercar; **to feel hemmed in** (fig)
sentirse acosado
he-man ['hiːmæn] n macho
hematology [hiːmə'tɔlədʒɪ] n (US)
= **haematology**
hemisphere ['hɛmɪsfɪə'] n hemisferio

hemline ['hɛmlaɪn] n bajo (del vestido)
hemlock ['hɛmlɔk] n cicuta
hemoglobin [hiːmə'gləubɪn] n (US)
= **haemoglobin**
hemophilia [hiːmə'fɪlɪə] n (US)
= **haemophilia**
hemorrhage ['hɛmərɪdʒ] n (US)
= **haemorrhage**
hemorrhoids ['hɛmərɔɪdz] npl (US)
= **haemorrhoids**
hemp [hɛmp] n cáñamo
hen [hɛn] n gallina; (female bird) hembra
hence [hɛns] adv (therefore) por lo tanto;
two years ~ de aquí a dos años
henceforth [hɛns'fɔːθ] adv de hoy en
adelante
henchman ['hɛntʃmən] n (pej) secuaz m
henna ['hɛnə] n alheña
hen night n (col) despedida de soltera
hen party n (col) reunión f de mujeres
henpecked ['hɛnpɛkt] adj: **to be ~** ser un
calzonazos
hepatitis [hɛpə'taɪtɪs] n hepatitis f inv
her [həː'] pron (direct) la; (indirect) le; (stressed,
after prep) ella ▪ adj su; see also **me; my**
herald ['hɛrəld] n (forerunner) precursor(a) m(f)
▪ vt anunciar
heraldic [hɛ'rældɪk] adj heráldico
heraldry ['hɛrəldrɪ] n heráldica
herb [həːb] n hierba
herbaceous [həː'beɪʃəs] adj herbáceo
herbal ['həːbl] adj de hierbas
herbicide ['həːbɪsaɪd] n herbicida m
herd [həːd] n rebaño; (of wild animals, swine)
piara ▪ vt (drive, gather: animals) llevar en
manada; (: people) reunir
▸ **herd together** vt agrupar, reunir ▪ vi
apiñarse, agruparse
here [hɪə'] adv aquí; **~!** (present) ¡presente!;
~ is/are aquí está/están; **~ she is** aquí está;
come ~! ¡ven aquí or acá!; **~ and there** aquí
y allá
hereabouts ['hɪərə'bauts] adv por aquí
(cerca)
hereafter [hɪər'aːftə'] adv en el futuro
▪ n: **the ~** el más allá
hereby [hɪə'baɪ] adv (in letter) por la presente
hereditary [hɪ'rɛdɪtrɪ] adj hereditario
heredity [hɪ'rɛdɪtɪ] n herencia
heresy ['hɛrəsɪ] n herejía
heretic ['hɛrətɪk] n hereje m/f
heretical [hɪ'rɛtɪkəl] adj herético
herewith [hɪə'wɪð] adv: **I send you ~ ...**
le mando adjunto ...
heritage ['hɛrɪtɪdʒ] n (gen) herencia; (fig)
patrimonio; **our national ~** nuestro
patrimonio nacional

hermetically [hə'mɛtɪkəlɪ] adv: ~ **sealed**
herméticamente cerrado
hermit ['hə:mɪt] n ermitaño(-a)
hernia ['hə:nɪə] n hernia
hero (pl **heroes**) ['hɪərəu] n héroe m; (in book,
film) protagonista m
heroic [hɪ'rəuɪk] adj heroico
heroin ['hɛrəuɪn] n heroína
heroin addict n heroinómano(-a), adicto(-a)
a la heroína
heroine ['hɛrəuɪn] n heroína; (in book, film)
protagonista
heroism ['hɛrəuɪzm] n heroísmo
heron ['hɛrən] n garza
hero worship n veneración f
herring ['hɛrɪŋ] n arenque m
hers [hə:z] pron (el) suyo/(la) suya etc;
a friend of ~ un amigo suyo; **this is** ~ esto es
suyo or de ella; see also **mine**
herself [hə:'sɛlf] pron (reflexive) se; (emphatic) ella
misma; (after prep) sí (misma); see also **oneself**
Herts abbr (Brit) = **Hertfordshire**
he's [hi:z] = **he is; he has**
hesitant ['hɛzɪtənt] adj indeciso; **to be** ~
about doing sth no decidirse a hacer algo
hesitate ['hɛzɪteɪt] vi dudar, vacilar; **don't** ~
to ask (me) no dudes en pedírmelo
hesitation [hɛzɪ'teɪʃən] n indecisión f; **I have
no** ~ **in saying (that)** ... no tengo el menor
reparo en afirmar que ...
hesslan ['hɛsɪən] n arpillera
heterogeneous ['hɛtərə'dʒi:nɪəs] adj
heterogéneo
heterosexual [hɛtərəu'sɛksjuəl] adj, n
heterosexual m/f
het up [hɛt'ʌp] adj (col) agitado, nervioso
HEW n abbr (US: = Department of Health,
Education, and Welfare) ministerio de sanidad,
educación y bienestar público
hew [hju:] vt cortar
hex [hɛks] (US) n maleficio, mal m de ojo
■ vt embrujar
hexagon ['hɛksəgən] n hexágono
hexagonal [hɛk'sægənl] adj hexagonal
hey [heɪ] excl ¡oye!, ¡oiga!
heyday ['heɪdeɪ] n: **the** ~ **of** el apogeo de
HF n abbr = **high frequency**
HGV n abbr = **heavy goods vehicle**
HI abbr (US) = **Hawaii**
hi [haɪ] excl ¡hola!
hiatus [haɪ'eɪtəs] n vacío, interrupción f;
(Ling) hiato
hibernate ['haɪbəneɪt] vi invernar
hibernation [haɪbə'neɪʃən] n hibernación f
hiccough, hiccup ['hɪkʌp] vi hipar;
hiccoughs npl hipo sg
hick [hɪk] n (US col) paleto(-a)

hid [hɪd] pt of **hide**
hidden ['hɪdn] pp of **hide** ■ adj: **there are no**
~ **extras** no hay suplementos ocultos;
~ **agenda** plan m encubierto
hide [haɪd] (pt **hid**, pp **hidden**) n (skin) piel
f ■ vt esconder, ocultar; (feelings, truth)
encubrir, ocultar ■ vi: **to** ~ **(from sb)**
esconderse or ocultarse (de algn)
hide-and-seek ['haɪdən'si:k] n escondite m
hideaway ['haɪdəweɪ] n escondite m
hideous ['hɪdɪəs] adj horrible
hideously ['hɪdɪəslɪ] adv horriblemente
hide-out ['haɪdaut] n escondite m, refugio
hiding ['haɪdɪŋ] n (beating) paliza; **to be in** ~
(concealed) estar escondido
hiding place n escondrijo
hierarchy ['haɪərɑ:kɪ] n jerarquía
hieroglyphic [haɪərə'glɪfɪk] adj jeroglífico
■ n: **hieroglyphics** jeroglíficos mpl
hi-fi ['haɪfaɪ] abbr (= high fidelity) n estéreo,
hifi m ■ adj de alta fidelidad
higgledy-piggledy ['hɪgldɪ'pɪgldɪ] adv en
desorden, de cualquier modo
high [haɪ] adj alto; (speed, number) grande,
alto, (price) elevado, (wind) fuerte, (voice)
agudo; (col: on drugs) colocado; (: on drink)
borracho; (Culin: meat, game) pasado;
(: spoilt) estropeado ■ adv alto, a gran
altura ■ n: **exports have reached a new**
~ las exportaciones han alcanzado niveles
inusitados; **it is 20 m** ~ tiene 20 m de altura;
~ **in the air** en las alturas; **to pay a** ~ **price
for sth** pagar algo muy caro
highball ['haɪbɔ:l] n (US: drink) whisky m soda,
highball m (LAm), jaibol m (LAm)
highboy ['haɪbɔɪ] n (US) cómoda alta
highbrow ['haɪbrau] adj culto
highchair ['haɪtʃɛəʳ] n silla alta (para niños)
high-class ['haɪ'klɑ:s] adj (neighbourhood) de alta
sociedad; (hotel) de lujo; (person) distinguido, de
categoría; (food) de alta categoría
High Court n (Law) tribunal m supremo; ver
nota

● **HIGH COURT**

● En el sistema legal de Inglaterra y Gales
● High Court es la forma abreviada de "High
● Court of Justice", tribunal superior que
● junto con el de apelación ("Court of
● Appeal") forma el Tribunal Supremo
● ("Supreme Court of Judicature"). En
● el sistema legal escocés es la forma
● abreviada de "High Court of Justiciary",
● tribunal con jurado que juzga los delitos
● más serios, que pueden dar lugar a una
● pena de gran severidad.

higher ['haɪəʳ] *adj (form of life, study etc)*
superior ■ *adv* más alto ■ *n (Scottish Scol)*:
H~ *cada una de las asignaturas que se estudian
entre los 16 y los 17 años generalmente, así como el
certificado de haberlas probado*
higher education *n* educación *f or*
enseñanza superior
high explosive *n* explosivo de gran potencia
highfalutin [haɪfəˈluːtɪn] *adj (col)* de altos
vuelos, encopetado
high finance *n* altas finanzas *fpl*
high-flier, high-flyer [haɪˈflaɪəʳ] *n*
ambicioso(-a)
high-handed [haɪˈhændɪd] *adj* despótico
high-heeled [haɪˈhiːld] *adj* de tacón alto
highjack ['haɪdʒæk] = **hijack**
high jump *n (Sport)* salto de altura
highlands ['haɪləndz] *npl* tierras *fpl* altas;
the H~ *(in Scotland)* las Tierras Altas de Escocia
high-level ['haɪlɛvl] *adj (talks etc)* de alto nivel
highlight ['haɪlaɪt] *n (fig: of event)* punto
culminante ■ *vt* subrayar
highly ['haɪlɪ] *adv* sumamente; **~ paid** muy
bien pagado; **to speak ~ of** hablar muy bien
de; **~ strung** muy excitable
High Mass *n* misa mayor
highness ['haɪnɪs] *n* altura; **Her** *or* **His H~**
Su Alteza
high-pitched [haɪˈpɪtʃt] *adj* agudo
high point *n*: **the ~** el punto culminante
high-powered ['haɪˈpauəd] *adj (engine)* de
gran potencia; *(fig: person)* importante
high-pressure ['haɪprɛʃəʳ] *adj* de alta
presión; *(fig: salesman etc)* enérgico
high-rise ['haɪraɪz] *n (also:* **high-rise block,
high-rise building)** torre *f* de pisos
high school *n* centro de enseñanza
secundaria, ≈ Instituto Nacional de
Bachillerato (SP), liceo (LAm); *ver nota*

● **HIGH SCHOOL**
●
● El término *high school* se aplica en
● Estados Unidos a dos tipos de centros
● de educación secundaria: "Junior
● High Schools", en los que se imparten
● normalmente del 7° al 9° curso (llamado
● "grade") y "Senior High Schools", que
● abarcan los cursos 10°, 11° y 12° y en
● ocasiones el 9°. Aquí pueden estudiarse
● asignaturas tanto de contenido
● académico como profesional. En
● Gran Bretaña también se llaman *high
● school* algunos centros de enseñanza
● secundaria.

high season *n (Brit)* temporada alta

high-speed ['haɪspiːd] *adj* de alta velocidad
high-spirited [haɪˈspɪrɪtɪd] *adj* animado
high spirits *npl* ánimos *mpl*
high street *n (Brit)* calle *f* mayor
high tide *n* marea alta
highway ['haɪweɪ] *n* carretera; *(US)*
autopista
Highway Code *n (Brit)* código de la
circulación
highwayman ['haɪweɪmən] *n* salteador *m*
de caminos
hijack ['haɪdʒæk] *vt* secuestrar ■ *n (also:*
hijacking) secuestro
hijacker ['haɪdʒækəʳ] *n* secuestrador(a) *m(f)*
hike [haɪk] *vi (go walking)* ir de excursión (a
pie); *(tramp)* caminar ■ *n* caminata; *(col: in
prices etc)* aumento
▶ **hike up** *vt (raise)* aumentar
hiker ['haɪkəʳ] *n* excursionista *m/f*
hilarious [hɪˈlɛərɪəs] *adj* divertidísimo
hilarity [hɪˈlærɪtɪ] *n (laughter)* risas *fpl*,
carcajadas *fpl*
hill [hɪl] *n* colina; *(high)* montaña; *(slope)* cuesta
hillbilly ['hɪlbɪlɪ] *n (US)* rústico(-a)
montañés(-esa); *(pej)* palurdo(-a)
hillock ['hɪlək] *n* montecillo, altozano
hillside ['hɪlsaɪd] *n* ladera
hilltop ['hɪltɔp] *n* cumbre *f*
hilly ['hɪlɪ] *adj* montañoso; *(uneven)*
accidentado
hilt [hɪlt] *n (of sword)* empuñadura; **to the
~** *(fig: support)* incondicionalmente; **to be
in debt up to the ~** estar hasta el cuello de
deudas
him [hɪm] *pron (direct)* le, lo; *(indirect)* le;
(stressed, after prep) él; *see also* **me**
Himalayas [hɪməˈleɪəz] *npl*: **the ~** el
Himalaya
himself [hɪmˈsɛlf] *pron (reflexive)* se; *(emphatic)*
él mismo; *(after prep)* sí (mismo); *see also*
oneself
hind [haɪnd] *adj* posterior ■ *n* cierva
hinder ['hɪndəʳ] *vt* estorbar, impedir
hindquarters ['haɪndkwɔːtəz] *npl (Zool)*
cuartos *mpl* traseros
hindrance ['hɪndrəns] *n* estorbo, obstáculo
hindsight ['haɪndsaɪt] *n* percepción *f* tardía
or retrospectiva; **with the benefit of ~** con la
perspectiva del tiempo transcurrido
Hindu ['hɪnduː] *n* hindú *m/f*
hinge [hɪndʒ] *n* bisagra, gozne *m* ■ *vi (fig)*:
to ~ on depender de
hint [hɪnt] *n* indirecta; *(advice)* consejo ■ *vt*:
to ~ that insinuar que ■ *vi*: **to ~ at** aludir a;
to drop a ~ soltar *or* tirar una indirecta; **give
me a ~** dame una pista
hip [hɪp] *n* cadera; *(Bot)* escaramujo

hip flask *n* petaca
hip-hop ['hɪphɔp] *n* hip hop *m*
hippie ['hɪpɪ] *n* hippie *m/f*, jipi *m/f*
hip pocket *n* bolsillo de atrás
hippopotamus (*pl* **hippopotamuses** *or*
  hippopotami) *n* [hɪpə'pɔtəməs, -'pɔtəmaɪ]
  hipopótamo
hippy ['hɪpɪ] *n* = **hippie**
hire ['haɪəʳ] *vt* (*Brit: car, equipment*) alquilar;
  (*worker*) contratar ■ *n* alquiler *m*; **for** ~ se
  alquila; (*taxi*) libre; **on** ~ de alquiler
  ▶ **hire out** *vt* alquilar, arrendar
hire car, hired car *n* (*Brit*) coche *m* de alquiler
hire purchase *n* (*Brit*) compra a plazos;
  to buy sth on ~ comprar algo a plazos
his [hɪz] *pron* (el) suyo/(la) suya *etc* ■ *adj* su;
  this is ~ esto es suyo *or* de él; *see also* **my**; **mine**
Hispanic [hɪs'pænɪk] *adj* hispánico
hiss [hɪs] *vi* sisear; (*in protest*) silbar ■ *n* siseo;
  silbido
histogram ['hɪstəgræm] *n* histograma *m*
historian [hɪ'stɔːrɪən] *n* historiador(a) *m(f)*
historic [hɪ'stɔrɪk], **historical** [hɪ'stɔrɪkl] *adj*
  histórico
history ['hɪstərɪ] *n* historia; **there's a**
  long ~ **of that illness in his family** esa
  enfermedad corre en su familia
histrionics [hɪstrɪ'ɔnɪks] *npl* histrionismo
hit [hɪt] *vt* (*pt, pp* **hit**) (*strike*) golpear, pegar;
  (*reach: target*) alcanzar; (*collide with: car*) chocar
  contra; (*fig: affect*) afectar ■ *n* golpe *m*;
  (*success*) éxito; **to** ~ **the headlines** salir en
  primera plana; **to** ~ **the road** (*col*) largarse;
  to ~ **it off with sb** llevarse bien con algn
  ▶ **hit back** *vi* defenderse; (*fig*) devolver golpe
  por golpe
  ▶ **hit out at** *vt fus* asestar un golpe a; (*fig*)
  atacar
  ▶ **hit (up)on** *vt fus* (*answer*) dar con; (*solution*)
  hallar, encontrar
hit and miss *adj*: **it's very** ~, **it's a** ~ **affair** es
  cuestión de suerte
hit-and-run driver ['hɪtən'rʌn-] *n conductor*
  que tras atropellar a algn se da a la fuga
hitch [hɪtʃ] *vt* (*fasten*) atar, amarrar; (*also:*
  hitch up) arremangarse ■ *n* (*difficulty*)
  problema, pega; **to** ~ **a lift** hacer autostop;
  technical ~ problema *m* técnico
  ▶ **hitch up** *vt* (*horse, cart*) enganchar, uncir
hitch-hike ['hɪtʃhaɪk] *vi* hacer autostop
hitch-hiker ['hɪtʃhaɪkəʳ] *n* autostopista *m/f*
hi-tech [haɪ'tɛk] *adj* de alta tecnología
hitherto ['hɪðə'tuː] *adv* hasta ahora, hasta aquí
hit list *n* lista negra
hitman ['hɪtmæn] *n* asesino a sueldo
hit or miss ['hɪtə'mɪs] *adj* = **hit and miss**
hit parade *n*: **the** ~ los cuarenta principales

HIV *n abbr* (= *human immunodeficiency virus*) VIH
  m; ~-**negative** no portador(a) del virus del
  sida, no seropositivo; ~-**positive** portador(a)
  del virus del sida, seropositivo
hive [haɪv] *n* colmena; **the shop was a** ~
  of activity (*fig*) la tienda era una colmena
  humana
  ▶ **hive off** *vt* (*col: separate*) separar; (*: privatize*)
  privatizar
hl *abbr* (= *hectolitre*) hl
HM *abbr* (= *His (or Her) Majesty*) S.M.
HMG *abbr* (*Brit*) = **His (or Her) Majesty's**
  Government
HMI *n abbr* (*Brit Scol*) = **His (or Her) Majesty's**
  Inspector
HMO *n abbr* (*US*: = *Health Maintenance*
  Organization) seguro médico global
HMS *abbr* = **His (or Her) Majesty's Ship**
HMSO *n abbr* (*Brit*: = *His (or Her) Majesty's*
  Stationery Office) distribuidor oficial de las
  publicaciones del gobierno del Reino Unido
HNC *n abbr* (*Brit*: = *Higher National Certificate*)
  título académico
HND *n abbr* (*Brit*: = *Higher National Diploma*) título
  académico
hoard [hɔːd] *n* (*treasure*) tesoro; (*stockpile*)
  provisión *f* ■ *vt* acumular
hoarding ['hɔːdɪŋ] *n* (*for posters*) valla
  publicitaria
hoarfrost ['hɔːfrɔst] *n* escarcha
hoarse [hɔːs] *adj* ronco
hoax [həuks] *n* engaño
hob [hɔb] *n* quemador *m*
hobble ['hɔbl] *vi* cojear
hobby ['hɔbɪ] *n* pasatiempo, afición *f*
hobby-horse ['hɔbɪhɔːs] *n* (*fig*) tema
  preferido
hobnob ['hɔbnɔb] *vi*: **to** ~ **(with)** alternar
  (con)
hobo ['həubəu] *n* (*US*) vagabundo
hock [hɔk] *n* corvejón *m*; (*col*): **to be in**
  ~ (*person*) estar empeñado *or* endeudado;
  (*object*) estar empeñado
hockey ['hɔkɪ] *n* hockey *m*
hocus-pocus [həukəs'pəukəs] *n* (*trickery*)
  engañifa; (*words: of magician*) abracadabra *m*
hod [hɔd] *n* capacho
hodge-podge ['hɔdʒpɔdʒ] *n* (*US*)
  = **hotchpotch**
hoe [həu] *n* azadón *m* ■ *vt* azadonar
hog [hɔg] *n* cerdo, puerco ■ *vt* (*fig*) acaparar;
  to go the whole ~ echar el todo por el todo
Hogmanay [hɔgmə'neɪ] *n* (*Scottish*)
  Nochevieja
hoist [hɔɪst] *n* (*crane*) grúa ■ *vt* levantar, alzar
hoity-toity [hɔɪtɪ'tɔɪtɪ] *adj* (*col*): **to be** ~ darse
  humos

595

hold [həuld] (pt, pp **held**) vt tener; (contain) contener; (keep back) retener; (believe) sostener; (take hold of) coger (SP), agarrar (LAm); (bear: weight) soportar; (meeting) celebrar ■ vi (withstand: pressure) resistir; (be valid) ser válido; (stick) pegarse ■ n (grasp) asimiento; (fig) dominio; (Wrestling) presa; (Naut) bodega; ~ **the line!** (Tel) ¡no cuelgue!; **to ~ one's own** (fig) defenderse; **to ~ office** (Pol) ocupar un cargo; **to ~ firm** or **fast** mantenerse firme; **he holds the view that ...** opina or es su opinión que ...; **to ~ sb responsible for sth** culpar or echarle la culpa a algn de algo; **where can I get ~ of ...?** ¿dónde puedo encontrar (a) ...?; **to catch** or **get (a) ~ of** agarrarse or asirse de
▶ **hold back** vt retener; (secret) ocultar; **to ~ sb back from doing sth** impedir a algn hacer algo, impedir que algn haga algo
▶ **hold down** vt (person) sujetar; (job) mantener
▶ **hold forth** vi perorar
▶ **hold off** vt (enemy) rechazar ■ vi: **if the rain holds off** si no llueve
▶ **hold on** vi agarrarse bien; (wait) esperar
▶ **hold on to** vt fus agarrarse a; (keep) guardar
▶ **hold out** vt ofrecer ■ vi (resist) resistir; **to ~ out (against)** resistir (a), sobrevivir
▶ **hold over** vt (meeting etc) aplazar
▶ **hold up** vt (raise) levantar; (support) apoyar; (delay) retrasar; (: traffic) demorar; (rob: bank) asaltar, atracar
holdall ['həuldɔːl] n (Brit) bolsa
holder ['həuldər] n (of ticket, record) poseedor(a) m(f); (of passport, post, office, title etc) titular m/f
holding ['həuldɪŋ] n (share) participación f
holding company n holding m
holdup ['həuldʌp] n (robbery) atraco; (delay) retraso; (Brit: in traffic) embotellamiento
hole [həul] n agujero ■ vt agujerear; **~ in the heart** (Med) boquete m en el corazón; **to pick holes in** (fig) encontrar defectos en; **the ship was holed** se abrió una vía de agua en el barco
▶ **hole up** vi esconderse
holiday ['hɔlədɪ] n vacaciones fpl; (day off) (día m de) fiesta, día m festivo or feriado (LAm); **on ~** de vacaciones; **to be on ~** estar de vacaciones
holiday camp n colonia or centro vacacional; (for children) colonia veraniega infantil
holiday home n residencia vacacional
holiday job n (Brit) trabajo para las vacaciones
holidaymaker ['hɔlədɪmeɪkər] n (Brit) turista m/f
holiday pay n paga de las vacaciones

holiday resort n centro turístico
holiday season n temporada de vacaciones
holiness ['həulɪnɪs] n santidad f
holistic [həu'lɪstɪk] adj holístico
Holland ['hɔlənd] n Holanda
holler ['hɔlər] vi (col) gritar, vocear
hollow ['hɔləu] adj hueco; (fig) vacío; (eyes) hundido; (sound) sordo ■ n (gen) hueco; (in ground) hoyo ■ vt: **to ~ out** ahuecar
holly ['hɔlɪ] n acebo
hollyhock ['hɔlɪhɔk] n malva loca
Hollywood ['hɔlɪwud] Hollywood m
holocaust ['hɔləkɔːst] n holocausto
hologram ['hɔləgræm] n holograma m
holster ['həulstər] n pistolera
holy ['həulɪ] adj (gen) santo, sagrado; (water) bendito; **the H~ Father** el Santo Padre
Holy Communion n Sagrada Comunión f
Holy Ghost, Holy Spirit n Espíritu m Santo
homage ['hɔmɪdʒ] n homenaje m; **to pay ~ to** rendir homenaje a
home [həum] n casa; (country) patria; (institution) asilo; (Comput) punto inicial or de partida ■ adj (domestic) casero, de casa; (Econ, Pol) nacional; (Sport: team) de casa; (: match, win) en casa ■ adv (direction) a casa; **at ~** en casa; **to go/come ~** ir/volver a casa; **make yourself at ~** ¡estás en tu casa!; **it's near my ~** está cerca de mi casa
▶ **home in on** vt fus (missile) dirigirse hacia
home address n domicilio
home-brew [həum'bruː] n cerveza etc casera
homecoming ['həumkʌmɪŋ] n regreso (al hogar)
home computer n ordenador m doméstico
Home Counties npl condados que rodean Londres
home economics n economía doméstica
home ground n: **to be on ~** estar en su etc terreno
home-grown ['həumgrəun] adj de cosecha propia
home help n (Brit) trabajador(a) m(f) del servicio de atención domiciliaria
homeland ['həumlænd] n tierra natal
homeless ['həumlɪs] adj sin hogar, sin casa ■ npl: **the ~** las personas sin hogar
home loan n préstamo para la vivienda
homely ['həumlɪ] adj (domestic) casero; (simple) sencillo
home-made [həum'meɪd] adj hecho en casa
Home Office n (Brit) Ministerio del Interior
homeopathy etc [həumɪ'ɔpəθɪ] (US) = **homoeopathy** etc
home page n (Comput) página de inicio
home rule n autonomía
Home Secretary n (Brit) Ministro del Interior

homesick ['həumsɪk] *adj*: **to be ~** tener
morriña *or* nostalgia
homestead ['həumstɛd] *n* hacienda
home town *n* ciudad *f* natal
home truth *n*: **to tell sb a few home truths**
decir cuatro verdades a algn
homeward ['həumwəd] *adj* (*journey*) de vuelta
■ *adv* hacia casa
homewards ['həumwədz] *adv* hacia casa
homework ['həumwɔːk] *n* deberes *mpl*
homicidal [hɒmɪˈsaɪdl] *adj* homicida
homicide ['hɒmɪsaɪd] *n* (*US*) homicidio
homily ['hɒmɪlɪ] *n* homilía
homing ['həumɪŋ] *adj* (*device, missile*)
buscador(a); **~ pigeon** paloma mensajera
homoeopath, homeopath (*US*)
['həumɪəupæθ] *n* homeópata *m/f*
homoeopathic, homeopathic (*US*)
[həumɪəuˈpæθɪk] *adj* homeopático
homoeopathy, homeopathy (*US*)
[həumɪˈɒpəθɪ] *n* homeopatía
homogeneous [hɒməˈdʒiːnɪəs] *adj*
homogéneo
homogenize [həˈmɒdʒənaɪz] *vt*
homogeneizar
homosexual [hɒməuˈsɛksjuəl] *adj, n*
homosexual *m/f*
Hon *abbr* (= *honourable, honorary*) *en títulos*
Honduras [hɒnˈdjuərəs] *n* Honduras *fpl*
hone [həun] *vt* (*sharpen*) afilar; (*fig*)
perfeccionar
honest ['ɒnɪst] *adj* honrado; (*sincere*) franco,
sincero; **to be quite ~ with you ...** para serte
franco ...
honestly ['ɒnɪstlɪ] *adv* honradamente;
francamente, de verdad
honesty ['ɒnɪstɪ] *n* honradez *f*
honey ['hʌnɪ] *n* miel *f*; (*US col*) cariño;
(: *to strangers*) guapo, linda
honeycomb ['hʌnɪkəum] *n* panal *m*; (*fig*)
laberinto
honeymoon ['hʌnɪmuːn] *n* luna de miel
honeysuckle ['hʌnɪsʌkl] *n* madreselva
Hong Kong ['hɒŋ'kɒŋ] *n* Hong-Kong *m*
honk [hɒŋk] *vi* (*Aut*) tocar la bocina
Honolulu [hɒnəˈluːluː] *n* Honolulú *m*
honorary ['ɒnərərɪ] *adj* no remunerado;
(*duty, title*) honorario
honour, honor (*US*) ['ɒnəʳ] *vt* honrar ■ *n*
honor *m*, honra; **in ~ of** en honor de; **it's a**
great ~ es un gran honor
honourable, honorable (*US*) ['ɒnərəbl] *adj*
honrado, honorable
honour-bound, honor-bound (*US*)
['ɒnə'baund] *adj* moralmente obligado
honours degree *n* (*Univ*) *licenciatura superior*;
ver nota

honours list *n* (*Brit*) *lista de distinciones*
honoríficas que entrega la reina; *ver nota*

Hons. [ɒnz] *abbr* (*Univ*) = **hono(u)rs degree**
hood [hud] *n* capucha; (*Brit Aut*) capota;
(*US Aut*) capó *m*; (*US col*) matón *m*
hooded ['hudɪd] *adj* (*robber*) encapuchado
hoodie ['hudɪ] *n* (*pullover*) sudadera *f* con
capucha; (*young person*) capuchero(-a) *m(f)*
hoodlum ['huːdləm] *n* matón *m*
hoodwink ['hudwɪŋk] *vt* (*Brit*) timar,
engañar
hoof (*pl* **hoofs** *or* **hooves**) [huːf, huːvz] *n*
pezuña
hook [huk] *n* gancho; (*on dress*) corchete
m, broche *m*; (*for fishing*) anzuelo ■ *vt*
enganchar; **hooks and eyes** corchetes *mpl*,
macho y hembra *m*; **by ~ or by crook** por las
buenas o por las malas, cueste lo que cueste;
to be hooked on (*col*) estar enganchado a
▶ **hook up** *vt* (*Radio, TV*) transmitir en cadena
hooligan ['huːlɪgən] *n* gamberro
hooliganism ['huːlɪgənɪzəm] *n* gamberrismo
hoop [huːp] *n* aro
hoot [huːt] *vi* (*Brit Aut*) tocar la bocina; (*siren*)
sonar; (*owl*) ulular ■ *n* bocinazo, toque *m* de
sirena; **to ~ with laughter** morirse de risa

hooter ['huːtə^r] n (Brit Aut) bocina; (of ship, factory) sirena
hoover® ['huːvə^r] (Brit) n aspiradora ∎ vt pasar la aspiradora por
hooves [huːvz] pl of **hoof**
hop [hɔp] vi saltar, brincar; (on one foot) saltar con un pie ∎ n salto, brinco; see also **hops**
hope [həup] vt, vi esperar ∎ n esperanza; **I ~ so/not** espero que sí/no
hopeful ['həupful] adj (person) optimista; (situation) prometedor(a); **I'm ~ that she'll manage to come** confío en que podrá venir
hopefully ['həupfulɪ] adv con optimismo, con esperanza
hopeless ['həuplɪs] adj desesperado
hopelessly ['həuplɪslɪ] adv (live etc) sin esperanzas; **I'm ~ confused/lost** estoy totalmente despistado/perdido
hopper ['hɔpə^r] n (chute) tolva
hops [hɔps] npl lúpulo sg
horde [hɔːd] n horda
horizon [hə'raɪzn] n horizonte m
horizontal [hɔrɪ'zɔntl] adj horizontal
hormone ['hɔːməun] n hormona
hormone replacement therapy n terapia hormonal sustitutiva
horn [hɔːn] n cuerno, cacho (LAm); (Mus: also: **French horn**) trompa; (Aut) bocina, claxon m
horned [hɔːnd] adj con cuernos
hornet ['hɔːnɪt] n avispón m
horny ['hɔːnɪ] adj (material) córneo; (hands) calloso; (US col) cachondo
horoscope ['hɔrəskəup] n horóscopo
horrendous [hə'rendəs] adj horrendo
horrible ['hɔrɪbl] adj horrible
horribly ['hɔrɪblɪ] adv horriblemente
horrid ['hɔrɪd] adj horrible, horroroso
horridly ['hɔrɪdlɪ] adv (behave) tremendamente mal
horrific [hɔ'rɪfɪk] adj (accident) horroroso; (film) horripilante
horrify ['hɔrɪfaɪ] vt horrorizar
horrifying ['hɔrɪfaɪɪŋ] adj horroroso
horror ['hɔrə^r] n horror m
horror film n película de terror or miedo
horror-struck ['hɔrəstrʌk], **horror-stricken** ['hɔrəstrɪkn] adj horrorizado
hors d'œuvre [ɔː'dəːvrə] n entremeses mpl
horse [hɔːs] n caballo
horseback ['hɔːsbæk] n: **on ~** a caballo
horsebox ['hɔːsbɔks] n remolque m para transportar caballos
horse chestnut n (tree) castaño de Indias
horsedrawn ['hɔːsdrɔːn] adj de tracción animal
horsefly ['hɔːsflaɪ] n tábano
horseman ['hɔːsmən] n jinete m

horsemanship ['hɔːsmənʃɪp] n equitación f, manejo del caballo
horseplay ['hɔːspleɪ] n pelea amistosa
horsepower ['hɔːspauə^r] n caballo (de fuerza), potencia en caballos
horse-racing ['hɔːsreɪsɪŋ] n carreras fpl de caballos
horseradish ['hɔːsrædɪʃ] n rábano picante
horseshoe ['hɔːsʃuː] n herradura
horse show n concurso hípico
horse-trader ['hɔːstreɪdə^r] n chalán(-ana) m(f)
horse trials npl = **horse show**
horsewhip ['hɔːswɪp] vt azotar
horsewoman ['hɔːswumən] n amazona
horsey ['hɔːsɪ] adj (col: person) aficionado a los caballos
horticulture ['hɔːtɪkʌltʃə^r] n horticultura
hose [həuz] n (also: **hosepipe**) manguera
▸ **hose down** vt limpiar con manguera
hosiery ['həuzɪərɪ] n calcetería
hospice ['hɔspɪs] n hospicio
hospitable ['hɔspɪtəbl] adj hospitalario
hospital ['hɔspɪtl] n hospital m
hospitality [hɔspɪ'tælɪtɪ] n hospitalidad f
hospitalize ['hɔspɪtəlaɪz] vt hospitalizar
host [həust] n anfitrión m; (TV, Radio) presentador(a) m(f); (of inn etc) mesonero; (Rel) hostia; (large number): **a ~ of** multitud de
hostage ['hɔstɪdʒ] n rehén m
hostel ['hɔstl] n hostal m; (for students, nurses etc) residencia; (also: **youth hostel**) albergue m juvenil; (for homeless people) hospicio
hostelling ['hɔstlɪŋ] n: **to go (youth) ~** hospedarse en albergues
hostess ['həustɪs] n anfitriona; (Brit: air hostess) azafata; (in night-club) señorita de compañía
hostile ['hɔstaɪl] adj hostil
hostility [hɔ'stɪlɪtɪ] n hostilidad f
hot [hɔt] adj caliente; (weather) caluroso, de calor; (as opposed to only warm) muy caliente; (spicy) picante; (fig) ardiente, acalorado; **to be ~** (person) tener calor; (object) estar caliente; (weather) hacer calor
▸ **hot up** vi (col: situation) ponerse difícil or apurado; (: party) animarse ∎ vt (col: pace) apretar; (: engine) aumentar la potencia de
hot air n (col) palabras fpl huecas
hot-air balloon [hɔt'ɛə-] n (Aviat) globo aerostático or de aire caliente
hotbed ['hɔtbed] n (fig) semillero
hot-blooded [hɔt'blʌdɪd] adj impetuoso
hotchpotch ['hɔtʃpɔtʃ] n mezcolanza, baturrillo
hot dog n perrito caliente
hotel [həu'tel] n hotel m

hotelier [həu'tɛlɪəʳ] n hotelero
hotel industry n industria hotelera
hotel room n habitación f de hotel
hot flush n (Brit) sofoco
hotfoot ['hɔtfut] adv a toda prisa
hothead ['hɔthɛd] n (fig) exaltado(-a)
hotheaded [hɔt'hɛdɪd] adj exaltado
hothouse ['hɔthaus] n invernadero
hot line n (Pol) teléfono rojo, línea directa
hotly ['hɔtlɪ] adv con pasión, apasionadamente
hotplate ['hɔtpleɪt] n (on cooker) hornillo
hotpot ['hɔtpɔt] n (Brit Culin) estofado
hot potato n (Brit col) asunto espinoso;
   to drop sth/sb like a ~ no querer saber ya nada de algo/algn
hot seat n primera fila
hotspot ['hɔt'spɔt] n (Comput: also: **wireless hotspot**) punto de acceso inalámbrico
hot spot n (trouble spot) punto caliente; (night club etc) lugar m popular
hot spring n terma, fuente f de aguas termales
hot-tempered ['hɔt'tɛmpəd] adj de mal genio or carácter
hot-water bottle [hɔt'wɔːtə] n bolsa de agua caliente
hot-wire ['hɔtwaɪəʳ] vt (col: car) hacer el puente en
hound [haund] vt acosar ■ n perro de caza
hour ['auəʳ] n hora, **at 30 miles an ~** a 30 millas por hora; **lunch ~** la hora del almuerzo or de comer; **to pay sb by the ~** pagar a algn por horas
hourly ['auəlɪ] adj (de) cada hora; (rate) por hora ■ adv cada hora
house n [haus] (pl **houses** ['hauzɪz]) casa; (Pol) cámara; (Theat) sala ■ vt [hauz] (person) alojar; **at/to my ~** en/a mi casa; **the H~ (of Commons/Lords)** (Brit) la Cámara de los Comunes/Lores; **the H~ (of Representatives)** (US) la Cámara de Representantes; **it's on the ~** (fig) la casa invita
house arrest n arresto domiciliario
houseboat ['hausbəut] n casa flotante
housebound ['hausbaund] adj confinado en casa
housebreaking ['hausbreɪkɪŋ] n allanamiento de morada
house-broken ['hausbrəukən] adj (US) = **house-trained**
housecoat ['hauskəut] n bata
household ['haushəuld] n familia
householder ['haushəuldəʳ] n propietario(-a); (head of house) cabeza de familia
househunting ['haushʌntɪŋ] n: **to go ~** ir en busca de vivienda

housekeeper ['hauskiːpəʳ] n ama de llaves
housekeeping ['hauskiːpɪŋ] n (work) trabajos mpl domésticos; (Comput) gestión f interna; (also: **housekeeping money**) dinero para gastos domésticos
houseman ['hausmən] n (Brit Med) médico residente
house-owner ['hausəunəʳ] n propietario(-a) de una vivienda
house plant n planta de interior
house-proud ['hauspraud] adj preocupado por el embellecimiento de la casa
house-to-house ['haustə'haus] adj; (search) casa por casa; (collection) de casa en casa
house-train ['haustreɪn] vt (pet) enseñar (a hacer sus necesidades en el sitio apropiado)
house-trained ['haustreɪnd] adj (Brit: animal) enseñado
house-warming ['hauswɔːmɪŋ] n (also: **house-warming party**) fiesta de estreno de una casa
housewife ['hauswaɪf] n ama de casa
housework ['hauswəːk] n faenas fpl (de la casa)
housing ['hauzɪŋ] n (act) alojamiento; (houses) viviendas fpl ■ cpd (problem, shortage) de (la) vivienda
housing association n asociación f de la vivienda
housing benefit n (Brit) subsidio por alojamiento
housing conditions npl condiciones fpl de habitabilidad
housing development, (Brit) housing estate n urbanización f
hovel ['hɔvl] n casucha
hover ['hɔvəʳ] vi flotar (en el aire); (helicopter) cernerse; **to ~ on the brink of disaster** estar al borde mismo del desastre
hovercraft ['hɔvəkrɑːft] n aerodeslizador m, hovercraft m
hoverport ['hɔvəpɔːt] n puerto de aerodeslizadores
how [hau] adv cómo; **~ are you?** ¿cómo está usted?, ¿cómo estás?; **~ do you do?** encantado, mucho gusto; **~ far is it to ...?** ¿qué distancia hay de aquí a ...?; **~ long have you been here?** ¿cuánto (tiempo) hace que estás aquí?, ¿cuánto (tiempo) llevas aquí?; **~ lovely!** ¡qué bonito!; **~ many/much?** ¿cuántos/cuánto?; **~ old are you?** ¿cuántos años tienes?; **~ is school?** ¿qué tal la escuela?; **~ about a drink?** ¿te gustaría algo de beber?, ¿qué te parece una copa?
however [hau'ɛvəʳ] adv de cualquier manera; (+ adjective) por muy ... que; (in questions) cómo ■ conj sin embargo, no obstante

h

howitzer ['hauɪtsəʳ] n (Mil) obús m
howl [haul] n aullido ■ vi aullar
howler ['hauləʳ] n plancha, falta garrafal
howling ['haulɪŋ] adj (wind) huracanado
HP n abbr (Brit) = **hire purchase**
hp abbr (Aut) = **horsepower**
HQ n abbr = **headquarters**
HR n abbr (US) = **House of Representatives**;
human resources
hr, hrs abbr (= hour(s)) h
HRH abbr (= His (or Her) Royal Highness) S.A.R.
HRT n abbr = **hormone replacement therapy**
HS abbr (US) = **high school**
HST abbr (US: = Hawaiian Standard Time) hora de
Hawai
HT abbr = **high tension**
HTML n abbr (Comput: = hypertext markup
language) HTML m
hub [hʌb] n (of wheel) cubo; (fig) centro
hubbub ['hʌbʌb] n barahúnda, barullo
hubcap ['hʌbkæp] n tapacubos m inv
HUD n abbr (US: = Department of Housing and
Urban Development) ministerio de la vivienda y
urbanismo
huddle ['hʌdl] vi: **to ~ together** amontonarse
hue [hju:] n color m, matiz m; **~ and cry** n
protesta
huff [hʌf] n: **in a ~** enojado
huffy ['hʌfɪ] adj (col) mosqueado
hug [hʌg] vt abrazar ■ n abrazo
huge [hju:dʒ] adj enorme
hulk [hʌlk] n (ship) barco viejo; (person, building
etc) mole f
hulking ['hʌlkɪŋ] adj pesado
hull [hʌl] n (of ship) casco
hullabaloo ['hʌləbə'lu:] n (col: noise)
algarabía, jaleo
hullo [hə'ləu] excl = **hello**
hum [hʌm] vt tararear, canturrear ■ vi
tararear, canturrear; (insect) zumbar ■ n
(Elec) zumbido; (of traffic, machines) zumbido,
ronroneo; (of voices etc) murmullo
human ['hju:mən] adj humano ■ n (also:
human being) ser m humano
humane [hju:'meɪn] adj humano,
humanitario
humanism ['hju:mənɪzəm] n humanismo
humanitarian [hju:mænɪ'tɛərɪən] adj
humanitario
humanity [hju:'mænɪtɪ] n humanidad f
humanly ['hju:mənlɪ] adv humanamente
humanoid ['hju:mənɔɪd] adj, n humanoide
m/f
human relations npl relaciones fpl humanas
human rights npl derechos mpl humanos
humble ['hʌmbl] adj humilde ■ vt humillar
humbly ['hʌmblɪ] adv humildemente

humbug ['hʌmbʌg] n patrañas fpl; (Brit:
sweet) caramelo de menta
humdrum ['hʌmdrʌm] adj (boring) monótono,
aburrido; (routine) rutinario
humid ['hju:mɪd] adj húmedo
humidifier [hju:'mɪdɪfaɪəʳ] n humectador m
humidity [hju:'mɪdɪtɪ] n humedad f
humiliate [hju:'mɪlɪeɪt] vt humillar
humiliation [hju:mɪlɪ'eɪʃən] n humillación f
humility [hju:'mɪlɪtɪ] n humildad f
humorist ['hju:mərɪst] n humorista m/f
humorous ['hju:mərəs] adj gracioso,
divertido
humour, humor (US) ['hju:məʳ] n
humorismo, sentido del humor; (mood)
humor m ■ vt (person) complacer; **sense of**
~ sentido del humor; **to be in a good/bad ~**
estar de buen/mal humor
humourless, humorless (US) ['hju:məlɪs]
adj serio
hump [hʌmp] n (in ground) montículo;
(camel's) giba
humus ['hju:məs] n (Bio) humus m
hunch [hʌntʃ] n (premonition) presentimiento;
I have a ~ that tengo la corazonada or el
presentimiento de que
hunchback ['hʌntʃbæk] n jorobado(-a)
hunched [hʌntʃt] adj jorobado
hundred ['hʌndrəd] num ciento; (before n)
cien; **about a ~ people** unas cien personas,
alrededor de cien personas; **hundreds**
of centenares de; **hundreds of people**
centenares de personas; **I'm a ~ per cent**
sure estoy completamente seguro
hundredweight ['hʌndrədweɪt] n (Brit) = 50.8
kg; 112 lb; (US) = 45.3 kg; 100 lb
hung [hʌŋ] pt, pp of **hang**
Hungarian [hʌŋ'gɛərɪən] adj húngaro
■ n húngaro(-a) m(f); (Ling) húngaro
Hungary ['hʌŋgərɪ] n Hungría
hunger ['hʌŋgəʳ] n hambre f ■ vi: **to ~ for**
(fig) tener hambre de, anhelar
hunger strike n huelga de hambre
hungover [hʌŋ'əuvəʳ] adj (col): **to be ~** tener
resaca
hungrily ['hʌŋgrəlɪ] adv ávidamente, con
ganas
hungry ['hʌŋgrɪ] adj hambriento; **to be ~**
tener hambre; **~ for** (fig) sediento de
hunk [hʌŋk] n (of bread etc) trozo, pedazo
hunt [hʌnt] vt (seek) buscar; (Sport) cazar
■ vi cazar ■ n caza, cacería
▶ **hunt down** vt acorralar, seguir la pista a
hunter ['hʌntəʳ] n cazador(a) m(f); (horse)
caballo de caza
hunting ['hʌntɪŋ] n caza
hurdle ['hə:dl] n (Sport) valla; (fig) obstáculo

hurl [hə:l] vt lanzar, arrojar
hurling ['hə:lɪŋ] n (Sport) juego irlandés semejante
al hockey
hurly-burly ['hə:lɪ'bə:lɪ] n jaleo, follón m
hurrah [hu'rɑ:], **hurray** [hu'reɪ] n ¡viva!,
¡hurra!
hurricane ['hʌrɪkən] n huracán m
hurried ['hʌrɪd] adj (fast) apresurado; (rushed)
hecho de prisa
hurriedly ['hʌrɪdlɪ] adv con prisa,
apresuradamente
hurry ['hʌrɪ] n prisa ■ vb (also: **hurry up**)
■ vi apresurarse, darse prisa, apurarse (LAm)
■ vt (person) dar prisa a; (work) apresurar,
hacer de prisa; **to be in a ~** tener prisa, tener
apuro (LAm), estar apurado (LAm); **to ~ back/
home** darse prisa en volver/volver a casa
▶ **hurry along** vi pasar de prisa
▶ **hurry away, hurry off** vi irse corriendo
▶ **hurry on** vi: **to ~ on to say** apresurarse a
decir
▶ **hurry up** vi darse prisa, apurarse (LAm)
hurt [hə:t] (pl **hurt**) vt hacer daño a; (business,
interests etc) perjudicar ■ vi doler ■ adj
lastimado; **I ~ my arm** me lastimé el brazo;
where does it ~? ¿dónde te duele?
hurtful ['hə:tful] adj (remark etc) hiriente,
dañino
hurtle ['hə:tl] vi: **to ~ past** pasar como
un rayo
husband ['hʌzbənd] n marido
hush [hʌʃ] n silencio ■ vt hacer callar;
(cover up) encubrir; **~!** ¡chitón!, ¡cállate!
▶ **hush up** vt (fact) encubrir, callar
hushed [hʌʃt] adj (voice) bajo
hush-hush [hʌʃ'hʌʃ] adj (col) muy secreto
husk [hʌsk] n (of wheat) cáscara
husky ['hʌskɪ] adj ronco; (burly) fornido
■ n perro esquimal
hustings ['hʌstɪŋz] npl (Pol) mítin msg
preelectoral
hustle ['hʌsl] vt (push) empujar; (hurry) dar
prisa a ■ n bullicio, actividad f febril; **~ and
bustle** ajetreo
hut [hʌt] n cabaña; (shed) cobertizo
hutch [hʌtʃ] n conejera
hyacinth ['haɪəsɪnθ] n jacinto
hybrid ['haɪbrɪd] adj, n híbrido
hydrant ['haɪdrənt] n (also: **fire hydrant**) boca
de incendios
hydraulic [haɪ'drɔ:lɪk] adj hidráulico

hydraulics [haɪ'drɔ:lɪks] n hidráulica
hydrochloric ['haɪdrəu'klɔrɪk] adj: **~ acid**
ácido clorhídrico
hydroelectric [haɪdrəuɪ'lɛktrɪk] adj
hidroeléctrico
hydrofoil ['haɪdrəfɔɪl] n aerodeslizador m
hydrogen ['haɪdrədʒən] n hidrógeno
hydrogen bomb n bomba de hidrógeno
hydrophobia [haɪdrə'fəubɪə] n hidrofobia
hydroplane ['haɪdrəpleɪn] n hidroavión m,
hidroavioneta
hyena [haɪ'i:nə] n hiena
hygiene ['haɪdʒi:n] n higiene f
hygienic [haɪ'dʒi:nɪk] adj higiénico
hymn [hɪm] n himno
hype [haɪp] n (col) bombo
hyperactive [haɪpər'æktɪv] adj hiperactivo
hyperlink ['haɪpəlɪnk] n hiperlink m
hypermarket ['haɪpəmɑ:kɪt] n
hipermercado
hypertension ['haɪpə'tɛnʃən] n
hipertensión f
hypertext ['haɪpə'tɛkst] n (Comput)
hipertexto m
hyphen ['haɪfn] n guión m
hypnosis [hɪp'nəusɪs] n hipnosis f
hypnotic [hɪp'nɔtɪk] adj hipnótico
hypnotism ['hɪpnətɪzəm] n hipnotismo
hypnotist ['hɪpnətɪst] n hipnotista m/f
hypnotize ['hɪpnətaɪz] vt hipnotizar
hypoallergenic ['haɪpəuælə'dʒɛnɪk] adj
hipoalérgeno
hypochondriac [haɪpəu'kɔndrɪæk] n
hipocondríaco(-a)
hypocrisy [hɪ'pɔkrɪsɪ] n hipocresía
hypocrite ['hɪpəkrɪt] n hipócrita m/f
hypocritical [hɪpə'krɪtɪkl] adj hipócrita
hypodermic [haɪpə'də:mɪk] adj hipodérmico
■ n (syringe) aguja hipodérmica
hypotenuse [haɪ'pɔtɪnju:z] n hipotenusa
hypothermia [haɪpəu'θə:mɪə] n hipotermia
hypothesis, hypotheses [haɪ'pɔθɪsɪs, -si:z]
n hipótesis f inv
hypothetical [haɪpə'θɛtɪkl] adj hipotético
hysterectomy [hɪstə'rɛktəmɪ] n
histerectomía
hysteria [hɪ'stɪərɪə] n histeria
hysterical [hɪ'stɛrɪkl] adj histérico
hysterics [hɪ'stɛrɪks] npl histeria sg,
histerismo sg; **to have ~** ponerse histérico
Hz abbr (= Hertz) Hz

h

I i

I, i [aɪ] n (*letter*) I, i f; **I for Isaac,** (*US*) **I for Item** I de Inés, I de Israel
I [aɪ] *pron* yo ■ *abbr* = **island; isle**
IA, Ia. *abbr* (*US*) = **Iowa**
IAEA n *abbr* = **International Atomic Energy Agency**
ib., ibid. *abbr* (= *ibidem: from the same source*) ibídem
IBA n *abbr* (*Brit:* = *Independent Broadcasting Authority*) *see* **ITV**
Iberian [aɪˈbɪərɪən] *adj* ibero, ibérico
Iberian Peninsula n: **the ~** la Península Ibérica
IBEW n *abbr* (*US:* = *International Brotherhood of Electrical Workers*) sindicato internacional de electricistas
i/c *abbr* (*Brit*) = **in charge**
ICBM n *abbr* (= *intercontinental ballistic missile*) misil m balístico intercontinental
ICC n *abbr* (= *International Chamber of Commerce*) CCI f; (*US*) = **Interstate Commerce Commission**
ice [aɪs] n hielo ■ vt (*cake*) alcorzar ■ vi (*also:* **ice over, ice up**) helarse; **to keep sth on ~** (*fig: plan, project*) tener algo en reserva
ice age n período glaciar
ice axe n piqueta (de alpinista)
iceberg [ˈaɪsbəːg] n iceberg m; **the tip of the ~** la punta del iceberg
icebox [ˈaɪsbɔks] n (*Brit*) congelador m; (*US*) nevera, refrigeradora (*LAm*)
icebreaker [ˈaɪsbreɪkəʳ] n rompehielos m inv
ice bucket n cubo para el hielo
icecap [ˈaɪskæp] n casquete m polar
ice-cold [aɪsˈkəuld] *adj* helado
ice cream n helado
ice-cream soda n soda mezclada con helado
ice cube n cubito de hielo
iced [aɪst] *adj* (*drink*) con hielo; (*cake*) escarchado
ice hockey n hockey m sobre hielo
Iceland [ˈaɪslənd] n Islandia

Icelander [ˈaɪsləndəʳ] n islandés(-esa) m(f)
Icelandic [aɪsˈlændɪk] *adj* islandés(-esa) ■ n (*Ling*) islandés m
ice lolly n (*Brit*) polo
ice pick n piolet m
ice rink n pista de hielo
ice-skate [ˈaɪsskeɪt] n patín m de hielo ■ vi patinar sobre hielo
ice-skating [ˈaɪsskeɪtɪŋ] n patinaje m sobre hielo
icicle [ˈaɪsɪkl] n carámbano
icing [ˈaɪsɪŋ] n (*Culin*) alcorza; (*Aviat etc*) formación f de hielo
icing sugar n (*Brit*) azúcar m glas(eado)
ICJ n *abbr* = **International Court of Justice**
icon [ˈaɪkɔn] n (*gen*) icono; (*Comput*) icono
ICR n *abbr* (*US*) = **Institute for Cancer Research**
ICT n *abbr* (= *Information and Communication(s) Technology*) TIC f, tecnología de la información; (*Brit Scol*) informática
ICU n *abbr* (= *intensive care unit*) UVI f
icy [ˈaɪsɪ] *adj* (*road*) helado; (*fig*) glacial
ID *abbr* (*US: Post*) = **Idaho**
I'd [aɪd] = **I would; I had**
Ida. *abbr* (*US: Post*) = **Idaho**
ID card n (*identity card*) DNI m
IDD n *abbr* (*Brit Tel:* = *international direct dialling*) servicio automático internacional
idea [aɪˈdɪə] n idea; **good ~!** ¡buena idea!; **to have an ~ that …** tener la impresión de que …; **I haven't the least ~** no tengo ni (la más remota) idea
ideal [aɪˈdɪəl] n ideal m ■ *adj* ideal
idealism [aɪˈdɪəlɪzəm] n idealismo
idealist [aɪˈdɪəlɪst] n idealista m/f
ideally [aɪˈdɪəlɪ] *adv* perfectamente; **~, the book should have …** idealmente, el libro debería tener …
identical [aɪˈdɛntɪkl] *adj* idéntico
identification [aɪdɛntɪfɪˈkeɪʃən] n identificación f; **means of ~** documentos mpl personales

identify [aɪ'dɛntɪfaɪ] vt identificar ■ vi: to ~ with identificarse con

Identikit® [aɪ'dɛntɪkɪt] n: ~ (picture) retrato-robot m

identity [aɪ'dɛntɪtɪ] n identidad f

identity card n carnet m de identidad, cédula (de identidad) (LAm)

identity papers npl documentos mpl (de identidad), documentación fsg

identity parade n identificación f de acusados

ideological [aɪdɪə'lɔdʒɪkəl] adj ideológico

ideology [aɪdɪ'ɔlədʒɪ] n ideología

idiocy ['ɪdɪəsɪ] n idiotez f; (stupid act) estupidez f

idiom ['ɪdɪəm] n modismo; (style of speaking) lenguaje m

idiomatic [ɪdɪə'mætɪk] adj idiomático

idiosyncrasy [ɪdɪəu'sɪŋkrəsɪ] n idiosincrasia

idiot ['ɪdɪət] n (gen) idiota m/f; (fool) tonto(-a)

idiotic [ɪdɪ'ɔtɪk] adj idiota; tonto

idle ['aɪdl] adj (lazy) holgazán(-ana); (unemployed) parado, desocupado; (talk) frívolo ■ vi (machine) funcionar or marchar en vacío; ~ capacity (Comm) capacidad f sin utilizar; ~ money (Comm) capital m improductivo; ~ time (Comm) tiempo de paro
▶ idle away vt: to ~ away one's time malgastar or desperdiciar el tiempo

idleness ['aɪdlnɪs] n holgazanería; paro, desocupación f

idler ['aɪdlər] n holgazán(-ana) m(f), vago(-a)

idol ['aɪdl] n ídolo

idolize ['aɪdəlaɪz] vt idolatrar

idyllic [ɪ'dɪlɪk] adj idílico

i.e. abbr (~ id est: that is) es decir

if [ɪf] conj si ■ n: there are a lot of ifs and buts hay muchas dudas sin resolver; (even) if aunque, si bien; I'd be pleased if you could do it yo estaría contento si pudieras hacerlo; if necessary si resultase necesario; if only si solamente; as if como si

iffy ['ɪfɪ] adj (col) dudoso

igloo ['ɪgluː] n iglú m

ignite [ɪg'naɪt] vt (set fire to) encender ■ vi encenderse

ignition [ɪg'nɪʃən] n (Aut) encendido; to switch on/off the ~ arrancar/apagar el motor

ignition key n (Aut) llave f de contacto

ignoble [ɪg'nəubl] adj innoble, vil

ignominious [ɪgnə'mɪnɪəs] adj ignominioso, vergonzoso

ignoramus [ɪgnə'reɪməs] n ignorante m/f, inculto(-a)

ignorance ['ɪgnərəns] n ignorancia; to keep sb in ~ of sth ocultarle algo a algn

ignorant ['ɪgnərənt] adj ignorante; to be ~ of (subject) desconocer; (events) ignorar

ignore [ɪg'nɔːr] vt (person) no hacer caso de; (fact) pasar por alto

ikon ['aɪkɔn] n = icon

IL abbr (US: Post) = Illinois

ILA n abbr (US: = International Longshoremen's Association) sindicato internacional de trabajadores portuarios

ill [ɪl] adj enfermo, malo ■ n mal m; (fig) infortunio ■ adv mal; to take or be taken ~ caer or ponerse enfermo; to feel ~ (with) encontrarse mal (de); to speak/think ~ of sb hablar/pensar mal de algn; see also ills

Ill. abbr (US: Post) = Illinois

I'll [aɪl] = I will; I shall

ill-advised [ɪləd'vaɪzd] adj poco recomendable; he was ~ to go se equivocaba al ir

ill-at-ease [ɪlət'iːz] adj incómodo

ill-considered [ɪlkən'sɪdəd] adj (plan) poco pensado

ill-disposed [ɪldɪs'pəuzd] adj: to be ~ towards sb/sth estar maldispuesto hacia algn/algo

illegal [ɪ'liːgl] adj ilegal

illegible [ɪ'lɛdʒɪbl] adj ilegible

illegitimate [ɪlɪ'dʒɪtɪmət] adj ilegítimo

ill-fated [ɪl'feɪtɪd] adj malogrado

ill-favoured, ill-favored (US) [ɪl'feɪvəd] adj poco agraciado

ill feeling n rencor m

ill-gotten ['ɪlgɔtn] adj (gains etc) mal adquirido

ill health n mala salud f; to be in ~ estar mal de salud

illicit [ɪ'lɪsɪt] adj ilícito

ill-informed [ɪlɪn'fɔːmd] adj (judgement) erróneo; (person) mal informado

illiterate [ɪ'lɪtərət] adj analfabeto

ill-mannered [ɪl'mænəd] adj mal educado

illness ['ɪlnɪs] n enfermedad f

illogical [ɪ'lɔdʒɪkl] adj ilógico

ills [ɪlz] npl males mpl

ill-suited [ɪl'suːtɪd] adj (couple) incompatible; he is ~ to the job no es la persona indicada para el trabajo

ill-timed [ɪl'taɪmd] adj inoportuno

ill-treat [ɪl'triːt] vt maltratar

ill-treatment [ɪl'triːtmənt] n malos tratos mpl

illuminate [ɪ'luːmɪneɪt] vt (room, street) iluminar, alumbrar; (subject) aclarar; illuminated sign letrero luminoso

illuminating [ɪ'luːmɪneɪtɪŋ] adj revelador(a)

illumination [ɪluːmɪ'neɪʃən] n alumbrado; illuminations npl luminarias fpl, luces fpl

illusion [ɪˈluːʒən] n ilusión f; **to be under the ~ that ...** estar convencido de que ...
illusive [ɪˈluːsɪv], **illusory** [ɪˈluːsərɪ] adj ilusorio
illustrate [ˈɪləstreɪt] vt ilustrar
illustration [ɪləˈstreɪʃən] n (example) ejemplo, ilustración f; (in book) lámina, ilustración f
illustrator [ˈɪləstreɪtəʳ] n ilustrador(a) m(f)
illustrious [ɪˈlʌstrɪəs] adj ilustre
ill will n rencor m
ILO n abbr (= International Labour Organization) OIT f
IM n abbr (= instant messaging) IM f ■ vt enviar un mensaje instantáneo
I'm [aɪm] = **I am**
image [ˈɪmɪdʒ] n imagen f
imagery [ˈɪmɪdʒərɪ] n imágenes fpl
imaginable [ɪˈmædʒɪnəbl] adj imaginable
imaginary [ɪˈmædʒɪnərɪ] adj imaginario
imagination [ɪmædʒɪˈneɪʃən] n imaginación f; (inventiveness) inventiva; (illusion) fantasía
imaginative [ɪˈmædʒɪnətɪv] adj imaginativo
imagine [ɪˈmædʒɪn] vt imaginarse; (suppose) suponer
imbalance [ɪmˈbæləns] n desequilibrio
imbecile [ˈɪmbəsiːl] n imbécil m/f
imbue [ɪmˈbjuː] vt: **to ~ sth with** imbuir algo de
IMF n abbr (= International Monetary Fund) FMI m
imitate [ˈɪmɪteɪt] vt imitar
imitation [ɪmɪˈteɪʃən] n imitación f; (copy) copia; (pej) remedo
imitator [ˈɪmɪteɪtəʳ] n imitador(a) m(f)
immaculate [ɪˈmækjulət] adj limpísimo, inmaculado; (Rel) inmaculado
immaterial [ɪməˈtɪərɪəl] adj incorpóreo; **it is ~ whether ...** no importa si ...
immature [ɪməˈtjuəʳ] adj (person) inmaduro; (of one's youth) joven
immaturity [ɪməˈtjuərɪtɪ] n inmadurez f
immeasurable [ɪˈmeʒrəbl] adj inconmensurable
immediacy [ɪˈmiːdɪəsɪ] n urgencia, proximidad f
immediate [ɪˈmiːdɪət] adj inmediato; (pressing) urgente, apremiante; **in the ~ future** en un futuro próximo
immediately [ɪˈmiːdɪətlɪ] adv (at once) en seguida; **~ next to** justo al lado de
immense [ɪˈmens] adj inmenso, enorme
immensity [ɪˈmensɪtɪ] n (of size, difference) inmensidad f; (of problem) enormidad f
immerse [ɪˈməːs] vt (submerge) sumergir; **to be immersed in** (fig) estar absorto en
immersion heater [ɪˈməːʃən-] n (Brit) calentador m de inmersión
immigrant [ˈɪmɪgrənt] n inmigrante m/f
immigrate [ˈɪmɪgreɪt] vi inmigrar

immigration [ɪmɪˈgreɪʃən] n inmigración f
immigration authorities npl servicio sg de inmigración
immigration laws npl leyes fpl de inmigración
imminent [ˈɪmɪnənt] adj inminente
immobile [ɪˈməubaɪl] adj inmóvil
immobilize [ɪˈməubɪlaɪz] vt inmovilizar
immoderate [ɪˈmɔdərɪt] adj (person) desmesurado; (opinion, demand) excesivo
immodest [ɪˈmɔdɪst] adj (indecent) desvergonzado, impúdico; (boasting) jactancioso
immoral [ɪˈmɔrl] adj inmoral
immorality [ɪmɔˈrælɪtɪ] n inmoralidad f
immortal [ɪˈmɔːtl] adj inmortal
immortality [ɪmɔːˈtælɪtɪ] n inmortalidad f
immortalize [ɪˈmɔːtlaɪz] vt inmortalizar
immovable [ɪˈmuːvəbl] adj (object) imposible de mover; (person) inconmovible
immune [ɪˈmjuːn] adj: **~ (to)** inmune (a)
immune system n sistema m inmunitario
immunity [ɪˈmjuːnɪtɪ] n (Med, of diplomat) inmunidad f; (Comm) exención f
immunization [ɪmjunaɪˈzeɪʃən] n inmunización f
immunize [ˈɪmjunaɪz] vt inmunizar
imp [ɪmp] n (small devil, child) diablillo
impact [ˈɪmpækt] n (gen) impacto
impair [ɪmˈpɛəʳ] vt perjudicar
-impaired [ɪmˈpɛəd] suff: **visually-impaired** con defectos de visión
impale [ɪmˈpeɪl] vt (with sword) atravesar
impart [ɪmˈpɑːt] vt comunicar; (make known) participar; (bestow) otorgar
impartial [ɪmˈpɑːʃl] adj imparcial
impartiality [ɪmpɑːʃɪˈælɪtɪ] n imparcialidad f
impassable [ɪmˈpɑːsəbl] adj (barrier) infranqueable; (road) intransitable
impasse [ɪmˈpɑːs] n callejón m sin salida; **to reach an ~** llegar a un punto muerto
impassioned [ɪmˈpæʃənd] adj apasionado, exaltado
impassive [ɪmˈpæsɪv] adj impasible
impatience [ɪmˈpeɪʃəns] n impaciencia
impatient [ɪmˈpeɪʃənt] adj impaciente; **to get** or **grow ~** impacientarse
impatiently [ɪmˈpeɪʃəntlɪ] adv con impaciencia
impeachment [ɪmˈpiːtʃmənt] n denuncia, acusación f
impeccable [ɪmˈpɛkəbl] adj impecable
impecunious [ɪmpɪˈkjuːnɪəs] adj sin dinero
impede [ɪmˈpiːd] vt estorbar, dificultar
impediment [ɪmˈpɛdɪmənt] n obstáculo, estorbo; (also: **speech impediment**) defecto (del habla)

impel [ɪm'pɛl] vt (force): **to ~ sb (to do sth)** obligar a algn (a hacer algo)

impending [ɪm'pɛndɪŋ] adj inminente

impenetrable [ɪm'pɛnɪtrəbl] adj (jungle, fortress) impenetrable; (unfathomable) insondable

imperative [ɪm'pɛrətɪv] adj (tone) imperioso; (necessary) imprescindible ▪ n (Ling) imperativo

imperceptible [ɪmpə'sɛptɪbl] adj imperceptible

imperfect [ɪm'pə:fɪkt] adj imperfecto; (goods etc) defectuoso

imperfection [ɪmpə'fɛkʃən] n (blemish) desperfecto; (fault, flaw) defecto

imperial [ɪm'pɪərɪəl] adj imperial

imperialism [ɪm'pɪərɪəlɪzəm] n imperialismo

imperil [ɪm'pɛrɪl] vt poner en peligro

imperious [ɪm'pɪərɪəs] adj señorial, apremiante

impersonal [ɪm'pə:sənl] adj impersonal

impersonate [ɪm'pə:səneɪt] vt hacerse pasar por

impersonation [ɪmpə:sə'neɪʃən] n imitación f

impersonator [ɪm'pə:səneɪtər] n (Theat etc) imitador(a) m(f)

impertinence [ɪm'pə:tɪnəns] n impertinencia, insolencia

impertinent [ɪm'pə:tɪnənt] adj impertinente, insolente

imperturbable [ɪmpə'tə:bəbl] adj imperturbable, impasible

impervious [ɪm'pə:vɪəs] adj impermeable; (fig): **~ to** insensible a

impetuous [ɪm'pɛtjuəs] adj impetuoso

impetus ['ɪmpətəs] n ímpetu m; (fig) impulso

impinge [ɪm'pɪndʒ]: **to ~ on** vt fus (affect) afectar a

impish ['ɪmpɪʃ] adj travieso

implacable [ɪm'plækəbl] adj implacable

implant [ɪm'plɑ:nt] vt (Med) injertar, implantar; (fig: idea, principle) inculcar

implausible [ɪm'plɔ:zɪbl] adj implausible

implement n ['ɪmplɪmənt] instrumento, herramienta ▪ vt ['ɪmplɪmɛnt] hacer efectivo; (carry out) realizar

implicate ['ɪmplɪkeɪt] vt (compromise) comprometer; (involve) enredar; **to ~ sb in sth** comprometer a algn en algo

implication [ɪmplɪ'keɪʃən] n consecuencia; **by ~** indirectamente

implicit [ɪm'plɪsɪt] adj (gen) implícito; (complete) absoluto

implicitly [ɪm'plɪsɪtlɪ] adv implícitamente

implore [ɪm'plɔ:r] vt (person) suplicar

imploring [ɪm'plɔ:rɪŋ] adj de súplica

imply [ɪm'plaɪ] vt (involve) implicar, suponer; (hint) insinuar

impolite [ɪmpə'laɪt] adj mal educado

impolitic [ɪm'pɔlɪtɪk] adj poco diplomático

imponderable [ɪm'pɔndərəbl] adj imponderable

import vt [ɪm'pɔ:t] importar ▪ n ['ɪmpɔ:t] (Comm) importación f; (meaning) significado, sentido ▪ cpd (duty, licence etc) de importación

importance [ɪm'pɔ:təns] n importancia; **to be of great/little ~** tener mucha/poca, importancia

important [ɪm'pɔ:tənt] adj importante; **it's not ~** no importa, no tiene importancia; **it is ~ that** es importante que

importantly [ɪm'pɔ:təntlɪ] adv (pej) dándose importancia; **but, more ~ ...,** pero, lo que es aún más importante ...

import duty n derechos mpl de importación

imported [ɪm'pɔ:tɪd] adj importado

importer [ɪm'pɔ:tər] n importador(a) m(f)

import licence, import license (US) n licencia de importación

impose [ɪm'pəuz] vt imponer ▪ vi: **to ~ on sb** abusar de algn

imposing [ɪm'pəuzɪŋ] adj imponente, impresionante

imposition [ɪmpə'zɪʃn] n (of tax etc) imposición f; **to be an ~** (on person) molestar

impossibility [ɪmpɔsə'bɪlɪtɪ] n imposibilidad f

impossible [ɪm'pɔsɪbl] adj imposible; (person) insoportable; **it is ~ for me to leave now** me es imposible salir ahora

impossibly [ɪm'pɔsɪblɪ] adv imposiblemente

impostor [ɪm'pɔstər] n impostor(a) m(f)

impotence ['ɪmpətəns] n impotencia

impotent ['ɪmpətənt] adj impotente

impound [ɪm'paund] vt embargar

impoverished [ɪm'pɔvərɪʃt] adj necesitado; (land) agotado

impracticable [ɪm'præktɪkəbl] adj no factible, irrealizable

impractical [ɪm'præktɪkl] adj (person) poco práctico

imprecise [ɪmprɪ'saɪs] adj impreciso

impregnable [ɪm'prɛgnəbl] adj invulnerable; (castle) inexpugnable

impregnate ['ɪmprɛgneɪt] vt (gen) impregnar; (soak) empapar; (fertilize) fecundar

impresario [ɪmprɪ'sɑ:rɪəu] n empresario(-a)

impress [ɪm'prɛs] vt impresionar; (mark) estampar ▪ vi causar buena impresión; **to ~ sth on sb** convencer a algn de la importancia de algo

605

impression [ɪmˈprɛʃən] n impresión f; (footprint etc) huella; (print run) edición f; **to be under the ~ that** tener la idea de que; **to make a good/bad ~ on sb** causar buena/mala impresión a algn

impressionable [ɪmˈprɛʃnəbl] adj impresionable

impressionist [ɪmˈprɛʃənɪst] n impresionista m/f

impressive [ɪmˈprɛsɪv] adj impresionante

imprint [ˈɪmprɪnt] n (Publishing) pie m de imprenta; (fig) sello

imprison [ɪmˈprɪzn] vt encarcelar

imprisonment [ɪmˈprɪznmənt] n encarcelamiento; (term of imprisonment) cárcel f; **life ~** cadena perpetua

improbable [ɪmˈprɔbəbl] adj improbable, inverosímil

impromptu [ɪmˈprɔmptjuː] adj improvisado ■ adv de improviso

improper [ɪmˈprɔpəʳ] adj (incorrect) impropio; (unseemly) indecoroso; (indecent) indecente

impropriety [ɪmprəˈpraɪətɪ] n falta de decoro; (indecency) indecencia; (of language) impropiedad f

improve [ɪmˈpruːv] vt mejorar; (foreign language) perfeccionar ■ vi mejorar
▶ **improve (up)on** vt fus (offer) mejorar

improvement [ɪmˈpruːvmənt] n mejora; perfeccionamiento; **to make improvements to** mejorar

improvise [ˈɪmprəvaɪz] vt, vi improvisar

imprudence [ɪmˈpruːdns] n imprudencia

imprudent [ɪmˈpruːdnt] adj imprudente

impudent [ˈɪmpjudnt] adj descarado, insolente

impugn [ɪmˈpjuːn] vt impugnar

impulse [ˈɪmpʌls] n impulso; **to act on ~** actuar sin reflexionar, dejarse llevar por el impulso

impulse buying n compra impulsiva

impulsive [ɪmˈpʌlsɪv] adj irreflexivo, impulsivo

impunity [ɪmˈpjuːnɪtɪ] n: **with ~** impunemente

impure [ɪmˈpjuəʳ] adj (adulterated) adulterado; (morally) impuro

impurity [ɪmˈpjuərɪtɪ] n impureza

IN abbr (US: Post) = **Indiana**

 KEYWORD

in [ɪn] prep **1** (indicating place, position, with place names) en; **in the house/garden** en (la) casa/el jardín; **in here/there** aquí/ahí or allí dentro; **in London/England** en Londres/Inglaterra; **in town** en el centro (de la ciudad)

2 (indicating time) en; **in spring** en (la) primavera; **in 1988/May** en 1988/mayo; **in the afternoon** por la tarde; **at four o'clock in the afternoon** a las cuarto de la tarde; **I did it in three hours/days** lo hice en tres horas/días; **I'll see you in two weeks** or **in two weeks' time** te veré dentro de dos semanas; **once in a hundred years** una vez cada cien años

3 (indicating manner etc) en; **in a loud/soft voice** en voz alta/baja; **in pencil/ink** a lápiz/bolígrafo; **the boy in the blue shirt** el chico de la camisa azul; **in writing** por escrito; **to pay in dollars** pagar en dólares

4 (indicating circumstances): **in the sun/shade** al sol/a la sombra; **in the rain** bajo la lluvia; **a change in policy** un cambio de política; **a rise in prices** un aumento de precios

5 (indicating mood, state): **in tears** llorando; **in anger/despair** enfadado/desesperado; **to live in luxury** vivir lujosamente

6 (with ratios, numbers): **1 in 10 households, 1 household in 10** una de cada 10 familias; **20 pence in the pound** 20 peniques por libra; **they lined up in twos** se alinearon de dos en dos; **in hundreds** a or por centenares

7 (referring to people, works) en; entre; **the disease is common in children** la enfermedad es común entre los niños; **in (the works of) Dickens** en (las obras de) Dickens

8 (indicating profession etc): **to be in teaching** dedicarse a la enseñanza

9 (after superlative) de; **the best pupil in the class** el/la mejor alumno(-a) de la clase

10 (with present participle): **in saying this** al decir esto

■ adv: **to be in** (person: at home) estar en casa; (: at work) estar; (train, ship, plane) haber llegado; (in fashion) estar de moda; **she'll be in later today** llegará más tarde hoy; **to ask sb in** hacer pasar a algn; **to run/limp etc in** entrar corriendo/cojeando etc; **in that** conj ya que

■ npl: **the ins and outs** (of proposal, situation etc) los detalles

in., ins abbr = **inch; inches**

inability [ɪnəˈbɪlɪtɪ] n incapacidad f; **~ to pay** insolvencia en el pago

inaccessible [ɪnækˈsɛsɪbl] adj inaccesible

inaccuracy [ɪnˈækjurəsɪ] n inexactitud f

inaccurate [ɪnˈækjurət] adj inexacto, incorrecto

inaction [ɪnˈækʃən] n inacción f

inactive [ɪnˈæktɪv] adj inactivo

inactivity [ɪnækˈtɪvɪtɪ] n inactividad f

inadequacy [ɪn'ædɪkwəsɪ] n insuficiencia; incapacidad f
inadequate [ɪn'ædɪkwət] adj (insufficient) insuficiente; (unsuitable) inadecuado; (person) incapaz
inadmissible [ɪnəd'mɪsəbl] adj improcedente, inadmisible
inadvertent [ɪnəd'və:tənt] adj descuidado, involuntario
inadvertently [ɪnəd'və:tntlɪ] adv por descuido
inadvisable [ɪnəd'vaɪzəbl] adj poco aconsejable
inane [ɪ'neɪn] adj necio, fatuo
inanimate [ɪn'ænɪmət] adj inanimado
inapplicable [ɪn'æplɪkəbl] adj inaplicable
inappropriate [ɪnə'prəuprɪət] adj inadecuado
inapt [ɪn'æpt] adj impropio
inaptitude [ɪn'æptɪtju:d] n incapacidad f
inarticulate [ɪnɑ:'tɪkjulət] adj (person) incapaz de expresarse; (speech) mal pronunciado
inartistic [ɪnɑ:'tɪstɪk] adj antiestético
inasmuch as [ɪnəz'mʌtʃ-] adv en la medida en que
inattention [ɪnə'tenʃən] n desatención f
inattentive [ɪnə'tentɪv] adj distraído
inaudible [ɪn'ɔ:dɪbl] adj inaudible
inaugural [ɪ'nɔ:gjurəl] adj inaugural; (speech) de apertura
inaugurate [ɪ'nɔ:gjureɪt] vt inaugurar; (president, official) investir
inauguration [ɪnɔ:gju'reɪʃən] n inauguración f; (of official) investidura; (of event) ceremonia de apertura
inauspicious [ɪnɔ:s'pɪʃəs] adj poco propicio, inoportuno
in-between [ɪnbɪ'twi:n] adj intermedio
inborn [ɪn'bɔ:n] adj (feeling) innato
inbred [ɪn'brɛd] adj innato; (family) consanguíneo
inbreeding [ɪn'bri:dɪŋ] n endogamia
Inc. abbr = **incorporated**
Inca ['ɪŋkə] adj (also: **Incan**) inca, de los incas ■ n inca m/f
incalculable [ɪn'kælkjuləbl] adj incalculable
incapability [ɪnkeɪpə'bɪlɪtɪ] n incapacidad f
incapable [ɪn'keɪpəbl] adj: ~ (of doing sth) incapaz (de hacer algo)
incapacitate [ɪnkə'pæsɪteɪt] vt: to ~ sb incapacitar a algn
incapacitated [ɪnkə'pæsɪteɪtɪd] adj incapacitado
incapacity [ɪnkə'pæsɪtɪ] n (inability) incapacidad f
incarcerate [ɪn'kɑ:səreɪt] vt encarcelar

incarnate adj [ɪn'kɑ:nɪt] en persona ■ vt ['ɪnkɑ:neɪt] encarnar
incarnation [ɪnkɑ:'neɪʃən] n encarnación f
incendiary [ɪn'sɛndɪərɪ] adj incendiario ■ n (bomb) bomba incendiaria
incense n ['ɪnsɛns] incienso ■ vt [ɪn'sɛns] (anger) indignar, encolerizar
incentive [ɪn'sɛntɪv] n incentivo, estímulo
incentive bonus n prima
incentive scheme n plan m de incentivos
inception [ɪn'sɛpʃən] n comienzo, principio
incessant [ɪn'sɛsnt] adj incesante, continuo
incessantly [ɪn'sɛsntlɪ] adv constantemente
incest ['ɪnsɛst] n incesto
inch [ɪntʃ] n pulgada; **to be within an ~ of** estar a dos dedos de; **he didn't give an ~** no hizo la más mínima concesión; **a few inches** unas pulgadas
▸ **inch forward** vi avanzar palmo a palmo
incidence ['ɪnsɪdns] n (of crime, disease) incidencia
incident ['ɪnsɪdnt] n incidente m; (in book) episodio
incidental [ɪnsɪ'dentl] adj circunstancial, accesorio; (unplanned) fortuito; ~ **to** relacionado con; ~ **expenses** (gastos mpl) imprevistos mpl
incidentally [ɪnsɪ'dentəlɪ] adv (by the way) por cierto
incidental music n música de fondo
incident room n (Police) centro de coordinación
incinerate [ɪn'sɪnəreɪt] vt incinerar, quemar
incinerator [ɪn'sɪnəreɪtər] n incinerador m, incineradora
incipient [ɪn'sɪpɪənt] adj incipiente
incision [ɪn'sɪʒən] n incisión f
incisive [ɪn'saɪsɪv] adj (mind) penetrante; (remark etc) incisivo
incisor [ɪn'saɪzər] n incisivo
incite [ɪn'saɪt] vt provocar, incitar
incl. abbr = **including; inclusive (of)**
inclement [ɪn'klɛmənt] adj inclemente
inclination [ɪnklɪ'neɪʃən] n (tendency) tendencia, inclinación f
incline [n 'ɪnklaɪn, vb ɪn'klaɪn] n pendiente f, cuesta ■ vt (slope) inclinar; (head) poner de lado ■ vi inclinarse; **to be inclined to** (tend) ser propenso a; (be willing) estar dispuesto a
include [ɪn'klu:d] vt incluir, comprender; (in letter) adjuntar; **the tip is/is not included** la propina está/no está incluida
including [ɪn'klu:dɪŋ] prep incluso, inclusive; ~ **tip** propina incluida
inclusion [ɪn'klu:ʒən] n inclusión f
inclusive [ɪn'klu:sɪv] adj inclusivo ■ adv

inclusive; ~ **of tax** incluidos los impuestos; **$50, ~ of all surcharges** 50 dólares, incluidos todos los recargos

incognito [ɪnkɒgˈniːtəu] adv de incógnito

incoherent [ɪnkəuˈhɪərənt] adj incoherente

income [ˈɪnkʌm] n (personal) ingresos mpl; (from property etc) renta; (profit) rédito; **gross/ net** ~ ingresos mpl brutos/netos; ~ **and expenditure account** cuenta de gastos e ingresos

income bracket n categoría económica

income support n (Brit) = ayuda familiar

income tax n impuesto sobre la renta

income tax inspector n inspector(a) m(f) de Hacienda

income tax return n declaración f de ingresos

incoming [ˈɪnkʌmɪŋ] adj (passengers, flight) de llegada; (government) entrante; (tenant) nuevo

incommunicado [ˈɪnkəmjunɪˈkɑːdəu] adj: **to hold sb** ~ mantener incomunicado a algn

incomparable [ɪnˈkɒmpərəbl] adj incomparable, sin par

incompatible [ɪnkəmˈpætɪbl] adj incompatible

incompetence [ɪnˈkɒmpɪtəns] n incompetencia

incompetent [ɪnˈkɒmpɪtənt] adj incompetente

incomplete [ɪnkəmˈpliːt] adj incompleto; (unfinished) sin terminar

incomprehensible [ɪnkɒmprɪˈhɛnsɪbl] adj incomprensible

inconceivable [ɪnkənˈsiːvəbl] adj inconcebible

inconclusive [ɪnkənˈkluːsɪv] adj sin resultado (definitivo); (argument) poco convincente

incongruity [ɪnkɒnˈgruːɪtɪ] n incongruencia

incongruous [ɪnˈkɒŋgruəs] adj discordante

inconsequential [ɪnkɒnsɪˈkwɛnʃl] adj intrascendente

inconsiderable [ɪnkənˈsɪdərəbl] adj insignificante

inconsiderate [ɪnkənˈsɪdərət] adj desconsiderado; **how ~ of him!** ¡qué falta de consideración (de su parte)!

inconsistency [ɪnkənˈsɪstənsɪ] n inconsecuencia; (of actions etc) falta de lógica; (of work) carácter m desigual, inconsistencia; (of statement etc) contradicción f

inconsistent [ɪnkənˈsɪstnt] adj inconsecuente; ~ **with** que no concuerda con

inconsolable [ɪnkənˈsəuləbl] adj inconsolable

inconspicuous [ɪnkənˈspɪkjuəs] adj (discreet) discreto; (person) que llama poco la atención

inconstancy [ɪnˈkɒnstənsɪ] n inconstancia

inconstant [ɪnˈkɒnstənt] adj inconstante

incontinence [ɪnˈkɒntɪnəns] n incontinencia

incontinent [ɪnˈkɒntɪnənt] adj incontinente

incontrovertible [ɪnkɒntrəˈvəːtəbl] adj incontrovertible

inconvenience [ɪnkənˈviːnjəns] n (gen) inconvenientes mpl; (trouble) molestia ■ vt incomodar; **to put sb to great** ~ causar mucha molestia a algn; **don't ~ yourself** no se moleste

inconvenient [ɪnkənˈviːnjənt] adj incómodo, poco práctico; (time, place) inoportuno; **that time is very ~ for me** esa hora no me es muy inconveniente

incorporate [ɪnˈkɔːpəreɪt] vt incorporar; (contain) comprender; (add) agregar

incorporated [ɪnˈkɔːpəreɪtɪd] adj: ~ **company** (US) = Sociedad f Anónima (S.A.)

incorrect [ɪnkəˈrɛkt] adj incorrecto

incorrigible [ɪnˈkɒrɪdʒəbl] adj incorregible

incorruptible [ɪnkəˈrʌptɪbl] adj incorruptible

increase [n ˈɪnkriːs, vb ɪnˈkriːs] n aumento
■ vi aumentar; (grow) crecer; (price) subir
■ vt aumentar; **an** ~ **of 5%** un aumento de 5%; **to be on the** ~ ir en aumento

increasing [ɪnˈkriːsɪŋ] adj (number) creciente, que va en aumento

increasingly [ɪnˈkriːsɪŋlɪ] adv cada vez más

incredible [ɪnˈkrɛdɪbl] adj increíble

incredibly [ɪnˈkrɛdɪblɪ] adv increíblemente

incredulity [ɪnkrɪˈdjuːlɪtɪ] n incredulidad f

incredulous [ɪnˈkrɛdjuləs] adj incrédulo

increment [ˈɪnkrɪmənt] n aumento, incremento

incriminate [ɪnˈkrɪmɪneɪt] vt incriminar

incriminating [ɪnˈkrɪmɪneɪtɪŋ] adj incriminatorio

incrust [ɪnˈkrʌst] vt = **encrust**

incubate [ˈɪnkjubeɪt] vt (egg) incubar, empollar ■ vi (egg, disease) incubar

incubation [ɪnkjuˈbeɪʃən] n incubación f

incubation period n período de incubación

incubator [ˈɪnkjubeɪtəʳ] n incubadora

inculcate [ˈɪnkʌlkeɪt] vt: **to** ~ **sth in sb** inculcar algo en algn

incumbent [ɪnˈkʌmbənt] n ocupante m/f
■ adj: **it is** ~ **on him to ...** le incumbe ...

incur [ɪnˈkəːʳ] vt (expenses) incurrir en; (loss) sufrir

incurable [ɪnˈkjuərəbl] adj incurable

incursion [ɪnˈkəːʃən] n incursión f

Ind. abbr (US) = **Indiana**

indebted [ɪnˈdɛtɪd] adj: **to be** ~ **to sb** estar agradecido a algn

indecency [ɪnˈdiːsnsɪ] n indecencia

indecent [ɪn'diːsnt] *adj* indecente
indecent assault *n* (*Brit*) atentado contra el pudor
indecent exposure *n* exhibicionismo
indecipherable [ɪndɪ'saɪfərəbl] *adj* indescifrable
indecision [ɪndɪ'sɪʒən] *n* indecisión *f*
indecisive [ɪndɪ'saɪsɪv] *adj* indeciso; (*discussion*) no resuelto, inconcluyente
indeed [ɪn'diːd] *adv* efectivamente, en realidad; **yes ~!** ¡claro que sí!
indefatigable [ɪndɪ'fætɪɡəbl] *adj* incansable, infatigable
indefensible [ɪndɪ'fɛnsəbl] *adj* (*conduct*) injustificable
indefinable [ɪndɪ'faɪnəbl] *adj* indefinible
indefinite [ɪn'dɛfɪnɪt] *adj* indefinido; (*uncertain*) incierto
indefinitely [ɪn'dɛfɪnɪtlɪ] *adv* (*wait*) indefinidamente
indelible [ɪn'dɛlɪbl] *adj* imborrable
indelicate [ɪn'dɛlɪkɪt] *adj* (*tactless*) indiscreto, inoportuno; (*not polite*) poco delicado
indemnify [ɪn'dɛmnɪfaɪ] *vt* indemnizar, resarcir
indemnity [ɪn'dɛmnɪtɪ] *n* (*insurance*) indemnidad *f*; (*compensation*) indemnización *f*
indent [ɪn'dɛnt] *vt* (*text*) sangrar
indentation [ɪndɛn'teɪʃən] *n* mella; (*Typ*) sangría
indenture [ɪn'dɛntʃəʳ] *n* escritura, instrumento
independence [ɪndɪ'pɛndns] *n* independencia
Independence Day *n* Día *m* de la Independencia

● **INDEPENDENCE DAY**

El cuatro de julio es la fiesta nacional de los Estados Unidos, *Independence Day*, en conmemoración de la Declaración de Independencia escrita por Thomas Jefferson y adoptada en 1776. En ella se proclamaba la ruptura total con Gran Bretaña de las trece colonias americanas que fueron el origen de los Estados Unidos de América.

independent [ɪndɪ'pɛndənt] *adj* independiente; **to become ~** independizarse
in-depth ['ɪndɛpθ] *adj* en profundidad, a fondo
indescribable [ɪndɪ'skraɪbəbl] *adj* indescriptible
indestructible [ɪndɪs'trʌktəbl] *adj* indestructible

indeterminate [ɪndɪ'təːmɪnɪt] *adj* indeterminado
index ['ɪndɛks] *n* (*pl* **indexes**) (*in book*) índice *m*; (*in library etc*) catálogo; (*pl* **indices**) ['ɪndɪsiːz] (*ratio, sign*) exponente *m*
index card *n* ficha
index finger *n* índice *m*
index-linked ['ɪndɛks'lɪŋkt], (*US*) **indexed** ['ɪndɛkst] *adj* indexado
India ['ɪndɪə] *n* la India
Indian ['ɪndɪən] *adj, n* indio(-a) *m(f)*; (*also:* **American Indian**) indio(-a) *m(f)* de América, amerindio(-a) *m(f)*; (*pej*): **Red ~** piel roja *m/f*
Indian Ocean *n*: **the ~** el Océano Índico, el Mar de las Indias
Indian summer *n* (*fig*) veranillo de San Martín
india rubber *n* caucho
indicate ['ɪndɪkeɪt] *vt* indicar ■ *vi* (*Brit Aut*): **to ~ left/right** indicar a la izquierda/a la derecha
indication [ɪndɪ'keɪʃən] *n* indicio, señal *f*
indicative [ɪn'dɪkətɪv] *adj*: **to be ~ of sth** indicar algo ■ *n* (*Ling*) indicativo
indicator ['ɪndɪkeɪtəʳ] *n* (*gen*) indicador *m*; (*Aut*) intermitente *m*, direccional *m* (*LAm*)
indices ['ɪndɪsiːz] *npl of* **index**
indict [ɪn'daɪt] *vt* acusar
indictable [ɪn'daɪtəbl] *adj*: **~ offence** delito procesable
indictment [ɪn'daɪtmənt] *n* acusación *f*
indifference [ɪn'dɪfrəns] *n* indiferencia
indifferent [ɪn'dɪfrənt] *adj* indiferente; (*poor*) regular
indigenous [ɪn'dɪdʒɪnəs] *adj* indígena
indigestible [ɪndɪ'dʒɛstɪbl] *adj* indigesto
indigestion [ɪndɪ'dʒɛstʃən] *n* indigestión *f*
indignant [ɪn'dɪɡnənt] *adj*: **to be ~ about sth** indignarse por algo
indignation [ɪndɪɡ'neɪʃən] *n* indignación *f*
indignity [ɪn'dɪɡnɪtɪ] *n* indignidad *f*
indigo ['ɪndɪɡəu] *adj* (*colour*) (de color) añil ■ *n* añil *m*
indirect [ɪndɪ'rɛkt] *adj* indirecto
indirectly [ɪndɪ'rɛktlɪ] *adv* indirectamente
indiscernible [ɪndɪ'səːnəbl] *adj* imperceptible
indiscreet [ɪndɪ'skriːt] *adj* indiscreto, imprudente
indiscretion [ɪndɪ'skrɛʃən] *n* indiscreción *f*, imprudencia
indiscriminate [ɪndɪ'skrɪmɪnət] *adj* indiscriminado
indispensable [ɪndɪ'spɛnsəbl] *adj* indispensable, imprescindible
indisposed [ɪndɪ'spəuzd] *adj* (*unwell*) indispuesto

indisposition [ɪndɪspəˈzɪʃən] n
indisposición f
indisputable [ɪndɪˈspjuːtəbl] adj
incontestable
indistinct [ɪndɪˈstɪŋkt] adj indistinto
indistinguishable [ɪndɪˈstɪŋgwɪʃəbl] adj
indistinguible
individual [ɪndɪˈvɪdjuəl] n individuo ▪ adj
individual; (personal) personal; (for/of one only)
particular
individualist [ɪndɪˈvɪdjuəlɪst] n
individualista m/f
individuality [ɪndɪvɪdjuˈælɪtɪ] n
individualidad f
individually [ɪndɪˈvɪdjuəlɪ] adv
individualmente; particularmente
indivisible [ɪndɪˈvɪzəbl] adj indivisible
Indo-China [ˈɪndəuˈtʃaɪnə] n Indochina
indoctrinate [ɪnˈdɒktrɪneɪt] vt adoctrinar
indoctrination [ɪndɒktrɪˈneɪʃən] n
adoctrinamiento
indolence [ˈɪndələns] n indolencia
indolent [ˈɪndələnt] adj indolente, perezoso
Indonesia [ɪndəˈniːzɪə] n Indonesia
Indonesian [ɪndəˈniːzɪən] adj indonesio
▪ n indonesio(-a); (Ling) indonesio
indoor [ˈɪndɔː'] adj (swimming pool) cubierto;
(plant) de interior; (sport) bajo cubierta
indoors [ɪnˈdɔːz] adv dentro; (at home) en casa
indubitable [ɪnˈdjuːbɪtəbl] adj indudable
indubitably [ɪnˈdjuːbɪtəblɪ] adv
indudablemente
induce [ɪnˈdjuːs] vt inducir, persuadir; (bring
about) producir; **to ~ sb to do sth** persuadir a
algn a que haga algo
inducement [ɪnˈdjuːsmənt] n (incentive)
incentivo, aliciente m
induct [ɪnˈdʌkt] vt iniciar; (in job, rank, position)
instalar
induction [ɪnˈdʌkʃən] n (Med: of birth)
inducción f
induction course n (Brit) cursillo
introductorio or de iniciación
indulge [ɪnˈdʌldʒ] vt (whim) satisfacer;
(person) complacer; (child) mimar ▪ vi: **to ~ in**
darse el gusto de
indulgence [ɪnˈdʌldʒəns] n vicio
indulgent [ɪnˈdʌldʒənt] adj indulgente
industrial [ɪnˈdʌstrɪəl] adj industrial
industrial action n huelga
industrial estate n (Brit) polígono or (LAm)
zona industrial
industrial goods npl bienes mpl de
producción
industrialist [ɪnˈdʌstrɪəlɪst] n industrial m/f
industrialize [ɪnˈdʌstrɪəlaɪz] vt
industrializar

industrial park n (US) = **industrial estate**
industrial relations npl relaciones fpl
empresariales
industrial tribunal n magistratura de
trabajo, tribunal m laboral
industrial unrest n (Brit) agitación f obrera
industrious [ɪnˈdʌstrɪəs] adj (gen)
trabajador(a); (student) aplicado
industry [ˈɪndəstrɪ] n industria; (diligence)
aplicación f
inebriated [ɪˈniːbrɪeɪtɪd] adj borracho
inedible [ɪnˈɛdɪbl] adj incomible; (plant etc) no
comestible
ineffective [ɪnɪˈfɛktɪv], **ineffectual**
[ɪnɪˈfɛktʃuəl] adj ineficaz, inútil
inefficiency [ɪnɪˈfɪʃənsɪ] n ineficacia
inefficient [ɪnɪˈfɪʃənt] adj ineficaz, ineficiente
inelegant [ɪnˈɛlɪgənt] adj poco elegante
ineligible [ɪnˈɛlɪdʒɪbl] adj inelegible
inept [ɪˈnɛpt] adj incompetente, incapaz
ineptitude [ɪˈnɛptɪtjuːd] n incapacidad f,
ineptitud f
inequality [ɪnɪˈkwɒlɪtɪ] n desigualdad f
inequitable [ɪnˈɛkwɪtəbl] adj injusto
ineradicable [ɪnɪˈrædɪkəbl] adj inextirpable
inert [ɪˈnəːt] adj inerte, inactivo; (immobile)
inmóvil
inertia [ɪˈnəːʃə] n inercia; (laziness) pereza
inertia-reel seat-belt [ɪˈnəːʃəˈriːl-] n
cinturón m de seguridad retráctil
inescapable [ɪnɪˈskeɪpəbl] adj ineludible,
inevitable
inessential [ɪnɪˈsɛnʃl] adj no esencial
inestimable [ɪnˈɛstɪməbl] adj inestimable
inevitability [ɪnɛvɪtəˈbɪlɪtɪ] n inevitabilidad f
inevitable [ɪnˈɛvɪtəbl] adj inevitable;
(necessary) forzoso
inevitably [ɪnˈɛvɪtəblɪ] adv inevitablemente;
as ~ happens ... como siempre pasa ...
inexact [ɪnɪgˈzaekt] adj inexacto
inexcusable [ɪnɪksˈkjuːzəbl] adj
imperdonable
inexhaustible [ɪnɪgˈzɔːstɪbl] adj inagotable
inexorable [ɪnˈɛksərəbl] adj inexorable,
implacable
inexpensive [ɪnɪkˈspɛnsɪv] adj económico
inexperience [ɪnɪkˈspɪərɪəns] n falta de
experiencia
inexperienced [ɪnɪkˈspɪərɪənst] adj
inexperto; **to be ~ in sth** no tener
experiencia en algo
inexplicable [ɪnɪkˈsplɪkəbl] adj inexplicable
inexpressible [ɪnɪkˈsprɛsəbl] adj
inexpresable
inextricable [ɪnɪksˈtrɪkəbl] adj inseparable
inextricably [ɪnɪksˈtrɪkəblɪ] adv
indisolublemente

infallibility [ɪnfælə'bɪlɪtɪ] n infalibilidad f
infallible [ɪn'fælɪbl] adj infalible
infamous ['ɪnfəməs] adj infame
infamy ['ɪnfəmɪ] n infamia
infancy ['ɪnfənsɪ] n infancia
infant ['ɪnfənt] n niño(-a)
infantile ['ɪnfəntaɪl] adj infantil; (pej)
aniñado
infant mortality n mortalidad f infantil
infantry ['ɪnfəntrɪ] n infantería
infantryman ['ɪnfəntrɪmən] n soldado de
infantería
infant school n (Brit) escuela de párvulos; see
also **primary school**
infatuated [ɪn'fætjueɪtɪd] adj: ~ **with**
(in love) loco por; **to become ~ (with sb)**
enamoriscarse (de algn), encapricharse
(con algn)
infatuation [ɪnfætju'eɪʃən] n
enamoramiento
infect [ɪn'fɛkt] vt (wound) infectar; (person)
contagiar; (fig: pej) corromper; **infected
with** (illness) contagiado de; **to become
infected** (wound) infectarse
infection [ɪn'fɛkʃən] n infección f; (fig)
contagio
infectious [ɪn'fɛkʃəs] adj contagioso; (fig)
infeccioso
infer [ɪn'fɜː'] vt deducir, inferir; **to ~ (from)**
inferir (de), deducir (de)
inference ['ɪnfərəns] n deducción f,
inferencia
inferior [ɪn'fɪərɪə'] adj, n inferior m/f; **to feel ~**
sentirse inferior
inferiority [ɪnfɪərɪ'ɒrɪtɪ] n inferioridad f
inferiority complex n complejo de
inferioridad
infernal [ɪn'fɜːnl] adj infernal
inferno [ɪn'fɜːnəu] n infierno; (fig) hoguera
infertile [ɪn'fɜːtaɪl] adj estéril; (person)
infecundo
infertility [ɪnfɜː'tɪlɪtɪ] n esterilidad f;
infecundidad f
infest [ɪn'fɛst] vt infestar
infested [ɪn'fɛstɪd] adj: ~ **(with)** plagado (de)
infidel ['ɪnfɪdəl] n infiel m/f
infidelity [ɪnfɪ'dɛlɪtɪ] n infidelidad f
in-fighting ['ɪnfaɪtɪŋ] n (fig) lucha(s) f(pl)
interna(s)
infiltrate ['ɪnfɪltreɪt] vt (troops etc) infiltrarse
en ■ vi infiltrarse
infinite ['ɪnfɪnɪt] adj infinito; **an ~ amount
of money/time** un sinfín de dinero/tiempo
infinitely ['ɪnfɪnɪtlɪ] adv infinitamente
infinitesimal [ɪnfɪnɪ'tɛsɪməl] adj
infinitésimo
infinitive [ɪn'fɪnɪtɪv] n infinitivo

infinity [ɪn'fɪnɪtɪ] n (Math) infinito; **an ~**
infinidad f
infirm [ɪn'fɜːm] adj enfermizo, débil
infirmary [ɪn'fɜːmərɪ] n hospital m
infirmity [ɪn'fɜːmɪtɪ] n debilidad f; (illness)
enfermedad f, achaque m
inflame [ɪn'fleɪm] vt inflamar
inflamed [ɪn'fleɪmd] adj: **to become ~**
inflamarse
inflammable [ɪn'flæməbl] adj (Brit)
inflamable; (situation etc) explosivo
inflammation [ɪnflə'meɪʃən] n inflamación f
inflammatory [ɪn'flæmətərɪ] adj (speech)
incendiario
inflatable [ɪn'fleɪtəbl] adj inflable
inflate [ɪn'fleɪt] vt (tyre) inflar; (fig) hinchar
inflated [ɪn'fleɪtɪd] adj (tyre etc) inflado; (price,
self-esteem etc) exagerado
inflation [ɪn'fleɪʃən] n (Econ) inflación f
inflationary [ɪn'fleɪʃnərɪ] adj inflacionario
inflationary spiral n espiral f inflacionista
inflexible [ɪn'flɛksɪbl] adj inflexible
inflict [ɪn'flɪkt] vt: **to ~ on** infligir en; (tax etc)
imponer a
in flight ['ɪnflaɪt] adj durante el vuelo
inflow ['ɪnfləu] n afluencia
influence ['ɪnfluəns] n influencia ■ vt
influir en, influenciar; **under the ~ of
alcohol** en estado de embriaguez
influential [ɪnflu'ɛnʃl] adj influyente
influenza [ɪnflu'ɛnzə] n gripe f
influx ['ɪnflʌks] n afluencia
inform [ɪn'fɔːm] vt: **to ~ sb of sth** informar
a algn sobre or de algo; (warn) avisar a algn
de algo; (communicate) comunicar algo a algn
■ vi: **to ~ on sb** delatar a algn
informal [ɪn'fɔːml] adj (manner, tone)
desenfadado; (dress, occasion) informal
informality [ɪnfɔː'mælɪtɪ] n falta de
ceremonia; (intimacy) intimidad f; (familiarity)
familiaridad f; (ease) afabilidad f
informally [ɪn'fɔːməlɪ] adv sin ceremonia;
(invite) informalmente
informant [ɪn'fɔːmənt] n informante m/f
informatics [ɪnfɔː'mætɪks] n informática
information [ɪnfə'meɪʃən] n información f;
(news) noticias fpl; (knowledge) conocimientos
mpl; (Law) delación f; **a piece of ~** un dato;
for your ~ para su información
**information and communication
technology, information and
communications technology** n (gen)
tecnología de la información y de las
comunicaciones; (Brit Scol) informática
information bureau n oficina de información
information processing n procesamiento
de datos

i

information retrieval n recuperación f de información

information science n gestión f de la información

information technology n informática

informative [ɪn'fɔːmətɪv] adj informativo

informed [ɪn'fɔːmd] adj (observer) informado, al corriente; **an ~ guess** una opinión bien fundamentada

informer [ɪn'fɔːmə^r] n delator(a) m(f); (also: **police informer**) soplón(-ona) m(f)

infra dig ['ɪnfrə'dɪg] adj abbr (col: = infra dignitatem: = beneath one's dignity) denigrante

infra-red [ɪnfrə'rɛd] adj infrarrojo

infrastructure ['ɪnfrəstrʌktʃə^r] n infraestructura

infrequent [ɪn'friːkwənt] adj infrecuente

infringe [ɪn'frɪndʒ] vt infringir, violar ▪ vi: **to ~ on** invadir

infringement [ɪn'frɪndʒmənt] n infracción f; (of rights) usurpación f; (Sport) falta

infuriate [ɪn'fjuərɪeɪt] vt: **to become infuriated** ponerse furioso

infuriating [ɪn'fjuərɪeɪtɪŋ] adj: **I find it ~** me saca de quicio

infuse [ɪn'fjuːz] vt (with courage, enthusiasm): **to ~ sb with sth** infundir algo a algn

infusion [ɪn'fjuːʒən] n (tea etc) infusión f

ingenious [ɪn'dʒiːnjəs] adj ingenioso

ingenuity [ɪndʒɪ'njuːɪtɪ] n ingeniosidad f

ingenuous [ɪn'dʒɛnjuəs] adj ingenuo

ingot ['ɪŋgət] n lingote m, barra

ingrained [ɪn'greɪnd] adj arraigado

ingratiate [ɪn'greɪʃɪeɪt] vt: **to ~ o.s. with** congraciarse con

ingratiating [ɪn'greɪʃɪeɪtɪŋ] adj (smile, speech) insinuante; (person) zalamero, congraciador(a)

ingratitude [ɪn'grætɪtjuːd] n ingratitud f

ingredient [ɪn'griːdɪənt] n ingrediente m

ingrowing ['ɪngrəʊɪŋ] adj: **~ (toe)nail** uña encarnada

inhabit [ɪn'hæbɪt] vt vivir en; (occupy) ocupar

inhabitable [ɪn'hæbɪtəbl] adj habitable

inhabitant [ɪn'hæbɪtənt] n habitante m/f

inhale [ɪn'heɪl] vt inhalar ▪ vi (in smoking) tragar

inhaler [ɪn'heɪlə^r] n inhalador m

inherent [ɪn'hɪərənt] adj: **~ in** or **to** inherente a

inherently [ɪn'hɪərəntlɪ] adv intrínsecamente

inherit [ɪn'hɛrɪt] vt heredar

inheritance [ɪn'hɛrɪtəns] n herencia; (fig) patrimonio

inhibit [ɪn'hɪbɪt] vt inhibir, impedir; **to ~ sb from doing sth** impedir a algn hacer algo

inhibited [ɪn'hɪbɪtɪd] adj (person) cohibido

inhibition [ɪnhɪ'bɪʃən] n cohibición f

inhospitable [ɪnhɔs'pɪtəbl] adj (person) inhospitalario; (place) inhóspito

in-house ['ɪnhaus] adj dentro de la empresa

inhuman [ɪn'hjuːmən] adj inhumano

inhumane [ɪnhjuː'meɪn] adj inhumano

inimitable [ɪ'nɪmɪtəbl] adj inimitable

iniquity [ɪ'nɪkwɪtɪ] n iniquidad f; (injustice) injusticia

initial [ɪ'nɪʃl] adj inicial; (first) primero ▪ n inicial f ▪ vt firmar con las iniciales; **initials** npl iniciales fpl; (abbreviation) siglas fpl

initialize [ɪ'nɪʃəlaɪz] vt (Comput) inicializar

initially [ɪ'nɪʃəlɪ] adv en un principio

initiate [ɪ'nɪʃɪeɪt] vt (start) iniciar; **to ~ sb into a secret** iniciar a algn en un secreto; **to ~ proceedings against sb** (Law) poner una demanda contra algn

initiation [ɪnɪʃɪ'eɪʃən] n (into secret etc) iniciación f; (beginning) comienzo

initiative [ɪ'nɪʃətɪv] n iniciativa; **to take the ~** tomar la iniciativa

inject [ɪn'dʒɛkt] vt inyectar; (money, enthusiasm) aportar

injection [ɪn'dʒɛkʃən] n inyección f; **to have an ~** ponerse una inyección

injudicious [ɪndʒuː'dɪʃəs] adj imprudente, indiscreto

injunction [ɪn'dʒʌŋkʃən] n entredicho, interdicto

injure ['ɪndʒə^r] vt herir; (hurt) lastimar; (fig: reputation etc) perjudicar; (feelings) herir; **to ~ o.s.** hacerse daño, lastimarse

injured ['ɪndʒəd] adj (also fig) herido; **~ party** (Law) parte f perjudicada

injurious [ɪn'dʒuərɪəs] adj: **~ (to)** perjudicial (para)

injury ['ɪndʒərɪ] n herida, lesión f; (wrong) perjuicio, daño; **to escape without ~** salir ileso

injury time n (Sport) descuento

injustice [ɪn'dʒʌstɪs] n injusticia; **you do me an ~** usted es injusto conmigo

ink [ɪŋk] n tinta

ink-jet printer ['ɪŋkdʒɛt-] n impresora de chorro de tinta

inkling ['ɪŋklɪŋ] n sospecha; (idea) idea

inkpad ['ɪŋkpæd] n almohadilla

inlaid ['ɪnleɪd] adj (wood) taraceado; (tiles) entarimado

inland adj ['ɪnlənd] interior; (town) del interior ▪ adv [ɪn'lænd] tierra adentro

Inland Revenue n (Brit) ≈ Hacienda

in-laws ['ɪnlɔːz] npl suegros mpl

inlet ['ɪnlɛt] n (Geo) ensenada, cala; (Tech) admisión f, entrada

inmate ['ɪnmeɪt] n (in prison) preso(-a), presidiario(-a); (in asylum) internado(-a)
inmost ['ɪnməʊst] adj más íntimo, más secreto
inn [ɪn] n posada, mesón m; **the Inns of Court** see **barrister**
innards ['ɪnədz] npl (col) tripas fpl
innate [ɪ'neɪt] adj innato
inner ['ɪnə'] adj interior, interno
inner city n barrios deprimidos del centro de una ciudad
innermost ['ɪnəməʊst] adj más íntimo, más secreto
inner tube n (of tyre) cámara, llanta (LAm)
innings ['ɪnɪŋz] n (Cricket) entrada, turno
innocence ['ɪnəsns] n inocencia
innocent ['ɪnəsnt] adj inocente
innocuous [ɪ'nɔkjuəs] adj inocuo
innovation [ɪnəu'veɪʃən] n novedad f
innuendo (pl **innuendoes**) [ɪnju'ɛndəu, -əuz] n indirecta
innumerable [ɪ'njuːmrəbl] adj innumerable
inoculate [ɪ'nɔkjuleɪt] vt: **to ~ sb with sth/against sth** inocular or vacunar a algn con algo/contra algo
inoculation [ɪnɔkju'leɪʃən] n inoculación f
inoffensive [ɪnə'fɛnsɪv] adj inofensivo
inopportune [ɪn'ɔpətjuːn] adj inoportuno
inordinate [ɪ'nɔːdɪnət] adj excesivo, desmesurado
inordinately [ɪ'nɔːdɪnətlɪ] adv excesivamente, desmesuradamente
inorganic [ɪnɔː'gænɪk] adj inorgánico
in-patient ['ɪnpeɪʃənt] n (paciente m/f) interno(-a)
input ['ɪnput] n (Elec) entrada; (Comput) entrada de datos ▪ vt (Comput) introducir, entrar
inquest ['ɪnkwɛst] n (coroner's) investigación f post-mortem
inquire [ɪn'kwaɪə'] vi preguntar ▪ vt: **to ~ when/where/whether** preguntar cuándo/dónde/si; **to ~ about** (person) preguntar por; (fact) informarse de
  ▶ **inquire into** vt fus: **to ~ into sth** investigar or indagar algo
inquiring [ɪn'kwaɪərɪŋ] adj (mind) inquieto; (look) interrogante
inquiry [ɪn'kwaɪərɪ] n pregunta; (Law) investigación f, pesquisa; (commission) comisión f investigadora; **to hold an ~ into sth** emprender una investigación sobre algo
inquiry desk n mesa de información
inquiry office n (Brit) oficina de información
inquisition [ɪnkwɪ'zɪʃən] n inquisición f
inquisitive [ɪn'kwɪzɪtɪv] adj (mind) inquisitivo; (person) fisgón(-ona)

inroad ['ɪnrəud] n incursión f; (fig) invasión f; **to make inroads into** (time) ocupar parte de; (savings, supplies) agotar parte de
insane [ɪn'seɪn] adj loco; (Med) demente
insanitary [ɪn'sænɪtərɪ] adj insalubre
insanity [ɪn'sænɪtɪ] n demencia, locura
insatiable [ɪn'seɪʃəbl] adj insaciable
inscribe [ɪn'skraɪb] vt inscribir; (book etc): **to ~ (to sb)** dedicar (a algn)
inscription [ɪn'skrɪpʃən] n (gen) inscripción f; (in book) dedicatoria
inscrutable [ɪn'skruːtəbl] adj inescrutable, insondable
inseam measurement ['ɪnsiːm-] n (US) **= inside leg measurement**
insect ['ɪnsɛkt] n insecto
insect bite n picadura
insecticide [ɪn'sɛktɪsaɪd] n insecticida m
insect repellent n loción f contra los insectos
insecure [ɪnsɪ'kjuə'] adj inseguro
insecurity [ɪnsɪ'kjuərɪtɪ] n inseguridad f
insemination [ɪnsɛmɪ'neɪʃn] n: **artificial ~** inseminación f artificial
insensible [ɪn'sɛnsɪbl] adj inconsciente; (unconscious) sin conocimiento
insensitive [ɪn'sɛnsɪtɪv] adj insensible
insensitivity [ɪnsɛnsɪ'tɪvɪtɪ] n insensibilidad f
inseparable [ɪn'sɛprəbl] adj inseparable; **they were ~ friends** los unía una estrecha amistad
insert vt [ɪn'səːt] (into sth) introducir; (Comput) insertar ▪ n ['ɪnsəːt] encarte m
insertion [ɪn'səːʃən] n inserción f
in-service [ɪn'səːvɪs] adj (training, course) en el trabajo, a cargo de la empresa
inshore [ɪn'ʃɔː'] adj: **~ fishing** pesca f costera ▪ adv (fish) a lo largo de la costa; (move) hacia la orilla
inside ['ɪn'saɪd] n interior m; (lining) forro; (of road: Brit) izquierdo; (: in US, Europe etc) derecho ▪ adj interior, interno ▪ adv (within) (por) dentro, adentro (esp LAm); (with movement) hacia dentro; (col: in prison) en chirona ▪ prep dentro de; (of time): **~ 10 minutes** en menos de 10 minutos; **insides** npl (col) tripas fpl; **~ out** adv (turn) al revés; (know) a fondo
inside forward n (Sport) interior m
inside information n información f confidencial
inside lane n (Aut: Brit) carril m izquierdo; (: in US, Europe etc) carril m derecho
inside leg measurement n medida de pernera
insider [ɪn'saɪdə'] n enterado(-a)
insider dealing, insider trading n (Stock Exchange) abuso de información privilegiada

inside story n historia íntima
insidious [ɪnˈsɪdɪəs] adj insidioso
insight [ˈɪnsaɪt] n perspicacia, percepción f; **to gain** or **get an ~ into sth** comprender algo mejor
insignia [ɪnˈsɪɡnɪə] npl insignias fpl
insignificant [ɪnsɪɡˈnɪfɪknt] adj insignificante
insincere [ɪnsɪnˈsɪəʳ] adj poco sincero
insincerity [ɪnsɪnˈsɛrɪtɪ] n falta de sinceridad, doblez f
insinuate [ɪnˈsɪnjueɪt] vt insinuar
insinuation [ɪnsɪnjuˈeɪʃən] n insinuación f
insipid [ɪnˈsɪpɪd] adj soso, insulso
insist [ɪnˈsɪst] vi insistir; **to ~ on doing** empeñarse en hacer; **to ~ that** insistir en que; (claim) exigir que
insistence [ɪnˈsɪstəns] n insistencia; (stubbornness) empeño
insistent [ɪnˈsɪstənt] adj insistente; empeñado
insofar as [ɪnsəʊˈfɑː-] conj en la medida en que, en tanto que
insole [ˈɪnsəʊl] n plantilla
insolence [ˈɪnsələns] n insolencia, descaro
insolent [ˈɪnsələnt] adj insolente, descarado
insoluble [ɪnˈsɒljubl] adj insoluble
insolvency [ɪnˈsɒlvənsɪ] n insolvencia
insolvent [ɪnˈsɒlvənt] adj insolvente
insomnia [ɪnˈsɒmnɪə] n insomnio
insomniac [ɪnˈsɒmnɪæk] n insomne m/f
inspect [ɪnˈspɛkt] vt inspeccionar, examinar; (troops) pasar revista a
inspection [ɪnˈspɛkʃən] n inspección f, examen m
inspector [ɪnˈspɛktəʳ] n inspector(a) m(f); (Brit: on buses, trains) revisor(a) m(f)
inspiration [ɪnspəˈreɪʃən] n inspiración f
inspire [ɪnˈspaɪəʳ] vt inspirar; **to ~ sb (to do sth)** alentar a algn (a hacer algo)
inspired [ɪnˈspaɪəd] adj (writer, book etc) inspirado, genial, iluminado; **in an ~ moment** en un momento de inspiración
inspiring [ɪnˈspaɪərɪŋ] adj inspirador(a)
inst. [ɪnst] abbr (Brit Comm: = instant, of the present month) cte
instability [ɪnstəˈbɪlɪtɪ] n inestabilidad f
install [ɪnˈstɔːl] vt instalar
installation [ɪnstəˈleɪʃən] n instalación f
installment plan n (US) compra a plazos
instalment, (US) **installment** [ɪnˈstɔːlmənt] n plazo; (of story) entrega; (of TV serial etc) capítulo; **in instalments** (pay, receive) a plazos; **to pay in instalments** pagar a plazos or por abonos
instance [ˈɪnstəns] n ejemplo, caso; **for ~** por ejemplo; **in the first ~** en primer lugar; **in that ~** en ese caso

instant [ˈɪnstənt] n instante m, momento ■ adj inmediato; (coffee) instantáneo
instantaneous [ɪnstənˈteɪnɪəs] adj instantáneo
instantly [ˈɪnstəntlɪ] adv en seguida, al instante
instant messaging [-ˈmɛsədʒɪŋ] n mensajería instantánea
instant replay n (US TV) repetición f de la jugada
instead [ɪnˈstɛd] adv en cambio; **~ of** en lugar de, en vez de
instep [ˈɪnstɛp] n empeine m
instigate [ˈɪnstɪɡeɪt] vt (rebellion, strike, crime) instigar; (new ideas etc) fomentar
instigation [ɪnstɪˈɡeɪʃən] n instigación f; **at sb's ~** a instigación de algn
instil [ɪnˈstɪl] vt: **to ~ into** inculcar a
instinct [ˈɪnstɪŋkt] n instinto
instinctive [ɪnˈstɪŋktɪv] adj instintivo
instinctively [ɪnˈstɪŋktɪvlɪ] adv por instinto
institute [ˈɪnstɪtjuːt] n instituto; (professional body) colegio ■ vt (begin) iniciar, empezar; (proceedings) entablar
institution [ɪnstɪˈtjuːʃən] n institución f; (beginning) iniciación f; (Med: home) asilo; (asylum) manicomio; (custom) costumbre f arraigada
institutional [ɪnstɪˈtjuːʃənl] adj institucional
instruct [ɪnˈstrʌkt] vt: **to ~ sb in sth** instruir a algn en or sobre algo; **to ~ sb to do sth** dar instrucciones a algn de or mandar a algn hacer algo
instruction [ɪnˈstrʌkʃən] n (teaching) instrucción f; **instructions** npl órdenes fpl; **instructions (for use)** modo sg de empleo
instruction book n manual m
instructive [ɪnˈstrʌktɪv] adj instructivo
instructor [ɪnˈstrʌktəʳ] n instructor(a) m(f)
instrument [ˈɪnstrəmənt] n instrumento
instrumental [ɪnstrəˈmɛntl] adj (Mus) instrumental; **to be ~ in** ser el artífice de; **to be ~ in sth/in doing sth** ser responsable de algo/de hacer algo
instrumentalist [ɪnstrəˈmɛntəlɪst] n instrumentista m/f
instrument panel n tablero (de instrumentos)
insubordinate [ɪnsəˈbɔːdənɪt] adj insubordinado
insubordination [ɪnsəbɔːdəˈneɪʃən] n insubordinación f
insufferable [ɪnˈsʌfrəbl] adj insoportable
insufficient [ɪnsəˈfɪʃənt] adj insuficiente
insular [ˈɪnsjuləʳ] adj insular; (outlook) estrecho de miras

insularity [ɪnsjuˈlærɪtɪ] n insularidad f
insulate [ˈɪnsjuleɪt] vt aislar
insulating tape [ˈɪnsjuleɪtɪŋ-] n cinta
aislante
insulation [ɪnsjuˈleɪʃən] n aislamiento
insulator [ˈɪnsjuleɪtəʳ] n aislante m
insulin [ˈɪnsjulɪn] n insulina
insult n [ˈɪnsʌlt] insulto; (offence) ofensa
■ vt [ɪnˈsʌlt] insultar; ofender
insulting [ɪnˈsʌltɪŋ] adj insultante; ofensivo
insuperable [ɪnˈsjuːprəbl] adj insuperable
insurance [ɪnˈʃuərəns] n seguro; **fire/life**
~ seguro de incendios/vida; **to take out** ~
(against) hacerse un seguro (contra)
insurance agent n agente m/f de seguros
insurance broker n corredor(a) m(f) or agente
m/f de seguros
insurance policy n póliza (de seguros)
insurance premium n prima de seguros
insure [ɪnˈʃuəʳ] vt asegurar; **to** ~ **sb** or **sb's**
life hacer un seguro de vida a algn; **to** ~
(against) asegurar (contra); **to be insured**
for £5000 tener un seguro de 5000 libras
insured [ɪnˈʃuəd] n: **the** ~ el/la asegurado(-a)
insurer [ɪnˈʃuərəʳ] n asegurador(a)
insurgent [ɪnˈsɜːdʒənt] adj, n insurgente m/f,
insurrecto(-a) m(f)
insurmountable [ɪnsəˈmauntəbl] adj
insuperable
insurrection [ɪnsəˈrɛkʃən] n insurrección f
intact [ɪnˈtækt] adj íntegro; (untouched)
intacto
intake [ˈɪnteɪk] n (Tech) entrada, toma; (: pipe)
tubo de admisión; (of food) ingestión f; (Brit
Scol): **an** ~ **of 200 a year** 200 matriculados
al año
intangible [ɪnˈtændʒɪbl] adj intangible
integer [ˈɪntɪdʒəʳ] n (número) entero
integral [ˈɪntɪɡrəl] adj (whole) íntegro; (part)
integrante
integrate [ˈɪntɪɡreɪt] vt integrar ■ vi
integrarse
integrated circuit [ˈɪntɪɡreɪtɪd-] n (Comput)
circuito integrado
integration [ɪntɪˈɡreɪʃən] n integración f;
racial ~ integración de razas
integrity [ɪnˈtɛɡrɪtɪ] n honradez f, rectitud f;
(Comput) integridad f
intellect [ˈɪntəlɛkt] n intelecto
intellectual [ɪntəˈlɛktjuəl] adj, n intelectual
m/f
intelligence [ɪnˈtɛlɪdʒəns] n inteligencia
intelligence quotient n coeficiente m
intelectual
Intelligence Service n Servicio de
Inteligencia
intelligence test n prueba de inteligencia

intelligent [ɪnˈtɛlɪdʒənt] adj inteligente
intelligently [ɪnˈtɛlɪdʒəntlɪ] adv
inteligentemente
intelligentsia [ɪntɛlɪˈdʒɛntsɪə] n
intelectualidad f
intelligible [ɪnˈtɛlɪdʒɪbl] adj inteligible,
comprensible
intemperate [ɪnˈtɛmpərət] adj inmoderado
intend [ɪnˈtɛnd] vt (gift etc): **to** ~ **sth for**
destinar algo a; **to** ~ **to do sth** tener
intención de or pensar hacer algo
intended [ɪnˈtɛndɪd] adj (effect) deseado
intense [ɪnˈtɛns] adj intenso; **to be** ~ (person)
tomárselo todo muy en serio
intensely [ɪnˈtɛnslɪ] adv intensamente; (very)
sumamente
intensify [ɪnˈtɛnsɪfaɪ] vt intensificar;
(increase) aumentar
intensity [ɪnˈtɛnsɪtɪ] n (gen) intensidad f
intensive [ɪnˈtɛnsɪv] adj intensivo
intensive care n: **to be in** ~ estar bajo
cuidados intensivos; ~ **unit** n unidad f de
vigilancia intensiva
intensively [ɪnˈtɛnsɪvlɪ] adv intensamente
intent [ɪnˈtɛnt] n propósito ■ adj (absorbed)
absorto; (attentive) atento; **to all intents**
and purposes a efectos prácticos; **to be** ~
on doing sth estar resuelto or decidido a
hacer algo
intention [ɪnˈtɛnʃən] n intención f, propósito
intentional [ɪnˈtɛnʃənl] adj deliberado
intentionally [ɪnˈtɛnʃnəlɪ] adv a propósito
intently [ɪnˈtɛntlɪ] adv atentamente,
fijamente
inter [ɪnˈtɜːʳ] vt enterrar, sepultar
inter- [ˈɪntəʳ] pref inter-
interact [ɪntərˈækt] vi (substances) influirse
mutuamente; (people) relacionarse
interaction [ɪntərˈækʃən] n interacción f,
acción f recíproca
interactive [ɪntərˈæktɪv] adj (Comput)
interactivo
intercede [ɪntəˈsiːd] vi (also: **to intercede**
(with)) interceder (con); **to** ~ **with sb/on**
behalf of sb interceder con algn/en nombre
de algn
intercept [ɪntəˈsɛpt] vt interceptar; (stop)
detener
interception [ɪntəˈsɛpʃən] n interceptación
f; detención f
interchange n [ˈɪntətʃeɪndʒ] intercambio;
(on motorway) intersección f ■ vt
[ɪntəˈtʃeɪndʒ] intercambiar
interchangeable [ɪntəˈtʃeɪndʒəbl] adj
intercambiable
intercity [ɪntəˈsɪtɪ] adj: ~ **(train)** (tren m)
intercity m

intercom ['ɪntəkɔm] n interfono
interconnect [ɪntəkə'nɛkt] vi (rooms) comunicar(se)
intercontinental ['ɪntəkɔntɪ'nɛntl] adj intercontinental
intercourse ['ɪntəkɔ:s] n (also: **sexual intercourse**) relaciones fpl sexuales, contacto sexual; (social) trato
interdependence [ɪntədɪ'pɛndəns] n interdependencia
interdependent [ɪntədɪ'pɛndənt] adj interdependiente
interest ['ɪntrɪst] n (Comm) interés m ▪ vt interesar; **compound/simple ~** interés compuesto/simple; **business interests** negocios mpl; **British interests in the Middle East** los intereses británicos en el Medio Oriente
interested ['ɪntrɪstɪd] adj interesado; **to be ~ in** interesarse por
interest-free ['ɪntrɪst'fri:] adj libre de interés
interesting ['ɪntrɪstɪŋ] adj interesante
interest rate n tipo de interés
interface ['ɪntəfeɪs] n (Comput) junción f, interface m
interfere [ɪntə'fɪər] vi: **to ~ in** (quarrel, other people's business) entrometerse en; **to ~ with** (hinder) estorbar; (damage) estropear; (Radio) interferir con
interference [ɪntə'fɪərəns] n (gen) intromisión f; (Radio, TV) interferencia
interfering [ɪntə'fɪərɪŋ] adj entrometido
interim ['ɪntərɪm] adj: **~ dividend** dividendo parcial ▪ n: **in the ~** en el ínterin
interior [ɪn'tɪərɪər] n interior m ▪ adj interior
interior decorator, interior designer n interiorista m/f, diseñador(a) m(f) de interiores
interjection [ɪntə'dʒɛkʃən] n interrupción f
interlock [ɪntə'lɔk] vi entrelazarse; (wheels etc) endentarse
interloper ['ɪntələupə'] n intruso(-a)
interlude ['ɪntəlu:d] n intervalo; (rest) descanso; (Theat) intermedio
intermarriage [ɪntə'mærɪdʒ] n endogamia
intermarry [ɪntə'mærɪ] vi casarse (entre parientes)
intermediary [ɪntə'mi:dɪərɪ] n intermediario(-a)
intermediate [ɪntə'mi:dɪət] adj intermedio
interminable [ɪn'tə:mɪnəbl] adj inacabable
intermission [ɪntə'mɪʃən] n (Theat) descanso
intermittent [ɪntə'mɪtnt] adj intermitente
intermittently [ɪntə'mɪtntlɪ] adv intermitentemente
intern vt [ɪn'tə:n] internar; (enclose) encerrar ▪ n ['ɪntə:n] (US) médico(-a) m(f) interno(-a)

internal [ɪn'tə:nl] adj interno, interior; **~ injuries** heridas fpl or lesiones fpl internas
internally [ɪn'tə:nəlɪ] adv interiormente; **"not to be taken ~"** "uso externo"
Internal Revenue Service n (US) ≈ Hacienda
international [ɪntə'næʃənl] adj internacional; **~ (game)** partido internacional; **~ (player)** jugador(a) m(f) internacional
International Atomic Energy Agency n Organismo Internacional de Energía Atómica
International Chamber of Commerce n Cámara de Comercio Internacional
International Court of Justice n Corte f Internacional de Justicia
international date line n línea de cambio de fecha
internationally [ɪntə'næʃnəlɪ] adv internacionalmente
International Monetary Fund n Fondo Monetario Internacional
internecine [ɪntə'ni:saɪn] adj de aniquilación mutua
internee [ɪntə'ni:] n interno(-a), recluso(-a)
Internet ['ɪntənɛt] n: **the ~** (el or la) Internet
Internet café n cibercafé m
Internet Service Provider n proveedor m de (acceso a) Internet
Internet user n internauta m/f
internment [ɪn'tə:nmənt] n internamiento
interplanetary [ɪntə'plænɪtərɪ] adj interplanetario
interplay ['ɪntəpleɪ] n interacción f
Interpol ['ɪntəpɔl] n Interpol f
interpret [ɪn'tə:prɪt] vt interpretar; (translate) traducir; (understand) entender ▪ vi hacer de intérprete
interpretation [ɪntə:prɪ'teɪʃən] n interpretación f; traducción f
interpreter [ɪn'tə:prɪtə'] n intérprete m/f
interrelated [ɪntərɪ'leɪtɪd] adj interrelacionado
interrogate [ɪn'tɛrəugeɪt] vt interrogar
interrogation [ɪntɛrəu'geɪʃən] n interrogatorio
interrogative [ɪntə'rɔgətɪv] adj interrogativo
interrupt [ɪntə'rʌpt] vt, vi interrumpir
interruption [ɪntə'rʌpʃən] n interrupción f
intersect [ɪntə'sɛkt] vt cruzar ▪ vi (roads) cruzarse
intersection [ɪntə'sɛkʃən] n intersección f; (of roads) cruce m
intersperse [ɪntə'spə:s] vt: **to ~ with** salpicar de
intertwine [ɪntə'twaɪn] vt entrelazar ▪ vi entrelazarse

interval ['ɪntəvl] n intervalo; (Brit Theat, Sport) descanso; **at intervals** a ratos, de vez en cuando; **sunny intervals** (Meteorology) claros mpl

intervene [ɪntə'viːn] vi intervenir; (take part) participar; (occur) sobrevenir

intervening [ɪntə'viːnɪŋ] adj intermedio

intervention [ɪntə'vɛnʃən] n intervención f

interview ['ɪntəvjuː] n (Radio, TV etc) entrevista ▪ vt entrevistar a

interviewee [ɪntəvjuː'iː] n entrevistado(-a)

interviewer ['ɪntəvjuːəʳ] n entrevistador(a) m(f)

intestate [ɪn'tɛsteɪt] adj intestado

intestinal [ɪn'tɛstɪnl] adj intestinal

intestine [ɪn'tɛstɪn] n: **large/small ~** intestino grueso/delgado

intimacy ['ɪntɪməsɪ] n intimidad f; (relations) relaciones fpl íntimas

intimate adj ['ɪntɪmət] íntimo; (friendship) estrecho; (knowledge) profundo ▪ vt ['ɪntɪmeɪt] (announce) dar a entender

intimately ['ɪntɪmətlɪ] adv íntimamente

intimidate [ɪn'tɪmɪdeɪt] vt intimidar, amedrentar

intimidation [ɪntɪmɪ'deɪʃən] n intimidación f

into ['ɪntuː] prep (gen) en; (towards) a; (inside) hacia el interior de; **~ three pieces/French** en tres pedazos/al francés; **to change pounds ~ euros** cambiar libras por euros

intolerable [ɪn'tɔlərəbl] adj intolerable, insoportable

intolerance [ɪn'tɔlərəns] n intolerancia

intolerant [ɪn'tɔlərənt] adj: **~ (of)** intolerante (con)

intonation [ɪntəu'neɪʃən] n entonación f

intoxicate [ɪn'tɔksɪkeɪt] vt embriagar

intoxicated [ɪn'tɔksɪkeɪtɪd] adj embriagado

intoxication [ɪntɔksɪ'keɪʃən] n embriaguez f

intractable [ɪn'træktəbl] adj (person) intratable; (problem) irresoluble; (illness) incurable

intranet ['ɪntrənɛt] n intranet f

intransigence [ɪn'trænsɪdʒəns] n intransigencia

intransigent [ɪn'trænsɪdʒənt] adj intransigente

intransitive [ɪn'trænsɪtɪv] adj intransitivo

intravenous [ɪntrə'viːnəs] adj intravenoso

in-tray ['ɪntreɪ] n bandeja de entrada

intrepid [ɪn'trɛpɪd] adj intrépido

intricacy ['ɪntrɪkəsɪ] n complejidad f

intricate ['ɪntrɪkət] adj intrincado; (plot, problem) complejo

intrigue [ɪn'triːg] n intriga ▪ vt fascinar ▪ vi andar en intrigas

intriguing [ɪn'triːgɪŋ] adj fascinante

intrinsic [ɪn'trɪnsɪk] adj intrínseco

introduce [ɪntrə'djuːs] vt introducir, meter; **to ~ sb (to sb)** presentar algn (a algn); **to ~ sb to** (pastime, technique) introducir a algn a; **may I ~ ...?** permítame presentarle a ...

introduction [ɪntrə'dʌkʃən] n introducción f; (of person) presentación f; **a letter of ~** una carta de recomendación

introductory [ɪntrə'dʌktərɪ] adj introductorio; **an ~ offer** una oferta introductoria; **~ remarks** comentarios mpl preliminares

introspection [ɪntrəu'spɛkʃən] n introspección f

introspective [ɪntrəu'spɛktɪv] adj introspectivo

introvert ['ɪntrəuvəːt] adj, n introvertido(-a) m(f)

intrude [ɪn'truːd] vi (person) entrometerse; **to ~ on** estorbar

intruder [ɪn'truːdəʳ] n intruso(-a)

intrusion [ɪn'truːʒən] n invasión f

intrusive [ɪn'truːsɪv] adj intruso

intuition [ɪntjuː'ɪʃən] n intuición f

intuitive [ɪn'tjuːɪtɪv] adj intuitivo

intuitively [ɪn'tjuːɪtɪvlɪ] adv por intuición, intuitivamente

inundate ['ɪnʌndeɪt] vt: **to ~ with** inundar de

inure [ɪn'juəʳ] vt: **to ~ (to)** acostumbrar or habituar (a)

invade [ɪn'veɪd] vt invadir

invader [ɪn'veɪdəʳ] n invasor(a) m(f)

invalid n ['ɪnvəlɪd] minusválido(-a) ▪ adj [ɪn'vælɪd] (not valid) inválido, nulo

invalidate [ɪn'vælɪdeɪt] vt invalidar, anular

invalid chair n silla de ruedas

invaluable [ɪn'væljuəbl] adj inestimable

invariable [ɪn'vɛərɪəbl] adj invariable

invariably [ɪn'vɛərɪəblɪ] adv sin excepción, siempre; **she is ~ late** siempre llega tarde

invasion [ɪn'veɪʒən] n invasión f

invective [ɪn'vɛktɪv] n invectiva

inveigle [ɪn'viːgl] vt: **to ~ sb into (doing) sth** embaucar or engatusar a algn para (que haga) algo

invent [ɪn'vɛnt] vt inventar

invention [ɪn'vɛnʃən] n invento; (inventiveness) inventiva; (lie) invención f

inventive [ɪn'vɛntɪv] adj inventivo

inventiveness [ɪn'vɛntɪvnɪs] n ingenio, inventiva

inventor [ɪn'vɛntəʳ] n inventor(a) m(f)

inventory ['ɪnvəntrɪ] n inventario

inventory control n control m de existencias

inverse [ɪn'vəːs] adj, n inverso; **in ~ proportion (to)** en proporción inversa (a)

i

inversely [ɪn'vɜːslɪ] *adv* a la inversa
invert [ɪn'vɜːt] *vt* invertir
invertebrate [ɪn'vɜːtɪbrət] *n* invertebrado
inverted commas [ɪn'vɜːtɪd-] *npl* (Brit) comillas *fpl*
invest [ɪn'vɛst] *vt* invertir; (fig: time, effort) dedicar ▪ *vi* invertir; **to ~ sb with sth** conferir algo a algn
investigate [ɪn'vɛstɪgeɪt] *vt* investigar; (study) estudiar, examinar
investigation [ɪnvɛstɪ'geɪʃən] *n* investigación *f*, pesquisa; examen *m*
investigative journalism [ɪn'vɛstɪgətɪv-] *n* periodismo de investigación
investigator [ɪn'vɛstɪgeɪtər] *n* investigador(a) *m(f)*; **private ~** investigador(a) *m(f)* privado(-a)
investiture [ɪn'vɛstɪtʃər] *n* investidura
investment [ɪn'vɛstmənt] *n* inversión *f*
investment grant *n* subvención *f* para la inversión
investment income *n* ingresos *mpl* procedentes de inversiones
investment portfolio *n* cartera de inversiones
investment trust *n* compañía inversionista, sociedad *f* de cartera
investor [ɪn'vɛstər] *n* inversor(a) *m(f)*
inveterate [ɪn'vɛtərət] *adj* empedernido
invidious [ɪn'vɪdɪəs] *adj* odioso
invigilate [ɪn'vɪdʒɪleɪt] *vt, vi* (in exam) vigilar
invigilator [ɪn'vɪdʒɪleɪtər] *n* celador(a) *m(f)*
invigorating [ɪn'vɪgəreɪtɪŋ] *adj* vigorizante
invincible [ɪn'vɪnsɪbl] *adj* invencible
inviolate [ɪn'vaɪələt] *adj* inviolado
invisible [ɪn'vɪzɪbl] *adj* invisible
invisible assets *npl* activo invisible
invisible ink *n* tinta simpática
invisible mending *n* puntada invisible
invitation [ɪnvɪ'teɪʃən] *n* invitación *f*; **by ~ only** solamente por invitación
invite [ɪn'vaɪt] *vt* invitar; (opinions etc) solicitar, pedir; (trouble) buscarse; **to ~ sb (to do)** invitar a algn (a hacer); **to ~ sb to dinner** invitar a algn a cenar
  ▸ **invite out** *vt* invitar a salir
  ▸ **invite over** *vt* invitar a casa
inviting [ɪn'vaɪtɪŋ] *adj* atractivo; (look) provocativo; (food) apetitoso
invoice ['ɪnvɔɪs] *n* factura ▪ *vt* facturar; **to ~ sb for goods** facturar a algn las mercancías
invoicing ['ɪnvɔɪsɪŋ] *n* facturación *f*
invoke [ɪn'vəʊk] *vt* invocar; (aid) pedir; (law) recurrir a
involuntary [ɪn'vɒləntrɪ] *adj* involuntario
involve [ɪn'vɒlv] *vt* (entail) suponer, implicar; **to ~ sb (in)** involucrar a algn (en)

involved [ɪn'vɒlvd] *adj* complicado; **to be/become ~ in sth** estar involucrado/ involucrarse en algo
involvement [ɪn'vɒlvmənt] *n* (gen) enredo; (obligation) compromiso; (difficulty) apuro
invulnerable [ɪn'vʌlnərəbl] *adj* invulnerable
inward ['ɪnwəd] *adj* (movement) interior, interno; (thought, feeling) íntimo ▪ *adv* hacia dentro
inwardly ['ɪnwədlɪ] *adv* (feel, think etc) para sí, para dentro
inwards ['ɪnwədz] *adv* hacia dentro
I/O *abbr* (Comput: = input/output) E/S; **~ error** error *m* de E/S
IOC *n abbr* (= International Olympic Committee) COI *m*
iodine ['aɪəʊdiːn] *n* yodo
IOM *abbr* (Brit) = **Isle of Man**
ion ['aɪən] *n* ion *m*
Ionian Sea [aɪ'əʊnɪən-] *n*: **the ~** el Mar Jónico
ioniser ['aɪənaɪzər] *n* ionizador *m*
iota [aɪ'əʊtə] *n* (fig) jota, ápice *m*
IOU *n abbr* (= I owe you) pagaré *m*
IOW *abbr* (Brit) = **Isle of Wight**
IPA *n abbr* (= International Phonetic Alphabet) AFI *m*
iPod® ['aɪpɒd] *n* iPod® *m*
IQ *n abbr* (= intelligence quotient) C.I. *m*
IRA *n abbr* (= Irish Republican Army) IRA *m*; (US) = **individual retirement account**
Iran [ɪ'rɑːn] *n* Irán *m*
Iranian [ɪ'reɪnɪən] *adj* iraní ▪ *n* iraní *m/f*; (Ling) iraní *m*
Iraq [ɪ'rɑːk] *n* Irak *m*
Iraqi [ɪ'rɑːkɪ] *adj, n* irakí *m/f*
irascible [ɪ'ræsɪbl] *adj* irascible
irate [aɪ'reɪt] *adj* enojado, airado
Ireland ['aɪələnd] *n* Irlanda; **Republic of ~** República de Irlanda
iris (pl **irises**) ['aɪrɪs, -ɪz] *n* (Anat) iris *m*; (Bot) lirio
Irish ['aɪrɪʃ] *adj* irlandés(-esa) ▪ *n* (Ling) irlandés *m*; **the ~** *npl* los irlandeses
Irishman ['aɪrɪʃmən] *n* irlandés *m*
Irish Sea *n*: **the ~** el Mar de Irlanda
Irishwoman ['aɪrɪʃwumən] *n* irlandesa
irk [əːk] *vt* fastidiar
irksome ['əːksəm] *adj* fastidioso
IRN *n abbr* (= Independent Radio News) servicio de noticias en las cadenas de radio privadas
IRO *n abbr* (US) = **International Refugee Organization**
iron ['aɪən] *n* hierro; (for clothes) plancha ▪ *adj* de hierro ▪ *vt* (clothes) planchar; **irons** *npl* (chains) grilletes *mpl*
  ▸ **iron out** *vt* (crease) quitar; (fig) allanar, resolver

Iron Curtain n: **the ~** el Telón de Acero
iron foundry n fundición f, fundidora
ironic [aɪ'rɒnɪk], **ironical** [aɪ'rɒnɪkl] adj
irónico
ironically [aɪ'rɒnɪklɪ] adv irónicamente
ironing ['aɪənɪŋ] n (act) planchado; (ironed
clothes) ropa planchada; (clothes to be ironed)
ropa por planchar
ironing board n tabla de planchar
iron lung n (Med) pulmón m de acero
ironmonger ['aɪənmʌŋgəʳ] n (Brit)
ferretero(-a); **~'s (shop)** ferretería
iron ore n mineral m de hierro
ironworks ['aɪənwəːks] n fundición f
irony ['aɪrənɪ] n ironía; **the ~ of it is that ...**
lo irónico del caso es que ...
irrational [ɪ'ræʃənl] adj irracional
irreconcilable [ɪrɛkən'saɪləbl] adj
inconciliable; (enemies) irreconciliable
irredeemable [ɪrɪ'diːməbl] adj irredimible
irrefutable [ɪrɪ'fjuːtəbl] adj irrefutable
irregular [ɪ'rɛgjuləʳ] adj irregular; (surface)
desigual
irregularity [ɪrɛgju'lærɪtɪ] n irregularidad f;
desigualdad f
irrelevance [ɪ'rɛləvəns] n irrelevancia
irrelevant [ɪ'rɛləvənt] adj irrelevante; **to be ~**
estar fuera de lugar, no venir al caso
irreligious [ɪrɪ'lɪdʒəs] adj irreligioso
irreparable [ɪ'rɛprəbl] adj irreparable
irreplaceable [ɪrɪ'pleɪsəbl] adj irremplazable
irrepressible [ɪrɪ'prɛsəbl] adj incontenible
irreproachable [ɪrɪ'prəutʃəbl] adj
irreprochable
irresistible [ɪrɪ'zɪstɪbl] adj irresistible
irresolute [ɪ'rɛzəluːt] adj indeciso
irrespective [ɪrɪ'spɛktɪv]: **~ of** prep sin tener
en cuenta, no importa
irresponsibility [ɪrɪsponsɪ'bɪlɪtɪ] n
irresponsabilidad f
irresponsible [ɪrɪ'sponsɪbl] adj (act)
irresponsable; (person) poco serio
irretrievable [ɪrɪ'triːvəbl] adj (object)
irrecuperable; (loss, damage) irremediable,
irreparable
irretrievably [ɪrɪ'triːvəblɪ] adv
irremisiblemente
irreverence [ɪ'rɛvərns] n irreverencia
irreverent [ɪ'rɛvərnt] adj irreverente,
irrespetuoso
irrevocable [ɪ'rɛvəkəbl] adj irrevocable
irrigate ['ɪrɪgeɪt] vt regar
irrigation [ɪrɪ'geɪʃən] n riego
irritability [ɪrɪtə'bɪlɪtɪ] n irritabilidad f
irritable ['ɪrɪtəbl] adj (person: temperament)
irritable; (: mood) de mal humor
irritant ['ɪrɪtənt] n agente m irritante

irritate ['ɪrɪteɪt] vt fastidiar; (Med) picar
irritating ['ɪrɪteɪtɪŋ] adj fastidioso
irritation [ɪrɪ'teɪʃən] n fastidio; picazón f,
picor m
IRS n abbr (US) = **Internal Revenue
Service**
is [ɪz] vb see **be**
ISA ['aɪsə] n abbr (Brit: = individual savings
account) plan de ahorro personal para pequeños
inversores con fiscalidad cero
ISBN n abbr (= International Standard Book
Number) ISBN m
ISDN n abbr (= Integrated Services Digital Network)
RDSI f
Islam ['ɪzlɑːm] n Islam m
island ['aɪlənd] n isla; (also: **traffic island**)
isleta
islander ['aɪləndəʳ] n isleño(-a)
Isle [aɪl] n isla
isn't ['ɪznt] = **is not**
isobar ['aɪsəubɑːʳ] n isobara
isolate ['aɪsəleɪt] vt aislar
isolated ['aɪsəleɪtɪd] adj aislado
isolation [aɪsə'leɪʃən] n aislamiento
isolationism [aɪsə'leɪʃənɪzəm] n
aislacionismo
isolation ward n pabellón m de
aislamiento
isotope ['aɪsəutəup] n isótopo
ISP n abbr = **Internet service provider**
Israel ['ɪzreɪl] n Israel m
Israeli [ɪz'reɪlɪ] adj, n israelí m/f
issue ['ɪsjuː] n cuestión f, asunto; (outcome)
resultado; (of banknotes etc) emisión f; (of
newspaper etc) número; (offspring) sucesión
f, descendencia ◼ vt (rations, equipment)
distribuir, repartir; (orders) dar; (certificate,
passport) expedir; (decree) promulgar;
(magazine) publicar; (cheque) extender;
(banknotes, stamp) emitir ◼ vi: **to ~
(from)** derivar (de), brotar (de); **at ~**
en cuestión; **to take ~ with sb (over)**
disentir con algn (en); **to avoid the ~**
andarse con rodeos; **to confuse** or
obscure the ~ confundir las cosas;
to make an ~ of sth dar a algo más
importancia de lo necesario; **to ~ sth to sb,
~ sb with sth** entregar algo a algn
Istanbul [ɪstæn'buːl] n Estambul m
isthmus ['ɪsməs] n istmo
IT n abbr = **information technology**

 KEYWORD

it [ɪt] pron **1** (specific: subject: not generally
translated) él/ella; (: direct object) lo/la; (: indirect
object) le; (after prep) él/ella; (abstract concept)

619

ello; **it's on the table** está en la mesa;
I can't find it no lo (or la) encuentro; **give
it to me** dámelo (or dámela); **I spoke to
him about it** le hablé del asunto; **what did
you learn from it?** ¿qué aprendiste de él
(or ella)?; **did you go to it?** (party, concert etc)
¿fuiste?

2 (impersonal): **it's raining** llueve, está
lloviendo; **it's 6 o'clock/the 10th of
August** son las 6/es el 10 de agosto; **how far
is it? — it's 10 miles/2 hours on the
train** ¿a qué distancia está? — a 10 millas/
2 horas en tren; **who is it? — it's me** ¿quién
es? — soy yo

ITA n abbr (Brit: = initial teaching alphabet)
alfabeto parcialmente fonético, ayuda para enseñar
a leer

Italian [ɪ'tæljən] adj italiano ∎ n
italiano(-a); (Ling) italiano

italic [ɪ'tælɪk] adj cursivo; **italics** npl
cursiva sg

Italy ['ɪtəlɪ] n Italia

ITC n abbr (Brit) = **Independent Television
Commission**

itch [ɪtʃ] n picazón f; (fig) prurito ∎ vi (person)
sentir or tener comezón; (part of body) picar;
to be itching to do sth rabiar por or morirse
de ganas de hacer algo

itching ['ɪtʃɪŋ] n picazón f, comezón f

itchy ['ɪtʃɪ] adj: **to be ~** picar

it'd ['ɪtd] = **it would; it had**

item ['aɪtəm] n artículo; (on agenda) asunto
(a tratar); (in programme) número; (also: **news
item**) noticia; **items of clothing** prendas fpl
de vestir

itemize ['aɪtəmaɪz] vt detallar

itemized bill ['aɪtəmaɪzd-] n recibo detallado

itinerant [ɪ'tɪnərənt] adj ambulante

itinerary [aɪ'tɪnərərɪ] n itinerario

it'll ['ɪtl] = **it will; it shall**

ITN n abbr (Brit) = **Independent Television News**

its [ɪts] adj su

it's [ɪts] = **it is; it has**

itself [ɪt'self] pron (reflexive) sí mismo(-a);
(emphatic) él/ella mismo(-a)

ITV n abbr (Brit: = Independent Television) ver nota

⬤ **ITV**
⬤
⬤ En el Reino Unido la ITV ("Independent
⬤ Television") es una cadena de
⬤ emisoras comerciales regionales con
⬤ licencia exclusiva para emitir en su
⬤ región. Suelen producir sus propios
⬤ programas, se financian con publicidad
⬤ y están bajo el control del organismo
⬤ oficial independiente "Independent
⬤ Broadcasting Authority" ("IBA").
⬤ El servicio de noticias nacionales e
⬤ internacionales, "ITN" ("Independent
⬤ Television News"), funciona como
⬤ una compañía productora para toda la
⬤ cadena.

IUD n abbr (= intra-uterine device) DIU m

I've [aɪv] = **I have**

ivory ['aɪvərɪ] n marfil m

Ivory Coast n: **the ~** la Costa de Marfil

ivory tower n (fig) torre f de marfil

ivy ['aɪvɪ] n hiedra

Ivy League n (US) ver nota

⬤ **IVY LEAGUE**
⬤
⬤ Las ocho universidades más prestigiosas
⬤ del nordeste de los Estados Unidos
⬤ reciben el nombre colectivo de Ivy
⬤ League, por sus muros cubiertos de
⬤ hiedra. Son: Brown, Columbia, Cornell,
⬤ Dartmouth College, Harvard, Princeton,
⬤ la universidad de Pennsylvania y Yale.
⬤ También se llaman así las competiciones
⬤ deportivas que celebran entre ellas.

Jj

J, j [dʒeɪ] n (letter) J, j f; **J for Jack**, (US) **J for Jig** J de José

JA n abbr = **judge advocate**

J/A abbr = **joint account**

jab [dʒæb] vt (elbow) dar un codazo a; (punch) dar un golpe rápido a ■ vi: **to ~ at** intentar golpear a; **to ~ sth into sth** clavar algo en algo ■ n codazo; golpe m (rápido); (Med: col) pinchazo

jabber ['dʒæbə^r] vt, vi farfullar

jack [dʒæk] n (Aut) gato; (Bowls) boliche m; (Cards) sota
  ▶ **jack in** vt (col) dejar
  ▶ **jack up** vt (Aut) levantar con el gato

jackal ['dʒækl] n (Zool) chacal m

jackass ['dʒækæs] n (also fig) asno, burro

jackdaw ['dʒækdɔ:] n grajo(-a), chova

jacket ['dʒækɪt] n chaqueta, americana, saco (LAm); (of boiler etc) camisa; (of book) sobrecubierta

jacket potato n patata asada (con piel)

jack-in-the-box ['dʒækɪnðəbɒks] n caja sorpresa, caja de resorte

jack-knife ['dʒæknaɪf] vi colear

jack-of-all-trades ['dʒækəv'ɔ:ltreɪdz] n aprendiz m de todo

jack plug n (Elec) enchufe m de clavija

jackpot ['dʒækpɒt] n premio gordo

Jacuzzi® [dʒə'ku:zɪ] n jacuzzi® m

jade [dʒeɪd] n (stone) jade m

jaded ['dʒeɪdɪd] adj (tired) cansado; (fed up) hastiado

jagged ['dʒægɪd] adj dentado

jaguar ['dʒægjuə^r] n jaguar m

jail [dʒeɪl] n cárcel f ■ vt encarcelar

jailbird ['dʒeɪlbə:d] n preso(-a) reincidente

jailbreak ['dʒeɪlbreɪk] n fuga or evasión f (de la cárcel)

jailer ['dʒeɪlə^r] n carcelero(-a)

jalopy [dʒə'lɒpɪ] n (col) cacharro, armatoste m

jam [dʒæm] n mermelada; (also: **traffic jam**) atasco, embotellamiento; (difficulty) apuro
  ■ vt (passage etc) obstruir; (mechanism, drawer etc) atascar; (Radio) interferir ■ vi atascarse,

trabarse; **to get sb out of a ~** sacar a algn del paso or de un apuro; **to ~ sth into sth** meter algo a la fuerza en algo; **the telephone lines are jammed** las líneas están saturadas

Jamaica [dʒə'meɪkə] n Jamaica

Jamaican [dʒə'meɪkən] adj, n jamaicano(-a) m(f)

jamb [dʒæm] n jamba

jamboree [dʒæmbə'ri:] n congreso de niños exploradores

jam-packed [dʒæm'pækt] adj: **(with)** atestado (de)

jam session n concierto improvisado de jazz/rock etc

Jan. abbr (= January) ene

jangle ['dʒæŋgl] vi sonar (de manera) discordante

janitor ['dʒænɪtə^r] n (caretaker) portero, conserje m

January ['dʒænjuərɪ] n enero; see also **July**

Japan [dʒə'pæn] n (el) Japón

Japanese [dʒæpə'ni:z] adj japonés(-esa) ■ n (pl inv) japonés(-esa) m(f); (Ling) japonés m

jar [dʒɑ:^r] n (glass: large) jarra; (: small) tarro ■ vi (sound) chirriar; (colours) desentonar

jargon ['dʒɑ:gən] n jerga

jarring ['dʒɑ:rɪŋ] adj (sound) discordante, desafinado; (colour) chocante

Jas. abbr = **James**

jasmine, jasmin ['dʒæzmɪn] n jazmín m

jaundice ['dʒɔ:ndɪs] n ictericia

jaundiced ['dʒɔ:ndɪst] adj (fig: embittered) amargado; (: disillusioned) desilusionado

jaunt [dʒɔ:nt] n excursión f

jaunty ['dʒɔ:ntɪ] adj alegre; (relaxed) desenvuelto

Java ['dʒɑ:və] n Java

javelin ['dʒævlɪn] n jabalina

jaw [dʒɔ:] n mandíbula; **jaws** npl (Tech: of vice etc) mordaza sg

jawbone ['dʒɔ:bəun] n mandíbula, quijada

jay [dʒeɪ] n (Zool) arrendajo

jaywalker ['dʒeɪwɔ:kə^r] n peatón(-ona) m(f) imprudente

jazz [dʒæz] n jazz m
▸ jazz up vt (liven up) animar
jazz band n orquesta de jazz
jazzy ['dʒæzɪ] adj de colores llamativos
JCB® n abbr excavadora
JCS n abbr (US) = Joint Chiefs of Staff
JD n abbr (US: = Doctor of Laws) título universitario;
(= Justice Department) Ministerio de Justicia
jealous ['dʒɛləs] adj (gen) celoso; (envious)
envidioso; to be ~ tener celos
jealously ['dʒɛləslɪ] adv (enviously)
envidiosamente; (watchfully) celosamente
jealousy ['dʒɛləsɪ] n celos mpl; envidia
jeans [dʒiːnz] npl (pantalones mpl) vaqueros
mpl or tejanos mpl, bluejean m inv (LAm)
Jeep® [dʒiːp] n jeep m
jeer [dʒɪəʳ] vi: to ~ (at) (boo) abuchear; (mock)
mofarse (de)
jeering ['dʒɪərɪŋ] adj (crowd) insolente,
ofensivo ■ n protestas fpl; (mockery)
burlas fpl
jelly ['dʒɛlɪ] n gelatina, jalea
jellyfish ['dʒɛlɪfɪʃ] n medusa
jemmy ['dʒɛmɪ] n palanqueta
jeopardize ['dʒɛpədaɪz] vt arriesgar, poner
en peligro
jeopardy ['dʒɛpədɪ] n: to be in ~ estar en
peligro
jerk [dʒəːk] n (jolt) sacudida; (wrench) tirón m;
(US col) imbécil m/f, pendejo(-a) (LAm) ■ vt
dar una sacudida a; tirar bruscamente de
■ vi (vehicle) dar una sacudida
jerkin ['dʒəːkɪn] n chaleco
jerky ['dʒəːkɪ] adj espasmódico
jerry-built ['dʒɛrɪbɪlt] adj mal construido
jerry can ['dʒɛrɪ-] n bidón m
Jersey ['dʒəːzɪ] n Jersey m
jersey ['dʒəːzɪ] n jersey m; (fabric) tejido de
punto
Jerusalem [dʒəˈruːsləm] n Jerusalén m
jest [dʒɛst] n broma
jester ['dʒɛstəʳ] n bufón m
Jesus ['dʒiːzəs] n Jesús m; ~ Christ Jesucristo
jet [dʒɛt] n (of gas, liquid) chorro; (Aviat) avión
m a reacción
jet-black ['dʒɛt'blæk] adj negro como el
azabache
jet engine n motor m a reacción
jet lag n desorientación f por desfase horario
jetsam ['dʒɛtsəm] n echazón f
jet-setter ['dʒɛtsɛtəʳ] n personaje m de la jet
jettison ['dʒɛtɪsn] vt desechar
jetty ['dʒɛtɪ] n muelle m, embarcadero
Jew [dʒuː] n judío
jewel ['dʒuːəl] n joya; (in watch) rubí m
jeweller, jeweler (US) ['dʒuːələʳ] n joyero(-a);
~'s (shop) joyería

jewellery, jewelry (US) ['dʒuːəlrɪ] n joyas fpl,
alhajas fpl
Jewess ['dʒuːɪs] n judía
Jewish ['dʒuːɪʃ] adj judío
JFK n abbr (US) = John Fitzgerald Kennedy
International Airport
jib [dʒɪb] vi (horse) plantarse; to ~ at doing
sth resistirse a hacer algo
jibe [dʒaɪb] n mofa
jiffy ['dʒɪfɪ] n (col): in a ~ en un santiamén
jig [dʒɪg] n (dance, tune) giga
jigsaw ['dʒɪgsɔː] n (also: jigsaw puzzle)
rompecabezas m inv; (tool) sierra de vaivén
jilt [dʒɪlt] vt dejar plantado a
jingle ['dʒɪŋgl] n (advert) musiquilla
■ vi tintinear
jingoism ['dʒɪŋgəuɪzəm] n patriotería,
jingoísmo
jinx [dʒɪŋks] n: there's a ~ on it está gafado
jitters ['dʒɪtəz] npl (col): to get the ~ ponerse
nervioso
jittery ['dʒɪtərɪ] adj (col) agitado
jiujitsu [dʒuːˈdʒɪtsuː] n jiujitsu m
job [dʒɔb] n trabajo; (task) tarea; (duty) deber
m; (post) empleo; (col: difficulty) dificultad f;
it's a good ~ that ... menos mal que ...; just
the ~! ¡justo lo que necesito!; a part-time/
full-time ~ un trabajo a tiempo parcial/
tiempo completo; that's not my ~ eso no me
incumbe or toca a mí; he's only doing his ~
está cumpliendo nada más
job centre n (Brit) oficina de empleo
job creation scheme n plan m de creación de
puestos de trabajo
job description n descripción f del puesto de
trabajo
jobless ['dʒɔblɪs] adj sin trabajo ■ n: the ~
los parados
job lot n lote m de mercancías, saldo
job satisfaction n satisfacción f en el trabajo
job security n garantía de trabajo
job specification n especificación f del
trabajo, profesiograma m
Jock n (col: Scotsman) escocés m
jockey ['dʒɔkɪ] n jockey m/f ■ vi: to ~ for
position maniobrar para sacar delantera
jockey box n (US Aut) guantera
jockstrap ['dʒɔkstræp] n suspensorio
jocular ['dʒɔkjuləʳ] adj (humorous) gracioso;
(merry) alegre
jodhpurs ['dʒɔdpəːz] npl pantalón msg de
montar
jog [dʒɔg] vt empujar (ligeramente) ■ vi (run)
hacer footing; to ~ along (fig) ir tirando; to ~
sb's memory refrescar la memoria a algn
jogger ['dʒɔgəʳ] n corredor(a) m(f)
jogging ['dʒɔgɪŋ] n footing m

john [dʒɒn] n (US col) wáter m
join [dʒɔɪn] vt (things) unir, juntar; (become
member of: club) hacerse socio de; (Pol: party)
afiliarse a; (meet: people) reunirse con; (fig)
unirse a ▪ vi (roads) empalmar; (rivers)
confluir ▪ n juntura; **will you ~ us for
dinner?** ¿quieres cenar con nosotros?;
I'll ~ you later me reuniré contigo luego;
to ~ forces (with) aliarse (con)
▸ **join in** vi tomar parte, participar ▪ vt fus
tomar parte or participar en
▸ **join up** vi unirse; (Mil) alistarse
joiner ['dʒɔɪnə'] n carpintero(-a)
joinery ['dʒɔɪnərɪ] n carpintería
joint [dʒɔɪnt] n (Tech) juntura, unión f; (Anat)
articulación f; (Brit Culin) pieza de carne
(para asar); (col: place) garito ▪ adj (common)
común; (combined) conjunto; (responsibility)
compartido; (committee) mixto
joint account n (with bank etc) cuenta
común
jointly ['dʒɔɪntlɪ] adv (gen) en común;
(together) conjuntamente
joint owners npl copropietarios mpl
joint ownership n copropiedad f, propiedad
f común
joint-stock bank ['dʒɔɪntstɔk-] n banco por
acciones
joint-stock company ['dʒɔɪntstɔk-] n
sociedad f anónima
joint venture n empresa conjunta
joist [dʒɔɪst] n viga
joke [dʒəuk] n chiste m; (also: **practical joke**)
broma ▪ vi bromear; **to play a ~ on** gastar
una broma a
joker ['dʒəukə'] n chistoso(-a), bromista m/f;
(Cards) comodín m
joking ['dʒəukɪŋ] n bromas fpl
jokingly ['dʒəukɪŋlɪ] adv en broma
jollity ['dʒɔlɪtɪ] n alegría
jolly ['dʒɔlɪ] adj (merry) alegre; (enjoyable)
divertido ▪ adv (col) muy, la mar de ▪ vt:
to ~ sb along animar or darle ánimos a algn;
~ good! ¡estupendo!
jolt [dʒəult] n (shake) sacudida; (blow) golpe m;
(shock) susto ▪ vt sacudir
Jordan ['dʒɔːdən] n (country) Jordania; (river)
Jordán m
joss stick [dʒɔs-] n barrita de incienso,
pebete m
jostle ['dʒɔsl] vt dar empujones or
empellones a
jot [dʒɔt] n: **not one ~** ni pizca, ni un ápice
▸ **jot down** vt apuntar
jotter ['dʒɔtə'] n (Brit) bloc m
journal ['dʒəːnl] n (paper) periódico; (magazine)
revista; (diary) diario

journalese [dʒəːnə'liːz] n (pej) lenguaje m
periodístico
journalism ['dʒəːnəlɪzəm] n periodismo
journalist ['dʒəːnəlɪst] n periodista m/f
journey ['dʒəːnɪ] n viaje m; (distance covered)
trayecto ▪ vi viajar; **return ~** viaje de
regreso; **a five-hour ~** un viaje de cinco
horas
jovial ['dʒəuvɪəl] adj risueño, alegre
jowl [dʒaul] n quijada
joy [dʒɔɪ] n alegría
joyful ['dʒɔɪful] adj alegre
joyfully ['dʒɔɪfulɪ] adv alegremente
joyous ['dʒɔɪəs] adj alegre
joyride ['dʒɔɪraɪd] n: **to go for a ~** darse una
vuelta en un coche robado
joyrider ['dʒɔɪraɪdə'] n persona que se da una
vuelta en un coche robado
joystick ['dʒɔɪstɪk] n (Aviat) palanca de
mando; (Comput) palanca de control
JP n abbr see **Justice of the Peace**
Jr abbr = **junior**
JTPA n abbr (US: = Job Training Partnership Act)
programa gubernamental de formación profesional
jubilant ['dʒuːbɪlnt] adj jubiloso
jubilation [dʒuːbɪ'leɪʃən] n júbilo
jubilee ['dʒuːbɪliː] n aniversario; **silver ~**
vigésimo quinto aniversario
judge [dʒʌdʒ] n juez m/f ▪ vt juzgar;
(competition) actuar de or ser juez en; (estimate)
considerar; (: weight, size etc) calcular ▪ vi:
judging or **to ~ by his expression** a juzgar
por su expresión; **as far as I can ~** por lo que
puedo entender, a mi entender; **I judged
it necessary to inform him** consideré
necesario informarle
judge advocate n (Mil) auditor m de guerra
judgment, judgement ['dʒʌdʒmənt] n
juicio; (punishment) sentencia, fallo; **to
pass judg(e)ment (on)** (Law) pronunciar
or dictar sentencia (sobre); (fig) emitir un
juicio crítico or dictaminar (sobre); **in my
judg(e)ment** a mi juicio
judicial [dʒuː'dɪʃl] adj judicial
judiciary [dʒuː'dɪʃɪərɪ] n poder m judicial,
magistratura
judicious [dʒuː'dɪʃəs] adj juicioso
judo ['dʒuːdəu] n judo
jug [dʒʌg] n jarro
jugged hare [dʒʌgd-] n (Brit) estofado de
liebre
juggernaut ['dʒʌgənɔːt] n (Brit: huge truck)
camión m de carga pesada
juggle ['dʒʌgl] vi hacer juegos malabares
juggler ['dʒʌglə'] n malabarista m/f
Jugoslav etc ['juːgəuslɑːv] = **Yugoslav** etc
jugular ['dʒʌgjulə'] adj: **~ vein** (vena) yugular f

623

juice [dʒu:s] n jugo, zumo (SP); (of meat) jugo; (col: petrol): **we've run out of** ~ se nos acabó la gasolina
juiciness ['dʒu:sınıs] n jugosidad f
juicy ['dʒu:sı] adj jugoso
juijitsu, jujitsu [dʒu:'dʒıtsu:] n jujitsu m
jukebox ['dʒu:kbɔks] n máquina de discos
Jul. (= July) jul
July [dʒu:'laı] n julio; **the first of** ~ el uno or primero de julio; **during** ~ en el mes de julio; **in** ~ **of next year** en julio del año que viene
jumble ['dʒʌmbl] n revoltijo ■ vt (also: **jumble together, jumble up**: mix up) revolver; (: disarrange) mezclar
jumble sale n (Brit) mercadillo; ver nota

◉ **JUMBLE SALE**

◉ En cada jumble sale pueden comprarse
◉ todo tipo de objetos baratos de segunda
◉ mano, especialmente ropa, juguetes,
◉ libros, vajillas y muebles. Suelen
◉ organizarse en los locales de un colegio,
◉ iglesia, ayuntamiento o similar, con
◉ fines benéficos, bien en ayuda de una
◉ organización benéfica conocida o para
◉ solucionar problemas más concretos de la
◉ comunidad.

jumbo ['dʒʌmbəu], **jumbo jet** n jumbo
jump [dʒʌmp] vi saltar, dar saltos; (start) sobresaltarse; (increase) aumentar ■ vt saltar ■ n salto; (fence) obstáculo; (increase) aumento; **to** ~ **the queue** (Brit) colarse
▶**jump about** vi dar saltos, brincar
▶**jump at** vt fus (fig) apresurarse a aprovechar; **he jumped at the offer** se apresuró a aceptar la oferta
▶**jump down** vi bajar de un salto, saltar a tierra
▶**jump up** vi levantarse de un salto
jumped-up ['dʒʌmptʌp] adj (pej) engreído
jumper ['dʒʌmpəʳ] n (Brit: pullover) jersey m, suéter m; (US: pinafore dress) pichi m; (Sport) saltador(a) m(f)
jump leads, (US) **jumper cables** npl cables mpl puente de batería
jump-start ['dʒʌmpstɑ:t] vt (car) arrancar con ayuda de otra batería or empujando; (fig: economy) reactivar
jump suit n mono
jumpy ['dʒʌmpı] adj nervioso
Jun. abbr = **junior**; (= June) jun
junction ['dʒʌŋkʃən] n (Brit: of roads) cruce m; (Rail) empalme m
juncture ['dʒʌŋktʃəʳ] n: **at this** ~ en este momento, en esta coyuntura

June [dʒu:n] n junio; see also **July**
jungle ['dʒʌŋgl] n selva, jungla
junior ['dʒu:nɪəʳ] adj (in age) menor, más joven; (competition) juvenil; (position) subalterno ■ n menor m/f, joven m/f; **he's** ~ **to me** es menor que yo
junior executive n ejecutivo/a subalterno/a
junior high school n (US) centro de educación secundaria; see also **high school**
junior school n (Brit) escuela primaria; see also **primary school**
junk [dʒʌŋk] n (cheap goods) baratijas fpl; (lumber) trastos mpl viejos; (rubbish) basura; (ship) junco ■ vt (esp US) deshacerse de
junk bond n (Comm) obligación f basura inv
junk dealer n vendedor(a) m(f) de objetos usados
junket ['dʒʌŋkıt] n (Culin) dulce de leche cuajada; (Brit col): **to go on a** ~, **go junketing** viajar a costa ajena or del erario público
junk food n comida basura or de plástico
junkie ['dʒʌŋkı] n (col) yonqui m/f, heroinómano(-a)
junk mail n propaganda (buzoneada), correo m basura inv
junk room n trastero
junk shop n tienda de objetos usados
junta ['dʒʌntə] n junta militar
Jupiter ['dʒu:pɪtəʳ] n (Mythology, Astro) Júpiter m
jurisdiction [dʒuərɪs'dıkʃən] n jurisdicción f; **it falls** or **comes within/outside our** ~ es/no es de nuestra competencia
jurisprudence [dʒuərɪs'pru:dəns] n jurisprudencia
juror ['dʒuərəʳ] n jurado
jury ['dʒuərı] n jurado
jury box n tribuna del jurado
juryman ['dʒuərımən] n miembro del jurado
just [dʒʌst] adj justo ■ adv (exactly) exactamente; (only) sólo, solamente, no más (LAm); **he's** ~ **done it/left** acaba de hacerlo/ irse; **I've** ~ **seen him** acabo de verle; ~ **right** perfecto; ~ **two o'clock** las dos en punto; **she's** ~ **as clever as you** es tan lista como tú; ~ **as well that ...** menos mal que ...; **it's** ~ **as well you didn't go** menos mal que no fuiste; **it's** ~ **as good (as)** es igual (que), es tan bueno (como); ~ **as he was leaving** en el momento en que se marchaba; **we were** ~ **going** ya nos íbamos; **I was** ~ **about to phone** estaba a punto de llamar; ~ **before/ enough** justo antes/lo suficiente; ~ **here** aquí mismo; **he** ~ **missed** falló por poco; ~ **listen to this** escucha esto un momento; ~ **ask someone the way** simplemente

pregúntale a alguien por dónde se va; **not ~ now** ahora no

justice ['dʒʌstɪs] *n* justicia; **this photo doesn't do you ~** esta foto no te favorece

Justice of the Peace *n* juez *m/f* de paz; *see also* **Crown Court**

justifiable [dʒʌstɪ'faɪəbl] *adj* justificable, justificado

justifiably [dʒʌstɪ'faɪəblɪ] *adv* justificadamente, con razón

justification [dʒʌstɪfɪ'keɪʃən] *n* justificación *f*

justify ['dʒʌstɪfaɪ] *vt* justificar; (*text*) alinear, justificar; **to be justified in doing sth**

tener motivo para *or* razón al hacer algo

justly ['dʒʌstlɪ] *adv* (*gen*) justamente; (*with reason*) con razón

justness ['dʒʌstnɪs] *n* justicia

jut [dʒʌt] *vi* (*also*: **jut out**) sobresalir

jute [dʒuːt] *n* yute *m*

juvenile ['dʒuːvənaɪl] *adj* juvenil; (*court*) de menores ■ *n* joven *m/f*, menor *m/f* de edad

juvenile delinquency *n* delincuencia juvenil

juvenile delinquent *n* delincuente *m/f* juvenil

juxtapose ['dʒʌkstəpəuz] *vt* yuxtaponer

juxtaposition ['dʒʌkstəpə'zɪʃən] *n* yuxtaposición *f*

j

Kk

K, k [keɪ] *n* (*letter*) K, k *f*; **K for King** K de Kilo
K *n abbr* (= *one thousand*) mille ■ *abbr* (*Brit*:
= *Knight*) *título*; (= *kilobyte*) K
kaftan ['kæftæn] *n* caftán *m*
Kalahari Desert [kælə'hɑːrɪ-] *n* desierto de
Kalahari
kale [keɪl] *n* col *f* rizada
kaleidoscope [kə'laɪdəskəup] *n* calidoscopio
kamikaze [kæmɪ'kɑːzɪ] *adj* kamikaze
Kampala [kæm'pɑːlə] *n* Kampala
Kampuchea [kæmpu'tʃɪə] *n* Kampuchea
kangaroo [kæŋɡə'ruː] *n* canguro
Kans. *abbr* (*US*) = **Kansas**
kaput [kə'put] *adj* (*col*) roto, estropeado
karaoke [kɑːrə'əukɪ] *n* karaoke
karate [kə'rɑːtɪ] *n* karate *m*
Kashmir [kæʃ'mɪəʳ] *n* Cachemira
kayak ['kaɪæk] *n* kayak *m*
Kazakhstan [kɑːzɑːk'stæn] *n* Kazajstán *m*
KC *n abbr* (*Brit Law*: = *King's Counsel*) título
concedido a determinados abogados
kebab [kə'bæb] *n* pincho moruno, brocheta
keel [kiːl] *n* quilla; **on an even ~** (*fig*)
en equilibrio
▶ **keel over** *vi* (*Naut*) zozobrar, volcarse;
(*person*) desplomarse
keen [kiːn] *adj* (*interest, desire*) grande, vivo;
(*eye, intelligence*) agudo; (*competition*) intenso;
(*edge*) afilado; (*Brit: eager*) entusiasta; **to be
~ to do** *or* **on doing sth** tener muchas ganas
de hacer algo; **to be ~ on sth/sb** interesarse
por algo/algn; **I'm not ~ on going** no tengo
ganas de ir
keenly ['kiːnlɪ] *adv* (*enthusiastically*) con
entusiasmo; (*acutely*) vivamente; (*intensely*)
intensamente
keenness ['kiːnnɪs] *n* (*eagerness*) entusiasmo,
interés *m*
keep [kiːp] (*pt, pp* **kept**) *vt* (*retain, preserve*)
guardar; (*hold back*) quedarse con; (*shop*) ser
propietario de; (*feed: family etc*) mantener;
(*promise*) cumplir; (*chickens, bees etc*) criar ■ *vi*
(*food*) conservarse; (*remain*) seguir, continuar

■ *n* (*of castle*) torreón *m*; (*food etc*) comida,
sustento; **to ~ doing sth** seguir haciendo
algo; **to ~ sb from doing sth** impedir a
algn hacer algo; **to ~ sth from happening**
impedir que algo ocurra; **to ~ sb happy**
tener a algn contento; **to ~ sb waiting** hacer
esperar a algn; **to ~ a place tidy** mantener
un lugar limpio; **to ~ sth to o.s.** no decirle
algo a nadie; **to ~ time** (*clock*) mantener la
hora exacta; **~ the change** quédese con la
vuelta; **to ~ an appointment** acudir a una
cita; **to ~ a record** *or* **note of sth** tomar nota
de *or* apuntar algo; *see also* **keeps**
▶ **keep away** *vt*: **to ~ sth/sb away from sb**
mantener algo/a algn apartado de algn ■ *vi*:
to ~ away (from) mantenerse apartado (de)
▶ **keep back** *vt* (*crowd, tears*) contener; (*money*)
quedarse con; (*conceal: information*): **to ~ sth
back from sb** ocultar algo a algn
■ *vi* hacerse a un lado
▶ **keep down** *vt* (*control: prices, spending*)
controlar; (*retain: food*) retener ■ *vi* seguir
agachado, no levantar la cabeza
▶ **keep in** *vt* (*invalid, child*) impedir que salga,
no dejar salir; (*Scol*) castigar (a quedarse en el
colegio) ■ *vi* (*col*): **to ~ in with sb** mantener
la relación con algn
▶ **keep off** *vt* (*dog, person*) mantener a distancia
■ *vi* evitar; **~ your hands off!** ¡no toques!;
"~ off the grass" "prohibido pisar el césped"
▶ **keep on** *vi* seguir, continuar
▶ **keep out** *vi* (*stay out*) permanecer fuera;
"~ out" "prohibida la entrada"
▶ **keep up** *vt* mantener, conservar ■ *vi* no
rezagarse; (*fig: in comprehension*) seguir (el
hilo); **to ~ up with** (*pace*) ir al paso de; (*level*)
mantenerse a la altura de; **to ~ up with sb**
seguir el ritmo a algn; (*fig*) seguir a algn
keeper ['kiːpəʳ] *n* guarda *m/f*
keep-fit [kiːp'fɪt] *n* gimnasia (de
mantenimiento)
keeping ['kiːpɪŋ] *n* (*care*) cuidado; **in ~ with**
de acuerdo con

keeps [ki:ps] *n*: **for ~** (*col*) para siempre
keepsake ['ki:pseɪk] *n* recuerdo
keg [kɛg] *n* barrilete *m*, barril *m*
Ken. *abbr* (*US*) = **Kentucky**
kennel ['kɛnl] *n* perrera; **kennels** *npl* perrera
Kenya ['kɛnjə] *n* Kenia
Kenyan ['kɛnjən] *adj, n* keniata *m/f*, keniano(-a) *m(f)*
kept [kɛpt] *pt, pp of* **keep**
kerb [kə:b] *n* (*Brit*) bordillo
kerb crawler [-krɔ:lə^r] *n conductor en busca de prostitutas desde su coche*
kernel ['kə:nl] *n* (*nut*) fruta; (*fig*) meollo
kerosene ['kɛrəsi:n] *n* keroseno
kestrel ['kɛstrəl] *n* cernícalo
ketchup ['kɛtʃəp] *n* salsa de tomate, ketchup *m*
kettle ['kɛtl] *n* hervidor *m*
kettle drum *n* (*Mus*) timbal *m*
key [ki:] *n* (*gen*) llave *f*; (*Mus*) tono; (*of piano, typewriter*) tecla; (*on map*) clave *f* ▪ *cpd* (*vital: position, industry etc*) clave ▪ *vt* (*also*: **key in**) teclear
keyboard ['ki:bɔ:d] *n* teclado ▪ *vt* (*text*) teclear
keyboarder ['ki:bɔ:də^r] *n* teclista *m/f*
keyed up [ki:d-] *adj* (*person*) nervioso; **to be (all) ~** estar nervioso *or* emocionado
keyhole ['ki:həul] *n* ojo (de la cerradura)
keyhole surgery *n* cirugía cerrada *or* no invasiva
key man *n* hombre *m* clave
keynote ['ki:nəut] *n* (*Mus*) tónica; (*fig*) idea fundamental
keynote speech *n* discurso de apertura
keypad ['ki:pæd] *n* teclado numérico
keyring ['ki:rɪŋ] *n* llavero
keystone ['ki:stəun] *n* piedra clave
keystroke ['ki:strəuk] *n* pulsación *f* (de una tecla)
kg *abbr* (= *kilogram*) kg
KGB *n abbr* KGB *m*
khaki ['ka:kɪ] *n* caqui
kibbutz, kibbutzim [kɪ'buts, -ɪm] *n* kibutz *m*
kick [kɪk] *vt* (*person*) dar una patada a; (*ball*) dar un puntapié a ▪ *vi* (*horse*) dar coces *or* patadas; puntapié *m*, tiro; (*of rifle*) culetazo; (*col: thrill*): **he does it for kicks** lo hace por pura diversión
  ▶ **kick around** *vt* (*idea*) dar vueltas a; (*person*) tratar a patadas a
  ▶ **kick off** *vi* (*Sport*) hacer el saque inicial
kick-start ['kɪksta:t] *n* (*also*: **kick-starter**) (pedal *m* de) arranque *m*
kid [kɪd] *n* (*col: child*) niño(-a), chiquillo(-a); (*animal*) cabrito; (*leather*) cabritilla ▪ *vi* (*col*) bromear

kid gloves *npl*: **to treat sb with ~** andarse con pies de plomo con algn
kidnap ['kɪdnæp] *vt* secuestrar
kidnapper ['kɪdnæpə^r] *n* secuestrador(a) *m(f)*
kidnapping ['kɪdnæpɪŋ] *n* secuestro
kidney ['kɪdnɪ] *n* riñón *m*
kidney bean *n* judía, alubia
kidney machine *n* riñón *m* artificial
kill [kɪl] *vt* matar; (*murder*) asesinar; (*fig: rumour, conversation*) acabar con ▪ *n* matanza; **to ~ time** matar el tiempo
  ▶ **kill off** *vt* exterminar, terminar con; (*fig*) echar por tierra
killer ['kɪlə^r] *n* asesino(-a)
killer app [- 'æp] *n abbr* (*col*: = *killer application*) aplicación *f* rompedora, aplicación *f* excelente rendimiento
killer instinct *n*: **to have the ~** ir a por todas
killing ['kɪlɪŋ] *n* (*one*) asesinato; (*several*) matanza; (*Comm*): **to make a ~** tener un gran éxito financiero
killjoy ['kɪldʒɔɪ] *n* (*Brit*) aguafiestas *m/f inv*
kiln [kɪln] *n* horno
kilo ['ki:ləu] *n abbr* (= *kilogram(me)*) kilo
kilobyte ['kɪləubaɪt] *n* (*Comput*) kilobyte *m*
kilogram, kilogramme ['kɪləugræm] *n* kilogramo
kilometre, (*US*) **kilometer** ['kɪləmi:tə^r] *n* kilómetro
kilowatt ['kɪləuwɔt] *n* kilovatio
kilt [kɪlt] *n* falda escocesa
kilter ['kɪltə^r] *n*: **out of ~** desbaratado
kimono [kɪ'məunəu] *n* quimono
kin [kɪn] *n* parientes *mpl*
kind [kaɪnd] *adj* (*treatment*) bueno, cariñoso; (*person, act, word*) amable, atento ▪ *n* clase *f*, especie *f*; (*species*) género; **in ~** (*Comm*) en especie; **a ~ of** una especie de; **to be two of a ~** ser tal para cual; **would you be ~ enough to ...?, would you be so ~ as to ...?** ¿me hace el favor de ...?; **it's very ~ of you (to do)** le agradezco mucho (el que haya hecho)
kindergarten ['kɪndəga:tn] *n* jardín *m* de infancia
kind-hearted [kaɪnd'ha:tɪd] *adj* bondadoso, de buen corazón
kindle ['kɪndl] *vt* encender
kindliness ['kaɪndlɪnəs] *n* bondad *f*, amabilidad *f*
kindling ['kɪndlɪŋ] *n* leña (menuda)
kindly ['kaɪndlɪ] *adj* bondadoso; (*gentle*) cariñoso ▪ *adv* bondadosamente, amablemente; **will you ~ ...** sería usted tan amable de ...
kindness ['kaɪndnɪs] *n* bondad *f*, amabilidad *f*
kindred ['kɪndrɪd] *n* familia, parientes *mpl* ▪ *adj*: **~ spirits** almas *fpl* gemelas

k

kinetic [kɪ'nɛtɪk] adj cinético
king [kɪŋ] n rey m
kingdom ['kɪŋdəm] n reino
kingfisher ['kɪŋfɪʃər] n martín m pescador
kingpin ['kɪŋpɪn] n (Tech) perno real or
pinzote; (fig) persona clave
king-size ['kɪŋsaɪz], **king-sized** ['kɪŋsaɪzd]
adj de tamaño gigante; (cigarette) extra largo
kink [kɪŋk] n (in rope etc) enroscadura; (in hair)
rizo; (fig: emotional, psychological) manía
kinky ['kɪŋkɪ] adj (pej) perverso
kinship ['kɪnʃɪp] n parentesco; (fig) afinidad f
kinsman ['kɪnzmən] n pariente m
kinswoman ['kɪnzwumən] n parienta
kiosk ['kiːɔsk] n quiosco; (Brit Tel) cabina;
newspaper ~ quiosco, kiosco
kipper ['kɪpər] n arenque m ahumado
Kirghizia [kə'gɪzɪə] n Kirguizistán m
kiss [kɪs] n beso ■ vt besar; ~ **of life** (artificial
respiration) respiración f artificial; **to ~ sb**
goodbye dar un beso de despedida a algn;
to ~ (each other) besarse
kissogram ['kɪsəgræm] n servicio de
felicitaciones mediante el que se envía a una persona
vestida de manera sugerente para besar a algn
kit [kɪt] n equipo; (set of tools etc) (caja
de) herramientas fpl; (assembly kit) juego
de armar; **tool** ~ juego or estuche m de
herramientas
   ▸ **kit out** vt equipar
kitbag ['kɪtbæg] n (Mil) macuto
kitchen ['kɪtʃɪn] n cocina
kitchen garden n huerto
kitchen sink n fregadero
kitchen unit n módulo de cocina
kitchenware ['kɪtʃɪnwɛər] n batería de cocina
kite [kaɪt] n (toy) cometa
kith [kɪθ] n: ~ **and kin** parientes mpl y
allegados
kitten ['kɪtn] n gatito(-a)
kitty ['kɪtɪ] n (pool of money) fondo común;
(Cards) bote m
kiwi ['kiːwiː] n (col: New Zealander)
neozelandés(-esa) m(f); (also: **kiwi fruit**)
kiwi m
KKK n abbr (US) = **Ku Klux Klan**
kleptomaniac [klɛptəu'meɪnɪæk] n
cleptómano(-a)
km abbr (= kilometre) km
km/h abbr (= kilometres per hour) km/h
knack [næk] n: **to have the ~ of doing sth**
tener facilidad para hacer algo
knackered ['nækəd] adj (col) hecho polvo
knapsack ['næpsæk] n mochila
knead [niːd] vt amasar
knee [niː] n rodilla
kneecap ['niːkæp] vt destrozar a tiros la

rótula de ■ n rótula
knee-deep ['niː'diːp] adj: **the water was** ~
el agua llegaba hasta la rodilla
kneel [niːl] (pt, pp **knelt** [nɛlt]) vi (also: **kneel**
down) arrodillarse
kneepad ['niːpæd] n rodillera
knell [nɛl] n toque m de difuntos
knelt [nɛlt] pt, pp of **kneel**
knew [njuː] pt of **know**
knickers ['nɪkəz] npl (Brit) bragas fpl, calzones
mpl (LAm)
knick-knack ['nɪknæk] n chuchería, baratija
knife [naɪf] (pl **knives**) n cuchillo ■ vt
acuchillar; ~, **fork and spoon** cubiertos mpl
knife edge n: **to be on a** ~ estar en la cuerda
floja
knight [naɪt] n caballero; (Chess) caballo
knighthood ['naɪthud] n (title): **to get a** ~
recibir el título de Sir
knit [nɪt] vt tejer, tricotar; (brows) fruncir;
(fig): **to ~ together** unir, juntar ■ vi hacer
punto, tejer, tricotar; (bones) soldarse
knitted ['nɪtɪd] adj de punto
knitting ['nɪtɪŋ] n labor f de punto
knitting machine n máquina de tricotar
knitting needle, **knit pin** (US) n aguja de
hacer punto or tejer
knitting pattern n patrón m para tricotar
knitwear ['nɪtwɛər] n prendas fpl de punto
knives [naɪvz] pl of **knife**
knob [nɔb] n (of door) pomo; (of stick) puño;
(lump) bulto; (fig): **a ~ of butter** (Brit) un
pedazo de mantequilla
knobbly ['nɔblɪ], **knobby** (US) ['nɔbɪ] adj
(wood, surface) nudoso; (knee) huesudo
knock [nɔk] vt (strike) golpear; (bump into)
chocar contra; (fig: col) criticar ■ vi (at door
etc): **to ~ at/on** llamar a ■ n golpe m; (on door)
llamada; **he knocked at the door** llamó a
la puerta
   ▸ **knock down** vt (pedestrian) atropellar; (price)
rebajar
   ▸ **knock off** vi (col: finish) salir del trabajo
■ vt (col: steal) birlar; (strike off) quitar; (fig:
from price, record): **to ~ off £10** rebajar en £10
   ▸ **knock out** vt dejar sin sentido; (Boxing)
poner fuera de combate, dejar K.O.; (stop)
estropear, dejar fuera de servicio
   ▸ **knock over** vt (object) derribar, tirar;
(pedestrian) atropellar
knockdown ['nɔkdaun] adj (price) de saldo
knocker ['nɔkər] n (on door) aldaba
knocking ['nɔkɪŋ] n golpes mpl, golpeteo
knock-kneed [nɔk'niːd] adj patizambo
knockout ['nɔkaut] n (Boxing) K.O. m,
knockout m
knock-up ['nɔkʌp] n (Tennis) peloteo

knot [nɔt] n (gen) nudo ■ vt anudar; **to tie a ~** hacer un nudo

knotted ['nɔtɪd] adj anudado

knotty ['nɔtɪ] adj (fig) complicado

know [nəu] (pt **knew**, pp **known**) [njuː, nəun] vt (gen) saber; (person, author, place) conocer ■ vi: **as far as I ~ ...** que yo sepa ...; **yes, I ~** sí, ya lo sé; **I don't ~** no lo sé; **to ~ how to do** saber hacer; **to ~ how to swim** saber nadar; **to ~ about** or **of sb/sth** saber de algn/algo; **to get to ~ sth** enterarse de algo; **I ~ nothing about it** no sé nada de eso; **I don't ~ him** no lo or le conozco; **to ~ right from wrong** saber distinguir el bien del mal

know-all ['nəuɔːl] n (Brit pej) sabelotodo m/f inv, sabihondo(-a)

know-how ['nəuhau] n conocimientos mpl

knowing ['nəuɪŋ] adj (look etc) de complicidad

knowingly ['nəuɪŋlɪ] adv (purposely) a sabiendas; (smile, look) con complicidad

know-it-all ['nəuɪtɔːl] n (US) = **know-all**

knowledge ['nɔlɪdʒ] n (gen) conocimiento; (learning) saber m, conocimientos mpl; **to have no ~ of** no saber nada de; **with my ~** con mis conocimientos, sabiéndolo; **to (the best of) my ~** a mi entender, que yo sepa; **not to my ~** que yo sepa, no; **it is common ~ that ...** es del dominio público que ..., it has come to my ~ that ...** me he enterado de que ...; **to have a working ~ of Spanish** defenderse con el español

knowledgeable ['nɔlɪdʒəbl] adj entendido, erudito

known [nəun] pp of **know** ■ adj (thief, facts) conocido; (expert) reconocido

knuckle ['nʌkl] n nudillo

▶ **knuckle down** vi (col) ponerse a trabajar en serio

▶ **knuckle under** vi someterse

knuckleduster ['nʌkldʌstə] n puño de hierro

KO abbr (= knock out) K.O. m ■ vt (knock out) dejar K.O.

koala [kəu'ɑːlə] n (also: **koala bear**) koala m

kook [kuːk] n (US col) chiflado(-a) m(f), majareta m/f

Koran [kɔ'rɑːn] n Corán m

Korea [kə'rɪə] n Corea; **North/South ~** Corea del Norte/Sur

Korean [kə'rɪən] adj, n coreano(-a) m(f)

kosher ['kəuʃə] adj autorizado por la ley judía

Kosovan ['kɒsɒvɒn], **Kosovar** ['kɒsəvɑː] adj kosovar

Kosovo ['kɒsəvəu] n Kosovo m

kowtow ['kau'tau] vi: **to ~ to sb** humillarse ante algn

KS abbr (US) = **Kansas**

Kt abbr (Brit: = Knight) caballero de una orden

Kuala Lumpur ['kwɑːlə'lumpuə] n Kuala Lumpur m

kudos ['kjuːdɒs] n gloria, prestigio

Kurd [kəːd] n kurdo(-a)

Kuwait [ku'weɪt] n Kuwait m

Kuwaiti [ku'weɪtɪ] adj, n Kuwaití m/f

kW abbr (= kilowatt) Kv

KY, Ky. abbr (US) = **Kentucky**

k

Ll

L, l [ɛl] n (letter) L, l f; **L for Lucy**, (US) **L for Love** L de Lorenzo

L abbr (on maps etc) = **lake**; **large**; (= left) izq.; (Brit Aut: = learner) L

l abbr = **litre**

LA n abbr (US: = Los Angeles) ■ abbr (US) = **Louisiana**

La. abbr (US) = **Louisiana**

lab [læb] n abbr = **laboratory**

Lab. abbr (Canada) = **Labrador**

label ['leɪbl] n etiqueta; (brand: of record) sello (discográfico) ■ vt poner una etiqueta a, etiquetar

labor ['leɪbər] (US) = **labour**

laboratory [ləˈbɔrətərɪ] n laboratorio

Labor Day n (US) día m de los trabajadores (primer lunes de septiembre)

laborious [ləˈbɔːrɪəs] adj penoso

laboriously [ləˈbɔːrɪəslɪ] adv penosamente

labor union n (US) sindicato

labor unrest n (US) conflictividad f laboral

Labour ['leɪbər] n (Brit Pol: also: **the Labour Party**) el partido laborista, los laboristas

labour, labor (US) ['leɪbər] n (task) trabajo; (also: **labour force**) mano f de obra; (workers) trabajadores mpl; (Med) (dolores mpl de) parto ■ vi: **to ~ (at)** trabajar (en) ■ vt insistir en; **hard ~** trabajos mpl forzados; **to be in ~** estar de parto

labour cost, labor cost (US) n costo de la mano de obra

labour dispute, labor dispute (US) n conflicto laboral

laboured, labored (US) ['leɪbəd] adj (breathing) fatigoso; (style) forzado, pesado

labourer, laborer (US) ['leɪbərər] n peón m; (on farm) peón m, obrero; (day labourer) jornalero

labour force, labor force (US) n mano f de obra

labour-intensive, labor-intensive (US) [leɪbərɪnˈtɛnsɪv] adj que necesita mucha mano de obra

labour relations, labor relations (US) npl relaciones fpl laborales

labour-saving, labor-saving (US) ['leɪbəseɪvɪŋ] adj que ahorra trabajo

laburnum [ləˈbəːnəm] n codeso

labyrinth ['læbɪrɪnθ] n laberinto

lace [leɪs] n encaje m; (of shoe etc) cordón m ■ vt (shoes: also: **lace up**) atarse; (drink: fortify with spirits) echar licor a

lacemaking ['leɪsmeɪkɪŋ] n obra de encaje

lacerate ['læsəreɪt] vt lacerar

laceration [læsəˈreɪʃən] n laceración f

lace-up ['leɪsʌp] adj (shoes etc) con cordones

lack [læk] n (absence) falta, carencia; (scarcity) escasez f ■ vt faltarle a algn, carecer de; **through** or **for ~ of** por falta de; **to be lacking** faltar, no haber

lackadaisical [lækəˈdeɪzɪkl] adj (careless) descuidado; (indifferent) indiferente

lackey ['lækɪ] n (also fig) lacayo

lacklustre, lackluster (US) ['læklʌstər] adj (surface) deslustrado, deslucido; (style) inexpresivo; (eyes) apagado

laconic [ləˈkɒnɪk] adj lacónico

lacquer ['lækər] n laca; **hair ~** laca para el pelo

lacrosse [ləˈkrɒs] n lacrosse f

lacy ['leɪsɪ] adj (like lace) parecido al encaje

lad [læd] n muchacho, chico; (in stable etc) mozo

ladder ['lædər] n escalera (de mano); (Brit: in tights) carrera ■ vt (Brit: tights) hacer una carrera en

laden ['leɪdn] adj: **~ (with)** cargado (de); **fully ~** (truck, ship) cargado hasta el tope

ladle ['leɪdl] n cucharón m

lady ['leɪdɪ] n señora; (distinguished, noble) dama; **young ~** señorita; **the ladies' (room)** los servicios de señoras

ladybird ['leɪdɪbəːd], **ladybug** (US) ['leɪdɪbʌg] n mariquita

lady doctor n médica, doctora

lady-in-waiting ['leɪdɪɪnˈweɪtɪŋ] n dama de honor

ladykiller ['leɪdɪkɪlər] n robacorazones m inv
ladylike ['leɪdɪlaɪk] adj fino
Ladyship ['leɪdɪʃɪp] n: **your ~** su Señoría
LAFTA n abbr (= *Latin American Free Trade Association*) ALALC f
lag [læg] vi (*also*: **lag behind**) retrasarse, quedarse atrás ■ vt (*pipes*) revestir
lager ['lɑːgər] n cerveza (rubia)
lager lout n (*Brit col*) gamberro borracho
lagging ['lægɪŋ] n revestimiento
lagoon [lə'guːn] n laguna
Lagos ['leɪgɔs] n Lagos m
laid [leɪd] pt, pp of **lay**
laid-back [leɪd'bæk] adj (*col*) tranquilo, relajado
laid up adj: **to be ~** (*person*) tener que guardar cama
lain [leɪn] pp of **lie**
lair [lɛər] n guarida
laissez-faire [lɛseɪ'fɛər] n laissez-faire m
laity ['leɪtɪ] n laicado
lake [leɪk] n lago
Lake District n (*Brit*): **the ~** la Región de los Lagos
lamb [læm] n cordero; (*meat*) carne f de cordero
lamb chop n chuleta de cordero
lambswool ['læmzwul] n lana de cordero
lame [leɪm] adj cojo, rengo (*LAm*); (*weak*) débil, poco convincente; **~ duck** (*fig: person*) inútil m/f; (: *firm*) empresa en quiebra
lamely ['leɪmlɪ] adv (*fig*) sin convicción
lament [lə'mɛnt] n lamento ■ vt lamentarse de
lamentable ['læməntəbl] adj lamentable
lamentation [læmən'teɪʃən] n lamento
laminated ['læmɪneɪtɪd] adj laminado
lamp [læmp] n lámpara
lamplight ['læmplaɪt] n: **by ~** a la luz de la lámpara
lampoon [læm'puːn] vt satirizar
lamppost ['læmppəust] n (*Brit*) farola
lampshade ['læmpʃeɪd] n pantalla
lance [lɑːns] n lanza ■ vt (*Med*) abrir con lanceta
lance corporal n (*Brit*) soldado de primera clase
lancet ['lɑːnsɪt] n (*Med*) lanceta
Lancs [læŋks] abbr (*Brit*) = **Lancashire**
land [lænd] n tierra; (*country*) país m; (*piece of land*) terreno; (*estate*) tierras fpl, finca; (*Agr*) campo ■ vi (*from ship*) desembarcar; (*Aviat*) aterrizar; (*fig: fall*) caer ■ vt (*obtain*) conseguir; (*passengers, goods*) desembarcar; **to go/travel by ~** ir/viajar por tierra; **to own ~** ser dueño de tierras; **to ~ on one's feet** caer de pie; (*fig: to be lucky*) salir bien parado

▶ **land up** vi: **to ~ up in/at** ir a parar a/en
landed ['lændɪd] adj: **~ gentry** terratenientes mpl
landfill site ['lændfɪl-] n vertedero
landing ['lændɪŋ] n desembarco; aterrizaje m; (*of staircase*) rellano
landing card n tarjeta de desembarque
landing craft n lancha de desembarco
landing gear n (*Aviat*) tren m de aterrizaje
landing stage n (*Brit*) desembarcadero
landing strip n pista de aterrizaje
landlady ['lændleɪdɪ] n (*of boarding house*) patrona; (*owner*) dueña
landlocked ['lændlɔkt] adj cercado de tierra
landlord ['lændlɔːd] n propietario; (*of pub etc*) patrón m
landlubber ['lændlʌbər] n marinero de agua dulce
landmark ['lændmɑːk] n lugar m conocido; **to be a ~** (*fig*) hacer época
landowner ['lændəunər] n terrateniente m/f
landscape ['lænskeɪp] n paisaje m
landscape architecture n arquitectura paisajista
landscaped ['lænskeɪpt] adj reformado artísticamente
landscape gardener n diseñador(-a) m(f) de paisajes
landscape gardening n jardinería paisajista
landscape painting n (*Art*) paisaje m
landslide ['lændslaɪd] n (*Geo*) corrimiento de tierras; (*fig: Pol*) victoria arrolladora
lane [leɪn] n (*in country*) camino; (*in town*) callejón m; (*Aut*) carril m; (*in race*) calle f; (*for air or sea traffic*) ruta; **shipping ~** ruta marina
language ['læŋgwɪdʒ] n lenguaje m; (*national tongue*) idioma m, lengua; **bad ~** palabrotas fpl
language laboratory n laboratorio de idiomas
language studies npl estudios mpl filológicos
languid ['læŋgwɪd] adj lánguido
languish ['læŋgwɪʃ] vi languidecer
languor ['læŋgər] n languidez f
languorous ['læŋgərəs] adj lánguido
lank [læŋk] adj (*hair*) lacio
lanky ['læŋkɪ] adj larguirucho
lanolin, lanoline ['lænəlɪn] n lanolina
lantern ['læntn] n linterna, farol m
lanyard ['lænjed] n acollador m
Laos [laus] n Laos m
lap [læp] n (*of track*) vuelta; (*of body*): **to sit on sb's ~** sentarse en las rodillas de algn ■ vt (*also*: **lap up**) beber a lengüetadas *or* con la lengua ■ vi (*waves*) chapotear

▶ **lap up** vt beber a lengüetadas *or* con la lengua; (*fig: compliments, attention*) disfrutar; (: *lies etc*) tragarse

La Paz [læ'pæz] *n* La Paz
lapdog ['læpdɔg] *n* perro faldero
lapel [lə'pɛl] *n* solapa
Lapland ['læplænd] *n* Laponia
Laplander ['læplændə^r] *n* lapón(-ona) *m(f)*
lapse [læps] *n* (*fault*) error *m*, fallo; (*moral*) desliz *m* ■ *vi* (*expire*) caducar; (*morally*) cometer un desliz; (*time*) pasar, transcurrir; **to ~ into bad habits** volver a las andadas; **~ of time** lapso, período; **a ~ of memory** un lapsus de memoria
laptop ['læptɔp] *n* (*also*: **laptop computer**) (ordenador *m*) portátil *m*
larceny ['lɑːsənɪ] *n* latrocinio
lard [lɑːd] *n* manteca (de cerdo)
larder ['lɑːdə^r] *n* despensa
large [lɑːdʒ] *adj* grande ■ *adv*: **by and ~** en general, en términos generales; **at ~** (*free*) en libertad; (*generally*) en general; **to make ~(r)** hacer mayor *or* más extenso; **a ~ number of people** una gran cantidad de personas; **on a ~ scale** a gran escala
largely ['lɑːdʒlɪ] *adv* en gran parte
large-scale ['lɑːdʒ'skeɪl] *adj* (*map, drawing*) a gran escala; (*reforms, business activities*) importante
largesse [lɑː'ʒɛs] *n* generosidad *f*
lark [lɑːk] *n* (*bird*) alondra; (*joke*) broma
▶ **lark about** *vi* bromear, hacer el tonto
larva (*pl* **larvae**) ['lɑːvə, -iː] *n* larva
laryngitis [lærɪn'dʒaɪtɪs] *n* laringitis *f*
larynx ['lærɪŋks] *n* laringe *f*
lasagne [lə'zænjə] *n* lasaña
lascivious [lə'sɪvɪəs] *adj* lascivo
laser ['leɪzə^r] *n* láser *m*
laser beam *n* rayo láser
laser printer *n* impresora láser
lash [læʃ] *n* latigazo; (*punishment*) azote *m*; (*also*: **eyelash**) pestaña ■ *vt* azotar; (*tie*) atar
▶ **lash down** *vt* sujetar con cuerdas ■ *vi* (*rain*) caer a trombas
▶ **lash out** *vi* (*col: spend*) gastar a la loca; **to ~ out at** *or* **against sb** (*fig*) lanzar invectivas contra algn
lashing ['læʃɪŋ] *n* (*beating*) azotaina, flagelación *f*; **lashings of** (*col*) montones *mpl* de
lass [læs] *n* chica
lassitude ['læsɪtjuːd] *n* lasitud *f*
lasso [læ'suː] *n* lazo ■ *vt* coger con lazo
last [lɑːst] *adj* (*gen*) último; (*final*) último, final ■ *adv* por último ■ *vi* (*endure*) durar; (*continue*) continuar, seguir; **~ night** anoche; **~ week** la semana pasada; **at ~** por fin; **~ but one** penúltimo; **~ time** la última vez; **it lasts (for) two hours** dura dos horas
last-ditch ['lɑːst'dɪtʃ] *adj* (*attempt*) de último recurso, último, desesperado

lasting ['lɑːstɪŋ] *adj* duradero
lastly ['lɑːstlɪ] *adv* por último, finalmente
last-minute ['lɑːstmɪnɪt] *adj* de última hora
latch [lætʃ] *n* picaporte *m*, pestillo
▶ **latch on to** *vt fus* (*cling to: person*) pegarse a; (: *idea*) agarrarse de
latchkey ['lætʃkiː] *n* llavín *m*
latchkey child *n* niño cuyos padres trabajan
late [leɪt] *adj* (*not on time*) tarde, atrasado; (*towards end of period, life*) tardío; (*hour*) avanzado; (*deceased*) fallecido ■ *adv* tarde; (*behind time, schedule*) con retraso; **to be (10 minutes) ~** llegar con (10 minutos de) retraso; **to be ~ with** estar atrasado con; **~ delivery** entrega tardía; **~ in life** a una edad avanzada; **of ~** últimamente; **in ~ May** hacia fines de mayo; **the ~ Mr X** el difunto Sr. X; **to work ~** trabajar hasta tarde
latecomer ['leɪtkʌmə^r] *n* recién llegado(-a)
lately ['leɪtlɪ] *adv* últimamente
lateness ['leɪtnɪs] *n* (*of person*) demora; (*of event*) tardanza
latent ['leɪtnt] *adj* latente; **~ defect** defecto latente
later ['leɪtə^r] *adj* (*date etc*) posterior; (*version etc*) más reciente ■ *adv* más tarde, después; **~ on today** hoy más tarde
lateral ['lætərl] *adj* lateral
latest ['leɪtɪst] *adj* último; **at the ~** a más tardar
latex ['leɪtɛks] *n* látex *m*
lathe [leɪð] *n* torno
lather ['lɑːðə^r] *n* espuma (de jabón) ■ *vt* enjabonar
Latin ['lætɪn] *n* latín *m* ■ *adj* latino
Latin America *n* América Latina, Latinoamérica
Latin American *adj, n* latinoamericano(-a) *m(f)*
Latino [læ'tiːnəu] *adj, n* latino(-a) *m(f)*
latitude ['lætɪtjuːd] *n* latitud *f*; (*fig: freedom*) libertad *f*
latrine [lə'triːn] *n* letrina
latter ['lætə^r] *adj* último; (*of two*) segundo ■ *n*: **the ~** el último, éste
latter-day ['lætədeɪ] *adj* moderno
latterly ['lætəlɪ] *adv* últimamente
lattice ['lætɪs] *n* enrejado
lattice window *n* ventana enrejada *or* de celosía
lattice work *n* enrejado
Latvia ['lætvɪə] *n* Letonia
Latvian ['lætvɪən] *adj* letón(-ona) ■ *n* letón(-ona) *m(f)*; (*Ling*) letón *m*
laudable ['lɔːdəbl] *adj* loable
laugh [lɑːf] *n* risa; (*loud*) carcajada ■ *vi* reírse, reír; reírse a carcajadas

▶ **laugh at** *vt fus* reírse de
▶ **laugh off** *vt* tomar a risa
laughable ['lɑ:fəbl] *adj* ridículo
laughing ['lɑ:fɪŋ] *adj* risueño ∎ *n*: **it's no ~ matter** no es cosa de risa
laughing gas *n* gas *m* hilarante
laughing stock *n*: **to be the ~ of the town** ser el hazmerreír de la ciudad
laughter ['lɑ:ftə^r] *n* risa
launch [lɔ:ntʃ] *n* (*boat*) lancha; *see also* **launching** ∎ *vt* (*ship*) botar; (*rocket, plan*) lanzar
▶ **launch forth** *vi*: **to ~ forth (into)** lanzarse a *or* en, emprender
▶ **launch out** *vi* = **launch forth**
launching ['lɔ:ntʃɪŋ] *n* (*of rocket etc*) lanzamiento; (*inauguration*) estreno
launching pad, launch pad *n* plataforma de lanzamiento
launder ['lɔ:ndə^r] *vt* lavar
Launderette® [lɔ:n'drɛt], **Laundromat®** (*US*) ['lɔ:ndrəmæt] *n* lavandería (automática)
laundry ['lɔ:ndrɪ] *n* lavandería; (*clothes*) ropa sucia; **to do the ~** hacer la colada
laureate ['lɔ:rɪət] *adj see* **poet**
laurel ['lɔrl] *n* laurel *m*; **to rest on one's laurels** dormirse *or* sobre los laureles
lava ['lɑ:və] *n* lava
lavatory ['lævətərɪ] *n* wáter *m*; **lavatories** *npl* servicios *mpl*, aseos *mpl*, sanitarios *mpl* (*LAm*)
lavatory paper *n* papel *m* higiénico
lavender ['lævəndə^r] *n* lavanda
lavish ['lævɪʃ] *adj* abundante; (*giving freely*): **~ with** pródigo en ∎ *vt*: **to ~ sth on sb** colmar a algn de algo
lavishly ['lævɪʃlɪ] *adv* (*give, spend*) generosamente; (*furnished*) lujosamente
law [lɔ:] *n* ley *f*; (*study*) derecho; (*of game*) regla; **against the ~** contra la ley; **to study ~** estudiar derecho; **to go to ~** recurrir a la justicia
law-abiding ['lɔ:əbaɪdɪŋ] *adj* respetuoso con la ley
law and order *n* orden *m* público
lawbreaker ['lɔ:breɪkə^r] *n* infractor(a) *m(f)* de la ley
law court *n* tribunal *m* (de justicia)
lawful ['lɔ:ful] *adj* legítimo, lícito
lawfully ['lɔ:fulɪ] *adv* legalmente
lawless ['lɔ:lɪs] *adj* (*act*) ilegal; (*person*) rebelde; (*country*) ingobernable
Law Lord *n* (*Brit*) *miembro de la Cámara de los Lores y del más alto tribunal de apelación*
lawmaker ['lɔ:meɪkə^r] *n* legislador(a) *m(f)*
lawn [lɔ:n] *n* césped *m*

lawnmower ['lɔ:nməuə^r] *n* cortacésped *m*
lawn tennis *n* tenis *m* sobre hierba
law school *n* (*US*) facultad *f* de derecho
law student *n* estudiante *m/f* de derecho
lawsuit ['lɔ:su:t] *n* pleito; **to bring a ~ against** entablar un pleito contra
lawyer ['lɔ:jə^r] *n* abogado(-a); (*for sales, wills etc*) notario(-a)
lax [læks] *adj* (*discipline*) relajado; (*person*) negligente
laxative ['læksətɪv] *n* laxante *m*
laxity ['læksɪtɪ] *n* flojedad *f*; (*moral*) relajamiento; (*negligence*) negligencia
lay [leɪ] *pt of* **lie** ∎ *adj* laico; (*not expert*) lego ∎ *vt* (*pt, pp* **laid** [leɪd]) (*place*) colocar; (*eggs, table*) poner; (*trap*) tender; **to ~ the facts/ one's proposals before sb** presentar los hechos/sus propuestas a algn
▶ **lay aside, lay by** *vt* dejar a un lado
▶ **lay down** *vt* (*pen etc*) dejar; (*arms*) rendir; (*policy*) trazar; **to ~ down the law** imponer las normas
▶ **lay in** *vt* abastecerse de
▶ **lay into** *vt fus* (*col: attack, scold*) arremeter contra
▶ **lay off** *vt* (*workers*) despedir
▶ **lay on** *vt* (*water, gas*) instalar; (*meal, facilities*) proveer
▶ **lay out** *vt* (*plan*) trazar; (*display*) exponer; (*spend*) gastar
▶ **lay up** *vt* (*store*) guardar; (*ship*) desarmar; (*illness*) obligar a guardar cama
layabout ['leɪəbaut] *n* vago(-a)
lay-by ['leɪbaɪ] *n* (*Brit Aut*) apartadero
lay days *npl* días *mpl* de inactividad
layer ['leɪə^r] *n* capa
layette [leɪ'et] *n* ajuar *m* (de niño)
layman ['leɪmən] *n* lego
lay-off ['leɪɔf] *n* despido, paro forzoso
layout ['leɪaut] *n* (*design*) plan *m*, trazado; (*disposition*) disposición *f*; (*Press*) composición *f*
laze [leɪz] *vi* no hacer nada; (*pej*) holgazanear
lazily ['leɪzɪlɪ] *adv* perezosamente
laziness ['leɪzɪnɪs] *n* pereza
lazy ['leɪzɪ] *adj* perezoso, vago, flojo (*LAm*)
LB *abbr* (*Canada*) = **Labrador**
lb. *abbr* = **pound** (*weight*)
lbw *abbr* (*Cricket*) = **leg before wicket**
LC *n abbr* (*US*) = **Library of Congress**
lc *abbr* (*Typ*: = *lower case*) min
L/C *abbr* = **letter of credit**
LCD *n abbr see* **liquid crystal display**
Ld *abbr* (*Brit*: = *Lord*) título de nobleza
LDS *n abbr* (= *Licentiate in Dental Surgery*) diploma universitario; (= *Latter-day Saints*) Iglesia de Jesucristo de los Santos del último día

LEA *n abbr* (Brit: = *local education authority*) organismo local encargado de la enseñanza

lead [li:d] (*pt, pp* **led** [lɛd]) *n* (*front position*) delantera; (*distance, time ahead*) ventaja; (*clue*) pista; (*Elec*) cable *m*; (*for dog*) correa; (*Theat*) papel *m* principal; (*metal*) plomo; (*in pencil*) mina ■ *vt* conducir; (*life*) llevar; (*be leader of*) dirigir; (*Sport*) ir en cabeza de; (*orchestra: Brit*) ser el primer violín en; (: *US*) dirigir ■ *vi* ir primero; **to be in the ~** (*Sport*) llevar la delantera; (*fig*) ir a la cabeza; **to take the ~** (*Sport*) tomar la delantera; (*fig*) tomar la iniciativa; **to ~ sb to believe that ...** hacer creer a algn que ...; **to ~ sb to do sth** llevar a algn a hacer algo
▸ **lead astray** *vt* llevar por mal camino
▸ **lead away** *vt* llevar
▸ **lead back** *vt* hacer volver
▸ **lead off** *vt* llevar ■ *vi* (*in game*) abrir
▸ **lead on** *vt* (*tease*) engañar; **to ~ sb on to** (*induce*) incitar a algn a
▸ **lead to** *vt fus* producir, provocar
▸ **lead up to** *vt fus* conducir a

leaded ['lɛdɪd] *adj*: **~ windows** ventanas *fpl* emplomadas

leaden ['lɛdn] *adj* (*sky, sea*) plomizo; (*heavy: footsteps*) pesado

leader ['li:də⁺] *n* jefe(-a) *m(f)*, líder *m*; (*of union etc*) dirigente *m/f*; (*guide*) guía *m/f*; (*of newspaper*) editorial *m*; **they are leaders in their field** (*fig*) llevan la delantera en su especialidad

leadership ['li:dəʃɪp] *n* dirección *f*; **qualities of ~** iniciativa *sg*; **under the ~ of ...** bajo la dirección de ..., al mando de ...

lead-free ['lɛdfri:] *adj* sin plomo

leading ['li:dɪŋ] *adj* (*main*) principal; (*outstanding*) destacado; (*first*) primero; (*front*) delantero; **a ~ question** una pregunta tendenciosa

leading lady *n* (*Theat*) primera actriz *f*

leading light *n* (*fig: person*) figura principal

leading man *n* (*Theat*) primer actor *m*

leading role *n* papel *m* principal

lead pencil *n* lápiz *m*

lead poisoning *n* envenenamiento plúmbico

lead time *n* (*Comm*) plazo de entrega

lead-up ['li:dʌp] *n*: **in the ~ to the election** cuando falta *etc* poco para las elecciones

lead weight *n* peso de plomo

leaf (*pl* **leaves**) [li:f, li:vz] *n* hoja; **to turn over a new ~** (*fig*) volver la hoja, hacer borrón y cuenta nueva; **to take a ~ out of sb's book** (*fig*) seguir el ejemplo de algn
▸ **leaf through** *vt fus* (*book*) hojear

leaflet ['li:flɪt] *n* folleto

leafy ['li:fɪ] *adj* frondoso

league [li:g] *n* sociedad *f*; (*Football*) liga; **to be in ~ with** estar confabulado con

league table *n* clasificación *f*

leak [li:k] *n* (*of liquid, gas*) escape *m*, fuga; (*in pipe*) agujero; (*in roof*) gotera; (*fig: of information, in security*) filtración *f* ■ *vi* (*ship*) hacer agua; (*shoes*) tener un agujero; (*pipe*) tener un escape; (*roof*) tener goteras; (*also*: **leak out**: *liquid, gas*) escaparse, salirse; (*fig: news*) trascender, divulgarse ■ *vt* (*gen*) dejar escapar; (*fig: information*) filtrar

leakage ['li:kɪdʒ] *n* (*of water, gas etc*) escape *m*, fuga

leaky ['li:kɪ] *adj* (*roof*) con goteras; (*bucket, shoe*) con agujeros; (*pipe*) con un escape; (*boat*) que hace agua

lean [li:n] (*pt, pp* **leaned** *or* **leant**) *adj* (*thin*) flaco; (*meat*) magro ■ *vt*: **to ~ sth on sth** apoyar algo en algo ■ *vi* (*slope*) inclinarse; (*rest*): **to ~ against** apoyarse contra; **to ~ on** apoyarse en
▸ **lean back** *vi* inclinarse hacia atrás
▸ **lean forward** *vi* inclinarse hacia adelante
▸ **lean out** *vi*: **to ~ out (of)** asomarse (a)
▸ **lean over** *vi* inclinarse

leaning ['li:nɪŋ] *adj* inclinado ■ *n*: **~ (towards)** inclinación *f* (hacia); **the L~ Tower of Pisa** la Torre Inclinada de Pisa

leant [lɛnt] *pt, pp of* **lean**

lean-to ['li:ntu:] *n* (*roof*) tejado de una sola agua; (*building*) cobertizo

leap [li:p] *n* salto ■ *vi* (*pt, pp* **leaped** *or* **leapt** [lɛpt] saltar; **to ~ at an offer** apresurarse a aceptar una oferta
▸ **leap up** *vi* (*person*) saltar

leapfrog ['li:pfrɔg] *n* pídola ■ *vi*: **to ~ over sb/sth** saltar por encima de algn/algo

leapt [lɛpt] *pt, pp of* **leap**

leap year *n* año bisiesto

learn (*pt, pp* **learned** *or* **learnt**) [lə:n, -t] *vt* (*gen*) aprender; (*come to know of*) enterarse de ■ *vi* aprender; **to ~ how to do sth** aprender a hacer algo; **to ~ that ...** enterarse *or* informarse de que ...; **to ~ about sth** (*Scol*) aprender algo; (*hear*) enterarse *or* informarse de algo; **we were sorry to ~ that ...** nos dio tristeza saber que ...

learned ['lə:nɪd] *adj* erudito

learner ['lə:nə⁺] *n* principiante *m/f*; (*Brit: also*: **learner driver**) conductor(a) *m(f)* en prácticas; *see also* **L-plates**

learning ['lə:nɪŋ] *n* saber *m*, conocimientos *mpl*

learnt [lə:nt] *pp of* **learn**

lease [li:s] *n* arriendo ■ *vt* arrendar; **on ~** en arriendo
▸ **lease back** *vt* subarrendar

leaseback ['liːsbæk] *n* subarriendo
leasehold ['liːshəuld] *n* (*contract*) derechos *mpl* de arrendamiento ■ *adj* arrendado
leash [liːʃ] *n* correa
least [liːst] *adj* (*slightest*) menor, más pequeño; (*smallest amount of*) mínimo ■ *adv* menos ■ *n*: **the ~** lo menos; **the ~ expensive car** el coche menos caro; **at ~** por lo menos, al menos; **not in the ~** en absoluto
leather ['lɛðəʳ] *n* cuero ■ *cpd*: **~ goods** artículos *mpl* de cuero *or* piel
leathery ['lɛðərɪ] *adj* (*skin*) curtido
leave [liːv] (*pt, pp* **left**) *vt* dejar; (*go away from*) abandonar ■ *vi* irse; (*train*) salir ■ *n* permiso; **to ~ school** dejar la escuela *or* el colegio; **~ it to me!** ¡yo me encargo!; **he's already left for the airport** ya se ha marchado al aeropuerto; **to be left** quedar, sobrar; **there's some milk left over** sobra *or* queda algo de leche; **on ~** de permiso; **to take one's ~ of** despedirse de
▶ **leave behind** *vt* (*on purpose*) dejar (atrás); (*accidentally*) olvidar
▶ **leave off** *vt* (*lid*) no poner; (*switch*) no encender; (*col: stop*): **to ~ off doing sth** dejar de hacer algo
▶ **leave on** *vt* (*lid*) dejar puesto; (*light, fire, cooker*) dejar encendido
▶ **leave out** *vt* omitir
▶ **leave over** *vt* (*postpone*) dejar, aplazar
leave of absence *n* excedencia
leaves [liːvz] *pl of* **leaf**
leavetaking ['liːvteɪkɪŋ] *n* despedida
Lebanon ['lɛbənən] *n*: **the ~** el Líbano
lecherous ['lɛtʃərəs] *adj* lascivo
lectern ['lɛktəːn] *n* atril *m*
lecture ['lɛktʃəʳ] *n* conferencia; (*Scol*) clase *f* ■ *vi* dar clase(s) ■ *vt* (*scold*) sermonear; (*reprove*) echar una reprimenda a; **to give a ~ on** dar una conferencia sobre
lecture hall *n* sala de conferencias; (*Univ*) aula
lecturer ['lɛktʃərəʳ] *n* conferenciante *m/f*; (*Brit: at university*) profesor(a) *m(f)*
lecture theatre *n* = **lecture hall**
LED *n abbr* (*Elec*: = *light-emitting diode*) LED *m*
led [lɛd] *pt, pp of* **lead**
ledge [lɛdʒ] *n* (*of window, on wall*) repisa, reborde *m*; (*of mountain*) saliente *m*
ledger ['lɛdʒəʳ] *n* libro mayor
lee [liː] *n* sotavento; **in the ~ of** al abrigo de
leech [liːtʃ] *n* sanguijuela
leek [liːk] *n* puerro
leer [lɪəʳ] *vi*: **to ~ at sb** mirar de manera lasciva a algn
leeway ['liːweɪ] *n* (*fig*): **to have some ~** tener cierta libertad de acción

left [lɛft] *pt, pp of* **leave** ■ *adj* izquierdo ■ *n* izquierda ■ *adv* a la izquierda; **on** *or* **to the ~** a la izquierda; **the L-** (*Pol*) la izquierda
left-click ['lɛftklɪk] *vi* clicar con el botón izquierdo del ratón ■ *vt*: **to ~ an icon** clicar en un icono con el botón izquierdo del ratón
left-hand drive ['lɛfthænd-] *n* conducción *f* por la izquierda
left-handed [lɛft'hændɪd] *adj* zurdo; **~ scissors** tijeras *fpl* zurdas *or* para zurdos
left-hand side ['lɛfthænd-] *n* izquierda
leftie ['lɛftɪ] *n* = **lefty**
leftist ['lɛftɪst] *adj* (*Pol*) izquierdista
left-luggage [lɛft'lʌgɪdʒ], **left-luggage office** *n* (*Brit*) consigna
left-overs ['lɛftəuvəz] *npl* sobras *fpl*
left-wing [lɛft'wɪŋ] *adj* (*Pol*) de izquierda(s), izquierdista
left-winger [lɛft'wɪŋəʳ] *n* (*Pol*) izquierdista *m/f*
lefty ['lɛftɪ] *n* (*col: Pol*) rojillo(-a)
leg [lɛg] *n* pierna; (*of animal, chair*) pata; (*Culin: of meat*) pierna; (*of journey*) etapa; **1st/2nd ~** (*Sport*) partido de ida/de vuelta; **to pull sb's ~** tomar el pelo a algn; **to stretch one's legs** dar una vuelta
legacy ['lɛgəsɪ] *n* herencia; (*fig*) herencia, legado
legal ['liːgl] *adj* (*permitted by law*) lícito; (*of law*) legal; (*inquiry etc*) jurídico; **to take ~ action** *or* **proceedings against sb** entablar *or* levantar un pleito contra algn
legal adviser *n* asesor(a) *m(f)* jurídico(-a)
legal holiday *n* (*US*) fiesta oficial
legality [lɪ'gælɪtɪ] *n* legalidad *f*
legalize ['liːgəlaɪz] *vt* legalizar
legally ['liːgəlɪ] *adv* legalmente; **~ binding** con fuerza legal
legal tender *n* moneda de curso legal
legend ['lɛdʒənd] *n* leyenda
legendary ['lɛdʒəndərɪ] *adj* legendario
-legged ['lɛgɪd] *suff*: **two~** (*table etc*) de dos patas
leggings ['lɛgɪŋz] *npl* mallas *fpl*, leggins *mpl*
leggy ['lɛgɪ] *adj* de piernas largas
legibility [lɛdʒɪ'bɪlɪtɪ] *n* legibilidad *f*
legible ['lɛdʒəbl] *adj* legible
legibly ['lɛdʒəblɪ] *adv* legiblemente
legion ['liːdʒən] *n* legión *f*
legionnaire [liːdʒə'nɛəʳ] *n* legionario
legionnaire's disease *n* enfermedad *f* del legionario
legislation [lɛdʒɪs'leɪʃən] *n* legislación *f*; **a piece of ~** (*bill*) un proyecto de ley; (*act*) una ley
legislative ['lɛdʒɪslətɪv] *adj* legislativo
legislator ['lɛdʒɪsleɪtəʳ] *n* legislador(a) *m(f)*

legislature ['lɛdʒɪslətʃəʳ] n cuerpo legislativo
legitimacy [lɪ'dʒɪtɪməsɪ] n legitimidad f
legitimate [lɪ'dʒɪtɪmət] adj legítimo
legitimize [lɪ'dʒɪtɪmaɪz] vt legitimar
legless ['lɛglɪs] adj (Brit col) mamado
leg-room ['lɛgruːm] n espacio para las piernas
Leics abbr (Brit) = **Leicestershire**
leisure ['lɛʒəʳ] n ocio, tiempo libre; **at ~** con tranquilidad
leisure centre n centro recreativo
leisurely ['lɛʒəlɪ] adj sin prisa; lento
leisure suit n conjunto tipo chandal
lemon ['lɛmən] n limón m
lemonade [lɛmə'neɪd] n (fruit juice) limonada; (fizzy) gaseosa
lemon cheese, lemon curd n queso de limón
lemon juice n zumo de limón
lemon tea n té m con limón
lend [lɛnd] (pt, pp **lent** [lɛnt]) vt: **to ~ sth to sb** prestar algo a algn
lender ['lɛndəʳ] n prestamista m/f
lending library ['lɛndɪŋ-] n biblioteca de préstamo
length [lɛŋθ] n (size) largo, longitud f; (section: of road, pipe) tramo; (: of rope etc) largo; **at ~** (at last) por fin, finalmente; (lengthily) largamente; **it is two metres in ~** tiene dos metros de largo; **what ~ is it?** ¿cuánto tiene de largo?; **to fall full ~** caer de bruces; **to go to any ~(s) to do sth** ser capaz de hacer cualquier cosa para hacer algo
lengthen ['lɛŋθn] vt alargar ▪ vi alargarse
lengthways ['lɛŋθweɪz] adv a lo largo
lengthy ['lɛŋθɪ] adj largo, extenso; (meeting) prolongado
lenient ['liːnɪənt] adj indulgente
lens [lɛnz] n (of spectacles) lente f; (of camera) objetivo
Lent [lɛnt] n Cuaresma
lent [lɛnt] pt, pp of **lend**
lentil ['lɛntl] n lenteja
Leo ['liːəu] n Leo
leopard ['lɛpəd] n leopardo
leotard ['liːətaːd] n leotardo
leper ['lɛpəʳ] n leproso(-a)
leper colony n colonia de leprosos
leprosy ['lɛprəsɪ] n lepra
lesbian ['lɛzbɪən] adj lesbiano ▪ n lesbiana
lesion ['liːʒən] n (Med) lesión f
Lesotho [lɪ'suːtuː] n Lesotho
less [lɛs] adj (in size, degree etc) menor; (in quantity) menos ▪ pron, adv menos; **~ than half** menos de la mitad; **~ than £1/a kilo/3 metres** menos de una libra/un kilo/3 metros; **~ than ever** menos que nunca; **~ 5%**

menos el cinco por ciento; **~ and ~** cada vez menos; **the ~ he works ...** cuanto menos trabaja ...
lessee [lɛ'siː] n inquilino(-a), arrendatario(-a)
lessen ['lɛsn] vi disminuir, reducirse ▪ vt disminuir, reducir
lesser ['lɛsəʳ] adj menor; **to a ~ extent** or **degree** en menor grado
lesson ['lɛsn] n clase f; **a maths ~** una clase de matemáticas; **to give lessons in** dar clases de; **it taught him a ~** (fig) le sirvió de lección
lessor ['lɛsɔːʳ, lɛ'sɔːʳ] n arrendador(a) m(f)
lest [lɛst] conj: **~ it happen** para que no pase
let (pt, pp **let**) [lɛt] vt (allow) dejar, permitir; (Brit: lease) alquilar; **to ~ sb do sth** dejar que algn haga algo; **to ~ sb have sth** dar algo a algn; **to ~ sb know sth** comunicar algo a algn; **~'s go** ¡vamos!; **~ him come** que venga; **"to ~"** "se alquila"
  ▶ **let down** vt (lower) bajar; (dress) alargar; (tyre) desinflar; (hair) soltar; (disappoint) defraudar
  ▶ **let go** vi soltar; (fig) dejarse ir ▪ vt soltar
  ▶ **let in** vt dejar entrar; (visitor etc) hacer pasar; **what have you ~ yourself in for?** ¿en qué te has metido?
  ▶ **let off** vt dejar escapar; (firework etc) disparar; (bomb) accionar; (passenger) dejar, bajar; **to ~ off steam** (fig, col) desahogarse, desfogarse
  ▶ **let on** vi: **to ~ on that ...** revelar que ...
  ▶ **let out** vt dejar salir; (dress) ensanchar; (rent out) alquilar
  ▶ **let up** vi disminuir; (rain etc) amainar
let-down ['lɛtdaun] n (disappointment) decepción f
lethal ['liːθl] adj (weapon) mortífero; (poison, wound) mortal
lethargic [lɛ'θaːdʒɪk] adj aletargado
lethargy ['lɛθədʒɪ] n letargo
letter ['lɛtəʳ] n (of alphabet) letra; (correspondence) carta; **letters** npl (literature, learning) letras fpl; **small/capital ~** minúscula/mayúscula; **covering ~** carta adjunta
letter bomb n carta-bomba
letterbox ['lɛtəbɒks] n (Brit) buzón m
letterhead ['lɛtəhɛd] n membrete m, encabezamiento
lettering ['lɛtərɪŋ] n letras fpl
letter of credit n carta de crédito; **documentary ~** carta de crédito documentaria; **irrevocable ~** carta de crédito irrevocable
letter-opener ['lɛtərəupnəʳ] n abrecartas m inv

letterpress ['lɛtəprɛs] n (method) prensa de copiar; (printed page) impresión f tipográfica
letter quality n calidad f de correspondencia
letters patent npl letra sg de patente
lettuce ['lɛtɪs] n lechuga
let-up ['lɛtʌp] n descanso, tregua
leukaemia, (US) **leukemia** [lu:'ki:mɪə] n leucemia
level ['lɛvl] adj (flat) llano; (flattened) nivelado; (uniform) igual ■ adv a nivel ■ n nivel m ■ vt nivelar, allanar; (gun) apuntar; (accusation): **to ~ (against)** levantar (contra) ■ vi (col): **to ~ with sb** ser franco con algn; **to be ~ with** estar a nivel de; **a ~ spoonful** (Culin) una cucharada rasa; **to draw ~ with** (team) igualar; (runner, car) alcanzar a; **O levels** npl (Brit: formerly) ≈ bachillerato sg elemental, octavo sg de Básica; **on the ~** (fig: honest) en serio; **talks at ministerial ~** charlas fpl a nivel ministerial
▶ **level off** or **out** vi (prices etc) estabilizarse; (ground) nivelarse; (aircraft) ponerse en una trayectoria horizontal
level crossing n (Brit) paso a nivel
level-headed [lɛvl'hɛdɪd] adj sensato
levelling, leveling (US) ['lɛvlɪŋ] adj (process, effect) de nivelación ■ n igualación f, allanamiento
level playing field n situación f de igualdad; **to compete on a ~** competir en igualdad de condiciones
lever ['li:vər] n palanca ■ vt: **to ~ up** levantar con palanca
leverage ['li:vərɪdʒ] n (fig: influence) influencia
levity ['lɛvɪtɪ] n frivolidad f, informalidad f
levy ['lɛvɪ] n impuesto ■ vt exigir, recaudar
lewd [lu:d] adj lascivo, obsceno, colorado (LAm)
lexicographer [lɛksɪ'kɔgrəfər] n lexicógrafo(-a) m(f)
lexicography [lɛksɪ'kɔgrəfɪ] n lexicografía
LGV n abbr (= Large Goods Vehicle) vehículo pesado
LI abbr (US) = **Long Island**
liabilities [laɪə'bɪlətɪz] npl obligaciones fpl; pasivo sg
liability [laɪə'bɪlətɪ] n responsabilidad f; (handicap) desventaja
liable ['laɪəbl] adj (subject): **~ to** sujeto a; (responsible): **~ for** responsable de; (likely): **~ to do** propenso a hacer; **to be ~ to a fine** exponerse a una multa
liaise [li:'eɪz] vi: **to ~ (with)** colaborar (con); **to ~ with sb** mantener informado a algn

liaison [li:'eɪzɔn] n (coordination) enlace m; (affair) relación f
liar ['laɪər] n mentiroso(-a)
libel ['laɪbl] n calumnia ■ vt calumniar
libellous ['laɪbləs] adj difamatorio, calumnioso
liberal ['lɪbərl] adj (gen) liberal; (generous): **~ with** generoso con ■ n: **L~** (Pol) liberal m/f
Liberal Democrat n (Brit) demócrata m/f liberal
liberality [lɪbə'rælɪtɪ] n (generosity) liberalidad f, generosidad f
liberalize ['lɪbərəlaɪz] vt liberalizar
liberally ['lɪbərəlɪ] adv liberalmente
liberal-minded ['lɪbərl'maɪndɪd] adj de miras anchas, liberal
liberate ['lɪbəreɪt] vt liberar
liberation [lɪbə'reɪʃən] n liberación f
liberation theology n teología de la liberación
Liberia [laɪ'bɪərɪə] n Liberia
Liberian [laɪ'bɪərɪən] adj, n liberiano(-a) m(f)
liberty ['lɪbətɪ] n libertad f; **to be at ~ to do** estar libre para hacer; **to take the ~ of doing sth** tomarse la libertad de hacer algo
libido [lɪ'bi:dəu] n libido
Libra ['li:brə] n Libra
librarian [laɪ'brɛərɪən] n bibliotecario(-a)
library ['laɪbrərɪ] n biblioteca
library book n libro de la biblioteca
libretto [lɪ'brɛtəu] n libreto
Libya ['lɪbɪə] n Libia
Libyan ['lɪbɪən] adj, n libio(-a) m(f)
lice [laɪs] pl of **louse**
licence, license (US) ['laɪsns] n licencia; (permit) permiso; (also: **driving licence,** (US) **driver's license**) carnet m de conducir; (excessive freedom) libertad f; **import ~** licencia or permiso de importación; **produced under ~** elaborado bajo licencia
licence number n (número de) matrícula
licence plate n (placa de) matrícula
license ['laɪsns] (US) = **licence**; vt autorizar, dar permiso a; (car) sacar la matrícula de or (LAm) la patente de
licensed ['laɪsnst] adj (for alcohol) autorizado para vender bebidas alcohólicas
licensed trade n comercio or negocio autorizado
licensee [laɪsən'si:] n (in a pub) concesionario(-a), dueño(-a) de un bar
licentious [laɪ'sɛnʃəs] adj licencioso
lichen ['laɪkən] n liquen m
lick [lɪk] vt lamer; (col: defeat) dar una paliza a ■ n lamedura; **a ~ of paint** una mano de pintura
licorice ['lɪkərɪs] n = **liquorice**

lid [lɪd] n (of box, case) tapa; (of pan) cobertera; **to take the ~ off sth** (fig) exponer algo a la luz pública

lido ['laɪdəu] n (Brit) piscina, alberca (LAm)

lie [laɪ] n mentira ■ vi mentir; (pt **lay**, pp **lain**) [leɪ, leɪn] (rest) estar echado, estar acostado; (of object: be situated) estar, encontrarse; **to tell lies** mentir; **to ~ low** (fig) mantenerse a escondidas
▸ **lie about, lie around** vi (things) estar tirado; (Brit: people) estar acostado or tumbado
▸ **lie back** vi recostarse
▸ **lie down** vi echarse, tumbarse
▸ **lie up** vi (hide) esconderse

Liechtenstein ['lɪktənstaɪn] n Liechtenstein m

lie detector n detector m de mentiras

lie-down ['laɪdaun] n (Brit): **to have a ~** echarse (una siesta)

lie-in ['laɪɪn] n (Brit): **to have a ~** quedarse en la cama

lieu [luː]: **in ~ of** prep en lugar de

Lieut. abbr = **lieutenant**

lieutenant [lɛf'tɛnənt, (US) luː'tɛnənt] n (Mil) teniente m

lieutenant colonel n teniente m coronel

life (pl **lives**) [laɪf, laɪvz] n vida; (of licence etc) vigencia; **to be sent to prison for ~** ser condenado a cadena perpetua; **country/city ~** la vida en el campo/en la ciudad; **true to ~** fiel a la realidad; **to paint from ~** pintar del natural; **to put** or **breathe new ~ into** (person) reanimar; (project, area etc) infundir nueva vida a

life assurance n (Brit) seguro de vida

lifebelt ['laɪfbɛlt] n (Brit) cinturón m salvavidas

lifeblood ['laɪfblʌd] n (fig) alma, nervio

lifeboat ['laɪfbəut] n lancha de socorro

life-buoy ['laɪfbɔɪ] n boya or guindola salvavidas

life coach n profesional encargado de mejorar la situación laboral y personal de sus clientes

life expectancy n esperanza de vida

lifeguard ['laɪfgɑːd] n vigilante m/f

life imprisonment n cadena perpetua

life insurance n = **life assurance**

life jacket n chaleco salvavidas

lifeless ['laɪflɪs] adj sin vida; (dull) soso

lifelike ['laɪflaɪk] adj natural

lifeline ['laɪflaɪn] n (fig) cordón m umbilical

lifelong ['laɪflɔŋ] adj de toda la vida

life preserver n (US) = **lifebelt**

lifer ['laɪfəʳ] n (col) condenado(-a) m(f) a cadena perpetua

life-saver ['laɪfseɪvəʳ] n socorrista m/f

life sentence n cadena perpetua

life-sized ['laɪfsaɪzd] adj de tamaño natural

life span n vida

lifestyle ['laɪfstaɪl] n estilo de vida

life support system n (Med) sistema m de respiración asistida

lifetime ['laɪftaɪm] n: **in his ~** durante su vida; **once in a ~** una vez en la vida; **the chance of a ~** una oportunidad única

lift [lɪft] vt levantar; (copy) plagiar ■ vi (fog) disiparse ■ n (Brit: elevator) ascensor m, elevador m (LAm); **to give sb a ~** (Brit) llevar a algn en coche
▸ **lift off** vt levantar, quitar ■ vi (rocket, helicopter) despegar
▸ **lift out** vt sacar; (troops, evacuees etc) evacuar
▸ **lift up** vt levantar

lift-off ['lɪftɔf] n despegue m

ligament ['lɪgəmənt] n ligamento

light [laɪt] n luz f; (flame) lumbre f; (lamp) luz f, lámpara; (daylight) luz f del día; (headlight) faro; (rear light) luz f trasera; (for cigarette etc): **have you got a ~?** ¿tienes fuego? ■ vt (pt, pp **lighted**, pt, pp **lit** [lɪt]) (candle, cigarette, fire) encender; (room) alumbrar ■ adj (colour) claro ligero, liviano (LAm); (room) alumbrado ■ adv (travel) con poco equipaje; **to turn the ~ on/off** encender/apagar la luz; **in the ~ of** a la luz de; **to come to ~** salir a la luz; **to cast** or **shed** or **throw ~ on** arrojar luz sobre; **to make ~ of sth** (fig) no dar importancia a algo
▸ **light up** vi (smoke) encender un cigarrillo; (face) iluminarse ■ vt (illuminate) iluminar, alumbrar

light bulb n bombilla, bombillo (LAm), foco (LAm)

lighten ['laɪtn] vi (grow light) clarear ■ vt (give light to) iluminar; (make lighter) aclarar; (make less heavy) aligerar

lighter ['laɪtəʳ] n (also: **cigarette lighter**) encendedor m (LAm), mechero

light-fingered [laɪt'fɪŋgəd] adj de manos largas

light-headed [laɪt'hɛdɪd] adj (dizzy) mareado; (excited) exaltado; (by nature) atolondrado

light-hearted [laɪt'hɑːtɪd] adj alegre

lighthouse ['laɪthaus] n faro

lighting ['laɪtɪŋ] n (act) iluminación f; (system) alumbrado

lighting-up time [laɪtɪŋ'ʌp-] n (Brit) hora de encendido del alumbrado

lightly ['laɪtlɪ] adv ligeramente; (not seriously) con poca seriedad; **to get off ~** ser castigado con poca severidad

light meter n (Phot) fotómetro

lightness ['laɪtnɪs] n claridad f; (in weight) ligereza

lightning ['laɪtnɪŋ] n relámpago, rayo
lightning conductor, lightning rod (US) n pararrayos m inv
lightning strike n huelga relámpago
lightweight ['laɪtweɪt] adj (suit) ligero ■ n (Boxing) peso ligero
light year n año luz
like [laɪk] vt (person) querer a; (thing):
I ~ **swimming/apples** me gusta nadar/me gustan las manzanas ■ prep como ■ adj parecido, semejante ■ n: **did you ever see the ~ (of it)?** ¿has visto cosa igual?; **his likes and dislikes** sus gustos y aversiones; **the likes of him** personas como él; **I would ~, I'd ~** me gustaría; (for purchase) quisiera; **would you ~ a coffee?** ¿te apetece un café?; **to be** or **look ~ sb/sth** parecerse a algn/algo; **that's just ~ him** es muy de él, es típico de él; **do it ~ this** hazlo así; **it is nothing ~** ... no tiene parecido alguno con ...; **what's he ~?** ¿cómo es (él)?; **what's the weather ~?** ¿qué tiempo hace?; **something ~** that algo así or por el estilo; **I feel ~ a drink** me apetece algo de beber; **if you ~** si quieres
likeable ['laɪkəbl] adj simpático, agradable
likelihood ['laɪklɪhud] n probabilidad f; **in all** ~ según todas las probabilidades
likely ['laɪklɪ] adj probable, capaz (LAm); **he's ~ to leave** es probable or (LAm) capaz que se vaya; **not ~!** ¡ni hablar!
like-minded [laɪk'maɪndɪd] adj de la misma opinión
liken ['laɪkən] vt: **to ~ to** comparar con
likeness ['laɪknɪs] n (similarity) semejanza, parecido
likewise ['laɪkwaɪz] adv igualmente
liking ['laɪkɪŋ] n: ~ **(for)** (person) cariño (a); (thing) afición (a); **to take a ~ to sb** tomar cariño a algn; **to be to sb's ~** ser del gusto de algn
lilac ['laɪlək] n lila ■ adj (colour) de color lila
Lilo® ['laɪləu] n colchoneta inflable
lilt [lɪlt] n deje m
lilting ['lɪltɪŋ] adj melodioso
lily ['lɪlɪ] n lirio, azucena
lily of the valley n lirio de los valles
Lima ['liːmə] n Lima
limb [lɪm] n miembro; (of tree) rama; **to be out on a ~** (fig) estar aislado
limber up ['lɪmbər-] vi (fig) entrenarse; (Sport) hacer (ejercicios de) precalentamiento
limbo ['lɪmbəu] n: **to be in ~** (fig) quedar a la expectativa
lime [laɪm] n (tree) limero; (fruit) lima; (Geo) cal f
lime juice n zumo (SP) or jugo de lima
limelight ['laɪmlaɪt] n: **to be in the ~** (fig) ser el centro de atención

limerick ['lɪmərɪk] n quintilla humorística
limestone ['laɪmstəun] n piedra caliza
limit ['lɪmɪt] n límite m ■ vt limitar; **weight/speed ~** peso máximo/velocidad f máxima; **within limits** entre límites
limitation [lɪmɪ'teɪʃən] n limitación f
limited ['lɪmɪtɪd] adj limitado; **to be ~ to** limitarse a; ~ **edition** edición limitada
limited company, limited liability company n (Brit) sociedad f anónima
limitless ['lɪmɪtlɪs] adj sin límites
limousine ['lɪməziːn] n limusina
limp [lɪmp] n: **to have a ~** tener cojera ■ vi cojear, renguear (LAm) ■ adj flojo
limpet ['lɪmpɪt] n lapa
limpid ['lɪmpɪd] adj (poetic) límpido, cristalino
limply ['lɪmplɪ] adv desmayadamente; **to say ~** decir débilmente
linchpin ['lɪntʃpɪn] n pezonera; (fig) eje m
Lincs [lɪŋks] abbr (Brit) = **Lincolnshire**
line [laɪn] n (Comm) línea; (straight line) raya; (rope) cuerda; (for fishing) sedal m; (wire) hilo; (row, series) fila, hilera; (of writing) renglón m; (on face) arruga; (speciality) rama ■ vt (Sewing): **to ~ (with)** forrar (de); **to ~ the streets** ocupar las aceras; **in ~ with** de acuerdo con; **she's in ~ for promotion** (fig) tiene muchas posibilidades de que la asciendan; **to bring sth into ~ with sth** poner algo de acuerdo con algo; ~ **of research/business** campo de investigación/comercio; **to take the ~ that ...** ser de la opinión que ...; **hold the ~** (Tel) no cuelgue usted, por favor; **to draw the ~ at doing sth** negarse a hacer algo; no permitir que se haga algo; **on the right lines** por buen camino; **a new ~ in cosmetics** una nueva línea en cosméticos; see also **lines**
▶ **line up** vi hacer cola ■ vt alinear, poner en fila; **to have sth lined up** tener algo arreglado
linear ['lɪnɪər] adj lineal
lined [laɪnd] adj (face) arrugado; (paper) rayado; (clothes) forrado
line editing n (Comput) corrección f por líneas
line feed n (Comput) avance m de línea
lineman ['laɪnmən] n (US) técnico de las líneas; (Football) delantero
linen ['lɪnɪn] n ropa blanca; (cloth) lino
line printer n impresora f de línea
liner ['laɪnər] n vapor m de línea transatlántico; **dustbin ~** bolsa de la basura
lines [laɪnz] npl (Rail) vía sg, raíles mpl
linesman ['laɪnzmən] n (Sport) juez m de línea
line-up ['laɪnʌp] n alineación f
linger ['lɪŋgər] vi retrasarse, tardar en marcharse; (smell, tradition) persistir

lingerie ['lænʒəri:] *n* ropa interior *or* íntima (de mujer)

lingering ['lɪŋgərɪŋ] *adj* persistente; (*death*) lento

lingo (*pl* **lingoes**) ['lɪŋgəu, -gəuz] *n* (*pej*) jerga

linguist ['lɪŋgwɪst] *n* lingüista *m/f*

linguistic [lɪŋ'gwɪstɪk] *adj* lingüístico

linguistics [lɪŋ'gwɪstɪks] *n* lingüística

liniment ['lɪnɪmənt] *n* linimento

lining ['laɪnɪŋ] *n* forro; (*Tech*) revestimiento; (*of brake*) guarnición *f*

link [lɪŋk] *n* (*of chain*) eslabón *m*; (*connection*) conexión *f*; (*bond*) vínculo, lazo; (*Internet*) enlace *m* ▪ *vt* vincular, unir; **rail ~** línea de ferrocarril, servicio de trenes
  ▶ **link up** *vt* acoplar ▪ *vi* unirse

links [lɪŋks] *npl* (*Golf*) campo *sg* de golf

link-up ['lɪŋkʌp] *n* (*gen*) unión *f*; (*meeting*) encuentro, reunión *f*; (*of roads*) empalme *m*; (*of spaceships*) acoplamiento; (*Radio, TV*) enlace *m*

lino ['laɪnəu], (*Brit*) **linoleum** [lɪ'nəuliəm] *n* linóleo

linseed oil ['lɪnsi:d-] *n* aceite *m* de linaza

lint [lɪnt] *n* gasa

lintel ['lɪntl] *n* dintel *m*

lion ['laɪən] *n* león *m*

lioness ['laɪənɪs] *n* leona

lip [lɪp] *n* labio; (*of jug*) pico; (*of cup etc*) borde *m*

liposuction ['lɪpəusʌkʃən] *n* liposucción *f*

lipread ['lɪpri:d] *vi* leer los labios

lip salve *n* crema protectora para labios

lip service *n*: **to pay ~ to sth** alabar algo pero sin hacer nada

lipstick ['lɪpstɪk] *n* lápiz *m or* barra de labios, carmín *m*

liquefy ['lɪkwɪfaɪ] *vt* licuar ▪ *vi* licuarse

liqueur [lɪ'kjuər] *n* licor *m*

liquid ['lɪkwɪd] *adj, n* líquido

liquidate ['lɪkwɪdeɪt] *vt* liquidar

liquidation [lɪkwɪ'deɪʃən] *n* liquidación *f*; **to go into ~** entrar en liquidación

liquid crystal display *n* pantalla de cristal líquido

liquidity [lɪ'kwɪdɪtɪ] *n* (*Comm*) liquidez *f*

liquidize ['lɪkwɪdaɪz] *vt* (*Culin*) licuar

liquidizer ['lɪkwɪdaɪzər] *n* (*Culin*) licuadora

liquor ['lɪkər] *n* licor *m*, bebidas *fpl* alcohólicas

liquorice ['lɪkərɪs] *n* regaliz *m*

liquor store *n* (*US*) bodega, *tienda de vinos y bebidas alcohólicas*

Lisbon ['lɪzbən] *n* Lisboa

lisp [lɪsp] *n* ceceo

lissom ['lɪsəm] *adj* ágil

list [lɪst] *n* lista; (*of ship*) inclinación *f* ▪ *vt* (*write down*) hacer una lista de; (*enumerate*) catalogar; (*Comput*) hacer un listado de ▪ *vi*

(*ship*) inclinarse; **shopping ~** lista de las compras; *see also* **lists**

listed building ['lɪstɪd-] *n* (*Arch*) edificio de interés histórico-artístico

listed company ['lɪstɪd-] *n* compañía cotizable

listen ['lɪsn] *vi* escuchar, oír; (*pay attention*) atender

listener ['lɪsnər] *n* oyente *m/f*

listeria [lɪs'tɪərɪə] *n* listeria

listing ['lɪstɪŋ] *n* (*Comput*) listado

listless ['lɪstlɪs] *adj* apático, indiferente

listlessly ['lɪstlɪslɪ] *adv* con indiferencia

listlessness ['lɪstlɪsnɪs] *n* indiferencia, apatía

list price *n* precio de catálogo

lists [lɪsts] *npl* (*History*) liza *sg*; **to enter the ~ (against sb/sth)** salir a la palestra (contra algn/algo)

lit [lɪt] *pt, pp of* **light**

litany ['lɪtənɪ] *n* letanía

liter ['li:tər] *n* (*US*) = **litre**

literacy ['lɪtərəsɪ] *n* capacidad *f* de leer y escribir

literacy campaign *n* campaña de alfabetización

literal ['lɪtərl] *adj* literal

literally ['lɪtrəlɪ] *adv* literalmente

literary ['lɪtərərɪ] *adj* literario

literate ['lɪtərət] *adj* que sabe leer y escribir; (*fig*) culto

literature ['lɪtərɪtʃər] *n* literatura; (*brochures etc*) folletos *mpl*

lithe [laɪð] *adj* ágil

lithography [lɪ'θɔgrəfɪ] *n* litografía

Lithuania [lɪθju'eɪnɪə] *n* Lituania

Lithuanian [lɪθju'eɪnɪən] *adj* lituano ▪ *n* lituano(-a); (*Ling*) lituano

litigate ['lɪtɪgeɪt] *vi* litigar

litigation [lɪtɪ'geɪʃən] *n* litigio

litmus paper ['lɪtməs-] *n* papel *m* de tornasol

litre, liter (*US*) ['li:tər] *n* litro

litter ['lɪtər] *n* (*rubbish*) basura; (*paper*) papeles *mpl* (tirados); (*young animals*) camada, cría

litter bin *n* (*Brit*) papelera

littered ['lɪtəd] *adj*: **~ with** lleno de

litter lout, litterbug (*US*) ['lɪtəbʌg] *n persona que tira papeles usados en la vía pública*

little ['lɪtl] *adj* (*small*) pequeño, chico (*LAm*); (*not much*) poco; (*often translated by suffix, eg*): **~ house** casita ▪ *adv* poco; **a ~** un poco (de); **~ by ~** poco a poco; **~ finger** (dedo) meñique *m*; **for a ~ while** (durante) un rato; **with ~ difficulty** sin problema *or* dificultad; **as ~ as possible** lo menos posible

little-known ['lɪtl'nəun] *adj* poco conocido

liturgy ['lɪtədʒɪ] *n* liturgia

live [*vb* lɪv, *adj* laɪv] *vi* vivir ■ *vt* (*a life*) llevar; (*experience*) vivir ■ *adj* (*animal*) vivo; (*wire*) conectado; (*broadcast*) en directo; (*issue*) de actualidad; (*unexploded*) sin explotar; **to ~ in London** vivir en Londres; **to ~ together** vivir juntos
▸ **live down** *vt* hacer olvidar
▸ **live off** *vt fus* (*land, fish etc*) vivir de; (*pej: parents etc*) vivir a costa de
▸ **live on** *vt fus* (*food*) vivir de, alimentarse de; **to ~ on £50 a week** vivir con 50 libras semanales *or* a la semana
▸ **live out** *vi* (*student*) ser externo ■ *vt*: **to ~ out one's days** *or* **life** pasar el resto de la vida
▸ **live up** *vt*: **to ~ it up** (*col*) tirarse la gran vida
▸ **live up to** *vt fus* (*fulfil*) cumplir con; (*justify*) justificar
live-in ['lɪvɪn] *adj*: **~ partner** pareja, compañero(-a) sentimental; **~ maid** asistenta interna
livelihood ['laɪvlɪhud] *n* sustento
liveliness ['laɪvlɪnɪs] *n* viveza
lively ['laɪvlɪ] *adj* (*gen*) vivo; (*talk*) animado; (*pace*) rápido; (*party, tune*) alegre
liven up ['laɪvn-] *vt* (*discussion, evening*) animar
liver ['lɪvə'] *n* hígado
liverish ['lɪvərɪʃ] *adj*: **to feel ~** sentirse *or* encontrarse mal, no estar muy católico
Liverpudlian [lɪvə'pʌdlɪən] *adj* de Liverpool ■ *n* nativo(-a) *or* habitante *m(f)* de Liverpool
livery ['lɪvərɪ] *n* librea
lives [laɪvz] *npl of* **life**
livestock ['laɪvstɔk] *n* ganado
live wire [laɪv-] *n* (*fig, col*): **he's a real ~!** ¡tiene una marcha!
livid ['lɪvɪd] *adj* lívido; (*furious*) furioso
living ['lɪvɪŋ] *adj* (*alive*) vivo ■ *n*: **to earn** *or* **make a ~** ganarse la vida; **cost of ~** coste *m* de la vida; **in ~ memory** que se recuerde *or* recuerda
living conditions *npl* condiciones *fpl* de vida
living expenses *npl* gastos *mpl* de mantenimiento
living room *n* sala (de estar), living *m* (*LAm*)
living standards *npl* nivel *msg* de vida
living wage *n* sueldo suficiente para vivir
lizard ['lɪzəd] *n* lagartija
llama ['lɑːmə] *n* llama
LLB *n abbr* (= *Bachelor of Laws*) Ldo.(-a.) en Dcho.; *see also* **Bachelor's Degree**
LLD *n abbr* (= *Doctor of Laws*) Dr(a). en Dcho.
LMT *n abbr* (*US*: = *Local Mean Time*) hora local
load [ləud] *n* (*gen*) carga; (*weight*) peso ■ *vt* (*Comput*) cargar; (*also*: **load up**): **to ~ (with)** cargar (con *or* de); **a ~ of, loads of** (*fig*) (gran) cantidad de, montones de

loaded ['ləudɪd] *adj* (*dice*) cargado; (*question*) intencionado; (*col: rich*) forrado (de dinero)
loading ['ləudɪŋ] *n* (*Comm*) sobreprima
loading bay *n* área de carga y descarga
loaf (*pl* **loaves**) [ləuf, ləuvz] *n* (barra de) pan *m* ■ *vi* (*also*: **loaf about, loaf around**) holgazanear
loam [ləum] *n* marga
loan [ləun] *n* préstamo; (*Comm*) empréstito ■ *vt* prestar; **on ~** (*book, painting*) prestado; **to raise a ~** (*money*) procurar un empréstito
loan account *n* cuenta de crédito
loan capital *n* empréstito
loan shark *n* (*col: pej*) prestamista *m/f* sin escrúpulos
loath [ləuθ] *adj*: **to be ~ to do sth** ser reacio a hacer algo
loathe [ləuð] *vt* aborrecer; (*person*) odiar
loathing ['ləuðɪŋ] *n* aversión *f*, odio
loathsome ['ləuðsəm] *adj* asqueroso, repugnante; (*person*) odioso
loaves [ləuvz] *pl of* **loaf**
lob [lɔb] *vt* (*ball*) volear por alto
lobby ['lɔbɪ] *n* vestíbulo, sala de espera; (*Pol: pressure group*) grupo de presión ■ *vt* presionar
lobbyist ['lɔbɪɪst] *n* cabildero(-a)
lobe [ləub] *n* lóbulo
lobster ['lɔbstə'] *n* langosta
lobster pot *n* nasa, langostera
local ['ləukl] *adj* local ■ *n* (*pub*) bar *m*; **the locals** *npl* los vecinos, los del lugar
local anaesthetic *n* (*Med*) anestesia local
local authority *n* municipio, ayuntamiento (*SP*)
local call *n* (*Tel*) llamada local
local government *n* gobierno municipal
locality [ləu'kælɪtɪ] *n* localidad *f*
localize ['ləukəlaɪz] *vt* localizar
locally ['ləukəlɪ] *adv* en la vecindad
locate [ləu'keɪt] *vt* (*find*) localizar; (*situate*) situar, ubicar (*LAm*)
location [ləu'keɪʃən] *n* situación *f*; **on ~** (*Cine*) en exteriores, fuera del estudio
loch [lɔx] *n* lago
lock [lɔk] *n* (*of door, box*) cerradura, chapa (*LAm*); (*of canal*) esclusa; (*of hair*) mechón *m* ■ *vt* (*with key*) cerrar con llave; (*immobilize*) inmovilizar ■ *vi* (*door etc*) cerrarse con llave; (*wheels*) trabarse; **~, stock and barrel** (*fig*) por completo *or* entero; **on full ~** (*Aut*) con el volante girado al máximo
▸ **lock away** *vt* (*valuables*) guardar bajo llave; (*criminal*) encerrar
▸ **lock out** *vt*: **the workers were locked out** los trabajadores tuvieron que enfrentarse con un cierre patronal

▶ **lock up** vi echar la llave
locker ['lɔkə^r] n casillero
locker-room ['lɔkərum] n (US Sport) vestuario
locket ['lɔkɪt] n medallón m
lockout ['lɔkaut] n (Industry) paro or cierre m patronal, lockout m
locksmith ['lɔksmɪθ] n cerrajero(-a)
lock-up ['lɔkʌp] n (prison) cárcel f; (cell) jaula; (also: **lock-up garage**) jaula, cochera
locomotive [ləukə'məutɪv] n locomotora
locum ['ləukəm] n (Med) (médico(-a)) suplente m(f)
locust ['ləukəst] n langosta
lodge [lɔdʒ] n casa del guarda; (porter's) portería; (Freemasonry) logia ■ vi (person): **to ~ (with)** alojarse (en casa de) ■ vt (complaint) presentar
lodger ['lɔdʒə^r] n huésped(a) m(f)
lodging house ['lɔdʒɪŋ-] n pensión f, casa de huéspedes
lodgings ['lɔdʒɪŋz] npl alojamiento sg; (house) casa sg de huéspedes
loft [lɔft] n desván m
lofty ['lɔftɪ] adj alto; (haughty) altivo, arrogante; (sentiments, aims) elevado, noble
log [lɔg] n (of wood) leño, tronco; (book) = **logbook** ■ n abbr (= logarithm) log ■ vt anotar, registrar
▶ **log in, log on** vi (Comput) iniciar la (or una) sesión
▶ **log off, log out** vi (Comput) finalizar la sesión
logarithm ['lɔgərɪðəm] n logaritmo
logbook ['lɔgbuk] n (Naut) diario de a bordo; (Aviat) libro de vuelo; (of car) documentación f (del coche)
log cabin n cabaña de troncos
log fire n fuego de leña
logger ['lɔgə^r] n leñador(a) m(f)
loggerheads ['lɔgəhɛdz] npl: **at ~ (with)** de pique (con)
logic ['lɔdʒɪk] n lógica
logical ['lɔdʒɪkl] adj lógico
logically ['lɔdʒɪkəlɪ] adv lógicamente
login ['lɔgɪn] n login m
logistics [lɔ'dʒɪstɪks] n logística
log jam n: **to break the ~** poner fin al estancamiento
logo ['ləugəu] n logotipo
loin [lɔɪn] n (Culin) lomo, solomillo; **loins** npl lomos mpl
loin cloth n taparrabos m inv
loiter ['lɔɪtə^r] vi vagar; (pej) merodear
lol abbr (Internet, Tel: = laugh out loud) lol (muerto de risa)
loll [lɔl] vi (also: **loll about**) repantigarse
lollipop ['lɔlɪpɔp] n pirulí m; (iced) polo
lollipop man/lady n (Brit) ver nota

lollop ['lɔləp] vi (Brit) moverse desgarbadamente
lolly ['lɔlɪ] n (col: ice cream) polo; (: lollipop) piruleta; (: money) guita
London ['lʌndən] n Londres m
Londoner ['lʌndənə^r] n londinense m/f
lone [ləun] adj solitario
loneliness ['ləunlɪnɪs] n soledad f, aislamiento
lonely ['ləunlɪ] adj solitario, solo
lonely hearts adj: **~ ad** anuncio de la sección de contactos; **~ column** sección f de contactos
lone parent family n familia monoparental
loner ['ləunə^r] n solitario(-a)
lonesome ['ləunsəm] adj (esp US) = **lonely**
long [lɔŋ] adj largo ■ adv mucho tiempo, largamente ■ vi: **to ~ for sth** anhelar algo ■ n: **the ~ and the short of it is that ...** (fig) en resumidas cuentas ...; **in the ~ run** a la larga; **so** or **as ~ as** mientras, con tal de que; **don't be ~!** ¡no tardes!, ¡vuelve pronto!; **how ~ is the street?** ¿cuánto tiene la calle de largo?; **how ~ is the lesson?** ¿cuánto dura la clase?; **six metres ~** que mide seis metros, de seis metros de largo; **six months ~** que dura seis meses, de seis meses de duración; **all night ~** toda la noche; **~ ago** hace mucho (tiempo); **he no longer comes** ya no viene; **~ before** mucho antes; **before ~** (+ future) dentro de poco; (+ past) poco tiempo después; **at ~ last** al fin, por fin; **I shan't be ~** termino pronto
long-distance [lɔŋ'dɪstəns] adj (race) de larga distancia; (call) interurbano
longevity [lɔn'dʒɛvɪtɪ] n longevidad f
long-haired ['lɔŋ'hɛəd] adj de pelo largo
longhand ['lɔŋhænd] n escritura (corriente)
longing ['lɔŋɪŋ] n anhelo, ansia; (nostalgia) nostalgia ■ adj anhelante
longingly ['lɔŋɪŋlɪ] adv con ansia
longitude ['lɔŋgɪtjuːd] n longitud f
long jump n salto de longitud
long-lost ['lɔŋlɔst] adj desaparecido hace mucho tiempo

long-playing record ['lɔŋpleɪɪŋ-] n elepé m, disco de larga duración

long-range ['lɔŋ'reɪndʒ] adj de gran alcance; (weather forecast) a largo plazo

longshoreman ['lɔŋʃɔːmən] n (US) estibador m

long-sighted ['lɔŋ'saɪtɪd] adj (Brit) présbita

long-standing ['lɔŋ'stændɪŋ] adj de mucho tiempo

long-suffering [lɔŋ'sʌfərɪŋ] adj sufrido

long-term ['lɔŋtəːm] adj a largo plazo

long wave n onda larga

long-winded [lɔŋ'wɪndɪd] adj prolijo

loo [luː] n (Brit: col) wáter m

loofah ['luːfə] n esponja de lufa

look [luk] vi mirar; (seem) parecer; (building etc): **to ~ south/on to the sea** dar al sur/al mar ■ n mirada; (glance) vistazo; (appearance) aire m, aspecto; **looks** npl físico sg, belleza sg; **to ~ ahead** mirar hacia delante; **it looks about four metres long** yo calculo que tiene unos cuarto metros de largo; **it looks all right to me** a mí me parece que está bien; **to have a ~ at sth** echar un vistazo a algo; **to have a ~ for sth** buscar algo
▶ **look after** vt fus cuidar
▶ **look around** vi echar una mirada alrededor
▶ **look at** vt fus mirar; (consider) considerar
▶ **look back** vi mirar hacia atrás; **to ~ back at sb/sth** mirar hacia atrás algo/a algn; **to ~ back on** (event, period) recordar
▶ **look down on** vt fus (fig) despreciar, mirar con desprecio
▶ **look for** vt fus buscar
▶ **look forward to** vt fus esperar con ilusión; (in letters): **we ~ forward to hearing from you** quedamos a la espera de su respuesta or contestación; **I'm not looking forward to it** no tengo ganas de eso, no me hace ilusión
▶ **look in** vi: **to ~ in on sb** (visit) pasar por casa de algn
▶ **look into** vt fus investigar
▶ **look on** vi mirar (como espectador)
▶ **look out** vi (beware): **to ~ out (for)** tener cuidado (de)
▶ **look out for** vt fus (seek) buscar; (await) esperar
▶ **look over** vt (essay) revisar; (town, building) inspeccionar, registrar; (person) examinar
▶ **look round** vi (turn) volver la cabeza; **to ~ round for sth** buscar algo
▶ **look through** vt fus (papers, book) hojear; (briefly) echar un vistazo a; (telescope) mirar por
▶ **look to** vt fus ocuparse de; (rely on) contar con
▶ **look up** vi mirar hacia arriba; (improve)

mejorar ■ vt (word) buscar; (friend) visitar
▶ **look up to** vt fus admirar

look-out ['lukaut] n (tower etc) puesto de observación; (person) vigía m/f; **to be on the ~ for sth** estar al acecho de algo

look-up table ['lukʌp-] n (Comput) tabla de consulta

loom [luːm] n telar m ■ vi (threaten) amenazar

loony ['luːnɪ] adj, n (col) loco(-a) m(f)

loop [luːp] n lazo; (bend) vuelta, recodo; (Comput) bucle m

loophole ['luːphəul] n laguna

loose [luːs] adj (gen) suelto; (not tight) flojo; (wobbly etc) movedizo; (clothes) ancho; (morals, discipline) relajado ■ vt (free) soltar; (slacken) aflojar; (also: **loose off**: arrow) disparar, soltar; **~ connection** (Elec) hilo desempalmado; **to be at a ~ end** or (US) **at ~ ends** no saber qué hacer; **to tie up ~ ends** (fig) no dejar ningún cabo suelto, atar cabos

loose change n cambio

loose chippings [-'tʃɪpɪŋz] npl (on road) gravilla sg suelta

loose-fitting ['luːsfɪtɪŋ] adj suelto

loose-leaf ['luːsliːf] adj: **~ binder** or **folder** carpeta de anillas

loose-limbed ['luːslɪmd] adj ágil, suelto

loosely ['luːslɪ] adv libremente, aproximadamente

loosely-knit [-nɪt] adj de estructura abierta

loosen ['luːsn] vt (free) soltar; (untie) desatar; (slacken) aflojar
▶ **loosen up** vi (before game) hacer (ejercicios de) precalentamiento; (col: relax) soltarse, relajarse

looseness ['luːsnɪs] n soltura; flojedad f

loot [luːt] n botín m ■ vt saquear

looter ['luːtəʳ] n saqueador(a) m(f)

looting ['luːtɪŋ] n pillaje m

lop [lɔp] n: **to ~ off** vt cortar; (branches) podar

lop-sided ['lɔp'saɪdɪd] adj desequilibrado

lord [lɔːd] n señor m; **L~ Smith** Lord Smith; **the L~** el Señor; **the (House of) Lords** (Brit) la Cámara de los Lores

lordly ['lɔːdlɪ] adj señorial

Lordship ['lɔːdʃɪp] n: **your ~** su Señoría

lore [lɔːʳ] n saber m popular, tradiciones fpl

lorry ['lɔrɪ] n (Brit) camión m

lorry driver n camionero(-a)

lorry load n carga

lose (pt, pp **lost**) [luːz, lɔst] vt perder ■ vi perder, ser vencido; **to ~ (time)** (clock) atrasarse; **to ~ no time (in doing sth)** no tardar (en hacer algo); **to get lost** (object) extraviarse; (person) perderse
▶ **lose out** vi salir perdiendo

loser ['lu:zər] n perdedor(a) m(f); **to be a bad ~** no saber perder

losing ['lu:zɪŋ] adj (team etc) vencido, perdedor(a)

loss [lɔs] n pérdida; **heavy losses** (Mil) grandes pérdidas fpl; **to be at a ~** no saber qué hacer; **to be a dead ~** ser completamente inútil; **to cut one's losses** reducir las pérdidas; **to sell sth at a ~** vender algo perdiendo dinero

loss adjuster n (Insurance) perito(-a) m(f) or tasador(-a) m/f de pérdidas

loss leader n (Comm) artículo de promoción

lost [lɔst] pt, pp of **lose** ■ adj perdido; **~ in thought** absorto, ensimismado

lost and found n (US) = **lost property**; **lost property office** or **department**

lost cause n causa perdida

lost property n (Brit) objetos mpl perdidos

lost property office or **department** n (Brit) departamento de objetos perdidos

lot [lɔt] n (at auction) lote m; (destiny) suerte f; **the ~** el todo, todos mpl, todas fpl; **a ~** mucho, bastante; **a ~ of**, **lots of** muchos(-as), mucho(-a) adj sg; **I read a ~** leo bastante; **to draw lots (for sth)** echar suertes (para decidir algo)

lotion ['ləuʃən] n loción f

lottery ['lɔtərɪ] n lotería

loud [laud] adj (voice, sound) fuerte; (laugh, shout) estrepitoso; (gaudy) chillón(-ona) ■ adv (speak etc) fuerte; **out ~** en voz alta

loudhailer [laud'heɪlər] n (Brit) megáfono

loudly ['laudlɪ] adv (noisily) fuerte; (aloud) en alta voz

loudness ['laudnɪs] n (of sound etc) fuerza

loudspeaker [laud'spi:kər] n altavoz m

lounge [laundʒ] n salón m, sala de estar; (of hotel) salón m; (of airport) sala de embarque ■ vi (also: **lounge about**, **lounge around**) holgazanear, no hacer nada; see also **pub**

lounge bar n salón m

lounge suit n (Brit) traje m de calle

louse (pl **lice**) [laus, laɪs] n piojo
  ▶ **louse up** vt (col) echar a perder

lousy ['lauzɪ] adj (fig) vil, asqueroso

lout [laut] n gamberro(-a)

louvre, **louver** (US) ['lu:vər] adj: **~ door** puerta de rejilla; **~ window** ventana de libro

lovable ['lʌvəbl] adj amable, simpático

love [lʌv] n amor m ■ vt amar, querer; **to send one's ~ to sb** dar sus recuerdos a algn; **~ from Anne** (in letter) con cariño de Anne; **I ~ to read** me encanta leer; **to be in ~ with** estar enamorado de; **to make ~** hacer el amor; **for the ~ of** por amor a; **"15 ~"** (Tennis) "15 a cero"; **I ~ paella** me encanta la paella; **I'd ~**

to come me gustaría muchísimo venir

love affair n aventura sentimental or amorosa

love child n hijo(-a) natural

loved ones ['lʌvdwʌnz] npl seres mpl queridos

love-hate relationship ['lʌvheɪt-] n relación f de amor y odio

love letter n carta de amor

love life n vida sentimental

lovely ['lʌvlɪ] adj (delightful) precioso, encantador(a), lindo (esp LAm); (beautiful) hermoso, lindo (esp LAm); **we had a ~ time** lo pasamos estupendo

lovemaking ['lʌvmeɪkɪŋ] n relaciones fpl sexuales

lover ['lʌvər] n amante m/f; (amateur): **a ~ of** un(a) aficionado(-a) or un(a) amante de

lovesick ['lʌvsɪk] adj enfermo de amor, amartelado

lovesong ['lʌvsɔŋ] n canción f de amor

loving ['lʌvɪŋ] adj amoroso, cariñoso

lovingly ['lʌvɪŋlɪ] adv amorosamente, cariñosamente

low [ləu] adj, adv bajo ■ n (Meteorology) área de baja presión ■ vi (cow) mugir; **to feel ~** sentirse deprimido; **to turn (down) ~** bajar; **to reach a new** or **an all-time ~** llegar a su punto más bajo

low-alcohol [ləu'ælkəhɔl] adj bajo en alcohol

lowbrow ['ləubrau] adj (person) de poca cultura

low-calorie ['ləu'kælərɪ] adj bajo en calorías

low-cut ['ləukʌt] adj (dress) escotado

low-down ['ləudaun] n (col): **he gave me the ~ on it** me puso al corriente ■ adj (mean) vil, bajo

lower ['ləuər] vt bajar; (reduce: price) reducir, rebajar; (: resistance) debilitar; **to ~ o.s. to** (fig) rebajarse a ■ vi ['lauər]: **to ~ (at sb)** fulminar (a algn) con la mirada

lower case n (Typ) minúscula

Lower House n (Pol): **the ~** la Cámara baja

lowering ['lauərɪŋ] adj (sky) amenazador(a)

low-fat ['ləu'fæt] adj (milk, yoghurt) desnatado; (diet) bajo en calorías

low-key ['ləu'ki:] adj de mínima intensidad; (operation) de poco perfil

lowland ['ləulənd] n tierra baja

low-level ['ləulevl] adj de bajo nivel; (flying) a poca altura

low-loader ['ləuləudər] n camión m de caja a bajo nivel

lowly ['ləulɪ] adj humilde

low-lying [ləu'laɪɪŋ] adj bajo

low-rise ['ləuraɪz] adj bajo

low-tech ['ləutɛk] adj de baja tecnología, tradicional

loyal ['lɔɪəl] *adj* leal
loyalist ['lɔɪəlɪst] *n* legitimista *m/f*
loyally ['lɔɪəlɪ] *adv* lealmente
loyalty ['lɔɪəltɪ] *n* lealtad *f*
loyalty card *n* (Brit) tarjeta cliente
lozenge ['lɔzɪndʒ] *n* (*Med*) pastilla
LP *n abbr* (= *long-playing record*) elepé *m*
LPG *n abbr* (= *liquefied petroleum gas*) GLP *m*
(= *Gas Licuado de Petróleo*)
L-plates ['ɛlpleɪts] *npl* (Brit) (placas *fpl* de)
la L; *ver nota*

● **L-PLATES**
●
● En el Reino Unido las personas que
● están aprendiendo a conducir han de
● llevar indicativos blancos con una L en
● rojo llamados normalmente *L-plates* (de
● "learner") en la parte delantera y trasera
● de los automóviles que conducen. No
● tienen que ir a clases teóricas, sino que
● desde el principio se les entrega un carnet
● de conducir provisional ("provisional
● driving licence") para que realicen sus
● prácticas, que han de estar supervisadas
● por un conductor con carnet definitivo
● ("full driving licence"). Tampoco se les
● permite hacer prácticas en autopistas
● aunque vayan acompañados.

LPN *n abbr* (US: = *Licensed Practical Nurse*)
enfermero(-a) practicante
LRAM *n abbr* (Brit) = **Licentiate of the Royal
Academy of Music**
LSAT *n abbr* (US) = **Law School Admissions
Test**
LSD *n abbr* (= *lysergic acid diethylamide*) LSD
m; (Brit: = *pounds, shillings and pence*) sistema
monetario usado en Gran Bretaña hasta 1971
LSE *n abbr* = **London School of Economics**
LT *abbr* (Elec) = **low tension**
Ll. *abbr* (= *lieutenant*) Tte.
Ltd *abbr* (Comm) = **limited**
lubricant ['lu:brɪkənt] *n* lubricante *m*
lubricate ['lu:brɪkeɪt] *vt* lubricar, engrasar
lubrication [lu:brɪ'keɪʃən] *n* lubricación *f*
lucid ['lu:sɪd] *adj* lúcido
lucidity [lu:'sɪdɪtɪ] *n* lucidez *f*
lucidly ['lu:sɪdlɪ] *adv* lúcidamente
luck [lʌk] *n* suerte *f*; **good/bad** ~ buena/mala
suerte; **good** ~! ¡(que tengas) suerte!; **to be
in** ~ estar de suerte; **to be out of** ~ tener
mala suerte
luckily ['lʌkɪlɪ] *adv* afortunadamente
luckless ['lʌklɪs] *adj* desafortunado
lucky ['lʌkɪ] *adj* afortunado
lucrative ['lu:krətɪv] *adj* lucrativo

ludicrous ['lu:dɪkrəs] *adj* absurdo
ludo ['lu:dəu] *n* parchís *m*
lug [lʌg] *vt* (*drag*) arrastrar
luggage ['lʌgɪdʒ] *n* equipaje *m*
luggage rack *n* (*in train*) rejilla, redecilla;
(*on car*) baca, portaequipajes *m inv*
luggage van *n* furgón *m or* vagón *m* de
equipaje
lugubrious [lu'gu:brɪəs] *adj* lúgubre
lukewarm ['lu:kwɔ:m] *adj* tibio, templado
lull [lʌl] *n* tregua ■ *vt* (*child*) acunar; (*person,
fear*) calmar
lullaby ['lʌləbaɪ] *n* nana
lumbago [lʌm'beɪgəu] *n* lumbago
lumber ['lʌmbəʳ] *n* (*junk*) trastos *mpl* viejos;
(*wood*) maderos *mpl* ■ *vt* (*Brit col*): **to** ~ **sb
with sth/sb** hacer que algn cargue con algo/
algn ■ *vi* (*also:* **lumber about, lumber along**)
moverse pesadamente
lumberjack ['lʌmbədʒæk] *n* maderero
lumber room *n* (Brit) cuarto trastero
lumber yard *n* (US) almacén *m* de madera
luminous ['lu:mɪnəs] *adj* luminoso
lump [lʌmp] *n* terrón *m*; (*fragment*) trozo;
(*in sauce*) grumo; (*in throat*) nudo; (*swelling*)
bulto ■ *vt* (*also:* **lump together**) juntar;
(*persons*) poner juntos
lump sum *n* suma global
lumpy ['lʌmpɪ] *adj* (*sauce*) lleno de grumos
lunacy ['lu:nəsɪ] *n* locura
lunar ['lu:nəʳ] *adj* lunar
lunatic ['lu:nətɪk] *adj, n* loco(-a) *m(f)*
lunatic asylum *n* manicomio
lunch [lʌntʃ] *n* almuerzo, comida ■ *vi*
almorzar; **to invite sb to** *or* **for** ~ invitar a
algn a almorzar
lunch break, lunch hour *n* hora del
almuerzo
luncheon ['lʌntʃən] *n* almuerzo
luncheon meat *n* tipo de fiambre
luncheon voucher *n* vale *m* de comida
lunchtime ['lʌntʃtaɪm] *n* hora del almuerzo
or de comer
lung [lʌŋ] *n* pulmón *m*
lung cancer *n* cáncer *m* del pulmón
lunge [lʌndʒ] *vi* (*also:* **lunge forward**)
abalanzarse; **to** ~ **at** arremeter contra
lupin ['lu:pɪn] *n* altramuz *m*
lurch [lə:tʃ] *vi* dar sacudidas ■ *n* sacudida;
to leave sb in the ~ dejar a algn plantado
lure [luəʳ] *n* (*bait*) cebo; (*decoy*) señuelo ■ *vt*
convencer con engaños
lurid ['luərɪd] *adj* (*colour*) chillón(-ona);
(*account*) sensacional; (*detail*) horripilante
lurk [lə:k] *vi* (*hide*) esconderse; (*wait*) estar al
acecho
luscious ['lʌʃəs] *adj* delicioso

lush [lʌʃ] *adj* exuberante
lust [lʌst] *n* lujuria; (*greed*) codicia
▶ lust after *vt fus* codiciar
lustful ['lʌstful] *adj* lascivo, lujurioso
lustre, luster (US) ['lʌstə^r] *n* lustre *m*, brillo
lustrous ['lʌstrəs] *adj* brillante
lusty ['lʌstɪ] *adj* robusto, fuerte
lute [luːt] *n* laúd *m*
Luxembourg ['lʌksəmbəːg] *n* Luxemburgo
luxuriant [lʌg'zjuərɪənt] *adj* exuberante
luxurious [lʌg'zjuərɪəs] *adj* lujoso
luxury ['lʌkʃərɪ] *n* lujo ■ *cpd* de lujo

luxury tax *n* impuesto de lujo
LV *n abbr* (Brit) = **luncheon voucher**
LW *abbr* (Radio) = **long wave**
Lycra® ['laɪkrə] *n* licra®
lying ['laɪɪŋ] *n* mentiras *fpl* ■ *adj* (*statement, story*) falso; (*person*) mentiroso
lynch [lɪntʃ] *vt* linchar
lynx [lɪnks] *n* lince *m*
Lyons ['laɪənz] *n* Lyón *m*
lyre ['laɪə^r] *n* lira
lyric ['lɪrɪk] *adj* lírico; lyrics *npl* (*of song*) letra *sg*
lyrical ['lɪrɪkl] *adj* lírico

Mm

M, m [ɛm] *n* (*letter*) M, m *f*; **M for Mary,**
(US) **M for Mike** M de Madrid
M *n abbr* (*Brit*: = *motorway*): **the M8** = la A8;
= **million; millions** ■ *abbr* (= *medium*) M
m *abbr* (= *metre*) m.; = **mile; miles**
MA *n abbr* (*Scol*) *see* **Master of Arts**;
(US) = **Military Academy** ■ *abbr* (US)
= **Massachusetts**
mac [mæk] *n* (*Brit*) impermeable *m*
macabre [mə'kɑːbrə] *adj* macabro
macaroni [mækə'rəunɪ] *n* macarrones *mpl*
macaroon [mækə'ruːn] *n* macarrón *m*,
mostachón *m*
mace [meɪs] *n* (*weapon, ceremonial*) maza;
(*spice*) macis *f*
Macedonia [mæsɪ'dəunɪə] *n* Macedonia
Macedonian [mæsɪ'dəunɪən] *adj*
macedonio ■ *n* macedonio(-a), (*Ling*)
macedonio
machinations [mæʃɪ'neɪʃənz] *npl* intrigas *fpl*,
maquinaciones *fpl*
machine [mə'ʃiːn] *n* máquina ■ *vt* (*dress etc*)
coser a máquina; (*Tech*) trabajar a máquina
machine code *n* (*Comput*) código máquina
machine gun *n* ametralladora
machine language *n* (*Comput*) lenguaje *m*
máquina
machine readable *adj* (*Comput*) legible por
máquina
machinery [mə'ʃiːnərɪ] *n* maquinaria; (*fig*)
mecanismo
machine shop *n* taller *m* de máquinas
machine tool *n* máquina herramienta
machine translation *n* traducción *f*
automática
machine washable *adj* lavable a máquina
machinist [mə'ʃiːnɪst] *n* operario(-a) *m(f)* (de
máquina)
macho [m'mætʃəu] *adj* macho
mackerel ['mækrl] *n pl inv* caballa
mackintosh ['mækɪntɔʃ] *n* (*Brit*)
impermeable *m*
macro ... ['mækrəu] *pref* macro...

macro-economics ['mækrəuiːkə'nɔmɪks] *n*
macroeconomía
mad [mæd] *adj* loco; (*idea*) disparatado;
(*angry*) furioso, enojado (*LAm*); ~ (**at** or **with**
sb) furioso (con algn); **to be ~ (keen) about**
or **on sth** estar loco por algo; **to go ~** volverse
loco, enloquecer(se)
madam ['mædəm] *n* señora; **can I help you,**
~? ¿le puedo ayudar, señora?; **M~ Chairman**
señora presidenta
madcap ['mædkæp] *adj* (*col*) alocado,
disparatado
mad cow disease *n* encefalopatía
espongiforme bovina
madden ['mædn] *vt* volver loco
maddening ['mædnɪŋ] *adj* enloquecedor(a)
made [meɪd] *pt, pp of* **make**
Madeira [mə'dɪərə] *n* (*Geo*) Madeira; (*wine*)
madeira *m*
made-to-measure ['meɪdtəmeʒəʳ] *adj* (*Brit*)
hecho a la medida
made-up ['meɪdʌp] *adj* (*story*) ficticio
madhouse ['mædhaus] *n* (*also fig*)
manicomio
madly ['mædlɪ] *adv* locamente
madman ['mædmən] *n* loco
madness ['mædnɪs] *n* locura
Madonna [mə'dɔnə] *n* Virgen *f*
Madrid [mə'drɪd] *n* Madrid *m*
madrigal ['mædrɪgəl] *n* madrigal *m*
Mafia ['mæfɪə] *n* Mafia
mag [mæg] *n abbr* (*Brit col*) = **magazine**
magazine [mægə'ziːn] *n* revista; (*Mil: store*)
almacén *m*; (*of firearm*) recámara
maggot ['mægət] *n* gusano
magic ['mædʒɪk] *n* magia ■ *adj* mágico
magical ['mædʒɪkəl] *adj* mágico
magician [mə'dʒɪʃən] *n* mago(-a)
magistrate ['mædʒɪstreɪt] *n* juez *m/f*
(*municipal*); **Magistrates' Court** (*Brit*)
see **crown court**
magnanimity [mægnə'nɪmɪtɪ] *n*
magnanimidad *f*

magnanimous [mæg'nænɪməs] *adj*
magnánimo
magnate ['mægneɪt] *n* magnate *m/f*
magnesium [mæg'niːzɪəm] *n* magnesio
magnet ['mægnɪt] *n* imán *m*
magnetic [mæg'netɪk] *adj* magnético
magnetic disk *n* (*Comput*) disco magnético
magnetic tape *n* cinta magnética
magnetism ['mægnɪtɪzəm] *n* magnetismo
magnification [mægnɪfɪ'keɪʃən] *n* aumento
magnificence [mæg'nɪfɪsns] *n*
magnificencia
magnificent [mæg'nɪfɪsnt] *adj* magnífico
magnificently [mæg'nɪfɪsntlɪ] *adv*
magníficamente
magnify ['mægnɪfaɪ] *vt* aumentar; (*fig*)
exagerar
magnifying glass ['mægnɪfaɪɪŋ-] *n* lupa
magnitude ['mægnɪtjuːd] *n* magnitud *f*
magnolia [mæg'nəʊlɪə] *n* magnolia
magpie ['mægpaɪ] *n* urraca
maharajah [mɑːhə'rɑːdʒə] *n* maharajá *m*
mahogany [mə'hɒgənɪ] *n* caoba ■ *cpd* de
caoba
maid [meɪd] *n* criada; **old ~** (*pej*) solterona
maiden ['meɪdn] *n* doncella ■ *adj* (*aunt etc*)
solterona; (*speech, voyage*) inaugural
maiden name *n* apellido de soltera
mail [meɪl] *n* correo; (*letters*) cartas *fpl* ■ *vt*
(*post*) echar al correo; (*send*) mandar por
correo; **by ~** por correo
mailbox ['meɪlbɒks] *n* (*US: for letters etc:*
Comput) buzón *m*
mailing list ['meɪlɪŋ-] *n* lista de direcciones
mailman ['meɪlmæn] *n* (*US*) cartero
mail-order ['meɪlɔːdər] *n* pedido postal;
(*business*) venta por correo ■ *adj*: **~ firm** or
house casa de venta por correo
mailshot ['meɪlʃɒt] *n* mailing *m inv*
mailtrain ['meɪltreɪn] *n* tren *m* correo
mail van, mail truck (*US*) *n* (*Aut*) camioneta
de correos *or* de reparto
maim [meɪm] *vt* mutilar, lisiar
main [meɪn] *adj* principal, mayor ■ *n*
(*pipe*) cañería principal *or* maestra; (*US*)
red *f* eléctrica; **the mains** (*Brit Elec*) la red
eléctrica; **in the ~** en general
main course *n* (*Culin*) plato principal
mainframe ['meɪnfreɪm] *n* (*also:* **mainframe**
computer) ordenador *m or* computadora
central
mainland ['meɪnlənd] *n* continente *m*
main line *n* línea principal
mainly ['meɪnlɪ] *adv* principalmente, en su
mayoría
main road *n* carretera principal
mainstay ['meɪnsteɪ] *n* (*fig*) pilar *m*

mainstream ['meɪnstriːm] *n* (*fig*) corriente *f*
principal
main street *n* calle *f* mayor
maintain [meɪn'teɪn] *vt* mantener; (*affirm*)
sostener; **to ~ that ...** mantener *or* sostener
que ...
maintenance ['meɪntənəns] *n*
mantenimiento; (*alimony*) pensión *f*
alimenticia
maintenance contract *n* contrato de
mantenimiento
maintenance order *n* (*Law*) obligación *f* de
pagar una pensión alimenticia al cónyuge
maisonette [meɪzə'nɛt] *n* dúplex *m*
maize [meɪz] *n* (*Brit*) maíz *m*, choclo (*LAm*)
Maj. *abbr* (*Mil*) = **major**
majestic [mə'dʒɛstɪk] *adj* majestuoso
majesty ['mædʒɪstɪ] *n* majestad *f*
major ['meɪdʒər] *n* (*Mil*) comandante *m*
■ *adj* principal; (*Mus*) mayor ■ *vi* (*US Univ*):
to ~ in especializarse en; **a ~ operation**
una operación *or* intervención de gran
importancia
Majorca [mə'jɔːkə] *n* Mallorca
major general *n* (*Mil*) general *m* de división
majority [mə'dʒɒrɪtɪ] *n* mayoría ■ *cpd*
(*verdict*) mayoritario
majority holding *n* (*Comm*): **to have a ~** tener
un interés mayoritario
make [meɪk] *vt* (*pt, pp* **made** [meɪd]) hacer;
(*manufacture*) hacer, fabricar; (*cause to be*): **to**
~ sb sad poner triste *or* entristecer a algn;
(*force*): **to ~ sb do sth** obligar a algn a hacer
algo; (*equal*): **2 and 2 = 4** 2 y 2 son 4 ■ *n* marca;
to ~ a fool of sb poner a algn en ridículo;
to ~ a profit/loss obtener ganancias/sufrir
pérdidas; **to ~ a profit of £500** sacar una
ganancia de 500 libras; **to ~ it** (*arrive*)
llegar; (*achieve sth*) tener éxito; **what time**
do you ~ it? ¿qué hora tienes?; **to ~ do with**
contentarse con
▶ **make for** *vt fus* (*place*) dirigirse a
▶ **make off** *vi* largarse
▶ **make out** *vt* (*decipher*) descifrar;
(*understand*) entender; (*see*) distinguir; (*write:*
cheque) extender; **to ~ out (that)** (*claim, imply*)
dar a entender (que); **to ~ out a case for sth**
dar buenas razones en favor de algo
▶ **make over** *vt* (*assign*): **to ~ over (to)** ceder *or*
traspasar (a)
▶ **make up** *vt* (*invent*) inventar; (*parcel*)
hacer ■ *vi* reconciliarse; (*with cosmetics*)
maquillarse; **to be made up of** estar
compuesto de
▶ **make up for** *vt fus* compensar
make-believe ['meɪkbɪliːv] *n* ficción *f*,
fantasía

makeover ['meɪkəuvə^r] n cambio de imagen; **to give sb a ~** hacerle a algn un cambio de imagen

maker ['meɪkə^r] n fabricante m/f

makeshift ['meɪkʃɪft] adj improvisado

make-up ['meɪkʌp] n maquillaje m

make-up bag n bolsita del maquillaje or de los cosméticos

make-up remover n desmaquillador m

making ['meɪkɪŋ] n (fig): **in the ~** en vías de formación; **to have the makings of** (person) tener madera de

maladjusted [mælə'dʒʌstɪd] adj inadaptado

maladroit [maelə'drɔɪt] adj torpe

malaise [mæ'leɪz] n malestar m

malaria [mə'lɛərɪə] n malaria

Malawi [mə'lɑːwɪ] n Malawi m

Malay [mə'leɪ] adj malayo ■ n malayo(-a); (Ling) malayo

Malaya [mə'leɪə] n Malaya, Malaca

Malayan [mə'leɪən] adj, n = **Malay**

Malaysia [mə'leɪzɪə] n Malaisia, Malaysia

Malaysian [mə'leɪzɪən] adj, n malaisio(-a) m(f), malaysio(-a) m(f)

Maldives ['mɔːldɪːvz] npl: **the ~** las Maldivas

male [meɪl] n (Biol, Elec) macho ■ adj (sex, attitude) masculino; (child etc) varón

male chauvinist n machista m

male nurse n enfermero

malevolence [mə'lɛvələns] n malevolencia

malevolent [mə'lɛvələnt] adj malévolo

malfunction [mæl'fʌŋkʃən] n mal funcionamiento

malice ['mælɪs] n (ill will) malicia; (rancour) rencor m

malicious [mə'lɪʃəs] adj malicioso; rencoroso

maliciously [mə'lɪʃəslɪ] adv con malevolencia, con malicia; rencorosamente

malign [mə'laɪn] vt difamar, calumniar ■ adj maligno

malignant [mə'lɪgnənt] adj (Med) maligno

malinger [mə'lɪŋgə^r] vi fingirse enfermo

malingerer [mə'lɪŋgərə^r] n enfermo(-a) fingido(-a)

mall [mɔːl] n (US: also: **shopping mall**) centro comercial

malleable ['mælɪəbl] adj maleable

mallet ['mælɪt] n mazo

malnutrition [mælnjuː'trɪʃən] n desnutrición f

malpractice [mæl'præktɪs] n negligencia profesional

malt [mɔːlt] n malta

Malta ['mɔːltə] n Malta

Maltese [mɔːl'tiːz] adj maltés(-esa) ■ n (pl inv) maltés(-esa) m(f); (Ling) maltés m

maltreat [mæl'triːt] vt maltratar

mammal ['mæml] n mamífero

mammoth ['mæməθ] n mamut m ■ adj gigantesco

man (pl **men**) [mæn, mɛn] n hombre m; (Chess) pieza ■ vt (Naut) tripular; (Mil) defender; **an old ~** un viejo; **~ and wife** marido y mujer

Man. abbr (Canada) = **Manitoba**

manacle ['mænəkl] n esposa, manilla; **manacles** npl grillos mpl

manage ['mænɪdʒ] vi arreglárselas ■ vt (be in charge of) dirigir; (person etc) manejar; **to ~ to do sth** conseguir hacer algo; **to ~ without sth/sb** poder prescindir de algo/algn

manageable ['mænɪdʒəbl] adj manejable

management ['mænɪdʒmənt] n dirección f, administración f; **"under new ~"** "bajo nueva dirección"

management accounting n contabilidad f de gestión

management buyout n adquisición f por parte de la dirección

management consultant n consultor(a) m(f) en dirección de empresas

manager ['mænɪdʒə^r] n director(a) m(f); (Sport) entrenador(a) m(f); **sales ~** jefe(-a) m(f) de ventas

manageress ['mænɪdʒərɛs] n directora; (Sport) entrenadora

managerial [mænə'dʒɪərɪəl] adj directivo

managing director ['mænɪdʒɪŋ-] n director(a) m(f) general

Mancunian [mæŋ'kjuːnɪən] adj de Manchester ■ n nativo(-a) or habitante m(f) de Manchester

mandarin ['mændərɪn] n (also: **mandarin orange**) mandarina; (person) mandarín m

mandate ['mændeɪt] n mandato

mandatory ['mændətərɪ] adj obligatorio

mandolin, mandoline ['mændəlɪn] n mandolina

mane [meɪn] n (of horse) crin f; (of lion) melena

maneuver [mə'nuːvə^r] (US) = **manoeuvre**

manful ['mænful] adj resuelto

manfully ['mænfəlɪ] adv resueltamente

mangetout [mɔnʒ'tuː] n tirabeque m

mangle ['mæŋgl] vt mutilar, destrozar ■ n escurridor m

mango (pl **mangoes**) ['mæŋgəu] n mango

mangrove ['mæŋgrəuv] n mangle m

mangy ['meɪndʒɪ] adj roñoso; (Med) sarnoso

manhandle ['mænhændl] vt maltratar; (move by hand: goods) manipular

manhole ['mænhəul] n boca de acceso

manhood ['mænhud] n edad f viril; (manliness) virilidad f

man-hour ['mæn'auə^r] n hora-hombre f

manhunt ['mænhʌnt] n caza de hombre

m

mania ['meɪnɪə] n manía
maniac ['meɪnɪæk] n maníaco(-a); (fig) maniático
manic ['mænɪk] adj (behaviour, activity) frenético
manic-depressive ['mænɪkdɪ'prɛsɪv] adj, n maniacodepresivo(-a) m(f)
manicure ['mænɪkjuəʳ] n manicura
manicure set n estuche m de manicura
manifest ['mænɪfɛst] vt manifestar, mostrar ■ adj manifiesto ■ n manifiesto
manifestation [mænɪfɛs'teɪʃən] n manifestación f
manifestly ['mænɪfɛstlɪ] adv evidentemente
manifesto [mænɪ'fɛstəu] n manifiesto
manifold ['mænɪfəuld] adj múltiples ■ n (Aut etc): **exhaust ~** colector m de escape
Manila [mə'nɪlə] n Manila
manila, manilla [mə'nɪlə] n (paper, envelope) manila
manipulate [mə'nɪpjuleɪt] vt manipular
manipulation [mənɪpju'leɪʃən] n manipulación f, manejo
mankind [mæn'kaɪnd] n humanidad f, género humano
manliness ['mænlɪnɪs] n virilidad f, hombría
manly ['mænlɪ] adj varonil
man-made ['mæn'meɪd] adj artificial
manna ['mænə] n maná m
mannequin ['mænɪkɪn] n (dummy) maniquí m; (fashion model) maniquí m/f
manner ['mænəʳ] n manera, modo; (behaviour) conducta, manera de ser; (type) clase f; **manners** npl modales mpl, educación fsg; **(good) manners** (buena) educación fsg, (buenos) modales mpl; **bad manners** falta sg de educación, pocos modales mpl; **all ~ of** toda clase or suerte de
mannerism ['mænərɪzəm] n gesto típico
mannerly ['mænəlɪ] adj bien educado, formal
manoeuvrable, maneuvrable (US) [mə'nu:vrəbl] adj (car etc) manejable
manoeuvre, maneuver (US) [mə'nu:vəʳ] vt, vi maniobrar ■ n maniobra; **to ~ sb into doing sth** manipular a algn para que haga algo
manor ['mænəʳ] n (also: **manor house**) casa solariega
manpower ['mænpauəʳ] n mano f de obra
Manpower Services Commission n (Brit) comisión para el aprovechamiento de los recursos humanos
manservant ['mænsə:vənt] n criado
mansion ['mænʃən] n mansión f
manslaughter ['mænslɔ:təʳ] n homicidio involuntario

mantelpiece ['mæntlpi:s] n repisa de la chimenea
mantle ['mæntl] n manto
man-to-man ['mæntə'mæn] adj de hombre a hombre
manual ['mænjuəl] adj manual ■ n manual m; **~ worker** obrero(-a), trabajador(a) m(f) manual
manufacture [mænju'fæktʃəʳ] vt fabricar ■ n fabricación f
manufactured goods [mænju'fæktʃəd-] npl manufacturas fpl, bienes mpl manufacturados
manufacturer [mænju'fæktʃərəʳ] n fabricante m/f
manufacturing industries [mænju'fæktʃərɪŋ-] npl industrias fpl manufactureras
manure [mə'njuəʳ] n estiércol m, abono
manuscript ['mænjuskrɪpt] n manuscrito
Manx [mæŋks] adj de la Isla de Man
many ['mɛnɪ] adj muchos(-as) ■ pron muchos(-as); **a great ~** muchísimos, un buen número de; **~ a time** muchas veces; **too ~ difficulties** demasiadas dificultades; **twice as ~** el doble; **how ~?** ¿cuántos?
Maori ['maurɪ] adj, n maorí m/f
map [mæp] n mapa m ■ vt trazar el mapa de
▶ **map out** vt (fig: career, holiday, essay) proyectar, planear
maple ['meɪpl] n arce m, maple m (LAm)
mar [mɑ:ʳ] vt estropear
Mar abbr (= March) mar
marathon ['mærəθən] n maratón m ■ adj: **a ~ session** una sesión maratoniana
marathon runner n corredor(a) m(f) de maratones
marauder [mə'rɔ:dəʳ] n merodeador(a) m(f)
marble ['mɑ:bl] n mármol m; (toy) canica
March [mɑ:tʃ] n marzo; see also **July**
march [mɑ:tʃ] vi (Mil) marchar; (fig) caminar con resolución ■ n marcha; (demonstration) manifestación f
marcher ['mɑ:tʃəʳ] n manifestante m/f
marching ['mɑ:tʃɪŋ] n: **to give sb his ~ orders** (fig) mandar a paseo a algn; (employee) poner de patitas en la calle a algn
march-past ['mɑ:tʃpɑ:st] n desfile m
mare [mɛəʳ] n yegua
margarine [mɑ:dʒə'ri:n] n margarina
marg(e) [mɑ:dʒ] n abbr (col) = **margarine**
margin ['mɑ:dʒɪn] n margen m
marginal ['mɑ:dʒɪnl] adj marginal
marginally ['mɑ:dʒɪnəlɪ] adv ligeramente
marginal seat n (Pol) circunscripción f políticamente no definida
marigold ['mærɪgəuld] n caléndula

marijuana [mærɪ'wɑːnə] n marihuana
marina [mə'riːnə] n marina
marinade [mærɪ'neɪd] n adobo
marinate ['mærɪneɪt] vt adobar
marine [mə'riːn] adj marino ■ n soldado de
infantería de marina
marine insurance n seguro marítimo
mariner ['mærɪnəʳ] n marinero, marino
marionette [mærɪə'nɛt] n marioneta, títere m
marital ['mærɪtl] adj matrimonial; ~ status
estado civil
maritime ['mærɪtaɪm] adj marítimo
marjoram ['mɑːdʒərəm] n mejorana
mark [mɑːk] n marca, señal f; (imprint)
huella; (stain) mancha; (Brit Scol) nota;
(currency) marco ■ vt (Sport: player) marcar;
(stain) manchar; (Brit Scol) calificar,
corregir; punctuation marks signos mpl de
puntuación; to be quick off the ~ (fig) ser
listo; up to the ~ (in efficiency) a la altura de
las circunstancias; to ~ time marcar el paso
▶ mark down vt (reduce: prices, goods) rebajar
▶ mark off vt (tick) indicar, señalar
▶ mark out vt trazar
▶ mark up vt (price) aumentar
marked [mɑːkt] adj marcado, acusado
markedly ['mɑːkɪdlɪ] adv marcadamente,
apreciablemente
marker ['mɑːkəʳ] n (sign) marcador m;
(bookmark) registro
market ['mɑːkɪt] n mercado ■ vt (Comm)
comercializar; (promote) publicitar; open ~
mercado libre; to be on the ~ estar en venta;
to play the ~ jugar a la bolsa
marketable ['mɑːkɪtəbl] adj comerciable
market analysis n análisis m del mercado
market day n día m de mercado
market demand n demanda de mercado
market economy n economía de mercado
market forces npl tendencias fpl del mercado
market garden n (Brit) huerto
marketing ['mɑːkɪtɪŋ] n marketing m,
mercadotecnia
marketing manager n director m de
marketing
market leader n líder m de ventas
marketplace ['mɑːkɪtpleɪs] n mercado
market price n precio de mercado
market research n (Comm) estudios mpl de
mercado
market value n valor m en el mercado
marking ['mɑːkɪŋ] n (on animal) pinta; (on
road) señal f
marking ink n tinta indeleble or de marcar
marksman ['mɑːksmən] n tirador m
marksmanship ['mɑːksmənʃɪp] n puntería
mark-up ['mɑːkʌp] n (Comm: margin) margen

m de beneficio; (: increase) aumento
marmalade ['mɑːməleɪd] n mermelada de
naranja
maroon [mə'ruːn] vt: to be marooned
(shipwrecked) naufragar; (fig) quedar
abandonado ■ adj granate inv
marquee [mɑː'kiː] n carpa, entoldado
marquess, marquis ['mɑːkwɪs] n marqués m
Marrakech, Marrakesh [mærə'kɛʃ] n
Marrakech m
marriage ['mærɪdʒ] n (state) matrimonio;
(wedding) boda; (act) casamiento
marriage bureau n agencia matrimonial
marriage certificate n partida de
casamiento
marriage guidance, marriage counseling
(US) n orientación f matrimonial
marriage of convenience n matrimonio de
conveniencia
married ['mærɪd] adj casado; (life, love)
conyugal
marrow ['mærəu] n médula; (vegetable)
calabacín m
marry ['mærɪ] vt casarse con; (father, priest etc)
casar ■ vi (also: get married) casarse
Mars [mɑːz] n Marte m
Marseilles [mɑː'seɪ] n Marsella
marsh [mɑːʃ] n pantano; (salt marsh)
marisma
marshal ['mɑːʃl] n (Mil) mariscal m; (at sports
meeting, demonstration etc) oficial m; (US: at
police, fire department) jefe(-a) m(f) ■ vt (facts)
ordenar; (soldiers) formar
marshalling yard ['mɑːʃəlɪŋ-] n (Rail)
estación f clasificadora
marshmallow ['mɑːʃmæləu] n (Bot)
malvavisco; (sweet) esponja, dulce m de
merengue blando
marshy ['mɑːʃɪ] adj pantanoso
marsupial [mɑː'suːpɪəl] adj, n marsupial m
martial ['mɑːʃl] adj marcial
martial arts npl artes fpl marciales
martial law n ley f marcial
martin ['mɑːtɪn] n (also: house martin) avión m
martyr ['mɑːtəʳ] n mártir m/f ■ vt martirizar
martyrdom ['mɑːtədəm] n martirio
marvel ['mɑːvl] n maravilla, prodigio ■ vi:
to ~ (at) maravillarse (de)
marvellous, (US) marvelous ['mɑːvləs] adj
maravilloso
marvellously, (US) marvelously ['mɑːvləslɪ]
adv maravillosamente
Marxism ['mɑːksɪzəm] n marxismo
Marxist ['mɑːksɪst] adj, n marxista m/f
marzipan ['mɑːzɪpæn] n mazapán m
mascara [mæs'kɑːrə] n rímel m
mascot ['mæskət] n mascota

m

masculine ['mæskjulın] *adj* masculino
masculinity [mæskju'lınıtı] *n* masculinidad *f*
MASH [mæʃ] *n abbr (US Mil)* = **mobile army surgical hospital**
mash [mæʃ] *n (mix)* mezcla; *(Culin)* puré *m*; *(pulp)* amasijo
mashed potatoes [mæʃt-] *npl* puré *m* de patatas *or (LAm)* papas
mask [mɑːsk] *n (Elec)* máscara ▪ *vt* enmascarar
masochism ['mæsəkızəm] *n* masoquismo
masochist ['mæsəukıst] *n* masoquista *m/f*
mason ['meısn] *n (also:* **stonemason**) albañil *m*; *(also:* **freemason**) masón *m*
masonic [mə'sɔnık] *adj* masónico
masonry ['meısnrı] *n* masonería; *(building)* mampostería
masquerade [mæskə'reıd] *n* baile *m* de máscaras; *(fig)* mascarada ▪ *vi:* **to ~ as** disfrazarse de, hacerse pasar por
mass [mæs] *n (people)* muchedumbre *f*; *(Physics)* masa; *(Rel)* misa; *(great quantity)* montón *m* ▪ *vi* reunirse; *(Mil)* concentrarse; **the masses** las masas; **to go to ~** ir a *or* oír misa
Mass. *abbr (US)* = **Massachusetts**
massacre ['mæsəkəʳ] *n* masacre *f* ▪ *vt* masacrar
massage ['mæsɑːʒ] *n* masaje *m* ▪ *vt* dar masajes *or* un masaje a
masseur [mæ'səːʳ] *n* masajista *m*
masseuse [mæ'səːz] *n* masajista *f*
massive ['mæsıv] *adj* enorme; *(support, intervention)* masivo
mass media *npl* medios *mpl* de comunicación de masas
mass meeting *n (of everyone concerned)* reunión *f* en masa; *(huge)* mitin *m*
mass-produce ['mæsprə'djuːs] *vt* fabricar en serie
mass-production ['mæsprə'dʌkʃən] *n* fabricación *f or* producción *f* en serie
mast [mɑːst] *n (Naut)* mástil *m*; *(Radio etc)* torre *f*, antena
mastectomy [mæs'tɛktəmı] *n* mastectomía
master ['mɑːstəʳ] *n (of servant, animal)* amo; *(fig: of situation)* dueño; *(Art, Mus)* maestro; *(in secondary school)* profesor *m*; *(title for boys):* **M~ X** Señorito X ▪ *vt* dominar
master disk *n (Comput)* disco maestro
masterful ['mɑːstəful] *adj* magistral, dominante
master key *n* llave *f* maestra
masterly ['mɑːstəlı] *adj* magistral
mastermind ['mɑːstəmaınd] *n* inteligencia superior ▪ *vt* dirigir, planear
Master of Arts *n* licenciatura superior en

Letras; *see also* **master's degree**
Master of Ceremonies *n* encargado de protocolo
Master of Science *n* licenciatura superior en Ciencias; *see also* **master's degree**
masterpiece ['mɑːstəpiːs] *n* obra maestra
master plan *n* plan *m* rector
master's degree *n* máster *m*

● **MASTER'S DEGREE**
●
● Los estudios de postgrado británicos
● que llevan a la obtención de un *master's*
● *degree* consisten generalmente en una
● combinación de curso(s) académico(s)
● y tesina ("dissertation") sobre un
● tema original, o bien únicamente la
● redacción de una tesina. El primer caso
● es el más frecuente para los títulos
● de "MA" ("Master of Arts") y "MSc"
● ("Master of Science"), mientras que
● los de "MLitt" ("Master of Letters") o
● "MPhil" ("Master of Philosophy") se
● obtienen normalmente mediante tesina.
● En algunas universidades, como las
● escocesas, el título de *master's degree* no es
● de postgrado, sino que corresponde a la
● licenciatura.

master stroke *n* golpe *m* maestro
mastery ['mɑːstərı] *n* maestría
mastiff ['mæstıf] *n* mastín *m*
masturbate ['mæstəbeıt] *vi* masturbarse
masturbation [mæstə'beıʃən] *n* masturbación *f*
mat [mæt] *n* alfombrilla; *(also:* **doormat**) felpudo ▪ *adj* = **matt**
MAT *n abbr (= machine-assisted translation)* TAO
match [mætʃ] *n* cerilla, fósforo; *(game)* partido; *(fig)* igual *m/f* ▪ *vt* emparejar; *(go well with)* hacer juego con; *(equal)* igualar ▪ *vi* hacer juego; **to be a good ~** hacer buena pareja
matchbox ['mætʃbɔks] *n* caja de cerillas
matching ['mætʃıŋ] *adj* que hace juego
matchless ['mætʃlıs] *adj* sin par, incomparable
matchmaker ['mætʃmeıkəʳ] *n* casamentero
mate [meıt] *n (workmate)* compañero(-a), colega *m/f*; *(col: friend)* amigo(-a), compadre *m/f* (*LAm*); *(animal)* macho/hembra; *(in merchant navy)* primer oficial *m* ▪ *vi* acoplarse, parearse ▪ *vt* acoplar, parear
maté ['mɑːteı] *n* mate *m* (cocido), yerba mate
material [mə'tıərıəl] *n (substance)* materia; *(equipment)* material *m*; *(cloth)* tela, tejido ▪ *adj* material; *(important)* esencial;

materials *npl* materiales *mpl*; *(equipment etc)* artículos *mpl*

materialistic [mətɪərɪə'lɪstɪk] *adj* materialista

materialize [mə'tɪərɪəlaɪz] *vi* materializarse

materially [mə'tɪərɪəlɪ] *adv* materialmente

maternal [mə'tə:nl] *adj* maternal; ~ **grandmother** abuela materna

maternity [mə'tə:nɪtɪ] *n* maternidad *f*

maternity benefit *n* subsidio por maternidad

maternity dress *n* vestido premamá

maternity hospital *n* hospital *m* de maternidad

maternity leave *n* baja por maternidad

math [mæθ] *n abbr (US:* = *mathematics)* matemáticas *fpl*

mathematical [mæθə'mætɪkl] *adj* matemático

mathematically [mæθɪ'mætɪklɪ] *adv* matemáticamente

mathematician [mæθəmə'tɪʃən] *n* matemático

mathematics [mæθə'mætɪks] *n* matemáticas *fpl*

maths [mæθs] *n abbr (Brit:* = *mathematics)* matemáticas *fpl*

matinée ['mætɪneɪ] *n* función *f* de la tarde, vermú(t) *m* (*LAm*)

mating ['meɪtɪŋ] *n* apareamiento

mating call *n* llamada del macho

mating season *n* época de celo

matins ['mætɪnz] *n* maitines *mpl*

matriarchal [meɪtrɪ'ɑːkl] *adj* matriarcal

matrices ['meɪtrɪsiːz] *pl of* **matrix**

matriculation [mətrɪkju'leɪʃən] *n* matriculación *f*, matrícula

matrimonial [mætrɪ'məunɪəl] *adj* matrimonial

matrimony ['mætrɪmənɪ] *n* matrimonio

matrix (*pl* **matrices**) ['meɪtrɪks, 'meɪtrɪsiːz] *n* matriz *f*

matron ['meɪtrən] *n (in hospital)* enfermera jefe; *(in school)* ama de llaves

matronly ['meɪtrənlɪ] *adj* de matrona; *(fig: figure)* corpulento

matt [mæt] *adj* mate

matted ['mætɪd] *adj* enmarañado

matter ['mætər] *n* cuestión *f*, asunto; *(Physics)* sustancia, materia; *(content)* contenido; *(Med: pus)* pus *m* ▪ *vi* importar; **it doesn't ~** no importa; **what's the ~?** ¿qué pasa?; **no ~ what** pase lo que pase; **as a ~ of course** por rutina; **as a ~ of fact** en realidad; **printed ~** impresos *mpl*; **reading ~** material *m* de lectura, lecturas *fpl*

matter-of-fact ['mætərəv'fækt] *adj (style)* prosaico; *(person)* práctico; *(voice)* neutro

mattress ['mætrɪs] *n* colchón *m*

mature [mə'tjuər] *adj* maduro ▪ *vi* madurar

mature student *n* estudiante de más de 21 años

maturity [mə'tjuərɪtɪ] *n* madurez *f*

maudlin ['mɔːdlɪn] *adj* llorón(-ona)

maul [mɔːl] *vt* magullar

Mauritania [mɔːrɪ'teɪnɪə] *n* Mauritania

Mauritius [mə'rɪʃəs] *n* Mauricio

mausoleum [mɔːsə'lɪəm] *n* mausoleo

mauve [məuv] *adj* de color malva

maverick ['mævrɪk] *n (fig)* inconformista *m/f*, persona independiente

mawkish ['mɔːkɪʃ] *adj* sensiblero, empalagoso

max *abbr* = **maximum**

maxim ['mæksɪm] *n* máxima

maxima ['mæksɪmə] *pl of* **maximum**

maximize ['mæksɪmaɪz] *vt (profits etc)* llevar al máximo; *(chances)* maximizar

maximum ['mæksɪməm] *adj* máximo ▪ *n* (*pl* **maxima**) ['mæksɪmə] máximo

May [meɪ] *n* mayo; *see also* **July**

may [meɪ] *vi (conditional* **might**) *(indicating possibility):* **he ~ come** puede que venga; *(be allowed to):* ~ **I smoke?** ¿puedo fumar?, *(wishes):* ~ **God bless you!** ¡que Dios le bendiga!; ~ **I sit here?** ¿me puedo sentar aquí?

maybe ['meɪbiː] *adv* quizá(s); ~ **not** quizá(s) no

May Day *n* el primero de Mayo

mayday ['meɪdeɪ] *n* señal *f* de socorro

mayhem ['meɪhem] *n* caos *m* total

mayonnaise [meɪə'neɪz] *n* mayonesa

mayor [meər] *n* alcalde *m*

mayoress ['meəres] *n* alcaldesa

maypole ['meɪpəul] *n* mayo

maze [meɪz] *n* laberinto

MB *abbr (Comput)* = **megabyte**; *(Canada)* = **Manitoba**

MBA *n abbr* (= *Master of Business Administration*) título universitario

MBBS, MBChB *n abbr (Brit:* = *Bachelor of Medicine and Surgery)* título universitario

MBE *n abbr (Brit:* = *Member of the Order of the British Empire)* título ceremonial

MBO *n abbr see* **management buyout**

MC *n abbr* (= *master of ceremonies*) e.p.; *(US:* = *Member of Congress)* diputado del Congreso de los Estados Unidos

MCAT *n abbr (US:* = *Medical College Admissions Test)* examen de ingreso en los estudios superiores de Medicina

MD *n abbr* (= *Doctor of Medicine*) título universitario; *(Comm)* = **managing director**; (= *MiniDisc®*) MiniDisc® *m*, minidisc *m* ▪ *abbr (US)* = **Maryland**

Md. abbr (US) = **Maryland**

MD player n MiniDisc® m, minidisc m

MDT n abbr (US: = Mountain Daylight Time) hora de verano de las Montañas Rocosas

ME abbr (US Post: = Maine) ∎ n abbr (US Med: = medical examiner); (Med: = myalgic encephalomyelitis) encefalomielitis f miálgica

me [miː] pron (direct) me; (stressed, after pronoun) mí; **can you hear me? ¿**me oyes?; **he heard ME!** me oyó a mí; **it's me** soy yo; **give them to me** dámelos; **with/without me** conmigo/sin mí; **it's for me** es para mí

meadow ['mɛdəʊ] n prado, pradera

meagre, (US) **meager** ['miːgəʳ] adj escaso, pobre

meal [miːl] n comida; (flour) harina; **to go out for a ~** salir a comer

meals on wheels nsg (Brit) servicio de alimentación a domicilio para necesitados y tercera edad

mealtime ['miːltaɪm] n hora de comer

mealy-mouthed ['miːlɪmaʊðd] adj: **to be ~** no decir nunca las cosas claras

mean [miːn] adj (with money) tacaño; (unkind) mezquino, malo; (average) medio; (US: vicious: animal) resabiado; (: person) malicioso ∎ vt (pt, pp **meant** [mɛnt]) (signify) querer decir, significar; (intend): **to ~ to do sth** tener la intención de or pensar hacer algo ∎ n medio, término medio; **do you ~ it? ¿**lo dices en serio?; **what do you ~?** ¿qué quiere decir?; **to be meant for sb/sth** ser para algn/algo; see also **means**

meander [mɪ'ændəʳ] vi (river) serpentear; (person) vagar

meaning ['miːnɪŋ] n significado, sentido

meaningful ['miːnɪŋful] adj significativo

meaningless ['miːnɪŋlɪs] adj sin sentido

meanness ['miːnnɪs] n (with money) tacañería; (unkindness) maldad f, mezquindad f

means [miːnz] npl medio sg, manera sg; (resource) recursos mpl, medios mpl; **by ~ of** mediante, por medio de; **by all ~!** ¡naturalmente!, ¡claro que sí!

means test n control m de los recursos económicos

meant [mɛnt] pt, pp of **mean**

meantime ['miːntaɪm], **meanwhile** ['miːnwaɪl] adv (also: **in the meantime**) mientras tanto

measles ['miːzlz] n sarampión m

measly ['miːzlɪ] adj (col) miserable

measurable ['mɛʒərəbl] adj mensurable, que se puede medir

measure ['mɛʒəʳ] vt medir; (for clothes etc) tomar las medidas a ∎ vi medir ∎ n

medida; (ruler) cinta métrica, metro; **a litre ~** una medida de un litro; **some ~ of success** cierto éxito; **to take measures to do sth** tomar medidas para hacer algo

▶ **measure up** vi: **to ~ up (to)** estar a la altura (de)

measured ['mɛʒəd] adj moderado; (tone) mesurado

measurement ['mɛʒəmənt] n (measure) medida; (act) medición f; **to take sb's measurements** tomar las medidas a algn

meat [miːt] n carne f; **cold meats** fiambres mpl; **crab ~** carne f de cangrejo

meatball ['miːtbɔːl] n albóndiga

meat pie n pastel m de carne

meaty ['miːtɪ] adj (person) fuerte, corpulento; (role) sustancioso; **a ~ meal** una comida con bastante carne

Mecca ['mɛkə] n (city) la Meca; (fig) meca

mechanic [mɪ'kænɪk] n mecánico(-a)

mechanical [mɪ'kænɪkl] adj mecánico

mechanical engineering n (science) ingeniería mecánica; (industry) construcción f mecánica

mechanics [mə'kænɪks] n mecánica ∎ npl mecanismo sg

mechanism ['mɛkənɪzəm] n mecanismo

mechanization [mɛkənaɪ'zeɪʃən] n mecanización f

mechanize ['mɛkənaɪz] vt mecanizar; (factory etc) automatizar

MEd n abbr (= Master of Education) título universitario

medal ['mɛdl] n medalla

medallion [mɪ'dælɪən] n medallón m

medallist, (US) **medalist** ['mɛdlɪst] n (Sport) medallista m/f

meddle ['mɛdl] vi: **to ~ in** entrometerse en; **to ~ with sth** manosear algo

meddlesome ['mɛdlsəm], **meddling** ['mɛdlɪŋ] adj (interfering) entrometido; (touching things) curioso

media ['miːdɪə] npl medios mpl de comunicación

media circus n excesivo despliegue informativo

mediaeval [mɛdɪ'iːvl] adj = **medieval**

median ['miːdɪən] n (US: also: **median strip**) mediana

media research n estudio de los medios de publicidad

mediate ['miːdɪeɪt] vi mediar

mediation [miːdɪ'eɪʃən] n mediación f

mediator ['miːdɪeɪtəʳ] n mediador(a) m(f)

Medicaid ['mɛdɪkeɪd] n (US) programa de ayuda médica

medical ['mɛdɪkl] adj médico ∎ n (also: **medical examination**) reconocimiento médico

medical certificate n certificado m médico
Medicare ['mɛdɪkɛəʳ] n (US) seguro médico del Estado
medicated ['mɛdɪkeɪtɪd] adj medicinal
medication [mɛdɪ'keɪʃən] n (drugs etc) medicación f
medicinal [mɛ'dɪsɪnl] adj medicinal
medicine ['mɛdsɪn] n medicina; (drug) medicamento
medicine chest n botiquín m
medicine man n hechicero
medieval [mɛdɪ'iːvl] adj medieval
mediocre [miːdɪ'əukəʳ] adj mediocre
mediocrity [miːdɪ'ɔkrɪtɪ] n mediocridad f
meditate ['mɛdɪteɪt] vi meditar
meditation [mɛdɪ'teɪʃən] n meditación f
Mediterranean [mɛdɪtə'reɪnɪən] adj mediterráneo; **the ~ (Sea)** el (Mar m) Mediterráneo
medium ['miːdɪəm] adj mediano; (level, height) medio ■ n (pl **media**) (means) medio (pl **mediums**) (person) médium m/f; **happy ~** punto justo
medium-dry ['miːdɪəm'draɪ] adj semiseco
medium-sized ['miːdɪəm'saɪzd] adj de tamaño mediano; (clothes) de (la) talla mediana
medium wave n onda media
medley ['mɛdlɪ] n mezcla; (Mus) popurrí m
meek [miːk] adj manso, sumiso
meekly ['miːklɪ] adv mansamente, dócilmente
meet [miːt] (pt, pp **met**) vt encontrar; (accidentally) encontrarse con; (by arrangement) reunirse con; (for the first time) conocer; (go and fetch) ir a buscar; (opponent) enfrentarse con; (obligations) cumplir; (bill, expenses) pagar, costear ■ vi encontrarse; (in session) reunirse; (join: objects) unirse; (get to know) conocerse ■ n (Brit Hunting) cacería; (US Sport) encuentro; **pleased to ~ you!** ¡encantado (de conocerle)!, ¡mucho gusto!
► **meet up** vi: **to ~ up with sb** reunirse con algn
► **meet with** vt fus reunirse con, (difficulty) tropezar con
meeting ['miːtɪŋ] n (also Sport: rally) encuentro; (arranged) cita, compromiso (LAm); (formal session, business meeting) reunión f; (Pol) mitin m; **to call a ~** convocar una reunión
meeting place n lugar m de reunión or encuentro
megabyte ['mɛgə'baɪt] n (Comput) megabyte m, megaocteto
megalomaniac [mɛgələu'meɪnɪæk] adj, n megalómano(-a) m(f)

megaphone ['mɛgəfəun] n megáfono
megawatt ['mɛgəwɔt] n megavatio
meh [mɛ] excl ¡bah!
melancholy ['mɛlənkəlɪ] n melancolía ■ adj melancólico
melee ['mɛleɪ] n refriega
mellow ['mɛləu] adj (wine) añejo; (sound, colour) suave; (fruit) maduro ■ vi (person) madurar
melodious [mɪ'ləudɪəs] adj melodioso
melodrama ['mɛləudrɑːmə] n melodrama m
melodramatic [mɛləudrə'mætɪk] adj melodramático
melody ['mɛlədɪ] n melodía
melon ['mɛlən] n melón m
melt [mɛlt] vi (metal) fundirse; (snow) derretirse; (fig) ablandarse ■ vt (also: **melt down**) fundir; **melted butter** mantequilla derretida
► **melt away** vi desvanecerse
meltdown ['mɛltdaun] n (in nuclear reactor) fusión f (de un reactor nuclear)
melting point ['mɛltɪŋ-] n punto de fusión
melting pot ['mɛltɪŋ-] n (fig) crisol m; **to be in the ~** estar sobre el tapete
member ['mɛmbəʳ] n (of political party) miembro; (of club) socio(-a); **M~ of Parliament (MP)** (Brit) diputado(-a); **M~ of the European Parliament (MEP)** (Brit) eurodiputado(-a); **M~ of the House of Representatives (MHR)** (US) diputado(a) del Congreso de los Estados Unidos; **M~ of the Scottish Parliament (MSP)** (Brit) diputado(-a) m(f) del Parlamento escocés
membership ['mɛmbəʃɪp] n (members) miembros mpl; socios mpl; (numbers) número de miembros or socios; **to seek ~ of** pedir el ingreso a
membership card n carnet m de socio
membrane ['mɛmbreɪn] n membrana
memento [mə'mɛntəu] n recuerdo
memo ['mɛməu] n abbr (= memorandum) nota (de servicio)
memoirs ['mɛmwɑːz] npl memorias fpl
memo pad n bloc m de notas
memorable ['mɛmərəbl] adj memorable
memorandum (memoranda) [mɛmə'rændəm, -də] n nota (de servicio); (Pol) memorándum m
memorial [mɪ'mɔːrɪəl] n monumento conmemorativo ■ adj conmemorativo
Memorial Day n (US) día de conmemoración de los caídos en la guerra
memorize ['mɛməraɪz] vt aprender de memoria
memory ['mɛmərɪ] n memoria; (recollection) recuerdo; (Comput) memoria; **to have a**

good/bad ~ tener buena/mala memoria; **loss of ~** pérdida de memoria

memory stick n (Comput) barra de memoria

men [mɛn] pl of **man**

menace ['mɛnəs] n amenaza; (col: nuisance) lata ■ vt amenazar; **a public ~** un peligro público

menacing ['mɛnɪsɪŋ] adj amenazador(-a)

menacingly ['mɛnɪsɪŋlɪ] adv amenazadoramente

menagerie [mɪ'nædʒərɪ] n casa de fieras

mend [mɛnd] vt reparar, arreglar; (darn) zurcir ■ vi reponerse ■ n (gen) remiendo; (darn) zurcido; **to be on the ~** ir mejorando

mending ['mɛndɪŋ] n arreglo, reparación f; (clothes) ropa por remendar

menial ['miːnɪəl] adj (pej) bajo, servil

meningitis [mɛnɪn'dʒaɪtɪs] n meningitis f

menopause ['mɛnəʊpɔːz] n menopausia

men's room n (US): **the ~** el servicio de caballeros

menstrual ['mɛnstruəl] adj menstrual

menstruate ['mɛnstrueɪt] vi menstruar

menstruation [mɛnstru'eɪʃən] n menstruación f

menswear ['mɛnzwɛər] n confección f de caballero

mental ['mɛntl] adj mental; **~ illness** enfermedad f mental

mental hospital n (hospital m) psiquiátrico

mentality [mɛn'tælɪtɪ] n mentalidad f

mentally ['mɛntlɪ] adv: **to be ~ handicapped** ser un disminuido mental

menthol ['mɛnθɒl] n mentol m

mention ['mɛnʃən] n mención f ■ vt mencionar; (speak of) hablar de; **don't ~ it!** ¡de nada!; **I need hardly ~ that ...** huelga decir que ...; **not to ~,without mentioning** sin contar

mentor ['mɛntɔːʳ] n mentor m

menu ['mɛnjuː] n (set menu) menú m; (printed) carta; (Comput) menú m

menu-driven ['mɛnjuːdrɪvn] adj (Comput) guiado por menú

MEP n abbr = **Member of the European Parliament**

mercantile ['mɜːkəntaɪl] adj mercantil

mercenary ['mɜːsɪnərɪ] adj, n mercenario(-a)

merchandise ['mɜːtʃəndaɪz] n mercancías fpl

merchandiser ['mɜːtʃəndaɪzəʳ] n comerciante m/f, tratante m

merchant ['mɜːtʃənt] n comerciante m/f

merchant bank n (Brit) banco comercial

merchantman ['mɜːtʃəntmən] n buque m mercante

merchant navy, (US) **merchant marine** n marina mercante

merciful ['mɜːsɪfʊl] adj compasivo

mercifully ['mɜːsɪfʊlɪ] adv con compasión; (fortunately) afortunadamente

merciless ['mɜːsɪlɪs] adj despiadado

mercilessly ['mɜːsɪlɪslɪ] adv despiadadamente, sin piedad

mercurial [mɜː'kjʊərɪəl] adj veleidoso, voluble

mercury ['mɜːkjʊrɪ] n mercurio

mercy ['mɜːsɪ] n compasión f; (Rel) misericordia; **at the ~ of** a la merced de

mercy killing n eutanasia

mere [mɪəʳ] adj simple, mero

merely ['mɪəlɪ] adv simplemente, sólo

merge [mɜːdʒ] vt (join) unir; (mix) mezclar; (fuse) fundir; (Comput: files, text) intercalar ■ vi unirse; (Comm) fusionarse

merger ['mɜːdʒəʳ] n (Comm) fusión f

meridian [mə'rɪdɪən] n meridiano

meringue [mə'ræŋ] n merengue m

merit ['mɛrɪt] n mérito ■ vt merecer

meritocracy [mɛrɪ'tɒkrəsɪ] n meritocracia

mermaid ['mɜːmeɪd] n sirena

merriment ['mɛrɪmənt] n alegría

merry ['mɛrɪ] adj alegre; **M~ Christmas!** ¡Felices Pascuas!

merry-go-round ['mɛrɪgəʊraʊnd] n tiovivo

mesh [mɛʃ] n malla; (Tech) engranaje m ■ vi (gears) engranar; **wire ~** tela metálica

mesmerize ['mɛzməraɪz] vt hipnotizar

mess [mɛs] n confusión f; (of objects) revoltijo; (tangle) lío; (Mil) comedor m; **to be (in) a ~** (room) estar revuelto; **to be/get o.s. in a ~** estar/meterse en un lío

▶ **mess about, mess around** vi (col) perder el tiempo; (pass the time) pasar el rato

▶ **mess about** or **around with** vt fus (col: play with) divertirse con; (: handle) manosear

▶ **mess up** vt (disarrange) desordenar; (spoil) estropear; (dirty) ensuciar

message ['mɛsɪdʒ] n recado, mensaje m; **to get the ~** (fig, col) enterarse

message switching n (Comput) conmutación f de mensajes

messenger ['mɛsɪndʒəʳ] n mensajero(-a)

Messiah [mɪ'saɪə] n Mesías m

Messrs, Messrs. abbr (on letters: = Messieurs) Sres

messy ['mɛsɪ] adj (dirty) sucio; (untidy) desordenado; (confused: situation etc) confuso

Met [mɛt] n abbr (US) = **Metropolitan Opera**

met [mɛt] pt, pp of **meet** ■ adj abbr = **meteorological**

metabolism [mɛ'tæbəlɪzəm] n metabolismo

metal ['mɛtl] n metal m

metallic [mɛ'tælɪk] adj metálico

metallurgy [mɛ'tælədʒɪ] n metalurgia

metalwork ['mɛtlwəːk] n (craft) metalistería
metamorphosis (pl **metamorphoses**)
　[mɛtə'mɔːfəsɪs, -siːz] n metamorfosis f inv
metaphor ['mɛtəfəʳ] n metáfora
metaphorical [mɛtə'fɒrɪkl] adj metafórico
metaphysics [mɛtə'fɪzɪks] n metafísica
mete [miːt]: **to ~ out** vt fus (punishment)
　imponer
meteor ['miːtɪəʳ] n meteoro
meteoric [miːtɪ'ɒrɪk] adj (fig) meteórico
meteorite ['miːtɪəraɪt] n meteorito
meteorological [miːtɪərə'lɒdʒɪkl] adj
　meteorológico
meteorology [miːtɪə'rɒlədʒɪ] n meteorología
meter ['miːtəʳ] n (instrument) contador m;
　(US: unit) = **metre** ■ vt (US Post) franquear;
　parking ~ parquímetro
methane ['miːθeɪn] n metano
method ['mɛθəd] n método; **~ of payment**
　método de pago
methodical [mɪ'θɒdɪkl] adj metódico
Methodist ['mɛθədɪst] adj, n metodista m/f
methodology [mɛθə'dɒlədʒɪ] n metodología
meths [mɛθs] n (Brit) = **methylated spirit**
methylated spirit ['mɛθɪleɪtɪd-] n (Brit)
　alcohol m metilado or desnaturalizado
meticulous [mɛ'tɪkjuləs] adj meticuloso
metre, meter (US) ['miːtəʳ] n metro
metric ['mɛtrɪk] adj métrico; **to go ~** pasar al
　sistema métrico
metrication [mɛtrɪ'keɪʃən] n conversión f al
　sistema métrico
metric system n sistema m métrico
metric ton n tonelada métrica
metronome ['mɛtrənəum] n metrónomo
metropolis [mɪ'trɒpəlɪs] n metrópoli(s) f
metropolitan [mɛtrə'pɒlɪtən] adj
　metropolitano
Metropolitan Police n (Brit): **the ~** la policía
　londinense
mettle ['mɛtl] n valor m, ánimo
mew [mjuː] vi (cat) maullar
mews [mjuːz] (Brit) n: **~ cottage** casa
　acondicionada en antiguos establos o cocheras;
　~ flat piso en antiguos establos o cocheras
Mexican ['mɛksɪkən] adj, n mejicano(-a) m(f),
　mexicano(-a) m(f) (LAm)
Mexico ['mɛksɪkəu] n Méjico, México (LAm)
Mexico City n Ciudad f de Méjico or (LAm)
　México
mezzanine ['mɛtsəniːn] n entresuelo
MFA n abbr (US: = Master of Fine Arts) título
　universitario
mfr abbr (= manufacturer) fab; = **manufacture**
mg abbr (= milligram) mg
Mgr abbr (= Monseigneur, Monsignor) Mons;
　(Comm) = **manager**

mgr abbr = **manager**
MHR n abbr (US) see **Member of the House of
　Representatives**
MHz abbr (= megahertz) MHz
MI abbr (US) = **Michigan**
MI5 n abbr (Brit: = Military Intelligence, section five)
　servicio de contraespionaje del gobierno británico
MI6 n abbr (Brit: = Military Intelligence, section six)
　servicio de inteligencia del gobierno británico
MIA abbr (Mil: = missing in action) desaparecido
miaow [miː'au] vi maullar
mice [maɪs] pl of **mouse**
Mich. abbr (US) = **Michigan**
mickey ['mɪkɪ] n: **to take the ~ out of sb**
　tomar el pelo a algn
micro ['maɪkrəu] n = **microcomputer**
micro... [maɪkrəu] pref micro...
microbe ['maɪkrəub] n microbio
microbiology [maɪkrəubaɪ'ɒlədʒɪ] n
　microbiología
microchip ['maɪkrəutʃɪp] n microchip m,
　microplaqueta
microcomputer ['maɪkrəukəm'pjuːtəʳ] n
　microordenador m, microcomputador m
　(LAm)
microcosm ['maɪkrəukɒzəm] n microcosmo
microeconomics ['maɪkrəui:kə'nɒmɪks] n
　microeconomía
microfiche ['maɪkrəufiːʃ] n microficha
microfilm ['maɪkrəufɪlm] n microfilm m
microlight ['maɪkrəulaɪt] n ultraligero
micrometer [maɪ'krɒmɪtəʳ] n micrómetro
microphone ['maɪkrəfəun] n micrófono
microprocessor ['maɪkrəu'prəusɛsəʳ] n
　microprocesador m
microscope ['maɪkrəskəup] n microscopio;
　under the ~ al microscopio
microscopic [maɪkrə'skɒpɪk] adj
　microscópico
microwave ['maɪkrəweɪv] n (also:
　microwave oven) horno microondas
mid [mɪd] adj: **in ~ May** a mediados de mayo;
　in ~ afternoon a media tarde; **in ~ air** en
　el aire; **he's in his ~ thirties** tiene unos
　treinta y cinco años
midday [mɪd'deɪ] n mediodía m
middle ['mɪdl] n medio, centro; (waist)
　cintura ■ adj de en medio; **in the ~ of
　the night** en plena noche; **I'm in the ~ of
　reading it** lo estoy leyendo ahora mismo
middle-aged [mɪdl'eɪdʒd] adj de mediana
　edad
Middle Ages npl: **the ~** la Edad sg Media
middle class n: **the ~(es)** la clase media
　■ adj: **middle-class** de clase media
Middle East n Oriente m Medio
middleman ['mɪdlmæn] n intermediario

middle management *n* dirección *f* de nivel medio

middle name *n* segundo nombre *m*

middle-of-the-road ['mɪdləvðə'rəud] *adj* moderado

middleweight ['mɪdlweɪt] *n* (*Boxing*) peso medio

middling ['mɪdlɪŋ] *adj* mediano

Middx *abbr* (*Brit*) = **Middlesex**

midge [mɪdʒ] *n* mosquito

midget ['mɪdʒɪt] *n* enano(-a)

midi system *n* cadena midi

Midlands ['mɪdləndz] *npl* *región central de Inglaterra*

midnight ['mɪdnaɪt] *n* medianoche *f*; **at ~** a medianoche

midriff ['mɪdrɪf] *n* diafragma *m*

midst [mɪdst] *n*: **in the ~ of** entre, en medio de

midsummer [mɪd'sʌmər] *n*: **a ~ day** un día de pleno verano

Midsummer's Day *n* Día *m* de San Juan

midway [mɪd'weɪ] *adj, adv*: **~ (between)** a mitad de camino *or* a medio camino (entre)

midweek [mɪd'wiːk] *adv* entre semana

midwife (*pl* **midwives**) ['mɪdwaɪf, -waɪvz] *n* comadrona

midwifery ['mɪdwɪfərɪ] *n* tocología

midwinter [mɪd'wɪntər] *n*: **in ~** en pleno invierno

miffed [mɪft] *adj* (*col*) mosqueado

might [maɪt] *vb see* **may** ■ *n* fuerza, poder *m*; **he ~ be there** puede que esté allí, a lo mejor está allí; **I ~ as well go** más vale que vaya; **you ~ like to try** podría intentar

mightily ['maɪtɪlɪ] *adv* fuertemente, poderosamente; **I was ~ surprised** me sorprendí enormemente

mightn't ['maɪtnt] = **might not**

mighty ['maɪtɪ] *adj* fuerte, poderoso

migraine ['miːɡreɪn] *n* jaqueca

migrant ['maɪɡrənt] *adj* migratorio ■ *n* (*bird*) ave *f* migratoria; (*worker*) emigrante *m/f*

migrate [maɪ'ɡreɪt] *vi* emigrar

migration [maɪ'ɡreɪʃən] *n* emigración *f*

mike [maɪk] *n abbr* (= *microphone*) micro

Milan [mɪ'læn] *n* Milán *m*

mild [maɪld] *adj* (*person*) apacible; (*climate*) templado; (*slight*) ligero; (*taste*) suave; (*illness*) leve

mildew ['mɪldjuː] *n* moho

mildly ['maɪldlɪ] *adv* ligeramente; suavemente; **to put it ~** por no decir algo peor

mildness ['maɪldnɪs] *n* suavidad *f*; (*of illness*) levedad *f*

mile [maɪl] *n* milla; **to do 20 miles per**

gallon hacer 20 millas por galón

mileage ['maɪlɪdʒ] *n* número de millas; (*Aut*) kilometraje *m*

mileage allowance *n* ≈ asignación *f* por kilometraje

mileometer [maɪ'lɔmɪtər] *n* (*Brit*) = **milometer**

milestone ['maɪlstəun] *n* mojón *m*; (*fig*) hito

milieu ['miːljəː] *n* (medio) ambiente *m*, entorno

militant ['mɪlɪtnt] *adj, n* militante *m/f*

militarism ['mɪlɪtərɪzəm] *n* militarismo

militaristic [mɪlɪtə'rɪstɪk] *adj* militarista

military ['mɪlɪtərɪ] *adj* militar

military service *n* servicio militar

militate ['mɪlɪteɪt] *vi*: **to ~ against** militar en contra de

militia [mɪ'lɪʃə] *n* milicia

milk [mɪlk] *n* leche *f* ■ *vt* (*cow*) ordeñar; (*fig*) chupar

milk chocolate *n* chocolate *m* con leche

milk float *n* (*Brit*) furgoneta de la leche

milking ['mɪlkɪŋ] *n* ordeño

milkman ['mɪlkmən] *n* lechero, repartidor *m* de la leche

milk shake *n* batido, malteada (*LAm*)

milk tooth *n* diente *m* de leche

milk truck *n* (*US*) = **milk float**

milky ['mɪlkɪ] *adj* lechoso

Milky Way *n* Vía Láctea

mill [mɪl] *n* (*windmill etc*) molino; (*coffee mill*) molinillo; (*factory*) fábrica; (*spinning mill*) hilandería ■ *vt* moler ■ *vi* (*also*: **mill about**) arremolinarse

milled [mɪld] (*grain*) molido; (*coin, edge*) acordonado

millennium (*pl* **millenniums** *or* **millennia**) [mɪ'lɛnɪəm, 'lɛnɪə] *n* milenio, milenario

millennium bug *n* (*Comput*): **the ~** el (problema del) efecto 2000

miller ['mɪlər] *n* molinero

millet ['mɪlɪt] *n* mijo

milli... ['mɪlɪ] *pref* mili...

milligram, milligramme ['mɪlɪɡræm] *n* miligramo

millilitre, (US) milliliter ['mɪlɪliːtər] *n* mililitro

millimetre, (US) millimeter ['mɪlɪmiːtər] *n* milímetro

milliner ['mɪlɪnər] *n* sombrerero(-a)

millinery ['mɪlɪnərɪ] *n* sombrerería

million ['mɪljən] *n* millón *m*; **a ~ times** un millón de veces

millionaire [mɪljə'nɛər] *n* millonario(-a)

millipede ['mɪlɪpiːd] *n* milpiés *m inv*

millstone ['mɪlstəun] *n* piedra de molino

millwheel ['mɪlwiːl] *n* rueda de molino

milometer [mar'lɔmɪtəʳ] n (Brit)
cuentakilómetros m inv

mime [maɪm] n mímica; (actor) mimo(-a)
■ vt remedar ■ vi actuar de mimo

mimic ['mɪmɪk] n imitador(a) m(f) ■ adj
mímico ■ vt remedar, imitar

mimicry ['mɪmɪkrɪ] n imitación f

Min abbr (Brit Pol: = Ministry) Min

min. abbr (= minute(s)) m.; = **minimum**

minaret [mɪnə'rɛt] n alminar m, minarete m

mince [mɪns] vt picar ■ vi (in walking) andar
con pasos menudos ■ n (Brit Culin) carne f
picada, picadillo

mincemeat ['mɪnsmi:t] n conserva de fruta
picada

mince pie n pastelillo relleno de fruta picada

mincer ['mɪnsəʳ] n picadora de carne

mincing ['mɪnsɪŋ] adj afectado

mind [maɪnd] n (gen) mente f, (contrasted
with matter) espíritu m ■ vt (attend to, look
after) ocuparse de, cuidar; (be careful of) tener
cuidado con; (object to): **I don't ~ the noise**
no me molesta el ruido; **it is on my ~** me
preocupa; **to my ~** a mi parecer or juicio;
to change one's ~ cambiar de idea or de
parecer; **to bring** or **call sth to ~** recordar
algo; **to have sth/sb in ~** tener algo/a
algn en mente; **to be out of one's ~** haber
perdido el juicio; **to bear sth in ~** tomar or
tener algo en cuenta; **to make up one's ~**
decidirse; **it went right out of my ~** se me
fue por completo (de la cabeza); **to be in two
minds about sth** estar indeciso or dudar
ante algo; **I don't ~** me es igual; **~ you, ...**
te advierto que ...; **never ~!** ¡es igual!, ¡no
importa!; (don't worry) ¡no te preocupes!;
'~ the step' 'cuidado con el escalón'

mind-boggling ['maɪndbɔglɪŋ] adj (col)
alucinante, increíble

-minded [-maɪndɪd] adj: **fair~** imparcial;
an industrially~ nation una nación
orientada a la industria

minder ['maɪndəʳ] n guardaespaldas m inv

mindful ['maɪndful] adj: **~ of** consciente de

mindless ['maɪndlɪs] adj (violence, crime) sin
sentido; (work) de autómata

mine [maɪn] pron (el) mío/(la) mía etc;
a friend of ~ un(a) amigo(-a) mío/mía ■ adj:
this book is ~ este libro es mío ■ n mina
■ vt (coal) extraer; (ship, beach) minar

mine detector n detector m de minas

minefield ['maɪnfi:ld] n campo de minas

miner ['maɪnəʳ] n minero(-a)

mineral ['mɪnərəl] adj mineral ■ n mineral
m; **minerals** npl (Brit: soft drinks) refrescos mpl
con gas

mineral water n agua mineral

minesweeper ['maɪnswi:pəʳ] n dragaminas
m inv

mingle ['mɪŋgl] vi: **to ~ with** mezclarse con

mingy ['mɪndʒɪ] adj (col) tacaño

mini ... [mɪnɪ] pref mini..., micro...

miniature ['mɪnətʃəʳ] adj (en) miniatura ■ n
miniatura

minibus ['mɪnɪbʌs] n microbús m

minicab ['mɪnɪkæb] n taxi m (que sólo puede
pedirse por teléfono)

minicomputer ['mɪnɪkəm'pjuːtəʳ] n
miniordenador m, minicomputador m (LAm)

MiniDisc® ['mɪnɪdɪsk] n MiniDisc® m

minim ['mɪnɪm] n (Brit Mus) blanca

minimal ['mɪnɪml] adj mínimo

minimalist ['mɪnɪməlɪst] adj, n minimalista
m/f

minimize ['mɪnɪmaɪz] vt minimizar

minimum ['mɪnɪməm] n (pl **minima**)
['mɪnɪmə] mínimo ■ adj mínimo; **to
reduce to a ~** reducir algo al mínimo; **~
wage** salario mínimo

minimum lending rate n tipo de interés
mínimo

mining ['maɪnɪŋ] n minería ■ adj minero

minion ['mɪnjən] n secuaz m

mini-series ['mɪnɪsɪərɪːz] n serie f de pocos
capítulos, miniserie f

miniskirt ['mɪnɪskəːt] n minifalda

minister ['mɪnɪstəʳ] n (Brit Pol) ministro(-a);
(Rel) pastor m ■ vi: **to ~ to** atender a

ministerial [mɪnɪs'tɪərɪəl] adj (Brit Pol)
ministerial

ministry ['mɪnɪstrɪ] n (Brit Pol) ministerio;
(Rel) sacerdocio; **M~ of Defence** Ministerio
de Defensa

mink [mɪŋk] n visón m

mink coat n abrigo de visón

Minn. abbr (US) = **Minnesota**

minnow ['mɪnəu] n pececillo (de agua dulce)

minor ['maɪnəʳ] adj (unimportant) secundario;
(Mus) menor ■ n (Law) menor m/f de edad

Minorca [mɪ'nɔːkə] n Menorca

minority [maɪ'nɔrɪtɪ] n minoría; **to be in a ~**
estar en or ser minoría

minority interest n participación f
minoritaria

minster ['mɪnstəʳ] n catedral f

minstrel ['mɪnstrəl] n juglar m

mint [mɪnt] n (plant) menta, hierbabuena;
(sweet) caramelo de menta ■ vt (coins) acuñar;
the (Royal) M~, (US) **the (US) M~** la Casa de
la Moneda; **in ~ condition** en perfecto estado

mint sauce n salsa de menta

minuet [mɪnju'ɛt] n minué m

minus ['maɪnəs] n (also: **minus sign**) signo
menos ■ prep menos

minuscule ['mɪnəskjuːl] *adj* minúsculo
minute *n* ['mɪnɪt] minuto; *(fig)* momento;
 minutes *npl (of meeting)* actas *fpl* ■ *adj*
 [maɪ'njuːt] diminuto; *(search)* minucioso;
 it is 5 minutes past 3 son las 3 y 5 (minutos);
 at the last ~ a última hora; **wait a ~!** ¡espera
 un momento!; **up to the ~** de última hora;
 in ~ detail con todo detalle
minute book *n* libro de actas
minute hand *n* minutero
minutely [maɪ'njuːtlɪ] *adv (by a small amount)*
 por muy poco; *(in detail)* detalladamente,
 minuciosamente
minutiae [mɪ'njuːʃiː] *npl* minucias *fpl*
miracle ['mɪrəkl] *n* milagro
miracle play *n* auto, milagro
miraculous [mɪ'rækjuləs] *adj* milagroso
miraculously [mɪ'rækjuləslɪ] *adv*
 milagrosamente
mirage ['mɪrɑːʒ] *n* espejismo
mire [maɪəʳ] *n* fango, lodo
mirror ['mɪrəʳ] *n* espejo; *(in car)* retrovisor *m*
 ■ *vt* reflejar
mirror image *n* reflejo inverso
mirth [məːθ] *n* alegría; *(laughter)* risa, risas *fpl*
misadventure [mɪsəd'vɛntʃəʳ] *n* desventura;
 death by ~ muerte *f* accidental
misanthropist [mɪ'zænθrəpɪst] *n*
 misántropo(-a)
misapply [mɪsə'plaɪ] *vt* emplear mal
misapprehension ['mɪsæprɪ'hɛnʃən] *n*
 equivocación *f*
misappropriate [mɪsə'prəuprɪeɪt] *vt (funds)*
 malversar
misappropriation ['mɪsəprəuprɪ'eɪʃən] *n*
 malversación *f*, desfalco
misbehave [mɪsbɪ'heɪv] *vi* portarse mal
misbehaviour, misbehavior *(US)*
 [mɪsbɪ'heɪvjəʳ] *n* mala conducta
misc. *abbr* = **miscellaneous**
miscalculate [mɪs'kælkjuleɪt] *vt* calcular mal
miscalculation [mɪskælkju'leɪʃən] *n* error *m*
 (de cálculo)
miscarriage ['mɪskærɪdʒ] *n (Med)* aborto (no
 provocado); **~ of justice** error *m* judicial
miscarry [mɪs'kærɪ] *vi (Med)* abortar
 (de forma natural); *(fail: plans)* fracasar,
 malograrse
miscellaneous [mɪsɪ'leɪnɪəs] *adj* varios(-as),
 diversos(-as); **~ expenses** gastos diversos
miscellany [mɪ'sɛlənɪ] *n* miscelánea
mischance [mɪs'tʃɑːns] *n* desgracia, mala
 suerte *f*; **by (some) ~** por (alguna) desgracia
mischief ['mɪstʃɪf] *n (naughtiness)* travesura;
 (harm) mal *m*, daño; *(maliciousness)* malicia
mischievous ['mɪstʃɪvəs] *adj* travieso;
 dañino; *(playful)* malicioso

mischievously ['mɪstʃɪvəslɪ] *adv* por
 travesura; maliciosamente
misconception ['mɪskən'sɛpʃən] *n* concepto
 erróneo; equivocación *f*
misconduct [mɪs'kɔndʌkt] *n* mala conducta;
 professional ~ falta profesional
misconstrue [mɪskən'struː] *vt* interpretar
 mal
miscount [mɪs'kaunt] *vt, vi* contar mal
misdeed [mɪs'diːd] *n (old)* fechoría, delito
misdemeanour, misdemeanor *(US)*
 [mɪsdɪ'miːnəʳ] *n* delito, ofensa
misdirect [mɪsdɪ'rɛkt] *vt (person)* informar
 mal; *(letter)* poner señas incorrectas en
miser ['maɪzəʳ] *n* avaro(-a)
miserable ['mɪzərəbl] *adj (unhappy)* triste,
 desgraciado; *(wretched)* miserable; **to feel ~**
 sentirse triste
miserably ['mɪzərəblɪ] *adv (smile, answer)*
 tristemente; *(fail)* rotundamente; **to pay ~**
 pagar una miseria
miserly ['maɪzəlɪ] *adj* avariento, tacaño
misery ['mɪzərɪ] *n (unhappiness)* tristeza;
 (wretchedness) miseria, desdicha
misfire [mɪs'faɪəʳ] *vt* fallar
misfit ['mɪsfɪt] *n (person)* inadaptado(-a)
misfortune [mɪs'fɔːtʃən] *n* desgracia
misgiving [mɪs'gɪvɪŋ] *n*, **misgivings**
 [mɪs'gɪvɪŋz] *npl (mistrust)* recelo;
 (apprehension) presentimiento; **to have
 misgivings about sth** tener dudas sobre
 algo
misguided [mɪs'gaɪdɪd] *adj* equivocado
mishandle [mɪs'hændl] *vt (treat roughly)*
 maltratar; *(mismanage)* manejar mal
mishap ['mɪshæp] *n* desgracia, contratiempo
mishear [mɪs'hɪəʳ] *vt, vi (irreg: like* **hear***)* oír
 mal
mishmash ['mɪʃmæʃ] *n (col)* revoltijo
misinform [mɪsɪn'fɔːm] *vt* informar mal
misinterpret [mɪsɪn'təːprɪt] *vt* interpretar
 mal
misinterpretation ['mɪsɪntəːprɪ'teɪʃən] *n*
 mala interpretación *f*
misjudge [mɪs'dʒʌdʒ] *vt* juzgar mal
mislay [mɪs'leɪ] *vt (irreg: like* **lay***)* extraviar,
 perder
mislead [mɪs'liːd] *vt (irreg: like* **lead***)* llevar a
 conclusiones erróneas; *(deliberately)* engañar
misleading [mɪs'liːdɪŋ] *adj* engañoso
misled [mɪs'lɛd] *pt, pp of* **mislead**
mismanage [mɪs'mænɪdʒ] *vt* administrar
 mal
mismanagement [mɪs'mænɪdʒmənt] *n*
 mala administración *f*
misnomer [mɪs'nəuməʳ] *n* término
 inapropiado *or* equivocado

misogynist [mɪ'sɔdʒɪnɪst] n misógino
misplace [mɪs'pleɪs] vt (lose) extraviar; **misplaced** (trust etc) inmerecido
misprint ['mɪsprɪnt] n errata, error m de imprenta
mispronounce [mɪsprə'naʊns] vt pronunciar mal
misquote ['mɪs'kwəʊt] vt citar incorrectamente
misread [mɪs'riːd] vt (irreg: like read) leer mal
misrepresent [mɪsrɛprɪ'zɛnt] vt falsificar
misrepresentation [mɪsrɛprɪzɛn'teɪʃən] n (Law) falsa declaración f
Miss [mɪs] n Señorita; **Dear ~ Smith** Estimada Señorita Smith
miss [mɪs] vt (train etc) perder; (shot) errar, fallar; (appointment, class) faltar a; (escape, avoid) evitar; (notice loss of: money etc) notar la falta de, echar en falta; (regret the absence of): **I ~ him** le echo de menos ■ vi fallar ■ n (shot) tiro fallido; **the bus just missed the wall** faltó poco para que el autobús se estrella contra el muro; **you're missing the point** no has entendido la idea
▶ **miss out** vt (Brit) omitir
▶ **miss out on** vt fus (fun, party, opportunity) perderse
Miss. abbr (US) = **Mississippi**
missal ['mɪsl] n misal m
misshapen [mɪs'ʃeɪpən] adj deforme
missile ['mɪsaɪl] n (Aviat) misil m; (object thrown) proyectil m
missile base n base f de misiles
missile launcher n lanzamisiles m inv
missing ['mɪsɪŋ] adj (pupil) ausente, que falta; (thing) perdido; (Mil) desaparecido; **to be ~** faltar; **~ person** desaparecido(-a)
mission ['mɪʃən] n misión f; **on a ~ for sb** en una misión para algn
missionary ['mɪʃənrɪ] n misionero(-a)
misspell [mɪs'spɛl] vt (irreg: like spell) escribir mal
misspent ['mɪs'spɛnt] adj: **his ~ youth** su juventud disipada
mist [mɪst] n (light) neblina; (heavy) niebla; (at sea) bruma ■ vi (also: **mist over, mist up**: weather) nublarse; (Brit: windows) empañarse
mistake [mɪs'teɪk] n error m ■ vt (irreg: like take) entender mal; **by ~** por equivocación; **to make a ~** (about sb/sth) equivocarse; (in writing, calculating etc) cometer un error; **to ~ A for B** confundir A con B
mistaken [mɪs'teɪkən] pp of **mistake** ■ adj (idea etc) equivocado; **to be ~** equivocarse, engañarse; **~ identity** identificación f errónea
mistakenly [mɪs'teɪkənlɪ] adv erróneamente

mister ['mɪstəʳ] n (col) señor m; see **Mr**
mistletoe ['mɪsltəʊ] n muérdago
mistook [mɪs'tuk] pt of **mistake**
mistranslation [mɪstræns'leɪʃən] n mala traducción f
mistreat [mɪs'triːt] vt maltratar, tratar mal
mistress ['mɪstrɪs] n (lover) amante f; (of house) señora (de la casa); (Brit: in primary school) maestra; (in secondary school) profesora; see also **Mrs**
mistrust [mɪs'trʌst] vt desconfiar de ■ n: **~ (of)** desconfianza (de)
mistrustful [mɪs'trʌstful] adj: **~ (of)** desconfiado (de), receloso (de)
misty ['mɪstɪ] adj nebuloso, brumoso; (day) de niebla; (glasses) empañado
misty-eyed ['mɪstɪ'aɪd] adj sentimental
misunderstand [mɪsʌndə'stænd] vt, vi (irreg: like **understand**) entender mal
misunderstanding [mɪsʌndə'stændɪŋ] n malentendido
misunderstood [mɪsʌndə'stud] pt, pp of **misunderstand** ■ adj (person) incomprendido
misuse n [mɪs'juːs] mal uso; (of power) abuso ■ vt [mɪs'juːz] abusar de; (funds) malversar
MIT n abbr (US) = **Massachusetts Institute of Technology**
mite [maɪt] n (small quantity) pizca; **poor ~!** ¡pobrecito!
mitigate ['mɪtɪgeɪt] vt mitigar; **mitigating circumstances** circunstancias fpl atenuantes
mitigation [mɪtɪ'geɪʃən] n mitigación f, alivio
mitre, (US) **miter** ['maɪtəʳ] n mitra
mitt ['mɪt], **mitten** ['mɪtn] n manopla
mix [mɪks] vt (gen) mezclar; (combine) unir ■ vi mezclarse; (people) llevarse bien ■ n mezcla; **to ~ sth with sth** mezclar algo con algo; **to ~ business with pleasure** combinar los negocios con el placer; **cake ~** preparado para pastel
▶ **mix in** vt (eggs etc) añadir
▶ **mix up** vt mezclar; (confuse) confundir; **to be mixed up in sth** estar metido en algo
mixed [mɪkst] adj (assorted) variado, surtido; (school, marriage etc) mixto
mixed-ability ['mɪkstə'bɪlɪtɪ] adj (class etc) de alumnos de distintas capacidades
mixed blessing n: **it's a ~** tiene su lado bueno y su lado malo
mixed doubles n (Sport) mixtos mpl
mixed economy n economía mixta
mixed grill n (Brit) parrillada mixta
mixed-up [mɪkst'ʌp] adj (confused) confuso, revuelto

661

mixer ['mɪksə^r] n (for food) batidora; (person): **he's a good ~** tiene don de gentes

mixer tap n (grifo) monomando

mixture ['mɪkstʃə^r] n mezcla

mix-up ['mɪksʌp] n confusión f

Mk abbr (Brit Tech: = mark) Mk

mkt abbr = **market**

MLA n abbr (Brit Pol: Northern Ireland: = Member of the Legislative Assembly) miembro de la asamblea legislativa

MLitt n abbr (= Master of Literature, Master of Letters) título universitario de postgrado; see also **master's degree**

MLR n abbr (Brit) = **minimum lending rate**

mm abbr (= millimetre) mm

MMR vaccine n (against measles, mumps, rubella) vacuna triple vírica

MMS n abbr (= multimedia messaging service) MMS m

MN abbr (Brit) = **Merchant Navy**; (US) = **Minnesota**

MO n abbr (Med) = **medical officer**; (US col) = **modus operandi** ▪ abbr (US) = **Missouri**

Mo. abbr (US) = **Missouri**

m.o. abbr (= money order) g/

moan [məun] n gemido ▪ vi gemir; (col: complain): **to ~ (about)** quejarse (de)

moaning ['məunɪŋ] n gemidos mpl; quejas fpl

moat [məut] n foso

mob [mɔb] n multitud f; (pej): **the ~** el populacho ▪ vt acosar

mobile ['məubaɪl] adj móvil ▪ n móvil m

mobile home n caravana

mobile phone n teléfono móvil

mobility [məu'bɪlɪtɪ] n movilidad f; **~ of labour** or (US) **labor** movilidad f de la mano de obra

mobilize ['məubɪlaɪz] vt movilizar

moccasin ['mɔkəsɪn] n mocasín m

mock [mɔk] vt (make ridiculous) ridiculizar; (laugh at) burlarse de ▪ adj fingido

mockery ['mɔkərɪ] n burla; **to make a ~ of** desprestigiar

mocking ['mɔkɪŋ] adj (tone) burlón(-ona)

mockingbird ['mɔkɪŋbəːd] n sinsonte m (LAm), zenzontle m (LAm)

mock-up ['mɔkʌp] n maqueta

MOD n abbr (Brit) = **Ministry of Defence**; see **defence**

mod cons ['mɔd'kɔnz] npl abbr (= modern conveniences) see **convenience**

mode [məud] n modo; (of transport) medio; (Comput) modo, modalidad f

model ['mɔdl] n (gen) modelo; (Arch) maqueta; (person: for fashion, art) modelo m/f ▪ adj modelo inv ▪ vt modelar ▪ vi ser modelo; **~ railway** ferrocarril m de juguete; **to ~ clothes** pasar modelos, ser modelo; **to ~ on** crear a imitación de

modelling, (US) **modeling** ['mɔdlɪŋ] n (modelmaking) modelado

modem ['məudəm] n módem m

moderate [adj, n 'mɔdərət, vb 'mɔdəreɪt] adj, n moderado(-a) m(f) ▪ vi moderarse, calmarse ▪ vt moderar

moderately ['mɔdərətlɪ] adv (act) con moderación; (expensive, difficult) medianamente; (pleased, happy) bastante

moderation [mɔdə'reɪʃən] n moderación f; **in ~** con moderación

moderator ['mɔdəreɪtə^r] n (mediator) moderador(a) m(f)

modern ['mɔdən] adj moderno; **~ languages** lenguas fpl modernas

modernity [mə'dəːnɪtɪ] n modernidad f

modernization [mɔdənaɪ'zeɪʃən] n modernización f

modernize ['mɔdənaɪz] vt modernizar

modest ['mɔdɪst] adj modesto

modestly ['mɔdɪstlɪ] adv modestamente

modesty ['mɔdɪstɪ] n modestia

modicum ['mɔdɪkəm] n: **a ~ of** un mínimo de

modification [mɔdɪfɪ'keɪʃən] n modificación f; **to make modifications** hacer cambios or modificaciones

modify ['mɔdɪfaɪ] vt modificar

modish ['məudɪʃ] adj de moda

Mods [mɔdz] n abbr (Brit: = (Honour) Moderations) examen de licenciatura de la universidad de Oxford

modular ['mɔdjulə^r] adj (filing, unit) modular

modulate ['mɔdjuleɪt] vt modular

modulation [mɔdju'leɪʃən] n modulación f

module ['mɔdjuːl] n módulo

modus operandi ['məudəsɔpə'rændiː] n manera de actuar

Mogadishu [mɔgə'dɪʃuː] n Mogadiscio

mogul ['məugəl] n (fig) magnate m

MOH n abbr (Brit) = **Medical Officer of Health**

mohair ['məuhɛə^r] n mohair m

Mohammed [mə'hæmɛd] n Mahoma m

moist [mɔɪst] adj húmedo

moisten ['mɔɪsn] vt humedecer

moisture ['mɔɪstʃə^r] n humedad f

moisturize ['mɔɪstʃəraɪz] vt (skin) hidratar

moisturizer ['mɔɪstʃəraɪzə^r] n crema hidratante

molar ['məulə^r] n muela

molasses [məu'læsɪz] n melaza

mold [məuld] n, vt (US) = **mould**

Moldavia [mɔl'deɪvɪə], **Moldova** [mɔl'dəuvə] n Moldavia, Moldova

Moldavian [mɔl'deɪvɪən], **Moldovan** [mɔl'dəuvən] adj, n moldavo(-a) m(f)

mole [məul] n (animal) topo; (spot) lunar m
molecular [mə'lɛkjuləʳ] adj molecular
molecule ['mɔlɪkjuːl] n molécula
molest [məu'lɛst] vt importunar; (sexually) abordar con propósitos deshonestos
moll [mɔl] n (slang) amiga
mollusc, mollusk (US) ['mɔləsk] n molusco
mollycoddle ['mɔlɪkɔdl] vt mimar
Molotov cocktail ['mɔlətɔf-] n cóctel m Molotov
molt [məult] vi (US) = moult
molten ['məultən] adj fundido; (lava) líquido
mom [mɔm] n (US) = mum
moment ['məumənt] n momento; at or for the ~ de momento, por el momento, por ahora; in a ~ dentro de un momento
momentarily ['məumntrɪlɪ] adv momentáneamente; (US: very soon) de un momento a otro
momentary ['məumntərɪ] adj momentáneo
momentous [məu'mɛntəs] adj trascendental, importante
momentum [məu'mɛntəm] n momento; (fig) ímpetu m; to gather ~ cobrar velocidad; (fig) cobrar fuerza
mommy ['mɔmɪ] n (US) = mummy
Mon abbr (= Monday) lun
Monaco ['mɔnəkəu] n Mónaco
monarch ['mɔnək] n monarca m/f
monarchist ['mɔnəkɪst] n monárquico(-a)
monarchy ['mɔnəkɪ] n monarquía
monastery ['mɔnəstərɪ] n monasterio
monastic [mə'næstɪk] adj monástico
Monday ['mʌndɪ] n lunes m inv; see also Tuesday
Monegasque [mɔnɪ'gæsk] adj, n monegasco(-a) m(f)
monetarist ['mʌnɪtərɪst] n monetarista m/f
monetary ['mʌnɪtərɪ] adj monetario
monetary policy n política monetaria
money ['mʌnɪ] n dinero, plata (LAm); to make ~ ganar dinero; I've got no ~ left no me queda dinero
moneyed ['mʌnɪd] adj adinerado
moneylender ['mʌnɪlɛndəʳ] n prestamista m/f
moneymaker ['mʌnɪmeɪkəʳ] n (Brit col: business) filón m
moneymaking ['mʌnɪmeɪkɪŋ] adj rentable
money market n mercado monetario
money order n giro
money-spinner ['mʌnɪspɪnəʳ] n (col: person, idea, business) filón m
money supply n oferta monetaria, medio circulante, volumen m monetario
Mongol ['mɔŋgəl] n mongol(a) m(f); (Ling)

mongol m
mongol ['mɔŋgəl] adj, n (Med) mongólico
Mongolia [mɔŋ'gəulɪə] n Mongolia
Mongolian [mɔŋ'gəulɪən] adj mongol(a) ■ n mongol(a) m(f); (Ling) mongol m
mongoose ['mɔŋguːs] n mangosta
mongrel ['mʌŋgrəl] n (dog) perro cruzado
monitor ['mɔnɪtəʳ] n monitor m ■ vt controlar; (foreign station) escuchar
monk [mʌŋk] n monje m
monkey ['mʌŋkɪ] n mono
monkey business n, monkey tricks ■ npl tejemanejes mpl
monkey nut n (Brit) cacahuete m, maní m (LAm)
monkey wrench n llave f inglesa
mono ['mɔnəu] adj (broadcast etc) mono inv
mono... [mɔnəu] pref mono ...
monochrome ['mɔnəukrəum] adj monocromo
monocle ['mɔnəkl] n monóculo
monogamous [mə'nɔgəməs] adj monógamo
monogram ['mɔnəgræm] n monograma m
monolith ['mɔnəlɪθ] n monolito
monolithic [mɔnə'lɪθɪk] adj monolítico
monologue ['mɔnələg] n monólogo
monoplane ['mɔnəpleɪn] n monoplano
monopolist [mə'nɔpəlɪst] n monopolista m/f
monopolize [mə'nɔpəlaɪz] vt monopolizar
monopoly [mə'nɔpəlɪ] n monopolio;
Monopolies and Mergers Commission (Brit) comisión reguladora de monopolios y fusiones
monorail ['mɔnəureɪl] n monocarril m, monorraíl m
monosodium glutamate [mɔnə'səudɪəm 'gluːtəmeɪt] n glutamato monosódico
monosyllabic [mɔnəsɪ'læbɪk] adj monosílabo
monosyllable ['mɔnəsɪləbl] n monosílabo
monotone ['mɔnətəun] n voz f (or tono) monocorde
monotonous [mə'nɔtənəs] adj monótono
monotony [mə'nɔtənɪ] n monotonía
monoxide [mə'nɔksaɪd] n: carbon ~ monóxido de carbono
monseigneur [mɔnsen'jəːʳ], monsignor [mɔn'siːnjəʳ] n monseñor m
monsoon [mɔn'suːn] n monzón m
monster ['mɔnstəʳ] n monstruo
monstrosity [mɔns'trɔsɪtɪ] n monstruosidad f
monstrous ['mɔnstrəs] adj (huge) enorme; (atrocious) monstruoso
Mont. abbr (US) = Montana
montage [mɔn'tɑːʒ] n montaje m
Mont Blanc [mɔ̃'blɑ̃] n Mont Blanc m
month [mʌnθ] n mes m; 300 dollars a ~ 300 dólares al mes; every ~ cada mes

monthly ['mʌnθlɪ] *adj* mensual ▪ *adv*
mensualmente ▪ *n* (*magazine*) revista,
mensual; **twice** ~ dos veces al mes;
~ **instalment** mensualidad *f*
monument ['mɔnjumənt] *n* monumento
monumental [mɔnju'mɛntl] *adj*
monumental
moo [mu:] *vi* mugir
mood [mu:d] *n* humor *m*; **to be in a good/
bad** ~ estar de buen/mal humor
moodily ['mu:dɪlɪ] *adv* malhumoradamente
moodiness ['mu:dɪnɪs] *n* humor *m*
cambiante; (*bad mood*) mal humor *m*
moody ['mu:dɪ] *adj* (*variable*) de humor
variable; (*sullen*) malhumorado
moon [mu:n] *n* luna
moonbeam ['mu:nbi:m] *n* rayo de luna
moon landing *n* alunizaje *m*
moonless ['mu:nlɪs] *adj* sin luna
moonlight ['mu:nlaɪt] *n* luz *f* de la luna ▪ *vi*
hacer pluriempleo
moonlighting ['mu:nlaɪtɪŋ] *n* pluriempleo
moonlit ['mu:nlɪt] *adj*: **a** ~ **night** una noche
de luna
moonshot ['mu:nʃɔt] *n* lanzamiento de una
astronave a la luna
moonstruck ['mu:nstrʌk] *adj* chiflado
moony ['mu:nɪ] *adj*: **to have** ~ **eyes** estar
soñando despierto, estar pensando en las
musarañas
Moor [muəʳ] *n* moro(-a)
moor [muəʳ] *n* páramo ▪ *vt* (*ship*) amarrar
▪ *vi* echar las amarras
moorings ['muərɪŋz] *npl* (*chains*) amarras *fpl*;
(*place*) amarradero *sg*
Moorish ['muərɪʃ] *adj* moro; (*architecture*)
árabe
moorland ['muələnd] *n* páramo, brezal *m*
moose [mu:s] *n pl inv* alce *m*
moot [mu:t] *vt* proponer para la discusión,
sugerir ▪ *adj*: ~ **point** punto discutible
mop [mɔp] *n* fregona; (*of hair*) greñas *fpl* ▪ *vt*
fregar
▸ **mop up** *vt* limpiar
mope [məup] *vi* estar deprimido
▸ **mope about, mope around** *vi* andar
abatido
moped ['məupɛd] *n* ciclomotor *m*
moquette [mɔ'kɛt] *n* moqueta
MOR *adj abbr* (*Mus*: = *middle-of-the-road*) para el
gran público
moral ['mɔrl] *adj* moral ▪ *n* moraleja;
morals *npl* moralidad *f*, moral *f*
morale [mɔ'rɑːl] *n* moral *f*
morality [mə'rælɪtɪ] *n* moralidad *f*
moralize ['mɔrəlaɪz] *vi*: **to** ~ **(about)**
moralizar (sobre)

morally ['mɔrəlɪ] *adv* moralmente
moral victory *n* victoria moral
morass [mə'ræs] *n* pantano
moratorium [mɔrə'tɔːrɪəm] *n* moratoria
morbid ['mɔːbɪd] *adj* (*interest*) morboso; (*Med*)
mórbido

 KEYWORD

more [mɔːʳ] *adj* **1** (*greater in number etc*) más;
more people/work than before más gente/
trabajo que antes
2 (*additional*) más; **do you want (some)
more tea?** ¿quieres más té?; **is there any
more wine?** ¿queda vino?; **it'll take a few
more weeks** tardará unas semanas más;
it's 2 kms more to the house faltan 2 kms
para la casa; **more time/letters than we
expected** más tiempo del que/más cartas
de las que esperábamos; **I have no more
money, I don't have any more money** (ya)
no tengo más dinero
▪ *pron* (*greater amount, additional amount*) más;
more than 10 más de 10; **it cost more than
the other one/than we expected** costó
más que el otro/más de lo que esperábamos;
is there any more? ¿hay más?; **I want
more** quiero más; **and what's more ...** y
además ...; **many/much more** muchos(-as)/
mucho(-a) más
▪ *adv* más; **more dangerous/easily (than)**
más peligroso/fácilmente (que); **more and
more expensive** cada vez más caro; **more
or less** más o menos; **more than ever** más
que nunca; **she doesn't live here any more**
ya no vive aquí

moreover [mɔː'rəuvəʳ] *adv* además, por otra
parte
morgue [mɔːg] *n* depósito de cadáveres
MORI ['mɔːrɪ] *n abbr* (*Brit*) = **Market and
Opinion Research Institute**
moribund ['mɔrɪbʌnd] *adj* moribundo
Mormon ['mɔːmən] *n* mormón(-ona) *m(f)*
morning ['mɔːnɪŋ] *n* (*gen*) mañana; (*early
morning*) madrugada; **in the** ~ por la mañana;
7 o'clock in the ~ las 7 de la mañana; **this** ~
esta mañana
morning-after pill ['mɔːnɪŋ'ɑːftə-] *n* píldora
del día después
morning sickness *n* (*Med*) náuseas *fpl* del
embarazo
Moroccan [mə'rɔkən] *adj, n* marroquí *m/f*
Morocco [mə'rɔkəu] *n* Marruecos *m*
moron ['mɔːrɔn] *n* imbécil *m/f*
morose [mə'rəus] *adj* hosco, malhumorado
morphine ['mɔːfiːn] *n* morfina

morris dancing ['mɔrɪs-] n (Brit) baile tradicional inglés en el que se llevan cascabeles en la ropa

Morse [mɔːs] n (also: **Morse code**) (alfabeto) morse m

morsel ['mɔːsl] n (of food) bocado

mortal ['mɔːtl] adj, n mortal m

mortality [mɔːˈtælɪtɪ] n mortalidad f

mortality rate n tasa de mortalidad

mortally ['mɔːtəlɪ] adv mortalmente

mortar ['mɔːtəʳ] n argamasa; (implement) mortero

mortgage ['mɔːgɪdʒ] n hipoteca ■ vt hipotecar; **to take out a** ~ sacar una hipoteca

mortgage company n (US) ≈ banco hipotecario

mortgagee [mɔːgəˈdʒiː] n acreedor(a) m(f) hipotecario(-a)

mortgager ['mɔːgədʒəʳ] n deudor(a) m(f) hipotecario(-a)

mortice ['mɔːtɪs] = **mortise**

mortician [mɔːˈtɪʃən] n (US) director(a) m(f) de pompas fúnebres

mortification ['mɔːtɪfɪˈkeɪʃən] n mortificación f, humillación f

mortified ['mɔːtɪfaɪd] adj: **I was** ~ me dio muchísima vergüenza

mortise ['mɔːtɪs], **mortise lock** n cerradura de muesca

mortuary ['mɔːtjuərɪ] n depósito de cadáveres

mosaic [məuˈzeɪɪk] n mosaico

Moscow ['mɔskəu] n Moscú m

Moslem ['mɔzləm] adj, n = **Muslim**

mosque [mɔsk] n mezquita

mosquito (pl **mosquitoes**) [mɔsˈkiːtəu] n mosquito

moss [mɔs] n musgo

mossy ['mɔsɪ] adj musgoso, cubierto de musgo

most [məust] adj la mayor parte de, la mayoría de ■ pron la mayor parte, la mayoría ■ adv el más; (very) muy; **the** ~ (also: + adjective) el más; ~ **of them** la mayor parte de ellos; **I saw the** ~ yo fui el que más vi; **at the (very)** ~ a lo sumo, todo lo más; **to make the** ~ **of** aprovechar (al máximo); **a** ~ **interesting book** un libro interesantísimo

mostly ['məustlɪ] adv en su mayor parte, principalmente

MOT n abbr (Brit: = Ministry of Transport): **the** ~ **(test)** ≈ la ITV

motel [məuˈtɛl] n motel m

moth [mɔθ] n mariposa nocturna; (clothes moth) polilla

mothball ['mɔθbɔːl] n bola de naftalina

moth-eaten ['mɔθiːtn] adj apolillado

mother ['mʌðəʳ] n madre f ■ adj materno ■ vt (care for) cuidar (como una madre)

mother board n (Comput) placa madre

motherhood ['mʌðəhud] n maternidad f

mother-in-law ['mʌðərɪnlɔː] n suegra

motherly ['mʌðəlɪ] adj maternal

mother-of-pearl ['mʌðərəv'pəːl] n nácar m

mother's help n niñera

mother-to-be ['mʌðətə'biː] n futura madre

mother tongue n lengua materna

mothproof ['mɔθpruːf] adj a prueba de polillas

motif [məuˈtiːf] n motivo; (theme) tema m

motion ['məuʃən] n movimiento; (gesture) ademán m, señal f; (at meeting) moción f; (Brit: also: **bowel motion**) evacuación f intestinal ■ vt, vi: **to** ~ **(to) sb to do sth** hacer señas a algn para que haga algo; **to be in** ~ (vehicle) estar en movimiento; **to set in** ~ poner en marcha; **to go through the motions of doing sth** (fig) hacer algo mecánicamente or sin convicción

motionless ['məuʃənlɪs] adj inmóvil

motion picture n película

motivate ['məutɪveɪt] vt motivar

motivated ['məutɪveɪtɪd] adj motivado

motivation [məutɪˈveɪʃən] n motivación f

motivational research [məutɪˈveɪʃənl-] n estudios mpl de motivación

motive ['məutɪv] n motivo; **from the best motives** con las mejores intenciones

motley ['mɔtlɪ] adj variopinto

motor ['məutəʳ] n motor m; (Brit: col: vehicle) coche m, carro (LAm), automóvil m, auto m (LAm) ■ adj motor/motora, motriz

motorbike ['məutəbaɪk] n moto f

motorboat ['məutəbəut] n lancha motora

motorcade ['məutəkeɪd] n desfile m de automóviles

motorcar ['məutəkaːʳ] n (Brit) coche m, carro (LAm), automóvil m, auto m (LAm)

motorcoach ['məutəkəutʃ] n autocar m, autobús m, camión m (LAm)

motorcycle ['məutəsaɪkl] n motocicleta

motorcycle racing n motociclismo

motorcyclist ['məutəsaɪklɪst] n motociclista m/f

motoring ['məutərɪŋ] n (Brit) automovilismo ■ adj (accident, offence) de tráfico or tránsito

motorist ['məutərɪst] n conductor(a) m(f), automovilista m/f

motorize ['məutəraɪz] vt motorizar

motor oil n aceite m para motores

motor racing n (Brit) carreras fpl de coches, automovilismo

motor scooter n vespa®
motor vehicle n automóvil m
motorway ['məutəweɪ] n (Brit) autopista
mottled ['mɔtld] adj moteado
motto (pl **mottoes**) ['mɔtəu] n lema m; (watchword) consigna
mould, mold (US) [məuld] n molde m; (mildew) moho ■ vt moldear; (fig) formar
moulder, molder (US) ['məuldə'] vi (decay) decaer
moulding, molding (US) ['məuldɪŋ] n (Arch) moldura
mouldy, moldy (US) ['məuldɪ] adj enmohecido
moult, molt (US) [məult] vi mudar la piel; (bird) mudar las plumas
mound [maund] n montón m, montículo
mount [maunt] n monte m; (horse) montura; (for jewel etc) engarce m; (for picture) marco ■ vt montar en, subir a; (stairs) subir; (exhibition) montar; (attack) lanzar; (stamp) pegar, fijar; (picture) enmarcar ■ vi (also: **mount up**) subirse, montarse
mountain ['mauntɪn] n montaña ■ cpd de montaña; **to make a ~ out of a molehill** hacer una montaña de un grano de arena
mountain bike n bicicleta de montaña
mountaineer [mauntɪ'nɪə'] n montañero(-a), alpinista m/f, andinista m/f (LAm)
mountaineering [mauntɪ'nɪərɪŋ] n montañismo, alpinismo, andinismo (LAm)
mountainous ['mauntɪnəs] adj montañoso
mountain range n sierra
mountain rescue team n equipo de rescate de montaña
mountainside ['mauntɪnsaɪd] n ladera de la montaña
mounted ['mauntɪd] adj montado
Mount Everest n Monte m Everest
mourn [mɔːn] vt llorar, lamentar ■ vi: **to ~ for** llorar la muerte de, lamentarse por
mourner ['mɔːnə'] n doliente m/f
mournful ['mɔːnful] adj triste, lúgubre
mourning ['mɔːnɪŋ] n luto ■ cpd (dress) de luto; **in ~** de luto
mouse (pl **mice**) [maus, maɪs] n (also Comput) ratón m
mouse mat, mouse pad n (Comput) alfombrilla, almohadilla
mousetrap ['maustræp] n ratonera
mousse [muːs] n (Culin) mousse f; (for hair) espuma (moldeadora)
moustache [məs'tɑːʃ], (US) **mustache** ['mʌstæʃ] n bigote m
mousy ['mausɪ] adj (person) tímido; (hair) pardusco

mouth (pl **mouths**) [mauθ, -ðz] n boca; (of river) desembocadura
mouthful ['mauθful] n bocado
mouth organ n armónica
mouthpiece ['mauθpiːs] n (of musical instrument) boquilla; (Tel) micrófono; (spokesman) portavoz m/f
mouth-to-mouth ['mauθtə'mauθ] adj (also: **mouth-to-mouth resuscitation**) boca a boca m
mouthwash ['mauθwɔʃ] n enjuague m bucal
mouth-watering ['mauθwɔːtərɪŋ] adj apetitoso
movable ['muːvəbl] adj movible
move [muːv] n (movement) movimiento; (in game) jugada; (: turn to play) turno; (change of house) mudanza ■ vt mover; (emotionally) conmover; (Pol: resolution etc) proponer ■ vi (gen) moverse; (traffic) circular; (Brit: also: **move house**) trasladarse, mudarse; **to ~ sb to do sth** mover a algn a hacer algo; **to be moved** estar conmovido; **to get a ~ on** darse prisa
▸ **move about** or **around** vi moverse; (travel) viajar
▸ **move along** vi (stop loitering) circular; (along seat etc) correrse
▸ **move away** vi (leave) marcharse
▸ **move back** vi (return) volver
▸ **move down** vt (demote) degradar
▸ **move forward** vi avanzar ■ vt adelantar
▸ **move in** vi (to a house) instalarse
▸ **move off** vi ponerse en camino
▸ **move on** vi seguir viaje ■ vt (onlookers) hacer circular
▸ **move out** vi (of house) mudarse
▸ **move over** vi hacerse a un lado, correrse
▸ **move up** vi subir; (employee) ascender
movement ['muːvmənt] n movimiento; (Tech) mecanismo; **~ (of the bowels)** (Med) evacuación f
mover ['muːvə'] n proponente m/f
movie ['muːvɪ] n película; **to go to the movies** ir al cine
movie camera n cámara cinematográfica
moviegoer ['muːvɪɡəuə'] n (US) aficionado(-a) al cine
moving ['muːvɪŋ] adj (emotional) conmovedor(a); (that moves) móvil; (instigating) motor(a)
mow (pt **mowed**, pp **mowed** or **mown**) [məu, -n] vt (grass) cortar; (corn) segar; (also: **mow down**: shoot) acribillar
mower ['məuə'] n (also: **lawnmower**) cortacésped m
Mozambique [məuzæm'biːk] n Mozambique m

MP n abbr (= Military Police) PM; (Brit)
= **Member of Parliament**; (Canada)
= **Mounted Police**
mpg n abbr (= miles per gallon) 30 mpg = 9.4 l. per
100 km
mph abbr (= miles per hour) 60 mph = 96 km/h
MPhil n abbr (= Master of Philosophy) título
universitario de postgrado; see also **master's
degree**
MPS n abbr (Brit) = **Member of the
Pharmaceutical Society**
MP3 ['empi:'θri:] n MP3 m
MP3 player n reproductor m MP3
Mr, Mr. ['mɪstər] n: **Mr Smith** (el) Sr. Smith
MRC n abbr (Brit: = Medical Research Council)
departamento estatal que controla la investigación
médica
MRCP n abbr (Brit) = **Member of the Royal
College of Physicians**
MRCS n abbr (Brit) = **Member of the Royal
College of Surgeons**
MRCVS n abbr (Brit) = **Member of the Royal
College of Veterinary Surgeons**
Mrs, Mrs. ['mɪsɪz] n: ~ **Smith** (la) Sra. de
Smith
MS n abbr (= manuscript) MS; = **multiple
sclerosis**; (US: = Master of Science) título
universitario ▪ abbr (US) = **Mississippi**
Ms, Ms. [mɪz] n (Miss or Mrs) abreviatura con la
que se evita hacer expreso el estado civil de una mujer
MSA n abbr (US: = Master of Science in Agriculture)
título universitario
MSc abbr see **Master of Science**
MSG n abbr = **monosodium glutamate**
MSP n abbr (Brit) = **Member of the Scottish
Parliament**
MST abbr (US: = Mountain Standard Time) hora de
invierno de las Montañas Rocosas
MSW n abbr (US: = Master of Social Work) título
universitario
MT abbr (US: = Montana) ▪ n abbr = **machine
translation**
Mt abbr (Geo: = mount) m
mth abbr (= month) m
MTV n abbr = **music television**
much [mʌtʃ] adj mucho ▪ adv, n, pron mucho;
(before pp) muy; **how ~ is it?** ¿cuánto es?,
¿cuánto cuesta?; **too ~** demasiado; **so ~**
tanto; **it's not ~** no es mucho; **as ~ as** tanto
como; **however ~ he tries** por mucho que
se esfuerce; **I like it very/so ~** me gusta
mucho/tanto; **thank you very ~** muchas
gracias, muy agradecido
muck [mʌk] n (dirt) suciedad f; (fig) porquería
▸ **muck about** or **around** vi (col) perder el
tiempo; (enjoy o.s.) entretenerse; (tinker)
manosear

▸ **muck in** vi (col) arrimar el hombro
▸ **muck out** vt (stable) limpiar
▸ **muck up** vt (col: dirty) ensuciar; (: spoil)
echar a perder; (: ruin) estropear
muckraking ['mʌkreɪkɪŋ] (fig col) n
amarillismo ▪ adj especializado en
escándalos
mucky ['mʌkɪ] adj (dirty) sucio
mucus ['mju:kəs] n mucosidad f, moco
mud [mʌd] n barro, lodo
muddle ['mʌdl] n desorden m, confusión f;
(mix-up) embrollo, lío ▪ vt (also: **muddle up**)
embrollar, confundir
▸ **muddle along, muddle on** vi
arreglárselas de alguna manera
▸ **muddle through** vi salir del paso
muddle-headed [mʌdl'hɛdɪd] adj (person)
despistado, confuso
muddy ['mʌdɪ] adj fangoso, cubierto de lodo
mudguard ['mʌdɡɑ:d] n guardabarros m inv
mudpack ['mʌdpæk] n mascarilla
mud-slinging ['mʌdslɪŋɪŋ] n injurias fpl,
difamación f
muesli ['mju:zlɪ] n muesli m
muff [mʌf] n manguito ▪ vt (chance)
desperdiciar; (lines) estropear; (shot, catch etc)
fallar; **to ~ it** fracasar
muffin ['mʌfɪn] n bollo
muffle ['mʌfl] vt (sound) amortiguar; (against
cold) abrigar
muffled ['mʌfld] adj sordo, apagado
muffler ['mʌflər] n (scarf) bufanda; (US Aut)
silenciador m; (on motorbike) silenciador m,
mofle m
mufti ['mʌftɪ] n: **in ~** (vestido) de paisano
mug [mʌɡ] n (cup) taza alta; (for beer) jarra;
(col: face) jeta; (: fool) bobo ▪ vt (assault)
atracar; **it's a ~'s game** es cosa de bobos
▸ **mug up** vt (col: also: **mug up on**) empollar
mugger ['mʌɡər] n atracador(a) m(f)
mugging ['mʌɡɪŋ] n atraco callejero
muggins ['mʌɡɪnz] nsg (col) tonto(-a) el bote
muggy ['mʌɡɪ] adj bochornoso
mug shot n (col) foto f (para la ficha policial)
mulatto (pl **mulattoes**) [mju:'lætəu] n
mulato(-a)
mulberry ['mʌlbrɪ] n (fruit) mora; (tree)
morera, moral m
mule [mju:l] n mula
mull [mʌl] **to ~ over** vt meditar sobre
mulled [mʌld] adj: ~ **wine** vino caliente (con
especias)
mullioned ['mʌlɪənd] adj (window) dividido
por parteluces
multi... [mʌltɪ] pref multi...
multi-access ['mʌltɪækses] adj (Comput)
multiacceso, de acceso múltiple

667

multicoloured, (US) **multicolored** ['mʌltɪkʌləd] adj multicolor

multifarious [mʌltɪ'fɛərɪəs] adj múltiple, vario

multilateral [mʌltɪ'lætərl] adj (Pol) multilateral

multi-level [mʌltɪ'lɛvl] adj (US) = **multi-storey**

multimillionaire [mʌltɪmɪljə'nɛəʳ] n multimillonario(-a)

multinational [mʌltɪ'næʃənl] n multinacional f ■ adj multinacional

multiple ['mʌltɪpl] adj múltiple ■ n múltiplo; (Brit: also: **multiple store**) (cadena de) grandes almacenes mpl

multiple choice n examen m de tipo test

multiple crash n colisión f en cadena

multiple sclerosis [-sklɪ'rəusɪs] n esclerosis f múltiple

multiplex ['mʌltɪplɛks] n (also: **multiplex cinema**) multicines m inv

multiplication [mʌltɪplɪ'keɪʃən] n multiplicación f

multiplication table n tabla de multiplicar

multiplicity [mʌltɪ'plɪsɪtɪ] n multiplicidad f

multiply ['mʌltɪplaɪ] vt multiplicar ■ vi multiplicarse

multiracial [mʌltɪ'reɪʃl] adj multirracial

multistorey [mʌltɪ'stɔːrɪ] adj (Brit: building, car park) de muchos pisos

multi-tasking ['mʌltɪtɑːskɪŋ] n (Comput) ejecución f de tareas múltiples, multitarea

multitude ['mʌltɪtjuːd] n multitud f

mum [mʌm] n (Brit) mamá ■ adj: **to keep ~ (about sth)** no decir ni mu (de algo)

mumble ['mʌmbl] vt decir entre dientes ■ vi hablar entre dientes, musitar

mumbo jumbo ['mʌmbəu-] n (col) galimatías m inv

mummify ['mʌmɪfaɪ] vt momificar

mummy ['mʌmɪ] n (Brit: mother) mamá; (embalmed) momia

mumps [mʌmps] n paperas fpl

munch [mʌntʃ] vt, vi mascar

mundane [mʌn'deɪn] adj mundano

municipal [mju:'nɪsɪpl] adj municipal

municipality [mju:nɪsɪ'pælɪtɪ] n municipio

munificence [mu:'nɪfɪsns] n munificencia

munitions [mju:'nɪʃənz] npl municiones fpl

mural ['mjuərl] n (pintura) mural m

murder ['mə:dəʳ] n asesinato; (in law) homicidio ■ vt asesinar, matar; **to commit ~** cometer un asesinato or homicidio

murderer ['mə:dərəʳ] n asesino

murderess ['mə:dərɪs] n asesina

murderous ['mə:dərəs] adj homicida

murk [mə:k] n oscuridad f, tinieblas fpl

murky ['mə:kɪ] adj (water, past) turbio; (room) sombrío

murmur ['mə:məʳ] n murmullo ■ vt, vi murmurar; **heart ~** soplo cardíaco

MusB, MusBac n abbr (= Bachelor of Music) título universitario

muscle ['mʌsl] n músculo
▸ **muscle in** vi entrometerse

muscular ['mʌskjuləʳ] adj muscular; (person) musculoso

muscular dystrophy n distrofia muscular

MusD, MusDoc n abbr (= Doctor of Music) título universitario

muse [mju:z] vi meditar ■ n musa

museum [mju:'zɪəm] n museo

mush [mʌʃ] n gachas fpl

mushroom ['mʌʃrum] n (gen) seta, hongo; (small) champiñón m ■ vi (fig) crecer de la noche a la mañana

mushy ['mʌʃɪ] adj (vegetables) casi hecho puré; (story) sentimentaloide

music ['mju:zɪk] n música

musical ['mju:zɪkl] adj melodioso; (person) musical ■ n (show) (comedia) musical m

musical box n = **music box**

musical chairs n juego de las sillas; (fig): **to play ~** cambiar de puesto continuamente

musical instrument n instrumento musical

musically ['mju:zɪklɪ] adv melodiosamente, armoniosamente

music box n caja de música

music centre n equipo de música

music hall n teatro de variedades

musician [mju:'zɪʃən] n músico(-a)

music stand n atril m

musk [mʌsk] n (perfume m de) almizcle m

musket ['mʌskɪt] n mosquete m

musk rat n ratón m almizclero

musk rose n (Bot) rosa almizcleña

Muslim ['mʌzlɪm] adj, n musulmán(-ana) m(f)

muslin ['mʌzlɪn] n muselina

musquash ['mʌskwɔʃ] n (fur) piel f del ratón almizclero

muss [mʌs] vt (col: hair) despeinar; (: dress) arrugar

mussel ['mʌsl] n mejillón m

must [mʌst] aux vb (obligation): **I ~ do it** debo hacerlo, tengo que hacerlo; (probability): **he ~ be there by now** ya debe (de) estar allí ■ n: **it's a ~** es imprescindible

mustache ['mʌstæʃ] n (US) = **moustache**

mustard ['mʌstəd] n mostaza

mustard gas n gas m mostaza

muster ['mʌstəʳ] vt juntar, reunir; (also: **muster up**) reunir; (: courage) armarse de

mustiness ['mʌstɪnɪs] n olor m a cerrado

mustn't ['mʌsnt] = **must not**

musty ['mʌstɪ] *adj* mohoso, que huele a humedad
mutant ['mju:tənt] *adj*, *n* mutante *m*
mutate [mju:'teɪt] *vi* sufrir mutación, transformarse
mutation [mju:'teɪʃən] *n* mutación *f*
mute [mju:t] *adj*, *n* mudo(-a) *m(f)*
muted ['mju:tɪd] *adj* (*noise*) sordo; (*criticism*) callado
mutilate ['mju:tɪleɪt] *vt* mutilar
mutilation [mju:tɪ'leɪʃən] *n* mutilación *f*
mutinous ['mju:tɪnəs] *adj* (*troops*) amotinado; (*attitude*) rebelde
mutiny ['mju:tɪnɪ] *n* motín *m* ◼ *vi* amotinarse
mutter ['mʌtəʳ] *vt*, *vi* murmurar
mutton ['mʌtn] *n* (carne *f* de) cordero
mutual ['mju:tʃuəl] *adj* mutuo; (*friend*) común
mutually ['mju:tʃuəlɪ] *adv* mutuamente
Muzak® ['mju:zæk] *n* hilo musical
muzzle ['mʌzl] *n* hocico; (*protective device*) bozal *m*; (*of gun*) boca ◼ *vt* amordazar; (*dog*) poner un bozal a
MV *abbr* = **motor vessel**
MVP *n abbr* (*US Sport*) = **most valuable player**
MW *abbr* (Radio: – *medium wave*) onda media
my [maɪ] *adj* mi(s); **my house/brother/**
sisters mi casa/hermano/mis hermanas;
I've washed my hair/cut my finger me he lavado el pelo/cortado un dedo; **is this my pen or yours?** ¿este bolígrafo es mío o tuyo?
Myanmar ['maɪænmɑ:ʳ] *n* Myanmar
myopic [maɪ'ɒpɪk] *adj* miope
myriad ['mɪrɪəd] *n* (*of people, things*) miríada
myrrh [mə:ʳ] *n* mirra
myself [maɪ'sɛlf] *pron* (*reflexive*) me; (*emphatic*) yo mismo; (*after prep*) mí (mismo); *see also* **oneself**
mysterious [mɪs'tɪərɪəs] *adj* misterioso
mysteriously [mɪs'tɪərɪəslɪ] *adv* misteriosamente
mystery ['mɪstərɪ] *n* misterio
mystery play *n* auto, misterio
mystic ['mɪstɪk] *adj*, *n* místico(-a) *m(f)*
mystical ['mɪstɪkl] *adj* místico
mysticism ['mɪstɪsɪzəm] *n* misticismo
mystification [mɪstɪfɪ'keɪʃən] *n* perplejidad *f*; desconcierto
mystify ['mɪstɪfaɪ] *vt* (*perplex*) dejar perplejo; (*disconcert*) desconcertar
mystique [mɪs'ti:k] *n* misterio
myth [mɪθ] *n* mito
mythical ['mɪθɪkl] *adj* mítico
mythological [mɪθə'lɒdʒɪkl] *adj* mitológico
mythology [mɪ'θɒlədʒɪ] *n* mitología

m

Nn

N, n [ɛn] *n (letter)* N, n *f*; **N for Nellie**, *(US)*
N for Nan N de Navarra

N *abbr* (= *North*) N

NA *n abbr* (US: = *Narcotics Anonymous*) *organización de ayuda a los drogadictos*; *(US)* = **National Academy**

n/a *abbr* (= *not applicable*) no interesa; *(Comm etc)* = **no account**

NAACP *n abbr* (US) = **National Association for the Advancement of Colored People**

NAAFI ['næfɪ] *n abbr* (Brit: = *Navy, Army & Air Force Institutes*) *servicio de cantinas etc para las fuerzas armadas*

nab [næb] *vt (col: grab)* coger (SP), agarrar (LAm); *(: catch out)* pillar

NACU *n abbr* (US) = **National Association of Colleges and Universities**

nadir ['neɪdɪəʳ] *n (Astro)* nadir *m*; *(fig)* punto más bajo

NAFTA ['næftə] *n abbr* (= *North Atlantic Free Trade Agreement*) TLC *m*

nag [næg] *n (pej: horse)* rocín *m* ■ *vt (scold)* regañar; *(annoy)* fastidiar

nagging ['nægɪŋ] *adj (doubt)* persistente; *(pain)* continuo ■ *n* quejas *fpl*

nail [neɪl] *n (human)* uña; *(metal)* clavo ■ *vt* clavar; *(fig: catch)* coger (SP), pillar; **to pay cash on the ~** pagar a tocateja; **to ~ sb down to a date/price** hacer que algn se comprometa a una fecha/un precio

nailbrush ['neɪlbrʌʃ] *n* cepillo para las uñas

nailfile ['neɪlfaɪl] *n* lima para las uñas

nail polish *n* esmalte *m or* laca para las uñas

nail polish remover *n* quitaesmalte *m*

nail scissors *npl* tijeras *fpl* para las uñas

nail varnish *n* (Brit) = **nail polish**

Nairobi [naɪˈrəʊbɪ] *n* Nairobi *m*

naïve [naɪˈiːv] *adj* ingenuo

naïvely [naɪˈiːvlɪ] *adv* ingenuamente

naïveté [naːˈiːvteɪ], **naivety** [naɪˈiːvɪtɪ] *n* ingenuidad *f*, candidez *f*

naked ['neɪkɪd] *adj (nude)* desnudo; *(flame)* expuesto al aire; **with the ~ eye** a simple vista

NAM *n abbr* (US) = **National Association of Manufacturers**

name [neɪm] *n (gen)* nombre *m*; *(surname)* apellido; *(reputation)* fama, renombre *m* ■ *vt (child)* poner nombre a; *(appoint)* nombrar; **by ~** de nombre; **in the ~ of** en nombre de; **what's your ~?** ¿cómo se llama usted?; **my ~ is Peter** me llamo Pedro; **to give one's ~ and address** dar sus señas; **to take sb's ~ and address** apuntar las señas de algn; **to make a ~ for o.s.** hacerse famoso; **to get (o.s.) a bad ~** forjarse una mala reputación

name-drop ['neɪmdrɒp] *vi*: **he's always name-dropping** siempre está presumiendo de la gente que conoce

nameless ['neɪmlɪs] *adj* anónimo, sin nombre

namely ['neɪmlɪ] *adv* a saber

nameplate ['neɪmpleɪt] *n (on door etc)* placa

namesake ['neɪmseɪk] *n* tocayo(-a)

nan bread [naːn-] *n* pan indio sin apenas levadura

nanny ['nænɪ] *n* niñera

nap [næp] *n (sleep)* sueñecito, siesta; **they were caught napping** les pilló desprevenidos

NAPA *n abbr* (US: = *National Association of Performing Artists*) *sindicato de trabajadores del espectáculo*

napalm ['neɪpaːm] *n* napalm *m*

nape [neɪp] *n*: **~ of the neck** nuca, cogote *m*

napkin ['næpkɪn] *n (also:* **table napkin***)* servilleta

Naples ['neɪplz] *n* Nápoles

nappy ['næpɪ] *n (Brit)* pañal *m*

nappy liner *n* gasa

nappy rash *n* prurito

narcissism [naːˈsɪsɪzəm] *n* narcisismo

narcissus *(pl* **narcissi***)* [naːˈsɪsəs, -saɪ] *n* narciso

narcotic [naːˈkɒtɪk] *adj, n* narcótico

narrate [nəˈreɪt] *vt* narrar, contar

narration [nəˈreɪʃən] *n* narración *f*, relato

narrative ['nærətɪv] *n* narrativa ■ *adj* narrativo

narrator [nəˈreɪtə^r] n narrador(a) m(f)
narrow [ˈnærəu] adj estrecho; (resources, means) escaso ■ vi estrecharse; (diminish) reducirse; **to have a ~ escape** escaparse por los pelos; **to ~ sth down** reducir algo
narrow gauge adj (Rail) de vía estrecha
narrowly [ˈnærəlɪ] adv (miss) por poco
narrow-minded [nærəuˈmaɪndɪd] adj de miras estrechas
narrow-mindedness [ˈnærəuˈmaɪndɪdnɪs] n estrechez f de miras
NAS n abbr (US) = **National Academy of Sciences**
NASA n abbr (US: = National Aeronautics and Space Administration) NASA f
nasal [ˈneɪzl] adj nasal
Nassau [ˈnæsɔ:] n (in Bahamas) Nassau m
nastily [ˈnɑ:stɪlɪ] adv (unpleasantly) de mala manera; (spitefully) con rencor
nastiness [ˈnɑ:stɪnɪs] n (malice) malevolencia; (rudeness) grosería; (of person, remark) maldad f; (spitefulness) rencor m
nasturtium [nəsˈtə:ʃəm] n capuchina
nasty [ˈnɑ:stɪ] adj (remark) feo; (person) antipático; (revolting: taste, smell) asqueroso; (wound, disease etc) peligroso, grave; **to turn ~** (situation) ponerse feo; (weather) empeorar; (person) ponerse negro
NAS/UWT n abbr (Brit: = National Association of Schoolmasters/Union of Women Teachers) sindicato de profesores
nation [ˈneɪʃən] n nación f
national [ˈnæʃənl] adj nacional ■ n súbdito(-a)
national anthem n himno nacional
National Curriculum n (Brit) plan m general de estudios (en Inglaterra y Gales)
national debt n deuda pública
national dress n traje m típico del país
National Guard n (US) Guardia Nacional
National Health Service n (Brit) servicio nacional de sanidad, ≈ INSALUD m (SP)
National Insurance n (Brit) seguro social nacional, ≈ Seguridad f Social
nationalism [ˈnæʃnəlɪzəm] n nacionalismo
nationalist [ˈnæʃnəlɪst] adj, n nacionalista m/f
nationality [næʃəˈnælɪtɪ] n nacionalidad f
nationalization [næʃnəlaɪˈzeɪʃən] n nacionalización f
nationalize [ˈnæʃnəlaɪz] vt nacionalizar; **nationalized industry** industria nacionalizada
nationally [ˈnæʃnəlɪ] adv (nationwide) a escala nacional; (as a nation) como nación
national press n prensa nacional
national service n (Mil) servicio militar

National Trust n (Brit) organización encargada de preservar el patrimonio histórico británico
nationwide [ˈneɪʃənwaɪd] adj a escala nacional
native [ˈneɪtɪv] n (local inhabitant) natural m/f; (in colonies) indígena m/f, nativo(-a) ■ adj (indigenous) indígena; (country) natal; (innate) natural, innato; **a ~ of Russia** un(a) natural de Rusia; **~ language** lengua materna; **a ~ speaker of French** un hablante nativo de francés
Native American adj, n americano(-a) indígena m(f), amerindio(-a) m(f)
Nativity [nəˈtɪvɪtɪ] n: **the ~** Navidad f
nativity play n auto del nacimiento
NATO [ˈneɪtəu] n abbr (= North Atlantic Treaty Organization) OTAN f
natter [ˈnætə^r] vi (Brit) charlar ■ n: **to have a ~** charlar
natural [ˈnætʃrəl] adj natural; **death from ~ causes** (Law) muerte f por causas naturales
natural childbirth n parto natural
natural gas n gas m natural
natural history n historia natural
naturalist [ˈnætʃrəlɪst] n naturalista m/f
naturalization [nætʃrəlaɪˈzeɪʃən] n naturalización f
naturalize [ˈnætʃrəlaɪz] vt: **to become naturalized** (person) naturalizarse; (plant) aclimatarse
naturally [ˈnætʃrəlɪ] adv (speak etc) naturalmente; (of course) desde luego, por supuesto, ¡cómo no! (LAm); (instinctively) por naturaleza
naturalness [ˈnætʃrəlnɪs] n naturalidad f
natural resources npl recursos mpl naturales
natural selection n selección f natural
natural wastage n (Industry) desgaste m natural
nature [ˈneɪtʃə^r] n naturaleza; (group, sort) género, clase f; (character) modo de ser, carácter m; **by ~** por naturaleza; **documents of a confidential ~** documentos mpl de tipo confidencial
-natured [ˈneɪtʃəd] suff: **ill~** malhumorado
nature reserve n reserva natural
nature trail n camino forestal educativo
naturist [ˈneɪtʃərɪst] n naturista m/f
naught [nɔ:t] = **nought**
naughtily [ˈnɔ:tɪlɪ] adv (behave) mal; (say) con malicia
naughtiness [ˈnɔ:tɪnɪs] n travesuras fpl
naughty [ˈnɔ:tɪ] adj (child) travieso; (story, film) picante, escabroso, colorado (LAm)
nausea [ˈnɔ:sɪə] n náusea
nauseate [ˈnɔ:sɪeɪt] vt dar náuseas a; (fig) dar asco a

n

nauseating ['nɔ:sieitiŋ] *adj* nauseabundo; (*fig*) asqueroso, repugnante

nauseous ['nɔ:siəs] *adj* nauseabundo; **to feel ~** sentir náuseas

nautical ['nɔ:tikl] *adj* náutico, marítimo; **~ mile** milla marina

naval ['neivl] *adj* naval, de marina

naval officer *n* oficial *m/f* de marina

nave [neiv] *n* nave *f*

navel ['neivl] *n* ombligo

navigable ['nævigəbl] *adj* navegable

navigate ['nævigeit] *vt* (*ship*) gobernar; (*river etc*) navegar por ▪ *vi* navegar; (*Aut*) hacer de copiloto

navigation [nævi'geiʃən] *n* (*action*) navegación *f*; (*science*) náutica

navigator ['nævigeitər] *n* navegante *m/f*

navvy ['nævi] *n* (*Brit*) peón *m* caminero

navy ['neivi] *n* marina de guerra; (*ships*) armada, flota ▪ *adj* azul marino

navy-blue ['neivi'blu:] *adj* azul marino

Nazareth ['næzəriθ] *n* Nazaret *m*

Nazi ['nɑ:tsi] *adj, n* nazi *m/f*

NB *abbr* (= *nota bene*) nótese; (*Canada*) = **New Brunswick**

NBA *n abbr* (*US*) = **National Basketball Association; National Boxing Association**

NBC *n abbr* (*US*: = *National Broadcasting Company*) *cadena de televisión*

NBS *n abbr* (*US*: = *National Bureau of Standards*) ≈ Oficina Nacional de Normalización

NC *abbr* (*Comm etc*: = *no charge*: *US*) = **North Carolina**

NCC *n abbr* (*Brit*: = *Nature Conservancy Council*) ≈ ICONA *m*; (*US*) = **National Council of Churches**

NCCL *n abbr* (*Brit*: = *National Council for Civil Liberties*) *asociación para la defensa de las libertades públicas*

NCO *n abbr* = **non-commissioned officer**

ND, N. Dak. *abbr* (*US*) = **North Dakota**

NE *abbr* (*US*) = **Nebraska; New England**

NEA *n abbr* (*US*) = **National Education Association**

Neapolitan [niə'pɔlitən] *adj, n* napolitano(-a) *m(f)*

neap tide [ni:p-] *n* marea muerta

near [niər] *adj* (*place, relation*) cercano; (*time*) próximo ▪ *adv* cerca ▪ *prep* (*also*: **near to**: *space*) cerca de, junto a; (: *time*) cerca de ▪ *vt* acercarse a, aproximarse a; **~ here/there** cerca de aquí/de allí; **£25,000 or nearest offer** 25,000 libras o precio a discutir; **in the ~ future** en fecha próxima; **the building is nearing completion** el edificio está casi terminado

nearby [niə'bai] *adj* cercano, próximo

▪ *adv* cerca

nearly ['niəli] *adv* casi, por poco; **I ~ fell** por poco me caigo; **not ~** ni mucho menos, ni con mucho

near miss *n* (*shot*) tiro casi en el blanco; (*Aviat*) *accidente evitado por muy poco*

nearness ['niənis] *n* cercanía, proximidad *f*

nearside ['niəsaid] *n* (*Aut*: *right-hand drive*) lado izquierdo; (: *left-hand drive*) lado derecho

near-sighted [niə'saitid] *adj* miope, corto de vista

neat [ni:t] *adj* (*place*) ordenado, bien cuidado; (*person*) pulcro; (*plan*) ingenioso; (*spirits*) solo

neatly ['ni:tli] *adv* (*tidily*) con esmero; (*skilfully*) ingeniosamente

neatness ['ni:tnis] *n* (*tidiness*) orden *m*; (*skilfulness*) destreza, habilidad *f*

Nebr. *abbr* (*US*) = **Nebraska**

nebulous ['nɛbjuləs] *adj* (*fig*) vago, confuso

necessarily ['nɛsisrili] *adv* necesariamente; **not ~** no necesariamente

necessary ['nɛsisri] *adj* necesario, preciso; **he did all that was ~** hizo todo lo necesario; **if ~** si es necesario

necessitate [ni'sɛsiteit] *vt* necesitar, precisar

necessity [ni'sɛsiti] *n* necesidad *f*; **necessities** *npl* artículos *mpl* de primera necesidad; **in case of ~** en caso de urgencia

neck [nɛk] *n* (*Anat*) cuello; (*of animal*) pescuezo ▪ *vi* besuquearse; **~ and ~** parejos; **to stick one's ~ out** (*col*) arriesgarse

necklace ['nɛklis] *n* collar *m*

neckline ['nɛklain] *n* escote *m*

necktie ['nɛktai] *n* (*US*) corbata

nectar ['nɛktər] *n* néctar *m*

nectarine ['nɛktərin] *n* nectarina

née [nei] *adj*: **~ Scott** de soltera Scott

need [ni:d] *n* (*lack*) escasez *f*, falta; (*necessity*) necesidad *f* ▪ *vt* (*require*) necesitar; **in case of ~** en caso de necesidad; **there's no ~ for ...** no hace(n) falta ...; **to be in ~ of, have ~ of** necesitar; **10 will meet my immediate needs** 10 satisfacerán mis necesidades más apremiantes; **the needs of industry** las necesidades de la industria; **I ~ it** lo necesito; **a signature is needed** se requiere una firma; **I ~ to do it** tengo que hacerlo; **you don't ~ to go** no hace falta que vayas

needle ['ni:dl] *n* aguja ▪ *vt* (*fig: col*) picar, fastidiar

needless ['ni:dlis] *adj* innecesario, inútil; **~ to say** huelga decir que

needlessly ['ni:dlisli] *adv* innecesariamente, inútilmente

needlework ['ni:dlwə:k] *n* (*activity*) costura, labor *f* de aguja

needn't ['niːdnt] = **need not**
needy ['niːdɪ] adj necesitado
negation [nɪ'geɪʃən] n negación f
negative ['nɛgətɪv] n (Phot) negativo; (answer) negativa; (Ling) negación f ▪ adj negativo
negative cash flow n flujo negativo de efectivo
negative equity n situación en la que el valor de la vivienda es menor que el de la hipoteca que pesa sobre ella
neglect [nɪ'glɛkt] vt (one's duty) faltar a, no cumplir con; (child) descuidar, desatender ▪ n (state) abandono; (personal) dejadez f; (of duty) incumplimiento; **to ~ to do sth** olvidarse de hacer algo
neglected [nɪ'glɛktɪd] adj abandonado
neglectful [nɪ'glɛktful] adj negligente; **to be ~ of sth/sb** desatender algo/a algn
negligee ['nɛglɪʒeɪ] n salto de cama
negligence ['nɛglɪdʒəns] n negligencia
negligent ['nɛglɪdʒənt] adj negligente; (casual) descuidado
negligently ['nɛglɪdʒəntlɪ] adv negligentemente; (casually) con descuido
negligible ['nɛglɪdʒɪbl] adj insignificante, despreciable
negotiable [nɪ'gəuʃɪəbl] adj negociable; **not ~** (cheque) no trasferible
negotiate [nɪ'gəuʃɪeɪt] vt (treaty, loan) negociar; (obstacle) franquear; (bend in road) tomar ▪ vi: **to ~ (with)** negociar (con); **to with sb for sth** tratar or negociar con algn por algo
negotiating table [nɪ'gəuʃɪeɪtɪŋ-] n mesa de negociaciones
negotiation [nɪgəuʃɪ'eɪʃən] n negociación f, gestión f; **to enter into negotiations with sb** entrar en negociaciones con algn
negotiator [nɪ'gəuʃɪeɪtər] n negociador(a) m(f)
Negress ['niːgrɪs] n negra
Negro ['niːgrəu] adj, n negro
neigh [neɪ] n relincho ▪ vi relinchar
neighbour, neighbor (US) ['neɪbər] n vecino(-a)
neighbourhood, neighborhood (US) ['neɪbəhud] n (place) vecindad f, barrio; (people) vecindario
neighbourhood watch n (Brit: also: **neighbourhood watch scheme**) vigilancia del barrio por los propios vecinos
neighbouring, neighboring (US) ['neɪbərɪŋ] adj vecino
neighbourly, neighborly (US) ['neɪbəlɪ] adj amigable, sociable
neither ['naɪðər] adj ni ▪ conj: **I didn't move and ~ did John** no me he movido, ni

Juan tampoco ▪ pron ninguno; **~ is true** ninguno(-a) de los/las dos es cierto(-a) ▪ adv: **~ good nor bad** ni bueno ni malo
neo ... [niːəu] pref neo...
neolithic [niːəu'lɪθɪk] adj neolítico
neologism [nɪ'ɔlədʒɪzəm] n neologismo
neon ['niːɔn] n neón m
neon light n lámpara de neón
Nepal [nɪ'pɔːl] n Nepal m
nephew ['nɛvjuː] n sobrino
nepotism ['nɛpətɪzəm] n nepotismo
nerd [nəːd] n (col) primo(-a)
nerve [nəːv] n (Anat) nervio; (courage) valor m; (impudence) descaro, frescura; **a fit of nerves** un ataque de nervios; **to lose one's ~** (self-confidence) perder el valor
nerve centre n (Anat) centro nervioso; (fig) punto neurálgico
nerve gas n gas m nervioso
nerve-racking ['nəːvrækɪŋ] adj angustioso
nervous ['nəːvəs] adj (anxious) nervioso; (Anat) nervioso; (timid) tímido, miedoso
nervous breakdown n crisis f nerviosa
nervously ['nəːvəslɪ] adv nerviosamente; tímidamente
nervousness ['nəːvəsnɪs] n nerviosismo; timidez f
nervous wreck n (col): **to be a ~** estar de los nervios
nervy ['nəːvɪ] adj: **to be ~** estar nervioso
nest [nɛst] n (of bird) nido ▪ vi anidar
nest egg n (fig) ahorros mpl
nestle ['nɛsl] vi: **to ~ down** acurrucarse
nestling ['nɛstlɪŋ] n pajarito
Net ['nɛt] n (Comput) Internet m or f
net [nɛt] n (gen) red f; (fabric) tul m ▪ adj (Comm) neto, líquido; (weight, price, salary) neto ▪ vt coger (SP) or agarrar (LAm) con red; (money: person) cobrar; (: deal, sale) conseguir; (Sport) marcar; **~ of tax** neto; **he earns £10,000 ~ per year** gana 10,000 libras netas por año; **the N~** (Internet) la Red
netball ['nɛtbɔːl] n básquet m
net curtain n visillo
Netherlands ['nɛðələndz] npl: **the ~** los Países Bajos
net income n renta neta
netiquette ['nɛtɪkɛt] n netiqueta
net loss n pérdida neta
net profit n beneficio neto
nett [nɛt] adj = **net**
netting ['nɛtɪŋ] n red f, redes fpl
nettle ['nɛtl] n ortiga
network ['nɛtwəːk] n red f ▪ vt (Radio, TV) difundir por la red de emisores; **local area ~** red local; **there's no ~ coverage here** (Tel) aquí no hay cobertura

neuralgia [njuə'rældʒə] n neuralgia
neurological [njuərə'lodʒɪkl] adj neurológico
neurosis (pl -ses) [njuə'rəusɪs, -si:z] n neurosis f inv
neurotic [njuə'rɒtɪk] adj, n neurótico(-a) m(f)
neuter ['nju:tər] adj (Ling) neutro ▪ vt castrar, capar
neutral ['nju:trəl] adj (person) neutral; (colour etc) neutro; (Elec) neutro ▪ n (Aut) punto muerto
neutrality [nju:'trælɪtɪ] n neutralidad f
neutralize ['nju:trəlaɪz] vt neutralizar
neutron ['nju:trɒn] n neutrón m
neutron bomb n bomba de neutrones
Nev. abbr (US) = **Nevada**
never ['nevər] adv nunca, jamás; **I ~ went** no fui nunca; **~ in my life** jamás en la vida; see also **mind**
never-ending [nevər'endɪŋ] adj interminable, sin fin
nevertheless [nevəðə'les] adv sin embargo, no obstante
New Age n Nueva era
new [nju:] adj nuevo; (recent) reciente; **as good as ~** como nuevo
newbie ['nju:bɪ] n recién llegado(-a) m(f)
newborn ['nju:bɔ:n] adj recién nacido
newcomer ['nju:kʌmər] n recién venido or llegado
new-fangled ['nju:fæŋgld] adj (pej) modernísimo
new-found ['nju:faund] adj (friend) nuevo; (enthusiasm) recién adquirido
New Guinea n Nueva Guinea
newly ['nju:lɪ] adv recién
newly-weds ['nju:lɪwedz] npl recién casados
new moon n luna nueva
newness ['nju:nɪs] n novedad f; (fig) inexperiencia
news [nju:z] n noticias fpl; **a piece of ~** una noticia; **the ~** (Radio, TV) las noticias fpl, el telediario; **good/bad ~** buenas/malas noticias fpl; **financial ~** noticias fpl financieras
news agency n agencia de noticias
newsagent ['nju:zeɪdʒənt] n (Brit) vendedor(a) m(f) de periódicos
news bulletin n (Radio, TV) noticiario
newscaster ['nju:zkɑ:stər] n presentador(a) m(f), locutor(a) m(f)
news dealer n (US) = **newsagent**
news flash n noticia de última hora
newsletter ['nju:zletər] n hoja informativa, boletín m
newspaper ['nju:zpeɪpər] n periódico, diario; **daily ~** diario; **weekly ~** periódico semanal
newsprint ['nju:zprɪnt] n papel m de periódico

newsreader ['nju:zri:dər] n = **newscaster**
newsreel ['nju:zri:l] n noticiario
newsroom ['nju:zru:m] n (Press, Radio, TV) sala de redacción
news stand n quiosco or puesto de periódicos
newsworthy ['nju:zwə:ðɪ] adj: **to be ~** ser de interés periodístico
newt [nju:t] n tritón m
new town n (Brit) ciudad f nueva
New Year n Año Nuevo; **Happy ~!** ¡Feliz Año Nuevo!; **to wish sb a happy ~** desear a algn un feliz año nuevo
New Year's Day n Día m de Año Nuevo
New Year's Eve n Nochevieja
New York [-'jɔ:k] n Nueva York
New Zealand [-'zi:lənd] n Nueva Zelanda (SP), Nueva Zelandia (LAm) ▪ adj neozelandés(-esa)
New Zealander [-'zi:ləndər] n neozelandés(-esa) m(f)
next [nekst] adj (house, room) vecino, de al lado; (meeting) próximo; (page) siguiente ▪ adv después; **the ~ day** el día siguiente; **~ time** la próxima vez; **~ year** el año próximo or que viene; **~ month** el mes que viene or entrante; **the week after ~** no la semana que viene sino la otra; **"turn to the ~ page"** "vuelva a la página siguiente"; **you're ~** le toca; **~ to** prep junto a, al lado de; **~ to nothing** casi nada
next door adv en la casa de al lado ▪ adj vecino, de al lado
next-of-kin ['nekstəv'kɪn] n pariente(s) m(pl) más cercano(s)
NF n abbr (Brit Pol: = National Front) partido político de la extrema derecha ▪ abbr (Canada) = **Newfoundland**
NFL n abbr (US) = **National Football League**
Nfld. abbr (Canada) = **Newfoundland**
NG abbr (US) = **National Guard**
NGO n abbr (= non-governmental organization) ONG f
NH abbr (US) = **New Hampshire**
NHL n abbr (US) = **National Hockey League**
NHS n abbr (Brit) = **National Health Service**
NI abbr = **Northern Ireland**; (Brit) = **National Insurance**
nib [nɪb] n plumilla
nibble ['nɪbl] vt mordisquear
Nicaragua [nɪkə'rægjuə] n Nicaragua
Nicaraguan [nɪkə'rægjuən] adj, n nicaragüense m/f, nicaragüeño(-a) m(f)
Nice [ni:s] n Niza
nice [naɪs] adj (likeable) simpático, majo; (kind) amable; (pleasant) agradable; (attractive) bonito, mono; (distinction) fino; (taste, smell, meal) rico

nice-looking ['naɪslukɪŋ] *adj* guapo
nicely ['naɪslɪ] *adv* amablemente; *(of health etc)* bien; **that will do ~** perfecto
niceties ['naɪsɪtɪz] *npl* detalles *mpl*
niche [niːʃ] *n* (*Arch*) nicho, hornacina
nick [nɪk] *n* (*wound*) rasguño; (*cut, indentation*) mella, muesca ■ *vt* (*cut*) cortar; (*col*) birlar, mangar; (: *arrest*) pillar; **in the ~ of time** justo a tiempo; **in good ~** en buen estado; **to ~ o.s.** cortarse
nickel ['nɪkl] *n* níquel *m*; (*US*) *moneda de 5 centavos*
nickname ['nɪkneɪm] *n* apodo, mote *m* ■ *vt* apodar
Nicosia [nɪkə'siːə] *n* Nicosia
nicotine ['nɪkətiːn] *n* nicotina
nicotine patch *n* parche *m* de nicotina
niece [niːs] *n* sobrina
nifty ['nɪftɪ] *adj* (*col: car, jacket*) elegante, chulo; (: *gadget, tool*) ingenioso
Niger ['naɪdʒəʳ] *n* (*country, river*) Níger *m*
Nigeria [naɪ'dʒɪərɪə] *n* Nigeria
Nigerian [naɪ'dʒɪərɪən] *adj, n* nigeriano(-a) *m(f)*
niggardly ['nɪgədlɪ] *adj* (*person*) avaro, tacaño, avariento; (*allowance, amount*) miserable
nigger ['nɪgəʳ] *n* (*col!: highly offensive*) negro(-a)
niggle ['nɪgl] *vt* preocupar ■ *vi* (*complain*) quejarse; (*fuss*) preocuparse por minucias
niggling ['nɪglɪŋ] *adj* (*detail: trifling*) nimio, insignificante; (*annoying*) molesto; (*doubt, pain*) constante
night [naɪt] *n* (*gen*) noche *f*; (*evening*) tarde *f*; **last ~** anoche; **the ~ before last** anteanoche, antes de ayer por la noche; **at ~**, **by ~** de noche, por la noche; **in the ~**, **during the ~** durante la noche, por la noche
night-bird ['naɪtbəːd] *n* (*fig*) trasnochador(a) *m(f)*, madrugador(a) *m(f)* (*LAm*)
nightcap ['naɪtkæp] *n* (*drink*) *bebida que se toma antes de acostarse*
night club *n* club nocturno, discoteca
nightdress ['naɪtdres] *n* (*Brit*) camisón *m*
nightfall ['naɪtfɔːl] *n* anochecer *m*
nightgown ['naɪtgaun], **nightie** ['naɪtɪ] (*Brit*) *n* = **nightdress**
nightingale ['naɪtɪŋgeɪl] *n* ruiseñor *m*
night life *n* vida nocturna
nightly ['naɪtlɪ] *adj* de todas las noches ■ *adv* todas las noches, cada noche
nightmare ['naɪtmɛəʳ] *n* pesadilla
night porter *n* guardián *m* nocturno
night safe *n* caja fuerte
night school *n* clase(s) *f(pl)* nocturna(s)
nightshade ['naɪtʃeɪd] *n*: **deadly ~** (*Bot*) belladona
night shift *n* turno nocturno *or* de noche

night-time ['naɪttaɪm] *n* noche *f*
night watchman *n* vigilante *m* nocturno, sereno
nihilism ['naɪɪlɪzəm] *n* nihilismo
nil [nɪl] *n* (*Brit Sport*) cero, nada
Nile [naɪl] *n*: **the ~** el Nilo
nimble ['nɪmbl] *adj* (*agile*) ágil, ligero; (*skilful*) diestro
nimbly ['nɪmblɪ] *adv* ágilmente; con destreza
nine [naɪn] *num* nueve
9-11, Nine-Eleven [naɪnɪ'lɛvn] *n* 11-S *m*
nineteen ['naɪn'tiːn] *num* diecinueve
nineteenth [naɪn'tiːnθ] *adj* decimonoveno, decimonono
ninety ['naɪntɪ] *num* noventa
ninth [naɪnθ] *adj* noveno
nip [nɪp] *vt* (*pinch*) pellizcar; (*bite*) morder ■ *vi* (*Brit col*): **to ~ out/down/up** salir/bajar/subir un momento ■ *n* (*drink*) trago
nipple ['nɪpl] *n* (*Anat*) pezón *m*; (*of bottle*) tetilla; (*Tech*) boquilla, manguito
nippy ['nɪpɪ] *adj* (*Brit: person*) rápido; (*taste*) picante; **it's a very ~ car** es un coche muy potente para el tamaño que tiene
nit [nɪt] *n* (*of louse*) liendre *f*; (*col: idiot*) imbécil *m/f*
nit-pick ['nɪtpɪk] *vi* (*col*) sacar punta a todo
nitrogen ['naɪtrədʒən] *n* nitrógeno
nitroglycerin, nitroglycerine ['naɪtrəu'glɪsəriːn] *n* nitroglicerina
nitty-gritty ['nɪtɪ'grɪtɪ] *n* (*col*): **to get down to the ~** ir al grano
nitwit ['nɪtwɪt] *n* cretino(-a)
NJ *abbr* (*US*) = **New Jersey**
NLF *n abbr* (= *National Liberation Front*) FLN *m*
NLRB *n abbr* (*US*: = *National Labor Relations Board*) *organismo de protección al trabajador*
NM, N. Mex. *abbr* (*US*) = **New Mexico**

 KEYWORD

no [nəu] (*pl* **noes**) *adv* (*opposite of "yes"*) no; **are you coming? — no (I'm not)** ¿vienes? — no; **would you like some more? — no thank you** ¿quieres más? — no gracias
■ *adj* (*not any*): **I have no money/time/books** no tengo dinero/tiempo/libros; **no other man would have done it** ningún otro lo hubiera hecho; **"no entry"** "prohibido el paso"; **"no smoking"** "prohibido fumar"
■ *n* no *m*

no. *abbr* (= *number*) nº, núm
nobble ['nɔbl] *vt* (*Brit col: bribe*) sobornar; (: *catch*) pescar; (: *Racing*) drogar
Nobel prize [nəu'bɛl-] *n* premio Nobel
nobility [nəu'bɪlɪtɪ] *n* nobleza

noble ['nəubl] *adj (person)* noble; *(title)* de nobleza

nobleman ['nəublmən] *n* noble *m*

nobly ['nəublı] *adv (selflessly)* noblemente

nobody ['nəubədı] *pron* nadie

no-claims bonus ['nəukleımz-] *n* bonificación *f* por carencia de reclamaciones

nocturnal [nɔk'təːnl] *adj* nocturno

nod [nɔd] *vi* saludar con la cabeza; *(in agreement)* asentir con la cabeza ■ *vt*: **to ~ one's head** inclinar la cabeza ■ *n* inclinación *f* de cabeza; **they nodded their agreement** asintieron con la cabeza
▶ **nod off** *vi* cabecear

no-fly zone [nəu'flaı-] *n* zona de exclusión aérea

noise [nɔız] *n* ruido; *(din)* escándalo, estrépito

noisily ['nɔızılı] *adv* ruidosamente, estrepitosamente

noisy ['nɔızı] *adj (gen)* ruidoso; *(child)* escandaloso

nomad ['nəumæd] *n* nómada *m/f*

nomadic [nəu'mædık] *adj* nómada

no man's land *n* tierra de nadie

nominal ['nɔmınl] *adj* nominal

nominate ['nɔmıneıt] *vt (propose)* proponer; *(appoint)* nombrar

nomination [nɔmı'neıʃən] *n* propuesta; nombramiento

nominee [nɔmı'niː] *n* candidato(-a)

non... [nɔn] *pref* no, des..., in...

nonalcoholic [nɔnælkə'hɔlık] *adj* sin alcohol

nonaligned [nɔnə'laınd] *adj* no alineado

nonarrival [nɔnə'raıvl] *n* falta de llegada

nonce word [nɔns-] *n* hápax *m*

nonchalant ['nɔnʃələnt] *adj* indiferente

noncommissioned [nɔnkə'mıʃənd] *adj*: **~ officer** suboficial *m/f*

noncommittal ['nɔnkə'mıtl] *adj (reserved)* reservado; *(uncommitted)* evasivo

nonconformist [nɔnkən'fɔːmıst] *adj* inconformista ■ *n* inconformista *m/f*; *(Brit Rel)* no conformista *m/f*

noncontributory [nɔnkən'trıbjutərı] *adj*: **~ pension scheme** *or (US)* **plan** fondo de pensiones no contributivo

noncooperation ['nɔnkəuɔpə'reıʃən] *n* no cooperación *f*

nondescript ['nɔndıskrıpt] *adj* anodino, soso

none [nʌn] *pron* ninguno(-a) ■ *adv* de ninguna manera; **~ of you** ninguno de vosotros; **I've ~ left** no me queda ninguno(-a); **he's ~ the worse for it** no le ha perjudicado; **I have ~** no tengo ninguno; **~ at all** *(not one)* ni uno

nonentity [nɔ'nɛntıtı] *n* cero a la izquierda, nulidad *f*

nonessential [nɔnı'sɛnʃl] *adj* no esencial ■ *n*: **nonessentials** cosas *fpl* secundarias *or* sin importancia

nonetheless [nʌnðə'lɛs] *adv* sin embargo, no obstante, aún así

non-EU [nɔni'juː] *adj (citizen, passport)* no comunitario; *(imports)* de fuera de la Unión Europea

non-event [nɔnı'vɛnt] *n* acontecimiento sin importancia; **it was a ~** no pasó absolutamente nada

nonexecutive [nɔnıg'zɛkjutıv] *adj*: **~ director** director *m* no ejecutivo

nonexistent [nɔnıg'zıstənt] *adj* inexistente

nonfiction [nɔn'fıkʃən] *n* no ficción *f*

nonintervention [nɔnıntə'vɛnʃən] *n* no intervención *f*

no-no ['nəunəu] *n (col)*: **it's a ~** de eso ni hablar

non obst. *abbr* (= *non obstante*: notwithstanding) no obstante

no-nonsense [nəu'nɔnsəns] *adj* sensato

nonpayment [nɔn'peımənt] *n* falta de pago

nonplussed [nɔn'plʌst] *adj* perplejo

non-profit-making [nɔn'prɔfıtmeıkıŋ] *adj* no lucrativo

nonsense ['nɔnsəns] *n* tonterías *fpl*, disparates *fpl*; **~!** ¡qué tonterías!; **it is ~ to say that ...** es absurdo decir que ...

nonsensical [nɔn'sɛnsıkl] *adj* disparatado, absurdo

nonshrink [nɔn'ʃrıŋk] *adj* que no encoge

nonskid [nɔn'skıd] *adj* antideslizante

nonsmoker ['nɔn'sməukə'] *n* no fumador(a) *m(f)*

nonstarter [nɔn'staːtə'] *n*: **it's a ~** no tiene futuro

nonstick ['nɔn'stık] *adj (pan, surface)* antiadherente

nonstop ['nɔn'stɔp] *adj* continuo; *(Rail)* directo ■ *adv* sin parar

nontaxable [nɔn'tæksəbl] *adj*: **~ income** renta no imponible

non-U ['nɔnjuː] *adj abbr (Brit col*: = *non-upper class)* que no pertenece a la clase alta

nonvolatile [nɔn'vɔlətaıl] *adj*: **~ memory** *(Comput)* memoria permanente

nonvoting [nɔn'vəutıŋ] *adj*: **~ shares** acciones *fpl* sin derecho a voto

nonwhite ['nɔn'waıt] *adj* de color ■ *n (person)* persona de color

noodles ['nuːdlz] *npl* tallarines *mpl*

nook [nuk] *n* rincón *m*; **nooks and crannies** escondrijos *mpl*

noon [nuːn] *n* mediodía *m*

no-one ['nəuwʌn] *pron* = **nobody**

noose [nuːs] *n* lazo corredizo

nor [nɔːʳ] *conj* = **neither** ■ *adv see* **neither**
Norf *abbr* (*Brit*) = **Norfolk**
norm [nɔːm] *n* norma
normal ['nɔːml] *adj* normal; **to return to ~**
volver a la normalidad
normality [nɔː'mælɪtɪ] *n* normalidad *f*
normally ['nɔːməlɪ] *adv* normalmente
Normandy ['nɔːməndɪ] *n* Normandía
north [nɔːθ] *n* norte *m* ■ *adj* del norte ■ *adv*
al *or* hacia el norte
North Africa *n* África del Norte
North African *adj, n* norteafricano(-a) *m(f)*
North America *n* América del Norte
North American *adj, n* norteamericano(-a)
m(f)
Northants [nɔː'θænts] *abbr* (*Brit*)
= **Northamptonshire**
northbound ['nɔːθbaund] *adj* (*traffic*) que
se dirige al norte; (*carriageway*) de dirección
norte
Northd *abbr* (*Brit*) = **Northumberland**
north-east [nɔːθ'iːst] *n* nor(d)este *m*
northerly ['nɔːðəlɪ] *adj* (*point, direction*) hacia
el norte, septentrional; (*wind*) del norte
northern ['nɔːðən] *adj* norteño, del norte
Northern Ireland *n* Irlanda del Norte
North Korea *n* Corea del Norte
North Pole *n*: **the ~** el Polo Norte
North Sea *n*: **the ~** el Mar del Norte
North Sea oil *n* petróleo del Mar del Norte
northward ['nɔːθwəd], **northwards**
['nɔːθwədz] *adv* hacia el norte
north-west [nɔːθ'wɛst] *n* noroeste *m*
Norway ['nɔːweɪ] *n* Noruega
Norwegian [nɔː'wiːdʒən] *adj* noruego
■ *n* noruego(-a); (*Ling*) noruego
nos. *abbr* (= *numbers*) núms.
nose [nəuz] *n* (*Anat*) nariz *f*; (*Zool*) hocico;
(*sense of smell*) olfato ■ *vi* (*also*: **nose one's
way**) avanzar con cautela; **to pay through
the ~ (for sth)** (*col*) pagar un dineral (por algo)
  ▶ **nose about, nose around** *vi* curiosear
nosebleed ['nəuzbliːd] *n* hemorragia, nasal
nose-dive ['nəuzdaɪv] *n* picado vertical
nose drops *npl* gotas *fpl* para la nariz
nosey ['nəuzɪ] *adj* curioso, fisgón(-ona)
nostalgia [nɔs'tældʒɪə] *n* nostalgia
nostalgic [nɔs'tældʒɪk] *adj* nostálgico
nostril ['nɔstrɪl] *n* ventana *or* orificio de la
nariz
nosy ['nəuzɪ] *adj* = **nosey**
not [nɔt] *adv* no; **~ at all** no ... en absoluto; **~
that** ... no es que ...; **it's too late, isn't it?** es
demasiado tarde, ¿verdad?; **~ yet** todavía no;
~ now ahora no; **why ~?** ¿por qué no?; **I hope
~** espero que no; **~ at all** no ... nada; (*after
thanks*) de nada

notable ['nəutəbl] *adj* notable
notably ['nəutəblɪ] *adv* especialmente;
(*in particular*) sobre todo
notary ['nəutərɪ] *n* (*also*: **notary public**)
notario(a)
notation [nəu'teɪʃən] *n* notación *f*
notch [nɔtʃ] *n* muesca, corte *m*
  ▶ **notch up** *vt* (*score, victory*) apuntarse
note [nəut] *n* (*Mus, record, letter*) nota;
(*banknote*) billete *m*; (*tone*) tono ■ *vt* (*observe*)
notar, observar; (*write down*) apuntar,
anotar; **delivery ~** nota de entrega; **to
compare notes** (*fig*) cambiar impresiones;
of ~ conocido, destacado; **to take ~** prestar
atención a; **just a quick ~ to let you know
that ...** sólo unas líneas para informarte
que ...
notebook ['nəutbuk] *n* libreta, cuaderno;
(*for shorthand*) libreta
notecase ['nəutkeɪs] *n* (*Brit*) cartera, billetero
noted ['nəutɪd] *adj* célebre, conocido
notepad ['nəutpæd] *n* bloc *m*
notepaper ['nəutpeɪpə] *n* papel *m* para cartas
noteworthy ['nəutwəːðɪ] *adj* notable, digno
de atención
nothing ['nʌθɪŋ] *n* nada; (*zero*) cero; **he does
~ no hace nada; ~ new** nada nuevo; **for ~**
(*free*) gratis; (*in vain*) en balde; **~ at all** nada
en absoluto
notice ['nəutɪs] *n* (*announcement*) anuncio;
(*dismissal*) despido; (*resignation*) dimisión *f*;
(*review: of play etc*) reseña ■ *vt* (*observe*) notar,
observar; **to take ~ of** hacer caso de, prestar
atención a; **at short ~** con poca antelación;
without ~ sin previo aviso; **advance ~** previo
aviso; **until further ~** hasta nuevo aviso; **to
give sb ~ of sth** avisar a algn de algo; **to give
~, hand in one's ~** dimitir, renunciar; **it has
come to my ~ that ...** he llegado a saber que
...; **to escape** *or* **avoid ~** pasar inadvertido
noticeable ['nəutɪsəbl] *adj* evidente, obvio
notice board *n* (*Brit*) tablón *m* de anuncios
notification [nəutɪfɪ'keɪʃən] *n* aviso;
(*announcement*) anuncio
notify ['nəutɪfaɪ] *vt*: **to ~ sb (of sth)**
comunicar (algo) a algn
notion ['nəuʃən] *n* noción *f*, concepto;
(*opinion*) opinión *f*
notions ['nəuʃənz] *npl* (*US*) mercería
notoriety [nəutə'raɪətɪ] *n* notoriedad *f*, mala
fama
notorious [nəu'tɔːrɪəs] *adj* notorio,
tristemente célebre
notoriously [nəu'tɔːrɪəslɪ] *adv* notoriamente
Notts [nɔts] *abbr* (*Brit*) = **Nottinghamshire**
notwithstanding [nɔtwɪθ'stændɪŋ] *adv* no
obstante, sin embargo; **~ this** a pesar de esto

n

nougat ['nu:gɑ:] n turrón m
nought [nɔ:t] n cero
noun [naun] n nombre m, sustantivo
nourish ['nʌrɪʃ] vt nutrir, alimentar; (fig) fomentar, nutrir
nourishing ['nʌrɪʃɪŋ] adj nutritivo, rico
nourishment ['nʌrɪʃmənt] n alimento, sustento
Nov. abbr (= November) nov
novel ['nɔvl] n novela ∎ adj (new) nuevo, original; (unexpected) insólito
novelist ['nɔvəlɪst] n novelista m/f
novelty ['nɔvəltɪ] n novedad f
November [nəu'vɛmbəʳ] n noviembre m; see also **July**
novice ['nɔvɪs] n principiante m/f, novato(-a); (Rel) novicio(-a)
NOW [nau] n abbr (US) = **National Organization for Women**
now [nau] adv (at the present time) ahora; (these days) actualmente, hoy día ∎ conj: ~ (**that**) ya que, ahora que; **right ~** ahora mismo; **by ~** ya; **just ~: I'll do it just now** ahora mismo lo hago; **~ and then, ~ and again** de vez en cuando; **from ~ on** de ahora en adelante; **between ~ and Monday** entre hoy y el lunes; **in 3 days from ~** de hoy en 3 días; **that's all for ~** eso es todo por ahora
nowadays ['nauədeɪz] adv hoy (en) día, actualmente
nowhere ['nəuwɛəʳ] adv (direction) a ninguna parte; (location) en ninguna parte; **~ else** en or a ninguna otra parte
no-win situation [nəu'wɪn-] n: **I'm in a ~** haga lo que haga, llevo las de perder
noxious ['nɔkʃəs] adj nocivo
nozzle ['nɔzl] n boquilla
NP n abbr = **notary public**
NS abbr (Canada) = **Nova Scotia**
NSC n abbr (US) = **National Security Council**
NSF n abbr (US) = **National Science Foundation**
NSPCC n abbr (Brit) = **National Society for the Prevention of Cruelty to Children**
NSW abbr (Australia) = **New South Wales**
NT n abbr (= New Testament) ∎ abbr (Canada) = **Northwest Territories**
nth [ɛnθ] adj: **for the ~ time** (col) por enésima vez
nuance ['nju:ɑ:ns] n matiz m
nubile ['nju:baɪl] adj núbil
nuclear ['nju:klɪəʳ] adj nuclear
nuclear disarmament n desarme m nuclear
nuclear family n familia nuclear
nuclear-free zone ['nju:klɪə'fri:-] n zona desnuclearizada
nucleus (pl **nuclei**) ['nju:klɪəs, 'nju:klɪaɪ] n núcleo

NUCPS n abbr (Brit: = National Union of Civil and Public Servants) sindicato de funcionarios
nude [nju:d] adj, n desnudo(-a) m(f); **in the ~** desnudo
nudge [nʌdʒ] vt dar un codazo a
nudist ['nju:dɪst] n nudista m/f
nudist colony n colonia de desnudistas
nudity ['nju:dɪtɪ] n desnudez f
nugget ['nʌgɪt] n pepita
nuisance ['nju:sns] n molestia, fastidio; (person) pesado, latoso; **what a ~!** ¡qué lata!
NUJ n abbr (Brit: = National Union of Journalists) sindicato de periodistas
nuke [nju:k] (col) n bomba atómica ∎ vt atacar con arma nuclear
null [nʌl] adj: **~ and void** nulo y sin efecto
nullify ['nʌlɪfaɪ] vt anular, invalidar
NUM n abbr (Brit: = National Union of Mineworkers) sindicato de mineros
numb [nʌm] adj entumecido; (fig) insensible ∎ vt quitar la sensación a, entumecer, entorpecer; **to be ~ with cold** estar entumecido de frío; **~ with fear/grief** paralizado de miedo/dolor
number ['nʌmbəʳ] n número; (numeral) número, cifra ∎ vt (pages etc) numerar, poner número a; (amount to) sumar, ascender a; **reference ~** número de referencia; **telephone ~** número de teléfono; **wrong ~** (Tel) número equivocado; **opposite ~** (person) homólogo(-a); **to be numbered among** figurar entre; **a ~ of** varios, algunos; **they were ten in ~** eran diez
number plate n (Brit) matrícula, placa
Number Ten n (Brit: 10 Downing Street) residencia del primer ministro
numbness ['nʌmnɪs] n insensibilidad f, parálisis f inv; (due to cold) entumecimiento
numbskull ['nʌmskʌl] n (col) papanatas m/f inv
numeral ['nju:mərəl] n número, cifra
numerate ['nju:mərɪt] adj competente en aritmética
numerical [nju:'mɛrɪkl] adj numérico
numerous ['nju:mərəs] adj numeroso, muchos
nun [nʌn] n monja, religiosa
nunnery ['nʌnərɪ] n convento de monjas
nuptial ['nʌpʃəl] adj nupcial
nurse [nə:s] n enfermero(-a); (nanny) niñera ∎ vt (patient) cuidar, atender; (baby: Brit) mecer; (: US) criar, amamantar; **male ~** enfermero
nursery ['nə:sərɪ] n (institution) guardería infantil; (room) cuarto de los niños; (for plants) criadero, semillero
nursery rhyme n canción f infantil
nursery school n escuela de preescolar

nursery slope n (Brit Ski) cuesta para principiantes
nursing ['nə:sɪŋ] n (profession) profesión f de enfermera; (care) asistencia, cuidado ▪ adj (mother) lactante
nursing home n clínica de reposo
nurture ['nə:tʃəʳ] vt (child, plant) alimentar, nutrir
NUS n abbr (Brit: = National Union of Students) sindicato de estudiantes
NUT n abbr (Brit: = National Union of Teachers) sindicato de profesores
nut [nʌt] n (Tech) tuerca; (Bot) nuez f ▪ adj (chocolate etc) con nueces; **nuts** (Culin) frutos secos
nutcrackers ['nʌtkrækəz] npl cascanueces m inv
nutmeg ['nʌtmɛg] n nuez f moscada
nutrient ['nju:trɪənt] adj nutritivo ▪ n elemento nutritivo
nutrition [nju:'trɪʃən] n nutrición f,

alimentación f
nutritionist [nju:'trɪʃənɪst] n dietista m/f
nutritious [nju:'trɪʃəs] adj nutritivo
nuts [nʌts] adj (col) chiflado
nutshell ['nʌtʃɛl] n cáscara de nuez; **in a ~** en resumidas cuentas
nutty ['nʌtɪ] adj (flavour) a frutos secos; (col: foolish) chalado
nuzzle ['nʌzl] vi: **to ~ up to** arrimarse a
NV abbr (US) = **Nevada**
NVQ n abbr (Brit: = national vocational qualification) título de formación profesional
NWT abbr (Canada) = **Northwest Territories**
NY abbr (US) = **New York**
NYC abbr (US) = **New York City**
nylon ['naɪlɔn] n nylon m, nilón m ▪ adj de nylon or nilón
nymph [nɪmf] n ninfa
nymphomaniac ['nɪmfəu'meɪnɪæk] adj, n ninfómana
NYSE n abbr (US) = **New York Stock Exchange**

n

Oo

O, o [əu] *n* (*letter*) O, o *f;* **O for Oliver,** (*US*)
  O for Oboe O de Oviedo
oaf [əuf] *n* zoquete *m/f*
oak [əuk] *n* roble *m* ▪ *adj* de roble
O & M *n abbr* = **organization and method**
OAP *n abbr* (*Brit*) = **old-age pensioner**
oar [ɔːʳ] *n* remo; **to put** *or* **shove one's ~ in**
  (*fig col*) entrometerse
oarsman ['ɔːzmən] *n* remero
OAS *n abbr* (= *Organization of American States*) OEA *f*
oasis (*pl* **oases**) [əu'eisis, əu'eisi:z] *n* oasis
  m inv
oath [əuθ] *n* juramento; (*swear word*)
  palabrota; **on** (*Brit*) *or* **under ~** bajo
  juramento
oatmeal ['əutmi:l] *n* harina de avena
oats [əuts] *n* avena
OAU *n abbr* (= *Organization of African Unity*) OUA *f*
obdurate ['ɔbdjurit] *adj* (*stubborn*) terco,
  obstinado; (*sinner*) empedernido; (*unyielding*)
  inflexible, firme
OBE *n abbr* (*Brit*: = *Order of the British Empire*) título
  ceremonial
obedience [ə'bi:diəns] *n* obediencia; **in ~ to**
  de acuerdo con
obedient [ə'bi:diənt] *adj* obediente
obelisk ['ɔbilisk] *n* obelisco
obese [əu'bi:s] *adj* obeso
obesity [əu'bi:siti] *n* obesidad *f*
obey [ə'bei] *vt* obedecer; (*instructions*) cumplir
obituary [ə'bitjuəri] *n* necrología
object ['ɔbdʒikt] *n* (*gen*) objeto; (*purpose*)
  objeto, propósito; (*Ling*) objeto,
  complemento ▪ *vi* [əb'dʒɛkt]: **to ~ to**
  (*attitude*) protestar contra; (*proposal*) oponerse
  a; **expense is no ~** no importan los gastos;
  I ~! ¡protesto!; **to ~ that** objetar que
objection [əb'dʒɛkʃən] *n* objeción *f;* **I have no**
  ~ to ... no tengo inconveniente en, que ...
objectionable [əb'dʒɛkʃənəbl] *adj* (*gen*)
  desagradable; (*conduct*) censurable
objective [əb'dʒɛktiv] *adj, n* objetivo
objectively [əb'dʒɛktivli] *adv* objetivamente

objectivity [ɔbdʒik'tiviti] *n* objetividad *f*
object lesson *n* (*fig*) (buen) ejemplo
objector [əb'dʒɛktəʳ] *n* objetor(a) *m(f)*
obligation [ɔbli'geiʃən] *n* obligación *f;* (*debt*)
  deber *m;* **"without ~"** "sin compromiso";
  to be under an ~ to sb/to do sth estar
  comprometido con algn/a hacer algo
obligatory [ə'bligətəri] *adj* obligatorio
oblige [ə'blaidʒ] *vt* (*do a favour for*) complacer,
  hacer un favor a; **to ~ sb to do sth** obligar
  a algn a hacer algo; **to be obliged to sb**
  for sth estarle agradecido a algn por algo;
  anything to ~! todo sea por complacerte
obliging [ə'blaidʒiŋ] *adj* servicial, atento
oblique [ə'bli:k] *adj* oblicuo; (*allusion*)
  indirecto ▪ *n* (*Typ*) barra
obliterate [ə'blitəreit] *vt* arrasar; (*memory*)
  borrar
oblivion [ə'bliviən] *n* olvido
oblivious [ə'bliviəs] *adj:* **~ of** inconsciente de
oblong ['ɔblɔŋ] *adj* rectangular ▪ *n*
  rectángulo
obnoxious [əb'nɔkʃəs] *adj* odioso, detestable;
  (*smell*) nauseabundo
o.b.o. *abbr* (*US:* = *or best offer: in classified ads*)
  abierto ofertas
oboe ['əubəu] *n* oboe *m*
obscene [əb'si:n] *adj* obsceno
obscenity [əb'seniti] *n* obscenidad *f*
obscure [əb'skjuəʳ] *adj* oscuro ▪ *vt* oscurecer;
  (*hide: sun*) ocultar
obscurity [əb'skjuəriti] *n* oscuridad *f;* (*obscure*
  point) punto oscuro; **to rise from ~** salir de
  la nada
obsequious [əb'si:kwiəs] *adj* servil
observable [əb'zə:vəbl] *adj* observable,
  perceptible
observance [əb'zə:vns] *n* observancia,
  cumplimiento; (*ritual*) práctica; **religious**
  observances *fpl* religiosas
observant [əb'zə:vnt] *adj* observador(a)
observation [ɔbzə'veiʃən] *n* (*Med*)
  observación *f;* (*by police etc*) vigilancia

observation post n (Mil) puesto de observación

observatory [əb'zə:vətrɪ] n observatorio

observe [əb'zə:v] vt (gen) observar; (rule) cumplir

observer [əb'zə:vəʳ] n observador(a) m(f)

obsess [əb'sɛs] vt obsesionar; **to be obsessed by** or **with sb/sth** estar obsesionado con algn/algo

obsession [əb'sɛʃən] n obsesión f

obsessive [əb'sɛsɪv] adj obsesivo

obsolescence [ɔbsə'lɛsns] n obsolescencia

obsolescent [ɔbsə'lɛsnt] adj que está cayendo en desuso

obsolete ['ɔbsəli:t] adj obsoleto

obstacle ['ɔbstəkl] n obstáculo; (nuisance) estorbo

obstacle race n carrera de obstáculos

obstetrician [ɔbstə'trɪʃən] n obstetra m/f

obstetrics [ɔb'stɛtrɪks] n obstetricia

obstinacy ['ɔbstɪnəsɪ] n terquedad f, obstinación f; tenacidad f

obstinate ['ɔbstɪnɪt] adj terco, obstinado; (determined) tenaz

obstinately ['ɔbstɪnɪtlɪ] adv tercamente, obstinadamente

obstreperous [əb'strɛpərəs] adj ruidoso; (unruly) revoltoso

obstruct [əb'strʌkt] vt (block) obstruir; (hinder) estorbar, obstaculizar

obstruction [əb'strʌkʃən] n obstrucción f; estorbo, obstáculo

obstructive [əb'strʌktɪv] adj obstruccionista; **stop being ~!** ¡deja de poner peros!

obtain [əb'teɪn] vt (get) obtener; (achieve) conseguir; **to ~ sth (for o.s.)** conseguir or adquirir algo

obtainable [əb'teɪnəbl] adj asequible

obtrusive [əb'tru:sɪv] adj (person) importuno; (: interfering) entrometido; (building etc) demasiado visible

obtuse [əb'tju:s] adj obtuso

obverse ['ɔbvə:s] n (of medal) anverso; (fig) complemento

obviate ['ɔbvɪeɪt] vt obviar, evitar

obvious ['ɔbvɪəs] adj (clear) obvio, evidente; (unsubtle) poco sutil; **it's ~ that ...** está claro que ..., es evidente que ...

obviously ['ɔbvɪəslɪ] adv obviamente, evidentemente; **~ not!** ¡por supuesto que no!; **he was ~ not drunk** era evidente que no estaba borracho; **he was not ~ drunk** no se le notaba que estaba borracho

OCAS n abbr (= Organization of Central American States) ODECA f

occasion [ə'keɪʒən] n oportunidad f, ocasión f; (event) acontecimiento ▪ vt ocasionar,

causar; **on that ~** esa vez, en aquella ocasión; **to rise to the ~** ponerse a la altura de las circunstancias

occasional [ə'keɪʒənl] adj poco frecuente, ocasional

occasionally [ə'keɪʒənlɪ] adv de vez en cuando; **very ~** muy de tarde en tarde, en muy contadas ocasiones

occasional table n mesita

occult [ɔ'kʌlt] adj (gen) oculto

occupancy ['ɔkjupənsɪ] n ocupación f

occupant ['ɔkjupənt] n (of house) inquilino(-a); (of boat, car) ocupante m/f

occupation [ɔkju'peɪʃən] n (of house) tenencia; (job) trabajo; (calling) oficio

occupational accident [ɔkju'peɪʃənl-] n accidente m laboral

occupational guidance n orientación f profesional

occupational hazard n gajes mpl del oficio

occupational pension scheme n plan m profesional de jubilación

occupational therapy n terapia ocupacional

occupier ['ɔkjupaɪəʳ] n inquilino(-a)

occupy ['ɔkjupaɪ] vt (seat, post, time) ocupar; (house) habitar; **to ~ o.s. with** or **by doing** (as job) dedicarse a hacer; (to pass time) entretenerse haciendo; **to be occupied with sth/in doing sth** estar ocupado con algo/haciendo algo

occur [ə'kə:ʳ] vi ocurrir, suceder; **to ~ to sb** ocurrírsele a algn

occurrence [ə'kʌrəns] n suceso

ocean ['əuʃən] n océano; **oceans of** (col) la mar de

ocean bed n fondo del océano

ocean-going ['əuʃəngəuɪŋ] adj de alta mar

Oceania [əuʃɪ'ɑ:nɪə] n Oceanía

ocean liner n buque m transoceánico

ochre, (US) **ocher** ['əukəʳ] n ocre m

o'clock [ə'klɔk] adv: **it is five ~** son las cinco

OCR n abbr = **optical character recognition/ reader**

Oct. abbr (= October) oct

octagonal [ɔk'tægənl] adj octagonal

octane ['ɔkteɪn] n octano; **high ~ petrol** or (US) **gas** gasolina de alto octanaje

octave ['ɔktɪv] n octava

October [ɔk'təubəʳ] n octubre m; see also **July**

octogenarian ['ɔktəudʒɪ'nɛərɪən] n octogenario(-a)

octopus ['ɔktəpəs] n pulpo

oculist ['ɔkjulɪst] n oculista m/f

odd [ɔd] adj (strange) extraño, raro; (number) impar; (left over) sobrante, suelto; **60-~** 60 y pico; **at ~ times** de vez en cuando; **to be**

o

681

the ~ one out estar de más; **if you have the ~ minute** si tienes unos minutos libres; *see also* **odds**

oddball ['ɔdbɔ:l] *n* (*col*) bicho raro

oddity ['ɔdɪtɪ] *n* rareza; (*person*) excéntrico(-a)

odd-job man [ɔd'dʒɔb-] *n* hombre *m* que hace chapuzas

odd jobs *npl* chapuzas *fpl*

oddly ['ɔdlɪ] *adv* extrañamente

oddments ['ɔdmənts] *npl* (*Brit Comm*) restos *mpl*

odds [ɔdz] *npl* (*in betting*) puntos *mpl* de ventaja; **it makes no ~** da lo mismo; **at ~** reñidos(-as); **to succeed against all the ~** tener éxito contra todo pronóstico; **~ and ends** cachivaches *mpl*

odds-on [ɔdz'ɔn] *adj* (*col*): **the ~ favourite** el máximo favorito; **it's ~ he'll come** seguro que viene

ode [əud] *n* oda

odious ['əudɪəs] *adj* odioso

odometer [ɔ'dɔmɪtəʳ] *n* (*US*) cuentakilómetros *m inv*

odour, odor (*US*) ['əudəʳ] *n* olor *m*; (*perfume*) perfume *m*

odourless, odorless (*US*) ['əudəlɪs] *adj* sin olor

OECD *n abbr* (= *Organization for Economic Cooperation and Development*) OCDE *f*

oesophagus, esophagus (*US*) [i:'sɔfəgəs] *n* esófago

oestrogen, estrogen (*US*) ['i:strədʒən] *n* estrógeno

 KEYWORD

of [ɔv, əv] *prep* **1** (*gen*) de; **a friend of ours** un amigo nuestro; **a boy of 10** un chico de 10 años; **that was kind of you** eso fue muy amable de tu parte

2 (*expressing quantity, amount, dates etc*) de; **a kilo of flour** un kilo de harina; **there were three of them** había tres; **three of us went** tres de nosotros fuimos; **the 5th of July** el 5 de julio; **a quarter of four** (*US*) las cuarto menos cuarto

3 (*from, out of*) de; **made of wood** (hecho) de madera

Ofcom ['ɔfkɔm] *n abbr* (*Brit*) = **Office of Communications**

off [ɔf] *adj, adv* (*engine, light*) apagado; (*tap*) cerrado; (*Brit: food: bad*) pasado, malo; (: *milk*) cortado; (*cancelled*) suspendido; (*removed*): **the lid was ~** no estaba puesta la tapadera ◼ *prep* de; **to be ~** (*leave*) irse, marcharse; **to be ~ sick** estar enfermo *or* de baja; **a day ~** un día libre; **to have an ~ day** tener un mal día;

he had his coat ~ se había quitado el abrigo; **10% ~** (*Comm*) (con el) 10% de descuento; **it's a long way ~** está muy lejos; **5 km ~ (the road)** a 5 km (de la carretera); **~ the coast** frente a la costa; **I'm ~ meat** (*no longer eat/like it*) paso de la carne; **on the ~ chance** por si acaso; **~ and on, on and ~** de vez en cuando; **I must be ~** tengo que irme; **to be well/badly ~** andar bien/mal de dinero; **I'm afraid the chicken is ~** desgraciadamente ya no queda pollo; **that's a bit ~, isn't it?** (*fig, col*) ¡eso no se hace!

offal ['ɔfl] *n* (*Brit Culin*) menudillos *mpl*, asaduras *fpl*

off-centre, (*US*) **off-center** [ɔf'sɛntəʳ] *adj* descentrado, ladeado

off-colour ['ɔf'kʌləʳ] *adj* (*Brit: ill*) indispuesto; **to feel ~** sentirse *or* estar mal

offence, offense (*US*) [ə'fɛns] *n* (*crime*) delito; (*insult*) ofensa; **to take ~ at** ofenderse por; **to commit an ~** cometer un delito

offend [ə'fɛnd] *vt* (*person*) ofender ◼ *vi*: **to ~ against** (*law, rule*) infringir

offender [ə'fɛndəʳ] *n* delincuente *m/f*; (*against regulations*) infractor(a) *m(f)*

offending [ə'fɛndɪŋ] *adj* culpable; (*object*) molesto; (*word*) problemático

offense [ə'fɛns] *n* (*US*) = **offence**

offensive [ə'fɛnsɪv] *adj* ofensivo; (*smell etc*) repugnante ◼ *n* (*Mil*) ofensiva

offer ['ɔfəʳ] *n* (*gen*) oferta, ofrecimiento; (*proposal*) propuesta ◼ *vt* ofrecer; **"on ~ "** (*Comm*) "en oferta"; **to make an ~ for sth** hacer una oferta por algo; **to ~ sth to sb, ~ sb sth** ofrecer algo a algn; **to ~ to do sth** ofrecerse a hacer algo

offering ['ɔfərɪŋ] *n* (*Rel*) ofrenda

offer price *n* precio de oferta

offertory ['ɔfətrɪ] *n* (*Rel*) ofertorio

offhand [ɔf'hænd] *adj* informal; (*brusque*) desconsiderado ◼ *adv* de improviso, sin pensarlo; **I can't tell you ~** no te lo puedo decir así de improviso *or* (*LAm*) así nomás

office ['ɔfɪs] *n* (*place*) oficina; (*room*) despacho; (*position*) cargo, oficio; **doctor's ~** (*US*) consultorio; **to take ~** entrar en funciones; **through his good offices** gracias a sus buenos oficios; **O~ of Fair Trading** (*Brit*) *oficina que regula normas comerciales*

office automation *n* ofimática, buromática

office bearer *n* (*of club etc*) titular *m/f* (de una cartera)

office block, office building (*US*) *n* bloque *m* de oficinas

office boy *n* ordenanza *m*

office hours *npl* horas *fpl* de oficina; (*US Med*) horas *fpl* de consulta

office manager n jefe(-a) m(f) de oficina

officer ['ɔfɪsəʳ] n (Mil etc) oficial m/f; (of organization) director(a) m(f); (also: **police officer**) agente m/f de policía

office work n trabajo de oficina

office worker n oficinista m/f

official [ə'fɪʃl] adj (authorized) oficial, autorizado; (strike) oficial ▪ n funcionario(-a)

officialdom [ə'fɪʃldəm] n burocracia

officially [ə'fɪʃəlɪ] adv oficialmente

official receiver n síndico

officiate [ə'fɪʃɪeɪt] vi (Rel) oficiar; **to ~ as Mayor** ejercer las funciones de alcalde; **to ~ at a marriage** celebrar una boda

officious [ə'fɪʃəs] adj oficioso

offing ['ɔfɪŋ] n: **in the ~** (fig) en perspectiva

off-key [ɔf'kiː] adj desafinado ▪ adv desafinadamente

off-licence ['ɔflaɪsns] n (Brit: shop) tienda de bebidas alcohólicas; ver nota

○ **OFF-LICENCE**
○
○ En el Reino Unido una off-licence es una
○ tienda especializada en la venta de
○ bebidas alcohólicas para el consumo
○ fuera del establecimiento. De ahí su
○ nombre, pues se necesita un permiso
○ especial para tal venta, que está
○ estrictamente regulada. Suelen vender
○ además bebidas sin alcohol, tabaco,
○ chocolate, patatas fritas etc y a menudo
○ son parte de grandes cadenas nacionales.

off-limits [ɔf'lɪmɪts] adj (US Mil) prohibido al personal militar

off line adj, adv (Comput) fuera de línea; (switched off) desconectado

off-load ['ɔfləud] vt descargar, desembarcar

off-peak ['ɔf'piːk] adj (holiday) de temporada baja; (electricity) de banda económica

off-putting ['ɔfputɪŋ] adj (Brit: person) poco amable, difícil; (behaviour) chocante

off-season ['ɔf'siːzn] adj, adv fuera de temporada

offset ['ɔfsɛt] vt (irreg: like **set**) (counteract) contrarrestar, compensar ▪ n (also: **offset printing**) offset m

offshoot ['ɔfʃuːt] n (Bot) vástago; (fig) ramificación f

offshore [ɔf'ʃɔːʳ] adj (breeze, island) costero; (fishing) de bajura; **~ oilfield** campo petrolífero submarino

offside ['ɔf'saɪd] n (Aut: with right-hand drive) lado derecho; (: with left-hand drive) lado izquierdo ▪ adj (Sport) fuera de juego; (Aut)

del lado derecho; del lado izquierdo

offspring ['ɔfsprɪŋ] n descendencia

offstage [ɔf'steɪdʒ] adv entre bastidores

off-the-cuff [ɔfðə'kʌf] adj espontáneo

off-the-job [ɔfðə'dʒɔb] adj: **~ training** formación f fuera del trabajo

off-the-peg [ɔfðə'pɛg], (US) **off-the-rack** [ɔfðə'ræk] adv confeccionado

off-the-record ['ɔfðə'rɛkɔːd] adj extraoficial, confidencial ▪ adv extraoficialmente, confidencialmente

off-white ['ɔfwaɪt] adj blanco grisáceo

Ofgas ['ɔfgæs] n abbr (Brit: = Office of Gas Supply) organismo que controla a las empresas del gas en Gran Bretaña

Ofgem ['ɔfdʒɛm] n abbr (Brit) **= Office of Gas and Electricity Markets**

Oftel ['ɔftɛl] n abbr (Brit: = Office of Telecommunications) organismo que controla las telecomunicaciones británicas

often ['ɔfn] adv a menudo, con frecuencia, seguido (LAm); **how ~ do you go?** ¿cada cuánto vas?

Ofwat ['ɔfwɔt] n abbr (Brit: = Office of Water Services) organismo que controla a las empresas suministradoras del agua en Inglaterra y Gales

ogle ['əugl] vt comerse con los ojos a

ogre ['əugəʳ] n ogro

OH abbr (US) **= Ohio**

oh [əu] excl ¡ah!

OHMS abbr (Brit) **= On His (or Her) Majesty's Service**

oil [ɔɪl] n aceite m; (petroleum) petróleo ▪ vt (machine) engrasar; **fried in ~** frito en aceite

oilcan ['ɔɪlkæn] n lata de aceite

oilfield ['ɔɪlfiːld] n campo petrolífero

oil filter n (Aut) filtro de aceite

oil-fired ['ɔɪlfaɪəd] adj de fuel-oil

oil gauge n indicador m del aceite

oil industry n industria petrolífera

oil level n nivel m del aceite

oil painting n pintura al óleo

oil refinery n refinería de petróleo

oil rig n torre f de perforación

oilskins ['ɔɪlskɪnz] npl impermeable msg, chubasquero sg

oil tanker n petrolero

oil well n pozo (de petróleo)

oily ['ɔɪlɪ] adj aceitoso; (food) grasiento

ointment ['ɔɪntmənt] n ungüento

OK abbr (US) **= Oklahoma**

O.K., okay ['əu'keɪ] excl O.K., ¡está bien!, ¡vale! ▪ adj bien ▪ n: **to give sth one's O.K.** dar el visto bueno a or aprobar algo ▪ vt dar el visto bueno a; **it's O.K. with** or **by me** estoy de acuerdo, me parece bien; **are you O.K. for money?** ¿andas or vas bien de dinero?

Okla. *abbr* (*US*) = **Oklahoma**
old [əʊld] *adj* viejo; (*former*) antiguo; **how ~ are you?** ¿cuántos años tienes?, ¿qué edad tienes?; **he's 10 years ~** tiene 10 años; **older brother** hermano mayor; **any ~ thing will do** sirve cualquier cosa
old age *n* vejez *f*
old-age pension ['əʊldeɪdʒ-] *n* (*Brit*) jubilación *f*, pensión *f*
old-age pensioner ['əʊldeɪdʒ-] *n* (*Brit*) jubilado(-a)
olden ['əʊldən] *adj* antiguo
old-fashioned ['əʊld'fæʃənd] *adj* anticuado, pasado de moda
old maid *n* solterona
old-style ['əʊldstaɪl] *adj* tradicional, chapado a la antigua
old-time ['əʊld'taɪm] *adj* antiguo, de antaño
old-timer [əʊld'taɪməʳ] *n* veterano(-a); (*old person*) anciano(-a)
old wives' tale *n* cuento de viejas, patraña
olive ['ɒlɪv] *n* (*fruit*) aceituna; (*tree*) olivo ■ *adj* (*also:* **olive-green**) verde oliva *inv*
olive branch *n* (*fig*): **to offer an ~ to sb** ofrecer hacer las paces con algn
olive oil *n* aceite *m* de oliva
Olympic [əʊ'lɪmpɪk] *adj* olímpico; **the ~ Games, the Olympics** *npl* las Olimpíadas
OM *n abbr* (*Brit*: = *Order of Merit*) *título ceremonial*
Oman [əʊ'mɑːn] *n* Omán *m*
OMB *n abbr* (*US*: = *Office of Management and Budget*) *servicio que asesora al presidente en materia presupuestaria*
omelette, omelet ['ɒmlɪt] *n* tortilla, tortilla de huevo (*LAm*)
omen ['əʊmən] *n* presagio
ominous ['ɒmɪnəs] *adj* de mal agüero, amenazador(a)
omission [əʊ'mɪʃən] *n* omisión *f*; (*error*) descuido
omit [əʊ'mɪt] *vt* omitir; (*by mistake*) olvidar, descuidar; **to ~ to do sth** olvidarse *or* dejar de hacer algo
omnivorous [ɒm'nɪvərəs] *adj* omnívoro
ON *abbr* (*Canada*) = **Ontario**

 KEYWORD

on [ɒn] *prep* **1** (*indicating position*) en; sobre; **on the wall** en la pared; **it's on the table** está sobre *or* en la mesa; **on the left** a la izquierda; **I haven't got any money on me** no llevo dinero encima
2 (*indicating means, method, condition etc*): **on foot** a pie; **on the train/plane** (*go*) en tren/avión; (*be*) en el tren/el avión; **on the radio/television** por *or* en la radio/televisión; **on the telephone** al teléfono; **to be on drugs** drogarse; (*Med*) estar a tratamiento; **to be on holiday/business** estar de vacaciones/en viaje de negocios; **we're on irregular verbs** estamos con los verbos irregulares
3 (*referring to time*): **on Friday** el viernes; **on Fridays** los viernes; **on June 20th** el 20 de junio; **a week on Friday** del viernes en una semana; **on arrival** al llegar; **on seeing this** al ver esto
4 (*about, concerning*) sobre, acerca de; **a book on physics** un libro de *or* sobre física
5 (*at the expense of*): **this round's on me** esta ronda la pago yo, invito yo a esta ronda; (*earning*): **he's on sixteen thousand pounds a year** gana dieciséis mil libras al año
■ *adv* **1** (*referring to dress*): **to have one's coat on** tener *or* llevar el abrigo puesto; **she put her gloves on** se puso los guantes
2 (*referring to covering*): **"screw the lid on tightly"** "cerrar bien la tapa"
3 (*further, continuously*): **to walk/run** *etc* **on** seguir caminando/corriendo *etc*; **from that day on** desde aquel día; **it was well on in the evening** estaba ya entrada la tarde
4 (*in phrases*): **I'm on to sth** creo haber encontrado algo; **my father's always on at me to get a job** (*col*) mi padre siempre me está dando la lata para que me ponga a trabajar
■ *adj* **1** (*functioning, in operation: machine, radio, TV, light*) encendido(-a) (*SP*), prendido(-a) (*LAm*); (: *tap*) abierto(-a); (: *brakes*) echado(-a), puesto(-a); **is the meeting still on?** (*in progress*) ¿todavía continúa la reunión?; (*not cancelled*) ¿va a haber reunión al fin?; **there's a good film on at the cinema** ponen una buena película en el cine
2: **that's not on!** (*col: not possible*) ¡eso ni hablar!; (: *not acceptable*) ¡eso no se hace!

ONC *n abbr* (*Brit*: = *Ordinary National Certificate*) *título escolar*
once [wʌns] *adv* una vez; (*formerly*) antiguamente ■ *conj* una vez que; **~ he had left/it was done** una vez que se había marchado/se hizo; **at ~** en seguida, inmediatamente; (*simultaneously*) a la vez; **~ a week** una vez a la semana; **~ more** otra vez; **~ and for all** de una vez por todas; **~ upon a time** érase una vez; **I knew him ~** le conocía hace tiempo
oncoming ['ɒnkʌmɪŋ] *adj* (*traffic*) que viene de frente
OND *n abbr* (*Brit*: = *Ordinary National Diploma*) *título escolar*

○ KEYWORD

one [wʌn] *num* un/una; **one hundred and fifty** ciento cincuenta; **one by one** uno a uno; **it's one (o'clock)** es la una
■ *adj* **1** (*sole*) único; **the one book which** el único libro que; **the one man who** el único que
2 (*same*) mismo(-a); **they came in the one car** vinieron en un solo coche
■ *pron* **1**: **this one** éste/ésta; **that one** ése/ésa; (*more remote*) aquél/aquélla; **I've already got (a red) one** ya tengo uno(-a) (rojo(-a)); **one by one** uno(-a) por uno(-a); **to be one up on sb** llevar ventaja a algn; **to be at one (with sb)** estar completamente de acuerdo (con algn)
2: **one another** (*US*) nos; (*you*) os (*SP*); (*you: polite: them*) se; **do you two ever see one another?** ¿os veis alguna vez? (*SP*), ¿se ven alguna vez?; **the two boys didn't dare look at one another** los dos chicos no se atrevieron a mirarse (el uno al otro); **they all kissed one another** se besaron unos a otros
3 (*impers*): **one never knows** nunca se sabe; **to cut one's finger** cortarse el dedo; **one needs to eat** hay que comer

one-armed bandit ['wʌnɑːmd-] *n* máquina tragaperras
one-day excursion ['wʌndeɪ-] *n* (*US*) billete *m* de ida y vuelta en un día
One-hundred share index ['wʌnhʌndrəd-] *n* índice *m* bursátil (*del Financial Times*)
one-man ['wʌn'mæn] *adj* (*business*) individual
one-man band *n* hombre-orquesta *m*
one-off [wʌn'ɔf] *n* (*Brit col*: *object*) artículo único; (: *event*) caso especial
one-parent family ['wʌnpɛərənt-] *n* familia monoparental
one-piece ['wʌnpiːs] *adj* (*bathing suit*) de una pieza
onerous ['ɔnərəs] *adj* (*task, duty*) pesado; (*responsibility*) oneroso
oneself [wʌn'sɛlf] *pron* uno mismo; (*after prep, also emphatic*) sí (mismo(-a)); **to do sth by ~** hacer algo solo *or* por sí solo
one-shot [wʌn'ʃɔt] *n* (*US*) = **one-off**
one-sided [wʌn'saɪdɪd] *adj* (*argument*) parcial; (*decision, view*) unilateral; (*game, contest*) desigual
one-time ['wʌntaɪm] *adj* antiguo, ex-
one-to-one ['wʌntəwʌn] *adj* (*relationship*) individualizado
one-upmanship [wʌn'ʌpmənʃɪp] *n*: **the art of ~** el arte de quedar siempre por encima

one-way ['wʌnweɪ] *adj* (*street, traffic*) de dirección única; (*ticket*) sencillo
ongoing ['ɔngəuɪŋ] *adj* continuo
onion ['ʌnjən] *n* cebolla
online *adj, adv* (*Comput*) en línea; (*switched on*) conectado
onlooker ['ɔnlukə'] *n* espectador(a) *m(f)*
only ['əunlɪ] *adv* solamente, sólo, nomás (*LAm*) ■ *adj* único, solo ■ *conj* solamente que, pero; **an ~ child** un hijo único; **not ~ ... but also ...** no sólo ... sino también ...; **I'd be ~ too pleased to help** encantado de ayudarles; **I saw her ~ yesterday** le vi ayer mismo; **I would come, ~ I'm very busy** iría, sólo que estoy muy atareado
ono *abbr* (= *or nearest offer*: *in classified ads*) abierto ofertas
onset ['ɔnsɛt] *n* comienzo
onshore ['ɔnʃɔː'] *adj* (*wind*) que sopla del mar hacia la tierra
onslaught ['ɔnslɔːt] *n* ataque *m*, embestida
Ont. *abbr* (*Canada*) = **Ontario**
on-the-job ['ɔnðə'dʒɔb] *adj*: **~ training** formación *f* en el trabajo *or* sobre la práctica
onto ['ɔntu] *prep* = **on to**
onus ['əunəs] *n* responsabilidad *f*; **the ~ is upon him to prove it** le incumbe a él demostrarlo
onward ['ɔnwəd], **onwards** ['ɔnwədz] *adv* (*move*) (hacia) adelante
onyx ['ɔnɪks] *n* ónice *m*, onyx *m*
oops [ups] *excl* (*also*: **oops-a-daisy!**) ¡huy!
ooze [uːz] *vi* rezumar
opal ['əupl] *n* ópalo
opaque [əu'peɪk] *adj* opaco
OPEC ['əupɛk] *n abbr* (= *Organization of Petroleum-Exporting Countries*) OPEP *f*
open ['əupn] *adj* abierto; (*car*) descubierto; (*road, view*) despejado; (*meeting*) público; (*admiration*) manifiesto ■ *vt* abrir ■ *vi* (*flower, eyes, door, debate*) abrirse; (*book etc*: *commence*) comenzar; **in the ~ (air)** al aire libre; **~ verdict** veredicto inconcluso; **~ ticket** billete *m* sin fecha; **~ ground** (*among trees*) claro; (*waste ground*) solar *m*; **to have an ~ mind (on sth)** estar sin decidirse aún (sobre algo); **to ~ a bank account** abrir una cuenta en el banco
▶ **open on to** *vt fus* (*room, door*) dar a
▶ **open out** *vt* abrir ■ *vi* (*person*) abrirse
▶ **open up** *vt* abrir; (*blocked road*) despejar ■ *vi* abrirse
open-and-shut ['əupənən'ʃʌt] *adj*: **~ case** caso claro *or* evidente
open day *n* (*Brit*) jornada de puertas abiertas *or* acceso público

O

open-ended [əupn'ɛndɪd] *adj* (*fig*) indefinido, sin definir

opener ['əupnəʳ] *n* (*also*: **can opener, tin opener**) abrelatas *m inv*

open-heart surgery [əupn'hɑːt-] *n* cirugía a corazón abierto

opening ['əupnɪŋ] *n* abertura; (*beginning*) comienzo; (*opportunity*) oportunidad *f*; (*job*) puesto vacante, vacante *f*

opening night *n* estreno

open learning *n* enseñanza flexible a tiempo parcial

openly ['əupnlɪ] *adv* abiertamente

open-minded [əupn'maɪndɪd] *adj* de amplias miras, sin prejuicios

open-necked ['əupnnɛkt] *adj* sin corbata

openness ['əupnnɪs] *n* (*frankness*) franqueza

open-plan ['əupn'plæn] *adj* sin tabiques, de plan abierto

open prison *n* centro penitenciario de régimen abierto

open return *n* vuelta con fecha abierta

open shop *n* empresa que contrata a mano de obra no afiliada a ningún sindicato

Open University *n* (*Brit*) ≈ Universidad *f* Nacional de Enseñanza a Distancia, UNED *f*; *ver nota*

● **OPEN UNIVERSITY**

La *Open University*, fundada en 1969, está especializada en impartir cursos a distancia y a tiempo parcial con sus propios materiales de apoyo diseñados para tal fin, entre ellos programas de radio y televisión emitidos por la "BBC". Los trabajos se envían por correo y se complementan con la asistencia obligatoria a cursos de verano. Para obtener la licenciatura es necesario estudiar un mínimo de módulos y alcanzar un determinado número de créditos.

opera ['ɔpərə] *n* ópera

opera glasses *npl* gemelos *mpl*

opera house *n* teatro de la ópera

opera singer *n* cantante *m/f* de ópera

operate ['ɔpəreɪt] *vt* (*machine*) hacer funcionar; (*company*) dirigir ■ *vi* funcionar; (*drug*) hacer efecto; **to ~ on sb** (*Med*) operar a algn

operatic [ɔpə'rætɪk] *adj* de ópera

operating costs ['ɔpəreɪtɪŋ-] *npl* gastos *mpl* operacionales

operating profit *n* beneficio de explotación

operating room *n* (*US*) quirófano, sala de operaciones

operating table *n* mesa de operaciones

operating theatre *n* quirófano, sala de operaciones

operation [ɔpə'reɪʃən] *n* (*gen*) operación *f*; (*of machine*) funcionamiento; **to be in ~** estar funcionando *or* en funcionamiento; **to have an ~** (*Med*) ser operado; **to have an ~ for** operarse de; **the company's operations during the year** las actividades de la compañía durante el año

operational [ɔpə'reɪʃənl] *adj* operacional, en buen estado; (*Comm*) en condiciones de servicio; (*ready for use or action*) en condiciones de funcionar; **when the service is fully ~** cuando el servicio esté en pleno funcionamiento

operative ['ɔpərətɪv] *adj* (*measure*) en vigor; **the ~ word** la palabra clave

operator ['ɔpəreɪtəʳ] *n* (*of machine*) operario(-a); (*Tel*) operador(a) *m(f)*, telefonista *m/f*

operetta [ɔpə'rɛtə] *n* opereta

ophthalmic [ɔf'θælmɪk] *adj* oftálmico

ophthalmologist [ɔfθæl'mɔlədʒɪst] *n* oftalmólogo(-a)

opinion [ə'pɪnjən] *n* (*gen*) opinión *f*; **in my ~** en mi opinión, a mi juicio; **to seek a second ~** pedir una segunda opinión

opinionated [ə'pɪnjəneɪtɪd] *adj* testarudo

opinion poll *n* encuesta, sondeo

opium ['əupɪəm] *n* opio

opponent [ə'pəunənt] *n* adversario(-a), contrincante *m/f*

opportune ['ɔpətjuːn] *adj* oportuno

opportunism [ɔpə'tjuːnɪzm] *n* oportunismo

opportunist [ɔpə'tjuːnɪst] *n* oportunista *m/f*

opportunity [ɔpə'tjuːnɪtɪ] *n* oportunidad *f*, chance *m or f* (*LAm*); **to take the ~ to do** *or* **of doing** aprovechar la ocasión para hacer

oppose [ə'pəuz] *vt* oponerse a; **to be opposed to sth** oponerse a algo; **as opposed to** en vez de; (*unlike*) a diferencia de

opposing [ə'pəuzɪŋ] *adj* (*side*) opuesto, contrario

opposite ['ɔpəzɪt] *adj* opuesto, contrario; (*house etc*) de enfrente ■ *adv* en frente ■ *prep* en frente de, frente a ■ *n* lo contrario; **the ~ sex** el otro sexo, el sexo opuesto

opposite number *n* (*Brit*) homólogo(-a)

opposition [ɔpə'zɪʃən] *n* oposición *f*

oppress [ə'prɛs] *vt* oprimir

oppression [ə'prɛʃən] *n* opresión *f*

oppressive [ə'prɛsɪv] *adj* opresivo

opprobrium [ə'prəubrɪəm] *n* (*formal*) oprobio

opt [ɔpt] *vi*: **to ~ for** optar por; **to ~ to do** optar por hacer; **to ~ out** (*of NHS etc*) salirse

optical ['ɔptɪkl] *adj* óptico
optical character reader *n* lector *m* óptico de caracteres
optical character recognition *n* reconocimiento *m* óptico de caracteres
optical fibre *n* fibra óptica
optician [ɔp'tɪʃən] *n* óptico *m/f*
optics ['ɔptɪks] *n* óptica
optimism ['ɔptɪmɪzəm] *n* optimismo
optimist ['ɔptɪmɪst] *n* optimista *m/f*
optimistic [ɔptɪ'mɪstɪk] *adj* optimista
optimum ['ɔptɪməm] *adj* óptimo
option ['ɔpʃən] *n* opción *f*; **to keep one's options open** (*fig*) mantener las opciones abiertas; **I have no** ~ no tengo más *or* otro remedio
optional ['ɔpʃənl] *adj* opcional; (*course*) optativo; ~ **extras** opciones *fpl* extras
opulence ['ɔpjuləns] *n* opulencia
opulent ['ɔpjulənt] *adj* opulento
OR *abbr* (*US*) = **Oregon**
or [ɔːʳ] *conj* o; (*before o, ho*) u; (*with negative*): **he hasn't seen or heard anything** no ha visto ni oído nada; **or else** si no; **let me go or I'll scream!** ¡suélteme, o me pongo a gritar!
oracle ['ɔrəkl] *n* oráculo
oral ['ɔːrəl] *adj* oral ■ *n* examen *m* oral
orange ['ɔrɪndʒ] *n* (*fruit*) naranja ■ *adj* (de color) naranja
orangeade [ɔrɪndʒ'eɪd] *n* naranjada, refresco de naranja
orange squash *n* zumo (*SP*) *or* jugo de naranja
orang-outang, orang-utan [ɔ'ræŋuː'tæn] *n* orangután *m*
oration [ɔː'reɪʃən] *n* discurso solemne; **funeral** ~ oración *f* fúnebre
orator ['ɔrətəʳ] *n* orador(a) *m(f)*
oratorio [ɔrə'tɔːrɪəu] *n* oratorio
orbit ['ɔːbɪt] *n* órbita ■ *vt, vi* orbitar; **to be in/go into** ~ **(round)** estar en/entrar en órbita (alrededor de)
orbital ['ɔːbɪtl] *n* (*also*: **orbital motorway**) autopista de circunvalación
orchard ['ɔːtʃəd] *n* huerto; **apple** ~ manzanar *m*, manzanal *m*
orchestra ['ɔːkɪstrə] *n* orquesta; (*US: seating*) platea
orchestral [ɔː'kestrəl] *adj* de orquesta
orchestrate ['ɔːkɪstreɪt] *vt* orquestar
orchid ['ɔːkɪd] *n* orquídea
ordain [ɔː'deɪn] *vt* (*Rel*) ordenar
ordeal [ɔː'diːl] *n* experiencia terrible
order ['ɔːdəʳ] *n* orden *m*; (*command*) orden *f*; (*type, kind*) clase *f*; (*state*) estado; (*Comm*) pedido, encargo ■ *vt* (*also*: **put in order**) ordenar, poner en orden; (*Comm*) encargar,

pedir; (*command*) mandar, ordenar; **in** ~ (*gen*) en orden; (*of document*) en regla; **in (working)** ~ en funcionamiento; **a machine in working** ~ una máquina en funcionamiento; **to be out of** ~ (*machine, toilets*) estar estropeado *or* (*LAm*) descompuesto; **in** ~ **to do** para hacer; **in** ~ **that** para que + *subjun*; **on** ~ (*Comm*) pedido; **to be on** ~ estar pedido; **we are under orders to do it** tenemos orden de hacerlo; **a point of** ~ una cuestión de procedimiento; **to place an** ~ **for sth with sb** hacer un pedido de algo a algn; **made to** ~ hecho a la medida; **his income is of the** ~ **of £24,000 per year** sus ingresos son del orden de 24 mil libras al año; **to the** ~ **of** (*Banking*) a la orden de; **to** ~ **sb to do sth** mandar a algn hacer algo
order book *n* cartera de pedidos
order form *n* hoja de pedido
orderly ['ɔːdəlɪ] *n* (*Mil*) ordenanza *m*; (*Med*) auxiliar *m/f* (de hospital) ■ *adj* ordenado
orderly officer *n* (*Mil*) oficial *m* del día
order number *n* número de pedido
ordinal ['ɔːdɪnl] *adj* ordinal
ordinarily ['ɔːdnrɪlɪ] *adv* por lo común
ordinary ['ɔːdnrɪ] *adj* corriente, normal; (*pej*) común y corriente; **out of the** ~ fuera de lo común, extraordinario
ordinary degree *n* (*Brit*) diploma *m*; *ver nota*

O

ⓞ **ORDINARY DEGREE**

ⓞ Después de tres años de estudios, algunos
ⓞ universitarios obtienen la titulación
ⓞ de *ordinary degree*. Esto ocurre en el caso
ⓞ poco frecuente de que no aprueben los
ⓞ exámenes que conducen al título de
ⓞ "honours degree" pero sus examinadores
ⓞ consideran que a lo largo de la carrera
ⓞ han logrado unos resultados mínimos
ⓞ satisfactorios. También es una opción
ⓞ que tienen los estudiantes de las
ⓞ universidades escocesas no interesados
ⓞ en estudiar en la universidad más de tres
ⓞ años.

ordinary seaman *n* (*Brit*) marinero
ordinary shares *npl* acciones *fpl* ordinarias
ordination [ɔːdɪ'neɪʃən] *n* ordenación *f*
ordnance ['ɔːdnəns] *n* (*Mil: unit*) artillería
ordnance factory *n* fábrica de artillería
Ordnance Survey *n* (*Brit*) *servicio oficial de topografía y cartografía*
ore [ɔːʳ] *n* mineral *m*
Ore., Oreg. *abbr* (*US*) = **Oregon**
organ ['ɔːgən] *n* órgano

organic [ɔː'gænɪk] *adj* orgánico; (*vegetables, produce*) biológico
organism ['ɔːgənɪzəm] *n* organismo
organist ['ɔːgənɪst] *n* organista *m/f*
organization [ɔːgənaɪ'zeɪʃən] *n* organización *f*
organization chart *n* organigrama *m*
organize ['ɔːgənaɪz] *vt* organizar; **to get organized** organizarse
organized crime *n* crimen organizado
organizer ['ɔːgənaɪzəʳ] *n* organizador(-a) *m(f)*
orgasm ['ɔːgæzəm] *n* orgasmo
orgy ['ɔːdʒɪ] *n* orgía
Orient ['ɔːrɪənt] *n* Oriente *m*
oriental [ɔːrɪ'ɛntl] *adj* oriental
orientate ['ɔːrɪənteɪt] *vt* orientar
origin ['ɒrɪdʒɪn] *n* origen *m*; (*point of departure*) procedencia
original [ə'rɪdʒɪnl] *adj* original; (*first*) primero; (*earlier*) primitivo ▪ *n* original *m*
originality [ərɪdʒɪ'nælɪtɪ] *n* originalidad *f*
originally [ə'rɪdʒɪnəlɪ] *adv* (*at first*) al principio; (*with originality*) con originalidad
originate [ə'rɪdʒɪneɪt] *vi*: **to ~ from, to ~ in** surgir de, tener su origen en
originator [ə'rɪdʒɪneɪtəʳ] *n* inventor(a) *m(f)*, autor(a) *m(f)*
Orkneys ['ɔːknɪz] *npl*: **the ~** (*also*: **the Orkney Islands**) las Orcadas
ornament ['ɔːnəmənt] *n* adorno
ornamental [ɔːnə'mɛntl] *adj* decorativo, de adorno
ornamentation [ɔːnəmɛn'teɪʃən] *n* ornamentación *f*
ornate [ɔː'neɪt] *adj* recargado
ornithologist [ɔːnɪ'θɔlədʒɪst] *n* ornitólogo(-a)
ornithology [ɔːnɪ'θɔlədʒɪ] *n* ornitología
orphan ['ɔːfn] *n* huérfano(-a) ▪ *vt*: **to be orphaned** quedar huérfano(-a)
orphanage ['ɔːfənɪdʒ] *n* orfanato
orthodox ['ɔːθədɔks] *adj* ortodoxo
orthodoxy ['ɔːθədɔksɪ] *n* ortodoxia
orthopaedic, orthopedic (*US*) [ɔːθə'piːdɪk] *adj* ortopédico
orthopaedics, orthopedics (*US*) [ɔːθə'piːdɪks] *n* ortopedia
OS *abbr* (*Brit*: = *Ordnance Survey*) servicio oficial de topografía y cartografía; (: *Dress*) = **outsize**
O.S. *abbr* = **out of stock**
Oscar ['ɔskəʳ] *n* óscar *m*
oscillate ['ɔsɪleɪt] *vi* oscilar; (*person*) vacilar
oscillation [ɔsɪ'leɪʃən] *n* oscilación *f*; (*of prices*) fluctuación *f*
OSHA *n abbr* (*US*: = *Occupational Safety and Health Administration*) oficina de la higiene y la seguridad en el trabajo
Oslo ['ɔzləu] *n* Oslo

ostensible [ɔs'tɛnsɪbl] *adj* aparente
ostensibly [ɔs'tɛnsɪblɪ] *adv* aparentemente
ostentatious [ɔstɛn'teɪʃəs] *adj* pretencioso, aparatoso; (*person*) ostentativo
osteopath ['ɔstɪəpæθ] *n* osteópata *m/f*
ostracize ['ɔstrəsaɪz] *vt* hacer el vacío a
ostrich ['ɔstrɪtʃ] *n* avestruz *m*
OT *n abbr* (= *Old Testament*) A.T. *m*
OTB *n abbr* (*US*: = *off-track betting*) apuestas hechas fuera del hipódromo
OTE *abbr* (= *on-target earnings*) beneficios según objetivos
other ['ʌðəʳ] *adj* otro ▪ *pron*: **the ~** (*one*) el/la otro(-a); **others** (*other people*) otros; **~ than** (*apart from*) aparte de; **the ~ day** el otro día; **some ~ people have still to arrive** quedan por llegar otros; **some actor or ~** un actor cualquiera; **somebody or ~** alguien, alguno; **it was no ~ than the bishop** no era otro que el obispo
otherwise ['ʌðəwaɪz] *adv, conj* de otra manera; (*if not*) si no; **an ~ good piece of work** un trabajo que, quitando eso, es bueno
OTT *abbr* (*col*) = **over the top**; *see* **top**
otter ['ɔtəʳ] *n* nutria
OU *n abbr* (*Brit*) = **Open University**
ouch [autʃ] *excl* ¡ay!
ought (*pt* **ought**) [ɔːt] *aux vb*: **I ~ to do it** debería hacerlo; **this ~ to have been corrected** esto debiera de haberse corregido; **he ~ to win** (*probability*) debiera ganar; **you ~ to go and see it** vale la pena ir a verlo
ounce [auns] *n* onza (28.35g: 16 in a pound)
our ['auəʳ] *adj* nuestro; *see also* **my**
ours ['auəz] *pron* (el) nuestro/(la) nuestra *etc*; *see also* **mine**
ourselves [auə'sɛlvz] *pron pl* (*reflexive, after prep*) nosotros; (*emphatic*) nosotros mismos; **we did it (all) by ~** lo hicimos nosotros solos; *see also* **oneself**
oust [aust] *vt* desalojar
out [aut] *adv* fuera, afuera; (*not at home*) fuera (de casa); (*light, fire*) apagado; (*on strike*) en huelga ▪ *vt*: **to ~ sb** revelar públicamente la homosexualidad de algn; **~ there** allí (fuera); **he's ~** (*absent*) no está, ha salido; **to be ~ in one's calculations** equivocarse (en sus cálculos); **to run ~** salir corriendo; **~ loud** en alta voz; **~ of** *prep* (*outside*) fuera de; (*because of: anger etc*) por; **to look ~ of the window** mirar por la ventana; **to drink ~ of a cup** beber de una taza; **made ~ of wood** de madera; **~ of petrol** sin gasolina; **"~ of order"** "no funciona", **it's ~ of stock** (*Comm*) está agotado; **to be ~ and about again** estar repuesto y levantado; **the journey ~** el viaje de ida; **the boat was 10**

km ~ el barco estaba a 10 kilómetros de la costa; **before the week was** ~ antes del fin de la semana; **he's** ~ **for all he can get** busca sus propios fines, anda detrás de lo suyo

out-and-out ['autəndaut] *adj* (*liar, thief etc*) redomado, empedernido

outback ['autbæk] *n* interior *m*

outbid [aut'bɪd] *vt* pujar más alto que, sobrepujar

outboard ['autbɔːd] *adj*: ~ **motor** (motor *m*) fuera borda *m*

outbound ['autbaund] *adj*: ~ **from/for** con salida de/hacia

outbreak ['autbreɪk] *n* (*of war*) comienzo; (*of disease*) epidemia; (*of violence etc*) ola

outbuilding ['autbɪldɪŋ] *n* dependencia; (*shed*) cobertizo

outburst ['autbəːst] *n* explosión *f*, arranque *m*

outcast ['autkɑːst] *n* paria *m/f*

outclass [aut'klɑːs] *vt* aventajar, superar

outcome ['autkʌm] *n* resultado

outcrop ['autkrɔp] *n* (*of rock*) afloramiento

outcry ['autkraɪ] *n* protestas *fpl*

outdated [aut'deɪtɪd] *adj* anticuado

outdistance [aut'dɪstəns] *vt* dejar atrás

outdo [aut'duː] *vt* (*irreg: like* **do**) superar

outdoor [aut'dɔːr] *adj* al aire libre

outdoors [aut'dɔːz] *adv* al aire libre

outer ['autər] *adj* exterior, externo

outer space *n* espacio exterior

outfit ['autfɪt] *n* equipo; (*clothes*) traje *m*; (*col: organization*) grupo, organización *f*

outfitter's ['autfɪtəz] *n* (Brit) sastrería

outgoing ['autgəuɪŋ] *adj* (*president, tenant*) saliente; (*means of transport*) que sale; (*character*) extrovertido

outgoings ['autgəuɪŋz] *npl* (Brit) gastos *mpl*

outgrow [aut'grəu] *vt* (*irreg: like* **grow**) **he has outgrown his clothes** su ropa le queda pequeña ya

outhouse ['authaus] *n* dependencia

outing ['autɪŋ] *n* excursión *f*, paseo

outlandish [aut'lændɪʃ] *adj* estrafalario

outlast [aut'lɑːst] *vt* durar más tiempo que, sobrevivir a

outlaw ['autlɔː] *n* proscrito(-a) ■ *vt* (*person*) declarar fuera de la ley; (*practice*) declarar ilegal

outlay ['autleɪ] *n* inversión *f*

outlet ['autlɛt] *n* salida; (*of pipe*) desagüe *m*; (US Elec) toma de corriente; (*for emotion*) desahogo; (*also*: **retail outlet**) punto de venta

outline ['autlaɪn] *n* (*shape*) contorno, perfil *m*; **in** ~ (*fig*) a grandes rasgos

outlive [aut'lɪv] *vt* sobrevivir a

outlook ['autluk] *n* perspectiva; (*opinion*) punto de vista

outlying ['autlaɪɪŋ] *adj* remoto, aislado

outmanoeuvre, (*US*) **outmaneuver** [autmə'nuːvər] *vt* (Mil: *fig*) superar en la estrategia

outmoded [aut'məudɪd] *adj* anticuado, pasado de moda

outnumber [aut'nʌmbər] *vt* exceder *or* superar en número

out of bounds [autəv'baundz] *adj*: **it's** ~ está prohibido el paso

out-of-court [autəv'kɔːt] *adj, adv* sin ir a juicio

out-of-date [autəv'deɪt] *adj* (*passport*) caducado, vencido; (*theory, idea*) anticuado; (*clothes, customs*) pasado de moda

out-of-doors [autəv'dɔːz] *adv* al aire libre

out-of-the-way [autəvðə'weɪ] *adj* (*remote*) apartado; (*unusual*) poco común *or* corriente

out-of-touch [autəv'tʌtʃ] *adj*: **to be** ~ estar desconectado

outpatient ['autpeɪʃənt] *n* paciente *m/f* externo(-a)

outpost ['autpəust] *n* puesto avanzado

outpouring ['autpɔːrɪŋ] *n* (*fig*) efusión *f*

output ['autput] *n* (*volumen m de*) producción *f*, rendimiento; (Comput) salida ■ *vt* (Comput: *to power*) imprimir

outrage ['autreɪdʒ] *n* (*scandal*) escándalo; (*atrocity*) atrocidad *f* ■ *vt* ultrajar

outrageous [aut'reɪdʒəs] *adj* (*clothes*) extravagante; (*behaviour*) escandaloso

outright [aut'raɪt] *adv* (*win*) de manera absoluta; (*be killed*) en el acto; (*ask*) abiertamente; (*completely*) completamente ■ *adj* ['autraɪt] completo; (*winner*) absoluto; (*refusal*) rotundo

outrun [aut'rʌn] *vt* (*irreg: like* **run**) correr más que, dejar atrás

outset ['autsɛt] *n* principio

outshine [aut'ʃaɪn] *vt* (*irreg: like* **shine**) (*fig*) eclipsar, brillar más que

outside [aut'saɪd] *n* exterior *m* ■ *adj* exterior, externo ■ *adv* fuera, afuera (LAm) ■ *prep* fuera de; (*beyond*) más allá de; **at the** ~ (*fig*) a lo sumo; **an** ~ **chance** una posibilidad remota; ~ **left/right** (*esp Football*) extremo izquierdo/derecho

outside broadcast *n* (Radio, TV) emisión *f* exterior

outside contractor *n* contratista *m/f* independiente

outside lane *n* (Aut) carril *m* de adelantamiento

outside line *n* (Tel) línea (exterior)

outsider [aut'saɪdər] *n* (*stranger*) forastero(-a)

outsize ['autsaɪz] *adj* (*clothes*) de talla grande

outskirts ['autskəːts] *npl* alrededores *mpl*, afueras *fpl*

O

outsmart [autˈsmɑːt] *vt* ser más listo que
outspoken [autˈspəukən] *adj* muy franco
outspread [autˈsprɛd] *adj* extendido; (*wings*) desplegado
outstanding [autˈstændɪŋ] *adj* excepcional, destacado; (*unfinished*) pendiente
outstay [autˈsteɪ] *vt*: **to ~ one's welcome** quedarse más de la cuenta
outstretched [autˈstrɛtʃt] *adj* (*arm*) extendido
outstrip [autˈstrɪp] *vt* (*competitors, demand: also* *fig*) dejar atrás, aventajar
out-tray [ˈauttreɪ] *n* bandeja de salida
outvote [autˈvəut] *vt*: **it was outvoted (by ...)** fue rechazado en el voto (por ...)
outward [ˈautwəd] *adj* (*sign, appearances*) externo; (*journey*) de ida
outwardly [ˈautwədlɪ] *adv* por fuera
outweigh [autˈweɪ] *vt* pesar más que
outwit [autˈwɪt] *vt* ser más listo que
outworn [autˈwɔːn] *adj* (*expression*) cansado
oval [ˈəuvl] *adj* ovalado ■ *n* óvalo
ovarian [əuˈvɛərɪən] *adj* ovárico; (*cancer*) de ovario
ovary [ˈəuvərɪ] *n* ovario
ovation [əuˈveɪʃən] *n* ovación *f*
oven [ˈʌvn] *n* horno
ovenproof [ˈʌvnpruːf] *adj* refractario, resistente al horno
oven-ready [ˈʌvnrɛdɪ] *adj* listo para el horno
ovenware [ˈʌvnwɛəʳ] *n* artículos *mpl* para el horno
over [ˈəuvəʳ] *adv* encima, por encima ■ *adj* (*finished*) terminado; (*surplus*) de sobra; (*excessively*) demasiado ■ *prep* (*por*) encima de; (*above*) sobre; (*on the other side of*) al otro lado de; (*more than*) más de; (*during*) durante; (*about, concerning*): **they fell out ~ money** riñeron por una cuestión de dinero; **~ here** (por) aquí; **~ there** (por) allí or allá; **all ~** (*everywhere*) por todas partes; **~ and ~ (again)** una y otra vez; **~ and above** además de; **to ask sb ~** invitar a algn a casa; **to bend ~** inclinarse; **now ~ to our Paris correspondent** damos la palabra a nuestro corresponsal de París; **the world ~** en todo el mundo, en el mundo entero; **she's not ~ intelligent** no es muy lista que digamos
over... [ˈəuvəʳ] *pref* sobre..., super...
overact [əuvərˈækt] *vi* (*Theat*) exagerar el papel
overall [ˈəuvərɔːl] *adj* (*length*) total; (*study*) de conjunto ■ *adv* [əuvərˈɔːl] en conjunto ■ *n* (Brit) guardapolvo; **overalls** *npl* mono *sg*, overol *msg* (*LAm*)
overall majority *n* mayoría absoluta
overanxious [əuvərˈæŋkʃəs] *adj* demasiado preocupado *or* ansioso
overawe [əuvərˈɔː] *vt* intimidar
overbalance [əuvəˈbæləns] *vi* perder el equilibrio
overbearing [əuvəˈbɛərɪŋ] *adj* autoritario, imperioso
overboard [ˈəuvəbɔːd] *adv* (*Naut*) por la borda; **to go ~ for sth** (*fig*) enloquecer por algo
overbook [əuvəˈbuk] *vt* sobrereservar, reservar con exceso
overcapitalize [əuvəˈkæpɪtəlaɪz] *vi* sobrecapitalizar
overcast [ˈəuvəkɑːst] *adj* encapotado
overcharge [əuvəˈtʃɑːdʒ] *vt*: **to ~ sb** cobrar un precio excesivo a algn
overcoat [ˈəuvəkəut] *n* abrigo
overcome [əuvəˈkʌm] *vt* (*irreg: like* **come**) (*gen*) vencer; (*difficulty*) superar; **she was quite ~ by the occasion** la ocasión le conmovió mucho
overconfident [əuvəˈkɔnfɪdənt] *adj* demasiado confiado
overcrowded [əuvəˈkraudɪd] *adj* atestado de gente; (*city, country*) superpoblado
overcrowding [əuvəˈkraudɪŋ] *n* (*in town, country*) superpoblación *f*; (*in bus etc*) hacinamiento, apiñamiento
overdo [əuvəˈduː] *vt* (*irreg: like* **do**) exagerar; (*overcook*) cocer demasiado; **to ~ it, ~ things** (*work too hard*) trabajar demasiado
overdose [ˈəuvədəus] *n* sobredosis *f inv*
overdraft [ˈəuvədrɑːft] *n* saldo deudor
overdrawn [əuvəˈdrɔːn] *adj* (*account*) en descubierto
overdrive [ˈəuvədraɪv] *n* (*Aut*) sobremarcha, superdirecta
overdue [əuvəˈdjuː] *adj* retrasado; (*recognition*) tardío; (*bill*) vencido y no pagado; **that change was long ~** ese cambio tenía que haberse hecho hace tiempo
overemphasis [əuvərˈɛmfəsɪs] *n*: **to put an ~ on** poner énfasis excesivo en
overenthusiastic [ˈəuvərənθuːzɪˈæstɪk] *adj* demasiado entusiasta
overestimate [əuvərˈɛstɪmeɪt] *vt* sobreestimar
overexcited [əuvərɪkˈsaɪtɪd] *adj* sobreexcitado
overexertion [əuvərɪgˈzəːʃən] *n* agotamiento, fatiga
overexpose [əuvərɪkˈspəuz] *vt* (*Phot*) sobreexponer
overflow [əuvəˈfləu] *vi* desbordarse ■ *n* [ˈəuvəfləu] (*excess*) exceso; (*of river*) desbordamiento; (*also:* **overflow pipe**) (cañería de) desagüe *m*
overfly [əuvəˈflaɪ] *vt* (*irreg: like* **fly**) sobrevolar

overgenerous [əʊvə'dʒɛnərəs] *adj*
demasiado generoso

overgrown [əʊvə'grəun] *adj (garden)* cubierto
de hierba; **he's just an ~ schoolboy** es un
niño en grande

overhang [əʊvə'hæŋ] *vt (irreg: like hang)*
sobresalir por encima de ■ *vi* sobresalir

overhaul *vt* [əʊvə'hɔːl] revisar, repasar ■ *n*
['əʊvəhɔːl] revisión *f*

overhead *adv* [əʊvə'hɛd] por arriba or
encima ■ *adj* ['əʊvəhɛd] *(cable)* aéreo;
(railway) elevado, aéreo ■ *n* ['əʊvəhɛd] *(US)*
= **overheads**

overheads ['əʊvəhɛdz] *npl (Brit)* gastos *mpl*
generales

overhear [əʊvə'hɪəʳ] *vt (irreg: like hear)* oír por
casualidad

overheat [əʊvə'hiːt] *vi (engine)* recalentarse

overjoyed [əʊvə'dʒɔɪd] *adj* encantado, lleno
de alegría

overkill ['əʊvəkɪl] *n (Mil)* capacidad *f* excesiva
de destrucción; *(fig)* exceso

overland ['əʊvəlænd] *adj, adv* por tierra

overlap *vi* [əʊvə'læp] superponerse ■ *n*
['əʊvəlæp] superposición *f*

overleaf [əʊvə'liːf] *adv* al dorso

overload [əʊvə'ləud] *vt* sobrecargar

overlook [əʊvə'luk] *vt (have view of)* dar a,
tener vistas a; *(miss)* pasar por alto; *(forgive)*
hacer la vista gorda a

overlord ['əʊvəlɔːd] *n* señor *m*

overmanning [əʊvə'mænɪŋ] *n* exceso de
mano de obra; *(in organization)* exceso de
personal

overnight [əʊvə'naɪt] *adv* durante la noche;
(fig) de la noche a la mañana ■ *adj* de noche;
to stay ~ pasar la noche

overnight bag *n* fin *m* de semana, neceser
m de viaje

overnight stay *n* estancia de una noche

overpass ['əʊvəpɑːs] *n (US)* paso elevado or a
desnivel

overpay [əʊvə'peɪ] *vt:* **to ~ sb by £50** pagar
50 libras de más a algn

overplay [əʊvə'pleɪ] *vt* exagerar; **to ~ one's
hand** desmedirse

overpower [əʊvə'pauəʳ] *vt* dominar; *(fig)*
embargar

overpowering [əʊvə'pauərɪŋ] *adj (heat)*
agobiante; *(smell)* penetrante

overproduction [əʊvəprə'dʌkʃən] *n*
superproducción *f*

overrate [əʊvə'reɪt] *vt* sobrevalorar

overreach [əʊvə'riːtʃ] *vt:* **to ~ o.s.** ir
demasiado lejos, pasarse

override [əʊvə'raɪd] *vt (irreg: like ride) (order,
objection)* no hacer caso de

overriding [əʊvə'raɪdɪŋ] *adj* predominante

overrule [əʊvə'ruːl] *vt (decision)* anular;
(claim) denegar

overrun [əʊvə'rʌn] *vt (irreg: like run) (Mil:
country)* invadir; *(time limit)* rebasar, exceder
■ *vi* rebasar el límite previsto; **the town is
~ with tourists** el pueblo está inundado de
turistas

overseas [əʊvə'siːz] *adv* en ultramar; *(abroad)*
en el extranjero ■ *adj (trade)* exterior; *(visitor)*
extranjero

oversee [əʊvə'siː] *vt* supervisar

overseer ['əʊvəsɪəʳ] *n (in factory)* supervisor(a)
m(f); *(foreman)* capataz *m*

overshadow [əʊvə'ʃædəu] *vt (fig)* eclipsar

overshoot [əʊvə'ʃuːt] *vt (irreg: like shoot)*
excederse

oversight ['əʊvəsaɪt] *n* descuido; **due to an ~**
a causa de un descuido or una equivocación

oversimplify [əʊvə'sɪmplɪfaɪ] *vt* simplificar
demasiado

oversleep [əʊvə'sliːp] *vi (irreg: like sleep)*
dormir más de la cuenta, no despertarse a
tiempo

overspend [əʊvə'spɛnd] *vi* gastar más de la
cuenta; **we have overspent by five dollars**
hemos excedido el presupuesto en cinco
dólares

overspill ['əʊvəspɪl] *n* exceso de población

overstaffed [əʊvə'stɑːft] *adj:* **to be ~** tener
exceso de plantilla

overstate [əʊvə'steɪt] *vt* exagerar

overstatement ['əʊvəsteɪtmənt] *n*
exageración *f*

overstay [əʊvə'steɪ] *vt:* **to ~ one's time** *or*
welcome quedarse más de lo conveniente

overstep [əʊvə'stɛp] *vt:* **to ~ the mark** *or* **the
limits** pasarse de la raya

overstock [əʊvə'stɔk] *vt* abarrotar

overstretched [əʊvə'strɛtʃt] *adj* utilizado por
encima de su capacidad

overstrike *n* ['əʊvəstraɪk] *(on printer)*
superposición *f* ■ *vt (irreg: like strike)*
[əʊvə'straɪk] superponer

oversubscribed [əʊvəsəb'skraɪbd] *adj*
suscrito en exceso

overt [əu'vəːt] *adj* abierto

overtake [əʊvə'teɪk] *vt (irreg: like take)*
sobrepasar; *(Brit Aut)* adelantar

overtax [əʊvə'tæks] *vt (Econ)* exigir
contribuciones *fpl* excesivas *or* impuestos
mpl excesivos a; *(fig: strength)* poner a prueba;
(patience) agotar, abusar de; **to ~ o.s.** fatigarse
demasiado

overthrow [əʊvə'θrəu] *vt (irreg: like throw)*
(government) derrocar

overtime ['əʊvətaɪm] *n* horas *fpl*

extraordinarias; **to do** or **work** ~ hacer or
trabajar horas extraordinarias or extras
overtime ban n prohibición f de (hacer)
horas extraordinarias
overtone ['əuvətəun] n (fig) tono
overture ['əuvətʃuə^r] n (Mus) obertura; (fig)
propuesta
overturn [əuvə'tə:n] vt, vi volcar
overview ['əuvəvju:] n visión f de conjunto
overweight [əuvə'weɪt] adj demasiado gordo
or pesado
overwhelm [əuvə'wɛlm] vt aplastar
overwhelming [əuvə'wɛlmɪŋ] adj (victory,
defeat) arrollador(a); (desire) irresistible;
one's ~ impression is of heat lo que más
impresiona es el calor
overwhelmingly [əuvə'wɛlmɪŋlɪ] adv
abrumadoramente
overwork [əuvə'wə:k] n trabajo excesivo
■ vt hacer trabajar demasiado ■ vi trabajar
demasiado
overwrite [əuvə'raɪt] vt (irreg: like **write**)
(Comput) sobreescribir
overwrought [əuvə'rɔ:t] adj sobreexcitado
ovulation [ɔvju'leɪʃən] n ovulación f
owe [əu] vt deber; **to ~ sb sth**, **~ sth to sb**
deber algo a algn
owing to ['əuɪŋtu:] prep debido a, por causa de
owl [aul] n (also: **long-eared owl**) búho; (also:
barn owl) lechuza
own [əun] vt tener, poseer ■ vi: **to ~ to sth/
to having done sth** confesar or reconocer
algo/haber hecho algo ■ adj propio; **a room
of my ~** mi propia habitación; **to get one's ~
back** tomarse la revancha; **on one's ~** solo, a
solas; **can I have it for my (very)~?** ¿puedo
quedarme con él?; **to come into one's ~**
llegar a realizarse
▶ **own up** vi confesar
own brand n (Comm) marca propia
owner ['əunə^r] n dueño(-a)

owner-occupier ['əunər'ɔkjupaɪə^r] n
ocupante propietario(-a) m(f)
ownership ['əunəʃɪp] n posesión f; **it's
under new** ~ está bajo nueva dirección
own goal n (Sport) autogol m; **to score an** ~
marcar un gol en propia puerta, marcar un
autogol
ox (pl **oxen**) [ɔks, 'ɔksn] n buey m
Oxbridge ['ɔksbrɪdʒ] n universidades de Oxford y
Cambridge; ver nota

● **OXBRIDGE**

● El término Oxbridge es una fusión
● de Ox(ford) y (Cam)bridge, las dos
● universidades británicas más antiguas y
● con mayor prestigio académico y social.
● Muchos miembros destacados de la clase
● dirigente del país son antiguos alumnos
● de una de las dos. El mismo término suele
● aplicarse a todo lo que ambas representan
● en cuestión de prestigio y privilegios
● sociales.

Oxfam ['ɔksfæm] n abbr (Brit: = Oxford
Committee for Famine Relief) OXFAM
oxide ['ɔksaɪd] n óxido
Oxon. ['ɔksn] abbr (Brit) = **Oxoniensis; of
Oxford**
oxtail ['ɔksteɪl] n: ~ **soup** sopa de rabo de
buey
oxyacetylene ['ɔksɪə'sɛtɪli:n] adj
oxiacetilénico; ~ **burner**, ~ **torch** soplete m
oxiacetilénico
oxygen ['ɔksɪdʒən] n oxígeno
oxygen mask n máscara de oxígeno
oxygen tent n tienda de oxígeno
oyster ['ɔɪstə^r] n ostra
oz. abbr = **ounce; ounces**
ozone ['əuzəun] n ozono
ozone layer n capa de ozono

Pp

P, p [piː] n (letter) P, p f; **P for Peter** P de París
P abbr = **president; prince**
p abbr (= page) pág.; (Brit) = **penny; pence**
PA n abbr see **personal assistant; public
address system** ▪ abbr (US) = **Pennsylvania**
pa [pɑː] n (col) papá m
p.a. abbr = **per annum**
PAC n abbr (US) = **political action committee**
pace [peɪs] n paso; (rhythm) ritmo ▪ vi:
to ~ up and down pasearse de un lado a
otro; **to keep ~ with** llevar el mismo paso
que; (events) mantenerse a la altura de or al
corriente de; **to set the ~** (running) marcar
el paso; (fig) marcar la pauta; **to put sb
through his paces** (fig) poner a algn a prueba
pacemaker ['peɪsmeɪkəʳ] n (Med) marcapasos
m inv
pacific [pə'sɪfɪk] adj pacífico ▪ n: **the P~
(Ocean)** el (Océano) Pacífico
pacification [pæsɪfɪ'keɪʃən] n pacificación f
pacifier ['pæsɪfaɪəʳ] n (US: dummy) chupete m
pacifism ['pæsɪfɪzəm] n pacifismo
pacifist ['pæsɪfɪst] n pacifista m/f
pacify ['pæsɪfaɪ] vt (soothe) apaciguar;
(country) pacificar
pack [pæk] n (packet) paquete m; (Comm)
embalaje m; (of hounds) jauría; (of wolves)
manada; (of thieves etc) banda; (of cards)
baraja; (bundle) fardo; (US: of cigarettes)
paquete m, cajetilla ▪ vt (wrap) empaquetar;
(fill) llenar; (in suitcase etc) meter, poner;
(cram) llenar, atestar; (fig: meeting etc) llenar
de partidarios; (Comput) comprimir; **to ~
(one's bags)** hacer las maletas; **to - sb off**
despachar a algn; **the place was packed**
el local estaba (lleno) hasta los topes; **to
send sb packing** (col) echar a algn con cajas
destempladas
▸ **pack in** vi (break down: watch, car) estropearse
▪ vt (col) dejar; **- it in!** ¡para!, ¡basta ya!
▸ **pack up** vi (col: machine) estropearse;
(person) irse ▪ vt (belongings, clothes) recoger;
(goods, presents) empaquetar, envolver

package ['pækɪdʒ] n paquete m; (bulky)
bulto; (Comput) paquete m (de software); (also:
package deal) acuerdo global ▪ vt (Comm:
goods) envasar, embalar
package holiday n viaje m organizado (con
todo incluido)
package tour n viaje m organizado
packaging ['pækɪdʒɪŋ] n envase m
packed lunch [pækt-] n almuerzo frío
packer ['pækəʳ] n (person) empacador(a) m(f)
packet ['pækɪt] n paquete m
packet switching [-'swɪtʃɪŋ] n (Comput)
conmutación f por paquetes
packhorse ['pækhɔːs] n caballo de carga
pack ice n banco de hielo
packing ['pækɪŋ] n embalaje m
packing case n cajón m de embalaje
pact [pækt] n pacto
pad [pæd] n (of paper) bloc m; (cushion)
cojinete m; (launching pad) plataforma (de
lanzamiento); (col: flat) casa ▪ vt rellenar
padded cell ['pædɪd-] n celda acolchada
padding ['pædɪŋ] n relleno; (fig) paja
paddle ['pædl] n (oar) canalete m, pala; (US:
for table tennis) pala ▪ vt remar ▪ vi (with feet)
chapotear
paddle steamer n vapor m de ruedas
paddling pool ['pædlɪŋ-] n (Brit) piscina para
niños
paddock ['pædək] n (field) potrero
paddy field ['pædɪ-] n arrozal m
padlock ['pædlɔk] n candado ▪ vt cerrar con
candado
padre ['pɑːdrɪ] n capellán m
paediatrician, (US) **pediatrician** [piːdɪə'trɪʃən]
n pediatra m/f
paediatrics, (US) **pediatrics** [piːdɪ'ætrɪks] n
pediatría
paedophile, (US) **pedophile** ['piːdəufaɪl] adj
de pedófilos ▪ n pedófilo(-a)
pagan ['peɪgən] adj, n pagano(-a) m(f)
page [peɪdʒ] n página; (also: **page boy**) paje m
▪ vt (in hotel etc) llamar por altavoz a

p

pageant ['pædʒənt] *n* (*procession*) desfile *m*; (*show*) espectáculo

pageantry ['pædʒəntrɪ] *n* pompa

page break *n* límite *m* de la página

pager ['peɪdʒəʳ] *n* busca *m*

paginate ['pædʒɪneɪt] *vt* paginar

pagination [pædʒɪ'neɪʃən] *n* paginación *f*

pagoda [pə'gəudə] *n* pagoda

paid [peɪd] *pt, pp of* **pay** ■ *adj* (*work*) remunerado; (*official*) asalariado; **to put ~ to** (*Brit*) acabar con

paid-up ['peɪdʌp], **paid-in** (*US*) ['peɪdɪn] *adj* (*member*) con sus cuotas pagadas *or* al día; (*share*) liberado; **~ capital** capital *m* desembolsado

pail [peɪl] *n* cubo, balde *m*

pain [peɪn] *n* dolor *m*; **to be in ~** sufrir; **on ~ of death** so *or* bajo pena de muerte; *see also* **pains**

pained [peɪnd] *adj* (*expression*) afligido

painful ['peɪnful] *adj* doloroso; (*difficult*) penoso; (*disagreeable*) desagradable

painfully ['peɪnfəlɪ] *adv* (*fig: very*) terriblemente

painkiller ['peɪnkɪləʳ] *n* analgésico

painless ['peɪnlɪs] *adj* sin dolor; (*method*) fácil

pains [peɪnz] *npl* (*efforts*) esfuerzos *mpl*; **to take ~ to do sth** tomarse trabajo en hacer algo

painstaking ['peɪnzteɪkɪŋ] *adj* (*person*) concienzudo, esmerado

paint [peɪnt] *n* pintura ■ *vt* pintar; **a tin of ~** un bote de pintura; **to ~ the door blue** pintar la puerta de azul

paintbox ['peɪntbɔks] *n* caja de pinturas

paintbrush ['peɪntbrʌʃ] *n* (*artist's*) pincel *m*; (*decorator's*) brocha

painter ['peɪntəʳ] *n* pintor(a) *m(f)*

painting ['peɪntɪŋ] *n* pintura

paintwork ['peɪntwəːk] *n* pintura

pair [peəʳ] *n* (*of shoes, gloves etc*) par *m*; (*of people*) pareja; **a ~ of scissors** unas tijeras; **a ~ of trousers** unos pantalones, un pantalón
▶ **pair off** *vi*: **to ~ off (with sb)** hacer pareja (con algn)

pajamas [pɪ'dʒɑːməz] *npl* (*US*) pijama *msg*, piyama *msg* (*LAm*)

Pakistan [pɑːkɪ'stɑːn] *n* Paquistán *m*

Pakistani [pɑːkɪ'stɑːnɪ] *adj, n* paquistaní *m/f*

PAL [pæl] *n abbr* (*TV*) = **phase alternation line**

pal [pæl] *n* (*col*) amiguete(-a) *m(f)*, colega *m/f*

palace ['pæləs] *n* palacio

palatable ['pælɪtəbl] *adj* sabroso; (*acceptable*) aceptable

palate ['pælɪt] *n* paladar *m*

palatial [pə'leɪʃəl] *adj* (*surroundings, residence*) suntuoso, espléndido

palaver [pə'lɑːvəʳ] *n* (*fuss*) lío

pale [peɪl] *adj* (*gen*) pálido; (*colour*) claro ■ *n*: **to be beyond the ~** pasarse de la raya ■ *vi* palidecer; **to grow** *or* **turn ~** palidecer; **to ~ into insignificance (beside)** no poderse comparar (con)

paleness ['peɪlnɪs] *n* palidez *f*

Palestine ['pælɪstaɪn] *n* Palestina

Palestinian [pælɪs'tɪnɪən] *adj, n* palestino(-a) *m(f)*

palette ['pælɪt] *n* paleta

paling ['peɪlɪŋ] *n* (*stake*) estaca; (*fence*) valla

palisade [pælɪ'seɪd] *n* palizada

pall [pɔːl] *n* (*of smoke*) cortina ■ *vi* cansar

pallbearer ['pɔːlbɛərəʳ] *n* portador *m* del féretro

pallet ['pælɪt] *n* (*for goods*) pallet *m*

palletization [pælɪtaɪ'zeɪʃən] *n* paletización *f*

palliative ['pælɪətɪv] *n* paliativo

pallid ['pælɪd] *adj* pálido

pallor ['pæləʳ] *n* palidez *f*

pally ['pælɪ] *adj* (*col*): **to be very ~ with sb** ser muy amiguete de algn

palm [pɑːm] *n* (*Anat*) palma; (*also:* **palm tree**) palmera, palma ■ *vt*: **to ~ sth off on sb** (*Brit col*) endosarle algo a algn

palmist ['pɑːmɪst] *n* quiromántico(-a), palmista *m/f*

Palm Sunday *n* Domingo de Ramos

palpable ['pælpəbl] *adj* palpable

palpably ['pælpəblɪ] *adv* obviamente

palpitation [pælpɪ'teɪʃən] *n* palpitación *f*

paltry ['pɔːltrɪ] *adj* (*amount etc*) miserable; (*insignificant: person*) insignificante

pamper ['pæmpəʳ] *vt* mimar

pamphlet ['pæmflət] *n* folleto; (*political:* *handed out in street*) panfleto

pan [pæn] *n* (*also:* **saucepan**) cacerola, cazuela, olla; (*also:* **frying pan**) sartén *m*; (*of lavatory*) taza ■ *vi* (*Cine*) tomar panorámicas; **to ~ for gold** cribar oro

pan- [pæn] *pref* pan-

panacea [pænə'sɪə] *n* panacea

panache [pə'næʃ] *n* gracia, garbo

Panama [pænə'mɑː] *n* Panamá *m*

Panama Canal *n* el Canal de Panamá

pancake ['pænkeɪk] *n* crepe *f*, panqueque *m* (*LAm*)

Pancake Day *n* martes *m* de carnaval

pancake roll *n* rollito de primavera

pancreas ['pæŋkrɪəs] *n* páncreas *m*

panda ['pændə] *n* panda *m*

panda car *n* (*Brit*) coche *m* de la policía

pandemic [pæn'demɪk] *n* pandemia

pandemonium [pændɪ'məunɪəm] *n* (*noise*): **there was ~** se armó un tremendo jaleo; (*mess*) caos *m*

pander ['pændəʳ] *vi*: **to ~ to** complacer a

p & h *abbr* (US: = *postage and handling*) gastos de
envío
P & L *abbr* = **profit and loss**
p & p *abbr* (Brit: = *postage and packing*) gastos de
envío
pane [peɪn] *n* cristal *m*
panel ['pænl] *n* (*of wood*) panel *m*; (*of cloth*)
paño; (*Radio, TV*) panel *m* de invitados
panel game *n* (TV) programa *m* concurso
para equipos
panelling, (US) **paneling** ['pænəlɪŋ] *n*
paneles *mpl*
panellist, panelist (US) ['pænəlɪst] *n*
miembro del jurado
pang [pæŋ] *n*: **pangs of conscience**
remordimientos *mpl*; **pangs of hunger**
dolores *mpl* del hambre
panhandler ['pænhændlə'] *n* (*US col*)
mendigo(-a)
panic ['pænɪk] *n* pánico ■ *vi* dejarse llevar
por el pánico
panic buying [-baɪɪŋ] *n* compras masivas por
miedo a futura escasez
panicky ['pænɪkɪ] *adj* (*person*) asustadizo
panic-stricken ['pænɪkstrɪkən] *adj* preso del
pánico
pannier ['pænɪə'] *n* (*on bicycle*) cartera;
(*on mule etc*) alforja
panorama [pænə'rɑ:mə] *n* panorama *m*
panoramic [pænə'ræmɪk] *adj* panorámico
pansy ['pænzɪ] *n* (*Bot*) pensamiento; (*col; pej*)
maricón *m*
pant [pænt] *vi* jadear
panther ['pænθə'] *n* pantera
panties ['pæntɪz] *npl* bragas *fpl*
pantihose ['pæntɪhəʊz] *n* (US) medias *fpl*,
panties *mpl*
panto ['pæntəʊ] *n* (Brit col) = **pantomime**
pantomime ['pæntəmaɪm] *n* (Brit)
representación musical navideña *ver nota*

● **PANTOMIME**
●
● En época navideña los teatros británicos
● ponen en escena representaciones
● llamadas *pantomimes*, versiones libres de
● cuentos tradicionales como Aladino o
● El gato con botas. En ella nunca faltan
● personajes como la dama ("dame"),
● papel que siempre interpreta un actor;
● el protagonista joven ("principal boy"),
● normalmente interpretado por una
● actriz, y el malvado ("villain"). Es un
● espectáculo familiar dirigido a los
● niños pero con grandes dosis de humor
● para adultos en el que se alienta la
● participación del público.

pantry ['pæntrɪ] *n* despensa
pants [pænts] *npl* (Brit: *underwear: woman's*)
bragas *fpl*; (: *man's*) calzoncillos *mpl*; (US:
trousers) pantalones *mpl*
pantsuit ['pæntsjuːt] *n* (US) traje *m* de
chaqueta y pantalón
papal ['peɪpəl] *adj* papal
paparazzi [pæpə'rætsɪ] *npl* paparazzi *mpl*
paper ['peɪpə'] *n* papel *m*; (*also:* **newspaper**)
periódico, diario; (*study, article*) artículo;
(*exam*) examen *m* ■ *adj* de papel ■ *vt*
empapelar; (**identity**) **papers** *npl* papeles
mpl, documentos *mpl*; **a piece of** ~ un papel;
to put sth down on ~ poner algo por escrito
paper advance *n* (*on printer*) avance *m* de
papel
paperback ['peɪpəbæk] *n* libro de bolsillo
paper bag *n* bolsa de papel
paperboy ['peɪpəbɔɪ] *n* (*selling*) vendedor *m*
de periódicos; (*delivering*) repartidor *m* de
periódicos
paper clip *n* clip *m*
paper hankie *n* pañuelo de papel
paper money *n* papel *m* moneda
paper profit *n* beneficio no realizado
paper shop *n* (Brit) tienda de periódicos
paperweight ['peɪpəweɪt] *n* pisapapeles *m inv*
paperwork ['peɪpəwɜːk] *n* trabajo
administrativo; (*pej*) papeleo
papier-mâché ['pæpɪeɪ'mæʃeɪ] *n* cartón *m*
piedra
paprika ['pæprɪkə] *n* pimentón *m*
Pap test ['pæp-] *n* (*Med*) frotis *m* (cervical)
papyrus [pə'paɪərəs] *n* papiro
par [pɑː'] *n* par *f*; (*Golf*) par *m* ■ *adj* a la par;
to be on a ~ **with** estar a la par con; **at** ~ a la
par; **to be above/below** ~ estar sobre/bajo
par; **to feel under** ~ sentirse en baja forma
parable ['pærəbl] *n* parábola
parachute ['pærəʃuːt] *n* paracaídas *m inv* ■ *vi*
lanzarse en paracaídas
parachutist ['pærəʃuːtɪst] *n* paracaidista *m/f*
parade [pə'reɪd] *n* desfile *m* ■ *vt* (*gen*)
recorrer, desfilar por; (*show off*) hacer alarde
de ■ *vi* desfilar; (*Mil*) pasar revista; **a**
fashion ~ un desfile de modelos
parade ground *n* plaza de armas
paradise ['pærədaɪs] *n* paraíso
paradox ['pærədɔks] *n* paradoja
paradoxical [pærə'dɔksɪkl] *adj* paradójico
paradoxically [pærə'dɔksɪklɪ] *adv*
paradójicamente
paraffin ['pærəfɪn] *n* (Brit): ~ (**oil**) parafina
paraffin heater *n* estufa de parafina
paraffin lamp *n* quinqué *m*
paragon ['pærəgən] *n* modelo
paragraph ['pærəgrɑːf] *n* párrafo, acápite *m*

(LAm); **new** ~ punto y aparte, punto acápite (LAm)

Paraguay ['pærəgwaı] n Paraguay m

Paraguayan [pærə'gwaıən] adj, n paraguayo(-a) m(f), paraguayano(-a) m(f)

parallel ['pærəlɛl] adj: ~ **(with/to)** en paralelo (con/a); (fig) semejante (a) ■ n (line) paralela; (fig) paralelo; (Geo) paralelo

paralysis [pə'rælısıs] n parálisis f inv

paralytic [pærə'lıtık] adj paralítico

paralyze ['pærəlaız] vt paralizar

paramedic [pærə'mɛdık] n auxiliar m/f sanitario(-a)

parameter [pə'ræmıtəʳ] n parámetro

paramilitary [pærə'mılıtərı] adj (organization, operations) paramilitar

paramount ['pærəmaunt] adj: **of** ~ **importance** de suma importancia

paranoia [pærə'nɔıə] n paranoia

paranoid ['pærənɔıd] adj (person, feeling) paranoico

paranormal [pærə'nɔ:ml] adj paranormal

parapet ['pærəpıt] n parapeto

paraphernalia [pærəfə'neılıə] n parafernalia

paraphrase ['pærəfreız] vt parafrasear

paraplegic [pærə'pli:dʒık] n parapléjico(-a)

parapsychology [pærəsaı'kɔlədʒı] n parasicología

parasite ['pærəsaıt] n parásito(-a)

parasol ['pærəsɔl] n sombrilla, quitasol m

paratrooper ['pærətru:pəʳ] n paracaidista m/f

parcel ['pa:sl] n paquete m ■ vt (also: **parcel up**) empaquetar, embalar; **to be part and** ~ **of** ser parte integrante de
▶ **parcel out** vt parcelar, repartir

parcel bomb n paquete m bomba

parcel post n servicio de paquetes postales

parch [pa:tʃ] vt secar, resecar

parched [pa:tʃt] adj (person) muerto de sed

parchment ['pa:tʃmənt] n pergamino

pardon ['pa:dn] n perdón m; (Law) indulto
■ vt perdonar; indultar; ~ **me!, I beg your** ~! ¡perdone usted!; **(I beg your)** ~?, (US) ~ **me?** ¿cómo (dice)?

pare [pɛəʳ] vt (nails) cortar; (fruit etc) pelar

parent ['pɛərənt] n: **parents** npl padres mpl

parentage ['pɛərəntıdʒ] n familia, linaje m; **of unknown** ~ de padres desconocidos

parental [pə'rɛntl] adj paternal/maternal

parent company n casa matriz

parenthesis (pl **parentheses**) [pə'rɛnθısıs, -θısı:z] n paréntesis m inv; **in parentheses** entre paréntesis

parenthood ['pɛərənthud] n el ser padres

parent ship n buque m nodriza

Paris ['pærıs] n París m

parish ['pærıʃ] n parroquia

parish council n consejo parroquial

parishioner [pə'rıʃənəʳ] n feligrés(-esa) m(f)

Parisian [pə'rızıən] adj, n parisino(-a) m(f), parisiense m/f

parity ['pærıtı] n paridad f, igualdad f

park [pa:k] n parque m, jardín m público ■ vt aparcar, estacionar ■ vi aparcar, estacionar

parka ['pa:kə] n parka

parking ['pa:kıŋ] n aparcamiento, estacionamiento; **"no** ~**"** "prohibido aparcar or estacionarse"

parking lights npl luces fpl de estacionamiento

parking lot n (US) parking m, aparcamiento, playa f de estacionamiento (LAm)

parking meter n parquímetro

parking offence, (US) **parking violation** n ofensa por aparcamiento indebido

parking place n sitio para aparcar, aparcamiento

parking ticket n multa de aparcamiento

Parkinson's n (also: **Parkinson's disease**) (enfermedad f de) Parkinson m

parkway ['pa:kweı] n (US) alameda

parlance ['pa:ləns] n lenguaje m; **in common/modern** ~ en lenguaje corriente/ moderno

parliament ['pa:ləmənt] n parlamento; (Spanish) las Cortes fpl; ver nota

● **PARLIAMENT**
●
● El Parlamento británico (Parliament) tiene
● como sede el palacio de Westminster,
● también llamado "Houses of Parliament".
● Consta de dos cámaras: la Cámara de los
● Comunes ("House of Commons") está
● formada por 650 diputados ("Members
● of Parliament") que acceden a ella tras
● ser elegidos por sufragio universal en
● su respectiva área o circunscripción
● electoral ("constituency"). Se reúne 175
● días al año y sus sesiones son presididas
● y moderadas por el Presidente de la
● Cámara ("Speaker"). La cámara alta es la
● Cámara de los Lores ("House of Lords")
● y sus miembros son nombrados por el
● monarca o bien han heredado su escaño.
● Su poder es limitado, aunque actúa como
● tribunal supremo de apelación, excepto
● en Escocia.

parliamentary [pa:lə'mɛntərı] adj parlamentario

parlour, parlor (US) ['pa:ləʳ] n salón m, living m (LAm)

parlous ['pɑːləs] *adj* peligroso, alarmante

Parmesan [pɑːmɪ'zæn] *n* (*also*: **Parmesan cheese**) queso parmesano

parochial [pə'rəukɪəl] *adj* parroquial; (*pej*) de miras estrechas

parody ['pærədɪ] *n* parodia ▪ *vt* parodiar

parole [pə'rəul] *n*: **on ~** en libertad condicional

paroxysm ['pærəksɪzəm] *n* (*Med*) paroxismo, ataque *m*; (*of anger, laughter, coughing*) ataque *m*; (*of grief*) crisis *f*

parquet ['pɑːkeɪ] *n*: **~ floor(ing)** parquet *m*

parrot ['pærət] *n* loro, papagayo

parrot fashion *adv* como un loro

parry ['pærɪ] *vt* parar

parsimonious [pɑːsɪ'məunɪəs] *adj* tacaño

parsley ['pɑːslɪ] *n* perejil *m*

parsnip ['pɑːsnɪp] *n* chirivía

parson ['pɑːsn] *n* cura *m*

part [pɑːt] *n* (*gen*) parte *f*; (*Mus*) parte *f*; (*bit*) trozo; (*of machine*) pieza; (*Theat etc*) papel *m*; (*of serial*) entrega; (*US: in hair*) raya ▪ *adv* = **partly** ▪ *vt* separar; (*break*) partir ▪ *vi* (*people*) separarse; (*roads*) bifurcarse; (*crowd*) apartarse; (*break*) romperse; **to take ~ in** participar or tomar parte en; **to take sb's ~** tomar partido por algn; **for my ~** por mi parte; **for the most ~** en su mayor parte; (*people*) en su mayoría; **for the better ~ of the day** durante la mayor parte del día; **~ of speech** (*Ling*) categoría gramatical, parte *f* de la oración; **to take sth in good/bad ~** aceptar algo bien/tomarse algo a mal
  ▸ **part with** *vt fus* ceder, entregar; (*money*) pagar; (*get rid of*) deshacerse de

partake [pɑː'teɪk] *vi* (*irreg: like* **take**) (*formal*): **to ~ of sth** (*food*) comer algo; (*drink*) tomar or beber algo

part exchange *n* (*Brit*): **in ~** como parte del pago

partial ['pɑːʃl] *adj* parcial; **to be ~ to** (*like*) ser aficionado a

partially ['pɑːʃəlɪ] *adv* en parte, parcialmente

participant [pɑː'tɪsɪpənt] *n* (*in competition*) concursante *m/f*

participate [pɑː'tɪsɪpeɪt] *vi*: **to ~ in** participar en

participation [pɑːtɪsɪ'peɪʃən] *n* participación *f*

participle ['pɑːtɪsɪpl] *n* participio

particle ['pɑːtɪkl] *n* partícula; (*of dust*) mota; (*fig*) pizca

particular [pə'tɪkjulə^r] *adj* (*special*) particular; (*concrete*) concreto; (*given*) determinado; (*detailed*) detallado, minucioso; (*fussy*) quisquilloso, exigente; **particulars** *npl* (*information*) datos *mpl*, detalles *mpl*; (*details*)

pormenores *mpl*; **in ~** en particular; **to be very ~ about** ser muy exigente en cuanto a; **I'm not ~** me es or da igual

particularly [pə'tɪkjuləlɪ] *adv* especialmente, en particular

parting ['pɑːtɪŋ] *n* (*act of*) separación *f*; (*farewell*) despedida; (*Brit: in hair*) raya ▪ *adj* de despedida; **~ shot** (*fig*) golpe *m* final

partisan [pɑːtɪ'zæn] *adj* partidista ▪ *n* partidario(-a); (*fighter*) partisano(-a)

partition [pɑː'tɪʃən] *n* (*Pol*) división *f*; (*wall*) tabique *m* ▪ *vt* dividir; dividir con tabique

partly ['pɑːtlɪ] *adv* en parte

partner ['pɑːtnə^r] *n* (*Comm*) socio(-a); (*Sport*) pareja; (*at dance*) pareja; (*spouse*) cónyuge *m/f*; (*friend etc*) compañero(-a) ▪ *vt* acompañar

partnership ['pɑːtnəʃɪp] *n* (*gen*) asociación *f*; (*Comm*) sociedad *f*; **to go into ~ (with), form a ~ (with)** asociarse (con)

part payment *n* pago parcial

partridge ['pɑːtrɪdʒ] *n* perdiz *f*

part-time ['pɑːt'taɪm] *adj, adv* a tiempo parcial

part-timer [pɑːt'taɪmə^r] *n* trabajador(a) *m(f)* a tiempo parcial

party ['pɑːtɪ] *n* (*Pol*) partido; (*celebration*) fiesta; (*group*) grupo; (*Law*) parte *f*, interesado ▪ *adj* (*Pol*) de partido; (*dress etc*) de fiesta, de gala; **to have** *or* **give** *or* **throw a ~** organizar una fiesta; **dinner ~** cena; **to be a ~ to a crime** ser cómplice *m/f* de un crimen

party line *n* (*Pol*) línea política del partido; (*Tel*) línea compartida

party piece *n*: **to do one's ~** hacer su numerito (de fiesta)

party political broadcast *n* = espacio electoral

pass [pɑːs] *vt* (*time, object*) pasar; (*place*) pasar por; (*exam, law*) aprobar; (*overtake, surpass*) rebasar; (*approve*) aprobar ▪ *vi* pasar; (*Scol*) aprobar ▪ *n* (*permit*) permiso, pase *m*; (*membership card*) carnet *m*; (*in mountains*) puerto; (*Sport*) pase *m*; (*Scol: also*: **pass mark**) aprobado; **to ~ sth through sth** pasar algo por algo; **to ~ the time of day with sb** pasar el rato con algn; **things have come to a pretty ~!** ¡hasta dónde hemos llegado!; **to make a ~ at sb** (*col*) insinuársele a algn
  ▸ **pass away** *vi* fallecer
  ▸ **pass by** *vi* pasar ▪ *vt* (*ignore*) pasar por alto
  ▸ **pass down** *vt* (*customs, inheritance*) pasar, transmitir
  ▸ **pass for** *vt fus* pasar por; **she could ~ for 25** se podría creer que sólo tiene 25 años
  ▸ **pass on** *vi* (*die*) fallecer, morir ▪ *vt* (*hand on*): **to ~ on (to)** transmitir (a); (*cold, illness*) pegar (a); (*benefits*) dar (a); (*price rises*) pasar (a)

▶ **pass out** vi desmayarse; (Mil) graduarse
▶ **pass over** vi (die) fallecer ■ vt omitir, pasar por alto
▶ **pass up** vt (opportunity) dejar pasar, no aprovechar
passable ['pɑːsəbl] adj (road) transitable; (tolerable) pasable
passably ['pɑːsəblɪ] adv pasablemente
passage ['pæsɪdʒ] n pasillo; (act of passing) tránsito; (fare, in book) pasaje m; (by boat) travesía
passageway ['pæsɪdʒweɪ] n (in house) pasillo, corredor m; (between buildings etc) pasaje m, pasadizo
passenger ['pæsɪndʒəʳ] n pasajero(-a), viajero(-a)
passer-by [pɑːsə'baɪ] n transeúnte m/f
passing ['pɑːsɪŋ] adj (fleeting) pasajero; **in ~** de paso
passing place n (Aut) apartadero
passion ['pæʃən] n pasión f
passionate ['pæʃənɪt] adj apasionado
passionately ['pæʃənɪtlɪ] adv apasionadamente, con pasión
passion fruit n fruta de la pasión, granadilla
passion play n drama m de la Pasión
passive ['pæsɪv] adj (also Ling) pasivo
passive smoking n efectos del tabaco en fumadores pasivos
passkey ['pɑːskiː] n llave f maestra
Passover ['pɑːsəuvəʳ] n Pascua (de los judíos)
passport ['pɑːspɔːt] n pasaporte m
passport control n control m de pasaporte
password ['pɑːswɜːd] n (also Comput) contraseña
past [pɑːst] prep (further than) más allá de; (later than) después de ■ adj pasado; (president etc) antiguo ■ n (time) pasado; (of person) antecedentes mpl; **quarter/half ~ four** las cuatro y cuarto/media; **he's ~ forty** tiene más de cuarenta años; **I'm ~ caring** ya no me importa; **to be ~ it** (col: person) estar acabado; **for the ~ few/three days** durante los últimos días/últimos tres días; **to run ~** pasar corriendo por; **in the ~** en el pasado, antes
pasta ['pæstə] n pasta
paste [peɪst] n (gen) pasta; (glue) engrudo ■ vt (stick) pegar; (glue) engomar; **tomato ~** tomate concentrado
pastel ['pæstl] adj pastel; (painting) al pastel
pasteurized ['pæstəraɪzd] adj pasteurizado
pastille ['pæstl] n pastilla
pastime ['pɑːstaɪm] n pasatiempo
past master n: **to be a ~ at** ser un maestro en
pastor ['pɑːstəʳ] n pastor m
pastoral ['pɑːstərl] adj pastoral

pastry ['peɪstrɪ] n (dough) pasta; (cake) pastel m
pasture ['pɑːstʃəʳ] n (grass) pasto
pasty n ['pæstɪ] empanada ■ adj ['peɪstɪ] pastoso; (complexion) pálido
pat [pæt] vt dar una palmadita a; (dog etc) acariciar ■ n (of butter) porción f ■ adj: **he knows it (off) ~** se lo sabe de memoria or al dedillo; **to give sb/o.s. a ~ on the back** (fig) felicitar a algn/felicitarse
patch [pætʃ] n (of material) parche m; (mended part) remiendo; (of land) terreno; (Comput) ajuste m ■ vt (clothes) remendar; **(to go through) a bad ~** (pasar por) una mala racha
▶ **patch up** vt (mend temporarily) reparar; **to ~ up a quarrel** hacer las paces
patchwork ['pætʃwɜːk] n labor f de retales
patchy ['pætʃɪ] adj desigual
pate [peɪt] n: **bald ~** calva
pâté ['pæteɪ] n paté m
patent ['peɪtnt] n patente f ■ vt patentar ■ adj patente, evidente
patent leather n charol m
patently ['peɪtntlɪ] adv evidentemente
patent medicine n específico
patent office n oficina de patentes y marcas
patent rights npl derechos mpl de patente
paternal [pə'tɜːnl] adj paternal; (relation) paterno
paternalistic [pətɜːnə'lɪstɪk] adj paternalista
paternity [pə'tɜːnɪtɪ] n paternidad f
paternity suit n (Law) caso de paternidad
path [pɑːθ] n camino, sendero; (trail, track) pista; (of missile) trayectoria
pathetic [pə'θetɪk] adj (pitiful) penoso, patético; (very bad) malísimo; (moving) conmovedor(a)
pathetically [pə'θetɪklɪ] adv penosamente, patéticamente; (very badly) malísimamente mal, de pena
pathological [pæθə'lɔdʒɪkəl] adj patológico
pathologist [pə'θɔlədʒɪst] n patólogo(-a)
pathology [pə'θɔlədʒɪ] n patología
pathos ['peɪθɔs] n patetismo
pathway ['pɑːθweɪ] n sendero, vereda
patience ['peɪʃns] n paciencia; (Brit Cards) solitario; **to lose one's ~** perder la paciencia
patient ['peɪʃnt] n paciente m/f ■ adj paciente, sufrido; **to be ~ with sb** tener paciencia con algn
patiently ['peɪʃntlɪ] adv pacientemente, con paciencia
patio ['pætɪəu] n patio
patriot ['peɪtrɪət] n patriota m/f
patriotic [pætrɪ'ɔtɪk] adj patriótico
patriotism ['pætrɪətɪzəm] n patriotismo
patrol [pə'trəul] n patrulla ■ vt patrullar por; **to be on ~** patrullar, estar de patrulla

patrol boat n patrullero, patrullera
patrol car n coche m patrulla
patrolman [pə'trəulmən] n (US) policía m
patron ['peɪtrən] n (in shop) cliente m/f; (of charity) patrocinador(a) m(f); ~ **of the arts** mecenas m
patronage ['pætrənɪdʒ] n patrocinio, protección f
patronize ['pætrənaɪz] vt (shop) ser cliente de; (look down on) tratar con condescendencia a
patronizing ['pætrənaɪzɪŋ] adj condescendiente
patron saint n santo(-a) patrón(-ona)
patter ['pætər] n golpeteo; (sales talk) labia ■ vi (rain) tamborilear
pattern ['pætən] n (Sewing) patrón m; (design) dibujo; (behaviour, events) esquema m; ~ **of events** curso de los hechos; **behaviour patterns** modelos mpl de comportamiento
patterned ['pætənd] adj (material) estampado
paucity ['pɔːsɪtɪ] n escasez f
paunch [pɔːntʃ] n panza, barriga
pauper ['pɔːpər] n pobre m/f
pause [pɔːz] n pausa; (interval) intervalo ■ vi hacer una pausa; **to ~ for breath** detenerse para tomar aliento
pave [peɪv] vt pavimentar; **to ~ the way for** preparar el terreno para
pavement ['peɪvmənt] n (Brit) acera, vereda (LAm), andén m (LAm), banqueta (LAm); (US) calzada, pavimento
pavilion [pə'vɪlɪən] n pabellón m; (Sport) vestuarios mpl
paving ['peɪvɪŋ] n pavimento
paving stone n losa
paw [pɔː] n pata; (claw) garra ■ vt (animal) tocar con la pata; (pej: touch) tocar, manosear
pawn [pɔːn] n (Chess) peón m; (fig) instrumento ■ vt empeñar
pawnbroker ['pɔːnbrəukər] n prestamista m/f
pawnshop ['pɔːnʃɔp] n casa de empeños
pay [peɪ] (pt, pp **paid**) n paga; (wage etc) sueldo, salario ■ vt pagar; (visit) hacer; (respect) ofrecer ■ vi pagar; (be profitable) rendir, compensar, ser rentable; **to be in sb's ~** estar al servicio de algn; **to ~ attention (to)** prestar atención (a); **I paid £5 for that record** pagué 5 libras por ese disco; **how much did you ~ for it?** ¿cuánto pagaste por él?; **to ~ one's way** (contribute one's share) pagar su parte; (remain solvent: company) ser solvente; **to ~ dividends** (Comm) pagar dividendos; (fig) compensar; **it won't ~ you to do that** no te merece la pena hacer eso; **to put paid to** (plan, person) acabar con
▶ **pay back** vt (money) devolver, reembolsar; (person) pagar

▶ **pay for** vt fus pagar
▶ **pay in** vt ingresar
▶ **pay off** vt liquidar; (person) pagar; (debts) liquidar, saldar; (creditor) cancelar, redimir; (workers) despedir; (mortgage) cancelar, redimir ■ vi (scheme, decision) dar resultado; **to ~ sth off in instalments** pagar algo a plazos
▶ **pay out** vt (rope) ir dando; (money) gastar, desembolsar
▶ **pay up** vt pagar
payable ['peɪəbl] adj pagadero; **to make a cheque ~ to sb** extender un cheque a favor de algn
pay-as-you-go [peɪəzjə'gəu] adj (mobile phone) (de) prepago
pay award n aumento de sueldo
pay day n día m de paga
PAYE n abbr (Brit: = pay as you earn) sistema de retención fiscal en la fuente de ingresos
payee [peɪ'iː] n portador(a) m(f)
pay envelope n (US) = **pay packet**
paying ['peɪɪŋ] adj: ~ **guest** huésped(a) m(f) que la paga
payload ['peɪləud] n carga útil
payment ['peɪmənt] n pago; **advance ~** (part sum) anticipo, adelanto; (total sum) saldo; **monthly ~** mensualidad f; **deferred ~**, ~ **by instalments** pago a plazos or diferido; **on ~ of £5** mediante pago de or pagando £5; **in ~ for** en pago de
pay packet n (Brit) sobre m (de la paga)
pay-phone ['peɪfəun] n teléfono público
payroll ['peɪrəul] n nómina; **to be on a firm's ~** estar en la nómina de una compañía
pay slip n hoja del sueldo
pay station n (US) teléfono público
PBS n abbr (US: = Public Broadcasting Service) agrupación de ayuda a la realización de emisiones para la TV pública
PBX abbr (Tel) = **private branch exchange**
PC n abbr (= personal computer) PC m, OP m; (Brit) = **police constable** ■ abbr (Brit) = **Privy Councillor** ■ adj abbr = **politically correct**
pc abbr = **per cent; postcard**
p/c abbr = **petty cash**
PCB n abbr (= printed circuit board) TCI f
pcm abbr = **per calendar month**
PD n abbr (US) = **police department**
pd abbr = **paid**
PDA n abbr (= personal digital assistant) agenda electrónica
PDSA n abbr (Brit) = **People's Dispensary for Sick Animals**
PDT n abbr (US: = Pacific Daylight Time) hora de verano del Pacífico

PE *n abbr* (= *physical education*) ed. física ■ *abbr* (*Canada*) = **Prince Edward Island**

pea [pi:] *n* guisante *m*, chícharo (*LAm*), arveja (*LAm*)

peace [pi:s] *n* paz *f*; (*calm*) paz *f*, tranquilidad *f*; **to be at ~ with sb/sth** estar en paz con algn/algo; **to keep the ~** (*policeman*) mantener el orden; (*citizen*) guardar el orden

peaceable ['pi:səbl] *adj* pacífico

peaceably [pi:səblı] *adv* pacíficamente

peaceful ['pi:sful] *adj* (*gentle*) pacífico; (*calm*) tranquilo, sosegado

peacekeeping ['pi:ski:pɪŋ] *adj* de pacificación ■ *n* pacificación *f*

peacekeeping force *n* fuerza de pacificación

peace offering *n* (*fig*) prenda de paz

peacetime ['pi:staɪm] *n*: **in ~** en tiempo de paz

peach [pi:tʃ] *n* melocotón *m*, durazno (*LAm*)

peacock ['pi:kɔk] *n* pavo real

peak [pi:k] *n* (*of mountain: top*) cumbre *f*, cima; (: *point*) pico; (*of cap*) visera; (*fig*) cumbre *f*

peak-hour ['pi:kauə^r] *adj* (*traffic etc*) de horas punta

peak hours *npl*, **peak period** ■ *n* horas *fpl* punta

peak rate *n* tarifa máxima

peaky ['pi:kı] *adj* (*Brit col*) pálido, paliducho; **I'm feeling a bit ~** estoy malucho, no me encuentro bien

peal [pi:l] *n* (*of bells*) repique *m*; **~ of laughter** carcajada

peanut ['pi:nʌt] *n* cacahuete *m*, maní *m* (*LAm*)

peanut butter *n* mantequilla de cacahuete

pear [peə^r] *n* pera

pearl [pə:l] *n* perla

peasant ['peznt] *n* campesino(-a)

peat [pi:t] *n* turba

pebble ['pebl] *n* guijarro

peck [pek] *vt* (*also*: **peck at**) picotear; (*food*) comer sin ganas ■ *n* picotazo; (*kiss*) besito

pecking order ['pekɪŋ-] *n* orden *m* de jerarquía

peckish ['pekɪʃ] *adj* (*Brit col*): **I feel ~** tengo ganas de picar algo

peculiar [pɪ'kju:lıə^r] *adj* (*odd*) extraño, raro; (*typical*) propio, característico; (*particular*: *importance, qualities*) particular; **~ to** propio de

peculiarity [pɪkju:lɪ'ærıtı] *n* peculiaridad *f*, característica

peculiarly [pɪ'kju:lıəlı] *adv* extrañamente; particularmente

pedal ['pedl] *n* pedal *m* ■ *vi* pedalear

pedal bin *n* cubo de la basura con pedal

pedant ['pedənt] *n* pedante *m/f*

pedantic [pɪ'dæntık] *adj* pedante

pedantry ['pedəntrı] *n* pedantería

peddle ['pedl] *vt* (*goods*) ir vendiendo *or* vender de puerta en puerta; (*drugs*) traficar con; (*gossip*) divulgar

peddler ['pedlə^r] *n* vendedor(a) *m(f)* ambulante

pedestal ['pedəstl] *n* pedestal *m*

pedestrian [pɪ'destrıən] *n* peatón *m* ■ *adj* pedestre

pedestrian crossing *n* (*Brit*) paso de peatones

pedestrian precinct *n* zona reservada para peatones

pediatrics [pi:dɪ'ætrıks] *n* (*US*) = **paediatrics**

pedigree ['pedɪgri:] *n* genealogía; (*of animal*) pedigrí *m* ■ *cpd* (*animal*) de raza, de casta

pedlar ['pedlə^r] *n* (*Brit*) = **peddler**

pee [pi:] *vi* (*col*) mear

peek [pi:k] *vi* mirar a hurtadillas; (*Comput*) inspeccionar

peel [pi:l] *n* piel *f*; (*of orange, lemon*) cáscara; (: *removed*) peladuras *fpl* ■ *vt* pelar ■ *vi* (*paint etc*) desconcharse; (*wallpaper*) despegarse, desprenderse
  ▶ **peel back** *vt* pelar

peeler ['pi:lə^r] *n*: **potato ~** mondador *m or* pelador *m* de patatas, pelapatatas *m inv*

peep [pi:p] *n* (*Brit: look*) mirada furtiva; (*sound*) pío ■ *vi* (*Brit*) piar
  ▶ **peep out** *vi* asomar la cabeza

peephole ['pi:phəul] *n* mirilla

peer [pıə^r] *vi*: **to ~ at** escudriñar ■ *n* (*noble*) par *m*; (*equal*) igual *m*

peerage ['pıərıdʒ] *n* nobleza

peerless ['pıəlıs] *adj* sin par, incomparable, sin igual

peeved [pi:vd] *adj* enojado

peevish ['pi:vıʃ] *adj* malhumorado

peevishness ['pi:vıʃnıs] *n* mal humor *m*

peg [peg] *n* clavija; (*for coat etc*) gancho, colgador *m*; (*Brit: also*: **clothes peg**) pinza; (*also*: **tent peg**) estaca ■ *vt* (*clothes*) tender; (*groundsheet*) fijar con estacas; (*fig: wages, prices*) fijar

pejorative [pɪ'dʒɔrətıv] *adj* peyorativo

Pekin [pi:'kın], **Peking** [pi:'kıŋ] *n* Pekín *m*

pekinese [pi:kı'ni:z] *n* pequinés(-esa) *m(f)*

pelican ['pelıkən] *n* pelícano

pelican crossing *n* (*Brit Aut*) paso de peatones señalizado

pellet ['pelıt] *n* bolita; (*bullet*) perdigón *m*

pell-mell ['pel'mel] *adv* en tropel

pelmet ['pelmıt] *n* galería

pelt [pelt] *vt*: **to ~ sb with sth** arrojarle algo a algn ■ *vi* (*rain: also*: **pelt down**) llover a cántaros ■ *n* pellejo

pelvis ['pelvıs] *n* pelvis *f*

pen [pen] *n* (*also*: **ballpoint pen**) bolígrafo;

(also: **fountain pen**) pluma; (for sheep) redil
m; (US col: prison) cárcel f, chirona; **to put ~ to
paper** tomar la pluma
penal ['piːnl] adj penal; ~ **servitude** trabajos
mpl forzados
penalize ['piːnəlaɪz] vt (punish) castigar;
(Sport) sancionar, penalizar
penalty ['pɛnltɪ] n (gen) pena; (fine) multa;
(Sport) sanción f; (also: **penalty kick**: Football)
penalty m
penalty area n (Brit Sport) área de castigo
penalty clause n cláusula de penalización
penalty shoot-out [-'ʃuːtaut] n (Football)
tanda de penaltis
penance ['penəns] n penitencia
pence [pɛns] pl of **penny**
penchant ['pãːʃãːŋ] n predilección f,
inclinación f
pencil ['pɛnsl] n lápiz m, lapicero (LAm) ■ vt
(also: **pencil in**) escribir con lápiz
pencil case n estuche m
pencil sharpener n sacapuntas m inv
pendant ['pɛndnt] n pendiente m
pending ['pɛndɪŋ] prep antes de ■ adj
pendiente; ~ **the arrival of** ... hasta que
llegue ..., hasta llegar ...
pendulum ['pɛndjuləm] n péndulo
penetrate ['pɛnɪtreɪt] vt penetrar
penetrating ['pɛnɪtreɪtɪŋ] adj penetrante
penetration [pɛnɪ'treɪʃən] n penetración f
penfriend ['pɛnfrɛnd] n (Brit) amigo(-a) por
correspondencia
penguin ['pɛŋgwɪn] n pingüino
penicillin [pɛnɪ'sɪlɪn] n penicilina
peninsula [pə'nɪnsjulə] n península
penis ['piːnɪs] n pene m
penitence ['pɛnɪtns] n penitencia
penitent ['pɛnɪtnt] adj arrepentido; (Rel)
penitente
penitentiary [pɛnɪ'tɛnʃərɪ] n (US) cárcel f,
presidio
penknife ['pɛnnaɪf] n navaja
Penn., Penna. abbr (US) = **Pennsylvania**
pen name n seudónimo
pennant ['pɛnənt] n banderola; banderín m
penniless ['pɛnɪlɪs] adj sin dinero
Pennines ['pɛnaɪnz] npl (Montes mpl)
Peninos mpl
penny (pl **pennies** or (BRIT) **pence**) ['pɛnɪ,
'pɛnɪz, pɛns] n (Brit) penique m; (US) centavo
penpal ['pɛnpæl] n amigo(-a) por
correspondencia
penpusher ['pɛnpuʃər] n (pej) chupatintas
m/f inv
pension ['pɛnʃən] n (allowance, state payment)
pensión f; (old-age) jubilación f
▶ **pension off** vt jubilar

pensioner ['pɛnʃənər] n (Brit) jubilado(-a)
pension fund n fondo de pensiones
pensive ['pɛnsɪv] adj pensativo; (withdrawn)
preocupado
pentagon ['pɛntəgən] n pentágono; **the P~**
(US Pol) el Pentágono

Pentecost ['pɛntɪkɔst] n Pentecostés m
penthouse ['pɛnthaus] n ático (de lujo)
pent-up ['pɛntʌp] adj (feelings) reprimido
penultimate [pɛ'nʌltɪmət] adj penúltimo
penury ['pɛnjurɪ] n miseria, pobreza
people ['piːpl] npl gente f; (citizens) pueblo
sg, ciudadanos mpl ■ n (nation, race) pueblo,
nación f ■ vt poblar; **several ~ came**
vinieron varias personas; ~ **say that** ... dice
la gente que ...; **old/young** ~ los ancianos/
jóvenes; ~ **at large** la gente en general;
a man of the ~ un hombre del pueblo
PEP [pɛp] n abbr (= personal equity plan) plan
personal de inversión con desgravación fiscal
pep [pɛp] n (col) energía
▶ **pep up** vt animar
pepper ['pɛpər] n (spice) pimienta; (vegetable)
pimiento, ají m (LAm), chile m (LAm) ■ vt (fig)
salpicar
peppermint ['pɛpəmɪnt] n menta; (sweet)
pastilla de menta
pepperoni [pɛpə'rəunɪ] n ≈ salchichón m
picante
pepperpot ['pɛpəpɔt] n pimentero
peptalk ['pɛptɔːk] n (col): **to give sb a** ~ darle
a algn una inyección de ánimo
per [pəːr] prep por; ~ **day/person** por día/
persona; **as ~ your instructions** de acuerdo
con sus instrucciones
per annum adv al año
per capita adj, adv per cápita
perceive [pə'siːv] vt percibir; (realize) darse
cuenta de
per cent, (US) **percent** [pə'sɛnt] n por ciento;
a 20 ~ discount un descuento del 20 por
ciento
percentage [pə'sɛntɪdʒ] n porcentaje m;
to get a ~ on all sales percibir un tanto por
ciento sobre todas las ventas; **on a ~ basis** a
porcentaje

percentage point *n* punto (porcentual)
perceptible [pə'sɛptəbl] *adj* perceptible; (*notable*) sensible
perception [pə'sɛpʃən] *n* percepción *f*; (*insight*) perspicacia
perceptive [pə'sɛptɪv] *adj* perspicaz
perch [pə:tʃ] *n* (*fish*) perca; (*for bird*) percha ■ *vi* posarse
percolate ['pə:kəleɪt] *vt* (*coffee*) filtrar ■ *vi* (*coffee*) filtrarse; (*fig*) filtrarse
percolator ['pə:kəleɪtəʳ] *n* cafetera de filtro
percussion [pə'kʌʃən] *n* percusión *f*
percussionist [pə'kʌʃənɪst] *n* percusionista *m/f*
peremptory [pə'rɛmptərɪ] *adj* perentorio
perennial [pə'rɛnɪəl] *adj* perenne
perfect *adj* ['pə:fɪkt] perfecto ■ *n* (*also:* **perfect tense**) perfecto ■ *vt* [pə'fɛkt] perfeccionar; **he's a ~ stranger to me** no le conozco de nada, me es completamente desconocido
perfection [pə'fɛkʃən] *n* perfección *f*
perfectionist [pə'fɛkʃənɪst] *n* perfeccionista *m/f*
perfectly ['pə:fɪktlɪ] *adv* perfectamente; **I'm ~ happy with the situation** estoy muy contento con la situación; **you know ~ well** lo sabes muy bien *or* perfectamente
perforate ['pə:fəreɪt] *vt* perforar
perforated ulcer *n* úlcera perforada
perforation [pə:fə'reɪʃən] *n* perforación *f*
perform [pə'fɔ:m] *vt* (*carry out*) realizar, llevar a cabo; (*Theat*) representar; (*piece of music*) interpretar ■ *vi* (*Theat*) actuar; (*Tech*) funcionar
performance [pə'fɔ:məns] *n* (*of task*) realización *f*; (*of a play*) representación *f*; (*of player etc*) actuación *f*; (*of engine*) rendimiento; (*of car*) prestaciones *fpl*; (*of function*) desempeño; **the team put up a good ~** el equipo se defendió bien
performer [pə'fɔ:məʳ] *n* (*actor*) actor *m*, actriz *f*; (*Mus*) intérprete *m/f*
performing [pə'fɔ:mɪŋ] *adj* (*animal*) amaestrado
performing arts *npl*: **the ~** las artes teatrales
perfume ['pə:fju:m] *n* perfume *m*
perfunctory [pə'fʌŋktərɪ] *adj* superficial
perhaps [pə'hæps] *adv* quizá(s), tal vez; **~ so/ not** puede que sí/no
peril ['pɛrɪl] *n* peligro, riesgo
perilous ['pɛrɪləs] *adj* peligroso
perilously ['pɛrɪləslɪ] *adv*: **they came ~ close to being caught** por poco les cogen *or* agarran
perimeter [pə'rɪmɪtəʳ] *n* perímetro
period ['pɪərɪəd] *n* período, periodo; (*History*)

época; (*Scol*) clase *f*; (*full stop*) punto; (*Med*) regla, periodo; (*US Sport*) tiempo ■ *adj* (*costume, furniture*) de época; **for a ~ of three weeks** durante (un período de) tres semanas; **the holiday ~** el período de vacaciones
periodic [pɪərɪ'ɔdɪk] *adj* periódico
periodical [pɪərɪ'ɔdɪkl] *adj* periódico ■ *n* revista, publicación *f* periódica
periodically [pɪərɪ'ɔdɪklɪ] *adv* de vez en cuando, cada cierto tiempo
period pains *npl* dolores *mpl* de la regla *or* de la menstruación
peripatetic [pɛrɪpə'tɛtɪk] *adj* (*salesman*) ambulante; (*teacher*) con trabajo en varios colegios
peripheral [pə'rɪfərəl] *adj* periférico ■ *n* (*Comput*) periférico, unidad *f* periférica
periphery [pə'rɪfərɪ] *n* periferia
periscope ['pɛrɪskəup] *n* periscopio
perish ['pɛrɪʃ] *vi* perecer; (*decay*) echarse a perder
perishable ['pɛrɪʃəbl] *adj* perecedero
perishables ['pɛrɪʃəblz] *npl* productos *mpl* perecederos
peritonitis [pɛrɪtə'naɪtɪs] *n* peritonitis *f*
perjure ['pə:dʒəʳ] *vt*: **to ~ o.s.** perjurar
perjury ['pə:dʒərɪ] *n* (*Law*) perjurio
perk [pə:k] *n* beneficio, extra *m*
  ▶ **perk up** *vi* (*cheer up*) animarse
perky ['pə:kɪ] *adj* alegre, animado
perm [pə:m] *n* permanente *f* ■ *vt*: **to have one's hair permed** hacerse una permanente
permanence ['pə:mənəns] *n* permanencia
permanent ['pə:mənənt] *adj* permanente; (*job, position*) fijo; (*dye, ink*) indeleble; **~ address** domicilio permanente; **I'm not ~ here** no estoy fijo aquí
permanently ['pə:mənəntlɪ] *adv* (*lastingly*) para siempre, de modo definitivo; (*all the time*) permanentemente
permeate ['pə:mɪeɪt] *vi* penetrar, trascender ■ *vt* penetrar, trascender a
permissible [pə'mɪsɪbl] *adj* permisible, lícito
permission [pə'mɪʃən] *n* permiso; **to give sb ~ to do sth** autorizar a algn para que haga algo; **with your ~** con su permiso
permissive [pə'mɪsɪv] *adj* permisivo
permit *n* ['pə:mɪt] permiso, licencia; (*entrance pass*) pase *m* ■ *vt* [pə'mɪt] permitir; (*accept*) tolerar ■ *vi* [pə'mɪt]: **weather permitting** si el tiempo lo permite; **fishing ~** permiso de pesca; **building/export ~** licencia *or* permiso de construcción/exportación
permutation [pə:mju'teɪʃən] *n* permutación *f*
pernicious [pə:'nɪʃəs] *adj* nocivo; (*Med*) pernicioso

pernickety [pə'nɪkɪtɪ] *adj* (*col: person*) quisquilloso; (*: task*) delicado
perpendicular [pə:pən'dɪkjuləʳ] *adj* perpendicular
perpetrate ['pə:pɪtreɪt] *vt* cometer
perpetual [pə'pɛtjuəl] *adj* perpetuo
perpetually [pə'pɛtjuəlɪ] *adv* (*eternally*) perpetuamente; (*continuously*) constantemente, continuamente
perpetuate [pə'pɛtjueɪt] *vt* perpetuar
perpetuity [pə:pɪ'tʃuɪtɪ] *n*: **in ~ a** perpetuidad
perplex [pə'plɛks] *vt* dejar perplejo
perplexed [pə'plɛkst] *adj* perplejo, confuso
perplexing [pə'plɛksɪŋ] *adj* que causa perplejidad
perplexity [pə'plɛksɪtɪ] *n* perplejidad *f*, confusión *f*
perquisites ['pə:kwɪzɪts] *npl* (*also*: **perks**) beneficios *mpl*
persecute ['pə:sɪkju:t] *vt* (*pursue*) perseguir; (*harass*) acosar
persecution [pə:sɪ'kju:ʃən] *n* persecución *f*
perseverance [pə:sɪ'vɪərəns] *n* perseverancia
persevere [pə:sɪ'vɪəʳ] *vi* perseverar
Persia ['pə:ʃə] *n* Persia
Persian ['pə:ʃən] *adj, n* persa *m/f* ■ *n* (*Ling*) persa *m*; **the ~ Gulf** el Golfo Pérsico
Persian cat *n* gato persa
persist [pə'sɪst] *vi* persistir; **to ~ in doing sth** empeñarse en hacer algo
persistence [pə'sɪstəns] *n* empeño
persistent [pə'sɪstənt] *adj* (*lateness, rain*) persistente; (*determined*) porfiado; (*continuing*) constante; **~ offender** (*Law*) multirreincidente *m/f*
persistently [pə'sɪstəntlɪ] *adv* persistentemente; (*continually*) constantemente
persnickety [pə'snɪkətɪ] *adj* (*US col*) = **pernickety**
person ['pə:sn] *n* persona; **in ~** en persona; **on** *or* **about one's ~** encima; **a ~ to ~ call** una llamada (de) persona a persona
personable ['pə:snəbl] *adj* atractivo
personal ['pə:snl] *adj* personal, individual; (*visit*) en persona; (*Brit Tel*) (de) persona a persona
personal allowance *n* desgravación *f* personal
personal assistant *n* ayudante *m/f* personal
personal belongings *npl* efectos *mpl* personales
personal column *n* anuncios *mpl* personales
personal computer *n* ordenador *m* personal
personal effects *npl* efectos *mpl* personales

personal identification number *n* número personal de identificación
personality [pə:sə'nælɪtɪ] *n* personalidad *f*
personally ['pə:snlɪ] *adv* personalmente
personal organizer *n* agenda (profesional); (*electronic*) organizador *m* personal
personal property *n* bienes *mpl* muebles
personal, social and health education *n* (*Brit Scol*) formación social y sanitaria para la vida adulta
personal stereo *n* walkman® *m*
personification [pə:sɔnɪfɪ'keɪʃən] *n* personificación *f*
personify [pə:'sɔnɪfaɪ] *vt* encarnar, personificar
personnel [pə:sə'nɛl] *n* personal *m*
personnel department *n* departamento de personal
personnel management *n* gestión *f* de personal
personnel manager *n* jefe *m* de personal
perspective [pə'spɛktɪv] *n* perspectiva; **to get sth into ~** ver algo en perspectiva *or* como es
Perspex® ['pə:spɛks] *n* (*Brit*) vidrio acrílico, plexiglás® *m*
perspiration [pə:spɪ'reɪʃən] *n* transpiración *f*, sudor *m*
perspire [pə'spaɪəʳ] *vi* transpirar, sudar
persuade [pə'sweɪd] *vt*: **to ~ sb to do sth** persuadir a algn para que haga algo; **to ~ sb of sth/that** persuadir *or* convencer a algn de algo/de que; **I am persuaded that ...** estoy convencido de que ...
persuasion [pə'sweɪʒən] *n* persuasión *f*; (*persuasiveness*) persuasiva; (*creed*) creencia
persuasive [pə'sweɪsɪv] *adj* persuasivo
persuasively [pə'sweɪsɪvlɪ] *adv* de modo persuasivo
pert [pə:t] *adj* impertinente, fresco, atrevido
pertaining [pə:'teɪnɪŋ]: **~ to** *prep* relacionado con
pertinent ['pə:tɪnənt] *adj* pertinente, a propósito
perturb [pə'tə:b] *vt* perturbar
perturbing [pə'tə:bɪŋ] *adj* inquietante, perturbador(a)
Peru [pə'ru:] *n* el Perú
perusal [pə'ru:zəl] *n* (*quick*) lectura somera; (*careful*) examen *m*
peruse [pə'ru:z] *vt* (*examine*) leer con detención, examinar; (*glance at*) mirar por encima
Peruvian [pə'ru:vɪən] *adj, n* peruano(-a) *m(f)*
pervade [pə'veɪd] *vt* impregnar; (*influence, ideas*) extenderse por
pervasive [pə'veɪsɪv] *adj* (*smell*) penetrante;

(*influence*) muy extendido; (*gloom, feelings, ideas*) reinante

perverse [pə'və:s] *adj* perverso; (*stubborn*) terco; (*wayward*) travieso

perversely [pə'və:slɪ] *adv* perversamente; tercamente; traviesamente

perverseness [pə'və:snɪs] *n* perversidad *f*; terquedad *f*; travesura

perversion [pə'və:ʃən] *n* perversión *f*

pervert *n* ['pə:və:t] pervertido(-a) ▪ *vt* [pə'və:t] pervertir

pessary ['pɛsərɪ] *n* pesario

pessimism ['pɛsɪmɪzəm] *n* pesimismo

pessimist ['pɛsɪmɪst] *n* pesimista *m/f*

pessimistic [pɛsɪ'mɪstɪk] *adj* pesimista

pest [pɛst] *n* (*insect*) insecto nocivo; (*fig*) lata, molestia; **pests** *npl* plaga

pest control *n* control *m* de plagas

pester ['pɛstər] *vt* molestar, acosar

pesticide ['pɛstɪsaɪd] *n* pesticida *m*

pestilence ['pɛstɪləns] *n* pestilencia

pestle ['pɛsl] *n* mano *f* de mortero *or* de almirez

pet [pɛt] *n* animal *m* doméstico; (*favourite*) favorito(-a) ▪ *vt* acariciar ▪ *vi* (*col*) besuquearse ▪ *cpd*: **my ~ aversion** mi manía

petal ['pɛtl] *n* pétalo

peter ['pi:tər]: **to ~ out** *vi* agotarse, acabarse

petite [pə'ti:t] *adj* menuda, chiquita

petition [pə'tɪʃən] *n* petición *f* ▪ *vt* presentar una petición a ▪ *vi*: **to ~ for divorce** pedir el divorcio

pet name *n* nombre *m* cariñoso, apodo

petrified ['pɛtrɪfaɪd] *adj* (*fig*) pasmado, horrorizado

petrochemical [pɛtrə'kɛmɪkl] *adj* petroquímico

petrodollars ['pɛtrəudɔləz] *npl* petrodólares *mpl*

petrol ['pɛtrəl] (*Brit*) *n* gasolina; (*for lighter*) bencina; **two/four-star ~** gasolina normal/súper

petrol bomb *n* cóctel *m* Molotov

petrol can *n* bidón *m* de gasolina

petrol engine *n* (*Brit*) motor *m* de gasolina

petroleum [pə'trəulɪəm] *n* petróleo

petroleum jelly *n* vaselina

petrol pump *n* (*Brit: in car*) bomba de gasolina; (*in garage*) surtidor *m* de gasolina

petrol station *n* (*Brit*) gasolinera

petrol tank *n* (*Brit*) depósito (de gasolina)

petticoat ['pɛtɪkəut] *n* combinación *f*, enagua(s) *f(pl)* (*LAm*)

pettifogging ['pɛtɪfɔgɪŋ] *adj* quisquilloso

pettiness ['pɛtɪnɪs] *n* mezquindad *f*

petty ['pɛtɪ] *adj* (*mean*) mezquino; (*unimportant*) insignificante

petty cash *n* dinero para gastos menores

petty cash book *n* libro de caja auxiliar

petty officer *n* contramaestre *m*

petulant ['pɛtjulənt] *adj* malhumorado

pew [pju:] *n* banco

pewter ['pju:tər] *n* peltre *m*

Pfc *abbr* (*US Mil*) = **private first class**

PG *n abbr* (*Cine*) = **parental guidance**

PG 13 *abbr* (*US: Cine*: = *Parental Guidance 13*) no apto para menores de 13 años

PGA *n abbr* = **Professional Golfers' Association**

PH *n abbr* (*US Mil*: = *Purple Heart*) *decoración otorgada a los heridos de guerra*

pH *n abbr* (= *pH value*) pH

PHA *n abbr* (*US*) = **Public Housing Administration**

phallic ['fælɪk] *adj* fálico

phantom ['fæntəm] *n* fantasma *m*

Pharaoh ['fɛərəu] *n* faraón *m*

pharmaceutical [fɑ:mə'sju:tɪkl] *adj* farmacéutico

pharmacist ['fɑ:məsɪst] *n* farmacéutico(-a)

pharmacy ['fɑ:məsɪ] *n* (*US*) farmacia

phase [feɪz] *n* fase *f* ▪ *vt*: **to ~ sth in/out** introducir/retirar algo por etapas; **phased withdrawal** retirada progresiva

PhD *abbr* = **Doctor of Philosophy**

pheasant ['fɛznt] *n* faisán *m*

phenomenal [fɪ'nɔmɪnl] *adj* fenomenal, extraordinario

phenomenally [fɪ'nɔmɪnlɪ] *adv* extraordinariamente

phenomenon (*pl* **phenomena**) [fə'nɔmɪnən, -nə] *n* fenómeno

phial ['faɪəl] *n* ampolla

philanderer [fɪ'lændərər] *n* donjuán *m*, don Juan *m*

philanthropic [fɪlən'θrɔpɪk] *adj* filantrópico

philanthropist [fɪ'lænθrəpɪst] *n* filántropo(-a)

philatelist [fɪ'lætəlɪst] *n* filatelista *m/f*

philately [fɪ'lætəlɪ] *n* filatelia

Philippines ['fɪlɪpi:nz] *npl*: **the ~** (las Islas) Filipinas

philosopher [fɪ'lɔsəfər] *n* filósofo(-a)

philosophical [fɪlə'sɔfɪkl] *adj* filosófico

philosophy [fɪ'lɔsəfɪ] *n* filosofía

phishing ['fɪʃɪŋ] *n* phishing *m*, *método de estafa a través de Internet*

phlegm [flɛm] *n* flema

phlegmatic [flɛg'mætɪk] *adj* flemático

phobia ['fəubjə] *n* fobia

phone [fəun] *n* teléfono ▪ *vt* telefonear, llamar por teléfono; **to be on the ~** tener teléfono; (*be calling*) estar hablando por teléfono

▶ **phone back** vt, vi volver a llamar
▶ **phone up** vt, vi llamar por teléfono
phone book n guía telefónica
phone box, phone booth n cabina
telefónica
phone call n llamada (telefónica)
phonecard ['fəunkɑːd] n tarjeta telefónica
phone-in ['fəunɪn] n (Brit Radio, TV) programa
de radio o televisión con las líneas abiertas al público
phone tapping [-tæpɪŋ] n escuchas
telefónicas
phonetics [fə'netɪks] n fonética
phoney ['fəunɪ] adj = **phony**
phonograph ['fəunəɡræf] n (US) fonógrafo,
tocadiscos m inv
phonology [fəu'nɔlədʒɪ] n fonología
phony ['fəunɪ] adj falso ▪ n (person) farsante
m/f
phosphate ['fɔsfeɪt] n fosfato
phosphorus ['fɔsfərəs] n fósforo
photo ['fəutəu] n foto f
photo... ['fəutəu] pref foto...
photocall ['fəutəukɔːl] n sesión f fotográfica
para la prensa
photocopier ['fəutəukɔpɪəʳ] n fotocopiadora
photocopy ['fəutəukɔpɪ] n fotocopia ▪ vt
fotocopiar
photoelectric [fəutəuɪ'lektrɪk] adj ▪ **cell**
célula fotoeléctrica
photo finish n resultado comprobado por
fotocontrol
Photofit® ['fəutəufɪt] n (also: **Photofit
picture**) retrato robot
photogenic [fəutəu'dʒenɪk] adj fotogénico
photograph ['fəutəɡræf] n fotografía ▪ vt
fotografiar; **to take a ~ of sb** sacar una foto
de algn
photographer [fə'tɔɡrəfəʳ] n fotógrafo
photographic [fəutə'ɡræfɪk] adj fotográfico
photography [fə'tɔɡrəfɪ] n fotografía
photo opportunity n oportunidad de salir en
la foto
Photostat® ['fəutəustæt] n fotóstato
photosynthesis [fəutəu'sɪnθəsɪs] n
fotosíntesis f
phrase [freɪz] n frase f ▪ vt (letter) expresar,
redactar
phrase book n libro de frases
physical ['fɪzɪkl] adj físico; **~ examination**
reconocimiento médico; **~ exercises**
ejercicios mpl físicos
physical education n educación f física
physically ['fɪzɪklɪ] adv físicamente
physical training n gimnasia
physician [fɪ'zɪʃən] n médico(-a)
physicist ['fɪzɪsɪst] n físico(-a)
physics ['fɪzɪks] n física

physiological [fɪzɪə'lɔdʒɪkl] adj fisiológico
physiology [fɪzɪ'ɔlədʒɪ] n fisiología
physiotherapy [fɪzɪəu'θerəpɪ] n fisioterapia
physique [fɪ'ziːk] n físico
pianist ['pɪənɪst] n pianista m/f
piano [pɪ'ænəu] n piano
piano accordion n (Brit) acordeón-piano m
piccolo ['pɪkələu] n (Mus) flautín m
pick [pɪk] n (tool: also: **pick-axe**) pico, piqueta
▪ vt (select) elegir, escoger; (gather) coger (SP),
recoger (LAm); (lock) abrir con ganzúa; (scab,
spot) rascar ▪ vi: **to ~ and choose** ser muy
exigente; **take your ~** escoja lo que quiera;
the ~ of lo mejor de; **to ~ one's nose/teeth**
hurgarse las narices/escarbarse los dientes;
to ~ pockets ratear, ser carterista; **to ~
one's way through** andar a tientas, abrirse
camino; **to ~ a fight/quarrel with sb** buscar
pelea/camorra con algn; **to ~ sb's brains**
aprovecharse de los conocimientos de algn
▶ **pick at** vt fus: **to ~ at one's food** comer con
poco apetito
▶ **pick off** vt (kill) matar de un tiro
▶ **pick on** vt fus (person) meterse con
▶ **pick out** vt escoger; (distinguish) identificar
▶ **pick up** vi (improve: sales) ir mejor; (: patient)
reponerse; (: Finance) recobrarse ▪ vt (from
floor) recoger; (buy) comprar; (find) encontrar;
(learn) aprender; (Radio, TV, Tel) captar; **to ~
up speed** acelerarse; **to ~ o.s. up** levantarse;
to ~ up where one left off volver a empezar
algo donde lo había dejado
pickaxe, pickax (US) ['pɪkæks] n pico,
zapapico
picket ['pɪkɪt] n (in strike) piquete m ▪ vt
hacer un piquete en, piquetear; **to be on ~
duty** estar de piquete
picketing ['pɪkɪtɪŋ] n organización f de
piquetes
picket line n piquete m
pickings ['pɪkɪŋz] npl (pilferings): **there are
good ~ to be had here** se pueden sacar
buenas ganancias de aquí
pickle ['pɪkl] n (also: **pickles**: as condiment)
escabeche m; (fig: mess) apuro ▪ vt conservar
en escabeche; (in vinegar) conservar en
vinagre; **in a ~** en un lío, en apuros
pick-me-up ['pɪkmɪʌp] n reconstituyente m
pickpocket ['pɪkpɔkɪt] n carterista m/f
pickup ['pɪkʌp] n (also: **pickup truck, pickup
van**) furgoneta
picnic ['pɪknɪk] n picnic m, merienda ▪ vi
merendar en el campo
pictorial [pɪk'tɔːrɪəl] adj pictórico; (magazine
etc) ilustrado
picture ['pɪktʃəʳ] n cuadro; (painting) pintura;
(photograph) fotografía; (film) película; (TV)

p

imagen f ■ vt pintar; **the pictures** (Brit) el cine; **we get a good ~ here** captamos bien la imagen aquí; **to take a ~ of sb/sth** hacer or sacar una foto a algn/de algo; **the garden is a ~ in June** el jardín es una preciosidad en junio; **the overall ~** la impresión general; **to put sb in the ~** poner a algn al corriente or al tanto

picture book n libro de dibujos

picture message n mensaje m con foto

picture messaging n (envío de) mensajes mpl con imágenes

picturesque [pɪktʃə'resk] adj pintoresco

piddling ['pɪdlɪŋ] adj insignificante

pidgin ['pɪdʒɪn] adj: **~ English** lengua franca basada en el inglés

pie [paɪ] n (of meat etc: large) pastel m; (: small) empanada; (sweet) tarta

piebald ['paɪbɔːld] adj pío

piece [piːs] n pedazo, trozo; (of cake) trozo; (Draughts etc) ficha; (Chess) pieza; (part of a set) pieza; (item): **a ~ of furniture/advice** un mueble/un consejo ■ vt: **to ~ together** juntar; (Tech) armar; **to take to pieces** desmontar; **a ~ of news** una noticia; **a 10p ~** una moneda de 10 peniques; **a six-~ band** un conjunto de seis (músicos); **in one ~** (object) de una sola pieza; **~ by ~** pieza por or a pieza; **to say one's ~** decir su parecer

piecemeal ['piːsmiːl] adv poco a poco

piece rate n tarifa a destajo

piecework ['piːswəːk] n trabajo a destajo

pie chart n gráfico de sectores or de tarta

pier [pɪəʳ] n muelle m, embarcadero

pierce [pɪəs] vt penetrar en, perforar; **to have one's ears pierced** hacerse los agujeros de las orejas

piercing ['pɪəsɪŋ] adj (cry) penetrante ■ n (body art) piercing m

piety ['paɪətɪ] n piedad f

pig [pɪɡ] n cerdo, puerco, chancho (LAm); (person: greedy) tragón(-ona) m(f), comilón(-ona) m(f); (nasty) cerdo(-a)

pigeon ['pɪdʒən] n paloma; (as food) pichón m

pigeonhole ['pɪdʒənhəul] n casilla

piggy bank ['pɪɡɪbæŋk] n hucha (en forma de cerdito)

pigheaded ['pɪɡ'hedɪd] adj terco, testarudo

piglet ['pɪɡlɪt] n cerdito, cochinillo

pigment ['pɪɡmənt] n pigmento

pigmentation [pɪɡmən'teɪʃən] n pigmentación f

pigmy ['pɪɡmɪ] n = **pygmy**

pigskin ['pɪɡskɪn] n piel f de cerdo

pigsty ['pɪɡstaɪ] n pocilga

pigtail ['pɪɡteɪl] n (girl's) trenza; (Chinese) coleta; (Taur) coleta

pike [paɪk] n (spear) pica; (fish) lucio

pilchard ['pɪltʃəd] n sardina

pile [paɪl] n (heap) montón m; (of carpet) pelo; (vb: also: **pile up**) ■ vt amontonar; (fig) acumular ■ vi amontonarse; **in a ~** en un montón; **to ~ into** (car) meterse en
▶ **pile on** vt: **to ~ it on** (col) exagerar

piles [paɪlz] npl (Med) almorranas fpl, hemorroides mpl

pile-up ['paɪlʌp] n (Aut) accidente m múltiple

pilfer ['pɪlfəʳ] vt, vi ratear, robar, sisar

pilfering ['pɪlfərɪŋ] n ratería

pilgrim ['pɪlɡrɪm] n peregrino(-a); **the P~ Fathers** or **Pilgrims** los primeros colonos norteamericanos; see also **Thanksgiving**

pilgrimage ['pɪlɡrɪmɪdʒ] n peregrinación f, romería

pill [pɪl] n píldora; **the ~** la píldora; **to be on the ~** tomar la píldora (anticonceptiva)

pillage ['pɪlɪdʒ] vt pillar, saquear

pillar ['pɪləʳ] n pilar m, columna

pillar box n (Brit) buzón m

pillion ['pɪljən] n (of motorcycle) asiento trasero; **to ride ~** ir en el asiento trasero

pillion passenger n pasajero que va detrás

pillory ['pɪlərɪ] vt poner en ridículo

pillow ['pɪləu] n almohada

pillowcase ['pɪləukeɪs], **pillowslip** ['pɪləuslɪp] n funda (de almohada)

pilot ['paɪlət] n piloto inv ■ adj (scheme etc) piloto ■ vt pilotar; (fig) guiar, conducir

pilot light n piloto

pimento [pɪ'mentəu] n pimiento morrón

pimp [pɪmp] n chulo, cafiche m (LAm)

pimple ['pɪmpl] n grano

pimply ['pɪmplɪ] adj lleno de granos

PIN n abbr (= personal identification number) NPI m

pin [pɪn] n alfiler m; (Elec: of plug) clavija; (Tech) perno; (: wooden) clavija; (drawing pin) chincheta; (in grenade) percutor m ■ vt prender con (alfiler); sujetar con perno; **pins and needles** hormigueo sg; **to ~ sth on sb** (fig) cargar a algn con la culpa de algo
▶ **pin down** vt (fig): **there's something strange here, but I can't quite ~ it down** aquí hay algo raro pero no puedo precisar qué es; **to ~ sb down** hacer que algn concrete

pinafore ['pɪnəfɔːʳ] n delantal m

pinafore dress n (Brit) pichi m

pinball ['pɪnbɔːl] n (also: **pinball machine**) millón m, fliper m

pincers ['pɪnsəz] npl pinzas fpl, tenazas fpl

pinch [pɪntʃ] n pellizco; (of salt etc) pizca ■ vt pellizcar; (col: steal) birlar ■ vi (shoe) apretar; **at a ~** en caso de apuro; **to feel the ~** (fig) pasar apuros or estrecheces

pinched [pɪntʃt] adj (drawn) cansado; **~ with**

cold transido de frío; **~ for money/space** mal *or* falto de dinero/espacio *or* sitio

pincushion ['pɪnkuʃən] *n* acerico

pine [paɪn] *n* (*also:* **pine tree**) pino ■ *vi:* **to ~ for** suspirar por

▸ **pine away** *vi* morirse de pena

pineapple ['paɪnæpl] *n* piña, ananá(s) *m* (*LAm*)

pine cone *n* piña

pine needle *n* aguja de pino

Ping-Pong® ['pɪŋpɔn] *n* pingpong *m*

pink [pɪŋk] *adj* (de color) rosa ■ *n* (*colour*) rosa; (*Bot*) clavel *m*

pinking shears ['pɪŋkɪŋ-] *npl* tijeras *fpl* dentadas

pin money *n* dinero para gastos extra

pinnacle ['pɪnəkl] *n* cumbre *f*

pinpoint ['pɪnpɔɪnt] *vt* precisar

pinstripe ['pɪnstraɪp] *adj:* **~ suit** traje *m* a rayas

pint [paɪnt] *n* (*Brit*) pinta (= 0,57 l); (*US*) pinta (= 0,47 l); (*Brit col: of beer*) pinta de cerveza, ≈ jarra (*SP*)

pin-up ['pɪnʌp] *n* (*picture*) *fotografía de mujer u hombre medio desnudos;* **~ (girl)** ≈ chica de calendario

pioneer [paɪə'nɪəʳ] *n* pionero(a) ■ *vt* promover

pious ['paɪəs] *adj* piadoso, devoto

pip [pɪp] *n* (*seed*) pepita; **the pips** (*Brit Tel*) la señal

pipe [paɪp] *n* tubería, cañería; (*for smoking*) pipa, cachimba (*LAm*), cachimbo (*LAm*) ■ *vt* conducir en cañerías; **(bag)pipes** *npl* gaita *sg*

▸ **pipe down** *vi* (*col*) callarse

pipe cleaner *n* limpiapipas *m inv*

piped music [paɪpt-] *n* música ambiental

pipe dream *n* sueño imposible

pipeline ['paɪplaɪn] *n* tubería, cañería; (*for oil*) oleoducto; (*for natural gas*) gaseoducto; **it is in the ~** (*fig*) está en trámite

piper ['paɪpəʳ] *n* (*gen*) flautista *m/f*; (*with bagpipes*) gaitero(-a)

pipe tobacco *n* tabaco de pipa

piping ['paɪpɪŋ] *adv:* **to be ~ hot** estar calentito

piquant ['piːkənt] *adj* picante

pique [piːk] *n* pique *m*, resentimiento

pirate ['paɪərət] *n* pirata *m/f* ■ *vt* (*record, video, book*) hacer una copia pirata de

pirated ['paɪərətɪd] *adj* (*book, record etc*) pirata *inv*

pirate radio *n* (*Brit*) emisora pirata

pirouette [pɪru'ɛt] *n* pirueta ■ *vi* piruetear

Pisces ['paɪsiːz] *n* Piscis *m*

piss [pɪs] *vi* (*col*) mear

pissed [pɪst] *adj* (*col: drunk*) mamado

pistol ['pɪstl] *n* pistola

piston ['pɪstən] *n* pistón *m*, émbolo

pit [pɪt] *n* hoyo; (*also:* **coal pit**) mina; (*in garage*) foso de inspección; (*also:* **orchestra pit**) foso de la orquesta; (*quarry*) cantera ■ *vt* (*chickenpox*) picar; (*rust*) comer; **to ~ A against B** oponer A a B; **pits** *npl* (*Aut*) box *msg*; **pitted with** (*chickenpox*) picado de

pitapat ['pɪtə'pæt] *adv:* **to go ~** (*heart*) latir rápidamente; (*rain*) golpetear

pitch [pɪtʃ] *n* (*throw*) lanzamiento; (*Mus*) tono; (*Brit Sport*) campo, terreno; (*tar*) brea; (*in market etc*) puesto; (*fig: degree*) nivel *m*, grado ■ *vt* (*throw*) arrojar, lanzar ■ *vi* (*fall*) caer(se); (*Naut*) cabecear; **I can't keep working at this ~** no puedo seguir trabajando a este ritmo; **at its (highest) ~** en su punto máximo; **his anger reached such a ~ that** ... su ira or cólera llegó a tal extremo que ...; **to ~ a tent** montar una tienda (de campaña); **to ~ one's aspirations too high** tener ambiciones desmesuradas

pitch-black ['pɪtʃ'blæk] *adj* negro como boca de lobo

pitched battle [pɪtʃt-] *n* batalla campal

pitcher ['pɪtʃəʳ] *n* cántaro, jarro

pitchfork ['pɪtʃfɔːk] *n* horca

piteous ['pɪtɪəs] *adj* lastimoso

pitfall ['pɪtfɔːl] *n* riesgo

pith [pɪθ] *n* (*of orange*) piel *f* blanca; (*fig*) meollo

pithead ['pɪthɛd] *n* (*Brit*) bocamina

pithy ['pɪθɪ] *adj* jugoso

pitiful ['pɪtɪful] *adj* (*touching*) lastimoso, conmovedor(a); (*contemptible*) lamentable

pitifully ['pɪtɪfəlɪ] *adv:* **it's ~ obvious** es tan evidente que da pena

pitiless ['pɪtɪlɪs] *adj* despiadado, implacable

pitilessly ['pɪtɪlɪslɪ] *adv* despiadadamente, implacablemente

pittance ['pɪtns] *n* miseria

pity ['pɪtɪ] *n* (*compassion*) compasión *f*, piedad *f*; (*shame*) lástima ■ *vt* compadecer(se de); **to have** *or* **take ~ on sb** compadecerse de algn; **what a ~!** ¡qué pena!; **it is a ~ that you can't come** ¡qué pena que no puedas venir!

pitying ['pɪtɪɪŋ] *adj* compasivo, de lástima

pivot ['pɪvət] *n* eje *m* ■ *vi:* **to ~ on** girar sobre; (*fig*) depender de

pixel ['pɪksl] *n* (*Comput*) pixel *m*, punto

pixie ['pɪksɪ] *n* duendecillo

pizza ['piːtsə] *n* pizza

placard ['plækɑːd] *n* (*in march etc*) pancarta

placate [plə'keɪt] *vt* apaciguar

place [pleɪs] *n* lugar *m*, sitio; (*rank*) rango; (*seat*) plaza, asiento; (*post*) puesto; (*in street names*) plaza; (*home*): **at/to his ~** en/a su casa ▪ vt (object) poner, colocar; (identify) reconocer; (find a post for) dar un puesto a, colocar; (goods) vender; **to take** ~ tener lugar; **to be placed** (in race, exam) colocarse; **out of** ~ (not suitable) fuera de lugar; **in the first** ~ (first of all) en primer lugar; **to change places with sb** cambiarse de sitio con algn; **from** ~ **to** ~ de un sitio a or para otro; **all over the** ~ por todas partes; **he's going places** (fig, col) llegará lejos; **I feel rather out of** ~ **here** me encuentro algo desplazado; **to put sb in his** ~ (fig) poner a algn en su lugar; **it is not my** ~ **to do it** no me incumbe a mí hacerlo; **to** ~ **an order with sb (for)** hacer un pedido a algn (de); **we are better placed than a month ago** estamos en mejor posición que hace un mes

placebo [plə'si:bəu] n placebo

place mat n (wooden etc) salvamanteles m inv; (in linen etc) mantel m individual

placement ['pleɪsmənt] n colocación f

place name n topónimo

placid ['plæsɪd] adj apacible, plácido

placidity [plæ'sɪdɪtɪ] n placidez f

plagiarism ['pleɪdʒjərɪzm] n plagio

plagiarist ['pleɪdʒjərɪst] n plagiario(-a)

plagiarize ['pleɪdʒjəraɪz] vt plagiar

plague [pleɪg] n plaga; (Med) peste f ▪ vt (fig) acosar, atormentar; **to** ~ **sb with questions** acribillar a algn a preguntas

plaice [pleɪs] n pl inv platija

plaid [plæd] n (material) tela de cuadros

plain [pleɪn] adj (clear) claro, evidente; (simple) sencillo; (frank) franco, abierto; (not handsome) poco atractivo; (pure) natural, puro ▪ adv claramente ▪ n llano, llanura; **in** ~ **clothes** (police) vestido de paisano; **to make sth** ~ **to sb** dejar algo en claro a algn

plain chocolate n chocolate m oscuro or amargo

plainly ['pleɪnlɪ] adv claramente, evidentemente; (frankly) francamente

plainness ['pleɪnnɪs] n (clarity) claridad f; (simplicity) sencillez f; (of face) falta de atractivo

plain speaking n: **there has been some** ~ se ha hablado claro

plaintiff ['pleɪntɪf] n demandante m/f

plaintive ['pleɪntɪv] adj (cry, voice) lastimero, quejumbroso; (look) que da lástima

plait [plæt] n trenza ▪ vt trenzar

plan [plæn] n (drawing) plano; (scheme) plan m, proyecto ▪ vt (think) pensar; (prepare) proyectar, planear; (intend) pensar, tener la intención de ▪ vi hacer proyectos; **have you any plans for today?** ¿piensas hacer algo hoy?; **to** ~ **to do** pensar hacer; **how long**

do you ~ **to stay?** ¿cuánto tiempo piensas quedarte?; **to** ~ **(for)** planear, proyectar
▶ **plan out** vt planear detalladamente

plane [pleɪn] n (Aviat) avión m; (tree) plátano; (tool) cepillo; (Math) plano

planet ['plænɪt] n planeta m

planetarium [plænɪ'tɛərɪəm] n planetario

planetary ['plænɪtərɪ] adj planetario

plank [plæŋk] n tabla

plankton ['plæŋktən] n plancton m

planned economy [plænd-] n economía planificada

planner ['plænə'] n planificador(-a) m(f); (chart) diagrama m de planificación; **town** ~ urbanista m/f

planning ['plænɪŋ] n (Pol, Econ) planificación f; **family** ~ planificación familiar

planning committee n (in local government) comité m de planificación

planning permission n licencia de obras

plant [plɑ:nt] n planta; (machinery) maquinaria; (factory) fábrica ▪ vt plantar; (field) sembrar; (bomb) colocar

plantain ['plænteɪn] n llantén m

plantation [plæn'teɪʃən] n plantación f; (estate) hacienda

planter ['plɑ:ntə'] n hacendado

plant pot n maceta, tiesto

plaque [plæk] n placa

plasma ['plæzmə] n plasma m

plaster ['plɑ:stə'] n (for walls) yeso; (also: **plaster of Paris**) yeso mate; (Med: for broken leg etc) escayola; (Brit: also: **sticking plaster**) tirita, esparadrapo ▪ vt enyesar; (cover): **to** ~ **with** llenar or cubrir de; **to be plastered with mud** estar cubierto de barro

plasterboard ['plɑ:stəbɔ:d] n cartón m yeso

plaster cast n (Med) escayola; (model, statue) vaciado de yeso

plastered ['plɑ:stəd] adj (col) borracho

plasterer ['plɑ:stərə'] n yesero

plastic ['plæstɪk] n plástico ▪ adj de plástico

plastic bag n bolsa de plástico

plastic bullet n bala de goma

plastic explosive n goma 2®

plasticine® ['plæstɪsi:n] n (Brit) plastilina®

plastic surgery n cirugía plástica

plastinate ['plæstɪneɪt] vt plastinar

plate [pleɪt] n (dish) plato; (metal, in book) lámina; (Phot) placa; (on door) placa; (Aut: also: **number plate**) matrícula

plateau [pl **plateaus** or **plateaux**] ['plætəu, -z] n meseta, altiplanicie f

plateful ['pleɪtful] n plato

plate glass n vidrio or cristal m cilindrado

platen ['plætən] n (on typewriter, printer) rodillo

plate rack n escurreplatos m inv

platform ['plætfɔːm] n (Rail) andén m;
(stage) plataforma; (at meeting) tribuna; (Pol)
programa m (electoral); **the train leaves
from ~ seven** el tren sale del andén número
siete
platform ticket n (Brit) billete m de andén
platinum ['plætɪnəm] n platino
platitude ['plætɪtjuːd] n tópico, lugar m
común
platonic [plə'tɒnɪk] adj platónico
platoon [plə'tuːn] n pelotón m
platter ['plætəʳ] n fuente f
plaudits ['plɔːdɪts] npl aplausos mpl
plausibility [plɔːzɪ'bɪlɪtɪ] n verosimilitud f,
credibilidad f
plausible ['plɔːzɪbl] adj verosímil; (person)
convincente
play [pleɪ] n (gen) juego; (Theat) obra ◼ vt
(game) jugar; (instrument) tocar; (Theat)
representar; (: part) hacer el papel de; (fig)
desempeñar ◼ vi jugar; (frolic) juguetear;
to ~ safe ir a lo seguro; **to bring** or **call into ~**
poner en juego; **to ~ a trick on sb** gastar una
broma a algn; **they're playing at soldiers**
están jugando a (los) soldados; **to ~ for time**
(fig) tratar de ganar tiempo; **to ~ into sb's
hands** (fig) hacerle el juego a algn; **a smile
played on his lips** una sonrisa le bailaba en
los labios
▸ **play about, play around** vi (person) hacer
el tonto; **to ~ about** or **around with** (fiddle
with) juguetear con; (idea) darle vueltas a
▸ **play along** vi: **to ~ along with** seguirle el
juego a ◼ vt: **to ~ sb along** (fig) jugar con
algn
▸ **play back** vt poner
▸ **play down** vt quitar importancia a
▸ **play on** vt fus (sb's feelings, credulity)
aprovecharse de; **to ~ on sb's nerves**
atacarle los nervios a algn
▸ **play up** vi (cause trouble) dar guerra
playact ['pleɪækt] vi (fig) hacer comedia or
teatro
play-acting ['pleɪæktɪŋ] n teatro
playboy ['pleɪbɔɪ] n playboy m
player ['pleɪəʳ] n jugador(a) m(f); (Theat) actor
m, actriz f; (Mus) músico(-a) m(f)
playful ['pleɪful] adj juguetón(-ona)
playground ['pleɪgraund] n (in school) patio
de recreo
playgroup ['pleɪgruːp] n jardín m de
infancia
playing card ['pleɪɪŋ-] n naipe m, carta
playing field n campo de deportes
playmaker ['pleɪmeɪkəʳ] n (Sport) jugador
encargado de facilitar buenas jugadas a sus
compañeros

playmate ['pleɪmeɪt] n compañero(-a) de
juego
play-off ['pleɪɔf] n (Sport) (partido de)
desempate m
playpen ['pleɪpɛn] n corral m
playroom ['pleɪruːm] n cuarto de juego
playschool ['pleɪskuːl] n = **playgroup**
plaything ['pleɪθɪŋ] n juguete m
playtime ['pleɪtaɪm] n (Scol) (hora de) recreo
playwright ['pleɪraɪt] n dramaturgo(-a)
plc abbr (Brit: = public limited company) S.A.
plea [pliː] n (request) súplica, petición f;
(excuse) pretexto, disculpa; (Law) alegato,
defensa
plea bargaining n (Law) acuerdo entre fiscal y
defensor para agilizar los trámites judiciales
plead [pliːd] vt (Law): **to ~ sb's case** defender
a alguien; (give as excuse) poner como pretexto
◼ vi (Law) declararse; (beg). **to ~ with sb**
suplicar or rogar a algn; **to ~ guilty/not
guilty** (defendant) declararse culpable/
inocente; **to ~ for sth** (beg for) suplicar algo
pleasant ['plɛznt] adj agradable
pleasantly ['plɛzntlɪ] adv agradablemente
pleasantries ['plɛzntrɪz] npl (polite remarks)
cortesías fpl; **to exchange ~** conversar
amablemente
please [pliːz] vt (give pleasure to) dar gusto a,
agradar ◼ vi (think fit): **do as you ~** haz lo que
quieras or lo que te dé la gana; **to ~ o.s.** hacer
lo que le parezca; **~! ¡por favor!; ~ yourself!**
¡haz lo que quieras!, ¡como quieras!; **~ don't
cry!** ¡no llores! te lo ruego
pleased [pliːzd] adj (happy) alegre, contento;
(satisfied): **~ (with)** satisfecho (de); **~ to meet
you** (col) ¡encantado!, ¡tanto or mucho
gusto!; **to be ~ (about sth)** alegrarse (de
algo); **we are ~ to inform you that ...**
tenemos el gusto de comunicarle que ...
pleasing ['pliːzɪŋ] adj agradable, grato
pleasurable ['plɛʒərəbl] adj agradable, grato
pleasurably ['plɛʒərəblɪ] adv
agradablemente, gratamente
pleasure ['plɛʒəʳ] n placer m, gusto; (will)
voluntad f ◼ cpd de recreo; **"it's a ~"**
"el gusto es mío"; **it's a ~ to see him** da
gusto verle; **I have much ~ in informing
you that ...** tengo el gran placer de
comunicarles que ...; **with ~** con mucho or
todo gusto; **is this trip for business or ~?**
¿este viaje es de negocios o de placer?
pleasure cruise n crucero de placer
pleasure ground n parque m de atracciones
pleasure-seeking ['plɛʒəsiːkɪŋ] adj
hedonista
pleat [pliːt] n pliegue m
pleb [plɛb] n: **the plebs** la gente baja, la plebe

709

plebeian [plɪˈbiːən] n plebeyo(-a) ▪ adj
plebeyo; (pej) ordinario
plebiscite [ˈplɛbɪsɪt] n plebiscito
plectrum [ˈplɛktrəm] n plectro
pledge [plɛdʒ] n (object) prenda; (promise)
promesa, voto ▪ vt (pawn) empeñar; (promise)
prometer; **to ~ support for sb** prometer su
apoyo a algn; **to ~ sb to secrecy** hacer jurar
a algn que guardará el secreto
plenary [ˈpliːnərɪ] adj: **in ~ session** en sesión
plenaria
plentiful [ˈplɛntɪful] adj copioso, abundante
plenty [ˈplɛntɪ] n abundancia; **~ of**
mucho(s)(-a(s)); **we've got ~ of time to get
there** tenemos tiempo de sobra para llegar
plethora [ˈplɛθərə] n plétora
pleurisy [ˈpluərɪsɪ] n pleuresía
pliability [plaɪəˈbɪlɪtɪ] n flexibilidad f
pliable [ˈplaɪəbl] adj flexible
pliers [ˈplaɪəz] npl alicates mpl, tenazas fpl
plight [plaɪt] n condición f or situación f
difícil
plimsolls [ˈplɪmsəlz] npl (Brit) zapatillas fpl
de tenis
plinth [plɪnθ] n plinto
PLO n abbr (= Palestine Liberation Organization)
OLP f
plod [plɔd] vi caminar con paso pesado; (fig)
trabajar laboriosamente
plodder [ˈplɔdər] n trabajador(a) diligente pero
lento/a
plodding [ˈplɔdɪŋ] adj (student)
empollón(-ona); (worker) más aplicado que
brillante
plonk [plɔŋk] (col) n (Brit: wine) vino peleón
▪ vt: **to ~ sth down** dejar caer algo
plot [plɔt] n (scheme) complot m, conjura;
(of story, play) argumento; (of land) terreno,
parcela ▪ vt (mark out) trazar; (conspire)
tramar, urdir ▪ vi conspirar; **a vegetable ~**
un cuadro de hortalizas
plotter [ˈplɔtər] n (instrument) trazador m (de
gráficos)
plotting [ˈplɔtɪŋ] n conspiración f, intrigas fpl
plough, plow (US) [plau] n arado ▪ vt (earth)
arar
 ▸ **plough back** vt (Comm) reinvertir
 ▸ **plough through** vt fus (crowd) abrirse paso
a la fuerza por
ploughing [ˈplauɪŋ] n labranza
ploughman [ˈplaumən] n: **~'s lunch** pan m
con queso y cebolla
plow [plau] (US) = **plough**
ploy [plɔɪ] n truco, estratagema
pluck [plʌk] vt (fruit) coger (SP), recoger (LAm);
(musical instrument) puntear; (bird) desplumar
▪ n valor m, ánimo; **to ~ up courage** hacer

de tripas corazón; **to ~ one's eyebrows**
depilarse las cejas
plucky [ˈplʌkɪ] adj valiente
plug [plʌg] n tapón m; (Elec) enchufe m,
clavija; (Aut: also: **spark(ing) plug**) bujía ▪ vt
(hole) tapar; (col: advertise) dar publicidad a; **to
give sb/sth a ~** dar publicidad a algn/algo;
to ~ a lead into a socket enchufar un hilo
en una toma
 ▸ **plug in** vt, vi (Elec) enchufar
plughole [ˈplʌghəul] n desagüe m
plum [plʌm] n (fruit) ciruela; (also: **plum job**)
chollo
plumage [ˈpluːmɪdʒ] n plumaje m
plumb [plʌm] adj vertical ▪ n plomo ▪ adv
(exactly) exactamente, en punto ▪ vt sondar;
(fig) sondear
 ▸ **plumb in** vt (washing machine) conectar
plumber [ˈplʌmər] n fontanero(-a),
plomero(-a) (LAm)
plumbing [ˈplʌmɪŋ] n (trade) fontanería,
plomería (LAm); (piping) cañerías
plume [pluːm] n (gen) pluma; (on helmet)
penacho
plummet [ˈplʌmɪt] vi: **to ~ (down)** caer a
plomo
plump [plʌmp] adj rechoncho, rollizo ▪ vt:
to ~ sth (down) on dejar caer algo en
 ▸ **plump for** vt fus (col: choose) optar por
 ▸ **plump up** vt ahuecar
plumpness [ˈplʌmpnɪs] n gordura
plunder [ˈplʌndər] n pillaje m; (loot) botín m
▪ vt saquear, pillar
plunge [plʌndʒ] n zambullida ▪ vt
sumergir, hundir ▪ vi (fall) caer; (dive) saltar;
(person) arrojarse; (sink) hundirse; **to take
the ~** lanzarse; **to ~ a room into darkness**
sumir una habitación en la oscuridad
plunger [ˈplʌndʒər] n émbolo; (for drain)
desatascador m
plunging [ˈplʌndʒɪŋ] adj (neckline) escotado
pluperfect [pluːˈpəːfɪkt] n pluscuamperfecto
plural [ˈpluərl] n plural m
plus [plʌs] n (also: **plus sign**) signo más; (fig)
punto a favor ▪ adj: **a ~ factor** (fig) un factor
m a favor ▪ prep más, y, además de; **ten/
twenty ~** más de diez/veinte
plush [plʌʃ] adj de felpa
plutonium [pluːˈtəunɪəm] n plutonio
ply [plaɪ] vt (a trade) ejercer ▪ vi (ship) ir y
venir; (for hire) ofrecerse (para alquilar);
three ~ (wool) de tres cabos; **to ~ sb with
drink** no dejar de ofrecer copas a algn
plywood [ˈplaɪwud] n madera
contrachapada
PM n abbr (Brit) see **Prime Minister**
p.m. adv abbr (= post meridiem) de la tarde or noche

PMS n abbr (= premenstrual syndrome) SPM m
PMT n abbr (= premenstrual tension) SPM m
pneumatic [nju:'mætɪk] adj neumático
pneumatic drill n taladradora neumática
pneumonia [nju:'məunɪə] n pulmonía, neumonía
PO n abbr (= Post Office) Correos mpl; (Naut) = **petty officer**
po abbr = **postal order**
POA n abbr (Brit) = **Prison Officers' Association**
poach [pəutʃ] vt (cook) escalfar; (steal) cazar/pescar en vedado ▪ vi cazar/pescar en vedado
poached [pəutʃt] adj (egg) escalfado
poacher ['pəutʃər] n cazador(a) m(f) furtivo(-a)
poaching ['pəutʃɪŋ] n caza/pesca furtiva
PO Box n abbr see **Post Office Box**
pocket ['pɒkɪt] n bolsillo; (of air,: Geo) bolsa; (fig) bolsa; (Billiards) tronera ▪ vt meter en el bolsillo; (steal) embolsarse; (Billiards) entronerar; **breast ~** bolsillo de pecho; **~ of resistance** foco de resistencia; **~ of warm air** bolsa de aire caliente; **to be out of ~** salir perdiendo; **to be f5 in/out of ~** salir ganando/perdiendo 5 libras
pocketbook ['pɒkɪtbuk] n (US: wallet) cartera; (: handbag) bolso
pocketful ['pɒkɪtful] n bolsillo lleno
pocket knife n navaja
pocket money n asignación f
pockmarked ['pɒkmɑːkt] adj (face) picado de viruelas
pod [pɒd] n vaina
podcast ['pɒdkɑːst] n podcast m ▪ vi podcastear
podcasting ['pɒdkɑːstɪŋ] n podcasting m
podgy ['pɒdʒɪ] adj gordinflón(-ona)
podiatrist [pɒ'diːətrɪst] n (US) podólogo(-a)
podiatry [pɒ'diːətrɪ] n (US) podología
podium ['pəudɪəm] n podio
POE n abbr = **port of embarkation; port of entry**
poem ['pəuɪm] n poema m
poet ['pəuɪt] n poeta m/f
poetic [pəu'etɪk] adj poético
poet laureate [-'lɔːrɪɪt] n poeta m laureado; ver nota

● **POET LAUREATE**
●
● El poeta de la corte, denominado Poet
● Laureate, ocupa como tal un puesto
● vitalicio al servicio de la Casa Real
● británica. Era tradición que escribiera
● poemas conmemorativos para ocasiones

● oficiales, aunque hoy día esto es poco
● frecuente. El primer poeta así distinguido
● fue Ben Jonson, en 1616.

poetry ['pəuɪtrɪ] n poesía
poignant ['pɔɪnjənt] adj conmovedor(a)
poignantly ['pɔɪnjəntlɪ] adv de modo conmovedor
point [pɔɪnt] n punto; (tip) punta; (purpose) fin m, propósito; (Brit Elec: also: **power point**) toma de corriente, enchufe m; (use) utilidad f; (significant part) lo esencial; (place) punto, lugar m; (also: **decimal point**): **2 ~ 3 (2.3)** coma tres (2,3) ▪ vt (gun etc): **to ~ sth at sb** apuntar con algo a algn ▪ vi señalar con el dedo; **points** npl (Aut) contactos mpl; (Rail) agujas fpl; **to be on the ~ of doing sth** estar a punto de hacer algo; **to make a ~ of doing sth** poner empeño en hacer algo; **to get the ~** comprender; **to come to the ~** ir al meollo; **there's no ~ (in doing)** no tiene sentido (hacer); **~ of departure** (also fig) punto de partida; **~ of order** cuestión f de procedimiento; **~ of sale** (Comm) punto de venta; **~-of-sale advertising** publicidad f en el punto de venta; **the train stops at Carlisle and all points south** el tren para en Carlisle, y en todas las estaciones al sur; **when it comes to the ~** a la hora de la verdad; **in ~ of fact** en realidad; **that's the whole ~!** ¡de eso se trata!; **to be beside the ~** no venir al caso; **you've got a ~ there!** ¡tienes razón!
▸ **point out** vt señalar
▸ **point to** vt fus indicar con el dedo; (fig) indicar, señalar
point-blank ['pɔɪnt'blæŋk] adv (also: **at point-blank range**) a quemarropa
point duty n (Brit) control m de circulación
pointed ['pɔɪntɪd] adj (shape) puntiagudo, afilado; (remark) intencionado
pointedly ['pɔɪntɪdlɪ] adv intencionadamente
pointer ['pɔɪntər] n (stick) puntero; (needle) aguja, indicador m; (clue) indicación f, pista; (advice) consejo
pointless ['pɔɪntlɪs] adj sin sentido
pointlessly ['pɔɪntlɪslɪ] adv inútilmente, sin motivo
point of view n punto de vista
poise [pɔɪz] n (of head, body) porte m; (calmness) aplomo
poised [pɔɪzd] adj (in temperament) sereno
poison ['pɔɪzn] n veneno ▪ vt envenenar
poisoning ['pɔɪznɪŋ] n envenenamiento
poisonous ['pɔɪznəs] adj venenoso; (fumes etc) tóxico; (fig: ideas, literature) pernicioso; (: rumours, individual) nefasto

p

poke [pəʊk] vt (fire) hurgar, atizar; (jab with finger, stick etc) dar; (Comput) almacenar; (put): **to ~ sth in(to)** introducir algo en ■ n (jab) empujoncito; (with elbow) codazo; **to ~ one's head out of the window** asomar la cabeza por la ventana; **to ~ fun at sb** ridiculizar a algn; **to give the fire a ~** atizar el fuego
▶ **poke about** vi fisgonear
poker ['pəʊkər] n atizador m; (Cards) póker m
poker-faced ['pəʊkəˈfeɪst] adj de cara impasible
poky ['pəʊkɪ] adj estrecho
Poland ['pəʊlənd] n Polonia
polar ['pəʊlər] adj polar
polar bear n oso polar
polarization [pəʊləraɪˈzeɪʃən] n polarización f
polarize ['pəʊləraɪz] vt polarizar
Pole [pəʊl] n polaco(-a)
pole [pəʊl] n palo; (Geo) polo; (Tel) poste m; (flagpole) asta; (tent pole) mástil m
poleaxe ['pəʊlæks] vt (fig) desnucar
pole bean n (US) judía trepadora
polecat ['pəʊlkæt] n (Brit) turón m; (US) mofeta
Pol. Econ. ['pɒlɪkɒn] n abbr = **political economy**
polemic [pɒˈlemɪk] n polémica
polemicist [pɒˈlemɪsɪst] n polemista m/f
pole star n estrella polar
pole vault n salto con pértiga
police [pəˈliːs] n policía ■ vt (streets, city, frontier) vigilar
police car n coche-patrulla m
police constable n (Brit) guardia m, policía m
police department n (US) policía
police force n cuerpo de policía
policeman [pəˈliːsmən] n guardia m, policía m, agente m (LAm)
police officer n guardia m, policía m
police record n: **to have a ~** tener antecedentes penales
police state n estado policial
police station n comisaría
policewoman [pəˈliːswʊmən] n mujer f policía
policy ['pɒlɪsɪ] n política; (also: **insurance policy**) póliza; (of newspaper, company) política; **it is our ~ to do that** tenemos por norma hacer eso; **to take out a ~** sacar una póliza, hacerse un seguro
policy holder n asegurado(-a)
policy-making ['pɒlɪsɪmeɪkɪŋ] n elaboración f de directrices generales
policy-making body n organismo encargado de elaborar las directrices generales
polio ['pəʊlɪəʊ] n polio f

Polish ['pəʊlɪʃ] adj polaco ■ n (Ling) polaco
polish ['pɒlɪʃ] n (for shoes) betún m; (for floor) cera (de lustrar); (for nails) esmalte m; (shine) brillo, lustre m; (fig: refinement) refinamiento ■ vt (shoes) limpiar; (make shiny) pulir, sacar brillo a; (fig: improve) perfeccionar, refinar
▶ **polish off** vt (work) terminar; (food) despachar
▶ **polish up** vt (shoes, furniture etc) limpiar, sacar brillo a; (fig: language) perfeccionar
polished ['pɒlɪʃt] adj (fig: person) refinado
polite [pəˈlaɪt] adj cortés, atento; (formal) correcto; **it's not ~ to do that** es de mala educación hacer eso
politely [pəˈlaɪtlɪ] adv cortésmente
politeness [pəˈlaɪtnɪs] n cortesía
politic ['pɒlɪtɪk] adj prudente
political [pəˈlɪtɪkl] adj político
political asylum n asilo político
politically [pəˈlɪtɪkəlɪ] adv políticamente
politically correct adj políticamente correcto
politician [pɒlɪˈtɪʃən] n político(-a)
politics ['pɒlɪtɪks] n política
polka ['pɒlkə] n polca
polka dot n lunar m
poll [pəʊl] n (votes) votación f, votos mpl; (also: **opinion poll**) sondeo, encuesta ■ vt (votes) obtener; (in opinion poll) encuestar; **to go to the polls** (voters) votar; (government) acudir a las urnas
pollen ['pɒlən] n polen m
pollen count n índice m de polen
pollination [pɒlɪˈneɪʃən] n polinización f
polling ['pəʊlɪŋ] n (Brit Pol) votación f; (Tel) interrogación f
polling booth n cabina de votar
polling day n día m de elecciones
polling station n centro electoral
pollster ['pəʊlstər] n (person) encuestador(a) m(f); (organization) empresa de encuestas or sondeos
poll tax n (Brit) contribución f municipal (no progresiva)
pollutant [pəˈluːtənt] n (agente m) contaminante m
pollute [pəˈluːt] vt contaminar
pollution [pəˈluːʃən] n contaminación f, polución f
polo ['pəʊləʊ] n (sport) polo
polo-neck ['pəʊləʊnɛk] adj de cuello vuelto ■ n (sweater) suéter m de cuello vuelto
poly ['pɒlɪ] n abbr (Brit) = **polytechnic**
poly... [pɒlɪ] pref poli...
poly bag n (Brit col) bolsa de plástico
polyester [pɒlɪˈɛstər] n poliéster m
polyethylene [pɒlɪˈɛθɪliːn] n (US) polietileno

polygamy [pə'lɪgəmɪ] n poligamia
polygraph ['pɒlɪgrɑːf] n polígrafo
Polynesia [pɒlɪ'niːzɪə] n Polinesia
Polynesian [pɒlɪ'niːzɪən] adj, n polinesio(-a) m(f)
polyp ['pɒlɪp] n (Med) pólipo
polystyrene [pɒlɪ'staɪriːn] n poliestireno
polytechnic [pɒlɪ'tɛknɪk] n escuela politécnica
polythene ['pɒlɪθiːn] n (Brit) polietileno
polythene bag n bolsa de plástico
polyurethane [pɒlɪ'juərɪθeɪn] n poliuretano
pomegranate ['pɒmɪgrænɪt] n granada
pommel ['pɒml] n pomo ▪ vt = **pummel**
pomp [pɒmp] n pompa
pompom ['pɒmpɒm] n borla
pompous ['pɒmpəs] adj pomposo; (person) presumido
pond [pɒnd] n (natural) charca; (artificial) estanque m
ponder ['pɒndər] vt meditar
ponderous ['pɒndərəs] adj pesado
pong [pɒŋ] n (Brit col) peste f ▪ vi (Brit col) apestar
pontiff ['pɒntɪf] n pontífice m
pontificate [pɒn'tɪfɪkeɪt] vi (fig): **to ~ (about)** pontificar (sobre)
pontoon [pɒn'tuːn] n pontón m; (Brit: card game) veintiuna
pony ['pəunɪ] n poney m, potro
ponytail ['pəunɪteɪl] n coleta, cola de caballo
pony trekking n (Brit) excursión f a caballo
poodle ['puːdl] n caniche m
pool [puːl] n (natural) charca; (pond) estanque m; (also: **swimming pool**) piscina, alberca (LAm); (billiards) billar m americano; (Comm: consortium) consorcio; (: US: monopoly trust) trust m ▪ vt juntar; **typing ~** servicio de mecanografía; **(football) pools** npl quinielas fpl
poor [puər] adj pobre; (bad) malo ▪ npl: **the ~** los pobres
poorly ['puəlɪ] adj mal, enfermo
pop [pɒp] n ¡pum!; (sound) ruido seco; (Mus) (música) pop m; (US col: father) papá m; (col: drink) gaseosa ▪ vt (burst) hacer reventar ▪ vi reventar; (cork) saltar; **she popped her head out (of the window)** sacó de repente la cabeza (por la ventana)
  ▶ **pop in** vi entrar un momento
  ▶ **pop out** vi salir un momento
  ▶ **pop up** vi aparecer inesperadamente
pop concert n concierto pop
popcorn ['pɒpkɔːn] n palomitas fpl (de maíz)
pope [pəup] n papa m
poplar ['pɒplər] n álamo
poplin ['pɒplɪn] n popelina

popper ['pɒpər] n corchete m, botón m automático
poppy ['pɒpɪ] n amapola; see also **Remembrance Sunday**
poppycock ['pɒpɪkɒk] n (col) tonterías fpl
Popsicle® ['pɒpsɪkl] n (US) polo
populace ['pɒpjuləs] n pueblo
popular ['pɒpjulər] adj popular; **a ~ song** una canción popular; **to be ~ (with)** (person) caer bien (a); (decision) ser popular (entre)
popularity [pɒpju'lærɪtɪ] n popularidad f
popularize ['pɒpjuləraɪz] vt popularizar; (disseminate) vulgarizar
populate ['pɒpjuleɪt] vt poblar
population [pɒpju'leɪʃən] n población f
population explosion n explosión f demográfica
populous ['pɒpjuləs] adj populoso
pop-up menu ['pɒpʌp-] n (Comput) menú m emergente
porcelain ['pɔːslɪn] n porcelana
porch [pɔːtʃ] n pórtico, entrada
porcupine ['pɔːkjupaɪn] n puerco m espín
pore [pɔːr] n poro ▪ vi: **to ~ over** enfrascarse en
pork [pɔːk] n (carne f de) cerdo or chancho (LAm)
pork chop n chuleta de cerdo
porn [pɔːn] adj (col) porno inv ▪ n porno
pornographic [pɔːnə'græfɪk] adj pornográfico
pornography [pɔː'nɒgrəfɪ] n pornografía
porous ['pɔːrəs] adj poroso
porpoise ['pɔːpəs] n marsopa
porridge ['pɒrɪdʒ] n gachas fpl de avena
port [pɔːt] n (harbour) puerto; (Naut: left side) babor m; (wine) oporto; (Comput) puerta, puerto, port m; **~ of call** puerto de escala
portable ['pɔːtəbl] adj portátil
portal ['pɔːtl] n puerta (grande), portalón m
port authorities npl autoridades fpl portuarias
portcullis [pɔːt'kʌlɪs] n rastrillo
portend [pɔː'tɛnd] vt presagiar, anunciar
portent ['pɔːtɛnt] n presagio, augurio
porter ['pɔːtər] n (for luggage) maletero; (doorkeeper) portero(-a), conserje m/f; (US Rail) mozo de los coches-cama
portfolio [pɔːt'fəulɪəu] n (case, of artist) cartera, carpeta; (Pol, Finance) cartera
porthole ['pɔːthəul] n portilla
portico ['pɔːtɪkəu] n pórtico
portion ['pɔːʃən] n porción f; (helping) ración f
portly ['pɔːtlɪ] adj corpulento
portrait ['pɔːtreɪt] n retrato
portray [pɔː'treɪ] vt retratar; (in writing) representar

portrayal [pɔ:'treɪəl] n representación f
Portugal ['pɔ:tjugl] n Portugal m
Portuguese [pɔ:tju'gi:z] adj portugués(-esa)
■ n pl inv portugués(-esa) m(f); (Ling)
portugués m
Portuguese man-of-war [-mænəu'wɔ:ʳ] n
(jellyfish) especie de medusa
pose [pəuz] n postura, actitud f; (pej)
afectación f, pose f ■ vi posar; (pretend): **to ~
as** hacerse pasar por ■ vt (question) plantear;
to strike a ~ tomar or adoptar una pose or
actitud
poser ['pəuzəʳ] n problema m/pregunta
difícil; (person) = **poseur**
poseur [pəu'zɜ:ʳ] n presumido(-a), persona
afectada
posh [pɔʃ] adj (col) elegante, de lujo ■ adv
(col): **to talk ~** hablar con acento afectado
position [pə'zɪʃən] n posición f; (job) puesto
■ vt colocar; **to be in a ~ to do sth** estar en
condiciones de hacer algo
positive ['pɔzɪtɪv] adj positivo; (certain)
seguro; (definite) definitivo; **we look
forward to a ~ reply** (Comm) esperamos que
pueda darnos una respuesta en firme;
~ cash flow (Comm) flujo positivo de efectivo
positively ['pɔzɪtɪvlɪ] adv (affirmatively,
enthusiastically) de forma positiva; (col: really)
absolutamente
posse ['pɔsɪ] n (US) pelotón m
possess [pə'zɛs] vt poseer; **like one
possessed** como un poseído; **whatever can
have possessed you?** ¿cómo se te ocurrió?
possessed [pə'zɛst] adj poseso, poseído
possession [pə'zɛʃən] n posesión f; **to take ~
of sth** tomar posesión de algo
possessive [pə'zɛsɪv] adj posesivo
possessiveness [pə'zɛsɪvnɪs] n posesividad f
possessor [pə'zɛsəʳ] n poseedor(a) m(f),
dueño(-a)
possibility [pɔsɪ'bɪlɪtɪ] n posibilidad f; **he's
a ~ for the part** es uno de los posibles para
el papel
possible ['pɔsɪbl] adj posible; **as big as ~**
lo más grande posible; **it is ~ to do it** es
posible hacerlo; **as far as ~** en la medida
de lo posible; **a ~ candidate** un(a) posible
candidato(-a)
possibly ['pɔsɪblɪ] adv (perhaps) posiblemente,
tal vez; **I cannot ~ come** me es imposible
venir; **could you ~ ...?** ¿podrías ...?
post [pəust] n (Brit: letters, delivery) correo;
(job, situation) puesto; (trading post) factoría;
(pole) poste m; (on internet forum) anuncio, post
m ■ vt (Brit: send by post) mandar por correo;
(: put in mailbox) echar al correo; (Mil) apostar;
(bills) fijar, pegar; (to internet) colgar; (Brit:

appoint): **to ~ to** destinar a; **by ~** por correo;
by return of ~ a vuelta de correo; **to keep sb
posted** tener a algn al corriente
post ... [pəust] pref post..., pos...; **post 1950**
pos(t)1950
postage ['pəustɪdʒ] n porte m, franqueo
postage stamp n sello (de correo)
postal ['pəustl] adj postal, de correos
postal order n giro postal
postbag ['pəustbæg] n (Brit)
correspondencia, cartas fpl
postbox ['pəustbɔks] n (Brit) buzón m
postcard ['pəustkɑ:d] n (tarjeta) postal f
postcode ['pəustkəud] n (Brit) código postal
postdate [pəust'deɪt] vt (cheque) poner fecha
adelantada a
poster ['pəustəʳ] n cartel m, afiche m (LAm)
poste restante [pəust'rɛstɔnt] n (Brit) lista
de correos
posterior [pɔs'tɪərɪəʳ] n (col) trasero
posterity [pɔs'tɛrɪtɪ] n posteridad f
poster paint n pintura al agua
post-free [pəust'fri:] adj (con) porte pagado
postgraduate ['pəust'grædjuɪt] n
posgraduado(-a)
posthumous ['pɔstjuməs] adj póstumo
posthumously ['pɔstjuməslɪ] adv
póstumamente, con carácter póstumo
posting ['pəustɪŋ] n destino
postman ['pəustmən] n cartero
postmark ['pəustmɑ:k] n matasellos m inv
postmaster ['pəustmɑ:stəʳ] n administrador
m de correos
Postmaster General n director m general
de correos
postmistress ['pəustmɪstrɪs] n
administradora de correos
post-mortem [pəust'mɔ:təm] n autopsia
postnatal ['pəust'neɪtl] adj postnatal,
postparto
post office n (building) (oficina de)
correos m; (organization): **the Post Office**
Administración f General de Correos
Post Office Box n apartado postal, casilla de
correos (LAm)
post-paid ['pəust'peɪd] adj porte pagado
postpone [pəs'pəun] vt aplazar, postergar
(LAm)
postponement [pəs'pəunmənt] n
aplazamiento
postscript ['pəustskrɪpt] n posdata
postulate ['pɔstjuleɪt] vt postular
posture ['pɔstʃəʳ] n postura, actitud f
postwar [pəust'wɔ:ʳ] adj de la posguerra
posy ['pəuzɪ] n ramillete m (de flores)
pot [pɔt] n (for cooking) olla; (for flowers)
maceta; (for jam) tarro, pote m (LAm); (piece of

pottery) cacharro; (*col: marijuana*) costo ■ *vt* (*plant*) poner en tiesto; (*conserve*) conservar (en tarros); **pots of** (*col*) montones de; **to go to ~** (*col: work, performance*) irse al traste

potash ['pɔtæʃ] *n* potasa

potassium [pə'tæsɪəm] *n* potasio

potato (*pl* **potatoes**) [pə'teɪtəu] *n* patata, papa (*LAm*)

potato crisps, potato chips (*US*) *npl* patatas *fpl or* papas *fpl* (*LAm*)

potato peeler *n* pelapatatas *m inv*

potbellied ['pɔtbelɪd] *adj* (*from overeating*) barrigón(-ona); (*from malnutrition*) con el vientre hinchado

potency ['pəutnsɪ] *n* potencia

potent ['pəutnt] *adj* potente, poderoso; (*drink*) fuerte

potentate ['pəutnteɪt] *n* potentado

potential [pə'tenʃl] *adj* potencial, posible ■ *n* potencial *m*; **to have ~** prometer

potentially [pə'tenʃəlɪ] *adv* en potencia

pothole ['pɔthəul] *n* (*in road*) bache *m*; (*Brit: underground*) gruta

potholer ['pɔthəulər] *n* (*Brit*) espeleólogo(-a)

potholing ['pɔthəulɪŋ] *n* (*Brit*): **to go ~** dedicarse a la espeleología

potion ['pəuʃən] *n* poción *f*, pócima

potluck [pɔt'lʌk] *n*: **to take ~** conformarse con lo que haya

pot roast *n* carne *f* asada

potshot ['pɔtʃɔt] *n*: **to take a ~ at sth** tirar a algo sin apuntar

potted ['pɔtɪd] *adj* (*food*) en conserva; (*plant*) en tiesto *or* maceta; (*fig: shortened*) resumido

potter ['pɔtər] *n* alfarero(-a) ■ *vi*: **to ~ around, ~ about** entretenerse haciendo cosillas; **to ~ round the house** estar en casa haciendo cosillas; **~'s wheel** torno de alfarero

pottery ['pɔtərɪ] *n* cerámica, alfarería; **a piece of ~** un objeto de cerámica

potty ['pɔtɪ] *adj* (*col: mad*) chiflado ■ *n* orinal *m* de niño

potty-trained ['pɔtɪtreɪnd] *adj* que ya no necesita pañales

pouch [pautʃ] *n* (*Zool*) bolsa; (*for tobacco*) petaca

pouf, pouffe [pu:f] *n* (*stool*) pouf *m*

poultry ['pəultrɪ] *n* aves *fpl* de corral; (*dead*) pollos *mpl*

poultry farm *n* granja avícola

poultry farmer *n* avicultor(-a) *m(f)*

pounce [pauns] *vi*: **to ~ on** precipitarse sobre ■ *n* salto, ataque *m*

pound [paund] *n* libra; (*for dogs*) perrera; (*for cars*) depósito ■ *vt* (*beat*) golpear; (*crush*) machacar ■ *vi* (*beat*) dar golpes; **half a ~**

media libra; **a one ~ note** un billete de una libra

pounding ['paundɪŋ] *n*: **to take a ~** (*team*) recibir una paliza

pound sterling *n* libra esterlina

pour [pɔ:r] *vt* echar; (*tea*) servir ■ *vi* correr, fluir; (*rain*) llover a cántaros

▶ **pour away, pour off** *vt* vaciar, verter

▶ **pour in** *vi* (*people*) entrar en tropel; **to come pouring in** (*water*) entrar a raudales; (*letters*) llegar a montones; (*cars, people*) llegar en tropel

▶ **pour out** *vi* (*people*) salir en tropel ■ *vt* (*drink*) echar, servir

pouring ['pɔ:rɪŋ] *adj*: **~ rain** lluvia torrencial

pout [paut] *vi* hacer pucheros

poverty ['pɔvətɪ] *n* pobreza, miseria; (*fig*) falta, escasez *f*

poverty line *n*: **below the ~** por debajo del umbral de pobreza

poverty-stricken ['pɔvətɪstrɪkn] *adj* necesitado

poverty trap *n* trampa de la pobreza

POW *n abbr* = **prisoner of war**

powder ['paudər] *n* polvo; (*also*: **face powder**) polvos *mpl*; (*also*: **gun powder**) pólvora ■ *vt* empolvar; **to ~ one's face** ponerse polvos; **to ~ one's nose** empolvarse la nariz, ponerse polvos; (*euphemism*) ir al baño

powder compact *n* polvera

powdered milk ['paudəd-] *n* leche *f* en polvo

powder keg *n* (*fig*) polvorín *m*

powder puff *n* borla (para empolvarse)

powder room *n* aseos *mpl*

powdery ['paudərɪ] *adj* polvoriento

power ['pauər] *n* poder *m*; (*strength*) fuerza; (*nation*) potencia; (*drive*) empuje *m*; (*Tech*) potencia; (*Elec*) energía ■ *vt* impulsar; **to be in ~** (*Pol*) estar en el poder; **to do all in one's ~ to help sb** hacer todo lo posible por ayudar a algn; **the world powers** las potencias mundiales

powerboat ['pauəbəut] *n* lancha a motor

power cut *n* (*Brit*) apagón *m*

powered ['pauəd] *adj*: **~ by** impulsado por; **nuclear-~ submarine** submarino nuclear

power failure *n* = **power cut**

powerful ['pauəful] *adj* poderoso; (*engine*) potente; (*strong*) fuerte; (*play, speech*) conmovedor(a)

powerhouse ['pauəhaus] *n* (*fig: person*) fuerza motriz; **a ~ of ideas** una cantera de ideas

powerless ['pauəlɪs] *adj* impotente, ineficaz

power line *n* línea de conducción eléctrica

power of attorney *n* poder *m*, procuración *f*

power point *n* (*Brit*) enchufe *m*

power station *n* central *f* eléctrica

P

power steering n (Aut) dirección f asistida
powwow ['pauwau] n conferencia ▪ vi
conferenciar
pp abbr (= per procurationem: by proxy) p.p.;
= **pages**
PPE n abbr (Brit Scol) = **philosophy, politics,
and economics**
PPS n abbr (= post postscriptum) posdata adicional;
(Brit: = Parliamentary Private Secretary) ayudante
de un ministro
PQ abbr (Canada) = **Province of Quebec**
PR n abbr see **proportional representation**;
(= public relations) relaciones fpl públicas
▪ abbr (US) = **Puerto Rico**
Pr. abbr (= prince) P
practicability [præktɪkə'bɪlɪtɪ] n
factibilidad f
practicable ['præktɪkəbl] adj (scheme) factible
practical ['præktɪkl] adj práctico
practicality [præktɪ'kælɪtɪ] n (of situation etc)
aspecto práctico
practical joke n broma pesada
practically ['præktɪklɪ] adv (almost) casi,
prácticamente
practice ['præktɪs] n (habit) costumbre f;
(exercise) práctica; (training) adiestramiento;
(Med) clientela ▪ vt, vi (US) = **practise**;
in ~ (in reality) en la práctica; **out of ~**
desentrenado; **to put sth into ~** poner algo
en práctica; **it's common ~** es bastante
corriente; **target ~** práctica de tiro; **he has a
small ~** (doctor) tiene pocos pacientes; **to set
up in ~ as** establecerse como
practise, practice (US) ['præktɪs] vt (carry
out) practicar; (profession) ejercer; (train at)
practicar ▪ vi ejercer; (train) practicar
practised, (US) **practiced** ['præktɪst] adj
(person) experto; (performance) bien ensayado;
(liar) consumado; **with a ~ eye** con ojo
experto
practising, practicing (US) ['præktɪsɪŋ] adj
(Christian etc) practicante; (lawyer) que ejerce;
(homosexual) activo
practitioner [præk'tɪʃənər] n practicante m/f;
(Med) médico(-a)
pragmatic [præg'mætɪk] adj pragmático
pragmatism ['prægmətɪzəm] n
pragmatismo
pragmatist ['prægmətɪst] n pragmatista m/f
Prague [prɑːg] n Praga
prairie ['prɛərɪ] n (US) pampa
praise [preɪz] n alabanza(s) f(pl), elogio(s)
m(pl)
praiseworthy ['preɪswəːðɪ] adj loable
pram [præm] n (Brit) cochecito de niño
prance [prɑːns] vi (horse) hacer cabriolas
prank [præŋk] n travesura

prat [præt] n (Brit col) imbécil m/f
prattle ['prætl] vi parlotear; (child) balbucear
prawn [prɔːn] n gamba
pray [preɪ] vi rezar; **to ~ for forgiveness**
pedir perdón
prayer [prɛər] n oración f, rezo; (entreaty)
ruego, súplica
prayer book n devocionario, misal m
pre- ['priː] pref pre..., ante-; **~1970** pre 1970
preach [priːtʃ] vi predicar
preacher ['priːtʃər] n predicador(a) m(f); (US:
minister) pastor(a) m(f)
preamble [prɪ'æmbl] n preámbulo
prearrange [priːə'reɪndʒ] vt organizar or
acordar de antemano
prearrangement [priːə'reɪndʒmənt] n: **by ~**
por previo acuerdo
precarious [prɪ'kɛərɪəs] adj precario
precariously [prɪ'kɛərɪəslɪ] adv
precariamente
precaution [prɪ'kɔːʃən] n precaución f
precautionary [prɪ'kɔːʃənrɪ] adj (measure) de
precaución
precede [prɪ'siːd] vt, vi preceder
precedence ['prɛsɪdəns] n precedencia;
(priority) preferencia
precedent ['prɛsɪdənt] n precedente m;
to establish or **set a ~** sentar un precedente
preceding [prɪ'siːdɪŋ] adj precedente
precept ['priːsɛpt] n precepto
precinct ['priːsɪŋkt] n recinto; (US: district)
distrito, barrio; **precincts** npl recinto;
pedestrian ~ (Brit) zona peatonal; **shopping
~** (Brit) centro comercial
precious ['prɛʃəs] adj precioso; (treasured)
querido; (stylized) afectado ▪ adv (col):
~ little/few muy poco/pocos; **your ~ dog**
(ironic) tu querido perro
precipice ['prɛsɪpɪs] n precipicio
precipitate [prɪ'sɪpɪtɪt] (hasty) precipitado
▪ vt [prɪ'sɪpɪteɪt] precipitar
precipitation [prɪsɪpɪ'teɪʃən] n
precipitación f
precipitous [prɪ'sɪpɪtəs] adj (steep) escarpado;
(hasty) precipitado
précis ['preɪsiː] n resumen m
precise [prɪ'saɪs] adj preciso, exacto; (person)
escrupuloso
precisely [prɪ'saɪslɪ] adv exactamente,
precisamente
precision [prɪ'sɪʒən] n precisión f
preclude [prɪ'kluːd] vt excluir
precocious [prɪ'kəʊʃəs] adj precoz
preconceived [priːkən'siːvd] adj (idea)
preconcebido
preconception [priːkən'sɛpʃən] n (idea) idea
preconcebida

precondition [priːkənˈdɪʃən] n condición f previa

precursor [priːˈkəːsəʳ] n precursor(a) m(f)

predate [priːˈdeɪt] vt (precede) preceder

predator [ˈprɛdətəʳ] n depredador m

predatory [ˈprɛdətərɪ] adj depredador(a)

predecessor [ˈpriːdɪsɛsəʳ] n antecesor(a) m(f)

predestination [priːdɛstɪˈneɪʃən] n predestinación f

predestine [priːˈdɛstɪn] vt predestinar

predetermine [priːdɪˈtəːmɪn] vt predeterminar

predicament [prɪˈdɪkəmənt] n apuro

predicate [ˈprɛdɪkɪt] n predicado

predict [prɪˈdɪkt] vt predecir, pronosticar

predictable [prɪˈdɪktəbl] adj previsible

predictably [prɪˈdɪktəblɪ] adv (behave, react) de forma previsible; ~ **she didn't arrive** como era de prever, no llegó

prediction [prɪˈdɪkʃən] n pronóstico, predicción f

predispose [ˈpriːdɪsˈpəuz] vt predisponer

predominance [prɪˈdɔmɪnəns] n predominio

predominant [prɪˈdɔmɪnənt] adj predominante

predominantly [prɪˈdɔmɪnəntlɪ] adv en su mayoría

predominate [prɪˈdɔmɪneɪt] vi predominar

pre-eminent [priːˈɛmɪnənt] adj preeminente

pre-empt [priːˈɛmt] vt (Brit) adelantarse a

pre-emptive [priːˈɛmtɪv] adj: ~ **strike** ataque m preventivo

preen [priːn] vt: **to ~ itself** (bird) limpiarse las plumas; **to ~ o.s.** pavonearse

prefab [ˈpriːfæb] n casa prefabricada

prefabricated [priːˈfæbrɪkeɪtɪd] adj prefabricado

preface [ˈprɛfəs] n prefacio

prefect [ˈpriːfɛkt] n (Brit: in school) monitor(a) m(f)

prefer [prɪˈfəːʳ] vt preferir; (Law: charges, complaint) presentar; (: action) entablar; **to ~ coffee to tea** preferir el café al té

preferable [ˈprɛfrəbl] adj preferible

preferably [ˈprɛfrəblɪ] adv preferentemente, más bien

preference [ˈprɛfrəns] n preferencia; **in ~ to sth** antes que algo

preference shares npl acciones fpl privilegiadas

preferential [prɛfəˈrɛnʃəl] adj preferente

prefix [ˈpriːfɪks] n prefijo

pregnancy [ˈprɛgnənsɪ] n embarazo

pregnancy test n prueba del embarazo

pregnant [ˈprɛgnənt] adj embarazada; **3 months ~** embarazada de tres meses; **~ with meaning** cargado de significado

prehistoric [ˈpriːhɪsˈtɔrɪk] adj prehistórico

prehistory [priːˈhɪstərɪ] n prehistoria

prejudge [priːˈdʒʌdʒ] vt prejuzgar

prejudice [ˈprɛdʒudɪs] n (bias) prejuicio; (harm) perjuicio ■ vt (bias) predisponer; (harm) perjudicar; **to ~ sb in favour of/against** (bias) predisponer a algn a favor de/en contra de

prejudiced [ˈprɛdʒudɪst] adj (person) predispuesto; (view) parcial, interesado; **to be ~ against sb/sth** estar predispuesto en contra de algn/algo

prelate [ˈprɛlət] n prelado

preliminaries [prɪˈlɪmɪnərɪz] npl preliminares mpl, preparativos mpl

preliminary [prɪˈlɪmɪnərɪ] adj preliminar

prelude [ˈprɛljuːd] n preludio

premarital [ˈpriːˈmærɪtl] adj prematrimonial, premarital

premature [ˈprɛmətʃuəʳ] adj (arrival etc) prematuro; **you are being a little ~** te has adelantado

prematurely [prɛməˈtʃuəlɪ] adv prematuramente, antes de tiempo

premeditate [priːˈmɛdɪteɪt] vt premeditar

premeditated [priːˈmɛdɪteɪtɪd] adj premeditado

premeditation [priːmɛdɪˈteɪʃən] n premeditación f

premenstrual [priːˈmɛnstruəl] adj premenstrual

premenstrual tension n (Med) tensión f premenstrual

premier [ˈprɛmɪəʳ] adj primero, principal ■ n (Pol) primer(a) ministro(-a)

première [ˈprɛmɪɛəʳ] n estreno

premise [ˈprɛmɪs] n premisa

premises [ˈprɛmɪsɪs] npl local msg; **on the ~** en el lugar mismo; **business ~** locales mpl comerciales

premium [ˈpriːmɪəm] n prima; **to be at a ~** estar muy solicitado; **to sell at a ~** (shares) vender caro

premium bond n (Brit) bono del estado que participa en una lotería nacional; ver nota

---

● **PREMIUM BOND**
●
● Se conoce como Premium Bonds o Premium
● Savings Bonds a los bonos emitidos por
● el Ministerio de Economía británico
● (Treasury) en los que se pueden invertir los
● ahorros. No producen intereses, pero dan
● acceso a un sorteo mensual de premios en
● metálico.

premium deal n (*Comm*) oferta extraordinaria
premium gasoline n (*US*) (gasolina) súper m
premonition [prɛmə'nɪʃən] n presentimiento
preoccupation [priːɔkju'peɪʃən] n preocupación f
preoccupied [priː'ɔkjupaɪd] adj (*worried*) preocupado; (*absorbed*) ensimismado
prep [prɛp] adj abbr: ~ **school** = **preparatory school** ■ n abbr (*Scol*: = *preparation*) deberes mpl
prepaid [priː'peɪd] adj porte pagado; ~ **envelope** sobre m de porte pagado
preparation [prɛpə'reɪʃən] n preparación f; **preparations** npl preparativos mpl; **in ~ for sth** en preparación para algo
preparatory [prɪ'pærətərɪ] adj preparatorio, preliminar; ~ **to sth/to doing sth** como preparación para algo/para hacer algo
preparatory school n (*Brit*) *colegio privado de enseñanza primaria*; (*US*) *colegio privado de enseñanza secundaria*; *see also* **public school**
prepare [prɪ'pɛəʳ] vt preparar, disponer ■ vi: **to ~ for** prepararse *or* disponerse para; (*make preparations*) hacer preparativos para
prepared [prɪ'pɛəd] adj (*willing*): **to be ~ to help sb** estar dispuesto a ayudar a algn
preponderance [prɪ'pɔndərns] n preponderancia, predominio
preposition [prɛpə'zɪʃən] n preposición f
prepossessing [priːpə'zɛsɪŋ] adj agradable, atractivo
preposterous [prɪ'pɔstərəs] adj absurdo, ridículo
prerecorded ['priːrɪ'kɔːdɪd] adj: ~ **broadcast** programa m grabado de antemano; ~ **cassette** cassette f pregrabada
prerequisite [priː'rɛkwɪzɪt] n requisito previo
prerogative [prɪ'rɔgətɪv] n prerrogativa
Presbyterian [prɛzbɪ'tɪərɪən] adj, n presbiteriano(-a) m(f)
presbytery ['prɛzbɪtərɪ] n casa parroquial
preschool ['priː'skuːl] adj (*child, age*) preescolar
prescribe [prɪ'skraɪb] vt prescribir; (*Med*) recetar; **prescribed books** (*Brit Scol*) libros mpl del curso
prescription [prɪ'skrɪpʃən] n (*Med*) receta; **to make up** *or* (*US*) **fill a ~** preparar una receta; **only available on ~** se vende solamente con receta (médica)
prescription charges npl (*Brit*) precio sg de las recetas
prescriptive [prɪ'skrɪptɪv] adj normativo
presence ['prɛzns] n presencia; (*attendance*) asistencia

presence of mind n aplomo
present adj ['prɛznt] (*in attendance*) presente; (*current*) actual ■ n (*gift*) regalo; (*actuality*) actualidad f, presente m ■ vt [prɪ'zɛnt] (*introduce*) presentar; (*expound*) exponer; (*give*) presentar, dar, ofrecer; (*Theat*) representar; **to be ~ at** asistir a, estar presente en; **those ~** los presentes; **to give sb a ~, make sb a ~ of sth** regalar algo a algn; **at ~** actualmente; **to ~ o.s. for an interview** presentarse a una entrevista; **may I ~ Miss Clark** permítame presentarle *or* le presento a la Srta Clark
presentable [prɪ'zɛntəbl] adj: **to make o.s. ~** arreglarse
presentation [prɛzn'teɪʃən] n presentación f; (*gift*) obsequio; (*of case*) exposición f; (*Theat*) representación f; **on ~ of the voucher** al presentar el vale
present-day ['prɛzntdeɪ] adj actual
presenter [prɪ'zɛntəʳ] n (*Radio, TV*) locutor(a) m(f)
presently ['prɛzntlɪ] adv (*soon*) dentro de poco; (*US: now*) ahora
present participle n participio (de) presente
present tense n (tiempo) presente m
preservation [prɛzə'veɪʃən] n conservación f
preservative [prɪ'zəːvətɪv] n conservante m
preserve [prɪ'zəːv] vt (*keep safe*) preservar, proteger; (*maintain*) mantener; (*food*) conservar; (*in salt*) salar ■ n (*for game*) coto, vedado; (*often pl: jam*) confitura
preshrunk [prɪ'ʃrʌŋk] adj inencogible
preside [prɪ'zaɪd] vi presidir
presidency ['prɛzɪdənsɪ] n presidencia
president ['prɛzɪdənt] n presidente m/f; (*US: of company*) director(a) m(f)
presidential [prɛzɪ'dɛnʃl] adj presidencial
press [prɛs] n (*tool, machine, newspapers*) prensa; (*printer's*) imprenta; (*of hand*) apretón m ■ vt (*push*) empujar; (*squeeze*) apretar; (*grapes*) pisar; (*clothes: iron*) planchar; (*pressure*) presionar; (*doorbell*) apretar, pulsar, tocar; (*insist*): **to ~ sth on sb** insistir en que algn acepte algo ■ vi (*squeeze*) apretar; (*pressurize*) ejercer presión; **to go to ~** (*newspaper*) entrar en prensa; **to be in the ~** (*being printed*) estar en prensa; (*in the newspapers*) aparecer en la prensa; **we are pressed for time** tenemos poco tiempo; **to ~ sb to do** *or* **into doing sth** (*urge, entreat*) presionar a algn para que haga algo; **to ~ sb for an answer** insistir a algn para que conteste; **to ~ charges against sb** (*Law*) demandar a algn
▶ **press ahead** vi seguir adelante
▶ **press on** vi avanzar; (*hurry*) apretar el paso
press agency n agencia de prensa
press clipping n = **press cutting**

press conference n rueda de prensa
press cutting n recorte m (de periódico)
pressing ['prɛsɪŋ] adj apremiante
pressman ['prɛsmæn] n periodista m
press officer n jefe(-a) m(f) de prensa
press release n comunicado de prensa
press stud n (Brit) botón m de presión
press-up ['prɛsʌp] n (Brit) flexión f
pressure ['prɛʃəʳ] n presión f; (urgency)
apremio, urgencia; (influence) influencia;
high/low ~ alta/baja presión; **to put ~ on sb**
presionar a algn, hacer presión sobre algn
pressure cooker n olla a presión
pressure gauge n manómetro
pressure group n grupo de presión
pressurize ['prɛʃəraɪz] vt presurizar; **to ~ sb
(into doing sth)** presionar a algn (para que
haga algo)
pressurized ['prɛʃəraɪzd] adj (container) a
presión
Prestel® ['prɛstɛl] n videotex m
prestige [prɛs'tiːʒ] n prestigio
prestigious [prɛs'tɪdʒəs] adj prestigioso
presumably [prɪ'zjuːməblɪ] adv es de
suponer que, cabe presumir que; ~ **he did it**
es de suponer que lo hizo él
presume [prɪ'zjuːm] vt suponer, presumir;
to ~ to do (dare) atreverse a hacer
presumption [prɪ'zʌmpʃən] n suposición f;
(pretension) presunción f
presumptuous [prɪ'zʌmptjuəs] adj
presumido
presuppose [priːsə'pəʊz] vt presuponer
presupposition [priːsʌpə'zɪʃən] n
presuposición f
pre-tax [priː'tæks] adj anterior al impuesto
pretence, pretense (US) [prɪ'tɛns] n (claim)
pretensión f; (pretext) pretexto; (make-believe)
fingimiento; **on** or **under the ~ of doing sth**
bajo or con el pretexto de hacer algo; **she is
devoid of all ~** no es pretenciosa
pretend [prɪ'tɛnd] vt (feign) fingir ■ vi (feign)
fingir; (claim): **to ~ to sth** pretender a algo
pretense [prɪ'tɛns] n (US) = **pretence**
pretension [prɪ'tɛnʃən] n (claim) pretensión f;
to have no pretensions to sth/to being sth
no engañarse en cuanto a algo/a ser algo
pretentious [prɪ'tɛnʃəs] adj pretencioso
pretext ['priːtɛkst] n pretexto; **on** or **under
the ~ of doing sth** con el pretexto de hacer
algo
prettily ['prɪtɪlɪ] adv encantadoramente, con
gracia
pretty ['prɪtɪ] adj (gen) bonito, lindo (LAm)
■ adv bastante
prevail [prɪ'veɪl] vi (gain mastery) prevalecer;
(be current) predominar; (persuade): **to ~**

(up)on sb to do sth persuadir a algn para
que haga algo
prevailing [prɪ'veɪlɪŋ] adj (dominant)
predominante
prevalent ['prɛvələnt] adj (dominant)
dominante; (widespread) extendido;
(fashionable) de moda
prevarication [prɪværɪ'keɪʃən] n evasivas fpl
prevent [prɪ'vɛnt] vt: **to ~ (sb) from doing
sth** impedir (a algn) hacer algo
preventable [prɪ'vɛntəbl] adj evitable
preventative [prɪ'vɛntətɪv] adj preventivo
prevention [prɪ'vɛnʃən] n prevención f
preventive [prɪ'vɛntɪv] adj preventivo
preview ['priːvjuː] n (of film) preestreno
previous ['priːvɪəs] adj previo, anterior;
he has no ~ experience in that field no
tiene experiencia previa en ese campo;
I have a ~ engagement tengo un
compromiso anterior
previously ['priːvɪəslɪ] adv antes
prewar [priː'wɔːʳ] adj antes de la guerra
prey [preɪ] n presa ■ vi: **to ~ on** vivir a costa
de; (feed on) alimentarse de; **it was preying
on his mind** le obsesionaba
price [praɪs] n precio; (Betting: odds) puntos
mpl de ventaja ■ vt (goods) fijar el precio de;
to go up or **rise in ~** subir de precio; **what
is the ~ of ...?** ¿qué precio tiene ...?; **to put
a ~ on sth** poner precio a algo; **what ~ his
promises now?** ¿para qué sirven ahora sus
promesas?; **he regained his freedom,
but at a ~** recobró su libertad, pero le había
costado caro; **to be priced out of the
market** (article) no encontrar comprador por
ese precio; (nation) no ser competitivo
price control n control m de precios
price-cutting ['praɪskʌtɪŋ] n reducción f de
precios
priceless ['praɪslɪs] adj que no tiene precio;
(col: amusing) divertidísimo
price list n tarifa
price range n gama de precios; **it's within
my ~** está al alcance de mi bolsillo
price tag n etiqueta
price war n guerra de precios
pricey ['praɪsɪ] adj (Brit col) caro
prick [prɪk] n pinchazo; (with pin) alfilerazo;
(sting) picadura ■ vt pinchar; picar; **to ~ up
one's ears** aguzar el oído
prickle ['prɪkl] n (sensation) picor m; (Bot)
espina; (Zool) púa
prickly ['prɪklɪ] adj espinoso; (fig: person)
enojadizo
prickly heat n sarpullido causado por exceso
de calor
prickly pear n higo chumbo

pride [praɪd] *n* orgullo; *(pej)* soberbia ■ *vt*: **to ~ o.s. on** enorgullecerse de; **to take (a) ~ in** enorgullecerse de; **her ~ and joy** su orgullo; **to have ~ of place** tener prioridad

priest [priːst] *n* sacerdote *m*

priestess ['priːstɪs] *n* sacerdotisa

priesthood ['priːsthud] *n* *(practice)* sacerdocio; *(priests)* clero

prig [prɪg] *n* gazmoño(-a)

prim [prɪm] *adj (demure)* remilgado; *(prudish)* gazmoño

primacy ['praɪməsɪ] *n* primacía

prima donna ['priːmə'dɔnə] *n* primadonna, diva

prima facie ['praɪmə'feɪʃɪ] *adj*: **to have a ~ case** *(Law)* tener razón a primera vista

primal ['praɪməl] *adj* original; *(important)* principal

primarily ['praɪmərɪlɪ] *adv (above all)* ante todo, primordialmente

primary ['praɪmərɪ] *adj* primario; *(first in importance)* principal ■ *n* (US: also: **primary election**) (elección *f*) primaria; *ver nota*

Las elecciones primarias *(primaries)* sirven para preseleccionar a los candidatos de los partidos Demócrata ("Democratic") y Republicano ("Republican") durante la campaña que precede a las elecciones a presidente de los Estados Unidos. Se inician en New Hampshire y tienen lugar en 35 estados de febrero a junio. El número de votos obtenidos por cada candidato determina el número de delegados que votarán en el congreso general ("National Convention") de julio y agosto, cuando se decide el candidato definitivo de cada partido.

primary colour, *(US)* **primary color** *n* color *m* primario

primary education *n* enseñanza primaria

primary school *n* *(Brit)* escuela primaria; *ver nota*

En el Reino Unido la escuela a la que van los niños entre cinco y once años se llama *primary school*, a menudo dividida en "infant school" (entre cinco y siete años de edad) y "junior school" (entre siete y once).

primate *n* ['praɪmɪt] *(Rel)* primado; ['praɪmeɪt] *(Zool)* primate *m*

prime [praɪm] *adj* primero, principal; *(basic)* fundamental; *(excellent)* selecto, de primera clase ■ *n*: **in the ~ of life** en la flor de la vida ■ *vt (gun, pump)* cebar; *(fig)* preparar

Prime Minister *n* primer(a) ministro(-a); *see also* **Downing Street**

primer ['praɪmə'] *n* *(book)* texto elemental; *(paint)* capa preparatoria

prime time *n* *(Radio, TV)* horas *fpl* de mayor audiencia

primeval [praɪ'miːvəl] *adj* primitivo

primitive ['prɪmɪtɪv] *adj* primitivo; *(crude)* rudimentario; *(uncivilized)* inculto

primly ['prɪmlɪ] *adv* remilgadamente; con gazmoñería

primrose ['prɪmrəuz] *n* primavera, prímula

primus® ['praɪməs], **primus stove** *n* *(Brit)* hornillo de camping

prince [prɪns] *n* príncipe *m*

prince charming *n* príncipe *m* azul

princess [prɪn'ses] *n* princesa

principal ['prɪnsɪpl] *adj* principal ■ *n* director(a) *m(f)*; *(in play)* protagonista principal *m/f*; *(Comm)* capital *m*, principal *m*; *see also* **pantomime**

principality [prɪnsɪ'pælɪtɪ] *n* principado

principle ['prɪnsɪpl] *n* principio; **in ~** en principio; **on ~** por principio

print [prɪnt] *n* *(impression)* marca, impresión *f*; huella; *(letters)* letra de molde; *(fabric)* estampado; *(Art)* grabado; *(Phot)* impresión *f* ■ *vt (gen)* imprimir; *(on mind)* grabar; *(write in capitals)* escribir en letras de molde; **out of ~** agotado

▶ **print out** *vt (Comput)* imprimir

printed circuit ['prɪntɪd-] *n* circuito impreso

printed circuit board *n* tarjeta de circuito impreso

printed matter *n* impresos *mpl*

printer ['prɪntə'] *n* *(person)* impresor(a) *m(f)*; *(machine)* impresora

printhead ['prɪnthed] *n* cabeza impresora

printing ['prɪntɪŋ] *n* *(art)* imprenta; *(act)* impresión *f*; *(quantity)* tirada

printing press *n* prensa

printout ['prɪntaut] *n* *(Comput)* printout *m*

print wheel *n* rueda impresora

prior ['praɪə'] *adj* anterior, previo ■ *n* prior *m*; **~ to doing** antes de *or* hasta hacer; **without ~ notice** sin previo aviso; **to have a ~ claim to sth** tener prioridad en algo

prioress [praɪə'res] *n* priora

priority [praɪ'ɔrɪtɪ] *n* prioridad *f*; **to have *or* take ~ over sth** tener prioridad sobre algo

priory ['praɪərɪ] *n* priorato

prise, prize (US) [praɪz] vt: **to ~ open** abrir con palanca

prism ['prɪzəm] n prisma m

prison ['prɪzn] n cárcel f, prisión f ◼ cpd carcelario

prison camp n campamento para prisioneros

prisoner ['prɪznəʳ] n (in prison) preso(-a); (under arrest) detenido(-a); (in dock) acusado(-a); **the ~ at the bar** el/la acusado(-a); **to take sb ~** hacer or tomar prisionero a algn

prisoner of war n prisionero(-a) or preso(-a) de guerra

prissy ['prɪsɪ] adj remilgado

pristine ['prɪstiːn] adj pristino

privacy ['prɪvəsɪ] n (seclusion) soledad f; (intimacy) intimidad f; **in the strictest ~** con el mayor secreto

private ['praɪvɪt] adj (personal) particular; (confidential) secreto, confidencial; (intimate) privado, íntimo; (sitting etc) a puerta cerrada ◼ n soldado raso; **"~"** (on envelope) "confidencial"; (on door) "privado"; **in ~** en privado; **in (his) ~ life** en su vida privada; **to be in ~ practice** tener consulta particular

private enterprise n la empresa privada

private eye n detective m/f privado(-a)

private hearing n (Law) vista a puerta cerrada

private limited company n (Brit) sociedad f de responsabilidad limitada

privately ['praɪvɪtlɪ] adv en privado; (in o.s.) en secreto

private parts npl partes fpl pudendas

private property n propiedad f privada

private school n colegio privado

privation [praɪ'veɪʃən] n (state) privación f; (hardship) privaciones fpl, estrecheces fpl

privatize ['praɪvɪtaɪz] vt privatizar

privet ['prɪvɪt] n alheña

privilege ['prɪvɪlɪdʒ] n privilegio; (prerogative) prerrogativa

privileged ['prɪvɪlɪdʒd] adj privilegiado; **to be ~ to do sth** gozar del privilegio de hacer algo

privy ['prɪvɪ] adj: **to be ~ to** estar enterado de

Privy Council n consejo privado (de la Corona); ver nota

⊜ **PRIVY COUNCIL**
⊜
⊜ El consejo de asesores de la Corona
⊜ conocido como Privy Council tuvo su origen
⊜ en la época de los normandos, y fue
⊜ adquiriendo mayor importancia hasta
⊜ ser substituido en 1688 por el actual
⊜ Consejo de Ministros ("Cabinet"). Hoy
⊜ día sigue existiendo con un carácter

⊜ fundamentalmente honorífico y
⊜ los ministros del gobierno y otras
⊜ personalidades políticas, eclesiásticas
⊜ y jurídicas adquieren el rango de "privy
⊜ councillors" de manera automática.

prize [praɪz] n premio ◼ adj (first class) de primera clase ◼ vt apreciar, estimar; (US) **= prise**

prize fighter n boxeador m profesional

prize fighting n boxeo m profesional

prize-giving ['praɪzgɪvɪŋ] n distribución f de premios

prize money n (Sport) bolsa

prizewinner ['praɪzwɪnəʳ] n premiado(-a)

prizewinning ['praɪzwɪnɪŋ] adj (novel, essay) premiado

PRO n abbr = **public relations officer**

pro [prəu] n (Sport) profesional m/f; **the pros and cons** los pros y los contras

pro- [prəu] pref (in favour of) pro, en pro de; **~Soviet** pro-soviético

proactive [prəu'æktɪv] adj: **to be ~** impulsar la actividad

probability [prɔbə'bɪlɪtɪ] n probabilidad f; **in all ~** lo más probable

probable ['prɔbəbl] adj probable; **it is ~/hardly ~ that** es probable/poco probable que

probably ['prɔbəblɪ] adv probablemente

probate ['prəubeɪt] n (Law) legalización f de un testamento

probation [prə'beɪʃən] n: **on ~** (employee) a prueba; (Law) en libertad condicional

probationary [prə'beɪʃənrɪ] adj: **~ period** período de prueba

probationer [prə'beɪʃənəʳ] n (Law) persona en libertad condicional; (nurse) ≈ ATS m/f (SP) or enfermero(-a) en prácticas

probation officer n persona a cargo de los presos en libertad condicional

probe [prəub] n (Med, Space) sonda; (enquiry) investigación f ◼ vt sondar; (investigate) investigar

probity ['prəubɪtɪ] n probidad f

problem ['prɔbləm] n problema m; **what's the ~?** ¿cuál es el problema?, ¿qué pasa?; **no ~!** ¡por supuesto!; **to have problems with the car** tener problemas con el coche

problematic [prɔblə'mætɪk], **problematical** [prɔblə'mætɪkl] adj problemático

problem-solving [prɔbləm'sɔlvɪŋ] n resolución f de problemas; **~ skills** técnicas de resolución de problemas

procedural [prəu'siːdʒərəl] adj de procedimiento; (Law) procesal

procedure [prə'siːdʒəʳ] n procedimiento; (bureaucratic) trámites mpl; **cashing a cheque**

P

is a simple ~ cobrar un cheque es un trámite sencillo

proceed [prə'si:d] vi proceder; (*continue*): **to ~ (with)** continuar (con); **to ~ against sb** (*Law*) proceder contra algn; **I am not sure how to ~** no sé cómo proceder; *see also* **proceeds**

proceedings [prə'si:dɪŋz] npl acto sg, actos mpl; (*Law*) proceso sg; (*meeting*) función fsg; (*records*) actas fpl

proceeds ['prəusi:dz] npl ganancias fpl, ingresos mpl

process ['prəusɛs] n proceso; (*method*) método, sistema m; (*proceeding*) procedimiento ▪ vt tratar, elaborar ▪ vi [prə'sɛs] (*Brit: formal: go in procession*) desfilar; **in ~** en curso; **we are in the ~ of moving to ...** estamos en vías de mudarnos a ...

processed cheese ['prəusɛst-], (US) **process cheese** n queso fundido

processing ['prəusɛsɪŋ] n elaboración f

procession [prə'sɛʃən] n desfile m; **funeral ~** cortejo fúnebre

pro-choice [prəu'tʃɔɪs] adj en favor del derecho de elegir de la madre

proclaim [prə'kleɪm] vt proclamar; (*announce*) anunciar

proclamation [prɔklə'meɪʃən] n proclamación f; (*written*) proclama

proclivity [prə'klɪvɪtɪ] n propensión f, inclinación f

procrastinate [prəu'kræstɪneɪt] vi demorarse

procrastination [prəukræstɪ'neɪʃən] n dilación f

procreation [prəukrɪ'eɪʃən] n procreación f

Procurator Fiscal ['prɔkjureɪtə-] n (*Scottish*) fiscal m/f

procure [prə'kjuə'] vt conseguir, obtener

procurement [prə'kjuəmənt] n obtención f

prod [prɔd] vt (*push*) empujar; (*with elbow*) dar un codazo a ▪ n empujoncito; codazo

prodigal ['prɔdɪgl] adj pródigo

prodigious [prə'dɪdʒəs] adj prodigioso

prodigy ['prɔdɪdʒɪ] n prodigio

produce n ['prɔdju:s] (*Agr*) productos mpl agrícolas ▪ vt [prə'dju:s] producir; (*yield*) rendir; (*bring*) sacar; (*show*) presentar, mostrar; (*proof of identity*) enseñar, presentar; (*Theat*) presentar, poner en escena; (*offspring*) dar a luz

produce dealer n (US) verdulero(-a)

producer [prə'dju:sə'] n (*Theat*) director(a) m(f); (*Agr, Cine*) productor(a) m(f)

product ['prɔdʌkt] n producto

production [prə'dʌkʃən] n (*act*) producción f; (*Theat*) representación f, montaje m; **to put**

into ~ lanzar a la producción

production agreement n (US) acuerdo de productividad

production line n línea de producción

production manager n jefe/jefa m/f de producción

productive [prə'dʌktɪv] adj productivo

productivity [prɔdʌk'tɪvɪtɪ] n productividad f

productivity agreement n (*Brit*) acuerdo de productividad

productivity bonus n bono de productividad

Prof. [prɔf] abbr (= *professor*) Prof

profane [prə'feɪn] adj profano

profess [prə'fɛs] vt profesar; **I do not ~ to be an expert** no pretendo ser experto

professed [prə'fɛst] adj (*self-declared*) declarado

profession [prə'fɛʃən] n profesión f

professional [prə'fɛʃnl] n profesional m/f ▪ adj profesional; (*by profession*) de profesión; **to take ~ advice** buscar un consejo profesional

professionalism [prə'fɛʃnəlɪzm] n profesionalismo

professionally [prə'fɛʃnəlɪ] adv: **I only know him ~** sólo le conozco por nuestra relación de trabajo

professor [prə'fɛsə'] n (*Brit*) catedrático(-a) m(f); (*US: teacher*) profesor(a) m(f)

professorship [prə'fɛsəʃɪp] n cátedra

proffer ['prɔfə'] vt ofrecer

proficiency [prə'fɪʃənsɪ] n capacidad f, habilidad f

proficiency test n prueba de capacitación

proficient [prə'fɪʃənt] adj experto, hábil

profile ['prəufaɪl] n perfil m; **to keep a high/ low ~** tratar de llamar la atención/pasar inadvertido

profit ['prɔfɪt] n (*Comm*) ganancia; (*fig*) provecho ▪ vi: **to ~ by** or **from** aprovechar or sacar provecho de; **~ and loss account** cuenta de ganancias y pérdidas; **with profits endowment assurance** seguro dotal con beneficios; **to sell sth at a ~** vender algo con ganancia

profitability [prɔfɪtə'bɪlɪtɪ] n rentabilidad f

profitable ['prɔfɪtəbl] adj (*Econ*) rentable; (*beneficial*) provechoso, útil

profitably ['prɔfɪtəblɪ] adv rentablemente; provechosamente

profit centre, (US) **profit center** n centro de beneficios

profiteering [prɔfɪ'tɪərɪŋ] n (*pej*) explotación f

profit-making ['prɔfɪtmeɪkɪŋ] adj rentable

profit margin n margen m de ganancia

profit-sharing ['prɔfɪtʃɛərɪŋ] n participación f de empleados en los beneficios

profits tax n impuesto sobre los beneficios

profligate ['prɔfligɪt] adj (dissolute: behaviour, act) disoluto; (: person) libertino; (extravagant): **he's very ~ with his money** es muy derrochador

pro forma ['prəu'fɔ:mə] adj: **~ invoice** factura pro-forma

profound [prə'faund] adj profundo

profoundly [prə'faundlɪ] adv profundamente

profusely [prə'fju:slɪ] adv profusamente

profusion [prə'fju:ʒən] n profusión f, abundancia

progeny ['prɔdʒɪnɪ] n progenie f

programme, program (US) ['prəugræm] n programa m ■ vt programar

programmer, program (US) ['prəugræmər] n programador(a) m(f)

programming, program (US) ['prəugræmɪŋ] n programación f

programming language, programing language (US) n lenguaje m de programación

progress n ['prəugres] progreso; (development) desarrollo ■ vi [prə'grɛs] progresar, avanzar; desarrollarse; **in ~** (meeting, work etc) en curso; **as the match progressed** a medida que avanzaba el partido

progression [prə'grɛʃən] n progresión f

progressive [prə'grɛsɪv] adj progresivo; (person) progresista

progressively [prə'grɛsɪvlɪ] adv progresivamente, poco a poco

progress report n (Med) informe m sobre el estado del paciente; (Admin) informe m sobre la marcha del trabajo

prohibit [prə'hɪbɪt] vt prohibir; **to ~ sb from doing sth** prohibir a algn hacer algo; **"smoking prohibited"** "prohibido fumar"

prohibition [prəuɪ'bɪʃən] n (US) prohibicionismo

prohibitive [prə'hɪbɪtɪv] adj (price etc) prohibitivo

project [n 'prɔdʒɛkt, vb prə'dʒɛkt] n proyecto; (Scol, Univ: research) trabajo, proyecto ■ vt proyectar ■ vi (stick out) salir, sobresalir

projectile [prə'dʒɛktaɪl] n proyectil m

projection [prə'dʒɛkʃən] n proyección f; (overhang) saliente m

projectionist [prə'dʒɛkʃənɪst] n (Cine) operador(a) m(f) de cine

projection room n (Cine) cabina de proyección

projector [prə'dʒɛktər] n proyector m

proletarian [prəulɪ'tɛərɪən] adj proletario

proletariat [prəulɪ'tɛərɪət] n proletariado

pro-life [prəu'laɪf] adj pro-vida

proliferate [prə'lɪfəreɪt] vi proliferar, multiplicarse

proliferation [prəlɪfə'reɪʃən] n proliferación f

prolific [prə'lɪfɪk] adj prolífico

prologue, (US) prolog ['prəulɔg] n prólogo

prolong [prə'lɔŋ] vt prolongar, extender

prom [prɔm] n abbr (Brit) = **promenade; promenade concert;** (US: ball) baile m de gala; ver nota

---

● **PROM**
●
● Los conciertos de música clásica más
● conocidos en Inglaterra son los llamados
● Proms (o promenade concerts), que tienen
● lugar en el "Royal Albert Hall" de Londres,
● aunque también se llama así a cualquier
● concierto de esas características. Su
● nombre se debe al hecho de que en un
● principio el público paseaba durante las
● actuaciones; en la actualidad parte de
● la gente que acude a ellos permanece de
● pie. En Estados Unidos se llama prom a un
● baile de gala en un colegio o universidad.

---

promenade [prɔmə'na:d] n (by sea) paseo marítimo ■ vi (stroll) pasearse

promenade concert n concierto (en que parte del público permanece de pie)

promenade deck n cubierta de paseo

prominence ['prɔmɪnəns] n (fig) importancia

prominent ['prɔmɪnənt] adj (standing out) saliente; (important) eminente, importante; **he is ~ in the field of ...** destaca en el campo de ...

prominently ['prɔmɪnəntlɪ] adv (display, set) muy a la vista; **he figured ~ in the case** desempeñó un papel destacado en el juicio

promiscuity [prɔmɪs'kju:ɪtɪ] n promiscuidad f

promiscuous [prə'mɪskjuəs] adj (sexually) promiscuo

promise ['prɔmɪs] n promesa ■ vt, vi prometer; **to make sb a ~** prometer algo a algn; **a young man of ~** un joven con futuro; **to ~ (sb) to do sth** prometer (a algn) hacer algo; **to ~ well** ser muy prometedor

promising ['prɔmɪsɪŋ] adj prometedor(a)

promissory note ['prɔmɪsərɪ-] n pagaré m

promontory ['prɔməntrɪ] n promontorio

promote [prə'məut] vt promover; (new product) dar publicidad a, lanzar; (Mil) ascender; **the team was promoted to the second division** (Brit Football) el equipo ascendió a la segunda división

p

723

promoter [prə'məutə^r] n (of sporting event) promotor(a) m(f); (of company, business) patrocinador(a) m(f)

promotion [prə'məuʃən] n (gen) promoción f; (Mil) ascenso

prompt [prɔmpt] adj pronto ▪ adv: **at six o'clock ~** a las seis en punto ▪ n (Comput) aviso, guía ▪ vt (urge) mover, incitar; (Theat) apuntar; **to ~ sb to do sth** instar a algn a hacer algo; **to be ~ to do sth** no tardar en hacer algo; **they're very ~** (punctual) son muy puntuales

prompter ['prɔmptə^r] n (Theat) apuntador(a) m(f)

promptly ['prɔmptlɪ] adv (punctually) puntualmente; (rapidly) rápidamente

promptness ['prɔmptnɪs] n puntualidad f; rapidez f

promulgate ['prɔməlgeɪt] vt promulgar

prone [prəun] adj (lying) postrado; **~ to** propenso a

prong [prɔŋ] n diente m, punta

pronoun ['prəunaun] n pronombre m

pronounce [prə'nauns] vt pronunciar; (declare) declarar ▪ vi: **to ~ (up)on** pronunciarse sobre; **they pronounced him unfit to plead** le declararon incapaz de defenderse

pronounced [prə'naunst] adj (marked) marcado

pronouncement [prə'naunsmənt] n declaración f

pronunciation [prənʌnsɪ'eɪʃən] n pronunciación f

proof [pru:f] n prueba; **70° ~** graduación f del 70 por 100 ▪ adj: **~ against** a prueba de ▪ vt (tent, anorak) impermeabilizar

proofreader ['pru:fri:də^r] n corrector(a) m(f) de pruebas

prop [prɔp] n apoyo; (fig) sostén m ▪ vt (also: **prop up**) apoyar; (lean): **to ~ sth against** apoyar algo contra

Prop. abbr (Comm) = **proprietor**

propaganda [prɔpə'gændə] n propaganda

propagate ['prɔpəgeɪt] vt propagar

propagation [prɔpə'geɪʃən] n propagación f

propel [prə'pɛl] vt impulsar, propulsar

propeller [prə'pɛlə^r] n hélice f

propelling pencil [prə'pɛlɪŋ-] n (Brit) lapicero

propensity [prə'pɛnsɪtɪ] n propensión f

proper ['prɔpə^r] adj (suited, right) propio; (exact) justo; (apt) apropiado, conveniente; (timely) oportuno; (seemly) correcto, decente; (authentic) verdadero; (col: real) auténtico; **to go through the ~ channels** (Admin) ir por la vía oficial

properly ['prɔpəlɪ] adv (adequately) correctamente; (decently) decentemente

proper noun n nombre m propio

properties ['prɔpətɪz] npl (Theat) accesorios mpl, atrezzo msg

property ['prɔpətɪ] n propiedad f; (estate) finca; **lost ~** objetos mpl perdidos; **personal ~** bienes mpl muebles

property developer n promotor(a) m(f) de construcciones

property owner n dueño(-a) de propiedades

property tax n impuesto sobre la propiedad

prophecy ['prɔfɪsɪ] n profecía

prophesy ['prɔfɪsaɪ] vt profetizar; (fig) predecir

prophet ['prɔfɪt] n profeta m/f

prophetic [prə'fɛtɪk] adj profético

proportion [prə'pɔ:ʃən] n proporción f; (share) parte f; **to be in/out of ~ to** or **with sth** estar en/no guardar proporción con algo; **to see sth in ~** (fig) ver algo en su justa medida

proportional [prə'pɔ:ʃənl] adj proporcional

proportionally [prəpɔ:'ʃnəlɪ] adv proporcionalmente, en proporción

proportional representation n (Pol) representación f proporcional

proportional spacing n (on printer) espaciado proporcional

proportionate [prə'pɔ:ʃənɪt] adj proporcionado

proportionately [prə'pɔ:ʃnɪtlɪ] adv proporcionadamente, en proporción

proportioned [prə'pɔ:ʃənd] adj proporcionado

proposal [prə'pəuzl] n propuesta; (offer of marriage) oferta de matrimonio; (plan) proyecto; (suggestion) sugerencia

propose [prə'pəuz] vt proponer; (have in mind): **to ~ sth/to do** or **doing sth** proponer algo/proponerse hacer algo ▪ vi declararse

proposer [prə'pəuzə^r] n (of motion) proponente m/f

proposition [prɔpə'zɪʃən] n propuesta, proposición f; **to make sb a ~** proponer algo a algn

propound [prə'paund] vt (theory) exponer

proprietary [prə'praɪətərɪ] adj (Comm): **~ article** artículo de marca; **~ brand** marca comercial

proprietor [prə'praɪətə^r] n propietario(-a), dueño(-a)

propriety [prə'praɪətɪ] n decoro

propulsion [prə'pʌlʃən] n propulsión f

pro rata [prəu'rɑ:tə] adv a prorrata

prosaic [prəu'zeɪɪk] adj prosaico

Pros. Atty. abbr (US) = **prosecuting attorney**

proscribe [prə'skraɪb] vt proscribir

prose [prəuz] n prosa; (Scol) traducción f inversa

prosecute ['prɔsɪkjuːt] vt (Law) procesar; **"trespassers will be prosecuted"** (Law) "se procesará a los intrusos"

prosecution [prɔsɪ'kjuːʃən] n proceso, causa; (accusing side) acusación f

prosecutor ['prɔsɪkjuːtər] n acusador(a) m(f); (also: **public prosecutor**) fiscal m/f

prospect [n 'prɔspɛkt, vb prə'spɛkt] n (chance) posibilidad f; (outlook) perspectiva; (hope) esperanza ■ vt explorar ■ vi buscar; **prospects** npl (for work etc) perspectivas fpl; **to be faced with the ~ of** tener que enfrentarse a la posibilidad de que ...; **we were faced with the ~ of leaving early** se nos planteó la posibilidad de marcharnos pronto; **there is every ~ of an early victory** hay buenas perspectivas de una pronta victoria

prospecting [prə'spɛktɪŋ] n prospección f

prospective [prə'spɛktɪv] adj (possible) probable, eventual; (certain) futuro; (buyer) presunto; (legislation, son-in-law) futuro

prospector [prə'spɛktər] n explorador(a) m(f); **gold ~** buscador m de oro

prospectus [prə'spɛktəs] n prospecto

prosper ['prɔspər] vi prosperar

prosperity [prɔ'spɛrɪtɪ] n prosperidad f

prosperous ['prɔspərəs] adj próspero

prostate ['prɔsteɪt] n (also: **prostate gland**) próstata

prostitute ['prɔstɪtjuːt] n prostituta; **male ~** prostituto

prostitution [prɔstɪ'tjuːʃən] n prostitución f

prostrate ['prɔstreɪt] adj postrado; (fig) abatido ■ vt: **to ~ o.s.** postrarse

protagonist [prə'tægənɪst] n protagonista m/f

protect [prə'tɛkt] vt proteger

protection [prə'tɛkʃən] n protección f; **to be under sb's ~** estar amparado por algn

protectionism [prə'tɛkʃənɪzəm] n proteccionismo

protection racket n chantaje m

protective [prə'tɛktɪv] adj protector(a); **~ custody** (Law) detención f preventiva

protector [prə'tɛktər] n protector(a) m(f)

protégé ['prəutɛʒeɪ] n protegido(-a)

protein ['prəutiːn] n proteína

pro tem [prəu'tɛm] adv abbr (= pro tempore: for the time being) provisionalmente

protest [n 'prəutɛst, vb prə'tɛst] n protesta ■ vi protestar ■ vt (affirm) afirmar, declarar; **to do sth under ~** hacer algo bajo protesta; **to ~ against/about** protestar en contra de/por

Protestant ['prɔtɪstənt] adj, n protestante m/f

protester, protestor [prə'tɛstər] n (in demonstration) manifestante m/f

protest march n manifestación f or marcha (de protesta)

protocol ['prəutəkɔl] n protocolo

prototype ['prəutətaɪp] n prototipo

protracted [prə'træktɪd] adj prolongado

protractor [prə'træktər] n (Geom) transportador m

protrude [prə'truːd] vi salir, sobresalir

protuberance [prə'tjuːbərəns] n protuberancia

proud [praud] adj orgulloso; (pej) soberbio, altanero ■ adv: **to do sth** ~ tratar a algn a cuerpo de rey; **to do o.s.** ~ no privarse de nada; **to be ~ to do sth** estar orgulloso de hacer algo

proudly ['praudlɪ] adv orgullosamente, con orgullo; (pej) con soberbia, con altanería

prove [pruːv] vt probar; (verify) comprobar; (show) demostrar ■ vi: **to ~ correct** resultar correcto; **to ~ o.s.** ponerse a prueba; **he was proved right in the end** al final se vio que tenía razón

proverb ['prɔvəːb] n refrán m

proverbial [prə'vəːbɪəl] adj proverbial

proverbially [prə'vəːbɪəlɪ] adv proverbialmente

provide [prə'vaɪd] vt proporcionar, dar; **to ~ sb with sth** proveer a algn de algo; **to be provided with** ser provisto de

▶ **provide for** vt fus (person) mantener a; (problem etc) tener en cuenta

provided [prə'vaɪdɪd] conj: **~ (that)** con tal de que, a condición de que

Providence ['prɔvɪdəns] n Divina Providencia

providing [prə'vaɪdɪŋ] conj a condición de que, con tal de que

province ['prɔvɪns] n provincia; (fig) esfera

provincial [prə'vɪnʃəl] adj provincial; (pej) provinciano

provision [prə'vɪʒən] n provisión f; (supply) suministro, abastecimiento; **provisions** npl provisiones fpl, víveres mpl; **to make ~ for** (one's family, future) atender las necesidades de

provisional [prə'vɪʒənl] adj provisional, provisorio (LAm); (temporary) interino ■ n: **P~** (Ireland Pol) Provisional m (miembro de la tendencia activista del IRA)

provisional driving licence n (Brit Aut) carnet m de conducir provisional; see also **L-plates**

proviso [prə'vaɪzəu] n condición f, estipulación f; **with the ~ that** a condición de que

Provo ['prɔvəu] n abbr (col) = **Provisional**

725

provocation [prɔvə'keɪʃən] n provocación f
provocative [prə'vɔkətɪv] adj provocativo
provoke [prə'vəuk] vt (arouse) provocar,
  incitar; (cause) causar, producir; (anger)
  enojar; **to ~ sb to sth/to do** or **into doing
  sth** provocar a algn a algo/a hacer algo
provoking [prə'vəukɪŋ] adj provocador(a)
provost ['prɔvəst] n (Brit: of university) rector(a)
  m(f); (Scottish) alcalde(-esa) m(f)
prow [prau] n proa
prowess ['prauɪs] n (skill) destreza, habilidad f;
  (courage) valor m; **his ~ as a footballer** (skill)
  su habilidad como futbolista
prowl [praul] vi (also: **prowl about, prowl
  around**) merodear ■ n: **on the ~** de
  merodeo, merodeando
prowler ['praulə'] n merodeador(a) m(f)
proximity [prɔk'sɪmɪtɪ] n proximidad f
proxy ['prɔksɪ] n poder m; (person)
  apoderado(-a); **by ~** por poderes
PRP n abbr (= performance related pay) retribución en
  función del rendimiento en el trabajo
prude [pru:d] n gazmoño(-a), mojigato(-a)
prudence ['pru:dns] n prudencia
prudent ['pru:dnt] adj prudente
prudently ['pru:dntlɪ] adv prudentemente,
  con prudencia
prudish ['pru:dɪʃ] adj gazmoño
prudishness [pru:dɪʃnɪs] n gazmoñería
prune [pru:n] n ciruela pasa ■ vt podar
pry [praɪ] vi: **to ~ into** entrometerse en
PS abbr (= postscript) P.D.
psalm [sɑ:m] n salmo
PSAT n abbr (US) = **Preliminary Scholastic
  Aptitude Test**
PSBR n abbr (Brit: = public sector borrowing
  requirement) necesidades de endeudamiento del
  sector público
pseud [sju:d] n (Brit col: intellectually) farsante
  m/f; (: socially) pretencioso(-a)
pseudo... [sju:dəu] pref seudo...
pseudonym ['sju:dənɪm] n seudónimo
PSHE n abbr (Brit Scol: = personal, social, and health
  education) formación social y sanitaria para la vida
  adulta
PST n abbr (US: = Pacific Standard Time) hora de
  invierno del Pacífico
PSV n abbr (Brit) see **public service vehicle**
psyche ['saɪkɪ] n psique f
psychiatric [saɪkɪ'ætrɪk] adj psiquiátrico
psychiatrist [saɪ'kaɪətrɪst] n psiquiatra m/f
psychiatry [saɪ'kaɪətrɪ] n psiquiatría
psychic ['saɪkɪk] adj (also: **psychical**) psíquico
psycho ['saɪkəu] n (col) psicópata m/f,
  pirado(-a)
psychoanalyse, psychoanalyze
  [saɪkəu'ænəlaɪz] vt psicoanalizar

psychoanalysis (pl **psychoanalyses**)
  [saɪkəuə'nælɪsɪs, -sɪ:z] n psicoanálisis m inv
psychoanalyst [saɪkəu'ænəlɪst] n
  psicoanalista m/f
psychological [saɪkə'lɔdʒɪkl] adj psicológico
psychologically [saɪkə'lɔdʒɪklɪ] adv
  psicológicamente
psychologist [saɪ'kɔlədʒɪst] n psicólogo(-a)
psychology [saɪ'kɔlədʒɪ] n psicología
psychopath ['saɪkəupæθ] n psicópata m/f
psychosis (pl **psychoses**) [saɪ'kəusɪs, -sɪ:z] n
  psicosis f inv
psychosomatic ['saɪkəusə'mætɪk] adj
  psicosomático
psychotherapy [saɪkəu'θɛrəpɪ] n
  psicoterapia
psychotic [saɪ'kɔtɪk] adj, n psicótico(-a)
PT n abbr (Brit: = physical training) Ed. Fís.
pt abbr = **pint; pints; point; points**
Pt. abbr (Geo: in place names: = Point) Pta
PTA n abbr (Brit: = Parent-Teacher Association)
  = Asociación f de Padres de Alumnos
Pte. abbr (Brit Mil) = **private**
PTO abbr (= please turn over) sigue
PTV n abbr (US) = **pay television; public
  television**
pub [pʌb] n abbr (= public house) pub m, bar m;
  ver nota

> **PUB**
>
> En un pub (o public house) se pueden
> consumir fundamentalmente bebidas
> alcohólicas, aunque en la actualidad
> también se sirven platos ligeros durante
> el almuerzo. Es, además, un lugar de
> encuentro donde se juega a los dardos o al
> billar, entre otras actividades. La estricta
> regulación sobre la venta de alcohol
> controla las horas de apertura, aunque
> éstas son más flexibles desde hace unos
> años. No se puede servir alcohol a los
> menores de 18 años.

pub crawl n (col): **to go on a ~** ir a recorrer
  bares
puberty ['pju:bətɪ] n pubertad f
pubic ['pju:bɪk] adj púbico
public ['pʌblɪk] adj, n público; **in ~** en público;
  to make sth ~ revelar or hacer público algo;
  to be ~ knowledge ser del dominio público;
  to go ~ (Comm) proceder a la venta pública
  de acciones
public address system n megafonía,
  sistema m de altavoces
publican ['pʌblɪkən] n dueño(-a) or
  encargado(-a) de un bar

publication [pʌblɪ'keɪʃən] n publicación f
public company n sociedad f anónima
public convenience n (Brit) aseos mpl
públicos, sanitarios mpl (LAm)
public holiday n día m de fiesta, (día) feriado
(LAm)
public house n (Brit) bar m, pub m
publicity [pʌb'lɪsɪtɪ] n publicidad f
publicize ['pʌblɪsaɪz] vt publicitar; (advertise)
hacer propaganda para
public limited company n sociedad f
anónima (S.A.)
publicly ['pʌblɪklɪ] adv públicamente, en
público
public opinion n opinión f pública
public ownership n propiedad f pública;
to be taken into ~ ser nacionalizado
Public Prosecutor n Fiscal m/f del Estado
public relations n relaciones fpl públicas
public relations officer n encargado(-a) de
relaciones públicas
public school n (Brit) colegio privado; (US)
instituto; ver nota

⬛ **PUBLIC SCHOOL**

En Inglaterra el término public school se
usa para referirse a un colegio privado
de pago, generalmente de alto prestigio
social y en régimen de internado.
Algunos de los más conocidos son Eton
o Harrow. Muchos de sus alumnos
estudian previamente hasta los 13 años
en un centro privado de pago llamado
"prep(aratory) school" y al terminar
el bachiller pasan a estudiar en las
universidades de Oxford y Cambridge.
En otros lugares como Estados Unidos
el mismo término se refiere a una
escuela pública de enseñanza gratuita
administrada por el Estado.

public sector n sector m público
public service vehicle n vehículo de servicio
público
public-spirited [pʌblɪk'spɪrɪtɪd] adj cívico
public transport, public transportation
(US) n transporte m público
public utility n servicio público
public works npl obras fpl públicas
publish ['pʌblɪʃ] vt publicar
publisher ['pʌblɪʃər] n (person) editor(a) m(f);
(firm) editorial f
publishing ['pʌblɪʃɪŋ] n (industry) industria
del libro
publishing company n (casa) editorial f
puce [pjuːs] adj de color pardo rojizo

puck [pʌk] n (ice hockey) puck m
pucker ['pʌkər] vt (pleat) arrugar; (brow etc)
fruncir
pudding ['pudɪŋ] n pudín m; (Brit: sweet)
postre m; **black ~** morcilla; **rice ~** arroz m
con leche
puddle ['pʌdl] n charco
puerile ['pjuəraɪl] adj pueril
Puerto Rican ['pwəːtəu'riːkən] adj, n
puertorriqueño(-a) m(f)
Puerto Rico [-'riːkəu] n Puerto Rico
puff [pʌf] n soplo; (of smoke) bocanada; (of
breathing, engine) resoplido; (also: **powder puff**)
borla ▪ vt: **to ~ one's pipe** dar chupadas a
la pipa; (also: **puff out**: sails, cheeks) hinchar,
inflar ▪ vi (gen) soplar; (pant) jadear; **to ~
out smoke** echar humo
puffed [pʌft] adj (col: out of breath) sin aliento
puffin ['pʌfɪn] n frailecillo
puff pastry, puff paste (US) n hojaldre m
puffy ['pʌfɪ] adj hinchado
pull [pul] n (tug): **to give sth a ~** dar un tirón
a algo; (fig: advantage) ventaja; (: influence)
influencia ▪ vt tirar de, jalar (LAm); (haul)
tirar, jalar (LAm), arrastrar; (strain): **to ~ a
muscle** sufrir un tirón ▪ vi tirar, jalar (LAm);
to ~ to pieces hacer pedazos; **to ~ one's
punches** andarse con bromas; **to ~ one's
weight** hacer su parte; **to ~ o.s. together**
tranquilizarse; **to ~ sb's leg** tomar el pelo a
algn; **to ~ strings (for sb)** enchufar (a algn)
▶ **pull about** vt (handle roughly: object)
manosear; (: person) maltratar
▶ **pull apart** vt (take apart) desmontar
▶ **pull down** vt (house) derribar
▶ **pull in** vi (Aut: at the kerb) parar (junto a la
acera); (Rail) llegar
▶ **pull off** vt (deal etc) cerrar
▶ **pull out** vi irse, marcharse; (Aut: from kerb)
salir ▪ vt sacar, arrancar
▶ **pull over** vi (Aut) hacerse a un lado
▶ **pull round, pull through** vi salvarse; (Med)
recobrar la salud
▶ **pull up** vi (stop) parar ▪ vt (uproot) arrancar,
desarraigar; (stop) parar
pulley ['pulɪ] n polea
pull-out ['pulaut] n suplemento ▪ cpd (pages,
magazine) separable
pullover ['puləuvər] n jersey m, suéter m
pulp [pʌlp] n (of fruit) pulpa; (for paper) pasta;
(pej: also: **pulp magazines** etc) prensa amarilla;
to reduce sth to ~ hacer algo papilla
pulpit ['pulpɪt] n púlpito
pulsate [pʌl'seɪt] vi pulsar, latir
pulse [pʌls] n (Anat) pulso; (of music, engine)
pulsación f; (Bot) legumbre f; **to feel** or **take
sb's ~** tomar el pulso a algn

P

pulverize ['pʌlvəraɪz] vt pulverizar; (fig) hacer polvo

puma ['pju:mə] n puma m

pumice ['pʌmɪs], **pumice stone** n piedra pómez

pummel ['pʌml] vt aporrear

pump [pʌmp] n bomba; (shoe) zapatilla de tenis ■ vt sacar con una bomba; (fig: col) (son)sacar; **to ~ sb for information** (son)sacarle información a algn
▶ **pump up** vt inflar

pumpkin ['pʌmpkɪn] n calabaza

pun [pʌn] n juego de palabras

punch [pʌntʃ] n (blow) golpe m, puñetazo; (tool) punzón m; (for paper) perforadora; (for tickets) taladro; (drink) ponche m ■ vt (hit): **to ~ sb/sth** dar un puñetazo or golpear a algn/algo; (make a hole in) punzar; perforar

punch card, punched card [pʌntʃt-] n tarjeta perforada

punch-drunk ['pʌntʃdrʌŋk] adj (Brit) grogui, sonado

punch line n (of joke) remate m

punch-up ['pʌntʃʌp] n (Brit col) riña

punctual ['pʌŋktjuəl] adj puntual

punctuality [pʌŋktju'ælɪtɪ] n puntualidad f

punctually ['pʌŋktjuəlɪ] adv: **it will start ~ at six** empezará a las seis en punto

punctuate ['pʌŋktjueɪt] vt puntuar; (fig) interrumpir

punctuation [pʌŋktju'eɪʃən] n puntuación f

punctuation mark n signo de puntuación

puncture ['pʌŋktʃəʳ] (Brit) n pinchazo ■ vt pinchar; **to have a ~** tener un pinchazo

pundit ['pʌndɪt] n experto(-a)

pungent ['pʌndʒənt] adj acre

punish ['pʌnɪʃ] vt castigar; **to ~ sb for sth/ for doing sth** castigar a algn por algo/por haber hecho algo

punishable ['pʌnɪʃəbl] adj punible, castigable

punishing ['pʌnɪʃɪŋ] adj (fig: exhausting) agotador(a)

punishment ['pʌnɪʃmənt] n castigo; (fig, col): **to take a lot of ~** (boxer) recibir una paliza; (car) ser maltratado

punitive ['pju:nɪtɪv] adj punitivo

punk [pʌŋk] n (also: **punk rocker**) punki m/f; (also: **punk rock**) música punk; (US col: hoodlum) matón m

punt [pʌnt] n (boat) batea; (Ireland) libra irlandesa ■ vi (bet) apostar

punter ['pʌntəʳ] n (gambler) jugador(a) m(f)

puny ['pju:nɪ] adj enclenque

pup [pʌp] n cachorro

pupil ['pju:pl] n alumno(-a); (of eye) pupila

puppet ['pʌpɪt] n títere m

puppet government n gobierno títere

puppy ['pʌpɪ] n cachorro, perrito

purchase ['pə:tʃɪs] n compra; (grip) agarre m, asidero ■ vt comprar

purchase order n orden f de compra

purchase price n precio de compra

purchaser ['pə:tʃɪsəʳ] n comprador(a) m(f)

purchase tax n (Brit) impuesto sobre la venta

purchasing power ['pə:tʃɪsɪŋ-] n poder m adquisitivo

pure [pjuəʳ] adj puro; **a ~ wool jumper** un jersey de pura lana; **it's laziness, ~ and simple** es pura vagancia

purebred ['pjuəbrɛd] adj de pura sangre

purée ['pjuəreɪ] n puré m

purely ['pjuəlɪ] adv puramente

purgatory ['pə:gətərɪ] n purgatorio

purge [pə:dʒ] n (Med, Pol) purga ■ vt purgar

purification [pjuərɪfɪ'keɪʃən] n purificación f, depuración f

purify ['pjuərɪfaɪ] vt purificar, depurar

purist ['pjuərɪst] n purista m/f

puritan ['pjuərɪtən] n puritano(-a)

puritanical [pjuərɪ'tænɪkl] adj puritano

purity ['pjuərɪtɪ] n pureza

purl [pə:l] n punto del revés

purloin [pə:'lɔɪn] vt hurtar, robar

purple ['pə:pl] adj morado

purport [pə:'pɔ:t] vi: **to ~ to be/do** dar a entender que es/hace

purpose ['pə:pəs] n propósito; **on ~** a propósito, adrede; **to no ~** para nada, en vano; **for teaching purposes** con fines pedagógicos; **for the purposes of this meeting** para los fines de esta reunión

purpose-built ['pə:pəs'bɪlt] adj (Brit) construido especialmente

purposeful ['pə:pəsful] adj resuelto, determinado

purposely ['pə:pəslɪ] adv a propósito, adrede

purr [pə:ʳ] n ronroneo ■ vi ronronear

purse [pə:s] n monedero; (US: handbag) bolso ■ vt fruncir

purser ['pə:səʳ] n (Naut) comisario(-a)

purse snatcher [-snætʃəʳ] n (US) persona que roba por el procedimiento del tirón

pursue [pə'sju:] vt seguir; (harass) perseguir; (profession) ejercer; (pleasures) buscar; (inquiry, matter) seguir

pursuer [pə'sju:əʳ] n perseguidor(a) m(f)

pursuit [pə'sju:t] n (chase) caza; (of pleasure etc) busca; (occupation) actividad f; **in (the) ~ of sth** en busca de algo

purveyor [pə'veɪəʳ] n proveedor(a) m(f)

pus [pʌs] n pus m

push [pʊʃ] n empujón m; (Mil) ataque m; (drive) empuje m ■ vt empujar; (button)

apretar; (*promote*) promover; (*fig: press,
advance: views*) fomentar; (*thrust*): **to ~ sth
(into)** meter algo a la fuerza (en) ■ *vi*
empujar; (*fig*) hacer esfuerzos; **at a ~** (*col*)
a duras penas; **she is pushing 50** (*col*) raya
en los 50; **to be pushed for time/money**
andar justo de tiempo/escaso de dinero; **to
~ a door open/shut** abrir/cerrar una puerta
empujándola; **to ~ for** (*better pay, conditions*)
reivindicar; **"~"** (*on door*) "empujar"; (*on bell*)
"pulse"
▶ **push aside** *vt* apartar con la mano
▶ **push in** *vi* colarse
▶ **push off** *vi* (*col*) largarse
▶ **push on** *vi* (*continue*) seguir adelante
▶ **push through** *vt* (*measure*) despachar
▶ **push up** *vt* (*total, prices*) hacer subir
push-bike ['puʃbaɪk] *n* (*Brit*) bicicleta
push-button ['puʃbʌtn] *adj* con botón de
mando
pushchair ['puʃtʃeəʳ] *n* (*Brit*) silla de niño
pusher ['puʃəʳ] *n* (*also*: **drug pusher**)
traficante *m/f* de drogas
pushover ['puʃəuvəʳ] *n* (*col*): **it's a ~** está
tirado
push-up ['puʃʌp] *n* (*US*) flexión *f*
pushy ['puʃɪ] *adj* (*pej*) agresivo
puss [pus], **pussy** ['pusɪ], **pussy-cat**
['pusɪkæt] *n* minino
put [put] (*pt, pp* **put**) *vt* (*place*) poner, colocar;
(*put into*) meter; (*express, say*) expresar; (*a
question*) hacer; (*estimate*) calcular; (*cause to
be*): **to ~ sb in a good/bad mood** poner a
algn de buen/mal humor; **to ~ a lot of time
into sth** dedicar mucho tiempo a algo; **to
~ money on a horse** apostar dinero en
un caballo; **to ~ money into a company**
invertir dinero en una compañía; **to ~ sb to
a lot of trouble** causar mucha molestia a
algn; **we ~ the children to bed** acostamos
a los niños; **how shall I ~ it?** ¿cómo puedo
explicarlo *or* decirlo?; **I ~ it to you that ...** le
sugiero que ...; **to stay ~** no moverse
▶ **put about** *vi* (*Naut*) virar ■ *vt* (*rumour*)
hacer correr
▶ **put across** *vt* (*ideas etc*) comunicar
▶ **put aside** *vt* (*lay down: book etc*) dejar *or*
poner a un lado; (*save*) ahorrar; (*in shop*)
guardar
▶ **put away** *vt* (*store*) guardar
▶ **put back** *vt* (*replace*) devolver a su lugar;
(*postpone*) posponer; (*set back: watch, clock*)
retrasar; **this will ~ us back 10 years** esto
nos retrasará 10 años
▶ **put by** *vt* (*money*) guardar
▶ **put down** *vt* (*on ground*) poner en el suelo;
(*animal*) sacrificar; (*in writing*) apuntar;

(*suppress: revolt etc*) sofocar; (*attribute*) atribuir;
~ me down for £15 apúntame por 15 libras;
~ it down on my account (*Comm*) póngalo
en mi cuenta
▶ **put forward** *vt* (*ideas*) presentar, proponer;
(*date*) adelantar
▶ **put in** *vt* (*application, complaint*) presentar
▶ **put in for** *vt fus* (*job*) solicitar; (*promotion*)
pedir
▶ **put off** *vt* (*postpone*) aplazar; (*discourage*)
desanimar, quitar las ganas a
▶ **put on** *vt* (*clothes, lipstick etc*) ponerse; (*light
etc*) encender; (*play etc*) presentar; (*brake*)
echar; (*assume: accent, manner*) afectar, fingir;
(*airs*) adoptar, darse; (*concert, exhibition etc*)
montar; (*extra bus, train etc*) poner; (*col:
kid, have on: esp US*) tomar el pelo a; (*inform,
indicate*): **to ~ sb on to sb/sth** informar a algn
de algn/algo; **to ~ on weight** engordar
▶ **put out** *vt* (*fire, light*) apagar; (*one's hand*)
alargar; (*news, rumour*) hacer circular; (*tongue
etc*) sacar; (*person: inconvenience*) molestar,
fastidiar; (*dislocate: shoulder, vertebra, knee*)
dislocar(se); (*vi: Naut*): **to ~ out to sea**
hacerse a la mar; **to ~ out from Plymouth**
salir de Plymouth
▶ **put through** *vt* (*call*) poner; **~ me through
to Mr Low** póngame *or* comuníqueme (*LAm*)
con el Señor Low
▶ **put together** *vt* unir, reunir; (*assemble:
furniture*) armar, montar; (*meal*) preparar
▶ **put up** *vt* (*raise*) levantar, alzar; (*hang*)
colgar; (*build*) construir; (*increase*) aumentar;
(*accommodate*) alojar; (*incite*): **to ~ sb up to
doing sth** instar *or* incitar a algn a hacer
algo; **to ~ sth up for sale** poner algo a la
venta
▶ **put upon** *vt fus*: **to be ~ upon** (*imposed upon*)
dejarse explotar
▶ **put up with** *vt fus* aguantar
putrid ['pju:trɪd] *adj* podrido
putsch [putʃ] *n* golpe *m* de estado
putt [pʌt] *vt* hacer un putt ■ *n* putt *m*
putter ['pʌtəʳ] *n* putter *m*
putting green ['pʌtɪŋ-] *n* green *m*, minigolf *m*
putty ['pʌtɪ] *n* masilla
put-up ['putʌp] *adj*: **~ job** (*Brit*) estafa
puzzle ['pʌzl] *n* (*riddle*) acertijo; (*jigsaw*)
rompecabezas *m inv*; (*also*: **crossword puzzle**)
crucigrama *m*; (*mystery*) misterio ■ *vt*
dejar perplejo, confundir ■ *vi*: **to ~ about**
quebrar la cabeza por; **to ~ over** (*sb's actions*)
quebrarse la cabeza por; (*mystery, problem*)
devanarse los sesos sobre; **to be puzzled
about sth** no llegar a entender algo
puzzling ['pʌzlɪŋ] *adj* (*question*) misterioso,
extraño; (*attitude, instructions*) extraño

P

PVC *n abbr* (= *polyvinyl chloride*) P.V.C. *m*
Pvt. *abbr* (*US Mil*) = **private**
PW *n abbr* (*US*) = **prisoner of war**
pw *abbr* (= *per week*) por semana
PX *n abbr* (*US Mil*: = *post exchange*) economato militar
pygmy ['pɪgmɪ] *n* pigmeo(-a)
pyjamas, pajamas (*US*) [pɪ'dʒɑːməz] *npl* pijama *m*, piyama *m* (*LAm*); **a pair of ~** un

pijama
pylon ['paɪlən] *n* torre *f* de conducción eléctrica
pyramid ['pɪrəmɪd] *n* pirámide *f*
Pyrenean [pɪrə'niːən] *adj* pirenaico
Pyrenees [pɪrə'niːz] *npl*: **the ~** los Pirineos
Pyrex® ['paɪreks] *n* pírex *m* ■ *cpd*: ~ **casserole** cazuela de pírex
python ['paɪθən] *n* pitón *m*

Qq

Q, q [kjuː] n (letter) Q, q f; **Q for Queen** Q de Quebec

Qatar [kæ'tɑː] n Qatar m

QC n abbr (Brit: ~ Queen's Counsel) título concedido a determinados abogados

QCA n abbr (Brit: = Qualifications and Curriculum Authority) organismo que se encarga del currículum educativo en Inglaterra

QED abbr (= quod erat demonstrandum) Q.E.D.

QM n abbr see **quartermaster**

q.t. n abbr (col: = quiet): **on the q.t.** a hurtadillas

qty abbr (= quantity) cantidad

quack [kwæk] n (of duck) graznido; (pej: doctor) curandero(-a), matasanos m inv ■ vi graznar

quad [kwɔd] abbr = **quadrangle**; **quadruple**; **quadruplet**

quadrangle ['kwɔdræŋgl] n (Brit: courtyard: abbr: quad) patio

quadruple [kwɔ'druːpl] vt, vi cuadruplicar

quadruplet [kwɔ'druːplɪt] n cuatrillizo

quagmire ['kwægmaɪəʳ] n lodazal m, cenegal m

quail [kweɪl] n (bird) codorniz f ■ vi amedrentarse

quaint [kweɪnt] adj extraño; (picturesque) pintoresco

quaintly ['kweɪntlɪ] adv extrañamente; pintorescamente

quaintness ['kweɪntnɪs] n lo pintoresco, tipismo

quake [kweɪk] vi temblar ■ n abbr = **earthquake**

Quaker ['kweɪkəʳ] n cuáquero(-a)

qualification [kwɔlɪfɪ'keɪʃən] n (reservation) reserva; (modification) modificación f; (act) calificación f; (paper qualification) título; **what are your qualifications?** ¿qué títulos tienes?

qualified ['kwɔlɪfaɪd] adj (trained) cualificado; (fit) capacitado; (limited) limitado; (professionally) titulado; ~ **for/to do sth** capacitado para/para hacer algo; **he's not ~ for the job** no está capacitado para ese trabajo; **it was a ~ success** fue un éxito relativo

qualify ['kwɔlɪfaɪ] vt (Ling) calificar a; (capacitate) capacitar; (modify) matizar; (limit) moderar ■ vi (Sport) clasificarse; **to ~ (as)** calificarse (de), graduarse (en), recibirse (de) (LAm); **to ~ (for)** reunir los requisitos (para); **to ~ as an engineer** sacar el título de ingeniero

qualifying ['kwɔlɪfaɪɪŋ] adj (exam, round) eliminatorio

qualitative ['kwɔlɪtətɪv] adj cualitativo

quality ['kwɔlɪtɪ] n calidad f; (moral) cualidad f; **of good/poor ~** de buena or alta/poca calidad

quality control n control m de calidad

quality of life n calidad f de vida

quality press n prensa seria; ver nota

● QUALITY PRESS

La expresión quality press se refiere los periódicos que dan un tratamiento serio de las noticias, ofreciendo información detallada sobre un amplio espectro de temas y análisis en profundidad de la actualidad. Por su tamaño, considerablemente mayor que el de los periódicos sensacionalistas, se les llama también "broadsheets".

---

qualm [kwɑːm] n escrúpulo; **to have qualms about sth** sentir escrúpulos por algo

quandary ['kwɔndrɪ] n: **to be in a ~** verse en un dilema

quango ['kwæŋgəu] n abbr (Brit: = quasi-autonomous non-governmental organization) organismo semiautónomo de subvención estatal

quantifiable [kwɔntɪ'faɪəbl] adj cuantificable

quantitative ['kwɔntɪtətɪv] adj cuantitativo

quantity ['kwɔntɪtɪ] n cantidad f; **in ~** en grandes cantidades

quantity surveyor n aparejador(a) m(f)

q

quantum leap ['kwɔntəm-] n (fig) avance m
espectacular
quarantine ['kwɔrnti:n] n cuarentena
quark [kwɑ:k] n cuark m
quarrel ['kwɔrl] n riña, pelea ▪ vi reñir,
pelearse; **to have a ~ with sb** reñir or
pelearse con algn; **I can't ~ with that** no le
veo pegas
quarrelsome ['kwɔrəlsəm] adj pendenciero
quarry ['kwɔrɪ] n (for stone) cantera; (animal)
presa
quart [kwɔ:t] n cuarto de galón = 1.136 l
quarter ['kwɔ:təʳ] n cuarto, cuarta parte
f; (of year) trimestre m; (district) barrio; (US,
Canada: 25 cents) cuarto de dólar ▪ vt dividir
en cuartos; (Mil: lodge) alojar; **quarters**
npl (barracks) cuartel m; (living quarters)
alojamiento sg; **a ~ of an hour** un cuarto de
hora; **to pay by the ~** pagar trimestralmente
or cada tres meses; **it's a ~ to** or (US) **of three**
son las tres menos cuarto; **it's a ~ past** or
(US) **after three** son las tres y cuarto; **from
all quarters** de todas partes; **at close
quarters** de cerca
quarterback ['kwɔ:təbæk] n (US: football)
mariscal m de campo
quarter-deck ['kwɔ:tədɛk] n (Naut) alcázar m
quarter final n cuarto de final
quarterly ['kwɔ:təlɪ] adj trimestral ▪ adv
cada 3 meses, trimestralmente
quartermaster ['kwɔ:təmɑ:stəʳ] n (Mil)
comisario, intendente m militar
quartet, quartette [kwɔ:'tɛt] n cuarteto
quarto ['kwɔ:təu] n tamaño holandés ▪ adj
de tamaño holandés
quartz [kwɔ:ts] n cuarzo
quash [kwɔʃ] vt (verdict) anular, invalidar
quasi- ['kweɪzaɪ] pref cuasi
quaver ['kweɪvəʳ] n (Brit Mus) corchea ▪ vi
temblar
quay [ki:] n (also: **quayside**) muelle m
Que. abbr (Canada) = **Quebec**
queasiness ['kwi:zɪnɪs] n malestar m,
náuseas fpl
queasy ['kwi:zɪ] adj: **to feel ~** tener náuseas
Quebec [kwɪ'bɛk] n Quebec m
queen [kwi:n] n reina; (Cards etc) dama
queen mother n reina madre
Queen's Speech n ver nota

▪ **QUEEN'S SPEECH**
▪
▪ Se llama Queen's Speech (o "King's
▪ Speech") al discurso que pronuncia el
▪ monarca durante la sesión de apertura
▪ del Parlamento británico, en el que
▪ se expresan las líneas generales de la
▪ política del gobierno para la nueva
▪ legislatura. El Primer Ministro se encarga
▪ de redactarlo con la ayuda del Consejo
▪ de Ministros y es leído en la Cámara
▪ de los Lores ("House of Lords") ante los
▪ miembros de ambas cámaras.

queer [kwɪəʳ] adj (odd) raro, extraño ▪ n (pej:
col) marica m
quell [kwɛl] vt calmar; (put down) sofocar
quench [kwɛntʃ] vt (flames) apagar; **to ~
one's thirst** apagar la sed
querulous ['kwɛrələs] adj (person, voice)
quejumbroso
query ['kwɪərɪ] n (question) pregunta; (doubt)
duda ▪ vt preguntar; (disagree with, dispute)
no estar conforme con, dudar de
quest [kwɛst] n busca, búsqueda
question ['kwɛstʃən] n pregunta; (matter)
asunto, cuestión f ▪ vt (doubt) dudar de;
(interrogate) interrogar, hacer preguntas
a; **to ask sb a ~**, **put a ~ to sb** hacerle una
pregunta a algn; **the ~ is ...** el asunto es ...;
to bring or **call sth into ~** poner algo en (tela
de) duda; **beyond ~** fuera de toda duda;
it's out of the ~ imposible, ni hablar
questionable ['kwɛstʃənəbl] adj discutible;
(doubtful) dudoso
questioner ['kwɛstʃənəʳ] n interrogador(a)
m(f)
questioning ['kwɛstʃənɪŋ] adj inquisitivo
▪ n preguntas fpl; (by police etc) interrogatorio
question mark n punto de interrogación
questionnaire [kwɛstʃə'nɛəʳ] n cuestionario
queue [kju:] n (Brit) cola ▪ vi hacer cola;
to jump the ~ colarse
quibble ['kwɪbl] vi andarse con sutilezas
quick [kwɪk] adj rápido; (temper) vivo; (agile)
ágil; (mind) listo; (eye) agudo; (ear) fino ▪ n:
cut to the ~ (fig) herido en lo más vivo;
be ~! ¡date prisa!; **to be ~ to act** obrar con
prontitud; **she was ~ to see that** se dio
cuenta de eso en seguida
quicken ['kwɪkən] vt apresurar ▪ vi
apresurarse, darse prisa
quick-fire ['kwɪkfaɪəʳ] adj (questions etc)
rápido, (hecho) a quemarropa
quick fix n (pej) parche m
quickly ['kwɪklɪ] adv rápidamente, de prisa;
we must act ~ tenemos que actuar cuanto
antes
quickness ['kwɪknɪs] n rapidez f; (of temper)
viveza; (agility) agilidad f; (of mind, eye etc)
agudeza
quicksand ['kwɪksænd] n arenas fpl
movedizas
quickstep ['kwɪkstɛp] n baile de ritmo rápido

quick-tempered [kwɪk'tɛmpəd] *adj* de genio vivo

quick-witted [kwɪk'wɪtɪd] *adj* listo, despabilado

quid [kwɪd] *n pl inv* (*Brit: col*) libra

quid pro quo ['kwɪdprəu'kwəu] *n* quid pro quo *m*, compensación *f*

quiet ['kwaɪət] *adj* (*not busy: day*) tranquilo; (*silent*) callado; (*reserved*) reservado; (*discreet*) discreto; (*not noisy: engine*) silencioso ■ *n* tranquilidad *f* ■ *vt, vi* (*US*) = **quieten; keep ~!** ¡cállate!, ¡silencio!; **business is ~ at this time of year** hay poco movimiento en esta época

quieten ['kwaɪətn] (*also:* **quieten down**) *vi* (*grow calm*) calmarse; (*grow silent*) callarse ■ *vt* calmar; hacer callar

quietly ['kwaɪətlɪ] *adv* tranquilamente; (*silently*) silenciosamente

quietness ['kwaɪətnɪs] *n* (*silence*) silencio; (*calm*) tranquilidad *f*

quill [kwɪl] *n* (*of porcupine*) púa; (*pen*) pluma

quilt [kwɪlt] *n* (*Brit*) edredón *m*

quin [kwɪn] *n abbr* = **quintuplet**

quince [kwɪns] *n* membrillo

quinine [kwɪ'niːn] *n* quinina

quintet, quintette [kwɪn'tɛt] *n* quinteto

quintuplet [kwɪn'tjuːplɪt] *n* quintillizo

quip [kwɪp] *n* ocurrencia ■ *vi* decir con ironía

quire ['kwaɪəʳ] *n* mano *f* de papel

quirk [kwəːk] *n* peculiaridad *f*; **by some ~ of fate** por algún capricho del destino

quit (*pt, pp ~* **or quitted**) [kwɪt] *vt* dejar, abandonar; (*premises*) desocupar; (*Comput*) abandonar ■ *vi* (*give up*) renunciar; (*go away*) irse; (*resign*) dimitir; **~ stalling!** (*US col*)

¡déjate de evasivas!

quite [kwaɪt] *adv* (*rather*) bastante; (*entirely*) completamente; **~ a few of them** un buen número de ellos; **~ (so)!** ¡así es!, ¡exactamente!; **~ new** bastante nuevo; **that's not ~ right** eso no está del todo bien; **not ~ as many as last time** no tantos como la última vez; **she's ~ pretty** es bastante guapa

Quito ['kiːtəu] *n* Quito

quits [kwɪts] *adj:* **~ (with)** en paz (con); **let's call it ~** quedamos en paz

quiver ['kwɪvəʳ] *vi* estremecerse ■ *n* (*for arrows*) carcaj *m*

quiz [kwɪz] *n* (*game*) concurso; (*: TV, Radio*) programa-concurso; (*questioning*) interrogatorio ■ *vt* interrogar

quizzical ['kwɪzɪkl] *adj* burlón(-ona)

quoits [kwɔɪts] *npl* juego de aros

quorum ['kwɔːrəm] *n* quórum *m*

quota ['kwəutə] *n* cuota

quotation [kwəu'teɪʃən] *n* cita; (*estimate*) presupuesto

quotation marks *npl* comillas *fpl*

quote [kwəut] *n* cita ■ *vt* (*sentence*) citar; (*Comm: sum, figure*) cotizar ■ *vi:* **to ~ from** citar de; **quotes** *npl* (*inverted commas*) comillas *fpl*; **in quotes** entre comillas; **the figure quoted for the repairs** el presupuesto dado para las reparaciones; **~ ... unquote** (*in dictation*) comillas iniciales ... finales

quotient ['kwəuʃənt] *n* cociente *m*

qv *n abbr* (= *quod vide: which see*) q.v.

qwerty keyboard ['kwəːtɪ-] *n* teclado QWERTY

q

Rr

R, r [ɑːʳ] *n* (*letter*) R, r f; **R for Robert,** (*US*)
  R for Roger R de Ramón
R *abbr* (= *right*) dcha.; (= *river*) R.; (= *Réaumur*
  (*scale*)) R; (*US Cine*: = *restricted*) sólo mayores; (*US*
  Pol: = *republican*; *Brit*: = *Rex, Regina*) R
RA *abbr* = **rear admiral** ▪ *n abbr* (*Brit*) = **Royal**
  Academy; Royal Academician
RAAF *n abbr* = **Royal Australian Air Force**
Rabat [rə'bɑːt] *n* Rabat *m*
rabbi ['ræbaɪ] *n* rabino
rabbit ['ræbɪt] *n* conejo ▪ *vi*: **to ~ (on)** (*Brit*
  col) hablar sin ton ni son
rabbit hutch *n* conejera
rabble ['ræbl] *n* (*pej*) chusma, populacho
rabies ['reɪbiːz] *n* rabia
RAC *n abbr* (*Brit*: = *Royal Automobile Club*) ≈ RACE
  m (*SP*)
raccoon [rə'kuːn] *n* mapache *m*
race [reɪs] *n* carrera; (*species*) raza ▪ *vt* (*horse*)
  hacer correr; (*person*) competir contra;
  (*engine*) acelerar ▪ *vi* (*compete*) competir;
  (*run*) correr; (*pulse*) latir a ritmo acelerado;
  the arms ~ la carrera armamentista; **the**
  human ~ el género humano; **he raced**
  across the road cruzó corriendo la carretera;
  to ~ in/out entrar/salir corriendo
race car *n* (*US*) = **racing car**
race car driver *n* (*US*) = **racing driver**
racecourse ['reɪskɔːs] *n* hipódromo
racehorse ['reɪshɔːs] *n* caballo de carreras
race meeting *n* concurso hípico
race relations *npl* relaciones *fpl* raciales
racetrack ['reɪstræk] *n* hipódromo; (*for cars*)
  circuito de carreras
racial ['reɪʃl] *adj* racial
racial discrimination *n* discriminación *f*
  racial
racial integration *n* integración *f* racial
racialism ['reɪʃəlɪzəm] *n* racismo
racialist ['reɪʃəlɪst] *adj, n* racista *m/f*
racing ['reɪsɪŋ] *n* carreras *fpl*
racing car *n* (*Brit*) coche *m* de carreras
racing driver *n* (*Brit*) corredor(a) *m(f)* de coches

racism ['reɪsɪzəm] *n* racismo
racist ['reɪsɪst] *adj, n* racista *m/f*
rack [ræk] *n* (*also*: **luggage rack**) rejilla
  (portaequipajes); (*shelf*) estante *m*; (*also*:
  roof rack) baca; (*also*: **clothes rack**) perchero
  ▪ *vt* (*cause pain to*) atormentar; **to go to ~**
  and ruin venirse abajo; **to ~ one's brains**
  devanarse los sesos
  ▶ **rack up** *vt* conseguir, ganar
racket ['rækɪt] *n* (*for tennis*) raqueta; (*noise*)
  ruido, estrépito; (*swindle*) estafa, timo
racketeer [rækɪ'tɪəʳ] *n* (*esp US*) estafador(a)
  m(f)
racoon [rə'kuːn] *n* = **raccoon**
racquet ['rækɪt] *n* raqueta
racy ['reɪsɪ] *adj* picante, subido
RADA ['rɑːdə] *n abbr* (*Brit*) = **Royal Academy**
  of Dramatic Art
radar ['reɪdɑːʳ] *n* radar *m*
radar trap *n* trampa radar
radial ['reɪdɪəl] *adj* (*tyre*: *also*: **radial-ply**) radial
radiance ['reɪdɪəns] *n* brillantez *f*, resplandor *m*
radiant ['reɪdɪənt] *adj* brillante,
  resplandeciente
radiate ['reɪdɪeɪt] *vt* (*heat*) radiar, irradiar
  ▪ *vi* (*lines*) extenderse
radiation [reɪdɪ'eɪʃən] *n* radiación *f*
radiation sickness *n* enfermedad *f* de
  radiación
radiator ['reɪdɪeɪtəʳ] *n* (*Aut*) radiador *m*
radiator cap *n* tapón *m* de radiador
radiator grill *n* (*Aut*) rejilla del radiador
radical ['rædɪkl] *adj* radical
radically ['rædɪkəlɪ] *adv* radicalmente
radii ['reɪdɪaɪ] *npl of* **radius**
radio ['reɪdɪəu] *n* radio *f* or *m* (*LAm*) ▪ *vi*:
  to ~ to sb mandar un mensaje por radio a
  algn ▪ *vt* (*information*) radiar, transmitir por
  radio; (*one's position*) indicar por radio; (*person*)
  llamar por radio; **on the ~** en or por la radio
radioactive [reɪdɪəu'æktɪv] *adj* radi(o)activo
radioactivity [reɪdɪəuæk'tɪvɪtɪ] *n*
  radi(o)actividad *f*

radio announcer n locutor(a) m(f) de radio
radio-controlled [ˌreɪdɪəʊkən'trəʊld] adj teledirigido
radiographer [reɪdɪ'ɒgrəfəʳ] n radiógrafo(-a)
radiography [reɪdɪ'ɒgrəfɪ] n radiografía
radiology [reɪdɪ'ɒlədʒɪ] n radiología
radio station n emisora
radio taxi n radio taxi m
radiotelephone [reɪdɪəʊ'tɛlɪfəʊn] n radioteléfono
radiotelescope [reɪdɪəʊ'tɛlɪskəʊp] n radiotelescopio
radiotherapist [reɪdɪəʊ'θɛrəpɪst] n radioterapeuta m/f
radiotherapy ['reɪdɪəʊθɛrəpɪ] n radioterapia
radish ['rædɪʃ] n rábano
radium ['reɪdɪəm] n radio
radius (pl **radii**) ['reɪdɪəs, -ɪaɪ] n radio; **within a ~ of 50 miles** en un radio de 50 millas
RAF n abbr (Brit) see **Royal Air Force**
raffia ['ræfɪə] n rafia
raffle ['ræfl] n rifa, sorteo ■ vt (object) rifar
raft [rɑːft] n (craft) balsa; (also: **life raft**) balsa salvavidas
rafter ['rɑːftəʳ] n viga
rag [ræg] n (piece of cloth) trapo; (torn cloth) harapo; (pej: newspaper) periodicucho; (for charity) actividades estudiantiles benéficas ■ vt (Brit) tomar el pelo a; **rags** npl harapos mpl; **in rags** en harapos, hecho jirones
rag-and-bone man [rægən'bəʊnmæn] n (Brit) trapero
rag doll n muñeca de trapo
rage [reɪdʒ] n (fury) rabia, furor m ■ vi (person) rabiar, estar furioso; (storm) bramar; **to fly into a ~** montar en cólera; **it's all the ~** es lo último
ragged ['rægɪd] adj (edge) desigual, mellado; (cuff) roto; (appearance) andrajoso, harapiento; **~ left/right** (text) margen m izquierdo/derecho irregular
raging ['reɪdʒɪŋ] adj furioso; **in a ~ temper** de un humor de mil demonios
rag trade n: **the ~** (col) el ramo de la confección
rag week n ver nota

● chistes más bien picantes para vender a
● los transeúntes, e incluso un baile de gala
● ("rag ball").

raid [reɪd] n (Mil) incursión f; (criminal) asalto; (by police) redada, allanamiento (LAm) ■ vt invadir, atacar; asaltar
raider ['reɪdəʳ] n invasor(a) m(f)
rail [reɪl] n (on stair) barandilla, pasamanos m inv; (on bridge) pretil m; (of balcony, ship) barandilla; (for train) riel m, carril m; **rails** npl vía sg; **by ~** por ferrocarril, en tren
railcard ['reɪlkɑːd] n (Brit) tarjeta para obtener descuentos en el tren; **Young Person's ~** = Tarjeta joven (SP)
railing ['reɪlɪŋ] n, **railings** ['reɪlɪŋz] npl verja sg
railway ['reɪlweɪ], (US) **railroad** ['reɪlrəʊd] n ferrocarril m, vía férrea
railway engine n (máquina) locomotora
railway line n (Brit) línea (de ferrocarril)
railwayman ['reɪlweɪmən] n (Brit) ferroviario
railway station n (Brit) estación f de ferrocarril
rain [reɪn] n lluvia ■ vi llover; **in the ~** bajo la lluvia; **it's raining** llueve, está lloviendo; **it's raining cats and dogs** está lloviendo a cántaros or a mares
rainbow ['reɪnbəʊ] n arco iris
raincoat ['reɪnkəʊt] n impermeable m
raindrop ['reɪndrɒp] n gota de lluvia
rainfall ['reɪnfɔːl] n lluvia
rainforest ['reɪnfɒrɪst] n selva tropical
rainproof ['reɪnpruːf] adj impermeable, a prueba de lluvia
rainstorm ['reɪnstɔːm] n temporal m (de lluvia)
rainwater ['reɪnwɔːtəʳ] n agua de lluvia
rainy ['reɪnɪ] adj lluvioso
raise [reɪz] n aumento ■ vt (lift) levantar; (build) erigir, edificar; (increase) aumentar; (doubts) suscitar; (a question) plantear; (cattle, family) criar; (crop) cultivar; (army) reclutar; (funds) reunir; (loan) obtener; (end: embargo) levantar; **to ~ one's voice** alzar la voz; **to ~ one's glass to sb/sth** brindar por algn/algo; **to ~ a laugh/a smile** provocar risa/una sonrisa; **to ~ sb's hopes** dar esperanzas a algn
raisin ['reɪzn] n pasa de Corinto
rake [reɪk] n (tool) rastrillo; (person) libertino ■ vt (garden) rastrillar; (fire) hurgar; (with machine gun) barrer
▶ **rake in, rake together** vt sacar
rake-off ['reɪkɔf] n (col) comisión f, tajada
rakish ['reɪkɪʃ] adj (dissolute) libertino; **at a ~ angle** (hat) echado a un lado, de lado

r

rally ['rælɪ] n reunión f; (Pol) mitin m; (Aut) rallye m; (Tennis) peloteo ∎ vt reunir ∎ vi reunirse; (sick person) recuperarse; (Stock Exchange) recuperarse
▸ **rally round** vt fus (fig) dar apoyo a
rallying point ['rælɪɪŋ-] n (Pol, Mil) punto de reunión
RAM [ræm] n abbr (Comput: = random access memory) RAM f
ram [ræm] n carnero; (Tech) pisón m ∎ vt (crash into) dar contra, chocar con; (tread down) apisonar
Ramadan ['ræmədæn] n Ramadán m
ramble ['ræmbl] n caminata, excursión f en el campo ∎ vi (pej: also: **ramble on**) divagar
rambler ['ræmblə^r] n excursionista m/f; (Bot) trepadora
rambling ['ræmblɪŋ] adj (speech) inconexo; (Bot) trepador(a); (house) laberíntico
rambunctious [ræm'bʌŋkʃəs] adj (US) = **rumbustious**
RAMC n abbr (Brit) = **Royal Army Medical Corps**
ramification [ræmɪfɪ'keɪʃən] n ramificación f
ramp [ræmp] n rampa; **on/off** ~ n (US Aut) vía de acceso/salida; **"~"** (Aut) "rampa"
rampage [ræm'peɪdʒ] n: **to be on the** ~ desmandarse
rampant ['ræmpənt] adj (disease etc): **to be** ~ estar muy extendido
rampart ['ræmpɑ:t] n terraplén m; (wall) muralla
ram raid vt atracar (rompiendo el escaparate con un coche)
ramshackle ['ræmʃækl] adj destartalado
RAN n abbr = **Royal Australian Navy**
ran [ræn] pt of **run**
R & B n abbr = **rhythm and blues**
ranch [rɑ:ntʃ] n (US) hacienda, estancia
rancher ['rɑ:ntʃə^r] n ganadero
rancid ['rænsɪd] adj rancio
rancour, rancor (US) ['ræŋkə^r] n rencor m
R & D n abbr (= research and development) I + D
random ['rændəm] adj fortuito, sin orden; (Comput, Math) aleatorio ∎ n: **at** ~ al azar
random access n (Comput) acceso aleatorio
R & R n abbr (also US Mil) = **rest and recreation**
randy ['rændɪ] adj (Brit col) cachondo, caliente
rang [ræŋ] pt of **ring**
range [reɪndʒ] n (of mountains) cadena de montañas, cordillera; (of missile) alcance m; (of voice) registro; (series) serie f; (of products) surtido; (Mil: also: **shooting range**) campo de tiro; (also: **kitchen range**) fogón m ∎ vt (place) colocar; (arrange) arreglar ∎ vi: **to** ~ **over** (wander) recorrer; (extend) extenderse

por; **within (firing)** ~ a tiro;
do you have anything else in this price ~? ¿tiene algo más de esta gama de precios?; **intermediate-/short-~ missile** proyectil m de medio/corto alcance; **to** ~ **from ... to ...** oscilar entre ... y ...; **ranged left/right** (text) alineado a la izquierda/derecha
ranger [reɪndʒə^r] n guardabosques m inv
Rangoon [ræŋ'gu:n] n Rangún m
rangy ['reɪndʒɪ] adj alto y delgado
rank [ræŋk] n (row) fila; (Mil) rango; (status) categoría; (Brit: also: **taxi rank**) parada ∎ vi: **to** ~ **among** figurar entre ∎ adj (stinking) fétido, rancio; (hypocrisy, injustice etc) manifiesto; **the** ~ **and file** (fig) las bases; **to close ranks** (Mil) cerrar filas; (fig) hacer un frente común; ~ **outsider** participante m/f sin probabilidades de vencer; **I** ~ **him sixth** yo le pongo en sexto lugar
rankle ['ræŋkl] vi (insult) doler
ransack ['rænsæk] vt (search) registrar; (plunder) saquear
ransom ['rænsəm] n rescate m; **to hold sb to** ~ (fig) poner a algn entre la espada y la pared
rant [rænt] vi despotricar
ranting ['ræntɪŋ] n desvaríos mpl
rap [ræp] vt golpear, dar un golpecito en
rape [reɪp] n violación f; (Bot) colza ∎ vt violar
rape oil, rapeseed oil ['reɪpsi:d-] n aceite m de colza
rapid ['ræpɪd] adj rápido
rapidity [rə'pɪdɪtɪ] n rapidez f
rapidly ['ræpɪdlɪ] adv rápidamente
rapids ['ræpɪdz] npl (Geo) rápidos mpl
rapier ['reɪpɪə^r] n estoque m
rapist ['reɪpɪst] n violador m
rapport [ræ'pɔ:^r] n entendimiento
rapprochement [ræ'prɔʃmɑ:ŋ] n acercamiento
rapt [ræpt] adj (attention) profundo; **to be** ~ **in contemplation** estar ensimismado
rapture ['ræptʃə^r] n éxtasis m
rapturous ['ræptʃərəs] adj extático; (applause) entusiasta; **a** ~ **(party)** macrofiesta con música máquina; ~ **music** música máquina
rare [reə^r] adj raro, poco común; (Culin: steak) poco hecho; **it is** ~ **to find that ...** es raro descubrir que ...
rarefied ['reərɪfaɪd] adj (air, atmosphere) enrarecido
rarely ['reəlɪ] adv rara vez, pocas veces
raring ['reərɪŋ] adj: **to be** ~ **to go** (col) tener muchas ganas de empezar
rarity ['reərɪtɪ] n rareza
rascal ['rɑ:skl] n pillo(-a), pícaro(-a)

rash [ræʃ] *adj* imprudente, precipitado
∎ *n* (*Med*) salpullido, erupción *f* (cutánea);
to come out in a ~ salir salpullidos
rasher ['ræʃər] *n* loncha
rashly ['ræʃlɪ] *adv* imprudentemente,
precipitadamente
rashness ['ræʃnɪs] *n* imprudencia,
precipitación *f*
rasp [rɑːsp] *n* (*tool*) escofina ∎ *vt* (*speak: also:*
rasp out) decir con voz áspera
raspberry ['rɑːzbərɪ] *n* frambuesa
rasping ['rɑːspɪŋ] *adj*: **a ~ noise** un ruido
áspero
Rastafarian [ræstə'fɛərɪən] *adj*, *n* rastafari
m/f
rat [ræt] *n* rata
ratchet ['rætʃɪt] *n* (*Tech*) trinquete *m*
rate [reɪt] *n* (*ratio*) razón *f*; (*percentage*) tanto
por ciento; (*price*) precio; (*: of hotel*) tarifa,
(*of interest*) tipo; (*speed*) velocidad *f* ∎ *vt*
(*value*) tasar; (*estimate*) estimar; **to ~ as** ser
considerado como; **rates** *npl* (*Brit*) impuesto
sg municipal; (*fees*) tarifa *sg*; **failure ~**
porcentaje *m* de fallos; **pulse ~** pulsaciones
fpl por minuto; **~ of pay** tipos *mpl* de sueldo;
at a ~ of 60 kph a una velocidad de 60 kph;
~ of growth ritmo de crecimiento; **~ of
return** (*Comm*) tasa de rendimiento; **bank ~**
tipo or tasa de interés bancario; **at any ~** en
todo caso; **to ~ sb/sth highly** tener a algn/
algo en alta estima; **the house is rated at
£84 per annum** (*Brit*) la casa está tasada en
84 libras al año
rateable value ['reɪtəbl-] *n* (*Brit*) valor *m*
impuesto
rate-capping ['reɪtkæpɪŋ] *n* (*Brit*) fijación *f*
de las contribuciones
ratepayer ['reɪtpeɪər] *n* (*Brit*) contribuyente
m/f
rather ['rɑːðər] *adv* antes, más bien;
(*somewhat*) algo, un poco; (*quite*) bastante;
it's ~ expensive es algo caro; (*too much*)
es demasiado caro; **there's ~ a lot** hay
bastante; **I would** or **I'd ~ go** preferiría ir;
I'd ~ not prefiero que no; **I ~ think he won't
come** me inclino a creer que no vendrá; **or ~**
(*more accurately*) o mejor dicho
ratification [rætɪfɪ'keɪʃən] *n* ratificación *f*
ratify ['rætɪfaɪ] *vt* ratificar
rating ['reɪtɪŋ] *n* (*valuation*) tasación
f; (*standing*) posición *f*; (*Brit Naut: sailor*)
marinero; **ratings** *npl* (*Radio, TV*)
clasificación *f*
ratio ['reɪʃɪəu] *n* razón *f*; **in the ~ of 100 to 1**
a razón de or en la proporción de 100 a 1
ration ['ræʃən] *n* ración *f*; **rations** *npl* víveres
mpl ∎ *vt* racionar

rational ['ræʃənl] *adj* racional; (*solution,
reasoning*) lógico, razonable; (*person*) cuerdo,
sensato
rationale [ræʃə'nɑːl] *n* razón *f* fundamental
rationalism ['ræʃnəlɪzəm] *n* racionalismo
rationalization [ræʃnəlaɪ'zeɪʃən] *n*
racionalización *f*
rationalize ['ræʃnəlaɪz] *vt* (*reorganize: industry*)
racionalizar
rationally ['ræʃnəlɪ] *adv* racionalmente;
(*logically*) lógicamente
rationing ['ræʃnɪŋ] *n* racionamiento
ratpack ['rætpæk] *n* (*Brit col*) periodistas que
persiguen a los famosos
rat race *n* lucha incesante por la supervivencia
rattan [ræ'tæn] *n* rota, caña de Indias
rattle ['rætl] *n* golpeteo; (*of train etc*) traqueteo;
(*object: of baby*) sonaja, sonajero; (*: of sports
fan*) matraca ∎ *vi* sonar, golpear; traquetear;
(*small objects*) castañetear ∎ *vt* hacer sonar
agitando; (*col: disconcert*) poner nervioso a
rattlesnake ['rætlsneɪk] *n* serpiente *f* de
cascabel
ratty ['rætɪ] *adj* (*col*) furioso; **to get ~**
mosquearse
raucous ['rɔːkəs] *adj* estridente, ronco
raucously ['rɔːkəslɪ] *adv* de modo estridente,
roncamente
raunchy ['rɔːntʃɪ] *adj* (*col*) lascivo
ravage ['rævɪdʒ] *vt* hacer estragos en,
destrozar; **ravages** *npl* estragos *mpl*
rave [reɪv] *vi* (*in anger*) encolerizarse; (*with
enthusiasm*) entusiasmarse; (*Med*) delirar,
desvariar ∎ *cpd*: **~ review** reseña entusiasta;
a ~ (*party*) macrofiesta con música máquina;
~ music música máquina
raven ['reɪvən] *n* cuervo
ravenous ['rævənəs] *adj*: **to be ~** tener un
hambre canina
ravine [rə'viːn] *n* barranco
raving ['reɪvɪŋ] *adj*: **~ lunatic** loco de atar
ravings ['reɪvɪŋz] *npl* desvaríos *mpl*
ravioli [rævɪ'əulɪ] *n* ravioles *mpl*, ravioli *mpl*
ravish ['rævɪʃ] *vt* (*charm*) encantar, embelesar;
(*rape*) violar
ravishing ['rævɪʃɪŋ] *adj* encantador(a)
raw [rɔː] *adj* (*uncooked*) crudo; (*not processed*)
bruto; (*sore*) vivo; (*inexperienced*) novato,
inexperto
Rawalpindi [rɔːl'pɪndɪ] *n* Rawalpindi *m*
raw data *n* (*Comput*) datos *mpl* en bruto
raw deal *n* (*col: bad deal*) mala pasada or
jugada; (*: harsh treatment*) injusticia
raw material *n* materia prima
ray [reɪ] *n* rayo; **~ of hope** (rayo de)
esperanza
rayon ['reɪɔn] *n* rayón *m*

r

raze [reɪz] vt (also: **raze to the ground**)
arrasar, asolar
razor ['reɪzəʳ] n (open) navaja; (safety razor)
máquina de afeitar
razor blade n hoja de afeitar
razzle ['ræzl], **razzle-dazzle** ['ræzl'dæzl] n
(Brit col): **to be/go on the ~(-dazzle)** estar/
irse de juerga
razzmatazz ['ræzmə'tæz] n (col) animación f,
bullicio
RC abbr = **Roman Catholic**
RCAF n abbr = **Royal Canadian Air Force**
RCMP n abbr = **Royal Canadian Mounted
Police**
RCN n abbr = **Royal Canadian Navy**
RD abbr (US Post) = **rural delivery**
Rd abbr = **road**
RDC n abbr (Brit) = **rural district council**
RE n abbr (Brit: = religious education) (Brit Mil)
= **Royal Engineers**
re [riː] prep con referencia a
re... [riː] pref re...
reach [riːtʃ] n alcance m; (Boxing)
envergadura; (of river etc) extensión f entre
dos recodos ■ vt alcanzar, llegar a; (achieve)
lograr ■ vi extenderse; (stretch out hand: also:
reach down, reach over: also: **reach across**
etc) tender la mano; **within ~** al alcance
(de la mano); **out of ~** fuera del alcance;
to ~ out for sth alargar or tender la mano
para tomar algo; **can I ~ you at your hotel?**
¿puedo localizarte en tu hotel?; **to ~ sb by
phone** comunicarse con algn por teléfono
react [riː'ækt] vi reaccionar
reaction [riː'ækʃən] n reacción f
reactionary [riː'ækʃənrɪ] adj, n
reaccionario(-a) m(f)
reactor [riː'æktəʳ] n reactor m
read (pt, pp ~) [riːd, rɛd] vi leer ■ vt leer;
(understand) entender; (study) estudiar;
to take sth as ~ (fig) dar algo por sentado;
do you ~ me? (Tel) ¿me escucha?; **to ~
between the lines** leer entre líneas
▶ **read out** vt leer en alta voz
▶ **read over** vt repasar
▶ **read through** vt (quickly) leer rápidamente,
echar un vistazo a; (thoroughly) leer con
cuidado or detenidamente
▶ **read up** vt, **read up on** vt fus
documentarse sobre
readable ['riːdəbl] adj (writing) legible; (book)
que merece la pena leer
reader ['riːdəʳ] n lector(a) m(f); (book) libro de
lecturas; (Brit: at university) profesor(a) m(f)
readership ['riːdəʃɪp] n (of paper etc) número
de lectores
readily ['rɛdɪlɪ] adv (willingly) de buena gana;

(easily) fácilmente; (quickly) en seguida
readiness ['rɛdɪnɪs] n buena voluntad;
(preparedness) preparación f; **in ~** (prepared)
listo, preparado
reading ['riːdɪŋ] n lectura; (understanding)
comprensión f; (on instrument) indicación f
reading lamp n lámpara portátil
reading matter n lectura
reading room n sala de lectura
readjust [riːə'dʒʌst] vt reajustar ■ vi (person):
to ~ to reajustarse a
readjustment [riːə'dʒʌstmənt] n reajuste m
ready ['rɛdɪ] adj listo, preparado; (willing)
dispuesto; (available) disponible ■ n: **at the
~** (Mil) listo para tirar; **~ for use** listo para
usar; **to be ~ to do sth** estar listo para hacer
algo; **to get ~** vi prepararse ■ vt preparar
ready cash n efectivo
ready-made ['rɛdɪ'meɪd] adj confeccionado
ready money n dinero contante
ready reckoner n tabla de cálculos hechos
ready-to-wear ['rɛdɪtə'wɛəʳ] adj
confeccionado
reaffirm [riːə'fəːm] vt reafirmar
reagent [riː'eɪdʒənt] n reactivo
real [rɪəl] adj verdadero, auténtico; **in ~
terms** en términos reales; **in ~ life** en la vida
real, en la realidad
real ale n cerveza elaborada
tradicionalmente
real estate n bienes mpl raíces
real estate agency n = **estate agency**
realism ['rɪəlɪzəm] n (also Art) realismo
realist ['rɪəlɪst] n realista m/f
realistic [rɪə'lɪstɪk] adj realista
realistically [rɪə'lɪstɪklɪ] adv de modo realista
reality [riː'ælɪtɪ] n realidad f; **in ~** en realidad
reality TV n telerrealidad f
realization [rɪəlaɪ'zeɪʃən] n comprensión
f; (of a project) realización f; (Comm: of assets)
realización f
realize ['rɪəlaɪz] vt (understand) darse cuenta
de; (a project) realizar; (Comm: asset) realizar;
I ~ that ... comprendo or entiendo que ...
really ['rɪəlɪ] adv realmente; **~?** ¿de veras?
realm [rɛlm] n reino; (fig) esfera
real time n (Comput) tiempo real
Realtor® ['rɪəltɔːʳ] n (US) corredor(a) m(f) de
bienes raíces
ream [riːm] n resma; **reams** (fig, col)
montones mpl
reap [riːp] vt segar; (fig) cosechar, recoger
reaper ['riːpəʳ] n segador(a) m(f)
reappear [riːə'pɪəʳ] vi reaparecer
reappearance [riːə'pɪərəns] n reaparición f
reapply [riːə'plaɪ] vi volver a presentarse,
hacer or presentar una nueva solicitud

reappoint [riːəˈpɔɪnt] vt volver a nombrar
reappraisal [riːəˈpreɪzl] n revaluación f
rear [rɪəʳ] adj trasero ■ n parte f trasera ■ vt
(cattle, family) criar ■ vi (also: **rear up**: animal)
encabritarse
rear-engined [ˈrɪərˈɛndʒɪnd] adj (Aut) con
motor trasero
rearguard [ˈrɪəgɑːd] n retaguardia
rearm [riːˈɑːm] vt rearmar ■ vi rearmarse
rearmament [riːˈɑːməmənt] n rearme m
rearrange [riːəˈreɪndʒ] vt ordenar or arreglar
de nuevo
rear-view [ˈrɪəvjuː]: ~ **mirror** n (Aut) espejo
retrovisor
reason [ˈriːzn] n razón f ■ vi: **to ~ with sb**
tratar de que algn entre en razón; **it stands
to ~ that** es lógico que; **the ~ for/why** la
causa de/la razón por la cual; **she claims
with good ~ that she's underpaid** dice con
razón que está mal pagada; **all the more ~
why you should not sell it** razón de más
para que no lo vendas
reasonable [ˈriːznəbl] adj razonable; (sensible)
sensato
reasonably [ˈriːznəblɪ] adv razonablemente;
a ~ accurate report un informe bastante
exacto
reasoned [ˈriːznd] adj (argument) razonado
reasoning [ˈriːznɪŋ] n razonamiento,
argumentos mpl
reassemble [riːəˈsɛmbl] vt volver a reunir;
(machine) montar de nuevo ■ vi volver a
reunirse
reassert [riːəˈsəːt] vt reafirmar, reiterar
reassurance [riːəˈʃuərəns] n consuelo
reassure [riːəˈʃuəʳ] vt tranquilizar; **to ~ sb
that** tranquilizar a algn asegurándole que
reassuring [riːəˈʃuərɪŋ] adj tranquilizador(a)
reawakening [riːəˈweɪknɪŋ] n despertar m
rebate [ˈriːbeɪt] n (on product) rebaja; (on tax
etc) desgravación f; (repayment) reembolso
rebel [ˈrɛbl] n rebelde m/f ■ vi [rɪˈbɛl]
rebelarse, sublevarse
rebellion [rɪˈbɛljən] n rebelión f,
sublevación f
rebellious [rɪˈbɛljəs] adj rebelde; (child)
revoltoso
rebirth [riːˈbəːθ] n renacimiento
rebound [rɪˈbaʊnd] vi (ball) rebotar ■ n
[ˈriːbaʊnd] rebote m
rebuff [rɪˈbʌf] n desaire m, rechazo ■ vt
rechazar
rebuild [riːˈbɪld] vt (irreg: like **build**)
reconstruir
rebuke [rɪˈbjuːk] n reprimenda ■ vt
reprender
rebut [rɪˈbʌt] vt rebatir

recalcitrant [rɪˈkælsɪtrənt] adj reacio
recall [rɪˈkɔːl] vt (remember) recordar;
(ambassador etc) retirar; (Comput) volver a
llamar ■ n recuerdo
recant [rɪˈkænt] vi retractarse
recap [ˈriːkæp] vt, vi recapitular
recapitulate [riːkəˈpɪtjuleɪt] vt, vi = **recap**
recapture [riːˈkæptʃəʳ] vt (town) reconquistar;
(atmosphere) hacer revivir
recd., rec'd abbr (= received) recibido
recede [rɪˈsiːd] vi retroceder
receding [rɪˈsiːdɪŋ] adj (forehead, chin)
hundido; ~ **hairline** entradas fpl
receipt [rɪˈsiːt] n (document) recibo; (act of
receiving) recepción f; **receipts** npl (Comm)
ingresos mpl; **to acknowledge ~ of** acusar
recibo de; **we are in ~ of** ... obra en nuestro
poder ...
receivable [rɪˈsiːvəbl] adj (Comm) a cobrar
receive [rɪˈsiːv] vt recibir; (guest) acoger;
(wound) sufrir; **"received with thanks"**
"recibí"
Received Pronunciation [rɪˈsiːvd-] n see **RP**
receiver [rɪˈsiːvəʳ] n (Tel) auricular m; (Radio)
receptor m; (of stolen goods) perista m/f; (Law)
administrador m jurídico
receivership [rɪˈsiːvəʃɪp] n: **to go into ~**
entrar en liquidación
recent [ˈriːsnt] adj reciente; **in ~ years** en los
últimos años
recently [ˈriːsntlɪ] adv recientemente, recién
(LAm); ~ **arrived** recién llegado; **until ~**
hasta hace poco
receptacle [rɪˈsɛptɪkl] n receptáculo
reception [rɪˈsɛpʃən] n (in building, office etc)
recepción f; (welcome) acogida
reception centre n (Brit) centro de recepción
reception desk n recepción f
receptionist [rɪˈsɛpʃənɪst] n recepcionista m/f
receptive [rɪˈsɛptɪv] adj receptivo
recess [rɪˈsɛs] n (in room) hueco; (for bed)
nicho; (secret place) escondrijo; (Pol etc: holiday)
período vacacional; (US Law: short break)
descanso; (Scol: esp US) recreo
recession [rɪˈsɛʃən] n recesión f, depresión f
recessionista [rɪsɛʃəˈnɪstə] n recesionista m/f
recharge [riːˈtʃɑːdʒ] vt (battery) recargar
rechargeable [riːˈtʃɑːdʒəbl] adj recargable
recipe [ˈrɛsɪpɪ] n receta
recipient [rɪˈsɪpɪənt] n recibidor(a) m(f);
(of letter) destinatario(-a)
reciprocal [rɪˈsɪprəkl] adj recíproco
reciprocate [rɪˈsɪprəkeɪt] vt devolver,
corresponder a ■ vi corresponder
recital [rɪˈsaɪtl] n (Mus) recital m
recitation [rɛsɪˈteɪʃən] n (of poetry) recitado;
(of complaints etc) enumeración f, relación f

r

739

recite [rɪ'saɪt] vt (poem) recitar; (complaints etc) enumerar

reckless ['rɛkləs] adj temerario, imprudente; (speed) peligroso

recklessly ['rɛkləslɪ] adv imprudentemente; de modo peligroso

recklessness ['rɛkləsnɪs] n temeridad f, imprudencia

reckon ['rɛkən] vt (count) contar; (consider) considerar ▪ vi: **to ~ without sb/sth** dejar de contar con algn/algo; **he is somebody to be reckoned with** no se le puede descartar; **I ~ that** ... me parece que ..., creo que ...
▸ **reckon on** vt fus contar con

reckoning ['rɛkənɪŋ] n (calculation) cálculo

reclaim [rɪ'kleɪm] vt (land) recuperar; (: from sea) rescatar; (demand back) reclamar

reclamation [rɛklə'meɪʃən] n recuperación f; rescate m

recline [rɪ'klaɪn] vi reclinarse

reclining [rɪ'klaɪnɪŋ] adj (seat) reclinable

recluse [rɪ'klu:s] n recluso(-a)

recognition [rɛkəg'nɪʃən] n reconocimiento; **transformed beyond ~** irreconocible; **in ~ of** en reconocimiento de

recognizable ['rɛkəgnaɪzəbl] adj: **~ (by)** reconocible (por)

recognize ['rɛkəgnaɪz] vt reconocer, conocer; **to ~ (by/as)** reconocer (por/como)

recoil [rɪ'kɔɪl] vi (person): **to ~ from doing sth** retraerse de hacer algo ▪ n (of gun) retroceso

recollect [rɛkə'lɛkt] vt recordar, acordarse de

recollection [rɛkə'lɛkʃən] n recuerdo; **to the best of my ~** que yo recuerde

recommend [rɛkə'mɛnd] vt recomendar; **she has a lot to ~ her** tiene mucho a su favor

recommendation [rɛkəmɛn'deɪʃən] n recomendación f

recommended retail price n (Brit) precio (recomendado) de venta al público

recompense ['rɛkəmpɛns] vt recompensar ▪ n recompensa

reconcilable ['rɛkənsaɪləbl] adj (re)conciliable

reconcile ['rɛkənsaɪl] vt (two people) reconciliar; (two facts) conciliar; **to ~ o.s. to sth** resignarse or conformarse a algo

reconciliation [rɛkənsɪlɪ'eɪʃən] n reconciliación f

recondite [rɪ'kɔndaɪt] adj recóndito

recondition [ri:kən'dɪʃən] vt (machine) reparar, reponer

reconditioned [ri:kən'dɪʃənd] adj renovado, reparado

reconnaissance [rɪ'kɔnɪsns] n (Mil) reconocimiento

reconnoitre, (US) reconnoiter [rɛkə'nɔɪtər] vt, vi (Mil) reconocer

reconsider [ri:kən'sɪdər] vt repensar

reconstitute [ri:'kɔnstɪtju:t] vt reconstituir

reconstruct [ri:kən'strʌkt] vt reconstruir

reconstruction [ri:kən'strʌkʃən] n reconstrucción f

reconvene [ri:kən'vi:n] vt volver a convocar ▪ vi volver a reunirse

record n ['rɛkɔ:d] (Mus) disco; (of meeting etc) relación f; (register) registro, partida; (file) archivo; (also: **police** or **criminal record**) antecedentes mpl penales; (written) expediente m; (Sport) récord m; (Comput) registro ▪ vt [rɪ'kɔ:d] (set down) registrar; (Comput) registrar; (relate) hacer constar; (Mus: song etc) grabar; **in ~ time** en un tiempo récord; **public records** archivos mpl nacionales; **he is on ~ as saying that** ... hay pruebas de que ha dicho públicamente que ...; **Spain's excellent ~** el excelente historial de España; **off the ~** adj no oficial ▪ adv confidencialmente

record card n (in file) ficha

recorded delivery letter [rɪ'kɔ:dɪd-] n (Brit Post) carta de entrega con acuse de recibo

recorded music n música grabada

recorder [rɪ'kɔ:dər] n (Mus) flauta de pico; (Tech) contador m

record holder n (Sport) actual poseedor(a) m(f) del récord

recording [rɪ'kɔ:dɪŋ] n (Mus) grabación f

recording studio n estudio de grabación

record library n discoteca

record player n tocadiscos m inv

recount vt [rɪ'kaunt] contar

re-count ['ri:kaunt] n (Pol: of votes) segundo escrutinio, recuento ▪ vt [ri:'kaunt] volver a contar

recoup [rɪ'ku:p] vt: **to ~ one's losses** recuperar las pérdidas

recourse [rɪ'kɔ:s] n recurso; **to have ~ to** recurrir a

recover [rɪ'kʌvər] vt recuperar; (rescue) rescatar ▪ vi recuperarse

recovery [rɪ'kʌvərɪ] n recuperación f; rescate m; (Med): **to make a ~** restablecerse

recreate [ri:krɪ'eɪt] vt recrear

recreation [rɛkrɪ'eɪʃən] n recreación f; (amusement) recreo

recreational [rɛkrɪ'eɪʃənl] adj de, recreo

recreational drug n droga recreativa

recreational vehicle n (US) caravana or roulotte f pequeña

recrimination [rɪkrɪmɪ'neɪʃən] n recriminación f

recruit [rɪ'kru:t] n recluta m/f ▪ vt reclutar; (staff) contratar

recruiting office [rɪ'kru:tɪŋ-] n caja de reclutas

recruitment [rɪ'kru:tmənt] n reclutamiento
rectangle ['rɛktæŋgl] n rectángulo
rectangular [rɛk'tæŋgjuləʳ] adj rectangular
rectify ['rɛktɪfaɪ] vt rectificar
rector ['rɛktəʳ] n (Rel) párroco; (Scol) rector(a) m(f)
rectory ['rɛktərɪ] n casa del párroco
rectum ['rɛktəm] n (Anat) recto
recuperate [rɪ'ku:pəreɪt] vi reponerse, restablecerse
recur [rɪ'kə:'] vi repetirse; (pain, illness) producirse de nuevo
recurrence [rɪ'kə:rns] n repetición f
recurrent [rɪ'kə:rnt] adj repetido
recyclable [ri:'saɪkləbl] adj reciclable
recycle [ri:'saɪkl] vt reciclar
recycling [ri:'saɪklɪŋ] vt reciclaje m
red [red] n rojo ■ adj rojo; **to be in the ~** (account) estar en números rojos; (business) tener un saldo negativo; **to give sb the ~ carpet treatment** recibir a algn con todos los honores
red alert n alerta roja
red-blooded ['red'blʌdɪd] adj (col) viril
redbrick university ['redbrɪk-] n ver nota

⬤ **REDBRICK UNIVERSITY**

⬤ El término redbrick university se aplica a las
⬤ universidades construidas en los grandes
⬤ centros urbanos industriales como
⬤ Birmingham, Liverpool o Manchester a
⬤ finales del siglo XIX o principios del XX.
⬤ Deben su nombre a que sus edificios son
⬤ normalmente de ladrillo, a diferencia de
⬤ las universidades tradicionales de Oxford
⬤ y Cambridge, cuyos edificios suelen ser
⬤ de piedra.

Red Cross n Cruz f Roja
redcurrant ['redkʌrənt] n grosella
redden ['redn] vt enrojecer ■ vi enrojecerse
reddish ['redɪʃ] adj (hair) rojizo
redecorate [ri:'dɛkəreɪt] vt pintar de nuevo; volver a decorar
redecoration [ri:dɛkə'reɪʃən] n renovación f
redeem [rɪ'di:m] vt (sth in pawn) desempeñar; (Rel) rescatar; (fig) rescatar
redeemable [rɪ'di:məbl] adj canjeable
redeeming [rɪ'di:mɪŋ] adj: **~ feature** punto bueno or favorable
redefine [ri:dɪ'faɪn] vt redefinir
redemption [rɪ'dɛmpʃən] n (Rel) redención f; **to be past** or **beyond ~** no tener remedio
redeploy [ri:dɪ'plɔɪ] vt disponer de nuevo
redeployment [ri:dɪ'plɔɪmənt] n redistribución f

redevelop [ri:dɪ'vɛləp] vt reorganizar
redevelopment [ri:dɪ'vɛləpmənt] n reorganización f
red-handed [red'hændɪd] adj: **he was caught ~** le pillaron con las manos en la masa
redhead ['redhɛd] n pelirrojo(-a)
red herring n (fig) pista falsa
red-hot [red'hɔt] adj candente
redirect [ri:daɪ'rɛkt] vt (mail) reexpedir
rediscover [ri:dɪs'kʌvəʳ] vt redescubrir
rediscovery [ri:dɪs'kʌvərɪ] n redescubrimiento
redistribute [ri:dɪs'trɪbju:t] vt redistribuir, hacer una nueva distribución de
red-letter day [red'lɛtə-] n día m señalado, día m especial
red light n: **to go through** or **jump a ~** (Aut) saltarse un semáforo
red-light district n barrio chino, zona de tolerancia
red meat n carne f roja
redness ['rednɪs] n rojez f
redo [ri:'du:] vt (irreg: like do) rehacer
redolent ['redələnt] adj: **~ of** (smell) con fragancia a; **to be ~ of** (fig) evocar
redouble [ri:'dʌbl] vt: **to ~ one's efforts** redoblar los esfuerzos
redraft [ri:'drɑ:ft] vt volver a redactar
redress [rɪ'drɛs] n reparación f ■ vt reparar, corregir; **to ~ the balance** restablecer el equilibrio
Red Sea n: **the ~** el mar Rojo
redskin ['redskɪn] n piel roja m/f
red tape n (fig) trámites mpl, papeleo (fam)
reduce [rɪ'dju:s] vt reducir; (lower) rebajar; **to ~ sth by/to** reducir algo en/a; **to ~ sb to silence/despair/tears** hacer callar/ desesperarse/llorar a algn; **"~ speed now"** (Aut) "reduzca la velocidad"
reduced [rɪ'dju:st] adj (decreased) reducido, rebajado; **at a ~ price** con rebaja or descuento; **"greatly ~ prices"** "grandes rebajas"
reduction [rɪ'dʌkʃən] n reducción f; (of price) rebaja; (discount) descuento
redundancy [rɪ'dʌndənsɪ] n despido; (unemployment) desempleo; **voluntary ~** baja voluntaria
redundancy payment n indemnización f por desempleo
redundant [rɪ'dʌndənt] adj (Brit: worker) parado, sin trabajo; (detail, object) superfluo; **to be made ~** quedar(se) sin trabajo, perder el empleo
reed [ri:d] n (Bot) junco, caña; (Mus: of clarinet etc) lengüeta

r

re-educate [riː'ɛdjukeɪt] vt reeducar
reedy ['riːdɪ] adj (voice, instrument) aflautado
reef [riːf] n (at sea) arrecife m
reek [riːk] vi: to ~ (of) oler or apestar (a)
reel [riːl] n carrete m, bobina; (of film) rollo
▪ vt (Tech) devanar; (also: reel in) sacar ▪ vi
(sway) tambalear(se); my head is reeling me
da vueltas la cabeza
► reel off vt recitar de memoria
re-election [riː'ɪlɛkʃən] n reelección f
re-engage [riːɪn'geɪdʒ] vt contratar de
nuevo
re-enter [riː'ɛntəʳ] vt reingresar en, volver a
entrar en
re-entry [riː'ɛntrɪ] n reingreso, reentrada
re-examine [riːɪg'zæmɪn] vt reexaminar
re-export vt ['riːɪks'pɔːt] reexportar ▪ n
[riː'ɛkspɔːt] reexportación f
ref [rɛf] n abbr (col) = referee
ref. abbr (Comm: = with reference to) Ref
refectory [rɪ'fɛktərɪ] n comedor m
refer [rɪ'fəːʳ] vt (send) remitir; (ascribe) referir
a, relacionar con ▪ vi: to ~ to (allude to)
referirse a, aludir a; (apply to) relacionarse
con; (consult) remitirse a; he referred me to
the manager me envió al gerente
referee [rɛfə'riː] n árbitro; (for job
application) persona que da referencias de otro
▪ vt (match) arbitrar en
reference ['rɛfrəns] n (mention: in book)
referencia; (sending) remisión f; (relevance)
relación f; (for job application: letter) carta de
recomendación; with ~ to con referencia a;
(Comm: in letter) me remito a
reference book n libro de consulta
reference library n biblioteca de consulta
reference number n número de referencia
referendum (pl referenda) [rɛfə'rɛndəm, -də]
n referéndum m
referral [rɪ'fəːrəl] n remisión f
refill vt [riː'fɪl] rellenar ▪ n ['riːfɪl] repuesto,
recambio
refine [rɪ'faɪn] vt (sugar, oil) refinar
refined [rɪ'faɪnd] adj (person, taste) refinado,
culto
refinement [rɪ'faɪnmənt] n (of person)
cultura, educación f
refinery [rɪ'faɪnərɪ] n refinería
refit (also Naut) n ['riːfɪt] reparación f ▪ vt
[riː'fɪt] reparar
reflate [riː'fleɪt] vt (economy) reflacionar
reflation [riː'fleɪʃən] n reflación f
reflationary [riː'fleɪʃənrɪ] adj reflacionario
reflect [rɪ'flɛkt] vt (light, image) reflejar ▪ vi
(think) reflexionar, pensar; it reflects badly/
well on him le perjudica/le hace honor
reflection [rɪ'flɛkʃən] n (act) reflexión f;

(image) reflejo; (discredit) crítica; on ~
pensándolo bien
reflector [rɪ'flɛktəʳ] n (Aut) catafaros m inv;
(telescope) reflector m
reflex ['riːflɛks] adj, n reflejo
reflexive [rɪ'flɛksɪv] adj (Ling) reflexivo
reform [rɪ'fɔːm] n reforma ▪ vt reformar
reformat [riː'fɔːmæt] vt (Comput) recomponer
Reformation [rɛfə'meɪʃən] n: the ~ la
Reforma
reformatory [rɪ'fɔːmətərɪ] n (US)
reformatorio
reformer [rɪ'fɔːməʳ] n reformador(a) m(f)
refrain [rɪ'freɪn] vi: to ~ from doing
abstenerse de hacer ▪ n (Mus etc) estribillo
refresh [rɪ'frɛʃ] vt refrescar
refresher course [rɪ'frɛʃə-] n (Brit) curso de
repaso
refreshing [rɪ'frɛʃɪŋ] adj (drink) refrescante;
(sleep) reparador; (change etc) estimulante;
(idea, point of view) estimulante, interesante
refreshments [rɪ'frɛʃmənts] npl (drinks)
refrescos mpl
refrigeration [rɪfrɪdʒə'reɪʃən] n
refrigeración f
refrigerator [rɪ'frɪdʒəreɪtəʳ] n frigorífico,
refrigeradora (LAm), heladera (LAm)
refuel [riː'fjuəl] vi repostar (combustible)
refuelling, (US) refueling [riː'fjuəlɪŋ] n
reabastecimiento de combustible
refuge ['rɛfjuːdʒ] n refugio, asilo; to take ~
in refugiarse en
refugee [rɛfju'dʒiː] n refugiado(-a)
refugee camp n campamento para
refugiados
refund n ['riːfʌnd] reembolso ▪ vt [rɪ'fʌnd]
devolver, reembolsar
refurbish [riː'fəːbɪʃ] vt restaurar, renovar
refurnish [riː'fəːnɪʃ] vt amueblar de nuevo
refusal [rɪ'fjuːzəl] n negativa; first ~ primera
opción; to have first ~ on sth tener la
primera opción a algo
refuse [n 'rɛfjuːs, vb rɪ'fjuːz] n basura ▪ vt
(reject) rehusar; (say no to) negarse a ▪ vi
negarse; (horse) rehusar; to ~ to do sth
negarse a or rehusar hacer algo
refuse bin n cubo or bote m (LAm) or balde m
(LAm) de la basura
refuse collection n recogida de basuras
refuse disposal n eliminación f de basuras
refusenik [rɪ'fjuːznɪk] n judío/a que tenía
prohibido emigrar de la ex Unión Soviética
refuse tip n vertedero
refute [rɪ'fjuːt] vt refutar, rebatir
regain [rɪ'geɪn] vt recobrar, recuperar
regal ['riːgl] adj regio, real
regale [rɪ'geɪl] vt agasajar, entretener

regalia [rɪˈgeɪlɪə] *n* galas *fpl*
regard [rɪˈgɑːd] *n* (*gaze*) mirada; (*aspect*) respeto; (*esteem*) respeto, consideración *f* ■ *vt* (*consider*) considerar; (*look at*) mirar; **to give one's regards to** saludar de su parte a; **"(kind) regards"** "muy atentamente"; **"with kindest regards"** "con muchos recuerdos"; **regards to María, please give my regards to María** recuerdos a María, dele recuerdos a María de mi parte; **as regards, with ~ to** con respecto a, en cuanto a
regarding [rɪˈgɑːdɪŋ] *prep* con respecto a, en cuanto a
regardless [rɪˈgɑːdlɪs] *adv* a pesar de todo; **~ of** sin reparar en
regatta [rɪˈgætə] *n* regata
regency [ˈriːdʒənsɪ] *n* regencia
regenerate [rɪˈdʒɛnəreɪt] *vt* regenerar
regent [ˈriːdʒənt] *n* regente *m/f*
reggae [ˈrɛgeɪ] *n* reggae *m*
régime [reɪˈʒiːm] *n* régimen *m*
regiment *n* [ˈrɛdʒɪmənt] regimiento ■ *vt* [ˈrɛdʒɪmɛnt] reglamentar
regimental [rɛdʒɪˈmɛntl] *adj* militar
regimentation [rɛdʒɪmɛnˈteɪʃən] *n* regimentación *f*
region [ˈriːdʒən] *n* región *f*; **in the ~ of** (*fig*) alrededor de
regional [ˈriːdʒənl] *adj* regional
regional development *n* desarrollo, regional
register [ˈrɛdʒɪstər] *n* registro ■ *vt* registrar; (*birth*) declarar; (*letter*) certificar; (*instrument*) marcar, indicar ■ *vi* (*at hotel*) registrarse; (*sign on*) inscribirse; (*make impression*) producir impresión; **to ~ a protest** presentar una queja; **to ~ for a course** matricularse *or* inscribirse en un curso
registered [ˈrɛdʒɪstəd] *adj* (*design*) registrado; (*Brit: letter*) certificado; (*student*) matriculado; (*voter*) registrado
registered company *n* sociedad *f* legalmente constituida
registered nurse *n* (*US*) enfermero(-a) titulado(-a)
registered office *n* domicilio social
registered trademark *n* marca registrada
registrar [ˈrɛdʒɪstrɑːr] *n* secretario(-a) (del registro civil)
registration [rɛdʒɪsˈtreɪʃən] *n* (*act*) declaración *f*; (*Aut: also:* **registration number**) matrícula
registry [ˈrɛdʒɪstrɪ] *n* registro
registry office *n* (*Brit*) registro civil; **to get married in a ~** casarse por lo civil
regret [rɪˈgrɛt] *n* sentimiento, pesar *m*; (*remorse*) remordimiento ■ *vt* sentir,

lamentar; (*repent of*) arrepentirse de; **we ~ to inform you that ...** sentimos informarle que ...
regretful [rɪˈgrɛtful] *adj* pesaroso, arrepentido
regretfully [rɪˈgrɛtfəlɪ] *adv* con pesar, sentidamente
regrettable [rɪˈgrɛtəbl] *adj* lamentable; (*loss*) sensible
regrettably [rɪˈgrɛtəblɪ] *adv* desgraciadamente
regroup [riːˈgruːp] *vt* reagrupar ■ *vi* reagruparse
regt *abbr* = **regiment**
regular [ˈrɛgjulər] *adj* regular; (*soldier*) profesional; (*col: intensive*) verdadero; (*listener, reader*) asiduo, habitual ■ *n* (*client etc*) cliente(-a) *m(f)* habitual
regularity [rɛgjuˈlærɪtɪ] *n* regularidad *f*
regularly [ˈrɛgjuləlɪ] *adv* con regularidad
regulate [ˈrɛgjuleɪt] *vt* (*gen*) controlar; (*Tech*) regular, ajustar
regulation [rɛgjuˈleɪʃən] *n* (*rule*) regla, reglamento; (*adjustment*) regulación *f*
rehabilitate [riːəˈbɪlɪteɪt] *vt* rehabilitar
rehabilitation [ˈriːəbɪlɪˈteɪʃən] *n* rehabilitación *f*
rehash [riːˈhæʃ] *vt* (*col*) hacer un refrito de
rehearsal [rɪˈhəːsəl] *n* ensayo; **dress ~** ensayo general *or* final
rehearse [rɪˈhəːs] *vt* ensayar
rehouse [riːˈhauz] *vt* dar nueva vivienda a
reign [reɪn] *n* reinado; (*fig*) predominio ■ *vi* reinar; (*fig*) imperar
reigning [ˈreɪnɪŋ] *adj* (*monarch*) reinante, actual; (*predominant*) imperante
reiki [ˈreɪkɪ] *n* reiki *m*
reimburse [riːɪmˈbəːs] *vt* reembolsar
rein [reɪn] *n* (*for horse*) rienda; **to give sb free ~** dar rienda suelta a algn
reincarnation [riːɪnkɑːˈneɪʃən] *n* reencarnación *f*
reindeer [ˈreɪndɪər] *n* (*pl inv*) reno
reinforce [riːɪnˈfɔːs] *vt* reforzar
reinforced concrete [riːɪnˈfɔːst-] *n* hormigón *m* armado
reinforcement [riːɪnˈfɔːsmənt] *n* (*action*) refuerzo; **reinforcements** *npl* (*Mil*) refuerzos *mpl*
reinstate [riːɪnˈsteɪt] *vt* (*worker*) reintegrar (a su puesto)
reinstatement [riːɪnˈsteɪtmənt] *n* reintegración *f*
reissue [riːˈɪʃuː] *vt* (*record, book*) reeditar
reiterate [riːˈɪtəreɪt] *vt* reiterar, repetir
reject *n* [ˈriːdʒɛkt] (*thing*) desecho ■ *vt* [rɪˈdʒɛkt] rechazar; (*proposition, offer etc*) descartar

r

rejection [rɪ'dʒɛkʃən] n rechazo
rejoice [rɪ'dʒɔɪs] vi: **to ~ at** or **over** regocijarse or alegrarse de
rejoinder [rɪ'dʒɔɪndə'] n (retort) réplica
rejuvenate [rɪ'dʒuːvəneɪt] vt rejuvenecer
rekindle [riː'kɪndl] vt volver a encender; (fig) despertar
relapse [rɪ'læps] n (Med) recaída; (into crime) reincidencia
relate [rɪ'leɪt] vt (tell) contar, relatar; (connect) relacionar ▪ vi relacionarse; **to ~ to** (connect) relacionarse or tener que ver con
related [rɪ'leɪtɪd] adj afín; (person) emparentado; **~ to** con referencia a, relacionado con
relating [rɪ'leɪtɪŋ]: **~ to** prep referente a
relation [rɪ'leɪʃən] n (person) pariente m/f; (link) relación f; **in ~ to** en relación con, en lo que se refiere a; **to bear a ~ to** guardar relación con; **diplomatic relations** relaciones fpl diplomáticas
relationship [rɪ'leɪʃənʃɪp] n relación f; (personal) relaciones fpl; (also: **family relationship**) parentesco
relative ['rɛlətɪv] n pariente m/f, familiar m/f ▪ adj relativo
relatively ['rɛlətɪvlɪ] adv (fairly, rather) relativamente
relative pronoun n pronombre m relativo
relax [rɪ'læks] vi descansar; (quieten down) relajarse ▪ vt relajar; (grip) aflojar; **~!** (calm down) ¡tranquilo!
relaxation [riːlæk'seɪʃən] n (rest) descanso; (easing) relajación f, relajamiento m; (amusement) recreo; (entertainment) diversión f
relaxed [rɪ'lækst] adj relajado; (tranquil) tranquilo
relaxing [rɪ'læksɪŋ] adj relajante
relay n ['riːleɪ] (race) carrera de relevos ▪ vt [rɪ'leɪ] (Radio, TV) retransmitir; (pass on) retransmitir
release [rɪ'liːs] n (liberation) liberación f; (discharge) puesta en libertad f; (of gas etc) escape m; (of film etc) estreno ▪ vt (prisoner) poner en libertad; (film) estrenar; (book) publicar; (piece of news) difundir; (gas etc) despedir, arrojar; (free: from wreckage etc) liberar; (Tech: catch, spring etc) desenganchar; (let go) soltar, aflojar
relegate ['rɛləgeɪt] vt relegar; (Sport): **to be relegated to** bajar a
relent [rɪ'lɛnt] vi ceder, ablandarse; (let up) descansar
relentless [rɪ'lɛntlɪs] adj implacable
relentlessly [rɪ'lɛntlɪslɪ] adv implacablemente
relevance ['rɛləvəns] n relación f

relevant ['rɛləvənt] adj (fact) pertinente; **~ to** relacionado con
reliability [rɪlaɪə'bɪlɪtɪ] n fiabilidad f; seguridad f; veracidad f
reliable [rɪ'laɪəbl] adj (person, firm) de confianza, de fiar; (method, machine) seguro; (source) fidedigno
reliably [rɪ'laɪəblɪ] adv: **to be ~ informed that ...** saber de fuente fidedigna que ...
reliance [rɪ'laɪəns] n: **~ (on)** dependencia (de)
reliant [rɪ'laɪənt] adj: **to be ~ on sth/sb** depender de algo/algn
relic ['rɛlɪk] n (Rel) reliquia; (of the past) vestigio
relief [rɪ'liːf] n (from pain, anxiety) alivio, desahogo; (help, supplies) socorro, ayuda; (Art, Geo) relieve m; **by way of light ~** a modo de diversión
relief road n carretera de descongestionamiento
relieve [rɪ'liːv] vt (pain, patient) aliviar; (bring help to) ayudar, socorrer; (burden) aligerar; (take over from: gen) sustituir a; (: guard) relevar; **to ~ sb of sth** quitar algo a algn; **to ~ sb of his command** (Mil) relevar a algn de su mando; **to ~ o.s.** hacer sus necesidades; **I am relieved to hear you are better** me alivia saber que estás or te encuentras mejor
religion [rɪ'lɪdʒən] n religión f
religious [rɪ'lɪdʒəs] adj religioso
religious education n educación f religiosa
religiously [rɪ'lɪdʒəslɪ] adv religiosamente
relinquish [rɪ'lɪŋkwɪʃ] vt abandonar; (plan, habit) renunciar a
relish ['rɛlɪʃ] n (Culin) salsa; (enjoyment) entusiasmo; (flavour) sabor m, gusto ▪ vt (food, challenge etc) saborear; **to ~ doing** gozar haciendo
relive [riː'lɪv] vt vivir de nuevo, volver a vivir
relocate [riːləu'keɪt] vt trasladar ▪ vi trasladarse
reluctance [rɪ'lʌktəns] n desgana, renuencia
reluctant [rɪ'lʌktənt] adj reacio; **to be ~ to do sth** resistirse a hacer algo
reluctantly [rɪ'lʌktəntlɪ] adv de mala gana
rely [rɪ'laɪ]: **to ~ on** vt fus confiar en, fiarse de; (be dependent on) depender de; **you can ~ on my discretion** puedes contar con mi discreción
remain [rɪ'meɪn] vi (survive) quedar; (be left) sobrar; (continue) quedar(se), permanecer; **to ~ silent** permanecer callado; **I ~, yours faithfully** (in letters) le saluda atentamente
remainder [rɪ'meɪndə'] n resto
remaining [rɪ'meɪnɪŋ] adj sobrante
remains [rɪ'meɪnz] npl restos mpl

remand [rɪ'mɑːnd] *n*: **on ~** detenido (bajo custodia) ∎ *vt*: **to ~ in custody** mantener bajo custodia

remand home *n* (*Brit*) reformatorio

remark [rɪ'mɑːk] *n* comentario ∎ *vt* comentar; **to ~ on sth** hacer observaciones sobre algo

remarkable [rɪ'mɑːkəbl] *adj* notable; (*outstanding*) extraordinario

remarkably [rɪ'mɑːkəblɪ] *adv* extraordinariamente

remarry [riː'mærɪ] *vi* casarse por segunda vez, volver a casarse

remedial [rɪ'miːdɪəl] *adj*: **~ education** educación *f* de los niños atrasados

remedy ['rɛmədɪ] *n* remedio ∎ *vt* remediar, curar

remember [rɪ'mɛmbəʳ] *vt* recordar, acordarse de; (*bear in mind*) tener presente; **I ~ seeing it, I ~ having seen it** recuerdo haberlo visto; **she remembered doing it** se acordó de hacerlo; **~ me to your wife and children!** ¡déle recuerdos a su familia!

remembrance [rɪ'mɛmbrəns] *n* (*memory, souvenir*) recuerdo; **in ~ of** en conmemoración de

Remembrance Day, Remembrance Sunday *n* (*Brit*) ver nota

En el Reino Unido el domingo más cercano al 11 de noviembre es *Remembrance Day* o *Remembrance Sunday*, aniversario de la firma del armisticio de 1918 que puso fin a la Primera Guerra Mundial. Tal día se recuerda a todos aquellos que murieron en las dos guerras mundiales con dos minutos de silencio a las once de la mañana hora en que se firmó el armisticio durante los actos de conmemoración celebrados en los monumentos a los caídos. Allí se colocan coronas de amapolas, flor que también se suele llevar prendida en el pecho tras pagar un donativo para los inválidos de guerra.

remind [rɪ'maɪnd] *vt*: **to ~ sb to do sth** recordar a algn que haga algo; **to ~ sb of sth** recordar algo a algn; **she reminds me of her mother** me recuerda a su madre; **that reminds me!** ¡a propósito!

reminder [rɪ'maɪndəʳ] *n* notificación *f*; (*memento*) recuerdo

reminisce [rɛmɪ'nɪs] *vi* recordar (viejas historias)

reminiscences [rɛmɪ'nɪsnsɪz] *npl* reminiscencias *fpl*, recuerdos *mpl*

reminiscent [rɛmɪ'nɪsnt] *adj*: **to be ~ of sth** recordar algo

remiss [rɪ'mɪs] *adj* descuidado; **it was ~ of me** fue un descuido de mi parte

remission [rɪ'mɪʃən] *n* remisión *f*; (*of sentence*) reducción *f* de la pena

remit [rɪ'mɪt] *vt* (*send: money*) remitir, enviar

remittance [rɪ'mɪtns] *n* remesa, envío

remnant ['rɛmnənt] *n* resto; (*of cloth*) retal *m*, retazo; **remnants** *npl* (*Comm*) restos de serie

remonstrate ['rɛmənstreɪt] *vi* protestar

remorse [rɪ'mɔːs] *n* remordimientos *mpl*

remorseful [rɪ'mɔːsful] *adj* arrepentido

remorseless [rɪ'mɔːslɪs] *adj* (*fig*) implacable, inexorable

remorselessly [rɪ'mɔːslɪslɪ] *adv* implacablemente, inexorablemente

remote [rɪ'məut] *adj* remoto; (*distant*) lejano; (*person*) distante; **there is a ~ possibility that …** hay una posibilidad remota de que …

remote control *n* mando a distancia

remote-controlled [rɪ'məutkən'trəuld] *adj* teledirigido, con mando a distancia

remotely [rɪ'məutlɪ] *adv* remotamente; (*slightly*) levemente

remoteness [rɪ'məutnɪs] *n* alejamiento; distancia

remould ['riːməuld] *n* (*Brit: tyre*) neumático *or* llanta (*LAm*) recauchutado(-a)

removable [rɪ'muːvəbl] *adj* (*detachable*) separable

removal [rɪ'muːvəl] *n* (*taking away*) (el) quitar; (*Brit: from house*) mudanza; (*from office: dismissal*) destitución *f*; (*Med*) extirpación *f*

removal van *n* (*Brit*) camión *m* de mudanzas

remove [rɪ'muːv] *vt* quitar; (*employee*) destituir; (*name: from list*) tachar, borrar; (*doubt*) disipar; (*Tech*) retirar, separar; (*Med*) extirpar; **first cousin once removed** (*parent's cousin*) tío(-a) segundo(-a); (*cousin's child*) sobrino(-a) segundo(-a)

remover [rɪ'muːvəʳ] *n*: **make-up ~** desmaquilladora

remunerate [rɪ'mjuːnəreɪt] *vt* remunerar

remuneration [rɪmjuːnə'reɪʃən] *n* remuneración *f*

Renaissance [rɪ'neɪsɔ̃s] *n*: **the ~** el Renacimiento

rename [riː'neɪm] *vt* poner nuevo nombre a

render ['rɛndəʳ] *vt* (*thanks*) dar; (*aid*) proporcionar; (*honour*) dar, conceder; (*assistance*) dar, prestar; **to ~ sth** (*+ adj*) volver algo *+ adj*

rendering ['rɛndərɪŋ] *n* (*Mus etc*) interpretación *f*

rendez-vous ['rɒndɪvuː] n cita ▪ vi reunirse, encontrarse; (spaceship) efectuar una reunión espacial
rendition [rɛn'dɪʃən] n (Mus) interpretación f
renegade ['rɛnɪɡeɪd] n renegado(-a)
renew [rɪ'njuː] vt renovar; (resume) reanudar; (extend date) prorrogar; (negotiations) volver a
renewable [rɪ'njuːəbl] adj renovable; ~ energy, **renewables** energías renovables
renewal [rɪ'njuːəl] n renovación f; reanudación f; prórroga
renounce [rɪ'nauns] vt renunciar a; (right, inheritance) renunciar
renovate ['rɛnəveɪt] vt renovar
renovation [rɛnə'veɪʃən] n renovación f
renown [rɪ'naun] n renombre m
renowned [rɪ'naund] adj renombrado
rent [rɛnt] n alquiler m; (for house) arriendo, renta ▪ vt (also: **rent out**) alquilar
rental ['rɛntl] n (for television, car) alquiler m
rent boy n (Brit col) chapero
renunciation [rɪnʌnsɪ'eɪʃən] n renuncia
reopen [riː'əupən] vt volver a abrir, reabrir
reorder [riː'ɔːdəʳ] vt volver a pedir, repetir el pedido de; (rearrange) volver a ordenar or arreglar
reorganization [riːɔːɡənaɪ'zeɪʃən] n reorganización f
reorganize [riː'ɔːɡənaɪz] vt reorganizar
Rep abbr (US Pol) = **representative**; **Republican**
rep [rɛp] n abbr (Comm) = **representative**; (Theat) = **repertory**
repair [rɪ'pɛəʳ] n reparación f, arreglo; (patch) remiendo ▪ vt reparar, arreglar; **in good/bad ~** en buen/mal estado; **under ~** en obras
repair kit n caja de herramientas
repair man n mecánico
repair shop n taller m de reparaciones
repartee [rɛpɑː'tiː] n réplicas fpl agudas
repast [rɪ'pɑːst] n (formal) comida
repatriate [riː'pætrɪeɪt] vt repatriar
repay [riː'peɪ] vt (irreg: like **pay**) (money) devolver, reembolsar; (person) pagar; (debt) liquidar; (sb's efforts) devolver, corresponder a
repayment [riː'peɪmənt] n reembolso, devolución f; (sum of money) recompensa
repeal [rɪ'piːl] n revocación f ▪ vt revocar
repeat [rɪ'piːt] n (Radio, TV) reposición f ▪ vt repetir ▪ vi repetirse
repeatedly [rɪ'piːtɪdlɪ] adv repetidas veces
repeat order n (Comm): **to place a ~ for** renovar un pedido de
repel [rɪ'pɛl] vt repugnar
repellent [rɪ'pɛlənt] adj repugnante ▪ n: **insect ~** crema/loción f antiinsectos
repent [rɪ'pɛnt] vi: **to ~ (of)** arrepentirse (de)

repentance [rɪ'pɛntəns] n arrepentimiento
repercussion [riːpə'kʌʃən] n (consequence) repercusión f; **to have repercussions** repercutir
repertoire ['rɛpətwɑːʳ] n repertorio
repertory ['rɛpətərɪ] n (also: **repertory theatre**) teatro de repertorio
repertory company n compañía de repertorio
repetition [rɛpɪ'tɪʃən] n repetición f
repetitious [rɛpɪ'tɪʃəs] adj repetidor(a), que se repite
repetitive [rɪ'pɛtɪtɪv] adj (movement, work) repetitivo, reiterativo; (speech) lleno de repeticiones
rephrase [riː'freɪz] vt decir or formular de otro modo
replace [rɪ'pleɪs] vt (put back) devolver a su sitio; (take the place of) reemplazar, sustituir
replacement [rɪ'pleɪsmənt] n reemplazo; (act) reposición f; (thing) recambio; (person) suplente m/f
replacement cost n costo de sustitución
replacement part n repuesto
replacement value n valor m de sustitución
replay ['riːpleɪ] n (Sport) partido de desempate; (TV: playback) repetición f
replenish [rɪ'plɛnɪʃ] vt (tank etc) rellenar; (stock etc) reponer; (with fuel) repostar
replete [rɪ'pliːt] adj repleto, lleno
replica ['rɛplɪkə] n réplica, reproducción f
reply [rɪ'plaɪ] n respuesta, contestación f ▪ vi contestar, responder; **in ~** en respuesta; **there's no ~** (Tel) no contestan
reply coupon n cupón-respuesta m
reply-paid [rɪ'plaɪ'peɪd] adj: ~ **postcard** tarjeta postal con respuesta pagada
report [rɪ'pɔːt] n informe m; (Press etc) reportaje m; (Brit: also: **school report**) informe m escolar; (of gun) detonación f ▪ vt informar sobre; (Press etc) hacer un reportaje sobre; (notify: accident, culprit) denunciar ▪ vi (make a report) presentar un informe; (present o.s.): **to ~ (to sb)** presentarse (ante algn); **annual ~** (Comm) informe m anual; **to ~ (on)** hacer un informe (sobre); **it is reported from Berlin that ...** se informa desde Berlín que ...
report card n (US, Scottish) cartilla escolar
reportedly [rɪ'pɔːtɪdlɪ] adv según se dice, según se informa
reporter [rɪ'pɔːtəʳ] n (Press) periodista m/f, reportero(-a); (Radio, TV) locutor(a) m(f)
repose [rɪ'pəuz] n: **in ~** (face, mouth) en reposo
repossess [riːpə'zɛs] vt recuperar
repossession order [riːpə'zɛʃən-] n orden de devolución de la vivienda por el impago de la hipoteca

reprehensible [rɛprɪ'hɛnsɪbl] *adj*
reprensible, censurable
represent [rɛprɪ'zɛnt] *vt* representar; (*Comm*)
ser agente de
representation [rɛprɪzɛn'teɪʃən] *n*
representación *f*; (*petition*) petición *f*;
representations *npl* (*protest*) quejas *fpl*
representative [rɛprɪ'zɛntətɪv] *n* (*US
Pol*) representante *m/f*, diputado(-a);
(*Comm*) representante *m/f* ■ *adj*: ~ (**of**)
representativo (de)
repress [rɪ'prɛs] *vt* reprimir
repression [rɪ'prɛʃən] *n* represión *f*
repressive [rɪ'prɛsɪv] *adj* represivo
reprieve [rɪ'priːv] *n* (*Law*) indulto; (*fig*) alivio
■ *vt* indultar; (*fig*) salvar
reprimand ['rɛprɪmɑːnd] *n* reprimenda ■ *vt*
reprender
reprint ['riːprɪnt] *n* reimpresión *f* ■ *vt*
[riː'prɪnt] reimprimir
reprisal [rɪ'praɪzl] *n* represalia; **to take
reprisals** tomar represalias
reproach [rɪ'prəʊtʃ] *n* reproche *m* ■ *vt*: **to ~
sb with sth** reprochar algo a algn; **beyond
~** intachable
reproachful [rɪ'prəʊtʃful] *adj* de reproche, de
acusación
reproduce [riːprə'djuːs] *vt* reproducir ■ *vi*
reproducirse
reproduction [riːprə'dʌkʃən] *n* reproducción *f*
reproductive [riːprə'dʌktɪv] *adj*
reproductor(a)
reproof [rɪ'pruːf] *n* reproche *m*
reprove [rɪ'pruːv] *vt*: **to ~ sb for sth**
reprochar algo a algn
reptile ['rɛptaɪl] *n* reptil *m*
Repub. *abbr* (*US Pol*) = **Republican**
republic [rɪ'pʌblɪk] *n* república
republican [rɪ'pʌblɪkən] *adj*, *n*
republicano(-a) *m(f)*
repudiate [rɪ'pjuːdɪeɪt] *vt* (*accusation*)
rechazar; (*obligation*) negarse a reconocer
repudiation [rɪpjuːdɪ'eɪʃən] *n*
incumplimiento
repugnance [rɪ'pʌgnəns] *n* repugnancia
repugnant [rɪ'pʌgnənt] *adj* repugnante
repulse [rɪ'pʌls] *vt* rechazar
repulsion [rɪ'pʌlʃən] *n* repulsión *f*,
repugnancia
repulsive [rɪ'pʌlsɪv] *adj* repulsivo
repurchase [riː'pəːtʃəs] *vt* volver a comprar,
readquirir
reputable ['rɛpjutəbl] *adj* (*make etc*) de
renombre
reputation [rɛpju'teɪʃən] *n* reputación *f*;
he has a ~ for being awkward tiene fama
de difícil

repute [rɪ'pjuːt] *n* reputación *f*, fama
reputed [rɪ'pjuːtɪd] *adj* supuesto; **to be ~ to
be rich/intelligent** *etc* tener fama de rico/
inteligente *etc*
reputedly [rɪ'pjuːtɪdlɪ] *adv* según dicen *or*
se dice
request [rɪ'kwɛst] *n* solicitud *f*, petición
f ■ *vt*: **to ~ sth of** *or* **from sb** solicitar algo
a algn; **at the ~ of** a petición de; **"you are
requested not to smoke"** "se ruega no
fumar"
request stop *n* (*Brit*) parada discrecional
requiem ['rɛkwɪəm] *n* réquiem *m*
require [rɪ'kwaɪər] *vt* (*need: person*) necesitar,
tener necesidad de; (: *thing, situation*) exigir,
requerir; (*want*) pedir; (*demand*) insistir
en que; **to ~ sb to do sth/sth of sb** exigir
que algn haga algo; **what qualifications
are required?** ¿qué títulos se requieren?;
required by law requerido por la ley
requirement [rɪ'kwaɪəmənt] *n* requisito;
(*need*) necesidad *f*
requisite ['rɛkwɪzɪt] *n* requisito ■ *adj*
necesario, requerido
requisition [rɛkwɪ'zɪʃən] *n* solicitud *f*; (*Mil*)
requisa ■ *vt* (*Mil*) requisar
reroute [riː'ruːt] *vt* desviar
resale ['riːseɪl] *n* reventa
resale price maintenance *n*
mantenimiento del precio de venta
rescind [rɪ'sɪnd] *vt* (*Law*) abrogar; (*contract*)
rescindir; (*order etc*) anular
rescue ['rɛskjuː] *n* rescate *m* ■ *vt* rescatar;
to come/go to sb's ~ ir en auxilio de uno,
socorrer a algn; **to ~ from** librar de
rescue party *n* equipo de salvamento
rescuer ['rɛskjuər] *n* salvador(a) *m(f)*
research [rɪ'səːtʃ] *n* investigaciones *fpl*
■ *vt* investigar; **a piece of ~** un trabajo de
investigación; **to ~ (into sth)** investigar
(algo)
research and development *n* investigación
f y desarrollo
researcher [rɪ'səːtʃər] *n* investigador(a) *m(f)*
research work *n* investigación *f*
resell [riː'sɛl] *vt* revender
resemblance [rɪ'zɛmbləns] *n* parecido;
to bear a strong ~ to parecerse mucho a
resemble [rɪ'zɛmbl] *vt* parecerse a
resent [rɪ'zɛnt] *vt* resentirse por, ofenderse
por; **he resents my being here** le molesta
que esté aquí
resentful [rɪ'zɛntful] *adj* resentido
resentment [rɪ'zɛntmənt] *n* resentimiento
reservation [rɛzə'veɪʃən] *n* reserva; (*Brit*:
also: **central reservation**) mediana; **with
reservations** con reservas

reservation desk n (US: in hotel) recepción f
reserve [rɪ'zə:v] n reserva; (Sport) suplente
m/f ■ vt (seats etc) reservar; **reserves** npl
(Mil) reserva sg; **in ~** en reserva
reserve currency n divisa de reserva
reserved [rɪ'zə:vd] adj reservado
reserve price n (Brit) precio mínimo
reserve team n (Sport) equipo de reserva
reservist [ri'zə:vɪst] n (Mil) reservista m
reservoir ['rɛzəvwɑ:'] n (artificial lake) embalse
m, represa; (small) depósito
reset [ri:'sɛt] vt (Comput) reinicializar
reshape [ri:'ʃeɪp] vt (policy) reformar, rehacer
reshuffle [ri:'ʃʌfl] n: **Cabinet ~** (Pol)
remodelación f del gabinete
reside [rɪ'zaɪd] vi residir
residence ['rɛzɪdəns] n residencia; (formal:
home) domicilio; (length of stay) permanencia;
in ~ (doctor) residente; **to take up ~**
instalarse
residence permit n (Brit) permiso de
residencia
resident ['rɛzɪdənt] n vecino(-a); (in hotel)
huésped(a) m(f) ■ adj residente; (population)
permanente
residential [rɛzɪ'dɛnʃəl] adj residencial
residue ['rɛzɪdju:] n resto, residuo
resign [rɪ'zaɪn] vt (gen) renunciar a ■ vi: **to ~**
(from) dimitir (de), renunciar (a); **to ~ o.s.**
to (endure) resignarse a
resignation [rɛzɪg'neɪʃən] n dimisión f; (state
of mind) resignación f; **to tender one's ~**
presentar la dimisión
resigned [rɪ'zaɪnd] adj resignado
resilience [rɪ'zɪlɪəns] n (of material) elasticidad
f; (of person) resistencia
resilient [rɪ'zɪlɪənt] adj (person) resistente
resin ['rɛzɪn] n resina
resist [rɪ'zɪst] vt resistirse a; (temptation,
damage) resistir
resistance [rɪ'zɪstəns] n resistencia
resistant [rɪ'zɪstənt] adj: **~ (to)** resistente (a)
resolute ['rɛzəlu:t] adj resuelto
resolutely ['rɛzəlu:tlɪ] adv resueltamente
resolution [rɛzə'lu:ʃən] n (gen) resolución f;
(purpose) propósito; (Comput) definición f;
to make a ~ tomar una resolución
resolve [rɪ'zɔlv] n (determination) resolución
f; (purpose) propósito ■ vt resolver ■ vi
resolverse; **to ~ to do** resolver hacer
resolved [rɪ'zɔlvd] adj resuelto
resonance ['rɛzənəns] n resonancia
resonant ['rɛzənənt] adj resonante
resort [rɪ'zɔ:t] n (town) centro turístico;
(recourse) recurso ■ vi: **to ~ to** recurrir a;
in the last ~ como último recurso; **seaside/**
winter sports ~ playa, estación f balnearia/

centro de deportes de invierno
resound [rɪ'zaund] vi: **to ~ (with)** resonar
(con)
resounding [rɪ'zaundɪŋ] adj sonoro; (fig)
clamoroso
resource [rɪ'sɔ:s] n recurso; **resources** npl
recursos mpl; **natural resources** recursos
mpl naturales; **to leave sb to his/her own**
resources (fig) abandonar a algn/a sus
propios recursos
resourceful [rɪ'sɔ:sful] adj ingenioso
resourcefulness [rɪ'sɔ:sfulnɪs] n inventiva,
iniciativa
respect [rɪs'pɛkt] n (consideration) respeto;
(relation) respecto; **respects** npl recuerdos
mpl, saludos mpl ■ vt respetar; **with ~ to** con
respecto a; **in this ~** en cuanto a eso; **to have**
or **show ~ for** tener or mostrar respeto a; **out**
of ~ for por respeto a; **in some respects** en
algunos aspectos; **with due ~ I still think**
you're wrong con el respeto debido, sigo
creyendo que está equivocado
respectability [rɪspɛktə'bɪlɪtɪ] n
respetabilidad f
respectable [rɪs'pɛktəbl] adj respetable;
(quite big: amount etc) apreciable; (passable)
tolerable; (quite good: player, result etc) bastante
bueno
respected [rɪs'pɛktɪd] adj respetado,
estimado
respectful [rɪs'pɛktful] adj respetuoso
respectfully [rɪs'pɛktfulɪ] adv
respetuosamente; **Yours ~** Le saluda
atentamente
respecting [rɪs'pɛktɪŋ] prep (con) respecto a,
en cuanto a
respective [rɪs'pɛktɪv] adj respectivo
respectively [rɪs'pɛktɪvlɪ] adv
respectivamente
respiration [rɛspɪ'reɪʃən] n respiración f
respiratory [rɛs'pɪrətərɪ] adj respiratorio
respite ['rɛspaɪt] n respiro; (Law) prórroga
resplendent [rɪs'plɛndənt] adj
resplandeciente
respond [rɪs'pɔnd] vi responder; (react)
reaccionar
respondent [rɪs'pɔndənt] n (Law)
demandado(-a)
response [rɪs'pɔns] n respuesta; (reaction)
reacción f; **in ~ to** como respuesta a
responsibility [rɪspɔnsɪ'bɪlɪtɪ] n
responsabilidad f; **to take ~ for sth/sb**
admitir responsabilidad por algo/uno
responsible [rɪs'pɔnsɪbl] adj (liable): **~ (for)**
responsable (de); (character) serio, formal;
(job) de responsabilidad; **to be ~ to sb (for**
sth) ser responsable ante algn (de algo)

responsibly [rɪs'pɔnsɪblɪ] *adv* con seriedad
responsive [rɪs'pɔnsɪv] *adj* sensible
rest [rɛst] *n* descanso, reposo; (*Mus*) pausa, silencio; (*support*) apoyo; (*remainder*) resto ■ *vi* descansar; (*be supported*): **to ~ on** apoyarse en ■ *vt* (*lean*): **to ~ sth on/against** apoyar algo en *or* sobre/contra; **the ~ of them** (*people, objects*) los demás; **to set sb's mind at ~** tranquilizar a algn; **to ~ one's eyes** *or* **gaze on** fijar la mirada en; **it rests with him** depende de él; **~ assured that ...** tenga por seguro que ...
restaurant ['rɛstərɔŋ] *n* restaurante *m*
restaurant car *n* (*Brit*) coche-comedor *m*
restaurant owner *n* dueño(-a) *or* propietario(-a) de un restaurante
rest cure *n* cura de reposo
restful ['rɛstful] *adj* descansado, tranquilo
rest home *n* residencia de ancianos
restitution [rɛstɪ'tjuːʃən] *n*: **to make ~ to sb for sth** restituir algo a algn; (*paying*) indemnizar a algn por algo
restive ['rɛstɪv] *adj* inquieto; (*horse*) rebelón(-ona)
restless ['rɛstlɪs] *adj* inquieto; **to get ~** impacientarse
restlessly ['rɛstlɪslɪ] *adv* inquietamente, con inquietud *f*
restlessness ['rɛstlɪsnɪs] *n* inquietud *f*
restock [riː'stɔk] *vt* reaprovisionar
restoration [rɛstə'reɪʃən] *n* restauración *f*; (*giving back*) devolución *f*, restitución *f*
restorative [rɪ'stɔːrətɪv] *adj* reconstituyente, fortalecedor(a) ■ *n* reconstituyente *m*
restore [rɪ'stɔːʳ] *vt* (*building*) restaurar; (*sth stolen*) devolver, restituir; (*health*) restablecer
restorer [rɪ'stɔːrəʳ] *n* (*Art etc*) restaurador(a) *m(f)*
restrain [rɪs'treɪn] *vt* (*feeling*) contener, refrenar; (*person*): **to ~ (from doing)** disuadir (de hacer)
restrained [rɪs'treɪnd] *adj* (*style*) reservado
restraint [rɪs'treɪnt] *n* (*restriction*) freno, control *m*; (*of style*) reserva; **wage ~** control *m* de los salarios
restrict [rɪs'trɪkt] *vt* restringir, limitar
restricted [rɪs'trɪktɪd] *adj* restringido, limitado
restriction [rɪs'trɪkʃən] *n* restricción *f*, limitación *f*
restrictive [rɪs'trɪktɪv] *adj* restrictivo
restrictive practices *npl* (*Industry*) prácticas *fpl* restrictivas
rest room *n* (*US*) aseos *mpl*
restructure [riː'strʌktʃəʳ] *vt* reestructurar
result [rɪ'zʌlt] *n* resultado ■ *vi*: **to ~ in** terminar en, tener por resultado; **as a ~**

of a *or* como consecuencia de; **to ~ (from)** resultar (de)
resultant [rɪ'zʌltənt] *adj* resultante
resume [rɪ'zjuːm] *vt* (*work, journey*) reanudar; (*sum up*) resumir ■ *vi* (*meeting*) continuar
résumé ['reɪzjuːmeɪ] *n* resumen *m*
resumption [rɪ'zʌmpʃən] *n* reanudación *f*
resurgence [rɪ'səːdʒəns] *n* resurgimiento
resurrection [rɛzə'rɛkʃən] *n* resurrección *f*
resuscitate [rɪ'sʌsɪteɪt] *vt* (*Med*) resucitar
resuscitation [rɪsʌsɪ'teɪʃn] *n* resucitación *f*
retail ['riːteɪl] *n* venta al por menor ■ *cpd* al por menor ■ *vt* vender al por menor *or* al detalle ■ *vi*: **to ~ at** (*Comm*) tener precio de venta al público de
retailer ['riːteɪləʳ] *n* minorista *m/f*, detallista *m/f*
retail outlet *n* punto de venta
retail price *n* precio de venta al público, precio al detalle *or* al por menor
retail price index *n* índice *m* de precios al por menor
retain [rɪ'teɪn] *vt* (*keep*) retener, conservar; (*employ*) contratar
retainer [rɪ'teɪnəʳ] *n* (*servant*) criado; (*fee*) anticipo
retaliate [rɪ'tælɪeɪt] *vi*: **to ~ (against)** tomar represalias (contra)
retaliation [rɪtælɪ'eɪʃən] *n* represalias *fpl*; **in ~ for** como represalia por
retaliatory [rɪ'tælɪətərɪ] *adj* de represalia
retarded [rɪ'tɑːdɪd] *adj* retrasado
retch [rɛtʃ] *vi* darle a algn arcadas
retentive [rɪ'tentɪv] *adj* (*memory*) retentivo
rethink [riː'θɪŋk] *vt* repensar
reticence ['rɛtɪsns] *n* reticencia, reserva
reticent ['rɛtɪsnt] *adj* reticente, reservado
retina ['rɛtɪnə] *n* retina
retinue ['rɛtɪnjuː] *n* séquito, comitiva
retire [rɪ'taɪəʳ] *vi* (*give up work*) jubilarse; (*withdraw*) retirarse; (*go to bed*) acostarse
retired [rɪ'taɪəd] *adj* (*person*) jubilado
retirement [rɪ'taɪəmənt] *n* jubilación *f*; **early ~** jubilación *f* anticipada
retiring [rɪ'taɪərɪŋ] *adj* (*departing: chairman*) saliente; (*shy*) retraído
retort [rɪ'tɔːt] *n* (*reply*) réplica ■ *vi* replicar
retrace [riː'treɪs] *vt*: **to ~ one's steps** volver sobre sus pasos, desandar lo andado
retract [rɪ'trækt] *vt* (*statement*) retirar; (*claws*) retraer; (*undercarriage, aerial*) replegar ■ *vi* retractarse
retractable [rɪ'træktəbl] *adj* replegable
retrain [riː'treɪn] *vt* reciclar
retraining [riː'treɪnɪŋ] *n* reciclaje *m*, readaptación *f* profesional
retread ['riːtrɛd] *n* neumático *or* llanta (*LAm*) recauchutado(-a)

r

retreat [rɪ'triːt] *n* (*place*) retiro; (*Mil*) retirada ■ *vi* retirarse; (*flood*) bajar; **to beat a hasty ~** (*fig*) retirarse en desbandada

retrial ['riːtraɪəl] *n* nuevo proceso

retribution [rɛtrɪ'bjuːʃən] *n* desquite *m*

retrieval [rɪ'triːvəl] *n* recuperación *f*; **information retrieval** recuperación *f* de datos

retrieve [rɪ'triːv] *vt* recobrar; (*situation, honour*) salvar; (*Comput*) recuperar; (*error*) reparar

retriever [rɪ'triːvəʳ] *n* perro cobrador

retroactive [rɛtrəu'æktɪv] *adj* retroactivo

retrograde ['rɛtrəgreɪd] *adj* retrógrado

retrospect ['rɛtrəspɛkt] *n*: **in ~** retrospectivamente

retrospective [rɛtrə'spɛktɪv] *adj* retrospectivo; (*law*) retroactivo ■ *n* exposición *f* retrospectiva

return [rɪ'təːn] *n* (*going or coming back*) vuelta, regreso; (*of sth stolen etc*) devolución *f*; (*recompense*) recompensa; (*Finance: from land, shares*) ganancia, ingresos *mpl*; (*Comm: of merchandise*) devolución *f* ■ *cpd* (*journey*) de regreso; (*Brit: ticket*) de ida y vuelta; (*match*) de vuelta ■ *vi* (*person etc: come or go back*) volver, regresar; (*symptoms etc*) reaparecer ■ *vt* devolver; (*favour, love etc*) corresponder a; (*verdict*) pronunciar; (*Pol: candidate*) elegir; **returns** *npl* (*Comm*) ingresos *mpl*; **tax ~** declaración *f* de la renta; **in ~ (for)** a cambio (de); **by ~ of post** a vuelta de correo; **many happy returns (of the day)!** ¡feliz cumpleaños!

returnable [rɪ'təːnəbl] *adj*: **~ bottle** envase *m* retornable

returner [rɪ'təːnəʳ] *n* mujer que vuelve a trabajar tras un tiempo dedicada a la familia

returning officer [rɪ'təːnɪŋ-] *n* (*Brit Pol*) escrutador(a) *m(f)*

return key *n* (*Comput*) tecla de retorno

reunion [riː'juːnɪən] *n* reencuentro

reunite [riːjuː'naɪt] *vt* reunir; (*reconcile*) reconciliar

rev [rɛv] *n abbr* (*Aut*: = *revolution*) revolución *f* ■ *vt* (*also*: **rev up**) acelerar

Rev., Revd. *abbr* (= *reverend*) R., Rvdo

revaluation [riːvæljuː'eɪʃən] *n* revalorización *f*

revamp [riː'væmp] *vt* renovar

reveal [rɪ'viːl] *vt* (*make known*) revelar

revealing [rɪ'viːlɪŋ] *adj* revelador(a)

reveille [rɪ'vælɪ] *n* (*Mil*) diana

revel ['rɛvl] *vi*: **to ~ in sth/in doing sth** gozar de algo/haciendo algo

revelation [rɛvə'leɪʃən] *n* revelación *f*

reveller, (*US*) **reveler** ['rɛvləʳ] *n* jaranero, juerguista *m/f*

revelry ['rɛvlrɪ] *n* jarana, juerga

revenge [rɪ'vɛndʒ] *n* venganza; (*in sport*) revancha; **to take ~ on** vengarse de; **to get one's ~ (for sth)** vengarse (de algo)

revengeful [rɪ'vɛndʒful] *adj* vengativo

revenue ['rɛvənjuː] *n* ingresos *mpl*, rentas *fpl*

revenue account *n* cuenta de ingresos presupuestarios

revenue expenditure *n* gasto corriente

reverberate [rɪ'vəːbəreɪt] *vi* (*sound*) resonar, retumbar

reverberation [rɪvəːbə'reɪʃən] *n* resonancia

revere [rɪ'vɪəʳ] *vt* reverenciar, venerar

reverence ['rɛvərəns] *n* reverencia

Reverend ['rɛvərənd] *adj* (*in titles*): **the ~ John Smith** (*Anglican*) el Reverendo John Smith; (*Catholic*) el Padre John Smith; (*Protestant*) el Pastor John Smith

reverent ['rɛvərənt] *adj* reverente

reverie ['rɛvərɪ] *n* ensueño

reversal [rɪ'vəːsl] *n* (*of order*) inversión *f*; (*of policy*) cambio de rumbo; (*of decision*) revocación *f*

reverse [rɪ'vəːs] *n* (*opposite*) contrario; (*back: of cloth*) revés *m*; (: *of coin*) reverso; (: *of paper*) dorso; (*Aut: also*: **reverse gear**) marcha atrás ■ *adj* (*order*) inverso; (*direction*) contrario ■ *vt* (*decision*) dar marcha atrás a; (*Aut*) dar marcha atrás a; (*position, function*) invertir ■ *vi* (*Brit Aut*) poner en marcha atrás; **in ~ order** en orden inverso; **the ~** lo contrario; **to go into ~** dar marcha atrás

reverse-charge call [rɪ'vəːstʃɑː:dʒ-] *n* (*Brit*) llamada a cobro revertido

reverse video *n* vídeo inverso

reversible [rɪ'vəːsəbl] *adj* (*garment, procedure*) reversible

reversing lights [rɪ'vəːsɪŋ-] *npl* (*Brit Aut*) luces *fpl* de marcha atrás

revert [rɪ'vəːt] *vi*: **to ~ to** volver or revertir a

review [rɪ'vjuː] *n* (*magazine*) revista; (*Mil*) revista; (*of book, film*) reseña; (*US: examination*) repaso, examen *m* ■ *vt* repasar, examinar; (*Mil*) pasar revista a; (*book, film*) reseñar; **to come under ~** ser examinado

reviewer [rɪ'vjuːəʳ] *n* crítico(-a)

revile [rɪ'vaɪl] *vt* injuriar, vilipendiar

revise [rɪ'vaɪz] *vt* (*manuscript*) corregir; (*opinion*) modificar; (*Brit: study: subject*) repasar; (*look over*) revisar; **revised edition** edición *f* corregida

revision [rɪ'vɪʒən] *n* corrección *f*; modificación *f*; (*of subject*) repaso; (*revised version*) revisión *f*

revisit [riː'vɪzɪt] *vt* volver a visitar

revitalize [riː'vaɪtəlaɪz] *vt* revivificar

revival [rɪ'vaɪvəl] *n* (*recovery*) reanimación *f*;

(*Pol*) resurgimiento; (*of interest*)
renacimiento; (*Theat*) reestreno; (*of faith*)
despertar *m*

revive [rɪ'vaɪv] *vt* resucitar; (*custom*)
restablecer; (*hope, courage*) reanimar; (*play*)
reestrenar ■ *vi* (*person*) volver en sí; (*from
tiredness*) reponerse; (*business*) reactivarse

revoke [rɪ'vəuk] *vt* revocar

revolt [rɪ'vəult] *n* rebelión *f* ■ *vi* rebelarse,
sublevarse ■ *vt* dar asco a, repugnar; **to ~
(against sb/sth)** rebelarse (contra algn/algo)

revolting [rɪ'vəultɪŋ] *adj* asqueroso,
repugnante

revolution [revə'lu:ʃən] *n* revolución *f*

revolutionary [revə'lu:ʃənrɪ] *adj, n*
revolucionario(-a) *m(f)*

revolutionize [revə'lu:ʃənaɪz] *vt*
revolucionar

revolve [rɪ'vɔlv] *vi* dar vueltao, girar

revolver [rɪ'vɔlvə^r] *n* revólver *m*

revolving [rɪ'vɔlvɪŋ] *adj* (*chair, door etc*)
giratorio

revue [rɪ'vju:] *n* (*Theat*) revista

revulsion [rɪ'vʌlʃən] *n* asco, repugnancia

reward [rɪ'wɔːd] *n* premio, recompensa ■ *vt*:
to ~ (for) recompensar *or* premiar (por)

rewarding [rɪ'wɔːdɪŋ] *adj* (*fig*) gratificante;
financially ~ económicamente provechoso

rewind [riː'waɪnd] *vt* (*watch*) dar cuerda a;
(*wool etc*) devanar

rewire [riː'waɪə^r] *vt* (*house*) renovar la
instalación eléctrica de

reword [riː'wəːd] *vt* expresar en otras
palabras

rewritable [riː'raɪtəbl] *adj* reescribible

rewrite [riː'raɪt] *vt* (*irreg: like* **write**) reescribir

Reykjavik ['reɪkjəviːk] *n* Reykjavik *m*

RFD *abbr* (*US Post*) = **rural free delivery**

RGN *n abbr* (*Brit*) = **Registered General Nurse**

Rh *abbr* (= *rhesus*) Rh *m*

rhapsody ['ræpsədɪ] *n* (*Mus*) rapsodia; (*fig*):
to go into rhapsodies over extasiarse por

rhesus negative ['riːsəs-] *adj* (*Med*) Rh
negativo

rhesus positive *adj* (*Med*) Rh positivo

rhetoric ['retərɪk] *n* retórica

rhetorical [rɪ'tɔrɪkl] *adj* retórico

rheumatic [ruː'mætɪk] *adj* reumático

rheumatism ['ruːmətɪzəm] *n* reumatismo,
reúma

rheumatoid arthritis ['ruːmətɔɪd-] *n* reúma
m articular

Rhine [raɪn] *n*: **the ~** el (río) Rin

rhinestone ['raɪnstəun] *n* diamante *m* de
imitación

rhinoceros [raɪ'nɔsərəs] *n* rinoceronte *m*

Rhodes [rəudz] *n* Rodas *f*

rhododendron [rəudə'dendrn] *n* rododendro

Rhone [rəun] *n*: **the ~** el (río) Ródano

rhubarb ['ruːbaːb] *n* ruibarbo

rhyme [raɪm] *n* rima; (*verse*) poesía ■ *vi*: **to ~
(with)** rimar (con); **without ~ or reason** sin
ton ni son

rhythm ['rɪðm] *n* ritmo

rhythmic ['rɪðmɪk], **rhythmical** ['rɪðmɪkl]
adj rítmico

rhythmically ['rɪðmɪklɪ] *adv* rítmicamente

rhythm method *n* método (de) Ogino

RI *n abbr* (*Brit*: = *religious instruction*) ed. religiosa
■ *abbr* (*US: Post*) = **Rhode Island**

rib [rɪb] *n* (*Anat*) costilla ■ *vt* (*mock*) tomar el
pelo a

ribald ['rɪbəld] *adj* escabroso

ribbon ['rɪbən] *n* cinta; **in ribbons** (*torn*)
hecho trizas

rice [raɪs] *n* arroz *m*

ricefield ['raɪsfiːld] *n* arrozal *m*

rice pudding *n* arroz *m* con leche

rich [rɪtʃ] *adj* rico; (*soil*) fértil; (*food*) pesado;
(: *sweet*) empalagoso; **the rich** *npl* los ricos;
riches *npl* riqueza *sg*; **to be ~ in sth** abundar
en algo

richly ['rɪtʃlɪ] *adv* ricamente

richness ['rɪtʃnɪs] *n* riqueza; (*of soil*) fertilidad *f*

rickets ['rɪkɪts] *n* raquitismo

rickety ['rɪkɪtɪ] *adj* (*old*) desvencijado; (*shaky*)
tambaleante

rickshaw ['rɪkʃɔ:] *n* carro de culí

ricochet ['rɪkəʃeɪ] *n* rebote *m* ■ *vi* rebotar

rid (*pt, pp ~*) [rɪd] *vt*: **to ~ sb of sth** librar
a algn de algo; **to get ~ of** deshacerse *or*
desembarazarse de

riddance ['rɪdns] *n*: **good ~!** ¡y adiós muy
buenas!

ridden ['rɪdn] *pp of* **ride**

-ridden ['rɪdn] *suff*: **disease~** plagado de
enfermedades; **inflation~** minado por la
inflación

riddle ['rɪdl] *n* (*conundrum*) acertijo; (*mystery*)
enigma *m*, misterio ■ *vt*: **to be riddled
with** ser lleno *or* plagado de

ride [raɪd] (*pt* **rode**, *pp* **ridden**) *n* paseo;
(*distance covered*) viaje *m*, recorrido ■ *vi* (*on
horse: as sport*) montar; (*go somewhere: on horse,
bicycle*) dar un paseo, pasearse; (*journey: on
bicycle, motorcycle, bus*) viajar ■ *vt* (*a horse*)
montar a; (*distance*) viajar; **to ~ a bicycle**
andar en bicicleta; **to ~ at anchor** (*Naut*)
estar fondeado; **can you ~ a bike?** ¿sabes
montar en bici(cleta)?; **to go for a ~** dar un
paseo; **to take sb for a ~** (*fig*) tomar el pelo
a algn

▶ **ride out** *vt*: **to ~ out the storm** (*fig*) capear
el temporal

rider ['raɪdə^r] n (on horse) jinete m; (on bicycle) ciclista m/f; (on motorcycle) motociclista m/f
ridge [rɪdʒ] n (of hill) cresta; (of roof) caballete m; (wrinkle) arruga
ridicule ['rɪdɪkjuːl] n irrisión f, burla ■ vt poner en ridículo a, burlarse de; **to hold sth/ sb up to ~** poner algo/a algn en ridículo
ridiculous [rɪ'dɪkjuləs] adj ridículo
ridiculously [rɪ'dɪkjuləslɪ] adv ridículamente, de modo ridículo
riding ['raɪdɪŋ] n equitación f; **I like ~** me gusta montar a caballo
riding habit n traje m de montar
riding school n escuela de equitación
rife [raɪf] adj: **to be ~** ser muy común; **to be ~ with** abundar en
riffraff ['rɪfræf] n chusma, gentuza
rifle ['raɪfl] n rifle m, fusil m ■ vt saquear
▶ **rifle through** vt fus saquear
rifle range n campo de tiro; (at fair) tiro al blanco
rift [rɪft] n (fig: between friends) desavenencia; (: in party) escisión f
rig [rɪg] n (also: **oil rig**: on land) torre f de perforación; (: at sea) plataforma petrolera ■ vt (election etc) amañar los resultados de
▶ **rig out** vt (Brit) ataviar
▶ **rig up** vt improvisar
rigging ['rɪgɪŋ] n (Naut) aparejo
right [raɪt] adj (true, correct) correcto, exacto; (suitable) indicado, debido; (proper) apropiado, propio; (just) justo; (morally good) bueno; (not left) derecho ■ n (title, claim) derecho; (not left) derecha ■ adv (correctly) bien, correctamente; (straight) derecho, directamente; (not on the left) a la derecha; (to the right) hacia la derecha ■ vt (put straight) enderezar ■ excl ¡bueno!, ¡está bien!; **to be ~** (person) tener razón; **to get sth ~** acertar en algo; **you did the ~ thing** hiciste bien; **let's get it ~ this time!** ¡a ver si esta vez nos sale bien!; **to put a mistake ~** corregir un error; **the ~ time** la hora exacta; (fig) el momento oportuno; **by rights** en justicia; **~ and wrong** el bien y el mal; **film rights** derechos mpl de la película; **on the ~** a la derecha; **to be in the ~** tener razón; **~ now** ahora mismo; **~ before/after** inmediatamente antes/ después; **~ in the middle** exactamente en el centro; **~ away** en seguida; **to go ~ to the end of sth** llegar hasta el final de algo; **~, who's next?** bueno, ¿quién sigue?; **all ~!** ¡vale!; **I'm/I feel all ~ now** ya estoy bien
right angle n ángulo recto
right-click ['raɪtklɪk] vi clicar con el botón derecho del ratón ■ vt: **to ~ an icon** clicar en un icono con el botón derecho del ratón

righteous ['raɪtʃəs] adj justo, honrado; (anger) justificado
righteousness ['raɪtʃəsnɪs] n justicia
rightful ['raɪtful] adj (heir) legítimo
right-hand ['raɪthænd] adj (drive, turn) por la derecha
right-handed [raɪt'hændɪd] adj (person) que usa la mano derecha
right-hand man n brazo derecho
right-hand side n derecha
rightly ['raɪtlɪ] adv correctamente, debidamente; (with reason) con razón; **if I remember ~** si recuerdo bien
right-minded ['raɪt'maɪndɪd] adj (sensible) sensato; (decent) honrado
right of way n (on path etc) derecho de paso; (Aut) prioridad f de paso
right-wing [raɪt'wɪŋ] adj (Pol) de derechas, derechista
right-winger [raɪt'wɪŋə^r] n (Pol) persona de derechas, derechista m/f; (Sport) extremo derecha
rigid ['rɪdʒɪd] adj rígido; (person, ideas) inflexible
rigidity [rɪ'dʒɪdɪtɪ] n rigidez f; inflexibilidad f
rigidly ['rɪdʒɪdlɪ] adv rígidamente; (inflexibly) inflexiblemente
rigmarole ['rɪgmərəul] n galimatías m inv
rigor mortis ['rɪgə'mɔːtɪs] n rigidez f cadavérica
rigorous ['rɪgərəs] adj riguroso
rigorously ['rɪgərəslɪ] adv rigurosamente
rigour, rigor (US) ['rɪgə^r] n rigor m, severidad f
rile [raɪl] vt irritar
rim [rɪm] n borde m; (of spectacles) montura, aro; (of wheel) llanta
rimless ['rɪmlɪs] adj (spectacles) sin aros
rimmed [rɪmd] adj: **~ with** con un borde de, bordeado de
rind [raɪnd] n (of bacon, cheese) corteza; (of lemon etc) cáscara
ring [rɪŋ] n (pt **rang**, pp **rung**) (of metal) aro; (on finger) anillo; (of people) corro; (of objects) círculo; (gang) banda; (for boxing) cuadrilátero; (of circus) pista; (bull ring) ruedo, plaza; (sound of bell) toque m; (telephone call) llamada ■ vi (on telephone) llamar por teléfono; (large bell) repicar; (also: **ring out**: voice, words) sonar; (ears) zumbar ■ vt (Brit Tel: also: **ring up**) llamar; (bell etc) hacer sonar; (doorbell) tocar; **that has the ~ of truth about it** eso suena a verdad; **to give sb a ~** (Brit Tel) llamar por teléfono a algn, dar un telefonazo a algn; **the name doesn't ~ a bell (with me)** el nombre no me suena; **to ~ sb (up)** llamar a algn

▸ **ring back** vt, vi (Tel) devolver la llamada
▸ **ring off** vi (Brit Tel) colgar, cortar la comunicación
ring binder n carpeta de anillas
ring finger n (dedo) anular m
ringing ['rɪŋɪŋ] n (of bell) toque m, tañido; (of large bell) repique m; (in ears) zumbido
ringing tone n (Tel) tono de llamada
ringleader ['rɪŋliːdər] n cabecilla m/f
ringlets ['rɪŋlɪts] npl tirabuzones mpl, bucles mpl
ring road n (Brit) carretera periférica or de circunvalación
ringtone ['rɪŋtəun] n tono de llamada
rink [rɪŋk] n (also: **ice rink**) pista de hielo; (for roller-skating) pista de patinaje
rinse [rɪns] n (of dishes) enjuague m; (of clothes) aclarado; (of hair) reflejo ▪ vt enjuagar; aclarar; dar reflejos a
Rio ['riːəu], **Rio de Janeiro** ['riːəudədʒə'nɪərəu] n Río de Janeiro
riot ['raɪət] n motín m, disturbio ▪ vi amotinarse; **to run** ~ desmandarse
rioter ['raɪətər] n amotinado(-a)
riot gear n uniforme m antidisturbios inv
riotous ['raɪətəs] adj alborotado; (party) bullicioso; (uncontrolled) desenfrenado
riotously ['raɪətəslɪ] adv bulliciosamente
riot police n policía antidisturbios
RIP abbr (= requiescat or requiescant in pace: rest in peace) q.e.p.d.
rip [rɪp] n rasgón m, desgarrón m ▪ vt rasgar, desgarrar ▪ vi rasgarse
▸ **rip up** vt hacer pedazos
ripcord ['rɪpkɔːd] n cabo de desgarre
ripe [raɪp] adj (fruit) maduro
ripen ['raɪpən] vt, vi madurar
ripeness ['raɪpnɪs] n madurez f
rip-off ['rɪpɔf] n (col): **it's a ~!** ¡es una estafa!, ¡es un timo!
riposte [rɪ'pɔst] n respuesta aguda, réplica
ripple ['rɪpl] n onda, rizo; (sound) murmullo ▪ vi rizarse ▪ vt rizar
rise [raɪz] n (slope) cuesta, pendiente f; (hill) altura; (increase: in wages: Brit) aumento; (: in prices, temperature) subida, alza; (fig: to power etc) ascenso; (: ascendancy) auge m ▪ vi (pt **rose**, pp **risen**) [rəuz, 'rɪzn] (gen) elevarse; (prices) subir; (waters) crecer; (river) nacer; (sun) salir; (person: from bed etc) levantarse; (also: **rise up**: rebel) sublevarse; (in rank) ascender; ~ **to power** ascenso al poder; **to give ~ to** dar lugar or origen a; **to ~ to the occasion** ponerse a la altura de las circunstancias
rising ['raɪzɪŋ] adj (increasing: number) creciente; (: prices) en aumento or alza; (tide)

creciente; (sun, moon) naciente ▪ n (uprising) sublevación f
rising damp n humedad f de paredes
rising star n (fig) figura en alza
risk [rɪsk] n riesgo, peligro ▪ vt (gen) arriesgar; (dare) atreverse a; **to take** or **run the ~ of doing** correr el riesgo de hacer; **at ~** en peligro; **at one's own ~** bajo su propia responsabilidad; **fire/health/security ~** peligro de incendio/para la salud/para la seguridad
risk capital n capital m de riesgo
risky ['rɪskɪ] adj arriesgado, peligroso
risqué ['riːskeɪ] adj (joke) subido de color
rissole ['rɪsəul] n croqueta
rite [raɪt] n rito; **last rites** últimos sacramentos mpl
ritual ['rɪtjuəl] adj ritual ▪ n ritual m, rito
rival ['raɪvl] n rival m/f; (in business) competidor(a) m(f) ▪ adj rival, opuesto ▪ vt competir con
rivalry ['raɪvlrɪ] n rivalidad f, competencia
river ['rɪvər] n río ▪ cpd (port, traffic) de río, del río; **up/down** ~ río arriba/abajo
riverbank ['rɪvəbæŋk] n orilla (del río)
riverbed ['rɪvəbed] n lecho, cauce m
rivet ['rɪvɪt] n roblón m, remache m ▪ vt remachar; (fig) fascinar
riveting ['rɪvɪtɪŋ] adj (fig) fascinante
Riviera [rɪvɪ'eərə] n: **the (French)** ~ la Costa Azul, la Riviera (francesa); **the Italian** ~ la Riviera italiana
Riyadh [rɪ'jɑːd] n Riyadh m
RMT n abbr (= National Union of Rail, Maritime and Transport Workers) sindicato de transportes
RN n abbr (Brit) = **Royal Navy**; (US) = registered nurse
RNA n abbr (= ribonucleic acid) ARN m, RNA m
RNLI n abbr (Brit: = Royal National Lifeboat Institution) organización benéfica que proporciona un servicio de lanchas de socorro
RNZAF n abbr = **Royal New Zealand Air Force**
RNZN n abbr = **Royal New Zealand Navy**
road [rəud] n (gen) camino; (motorway etc) carretera; (in town) calle f; **major/minor** ~ carretera general/secundaria; **main** ~ carretera; **it takes four hours by** ~ se tarda cuatro horas por carretera; **on the ~ to success** camino del éxito
roadblock ['rəudblɔk] n barricada, control m, retén m (LAm)
road haulage n transporte m por carretera
roadhog ['rəudhɔg] n loco(-a) del volante
road map n mapa m de carreteras
road rage n conducta agresiva de los conductores
road safety n seguridad f vial
roadside ['rəudsaɪd] n borde m (del camino)

r

■ *cpd* al lado de la carretera; **by the ~** al borde del camino

roadsign ['rəudsaɪn] *n* señal *f* de tráfico

roadsweeper ['rəudswiːpəʳ] *n* (*Brit: person*) barrendero(-a)

road user *n* usuario(-a) de la vía pública

roadway ['rəudweɪ] *n* calzada

roadworks ['rəudwəːks] *npl* obras *fpl*

roadworthy ['rəudwəːðɪ] *adj* (*car*) en buen estado para circular

roam [rəum] *vi* vagar ■ *vt* vagar por

roar [rɔːʳ] *n* (*of animal*) rugido, bramido; (*of crowd*) clamor *m*, rugido; (*of vehicle, storm*) estruendo; (*of laughter*) carcajada ■ *vi* rugir, bramar; hacer estruendo; **to ~ with laughter** reírse a carcajadas

roaring ['rɔːrɪŋ] *adj*: **a ~ success** un tremendo éxito; **to do a ~ trade** hacer buen negocio

roast [rəust] *n* carne *f* asada, asado ■ *vt* (*meat*) asar; (*coffee*) tostar

roast beef *n* rosbif *m*

roasting ['rəustɪŋ] *n*: **to give sb a ~** (*col*) echar una buena bronca a algn

rob [rɔb] *vt* robar; **to ~ sb of sth** robar algo a algn; (*fig: deprive*) quitar algo a algn

robber ['rɔbəʳ] *n* ladrón(-ona) *m(f)*

robbery ['rɔbərɪ] *n* robo

robe [rəub] *n* (*for ceremony etc*) toga; (*also:* **bath robe**) bata

robin ['rɔbɪn] *n* petirrojo

robot ['rəubɔt] *n* robot *m*

robotics [rəu'bɔtɪks] *n* robótica

robust [rəu'bʌst] *adj* robusto, fuerte

rock [rɔk] *n* (*gen*) roca; (*boulder*) peña, peñasco; (*Brit: sweet*) ≈ pirulí *m* ■ *vt* (*swing gently*) mecer; (*shake*) sacudir ■ *vi* mecerse, balancearse; sacudirse; **on the rocks** (*drink*) con hielo; **their marriage is on the rocks** su matrimonio se está yendo a pique; **to ~ the boat** (*fig*) crear problemas

rock and roll *n* rock and roll *m*, rocanrol *m*

rock-bottom ['rɔk'bɔtəm] *adj* (*fig*) por los suelos; **to reach** *or* **touch ~** (*price*) estar por los suelos; (*person*) tocar fondo

rock cake *n* (*Brit*) *bollito de pasas con superficie rugosa*

rock climber *n* escalador(a) *m(f)*

rock climbing *n* (*Sport*) escalada

rockery ['rɔkərɪ] *n* cuadro alpino

rocket ['rɔkɪt] *n* cohete *m* ■ *vi* (*prices*) dispararse, ponerse por las nubes

rocket launcher *n* lanzacohetes *m inv*

rock face *n* pared *f* de roca

rocking chair ['rɔkɪŋ-] *n* mecedora

rocking horse *n* caballo de balancín

rocky ['rɔkɪ] *adj* (*gen*) rocoso; (*unsteady: table*) inestable

Rocky Mountains *npl*: **the ~** las Montañas Rocosas

rococo [rə'kəukəu] *adj* rococó *inv* ■ *n* rococó

rod [rɔd] *n* vara, varilla; (*Tech*) barra; (*also:* **fishing rod**) caña

rode [rəud] *pt of* **ride**

rodent ['rəudnt] *n* roedor *m*

rodeo ['rəudɪəu] *n* rodeo

roe [rəu] *n* (*species: also:* **roe deer**) corzo; (*of fish*): **hard/soft ~** hueva/lecha

rogue [rəug] *n* pícaro, pillo

roguish ['rəugɪʃ] *adj* (*child*) travieso; (*smile etc*) pícaro

role [rəul] *n* papel *m*, rol *m*

role-model ['rəulmɔdl] *n* modelo a imitar

role play *n* (*also:* **role playing**) juego de papeles *or* roles

roll [rəul] *n* rollo; (*of bank notes*) fajo; (*also:* **bread roll**) panecillo; (*register*) lista, nómina; (*sound: of drums etc*) redoble *m*; (*movement: of ship*) balanceo ■ *vt* hacer rodar; (*also:* **roll up:** *string*) enrollar; (: *sleeves*) arremangar; (*cigarettes*) liar; (*also:* **roll out:** *pastry*) aplanar ■ *vi* (*gen*) rodar; (*drum*) redoblar; (*in walking*) bambolearse; (*ship*) balancearse; **cheese ~** panecillo de queso

▸ **roll about, roll around** *vi* (*person*) revolcarse

▸ **roll by** *vi* (*time*) pasar

▸ **roll in** *vi* (*mail, cash*) entrar a raudales

▸ **roll over** *vi* dar una vuelta

▸ **roll up** *vi* (*col: arrive*) presentarse, aparecer ■ *vt* (*carpet, cloth, map*) arrollar; (*sleeves*) arremangar; **to ~ o.s. up into a ball** acurrucarse, hacerse un ovillo

roll call *n*: **to take a ~** pasar lista

rolled [rəuld] *adj* (*umbrella*) plegado

roller ['rəuləʳ] *n* rodillo; (*wheel*) rueda

roller blind *n* (*Brit*) persiana (enrollable)

roller coaster *n* montaña rusa

roller skates *npl* patines *mpl* de rueda

rollicking ['rɔlɪkɪŋ] *adj*: **we had a ~ time** nos divertimos una barbaridad

rolling ['rəulɪŋ] *adj* (*landscape*) ondulado

rolling mill *n* taller *m* de laminación

rolling pin *n* rodillo (de cocina)

rolling stock *n* (*Rail*) material *m* rodante

ROM [rɔm] *n abbr* (*Comput:* = *read-only memory*) (memoria) ROM *f*

Roman ['rəumən] *adj*, *n* romano(-a) *m(f)*

Roman Catholic *adj*, *n* católico(-a) *m(f)* (romano(-a))

romance [rə'mæns] *n* (*love affair*) amor *m*, idilio; (*charm*) lo romántico; (*novel*) novela de amor

romanesque [rəumə'nɛsk] *adj* románico

Romania [ruː'meɪnɪə] *n* = **Rumania**

Romanian [ru:'meɪnɪən] adj, n = **Rumanian**
Roman numeral n número romano
romantic [rə'mæntɪk] adj romántico
romanticism [rə'mæntɪsɪzəm] n romanticismo
Romany ['rəumənɪ] adj gitano ■ n (person) gitano(-a); (Ling) lengua gitana, caló (SP)
Rome [rəum] n Roma
romp [rɔmp] n retozo, jugueteo ■ vi (also: **romp about**) juguetear; **to ~ home** (horse) ganar fácilmente
rompers ['rɔmpəz] npl pelele m
roof [ru:f] n (gen) techo; (of house) tejado ■ vt techar, poner techo a; **~ of the mouth** paladar m
roofing ['ru:fɪŋ] n techumbre f
roof rack n (Aut) baca
rook [ruk] n (bird) graja; (Chess) torre f
rookie ['rukɪ] n (col) novato(-a); (Mil) chivo
room [ru:m] n (in house) cuarto, habitación f, pieza (esp LAm); (also: **bedroom**) dormitorio; (in school etc) sala; (space) sitio; **rooms** npl (lodging) alojamiento sg; **"rooms to let"**, (US) **"rooms for rent"** "se alquilan pisos or cuartos"; **single/double ~** habitación individual/doble or para dos personas; **is there ~ for this?** ¿cabe esto?; **to make ~ for sb** hacer sitio para algn; **there is ~ for improvement** podría mejorarse
roominess ['ru:mɪnɪs] n amplitud f, espaciosidad f
rooming house ['ru:mɪŋ-] n (US) pensión f
roommate ['ru:mmeɪt] n compañero(-a) de cuarto
room service n servicio de habitaciones
room temperature n temperatura ambiente
roomy ['ru:mɪ] adj espacioso
roost [ru:st] n percha ■ vi pasar la noche
rooster ['ru:stər] n gallo
root [ru:t] n (Bot, Math) raíz f ■ vi (plant, belief) arraigar(se); **to take ~** (plant) echar raíces; (idea) arraigar(se); **the ~ of the problem is that ...** la raíz del problema es que ...
  ▶ **root about** vi (fig) rebuscar
  ▶ **root for** vt fus apoyar a
  ▶ **root out** vt desarraigar
root beer n (US) refresco sin alcohol de extractos de hierbas
rooted ['ru:tɪd] adj enraizado; (opinions etc) arraigado
rope [rəup] n cuerda; (Naut) cable m ■ vt (box) atar or amarrar con (una) cuerda; (climbers: also: **rope together**) encordarse; **to ~ sb in** (fig) persuadir a algn a tomar parte; **to know the ropes** (fig) conocer los trucos (del oficio)
rope ladder n escala de cuerda

ropey ['rəupɪ] adj (col) chungo
rosary ['rəuzərɪ] n rosario
rose [rəuz] pt of **rise** ■ n rosa; (also: **rosebush**) rosal m; (on watering can) roseta ■ adj color de rosa
rosé ['rəuzeɪ] n vino rosado, clarete m
rosebed ['rəuzbɛd] n rosaleda
rosebud ['rəuzbʌd] n capullo de rosa
rosebush ['rəuzbʊʃ] n rosal m
rosemary ['rəuzmərɪ] n romero
rosette [rəu'zɛt] n rosctón m
ROSPA ['rɔspə] n abbr (Brit) = **Royal Society for the Prevention of Accidents**
roster ['rɔstər] n: **duty ~** lista de tareas
rostrum ['rɔstrəm] n tribuna
rosy ['rəuzɪ] adj rosado, sonrosado; **the future looks ~** el futuro parece prometedor
rot [rɔt] n (decay) putrefacción f, podredumbre f, (fig: pej) tonterías ¡pl ■ vt pudrir, corromper ■ vi pudrirse, corromperse; **it has rotted** está podrido; **to stop the ~** (fig) poner fin a las pérdidas
rota ['rəutə] n lista (de tareas)
rotary ['rəutərɪ] adj rotativo
rotate [rəu'teɪt] vt (revolve) hacer girar, dar vueltas a; (change round: crops) cultivar en rotación; (: jobs) alternar ■ vi (revolve) girar, dar vueltas
rotating [rəu'teɪtɪŋ] adj (movement) rotativo
rotation [rəu'teɪʃən] n rotación f; **in ~** por turno
rote [rəut] n: **by ~** de memoria
rotor ['rəutər] n rotor m
rotten ['rɔtn] adj (decayed) podrido; (: wood) carcomido; (fig) corrompido; (col: bad) pésimo; **to feel ~** (ill) sentirse fatal; **~ to the core** completamente podrido
rotund [rəu'tʌnd] adj rotundo
rouble, ruble (US) ['ru:bl] n rublo
rouge [ru:ʒ] n colorete m
rough [rʌf] adj (skin, surface) áspero; (terrain) accidentado; (road) desigual; (voice) bronco; (person, manner: coarse) tosco, grosero; (weather) borrascoso; (treatment) brutal; (sea) embravecido; (cloth) basto; (plan) preliminar; (guess) aproximado; (: crime) violento ■ n (Golf): **in the ~** en las hierbas altas; **to ~ it** vivir sin comodidades; **to sleep ~** (Brit) pasar la noche al raso; **the sea is ~ today** el mar está agitado hoy; **to have a ~ time (of it)** pasar una mala racha; **~ estimate** cálculo aproximado
roughage ['rʌfɪdʒ] n fibra(s) f(pl), forraje m
rough-and-ready ['rʌfən'rɛdɪ] adj improvisado, tosco
rough-and-tumble ['rʌfən'tʌmbl] n pelea
roughcast ['rʌfkɑ:st] n mezcla gruesa

rough copy, rough draft n borrador m
roughen ['rʌfn] vt (a surface) poner áspero
roughly ['rʌflɪ] adv (handle) torpemente;
(make) toscamente; (approximately)
aproximadamente; ~ **speaking** más o menos
roughness ['rʌfnɪs] n aspereza; tosquedad f;
brutalidad f
roughshod ['rʌfʃɒd] adv: **to ride ~ over**
(person) pisotear a; (objections) hacer caso
omiso de
rough work n (Scol etc) borrador m
roulette [ruːˈlɛt] n ruleta
Roumania [ruːˈmeɪnɪə] n = **Rumania**
round [raund] adj redondo ▪ n círculo;
(of policeman) ronda; (of milkman) recorrido;
(of doctor) visitas fpl; (game: in competition, cards)
partida; (of ammunition) cartucho; (Boxing)
asalto; (of talks) ronda ▪ vt (corner) doblar
▪ prep alrededor de ▪ adv: **all** ~ por todos
lados; **the long way** ~ por el camino menos
directo; **all the year** ~ durante todo el año;
it's just ~ **the corner** (fig) está a la vuelta
de la esquina; **to ask sb** ~ invitar a algn a
casa; **I'll be** ~ **at six o'clock** llegaré a eso de
las seis; **she arrived** ~ **(about) noon** llegó
alrededor del mediodía; ~ **the clock** adv las
24 horas; **to go** ~ **to sb's (house)** ir a casa de
algn; **to go** ~ **the back** pasar por atrás; **to
go** ~ **a house** visitar una casa; **enough to
go** ~ bastante (para todos); **in** ~ **figures** en
números redondos; **to go the rounds** (story)
divulgarse; **a** ~ **of applause** una salva de
aplausos; **a** ~ **of drinks/sandwiches** una
ronda de bebidas/bocadillos; **a** ~ **of toast**
(Brit) una tostada; **the daily** ~ la rutina
cotidiana
▸ **round off** vt (speech etc) acabar, poner
término a
▸ **round up** vt (cattle) acorralar; (people)
reunir; (prices) redondear
roundabout ['raundəbaut] n (Brit: Aut)
glorieta, rotonda; (: at fair) tiovivo ▪ adj
(route, means) indirecto
rounded ['raundɪd] adj redondeado, redondo
rounders ['raundəz] n (Brit: game) juego similar
al béisbol
roundly ['raundlɪ] adv (fig) rotundamente
round-robin ['raundrɒbɪn] n (Sport: also:
round-robin tournament) liguilla
round-shouldered ['raundʃəuldəd] adj
cargado de espaldas
round trip n viaje m de ida y vuelta
roundup ['raundʌp] n rodeo; (of criminals)
redada; **a** ~ **of the latest news** un resumen
de las últimas noticias
rouse [rauz] vt (wake up) despertar; (stir up)
suscitar

rousing ['rauzɪŋ] adj (applause) caluroso;
(speech) conmovedor(a)
rout [raut] n (Mil) derrota; (flight) desbandada
▪ vt derrotar
route [ruːt] n ruta, camino; (of bus) recorrido;
(of shipping) rumbo, derrota; **the best** ~ **to
London** el mejor camino or la mejor ruta
para a Londres; **en** ~ **from** ... **to** en el viaje
de ... a; **en** ~ **for** rumbo a, con destino en
route map n (Brit: for journey) mapa m de
carreteras
routine [ruːˈtiːn] adj (work) rutinario ▪ n
rutina; (Theat) número; (Comput) rutina; ~
procedure trámite m rutinario
rover ['rəuvər] n vagabundo(-a)
roving ['rəuvɪŋ] adj (wandering) errante;
(salesman) ambulante; (reporter) volante
row [rəu] n (line) fila, hilera; (Knitting) vuelta
[rau] (noise) escándalo; (dispute) bronca,
pelea; (fuss) jaleo; (scolding) reprimenda ▪ vi
(in boat) remar; [rau] reñir(se) ▪ vt (boat)
conducir remando; **four days in a** ~ cuarto
días seguidos; **to make a** ~ armar un lío; **to
have a** ~ pelearse, reñir
rowboat ['rəubəut] n (US) bote m de remos
rowdy ['raudɪ] adj (person: noisy) ruidoso;
(: quarrelsome) pendenciero; (occasion)
alborotado ▪ n pendenciero
rowdyism ['raudɪɪzəm] n gamberrismo
row houses npl (US) casas fpl adosadas
rowing ['rəuɪŋ] n remo
rowing boat n (Brit) bote m or barco de remos
rowlock ['rɒlək] n (Brit) chumacera
royal ['rɔɪəl] adj real
Royal Academy, Royal Academy of Arts
n (Brit) la Real Academia (de Bellas Artes);
ver nota

● **ROYAL ACADEMY (OF ARTS)**
●
● La Royal Academy (of Arts), fundada en
● 1768 durante el reinado de Jorge III, es
● una institución dedicada al fomento de
● la pintura, escultura y arquitectura en
● el Reino Unido. Además de dar cursos
● de arte, presenta una exposición anual
● de artistas contemporáneos en su sede
● de Burlington House, en el centro de
● Londres. No existe una institución
● equivalente a la Real Academia de la
● Lengua.

Royal Air Force n Fuerzas Aéreas Británicas
fpl
royal blue n azul m marino
royalist ['rɔɪəlɪst] adj, n monárquico(-a) m(f)
Royal Navy n (Brit) Marina Británica

royalty ['rɔɪəltɪ] n (royal persons) (miembros mpl de la) familia real; (payment to author) derechos mpl de autor

RP (n abbr: Brit: = Received Pronunciation) ver nota

> ● **RP**
> ●
> ● El acento con el que suelen hablar las
> ● clases medias y altas de Inglaterra se
> ● denomina RP (o Received Pronunciation).
> ● Es el acento estándar, sin variaciones
> ● regionales, que aún usan los locutores en
> ● los informativos nacionales de la "BBC".
> ● También suele tomarse como norma en
> ● la enseñanza del inglés británico como
> ● lengua extranjera. Todavía conserva un
> ● gran prestigio, aunque la gran mayoría
> ● de la población habla con el acento de su
> ● región, que puede ser más o menos fuerte
> ● según su educación o clase social.

rpm (abbr: = revolutions per minute) r.p.m.

RR abbr (US) = **railroad**

RRP n abbr (Brit: = recommended retail price) PVP m

RSA n abbr (Brit) = **Royal Society of Arts; Royal Scottish Academy**

RSI n abbr (Med: = repetitive strain injury) traumatismo producido por un esfuerzo continuado (como el de las mecanógrafas)

RSPB n abbr (Brit) = **Royal Society for the Protection of Birds**

RSPCA n abbr (Brit) = **Royal Society for the Prevention of Cruelty to Animals**

RSVP abbr (= répondez s'il vous plaît) SRC

RTA n abbr (= road traffic accident) accidente m de carretera

Rt. Hon. abbr (Brit: = Right Honourable) tratamiento honorífico de diputado

Rt. Rev. abbr (= Right Reverend) Rvdo.

rub [rʌb] vt (gen) frotar; (hard) restregar ■ n (gen) frotamiento; (touch) roce m; **to ~ sb up** or (US) **~ sb the wrong way** sacar de quicio a algn

▸ **rub down** vt (body) secar frotando; (horse) almohazar

▸ **rub in** vt (ointment) frotar

▸ **rub off** vt borrarse ■ vi quitarse (frotando); **to ~ off on sb** influir en algn, pegársele a algn

▸ **rub out** vt borrar ■ vi borrarse

rubber ['rʌbəʳ] n caucho, goma; (Brit: eraser) goma de borrar

rubber band n goma, gomita

rubber bullet n bala de goma

rubber plant n ficus m

rubber ring n (for swimming) flotador m

rubber stamp n sello (de caucho) ■ vt:

rubber-stamp (fig) aprobar maquinalmente

rubbery ['rʌbərɪ] adj (como) de goma

rubbish ['rʌbɪʃ] (Brit) n (from household) basura; (waste) desperdicios mpl; (fig: pej) tonterías fpl; (trash) basura, porquería ■ vt (col) poner por los suelos; **what you've just said is ~** lo que acabas de decir es una tontería

rubbish bin n cubo or bote m (LAm) de la basura

rubbish dump n (in town) vertedero, basurero

rubbishy ['rʌbɪʃɪ] adj de mala calidad, de pacotilla

rubble ['rʌbl] n escombros mpl

ruby ['ruːbɪ] n rubí m

RUC n abbr (= Royal Ulster Constabulary) fuerza de policía en Irlanda del Norte

rucksack ['rʌksæk] n mochila

ructions ['rʌkʃənz] npl: **there will be ~** se va a armar la gorda

ruddy ['rʌdɪ] adj (face) rubicundo; (col: damned) condenado

rude [ruːd] adj (impolite: person) grosero, maleducado; (: word, manners) rudo, grosero; (indecent) indecente; **to be ~ to sb** ser grosero con algn

rudeness ['ruːdnɪs] n grosería, tosquedad f

rudiment ['ruːdɪmənt] n rudimento

rudimentary [ruːdɪ'mentərɪ] adj rudimentario

rue [ruː] vt arrepentirse de

rueful ['ruːful] adj arrepentido

ruffian ['rʌfɪən] n matón m, criminal m

ruffle ['rʌfl] vt (hair) despeinar; (clothes) arrugar; (fig: person) agitar

rug [rʌg] n alfombra; (Brit: for knees) manta

rugby ['rʌgbɪ] n (also: **rugby football**) rugby m

rugged ['rʌgɪd] adj (landscape) accidentado, (features) robusto

rugger ['rʌgəʳ] n (Brit col) rugby m

ruin ['ruːɪn] n ruina ■ vt arruinar; (spoil) estropear; **ruins** npl ruinas fpl, restos mpl; **in ruins** en ruinas

ruinous ['ruːɪnəs] adj ruinoso

rule [ruːl] n (norm) norma, costumbre f; (regulation, ruler) regla; (government) dominio; (dominion etc): **under British ~** bajo el dominio británico ■ vt (country, person) gobernar; (decide) disponer; (draw lines) trazar ■ vi gobernar; (Law) fallar; **to ~ against/in favour of/on** fallar en contra de/a favor de/ sobre; **to ~ that ...** (umpire, judge) fallar que ...; **it's against the rules** está prohibido; **as a ~** por regla general, generalmente; **by ~ of thumb** por experiencia; **majority ~** (Pol) gobierno mayoritario

▸ **rule out** vt excluir

ruled [ruːld] adj (paper) rayado

ruler ['ruːləʳ] n (sovereign) soberano; (for measuring) regla
ruling ['ruːlɪŋ] adj (party) gobernante; (class) dirigente ▪ n (Law) fallo, decisión f
rum [rʌm] n ron m
Rumania [ruːˈmeɪnɪə] n Rumanía
Rumanian [ruːˈmeɪnɪən] adj, n rumano(-a) m(f)
rumble ['rʌmbl] n ruido sordo; (of thunder) redoble m ▪ vi retumbar, hacer un ruido sordo; (stomach, pipe) sonar
rumbustious [rʌmˈbʌstʃəs] adj (person) bullicioso
rummage ['rʌmɪdʒ] vi revolverlo todo
rumour, rumor (US) ['ruːməʳ] n rumor m ▪ vt: **it is rumoured that …** se rumorea que …; **~ has it that …** corre la voz de que …
rump [rʌmp] n (of animal) ancas fpl, grupa
rumple ['rʌmpl] vt (clothes) arrugar; (hair) despeinar
rump steak n filete m de lomo
rumpus ['rʌmpəs] n (col) lío, jaleo; (quarrel) pelea, riña; **to kick up a ~** armar un follón or armar bronca
run [rʌn] (pt **ran**, pp **~**) n (Sport) carrera; (outing) paseo, excursión f; (distance travelled) trayecto; (series) serie f; (Theat) temporada; (Ski) pista; (in tights, stockings) carrera ▪ vt (operate: business) dirigir; (: competition, course) organizar; (: hotel, house) administrar, llevar; (Comput: program) ejecutar; (to pass: hand) pasar; (bath): **to ~ a bath** llenar la bañera ▪ vi (gen) correr; (work: machine) funcionar, marchar; (bus, train: operate) circular, ir; (: travel) ir; (continue: play) seguir en cartel; (: contract) ser válido; (flow: river, bath) fluir; (colours, washing) desteñirse; (in election) ser candidato; **to go for a ~** ir a correr; **to make a ~ for it** echar(se) a correr, escapar(se), huir; **to have the ~ of sb's house** tener el libre uso de la casa de algn; **a ~ of luck** una racha de suerte; **there was a ~ on** (meat, tickets) hubo mucha demanda de; **in the long ~** a la larga; **on the ~** en fuga; **I'll ~ you to the station** te llevaré a la estación en coche; **to ~ a risk** correr un riesgo; **to ~ errands** hacer recados; **it's very cheap to ~** es muy económico; **to be ~ off one's feet** estar ocupadísimo; **to ~ for the bus** correr tras el autobús; **we shall have to ~ for it** tendremos que escapar; **the train runs between Gatwick and Victoria** el tren circula entre Gatwick y Victoria; **the bus runs every 20 minutes** el autobús pasa cada 20 minutos; **to ~ on petrol/on diesel/ off batteries** funcionar con gasolina/gasoil/ baterías; **my salary won't ~ to a car** mi sueldo no me da para comprarme un coche;

the car ran into the lamppost el coche chocó contra el farol
▶ **run about, run around** vi (children) correr por todos lados
▶ **run across** vt fus (find) dar or topar con
▶ **run away** vi huir
▶ **run down** vi (clock) pararse ▪ vt (reduce: production) ir reduciendo; (factory) restringir la producción de; (Aut) atropellar; (criticize) criticar; **to be ~ down** (person: tired) encontrarse agotado
▶ **run in** vt (Brit: car) rodar
▶ **run into** vt fus (meet: person, trouble) tropezar con; (collide with) chocar con; **to ~ into debt** contraer deudas, endeudarse
▶ **run off** vt (water) dejar correr ▪ vi huir corriendo
▶ **run out** vi (person) salir corriendo; (liquid) irse; (lease) caducar, vencer; (money) acabarse
▶ **run out of** vt fus quedar sin; **I've ~ out of petrol** se me acabó la gasolina
▶ **run over** vt (Aut) atropellar ▪ vt fus (revise) repasar
▶ **run through** vt fus (instructions) repasar
▶ **run up** vt (debt) incurrir en; **to ~ up against** (difficulties) tropezar con
run-around ['rʌnəraund] n: **to give sb the ~** traer a algn al retortero
runaway ['rʌnəweɪ] adj (horse) desbocado; (truck) sin frenos; (person) fugitivo
rundown ['rʌndaun] n (Brit: of industry etc) cierre m gradual
rung [rʌŋ] pp of **ring** ▪ n (of ladder) escalón m, peldaño
run-in ['rʌnɪn] n (col) altercado
runner ['rʌnəʳ] n (in race: person) corredor(a) m(f); (: horse) caballo; (on sledge) patín m; (wheel) ruedecilla
runner bean n (Brit) judía escarlata
runner-up [rʌnərˈʌp] n subcampeón(-ona) m(f)
running ['rʌnɪŋ] n (sport) atletismo; (race) carrera ▪ adj (costs, water) corriente; (commentary) en directo; **to be in/out of the ~ for sth** tener/no tener posibilidades de ganar algo; **6 days ~** 6 días seguidos
running costs npl (of business) gastos mpl corrientes; (of car) gastos mpl de mantenimiento
running head n (Typ) encabezamiento normal
running mate n (US Pol) candidato(-a) a la vicepresidencia
runny ['rʌnɪ] adj derretido
run-off ['rʌnɔf] n (in contest, election) desempate m; (extra race) carrera de desempate
run-of-the-mill ['rʌnəvðəˈmɪl] adj común y corriente

runt [rʌnt] n (also pej) enano
run-up ['rʌnʌp] n: ~ **to** (election etc) período previo a
runway ['rʌnweɪ] n (Aviat) pista (de aterrizaje)
rupee [ruː'piː] n rupia
rupture ['rʌptʃəʳ] n (Med) hernia ■ vt: **to ~ o.s.** causarse una hernia
rural ['ruərl] adj rural
ruse [ruːz] n ardid m
rush [rʌʃ] n ímpetu m; (hurry) prisa, apuro (LAm); (Comm) demanda repentina; (Bot) junco; (current) corriente f fuerte, ráfaga ■ vt apresurar; (work) hacer de prisa; (attack: town etc) asaltar ■ vi correr, precipitarse; **gold ~** fiebre f del oro; **we've had a ~ of orders** ha habido una gran demanda; **I'm in a ~ (to do)** tengo prisa or apuro (LAm) (por hacer); **is there any ~ for this?** ¿te corre prisa esto?; **to ~ sth off** hacer algo de prisa y corriendo
▶ **rush through** vt fus (meal) comer de prisa; (book) leer de prisa; (work) hacer de prisa;

(town) atravesar a toda velocidad ■ vt sep (Comm: order) despachar rápidamente
rush hour n horas fpl punta
rush job n (urgent) trabajo urgente
rusk [rʌsk] n bizcocho tostado
Russia ['rʌʃə] n Rusia
Russian ['rʌʃən] adj ruso ■ n ruso(-a); (Ling) ruso
rust [rʌst] n herrumbre f, moho ■ vi oxidarse
rustic ['rʌstɪk] adj rústico
rustle ['rʌsl] vi susurrar ■ vt (paper) hacer crujir; (US: cattle) hurtar, robar
rustproof ['rʌstpruːf] adj inoxidable
rusty ['rʌstɪ] adj oxidado
rut [rʌt] n surco; (Zool) celo; **to be in a ~** ser esclavo de la rutina
ruthless ['ruːθlɪs] adj despiadado
RV abbr (= revised version) traducción inglesa de la Biblia de 1855 ■ n abbr (US) = **recreational vehicle**
rye [raɪ] n centeno
rye bread n pan de centeno

Ss

S, s [ɛs] n (letter) S, s f; **S for Sugar** S de sábado
S abbr (= Saint) Sto.(-a.); (US Scol: mark:
  = satisfactory) suficiente; (= south) S; (on clothes)
  = **small**
SA n abbr = **South Africa; South America**
sabbath ['sæbəθ] n domingo; (Jewish) sábado
sabbatical [sə'bætɪkl] adj: ~ **year** año
  sabático
sabotage ['sæbətɑːʒ] n sabotaje m ■ vt
  sabotear
sabre, saber (US) ['seɪbər] n sable m
saccharin, saccharine ['sækərɪn] n sacarina
sachet ['sæʃeɪ] n sobrecito
sack [sæk] n (bag) saco, costal m ■ vt (dismiss)
  despedir, echar; (plunder) saquear; **to get the**
  ~ ser despedido; **to give sb the** ~ despedir or
  echar a algn
sackful ['sækful] n saco
sacking ['sækɪŋ] n (material) arpillera
sacrament ['sækrəmənt] n sacramento
sacred ['seɪkrɪd] adj sagrado, santo
sacred cow n (fig) vaca sagrada
sacrifice ['sækrɪfaɪs] n sacrificio ■ vt
  sacrificar; **to make sacrifices (for sb)**
  sacrificarse (por algn)
sacrilege ['sækrɪlɪdʒ] n sacrilegio
sacrosanct ['sækrəusæŋkt] adj sacrosanto
sad [sæd] adj (unhappy) triste; (deplorable)
  lamentable
sadden ['sædn] vt entristecer
saddle ['sædl] n silla (de montar); (of cycle)
  sillín m ■ vt (horse) ensillar; **to ~ sb with**
  sth (col: task, bill, name) cargar a algn con algo;
  (responsibility) gravar a algn con algo; **to be**
  saddled with sth (col) quedar cargado con
  algo
saddlebag ['sædlbæg] n alforja
sadism ['seɪdɪzm] n sadismo
sadist ['seɪdɪst] n sádico(-a)
sadistic [sə'dɪstɪk] adj sádico
sadly ['sædlɪ] adv tristemente; (regrettably)
  desgraciadamente; ~ **lacking (in)** muy
  deficiente (en)

sadness ['sædnɪs] n tristeza
sado-masochism [seɪdəu'mæsəkɪzɪm] n
  sadomasoquismo
sae abbr (Brit: = stamped addressed envelope) sobre
  con las propias señas de uno y con sello
safari [sə'fɑːrɪ] n safari m
safari park n safari m
safe [seɪf] adj (out of danger) fuera de peligro;
  (not dangerous, sure) seguro; (unharmed) ileso;
  (trustworthy) digno de confianza ■ n caja de
  caudales, caja fuerte; ~ **and sound** sano y
  salvo; **(just) to be on the** ~ **side** para mayor
  seguridad; ~ **journey!** ¡buen viaje!; **it is** ~
  to say that ... se puede decir con confianza
  que ...
safe bet n apuesta segura; **it's a** ~ **she'll**
  turn up seguro que viene
safe-breaker ['seɪfbreɪkər] n (Brit)
  ladrón(-ona) m(f) de cajas fuertes
safe-conduct [seɪf'kɒndʌkt] n salvoconducto
safe-cracker ['seɪfkrækər] n (US) = **safe-**
  breaker
safe-deposit ['seɪfdɪpɒzɪt] n (vault) cámara
  acorazada; (box) caja de seguridad or de
  caudales
safeguard ['seɪfgɑːd] n protección f, garantía
  ■ vt proteger, defender
safe haven n refugio
safekeeping ['seɪf'kiːpɪŋ] n custodia
safely ['seɪflɪ] adv seguramente, con
  seguridad; (without mishap) sin peligro;
  I can ~ **say** puedo decir or afirmar con toda
  seguridad
safeness ['seɪfnɪs] n seguridad f
safe passage n garantías fpl para marcharse
  en libertad
safe sex n sexo seguro or sin riesgo
safety ['seɪftɪ] n seguridad f ■ cpd de
  seguridad; **road** ~ seguridad f en carretera;
  ~ **first!** ¡precaución!
safety belt n cinturón m (de seguridad)
safety catch n seguro
safety net n red f (de seguridad)

safety pin n imperdible m, seguro (LAm)
safety valve n válvula de seguridad or de escape
saffron ['sæfrən] n azafrán m
sag [sæg] vi aflojarse
saga ['sɑːɡə] n (History) saga; (fig) epopeya
sage [seɪdʒ] n (herb) salvia; (man) sabio
Sagittarius [sædʒɪ'tɛərɪəs] n Sagitario
sago ['seɪɡəu] n sagú m
Sahara [sə'hɑːrə] n: **the ~ (Desert)** el Sáhara
Sahel [sæ'hɛl] n Sahel m
said [sɛd] pt, pp of **say**
Saigon [saɪ'ɡɔn] n Saigón m
sail [seɪl] n (on boat) vela ■ vt (boat) gobernar ■ vi (travel: ship) navegar; (passenger) pasear en barco; (set off: also: **to set sail**) zarpar; **to go for a ~** dar un paseo en barco; **they sailed into Copenhagen** arribaron a Copenhague
▶ **sail through** vt fus (exam) aprobar fácilmente
sailboat ['seɪlbəut] n (US) velero, barco de vela
sailing ['seɪlɪŋ] n (Sport) balandrismo; **to go ~** salir en balandro
sailing ship n barco de vela
sailor ['seɪlər] n marinero, marino
saint [seɪnt] n santo; **S~ John** San Juan
saintliness ['seɪntlɪnɪs] n santidad f
saintly ['seɪntlɪ] adj santo
sake [seɪk] n: **for the ~ of** por; **for the ~ of argument** digamos, es un decir; **art for art's** - el arte por el arte
salad ['sæləd] n ensalada; **tomato ~** ensalada de tomate
salad bowl n ensaladera
salad cream n (Brit) mayonesa
salad dressing n aliño
salad oil n aceite m para ensalada
salami [sə'lɑːmɪ] n salami m, salchichón m
salaried ['sælərɪd] adj asalariado
salary ['sælərɪ] n sueldo
salary earner n asalariado(-a)
salary scale n escala salarial
sale [seɪl] n venta; (at reduced prices) liquidación f, saldo; **"for ~"** "se vende"; **on ~** en venta; **on ~ or return** (goods) venta por reposición; **closing-down** or (US) **liquidation ~** liquidación f; **~ and lease back** venta y arrendamiento al vendedor
saleroom ['seɪlruːm] n sala de subastas
sales assistant n (Brit) dependiente(-a) m(f)
sales campaign n campaña de venta
sales clerk n (US) dependiente(-a) m(f)
sales conference n conferencia de ventas
sales drive n promoción f de ventas
sales figures npl cifras fpl de ventas
sales force n personal m de ventas

salesman ['seɪlzmən] n vendedor m; (in shop) dependiente m; (representative) viajante m
sales manager n gerente m/f de ventas
salesmanship ['seɪlzmənʃɪp] n arte m de vender
sales meeting n reunión f de ventas
sales tax n (US) = **purchase tax**
saleswoman ['seɪlzwumən] n vendedora; (in shop) dependienta; (representative) viajante f
salient ['seɪlɪənt] adj (features, points) sobresaliente
saline ['seɪlaɪn] adj salino
saliva [sə'laɪvə] n saliva
sallow ['sæləu] adj cetrino
sally forth, sally out ['sælɪ-] vi salir, ponerse en marcha
salmon ['sæmən] n (pl inv) salmón m
salon ['sælɔn] n (hairdressing salon, beauty salon) salón m
saloon [sə'luːn] n (US) bar m, taberna; (Brit Aut) (coche m de) turismo; (ship's lounge) cámara, salón m
SALT [sɔːlt] n abbr (= Strategic Arms Limitation Talks/Treaty) tratado SALT
salt [sɔːlt] n sal f ■ vt salar; (put salt on) poner sal en; **an old ~** un lobo de mar
▶ **salt away** vt (col: money) ahorrar
salt cellar n salero
salt mine n mina de sal
saltwater ['sɔːltwɔːtər] adj (fish etc) de agua salada, de mar
salty ['sɔːltɪ] adj salado
salubrious [sə'luːbrɪəs] adj sano; (fig: district etc) atractivo
salutary ['sæljutərɪ] adj saludable
salute [sə'luːt] n saludo; (of guns) salva ■ vt saludar
salvage ['sælvɪdʒ] n (saving) salvamento, recuperación f; (things saved) objetos mpl salvados ■ vt salvar
salvage vessel n buque m de salvamento
salvation [sæl'veɪʃən] n salvación f
Salvation Army n Ejército de Salvación
salve [sælv] n (cream etc) ungüento, bálsamo
salvo ['sælvəu] n (Mil) salva
Samaritan [sə'mærɪtən] n: **to call the Samaritans** llamar al teléfono de la esperanza
same [seɪm] adj mismo ■ pron: **the ~** el mismo/la misma; **the ~ book as** el mismo libro que; **on the ~ day** el mismo día; **at the ~ time** (at the same moment) al mismo tiempo; (yet) sin embargo; **all** or **just the ~** sin embargo, aun así; **they're one and the ~** (person) son la misma persona; (thing) son iguales; **to do the ~ (as sb)** hacer lo mismo (que otro); **and the ~ to you!** ¡igualmente!;

~ **here!** ¡yo también!; **the ~ again** (in bar etc)
otro igual
sampan ['sæmpæn] n sampán m
sample ['sɑːmpl] n muestra ▪ vt (food, wine)
probar; **to take a ~** tomar una muestra; **free**
~ muestra gratuita
sanatorium (pl **sanatoria**) [sænə'tɔːrɪəm,
-rɪə] n (Brit) sanatorio
sanctify ['sæŋktɪfaɪ] vt santificar
sanctimonious [sæŋktɪ'məunɪəs] adj
santurrón(-ona)
sanction ['sæŋkʃən] n sanción f ▪ vt
sancionar; **to impose economic**
sanctions on or **against** imponer sanciones
económicas a or contra
sanctity ['sæŋktɪtɪ] n (gen) santidad f;
(inviolability) inviolabilidad f
sanctuary ['sæŋktjuərɪ] n (gen) santuario;
(refuge) asilo, refugio
sand [sænd] n arena; (beach) playa ▪ vt (also:
sand down: wood etc) lijar
sandal ['sændl] n sandalia
sandalwood ['sændlwud] n sándalo
sandbag ['sændbæg] n saco de arena
sandblast ['sændblɑːst] vt limpiar con
chorro de arena
sandbox ['sændbɔks] n (US) = **sandpit**
sandcastle ['sændkɑːsl] n castillo de arena
sand dune n duna
sander ['sændər] n pulidora
sandpaper ['sændpeɪpər] n papel m de lija
sandpit ['sændpɪt] n (for children) cajón m de
arena
sands [sændz] npl playa sg de arena
sandstone ['sændstəun] n piedra arenisca
sandstorm ['sændstɔːm] n tormenta de
arena
sandwich ['sændwɪtʃ] n bocadillo (SP),
sandwich m (LAm) ▪ vt (also: **sandwich in**)
intercalar; **to be sandwiched between**
estar apretujado entre; **cheese/ham ~**
sandwich de queso/jamón
sandwich board n cartelón m
sandwich course n (Brit) programa que intercala
períodos de estudio con prácticas profesionales
sandy ['sændɪ] adj arenoso; (colour) rojizo
sane [seɪn] adj cuerdo, sensato
sang [sæŋ] pt of **sing**
sanitarium [sænɪ'tɛərɪəm] n (US)
= **sanatorium**
sanitary ['sænɪtərɪ] adj (system, arrangements)
sanitario; (clean) higiénico
sanitary towel, sanitary napkin (US) n
paño higiénico, compresa
sanitation [sænɪ'teɪʃən] n (in house) servicios
mpl higiénicos; (in town) servicio de
desinfección

sanitation department n (US)
departamento de limpieza y recogida de
basuras
sanity ['sænɪtɪ] n cordura; (of judgment)
sensatez f
sank [sæŋk] pt of **sink**
San Marino ['sænmə'riːnəu] n San Marino
Santa Claus [sæntə'klɔːz] n San Nicolás m,
Papá Noel m
Santiago [sæntɪ'ɑːgəu] n (also: **Santiago de**
Chile) Santiago (de Chile)
sap [sæp] n (of plants) savia ▪ vt (strength)
minar, agotar
sapling ['sæplɪŋ] n árbol nuevo or joven
sapphire ['sæfaɪər] n zafiro
Saragossa [særə'gɔsə] n Zaragoza
sarcasm ['sɑːkæzm] n sarcasmo
sarcastic [sɑː'kæstɪk] adj sarcástico; **to be ~**
ser sarcástico
sarcophagus, sarcophagi [sɑː'kɔfəgəs,
-gaɪ] n sarcófago
sardine [sɑː'diːn] n sardina
Sardinia [sɑː'dɪnɪə] n Cerdeña
Sardinian [sɑː'dɪnɪən] adj, n sardo(-a) m(f)
sardonic [sɑː'dɔnɪk] adj sardónico
sari ['sɑːrɪ] n sari m
SARS ['sɑːz] n abbr (= severe acute respiratory
syndrome) neumonía asiática, SARS m
SAS n abbr (Brit Mil: = Special Air Service) cuerpo del
ejército británico encargado de misiones clandestinas
SASE n abbr (US: = self-addressed stamped envelope)
sobre con las propias señas de uno y con sello
sash [sæʃ] n faja
Sask. abbr (Canada) = **Saskatchewan**
SAT n abbr (US) = **Scholastic Aptitude Test**
Sat. abbr (= Saturday) sáb
sat [sæt] pt, pp of **sit**
Satan ['seɪtn] n Satanás m
satanic [sə'tænɪk] adj satánico
satchel ['sætʃl] n bolsa; (child's) cartera,
mochila (LAm)
sated ['seɪtɪd] adj (appetite, person) saciado
satellite ['sætəlaɪt] n satélite m
satellite dish n (antena) parabólica
satellite navigation system n sistema m de
navegación por satélite
satellite television n televisión f por satélite
satiate ['seɪʃɪeɪt] vt saciar, hartar
satin ['sætɪn] n raso ▪ adj de raso; **with a ~**
finish satinado
satire ['sætaɪər] n sátira
satirical [sə'tɪrɪkl] adj satírico
satirist ['sætɪrɪst] n (writer etc) escritor(a) m(f)
satírico(-a); (cartoonist) caricaturista m/f
satirize ['sætɪraɪz] vt satirizar
satisfaction [sætɪs'fækʃən] n satisfacción f;
it gives me great ~ es para mí una gran

satisfacción; **has it been done to your ~?** ¿se ha hecho a su satisfacción?

satisfactorily [sætɪs'fæktərɪlɪ] *adv* satisfactoriamente, de modo satisfactorio

satisfactory [sætɪs'fæktərɪ] *adj* satisfactorio

satisfied ['sætɪsfaɪd] *adj* satisfecho; **to be ~ (with sth)** estar satisfecho (de algo)

satisfy ['sætɪsfaɪ] *vt* satisfacer; *(pay)* liquidar; *(convince)* convencer; **to ~ the requirements** llenar los requisitos; **to ~ sb that** convencer a algn de que; **to ~ o.s. of sth** convencerse de algo

satisfying ['sætɪsfaɪɪŋ] *adj* satisfactorio

satsuma [sæt'suːmə] *n* satsuma

saturate ['sætʃəreɪt] *vt:* **to ~ (with)** empapar *or* saturar (de)

saturated fat [sætʃəreɪtɪd-] *n* grasa saturada

saturation [sætʃə'reɪʃən] *n* saturación *f*

Saturday ['sætədɪ] *n* sábado; *see also* **Tuesday**

sauce [sɔːs] *n* salsa; *(sweet)* crema; *(fig: cheek)* frescura

saucepan ['sɔːspən] *n* cacerola, olla

saucer ['sɔːsə'] *n* platillo

saucily ['sɔːsɪlɪ] *adv* con frescura, descaradamente

sauciness ['sɔːsɪnɪs] *n* frescura, descaro

saucy ['sɔːsɪ] *adj* fresco, descarado

Saudi ['saʊdɪ] *adj, n* saudí *m/f*, saudita *m/f*

Saudi Arabia *n* Arabia Saudí *or* Saudita

Saudi Arabian *adj, n =* **Saudi**

sauna ['sɔːnə] *n* sauna

saunter ['sɔːntə'] *vi* deambular

sausage ['sɒsɪdʒ] *n* salchicha; *(salami etc)* salchichón *m*

sausage roll *n* empanadilla

sauté ['səʊteɪ] *adj (Culin: potatoes)* salteado; *(: onions)* dorado, rehogado ■ *vt* saltear; dorar

savage ['sævɪdʒ] *adj (cruel, fierce)* feroz, furioso; *(primitive)* salvaje ■ *n* salvaje *m/f* ■ *vt (attack)* embestir

savagely ['sævɪdʒlɪ] *adv* con ferocidad, furiosamente; de modo salvaje

savagery ['sævɪdʒrɪ] *n* ferocidad *f*; salvajismo

save [seɪv] *vt (rescue)* salvar, rescatar; *(money, time)* ahorrar; *(put by)* guardar; *(Comput)* salvar (y guardar); *(avoid: trouble)* evitar ■ *vi (also:* **save up)** ahorrar ■ *n (Sport)* parada ■ *prep* salvo, excepto; **to ~ face** salvar las apariencias; **God ~ the Queen!** ¡Dios guarde a la Reina!, ¡Viva la Reina!; **I saved you a piece of cake** te he guardado un trozo de tarta; **it will ~ me an hour** con ello ganaré una hora

saving ['seɪvɪŋ] *n (on price etc)* economía ■ *adj:* **the ~ grace of** el único mérito de;

savings *npl* ahorros *mpl*; **to make savings** economizar

savings account *n* cuenta de ahorros

savings bank *n* caja de ahorros

saviour, savior *(US)* ['seɪvjə'] *n* salvador(a) *m(f)*

savoir-faire ['sævwɑː'fɛə'] *n* don *m* de gentes

savour, savor *(US)* ['seɪvə'] *n* sabor *m*, gusto ■ *vt* saborear

savoury, savory *(US)* ['seɪvərɪ] *adj* sabroso; *(dish: not sweet)* salado

savvy ['sævɪ] *n (col)* conocimiento, experiencia

saw [sɔː] *pt of* **see** ■ *n (tool)* sierra ■ *vt (pt* **sawed,** *pp* **sawed** *or* **sawn** [sɔːn]) serrar; **to ~ sth up** (a)serrar algo

sawdust ['sɔːdʌst] *n (a)*serrín *m*

sawmill ['sɔːmɪl] *n* aserradero

sawn [sɔːn] *pp of* **saw**

sawn-off ['sɔːnɒf], **sawed-off** *(US)* ['sɔːdɒf] *adj:* **~ shotgun** escopeta de cañones recortados

saxophone ['sæksəfəʊn] *n* saxófono

say [seɪ] *n:* **to have one's ~** expresar su opinión; **to have a** *or* **some ~ in sth** tener voz y voto en algo ■ *vt, vi (pt, pp* **said** [sɛd]) decir; **to ~ yes/no** decir que sí/no; **my watch says 3 o'clock** mi reloj marca las tres; **that is to ~** es decir; **that goes without saying** ni que decir tiene; **she said (that) I was to give you this** me pidió que te diera esto; **I should ~ it's worth about £100** yo diría que vale unas 100 libras; **~ after me** repite lo que yo diga; **shall we ~ Tuesday?** ¿quedamos, por ejemplo, el martes?; **that doesn't ~ much for him** eso no dice nada a su favor; **when all is said and done** al fin y al cabo, a fin de cuentas; **there is something** *or* **a lot to be said for it** hay algo *or* mucho que decir a su favor

saying ['seɪɪŋ] *n* dicho, refrán *m*

say-so ['seɪsəʊ] *n (col)* autorización *f*

SBA *n abbr (US) =* **Small Business Administration**

SC *n abbr (US) =* **Supreme Court** ■ *abbr (US) =* **South Carolina**

s/c *abbr =* **self-contained**

scab [skæb] *n* costra; *(pej)* esquirol(a) *m(f)*

scaffold ['skæfəld] *n (for execution)* cadalso

scaffolding ['skæfəldɪŋ] *n* andamio, andamiaje *m*

scald [skɔːld] *n* escaldadura ■ *vt* escaldar

scalding ['skɔːldɪŋ] *adj (also:* **scalding hot)** hirviendo, que arde

scale [skeɪl] *n (gen)* escala; *(Mus)* escala; *(of fish)* escama; *(of salaries, fees etc)* escalafón *m* ■ *vt (mountain)* escalar; *(tree)* trepar; **scales**

S

npl (*small*) balanza *sg*; (*large*) báscula *sg*; **on a large** ~ a gran escala; ~ **of charges** tarifa, lista de precios; **pay** ~ escala salarial; **to draw sth to** ~ dibujar algo a escala
▶ **scale down** *vt* reducir
scaled-down [skeɪld'daun] *adj* reducido proporcionalmente
scale model *n* modelo a escala
scallop ['skɔləp] *n* (*Zool*) venera; (*Sewing*) festón *m*
scalp [skælp] *n* cabellera ■ *vt* escalpar
scalpel ['skælpl] *n* bisturí *m*
scam [skæm] *n* (*col*) estafa, timo
scamper ['skæmpəʳ] *vi*: **to** ~ **away,** ~ **off** escabullirse
scampi ['skæmpɪ] *npl* gambas *fpl*
scan [skæn] *vt* (*examine*) escudriñar; (*glance at quickly*) dar un vistazo a; (*TV, Radar*) explorar, registrar; (*Comput*) escanear ■ *n* (*Med*) examen *m* ultrasónico
scandal ['skændl] *n* escándalo; (*gossip*) chismes *mpl*
scandalize ['skændəlaɪz] *vt* escandalizar
scandalous ['skændələs] *adj* escandaloso
Scandinavia [skændɪ'neɪvɪə] *n* Escandinavia
Scandinavian [skændɪ'neɪvɪən] *adj, n* escandinavo(-a) *m(f)*
scanner ['skænəʳ] *n* (*Radar, Med, Comput*) escáner *m*
scant [skænt] *adj* escaso
scantily ['skæntɪlɪ] *adv*: ~ **clad** *or* **dressed** ligero de ropa
scantiness ['skæntɪnɪs] *n* escasez *f*, insuficiencia
scanty ['skæntɪ] *adj* (*meal*) insuficiente; (*clothes*) ligero
scapegoat ['skeɪpgəut] *n* cabeza de turco, chivo expiatorio
scar [skɑ:] *n* cicatriz *f* ■ *vt* marcar con una cicatriz ■ *vi* cicatrizarse
scarce [skɛəs] *adj* escaso
scarcely ['skɛəslɪ] *adv* apenas; ~ **anybody** casi nadie; **I can** ~ **believe it** casi no puedo creerlo
scarceness ['skɛəsnɪs], **scarcity** ['skɛəsɪtɪ] *n* escasez *f*
scarcity value *n* valor *m* de escasez
scare [skɛəʳ] *n* susto, sobresalto; (*panic*) pánico ■ *vt* asustar, espantar; **to** ~ **sb stiff** dar a algn un susto de muerte; **bomb** ~ amenaza de bomba
▶ **scare away, scare off** *vt* espantar, ahuyentar
scarecrow ['skɛəkrəu] *n* espantapájaros *m inv*
scared [skɛəd] *adj*: **to be** ~ asustarse, estar asustado

scaremonger ['skɛəmʌŋgəʳ] *n* alarmista *m/f*
scarf (*pl* **scarves**) [skɑ:f, skɑ:vz] *n* (*long*) bufanda; (*square*) pañuelo
scarlet ['skɑ:lɪt] *adj* escarlata
scarlet fever *n* escarlatina
scarper ['skɑ:pəʳ] *vi* (*Brit col*) largarse
scarred [skɑ:d] *adj* lleno de cicatrices
scarves [skɑ:vz] *npl of* **scarf**
scary ['skɛərɪ] *adj* (*col*) de miedo; **it's** ~ da miedo
scathing ['skeɪðɪŋ] *adj* mordaz; **to be** ~ **about sth** criticar algo duramente
scatter ['skætəʳ] *vt* (*spread*) esparcir, desparramar; (*put to flight*) dispersar ■ *vi* desparramarse; dispersarse
scatterbrained ['skætəbreɪnd] *adj* ligero de cascos
scavenge ['skævɪndʒ] *vi*: **to** ~ **(for)** (*person*) revolver entre la basura (para encontrar); **to** ~ **for food** (*hyenas etc*) nutrirse de carroña
scavenger ['skævɪndʒəʳ] *n* (*person*) mendigo/a que rebusca en la basura; (*Zool: animal*) animal *m* de carroña; (*: bird*) ave *f* de carroña
SCE *n abbr* = **Scottish Certificate of Education**
scenario [sɪ'nɑ:rɪəu] *n* (*Theat*) argumento; (*Cine*) guión *m*; (*fig*) escenario
scene [si:n] *n* (*Theat*) escena; (*of crime, accident*) escenario; (*sight, view*) vista, perspectiva; (*fuss*) escándalo; **the political** ~ **in Spain** el panorama político español; **behind the scenes** (*also fig*) entre bastidores; **to appear** *or* **come on the** ~ (*also fig*) aparecer, presentarse; **to make a** ~ (*col: fuss*) armar un escándalo
scenery ['si:nərɪ] *n* (*Theat*) decorado; (*landscape*) paisaje *m*
scenic ['si:nɪk] *adj* (*picturesque*) pintoresco
scent [sent] *n* perfume *m*, olor *m*; (*fig: track*) rastro, pista; (*sense of smell*) olfato ■ *vt* perfumar; (*suspect*) presentir; **to put** *or* **throw sb off the** ~ (*fig*) despistar a algn
sceptic, skeptic (*US*) ['skɛptɪk] *n* escéptico(-a)
sceptical, skeptical (*US*) ['skɛptɪkl] *adj* escéptico
scepticism, skepticism (*US*) ['skɛptɪsɪzm] *n* escepticismo
sceptre, scepter (*US*) ['sɛptəʳ] *n* cetro
schedule ['ʃedju:l], (*US*) ['skedju:l] *n* (*of trains*) horario; (*of events*) programa *m*; (*list*) lista ■ *vt* (*timetable*) establecer el horario de; (*list*) catalogar; (*visit*) fijar la hora de; **on** ~ a la hora, sin retraso; **to be ahead of/behind** ~ estar adelantado/retrasado; **we are working to a very tight** ~ tenemos un programa de trabajo muy apretado; **everything went according to** ~ todo salió según lo previsto;

the meeting is scheduled for seven or **to begin at seven** la reunión está fijada para las siete

scheduled ['ʃedjuːld], (US) ['skedjuːld] adj (date, time) fijado; (visit, event, bus, train) programado; (stop) previsto; **~ flight** vuelo regular

schematic [skɪ'mætɪk], adj (diagram etc) esquemático

scheme [skiːm] n (plan) plan m, proyecto; (method) esquema m; (plot) intriga; (trick) ardid m; (arrangement) disposición f; (pension scheme etc) sistema m ■ vt proyectar ■ vi (plan) hacer proyectos; (intrigue) intrigar; **colour ~** combinación f de colores

scheming ['skiːmɪŋ] adj intrigante

schism ['skɪzəm] n cisma m

schizophrenia [skɪtsə'friːnɪə] n esquizofrenia

schizophrenic [skɪtsə'frenɪk] adj esquizofrénico

scholar ['skɒlər] n (pupil) alumno(-a), estudiante m/f; (learned person) sabio(-a), erudito(-a)

scholarly ['skɒləlɪ] adj erudito

scholarship ['skɒləʃɪp] n erudición f; (grant) beca

school [skuːl] n (gen) escuela, colegio; (in university) facultad f; (of fish) banco ■ vt (animal) amaestrar; **to be at** or **go to ~** ir al colegio or a la escuela

school age n edad f escolar

schoolbook ['skuːlbʊk] n libro de texto

schoolboy ['skuːlbɔɪ] n alumno

schoolchild (pl **schoolchildren**) ['skuːltʃaɪld, -tʃɪldrən] n alumno(-a)

schooldays ['skuːldeɪz] npl años mpl del colegio

schoolgirl ['skuːlgəːl] n alumna

schooling ['skuːlɪŋ] n enseñanza

school-leaver ['skuːlliːvər] n (Brit) joven que ha terminado la educación secundaria

schoolmaster ['skuːlmɑːstər] n (primary) maestro; (secondary) profesor m

schoolmistress ['skuːlmɪstrɪs] n (primary) maestra; (secondary) profesora

schoolroom ['skuːlrʊm] n clase f

schoolteacher ['skuːltiːtʃər] n (primary) maestro(-a); (secondary) profesor(a) m(f)

schoolyard ['skuːljɑːd] n (US) patio del colegio

schooner ['skuːnər] n (ship) goleta

sciatica [saɪ'ætɪkə] n ciática

science ['saɪəns] n ciencia; **the sciences** las ciencias

science fiction n ciencia-ficción f

scientific [saɪən'tɪfɪk] adj científico

scientist ['saɪəntɪst] n científico(-a)

sci-fi ['saɪfaɪ] n abbr (col) = **science fiction**

Scilly Isles ['sɪlɪ-], **Scillies** ['sɪlɪz] npl: **the ~** las Islas Sorlingas

scintillating ['sɪntɪleɪtɪŋ] adj (wit, conversation, company) brillante, chispeante, ingenioso

scissors ['sɪzəz] npl tijeras fpl; **a pair of ~** unas tijeras

scoff [skɒf] vt (Brit col: eat) engullir ■ vi: **to ~ (at)** (mock) mofarse (de)

scold [skəʊld] vt regañar

scolding ['skəʊldɪŋ] n riña, reprimenda

scone [skɒn] n pastel de pan

scoop [skuːp] n cucharón m; (for flour etc) pala; (Press) exclusiva ■ vt (Comm: market) adelantarse a; (: profit) sacar; (Comm, Press: competitors) adelantarse a
▶ **scoop out** vt excavar
▶ **scoop up** vt recoger

scooter ['skuːtər] n (motor cycle) Vespa®; (toy) patinete m

scope [skəʊp] n (of plan, undertaking) ámbito; (reach) alcance m; (of person) competencia; (opportunity) libertad f (de acción); **there is plenty of ~ for improvement** hay bastante campo para efectuar mejoras

scorch [skɔːtʃ] vt (clothes) chamuscar; (earth, grass) quemar, secar

scorcher ['skɔːtʃər] n (col: hot day) día m abrasador

scorching ['skɔːtʃɪŋ] adj abrasador(a)

score [skɔːr] n (points etc) puntuación f; (Mus) partitura; (reckoning) cuenta; (twenty) veintena ■ vt (goal, point) ganar; (mark, cut) rayar ■ vi marcar un tanto; (Football) marcar un gol; (keep score) llevar el tanteo; **to keep (the) ~** llevar la cuenta; **to have an old ~ to settle with sb** (fig) tener cuentas pendientes con algn; **on that ~** en lo que se refiere a eso; **scores of people** (fig) muchísima gente, cantidad de gente; **to ~ 6 out of 10** obtener una puntuación de 6 sobre 10
▶ **score out** vt tachar

scoreboard ['skɔːbɔːd] n marcador m

scoreline ['skɔːlaɪn] n (Sport) resultado final

scorer ['skɔːrər] n marcador m; (keeping score) encargado(-a) del marcador

scorn [skɔːn] n desprecio ■ vt despreciar

scornful ['skɔːnful] adj desdeñoso, despreciativo

scornfully ['skɔːnfulɪ] adv desdeñosamente, con desprecio

Scorpio ['skɔːpɪəʊ] n Escorpión m

scorpion ['skɔːpɪən] n alacrán m, escorpión m

Scot [skɒt] n escocés(-esa) m(f)

Scotch [skɒtʃ] n whisky m escocés

765

scotch [skɔtʃ] *vt* (*rumour*) desmentir; (*plan*)
frustrar
Scotch tape® *n* (*US*) cinta adhesiva, celo,
scotch® *m*
scot-free [skɔt'fri:] *adv*: **to get off ~**
(*unpunished*) salir impune; (*unhurt*) salir ileso
Scotland ['skɔtlənd] *n* Escocia
Scots [skɔts] *adj* escocés(-esa)
Scotsman ['skɔtsmən] *n* escocés *m*
Scotswoman ['skɔtswumən] *n* escocesa
Scottish ['skɔtɪʃ] *adj* escocés(-esa); **the ~**
National Party partido político independista
escocés; **the ~ Parliament** el Parlamento
escocés
scoundrel ['skaundrəl] *n* canalla *m/f*,
sinvergüenza *m/f*
scour ['skauəʳ] *vt* (*clean*) fregar, estregar;
(*search*) recorrer, registrar
scourer ['skauərəʳ] *n* (*pad*) estropajo; (*powder*)
limpiador *m*
scourge [skə:dʒ] *n* azote *m*
scout [skaut] *n* explorador *m*
  ▶ **scout around** *vi* reconocer el terreno
scowl [skaul] *vi* fruncir el ceño; **to ~ at sb**
mirar con ceño a algn
scrabble ['skræbl] *vi* (*claw*): **to ~ (at)** arañar
  ■ *n*: **S~®** Scrabble® *m*, Intelect® *m*; **to ~**
  around for sth revolver todo buscando algo
scraggy ['skrægɪ] *adj* flaco, delgaducho
scram [skræm] *vi* (*col*) largarse
scramble ['skræmbl] *n* (*climb*) subida (difícil);
(*struggle*) pelea ■ *vi*: **to ~ out/through**
salir/abrirse paso con dificultad; **to ~ for**
pelear por; **to go scrambling** (*Sport*) hacer
motocrós
scrambled eggs ['skræmbld-] *npl* huevos *mpl*
revueltos
scrap [skræp] *n* (*bit*) pedacito; (*fig*) pizca;
(*fight*) riña, bronca; (*also*: **scrap iron**)
chatarra, hierro viejo ■ *vt* (*discard*) desechar,
descartar ■ *vi* reñir, armar (una) bronca;
scraps *npl* (*waste*) sobras *fpl*, desperdicios *mpl*;
to sell sth for ~ vender algo como chatarra
scrapbook ['skræpbuk] *n* álbum *m* de
recortes
scrap dealer *n* chatarrero(-a)
scrape [skreɪp] *n* (*fig*) lío, apuro ■ *vt* raspar;
(*skin etc*) rasguñar; (*also*: **scrape against**)
rozar
  ▶ **scrape through** *vi* (*succeed*) salvarse por los
  pelos; (*exam*) aprobar por los pelos
scraper ['skreɪpəʳ] *n* raspador *m*
scrap heap *n* (*fig*): **on the ~** desperdiciado;
to throw sth on the ~ desechar *or* descartar
algo
scrap iron *n* chatarra
scrap merchant *n* (*Brit*) chatarrero(-a)

scrap metal *n* chatarra, desecho de metal
scrap paper *n* pedazos *mpl* de papel
scrappy ['skræpɪ] *adj* (*essay etc*) deshilvanado;
(*education*) incompleto
scrap yard *n* depósito de chatarra; (*for cars*)
cementerio de coches
scratch [skrætʃ] *n* rasguño; (*from claw*)
arañazo ■ *adj*: **~ team** equipo improvisado
■ *vt* (*record*) rayar; (*with claw, nail*) rasguñar,
arañar; (*Comput*) borrar ■ *vi* rascarse; **to**
start from ~ partir de cero; **to be up to ~**
cumplir con los requisitos
scratchpad ['skrætʃpæd] *n* (*US*) bloc *m* de
notas
scrawl [skrɔ:l] *n* garabatos *mpl* ■ *vi* hacer
garabatos
scrawny ['skrɔ:nɪ] *adj* (*person, neck*) flaco
scream [skri:m] *n* chillido ■ *vi* chillar;
it was a ~ (*fig, col*) fue para morirse de risa
or muy divertido; **he's a ~** (*fig, col*) es muy
divertido *or* de lo más gracioso; **to ~ at sb (to**
do sth) gritarle a algn (para que haga algo)
scree [skri:] *n* cono de desmoronamiento
screech [skri:tʃ] *vi* chirriar
screen [skri:n] *n* (*Cine, TV*) pantalla; (*movable*)
biombo; (*wall*) tabique *m*; (*also*: **windscreen**)
parabrisas *m inv* ■ *vt* (*conceal*) tapar; (*from the*
wind etc) proteger; (*film*) proyectar; (*fig: person:*
for security) investigar; (*: for illness*) hacer una
exploración a
screen editing *n* (*Comput*) corrección *f* en
pantalla
screenful ['skri:nful] *n* pantalla
screening ['skri:nɪŋ] *n* (*of film*) proyección *f*;
(*for security*) investigación *f*; (*Med*)
exploración *f*
screen memory *n* (*Comput*) memoria de la
pantalla
screenplay ['skri:npleɪ] *n* guión *m*
screen saver [-seɪvəʳ] *n* (*Comput*)
salvapantallas *m inv*
screen test *n* prueba de pantalla
screw [skru:] *n* tornillo; (*propeller*) hélice *f*
■ *vt* atornillar; **to ~ sth to the wall** fijar algo
a la pared con tornillos
  ▶ **screw up** *vt* (*paper, material etc*) arrugar; (*col:*
  ruin) fastidiar; **to ~ up one's eyes** arrugar
  el entrecejo; **to ~ up one's face** torcer *or*
  arrugar la cara
screwdriver ['skru:draɪvəʳ] *n* destornillador
m
screwed-up ['skru:d'ʌp] *adj* (*col*): **she's**
totally ~ está trastornada
screwy ['skru:ɪ] *adj* (*col*) chiflado
scribble ['skrɪbl] *n* garabatos *mpl* ■ *vt*
escribir con prisa; **to ~ sth down** garabatear
algo

script [skrɪpt] n (Cine etc) guión m; (writing) escritura, letra

scripted ['skrɪptɪd] adj (Radio, TV) escrito

Scripture ['skrɪptʃəʳ] n Sagrada Escritura

scriptwriter ['skrɪptraɪtəʳ] n guionista m/f

scroll [skrəul] n rollo ▪ vt (Comput) desplazar

scrotum ['skrəutəm] n escroto

scrounge [skraundʒ] (col) vt: **to ~ sth off** or **from sb** gorronear algo a algn ▪ vi: **to ~ on sb** vivir a costa de algn

scrounger ['skraundʒəʳ] n gorrón(-ona) m(f)

scrub [skrʌb] n (clean) fregado; (land) maleza ▪ vt fregar, restregar; (reject) cancelar, anular

scrubbing brush ['skrʌbɪŋ-] n cepillo de fregar

scruff [skrʌf] n: **by the ~ of the neck** por el pescuezo

scruffy ['skrʌfɪ] adj desaliñado, desaseado

scrum ['skrʌm], **scrummage** ['skrʌmɪdʒ] n (Rugby) melée f

scruple ['skru:pl] n escrúpulo; **to have no scruples about doing sth** no tener reparos en or escrúpulos para hacer algo

scrupulous ['skru:pjuləs] adj escrupuloso

scrupulously ['skru:pjuləslɪ] adv escrupulosamente; **to be ~ fair/honest** ser sumamente justo/honesto

scrutinize ['skru:tɪnaɪz] vt escudriñar; (votes) escrutar

scrutiny ['skru:tɪnɪ] n escrutinio, examen m; **under the ~ of sb** bajo la mirada or el escrutinio de algn

scuba ['sku:bə] n escafandra autónoma

scuba diving n submarinismo

scuff [skʌf] vt (shoes, floor) rayar

scuffle ['skʌfl] n refriega

scullery ['skʌlərɪ] n trascocina

sculptor ['skʌlptəʳ] n escultor(a) m(f)

sculpture ['skʌlptʃəʳ] n escultura

scum [skʌm] n (on liquid) espuma; (pej: people) escoria

scupper ['skʌpəʳ] vt (Brit: boat) hundir; (: fig: plans etc) acabar con

scurrilous ['skʌrɪləs] adj difamatorio, calumnioso

scurry ['skʌrɪ] vi: **to ~ off** escabullirse

scurvy ['skə:vɪ] n escorbuto

scuttle ['skʌtl] n (also: **coal scuttle**) cubo, carbonera ▪ vt (ship) barrenar ▪ vi (scamper): **to ~ away, ~ off** escabullirse

scythe [saɪð] n guadaña

SD, S. Dak. abbr (US) = **South Dakota**

SDI n abbr (= Strategic Defense Initiative) IDE f

SDLP n abbr (Brit Pol) = **Social Democratic and Labour Party**

sea [si:] n mar m/f; **by ~** (travel) en barco; **on the ~** (boat) en el mar; (town) junto al mar; **to be all at ~** (fig) estar despistado; **out to** or **at ~** en alta mar; **to go by ~** ir en barco; **heavy** or **rough seas** marejada; **by** or **beside the ~** (holiday) en la playa; (village) a orillas del mar; **a ~ of faces** una multitud de caras

sea bed n fondo del mar

sea bird n ave f marina

seaboard ['si:bɔ:d] n litoral m

sea breeze n brisa de mar

seadog ['si:dɔg] n lobo de mar

seafarer ['si:fɛərəʳ] n marinero

seafaring ['si:fɛərɪŋ] adj (community) marinero; (life) de marinero

seafood ['si:fu:d] n mariscos mpl

sea front n (beach) playa; (prom) paseo marítimo

seagoing ['si:gəuɪŋ] adj (ship) de alta mar

seagull ['si:gʌl] n gaviota

seal [si:l] n (animal) foca; (stamp) sello ▪ vt (close) cerrar; (: with seal) sellar; (decide: sb's fate) decidir; (: bargain) cerrar; **~ of approval** sello de aprobación

▸ **seal off** vt obturar

seal cull n matanza de crías de foca

sea level n nivel m del mar

sealing wax ['si:lɪŋ-] n lacre m

sea lion n león m marino

sealskin ['si:lskɪn] n piel f de foca

seam [si:m] n costura; (of metal) juntura; (of coal) veta, filón m; **the hall was bursting at the seams** la sala rebosaba de gente

seaman ['si:mən] n marinero

seamanship ['si:mənʃɪp] n náutica

seamy ['si:mɪ] adj sórdido

seance ['seɪɔns] n sesión f de espiritismo

seaplane ['si:pleɪn] n hidroavión m

seaport ['si:pɔ:t] n puerto de mar

search [sə:tʃ] n (for person, thing) busca, búsqueda; (of drawer, pockets) registro; (inspection) reconocimiento ▪ vt (look in) buscar en; (examine) examinar; (person, place) registrar; (Comput) buscar ▪ vi: **to ~ for** buscar; **in ~ of** en busca de; **"~ and replace"** (Comput) "buscar y reemplazar"

▸ **search through** vt fus registrar

search engine n (Comput: Internet) buscador m

searcher ['sə:tʃəʳ] n buscador(a) m(f)

searching ['sə:tʃɪŋ] adj (question) penetrante

searchlight ['sə:tʃlaɪt] n reflector m

search party n equipo de salvamento

search warrant n mandamiento judicial

searing ['sɪərɪŋ] adj (heat) abrasador(a); (pain) agudo

seashore ['si:ʃɔ:ʳ] n playa, orilla del mar; **on the ~** a la orilla del mar

seasick ['si:sɪk] adj mareado; **to be ~** marearse

seaside ['si:saɪd] n playa, orilla del mar;
to go to the ~ ir a la playa
seaside resort n playa
season ['si:zn] n (of year) estación f; (sporting
etc) temporada; (gen) época, período ▪ vt
(food) sazonar; **to be in/out of ~** estar en
sazón/fuera de temporada; **the busy ~**
(for shops, hotels etc) la temporada alta; **the
open ~** (Hunting) la temporada de caza or de
pesca
seasonal ['si:znl] adj estacional
seasoned ['si:znd] adj (wood) curado; (fig:
worker, actor) experimentado; (troops) curtido;
~ campaigner veterano(-a)
seasoning ['si:znɪŋ] n condimento
season ticket n abono
seat [si:t] n (in bus, train: place) asiento; (chair)
silla; (Parliament) escaño; (buttocks) trasero;
(centre: of government etc) sede f ▪ vt sentar;
(have room for) tener cabida para; **are there
any seats left?** ¿quedan plazas?; **to take
one's ~** sentarse, tomar asiento; **to be
seated** estar sentado, sentarse
seat belt n cinturón m de seguridad
seating ['si:tɪŋ] n asientos mpl
seating arrangements npl distribución fsg
de los asientos
seating capacity n número de asientos,
aforo
SEATO ['si:təu] n abbr (= Southeast Asia Treaty
Organization) OTASE f
sea water n agua m del mar
seaweed ['si:wi:d] n alga marina
seaworthy ['si:wə:ðɪ] adj en condiciones de
navegar
SEC n abbr (US: = Securities and Exchange
Commission) comisión de operaciones bursátiles
sec. abbr = **second; seconds**
secateurs [sɛkə'tə:z] npl podadera sg
secede [sɪ'si:d] vi: **to ~ (from)** separarse (de)
secluded [sɪ'klu:dɪd] adj retirado
seclusion [sɪ'klu:ʒən] n retiro
second ['sɛkənd] adj segundo ▪ adv (in race
etc) en segundo lugar ▪ n (gen) segundo;
(Aut: also: **second gear**) segunda; (Comm)
artículo con algún desperfecto; (Brit Scol:
degree) título universitario de segunda clase
▪ vt (motion) apoyar [sɪ'kɔnd] (employee)
trasladar temporalmente; **~ floor** (Brit)
segundo piso; (US) primer piso; **Charles the
S~** Carlos Segundo; **to ask for a ~ opinion**
(Med) pedir una segunda opinión; **just a ~!**
¡un momento!; **to have ~ thoughts** cambiar
de opinión; **on ~ thoughts** or (US) **thought**
pensándolo bien; **~ mortgage** segunda
hipoteca
secondary ['sɛkəndərɪ] adj secundario

secondary education n enseñanza
secundaria
secondary school n escuela secundaria; ver
nota

second-best [sɛkənd'bɛst] n segundo
second-class ['sɛkənd'klɑ:s] adj de segunda
clase ▪ adv: **to send sth ~** enviar algo por
correo de segunda clase; **to travel ~** viajar
en segunda; **~ citizen** ciudadano(-a) de
segunda (clase)
second cousin n primo(-a) segundo(-a)
seconder ['sɛkəndər] n el/la que apoya una
moción
second-guess ['sɛkənd'gɛs] vt (evaluate)
juzgar (a posteriori); (anticipate): **to ~ sth/sb**
(intentar) adivinar algo/lo que va a hacer
algn
secondhand ['sɛkənd'hænd] adj de segunda
mano, usado ▪ adv: **to buy sth ~** comprar
algo de segunda mano; **to hear sth ~** oír
algo indirectamente
second hand n (on clock) segundero
second-in-command ['sɛkəndɪnkə'mɑ:
nd] n (Mil) segundo en el mando; (Admin)
segundo(-a), ayudante m/f
secondly ['sɛkəndlɪ] adv en segundo lugar
secondment [sɪ'kɔndmənt] n (Brit) traslado
temporal
second-rate ['sɛkənd'reɪt] adj de segunda
categoría
secrecy ['si:krəsɪ] n secreto
secret ['si:krɪt] adj, n secreto; **in ~** adv en
secreto; **to keep sth ~ (from sb)** ocultarle
algo (a algn); **to make no ~ of sth** no ocultar
algo
secret agent n agente m/f secreto(-a), espía
m/f
secretarial [sɛkrɪ'tɛərɪəl] adj (course) de
secretariado; (staff) de secretaría; (work,
duties) de secretaria
secretariat [sɛkrɪ'tɛərɪət] n secretaría
secretary ['sɛkrətərɪ] n secretario(-a); **S~ of
State** (Brit Pol) Ministro (con cartera)
secretary-general ['sɛkrətərɪ'dʒɛnərl] n
secretario(-a) general

secretary pool n (US) = **typing pool**
secrete [sɪ'kri:t] vt (Med, Anat, Bio) secretar;
(hide) ocultar, esconder
secretion [sɪ'kri:ʃən] n secreción f
secretive ['si:krətɪv] adj reservado, sigiloso
secretly ['si:krɪtlɪ] adv en secreto
secret police n policía secreta
secret service n servicio secreto
sect [sɛkt] n secta
sectarian [sɛk'tɛərɪən] adj sectario
section ['sɛkʃən] n sección f; (part) parte f;
(of document) artículo; (of opinion) sector m;
business ~ (Press) sección f de economía
sectional ['sɛkʃənl] adj (regional) regional,
local
sector ['sɛktər] n sector m
secular ['sɛkjulər] adj secular, seglar
secure [sɪ'kjuər] adj (free from anxiety) seguro;
(firmly fixed) firme, fijo ■ vt (fix) asegurar,
afianzar; (get) conseguir; (Comm: loan)
garantizar; **to make sth ~** afianzar algo;
to ~ sth for sb conseguir algo para algn
secured creditor [sɪ'kjuəd-] n acreedor(a)
m(f) con garantía
securely [sɪ'kjuəlɪ] adv firmemente; **it is ~
fastened** está bien sujeto
security [sɪ'kjuərɪtɪ] n seguridad f; (for loan)
fianza; (: object) prenda; **securities** npl
(Comm) valores mpl, títulos mpl; **~ of tenure**
tenencia asegurada; **to increase/tighten
~** aumentar/estrechar las medidas de
seguridad; **job ~** seguridad f en el empleo
Security Council n: **the ~** el Consejo de
Seguridad
security forces npl fuerzas fpl de seguridad
security guard n guardia m/f de seguridad
security risk n riesgo para la seguridad
secy. abbr (= secretary) Sec.
sedan [sɪ'dæn] n (US Aut) sedán m
sedate [sɪ'deɪt] adj tranquilo ■ vt
administrar sedantes a, sedar
sedation [sɪ'deɪʃən] n (Med) sedación f; **to be
under ~** estar bajo sedación
sedative ['sedɪtɪv] n sedante m, calmante m
sedentary ['sedntrɪ] adj sedentario
sediment ['sedɪmənt] n sedimento
sedimentary [sedɪ'mentərɪ] adj (Geo)
sedimentario
sedition [sɪ'dɪʃən] n sedición f
seduce [sɪ'dju:s] vt (gen) seducir
seduction [sɪ'dʌkʃən] n seducción f
seductive [sɪ'dʌktɪv] adj seductor(-a)
see [si:] (pt **saw**, pp **seen**) vt (gen) ver;
(understand) ver, comprender; (look at) mirar
■ vi ver ■ n sede f; **to ~ sb to the door**
acompañar a algn a la puerta; **to ~ that**
(ensure) asegurarse de que; **~ you soon/later/**

tomorrow! ¡hasta pronto/luego/mañana!;
as far as I can ~ por lo visto or por lo que veo;
there was nobody to be seen no se veía a
nadie; **let me ~** (show me) a ver; (let me think)
vamos a ver; **to go and ~ sb** ir a ver a algn;
~ for yourself compruébalo tú mismo;
I don't know what she sees in him no sé
qué le encuentra
▶ **see about** vt fus atender a, encargarse de
▶ **see off** vt despedir
▶ **see through** vt fus calar ■ vt llevar a cabo
▶ **see to** vt fus atender a, encargarse de
seed [si:d] n semilla; (in fruit) pepita; (fig)
germen m; (Tennis) preseleccionado(-a);
to go to ~ (plant) granar; (fig) descuidarse
seedless ['si:dlɪs] adj sin semillas or pepitas
seedling ['si:dlɪŋ] n planta de semillero
seedy ['si:dɪ] adj (person) desaseado; (place)
sórdido
seeing ['si:ɪŋ] conj: **~ (that)** visto que, en vista
de que
seek (pt, pp **sought**) [si:k, sɔ:t] vt (gen) buscar;
(post) solicitar; **to ~ advice/help from sb**
pedir consejos/solicitar ayuda a algn
▶ **seek out** vt (person) buscar
seem [si:m] vi parecer; **there seems to be ...**
parece que hay ...; **it seems (that)** ... parece
que ...; **what seems to be the trouble?** ¿qué
pasa?; **I did what seemed best** hice lo que
parecía mejor
seemingly ['si:mɪŋlɪ] adv aparentemente,
según parece
seen [si:n] pp of **see**
seep [si:p] vi filtrarse
seer [sɪər] n vidente m/f, profeta m/f
seersucker [sɪə'sʌkər] n sirsaca
seesaw ['si:sɔ:] n balancín m, subibaja m
seethe [si:ð] vi hervir; **to ~ with anger**
enfurecerse
see-through ['si:θru:] adj transparente
segment ['segmənt] n segmento
segregate ['segrɪgeɪt] vt segregar
segregation [segrɪ'geɪʃən] n segregación f
Seine [seɪn] n Sena m
seismic ['saɪzmɪk] adj sísmico
seize [si:z] vt (grasp) agarrar, asir; (take
possession of) secuestrar; (: territory) apoderarse
de; (opportunity) aprovecharse de
▶ **seize up** vi (Tech) agarrotarse
▶ **seize (up)on** vt fus valerse de
seizure ['si:ʒər] n (Med) ataque m; (Law)
incautación f
seldom ['seldəm] adv rara vez
select [sɪ'lɛkt] adj selecto, escogido; (hotel,
restaurant, clubs) exclusivo ■ vt escoger,
elegir; (Sport) seleccionar; **a ~ few** una
minoría selecta

S

selection [sɪˈlɛkʃən] n selección f, elección f; (Comm) surtido
selection committee n comisión f de nombramiento
selective [sɪˈlɛktɪv] adj selectivo
self [sɛlf] n (pl **selves**) [sɛlvz] uno mismo ■ pref auto...; **the ~** el yo
self-addressed [ˈsɛlfəˈdrɛst] adj: **~ envelope** sobre m con la dirección propia
self-adhesive [sɛlfədˈhiːzɪv] adj autoadhesivo, autoadherente
self-appointed [sɛlfəˈpɔɪntɪd] adj autonombrado
self-assurance [sɛlfəˈʃuərəns] n confianza en sí mismo
self-assured [sɛlfəˈʃuəd] adj seguro de sí mismo
self-catering [sɛlfˈkeɪtərɪŋ] adj (Brit) sin pensión or servicio de comida; **~ apartment** apartamento con cocina propia
self-centred, self-centered (US) [sɛlfˈsɛntəd] adj egocéntrico
self-cleaning [sɛlfˈkliːnɪŋ] adj autolimpiador
self-confessed [sɛlfkənˈfɛst] adj (alcoholic etc) confeso
self-confidence [sɛlfˈkɔnfɪdns] n confianza en sí mismo
self-confident [sɛlfˈkɔnfɪdnt] adj seguro de sí (mismo), lleno de confianza en sí mismo
self-conscious [sɛlfˈkɔnʃəs] adj cohibido
self-contained [sɛlfkənˈteɪnd] adj (gen) independiente; (Brit: flat) con entrada particular
self-control [sɛlfkənˈtrəul] n autodominio
self-defeating [sɛlfdɪˈfiːtɪŋ] adj contraproducente
self-defence, self-defense (US) [sɛlfdɪˈfɛns] n defensa propia
self-discipline [sɛlfˈdɪsɪplɪn] n autodisciplina
self-employed [sɛlfɪmˈplɔɪd] adj que trabaja por cuenta propia, autónomo
self-esteem [sɛlfɪˈstiːm] n amor m propio
self-evident [sɛlfˈɛvɪdnt] adj patente
self-explanatory [sɛlfɪksˈplænətərɪ] adj que no necesita explicación
self-financing [sɛlffaɪˈnænsɪŋ] adj autofinanciado
self-governing [sɛlfˈɡʌvənɪŋ] adj autónomo
self-help [ˈsɛlfˈhɛlp] n autosuficiencia, ayuda propia
self-importance [sɛlfɪmˈpɔːtns] n presunción f, vanidad f
self-important [sɛlfɪmˈpɔːtnt] adj vanidoso
self-indulgent [sɛlfɪnˈdʌldʒənt] adj indulgente consigo mismo

self-inflicted [sɛlfɪnˈflɪktɪd] adj infligido a sí mismo
self-interest [sɛlfˈɪntrɪst] n egoísmo
selfish [ˈsɛlfɪʃ] adj egoísta
selfishly [ˈsɛlfɪʃlɪ] adv con egoísmo, de modo egoísta
selfishness [ˈsɛlfɪʃnɪs] n egoísmo
selfless [ˈsɛlflɪs] adj desinteresado
selflessly [ˈsɛlflɪslɪ] adv desinteresadamente
self-made man [ˈsɛlfmeɪd-] n hombre que ha triunfado por su propio esfuerzo
self-pity [sɛlfˈpɪtɪ] n lástima de sí mismo
self-portrait [sɛlfˈpɔːtreɪt] n autorretrato
self-possessed [sɛlfpəˈzɛst] adj sereno, dueño de sí mismo
self-preservation [ˈsɛlfprɛzəˈveɪʃən] n propia conservación f
self-propelled [sɛlfprəˈpɛld] adj autopropulsado, automotor(-triz)
self-raising [sɛlfˈreɪzɪŋ], **self-rising** (US) [sɛlfˈraɪzɪŋ] adj: **~ flour** harina con levadura
self-reliant [sɛlfrɪˈlaɪənt] adj independiente, autosuficiente
self-respect [sɛlfrɪˈspɛkt] n amor m propio
self-respecting [sɛlfrɪˈspɛktɪŋ] adj que tiene amor propio
self-righteous [sɛlfˈraɪtʃəs] adj santurrón(-ona)
self-rising [sɛlfˈraɪzɪŋ] adj (US) = **self-raising**
self-sacrifice [sɛlfˈsækrɪfaɪs] n abnegación f
self-same [sɛlfseɪm] adj mismo, mismísimo
self-satisfied [sɛlfˈsætɪsfaɪd] adj satisfecho de sí mismo
self-service [sɛlfˈsəːvɪs] adj de autoservicio
self-styled [ˈsɛlfstaɪld] adj supuesto, sedicente
self-sufficient [sɛlfsəˈfɪʃənt] adj autosuficiente
self-supporting [sɛlfsəˈpɔːtɪŋ] adj económicamente independiente
self-tanning [sɛlfˈtænɪŋ] adj autobronceador
self-taught [sɛlfˈtɔːt] adj autodidacta
self-test [ˈsɛlftɛst] n (Comput) autocomprobación f
sell (pt, pp **sold**) [sɛl, səuld] vt vender ■ vi venderse; **to ~ at** or **for £10** venderse a 10 libras; **to ~ sb an idea** (fig) convencer a algn de una idea
  ▸ **sell off** vt liquidar
  ▸ **sell out** vi transigir, transar (LAm); **to ~ out (to sb/sth)** (Comm) vender su negocio (a algn/algo) ■ vt agotar las existencias de, venderlo todo; **the tickets are all sold out** las entradas están agotadas
  ▸ **sell up** vi (Comm) liquidarse
sell-by date [ˈsɛlbaɪ-] n fecha de caducidad

seller ['sɛlə'] n vendedor(a) m(f); **~'s market** mercado de demanda

selling price ['sɛlɪŋ-] n precio de venta

Sellotape® ['sɛləuteɪp] n (Brit) cinta adhesiva, celo, scotch® m

sellout ['sɛlaut] n traición f; **it was a ~** (Theat etc) fue un éxito de taquilla

selves [sɛlvz] npl of **self**

semantic [sɪ'mæntɪk] adj semántico

semaphore ['sɛməfɔ:'] n semáforo

semblance ['sɛmbləns] n apariencia

semen ['si:mən] n semen m

semester [sɪ'mɛstə'] n (US) semestre m

semi ['sɛmɪ] n = **semidetached house**

semi... [sɛmɪ] pref semi..., medio...

semicircle ['sɛmɪsə:kl] n semicírculo

semicircular ['sɛmɪ'sə:kjulə'] adj semicircular

semicolon [sɛmɪ'kəulən] n punto y coma

semiconductor [sɛmɪkən'dʌktə'] n semiconductor m

semiconscious [sɛmɪ'kɔnʃəs] adj semiconsciente

semidetached [sɛmɪdɪ'tætʃt], **semidetached house** n casa adosada

semi-final [sɛmɪ'faɪnl] n semifinal f

seminar ['sɛmɪnɑ:'] n seminario

seminary ['sɛmɪnərɪ] n (Rel) seminario

semiprecious stone [sɛmɪ'prɛʃəs-] n piedra semipreciosa

semiquaver ['sɛmɪkweɪvə'] n (Brit) semicorchea

semiskilled ['sɛmɪskɪld] adj (work, worker) semicualificado

semi-skimmed adj semidesnatado

semitone ['sɛmɪtəun] n semitono

semolina [sɛmə'li:nə] n sémola

Sen., sen. abbr = **senator; senior**

senate ['sɛnɪt] n senado; see also **Congress**

senator ['sɛnɪtə'] n senador(a) m(f)

send (pt, pp **sent**) [sɛnd, sɛnt] vt mandar, enviar; **to ~ by post** mandar por correo; **to ~ sb for sth** mandar a algn a buscar algo; **to ~ word that ...** avisar or mandar aviso de que ...; **she sends (you) her love** te manda or envía cariñosos recuerdos; **to ~ sb to sleep/ into fits of laughter** dormir/hacer reír a algn; **to ~ sb flying** echar a algn; **to ~ sth flying** tirar algo

▶ **send away** vt (letter, goods) despachar

▶ **send away for** vt fus pedir

▶ **send back** vt devolver

▶ **send for** vt fus mandar traer; (by post) escribir pidiendo algo

▶ **send in** vt (report, application, resignation) mandar

▶ **send off** vt (goods) despachar; (Brit Sport: player) expulsar

▶ **send on** vt (letter) mandar, expedir; (luggage etc: in advance) facturar

▶ **send out** vt (invitation) mandar; (emit: light, heat) emitir, difundir; (signal) emitir

▶ **send round** vt (letter, document etc) hacer circular

▶ **send up** vt (person, price) hacer subir; (Brit: parody) parodiar

sender ['sɛndə'] n remitente m/f

send-off ['sɛndɔf] n: **a good ~** una buena despedida

send-up ['sɛndʌp] n (col) parodia, sátira

Senegal [sɛnɪ'gɔ:l] n Senegal m

Senegalese [sɛnɪgə'li:z] adj, n senegalés(-esa) m(f)

senile ['si:naɪl] adj senil

senility [sɪ'nɪlɪtɪ] n senilidad f

senior ['si:nɪə'] adj (older) mayor, más viejo; (: on staff) más antiguo; (of higher rank) superior ■ n mayor m; **P. Jones ~** P. Jones padre

senior citizen n persona de la tercera edad

senior high school n (US) = instituto de enseñanza media; see also **high school**

seniority [si:nɪ'ɔrɪtɪ] n antigüedad f; (in rank) rango superior

sensation [sɛn'seɪʃən] n (physical feeling, impression) sensación f

sensational [sɛn'seɪʃənl] adj sensacional

sense [sɛns] n (faculty, meaning) sentido; (feeling) sensación f; (good sense) sentido común, juicio ■ vt sentir, percibir; **~ of humour** sentido del humor; **it makes ~** tiene sentido; **there is no ~ in (doing) that** no tiene sentido (hacer) eso; **to come to one's senses** (regain consciousness) volver en sí, recobrar el sentido; **to take leave of one's senses** perder el juicio

senseless ['sɛnslɪs] adj estúpido, insensato; (unconscious) sin conocimiento

senselessly ['sɛnslɪslɪ] adv estúpidamente, insensatamente

sensibility [sɛnsɪ'brɪlɪtɪ] n sensibilidad f; **sensibilities** npl delicadeza sg

sensible ['sɛnsɪbl] adj sensato; (reasonable) razonable, lógico

sensibly ['sɛnsɪblɪ] adv sensatamente; razonablemente, de modo lógico

sensitive ['sɛnsɪtɪv] adj sensible; (touchy) susceptible; **he is very ~ about it** es muy susceptible acerca de eso

sensitivity [sɛnsɪ'tɪvɪtɪ] n sensibilidad f; susceptibilidad f

sensual ['sɛnsjuəl] adj sensual

sensuous ['sɛnsjuəs] adj sensual

sent [sɛnt] pt, pp of **send**

sentence ['sɛntəns] n (Ling) frase f, oración f; (Law) sentencia, fallo ▪ vt: **to ~ sb to death/ to five years** condenar a algn a muerte/a cinco años de cárcel; **to pass ~ on sb** (also fig) sentenciar or condenar a algn

sentiment ['sɛntɪmənt] n sentimiento; (opinion) opinión f

sentimental [sɛntɪ'mɛntl] adj sentimental

sentimentality [sɛntɪmen'tælɪtɪ] n sentimentalismo, sensiblería

sentinel ['sɛntɪnl] n centinela m

sentry ['sɛntrɪ] n centinela m

sentry duty n: **to be on ~** estar de guardia, hacer guardia

Seoul [səul] n Seúl m

separable ['sɛpərəbl] adj separable

separate [adj 'sɛprɪt, vb 'sɛpəreɪt] adj separado; (distinct) distinto ▪ vt separar; (part) dividir ▪ vi separarse; **~ from** separado or distinto de; **under ~ cover** (Comm) por separado; **to ~ into** dividir or separar en; **he is separated from his wife, but not divorced** está separado de su mujer, pero no (está) divorciado

separately ['sɛprɪtlɪ] adv por separado

separates ['sɛprɪts] npl (clothes) coordinados mpl

separation [sɛpə'reɪʃən] n separación f

sepia ['si:pɪə] adj color sepia inv

Sept. abbr (= September) sep

September [sɛp'tɛmbəʳ] n se(p)tiembre m; see also **July**

septic ['sɛptɪk] adj séptico; **to go ~** ponerse séptico

septicaemia, septicemia (US) [sɛptɪ'si:mɪə] n septicemia

septic tank n fosa séptica

sequel ['si:kwl] n consecuencia, resultado; (of story) continuación f

sequence ['si:kwəns] n sucesión f, serie f; (Cine) secuencia; **in ~** en orden or serie

sequential [sɪ'kwɛnʃəl] adj: **~ access** (Comput) acceso en serie

sequin ['si:kwɪn] n lentejuela

Serb [sə:b] adj, n = **Serbian**

Serbia ['sə:bɪə] n Serbia

Serbian ['sə:bɪən] adj serbio ▪ n serbio(-a); (Ling) serbio

Serbo-Croat ['sə:bəu'krəuæt] n (Ling) serbocroata m

serenade [sɛrə'neɪd] n serenata ▪ vt dar serenata a

serene [sɪ'ri:n] adj sereno, tranquilo

serenely [sɪ'ri:nlɪ] adv serenamente, tranquilamente

serenity [sə'rɛnɪtɪ] n serenidad f, tranquilidad f

sergeant ['sɑ:dʒənt] n sargento

sergeant major n sargento mayor

serial ['sɪərɪəl] n novela por entregas; (TV) telenovela

serial access n (Comput) acceso en serie

serial interface n (Comput) interface m en serie

serialize ['sɪərɪəlaɪz] vt publicar/televisar por entregas

serial killer n asesino(-a) múltiple

serial number n número de serie

series ['sɪəri:z] n (pl inv) serie f

serious ['sɪərɪəs] adj serio; (grave) grave; **are you ~ (about it)?** ¿lo dices en serio?

seriously ['sɪərɪəslɪ] adv en serio; (ill, wounded etc) gravemente; (col: extremely) de verdad; **to take sth/sb ~** tomar algo/a algn en serio; **he's ~ rich** es una pasada de rico

seriousness ['sɪərɪəsnɪs] n seriedad f; gravedad f

sermon ['sə:mən] n sermón m

serpent ['sə:pənt] n serpiente f

serrated [sɪ'reɪtɪd] adj serrado, dentellado

serum ['sɪərəm] n suero

servant ['sə:vənt] n (gen) servidor(a) m(f); (also: **house servant**) criado(-a) m(f)

serve [sə:v] vt servir; (customer) atender; (train) tener parada en; (apprenticeship) hacer; (prison term) cumplir ▪ vi (servant, soldier etc) servir; (Tennis) sacar ▪ n (Tennis) saque m; **it serves him right** se lo merece, se lo tiene merecido; **to ~ a summons on sb** entregar una citación a algn; **it serves my purpose** me sirve para lo que quiero; **are you being served?** ¿le atienden?; **the power station serves the entire region** la central eléctrica abastece a toda la región; **to ~ as/for/to do** servir de/para/para hacer; **to ~ on a committee/a jury** ser miembro de una comisión/un jurado

▸ **serve out, serve up** vt (food) servir

service ['sə:vɪs] n (gen) servicio; (Rel: Catholic) misa; (: other) oficio (religioso); (Aut) mantenimiento; (of dishes) juego ▪ vt (car, washing machine) mantener; (: repair) reparar; **the Services** las fuerzas armadas; **funeral ~** exequias fpl; **to hold a ~** celebrar un oficio religioso; **the essential services** los servicios esenciales; **medical/social services** servicios mpl médicos/sociales; **the train ~ to London** los trenes a Londres; **to be of ~ to sb** ser útil a algn

serviceable ['sə:vɪsəbl] adj servible, utilizable

service area n (on motorway) área de servicios

service charge n (Brit) servicio

service industries npl industrias fpl del servicio
serviceman ['sə:vɪsmən] n militar m
service station n estación f de servicio
servicing ['sə:vɪsɪŋ] n (of car) revisión f; (of washing machine etc) servicio de reparaciones
serviette [sə:vɪ'ɛt] n (Brit) servilleta
servile ['sə:vaɪl] adj servil
session ['sɛʃən] n (sitting) sesión f; **to be in ~** estar en sesión
session musician n músico m/f de estudio
set [sɛt] (pt, pp ~) n juego; (Radio) aparato m; (TV) televisor m; (of utensils) batería; (of cutlery) cubierto; (of books) colección f; (Tennis) set m; (group of people) grupo; (Cine) plató m; (Theat) decorado; (Hairdressing) marcado ▪ adj (fixed) fijo; (ready) listo; (resolved) resuelto, decidido ▪ vt (place) poner, colocar; (fix) fijar; (adjust) ajustar, arreglar; (decide: rules etc) establecer, decidir; (assign: task) asignar; (: homework) poner ▪ vi (sun) ponerse; (jam, jelly) cuajarse; (concrete) fraguar; **a ~ of false teeth** una dentadura postiza; **a ~ of dining-room furniture** muebles mpl de comedor; **~ in one's ways** con costumbres arraigadas; **a ~ phrase** una frase hecha; **to be all ~ to do sth** estar listo para hacer algo; **to be ~ on doing sth** estar empeñado en hacer algo; **a novel ~ in Valencia** una novela ambientada en Valencia; **to ~ to music** poner música a; **to ~ on fire** incendiar, prender fuego a; **to ~ free** poner en libertad; **to ~ sth going** poner algo en marcha; **to ~ sail** zarpar, hacerse a la mar
  ▶ **set about** vt fus: **to ~ about doing sth** ponerse a hacer algo
  ▶ **set aside** vt poner aparte, dejar de lado
  ▶ **set back** vt (progress): **to ~ back (by)** retrasar (por); **a house ~ back from the road** una casa apartada de la carretera
  ▶ **set down** vt (bus, train) dejar; (record) poner por escrito
  ▶ **set in** vi (infection) declararse; (complications) comenzar; **the rain has ~ in for the day** parece que va a llover todo el día
  ▶ **set off** vi partir ▪ vt (bomb) hacer estallar; (cause to start) poner en marcha; (show up well) hacer resaltar
  ▶ **set out** vi: **to ~ out to do sth** proponerse hacer algo ▪ vt (arrange) disponer; (state) exponer; **to ~ out (from)** salir (de)
  ▶ **set up** vt (organization) establecer
setback ['sɛtbæk] n (hitch) revés m, contratiempo; (in health) recaída
set menu n menú m
set phrase n frase f hecha
set square n cartabón m

settee [sɛ'ti:] n sofá m
setting ['sɛtɪŋ] n (scenery) marco; (of jewel) engaste m, montadura
setting lotion n fijador m (para el pelo)
settle ['sɛtl] vt (argument, matter) resolver; (pay: bill, accounts) pagar, liquidar; (colonize: land) colonizar; (Med: calm) calmar, sosegar ▪ vi (dust etc) depositarse; (weather) estabilizarse; (also: **settle down**) instalarse; (calm down) tranquilizarse; **to ~ for sth** convenir en aceptar algo; **to ~ on sth** decidirse por algo; **that's settled then** bueno, está arreglado; **to ~ one's stomach** asentar el estómago
  ▶ **settle in** vi instalarse
  ▶ **settle up** vi: **to ~ up with sb** ajustar cuentas con algn
settlement ['sɛtlmənt] n (payment) liquidación f; (agreement) acuerdo, convenio; (village etc) poblado; **in ~ of our account** (Comm) en pago or liquidación de nuestra cuenta
settler ['sɛtlər] n colono(-a), colonizador(a) m(f)
setup ['sɛtʌp] n sistema m
seven ['sɛvn] num siete
seventeen [sɛvn'ti:n] num diez y siete, diecisiete
seventh ['sɛvnθ] adj séptimo
seventy ['sɛvntɪ] num setenta
sever ['sɛvər] vt cortar; (relations) romper
several ['sɛvərl] adj, pron varios(-as) m(f)pl, algunos(-as) m(f)pl; **~ of us** varios de nosotros; **~ times** varias veces
severance ['sɛvərəns] n (of relations) ruptura
severance pay n indemnización f por despido
severe [sɪ'vɪər] adj severo; (serious) grave; (hard) duro; (pain) intenso
severely [sɪ'vɪəlɪ] adv severamente; (wounded, ill) de gravedad, gravemente
severity [sɪ'vɛrɪtɪ] n severidad f; gravedad f; intensidad f
Seville [sə'vɪl] n Sevilla
sew (pt **sewed**, pp **sewn**) [səu, səud, səun] vt, vi coser
  ▶ **sew up** vt coser
sewage ['su:ɪdʒ] n (effluence) aguas fpl residuales; (system) alcantarillado
sewage works n estación f depuradora (de aguas residuales)
sewer ['su:ər] n alcantarilla, cloaca
sewing ['səuɪŋ] n costura
sewing machine n máquina de coser
sewn [səun] pp of **sew**
sex [sɛks] n sexo; **the opposite ~** el sexo opuesto; **to have ~ with sb** tener relaciones (sexuales) con algn

S

sex act n acto sexual, coito
sex appeal n sex-appeal m, gancho
sex education n educación f sexual
sexism ['sɛksɪzəm] n sexismo
sexist ['sɛksɪst] adj, n sexista m/f
sex life n vida sexual
sex object n objeto sexual
sextant ['sɛkstənt] n sextante m
sextet [sɛks'tɛt] n sexteto
sexual ['sɛksjuəl] adj sexual; **~ assault**
atentado contra el pudor; **~ harassment**
acoso sexual; **~ intercourse** relaciones fpl
sexuales
sexually ['sɛksjuəlɪ] adv sexualmente
sexy ['sɛksɪ] adj sexy
Seychelles [seɪ'ʃɛlz] npl: **the ~** las Seychelles
SF n abbr = **science fiction**
SG n abbr (US: = Surgeon General) jefe del servicio
federal de sanidad
Sgt. abbr (= sergeant) Sgto.
shabbily ['ʃæbɪlɪ] adv (treat) injustamente;
(dressed) pobremente
shabbiness ['ʃæbɪnɪs] n (of dress, person)
aspecto desharrapado; (of building) mal
estado
shabby ['ʃæbɪ] adj (person) desharrapado;
(clothes) raído, gastado
shack [ʃæk] n choza, chabola
shackle ['ʃækl] vt encadenar; (fig): **to be
shackled by sth** verse obstaculizado por
algo
shackles ['ʃæklz] npl grillos mpl, grilletes mpl
shade [ʃeɪd] n sombra; (for lamp) pantalla;
(for eyes) visera; (of colour) tono m, tonalidad f;
(US: window shade) persiana ■ vt dar sombra
a; **shades** npl (US: sunglasses) gafas fpl de sol;
in the ~ a la sombra; (small quantity): **a ~ of**
un poquito de; **a ~ smaller** un poquito más
pequeño
shadow ['ʃædəu] n sombra ■ vt (follow)
seguir y vigilar; **without** or **beyond a ~ of
doubt** sin lugar a dudas
shadow cabinet n (Brit Pol) gobierno en la
oposición
shadowy ['ʃædəuɪ] adj oscuro; (dim)
indistinto
shady ['ʃeɪdɪ] adj sombreado; (fig: dishonest)
sospechoso; (deal) turbio
shaft [ʃɑːft] n (of arrow, spear) astil m; (Aut, Tech)
eje m, árbol m; (of mine) pozo; (of lift) hueco,
caja; (of light) rayo; **ventilator ~** chimenea de
ventilación
shaggy ['ʃægɪ] adj peludo
shake [ʃeɪk] (pt **shook**, pp **shaken**) ['ʃeɪkn] vt
sacudir; (building) hacer temblar; (perturb)
inquietar, perturbar; (weaken) debilitar;
(alarm) trastornar ■ vi estremecerse;

(tremble) temblar ■ n (movement) sacudida;
to ~ one's head (in refusal) negar con la
cabeza; (in dismay) mover or menear la cabeza,
incrédulo; **to ~ hands with sb** estrechar
la mano a algn; **to ~ in one's shoes** (fig)
temblar de miedo
▸ **shake off** vt sacudirse; (fig) deshacerse de
▸ **shake up** vt agitar
shake-up ['ʃeɪkʌp] n reorganización f
shakily ['ʃeɪkɪlɪ] adv (reply) con voz temblorosa
or trémula; (walk) con paso vacilante; (write)
con mano temblorosa
shaky ['ʃeɪkɪ] adj (unstable) inestable, poco
firme; (trembling) tembloroso; (health)
delicado; (memory) defectuoso; (person: from
illness) temblando; (premise etc) incierto
shale [ʃeɪl] n esquisto
shall [ʃæl] aux vb: **I ~ go** iré
shallot [ʃə'lɔt] n (Brit) cebollita, chalote m
shallow ['ʃæləu] adj poco profundo; (fig)
superficial
shallows ['ʃæləuz] npl bajío sg, bajos mpl
sham [ʃæm] n fraude m, engaño ■ adj falso,
fingido ■ vt fingir, simular
shambles ['ʃæmblz] n desorden m, confusión
f; **the economy is (in) a complete ~** la
economía está en un estado desastroso
shambolic [ʃæm'bɔlɪk] adj (col) caótico
shame [ʃeɪm] n vergüenza; (pity) lástima,
pena ■ vt avergonzar; **it is a ~ that/to do**
es una lástima or pena que/hacer; **what a ~!**
¡qué lástima or pena!; **to put sth/sb to ~** (fig)
ridiculizar algo/a algn
shamefaced ['ʃeɪmfeɪst] adj avergonzado
shameful ['ʃeɪmful] adj vergonzoso
shamefully ['ʃeɪmfulɪ] adv vergonzosamente
shameless ['ʃeɪmlɪs] adj descarado
shampoo [ʃæm'puː] n champú m ■ vt lavar
con champú
shampoo and set n lavado y marcado
shamrock ['ʃæmrɔk] n trébol m
shandy ['ʃændɪ], **shandygaff** (US)
['ʃændɪgæf] n clara, cerveza con gaseosa
shan't [ʃɑːnt], **shall not**
shanty town ['ʃæntɪ-] n barrio de chabolas
SHAPE [ʃeɪp] n abbr (= Supreme Headquarters
Allied Powers, Europe) cuartel general de las fuerzas
aliadas en Europa
shape [ʃeɪp] n forma ■ vt formar, dar forma
a; (clay) modelar; (stone) labrar; (sb's ideas)
formar; (sb's life) determinar ■ vi (also: **shape
up**: events) desarrollarse; (person) formarse;
to take ~ tomar forma; **to get o.s. into ~**
ponerse en forma or en condiciones; **in the ~
of a heart** en forma de corazón; **I can't bear
gardening in any ~ or form** no aguanto la
jardinería de ningún modo

-shaped *suff*: **heart~** en forma de corazón

shapeless ['ʃeɪplɪs] *adj* informe, sin forma definida

shapely ['ʃeɪplɪ] *adj* bien formado *or* proporcionado

share [ʃɛəʳ] *n* (*part*) parte *f*, porción *f*; (*contribution*) cuota; (*Comm*) acción *f* ▪ *vt* dividir; (*fig: have in common*) compartir; **to have a ~ in the profits** tener una proporción de las ganancias; **he has a 50% ~ in a new business venture** tiene una participación del 50% en un nuevo negocio; **to ~ in** participar en; **to ~ out (among** *or* **between)** repartir (entre)

share capital *n* (*Comm*) capital *m* social en acciones

share certificate *n* certificado *or* título de una acción

shareholder ['ʃɛəhəʊldəʳ] *n* (*Brit*) accionista *m/f*

share index *n* (*Comm*) índice *m* de la bolsa

share issue *n* emisión *f* de acciones

share price *n* (*Comm*) cotización *f*

shark [ʃɑːk] *n* tiburón *m*

sharp [ʃɑːp] *adj* (*razor, knife*) afilado; (*point*) puntiagudo; (*outline*) definido; (*pain*) intenso; (*Mus*) desafinado; (*contrast*) marcado; (*voice*) agudo; (*curve, bend*) cerrado; (*person: quick-witted*) avispado; (·*dishonest*) poco escrupuloso ▪ *n* (*Mus*) sostenido ▪ *adv*: **at two o'clock ~** a las dos en punto; **to be ~ with sb** hablar a algn de forma brusca y tajante; **turn ~ left** tuerce del todo a la izquierda

sharpen ['ʃɑːpn] *vt* afilar; (*pencil*) sacar punta a; (*fig*) agudizar

sharpener ['ʃɑːpnəʳ] *n* (*gen*) afilador *m*; (*also*: **pencil sharpener**) sacapuntas *m inv*

sharp-eyed [ʃɑːp'aɪd] *adj* de vista aguda

sharpish ['ʃɑːpɪʃ] *adv* (*Brit col: quickly*) prontito, bien pronto

sharply ['ʃɑːplɪ] *adv* (*abruptly*) bruscamente; (*clearly*) claramente; (*harshly*) severamente

sharp-tempered [ʃɑːp'tɛmpəd] *adj* de genio arisco

sharp-witted [ʃɑːp'wɪtɪd] *adj* listo, despabilado

shatter ['ʃætəʳ] *vt* hacer añicos *or* pedazos; (*fig: ruin*) destruir, acabar con ▪ *vi* hacerse añicos

shattered ['ʃætəd] *adj* (*grief-stricken*) destrozado, deshecho; (*exhausted*) agotado, hecho polvo

shattering ['ʃætərɪŋ] *adj* (*experience*) devastador(a), anonadante

shatterproof ['ʃætəpruːf] *adj* inastillable

shave [ʃeɪv] *vt* afeitar, rasurar ▪ *vi* afeitarse ▪ *n*: **to have a ~** afeitarse

shaven ['ʃeɪvn] *adj* (*head*) rapado

shaver ['ʃeɪvəʳ] *n* (*also*: **electric shaver**) máquina de afeitar (eléctrica)

shaving ['ʃeɪvɪŋ] *n* (*action*) afeitado; **shavings** *npl* (*of wood etc*) virutas *fpl*

shaving brush *n* brocha (de afeitar)

shaving cream *n* crema (de afeitar)

shaving point *n* enchufe *m* para máquinas de afeitar

shaving soap *n* jabón *m* de afeitar

shawl [ʃɔːl] *n* chal *m*

she [ʃiː] *pron* ella; **there ~ is** allí está; **~-cat** gata, NB: *for ships, countries follow the gender of your translation*

sheaf (*pl* **sheaves**) [ʃiːf, ʃiːvz] *n* (*of corn*) gavilla; (*of arrows*) haz *m*; (*of papers*) fajo

shear [ʃɪəʳ] *vt* (*pt, pp* **sheared** *or* **shorn**) [ʃɔːn] (*sheep*) esquilar, trasquilar
  ▸ **shear off** *vi* romperse

shears [ʃɪəz] *npl* (*for hedge*) tijeras *fpl* de jardín

sheath [ʃiːθ] *n* vaina; (*contraceptive*) preservativo

sheath knife *n* cuchillo de monte

sheaves [ʃiːvz] *npl* of **sheaf**

shed [ʃɛd] *n* cobertizo; (*Industry, Rail*) nave *f* ▪ *vt* (*pt, pp* **shed**) (*skin*) mudar; (*tears*) derramar; **to ~ light on** (*problem, mystery*) aclarar, arrojar luz sobre

she'd [ʃiːd] = **she had; she would**

sheen [ʃiːn] *n* brillo, lustre *m*

sheep [ʃiːp] *n* (*pl inv*) oveja

sheepdog ['ʃiːpdɔg] *n* perro pastor

sheep farmer *n* ganadero (de ovejas)

sheepish ['ʃiːpɪʃ] *adj* tímido, vergonzoso

sheepskin ['ʃiːpskɪn] *n* piel *f* de carnero

sheepskin jacket *n* zamarra

sheer [ʃɪəʳ] *adj* (*utter*) puro, completo; (*steep*) escarpado; (*material*) diáfano ▪ *adv* verticalmente; **by ~ chance** de pura casualidad

sheet [ʃiːt] *n* (*on bed*) sábana; (*of paper*) hoja; (*of glass, metal*) lámina

sheet feed *n* (*on printer*) alimentador *m* de papel

sheet lightning *n* relámpago (difuso)

sheet metal *n* metal *m* en lámina

sheet music *n* hojas *fpl* de partitura

sheik, sheikh [ʃeɪk] *n* jeque *m*

shelf (*pl* **shelves**) [ʃɛlf, ʃɛlvz] *n* estante *m*

shelf life *n* (*Comm*) periodo de conservación antes de la venta

shell [ʃɛl] *n* (*on beach*) concha, caracol (*LAm*); (*of egg, nut etc*) cáscara; (*explosive*) proyectil *m*, obús *m*; (*of building*) armazón *m* ▪ *vt* (*peas*) desenvainar; (*Mil*) bombardear

S

▶ **shell out** vi (col): **to ~ out (for)** soltar el dinero (para), desembolsar (para)

she'll [ʃiːl] = **she will; she shall**

shellfish [ˈʃelfɪʃ] n pl inv crustáceo; (pl: as food) mariscos mpl

shellsuit [ˈʃelsuːt] n chándal m (de tactel®)

shelter [ˈʃeltəʳ] n abrigo, refugio ▪ vt (aid) amparar, proteger; (give lodging to) abrigar; (hide) esconder ▪ vi abrigarse, refugiarse; **to take ~ (from)** refugiarse or asilarse (de); **bus ~** parada de autobús cubierta

sheltered [ˈʃeltəd] adj (life) protegido; (spot) abrigado

shelve [ʃelv] vt (fig) dar carpetazo a

shelves [ʃelvz] npl of **shelf**

shelving [ˈʃelvɪŋ] n estantería

shepherd [ˈʃepəd] n pastor m ▪ vt (guide) guiar, conducir

shepherdess [ˈʃepədɪs] n pastora

shepherd's pie n pastel de carne y puré de patatas

sherbert [ˈʃəːbət] n (Brit: powder) polvos mpl azucarados; (US: water ice) sorbete m

sheriff [ˈʃerɪf] n (US) sheriff m

sherry [ˈʃerɪ] n jerez m

she's [ʃiːz] = **she is; she has**

Shetland [ˈʃetlənd] n (also: **the Shetlands, the Shetland Isles**) las Islas fpl Shetland

Shetland pony n pony m de Shetland

shield [ʃiːld] n escudo; (Tech) blindaje m ▪ vt: **to ~ (from)** proteger (de)

shift [ʃɪft] n (change) cambio; (at work) turno ▪ vt trasladar; (remove) quitar ▪ vi moverse; (change place) cambiar de sitio; **the wind has shifted to the south** el viento ha virado al sur; **a ~ in demand** (Comm) un desplazamiento de la demanda

shift key n (on typewriter) tecla de mayúsculas

shiftless [ˈʃɪftlɪs] adj (person) vago

shift work n (Brit) trabajo por turnos; **to do ~** trabajar por turnos

shifty [ˈʃɪftɪ] adj tramposo; (eyes) furtivo

Shiite [ˈʃiːaɪt] adj, n shiíta m/f

shilling [ˈʃɪlɪŋ] n (Brit) chelín m (= 12 old pence; 20 in a pound)

shilly-shally [ˈʃɪlɪʃælɪ] vi titubear, vacilar

shimmer [ˈʃɪməʳ] n reflejo trémulo ▪ vi relucir

shimmering [ˈʃɪmərɪŋ] adj reluciente; (haze) trémulo; (satin etc) lustroso

shin [ʃɪn] n espinilla ▪ vi: **to ~ down/up a tree** bajar de/trepar un árbol

shindig [ˈʃɪndɪg] n (col) fiesta, juerga

shine [ʃaɪn] (pt, pp **shone**) n brillo, lustre m ▪ vi brillar, relucir ▪ vt (shoes) lustrar, sacar brillo a; **to ~ a torch on sth** dirigir una linterna hacia algo

shingle [ˈʃɪŋgl] n (on beach) guijarras fpl

shingles [ˈʃɪŋglz] n (Med) herpes msg

shining [ˈʃaɪnɪŋ] adj (surface, hair) lustroso; (light) brillante

shiny [ˈʃaɪnɪ] adj brillante, lustroso

ship [ʃɪp] n buque m, barco ▪ vt (goods) embarcar; (oars) desarmar; (send) transportar or enviar por vía marítima; **~'s manifest** manifiesto del buque; **on board ~** a bordo

shipbuilder [ˈʃɪpbɪldəʳ] n constructor(a) m(f) naval

shipbuilding [ˈʃɪpbɪldɪŋ] n construcción f naval

ship canal n canal m de navegación

ship chandler [-ˈtʃɑːndləʳ] n proveedor m de efectos navales

shipment [ˈʃɪpmənt] n (act) embarque m; (goods) envío

shipowner [ˈʃɪpəunəʳ] n naviero, armador m

shipper [ˈʃɪpəʳ] n compañía naviera

shipping [ˈʃɪpɪŋ] n (act) embarque m; (traffic) buques mpl

shipping agent n agente m/f marítimo(-a)

shipping company n compañía naviera

shipping lane n ruta de navegación

shipping line n = **shipping company**

shipshape [ˈʃɪpʃeɪp] adj en buen orden

shipwreck [ˈʃɪprek] n naufragio ▪ vt: **to be shipwrecked** naufragar

shipyard [ˈʃɪpjɑːd] n astillero

shire [ˈʃaɪəʳ] n (Brit) condado

shirk [ʃəːk] vt eludir, esquivar; (obligations) faltar a

shirt [ʃəːt] n camisa; **in ~ sleeves** en mangas de camisa

shirty [ˈʃəːtɪ] adj (Brit col): **to be ~** estar de malas pulgas

shit [ʃɪt] (col!) n mierda (!); (nonsense) chorradas fpl; **to be a ~** ser un cabrón (!) ▪ excl ¡mierda! (!); **tough ~!** ¡te jodes! (!)

shiver [ˈʃɪvəʳ] vi temblar, estremecerse; (with cold) tiritar

shoal [ʃəul] n (of fish) banco

shock [ʃɔk] n (impact) choque m; (Elec) descarga (eléctrica); (emotional) conmoción f; (start) sobresalto, susto; (Med) postración f nerviosa ▪ vt dar un susto a; (offend) escandalizar; **to get a ~** (Elec) sentir una sacudida eléctrica; **to give sb a ~** dar un susto a algn; **to be suffering from ~** padecer una postración nerviosa; **it came as a ~ to hear that ...** me etc asombró descubrir que ...

shock absorber [-əbsɔːbəʳ] n amortiguador m

shocker [ˈʃɔkəʳ] n (col): **it was a real ~** fue muy fuerte

shocking [ˈʃɔkɪŋ] adj (awful: weather, handwriting) espantoso, horrible; (improper) escandaloso; (result) inesperado

shock therapy, shock treatment n (Med) terapia de choque

shock wave n onda expansiva or de choque

shod [ʃɔd] pt, pp of **shoe** ▪ adj calzado

shoddiness ['ʃɔdɪnɪs] n baja calidad f

shoddy ['ʃɔdɪ] adj de pacotilla

shoe [ʃuː] n zapato; (for horse) herradura; (brake shoe) zapata ▪ vt (pt, pp **shod**) [ʃɔd] (horse) herrar

shoebrush ['ʃuːbrʌʃ] n cepillo para zapatos

shoehorn ['ʃuːhɔːn] n calzador m

shoelace ['ʃuːleɪs] n cordón m

shoemaker ['ʃuːmeɪkəʳ] n zapatero(-a)

shoe polish n betún m

shoeshop ['ʃuːʃɔp] n zapatería

shoestring ['ʃuːstrɪŋ] n (shoelace) cordón m; (fig): **on a ~** con muy poco dinero, a lo barato

shone [ʃɔn] pt, pp of **shine**

shoo [ʃuː] excl ¡fuera!; (to animals) ¡zape! ▪ vt (also: **shoo away, shoo off**) ahuyentar

shook [ʃuk] pt of **shake**

shoot [ʃuːt] (pt, pp **shot**) n (on branch, seedling) retoño, vástago; (shooting party) cacería; (competition) concurso de tiro; (preserve) coto de caza ▪ vt disparar; (kill) matar a tiros; (execute) fusilar; (Cine: film, scene) rodar, filmar ▪ vi (Football) chutar; **to ~ (at)** tirar (a); **to ~ past** pasar como un rayo; **to ~ in/out** vi entrar corriendo/salir disparado

▶ **shoot down** vt (plane) derribar

▶ **shoot up** vi (prices) dispararse

shooting ['ʃuːtɪŋ] n (shots) tiros mpl, tiroteo; (Hunting) caza con escopeta; (act: murder) asesinato (a tiros); (Cine) rodaje m

shooting star n estrella fugaz

shop [ʃɔp] n tienda; (workshop) taller m ▪ vi (also: **go shopping**) ir de compras; **to talk ~** (fig) hablar del trabajo; **repair ~** taller m de reparaciones

▶ **shop around** vi comparar precios

shopaholic ['ʃɔpə'hɔlɪk] n (col) adicto(-a) a las compras

shop assistant n (Brit) dependiente(-a) m(f)

shop floor n (Brit fig) taller m, fábrica

shopkeeper ['ʃɔpkiːpəʳ] n (Brit) tendero(-a)

shoplift ['ʃɔplɪft] vi robar en las tiendas

shoplifter ['ʃɔplɪftəʳ] n ratero(-a)

shoplifting ['ʃɔplɪftɪŋ] n ratería, robo (en las tiendas)

shopper ['ʃɔpəʳ] n comprador(a) m(f)

shopping ['ʃɔpɪŋ] n (goods) compras fpl

shopping bag n bolsa (de compras)

shopping centre, shopping center (US) n centro comercial

shopping mall n centro comercial

shop-soiled ['ʃɔpsɔɪld] adj (Brit) usado

shop steward n (Brit Industry) enlace m/f sindical

shop window n escaparate m, vidriera (LAm)

shopworn ['ʃɔpwɔːn] adj (US) usado

shore [ʃɔːʳ] n (of sea, lake) orilla ▪ vt: **to ~ (up)** reforzar; **on ~** en tierra

shore leave n (Naut) permiso para bajar a tierra

shorn [ʃɔːn] pp of **shear**

short [ʃɔːt] adj (not long) corto; (in time) breve, de corta duración; (person) bajo; (curt) brusco, seco ▪ vi (Elec) ponerse en cortocircuito ▪ n (also: **short film**) cortometraje m; **(a pair of) shorts** (unos) pantalones mpl cortos; **to be ~ of sth** estar falto de algo; **in ~** en pocas palabras; **a ~ time ago** hace poco (tiempo); **in the ~ term** a corto plazo; **to be in ~ supply** escasear, haber escasez de; **I'm ~ of time** me falta tiempo; **~ of doing ...** a menos que hagamos etc ...; **everything ~ of ...** todo menos ...; **it is ~ for** es la forma abreviada de; **to cut ~** (speech, visit) interrumpir, terminar inesperadamente; **to fall ~ of** no alcanzar; **to run ~ of sth** acabársele algo; **to stop ~** parar en seco; **to stop ~ of** detenerse antes de

shortage ['ʃɔːtɪdʒ] n escasez f, falta

shortbread ['ʃɔːtbrɛd] n pasta de mantequilla

short-change [ʃɔːt'tʃeɪndʒ] vt: **to ~ sb** no dar el cambio completo a algn

short circuit [ʃɔːt'sɜːkɪt] n cortocircuito ▪ vt poner en cortocircuito ▪ vi ponerse, en cortocircuito

shortcoming ['ʃɔːtkʌmɪŋ] n defecto, deficiencia

shortcrust pastry ['ʃɔːtkrʌst-], **short pastry** n (Brit) pasta quebradiza

shortcut ['ʃɔːtkʌt] n atajo

shorten ['ʃɔːtn] vt acortar; (visit) interrumpir

shortfall ['ʃɔːtfɔːl] n déficit m, deficiencia

shorthand ['ʃɔːthænd] n (Brit) taquigrafía; **to take sth down in ~** taquigrafiar algo

shorthand notebook n cuaderno de taquigrafía

shorthand typist n (Brit) taquimecanógrafo(-a)

short list n (Brit: for job) lista de candidatos pre-seleccionados

short-lived ['ʃɔːt'lɪvd] adj efímero

shortly ['ʃɔːtlɪ] adv en breve, dentro de poco

shortness ['ʃɔːtnɪs] n (of distance) cortedad f; (of time) brevedad f; (manner) brusquedad f

short-sighted [ʃɔːt'saɪtɪd] adj (Brit) miope, corto de vista; (fig) imprudente

short-sightedness [ʃɔːt'saɪtɪdnɪs] n miopía; (fig) falta de previsión, imprudencia

S

777

short-staffed [ˌʃɔːtˈstɑːft] *adj* falto de personal

short story *n* cuento

short-tempered [ˌʃɔːtˈtɛmpəd] *adj* enojadizo

short-term [ˈʃɔːttəːm] *adj* (*effect*) a corto plazo

short time *n*: **to work ~**, **be on ~** (*Industry*) trabajar con sistema de horario reducido

short-time working [ˈʃɔːttaɪm-] *n* trabajo de horario reducido

short wave *n* (*Radio*) onda corta

shot [ʃɔt] *pt, pp of* **shoot** ■ *n* (*sound*) tiro, disparo; (*person*) tirador(a) *m(f)*; (*try*) tentativa; (*injection*) inyección *f*; (*Phot*) toma, fotografía; (*shotgun pellets*) perdigones *mpl*; **to fire a ~ at sb/sth** tirar *or* disparar contra algn/algo; **to have a ~ at (doing) sth** probar suerte con algo; **like a ~** (*without any delay*) como un rayo; **a big ~** (*col*) un pez gordo; **to get ~ of sth/sb** (*col*) deshacerse de algo/algn, quitarse algo/a algn de encima

shotgun [ˈʃɔtɡʌn] *n* escopeta

should [ʃud] *aux vb*: **I ~ go now** debo irme ahora; **he ~ be there now** debe de haber llegado (ya); **I ~ go if I were you** yo en tu lugar me iría; **I ~ like to** me gustaría; **~ he phone ...** si llamara ..., en caso de que llamase ...

shoulder [ˈʃəuldər] *n* hombro; (*Brit: of road*): **hard ~** arcén *m* ■ *vt* (*fig*) cargar con; **to look over one's ~** mirar hacia atrás; **to rub shoulders with sb** (*fig*) codearse con algn; **to give sb the cold ~** (*fig*) dar de lado a algn

shoulder bag *n* bolso de bandolera

shoulder blade *n* omóplato

shoulder strap *n* tirante *m*

shouldn't [ˈʃudnt] = **should not**

shout [ʃaut] *n* grito ■ *vt* gritar ■ *vi* gritar, dar voces
  ▶ **shout down** *vt* hundir a gritos

shouting [ˈʃautɪŋ] *n* griterío

shouting match *n* (*col*) discusión *f* a voz en grito

shove [ʃʌv] *n* empujón *m* ■ *vt* empujar; (*col: put*): **to ~ sth in** meter algo a empellones; **he shoved me out of the way** me quitó de en medio de un empujón
  ▶ **shove off** *vi* (*Naut*) alejarse del muelle; (*fig: col*) largarse

shovel [ˈʃʌvl] *n* pala; (*mechanical*) excavadora ■ *vt* mover con pala

show [ʃəu] (*pt* **showed**, *pp* **shown**) *n* (*of emotion*) demostración *f*; (*semblance*) apariencia; (*Comm, Tech: exhibition*) exhibición *f*, exposición *f*; (*Theat*) función *f*, espectáculo; (*organization*) negocio, empresa ■ *vt* mostrar, enseñar; (*courage etc*) mostrar, manifestar; (*exhibit*) exponer; (*film*) proyectar ■ *vi*

mostrarse; (*appear*) aparecer; **on ~** (*exhibits etc*) expuesto; **to be on ~** estar expuesto; **it's just for ~** es sólo para impresionar; **to ask for a ~ of hands** pedir una votación a mano alzada; **who's running the ~ here?** ¿quién manda aquí?; **to ~ a profit/loss** (*Comm*) arrojar un saldo positivo/negativo; **I have nothing to ~ for it** no saqué ningún provecho (de ello); **to ~ sb to his seat/to the door** acompañar a algn a su asiento/a la puerta; **as shown in the illustration** como se ve en el grabado; **it just goes to ~ that ...** queda demostrado que ...; **it doesn't ~** no se ve *or* nota
  ▶ **show in** *vt* (*person*) hacer pasar
  ▶ **show off** *vi* (*pej*) presumir ■ *vt* (*display*) lucir; (*pej*) hacer alarde de
  ▶ **show out** *vt*: **to ~ sb out** acompañar a algn a la puerta
  ▶ **show up** *vi* (*stand out*) destacar; (*col: turn up*) presentarse ■ *vt* descubrir; (*unmask*) desenmascarar

showbiz [ˈʃəubɪz] *n* (*col*) = **show business**

show business *n* el mundo del espectáculo

showcase [ˈʃəukeɪs] *n* vitrina; (*fig*) escaparate *m*

showdown [ˈʃəudaun] *n* crisis *f*, momento decisivo

shower [ˈʃauər] *n* (*rain*) chaparrón *m*, chubasco; (*of stones etc*) lluvia; (*also*: **shower bath**) ducha ■ *vi* llover ■ *vt*: **to ~ sb with sth** colmar a algn de algo; **to have** *or* **take a ~** ducharse

shower cap *n* gorro de baño

shower gel *n* gel de ducha

showerproof [ˈʃauəpruːf] *adj* impermeable

showery [ˈʃauərɪ] *adj* (*weather*) lluvioso

showground [ˈʃəugraund] *n* ferial *m*, real *m* (de la feria)

showing [ˈʃəuɪŋ] *n* (*of film*) proyección *f*

show jumping *n* hípica

showman [ˈʃəumən] *n* (*at fair, circus*) empresario (de espectáculos); (*fig*) actor *m* consumado

showmanship [ˈʃəumənʃɪp] *n* dotes *fpl* teatrales

shown [ʃəun] *pp of* **show**

show-off [ˈʃəuɔf] *n* (*col: person*) fantasmón(-ona) *m(f)*

showpiece [ˈʃəupiːs] *n* (*of exhibition etc*) objeto más valioso, joya; **that hospital is a ~** ese hospital es un modelo del género

showroom [ˈʃəuruːm] *n* sala de muestras

show trial *n* juicio propagandístico

showy [ˈʃəuɪ] *adj* ostentoso

shrank [ʃræŋk] *pt of* **shrink**

shrapnel [ˈʃræpnl] *n* metralla

shred [ʃrɛd] n (gen pl) triza, jirón m; (fig: of truth, evidence) pizca, chispa ▪ vt hacer trizas; (documents) triturar; (Culin) desmenuzar

shredder ['ʃrɛdə^r] n (vegetable shredder) picadora; (document shredder) trituradora (de papel)

shrewd [ʃruːd] adj astuto

shrewdly ['ʃruːdlɪ] adv astutamente

shrewdness ['ʃruːdnɪs] n astucia

shriek [ʃriːk] n chillido ▪ vt, vi chillar

shrill [ʃrɪl] adj agudo, estridente

shrimp [ʃrɪmp] n camarón m

shrine [ʃraɪn] n santuario, sepulcro

shrink (pt **shrank**, pp **shrunk**) [ʃrɪŋk, ʃræŋk, ʃrʌŋk] vi encogerse; (be reduced) reducirse ▪ vt encoger; **to ~ from (doing) sth** no atreverse a hacer algo
▸ **shrink away** vi retroceder, retirarse

shrinkage ['ʃrɪŋkɪdʒ] n encogimiento, reducción f; (Comm: in shops) pérdidas fpl

shrink-wrap ['ʃrɪŋkræp] vt empaquetar en envase termoretráctil

shrivel ['ʃrɪvl] (also: **shrivel up**) vt (dry) secar; (crease) arrugar ▪ vi secarse; arrugarse

shroud [ʃraud] n sudario ▪ vt: **shrouded in mystery** envuelto en el misterio

Shrove Tuesday ['ʃrəuv-] n martes m de carnaval

shrub [ʃrʌb] n arbusto

shrubbery ['ʃrʌbərɪ] n arbustos mpl

shrug [ʃrʌg] n encogimiento de hombros ▪ vt, vi: **to ~ (one's shoulders)** encogerse de hombros
▸ **shrug off** vt negar importancia a; (cold, illness) deshacerse de

shrunk [ʃrʌŋk] pp of **shrink**

shrunken ['ʃrʌŋkn] adj encogido

shudder ['ʃʌdə^r] n estremecimiento, escalofrío ▪ vi estremecerse

shuffle ['ʃʌfl] vt (cards) barajar; **to ~ (one's feet)** arrastrar los pies

shun [ʃʌn] vt rehuir, esquivar

shunt [ʃʌnt] vt (Rail) maniobrar

shunting yard ['ʃʌntɪŋ-] n estación f de maniobras

shut (pt, pp **~**) [ʃʌt] vt cerrar ▪ vi cerrarse
▸ **shut down** vt, vi cerrar; (machine) parar
▸ **shut off** vt (stop: power, water supply etc) interrumpir, cortar; (engine) parar
▸ **shut out** vt (person) excluir, dejar fuera; (noise, cold) no dejar entrar; (block: view) tapar; (memory) tratar de olvidar
▸ **shut up** vi (col: keep quiet) callarse ▪ vt (close) cerrar; (silence) callar

shutdown ['ʃʌtdaun] n cierre m

shutter ['ʃʌtə^r] n contraventana; (Phot) obturador m

shuttle ['ʃʌtl] n lanzadera; (also: **shuttle service**: Aviat) puente m aéreo ▪ vi (vehicle, person) ir y venir ▪ vt (passengers) transportar, trasladar

shuttlecock ['ʃʌtlkɔk] n volante m

shuttle diplomacy n viajes mpl diplomáticos

shy [ʃaɪ] adj tímido ▪ vi: **to ~ away from doing sth** (fig) rehusar hacer algo; **to be ~ of doing sth** esquivar hacer algo

shyly ['ʃaɪlɪ] adv tímidamente

shyness ['ʃaɪnɪs] n timidez f

Siam [saɪˈæm] n Siam m

Siamese [saɪəˈmiːz] adj siamés(-esa) ▪ n (person) siamés(-esa) m(f); (Ling) siamés m; **~ cat** gato siamés; **~ twins** gemelos(-as) m(f)pl siameses(-as)

Siberia [saɪˈbɪərɪə] n Siberia

sibling ['sɪblɪŋ] n (formal) hermano(-a)

Sicilian [sɪˈsɪlɪən] adj, n siciliano(-a) m(f)

Sicily ['sɪsɪlɪ] n Sicilia

sick [sɪk] adj (ill) enfermo; (nauseated) mareado; (humour) morboso; **to be ~** (Brit) vomitar; **to feel ~** estar mareado; **to be ~ of** (fig) estar harto de; **a ~ person** un(a) enfermo(-a); **to be (off) ~** estar ausente por enfermedad; **to fall** or **take ~** ponerse enfermo

sickbag ['sɪkbæg] n bolsa para el mareo

sick bay n enfermería

sickbed ['sɪkbɛd] n lecho de enfermo

sick building syndrome n enfermedad causada por falta de ventilación y luz natural en un edificio

sicken ['sɪkn] vt dar asco a ▪ vi enfermar; **to be sickening for** (cold, flu etc) mostrar síntomas de

sickening ['sɪknɪŋ] adj (fig) asqueroso

sickle ['sɪkl] n hoz f

sick leave n baja por enfermedad

sickle-cell anaemia ['sɪklsɛl-] n anemia de células falciformes, drepanocitosis f

sick list n: **to be on the ~** estar de baja

sickly ['sɪklɪ] adj enfermizo; (taste) empalagoso

sickness ['sɪknɪs] n enfermedad f, mal m; (vomiting) náuseas fpl

sickness benefit n subsidio de enfermedad

sick pay n prestación por enfermedad pagada por la empresa

sickroom ['sɪkruːm] n cuarto del enfermo

side [saɪd] n (gen) lado; (face, surface) cara; (of paper) cara; (slice of bread) rebanada; (of body) costado; (of animal) ijar m, ijada; (of lake) orilla; (part) lado; (aspect) aspecto; (team: Sport) equipo; (: Pol etc) partido; (of hill) ladera ▪ adj (door, entrance) lateral ▪ vi: **to ~ with sb** ponerse de parte de algn; **by the ~ of** al lado de; **~ by ~** juntos(-as); **from all sides**

de todos lados; **to take sides (with)** tomar
partido (por); ~ **of beef** flanco de vaca; **the
right/wrong** ~ el derecho/revés; **from** ~ **to** ~
de un lado a otro
sideboard ['saɪdbɔːd] *n* aparador *m*
sideboards ['saɪdbɔːdz], (*Brit*) **sideburns**
['saɪdbəːnz] *npl* patillas *fpl*
sidecar ['saɪdkɑːˈ] *n* sidecar *m*
side dish *n* entremés *m*
side drum *n* (*Mus*) tamboril *m*
side effect *n* efecto secundario
sidekick ['saɪdkɪk] *n* compinche *m*
sidelight ['saɪdlaɪt] *n* (*Aut*) luz *f* lateral
sideline ['saɪdlaɪn] *n* (*Sport*) línea lateral; (*fig*)
empleo suplementario
sidelong ['saɪdlɔŋ] *adj* de soslayo; **to give a** ~
glance at sth mirar algo de reojo
side plate *n* platito
side road *n* (*Brit*) calle *f* lateral
sidesaddle ['saɪdsædl] *adv* a la amazona
side show *n* (*stall*) caseta; (*fig*) atracción *f*
secundaria
sidestep ['saɪdstɛp] *vt* (*question*) eludir;
(*problem*) esquivar ■ *vi* (*Boxing etc*) dar un
quiebro
side street *n* calle *f* lateral
sidetrack ['saɪdtræk] *vt* (*fig*) desviar (de su
propósito)
sidewalk ['saɪdwɔːk] *n* (*US*) acera, vereda
(*LAm*), andén *m* (*LAm*), banqueta (*LAm*)
sideways ['saɪdweɪz] *adv* de lado
siding ['saɪdɪŋ] *n* (*Rail*) apartadero, vía
muerta
sidle ['saɪdl] *vi*: **to** ~ **up (to)** acercarse
furtivamente (a)
SIDS [sɪdz] *n abbr* (= *sudden infant death syndrome*)
(síndrome *m* de la) muerte *f* súbita
siege [siːdʒ] *n* cerco, sitio; **to lay** ~ **to** cercar,
sitiar
siege economy *n* economía de sitio *or* de
asedio
Sierra Leone [sɪˈɛrəlɪˈəun] *n* Sierra Leona
siesta [sɪˈɛstə] *n* siesta
sieve [sɪv] *n* colador *m* ■ *vt* cribar
sift [sɪft] *vt* cribar ■ *vi*: **to** ~ **through**
pasar por una criba; (*information*) analizar
cuidadosamente
sigh [saɪ] *n* suspiro ■ *vi* suspirar
sight [saɪt] *n* (*faculty*) vista; (*spectacle*)
espectáculo; (*on gun*) mira, alza ■ *vt* ver,
divisar; **in** ~ a la vista; **out of** ~ fuera de (la)
vista; **at** ~ a la vista; **at first** ~ a primera
vista; **to lose** ~ **of sth/sb** perder algo/a algn
de vista; **to catch** ~ **of sth/sb** divisar algo/a
algn; **I know her by** ~ la conozco de vista;
to set one's sights on (doing) sth aspirar a
or ambicionar (hacer) algo

sighted ['saɪtɪd] *adj* vidente, de vista normal;
partially ~ de vista limitada
sightseeing ['saɪtsiːɪŋ] *n* excursionismo,
turismo; **to go** ~ visitar monumentos
sightseer ['saɪtsiːəˈ] *n* excursionista *m/f*,
turista *m/f*
sign [saɪn] *n* (*with hand*) señal *f*, seña;
(*trace*) huella, rastro; (*notice*) letrero;
(*written*) signo; (*also*: **road sign**) indicador
m; (: *with instructions*) señal *f* de tráfico ■ *vt*
firmar; **as a** ~ **of** en señal de; **it's a good/
bad** ~ es buena/mala señal; **plus/minus** ~
signo de más/de menos; **to** ~ **one's name**
firmar
▶ **sign away** *vt* (*rights etc*) ceder
▶ **sign off** *vi* (*Radio, TV*) cerrar el programa
▶ **sign on** *vi* (*Mil*) alistarse; (*as unemployed*)
apuntarse al paro; (*employee*) firmar un
contrato ■ *vt* (*Mil*) alistar; (*employee*)
contratar; **to** ~ **on for a course** matricularse
en un curso
▶ **sign out** *vi* firmar el registro (al salir)
▶ **sign over** *vt*: **to** ~ **sth over to sb** traspasar
algo a algn
▶ **sign up** *vi* (*Mil*) alistarse ■ *vt* (*contract*)
contratar
signal ['sɪɡnl] *n* señal *f* ■ *vi* (*Aut*) señalizar
■ *vt* (*person*) hacer señas a; (*message*)
transmitir; **the engaged** ~ (*Tel*) la señal de
comunicando; **the** ~ **is very weak** (*TV*) no
captamos bien el canal; **to** ~ **a left/right
turn** (*Aut*) indicar que se va a doblar a la
izquierda/derecha; **to** ~ **to sb (to do sth)**
hacer señas a algn (para que haga algo)
signal box *n* (*Rail*) garita de señales
signalman ['sɪɡnlmən] *n* (*Rail*) guardavía *m*
signatory ['sɪɡnətərɪ] *n* firmante *m/f*
signature ['sɪɡnətfəˈ] *n* firma
signature tune *n* sintonía
signet ring ['sɪɡnət-] *n* (anillo de) sello
significance [sɪɡˈnɪfɪkəns] *n* significado;
(*importance*) trascendencia; **that is of no** ~
eso no tiene importancia
significant [sɪɡˈnɪfɪkənt] *adj* significativo;
trascendente; **it is** ~ **that** ... es significativo
que ...
significantly [sɪɡˈnɪfɪkəntlɪ] *adv* (*smile*)
expresivamente; (*improve, increase*)
sensiblemente; **and,** ~ ... y debe notarse
que ...
signify ['sɪɡnɪfaɪ] *vt* significar
sign language *n* mímica, lenguaje *m* por *or*
de señas
signpost ['saɪnpəust] *n* indicador *m*
silage ['saɪlɪdʒ] *n* ensilaje *m*
silence ['saɪlns] *n* silencio ■ *vt* hacer callar;
(*guns*) reducir al silencio

silencer ['saɪlnsəʳ] *n* silenciador *m*
silent ['saɪlnt] *adj* (*gen*) silencioso; (*not speaking*) callado; (*film*) mudo; **to keep** *or* **remain ~** guardar silencio
silently ['saɪlntlɪ] *adv* silenciosamente, en silencio
silent partner *n* (*Comm*) socio(-a) comanditario(-a)
silhouette [sɪluː'ɛt] *n* silueta; **silhouetted against** destacado sobre *or* contra
silicon ['sɪlɪkən] *n* silicio
silicon chip *n* chip *m*, plaqueta de silicio
silicone ['sɪlɪkəun] *n* silicona
silk [sɪlk] *n* seda ■ *cpd* de seda
silky ['sɪlkɪ] *adj* sedoso
sill [sɪl] *n* (*also*: **windowsill**) alféizar *m*; (*Aut*) umbral *m*
silliness ['sɪlɪnɪs] *n* (*of person*) necedad *f*; (*of idea*) lo absurdo
silly ['sɪlɪ] *adj* (*person*) tonto; (*idea*) absurdo; **to do sth ~** hacer una tontería
silo ['saɪləu] *n* silo
silt [sɪlt] *n* sedimento
silver ['sɪlvəʳ] *n* plata; (*money*) moneda suelta ■ *adj* de plata
silver paper, (*Brit*) **silver foil** *n* papel *m* de plata
silver-plated [sɪlvə'pleɪtɪd] *adj* plateado
silversmith ['sɪlvəsmɪθ] *n* platero(-a)
silverware ['sɪlvəwɛəʳ] *n* plata
silver wedding, silver wedding anniversary *n* (*Brit*) bodas *fpl* de plata
silvery ['sɪlvrɪ] *adj* plateado
SIM card ['sɪm-] *n* (*Tel*) SIM card *m* o *f*, tarjeta SIM
similar ['sɪmɪləʳ] *adj*: **~ to** parecido *or* semejante a
similarity [sɪmɪ'lærɪtɪ] *n* parecido, semejanza
similarly ['sɪmɪləlɪ] *adv* del mismo modo; (*in a similar way*) de manera parecida; (*equally*) igualmente
simile ['sɪmɪlɪ] *n* símil *m*
simmer ['sɪməʳ] *vi* hervir a fuego lento
▶ **simmer down** *vi* (*fig, col*) calmarse, tranquilizarse
simpering ['sɪmpərɪŋ] *adj* afectado; (*foolish*) bobo
simple ['sɪmpl] *adj* (*easy*) sencillo; (*foolish*) simple; (*Comm*) simple; **the ~ truth** la pura verdad
simple interest *n* (*Comm*) interés *m* simple
simple-minded [sɪmpl'maɪndɪd] *adj* simple, ingenuo
simpleton ['sɪmpltən] *n* inocentón(-ona) *m(f)*
simplicity [sɪm'plɪsɪtɪ] *n* sencillez *f*; (*foolishness*) ingenuidad *f*

simplification [sɪmplɪfɪ'keɪʃən] *n* simplificación *f*
simplify ['sɪmplɪfaɪ] *vt* simplificar
simply ['sɪmplɪ] *adv* (*in a simple way*: *live, talk*) sencillamente; (*just, merely*) sólo
simulate ['sɪmjuleɪt] *vt* simular
simulation [sɪmju'leɪʃən] *n* simulación *f*
simultaneous [sɪməl'teɪnɪəs] *adj* simultáneo
simultaneously [sɪməl'teɪnɪəslɪ] *adv* simultáneamente, a la vez
sin [sɪn] *n* pecado ■ *vi* pecar
since [sɪns] *adv* desde entonces ■ *prep* desde ■ *conj* (*time*) desde que; (*because*) ya que, puesto que; **~ then** desde entonces; **~ Monday** desde el lunes; (**ever**) **~ I arrived** desde que llegué
sincere [sɪn'sɪəʳ] *adj* sincero
sincerely [sɪn'sɪəlɪ] *adv* sinceramente; **yours ~** (*in letters*) le saluda (afectuosamente); **~ yours** (*US: in letters*) le saluda atentamente
sincerity [sɪn'sɛrɪtɪ] *n* sinceridad *f*
sinecure ['saɪnɪkjuəʳ] *n* chollo
sinew ['sɪnjuː] *n* tendón *m*
sinful ['sɪnful] *adj* (*thought*) pecaminoso; (*person*) pecador(a)
sing (*pt* **sang**, *pp* **sung**) [sɪŋ, sæŋ, sʌŋ] *vt* cantar ■ *vi* (*gen*) cantar; (*bird*) trinar; (*ears*) zumbar
Singapore [sɪŋə'pɔː'] *n* Singapur *m*
singe [sɪndʒ] *vt* chamuscar
singer ['sɪŋəʳ] *n* cantante *m/f*
Singhalese [sɪŋə'liːz] *adj* = **Sinhalese**
singing ['sɪŋɪŋ] *n* (*of person, bird*) canto; (*songs*) canciones *fpl*; (*in the ears*) zumbido; (*of kettle*) silbido
single ['sɪŋgl] *adj* único, solo; (*unmarried*) soltero; (*not double*) individual, sencillo ■ *n* (*Brit: also*: **single ticket**) billete *m* sencillo; (*record*) sencillo, single *m*; **singles** *npl* (*Tennis*) individual *msg*; **not a ~ one was left** no quedaba ni uno; **every ~ day** todos los días (sin excepción)
▶ **single out** *vt* (*choose*) escoger; (*point out*) singularizar
single bed *n* cama individual
single-breasted [sɪŋgl'brɛstɪd] *adj* (*jacket, suit*) recto, sin cruzar
single-entry book-keeping ['sɪŋglɛntrɪ-] *n* contabilidad *f* por partida simple
Single European Market *n*: **the ~** el Mercado Único Europeo
single file *n*: **in ~** en fila de uno
single-handed [sɪŋgl'hændɪd] *adv* sin ayuda
single-minded [sɪŋgl'maɪndɪd] *adj* resuelto, firme
single parent *n* (*mother*) madre *f* soltera; (*father*) padre *m* soltero

S

single-parent family ['sɪŋglpɛərənt-] n familia monoparental

single room n habitación f individual

singles bar n (esp US) bar m para solteros

single-sex school ['sɪŋglsɛks-] n escuela no mixta

single-sided [sɪŋg'saɪdɪd] adj (Comput: disk) de una cara

single spacing n (Typ): **in ~** a un espacio

singlet ['sɪŋglɪt] n camiseta

singly ['sɪŋglɪ] adv uno por uno

singsong ['sɪŋsɔŋ] adj (tone) cantarín(-ina) ▪ n (songs): **to have a ~** tener un concierto improvisado

singular ['sɪŋgjuləʳ] adj singular, extraordinario; (odd) extraño; (Ling) singular ▪ n (Ling) singular m; **in the feminine ~** en femenino singular

singularly ['sɪŋgjuləlɪ] adv singularmente, extraordinariamente

Sinhalese [sɪnhə'liːz] adj singhalese

sinister ['sɪnɪstəʳ] adj siniestro

sink [sɪŋk] (pt **sank**, pp **sunk**) n fregadero ▪ vt (ship) hundir, echar a pique; (foundations) excavar; (piles etc): **to ~ sth into** hundir algo en ▪ vi (gen) hundirse; **he sank into a chair/the mud** se dejó caer en una silla/se hundió en el barro; **the shares** or **share prices have sunk to three dollars** las acciones han bajado a tres dólares
  ▶ **sink in** vi (fig) penetrar, calar; **the news took a long time to ~ in** la noticia tardó mucho en hacer mella en él (or mí etc)

sinking ['sɪŋkɪŋ] adj: **that ~ feeling** la sensación esa de desmoralización

sinking fund n fondo de amortización

sink unit n fregadero

sinner ['sɪnəʳ] n pecador(a) m(f)

Sinn Féin [ʃɪn'feɪn] n partido político republicano de Irlanda del Norte

sinuous ['sɪnjuəs] adj sinuoso

sinus ['saɪnəs] n (Anat) seno

sip [sɪp] n sorbo ▪ vt sorber, beber a sorbitos

siphon ['saɪfən] n sifón m ▪ vt (also: **siphon off**: funds) desviar

sir [səːʳ] n señor m; **S~ John Smith** el Señor John Smith; **yes ~** sí, señor; **Dear S~** (in letter) Muy señor mío, Estimado Señor; **Dear Sirs** Muy señores nuestros, Estimados Señores

siren ['saɪərn] n sirena

sirloin ['səːlɔɪn] n solomillo

sirloin steak n filete m de solomillo

sisal ['saɪsəl] n pita, henequén m (LAm)

sissy ['sɪsɪ] n (col) marica m

sister ['sɪstəʳ] n hermana; (Brit: nurse) enfermera jefe

sister-in-law ['sɪstərɪnlɔː] n cuñada

sister organization n organización f hermana

sister ship n barco gemelo

sit (pt, pp **sat**) [sɪt, sæt] vi sentarse; (be sitting) estar sentado; (assembly) reunirse; (dress etc) caer, sentar ▪ vt (exam) presentarse a; **that jacket sits well** esa chaqueta sienta bien; **to ~ on a committee** ser miembro de una comisión or un comité
  ▶ **sit about, sit around** vi holgazanear
  ▶ **sit back** vi (in seat) recostarse
  ▶ **sit down** vi sentarse; **to be sitting down** estar sentado
  ▶ **sit in on** vt fus: **to ~ in on a discussion** asistir a una discusión
  ▶ **sit up** vi incorporarse; (not go to bed) no acostarse

sitcom ['sɪtkɔm] n abbr (TV: = situation comedy) telecomedia

sit-down ['sɪtdaun] adj: **~ strike** huelga de brazos caídos; **a ~ meal** una comida sentada

site [saɪt] n sitio; (also: **building site**) solar m ▪ vt situar

sit-in ['sɪtɪn] n (demonstration) sentada f

siting ['saɪtɪŋ] n (location) situación f, emplazamiento

sitter ['sɪtəʳ] n (Art) modelo m/f; (babysitter) canguro m/f

sitting ['sɪtɪŋ] n (of assembly etc) sesión f; (in canteen) turno

sitting member n (Pol) titular m/f de un escaño

sitting room n sala de estar

sitting tenant n inquilino con derechos de estancia en una vivienda

situate ['sɪtjueɪt] vt situar, ubicar (LAm)

situated ['sɪtjueɪtɪd] adj situado, ubicado (LAm)

situation [sɪtju'eɪʃən] n situación f; **"situations vacant"** (Brit) "ofertas de trabajo"

situation comedy n (TV, Radio) serie f cómica, comedia de situación

six [sɪks] num seis

six-pack ['sɪkspæk] n (esp US) paquete m de seis cervezas

sixteen [sɪks'tiːn] num dieciséis

sixth [sɪksθ] adj sexto; **the upper/lower ~** (Scol) el séptimo/sexto año

sixty ['sɪkstɪ] num sesenta

size [saɪz] n (gen) tamaño; (extent) extensión f; (of clothing) talla; (of shoes) número; **I take ~ 5 shoes** calzo el número cinco; **I take ~ 14** mi talla es la 42; **I'd like the small/large ~** (of soap powder etc) quisiera el tamaño pequeño/grande
  ▶ **size up** vt formarse una idea de

sizeable ['saɪzəbl] *adj* importante, considerable

sizzle ['sɪzl] *vi* crepitar

SK *abbr* (*Canada*) = **Saskatchewan**

skate [skeɪt] *n* patín *m*; (*fish: pl inv*) raya ■ *vi* patinar
▸ **skate over, skate round** *vt fus* (*problem, issue*) pasar por alto

skateboard ['skeɪtbɔːd] *n* monopatín *m*

skater ['skeɪtəʳ] *n* patinador(a) *m(f)*

skating ['skeɪtɪŋ] *n* patinaje *m*

skating rink *n* pista de patinaje

skeleton ['skelɪtn] *n* esqueleto; (*Tech*) armazón *m*; (*outline*) esquema *m*

skeleton key *n* llave *f* maestra

skeleton staff *n* personal *m* reducido

skeptic *etc* ['skeptɪk] (*US*) = **sceptic** *etc*

sketch [sketʃ] *n* (*drawing*) dibujo; (*outline*) esbozo, bosquejo; (*Theat*) pieza corta ■ *vt* dibujar; esbozar

sketch book *n* bloc *m* de dibujo

sketch pad *n* bloc *m* de dibujo

sketchy ['sketʃɪ] *adj* incompleto

skewer ['skjuːəʳ] *n* broqueta

ski [skiː] *n* esquí *m* ■ *vi* esquiar

ski boot *n* bota de esquí

skid [skɪd] *n* patinazo ■ *vi* patinar; **to go into a ~** comenzar a patinar

skid mark *n* señal *f* de patinazo

skier ['skiːəʳ] *n* esquiador(a) *m(f)*

skiing ['skiːɪŋ] *n* esquí *m*; **to go ~** practicar el esquí, (ir a) esquiar

ski instructor *n* instructor(a) *m(f)* de esquí

ski jump *n* pista para salto de esquí

skilful, skillful (*US*) ['skɪlful] *adj* diestro, experto

skilfully, skillfully (*US*) ['skɪlfulɪ] *adv* hábilmente, con destreza

ski lift *n* telesilla *m*, telesquí *m*

skill [skɪl] *n* destreza, pericia; (*technique*) arte *m*, técnica; **there's a certain ~ to doing it** se necesita cierta habilidad para hacerlo

skilled [skɪld] *adj* hábil, diestro; (*worker*) cualificado

skillet ['skɪlɪt] *n* sartén *f* pequeña

skillful *etc* ['skɪlful] (*US*) = **skilful** *etc*

skim [skɪm] *vt* (*milk*) desnatar; (*glide over*) rozar, rasar ■ *vi*: **to ~ through** (*book*) hojear

skimmed milk [skɪmd-] *n* leche *f* desnatada *or* descremada

skimp [skɪmp] *vt* (*work*) chapucear; (*cloth etc*) escatimar; **to ~ on** (*material etc*) economizar; (*work*) escatimar

skimpy ['skɪmpɪ] *adj* (*meagre*) escaso; (*skirt*) muy corto

skin [skɪn] *n* (*gen*) piel *f*; (*complexion*) cutis *m*; (*of fruit, vegetable*) piel *f*, cáscara; (*crust: on pudding, paint*) nata ■ *vt* (*fruit etc*) pelar; (*animal*) despellejar; **wet** *or* **soaked to the ~** calado hasta los huesos

skin cancer *n* cáncer *m* de piel

skin-deep ['skɪn'diːp] *adj* superficial

skin diver *n* buceador(a) *m(f)*

skin diving *n* buceo

skinflint ['skɪnflɪnt] *n* tacaño(-a), roñoso(-a)

skinhead ['skɪnhed] *n* cabeza *m/f* rapada, skin(head) *m/f*

skinny ['skɪnɪ] *adj* flaco, magro

skintight ['skɪntaɪt] *adj* (*dress etc*) muy ajustado

skip [skɪp] *n* brinco, salto; (*container*) contenedor *m* ■ *vi* brincar; (*with rope*) saltar a la comba ■ *vt* (*pass over*) omitir, saltar

ski pants *npl* pantalones *mpl* de esquí

ski pole *n* bastón *m* de esquiar

skipper ['skɪpəʳ] *n* (*Naut, Sport*) capitán *m*

skipping rope ['skɪpɪŋ-] *n* (*Brit*) comba, cuerda (de saltar)

ski resort *n* estación *f* de esquí

skirmish ['skɜːmɪʃ] *n* escaramuza

skirt [skɜːt] *n* falda, pollera (*LAm*) ■ *vt* (*surround*) ceñir, rodear; (*go round*) ladear

skirting board ['skɜːtɪŋ] *n* (*Brit*) rodapié *m*

ski run *n* pista de esquí

ski suit *n* traje *m* de esquiar

skit [skɪt] *n* sátira, parodia

ski tow *n* arrastre *m* (de esquí)

skittle ['skɪtl] *n* bolo; **skittles** (*game*) boliche *m*

skive [skaɪv] *vi* (*Brit: col*) gandulear

skulk [skʌlk] *vi* esconderse

skull [skʌl] *n* calavera; (*Anat*) cráneo

skullcap ['skʌlkæp] *n* (*worn by Jews*) casquete *m*; (*worn by Pope*) solideo

skunk [skʌŋk] *n* mofeta

sky [skaɪ] *n* cielo; **to praise sb to the skies** poner a algn por las nubes

sky-blue [skaɪ'bluː] *adj* (azul) celeste

skydiving ['skaɪdaɪvɪŋ] *n* paracaidismo acrobático

sky-high ['skaɪ'haɪ] *adj* (*col*) por las nubes ■ *adv* (*throw*) muy alto; **prices have gone ~** (*col*) los precios están por las nubes

skylark ['skaɪlɑːk] *n* (*bird*) alondra

skylight ['skaɪlaɪt] *n* tragaluz *m*, claraboya

skyline ['skaɪlaɪn] *n* (*horizon*) horizonte *m*; (*of city*) perfil *m*

Skype® ['skaɪp] (*Internet, Tel*) *n* skype® *m* ■ *vt* hablar con algn a través de skype

skyscraper ['skaɪskreɪpəʳ] *n* rascacielos *m inv*

slab [slæb] *n* (*stone*) bloque *m*; (*of wood*) tabla, plancha; (*flat*) losa; (*of cake*) trozo; (*of meat, cheese*) tajada, trozo

slack [slæk] *adj* (*loose*) flojo; (*slow*) de poca

S

actividad; (*careless*) descuidado; (*Comm*: *market*) poco activo; (: *demand*) débil; (*period*) bajo; **business is** ~ hay poco movimiento en el negocio

slacken ['slækn] (*also*: **slacken off**) *vi* aflojarse ▪ *vt* aflojar; (*speed*) disminuir

slackness ['slæknɪs] *n* flojedad *f*; negligencia

slacks [slæks] *npl* pantalones *mpl*

slag [slæg] *n* escoria, escombros *mpl*

slag heap *n* escorial *m*, escombrera

slain [sleɪn] *pp of* **slay**

slake [sleɪk] *vt* (*one's thirst*) apagar

slalom ['slɑːləm] *n* eslálom *m*

slam [slæm] *vt* (*door*) cerrar de golpe; (*throw*) arrojar (violentamente); (*criticize*) vapulear, vituperar ▪ *vi* cerrarse de golpe

slammer [slæmə^r] *n* (*col*): **the** ~ la trena, el talego

slander ['slɑːndə^r] *n* calumnia, difamación *f* ▪ *vt* calumniar, difamar

slanderous ['slɑːndərəs] *adj* calumnioso, difamatorio

slang [slæŋ] *n* argot *m*; (*jargon*) jerga

slanging match ['slæŋɪŋ-] *n* (*Brit col*) bronca gorda

slant [slɑːnt] *n* sesgo, inclinación *f*; (*fig*) punto de vista; **to get a new** ~ **on sth** obtener un nuevo punto de vista sobre algo

slanted ['slɑːntɪd], **slanting** ['slɑːntɪŋ] *adj* inclinado

slap [slæp] *n* palmada; (*in face*) bofetada ▪ *vt* dar una palmada/bofetada a ▪ *adv* (*directly*) de lleno

slapdash ['slæpdæʃ] *adj* chapucero

slaphead ['slæphɛd] *n* (*Brit col*) colgado(-a)

slapstick ['slæpstɪk] *n*: ~ **comedy** comedia de payasadas

slap-up ['slæpʌp] *adj*: **a** ~ **meal** (*Brit*) un banquetazo, una comilona

slash [slæʃ] *vt* acuchillar; (*fig*: *prices*) quemar

slat [slæt] *n* (*of wood, plastic*) tablilla, listón *m*

slate [sleɪt] *n* pizarra ▪ *vt* (*Brit*: *fig*: *criticize*) vapulear

slaughter ['slɔːtə^r] *n* (*of animals*) matanza; (*of people*) carnicería ▪ *vt* matar

slaughterhouse ['slɔːtəhaus] *n* matadero

Slav [slɑːv] *adj* eslavo

slave [sleɪv] *n* esclavo(-a) ▪ *vi* (*also*: **slave away**) trabajar como un negro; **to** ~ **(away) at sth** trabajar como un negro en algo

slave driver *n* (*col, pej*) tirano(-a)

slave labour, slave labor (*US*) *n* trabajo de esclavos

slaver ['slævə^r] *vi* (*dribble*) babear

slavery ['sleɪvərɪ] *n* esclavitud *f*

slavish ['sleɪvɪʃ] *adj* (*devotion*) de esclavo; (*imitation*) servil

slay (*pt* **slew**, *pp* **slain**) [sleɪ, sluː, sleɪn] *vt* (*literary*) matar

sleazy ['sliːzɪ] *adj* (*fig*: *place*) sórdido

sledge [slɛdʒ], **sled** (*US*) [slɛd] *n* trineo

sledgehammer ['slɛdʒhæmə^r] *n* mazo

sleek [sliːk] *adj* (*shiny*) lustroso

sleep [sliːp] (*pt, pp* **slept**) *n* sueño ▪ *vi* dormir ▪ *vt*: **we can** ~ **4** podemos alojar a 4, tenemos cabida para 4; **to go to** ~ dormirse; **to have a good night's** ~ dormir toda la noche; **to put to** ~ (*patient*) dormir; (*animal*: *euphemism*: *kill*) sacrificar; **to** ~ **lightly** tener el sueño ligero; **to** ~ **with sb** (*euphemism*) acostarse con algn
▸ **sleep in** *vi* (*oversleep*) quedarse dormido

sleeper ['sliːpə^r] *n* (*person*) durmiente *m/f*; (*Brit Rail*: *on track*) traviesa; (: *train*) coche-cama *m*

sleepiness ['sliːpɪnɪs] *n* somnolencia

sleeping bag ['sliːpɪŋ-] *n* saco de dormir

sleeping car *n* coche-cama *m*

sleeping partner *n* (*Comm*) socio(-a) comanditario(-a)

sleeping pill *n* somnífero

sleeping sickness *n* enfermedad *f* del sueño

sleepless ['sliːplɪs] *adj*: **a** ~ **night** una noche en blanco

sleeplessness ['sliːplɪsnɪs] *n* insomnio

sleepover ['sliːpəuvə^r] *n*: **we're having a** ~ **at Fiona's** pasamos la noche en casa de Fiona

sleepwalk ['sliːpwɔːk] *vi* caminar dormido; (*habitually*) ser sonámbulo

sleepwalker ['sliːpwɔːkə^r] *n* sonámbulo(-a)

sleepy ['sliːpɪ] *adj* soñoliento; **to be** *or* **feel** ~ tener sueño

sleet [sliːt] *n* aguanieve *f*

sleeve [sliːv] *n* manga; (*Tech*) manguito; (*of record*) funda

sleeveless ['sliːvlɪs] *adj* (*garment*) sin mangas

sleigh [sleɪ] *n* trineo

sleight [slaɪt] *n*: ~ **of hand** prestidigitación *f*

slender ['slɛndə^r] *adj* delgado; (*means*) escaso

slept [slɛpt] *pt, pp of* **sleep**

sleuth [sluːθ] *n* (*col*) detective *m/f*

slew [sluː] *vi* (*veer*) torcerse ▪ *pt of* **slay**

slice [slaɪs] *n* (*of meat*) tajada; (*of bread*) rebanada; (*of lemon*) rodaja; (*utensil*) paleta ▪ *vt* cortar, tajar; rebanar; **sliced bread** pan *m* de molde

slick [slɪk] *adj* (*skilful*) hábil, diestro ▪ *n* (*also*: **oil slick**) capa de aceite

slid [slɪd] *pt, pp of* **slide**

slide [slaɪd] (*pt, pp* **slid**) *n* (*in playground*) tobogán *m*; (*Phot*) diapositiva; (*microscope slide*) portaobjetos *m* inv, plaquilla de vidrio; (*Brit*: *also*: **hair slide**) pasador *m* ▪ *vt* correr, deslizar ▪ *vi* (*slip*) resbalarse; (*glide*) deslizarse; **to let things ~** (fig) dejar que ruede la bola

slide projector n (Phot) proyector m de diapositivas

slide rule n regla de cálculo

sliding ['slaɪdɪŋ] adj (door) corredizo; **~ roof** (Aut) techo de corredera

sliding scale n escala móvil

slight [slaɪt] adj (slim) delgado; (frail) delicado; (pain etc) leve; (trifling) insignificante; (small) pequeño ■ n desaire m ■ vt (offend) ofender, desairar; **a ~ improvement** una ligera mejora; **not in the slightest** en absoluto; **there's not the slightest possibility** no hay la menor or más mínima posibilidad

slightly ['slaɪtlɪ] adv ligeramente, un poco; **~ built** delgado

slim [slɪm] adj delgado, esbelto ■ vi adelgazar

slime [slaɪm] n limo, cieno

slimming ['slɪmɪŋ] n adelgazamiento ■ adj (diet, pills) adelgazante

slimness ['slɪmnɪs] n delgadez f

slimy ['slaɪmɪ] adj limoso; (covered with mud) fangoso; (also fig: person) adulón, zalamero

sling [slɪŋ] n (Med) cabestrillo; (weapon) honda ■ vt (pt, pp **slung**) [slʌŋ] tirar, arrojar; **to have one's arm in a ~** llevar el brazo en cabestrillo

slink (pt, pp **slunk**) [slɪŋk, slʌŋk] vi: **to ~ away, ~ off** escabullirse

slinky ['slɪŋkɪ] adj (clothing) pegado al cuerpo, superajustado

slip [slɪp] n (slide) resbalón m; (mistake) descuido; (underskirt) combinación f; (of paper) papelito ■ vt (slide) deslizar ■ vi (slide) deslizarse; (stumble) resbalar(se); (decline) decaer; (move smoothly): **to ~ into/out of** (room etc) colarse en/salirse de; **to let a chance ~ by** dejar escapar la oportunidad; **to ~ sth on/ off** ponerse/quitarse algo; **to ~ on a jumper** ponerse un jersey or un suéter; **it slipped from her hand** se la cayó de la mano; **to give sb the ~** dar esquinazo a algn; **wages ~** (Brit) hoja del sueldo; **a ~ of the tongue** un lapsus

▶ **slip away** vi escabullirse

▶ **slip in** vt meter ■ vi meterse, colarse

▶ **slip out** vi (go out) salir (un momento)

slip-on ['slɪpɔn] adj de quita y pon; (shoes) sin cordones

slipped disc [slɪpt-] n vértebra dislocada

slipper ['slɪpə'] n zapatilla, pantufla

slippery ['slɪpərɪ] adj resbaladizo

slip road n (Brit) carretera de acceso

slipshod ['slɪpʃɔd] adj descuidado, chapucero

slipstream ['slɪpstri:m] n viento de la hélice

slip-up ['slɪpʌp] n (error) desliz m

slipway ['slɪpweɪ] n grada, gradas fpl

slit [slɪt] n raja; (cut) corte m ■ vt (pt, pp **slit**) rajar, cortar; **to ~ sb's throat** cortarle el pescuezo a algn

slither ['slɪðə'] vi deslizarse

sliver ['slɪvə'] n (of glass, wood) astilla; (of cheese, sausage) lonja, loncha

slob [slɔb] n (col) patán(-ana) m(f), palurdo(-a) m(f)

slog [slɔg] (Brit) vi sudar tinta ■ n: **it was a ~** costó trabajo (hacerlo)

slogan ['sləugən] n eslogan m, lema m

slop [slɔp] vi (also: **slop over**) derramarse, desbordarse ■ vt derramar, verter

slope [sləup] n (up) cuesta, pendiente f; (down) declive m; (side of mountain) falda, vertiente f ■ vi: **to ~ down** estar en declive; **to ~ up** subir (en pendiente)

sloping ['sləupɪŋ] adj en pendiente; en declive

sloppily ['slɔpɪlɪ] adv descuidadamente; con descuido or desaliño

sloppiness ['slɔpɪnɪs] n descuido; desaliño

sloppy ['slɔpɪ] adj (work) descuidado; (appearance) desaliñado

slosh [slɔʃ] vi: **to ~ about** or **around** chapotear

sloshed [slɔʃt] adj (col: drunk): **to get ~** agarrar una trompa

slot [slɔt] n ranura; (fig: in timetable) hueco; (Radio, TV) espacio ■ vt: **to ~ into** encajar en

sloth [sləuθ] n (vice) pereza; (Zool) oso perezoso

slot machine n (Brit: vending machine) máquina expendedora; (for gambling) máquina tragaperras

slot meter n contador m

slouch [slautʃ] vi: **to ~ about, ~ around** (laze) gandulear

Slovak ['sləuvæk] adj eslovaco ■ n eslovaco(-a); (Ling) eslovaco; **the ~ Republic** Eslovaquia

Slovakia [sləu'vækɪə] n Eslovaquia

Slovakian [sləu'vækɪən] adj, n = **Slovak**

Slovene [sləu'vi:n] adj esloveno ■ n esloveno(-a); (Ling) esloveno

Slovenia [sləu'vi:nɪə] n Eslovenia

Slovenian [sləu'vi:nɪən] adj, n = **Slovene**

slovenly ['slʌvənlɪ] adj (dirty) desaliñado, desaseado; (careless) descuidado

slow [sləu] adj lento; (watch): **to be ~** estar atrasado ■ adv lentamente, despacio ■ vt (also: **slow down, slow up**) retardar; (engine, machine) reducir la marcha de ■ vi (also: **slow down, slow up**) ir más despacio; **"~"** (road sign) "disminuir la velocidad"; **at a ~**

speed a una velocidad lenta; **the ~ lane** el carril derecho; **business is ~** (*Comm*) hay poca actividad; **my watch is 20 minutes ~** mi reloj lleva 20 minutos de retraso; **bake in a ~ oven** cocer *or* asar en el horno a fuego lento; **to be ~ to act/decide** tardar en obrar/decidir; **to go ~** (*driver*) conducir despacio; (*in industrial dispute*) trabajar a ritmo lento

slow-acting [sləu'æktɪŋ] *adj* de efecto retardado

slowcoach ['sləukəutʃ] *n* (*Brit col*) tortuga

slowdown ['sləudaun] *n* (*US*) huelga de celo

slowly ['sləulɪ] *adv* lentamente, despacio; **to drive ~** conducir despacio; **~ but surely** lento pero seguro

slow motion *n*: **in ~** a cámara lenta

slow-moving ['sləu'mu:vɪŋ] *adj* lento

slowpoke ['sləupəuk] *n* (*US col*) = **slowcoach**

sludge [slʌdʒ] *n* lodo, fango

slug [slʌg] *n* babosa; (*bullet*) posta

sluggish ['slʌgɪʃ] *adj* (*slow*) lento; (*lazy*) perezoso; (*business, market, sales*) inactivo

sluggishly ['slʌgɪʃlɪ] *adv* lentamente

sluggishness ['slʌgɪʃnɪs] *n* lentitud *f*

sluice [slu:s] *n* (*gate*) esclusa; (*channel*) canal *m* ◼ *vt*: **to ~ down** *or* **out** regar

slum [slʌm] *n* (*area*) barrios *mpl* bajos; (*house*) casucha

slumber ['slʌmbəʳ] *n* sueño

slum clearance, slum clearance programme *n* (programa *m* de) deschabolización *f*

slump [slʌmp] *n* (*economic*) depresión *f* ◼ *vi* hundirse; **the ~ in the price of copper** la baja repentina del precio del cobre; **he was slumped over the wheel** se había desplomado encima del volante

slung [slʌŋ] *pt, pp of* **sling**

slunk [slʌŋk] *pt, pp of* **slink**

slur [slə:ʳ] *n* calumnia ◼ *vt* calumniar, difamar; (*word*) pronunciar mal; **to cast a ~ on sb** manchar la reputación de algn, difamar a algn

slurp [slə:p] *vt, vi* sorber ruidosamente

slurred [slə:d] *adj* (*pronunciation*) poco claro

slush [slʌʃ] *n* nieve *f* a medio derretir

slush fund *n* fondos *mpl* para sobornar

slushy ['slʌʃɪ] *adj* (*col: poetry etc*) sentimentaloide

slut [slʌt] *n* marrana

sly [slaɪ] *adj* (*clever*) astuto; (*nasty*) malicioso

slyly ['slaɪlɪ] *adv* astutamente; taimadamente

slyness ['slaɪnɪs] *n* astucia

SM *n abbr* = **sadomasochism**

smack [smæk] *n* (*slap*) manotada; (*blow*) golpe *m* ◼ *vt* dar una manotada a; golpear

con la mano ◼ *vi*: **to ~ of** saber a, oler a ◼ *adv*: **it fell ~ in the middle** (*col*) cayó justo en medio

smacker ['smækəʳ] *n* (*col: kiss*) besazo; (: *Brit: pound note*) billete *m* de una libra; (: *US: dollar bill*) billete *m* de un dólar

small [smɔ:l] *adj* pequeño, chico (*LAm*); (*in height*) bajo, chaparro (*LAm*); (*letter*) en minúscula ◼ *n*: **~ of the back** región *f* lumbar; **~ shopkeeper** pequeño(-a) comerciante *m(f)*; **to get** *or* **grow smaller** (*stain, town*) empequeñecer; (*debt, organization, numbers*) reducir, disminuir; **to make smaller** (*amount, income*) reducir; (*garden, object, garment*) achicar

small ads *npl* (*Brit*) anuncios *mpl* por palabras

small arms *npl* armas *fpl* cortas

small business *n* pequeño negocio; **small businesses** la pequeña empresa

small change *n* suelto, cambio

smallholder ['smɔ:lhəuldəʳ] *n* (*Brit*) granjero(-a), parcelero(-a)

smallholding ['smɔ:lhəuldɪŋ] *n* parcela, minifundio

small hours *npl*: **in the ~** a altas horas de la noche

smallish ['smɔ:lɪʃ] *adj* más bien pequeño

small-minded [smɔ:l'maɪndɪd] *adj* mezquino, de miras estrechas

smallness ['smɔ:lnɪs] *n* pequeñez *f*

smallpox ['smɔ:lpɔks] *n* viruela

small print *n* letra pequeña *or* menuda

small-scale ['smɔ:lskeɪl] *adj* (*map, model*) a escala reducida; (*business, farming*) en pequeña escala

small talk *n* cháchara

small-time ['smɔ:ltaɪm] *adj* (*col*) de poca categoría *or* monta; **a ~ thief** un(a) ratero(-a)

small-town ['smɔ:ltəun] *adj* de provincias

smarmy ['smɑ:mɪ] *adj* (*Brit pej*) pelotillero (*fam*)

smart [smɑ:t] *adj* elegante; (*clever*) listo, inteligente; (*quick*) rápido, vivo; (*weapon*) inteligente ◼ *vi* escocer, picar; **the ~ set** la gente de buen tono; **to look ~** estar elegante; **my eyes are smarting** me pican los ojos

smartcard ['smɑ:tkɑ:d] *n* tarjeta inteligente

smarten up ['smɑ:tn-] *vi* arreglarse ◼ *vt* arreglar

smartness ['smɑ:tnɪs] *n* elegancia; (*cleverness*) inteligencia

smart phone *n* smartphone *m*

smash [smæʃ] *n* (*also*: **smash-up**) choque *m*; (*sound*) estrépito ◼ *vt* (*break*) hacer pedazos; (*car etc*) estrellar; (*Sport: record*) batir ◼ *vi* hacerse pedazos; (*against wall etc*) estrellarse

▶ **smash up** vt (car) hacer pedazos; (room) destrozar

smash hit n exitazo

smashing ['smæʃɪŋ] adj (col) cojonudo

smattering ['smætərɪŋ] n: **a ~ of Spanish** algo de español

smear [smɪə^r] n mancha; (Med) frotis m inv (cervical); (insult) calumnia ■ vt untar; (fig) calumniar, difamar; **his hands were smeared with oil/ink** tenía las manos manchadas de aceite/tinta

smear campaign n campaña de calumnias

smear test n (Med) citología, frotis m inv (cervical)

smell [smel] (pt, pp **smelt** or **smelled**) n olor m; (sense) olfato ■ vt, vi oler; **it smells good/of garlic** huele bien/a ajo

smelly ['smelɪ] adj maloliente

smelt [smelt] vt (ore) fundir ■ pt, pp of **smell**

smile [smaɪl] n sonrisa ■ vi sonreír

smiley ['smaɪlɪ] n (in email etc) smiley m, emoticón m

smiling ['smaɪlɪŋ] adj sonriente, risueño

smirk [smə:k] n sonrisa falsa or afectada

smith [smɪθ] n herrero

smitten ['smɪtn] adj: **he's really ~ with her** está totalmente loco por ella

smock [smɔk] n blusón; (children's) babi m; (US: overall) guardapolvo, bata

smog [smɔg] n smog m

smoke [sməuk] n humo ■ vi fumar; (chimney) echar humo ■ vt (cigarettes) fumar; **to go up in ~** quemarse; (fig) quedar en agua de borrajas

smoked [sməukt] adj (bacon, glass) ahumado

smokeless fuel ['sməuklɪs-] n combustible m sin humo

smokeless zone ['sməuklɪs-] n zona libre de humo

smoker ['sməukə^r] n fumador(a) m(f)

smoke screen n cortina de humo

smoke shop n (US) estanco, tabaquería

smoking ['sməukɪŋ] n: **"no ~"** "prohibido fumar"; **he's given up ~** ha dejado de fumar

smoking compartment, smoking car (US) n departamento de fumadores

smoky ['sməukɪ] adj (room) lleno de humo

smolder ['sməuldə^r] vi (US) = **smoulder**

smoochy ['smu:tʃɪ] adj (col) blandengue

smooth [smu:ð] adj liso; (sea) tranquilo; (flavour, movement) suave; (person: pej) meloso ■ vt alisar; (also: **smooth out**: creases) alisar; (difficulties) allanar

▶ **smooth over** vt: **to ~ things over** (fig) limar las asperezas

smoothly ['smu:ðlɪ] adv (easily) fácilmente; **everything went ~** todo fue sobre ruedas

smoothness ['smu:ðnɪs] n (of skin, cloth) tersura; (of surface, flavour, movement) suavidad f

smother ['smʌðə^r] vt sofocar; (repress) contener

smoulder, smolder (US) ['sməuldə^r] vi arder sin llama

SMS n abbr (= short message service) SMS m

smudge [smʌdʒ] n mancha ■ vt manchar

smug [smʌg] adj engreído

smuggle ['smʌgl] vt pasar de contrabando; **to ~ in/out** (goods etc) meter/sacar de contrabando

smuggler ['smʌglə^r] n contrabandista m/f

smuggling ['smʌglɪŋ] n contrabando

smugly ['smʌglɪ] adv con suficiencia

smugness ['smʌgnɪs] n suficiencia

smut [smʌt] n (grain of soot) carbonilla, hollín m; (mark) tizne m; (in conversation etc) obscenidades fpl

smutty ['smʌtɪ] adj (fig) verde, obsceno

snack [snæk] n bocado, tentempié m; **to have a ~** tomar un bocado

snack bar n cafetería

snag [snæg] n problema m; **to run into** or **hit a ~** encontrar inconvenientes, dar con un obstáculo

snail [sneɪl] n caracol m

snake [sneɪk] n (gen) serpiente f; (harmless) culebra; (poisonous) víbora

snap [snæp] n (sound) chasquido; golpe m seco; (photograph) foto f ■ adj (decision) instantáneo ■ vt (fingers etc) castañetear; (break) partir, quebrar; (photograph) tomar una foto de ■ vi (break) partirse, quebrarse; (fig: person) contestar bruscamente; **to ~ (at sb)** (person) hablar con brusquedad (a algn); (dog) intentar morder (a algn); **to ~ shut** cerrarse de golpe; **to ~ one's fingers at sth/sb** (fig) burlarse de algo/uno; **a cold ~** (of weather) una ola de frío

▶ **snap off** vi (break) partirse

▶ **snap up** vt agarrar

snap fastener n (US) botón m de presión

snappy ['snæpɪ] adj (col: answer) instantáneo; (slogan) conciso; **make it ~!** (hurry up) ¡date prisa!

snapshot ['snæpʃɔt] n foto f (instantánea)

snare [snɛə^r] n trampa ■ vt cazar con trampa; (fig) engañar

snarl [snɑ:l] n gruñido ■ vi gruñir; **to get snarled up** (wool, plans) enmarañarse, enredarse; (traffic) quedar atascado

snatch [snætʃ] n (fig) robo; **snatches of trocitos mpl de** ■ vt (snatch away) arrebatar; (grasp) coger (SP), agarrar; **snatches of conversation** fragmentos mpl de

conversación; **to ~ a sandwich** comer un bocadillo a prisa; **to ~ some sleep** buscar tiempo para dormir; **don't ~!** ¡no me lo quites!
▸ **snatch up** *vt* agarrar
snazzy ['snæzɪ] *adj* (*col*) guapo
sneak [sni:k] *vi*: **to ~ in/out** entrar/salir a hurtadillas ■ *vt*: **to ~ a look at sth** mirar algo de reojo ■ *n* (*fam*) soplón(-ona) *m(f)*
sneakers ['sni:kəz] *npl* (*US*) zapatos *mpl* de lona, zapatillas *fpl*
sneaking ['sni:kɪŋ] *adj*: **to have a ~ feeling/ suspicion that ...** tener la sensación/ sospecha de que ...
sneaky ['sni:kɪ] *adj* furtivo
sneer [snɪəʳ] *n* sonrisa de desprecio ■ *vi* sonreír con desprecio; **to ~ at sth/sb** burlarse *or* mofarse de algo/uno
sneeze [sni:z] *n* estornudo ■ *vi* estornudar
snide [snaɪd] *adj* (*col: sarcastic*) sarcástico
sniff [snɪf] *vi* sorber (por la nariz) ■ *vt* husmear, oler; (*glue, drug*) esnifar
▸ **sniff at** *vt fus*: **it's not to be sniffed at** no es de despreciar
sniffer dog ['snɪfə-] *n* (*for drugs*) perro antidroga; (*for explosives*) perro antiexplosivos
snigger ['snɪɡəʳ] *n* risa disimulada ■ *vi* reírse con disimulo
snip [snɪp] *n* (*piece*) recorte *m*; (*bargain*) ganga ■ *vt* tijeretear
sniper ['snaɪpəʳ] *n* francotirador(a) *m(f)*
snippet ['snɪpɪt] *n* retazo
snivelling, sniveling (*US*) ['snɪvlɪŋ] *adj* llorón(-ona)
snob [snɔb] *n* (e)snob *m/f*
snobbery ['snɔbərɪ] *n* (e)snobismo
snobbish ['snɔbɪʃ] *adj* (e)snob
snobbishness ['snɔbɪʃnɪs] *n* (e)snobismo
snog [snɔɡ] *vi* (*Brit col*) besuquearse, morrear; **to ~ sb** besuquear a algn
snooker ['snu:kəʳ] *n* snooker *m*
snoop [snu:p] *vi*: **to ~ about** fisgonear
snooper ['snu:pəʳ] *n* fisgón(-ona) *m(f)*
snooty ['snu:tɪ] *adj* (e)snob
snooze [snu:z] *n* siesta ■ *vi* echar una siesta
snore [snɔːʳ] *vi* roncar ■ *n* ronquido
snoring ['snɔːrɪŋ] *n* ronquidos *mpl*
snorkel ['snɔːkl] *n* tubo de respiración
snort [snɔːt] *n* bufido ■ *vi* bufar ■ *vt* (*col: drugs*) esnifar
snotty ['snɔtɪ] *adj* (*col*) creído
snout [snaut] *n* hocico, morro
snow [snəu] *n* nieve *f* ■ *vi* nevar ■ *vt*: **to be snowed under with work** estar agobiado de trabajo
snowball ['snəubɔːl] *n* bola de nieve ■ *vi* ir aumentándose

snow-blind ['snəublaɪnd] *adj* cegado por la nieve
snowbound ['snəubaund] *adj* bloqueado por la nieve
snow-capped ['snəukæpt] *adj* (*peak*) cubierto de nieve, nevado
snowdrift ['snəudrɪft] *n* ventisquero
snowdrop ['snəudrɔp] *n* campanilla
snowfall ['snəufɔːl] *n* nevada
snowflake ['snəufleɪk] *n* copo de nieve
snowline ['snəulaɪn] *n* límite *m* de las nieves perpetuas
snowman ['snəumæn] *n* figura de nieve
snowplough, snowplow (*US*) ['snəuplau] *n* quitanieves *m inv*
snowshoe ['snəuʃu:] *n* raqueta (de nieve)
snowstorm ['snəustɔːm] *n* tormenta de nieve, nevasca
Snow White *n* Blancanieves *f*
snowy ['snəuɪ] *adj* de (mucha) nieve
SNP *n abbr* (*Brit Pol*) = **Scottish National Party**
snub [snʌb] *vt*: **to ~ sb** desairar a algn ■ *n* desaire *m*, repulsa
snub-nosed [snʌb'nəuzd] *adj* chato
snuff [snʌf] *n* rapé *m* ■ *vt* (*also*: **snuff out**: *candle*) apagar
snuffbox ['snʌfbɔks] *n* caja de rapé
snuff movie *n* (*col*) película porno (*que acaba con un asesinato real*)
snug [snʌɡ] *adj* (*cosy*) cómodo; (*fitted*) ajustado
snuggle ['snʌɡl] *vi*: **to ~ down in bed** hacerse un ovillo *or* acurrucarse en la cama; **to ~ up to sb** acurrucarse junto a algn
snugly ['snʌɡlɪ] *adv* cómodamente; **it fits ~** (*object in pocket etc*) cabe perfectamente; (*garment*) ajusta perfectamente
SO *abbr* (*Banking*) = **standing order**

 KEYWORD

so [səu] *adv* **1** (*thus, likewise*) así, de este modo; **if so** de ser así; **I like swimming — so do I** a mí me gusta nadar — a mí también; **I've got work to do — so has Paul** tengo trabajo que hacer — Paul también; **it's five o'clock — so it is!** son las cinco — ¡pues es verdad!; **I hope/think so** espero/creo que sí; **so far** hasta ahora; (*in past*) hasta este momento; **so to speak** por decirlo así
2 (*in comparisons etc: to such a degree*) tan; **so quickly (that)** tan rápido (que); **so big (that)** tan grande (que); **she's not so clever as her brother** no es tan lista como su hermano; **we were so worried** estábamos preocupadísimos
3: **so much** *adj* tanto(-a)

■ adv tanto; **so many** tantos(-as)
4 (phrases): **10 or so** unos 10, 10 o así; **so long!**
(col: goodbye) ¡hasta luego!; **so (what)?** (col)
¿y (qué)?
■ conj **1** (expressing purpose): **so as to do**
para hacer; **so (that)** para que + subjun; **we
hurried so (that) we wouldn't be late** nos
dimos prisa para no llegar tarde
2 (expressing result) así que; **so you see, I
could have gone** así que ya ves, (yo) podría
haber ido; **so that's the reason!** ¡así que es
por eso or por eso es!

soak [səuk] vt (drench) empapar; (put in water)
remojar ■ vi remojarse, estar a remojo
▶ **soak in** vi penetrar
▶ **soak up** vt absorber
soaking ['səukɪŋ] adj (also: **soaking wet**)
calado or empapado (hasta los huesos or el
tuétano)
so-and-so ['səuənsəu] n (somebody) fulano(-a)
de tal
soap [səup] n jabón m
soapbox ['səupbɔks] n tribuna improvisada
soapflakes ['səupfleɪks] npl jabón msg en
escamas
soap opera n (TV) telenovela; (Radio)
radionovela
soap powder n jabón m en polvo
soapsuds ['səupsʌdz] npl espuma sg
soapy ['səupɪ] adj jabonoso
soar [sɔːʳ] vi (on wings) remontarse; (building
etc) elevarse; (price) subir vertiginosamente;
(morale) elevarse
soaring ['sɔːrɪŋ] adj (flight) por lo alto; (prices)
en alza or aumento; **~ inflation** inflación f
altísima or en aumento
sob [sɔb] n sollozo ■ vi sollozar
s.o.b. n abbr (US col!: = son of a bitch) hijo de
puta (!)
sober ['səubəʳ] adj (moderate) moderado;
(serious) serio; (not drunk) sobrio; (colour, style)
discreto
▶ **sober up** vi pasársele a algn la borrachera
soberly ['səubəlɪ] adv sobriamente
sobriety [sə'braɪətɪ] n (not being drunk)
sobriedad f; (seriousness, sedateness) seriedad f,
sensatez f
sob story n (col, pej) dramón m
Soc. abbr (= society) S
so-called ['səu'kɔːld] adj presunto, supuesto
soccer ['sɔkəʳ] n fútbol m
soccer pitch n campo or cancha (LAm) de
fútbol
soccer player n jugador(a) m(f) de fútbol
sociability [səuʃə'bɪlɪtɪ] n sociabilidad f
sociable ['səuʃəbl] adj sociable

social ['səuʃl] adj social ■ n velada, fiesta
social class n clase f social
social climber n arribista m/f
social club n club m
Social Democrat n socialdemócrata m/f
social insurance n (US) seguro social
socialism ['səuʃəlɪzəm] n socialismo
socialist ['səuʃəlɪst] adj, n socialista m/f
socialite ['səuʃəlaɪt] n persona que alterna con la
buena sociedad
socialize ['səuʃəlaɪz] vi hacer vida social; **to ~
with** (colleagues) salir con
social life n vida social
socially ['səuʃəlɪ] adv socialmente
social networking [-'nɛtwəːkɪŋ] n
interacción f social a través de la red
social science n, **social sciences** npl
ciencias fpl sociales
social security n seguridad f social
social services npl servicios mpl sociales
social welfare n asistencia social
social work n asistencia social
social worker n asistente(-a) m(f) social
society [sə'saɪətɪ] n sociedad f; (club)
asociación f; (also: **high society**) buena
sociedad ■ cpd (party, column) social, de
sociedad
socio-economic ['səusɪəuiːkə'nɔmɪk] adj
socioeconómico
sociological [səusɪə'lɔdʒɪkəl] adj sociológico
sociologist [səusɪ'ɔlədʒɪst] n sociólogo(-a)
sociology [səusɪ'ɔlədʒɪ] n sociología
sock [sɔk] n calcetín m, media (LAm); **to
pull one's socks up** (fig) hacer esfuerzos,
despabilarse
socket ['sɔkɪt] n (Elec) enchufe m
sod [sɔd] n (of earth) césped m; (col!)
cabrón(-ona) m(f) (!) ■ excl: **~ off!** (col!) ¡vete
a la porra!
soda ['səudə] n (Chem) sosa; (also: **soda water**)
soda; (US: also: **soda pop**) gaseosa
sodden ['sɔdn] adj empapado
sodium ['səudɪəm] n sodio
sodium chloride n cloruro sódico or de sodio
sofa ['səufə] n sofá m
Sofia ['səufɪə] n Sofía
soft [sɔft] adj (teacher, parent) blando; (gentle,
not loud) suave; (stupid) bobo; **~ currency**
divisa blanda or débil
soft-boiled ['sɔftbɔɪld] adj (egg) pasado por
agua
soft copy n (Comput) copia transitoria
soft drink n bebida no alcohólica
soft drugs npl drogas fpl blandas
soften ['sɔfn] vt ablandar; suavizar ■ vi
ablandarse; suavizarse
softener ['sɔfnəʳ] n suavizante m

S

soft fruit n bayas fpl
soft furnishings npl tejidos mpl para el hogar
soft-hearted [sɔft'hɑːtɪd] adj bondadoso
softly ['sɔftlɪ] adv suavemente; (gently)
delicadamente, con delicadeza
softness ['sɔftnɪs] n blandura; suavidad f
soft option n alternativa fácil
soft sell n venta persuasiva
soft target n blanco or objetivo fácil
soft toy n juguete m de peluche
software ['sɔftwɛəʳ] n (Comput) software m
soft water n agua blanda
soggy ['sɔgɪ] adj empapado
soil [sɔɪl] n (earth) tierra, suelo ▪ vt ensuciar
soiled [sɔɪld] adj sucio, manchado
sojourn ['sɔdʒɜːn] n (formal) estancia
solace ['sɔlɪs] n consuelo
solar ['səʊləʳ] adj solar
solarium (pl solaria) [sə'lɛərɪəm, -rɪə] n
solario
solar panel n panel m solar
solar plexus [-'plɛksəs] n (Anat) plexo solar
solar power n energía solar
solar system n sistema m solar
sold [səʊld] pt, pp of sell
solder ['səʊldəʳ] vt soldar ▪ n soldadura
soldier ['səʊldʒəʳ] n (gen) soldado; (army man)
militar m ▪ vi: to ~ on seguir adelante; toy ~
soldadito de plomo
sold out adj (Comm) agotado
sole [səʊl] n (of foot) planta; (of shoe) suela;
(fish: pl inv) lenguado ▪ adj único; the ~
reason la única razón
solely ['səʊllɪ] adv únicamente, sólo,
solamente; I will hold you ~ responsible le
consideraré el único responsable
solemn ['sɔləm] adj solemne
sole trader n (Comm) comerciante m/f
exclusivo(-a)
solicit [sə'lɪsɪt] vt (request) solicitar ▪ vi
(prostitute) abordar clientes
solicitor [sə'lɪsɪtəʳ] n abogado(-a); see also
barrister
solid ['sɔlɪd] adj sólido; (gold etc) macizo; (line)
continuo; (vote) unánime ▪ n sólido; we
waited two ~ hours esperamos dos horas
enteras; to be on ~ ground estar en tierra
firme; (fig) estar seguro
solidarity [sɔlɪ'dærɪtɪ] n solidaridad f
solid fuel n combustible m sólido
solidify [sə'lɪdɪfaɪ] vi solidificarse
solidity [sə'lɪdɪtɪ] n solidez f
solidly ['sɔlɪdlɪ] adv sólidamente; (fig)
unánimemente
solid-state ['sɔlɪdsteɪt] adj (Elec) estado
sólido
soliloquy [sə'lɪləkwɪ] n soliloquio

solitaire [sɔlɪ'tɛəʳ] n (game, gem) solitario
solitary ['sɔlɪtərɪ] adj solitario, solo; (isolated)
apartado, aislado; (only) único
solitary confinement n incomunicación f;
to be in ~ estar incomunicado
solitude ['sɔlɪtjuːd] n soledad f
solo ['səʊləʊ] n solo
soloist ['səʊləʊɪst] n solista m/f
Solomon Islands ['sɔləmən-] npl: the ~ las
Islas Salomón
solstice ['sɔlstɪs] n solsticio
soluble ['sɔljubl] adj soluble
solution [sə'luːʃən] n solución f
solve [sɔlv] vt resolver, solucionar
solvency ['sɔlvənsɪ] n (Comm) solvencia
solvent ['sɔlvənt] adj (Comm) solvente ▪ n
(Chem) solvente m
solvent abuse n uso indebido de disolventes
Som. abbr (Brit) = Somerset
Somali [sə'mɑːlɪ] adj, n somalí m/f
Somalia [sə'mɑːlɪə] n Somalia
Somaliland [sə'mɑːlɪlænd] n Somaliland f
sombre, somber (US) ['sɔmbəʳ] adj sombrío

○ KEYWORD

some [sʌm] adj 1 (a certain amount or number of):
some tea/water/biscuits té/agua/(unas)
galletas; have some tea tómese un té;
there's some milk in the fridge hay
leche en el frigo; there were some people
outside había algunas personas fuera; I've
got some money, but not much tengo algo
de dinero, pero no mucho
2 (certain: in contrasts) algunos(-as); some
people say that ... hay quien dice que ...;
some films were excellent, but most were
mediocre hubo películas excelentes, pero la
mayoría fueron mediocres
3 (unspecified): some woman was asking
for you una mujer estuvo preguntando por
ti; some day algún día; some day next
week un día de la semana que viene; he
was asking for some book (or other) pedía
no se qué libro; in some way or other de
alguna que otra manera
4 (considerable amount of) bastante; some days
ago hace unos cuantos días; after some
time pasado algún tiempo; at some length
con mucho detalle
5 (col: intensive): that was some party!
¡menuda fiesta!
▪ pron 1 (a certain number): I've got some
(books etc) tengo algunos(-as)
2 (a certain amount): I've got some
(money, milk) tengo algo; would you like
some? (coffee etc) ¿quiere un poco?; (books

etc) ¿quiere alguno?; **could I have some of that cheese?** ¿me puede dar un poco de ese queso?; **I've read some of the book** he leído parte del libro ■ *adv*: **some 10 people** unas 10 personas, una decena de personas

somebody ['sʌmbədɪ] *pron* alguien; **~ or other** alguien

someday ['sʌmdeɪ] *adv* algún día

somehow ['sʌmhau] *adv* de alguna manera; *(for some reason)* por una u otra razón

someone ['sʌmwʌn] *pron* = **somebody**

someplace ['sʌmpleɪs] *adv (US)* = **somewhere**

somersault ['sʌməsɔːlt] *n (deliberate)* salto mortal; *(accidental)* vuelco ■ *vi* dar un salto mortal; dar vuelcos

something ['sʌmθɪŋ] *pron* algo ■ *adv*: **he's ~ like me** es un poco como yo; **~ to do** algo que hacer; **it's ~ of a problem** es bastante problemático

sometime ['sʌmtaɪm] *adv (in future)* algún día, en algún momento; **~ last month** durante el mes pasado; **I'll finish it ~** lo terminaré un día de éstos

sometimes ['sʌmtaɪmz] *adv* a veces

somewhat ['sʌmwɔt] *adv* algo

somewhere ['sʌmwɛəʳ] *adv (be)* en alguna parte; *(go)* a alguna parte; **~ else** *(be)* en otra parte; *(go)* a otra parte

son |sʌn| *n* hijo

sonar ['səunɑːʳ] *n* sonar *m*

sonata [sə'nɑːtə] *n* sonata

song [sɔŋ] *n* canción *f*

songwriter ['sɔŋraɪtəʳ] *n* compositor(a) *m(f)* de canciones

sonic ['sɔnɪk] *adj (boom)* sónico

son-in-law ['sʌnɪnlɔː] *n* yerno

sonnet ['sɔnɪt] *n* soneto

sonny ['sʌnɪ] *n (col)* hijo

soon [suːn] *adv* pronto, dentro de poco; **~ afterwards** poco después; **very/quite ~** muy/bastante pronto; **how ~ can you be ready?** ¿cuánto tardas en prepararte?; **it's too ~ to tell** es demasiado pronto para saber; **see you ~!** ¡hasta pronto!; *see also* **as**

sooner ['suːnəʳ] *adv (time)* antes, más temprano; **I would ~ do that** preferiría hacer eso; **~ or later** tarde o temprano; **no ~ said than done** dicho y hecho; **the ~ the better** cuanto antes mejor; **no ~ had we left than ...** apenas nos habíamos marchado cuando ...

soot [sut] *n* hollín *m*

soothe [suːð] *vt* tranquilizar; *(pain)* aliviar

soothing ['suːðɪŋ] *adj (ointment etc)* sedante;

(tone, words etc) calmante, tranquilizante

SOP *n abbr* = **standard operating procedure**

sophisticated [sə'fɪstɪkeɪtɪd] *adj* sofisticado

sophistication [səfɪstɪ'keɪʃən] *n* sofisticación *f*

sophomore ['sɔfəmɔːʳ] *n (US)* estudiante *m/f* de segundo año

soporific [sɔpə'rɪfɪk] *adj* soporífero

sopping ['sɔpɪŋ] *adj*: **~ (wet)** empapado

soppy ['sɔpɪ] *adj (pej)* bobo, tonto

soprano [sə'prɑːnəu] *n* soprano *f*

sorbet ['sɔːbeɪ] *n* sorbete *m*

sorcerer ['sɔːsərəʳ] *n* hechicero

sordid ['sɔːdɪd] *adj (place etc)* sórdido; *(motive etc)* mezquino

sore [sɔːʳ] *adj (painful)* doloroso, que duele; *(offended)* resentido ■ *n* llaga; **~ throat** dolor *m* de garganta; **my eyes are ~, I have ~ eyes** me duelen los ojos; **it's a ~ point** es un asunto delicado *or* espinoso

sorely *adv*: **I am ~ tempted to (do it)** estoy muy tentado a (hacerlo)

soreness ['sɔːnɪs] *n* dolor *m*

sorrel ['sɔrəl] *n (Bot)* acedera

sorrow ['sɔrəu] *n* pena, dolor *m*

sorrowful ['sɔrəuful] *adj* afligido, triste

sorrowfully ['sɔrəufulɪ] *adv* tristemente

sorry ['sɔrɪ] *adj (regretful)* arrepentido; *(condition, excuse)* lastimoso; *(sight, failure)* triste; **~!** ¡perdón!, ¡perdone!; **I am ~** lo siento; **I feel ~ for him** me da lástima *or* pena; **I'm ~ to hear that ...** siento saber que ...; **to be ~ about sth** lamentar algo

sort [sɔːt] *n* clase *f*, género, tipo; *(make: of coffee, car etc)* marca ■ *vt (also:* **sort out:** *papers)* clasificar; *(: problems)* arreglar, solucionar; *(Comput)* clasificar; **what ~ do you want?** *(make)* ¿qué marca quieres?; **what ~ of car?** ¿qué tipo de coche?; **I shall do nothing of the ~** no pienso hacer nada parecido; **it's ~ of awkward** *(col)* es bastante difícil

sortie ['sɔːtɪ] *n* salida

sorting office ['sɔːtɪŋ-] *n* oficina de clasificación del correo

SOS *n* SOS *m*

so-so ['səusəu] *adv* regular, así así

soufflé ['suːfleɪ] *n* suflé *m*

sought [sɔːt] *pt, pp of* **seek**

sought-after ['sɔːtɑːftəʳ] *adj* solicitado, codiciado

soul [səul] *n* alma *f*; **God rest his ~** Dios le reciba en su seno *or* en su gloria; **I didn't see a ~** no vi a nadie; **the poor ~ had nowhere to sleep** el pobre no tenía dónde dormir

soul-destroying ['səuldɪstrɔɪɪŋ] *adj (work)* deprimente

S

soulful ['səulful] *adj* lleno de sentimiento
soulmate ['səulmeɪt] *n* compañero(-a) del
 alma
soul-searching ['səulsə:tʃɪŋ] *n*: **after much**
 ~ después de pensarlo mucho, después de
 darle muchas vueltas
sound [saund] *adj* (*healthy*) sano; (*safe, not*
 damaged) en buen estado; (*valid: argument,*
 policy, claim) válido; (: *move*) acertado;
 (*dependable: person*) de fiar; (*sensible*) sensato,
 razonable ▪ *adv*: **~ asleep** profundamente
 dormido ▪ *n* (*noise*) sonido, ruido; (*Geo*)
 estrecho ▪ *vt* (*alarm*) sonar; (*also*: **sound**
 out: *opinions*) consultar, sondear ▪ *vi* sonar,
 resonar; (*fig: seem*) parecer; **to ~ like** sonar a;
 to be of ~ mind estar en su sano juicio;
 I don't like the ~ of it no me gusta nada;
 it sounds as if ... parece que ...
 ▸ **sound off** *vi* (*col*): **to ~ off (about)** (*give one's*
 opinions) despotricar (contra)
sound barrier *n* barrera del sonido
sound bite *n* cita jugosa
sound effects *npl* efectos *mpl* sonoros
sound engineer *n* ingeniero(-a) del sonido
sounding ['saundɪŋ] *n* (*Naut etc*) sondeo
sounding board *n* caja de resonancia
soundly ['saundlɪ] *adv* (*sleep*)
 profundamente; (*beat*) completamente
soundproof ['saundpru:f] *adj* insonorizado
sound system *n* equipo de sonido
soundtrack ['saundtræk] *n* (*of film*) banda
 sonora
sound wave *n* (*Physics*) onda sonora
soup [su:p] *n* (*thick*) sopa; (*thin*) caldo; **in the**
 ~ (*fig*) en apuros
soup kitchen *n* comedor *m* de beneficencia
soup plate *n* plato sopero
soupspoon ['su:pspu:n] *n* cuchara sopera
sour ['sauə^r] *adj* agrio; (*milk*) cortado; **it's**
 just ~ grapes! (*fig*) ¡pura envidia!, ¡están
 verdes!; **to go** *or* **turn ~** (*milk*) cortarse; (*wine*)
 agriarse; (*fig: relationship*) agriarse; (: *plans*)
 irse a pique
source [sɔ:s] *n* fuente *f*; **I have it from a**
 reliable ~ that ... sé de fuente fidedigna
 que ...
source language *n* (*Comput*) lenguaje *m*
 fuente *or* de origen
south [sauθ] *n* sur *m* ▪ *adj* del sur ▪ *adv* al
 sur, hacia el sur; **(to the) ~ of** al sur de; **the**
 S~ of France el Sur de Francia; **to travel ~**
 viajar hacia el sur
South Africa *n* Sudáfrica
South African *adj, n* sudafricano(-a) *m(f)*
South America *n* América del Sur,
 Sudamérica
South American *adj, n* sudamericano(-a) *m(f)*

southbound ['sauθbaund] *adj* (*con*) rumbo
 al sur
south-east [sauθ'i:st] *n* sudeste *m* ▪ *adj*
 (*counties etc*) (del) sudeste
Southeast Asia *n* Sudeste *m* asiático
southerly ['sʌðəlɪ] *adj* sur; (*from the south*)
 del sur
southern ['sʌðən] *adj* del sur, meridional;
 the ~ hemisphere el hemisferio sur
South Korea *n* Corea del Sur
South Pole *n* Polo Sur
South Sea Islands *npl*: **the ~** Oceanía
South Seas *npl*: **the ~** los Mares del Sur
South Vietnam *n* Vietnam *m* del Sur
southward ['sauθwəd], **southwards**
 ['sauθwədz] *adv* hacia el sur
south-west [sauθ'wɛst] *n* suroeste *m*
souvenir [su:və'nɪə^r] *n* recuerdo
sovereign ['sɔvrɪn] *adj, n* soberano(-a) *m(f)*
sovereignty ['sɔvrɪntɪ] *n* soberanía
soviet ['səuvɪət] *adj* soviético
Soviet Union *n*: **the ~** la Unión Soviética
sow [sau] *n* cerda, puerca ▪ *vt* [səu] (*pt*
 sowed, *pp* **sown**) [səun] (*gen*) sembrar;
 (*spread*) esparcir
soya ['sɔɪə], **soy** (*US*) [sɔɪ] *n* soja
soya bean, soy bean (*US*) *n* semilla de soja
soya sauce, soy sauce (*US*) *n* salsa de soja
sozzled ['sɔzld] *adj* (*Brit col*) mamado
spa [spɑ:] *n* balneario
space [speɪs] *n* espacio; (*room*) sitio ▪ *vt*
 (*also*: **space out**) espaciar; **to clear a ~ for**
 sth hacer sitio para algo; **in a confined ~**
 en un espacio restringido; **in a short ~**
 of time en poco *or* un corto espacio de
 tiempo; **(with)in the ~ of an hour/three**
 generations en el espacio de una hora/tres
 generaciones
space bar *n* (*on typewriter*) barra espaciadora
spacecraft ['speɪskrɑ:ft] *n* nave *f* espacial,
 astronave *f*
spaceman ['speɪsmæn] *n* astronauta *m*,
 cosmonauta *m*
spaceship ['speɪsʃɪp] *n* = **spacecraft**
space shuttle *n* transportador *m* espacial
spacesuit ['speɪssu:t] *n* traje *m* espacial
spacewoman ['speɪswumən] *n* astronauta,
 cosmonauta
spacing ['speɪsɪŋ] *n* espacio
spacious ['speɪʃəs] *adj* amplio
spade [speɪd] *n* (*tool*) pala; **spades** *npl* (*Cards*:
 British) picas *fpl*; (*Spanish*) espadas *fpl*
spadework ['speɪdwə:k] *n* (*fig*) trabajo
 preliminar
spaghetti [spə'gɛtɪ] *n* espaguetis *mpl*
Spain [speɪn] *n* España
spam [spæm] *n* (*junk email*) correo basura

span [spæn] n (of bird, plane) envergadura; (of hand) palmo; (of arch) luz f; (in time) lapso ■ vt extenderse sobre, cruzar; (fig) abarcar
Spaniard ['spænjəd] n español(a) m(f)
spaniel ['spænjəl] n perro de aguas
Spanish ['spænɪʃ] adj español(a) ■ n (Ling) español m, castellano; **the Spanish** npl (people) los españoles; ~ **omelette** tortilla española or de patata
spank [spæŋk] vt zurrar, dar unos azotes a
spanner ['spænər] n (Brit) llave f inglesa
spar [spɑː'] n palo, verga ■ vi (Boxing) entrenarse (en el boxeo)
spare [spɛə'] adj de reserva; (surplus) sobrante, de más ■ n (part) pieza de repuesto ■ vt (do without) pasarse sin; (afford to give) tener de sobra; (refrain from hurting) perdonar; (details etc) ahorrar; **to** ~ (surplus) sobrante, de sobra; **there are two going** ~ sobran or quedan dos; **to** ~ **no expense** no escatimar gastos; **can you** ~ **(me) £10?** ¿puedes prestarme or darme 10 libras?; **can you** ~ **the time?** ¿tienes tiempo?; **I've a few minutes to** ~ tengo unos minutos libres; **there is no time to** ~ no hay tiempo que perder
spare part n pieza de repuesto
spare room n cuarto de los invitados
spare time n ratos mpl de ocio, tiempo libre
spare tyre, spare tire (US) n (Aut) neumático or llanta (LAm) de recambio
spare wheel n (Aut) rueda de recambio
sparing ['spɛərɪŋ] adj: **to be** ~ **with** ser parco en
sparingly ['spɛərɪŋlɪ] adv escasamente
spark [spɑːk] n chispa; (fig) chispazo
sparking plug ['spɑːk(ɪŋ)-] n = **spark plug**
sparkle ['spɑːkl] n centelleo, destello ■ vi centellear; (shine) relucir, brillar
sparkler ['spɑːklə'] n bengala
sparkling ['spɑːklɪŋ] adj centelleante; (wine) espumoso
spark plug n bujía
sparring partner ['spɑːrɪŋ-] n sparring m; (fig) contrincante m/f
sparrow ['spærəu] n gorrión m
sparse [spɑːs] adj esparcido, escaso
sparsely ['spɑːslɪ] adv escasamente; **a** ~ **furnished room** un cuarto con pocos muebles
spartan ['spɑːtən] adj (fig) espartano
spasm ['spæzəm] n (Med) espasmo; (fig) arranque m, ataque m
spasmodic [spæz'mɔdɪk] adj espasmódico
spastic ['spæstɪk] n espástico(-a)
spat [spæt] pt, pp of **spit** ■ n (US) riña
spate [speɪt] n (fig): ~ **of** torrente m de; **in** ~ (river) crecido

spatial ['speɪʃl] adj espacial
spatter ['spætə'] vt: **to** ~ **with** salpicar de
spatula ['spætjulə] n espátula
spawn [spɔːn] vt (pej) engendrar ■ vi desovar, frezar ■ n huevas fpl
SPCA n abbr (US) = **Society for the Prevention of Cruelty to Animals**
SPCC n abbr (US) = **Society for the Prevention of Cruelty to Children**
speak (pt **spoke**, pp **spoken**) [spiːk, spəuk, 'spəukn] vt (language) hablar; (truth) decir ■ vi hablar; (make a speech) intervenir; **to** ~ **one's mind** hablar claro or con franqueza; **to** ~ **to sb/of** or **about sth** hablar con algn/de or sobre algo; **to** ~ **at a conference/in a debate** hablar en un congreso/un debate; **he has no money to** ~ **of** no tiene mucho dinero que digamos; **speaking!** ¡al habla!; ~ **up!** ¡habla más alto!
▸ **speak for** vt fus: **to** ~ **for sb** hablar por or en nombre de algn; **that picture is already spoken for** (in shop) ese cuadro está reservado
speaker ['spiːkə'] n (in public) orador(a) m(f); (also: **loudspeaker**) altavoz m; (for stereo etc) bafle m; (Pol): **the S**~ (Brit) el Presidente de la Cámara de los Comunes; (US) el Presidente del Congreso; **are you a Welsh** ~? ¿habla Ud galés?
speaking ['spiːkɪŋ] adj hablante
-speaking ['spiːkɪŋ] suff -hablante; **Spanish-people** los hispanohablantes
spear [spɪə'] n lanza; (for fishing) arpón m ■ vt alancear; arponear
spearhead ['spɪəhed] vt (attack etc) encabezar ■ n punta de lanza, vanguardia
spearmint ['spɪəmɪnt] n menta verde
spec [spɛk] n (col): **on** ~ por si acaso; **to buy on** ~ arriesgarse a comprar
special ['spɛʃl] adj especial; (edition etc) extraordinario; (delivery) urgente ■ n (train) tren m especial; **nothing** ~ nada de particular, nada extraordinario
special agent n agente m/f especial
special correspondent n corresponsal m/f especial
special delivery n (Post): **by** ~ por entrega urgente
special effects npl (Cine) efectos mpl especiales
specialist ['spɛʃəlɪst] n especialista m/f; **a heart** ~ (Med) un(-a) especialista del corazón
speciality [spɛʃɪ'ælɪtɪ], **specialty** (US) ['spɛʃəltɪ] n especialidad f
specialize ['spɛʃəlaɪz] vi: **to** ~ **(in)** especializarse (en)
specially ['spɛʃlɪ] adv especialmente

special offer n (Comm) oferta especial
special train n tren m especial
specialty ['spɛʃəltɪ] n (US) = **speciality**
species ['spiːʃiːz] n especie f
specific [spə'sɪfɪk] adj específico
specifically [spə'sɪfɪklɪ] adv (explicitly: state, warn) específicamente, expresamente; (especially: design, intend) especialmente
specification [spɛsɪfɪ'keɪʃən] n especificación f; **specifications** npl (plan) presupuesto sg; (of car, machine) descripción f técnica; (for building) plan msg detallado
specify ['spɛsɪfaɪ] vt, vi especificar, precisar; **unless otherwise specified** salvo indicaciones contrarias
specimen ['spɛsɪmən] n ejemplar m; (Med: of urine) espécimen m; (: of blood) muestra
specimen copy n ejemplar m de muestra
specimen signature n muestra de firma
speck [spɛk] n grano, mota
speckled ['spɛkld] adj moteado
specs [spɛks] npl (col) gafas fpl (SP), anteojos mpl
spectacle ['spɛktəkl] n espectáculo
spectacle case n estuche m or funda (de gafas)
spectacles ['spɛktəklz] npl (Brit) gafas fpl (SP), anteojos mpl
spectacular [spɛk'tækjulər] adj espectacular; (success) impresionante
spectator [spɛk'teɪtər] n espectador(a) m(f)
spectator sport n deporte m espectáculo
spectra ['spɛktrə] npl of **spectrum**
spectre, specter (US) ['spɛktər] n espectro, fantasma m
spectrum (pl **spectra**) ['spɛktrəm, -trə] n espectro
speculate ['spɛkjuleɪt] vi especular; (try to guess): **to ~ about** especular sobre
speculation [spɛkju'leɪʃən] n especulación f
speculative ['spɛkjulətɪv] adj especulativo
speculator ['spɛkjuleɪtər] n especulador(a) m(f)
sped [spɛd] pt, pp of **speed**
speech [spiːtʃ] n (faculty) habla; (formal talk) discurso; (words) palabras fpl; (manner of speaking) forma de hablar; (language) idioma m, lenguaje m
speech day n (Brit Scol) ≈ día de reparto de premios
speech impediment n defecto del habla
speechless ['spiːtʃlɪs] adj mudo, estupefacto
speech therapy n logopedia
speed [spiːd] n (also Aut, Tech: gear) velocidad f; (haste) prisa; (promptness) rapidez f ■ vi (pt, pp **sped**) (Aut: exceed speed limit) conducir con exceso de velocidad; **at full** or **top ~**

a máxima velocidad; **at a ~ of 70 km/h** a una velocidad de 70 km por hora; **at ~** a gran velocidad; **a five-~ gearbox** una caja de cambios de cinco velocidades; **shorthand/typing ~** rapidez f en taquigrafía/mecanografía; **the years sped by** los años pasaron volando
▶ **speed up** vi acelerarse ■ vt acelerar
speedboat ['spiːdbəut] n lancha motora
speedily ['spiːdɪlɪ] adv rápido, rápidamente
speeding ['spiːdɪŋ] n (Aut) exceso de velocidad
speed limit n límite m de velocidad, velocidad f máxima
speedometer [spɪ'dɔmɪtər] n velocímetro
speed trap n (Aut) control m de velocidades
speedway ['spiːdweɪ] n (Sport) pista de carrera
speedy ['spiːdɪ] adj (fast) veloz, rápido; (prompt) pronto
spell [spɛl] n (also: **magic spell**) encanto, hechizo; (period of time) rato, período; (turn) turno ■ vt (pt, pp **spelt** or **spelled**) [spɛlt, spɛld] (also: **spell out**) deletrear; (fig) anunciar, presagiar; **to cast a ~ on sb** hechizar a algn; **he can't ~** no sabe escribir bien, comete faltas de ortografía; **can you ~ it for me?** ¿cómo se deletrea or se escribe?; **how do you ~ your name?** ¿cómo se escribe tu nombre?
spellbound ['spɛlbaund] adj embelesado, hechizado
spellchecker n (Comput) corrector m (ortográfico)
spelling ['spɛlɪŋ] n ortografía
spelling mistake n falta de ortografía
spelt [spɛlt] pt, pp of **spell**
spend (pt, pp **spent**) [spɛnd, spɛnt] vt (money) gastar; (time) pasar; (life) dedicar; **to ~ time/money/effort on sth** gastar tiempo/dinero/energías en algo
spending ['spɛndɪŋ] n: **government ~** gastos mpl del gobierno
spending money n dinero para gastos
spending power n poder m adquisitivo
spendthrift ['spɛndθrɪft] n derrochador(a) m(f) manirroto(-a)
spent [spɛnt] pt, pp of **spend** ■ adj (cartridge, bullets, match) usado
sperm [spəːm] n esperma
sperm bank n banco de esperma
sperm whale n cachalote m
spew [spjuː] vt vomitar, arrojar
sphere [sfɪər] n esfera
spherical ['sfɛrɪkl] adj esférico
sphinx [sfɪŋks] n esfinge f
spice [spaɪs] n especia ■ vt especiar

spiciness ['spaɪsɪnɪs] *n* lo picante
spick-and-span ['spɪkən'spæn] *adj* impecable
spicy ['spaɪsɪ] *adj* picante
spider ['spaɪdər] *n* araña
spider's web *n* telaraña
spiel [ʃpi:l] *n* (col) rollo
spike [spaɪk] *n* (point) punta; (Zool) pincho, púa; (Bot) espiga; (Elec) pico parásito ▪ *vt*: **to ~ a quote** cancelar una cita; **spikes** *npl* (Sport) zapatillas *fpl* con clavos
spiky ['spaɪkɪ] *adj* (bush, branch) cubierto de púas; (animal) erizado
spill (pt, pp **spilt** or **spilled**) [spɪl, spɪlt, spɪld] *vt* derramar, verter; (blood) derramar ▪ *vi* derramarse; **to ~ the beans** (col) descubrir el pastel
  ▸ **spill out** *vi* derramarse, desparramarse
  ▸ **spill over** *vi* desbordarse
spillage ['spɪlɪdʒ] *n* (event) derrame *m*; (substance) vertidos
spin [spɪn] (pt, pp **spun**) *n* (revolution of wheel) vuelta, revolución *f*; (Aviat) barrena; (trip in car) paseo (en coche) ▪ *vt* (wool etc) hilar; (wheel) girar ▪ *vi* girar, dar vueltas; **the car spun out of control** el coche se descontroló y empezó a dar vueltas
  ▸ **spin out** *vt* alargar, prolongar
spina bifida ['spaɪnə'bɪfɪdə] *n* espina *f* bífida
spinach ['spɪnɪtʃ] *n* espinacas *fpl*
spinal ['spaɪnl] *adj* espinal
spinal column *n* columna vertebral
spinal cord *n* médula espinal
spin class *n* (Sport) clase *f* de spinning
spindly ['spɪndlɪ] *adj* (leg) zanquivano
spin doctor *n* (col) informador(a) parcial al servicio de un partido político
spin-dry ['spɪn'draɪ] *vt* centrifugar
spin-dryer [spɪn'draɪər] *n* (Brit) secadora centrífuga
spine [spaɪn] *n* espinazo, columna vertebral; (thorn) espina
spine-chilling ['spaɪntʃɪlɪŋ] *adj* terrorífico
spineless ['spaɪnlɪs] *adj* (fig) débil, flojo
spinet ['spɪnet] *n* espineta
spinning ['spɪnɪŋ] *n* (of thread) hilado; (art) hilandería; (Sport) spinning *m*
spinning top *n* peonza
spinning wheel *n* rueca, torno de hilar
spin-off ['spɪnɔf] *n* derivado, producto secundario
spinster ['spɪnstər] *n* soltera; (pej) solterona
spiral ['spaɪərl] *n* espiral *f* ▪ *adj* en espiral ▪ *vi* (prices) dispararse; **the inflationary ~** la espiral inflacionista
spiral staircase *n* escalera de caracol
spire ['spaɪər] *n* aguja, chapitel *m*

spirit ['spɪrɪt] *n* (soul) alma *f*; (ghost) fantasma *m*; (attitude) espíritu *m*; (courage) valor *m*, ánimo; **spirits** *npl* (drink) alcohol *msg*, bebidas *fpl* alcohólicas; **in good spirits** alegre, de buen ánimo; **Holy S~** Espíritu *m* Santo; **community ~**, **public ~** civismo
spirit duplicator *n* copiadora al alcohol
spirited ['spɪrɪtɪd] *adj* enérgico, vigoroso
spirit level *n* nivel *m* de aire
spiritual ['spɪrɪtjuəl] *adj* espiritual ▪ *n* (also: **Negro spiritual**) canción *f* religiosa, espiritual *m*
spiritualism ['spɪrɪtjuəlɪzəm] *n* espiritualismo
spit [spɪt] *n* (for roasting) asador *m*, espetón *m*; (spittle) esputo, escupitajo; (saliva) saliva ▪ *vi* (pt, pp **spat**) [spæt] escupir; (sound) chisporrotear
spite [spaɪt] *n* rencor *m*, ojeriza ▪ *vt* fastidiar; **in ~ of** a pesar de, pese a
spiteful ['spaɪtful] *adj* rencoroso, malévolo
spitting ['spɪtɪŋ] *n*: "**~ prohibited**" "se prohíbe escupir" ▪ *adj*: **to be the ~ image of sb** ser la viva imagen de algn
spittle ['spɪtl] *n* saliva, baba
splash [splæʃ] *n* (sound) chapoteo; (of colour) mancha ▪ *vt* salpicar de ▪ *vi* (also: **splash about**) chapotear; **to ~ paint on the floor** manchar el suelo de pintura
splashdown ['splæʃdaun] *n* amaraje *m*, amerizaje *m*
spleen [spli:n] *n* (Anat) bazo
splendid ['splendɪd] *adj* espléndido
splendidly ['splendɪdlɪ] *adv* espléndidamente; **everything went ~** todo fue a las mil maravillas
splendour, splendor (US) ['splendər] *n* esplendor *m*; (fig) brillo, gloria
splice [splaɪs] *vt* empalmar
splint [splɪnt] *n* tablilla
splinter ['splɪntər] *n* astilla ▪ *vi* astillarse, hacer astillas
splinter group *n* grupo disidente, facción *f*
split [splɪt] (pt, pp **~**) *n* hendedura, raja; (fig) división *f*; (Pol) escisión *f* ▪ *vt* partir, rajar; (party) dividir; (work, profits) repartir ▪ *vi* (divide) dividirse, escindirse; **to ~ the difference** partir la diferencia; **to do the splits** hacer el spagat; **to ~ sth down the middle** (also fig) dividir algo en dos
  ▸ **split up** *vi* (couple) separarse, romper; (meeting) acabarse
split-level ['splɪtlevl] *adj* (house) dúplex
split peas *npl* guisantes *mpl* secos
split personality *n* doble personalidad *f*
split second *n* fracción *f* de segundo
splitting ['splɪtɪŋ] *adj* (headache) horrible

S

795

splutter ['splʌtə^r] vi chisporrotear; (person) balbucear

spoil (pt, pp **spoilt** or **spoiled**) [spɔɪl, spɔɪlt, spɔɪld] vt (damage) dañar; (ruin) estropear, echar a perder; (child) mimar, consentir; (ballot paper) invalidar ■ vi: **to be spoiling for a fight** estar con ganas de lucha, andar con ganas de pelea

spoiled [spɔɪld] adj (US: food: bad) pasado, malo; (milk) cortado

spoils [spɔɪlz] npl despojo sg, botín msg

spoilsport ['spɔɪlspɔːt] n aguafiestas m inv

spoilt [spɔɪlt] pt, pp of **spoil** ■ adj (child) mimado, consentido; (ballot paper) invalidado

spoke [spəuk] pt of **speak** ■ n rayo, radio

spoken ['spəukn] pp of **speak**

spokesman ['spəuksmən] n portavoz m, vocero (LAm)

spokesperson ['spəukspə:sn] n portavoz m/f, vocero(-a) (LAm)

spokeswoman ['spəukswumən] n portavoz f, vocera (LAm)

sponge [spʌndʒ] n esponja; (Culin: also: **sponge cake**) bizcocho ■ vt (wash) lavar con esponja ■ vi: **to ~ on** or (US) **off sb** vivir a costa de algn

sponge bag n (Brit) neceser m

sponge cake n bizcocho, pastel m

sponger ['spʌndʒə^r] n gorrón(-ona) m(f)

spongy ['spʌndʒɪ] adj esponjoso

sponsor ['spɔnsə^r] n (Radio, TV) patrocinador(a) m(f); (for membership) padrino/madrina; (Comm) fiador(a) m(f), avalador(a) m(f) ■ vt patrocinar; apadrinar; (parliamentary bill) apoyar, respaldar; (idea etc) presentar, promover; **I sponsored him at 3p a mile** (in fund-raising race) me apunté para darle 3 peniques la milla

sponsorship ['spɔnsəʃɪp] n patrocinio

spontaneity [spɔntə'neɪtɪ] n espontaneidad f

spontaneous [spɔn'teɪnɪəs] adj espontáneo

spontaneously [spɔn'teɪnɪəslɪ] adv espontáneamente

spooky ['spuːkɪ] adj (col: place, atmosphere) espeluznante, horripilante

spool [spuːl] n carrete m; (of sewing machine) canilla

spoon [spuːn] n cuchara

spoon-feed ['spuːnfiːd] vt dar de comer con cuchara a; (fig) dárselo todo mascado a

spoonful ['spuːnful] n cucharada

sporadic [spə'rædɪk] adj esporádico

sport [spɔːt] n deporte m; (person) buen(a) perdedor(a) m/f; (amusement) juego, diversión f; **indoor/outdoor sports** deportes mpl en sala cubierta/al aire libre; **to say sth in ~** decir algo en broma

sport coat n (US) = **sports jacket**

sporting ['spɔːtɪŋ] adj deportivo; **to give sb a ~ chance** darle a algn su oportunidad

sports car n coche m sport

sports coat n (US) = **sports jacket**

sports ground n campo de deportes, centro deportivo

sports jacket, sport jacket (US) n chaqueta deportiva

sportsman ['spɔːtsmən] n deportista m

sportsmanship ['spɔːtsmənʃɪp] n deportividad f

sports pages npl páginas fpl deportivas

sportswear ['spɔːtswɛə^r] n ropa de deporte

sportswoman ['spɔːtswumən] n deportista

sporty ['spɔːtɪ] adj deportivo

spot [spɔt] n sitio, lugar m; (dot: on pattern) punto, mancha; (pimple) grano; (also: **advertising spot**) spot m; (small amount): **a ~ of** un poquito de ■ vt (notice) notar, observar ■ adj (Comm) inmediatamente efectivo; **on the ~** en el acto, acto seguido; (in difficulty) en un aprieto; **to do sth on the ~** hacer algo en el acto; **to put sb on the ~** poner a algn en un apuro

spot check n reconocimiento rápido

spotless ['spɔtlɪs] adj (clean) inmaculado; (reputation) intachable

spotlessly ['spɔtlɪslɪ] adv: **~ clean** limpísimo

spotlight ['spɔtlaɪt] n foco, reflector m; (Aut) faro auxiliar

spot-on [spɔt'ɔn] adj (Brit col) exacto

spot price n precio de entrega inmediata

spotted ['spɔtɪd] adj (pattern) de puntos

spotty ['spɔtɪ] adj (face) con granos

spouse [spauz] n cónyuge m/f

spout [spaut] n (of jug) pico; (pipe) caño ■ vi chorrear

sprain [spreɪn] n torcedura, esguince m ■ vt: **to ~ one's ankle** torcerse el tobillo

sprang [spræŋ] pt of **spring**

sprawl [sprɔːl] vi tumbarse ■ n: **urban ~** crecimiento urbano descontrolado; **to send sb sprawling** tirar a algn al suelo

sprawling ['sprɔːlɪŋ] adj (town) desparramado

spray [spreɪ] n rociada; (of sea) espuma; (container) atomizador m; (of paint) pistola rociadora; (of flowers) ramita ■ vt rociar; (crops) regar ■ cpd (deodorant) en atomizador

spread [sprɛd] (pt, pp **~**) n extensión f; (of idea) diseminación f; (col: food) comilona; (Press, Typ: two pages) plana ■ vt extender; diseminar; (butter) untar; (wings, sails) desplegar; (scatter) esparcir ■ vi extenderse; diseminarse; untarse; desplegarse;

esparcirse; **middle-age** ~ gordura de la
mediana edad; **repayments will be** ~ **over
18 months** los pagos se harán a lo largo de
18 meses
spread-eagled ['sprɛdi:gld] *adj*: **to be** ~ estar
despatarrado
spreadsheet ['sprɛdʃi:t] *n* (*Comput*) hoja de
cálculo
spree [spri:] *n*: **to go on a** ~ ir de juerga *or*
farra (*LAm*)
sprightly ['spraɪtlɪ] *adj* vivo, enérgico
spring [sprɪŋ] (*pt* **sprang**, *pp* **sprung**) *n* (*season*)
primavera; (*leap*) salto, brinco; (*coiled metal*)
resorte *m*; (*of water*) fuente *f*, manantial *m*;
(*bounciness*) elasticidad *f* ■ *vi* (*arise*) brotar,
nacer; (*leap*) saltar, brincar ■ *vt*: **to** ~ **a leak**
(*pipe etc*) empezar a hacer agua; **he sprang
the news on me** de repente me soltó la
noticia; **in (the)** ~ en (la) primavera; **to walk
with a** ~ **in one's step** andar dando saltos *or*
brincos; **to** ~ **into action** lanzarse a la acción
▶ **spring up** *vi* (*problem*) surgir
springboard ['sprɪŋbɔ:d] *n* trampolín *m*
spring-clean [sprɪŋ'kli:n] *n* (*also*: **spring-
cleaning**) limpieza general
spring onion *n* cebolleta
spring roll *n* rollito de primavera
springtime ['sprɪŋtaɪm] *n* primavera
springy ['sprɪŋɪ] *adj* elástico; (*grass*) mullido
sprinkle ['sprɪŋkl] *vt* (*pour*) rociar; **to** ~ **water
on,** ~ **with water** rociar *or* salpicar de agua
sprinkler ['sprɪŋkləʳ] *n* (*for lawn*) aspersor
m; (*to put out fire*) aparato de rociadura
automática
sprinkling ['sprɪŋklɪŋ] *n* (*of water*) rociada;
(*of salt, sugar*) un poco de
sprint [sprɪnt] *n* (*e*)sprint *m* ■ *vi* (*gen*) correr
a toda velocidad; (*Sport*) esprintar; **the 200
metres** ~ el (e)sprint de 200 metros
sprinter ['sprɪntəʳ] *n* velocista *m/f*
spritzer ['sprɪtsəʳ] *n* vino blanco con soda
sprocket ['sprɔkɪt] *n* (*on printer etc*) rueda
dentada
sprocket feed *n* avance *m* por rueda dentada
sprout [spraut] *vi* brotar, retoñar ■ *n*:
(Brussels) sprouts *npl* coles *fpl* de Bruselas
spruce [spru:s] *n* (*Bot*) pícea ■ *adj* aseado,
pulcro
▶ **spruce up** *vt* (*tidy*) arreglar, acicalar;
(*smarten up: room etc*) ordenar; **to** ~ **o.s. up**
arreglarse
sprung [sprʌŋ] *pp of* **spring**
spry [spraɪ] *adj* ágil, activo
SPUC *n abbr* (= *Society for the Protection of
Unborn Children*) ≈ Federación *f* Española de
Asociaciones Provida
spun [spʌn] *pt, pp of* **spin**

spur [spə:ʳ] *n* espuela; (*fig*) estímulo, aguijón
m ■ *vt* (*also*: **spur on**) estimular, incitar; **on
the** ~ **of the moment** de improviso
spurious ['spjuərɪəs] *adj* falso
spurn [spə:n] *vt* desdeñar, rechazar
spurt [spə:t] *n* chorro; (*of energy*) arrebato ■ *vi*
chorrear; **to put in** *or* **on a** ~ (*runner*) acelerar;
(*fig: in work etc*) hacer un gran esfuerzo
sputter ['spʌtəʳ] *vi* = **splutter**
spy [spaɪ] *n* espía *m/f* ■ *vi*: **to** ~ **on** espiar a
■ *vt* (*see*) divisar, lograr ver ■ *cpd* (*film, story*)
de espionaje
spying ['spaɪɪŋ] *n* espionaje *m*
Sq. *abbr* (*in address*: = *Square*) Pl.
sq. *abbr* (*Math etc*) = **square**
squabble ['skwɔbl] *n* riña, pelea ■ *vi* reñir,
pelear
squad [skwɔd] *n* (*Mil*) pelotón *m*; (*Police*)
brigada; (*Sport*) equipo, **flying** ~ (*Police*)
brigada móvil
squad car *n* (*Police*) coche-patrulla *m*
squaddie ['skwɔdɪ] *n* (*Mil: col*) chivo
squadron ['skwɔdrn] *n* (*Mil*) escuadrón *m*;
(*Aviat, Naut*) escuadra
squalid ['skwɔlɪd] *adj* miserable
squall [skwɔ:l] *n* (*storm*) chubasco; (*wind*)
ráfaga
squalor ['skwɔləʳ] *n* miseria
squander ['skwɔndəʳ] *vt* (*money*) derrochar,
despilfarrar; (*chances*) desperdiciar
square [skwɛəʳ] *n* cuadro; (*in town*) plaza;
(*US: block of houses*) manzana, cuadra (*LAm*)
■ *adj* cuadrado ■ *vt* (*arrange*) arreglar; (*Math*)
cuadrar; (*reconcile*): **can you** ~ **it with your
conscience?** ¿cómo se justifica ante sí
mismo? ■ *vi* cuadrar, conformarse; **all** ~
igual(es); **a** ~ **meal** una comida decente; **two
metres** ~ dos metros por dos; **one** ~ **metre**
un metro cuadrado; **to get one's accounts**
~ dejar las cuentas claras; **I'll** ~ **it with him**
(*col*) yo lo arreglo con él; **we're back to** ~ **one**
(*fig*) hemos vuelto al punto de partida
▶ **square up** *vi* (*settle*): **to** ~ **up (with sb)**
ajustar cuentas (con algn)
square bracket *n* (*Typ*) corchete *m*
squarely ['skwɛəlɪ] *adv* (*fully*) de lleno;
(*honestly, fairly*) honradamente, justamente
square root *n* raíz *f* cuadrada
squash [skwɔʃ] *n* (*vegetable*) calabaza; (*Sport*)
squash *m*; (*Brit: drink*): **lemon/orange** ~ zumo
(*SP*) *or* jugo (*LAm*) de limón/naranja ■ *vt*
aplastar
squat [skwɔt] *adj* achaparrado ■ *vi*
agacharse, sentarse en cuclillas; (*on property*)
ocupar ilegalmente
squatter ['skwɔtəʳ] *n* ocupante *m/f* ilegal,
okupa *m/f*

S

squawk [skwɔ:k] vi graznar

squeak [skwi:k] vi (hinge, wheel) chirriar, rechinar; (shoe, wood) crujir ∎ n (of hinge, wheel etc) chirrido, rechinamiento; (of shoes) crujir m; (of mouse etc) chillido

squeaky ['skwi:kɪ] adj que cruje; **to be ~ clean** (fig) ser superhonrado

squeal [skwi:l] vi chillar, dar gritos agudos

squeamish ['skwi:mɪʃ] adj delicado, remilgado

squeeze [skwi:z] n presión f; (of hand) apretón m; (Comm: credit squeeze) restricción f ∎ vt (lemon etc) exprimir; (hand, arm) apretar; **a ~ of lemon** unas gotas de limón; **to ~ past/under sth** colarse al lado de/por debajo de algo

▸ **squeeze out** vt exprimir; (fig) excluir

▸ **squeeze through** vi abrirse paso con esfuerzos

squelch [skwɛltʃ] vi chapotear

squid [skwɪd] n calamar m

squiggle ['skwɪgl] n garabato

squint [skwɪnt] vi entrecerrar los ojos ∎ n (Med) estrabismo; **to ~ at sth** mirar algo entornando los ojos

squire ['skwaɪəʳ] n (Brit) terrateniente m

squirm [skwə:m] vi retorcerse, revolverse

squirrel ['skwɪrəl] n ardilla

squirt [skwə:t] vi salir a chorros

Sr abbr = **senior**; (Rel) = **sister**

SRC n abbr (Brit: = Students' Representative Council) consejo de estudiantes

Sri Lanka [srɪ'læŋkə] n Sri Lanka m

SRO abbr (US) = **standing room only**

SS abbr (= steamship) M.V.

SSA n abbr (US: = Social Security Administration) = Seguro Social

SST n abbr (US) = **supersonic transport**

ST abbr (US: = Standard Time) hora oficial

St abbr (= saint) Sto.(-a); (= street) c/

stab [stæb] n (with knife etc) puñalada; (of pain) pinchazo; **to have a ~ at (doing) sth** (col) probar (a hacer) algo ∎ vt apuñalar; **to ~ sb to death** matar a algn a puñaladas

stabbing ['stæbɪŋ] n: **there's been a ~** han apuñalado a alguien ∎ adj (pain) punzante

stability [stə'bɪlɪtɪ] n estabilidad f

stabilization [steɪbəlaɪ'zeɪʃən] n estabilización f

stabilize ['steɪbəlaɪz] vt estabilizar ∎ vi estabilizarse

stabilizer ['steɪbəlaɪzəʳ] n (Aviat, Naut) estabilizador m

stable ['steɪbl] adj estable ∎ n cuadra, caballeriza; **riding stables** escuela hípica

staccato [stə'kɑ:təu] adj, adv staccato

stack [stæk] n montón m, pila; (col) mar f

∎ vt amontonar, apilar; **there's stacks of time to finish it** hay cantidad de tiempo para acabarlo

stacker ['stækəʳ] n (for printer) apiladora

stadium ['steɪdɪəm] n estadio

staff [stɑ:f] n (work force) personal m, plantilla; (Brit Scol: also: **teaching staff**) cuerpo docente; (stick) bastón m ∎ vt proveer de personal; **to be staffed by Asians/women** tener una plantilla asiática/femenina

staffroom ['stɑ:fru:m] n sala de profesores

Staffs abbr (Brit) = **Staffordshire**

stag [stæg] n ciervo, venado; (Brit Stock Exchange) especulador m con nuevas emisiones

stage [steɪdʒ] n escena; (point) etapa; (platform) plataforma; **the ~** el escenario, el teatro ∎ vt (play) poner en escena, representar; (organize) montar, organizar; (fig: perform: recovery etc) efectuar; **in stages** por etapas; **in the early/final stages** en las primeras/últimas etapas; **to go through a difficult ~** pasar una fase or etapa mala

stagecoach ['steɪdʒkəutʃ] n diligencia

stage door n entrada de artistas

stagehand ['steɪdʒhænd] n tramoyista m/f

stage-manage ['steɪdʒmænɪdʒ] vt (fig) manipular

stage manager n director(a) m(f) de escena

stagger ['stægəʳ] vi tambalear ∎ vt (amaze) asombrar; (hours, holidays) escalonar

staggering ['stægərɪŋ] adj (amazing) asombroso, pasmoso

staging post ['steɪdʒɪŋ-] n escala

stagnant ['stægnənt] adj estancado

stagnate [stæg'neɪt] vi estancarse; (fig: economy, mind) quedarse estancado

stagnation [stæg'neɪʃən] n estancamiento

stag night, stag party n despedida de soltero

staid [steɪd] adj (clothes) serio, formal

stain [steɪn] n mancha; (colouring) tintura ∎ vt manchar; (wood) teñir

stained glass window [steɪnd-] n vidriera de colores

stainless ['steɪnlɪs] adj (steel) inoxidable

stain remover n quitamanchas m inv

stair [stɛəʳ] n (step) peldaño, escalón m; **stairs** npl escaleras fpl

staircase ['stɛəkeɪs], **stairway** ['stɛəweɪ] n escalera

stairwell ['stɛəwɛl] n hueco or caja de la escalera

stake [steɪk] n estaca, poste m; (Betting) apuesta ∎ vt (bet) apostar; (also: **stake out**: area) cercar con estacas; **to be at ~** estar en juego; **to have a ~ in sth** tener interés

en algo; **to ~ a claim to (sth)** presentar
reclamación por or reclamar (algo)
stake-out ['steɪkaut] n vigilancia; **to be on
a ~** estar de vigilancia
stalactite ['stæləktaɪt] n estalactita
stalagmite ['stæləgmaɪt] n estalagmita
stale [steɪl] adj (bread) duro; (food) pasado
stalemate ['steɪlmeɪt] n tablas fpl; **to reach ~**
(fig) estancarse, alcanzar un punto muerto
stalk [stɔːk] n tallo, caña ■ vt acechar, cazar
al acecho; **to ~ off** irse airado
stall [stɔːl] n (in market) puesto; (in stable)
casilla (de establo) ■ vt (Aut) parar, calar
■ vi (Aut) pararse, calarse; (fig) buscar
evasivas; **stalls** npl (Brit: in cinema, theatre)
butacas fpl; **a newspaper ~** un quiosco (de
periódicos); **a flower ~** un puesto de flores
stallholder ['stɔːlhəʊldəʳ] n dueño(-a) de un
puesto
stallion ['stæliən] n semental m, garañón m
stalwart ['stɔːlwət] n partidario(-a)
incondicional
stamen ['steɪmən] n estambre m
stamina ['stæmɪnə] n resistencia
stammer ['stæməʳ] n tartamudeo, balbuceo
■ vi tartamudear, balbucir
stamp [stæmp] n sello, estampilla (LAm);
(mark) marca, huella; (on document) timbre
m ■ vi (also: **stamp one's foot**) patear ■ vt
patear, golpear con el pie; (letter) poner
sellos en; (with rubber stamp) marcar con sello;
stamped addressed envelope (sae) sobre m
sellado con las señas propias
▶ **stamp out** vt (fire) apagar con el pie; (crime,
opposition) acabar con
stamp album n álbum m para sellos
stamp collecting n filatelia
stamp duty n (Brit) derecho de timbre
stampede [stæm'piːd] n (of cattle) estampida
stamp machine n máquina (expendedora)
de sellos
stance [stæns] n postura
stand [stænd] (pt, pp **stood**) n (attitude)
posición f, postura; (for taxis) parada; (also:
music stand) atril m; (Sport) tribuna;
(at exhibition) stand m ■ vi (be) estar,
encontrarse; (be on foot) estar de pie; (rise)
levantarse; (remain) quedar en pie ■ vt (place)
poner, colocar; (tolerate, withstand) aguantar,
soportar; **to make a ~** resistir; (fig) mantener
una postura firme; **to take a ~ on an issue**
adoptar una actitud hacia una cuestión; **to
~ for parliament** (Brit) presentarse (como
candidato) a las elecciones; **nothing stands
in our way** nada nos lo impide; **to ~ still**
quedarse inmóvil; **to let sth ~ as it is** dejar
algo como está; **as things ~** tal como están

las cosas; **to ~ sb a drink/meal** invitar a
algn a una copa/a comer; **the company will
have to ~ the loss** la empresa tendrá que
hacer frente a las pérdidas; **I can't ~ him**
no le aguanto, no le puedo ver; **to ~ guard** or
watch (Mil) hacer guardia
▶ **stand aside** vi apartarse, mantenerse
aparte
▶ **stand by** vi (be ready) estar listo ■ vt fus
(opinion) mantener
▶ **stand down** vi (withdraw) ceder el puesto;
(Mil, Law) retirarse
▶ **stand for** vt fus (signify) significar; (tolerate)
aguantar, permitir
▶ **stand in for** vt fus suplir a
▶ **stand out** vi (be prominent) destacarse
▶ **stand up** vi (rise) levantarse, ponerse de pie
▶ **stand up for** vt fus defender
▶ **stand up to** vt fus hacer frente a
stand-alone ['stændələʊn] adj (Comput)
autónomo
standard ['stændəd] n patrón m, norma;
(flag) estandarte m ■ adj (size etc) normal,
corriente, estándar; **standards** npl (morals)
valores mpl morales; **the gold ~** (Comm) el
patrón oro; **high/low ~** de alto/bajo nivel;
below or **not up to ~** (work) de calidad
inferior; **to be** or **come up to ~** satisfacer los
requisitos; **to apply a double ~** aplicar un
doble criterio
Standard Grade n (Scottish Scol) certificado del
último ciclo de la enseñanza secundaria obligatoria
standardization [stændədaɪ'zeɪʃən] n
normalización f
standardize ['stændədaɪz] vt estandarizar
standard lamp n (Brit) lámpara de pie
standard model n modelo estándar
standard of living n nivel m de vida
standard practice n norma, práctica común
standard rate n tasa de imposición
standard time n hora oficial
stand-by ['stændbaɪ] n (alert) alerta, aviso;
(also: **stand-by ticket**: Theat) entrada reducida de
última hora; (: Aviat) billete m standby; **to be
on ~** estar preparado; (doctor) estar listo para
acudir; (Aviat) estar en la lista de espera
stand-by generator n generador m de
reserva
stand-by passenger n (Aviat) pasajero(-a) en
lista de espera
stand-by ticket n (Aviat) (billete m) standby m
stand-in ['stændɪn] n suplente m/f; (Cine)
doble m/f
standing ['stændɪŋ] adj (upright) derecho;
(on foot) de pie, en pie; (permanent:
committee) permanente; (: rule) fijo; (: army)
permanente, regular; (grievance) constante,

799

viejo ■ *n* reputación *f*; (*duration*): **of six months'** ~ que lleva seis meses; **of many years'** ~ que lleva muchos años; **he was given a ~ ovation** le dieron una calurosa ovación de pie; ~ **joke** motivo constante de broma; **a man of some ~** un hombre de cierta posición *or* categoría

standing order *n* (*Brit*: *at bank*) giro bancario; **standing orders** *npl* (*Mil*) reglamento *sg* general

standing room *n* sitio para estar de pie

stand-off ['stændɔf] *n* punto muerto

stand-offish [stænd'ɔfɪʃ] *adj* distante

standpipe ['stændpaɪp] *n* tubo vertical

standpoint ['stændpɔɪnt] *n* punto de vista

standstill ['stændstɪl] *n*: **at a ~** paralizado, en un punto muerto; **to come to a ~** pararse, quedar paralizado

stank [stæŋk] *pt of* **stink**

staple ['steɪpl] *n* (*for papers*) grapa; (*product*) producto *or* artículo de primeva necesidad ■ *adj* (*crop, industry, food etc*) básico ■ *vt* grapar

stapler ['steɪplər] *n* grapadora

star [stɑːr] *n* estrella; (*celebrity*) estrella, astro ■ *vi*: **to ~ in** ser la estrella de; **four-~ hotel** hotel *m* de cuatro estrellas; **4-~ petrol** gasolina extra

star attraction *n* atracción *f* principal

starboard ['stɑːbəd] *n* estribor *m*

starch [stɑːtʃ] *n* almidón *m*

starchy ['stɑːtʃɪ] *adj* (*food*) feculento

stardom ['stɑːdəm] *n* estrellato

stare [steər] *n* mirada fija ■ *vi*: **to ~ at** mirar fijo

starfish ['stɑːfɪʃ] *n* estrella de mar

stark [stɑːk] *adj* (*bleak*) severo, escueto; (*simplicity, colour*) austero; (*reality, truth*) puro; (*poverty*) absoluto ■ *adv*: ~ **naked** en cueros

starkers ['stɑːkəz] *adj* (*Brit col*): **to be ~** estar en cueros

starlet ['stɑːlɪt] *n* (*Cine*) actriz *f* principiante

starling ['stɑːlɪŋ] *n* estornino

starry ['stɑːrɪ] *adj* estrellado

starry-eyed [stɑːrɪ'aɪd] *adj* (*gullible, innocent*) inocentón(-ona), ingenuo; (*idealistic*) idealista; (*from wonder*) asombrado; (*from love*) enamoradísimo

Stars and Stripes *npl*: **the ~** las barras y las estrellas, la bandera de EEUU

star sign *n* signo del zodíaco

star-studded ['stɑːstʌdɪd] *adj*: **a ~ cast** un elenco estelar

start [stɑːt] *n* (*beginning*) principio, comienzo; (*departure*) salida; (*sudden movement*) sobresalto; (*advantage*) ventaja ■ *vt* empezar, comenzar; (*cause*) causar; (*found: business,*

newspaper) establecer, fundar; (*engine*) poner en marcha ■ *vi* (*begin*) comenzar, empezar; (*with fright*) asustarse, sobresaltarse; (*train etc*) salir; **to give sb a ~** dar un susto a algn; **at the ~** al principio; **for a ~** en primer lugar; **to make an early ~** ponerse en camino temprano; **the thieves had three hours' ~** los ladrones llevaban tres horas de ventaja; **to ~ a fire** provocar un incendio; **to ~ doing** *or* **to do sth** empezar a hacer algo; **to ~ (off) with ...** (*firstly*) para empezar; (*at the beginning*) al principio

▶ **start off** *vi* empezar, comenzar; (*leave*) salir, ponerse en camino

▶ **start over** *vi* (*US*) volver a empezar

▶ **start up** *vi* comenzar; (*car*) ponerse en marcha ■ *vt* comenzar; (*car*) poner en marcha

starter ['stɑːtər] *n* (*Aut*) botón *m* de arranque; (*Sport*: *official*) juez *m/f* de salida; (: *runner*) corredor(a) *m(f)*; (*Brit Culin*) entrada

starting point ['stɑːtɪŋ-] *n* punto de partida

starting price *n* (*Comm*) precio inicial

startle ['stɑːtl] *vt* asustar, sobresaltar

startling ['stɑːtlɪŋ] *adj* alarmante

star turn *n* (*Brit*) atracción *f* principal

starvation [stɑː'veɪʃən] *n* hambre *f*, hambruna (*LAm*); (*Med*) inanición *f*

starvation wages *npl* sueldo *sg* de hambre

starve [stɑːv] *vi* pasar hambre; (*to death*) morir de hambre ■ *vt* hacer pasar hambre; (*fig*) privar; **I'm starving** estoy muerto de hambre

stash [stæʃ] *vt*: **to ~ sth away** (*col*) poner algo a buen recaudo

state [steɪt] *n* estado; (*pomp*): **in ~** con mucha ceremonia ■ *vt* (*say, declare*) afirmar; (*a case*) presentar, exponer; ~ **of emergency** estado de excepción *or* emergencia; ~ **of mind** estado de ánimo; **to lie in ~** (*corpse*) estar de cuerpo presente; **to be in a ~** estar agitado

State Department *n* (*US*) Ministerio de Asuntos Exteriores

state education *n* (*Brit*) enseñanza pública

stateless ['steɪtlɪs] *adj* desnacionalizado

stately ['steɪtlɪ] *adj* majestuoso, imponente

statement ['steɪtmənt] *n* afirmación *f*; (*Law*) declaración *f*; (*Comm*) estado; **official ~** informe *m* oficial; ~ **of account, bank ~** estado de cuenta

state-of-the-art ['steɪtəvðɪ'ɑːt] *adj* (*technology etc*) puntero

state-owned ['steɪtəund] *adj* estatal, del estado

States [steɪts] *npl*: **the ~** los Estados Unidos

state school *n* escuela *or* colegio estatal

statesman ['steɪtsmən] n estadista m
statesmanship ['steɪtsmənʃɪp] n habilidad f política, arte m de gobernar
static ['stætɪk] n (Radio) parásitos mpl ∎ adj estático
static electricity n electricidad f estática
station ['steɪʃən] n (gen) estación f; (place) puesto, sitio; (Radio) emisora; (rank) posición f social ∎ vt colocar, situar; (Mil) apostar; **action stations!** ¡a los puestos de combate!; **to be stationed in** (Mil) estar estacionado en
stationary ['steɪʃnərɪ] adj estacionario, fijo
stationer ['steɪʃənər] n papelero(-a)
stationer's, stationer's shop n (Brit) papelería
stationery ['steɪʃənərɪ] n (writing paper) papel m de escribir; (writing materials) artículos mpl de escritorio
station master n (Rail) jefe m de estación
station wagon n (US) coche m familiar con ranchera
statistic [stə'tɪstɪk] n estadística
statistical [stə'tɪstɪkl] adj estadístico
statistics [stə'tɪstɪks] n (science) estadística
statue ['stætjuː] n estatua
statuette [stætjuː'et] n figurilla
stature ['stætʃər] n estatura; (fig) talla
status ['steɪtəs] n condición f, estado; (reputation) reputación f, estatus m; **the ~ quo** el statu quo
status line n (Comput) línea de situación or de estado
status symbol n símbolo de prestigio
statute ['stætjuːt] n estatuto, ley f
statute book n código de leyes
statutory ['stætjutrɪ] adj estatutario; **~ meeting** junta ordinaria
staunch [stɔːntʃ] adj leal, incondicional ∎ vt (flow, blood) restañar
stave [steɪv] vt: **to ~ off** (attack) rechazar; (threat) evitar
stay [steɪ] n (period of time) estancia; (Law): **~ of execution** aplazamiento de una sentencia ∎ vi (remain) quedar(se); (as guest) hospedarse; **to ~ put** seguir en el mismo sitio; **to ~ the night/5 days** pasar la noche/estar or quedarse 5 días
▶ **stay behind** vi quedar atrás
▶ **stay in** vi (at home) quedarse en casa
▶ **stay on** vi quedarse
▶ **stay out** vi (of house) no volver a casa; (strikers) no volver al trabajo
▶ **stay up** vi (at night) velar, no acostarse
staying power ['steɪɪŋ-] n resistencia, aguante m
STD n abbr (Brit: = subscriber trunk dialling) servicio de conferencias automáticas; (= sexually transmitted disease) ETS f

stead [sted] n: **in sb's ~** en lugar de algn; **to stand sb in good ~** ser muy útil a algn
steadfast ['stedfɑːst] adj firme, resuelto
steadily ['stedɪlɪ] adv (firmly) firmemente; (unceasingly) sin parar; (fixedly) fijamente; (walk) normalmente; (drive) a velocidad constante
steady ['stedɪ] adj (fixed) firme, fijo; (regular) regular; (boyfriend etc) formal, fijo; (person, character) sensato, juicioso ∎ vt (hold) mantener firme; (stabilize) estabilizar; (nerves) calmar; **to ~ o.s. on** or **against sth** afirmarse en algo
steak [steɪk] n (gen) filete m; (beef) bistec m
steal (pt **stole**, pp **stolen**) [stiːl, stəul, 'stəuln] vt, vi robar
▶ **steal away, steal off** vi marcharse furtivamente, escabullirse
stealth [stelθ] n: **by ~** a escondidas, sigilosamente
stealthy ['stelθɪ] adj cauteloso, sigiloso
steam [stiːm] n vapor m; (mist) vaho, humo ∎ vt (Culin) cocer al vapor ∎ vi echar vapor; (ship): **to ~ along** avanzar, ir avanzando; **under one's own ~** (fig) por sus propios medios or propias fuerzas; **to run out of ~** (fig: person) quedar(se) agotado, quemarse; **to let off ~** (fig) desahogarse
▶ **steam up** vi (window) empañarse; **to get steamed up about sth** (fig) ponerse negro por algo
steam engine n máquina de vapor
steamer ['stiːmər] n (buque m de) vapor m; (Culin) recipiente para cocinar al vapor
steam iron n plancha de vapor
steamroller ['stiːmrəulər] n apisonadora
steamship ['stiːmʃɪp] n = **steamer**
steamy ['stiːmɪ] adj (room) lleno de vapor; (window) empañado
steel [stiːl] n acero ∎ adj de acero
steel band n banda de percusión del Caribe
steel industry n industria siderúrgica
steel mill n fábrica de acero
steelworks ['stiːlwəːks] n acería, fundición f de acero
steely ['stiːlɪ] adj (determination) inflexible; (gaze) duro; (eyes) penetrante; **~ grey** gris m metálico
steelyard ['stiːljɑːd] n romana
steep [stiːp] adj escarpado, abrupto; (stair) empinado; (price) exorbitante, excesivo ∎ vt empapar, remojar
steeple ['stiːpl] n aguja, campanario
steeplechase ['stiːpltʃeɪs] n carrera de obstáculos

S

steeplejack ['sti:pldʒæk] n reparador(a) m(f) de chimeneas or de campanarios
steer [stɪəʳ] vt (car) conducir (SP), manejar (LAm); (person) dirigir, guiar ▪ vi conducir; **to ~ clear of sb/sth** (fig) esquivar a algn/ evadir algo
steering ['stɪərɪŋ] n (Aut) dirección f
steering committee n comisión f directiva
steering wheel n volante m
stellar ['stɛləʳ] adj estelar
stem [stɛm] n (of plant) tallo; (of glass) pie m; (of pipe) cañón m ▪ vt detener; (blood) restañar
▸ **stem from** vt fus ser consecuencia de
stem cell n célula madre
stench [stɛntʃ] n hedor m
stencil ['stɛnsl] n (typed) cliché m, clisé m; (lettering) plantilla ▪ vt hacer un cliché de
stenographer [stɛ'nɔgrəfəʳ] n (US) taquígrafo(-a)
step [stɛp] n paso; (sound) paso, pisada; (stair) peldaño, escalón m ▪ vi: **to ~ forward** dar un paso adelante; **steps** npl (Brit) = **stepladder**; **~ by ~** paso a paso; (fig) poco a poco; **to keep in ~ (with)** llevar el paso de; (fig) llevar el paso de, estar de acuerdo con; **to be in/out of ~ with** estar acorde con/estar en disonancia con; **to take steps to solve a problem** tomar medidas para resolver un problema
▸ **step down** vi (fig) retirarse
▸ **step in** vi entrar; (fig) intervenir
▸ **step off** vt fus bajar de
▸ **step on** vt fus pisar
▸ **step over** vt fus pasar por encima de
▸ **step up** vt (increase) aumentar
step aerobics npl step m
stepbrother ['stɛpbrʌðəʳ] n hermanastro
stepdaughter ['stɛpdɔːtəʳ] n hijastra
stepfather ['stɛpfɑːðəʳ] n padrastro
stepladder ['stɛplædəʳ] n escalera doble or de tijera
stepmother ['stɛpmʌðəʳ] n madrastra
stepping stone ['stɛpɪŋ-] n pasadera
step Reebok® [-'riːbɔk] n step m
stepsister ['stɛpsɪstəʳ] n hermanastra
stepson ['stɛpsʌn] n hijastro
stereo ['stɛrɪəu] n estéreo ▪ adj (also: **stereophonic**) estéreo, estereofónico; **in ~** en estéreo
stereotype ['stɛrɪətaɪp] n estereotipo ▪ vt estereotipar
sterile ['stɛraɪl] adj estéril
sterilization [stɛrɪlaɪ'zeɪʃən] n esterilización f
sterilize ['stɛrɪlaɪz] vt esterilizar
sterling ['stəːlɪŋ] adj (silver) de ley ▪ n (Econ) libras fpl esterlinas; **a pound ~** una libra esterlina; **he is of ~ character** tiene un carácter excelente
stern [stəːn] adj severo, austero ▪ n (Naut) popa
sternum ['stəːnəm] n esternón m
steroid ['stɪərɔɪd] n esteroide m
stethoscope ['stɛθəskəup] n estetoscopio
stevedore ['stiːvədɔːʳ] n estibador m
stew [stjuː] n cocido, estofado, guisado (LAm) ▪ vt, vi estofar, guisar; (fruit) cocer; **stewed fruit** compota de fruta
steward ['stjuːəd] n (Brit: gen) camarero; (shop steward) enlace m/f sindical
stewardess ['stjuːədəs] n azafata
stewardship ['stjuːədʃɪp] n tutela
stewing steak ['stjuːɪŋ-], **stew meat** (US) n carne f de vaca
St. Ex. abbr = **stock exchange**
stg abbr (= sterling) ester
stick [stɪk] (pt, pp **stuck**) n palo; (as weapon) porra; (also: **walking stick**) bastón m ▪ vt (glue) pegar; (col: put) meter; (: tolerate) aguantar, soportar ▪ vi pegarse; (come to a stop) quedarse parado; (get jammed: door, lift) atascarse; **to get hold of the wrong end of the ~** entender al revés; **to ~ to** (word, principles) atenerse a, ser fiel a; (promise) cumplir; **it stuck in my mind** se me quedó grabado; **to ~ sth into** clavar or hincar algo en
▸ **stick around** vi (col) quedarse
▸ **stick out** vi sobresalir ▪ vt: **to ~ it out** (col) aguantar
▸ **stick up** vi sobresalir
▸ **stick up for** vt fus defender
sticker ['stɪkəʳ] n (label) etiqueta adhesiva; (with slogan) pegatina
sticking plaster ['stɪkɪŋ-] n (Brit) esparadrapo
sticking point n (fig) punto de fricción
stick insect n insecto palo
stickler ['stɪkləʳ] n: **to be a ~ for** insistir mucho en
stick shift n (US Aut) palanca de cambios
stick-up ['stɪkʌp] n asalto, atraco
sticky ['stɪkɪ] adj pegajoso; (label) adhesivo; (fig) difícil
stiff [stɪf] adj rígido, tieso; (hard) duro; (difficult) difícil; (person) inflexible; (price) exorbitante; **to have a ~ neck/back** tener tortícolis/dolor de espalda; **the door's ~** la puerta está atrancada
stiffen ['stɪfn] vt hacer más rígido; (limb) entumecer ▪ vi endurecerse; (grow stronger) fortalecerse
stiffness ['stɪfnɪs] n rigidez f

stifle ['staɪfl] vt ahogar, sofocar
stifling ['staɪflɪŋ] adj (heat) sofocante,
bochornoso
stigma n (Bot, Med, Rel) (pl **stigmata**) (fig)
(pl **stigmas**) ['stɪgmə, stɪg'mɑːtə] ▪ n
estigma m
stile [staɪl] n escalera (para pasar una cerca)
stiletto [stɪ'letəu] n (Brit: also: **stiletto heel**)
tacón m de aguja
still [stɪl] adj inmóvil, quieto; (orange juice etc)
sin gas ▪ adv (up to this time) todavía; (even)
aún; (nonetheless) sin embargo, aun así ▪ n
(Cine) foto f fija; **keep ~!** ¡estate quieto!, ¡no
te muevas!; **he ~ hasn't arrived** todavía no
ha llegado
stillborn ['stɪlbɔːn] adj nacido muerto
still life n naturaleza muerta
stilt [stɪlt] n zanco; (pile) pilar m, soporte m
stilted ['stɪltɪd] adj afectado, artificial
stimulant ['stɪmjulənt] n estimulante m
stimulate ['stɪmjuleɪt] vt estimular
stimulating ['stɪmjuleɪtɪŋ] adj estimulante
stimulation [stɪmju'leɪʃən] n estímulo
stimulus (pl **stimuli**) ['stɪmjuləs, -laɪ] n
estímulo, incentivo
sting [stɪŋ] (pt, pp **stung**) n (wound) picadura;
(pain) escozor m, picazón m; (organ) aguijón
m; (col: confidence trick) timo ▪ vt picar ▪ vi
picar, escocer; **my eyes are stinging** me
pican or escuecen los ojos
stingy ['stɪndʒɪ] adj tacaño
stink [stɪŋk] n hedor m, tufo ▪ vi (pt **stank**, pp
stunk) [stæŋk, stʌŋk] heder, apestar
stinking ['stɪŋkɪŋ] adj hediondo, fétido;
(fig: col) horrible
stint [stɪnt] n tarea, destajo; **to do one's ~
(at sth)** hacer su parte (de algo), hacer lo que
corresponde (de algo) ▪ vi: **to ~ on** escatimar
stipend ['staɪpɛnd] n salario, remuneración f
stipendiary [staɪ'pɛndɪərɪ] adj: **~ magistrate**
magistrado(-a) estipendiario(-a)
stipulate ['stɪpjuleɪt] vt estipular
stipulation [stɪpju'leɪʃən] n estipulación f
stir [stəː] n (fig: agitation) conmoción f ▪ vt
(tea etc) remover; (fire) atizar; (move) agitar;
(fig: emotions) conmover ▪ vi moverse; **to
give sth a ~** remover algo; **to cause a ~**
causar conmoción or sensación
  ▸ **stir up** vt excitar; (trouble) fomentar
stir-fry ['stəːfraɪ] vt sofreír removiendo
▪ n plato preparado sofriendo y removiendo los
ingredientes
stirrup ['stɪrəp] n estribo
stitch [stɪtʃ] n (Sewing) puntada; (Knitting)
punto; (Med) punto (de sutura); (pain)
punzada ▪ vt coser; (Med) suturar
stoat [stəut] n armiño

stock [stɔk] n (Comm: reserves) existencias fpl,
stock m; (: selection) surtido; (Agr) ganado,
ganadería; (Culin) caldo; (fig: lineage) estirpe f,
cepa; (Finance) capital m; (: shares) acciones fpl;
(Rail: rolling stock) material m rodante ▪ adj
(Comm: goods, size) normal, de serie; (fig: reply
etc) clásico, trillado; (: greeting) acostumbrado
▪ n (have in stock) tener existencias de;
(supply) proveer, abastecer; **in ~** en existencia
or almacén; **to have sth in ~** tener
existencias de algo; **out of ~** agotado; **to
take ~ of** (fig) considerar, examinar; **stocks**
npl (History: punishment) cepo sg; **stocks and
shares** acciones y valores; **government ~**
papel m del Estado
  ▸ **stock up with** vt fus abastecerse de
stockbroker ['stɔkbrəukə'] n agente m/f or
corredor(a) m/f de bolsa
stock control n (Comm) control m de
existencias
stock cube n pastilla or cubito de caldo
stock exchange n bolsa
stockholder ['stɔkhəuldə'] n (US) accionista
m/f
Stockholm ['stɔkhəum] n Estocolmo
stocking ['stɔkɪŋ] n media
stock-in-trade ['stɔkɪn'treɪd] n (tools etc)
herramientas fpl; (stock) existencia de
mercancías; (fig): **it's his ~** es su
especialidad
stockist ['stɔkɪst] n (Brit) distribuidor(a) m(f)
stock market n bolsa (de valores)
stock phrase n vieja frase f
stockpile ['stɔkpaɪl] n reserva ▪ vt
acumular, almacenar
stockroom ['stɔkruːm] n almacén m,
depósito
stocktaking ['stɔkteɪkɪŋ] n (Brit Comm)
inventario, balance m
stocky ['stɔkɪ] adj (strong) robusto; (short)
achaparrado
stodgy ['stɔdʒɪ] adj indigesto, pesado
stoical ['stəuɪkəl] adj estoico
stoke [stəuk] vt atizar
stole [stəul] pt of **steal** ▪ n estola
stolen ['stəuln] pp of **steal**
stolid ['stɔlɪd] adj (person) imperturbable,
impasible
stomach ['stʌmək] n (Anat) estómago; (belly)
vientre m ▪ vt tragar, aguantar
stomach ache n dolor m de estómago
stomach pump n bomba gástrica
stomach ulcer n úlcera de estómago
stomp [stɔmp] vi: **to ~ in/out** entrar/salir
con pasos ruidosos
stone [stəun] n piedra; (in fruit) hueso; (Brit:
weight) = 6.348 kg; 14 pounds ▪ adj de piedra ▪ vt

803

apedrear; **within a ~'s throw of the station** a tiro de piedra or a dos pasos de la estación

Stone Age n: **the ~** la Edad de Piedra

stone-cold ['stəun'kəuld] adj helado

stoned [stəund] adj (col: drunk) trompa, borracho, colocado

stone-deaf ['stəun'dɛf] adj sordo como una tapia

stonemason ['stəunmeɪsən] n albañil m

stonewall [stəun'wɔːl] vi alargar la cosa innecesariamente ■ vt dar largas a

stonework ['stəunwəːk] n (art) cantería

stony ['stəunɪ] adj pedregoso; (glance) glacial

stood [stud] pt, pp of **stand**

stooge [stuːdʒ] n (col) hombre m de paja

stool [stuːl] n taburete m

stoop [stuːp] vi (also: **have a stoop**) ser cargado de espaldas; (bend) inclinarse, encorvarse; **to ~ to (doing) sth** rebajarse a (hacer) algo

stop [stɔp] n parada, alto; (in punctuation) punto ■ vt parar, detener; (break off) suspender; (block) tapar, cerrar; (prevent) impedir; (also: **put a stop to**) poner término a ■ vi pararse, detenerse; (end) acabarse; **to ~ doing sth** dejar de hacer algo; **to ~ sb (from) doing sth** impedir a algn hacer algo; **to ~ dead** pararse en seco; **~ it!** ¡basta ya!, ¡párate!

▶ **stop by** vi pasar por

▶ **stop off** vi interrumpir el viaje

▶ **stop up** vt (hole) tapar

stopcock ['stɔpkɔk] n llave f de paso

stopgap ['stɔpgæp] n interino; (person) sustituto(-a); (measure) medida provisional ■ cpd (situation) provisional

stoplights ['stɔplaɪts] npl (Aut) luces fpl de detención

stopover ['stɔpəuvəʳ] n parada intermedia; (Aviat) escala

stoppage ['stɔpɪdʒ] n (strike) paro; (temporary stop) interrupción f; (of pay) suspensión f; (blockage) obstrucción f

stopper ['stɔpəʳ] n tapón m

stop press n noticias fpl de última hora

stopwatch ['stɔpwɔtʃ] n cronómetro

storage ['stɔːrɪdʒ] n almacenaje m; (Comput) almacenamiento

storage capacity n espacio de almacenaje

store [stɔːʳ] n (stock) provisión f; (depot) almacén m; (Brit: large shop) almacén m; (US) tienda; (reserve) reserva, repuesto ■ vt (gen) almacenar; (Comput) almacenar; (keep) guardar; (in filing system) archivar; **stores** npl víveres mpl; **who knows what is in ~ for us** quién sabe lo que nos espera; **to set great/little ~ by sth** dar mucha/poca importancia

a algo, valorar mucho/poco algo

▶ **store up** vt acumular

storehouse ['stɔːhaus] n almacén m, depósito

storekeeper ['stɔːkiːpəʳ] n (US) tendero(-a)

storeroom ['stɔːruːm] n despensa

storey, story (US) ['stɔːrɪ] n piso

stork [stɔːk] n cigüeña

storm [stɔːm] n tormenta; (wind) vendaval m; (fig) tempestad f ■ vi (fig) rabiar ■ vt tomar por asalto, asaltar; **to take a town by ~** (Mil) tomar una ciudad por asalto

storm cloud n nubarrón m

storm door n contrapuerta

stormy ['stɔːmɪ] adj tempestuoso

story ['stɔːrɪ] n historia; (Press) artículo; (joke) cuento, chiste m; (plot) argumento; (lie) cuento; (US) = **storey**

storybook ['stɔːrɪbuk] n libro de cuentos

storyteller ['stɔːrɪtɛləʳ] n cuentista m/f

stout [staut] adj (strong) sólido; (fat) gordo, corpulento ■ n cerveza negra

stove [stəuv] n (for cooking) cocina; (for heating) estufa; **gas/electric ~** cocina de gas/eléctrica

stow [stəu] vt meter, poner; (Naut) estibar

stowaway ['stəuəweɪ] n polizón(-ona) m(f)

straddle ['strædl] vt montar a horcajadas

straggle ['strægl] vi (wander) vagar en desorden; (lag behind) rezagarse

straggler ['strægləʳ] n rezagado(-a)

straggling ['stræglɪŋ], **straggly** ['stræglɪ] adj (hair) desordenado

straight [streɪt] adj (direct) recto, derecho; (plain, uncomplicated) sencillo; (frank) franco, directo; (in order) en orden; (continuous) continuo; (Theat: part, play) serio; (person: conventional) recto, convencional; (: heterosexual) heterosexual ■ adv derecho, directamente; (drink) solo; **to put** or **get sth ~** dejar algo en claro; **10 ~ wins** 10 victorias seguidas; **to be (all) ~** (tidy) estar en orden; (clarified) estar claro; **I went ~ home** (me) fui directamente a casa; **~ away, ~ off** (at once) en seguida

straighten ['streɪtn] vt (also: **straighten out**) enderezar, poner derecho; **to ~ things out** poner las cosas en orden

straighteners ['streɪtnə] npl (for hair) plancha de pelo

straight-faced [streɪt'feɪst] adj serio ■ adv sin mostrar emoción, impávido

straightforward [streɪt'fɔːwəd] adj (simple) sencillo; (honest) sincero

strain [streɪn] n (gen) tensión f; (Tech) esfuerzo; (Med) distensión f, torcedura; (breed) raza; (lineage) linaje m; (of virus) variedad f ■ vt (back etc) distender, torcerse; (tire) cansar; (stretch) estirar; (filter) filtrar;

(*meaning*) tergiversar ■ *vi* esforzarse; **strains** *npl* (*Mus*) son *m*; **she's under a lot of ~** está bajo mucha tensión

strained [streɪnd] *adj* (*muscle*) torcido; (*laugh*) forzado; (*relations*) tenso

strainer ['streɪnər] *n* colador *m*

strait [streɪt] *n* (*Geo*) estrecho; **to be in dire straits** (*fig*) estar en un gran aprieto

straitjacket ['streɪtdʒækɪt] *n* camisa de fuerza

strait-laced [streɪt'leɪst] *adj* mojigato, gazmoño

strand [strænd] *n* (*of thread*) hebra; (*of rope*) ramal *m*; **a ~ of hair** un pelo

stranded ['strændɪd] *adj* (*person*) colgado

strange [streɪndʒ] *adj* (*not known*) desconocido; (*odd*) extraño, raro

stranger ['streɪndʒər] *n* desconocido(-a); (*from another area*) forastero(-a); **I'm a ~ here** no soy de aquí

strangle ['stræŋgl] *vt* estrangular

stranglehold ['stræŋglhəʊld] *n* (*fig*) dominio completo

strangulation [stræŋgju'leɪʃən] *n* estrangulación *f*

strap [stræp] *n* correa; (*of slip, dress*) tirante *m* ■ *vt* atar con correa

straphanging ['stræphæŋɪŋ] *n* viajar *m* de pie or parado (*LAm*)

strapless ['stræplɪs] *adj* (*bra, dress*) sin tirantes

strapped [stræpt] *adj*: **to be for cash** (*col*) andar mal de dinero

strapping ['stræpɪŋ] *adj* robusto, fornido

Strasbourg ['stræzbɜːg] *n* Estrasburgo

strata ['strɑːtə] *npl of* **stratum**

stratagem ['strætɪdʒəm] *n* estratagema

strategic [strə'tiːdʒɪk] *adj* estratégico

strategy ['strætɪdʒɪ] *n* estrategia

stratum, strata ['strɑːtəm, 'strɑːtə] *n* estrato

straw [strɔː] *n* paja; (*also*: **drinking straw**) caña, pajita; **that's the last ~!** ¡eso es el colmo!

strawberry ['strɔːbərɪ] *n* fresa, frutilla (*LAm*)

stray [streɪ] *adj* (*animal*) extraviado; (*bullet*) perdido; (*scattered*) disperso ■ *vi* extraviarse, perderse; (*wander: walker*) vagar, ir sin rumbo fijo; (*: speaker*) desvariar

streak [striːk] *n* raya; (*fig: of madness etc*) vena ■ *vt* rayar ■ *vi*: **to ~ past** pasar como un rayo; **to have streaks in one's hair** tener vetas en el pelo; **a winning/losing ~** una racha de buena/mala suerte

streaker ['striːkər] *n* corredor(a) *m(f)* desnudo(-a)

streaky ['striːkɪ] *adj* rayado

stream [striːm] *n* riachuelo, arroyo; (*jet*) chorro; (*flow*) corriente *f*; (*of people*) oleada ■ *vt* (*Scol*) dividir en grupos por habilidad ■ *vi* correr, fluir; **to ~ in/out** (*people*) entrar/salir en tropel; **against the ~** a contracorriente; **on ~** (*new power plant etc*) en funcionamiento

streamer ['striːmər] *n* serpentina

stream feed *n* (*on photocopier etc*) alimentación *f* continua

streamline ['striːmlaɪn] *vt* aerodinamizar; (*fig*) racionalizar

streamlined ['striːmlaɪnd] *adj* aerodinámico

street [striːt] *n* calle *f* ■ *adj* callejero; **the back streets** las callejuelas; **to be on the streets** (*homeless*) estar sin vivienda; (*as prostitute*) hacer la calle

streetcar ['striːtkɑː] *n* (*US*) tranvía *m*

street cred [-krɛd] *n* (*col*) imagen de estar en la onda

street lamp *n* farol *m*

street lighting *n* alumbrado público

street market *n* mercado callejero

street plan *n* plano callejero

streetwise ['striːtwaɪz] *adj* (*col*) pícaro

strength [streŋθ] *n* fuerza; (*of girder, knot etc*) resistencia; (*of chemical solution*) potencia; (*of wine*) graduación *f* de alcohol; **on the ~ of** a base de, en base a; **to be at full/below ~** tener/no tener completo el cupo

strengthen ['streŋθən] *vt* fortalecer, reforzar

strenuous ['strenjuəs] *adj* (*tough*) arduo; (*energetic*) enérgico; (*opposition*) firme, tenaz; (*efforts*) intensivo

stress [stres] *n* (*force, pressure*) presión *f*; (*mental strain*) estrés *m*, tensión *f*; (*accent, emphasis*) énfasis *m*, acento; (*Ling, Poetry*) acento; (*Tech*) tensión *f*, carga ■ *vt* subrayar, recalcar; **to be under ~** estar estresado; **to lay great ~ on sth** hacer hincapié en algo

stressful ['stresful] *adj* (*job*) estresante

stretch [stretʃ] *n* (*of sand etc*) trecho; (*of road*) tramo; (*of time*) período, tiempo ■ *vi* estirarse; (*extend*): **to ~ to** or **as far as** extenderse hasta; (*be enough: money, food*): **to ~ to** alcanzar para, dar de sí para ■ *vt* extender, estirar; (*make demands of*) exigir el máximo esfuerzo a; **to ~ one's legs** estirar las piernas

▶ **stretch out** *vi* tenderse ■ *vt* (*arm etc*) extender; (*spread*) estirar

stretcher ['stretʃər] *n* camilla

stretcher-bearer ['stretʃəbeərər] *n* camillero(-a)

stretch marks *npl* estrías *fpl*

strewn [struːn] *adj*: **~ with** cubierto or sembrado de

stricken ['strɪkən] *adj* (*person*) herido; (*city, industry etc*) condenado; ~ **with** (*arthritis, disease*) afligido por; **grief-~** destrozado por el dolor

strict [strɪkt] *adj* (*order, rule etc*) estricto; (*discipline, ban*) severo; **in ~ confidence** en la más absoluta confianza

strictly ['strɪktlɪ] *adv* estrictamente; (*totally*) terminantemente; ~ **confidential** estrictamente confidencial; ~ **speaking** en (el) sentido estricto (de la palabra); ~ **between ourselves** ... entre nosotros ...

stridden ['strɪdn] *pp of* **stride**

stride [straɪd] *n* zancada, tranco ■ *vi* (*pt* **strode**, *pp* **stridden**) [strəʊd, 'strɪdn] dar zancadas, andar a trancos; **to take in one's ~** (*fig: changes etc*) tomar con calma

strident ['straɪdnt] *adj* estridente; (*colour*) chillón(-ona)

strife [straɪf] *n* lucha

strike [straɪk] (*pt, pp* **struck**) *n* huelga; (*of oil etc*) descubrimiento; (*attack*) ataque *m*; (*Sport*) golpe *m* ■ *vt* golpear, pegar; (*oil etc*) descubrir; (*obstacle*) topar con; (*produce: coin, medal*) acuñar; (*: agreement, deal*) concertar ■ *vi* declarar la huelga; (*attack: Mil etc*) atacar; (*clock*) dar la hora; **on ~** (*workers*) en huelga; **to call a ~** declarar una huelga; **to go on** *or* **come out on ~** ponerse *or* declararse en huelga; **to ~ a match** encender una cerilla; **to ~ a balance** (*fig*) encontrar un equilibrio; **to ~ a bargain** cerrar un trato; **the clock struck nine o'clock** el reloj dio las nueve
  ▶ **strike back** *vi* (*Mil*) contraatacar; (*fig*) devolver el golpe
  ▶ **strike down** *vt* derribar
  ▶ **strike off** *vt* (*from list*) tachar; (*doctor etc*) suspender
  ▶ **strike out** *vt* borrar, tachar
  ▶ **strike up** *vt* (*Mus*) empezar a tocar; (*conversation*) entablar; (*friendship*) trabar

strikebreaker ['straɪkbreɪkə^r] *n* rompehuelgas *m/f inv*

striker ['straɪkə^r] *n* huelgista *m/f*; (*Sport*) delantero

striking ['straɪkɪŋ] *adj* (*colour*) llamativo; (*obvious*) notorio

Strimmer® ['strɪmə^r] *n* cortacéspedes *m inv* (*especial para los bordes*)

string [strɪŋ] *n* (*gen*) cuerda; (*row*) hilera; (*Comput*) cadena ■ *vt* (*pt, pp* **strung**) [strʌŋ]: **to ~ together** ensartar; **to ~ out** extenderse; **the strings** *npl* (*Mus*) los instrumentos de cuerda; **to pull strings** (*fig*) mover palancas; **to get a job by pulling strings** conseguir un trabajo por enchufe; **with no strings attached** (*fig*) sin compromiso

string bean *n* judía verde, habichuela

stringed instrument [strɪŋ(d)-], **string instrument** *n* (*Mus*) instrumento de cuerda

stringent ['strɪndʒənt] *adj* riguroso, severo

string quartet *n* cuarteto de cuerdas

strip [strɪp] *n* tira; (*of land*) franja; (*of metal*) cinta, lámina ■ *vt* desnudar; (*also*: **strip down**: *machine*) desmontar ■ *vi* desnudarse

strip cartoon *n* tira cómica, historieta (*LAm*)

stripe [straɪp] *n* raya; (*Mil*) galón *m*; **white with green stripes** blanco con rayas verdes

striped [straɪpt] *adj* a rayas, rayado

strip lighting *n* alumbrado fluorescente

stripper ['strɪpə^r] *n* artista *m/f* de striptease

strip-search ['strɪpsə:tʃ] *vt*: **to ~ sb** desnudar y registrar a algn

striptease ['strɪpti:z] *n* striptease *m*

strive (*pt* **strove**, *pp* **striven**) [straɪv, strəʊv, 'strɪvn] *vi*: **to ~ to do sth** esforzarse *or* luchar por hacer algo

strobe [strəʊb] *n* (*also*: **strobe light**) luz *f* estroboscópica

strode [strəʊd] *pt of* **stride**

stroke [strəʊk] *n* (*blow*) golpe *m*; (*Med*) apoplejía; (*caress*) caricia; (*of pen*) trazo; (*Swimming: style*) estilo; (*of piston*) carrera ■ *vt* acariciar; **at a ~** de golpe; **a ~ of luck** golpe de suerte; **two-~ engine** motor *m* de dos tiempos

stroll [strəʊl] *n* paseo, vuelta ■ *vi* dar un paseo *or* una vuelta; **to go for a ~**, **have** *or* **take a ~** dar un paseo

stroller ['strəʊlə^r] *n* (*US: pushchair*) cochecito

strong [strɒŋ] *adj* fuerte; (*bleach, acid*) concentrado ■ *adv*: **to be going ~** (*company*) marchar bien; (*person*) conservarse bien; **they are 50 ~** son 50

strong-arm ['strɒŋɑ:m] *adj* (*tactics, methods*) represivo

strongbox ['strɒŋbɒks] *n* caja fuerte

strong drink *n* bebida cargada *or* fuerte

stronghold ['strɒŋhəʊld] *n* fortaleza; (*fig*) baluarte *m*

strong language *n* lenguaje *m* fuerte

strongly ['strɒŋlɪ] *adv* fuertemente, con fuerza; (*believe*) firmemente; **to feel ~ about sth** tener una opinión firme sobre algo

strongman ['strɒŋmæn] *n* forzudo; (*fig*) hombre *m* robusto

strongroom ['strɒŋru:m] *n* cámara acorazada

stroppy ['strɒpɪ] *adj* (*Brit col*) borde; **to get ~** ponerse borde

strove [strəʊv] *pt of* **strive**

struck [strʌk] *pt, pp of* **strike**

structural ['strʌktʃərəl] *adj* estructural

structure ['strʌktʃəʳ] n estructura; (building) construcción f

struggle ['strʌgl] n lucha ▪ vi luchar; **to have a ~ to do sth** esforzarse por hacer algo

strum [strʌm] vt (guitar) rasguear

strung [strʌŋ] pt, pp of **string**

strut [strʌt] n puntal m ▪ vi pavonearse

strychnine ['strɪkniːn] n estricnina

stub [stʌb] n (of ticket etc) matriz f; (of cigarette) colilla ▪ vt: **to ~ one's toe on sth** dar con el dedo del pie contra algo
▶ **stub out** vt (cigarette) apagar

stubble ['stʌbl] n rastrojo; (on chin) barba (incipiente)

stubborn ['stʌbən] adj terco, testarudo

stucco ['stʌkəu] n estuco

stuck [stʌk] pt, pp of **stick** ▪ adj (jammed) atascado

stuck-up [stʌk'ʌp] adj engreído, presumido

stud [stʌd] n (shirt stud) corchete m, (of boot) taco; (of horses) caballeriza; (also: **stud horse**) caballo semental ▪ vt (fig): **studded with** salpicado de

student ['stjuːdənt] n estudiante m/f ▪ adj estudiantil; **a law/medical ~** un(a) estudiante de derecho/medicina

student driver n (US Aut) aprendiz(a) m(f) de conductor

students' union n (Brit: association) sindicato de estudiantes; (: building) centro de estudiantes

studio ['stjuːdɪəu] n estudio; (artist's) taller m

studio flat, studio apartment (US) n estudio

studious ['stjuːdɪəs] adj estudioso; (studied) calculado

studiously ['stjuːdɪəslɪ] adv (carefully) con esmero

study ['stʌdɪ] n estudio ▪ vt estudiar; (examine) examinar, investigar ▪ vi estudiar; **to make a ~ of sth** realizar una investigación de algo; **to ~ for an exam** preparar un examen

stuff [stʌf] n materia; (cloth) tela; (substance) material m, sustancia; (things, belongings) cosas fpl ▪ vt llenar; (Culin) rellenar; (animal: for exhibition) disecar; **my nose is stuffed up** tengo la nariz tapada; **stuffed toy** juguete m or muñeco de trapo

stuffing ['stʌfɪŋ] n relleno

stuffy ['stʌfɪ] adj (room) mal ventilado; (person) de miras estrechas

stumble ['stʌmbl] vi tropezar, dar un traspié
▶ **stumble across** vt fus (fig) tropezar con

stumbling block ['stʌmblɪŋ-] n tropiezo, obstáculo

stump [stʌmp] n (of tree) tocón m; (of limb) muñón m ▪ vt: **to be stumped** quedarse perplejo; **to be stumped for an answer** quedarse sin saber qué contestar

stun [stʌn] vt aturdir

stung [stʌŋ] pt, pp of **sting**

stunk [stʌŋk] pp of **stink**

stunning ['stʌnɪŋ] adj (fig) pasmoso

stunt [stʌnt] n (Aviat) vuelo acrobático; (also: **publicity stunt**) truco publicitario

stunted ['stʌntɪd] adj enano, achaparrado

stuntman ['stʌntmæn] n especialista m

stupefaction [stjuːpɪ'fækʃən] n estupefacción f

stupefy ['stjuːpɪfaɪ] vt dejar estupefacto

stupendous [stjuː'pɛndəs] adj estupendo, asombroso

stupid ['stjuːpɪd] adj estúpido, tonto

stupidity [stjuː'pɪdɪtɪ] n estupidez f

stupor ['stjuːpəʳ] n estupor m

sturdy ['stəːdɪ] adj robusto, fuerte

stutter ['stʌtəʳ] n tartamudeo ▪ vi tartamudear

sty [staɪ] n (for pigs) pocilga

stye [staɪ] n (Med) orzuelo

style [staɪl] n estilo; (fashion) moda; (of dress etc) hechura; (hair style) corte m; **in the latest ~** en el último modelo

stylish ['staɪlɪʃ] adj elegante, a la moda

stylist ['staɪlɪst] n (hair stylist) peluquero(-a)

stylus (pl **styli** or **styluses**) ['staɪləs, -laɪ] n (of record player) aguja

Styrofoam® ['staɪrəfəum] n (US) poliestireno ▪ adj (cup) de poliestireno

suave [swɑːv] adj cortés, fino

sub [sʌb] n abbr = **submarine; subscription**

sub... [sʌb] pref sub...

subcommittee ['sʌbkəmɪtɪ] n subcomisión f

subconscious [sʌb'kɒnʃəs] adj subconsciente ▪ n subconsciente m

subcontinent [sʌb'kɒntɪnənt] n: **the Indian ~** el subcontinente (de la India)

subcontract n ['sʌb'kɒntrækt] subcontrato ▪ vt ['sʌbkən'trækt] subcontratar

subcontractor ['sʌbkən'træktəʳ] n subcontratista m/f

subdivide [sʌbdɪ'vaɪd] vt subdividir

subdue [səb'djuː] vt sojuzgar; (passions) dominar

subdued [səb'djuːd] adj (light) tenue; (person) sumiso, manso

sub-editor ['sʌb'ɛdɪtəʳ] n (Brit) redactor(a) m(f)

subject n ['sʌbdʒɪkt] súbdito; (Scol) tema m, materia ▪ vt [səb'dʒɛkt]: **to ~ sb to sth** someter a algn a algo ▪ adj ['sʌbdʒɪkt]: **to be ~ to** (law) estar sujeto a; **~ to confirmation**

S

807

in writing sujeto a confirmación por escrito; to change the ~ cambiar de tema
subjective [səb'dʒɛktɪv] *adj* subjetivo
subject matter *n* materia; *(content)* contenido
sub judice [sʌb'dju:dɪsɪ] *adj* (*Law*) pendiente de resolución
subjugate ['sʌbdʒugeɪt] *vt* subyugar, sojuzgar
subjunctive [səb'dʒʌŋktɪv] *adj, n* subjuntivo
sublet [sʌb'lɛt] *vt, vi* subarrendar, realquilar
sublime [sə'blaɪm] *adj* sublime
subliminal [sʌb'lɪmɪnl] *adj* subliminal
submachine gun ['sʌbmə'ʃi:n-] *n* metralleta
submarine [sʌbmə'ri:n] *n* submarino
submerge [səb'mə:dʒ] *vt* sumergir; *(flood)* inundar ■ *vi* sumergirse
submersion [səb'mə:ʃən] *n* submersión *f*
submission [səb'mɪʃən] *n* sumisión *f*; *(to committee etc)* ponencia
submissive [səb'mɪsɪv] *adj* sumiso
submit [səb'mɪt] *vt* someter; *(proposal, claim)* presentar ■ *vi* someterse; **I ~ that ...** me permito sugerir que ...
subnormal [sʌb'nɔ:məl] *adj* subnormal
subordinate [sə'bɔ:dɪnət] *adj, n* subordinado(-a) *m(f)*
subpoena [səb'pi:nə] *(Law)* *n* citación *f* ■ *vt* citar
subroutine [sʌbru:'ti:n] *n* (*Comput*) subrutina
subscribe [səb'skraɪb] *vi* suscribir; **to ~ to** *(fund)* suscribir, aprobar; *(opinion)* estar de acuerdo con; *(newspaper)* suscribirse a
subscribed capital [səb'skraɪbd-] *n* capital *m* suscrito
subscriber [səb'skraɪbə'] *n* (*to periodical*) suscriptor(a) *m(f)*; *(to telephone)* abonado(-a)
subscript ['sʌbskrɪpt] *n* (*Typ*) subíndice *m*
subscription [səb'skrɪpʃən] *n* (*to club*) abono; *(to magazine)* suscripción *f*; **to take out a ~ to** suscribirse a
subsequent ['sʌbsɪkwənt] *adj* subsiguiente, posterior; **~ to** posterior a
subsequently ['sʌbsɪkwəntlɪ] *adv* posteriormente, más tarde
subservient [səb'sə:vɪənt] *adj*: **~ (to)** servil (a)
subside [səb'saɪd] *vi* hundirse; *(flood)* bajar; *(wind)* amainar
subsidence [səb'saɪdns] *n* hundimiento; *(in road)* socavón *m*
subsidiarity [səbsɪdɪ'ærɪtɪ] *n* (*Pol*) subsidiariedad *f*
subsidiary [səb'sɪdɪərɪ] *n* sucursal *f*, filial *f* ■ *adj* (*Univ: subject*) secundario
subsidize ['sʌbsɪdaɪz] *vt* subvencionar
subsidy ['sʌbsɪdɪ] *n* subvención *f*

subsist [səb'sɪst] *vi*: **to ~ on sth** subsistir a base de algo, sustentarse con algo
subsistence [səb'sɪstəns] *n* subsistencia
subsistence allowance *n* dietas *fpl*
subsistence level *n* nivel *m* de subsistencia
subsistence wage *n* sueldo de subsistencia
substance ['sʌbstəns] *n* sustancia; *(fig)* esencia; **to lack ~** *(argument)* no tener poco convincente; *(accusation)* no tener fundamento; *(film, book)* tener poca profundidad
substance abuse *n* uso indebido de sustancias tóxicas
substandard [sʌb'stændəd] *adj* (*goods*) inferior; *(housing)* deficiente
substantial [səb'stænʃl] *adj* sustancial, sustancioso; *(fig)* importante
substantially [səb'stænʃəlɪ] *adv* sustancialmente; **~ bigger** bastante más grande
substantiate [səb'stænʃɪeɪt] *vt* comprobar
substitute ['sʌbstɪtju:t] *n* (*person*) suplente *m/f*; *(thing)* sustituto ■ *vt*: **to ~ A for B** sustituir B por A, reemplazar A por B
substitution [sʌbstɪ'tju:ʃən] *n* sustitución *f*
subterfuge ['sʌbtəfju:dʒ] *n* subterfugio
subterranean [sʌbtə'reɪnɪən] *adj* subterráneo
subtitle ['sʌbtaɪtl] *n* subtítulo
subtle ['sʌtl] *adj* sutil
subtlety ['sʌtltɪ] *n* sutileza
subtly ['sʌtlɪ] *adv* sutilmente
subtotal [sʌb'təutl] *n* subtotal *m*
subtract [səb'trækt] *vt* restar; sustraer
subtraction [səb'trækʃən] *n* resta; sustracción *f*
suburb ['sʌbə:b] *n* barrio residencial; **the suburbs** las afueras (de la ciudad)
suburban [sə'bə:bən] *adj* suburbano; *(train etc)* de cercanías
suburbia [sə'bə:bɪə] *n* barrios *mpl* residenciales
subversion [səb'və:ʃən] *n* subversión *f*
subversive [səb'və:sɪv] *adj* subversivo
subway ['sʌbweɪ] *n* (*Brit*) paso subterráneo *or* inferior; (*US*) metro
sub-zero [sʌb'zɪərəu] *adj*: **~ temperatures** temperaturas *fpl* por debajo del cero
succeed [sək'si:d] *vi* (*person*) tener éxito; *(plan)* salir bien ■ *vt* suceder a; **to ~ in doing** lograr hacer
succeeding [sək'si:dɪŋ] *adj* (*following*) sucesivo; **~ generations** generaciones *fpl* futuras
success [sək'sɛs] *n* éxito; *(gain)* triunfo
successful [sək'sɛsful] *adj* (*venture*) de éxito, exitoso (*esp LAm*); **to be ~ (in doing)** lograr (hacer)

successfully [sək'sɛsfulɪ] *adv* con éxito
succession [sək'sɛʃən] *n (series)* sucesión
f, serie *f*; *(descendants)* descendencia; **in ~** sucesivamente
successive [sək'sɛsɪv] *adj* sucesivo, consecutivo; **on three ~ days** tres días seguidos
successor [sək'sɛsəʳ] *n* sucesor(a) *m(f)*
succinct [sək'sɪŋkt] *adj* sucinto
succulent ['sʌkjulənt] *adj* suculento ■ *n* (*Bot*); **succulents** *npl* plantas *fpl* carnosas
succumb [sə'kʌm] *vi* sucumbir
such [sʌtʃ] *adj* tal, semejante; *(of that kind)*: **~ a book** tal libro; **~ books** tales libros; *(so much)*: **~ courage** tanto valor ■ *adv* tan; **~ a long trip** un viaje tan largo; **~ a lot of** tanto; **~ as** *(like)* tal como; **a noise ~ as to** un ruido tal que; **~ books as I have** cuantos libros tengo; **I said no ~ thing** no dije tal cosa; **it's ~ a long time since we saw each other** hace tanto tiempo que no nos vemos; **~ a long time ago** hace tantísimo tiempo; **as ~** *adv* como tal
such-and-such ['sʌtʃənsʌtʃ] *adj* tal o cual
suchlike ['sʌtʃlaɪk] *pron (col)*: **and ~** y cosas por el estilo
suck [sʌk] *vt* chupar; *(bottle)* sorber; *(breast)* mamar; *(pump, machine)* aspirar
sucker ['sʌkəʳ] *n (Bot)* serpollo; *(Zool)* ventosa; *(col)* bobo, primo
sucrose ['su:krəuz] *n* sacarosa
suction ['sʌkʃən] *n* succión *f*
suction pump *n* bomba aspirante *or* de succión
Sudan [su'dæn] *n* Sudán *m*
Sudanese [su:də'ni:z] *adj, n* sudanés(-esa) *m(f)*
sudden ['sʌdn] *adj (rapid)* repentino, súbito; *(unexpected)* imprevisto; **all of a ~** de repente
sudden-death [sʌdn'dɛθ] *n (also:* **sudden-death play off)** desempate *m* instantáneo, muerte *f* súbita
suddenly ['sʌdnlɪ] *adv* de repente
sudoku [sʊ'dəuku:] *n* sudoku *m*
suds [sʌdz] *npl* espuma *sg* de jabón
sue [su:] *vt* demandar; **to ~ (for)** demandar (por); **to ~ for divorce** solicitar *or* pedir el divorcio; **to ~ for damages** demandar por daños y perjuicios
suede [sweɪd] *n* ante *m*, gamuza *(LAm)*
suet ['suɪt] *n* sebo
Suez Canal ['su:ɪz-] *n* Canal *m* de Suez
Suff. *abbr (Brit)* = **Suffolk**
suffer ['sʌfəʳ] *vt* sufrir, padecer; *(tolerate)* aguantar, soportar; *(undergo: loss, setback)* experimentar ■ *vi* sufrir, padecer; **to ~**

from sufrir, tener; **to ~ from the effects of alcohol/a fall** sufrir los efectos del alcohol/ resentirse de una caída
sufferance ['sʌfərns] *n*: **he was only there on ~** estuvo allí sólo porque se lo toleraron
sufferer ['sʌfərəʳ] *n* víctima *f*; *(Med)*: **~ from** enfermo(-a) de
suffering ['sʌfərɪŋ] *n (hardship, deprivation)* sufrimiento; *(pain)* dolor *m*
suffice [sə'faɪs] *vi* bastar, ser suficiente
sufficient [sə'fɪʃənt] *adj* suficiente, bastante
sufficiently [sə'fɪʃəntlɪ] *adv* suficientemente, bastante
suffix ['sʌfɪks] *n* sufijo
suffocate ['sʌfəkeɪt] *vi* ahogarse, asfixiarse
suffocation [sʌfə'keɪʃən] *n* sofocación *f*, asfixia
suffrage ['sʌfrɪdʒ] *n* sufragio
suffuse [sə'fju:z] *vt*: **to ~ (with)** *(colour)* bañar (de); **her face was suffused with joy** su cara estaba llena de alegría
sugar ['ʃugəʳ] *n* azúcar *m* ■ *vt* echar azúcar a, azucarar
sugar basin *n (Brit)* = **sugar bowl**
sugar beet *n* remolacha
sugar bowl *n* azucarero
sugar cane *n* caña de azúcar
sugar-coated [ʃugə'kəutɪd] *adj* azucarado
sugar lump *n* terrón *m* de azúcar
sugar refinery *n* refinería de azúcar
sugary ['ʃugərɪ] *adj* azucarado
suggest [sə'dʒɛst] *vt* sugerir; *(recommend)* aconsejar; **what do you ~ I do?** ¿qué sugieres que haga?; **this suggests that ...** esto hace pensar que ...
suggestion [sə'dʒɛstʃən] *n* sugerencia; **there's no ~ of ...** no hay indicación *or* evidencia de ...
suggestive [sə'dʒɛstɪv] *adj* sugestivo; *(pej: indecent)* indecente
suicidal ['suɪsaɪdl] *adj* suicida
suicide ['suɪsaɪd] *n* suicidio; *(person)* suicida *m/f*; **to commit ~** suicidarse
suicide attempt, suicide bid *n* intento de suicidio
suicide bomber *n* terrorista *m/f* suicida
suicide bombing *n* atentado *m* suicida
suit [su:t] *n (man's)* traje *m*; *(woman's)* traje de chaqueta; *(Law)* pleito; *(Cards)* palo ■ *vt* convenir; *(clothes)* sentar bien a, ir bien a; *(adapt)*: **to ~ sth to** adaptar *or* ajustar algo a; **to be suited to sth** *(suitable for)* ser apto para algo; **well suited** *(couple)* hechos el uno para el otro; **to bring a ~ against sb** entablar demanda contra algn; **to follow ~** *(Cards)* seguir el palo; *(fig)* seguir el ejemplo (de algn); **that suits me** me va bien

S

suitable ['su:təbl] *adj* conveniente; (*apt*) indicado
suitably ['su:təblɪ] *adv* convenientemente; (*appropriately*) en forma debida
suitcase ['su:tkeɪs] *n* maleta, valija (*LAm*)
suite [swi:t] *n* (*of rooms*) suite *f*; (*Mus*) suite *f*; (*furniture*): **bedroom/dining room** ~ (juego de) dormitorio/comedor *m*; **a three-piece** ~ un tresillo
suitor ['su:tər] *n* pretendiente *m*
sulfate ['sʌlfeɪt] *n* (*US*) = **sulphate**
sulfur ['sʌlfər] *n* (*US*) = **sulphur**
sulk [sʌlk] *vi* estar de mal humor
sulky ['sʌlkɪ] *adj* malhumorado
sullen ['sʌlən] *adj* hosco, malhumorado
sulphate, sulfate (*US*) ['sʌlfeɪt] *n* sulfato; **copper** ~ sulfato de cobre
sulphur, sulfur (*US*) ['sʌlfər] *n* azufre *m*
sulphur dioxide *n* dióxido de azufre
sultan ['sʌltən] *n* sultán *m*
sultana [sʌl'tɑ:nə] *n* (*fruit*) pasa de Esmirna
sultry ['sʌltrɪ] *adj* (*weather*) bochornoso; (*seductive*) seductor(a)
sum [sʌm] *n* suma; (*total*) total *m*
▶ **sum up** *vt* resumir; (*evaluate rapidly*) evaluar ▪ *vi* hacer un resumen
Sumatra [su'mɑ:trə] *n* Sumatra
summarize ['sʌmaraɪz] *vt* resumir
summary ['sʌmərɪ] *n* resumen *m* ▪ *adj* (*justice*) sumario
summer ['sʌmər] *n* verano ▪ *adj* de verano; **in (the)** ~ en (el) verano
summerhouse ['sʌməhaus] *n* (*in garden*) cenador *m*, glorieta
summertime ['sʌmətaɪm] *n* (*season*) verano
summer time *n* (*by clock*) hora de verano
summery ['sʌmərɪ] *adj* veraniego
summing-up [sʌmɪŋ'ʌp] *n* (*Law*) resumen *m*
summit ['sʌmɪt] *n* cima, cumbre *f*; (*also*: **summit conference**) (conferencia) cumbre *f*
summit conference *n* conferencia cumbre *f*
summon ['sʌmən] *vt* (*person*) llamar; (*meeting*) convocar; **to** ~ **a witness** citar a un testigo
▶ **summon up** *vt* (*courage*) armarse de
summons ['sʌmənz] *n* llamamiento, llamada ▪ *vt* citar, emplazar; **to serve a** ~ **on sb** citar a algn ante el juicio
sumo ['su:məu] *n* (*also*: **sumo wrestling**) sumo
sump [sʌmp] *n* (*Brit Aut*) cárter *m*
sumptuous ['sʌmptjuəs] *adj* suntuoso
sun [sʌn] *n* sol *m*; **they have everything under the** ~ no les falta nada, tienen de todo
Sun. *abbr* (= *Sunday*) dom
sunbathe ['sʌnbeɪð] *vi* tomar el sol
sunbeam ['sʌnbi:m] *n* rayo de sol
sunbed ['sʌnbɛd] *n* cama solar

sunburn ['sʌnbə:n] *n* (*painful*) quemadura del sol; (*tan*) bronceado
sunburnt ['sʌnbə:nt], **sunburned** ['sʌnbə:nd] *adj* (*tanned*) bronceado; (*painfully*) quemado por el sol
sundae ['sʌndeɪ] *n* helado con frutas y nueces
Sunday ['sʌndɪ] *n* domingo; *see also* **Tuesday**
Sunday paper *n* (*periódico*) dominical *m*
Sunday school *n* catequesis *f*
sundial ['sʌndaɪəl] *n* reloj *m* de sol
sundown ['sʌndaun] *n* anochecer *m*, puesta de sol
sundries ['sʌndrɪz] *npl* géneros *mpl* diversos
sundry ['sʌndrɪ] *adj* varios, diversos; **all and** ~ todos sin excepción
sunflower ['sʌnflauər] *n* girasol *m*
sung [sʌŋ] *pp of* **sing**
sunglasses ['sʌnglɑ:sɪz] *npl* gafas *fpl* de sol
sunk [sʌŋk] *pp of* **sink**
sunken ['sʌŋkn] *adj* (*bath*) hundido
sunlamp ['sʌnlæmp] *n* lámpara solar ultravioleta
sunlight ['sʌnlaɪt] *n* luz *f* del sol
sunlit ['sʌnlɪt] *adj* iluminado por el sol
sunny ['sʌnɪ] *adj* soleado; (*day*) de sol; (*fig*) alegre; **it is** ~ hace sol
sunrise ['sʌnraɪz] *n* salida del sol
sun roof *n* (*Aut*) techo corredizo *or* solar; (*on building*) azotea, terraza
sunscreen ['sʌnskri:n] *n* protector *m* solar
sunset ['sʌnset] *n* puesta del sol
sunshade ['sʌnʃeɪd] *n* (*over table*) sombrilla
sunshine ['sʌnʃaɪn] *n* sol *m*
sunstroke ['sʌnstrəuk] *n* insolación *f*
suntan ['sʌntæn] *n* bronceado
suntanned ['sʌntænd] *adj* bronceado
suntan oil *n* aceite *m* bronceador
super ['su:pər] *adj* (*col*) bárbaro
superannuation [su:pərænju'eɪʃən] *n* jubilación *f*, pensión *f*
superb [su:'pə:b] *adj* magnífico, espléndido
Super Bowl *n* (*US Sport*) super copa de fútbol americano
supercilious [su:pə'sɪlɪəs] *adj* (*disdainful*) desdeñoso; (*haughty*) altanero
superconductor [su:pəkən'dʌktər] *n* superconductor *m*
superficial [su:pə'fɪʃəl] *adj* superficial
superfluous [su'pə:fluəs] *adj* superfluo, de sobra
superglue ['su:pəglu:] *n* cola de contacto, supercola
superhighway ['su:pəhaɪweɪ] *n* (*US*) superautopista; **the information** ~ la superautopista de la información
superhuman [su:pə'hju:mən] *adj* sobrehumano

superimpose ['su:pərɪm'pəuz] vt sobreponer

superintend [su:pərɪn'tɛnd] vt supervisar

superintendent [su:pərɪn'tɛndənt] n director(a) m(f); (also: **police superintendent**) subjefe(-a) m(f)

superior [su'pɪərɪəʳ] adj superior; (smug: person) altivo, desdeñoso; (: smile, air) de suficiencia; (: remark) desdeñoso ■ n superior m; **Mother S~** (Rel) madre f superiora

superiority [supɪərɪ'ɔrɪtɪ] n superioridad f; desdén m

superlative [su'pə:lətɪv] adj, n superlativo

superman ['su:pəmæn] n superhombre m

supermarket ['su:pəmɑ:kɪt] n supermercado

supermodel ['su:pəmɔdl] n top model f, supermodelo f

supernatural [su:pə'nætʃərəl] adj sobrenatural

supernova [su:pə'nəuvə] n supernova

superpower ['su:pəpauəʳ] n (Pol) superpotencia

supersede [su:pə'si:d] vt suplantar

supersonic ['su:pə'sɔnɪk] adj supersónico

superstar ['su:pəstɑ:ʳ] n superestrella ■ adj de superestrella

superstition [su:pə'stɪʃən] n superstición f

superstitious [su:pə'stɪʃəs] adj supersticioso

superstore ['su:pəstɔ:ʳ] n (Brit) hipermercado

supertanker ['su:pətænkəʳ] n superpetrolero

supertax ['su:pətæks] n sobretasa, sobreimpuesto

supervise ['su:pəvaɪz] vt supervisar

supervision [su:pə'vɪʒən] n supervisión f

supervisor ['su:pəvaɪzəʳ] n supervisor(a) m(f)

supervisory ['su:pəvaɪzərɪ] adj de supervisión

supper ['sʌpəʳ] n cena; **to have ~** cenar

supplant [sə'plɑ:nt] vt suplantar, reemplazar

supple ['sʌpl] adj flexible

supplement n ['sʌplɪmənt] suplemento ■ vt [sʌplɪ'mɛnt] suplir

supplementary [sʌplɪ'mɛntərɪ] adj suplementario

supplementary benefit n (Brit) subsidio adicional de la seguridad social

supplier [sə'plaɪəʳ] n suministrador(a) m(f); (Comm) distribuidor(a) m(f)

supply [sə'plaɪ] vt (provide) suministrar; (information) facilitar; (fill: need, want) suplir, satisfacer; (equip): **to ~ (with)** proveer (de) ■ n provisión f; (of gas, water etc) suministro ■ adj (Brit: teacher etc) suplente; **supplies** npl (food) víveres mpl; (Mil) pertrechos mpl; **office supplies** materiales mpl para oficina; **to be in short ~** escasear, haber escasez de; **the electricity/water/gas ~** el suministro de electricidad/agua/gas; **~ and demand** la oferta y la demanda

support [sə'pɔ:t] n (moral, financial etc) apoyo; (Tech) soporte m ■ vt apoyar; (financially) mantener; (uphold) sostener; (Sport: team) seguir, ser hincha de; **they stopped work in ~ (of)** pararon de trabajar en apoyo (de); **to ~ o.s.** (financially) ganarse la vida

support buying [-'baɪɪŋ] n compra proteccionista

supporter [sə'pɔ:təʳ] n (Pol etc) partidario(-a); (Sport) aficionado(-a); (Football) hincha m/f

supporting [sə'pɔ:tɪŋ] adj (wall) de apoyo; **~ role** papel m secundario; **~ actor/actress** actor/actriz m/f secundario(-a)

supportive [sə'pɔ:tɪv] adj de apoyo; **I have a ~ family/wife** mi familia/mujer me apoya

suppose [sə'pəuz] vt, vi suponer; (imagine) imaginarse; **to be supposed to do sth** deber hacer algo; **I don't ~ she'll come** no creo que venga; **he's supposed to be an expert** se le supone un experto

supposedly [sə'pəuzɪdlɪ] adv según cabe suponer

supposing [sə'pəuzɪŋ] conj en caso de que; **always ~ (that) he comes** suponiendo que venga

supposition [sʌpə'zɪʃən] n suposición f

suppository [sə'pɔzɪtrɪ] n supositorio

suppress [sə'prɛs] vt suprimir; (yawn) ahogar

suppression [sə'prɛʃən] n represión f

supremacy [su'prɛməsɪ] n supremacía f

supreme [su'pri:m] adj supremo

Supreme Court n (US) Tribunal m Supremo, Corte f Suprema

supremo [su'pri:məu] n autoridad f máxima

Supt. abbr (Police) = **superintendent**

surcharge ['sə:tʃɑ:dʒ] n sobretasa, recargo

sure [ʃuəʳ] adj seguro; (definite, convinced) cierto; (aim) certero ■ adv: **that ~ is pretty, that's ~ pretty** (US) ¡qué bonito es!; **to be ~ of sth** estar seguro de algo; **to be ~ of o.s.** estar seguro de sí mismo; **to make ~ of sth/that** asegurarse de algo/asegurar que; **I'm not ~ how/why/when** no estoy seguro de cómo/por qué/cuándo; **~!** (of course) ¡claro!, ¡por supuesto!; **~ enough** efectivamente

sure-fire ['ʃuəfaɪəʳ] adj (col) infalible

sure-footed [ʃuə'futɪd] adj de pie firme

surely ['ʃuəlɪ] adv (certainly) seguramente; **~ you don't mean that!** ¡no lo dices en serio!

surety ['ʃuərətɪ] n fianza; (person) fiador(a) m(f); **to go** or **stand ~ for sb** ser fiador de algn, salir garante por algn

surf [sə:f] n olas fpl ■ vi hacer surf ■ vt (Internet): **to ~ the Net** navegar por Internet

surface ['sə:fɪs] n superficie f ▪ vt (road)
revestir ▪ vi salir a la superficie ▪ cpd (Mil,
Naut) de (la) superficie; **on the ~ it seems
that ...** (fig) a primera vista parece que ...
surface area n área de la superficie
surface mail n vía terrestre
surface-to-air ['sə:fɪstə'εə'] adj (Mil) tierra-
aire
surface-to-surface ['sə:fɪstə'sə:fɪs] adj (Mil)
tierra-tierra
surfboard ['sə:fbɔ:d] n plancha (de surf)
surfeit ['sə:fɪt] n: **a ~ of** un exceso de
surfer ['sə:fə'] n súrfer m/f
surfing ['sə:fɪŋ] n surf m
surge [sə:dʒ] n oleada, oleaje m; (Elec)
sobretensión f transitoria ▪ vi avanzar a
tropel; **to ~ forward** avanzar rápidamente
surgeon ['sə:dʒən] n cirujano(-a)
surgery ['sə:dʒərɪ] n cirugía; (Brit: room)
consultorio; (: Pol) horas en las que los electores
pueden reunirse personalmente con su diputado; **to
undergo ~** operarse; see also **constituency**
surgery hours npl (Brit) horas fpl de consulta
surgical ['sə:dʒɪkl] adj quirúrgico
surgical spirit n (Brit) alcohol m
surly ['sə:lɪ] adj hosco, malhumorado
surmount [sə:'maunt] vt superar, vencer
surname ['sə:neɪm] n apellido
surpass [sə:'pɑ:s] vt superar, exceder
surplus ['sə:pləs] n excedente m; (Comm)
superávit m ▪ adj (Comm) excedente,
sobrante; **to have a ~ of sth** tener
un excedente de algo; **it is ~ to our
requirements** nos sobra; **~ stock** saldos mpl
surprise [sə'praɪz] n sorpresa ▪ vt
sorprender; **to take by ~** (person) coger
desprevenido or por sorpresa a, sorprender a;
(Mil: town, fort) atacar por sorpresa
surprising [sə'praɪzɪŋ] adj sorprendente
surprisingly [sə'praɪzɪŋlɪ] adv (easy, helpful)
de modo sorprendente; **(somewhat) ~, he
agreed** para sorpresa de todos, aceptó
surrealism [sə'rɪəlɪzəm] n surrealismo
surrender [sə'rεndə'] n rendición f, entrega
▪ vi rendirse, entregarse ▪ vt renunciar
surrender value n valor m de rescate
surreptitious [sʌrəp'tɪʃəs] adj subrepticio
surrogate ['sʌrəgɪt] n (Brit) sustituto(-a)
surrogate mother n madre f de alquiler
surround [sə'raund] vt rodear, circundar;
(Mil etc) cercar
surrounding [sə'raundɪŋ] adj circundante
surroundings [sə'raundɪŋz] npl alrededores
mpl, cercanías fpl
surtax ['sə:tæks] n sobretasa, sobreimpuesto
surveillance [sə:'veɪləns] n vigilancia
survey n ['sə:veɪ] inspección f

reconocimiento; (inquiry) encuesta;
(comprehensive view: of situation etc) vista
de conjunto ▪ vt [sə:'veɪ] examinar,
inspeccionar; (Surveying: building)
inspeccionar; (: land) hacer un
reconocimiento de, reconocer; (look at)
mirar, contemplar; (make inquiries about)
hacer una encuesta de; **to carry out a ~ of**
inspeccionar, examinar
surveyor [sə'veɪə'] n (Brit: of building) perito
m/f; (of land) agrimensor(a) m(f)
survival [sə'vaɪvl] n supervivencia
survival course n curso de supervivencia
survival kit n equipo de emergencia
survive [sə'vaɪv] vi sobrevivir; (custom etc)
perdurar ▪ vt sobrevivir a
survivor [sə'vaɪvə'] n superviviente m/f
susceptibility [səsεptə'bɪlɪtɪ] n (to illness)
propensión f
susceptible [sə'sεptəbl] adj (easily influenced)
influenciable; (to disease, illness): **~ to**
propenso a
sushi [su:ʃɪ] n sushi m
suspect adj, n ['sʌspεkt] sospechoso(-a) m(f)
▪ vt [səs'pεkt] sospechar
suspected [səs'pεktɪd] adj presunto; **to have
a ~ fracture** tener una posible fractura
suspend [səs'pεnd] vt suspender
suspended animation [səs'pεndəd-] n: **in a
state of ~** en (estado de) hibernación
suspended sentence n (Law) libertad f
condicional
suspender belt [səs'pεndə'-] n (Brit) liguero,
portaligas m inv (LAm)
suspenders [səs'pεndəz] npl (Brit) ligas fpl;
(US) tirantes mpl
suspense [səs'pεns] n incertidumbre f, duda;
(in film etc) suspense m
suspension [səs'pεnʃən] n (gen) suspensión f;
(of driving licence) privación f
suspension bridge n puente m colgante
suspension file n archivador m colgante
suspicion [səs'pɪʃən] n sospecha; (distrust)
recelo; (trace) traza; **to be under ~** estar
bajo sospecha; **arrested on ~ of murder**
detenido bajo sospecha de asesinato
suspicious [səs'pɪʃəs] adj (suspecting) receloso;
(causing suspicion) sospechoso; **to be ~ of** or
about sb/sth tener sospechas de algn/algo
suss out [sʌs-] vt (Brit col) calar
sustain [səs'teɪn] vt sostener, apoyar; (suffer)
sufrir, padecer
sustainable [səs'teɪnəbl] adj sostenible;
~ development desarrollo sostenible
sustained [səs'teɪnd] adj (effort) sostenido
sustenance ['sʌstɪnəns] n sustento
suture ['su:tʃə'] n sutura

SUV [ˈɛsˈjuːˈviː] n abbr (= sports utility vehicle) todoterreno m inv

SVQ n abbr (= Scottish Vocational Qualification) titulación de formación profesional en Escocia

SW abbr = **short wave**

swab [swɔb] n (Med) algodón m, frotis m inv ■ vt (Naut: also: **swab down**) limpiar, fregar

swagger [ˈswægəʳ] vi pavonearse

swallow [ˈswɔləu] n (bird) golondrina; (of food) bocado; (of drink) trago ■ vt tragar
▶ **swallow up** vt (savings etc) consumir

swam [swæm] pt of **swim**

swamp [swɔmp] n pantano, ciénaga ■ vt abrumar, agobiar

swampy [ˈswɔmpɪ] adj pantanoso

swan [swɔn] n cisne m

swank [swæŋk] (col) n (vanity, boastfulness) fanfarronada ■ vi fanfarronear, presumir

swan song n (fig) canto del cisne

swap [swɔp] n canje m, trueque m ■ vt: **to ~ (for)** canjear (por)

SWAPO [ˈswɑːpəu] n abbr (= South-West Africa People's Organization) SWAPO f

swarm [swɔːm] n (of bees) enjambre m; (fig) multitud f ■ vi (fig) hormiguear, pulular

swarthy [ˈswɔːðɪ] adj moreno

swashbuckling [ˈswɔʃbʌklɪŋ] adj (person) aventurero; (film) de capa y espada

swastika [ˈswɔstɪkə] n esvástica, cruz f gamada

swat [swɔt] vt aplastar ■ n (also: **fly swat**) matamoscas m inv

SWAT [swɔt] n abbr (US: = Special Weapons and Tactics) unidad especial de la policía

swathe [sweɪð] vt: **to ~ in** (blankets) envolver en; (bandages) vendar en

sway [sweɪ] vi mecerse, balancearse ■ vt (influence) mover, influir en ■ n (rule, power): **~ (over)** dominio (sobre); **to hold ~ over sb** dominar a algn, mantener el dominio sobre algn

Swaziland [ˈswɑːzɪlænd] n Swazilandia

swear (pt **swore**, pp **sworn**) [sweəʳ, swɔːʳ, swɔːn] vi jurar; (with swearwords) decir tacos ■ vt: **to ~ an oath** prestar juramento, jurar; **to ~ to sth** declarar algo bajo juramento
▶ **swear in** vt tomar juramento (a)

swearword [ˈsweəwəːd] n taco, palabrota

sweat [swɛt] n sudor m ■ vi sudar

sweatband [ˈswɛtbænd] n (Sport: on head) banda; (: on wrist) muñequera

sweater [ˈswɛtəʳ] n suéter m

sweatshirt [ˈswɛtʃəːt] n sudadera

sweatshop [ˈswɛtʃɔp] n fábrica donde se explota al obrero

sweaty [ˈswɛtɪ] adj sudoroso

Swede [swiːd] n sueco(-a)

swede [swiːd] n (Brit) nabo

Sweden [ˈswiːdn] n Suecia

Swedish [ˈswiːdɪʃ] adj, n (Ling) sueco

sweep [swiːp] (pt, pp **swept**) n (act) barrida; (of arm) manotazo m; (curve) curva, alcance m; (also: **chimney sweep**) deshollinador(a) m(f) ■ vt barrer; (disease, fashion) recorrer ■ vi barrer
▶ **sweep away** vt barrer; (rub out) borrar
▶ **sweep past** vi pasar rápidamente; (brush by) rozar
▶ **sweep up** vi barrer

sweeper [ˈswiːpəʳ] n (person) barrendero(-a); (machine) barredora; (Football) líbero, libre m

sweeping [ˈswiːpɪŋ] adj (gesture) dramático; (generalized) generalizado; (changes, reforms) radical

sweepstake [ˈswiːpsteɪk] n lotería

sweet [swiːt] n (candy) dulce m, caramelo; (Brit: pudding) postre m ■ adj dulce; (sugary) azucarado; (charming: person) encantador(a); (: smile, character) dulce, amable, agradable ■ adv: **to smell/taste ~** oler/saber dulce

sweet and sour adj agridulce

sweetcorn [ˈswiːtkɔːn] n maíz m (dulce)

sweeten [ˈswiːtn] vt (person) endulzar; (add sugar to) poner azúcar a

sweetener [ˈswiːtnəʳ] n (Culin) edulcorante m

sweetheart [ˈswiːthɑːt] n amor m, novio(-a); (in speech) amor, cariño

sweetness [ˈswiːtnɪs] n (gen) dulzura

sweet pea n guisante m de olor

sweet potato n batata, camote m (LAm)

sweetshop [ˈswiːtʃɔp] n (Brit) confitería, bombonería

swell [swɛl] (pt **swelled**, pp **swollen** or **swelled**) n (of sea) marejada, oleaje m ■ adj (US: col: excellent) estupendo, fenomenal ■ vt hinchar, inflar ■ vi hincharse, inflarse

swelling [ˈswɛlɪŋ] n (Med) hinchazón f

sweltering [ˈswɛltərɪŋ] adj sofocante, de mucho calor

swept [swɛpt] pt, pp of **sweep**

swerve [swəːv] n regate m; (in car) desvío brusco ■ vi desviarse bruscamente

swift [swɪft] n (bird) vencejo ■ adj rápido, veloz

swiftly [ˈswɪftlɪ] adv rápidamente

swiftness [ˈswɪftnɪs] n rapidez f, velocidad f

swig [swɪg] n (col: drink) trago

swill [swɪl] n bazofia ■ vt (also: **swill out**, **swill down**) lavar, limpiar con agua

swim [swɪm] (pt **swam**, pp **swum**) n: **to go for a ~** ir a nadar or a bañarse ■ vi nadar; (head, room) dar vueltas ■ vt pasar a nado; **to go swimming** ir a nadar; **to ~ a length** nadar or hacer un largo

S

swimmer ['swɪmə'] n nadador(a) m(f)
swimming ['swɪmɪŋ] n natación f
swimming cap n gorro de baño
swimming costume n bañador m, traje m
de baño
swimmingly ['swɪmɪŋlɪ] adv: **to go ~**
(wonderfully) ir como una seda or sobre ruedas
swimming pool n piscina, alberca (LAm)
swimming trunks npl bañador msg
swimsuit ['swɪmsuːt] n = **swimming costume**
swindle ['swɪndl] n estafa ■ vt estafar
swine [swaɪn] n pl inv cerdo, puerco; (col!)
canalla m (!)
swine flu n gripe f porcina
swing [swɪŋ] (pt, pp **swung**) n (in playground)
columpio; (movement) balanceo, vaivén m;
(change of direction) viraje m; (rhythm) ritmo;
(Pol: in votes etc): **there has been a ~ towards/
away from Labour** ha habido un viraje en
favor/en contra del Partido Laborista ■ vt
balancear; (on a swing) columpiar; (also:
swing round) voltear, girar ■ vi balancearse,
columpiarse; (also: **swing round**) dar media
vuelta; **a ~ to the left** un movimiento hacia
la izquierda; **to be in full ~** estar en plena
marcha; **to get into the ~ of things** meterse
en situación; **the road swings south** la
carretera gira hacia el sur
swing bridge n puente m giratorio
swing door, swinging door (US) ['swɪŋɪŋ-]
n puerta giratoria
swingeing ['swɪndʒɪŋ] adj (Brit)
abrumador(a)
swipe [swaɪp] n golpe m fuerte ■ vt (hit)
golpear fuerte; (col: steal) guindar; (credit card
etc) pasar
swirl [swəːl] vi arremolinarse
swish [swɪʃ] n (sound: of whip) chasquido;
(: of skirts) frufrú m; (: of grass) crujido ■ adj
(col: smart) elegante ■ vi chasquear
Swiss [swɪs] adj, n (pl inv) suizo(-a) m(f)
switch [swɪtʃ] n (for light, radio etc) interruptor
m; (change) cambio ■ vt (change) cambiar
de; (invert: also: **switch round, switch over**)
intercambiar
▶ **switch off** vt apagar; (engine) parar
▶ **switch on** vt (Aut: ignition) encender,
prender (LAm); (engine, machine) arrancar;
(water supply) conectar
switchboard ['swɪtʃbɔːd] n (Tel) centralita
(de teléfonos), conmutador m (LAm)
Switzerland ['swɪtsələnd] n Suiza
swivel ['swɪvl] vi (also: **swivel round**) girar
swollen ['swəulən] pp of **swell**
swoon [swuːn] vi desmayarse
swoop [swuːp] n (by police etc) redada; (of bird
etc) descenso en picado, calada ■ vi (also:

swoop down) caer en picado
swop [swɔp] = **swap**
sword [sɔːd] n espada
swordfish ['sɔːdfɪʃ] n pez m espada
swore [swɔːʳ] pt of **swear**
sworn [swɔːn] pp of **swear**
swot [swɔt] (Brit) vt, vi empollar ■ n
empollón(-ona) m(f)
swum [swʌm] pp of **swim**
swung [swʌŋ] pt, pp of **swing**
sycamore ['sɪkəmɔːʳ] n sicomoro
sycophant ['sɪkəfænt] n adulador(a) m(f)
pelotillero(-a)
Sydney ['sɪdnɪ] n Sidney m
syllable ['sɪləbl] n sílaba
syllabus ['sɪləbəs] n programa m de estudios;
on the ~ en el programa de estudios
symbol ['sɪmbl] n símbolo
symbolic [sɪm'bɔlɪk], **symbolical**
[sɪm'bɔlɪkl] adj simbólico; **to be ~(al) of sth**
simbolizar algo
symbolism ['sɪmbəlɪzəm] n simbolismo
symbolize ['sɪmbəlaɪz] vt simbolizar
symmetrical [sɪ'metrɪkl] adj simétrico
symmetry ['sɪmɪtrɪ] n simetría
sympathetic [sɪmpə'θetɪk] adj compasivo;
(understanding) comprensivo; **to be ~ to a
cause** (well-disposed) apoyar una causa; **to be
~ towards** (person) ser comprensivo con
sympathize ['sɪmpəθaɪz] vi: **to ~ with
sb** compadecerse de algn; (understand)
comprender a algn
sympathizer ['sɪmpəθaɪzəʳ] n (Pol)
simpatizante m/f
sympathy ['sɪmpəθɪ] n (pity) compasión
f; (understanding) comprensión f; **with our
deepest ~** nuestro más sentido pésame
symphony ['sɪmfənɪ] n sinfonía
symposium [sɪm'pəuzɪəm] n simposio
symptom ['sɪmptəm] n síntoma m, indicio
symptomatic [sɪmptə'mætɪk] adj: **~ (of)**
sintomático (de)
synagogue ['sɪnəgɔg] n sinagoga
sync [sɪŋk] n (col): **to be in/out of ~ (with)**
ir/no ir al mismo ritmo (que); (fig: people)
conectar/no conectar con
synchromesh ['sɪŋkrəumeʃ] n cambio
sincronizado de velocidades
synchronize ['sɪŋkrənaɪz] vt sincronizar
■ vi: **to ~ with** sincronizarse con
synchronized swimming ['sɪŋkrənaɪzd-] n
natación f sincronizada
syncopated ['sɪŋkəpeɪtɪd] adj sincopado
syndicate ['sɪndɪkɪt] n (gen) sindicato; (Press)
agencia (de noticias)
syndrome ['sɪndrəum] n síndrome m
synonym ['sɪnənɪm] n sinónimo

synonymous [sɪˈnɔnɪməs] *adj:* ~ **(with)** sinónimo (con)
synopsis, synopses [sɪˈnɔpsɪs, -siːz] *n* sinopsis *f inv*
syntax [ˈsɪntæks] *n* sintaxis *f*
syntax error *n* (*Comput*) error *m* sintáctico
synthesis, syntheses [ˈsɪnθəsɪs, -siːz] *n* síntesis *f inv*
synthesizer [ˈsɪnθəsaɪzəʳ] *n* sintetizador *m*
synthetic [sɪnˈθɛtɪk] *adj* sintético ■ *n* sintético
syphilis [ˈsɪfɪlɪs] *n* sífilis *f*

syphon [ˈsaɪfən] = **siphon**
Syria [ˈsɪrɪə] *n* Siria
Syrian [ˈsɪrɪən] *adj, n* sirio(-a) *m(f)*
syringe [sɪˈrɪndʒ] *n* jeringa
syrup [ˈsɪrəp] *n* jarabe *m*, almíbar *m*
system [ˈsɪstəm] *n* sistema *m*; (*Anat*) organismo; **it was quite a shock to his** ~ fue un golpe para él
systematic [sɪstəˈmætɪk] *adj* sistemático; metódico
system disk *n* (*Comput*) disco del sistema
systems analyst *n* analista *m/f* de sistemas

S

Tt

T, t [tiː] *n* (*letter*) T, t *f*; **T for Tommy** T de
Tarragona
TA *n abbr* (*Brit*) = **Territorial Army**
ta [tɑː] *excl* (*Brit: col*) ¡gracias!
tab [tæb] *n abbr* = **tabulator** ■ *n* lengüeta;
(*label*) etiqueta; **to keep tabs on** (*fig*) vigilar
tabby ['tæbɪ] *n* (*also:* **tabby cat**) gato atigrado
tabernacle ['tæbənækl] *n* tabernáculo
table ['teɪbl] *n* mesa; (*chart: of statistics
etc*) cuadro, tabla ■ *vt* (*Brit: motion etc*)
presentar; **to lay** *or* **set the ~** poner la mesa;
to clear the ~ quitar *or* levantar la mesa;
league ~ (*Football, Rugby*) clasificación *f* del
campeonato; **~ of contents** índice *m* de
materias
tablecloth ['teɪblklɔθ] *n* mantel *m*
table d'hôte [tɑːbl'dəut] *n* menú *m*
table lamp *n* lámpara de mesa
tablemat ['teɪblmæt] *n* salvamanteles *m inv*,
posaplatos *m inv*
tablespoon ['teɪblspuːn] *n* cuchara grande;
(*also:* **tablespoonful:** *as measurement*)
cucharada
tablet ['tæblɪt] *n* (*Med*) pastilla, comprimido;
(*for writing*) bloc *m*; (*of stone*) lápida; **~ of soap**
pastilla de jabón
table talk *n* conversación *f* de sobremesa
table tennis *n* ping-pong *m*, tenis *m* de mesa
table wine *n* vino de mesa
tabloid ['tæblɔɪd] *n* (*newspaper*) periódico
popular sensacionalista
tabloid press *n* ver nota

taboo [tə'buː] *adj, n* tabú *m*
tabulate ['tæbjuleɪt] *vt* disponer en tablas
tabulator ['tæbjuleɪtəʳ] *n* tabulador *m*
tachograph ['tækəɡrɑːf] *n* tacógrafo
tachometer [tæ'kɔmɪtəʳ] *n* taquímetro
tacit ['tæsɪt] *adj* tácito
tacitly ['tæsɪtlɪ] *adv* tácitamente
taciturn ['tæsɪtəːn] *adj* taciturno
tack [tæk] *n* (*nail*) tachuela; (*stitch*) hilván
m; (*Naut*) bordada ■ *vt* (*nail*) clavar con
tachuelas; (*stitch*) hilvanar ■ *vi* virar; **to
~ sth on to (the end of) sth** (*of letter, book*)
añadir algo a(l final de) algo
tackle ['tækl] *n* (*gear*) equipo; (*fishing tackle, for
lifting*) aparejo; (*Football*) entrada, tackle *m*;
(*Rugby*) placaje *m* ■ *vt* (*difficulty*) enfrentarse
a, abordar; (*grapple with*) agarrar; (*Football*)
entrar a; (*Rugby*) placar
tacky ['tækɪ] *adj* pegajoso; (*fam*) hortera *inv*
tact [tækt] *n* tacto, discreción *f*
tactful ['tæktful] *adj* discreto, diplomático;
to be ~ tener tacto, actuar discretamente
tactfully ['tæktfulɪ] *adv* diplomáticamente,
con tacto
tactical ['tæktɪkl] *adj* táctico
tactical voting *n* voto útil
tactician [tæk'tɪʃən] *n* táctico(-a)
tactics ['tæktɪks] *n, npl* táctica *sg*
tactless ['tæktlɪs] *adj* indiscreto
tactlessly ['tæktlɪslɪ] *adv* indiscretamente,
sin tacto
tadpole ['tædpəul] *n* renacuajo
taffy ['tæfɪ] *n* (*US*) melcocha
tag [tæɡ] *n* (*label*) etiqueta; **price/name ~**
etiqueta del precio/con el nombre
▶ **tag along** *vi:* **to ~ along with sb**
engancharse a algn
tag question *n* pregunta coletilla

Tahiti [tɑːˈhiːtɪ] *n* Tahití *m*
tail [teɪl] *n* cola; (*Zool*) rabo; (*of shirt, coat*)
faldón *m* ▪ *vt* (*follow*) vigilar a; **heads or
tails** cara o cruz; **to turn ~** volver la espalda
▶ **tail away, tail off** *vi* (*in size, quality etc*) ir
disminuyendo
tailback [ˈteɪlbæk] *n* (*Brit Aut*) cola
tail coat *n* frac *m*
tail end *n* cola, parte *f* final
tailgate [ˈteɪlgeɪt] *n* (*Aut*) puerta trasera
tail light *n* (*Aut*) luz *f* trasera
tailor [ˈteɪləʳ] *n* sastre *m* ▪ *vt*: **to ~ sth (to)**
confeccionar algo a medida (para); **~'s
(shop)** sastrería
tailoring [ˈteɪlərɪŋ] *n* (*cut*) corte *m*; (*craft*)
sastrería
tailor-made [ˈteɪləˈmeɪd] *adj* (*also fig*) hecho a
(la) medida
tailwind [ˈteɪlwɪnd] *n* viento de cola
taint [teɪnt] *vt* (*meat, food*) contaminar;
(*fig: reputation*) manchar, tachar (*LAm*)
tainted [ˈteɪntɪd] *adj* (*water, air*) contaminado;
(*fig*) manchado
Taiwan [taɪˈwɑːn] *n* Taiwán *m*
Tajikistan [tɑːdʒɪkɪˈstɑːn] *n* Tayikistán *m*
take [teɪk] (*pt* **took**, *pp* **taken**) *vt* tomar; (*grab*)
coger (*SP*), agarrar (*LAm*); (*gain: prize*) ganar;
(*require: effort, courage*) exigir; (*support weight of*)
aguantar; (*hold: passengers etc*) tener cabida
para; (*accompany, bring, carry*) llevar; (*exam*)
presentarse a; (*conduct: meeting*) presidir ▪ *vi*
(*fire*) prender; (*dye*) coger (*SP*), agarrar, tomar
▪ *n* (*Cine*) toma; **to ~ sth from** (*drawer etc*)
sacar algo de; (*person*) coger algo a (*SP*); **to
~ sb's hand** tomar de la mano a algn; **to
~ notes** tomar apuntes; **to be taken ill**
ponerse enfermo; **~ the first on the left**
toma la primera a la izquierda; **I only took
Russian for one year** sólo estudié ruso un
año; **I took him for a doctor** le tenía por
médico; **it won't ~ long** durará poco; **it
will ~ at least five litres** tiene cabida por lo
menos para cinco litros; **to be taken with
sb/sth** (*attracted*) tomarle cariño a algn/
tomarle gusto a algo; **I ~ it that ...** supongo
que ...
▶ **take after** *vt fus* parecerse a
▶ **take apart** *vt* desmontar
▶ **take away** *vt* (*remove*) quitar; (*carry off*)
llevar ▪ *vi*: **to ~ away from** quitar mérito a
▶ **take back** *vt* (*return*) devolver; (*one's words*)
retractar
▶ **take down** *vt* (*building*) derribar; (*dismantle:
scaffolding*) desmantelar; (*message etc*)
apuntar, tomar nota de
▶ **take in** *vt* (*Brit: deceive*) engañar; (*understand*)
entender; (*include*) abarcar; (*lodger*) acoger,

recibir; (*orphan, stray dog*) recoger; (*Sewing*)
achicar
▶ **take off** *vi* (*Aviat*) despegar, decolar (*LAm*)
▪ *vt* (*remove*) quitar; (*imitate*) imitar, remedar
▶ **take on** *vt* (*work*) emprender; (*employee*)
contratar; (*opponent*) desafiar
▶ **take out** *vt* sacar; (*remove*) quitar; **don't ~
it out on me!** ¡no te desquites conmigo!
▶ **take over** *vt* (*business*) tomar posesión de
▪ *vi*: **to ~ over from sb** reemplazar a algn
▶ **take to** *vt fus* (*person*) coger cariño a (*SP*),
encariñarse con (*LAm*); (*activity*) aficionarse a;
to ~ to doing sth aficionarse a (hacer) algo
▶ **take up** *vt* (*a dress*) acortar; (*occupy: time,
space*) ocupar; (*engage in: hobby etc*) dedicarse a;
(*absorb: liquids*) absorber; (*accept: offer, challenge*)
aceptar ▪ *vi*: **to ~ up with sb** hacerse amigo
de algn
▶ **take upon** *vt*: **to ~ it upon o.s. to do sth**
encargarse de hacer algo
takeaway [ˈteɪkəweɪ] *adj* (*Brit: food*) para
llevar
take-home pay [ˈteɪkhəum-] *n* salario neto
taken [ˈteɪkən] *pp* of **take**
takeoff [ˈteɪkɒf] *n* (*Aviat*) despegue *m*,
decolaje *m* (*LAm*)
takeover [ˈteɪkəuvəʳ] *n* (*Comm*) absorción *f*
takeover bid *n* oferta pública de adquisición
takings [ˈteɪkɪnz] *npl* (*Comm*) ingresos *mpl*
talc [tælk] *n* (*also:* **talcum powder**) talco
tale [teɪl] *n* (*story*) cuento; (*account*) relación *f*;
to tell tales (*fig*) contar chismes
talent [ˈtælnt] *n* talento
talented [ˈtæləntɪd] *adj* talentoso, de talento
talisman [ˈtælɪzmən] *n* talismán *m*
talk [tɔːk] *n* charla; (*gossip*) habladurías *fpl*,
chismes *mpl*; (*conversation*) conversación *f*
▪ *vi* (*speak*) hablar; (*chatter*) charlar; **talks**
npl (*Pol etc*) conversaciones *fpl*; **to give a ~** dar
una charla or conferencia; **to ~ about** hablar
de; **to ~ sb into doing sth** convencer a algn
para que haga algo; **to ~ sb out of doing sth**
disuadir a algn de que haga algo; **to ~ shop**
hablar del trabajo; **talking of films, have
you seen ...?** hablando de películas, ¿has
visto ...?
▶ **talk over** *vt* discutir
talkative [ˈtɔːkətɪv] *adj* hablador(a)
talker [ˈtɔːkəʳ] *n* hablador(a) *m(f)*
talking point [ˈtɔːkɪŋ-] *n* tema *m* de
conversación
talking-to [ˈtɔːkɪŋtuː] *n*: **to give sb a good ~**
echar una buena bronca a algn
talk show *n* programa *m* magazine
tall [tɔːl] *adj* alto; (*tree*) grande; **to be 6 feet ~**
= medir 1 metro 80, tener 1 metro 80 de alto;
how ~ are you? ¿cuánto mides?

t

tallboy ['tɔːlbɔɪ] *n* (*Brit*) cómoda alta

tallness ['tɔːlnɪs] *n* altura

tall story *n* cuento chino

tally ['tælɪ] *n* cuenta ■ *vi*: **to ~ (with)** concordar (con), cuadrar (con); **to keep a ~ of sth** llevar la cuenta de algo

talon ['tælən] *n* garra

tambourine [tæmbə'riːn] *n* pandereta

tame [teɪm] *adj* (*mild*) manso; (*tamed*) domesticado; (*fig: story, style, person*) soso, anodino

tameness ['teɪmnɪs] *n* mansedumbre *f*

Tamil ['tæmɪl] *adj* tamil ■ *n* tamil *m/f*; (*Ling*) tamil *m*

tamper ['tæmpəʳ] *vi*: **to ~ with** (*lock etc*) intentar forzar; (*papers*) falsificar

tampon ['tæmpən] *n* tampón *m*

tan [tæn] *n* (*also*: **suntan**) bronceado ■ *vt* broncear ■ *vi* ponerse moreno ■ *adj* (*colour*) marrón; **to get a ~** broncearse, ponerse moreno

tandem ['tændəm] *n* tándem *m*

tandoori [tæn'duərɪ] *adj,n* tandoori *m* (*asado a la manera hindú, en horno de barro*)

tang [tæŋ] *n* sabor *m* fuerte

tangent ['tændʒənt] *n* (*Math*) tangente *f*; **to go off at a ~** (*fig*) salirse por la tangente

tangerine [tændʒə'riːn] *n* mandarina

tangible ['tændʒəbl] *adj* tangible; **~ assets** bienes *mpl* tangibles

Tangier [tæn'dʒɪəʳ] *n* Tánger *m*

tangle ['tæŋgl] *n* enredo; **to get in(to) a ~** enredarse

tango ['tæŋgəu] *n* tango

tank [tæŋk] *n* (*also*: **water tank**) depósito, tanque *m*; (*for fish*) acuario; (*Mil*) tanque *m*

tankard ['tæŋkəd] *n* bock *m*

tanker ['tæŋkəʳ] *n* (*ship*) petrolero; (*truck*) camión *m* cisterna

tankful ['tæŋkful] *n*: **to get a ~ of petrol** llenar el depósito de gasolina

tankini [tæn'kiːnɪ] *n* tankini *m*

tanned [tænd] *adj* (*skin*) moreno, bronceado

tannin ['tænɪn] *n* tanino

tanning ['tænɪŋ] *n* (*of leather*) curtido

tannoy® ['tænɔɪ] *n*: **over the ~** por el altavoz

tantalizing ['tæntəlaɪzɪŋ] *adj* tentador(a)

tantamount ['tæntəmaunt] *adj*: **~ to** equivalente a

tantrum ['tæntrəm] *n* rabieta; **to throw a ~** coger una rabieta

Tanzania [tænzə'nɪə] *n* Tanzania

Tanzanian [tænzə'nɪən] *adj,n* tanzano(-a) *m(f)*

tap [tæp] *n* (*Brit: on sink etc*) grifo, canilla (*LAm*); (*gentle blow*) golpecito; (*gas tap*) llave *f* ■ *vt* (*table etc*) tamborilear; (*shoulder etc*) dar palmaditas en; (*resources*) utilizar, explotar;

(*telephone conversation*) intervenir, pinchar; **on ~** (*fig: resources*) a mano; **beer on ~** cerveza de barril

tap-dancing ['tæpdɑːnsɪŋ] *n* claqué *m*

tape [teɪp] *n* cinta; (*also*: **magnetic tape**) cinta magnética; (*sticky tape*) cinta adhesiva ■ *vt* (*record*) grabar (en cinta); **on ~** (*song etc*) grabado (en cinta)

tape deck *n* pletina

tape measure *n* cinta métrica, metro

taper ['teɪpəʳ] *n* cirio ■ *vi* afilarse

tape-record ['teɪprɪkɔːd] *vt* grabar (en cinta)

tape recorder *n* grabadora

tapered ['teɪpəd], **tapering** ['teɪpərɪŋ] *adj* terminado en punta

tapestry ['tæpɪstrɪ] *n* (*object*) tapiz *m*; (*art*) tapicería

tape-worm ['teɪpwəːm] *n* solitaria, tenia

tapioca [tæpɪ'əukə] *n* tapioca

tappet ['tæpɪt] *n* excéntrica

tar [tɑːʳ] *n* alquitrán *m*, brea; **low/middle ~ cigarettes** cigarrillos con contenido bajo/medio de alquitrán

tarantula [tə'ræntjulə] *n* tarántula

tardy ['tɑːdɪ] *adj* (*late*) tardío; (*slow*) lento

tare [tɛəʳ] *n* (*Comm*) tara

target ['tɑːgɪt] *n* (*gen*) blanco; **to be on ~** (*project*) seguir el curso previsto

target audience *n* público al que va destinado un programa etc

target market *n* (*Comm*) mercado al que va destinado un producto etc

target practice *n* tiro al blanco

tariff ['tærɪf] *n* tarifa

tariff barrier *n* (*Comm*) barrera arancelaria

tarmac ['tɑːmæk] *n* (*Brit: on road*) alquitranado; (*Aviat*) pista (de aterrizaje)

tarn [tɑːn] *n* lago pequeño de montaña

tarnish ['tɑːnɪʃ] *vt* deslustrar

tarot ['tærəu] *n* tarot *m*

tarpaulin [tɑː'pɔːlɪn] *n* alquitranado

tarragon ['tærəgən] *n* estragón *m*

tarry ['tærɪ] *vi* entretenerse, quedarse atrás

tart [tɑːt] *n* (*Culin*) tarta; (*Brit col: pej: woman*) fulana ■ *adj* (*flavour*) agrio, ácido
▶ **tart up** *vt* (*room, building*) dar tono a

tartan ['tɑːtn] *n* tartán *m* ■ *adj* de tartán

tartar ['tɑːtəʳ] *n* (*on teeth*) sarro

tartar sauce *n* salsa tártara

tartly ['tɑːtlɪ] *adv* (*answer*) ásperamente

task [tɑːsk] *n* tarea; **to take to ~** reprender

task force *n* (*Mil, Police*) grupo de operaciones

taskmaster ['tɑːskmɑːstəʳ] *n*: **he's a hard ~** es muy exigente

tassel ['tæsl] *n* borla

taste [teɪst] *n* sabor *m*, gusto; (*also*: **aftertaste**) dejo; (*sip*) sorbo; (*fig: glimpse, idea*)

muestra, idea ■ *vt* probar ■ *vi*: **to ~ of** or
like *(fish etc)* saber a; **you can ~ the garlic
(in it)** se nota el sabor a ajo; **can I have a ~
of this wine?** ¿puedo probar este vino?; **to
have a ~ for sth** ser aficionado a algo; **in
good/bad ~** de buen/mal gusto; **to be in bad**
or **poor ~** ser de mal gusto
taste bud *n* papila gustativa or del gusto
tasteful ['teistful] *adj* de buen gusto
tastefully ['teistfuli] *adv* elegantemente, con
buen gusto
tasteless ['teistlis] *adj (food)* soso; *(remark)* de
mal gusto
tastelessly ['teistlisli] *adv* con mal gusto
tastily ['teistili] *adv* sabrosamente
tastiness ['teistinis] *n* (buen) sabor *m*, lo
sabroso
tasty ['teisti] *adj* sabroso, rico
ta-ta ['tæ'taː] *interj (Brit col)* hasta luego, adiós
tatters ['tætəz] *npl*. **In ~** *(also:* **tattered)**
hecho jirones
tattoo [tə'tuː] *n* tatuaje *m*; *(spectacle)*
espectáculo militar ■ *vt* tatuar
tatty ['tæti] *adj (Brit col)* cochambroso
taught [tɔːt] *pt, pp* of **teach**
taunt [tɔːnt] *n* pulla ■ *vt* lanzar pullas a
Taurus ['tɔːrəs] *n* Tauro
taut [tɔːt] *adj* tirante, tenso
tavern ['tævən] *n (old)* posada, fonda
tawdry ['tɔːdrɪ] *adj* de mal gusto
tawny ['tɔːnɪ] *adj* leonado
tax [tæks] *n* impuesto ■ *vt* gravar (con
un impuesto); *(fig: test)* poner a prueba;
(: patience) agotar; **before/after ~** impuestos
excluidos/incluidos; **free of ~** libre de
impuestos
taxable ['tæksəbl] *adj (income)* imponible,
sujeto a impuestos
tax allowance *n* desgravación *f* fiscal
taxation [tæk'seɪʃən] *n* impuestos *mpl*;
system of ~ sistema *m* tributario
tax avoidance *n* evasión *f* de impuestos
tax collector *n* recaudador(a) *m(f)*
tax disc *n (Brit Aut)* pegatina del impuesto de
circulación
tax evasion *n* evasión *f* fiscal
tax exemption *n* exención *f* de impuestos
tax-free ['tæksfriː] *adj* libre de impuestos
tax haven *n* paraíso fiscal
taxi ['tæksɪ] *n* taxi *m* ■ *vi (Aviat)* rodar por la
pista
taxidermist ['tæksɪdəːmɪst] *n* taxidermista
m/f
taxi driver *n* taxista *m/f*
tax inspector *n* inspector(a) *m(f)* de
Hacienda
taxi rank, *(Brit)* **taxi stand** *n* parada de taxis

tax payer *n* contribuyente *m/f*
tax rebate *n* devolución *f* de impuestos,
reembolso fiscal
tax relief *n* desgravación *f* fiscal
tax return *n* declaración *f* de la renta
tax shelter *n* protección *f* fiscal
tax year *n* año fiscal
TB *n abbr* = **tuberculosis**
tbc *abbr* (= *to be confirmed*) por confirmar
TD *n abbr (US)* = **Treasury Department**;
(: *Football*) = **touchdown**
tea [tiː] *n* té *m*; *(Brit: snack)* = merienda; **high ~**
(Brit) = merienda-cena
tea bag *n* bolsita de té
tea break *n (Brit)* descanso para el té
teacake ['tiːkeɪk] *n* bollito, queque *m (LAm)*
teach *(pt, pp* **taught)** [tiːtʃ, tɔːt] *vt*: **to ~ sb sth**,
~ sth to sb enseñar algo a algn ■ *vi* enseñar;
(be a teacher) ser profesor(a); **it taught him a
lesson** (eso) le sirvió de escarmiento
teacher ['tiːtʃəʳ] *n (in secondary school)*
profesor(a) *m(f)*; *(in primary school)*
maestro(-a); **Spanish ~** profesor(a) *m(f)* de
español
teacher training college *n (for primary schools)*
escuela normal; *(for secondary schools)* centro
de formación del profesorado
teach-in ['tiːtʃɪn] *n* seminario
teaching ['tiːtʃɪŋ] *n* enseñanza
teaching aids *npl* materiales *mpl*
pedagógicos
teaching hospital *n* hospital universitario
tea cosy *n* cubretetera *m*
teacup ['tiːkʌp] *n* taza de té
teak [tiːk] *n* (madera de) teca
tea leaves *npl* hojas *fpl* de té
team [tiːm] *n* equipo; *(of animals)* pareja
▶ **team up** *vi* asociarse
team spirit *n* espíritu *m* de equipo
teamwork ['tiːmwəːk] *n* trabajo en equipo
tea party *n* té *m*
teapot ['tiːpɒt] *n* tetera
tear [tɛəʳ] *(pt* **tore**, *pp* **torn)** *n* rasgón *m*,
desgarrón *m* [tɪəʳ] lágrima ■ *vb* [tɛəʳ] ■ *vt*
romper, rasgar ■ *vi* rasgarse; **in tears**
llorando; **to burst into tears** deshacerse
en lágrimas; **to ~ to pieces** or **to bits** or **to
shreds** *(also fig)* hacer pedazos, destrozar
▶ **tear along** *vi (rush)* precipitarse
▶ **tear apart** *vt (also fig)* hacer pedazos
▶ **tear away** *vt*: **to ~ o.s. away (from sth)**
alejarse (de algo)
▶ **tear out** *vt (sheet of paper, cheque)* arrancar
▶ **tear up** *vt (sheet of paper etc)* romper
tearaway ['tɛərəweɪ] *n (col)* gamberro(-a)
teardrop ['tɪədrɒp] *n* lágrima
tearful ['tɪəful] *adj* lloroso

t

819

tear gas *n* gas *m* lacrimógeno
tearing ['tɛərɪŋ] *adj*: **to be in a ~ hurry** tener
muchísima prisa
tearoom ['tiːruːm] *n* salón *m* de té
tease [tiːz] *n* bromista *m/f* ■ *vt* tomar el
pelo a
tea set *n* servicio de té
teashop ['tiːʃɔp] *n* café *m*, cafetería
Teasmaid® ['tiːzmeɪd] *n* tetera automática
teaspoon ['tiːspuːn] *n* cucharita; (*also*:
teaspoonful: *as measurement*) cucharadita
tea strainer *n* colador *m* de té
teat [tiːt] *n* (*of bottle*) boquilla, tetilla
teatime ['tiːtaɪm] *n* hora del té
tea towel *n* (*Brit*) paño de cocina
tea urn *n* tetera grande
tech [tɛk] *n abbr* (*col*) = **technology; technical
college**
technical ['tɛknɪkl] *adj* técnico
technical college *n* centro de formación
profesional
technicality [tɛknɪ'kælɪtɪ] *n* detalle *m*
técnico; **on a legal ~** por una cuestión
formal
technically ['tɛknɪklɪ] *adv* técnicamente
technician [tɛk'nɪʃn] *n* técnico(-a)
technique [tɛk'niːk] *n* técnica
techno ['tɛknəu] *n* (*Mus*) (música) tecno
technocrat ['tɛknəkræt] *n* tecnócrata *m/f*
technological [tɛknə'lɔdʒɪkl] *adj* tecnológico
technologist [tɛk'nɔlədʒɪst] *n* tecnólogo(-a)
technology [tɛk'nɔlədʒɪ] *n* tecnología
teddy ['tɛdɪ], **teddy bear** *n* osito de peluche
tedious ['tiːdɪəs] *adj* pesado, aburrido
tedium ['tiːdɪəm] *n* tedio
tee [tiː] *n* (*Golf*) tee *m*
teem [tiːm] *vi*: **to ~ with** rebosar de; **it is
teeming (with rain)** llueve a mares
teenage ['tiːneɪdʒ] *adj* (*fashions etc*) juvenil
teenager ['tiːneɪdʒə'] *n* adolescente *m/f*,
quinceañero(-a)
teens [tiːnz] *npl*: **to be in one's ~** ser
adolescente
tee-shirt ['tiːʃəːt] *n* = **T-shirt**
teeter ['tiːtə'] *vi* balancearse
teeth [tiːθ] *npl* of **tooth**
teethe [tiːð] *vi* echar los dientes
teething ring ['tiːðɪŋ-] *n* mordedor *m*
teething troubles ['tiːðɪŋ-] *npl* (*fig*)
dificultades *fpl* iniciales
teetotal ['tiːˈtəutl] *adj* (*person*) abstemio
teetotaller, teetotaler (US) ['tiːˈtəutlə'] *n*
(*person*) abstemio(-a)
TEFL ['tɛfl] *n abbr* (= *Teaching of English as a
Foreign Language*, *TEFL qualification*) *título para la
enseñanza del inglés como lengua extranjera*
Teflon® ['tɛflɔn] *n* teflón® *m*

Teheran [tɛəˈrɑːn] *n* Teherán *m*
tel. *abbr* (= *telephone*) tel
Tel Aviv ['tɛləˈviːv] *n* Tel Aviv *m*
telecast ['tɛlɪkɑːst] *vt, vi* transmitir por
televisión
telecommunications ['tɛlɪkəmjuːnɪ] *n*
telecomunicaciones *fpl*
teleconferencing ['tɛlɪkɒnfərənsɪŋ] *n*
teleconferencias *fpl*
telefax ['tɛlɪfæks] *n* telefax *m*
telegram ['tɛlɪgræm] *n* telegrama *m*
telegraph ['tɛlɪgrɑːf] *n* telégrafo
telegraphic [tɛlɪˈgræfɪk] *adj* telegráfico
telegraph pole *n* poste *m* telegráfico
telegraph wire *n* hilo telegráfico
telepathic [tɛlɪˈpæθɪk] *adj* telepático
telepathy [təˈlɛpəθɪ] *n* telepatía
telephone ['tɛlɪfəun] *n* teléfono ■ *vt* llamar
por teléfono, telefonear; **to be on the ~**
(*subscriber*) tener teléfono; (*be speaking*) estar
hablando por teléfono
telephone booth, (*Brit*) **telephone box** *n*
cabina telefónica
telephone call *n* llamada telefónica
telephone directory *n* guía telefónica
telephone exchange *n* central *f* telefónica
telephone number *n* número de teléfono
telephonist [təˈlɛfənɪst] *n* (*Brit*) telefonista
m/f
telephoto ['tɛlɪˈfəutəu] *adj*: **~ lens**
teleobjetivo
teleprinter ['tɛlɪprɪntə'] *n* teletipo,
teleimpresora
teleprompter® ['tɛlɪprɔmptə'] *n*
teleapuntador *m*
telesales ['tɛlɪseɪlz] *npl* televentas *fpl*
telescope ['tɛlɪskəup] *n* telescopio
telescopic [tɛlɪˈskɔpɪk] *adj* telescópico;
(*umbrella*) plegable
Teletext® ['tɛlɪtɛkst] *n* teletexto *m*
telethon ['tɛlɪθɔn] *n* telemaratón *m*, maratón
m televisivo (*con fines benéficos*)
televise ['tɛlɪvaɪz] *vt* televisar
television ['tɛlɪvɪʒən] *n* televisión *f*;
to watch ~ mirar *or* ver la televisión
television licence *n* impuesto por uso de
televisor
television set *n* televisor *m*
teleworking ['tɛlɪwɜːkɪŋ] *n* teletrabajo
telex ['tɛlɛks] *n* télex *m* ■ *vt* (*message*) enviar
por télex; (*person*) enviar un télex a ■ *vi*
enviar un télex
tell (*pt, pp* **told**) [tɛl, təuld] *vt* decir; (*relate*:
story) contar; (*distinguish*): **to ~ sth from**
distinguir algo de ■ *vi* (*talk*): **to ~ (of)** contar;
(*have effect*) tener efecto; **to ~ sb to do sth**
decir a algn que haga algo; **to ~ sb about**

sth contar algo a algn; **to ~ the time** dar or decir la hora; **can you ~ me the time?** ¿me puedes decir la hora?; **(I) ~ you what ...** fíjate ...; **I couldn't ~ them apart** no podía distinguirlos
▶ **tell off** vt: **to ~ sb off** regañar a algn
▶ **tell on** vt fus: **to ~ on sb** chivarse de algn
teller ['tɛlə'] n (in bank) cajero(-a)
telling ['tɛlɪŋ] adj (remark, detail) revelador(a)
telltale ['tɛlteɪl] adj (sign) indicador(a)
telly ['tɛlɪ] n (Brit col) tele f
temerity [tə'mɛrɪtɪ] n temeridad f
temp [tɛmp] n abbr (Brit: = temporary office worker) empleado(-a) eventual ■ vi trabajar como empleado(-a) eventual
temper ['tɛmpə'] n (mood) humor m; (bad temper) (mal) genio; (fit of anger) ira; (of child) rabieta ■ vt (moderate) moderar; **to be in a ~** estar furioso; **to lose one's ~** enfadarse, enojarse (LAm); **to keep one's ~** contenerse, no alterarse
temperament ['tɛmprəmənt] n (nature) temperamento
temperamental [tɛmprə'mɛntl] adj temperamental
temperance ['tɛmpərns] n moderación f; (in drinking) sobriedad f
temperate ['tɛmprət] adj moderado; (climate) templado
temperature ['tɛmprətʃə'] n temperatura; **to have** or **run a ~** tener fiebre
tempered ['tɛmpəd] adj (steel) templado
tempest ['tɛmpɪst] n tempestad f
tempestuous [tɛm'pɛstjuəs] adj (relationship, meeting) tempestuoso
tempi ['tɛmpiː] npl of **tempo**
template ['tɛmplɪt] n plantilla
temple ['tɛmpl] n (building) templo; (Anat) sien f
templet ['tɛmplɪt] n = **template**
tempo (pl **tempos** or **tempi**) ['tɛmpəu, 'tɛmpiː] n tempo; (fig: of life etc) ritmo
temporal ['tɛmpərl] adj temporal
temporarily ['tɛmpərərɪlɪ] adv temporalmente
temporary ['tɛmpərərɪ] adj provisional, temporal; (passing) transitorio; (worker) eventual; **~ teacher** maestro(-a) interino(-a)
tempt [tɛmpt] vt tentar; **to ~ sb into doing sth** tentar or inducir a algn a hacer algo; **to be tempted to do sth** (person) sentirse tentado de hacer algo
temptation [tɛmp'teɪʃən] n tentación f
tempting ['tɛmptɪŋ] adj tentador(a)
ten [tɛn] num diez; **tens of thousands** decenas fpl de miles
tenable ['tɛnəbl] adj sostenible

tenacious [tə'neɪʃəs] adj tenaz
tenaciously [tə'neɪʃəslɪ] adv tenazmente
tenacity [tə'næsɪtɪ] n tenacidad f
tenancy ['tɛnənsɪ] n alquiler m
tenant ['tɛnənt] n (rent-payer) inquilino(-a); (occupant) habitante m/f
tend [tɛnd] vt (sick etc) cuidar, atender; (cattle, machine) vigilar, cuidar ■ vi: **to ~ to do sth** tener tendencia a hacer algo
tendency ['tɛndənsɪ] n tendencia
tender ['tɛndə'] adj tierno, blando; (delicate) delicado; (sore) sensible; (affectionate) tierno, cariñoso ■ n (Comm: offer) oferta; (money): **legal ~** moneda de curso legal ■ vt ofrecer; **to put in a ~ (for)** hacer una oferta (para); **to put work out to ~** ofrecer un trabajo a contrata; **to ~ one's resignation** presentar la dimisión
tenderize ['tɛndəraɪz] vt (Culin) ablandar
tenderly ['tɛndəlɪ] adv tiernamente
tenderness ['tɛndənɪs] n ternura; (of meat) blandura
tendon ['tɛndən] n tendón m
tendril ['tɛndrɪl] n zarcillo
tenement ['tɛnəmənt] n casa or bloque m de pisos or vecinos (LAm)
Tenerife [tɛnə'riːf] n Tenerife m
tenet ['tɛnət] n principio
Tenn. abbr (US) = **Tennessee**
tenner ['tɛnə'] n (billete m de) diez libras fpl
tennis ['tɛnɪs] n tenis m
tennis ball n pelota de tenis
tennis club n club m de tenis
tennis court n cancha de tenis
tennis elbow n (Med) sinovitis f del codo
tennis match n partido de tenis
tennis player n tenista m/f
tennis racket n raqueta de tenis
tennis shoes npl zapatillas fpl de tenis
tenor ['tɛnə'] n (Mus) tenor m
tenpin bowling ['tɛnpɪn-] n bolos mpl
tense [tɛns] adj tenso; (stretched) tirante; (stiff) rígido, tieso; (person) nervioso ■ n (Ling) tiempo ■ vt (tighten: muscles) tensar
tensely ['tɛnslɪ] adv: **they waited ~** esperaban tensos
tenseness ['tɛnsnɪs] n tirantez f, tensión f
tension ['tɛnʃən] n tensión f
tent [tɛnt] n tienda (de campaña), carpa (LAm)
tentacle ['tɛntəkl] n tentáculo
tentative ['tɛntətɪv] adj (person) indeciso; (provisional) provisional
tentatively ['tɛntətɪvlɪ] adv con indecisión; (provisionally) provisionalmente
tenterhooks ['tɛntəhuks] npl: **on ~** sobre ascuas

t

tenth [tɛnθ] *adj* décimo
tent peg *n* clavija, estaca
tent pole *n* mástil *m*
tenuous ['tɛnjuəs] *adj* tenue
tenure ['tɛnjuəʳ] *n* posesión *f*, tenencia; **to have ~** tener posesión *or* título de propiedad
tepid ['tɛpɪd] *adj* tibio
Ter. *abbr* = **terrace**
term [tə:m] *n* (*limit*) límite *m*; (*Comm*) plazo; (*word*) término; (*period*) período; (*Scol*) trimestre *m* ■ *vt* llamar, calificar de; **terms** *npl* (*conditions*) condiciones *fpl*; (*Comm*) precio, tarifa; **in the short/long ~** a corto/largo plazo; **during his ~ of office** bajo su mandato; **to be on good terms with sb** llevarse bien con algn; **to come to terms with** (*problem*) aceptar; **in terms of ...** en cuanto a ..., en términos de ...
terminal ['tə:mɪnl] *adj* terminal ■ *n* (*Elec*) borne *m*; (*Comput*) terminal *m*; (*also*: **air terminal**) terminal *f*; (*Brit*: *also*: **coach terminal**) (estación *f*) terminal *f*
terminate ['tə:mɪneɪt] *vt* poner término a; (*pregnancy*) interrumpir ■ *vi*: **to ~ in** acabar en
termination [tə:mɪ'neɪʃən] *n* fin *m*; (*of contract*) terminación *f*; **~ of pregnancy** interrupción *f* del embarazo
termini ['tə:mɪnaɪ] *npl of* **terminus**
terminology [tə:mɪ'nɔlədʒɪ] *n* terminología
terminus (*pl* **termini**) ['tə:mɪnəs, 'tə:mɪnaɪ] *n* término, (estación *f*) terminal *f*
termite ['tə:maɪt] *n* termita, comején *m*
term paper *n* (*US Univ*) trabajo escrito trimestral *or* semestral
terrace ['tɛrəs] *n* terraza; (*Brit*: *row of houses*) hilera de casas adosadas; **the terraces** (*Brit Sport*) las gradas *fpl*
terraced ['tɛrəst] *adj* (*garden*) escalonado; (*house*) adosado
terracotta ['tɛrə'kɔtə] *n* terracota
terrain [tɛ'reɪn] *n* terreno
terrible ['tɛrɪbl] *adj* terrible, horrible; (*fam*) malísimo
terribly ['tɛrɪblɪ] *adv* terriblemente; (*very badly*) malísimamente
terrier ['tɛrɪəʳ] *n* terrier *m*
terrific [tə'rɪfɪk] *adj* fantástico, fenomenal, macanudo (*LAm*); (*wonderful*) maravilloso
terrify ['tɛrɪfaɪ] *vt* aterrorizar; **to be terrified** estar aterrado *or* aterrorizado
terrifying ['tɛrɪfaɪɪŋ] *adj* aterrador(a)
territorial [tɛrɪ'tɔ:rɪəl] *adj* territorial
territorial waters *npl* aguas *fpl* jurisdiccionales
territory ['tɛrɪtərɪ] *n* territorio
terror ['tɛrəʳ] *n* terror *m*
terror attack *n* atentado (terrorista)

terrorism ['tɛrərɪzəm] *n* terrorismo
terrorist ['tɛrərɪst] *n* terrorista *m/f*
terrorize ['tɛrəraɪz] *vt* aterrorizar
terse [tə:s] *adj* (*style*) conciso; (*reply*) brusco
tertiary ['tə:ʃərɪ] *adj* terciario; **~ education** enseñanza superior
Terylene® ['tɛrəli:n] *n* (*Brit*) terylene® *m*
TESL [tɛsl] *n abbr* = **Teaching of English as a Second Language**
TESSA ['tɛsə] *n abbr* (*Brit*: = *Tax Exempt Special Savings Account*) *plan de ahorro por el que se invierte a largo plazo a cambio de intereses libres de impuestos*
test [tɛst] *n* (*trial, check*) prueba; (: *of goods in factory*) control *m*; (*of courage etc*) prueba; (*Chem, Med*) prueba; (*of blood, urine*) análisis *m inv*; (*exam*) examen *m*, test *m*; (*also*: **driving test**) examen *m* de conducir ■ *vt* probar, poner a prueba; (*Med*) examinar; (: *blood*) analizar; **to put sth to the ~** someter algo a prueba; **to ~ sth for sth** analizar algo en busca de algo
testament ['tɛstəmənt] *n* testamento; **the Old/New T~** el Antiguo/Nuevo Testamento
test ban *n* (*also*: **nuclear test ban**) suspensión *f* de pruebas nucleares
test card *n* (*TV*) carta de ajuste
test case *n* juicio que sienta precedente
testes ['tɛsti:z] *npl* testes *mpl*
test flight *n* vuelo de ensayo
testicle ['tɛstɪkl] *n* testículo
testify ['tɛstɪfaɪ] *vi* (*Law*) prestar declaración; **to ~ to sth** atestiguar algo
testimonial [tɛstɪ'məunɪəl] *n* (*of character*) (carta de) recomendación *f*
testimony ['tɛstɪmənɪ] *n* (*Law*) testimonio, declaración *f*
testing ['tɛstɪŋ] *adj* (*difficult: time*) duro
test match *n* partido internacional
testosterone [tɛs'tɔstərəun] *n* testosterona
test paper *n* examen *m*, test *m*
test pilot *n* piloto *m/f* de pruebas
test tube *n* probeta
test-tube baby *n* bebé *m* probeta *inv*
testy ['tɛstɪ] *adj* irritable
tetanus ['tɛtənəs] *n* tétano
tetchy ['tɛtʃɪ] *adj* irritable
tether ['tɛðəʳ] *vt* atar ■ *n*: **to be at the end of one's ~** no aguantar más
Tex. *abbr* (*US*) = **Texas**
text [tɛkst] *n* texto; (*on mobile*) mensaje *m* de texto ■ *vt*: **to ~ sb** enviar un mensaje (de texto) a algn
textbook ['tɛkstbuk] *n* libro de texto
textiles ['tɛkstaɪlz] *npl* tejidos *mpl*
text message *n* mensaje *m* de texto
text messaging [-'mɛsɪdʒɪŋ] *n* (envío de) mensajes *mpl* de texto

textual ['tɛkstjuəl] *adj* del texto, textual
texture ['tɛkstʃəʳ] *n* textura
TGIF *abbr* (*col*) = **thank God it's Friday**
TGWU *n abbr* (*Brit*: = *Transport and General Workers' Union*) sindicato de transportistas
Thai [taɪ] *adj, n* tailandés(-esa) *m(f)*
Thailand ['taɪlænd] *n* Tailandia
thalidomide® [θə'lɪdəmaɪd] *n* talidomida®
Thames [tɛmz] *n*: **the** ~ el (río) Támesis
than [ðæn, ðən] *conj* que; (*with numerals*):
  more ~ **10/once** más de 10/una vez; **I have more/less** ~ **you** tengo más/menos que tú; **it is better to phone** ~ **to write** es mejor llamar por teléfono que escribir; **no sooner did he leave** ~ **the phone rang** en cuanto se marchó, sonó el teléfono
thank [θæŋk] *vt* dar las gracias a, agradecer;
  ~ **you** (**very much**) muchas gracias;
  ~ **heavens,** ~ **God!** ¡gracias a Dios!, ¡menos mal!
thankful ['θæŋkful] *adj*: ~ **for** agradecido (por)
thankfully ['θæŋkfəlɪ] *adv* (*gratefully*) con agradecimiento; (*with relief*) por suerte;
  ~ **there were few victims** afortunadamente hubo pocas víctimas
thankless ['θæŋklɪs] *adj* ingrato
thanks [θæŋks] *npl* gracias *fpl* ■ *excl* ¡gracias!; ~ **to** *prep* gracias a
Thanksgiving ['θæŋksgɪvɪŋ], **Thanksgiving Day** *n* día *m* de Acción de Gracias; *ver nota*

 **THANKSGIVING DAY**

En Estados Unidos el cuarto jueves de noviembre es *Thanksgiving Day*, fiesta oficial en la que se conmemora la celebración que tuvieron los primeros colonos norteamericanos ("Pilgrims" o "Pilgrim Fathers") tras la estupenda cosecha de 1621, por la que se dan gracias a Dios. En Canadá se celebra una fiesta semejante el segundo lunes de octubre, aunque no está relacionada con dicha fecha histórica.

 KEYWORD

that [ðæt] (*pl* **those**) *adj* (*demonstrative*) ese(-a), esos(-as) *pl*; (*more remote*) aquel/aquella/aquellos(-as) *m(f)pl*; **leave those books on the table** deja esos libros sobre la mesa;
  that one ése/ésa; (*more remote*) aquél/aquélla;
  that one over there ése/ésa de ahí; aquél/aquélla de allí
  ■ *pron* **1** (*demonstrative*) ése(-a), ésos(-as) *pl*; (*neuter*) eso; (*more remote*) aquél/aquélla *m/f*,

aquéllos(-as) *m(f)pl*, aquello *neuter*; **what's that?** ¿qué es eso (*or* aquello)?; **who's that?** ¿quién es?; (*pointing etc*) ¿quién es ése/a?; **is that you?** ¿eres tú?; **will you eat all that?** ¿vas a comer todo eso?; **that's my house** ésa es mi casa; **that's what he said** eso es lo que dijo; **that is (to say)** es decir; **at** *or* **with that she ...** en eso, ella ...; **do it like that** hazlo así
  2 (*relative: subject, object*) que; (*with preposition*) (el/la) que, el/la cual; **the book (that) I read** el libro que leí; **the books that are in the library** los libros que están en la biblioteca; **all (that) I have** todo lo que tengo; **the box (that) I put it in** la caja en la que *or* donde lo puse; **the people (that) I spoke to** la gente con la que hablé; **not that I know of** que yo sepa, no
  3 (*relative: of time*) que; **the day (that) he came** el día (en) que vino
  ■ *conj* que; **he thought that I was ill** creyó que yo estaba enfermo
  ■ *adv* (*demonstrative*): **I can't work that much** no puedo trabajar tanto; **I didn't realize it was that bad** no creí que fuera tan malo; **that high** así de alto

thatched [θætʃt] *adj* (*roof*) de paja; ~ **cottage** casita con tejado de paja
Thatcherism ['θætʃərɪzəm] *n* thatcherismo
thaw [θɔː] *n* deshielo ■ *vi* (*ice*) derretirse; (*food*) descongelarse ■ *vt* descongelar

 KEYWORD

the [ðiː, ðə] *def art* **1** (*gen*) el, la *f*, los *pl*, las *fpl* (*NB -el immediately before feminine noun beginning with stressed (h)a; a+el = al; de+el = del*): **the boy/girl** el chico/la chica; **the books/flowers** los libros/las flores; **to the postman/from the drawer** al cartero/del cajón; **I haven't the time/money** no tengo tiempo/dinero; **1.10 euros to the dollar** 1,10 euros por dólar; **paid by the hour** pagado por hora
  2 (+*adj to form noun*) los; lo; **the rich and the poor** los ricos y los pobres; **to attempt the impossible** intentar lo imposible
  3 (*in titles, surnames*): **Elizabeth the First** Isabel Primera; **Peter the Great** Pedro el Grande; **do you know the Smiths?** ¿conoce a los Smith?
  4 (*in comparisons*): **the more he works the more he earns** cuanto más trabaja más gana

theatre, theater (*US*) ['θɪətəʳ] *n* teatro
theatre-goer, theater-goer (*US*) ['θɪətəgəuəʳ] *n* aficionado(-a) al teatro

theatrical [θɪˈætrɪkl] *adj* teatral
theft [θɛft] *n* robo
their [ðɛəʳ] *adj* su
theirs [ðɛəz] *pron* (el) suyo/(la) suya *etc*; *see also* **my**; **mine**
them [ðɛm, ðəm] *pron* (*direct*) los/las; (*indirect*) les; (*stressed, after prep*) ellos/ellas; **I see** ~ los veo; **both of** ~ ambos(-as), los/las dos; **give me a few of** ~ dame algunos(-as); *see also* **me**
theme [θiːm] *n* tema *m*
theme park *n* parque *m* temático
theme song *n* tema *m* (musical)
themselves [ðəmˈsɛlvz] *pl pron* (*subject*) ellos mismos/ellas mismas; (*complement*) se; (*after prep*) sí (mismos(-as)); *see also* **oneself**
then [ðɛn] *adv* (*at that time*) entonces; (*next*) pues; (*later*) luego, después; (*and also*) además ■ *conj* (*therefore*) en ese caso, entonces ■ *adj*: **the** ~ **president** el entonces presidente; **from** ~ **on** desde entonces; **until** ~ hasta entonces; **and** ~ **what?** y luego, ¿qué?; **what do you want me to do,** ~? ¿entonces, qué quiere que haga?
theologian [θɪəˈləudʒən] *n* teólogo(-a)
theological [θɪəˈlɔdʒɪkl] *adj* teológico
theology [θɪˈɔlədʒɪ] *n* teología
theorem [ˈθɪərəm] *n* teorema *m*
theoretical [θɪəˈrɛtɪkl] *adj* teórico
theoretically [θɪəˈrɛtɪklɪ] *adv* teóricamente, en teoría
theorize [ˈθɪəraɪz] *vi* teorizar
theory [ˈθɪərɪ] *n* teoría
therapeutic [θɛrəˈpjuːtɪk], **therapeutical** [θɛrəˈpjuːtɪkl] *adj* terapéutico
therapist [ˈθɛrəpɪst] *n* terapeuta *m/f*
therapy [ˈθɛrəpɪ] *n* terapia

 KEYWORD

there [ˈðɛəʳ] *adv* **1**: **there is**, **there are** hay; **there is no-one here** no hay nadie aquí; **there is no bread left** no queda pan; **there has been an accident** ha habido un accidente
2 (*referring to place*) ahí; (*distant*) allí; **it's there** está ahí; **put it in/on/up/down there** ponlo ahí dentro/encima/arriba/abajo; **I want that book there** quiero ese libro de ahí; **there he is!** ¡ahí está!; **there's the bus** ahí *or* ya viene el autobús; **back/down there** allí atrás/abajo; **over there**, **through there** por allí
3: **there, there** (*esp to child*) ¡venga, venga!

thereabouts [ˈðɛərəˈbauts] *adv* por ahí
thereafter [ðɛərˈɑːftəʳ] *adv* después
thereby [ˈðɛəbaɪ] *adv* así, de ese modo

therefore [ˈðɛəfɔːʳ] *adv* por lo tanto
there's [ðɛəz] = **there is**; **there has**
thereupon [ðɛərəˈpɔn] *adv* (*at that point*) en eso, en seguida
thermal [ˈθəːml] *adj* termal
thermal paper *n* papel *m* térmico
thermal printer *n* termoimpresora
thermodynamics [ˈθəːmədaɪnæmɪks] *n* termodinámica
thermometer [θəˈmɔmɪtəʳ] *n* termómetro
thermonuclear [θəːməuˈnjuːklɪəʳ] *adj* termonuclear
Thermos® [ˈθəːməs] *n* (*also*: **Thermos flask**) termo
thermostat [ˈθəːməustæt] *n* termostato
thesaurus [θɪˈsɔːrəs] *n* tesoro, diccionario de sinónimos
these [ðiːz] *pl adj* estos(-as) ■ *pl pron* éstos(-as)
thesis (*pl* **theses**) [ˈθiːsɪs, -siːz] *n* tesis *f inv*; *see also* **doctorate**
they [ðeɪ] *pl pron* ellos/ellas; ~ **say that ...** (*it is said that*) se dice que ...
they'd [ðeɪd] = **they had**; **they would**
they'll [ðeɪl] = **they shall**; **they will**
they're [ðɛəʳ] = **they are**
they've [ðeɪv] = **they have**
thick [θɪk] *adj* (*wall, slice*) grueso; (*dense: liquid, smoke etc*) espeso; (*vegetation, beard*) tupido; (*stupid*) torpe ■ *n*: **in the** ~ **of the battle** en lo más reñido de la batalla; **it's 20 cm** ~ tiene 20 cm de espesor
thicken [ˈθɪkn] *vi* espesarse ■ *vt* (*sauce etc*) espesar
thicket [ˈθɪkɪt] *n* espesura
thickly [ˈθɪklɪ] *adv* (*spread*) en capa espesa; (*cut*) en rebanada gruesa; (*populated*) densamente
thickness [ˈθɪknɪs] *n* espesor *m*, grueso
thickset [θɪkˈsɛt] *adj* fornido
thickskinned [θɪkˈskɪnd] *adj* (*fig*) insensible
thief (*pl* **thieves**) [θiːf, θiːvz] *n* ladrón(-ona) *m(f)*
thieving [ˈθiːvɪŋ] *n* tobo, hurto ■ *adj* ladrón(-ona)
thigh [θaɪ] *n* muslo
thighbone [ˈθaɪbəun] *n* fémur *m*
thimble [ˈθɪmbl] *n* dedal *m*
thin [θɪn] *adj* delgado; (*wall, layer*) fino; (*watery*) aguado; (*light*) tenue; (*hair*) escaso; (*fog*) ligero; (*crowd*) disperso ■ *vt*: **to** ~ (**down**) (*sauce, paint*) diluir ■ *vi* (*fog*) aclararse; (*also*: **thin out**: *crowd*) dispersarse; **his hair is thinning** se está quedando calvo
thing [θɪŋ] *n* cosa; (*object*) objeto, artículo; (*contraption*) chisme *m*; (*mania*) manía; **things** *npl* (*belongings*) cosas *fpl*; **the best** ~ **would**

be to ... lo mejor sería ...; **the main ~ is ...** lo principal es ...; **first ~ (in the morning)** a primera hora (de la mañana); **last ~ (at night)** a última hora (de la noche); **the ~ is** ... lo que pasa es que ...; **how are things?** ¿qué tal van las cosas?; **she's got a ~ about mice** le dan no sé qué los ratones; **poor ~!** ¡pobre! *m/f*, ¡pobrecito(-a)!

think (*pl* **thought**) [θɪŋk, θɔːt] *vi* pensar ■ *vt* pensar, creer; (*imagine*) imaginar; **what did you ~ of it?** ¿qué te parece?; **what did you ~ of them?** ¿qué te parecieron?; **to ~ about sth/sb** pensar en algo/uno; **I'll ~ about it** lo pensaré; **to ~ of doing sth** pensar en hacer algo; **I ~ so/not** creo que sí/no; **~ again!** ¡piénsalo bien!; **to ~ aloud** pensar en voz alta; **to ~ well of sb** tener buen concepto de algn
▶ **think out** *vt* (*plan*) elaborar, tramar; (*solution*) encontrar
▶ **think over** *vt* reflexionar sobre, meditar; **I'd like to ~ things over** me gustaría pensármelo
▶ **think through** *vt* pensar bien
▶ **think up** *vt* imaginar

thinking ['θɪŋkɪŋ] *n*: **to my (way of) ~** a mi parecer

think tank *n* grupo de expertos

thinly ['θɪnlɪ] *adv* (*cut*) en lonchas finas; (*spread*) en una capa fina

thinness ['θɪnnɪs] *n* delgadez *f*

third [θəːd] *adj* (*before nmsg*) tercer; tercero ■ *n* tercero(-a); (*fraction*) tercio; (*Brit Scol: degree*) título universitario de tercera clase

third degree *adj* (*burns*) de tercer grado

thirdly ['θəːdlɪ] *adv* en tercer lugar

third party insurance *n* (*Brit*) seguro a terceros

third-rate ['θəː'd'reɪt] *adj* de poca calidad

Third World *n*: **the ~** el Tercer Mundo ■ *cpd* tercermundista

thirst [θəːst] *n* sed *f*

thirsty ['θəːstɪ] *adj* (*person*) sediento; **to be ~** tener sed

thirteen [θəː'tiːn] *num* trece

thirteenth [θəː'tiːnθ] *adj* decimotercero ■ *n* (*in series*) decimotercero(-a); (*fraction*) decimotercio

thirtieth ['θəːtɪəθ] *adj* trigésimo ■ *n* (*in series*) trigésimo(-a); (*fraction*) treintavo

thirty ['θəːtɪ] *num* treinta

🔵 **KEYWORD**

this [ðɪs] (*pl* **these**) *adj* (*demonstrative*) este(-a), estos(-as) *pl*, esto *neuter*; **this man/woman** este hombre/esta mujer; **these children/**flowers estos chicos/estas flores; **this way** por aquí; **this time last year** hoy hace un año; **this one (here)** éste(-a), esto (de aquí)
■ *pron* (*demonstrative*) éste(-a), éstos(-as) *pl*, esto *neuter*; **who is this?** ¿quién es éste/ésta?; **what is this?** ¿qué es esto?; **this is where I live** aquí vivo; **this is what he said** esto es lo que dijo; **this is Mr Brown** (*in introductions*) le presento al Sr. Brown; (*photo*) éste es el Sr. Brown; (*on telephone*) habla el Sr. Brown; **they were talking of this and that** hablaban de esto y lo otro
■ *adv* (*demonstrative*): **this high/long** así de alto/largo; **this far** hasta aquí

thistle ['θɪsl] *n* cardo

thong [θɔŋ] *n* correa

thorn [θɔːn] *n* espina

thorny ['θɔːnɪ] *adj* espinoso

thorough ['θʌrə] *adj* (*search*) minucioso; (*knowledge*) profundo; (*research*) a fondo

thoroughbred ['θʌrəbred] *adj* (*horse*) de pura sangre

thoroughfare ['θʌrəfɛəʳ] *n* calle *f*; **"no ~"** "prohibido el paso"

thoroughgoing ['θʌrəgəʊɪŋ] *adj* a fondo

thoroughly ['θʌrəlɪ] *adv* minuciosamente; a fondo

thoroughness ['θʌrənɪs] *n* minuciosidad *f*

those [ðəʊz] *pl pron* ésos/ésas; (*more remote*) aquéllos(-as) ■ *pl adj* esos/esas; aquellos(-as)

though [ðəʊ] *conj* aunque ■ *adv* sin embargo, aún así; **even ~** aunque; **it's not so easy, ~** sin embargo no es tan fácil

thought [θɔːt] *pt, pp of* **think** ■ *n* pensamiento; (*opinion*) opinión *f*; (*intention*) intención *f*; **to give sb some ~** pensar algo detenidamente; **after much ~** después de pensarlo bien; **I've just had a ~** se me acaba de ocurrir una idea

thoughtful ['θɔːtful] *adj* pensativo; (*considerate*) atento

thoughtfully ['θɔːtfəlɪ] *adv* pensativamente; atentamente

thoughtless ['θɔːtlɪs] *adj* desconsiderado

thoughtlessly ['θɔːtlɪslɪ] *adv* insensatamente

thought-provoking ['θɔːtprəvəʊkɪŋ] *adj* estimulante

thousand ['θaʊzənd] *num* mil; **two ~** dos mil; **thousands of** miles de

thousandth ['θaʊzəntθ] *num* milésimo

thrash [θræʃ] *vt* dar una paliza a
▶ **thrash about** *vi* revolverse
▶ **thrash out** *vt* discutir a fondo

thrashing ['θræʃɪŋ] *n*: **to give sb a ~** dar una paliza a algn

825

thread [θrɛd] n hilo; (of screw) rosca ■ vt
(needle) enhebrar

threadbare ['θrɛdbɛəʳ] adj raído

threat [θrɛt] n amenaza; **to be under ~ of**
estar amenazado de

threaten ['θrɛtn] vi amenazar ■ vt: **to ~ sb**
with sth/to do amenazar a algn con algo/
con hacer

threatening ['θrɛtnɪŋ] adj amenazador(a),
amenazante

three [θriː] num tres

three-dimensional [θriːdɪ'mɛnʃənl] adj
tridimensional

threefold ['θriːfəuld] adv: **to increase ~**
triplicar

three-piece ['θriːpiːs]: **~ suit** n traje m de
tres piezas

three-piece suite n tresillo

three-ply [θriː'plaɪ] adj (wood) de tres capas;
(wool) triple

three-quarter [θriː'kwɔːtəʳ] adj: **~ length**
sleeves mangas fpl tres cuartos

three-quarters [θriː'kwɔːtəz] npl tres cuartas
partes; **~ full** tres cuartas partes lleno

three-wheeler [θriː'wiːləʳ] n (car) coche m
cabina

thresh [θrɛʃ] vt (Agr) trillar

threshing machine ['θrɛʃɪŋ-] n trilladora

threshold ['θrɛʃhəuld] n umbral m; **to be on**
the ~ of (fig) estar al borde de

threshold agreement n convenio de nivel
crítico

threw [θruː] pt of **throw**

thrift [θrɪft] n economía

thrifty ['θrɪftɪ] adj económico

thrill [θrɪl] n (excitement) emoción f ■ vt
emocionar; **to be thrilled** (with gift etc) estar
encantado

thriller ['θrɪləʳ] n película/novela de suspense

thrilling ['θrɪlɪŋ] adj emocionante

thrive (pt **thrived, throve,** pp **thrived, thriven**)
[θraɪv, θrəuv, 'θrɪvn] vi (grow) crecer; (do well)
prosperar

thriving ['θraɪvɪŋ] adj próspero

throat [θrəut] n garganta; **I have a sore ~** me
duele la garganta

throb [θrɔb] n (of heart) latido; (of engine)
vibración f ■ vi latir; vibrar; (with pain) dar
punzadas; **my head is throbbing** la cabeza
me da punzadas

throes [θrəuz] npl: **in the ~ of** en medio de

thrombosis [θrɔm'bəusɪs] n trombosis f

throne [θrəun] n trono

throng [θrɔŋ] n multitud f, muchedumbre f
■ vt, vi apiñarse, agolparse

throttle ['θrɔtl] n (Aut) acelerador m ■ vt
estrangular

through [θruː] prep por, a través de; (time)
durante; (by means of) por medio de,
mediante; (owing to) gracias a ■ adj (ticket,
train) directo ■ adv completamente, de parte
a parte; de principio a fin; **(from) Monday ~**
Friday (US) de lunes a viernes; **to go ~ sb's**
papers mirar entre los papeles de algn;
I am halfway ~ the book voy por la mitad
del libro; **the soldiers didn't let us ~** los
soldados no nos dejaron pasar; **to put sb ~**
to sb (Tel) poner or pasar a algn con algn;
to be ~ (Tel) tener comunicación; (have
finished) haber terminado; **"no ~ road"** (Brit)
"calle sin salida"

throughout [θruː'aut] prep (place) por todas
partes de, por todo; (time) durante todo ■ adv
por or en todas partes

throughput ['θruːput] n (of goods, materials)
producción f; (Comput) capacidad f de
procesamiento

throve [θrəuv] pt of **thrive**

throw [θrəu] n tiro; (Sport) lanzamiento ■ vt
(pt **threw,** pp **thrown**) [θruː, θrəun] tirar,
echar, botar (LAm); (Sport) lanzar; (rider)
derribar; (fig) desconcertar; **to ~ a party** dar
una fiesta
  ▸ **throw about, throw around** vt (litter etc)
tirar, esparcir
  ▸ **throw away** vt tirar
  ▸ **throw off** vt deshacerse de
  ▸ **throw open** vt (doors, windows) abrir de par
en par; (house, gardens etc) abrir al público;
(competition, race) abrir a todos
  ▸ **throw out** vt tirar, botar (LAm)
  ▸ **throw together** vt (clothes) amontonar;
(meal) preparar a la carrera; (essay) hacer sin
cuidado
  ▸ **throw up** vi vomitar, devolver

throwaway ['θrəuəweɪ] adj para tirar,
desechable

throwback ['θrəubæk] n: **it's a ~ to** (fig) eso
nos lleva de nuevo a

throw-in ['θrəuɪn] n (Sport) saque m de banda

thrown [θrəun] pp of **throw**

thru [θruː] (US) = **through**

thrush [θrʌʃ] n zorzal m, tordo; (Med)
candiasis f

thrust [θrʌst] n (Tech) empuje m ■ vt (pt, pp
thrust) empujar; (push in) introducir

thrusting ['θrʌstɪŋ] adj (person) dinámico, con
empuje

thud [θʌd] n golpe m sordo

thug [θʌg] n gamberro(-a)

thumb [θʌm] n (Anat) pulgar m ■ vt: **to ~ a**
lift hacer dedo; **to give sth/sb the thumbs**
up/down aprobar/desaprobar algo/a algn
  ▸ **thumb through** vt fus (book) hojear

thumb index n uñero, índice m recortado

thumbnail ['θʌmneɪl] n uña del pulgar

thumbnail sketch n esbozo

thumbtack ['θʌmtæk] n (US) chincheta, chinche f

thump [θʌmp] n golpe m; (sound) ruido seco or sordo ■ vt, vi golpear

thumping ['θʌmpɪŋ] adj (col: huge) descomunal

thunder ['θʌndə'] n trueno; (of applause etc) estruendo ■ vi tronar; (train etc): **to ~ past** pasar como un trueno

thunderbolt ['θʌndəbəʊlt] n rayo

thunderclap ['θʌndəklæp] n trueno

thunderous ['θʌndərəs] adj ensordecedor(a), estruendoso

thunderstorm ['θʌndəstɔ:m] n tormenta

thunderstruck ['θʌndəstrʌk] adj pasmado

thundery ['θʌndərɪ] adj tormentoso

Thur., Thurs. abbr (= Thursday) juev

Thursday ['θə:zdɪ] n jueves m inv; see also **Tuesday**

thus [ðʌs] adv así, de este modo

thwart [θwɔ:t] vt frustrar

thyme [taɪm] n tomillo

thyroid ['θaɪrɔɪd] n tiroides m inv

tiara [tɪ'ɑ:rə] n tiara, diadema

Tiber ['taɪbə'] n Tíber m

Tibet [tɪ'bet] n el Tíbet

Tibetan [tɪ'betən] adj tibetano ■ n tibetano(-a); (Ling) tibetano

tibia ['tɪbɪə] n tibia

tic [tɪk] n tic m

tick [tɪk] n (sound: of clock) tictac m; (mark) señal f (de visto bueno), palomita (LAm); (Zool) garrapata; (Brit col): **in a ~** en un instante; (Brit col: credit): **to buy sth on ~** comprar algo a crédito ■ vi hacer tictac ■ vt marcar, señalar; **to put a ~ against sth** poner una señal en algo
   ▶ **tick off** vt marcar; (person) reñir
   ▶ **tick over** vi (Brit: engine) girar en marcha lenta; (: fig) ir tirando

ticker tape ['tɪkə-] n cinta perforada

ticket ['tɪkɪt] n billete m, tíquet m, boleto (LAm); (for cinema etc) entrada, boleto (LAm); (in shop: on goods) etiqueta; (for library) tarjeta; (US Pol) lista (de candidatos);
   to get a parking ~ (Aut) ser multado por estacionamiento ilegal

ticket agency n (Theat) agencia de venta de entradas

ticket collector n revisor(a) m(f)

ticket holder n poseedor(a) m(f) de billete or entrada

ticket inspector n revisor(a) m(f), inspector(a) m(f) de boletos (LAm)

ticket office n (Theat) taquilla, boletería (LAm); (Rail) despacho de billetes or boletos (LAm)

ticking-off ['tɪkɪŋ'ɔf] n (col): **to give sb a ~** echarle una bronca a algn

tickle ['tɪkl] n: **to give sb a ~** hacer cosquillas a algn ■ vt hacer cosquillas a

ticklish ['tɪklɪʃ] adj (which tickles: blanket) que pica; (: cough) irritante; **to be ~** tener cosquillas

tidal ['taɪdl] adj de marea

tidal wave n maremoto

tidbit ['tɪdbɪt] (US) = **titbit**

tiddlywinks ['tɪdlɪwɪŋks] n juego de la pulga

tide [taɪd] n marea; (fig: of events) curso, marcha ■ vt: **to ~ sb over** or **through (until)** sacar a algn del apuro (hasta); **high/low ~** marea alta/baja; **the ~ of public opinion** la tendencia de la opinión pública

tidily ['taɪdɪlɪ] adv bien, ordenadamente; **to arrange ~** ordenar; **to dress ~** vestir bien

tidiness ['taɪdɪnɪs] n (order) orden m; (cleanliness) aseo

tidy ['taɪdɪ] adj (room) ordenado; (drawing, work) limpio; (person) (bien) arreglado; (: in character) metódico; (mind) claro, metódico ■ vt (also: **tidy up**) ordenar, poner en orden

tie [taɪ] n (string etc) atadura; (Brit: necktie) corbata; (fig: link) vínculo, lazo; (Sport: draw) empate m ■ vt atar ■ vi (Sport) empatar; **family ties** obligaciones fpl familiares; **cup ~** (Sport: match) partido de copa; **to ~ in a bow** hacer un lazo; **to ~ a knot in sth** hacer un nudo en algo
   ▶ **tie down** vt atar; (fig): **to ~ sb down to** obligar a algn a
   ▶ **tie in** vi: **to ~ in (with)** (correspond) concordar (con)
   ▶ **tie on** vt (Brit: label etc) atar
   ▶ **tie up** vt (parcel) envolver; (dog) atar; (boat) amarrar; (arrangements) concluir; **to be tied up** (busy) estar ocupado

tie-break ['taɪbreɪk], **tie-breaker** ['taɪbreɪkə'] n (Tennis) tiebreak m, muerte f súbita; (in quiz) punto decisivo

tie-on ['taɪɔn] adj (Brit: label) para atar

tie-pin ['taɪpɪn] n (Brit) alfiler m de corbata

tier [tɪə'] n grada; (of cake) piso

tie tack n (US) alfiler m de corbata

tiff [tɪf] n (col) pelea, riña

tiger ['taɪgə'] n tigre m

tight [taɪt] adj (rope) tirante; (money) escaso; (clothes, budget) ajustado; (programme) apretado; (col: drunk) borracho ■ adv (squeeze) muy fuerte; (shut) herméticamente; **to be packed ~** (suitcase) estar completamente lleno; (people) estar apretados; **everybody hold ~!** ¡agárrense bien!

t

tighten ['taɪtn] vt (rope) tensar, estirar; (screw) apretar ■ vi estirarse; apretarse
tight-fisted [taɪt'fɪstɪd] adj tacaño
tight-lipped ['taɪt'lɪpt] adj: **to be ~** (silent) rehusar hablar; (angry) apretar los labios
tightly ['taɪtlɪ] adv (grasp) muy fuerte
tightness ['taɪtnɪs] n (of rope) tirantez f; (of clothes) estrechez f; (of budget) lo ajustado
tightrope ['taɪtrəup] n cuerda floja
tightrope walker n equilibrista m/f, funambulista m/f
tights [taɪts] npl (Brit) medias fpl, panties mpl
tigress ['taɪgrɪs] n tigresa
tilde ['tɪldə] n tilde f
tile [taɪl] n (on roof) teja; (on floor) baldosa; (on wall) azulejo ■ vt (floor) poner baldosas en; (wall) alicatar
tiled [taɪld] adj (floor) embaldosado; (wall, bathroom) alicatado; (roof) con tejas
till [tɪl] n caja (registradora) ■ vt (land) cultivar ■ prep, conj = **until**
tiller ['tɪləʳ] n (Naut) caña del timón
tilt [tɪlt] vt inclinar ■ vi inclinarse ■ n (slope) inclinación f; **to wear one's hat at a ~** llevar el sombrero echado a un lado or terciado; **(at) full ~** a toda velocidad or carrera
timber ['tɪmbəʳ] n (material) madera; (trees) árboles mpl
time [taɪm] n tiempo; (epoch: often pl) época; (by clock) hora; (moment) momento; (occasion) vez f; (Mus) compás m ■ vt calcular or medir el tiempo de; (race) cronometrar; (remark etc) elegir el momento para; **a long ~** mucho tiempo; **four at a ~** cuarto a la vez; **for the ~ being** de momento, por ahora; **at times** a veces, a ratos; **~ after ~, ~ and again** repetidas veces, una y otra vez; **from ~ to ~** de vez en cuando; **in ~** (soon enough) a tiempo; (after some time) con el tiempo; (Mus) al compás; **in a week's ~** dentro de una semana; **in no ~** en un abrir y cerrar de ojos; **any ~** cuando sea; **on ~** a la hora; **to be 30 minutes behind/ahead of ~** llevar media hora de retraso/adelanto; **to take one's ~** tomárselo con calma; **he'll do it in his own ~** (without being hurried) lo hará sin prisa; (out of working hours) lo hará en su tiempo libre; **by the ~ he arrived** cuando llegó; **5 times 5** 5 por 5; **what ~ is it?** ¿qué hora es?; **what ~ do you make it?** ¿qué hora es or tiene?; **to be behind the times** estar atrasado; **to carry three boxes at a ~** llevar tres cajas a la vez; **to keep ~** llevar el ritmo or el compás; **to have a good ~** pasarlo bien, divertirse; **to ~ sth well/badly** elegir un buen/mal momento para algo; **the bomb was timed to explode five minutes later** la bomba estaba programada para explotar cinco minutos más tarde

time-and-motion expert ['taɪmənd'məuʃən-] n experto(-a) en la ciencia de la producción
time-and-motion study ['taɪmənd'məuʃən-] n estudio de desplazamientos y tiempos
time bomb n bomba de relojería
time card n tarjeta de registro horario
time clock n reloj m registrador
time-consuming ['taɪmkənsju:mɪŋ] adj que requiere mucho tiempo
time frame n plazo
time-honoured, time-honored (US) ['taɪmɔnəd] adj consagrado
timekeeper ['taɪmki:pəʳ] n (Sport) cronómetro
time lag n desfase m
timeless ['taɪmlɪs] adj eterno
time limit n (gen) límite m de tiempo; (Comm) plazo
timely ['taɪmlɪ] adj oportuno
time off n tiempo libre
timer ['taɪməʳ] n (also: **timer switch**) interruptor m; (in kitchen) temporizador m; (Tech) temporizador m
time-saving ['taɪmseɪvɪŋ] adj que ahorra tiempo
time scale n escala de tiempo
time sharing n (Comput) tiempo compartido
time sheet n = **time card**
time signal n señal f horaria
time switch n (Brit) interruptor m (horario)
timetable ['taɪmteɪbl] n horario; (programme of events etc) programa m
time zone n huso horario
timid ['tɪmɪd] adj tímido
timidity [tɪ'mɪdɪtɪ] n timidez f
timidly ['tɪmɪdlɪ] adv tímidamente
timing ['taɪmɪŋ] n (Sport) cronometraje m; **the ~ of his resignation** el momento que eligió para dimitir
timpani ['tɪmpənɪ] npl tímpanos mpl
tin [tɪn] n estaño; (also: **tin plate**) hojalata; (Brit: can) lata
tinfoil ['tɪnfɔɪl] n papel m de estaño
tinge [tɪndʒ] n matiz m ■ vt: **tinged with** teñido de
tingle ['tɪŋgl] n hormigueo ■ vi (cheeks, skin: from cold) sentir comezón; (: from bad circulation) sentir hormigueo
tinker ['tɪŋkəʳ] n calderero(-a); (gipsy) gitano(-a)
  ▶ **tinker with** vt fus jugar con, tocar
tinkle ['tɪŋkl] vi tintinear
tin mine n mina de estaño

tinned [tɪnd] *adj* (*Brit: food*) en lata, en conserva

tinnitus ['tɪnɪtəs] *n* (*Med*) acufeno

tinny ['tɪnɪ] *adj* (*sound, taste*) metálico; (*pej: car*) poco sólido, de pacotilla

tin opener [-əupnəʳ] *n* (*Brit*) abrelatas *m inv*

tinsel ['tɪnsl] *n* oropel *m*

tint [tɪnt] *n* matiz *m*; (*for hair*) tinte *m* ▪ *vt* (*hair*) teñir

tinted ['tɪntɪd] *adj* (*hair*) teñido; (*glass, spectacles*) ahumado

tiny ['taɪnɪ] *adj* minúsculo, pequeñito

tip [tɪp] *n* (*end*) punta; (*gratuity*) propina; (*Brit: for rubbish*) vertedero; (*advice*) consejo ▪ *vt* (*waiter*) dar una propina a; (*tilt*) inclinar; (*empty: also:* **tip out**) vaciar, echar; (*predict: winner*) pronosticar; (*: horse*) recomendar; **he tipped out the contents of the box** volcó el contenido de la caja
  ► **tip off** *vt* avisar, poner sobre aviso a
  ► **tip over** *vt* volcar ▪ *vi* volcarse

tip-off ['tɪpɔf] *n* (*hint*) advertencia

tipped [tɪpt] *adj* (*Brit: cigarette*) con filtro

Tipp-Ex® ['tɪpɛks] *n* Tipp-Ex® *m*

tipple ['tɪpl] *n* (*Brit*): **his ~ is Cointreau** bebe Cointreau

tipster ['tɪpstəʳ] *n* (*Racing*) pronosticador(a) *m(f)*

tipsy ['tɪpsɪ] *adj* alegre, achispado

tiptoe ['tɪptəu] *n* (*Brit*): **on ~** de puntillas

tiptop ['tɪptɔp] *adj*: **in ~ condition** en perfectas condiciones

tirade [taɪ'reɪd] *n* diatriba

tire ['taɪəʳ] *n* (*US*) = **tyre** ▪ *vt* cansar ▪ *vi* (*gen*) cansarse; (*become bored*) aburrirse
  ► **tire out** *vt* agotar, rendir

tired ['taɪəd] *adj* cansado; **to be ~ of sth** estar harto de algo; **to be/feel/look ~** estar/sentirse/parecer cansado

tiredness ['taɪədnɪs] *n* cansancio

tireless ['taɪəlɪs] *adj* incansable

tirelessly ['taɪəlɪslɪ] *adv* incansablemente

tiresome ['taɪəsəm] *adj* aburrido

tiring ['taɪrɪŋ] *adj* cansado

tissue ['tɪʃuː] *n* tejido; (*paper handkerchief*) pañuelo de papel, kleenex® *m*

tissue paper *n* papel *m* de seda

tit [tɪt] *n* (*bird*) herrerillo común; **to give ~ for tat** dar ojo por ojo

titbit ['tɪtbɪt], **tidbit** (*US*) ['tɪdbɪt] *n* (*food*) golosina; (*news*) pedazo

titillate ['tɪtɪleɪt] *vt* estimular, excitar

titillation [tɪtɪ'leɪʃən] *n* estimulación *f*, excitación *f*

titivate ['tɪtɪveɪt] *vt* emperejilar

title ['taɪtl] *n* título; (*Law: right*): **~ (to)** derecho (a)

title deed *n* (*Law*) título de propiedad

title page *n* portada

title role *n* papel *m* principal

titter ['tɪtəʳ] *vi* reírse entre dientes

tittle-tattle ['tɪtltætl] *n* chismes *mpl*

titular ['tɪtjuləʳ] *adj* (*in name only*) nominal

T-junction ['tiːdʒʌŋkʃən] *n* cruce *m* en T

TM *abbr* (= *trademark*) marca de fábrica; = **transcendental meditation**

TN *abbr* (*US*) = **Tennessee**

TNT *n abbr* (= *trinitrotoluene*) TNT *m*

O KEYWORD

to [tuː, tə] *prep* **1** (*direction*) a; **to go to France/London/school/the station** ir a Francia/Londres/al colegio/a la estación; **to go to Claude's/the doctor's** ir a casa de Claude/al médico; **the road to Edinburgh** la carretera de Edimburgo; **to the left/right** a la izquierda/derecha

2 (*as far as*) hasta, a; **from here to London** de aquí a or hasta Londres; **to count to 10** contar hasta 10; **from 40 to 50 people** entre 40 y 50 personas

3 (*with expressions of time*): **a quarter/twenty to five** las cuarto menos cuarto/veinte

4 (*for, of*): **the key to the front door** la llave de la puerta principal; **she is secretary to the director** es la secretaria del director; **a letter to his wife** una carta a or para su mujer

5 (*expressing indirect object*) a; **to give sth to sb** darle algo a algn; **give it to me** dámelo; **to talk to sb** hablar con algn; **to be a danger to sb** ser un peligro para algn; **to carry out repairs to sth** hacer reparaciones en algo

6 (*in relation to*): **3 goals to 2** 3 goles a 2; **30 miles to the gallon** ≈ 9,4 litros a los cien (kilómetros); **8 apples to the kilo** 8 manzanas por kilo

7 (*purpose, result*): **to come to sb's aid** venir en auxilio or ayuda de algn; **to sentence sb to death** condenar a algn a muerte; **to my great surprise** con gran sorpresa mía ▪ *infin particle* **1** (*simple infin*): **to go/eat** ir/comer

2 (*following another vb; see also relevant vb*): **to want/try/start to do** querer/intentar/empezar a hacer

3 (*with vb omitted*): **I don't want to** no quiero

4 (*purpose, result*) para; **I did it to help you** lo hice para ayudarte; **he came to see you** vino a verte

5 (*equivalent to relative clause*): **I have things to do** tengo cosas que hacer; **the main thing is to try** lo principal es intentarlo

t

6 (*after adj etc*): **ready to go** listo para irse; **too old to** ... demasiado viejo (como) para ... ▪ *adv*: **pull/push the door to** tirar de/empujar la puerta; **to go to and fro** ir y venir

toad [təud] *n* sapo

toadstool ['təudstu:l] *n* seta venenosa

toady ['təudɪ] *n* pelota *m/f* ▪ *vi*: **to ~ to sb** hacer la pelota *or* dar coba a algn

toast [təust] *n* (*Culin: also*: **piece of toast**) tostada; (*drink, speech*) brindis *m inv* ▪ *vt* (*Culin*) tostar; (*drink to*) brindar

toaster ['təustər] *n* tostador *m*

toastmaster ['təustmɑ:stər] *n persona que propone brindis y anuncia a los oradores en un banquete*

toast rack *n* rejilla para tostadas

tobacco [tə'bækəu] *n* tabaco; **pipe ~** tabaco de pipa

tobacconist [tə'bækənɪst] *n* estanquero(-a), tabaquero(-a) (*LAm*); **~'s (shop)** (*Brit*) estanco, tabaquería (*LAm*)

tobacco plantation *n* plantación *f* de tabaco, tabacal *m*

Tobago [tə'beɪgəu] *n see* **Trinidad and Tobago**

toboggan [tə'bɔgən] *n* tobogán *m*

today [tə'deɪ] *adv, n* (*also fig*) hoy *m*; **what day is it ~?** ¿qué día es hoy?; **what date is it ~?** ¿a qué fecha estamos hoy?; **~ is the 4th of March** hoy es el 4 de marzo; **~'s paper** el periódico de hoy; **a fortnight ~** de hoy en 15 días, dentro de 15 días

toddle ['tɔdl] *vi* empezar a andar, dar los primeros pasos

toddler ['tɔdlər] *n* niño(-a) (que empieza a andar)

toddy ['tɔdɪ] *n* ponche *m*

to-do [tə'du:] *n* (*fuss*) lío

toe [təu] *n* dedo (del pie); (*of shoe*) punta ▪ *vt*: **to ~ the line** (*fig*) acatar las normas; **big/little ~** dedo gordo/pequeño del pie

TOEFL ['təufl] *n abbr* = **Test(ing) of English as a Foreign Language**

toehold ['təuhəuld] *n* punto de apoyo (para el pie)

toenail ['təuneɪl] *n* uña del pie

toffee ['tɔfɪ] *n* caramelo

toffee apple *n* (*Brit*) manzana de caramelo

tofu ['təufu:] *n* tofu *m*

toga ['təugə] *n* toga

together [tə'gɛðər] *adv* juntos; (*at same time*) al mismo tiempo, a la vez; **~ with** junto con

togetherness [tə'gɛðənɪs] *n* compañerismo

toggle switch ['tɔgl-] *n* (*Comput*) conmutador *m* de palanca

Togo ['təugəu] *n* Togo

togs [tɔgz] *npl* (*col: clothes*) atuendo, ropa

toil [tɔɪl] *n* trabajo duro, labor *f* ▪ *vi* esforzarse

toilet ['tɔɪlət] *n* (*Brit: lavatory*) servicios *mpl*, wáter *m* ▪ *cpd* (*bag, soap etc*) de aseo; **to go to the ~** ir al baño; *see also* **toilets**

toilet bag *n* neceser *m*, bolsa de aseo

toilet bowl *n* taza (de retrete)

toilet paper *n* papel *m* higiénico

toiletries ['tɔɪlətrɪz] *npl* artículos *mpl* de aseo; (*make-up etc*) artículos *mpl* de tocador

toilet roll *n* rollo de papel higiénico

toilets ['tɔɪləts] *npl* (*Brit*) servicios *mpl*

toilet soap *n* jabón *m* de tocador

toilet water *n* (agua de) colonia

to-ing and fro-ing ['tuɪŋən'frəuɪŋ] *n* vaivén *m*

token ['təukən] *n* (*sign*) señal *f*, muestra; (*souvenir*) recuerdo; (*voucher*) vale *m*; (*disc*) ficha ▪ *cpd* (*fee, strike*) nominal, simbólico; **book/record ~** (*Brit*) vale *m* para comprar libros/discos; **by the same ~** (*fig*) por la misma razón

tokenism ['təukənɪzəm] *n* (*Pol*) política simbólica *or* de fachada

Tokyo ['təukjəu] *n* Tokio, Tokío

told [təuld] *pt, pp of* **tell**

tolerable ['tɔlərəbl] *adj* (*bearable*) soportable; (*fairly good*) pasable

tolerably ['tɔlərəblɪ] *adv* (*good, comfortable*) medianamente

tolerance ['tɔlərns] *n* (*also Tech*) tolerancia

tolerant ['tɔlərnt] *adj*: **~ of** tolerante con

tolerantly ['tɔlərntlɪ] *adv* con tolerancia

tolerate ['tɔləreɪt] *vt* tolerar

toleration [tɔlə'reɪʃən] *n* tolerancia

toll [təul] *n* (*of casualties*) número de víctimas; (*tax, charge*) peaje *m* ▪ *vi* (*bell*) doblar

toll bridge *n* puente *m* de peaje

toll call *n* (*US Telec*) conferencia, llamada interurbana

toll-free *adj, adv* (*US*) gratis

toll road *n* carretera de peaje

tomato (*pl* **tomatoes**) [tə'mɑ:təu] *n* tomate *m*

tomato puree *n* puré *m* de tomate

tomb [tu:m] *n* tumba

tombola [tɔm'bəulə] *n* tómbola

tomboy ['tɔmbɔɪ] *n* marimacho

tombstone ['tu:mstəun] *n* lápida

tomcat ['tɔmkæt] *n* gato

tomorrow [tə'mɔrəu] *adv, n* (*also fig*) mañana; **the day after ~** pasado mañana; **~ morning** mañana por la mañana; **a week ~** de mañana en ocho (días)

ton [tʌn] *n* tonelada; **tons of** (*col*) montones de

tonal ['təunl] *adj* tonal

tone [təun] n tono ■ vi armonizar; **dialling ~** (Tel) señal f para marcar
▸ **tone down** vt (criticism) suavizar; (colour) atenuar
▸ **tone up** vt (muscles) tonificar
tone-deaf [təun'def] adj sin oído musical
toner ['təunəʳ] n (for photocopier) virador m
Tonga ['tɔŋə] n Islas fpl Tonga
tongs [tɔŋz] npl (for coal) tenazas fpl; (for hair) tenacillas fpl
tongue [tʌŋ] n lengua; **~ in cheek** adv en plan de broma
tongue-tied ['tʌŋtaɪd] adj (fig) mudo
tongue-twister ['tʌŋtwɪstəʳ] n trabalenguas m inv
tonic ['tɔnɪk] n (Med) tónico; (Mus) tónica; (also: **tonic water**) (agua) tónica
tonight [tə'naɪt] adv, n esta noche; **I'll see you ~** nos vemos esta noche
tonnage ['tʌnɪdʒ] n (Naut) tonelaje m
tonsil ['tɔnsl] n amígdala; **to have one's tonsils out** sacarse las amígdalas or anginas
tonsillitis [tɔnsɪ'laɪtɪs] n amigdalitis f
too [tu:] adv (excessively) demasiado; (very) muy; (also) también; (also: **it's too sweet**) está demasiado dulce; **I'm not ~ sure about that** no estoy muy seguro de eso; **I went ~** yo también fui; **~ much** adv, adj demasiado; **many** adj demasiados(-as); **~ bad!** ¡mala suerte!
took [tuk] pt of **take**
tool [tu:l] n herramienta; (fig: person) instrumento
toolbar ['tu:lbɑːʳ] n barra de herramientas
tool box n caja de herramientas
tool kit n juego de herramientas
tool shed n cobertizo (para herramientas)
toot [tu:t] n (of horn) bocinazo; (of whistle) silbido ■ vi (with car horn) tocar la bocina
tooth (pl **teeth**) [tu:θ, ti:θ] n (Anat, Tech) diente m; (molar) muela; **to clean one's teeth** lavarse los dientes; **to have a ~ out** sacarse una muela; **by the skin of one's teeth** por un pelo
toothache ['tu:θeɪk] n dolor m de muelas
toothbrush ['tu:θbrʌʃ] n cepillo de dientes
toothpaste ['tu:θpeɪst] n pasta de dientes
toothpick ['tu:θpɪk] n palillo
tooth powder n polvos mpl dentífricos
top [tɔp] n (of mountain) cumbre f, cima; (of head) coronilla; (of ladder) (lo) alto; (of cupboard, table) superficie f; (lid: of box, jar) tapa; (: of bottle) tapón m; (of list, table, queue, page) cabeza; (toy) peonza; (Dress: blouse) blusa; (: T-shirt) camiseta; (: of pyjamas) chaqueta ■ adj de arriba; (in rank) principal, primero; (best) mejor ■ vt (exceed) exceder; (be first in)

encabezar; **on ~ of** sobre, encima de; **from ~ to bottom** de pies a cabeza; **the ~ of the milk** la nata; **at the ~ of the stairs** en lo alto de la escalera; **at the ~ of the street** al final de la calle; **at the ~ of one's voice** (fig) a voz en grito; **at ~ speed** a máxima velocidad; **a ~ surgeon** un cirujano eminente; **over the ~** (col) excesivo, desmesurado; **to go over the ~** pasarse
▸ **top up**, (US) **top off** vt volver a llenar
topaz ['təupæz] n topacio
top-class ['tɔp'klɑːs] adj de primera clase
topcoat ['tɔpkəut] n sobretodo, abrigo
topflight ['tɔpflaɪt] adj de primera (categoría or clase)
top floor n último piso
top hat n sombrero de copa
top-heavy [tɔp'hɛvɪ] adj (object) con más peso en la parte superior
topic ['tɔpɪk] n tema m
topical ['tɔpɪkl] adj actual
topless ['tɔplɪs] adj (bather etc) topless
top-level ['tɔplɛvl] adj (talks) al más alto nivel
topmost ['tɔpməust] adj más alto
top-notch ['tɔp'nɔtʃ] adj (col) de primerísima categoría
topography [tə'pɔgrəfɪ] n topografía
topping ['tɔpɪŋ] n (Culin): **with a ~ of cream** con nata por encima
topple ['tɔpl] vt volcar, derribar ■ vi caerse
top-ranking ['tɔpræŋkɪŋ] adj de alto rango
top-secret [tɔp'si:krɪt] adj de alto secreto
top-security ['tɔpsɪ'kjuərɪtɪ] adj (Brit) de máxima seguridad
topsy-turvy ['tɔpsɪ'tə:vɪ] adj, adv patas arriba
top-up ['tɔpʌp] n: **would you like a ~?** ¿quiere que se lo vuelva a llenar?
top-up loan n (Brit) préstamo complementario
torch [tɔ:tʃ] n antorcha; (Brit: electric) linterna
tore [tɔ:ʳ] pt of **tear**
torment n ['tɔ:mɛnt] tormento ■ vt [tɔ:'mɛnt] atormentar; (fig: annoy) fastidiar
torn [tɔ:n] pp of **tear**
tornado (pl **tornadoes**) [tɔ:'neɪdəu] n tornado
torpedo (pl **torpedoes**) [tɔ:'pi:dəu] n torpedo
torpedo boat n torpedero, lancha torpedera
torpor ['tɔ:pəʳ] n letargo
torrent ['tɔrnt] n torrente m
torrential [tɔ'rɛnʃl] adj torrencial
torrid ['tɔrɪd] adj tórrido; (fig) apasionado
torso ['tɔ:səu] n torso
tortoise ['tɔ:təs] n tortuga
tortoiseshell ['tɔ:təʃɛl] adj de carey
tortuous ['tɔ:tjuəs] adj tortuoso
torture ['tɔ:tʃəʳ] n tortura ■ vt torturar; (fig) atormentar

t

torturer ['tɔ:tʃərərˈ] n torturador(a) m(f)
Tory ['tɔ:rɪ] adj, n (Brit Pol) conservador(a) m(f)
toss [tɔs] vt tirar, echar; (head) sacudir ■ n
(movement: of head etc) sacudida; (of coin)
tirada, echada, (LAm); **to ~ a coin** echar a cara
o cruz; **to ~ up for sth** jugar algo a cara o
cruz; **to ~ and turn** (in bed) dar vueltas (en la
cama); **to win/lose the ~** (also Sport) ganar/
perder (a cara o cruz)
tot [tɔt] n (Brit: drink) copita; (child) nene(-a)
m(f)
▸ **tot up** vt sumar
total ['təʊtl] adj total, entero ■ n total
m, suma ■ vt (add up) sumar; (amount to)
ascender a; **grand ~** cantidad f total; (cost)
importe m total; **in ~** en total, en suma
totalitarian [təʊtælɪˈtɛərɪən] adj totalitario
totality [təʊˈtælɪtɪ] n totalidad f
total loss n siniestra total
totally ['təʊtəlɪ] adv totalmente
tote bag n bolsa
totem pole ['təʊtəm-] n poste m totémico
totter ['tɔtərˈ] vi tambalearse
touch [tʌtʃ] n (sense) tacto; (contact) contacto;
(Football) fuera de juego ■ vt tocar;
(emotionally) conmover; **a ~ of** (fig) una
pizca or un poquito de; **to get in ~ with sb**
ponerse en contacto con algn; **I'll be in ~** le
llamaré/escribiré; **to lose ~** (friends) perder
contacto; **to be out of ~ with events** no
estar al corriente (de los acontecimientos);
the personal ~ el toque personal; **to put
the finishing touches to sth** dar el último
toque a algo
▸ **touch on** vt fus (topic) aludir (brevemente) a
▸ **touch up** vt (paint) retocar
touch-and-go ['tʌtʃən'gəʊ] adj arriesgado
touchdown ['tʌtʃdaʊn] n aterrizaje m; (US
Football) ensayo
touched [tʌtʃt] adj conmovido; (col) chiflado
touchiness ['tʌtʃɪnɪs] n susceptibilidad f
touching ['tʌtʃɪŋ] adj conmovedor(a)
touchline ['tʌtʃlaɪn] n (Sport) línea de banda
touch screen n (Tech) pantalla táctil;
~ mobile móvil m con pantalla táctil;
~ technology technología táctil
touch-sensitive ['tʌtʃ'sɛnsɪtɪv] adj sensible
al tacto
touch-type ['tʌtʃtaɪp] vi mecanografiar al
tacto
touchy ['tʌtʃɪ] adj (person) quisquilloso
tough [tʌf] adj (meat) duro; (journey) penoso;
(task, problem, situation) difícil; (resistant)
resistente; (person) fuerte; (: pej) bruto ■ n
(gangster etc) gorila m; **they got ~ with the
workers** se pusieron muy duros con los
trabajadores

toughen ['tʌfn] vt endurecer
toughness ['tʌfnɪs] n dureza; (resistance)
resistencia; (strictness) inflexibilidad f
toupée ['tu:peɪ] n peluquín m
tour ['tʊərˈ] n viaje m; (also: **package tour**)
viaje m con todo incluido; (of town, museum)
visita ■ vt viajar por; **to go on a ~ of** (region,
country) ir de viaje por; (museum, castle) visitar;
to go on ~ partir or ir de gira
touring ['tʊərɪŋ] n viajes mpl turísticos,
turismo
tourism ['tʊərɪzm] n turismo
tourist ['tʊərɪst] n turista m/f ■ cpd turístico;
the ~ trade el turismo
tourist class n (Aviat) clase f turista
tourist office n oficina de turismo
tournament ['tʊənəmənt] n torneo
tourniquet ['tʊənɪkeɪ] n (Med) torniquete m
tour operator n touroperador(a) m(f),
operador(a) m(f) turístico(-a)
tousled ['tauzld] adj (hair) despeinado
tout [taut] vi: **to ~ for business** solicitar
clientes ■ n: **ticket ~** revendedor(a) m(f)
tow [təʊ] n: **to give sb a ~** (Aut) remolcar a
algn ■ vt remolcar; **"on** or (US) **in ~"** (Aut)
"a remolque"
toward [tə'wɔːd], **towards** [tə'wɔːdz] prep
hacia; (of attitude) respecto a, con; (of purpose)
para; **~(s) noon** alrededor de mediodía;
~(s) the end of the year hacia finales de
año; **to feel friendly ~(s) sb** sentir amistad
hacia algn
towel ['tauəl] n toalla; **to throw in the ~** (fig)
darse por vencido, renunciar
towelling ['tauəlɪŋ] n (fabric) felpa
towel rail, towel rack (US) n toallero
tower ['tauəˈ] n torre f ■ vi (building, mountain)
elevarse; **to ~ above** or **over sth/sb** dominar
algo/destacarse sobre algn
tower block n (Brit) bloque m de pisos
towering ['tauərɪŋ] adj muy alto, imponente
town [taun] n ciudad f; **to go to ~** ir a la
ciudad; (fig) tirar la casa por la ventana;
in the ~ en la ciudad; **to be out of ~** estar
fuera de la ciudad
town centre n centro de la ciudad
town clerk n secretario(-a) del
Ayuntamiento
town council n Ayuntamiento, consejo
municipal
town crier [-kraɪəˈ] n (Brit) pregonero
town hall n ayuntamiento
townie ['taunɪ] n (Brit col) persona de la
ciudad
town plan n plano de la ciudad
town planner n urbanista m/f
town planning n urbanismo

township ['taunʃɪp] n *municipio habitado sólo por negros en Sudáfrica*
townspeople ['taunzpiːpl] npl *gente f de ciudad*
towpath ['təupɑːθ] n *camino de sirga*
towrope ['təurəup] n *cable m de remolque*
tow truck n *(US) camión m grúa*
toxic ['tɒksɪk] adj *tóxico*
toxic asset n *(Econ) activo tóxico*
toxic bank n *(Econ) banco malo*
toxin ['tɒksɪn] n *toxina*
toy [tɔɪ] n *juguete m*
 ▶ **toy with** vt fus *jugar con; (idea) acariciar*
toyshop ['tɔɪʃɒp] n *juguetería*
trace [treɪs] n *rastro* ■ vt *(draw) trazar, delinear; (locate) encontrar;* **there was no ~ of it** *no había ningún indicio de ello*
trace element n *oligoelemento*
trachea [trə'kɪə] n *(Anat) tráquea*
tracing paper ['treɪsɪŋ-] n *papel m de calco*
track [træk] n *(mark) huella, pista; (path: gen) camino, senda; (: of bullet etc) trayectoria; (: of suspect, animal) pista, rastro; (Rail) vía; (Comput, Sport) pista; (on album) canción f* ■ vt *seguir la pista de;* **to keep ~ of** *mantenerse al tanto de, seguir;* **a four-~ tape** *una cinta de cuatro pistas;* **the first ~ on the record/tape** *la primera canción en el disco/la cinta;* **to be on the right ~** *(fig) ir por buen camino*
 ▶ **track down** vt *(person) localizar; (sth lost) encontrar*
tracker dog ['trækə-] n *(Brit) perro rastreador*
track events npl *(Sport) pruebas fpl en pista*
tracking station ['trækɪŋ-] n *(Space) estación f de seguimiento*
track meet n *(US) concurso de carreras y saltos*
track record n: **to have a good ~** *(fig) tener un buen historial*
tracksuit ['træksuːt] n *chandal m*
tract [trækt] n *(Geo) región f; (pamphlet) folleto*
traction ['trækʃən] n *(Aut: power) tracción f;* **in ~** *(Med) en tracción*
traction engine n *locomotora de tracción*
tractor ['træktər] n *tractor m*
trade [treɪd] n *comercio, negocio; (skill, job) oficio, empleo; (industry) industria* ■ vi *negociar, comerciar;* **foreign ~** *comercio exterior*
 ▶ **trade in** vt *(old car etc) ofrecer como parte del pago*
trade barrier n *barrera comercial*
trade deficit n *déficit m comercial*
Trade Descriptions Act n *(Brit) ley sobre descripciones comerciales*
trade discount n *descuento comercial*

trade fair n *feria de muestras*
trade-in ['treɪdɪn] adj: **~ price/value** *precio/valor de un artículo usado que se descuenta del precio de otro nuevo*
trademark ['treɪdmɑːk] n *marca de fábrica*
trade mission n *misión f comercial*
trade name n *marca registrada*
trade-off n: **a ~ (between)** *un equilibrio (entre)*
trade price n *precio al detallista*
trader ['treɪdər] n *comerciante m/f*
trade reference n *referencia comercial*
trade secret n *secreto profesional*
tradesman ['treɪdzmən] n *(shopkeeper) comerciante m/f*
trade union n *sindicato*
trade unionist [-'juːnjənɪst] n *sindicalista m/f*
trade wind n *viento alisio*
trading ['treɪdɪŋ] n *comercio*
trading account n *cuenta de compraventa*
trading estate n *(Brit) polígono industrial*
trading stamp n *cupón m, sello de prima*
tradition [trə'dɪʃən] n *tradición f*
traditional [trə'dɪʃənl] adj *tradicional*
traditionally [trə'dɪʃənlɪ] adv *tradicionalmente*
traffic ['træfɪk] n *tráfico, circulación f, tránsito* ■ vi: **to ~ in** *(pej: liquor, drugs) traficar en;* **air ~** *tráfico aéreo*
traffic calming [-'kɑːmɪŋ] n *reducción f de la velocidad de la circulación*
traffic circle n *(US) glorieta de tráfico*
traffic island n *refugio, isleta*
traffic jam n *embotellamiento, atasco*
trafficker ['træfɪkər] n *traficante m/f*
traffic lights npl *semáforo sg*
traffic offence, traffic violation *(US) n infracción f de tráfico*
traffic warden n *guardia m/f de tráfico*
tragedy ['trædʒədɪ] n *tragedia*
tragic ['trædʒɪk] adj *trágico*
tragically ['trædʒɪkəlɪ] adv *trágicamente*
trail [treɪl] n *(tracks) rastro, pista; (path) camino, sendero; (dust, smoke) estela* ■ vt *(drag) arrastrar; (follow) seguir la pista de; (follow closely) vigilar* ■ vi *arrastrarse;* **to be on sb's ~** *seguir la pista de algn*
 ▶ **trail away, trail off** vi *(sound) desvanecerse; (interest, voice) desaparecer*
 ▶ **trail behind** vi *quedar a la zaga*
trailer ['treɪlər] n *(Aut) remolque m; (caravan) caravana; (Cine) trailer m, avance m*
trailer truck n *(US) camión articulado m*
train [treɪn] n *(tracks) tren m; (of dress) cola; (series):* **~ of events** *curso de los acontecimientos* ■ vt *(educate) formar; (teach skills to) adiestrar;*

t

(*sportsman*) entrenar; (*dog*) amaestrar; (*point: gun etc*): **to ~ on** apuntar a ◼ *vi* (*Sport*) entrenarse; (*be educated, learn a skill*) formarse; **to go by ~** ir en tren; **one's ~ of thought** el razonamiento de algn; **to ~ sb to do sth** enseñar a algn a hacer algo

train attendant *n* (*US Rail*) empleado(-a) de coches-cama

trained [treɪnd] *adj* (*worker*) cualificado; (*animal*) amaestrado

trainee [treɪ'niː] *n* trabajador(a) *m(f)* en prácticas ◼ *cpd*: **he's a ~ teacher** (*primary*) es estudiante de magisterio; (*secondary*) está haciendo las prácticas del I.C.E.

trainer ['treɪnəʳ] *n* (*Sport*) entrenador(a) *m(f)*; (*of animals*) domador(a) *m(f)*; **trainers** *npl* (*shoes*) zapatillas *fpl* (de deporte)

training ['treɪnɪŋ] *n* formación *f*; entrenamiento; **to be in ~** (*Sport*) estar entrenando; (: *fit*) estar en forma

training college *n* (*gen*) colegio de formación profesional; (*for teachers*) escuela normal

training course *n* curso de formación

train wreck *n* (*fig*) destrozo; **he's a complete ~** está completamente destrozado

traipse [treɪps] *vi* andar penosamente

trait [treɪt] *n* rasgo

traitor ['treɪtəʳ] *n* traidor(a) *m(f)*

trajectory [trə'dʒɛktərɪ] *n* trayectoria, curso

tram [træm] *n* (*Brit: also*: **tramcar**) tranvía *m*

tramline ['træmlaɪn] *n* carril *m* de tranvía

tramp [træmp] *n* (*person*) vagabundo(-a); (*col: offensive: woman*) puta ◼ *vi* andar con pasos pesados

trample ['træmpl] *vt*: **to ~ (underfoot)** pisotear

trampoline ['træmpəliːn] *n* trampolín *m*

trance [trɑːns] *n* trance *m*; **to go into a ~** entrar en trance

tranquil ['træŋkwɪl] *adj* tranquilo

tranquillity, tranquility (*US*) [træŋ'kwɪlɪtɪ] *n* tranquilidad *f*

tranquillizer, tranquilizer (*US*) ['træŋkwɪlaɪzəʳ] *n* (*Med*) tranquilizante *m*

trans- [trænz] *pref* trans-, tras-

transact [træn'zækt] *vt* (*business*) tramitar

transaction [træn'zækʃən] *n* transacción *f*, operación *f*; **cash transactions** transacciones al contado

transatlantic ['trænzət'læntɪk] *adj* transatlántico

transcend [træn'sɛnd] *vt* rebasar

transcendental [trænsɛn'dɛntl] *adj*: **~ meditation** meditación *f* transcendental

transcribe [træn'skraɪb] *vt* transcribir, copiar

transcript ['trænskrɪpt] *n* copia

transcription [træn'skrɪpʃən] *n* transcripción *f*

transept ['trænsɛpt] *n* crucero

transfer *n* ['trænsfəʳ] transferencia; (*Sport*) traspaso; (*picture, design*) calcomanía ◼ *vt* [træns'fəːʳ] trasladar, pasar; **to ~ the charges** (*Brit Tel*) llamar a cobro revertido; **by bank ~** por transferencia bancaria *or* giro bancario; **to ~ money from one account to another** transferir dinero de una cuenta a otra; **to ~ sth to sb's name** transferir algo al nombre de algn

transferable [træns'fəːrəbl] *adj*: **not ~** intransferible

transfix [træns'fɪks] *vt* traspasar; (*fig*): **transfixed with fear** paralizado por el miedo

transform [træns'fɔːm] *vt* transformar

transformation [trænsfə'meɪʃən] *n* transformación *f*

transformer [træns'fɔːməʳ] *n* (*Elec*) transformador *m*

transfusion [træns'fjuːʒən] *n* transfusión *f*

transgress [træns'grɛs] *vt* (*go beyond*) traspasar; (*violate*) violar, infringir

tranship [træn'ʃɪp] *vt* trasbordar

transient ['trænzɪənt] *adj* transitorio

transistor [træn'zɪstəʳ] *n* (*Elec*) transistor *m*

transistorized [træn'zɪstəraɪzd] *adj* (*circuit*) transistorizado

transistor radio *n* transistor *m*

transit ['trænzɪt] *n*: **in ~** en tránsito

transit camp *n* campamento de tránsito

transition [træn'zɪʃən] *n* transición *f*

transitional [træn'zɪʃənl] *adj* transitorio

transition period *n* período de transición

transitive ['trænzɪtɪv] *adj* (*Ling*) transitivo

transitively ['trænzɪtɪvlɪ] *adv* transitivamente

transitory ['trænzɪtərɪ] *adj* transitorio

transit visa *n* visado de tránsito

translate [trænz'leɪt] *vt*: **to ~ (from/into)** traducir (de/a)

translation [trænz'leɪʃən] *n* traducción *f*

translator [trænz'leɪtəʳ] *n* traductor(a) *m(f)*

translucent [trænz'luːsnt] *adj* traslúcido

transmission [trænz'mɪʃən] *n* transmisión *f*

transmit [trænz'mɪt] *vt* transmitir

transmitter [trænz'mɪtəʳ] *n* transmisor *m*; (*station*) emisora

transparency [træns'pɛərnsɪ] *n* (*Brit Phot*) diapositiva

transparent [træns'pærnt] *adj* transparente

transpire [træns'paɪəʳ] *vi* (*turn out*) resultar (ser); (*happen*) ocurrir, suceder; (*become known*): **it finally transpired that ...** por fin se supo que ...

transplant vt [træns'plɑ:nt] transplantar
■ n ['trænsplɑ:nt] (Med) transplante m;
to have a heart ~ hacerse un transplante
de corazón

transport n ['trænspɔ:t] transporte m ■ vt
[træns'pɔ:t] transportar; **public ~** transporte
m público

transportable [træns'pɔ:təbl] adj
transportable

transportation [trænspɔ:'teɪʃən] n
transporte m; (of prisoners) deportación f

transport café n (Brit) bar-restaurante m de
carretera

transpose [træns'pəuz] vt transponer

transsexual [trænz'sɛksjuəl] adj, n
transexual m/f

transverse ['trænzvɔ:s] adj transverso,
transversal

transvestite [trænz'vɛstaɪt] n travestí m/f

trap [træp] n (snare, trick) trampa; (carriage)
cabriolé m ■ vt coger (SP) or agarrar (LAm)
en una trampa; (immobilize) bloquear; (jam)
atascar; **to set** or **lay a ~ (for sb)** poner(le)
una trampa (a algn); **to ~ one's finger in
the door** pillarse el dedo en la puerta

trap door n escotilla

trapeze [trə'pi:z] n trapecio

trapper ['træpər] n trampero, cazador m

trappings ['træpɪŋz] npl adornos mpl

trash [træʃ] n basura; (nonsense) tonterías fpl

trash can n (US) cubo, balde m (LAm) or bote m
(LAm) de la basura

trash can liner n (US) bolsa de basura

trashy ['træʃɪ] adj (col) chungo

trauma ['trɔ:mə] n trauma m

traumatic [trɔ:'mætɪk] adj traumático

travel ['trævl] n viaje m ■ vi viajar ■ vt
(distance) recorrer; **this wine doesn't ~ well**
este vino pierde con los viajes

travel agency n agencia de viajes

travel agent n agente m/f de viajes

travel brochure n folleto turístico

traveller, traveler (US) ['trævlər] n
viajero(-a); (Comm) viajante m/f

traveller's cheque, traveler's check (US) n
cheque m de viaje

travelling, traveling (US) ['trævlɪŋ] n
los viajes, el viajar ■ adj (circus, exhibition)
ambulante ■ cpd (bag, clock) de viaje

travelling expenses, traveling expenses
(US) npl dietas fpl

travelling salesman, traveling salesman
(US) n viajante m

travelogue ['trævəlɒg] n (book) relación f de
viajes; (film) documental m de viajes; (talk)
recuento de viajes

travel sickness n mareo

traverse ['trævəs] vt atravesar

travesty ['trævəstɪ] n parodia

trawler ['trɔ:lər] n pesquero de arrastre

tray [treɪ] n (for carrying) bandeja; (on desk)
cajón m

treacherous ['trɛtʃərəs] adj traidor(a); **road
conditions are ~** el estado de las carreteras
es peligroso

treachery ['trɛtʃərɪ] n traición f

treacle ['tri:kl] n (Brit) melaza

tread [trɛd] n paso, pisada; (of tyre) banda de
rodadura ■ vi (pt **trod**, pp **trodden**) [trɒd,
'trɒdn] pisar
▶ **tread on** vt fus pisar

treas. abbr = **treasurer**

treason ['tri:zn] n traición f

treasure ['trɛʒər] n tesoro ■ vt (value)
apreciar, valorar

treasure hunt n caza del tesoro

treasurer ['trɛʒərər] n tesorero(-a)

treasury ['trɛʒərɪ] n: **the T~**, (US) **the T~
Department** = el Ministerio de Economía y
de Hacienda

treasury bill n bono del Tesoro

treat [tri:t] n (present) regalo; (pleasure) placer
m ■ vt tratar; (consider) considerar; **to give
sb a ~** hacer un regalo a algn; **to ~ sb to
sth** invitar a algn a algo; **to ~ sth as a joke**
tomar algo a broma

treatise ['tri:tɪz] n tratado

treatment ['tri:tmənt] n tratamiento; **to
have ~ for sth** recibir tratamiento por algo

treaty ['tri:tɪ] n tratado

treble ['trɛbl] adj triple ■ vt triplicar ■ vi
triplicarse

treble clef n (Mus) clave f de sol

tree [tri:] n árbol m

tree-lined ['tri:laɪnd] adj bordeado de árboles

tree trunk n tronco de árbol

trek [trɛk] n (long journey) expedición f; (tiring
walk) caminata

trellis ['trɛlɪs] n enrejado

tremble ['trɛmbl] vi temblar

trembling ['trɛmblɪŋ] n temblor m ■ adj
tembloroso

tremendous [trɪ'mɛndəs] adj tremendo;
(enormous) enorme; (excellent) estupendo

tremendously [trɪ'mɛndəslɪ] adv
enormemente, sobremanera; **he enjoyed it
~** lo disfrutó de lo lindo

tremor ['trɛmər] n temblor m; (also: **earth
tremor**) temblor m de tierra

trench [trɛntʃ] n zanja; (Mil) trinchera

trench coat n trinchera

trench warfare n guerra de trincheras

trend [trɛnd] n (tendency) tendencia; (of events)
curso; (fashion) moda; **~ towards/away from**

t

sth tendencia hacia/en contra de algo; **to set the ~** marcar la pauta

trendy ['trɛndɪ] *adj* de moda

trepidation [trɛpɪ'deɪʃən] *n* inquietud *f*

trespass ['trɛspəs] *vi*: **to ~ on** entrar sin permiso en; **"no trespassing"** "prohibido el paso"

trespasser ['trɛspəsəʳ] *n* intruso(-a) *m(f)*; **"trespassers will be prosecuted"** "se procesará a los intrusos"

tress [trɛs] *n* guedeja

trestle ['trɛsl] *n* caballete *m*

trestle table *n* mesa de caballete

tri- [traɪ] *pref* tri-

trial ['traɪəl] *n* (*Law*) juicio, proceso; (*test: of machine etc*) prueba; (*hardship*) desgracia; **trials** *npl* (*Athletics*) pruebas *fpl*; (*of horses*) pruebas *fpl*; **to bring sb to ~ (for a crime)** llevar a algn a juicio (por un delito); **~ by jury** juicio ante jurado; **to be sent for ~** ser remitido al tribunal; **by ~ and error** a fuerza de probar

trial balance *n* balance *m* de comprobación

trial basis *n*: **on a ~** a modo de prueba

trial offer *n* oferta de prueba

trial run *n* prueba

triangle ['traɪæŋgl] *n* (*Math, Mus*) triángulo

triangular [traɪ'æŋgjuləʳ] *adj* triangular

triathlon [traɪ'æθlən] *n* triatlón *m*

tribal ['traɪbəl] *adj* tribal

tribe [traɪb] *n* tribu *f*

tribesman ['traɪbzmən] *n* miembro de una tribu

tribulation [trɪbju'leɪʃən] *n* tribulación *f*

tribunal [traɪ'bju:nl] *n* tribunal *m*

tributary ['trɪbju:tərɪ] *n* (*river*) afluente *m*

tribute ['trɪbju:t] *n* homenaje *m*, tributo; **to pay ~ to** rendir homenaje a

trice [traɪs] *n*: **in a ~** en un santiamén

trick [trɪk] *n* trampa; (*conjuring trick, deceit*) truco; (*joke*) broma; (*Cards*) baza ■ *vt* engañar; **it's a ~ of the light** es una ilusión óptica; **to play a ~ on sb** gastar una broma a algn; **that should do the ~** eso servirá; **to ~ sb out of sth** quitarle algo a algn con engaños; **to ~ sb into doing sth** hacer que algn haga algo con engaños

trickery ['trɪkərɪ] *n* engaño

trickle ['trɪkl] *n* (*of water etc*) hilo ■ *vi* gotear

trick question *n* pregunta capciosa

trickster ['trɪkstəʳ] *n* estafador(a) *m(f)*

tricky ['trɪkɪ] *adj* difícil; (*problem*) delicado

tricycle ['traɪsɪkl] *n* triciclo

tried [traɪd] *adj* probado

trifle ['traɪfl] *n* bagatela; (*Culin*) *dulce de bizcocho, gelatina, fruta y natillas* ■ *adv*: **a ~ long** un pelín largo ■ *vi*: **to ~ with** jugar con

trifling ['traɪflɪŋ] *adj* insignificante

trigger ['trɪgəʳ] *n* (*of gun*) gatillo
► **trigger off** *vt* desencadenar

trigonometry [trɪgə'nɔmətrɪ] *n* trigonometría

trilby ['trɪlbɪ] *n* (*also:* **trilby hat**) sombrero flexible *or* tirolés

trill [trɪl] *n* (*of bird*) gorjeo; (*Mus*) trino

trilogy ['trɪlədʒɪ] *n* trilogía

trim [trɪm] *adj* (*elegant*) aseado; (*house, garden*) en buen estado; (*figure*): **to be ~** tener buen talle ■ *n* (*haircut etc*) recorte *m* ■ *vt* (*neaten*) arreglar; (*cut*) recortar; (*decorate*) adornar; (*Naut: a sail*) orientar; **to keep in (good) ~** mantener en buen estado

trimmings ['trɪmɪŋz] *npl* (*extras*) accesorios *mpl*; (*cuttings*) recortes *mpl*

Trinidad and Tobago ['trɪnɪdæd-] *n* Trinidad *f* y Tobago

Trinity ['trɪnɪtɪ] *n*: **the ~** la Trinidad

trinket ['trɪŋkɪt] *n* chuchería, baratija

trio ['tri:əu] *n* trío

trip [trɪp] *n* viaje *m*; (*excursion*) excursión *f*; (*stumble*) traspié *m* ■ *vi* (*stumble*) tropezar; (*go lightly*) andar a paso ligero; **on a ~** de viaje
► **trip over** *vt fus* tropezar con
► **trip up** *vi* tropezar, caerse ■ *vt* hacer tropezar *or* caer

tripartite [traɪ'pɑ:taɪt] *adj* (*agreement, talks*) tripartito

tripe [traɪp] *n* (*Culin*) callos *mpl*; (*pej: rubbish*) bobadas *fpl*

triple ['trɪpl] *adj* triple ■ *adv*: **~ the distance/the speed** 3 veces la distancia/la velocidad

triple jump *n* triple salto

triplets ['trɪplɪts] *npl* trillizos(-as) *m(f)pl*

triplicate ['trɪplɪkət] *n*: **in ~** por triplicado

tripod ['traɪpɔd] *n* trípode *m*

Tripoli ['trɪpəlɪ] *n* Trípoli *m*

tripper ['trɪpəʳ] *n* turista *m/f*, excursionista *m/f*

tripwire ['trɪpwaɪəʳ] *n* cable *m* de trampa

trite [traɪt] *adj* trillado

triumph ['traɪʌmf] *n* triunfo ■ *vi*: **to ~ (over)** vencer

triumphal [traɪ'ʌmfl] *adj* triunfal

triumphant [traɪ'ʌmfənt] *adj* triunfante

triumphantly [traɪ'ʌmfəntlɪ] *adv* triunfalmente, en tono triunfal

trivia ['trɪvɪə] *npl* trivialidades *fpl*

trivial ['trɪvɪəl] *adj* insignificante, trivial

triviality [trɪvɪ'ælɪtɪ] *n* insignificancia, trivialidad *f*

trivialize ['trɪvɪəlaɪz] *vt* trivializar

trod [trɔd] *pt of* **tread**

trodden ['trɔdn] *pp of* **tread**

trolley ['trɔlɪ] *n* carrito; (*in hospital*) camilla

trolley bus n trolebús m
trombone [trɔm'bəun] n trombón m
troop [truːp] n grupo, banda; *see also* **troops**
▶ **troop in** vi entrar en tropel
▶ **troop out** vi salir en tropel
troop carrier n (*plane*) transporte m
(militar); (*Naut: also*: **troopship**) (buque m de)
transporte m
trooper ['truːpəʳ] n (*Mil*) soldado (de
caballería); (*US: policeman*) policía m/f
montado(-a)
trooping the colour ['truːpɪŋ-] n (*ceremony*)
presentación f de la bandera
troopship ['truːpʃɪp] n (buque m de)
transporte m
trophy ['trəufɪ] n trofeo
tropic ['trɔpɪk] n trópico; **the tropics** los
trópicos, la zona tropical; **T- of Cancer/
Capricorn** trópico de Cáncer/Capricornio
tropical ['trɔpɪkl] adj tropical
trot [trɔt] n trote m ▪ vi trotar; **on the ~**
(*Brit fig*) seguidos(-as)
▶ **trot out** vt (*excuse, reason*) volver a usar;
(*names, facts*) sacar a relucir
trouble ['trʌbl] n problema m, dificultad
f; (*worry*) preocupación f; (*bother, effort*)
molestia, esfuerzo; (*unrest*) inquietud f;
(*with machine etc*) fallo, avería; (*Med*):
stomach ~ problemas mpl gástricos ▪ vt
molestar; (*worry*) preocupar, inquietar ▪ vi:
to ~ to do sth molestarse en hacer algo;
troubles npl (*Pol etc*) conflictos mpl; **to be
in ~** estar en un apuro; (*for doing wrong*) tener
problemas; **to have ~ doing sth** tener
dificultad en or para hacer algo; **to go to the
~ of doing sth** tomarse la molestia de hacer
algo; **what's the ~?** ¿qué pasa?; **the ~ is ...**
el problema es ..., lo que pasa es ...; **please
don't ~ yourself** por favor no se moleste
troubled ['trʌbld] adj (*person*) preocupado;
(*epoch, life*) agitado
trouble-free ['trʌblfriː] adj sin problemas or
dificultades
troublemaker ['trʌblmeɪkəʳ] n agitador(a)
m(f)
troubleshooter ['trʌblʃuːtəʳ] n (*in conflict*)
mediador(a) m(f)
troublesome ['trʌblsəm] adj molesto,
inoportuno
trouble spot n centro de fricción, punto
caliente
troubling ['trʌblɪŋ] adj (*thought*) preocupante;
these are ~ times son malos tiempos
trough [trɔf] n (*also*: **drinking trough**)
abrevadero; (*also*: **feeding trough**) comedero;
(*channel*) canal m
trounce [trauns] vt dar una paliza a

troupe [truːp] n grupo
trouser press n prensa para pantalones
trousers ['trauzəz] npl pantalones mpl; **short
~** pantalones mpl cortos
trouser suit n traje m de chaqueta y pantalón
trousseau (*pl* **trousseaux** or **trousseaus**)
['truːsəu, -z] n ajuar m
trout [traut] n (*pl inv*) trucha
trowel ['trauəl] n paleta
truant ['truənt] n: **to play ~** (*Brit*) hacer
novillos
truce [truːs] n tregua
truck [trʌk] n (*US*) camión m; (*Rail*) vagón m
truck driver n camionero(-a)
trucker ['trʌkəʳ] n (*esp US*) camionero(-a)
truck farm n (*US*) huerto de hortalizas
trucking ['trʌkɪŋ] n (*esp US*) transporte m en
camión
trucking company n (*US*) compañía de
transporte por carretera
truckload ['trʌkləud] n camión m lleno
truculent ['trʌkjulənt] adj agresivo
trudge [trʌdʒ] vi caminar penosamente
true [truː] adj verdadero; (*accurate*) exacto;
(*genuine*) auténtico; (*faithful*) fiel; (*wheel*)
centrado; (*wall*) a plomo; (*beam*) alineado;
~ to life verídico; **to come ~** realizarse,
cumplirse
truffle ['trʌfl] n trufa
truly ['truːlɪ] adv realmente; (*faithfully*)
fielmente; **yours ~** (*in letter-writing*)
atentamente
trump [trʌmp] n (*Cards*) triunfo; **to turn up
trumps** (*fig*) salir or resultar bien
trump card n triunfo; (*fig*) baza
trumped-up ['trʌmptʌp] adj inventado
trumpet ['trʌmpɪt] n trompeta
truncated [trʌŋ'keɪtɪd] adj truncado
truncheon ['trʌntʃən] n (*Brit*) porra
trundle ['trʌndl] vt, vi: **to ~ along** rodar
haciendo ruido
trunk [trʌŋk] n (*of tree, person*) tronco; (*of
elephant*) trompa; (*case*) baúl m; (*US Aut*)
maletero, baúl m (*LAm*); *see also* **trunks**
trunk call n (*Brit Tel*) llamada interurbana
trunk road n carretera principal
trunks [trʌŋks] npl (*also*: **swimming trunks**)
bañador m
truss [trʌs] n (*Med*) braguero ▪ vt: **to ~ (up)**
atar
trust [trʌst] n confianza; (*Comm*) trust
m; (*Law*) fideicomiso ▪ vt (*rely on*) tener
confianza en; (*entrust*): **to ~ sth to sb** confiar
algo a algn; (*hope*): **to ~ (that)** esperar (que);
in ~ en fideicomiso; **you'll have to take it
on ~** tienes que aceptarlo a ojos cerrados
trust company n banco fideicomisario

t

837

trusted ['trʌstɪd] *adj* de confianza, fiable, de fiar

trustee [trʌs'tiː] *n* (*Law*) fideicomisario

trustful ['trʌstful] *adj* confiado

trust fund *n* fondo fiduciario *or* de fideicomiso

trusting ['trʌstɪŋ] *adj* confiado

trustworthy ['trʌstwəːðɪ] *adj* digno de confianza, fiable, de fiar

trusty ['trʌstɪ] *adj* fiel

truth, truths [truːθ, truːðz] *n* verdad *f*

truthful ['truːθfəl] *adj* (*person*) sincero; (*account*) fidedigno

truthfully ['truːθfulɪ] *adv* (*answer*) con sinceridad

truthfulness ['truːθfulnɪs] *n* (*of account*) verdad *f*; (*of person*) sinceridad *f*

try [traɪ] *n* tentativa, intento; (*Rugby*) ensayo ■ *vt* (*Law*) juzgar, procesar; (*test: sth new*) probar, someter a prueba; (*attempt*) intentar; (*strain: patience*) hacer perder ■ *vi* probar; **to give sth a ~** intentar hacer algo; **to ~ one's (very) best** *or* **hardest** poner todo su empeño, esmerarse; **to ~ to do sth** intentar hacer algo

▸ **try on** *vt* (*clothes*) probarse

▸ **try out** *vt* probar, poner a prueba

trying ['traɪɪŋ] *adj* cansado; (*person*) pesado

tsar [zaːʳ] *n* zar *m*

T-shirt ['tiːʃəːt] *n* camiseta

TSO *n abbr* (*Brit*) = **The Stationery Office**

T-square ['tiːskwɛəʳ] *n* regla en T

tsunami [tsʊ'naːmɪ] *n* tsunami *m*

TT *adj abbr* (*Brit col*) = **teetotal** ■ *abbr* (*US*) = **Trust Territory**

tub [tʌb] *n* cubo (*SP*), balde *m* (*LAm*); (*bath*) bañera, tina (*LAm*)

tuba ['tjuːbə] *n* tuba

tubby ['tʌbɪ] *adj* regordete

tube [tjuːb] *n* tubo; (*Brit: underground*) metro; (*US col: television*) tele *f*

tubeless ['tjuːblɪs] *adj* (*tyre*) sin cámara

tuber ['tjuːbəʳ] *n* (*Bot*) tubérculo

tuberculosis [tjubəːkjuˈləusɪs] *n* tuberculosis *f inv*

tube station *n* (*Brit*) estación *f* de metro

tubing ['tjuːbɪŋ] *n* tubería (*SP*), cañería; **a piece of ~** un trozo de tubo

tubular ['tjuːbjuləʳ] *adj* tubular

TUC *n abbr* (*Brit*: = *Trades Union Congress*) *federación nacional de sindicatos*

tuck [tʌk] *n* (*Sewing*) pliegue *m* ■ *vt* (*put*) poner

▸ **tuck away** *vt* esconder

▸ **tuck in** *vt* meter; (*child*) arropar ■ *vi* (*eat*) comer con apetito

▸ **tuck up** *vt* (*child*) arropar

tuck shop *n* (*Scol*) tienda de golosinas

Tue., Tues. *abbr* (= *Tuesday*) mart

Tuesday ['tjuːzdɪ] *n* martes *m inv*; **on ~** el martes; **on Tuesdays** los martes; **every ~** todos los martes; **every other ~** cada dos martes, un martes sí y otro no; **last/next ~** el martes pasado/próximo; **a week/fortnight on ~, ~ week/fortnight** del martes en 8/15 días, del martes en una semana/dos semanas

tuft [tʌft] *n* mechón *m*; (*of grass etc*) manojo

tug [tʌg] *n* (*ship*) remolcador *m* ■ *vt* remolcar

tug-of-love [tʌgəv'lʌv] *n*: **~ children** hijos envueltos en el litigio de los padres por su custodia

tug-of-war [tʌgəv'wɔːʳ] *n* juego de la cuerda

tuition [tjuːˈɪʃən] *n* (*Brit*) enseñanza; (: *private tuition*) clases *fpl* particulares; (*US: school fees*) matrícula

tulip ['tjuːlɪp] *n* tulipán *m*

tumble ['tʌmbl] *n* (*fall*) caída ■ *vi* caerse, tropezar; **to ~ to sth** (*col*) caer en la cuenta de algo

tumbledown ['tʌmbldaun] *adj* ruinoso

tumble dryer *n* (*Brit*) secadora

tumbler ['tʌmbləʳ] *n* vaso

tummy ['tʌmɪ] *n* (*col*) barriga, vientre *m*

tumour, tumor (*US*) ['tjuːməʳ] *n* tumor *m*

tumult ['tjuːmʌlt] *n* tumulto

tumultuous [tjuːˈmʌltjuəs] *adj* tumultuoso

tuna ['tjuːnə] *n* (*pl inv: also*: **tuna fish**) atún *m*

tundra ['tʌndrə] *n* tundra

tune [tjuːn] *n* (*melody*) melodía ■ *vt* (*Mus*) afinar; (*Radio, TV, Aut*) sintonizar; **to be in/out of ~** (*instrument*) estar afinado/desafinado; (*singer*) afinar/desafinar; **to be in/out of ~ with** (*fig*) armonizar/desentonar con; **to the ~ of** (*fig: amount*) por (la) cantidad de

▸ **tune in** *vi* (*Radio, TV*): **to ~ in (to)** sintonizar (con)

▸ **tune up** *vi* (*musician*) afinar (su instrumento)

tuneful ['tjuːnful] *adj* melodioso

tuner ['tjuːnəʳ] *n* (*radio set*) sintonizador *m*; **piano ~** afinador(a) *m(f)* de pianos

tungsten ['tʌŋstn] *n* tungsteno

tunic ['tjuːnɪk] *n* túnica

tuning ['tjuːnɪŋ] *n* sintonización *f*; (*Mus*) afinación *f*

tuning fork *n* diapasón *m*

Tunis ['tjuːnɪs] *n* Túnez *m*

Tunisia [tjuːˈnɪzɪə] *n* Túnez *m*

Tunisian [tjuːˈnɪzɪən] *adj, n* tunecino(-a) *m(f)*

tunnel ['tʌnl] *n* túnel *m*; (*in mine*) galería ■ *vi* construir un túnel/una galería

tunnel vision *n* (*Med*) visión *f* periférica restringida; (*fig*) estrechez *f* de miras

tunny ['tʌnɪ] *n* atún *m*
turban ['tɜ:bən] *n* turbante *m*
turbid ['tɜ:bɪd] *adj* turbio
turbine ['tɜ:baɪn] *n* turbina
turbo ['tɜ:bəu] *n* turbo
turboprop ['tɜ:bəuprɔp] *n* turbohélice *m*
turbot ['tɜ:bət] *n* (*pl inv*) rodaballo
turbulence ['tɜ:bjuləns] *n* (*Aviat*) turbulencia
turbulent ['tɜ:bjulənt] *adj* turbulento
tureen [tə'ri:n] *n* sopera
turf [tɜ:f] *n* césped *m*; (*clod*) tepe *m* ▪ *vt* cubrir con césped
  ▸ **turf out** *vt* (*col*) echar a la calle
turf accountant *n* corredor(a) *m(f)* de apuestas
turgid ['tɜ:dʒɪd] *adj* (*prose*) pesado
Turin [tjuə'rɪn] *n* Turín *m*
Turk [tɜ:k] *n* turco(-a)
Turkey ['tɜ:kɪ] *n* Turquía
turkey ['tɜ:kɪ] *n* pavo
Turkish ['tɜ:kɪʃ] *adj* turco ▪ *n* (*Ling*) turco
Turkish bath *n* baño turco
turmeric ['tɜ:mərɪk] *n* cúrcuma
turmoil ['tɜ:mɔɪl] *n* desorden *m*, alboroto
turn [tɜ:n] *n* turno; (*in road*) curva; (*Theat*) número; (*Med*) ataque *m* ▪ *vt* girar, volver, voltear (*LAm*); (*collar, steak*) dar la vuelta a; (*shape: wood, metal*) tornear; (*change*): **to ~ sth into** convertir algo en ▪ *vi* volver, voltearse (*LAm*); (*person: look back*) volverse; (*reverse direction*) dar la vuelta, voltear (*LAm*); (*milk*) cortarse; (*change*) cambiar; (*become*): **to ~ into sth** convertirse or transformarse en algo; **a good ~** un favor; **it gave me quite a ~** me dio un susto; **"no left ~"** (*Aut*) "prohibido girar a la izquierda"; **it's your ~** te toca a ti; **in ~** por turnos; **to take turns** turnarse; **at the ~ of the year/century** a fin de año/a finales de siglo; **to take a ~ for the worse** (*situation, patient*) empeorar; **they turned him against us** le pusieron en contra nuestra; **the car turned the corner** el coche dobló la esquina; **to ~ left** (*Aut*) torcer or girar a la izquierda; **she has no-one to ~ to** no tiene a quién recurrir
  ▸ **turn away** *vi* apartar la vista ▪ *vt* (*reject: person, business*) rechazar
  ▸ **turn back** *vi* volverse atrás
  ▸ **turn down** *vt* (*refuse*) rechazar; (*reduce*) bajar; (*fold*) doblar
  ▸ **turn in** *vi* (*col: go to bed*) acostarse ▪ *vt* (*fold*) doblar hacia dentro
  ▸ **turn off** *vi* (*from road*) desviarse ▪ *vt* (*light, radio etc*) apagar; (*engine*) parar
  ▸ **turn on** *vt* (*light, radio etc*) encender, prender (*LAm*); (*engine*) poner en marcha
  ▸ **turn out** *vt* (*light, gas*) apagar; (*produce: goods, novel etc*) producir ▪ *vi* (*attend: troops*)

presentarse; (: *doctor*) atender; **to ~ out to be ... resultar ser ...**
  ▸ **turn over** *vi* (*person*) volverse ▪ *vt* (*mattress, card*) dar la vuelta a; (*page*) volver
  ▸ **turn round** *vi* volverse; (*rotate*) girar
  ▸ **turn to** *vt fus*: **to ~ to sb** acudir a algn
  ▸ **turn up** *vi* (*person*) llegar, presentarse; (*lost object*) aparecer ▪ *vt* (*radio*) subir, poner más alto; (*heat, gas*) poner más fuerte
turnabout ['tɜ:nəbaut], **turnaround** ['tɜ:nəraund] *n* (*fig*) giro total
turncoat ['tɜ:nkəut] *n* renegado(-a)
turned-up ['tɜ:ndʌp] *adj* (*nose*) respingón(-ona)
turning ['tɜ:nɪŋ] *n* (*side road*) bocacalle *f*; (*bend*) curva; **the first ~ on the right** la primera bocacalle a la derecha
turning point *n* (*fig*) momento decisivo
turnip ['tɜ:nɪp] *n* nabo
turnkey system ['tɜ:nki:-] *n* (*Comput*) sistema *m* de seguridad
turnout ['tɜ:naut] *n* asistencia, número de asistentes, público
turnover ['tɜ:nəuvəʳ] *n* (*Comm: amount of money*) facturación *f*; (*of goods*) movimiento; **there is a rapid ~ in staff** hay mucho movimiento de personal
turnpike ['tɜ:npaɪk] *n* (*US*) autopista de peaje
turnstile ['tɜ:nstaɪl] *n* torniquete *m*
turntable ['tɜ:nteɪbl] *n* plato
turn-up ['tɜ:nʌp] *n* (*Brit: on trousers*) vuelta
turpentine ['tɜ:pəntaɪn] *n* (*also*: **turps**) trementina
turquoise ['tɜ:kwɔɪz] *n* (*stone*) turquesa ▪ *adj* color turquesa
turret ['tʌrɪt] *n* torreón *m*
turtle ['tɜ:tl] *n* tortuga (marina)
turtleneck ['tɜ:tlnɛk], **turtleneck sweater** *n* (jersey *m* de) cuello cisne
Tuscany ['tʌskənɪ] *n* Toscana
tusk [tʌsk] *n* colmillo
tussle ['tʌsl] *n* lucha, pelea
tutor ['tju:təʳ] *n* profesor(a) *m(f)*
tutorial [tju:'tɔ:rɪəl] *n* (*Scol*) seminario
tuxedo [tʌk'si:dəu] *n* (*US*) smóking *m*, esmoquin *m*
TV [ti:'vi:] *n abbr* (= *television*) televisión *f*
TV dinner *n* cena precocinada
TV licence *n* licencia que se paga por el uso del televisor, destinada a financiar la BBC
twaddle ['twɔdl] *n* (*col*) tonterías *fpl*
twang [twæŋ] *n* (*of instrument*) tañido; (*of voice*) timbre *m* nasal
tweak [twi:k] *vt* (*nose, ear*) pellizcar; (*hair*) tirar
tweed [twi:d] *n* tweed *m*
tweezers ['twi:zəz] *npl* pinzas *fpl* (de depilar)

t

839

twelfth [twɛlfθ] *num* duodécimo
Twelfth Night *n* (Día *m* de) Reyes *mpl*
twelve [twɛlv] *num* doce; **at ~ o'clock**
(*midday*) a mediodía; (*midnight*) a medianoche
twentieth ['twɛntɪɪθ] *num* vigésimo
twenty ['twɛntɪ] *num* veinte
twerp [twə:p] *n* (*col*) idiota *m/f*
twice [twaɪs] *adv* dos veces; **~ as much** dos
veces más, el doble; **she is ~ your age** ella
te dobla edad; **~ a week** dos veces a la *or* por
semana
twiddle ['twɪdl] *vt, vi:* **to ~ (with) sth** dar
vueltas a algo; **to ~ one's thumbs** (*fig*) estar
de brazos cruzados
twig [twɪg] *n* ramita ▪ *vi* (*col*) caer en la
cuenta
twilight ['twaɪlaɪt] *n* crepúsculo; (*morning*)
madrugada; **in the ~** en la media luz
twill [twɪl] *n* sarga, estameña
twin [twɪn] *adj, n* gemelo(-a) *m(f)* ▪ *vt*
hermanar
twin-bedded room ['twɪn'bɛdɪd-] *n* = **twin
room**
twin beds *npl* camas *fpl* gemelas
twin-carburettor ['twɪnkɑːbjuˈrɛtəᵣ] *adj* de
dos carburadores
twine [twaɪn] *n* bramante *m* ▪ *vi* (*plant*)
enroscarse
twin-engined [twɪn'ɛndʒɪnd] *adj* bimotor;
~ aircraft avión *m* bimotor
twinge [twɪndʒ] *n* (*of pain*) punzada; (*of
conscience*) remordimiento
twinkle ['twɪŋkl] *n* centelleo ▪ *vi* centellear;
(*eyes*) parpadear
twin room *n* habitación *f* con dos camas
twin town *n* ciudad *f* hermanada *or* gemela
twirl [twə:l] *n* giro ▪ *vt* dar vueltas a ▪ *vi*
piruetear
twist [twɪst] *n* (*action*) torsión *f*; (*in road, coil*)
vuelta; (*in wire, flex*) doblez *f*; (*in story*) giro
▪ *vt* torcer, retorcer; (*roll around*) enrollar; (*fig*)
deformar ▪ *vi* serpentear; **to ~ one's ankle/
wrist** (*Med*) torcerse el tobillo/la muñeca
twisted ['twɪstɪd] *adj* (*wire, rope*) trenzado,
enroscado; (*ankle, wrist*) torcido; (*fig: logic,
mind*) retorcido
twit [twɪt] *n* (*col*) tonto
twitch [twɪtʃ] *n* sacudida; (*nervous*) tic *m*
nervioso ▪ *vi* moverse nerviosamente
Twitter® ['twɪtəᵣ] *n* Twitter® *m* ▪ *vi*
conectarse a Twitter
two [tu:] *num* dos; **~ by ~, in twos** de dos en
dos; **to put ~ and ~ together** (*fig*) atar cabos
two-bit [tu:'bɪt] *adj* (*esp US: col, pej*) de poca
monta, de tres al cuarto
two-door [tu:'dɔːᵣ] *adj* (*Aut*) de dos puertas

two-faced [tu:'feɪst] *adj* (*pej: person*) falso,
hipócrita
twofold ['tu:fəuld] *adv:* **to increase ~**
duplicarse ▪ *adj* (*increase*) doble; (*reply*) en
dos partes
two-piece [tu:'pi:s] *n* (*also:* **two-piece suit**)
traje *m* de dos piezas; (*also:* **two-piece
swimsuit**) dos piezas *m inv*, bikini *m*
two-seater [tu:'si:təᵣ] *n* (*plane, car*) avión *m/*
coche *m* de dos plazas, biplaza *m*
twosome ['tu:səm] *n* (*people*) pareja
two-stroke ['tu:strəuk] *n* (*also:* **two-stroke
engine**) motor *m* de dos tiempos ▪ *adj* de dos
tiempos
two-tone ['tu:təun] *adj* (*colour*) bicolor, de
dos tonos
two-way ['tu:weɪ] *adj:* **~ traffic** circulación
f de dos sentidos; **~ radio** radio *f* emisora y
receptora
TX *abbr* (*US*) = **Texas**
tycoon [taɪ'ku:n] *n:* **(business) ~** magnate
m/f
type [taɪp] *n* (*category*) tipo, género; (*model*)
modelo; (*Typ*) tipo, letra ▪ *vt* (*letter etc*)
escribir a máquina; **what ~ do you want?**
¿qué tipo quieres?; **in bold/italic ~** en
negrita/cursiva
type-cast ['taɪpkɑːst] *adj* (*actor*) encasillado
typeface ['taɪpfeɪs] *n* tipo de letra
typescript ['taɪpskrɪpt] *n* texto
mecanografiado
typeset ['taɪpset] *vt* (*irreg: like* **set**) componer
typesetter ['taɪpsetəᵣ] *n* cajista *m/f*
typewriter ['taɪpraɪtəᵣ] *n* máquina de
escribir
typewritten ['taɪprɪtn] *adj* mecanografiado
typhoid ['taɪfɔɪd] *n* (fiebre *f*) tifoidea
typhoon [taɪ'fu:n] *n* tifón *m*
typhus ['taɪfəs] *n* tifus *m*
typical ['tɪpɪkl] *adj* típico
typically ['tɪpɪklɪ] *adv* típicamente
typify ['tɪpɪfaɪ] *vt* tipificar
typing ['taɪpɪŋ] *n* mecanografía
typing pool *n* (*Brit*) servicio de mecanógrafos
typist ['taɪpɪst] *n* mecanógrafo(-a)
typography [taɪ'pɔgrəfɪ] *n* tipografía
tyranny ['tɪrənɪ] *n* tiranía
tyrant ['taɪərənt] *n* tirano(-a)
tyre, tire (*US*) ['taɪəᵣ] *n* neumático, llanta
(*LAm*)
tyre pressure *n* presión *f* de los neumáticos
Tyrol [tɪ'rəul] *n* Tirol *m*
Tyrolean [tɪrə'lɪən], **Tyrolese** [tɪrə'li:z] *adj*
tirolés(-esa)
Tyrrhenian Sea [tɪ'ri:nɪən-] *n* Mar *m* Tirreno
tzar [zɑːᵣ] *n* = **tsar**

Uu

U, u [ju:] *n* (*letter*) U, u *f*; **U for Uncle** U de
Uruguay

U *n abbr* (*Brit Cine*: = *universal*) todos los públicos

UAW *n abbr* (*US*) = **United Automobile
Workers**

UB40 *n abbr* (*Brit*: = *unemployment benefit form 40*)
número de referencia en la solicitud de inscripción en
la lista de parados por extensión, la tarjeta del paro o
su beneficiario

U-bend ['ju:bɛnd] *n* recodo

ubiquitous [ju:'bɪkwɪtəs] *adj* omnipresente,
ubicuo

UCAS ['ju:kæs] *n abbr* (*Brit*) = **Universities and
Colleges Admissions Service**

UDA *n abbr* (*Brit*: = *Ulster Defence Association*)
organización paramilitar protestante de Irlanda del
Norte

UDC *n abbr* (*Brit*) = **Urban District Council**

udder ['ʌdəʳ] *n* ubre *f*

UDI *n abbr* (*Brit Pol*) = **unilateral declaration of
independence**

UDR *n abbr* (*Brit*: = *Ulster Defence Regiment*) fuerza
de seguridad de Irlanda del Norte

UEFA [ju:'eɪfə] *n abbr* (= *Union of European
Football Associations*) U.E.F.A. *f*

UFO ['ju:fəu] *n abbr* (= *unidentified flying object*)
OVNI *m*

Uganda [ju:'gændə] *n* Uganda

Ugandan [ju:'gændən] *adj* de Uganda

UGC *n abbr* (*Brit*: = *University Grants Committee*)
entidad gubernamental que controla las finanzas de
las universidades

ugh [əːh] *excl* ¡uf!

ugliness ['ʌglɪnɪs] *n* tealdad *f*

ugly ['ʌglɪ] *adj* feo; (*dangerous*) peligroso

UHF *abbr* (= *ultra-high frequency*) UHF *f*

UHT *adj abbr* (= *ultra heat treated*): **~ milk** leche
f uperizada

UK *n abbr* (= *United Kingdom*) Reino Unido, R.U.

Ukraine [ju:'kreɪn] *n* Ucrania

Ukrainian [ju:'kreɪnɪən] *adj* ucraniano ■ *n*
ucraniano(-a); (*Ling*) ucraniano

ulcer ['ʌlsəʳ] *n* úlcera; **mouth ~** úlcera bucal

Ulster ['ʌlstəʳ] *n* Ulster *m*

ulterior [ʌl'tɪərɪəʳ] *adj* ulterior; **~ motive**
segundas intenciones *fpl*

ultimate ['ʌltɪmət] *adj* último, final;
(*greatest*) mayor ■ *n*: **the ~ in luxury** el
colmo del lujo

ultimately ['ʌltɪmətlɪ] *adv* (*in the end*) por
último, al final; (*fundamentally*) a fin de
cuentas

ultimatum (*pl* **ultimatums** *or* **ultimata**)
[ʌltɪ'meɪtəm, -tə] *n* ultimátum *m*

ultra- ['ʌltrə] *pref* ultra-

ultrasonic [ʌltrə'sɔnɪk] *adj* ultrasónico

ultrasound ['ʌltrəsaund] *n* (*Med*) ultrasonido

ultraviolet ['ʌltrə'vaɪəlɪt] *adj* ultravioleta

um [ʌm] *interj* (*col*: *in hesitation*) esto, este (*LAm*)

umbilical cord [ʌmbɪ'laɪkl-] *n* cordón *m*
umbilical

umbrage ['ʌmbrɪdʒ] *n*: **to take ~ (at)**
ofenderse (por)

umbrella [ʌm'brelə] *n* paraguas *m inv*; **under
the ~ of** (*fig*) bajo la protección de

umlaut ['umlaut] *n* diéresis *f inv*

umpire ['ʌmpaɪəʳ] *n* árbitro ■ *vt* arbitrar

umpteen [ʌmp'ti:n] *num* enésimos(-as);
for the umpteenth time por enésima vez

UMW *n abbr* (= *United Mineworkers of America*)
sindicato de mineros

UN *n abbr* (= *United Nations*) ONU *f*

un- [ʌn] *pref* in-; des-; no ...; (*XX*) poco ...; nada ...

unabashed [ʌnə'bæʃt] *adj* nada avergonzado

unabated [ʌnə'beɪtɪd] *adj*: **to continue ~**
seguir con la misma intensidad

unable [ʌn'eɪbl] *adj*: **to be ~ to do sth** no
poder hacer algo; (*not know how to*) ser incapaz
de hacer algo, no saber hacer algo

unabridged [ʌnə'brɪdʒd] *adj* íntegro

unacceptable [ʌnək'sɛptəbl] *adj* (*proposal,
behaviour, price*) inaceptable; **it's ~ that** no se
puede aceptar que

unaccompanied [ʌnə'kʌmpənɪd] *adj*
no acompañado; (*singing, song*) sin
acompañamiento

u

unaccountably [ʌnə'kauntəblɪ] *adv* inexplicablemente

unaccounted [ʌnə'kauntɪd] *adj*: **two passengers are ~ for** faltan dos pasajeros

unaccustomed [ʌnə'kʌstəmd] *adj*: **to be ~ to** no estar acostumbrado a

unacquainted [ʌnə'kweɪntɪd] *adj*: **to be ~ with** (*facts*) desconocer, ignorar

unadulterated [ʌnə'dʌltəreɪtɪd] *adj* (*gen*) puro; (*wine*) sin mezcla

unaffected [ʌnə'fɛktɪd] *adj* (*person, behaviour*) sin afectación, sencillo; (*emotionally*): **to be ~ by** no estar afectado por

unafraid [ʌnə'freɪd] *adj*: **to be ~** no tener miedo

unaided [ʌn'eɪdɪd] *adj* sin ayuda, por sí solo

unanimity [juːnə'nɪmɪtɪ] *n* unanimidad *f*

unanimous [juː'nænɪməs] *adj* unánime

unanimously [juː'nænɪməslɪ] *adv* unánimemente

unanswered [ʌn'ɑːnsəd] *adj* (*question, letter*) sin contestar; (*criticism*) incontestado

unappetizing [ʌn'æpɪtaɪzɪŋ] *adj* poco apetitoso

unappreciative [ʌnə'priːʃɪətɪv] *adj* desagradecido

unarmed [ʌn'ɑːmd] *adj* (*person*) desarmado; (*combat*) sin armas

unashamed [ʌnə'ʃeɪmd] *adj* desvergonzado

unassisted [ʌnə'sɪstɪd] *adj, adv* sin ayuda

unassuming [ʌnə'sjuːmɪŋ] *adj* modesto, sin pretensiones

unattached [ʌnə'tætʃt] *adj* (*person*) soltero; (*part etc*) suelto

unattended [ʌnə'tɛndɪd] *adj* (*car, luggage*) sin atender

unattractive [ʌnə'træktɪv] *adj* poco atractivo

unauthorized [ʌn'ɔːθəraɪzd] *adj* no autorizado

unavailable [ʌnə'veɪləbl] *adj* (*article, room, book*) no disponible; (*person*) ocupado

unavoidable [ʌnə'vɔɪdəbl] *adj* inevitable

unavoidably [ʌnə'vɔɪdəblɪ] *adv* (*detained*) por causas ajenas a su voluntad

unaware [ʌnə'wɛəʳ] *adj*: **to be ~ of** ignorar

unawares [ʌnə'wɛəz] *adv* de improviso

unbalanced [ʌn'bælənst] *adj* desequilibrado; (*mentally*) trastornado

unbearable [ʌn'bɛərəbl] *adj* insoportable

unbeatable [ʌn'biːtəbl] *adj* (*gen*) invencible; (*price*) inmejorable

unbeaten [ʌn'biːtn] *adj* (*team*) imbatido; (*army*) invicto; (*record*) no batido

unbecoming [ʌnbɪ'kʌmɪŋ] *adj* (*unseemly: language, behaviour*) indecoroso, impropio; (*unflattering: garment*) poco favorecedor(a)

unbeknown [ʌnbɪ'nəun], **unbeknownst**
[ʌnbɪ'nəunst] *adv*: **~(st) to me** sin saberlo yo

unbelief [ʌnbɪ'liːf] *n* incredulidad *f*

unbelievable [ʌnbɪ'liːvəbl] *adj* increíble

unbelievingly [ʌnbɪ'liːvɪŋlɪ] *adv* sin creer

unbend [ʌn'bɛnd] (*irreg: like* **bend**) *vi* (*fig: person*) relajarse ▪ *vt* (*wire*) enderezar

unbending [ʌn'bɛndɪŋ] *adj* (*fig*) inflexible

unbiased, unbiassed [ʌn'baɪəst] *adj* imparcial

unblemished [ʌn'blɛmɪʃt] *adj* sin mancha

unblock [ʌn'blɔk] *vt* (*pipe*) desatascar; (*road*) despejar

unborn [ʌn'bɔːn] *adj* que va a nacer

unbounded [ʌn'baundɪd] *adj* ilimitado, sin límite

unbreakable [ʌn'breɪkəbl] *adj* irrompible

unbridled [ʌn'braɪdld] *adj* (*fig*) desenfrenado

unbroken [ʌn'brəukən] *adj* (*seal*) intacto; (*series*) continuo, ininterrumpido; (*record*) no batido; (*spirit*) indómito

unbuckle [ʌn'bʌkl] *vt* desabrochar

unburden [ʌn'bəːdn] *vt*: **to ~ o.s.** desahogarse

unbusinesslike [ʌn'bɪznɪslaɪk] *adj* (*trader*) poco profesional; (*transaction*) incorrecto; (*fig: person*) poco práctico; (: *without method*) desorganizado

unbutton [ʌn'bʌtn] *vt* desabrochar

uncalled-for [ʌn'kɔːldfɔːʳ] *adj* gratuito, inmerecido

uncanny [ʌn'kænɪ] *adj* extraño, extraordinario

unceasing [ʌn'siːsɪŋ] *adj* incesante

unceremonious ['ʌnsɛrɪ'məunɪəs] *adj* (*abrupt, rude*) brusco, hosco

uncertain [ʌn'səːtn] *adj* incierto; (*indecisive*) indeciso; **it's ~ whether** no se sabe si; **in no ~ terms** sin dejar lugar a dudas

uncertainty [ʌn'səːtntɪ] *n* incertidumbre *f*

unchallenged [ʌn'tʃælɪndʒd] *adj* (*Law etc*) incontestado; **to go ~** no encontrar respuesta

unchanged [ʌn'tʃeɪndʒd] *adj* sin cambiar *or* alterar

uncharitable [ʌn'tʃærɪtəbl] *adj* (*remark, behaviour*) demasiado duro

uncharted [ʌn'tʃɑːtɪd] *adj* inexplorado

unchecked [ʌn'tʃɛkt] *adj* desenfrenado

uncivil [ʌn'sɪvɪl] *adj* descortés, grosero

uncivilized [ʌn'sɪvɪlaɪzd] *adj* (*gen*) inculto, poco civilizado; (*fig: behaviour etc*) bárbaro

uncle ['ʌŋkl] *n* tío

unclear [ʌn'klɪəʳ] *adj* poco claro; **I'm still ~ about what I'm supposed to do** todavía no tengo muy claro lo que tengo que hacer

uncoil [ʌn'kɔɪl] *vt* desenrollar ▪ *vi* desenrollarse

uncomfortable [ʌn'kʌmfətəbl] *adj* incómodo; (*uneasy*) inquieto

uncomfortably [ʌn'kʌmfətəblɪ] *adv* (*uneasily: say*) con inquietud; (: *think*) con remordimiento *or* nerviosismo

uncommitted [ʌnkə'mɪtɪd] *adj* (*attitude, country*) no comprometido; **to remain ~ to** (*policy, party*) no comprometerse a

uncommon [ʌn'kɔmən] *adj* poco común, raro

uncommunicative [ʌnkə'mjuːnɪkətɪv] *adj* poco comunicativo, reservado

uncomplicated [ʌn'kɔmplɪkeɪtɪd] *adj* sin complicaciones

uncompromising [ʌn'kɔmprəmaɪzɪŋ] *adj* intransigente

unconcerned [ʌnkən'səːnd] *adj* indiferente; **to be ~ about** ser indiferente a, no preocuparse de

unconditional [ʌnkən'dɪʃənl] *adj* incondicional

uncongenial [ʌnkən'dʒiːnɪəl] *adj* desagradable

unconnected [ʌnkə'nɛktɪd] *adj* (*unrelated*): **to be ~ with** no estar relacionado con

unconscious [ʌn'kɔnʃəs] *adj* sin sentido; (*unaware*) inconsciente ■ *n*: **the ~** el inconsciente; **to knock sb ~** dejar a algn sin sentido

unconsciously [ʌn'kɔnʃəslɪ] *adv* inconscientemente

unconsciousness [ʌn'kɔnʃəsnɪs] *n* inconsciencia

unconstitutional [ʌnkɔnstɪ'tjuːʃənl] *adj* anticonstitucional

uncontested [ʌnkən'tɛstɪd] *adj* (*champion*) incontestado; (*Parliament: seat*) ganado sin oposición

uncontrollable [ʌnkən'trəuləbl] *adj* (*temper*) indomable; (*laughter*) incontenible

uncontrolled [ʌnkən'trəuld] *adj* (*child, dog, emotion*) incontrolado; (*inflation, price rises*) desenfrenado

unconventional [ʌnkən'vɛnʃənl] *adj* poco convencional

unconvinced [ʌnkən'vɪnst] *adj*: **to be** *or* **remain ~** seguir sin convencerse

unconvincing [ʌnkən'vɪnsɪŋ] *adj* poco convincente

uncork [ʌn'kɔːk] *vt* descorchar

uncorroborated [ʌnkə'rɔbəreɪtɪd] *adj* no confirmado

uncouth [ʌn'kuːθ] *adj* grosero, inculto

uncover [ʌn'kʌvər] *vt* (*gen*) descubrir; (*take lid off*) destapar

undamaged [ʌn'dæmɪdʒd] *adj* (*goods*) en buen estado; (*fig: reputation*) intacto

undaunted [ʌn'dɔːntɪd] *adj*: **~ by** sin dejarse desanimar por

undecided [ʌndɪ'saɪdɪd] *adj* (*person*) indeciso; (*question*) no resuelto, pendiente

undelivered [ʌndɪ'lɪvəd] *adj* no entregado al destinatario; **if ~ return to sender** en caso de no llegar a su destino devolver al, remitente

undeniable [ʌndɪ'naɪəbl] *adj* innegable

undeniably [ʌndɪ'naɪəblɪ] *adv* innegablemente

under ['ʌndər] *prep* debajo de; (*less than*) menos de; (*according to*) según, de acuerdo con ■ *adv* debajo, abajo; **~ there** ahí debajo; **~ construction** en construcción; en obras; **~ the circumstances** dadas las circunstancias; **in ~ 2 hours** en menos de dos horas; **~ anaesthetic** bajo los efectos de la anestesia; **~ discussion** en discusión, sobre el tapete

under... [ʌndər] *pref* sub...

under-age [ʌndər'eɪdʒ] *adj* menor de edad

underarm ['ʌndərɑːm] *n* axila, sobaco ■ *cpd*: **~ deodorant** desodorante *m* corporal

undercapitalised [ʌndə'kæpɪtəlaɪzd] *adj* descapitalizado

undercarriage ['ʌndəkærɪdʒ] *n* (*Brit Aviat*) tren *m* de aterrizaje

undercharge [ʌndə'tʃɑːdʒ] *vt* cobrar de menos

underclass ['ʌndəklɑːs] *n* clase *f* marginada

underclothes ['ʌndəkləuðz] *npl* ropa *sg* interior *or* íntima (*LAm*)

undercoat ['ʌndəkəut] *n* (*paint*) primera mano

undercover [ʌndə'kʌvər] *adj* clandestino

undercurrent ['ʌndəkʌrnt] *n* corriente *f* submarina; (*fig*) tendencia oculta

undercut [ʌndəkʌt] *vt* (*irreg: like* **cut**) vender más barato que; fijar un precio más barato que

underdeveloped [ʌndədɪ'vɛləpt] *adj* subdesarrollado

underdog ['ʌndədɔg] *n* desvalido(-a)

underdone [ʌndə'dʌn] *adj* (*Culin*) poco hecho

underemployment [ʌndərɪm'plɔɪmənt] *n* subempleo

underestimate [ʌndər'ɛstɪmeɪt] *vt* subestimar

underexposed [ʌndərɪks'pəuzd] *adj* (*Phot*) subexpuesto

underfed [ʌndə'fɛd] *adj* subalimentado

underfoot [ʌndə'fut] *adv*: **it's wet ~** el suelo está mojado

underfunded [ʌndə'fʌndɪd] *adj* infradotado (económicamente)

undergo [ʌndə'gəu] *vt* (*irreg: like* **go**) sufrir;

u

undergraduate [ˈʌndəˈgrædjuət] *n* estudiante *m/f* ■ *cpd*: ~ **courses** cursos *mpl* de licenciatura

underground [ˈʌndəgraund] *n* (Brit: railway) metro; (Pol) movimiento clandestino ■ *adj* subterráneo

undergrowth [ˈʌndəgrəuθ] *n* maleza

underhand [ʌndəˈhænd], **underhanded** [ʌndəˈhændɪd] *adj* (fig) poco limpio

underinsured [ʌndərɪnˈʃuəd] *adj* insuficientemente asegurado

underlie [ʌndəˈlaɪ] *vt* (irreg: like **lie**) (fig) ser la razón fundamental de; **the underlying cause** la causa fundamental

underline [ʌndəˈlaɪn] *vt* subrayar

underling [ˈʌndəlɪŋ] *n* (pej) subalterno(-a)

undermanning [ʌndəˈmænɪŋ] *n* falta de personal

undermentioned [ʌndəˈmɛnʃənd] *adj* abajo citado

undermine [ʌndəˈmaɪn] *vt* socavar, minar

underneath [ʌndəˈniːθ] *adv* debajo ■ *prep* debajo de, bajo

undernourished [ʌndəˈnʌrɪʃt] *adj* desnutrido

underpaid [ʌndəˈpeɪd] *adj* mal pagado

underpants [ˈʌndəpænts] *npl* calzoncillos *mpl*

underpass [ˈʌndəpɑːs] *n* (Brit) paso subterráneo

underpin [ʌndəˈpɪn] *vt* (argument, case) secundar, sostener

underplay [ʌndəˈpleɪ] *vt* (Brit) minimizar

underpopulated [ʌndəˈpɔpjuleɪtɪd] *adj* poco poblado

underprice [ʌndəˈpraɪs] *vt* vender demasiado barato

underpriced [ʌndəˈpraɪst] *adj* con precio demasiado bajo

underprivileged [ʌndəˈprɪvɪlɪdʒd] *adj* desvalido

underrate [ʌndəˈreɪt] *vt* infravalorar, subestimar

underscore [ˈʌndəskɔːʳ] *vt* subrayar, sostener

underseal [ʌndəˈsiːl] *vt* (Aut) proteger contra la corrosión

undersecretary [ʌndəˈsɛkrətrɪ] *n* subsecretario(-a)

undersell [ʌndəˈsɛl] *vt* (competitors) vender más barato que

undershirt [ˈʌndəʃəːt] *n* (US) camiseta

undershorts [ˈʌndəʃɔːts] *npl* (US) calzoncillos *mpl*

underside [ˈʌndəsaɪd] *n* parte *f* inferior, revés *m*

undersigned [ˈʌndəsaɪnd] *adj, n*: **the** ~ el/la *etc* abajo firmante

underskirt [ˈʌndəskəːt] *n* (Brit) enaguas *fpl*

understaffed [ʌndəˈstɑːft] *adj* falto de personal

understand [ʌndəˈstænd] (irreg: like **stand**) *vt, vi* entender, comprender; (assume) tener entendido; **to make o.s. understood** hacerse entender; **I ~ you have been absent** tengo entendido que (usted) ha estado ausente

understandable [ʌndəˈstændəbl] *adj* comprensible

understanding [ʌndəˈstændɪŋ] *adj* comprensivo ■ *n* comprensión *f*, entendimiento; (agreement) acuerdo; **to come to an ~ with sb** llegar a un acuerdo con algn; **on the ~ that** a condición de que + *subjun*

understate [ʌndəˈsteɪt] *vt* minimizar

understatement [ʌndəˈsteɪtmənt] *n* subestimación *f*; (modesty) modestia (excesiva); **to say it was good is quite an ~** decir que estuvo bien es quedarse corto

understood [ʌndəˈstud] *pt, pp of* **understand** ■ *adj* entendido; (implied): **it is ~ that** se sobreentiende que

understudy [ˈʌndəstʌdɪ] *n* suplente *m/f*

undertake [ʌndəˈteɪk] *vt* (irreg: like **take**) emprender; **to ~ to do sth** comprometerse a hacer algo

undertaker [ˈʌndəteɪkəʳ] *n* director(a) *m(f)* de pompas fúnebres

undertaking [ˈʌndəteɪkɪŋ] *n* empresa; (promise) promesa

undertone [ˈʌndətəun] *n* (of criticism) connotación *f*; (low voice): **in an ~** en voz baja

undervalue [ʌndəˈvæljuː] *vt* (fig) subestimar, infravalorar; (Comm etc) valorizar por debajo de su precio

underwater [ʌndəˈwɔːtəʳ] *adv* bajo el agua ■ *adj* submarino

underwear [ˈʌndəwɛəʳ] *n* ropa interior *or* íntima (LAm)

underweight [ʌndəˈweɪt] *adj* de peso insuficiente; (person) demasiado delgado

underworld [ˈʌndəwəːld] *n* (of crime) hampa, inframundo

underwrite [ʌndəˈraɪt] *vt* (irreg: like **write**) (Comm) suscribir; (Insurance) asegurar (contra riesgos)

underwriter [ˈʌndəraɪtəʳ] *n* (Insurance) asegurador(a) *m(f)*

undeserving [ʌndɪˈzəːvɪŋ] *adj*: **to be ~ of** no ser digno de

undesirable [ʌndɪˈzaɪərəbl] *adj* indeseable

undeveloped [ʌndɪˈvɛləpt] *adj* (land, resources) sin explotar

undies ['ʌndɪz] npl (col) paños mpl menores
undiluted [ʌndaɪ'luːtɪd] adj (concentrate) concentrado
undiplomatic [ʌndɪplə'mætɪk] adj poco diplomático
undischarged [ʌndɪs'tʃɑːdʒd] adj:
~ **bankrupt** quebrado(-a) no rehabilitado(-a)
undisciplined [ʌn'dɪsɪplɪnd] adj indisciplinado
undiscovered [ʌndɪs'kʌvəd] adj no descubierto; (unknown) desconocido
undisguised [ʌndɪs'gaɪzd] adj franco, abierto
undisputed [ʌndɪ'spjuːtɪd] adj incontestable
undistinguished [ʌndɪs'tɪŋgwɪʃt] adj mediocre
undisturbed [ʌndɪs'tɜːbd] adj (sleep) ininterrumpido; **to leave sth ~** dejar algo tranquilo or como está
undivided [ʌndɪ'vaɪdɪd] adj: **I want your ~ attention** quiero su completa atención
undo [ʌn'duː] vt (irreg: like **do**) deshacer
undoing [ʌn'duːɪŋ] n ruina, perdición f
undone [ʌn'dʌn] pp of **undo** ■ adj: **to come ~** (clothes) desabrocharse; (parcel) desatarse
undoubted [ʌn'daʊtɪd] adj indudable
undoubtedly [ʌn'daʊtɪdlɪ] adv indudablemente, sin duda
undress [ʌn'drɛs] vi desnudarse, desvestirse (esp LAm)
undrinkable [ʌn'drɪŋkəbl] adj (unpalatable) imbebible; (poisonous) no potable
undue [ʌn'djuː] adj indebido, excesivo
undulating ['ʌndjuleɪtɪŋ] adj ondulante
unduly [ʌn'djuːlɪ] adv excesivamente, demasiado
undying [ʌn'daɪɪŋ] adj eterno
unearned [ʌn'ɜːnd] adj (praise, respect) inmerecido; ~ **income** ingresos mpl no ganados, renta no ganada or salarial
unearth [ʌn'ɜːθ] vt desenterrar
unearthly [ʌn'ɜːθlɪ] adj: ~ **hour** (col) hora intempestiva
unease [ʌn'iːz] n malestar m
uneasy [ʌn'iːzɪ] adj intranquilo; (worried) preocupado; **to feel ~ about doing sth** sentirse incómodo con la idea de hacer algo
uneconomic ['ʌniːkə'nɒmɪk], **uneconomical** ['ʌniːkə'nɒmɪkl] adj no económico
uneducated [ʌn'ɛdjukeɪtɪd] adj ignorante, inculto
unemployed [ʌnɪm'plɔɪd] adj parado, sin trabajo ■ n: **the ~** los parados
unemployment [ʌnɪm'plɔɪmənt] n paro, desempleo, cesantía (LAm)
unemployment benefit n (Brit) subsidio de desempleo or paro

unending [ʌn'ɛndɪŋ] adj interminable
unenviable [ʌn'ɛnvɪəbl] adj poco envidiable
unequal [ʌn'iːkwəl] adj (length, objects etc) desigual; (amounts) distinto; (division of labour) poco justo
unequalled, unequaled (US) [ʌn'iːkwəld] adj inigualado, sin par
unequivocal [ʌnɪ'kwɪvəkəl] adj (answer) inequívoco, claro; (person) claro
unerring [ʌn'ɜːrɪŋ] adj infalible
UNESCO [juː'nɛskəʊ] n abbr (= United Nations Educational, Scientific and Cultural Organization) UNESCO f
unethical [ʌn'ɛθɪkəl] adj (methods) inmoral; (doctor's behaviour) que infringe la ética profesional
uneven [ʌn'iːvn] adj desigual; (road etc) con baches
uneventful [ʌnɪ'vɛntful] adj sin incidentes
unexceptional [ʌnɪk'sɛpʃənl] adj sin nada de extraordinario, corriente
unexciting [ʌnɪk'saɪtɪŋ] adj (news) sin interés; (film, evening) aburrido
unexpected [ʌnɪk'spɛktɪd] adj inesperado
unexpectedly [ʌnɪk'spɛktɪdlɪ] adv inesperadamente
unexplained [ʌnɪks'pleɪnd] adj inexplicado
unexploded [ʌnɪks'pləʊdɪd] adj sin explotar
unfailing [ʌn'feɪlɪŋ] adj (support) indefectible; (energy) inagotable
unfair [ʌn'fɛər] adj: ~ **(to sb)** injusto (con algn); **it's ~ that ...** es injusto que ..., no es justo que ...
unfair dismissal n despido improcedente
unfairly [ʌn'fɛəlɪ] adv injustamente
unfaithful [ʌn'feɪθful] adj infiel
unfamiliar [ʌnfə'mɪlɪər] adj extraño, desconocido; **to be ~ with sth** desconocer or ignorar algo
unfashionable [ʌn'fæʃnəbl] adj (clothes) pasado or fuera de moda; (district) poco elegante
unfasten [ʌn'fɑːsn] vt desatar
unfathomable [ʌn'fæðəməbl] adj insondable
unfavourable, unfavorable (US) [ʌn'feɪvərəbl] adj desfavorable
unfavourably, unfavorably (US) [ʌn'feɪvrəblɪ] adv: **to look ~ upon** ser adverso a
unfeeling [ʌn'fiːlɪŋ] adj insensible
unfinished [ʌn'fɪnɪʃt] adj inacabado, sin terminar
unfit [ʌn'fɪt] adj en baja forma; (incompetent) incapaz; ~ **for work** no apto para trabajar
unflagging [ʌn'flægɪŋ] adj incansable
unflappable [ʌn'flæpəbl] adj imperturbable
unflattering [ʌn'flætərɪŋ] adj (dress, hairstyle) poco favorecedor

u

845

unflinching [ʌn'flɪntʃɪŋ] *adj* impávido
unfold [ʌn'fəuld] *vt* desdoblar; *(fig)* revelar ▪ *vi* abrirse; revelarse
unforeseeable [ʌnfɔː'siːəbl] *adj* imprevisible
unforeseen [ʌnfɔː'siːn] *adj* imprevisto
unforgettable [ʌnfə'ɡetəbl] *adj* inolvidable
unforgivable [ʌnfə'ɡɪvəbl] *adj* imperdonable
unformatted [ʌn'fɔːmætɪd] *adj (disk, text)* sin formatear
unfortunate [ʌn'fɔːtʃnət] *adj* desgraciado; *(event, remark)* inoportuno
unfortunately [ʌn'fɔːtʃnətlɪ] *adv* desgraciadamente, por desgracia
unfounded [ʌn'faundɪd] *adj* infundado
unfriendly [ʌn'frendlɪ] *adj* antipático
unfulfilled [ʌnful'fɪld] *adj (ambition)* sin realizar; *(prophecy, promise, terms of contract)* incumplido; *(desire, person)* insatisfecho
unfurl [ʌn'fəːl] *vt* desplegar
unfurnished [ʌn'fəːnɪʃt] *adj* sin amueblar
ungainly [ʌn'ɡeɪnlɪ] *adj (walk)* desgarbado
ungodly [ʌn'ɡɔdlɪ] *adj*: **at an ~ hour** a una hora intempestiva
ungrateful [ʌn'ɡreɪtful] *adj* ingrato
unguarded [ʌn'ɡɑːdɪd] *adj (moment)* de descuido
unhappily [ʌn'hæpɪlɪ] *adv (unfortunately)* desgraciadamente
unhappiness [ʌn'hæpɪnɪs] *n* tristeza
unhappy [ʌn'hæpɪ] *adj (sad)* triste; *(unfortunate)* desgraciado; *(childhood)* infeliz; **~ with** *(arrangements etc)* poco contento con, descontento de
unharmed [ʌn'hɑːmd] *adj (person)* ileso
UNHCR *n abbr* (= *United Nations High Commission for Refugees*) ACNUR *m*
unhealthy [ʌn'hɛlθɪ] *adj (gen)* malsano, insalubre; *(person)* enfermizo; *(interest)* morboso
unheard-of [ʌn'həːdɔv] *adj* inaudito, sin precedente
unhelpful [ʌn'hɛlpful] *adj (person)* poco servicial; *(advice)* inútil
unhesitating [ʌn'hɛzɪteɪtɪŋ] *adj (loyalty)* automático; *(reply, offer)* inmediato; *(person)* resuelto
unholy [ʌn'həulɪ] *adj*: **an ~ alliance** una alianza nefasta; **he returned at an ~ hour** volvió a una hora intempestiva
unhook [ʌn'huk] *vt* desenganchar; *(from wall)* descolgar; *(undo)* desabrochar
unhurt [ʌn'həːt] *adj* ileso
unhygienic [ʌnhaɪ'dʒiːnɪk] *adj* antihigiénico
UNICEF ['juːnɪsɛf] *n abbr* (= *United Nations International Children's Emergency Fund*) UNICEF *f*
unidentified [ʌnaɪ'dɛntɪfaɪd] *adj* no identificado; **~ flying object (UFO)** objeto volante no identificado

unification [juːnɪfɪ'keɪʃən] *n* unificación *f*
uniform ['juːnɪfɔːm] *n* uniforme *m* ▪ *adj* uniforme
uniformity [juːnɪ'fɔːmɪtɪ] *n* uniformidad *f*
unify ['juːnɪfaɪ] *vt* unificar, unir
unilateral [juːnɪ'lætərəl] *adj* unilateral
unimaginable [ʌnɪ'mædʒɪnəbl] *adj* inconcebible, inimaginable
unimaginative [ʌnɪ'mædʒɪnətɪv] *adj* falto de imaginación
unimpaired [ʌnɪm'pɛəd] *adj (unharmed)* intacto; *(not lessened)* no disminuido; *(unaltered)* inalterado
unimportant [ʌnɪm'pɔːtənt] *adj* sin importancia
unimpressed [ʌnɪm'prɛst] *adj* poco impresionado
uninhabited [ʌnɪn'hæbɪtɪd] *adj* desierto; *(country)* despoblado; *(house)* deshabitado, desocupado
uninhibited [ʌnɪn'hɪbɪtɪd] *adj* nada cohibido, desinhibido
uninjured [ʌn'ɪndʒəd] *adj (person)* ileso
uninspiring [ʌnɪn'spaɪərɪŋ] *adj* anodino
unintelligent [ʌnɪn'tɛlɪdʒənt] *adj* poco inteligente
unintentional [ʌnɪn'tɛnʃənəl] *adj* involuntario
unintentionally [ʌnɪn'tɛnʃnəlɪ] *adv* sin querer
uninvited [ʌnɪn'vaɪtɪd] *adj (guest)* sin invitación
uninviting [ʌnɪn'vaɪtɪŋ] *adj (place, offer)* poco atractivo; *(food)* poco apetecible
union ['juːnjən] *n* unión *f*; *(also*: **trade union**) sindicato ▪ *cpd* sindical; **the U~** *(US)* la Unión
union card *n* carnet *m* de sindicato
unionize ['juːnjənaɪz] *vt* sindicalizar
Union Jack *n* bandera del Reino Unido
Union of Soviet Socialist Republics *n* Unión *f* de Repúblicas Socialistas Soviéticas
union shop *n (US) empresa de afiliación sindical obligatoria*
unique [juː'niːk] *adj* único
unisex ['juːnɪsɛks] *adj* unisex
Unison ['juːnɪsn] *n (trade union) gran sindicato de funcionarios*
unison ['juːnɪsn] *n*: **in ~** en armonía
unissued capital [ʌn'ɪʃuːd-] *n* capital *m* no emitido
unit ['juːnɪt] *n* unidad *f*; *(team, squad)* grupo; **kitchen ~** módulo de cocina; **production ~** taller *m* de fabricación; **sink ~** fregadero
unit cost *n* costo unitario
unite [juː'naɪt] *vt* unir ▪ *vi* unirse
united [juː'naɪtɪd] *adj* unido

United Arab Emirates *npl* Emiratos *mpl* Árabes Unidos
United Kingdom *n* Reino Unido
United Nations, United Nations Organization *n* Naciones Unidas *fpl*
United States, United States of America *n* Estados Unidos *mpl* (de América)
unit price *n* precio unitario
unit trust *n* (Brit) bono fiduciario
unity ['ju:nɪtɪ] *n* unidad *f*
Univ. *abbr* = university
universal [ju:nɪ'vɜ:sl] *adj* universal
universally [ju:nɪ'vɜ:səlɪ] *adv* universalmente
universe ['ju:nɪvɜ:s] *n* universo
university [ju:nɪ'vɜ:sɪtɪ] *n* universidad *f* ■ *cpd* (*student, professor, education, degree*) universitario; (*year*) académico; to be at/go to ~ estudiar en/ir a la universidad
unjust [ʌn'dʒʌst] *adj* injusto
unjustifiable [ʌndʒʌstɪ'faɪəbl] *adj* injustificable
unjustified [ʌn'dʒʌstɪfaɪd] *adj* (*text*) no alineado *or* justificado
unkempt [ʌn'kempt] *adj* descuidado; (*hair*) despeinado
unkind [ʌn'kaɪnd] *adj* poco amable; (*comment etc*) cruel
unkindly [ʌn'kaɪndlɪ] *adv* (*speak*) severamente; (*treat*) cruelmente, mal
unknown [ʌn'nəʊn] *adj* desconocido ■ *adv*: ~ to me sin saberlo yo; ~ quantity incógnita
unladen [ʌn'leɪdən] *adj* (*weight*) vacío, sin cargamento
unlawful [ʌn'lɔ:ful] *adj* ilegal, ilícito
unleaded [ʌn'ledɪd] *n* (*also*: unleaded petrol) gasolina sin plomo
unleash [ʌn'li:ʃ] *vt* desatar
unleavened [ʌn'levənd] *adj* ácimo, sin levadura
unless [ʌn'les] *conj* a menos que; ~ he comes a menos que venga; ~ otherwise stated salvo indicación contraria; ~ I am mistaken si no mi equivoco
unlicensed [ʌn'laɪsənst] *adj* (*Brit: to sell alcohol*) no autorizado
unlike [ʌn'laɪk] *adj* distinto ■ *prep* a diferencia de
unlikelihood [ʌn'laɪklɪhud] *n* improbabilidad *f*
unlikely [ʌn'laɪklɪ] *adj* improbable
unlimited [ʌn'lɪmɪtɪd] *adj* ilimitado; ~ liability responsabilidad *f* ilimitada
unlisted [ʌn'lɪstɪd] *adj* (*US Tel*) que no figura en la guía; ~ company empresa sin cotización en bolsa
unlit [ʌn'lɪt] *adj* (*room*) oscuro, sin luz

unload [ʌn'ləʊd] *vt* descargar
unlock [ʌn'lɔk] *vt* abrir (con llave)
unlucky [ʌn'lʌkɪ] *adj* desgraciado; (*object, number*) que da mala suerte; to be ~ (*person*) tener mala suerte
unmanageable [ʌn'mænɪdʒəbl] *adj* (*unwieldy: tool, vehicle*) difícil de manejar; (*situation*) incontrolable
unmanned [ʌn'mænd] *adj* (*spacecraft*) sin tripulación
unmannerly [ʌn'mænəlɪ] *adj* mal educado, descortés
unmarked [ʌn'mɑ:kt] *adj* (*unstained*) sin mancha; ~ police car vehículo policial camuflado
unmarried [ʌn'mærɪd] *adj* soltero
unmask [ʌn'mɑ:sk] *vt* desenmascarar
unmatched [ʌn'mætʃt] *adj* incomparable
unmentionable [ʌn'menʃnəbl] *adj* (*topic, vice*) indecible; (*word*) que no se debe decir
unmerciful [ʌn'mə:sɪful] *adj* despiadado
unmistakable [ʌnmɪs'teɪkəbl] *adj* inconfundible
unmistakably [ʌnmɪs'teɪkəblɪ] *adv* de modo inconfundible
unmitigated [ʌn'mɪtɪgeɪtɪd] *adj* rematado, absoluto
unnamed [ʌn'neɪmd] *adj* (*nameless*) sin nombre; (*anonymous*) anónimo
unnatural [ʌn'nætʃrəl] *adj* (*gen*) antinatural; (*manner*) afectado; (*habit*) perverso
unnecessary [ʌn'nesəsərɪ] *adj* innecesario, inútil
unnerve [ʌn'nə:v] *vt* (*accident*) poner nervioso; (*hostile attitude*) acobardar; (*long wait, interview*) intimidar
unnoticed [ʌn'nəʊtɪst] *adj*: to go *or* pass ~ pasar desapercibido
UNO ['ju:nəʊ] *n abbr* (= United Nations Organization) ONU *f*
unobservant [ʌnəb'zə:vnt] *adj*: to be ~ ser poco observador, ser distraído
unobtainable [ʌnəb'teɪnəbl] *adj* inasequible; (*Tel*) inexistente
unobtrusive [ʌnəb'tru:sɪv] *adj* discreto
unoccupied [ʌn'ɔkjupaɪd] *adj* (*house etc*) libre, desocupado
unofficial [ʌnə'fɪʃl] *adj* no oficial; ~ strike huelga no oficial
unopened [ʌn'əʊpənd] *adj* (*letter, present*) sin abrir
unopposed [ʌnə'pəʊzd] *adv* (*enter, be elected*) sin oposición
unorthodox [ʌn'ɔ:θədɔks] *adj* poco ortodoxo
unpack [ʌn'pæk] *vi* deshacer las maletas, desempacar (*LAm*)
unpaid [ʌn'peɪd] *adj* (*bill, debt*) sin pagar,

u

impagado; (*Comm*) pendiente; (*holiday*) sin
sueldo; (*work*) sin pago, voluntario
unpalatable [ʌn'pælətəbl] *adj* (*truth*)
desagradable
unparalleled [ʌn'pærəlɛld] *adj* (*unequalled*)
sin par; (*unique*) sin precedentes
unpatriotic [ʌnpætrɪ'ɔtɪk] *adj* (*person*) poco
patriota; (*speech, attitude*) antipatriótico
unplanned [ʌn'plænd] *adj* (*visit*) imprevisto;
(*baby*) no planeado
unpleasant [ʌn'plɛznt] *adj* (*disagreeable*)
desagradable; (*person, manner*) antipático
unplug [ʌn'plʌg] *vt* desenchufar, desconectar
unpolluted [ʌnpə'lu:tɪd] *adj* impoluto, no
contaminado
unpopular [ʌn'pɔpjuləʳ] *adj* poco popular;
to be ~ with sb (*person, law*) no ser popular
con algn; **to make o.s. ~ (with)** hacerse
impopular (con)
unprecedented [ʌn'prɛsɪdəntɪd] *adj* sin
precedentes
unpredictable [ʌnprɪ'dɪktəbl] *adj*
imprevisible
unprejudiced [ʌn'prɛdʒudɪst] *adj* (*not biased*)
imparcial; (*having no prejudices*) sin prejuicio
unprepared [ʌnprɪ'pɛəd] *adj* (*person*)
desprevenido; (*speech*) improvisado
unprepossessing [ʌnpri:pə'zɛsɪŋ] *adj* poco
atractivo
unprincipled [ʌn'prɪnsɪpld] *adj* sin escrúpulos
unproductive [ʌnprə'dʌktɪv] *adj*
improductivo; (*discussion*) infructuoso
unprofessional [ʌnprə'fɛʃənl] *adj* poco
profesional; **~ conduct** negligencia
unprofitable [ʌn'prɔfɪtəbl] *adj* poco
provechoso, no rentable
UNPROFOR *n abbr* (= *United Nations Protection
Force*) FORPRONU *f*, Unprofor *f*
unprotected ['ʌnprə'tɛktɪd] *adj* (*sex*) sin
protección
unprovoked [ʌnprə'vəukt] *adj* no provocado
unpunished [ʌn'pʌnɪʃt] *adj*: **to go ~** quedar
sin castigo, salir impune
unqualified [ʌn'kwɔlɪfaɪd] *adj* sin título, no
cualificado; (*success*) total, incondicional
unquestionably [ʌn'kwɛstʃənəblɪ] *adv*
indiscutiblemente
unquestioning [ʌn'kwɛstʃənɪŋ] *adj* (*obedience,
acceptance*) incondicional
unravel [ʌn'rævl] *vt* desenmarañar
unreal [ʌn'rɪəl] *adj* irreal
unrealistic [ʌnrɪə'lɪstɪk] *adj* poco realista
unreasonable [ʌn'ri:znəbl] *adj* irrazonable;
to make ~ demands on sb hacer demandas
excesivas a algn
unrecognizable [ʌn'rɛkəgnaɪzəbl] *adj*
irreconocible

unrecognized [ʌn'rɛkəgnaɪzd] *adj* (*talent,
genius*) ignorado; (*Pol: regime*) no reconocido
unrecorded [ʌnrɪ'kɔ:dɪd] *adj* no registrado
unrefined [ʌnrɪ'faɪnd] *adj* (*sugar, petroleum*)
sin refinar
unrehearsed [ʌnrɪ'hə:st] *adj* (*Theat etc*)
improvisado; (*spontaneous*) espontáneo
unrelated [ʌnrɪ'leɪtɪd] *adj* sin relación;
(*family*) no emparentado
unrelenting [ʌnrɪ'lɛntɪŋ] *adj* implacable
unreliable [ʌnrɪ'laɪəbl] *adj* (*person*) informal;
(*machine*) poco fiable
unrelieved [ʌnrɪ'li:vd] *adj* (*monotony*)
constante
unremitting [ʌnrɪ'mɪtɪŋ] *adj* incesante
unrepeatable [ʌnrɪ'pi:təbl] *adj* irrepetible
unrepentant [ʌnrɪ'pɛntənt] *adj* (*smoker,
sinner*) impenitente; **to be ~ about sth** no
arrepentirse de algo
unrepresentative [ʌnrɛprɪ'zɛntətɪv] *adj*
(*untypical*) poco representativo
unreserved [ʌnrɪ'zə:vd] *adj* (*seat*) no
reservado; (*approval, admiration*) total
unreservedly [ʌnrɪ'zə:vɪdlɪ] *adv* sin reserva
unresponsive [ʌnrɪ'spɔnsɪv] *adj* insensible
unrest [ʌn'rɛst] *n* inquietud *f*, malestar *m*;
(*Pol*) disturbios *mpl*
unrestricted [ʌnrɪ'strɪktɪd] *adj* (*power, time*)
sin restricción; (*access*) libre
unrewarded [ʌnrɪ'wɔ:dɪd] *adj* sin
recompensa
unripe [ʌn'raɪp] *adj* verde, inmaduro
unrivalled, unrivaled (*US*) [ʌn'raɪvəld] *adj*
incomparable, sin par
unroll [ʌn'rəul] *vt* desenrollar
unruffled [ʌn'rʌfld] *adj* (*person*)
imperturbable; (*hair*) liso
unruly [ʌn'ru:lɪ] *adj* indisciplinado
unsafe [ʌn'seɪf] *adj* (*journey*) peligroso; (*car etc*)
inseguro; (*method*) arriesgado; **~ to drink/
eat** no apto para el consumo humano
unsaid [ʌn'sɛd] *adj*: **to leave sth ~** dejar algo
sin decir
unsaleable, unsalable (*US*) [ʌn'seɪləbl] *adj*
invendible
unsatisfactory ['ʌnsætɪs'fæktərɪ] *adj* poco
satisfactorio
unsatisfied [ʌn'sætɪsfaɪd] *adj* (*desire, need etc*)
insatisfecho
unsavoury, unsavory (*US*) [ʌn'seɪvərɪ] *adj*
(*fig*) repugnante
unscathed [ʌn'skeɪðd] *adj* ileso
unscientific [ʌnsaɪən'tɪfɪk] *adj* poco
científico
unscrew [ʌn'skru:] *vt* destornillar
unscrupulous [ʌn'skru:pjuləs] *adj* sin
escrúpulos

unseat [ʌn'siːt] vt (rider) hacer caerse de la silla a; (fig: official) hacer perder su escaño a
unsecured [ʌnsɪ'kjuəd] adj: ~ **creditor** acreedor(a) m(f) común
unseeded [ʌn'siːdɪd] adj (Sport) no preseleccionado
unseen [ʌn'siːn] adj (person, danger) oculto
unselfish [ʌn'sɛlfɪʃ] adj generoso, poco egoísta; (act) desinteresado
unsettled [ʌn'sɛtld] adj inquieto; (situation) inestable; (weather) variable
unsettling [ʌn'sɛtlɪŋ] adj perturbador(a), inquietante
unshakable, unshakeable [ʌn'ʃeɪkəbl] adj inquebrantable
unshaven [ʌn'ʃeɪvn] adj sin afeitar
unsightly [ʌn'saɪtlɪ] adj desagradable
unskilled [ʌn'skɪld] adj: ~ **workers** mano f de obra no cualificada
unsociable [ʌn'səʊʃəbl] adj insociable
unsocial [ʌn'səʊʃl] adj: ~ **hours** horario nocturno
unsold [ʌn'səʊld] adj sin vender
unsolicited [ʌnsə'lɪsɪtɪd] adj no solicitado
unsophisticated [ʌnsə'fɪstɪkeɪtɪd] adj (person) sencillo, ingenuo; (method) poco sofisticado
unsound [ʌn'saʊnd] adj (health) malo; (in construction, floor, foundations) defectuoso; (policy, advice, judgment) erróneo; (investment) poco seguro
unspeakable [ʌn'spiːkəbl] adj indecible; (awful) incalificable
unspoken [ʌn'spəʊkn] adj (words) sobreentendido; (agreement, approval) tácito
unstable [ʌn'steɪbl] adj inestable
unsteady [ʌn'stɛdɪ] adj inestable
unstinting [ʌn'stɪntɪŋ] adj (support etc) pródigo
unstuck [ʌn'stʌk] adj: **to come ~** despegarse; (fig) fracasar
unsubscribe [ʌnsəb'skraɪb] vt (Internet) borrarse
unsubstantiated [ʌnsəb'stænʃieɪtɪd] adj (rumour, accusation) no comprobado
unsuccessful [ʌnsək'sɛsful] adj (attempt) infructuoso; (writer, proposal) sin éxito; **to be ~** (in attempting sth) no tener éxito, fracasar
unsuccessfully [ʌnsək'sɛsfulɪ] adv en vano, sin éxito
unsuitable [ʌn'suːtəbl] adj inconveniente, inapropiado; (time) inoportuno
unsuited [ʌn'suːtɪd] adj: **to be ~ for** or **to** no ser apropiado para
unsung ['ʌnsʌŋ] adj: **an ~ hero** un héroe desconocido
unsupported [ʌnsə'pɔːtɪd] adj (claim) sin

fundamento; (theory) sin base firme
unsure [ʌn'ʃuəʳ] adj inseguro, poco seguro; **to be ~ of o.s.** estar poco seguro de sí mismo
unsuspecting [ʌnsə'spɛktɪŋ] adj confiado
unsweetened [ʌn'swiːtnd] adj sin azúcar
unsympathetic [ʌnsɪmpə'θɛtɪk] adj (attitude) poco comprensivo; (person) sin compasión; ~ **(to)** indiferente (a)
untangle [ʌn'tæŋgl] vt desenredar
untapped [ʌn'tæpt] adj (resources) sin explotar
untaxed [ʌn'tækst] adj (goods) libre de impuestos; (income) antes de impuestos
unthinkable [ʌn'θɪŋkəbl] adj inconcebible, impensable
unthinkingly [ʌn'θɪŋkɪŋlɪ] adv irreflexivamente
untidy [ʌn'taɪdɪ] adj (room) desordenado, en desorden; (appearance) desaliñado
untie [ʌn'taɪ] vt desatar
until [ən'tɪl] prep hasta ■ conj hasta que; ~ **he comes** hasta que venga; ~ **now** hasta ahora; ~ **then** hasta entonces; **from morning ~ night** de la mañana a la noche
untimely [ʌn'taɪmlɪ] adj inoportuno; (death) prematuro
untold [ʌn'təʊld] adj (story) nunca contado; (suffering) indecible; (wealth) incalculable
untouched [ʌn'tʌtʃt] adj (not used etc) intacto, sin tocar; (safe: person) indemne, ileso; (unaffected): ~ **by** insensible a
untoward [ʌntə'wɔːd] adj (behaviour) impropio; (event) adverso
untrained [ʌn'treɪnd] adj (worker) sin formación; (troops) no entrenado; **to the ~ eye** para los no entendidos
untrammelled, untrammeled (US) [ʌn'træməld] adj ilimitado
untranslatable [ʌntrænz'leɪtəbl] adj intraducible
untried [ʌn'traɪd] adj (plan) no probado
untrue [ʌn'truː] adj (statement) falso
untrustworthy [ʌn'trʌstwəːðɪ] adj (person) poco fiable
unusable [ʌn'juːzəbl] adj inservible
unused [ʌn'juːzd] adj sin usar, nuevo; **to be ~ to (doing) sth** no estar acostumbrado a (hacer) algo
unusual [ʌn'juːʒuəl] adj insólito, poco común
unusually [ʌn'juːʒuəlɪ] adv: **he arrived ~ early** llegó más temprano que de costumbre
unveil [ʌn'veɪl] vt (statue) descubrir
unwanted [ʌn'wɒntɪd] adj (person, effect) no deseado
unwarranted [ʌn'wɒrəntɪd] adj injustificado
unwary [ʌn'wɛərɪ] adj imprudente, incauto
unwavering [ʌn'weɪvərɪŋ] adj inquebrantable

u

unwelcome [ʌn'wɛlkəm] *adj* (*at a bad time*) inoportuno, molesto; **to feel ~** sentirse incómodo

unwell [ʌn'wɛl] *adj*: **to feel ~** estar indispuesto, sentirse mal

unwieldy [ʌn'wiːldɪ] *adj* difícil de manejar

unwilling [ʌn'wɪlɪŋ] *adj*: **to be ~ to do sth** estar poco dispuesto a hacer algo

unwillingly [ʌn'wɪlɪŋlɪ] *adv* de mala gana

unwind [ʌn'waɪnd] (*irreg: like* **wind**) *vt* desenvolver ■ *vi* (*relax*) relajarse

unwise [ʌn'waɪz] *adj* imprudente

unwitting [ʌn'wɪtɪŋ] *adj* inconsciente

unworkable [ʌn'wəːkəbl] *adj* (*plan*) impracticable

unworthy [ʌn'wəːðɪ] *adj* indigno; **to be ~ of sth/to do sth** ser indigno de algo/de hacer algo

unwrap [ʌn'ræp] *vt* deshacer

unwritten [ʌn'rɪtn] *adj* (*agreement*) tácito; (*rules, law*) no escrito

unzip [ʌn'zɪp] *vt* abrir la cremallera de; (*Comput*) descomprimir

 KEYWORD

up [ʌp] *prep*: **to go/be up sth** subir/estar subido en algo; **he went up the stairs/the hill** subió las escaleras/la colina; **we walked/climbed up the hill** subimos la colina; **they live further up the street** viven más arriba en la calle; **go up that road and turn left** sigue por esa calle y gira a la izquierda

■ *adv* **1** (*upwards, higher*) más arriba; **up in the mountains** en lo alto (de la montaña); **put it a bit higher up** ponlo un poco más arriba *or* alto; **to stop halfway up** pararse a la mitad del camino *or* de la subida; **up there** ahí *or* allí arriba; **up above** en lo alto, por encima, arriba; **"this side up"** "este lado hacia arriba"; **to live/go up North** vivir en el norte/ir al norte

2: **to be up** (*out of bed*) estar levantado; (*prices, level*) haber subido; (*building*) estar construido; (*tent*) estar montado; (*curtains, paper etc*) estar puesto; **time's up** se acabó el tiempo; **when the year was up** al terminarse el año; **he's well up in** *or* **on politics** (*Brit: knowledgeable*) está muy al día en política; **what's up?** (*wrong*) ¿qué pasa?; **what's up with him?** ¿qué le pasa?; **prices are up on last year** los precios han subido desde el año pasado

3: **up to** (*as far as*) hasta; **up to now** hasta ahora *or* la fecha

4: **to be up to** (*depending on*): **it's up to you** depende de ti; **he's not up to it** (*job, task etc*) no es capaz de hacerlo; **I don't feel up to it** no me encuentro con ánimos para ello; **his work is not up to the required standard** su trabajo no da la talla; (*col: be doing*): **what is he up to?** ¿qué estará tramando?

■ *vi* (*col*): **she upped and left** se levantó y se marchó

■ *vt* (*col: price*) subir

■ *n*: **ups and downs** altibajos *mpl*

up-and-coming [ʌpənd'kʌmɪŋ] *adj* prometedor(a)

upbeat ['ʌpbiːt] *n* (*Mus*) tiempo no acentuado; (*in economy, prosperity*) aumento ■ *adj* (*col*) optimista, animado

upbraid [ʌp'breɪd] *vt* censurar, reprender

upbringing ['ʌpbrɪŋɪŋ] *n* educación *f*

upcoming ['ʌpkʌmɪŋ] *adj* próximo

update [ʌp'deɪt] *vt* poner al día

upend [ʌp'ɛnd] *vt* poner vertical

upfront [ʌp'frʌnt] *adj* claro, directo ■ *adv* a las claras; (*pay*) por adelantado; **to be ~ about sth** admitir algo claramente

upgrade [ʌp'greɪd] *vt* ascender; (*Comput*) modernizar

upheaval [ʌp'hiːvl] *n* trastornos *mpl*; (*Pol*) agitación *f*

uphill [ʌp'hɪl] *adj* cuesta arriba; (*fig: task*) penoso, difícil ■ *adv*: **to go ~** ir cuesta arriba

uphold [ʌp'həʊld] *vt* (*irreg: like* **hold**) sostener

upholstery [ʌp'həʊlstərɪ] *n* tapicería

upkeep ['ʌpkiːp] *n* mantenimiento

upmarket [ʌp'mɑːkɪt] *adj* (*product*) de categoría

upon [ə'pɒn] *prep* sobre

upper ['ʌpər] *adj* superior, de arriba ■ *n* (*of shoe: also*: **uppers**) pala

upper case *n* (*Typ*) mayúsculas *fpl*

upper-class [ʌpə'klɑːs] *adj* (*district, people, accent*) de clase alta; (*attitude*) altivo

uppercut ['ʌpəkʌt] *n* uppercut *m*, gancho a la cara

upper hand *n*: **to have the ~** tener la sartén por el mango

Upper House *n* (*Pol*): **the ~** la Cámara alta

uppermost ['ʌpəməʊst] *adj* el más alto; **what was ~ in my mind** lo que me preocupaba más

Upper Volta [-'vəʊltə] *n* Alto Volta *m*

upright ['ʌpraɪt] *adj* vertical; (*fig*) honrado

uprising ['ʌpraɪzɪŋ] *n* sublevación *f*

uproar ['ʌprɔːr] *n* tumulto, escándalo

uproarious [ʌp'rɔːrɪəs] *adj* escandaloso; (*hilarious*) graciosísimo

uproot [ʌp'ruːt] *vt* desarraigar

upset *n* ['ʌpsɛt] (*to plan etc*) revés *m*,

contratiempo; (*Med*) trastorno ■ *vt*
[ʌp'sɛt] (*irreg: like* **set**) (*glass etc*) volcar; (*spill*)
derramar; (*plan*) alterar; (*person*) molestar,
perturbar ■ *adj* [ʌp'sɛt] preocupado,
perturbado; (*stomach*) revuelto; **to have a
stomach** ~ (*Brit*) tener el estómago revuelto;
to get ~ molestarse, llevarse un disgusto

upset price *n* (*US, Scottish*) precio mínimo *or*
de reserva

upsetting [ʌp'sɛtɪŋ] *adj* (*worrying*)
inquietante; (*offending*) ofensivo; (*annoying*)
molesto

upshot ['ʌpʃɔt] *n* resultado

upside-down ['ʌpsaɪd'daun] *adv* al revés

upstage ['ʌp'steɪdʒ] *vt* robar protagonismo a

upstairs [ʌp'stɛəz] *adv* arriba ■ *adj* (*room*) de
arriba ■ *n* el piso superior

upstart ['ʌpstɑːt] *n* advenedizo

upstream [ʌp'striːm] *adv* río arriba

upsurge ['ʌpsəːdʒ] *n* (*of enthusiasm etc*) arrebato

uptake ['ʌpteɪk] *n*: **he is quick/slow on the** ~
es muy listo/torpe

uptight [ʌp'taɪt] *adj* tenso, nervioso

up-to-date ['ʌptə'deɪt] *adj* moderno, actual;
to bring sb ~ **(on sth)** poner a algn al
corriente/tanto (de algo)

upturn ['ʌptəːn] *n* (*in luck*) mejora; (*Comm: in
market*) resurgimiento económico; (: *in value of
currency*) aumento

upturned ['ʌptəːnd] *adj*: ~ **nose** nariz *f*
respingona

upward ['ʌpwəd] *adj* ascendente ■ *adv* hacia
arriba

upwardly-mobile ['ʌpwədlɪ'məubaɪl] *adj*:
to be ~ mejorar socialmente

upwards ['ʌpwədz] *adv* hacia arriba

URA *n abbr* (*US*) – **Urban Renewal
Administration**

Ural Mountains ['juərəl-] *npl*: **the** ~ (*also*: **the
Urals**) los Montes Urales

uranium [juə'reɪnɪəm] *n* uranio

Uranus [juə'reɪnəs] *n* (*Astro*) Urano

urban ['əːbən] *adj* urbano

urbane [əː'beɪn] *adj* cortés, urbano

urbanization ['əːbənaɪ'zeɪʃən] *n*
urbanización *f*

urchin ['əːtʃɪn] *n* pilluelo, golfillo

Urdu ['uədu:] *n* urdu *m*

urge [əːdʒ] *n* (*force*) impulso; (*desire*) deseo
■ *vt*: **to** ~ **sb to do** animar a algn a hacer
▸ **urge on** *vt* animar

urgency ['əːdʒənsɪ] *n* urgencia

urgent ['əːdʒənt] *adj* (*earnest, persistent: plea*)
insistente; (: *tone*) urgente

urgently ['əːdʒəntlɪ] *adv* con urgencia,
urgentemente

urinal ['juərɪnl] *n* (*building*) urinario; (*vessel*)

orinal *m*

urinate ['juərɪneɪt] *vi* orinar

urine ['juərɪn] *n* orina

URL *n abbr* (= *uniform resource locator*) URL *m*

urn [əːn] *n* urna; (*also*: **tea urn**) tetera
(grande)

Uruguay ['juərəgwaɪ] *n* el Uruguay

Uruguayan [juərə'gwaɪən] *adj, n*
uruguayo(-a) *m(f)*

US *n abbr* (– *United States*) EE.UU.

us [ʌs] *pron* nos; (*after prep*) nosotros(-as); (*col:
me*): **give us a kiss** dame un beso; *see also* **me**

USA *n abbr* = **United States of America**; (*Mil*)
= **United States Army**

usable ['juːzəbl] *adj* utilizable

USAF *n abbr* – **United States Air Force**

usage ['juːzɪdʒ] *n* (*Ling*) uso; (*utilization*)
utilización *f*

USB key *n* llave *f* USB, memoria *f* USB

USCG *n abbr* = **United States Coast Guard**

USDA *n abbr* = **United States Department of
Agriculture**

USDAW ['ʌzdɔː] *n abbr* (*Brit*: = *Union of Shop,
Distributive, and Allied Workers*) sindicato de
empleados de comercio

USDI *n abbr* = **United States Department of
the Interior**

use *n* [juːs] uso, empleo; (*usefulness*) utilidad
f ■ *vt* [juːz] usar, emplear; **in** ~ en uso; **out
of** ~ en desuso; **to be of** ~ servir; **ready
for** ~ listo (para usar); **to make** ~ **of sth**
aprovecharse *or* servirse de algo; **it's no**
~ (*pointless*) es inútil; (*not useful*) no sirve;
what's this used for? ¿para qué sirve esto?;
to be used to estar acostumbrado a (*SP*),
acostumbrar; **to get used to** acostumbrarse
a; **she used to do it** (ella) solía *or*
acostumbraba hacerlo
▸ **use up** *vt* agotar

used [juːzd] *adj* (*car*) usado

useful ['juːsful] *adj* útil; **to come in** ~ ser útil

usefulness ['juːsfəlnɪs] *n* utilidad *f*

useless ['juːslɪs] *adj* inútil; (*unusable: object*)
inservible

uselessly ['juːslɪslɪ] *adv* inútilmente, en vano

uselessness ['juːslɪsnɪs] *n* inutilidad *f*

user ['juːzəʳ] *n* usuario(-a); (*of petrol, gas etc*)
consumidor(a) *m(f)*

user-friendly ['juːzə'frɛndlɪ] *adj* (*Comput*) fácil
de utilizar

USES *n abbr* = **United States Employment
Service**

usher ['ʌʃəʳ] *n* (*at wedding*) ujier *m*; (*in cinema
etc*) acomodador *m* ■ *vt*: **to** ~ **sb in** (*into room*)
hacer pasar a algn; **it ushered in a new era**
(*fig*) inició una nueva era

usherette [ʌʃə'rɛt] *n* (*in cinema*) acomodadora

u

USIA *n abbr* = United States Information Agency

USM *n abbr* = United States Mail; United States Mint

USN *n abbr* = United States Navy

USP *n abbr* = unique selling point *or* proposition

USPHS *n abbr* = United States Public Health Service

USPO *n abbr* = United States Post Office

USS *abbr* = United States Ship (*or* Steamer)

USSR *n abbr* (*History*): **the (former)** ~ la (antigua) U.R.S.S.; *see* Union of Soviet Socialist Republics

usu. *abbr* = **usually**

usual ['juːʒʊəl] *adj* normal, corriente; **as** ~ como de costumbre, como siempre

usually ['juːʒʊəlı] *adv* normalmente

usurer ['juːʒərəʳ] *n* usurero

usurp [juːˈzəːp] *vt* usurpar

usury ['juːʒərı] *n* usura

UT *abbr* (*US*) = **Utah**

utensil [juːˈtɛnsl] *n* utensilio; **kitchen utensils** batería de cocina

uterus ['juːtərəs] *n* útero

utilitarian [juːtılıˈtɛərıən] *adj* utilitario

utility [juːˈtılıtı] *n* utilidad *f*

utility room *n* trascocina

utilization [juːtılaıˈzeıʃən] *n* utilización *f*

utilize ['juːtılaız] *vt* utilizar

utmost ['ʌtməust] *adj* mayor ◼ *n*: **to do one's** ~ hacer todo lo posible; **it is of the** ~ **importance that ...** es de la mayor importancia que ...

utter ['ʌtəʳ] *adj* total, completo ◼ *vt* pronunciar, proferir

utterance ['ʌtərns] *n* palabras *fpl*, declaración *f*

utterly ['ʌtəlı] *adv* completamente, totalmente

U-turn ['juːˈtəːn] *n* cambio de sentido; (*fig*) giro de 180 grados

Uzbekistan [ʌzbɛkıˈstɑːn] *n* Uzbekistán *m*

V, v [viː] n (letter) V, v f; **V for Victor** V de Valencia

V. abbr (= verse) vers.°; (= vide: see) V, vid., vide; (= versus) vs.; = **volt**

VA, Va. abbr (US) = **Virginia**

vac [væk] n abbr (Brit col) = **vacation**

vacancy ['veɪkənsɪ] n (Brit: job) vacante f; (room) cuarto libre; **have you any vacancies?** ¿tiene or hay alguna habitación or algún cuarto libre?

vacant ['veɪkənt] adj desocupado, libre; (expression) distraído

vacant lot n (US) solar m

vacate [və'keɪt] vt (house) desocupar; (job) dejar (vacante)

vacation [və'keɪʃən] n vacaciones fpl; **on ~** de vacaciones; **to take a ~** (esp US) tomarse unas vacaciones

vacation course n curso de vacaciones

vacationer [və'keɪʃənəʳ], **vacationist** [və'keɪʃənɪst] n (US) turista m/f

vaccinate ['væksɪneɪt] vt vacunar

vaccination [væksɪ'neɪʃən] n vacunación f

vaccine ['væksiːn] n vacuna

vacuum ['vækjum] n vacío

vacuum bottle n (US) = **vacuum flask**

vacuum cleaner n aspiradora

vacuum flask n (Brit) termo

vacuum-packed ['vækjum'pækt] adj envasado al vacío

vagabond ['vægəbɔnd] n vagabundo(-a)

vagary ['veɪgərɪ] n capricho

vagina [və'dʒaɪnə] n vagina

vagrancy ['veɪgrənsɪ] n vagabundeo

vagrant ['veɪgrənt] n vagabundo(-a)

vague [veɪg] adj vago; (blurred: memory) borroso; (uncertain) incierto, impreciso; (person) distraído; **I haven't the vaguest idea** no tengo la más remota idea

vaguely ['veɪglɪ] adv vagamente

vagueness ['veɪgnɪs] n vaguedad f; imprecisión f; (absent-mindedness) despiste m

vain [veɪn] adj (conceited) presumido; (useless) vano, inútil; **in ~** en vano

vainly ['veɪnlɪ] adv (to no effect) en vano; (conceitedly) vanidosamente

valance ['væləns] n (for bed) volante alrededor de la colcha o sábana que cuelga hasta el suelo

valedictory [vælɪ'dɪktərɪ] adj de despedida

valentine ['væləntaɪn] n (also: **valentine card**) tarjeta del Día de los Enamorados

valet ['væleɪ] n ayuda m de cámara

valet service n (for clothes) planchado

valiant ['væljənt] adj valiente

valiantly ['væljəntlɪ] adv valientemente, con valor

valid ['vælɪd] adj válido; (ticket) valedero; (law) vigente

validate ['vælɪdeɪt] vt (contract, document) convalidar; (argument, claim) dar validez a

validity [və'lɪdɪtɪ] n validez f; vigencia

valise [və'liːz] n maletín m

valley ['vælɪ] n valle m

valour, valor (US) ['væləʳ] n valor m, valentía

valuable ['væljuəbl] adj (jewel) de valor; (time) valioso; **valuables** npl objetos mpl de valor

valuation [vælju'eɪʃən] n tasación f, valuación f

value ['væljuː] n valor m; (importance) importancia ■ vt (fix price of) tasar, valorar; (esteem) apreciar; **values** npl (moral) valores mpl morales; **to lose (in) ~** (currency) bajar; (property) desvalorizarse; **to gain (in) ~** (currency) subir; (property) revalorizarse; **you get good ~ (for money) in that shop** la relación calidad-precio es muy buena en esa tienda; **to be of great ~ to sb** ser de gran valor para algn; **it is valued at £8** está valorado en ocho libras

value added tax n (Brit) impuesto sobre el valor añadido or agregado (LAm)

valued ['væljuːd] adj (appreciated) apreciado

valueless ['væljuːlɪs] adj sin valor

valuer ['væljuəʳ] n tasador(a) m(f)

valve [vælv] n (Anat, Tech) válvula

vampire ['væmpaɪəʳ] n vampiro

V

van [væn] n (Aut) furgoneta, camioneta (LAm); (Brit Rail) furgón m (de equipajes)

V and A n abbr (Brit) = **Victoria and Albert Museum**

vandal ['vændl] n vándalo(-a)

vandalism ['vændəlɪzəm] n vandalismo

vandalize ['vændəlaɪz] vt dañar, destruir, destrozar

vanguard ['væŋgɑːd] n vanguardia

vanilla [və'nɪlə] n vainilla

vanish ['vænɪʃ] vi desaparecer, esfumarse

vanity ['vænɪtɪ] n vanidad f

vanity case n neceser m

vantage point ['vɑːntɪdʒ-] n posición f ventajosa

vaporize ['veɪpəraɪz] vt vaporizar ■ vi vaporizarse

vapour, vapor (US) ['veɪpəʳ] n vapor m; (on breath, window) vaho

vapour trail, vapor trail (US) n (Aviat) estela

variable ['vɛərɪəbl] adj variable ■ n variable f

variance ['vɛərɪəns] n: **to be at ~ (with)** estar en desacuerdo (con), no cuadrar (con)

variant ['vɛərɪənt] n variante f

variation [vɛərɪ'eɪʃən] n variación f

varicose ['værɪkəus] adj: **~ veins** varices fpl

varied ['vɛərɪd] adj variado

variety [və'raɪətɪ] n variedad f, diversidad f; (quantity) surtido; **for a ~ of reasons** por varias or diversas razones

variety show n espectáculo de variedades

various ['vɛərɪəs] adj varios(-as), diversos(-as); **at ~ times** (different) en distintos momentos; (several) varias veces

varnish ['vɑːnɪʃ] n (gen) barniz m; (also: **nail varnish**) esmalte m ■ vt (gen) barnizar; (nails) pintar (con esmalte)

vary ['vɛərɪ] vt variar; (change) cambiar ■ vi variar; (disagree) discrepar; **to ~ with** or **according to** variar según or de acuerdo con

varying ['vɛərɪɪŋ] adj diversos(-as)

vase [vɑːz] n florero

vasectomy [və'sɛktəmɪ] n vasectomía

Vaseline® ['væsɪliːn] n vaselina®

vast [vɑːst] adj enorme; (success) abrumador(a), arrollador(a)

vastly ['vɑːstlɪ] adv enormemente

vastness ['vɑːstnɪs] n inmensidad f

VAT [væt] n abbr (Brit: = value added tax) IVA m

vat [væt] n tina, tinaja

Vatican ['vætɪkən] n: **the ~** el Vaticano

vatman ['vætmæn] n (Brit col) inspector m or recaudador m del IVA; **"how to avoid the ~"** "cómo evitar pagar el IVA"

vaudeville ['vəudəvɪl] n (US) vodevil m

vault [vɔːlt] n (of roof) bóveda; (tomb) tumba;

(in bank) cámara acorazada ■ vt (also: **vault over**) saltar (por encima de)

vaunted ['vɔːntɪd] adj: **much ~** cacareado

VC n abbr = **vice-chairman; vice-chancellor;** (Brit: = Victoria Cross) condecoración militar

VCR n abbr = **video cassette recorder**

VD n abbr see **venereal disease**

VDU n abbr see **visual display unit**

veal [viːl] n ternera

veer [vɪəʳ] vi (ship) virar

veg. [vɛdʒ] n abbr (Brit col) = **vegetable(s)**

vegan ['viːgən] n vegetariano(-a) estricto(-a)

vegeburger, veggieburger ['vɛdʒɪbə:gəʳ] n hamburguesa vegetal

vegetable ['vɛdʒtəbl] n (Bot) vegetal m; (edible plant) legumbre f, hortaliza ■ adj vegetal;

vegetables npl (cooked) verduras fpl

vegetable garden n huerta, huerto

vegetarian [vɛdʒɪ'tɛərɪən] adj, n vegetariano(-a) m(f)

vegetate ['vɛdʒɪteɪt] vi vegetar

vegetation [vɛdʒɪ'teɪʃən] n vegetación f

vegetative ['vɛdʒɪtətɪv] adj vegetativo; (Bot) vegetal

vehemence ['viːɪməns] n vehemencia; violencia

vehement ['viːɪmənt] adj vehemente, apasionado; (dislike, hatred) violento

vehicle ['viːɪkl] n vehículo; (fig) vehículo, medio

vehicular [vɪ'hɪkjuləʳ] adj: **~ traffic** circulación f rodada

veil [veɪl] n velo ■ vt velar; **under a ~ of secrecy** (fig) en el mayor secreto

veiled [veɪld] adj (also fig) disimulado, velado

vein [veɪn] n vena; (of ore etc) veta

Velcro® ['vɛlkrəu] n velcro® m

vellum ['vɛləm] n (writing paper) papel m vitela

velocity [vɪ'lɒsɪtɪ] n velocidad f

velour [və'luəʳ] n terciopelo

velvet ['vɛlvɪt] n terciopelo ■ adj aterciopelado

vendetta [vɛn'dɛtə] n vendetta

vending machine ['vɛndɪŋ-] n máquina expendedora, expendedor m

vendor ['vɛndəʳ] n vendedor(a) m(f); **street ~** vendedor(a) m(f) callejero(-a)

veneer [və'nɪəʳ] n chapa, enchapado; (fig) barniz m

venereal [vɪ'nɪərɪəl] adj: **~ disease (VD)** enfermedad f venérea

Venetian blind [vɪ'niːʃən-] n persiana

Venezuela [vɛnɛ'zweɪlə] n Venezuela

Venezuelan [vɛnɛ'zweɪlən] adj, n venezolano(-a) m(f)

vengeance ['vɛndʒəns] n venganza; **with a ~** (fig) con creces

vengeful ['vɛndʒful] *adj* vengativo
Venice ['vɛnɪs] *n* Venecia
venison ['vɛnɪsn] *n* carne *f* de venado
venom ['vɛnəm] *n* veneno
venomous ['vɛnəməs] *adj* venenoso
venomously ['vɛnəməslɪ] *adv* con odio
vent [vɛnt] *n* (*opening*) abertura; (*air-hole*) respiradero; (*in wall*) rejilla (de ventilación) ■ *vt* (*fig*: *feelings*) desahogar
ventilate ['vɛntɪleɪt] *vt* ventilar
ventilation [vɛntɪ'leɪʃən] *n* ventilación *f*
ventilation shaft *n* pozo de ventilación
ventilator ['vɛntɪleɪtəʳ] *n* ventilador *m*
ventriloquist [vɛn'trɪləkwɪst] *n* ventrílocuo(-a)
venture ['vɛntʃəʳ] *n* empresa ■ *vt* arriesgar; (*opinion*) ofrecer ■ *vi* arriesgarse, lanzarse; **a business ~** una empresa comercial; **to ~ to do sth** aventurarse a hacer algo
venture capital *n* capital *m* arriesgado
venue ['vɛnjuː] *n* (*meeting place*) lugar *m* de reunión; (*for concert*) local *m*
Venus ['viːnəs] *n* (*Astro*) Venus *m*
veracity [və'ræsɪtɪ] *n* veracidad *f*
veranda, verandah [və'rændə] *n* terraza; (*with glass*) galería
verb [vəːb] *n* verbo
verbal ['vəːbl] *adj* verbal
verbally ['vəːbəlɪ] *adv* verbalmente, de palabra
verbatim [vəː'beɪtɪm] *adj, adv* al pie de la letra, palabra por palabra
verbose [vəː'bəus] *adj* prolijo
verdict ['vəːdɪkt] *n* veredicto, fallo; (*fig*: *opinion*) opinión *f*, juicio; **~ of guilty/not guilty** veredicto de culpabilidad/inocencia
verge [vəːdʒ] *n* (*Brit*) borde *m*; **to be on the ~ of doing sth** estar a punto de hacer algo
▶ **verge on** *vt fus* rayar en
verger ['vəːdʒəʳ] *n* sacristán *m*
verification [vɛrɪfɪ'keɪʃən] *n* comprobación *f*, verificación *f*
verify ['vɛrɪfaɪ] *vt* comprobar, verificar; (*prove the truth of*) confirmar
veritable ['vɛrɪtəbl] *adj* verdadero, auténtico
vermin ['vəːmɪn] *npl* (*animals*) bichos *mpl*; (*insects*) sabandijas *fpl*; (*fig*) sabandijas *fpl*
vermouth ['vəːməθ] *n* vermut *m*
vernacular [və'nækjuləʳ] *n* lengua vernácula
versatile ['vəːsətaɪl] *adj* (*person*) polifacético; (*machine, tool etc*) versátil
versatility [vəːsə'tɪlɪtɪ] *n* versatilidad *f*
verse [vəːs] *n* versos *mpl*, poesía; (*stanza*) estrofa; (*in bible*) versículo; **in ~** en verso
versed [vəːst] *adj*: **(well-)~ in** versado en
version ['vəːʃən] *n* versión *f*
versus ['vəːsəs] *prep* contra

vertebra (*pl* **vertebrae**) ['vəːtɪbrə, briː] *n* vértebra
vertebrate ['vəːtɪbrɪt] *n* vertebrado
vertical ['vəːtɪkl] *adj* vertical
vertically ['vəːtɪkəlɪ] *adv* verticalmente
vertigo ['vəːtɪgəu] *n* vértigo; **to suffer from ~** tener vértigo
verve [vəːv] *n* brío
very ['vɛrɪ] *adv* muy ■ *adj*: **the ~ book which** el mismo libro que; **the ~ last** el último (de todos); **at the ~ least** al menos; **~ much** muchísimo; **~ well/little** muy bien/poco; **~ high frequency** (*Radio*) frecuencia muy alta; **it's ~ cold** hace mucho frío; **the ~ thought (of it) alarms me** con sólo pensarlo me entra miedo
vespers ['vɛspəz] *npl* vísperas *fpl*
vessel ['vɛsl] *n* (*Anat*) vaso; (*ship*) barco; (*container*) vasija
vest [vɛst] *n* (*Brit*) camiseta; (*US*: *waistcoat*) chaleco
vested interests ['vɛstɪd-] *npl* (*Comm*) intereses *mpl* creados
vestibule ['vɛstɪbjuːl] *n* vestíbulo
vestige ['vɛstɪdʒ] *n* vestigio, rastro
vestry ['vɛstrɪ] *n* sacristía
Vesuvius [vɪ'suːvɪəs] *n* Vesubio
vet [vɛt] *n abbr* = **veterinary surgeon**; (*US*: *col*) = **veteran** ■ *vt* revisar; **to ~ sb for a job** someter a investigación a algn para un trabajo
veteran ['vɛtərn] *n* veterano(-a) ■ *adj*: **she is a ~ campaigner for ...** es una veterana de la campaña de ...
veteran car *n* coche *m* antiguo
veterinarian [vɛtrɪ'nɛərɪən] *n* (*US*) = **veterinary surgeon**
veterinary ['vɛtrɪnərɪ] *adj* veterinario
veterinary surgeon *n* (*Brit*) veterinario(-a)
veto ['viːtəu] *n* (*pl* **vetoes**) veto ■ *vt* prohibir, vedar; **to put a ~ on** vetar
vetting ['vɛtɪŋ] *n*: **positive ~** investigación gubernamental de los futuros altos cargos de la Administración
vex [vɛks] *vt* (*irritate*) fastidiar; (*make impatient*) impacientar
vexed [vɛkst] *adj* (*question*) controvertido
vexing ['vɛksɪŋ] *adj* molesto, engorroso
VFD *n abbr* (*US*) = **voluntary fire department**
VG *n abbr* (*Brit Scol etc*: = *very good*) S (= *sobresaliente*)
VHF *abbr* (= *very high frequency*) VHF *f*
VI *abbr* (*US*) = **Virgin Islands**
via ['vaɪə] *prep* por, por vía de
viability [vaɪə'bɪlɪtɪ] *n* viabilidad *f*
viable ['vaɪəbl] *adj* viable
viaduct ['vaɪədʌkt] *n* viaducto

V

vial ['vaɪəl] n frasco pequeño
vibes [vaɪbz] npl (col): **I got good/bad ~ me dio buen/mal rollo**
vibrant ['vaɪbrənt] adj (lively, bright) vivo; (full of emotion: voice) vibrante; (colour) fuerte
vibraphone ['vaɪbrəfəun] n vibráfono
vibrate [vaɪ'breɪt] vi vibrar
vibration [vaɪ'breɪʃən] n vibración f
vibrator [vaɪ'breɪtəʳ] n vibrador m
vicar ['vɪkəʳ] n párroco
vicarage ['vɪkərɪdʒ] n parroquia
vicarious [vɪ'kɛərɪəs] adj indirecto; (responsibility) delegado
vice [vaɪs] n (evil) vicio; (Tech) torno de banco
vice- [vaɪs] pref vice...
vice-chairman ['vaɪs'tʃɛəmən] n vicepresidente m
vice-chancellor [vaɪs'tʃɑːnsələʳ] n (Brit Univ) rector(a) m(f)
vice-president [vaɪs'prɛzɪdənt] n vicepresidente(-a) m(f)
viceroy ['vaɪsrɔɪ] n virrey m
vice versa ['vaɪsɪ'vəːsə] adv viceversa
vicinity [vɪ'sɪnɪtɪ] n (area) vecindad f; (nearness) proximidad f; **in the ~ (of)** cercano (a)
vicious ['vɪʃəs] adj (remark) malicioso; (blow) brutal; **a ~ circle** un círculo vicioso
viciousness ['vɪʃəsnɪs] n brutalidad f
vicissitudes [vɪ'sɪsɪtjuːdz] npl vicisitudes fpl, peripecias fpl
victim ['vɪktɪm] n víctima; **to be the ~ of** ser víctima de
victimization [vɪktɪmaɪ'zeɪʃən] n persecución f; (of striker etc) represalias fpl
victimize ['vɪktɪmaɪz] vt (strikers etc) tomar represalias contra
victor ['vɪktəʳ] n vencedor(a) m(f)
Victorian [vɪk'tɔːrɪən] adj victoriano
victorious [vɪk'tɔːrɪəs] adj vencedor(a)
victory ['vɪktərɪ] n victoria; **to win a ~ over sb** obtener una victoria sobre algn
video ['vɪdɪəu] cpd de vídeo ∎ n vídeo ∎ vt grabar (en vídeo)
video call n llamada de vídeo
video camera n videocámara, cámara de vídeo
video cassette n videocassette f
video cassette recorder n = **video recorder**
videodisk ['vɪdɪəudɪsk] n videodisco
video game n videojuego
video nasty n vídeo de violencia y/o porno duro
videophone ['vɪdɪəufəun] n videoteléfono, videófono
video recorder n vídeo, videocassette f
video recording n videograbación f
video tape n cinta de vídeo

vie [vaɪ] vi: **to ~ with** competir con
Vienna [vɪ'ɛnə] n Viena
Viennese [vɪə'niːz] adj, n vienés(-esa) m(f)
Vietnam, Viet Nam [vjɛt'næm] n Vietnam m
Vietnamese [vjɛtnə'miːz] adj vietnamita ∎ n (pl inv) vietnamita m/f; (Ling) vietnamita m
view [vjuː] n vista; (landscape) paisaje m; (opinion) opinión f, criterio ∎ vt (look at) mirar; (examine) examinar; (in museum etc) expuesto; **in full ~ of sb** a la vista de algn; **to be within ~ (of sth)** estar a la vista (de algo); **an overall ~ of the situation** una visión de conjunto de la situación; **in ~ of the fact that** en vista de que; **to take or hold the ~ that ...** opinar or pensar que ...; **with a ~ to doing sth** con miras or vistas a hacer algo
viewdata ['vjuːdeɪtə] n (Brit) videodatos mpl
viewer ['vjuːəʳ] n (small projector) visionadora; (TV) televidente m/f, telespectador(a) m(f)
viewfinder ['vjuːfaɪndəʳ] n visor m de imagen
viewpoint ['vjuːpɔɪnt] n punto de vista
vigil ['vɪdʒɪl] n vigilia; **to keep ~** velar
vigilance ['vɪdʒɪləns] n vigilancia
vigilance committee n (US) comité m de autodefensa
vigilant ['vɪdʒɪlənt] adj vigilante
vigilante [vɪdʒɪ'læntɪ] n vecino/a que se toma la justicia por su mano
vigorous ['vɪgərəs] adj enérgico, vigoroso
vigorously ['vɪgərəslɪ] adv enérgicamente, vigorosamente
vigour, vigor (US) ['vɪgəʳ] n energía, vigor m
vile [vaɪl] adj (action) vil, infame; (smell) repugnante
vilify ['vɪlɪfaɪ] vt denigrar, vilipendiar
villa ['vɪlə] n (country house) casa de campo; (suburban house) chalet m
village ['vɪlɪdʒ] n aldea
villager ['vɪlɪdʒəʳ] n aldeano(-a)
villain ['vɪlən] n (scoundrel) malvado(-a); (criminal) maleante m/f; see also **pantomime**
VIN n abbr (US) = **vehicle identification number**
vinaigrette [vɪneɪ'grɛt] n vinagreta
vindicate ['vɪndɪkeɪt] vt vindicar, justificar
vindication [vɪndɪ'keɪʃən] n: **in ~ of** en justificación de
vindictive [vɪn'dɪktɪv] adj vengativo
vine [vaɪn] n vid f
vinegar ['vɪnɪgəʳ] n vinagre m
vine-growing ['vaɪngrəuɪŋ] adj (region) viticultor(a)
vineyard ['vɪnjɑːd] n viña, viñedo
vintage ['vɪntɪdʒ] n (year) vendimia, cosecha; **the 1970 ~** la cosecha de 1970
vintage car n coche m antiguo or de época

vintage wine n vino añejo
vintage year n: **it's been a ~ for plays** ha
sido un año destacado en lo que a teatro se
refiere
vinyl ['vaɪnl] n vinilo
viola [vɪ'əulə] n (Mus) viola
violate ['vaɪəleɪt] vt violar
violation [vaɪə'leɪʃən] n violación f; **in ~ of
sth** en violación de algo
violence ['vaɪələns] n violencia; **acts of ~**
actos mpl de violencia
violent ['vaɪələnt] adj (gen) violento; (pain)
intenso; **a ~ dislike of sb/sth** una profunda
antipatía or manía a algn/algo
violently ['vaɪələntlɪ] adv (severely: ill, angry)
muy
violet ['vaɪələt] adj violado, violeta ■ n (plant)
violeta
violin [vaɪə'lɪn] n violín m
violinist [vaɪə'lɪnɪst] n violinista m/f
VIP n abbr (= very important person) VIP m
viper ['vaɪpəʳ] n víbora
viral ['vaɪərəl] adj vírico
virgin ['vɜːdʒɪn] n virgen m/f ■ adj virgen;
the Blessed V~ la Santísima Virgen
virginity [və'dʒɪnɪtɪ] n virginidad f
Virgo ['vɜːgəu] n Virgo
virile ['vɪraɪl] adj viril
virility [vɪ'rɪlɪtɪ] n virilidad f
virtual ['vɜːtjuəl] adj (also Comput, Phys)
virtual
virtually ['vɜːtjuəlɪ] adv (almost)
prácticamente, virtualmente; **it is ~
impossible** es prácticamente imposible
virtual reality n (Comput) realidad f virtual
virtue ['vɜːtjuː] n virtud f; **by ~ of** en virtud de
virtuosity [vɜːtju'ɒsɪtɪ] n virtuosismo
virtuoso [vɜːtju'əusəu] n virtuoso
virtuous ['vɜːtjuəs] adj virtuoso
virulence ['vɪruləns] n virulencia
virulent ['vɪrulənt] adj virulento, violento
virus ['vaɪərəs] n virus m inv
visa ['viːzə] n visado, visa (LAm)
vis-à-vis [viːzə'viː] prep con respecto a
viscount ['vaɪkaunt] n vizconde m
viscous ['vɪskəs] adj viscoso
vise [vaɪs] n (US Tech) = **vice**
visibility [vɪzɪ'bɪlɪtɪ] n visibilidad f
visible ['vɪzəbl] adj visible; **~ exports/
imports** exportaciones fpl/importaciones
fpl visibles
visibly ['vɪzɪblɪ] adv visiblemente
vision ['vɪʒən] n (sight) vista; (foresight: in
dream) visión f
visionary ['vɪʒənrɪ] n visionario(-a)
visit ['vɪzɪt] n visita ■ vt (person) visitar, hacer
una visita a; (place) ir a, (ir a) conocer; **to pay**

a ~ to (person) visitar a; **on a private/official
~ en** visita privada/oficial
visiting ['vɪzɪtɪŋ] adj (speaker, professor)
invitado; (team) visitante
visiting card n tarjeta de visita
visiting hours npl (in hospital etc) horas fpl de
visita
visitor n (gen) visitante m/f; (to one's
house) visita; (tourist) turista m/f; (tripper)
excursionista m/f; **to have visitors** (at home)
tener visita
visitors' book n libro de visitas
visor ['vaɪzəʳ] n visera
VISTA ['vɪstə] n abbr (= Volunteers In Service
to America) programa de ayuda voluntaria a los
necesitados
vista ['vɪstə] n vista, panorama
visual ['vɪzjuəl] adj visual
visual aid n medio visual
visual arts npl artes fpl plásticas
visual display unit n unidad f de despliegue
visual, monitor m
visualize ['vɪzjuəlaɪz] vt imaginarse; (foresee)
prever
visually ['vɪzjuəlɪ] adv: **~ handicapped** con
visión deficiente
vital ['vaɪtl] adj (essential) esencial,
imprescindible; (crucial) crítico; (person)
enérgico, vivo; (of life) vital; **of ~ importance
(to sb/sth)** de suma importancia (para
algn/algo)
vitality [vaɪ'tælɪtɪ] n energía, vitalidad f
vitally ['vaɪtlɪ] adv: **~ important** de suma
importancia
vital statistics npl (of population) estadísticas
fpl demográficas; (col: of woman) medidas fpl
(corporales)
vitamin ['vɪtəmɪn] n vitamina
vitamin pill n pastilla de vitaminas
vitreous ['vɪtrɪəs] adj (china, enamel) vítreo
vitriolic [vɪtrɪ'ɒlɪk] adj mordaz
viva ['vaɪvə] n (also: **viva voce**) examen m oral
vivacious [vɪ'veɪʃəs] adj vivaz, alegre
vivacity [vɪ'væsɪtɪ] n vivacidad f
vivid ['vɪvɪd] adj (account) gráfico; (light)
intenso; (imagination) vivo
vividly ['vɪvɪdlɪ] adv (describe) gráficamente;
(remember) como si fuera hoy
vivisection [vɪvɪ'sekʃən] n vivisección f
vixen ['vɪksn] n (Zool) zorra, raposa; (pej:
woman) arpía, bruja
viz abbr (= videlicet: namely) v.gr.
VLF abbr = **very low frequency**
V-neck ['viːnɛk] n cuello de pico
VOA n abbr (= Voice of America) Voz f de América
vocabulary [vəu'kæbjulərɪ] n vocabulario
vocal ['vəukl] adj vocal; (articulate) elocuente

V

vocal cords *npl* cuerdas *fpl* vocales
vocalist ['vəukəlıst] *n* cantante *m/f*
vocation [vəu'keıʃən] *n* vocación *f*
vocational [vəu'keıʃənl] *adj* vocacional;
~ **guidance** orientación *f* profesional; ~
training formación *f* profesional
vociferous [və'sıfərəs] *adj* vociferante
vociferously [və'sıfərəslı] *adv* a gritos
vodka ['vɔdkə] *n* vodka *m*
vogue [vəug] *n* boga, moda; **to be in ~, be
the ~** estar de moda *or* en boga
voice [vɔıs] *n* voz *f* ■ *vt* (*opinion*) expresar; **in
a loud/soft ~** en voz alta/baja; **to give ~ to**
expresar
voice mail *n* (*Tel*) fonobuzón *m*
voice-over ['vɔısəuvəʳ] *n* voz *f* en off
void [vɔıd] *n* vacío; (*hole*) hueco ■ *adj* (*invalid*)
nulo, inválido; (*empty*): ~ **of** carente *or*
desprovisto de
voile [vɔıl] *n* gasa
vol. *abbr* (= *volume*) t
volatile ['vɔlətaıl] *adj* volátil; (*Comput*:
memory) no permanente
volcanic [vɔl'kænık] *adj* volcánico
volcano (*pl* **volcanoes**) [vɔl'keınəu] *n* volcán *m*
volition [və'lıʃən] *n*: **of one's own** ~ por su
propia voluntad
volley ['vɔlı] *n* (*of gunfire*) descarga; (*of stones
etc*) lluvia; (*Tennis etc*) volea
volleyball *n* voleibol *m*, balonvolea *m*
volt [vəult] *n* voltio
voltage ['vəultıdʒ] *n* voltaje *m*; **high/low ~**
alto/bajo voltaje, alta/baja tensión
volte-face ['vɔlt'fɑːs] *n* viraje *m*
voluble ['vɔljubl] *adj* locuaz, hablador(a)
volume ['vɔljuːm] *n* (*of tank*) volumen
m; (*book*) tomo; ~ **one/two** (*of book*) tomo
primero/segundo; **volumes** *npl* (*great
quantities*) cantidad *fsg*; **his expression
spoke volumes** su expresión (lo) decía todo
volume control *n* (*Radio, TV*) (botón *m* del)
volumen *m*
volume discount *n* (*Comm*) descuento por
volumen de compras
voluminous [və'luːmınəs] *adj* (*large*)
voluminoso; (*prolific*) prolífico
voluntarily ['vɔləntrılı] *adv* libremente,
voluntariamente
voluntary ['vɔləntərı] *adj* voluntario,
espontáneo

voluntary liquidation *n* (*Comm*) liquidación
f voluntaria
voluntary redundancy *n* (*Brit*) despido
voluntario
volunteer [vɔlən'tıəʳ] *n* voluntario(-a)
■ *vi* ofrecerse (de voluntario); **to ~ to do**
ofrecerse a hacer
voluptuous [və'lʌptjuəs] *adj* voluptuoso
vomit ['vɔmıt] *n* vómito ■ *vt, vi* vomitar
voracious [və'reıʃəs] *adj* voraz; (*reader*) ávido
vote [vəut] *n* voto; (*votes cast*) votación *f*; (*right
to vote*) derecho a votar; (*franchise*) sufragio
■ *vt* (*chairman*) elegir ■ *vi* votar, ir a votar;
~ **of thanks** voto de gracias; **to put sth to
the ~, to take a ~ on sth** someter algo a
votación; ~ **for** *or* **in favour of/against** voto
a favor de/en contra de; **to ~ to do sth** votar
por hacer algo; **he was voted secretary** fue
elegido secretario por votación; **to pass a ~
of confidence/no confidence** aprobar un
voto de confianza/de censura
voter ['vəutəʳ] *n* votante *m/f*
voting ['vəutıŋ] *n* votación *f*
voting paper *n* (*Brit*) papeleta de votación
voting right *n* derecho a voto
vouch [vautʃ]: **to ~ for** *vt fus* garantizar,
responder de
voucher ['vautʃəʳ] *n* (*for meal, petrol*) vale *m*;
luncheon/travel ~ vale *m* de comida/de viaje
vow [vau] *n* voto ■ *vi* hacer voto; **to take**
or **make a ~ to do sth** jurar hacer algo,
comprometerse a hacer algo
vowel ['vauəl] *n* vocal *f*
voyage ['vɔııdʒ] *n* (*journey*) viaje *m*; (*crossing*)
travesía
voyeur [vwɑː'jəːʳ] *n* voyeur *m/f*, mirón(-ona)
m(f)
VP *n abbr* (= *vice-president*) V.P.
vs *abbr* (= *versus*) vs
VSO *n abbr* (*Brit*: = *Voluntary Service Overseas*)
organización que envía jóvenes voluntarios a trabajar
y enseñar en los países del Tercer Mundo
VT, Vt. *abbr* (*US*) = **Vermont**
vulgar ['vʌlgəʳ] *adj* (*rude*) ordinario, grosero;
(*in bad taste*) de mal gusto
vulgarity [vʌl'gærıtı] *n* grosería; mal gusto
vulnerability [vʌlnərə'bılıtı] *n*
vulnerabilidad *f*
vulnerable ['vʌlnərəbl] *adj* vulnerable
vulture ['vʌltʃəʳ] *n* buitre *m*, gallinazo (*LAm*)

Ww

W, w ['dʌblju:] n (letter) W, w f; **W for William** W de Washington

W abbr (= west) O; (Elec: = watt) v

WA abbr (US) = **Washington**

wad [wɔd] n (of cotton wool, paper) bolita; (of banknotes etc) fajo

wadding ['wɔdɪŋ] n relleno

waddle ['wɔdl] vi andar como un pato

wade [weɪd] vi: **to ~ through** caminar por el agua; (fig: a book) leer con dificultad

wading pool ['weɪdɪŋ-] n (US) piscina para niños

wafer ['weɪfəʳ] n (biscuit) barquillo; (Rel) oblea; (: consecrated) hostia; (Comput) oblea, microplaqueta

wafer-thin ['weɪfə'θɪn] adj finísimo

waffle ['wɔfl] n (Culin) gofre m ▪ vi meter el rollo

waffle iron n molde m para hacer gofres

waft [wɔft] vt llevar por el aire ▪ vi flotar

wag [wæg] vt menear, agitar ▪ vi moverse, menearse; **the dog wagged its tail** el perro meneó la cola

wage [weɪdʒ] n (also: **wages**) sueldo, salario ▪ vt: **to ~ war** hacer la guerra; **a day's ~** el sueldo de un día

wage claim n reivindicación f salarial

wage differential n diferencia salarial

wage earner n asalariado(-a)

wage freeze n congelación f de salarios

wage packet n sobre m de la paga

wager ['weɪdʒəʳ] n apuesta ▪ vt apostar

waggle ['wægl] vt menear, mover

wagon, waggon ['wægən] n (horse-drawn) carro; (Brit Rail) vagón m

wail [weɪl] n gemido ▪ vi gemir

waist [weɪst] n cintura, talle m

waistcoat ['weɪstkəut] n (Brit) chaleco

waistline ['weɪstlaɪn] n talle m

wait [weɪt] n espera; (interval) pausa ▪ vi esperar; **to lie in ~ for** acechar a; **I can't ~ to** (fig) estoy deseando; **to ~ for** esperar (a); **to keep sb waiting** hacer esperar a algn; **~ a**

moment! ¡un momento!, ¡un momentito!; **"repairs while you ~"** "reparaciones en el acto"

▶ **wait behind** vi quedarse

▶ **wait on** vt fus servir a

▶ **wait up** vi esperar levantado

waiter ['weɪtəʳ] n camarero

waiting ['weɪtɪŋ] n: **"no ~"** (Brit Aut) "prohibido estacionarse"

waiting list n lista de espera

waiting room n sala de espera

waitress ['weɪtrɪs] n camarera

waive [weɪv] vt suspender

waiver ['weɪvəʳ] n renuncia

wake [weɪk] (pt **woke** or **waked**, pp **woken** or **waked**) vt (also: **wake up**) despertar ▪ vi (also: **wake up**) despertarse ▪ n (for dead person) velatorio; (Naut) estela; **to ~ up to sth** (fig) darse cuenta de algo; **in the ~ of** tras, después de; **to follow in sb's ~** (fig) seguir las huellas de algn

waken ['weɪkn] vt, vi = **wake**

Wales [weɪlz] n País m de Gales

walk [wɔːk] n (stroll) paseo; (hike) excursión f a pie, caminata; (gait) paso, andar m; (in park etc) paseo ▪ vi andar, caminar; (for pleasure, exercise) pasearse ▪ vt (distance) recorrer a pie, andar; (dog) (sacar a) pasear; **to go for a ~** ir a dar un paseo; **10 minutes' ~ from here** a 10 minutos de aquí andando; **people from all walks of life** gente de todas las esferas; **to ~ in one's sleep** ser sonámbulo(-a); **I'll ~ you home** te acompañaré a casa

▶ **walk out** vi (go out) salir; (as protest) marcharse, salirse; (strike) declararse en huelga; **to ~ out on sb** abandonar a algn

walkabout ['wɔːkəbaut] n: **to go (on a) ~** darse un baño de multitudes

walker ['wɔːkəʳ] n (person) paseante m/f, caminante m/f

walkie-talkie ['wɔːkɪ'tɔːkɪ] n walkie-talkie m

walking ['wɔːkɪŋ] n (el) andar; **it's within ~ distance** se puede ir andando or a pie

w

walking stick n bastón m

Walkman® ['wɔːkmən] n walkman® m

walk-on ['wɔːkɔn] adj (Theat: part) de comparsa

walkout ['wɔːkaut] n (of workers) huelga

walkover ['wɔːkəuvəʳ] n (col) pan m comido

walkway ['wɔːkweɪ] n paseo

wall [wɔːl] n pared f; (exterior) muro; (city wall etc) muralla; **to go to the ~** (fig: firm etc) quebrar, ir a la bancarrota
  ▸ **wall in** vt (garden etc) cercar con una tapia

walled [wɔːld] adj (city) amurallado; (garden) con tapia

wallet ['wɔlɪt] n cartera, billetera (esp LAm)

wallflower ['wɔːlflauəʳ] n alhelí m; **to be a ~** (fig) comer pavo

wall hanging n tapiz m

wallop ['wɔləp] vt (col) zurrar

wallow ['wɔləu] vi revolcarse; **to ~ in one's grief** sumirse en su pena

wallpaper ['wɔːlpeɪpəʳ] n (for walls) papel m pintado; (Comput) fondo de escritorio

wall-to-wall ['wɔːltə'wɔːl] adj: **~ carpeting** moqueta

wally ['wɔlɪ] n (col) majadero(-a)

walnut ['wɔːlnʌt] n nuez f; (tree) nogal m

walrus (pl ~ or **walruses**) ['wɔːlrəs] n morsa

waltz [wɔːlts] n vals m ▪ vi bailar el vals

wan [wɔn] adj pálido

wand [wɔnd] n (also: **magic wand**) varita (mágica)

wander ['wɔndəʳ] vi (person) vagar; deambular; (thoughts) divagar; (get lost) extraviarse ▪ vt recorrer, vagar por

wanderer ['wɔndərəʳ] n vagabundo(-a)

wandering ['wɔndərɪŋ] adj (tribe) nómada; (minstrel, actor) ambulante; (path, river) sinuoso; (glance, mind) distraído

wane [weɪn] vi menguar

wangle ['wæŋgl] (Brit col) vt: **to ~ sth** agenciarse or conseguir algo ▪ n chanchullo

wanker ['wæŋkəʳ] n (col!) pajero(-a) (!); (as insult) mamón(-ona) (!) m/f

want [wɔnt] vt (wish for) querer, desear; (need) necesitar; (lack) carecer de ▪ n (poverty) pobreza; **for ~ of** por falta de; **wants** npl (needs) necesidades fpl; **to ~ to do** querer hacer; **to ~ sb to do sth** querer que algn haga algo; **you're wanted on the phone** te llaman al teléfono; **to be in ~** estar necesitado; **"cook wanted"** "se necesita cocinero(-a)"

want ads npl (US) anuncios mpl por palabras

wanting ['wɔntɪŋ] adj: **to be ~ (in)** estar falto (de); **to be found ~** no estar a la altura de las circunstancias

wanton ['wɔntɪn] adj (licentious) lascivo

WAP [wæp] n abbr (= wireless application protocol) WAP f

WAP phone n teléfono WAP

war [wɔːʳ] n guerra; **to make ~** hacer la guerra; **the First/Second World W~** la primera/segunda guerra mundial

warble ['wɔːbl] n (of bird) trino, gorjeo ▪ vi (bird) trinar

war cry n grito de guerra

ward [wɔːd] n (in hospital) sala; (Pol) distrito electoral; (Law: child) pupilo(-a)
  ▸ **ward off** vt desviar, parar; (attack) rechazar

warden ['wɔːdn] n (Brit: of institution) director(a) m(f); (of park, game reserve) guardián(-ana) m(f); (Brit: also: **traffic warden**) guardia m/f

warder ['wɔːdəʳ] n (Brit) guardián(-ana) m(f), carcelero(-a) m(f)

wardrobe ['wɔːdrəub] n armario, guardarropa, ropero, clóset/closet m (LAm)

warehouse ['wɛəhaus] n almacén m, depósito

wares [wɛəz] npl mercancías fpl

warfare ['wɔːfɛəʳ] n guerra

war game n juego de estrategia militar

warhead ['wɔːhɛd] n cabeza armada; **nuclear warheads** cabezas fpl nucleares

warily ['wɛərɪlɪ] adv con cautela, cautelosamente

warlike ['wɔːlaɪk] adj guerrero

warm [wɔːm] adj caliente; (person, greeting, heart) afectuoso, cariñoso; (supporter) entusiasta; (thanks, congratulations, apologies) efusivo; (clothes etc) que abriga; (welcome, day) caluroso; **it's ~** hace calor; **I'm ~** tengo calor; **to keep sth ~** mantener algo caliente
  ▸ **warm up** vi (room) calentarse; (person) entrar en calor; (athlete) hacer ejercicios de calentamiento; (discussion) acalorarse ▪ vt calentar

warm-blooded ['wɔːm'blʌdɪd] adj de sangre caliente

war memorial n monumento a los caídos

warm-hearted [wɔːm'hɑːtɪd] adj afectuoso

warmly ['wɔːmlɪ] adv afectuosamente

warmonger ['wɔːmʌŋgəʳ] n belicista m/f

warmongering ['wɔːmʌŋgrɪŋ] n belicismo

warmth [wɔːmθ] n calor m

warm-up ['wɔːmʌp] n (Sport) ejercicios mpl de calentamiento

warn [wɔːn] vt avisar, advertir; **to ~ sb not to do sth** or **against doing sth** aconsejar a algn que no haga algo

warning ['wɔːnɪŋ] n aviso, advertencia; **gale ~** (Meteorology) aviso de vendaval; **without (any) ~** sin aviso or avisar

warning light n luz f de advertencia

warning triangle n (Aut) triángulo
señalizador
warp [wɔːp] vi (wood) combarse
warpath ['wɔːpɑːθ] n: **to be on the ~** (fig)
estar en pie de guerra
warped [wɔːpt] adj (wood) alabeado; (fig:
character, sense of humour etc) pervertido
warrant ['wɔrnt] n (Law: to arrest) orden f
de detención; (: to search) mandamiento de
registro ■ vt (justify, merit) merecer
warrant officer n (Mil) brigada m; (Naut)
contramaestre m
warranty ['wɔrəntɪ] n garantía; **under ~**
(Comm) bajo garantía
warren ['wɔrən] n (of rabbits) madriguera;
(fig) laberinto
warring ['wɔːrɪŋ] adj (interests etc) opuesto;
(nations) en guerra
warrior ['wɔrɪər] n guerrero(-a)
Warsaw ['wɔːsɔː] n Varsovia
warship ['wɔːʃɪp] n buque m or barco de guerra
wart [wɔːt] n verruga
wartime ['wɔːtaɪm] n: **in ~** en tiempos de
guerra, en la guerra
wary ['wɛərɪ] adj cauteloso; **to be ~ about** or
of doing sth tener cuidado con hacer algo
was [wɒz] pt of **be**
wash [wɒʃ] vt lavar; (sweep, carry: sea etc)
llevar ■ vi lavarse ■ n (clothes etc) lavado;
(bath) baño; (of ship) estela; **he was washed
overboard** fue arrastrado del barco por las
olas; **to have a ~** lavarse
▸ **wash away** vt (stain) quitar lavando;
(river etc) llevarse; (fig) limpiar
▸ **wash down** vt lavar
▸ **wash off** vt quitar lavando
▸ **wash up** vi (Brit) fregar los platos; (US: have
a wash) lavarse
Wash. abbr (US) = **Washington**
washable ['wɒʃəbl] adj lavable
washbasin ['wɒʃbeɪsn], **washbowl** (US)
['wɒʃbəul] n lavabo
washcloth ['wɒʃklɔθ] n (US) manopla
washer ['wɒʃər] n (Tech) arandela
washing ['wɒʃɪŋ] n (dirty) ropa sucia; (clean)
colada
washing line n cuerda de (colgar) la ropa
washing machine n lavadora
washing powder n (Brit) detergente m (en
polvo)
Washington ['wɒʃɪŋtən] n (city, state)
Washington m
washing-up [wɒʃɪŋ'ʌp] n fregado; (dishes)
platos mpl (para fregar); **to do the ~** fregar
los platos
washing-up liquid n lavavajillas m inv
wash leather n gamuza

wash-out ['wɒʃaut] n (col) fracaso
washroom ['wɒʃrum] n servicios mpl
wasn't ['wɒznt] = **was not**
WASP, Wasp [wɒsp] n abbr (US col: = White
Anglo-Saxon Protestant) sobrenombre, en general
peyorativo, que se da a los americanos de origen
anglosajón, acomodados y de tendencia conservadora
wasp [wɒsp] n avispa
waspish ['wɒspɪʃ] adj (character) irascible;
(comment) mordaz, punzante
wastage ['weɪstɪdʒ] n desgaste m; (loss)
pérdida; **natural ~** desgaste natural
waste [weɪst] n derroche m, despilfarro;
(misuse) desgaste m; (of time) pérdida; (food)
sobras fpl; (rubbish) basura, desperdicios mpl
■ adj (material) de desecho; (left over) sobrante;
(energy, heat) desperdiciado; (land, ground: in
city) sin construir; (: in country) baldío ■ vt
(squander) malgastar, derrochar; (time)
perder; (opportunity) desperdiciar; **wastes**
npl (area of land) tierras fpl baldías; **to lay ~**
devastar, arrasar; **it's a ~ of money** es tirar
el dinero; **to go to ~** desperdiciarse
▸ **waste away** vi consumirse
wastebasket ['weɪstbɑːskɪt] n (esp US)
= **wastepaper basket**
waste disposal, waste disposal unit n
(Brit) triturador m de basura
wasteful ['weɪstful] adj derrochador(a);
(process) antieconómico
wastefully ['weɪstfulɪ] adv: **to spend money
~** derrochar dinero
waste ground n (Brit) terreno baldío
wasteland ['weɪstlənd] n (urban)
descampados mpl
wastepaper basket ['weɪstpeɪpə-] n
papelera; (Comput) papelera de reciclaje
waste pipe n tubo de desagüe
waste products npl (Industry) residuos mpl
waster ['weɪstər] n (col) gandul m/f
watch [wɒtʃ] n reloj m; (vigil) vigilia;
(vigilance) vigilancia; (Mil: guard) centinela
m; (Naut: spell of duty) guardia ■ vt (look at)
mirar, observar; (: match, programme) ver;
(spy on, guard) vigilar; (be careful of) cuidar,
tener cuidado de ■ vi ver, mirar; (keep guard)
montar guardia; **to keep a close ~ on sth/
sb** vigilar algo/a algn de cerca; **~ how you
drive/what you're doing** ten cuidado al
conducir/con lo que haces
▸ **watch out** vi cuidarse, tener cuidado
watch band n (US) pulsera (de reloj)
watchdog ['wɒtʃdɔg] n perro guardián; (fig)
organismo de control
watchful ['wɒtʃful] adj vigilante, sobre aviso
watchfully ['wɒtʃfulɪ] adv: **to stand ~**
permanecer vigilante

W

watchmaker ['wɔtʃmeɪkəʳ] n relojero(-a)
watchman n guardián m; (also: **night watchman**) sereno, vigilante m; (in factory) vigilante m nocturno
watch stem n (US) cuerda
watch strap n pulsera (de reloj)
watchword ['wɔtʃwə:d] n consigna, contraseña
water ['wɔ:təʳ] n agua ■ vt (plant) regar ■ vi (eyes) llorar; **I'd like a drink of ~** quisiera un vaso de agua; **in British waters** en aguas británicas; **to pass ~** orinar; **his mouth watered** se le hizo la boca agua
▶ **water down** vt (milk etc) aguar
water closet n wáter m
watercolour, watercolor (US) ['wɔ:təkʌləʳ] n acuarela
water-cooled ['wɔ:təku:ld] adj refrigerado (por agua)
watercress ['wɔ:təkrɛs] n berro
waterfall ['wɔ:təfɔ:l] n cascada, salto de agua
waterfront ['wɔ:təfrʌnt] n (seafront) parte f que da al mar; (at docks) muelles mpl
water heater n calentador m de agua
water hole n abrevadero
watering can ['wɔ:tərɪŋ-] n regadera
water level n nivel m del agua
water lily n nenúfar m
waterline ['wɔ:təlaɪn] n (Naut) línea de flotación
waterlogged ['wɔ:tələgd] adj (boat) anegado; (ground) inundado
water main n cañería del agua
watermark ['wɔ:təmɑ:k] n (on paper) filigrana
watermelon ['wɔ:təmɛlən] n sandía
water polo n waterpolo, polo acuático
waterproof ['wɔ:təpru:f] adj impermeable
water-repellent ['wɔ:tərɪ'pɛlənt] adj hidrófugo
watershed ['wɔ:təʃɛd] n (Geo) cuenca; (fig) momento crítico
water-skiing ['wɔ:təski:ɪŋ] n esquí m acuático
water softener n ablandador m de agua
water tank n depósito de agua
watertight ['wɔ:tətaɪt] adj hermético
water vapour, water vapor (US) n vapor m de agua
waterway ['wɔ:təweɪ] n vía fluvial or navegable
waterworks ['wɔ:təwə:ks] npl central fsg depuradora
watery ['wɔ:tərɪ] adj (colour) desvaído; (coffee) aguado; (eyes) lloroso
watt [wɔt] n vatio
wattage ['wɔtɪdʒ] n potencia en vatios

wattle ['wɔtl] n zarzo
wave [weɪv] n ola; (of hand) señal f con la mano; (Radio) onda; (in hair) onda; (fig: of enthusiasm, strikes) oleada ■ vi agitar la mano; (flag) ondear ■ vt (handkerchief, gun) agitar; **short/medium/long ~** (Radio) onda corta/media/larga; **the new ~** (Cine, Mus) la nueva ola; **to ~ goodbye to sb** decir adiós a algn con la mano; **he waved us over to his table** nos hizo señas (con la mano) para que nos acercásemos a su mesa
▶ **wave aside, wave away** vt (person): **to ~ sb aside** apartar a algn con la mano; (fig: suggestion, objection) rechazar; (doubts) desechar
waveband ['weɪvbænd] n banda de ondas
wavelength ['weɪvlɛŋθ] n longitud f de onda
waver ['weɪvəʳ] vi oscilar; (confidence) disminuir; (faith) flaquear
wavy ['weɪvɪ] adj ondulado
wax [wæks] n cera ■ vt encerar ■ vi (moon) crecer
waxen ['wæksn] adj (fig: pale) blanco como la cera
waxworks ['wækswə:ks] npl museo sg de cera
way [weɪ] n camino; (distance) trayecto, recorrido; (direction) dirección f, sentido; (manner) modo, manera; (habit) costumbre f; **which ~? — this ~** ¿por dónde? or ¿en qué dirección? — por aquí; **on the ~** (en route) en (el) camino; (expected) en camino; **to be on one's ~** estar en camino; **you pass it on your ~ home** está de camino a tu casa; **to be in the ~** bloquear el camino; (fig) estorbar; **to keep out of sb's ~** esquivar a algn; **to make ~ (for sb/sth)** dejar paso (a algn/algo); (fig) abrir camino (a algn/algo); **to go out of one's ~ to do sth** desvivirse por hacer algo; **to lose one's ~** perderse, extraviarse; **to be the wrong ~ round** estar del or al revés; **in a ~** en cierto modo or sentido; **by the ~** a propósito; **by ~ of** (via) pasando por; (as a sort of) como, a modo de; **"~ in"** (Brit) "entrada"; **"~ out"** (Brit) "salida"; **the ~ back** el camino de vuelta; **the village is rather out of the ~** el pueblo está un poco apartado or retirado; **it's a long ~ away** está muy lejos; **to get one's own ~** salirse con la suya; **"give ~"** (Brit Aut) "ceda el paso"; **no ~!** (col) ¡ni pensarlo!; **put it the right ~ up** ponlo boca arriba; **he's in a bad ~** está grave; **to be under ~** (work, project) estar en marcha
waybill ['weɪbɪl] n (Comm) hoja de ruta, carta de porte
waylay [weɪ'leɪ] vt (irreg: like **lay**) atacar
wayside ['weɪsaɪd] n borde m del camino; **to fall by the ~** (fig) fracasar

way station n (US Rail) apeadero
wayward ['weɪwəd] adj díscolo, caprichoso
WC ['dʌblju:'si:] n abbr (Brit: = water closet) wáter m
WCC n abbr = **World Council of Churches**
we [wi:] pl pron nosotros(-as); **we understand** (nosotros) entendemos; **here we are** aquí estamos
weak [wi:k] adj débil, flojo; (tea, coffee) flojo, aguado; **to grow ~(er)** debilitarse
weaken ['wi:kən] vi debilitarse; (give way) ceder ■ vt debilitar
weak-kneed [wi:k'ni:d] adj (fig) sin voluntad or carácter
weakling ['wi:klɪŋ] n debilucho(a)
weakly ['wi:klɪ] adj enfermizo, débil ■ adv débilmente
weakness ['wi:knɪs] n debilidad f; (fault) punto débil
wealth [welθ] n (money, resources) riqueza; (of details) abundancia
wealth tax n impuesto sobre el patrimonio
wealthy ['welθɪ] adj rico
wean [wi:n] vt destetar
weapon ['wepən] n arma; **weapons of mass destruction** armas de destrucción masiva
wear [weəʳ] (pt **wore**, pp **worn**) n (use) uso; (deterioration through use) desgaste m; (clothing): **sports/babywear** ropa de deportes/de niños ■ vt (clothes, beard) llevar; (shoes) calzar; (look, smile) tener; (damage: through use) gastar, usar ■ vi (last) durar; (rub through etc) desgastarse; **evening ~** (man's) traje m de etiqueta; (woman's) traje m de noche; **to ~ a hole in sth** hacer un agujero en algo
  ▶ **wear away** vt gastar ■ vi desgastarse
  ▶ **wear down** vt gastar; (strength) agotar
  ▶ **wear off** vi (pain, excitement etc) pasar, desaparecer
  ▶ **wear out** vt desgastar; (person, strength) agotar
wearable ['weərəbl] adj que se puede llevar, ponible
wear and tear n desgaste m
wearer ['weərəʳ] n: **the ~ of this jacket** el/la que lleva puesta esta chaqueta
wearily ['wɪərɪlɪ] adv con cansancio
weariness ['wɪərɪnɪs] n cansancio; abatimiento
wearisome ['wɪərɪsəm] adj (tiring) cansado, pesado; (boring) aburrido
weary ['wɪərɪ] adj (tired) cansado; (dispirited) abatido ■ vt cansar ■ vi: **to ~ of** cansarse de, aburrirse de
weasel ['wi:zl] n (Zool) comadreja
weather ['weðəʳ] n tiempo ■ vt (storm, crisis) hacer frente a; **under the ~** (fig: ill) mal, pachucho; **what's the ~ like?** ¿qué tiempo

hace?, ¿cómo hace?
weather-beaten ['weðəbi:tn] adj curtido
weathercock ['weðəkɔk] n veleta
weather forecast n boletín m meteorológico
weatherman ['weðəmæn] n hombre m del tiempo
weatherproof ['weðəpru:f] adj (garment) impermeable
weather report n parte m meteorológico
weather vane n = **weathercock**
weave (pt **wove**, pp **woven**) [wi:v, wəuv, 'wəuvn] vt (cloth) tejer; (fig) entretejer ■ vi (pt, pp **weaved**) (move in and out) zigzaguear
weaver ['wi:vəʳ] n tejedor(a) m(f)
weaving ['wi:vɪŋ] n tejeduría
web [web] n (of spider) telaraña; (on foot) membrana; (Comput: network) red f; **the (World Wide) W~** el or la Web
web address n dirección f de página web
webbed [webd] adj (foot) palmeado
webbing ['webɪŋ] n (on chair) cinchas fpl
webcam ['webkæm] n webcam f
weblog ['weblɔg] n weblog m
web page n página web
website ['websaɪt] n sitio web
wed [wed] vt (pt, pp **wedded**) casar ■ n: **the newly-weds** los recién casados
Wed. abbr (= Wednesday) miérc
we'd [wi:d] = **we had**; **we would**
wedded ['wedɪd] pt, pp of **wed**
wedding ['wedɪŋ] n boda, casamiento
wedding anniversary n aniversario de boda; **silver/golden ~** bodas fpl de plata/de oro
wedding day n día m de la boda
wedding dress n traje m de novia
wedding present n regalo de boda
wedding ring n alianza
wedge [wedʒ] n (of wood etc) cuña; (of cake) trozo ■ vt acuñar; (push) apretar
wedge-heeled ['wedʒ'hi:ld] adj con suela de cuña
wedlock ['wedlɔk] n matrimonio
Wednesday ['wednzdɪ] n miércoles m inv; see also **Tuesday**
wee [wi:] adj (Scottish) pequeñito
weed [wi:d] n mala hierba, maleza ■ vt escardar, desherbar
  ▶ **weed out** vt eliminar
weedkiller ['wi:dkɪləʳ] n herbicida m
weedy ['wi:dɪ] adj (person) debilucho
week [wi:k] n semana; **a ~ today** de hoy en ocho días; **Tuesday ~, a ~ on Tuesday** del martes en una semana; **once/twice a ~** una vez/dos veces a la semana; **this ~** esta semana; **in two weeks' time** dentro de dos semanas; **every other ~** cada dos semanas

W

weekday ['wiːkdeɪ] n día m laborable; **on weekdays** entre semana, en días laborables
weekend [wiːk'end] n fin m de semana
weekend case n neceser m
weekly ['wiːklɪ] adv semanalmente, cada semana ■ adj semanal ■ n semanario; ~ **newspaper** semanario
weep (pt, pp **wept**) [wiːp, wɛpt] vi, vt llorar; (Med: wound etc) supurar
weeping willow ['wiːpɪŋ-] n sauce m llorón
weepy ['wiːpɪ] n (col: film) película lacrimógena; (: story) historia lacrimógena
weft [wɛft] n (Textiles) trama
weigh [weɪ] vt, vi pesar; **to ~ anchor** levar anclas; **to ~ the pros and cons** pesar los pros y los contras
▶ **weigh down** vt sobrecargar; (fig: with worry) agobiar
▶ **weigh out** vt (goods) pesar
▶ **weigh up** vt pesar
weighbridge ['weɪbrɪdʒ] n báscula para camiones
weighing machine ['weɪɪŋ-] n báscula, peso
weight [weɪt] n peso; (on scale) pesa; **to lose/ put on ~** adelgazar/engordar; **weights and measures** pesas y medidas
weighting ['weɪtɪŋ] n (allowance): (**London**) ~ dietas (por residir en Londres)
weightlessness ['weɪtlɪsnɪs] n ingravidez f
weight lifter n levantador(a) m(f) de pesas
weight limit n límite m de peso
weight training n musculación f (con pesas)
weighty ['weɪtɪ] adj pesado
weir [wɪəʳ] n presa
weird [wɪəd] adj raro, extraño
weirdo ['wɪədəʊ] n (col) tio(-a) raro(-a)
welcome ['wɛlkəm] adj bienvenido ■ n bienvenida ■ vt dar la bienvenida a; (be glad of) alegrarse de; **to make sb ~** recibir or acoger bien a algn; **thank you — you're ~** gracias — de nada; **you're ~ to try** puede intentar cuando quiera; **we ~ this step** celebramos esta medida
weld [wɛld] n soldadura ■ vt soldar
welding ['wɛldɪŋ] n soldadura
welfare ['wɛlfɛəʳ] n bienestar m; (social aid) asistencia social; **W~** (US) subsidio de paro; **to look after sb's ~** cuidar del bienestar de algn
welfare state n estado del bienestar
welfare work n asistencia social
well [wɛl] n pozo ■ adv bien ■ adj: **to be ~** estar bien (de salud) ■ excl ¡vaya!, ¡bueno!; **as ~** (in addition) además, también; **as ~ as** además de; **you might as ~ tell me** más vale que me lo digas; **it would be as ~ to ask** más valdría preguntar; **~ done!** ¡bien

hecho!; **get ~ soon!** ¡que te mejores pronto!; **to do ~** (business) ir bien; **I did ~ in my exams** me han salido bien los exámenes; **they are doing ~ now** les va bien ahora; **to think ~ of sb** pensar bien de algn; **I don't feel ~** no me encuentro or siento bien; **~, as I was saying** ... bueno, como decía ...
▶ **well up** vi brotar
we'll [wiːl] = **we will; we shall**
well-behaved ['wɛlbɪ'heɪvd] adj: **to be ~** portarse bien
well-being ['wɛl'biːɪŋ] n bienestar m
well-bred ['wɛl'brɛd] adj bien educado
well-built ['wɛl'bɪlt] adj (person) fornido
well-chosen ['wɛl'tʃəuzn] adj (remarks, words) acertado
well-deserved ['wɛldɪ'zəːvd] adj merecido
well-developed ['wɛldɪ'vɛləpt] adj (arm, muscle etc) bien desarrollado; (sense) agudo, fino
well-disposed ['wɛldɪs'pəuzd] adj: ~ **to(wards)** bien dispuesto a
well-dressed ['wɛl'drɛst] adj bien vestido
well-earned ['wɛl'əːnd] adj (rest) merecido
well-groomed ['wɛl'gruːmd] adj de apariencia cuidada
well-heeled ['wɛl'hiːld] adj (col: wealthy) rico
well-informed ['wɛlɪn'fɔːmd] adj (having knowledge of sth) enterado, al corriente
Wellington ['wɛlɪŋtən] n Wellington m
wellingtons ['wɛlɪŋtənz] npl (also: **Wellington boots**) botas fpl de goma
well-kept ['wɛl'kɛpt] adj (secret) bien guardado; (hair, hands, house, grounds) bien cuidado
well-known ['wɛl'nəun] adj (person) conocido
well-mannered ['wɛl'mænəd] adj educado
well-meaning ['wɛl'miːnɪŋ] adj bienintencionado
well-nigh ['wɛl'naɪ] adv: ~ **impossible** casi imposible
well-off ['wɛl'ɔf] adj acomodado
well-read ['wɛl'rɛd] adj culto
well-spoken ['wɛl'spəukən] adj bienhablado
well-stocked ['wɛl'stɔkt] adj (shop, larder) bien surtido
well-timed ['wɛl'taɪmd] adj oportuno
well-to-do ['wɛltə'duː] adj acomodado
well-wisher ['wɛlwɪʃəʳ] n admirador(a) m(f)
well-woman clinic ['wɛlwumən-] n centro de prevención médica para mujeres
Welsh [wɛlʃ] adj galés(-esa) ■ n (Ling) galés m; **the Welsh** npl los galeses; **the ~ Assembly** el Parlamento galés
Welshman ['wɛlʃmən] n galés m
Welsh rarebit [-'rɛəbɪt] n pan m con queso tostado

Welshwoman ['wɛlʃwumən] *n* galesa
welter ['wɛltə^r] *n* mescolanza, revoltijo
went [wɛnt] *pt of* **go**
wept [wɛpt] *pt, pp of* **weep**
were [wə:^r] *pt of* **be**
we're [wɪə^r] = **we are**
weren't [wə:nt] = **were not**
werewolf (*pl* **werewolves**) ['wɪəwulf, -wulvz]
   n hombre *m* lobo
west [wɛst] *n* oeste *m* ▪ *adj* occidental, del
   oeste ▪ *adv* al *or* hacia el oeste; **the W~**
   Occidente *m*
westbound ['wɛstbaund] *adj* (*traffic,*
   carriageway) con rumbo al oeste
West Country *n*: **the ~** el suroeste de
   Inglaterra
westerly ['wɛstəlɪ] *adj* (*wind*) del oeste
western ['wɛstən] *adj* occidental ▪ *n* (*Cine*)
   película del oeste
westerner ['wɛstənə^r] *n* (*Pol*) occidental *m/f*
westernized ['wɛstənaɪzd] *adj*
   occidentalizado
West German (*formerly*) *adj* de Alemania
   Occidental ▪ *n* alemán(-ana) *m(f)* (de
   Alemania Occidental)
West Germany *n* (*formerly*) Alemania
   Occidental
West Indian *adj, n* antillano(-a) *m(f)*
West Indies [-'ɪndɪz] *npl*: **the ~** las Antillas
Westminster ['wɛstmɪnstə^r] *n* el parlamento
   británico, Westminster *m*
westward ['wɛstwəd], **westwards**
   ['wɛstwədz] *adv* hacia el oeste
wet [wɛt] *adj* (*damp*) húmedo; (*wet through*)
   mojado; (*rainy*) lluvioso ▪ *vt*: **to ~ one's**
   pants *or* **o.s.** mearse; **to get ~** mojarse;
   "~ paint" "recién pintado"
wet blanket *n*: **to be a ~** (*fig*) ser un/una
   aguafiestas
wetness ['wɛtnɪs] *n* humedad *f*
wet rot *n* putrefacción *f* por humedad
wet suit *n* traje *m* de buzo
we've [wi:v] = **we have**
whack [wæk] *vt* dar un buen golpe a
whale [weɪl] *n* (*Zool*) ballena
whaler ['weɪlə^r] *n* (*ship*) ballenero
whaling ['weɪlɪŋ] *n* pesca de ballenas
wharf (*pl* **wharves**) [wɔ:f, wɔ:vz] *n* muelle *m*

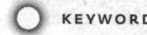 **KEYWORD**

what [wɔt] *adj* **1** (*in direct/indirect questions*)
   qué; **what size is he?** ¿qué talla usa?; **what**
   colour/shape is it? ¿de qué color/forma
   es?; **what books do you need?** ¿qué libros
   necesitas?
2 (*in exclamations*): **what a mess!** ¡qué

desastre!; **what a fool I am!** ¡qué tonto soy!
▪ *pron* **1** (*interrogative*) qué; **what are you**
   doing? ¿qué haces *or* estás haciendo?; **what**
   is happening? ¿qué pasa *or* está pasando?;
   what is it called? ¿cómo se llama?; **what**
   about me? ¿y yo qué?; **what about doing**
   ...? ¿qué tal si hacemos ...?; **what is his**
   address? ¿cuáles son sus señas?; **what will**
   it cost? ¿cuánto costará?
2 (*relative*) lo que; **I saw what you did/was on**
   the table vi lo que hiciste/había en la mesa;
   what I want is a cup of tea lo que quiero es
   una taza de té; **I don't know what to do** no
   sé qué hacer; **tell me what you're thinking**
   about dime en qué estás pensando
3 (*reported questions*): **she asked me what I**
   wanted me preguntó qué quería
▪ *excl* (*disbelieving*) ¡cómo!; **what, no coffee!**
   ¡que no hay café!

whatever [wɔt'ɛvə^r] *adj*: **~ book you choose**
   cualquier libro que elijas ▪ *pron*: **do ~ is**
   necessary haga lo que sea necesario; **no**
   reason ~ ninguna razón en absoluto; **no**
   nothing ~ nada en absoluto; **~ it costs**
   cueste lo que cueste
wheat [wi:t] *n* trigo
wheatgerm ['wi:tdʒə:m] *n* germen *m* de
   trigo
wheatmeal ['wi:tmi:l] *n* harina de trigo
wheedle ['wi:dl] *vt*: **to ~ sb into doing sth**
   engatusar a algn para que haga algo; **to ~**
   sth out of sb sonsacar algo a algn
wheel [wi:l] *n* rueda; (*Aut: also:* **steering**
   wheel) volante *m*; (*Naut*) timón *m* ▪ *vt* (*pram*
   etc) empujar ▪ *vi* (*also:* **wheel round**) dar la
   vuelta, girar; **four-~ drive** tracción *f* en las
   cuatro ruedas; **front-/rear-~ drive** tracción *f*
   delantera/trasera
wheelbarrow ['wi:lbærəu] *n* carretilla
wheelbase ['wi:lbeɪs] *n* batalla
wheelchair ['wi:ltʃeə^r] *n* silla de ruedas
wheel clamp *n* (*Aut*) cepo
wheeler-dealer ['wi:lə'di:lə^r] *n*
   chanchullero(-a)
wheelie-bin ['wi:lɪbɪn] *n* (*Brit*) contenedor *m*
   de basura
wheeling ['wi:lɪŋ] *n*: **~ and dealing** (*col*)
   chanchullos *mpl*
wheeze [wi:z] *vi* resollar
wheezy ['wi:zɪ] *adj* silbante

 KEYWORD

when [wɛn] *adv* cuando; **when did it**
   happen? ¿cuándo ocurrió?; **I know when it**
   happened sé cuándo ocurrió

865

W

■ *conj* **1** (*at, during, after the time that*) cuando; **be careful when you cross the road** ten cuidado al cruzar la calle; **that was when I needed you** entonces era cuando te necesitaba; **I'll buy you a car when you're 18** te compraré un coche cuando cumplas 18 años **2** (*on, at which*): **on the day when I met him** el día en qué le conocí **3** (*whereas*) cuando; **you said I was wrong when in fact I was right** dijiste que no tenía razón, cuando en realidad sí la tenía

whenever [wɛn'ɛvəʳ] *conj* cuando; (*every time*) cada vez que; **I go ~ I can** voy siempre *or* todas las veces que puedo
where [wɛəʳ] *adv* dónde ■ *conj* donde; **this is ~** aquí es donde; **~ possible** donde sea posible; **~ are you from?** ¿de dónde es usted?
whereabouts ['wɛərəbauts] *adv* dónde ■ *n*: **nobody knows his ~** nadie conoce su paradero
whereas [wɛər'æz] *conj* mientras
whereby [wɛə'baɪ] *adv* mediante el/la cual *etc*
whereupon [wɛərə'pɒn] *conj* con lo cual, después de lo cual
wherever [wɛər'ɛvəʳ] *adv* dondequiera que; (*interrogative*) dónde; **sit ~ you like** siéntese donde quiera
wherewithal ['wɛəwɪðɔːl] *n* recursos *mpl*; **the ~ (to do sth)** los medios económicos (para hacer algo)
whet [wɛt] *vt* estimular; (*appetite*) abrir
whether ['wɛðəʳ] *conj* si; **I don't know ~ to accept or not** no sé si aceptar o no; **~ you go or not** vayas o no vayas
whey [weɪ] *n* suero

○ **KEYWORD**

which [wɪtʃ] *adj* **1** (*interrogative: direct, indirect*) qué; **which picture(s) do you want?** ¿qué cuadro(s) quieres?; **which one?** ¿cuál?; **which one of you?** ¿cuál de vosotros?; **tell me which one you want** dime cuál (es el que) quieres
2: **in which case** en cuyo caso; **we got there at eight pm, by which time the cinema was full** llegamos allí a las ocho, cuando el cine estaba lleno
■ *pron* (*interrogative*) cual; **I don't mind which** el(-la) que sea; **which do you want?** ¿cuál quieres?
3 (*relative: replacing noun*) que; (*: replacing clause*) lo que; (*: after preposition*) (el(-la)) que, el(-la) cual; **the apple which you ate/which is on the table** la manzana que comiste/que está en la mesa; **the chair on which you**

are sitting la silla en la que estás sentado; **he didn't believe it, which upset me** no se lo creyó, lo cual *or* lo que me disgustó; **after which** después de lo cual

whichever [wɪtʃ'ɛvəʳ] *adj*: **take ~ book you prefer** coja el libro que prefiera; **~ book you take** cualquier libro que coja
whiff [wɪf] *n* bocanada; **to catch a ~ of sth** oler algo
while [waɪl] *n* rato, momento ■ *conj* durante; (*whereas*) mientras; (*although*) aunque ■ *vt*: **to ~ away the time** pasar el rato; **for a ~** durante algún tiempo; **in a ~** dentro de poco; **all the ~** todo el tiempo; **we'll make it worth your ~** te compensaremos generosamente
whilst [waɪlst] *conj* = **while**
whim [wɪm] *n* capricho
whimper ['wɪmpəʳ] *n* (*weeping*) lloriqueo; (*moan*) quejido ■ *vi* lloriquear; quejarse
whimsical ['wɪmzɪkl] *adj* (*person*) caprichoso
whine [waɪn] *n* (*of pain*) gemido; (*of engine*) zumbido ■ *vi* gemir; zumbar
whip [wɪp] *n* látigo; (*Brit: Pol*) *diputado encargado de la disciplina del partido en el parlamento* ■ *vt* azotar; (*snatch*) arrebatar; (*US Culin*) batir
▶ **whip up** *vt* (*cream etc*) batir (rápidamente); (*col: meal*) preparar rápidamente; (*: stir up: support, feeling*) avivar; *ver nota*

○ **WHIP**

○ En el Parlamento británico la
○ disciplina de partido (en concreto de
○ voto y de asistencia a la Cámara de los
○ Comunes) está a cargo de un grupo
○ de parlamentarios llamados *whips*,
○ encabezados por el "Chief Whip". Por lo
○ general todos ellos tienen también otros
○ cargos en la Administración del Estado si
○ pertenecen al partido en el poder.

whiplash ['wɪplæʃ] *n* (*Med: also*: **whiplash injury**) latigazo
whipped cream [wɪpt-] *n* nata montada
whipping boy ['wɪpɪŋ-] *n* (*fig*) cabeza de turco
whip-round ['wɪpraund] *n* (*Brit*) colecta
whirl [wəːl] *n* remolino ■ *vt* hacer girar, dar vueltas a ■ *vi* (*dancers*) girar, dar vueltas; (*leaves, dust, water etc*) arremolinarse
whirlpool ['wəːlpuːl] *n* remolino
whirlwind ['wəːlwɪnd] *n* torbellino
whirr [wəːʳ] *vi* zumbar
whisk [wɪsk] *n* (*Brit Culin*) batidor *m* ■ *vt* (*Brit Culin*) batir; **to ~ sb away** *or* **off** llevarse volando a algn

whiskers [ˈwɪskəz] npl (of animal) bigotes mpl; (of man) patillas fpl

whisky, whiskey (US, Ireland) [ˈwɪskɪ] n whisky m

whisper [ˈwɪspəʳ] n cuchicheo; (rumour) rumor m; (fig) susurro, murmullo ◼ vi cuchichear, hablar bajo; (fig) susurrar ◼ vt decir en voz muy baja; **to ~ sth to sb** decirle algo al oído a algn

whispering [ˈwɪspərɪŋ] n cuchicheo

whist [wɪst] n (Brit) whist m

whistle [ˈwɪsl] n (sound) silbido; (object) silbato ◼ vi silbar; **to ~ a tune** silbar una melodía

whistle-stop [ˈwɪslstɔp] adj: **~ tour** (US Pol) gira electoral rápida; (fig) recorrido rápido

Whit [wɪt] n Pentecostés m

white [waɪt] adj blanco; (pale) pálido ◼ n blanco; (of egg) clara; **to turn** or **go ~** (person) palidecer, ponerse blanco; (hair) encanecer; **the whites** (washing) la ropa blanca; **tennis whites** ropa f de tenis

whitebait [ˈwaɪtbeɪt] n chanquetes mpl

whiteboard [ˈwaɪtbɔːd] n pizarra blanca; **interactive ~** pizarra interactiva

white coffee n (Brit) café m con leche

white-collar worker [ˈwaɪtkɔlə-] n oficinista m/f

white elephant n (fig) maula

white goods npl (appliances) electrodomésticos mpl de línea blanca; (linen etc) ropa blanca

white-hot [waɪtˈhɔt] adj (metal) candente, calentado al (rojo) blanco

white lie n mentirijilla

whiteness [ˈwaɪtnɪs] n blancura

white noise n sonido blanco

whiteout [ˈwaɪtaut] n resplandor m sin sombras; (fig) masa confusa

white paper n (Pol) libro blanco

whitewash [ˈwaɪtwɔʃ] n (paint) cal f, jalbegue m ◼ vt encalar, blanquear; (fig) encubrir

whiting [ˈwaɪtɪŋ] n (pl inv: fish) pescadilla

Whit Monday n lunes m de Pentecostés

Whitsun [ˈwɪtsn] n (Brit) Pentecostés m

whittle [ˈwɪtl] vt: **to ~ away; whittle down** ir reduciendo

whizz [wɪz] vi: **to ~ past** or **by** pasar a toda velocidad

whizz kid n (col) prodigio(-a)

WHO n abbr (= World Health Organization) OMS f

 KEYWORD

who [huː] pron **1** (interrogative) quién; **who is it?, who's there?** ¿quién es?; **who are you looking for?** ¿a quién buscas?; **I told her who I was** le dije quién era yo

2 (relative) que; **the man/woman who spoke to me** el hombre/la mujer que habló conmigo; **those who can swim** los que saben or sepan nadar

whodunit, whodunnit [huːˈdʌnɪt] n (col) novela policíaca

whoever [huːˈɛvəʳ] pron: **~ finds it** cualquiera or quienquiera que lo encuentre; **ask ~ you like** pregunta a quien quieras; **~ he marries** se case con quien se case

whole [həul] adj (complete) todo, entero; (not broken) intacto ◼ n (total) total m; (sum) conjunto; **~ villages were destroyed** pueblos enteros fueron destruídos; **the ~ of the town** toda la ciudad, la ciudad entera; **on the ~, as a ~** en general

wholehearted [həulˈhaːtɪd] adj (support, approval) total; (sympathy) todo

wholeheartedly [həulˈhaːtɪdlɪ] adv con entusiasmo

wholemeal [ˈhəulmiːl] adj (Brit: flour, bread) integral

wholesale [ˈhəulseɪl] n venta al por mayor ◼ adj al por mayor; (destruction) sistemático

wholesaler [ˈhəulseɪləʳ] n mayorista m/f

wholesome [ˈhəulsəm] adj sano

wholewheat [ˈhəulwiːt] adj = wholemeal

wholly [ˈhəulɪ] adv totalmente, enteramente

 KEYWORD

whom [huːm] pron **1** (interrogative): **whom did you see?** ¿a quién viste?; **to whom did you give it?** ¿a quién se lo diste?; **tell me from whom you received it** dígame de quién lo recibiste

2 (relative) que; **to whom** a quien(es); **of whom** de quien(es), del/de la que; **the man whom I saw** el hombre qui vi; **the man to whom I wrote** el hombre a quien escribí; **the lady about whom I was talking** la señora de (la) que hablaba; **the lady with whom I was talking** la señora con quien or (la) que hablaba

whooping cough [ˈhuːpɪŋ-] n tos f ferina

whoops [wuːps] excl (also: **whoops-a-daisy!**) ¡huy!

whoosh [wuʃ] n: **it came out with a ~** (sauce etc) salió todo de repente; (air) salió con mucho ruido

whopper [ˈwɔpəʳ] n (col: lie) embuste m; (: large thing): **a ~** uno(-a) enorme

whopping [ˈwɔpɪŋ] adj (col) enorme

whore [hɔːʳ] n (col: pej) puta

W

KEYWORD

whose [hu:z] *adj* **1** (*possessive: interrogative*) de quién; **whose book is this?**, **whose is this book?** ¿de quién es este libro?; **whose pencil have you taken?** ¿de quién es el lápiz que has cogido?; **whose daughter are you?** ¿de quién eres hija?

2 (*possessive: relative*) cuyo(-a) *m(f)*, cuyos(-as) *m(f)pl*; **the man whose son they rescued** el hombre cuyo hijo rescataron; **the girl whose sister he was speaking to** la chica con cuya hermana estaba hablando; **those whose passports I have** aquellas personas cuyos pasaportes tengo; **the woman whose car was stolen** la mujer a quien le robaron el coche

■ *pron* de quién; **whose is this?** ¿de quién es esto?; **I know whose it is** sé de quién es

 KEYWORD

why [waɪ] *adv* por qué; **why not?** ¿por qué no?; **why not do it now?** ¿por qué no lo haces (*or* hacemos ahora?)

■ *conj*: **I wonder why he said that** me pregunto por qué dijo eso; **that's not why I'm here** no es por eso (por lo) que estoy aquí; **the reason why** la razón por la que

■ *excl* (*expressing surprise, shock, annoyance*) ¡hombre!, ¡vaya!; (*explaining*): **why, it's you!** ¡hombre, eres tú!; **why, that's impossible** ¡pero si eso es imposible!

whyever [waɪˈɛvəʳ] *adv* por qué
WI *n abbr* (Brit: = Women's Institute) asociación de amas de casa ■ *abbr* (Geo) = **West Indies**; (US) = **Wisconsin**
wick [wɪk] *n* mecha
wicked [ˈwɪkɪd] *adj* malvado, cruel
wicker [ˈwɪkəʳ] *n* mimbre *m*
wickerwork [ˈwɪkəwə:k] *n* artículos *mpl* de mimbre
wicket [ˈwɪkɪt] *n* (Cricket) palos *mpl*
wicket keeper *n* guardameta *m*
wide [waɪd] *adj* ancho; (*area, knowledge*) vasto, grande; (*choice*) grande ■ *adv*: **to open ~** abrir de par en par; **to shoot ~** errar el tiro; **it is three metres ~** tiene tres metros de ancho
wide-angle lens [ˈwaɪdæŋgl-] *n* (objetivo) gran angular *m*
wide-awake [waɪdəˈweɪk] *adj* bien despierto
wide-eyed [waɪdˈaɪd] *adj* con los ojos muy abiertos; (*fig*) ingenuo
widely [ˈwaɪdlɪ] *adv* (*differing*) muy; **it is ~ believed that ...** existe la creencia generalizada de que ...; **to be ~ read** (*author*)

ser muy leído; (*reader*) haber leído mucho
widen [ˈwaɪdn] *vt* ensanchar
wideness [ˈwaɪdnɪs] *n* anchura; amplitud *f*
wide open *adj* abierto de par en par
wide-ranging [waɪdˈreɪndʒɪŋ] *adj* (*survey, report*) de gran alcance; (*interests*) muy diversos
widespread [ˈwaɪdsprɛd] *adj* (*belief etc*) extendido, general
widget [ˈwɪdʒɪt] *n* (Comput) mini aplicación *f*, widget *m*
widow [ˈwɪdəu] *n* viuda
widowed [ˈwɪdəud] *adj* viudo
widower [ˈwɪdəuəʳ] *n* viudo
width [wɪdθ] *n* anchura; (*of cloth*) ancho; **it's seven metres in ~** tiene siete metros de ancho
widthways [ˈwɪdθweɪz] *adv* a lo ancho
wield [wi:ld] *vt* (*sword*) manejar; (*power*) ejercer
wife (*pl* **wives**) [waɪf, waɪvz] *n* mujer *f*, esposa
WiFi [ˈwaɪfaɪ] *n abbr* (= *wireless fidelity*) wi-fi *m*
■ *adj* (*hot spot, network etc*) wi-fi
wig [wɪg] *n* peluca
wigging [ˈwɪgɪŋ] *n* (Brit col) rapapolvo, bronca
wiggle [ˈwɪgl] *vt* menear ■ *vi* menearse
wiggly [ˈwɪglɪ] *adj* (*line*) ondulado
wigwam [ˈwɪgwæm] *n* tipi *m*, tienda india
wild [waɪld] *adj* (*animal*) salvaje; (*plant*) silvestre; (*rough*) furioso, violento; (*idea*) descabellado; (*col: angry*) furioso ■ *n*: **the ~** la naturaleza; **wilds** *npl* regiones *fpl* salvajes, tierras *fpl* vírgenes; **to be ~ about** (*enthusiastic*) estar *or* andar loco por; **in its ~ state** en estado salvaje
wild card *n* (Comput) comodín *m*
wildcat [ˈwaɪldkæt] *n* gato montés
wildcat strike *n* huelga salvaje
wilderness [ˈwɪldənɪs] *n* desierto; (*jungle*) jungla
wildfire [ˈwaɪldfaɪəʳ] *n*: **to spread like ~** correr como un reguero de pólvora
wild-goose chase [waɪldˈguːs-] *n* (*fig*) búsqueda inútil
wildlife [ˈwaɪldlaɪf] *n* fauna
wildly [ˈwaɪldlɪ] *adv* (*roughly*) violentamente; (*foolishly*) locamente; (*rashly*) descabelladamente
wiles [waɪlz] *npl* artimañas *fpl*, ardides *mpl*
wilful, willful (US) [ˈwɪlful] *adj* (*action*) deliberado; (*obstinate*) testarudo

 KEYWORD

will [wɪl] *aux vb* **1** (*forming future tense*): **I will finish it tomorrow** lo terminaré *or* voy a terminar mañana; **I will have finished it by tomorrow** lo habré terminado para mañana; **will you do it? — yes I will/no I**

won't ¿lo harás? — sí/no; **you won't lose it, will you?** no lo vayas a perder *or* no lo perderás ¿verdad?
2 (*in conjectures, predictions*): **he will** *or* **he'll be there by now** ya habrá llegado, ya debe (de) haber llegado; **that will be the postman** será el cartero, debe ser el cartero
3 (*in commands, requests, offers*): **will you be quiet!** ¿quieres callarte?; **will you help me?** ¿quieres ayudarme?; **will you have a cup of tea?** ¿te apetece un té?; **I won't put up with it!** ¡no lo soporto!
4 (*habits, persistence*): **the car won't start** el coche no arranca; **accidents will happen** son cosas que pasan
■ *vt* (*pt, pp* **willed**); **to will sb to do sth** desear que algn haga algo; **he willed himself to go on** con gran fuerza de voluntad, continuó
■ *n* **1** (*desire*) voluntad *f*; **against sb's will** contra la voluntad de algn; **he did it of his own free will** lo hizo por su propia voluntad
2 (*Law*) testamento; **to make a** *or* **one's will** hacer su testamento

willful ['wɪful] *adj* (*US*) = **wilful**
willing ['wɪlɪŋ] *adj* (*with goodwill*) de buena voluntad; complaciente; **he's ~ to do it** está dispuesto a hacerlo; **to show ~** mostrarse dispuesto
willingly ['wɪlɪŋlɪ] *adv* con mucho gusto
willingness ['wɪlɪŋnɪs] *n* buena voluntad
will-o'-the-wisp ['wɪləðə'wɪsp] *n* fuego fatuo; (*fig*) quimera
willow ['wɪləu] *n* sauce *m*
willpower ['wɪlpauəʳ] *n* fuerza de voluntad
willy-nilly [wɪlɪ'nɪlɪ] *adv* quiérase o no
wilt [wɪlt] *vi* marchitarse
Wilts *abbr* (*Brit*) = **Wiltshire**
wily ['waɪlɪ] *adj* astuto
wimp [wɪmp] *n* (*col*) enclenque *m/f*; (*character*) calzonazos *m inv*
win [wɪn] (*pt, pp* **won**) *n* (*in sports etc*) victoria, triunfo ■ *vt* ganar; (*obtain: contract etc*) conseguir, lograr ■ *vi* ganar
▶ **win over, win round** (*Brit*) *vt* convencer a
wince [wɪns] *vi* encogerse
winch [wɪntʃ] *n* torno
Winchester disk® ['wɪntʃɪstə-] *n* (*Comput*) disco Winchester®
wind [*n* wɪnd, *vb* waɪnd] (*pt, pp* **wound**) *n* viento; (*Med*) gases *mpl*; (*breath*) aliento ■ *vt* enrollar; (*wrap*) envolver; (*clock, toy*) dar cuerda a [wɪnd] (*take breath away from*) dejar sin aliento a ■ *vi* (*road, river*) serpentear; (*Brit*) **against the ~** contra el viento; **to get ~ into** *or* **against the ~** contra el viento; **to get ~ of sth** enterarse de algo; **to break ~** ventosear
▶ **wind down** *vt* (*car window*) bajar; (*fig*:

production, business) disminuir
▶ **wind up** *vt* (*clock*) dar cuerda a; (*debate*) concluir, terminar
windbreak ['wɪndbreɪk] *n* barrera contra el viento
windcheater ['wɪndtʃiːtəʳ], **windbreaker** (*US*) ['wɪndbreɪkəʳ] *n* cazadora
winder ['waɪndəʳ] *n* (*on watch*) cuerda
wind erosion *n* erosión *f* del viento
windfall ['wɪndfɔːl] *n* golpe *m* de suerte
wind farm *n* parque *m* eólico
winding ['waɪndɪŋ] *adj* (*road*) tortuoso
wind instrument *n* (*Mus*) instrumento de viento
windmill ['wɪndmɪl] *n* molino de viento
window ['wɪndəu] *n* ventana; (*in car, train*) ventana; (*in shop etc*) escaparate *m*, vitrina (*LAm*), vidriera (*LAm*); (*Comput*) ventana
window box *n* jardinera (de ventana)
window cleaner *n* (*person*) limpiacristales *m inv*
window dressing *n* decoración *f* de escaparates
window envelope *n* sobre *m* de ventanilla
window frame *n* marco de ventana
window ledge *n* alféizar *m*, repisa
window pane *n* cristal *m*
window-shopping [wɪndəu'ʃɒpɪŋ] *n*: **to go ~** ir a ver *or* mirar escaparates
windowsill ['wɪndəusɪl] *n* alféizar *m*, repisa
windpipe ['wɪndpaɪp] *n* tráquea
wind power *n* energía eólica
windscreen ['wɪndskriːn], **windshield** (*US*) ['wɪndʃiːld] *n* parabrisas *m inv*
windscreen washer, windshield washer (*US*) *n* lavaparabrisas *m inv*
windscreen wiper, windshield wiper (*US*) *n* limpiaparabrisas *m inv*
windsurfing ['wɪndsəːfɪŋ] *n* windsurf *m*
windswept ['wɪndswept] *adj* azotado por el viento
wind tunnel *n* túnel *m* aerodinámico
windy ['wɪndɪ] *adj* de mucho viento; **it's ~** hace viento
wine [waɪn] *n* vino ■ *vt*: **to ~ and dine sb** agasajar *or* festejar a algn
wine bar *n* bar *especializado en vinos*
wine cellar *n* bodega
wine glass *n* copa (de *or* para vino)
wine list *n* lista de vinos
wine merchant *n* vinatero
wine tasting *n* degustación *f* de vinos
wine waiter *n* escanciador *m*
wing [wɪŋ] *n* ala; (*Brit Aut*) aleta; **wings** *npl* (*Theat*) bastidores *mpl*
winger ['wɪŋəʳ] *n* (*Sport*) extremo
wing mirror *n* (*espejo*) retrovisor *m*

W

wing nut n tuerca (de) mariposa

wingspan ['wɪŋspaen], **wingspread** ['wɪŋsprɛd] n envergadura

wink [wɪŋk] n guiño; (blink) pestañeo ■ vi guiñar; (blink) pestañear; (light etc) parpadear

winkle ['wɪŋkl] n bígaro, bigarro

winner ['wɪnəʳ] n ganador(a) m(f)

winning ['wɪnɪŋ] adj (team) ganador(a); (goal) decisivo; (charming) encantador(a)

winning post n meta

winnings ['wɪnɪŋz] npl ganancias fpl

winter ['wɪntəʳ] n invierno ■ vi invernar

winter sports npl deportes mpl de invierno

wintry ['wɪntrɪ] adj invernal

wipe [waɪp] n: **to give sth a ~** pasar un trapo sobre algo ■ vt limpiar; **to ~ one's nose** limpiarse la nariz
  ▶ **wipe off** vt limpiar con un trapo
  ▶ **wipe out** vt (debt) liquidar; (memory) borrar; (destroy) destruir
  ▶ **wipe up** vt limpiar

wire ['waɪəʳ] n alambre m; (Elec) cable m (eléctrico); (Tel) telegrama m ■ vt (house) poner la instalación eléctrica en; (also: **wire up**) conectar

wire cutters npl cortaalambres msg inv

wireless ['waɪəlɪs] n (Brit) radio f ■ adj inalámbrico

wireless technology n tecnología inalámbrico

wire mesh, wire netting n tela metálica

wire service n (US) agencia de noticias

wire-tapping ['waɪə'tæpɪŋ] n intervención f telefónica

wiring ['waɪərɪŋ] n instalación f eléctrica

wiry ['waɪərɪ] adj enjuto y fuerte

Wis., Wisc. abbr (US) = **Wisconsin**

wisdom ['wɪzdəm] n sabiduría, saber m; (good sense) cordura

wisdom tooth n muela del juicio

wise [waɪz] adj sabio; (sensible) juicioso; **I'm none the wiser** sigo sin entender
  ▶ **wise up** vi (col): **to ~ up (to sth)** enterarse (de algo)

...wise [waɪz] suff: **timewise** en cuanto a or respecto al tiempo

wisecrack ['waɪzkræk] n broma

wish [wɪʃ] n (desire) deseo ■ vt desear; (want) querer; **best wishes** (on birthday etc) felicidades fpl; **with best wishes** (in letter) saludos mpl, recuerdos mpl; **he wished me well** me deseó mucha suerte; **to ~ sth on sb** imponer algo a algn; **to ~ to do/sb to do sth** querer hacer/que algn haga algo; **to ~ for** desear

wishbone ['wɪʃbəun] n espoleta (de la que tiran dos personas quien se quede con el hueso más largo pide un deseo)

wishful ['wɪʃful] adj: **it's ~ thinking** eso es hacerse ilusiones

wishy-washy ['wɪʃɪwɔʃɪ] adj (col: colour) desvaído; (: ideas, thinking) flojo

wisp [wɪsp] n mechón m; (of smoke) voluta

wistful ['wɪstful] adj pensativo; (nostalgic) nostálgico

wit [wɪt] n (wittiness) ingenio, gracia; (intelligence: also: **wits**) inteligencia; (person) chistoso(-a); **to have** or **keep one's wits about one** no perder la cabeza

witch [wɪtʃ] n bruja

witchcraft ['wɪtʃkrɑːft] n brujería

witch doctor n hechicero

witch-hunt ['wɪtʃhʌnt] n (Pol) caza de brujas

 KEYWORD

with [wɪð, wɪθ] prep **1** (accompanying, in the company of) con (con +mí, ti, sí = conmigo, contigo, consigo); **I was with him** estaba con él; **we stayed with friends** nos quedamos en casa de unos amigos
2 (descriptive, indicating manner etc) con; de; **a room with a view** una habitación con vistas; **the man with the grey hat/blue eyes** el hombre del sombrero gris/de los ojos azules; **red with anger** rojo de ira; **to shake with fear** temblar de miedo; **to fill sth with water** llenar algo de agua
3: **I'm with you/I'm not with you** (understand) ya te entiendo/no te entiendo; **I'm not really with it today** no doy pie con bola hoy

withdraw [wɪθ'drɔː] (irreg: like **draw**) vt retirar ■ vi retirarse; (go back on promise) retractarse; **to ~ money (from the bank)** retirar fondos (del banco); **to ~ into o.s.** ensimismarse

withdrawal [wɪθ'drɔːəl] n retirada

withdrawal symptoms npl síndrome m de abstinencia

withdrawn [wɪθ'drɔːn] adj (person) reservado, introvertido ■ pp of **withdraw**

wither ['wɪðəʳ] vi marchitarse

withered ['wɪðəd] adj marchito, seco

withhold [wɪθ'həuld] vt (irreg: like **hold**) (money) retener; (decision) aplazar; (permission) negar; (information) ocultar

within [wɪð'ɪn] prep dentro de ■ adv dentro; **~ reach** al alcance de la mano; **~ sight of** a la vista de; **~ the week** antes de que acabe la semana; **to be ~ the law** atenerse a la legalidad; **~ an hour from now** dentro de una hora

without [wɪð'aut] *prep* sin; **to go** *or* **do ~ sth** prescindir de algo; **~ anybody knowing** sin saberlo nadie

withstand [wɪθ'stænd] *vt* (*irreg: like* **stand**) resistir a

witness ['wɪtnɪs] *n* (*person*) testigo *m/f*; (*evidence*) testimonio ■ *vt* (*event*) presenciar, ser testigo de; (*document*) atestiguar la veracidad de; **~ for the prosecution/ defence** testigo de cargo/descargo; **to ~ to (having seen) sth** dar testimonio de (haber visto) algo

witness box, witness stand (US) *n* tribuna de los testigos

witticism ['wɪtɪsɪzm] *n* dicho ingenioso

wittily ['wɪtɪlɪ] *adv* ingeniosamente

witty ['wɪtɪ] *adj* ingenioso

wives [waɪvz] *npl of* **wife**

wizard ['wɪzəd] *n* hechicero

wizened ['wɪznd] *adj* arrugado, marchito

wk *abbr* = **week**

Wm. *abbr* = **William**

WMD *n abbr see* **weapons of mass destruction**

WO *n abbr* = **warrant officer**

wobble ['wɔbl] *vi* tambalearse

wobbly ['wɔblɪ] *adj* (*hand, voice*) tembloroso; (*table, chair*) tambaleante, cojo

woe [wəu] *n* desgracia

woeful ['wəuful] *adj* (*bad*) lamentable; (*sad*) apesadumbrado

wok [wɔk] *n* wok *m*

woke [wəuk] *pt of* **wake**

woken ['wəukn] *pp of* **wake**

wolf (*pl* **wolves**) [wulf, wulvz] *n* lobo

woman (*pl* **women**) ['wumən, 'wɪmɪn] *n* mujer *f*; **young ~** (*mujer f*) joven *f*; **women's page** (*Press*) sección *f* de la mujer

woman doctor *n* doctora

woman friend *n* amiga

womanize ['wumənaɪz] *vi* ser un mujeriego

womanly ['wumənlɪ] *adj* femenino

womb [wu:m] *n* (*Anat*) matriz *f*, útero

women ['wɪmɪn] *npl of* **woman**

Women's Liberation Movement, Women's Movement *n* (*also*: **women's lib**) Movimiento de liberación de la mujer

won [wʌn] *pt, pp of* **win**

wonder ['wʌndər] *n* maravilla, prodigio; (*feeling*) asombro ■ *vi*: **to ~ whether** preguntarse si; **to ~ at** asombrarse de; **to ~ about** pensar sobre *or* en; **it's no ~ that** no es de extrañar que

wonderful ['wʌndəful] *adj* maravilloso

wonderfully ['wʌndəfəlɪ] *adv* maravillosamente, estupendamente

wonky ['wɔŋkɪ] *adj* (*Brit col: unsteady*) poco seguro, cojo; (: *broken down*) estropeado

wont [wɔnt] *n*: **as is his/her ~** como tiene por costumbre

won't [wəunt] = **will not**

woo [wu:] *vt* (*woman*) cortejar

wood [wud] *n* (*timber*) madera; (*forest*) bosque *m* ■ *cpd* de madera

wood alcohol *n* (US) alcohol *m* desnaturalizado

wood carving *n* tallado en madera

wooded ['wudɪd] *adj* arbolado

wooden ['wudn] *adj* de madera; (*fig*) inexpresivo

woodland ['wudlənd] *n* bosque *m*

woodpecker ['wudpɛkər] *n* pájaro carpintero

wood pigeon *n* paloma torcaz

woodwind ['wudwɪnd] *n* (*Mus*) instrumentos *mpl* de viento de madera

woodwork ['wudwə:k] *n* carpintería

woodworm ['wudwɔ:m] *n* carcoma

woof [wuf] *n* (*of dog*) ladrido ■ *vi* ladrar; **~, ~!** ¡guau, guau!

wool [wul] *n* lana; **knitting ~** lana (de hacer punto); **to pull the ~ over sb's eyes** (*fig*) dar a algn gato por liebre

woollen, woolen (US) ['wulən] *adj* de lana ■ *n*: **woollens** géneros *mpl* de lana

woolly, wooly (US) ['wulɪ] *adj* de lana; (*fig: ideas*) confuso

woozy ['wu:zɪ] *adj* (*col*) mareado

word [wə:d] *n* palabra; (*news*) noticia; (*promise*) palabra (de honor) ■ *vt* redactar; **~ for ~** palabra por palabra; **what's the ~ for "pen" in Spanish?** ¿cómo se dice "pen" en español?; **to put sth into words** expresar algo en palabras; **to have a ~ with sb** hablar (dos palabras) con algn; **in other words** en otras palabras; **to break/keep one's ~** faltar a la palabra/cumplir la promesa; **to leave ~ (with/for sb) that ...** dejar recado (con/para algn) de que ...; **to have words with sb** (*quarrel with*) discutir or reñir con algn

wording ['wə:dɪŋ] *n* redacción *f*

word-of-mouth [wə:dəv'mauθ] *n*: **by** *or* **through ~** de palabra, por el boca a boca

word-perfect ['wə:d'pə:fɪkt] *adj* (*speech etc*) sin faltas de expresión

word processing *n* procesamiento *or* tratamiento de textos

word processor [-'prəusɛsər] *n* procesador *m* de textos

wordwrap ['wə:dræp] *n* (*Comput*) salto de línea automático

wordy ['wə:dɪ] *adj* verboso, prolijo

wore [wɔ:r] *pt of* **wear**

work [wə:k] *n* trabajo; (*job*) empleo, trabajo; (*Art, Lit*) obra ■ *vi* trabajar; (*mechanism*) funcionar, marchar; (*medicine*) ser eficaz,

W

surtir efecto ▪ vt (shape) trabajar; (stone etc)
tallar; (mine etc) explotar; (machine) manejar,
hacer funcionar; (cause) producir; **to go to
~** ir a trabajar or al trabajo; **to be at ~ (on
sth)** estar trabajando (en algo); **to set to
~, start ~** ponerse a trabajar; **to be out of
~** estar parado, no tener trabajo; **his life's
~** el trabajo de su vida; **to ~ hard** trabajar
mucho or duro; **to ~ to rule** (Industry)
hacer una huelga de celo; **to ~ loose** (part)
desprenderse; (knot) aflojarse; see also **works**
▶ **work off** vt: **to ~ off one's feelings**
desahogarse
▶ **work on** vt fus trabajar en, dedicarse a;
(principle) basarse en; **he's working on the
car** está reparando el coche
▶ **work out** vi (plans etc) salir bien, funcionar;
(Sport) hacer ejercicios ▪ vt (problem) resolver;
(plan) elaborar; **it works out at £100**
asciende a 100 libras
▶ **work up** vt: **he worked his way up in
the company** ascendió en la compañía
mediante sus propios esfuerzos
workable ['wə:kəbl] adj (solution) práctico,
factible
workaholic [wə:kə'hɔlɪk] n adicto(-a) al
trabajo
workbench ['wə:kbɛntʃ] n banco or mesa de
trabajo
worked up [wə:kt-] adj: **to get ~** excitarse
worker ['wə:kə'] n trabajador(a) m(f),
obrero(-a) m(f); **office ~** oficinista m/f
work force n mano f de obra
work-in ['wə:kɪn] n (Brit) ocupación f (de la
empresa sin interrupción del trabajo)
working ['wə:kɪŋ] adj (day, week) laborable;
(tools, conditions, clothes) de trabajo; (wife) que
trabaja; (partner) activo
working capital n (Comm) capital m
circulante
working class n clase f obrera ▪ adj:
working-class obrero
working knowledge n conocimientos mpl
básicos
working man n obrero
working order n: **in ~** en funcionamiento
working party n comisión f de
investigación, grupo de trabajo
working week n semana laboral
work-in-progress ['wə:kɪn'prəugrɛs] n
(Comm) trabajo en curso
workload ['wə:kləud] n cantidad f de trabajo
workman ['wə:kmən] n obrero
workmanship ['wə:kmənʃɪp] n (art) hechura;
(skill) habilidad f
workmate ['wə:kmeɪt] n compañero(-a) de
trabajo

workout ['wə:kaut] n (Sport) sesión f de
ejercicios
work permit n permiso de trabajo
works [wə:ks] nsg (Brit: factory) fábrica ▪ npl
(of clock, machine) mecanismo; **road ~** obras fpl
works council n comité m de empresa
worksheet ['wə:kʃiːt] n (Comput) hoja de
trabajo; (Scol) hoja de ejercicios
workshop ['wə:kʃɔp] n taller m
work station n estación f de trabajo
work study n estudio del trabajo
worktop ['wə:ktɔp] n encimera
work-to-rule ['wə:ktə'ruːl] n (Brit) huelga
de celo
world [wə:ld] n mundo ▪ cpd (champion) del
mundo; (power, war) mundial; **all over the
~** por todo el mundo, en el mundo entero;
the business ~ el mundo de los negocios;
what in the ~ is he doing? ¿qué diablos está
haciendo?; **to think the ~ of sb** (fig) tener
un concepto muy alto de algn; **to do sb a ~ of
good** sentar muy bien a algn; **W~ War One/
Two** la primera/segunda Guerra Mundial
World Cup n (Football): **the ~** el Mundial, los
Mundiales
world-famous [wə:ld'feɪməs] adj de fama
mundial, mundialmente famoso
worldly ['wə:ldlɪ] adj mundano
world music n música étnica
World Series n: **the ~** (US Baseball) el
campeonato nacional de béisbol de EEUU
World Service n see **BBC**
world-wide ['wə:ldwaɪd] adj mundial,
universal
worm [wə:m] n gusano; (earthworm) lombriz f
worn [wɔ:n] pp of **wear** ▪ adj usado
worn-out ['wɔ:naut] adj (object) gastado;
(person) rendido, agotado
worried ['wʌrɪd] adj preocupado; **to be ~
about sth** estar preocupado por algo
worrisome ['wʌrɪsəm] adj preocupante,
inquietante
worry ['wʌrɪ] n preocupación f ▪ vt
preocupar, inquietar ▪ vi preocuparse;
to ~ about or **over sth/sb** preocuparse por
algo/algn
worrying ['wʌrɪɪŋ] adj inquietante
worse [wə:s] adj, adv peor ▪ n el peor, lo peor;
a change for the ~ un empeoramiento; **so
much the ~ for you** tanto peor para ti; **he's
none the ~ for it** se ha quedado tan fresco or
tan tranquilo; **to get ~, to grow ~** empeorar
worsen ['wə:sn] vt, vi empeorar
worse off adj (fig): **you'll be ~ this way** de
esta forma estarás peor que antes
worship ['wə:ʃɪp] n (organized worship) culto;
(act) adoración f ▪ vt adorar; **Your W~** (Brit:

to mayor) su Ilustrísima; (: *to judge*) su señoría

worshipper, worshiper (US) ['wəːʃɪpəʳ] *n*
devoto(-a)

worst [wəːst] *adj* (el/la) peor ▪ *adv* peor ▪ *n*
lo peor; **at ~** en el peor de los casos; **to come
off ~** llevar la peor parte; **if the ~ comes to
the ~** en el peor de los casos

worst-case ['wəːstkeɪs] *adj*: **the ~ scenario** el
peor de los casos

worsted ['wustɪd] *n*: **(wool) ~** estambre *m*

worth [wəːθ] *n* valor *m* ▪ *adj*: **to be ~** valer;
how much is it ~? ¿cuánto vale?; **it's ~ it**
vale *or* merece la pena; **to be ~ one's while
(to do)** merecer la pena (hacer); **it's not ~
the trouble** no vale *or* merece la pena

worthless ['wəːθlɪs] *adj* sin valor; (*useless*)
inútil

worthwhile ['wəːθwaɪl] *adj* (*activity*) que
merece la pena; (*cause*) loable

worthy ['wəːðɪ] *adj* (*person*) respetable;
(*motive*) honesto; **~ of** digno de

 KEYWORD

would [wud] *aux vb* **1** (*conditional tense*): **if you
asked him he would do it** si se lo pidieras,
lo haría; **if you had asked him he would
have done it** si se lo hubieras pedido, lo
habría *or* hubiera hecho

2 (*in offers, invitations, requests*): **would you like
a biscuit?** ¿quieres una galleta?; (*formal*)
¿querría una galleta?; **would you ask him
to come in?** ¿quiere hacerle pasar?; **would
you open the window please?** ¿quiere *or*
podría abrir la ventana, por favor?

3 (*in indirect speech*): **I said I would do it** dije
que lo haría

4 (*emphatic*): **it WOULD have to snow today!**
¡tenía que nevar precisamente hoy!

5 (*insistence*): **she wouldn't behave** no quiso
comportarse bien

6 (*conjecture*): **it would have been midnight**
sería medianoche; **it would seem so** parece
ser que sí

7 (*indicating habit*): **he would go there on
Mondays** iba allí los lunes

would-be ['wudbiː] *adj* (*pej*) presunto

wouldn't ['wudnt] = **would not**

wound [*n* wuːnd, *vb* waund] *pt, pp of* **wind** ▪ *n*
herida ▪ *vt* herir

wove [wəuv] *pt of* **weave**

woven ['wəuvən] *pp of* **weave**

WP *n abbr* = **word processing; word processor**
▪ *abbr* (*Brit col*: = *weather permitting*) si lo
permite el tiempo

WPC *n abbr* (*Brit*) = **woman police constable**

wpm *abbr* (= *words per minute*) p.p.m.

WRAC *n abbr* (*Brit*: = *Women's Royal Army Corps*)
cuerpo auxiliar femenino del ejército de tierra

WRAF *n abbr* (*Brit*: = *Women's Royal Air Force*)
cuerpo auxiliar femenino del ejército del aire

wrangle ['ræŋgl] *n* riña ▪ *vi* reñir

wrap [ræp] *n* (*stole*) chal *m* ▪ *vt* (*also*: **wrap
up**) envolver; **under wraps** (*fig*: *plan, scheme*)
oculto, tapado

wrapper ['ræpəʳ] *n* (*Brit*: *of book*)
sobrecubierta; (*on chocolate etc*) envoltura

wrapping paper ['ræpɪŋ-] *n* papel *m* de
envolver

wrath [rɔθ] *n* cólera

wreak [riːk] *vt* (*destruction*) causar; **to ~ havoc
(on)** hacer *or* causar estragos (en); **to ~
vengeance (on)** vengarse (en)

wreath (*pl* **wreaths**) [riːθ, riːðz] *n* (*also*:
funeral wreath) corona; (*of flowers*) guirnalda

wreck [rɛk] *n* (*ship*: *destruction*) naufragio;
(: *remains*) restos *mpl* del barco; (*pej*: *person*)
ruina ▪ *vt* destrozar; **to be wrecked** (*Naut*)
naufragar

wreckage ['rɛkɪdʒ] *n* (*remains*) restos *mpl*;
(*of building*) escombros *mpl*

wrecker ['rɛkəʳ] *n* (*US*: *breakdown van*) camión
grúa *m*

WREN [rɛn] *n abbr* (*Brit*) miembro del WRNS

wren [rɛn] *n* (*Zool*) reyezuelo

wrench [rɛntʃ] *n* (*Tech*) llave *f* inglesa; (*tug*)
tirón *m* ▪ *vt* arrancar; **to ~ sth from sb**
arrebatar algo violentamente a algn

wrest [rɛst] *vt*: **to ~ sth from sb** arrebatar *or*
arrancar algo a algn

wrestle ['rɛsl] *vi*: **to ~ (with sb)** luchar (con *or*
contra algn)

wrestler ['rɛsləʳ] *n* luchador(a) *m(f)* (de lucha
libre)

wrestling ['rɛslɪŋ] *n* lucha libre

wrestling match *n* combate *m* de lucha libre

wretch [rɛtʃ] *n* desgraciado(-a), miserable
m/f; **little ~!** (*often humorous*) ¡granuja!

wretched ['rɛtʃɪd] *adj* miserable

wriggle ['rɪgl] *vi* serpentear

wring (*pt, pp* **wrung**) [rɪŋ, rʌŋ] *vt* torcer,
retorcer; (*wet clothes*) escurrir; (*fig*): **to ~ sth
out of sb** sacar algo por la fuerza a algn

wringer ['rɪŋəʳ] *n* escurridor *m*

wringing ['rɪŋɪŋ] *adj* (*also*: **wringing wet**)
empapado

wrinkle ['rɪŋkl] *n* arruga ▪ *vt* arrugar ▪ *vi*
arrugarse

wrinkled ['rɪŋkld], **wrinkly** ['rɪŋklɪ] *adj*
(*fabric, paper etc*) arrugado

wrist [rɪst] *n* muñeca

wristband ['rɪstbænd] *n* (*Brit*: *of shirt*) puño;
(: *of watch*) correa

W

wrist watch n reloj m de pulsera

writ [rɪt] n mandato judicial; **to serve a ~ on sb** notificar un mandato judicial a algn

writable ['raɪtəbl] adj (CD, DVD) escribible

write (pt **wrote**, pp **written**) [raɪt, rəut, 'rɪtn] vt, vi escribir; **to ~ sb a letter** escribir una carta a algn
- ▶ **write away** vi: **to ~ away for** (information, goods) pedir por escrito or carta
- ▶ **write down** vt escribir; (note) apuntar
- ▶ **write off** vt (debt) borrar (como incobrable); (fig) desechar por inútil; (smash up: car) destrozar
- ▶ **write out** vt escribir
- ▶ **write up** vt redactar

write-off ['raɪtɔf] n siniestro total; **the car is a ~** el coche es pura chatarra

write-protect ['raɪtprə'tɛkt] vt (Comput) proteger contra escritura

writer ['raɪtəʳ] n escritor(a) m(f)

write-up ['raɪtʌp] n (review) crítica, reseña

writhe [raɪð] vi retorcerse

writing ['raɪtɪŋ] n escritura; (handwriting) letra; (of author) obras fpl; **in ~** por escrito; **to put sth in ~** poner algo por escrito; **in my own ~** escrito por mí; see also **writings**

writing case n estuche m de papel de escribir

writing desk n escritorio

writing paper n papel m de escribir

writings npl obras fpl

written ['rɪtn] pp of **write**

WRNS n abbr (Brit: = Women's Royal Naval Service) cuerpo auxiliar femenino de la armada

wrong [rɔŋ] adj (wicked) malo; (unfair) injusto; (incorrect) equivocado, incorrecto; (not suitable) inoportuno, inconveniente ■ adv mal ■ n

mal m; (injustice) injusticia ■ vt ser injusto con; (hurt) agraviar; **to be ~** (answer) estar equivocado; (in doing, saying) equivocarse; **it's ~ to steal, stealing is ~** es mal robar; **you are ~ to do it** haces mal en hacerlo; **you are ~ about that, you've got it ~** en eso estás equivocado; **to be in the ~** no tener razón; (guilty) tener la culpa; **what's ~?** ¿qué pasa?; **what's ~ with the car?** ¿qué le pasa al coche?; **there's nothing ~** no pasa nada; **you have the ~ number** (Tel) se ha equivocado de número; **to go ~** (person) equivocarse; (plan) salir mal; (machine) estropearse

wrongdoer ['rɔŋduəʳ] n malhechor(a) m(f)

wrong-foot [rɔŋ'fut] vt (Sport) hacer perder el equilibrio a; (fig) poner en un aprieto a

wrongful ['rɔŋful] adj injusto; **~ dismissal** (Industry) despido improcedente

wrongly ['rɔŋlɪ] adv (answer, do, count) incorrectamente; (treat) injustamente

wrote [rəut] pt of **write**

wrought [rɔ:t] adj: **~ iron** hierro forjado

wrung [rʌŋ] pt, pp of **wring**

WRVS n abbr (Brit: = Women's Royal Voluntary Service) cuerpo de voluntarias al servicio de la comunidad

wry [raɪ] adj irónico

wt. abbr = **weight**

WV, W.Va. abbr (US) = **West Virginia**

WWW n abbr (= World Wide Web) WWW m or f

WY, Wyo. abbr (US) = **Wyoming**

WYSIWYG ['wɪzɪwɪg] abbr (Comput: = what you see is what you get) tipo de presentación en un procesador de textos

Xx

X, x [eks] *n* (*letter*) X, x f; (*Brit Cine: formerly*) no apto para menores de 18 años; **X for Xmas** X de Xiquena; **if you earn X dollars a year** si ganas X dólares al año

X-certificate ['ɛkssə'tɪfɪkɪt] *adj* (*Brit; film: formerly*) no apto para menores de 18 años

Xerox® ['zɪərɔks] *n* (*also:* **Xerox machine**) fotocopiadora; (*photocopy*) fotocopia ■ *vt* fotocopiar

XL *abbr* = **extra large**

Xmas ['ɛksməs] *n abbr* = **Christmas**

X-rated ['eks'reɪtɪd] *adj* (*US: film*) no apto para menores de 18 años

X-ray [eks'reɪ] *n* radiografía; **X-rays** *npl* rayos *mpl* X ■ *vt* radiografiar

xylophone ['zaɪləfəun] *n* xilófono

Yy

Y, y [waɪ] n (letter) Y, y f; **Y for Yellow,** (US)
Y for Yoke Y de Yegua

Y2K [ˌwaɪtuːˈkeɪ] abbr (= Year 2000): **the ~
problem** (Comput) el efecto 2000

yacht [jɔt] n yate m

yachting [ˈjɔtɪŋ] n (sport) balandrismo

yachtsman [ˈjɔtsmən] n balandrista m

yachtswoman [ˈjɔtswumən] n balandrista

yam [jæm] n ñame m; (sweet potato) batata,
camote m (LAm)

Yank [jæŋk], **Yankee** [ˈjæŋkɪ] n (pej) yanqui m/f

yank [jæŋk] vt tirar de, jalar de (LAm) ■ n
tirón m

yap [jæp] vi (dog) aullar

yard [jɑːd] n patio; (US: garden) jardín m;
(measure) yarda; **builder's ~** almacén m

yardstick [ˈjɑːdstɪk] n (fig) criterio, norma

yarn [jɑːn] n hilo; (tale) cuento (chino),
historia

yawn [jɔːn] n bostezo ■ vi bostezar

yawning [ˈjɔːnɪŋ] adj (gap) muy abierto

yd. abbr (= yard) yda

yeah [jeə] adv (col) sí

year [jɪəʳ] n año; (Scol, Univ) curso; **this ~**
este año; **~ in, ~ out** año tras año; **a** or **per
~** al año; **to be eight years old** tener ocho
años; **she's three years old** tiene tres años;
an eight-~-old child un niño de ocho años
(de edad)

yearbook [ˈjɪəbuk] n anuario

yearling [ˈjɪəlɪŋ] n (racehorse) potro de un año

yearly [ˈjɪəlɪ] adj anual ■ adv anualmente,
cada año; **twice ~** dos veces al año

yearn [jəːn] vi: **to ~ for sth** añorar algo,
suspirar por algo

yearning [ˈjəːnɪŋ] n ansia; (longing) añoranza

yeast [jiːst] n levadura

yell [jɛl] n grito, alarido ■ vi gritar

yellow [ˈjɛləu] adj, n amarillo

yellow fever n fiebre f amarilla

yellowish [ˈjɛləuɪʃ] adj amarillento

Yellow Pages® npl páginas fpl amarillas

Yellow Sea n: **the ~** el Mar Amarillo

yelp [jɛlp] n aullido ■ vi aullar

Yemen [ˈjɛmən] n Yemen m

Yemeni [ˈjɛmənɪ] adj, n yemení m/f,
yemenita m/f

yen [jɛn] n (currency) yen m

yeoman [ˈjəumən] n: **Y~ of the Guard**
alabardero de la Casa Real

yes [jɛs] adv, n sí m; **to say/answer ~** decir/
contestar que sí; **to say ~ (to)** decir que sí (a),
conformarse (con)

yes man n pelotillero

yesterday [ˈjɛstədɪ] adv, n ayer m; **~
morning/evening** ayer por la mañana/
tarde; **all day ~** todo el día de ayer; **the day
before ~** antes de ayer, anteayer

yet [jɛt] adv todavía ■ conj sin embargo, a
pesar de todo; **~ again** de nuevo; **it is not
finished ~** todavía no está acabado; **the best
~** el/la mejor hasta ahora; **as ~** hasta ahora,
todavía

yew [juː] n tejo

Y-fronts® [ˈwaɪfrʌnts] npl (Brit) calzoncillos
mpl, eslip msg tradicional

YHA n abbr (Brit: = Youth Hostel Association) ≈ Red
f Española de Albergues Juveniles

Yiddish [ˈjɪdɪʃ] n yiddish m

yield [jiːld] n producción f; (Agr) cosecha;
(Comm) rendimiento ■ vt producir, dar;
(profit) rendir ■ vi rendirse, ceder; (US Aut)
ceder el paso; **a ~ of 5%** un rédito del 5 por
ciento

YMCA n abbr (= Young Men's Christian Association)
Asociación f de Jóvenes Cristianos

yob [ˈjɔb], **yobbo** [ˈjɔbbəu] n (Brit col)
gamberro

yodel [ˈjəudl] vi cantar a la tirolesa

yoga [ˈjəugə] n yoga m

yoghurt, yogurt [ˈjəugət] n yogur m

yoke [jəuk] n (of oxen) yunta; (on shoulders)
balancín m; (fig) yugo ■ vt (also: **yoke
together**: oxen) uncir

yolk [jəuk] n yema (de huevo)

yonder [ˈjɔndəʳ] adv allá (a lo lejos)

yonks [jɔŋks] *npl (col)*: **I haven't seen him for** ~ hace siglos que no lo veo

Yorks [jɔːks] *abbr (Brit)* = **Yorkshire**

 KEYWORD

you [juː] *pron* **1** *(subject: familiar)* tú, vosotros(-as) *(SP) pl*, ustedes *(LAm)*; *(polite)* usted, ustedes *pl*; **you are very kind** eres/es *etc* muy amable; **you French enjoy your food** a vosotros *(or* ustedes*)* los franceses os *(or* les*)* gusta la comida; **you and I will go** iremos tú y yo

2 *(object: direct: familiar)* te, os *pl (SP)*, les *(LAm)*; *(polite)* lo *or* le; *(pl)* los *or* les; *(f)* la; *(pl)* las; **I know you** te/le *etc* conozco

3 *(object: indirect: familiar)* te, os *pl (SP)*, les *(LAm)*; *(polite)* le, les *pl*; **I gave the letter to you yesterday** te/os *etc* di la carta ayer

4 *(stressed)*: **I told YOU to do it** te dije a ti que lo hicieras, es a ti a quien dije que lo hicieras; *see also* **3, 5**

5 *(after prep: NB: con +ti = contigo: familiar)* ti, vosotros(-as) *pl (SP)*, ustedes *pl (LAm)*; *(: polite)* usted, ustedes *pl*; **it's for you** es para ti/vosotros *etc*

6 *(comparisons: familiar)* tú, vosotros(-as) *pl (SP)*, ustedes *pl (LAm)*; *(: polite)* usted, ustedes *pl*, **she's younger than you** es más joven que tú/vosotros *etc*

7 *(impersonal: one)*: **fresh air does you good** el aire puro (te) hace bien; **you never know** nunca se sabe; **you can't do that!** ¡eso no se hace!

you'd [juːd] = **you had**; **you would**

you'll [juːl] = **you will**; **you shall**

young [jʌŋ] *adj* joven ■ *npl (of animal)* cría; *(people)*: **the** ~ los jóvenes, la juventud; **a** ~ **man/lady** un(a) joven; **my younger brother** mi hermano menor *or* pequeño; **the younger generation** la nueva generación

youngster ['jʌŋstər] *n* joven *m/f*

your [jɔːr] *adj* tu, vuestro *pl*; *(formal)* su; ~ **house** tu *etc* casa; *see also* **my**

you're [juər] = **you are**

yours [jɔːz] *pron* tuyo, vuestro *pl*; *(formal)* suyo; **a friend of** ~ un amigo tuyo *etc*; *see also* **faithfully**; **mine**; **sincerely**

yourself [jɔːˈsɛlf] *pron (reflexive)* tú mismo; *(complement)* te; *(after prep)* ti (mismo); *(formal)* usted mismo; *(: complement)* se; *(: after prep)* sí (mismo); **you** ~ **told me** me lo dijiste tú mismo; **(all) by** ~ sin ayuda de nadie, solo; *see also* **oneself**

yourselves [jɔːˈsɛlvz] *pl pron* vosotros mismos; *(after prep)* vosotros (mismos); *(formal)* ustedes (mismos); *(: complement)* se; *(: after prep)* sí mismos

youth [juːθ] *n* juventud *f*; *(young man) (pl* **youths**) [juːðz] joven *m*; **in my** ~ en mi juventud

youth club *n* club *m* juvenil

youthful ['juːθful] *adj* juvenil

youthfulness ['juːθfəlnɪs] *n* juventud *f*

youth hostel *n* albergue *m* juvenil

youth movement *n* movimiento juvenil

you've [juːv] = **you have**

yowl [jaul] *n (of animal, person)* aullido ■ *vi* aullar

yr *abbr (= year)* a

YT *abbr (Canada)* = **Yukon Territory**

Yugoslav ['juːgəuslɑːv] *adj, n* yugoslavo(-a) *m(f)*

Yugoslavia [juːgəuˈslɑːvɪə] *n* Yugoslavia

Yugoslavian [juːgəuˈslɑːvɪən] *adj* yugoslavo(-a)

yuppie ['jʌpɪ] *(col) adj, n* yuppie *m/f*

YWCA *n abbr (= Young Women's Christian Association)* Asociación *f* de Jóvenes Cristianas

y

Zz

Z, z [zɛd] (US) [ziː] n (letter) Z, z f; **Z for Zebra**
Z de Zaragoza
Zaire [zɑːˈiːəʳ] n Zaire m
Zambia [ˈzæmbɪə] n Zambia
Zambian [ˈzæmbɪən] adj, n zambiano(-a) m(f)
zany [ˈzeɪnɪ] adj estrafalario
zap [zæp] vt (Comput) borrar
zeal [ziːl] n celo, entusiasmo
zealot [ˈzɛlət] n fanático(-a)
zealous [ˈzɛləs] adj celoso, entusiasta
zebra [ˈziːbrə] n cebra
zebra crossing n (Brit) paso de peatones
zenith [ˈzɛnɪθ] n (Astro) cénit m; (fig) apogeo
zero [ˈzɪərəu] n cero; **5 degrees below ~**
5 grados bajo cero
zero hour n hora cero
zero option n (Pol) opción f cero
zero-rated [ˈzɪərəureɪtɪd] adj (Brit) de tasa
cero
zest [zɛst] n entusiasmo; **~ for living** brío
zigzag [ˈzɪgzæg] n zigzag m ■ vi zigzaguear
Zimbabwe [zɪmˈbɑːbwɪ] n Zimbabwe m
Zimbabwean [zɪmˈbɑːbwɪən] adj, n
zimbabuo(-a) m(f)
Zimmer® [ˈzɪməʳ] n (also: **Zimmer frame**)
andador m, andaderas fpl

zinc [zɪŋk] n cinc m, zinc m
Zionism [ˈzaɪənɪzm] n sionismo
Zionist [ˈzaɪənɪst] adj, n sionista m/f
zip [zɪp] n (also: **zip fastener**; US: also: **zipper**)
cremallera, cierre m relámpago (LAm);
(energy) energía, vigor m ■ vt (Comput)
comprimir; (also: **zip up**) cerrar la cremallera
de ■ vi: **to ~ along to the shops** ir de
compras volando
zip code n (US) código postal
zip file n (Comput) archivo m comprimido
zither [ˈzɪðəʳ] n cítara
zodiac [ˈzəudɪæk] n zodíaco
zombie [ˈzɒmbɪ] n zombi m
zone [zəun] n zona
zonked [zɒŋkt] adj (col) hecho polvo
zoo [zuː] n zoo, (parque m) zoológico
zoological [zuːəˈlɒdʒɪkəl] adj zoológico
zoologist [zuˈɒlədʒɪst] n zoólogo(-a)
zoology [zuːˈɒlədʒɪ] n zoología
zoom [zuːm] vi: **to ~ past** pasar zumbando;
to ~ in (on sth/sb) (Phot, Cine) enfocar
(algo/a algn) con el zoom
zoom lens n zoom m
zucchini [zuːˈkiːnɪ] n(pl) (US) calabacín(ines)
m(pl)

Grammar
Gramática

Using the grammar

The Grammar section deals systematically and comprehensively with all the information you will need in order to communicate accurately in Spanish. The user-friendly layout explains the grammar point on a left hand page, leaving the facing page free for illustrative examples. The circled numbers, → ❶ etc, direct you to the relevant example in every case. Another strong point of the Grammar section is its comprehensive treatment of verbs. Regular verbs are fully explained, and 80 major irregular verbs are conjugated in their simple tenses. The irregular verbs are given in alphabetical order and laid out in tables, making them easy and efficient to consult. In addition, a verb index lists every Spanish verb in this dictionary each cross-referred to the appropriate conjugation model.

The Grammar section also provides invaluable guidance on the danger of translating English structures by identical structures in Spanish. Use of Numbers and Punctuation are important areas covered towards the end of the section. Finally, the index lists the main words and grammatical terms in both English and Spanish.

Abbreviations

cond.	conditional
fem.	feminine
masc.	masculine
plur.	plural
sing.	singular
subj	subjunctive
algn	alguien
sb	somebody
sth	something

Contents

Simple Tenses: Formation

In Spanish the simple tenses are:

Present → ❶
Imperfect → ❷
Future → ❸
Conditional → ❹
Preterite → ❺
Present Subjunctive → ❻
Imperfect Subjunctive → ❼

They are formed by adding endings to a verb stem. The endings show the number and person of the subject of the verb → ❽

The stem and endings of regular verbs are totally predictable. The following sections show all the patterns for regular verbs. For irregular verbs see page 80 onwards.

Regular Verbs

There are three regular verb patterns (called conjugations), each identifiable by the ending of the infinitive:

First conjugation verbs end in **-ar** e.g. **hablar** to speak.

Second conjugation verbs end in **-er** e.g. **comer** to eat.

Third conjugation verbs end in **-ir** e.g. **vivir** to live.

These three conjugations are treated in order on the following pages. The subject pronouns will appear in brackets because they are not always necessary in Spanish (see page 230).

Examples

1 (yo) hablo

I speak
I am speaking
I do speak

2 (yo) hablaba

I spoke
I was speaking
I used to speak

3 (yo) hablaré

I shall speak
I shall be speaking

4 (yo) hablaría

I should/would speak
I should/would be speaking

5 (yo) hablé

I spoke

6 (que) (yo) hable

(that) I speak

7 (que) (yo) hablara *or* hablase

(that) I spoke

8 (yo) hablo
(nosotros) hablamos
(yo) hablaria
(nosotros) hablaríamos

I speak
we speak
I would speak
we would speak

Simple Tenses: First Conjugation

The stem is formed as follows:

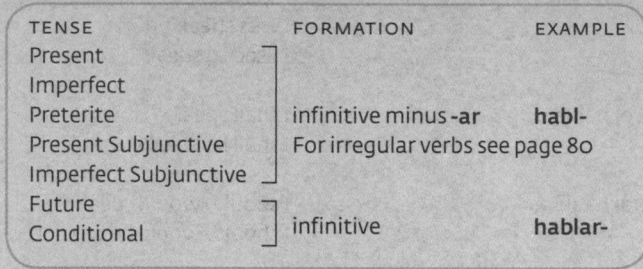

TENSE	FORMATION	EXAMPLE
Present		
Imperfect		
Preterite	infinitive minus **-ar**	**habl-**
Present Subjunctive	For irregular verbs see page 80	
Imperfect Subjunctive		
Future	infinitive	**hablar-**
Conditional		

To the appropriate stem add the following endings:

		❶ PRESENT	❷ IMPERFECT	❸ PRETERITE
	1st person	**-o**	-aba	-é
sing.	2nd person	**-as**	-abas	-aste
	3rd person	**-a**	-aba	-ó
	1st person	**-amos**	-ábamos	-amos
plur.	2nd person	**-áis**	-abais	-asteis
	3rd person	**-an**	-aban	-aron

		❹ PRESENT SUBJUNCTIVE	❺ IMPERFECT SUBJUNCTIVE
	1st person	**-e**	-ara *or* -ase
sing.	2nd person	**-es**	-aras *or* -ases
	3rd person	**-e**	-ara *or* -ase
	1st person	**-emos**	-áramos *or* -ásemos
plur.	2nd person	**-éis**	-arais *or* -aseis
	3rd person	**-en**	-aran *or* -asen

		❻ FUTURE	❼ CONDITIONAL
	1st person	**-é**	-ía
sing.	2nd person	**-ás**	-ías
	3rd person	**-á**	-ía
	1st person	**-emos**	-íamos
plur.	2nd person	**-éis**	-íais
	3rd person	**-án**	-ían

Examples

1 PRESENT

(yo)	hablo
(tú)	hablas
(él/ella/Vd)	habla
(nosotros/as)	hablamos
(vosotros/as)	habláis
(ellos/as/Vds)	hablan

2 IMPERFECT

hablaba
hablabas
hablaba
hablábamos
hablabais
hablaban

3 PRETERITE

hablé
hablaste
habló
hablamos
hablasteis
hablaron

4 PRESENT SUBJUNCTIVE

(yo)	hable
(tú)	hables
(él/ella/Vd)	hable
(nosotros/as)	hablemos
(vosotros/as)	habléis
(ellos/as/Vds)	hablen

5 IMPERFECT SUBJUNCTIVE

hablara or hablase
hablaras or hablases
hablara or hablase
habláramos or hablásemos
hablarais or hablaseis
hablaran or hablasen

6 FUTURE

(yo)	hablaré
(tú)	hablarás
(él/ella/Vd)	hablará
(nosotros/as)	hablaremos
(vosotros/as)	hablaréis
(ellos/as/Vds)	hablarán

7 CONDITIONAL

hablaría
hablarías
hablaría
hablaríamos
hablariais
hablarían

Simple Tenses: Second Conjugation

The stem is formed as follows:

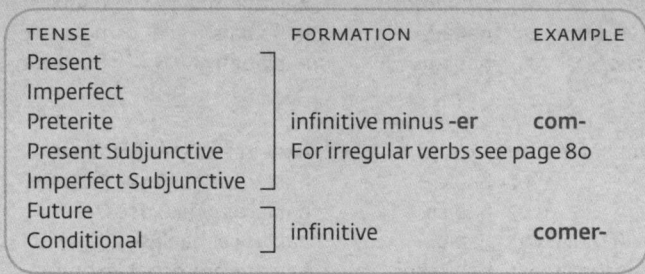

TENSE	FORMATION	EXAMPLE
Present		
Imperfect		
Preterite	infinitive minus **-er**	**com-**
Present Subjunctive	For irregular verbs see page 80	
Imperfect Subjunctive		
Future	infinitive	**comer-**
Conditional		

To the appropriate stem add the following endings:

		❶ PRESENT	❷ IMPERFECT	❸ PRETERITE
sing.	1st person	**-o**	**-ía**	**-í**
	2nd person	**-es**	**-ías**	**-iste**
	3rd person	**-e**	**-ía**	**-ió**
plur.	1st person	**-emos**	**-íamos**	**-imos**
	2nd person	**-éis**	**-íais**	**-isteis**
	3rd person	**-en**	**-ían**	**-ieron**

		❹ PRESENT SUBJUNCTIVE	❺ IMPERFECT SUBJUNCTIVE
sing.	1st person	**-a**	**-iera** or **-iese**
	2nd person	**-as**	**-ieras** or **-ieses**
	3rd person	**-a**	**-iera** or **-iese**
plur.	1st person	**-amos**	**-iéramos** or **-iésemos**
	2nd person	**-áis**	**-ierais** or **-ieseis**
	3rd person	**-an**	**-ieran** or **-iesen**

		❻ FUTURE	❼ CONDITIONAL
sing.	1st person	**-é**	**-ía**
	2nd person	**-ás**	**-ías**
	3rd person	**-á**	**-ía**
plur.	1st person	**-emos**	**-íamos**
	2nd person	**-éis**	**-íais**
	3rd person	**-án**	**-ían**

Examples

1 PRESENT

(yo)	como
(tú)	comes
(él/ella/Vd)	come
(nosotros/as)	comemos
(vosotros/as)	coméis
(ellos/as/Vds)	comen

2 IMPERFECT

comía
comías
comía
comíamos
comíais
comían

3 PRETERITE

comí
comiste
comió
comimos
comisteis
comieron

4 PRESENT SUBJUNCTIVE

(yo)	coma
(tú)	comas
(él/ella/Vd)	coma
(nosotros/as)	comamos
(vosotros/as)	comáis
(ellos/as/Vds)	coman

5 IMPERFECT SUBJUNCTIVE

comiera or comiese
comieras or comieses
comiera or comiese
comiéramos or comiésemos
comierais or comieseis
comieran or comiesen

6 FUTURE

(yo)	comeré
(tú)	comerás
(el/ella/Vd)	comerá
(nosotros/as)	comeremos
(vosotros/as)	comeréis
(ellos/as/Vds)	comerán

7 CONDITIONAL

comería
comerías
comería
comeríamos
comeríais
comerían

11

Simple Tenses: Third Conjugation

The stem is formed as follows:

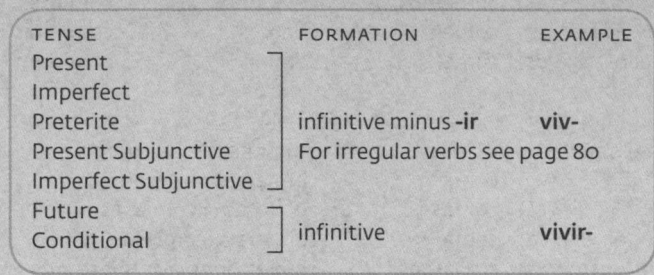

TENSE	FORMATION	EXAMPLE
Present		
Imperfect		
Preterite	infinitive minus **-ir**	**viv-**
Present Subjunctive	For irregular verbs see page 80	
Imperfect Subjunctive		
Future		
Conditional	infinitive	**vivir-**

To the appropriate stem add the following endings:

		❶ PRESENT	❷ IMPERFECT	❸ PRETERITE
	1ˢᵗ person	**-o**	**-ía**	**-í**
sing.	2ⁿᵈ person	**-es**	**-ías**	**-iste**
	3ʳᵈ person	**-e**	**-ía**	**-ió**
	1ˢᵗ person	**-imos**	**-íamos**	**-imos**
plur.	2ⁿᵈ person	**-ís**	**-íais**	**-isteis**
	3ʳᵈ person	**-en**	**-ían**	**-ieron**

		❹ PRESENT SUBJUNCTIVE	❺ IMPERFECT SUBJUNCTIVE
	1ˢᵗ person	**-a**	**-iera** or **-iese**
sing.	2ⁿᵈ person	**-as**	**-ieras** or **-ieses**
	3ʳᵈ person	**-a**	**-iera** or **-iese**
	1ˢᵗ person	**-amos**	**-iéramos** or **-iésemos**
plur.	2ⁿᵈ person	**-áis**	**-ierais** or **-ieseis**
	3ʳᵈ person	**-an**	**-ieran** or **-iesen**

		❻ FUTURE	❼ CONDITIONAL
	1ˢᵗ person	**-é**	**-ía**
sing.	2ⁿᵈ person	**-ás**	**-ías**
	3ʳᵈ person	**-á**	**-ía**
	1ˢᵗ person	**-emos**	**-íamos**
plur.	2ⁿᵈ person	**-éis**	**-íais**
	3ʳᵈ person	**-án**	**-ían**

Examples

❶ PRESENT

(yo)	vivo
(tú)	vives
(él/ella/Vd)	vive
(nosotros/as)	vivimos
(vosotros/as)	vivís
(ellos/as/Vds)	viven

❷ IMPERFECT

vivía
vivías
vivía
vivíamos
vivíais
vivían

❸ PRETERITE

viví
viviste
vivió
vivimos
vivisteis
vivieron

❹ PRESENT SUBJUNCTIVE

(yo)	viva
(tú)	vivas
(él/ella/Vd)	viva
(nosotros/as)	vivamos
(vosotros/as)	viváis
(ellos/as/Vds)	vivan

❺ IMPERFECT SUBJUNCTIVE

viviera or viviese
vivieras or vivieses
viviera or viviese
viviéramos or viviésemos
vivierais or vivieseis
vivieran or viviesen

❻ FUTURE

(yo)	viviré
(tú)	vivirás
(él/ella/Vd)	vivirá
(nosotros/as)	viviremos
(vosotros/as)	viviréis
(ellos/as/Vds)	vivirán

❼ CONDITIONAL

viviría
vivirías
viviría
viviríamos
viviríais
vivirían

13

The Imperative

The imperative is the form of the verb used to give commands or orders. It can be used politely, as in English 'Shut the door, please'.

In *positive* commands, the imperative forms for **Vd**, **Vds** and **nosotros** are the same as the subjunctive. The other forms are as follows:

> **tú** (same as 3rd person singular present indicative)
> **vosotros** (final **-r** of infinitive changes to **-d**) → ❶

(tú)	**habla** speak	**come** eat	**vive** live
(Vd)	**hable** speak	**coma** eat	**viva** live
(nosotros)	**hablemos** let's speak	**comamos** let's eat	**vivamos** let's live
(vosotros)	**hablad** speak	**comed** eat	**vivid** live
(Vds)	**hablen** speak	**coman** eat	**vivan** live

In *negative* commands, all the imperative forms are exactly the same as the present subjunctive.

The imperative of irregular verbs is given in the verb tables, pages 82 to 160.

Position of object pronouns with the imperative:
- in *positive* commands: they follow the verb and are attached to it. An accent is needed to show the correct position for stress (see page 296) → ❷
- in *negative* commands: they precede the verb and are not attached to it → ❸

For the order of object pronouns, see page 236.

Examples

1 cantar   to sing
   cantad   sing

2 Perdóneme   Excuse me
   Enviémoselos   Let's send them to him/her/
                   them

   Elíjanos   Choose us
   Explíquemelo   Explain it to me

   Esperémosla   Let's wait for her/it
   Devuélvaselo   Give it back to him/her/them

3 No me molestes   Don't disturb me
   No se la devolvamos   Let's not give it back to him/her/
                   them

   No les castiguemos   Let's not punish them
   No me lo mandes   Don't send it to me
   No las conteste   Don't answer them
   No nos lo hagan   Don't do it to us

The Imperative *continued*

For reflexive verbs – e.g. **levantarse** to get up – the object pronoun is the reflexive pronoun. It should be noted that the imperative forms need an accent to show the correct position for stress (see page 296). The forms **nosotros** and **vosotros** also drop the final **-s** and **-d** respectively before the pronoun → **1**

> BUT: **idos (vosotros)** go

(i) Note: For general instructions, the infinitive is used instead of the imperative → **2**, but when it is preceded by **vamos a** it often translates *let's ...* → **3**

Examples

① Levántate — Get up
No te levantes — Don't get up
Levántese (Vd) — Get up
No se levante (Vd) — Don't get up
Levantémonos — Let's get up
No nos levantemos — Let's not get up
Levantaos — Get up
No os levantéis — Don't get up
Levántense (Vds) — Get up
No se levanten (Vds) — Don't get up

Levántate	Get up
No te levantes	Don't get up
Levántese (Vd)	Get up
No se levante (Vd)	Don't get up
Levantémonos	Let's get up
No nos levantemos	Let's not get up
Levantaos	Get up
No os levantéis	Don't get up
Levántense (Vds)	Get up
No se levanten (Vds)	Don't get up

②
Ver pág ...	See page
No pasar	Do not pass ...

③
Vamos a ver	Let's see
Vamos a empezar	Let's start

Compound Tenses: formation

In Spanish the compound tenses are:
Perfect → ❶
Pluperfect → ❷
Future Perfect → ❸
Conditional Perfect → ❹
Past Anterior → ❺
Perfect Subjunctive → ❻
Pluperfect Subjunctive → ❼

They consist of the past participle of the verb together with the auxiliary verb **haber**.

Compound tenses are formed in exactly the same way for both regular and irregular verbs, the only difference being that irregular verbs may have an irregular past participle.

The Past Participle

For all compound tenses you need to know how to form the past participle of the verb. For regular verbs this is as follows:

First conjugation: replace the **-ar** of the infinitive by **-ado** → ❽

Second conjugation: replace the **-er** of the infinitive by **-ido** → ❾

Third conjugation: replace the **-ir** of the infinitive by **-ido** → ❿

Examples

1. (yo) he hablado — I have spoken

2. (yo) había hablado — I had spoken

3. (yo) habré hablado — I shall have spoken

4. (yo) habría hablado — I should/would have spoken

5. (yo) hube hablado — I had spoken

6. (que) (yo) haya hablado — (that) I spoke, have spoken

7. (que) (yo) hubiera/hubiese hablado — (that) I had spoken

8. **cantar** to sing → **cantado** sung

9. **comer** to eat → **comido** eaten

10. **vivir** to live → **vivido** lived

Compound Tenses: formation *continued*

PERFECT TENSE
The present tense of **haber** plus the past participle → ❶

PLUPERFECT TENSE
The imperfect tense of **haber** plus the past participle → ❷

FUTURE PERFECT
The future tense of **haber** plus the past participle → ❸

CONDITIONAL PERFECT
The conditional of **haber** plus the past participle → ❹

Examples

❶ PERFECT

(yo)	**he** hablado
(tú)	**has** hablado
(él/ella/Vd)	**ha** hablado
(nosotros/as)	**hemos** hablado
(vosotros/as)	**habéis** hablado
(ellos/as/Vds)	**han** hablado

❷ PLUPERFECT

(yo)	**había** hablado
(tú)	**habías** hablado
(él/ella/Vd)	**había** hablado
(nosotros/as)	**habíamos** hablado
(vosotros/as)	**habíais** hablado
(ellos/as/Vds)	**habían** hablado

❸ FUTURE PERFECT

(yo)	**habré** hablado
(tú)	**habrás** hablado
(él/ella/Vd)	**habrá** hablado
(nosotros/as)	**habremos** hablado
(vosotros/as)	**habréis** hablado
(ellos/as/Vds)	**habrán** hablado

❹ CONDITIONAL PERFECT

(yo)	**habría** hablado
(tú)	**habrías** hablado
(él/ella/Vd)	**habría** hablado
(nosotros/as)	**habríamos** hablado
(vosotros/as)	**habríais** hablado
(ellos/as/Vds)	**habrían** hablado

Compound Tenses: Formation *continued*

PAST ANTERIOR
The preterite of **haber** plus the past participle → ❶

PERFECT SUBJUNCTIVE
The present subjunctive of **haber** plus the past participle → ❷

PLUPERFECT SUBJUNCTIVE
The imperfect subjunctive of **haber** plus the past participle → ❸

For how to form the past participle of regular verbs see page 18.
The past participle of irregular verbs is given for each verb in the verb
tables, pages 82 to 160.

Examples

① PAST ANTERIOR

(yo)	**hube** hablado
(tú)	**hubiste** hablado
(él/ella/Vd)	**hubo** hablado
(nosotros/as)	**hubimos** hablado
(vosotros/as)	**hubisteis** hablado
(ellos/as/Vds)	**hubieron** hablado

② PERFECT SUBJUNCTIVE

(yo)	**haya** hablado
(tú)	**hayas** hablado
(él/ella/Vd)	**haya** hablado
(nosotros/as)	**hayamos** hablado
(vosotros/as)	**hayáis** hablado
(ellos/as/Vds)	**hayan** hablado

③ PLUPERFECT SUBJUNCTIVE

(yo)	**hubiera** or **hubiese** hablado
(tú)	**hubieras** or **hubieses** hablado
(él/ella/Vd)	**hubiera** or **hubiese** hablado
(nosotros/as)	**hubiéramos** or **hubiésemos** hablado
(vosotros/as)	**hubierais** or **hubieseis** hablado
(ellos/as/Vds)	**hubieran** or **hubiesen** hablado

Reflexive Verbs

A reflexive verb is one accompanied by a reflexive pronoun. The infinitive of a reflexive verb ends with the pronoun **se**, which is added to the verb form e.g. **levantarse** to get up; **lavarse** to wash (oneself)
The reflexive pronouns are:

	SINGULAR	PLURAL
1st person	me	nos
2nd person	te	os
3rd person	se	se

The reflexive pronoun 'reflects back' to the subject, but it is not always translated in English → ①

The plural pronouns are sometimes translated as 'one another', 'each other' (the *reciprocal* meaning) → ②

The reciprocal meaning may be emphasized by **el uno al otro/ la una a la otra (los unos a los otros/las unas a las otras)** → ③

Both simple and compound tenses of reflexive verbs are conjugated in exactly the same way as those of non-reflexive verbs, except that the reflexive pronoun is always used.

The only irregularity is in the 1st and 2nd person plural of the affirmative imperative (see page 16). A sample reflexive verb is conjugated in full on pages 28 to 31.

Position of reflexive pronouns

Except with the infinitive, gerund and positive commands, the pronoun comes before the verb → ④

In the infinitive, gerund and positive commands, the pronoun follows the verb and is attached to it (but see also page 232) → ⑤

Examples

1. Me visto
   Nos lavamos
   Se levanta

   I'm dressing (myself)
   We're washing (ourselves)
   He gets up

2. Nos queremos
   Se parecen

   We love each other
   They resemble one another

3. Se miraban el uno al otro

   They were looking at each other

4. Me acuesto temprano
   ¿Cómo se llama Vd?
   No se ha despertado
   No te levantes

   I go to bed early
   What is your name?
   He hasn't woken up
   Don't get up

5. Quiero irme
   Estoy levantándome
   Siéntense
   Vámonos

   I want to go away
   I am getting up
   Sit down
   Let's go

Reflexive Verbs *continued*

Some verbs have both a reflexive and non-reflexive form. When used reflexively, they have a different but closely related meaning, as shown in the following examples.

NON-REFLEXIVE	REFLEXIVE
acostar to put to bed	**acostarse** to go to bed
casar to marry (off)	**casarse** to get married
detener to stop	**detenerse** to come to a halt
dormir to sleep	**dormirse** to go to sleep
enfadar to annoy	**enfadarse** to get annoyed
hacer to make	**hacerse** to become
ir to go	**irse** to leave, go away
lavar to wash	**lavarse** to get washed
levantar to raise	**levantarse** to get up
llamar to call	**llamarse** to be called
poner to put	**ponerse** to put on (clothing), to become
sentir to feel (something)	**sentirse** to feel (sick, tired, *etc*)
vestir to dress (someone)	**vestirse** to get dressed
volver to return	**volverse** to turn round

Some other verbs exist only in the reflexive:

arrepentirse to repent   **jactarse** to boast
atreverse to dare   **quejarse** to complain

Some verbs acquire a different nuance when used reflexively:

caer to fall → ❶   **caerse** to fall down (by accident) → ❷

morir to die, be killed (by accident or on purpose) → ❸   **morirse** to die (from natural causes) → ❹

Often a reflexive verb can be used:
- to avoid the passive (see page 32) → ❺
- in impersonal expressions (see page 40) → ❻

Examples

1 El agua caía desde las rocas — Water fell from the rocks

2 Me caí y me rompí el brazo — I fell and broke my arm

3 Tres personas han muerto en un accidente/atentado terrorista — Three people were killed in an accident/a terrorist attack

4 Mi abuelo se murió a los ochenta años — My grandfather died at the age of eighty

5 Se perdió la batalla — The battle was lost
No se veían las casas — The houses could not be seen

6 Se dice que ... — (It is said that) People say that ...
No se puede entrar — You/One can't go in
No se permite — It is not allowed

Reflexive Verbs *continued*

Conjugation of: **lavarse** to wash oneself

1 SIMPLE TENSES

PRESENT

(yo)	**me** lav**o**
(tú)	**te** lav**as**
(él/ella/Vd)	**se** lav**a**
(nosotros/as)	**nos** lav**amos**
(vosotros/as)	**os** lav**áis**
(ellos/as/Vds)	**se** lav**an**

IMPERFECT

(yo)	**me** lav**aba**
(tú)	**te** lav**abas**
(él/ella/Vd)	**se** lav**aba**
(nosotros/as)	**nos** lav**ábamos**
(vosotros/as)	**os** lav**abais**
(ellos/as/Vds)	**se** lav**aban**

FUTURE

(yo)	**me** lavar**é**
(tú)	**te** lavar**ás**
(él/ella/Vd)	**se** lavar**á**
(nosotros/as)	**nos** lavar**emos**
(vosotros/as)	**os** lavar**éis**
(ellos/as/Vds)	**se** lavar**án**

CONDITIONAL

(yo)	**me** lavar**ía**
(tú)	**te** lavar**ías**
(él/ella/Vd)	**se** lavar**ía**
(nosotros/as)	**nos** lavar**íamos**
(vosotros/as)	**os** lavar**íais**
(ellos/as/Vds)	**se** lavar**ían**

Reflexive Verbs *continued*

Conjugation of: **lavarse** to wash oneself

1 SIMPLE TENSES

PRETERITE

(yo)	**me** lav**é**
(tú)	**te** lav**aste**
(él/ella/Vd)	**se** lav**ó**
(nosotros/as)	**nos** lav**amos**
(vosotros/as)	**os** lav**asteis**
(ellos/as/Vds)	**se** lav**aron**

PRESENT SUBJUNCTIVE

(yo)	**me** lav**e**
(tú)	**te** lav**es**
(él/ella/Vd)	**se** lav**e**
(nosotros/as)	**nos** lav**emos**
(vosotros/as)	**os** lav**éis**
(ellos/as/Vds)	**se** lav**en**

IMPERFECT SUBJUNCTIVE

(yo)	**me** lav**ara** *or* lav**ase**
(tú)	**te** lav**aras** *or* lav**ases**
(él/ella/Vd)	**se** lav**ara** *or* lav**ase**
(nosotros/as)	**nos** lav**áramos** *or* lav**ásemos**
(vosotros/as)	**os** lav**arais** *or* lav**aseis**
(ellos/as/Vds)	**se** lav**aran** *or* lav**asen**

Reflexive Verbs *continued*

Conjugation of: **lavarse** to wash oneself

2 COMPOUND TENSES

PERFECT

(yo)	**me he** lavado
(tú)	**te has** lavado
(él/ella/Vd)	**se ha** lavado
(nosotros/as)	**nos hemos** lavado
(vosotros/as)	**os habéis** lavado
(ellos/as/Vds)	**se han** lavado

PLUPERFECT

(yo)	**me había** lavado
(tú)	**te habías** lavado
(él/ella/Vd)	**se había** lavado
(nosotros/as)	**nos habíamos** lavado
(vosotros/as)	**os habíais** lavado
(ellos/as/Vds)	**se habían** lavado

FUTURE PERFECT

(yo)	**me habré** lavado
(tú)	**te habrás** lavado
(él/ella/Vd)	**se habrá** lavado
(nosotros/as)	**nos habremos** lavado
(vosotros/as)	**os habréis** lavado
(ellos/as/Vds)	**se habrán** lavado

Reflexive Verbs *continued*

Conjugation of: **lavarse** to wash oneself

2 COMPOUND TENSES

PAST ANTERIOR

(yo)	**me hube** lavado
(tú)	**te hubiste** lavado
(él/ella/Vd)	**se hubo** lavado
(nosotros/as)	**nos hubimos** lavado
(vosotros/as)	**os hubisteis** lavado
(ellos/as/Vds)	**se hubieron** lavado

PERFECT SUBJUNCTIVE

(yo)	**me haya** lavado
(tú)	**te hayas** lavado
(él/ella/Vd)	**se haya** lavado
(nosotros/as)	**nos hayamos** lavado
(vosotros/as)	**os hayáis** lavado
(ellos/as/Vds)	**se hayan** lavado

PLUPERFECT SUBJUNCTIVE

(yo)	**me hubiera** *or* **hubiese** lavado
(tú)	**te hubieras** *or* **hubieses** lavado
(él/ella/Vd)	**se hubiera** *or* **hubiese** lavado
(nosotros/as)	**nos hubiéramos** *or* **hubiésemos** lavado
(vosotros/as)	**os hubierais** *or* **hubieseis** lavado
(ellos/as/Vds)	**se hubieran** *or* **hubiesen** lavado

The Passive

In active sentences, the subject of a verb carries out the action of that verb, but in passive sentences the subject receives the action. Compare the following:

> The car hit Jane (*subject*: the car)
> Jane was hit by the car (*subject*: Jane)

English uses the verb 'to be' with the past participle to form passive sentences. Spanish forms them in the same way, i.e.:
> a tense of **ser** + *past participle*.

The past participle agrees in number and gender with the subject → ❶

A sample verb is conjugated in the passive voice on pages 36 to 39.

In English, the word 'by' usually introduces the agent through which the action of a passive sentence is performed. In Spanish this agent is preceded by **por** → ❷

The passive voice is used much less frequently in Spanish than English. It is, however, often used in expressions where the identity of the agent is unknown or unimportant → ❸

Examples

1. Pablo ha sido despedido — Paul has been sacked
   Su madre era muy admirada — His mother was greatly admired
   El palacio será vendido — The palace will be sold
   Las puertas habían sido cerradas — The doors had been closed

2. La casa fue diseñada por mi hermano — The house was designed by my brother

3. La ciudad fue conquistada tras un largo asedio — The city was conquered after a long siege
   Ha sido declarado el estado de excepción — A state of emergency has been declared

The Passive *continued*

In English the indirect object in an active sentence can become the subject of the related passive sentence, e.g.

> 'His mother gave him the book' (*indirect object*: him)
> He was given the book by his mother

This is not possible in Spanish. The indirect object remains as such, while the object of the active sentence becomes the subject of the passive sentence → **①**

Other ways to express a passive meaning

Since modern Spanish tends to avoid the passive, it uses various other constructions to replace it:

If the agent (person or object performing the action) is known, the active is often preferred where English might prefer the passive → **②**

The 3rd person plural of the active voice can be used. The meaning is equivalent to 'they' + *verb* → **③**

When the action of the sentence is performed on a person, the reflexive form of the verb can be used in the 3rd person singular, and the person becomes the object → **④**

When the action is performed on a thing, this becomes the subject of the sentence and the verb is made reflexive, agreeing in number with the subject → **⑤**

Examples

1 Su madre le regaló el libro

His mother gave him the book

BECOMES:

El libro le fue regalado por su madre

The book was given to him by his mother

2 La policía interrogó al sospechoso

The police questioned the suspect

RATHER THAN:

El sospechoso fue interrogado por la policía

3 Usan demasiada publicidad en la televisión

Too much advertising is used on television

4 Últimamente no se le/les ha visto mucho en público

He has/they have not been seen much in public recently

5 Esta palabra ya no se usa
Todos los libros se han vendido

This word is no longer used
All the books have been sold

The Passive *continued*

Conjugation of: **ser amado** to be loved

PRESENT

(yo)	**soy** amado(a)
(tú)	**eres** amado(a)
(él/ella/Vd)	**es** amado(a)
(nosotros/as)	**somos** amado(a)s
(vosotros/as)	**sois** amado(a)s
(ellos/as/Vds)	**son** amado(a)s

IMPERFECT

(yo)	**era** amado(a)
(tú)	**eras** amado(a)
(él/ella/Vd)	**era** amado(a)
(nosotros/as)	**éramos** amado(a)s
(vosotros/as)	**erais** amado(a)s
(ellos/as/Vds)	**eran** amado(a)s

FUTURE

(yo)	**seré** amado(a)
(tú)	**serás** amado(a)
(él/ella/Vd)	**será** amado(a)
(nosotros/as)	**seremos** amado(a)s
(vosotros/as)	**seréis** amado(a)s
(ellos/as/Vds)	**serán** amado(a)s

CONDITIONAL

(yo)	**sería** amado(a)
(tú)	**serías** amado(a)
(él/ella/Vd)	**sería** amado(a)
(nosotros/as)	**seríamos** amado(a)s
(vosotros/as)	**seríais** amado(a)s
(ellos/as/Vds)	**serían** amado(a)s

The Passive *continued*

Conjugation of: **ser amado** to be loved

PRETERITE

(yo)	**fui** amado(**a**)
(tú)	**fuiste** amado(**a**)
(él/ella/Vd)	**fue** amado(**a**)
(nosotros/as)	**fuimos** amado(**a**)**s**
(vosotros/as)	**fuisteis** amado(**a**)**s**
(ellos/as/Vds)	**fueron** amado(**a**)**s**

PRESENT SUBJUNCTIVE

(yo)	**sea** amado(**a**)
(tú)	**seas** amado(**a**)
(él/ella/Vd)	**sea** amado(**a**)
(nosotros/as)	**seamos** amado(**a**)**s**
(vosotros/as)	**seáis** amado(**a**)**s**
(ellos/as/Vds)	**sean** amado(**a**)**s**

IMPERFECT SUBJUNCTIVE

(yo)	**fuera** *or* **fuese** amado(**a**)
(tú)	**fueras** *or* **fueses** amado(**a**)
(él/ella/Vd)	**fuera** *or* **fuese** amado(**a**)
(nosotros/as)	**fuéramos** *or* **fuésemos** amado(**a**)**s**
(vosotros/as)	**fuerais** *or* **fueseis** amado(**a**)**s**
(ellos/as/Vds)	**fueran** *or* **fuesen** amado(**a**)**s**

The Passive *continued*

Conjugation of: **ser amado** to be loved

PERFECT

(yo)	**he sido** amado(a)
(tú)	**has sido** amado(a)
(él/ella/Vd)	**ha sido** amado(a)
(nosotros/as)	**hemos sido** amado(a)s
(vosotros/as)	**habéis sido** amado(a)s
(ellos/as/Vds)	**han sido** amado(a)s

PLUPERFECT

(yo)	**había sido** amado(a)
(tú)	**habías sido** amado(a)
(él/ella/Vd)	**había sido** amado(a)
(nosotros/as)	**habíamos sido** amado(a)s
(vosotros/as)	**habíais sido** amado(a)s
(ellos/as/Vds)	**habían sido** amado(a)s

FUTURE PERFECT

(yo)	**habré sido** amado(a)
(tú)	**habrás sido** amado(a)
(él/ella/Vd)	**habrá sido** amado(a)
(nosotros/as)	**habremos sido** amado(a)s
(vosotros/as)	**habréis sido** amado(a)s
(ellos/as/Vds)	**habrán sido** amado(a)s

CONDITIONAL PERFECT

(yo)	**habría sido** amado(a)
(tú)	**habrías sido** amado(a)
(él/ella/Vd)	**habría sido** amado(a)
(nosotros/as)	**habríamos sido** amado(a)s
(vosotros/as)	**habríais sido** amado(a)s
(ellos/as/Vds)	**habrían sido** amado(a)s

The Passive *continued*

Conjugation of: **ser amado** to be loved

PAST ANTERIOR

(yo)	**hube sido** amado(a)
(tú)	**hubiste sido** amado(a)
(él/ella/Vd)	**hubo sido** amado(a)
(nosotros/as)	**hubimos sido** amado(a)s
(vosotros/as)	**hubisteis sido** amado(a)s
(ellos/as/Vds)	**hubieron sido** amado(a)s

PERFECT SUBJUNCTIVE

(yo)	**haya sido** amado(a)
(tú)	**hayas sido** amado(a)
(él/ella/Vd)	**haya sido** amado(a)
(nosotros/as)	**hayamos sido** amado(a)s
(vosotros/as)	**hayáis sido** amado(a)s
(ellos/as/Vds)	**hayan sido** amado(a)s

PLUPERFECT SUBJUNCTIVE

(yo)	**hubiera/-se sido** amado(a)
(tú)	**hubieras/-ses sido** amado(a)
(él/ella/Vd)	**hubiera/-se sido** amado(a)
(nosotros/as)	**hubiéramos/-semos sido** amado(a)s
(vosotros/as)	**hubierais/-seis sido** amado(a)s
(ellos/as/Vds)	**hubieran/-sen sido** amado(a)s

Impersonal Verbs

Impersonal verbs are used only in the infinitive, the gerund, and in the 3rd person (usually singular); unlike English, Spanish does not use the subject pronoun with impersonal verbs, e.g.

> **llueve** it's raining
> **es fácil decir que ...** it's easy to say that ...

The most common impersonal verbs are:

INFINITIVE	CONSTRUCTION
amanecer	amanece/está amaneciendo
	it's daybreak
anochecer	anochece/está anocheciendo
	it's getting dark
granizar	graniza/está granizando
	it's hailing
llover	llueve/está lloviendo
	it's raining → ❶
lloviznar	llovizna/está lloviznando
	it's drizzling
nevar	nieva/está nevando
	it's snowing → ❶
tronar	truena/está tronando
	it's thundering

Some reflexive verbs are also used impersonally.
The most common are:

INFINITIVE	CONSTRUCTION
creerse	se cree que* + *indicative* → ❷
	it is thought that; people think that
decirse	se dice que* + *indicative* → ❸
	it is said that; people say that

Examples

1. Llovía a cántaros — It was raining cats and dogs
   Estaba nevando cuando salieron — It was snowing when they left

2. Se cree que llegarán mañana — It is thought they will arrive tomorrow

3. Se dice que ha sido el peor invierno en 50 años — People say it's been the worst winter in 50 years

Impersonal Verbs *continued*

INFINITIVE	CONSTRUCTION
poderse	**se puede** + *infinitive* → ❶
	one/people can, it is possible to
tratarse de	**se trata de** + *noun* → ❷
	it's a question/matter of something
	it's about something
	se trata de + *infinitive* → ❸
	it's a question/matter of doing; somebody must do
venderse	**se vende*** + *noun* → ❹
	to be sold; for sale

* This impersonal construction conveys the same meaning as the 3rd person plural of these verbs; **creen que, dicen que, venden**

The following verbs are also commonly used in impersonal constructions:

INFINITIVE	CONSTRUCTION
bastar	**basta con** + *infinitive* → ❺
	it is enough to do
	basta con + *noun* → ❻
	something is enough, it only takes something
faltar	**falta** + *infinitive* → ❼
	we still have to/one still has to
haber	**hay** + *noun* → ❽
	there is/are
	hay que + *infinitive* → ❾
	one has to/we have to
hacer	**hace** + *noun/adjective depicting weather/dark/light etc* → ❿
	it is
	hace + *time expression* + **que** + *indicative* → ⓫
	somebody has done *or* been doing something since ...
	hace + *time expression* + **que** + *negative indicative* → ⓬
	it is ... since

Examples

1. Aquí se puede aparcar — One can park here

2. No se trata de dinero — It isn't a question/matter of money

3. Se trata de poner fin al asunto — We must put an end to the matter

4. Se vende coche — Car for sale

5. Basta con telefonear para reservar un asiento — You need only phone to reserve a seat

6. Basta con un error para que todo se estropee — One single error is enough to ruin everything

7. Aún falta cerrar las maletas — We/One still have/has to close the suitcases

8. Hay una habitación libre — There is one spare room
   No había cartas esta mañana — There were no letters this morning

9. Hay que cerrar las puertas — We have/One has to shut the doors

10. Hace calor/viento/sol — It is hot/windy/sunny
    Mañana hará bueno — It'll be nice (weather) tomorrow

11. Hace seis meses que vivo/vivimos aquí — I/We have lived or been living here for six months

12. Hace tres años que no le veo — It is three years since I last saw him

Impersonal Verbs *continued*

INFINITIVE	CONSTRUCTION
hacer falta	**hace falta** + *noun object* (+ *indirect object*) → ❶
	(somebody) needs something; something is
	necessary (to somebody)
	hace falta + *infinitive* (+ *indirect object*) → ❷
	it is necessary to do
	hace falta que + *subjunctive* → ❸
	it is necessary to do, somebody must do
parecer	**parece que** (+ *indirect object*) + *indicative* → ❹
	it seems/appears that
ser	**es/son** + *time expression* → ❺
	it is
	es + **de día/noche** → ❻
	it is
	es + *adjective* + *infinitive* → ❼
	it is
ser mejor	**es mejor** + *infinitive* → ❽
	it's better to do
	es mejor que + *subjunctive* → ❾
	it's better if/that
valer más	**más vale** + *infinitive* → ❿
	it's better to do
	más vale que + *subjunctive* → ⓫
	it's better to do/that somebody does

Examples

1. Hace falta valor para hacer eso — One needs courage to do that/
   Courage is needed to do that

   Me hace falta otro vaso más — I need an extra glass

2. Hace falta volver — It is necessary to return/
   We/I/You must return*

   Me hacía falta volver — I had to return

3. Hace falta que Vd se vaya — You have to/must leave

4. (Me) parece que estás equivocado — It seems (to me) you are wrong

5. Son las tres y media — It is half past three
   Ya es primavera — It is spring now

6. Era de noche cuando llegamos — It was night when we arrived

7. Era inútil protestar — It was useless to complain

8. Es mejor no decir nada — It's better to keep quiet

9. Es mejor que lo pongas aquí — It's better if/that you put it here

10. Más vale prevenir que curar — Prevention is better than cure

11. Más valdría que no fuéramos — It would be better if we didn't go/
    We'd better not go

*The translation here obviously depends on context

The Infinitive

The infinitive is the form of the verb found in dictionary entries meaning 'to ...', e.g. **hablar** to speak, **vivir** to live.

The infinitive is used in the following ways:

After a preposition → ❶

As a verbal noun → ❷
In this use the article may precede the infinitive, especially when the infinitive is the subject and begins the sentence → ❸

As a dependent infinitive, in the following verbal constructions:
- with no linking preposition → ❹
- with the linking preposition **a** → ❺
  (see also page 66)
- with the linking preposition **de** → ❻
  (see also page 66)
- with the linking preposition **en** → ❼
  (see also page 66)
- with the linking preposition **con** → ❽
  (see also page 66)
- with the linking preposition **por** → ❾
  (see also page 66)

The following construction should also be noted:
  indefinite pronoun + **que** + *infinitive* → ❿

The object pronouns generally follow the infinitive and are attached to it. For exceptions see page 232.

Examples

1. Después de acabar el desayuno, salió de casa

   After finishing her breakfast she went out

   Al enterarse de lo ocurrido se puso furiosa

   When she found out what had happened she was furious

   Me hizo daño sin saberlo

   She hurt me without her knowing

2. Su deporte preferido es montar a caballo

   Her favourite sport is horse riding

   Ver es creer

   Seeing is believing

3. El viajar tanto me resulta cansado

   I find so much travelling tiring

4. ¿Quiere Vd esperar?

   Would you like to wait?

5. Aprenderán pronto a nadar

   They will soon learn to swim

6. Pronto dejará de llover

   It'll stop raining soon

7. La comida tarda en hacerse

   The meal is taking a long time to cook

8. Amenazó con denunciarles

   He threatened to report them (to the police)

9. Comience Vd por decirme su nombre

   Please start by giving me your name

10. Tengo algo que decirte

    I have something to tell you

The Infinitive *continued*

The verbs set out below are followed by the infinitive with no linking preposition.

deber, **poder**, **saber**, **querer** and **tener que** (**hay que** in impersonal constructions) → ❶

valer más, **hacer falta**: see Impersonal Verbs, page 44.

verbs of seeing or hearing, e.g. **ver** to see, **oír** to hear → ❷

hacer → ❸

dejar to let, allow → ❸

The following common verbs:
aconsejar to advise → ❹
conseguir to manage to → ❺
decidir to decide
desear to wish, want → ❻
esperar to hope → ❼
evitar to avoid → ❽
impedir to prevent → ❾
intentar to try → ❿
lograr to manage to → ❺

necesitar to need → ⓫
odiar to hate
olvidar to forget → ⓬
pensar to think → ⓭
preferir to prefer → ⓮
procurar to try → ❿
prohibir to forbid → ⓯
prometer to promise → ⓰
proponer to propose → ⓱

Examples

1. ¿Quiere Vd esperar?
   No puede venir

   Would you like to wait?
   She can't come

2. Nos ha visto llegar
   Se les oye cantar

   She saw us arriving
   You can hear them singing

3. No me hagas reír
   Déjeme pasar

   Don't make me laugh
   Let me past

4. Le aconsejamos dejarlo para
   mañana

   We advise you to leave it until
   tomorrow

5. Aún no he conseguido/logrado
   entenderlo

   I still haven't managed to
   understand it

6. No desea tener más hijos

   She doesn't want to have any
   more children

7. Esperamos ir de vacaciones
   este verano

   We are hoping to go on holiday
   this summer

8. Evite beber cuando conduzca

   Avoid drinking and driving

9. No pudo impedirle hablar

   He couldn't prevent him from
   speaking

10. Intentamos/procuramos pasar
    desapercibidos

    We tried not to be noticed

11. Necesitaba salir a la calle

    I/he/she needed to go out

12. Olvidó dejar su dirección

    He/she forgot to leave his/
    her address

13. ¿Piensan venir por Navidad?

    Are you thinking of coming for
    Christmas?

14. Preferiría elegirlo yo mismo

    I'd rather choose it myself

15. Prohibió fumar a los alumnos

    He forbade the pupils to smoke

16. Prometieron volver pronto

    They promised to come back soon

17. Propongo salir cuanto antes

    I propose to leave as soon as
    possible

The Infinitive: Set Expressions

The following are set in Spanish with the meaning shown:

dejar caer to drop → ❶
hacer entrar to show in → ❷
hacer saber to let know, make known → ❸
hacer salir to let out → ❹
hacer venir to send for → ❺
ir(se) a buscar to go for, go and get → ❻
mandar hacer to order → ❼
mandar llamar to send for → ❽
oír decir que to hear it said that → ❾
oír hablar de to hear of/about → ❿
querer decir to mean → ⓫

The Perfect Infinitive

The perfect infinitive is formed using the auxiliary verb **haber** with the past participle of the verb → ⓬

The perfect infinitive is found:
- following certain prepositions, especially **después de** after → ⓭
- following certain verbal constructions → ⓮

Examples

1. Al verlo, dejó caer lo que llevaba en las manos — When he saw him he dropped what he was carrying

2. Haz entrar a nuestros invitados — Show our guests in

3. Quiero hacerles saber que no serán bien recibidos — I want to let them know that they won't be welcome

4. Hágale salir, por favor — Please let him out

5. Le he hecho venir a Vd porque ... — I sent for you because ...

6. Vete a buscar los guantes — Go and get your gloves

7. Me he mandado hacer un traje — I have ordered a suit

8. Mandaron llamar al médico — They sent for the doctor

9. He oído decir que está enfermo — I've heard it said that he's ill

10. No he oído hablar más de él — I haven't heard anything more (said) of him

11. ¿Qué quiere decir eso? — What does that mean?

12. haber terminado — to have finished
    haberse vestido — to have got dressed

13. Después de haber comprado el regalo, volvió a casa — After buying/having bought the present, he went back home
    Después de haber madrugado tanto, el taxi se retrasó — After she got up so early, the taxi arrived late

14. perdonar a alguien por haber hecho — to forgive somebody for doing/having done
    dar las gracias a alguien por haber hecho — to thank somebody for doing/having done
    pedir perdón por haber hecho — to be sorry for doing/having done

The Gerund

Formation

First conjugation:
- replace the **-ar** of the infinitive by **-ando** → ❶

Second conjugation:
- replace the **-er** of the infinitive by **-iendo** → ❷

Third conjugation:
- replace the **-ir** of the infinitive by **-iendo** → ❸

For irregular gerunds, see irregular verbs, page 80 onwards.

Uses

After the verb **estar**, to form the continuous tenses → ❹

After the verbs **seguir** and **continuar** *to continue*, and **ir** when meaning to *happen gradually* → ❺

In time constructions, after **llevar** → ❻

When the action in the main clause needs to be complemented by another action → ❼

The position of object pronouns is the same as for the infinitive (see page 46).

The gerund is invariable and strictly verbal in sense.

The Present Participle

It is formed by replacing the **-ar** of the infinitive of 1st conjugation verbs by **-ante**, and the **-er** and **-ir** of the 2nd and 3rd conjugations by **-iente** → ❽

A very limited number of verbs have a present participle used either as an adjective or a noun → ❾/❿

Examples

① cantar to sing → cantando singing

② temer to fear → temiendo fearing

③ partir to leave → partiendo leaving

④ Estoy escribiendo una carta — I am writing a letter
Estaban esperándonos — They were waiting for us

⑤ Sigue viniendo todos los días — He/she is still coming every day
Continuarán subiendo los precios — Prices will continue to go up
El ejército iba avanzando poco a poco — The army was gradually advancing

⑥ Lleva dos años estudiando inglés — He/she has been studying English for two years

⑦ Pasamos el día tomando el sol en la playa — We spent the day sunbathing on the beach
Iba cojeando — He/she/I was limping
Salieron corriendo — They ran out

⑧ cantar to sing → cantante singing/singer
pender to hang → pendiente hanging
seguir to follow → siguiente following

⑨ agua corriente — running water

⑩ un estudiante — a student

Use of Tenses

The Present

Unlike English, Spanish often uses the same verb form for the simple present (e.g. I smoke, he reads, we live) and the continuous present (e.g. I am smoking, he is reading, we are living) → ❶

Normally, however, the continuous present is used to translate the Spanish:
estar haciendo to be doing → ❷

Spanish uses the present tense where English uses the perfect in the following cases:
- with certain prepositions of time – notably **desde** for/since – when an action begun in the past is continued in the present → ❸
  - ⓘ Note: The perfect can be used as in English when the verb is negative → ❹
- in the construction **acabar de hacer** to have just done → ❺

Like English, Spanish often uses the present where a future action is implied → ❻

The Future

The future is generally used as in English → ❼, but note the following:

Immediate future time is often expressed by means of the present tense of **ir** + **a** + infinitive → ❽

When 'will' or 'shall' mean 'wish to', 'are willing to', **querer** is used → ❾

The Future Perfect

Used as in English shall/will have done → ❿

It can also express conjecture, usually about things in the recent past → ⓫

Examples

1 Fumo I smoke *or* I am smoking
Lee He reads *or* He is reading
Vivimos We live *or* We are living

2 Está fumando   He is smoking

3 Linda estudia español desde   Linda's been learning Spanish for
  hace seis meses   six months (and still is)
Estoy de pie desde las siete   I've been up since seven
¿Hace mucho que esperan?   Have you been waiting long?
Ya hace dos semanas que   That's two weeks we've been
  estamos aquí   here (now)

4 No se han visto desde hace   They haven't seen each other for
  meses   months

5 Isabel acaba de salir   Isabel has just left

6 Mañana voy a Madrid   I am going to Madrid tomorrow

7 Lo haré mañana   I'll do it tomorrow

8 Te vas a caer si no tienes cuidado   You'll fall if you're not careful
Va a perder el tren   He's going to miss the train
Va a llevar una media hora   It'll take about half an hour

9 ¿Me quieres esperar un   Will you wait for me a second,
  momento, por favor?   please?

10 Lo habré acabado para mañana   I will have finished it for
                                                          tomorrow

11 Ya habrán llegado a casa   They must have arrived home by
                                                          now

Use of Tenses *continued*

The Imperfect

The imperfect describes:
- an action or state in the past without definite limits in time → ❶
- habitual action(s) in the past (often expressed in English by means of would or used to) → ❷

Spanish uses the imperfect tense where English uses the pluperfect in the following cases:
- with certain prepositions of time – notably **desde** for/since – when an action begun in the remoter past was continued in the more recent past → ❸
  - ⓘ Note: The pluperfect is used as in English when the verb is negative or the action has been completed → ❹
- in the construction **acabar de hacer** to have just done → ❺

Both the continuous and simple forms in English can be translated by the Spanish simple imperfect, but the continuous imperfect is used when the emphasis is on the fact that an action was going on at a precise moment in the past → ❻

The Perfect

The perfect is generally used as in English → ❼

The Preterite

The preterite generally corresponds to the English simple past in both written and spoken Spanish → ❽

However, while English can use the simple past to describe habitual actions or settings, Spanish uses the imperfect (see above) → ❾

The Past Anterior

This tense is only ever used in written, literary Spanish, to replace the pluperfect in time clauses where the verb in the main clause is in the preterite → ❿

Examples

1 Todos mirábamos en silencio   We were all watching in silence
Nuestras habitaciones daban a la playa   Our rooms overlooked the beach

2 En su juventud se levantaba de madrugada   In his youth he got up at dawn
Hablábamos sin parar durante horas   We would talk non-stop for hours on end
Mi hermano siempre me tomaba el pelo   My brother always used to tease me

3 Hacía dos años que vivíamos en Irlanda   We had been living in Ireland for two years
Estaba enfermo desde 1990   He had been ill since 1990
Hacía mucho tiempo que salían juntos   They had been going out together for a long time

4 Hacía un año que no le había visto   I hadn't seen him for a year
Hacía una hora que había llegado   She had arrived an hour before

5 Acababa de encontrármelos   I had just met them

6 Cuando llegué, todos estaban fumando   When I arrived, they were all smoking

7 Todavía no han salido   They haven't come out yet

8 Me desperté y salté de la cama   I woke up and jumped out of bed

9 Siempre iban en coche al trabajo   They always travelled to work by car

10 Apenas hubo acabado, se oyeron unos golpes en la puerta   She had scarcely finished when there was a knock at the door

The Subjunctive: when to use it

For how to form the subjunctive see page 6 onwards.

After verbs of:

- 'wishing'
  querer que ⎤
  desear que ⎦   to wish that, want → ❶

- 'emotion' (e.g. regret, surprise, shame, pleasure, etc)
  sentir que   to be sorry that → ❷
  sorprender que   to be surprised that → ❸
  alegrarse de que   to be pleased that → ❹

- 'asking' and 'advising'
  pedir que   to ask that → ❺
  aconsejar que   to advise that → ❻

In all the above constructions, when the subject of the verbs in the main and subordinate clause is the same, the infinitive is used, and the conjunction **que** omitted → ❼

- 'ordering', 'forbidding', 'allowing'
  mandar que* ⎤
  ordenar que ⎦   to order that → ❽

  permitir que* ⎤
  dejar que* ⎦   to allow that → ❾

  prohibir que*   to forbid that → ❿
  impedir que*   to prevent that → ⓫

  * With these verbs either the subjunctive or the infinitive is used when the object of the main verb is the subject of the subordinate verb → ⓬

Always after verbs expressing doubt or uncertainty, and verbs of opinion used negatively.

dudar que   to doubt that → ⓭

no creer que ⎤
no pensar que ⎦   not to think that → ⓮

Examples

① Queremos que esté contenta

We want her to be happy
(*literally*: We want that she is
  happy)

¿Desea Vd que lo haga yo?

Do you want me to do it?

② Sentí mucho que no vinieran

I was very sorry that they didn't
  come

③ Nos sorprendió que no les
  vieran Vds

We were surprised you didn't
  see them

④ Me alegro de que te gusten

I'm pleased that you like them

⑤ Sólo les pedimos que tengan
  cuidado

We're only asking you to take
  care

⑥ Le aconsejé que no llegara tarde

I advised him not to be late

⑦ Quiero que lo termines pronto
BUT:
Quiero terminarlo pronto

I want you to finish it soon

I want to finish it soon

⑧ Ha mandado que vuelvan
Ordenó que fueran castigados

He has ordered them to come back
He ordered them to be punished

⑨ No permitas que te tomen el pelo
No me dejó que la llevara a casa

Don't let them pull your leg
She didn't allow me to take her
  home

⑩ Te prohíbo que digas eso

I forbid you to say that

⑪ No les impido que vengan

I am not preventing them from
  coming

⑫ Les ordenó que salieran
or Les ordenó salir

She ordered them to go out

⑬ Dudo que lo sepan hacer

I doubt they can do it

⑭ No creo que sean tan listos

I don't think they are as clever
  as that

59

The Subjunctive: when to use it *continued*

In impersonal constructions which express necessity, possibility, etc:

hace falta que ⎤	it is necessary that → ①
es necesario que ⎦	
es posible que	it is possible that → ②
más vale que	it is better that → ③
es una lástima que	it is a pity that → ④

ⓘ Note: In impersonal constructions which state a fact or express certainty the indicative is used when the impersonal verb is affirmative. When it is negative, the subjunctive is used → ⑤

After certain conjunctions:

para que ⎤	so that → ⑥
a fin de que* ⎦	
como si	as if → ⑦
sin que*	without → ⑧
a condición de que* ⎤	
con tal (de) que* ⎥	provided that,
siempre que ⎦	on condition that → ⑨
a menos que ⎤	unless → ⑩
a no ser que ⎦	
antes (de) que*	before → ⑪
no sea que	lest/in case → ⑫
mientras (que) ⎤	as long as → ⑬
siempre que ⎦	
(el) que	the fact that → ⑭

*When the subject of both verbs is the same, the infinitive is used, and the final **que** is omitted → ⑧

Examples

❶	¿Hace falta que vaya Jaime?	Does James have to go?
❷	Es posible que tengan razón	It's possible that they are right
❸	Más vale que se quede Vd en su casa	It's better that you stay at home
❹	Es una lástima que haya perdido su perrito	It's a shame/pity that she has lost her puppy
❺	Es verdad que va a venir BUT: No es verdad que vayan a hacerlo	It's true that he's coming It's not true that they are going to do it
❻	Átalas bien para que no se caigan	Tie them up tightly so that they won't fall
❼	Hablaba como si no creyera en sus propias palabras	He talked as if he didn't believe in his own words
❽	Salimos sin que nos vieran BUT: Me fui sin esperarla	We left without them seeing us I went without waiting for her
❾	Lo haré con tal de que me cuentes todo lo que pasó	I'll do it provided you tell me all that happened
❿	Saldremos de paseo a menos que esté lloviendo	We'll go for a walk unless it's raining
⓫	Avísale antes de que sea demasiado tarde	Warn him before it's too late
⓬	Habla en voz baja, no sea que alguien nos oiga	Speak softly in case anyone hears us
⓭	Eso no pasará mientras yo sea el jefe aquí	That won't happen as long as I am the boss here
⓮	El que no me escribiera no me importaba demasiado	The fact that he didn't write didn't matter to me too much

The Subjunctive: when to use it *continued*

After the conjunctions:
    de modo que
    de forma que   so that (*indicating a purpose*) → ❶
    de manera que

> ⓘ Note: When these conjunctions introduce a result and not a
> purpose the subjunctive is not used → ❷

In relative clauses with an antecedent which is:
- negative → ❸
- indefinite → ❹
- non-specific → ❺

In main clauses, to express a wish or exhortation. The verb may be
preceded by expressions like **ojalá** or **que** → ❻

In the **si** clause of conditions where the English sentence contains a
conditional tense → ❼

In set expressions → ❽

In the following constructions which translate however:
- **por** + *adjective* + *subjunctive* → ❾
- **por** + *adverb* + *subjunctive* → ❿
- **por** + **mucho** + *subjunctive* → ⓫

Examples

1. Vuélvanse de manera que les vea bien

   Turn round so that I can see you properly

2. No quieren hacerlo, de manera que tendré que hacerlo yo

   They won't do it, so I'll have to do it myself

3. No he encontrado a nadie que la conociera

   I haven't met anyone who knows her

   No dijo nada que no supiéramos ya

   He/she didn't say anything we didn't already know

4. Necesito alguien que sepa conducir

   I need someone who can drive

   Busco algo que me distraiga

   I'm looking for something to take my mind off it

5. Busca una casa que tenga calefacción central

   He/she's looking for a house which has central heating
   (*subjunctive used since such a house may or may not exist*)

   El que lo haya visto tiene que decírmelo

   Anyone who has seen it must tell me
   (*subjunctive used since it is not known who has seen it*)

6. ¡Ojalá haga buen tiempo!

   Let's hope the weather will be good!

   ¡Que te diviertas!

   Have a good time!

7. Si fuéramos en coche llegaríamos a tiempo

   If we went by car we'd be there in time

8. Diga lo que diga ...

   Whatever he may say ...

   Sea lo que sea ...

   Be that as it may ...

   Pase lo que pase ...

   Come what may ...

   Sea como sea ...

   One way or another ...

9. Por cansado que esté, seguirá trabajando

   No matter how/however tired he may be, he'll go on working

10. Por lejos que viva, iremos a buscarle

    No matter how/however far away he lives, we'll go and look for him

11. Por mucho que lo intente, nunca lo conseguirá

    No matter how/however hard he tries, he'll never succeed

The Subjunctive: when to use it *continued*

Clauses taking either a subjunctive or an indicative

In certain constructions, a subjunctive is needed when the action refers to future events or hypothetical situations, whereas an indicative is used when stating a fact or experience → ❶

The commonest of these are:

The conjunctions:

cuando	when → ❶
en cuanto ⎤	
tan pronto como ⎦	as soon as → ❷
después (de) que*	after → ❸
hasta que	until → ❹
mientras	while → ❺
siempre que	whenever → ❻
aunque	even though → ❼

All conjunctions and pronouns ending in **-quiera** (*-ever*) → ❽

* ⓘ Note: If the subject of both verbs is the same, the subjunctive introduced by **después (de) que** may be replaced by **después de** + *infinitive* → ❾

Sequence of tenses in Subordinate Clauses

If the verb in the main clause is in the present, future or imperative, the verb in the dependent clause will be in the present or perfect subjunctive → ❿

If the verb in the main clause is in the conditional or any past tense, the verb in the dependent clause will be in the imperfect or pluperfect subjunctive → ⓫

Examples

1. Le aconsejé que oyera música
   cuando estuviera nervioso

   I advised him to listen to music
   when he felt nervous

   Me gusta nadar cuando hace
   calor

   I like to swim when it is warm

2. Te devolveré el libro tan pronto
   como lo haya leído

   I'll give you back the book as
   soon as I have read it

3. Te lo diré después de que te
   hayas sentado

   I'll tell you after you've sat down

4. Quédate aquí hasta que volvamos

   Stay here until we come back

5. No hablen en voz alta mientras
   estén ellos aquí

   Don't speak loudly while they
   are here

6. Vuelvan por aquí siempre que
   quieran

   Come back whenever you wish to

7. No le creeré aunque diga la
   verdad

   I won't believe him even if he
   tells the truth

8. La encontraré dondequiera
   que esté

   I will find her wherever she
   might be

9. Después de cenar nos fuimos
   al cine

   After dinner we went to the
   cinema

   Quiero que lo hagas
   (*pres + pres subj*)

   I want you to do it

   Temo que no haya venido
   (*pres + perf subj*)

   I fear he hasn't come (might not
   have come)

   Iremos por aquí para que no nos
   vean (*future + pres subj*)

   We'll go this way so that they
   won't see us

   Me gustaría que llegaras
   temprano (*cond + imperf subj*)

   I'd like you to arrive early

   Les pedí que me esperaran
   (*preterite + imperf subj*)

   I asked them to wait for me

   Sentiría mucho que hubiese
   muerto (*cond + pluperf subj*)

   I would be very sorry if he were
   dead

Verbs governing a, de, con, en, por and para

The following lists (pages 66 to 73) contain common verbal constructions using the prepositions **a**, **de**, **con**, **en**, **por** and **para**.

Note the following abbreviations:

infin.	*infinitive*
perf. infin.	*perfect infinitive**
algn	alguien
sb	somebody
sth	something

* For information see page 50.

aburrirse de + *infin.*	to get bored with doing → ❶
acabar con algo/algn	to put an end to sth/finish with sb → ❷
acabar de * + *infin.*	to have just done → ❸
acabar por + *infin.*	to end up doing → ❹
acercarse a algo/algn	to approach sth/sb
acordarse de algo/algn/de + *infin.*	to remember sth/sb/doing → ❺
acostumbrarse a algo/algn/a + *infin.*	to get used to sth/sb/to doing → ❻
acusar a algn de algo/de + *perf. infin*	to accuse sb of sth/of doing, having done. → ❼
advertir a algn de algo	to notify, warn sb about sth → ❽
aficionarse a algo/a + *infin.*	to grow fond of sth/of doing → ❾
alegrarse de algo/de + *perf. infin.*	to be glad about sth/of doing, having done → ❿
alejarse de algn/algo	to move away from sb/sth
amenazar a algn con algo/con + *infin.*	to threaten sb with sth/to do → ⓫
animar a algn a + *infin.*	to encourage sb to do
apresurarse a + *infin.*	to hurry to do → ⓬

* See also Use of Tenses, pages 54 and 56

Examples

1. Me aburría de no poder salir de casa — I used to get bored with not being able to leave the house

2. Quiso acabar con su vida — He wanted to put an end to his life

3. Acababan de llegar cuando ... — They had just arrived when ...

4. El acusado acabó por confesarlo todo — The accused ended up by confessing everything

5. Nos acordamos muy bien de aquellas vacaciones — We remember that holiday very well

6. Me he acostumbrado a levantarme temprano — I've got used to getting up early

7. Le acusó de haber mentido — She accused him of lying

8. Advertí a mi amigo del peligro que corría — I warned my friend about the danger he was in

9. Nos hemos aficionado a la música clásica — We've grown fond of classical music

10. Me alegro de haberle conocido — I'm glad I met him

11. Amenazó con denunciarles — He threatened to report them

12. Se apresuraron a coger sitio — They hurried to find a seat

Verbs governing a, de, con, en, por and para *continued*

aprender a + *infin.*	to learn to do → ❶
aprovecharse de algo/algn	to take advantage of sth/sb
aproximarse a algn/algo	to approach sb/sth
asistir a algo	to attend sth, be at sth
asomarse a/por	to lean out of → ❷
asombrarse de + *infin.*	to be surprised at doing → ❸
atreverse a + *infin.*	to dare to do
avergonzarse de algo/algn/de + *perf. infin.*	to be ashamed of sth/sb/of doing, having done → ❹
ayudar a algn a + *infin.*	to help sb to do → ❺
bajarse de (+ *place/vehicle*)	to get off/out of → ❻
burlarse de algn	to make fun of sb
cansarse de algo/algn/de + *infin.*	to tire of sth/sb/of doing
carecer de algo	to lack sth → ❼
cargar de algo	to load with sth → ❽
casarse con algn	to get married to sb → ❾
cesar de + *infin.*	to stop doing
chocar con algo	to crash/bump into sth → ❿
comenzar a + *infin.*	to begin to do
comparar con algn/algo	to compare with sb/sth
consentir en + *infin.*	to agree to do
consistir en + *infin.*	to consist of doing → ⓫
constar de algo	to consist of sth → ⓬
contar con algn/algo	to rely on sb/sth → ⓭
convenir en + *infin.*	to agree to do → ⓮
darse cuenta de algo	to realize sth
dejar de + *infin.*	to stop doing → ⓯
depender de algo/algn	to depend on sth/sb → ⓰
despedirse de algn	to say goodbye to sb
dirigirse a algn/+ place	to address sb/head for
disponerse a + *infin.*	to get ready to do
empezar a + *infin.*	to begin to do
empezar por + *infin.*	to begin by doing → ⓱

Examples

1. Me gustaría aprender a nadar — I'd like to learn to swim

2. No te asomes a la ventana — Don't lean out of the window

3. Nos asombramos mucho de verles ahí — We were very surprised at seeing them there

4. No me avergüenzo de haberlo hecho — I'm not ashamed of having done it

5. Ayúdeme a llevar estas maletas — Help me to carry these cases

6. Se bajó del coche — He got out of the car

7. La casa carecía de jardín — The house lacked (did not have) a garden

8. El carro iba cargado de paja — The cart was loaded with straw

9. Se casó con Andrés — She married Andrew

10. Enciende la luz, o chocarás con la puerta — Turn the light on, or you'll bump into the door

11. Mi plan consistía en vigilarles de cerca — My plan consisted of keeping a close eye on them

12. El examen consta de tres partes — The exam consists of three parts

13. Cuento contigo para que me ayudes a hacerlo — I rely on you to help me do it

14. Convinieron en reunirse al día siguiente — They agreed to meet the following day

15. ¿Quieres dejar de hablar? — Will you stop talking?

16. No depende de mí — It doesn't depend on me

17. Empieza por enterarte de lo que se trata — Begin by finding out what it is about

69

Verbs governing a, de, con, en, por and para *continued*

encontrarse con algn	to meet sb (by chance) → ❶
enfadarse con algn	to get annoyed with sb
enseñar a algn a + *infin.*	to teach sb to → ❷
enterarse de algo	to find out about sth → ❸
entrar en (+ *place*)	to enter, go into
esperar a + *infin.*	to wait until → ❹
estar de acuerdo con algn/algo	to agree with sb/sth
fiarse de algn/algo	to trust sb/sth
fijarse en algo/algn	to notice sth/sb → ❺
hablar con algn	to talk to sb → ❻
hacer caso a algn	to pay attention to sb
hartarse de algo/algn/de + *infin.*	to get fed up with sth/sb/with doing → ❼
interesarse por algo/algn	to be interested in sth/sb → ❽
invitar a algn a + *infin.*	to invite sb to do
jugar a (+ sports, games)	to play
luchar por algo/por + *infin.*	to fight, strive for/to do → ❾
llegar a + *infin./*(place)	to manage to do/to reach → ❿
llenar de algo	to fill with sth
negarse a + *infin.*	to refuse to do → ⓫
obligar a algn a + *infin.*	to make sb do → ⓬
ocuparse de algn/algo	to take care of sb/attend to sth
oler a algo	to smell of sth → ⓭
olvidarse de algo/algn/de + *infin.*	to forget sth/sb/to do → ⓮
oponerse a algo/a + *infin.*	to be opposed to sth/to doing
parecerse a algn/algo	to resemble sb/sth
pensar en algo/algn/en + *infin.*	to think about sth/sb/about doing → ⓯
preguntar por algn	to ask for/about sb
preocuparse de *or* **por algo/algn**	to worry about sth/sb → ⓰

Examples

1. Me encontré con ella al entrar en el banco — I met her as I was entering the bank

2. Le estoy enseñando a nadar — I am teaching him to swim

3. ¿Te has enterado del sitio adonde hay que ir? — Have you found out where we have to go?

4. Espera a saber lo que quiere antes de comprar el regalo — Wait until you know what he wants before buying the present

5. Me fijé en él cuando subía a su coche — I noticed him when he was getting into his car

6. ¿Puedo hablar con Vd un momento? — May I talk to you for a moment?

7. Me he hartado de escribirle — I've got fed up with writing to him

8. Me interesaba mucho por la arqueología — I was very interested in archaeology

9. Hay que luchar por mantener la paz — One must strive to preserve peace

10. Lo intenté sin llegar a conseguirlo — I tried without managing to do it

11. Se negó a hacerlo — He refused to do it

12. Le obligó a sentarse — He made him sit down

13. Este perfume huele a jazmín — This perfume smells of jasmine

14. Siempre me olvido de cerrar la puerta — I always forget to shut the door

15. No quiero pensar en eso — I don't want to think about that

16. Se preocupa mucho de/por su apariencia — He worries a lot about his appearance

Verbs governing a, de, con, en, por and para *continued*

prepararse a + *infin.*	to prepare to do
probar a + *infin.*	to try to do
quedar en + *infin.*	to agree to do → ❶
quedar por + *infin.*	to remain to be done → ❷
quejarse de algo	to complain of sth
referirse a algo	to refer to sth
reírse de algo/algn	to laugh at sth/sb
rodear de	to surround with → ❸
romper a + *infin.*	to (suddenly) start to do → ❹
salir de (+ *place*)	to leave
sentarse a (+ *table etc*)	to sit down at
subir(se) a (+ *vehicle/place*)	to get on, into/to climb → ❺
servir de algo a algn	to be useful to/serve sb as sth → ❻
servir para algo/para + *infin.*	to be good as sth/for doing → ❼
servirse de algo	to use sth → ❽
soñar con algn/algo/con + *infin.*	to dream about/of sb/sth/of doing
sorprenderse de algo	to be surprised at sth
tardar en + *infin.*	to take time to do → ❾
tener ganas de algo/de + *infin.*	to want sth/to do → ❿
tener miedo de algo	to be afraid of sth → ⓫
tener miedo a algn	to be afraid of sb → ⓬
terminar por + *infin.*	to end by doing
tirar de algo/algn	to pull sth/sb
trabajar de (+ *occupation*)	to work as → ⓭
trabajar en (+ *place of work*)	to work at/in → ⓮
traducir a (+ *language*)	to translate into
tratar de + *infin.*	to try to do → ⓯
tratarse de algo/algn/de + *infin.*	to be a question of sth/about sb/ about doing → ⓰
vacilar en + *infin.*	to hesitate to do → ⓱
volver a + *infin.*	to do again → ⓲

Examples

1. Habíamos quedado en encontrarnos a las 8 — We had agreed to meet at 8

2. Queda por averiguar dónde se ocultan — It remains to be discovered where they are hiding

3. Habían rodeado el jardín de un seto de cipreses — They had surrounded the garden with a hedge of cypress trees

4. Al apagarse la luz, el niño rompió a llorar — When the lights went out, the little boy suddenly started to cry

5. ¡De prisa, sube al coche! — Get into the car, quick!

6. Esto me servirá de bastón — This will serve me as a walking stick

7. No sirvo para (ser) jardinero — I'm no good as a gardener

8. Se sirvió de un destornillador para abrirlo — She used a screwdriver to open it

9. Tardaron mucho en salir — They took a long time to come out

10. Tengo ganas de volver a España — I want to go back to Spain

11. Mi hija tiene miedo de la oscuridad — My daughter is afraid of the dark

12. Nunca tuvieron miedo a su padre — They were never afraid of their father

13. Pedro trabaja de camarero en Londres — Peter works as a waiter in London

14. Trabajaba en una oficina — I used to work in an office

15. No trates de engañarme — Don't try to fool me

16. Se trata de nuestro nuevo vecino — It's about our new neighbour

17. Nunca vacilaban en pedir dinero — They never hesitated to borrow money

18. No vuelvas a hacerlo nunca más — Don't ever do it again

Ser and Estar

Spanish has two verbs – **ser** and **estar** – for 'to be'.

They are not interchangeable and each one is used in defined contexts.

ser is used:
- with an adjective, to express a permanent or inherent quality → ❶
- to express occupation or nationality → ❷
- to express possession → ❸
- to express origin or the material from which something is made → ❹
- with a noun, pronoun or infinitive following the verb → ❺
- to express the time and date → ❻
- to form the passive, with the past participle (see page 32).

ⓘ Note: This use emphasizes the action of the verb. If, however, the resultant state or condition needs to be emphasized, **estar** is used. The past participle then functions as an adjective (see page 208) and has to agree in gender and in number with the noun → ❼

estar is used:
- always, to indicate place or location → ❽
- with an adjective or adjectival phrase, to express a quality or state seen by the speaker as subject to change or different from expected → ❾
- when speaking of a person's state of health → ❿
- to form the continuous tenses, used with the gerund (see page 52) → ⓫
- with **de** + *noun*, to indicate a temporary occupation → ⓬

Examples

1. Mi hermano es alto
   María es inteligente

   My brother is tall
   Mary is intelligent

2. Javier es aviador
   Sus padres son italianos

   Javier is an airman
   His parents are Italian

3. La casa es de Miguel

   The house belongs to Michael

4. Mi hermana es de Granada
   Las paredes son de ladrillo

   My sister is from Granada
   The walls are made of brick

5. Andrés es un niño travieso
   Soy yo, Enrique
   Todo es proponérselo

   Andrew is a naughty boy
   It's me, Henry
   It's all a question of putting your
     mind to it

6. Son las tres y media
   Mañana es sábado

   It's half past three
   Tomorrow is Saturday

7. Las puertas eran cerradas
     sigilosamente
   Las puertas estaban cerradas

   The doors were being silently
     closed
   The doors were closed
   (resultant action)

8. La comida está en la mesa

   The meal is on the table

9. Su amigo está enfermo
   El lavabo está ocupado
   Hoy estoy de mal humor
   Las tiendas están cerradas

   Her friend is ill
   The toilet is engaged
   I'm in a bad mood today
   The shops are closed

10. ¿Cómo están Vds?
    Estamos todos bien

    How are you?
    We are all well

11. Estamos aprendiendo mucho

    We are learning a great deal

12. Mi primo está de médico en un
      pueblo

    My cousin works as a doctor in a
      village

Ser and Estar *continued*

With certain adjectives, both ser and estar can be used, although they are not interchangeable when used in this way:

- **ser** will express a permanent or inherent quality → **1**
- **estar** will express a temporary state or quality → **2**

Both **ser** and **estar** may also be used in set expressions.

The commonest of these are:

With **ser**

Sea como sea	Be that as it may
Es igual/Es lo mismo	It's all the same
llegar a ser	to become
¿Cómo fue eso?	How did that happen?
¿Qué ha sido de él?	What has become of him?
ser para (*with the idea of purpose*)	to be for → **3**

With **estar**

estar de pie/de rodillas	to be standing/kneeling
estar de viaje	to be travelling
estar de vacaciones	to be on holiday
estar de vuelta	to be back
estar de moda	to be in fashion
Está bien	It's all right
estar para	to be about to do sth/to be in a mood for → **4**
estar por	to be inclined to/to be (all) for → **5**
estar a punto de	to be just about to do sth → **6**

Examples

① Su hermana es muy joven/vieja — His sister is very young/old
Son muy ricos/pobres — They are very rich/poor
Su amigo era un enfermo — His friend was an invalid
Es un borracho — He is a drunkard
Mi hijo es bueno/malo — My son is good/naughty
Viajar es cansado — Travelling is tiring

② Está muy joven/vieja con ese vestido — She looks very young/old in that dress
Ahora están muy ricos/pobres — They have become very rich/poor lately

Estaba enfermo — He was ill
Está borracho — He is drunk
Está bueno/malo — He is well/ill
Hoy estoy cansada — I am tired today

③ Este paquete es para Vd — This parcel is for you
Esta caja es para guardar semillas — This box is for keeping seeds in

④ Están para llegar — They're about to arrive

⑤ Estoy por irme a vivir a España — I'm inclined to go and live in Spain

⑥ Las rosas están a punto de salir — The roses are about to come out

Verbal Idioms

Special Intransitive Verbs

With the following verbs the Spanish construction is the opposite of the English. The subject in English becomes the indirect object of the Spanish verb, while the object in English becomes the subject of the Spanish verb. Compare the following:

> I like that house (subject: I, object: that house)
> **Esa casa me gusta** (subject: **esa casa**, indirect object: **me**)

The commonest of these verbs are:

gustar	to like →	❶
gustar más	to prefer →	❷
encantar	(colloquial) to love →	❸
faltar	to need/to be short of/to have missing →	❹
quedar	to be/have left →	❺
doler	to have a pain in/to hurt, ache →	❻
interesar	to be interested in →	❼
importar	to mind →	❽

Examples

1 Me gusta este vestido

I like this dress (This dress pleases me)

2 Me gustan más éstas

I prefer these

3 Nos encanta hacer deporte

We love sport

4 Me faltaban 100 euros
Sólo le falta el toque final
Le faltaban tres dientes

I was short of 100 euros
It just needs the finishing touch
He/she had three teeth missing

5 Sólo nos quedan dos kilómetros

We only have two kilometres (left) to go

6 Me duele la cabeza

I have a headache

7 Nos interesa mucho la política

We are very interested in politics

8 No me importa la lluvia

I don't mind the rain

IrregularVerbs

The verbs listed opposite and conjugated on pages 82 to 160 provide the main patterns for irregular verbs. The verbs are grouped opposite according to their infinitive ending and are shown in the following tables in alphabetical order.

In the tables, the most important irregular verbs are given in their most common simple tenses, together with the imperative and the gerund.

The past participle is also shown for each verb, to enable you to form all the compound tenses, as on pages 18 to 23.

The pronouns **ella** and **Vd** take the same verb endings as **él**, while **ellas** and **Vds** take the same endings as **ellos**.

> All the verbs included in the tables differ from the three conjugations set out on pages 8 to 13. Many – e.g. **contar** – serve as models for groups of verbs, while others – e.g. **ir** – are unique. On pages 161–190 you will find every verb in this dictionary listed alphabetically and cross-referred either to the relevant basic conjugation or to the appropriate model in the verb tables.

Imperfect Subjunctive of IrregularVerbs

For verbs with an irregular root form in the preterite tense – e.g. **andar** → **anduvieron** – the imperfect subjunctive is formed by using the root form of the 3rd person plural of the preterite tense, and adding the imperfect subjunctive endings **-iera/-iese** etc where the verb has an 'i' in the preterite ending – e.g. andu**vieron** → andu**viera/iese**. Where the verb has no 'i' in the preterite ending, add **-era/-ese** etc – e.g. produj**eron** → produj**era/ese**.

Irregular Verbs

'-ar':

actuar	saber
almorzar	satisfacer
andar	ser
aullar	tener
avergonzar	torcer
averiguar	traer
contar	valer
cruzar	vencer
dar	ver
empezar	volver
enviar	
errar	**'-ir':** abolir
estar	abrir
jugar	adquirir
negar	bendecir
pagar	conducir
pensar	construir
rehusar	decir
rogar	dirigir
sacar	distinguir
volcar	dormir
	elegir
'-er': caber	erguir
caer	escribir
cocer	freír
coger	gruñir
crecer	ir
entender	lucir
haber	morir
hacer	oír
hay	pedir
leer	prohibir
llover	reír
mover	reñir
nacer	reunir
oler	salir
poder	seguir
poner	sentir
querer	venir
resolver	zurcir
romper	

abolir (to abolish)

	PRESENT*
nosotros	abol**imos**
vosotros	abol**ís**

* Present tense only
  used in persons shown

	IMPERFECT
yo	abol**ía**
tú	abol**ías**
él	abol**ía**
nosotros	abol**íamos**
vosotros	abol**íais**
ellos	abol**ían**

	FUTURE
yo	abolir**é**
tú	abolir**ás**
él	abolir**á**
nosotros	abolir**emos**
vosotros	abolir**éis**
ellos	abolir**án**

	CONDITIONAL
yo	abolir**ía**
tú	abolir**ías**
él	abolir**ía**
nosotros	abolir**íamos**
vosotros	abolir**íais**
ellos	abolir**ían**

PRESENT SUBJUNCTIVE
not used

	PRETERITE
yo	abol**í**
tú	abol**iste**
él	abol**ió**
nosotros	abol**imos**
vosotros	abol**isteis**
ellos	abol**ieron**

PAST PARTICIPLE
abol**ido**

IMPERATIVE
abol**id**

GERUND
abol**iendo**

abrir (to open)

	PRESENT		IMPERFECT
yo	abro	yo	abría
tú	abres	tú	abrías
él	abre	él	abría
nosotros	abrimos	nosotros	abríamos
vosotros	abrís	vosotros	abríais
ellos	abren	ellos	abrían

	FUTURE		CONDITIONAL
yo	abriré	yo	abriría
tú	abrirás	tú	abrirías
él	abrirá	él	abriría
nosotros	abriremos	nosotros	abriríamos
vosotros	abriréis	vosotros	abriríais
ellos	abrirán	ellos	abrirían

	PRESENT SUBJUNCTIVE		PRETERITE
yo	abra	yo	abrí
tú	abras	tú	abriste
él	abra	él	abrió
nosotros	abramos	nosotros	abrimos
vosotros	abráis	vosotros	abristeis
ellos	abran	ellos	abrieron

PAST PARTICIPLE	IMPERATIVE
abierto	abre
	abrid

GERUND
abriendo

actuar (to act)

	PRESENT		IMPERFECT
yo	**actúo**	yo	actu**aba**
tú	**actúas**	tú	actu**abas**
él	**actúa**	él	actu**aba**
nosotros	actu**amos**	nosotros	actu**ábamos**
vosotros	actu**áis**	vosotros	actu**abais**
ellos	**actúan**	ellos	actu**aban**

	FUTURE		CONDITIONAL
yo	actuar**é**	yo	actuar**ía**
tú	actuar**ás**	tú	actuar**ías**
él	actuar**á**	él	actuar**ía**
nosotros	actuar**emos**	nosotros	actuar**íamos**
vosotros	actuar**éis**	vosotros	actuar**íais**
ellos	actuar**án**	ellos	actuar**ían**

	PRESENT SUBJUNCTIVE		PRETERITE
yo	**actúe**	yo	actu**é**
tú	**actúes**	tú	actu**aste**
él	**actúe**	él	actu**ó**
nosotros	actu**emos**	nosotros	actu**amos**
vosotros	actu**éis**	vosotros	actu**asteis**
ellos	**actúen**	ellos	actu**aron**

PAST PARTICIPLE	IMPERATIVE
actu**ado**	**actúa**
	actua**d**

GERUND
actu**ando**

adquirir (to acquire)

	PRESENT		IMPERFECT
yo	adquiero	yo	adquiría
tú	adquieres	tú	adquirías
él	adquiere	él	adquiría
nosotros	adquirimos	nosotros	adquiríamos
vosotros	adquirís	vosotros	adquiríais
ellos	adquieren	ellos	adquirían

	FUTURE		CONDITIONAL
yo	adquiriré	yo	adquiriría
tú	adquirirás	tú	adquirirías
él	adquirirá	él	adquiriría
nosotros	adquiriremos	nosotros	adquiriríamos
vosotros	adquiriréis	vosotros	adquiriríais
ellos	adquirirán	ellos	adquirirían

	PRESENT SUBJUNCTIVE		PRETERITE
yo	adquiera	yo	adquirí
tú	adquieras	tú	adquiriste
él	adquiera	él	adquirió
nosotros	adquiramos	nosotros	adquirimos
vosotros	adquiráis	vosotros	adquiristeis
ellos	adquieran	ellos	adquirieron

PAST PARTICIPLE	IMPERATIVE
adquirido	adquiere
	adquirid

GERUND
adquiriendo

almorzar (to have lunch)

	PRESENT		IMPERFECT
yo	almuerzo	yo	almorzaba
tú	almuerzas	tú	almorzabas
él	almuerza	él	almorzaba
nosotros	almorzamos	nosotros	almorzábamos
vosotros	almorzáis	vosotros	almorzabais
ellos	almuerzan	ellos	almorzaban

	FUTURE		CONDITIONAL
yo	almorzaré	yo	almorzaría
tú	almorzarás	tú	almorzarías
él	almorzará	él	almorzaría
nosotros	almorzaremos	nosotros	almorzaríamos
vosotros	almorzaréis	vosotros	almorzaríais
ellos	almorzarán	ellos	almorzarían

	PRESENT SUBJUNCTIVE		PRETERITE
yo	almuerce	yo	almorcé
tú	almuerces	tú	almorzaste
él	almuerce	él	almorzó
nosotros	almorcemos	nosotros	almorzamos
vosotros	almorcéis	vosotros	almorzasteis
ellos	almuercen	ellos	almorzaron

PAST PARTICIPLE	IMPERATIVE
almorzado	almuerza
	almorzad

GERUND

almorzando

andar (to walk)

	PRESENT		IMPERFECT
yo	ando	yo	andaba
tú	andas	tú	andabas
él	anda	él	andaba
nosotros	andamos	nosotros	andábamos
vosotros	andáis	vosotros	andabais
ellos	andan	ellos	andaban

	FUTURE		CONDITIONAL
yo	andaré	yo	andaría
tú	andarás	tú	andarías
él	andará	él	andaría
nosotros	andaremos	nosotros	andaríamos
vosotros	andaréis	vosotros	andaríais
ellos	andarán	ellos	andarían

	PRESENT SUBJUNCTIVE		PRETERITE
yo	ande	yo	anduve
tú	andes	tú	anduviste
él	ande	él	anduvo
nosotros	andemos	nosotros	anduvimos
vosotros	andéis	vosotros	anduvisteis
ellos	anden	ellos	anduvieron

PAST PARTICIPLE	IMPERATIVE
andado	anda
	andad

GERUND
andando

aullar (to howl)

	PRESENT		IMPERFECT
yo	aúllo	yo	aullaba
tú	aúllas	tú	aullabas
él	aúlla	él	aullaba
nosotros	aullamos	nosotros	aullábamos
vosotros	aulláis	vosotros	aullabais
ellos	aúllan	ellos	aullaban

	FUTURE		CONDITIONAL
yo	aullaré	yo	aullaría
tú	aullarás	tú	aullarías
él	aullará	él	aullaría
nosotros	aullaremos	nosotros	aullaríamos
vosotros	aullaréis	vosotros	aullaríais
ellos	aullarán	ellos	aullarían

	PRESENT SUBJUNCTIVE		PRETERITE
yo	aúlle	yo	aullé
tú	aúlles	tú	aullaste
él	aúlle	él	aulló
nosotros	aullemos	nosotros	aullamos
vosotros	aulléis	vosotros	aullasteis
ellos	aúllen	ellos	aullaron

PAST PARTICIPLE	IMPERATIVE
aullado	aúlla
	aullad

GERUND

aullando

avergonzar (to shame)

	PRESENT		IMPERFECT
yo	avergüenzo	yo	avergonzaba
tú	avergüenzas	tú	avergonzabas
él	avergüenza	él	avergonzaba
nosotros	avergonzamos	nosotros	avergonzábamos
vosotros	avergonzáis	vosotros	avergonzabais
ellos	avergüenzan	ellos	avergonzaban

	FUTURE		CONDITIONAL
yo	avergonzaré	yo	avergonzaría
tú	avergonzarás	tú	avergonzarías
él	avergonzará	él	avergonzaría
nosotros	avergonzaremos	nosotros	avergonzaríamos
vosotros	avergonzaréis	vosotros	avergonzaríais
ellos	avergonzarán	ellos	avergonzarían

	PRESENT SUBJUNCTIVE		PRETERITE
yo	avergüence	yo	avergoncé
tú	avergüences	tú	avergonzaste
él	avergüence	él	avergonzó
nosotros	avergoncemos	nosotros	avergonzamos
vosotros	avergoncéis	vosotros	avergonzasteis
ellos	avergüencen	ellos	avergonzaron

PAST PARTICIPLE
avergonzado

IMPERATIVE
avergüenza
avergonzad

GERUND
avergonzando

averiguar (to find out)

	PRESENT		IMPERFECT
yo	averiguo	yo	averiguaba
tú	averiguas	tú	averiguabas
él	averigua	él	averiguaba
nosotros	averiguamos	nosotros	averiguábamos
vosotros	averiguáis	vosotros	averiguabais
ellos	averiguan	ellos	averiguaban

	FUTURE		CONDITIONAL
yo	averiguaré	yo	averiguaría
tú	averiguarás	tú	averiguarías
él	averiguará	él	averiguaría
nosotros	averiguaremos	nosotros	averiguaríamos
vosotros	averiguaréis	vosotros	averiguaríais
ellos	averiguarán	ellos	averiguarían

	PRESENT SUBJUNCTIVE		PRETERITE
yo	averigüe	yo	averigüé
tú	averigües	tú	averiguaste
él	averigüe	él	averiguó
nosotros	averigüemos	nosotros	averiguamos
vosotros	averigüéis	vosotros	averiguasteis
ellos	averigüen	ellos	averiguaron

PAST PARTICIPLE	IMPERATIVE
averiguado	averigua
	averiguad

GERUND
averiguando

bendecir (to bless)

	PRESENT		IMPERFECT
yo	bendigo	yo	bendecía
tú	bendices	tú	bendecías
él	bendice	él	bendecía
nosotros	bendecimos	nosotros	bendecíamos
vosotros	bendecís	vosotros	bendecíais
ellos	bendicen	ellos	bendecían

	FUTURE		CONDITIONAL
yo	bendeciré	yo	bendeciría
tú	bendecirás	tú	bendecirías
él	bendecirá	él	bendeciría
nosotros	bendeciremos	nosotros	bendeciríamos
vosotros	bendeciréis	vosotros	bendeciríais
ellos	bendecirán	ellos	bendecirían

	PRESENT SUBJUNCTIVE		PRETERITE
yo	bendiga	yo	bendije
tú	bendigas	tú	bendijiste
él	bendiga	él	bendijo
nosotros	bendigamos	nosotros	bendijimos
vosotros	bendigáis	vosotros	bendijisteis
ellos	bendigan	ellos	bendijeron

PAST PARTICIPLE
bendecido

IMPERATIVE
bendice
bendecid

GERUND
bendiciendo

caber (to fit)

	PRESENT		IMPERFECT
yo	quepo	yo	cabía
tú	cabes	tú	cabías
él	cabe	él	cabía
nosotros	cabemos	nosotros	cabíamos
vosotros	cabéis	vosotros	cabíais
ellos	caben	ellos	cabían

	FUTURE		CONDITIONAL
yo	cabré	yo	cabría
tú	cabrás	tú	cabrías
él	cabrá	él	cabría
nosotros	cabremos	nosotros	cabríamos
vosotros	cabréis	vosotros	cabríais
ellos	cabrán	ellos	cabrían

	PRESENT SUBJUNCTIVE		PRETERITE
yo	quepa	yo	cupe
tú	quepas	tú	cupiste
él	quepa	él	cupo
nosotros	quepamos	nosotros	cupimos
vosotros	quepáis	vosotros	cupisteis
ellos	quepan	ellos	cupieron

PAST PARTICIPLE	IMPERATIVE
cabido	cabe
	cabed

GERUND
cabiendo

caer (to fall)

	PRESENT		IMPERFECT
yo	caigo	yo	caía
tú	caes	tú	caías
él	cae	él	caía
nosotros	caemos	nosotros	caíamos
vosotros	caéis	vosotros	caíais
ellos	caen	ellos	caían

	FUTURE		CONDITIONAL
yo	caeré	yo	caería
tú	caerás	tú	caerías
él	caerá	él	caería
nosotros	caeremos	nosotros	caeríamos
vosotros	caeréis	vosotros	caeríais
ellos	caerán	ellos	caerían

	PRESENT SUBJUNCTIVE		PRETERITE
yo	caiga	yo	caí
tú	caigas	tú	caíste
él	caiga	él	cayó
nosotros	caigamos	nosotros	caímos
vosotros	caigáis	vosotros	caísteis
ellos	caigan	ellos	cayeron

PAST PARTICIPLE	IMPERATIVE
caído	cae
	caed

GERUND
cayendo

cocer (to boil)

	PRESENT		IMPERFECT
yo	cuezo	yo	cocía
tú	cueces	tú	cocías
él	cuece	él	cocía
nosotros	cocemos	nosotros	cocíamos
vosotros	cocéis	vosotros	cocíais
ellos	cuecen	ellos	cocían

	FUTURE		CONDITIONAL
yo	coceré	yo	cocería
tú	cocerás	tú	cocerías
él	cocerá	él	cocería
nosotros	coceremos	nosotros	coceríamos
vosotros	coceréis	vosotros	coceríais
ellos	cocerán	ellos	cocerían

	PRESENT SUBJUNCTIVE		PRETERITE
yo	cueza	yo	cocí
tú	cuezas	tú	cociste
él	cueza	él	coció
nosotros	cozamos	nosotros	cocimos
vosotros	cozáis	vosotros	cocisteis
ellos	cuezan	ellos	cocieron

PAST PARTICIPLE	IMPERATIVE
cocido	cuece
	coced

GERUND
cociendo

coger (to take)

	PRESENT			IMPERFECT
yo	cojo		yo	cogía
tú	coges		tú	cogías
él	coge		él	cogía
nosotros	cogemos		nosotros	cogíamos
vosotros	cogéis		vosotros	cogíais
ellos	cogen		ellos	cogían

	FUTURE			CONDITIONAL
yo	cogeré		yo	cogería
tú	cogerás		tú	cogerías
él	cogerá		él	cogería
nosotros	cogeremos		nosotros	cogeríamos
vosotros	cogeréis		vosotros	cogeríais
ellos	cogerán		ellos	cogerían

	PRESENT SUBJUNCTIVE			PRETERITE
yo	coja		yo	cogí
tú	cojas		tú	cogiste
él	coja		él	cogió
nosotros	cojamos		nosotros	cogimos
vosotros	cojáis		vosotros	cogisteis
ellos	cojan		ellos	cogieron

PAST PARTICIPLE
cogido

IMPERATIVE
coge
coged

GERUND
cogiendo

conducir (to drive, to lead)

	PRESENT			IMPERFECT
yo	conduzco		yo	conducía
tú	conduces		tú	conducías
él	conduce		él	conducía
nosotros	conducimos		nosotros	conducíamos
vosotros	conducís		vosotros	conducíais
ellos	conducen		ellos	conducían

	FUTURE			CONDITIONAL
yo	conduciré		yo	conduciría
tú	conducirás		tú	conducirías
él	conducirá		él	conduciría
nosotros	conduciremos		nosotros	conduciríamos
vosotros	conduciréis		vosotros	conduciríais
ellos	conducirán		ellos	conducirían

	PRESENT SUBJUNCTIVE			PRETERITE
yo	conduzca		yo	conduje
tú	conduzcas		tú	condujiste
él	conduzca		él	condujo
nosotros	conduzcamos		nosotros	condujimos
vosotros	conduzcáis		vosotros	condujisteis
ellos	conduzcan		ellos	condujeron

PAST PARTICIPLE	IMPERATIVE
conducido	conduce
	conducid

GERUND
conduciendo

construir (to build)

	PRESENT		IMPERFECT
yo	construyo	yo	construía
tú	construyes	tú	construías
él	construye	él	construía
nosotros	construimos	nosotros	construíamos
vosotros	construís	vosotros	construíais
ellos	construyen	ellos	construían

	FUTURE		CONDITIONAL
yo	construiré	yo	construiría
tú	construirás	tú	construirías
él	construirá	él	construiría
nosotros	construiremos	nosotros	construiríamos
vosotros	construiréis	vosotros	construiríais
ellos	construirán	ellos	construirían

	PRESENT SUBJUNCTIVE		PRETERITE
yo	construya	yo	construí
tú	construyas	tú	construiste
él	construya	él	construyó
nosotros	construyamos	nosotros	construimos
vosotros	construyáis	vosotros	construisteis
ellos	construyan	ellos	construyeron

PAST PARTICIPLE	IMPERATIVE
construido	construye
	construid

GERUND
construyendo

contar (to tell, to count)

	PRESENT		IMPERFECT
yo	cuento	yo	contaba
tú	cuentas	tú	contabas
él	cuenta	él	contaba
nosotros	contamos	nosotros	contábamos
vosotros	contáis	vosotros	contabais
ellos	cuentan	ellos	contaban

	FUTURE		CONDITIONAL
yo	contaré	yo	contaría
tú	contarás	tú	contarías
él	contará	él	contaría
nosotros	contaremos	nosotros	contaríamos
vosotros	contaréis	vosotros	contaríais
ellos	contarán	ellos	contarían

	PRESENT SUBJUNCTIVE		PRETERITE
yo	cuente	yo	conté
tú	cuentes	tú	contaste
él	cuente	él	contó
nosotros	contemos	nosotros	contamos
vosotros	contéis	vosotros	contasteis
ellos	cuenten	ellos	contaron

PAST PARTICIPLE	IMPERATIVE
contado	cuenta
	contad

GERUND
contando

crecer (to grow)

	PRESENT		IMPERFECT
yo	crezco	yo	crecía
tú	creces	tú	crecías
él	crece	él	crecía
nosotros	crecemos	nosotros	crecíamos
vosotros	crecéis	vosotros	crecíais
ellos	crecen	ellos	crecían

	FUTURE		CONDITIONAL
yo	creceré	yo	crecería
tú	crecerás	tú	crecerías
él	crecerá	él	crecería
nosotros	creceremos	nosotros	creceríamos
vosotros	creceréis	vosotros	creceríais
ellos	crecerán	ellos	crecerían

	PRESENT SUBJUNCTIVE		PRETERITE
yo	crezca	yo	crecí
tú	crezcas	tú	creciste
él	crezca	él	creció
nosotros	crezcamos	nosotros	crecimos
vosotros	crezcáis	vosotros	crecisteis
ellos	crezcan	ellos	crecieron

PAST PARTICIPLE	IMPERATIVE
crecido	crece
	creced

GERUND
creciendo

cruzar (to cross)

	PRESENT			IMPERFECT
yo	cruzo		yo	cruzaba
tú	cruzas		tú	cruzabas
él	cruza		él	cruzaba
nosotros	cruzamos		nosotros	cruzábamos
vosotros	cruzáis		vosotros	cruzabais
ellos	cruzan		ellos	cruzaban

	FUTURE			CONDITIONAL
yo	cruzaré		yo	cruzaría
tú	cruzarás		tú	cruzarías
él	cruzará		él	cruzaría
nosotros	cruzaremos		nosotros	cruzaríamos
vosotros	cruzaréis		vosotros	cruzaríais
ellos	cruzarán		ellos	cruzarían

	PRESENT SUBJUNCTIVE			PRETERITE
yo	cruce		yo	crucé
tú	cruces		tú	cruzaste
él	cruce		él	cruzó
nosotros	crucemos		nosotros	cruzamos
vosotros	crucéis		vosotros	cruzasteis
ellos	crucen		ellos	cruzaron

PAST PARTICIPLE	IMPERATIVE
cruzado	cruza
	cruzad

GERUND

cruzando

dar (to give)

	PRESENT			IMPERFECT
yo	doy		yo	daba
tú	das		tú	dabas
él	da		él	daba
nosotros	damos		nosotros	dábamos
vosotros	dais		vosotros	dabais
ellos	dan		ellos	daban

	FUTURE			CONDITIONAL
yo	daré		yo	daría
tú	darás		tú	darías
él	dará		él	daría
nosotros	daremos		nosotros	daríamos
vosotros	daréis		vosotros	daríais
ellos	darán		ellos	darían

	PRESENT SUBJUNCTIVE			PRETERITE
yo	dé		yo	di
tú	des		tú	diste
él	dé		él	dio
nosotros	demos		nosotros	dimos
vosotros	deis		vosotros	disteis
ellos	den		ellos	dieron

PAST PARTICIPLE	IMPERATIVE
dado	da
	dad

GERUND
dando

decir (to say)

	PRESENT		IMPERFECT
yo	digo	yo	decía
tú	dices	tú	decías
él	dice	él	decía
nosotros	decimos	nosotros	decíamos
vosotros	decís	vosotros	decíais
ellos	dicen	ellos	decían

	FUTURE		CONDITIONAL
yo	diré	yo	diría
tú	dirás	tú	dirías
él	dirá	él	diría
nosotros	diremos	nosotros	diríamos
vosotros	diréis	vosotros	diríais
ellos	dirán	ellos	dirían

	PRESENT SUBJUNCTIVE		PRETERITE
yo	diga	yo	dije
tú	digas	tú	dijiste
él	diga	él	dijo
nosotros	digamos	nosotros	dijimos
vosotros	digáis	vosotros	dijisteis
ellos	digan	ellos	dijeron

PAST PARTICIPLE	IMPERATIVE
dicho	di
	decid

GERUND

diciendo

dirigir (to direct)

	PRESENT		IMPERFECT
yo	dirijo	yo	dirigía
tú	diriges	tú	dirigías
él	dirige	él	dirigía
nosotros	dirigimos	nosotros	dirigíamos
vosotros	dirigís	vosotros	dirigíais
ellos	dirigen	ellos	dirigían

	FUTURE		CONDITIONAL
yo	dirigiré	yo	dirigiría
tú	dirigirás	tú	dirigirías
él	dirigirá	él	dirigiría
nosotros	dirigiremos	nosotros	dirigiríamos
vosotros	dirigiréis	vosotros	dirigiríais
ellos	dirigirán	ellos	dirigirían

	PRESENT SUBJUNCTIVE		PRETERITE
yo	dirija	yo	dirigí
tú	dirijas	tú	dirigiste
él	dirija	él	dirigió
nosotros	dirijamos	nosotros	dirigimos
vosotros	dirijáis	vosotros	dirigisteis
ellos	dirijan	ellos	dirigieron

PAST PARTICIPLE	IMPERATIVE
dirigido	dirige
	dirigid

GERUND
dirigiendo

distinguir (to distinguish)

	PRESENT		IMPERFECT
yo	distingo	yo	distinguía
tú	distingues	tú	distinguías
él	distingue	él	distinguía
nosotros	distinguimos	nosotros	distinguíamos
vosotros	distinguís	vosotros	distinguíais
ellos	distinguen	ellos	distinguían

	FUTURE		CONDITIONAL
yo	distinguiré	yo	distinguiría
tú	distinguirás	tú	distinguirías
él	distinguirá	él	distinguiría
nosotros	distinguiremos	nosotros	distinguiríamos
vosotros	distinguiréis	vosotros	distinguiríais
ellos	distinguirán	ellos	distinguirían

	PRESENT SUBJUNCTIVE		PRETERITE
yo	distinga	yo	distinguí
tú	distingas	tú	distinguiste
él	distinga	él	distinguió
nosotros	distingamos	nosotros	distinguimos
vosotros	distingáis	vosotros	distinguisteis
ellos	distingan	ellos	distinguieron

PAST PARTICIPLE	IMPERATIVE
distinguido	distingue
	distinguid

GERUND
distinguiendo

dormir (to sleep)

	PRESENT		IMPERFECT
yo	duermo	yo	dormía
tú	duermes	tú	dormías
él	duerme	él	dormía
nosotros	dormimos	nosotros	dormíamos
vosotros	dormís	vosotros	dormíais
ellos	duermen	ellos	dormían

	FUTURE		CONDITIONAL
yo	dormiré	yo	dormiría
tú	dormirás	tú	dormirías
él	dormirá	él	dormiría
nosotros	dormiremos	nosotros	dormiríamos
vosotros	dormiréis	vosotros	dormiríais
ellos	dormirán	ellos	dormirían

	PRESENT SUBJUNCTIVE		PRETERITE
yo	duerma	yo	dormí
tú	duermas	tú	dormiste
él	duerma	él	durmió
nosotros	durmamos	nosotros	dormimos
vosotros	durmáis	vosotros	dormisteis
ellos	duerman	ellos	durmieron

PAST PARTICIPLE	IMPERATIVE
dormido	duerme
	dormid

GERUND
durmiendo

elegir (to choose)

	PRESENT		IMPERFECT
yo	elijo	yo	elegía
tú	eliges	tú	elegías
él	elige	él	elegía
nosotros	elegimos	nosotros	elegíamos
vosotros	elegís	vosotros	elegíais
ellos	eligen	ellos	elegían

	FUTURE		CONDITIONAL
yo	elegiré	yo	elegiría
tú	elegirás	tú	elegirías
él	elegirá	él	elegiría
nosotros	elegiremos	nosotros	elegiríamos
vosotros	elegiréis	vosotros	elegiríais
ellos	elegirán	ellos	elegirían

	PRESENT SUBJUNCTIVE		PRETERITE
yo	elija	yo	elegí
tú	elijas	tú	elegiste
él	elija	él	eligió
nosotros	elijamos	nosotros	elegimos
vosotros	elijáis	vosotros	elegisteis
ellos	elijan	ellos	eligieron

PAST PARTICIPLE	IMPERATIVE
elegido	elige
	elegid

GERUND

eligiendo

empezar (to begin)

	PRESENT			IMPERFECT
yo	empiezo		yo	empezaba
tú	empiezas		tú	empezabas
él	empieza		él	empezaba
nosotros	empezamos		nosotros	empezábamos
vosotros	empezáis		vosotros	empezabais
ellos	empiezan		ellos	empezaban

	FUTURE			CONDITIONAL
yo	empezaré		yo	empezaría
tú	empezarás		tú	empezarías
él	empezará		él	empezaría
nosotros	empezaremos		nosotros	empezaríamos
vosotros	empezaréis		vosotros	empezaríais
ellos	empezarán		ellos	empezarían

	PRESENT SUBJUNCTIVE			PRETERITE
yo	empiece		yo	empecé
tú	empieces		tú	empezaste
él	empiece		él	empezó
nosotros	empecemos		nosotros	empezamos
vosotros	empecéis		vosotros	empezasteis
ellos	empiecen		ellos	empezaron

PAST PARTICIPLE	IMPERATIVE
empezado	empieza
	empezad

GERUND
empezando

entender (to understand)

	PRESENT		IMPERFECT
yo	entiendo	yo	entendía
tú	entiendes	tú	entendías
él	entiende	él	entendía
nosotros	entendemos	nosotros	entendíamos
vosotros	entendéis	vosotros	entendíais
ellos	entienden	ellos	entendían

	FUTURE		CONDITIONAL
yo	entenderé	yo	entendería
tú	entenderás	tú	entenderías
él	entenderá	él	entendería
nosotros	entenderemos	nosotros	entenderíamos
vosotros	entenderéis	vosotros	entenderíais
ellos	entenderán	ellos	entenderían

	PRESENT SUBJUNCTIVE		PRETERITE
yo	entienda	yo	entendí
tú	entiendas	tú	entendiste
él	entienda	él	entendió
nosotros	entendamos	nosotros	entendimos
vosotros	entendáis	vosotros	entendisteis
ellos	entiendan	ellos	entendieron

PAST PARTICIPLE	IMPERATIVE
entendido	entiende
	entended

GERUND

entendiendo

enviar (to send)

	PRESENT			IMPERFECT
yo	envío		yo	enviaba
tú	envías		tú	enviabas
él	envía		él	enviaba
nosotros	enviamos		nosotros	enviábamos
vosotros	enviáis		vosotros	enviabais
ellos	envían		ellos	enviaban

	FUTURE			CONDITIONAL
yo	enviaré		yo	enviaría
tú	enviarás		tú	enviarías
él	enviará		él	enviaría
nosotros	enviaremos		nosotros	enviaríamos
vosotros	enviaréis		vosotros	enviaríais
ellos	enviarán		ellos	enviarían

	PRESENT SUBJUNCTIVE			PRETERITE
yo	envíe		yo	envié
tú	envíes		tú	enviaste
él	envíe		él	envió
nosotros	enviemos		nosotros	enviamos
vosotros	enviéis		vosotros	enviasteis
ellos	envíen		ellos	enviaron

PAST PARTICIPLE	IMPERATIVE
enviado	envía
	enviad

GERUND
enviando

erguir (to erect)

	PRESENT		IMPERFECT
yo	yergo	yo	erguía
tú	yergues	tú	erguías
él	yergue	él	erguía
nosotros	erguimos	nosotros	erguíamos
vosotros	erguís	vosotros	erguíais
ellos	yerguen	ellos	erguían

	FUTURE		CONDITIONAL
yo	erguiré	yo	erguiría
tú	erguirás	tú	erguirías
él	erguirá	él	erguiría
nosotros	erguiremos	nosotros	erguiríamos
vosotros	erguiréis	vosotros	erguiríais
ellos	erguirán	ellos	erguirían

	PRESENT SUBJUNCTIVE		PRETERITE
yo	yerga	yo	erguí
tú	yergas	tú	erguiste
él	yerga	él	irguió
nosotros	irgamos	nosotros	erguimos
vosotros	irgáis	vosotros	erguisteis
ellos	yergan	ellos	irguieron

PAST PARTICIPLE	IMPERATIVE
erguido	yergue
	erguid

GERUND
irguiendo

errar (to err)

	PRESENT		IMPERFECT
yo	yerro	yo	erraba
tú	yerras	tú	errabas
él	yerra	él	erraba
nosotros	erramos	nosotros	errábamos
vosotros	erráis	vosotros	errabais
ellos	yerran	ellos	erraban

	FUTURE		CONDITIONAL
yo	erraré	yo	erraría
tú	errarás	tú	errarías
él	errará	él	erraría
nosotros	erraremos	nosotros	erraríamos
vosotros	erraréis	vosotros	erraríais
ellos	errarán	ellos	errarían

	PRESENT SUBJUNCTIVE		PRETERITE
yo	yerre	yo	erré
tú	yerres	tú	erraste
él	yerre	él	erró
nosotros	erremos	nosotros	erramos
vosotros	erréis	vosotros	errasteis
ellos	yerren	ellos	erraron

PAST PARTICIPLE	IMPERATIVE
errado	yerra
	errad

GERUND
errando

escribir (to write)

	PRESENT		IMPERFECT
yo	escribo	yo	escribía
tú	escribes	tú	escribías
él	escribe	él	escribía
nosotros	escribimos	nosotros	escribíamos
vosotros	escribís	vosotros	escribíais
ellos	escriben	ellos	escribían

	FUTURE		CONDITIONAL
yo	escribiré	yo	escribiría
tú	escribirás	tú	escribirías
él	escribirá	él	escribiría
nosotros	escribiremos	nosotros	escribiríamos
vosotros	escribiréis	vosotros	escribiríais
ellos	escribirán	ellos	escribirían

	PRESENT SUBJUNCTIVE		PRETERITE
yo	escriba	yo	escribí
tú	escribas	tú	escribiste
él	escriba	él	escribió
nosotros	escribamos	nosotros	escribimos
vosotros	escribáis	vosotros	escribisteis
ellos	escriban	ellos	escribieron

PAST PARTICIPLE
escrito

IMPERATIVE
escrib**e**
escrib**id**

GERUND
escrib**iendo**

estar (to be)

	PRESENT			IMPERFECT
yo	estoy		yo	estaba
tú	estás		tú	estabas
él	está		él	estaba
nosotros	estamos		nosotros	estábamos
vosotros	estáis		vosotros	estabais
ellos	están		ellos	estaban

	FUTURE			CONDITIONAL
yo	estaré		yo	estaría
tú	estarás		tú	estarías
él	estará		él	estaría
nosotros	estaremos		nosotros	estaríamos
vosotros	estaréis		vosotros	estaríais
ellos	estarán		ellos	estarían

	PRESENT SUBJUNCTIVE			PRETERITE
yo	esté		yo	estuve
tú	estés		tú	estuviste
él	esté		él	estuvo
nosotros	estemos		nosotros	estuvimos
vosotros	estéis		vosotros	estuvisteis
ellos	estén		ellos	estuvieron

PAST PARTICIPLE
estado

IMPERATIVE
está
estad

GERUND
estando

freír (to fry)

	PRESENT		IMPERFECT
yo	frío	yo	freía
tú	fríes	tú	freías
él	fríe	él	freía
nosotros	freímos	nosotros	freíamos
vosotros	freís	vosotros	freíais
ellos	fríen	ellos	freían

	FUTURE		CONDITIONAL
yo	freiré	yo	freiría
tú	freirás	tú	freirías
él	freirá	él	freiría
nosotros	freiremos	nosotros	freiríamos
vosotros	freiréis	vosotros	freiríais
ellos	freirán	ellos	freirían

	PRESENT SUBJUNCTIVE		PRETERITE
yo	fría	yo	freí
tú	frías	tú	freíste
él	fría	él	frió
nosotros	friamos	nosotros	freímos
vosotros	friáis	vosotros	freísteis
ellos	frían	ellos	frieron

PAST PARTICIPLE	IMPERATIVE
frito	fríe
	freíd

GERUND
friendo

gruñir (to grunt)

	PRESENT		IMPERFECT
yo	gruño	yo	gruñía
tú	gruñes	tú	gruñías
él	gruñe	él	gruñía
nosotros	gruñimos	nosotros	gruñíamos
vosotros	gruñís	vosotros	gruñíais
ellos	gruñen	ellos	gruñían

	FUTURE		CONDITIONAL
yo	gruñiré	yo	gruñiría
tú	gruñirás	tú	gruñirías
él	gruñirá	él	gruñiría
nosotros	gruñiremos	nosotros	gruñiríamos
vosotros	gruñiréis	vosotros	gruñiríais
ellos	gruñirán	ellos	gruñirían

	PRESENT SUBJUNCTIVE		PRETERITE
yo	gruña	yo	gruñí
tú	gruñas	tú	gruñiste
él	gruña	él	gruñó
nosotros	gruñamos	nosotros	gruñimos
vosotros	gruñáis	vosotros	gruñisteis
ellos	gruñan	ellos	gruñeron

PAST PARTICIPLE	IMPERATIVE
gruñido	gruñe
	gruñid

GERUND

gruñendo

haber (to have, *auxiliary*)

	PRESENT		IMPERFECT
yo	**he**	yo	**hab**ía
tú	**has**	tú	**hab**ías
él	**ha**	él	**hab**ía
nosotros	**hemos**	nosotros	**hab**íamos
vosotros	**hab**éis	vosotros	**hab**íais
ellos	**han**	ellos	**hab**ían

	FUTURE		CONDITIONAL
yo	**habré**	yo	**habría**
tú	**habrás**	tú	**habrías**
él	**habrá**	él	**habría**
nosotros	**habremos**	nosotros	**habríamos**
vosotros	**habréis**	vosotros	**habríais**
ellos	**habrán**	ellos	**habrían**

	PRESENT SUBJUNCTIVE		PRETERITE
yo	**haya**	yo	**hube**
tú	**hayas**	tú	**hubiste**
él	**haya**	él	**hubo**
nosotros	**hayamos**	nosotros	**hubimos**
vosotros	**hayáis**	vosotros	**hubisteis**
ellos	**hayan**	ellos	**hubieron**

PAST PARTICIPLE	IMPERATIVE
hab**ido**	*not used*

GERUND
hab**iendo**

hacer (to do, to make)

	PRESENT		IMPERFECT
yo	hago	yo	hacía
tú	haces	tú	hacías
él	hace	él	hacía
nosotros	hacemos	nosotros	hacíamos
vosotros	hacéis	vosotros	hacíais
ellos	hacen	ellos	hacían

	FUTURE		CONDITIONAL
yo	haré	yo	haría
tú	harás	tú	harías
él	hará	él	haría
nosotros	haremos	nosotros	haríamos
vosotros	haréis	vosotros	haríais
ellos	harán	ellos	harían

	PRESENT SUBJUNCTIVE		PRETERITE
yo	haga	yo	hice
tú	hagas	tú	hiciste
él	haga	él	hizo
nosotros	hagamos	nosotros	hicimos
vosotros	hagáis	vosotros	hicisteis
ellos	hagan	ellos	hicieron

PAST PARTICIPLE
hecho

IMPERATIVE
haz
haced

GERUND
haciendo

hay (there is, there are)

PRESENT hay	**IMPERFECT** había
FUTURE habrá	**CONDITIONAL** habría
PRESENT SUBJUNCTIVE haya	**PRETERITE** hubo

PAST PARTICIPLE hab**ido**	**IMPERATIVE** *not used*
GERUND hab**iendo**	

ir (to go)

	PRESENT		IMPERFECT
yo	**voy**	yo	**iba**
tú	**vas**	tú	**ibas**
él	**va**	él	**iba**
nosotros	**vamos**	nosotros	**íbamos**
vosotros	**vais**	vosotros	**ibais**
ellos	**van**	ellos	**iban**

	FUTURE		CONDITIONAL
yo	**iré**	yo	**iría**
tú	**irás**	tú	**irías**
él	**irá**	él	**iría**
nosotros	**iremos**	nosotros	**iríamos**
vosotros	**iréis**	vosotros	**iríais**
ellos	**irán**	ellos	**irían**

	PRESENT SUDJUNCTIVE		PRETERITE
yo	**vaya**	yo	**fui**
tú	**vayas**	tú	**fuiste**
él	**vaya**	él	**fue**
nosotros	**vayamos**	nosotros	**fuimos**
vosotros	**vayáis**	vosotros	**fuisteis**
ellos	**vayan**	ellos	**fueron**

PAST PARTICIPLE	IMPERATIVE
ido	**ve**
	id

GERUND
yendo

jugar (to play)

	PRESENT		IMPERFECT
yo	juego	yo	jugaba
tú	juegas	tú	jugabas
él	juega	él	jugaba
nosotros	jugamos	nosotros	jugábamos
vosotros	jugáis	vosotros	jugabais
ellos	juegan	ellos	jugaban

	FUTURE		CONDITIONAL
yo	jugaré	yo	jugaría
tú	jugarás	tú	jugarías
él	jugará	él	jugaría
nosotros	jugaremos	nosotros	jugaríamos
vosotros	jugaréis	vosotros	jugaríais
ellos	jugarán	ellos	jugarían

	PRESENT SUBJUNCTIVE		PRETERITE
yo	juegue	yo	jugué
tú	juegues	tú	jugaste
él	juegue	él	jugó
nosotros	juguemos	nosotros	jugamos
vosotros	juguéis	vosotros	jugasteis
ellos	jueguen	ellos	jugaron

PAST PARTICIPLE	IMPERATIVE
jugado	juega
	jugad

GERUND
jugando

leer (to read)

	PRESENT		IMPERFECT
yo	leo	yo	leía
tú	lees	tú	leías
él	lee	él	leía
nosotros	leemos	nosotros	leíamos
vosotros	leéis	vosotros	leíais
ellos	leen	ellos	leían

	FUTURE		CONDITIONAL
yo	leeré	yo	leería
tú	leerás	tú	leerías
él	leerá	él	leería
nosotros	leeremos	nosotros	leeríamos
vosotros	leeréis	vosotros	leeríais
ellos	leerán	ellos	leerían

	PRESENT SUBJUNCTIVE		PRETERITE
yo	lea	yo	leí
tú	leas	tú	leíste
él	lea	él	leyó
nosotros	leamos	nosotros	leímos
vosotros	leáis	vosotros	leísteis
ellos	lean	ellos	leyeron

PAST PARTICIPLE	IMPERATIVE
leído	lee
	leed

GERUND
leyendo

lucir (to shine)

	PRESENT		IMPERFECT
yo	luzco	yo	lucía
tú	luces	tú	lucías
él	luce	él	lucía
nosotros	lucimos	nosotros	lucíamos
vosotros	lucís	vosotros	lucíais
ellos	lucen	ellos	lucían

	FUTURE		CONDITIONAL
yo	luciré	yo	luciría
tú	lucirás	tú	lucirías
él	lucirá	él	luciría
nosotros	luciremos	nosotros	luciríamos
vosotros	luciréis	vosotros	luciríais
ellos	lucirán	ellos	lucirían

	PRESENT SUBJUNCTIVE		PRETERITE
yo	luzca	yo	lucí
tú	luzcas	tú	luciste
él	luzca	él	lució
nosotros	luzcamos	nosotros	lucimos
vosotros	luzcáis	vosotros	lucisteis
ellos	luzcan	ellos	lucieron

PAST PARTICIPLE	IMPERATIVE
lucido	luce
	lucid

GERUND
luciendo

llover (to rain)

PRESENT
llueve

IMPERFECT
llovía

FUTURE
lloverá

CONDITIONAL
llovería

PRESENT SUBJUNCTIVE
llueva

PRETERITE
llovió

PAST PARTICIPLE
llovido

IMPERATIVE
not used

GERUND
lloviendo

morir (to die)

	PRESENT			IMPERFECT
yo	**muero**		yo	mor**ía**
tú	**mueres**		tú	mor**ías**
él	**muere**		él	mor**ía**
nosotros	mor**imos**		nosotros	mor**íamos**
vosotros	mor**ís**		vosotros	mor**íais**
ellos	**mueren**		ellos	mor**ían**

	FUTURE			CONDITIONAL
yo	morir**é**		yo	morir**ía**
tú	morir**ás**		tú	morir**ías**
él	morir**á**		él	morir**ía**
nosotros	morir**emos**		nosotros	morir**íamos**
vosotros	morir**éis**		vosotros	morir**íais**
ellos	morir**án**		ellos	morir**ían**

	PRESENT SUBJUNCTIVE			PRETERITE
yo	**muera**		yo	mor**í**
tú	**mueras**		tú	mor**iste**
él	**muera**		él	**murió**
nosotros	**muramos**		nosotros	mor**imos**
vosotros	**muráis**		vosotros	mor**isteis**
ellos	**mueran**		ellos	**murieron**

PAST PARTICIPLE	IMPERATIVE
muerto	**muere**
	mori**d**

GERUND
muriendo

mover (to move)

	PRESENT		IMPERFECT
yo	muevo	yo	movía
tú	mueves	tú	movías
él	mueve	él	movía
nosotros	movemos	nosotros	movíamos
vosotros	movéis	vosotros	movíais
ellos	mueven	ellos	movían

	FUTURE		CONDITIONAL
yo	moveré	yo	movería
tú	moverás	tú	moverías
él	moverá	él	movería
nosotros	moveremos	nosotros	moveríamos
vosotros	moveréis	vosotros	moveríais
ellos	moverán	ellos	moverían

	PRESENT SUBJUNCTIVE		PRETERITE
yo	mueva	yo	moví
tú	muevas	tú	moviste
él	mueva	él	movió
nosotros	movamos	nosotros	movimos
vosotros	mováis	vosotros	movisteis
ellos	muevan	ellos	movieron

PAST PARTICIPLE
movido

IMPERATIVE
mueve
moved

GERUND
moviendo

nacer (to be born)

	PRESENT		IMPERFECT
yo	nazco	yo	nacía
tú	naces	tú	nacías
él	nace	él	nacía
nosotros	nacemos	nosotros	nacíamos
vosotros	nacéis	vosotros	nacíais
ellos	nacen	ellos	nacían

	FUTURE		CONDITIONAL
yo	naceré	yo	nacería
tú	nacerás	tú	nacerías
él	nacerá	él	nacería
nosotros	naceremos	nosotros	naceríamos
vosotros	naceréis	vosotros	naceríais
ellos	nacerán	ellos	nacerían

	PRESENT SUBJUNCTIVE		PRETERITE
yo	nazca	yo	nací
tú	nazcas	tú	naciste
él	nazca	él	nació
nosotros	nazcamos	nosotros	nacimos
vosotros	nazcáis	vosotros	nacisteis
ellos	nazcan	ellos	nacieron

PAST PARTICIPLE	IMPERATIVE
nacido	nace
	naced

GERUND

naciendo

negar (to deny)

	PRESENT		IMPERFECT
yo	niego	yo	negaba
tú	niegas	tú	negabas
él	niega	él	negaba
nosotros	negamos	nosotros	negábamos
vosotros	negáis	vosotros	negabais
ellos	niegan	ellos	negaban

	FUTURE		CONDITIONAL
yo	negaré	yo	negaría
tú	negarás	tú	negarías
él	negará	él	negaría
nosotros	negaremos	nosotros	negaríamos
vosotros	negaréis	vosotros	negaríais
ellos	negarán	ellos	negarían

	PRESENT SUBJUNCTIVE		PRETERITE
yo	niegue	yo	negué
tú	niegues	tú	negaste
él	niegue	él	negó
nosotros	nieguemos	nosotros	negamos
vosotros	neguéis	vosotros	negasteis
ellos	nieguen	ellos	negaron

PAST PARTICIPLE	IMPERATIVE
negado	niega
	negad

GERUND
negando

Oír (to hear)

	PRESENT		IMPERFECT
yo	oigo	yo	oía
tú	oyes	tú	oías
él	oye	él	oía
nosotros	oímos	nosotros	oíamos
vosotros	oís	vosotros	oíais
ellos	oyen	ellos	oían

	FUTURE		CONDITIONAL
yo	oiré	yo	oiría
tú	oirás	tú	oirías
él	oirá	él	oiría
nosotros	oiremos	nosotros	oiríamos
vosotros	oiréis	vosotros	oiríais
ellos	oirán	ellos	oirían

	PRESENT SUBJUNCTIVE		PRETERITE
yo	oiga	yo	oí
tú	oigas	tú	oíste
él	oiga	él	oyó
nosotros	oigamos	nosotros	oímos
vosotros	oigáis	vosotros	oísteis
ellos	oigan	ellos	oyeron

PAST PARTICIPLE	IMPERATIVE
oído	oye
	oíd

GERUND
oyendo

oler (to smell)

	PRESENT		IMPERFECT
yo	huelo	yo	olía
tú	hueles	tú	olías
él	huele	él	olía
nosotros	olemos	nosotros	olíamos
vosotros	oléis	vosotros	olíais
ellos	huelen	ellos	olían

	FUTURE		CONDITIONAL
yo	oleré	yo	olería
tú	olerás	tú	olerías
él	olerá	él	olería
nosotros	oleremos	nosotros	oleríamos
vosotros	oleréis	vosotros	oleríais
ellos	olerán	ellos	olerían

	PRESENT SUBJUNCTIVE		PRETERITE
yo	huela	yo	olí
tú	huelas	tú	oliste
él	huela	él	olió
nosotros	olamos	nosotros	olimos
vosotros	oláis	vosotros	olisteis
ellos	huelan	ellos	olieron

PAST PARTICIPLE	IMPERATIVE
olido	huele
	oled

GERUND
oliendo

pagar (to pay)

	PRESENT		IMPERFECT
yo	pago	yo	pagaba
tú	pagas	tú	pagabas
él	paga	él	pagaba
nosotros	pagamos	nosotros	pagábamos
vosotros	pagáis	vosotros	pagabais
ellos	pagan	ellos	pagaban

	FUTURE		CONDITIONAL
yo	pagaré	yo	pagaría
tú	pagarás	tú	pagarías
él	pagará	él	pagaría
nosotros	pagaremos	nosotros	pagaríamos
vosotros	pagaréis	vosotros	pagaríais
ellos	pagarán	ellos	pagarían

	PRESENT SUBJUNCTIVE		PRETERITE
yo	pague	yo	pagué
tú	pagues	tú	pagaste
él	pague	él	pagó
nosotros	paguemos	nosotros	pagamos
vosotros	paguéis	vosotros	pagasteis
ellos	paguen	ellos	pagaron

PAST PARTICIPLE	IMPERATIVE
pagado	paga
	pagad

GERUND

pagando

pedir (to ask for)

	PRESENT			IMPERFECT
yo	pido		yo	pedía
tú	pides		tú	pedías
él	pide		él	pedía
nosotros	pedimos		nosotros	pedíamos
vosotros	pedís		vosotros	pedíais
ellos	piden		ellos	pedían

	FUTURE			CONDITIONAL
yo	pediré		yo	pediría
tú	pedirás		tú	pedirías
él	pedirá		él	pediría
nosotros	pediremos		nosotros	pediríamos
vosotros	pediréis		vosotros	pediríais
ellos	pedirán		ellos	pedirían

	PRESENT SUBJUNCTIVE			PRETERITE
yo	pida		yo	pedí
tú	pidas		tú	pediste
él	pida		él	pidió
nosotros	pidamos		nosotros	pedimos
vosotros	pidáis		vosotros	pedisteis
ellos	pidan		ellos	pidieron

PAST PARTICIPLE	IMPERATIVE
pedido	pide
	pedid

GERUND
pidiendo

pensar (to think)

	PRESENT		IMPERFECT
yo	**pienso**	yo	pens**aba**
tú	**piensas**	tú	pens**abas**
él	**piensa**	él	pens**aba**
nosotros	pens**amos**	nosotros	pens**ábamos**
vosotros	pens**áis**	vosotros	pens**abais**
ellos	**piensan**	ellos	pens**aban**

	FUTURE		CONDITIONAL
yo	pensar**é**	yo	pensar**ía**
tú	pensar**ás**	tú	pensar**ías**
él	pensar**á**	él	pensar**ía**
nosotros	pensar**emos**	nosotros	pensar**íamos**
vosotros	pensar**éis**	vosotros	pensar**íais**
ellos	pensar**án**	ellos	pensar**ían**

	PRESENT SUBJUNCTIVE		PRETERITE
yo	**piense**	yo	pens**é**
tú	**pienses**	tú	pens**aste**
él	**piense**	él	pens**ó**
nosotros	pens**emos**	nosotros	pens**amos**
vosotros	pens**éis**	vosotros	pens**asteis**
ellos	**piensen**	ellos	pens**aron**

PAST PARTICIPLE	IMPERATIVE
pens**ado**	**piensa**
	pensa**d**

GERUND
pens**ando**

poder (to be able)

	PRESENT			IMPERFECT
yo	puedo		yo	podía
tú	puedes		tú	podías
él	puede		él	podía
nosotros	podemos		nosotros	podíamos
vosotros	podéis		vosotros	podíais
ellos	pueden		ellos	podían

	FUTURE			CONDITIONAL
yo	podré		yo	podría
tú	podrás		tú	podrías
él	podrá		él	podría
nosotros	podremos		nosotros	podríamos
vosotros	podréis		vosotros	podríais
ellos	podrán		ellos	podrían

	PRESENT SUBJUNCTIVE			PRETERITE
yo	pueda		yo	pude
tú	puedas		tú	pudiste
él	pueda		él	pudo
nosotros	podamos		nosotros	pudimos
vosotros	podáis		vosotros	pudisteis
ellos	puedan		ellos	pudieron

PAST PARTICIPLE	IMPERATIVE
podido	puede
	poded

GERUND
pudiendo

poner (to put)

	PRESENT		IMPERFECT
yo	pongo	yo	ponía
tú	pones	tú	ponías
él	pone	él	ponía
nosotros	ponemos	nosotros	poníamos
vosotros	ponéis	vosotros	poníais
ellos	ponen	ellos	ponían

	FUTURE		CONDITIONAL
yo	pondré	yo	pondría
tú	pondrás	tú	pondrías
él	pondrá	él	pondría
nosotros	pondremos	nosotros	pondríamos
vosotros	pondréis	vosotros	pondríais
ellos	pondrán	ellos	pondrían

	PRESENT SUBJUNCTIVE		PRETERITE
yo	ponga	yo	puse
tú	pongas	tú	pusiste
él	ponga	él	puso
nosotros	pongamos	nosotros	pusimos
vosotros	pongáis	vosotros	pusisteis
ellos	pongan	ellos	pusieron

PAST PARTICIPLE	IMPERATIVE
puesto	pon
	poned

GERUND

poniendo

prohibir (to forbid)

	PRESENT			IMPERFECT
yo	prohíbo		yo	prohibía
tú	prohíbes		tú	prohibías
él	prohíbe		él	prohibía
nosotros	prohibimos		nosotros	prohibíamos
vosotros	prohibís		vosotros	prohibíais
ellos	prohíben		ellos	prohibían

	FUTURE			CONDITIONAL
yo	prohibiré		yo	prohibiría
tú	prohibirás		tú	prohibirías
él	prohibirá		él	prohibiría
nosotros	prohibiremos		nosotros	prohibiríamos
vosotros	prohibiréis		vosotros	prohibiríais
ellos	prohibirán		ellos	prohibirían

	PRESENT SUBJUNCTIVE			PRETERITE
yo	prohíba		yo	prohibí
tú	prohíbas		tú	prohibiste
él	prohíba		él	prohibió
nosotros	prohibamos		nosotros	prohibimos
vosotros	prohibáis		vosotros	prohibisteis
ellos	prohíban		ellos	prohibieron

PAST PARTICIPLE	IMPERATIVE
prohibido	prohíbe
	prohibid

GERUND

prohibiendo

querer (to want)

	PRESENT		IMPERFECT
yo	quiero	yo	quería
tú	quieres	tú	querías
él	quiere	él	quería
nosotros	queremos	nosotros	queríamos
vosotros	queréis	vosotros	queríais
ellos	quieren	ellos	querían

	FUTURE		CONDITIONAL
yo	querré	yo	querría
tú	querrás	tú	querrías
él	querrá	él	querría
nosotros	querremos	nosotros	querríamos
vosotros	querréis	vosotros	querríais
ellos	querrán	ellos	querrían

	PRESENT SUBJUNCTIVE		PRETERITE
yo	quiera	yo	quise
tú	quieras	tú	quisiste
él	quiera	él	quiso
nosotros	queramos	nosotros	quisimos
vosotros	queráis	vosotros	quisisteis
ellos	quieran	ellos	quisieron

PAST PARTICIPLE	IMPERATIVE
querido	quiere
	quered

GERUND

queriendo

rehusar (to refuse)

	PRESENT		IMPERFECT
yo	rehúso	yo	rehusaba
tú	rehúsas	tú	rehusabas
él	rehúsa	él	rehusaba
nosotros	rehusamos	nosotros	rehusábamos
vosotros	rehusáis	vosotros	rehusabais
ellos	rehúsan	ellos	rehusaban

	FUTURE		CONDITIONAL
yo	rehusaré	yo	rehusaría
tú	rehusarás	tú	rehusarías
él	rehusará	él	rehusaría
nosotros	rehusaremos	nosotros	rehusaríamos
vosotros	rehusaréis	vosotros	rehusaríais
ellos	rehusarán	ellos	rehusarían

	PRESENT SUBJUNCTIVE		PRETERITE
yo	rehúse	yo	rehusé
tú	rehúses	tú	rehusaste
él	rehúse	él	rehusó
nosotros	rehusemos	nosotros	rehusamos
vosotros	rehuséis	vosotros	rehusasteis
ellos	rehúsen	ellos	rehusaron

PAST PARTICIPLE	IMPERATIVE
rehusado	rehúsa
	rehusad

GERUND
rehusando

reír (to laugh)

	PRESENT			IMPERFECT
yo	río		yo	reía
tú	ríes		tú	reías
él	ríe		él	reía
nosotros	reímos		nosotros	reíamos
vosotros	reís		vosotros	reíais
ellos	ríen		ellos	reían

	FUTURE			CONDITIONAL
yo	reiré		yo	reiría
tú	reirás		tú	reirías
él	reirá		él	reiría
nosotros	reiremos		nosotros	reiríamos
vosotros	reiréis		vosotros	reiríais
ellos	reirán		ellos	reirían

	PRESENT SUBJUNCTIVE			PRETERITE
yo	ría		yo	reí
tú	rías		tú	reíste
él	ría		él	rió
nosotros	riamos		nosotros	reímos
vosotros	riáis		vosotros	reísteis
ellos	rían		ellos	rieron

PAST PARTICIPLE	IMPERATIVE
reído	ríe
	reíd

GERUND
riendo

reñir (to scold)

	PRESENT		IMPERFECT
yo	riño	yo	reñía
tú	riñes	tú	reñías
él	riñe	él	reñía
nosotros	reñimos	nosotros	reñíamos
vosotros	reñís	vosotros	reñíais
ellos	riñen	ellos	reñían

	FUTURE		CONDITIONAL
yo	reñiré	yo	reñiría
tú	reñirás	tú	reñirías
él	reñirá	él	reñiría
nosotros	reñiremos	nosotros	reñiríamos
vosotros	reñiréis	vosotros	reñiríais
ellos	reñirán	ellos	reñirían

	PRESENT SUBJUNCTIVE		PRETERITE
yo	riña	yo	reñí
tú	riñas	tú	reñiste
él	riña	él	riñó
nosotros	riñamos	nosotros	reñimos
vosotros	riñáis	vosotros	reñisteis
ellos	riñan	ellos	riñeron

PAST PARTICIPLE	IMPERATIVE
reñido	ríñe
	reñid

GERUND
riñendo

resolver (to solve)

	PRESENT		IMPERFECT
yo	resuelvo	yo	resolvía
tú	resuelves	tú	resolvías
él	resuelve	él	resolvía
nosotros	resolvemos	nosotros	resolvíamos
vosotros	resolvéis	vosotros	resolvíais
ellos	resuelven	ellos	resolvían

	FUTURE		CONDITIONAL
yo	resolveré	yo	resolvería
tú	resolverás	tú	resolverías
él	resolverá	él	resolvería
nosotros	resolveremos	nosotros	resolveríamos
vosotros	resolveréis	vosotros	resolveríais
ellos	resolverán	ellos	resolverían

	PRESENT SUBJUNCTIVE		PRETERITE
yo	resuelva	yo	resolví
tú	resuelvas	tú	resolviste
él	resuelva	él	resolvió
nosotros	resolvamos	nosotros	resolvimos
vosotros	resolváis	vosotros	resolvisteis
ellos	resuelvan	ellos	resolvieron

PAST PARTICIPLE	IMPERATIVE
resuelto	resuelve
	resolved

GERUND
resolviendo

reunir (to put together, to gather)

	PRESENT		IMPERFECT
yo	reúno	yo	reunía
tú	reúnes	tú	reunías
él	reúne	él	reunía
nosotros	reunimos	nosotros	reuníamos
vosotros	reunís	vosotros	reuníais
ellos	reúnen	ellos	reunían

	FUTURE		CONDITIONAL
yo	reuniré	yo	reuniría
tú	reunirás	tú	reunirías
él	reunirá	él	reuniría
nosotros	reuniremos	nosotros	reuniríamos
vosotros	reuniréis	vosotros	reuniríais
ellos	reunirán	ellos	reunirían

	PRESENT SUBJUNCTIVE		PRETERITE
yo	reúna	yo	reuní
tú	reúnas	tú	reuniste
él	reúna	él	reunió
nosotros	reunamos	nosotros	reunimos
vosotros	reunáis	vosotros	reunisteis
ellos	reúnan	ellos	reunieron

PAST PARTICIPLE	IMPERATIVE
reunido	reúne
	reunid

GERUND
reuniendo

rogar (to beg)

	PRESENT		IMPERFECT
yo	ruego	yo	rogaba
tú	ruegas	tú	rogabas
él	ruega	él	rogaba
nosotros	rogamos	nosotros	rogábamos
vosotros	rogáis	vosotros	rogabais
ellos	ruegan	ellos	rogaban

	FUTURE		CONDITIONAL
yo	rogaré	yo	rogaría
tú	rogarás	tú	rogarías
él	rogará	él	rogaría
nosotros	rogaremos	nosotros	rogaríamos
vosotros	rogaréis	vosotros	rogaríais
ellos	rogarán	ellos	rogarían

	PRESENT SUBJUNCTIVE		PRETERITE
yo	ruegue	yo	rogué
tú	ruegues	tú	rogaste
él	ruegue	él	rogó
nosotros	roguemos	nosotros	rogamos
vosotros	roguéis	vosotros	rogasteis
ellos	rueguen	ellos	rogaron

PAST PARTICIPLE	IMPERATIVE
rogado	ruega
	rogad

GERUND

rogando

romper (to break)

	PRESENT			IMPERFECT
yo	rompo		yo	rompía
tú	rompes		tú	rompías
él	rompe		él	rompía
nosotros	rompemos		nosotros	rompíamos
vosotros	rompéis		vosotros	rompíais
ellos	rompen		ellos	rompían

	FUTURE			CONDITIONAL
yo	romperé		yo	rompería
tú	romperás		tú	romperías
él	romperá		él	rompería
nosotros	romperemos		nosotros	romperíamos
vosotros	romperéis		vosotros	romperíais
ellos	romperán		ellos	romperían

	PRESENT SUBJUNCTIVE			PRETERITE
yo	rompa		yo	rompí
tú	rompas		tú	rompiste
él	rompa		él	rompió
nosotros	rompamos		nosotros	rompimos
vosotros	rompáis		vosotros	rompisteis
ellos	rompan		ellos	rompieron

PAST PARTICIPLE
roto

IMPERATIVE
rompe
romped

GERUND
rompiendo

saber (to know)

	PRESENT		IMPERFECT
yo	**sé**	yo	sab**ía**
tú	sab**es**	tú	sab**ías**
él	sab**e**	él	sab**ía**
nosotros	sab**emos**	nosotros	sab**íamos**
vosotros	sab**éis**	vosotros	sab**íais**
ellos	sab**en**	ellos	sab**ían**

	FUTURE		CONDITIONAL
yo	**sabré**	yo	**sabría**
tú	**sabrás**	tú	**sabrías**
él	**sabrá**	él	**sabría**
nosotros	**sabremos**	nosotros	**sabríamos**
vosotros	**sabréis**	vosotros	**sabríais**
ellos	**sabrán**	ellos	**sabrían**

	PRESENT SUBJUNCTIVE		PRETERITE
yo	**sepa**	yo	**supe**
tú	**sepas**	tú	**supiste**
él	**sepa**	él	**supo**
nosotros	**sepamos**	nosotros	**supimos**
vosotros	**sepáis**	vosotros	**supisteis**
ellos	**sepan**	ellos	**supieron**

PAST PARTICIPLE	IMPERATIVE
sab**ido**	sab**e**
	sab**ed**

GERUND

sab**iendo**

sacar (to take out)

	PRESENT		IMPERFECT
yo	saco	yo	sacaba
tú	sacas	tú	sacabas
él	saca	él	sacaba
nosotros	sacamos	nosotros	sacábamos
vosotros	sacáis	vosotros	sacabais
ellos	sacan	ellos	sacaban

	FUTURE		CONDITIONAL
yo	sacaré	yo	sacaría
tú	sacarás	tú	sacarías
él	sacará	él	sacaría
nosotros	sacaremos	nosotros	sacaríamos
vosotros	sacaréis	vosotros	sacaríais
ellos	sacarán	ellos	sacarían

	PRESENT SUBJUNCTIVE		PRETERITE
yo	saque	yo	saqué
tú	saques	tú	sacaste
él	saque	él	sacó
nosotros	saquemos	nosotros	sacamos
vosotros	saqueís	vosotros	sacasteis
ellos	saquen	ellos	sacaron

PAST PARTICIPLE	IMPERATIVE
sacado	saca
	sacad

GERUND
sacando

salir (to go out)

	PRESENT			IMPERFECT
yo	salgo		yo	salía
tú	sales		tú	salías
él	sale		él	salía
nosotros	salimos		nosotros	salíamos
vosotros	salís		vosotros	salíais
ellos	salen		ellos	salían

	FUTURE			CONDITIONAL
yo	saldré		yo	saldría
tú	saldrás		tú	saldrías
él	saldrá		él	saldría
nosotros	saldremos		nosotros	saldríamos
vosotros	saldréis		vosotros	saldríais
ellos	saldrán		ellos	saldrían

	PRESENT SUBJUNCTIVE			PRETERITE
yo	salga		yo	salí
tú	salgas		tú	saliste
él	salga		él	salió
nosotros	salgamos		nosotros	salimos
vosotros	salgáis		vosotros	salisteis
ellos	salgan		ellos	salieron

PAST PARTICIPLE	IMPERATIVE
salido	sal
	salid

GERUND
saliendo

satisfacer (to satisfy)

	PRESENT			IMPERFECT
yo	satisfago		yo	satisfacía
tú	satisfaces		tú	satisfacías
él	satisface		él	satisfacía
nosotros	satisfacemos		nosotros	satisfacíamos
vosotros	satisfacéis		vosotros	satisfacíais
ellos	satisfacen		ellos	satisfacían

	FUTURE			CONDITIONAL
yo	satisfaré		yo	satisfaría
tú	satisfarás		tú	satisfarías
él	satisfará		él	satisfaría
nosotros	satisfaremos		nosotros	satisfaríamos
vosotros	satisfaréis		vosotros	satisfaríais
ellos	satisfarán		ellos	satisfarían

	PRESENT SUBJUNCTIVE			PRETERITE
yo	satisfaga		yo	satisfice
tú	satisfagas		tú	satisficiste
él	satisfaga		él	satisfizo
nosotros	satisfagamos		nosotros	satisficimos
vosotros	satisfagáis		vosotros	satisficisteis
ellos	satisfagan		ellos	satisficieron

PAST PARTICIPLE	IMPERATIVE
satisfecho	satisfaz/satisface
	satisfaced

GERUND
satisfaciendo

seguir (to follow)

	PRESENT		IMPERFECT
yo	**sigo**	yo	seguía
tú	**sigues**	tú	seguías
él	**sigue**	él	seguía
nosotros	segu**imos**	nosotros	seguíamos
vosotros	segu**ís**	vosotros	seguíais
ellos	**siguen**	ellos	seguían

	FUTURE		CONDITIONAL
yo	seguir**é**	yo	seguir**ía**
tú	seguir**ás**	tú	seguir**ías**
él	seguir**á**	él	seguir**ía**
nosotros	seguir**emos**	nosotros	seguir**íamos**
vosotros	seguir**éis**	vosotros	seguir**íais**
ellos	seguir**án**	ellos	seguir**ían**

	PRESENT SUBJUNCTIVE		PRETERITE
yo	**siga**	yo	segu**í**
tú	**sigas**	tú	segu**iste**
él	**siga**	él	**siguió**
nosotros	**sigamos**	nosotros	segu**imos**
vosotros	**sigáis**	vosotros	segu**isteis**
ellos	**sigan**	ellos	**siguieron**

PAST PARTICIPLE	IMPERATIVE
segu**ido**	**sigue**
	segu**id**

GERUND
siguiendo

sentir (to feel)

	PRESENT			IMPERFECT
yo	siento		yo	sentía
tú	sientes		tú	sentías
él	siente		él	sentía
nosotros	sentimos		nosotros	sentíamos
vosotros	sentís		vosotros	sentíais
ellos	sienten		ellos	sentían

	FUTURE			CONDITIONAL
yo	sentiré		yo	sentiría
tú	sentirás		tú	sentirías
él	sentirá		él	sentiría
nosotros	sentiremos		nosotros	sentiríamos
vosotros	sentiréis		vosotros	sentiríais
ellos	sentirán		ellos	sentirían

	PRESENT SUBJUNCTIVE			PRETERITE
yo	sienta		yo	sentí
tú	sientas		tú	sentiste
él	sienta		él	sintió
nosotros	sintamos		nosotros	sentimos
vosotros	sintáis		vosotros	sentisteis
ellos	sientan		ellos	sintieron

PAST PARTICIPLE	IMPERATIVE
sentido	siente
	sentid

GERUND
sintiendo

149

ser (to be)

	PRESENT		IMPERFECT
yo	**soy**	yo	**era**
tú	**eres**	tú	**eras**
él	**es**	él	**era**
nosotros	**somos**	nosotros	**éramos**
vosotros	**sois**	vosotros	**erais**
ellos	**son**	ellos	**eran**

	FUTURE		CONDITIONAL
yo	**seré**	yo	**sería**
tú	**serás**	tú	**serías**
él	**será**	él	**sería**
nosotros	**seremos**	nosotros	**seríamos**
vosotros	**seréis**	vosotros	**seríais**
ellos	**serán**	ellos	**serían**

	PRESENT SUBJUNCTIVE		PRETERITE
yo	**sea**	yo	**fui**
tú	**seas**	tú	**fuiste**
él	**sea**	él	**fue**
nosotros	**seamos**	nosotros	**fuimos**
vosotros	**seáis**	vosotros	**fuisteis**
ellos	**sean**	ellos	**fueron**

PAST PARTICIPLE	IMPERATIVE
sido	**sé**
	sed

GERUND

siendo

tener (to have)

	PRESENT			IMPERFECT
yo	tengo		yo	tenía
tú	tienes		tú	tenías
él	tiene		él	tenía
nosotros	tenemos		nosotros	teníamos
vosotros	tenéis		vosotros	teníais
ellos	tienen		ellos	tenían

	FUTURE			CONDITIONAL
yo	tendré		yo	tendría
tú	tendrás		tú	tendrías
él	tendrá		él	tendría
nosotros	tendremos		nosotros	tendríamos
vosotros	tendréis		vosotros	tendríais
ellos	tendrán		ellos	tendrían

	PRESENT SUBJUNCTIVE			PRETERITE
yo	tenga		yo	tuve
tú	tengas		tú	tuviste
él	tenga		él	tuvo
nosotros	tengamos		nosotros	tuvimos
vosotros	tengáis		vosotros	tuvisteis
ellos	tengan		ellos	tuvieron

PAST PARTICIPLE	IMPERATIVE
tenido	ten
	tened

GERUND

teniendo

torcer (to twist)

	PRESENT		IMPERFECT
yo	**tuerzo**	yo	torc**ía**
tú	**tuerces**	tú	torc**ías**
él	**tuerce**	él	torc**ía**
nosotros	torc**emos**	nosotros	torc**íamos**
vosotros	toc**éis**	vosotros	torc**íais**
ellos	**tuercen**	ellos	torc**ían**

	FUTURE		CONDITIONAL
yo	torcer**é**	yo	torcer**ía**
tú	torcer**ás**	tú	torcer**ías**
él	torcer**á**	él	torcer**ía**
nosotros	torcer**emos**	nosotros	torcer**íamos**
vosotros	torcer**éis**	vosotros	torcer**íais**
ellos	torcer**án**	ellos	torcer**ían**

	PRESENT SUBJUNCTIVE		PRETERITE
yo	**tuerza**	yo	torc**í**
tú	**tuerzas**	tú	torc**iste**
él	**tuerza**	él	torc**ió**
nosotros	**tuerzamos**	nosotros	torc**imos**
vosotros	**tuerzáis**	vosotros	torc**isteis**
ellos	**tuerzan**	ellos	torc**ieron**

PAST PARTICIPLE	IMPERATIVE
torc**ido**	**tuerce**
	torc**ed**

GERUND

torc**iendo**

traer (to bring)

	PRESENT			IMPERFECT
yo	traigo		yo	traía
tú	traes		tú	traías
él	trae		él	traía
nosotros	traemos		nosotros	traíamos
vosotros	traéis		vosotros	traíais
ellos	traen		ellos	traían

	FUTURE			CONDITIONAL
yo	traeré		yo	traería
tú	traerás		tú	traerías
él	traerá		él	traería
nosotros	traeremos		nosotros	traeríamos
vosotros	traeréis		vosotros	traeríais
ellos	traerán		ellos	traerían

	PRESENT SUBJUNCTIVE			PRETERITE
yo	traiga		yo	traje
tú	traigas		tú	trajiste
él	traiga		él	trajo
nosotros	traigamos		nosotros	trajimos
vosotros	traigáis		vosotros	trajisteis
ellos	traigan		ellos	trajeron

PAST PARTICIPLE	IMPERATIVE
traído	trae
	traed

GERUND
trayendo

valer (to be worth)

	PRESENT		IMPERFECT
yo	valgo	yo	valía
tú	vales	tú	valías
él	vale	él	valía
nosotros	valemos	nosotros	valíamos
vosotros	valéis	vosotros	valíais
ellos	valen	ellos	valían

	FUTURE		CONDITIONAL
yo	valdré	yo	valdría
tú	valdrás	tú	valdrías
él	valdrá	él	valdría
nosotros	valdremos	nosotros	valdríamos
vosotros	valdréis	vosotros	valdríais
ellos	valdrán	ellos	valdrían

	PRESENT SUBJUNCTIVE		PRETERITE
yo	valga	yo	valí
tú	valgas	tú	valiste
él	valga	él	valió
nosotros	valgamos	nosotros	valimos
vosotros	valgáis	vosotros	valisteis
ellos	valgan	ellos	valieron

PAST PARTICIPLE
valido

IMPERATIVE
vale
valed

GERUND
valiendo

vencer (to win)

	PRESENT		IMPERFECT
yo	venzo	yo	vencía
tú	vences	tú	vencías
él	vence	él	vencía
nosotros	vencemos	nosotros	vencíamos
vosotros	vencéis	vosotros	vencíais
ellos	vencen	ellos	vencían

	FUTURE		CONDITIONAL
yo	venceré	yo	vencería
tú	vencerás	tú	vencerías
él	vencerá	él	vencería
nosotros	venceremos	nosotros	venceríamos
vosotros	venceréis	vosotros	venceríais
ellos	vencerán	ellos	vencerían

	PRESENT SUBJUNCTIVE		PRETERITE
yo	venza	yo	vencí
tú	venzas	tú	venciste
él	venza	él	venció
nosotros	venzamos	nosotros	vencimos
vosotros	venzáis	vosotros	vencisteis
ellos	venzan	ellos	vencieron

PAST PARTICIPLE	IMPERATIVE
vencido	vence
	venced

GERUND

venciendo

venir (to come)

	PRESENT		IMPERFECT
yo	**vengo**	yo	ven**ía**
tú	**vienes**	tú	ven**ías**
él	**viene**	él	ven**ía**
nosotros	ven**imos**	nosotros	ven**íamos**
vosotros	ven**ís**	vosotros	ven**íais**
ellos	**vienen**	ellos	ven**ían**

	FUTURE		CONDITIONAL
yo	**vendré**	yo	**vendría**
tú	**vendrás**	tú	**vendrías**
él	**vendrá**	él	**vendría**
nosotros	**vendremos**	nosotros	**vendríamos**
vosotros	**vendréis**	vosotros	**vendríais**
ellos	**vendrán**	ellos	**vendrían**

	PRESENT SUBJUNCTIVE		PRETERITE
yo	**venga**	yo	**vine**
tú	**vengas**	tú	**viniste**
él	**venga**	él	**vino**
nosotros	**vengamos**	nosotros	**vinimos**
vosotros	**vengáis**	vosotros	**vinisteis**
ellos	**vengan**	ellos	**vinieron**

PAST PARTICIPLE	IMPERATIVE
ven**ido**	**ven**
	veni**d**

GERUND
viniendo

ver (to see)

	PRESENT		IMPERFECT
yo	veo	yo	veía
tú	ves	tú	veías
él	ve	él	veía
nosotros	vemos	nosotros	veíamos
vosotros	veis	vosotros	veíais
ellos	ven	ellos	veían

	FUTURE		CONDITIONAL
yo	veré	yo	vería
tú	verás	tú	verías
él	verá	él	vería
nosotros	veremos	nosotros	veríamos
vosotros	veréis	vosotros	veríais
ellos	verán	ellos	verían

	PRESENT SUBJUNCTIVE		PRETERITE
yo	vea	yo	vi
tú	veas	tú	viste
él	vea	él	vio
nosotros	veamos	nosotros	vimos
vosotros	veáis	vosotros	visteis
ellos	vean	ellos	vieron

PAST PARTICIPLE	IMPERATIVE
visto	ve
	ved

GERUND
viendo

volcar (to overturn)

	PRESENT		IMPERFECT
yo	**vuelco**	yo	volc**aba**
tú	**vuelcas**	tú	volc**abas**
él	**vuelca**	él	volc**aba**
nosotros	volc**amos**	nosotros	volc**ábamos**
vosotros	volc**áis**	vosotros	volc**abais**
ellos	**vuelcan**	ellos	volc**aban**

	FUTURE		CONDITIONAL
yo	volcar**é**	yo	volcar**ía**
tú	volcar**ás**	tú	volcar**ías**
él	volcar**á**	él	volcar**ía**
nosotros	volcar**emos**	nosotros	volcar**íamos**
vosotros	volcar**éis**	vosotros	volcar**íais**
ellos	volcar**án**	ellos	volcar**ían**

	PRESENT SUBJUNCTIVE		PRETERITE
yo	**vuelque**	yo	**volqué**
tú	**vuelques**	tú	volc**aste**
él	**vuelque**	él	volc**ó**
nosotros	**volquemos**	nosotros	volc**amos**
vosotros	**volquéis**	vosotros	volc**asteis**
ellos	**vuelquen**	ellos	volc**aron**

PAST PARTICIPLE	IMPERATIVE
volc**ado**	**vuelca**
	volc**ad**

GERUND

volc**ando**

volver (to return)

	PRESENT		IMPERFECT
yo	**vuelvo**	yo	volv**ía**
tú	**vuelves**	tú	volv**ías**
él	**vuelve**	él	volv**ía**
nosotros	volv**emos**	nosotros	volv**íamos**
vosotros	volv**éis**	vosotros	volv**íais**
ellos	**vuelven**	ellos	volv**ían**

	FUTURE		CONDITIONAL
yo	volver**é**	yo	volver**ía**
tú	volver**ás**	tú	volver**ías**
él	volver**á**	él	volver**ía**
nosotros	volver**emos**	nosotros	volver**íamos**
vosotros	volver**éis**	vosotros	volver**íais**
ellos	volver**án**	ellos	volver**ían**

	PRESENT SUBJUNCTIVE		PRETERITE
yo	**vuelva**	yo	volv**í**
tú	**vuelvas**	tú	volv**iste**
él	**vuelva**	él	volv**ió**
nosotros	volv**amos**	nosotros	volv**imos**
vosotros	volv**áis**	vosotros	volv**isteis**
ellos	**vuelvan**	ellos	volv**ieron**

PAST PARTICIPLE	IMPERATIVE
vuelto	**vuelve**
	volv**ed**

GERUND

volv**iendo**

zurcir (to darn)

	PRESENT			IMPERFECT
yo	zurzo		yo	zurcía
tú	zurces		tú	zurcías
él	zurce		él	zurcía
nosotros	zurcimos		nosotros	zurcíamos
vosotros	zurcís		vosotros	zurcíais
ellos	zurcen		ellos	zurcían

	FUTURE			CONDITIONAL
yo	zurciré		yo	zurciría
tú	zurcirás		tú	zurcirías
él	zurcirá		él	zurciría
nosotros	zurciremos		nosotros	zurciríamos
vosotros	zurciréis		vosotros	zurciríais
ellos	zurcirán		ellos	zurcirían

	PRESENT SUBJUNCTIVE			PRETERITE
yo	zurza		yo	zurcí
tú	zurzas		tú	zurciste
él	zurza		él	zurció
nosotros	zurzamos		nosotros	zurcimos
vosotros	zurzáis		vosotros	zurcisteis
ellos	zurzan		ellos	zurcieron

PAST PARTICIPLE	IMPERATIVE
zurcido	zurce
	zurcid

GERUND

zurciendo

Verb Index

The following pages, 162 to 190, contain an index of all the Spanish verbs in this dictionary cross-referred to the appropriate conjugation model:

- Regular verbs belonging to the first, second and third conjugation are numbered 1, 2 and 3 respectively. For the regular conjugations see pages 6 to 13.

- Irregular verbs are numerically cross-referred to the appropriate model as conjugated on pages 82 to 160. Thus, **alzar** is cross-referred to page 100 where **cruzar**, the model for this verb group, is conjugated.

- Verbs which are most commonly used in the reflexive form – e.g. **amodorrarse** – have been cross-referred to the appropriate non-reflexive model. For the full conjugation of a reflexive verb, see pages 28 to 31.

- Verbs printed in **bold** – e.g. **abrir** – are themselves models.

- Superior numbers refer you to notes on page 191 which indicate how the verb differs from its model.

Verb Index

Verb Index

Verb Index

Verb Index

Verb Index

Verb index

Verb Index

Verb Index

Verb Index

Verb Index

Verb Index

Verb Index

Verb Index

Verb Index

Notes

The notes below indicate special peculiarities of individual verbs.
When only some forms of a given tense are affected, all these are shown.
When all forms of the tense are affected, only the 1st and 2nd persons are
shown, followed by *etc*.

1 Gerund 2 Past Participle 3 Present 4 Preterite 5 Present Subjunctive
6 Imperfect Subjunctive

1   **acaecer, acontecer, amanecer, anochecer, competer, deshelar,
    escampar, granizar, helar, nevar, nublar, relampaguear, tronar,
    verdear**: used almost exclusively in infinitive and 3rd person singular
2   **asir** 3 asgo 5 asga, asgar *etc*
3   **atañer, -tañer** 1 atañendo 4 atañó: see also 1 above
4   **balbucir** 3 balbuceo 5 balbucee, balbucees *etc*
5   **concernir** 3 concierne, conciernen 5 concierna, conciernan:
    only used in 3rd person
6   **degollar** 3 degüello, degüellas, degüella, degüellan 5 degüelle,
    degüelles, degüellen
7   **delinquir** 3 delinco 5 delinca, delincas *etc*
8   **desasir** 3 desasgo 5 desasga, desasgas *etc*
9   **discernir** 3 discierno, disciernes, discierne, disciernen 5 discierna,
    disciernas, disciernan
10 **enraizar** 3 enraízo, enraízas, enraíza, enraízan 5 enraíce, enraíces,
    enraícen
11 **pudrir** 2 podrido
12 **rehuir** 3 rehúyo, rehúyes, rehúye, rehúyen 5 rehúya, rehúyas,
    rehúyan
13 **roer** 4 royó, royeron 6 royera, royeras *etc*
14 **soler**: used only in present and imperfect indicative
15 **yacer** 3 yazgo *or* yazco *or* yago 5 yazga *etc or* yazca *etc or* yaga *etc*

The Gender of Nouns

In Spanish, all nouns are either masculine or feminine, whether denoting people, animals or things. Gender is largely unpredictable and has to be learnt for each noun. However, the following guidelines will help you determine the gender for certain types of nouns:

Nouns denoting male people and animals are usually – but not always – masculine, e.g.

un hombre a man
un toro a bull
un enfermero a (*male*) nurse
un semental a stallion

Nouns denoting female people and animals are usually – but not always – feminine, e.g.

una niña a girl
una vaca a cow
una enfermera a nurse
una yegua a mare

Some nouns are masculine *or* feminine depending on the sex of the person to whom they refer, e.g.

un camarada a (*male*) comrade
una camarada a (*female*) comrade
un belga a Belgian (*man*)
una belga a Belgian (*woman*)
un marroquí a Moroccan (*man*)
una marroquí a Moroccan (*woman*)

Other nouns referring to either men *or* women have only one gender which applies to both, e.g.

una persona a person
una visita a visitor
una víctima a victim
una estrella a star

Often the ending of a noun indicates its gender. Shown opposite are some of the most important to guide you.

Often the ending of the noun indicates its gender. Shown below are some of the most important to guide you:

Masculine endings

-o	**un clavo** a nail, **un plátano** a banana EXCEPTIONS: **mano** hand, **foto** photograph, **moto(cicleta)** motorbike
-l	**un tonel** a barrel, **un hotel** a hotel EXCEPTIONS: **cal** lime, **cárcel** prison, **catedral** cathedral, **col** cabbage, **miel** honey, **piel** skin, **sal** salt, **señal** sign
-r	**un tractor** a tractor, **el altar** the altar EXCEPTIONS: **coliflor** cauliflower, **flor** flower, **labor** task
-y	**el rey** the king, **un buey** an ox EXCEPTION: **ley** law

Feminine endings

-a	**un casa** a house, **la cara** the face EXCEPTIONS: **día** day, **mapa** map, **planeta** planet, **tranvía** tram, and most words ending in -ma (**tema** subject, **problema** problem, *etc*)
-ión	**una canción** a song, **una procesión** a procession EXCEPTIONS: most nouns not ending in -ción or -sión, e.g. **avión** aeroplane, **camión** lorry, **gorrión** sparrow
-dad, -tad, -tud	**una ciudad** a town, **la libertad** freedom, **una multitud** a crowd
-ed	**una pared** a wall, **la sed** thirst EXCEPTION: **césped** lawn
-itis	**una faringitis** pharyngitis, **la celulitis** cellulitis
-iz	**una perdiz** a partridge, **una matriz** a matrix EXCEPTIONS: **lápiz** pencil, **maíz** corn, **tapiz** tapestry
-sis	**una tesis** a thesis, **una dosis** a dose EXCEPTIONS: **análisis** analysis, **énfasis** emphasis, **paréntesis** parenthesis
-umbre	**la podredumbre** rot, **la muchedrume** crowd

The Gender of Nouns *continued*

Some nouns change meaning according to gender. The most common are set out below:

	MASCULINE	FEMININE
capital	capital (*money*)	capital (*city*) → ①
clave	harpsichord	clue
cólera	cholera	anger → ②
cometa	comet	kite
corriente	current month	current
corte	cut	court (*royal*) → ③
coma	coma	comma → ④
cura	priest	cure → ⑤
frente	front (*in war*)	forehead → ⑥
guardia	guard(sman)	guard → ⑦
guía	guide (*person*)	guide(book) → ⑧
moral	mulberry tree	morals
orden	order (*arrangement*)	order (*command*) → ⑨
ordenanza	office boy	ordinance
papa	Pope	potato
parte	dispatch	part → ⑩
pendiente	earring	slope
pez	fish	pitch
policía	policeman	police
radio	radius, radium	radio

Examples

① Invirtieron mucho capital
   La capital es muy fea

   They invested a lot of capital
   The capital city is very ugly

② Es difícil luchar contra el cólera
   Montó en cólera

   Cholera is difficult to combat
   He got angry

③ Me encanta tu corte de pelo
   Se trasladó la corte a Madrid

   I love your haircut
   The court was moved to Madrid

④ Entró en un coma profundo
   Aquí hace falta una coma

   He went into a deep coma
   You need to put a comma here

⑤ ¿Quién es? – El cura
   No tiene cura

   Who is it? – The priest
   It's hopeless

⑥ Han mandado a su hijo al
   frente
   Tiene la frente muy ancha

   Her son has been sent to the
   front
   She has a very broad forehead

⑦ Vino un guardia de tráfico
   Están relevando la guardia ahora

   A traffic policeman came
   They're changing the guard now

⑧ Nuestro guía nos hizo reír a
   carcajadas
   Busco una guía turística

   Our guide had us falling about
   laughing
   I'm looking for a guidebook

⑨ Están en orden alfabético
   No hemos recibido la orden
   de pago

   They're in alphabetical order
   We haven't had the payment
   order

⑩ Le mandó un parte al general
   En alguna parte debe estar

   He sent a dispatch to the general
   It must be somewhere or other

Gender: the Formation of Feminines

As in English, male and female are sometimes differentiated by the use of two quite separate words, e.g.

> **mi marido** my husband
> **mi mujer** my wife
> **un toro** a bull
> **una vaca** a cow

There are, however, some words in Spanish which show this distinction by the form of their ending:

> Nouns ending in **-o** change to **-a** to form the feminine → ❶

> If the masculine singular form already ends in **-a**, no further **-a** is added to the feminine → ❷

> If the last letter of the masculine singular form is a consonant, an **-a** is normally added in the feminine* → ❸

Feminine forms to note

MASCULINE	FEMININE	
el abad	la abadesa	abbot/abbess
un actor	una actriz	actor/actress
el alcalde	la alcaldesa	mayor/mayoress
el conde	la condesa	count/countess
el duque	la duquesa	duke/duchess
el emperador	la emperatriz	emperor/empress
un poeta	una poetisa	poet/poetess
el príncipe	la princesa	prince/princess
el rey	la reina	king/queen
un sacerdote	una sacerdotisa	priest/priestess
un tigre	una tigresa	tiger/tigress
el zar	la zarina	tzar/tzarina

* If the last syllable has an accent, it disappears in the feminine (see page 296) → ❹

Examples

① un amigo a (*male*) friend
   un empleado a (*male*) employee
   un gato a cat

una amiga a (*female*) friend
una empleada a (*female*) employee
una gata a (*female*) cat

② un deportista a sportsman
   un colega a (*male*) colleague
   un camarada a (*male*) comrade

una deportista a sportswoman
una colega a (*female*) colleague
una camarada a (*female*) comrade

③ un español a Spaniard,
     a Spanish man
   un vendedor a salesman
   un jugador a (*male*) player

una española a Spanish woman

una vendedora a saleswoman
una jugadora a (*female*) player

④ un lapón a Laplander (*man*)
   un león a lion
   un neocelandés
     a New Zealander (*man*)

una lapona a Laplander (*woman*)
una leona a lioness
una neocelandesa
  a New Zealander (*woman*)

The Formation of Plurals

Nouns ending in an unstressed vowel add **-s** to the singular form → ❶

Nouns ending in a consonant or a stressed vowel add **-es** to the singular form → ❷

   ⓘ BUT: **café** coffee shop (*plural*: **cafés**)
         mamá mummy (*plural*: **mamás**)
         papá daddy (*plural*: **papás**)
         pie foot (*plural*: **pies**)
         sofá sofa (*plural*: **sofás**)
         té tea (*plural*: **tes**)

and words of foreign origin ending in a consonant, e.g.:

         coñac brandy (*plural*: **coñacs**)
         jersey jumper (*plural*: **jerseys**)

ⓘ Note:

- nouns ending in **-n** or **-s** with an accent on the last syllable drop this accent in the plural (see page 296) → ❸
- nouns ending in **-n** with the stress on the second-last syllable in the singular add an accent to that syllable in the plural in order to show the correct position for stress (see page 296) → ❹
- nouns ending in **-z** change this to **c** in the plural → ❺

Nouns with an unstressed final syllable ending in **-s** do not change in the plural → ❻

Examples

1. la casa the house   las casas the houses
   el libro the book   los libros the books

2. un rumor a rumour   unos rumores (some) rumours
   un jabalí a boar   unos jabalíes (some) boars

3. la canción the song   las canciones the songs
   el autobús the bus   los autobuses the buses

4. un examen an exam   unos exámenes (some) exams
   un crimen a crime   unos crímenes (some) crimes

5. la luz the light   las luces the lights

6. un paraguas an umbrella   unos paraguas (some) umbrellas
   la dosis the dose   las dosis the doses
   el lunes Monday   los lunes Mondays

The Definite Article

	WITH MASC. NOUN	WITH FEM. NOUN	
SING.	el	la	the
PLUR.	los	las	the

The gender and number of the noun determine the form of the article → ❶

> ⓘ Note: However, if the article comes directly before a feminine singular noun which starts with a stressed a- or ha-, the masculine form el is used instead of the feminine la → ❷

For uses of the definite article see page 203.

a + el becomes al → ❸

de + el becomes del → ❹

Examples

1   el tren   the train   la estación   the station
     el actor   the actor   la actriz   the actress
     los hoteles   the hotels   las escuelas   the schools
     los profesores   the teachers   las mujeres   the women

2   el agua   the water
     BUT:
     la misma agua   the same water

     el hacha   the axe
     BUT:
     la mejor hacha   the best axe

3   al cine   to the cinema
     al empleado   to the employee
     al hospital   to the hospital

4   del departamento   from/of the department
     del autor   from/of the author
     del presidente   from/of the president

Uses of the Definite Article

While the definite article is used in much the same way in Spanish as it is in English, its use is more widespread in Spanish. Unlike English the definite article is also used:

with abstract nouns, except when following certain prepositions → ❶

in generalizations, especially with plural or uncountable* nouns → ❷

with parts of the body → ❸
'Ownership' is often indicated by an indirect object pronoun or a reflexive pronoun → ❹

with titles/ranks/professions followed by a proper name → ❺
EXCEPTIONS: with **Don/Doña**, **San/Santo(a)** → ❻

before nouns of official, academic and religious buildings, and names of meals and games → ❼

The definite article is *not* used with nouns in apposition unless those nouns are individualized → ❽

* An uncountable noun is one which cannot be used in the plural or with an indefinite article, e.g. **el acero** steel; **la leche** milk.

Examples

① Los precios suben   Prices are rising
El tiempo es oro   Time is money
BUT:
con pasión   with passion
sin esperanza   without hope

② No me gusta el café   I don't like coffee
Los niños necesitan ser queridos   Children need to be loved

③ Vuelva la cabeza hacia la izquierda   Turn your head to the left
No puedo mover las piernas   I can't move my legs

④ La cabeza me da vueltas   My head is spinning
Lávate las manos   Wash your hands

⑤ El rey Jorge III   King George III
el capitán Menéndez   Captain Menéndez
el doctor Ochoa   Doctor Ochoa
el señor Ramírez   Mr Ramírez

⑥ Don Arturo Ruiz   Mr Arturo Ruiz
Santa Teresa   Saint Teresa

⑦ en la cárcel   in prison
en la universidad   at university
en la iglesia   at church
la cena   dinner
el tenis   tennis
el ajedrez   chess

⑧ Madrid, capital de España,   Madrid, the capital of Spain,
  es la ciudad que ...   is the city which ...
BUT:
Maria Callas, la famosa cantante   Maria Callas, the famous opera
  de ópera ...   singer ...

The Indefinite Article

	WITH MASC. NOUN	WITH FEM. NOUN	
SING.	un	una	a
PLUR.	unos	unas	some

The indefinite article is used in Spanish largely as it is in English.

BUT:

There is no article when a person's profession is being stated → ❶

The article is used, however, when the profession is qualified by an adjective → ❷

The article is not used with the following words:

otro	another	→ ❸
cierto	certain	→ ❹
semejante	such (a)	→ ❺
tal	such (a)	→ ❻
cien	a hundred	→ ❼
mil	a thousand	→ ❽
sin	without	→ ❾
qué	what a	→ ❿

There is no article with a noun in apposition → ⓫. When an abstract noun is qualified by an adjective, the indefinite article is used, but is not translated in English → ⓬

Examples

① Es profesor   He's a teacher
 Mi madre es enfermera My mother is a nurse

② Es un buen médico   He's a good doctor
 Se hizo una escritora célebre She became a famous writer

③ otro libro   another book

④ cierta calle   a certain street

⑤ semejante ruido   such a noise

⑥ tal mentira   such a lie

⑦ cien soldados   a hundred soldiers

⑧ mil años   a thousand years

⑨ sin casa   without a house

⑩ ¡Qué sorpresa!   What a surprise!

⑪ Baroja, gran escritor de la Baroja, a great writer of the
 Generación del 98 'Generación del 98'

⑫ con una gran sabiduría/un valor with great wisdom/admirable
 admirable   courage
 Dieron pruebas de una sangre They showed incredible coolness
 fría increíble
 una película de un mal gusto a film in appallingly bad taste
 espantoso

The Article 'lo'

This is never used with a noun. Instead, it is used in the following ways:

as an intensifier before an adjective or adverb in the construction

lo + adjective/adverb + **que** → ❶

ⓘ Note: The adjective agrees with the noun it refers to → ❷

With an adjective or participle to form an abstract noun → ❸

In the phrase **lo de** to refer to a subject of which speaker and listener are already aware. It can often be translated as *the business/affair of/about* ... → ❹

In set expressions, the commonest of which are:

a lo mejor	maybe, perhaps	→ ❺
a lo lejos	in the distance	→ ❻
a lo largo de	along, through	→ ❼
por lo menos	at least	→ ❽
por lo tanto	therefore, so	→ ❾
por lo visto	apparently	→ ❿

Examples

1 No sabíamos lo pequeña que era la casa
We didn't know how small the house was

Sé lo mucho que te gusta la música
I know how much you like music

2 No te imaginas lo simpáticos que son
You can't imagine how nice they are

Ya sabes lo buenas que son estas manzanas
You already know how good these apples are

3 Lo bueno de eso es que ...
The good thing about it is that ...

Sentimos mucho lo ocurrido
We are very sorry about what happened

4 Lo de ayer es mejor que lo olvides
It's better if you forget what happened yesterday

Lo de tu hermano me preocupa mucho
The business about your brother worries me very much

5 A lo mejor ha salido
Perhaps he's gone out

6 A lo lejos se veían unas casas
Some houses could be seen in the distance

7 A lo largo de su vida
Throughout his life

A lo largo de la carretera
Along the road

8 Hubo por lo menos cincuenta heridos
At least fifty people were injured

9 No hemos recibido ninguna instrucción al respecto, y por lo tanto no podemos ...
We have not received any instructions about it, therefore we cannot ...

10 Por lo visto, no viene
Apparently he's not coming or: He's not coming, it seems

Adjectives

Most adjectives agree in number and in gender with the noun or pronoun.

ⓘ Note that:

- if the adjective refers to two or more singular nouns of the same gender, a plural ending of that gender is required → ❶
- if the adjective refers to two or more singular nouns of different genders, a masculine plural ending is required → ❷

The formation of feminines

Adjectives ending in **-o** change to **-a** → ❸

Some groups of adjectives add **-a**:
- adjectives of nationality or geographical origin → ❹
- adjectives ending in **-or** (except irregular comparatives: see page 214), **-án**, **-ón**, **-ín** → ❺

ⓘ Note: When there is an accent on the last syllable, it disappears in the feminine (see page 296).

Other adjectives do not change → ❻

The formation of plurals

Adjectives ending in an unstressed vowel add **-s** → ❼

Adjectives ending in a stressed vowel or a consonant add **-es** → ❽

ⓘ Note:

- if there is an accent on the last syllable of a word ending in a consonant, it will disappear in the plural (see page 296) → ❾
- if the last letter is a **z** it will become a **c** in the plural → ❿

Examples

❶	la lengua y la literatura españolas	(the) Spanish language and literature
❷	Nunca había visto árboles y flores tan raros	I had never seen such strange trees and flowers
❸	mi hermano pequeño mi hermana pequeña	my little brother my little sister
❹	un chico español una chica española el equipo barcelonés la vida barcelonesa	a Spanish boy a Spanish girl the team from Barcelona the Barcelona way of life
❺	un niño encantador una niña encantadora un hombre holgazán una mujer holgazana un gesto burlón una sonrisa burlona un chico cantarín una chica cantarina	a charming little boy a charming little girl an idle man an idle woman a mocking gesture a mocking smile a boy fond of singing a girl fond of singing
❻	un final feliz una infancia feliz mi amigo belga mi amiga belga el vestido verde la blusa verde	a happy ending a happy childhood my Belgian (*male*) friend my Belgian (*female*) friend the green dress the green blouse
❼	el último tren los últimos trenes una casa vieja unas casas viejas	the last train the last trains an old house (some) old houses
❽	un médico iraní unos médicos iraníes un examen fácil unos exámenes fáciles	an Iranian doctor (some) Iranian doctors easy exam (some) easy exams
❾	un río francés unos ríos franceses	a French river (some) French rivers
❿	un día feliz unos días felices	a happy day (some) happy days

Adjectives

Invariable Adjectives

Some adjectives and other parts of speech when used adjectivally never change in the feminine or plural.

The commonest of these are:
- nouns denoting colour → ①
- compound adjectives → ②
- nouns used as adjectives → ③

Shortening of adjectives

The following drop the final **-o** before a masculine singular noun:

bueno good → ④
malo bad
alguno* some → ⑤
ninguno* none
uno one → ⑥
primero first → ⑦
tercero third
postrero last → ⑧

* ⓘ Note: An accent is required to show the correct position for stress.

Grande *big, great* is usually shortened to **gran** before a masculine *or* feminine singular noun → ⑨

Santo *Saint* changes to **San** except with saints' names beginning with **Do-** *or* **To-** → ⑩

Ciento *a hundred* is shortened to **cien** before a masculine *or* feminine plural noun → ⑪

Cualquiera drops the final **-a** before a masculine *or* feminine singular noun → ⑫

Examples

1. los vestidos naranja — the orange dresses

2. las chaquetas azul marino — the navy blue jackets

3. bebés probeta — test-tube babies
   mujeres soldado — women soldiers

4. un buen libro — a good book

5. algún libro — some book

6. cuarenta y un años — forty-one years

7. el primer hijo — the first child

8. un postrer deseo — a last wish

9. un gran actor — a great actor
   una gran decepción — a great disappointment

10. San Antonio — Saint Anthony
    Santo Tomás — Saint Thomas

11. cien años — a hundred years
    cien millones — a hundred million

12. cualquier día — any day
    a cualquier hora — any time

Comparatives and Superlatives

Comparatives

These are formed using the following constructions:

más ... (que) more ... (than) → ❶
menos ... (que) less ... (than) → ❷
tanto ... como as ... as → ❸
tan ... como as ... as → ❹
tan ... que so ... that → ❺

demasiado ... ⎤   too ... ⎤
bastante ...   **para**   enough ... **to** → ❻
suficiente ... ⎦   enough ... ⎦

'Than' followed by a clause is translated by **de lo que** → ❼

Superlatives

These are formed using the following constructions:

el/la/los/las más ... (que) the most ... (that) → ❽
el/la/los/las menos ... (que) the least ... (that) → ❾

After a superlative the preposition **de** is often translated as 'in' → ❿

The absolute superlative (*very, most, extremely + adjective*) is expressed in Spanish by **muy** + adjective, or by adding **-ísimo/a/os/as** to the adjective when it ends in a consonant, or to its stem (adjective minus final vowel) when it ends in a vowel → ⓫

ⓘ Note: It is sometimes necessary to change the spelling of the adjective when **-ísimo** is added, in order to maintain the same sound (see page 300) → ⓬

Examples

1. una razón más seria — a more serious reason
   Es más alto que mi hermano — He's taller than my brother

2. una película menos conocida — a less well known film
   Luis es menos tímido que tú — Luis is less shy than you

3. Pablo tenía tanto miedo como yo — Paul was as frightened as I was

4. No es tan grande como creía — It isn't as big as I thought

5. El examen era tan difícil que nadie aprobó — The exam was so difficult that nobody passed

6. No tengo suficiente dinero para comprarlo — I haven't got enough money to buy it

7. Está más cansada de lo que parece — She is more tired than she seems

8. el caballo más veloz — the fastest horse
   la casa más pequeña — the smallest house
   los días más lluviosos — the wettest days
   las manzanas más maduras — the ripest apples

9. el hombre menos simpático — the least likeable man
   la niña menos habladora — the least talkative girl
   los cuadros menos bonitos — the least attractive paintings
   las camisas menos viejas — the least old shirts

10. la estación más ruidosa de Londres — the noisiest station in London

11. Este libro es muy interesante — This book is very interesting

12. Tienen un coche rapidísimo — They have an extremely fast car
    Era facilísimo de hacer — It was very easy to make
    Mi tío era muy rico — My uncle was very rich
    Se hizo riquísimo — He became extremely rich
    un león muy feroz — a very ferocious lion
    un tigre ferocísimo — an extremely ferocious tiger

Comparatives and Superlatives *continued*

Adjectives with irregular comparatives/superlatives

ADJECTIVE	COMPARATIVE	SUPERLATIVE
bueno	**mejor**	**el mejor**
good	better	the best
malo	**peor**	**el peor**
bad	worse	the worst
grande	**mayor** *or* **más grande**	**el más grande**
big	bigger; older	the biggest; the oldest
pequeño	**menor** *or* **más pequeño**	**el más pequeño**
small	smaller; younger; lesser	the smallest; the youngest; the least

The irregular comparative and superlative forms of **grande** and **pequeño** are used mainly to express:
- age, in which case they come after the noun → ❶
- abstract size and degrees of importance, in which case they come before the noun → ❷

The regular forms are used mainly to express physical size → ❸

Irregular comparatives and superlatives have one form for both masculine and feminine, but always agree in number with the noun → ❶

Examples

1 mis hermanos mayores   my older brothers
   la hija menor   the youngest daughter

2 el menor ruido   the slightest sound
   las mayores dificultades   the biggest difficulties

3 Este plato es más grande que   This plate is bigger than that
    aquél   one
   Mi casa es más pequeña que   My house is smaller than yours
    la tuya

Demonstrative Adjectives

	MASCULINE	FEMININE	
SING.	este	esta	this
	ese	esa	that
	aquel	aquella	
PLUR.	estos	estas	these
	esos	esas	those
	aquellos	aquellas	

Demonstrative adjectives normally precede the noun and always agree in number and in gender → ❶

The forms **ese/a/os/as** are used:
- to indicate distance from the speaker but proximity to the person addressed → ❷
- to indicate a not too remote distance → ❸

The forms **aquel/la/los/las** are used to indicate distance, in space or time → ❹

Examples

1. Este bolígrafo no escribe · · · · · · · · · This pen is not working
   Esa revista es muy mala · · · · · · · · · That is a very bad magazine
   Aquella montaña es muy alta · · · · · · That mountain (over there) is
   · very high

   ¿Conoces a esos señores? · · · · · · · · Do you know those gentlemen?
   Siga Vd hasta aquellos edificios · · · Carry on until you come to those
   · buildings

   ¿Ves aquellas personas? · · · · · · · · · Can you see those people
   · (over there)?

2. Ese papel en donde escribes ... · · · That paper you are writing on ...

3. No me gustan esos cuadros · · · · · · · I don't like those pictures

4. Aquella calle parece muy ancha · · · That street (over there) looks
   · very wide

   Aquellos años sí que fueron felices · Those were really happy years

Interrogative Adjectives

		MASCULINE	FEMININE	
SING.	⌈	¿qué?	¿qué?	what?, which?
	⌊	¿cuánto?	¿cuánta?	how much?, how many?
PLUR.	⌈	¿qué?	¿qué?	what?, which?
	⌊	¿cuántos?	¿cuántas?	how much?, how many?

Interrogative adjectives, when not invariable, agree in number and gender with the noun → ①

The forms shown above are also used in indirect questions → ②

Exclamatory Adjectives

		MASCULINE	FEMININE	
SING.	⌈	¡qué!	¡qué!	what (a)
	⌊	¡cuánto!	¡cuánta!	what (a lot of)
PLUR.	⌈	¡qué!	¡qué!	what
	⌊	¡cuántos!	¡cuántas!	what (a lot of)

Exclamatory adjectives, when not invariable, agree in number and gender with the noun → ③

Examples

❶ ¿Qué libro te gustó más?   Which book did you like most?

¿Qué clase de hombre es?   What type of man is he?

¿Qué instrumentos toca Vd?   What instruments do you play?

¿Qué ofertas ha recibido Vd?   What offers have you received?

¿Cuánto dinero te queda?   How much money have you got left?

¿Cuánta lluvia ha caído?   How much rain have we had?

¿Cuántos vestidos quieres comprar?   How many dresses do you want to buy?

¿Cuántas personas van a venir?   How many people are coming?

❷ No sé a qué hora llegó   I don't know at what time she arrived

Dígame cuántas postales quiere   Tell me how many postcards you'd like

❸ ¡Qué pena!   What a pity!

¡Qué tiempo tan/más malo!   What lousy weather!

¡Cuánto tiempo!   What a long time!

¡Cuánta pobreza!   What poverty!

¡Cuántos autobuses!   What a lot of buses!

¡Cuántas mentiras!   What a lot of lies!

Possessive Adjectives

Weak forms

WITH SING. NOUN		WITH PLUR. NOUN		
MASC.	FEM.	MASC.	FEM.	
mi	mi	mis	mis	my
tu	tu	tus	tus	your
su	su	sus	sus	his; her; its; your (of **Vd**)
nuestro	nuestra	nuestros	nuestras	our
vuestro	vuestra	vuestros	vuestras	your
su	su	sus	sus	their; your (of **Vds**)

All possessive adjectives agree in number and (when applicable) in gender with the noun, not with the owner → ❶
The weak forms always precede the noun → ❶

Since the form **su(s)** can mean his, her, your (of **Vd**, **Vds**) or their, clarification is often needed. This is done by adding **de él**, **de ella**, **de Vds** etc to the noun, and usually (but not always) changing the possessive to a definite article → ❷

Examples

1   Pilar no ha traído nuestros libros   Pilar hasn't brought our books
Antonio irá a vuestra casa   Anthony will go to your house
¿Han vendido su coche tus   Have your neighbours sold their
   vecinos?   car?
Mi hermano y tu primo no se   My brother and your cousin
   llevan bien   don't get on

2   su casa → la casa de él   his house
sus amigos → los amigos de Vd   your friends
sus coches → los coches de ellos   their cars
su abrigo → el abrigo de ella   her coat

Possessive Adjectives *continued*

Strong forms

WITH SING. NOUN		WITH PLUR. NOUN		
MASC.	FEM.	MASC.	FEM.	
mío	mía	míos	mías	my
tuyo	tuya	tuyos	tuyas	your
suyo	suya	suyos	suyas	his; her; its; your (of **Vd**)
nuestro	nuestra	nuestros	nuestras	our
vuestro	vuestra	vuestros	vuestras	your
suyo	suya	suyos	suyas	their; your (of **Vds**)

The strong forms agree in the same way as the weak forms
(see page 220)

The strong forms always follow the noun, and they are used:
- to translate the English *of mine, of yours*, etc → ❶
- to address people → ❷

Examples

1. Es un capricho suyo   It's a whim of hers
   un amigo nuestro   a friend of ours
   una revista tuya   a magazine of yours

2. Muy señor mío (in letters)   Dear Sir
   hija mía   my daughter
   ¡Dios mío!   My God!
   Amor mío   Darling/My love

Indefinite Adjectives

alguno(a)s	some
ambos(as)	both
cada	each; every
cierto(a)s	certain; definite
cualquiera plural cualesquiera	some; any
los (las) demás	the others; the remainder
mismo(a)s	same; -self
mucho(a)s	many; much
ningún, ninguna plural ningunos, ningunas	any; no
otro(a)s	other; another
poco(a)s	few; little
tal(es)	such (a)
tanto(a)s	so much; so many
todo(a)s	all; every
varios(as)	several; various

Unless invariable, all indefinite adjectives agree in number and gender with the noun → ❶

alguno
Before a masculine singular noun, this drops the final **-o** and adds an accent to show the correct position for stress → ❷ (see also page 296)

ambos
This is usually only used in written Spanish. The spoken language prefers the form **los dos/las dos** → ❸

cierto and **mismo**
These change their meaning according to their position in relation to the noun (see also Position of Adjectives, page 228) → ❹

cualquiera
This drops the final **-a** before a masculine or feminine noun → ❺

Examples

1 el mismo día   the same day
las mismas películas   the same films
mucha/poca gente   many/few people
mucho/poco dinero   much/little money

2 algún día   some day
alguna razón   some reason

3 Me gustan los dos cuadros   I like both pictures
¿Conoces a las dos enfermeras?   Do you know both nurses?

4 cierto tiempo   a certain time
BUT:
éxito cierto   sure success
el mismo color   the same colour
BUT:
en la iglesia misma   in the church itself

5 cualquier casa   any house
BUT:
una revista cualquiera   any magazine

Indefinite Adjectives *continued*

ningún is only used in negative sentences or phrases → **1**

otro is never preceded by an indefinite article → **2**

tal is never followed by an indefinite article → **3**

todo can be followed by a definite article, a demonstrative or possessive adjective or a place name → **4**

    EXCEPTIONS:
- when **todo** in the singular means any, every, or each → **5**
- in some set expressions → **6**

Examples

1 No es ninguna tonta — She's no fool
¿No tienes parientes? — Haven't you any relatives?
— No, ninguno — — No, none

2 ¿Me das otra manzana? — Will you give me another apple?
Prefiero estos otros zapatos — I prefer these other shoes

3 Nunca dije tal cosa — I never said such a thing

4 Estudian durante toda la noche — They study all night
Ha llovido toda esta semana — It has rained all this week
Pondré en orden todos mis libros — I'll sort out all my books
Lo sabe todo Madrid — All Madrid knows it

5 Podrá entrar toda persona que — Any person who wishes to enter
 lo desee — may do so
BUT:
Vienen todos los días — They come every day

6 de todos modos — anyway
a toda velocidad — at full/top speed
por todas partes ⎤
por todos lados ⎟
a/en todas partes ⎟ everywhere
a/en todos lados ⎦

Position of Adjectives

Spanish adjectives usually follow the noun → ❶, ❷

Note that when used figuratively or to express a quality already inherent in the noun, adjectives can precede the noun → ❸

As in English, demonstrative, possessive (weak forms), numerical, interrogative and exclamatory adjectives precede the noun → ❹

Indefinite adjectives also usually precede the noun → ❺

> ⓘ Note: **alguno** *some* in negative expressions follows the noun → ❻

Some adjectives can precede or follow the noun, but their meaning varies according to their position:

	BEFORE NOUN	AFTER NOUN
antiguo	former	old, ancient → ❼
diferente	various	different → ❽
grande	great	big → ❾
medio	half	average → ❿
mismo	same	-self, very/precisely → ⑪
nuevo	new, another, fresh	brand new → ⑫
pobre	poor (wretched)	poor (not rich) → ⑬
puro	sheer, mere	pure (clear) → ⑭
varios	several	various, different → ⑮
viejo	old (long known, etc)	old (aged) → ⑯

Adjectives following the noun are linked by **y** → ⑰

Examples

1. la página siguiente — the following page
   la hora exacta — the right time

2. una corbata azul — a blue tie
   una palabra española — a Spanish word

3. un dulce sueño — a sweet dream
   un terrible desastre — a terrible disaster
   (*all disasters are terrible*)

4. este sombrero — this hat
   mi padre — my father
   ¿qué hombre? — what man?

5. cada día — every day
   otra vez — another time
   poco dinero — little money

6. sin duda alguna — without any doubt

7. un antiguo colega — a former colleague
   la historia antigua — ancient history

8. diferentes capítulos — various chapters
   personas diferentes — different people

9. un gran pintor — a great painter
   una casa grande — a big house

10. medio melón — half a melon
    velocidad media — average speed

11. la misma respuesta — the same answer
    yo mismo — myself
    eso mismo — precisely that

12. mi nuevo coche — my new car
    unos zapatos nuevos — (some) brand new shoes

13. esa pobre mujer — that poor woman
    un país pobre — a poor country

14. la pura verdad — the plain truth
    aire puro — fresh air

15. varios caminos — several ways/paths
    artículos varios — various items

16. un viejo amigo — an old friend
    esas toallas viejas — those old towels

17. una acción cobarde y falsa — a cowardly, deceitful act

Personal Pronouns

	SUBJECT PRONOUNS		
	SINGULAR	PLURAL	
1st person	**yo** I	**nosotros** we	*(masc./masc. + fem.)*
		nosotras we	*(all fem.)*
2nd person	**tú** you	**vosotros** you	*(masc./masc. + fem.)*
		vosotras you	*(all fem.)*
3rd person	**él** he; it	**ellos** they	*(masc./masc. + fem.)*
	ella she; it	**ellas** they	*(all fem.)*
	usted (Vd) you	**ustedes (Vds)** you	

Subject pronouns have a limited usage in Spanish. Normally they are only used:

- for emphasis → **❶**
- for clarity → **❷**

BUT: **Vd** and **Vds** should always be used for politeness, whether they are otherwise needed or not → **❸**

It as subject and *they*, referring to things, are never translated into Spanish → **❹**

tú/usted
As a general rule, you should use **tú** (or **vosotros**, if plural) when addressing a friend, a child, a relative, someone you know well, or when invited to do so. In all other cases, use **usted** (or **ustedes**).

nosotros/as; vosotros/as; él/ella; ellos/ellas
All these forms reflect the number and gender of the noun(s) they replace. **Nosotros**, **vosotros** and **ellos** also replace a combination of masculine and feminine nouns.

Examples

1. Ellos sí que llegaron tarde
   Tú no tienes por qué venir

   Ella jamás creería eso

   They really did arrive late
   There is no reason for you to come

   She would never believe that

2. Yo estudio español pero él estudia francés
   Ella era muy deportista pero él prefería jugar a las cartas
   Vosotros saldréis primero y nosotros os seguiremos

   I study Spanish but he studies French
   She was a sporty type but he preferred to play cards
   You leave first and we will follow you

3. Pase Vd por aquí
   ¿Habían estado Vds antes en esta ciudad?

   Please come this way
   Had you been to this town before?

4. ¿Qué es? — Es una sorpresa
   ¿Qué son? — Son abrelatas

   What is it? — It's a surprise
   What are they? — They are tin-openers

Personal Pronouns *continued*

	DIRECT OBJECT PRONOUNS	
	SINGULAR	PLURAL
1st person	**me** me	**nos** us
2nd person	**te** you	**os** you
3rd person (*masc.*)	**lo** him; it; you (of **Vd**)	**los** them; you (of **Vds**)
(*fem.*)	**la** her; it; you (of **Vd**)	**las** them; you (of **Vds**)

lo sometimes functions as a 'neuter' pronoun, referring to an idea or information contained in a previous statement or question. It is often not translated → ❶

Position of direct object pronouns

In constructions other than the imperative affirmative, infinitive or gerund, the pronoun always comes before the verb → ❷

> In the imperative affirmative, infinitive and gerund, the pronoun follows the verb and is attached to it. An accent is needed in certain cases to show the correct position for stress (see also page 296) → ❸

Where an infinitive or gerund depends on a previous verb, the pronoun may be used either after the infinitive or gerund, or before the main verb → ❹

> ⓘ Note: see how this applies to reflexive verbs → ❹

For further information, see Order of Object Pronouns, page 236.

Reflexive Pronouns

These are dealt with under reflexive verbs, page 24.

① ¿Va a venir María? — No lo sé   Is Maria coming? — I don't know
Hay que regar las plantas   The plants need watering
— Yo lo haré   — I'll do it
Habían comido ya pero no nos   They had already eaten, but they
lo dijeron   didn't tell us
Yo conduzco de prisa pero él lo   I drive fast but he drives slowly
hace despacio

② Te quiero   I love you
¿Las ve Vd?   Can you see them?
¿No me oyen Vds?   Can't you hear me?
Tu hija no nos conoce   Your daughter doesn't know us
No los toques   Don't touch them

③ Ayúdame   Help me
Acompáñenos   Come with us
Quiero decirte algo   I want to tell you something
Estaban persiguiéndonos   They were coming after us

④ Lo está comiendo or   She is eating it
Está comiéndolo
Nos vienen a ver or   They are coming to see us
Vienen a vernos
No quería levantarse or   He didn't want to get up
No se quería levantar
Estoy afeitándome or   I'm shaving
Me estoy afeitando

Personal Pronouns *continued*

	INDIRECT OBJECT PRONOUNS	
	SINGULAR	PLURAL
1st person	me	nos
2nd person	te	os
3rd person	le	les

The pronouns shown in the above table replace the preposition **a** + noun → ①

Position of indirect object pronouns

In constructions other than the imperative affirmative, the infinitive or the gerund, the pronoun comes before the verb → ②

In the imperative affirmative, infinitive and gerund, the pronoun follows the verb and is attached to it. An accent is needed in certain cases to show the correct position for stress (see also page 296) → ③

Where an infinitive or gerund depends on a previous verb, the pronoun may be used either after the infinitive or gerund, or before the main verb → ④

For further information, see Order of Object Pronouns, page 236.

Reflexive Pronouns

These are dealt with under reflexive verbs, page 24.

Examples

① Estoy escribiendo a Teresa — I am writing to Teresa
Le estoy escribiendo — I am writing to her
Da de comer al gato — Give the cat some food
Dale de comer — Give it some food

② Sofía os ha escrito — Sophie has written to you
¿Os ha escrito Sofía? — Has Sophie written to you?
Carlos no nos habla — Charles doesn't speak to us
¿Qué te pedían? — What were they asking you for?
No les haga caso Vd — Don't take any notice of them

③ Respóndame Vd — Answer me
Díganos Vd la respuesta — Tell us the answer
No quería darte la noticia todavía — I didn't want to tell you the news yet
Llegaron diciéndome que ... — They came telling me that ...

④ Estoy escribiéndole or — I am writing to him/her
Le estoy escribiendo
Les voy a hablar or — I'm going to talk to them
Voy a hablarles

Personal Pronouns *continued*

Order of object pronouns

When two object pronouns of different persons are combined, the order is: indirect before direct, i.e.

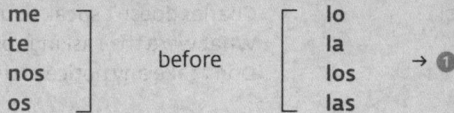

ⓘ Note: When two 3rd person object pronouns are combined, the first (i.e. the indirect object pronoun) becomes **se** → ❷

Points to note on object pronouns

As **le/les** can refer to either gender, and **se** to either gender, singular or plural, sometimes clarification is needed. This is done by adding **a él** *to him*, **a ella** *to her*, **a Vd** *to you* etc to the phrase, usually after the verb → ❸

When a noun object precedes the verb, the corresponding object pronoun must be used too → ❹

Indirect object pronouns are often used instead of possessive adjectives with parts of the body or clothing to indicate 'ownership', and also in certain common constructions involving reflexive verbs (see also The Indefinite Article, page 202) → ❺

Le and **les** are often used in Spanish instead of **lo** and **los** when referring to people. Equally **la** is sometimes used instead of **le** when referring to a feminine person or animal, although this usage is considered incorrect by some speakers of Spanish → ❻

Examples

1 Paloma os lo mandará mañana — Paloma is sending it to you tomorrow

¿Te los ha enseñado mi hermana? — Has my sister shown them to you?

No me lo digas — Don't tell me (that)

Todos estaban pidiéndotelo — They were all asking you for it

No quiere prestárnosla — He won't lend it to us

2 Se lo di ayer — I gave it to him/her/them yesterday

3 Le escriben mucho a ella — They write to her often

Se lo van a mandar pronto a ellos — They will be sending it to them soon

4 A tu hermano lo conozco bien — I know your brother well

A María la vemos algunas veces — We sometimes see Maria

5 La chaqueta le estaba ancha — His jacket was too loose

Me duele el tobillo — My ankle is aching

Se me ha perdido el bolígrafo — I have lost my pen

6 Le/lo encontraron en el cine — They met him at the cinema

Les/los oímos llegar — We heard them coming

Le/la escribimos una carta — We wrote a letter to her

Personal Pronouns *continued*

Pronouns after prepositions

These are the same as the subject pronouns, except for the forms
mí me, **ti** you (*singular*), and the reflexive **sí** himself, herself, themselves,
yourselves → ❶

Con with combines with **mí**, **ti** and **sí** to form

conmigo	with me → ❷
contigo	with you
consigo	with himself/herself *etc*

The following prepositions always take a subject pronoun:

entre	between, among → ❸
hasta ⎤	
incluso ⎦	even, including → ❹
salvo ⎤	
menos ⎦	except → ❺
según	according to → ❻

These pronouns are used for emphasis, especially where contrast is
involved → ❼

Ello it, that is used after a preposition when referring to an idea already
mentioned, but never to a concrete noun → ❼

A él, de él never contract → ❾

Examples

1. Pienso en ti   I think about you
   ¿Son para mí?   Are they for me?
   Es para ella   This is for her
   Iban hacia ellos   They were going towards them
   Volveréis sin nosotros   You'll come back without us
   Volaban sobre vosotros   They were flying above you
   Hablaba para si   He was talking to himself

2. Venid conmigo   Come with me
   Lo trajeron consigo   They brought it/him with them
   BUT:
   ¿Hablaron con vosotros?   Did they talk to you?

3. entre tú y ella   between you and her

4. Hasta yo puedo hacerlo   Even I can do it

5. todos menos yo   everybody except me

6. según tú   according to you

7. ¿A ti no te escriben?   Don't they write to you?
   Me lo manda a mí, no a ti   She is sending it to me, not to you

8. Nunca pensaba en ello   He never thought about it
   Por todo ello me parece que ...   For all those reasons it seems to me that ...

9. A él no lo conozco   I don't know him
   No he sabido nada de él   I haven't heard from him

Indefinite Pronouns

algo	something, anything → ①
alguien	somebody, anybody → ②
alguno/a/os/as	some, a few → ③
cada uno/a	each (one) → ④
	everybody
cualquiera	anybody; any → ⑤
los/las demás	the others
	the rest → ⑥
mucho/a/os/as	many; much → ⑦
nada	nothing → ⑧
nadie	nobody → ⑨
ninguno/a	none, not any → ⑩
poco/a/os/as	few; little → ⑪
tanto/a/os/as	so much; so many → ⑫
todo/a/os/as	all; everything → ⑬
uno ... (el) otro	(the) one ... the other
una ... (la) otra	
	→ ⑭
unos ... (los) otros	some ... (the) others
unas ... (las) otras	
varios/as	several → ⑮

algo, alguien, alguno

They can never be used after a negative. The appropriate negative pronouns are used instead: **nada**, **nadie**, **ninguno** (see also negatives, page 276) → ⑯

Examples

1	Tengo algo para ti	I have something for you
	¿Viste algo?	Did you see anything?
2	Alguien me lo ha dicho	Somebody said it to me
	¿Has visto a alguien?	Have you seen anybody?
3	Algunos de los niños ya sabían leer	Some of the children could read already
4	Le dió una manzana a cada uno	She gave each of them an apple
	!Cada uno a su casa!	Everybody go home!
5	Cualquiera puede hacerlo	Anybody can do it
	Cualquiera de las explicaciones vale	Any of the explanations is a valid one
6	Yo me fui, los demás se quedaron	I went, the others stayed
7	Muchas de las casas no tenían jardín	Many of the houses didn't have a garden
8	¿Qué tienes en la mano?	What have you got in your hand?
	— Nada	— Nothing
9	¡A quién ves? — A nadie	Who can you see? — Nobody
10	¿Cuántas tienes? — Ninguna	How many have you got? — None
11	Había muchos cuadros, pero vi pocos que me gustaran	There were many pictures, but I saw few I liked
12	¿Se oía mucho ruido? — No tanto	Was it very noisy? — Not so very
13	Lo ha estropeado todo	He has spoiled everything
	Todo va bien	All is going well
14	Unos cuestan 30 euros, los otros 40 euros	Some cost 30 euros, the others 40 euros
15	Varios de ellos me gustaron mucho	I liked several of them very much
16	Veo a alguien	I can see somebody
	No veo a nadie	I can't see anybody
	Tengo algo que hacer	I have something to do
	No tengo nada que hacer	I don't have anything to do

Relative Pronouns

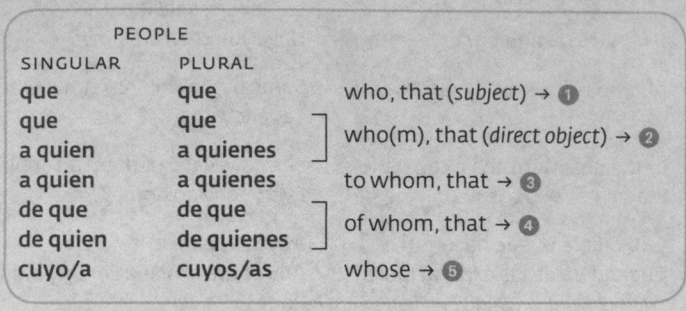

PEOPLE		
SINGULAR	PLURAL	
que	que	who, that (*subject*) → ❶
que	que	who(m), that (*direct object*) → ❷
a quien	a quienes	
a quien	a quienes	to whom, that → ❸
de que	de que	of whom, that → ❹
de quien	de quienes	
cuyo/a	cuyos/as	whose → ❺

THINGS	
SINGULAR AND PLURAL	
que	which, that (*subject*) → ❻
que	which, that (*direct object*) → ❼
a que	to which, that → ❽
de que	of which, that → ❾
cuyo	whose → ❿

ⓘ Note: These forms can also refer to people.

cuyo agrees with the noun it accompanies, not with the owner → ❺/❿

You cannot omit the relative pronoun in Spanish as you can in English → ❷/❼

❶	Mi hermano, que tiene veinte años, es el más joven	My brother, who is twenty, is the youngest
❷	Los amigos que más quiero son ...	The friends (that) I like best are ...
	María, a quien Daniel admira tanto, es ...	Maria, whom Daniel admires so much, is ...
❸	Mis abogados, a quienes he escrito hace poco, están ...	My lawyers, to whom I wrote recently, are ...
❹	La chica de que te hablé llega mañana	The girl (that) I told you about is coming tomorrow
	los niños de quienes se ocupa Vd	the children (that) you look after
❺	Vendrá la mujer cuyo hijo está enfermo	The woman whose son is ill will be coming
❻	Hay una escalera que lleva a la buhardilla	There's a staircase which leads to the loft
❼	La casa que hemos comprado tiene ...	The house (which) we've bought has ...
	Este es el regalo que me ha mandado mi amiga	This is the present (that) my friend has sent to me
❽	la tienda a que siempre va	the shop (which) she always goes to
❾	las injusticias de que se quejan	the injustices (that) they're complaining about
❿	la ventana cuyas cortinas están corridas	the window whose curtains are drawn

Relative Pronouns *continued*

el cual, el que
These are used when the relative is separated from the word it refers to, or when it would otherwise be unclear which word it referred to. The pronouns always agree in number and gender with the noun → ❶

> **El cual** may also be used when the verb in the relative clause is separated from the relative pronoun → ❷

lo que, lo cual
The neuter form **lo** is normally used when referring to an idea, statement or abstract noun. In certain expressions, the form **lo cual** may also be used as the subject of the relative clause → ❸

Relative pronouns after prepositions

Que and **quienes** are generally used after the prepositions:

a	to	→ ❹
con	with	→ ❺
de	from, about, of	→ ❻
en	in, on, into	→ ❼

It should be noted that **en que** can sometimes be translated by:
- *where*. In this case it can also be replaced by **en donde** or **donde** → ❽
- *when*. Sometimes here it can be replaced by **cuando** → ❾

El que or **el cual** are used after other prepositions, and they always agree → ❿

Examples

1. El padre de Elena, el cual tiene mucho dinero, es ...

   Elena's father, who has a lot of money, is ...

   (el cual *is used here since* que *or* quien *might equally refer to Elena*)

   Su hermana, a la cual/la que hacía mucho que no veía, estaba también allí

   His sister, whom I hadn't seen for a long time, was also there

2. Vieron a su tío, el cual, después de levantarse, salió

   They saw their uncle, who, after having got up, went out

3. No sabe lo que hace

   He doesn't know what he is doing

   Lo que dijiste fue una tontería

   What you said was foolish

   Todo estaba en silencio, lo que (*or* lo cual) me pareció muy raro

   All was silent, which I thought most odd

4. las tiendas a (las) que íbamos

   the shops we used to go to

5. la chica con quien (*or* la que) sale

   the girl he's going out with

6. el libro de(l) que te hablé

   the book I told you about

7. el lío en (el) que te has metido

   the trouble you've got yourself into

8. el sitio en que (en donde/donde) se escondía

   the place where he/she was hiding

9. el año en que naciste

   the year (when) you were born

10. el puente debajo del que/cual pasa el río

    the bridge under which the river flows

    las obras por las cuales/que es famosa

    the plays for which she is famous

Relative Pronouns *continued*

el que, la que; los que, las que
These mean *the one(s) who/which, those who* → ❶

> ⓘ Note: **quien(es)** can replace **el que** *etc* when used in a general sense → ❷

todos los que, todas las que
These mean *all who, all those/the ones which* → ❸

todo lo que
This translates *all that, everything that* → ❹

el de, la de; los de, las de
These can mean:
- *the one(s) of, that/those of* → ❺
- *the one(s) with* → ❻

Examples

① Esa película es la que quiero ver
That film is the one I want to see

¿Te acuerdas de ese amigo?
Do you remember that friend?

El que te presenté ayer
The one I introduced you to yesterday

Los que quieran entrar tendrán que pagar
Those who want to go in will have to pay

② Quien (or el que) llegue antes ganará el premio
He who arrives first will win the prize

③ Todos los que salían iban de negro
All those who were coming out were dressed in black

¿Qué autobuses puedo tomar?
Which buses can I take?

– Todos los que pasen por aquí
– Any (All those) that come this way

④ Quiero saber todo lo que ha pasado
I want to know all that has happened

⑤ Trae la foto de tu novio y la de tu hermano
Bring the photo of your boyfriend and the one of your brother

Viajamos en mi coche y en el de María
We travelled in my car and Maria's

Te doy estos libros y también los de mi hermana
I'll give you these books and my sister's too

⑥ Tu amigo, el de las gafas, me lo contó
Your friend, the one with glasses, told me

Interrogative Pronouns

¿qué? what?; which?
¿cuál(es)? which?; what?
¿quién(es)? who?

qué

It always translates *what* → **1**

ⓘ Note: **por** + **qué** is normally translated by *why* → **2**

cuál

It normally implies a choice, and translates *which* → **3**

ⓘ EXCEPT: when no choice is implied or more specific information is required → **4**

ⓘ Note: Whilst the pronoun **qué** can also work as an adjective, **cuál** only works as a pronoun → **5**

quién

SUBJECT *or* AFTER PREPOSITION	**quién(es)**	who → **6**
OBJECT	**a quién(es)**	whom → **7**
	de quién(es)	whose → **8**

All the forms shown above are also used in indirect questions → **9**

Examples

① ¿Qué estan haciendo?   What are they doing?
¿Qué dices?   What are you saying?
¿Para qué lo quieres?   What do you want it for?

② ¿Por qué no llegaron Vds antes?   Why didn't you arrive earlier?

③ ¿Cuál de estos vestidos te gusta más?   Which of these dresses do you like best?
¿Cuáles viste?   Which ones did you see?

④ ¿Cuál es la capital de España?   What is the capital of Spain?
¿Cuál es tu consejo?   What is your advice?
¿Cuál es su fecha de nacimiento?   What is your date of birth?

⑤ ¿Qué libro es más interesante?   Which book is more interesting?
¿Cuál (de estos libros) es más interesante?   Which (of these books) is more interesting?

⑥ ¿Quién ganó la carrera?   Who won the race?
¿Con quiénes los viste?   Who did you see them with?

⑦ ¿A quiénes ayudaste?   Who(m) did you help?
¿A quién se lo diste?   Who did you give it to?

⑧ ¿De quién es este libro?   Whose is this book?

⑨ Le pregunté para qué lo quería   I asked him/her what he/she wanted it for

No me dijeron cuáles preferían   They didn't tell me which ones they preferred

No sabía a quién acudir   I didn't know who to turn to

Possessive Pronouns

These are the same as the strong forms of the possessive adjectives, but they are always accompanied by the definite article.

Singular:

MASCULINE	FEMININE	
el mío	la mía	mine
el tuyo	la tuya	yours (of **tú**)
el suyo	la suya	his; hers; its; yours (of **Vd**)
el nuestro	la nuestra	ours
el vuestro	la vuestra	yours (of **vosotros**)
el suyo	la suya	theirs; yours (of **Vds**)

Plural:

MASCULINE	FEMININE	
los míos	las mías	mine
los tuyos	las tuyas	yours (of **tú**)
los suyos	las suyas	his; hers; its; yours (of **Vd**)
los nuestros	las nuestras	ours
los vuestros	las vuestras	yours (of **vosotros**)
los suyos	las suyas	theirs; yours (of **Vds**)

The pronoun agrees in number and gender with the noun it replaces, not with the owner → **1**

Alternative translations are 'my own', 'your own' *etc* → **2**

After the prepositions **a** and **de** the article **el** is contracted in the normal way (see page 200):

> a + el mío → al mío → **3**
> de + el mío → del mío → **4**

Examples

① Pregunta a Cristina si este bolígrafo es el suyo

Ask Christine if this pen is hers

¿Qué equipo ha ganado, el suyo o el nuestro?

Which team won – theirs or ours?

Mi perro es más joven que el tuyo

My dog is younger than yours

Daniel pensó que esos libros eran los suyos

Daniel thought those books were his

Si no tienes discos, te prestaré los míos

If you don't have any records, I'll lend you mine

Las habitaciones son menos amplias que las vuestras

The rooms are smaller than yours

② ¿Es su familia tan grande como la tuya?

Is his/her/their family as big as your own?

Sus precios son más bajos que los nuestros

Their prices are lower than our own

③ ¿Por qué prefieres este sombrero al mío?

Why do you prefer this hat to mine?

Su coche se parece al vuestro

His/her/their car looks like yours

④ Mi libro está encima del tuyo

My book is on top of yours

Su padre vive cerca del nuestro

His/her/their father lives near ours

Demonstrative Pronouns

	MASCULINE	FEMININE	NEUTER	
SING.	éste	ésta	esto	this
	ése	ésa	eso	that
	aquél	aquélla	aquello	
PLUR.	éstos	éstas		these
	ésos	ésas		those
	aquéllos	aquéllas		

The pronoun agrees in number and gender with the noun it replaces → ❶

The difference in meaning between the forms **ése** and **aquél** is the same as between the corresponding adjectives (see page 216).

The masculine and feminine forms have an accent, which is the only thing that differentiates them from the corresponding adjectives.

The neuter forms always refer to an idea or a statement or to an object when we want to identify it, etc, but never to specified nouns → ❷

An additional meaning of **aquél** is *the former*, and of **éste** *the latter* → ❸

Examples

1 ¿Qué abrigo te gusta más?
— Éste de aquí
Aquella casa era más grande
que ésta
estos libros y aquéllos

Quiero estas sandalias y ésas

Which coat do you like best?
— This one here
That house was bigger than
this one
these books and those (over
there)
I'd like these sandals and those
ones

2 No puedo creer que esto me
esté pasando a mí
Eso de madrugar es algo que
no le gusta

Aquello sí que me gustó
Esto es una bicicleta

I can't believe this is really
happening to me
(This business of) getting up
early is something she doesn't
like
I really did like that
This is a bicycle

3 Hablaban Jaime y Andrés, éste a
voces y aquél casi en un susurro

James and Andrew were talking,
the latter in a loud voice and
the former almost in a whisper

Adverbs

Formation

Most adverbs are formed by adding **-mente** to the feminine form of the adjective. Accents on the adjective are not affected since the suffix **-mente** is stressed independently → ①

> ⓘ Note: **-mente** is omitted:
> - in the first of two or more of these adverbs when joined by a conjunction → ②
> - in **recientemente** *recently* when immediately preceding a past participle → ③
>   An accent is then needed on the last syllable (see page 296)

The following adverbs are formed in an irregular way:

bueno	→	**bien**
good		well
malo	→	**mal**
bad		badly

Adjectives used as adverbs

Certain adjectives are used adverbially. These include:
alto, **bajo**, **barato**, **caro**, **claro**, **derecho**, **fuerte** and **rápido** → ④

> ⓘ Note: Other adjectives used as adverbs agree with the subject, and can normally be replaced by the adverb ending in **-mente** or an adverbial phrase → ⑤

Position of adverbs

When the adverb accompanies a verb, it may either immediately follow it or precede it for emphasis → ⑥

> ⓘ Note: The adverb can never be placed between **haber** and the past participle in compound tenses → ⑦

When the adverb accompanies an adjective or another adverb, it generally precedes the adjective or adverb → ⑧

Examples

1 FEM ADJECTIVE

lenta slow	lentamente slowly
franca frank	francamente frankly
feliz happy	felizmente happily
fácil easy	fácilmente easily

ADVERB

2 Lo hicieron lenta pero eficazmente — They did it slowly but efficiently

3 El pan estaba recién hecho — The bread had just been baked

4
hablar alto/bajo	to speak loudly/softly
cortar derecho	to cut (in a) straight (line)
costar barato/caro	to be cheap/expensive
Habla muy fuerte	He talks very loudly
ver claro	to see clearly
correr rápido	to run fast

5
Esperaban impacientes (or impacientemente/ con impaciencia)	They were waiting impatiently
Vivieron muy felices (or muy felizmente)	They lived very happily

6
No conocemos aún al nuevo médico	We still haven't met the new doctor
Aún estoy esperando	I'm still waiting
Han hablado muy bien	They have spoken very well
Siempre le regalaban flores	They always gave her flowers

7
Lo he hecho ya	I've already done it
No ha estado nunca en Italia	She's never been to Italy

8
un sombrero muy bonito	a very nice hat
hablar demasiado alto	to talk too loud
mañana temprano	early tomorrow
hoy mismo	today

Comparatives and Superlatives

Comparatives

These are formed using the following constructions:

más ... (que) more ... (than) → ❶
menos ... (que) less ... (than) → ❷
tanto como as much as → ❸
tan ... como as ... as → ❹
tan ... que so ... that → ❺
demasiado ... para too ... to → ❻
(lo) bastante ...
(lo) suficientemente ... ⎤ **para** enough to → ❼
cada vez más/menos more and more/less and less → ❽

Superlatives

These are formed by placing **más/menos** *the most/the least* before the adverb → ❾

lo is added before a superlative which is qualified → ❿

The absolute superlative (*very, most, extremely* + adverb) is formed by placing **muy** before the adverb. The form **-ísimo** (see also page 296) is also occasionally found → ⓫

Adverbs with irregular comparatives/superlatives

ADVERB	COMPARATIVE	SUPERLATIVE
bien well	**mejor*** better	**(lo) mejor** (the) best
mal badly	**peor** worse	**(lo) peor** (the) worst
mucho a lot	**más** more	**(lo) más** (the) most
poco little	**menos** less	**(lo) menos** (the) least

* **más bien** also exists, meaning *rather* → ⓬

Examples

1 más de prisa   more quickly
más abiertamente   more openly
Mi hermana canta más fuerte que yo   My sister sings louder than me

2 menos fácilmente   less easily
menos a menudo   less often
Nos vemos menos frecuentemente que antes   We see each other less frequently than before

3 Daniel no lee tanto como Andrés   Daniel doesn't read as much as Andrew

4 Hágalo tan rápido como le sea posible   Do it as quickly as you can
Ganan tan poco como nosotros   They earn as little as we do

5 Llegaron tan pronto que tuvieron que esperarnos   They arrived so early that they had to wait for us

6 Es demasiado tarde para ir al cine   It's too late to go to the cinema

7 Eres (lo) bastante grande para hacerlo solo   You're old enough to do it by yourself

8 Me gusta el campo cada vez más   I like the countryside more and more

9 María es la que corre más rápido   María is the one who runs fastest
El que llegó menos tarde fue Miguel   Miguel was the one to arrive the least late

10 Lo hice lo más de prisa que pude   I did it as quickly as I could

11 muy lentamente   very slowly
tempranísimo   extremely early
muchísimo   very much

12 Era un hombre más bien bajito   He was a rather short man
Estaba más bien inquieta que impaciente   I was restless rather than impatient

Common Adverbs and their Usage

Some common adverbs:

bastante	enough; quite → ①
bien	well → ②
cómo	how → ③
cuánto	how much → ④
demasiado	too much; too → ⑤
más	more → ⑥
menos	less → ⑦
mucho	a lot; much → ⑧
poco	little, not much; not very → ⑨
siempre	always → ⑩
también	also, too → ⑪
tan	as → ⑫
tanto	as much → ⑬
todavía/aún	still; yet; even → ⑭
ya	already → ⑮

bastante, cuánto, demasiado, mucho, poco and **tanto** are also used as adjectives that agree with the noun they qualify (see indefinite adjectives, page 224 and interrogative adjectives, page 218)

1. Es bastante tarde — It's quite late

2. ¡Bien hecho! — Well done!

3. ¡Cómo me ha gustado! — How I liked it!

4. ¿Cuánto cuesta este libro? — How much is this book?

5. He comido demasiado — I've eaten too much
   Es demasiado caro — It's too expensive

6. Mi hermano trabaja más ahora — My brother works more now
   Es más tímida que Sofía — She is shyer than Sophie

7. Se debe beber menos — One must drink less
   Estoy menos sorprendida que tú — I'm less surprised than you are

8. ¿Lees mucho? — Do you read a lot?
   ¿Está mucho más lejos? — Is it much further?

9. Comen poco — They don't eat (very) much
   María es poco decidida — Maria is not very daring

10. Siempre dicen lo mismo — They always say the same (thing)

11. A mí también me gusta — I like it too

12. Ana es tan alta como yo — Ana is as tall as I am

13. Nos aburrimos tanto como vosotros — We got as bored as you did

14. Todavía/aún tengo dos — I've still got two
    Todavía/aún no han llegado — They haven't arrived yet
    Mejor aún/todavía — Even better

15. Ya lo he hecho — I've done it already

Prepositions

On the following pages you will find some of the most frequent uses
of prepositions in Spanish. Particular attention is paid to cases where
usage differs markedly from English. It is often difficult to give an English
equivalent for Spanish prepositions, since usage *does* vary so much
between the two languages. In the list below, the broad meaning of
the preposition is given on the left, with examples of usage following.
Prepositions are dealt with in alphabetical order, except **a**, **de**, **en** and **por**
which are shown first.

a

at	**echar algo a algn** to throw sth at sb
	a 50 euros el kilo (at) 50 euros a kilo
	a 100 km por hora at 100 km per hour
	sentarse a la mesa to sit down at the table
in	**al sol** in the sun
	a la sombra in the shade
onto	**cayeron al suelo** they fell onto the floor
	pegar una foto al álbum to stick a photo into the album
to	**ir al cine** to go to the cinema
	dar algo a algn to give sth to sb
	venir a hacer to come to do
from	**quitarle algo a algn** to take sth from sb
	robarle algo a algn to steal sth from sb
	arrebatarle algo a algn to snatch sth from sb
	comprarle algo a algn to buy sth from/for sb*
	esconderle algo a algn to hide sth from sb
means	**a mano** by hand
	a caballo on horseback
	(*but note other forms of transport used with* **en** *and* **por**)
	a pie on foot

*The translation here obviously depends on the context.

Prepositions

manner	**a la inglesa** in the English manner
	a pasos lentos with slow steps
	poco a poco little by little
	a ciegas blindly
time, date:	**a medianoche** at midnight
at, on	**a las dos y cuarto** at quarter past two
	a tiempo on time
	a final/fines de mes at the end of the month
	a veces at times
distance	**a 8 km de aquí** (at a distance of) 8 kms from here
	a dos pasos de mi casa just a step from my house
	a lo lejos in the distance
with el + infin.	**al levantarse** on getting up
	al abrir la puerta on opening the door
after certain adjectives	**dispuesto a todo** ready for anything
	parecido a esto similar to this
	obligado a ello obliged to (do) that
after certain verbs	see page 66

Personal a

When the direct object of a verb is a person or pet animal, **a** must always be placed immediately before it.

EXAMPLES: **querían mucho a sus hijos**
    they loved their children dearly
el niño miraba a su perro con asombro
    the boy kept looking at his dog in astonishment

EXCEPTIONS: **tener**
    to have
tienen dos hijos
    they have two children

261

de

from	**venir de Londres** to come from London
	un médico de Valencia a doctor from Valencia
	de la mañana a la noche from morning till night
	de 10 a 15 from 10 to 15
belonging to, of	**el sombrero de mi padre** my father's hat
	las lluvias de abril April showers
contents, composition, material	**una caja de cerillas** a box of matches
	una taza de té a cup of tea; a tea-cup
	un vestido de seda a silk dress
destined for	**una silla de cocina** a kitchen chair
	un traje de noche an evening dress
descriptive	**la mujer del sombrero verde** the woman with the green hat
	el vecino de al lad/lado the next door neighbour
manner	**de manera irregular** in an irregular way
	de una puñalada by stabbing
quality	**una mujer de edad** an aged lady
	objetos de valor valuable items
comparative + a number	**había más/menos de 100 personas** there were more/fewer than 100 people
in (*after superlatives*)	**la ciudad más/menos bonita del mundo** the most/least beautiful city in the world
after certain adjectives	**contento de ver** pleased to see
	fácil/difícil de entender easy/difficult to understand
	capaz de hacer capable of doing
after certain verbs	see page 66

Prepositions

en

in, at	**en el campo** in the country
	en Londres in London
	en la cama in bed
	con un libro en la mano with a book in his hand
	en voz baja in a low voice
	en la escuela in/at school
into	**entra en la casa** go into the house
	metió la mano en su bolso
	she put her hand into her handbag
on	**un cuadro en la pared** a picture on the wall
	sentado en una silla sitting on a chair
	en la planta baja on the ground floor
time, dates, months:	**en este momento** at this moment
at, in	**en 1994** in 1994
	en enero in January
transport:	**en coche** by car
by	**en avión** by plane
	en tren by train (but see also **por**)
language	**en español** in Spanish
duration	**lo haré en una semana** I'll do it in one week
after certain adjectives	**es muy buena/mala en geografía**
	she is very good/bad at geography
	fueron los primeros/últimos/únicos en + *infin.*
	they were the first/last/only ones + *infin.*
after certain verbs	see page 66

Prepositions

por

motion: along, through, around	**vaya por ese camino** go along that path **por el túnel** through the tunnel **pasear por el campo** to walk around the countryside
vague location	**tiene que estar por aquí** it's got to be somewhere around here **le busqué por todas partes** I looked for him everywhere
vague time	**por la tarde** in the afternoon **por aquellos días** in those days
rate	**90 km por hora** 90 km per hour **un cinco por ciento** five per cent **ganaron por 3 a 0** they won by 3 to 0
by (*agent of passive*)	**descubierto por unos niños** discovered by some children **odiado por sus enemigos** hated by his enemies
by (*means of*)	**por barco** by boat **por tren** by train (freight) **por correo aéreo** by airmail **llamar por teléfono** to telephone
cause, reason: for, because	**¿por qué?** why?, for what reason? **por todo eso** because of all that **por lo que he oído** judging by what I've heard
+ *infinitive:* to	**libros por leer** books to be read **cuentas por pagar** bills to be paid
equivalence	**¿me tienes por tonto?** do you think I'm stupid?
+ *adjective/*+ *adverb* + **que:** however	**por buenos que sean** however good they are **por mucho que lo quieras** however much you want it

Prepositions

for	**¿cuanto me darán por este libro?** how much will they give me for this book?
	te lo cambio por éste I'll swap you this one for it
	no siento nada por ti I feel nothing for you
	si no fuera por ti if it weren't for you
	¡Por Dios! For God's sake!
for the benefit of	**lo hago por ellos** I do it for their benefit
on behalf of	**firma por mí** sign on my behalf

por also combines with other prepositions to form double prepositions usually conveying the idea of movement. The commonest of these are:

over	**saltó por encima de la mesa** she jumped over the table
under	**nadamos por debajo del puente** we swam under the bridge
past	**pasaron por delante de Correos** they went past the post office
behind	**por detrás de la puerta** behind the door
through	**la luz entraba por entre las cortinas** light was coming in through the curtains
+ donde	**¿por dónde has venido?** which way did you come?

ante

faced with, before	**lo hicieron ante mis propios ojos** they did it before my very eyes
	ante eso no se puede hacer nada one can't do anything when faced with that
preference	**la salud ante todo** health above all things

antes de

before (*time*)	**antes de las 5** before 5 o'clock

bajo/debajo de

These are usually equivalent, although **bajo** is used more frequently in a figurative sense and with temperatures.

under	**bajo/debajo de la cama** under the bed
	bajo el dominio romano under Roman rule
below	**un grado bajo cero** one degree below zero

con

with	**vino con su amigo** she came with her friend
after certain adjectives	**enfadado con ellos** angry with them
	magnánimo con sus súbditos
	magnanimous with his subjects

contra

against	**no tengo nada contra ti** I've nothing against you
	apoyado contra la pared leaning against the wall

delante de

in front of	**iba delante de mí** she was walking in front of me

desde

from	**desde aquí se puede ver** you can see it from here
	llamaban desde España
	they were phoning from Spain
	desde otro punto de vista
	from a different point of view
	desde la 1 hasta las 6 from 1 till 6
	desde entonces from then onwards
since	**desde que volvieron** since they returned

for	**viven en esa casa desde hace 3 años**
	they've been living in that house for 3 years
	(*note tense*)

detrás de

| behind | **están detrás de la puerta** they are behind the door |

durante

| during | **durante la guerra** during the war |
| for | **anduvieron durante 3 días** they walked for 3 days |

entre

between	**entre 8 y 10** between 8 and 10
among	**María y Elena, entre otras**
	Maria and Elena, among others
reciprocal	**ayudarse entre sí** to help each other

excepto

| except (for) | **todos excepto tú** everybody except you |

hacia

towards	**van hacia ese edificio**
	they're going towards that building
around (*time*)	**hacia las 3** at around 3 (o'clock)
	hacia fines de enero around the end of January

Hacia can also combine with some adverbs to convey a sense of motion in a particular direction:

> **hacia arriba** upwards
> **hacia abajo** downwards
> **hacia adelante** forwards
> **hacia atrás** backwards
> **hacia adentro** inwards
> **hacia afuera** outwards

hasta

until	**hasta la noche** until night
as far as	**viajaron hasta Sevilla** they travelled as far as Seville
up to	**conté hasta 300 ovejas** I counted up to 300 lambs **hasta ahora no los había visto** up to now I hadn't seen them
even	**hasta un tonto lo entendería** even an imbecile would understand that

para

for	**es para ti** it's for you
	es para mañana it's for tomorrow
	una habitación para dos noches
	  a room for two nights
	para ser un niño, lo hace muy bien
	  for a child he is very good at it
	salen para Cádiz they are leaving for Cádiz
	se conserva muy bien para sus años
	  he keeps very well for his age

+ *infinitive*: (in order) to	**es demasiado torpe para comprenderlo** he's too stupid to understand
+ **sí**: to oneself	**hablar para sí** to talk to oneself **reír para sí** to laugh to oneself
with time	**todavía tengo para 1 hora** I'll be another hour (at it) yet

Prepositions

salvo

except (for)	**todos salvo él** all except him **salvo cuando llueve** except when it's raining
barring	**salvo imprevistos** barring the unexpected **salvo contraorden** unless you hear to the contrary

según

according to	**según su consejo** according to her advice **según lo que me dijiste** according to what you told me

sin

without	**sin agua/dinero** without water/money **sin mi marido** without my husband
+ *infinitive*	**sin contar a los otros** without counting the others

sobre

on	**sobre la cama** on the bed **sobre el armario** on (top of) the wardrobe
on (to)	**póngalo sobre la mesa** put it on the table
about, on	**un libro sobre Eva Perón** a book about Eva Perón
above, over	**volábamos sobre el mar** we were flying over the sea **la nube sobre aquella montaña** the cloud above that mountain
approximately	**vendré sobre las 4** I'll come about 4 o'clock
about	**Madrid tiene sobre 4 millones de habitantes** Madrid has about 4 million inhabitants

tras

behind	**está tras el asiento** it's behind the seat
after	**uno tras otro** one after another **día tras día** day after day **corrieron tras el ladrón** they ran after the thief

Conjunctions

There are conjunctions which introduce a main clause, such as **y** (*and*),
pero (*but*), **si** (*if*), **o** (*or*) etc, and those which introduce subordinate
clauses like **porque** (*because*), **mientras que** (*while*), **después de que**
(*after*) etc. They are all used in much the same way as in English, but the
following points are of note:

Some conjunctions in Spanish require a following subjunctive,
see pages 60 to 63.

Some conjunctions are 'split' in Spanish like 'both ... and',
'either ... or' in English:

tanto ... como both ... and → ❶
ni ... ni neither ... nor → ❷
o (bien) ... o (bien) either ... or (else) → ❸
sea ... sea either ... or, whether ... or → ❹

y
- Before words beginning with **i-** or **hi-** + consonant it becomes
  e → ❺

o
- Before words beginning with **o-** or **ho-** it becomes **u** → ❻
- Between numerals it becomes **ó** → ❼

que
- meaning *that* → ❽
- in comparisons, meaning *than* → ❾
- followed by the subjunctive, see page 58.

porque (Not to be confused with **por qué** *why*)
- como should be used instead at the beginning of a
  sentence → ❿

pero, sino
- pero normally translates *but* → ⓫
- sino is used when there is a direct contrast after a
  negative → ⓬

Examples

1 Estas flores crecen tanto
en verano como en invierno

These flowers grow in both
summer and winter

2 Ni él ni ella vinieron
No tengo ni dinero ni comida

Neither he nor she came
I have neither money nor food

3 Debe de ser o ingenua o tonta

She must be either naïve or
stupid

O bien me huyen o bien no me
reconocen

Either they're avoiding me or
else they don't recognize me

4 Sea en verano, sea en invierno,
siempre me gusta andar

I always like walking, whether
in summer or in winter

5 Diana e Isabel
madre e hija
BUT:
árboles y hierba

Diana and Isabel
mother and daughter

trees and grass

6 diez u once
minutos u horas

ten or eleven
minutes or hours

7 37 ó 38

37 or 38

8 Dicen que te han visto
¿Sabías que estábamos allí?

They say (that) they've seen you
Did you know that we were
there?

9 Le gustan más que nunca
María es menos guapa que su
hermana

He likes them more than ever
Maria is less attractive than her
sister

10 Como estaba lloviendo no
pudimos salir
(Compare with: No pudimos salir
porque estaba lloviendo)

Because/As it was raining we
couldn't go out

11 Me gustaría ir, pero estoy muy
cansada

I'd like to go, but I am very tired

12 No es escocesa sino irlandesa

She is not Scottish but Irish

271

Augmentative, Diminutive and Pejorative Suffixes

These can be used after nouns, adjectives and some adverbs. They are attached to the end of the word after any final vowel has been removed:

> e.g. puerta → puertita
> doctor → doctorcito

> ⓘ Note: Further changes sometimes take place (see page 300).

Augmentatives

These are used mainly to imply largeness, but they can also suggest clumsiness, ugliness or grotesqueness. The commonest augmentatives are:
ón/ona → ❶
azo/a → ❷
ote/a → ❸

Diminutives

These are used mainly to suggest smallness or to express a feeling of affection. Occasionally they can be used to express ridicule or contempt. The commonest diminutives are:
ito/a → ❹
(e)cito/a → ❺
(ec)illo/a → ❻
(z)uelo/a → ❼

Pejoratives

These are used to convey the idea that something is unpleasant or to express contempt. The commonest suffixes are:
ucho/a → ❽
acho/a → ❾
uzo/a → ❿
uco/a → ⑪
astro/a → ⑫

Examples

ORIGINAL WORD	DERIVED FORM
① un hombre a man	un hombrón a big man
② bueno good	buenazo (person) easily imposed on
un perro a dog	un perrazo a really big dog
gripe flu	un gripazo a really bad bout of flu
③ grande big	grandote huge
palabra word	palabrota swear word
amigo friend	amigote old pal
④ una casa a house	una casita a cottage
un poco a little	un poquito a little bit
un rato a while	un ratito a little while
mi hija my daughter	mi hijita my dear sweet daughter
despacio slowly	despacito nice and slowly
⑤ un viejo an old man	un viejecito a little old man
un pueblo a village	un pueblecito a small village
una voz a voice	una vocecita a sweet little voice
⑥ una ventana a window	una ventanilla a small window (car, train etc)
un chico a boy	un chiquillo a small boy
una campana a bell	una campanilla a small bell
un palo a stick	un palillo a toothpick
un médico a doctor	un mediquillo a quack (doctor)
⑦ los pollos the chickens	los polluelos the little chicks
hoyos hollows	hoyuelos dimples
un ladrón a thief	un ladronzuelo a petty thief
una mujer a woman	una mujerzuela a whore
⑧ un animal an animal	un animalucho a wretched animal
un cuarto a room	un cuartucho a poky little room
una casa a house	una casucha a shack
⑨ rico rich	ricacho nouveau riche
⑩ gente people	gentuza scum
⑪ una ventana a window	un ventanuco a miserable little window
⑫ un político a politician	un politicastro a third-rate politician

Word Order

Word order in Spanish is much more flexible than in English. You can often find the subject placed after the verb or the object before the verb, either for emphasis or for stylistic reasons → ❶

There are some cases, however, where the order is always different from English. Most of these have already been dealt with under the appropriate part of speech, but are summarized here along with other instances not covered elsewhere.

Object pronouns nearly always come before the verb → ❷
For details, see pages 232 to 235.

Qualifying adjectives nearly always come after the noun → ❸
For details, see page 228.

Following direct speech the subject always follows the verb → ❹

For word order in negative sentences, see page 276.

For word order in interrogative sentences, see page 280 → ❶

Examples

1. Ese libro te lo di yo   I gave you that book
   No nos vio nadie   Nobody saw us

2. Ya los veo   I can see them now
   Me lo dieron ayer   They gave it to me yesterday

3. Ya los veo   I can see them now
   Me lo dieron ayer   They gave it to me yesterday

4. una ciudad española   a Spanish town
   vino tinto   red wine

5. – Pienso que sí – dijo María   'I think so,' said Maria
   – No importa – replicó Daniel   'It doesn't matter,' Daniel replied

Negatives

A sentence is made negative by adding **no** between the subject and the verb (and any preceding object pronouns) → ❶

There are, however, some points to note:
- in phrases like *not her, not now,* etc the Spanish **no** usually comes after the word it qualifies → ❷
- with verbs of saying, hoping, thinking etc *not* is translated by **que no** → ❸

Double negatives

The following are the most common negative pairs:

> no ... **nada** nothing (*not ... anything*)
> no ... **nadie** nobody (*not ... anybody*)
> no ... **más** no longer (*not ... any more*)
> no ... **nunca** never (*not ... ever*)
> no ... **jamás** never (stronger) (*not ... ever*)
> no ... **más que** only (*not ... more than*)
> no ... **ningún(o)(a)** no (*not any*)
> no ... **tampoco** not ... either
> no ... **ni ... ni** neither ... nor
> no ... **ni siquiera** not even

Word order

No precedes the verb (and any object pronouns) in both simple and compound tenses, and the second element follows the verb → ❹

Sometimes the above negatives are placed before the verb (with the exception of **más** and **más que**), and **no** is then dropped → ❺

For use of **nada**, **nadie** and **ninguno** as pronouns, see page 240.

Examples

	AFFIRMATIVE		NEGATIVE

① El coche es suyo → El coche no es suyo
The car is his · The car is not his
Yo me lo pondré → Yo no me lo pondré
I will put it on · I will not put it on

② ¿Quién lo ha hecho? — Ella no · Who did it? — Not her
¿Quieres un cigarrillo? · Do you want a cigarette?
 — Ahora no · — Not now
Dame ese libro, el que está a tu · Give me that book, not the one
 lado no, el otro · near you, the other one

③ Opino que no · I think not
Dijeron que no · They said not

④ No dicen nada · They don't say anything
No han visto a nadie · They haven't seen anybody
No me veréis más · You won't see me any more
No te olvidaré nunca/jamás · I'll never forget you
No habían recorrido más que · They hadn't travelled more than
 40 kms cuando ... · 40 kms when ...
No se me ha ocurrido ninguna idea · I haven't had any ideas
No les estaban esperando ni mi · Neither my son nor my daughter
 hijo ni mi hija · were waiting for them
No ha venido ni siquiera Juan · Even John hasn't come

⑤ Nadie ha venido hoy · Nobody came today
Nunca me han gustado · I've never liked them
Ni mi hermano ni mi hermana · Neither my brother nor my sister
 fuman · smokes

Negatives *continued*

Negatives in short replies

No *no* is the usual negative response to a question → ①

> ⓘ Note: It is often translated as 'not' → ②
> (see also page 276)

Nearly all the other negatives listed on page 276 may be used without a verb in a short reply → ③

Combination of negatives

These are the most common combinations of negative particles:
>   no ... nunca más → ④
>   no ... nunca a nadie → ⑤
>   no ... nunca nada/nada nunca → ⑥
>   no ... nunca más que → ⑦
>   no ... ni ... nunca ... → ⑧

Examples

1 ¿Quieres venir con nosotros?
— No

Do you want to come with us?
— No

2 ¿Vienes o no?

Are you coming or not?

3 ¿Ha venido alguien? — ¡Nadie!
¿Has ido al Japón alguna vez?
— Nunca

Has anyone come? — Nobody!
Have you ever been to Japan?
— Never

4 No lo haré nunca más

I'll never do it again

5 No se ve nunca a nadie por allí

You never see anybody around there

6 No cambiaron nada nunca

They never changed anything

7 No he hablado nunca más que con su mujer

I've only ever spoken to his wife

8 No me ha escrito ni llamado por teléfono nunca

He/she has never written to me or phoned me

Question Forms

Direct

There are two ways of forming direct questions in Spanish:

by inverting the normal word order so that
subject + verb → *verb + subject* → **1**

by maintaining the word order *subject + verb*, but by using a rising intonation at the end of the sentence → **2**

ⓘ Note: In compound tenses the auxiliary may never be separated from the past participle, as happens in English → **3**

Indirect

An indirect question is one that is 'reported', e.g. he asked me 'what the time was', tell me 'which way to go'. Word order in indirect questions can adopt one of the two following patterns:

interrogative word + subject + verb → **4**

interrogative word + verb + subject → **5**

¿verdad?, ¿no?

These are used wherever English would use 'isn't it?', 'don't they?', 'weren't we?', 'is it?' etc tagged on to the end of a sentence → **6**

sí

Sí is the word for 'yes' in answer to a question put either in the affirmative or in the negative → **7**

Examples

1 ¿Vendrá tu madre? — Will your mother come?
¿Lo trajo Vd? — Did you bring it?
¿Es posible eso? — Is it possible?
¿Cuándo volverán Vds? — When will you come back?

2 El gato, ¿se bebió toda la leche? — Did the cat drink up all his milk?
Andrés, ¿va a venir? — Is Andrew coming?

3 ¿Lo ha terminado Vd? — Have you finished it?
¿Había llegado tu amigo? — Had your friend arrived?

4 Dime qué autobuses pasan por aquí — Tell me which buses come this way
No sé cuántas personas vendrán — I don't know how many people will turn up

5 Me preguntó dónde trabajaba mi hermano — He asked me where my brother worked
No sabemos a qué hora empieza la película — We don't know what time the film starts

6 Hace calor, ¿verdad? — It's warm, isn't it?
No se olvidará Vd, ¿verdad? — You won't forget, will you?
Estaréis cansados, ¿no? — You will be tired, won't you?
Te lo dijo María, ¿no? — Maria told you, didn't she?

7 ¿Lo has hecho? — Sí — Have you done it? — Yes (I have)
¿No lo has hecho? — Sí — Haven't you done it? — Yes (I have)

Beware of translating word by word. While on occasions this is possible, quite often it is not. The need for caution is illustrated by the following:

English phrasal verbs (i.e. verbs followed by a preposition), e.g. 'to run away', 'to fall down', are often translated by one word in Spanish → ➊

English verbal constructions often contain a preposition where none exists in Spanish, or vice versa → ➋

Two or more prepositions in English may have a single rendering in Spanish → ➌

A word which is singular in English may be plural in Spanish, or vice versa → ➍

Spanish has no equivalent of the possessive construction denoted by ...'s/...s' → ➎

Problems

-ing

This is translated in a variety of ways in Spanish:

'to be ... -ing' can sometimes be translated by a simple tense (see also pages 54 to 56) → ➏
But, when a physical position is denoted, a past participle is used → ➐

in the construction 'to see/hear sb ... -ing', use an infinitive → ➑
'-ing' can also be translated by:
- an infinitive, see page 46 → ➒
- a perfect infinitive, see page 50 → ➓
- a gerund, see page 52 → ⑪
- a noun → ⑫

Examples

1. huir — to run away
   caerse — to fall down
   ceder — to give in

2. pagar — to pay for
   mirar — to look at
   escuchar — to listen to
   encontrarse con — to meet
   fijarse en — to notice
   servirse de — to use

3. extrañarse de — to be surprised at
   harto de — fed up with
   soñar con — to dream of
   contar con — to count on

4. unas vacaciones — a holiday
   sus cabellos — his/her hair
   la gente — people
   mi pantalón — my trousers

5. el coche de mi hermano — my brother's car
     (*literally*: ... of my brother)

   el cuarto de las niñas — the children's bedroom
     (*literally*: ... of the children)

6. Se va mañana — He/she is leaving tomorrow
   ¿Qué haces? — What are you doing?

7. Está sentado ahí — He is sitting over there
   Estaba tendida en el suelo — She was lying on the ground

8. Les veo venir — I can see them coming
   La he oído cantar — I've heard her singing

9. Me gusta ir al cine — I like going to the cinema

10. ¡Deja de hablar! — Stop talking!
    En vez de contestar — Instead of answering
    Antes de salir — Before leaving
    Después de haber abierto la caja, Maria ... — After opening the box, Maria ...

11. Pasamos la tarde fumando y charlando — We spent the afternoon smoking and chatting

12. El esquí me mantiene en forma — Skiing keeps me fit

to be (*See also Verbal Idioms*, pages 74 to 76)

In set expressions, describing physical and emotional conditions, **tener** is used:

> **tener calor/frío** to be warm/cold
> **tener hambre/sed** to be hungry/thirsty
> **tener miedo** to be afraid
> **tener razón** to be right

Describing the weather, e.g. 'what's the weather like?', 'it's windy/sunny', use **hacer** → ❶

For ages, e.g. 'he is 6', use **tener** (see also page 310) → ❷

there is/there are

Both are translated by **hay** → ❸

can, be able

Physical ability is expressed by **poder** → ❹

If the meaning is 'to know how to', use **saber** → ❺

'Can' + a 'verb of hearing or seeing etc' in English is not translated in Spanish → ❻

to

Generally translated by **a** → ❼

In time expressions, e.g. 10 to 6, use **menos** → ❽

When the meaning is 'in order to', use **para** → ❾

Following a verb, as in 'to try to do', 'to like to do', see pages 46 and 48.

'easy/difficult/impossible' etc 'to do' are translated by **fácil/difícil/imposible** etc **de hacer** → ❿

Examples

1.   ¿Qué tiempo hace?
    Hace bueno/malo/viento

    What's the weather like?
    It's lovely/miserable/windy

2.   ¿Cuántos años tienes?
    Tengo quince (años)

    How old are you?
    I'm fifteen

3.   Hay un señor en la puerta
    Hay cinco libros en la mesa

    There's a gentleman at the door
    There are five books on the table

4.   No puedo salir contigo

    I can't go out with you

5.   ¿Sabes nadar?

    Can you swim?

6.   No veo nada
    ¿Es que no me oyes?

    I can't see anything
    Can't you hear me?

7.   Dale el libro a Isabel

    Give the book to Isabel

8.   las diez menos cinco
    a las siete menos cuarto

    five to ten
    at a quarter to seven

9.   Lo hice para ayudaros
    Se inclinó para atarse el cordón
     de zapato

    I did it to help you
    He bent down to tie his
     shoe-lace

10. Este libro es fácil/difícil de leer

    This book is easy/difficult to read

must

When *must* expresses an assumption, **deber de** is often used → **1**

> ⓘ Note: This meaning is also often expressed by **deber** directly
> followed by the infinitive → **2**

When it expresses obligation, there are three possible translations:
- **tener que** → **3**
- **deber** → **4**
- **hay que** (impersonal) → **5**

may

If *may* expresses possibility, it can be translated by:
- **poder** → **6**
- **puede (ser) que** + *subjunctive*

To express permission, use **poder** → **7**

will

If *will* expresses willingness or desire rather than the future, the present
tense of **querer** is used → **8**

would

If *would* expresses willingness, use the preterite or imperfect of
querer → **9**

When a repeated or habitual action in the past is referred to, use
- the imperfect → **10**
- the imperfect of **soler** + *infinitive* → **11**

Examples

① Ha debido de mentir   He must have lied
Debe de gustarle   She must like it

② Debe estar por aquí cerca   It must be near here
Debo haberlo dejado en el tren   I must have left it on the train

③ Tenemos que salir temprano mañana   We must leave early tomorrow
Tengo que irme   I must go

④ Debo visitarles   I must visit them
Debéis escuchar lo que se os dice   You must listen to what is said to you

⑤ Hay que entrar por ese lado   One (We etc) must get in that way

⑥ Todavía puede cambiar de opinión   He may still change his mind
Creo que puede llover esta tarde   I think it may rain this afternoon
Puede (ser) que no lo sepa   She may not know

⑦ ¿Puedo irme?   May I go?
Puede sentarse   You may sit down

⑧ Quiere Vd esperar un momento, por favor?   Will you wait a moment, please?
No quiere ayudarme   He won't help me

⑨ No quisieron venir   They wouldn't come

⑩ Las miraba hora tras hora   She would watch them for hours on end

⑪ Últimamente solía comer muy poco   Latterly he would eat very little

Pronunciation of Vowels

Spanish vowels are always clearly pronounced and not relaxed in unstressed syllables as happens in English.

	EXAMPLES	HINTS ON PRONUNCIATION
[a]	casa	Between English *a* as in *hat* and *u* as in *hut*
[e]	pensar	Similar to English *e* in *pet*
[i]	filo	Between English *i* as in *pin* and *ee* as in *been*
[o]	loco	Similar to English *o* in *hot*
[u]	luna	Between English *ew* as in *few* and *u* as in *put*

Pronunciation of Diphthongs

All these diphthongs are shorter than similar English diphthongs.

[ai]	baile hay	Like *i* in *side*
[au]	causa	Like *ou* in *sound*
[ei]	peine rey	Like *ey* in *grey*
[eu]	deuda	Like the vowel sounds in English *may you*, but without the sound of the *y*
[oi]	boina voy	Like *oy* in *boy*

Semi-consonants

[j]	hacia ya tiene yeso labio yo	*i* following a consonant and preceding a vowel, and *y* preceding a vowel are pronounced as *y* inEnglish yet
[w]	agua bueno arduo ruido	*u* following a consonant and preceding a vowel is pronounced as *w* in English *walk*

EXCEPTIONS: **gue, gui** (see page 290)

Pronunciation

Pronunciation of Consonants

Some consonants are pronounced almost exactly as in English:
[l, m, n, f, k, and in some cases g].

Others, listed below, are similar to English, but differences should be noted.

	EXAMPLES	HINTS ON PRONUNCIATION
[p]	padre	They are not aspirated, unlike
[k]	coco	English *pot*, *cook* and *ten*.
[t]	tan	
[t]	todo tú	Pronounced with the tip of the
[d]	doy balde	tongue touching the upper front teeth and not the roof of the mouth as in English.

The following consonants are not heard in English:

[β]	labio	This is pronounced between upper and lower lips, which do not touch, unlike English *b* as in *bend*.
[ɣ]	haga	Similar to English *g* as in *gate*, but tongue does not touch the soft palate.
[ɲ]	año	Similar to *ni* in o*ni*on
[x]	jota	Like the guttural *ch* in lo*ch*
[ɾ]	pera	A single trill with the tip of the tongue against the teeth ridge.
[rr]	rojo perro	A multiple trill with the tip of the tongue against the teeth ridge.

From Spelling to Sounds

Note the pronunciation of the following (groups of) letters.

LETTER	PRONOUNCED	EXAMPLES
b,v	[b]	These letters have the same value. At the start of a breath group, and after written **m** and **n**, the sound is similar to English *boy* → ❶
	[β]	in all other positions, the sound is unknown in English (see page 289) → ❷
c	[k]	Before **a**, **o**, **u** or a consonant, like English *keep*, but not aspirated → ❸
	[θ/s]	Before **e**, **i** like English *thin*, or, in Latin America and parts of Spain, like English *same* → ❹
ch	[tʃ]	Like English *church* → ❺
d	[d]	At the start of the breath group and after **l** or **n**, it is pronounced similar to English *deep* (see page 289) → ❻
	[ð]	Between vowels and after consonants (except **l** or **n**), it is pronounced very like English *though* → ❼
	[(ð)]	At the end of words, and in the verb ending **-ado**, it is often not pronounced → ❽
g	[x]	Before **e**, **i**, pronounced gutturally, similar to English lo*ch* → ❾
	[g]	At the start of the breath group and after **n**, it is pronounced like English *get* → ❿
	[ɣ]	In other positions the sound is unknown in English → ⑪
gue gui	[ge/ɣe] [gi/ɣi]	The **u** is silent → ⑫
güe güi	[gwe/ɣwe] [gwi/ɣwi]	The **u** is pronounced like English *walk* → ⑬

Examples

1. bomba ['bomba]   voy [boi]   vicio ['biθjo]

2. hubo ['uβo]   de veras [de 'βeras]   lavar [la'βar]

3. casa ['kasa]   coco ['koko]   cumbre ['kumbre]

4. cero ['θero/'sero]   cinco ['θiŋko/'siŋko]

5. mucho ['mutʃo]   chuchería [tʃutʃe'ria]

6. doy [doi]   balde ['balde]   bondad [bon'dað]

7. modo ['moðo]   ideal [iðe'al]

8. Madrid [ma'ðri(ð)]   comprado [kom'pra(ð)o]

9. gente ['xente]   giro ['xiro]   general [xene'ral]

10. ganar [ga'nar]   pongo ['poŋgo]

11. agua ['aɣwa]   agrícola [a'ɣrikola]

12. guija ['gixa]   guerra ['gerra]   pague ['paɣe]

13. agüero [a'ɣwero]   argüir [ar'ɣwir]

From Spelling to Sounds *continued*

LETTER	PRONOUNCED	EXAMPLES
h	[-]	This is always silent → ①
j	[x]	Like the guttural sound in English lo*ch*, but often aspirated at the end of a word → ②
ll	[ʎ]	Similar to English -*ll*- in mi*ll*ion → ③
	[j/ʒ]	In some parts of Spain and in Latin America, like English *y*et or plea*s*ure → ④
-nv-	[mb]	This combination of letters is pronounced as in English i*mb*ibe → ⑤
ñ	[ɲ]	As in English o*ni*on → ⑥
q	[k]	Always followed by silent letter u, and pronounced as in English *k*eep, but not aspirated → ⑦
s	[s]	Except where mentioned below, like English *s*ing → ⑧
	[z]	When followed by b, d, g, l, m, n like English *z*oo → ⑨
w	[w]	Like English *v*, *w* → ⑩
x	[ks]	Between vowels, often like English e*x*it → ⑪
	[s]	Before a consonant, and, increasingly, even between vowels, like English *s*end → ⑫
y	[j]	Like English *y*es → ⑬
	[ʒ]	In some parts of Latin America, like English lei*s*ure → ⑭
z	[θ]	Like English *th*in → ⑮
	[s]	In some parts of Spain and in Latin America, like English *s*end → ⑯

Examples

1. hombre ['ombre]　　hoja ['oxa]　　ahorrar [ao'rrar]

2. jota ['xota]　　tejer [te'xer]　　reloj [re'lo(h)]

3. calle ['kaʎe]　　llamar [ʎa'mar]

4. pillar [pi'jar/pi'ʒar]　　olla ['oja/'oʒa]

5. enviar [em'bjar]　　sin valor ['sim ba'lor]

6. uña ['uɲa]　　bañar [ba'ɲar]

7. aquel [a'kel]　　querer [ke'rer]

8. está [es'ta]　　serio ['serjo]

9. desde ['dezðe]　　mismo ['mizmo]　　asno ['azno]

10. wáter ['bater]　　Walkman® [wak'man]

11. éxito ['eksito]　　máximo ['maksimo]

12. extra ['estra]　　sexto ['sesto]

13. yo [jo]　　yedra ['jeðra]

14. yeso ['ʒeso]　　yerno ['ʒerno]

15. zapato [θa'pato]　　zona ['θona]　　luz [luθ]

16. zaguán [sa'ʎwan]　　zueco ['sweko]　　pez [pes]

Normal Word Stress

There are simple rules to establish which syllable in a Spanish word is stressed. When an exception to these rules occurs an acute accent (stress-mark) is needed (see page 296). These rules are as follows:

- words ending in a vowel or combination of vowels, or with the consonants -s or -n are stressed on the next to last syllable. The great majority of Spanish words fall into this category → **1**
- words ending in a consonant other than -s or -n bear the stress on the last syllable → **2**
- a minority of words bear the stress on the second to last syllable, and these always need an accent → **3**
- some nouns change their stress from singular to plural → **4**

Stress in Diphthongs

In the case of diphthongs there are rules to establish which of the vowels is stressed (see page 288 for pronunciation). These rules are as follows:

- diphthongs formed by the combination of a 'weak' vowel (i, u) and a 'strong' vowel (a, e or o) bear the stress on the strong vowel → **5**
- diphthongs formed by the combination of two 'weak' vowels bear the stress on the second vowel → **6**

- (i) Note: Two 'strong' vowels don't form a diphthong but are pronounced as two separate vowels. In these cases stress follows the normal rules → **7**

Examples

❶ **ca**sa house
corre he runs
pala**b**ra word
crisis crisis

casas houses
corren they run
pala**b**ras words
crisis crises

❷ relo**j** watch
ver**dad** truth
bati**dor** beater

❸ mur**cié**lago bat
pájaro bird

❹ ca**rác**ter character
régimen regime

carac**te**res characters
reg**í**menes regimes

❺ **ba**ile dance
boina beret
peine comb
causa cause
reina queen

❻ fu**i** I went
vi**u**do widower

❼ me ma**re**o I feel dizzy
ca**er** to fall
caos chaos
cor**re**a leash

The Acute Accent (´)

This is used in writing to show that a word is stressed contrary to the normal rules for stress (see page 294) → ①

The following points should be noted:

The same syllable is stressed in the plural form of adjectives and nouns as in the singular. To show this, it is necessary to
- add an accent in the case of unaccented nouns and adjectives ending in -n → ②
- drop the accent from nouns and adjectives ending in -n or -s which have an accent on the last syllable → ③

The feminine form of accented nouns or adjectives does not have an accent → ④

When object pronouns are added to certain verb forms an accent is required to show that the syllable stressed in the verb form does not change. These verb forms are:
- the gerund → ⑤
- the infinitive, when followed by two pronouns → ⑥
- imperative forms, except for the 2nd person plural → ⑦

The absolute superlative forms of adjectives are always accented → ⑧

Accents on adjectives are not affected by the addition of the adverbial suffix -mente → ⑨

1 autobús
bus
relámpago
lightning

revolución
revolution
árboles
trees

2 orden → órdenes
order orders
examen → exámenes
examination examinations
joven → jóvenes
young young

3 revolución → revoluciones
revolution revolutions
autobús → autobuses
bus buses
parlanchín → parlanchines
chatty chatty

4 marqués → marquesa
marquis marchioness
francés → francesa
French (*masc*) French (*fem*)

5 comprando → comprándo(se)lo
buying buying it (for him/her/them)

6 vender → vendérselas
to sell to sell them to him/her/them

7 compra → cómpralo
buy buy it
hagan → háganselo
do do it for him/her/them

8 viejo → viejísimo
old ancient
caro → carísimo
expensive very expensive

9 fácil → fácilmente
easy easily

The Acute Accent *continued*

It is also used to distinguish between the written forms of words which are pronounced the same but have a different meaning or function. These are as follows:

Possessive adjectives/personal pronouns → ①

Demonstrative adjectives/demonstrative pronouns → ②

Interrogative and exclamatory forms of adverbs, pronouns and adjectives → ③

ⓘ Note: The accent is used in indirect as well as direct questions and exclamations → ④

The pronoun **él** and the article **el** → ⑤

A small group of words which could otherwise be confused. These are:

de	of, from	dé	give (*pres. subj.*)
mas	but	más	more
si	if	sí	yes; himself etc → ⑥
solo/a	alone	sólo	only → ⑦
te	you	té	tea

The Dieresis (¨)

This is used only in the combinations **güi** or **güe** to show that the **u** is pronounced as a semi-consonant (see page 288) → ⑧

Examples

1
Han robado mi coche	They've stolen my car
A mí no me vio	He didn't see me
¿Te gusta tu trabajo?	Do you like your job?
Tú, ¿que opinas?	What do you think?

2
Me gusta esta casa	I like this house
Me quedo con ésta	I'll take this one
¿Ves aquellos edificios?	Can you see those buildings?
Aquéllos son más bonitos	Those are prettier

3
El chico con quien viajé	The boy I travelled with
¿Con quién viajaste?	Who did you travel with?
Donde quieras	Wherever you want
¿Dónde encontraste eso?	Where did you find that?

4
¿Cómo se abre?	How does it open?
No sé cómo se abre	I don't know how it opens

5
El puerto queda cerca	The harbour's nearby
Él no quiso hacerlo	He refused to do it

6
si no viene	if he doesn't come
Sí que lo sabe	Yes he *does* know

7
Vino solo	He came by himself
Sólo lo sabe él	Only he knows

8
¡Qué vergüenza!	How shocking!
En seguida averigüé dónde estaba	I found out straight away where it was

Regular Spelling Changes

The consonants **c**, **g** and **z** are modified by the addition of certain verb or plural endings and by some suffixes. Most of the cases where this occurs have already been dealt with under the appropriate part of speech, but are summarized here along with other instances not covered elsewhere.

Verbs

The changes set out below occur so that the consonant of the verb stem is always pronounced the same as in the infinitive. For verbs affected by these changes see the list of verbs on page 81.

INFINITIVE	CHANGE			TENSES AFFECTED
-car	**c + e**	→	**-que**	Present subj, pret → 1
-cer, -cir	**c + a, o**	→	**-za, -zo**	Present, pres subj → 2
-gar	**g + e, i**	→	**-gue**	Present subj, pret → 3
-guar	**gu + e**	→	**-güe**	Present subj, pret → 4
-ger, -gir	**g + a, o**	→	**-ja, -jo**	Present, pres subj → 5
-guir	**gu + a, o**	→	**-ga, -go**	Present, pres subj → 6
-zar	**z + e**	→	**-ce**	Present subj, pret → 7

Noun and adjective plurals

SINGULAR		PLURAL
vowel + **z**	→	**-ces** → 8

Nouns and adjectives + suffixes

ENDING	SUFFIX	NEW ENDING
vowel + **z** +	**-cito**	**-cecito** → 9
-go, -ga +	**-ito, -illo**	**-guito/a, -guillo/a** → 10
-co, -ca +	**-ito, -illo**	**-quito/a, -quillo/a** → 11

Adjective absolute superlatives

ENDING	SUPERLATVE
-co	**-quísimo** → 12
-go	**-guísimo** → 13
vowel + **z**	**-císimo** → 14

Examples

1 Es inútil que lo busques aquí — It's no good looking for it here
Saqué dos entradas — I got two tickets

2 Hace falta que venzas tu miedo — You must overcome your fear

3 No creo que lleguemos antes — I don't think we'll be there any sooner

Ya le pagué — I've already paid her

4 Averigüé dónde estaba la casa — I found out where the house was

5 Cojo el autobús, es más barato — I take the bus, it's cheaper

6 ¿Sigo? — Shall I go on?

7 No permiten que se cruce la frontera — They don't allow people to cross the border
Nunca simpaticé mucho con él — I never got on very well with him

8

voz →	voces	luz →	luces
voice	**voices**	light	lights
veloz →	veloces	capaz →	capaces
quick		capable	

9 luz → lucecita
light little light

10 amigo → amiguito
friend chum

11 chico → chiquillo
boy little boy

12 rico → riquísimo
rich extremely rich

13 largo → larguísimo
long very, very long

14 feroz → ferocísimo
fierce extremely fierce

301

The Alphabet

A, a [a]	J, j ['xota]	R, r ['erre]
B, b [be]	K, k [ka]	S, s ['ese]
C, c [θe]	L, l ['ele]	T, t [te]
Ch, ch [tʃe]	Ll, ll ['eʎe]	U, u [u]
D, d [de]	M, m ['eme]	V, v ['uβe]
E, e [e]	N, n ['ene]	W, w ['uβe'doble]
F, f ['efe]	Ñ, ñ ['eɲe]	X, x ['ekis]
G, g [xe]	O, o [o]	Y, y [i'ɣrjeɣa]
H, h ['atʃe]	P, p [pe]	Z, z ['θeta]
I, i [i]	Q, q [ku]	

The letters are feminine and you therefore talk of **una a**, or **la a**.

Capital letters are used as in English except for the following:

adjectives of nationality:
e.g. **una ciudad alemana** a German town
un autor español a Spanish author

languages:
e.g. **¿Habla Vd inglés?** Do you speak English?
Hablan español e italiano They speak Spanish and Italian

days of the week:

lunes Monday	**viernes** Friday
martes Tuesday	**sábado** Saturday
miércoles Wednesday	**domingo** Sunday
jueves Thursday	

months of the year:

enero January	**julio** July
febrero February	**agosto** August
marzo March	**se(p)tiembre** September
abril April	**octubre** October
mayo May	**noviembre** November
junio June	**diciembre** December

Punctuation

Spanish punctuation differs from English in the following ways:

Question marks

There are inverted question marks and exclamation marks at the beginning of a question or exclamation, as well as upright ones at the end.

Indications of dialogue

Dashes are used to indicate dialogue, and are equivalent to the English inverted commas:

> – ¿Vendrás conmigo? – le preguntó María
> 'Will you come with me?' Maria asked him

ⓘ Note: When no expression of saying, replying etc follows, only one dash is used at the beginning:
> – Sí. 'Yes.'

Letter headings

At the beginning of a letter, a colon is used instead of the English comma:

> Querida Cristina: Dear Cristina, Muy Sr. mío: Dear Sir,

Punctuation terms in Spanish

.	punto	!	se cierra admiración
,	coma	" "	comillas (used as '...')
;	punto y coma	"	se abren comillas
:	dos puntos	"	se cierran comillas
...	puntos suspensivos	( )	paréntesis
¿?	interrogación	(	se abre paréntesis
¿	se abre interrogación	)	se cierra paréntesis
?	se cierra interrogación	–	guión
¡!	admiración		
¡	se abre admiración punto y aparte	new paragraph
		punto final	last full stop

303

Cardinal (one, two, three *etc*)

cero	0	setenta	70
uno (un, una)	1	ochenta	80
dos	2	noventa	90
tres	3	cien (ciento)	100
cuatro	4	ciento uno(una)	101
cinco	5	ciento dos	102
seis	6	ciento diez	110
siete	7	ciento cuarenta y dos	142
ocho	8	doscientos(as)	200
nueve	9	doscientos(as) uno(una)	201
diez	10	doscientos(as) dos	202
once	11	trescientos(as)	300
doce	12	cuatrocientos(as)	400
trece	13	quinientos(as)	500
catorce	14	seiscientos(as)	600
quince	15	setecientos(as)	700
dieciséis	16	ochocientos(as)	800
diecisiete	17	novecientos(as)	900
dieciocho	18	mil	1.000
diecinueve	19	mil uno(una)	1.001
veinte	20	mil dos	1.002
veintiuno	21	mil doscientos veinte	1.220
veintidós	22	dos mil	2.000
treinta	30	cien mil	100.000
treinta y uno	31	doscientos(as) mil	200.000
cuarenta	40	un millón	1.000.000
cincuenta	50	dos millones	2.000.000
sesenta	60	un billón	1.000.000.000.000

Fractions

un medio; medio(a)	½
un tercio	⅓
dos tercios	⅔
un cuarto	¼
tres cuartos	¾
un quinto	⅕
cinco y tres cuartos	5¾

Others

cero coma cinco	0,5
uno coma tres	1,3
(el, un) diez por ciento	10%
dos más/y dos	2 + 2
dos menos dos	2 − 2
dos por dos	2 × 2
dos dividido por dos	2 ÷ 2

Numbers

Points to note on cardinals

uno drops the o before masculine nouns, and the same applies when in compound numerals:
- **un libro** 1 book, **treinta y un niños** 31 children

1, 21, 31 etc and 200, 300, 400 etc have feminine forms:
- **cuarenta y una euros** 41 euros, **quinientas libras** £500

ciento is used before numbers smaller than 100, otherwise **cien** is used:
- **ciento cuatro** 104 but **cien euros** 100 euros, **cien mil** 100,000 (see also page 210)

millón takes **de** before a noun:
- **un millón de personas** 1,000,000 people

mil is only found in the plural when meaning thousands of:
- **miles de solicitantes** thousands of applicants

cardinals normally precede ordinals:
- **los tres primeros pisos** the first three floors

ⓘ Note: The full stop is used with numbers over one thousand and the comma with decimals i.e. the opposite of English usage.

Ordinal Numbers (first, second, third *etc*)

primero (primer, primera)	1°,1ª	undécimo(a)	11°,11ª
segundo(a)	2°,2ª	duodécimo(a)	12°,12ª
tercero (tercer, tercera)	3°,3ª	decimotercer(o)(a)	13°,13ª
cuarto(a)	4°,4ª	decimocuarto(a)	14°,14ª
quinto(a)	5°,5ª	decimoquinto(a)	15°,15ª
sexto(a)	6°,6ª	decimosexto(a)	16°,16ª
séptimo(a)	7°,7ª	decimoséptimo(a)	17°,17ª
octavo(a)	8°,8ª	decimoctavo(a)	18°,18ª
noveno(a)	9°,9ª	decimonoveno(a)	19°,19ª
décimo(a)	10°,10ª	vigésimo(a)	20°,20ª

Points to note on ordinals

They agree in gender and in number with the noun, which they normally precede, except with royal titles:

> **la primera vez** the first time
> **Felipe segundo** Philip II

primero and **tercero** drop the **o** before a masculine singular noun:

> **el primer premio** the first prize
> **el tercer día** the third day

Beyond **décimo** ordinal numbers are rarely used, and they are replaced by the cardinal number placed immediately after the noun:

> **el siglo diecisiete** the seventeenth century
> **Alfonso doce** Alfonso XII
> **en el piso trece** on the 13th floor

> BUT: **vigésimo(a)** 20th
> (but not with royal titles or centuries)
> **centésimo(a)** 100th
> **milésimo(a)** 1,000th
> **millonésimo(a)** 1,000,000th

Other Uses

collective numbers:

un par	2, a couple
una decena (de personas)	about 10 (people)
una docena (de niños)	(about) a dozen (children)
una quincena (de hombres)	about fifteen (men)
una veintena* (de coches)	about twenty (cars)
un centenar, una centena (de casas)	about a hundred (houses)
cientos/centenares de personas	hundreds of people
un millar (de soldados)	about a thousand (soldiers)
miles/millares de moscas	thousands of flies

* 20, 30, 40, 50 can also be converted in the same way.

measurements:

veinte metros cuadrados	20 square metres
veinte metros cúbicos	20 cubic metres
un puente de cuarenta metros de largo/longitud	a bridge 40 metres long

distance:

De aquí a Madrid hay 400 km	Madrid is 400 km away
a siete km de aquí	7 km from here

Telephone numbers

Póngame con Madrid, el cuatro, cincuenta y ocho, veintidós, noventa y tres
  I would like Madrid 458 22 93
Me da Valencia, el veinte, cincuenta y uno, setenta y tres
  Could you get me Valencia 20 51 73
Extensión tres, tres, cinco/trescientos treinta y cinco
  Extension number 335

ⓘ Note: In Spanish telephone numbers may be read out individually, but more frequently they are broken down into groups of two. They are written in groups of two or three numbers (never four).

The Time

¿Qué hora es? *What time is it?*
Es ... *(1 o'clock, midnight, noon)* ⎤ It's ...
Son las ... *(other times)* ⎦
Es la una y cuarto   It's 1.15
Son las diez menos cinco   It's 9.55

00.00	**medianoche; las doce (de la noche)**	midnight, twelve o'clock
00.10	**las doce y diez (de la noche)**	
00.15	**las doce y cuarto**	
00.30	**las doce y media**	
00.45	**la una menos cuarto**	
01.00	**la una (de la madrugada)**	one a.m., one o'clock in the morning
01.10	**la una y diez (de la madrugada)**	
02.45	**las tres menos cuarto**	
07.00	**las siete (de la mañana)**	
07.50	**las ocho menos diez**	
12.00	**mediodía; las doce (de la mañana)**	noon, twelve o'clock
13.00	**la una (de la tarde)**	one p.m., one o'clock in the afternoon
19.00	**las siete (de la tarde)**	seven p.m., seven o'clock in the evening
21.00	**las nueve (de la noche)**	nine p.m., nine o'clock at night

ⓘ Note: When referring to a timetable, the 24 hour clock is used:

las dieciséis cuarenta y cinco   16.45
las veintiuna quince   21.15

¿A qué hora vas a venir?	What time are you coming?
— A las siete	— At seven o'clock
Las oficinas cierran de dos a cuatro	The offices are closed from two until four
Vendré a eso de/hacia las siete y media	I'll come at around 7.30
a las seis y pico	just after 6 o'clock
a las cinco en punto	at 5 o'clock sharp
entre las ocho y las nueve	between 8 and 9 o'clock
Son más de las tres y media	It's after half past three
Hay que estar allí lo más tarde a las diez	You have to be there by ten o'clock at the latest
Tiene para media hora	He'll be half an hour (at it)
Estuvo sin conocimiento durante un cuarto de hora	She was unconscious for a quarter of an hour
Les estoy esperando desde hace una hora/desde las dos	I've been waiting for them for an hour/since two o'clock
Se fueron hace unos minutos	They left a few minutes ago
Lo hice en veinte minutos	I did it in twenty minutes
El tren llega dentro de una hora	The train arrives in an hour('s time)
¿Cuánto (tiempo) dura la película?	How long does the film last?
por la mañana/tarde/noche	in the morning/afternoon or evening/at night
mañana por la mañana	tomorrow morning
ayer por la tarde	yesterday afternoon or evening
anoche	last night
anteayer	the day before yesterday
pasado mañana	the day after tomorrow

Dates

¿Qué día es hoy? ¿A qué día estamos?	What's the date today?
Es (el) ... Estamos a ...	It's the ...
uno/primero de mayo	1st of May
dos de mayo	2nd of May
veintiocho de mayo	28th of May
lunes tres de octubre	Monday the 3rd of October
Vienen el siete de marzo	They're coming on the 7th of March

ⓘ Note: Use cardinal numbers for dates. Only for the first of the month can the ordinal number sometimes be used.

Years

Nací en 1970	I was born in 1970
el veinte de enero de mil novecientos setenta	(on) 20th January 1970

Other expressions

en los años cincuenta	during the fifties
en el siglo veinte	in the twentieth century
en mayo	in May
lunes (quince)	Monday (the 15th)
el quince de marzo	on March the 15th
el/los lunes	on Monday/Mondays
dentro de diez días	in 10 days' time
hace diez días	10 days ago

Age

¿Qué edad tiene? ¿Cuántos años tiene?	How old is he/she?
Tiene 23 (años)	He/She is 23
Tiene unos 40 años	He/She is around 40
A los 21 años	At the age of 21

Index

The following index lists comprehensively both grammatical terms and key words in English and Spanish.

Index

Index